VIIIIKE a
Leō m̄e p̄te k̄ore ma
ACOBVS d
ih̄u x̄p̄i seruus: duo
quę sunt in dispsion
ETCETERA: Serouc
yonia
bi vig̃t
sr̃s desid

recolim̄? dignū est ut
xp̄i laudes n̄rarū ling
non sileant; Jacobus d
ih̄u xp̄i seruum inp̄n
suę se ē̄ asserit: & salu
p mittit: ut demonstr̄e
in dei seruicio usq: in̄
uerit: p̄cul dubio inp̄
erit; Dirit de hoc iacobo: ap̄l's paulus; Jacobus ce
qui uidebā̄ columne ē̄: dertras dederīt m̄ ibarr

St. John, from the Codex Calixtinus.
(© Gianni Dagli Orti/CORBIS)

NEW
CATHOLIC
ENCYCLOPEDIA

NEW CATHOLIC ENCYCLOPEDIA

SECOND EDITION

7

Hol–Jub

GALE®

THOMSON

^{TM}

GALE

Detroit • New York • San Diego • San Francisco • Cleveland • New Haven, Conn. • Waterville, Maine • London • Munich

in association with
THE CATHOLIC UNIVERSITY OF AMERICA • WASHINGTON, D.C.

The New Catholic Encyclopedia, Second Edition

Project Editors
Thomas Carson, Joann Cerrito

Editorial
Erin Bealmear, Jim Craddock, Stephen Cusack,
Miranda Ferrara, Kristin Hart, Melissa Hill,
Margaret Mazurkiewicz, Carol Schwartz,
Christine Tomassini, Michael J. Tyrkus

Permissions
Edna Hedblad, Shalice Shah-Caldwell

Imaging and Multimedia
Randy Bassett, Dean Dauphinais, Robert
Duncan, Leitha Etheridge-Sims, Mary K.
Grimes, Lezlie Light, Dan Newell, David G.
Oblender, Christine O'Bryan, Luke
Rademacher, Pamela Reed

Product Design
Michelle DiMercurio

Data Capture
Civie Green

Manufacturing
Rhonda Williams

Indexing
Victoria Agee, Victoria Baker, Lynne Maday,
Do Mi Stauber, Amy Suchowski

While every effort has been made to ensure
the reliability of the information presented in
this publication, The Gale Group, Inc. does
not guarantee the accuracy of the data contained herein. The Gale Group, Inc. accepts
no payment for listing; and inclusion in the
publication of any organization, agency, institution, publication, service, or individual does
not imply endorsement of the editors or publisher. Errors brought to the attention of the
publisher and verified to the satisfaction of
the publisher will be corrected in future editions.

LIBRARY OF CONGRESS CATALOGING-IN-PUBLICATION DATA

New Catholic encyclopedia.—2nd ed.
    p. cm.
      Includes bibliographical references and indexes.
      ISBN 0-7876-4004-2
      1. Catholic Church—Encyclopedias. I. Catholic University of America.
BX841 .N44 2002
282' .03—dc21
2002000924

ISBN: 0-7876-4004-2 (set)
0-7876-4005-0 (v. 1)
0-7876-4006-9 (v. 2)
0-7876-4007-7 (v. 3)
0-7876-4008-5 (v. 4)

0-7876-4009-3 (v. 5)
0-7876-4010-7 (v. 6)
0-7876-4011-5 (v. 7)
0-7876-4012-3 (v. 8)
0-7876-4013-1 (v. 9)

0-7876-4014-x (v. 10)
0-7876-4015-8 (v. 11)
0-7876-4016-6 (v. 12)
0-7876-4017-4 (v. 13)
0-7876-4018-2 (v. 14)
0-7876-4019-0 (v. 15)

Printed in the United States of America
10 9 8 7 6 5 4 3 2 1

For The Catholic University of America Press

Foreword

This revised edition of the *New Catholic Encyclopedia* represents a third generation in the evolution of the text that traces its lineage back to the *Catholic Encyclopedia* published from 1907 to 1912. In 1967, sixty years after the first volume of the original set appeared, The Catholic University of America and the McGraw-Hill Book Company joined together in organizing a small army of editors and scholars to produce the *New Catholic Encyclopedia*. Although planning for the *NCE* had begun before the Second Vatican Council and most of the 17,000 entries were written before Council ended, Vatican II enhanced the encyclopedia's value and importance. The research and the scholarship that went into the articles witnessed to the continuity and richness of the Catholic Tradition given fresh expression by Council. In order to keep the *NCE* current, supplementary volumes were published in 1972, 1978, 1988, and 1995. Now, at the beginning of the third millennium, The Catholic University of America is proud to join with The Gale Group in presenting a new edition of the *New Catholic Encyclopedia*. It updates and incorporates the many articles from the 1967 edition and its supplements that have stood the test of time and adds hundreds of new entries.

As the president of The Catholic University of America, I cannot but be pleased at the reception the *NCE* has received. It has come to be recognized as an authoritative reference work in the field of religious studies and is praised for its comprehensive coverage of the Church's history and institutions. Although Canon Law no longer requires encyclopedias and reference works of this kind to receive an *imprimatur* before publication, I am confident that this new edition, like the original, reports accurate information about Catholic beliefs and practices. The editorial staff and their consultants were careful to present official Church teachings in a straightforward manner, and in areas where there are legitimate disputes over fact and differences in interpretation of events, they made every effort to insure a fair and balanced presentation of the issues.

The way for this revised edition was prepared by the publication, in 2000, of a Jubilee volume of the *NCE,* heralding the beginning of the new millennium. In my foreword to that volume I quoted Pope John Paul II's encyclical on Faith and Human Reason in which he wrote that history is "the arena where we see what God does for humanity." The *New Catholic Encyclopedia* describes that arena. It reports events, people, and ideas—"the things we know best and can verify most easily, the things of our everyday life, apart from which we cannot understand ourselves" *(Fides et ratio,* 12).

Finally, I want to express appreciation on my own behalf and on the behalf of the readers of these volumes to everyone who helped make this revision a reality. We are all indebted to The Gale Group and the staff of The Catholic University of America Press for their dedication and the alacrity with which they produced it.

Very Reverend David M. O'Connell, C.M., J.C.D.
President
The Catholic University of America

Preface to the Revised Edition

When first published in 1967 the *New Catholic Encyclopedia* was greeted with enthusiasm by librarians, researchers, and general readers interested in Catholicism. In the United States the *NCE* has been recognized as the standard reference work on matters of special interest to Catholics. In an effort to keep the encyclopedia current, supplementary volumes were published in 1972, 1978, 1988, and 1995. However, it became increasingly apparent that further supplements would not be adequate to this task. The publishers subsequently decided to undertake a thorough revision of the *NCE,* beginning with the publication of a Jubilee volume at the start of the new millennium.

Like the biblical scribe who brings from his storeroom of knowledge both the new and the old, this revised edition of the *New Catholic Encyclopedia* incorporates material from the 15-volume original edition and the supplement volumes. Entries that have withstood the test of time have been edited, and some have been amended to include the latest information and research. Hundreds of new entries have been added. For all practical purposes, it is an entirely new edition intended to serve as a comprehensive and authoritative work of reference reporting on the movements and interests that have shaped Christianity in general and Catholicism in particular over two millennia.

SCOPE

The title reflects its outlook and breadth. It is the *New Catholic Encyclopedia,* not merely a new encyclopedia of Catholicism. In addition to providing information on the doctrine, organization, and history of Christianity over the centuries, it includes information about persons, institutions, cultural phenomena, religions, philosophies, and social movements that have affected the Catholic Church from within and without. Accordingly, the *NCE* attends to the history and particular traditions of the Eastern Churches and the Churches of the Protestant Reformation, and other ecclesial communities. Christianity cannot be understood without exploring its roots in ancient Israel and Judaism, nor can the history of the medieval and modern Church be understood apart from its relationship with Islam. Interfaith dialogue requires an appreciation of Buddhism and other world religions, as well as some knowledge of the history of religion in general.

On the assumption that most readers and researchers who use the *NCE* are individuals interested in Catholicism in general and the Church in North America in particular, its editorial content gives priority to the Western Church, while not neglecting the churches in the East; to Roman Catholicism, acknowledging much common history with Protestantism; and to Catholicism in the United States, recognizing that it represents only a small part of the universal Church.

Scripture, Theology, Patrology, Liturgy. The many and varied articles dealing with Sacred Scripture and specific books of the Bible reflect contemporary biblical scholarship and its concerns. The *NCE* highlights official church teachings as expressed by the Church's magisterium. It reports developments in theology, explains issues and introduces ecclesiastical writers from the early Church Fathers to present-day theologians whose works exercise major influence on the development of Christian thought. The *NCE* traces the evolution of the Church's worship with special emphasis on rites and rituals consequent to the liturgical reforms and renewal initiated by the Second Vatican Council.

Church History. From its inception Christianity has been shaped by historical circumstances and itself has become a historical force. The *NCE* presents the Church's history from a number of points of view against the background of general political and cultural history. The revised edition reports in some detail the Church's missionary activity as it grew from a small community in Jerusalem to the worldwide phenomenon it is today. Some entries, such as those dealing with the Middle Ages, the Reformation, and the Enlightenment, focus on major time-periods and movements that cut across geographical boundaries. Other articles describe the history and structure of the Church in specific areas, countries, and regions. There are separate entries for many dioceses and monasteries which by reason of antiquity, size, or influence are of special importance in ecclesiastical history, as there are for religious orders and congregations. The *NCE* rounds out its comprehensive history of the Church with articles on religious movements and biographies of individuals.

Canon and Civil Law. The Church inherited and has safeguarded the precious legacy of ancient Rome, described by Virgil, "to rule people under law, [and] to establish the way of peace." The *NCE* deals with issues of ecclesiastical jurisprudence and outlines the development of legislation governing communal practices and individual obligations, taking care to incorporate and reference the 1983 *Code of Canon Law* throughout and, where appropriate, the *Code of Canons for the Eastern Churches*. It deals with issues of Church-State relations and with civil law as it impacts on the Church and Church's teaching regarding human rights and freedoms.

Philosophy. The Catholic tradition from its earliest years has investigated the relationship between faith and reason. The *NCE* considers at some length the many and varied schools of ancient, medieval, and modern philosophy with emphasis, when appropriate, on their relationship to theological positions. It pays particular attention to the scholastic tradition, particularly Thomism, which is prominent in Catholic intellectual history. Articles on many major and lesser philosophers contribute to a comprehensive survey of philosophy from pre-Christian times to the present.

Biography and Hagiography. The *NCE*, making an exception for the reigning pope, leaves to other reference works biographical information about living persons. This revised edition presents biographical sketches of hundreds of men and women, Christian and non-Christian, saints and sinners, because of their significance for the Church. They include: Old and New Testament figures; the Fathers of the Church and ecclesiastical writers; pagan and Christian emperors; medieval and modern kings; heads of state and other political figures; heretics and champions of orthodoxy; major and minor figures in the Reformation and Counter Reformation; popes, bishops, and priests; founders and members of religious orders and congregations; lay men and lay women; scholars, authors, composers, and artists. The *NCE* includes biographies of most saints whose feasts were once celebrated or are currently celebrated by the universal church. The revised edition relies on Butler's *Lives of the Saints* and similar reference works to give accounts of many saints, but the *NCE* also

provides biographical information about recently canonized and beatified individuals who are, for one reason or another, of special interest to the English-speaking world.

Social Sciences. Social sciences came into their own in the twentieth century. Many articles in the *NCE* rely on data drawn from anthropology, economics, psychology and sociology for a better understanding of religious structures and behaviors. Papal encyclicals and pastoral letters of episcopal conferences are the source of principles and norms for Christian attitudes and practice in the field of social action and legislation. The *NCE* draws attention to the Church's organized activities in pursuit of peace and justice, social welfare and human rights. The growth of the role of the laity in the work of the Church also receives thorough coverage.

ARRANGEMENT OF ENTRIES

The articles in the *NCE* are arranged alphabetically by the first substantive word using the word-by-word method of alphabetization; thus "New Zealand" precedes "Newman, John Henry," and "Old Testament Literature" precedes "Oldcastle, Sir John." Monarchs, patriarchs, popes, and others who share a Christian name and are differentiated by a title and numerical designation are alphabetized by their title and then arranged numerically. Thus, entries for Byzantine emperors Leo I through IV precede those for popes of the same name, while "Henry VIII, King of England" precedes "Henry IV, King of France."

Maps, Charts, and Illustrations. The *New Catholic Encyclopedia* contains nearly 3,000 illustrations, including photographs, maps, and tables. Entries focusing on the Church in specific countries contain a map of the country as well as easy-to-read tables giving statistical data and, where helpful, lists of archdioceses and dioceses. Entries on the Church in U.S. states also contain tables listing archdioceses and dioceses where appropriate. The numerous photographs appearing in the *New Catholic Encyclopedia* help to illustrate the history of the Church, its role in modern societies, and the many magnificent works of art it has inspired.

SPECIAL FEATURES

Subject Overview Articles. For the convenience and guidance of the reader, the *New Catholic Encyclopedia* contains several brief articles outlining the scope of major fields: "Theology, Articles on," "Liturgy, Articles on," "Jesus Christ, Articles on," etc.

Cross-References. The cross-reference system in the *NCE* serves to direct the reader to related material in other articles. The appearance of a name or term in small capital letters in text indicates that there is an article of that title elsewhere in the encyclopedia. In some cases, the name of the related article has been inserted at the appropriate point as a *see* reference: (*see* THOMAS AQUINAS, ST.). When a further aspect of the subject is treated under another title, a *see also* reference is placed at the end of the article. In addition to this extensive cross-reference system, the comprehensive index in volume 15 will greatly increase the reader's ability to access the wealth of information contained in the encyclopedia.

Abbreviations List. Following common practice, books and versions of the Bible as well as other standard works by selected authors have been abbreviated throughout the text. A guide to these abbreviations follows this preface.

The Editors

Abbreviations

The system of abbreviations used for the works of Plato, Aristotle, St. Augustine, and St. Thomas Aquinas is as follows: Plato is cited by book and Stephanus number only, e.g., Phaedo 79B; Rep. 480A. Aristotle is cited by book and Bekker number only, e.g., Anal. post. 72b 8–12; Anim. 430a 18. St. Augustine is cited as in the Thesaurus Linguae Latinae, e.g., C. acad. 3.20.45; Conf. 13.38.53, with capitalization of the first word of the title. St. Thomas is cited as in scholarly journals, but using Arabic numerals. In addition, the following abbreviations have been used throughout the encyclopedia for biblical books and versions of the Bible.

Books

Acts	Acts of the Apostles
Am	Amos
Bar	Baruch
1–2 Chr	1 and 2 Chronicles (1 and 2 Paralipomenon in Septuagint and Vulgate)
Col	Colossians
1–2 Cor	1 and 2 Corinthians
Dn	Daniel
Dt	Deuteronomy
Eccl	Ecclesiastes
Eph	Ephesians
Est	Esther
Ex	Exodus
Ez	Ezekiel
Ezr	Ezra (Esdras B in Septuagint; 1 Esdras in Vulgate)
Gal	Galatians
Gn	Genesis
Hb	Habakkuk
Heb	Hebrews
Hg	Haggai
Hos	Hosea
Is	Isaiah
Jas	James
Jb	Job
Jdt	Judith
Jer	Jeremiah
Jgs	Judges
Jl	Joel
Jn	John
1–3 Jn	1, 2, and 3 John
Jon	Jonah
Jos	Joshua
Jude	Jude
1–2 Kgs	1 and 2 Kings (3 and 4 Kings in Septuagint and Vulgate)
Lam	Lamentations
Lk	Luke
Lv	Leviticus
Mal	Malachi (Malachias in Vulgate)
1–2 Mc	1 and 2 Maccabees
Mi	Micah
Mk	Mark
Mt	Matthew
Na	Nahum
Neh	Nehemiah (2 Esdras in Septuagint and Vulgate)
Nm	Numbers
Ob	Obadiah
Phil	Philippians
Phlm	Philemon
Prv	Proverbs
Ps	Psalms
1–2 Pt	1 and 2 Peter
Rom	Romans
Ru	Ruth
Rv	Revelation (Apocalypse in Vulgate)
Sg	Song of Songs
Sir	Sirach (Wisdom of Ben Sira; Ecclesiasticus in Septuagint and Vulgate)
1–2 Sm	1 and 2 Samuel (1 and 2 Kings in Septuagint and Vulgate)
Tb	Tobit
1–2 Thes	1 and 2 Thessalonians
Ti	Titus
1–2 Tm	1 and 2 Timothy
Wis	Wisdom
Zec	Zechariah
Zep	Zephaniah

Versions

Apoc	Apocrypha
ARV	American Standard Revised Version
ARVm	American Standard Revised Version, margin
AT	American Translation
AV	Authorized Version (King James)
CCD	Confraternity of Christian Doctrine
DV	Douay-Challoner Version

ERV	English Revised Version	NJB	New Jerusalem Bible
ERVm	English Revised Version, margin	NRSV	New Revised Standard Version
EV	English Version(s) of the Bible	NT	New Testament
JB	Jerusalem Bible	OT	Old Testament
LXX	Septuagint	RSV	Revised Standard Version
MT	Masoretic Text	RV	Revised Version
NAB	New American Bible	RVm	Revised Version, margin
NEB	New English Bible	Syr	Syriac
NIV	New International Version	Vulg	Vulgate

H

HOLAIND, RENÉ

Educator, author; b. Moulins, France, July 27, 1836; d. Woodstock, Md., April 20, 1906. He entered the Jesuit novitiate at Avignon, France, in 1851 and taught at Avignon and Dôle, France, before immigrating to the U.S. in 1861. After theological studies at Boston College, Mass., and Spring Hill College, Mobile, Ala., he taught for 13 years at Jesuit schools in Alabama and Louisiana and for five years was a parish priest at Selma, Ala. He was professor of ethics at Woodstock College, Woodstock, Md., from 1885 until 1898. After a brief time as a chaplain with the U.S. Army, he taught ethics and jurisprudence at Georgetown University, Washington, D.C., until he retired to Woodstock in 1905. Holaind's interests included music, architecture, and the classics of ancient and modern literature. He published a defense of the right of private property, *Ownership and Natural Right* (1887), and a textbook on jurisprudence, *Natural Law and Legal Practice* (1889). During the Catholic controversy in the 1890s over the role of public and parochial schools, he opposed the party led by Abp. John Ireland (*see* FARIBAULT PLAN). His strong defense of parochial schools, *The Parent First* (1891), was probably written at the suggestion of Ireland's opponent, Abp. Michael A. Corrigan of New York. Holaind's critics, condemning his pamphlet as reactionary and attuned to the situation in Europe rather than to American conditions, generally sided with Thomas J. BOUQUILLON of The Catholic University of America, Washington, D.C., who defended the rights of the state in education.

Bibliography: P. J. DOOLEY, *Woodstock and Its Makers* (Woodstock, Md. 1927). J. T. ELLIS, *The Life of James Cardinal Gibbons*, 2 v. (Milwaukee 1952) 1:653–707.

[J. J. HENNESEY]

HOLBACH, PAUL HEINRICH DIETRICH

Also known as Paul Thiry, Baron d'Holbach, French encyclopedist; b. Heidesheim in the Palatinate, 1723; d. Paris, Jan. 21, 1789. Holbach, educated at the University of Leyden, where he pursued his early interests in science, contributed approximately 400 articles to the *Encyclopédie*. Most of these pertained to science and were merely translations from German texts. Between 1760 and 1770 Holbach published French translations of the writings of several English deists, including passages written by himself but attributed to them. He produced numerous volumes dedicated to the destruction of religion, many attributed on their title page to deceased Frenchmen of note: e.g., *Christianisme dévoilé* (1761), to N. A. Boulanger; and *Essai sur les préjugés* (1769), to C. C. Dumarsais. His most widely read work, *Système de la nature, ou des Lois du monde physique et du monde moral* (1770), published as the work of J. B. Mirabaud, is a systematic explanation of the universe in terms of ATHEISM, MATERIALISM, determinism, and utilitarianism.

See Also: ENCYCLOPEDISTS; DEISM.

Bibliography: C. CAPONE BRAGA, *Enciclopedia filosofica*, 4 v. (Venice-Rome 1957) 2:1103–06. V. W. TOPAZIO, *D'Holbach's Moral Philosophy* (Geneva 1956).

[R. Z. LAUER]

HOLDEN, HENRY

Theologian and controversialist; b. Chagley, Lancashire, England, 1596; d. Paris, March 1662. In 1618 he entered the seminary at Douai under the assumed name of Johnson and he remained there until 1623. Later, as a priest, he studied at the Sorbonne, was awarded the degree of doctor of theology by that institution, and was given a position on the faculty. About the same time, he received an appointment as a vicar-general of the archbishop of Paris. For a while he was superior of the seminary of St. Gregory in Paris, but he was not a success as a financial administrator and in 1655 had to be replaced. In 1659 he was appointed superior of a famous community at Paris known as the "Blue Nuns," whose rule had originally been Franciscan but had been changed to that of the Immaculate Conception of Our Lady.

In the controversy that developed in the 17th century between the regular and secular clergy over the timeliness of having a bishop present in England, Holden was an active supporter of the secular argument. He wrote prominently on the subject, and in 1631 he went to Rome as a representative of the secular position. As a professor at the Sorbonne he could not escape being influenced by Gallican ideas concerning the authority of the pope, but his orthodoxy in relation to the religious controversies of his day, as well as his learning, is attested to by his position and his works, such as *Divinae fidei analysis, seu de fidei Christianae resolutione, libri duo . . .* (Paris 1652), and his letters concerning the condemned writings of Thomas WHITE, alias Blacklo.

Bibliography: H. TOOTELL, *Dodd's Church History of England,* ed. M. A. TIERNEY, 5 v. (London 1839–43). J. GILLOW and R. TRAPPES-LOMAX, eds., *The Diary of the 'Blue Nuns' or Order of the Immaculate Conception of Our Lady, at Paris. 1658–1810* (London 1910). C. BUTLER, *Historical Memoirs Respecting the English, Irish and Scottish Catholics from the Reformation to the Present Time,* 4 v. (London 1819–21). J. GILLOW, *A Literary and Biographical History or Bibliographical Dictionary of the English Catholics from 1534 to the Present time,* 5 v. (London-New York 1885–1902; repr. New York 1961) 3:332–339. P. FERET, *La Faculté de Théologie de Paris . . . époque moderne,* 7 v. (Paris 1900–10) 3:220, 224. J. G. ALGER, *The Dictionary of National Biography from the Earliest Times to 1900,* 63 v. (London 1885–1900) 9:1013–14. A. GATARD, *Dictionnaire de théologie catholique,* ed. A. VACANT et al., 15 v. (Paris 1903–50; Tables Générales 1951–) 7.1:31–32.

[V. PONKO, JR.]

HOLIDAY, RICHARD, BL.

Priest, martyr; b. in Yorkshire, England; d. May 27, 1590, hanged, drawn, and quartered at Durham. He went to Rheims to study at the English College on Sept. 6, 1584, but was not ordained a priest until 1589. He was arrested and condemned for his priesthood with Bl. Edmund DUKE, Richard HILL, and John HOGG almost immediately upon arrival in England. They were beatified by Pope John Paul II on Nov. 22, 1987 with George Haydock and Companions.

Feast of the English Martyrs: May 4 (England).

See Also: ENGLAND, SCOTLAND, AND WALES, MARTYRS OF.

Bibliography: R. CHALLONER, *Memoirs of Missionary Priests,* ed. J. H. POLLEN (rev. ed. London 1924). J. H. POLLEN, *Acts of English Martyrs* (London 1891).

[K. I. RABENSTEIN]

HOLINESS

Sanctity, the state or character a thing has by being set apart and specially dedicated to God and His service.

St. Thomas Aquinas made sanctity equivalent to the virtue of religion (*Summa Theologiae* 2a2ae, 32.8; *see* RELIGION, VIRTUE OF), sanctity being the referral by man of his spiritual capabilities to God by the practice of virtue, and religion being the devotion to divine worship by acts of liturgical sacrifice, offerings, prayer, and vows. Among Christian writers the terms holiness and sanctity are sometimes used equivalently with Christian perfection, which consists properly in the development of the virtue of charity (*see* PERFECTION, SPIRITUAL) and with saintliness or the practice of heroic virtue (*see* VIRTUE, HEROIC).

St. Thomas used etymological considerations to show that two notions are involved in the idea of sanctity: cleanness (from the Greek equivalent ἅγιος, or the *sanguine tinctus* suggested by Isidore), and firmness (if the term is seen as derived from *sancire*). Although the etymological argument here is of dubious value, it cannot be doubted that sanctity embraces both notions. Since sanctity is attributed to what is dedicated to the divine cult, only that can be fitly dedicated to God which is free of all sordidness, and its application to the service of God, the unchangeable First Principle and Last End of all things, should, from the nature of its term, be characterized by immutability and firmness.

Although the term holy may be applied to objects such as churches and to the vessels and vestments used in divine worship, it is properly the characteristic of man.

Bibliography: THOMAS AQUINAS, *Summa Theologiae* 2a2ae, 81.8. B. H. MERKELBACH, *summa theologiae moralis,* 3 v. (8th ed. Paris 1949) 2:645–648. D. M. PRÜMMER, *Manuale theologiae moralis* (Freiburg-Barcelona 1955) 2:323–327.

[J. D. FEARON]

HOLINESS (IN THE BIBLE)

Holiness is the English word for *qōdeš,* derived from the Hebrew root *qdš,* common to all Semitic languages and having essentially the same meaning. The concept of holiness is not established etymologically from the root; it comes from the sense in which its derivatives are used. Hence it signifies ''separateness'' from the nonholy or profane. What is ''clean'' or ''pure'' is also related to ''holy'' in a ritual sense, i.e., free from defilement by the profane and in a potentially holy state. The profoundest sense of holiness is that proper to God, absolute holiness consisting in His ''otherness'' or His uncreated transcendence and majesty, a meaning related to His GLORY. Dependent on this is holiness in the cultic and moral senses. In the cultic sense, it is a quality of an object that is withdrawn from the profane and consecrated to God; in the moral sense, it can be ascribed, to God, to angels, or to men.

Holiness in the Old Testament Unlike those religions that attach the term "holy" to cultic objects and seldom to the diety, the OT authors often use it of God.

Sanctity of God. "Holy" in an absolute sense is used exclusively of God's "otherness" or uncreated and inaccessible majesty in relation to which all else is unholy: "Who shall be able to stand before the Lord, this holy God?" (1 Sm 6.20). The canticles of Moses and of Anna depict God's holiness as something unattainable and beyond all creatures: "Who is like to you among the gods, O Lord? Who is like to you, magnificent in holiness? O terrible in renown, worker of wonders" (Ex 15.11); "There is none holy as the Lord is; for there is no other besides thee, and there is none strong like our God" (1 Sm 2.2; see also Is 6.3). God's name is holy, as He Himself is holy: "Let them praise your great and awesome name; holy is he" [Ps 98(99).3; see also Lv 11.44; 19.2; 20.26; Is 40.25; etc.]. In comparison to Him none is holy, neither angels nor men: "If in his holy ones God places no confidence, and if the heavens are not clean in his sight, how much less so is the abominable, the corrupt: man, who drinks in iniquity like water!" (Jb 15.15–16). God's holiness can be considered as His infinite omnipotence manifesting itself exteriorly in glory: "Deliver us by your wonders, and bring glory to your name, O Lord" (Dn 3.43).

The moral aspect of God's holiness, which He allows man to share, is totally opposed to man's sinfulness. This aspect did not evolve only with the Prophets, even though they strongly stressed it. It preceded them and was applied to God in Gn 6.3, 5–7, as well as in the story of Sodom and Gomorra (Gn 18.16–19.29), which was later used by the Prophets (Is 1.9; Jer 49.18; Am 4.11). In His appearance to Moses, God revealed His holiness as opposed to Moses' sinfulness (Ex 3.5–6); when He made His covenant, He demanded holiness of His "kingdom of priests, a holy nation" (Ex 19.3–7). The Prophets stressed both the moral aspect of God's holiness, and His holiness in the absolute sense. God's holiness demands that man be free from sin and share in God's justice (Is 6.3–7). His holiness is the very reason for the people's holiness (Lv 19.2). God by His holiness is above sin in spite of the infidelities and sins of His own people (Am 2.7). Because of His sanctity Yahweh abhors sin: "For you, O God, delight not in wickedness; . . . You hate evildoers" (Ps 5.5). The justice of the Holy One of Israel is coupled with redemptive mercy and love: "Fear not, O worm Jacob, O maggot Israel; I will help you, says the Lord; your redeemer is the Holy One of Israel" (Is 41.14; 43.3, 14; Hos 11.9).

Holiness of Men. Man's holiness finds its reason and norm in that of God: "Be holy, for I, the Lord, your God, am holy" (Lv 19.2; cf. 11.44; 20.26). Yahweh demands holiness of His people, since they are bound to Him by the Covenant. They are to live according to His word, avoiding any contact with pagan idols (Is 52.1). Israel must be holy because Yahweh has made them "a people peculiarly his own" (Dt 7.6).

To safeguard and develop moral holiness, cultic holiness was prescribed. It was the duty of the priest to foster external and material holiness; he was to distinguish the sacred from the profane (Lv 10.10). The priests especially had to be holy. Whoever and whatever was consecrated to God was separate and holy: the NAZIRITES by their vows (Nm 6.1–21); places, like the heavens, God's abode; the Meeting Tent (Ex 28.43), especially the Holy of Holies (Ex 26.33); certain times, such as the Sabbath (Gn 2.3) and feasts (Ex 12.16; Lv 23.4; etc.).

Holiness in the New Testament. In the NT the ritual or cultic aspect of holiness disappears; what is left is type and figure (Heb 8.5). The emphasis is on the personal, moral aspect of holiness; material objects still have their role, especially in the Sacraments, but on a spiritual level. The NT does use, however, the doctrine and vocabulary of the OT. God is the Holy Father (Jn 17.11); His Name (Lk 1.49), His Law (Rom 7.12), and His Covenant (Lk 1.73) are holy. Holy too are His angels (Mk 8.38), His Prophets (Lk 1.70; Mk 6.20); holy is His new temple, the people of God, and the New Jerusalem (1 Cor 3.17; Rv 21.2). His elect are to be holy (1 Pt 1.15–16). The holiness of His Name ought to be manifested in the coming of His Kingdom (Mt 6.9). Pentecost and the manifestation of the "Holy" Spirit brings the specifical holiness of the NT.

Holiness of Christ. Christ's holiness is based on His divine sonship and the presence of the Spirit of God in Him; He is conceived by the Holy Spirit and will be called the Holy One, the Son of God (Lk 1.35; Mt 1.18). At His Baptism the beloved Son is anointed by the Holy Spirit (Acts 10.38; Lk 3.22). Jesus drives out unholy or unclean spirits from men while they proclaim Him "the Holy One of God" (Lk 5.33–35); Christ manifests Himself through His works, miracles, and signs of His holiness.

As the "holy servant" of God (Acts 4.27, 30), who suffered death even though He was the author of life, He is uniquely consecrated and holy. For this reason God has exalted Him (Phil 2.9); "in keeping with the holiness of his spirit," by His Resurrection, He is revealed as God's Son (Rom 1.4). He is not of this world (Jn 17.11). Seated at the right hand of the Father, He is the Holy One, like Yahweh (Rv 3.7). The holiness of Christ is then far beyond that of the holy persons of the OT, and the same as that of His Father. Its manifest effects are the same—

spiritual power and miraculous events. He loves His own and communicates to them the glory He received from the Father by sacrificing Himself for them: "They are not of the world, even as I am not of the world. Sanctify them in the truth. . . . And for them I sanctify myself, that they also may be sanctified in truth . . . Father, I will that where I am they also whom thou hast given me may be with me; in order that they may behold my glory, which thou hast given me, because thou hast loved me before the creation of the world" (Jn 17.16–19, 24).

The Holy Spirit. The term "holy" is used of God primarily because it is His specific function to make the Christian "holy" as He made Christ holy in His conception and His baptism. As the unique possession of the Christian community (Acts 2.4; 4.31), He sanctifies the faithful (Rom 15.16; 2 Thes 2.13); He makes them one in His Spirit's holiness and unity (Eph 3.16; 4.3–4). His presence is permanent, making Christians "temples of the Holy Spirit," "temples of God" (1 Cor 6.11, 19–20; 3.16–17); "For whoever are led by the Spirit of God, they are the sons of God" (Rom 8.14); "And because you are sons, God has sent the Spirit of His Son into our hearts, crying 'Abba, Father'" (Gal 4.7).

Holiness of Christians. Christians are the new people of God, the worshipping community of the new covenant, the new creation, newly born of water and the Holy Spirit, with a new heart, no longer encumbered with detailed external ritual but worshipping in spirit and truth. They are a "chosen race, a royal priesthood, a holy nation, a purchased people" (1 Pt 2.9). No longer limited by nationality, the holy people are united through the ministry of Christ (Rom 15.7–12), sanctified in Him (1 Cor 1.2), and in fact, "saints" by vocation (1 Rom 1.7; 15.25). To be holy means to be separated from the world of sin, darkness, and the devil by faith in the Lord Jesus (Acts 26.18), to be "God's chosen ones, holy and beloved" (Col 3.12), and to inherit the riches of His glory (Eph 1.18).

Upon reception into the new community, personal holiness comes with the forgiveness of sins (1 Cor 6.11) and reconciliation with the Holy One (Rom 5.5–11; 2 Cor 5.18) by means of faith (Rom 3.21–31) and Baptism (Eph 5.25–27). Thus the Christian partakes of Christ's own holy life, His Passion, Death, and Resurrection: "Do you not know that all who have been baptized into Christ Jesus, have been baptized into his death? . . . just as Christ has risen from the dead through the glory of the Father, so we also may walk in newness of life" (Rom 6.3–4). It follows that the Christian must die to sin and live to God in Christ Jesus (Rom 6.11).

Through the Holy Spirit, who is given, the Christian participates in true divine holiness. As a member of the "holy people" and the royal priesthood, a membership making him a temple of God and the Holy Spirit, he renders God true cult in offering himself with Christ a "holy sacrifice": "I exhort you . . . to present your bodies as a sacrifice, living, holy, pleasing to God—your spiritual service" (Rom 12.1; cf. 15.16; Phil 2.17).

The NT, with its special emphasis on personal purity, has a more spiritual and moral character than OT holiness. In the SERMON on the Mount Jesus proclaims: "Blessed are the clean of heart, for they shall see God" (Mt 5.8). A pure heart is demanded of Christians (1 Tm 1.5; 2 Tm 2.4). Sanctification is the purification in which Christian life consists: "Having therefore these promises, beloved, let us cleanse ourselves from all defilement of the flesh and of the spirit, perfecting holiness in the fear of God" (2 Cor 7.1).

The vocabulary of holiness indicates the religious quality of the NT concept: ἁγιασμός; is not only the process of becoming holy, but also the state of being holy (Rom 6.19, 22; 1 Thes 4.7; Heb 12.14); ἁγιότης is the state of holiness proper to God that man shares by moral purity [2 Cor 1.12 (variant reading); Heb 12.10]; ἁγιωσύνη is rather the dynamic quality of holiness than a mere state (proper to St. Paul: Rom 1.4; 2 Cor 7.1; 1 Thes 3.13).

Bibliography: *Encyclopedic Dictionary of the Bible,* tr. and adap. by L. HARTMAN (New York 1963) 1012–18. J. MUILENBURG, *The Interpreters' Dictionary of the Bible,* ed. G. A. BUTTRICK (Nashville, Tenn. 1962) 2:616–625. J. HASTINGS and J. A. SELBIA, eds. *Dictionary of the Bible* (New York 1963) 387–388. X. LÉON-DUFOUR et al., *Vocabulaire de théologie biblique* (Paris 1962) 981–987.

[J. LACHOWSKI]

HOLINESS (PAPAL TITLE)

Although only God is holy in the full sense (cf. Mt 19.17), those whom God sanctifies or through whom He mediates Christ's salvation are derivatively called holy. Thus the HOLINESS OF THE CHURCH refers as much to its function of mediating holiness as to its condition of being holy. As the title holy see, though at first used of sees founded by the Apostles, was later restricted to Rome as the see of Peter, so too the title "His Holiness" has become restricted in Catholic practice to the pope. The use of this title has no bearing on the personal sanctity of the pope.

[B. FORSHAW]

HOLINESS, LAW OF

The body of legislation comprising ch. 17 to 26 of the Book of LEVITICUS was named the Law of Holiness

(*Heiligkeitsgesetz*) by A. Klostermann in 1877. Though it is rooted in Israelite priestly circles and manifests many traits of the *Priestercodex* (*see* PRIESTLY WRITERS, PENTATEUCHAL), the Law of Holiness has its own distinctive features setting it off from the rest of the Book of Leviticus. The division, the characteristic, and the laws of the Holiness Code are considered in this article.

Division. Like the Covenant (Ex 20.22–23.19) and Deuteronomic (Dt 12–26) Codes, the Code of Holiness has an initial section on sacrifice (Lv 17) and an exhortatory conclusion (26). Regulations regarding moral (18–20) and ritual (21) sanctity, especially as related to sacrifice (22) and festival observance (23), are followed by additional rubrical and moral considerations (24) and by a treatment of the holy years and their social ramifications (25).

Characteristic of the Law of Holiness. The code's most singular characteristic is its stress on holiness. In its original sense of separation or detachment, holiness is proper first to Yahweh, the One utterly transcendent or "wholly other," set apart from the world of men [*see* HOLINESS (IN THE BIBLE)]. His sacred character is to be respected (22.32) and imitated (20.7, 26; 21.6) by His chosen people. In the exodus from Egypt, Yahweh has separated (sanctified) the Israelites and He always remains the cause of whatever holiness they possess (20.8; 21.15; 22.33). Their election requires that they be completely divorced from the profane or unseemly by the preservation of ritual cleanness and moral rectitude. In this way Israel is to mirror the "otherness" of the Lord.

Laws. Many of the laws in the Holiness Code are of ancient vintage, existing originally in separate form or in small collections as decisions of priests who were attached to one or more sanctuaries. These were preserved and eventually edited by members of the Jerusalem clergy at a date best identified with the final years of the monarchy.

Because of the variety of its laws, the contents of the code do not lend themselves to summarization. The laws in ch. 17, motivated by respect for blood and the desire to eliminate or forestall idolatrous practice, require that all animal slaughter, properly sacrificial or not, be done in the temple area.

The moral laws and sanctions of ch. 18–20 protect the sacredness of the lifegiving act by forbidding sexual commerce within determined degrees of consanguinity and affinity, as well as other forms of promiscuity. The miscellaneous laws in ch. 19 concern worship, justice, chastity, and charity. The mainly ritual content of ch. 21–22 prohibits uncleanness among the priests, lists the norms by which their wives are chosen, excludes from priestly functions those with physical defects, restricts participation in the sacrificial meal, and specifies unacceptable animal offerings.

In its original pre-Exilic form, the liturgical calendar of ch. 23 lists only the three great pilgrimage feasts: the Feast of the PASSOVER, which was held in connection with the Feast of the Unleavened Bread; the Feast of Weeks; and the Feast of BOOTHS (Tabernacles). The later additions, which perhaps contain some ancient elements, concern: the SABBATH, The Feast of the First Sheaf, the Feast of the New Year, the Day of ATONEMENT (Yom Kippur), and a different ritual for the Feast of Booths.

Ritual and moral directives are found in ch. 24: care of the sanctuary light and showbread, blasphemy and its punishment, and the law of retaliation. The Holy Years are treated in ch. 25 (the SABBATH YEAR occurred every 7th year during which the land lay fallow). The JUBILEE YEAR, which occurred every 50th year, was marked by the repossession of ancestral property, remission of debts, and liberation of slaves, in addition to the regular Sabbatical observance.

The curses and blessings concluding the Code in ch. 26 are strikingly similar to those that terminate the Law of Deuteronomy (Dt 28).

Bibliography: S. R. DRIVER, *An Introduction to the Literature of the Old Testament* (11th ed. rev. and enl. New York 1905; Meridian Book, 1956) 47–59. W. KORNFELD, Studien zum Heiligkeitsgesetz (Vienna 1952).

[R. J. FALEY]

HOLINESS, UNIVERSAL CALL TO

A prominent element in the current resurgence of theological concern for the laity in the Church is the theme of genuine sanctity as meant for everyone. The egalitarian atmosphere of the day was a natural preparation for the emphasis of VATICAN COUNCIL II on the biblical idea of complete holiness to be found in all vocations of life. The doctrine of the universal call is not new in the Church. Early patristic literature commonly assumes that all biblical themes (except radical poverty and dedicated virginity) are meant for all classes of people. However, with the rise of the religious orders many people began to identify the highest reaches of holiness with those persons who renounced property and family for a single-minded pursuit of the kingdom. This popular identification never became part of Catholic teaching, but at the same time the universal call to holiness was not prominent in the ordinary proclamation of the Church in everyday parish life. Yet it was implied in the canonization of lay saints and it was explicit in the liturgical texts. For example, the original Latin text for the feast of St. Teresa of Avila prays that we, all of us, "always be nourished by the food of her heavenly teaching and enkindled by it with the desire for true sanctity," and on the feast of St. John of the Cross the liturgy prays that we may "imitate him always." Likewise the declaration of these saints as universal doctors indicates the universal applicability of their teaching. Nonetheless, the popular preaching in typical parishes hardly emphasized the Church's genuine mind.

Teaching of Vatican Council II. The Council devoted the whole of Chapter 5 in *Lumen gentium* to the universal call to holiness; this same teaching is also found repeatedly and with a rich diversity of expression in other documents. All the disciples are to be holy and give the witness of a holy life (*Lumen gentium* 10, 32, 39). The faithful of every condition are called to that perfect holiness by which the Father is perfect (ibid. 11). They have the obligation, not simply an invitation, to strive for the perfection of their own state in life (ibid. 42; *Unitatis redintegratio* 4), and they are therefore to grow to the mature measure of the fullness of Christ himself (*Sacrosanctum Concilium* 2). The Council presents Jesus as the author and consummator of the universal call in his teaching that everyone is to be perfect (Mt 5.48) and in the greatest of all commandments addressed to all men, a total love for God with entire heart, soul and mind (Lk 10.27). All the faithful are to practice the spirit of evangelical poverty and therefore to achieve a detachment from this world and its riches (*Lumen gentium* 42). They are to come to the aid of the poor not only from their superfluities but also from their needed resources, a radical doctrine indeed (*Gaudium et spes* 69, 88). The Decree on the Laity states that they are consecrated as holy people both to offer spiritual sacrifices in everything and also to witness to Christ throughout the world (*Apostolicam actuositatem* 3). They too are to progress in holiness through a generous dedication to spreading the kingdom, through meditation on the word of God and through the other spiritual aids available in the Church (ibid. 4; *Dei Verbum* 25). They are likewise to carry the cross and live the spirit of the beatitudes (*Apostolicam actuositatem* 4).

This universal call is implied in another conciliar theme, namely, that the Church herself is filled with holiness because she has Christ. He fills the whole body of the Church with the riches of his glory, and so she receives her "full growth in God" (Col 2.19). Because in Jesus resides the fullness of divinity, each of us is to attain our fulfillment in him, not just a partial perfection (Col 2.9). The Ephesians are to be filled with "the utter fullness of God" (Eph 3.19; *Lumen gentium* 7). Even here on earth the members of the Church are to experience divine mysteries, "the things that are above." (Ps

34.8; 1 Pt 1.8; 2.3; *Lumen gentium* 6; *Sacrosanctum Concilium* 10).

Conciliar teaching also points to a striking, specific theme: each vocation is to be the locus of profound intimacy with God, for the Council assumes mystical prayer to be found in all classes in the Church as a normal development of the grace life. The modern layperson must be concerned with developing the life of contemplation (*Gaudium et spes* 56, 59); the new creation and genuine holiness are to be found in the laity (*Ad gentes* 21). The first and most important obligation of lay people is to live a profoundly Christian life (ibid. 36). They as well as all others in the Church pray continually (*Sacrosanctum Concilium* 12), burn with love during the liturgical celebrations, and taste fully the paschal mysteries (ibid. 10). Active religious no less than the cloistered are assumed to be "thoroughly enriched with mystical treasures" (*Ad gentes* 18), while all priests are to "abound in contemplation" (*Lumen gentium* 41). Though all priests and laity can and must seek perfection, yet the former are bound to acquire that perfection under the new title of their configuration to Christ in the Sacrament of Ordination and in their sacred ministry (*Presbyterorum ordinis* 12). Seminarians are to learn to live in intimate familiarity with the indwelling Trinity (*Optatam totius* 8) and the entirety of seminary life is to be penetrated with prayerful silence as a preparation for the kind of life priests themselves are to live (ibid. 11). The Council again speaks of mystical experience for all in the Church when it describes all the faithful as growing in understanding divine realities through their contemplation and study and experience of them (*Dei Verbum* 8). No ecumenical council of the past approaches this last one in the frequency of mention and the strength of what it says about contemplation and mysticism in the Church's life.

Nature of This Holiness. The universal call does not bear simply on a moral rectitude. According to Scripture it is a transformation, a deification, a revolution, an exchange, a losing of one's old self to find a new self. It is a being filled with a divine knowledge, love, joy, peace that surpasses understanding (Phil 4.4,7; 1 Pt 1.8). It is a new creation which eye has not seen nor ear heard, nor the heart imagined (1 Cor 2.9). It is an "utter and blissful perfection" to which men come freely (*Gaudium et spes* 17). It is one and the same holiness in all persons, even though there are differing degrees of it and vocational paths which lead to it (*Lumen gentium* 41).

By definition holiness is not mediocrity. To speak of the universal call to holiness is to speak of a universal call to saintliness. It is a call to what traditionally has been described as heroic virtue. That man or woman is holy who lives the theological virtues (faith, hope, love) and the moral virtues (humility, fortitude, chastity, justice, patience and the others) to an eminent degree not attainable by human resources alone. The canonized saints are exemplars of this heroic goodness. Their lives are replete with illustrations of the joyous fullness with which men are to live. When the Church canonizes men and women and when she celebrates them in the liturgy and calls for the imitation of their goodness, she is reiterating the universal call to holiness. What this universal call means in the concrete can also be seen in the mystic's description of the transformation that occurs in the person who has grown to the highest development of prayerful contemplation. St. John of the Cross describes traits of this growth: one loves God in everything; his excessive impulses disappear; his emotions are peaceful and he loses useless desires; he enjoys an undisturbable peace and a habitual joy in the divine presence; his actions are "bathed in love" and are done with an amazing strength; his union with God is as the union of a candle flame with the sun.

Implications. Both Scripture and Vatican Council II make it clear that there is only one way to complete holiness, a way to which all men and women are invited. It is a way that has active and passive elements, ascetical and mystical developments. However, both Scripture and Vatican II (as well as the Council of Trent) do teach that there are different vocational paths leading to the one holiness and that those paths differ in effectiveness. Virginity consecrated to Christ more easily enables one to give the Lord undivided attention, to pursue the radical demands of the kingdom (1 Cor 7.32–35; Lk 18.29–30; *Optatam totius* 10). The Church does not say that a given religious is superior in holiness to a given married person, but she does say that the radical surrender of all that the world yearns for is a privileged, superior way of life because it bestows an immense freedom from impediments to achieving the "one thing necessary."

The holiness to which all are called is ecclesial and objective, not simply individual and subjective. The universal call includes the objective call and obligation to enter and remain in the Catholic Church which Christ has made necessary for salvation (*Lumen gentium* 14). It is true that the Holy Spirit does operate with his sanctifying power outside the boundaries of the Church (ibid. 15) and that he can lead to holiness those in good faith. Yet in objective fact one may not try to separate adherence to Christ from adherence to his Church: "he who hears you, hears me; he who rejects you, rejects me" (Lk 10:16).

The diverse spiritualities in the Church (religious—and its kinds—married, priestly, charismatic, etc.) include all elements of evangelical holiness; they are characterized by differing emphases and life styles, but all lead to the one holiness.

Bibliography: Paul VI, *Osservatore Romano,* Eng. ed., July 17, 1975, 1; Oct. 16, 1975, 10. K. TRUHLAR, J. SPLETT and K. HEMMERLE, *Encyclopedia of Theology* 635–641. T. DUBAY, *Authenticity* (Denville, N.J. 1977).

[T. DUBAY]

HOLINESS CHURCHES

The holiness spirit in Protestantism stems from the teaching of John WESLEY, who believed there were two stages in the process of justification: freedom from sin and sanctification or the second blessing. With the decline of strictly Wesleyan principles among American METHODISTS, groups of perfectionists were organized to preserve and foster the idea of holiness as an essential part of the Methodist tradition. About 30 denominations in the U.S. qualify as Holiness bodies, even though the term does not appear in their official names.

One of the earliest Holiness groups was founded in 1860 as the Free Methodist Church of North America. The largest Holiness body in America is the CHURCH OF THE NAZARENE, established in 1908 by a merger of the PENTECOSTAL, Nazarene, and Holiness Churches. In 1919 the word "Pentecostal" was dropped from the name to disclaim any connection with the more radical forms of the movement. Moreover, none of six affiliated colleges and one seminary retained "Holiness" in its title although the basic emphasis on perfectionism did not change. A typically conservative group is the PILGRIM HOLINESS CHURCH, organized in 1897 to restore primitive Wesleyan doctrine on "apostolic practices, methods, power and success."

The pattern of Holiness theology is fundamentalist, which entails acceptance of Christ's divinity, the virgin birth, substitutionary atonement through Christ's death, and final resurrection from the dead. More specifically, Holiness Churches may be characterized by five main features, which, taken collectively, identify this form of modern Protestantism. 1. Besides justification, which is a sense of security that past sins are forgiven, there is a "second blessing" in which the faithful Christian feels himself close to God. 2. There is an emotional experience produced in the heart by a direct action of the Holy Spirit. Although instantaneous, the "second blessing" may require years of preparation. It may be lost and regained and may be increased in efficacy, but there is no mistaking the presence of the Spirit when He comes. More extreme sects identify the Spirit's coming with the infusion of extraordinary gifts, such as speaking with tongues or sudden healing. The milder Holiness churches recognize the Spirit by an exalted feeling, inner impression, bodily emotion, and a deepened sense of awareness of God's loving kindness. 3. As a group, Holiness bodies depreciate the teachings and practices of the larger denominations for having abandoned the true faith and for compromising with modernism. Their theology is literally biblical. 4. The favorite method of preaching is the popular revival, always for making converts; and often REVIVALISM is the essence of a Holiness denomination. 5. Most Holiness churches profess, without always stressing, the early Second Coming of Christ, which is to inaugurate a millennium of earthly peace and happiness before the last day.

The Holiness movement in the U.S. is a fluctuating phenomenon. After the Civil War and until the early 20th century, perfectionist churches came into existence in the westward drive of the Methodist circuit riders. Since then the emphasis has changed. Instead of perfectionism, it is now pentecostalism that holds sway. In the same basic tradition, the latest development shows a reaction against the cold formalism and bureaucracy of established churches, in favor of a more spontaneous (if extreme) religious experience.

Bibliography: J. B. CHAPMAN, *The Nazarene Primer* (Kansas City, Mo. 1955). C. T. CORBETT, *Our Pioneer Nazarenes* (Kansas City, Mo. 1958). J. L. PETERS, *Christian Perfection and American Methodism* (Nashville 1956). T. L. SMITH, *Called unto Holiness* (Kansas City, Mo. 1962); *Revivalism and Social Reform in Mid-Nineteenth-Century America* (Nashville 1957).

[J. A. HARDON]

HOLINESS OF GOD

Biblical Basis. In the Old Testament God identifies himself as "the Holy One" (Is 40:25; Jer 50:29). As holy God transcends the world contaminated by sin, and yet the places where he reveals himself become holy places, and thus the place where God appeared to Moses in the burning bush is designated "holy ground" (Ex 3:5). To experience God, as did Isaiah, is to experience above all his holiness and one's own sinfulness, for the eternal angelic hymn that resounds eternally is "Holy, holy, holy is the Lord God of host." (Is 6:3, Rev 4:8). The innermost sanctuary where the Holy God abides, hidden by a curtain that separates him from humankind contaminated by sin and so not holy, is designated the Holy of Holies. As holy God cannot sin (1 Sm 2:2; Jb 4:17; 25:5). Rather he has an absolute hatred for sin (Ps 5:5; 44/45:8). He takes vengeance on crime (Ez 28:22; 38:22); He makes his righteousness appear among the enemies of Israel (Jgs 4:15; 7.22; Ps 82/83.10–12). Positively, the Old Testament reveals God's holiness as the reason and norm for man's holiness (Lv 11:44; 19:2; 20:26), and God demands it of men (Jos 24:19; Dt 7:6; Is 63:18; Jer 2:3). God makes a covenant with his people precisely to make them like himself, holy. "You shall be holy to me; for I the Lord am holy, and have separated you from the peoples, that you should be mine" (Lv 20:26). God "will vindicate his holiness" by cleansing his people of their sin and by placing within them his very own Spirit" (Ez 36:22–36). In contrast to the god of Platonic and Aristotelian philosophy, whose transcendence protects him from being contaminated by the world of evil and material change, God in the Old Testament reveals that he comes in contact with humankind so as to make it holy. This is most dramatically seen within the Incarnation. The holy Son of God assumes (touches) sinful human flesh so as to purge it of sin and so make it holy. From all eternity the Father chose us in Christ "to be holy and blameless before him," that is, to be holy sons as his Son is holy (Eph 1:3–5). The first gift of salvation, won through the cross, is the Holy Spirit by whom all who believe and are baptized are conformed into the likeness of Christ and so made holy children of the Father (Rom 8:14–17, Gal 4:4–7). Christians are holy because they are consecrated to God and so participate in divine holiness (Rom 1:7; 1 Cor 1:2; 2 Cor 1:1; 2 Pt 2:21; 1 Jn 3:1–3). Their very own bodies are the new temples of God where the Holy Spirit abides (1 Cor 3:16–17; 6:19). Thus they are newly called to be holy because God is holy (1 Pt 1:15–16; 2:9; Rev 4:8; 15:4).

Christian Tradition. The holiness of God is defined both positively and negatively. Negatively, it specifies that God in himself is devoid of all evil both in thought and action. Sin and evil are completely absent from God and it is completely impossible for him to turn away from his own perfect goodness. Nor can anything deprive God of his holiness for nothing can deprive him of his infinite perfection. God hates what is evil and sinful for such are completely contrary and opposed to his holiness. Positively, God's holiness entails his complete perfection, especially that of his goodness and love. God is goodness itself and the very nature of God is to love the goodness that he is as well as the good that resides in what he creates and recreates through grace. Because God's very nature is be eternally all-perfect and unchangeable in his goodness and love, he is substantially or ontologically holy. The human response to such holiness does not reside primarily in knowing it, but in prostrating oneself in awe, reverence, praise, and holy fear before the all-holy God. As all-holy, God is the exemplar of holiness and only he can make holy (Mt 5:48). "He who called you is holy, be holy yourselves in all your conduct; since it is written, 'You shall be holy for I am holy'" (1 Pt 1:15–16; Lv 11:44–45).

The Christian tradition has also consistently interpreted the angelic hymn in Isaiah 6:3 and Revelation 4:8

as referring to the three divine persons of the Father, the Son, and the Holy Spirit (Athanasius, *The Incarnation of the Word of God and Against the Arians*, 10; Augustine, *Letter* 55.29). This tradition finds its expression within the *Sanctus* at Mass. God, as an eternal trinity of co-equal persons, is thrice holy and therefore perfect in holiness.

See Also: HOLINESS; HOLINESS (IN THE BIBLE); INEFFABILITY OF GOD; JUSTICE OF GOD; SACRED AND PROFANE; GOD, ARTICLES ON.

Bibliography: D. P. WRIGHT, "Holiness (OT)," *The Anchor Bible Dictionary*, v.3, ed. D. N. FREEDMAN (New York 1992) 237–49. R. HODGSON, JR., "Holiness (NT)," *The Anchor Bible Dictionary,* v.3, 249–54. R. OTTO, *The Idea of the Holy* (Oxford 1950). D. NICHOLL, *Holiness* (London 1996). P. SHELDRAKE, *Images of Holiness: Explorations in Contemporary Spirituality* (London 1987).

[T. G. WEINANDY]

HOLINESS OF THE CHURCH

Among the marks of the Church the oldest ascribed to it is holiness. In the Apostles Creed, whose origin is rooted in the 1st or 2nd century after Christ, is found: "I believe in the Holy Ghost, the holy catholic church, the communion of saints . . . ." Actually, Scripture gives the basis for this designation, for in the New Testament the Greek word for Church—ἐκκλησία—signifies the assembly of God. It refers to the calling out or selecting by God of His holy ones (Rom 1.7; Eph 1.4). These are to be erected by God into a holy living temple, His Church (Eph 2.19–21; *see* CHURCH, ARTICLES ON).

Cause of Church's Holiness. Only God is essentially holy (*see* HOLINESS OF GOD). Creatures can only reflect or share His inimitable holiness. The Church is holy precisely because it is the bride of Christ, called into existence by God in order to manifest the divine holiness in an increasing manner in time through the gradual incorporation of all creation within its holy unity. This fundamental statement indicates the four-fold special relationship to God that makes the Church holy. First, in and through Christ the Church has received from the Father the holy mission to sanctify all men (Mt 28.16–20; Mk 16.15–16). Second, in and through the redeeming actions of Christ, God has given the Church its essential structure—hierarchy of persons, doctrine, sacramental rites—and the sanctifying efficacy of its essential activity. Third, the all-holy God dwells within individual members (*see* INDWELLING, DIVINE) and in the Church as a whole (Jn 14.16, 23–24, 26; Mt 28.20; 1 Cor 3.16–17; 6.19–20; Eph 2.19–22). Fourth, the Church is a virgin bride (2 Cor 11.2), worthy of her lord, and living in perfect fidelity (*Lumen gentium* 6, 9). Although individuals fail, the Church itself never fails in the integrity of its faith, hope, and love. Through the gifts in her members she is a spouse adorned for her husband (Rv 21.2; *Perfectae caritatis* 1).

Temporal Realization of the Church's Holiness. In the present age the Church can be said to be holy in two senses. First, the Church is the aggregate of things and persons constituted by God in Christ as the great visible sign through which the divine holiness is imparted to men. God has so wedded Himself to the essential structure and activity of the Church that through them He continuously sanctifies the world. Thus, the Church is holy because it is the *means* of holiness. It "is spotless in the Sacraments, by which it gives birth to and nourishes its children; in the faith which it has always preserved inviolate; in its sacred laws imposed on all; in the evangelical counsels which it recommends; in those heavenly gifts and extraordinary graces through which, with inexhaustible fecundity, it generates hosts of martyrs, virgins, and confessors" (Pius XII *Mystici Corporis*, par. 65). Thus, the great ecclesial activities are continuously impregnated with the holiness-making power of God. Members become holy by allowing God to sanctify them through these activities.

Second, the Church is holy in that its members actually possess a participation in the divine holiness. "You . . . are a chosen race . . . a holy nation, a purchased people; that you may proclaim the perfections of him who has called you out of darkness into his marvellous light" (1 Pt 2.9). God wills that there be holiness in varying degrees in the members of the Church. He willed that Jesus Christ, as head of the Church, be substantially holy (*see* HYPOSTATIC UNION); He willed that Mary, Blessed Virgin, be the full and totally human realization of the holiness possible in the Church; and He wills that in every age in varying degrees saints shall concretely manifest aspects of that one holiness coming from God in Christ. Though this holiness is essentially internal by GRACE, it is willed by God to be manifested externally; and in every age the great saints supremely manifest this holiness, thus constituting in their persons the apologetic mark of holiness by which the true Church can be recognized. Moreover, not only is the Church holy in its members but also all true holiness that is in the world—even the holiness of those who know not the Church—is ordained to the Church so that outside the Church (or apart from the Church) there is no holiness and no SALVATION (*see* SALVATION, NECESSITY OF THE CHURCH FOR).

Paradoxically the Church is holy and yet needing to be purified and renewed (*Lumen gentium* 8; *Unitatis redintegratio* 6). Failure of the members to live fervently dims the radiance of the Church's image in the world (ibid. 4) and so her sanctity, while real, is imperfect on earth (*Lumen gentium* 48). It is a growing holiness, for the Holy Spirit purifies and renews her ceaselessly (ibid. 3, 5; *Sacrosanctum Concilium* 2; *Gaudium et spes* 21). Yet at the same time the Church is the "spotless spouse of the spotless Lamb" and "indefectibly holy" (*Lumen gentium* 6, 39).

Eternal Fulfillment of Church's Holiness. While time lasts, the holiness of the Church will be imperfectly realized. The Blessed Virgin excepted, all members of the earthly Church resist to some extent the active sanctifying power of God working in the ecclesiastical body. Thus, they are sinners, not because of the Church, but because of their free-willed capacity to resist the sanctifying efficacy of the Church's activity. However, at the end of time the holiness of the Church will reach completion. The visible elements through which God sanctifies men in the temporal Church—the priesthood, Sacraments, teaching authority—will be replaced by the direct sanctification of God in the BEATIFIC VISION. This ultimate realization of the Church's holiness—a social holiness that will encompass every fiber of men's beings and will be reflected even in the renewed material creation (Rom 8.18–21)—is described in imagery in Revelation. The Church triumphant is pictured as the Holy City coming down from God (21.2), as the dwelling place of God with men (21.3), as the new Jerusalem that has no need of a temple because God Himself and His Son constitute the real temple thereof (21.22), as the city from which all evil and evil-doers have been banished (21.8, 27).

See Also: MIRACLE, MORAL (THE CHURCH); MYSTICAL BODY OF CHRIST.

Bibliography: A. MICHEL, *Dictionnaire de théologie catholique*, ed. A. VACANT et al., 15 v. Paris 1903–50; Tables générales 1951 14.1:841–860. F. HOFMANN, *Lexikon für Theologie und Kirche*[2], ed. J. HOFER and K. RAHNER, 10 v. (Freiburg 1957–65) 5:128–129. C. JOURNET, *L'Église du Verbe Incarné*, 2 v. (Bruges 1954–62) 2:893–934; *Théologie de l'Église* (Bruges 1958) 235–263. M. SCHMAUS, *Katholische Dogmatik* (Munich 1953–59) 3.1:630–638. Y. M. J. CONGAR, *The Mystery of the Temple*, tr. R. F. TREVETT (Westminster, Md. 1962). J. JUNGMANN, "The Holy Church," *The Church: Readings in Theology* (New York 1963) 30–39. F. MALMBERG, *Ein Leib - Ein Geist: Vom Mysterium der Kirche*, tr. R. E. TORFS (Freiburg 1960). Y. DE MONTCHEUIL, *Aspects of the Church*, tr. A. J. LAMOTHE (Chicago 1955). O. PROCKSCH, in *Theological Dictionary of the New Testament*, ed. G. KITTEL, tr. and ed. G. W. BROMILEY (Grand Rapids 1964) 1:105–110. K. RAHNER, *Schriften zur Theologie*, 5 v. (Einsiedeln 1954–62) 3:111–126. W. J. BURGHARDT, "A Holy Church," *Way* 3 (1963) 22–31. B. KLOPPENBURG, *Ecclesiology of Vatican II* (Chicago 1974); R. LAWLER, D. WUERL, and T. LAWLER, *The Teaching of Christ* (Huntington, Ind. 1976) 196–200.

[P. F. CHIRICO/T. DUBAY]

HOLLAZ, DAVID

Lutheran theologian and dogmatician; b. Wulkow, near Stargard, Pomerania, 1648?; d. Jakobshagen, Pomerania, April 17, 1713. Hollaz (Hollatz or Hollatius) studied at Erfurt and Wittenberg and held the following ecclesiastical positions: preacher at Putzerlin near Stargard (1670), preacher at Stargard (1681), assistant rector at Stargard (1683), rector at Colberg (1684), and pastor at Jakobshagen (1692–1713). His principal work is his *Examen theologicum acroamaticum* (Rostock and Leipsic 1717), which is considered the last of the great textbooks of the period of Lutheran orthodoxy, despite its considerable modification by growing Pietistic (*see* PIETISM) influences. It is the last of the strict Lutheran attempts at systematizing dogma. Although Hollaz does not mention Pietism as such, it is obvious from his ardent refutation of mysticism that he was aware of its development. The work owes its reputation not to originality but to the clearness of its definitions and the excellence of its arrangements, and to its prevailing devotional spirit. In addition to a collection of sermons, his published works include *Scrutinium veritatis in mysticorum dogmata* (Wittenberg 1711) and *Ein gottgeheiligt dreifaches Kleeblatt,* or *Leidender Jesus* (1713).

Bibliography: J. C. ERDMANN, *Lebensbeschreibungen und litterarische Nachrichten von den wittenbergschen Theologen* (Wittenberg 1804). F. A. G. THOLUCK, *Der Geist der lutherischen Theologen Wittenbergs* (Hamburg 1852). E. WOLF, *Die Religion in Geschichte und Gegenwart*, 7 v. (3d ed. Tübingen 1957–65) 3: 433–434.

[C. J. BERSCHNEIDER]

HOLLIS, (MAURICE) CHRISTOPHER

Writer, editor, politician; b. Axbridge, England, March 2, 1903; d. Mells, Somerset, England, May 6, 1977. His father, Anglican bishop of Taunton, England, had been headmaster of Wells Theological College; his mother was a writer of Anglican histories and stories which continue to command an audience. Hollis went to Eton on scholarship and, while there, won further scholarships to Oxford. As a student at the university (Balliol College), he fell under the influence of Bernard Shaw, and, especially, of Belloc and Chesterton. During his last year at Oxford, at 22, he became a Catholic. He next took part in an extended debating tour as a member of the Oxford Union in company with Douglas Woodruff and Malcolm McDonald, visiting the United States, New Zealand, and Australia. For the ten years following, 1925–35, he was an instructor at Stonyhurst, a Jesuit college in Lancashire.

His first book, *The American Heresy* (1930), about assorted American political figures, belongs to this period, as do his *Thomas More* (1934), *St. Ignatius* (1931), and *The Monstrous Regiment* (1930) on Queen Elizabeth and her times. His next two books marked the economic phase of his miscellaneous interests. *On the Breakdown of Money* (1937) and *The Two Nations* (1935) were effects of the influence on his mind of McNair Wilson, then a correspondent of the *Times*. These led to his "American period," 1935–39, when he was lecturing in economics at the University of Notre Dame. These years also saw the appearance of a series of letters on foreign issues of the day: *Foreigners Aren't Fools; Foreigners Aren't Knaves*; and *We Aren't So Dumb*. The war brought him back to England. After a term as instructor at Downside Abbey School, he entered the Royal Air Force. By a rather unusual arrangement, he worked as an intelligence officer by night, and supervised the Catholic publishing house, Burns & Oates by day. Somehow, at the same time, he wrote his most successful work, *Death of a Gentleman* (1945).

At war's end, Hollis joined with Douglas Jerrold, who had brought Hollis into Burns & Oates, in forming a company, Hollis and Carter, for the publication of books on education. This also was the political phase of his life; he became the Conservative member of parliament for Devizes, held the seat for ten years, and then gave it up, undefeated. As an MP he had played a part in the abolition of capital punishment for murder. In his last years he joined the Liberal Party. From 1936 until his death, he was a director of the London *Tablet* and up to a few weeks before his death, he contributed numerous signed articles and reviews to that publication. Meanwhile he was a regular contributor to the obituary columns of the *London Times*. For years, under Malcolm Muggeridge, he was on the board of *Punch*, writing a parliamentary sketch.

His literary output, mostly Catholic in character, was very extensive. Among his better known works are *Erasmus* (Milwaukee 1933); *Lenin* (Milwaukee 1938); *G.K. Chesterton* (London 1950); *Evelyn Waugh* (London and New York 1954); *The Achievements of Vatican II* (New York 1967); *Newman and the Modern World* (New York 1968); and *The Mind of Chesterton* (Coral Gables, Fla. 1970).

Bibliography: *Tablet* (London), May 14, 1977, 466–467; *Times* (London), May 9, 1977, 16.

[P. F. MULHERN]

HOLLWECK, JOSEF

Canonist; b. Pfaffenhofen (Bavaria), Jan. 16, 1854; d. Eichstätt, March 10, 1926. He was ordained in 1879, and from 1892 until his death he was professor of Canon Law at the episcopal lyceum in Eichstätt. On occasion he also gave courses in homilectics, patrology, catachetics, and Church history. In 1906 he became dean of the cathedral chapter of Eichstätt. He was particularly active as a consultor in the codification of Canon Law. Although the author of a number of historical works, he is noted especially for his works on Canon Law, which include *Die kirchlichen Strajgesetze* (Mainz 1899), *Das kirchliche Bücherverbot* (Mainz 1897), *Das Testament des Geistlichen* (Mainz 1901), and *Lehrbuch des kath. Kirchenrechts* (Mainz 1900; ed. P. Hergenröhter in 1905).

Bibliography: M. RACKL, *Jahrbücher der Bischof philosophischtheologisch Hochschule* (Eichstätt 1926) 6–9. A. BRIDE, *Catholicisme* 5:822–823. J. LEDERER, *Lexikon für Theologie und Kirche*, ed. J. HOFER and K. RAHNER, 10 v. (2d, new ed. Freiburg 1957–65) 5:456.

[E. LEWIS]

HOLOCAUST

The OT sacrifice in which the offering, preferably an unblemished male animal, was wholly burnt on the altar in worship of Yahweh. Due to the notion in postexilic theology that this sacrifice had propitiatory value, laws concerning holocausts dominated cultic legislation of the Pentateuchal priestly writers. The Hebrew term for holocaust, '*ôlâ* (literally, "that which goes up," i.e., in smoke), is regularly translated in the Septuagint (LXX) by the noun ὁλοκαύτωμα (literally "complete burning"); from the related verbal adjective ὁλόκαυστος (completely burnt) the English word holocaust is derived. This sacrifice is referred to also as *kālîl*, "total" sacrifice (Dt 33.10) and '*ôlâ kālîl*, "total burnt-offering" [1 Sm 7.9; Ps 50(51).21]. The prescriptions of the Priestly Code concerning the material and ceremonies of the holocaust are given in Lv 1.3–17, while the duties of the officiating priest are treated in Lv 6.8–13. Acceptable victims for the holocaust had to be unblemished males from the herd or flock (Lv 1.3), although, as a concession, pigeons or doves could be offered by the poor (Lv 5.7; 12.8; 14.22). After the laying on of hands, the victim was slaughtered, cut up, and laid on the altar, and the blood was poured around the altar; the whole victim (except the hide) was then burned up "as a sweet-smelling oblation to the Lord" (Lv 1.13, 17). The Levitical liturgy made extensive use of holocausts, prescribing its offering every morning and evening in the Temple of Jerusalem (Nm 28.3), with additional holocausts on days of the Sabbath (Nm 28.9–10), the Feast of Booths (Lv 23.36), and New Year's Day (Nm 29.2), as well as on special occasions, such as purification after childbirth (Lv 12.6–8), cure of leprosy (Lv 14.10–13), and consecration of the high

Jews captured during the Warsaw ghetto uprising are lead by Waffen SS. for deportation. (National Archives/USHMM Photo Archives)

priest (Lv 8.18). Holocaust is an act principally of homage expressed through total sacrifice to God. An expiatory value beyond that of other sacrifices was later attributed to the holocaust (Lv 1.4). The only NT references to holocaust are citations from the LXX (Mk 12.33; Heb 10.6, 8).

Bibliography: R. DE VAUX, *Ancient Israel, Its Life and Institutions,* tr. J. MCHUGH (New York 1961) 415–417. G. B. GRAY, *Sacrifice in the O.T.* (Oxford 1925). W. O. E. OESTERLEY, *Sacrifices in Ancient Israel* (London 1937).

[J. B. FREUND]

HOLOCAUST (SHOAH)

The Holocaust (*Shoah*, Hebrew for "catastrophe") refers to the carefully planned genocide of the Jewish people by the Nazis, the "Final Solution," from 1933–45. It is the most extreme form of racism the world had known until then. The Holocaust differs from other mass murders and forms of brutality in the motivation of the perpetrators (the destruction of a human group for no other reason than that it was considered subhuman in Nazi racist ideology) and the means used (a long process of extreme dehumanization, culminating in gas chambers and death camps). Only with the total defeat of Germany at the end of World War II (May 1945) did the slaughter come to an end. By that time nearly 6,000,000 Jews were dead, among them more than one million children, and Europe's ancient Jewish communities had vanished forever. The Nuremberg War Crimes Trial, conducted by the Allies after the war, were an attempt to punish the criminals.

The Holocaust can be divided into two periods: from Hitler's rise to power (Jan. 30, 1933) to the outbreak of World War II in Europe (Sept. 1, 1939), during which time the foundations were laid for the eventual destruction of the Jews; and the wartime period.

Using "legal" means, the German government passed a body of legislation that defined a Jew (anyone with three Jewish grandparents), and progressively excluded Jews from civic life. They were deprived of citizenship and all constitutional rights, becoming pariahs. Emigration was still possible in those years, but was made difficult by the severe restrictions imposed by the Nazis and by the reluctance of the free world to take in large numbers of Jews. Adolf Eichmann was the Nazi official in charge of emigration (he was brought to trial by the Israeli government in 1961 and executed).

With the outbreak of war escape became almost impossible. The German government then developed an intricate machinery of destruction, which was constantly ''refined'' by modern technology. The shooting of hundreds of thousands of Jews at the Russian front by the Mobile Killing Units (*Einsatzgruppen*) soon proved too slow and in efficient, and was replaced in 1942 by gas chambers and death camps. The largest of these was Auschwitz-Birkenau. A network of concentration, labor, and death camps covered Nazi-occupied Europe. The destruction was greatest in eastern Europe: in Poland alone 3,000,000 Jews perished.

The Holocaust became one of the dominant events of Jewish consciousness. The savagery and extent of the genocide prompted some Jewish and non-Jewish thinkers alike, led by concentration camp survivor Elie Wiesel, to ask whether it is possible to do theology after the Holocaust. Christian reflection on the Holocaust in the second half of the 20th century focused on two points: the theological meaning of the event and Christian responsibility for its occurrence.

Church Statements. In 1975 the Commission for Religious Relations with Jews, established by Pope Paul VI, published a series of ''guidelines and suggestions'' for implementing Vatican II's Declaration on Non-Christian Religions, *Nostra aetate*. According to the Commission, ''the memory of the persecution and massacre of Jews which took place in Europe just before and during the Second World War'' provided the historical context for the section dealing with Judaism (n. 4) in that document. In 1985 the same Commission issued ''Notes on the correct way to present the Jews and Judaism in preaching and catechesis in the Roman Catholic Church.'' After stating that ''the permanence of Israel (while so many ancient peoples have disappeared without trace) is a historic fact and a sign to be interpreted within God's design,'' the Commission directs that catechesis should ''help in understanding the meaning for the Jews of the extermination during the years 1939–1945'' (n. 25).

In June 1979, Pope John Paul II visited Auschwitz (Oswiecim), the site where millions of Polish Jews perished. He recalled that visit in several public declarations. In an address to the United Nations Assembly, Oct. 2, 1985, he contrasted the U.N. Declaration on Human Rights with the contempt for fundamental rights evident in Auschwitz and similar ''extermination'' camps scattered over the continent of Europe. ''This declaration,'' he said, ''was paid for by millions of our brothers and sisters at the cost of their suffering and sacrifice, brought by

An anti-Semitic campaign poster from Germany in 1933 for the Nazis reads: ''Do you wish to be free? (From Jewish Domination) Then vote the Nationalist Block!'' (©CORBIS)

the brutalization that darkened and made insensitive the human consciences of their oppressors and of those who carried out a real genocide.'' On his visit to Rome's main synagogue in April, 1986, again recalling his visit to Auschwitz, he expressed ''abhorrence for the genocide decreed against the Jewish people during the last war, which led to the holocaust of millions of innocent victims.'' Speaking of the ''terrible reality of the extermination—the unconditional extermination—of your people, and extermination carried out with premeditation'' to Jewish leaders in Warsaw in June of 1987, the pope stated: ''I think that today the people of Israel, perhaps more than ever before, finds itself at the center of the attention of the nations of the world, above all because of this terrible experience, through which you have become a loud warning voice for all humanity. More than any else, it is precisely you who have become this saving warning. I think that in this sense you continue your particular vocation, showing yourselves to be still the heirs of that election to which God is faithful. This is your mission in the contemporary world before the peoples, the nations, all of humanity, the Church. And in this Church all peoples and nations feel united to you in this mission. . . . In your name, the pope, too, lifts up his voice in this warning.''

Park Bench in Berlin, reads "Nicht für Juden (Not for Jews)," 1945. (©Hulton-Deutsch Collection/CORBIS)

Receiving the first ambassador to the Vatican of the newly reunited Germany, the Polish pope raised with him "the tragedy of the Jews. For Christians the heavy burden of guilt for the murder of the Jewish people must be an enduring call to repentance; thereby we can overcome every form of anti-Semitism and establish a new relationship with our kindred nation of the Ancient Covenant." "Guilt," he reminded Christians, "should not oppress and lead to self-agonizing thoughts, but must always be the point of departure for conversion."

The pope's call for universal Christian repentance for the role of Christian teaching in preparing the way for the Shoah, and for the involvement of so many Christians in actually perpetrating it, led in the mid-1990s to a series of statements on the Church and the Shoah by bishop conferences throughout Europe as well as the U.S. These culminated in the 1998 document of the Holy See's Commission, *We Remember: A Reflection on the Shoah*. The document concluded by expressing the Church's "deep

sorrow for the failures of her sons and daughters in every age" and identified this as "an act of repentance (*teshuvah*), since, as members of the Church we are linked with the sins as well as the merits of her children."

During the Jubilee Year, the pope lead a Liturgy of Repentance in which he articulated the Church's sorrow over seven major categories of pervasive Christian sin over the centuries. One was devoted entirely to contrition for sins against the Jews, including, as a statement of the International Theological Commission issued days before the liturgy explained, guilt for the sins of omission and commission by Catholics on all levels of the Church's life during the Holocaust. In March of that year the pope made the first extensive visit by a pope to Israel. He visited Yad VaShem, Israel's memorial to the six million victims of the Holocaust, prayed there and met with a group of survivors which included people from his own home town in Poland. Finally, he went to the Western (or Wailing) Wall, the last remnant of the Jerusalem Temple.

Main entrance to the Auschwitz camp of Auschwitz-Birken, the largest concentration and extermination camp in operation during World War II. The sign overhead translates to ''Work will make you free,'' Auschwitz, Poland. (©Michael St. Maur Sheil/CORBIS)

There, like millions of humble Jews before him, he prayed and placed a prayer of petition to the God of Israel in a crack between the gigantic stones of the wall. The prayer reiterated the pope's prayer for forgiveness from the liturgy of repentance at the Vatican.

A 2001 statement by the U.S. Conference of Catholic Bishops, *Catholic Teaching on the Shoah: Implementing ''We Remember,''* interpreted the Vatican document for American Catholics. The document makes clear the distinction and connectedness between the traditional Christian teaching of contempt and the modern, racial anti-Semitism of pagan Nazi ideology: ''Christian anti-Judaism did lay the groundwork for racial, genocidal anti-Semitism by stigmatizing not only Judaism but Jews themselves for opprobrium and contempt. So the Nazi theories tragically found fertile soil in which to plant the horror of an unprecedented attempt at genocide. One way to put the ''connectedness'' between the Christian teach-

ing of anti-Judaism (leading to anti-Jewishness) and Nazi anti-Semitism is that the former is a ''necessary cause'' to consider in explaining the development and success of the latter in the 20th century, but not a ''sufficient cause.'' To account for the Holocaust, one must acknowledge the historical role of Christian anti-Judaism. But Christian anti-Judaism alone cannot account for the Holocaust. Semi-scientific racial theories and specific historical, ideological, economic, and social realities within Germany must also be taken into account to begin grappling with why Nazism succeeded in mobilizing virtually the entire intellectual and technological apparatus of a modern industrial state to its warped purpose of eliminating from human history God's People, the Jews.''

Bibliography: *Encyclopedia Judaica*, v. 8, ''Holocaust'' (a lengthy article dealing with many major aspects of the Holocaust). N. LEVIN, *The Holocaust* (New York 1974). D. WYMAN, *The Abandonment of the Jews* (New York 1984). Non-Jews who tried to save Jews: C. RITTNER and S. MYERS, *The Courage to Care* (New York

Edith Stein, a Carmelite nun who was killed at Auschwitz after she refused to renounce her Jewish heritage. She was canonized by Pope John Paul II on Oct. 11, 1998. (©Bettmann/CORBIS)

1986). Y. SUHL, *They Fought Back* (New York 1967). E. WIESEL, *Night* (New York 1958). E. FLANNERY, *The Anguish of the Jews,* (rev. ed. Mahwah, N.J. 1985). E. FISHER and L. KLENICKI, eds., *Spiritual Pilgrimage: Pope John Paul II on Jews and Judaism 1979–1995* (New York 1995). J. M. SANCHEZ, *Pius XII and the Holocaust: Understanding the Controversy* (Washington, D.C. 2001). *Yad Vashem* located on the outskirts of Jerusalem, contains extensive archives and a museum, as does the U.S. Holocaust Memorial Museum in Washington, D.C.

[E. FLEISCHNER/E. FISHER/EDS.]

HOLTZMANN, HEINRICH JULIUS

The leading NT scholar of the liberal school of his time in Germany; b. Karlsruhe, June 17, 1832; d. Baden-Baden, Oct. 4, 1910. Holtzmann taught at Heidelberg from 1858 to 1874 and at Strassburg from 1874 to 1904. He was an influential scholar and teacher of unusual versatility and productivity. The most important of his numerous works are *Kanon und Tradition* (Ludwigsburg 1859); *Die synoptischen Evangelien* (Leipzig 1863); *Die Pastoralbriefe* (Leipzig 1880); *Lehrbuch der historisch-kritischen Einleitung in das NT* (Freiburg 1885; 3d ed. 1892); and *Lehrbuch der neutest. Theologie* (Freiburg and Tübingen 1896–97; 2d ed. 1911), his masterpiece. In

the series *Hand-Commentar zum NT,* which he founded and which he edited together with R. A. Lipsius, P. W. Schmiedel, and H. von Soden, he himself wrote *Die synopt. Evangelien* (Freiburg 1889; 3d ed. 1901), *Die Apostelgeschichte* (Freiburg 1891; 3d ed. 1901), and *Die johanneischen Schriften* (Freiburg 1891; 3d ed., ed. W. Bauer 1908). He was also the editor of volumes 12 to 19 of the *Theol. Jahresbericht* (1892–99).

Bibliography: W. BAUER, *Heinrich Julius Holtzmann* (Giessen 1932). W. G. KÜMMEL, *Das Neue Testament: Geschichte der Erforschung seiner Probleme* (Freiburg 1958) 185–191, 239–242. J. J. HERZOG and A. HAUCK, eds., *Realencyklopädie für protestantische Theologie,* 24 v. (3d ed. Leipzig 1896–1913) 23:655–660. A. FAUX, *Dictionnaire de la Bible,* suppl. ed. L. PIROT, et al. (Paris 1928–) 4:112–116.

[J. SCHMID]

HOLTZMANN, WALTHER

Medievalist, historian of the papacy; b. Eberbach-Neckar, Germany, Dec. 31, 1891; d. Bonn, Germany, Nov. 25, 1963. From 1922 to 1924 he was an assistant to Paul KEHR, who greatly influenced him. In 1924–25 Holtzmann was active in the newly revived Prussian Historical Institute in Rome, and then qualified for university lecturing at Berlin in 1926. He was ordinary professor of medieval history at Halle from 1931 to 1936 and at Bonn from 1936 to 1955. From 1953 to 1961 he was director of the German Historical Institute in Rome, which he had revived. Holtzmann's scholarly publications consist of a number of critical editions of sources and a series of research papers, for the most part connected with his source editions, e.g., several reports on discoveries in English archives connected with his research monographs on English history in the Middle Ages, and his important works on the papacy of the high Middle Ages, written to a large extent as byproduct of the continuation of the *Regesta Pontificum Romanorum: Italia pontificia* begun by Kehr.

Bibliography: W. HOLTZMANN, *Papsturkunden in England,* 3 v. (*Abhandlungen der Akademie* NS 25, 3d ser. 14–15, 33; Berlin-Göttingen 1930–52); "Papst-, Kaiser- und Normannenurkunden aus Unteritalien," *Quellen und Forschungen aus italienischen Archiven und Bibliotheken* (Rome 1897–) 35 (1955) 46–85; 36 (1956) 1–85; 42–43 (1963) 56–103; *Beiträge zur Reichs- und Papstgeschichte des hohen Mittelalters: Ausgewählte Aufsätze* (Bonn 1957) 235–238, bibliog. of Holtzmann's works; ed., *Kanonistische Ergänzungen zur Italia pontificia* (Tübingen 1959); *Samnium, Apulia, Lucania* (Berlin 1962) v.9 of P. F. KEHR, *Regesta Pontificum Romanorum. Italia Pontificia,* 8 v. (Berlin 1906–35). P. E. HÜBINGER "Nachruf auf W. H.," *Mitteilungsblatt der Arbeitsgemeinschaft für Forschung des Landes Nordrhein-Westfalen* 18 (1964) 13–21, life of Holtzmann and bibliog. of his last works.

[K. H. SCHWARTE]

HOLWECK, FREDERICK G.

Author, editor; b. Baden, Germany, Dec. 29, 1856; d. St. Louis, Mo., Feb. 15, 1927. After studying at Freiburg and Karlsruhe, Germany, he arrived in the U.S. when he was 20 years old. He entered St. Francis Seminary, Milwaukee, Wis., and was ordained on June 27, 1880. Thereafter, he worked in parishes in the Archdiocese of St. Louis. In 1924, after many years of research, he published the *Biographical Dictionary of the Saints.* The following year he published the *Calendarium liturgicum festorum Dei et Dei Matris,* an enlarged edition of his *Fasti Mariani* (1892). A frequent contributor to periodicals and newspapers, he was editor (1905–25) of the *Pastoral-Blatt,* a review sponsored by the German clergy in St. Louis, and contributing editor (1918–23) of the *St. Louis Catholic Historical Review.* Honored with a doctorate in theology from the University of Freiburg, Germany, Holweck was elevated to the rank of domestic prelate in 1923. On Jan. 6, 1926, Abp. John J. Glennon appointed him vicar-general of St. Louis.

Bibliography: J. ROTHENSTEINER, *History of the Archdiocese of St. Louis* (St. Louis 1928).

[J. J. LEIBRECHT]

HOLY ALLIANCE

A declaration, in the form of a treaty, signed Sept. 26, 1815, by the Orthodox Czar of Russia, the Protestant King of Prussia, and the Catholic Emperor of Austria after the final victory of the Allies over NAPOLEON I. Considered one of the most extraordinary documents in Europe's diplomatic history, it proclaimed the resolution to abide by the Biblical precept that all men are brothers. The sovereigns declared that they would on all occasions lend each other aid and assistance and would act toward their subjects and armies as fathers of families. The Holy Alliance went on to promise that governments and subjects alike would consider themselves as members of the same Christian nation and would admit no other sovereign but "God, our Divine Saviour, Jesus Christ, the Almighty's Word, the Word of life." Inspiration for this compact was once generally credited to Baroness Julie von Krüdener, a pietistic Protestant lady with great influence over ALEXANDER I; but it is now recognized that the Czar had been nurturing for some time the idea of breaking away from the Machiavellian conception of international relations, based upon egotistical interests and power politics. Francis I, Emperor of Austria, and Frederick William III, King of Prussia, to whom the treaty was first proposed, were bewildered by its high-flown mystic tone, but signed it because they did not dare to displease

their friend and ally. Afterward the treaty was countersigned by most European rulers. The Prince Regent of England, however, declined to sign an agreement that could not be submitted for approval to Parliament, where the foreign secretary, Viscount Castlereagh, had called it "a piece of sublime mysticism and nonsense." Pope Pius VII refused to sign because the manifesto considered meaningless any distinction between Catholics, Protestants, and Orthodox. The Holy Alliance had no practical consequence, but the name became widely, if erroneously, used to designate the coalition of Great Powers established by the treaties of Paris (Nov. 25, 1815) in order to preserve peace upon the bases of the Congress of Vienna and the Paris agreement. Revolutionaries and liberals everywhere gave it the sinister connotation of a conspiracy of reactionary powers against freedom-loving peoples. The rise of international organizations in the 20th century led to new historical appraisals, which regarded the Alliance as a first attempt toward a world order governed by principles of Christian justice.

Bibliography: M. BOURQUIN, *Histoire de la Sainte Alliance* (Geneva 1954), the best work. J. H. PIRENNE, *La Sainte-Alliance,* 2 v. (Neuchâtel 1946–49), tries unconvincingly to prove that Alexander I used the Holy Alliance to frustrate British hegemony.

[G. DE BERTIER DE SAUVIGNY]

HOLY CHILD JESUS, SOCIETY OF THE

(SHCJ; Official Catholic Directory #4060); a congregation of women religious bound by simple perpetual vows and devoted to a variety of educational works. The Society of the Holy Child Jesus was founded in Derby, England in 1846 by an American convert, Cornelia Connelly. The motherhouse is in Rome, and the society is comprised of European, American, and African provinces.

Mother Connelly responded to an appeal from Bp. (later Cardinal) Nicholas Wiseman of Oscott, England, to assist in the Catholic revival there by improving Catholic education, especially for girls. She soon developed an educational tradition that utilized the resources of Christian humanism, drew upon the educational theory of the time, and exhibited remarkable flexibility in meeting the needs of the individual and the demands of the age. Mother Connelly adapted the rule of St. Ignatius to her congregation, finding inspiration also in the spiritual teachings of St. Francis de Sales, St. Gertrude, St. Teresa, and St. Francis of Assisi.

Her most effective spiritual instruction lay in the example of her own fidelity to the will of God throughout lifelong suffering, occasioned by the apostasy of her husband (who had become a priest), his alienation of their three children from her and from the Church, and his attempts to interfere in the government of her society. His activities contributed largely to the delay in papal approbation of her rule until 1893, after her death. Despite these obstacles, Mother Connelly was able to expand her apostolate in England and to extend it to the United States in 1862 and to France in 1870. It was in 1923 that the motherhouse of the Society was transferred from England to Rome. The former English Province has become the European Province.

From the time of its American foundation at Towanda, PA, in 1862, and in the Philadelphia area, the society across the United States has opened both private and parochial schools, and now has ministries in parish, hospital, college, and legal settings. In 1967, the American Province established a parish and school ministry in Santiago, Chile, and is present in several similar locations in other countries. The Provincial Offices are located in Drexel Hill, PA.

Beginning in 1930 in Nigeria and in 1947 in Ghana, sisters from the European and American Provinces have founded an ever-growing number of schools, including teacher-training colleges. An African sisterhood, the Handmaids of the Holy Child Jesus, had been established by the society in 1937 and given independent status in 1960. During the 1980s, the former African vicariate became the African Province of the SHCJ.

Following upon Vatican II, and in response to its directives, a special general chapter of the SHCJ was held in 1968. A period of experimentation was begun with a study of the original charism of Cornelia Connelly, and led eventually to revision of the SHCJ Constitutions. Many sisters returned to their Baptismal names, religious habits were modified, superiors, and their councillors became known as leaders and leadership teams. At this time, two censors, who had been appointed by the Congregation of Rites to examine Cornelia Connelly's writings, completed their report. It was in 1992 that she was declared Venerable by Pope John Paul II.

[M. C. MCCARTHY/H. G. MAYER]

HOLY CROSS, ABBEY OF

Former Cistercian monastery on the river Suir, near Thurles, County Tipperary, Ireland. It was founded *c.* 1180 by Domnall Mór O'Brien, king of Thomond, to house a relic of the true cross, said to have been sent by Pope Paschal II to an earlier O'Brien king. Domnall's son, Donnchad Cairbrech O'Brien, was a great benefac-

tor of the growing monastery; King John of England confirmed the previous grants and added to the abbey's privileges. Much of the church was rebuilt in the 15th century. William O'Dwyer was the last abbot, but even after the suppression by King HENRY VIII the site was held in veneration because of the precious relic. Hugh O'NEILL, earl of Tyrone, visited Holy Cross in 1600, as did Hugh Roe O'DONNELL in 1601. Queen Elizabeth I conferred the abbey and its lands on the Butler family of Ormond, under whose powerful protection some monks were able to maintain a precarious connection with the buildings into the 17th century. The Butlers acquired the relic; but when the earl abandoned the Catholic faith, he transferred the relic to a Catholic friend. In 1801, after many vicissitudes, the relic passed to the bishop of Cork, who deposited it in the local Ursuline convent, where it remains. The abbey is now in ruins.

Bibliography: M. HARTRY, *Triumphalia chronologica monasterii Sanctae Crucis in Hibernia,* ed. and tr. D. MURPHY (Dublin 1891). A. THOMPSON et al., "The Cistercian Order in Ireland," *Archaeological Journal* 88 (1931). *Journal of the Royal Society of Antiquaries of Ireland* (Dublin 1849–), refs. in various v. from 1–67. E. CURTIS, ed., *Calendar of Ormond Deeds,* 6 v. (Dublin 1932–43).

[J. RYAN]

HOLY CROSS, CONGREGATION OF

Founded in France in 1837, its members include priests and brothers dedicated to parochial education, social justice, spiritual renewal, and foreign mission work. The congregation has a generalate in Rome, six provinces in the U. S., three in Canada, two in Bangladesh and one in India.

Origin and Development. The Congregation of Holy Cross was founded March 1, 1837, at Le Mans, Sarthe, France, by Basil Anthony MOREAU, who united into one religious institute the Congregation of the Brothers of St. Joseph—founded in 1820 at Ruillé-sur-Loir, Diocese of Le Mans, by Canon Jacques-François Dujarié—and the Auxiliary Priests of Le Mans—which Moreau himself had founded in 1835. The Brothers of St. Joseph had been established to provide primary education for children in rural villages where the French Revolution had practically destroyed the previously existing system for the education of the children of the common people. To counteract the evil influences of the Revolution in the more strictly religious and spiritual order, the Auxiliary Priests had taken as their specific aim assistance of the parish clergy in different dioceses, particularly by preaching parish missions and retreats.

In 1835, Dujarié's ill health led Bp. Jean-Baptiste Bouvier of Le Mans to entrust to Moreau the direction of

Moreau Seminary, dedicated May 13, 1957, Congregation of the Holy Cross, Indiana.

the Brothers of St. Joseph. After first attempting to govern the two communities separately, Moreau united them into one institute. The Brothers of St. Joseph had some time earlier begun to adopt perpetual religious vows, whereas the Auxiliary Priests were still diocesan priests living in community while engaging in joint apostolic activities under the direction of their superior. However, on Aug. 15, 1840, Moreau pronounced his perpetual vows in the presence of Bouvier and was followed by several of his first collaborators, among whom was Edward F. Sorin, CSC, first superior of the congregation in the U. S. and first president of the University of Notre Dame, Ind.

The congregation composed of priests and brothers was granted a papal decree of praise on June 18, 1855, and definitive approval was decreed on May 13, 1857. It had been Moreau's original intention to include in the organization a congregation of religious women that he had founded as the Marianite Sisters of Holy Cross. However,

the sisters were eventually excluded from the approval granted by Rome, and Moreau was instructed to govern them as a separate and autonomous community. They later developed three distinct congregations, in France, the U. S., and Canada. From the beginning the apostolate of the Brothers of Holy Cross, formerly the Brothers of St. Joseph, was confined to education, especially on the primary level, in France. The Priests of Holy Cross, on the other hand, devoted themselves to both teaching and the works of the sacred ministry.

Early in its history, the Congregation of Holy Cross extended its activities outside France, establishing houses in Algeria (1840), the U. S. (1842), Canada (1847), Italy (1850), and India (1853), in addition to scattered temporary foundations in Poland and the French Caribbean possessions. In 2001 foundations existed in Bangladesh, Brazil, Canada, Chile, France, Ghana, Haiti, India, Ireland, Italy, Kenya, Mexico, Peru, Tanzania, and the U.

S., organized into thirteen provinces and seven religious religious districts.

Special Characteristics. According to its pontifically approved constitutions, the Congregation of Holy Cross is a clerical institute of pontifical right, composed of two societies that, while canonically united, remain nevertheless distinct and, within the limits determined by the constitutions, autonomous. The distinction of the two societies within the congregation is established on the provincial and local levels, where each society has its own government and administration. Union between the two societies is maintained by the same general administration, under a priest as superior general, and a general council composed of an equal number of priests and brothers; by the observance of the same constitutions and the use of the same manual of prayers and religious practices; and by the canonical visitation of all the houses of the congregation by the superior general or his delegate.

In the priests' society there are two canonical classes of religious, namely, priests or clerics and brothers. The brothers' society has only one class of religious, engaged either in teaching or in other activities. All the perpetually professed members of the congregation enjoy full active and passive voice in the government of the congregation, irrespective of occupation. The members of each society have a special name: Priests of Holy Cross (earlier called Salvatorists) and Brothers of Holy Cross (formerly known as Josephites). Under the general name of Religious of Holy Cross, all belong to the same religious institute known as the Congregation of Holy Cross or *Congregatio a Sancta Cruce* (CSC). The name of the congregation does not come from the Holy Cross, but from the suburb of Le Mans, called Sainte-Croix (Holy Cross), where Moreau established the first motherhouse of the congregation.

Local houses, provinces, and religious districts are, in principle, autonomous according to the prescriptions contained in the constitutions, i.e., they are composed of members of the two societies of the congregation, and are governed by superiors chosen from among the religious of that society which has jurisdiction. It pertains to the provincial superiors to establish coordination between the activities proper to each society or common to both, and to determine what assistance shall be provided by each society in its respective provinces.

Because of this common direction and pooling of efforts, the members of one society may be employed in the houses or activities of the other society. The priests of the congregation often serve as chaplains in the houses of the brothers, according to ordinances drawn up by the respective provincial superiors regulating the residence, duties, and rights of these chaplains.

Purpose and Constitutions. The congregation has as its general goal the glory of God and the perfection of its individual members through the practice of the simple vows of poverty, chastity and obedience. The nature of the vows is, in general, identical with the traditional significance of the vows in similar congregations.

The special goals of the congregation, as specified in the constitutions, are: to follow Christ, to serve all people, believers and unbelievers alike, and to spread the Gospel and to work for the development of a more just and humane society.

In the first years of the congregation, each society of priests, brothers, and sisters had its own particular constitutions. At the time of papal approval in 1857 there existed only one summary text of constitutions for both priests and brothers. Each society nevertheless retained its own particular capitular rules, which were more detailed than the constitutions and served as a commentary on them. Some years later, the capitular rules were likewise unified into one volume for both societies. The text of both the constitutions and the capitular rules underwent successive modifications over the years. Finally, the general chapter of 1950 undertook a complete revision of the rules and constitutions, synthesizing them into one text henceforth known as the *Constitutions of the Congregation of Holy Cross.*

The constitutions were revised by the general chapter of 1968 to bring them into accord with the Second Vatican Council's call for the renewal of religious life. They were again separated into constitutions, which can be amended only with the approval of the Holy See, and statutes, which can be amended by an absolute majority of the general chapter. The governance of the congregation was decentralized so that the superior general was henceforth elected to a six-year term renewable once. His role became to ''guide and govern,'' and many of his powers were given to the provincial superiors and their councils. After 1968, only a general chapter, not the superior general, could establish and suppress provinces.

The 1974 general chapter established an annual meeting of provincial superiors with the general administration as the Council of the Congregation. The general chapter of 1980 proposed that the office of superior general should not be restricted to priests, but should be open to any member of the congregation professed for at least ten years. This proposal was repeated by the general chapters of 1986, 1992 and 1998, but was not approved by the Holy See. The general chapter of 1986 rewrote the constitutions in an exhortative rather than a canonical style.

Activities. The congregation developed extensively in the U. S. where, in 2001, it had its greatest number of members and apostolic works. Three provinces of priests have headquarters located respectively at Notre Dame, Indiana, Bridgeport, Connecticut, and Austin, Texas; three provinces of brothers have administrative centers at Notre Dame, Indiana, New Rochelle, New York, and Austin, Texas. The Notre Dame province of priests is affiliated with the University of Notre Dame and the University of Portland in Oregon. It also owns Ave Maria Press, which publishes spiritual books and religious educationaal materials, and is engaged in multiple other phases of educational, parochial, social justice, and spiritual renewal in the U. S. The Bridgeport province is affiliated with King's College in Wilkes-Barre, Pennsylvania, and Stonehill College, in North Easton, Massachusetts, in addition to parish and spiritual renewal ministry. The province is also responsible for Holy Cross Family Ministries, founded as the Family Rosary Crusade by Rev. Patrick J. Peyton. The Austin province is engaged in parochial work in Louisiana, Texas, and Mexico.

The Notre Dame brothers' province conducts high schools in two dioceses and Holy Cross College at Notre Dame, Indiana, and directs schools for exceptional and needy boys in the U. S. The brothers' provinces of New Rochelle (four dioceses) and Austin (four dioceses) engage in the same general type of apostolic work; St. Edward's University, Austin, is affiliated with the brothers of that province.

In Canada, the chief houses of the priests' province is the Oratory of St. Joseph in Montreal, made famous by Brother André Besette, CSC, as an international center of devotion and pilgrimage in honor of St. Joseph. The Collège Notre-Dame, Montreal, is under the direction of the Canadian brothers' province. There are also other educational, parochial and missionary activities in other localities throughout the Provinces of Quebec and New Brunswick. The Canadian priests' province directs the Fides publishing house, one of the largest religious publishers in Canada. The English Canadian priests' province is engaged in education, sponsoring schools in Welland and St. Catherine's in Ontario, and in parish work in Nova Scotia, Ontario and Alberta.

Just as in the U. S. and Canada, the congregation carries out a twofold apostolate of education and parish ministry elsewhere in the world. In Bangladesh, the priests' province conducts Notre Dame College in Dhaka and staffs parishes throughout the country. The brothers' province conducts high schools in Dhaka and Chittagong. In India, the priests' province is engaged in education and parish ministry in the North East Territory, while the brothers conduct several schools in southern India.

There is one novitiate in Cascade, Colorado, used by all the provinces in North America. Other novitiates are located in India, Bangladesh, Ghana, Haiti Peru, and Uganda. Houses of studies are maintained in Montreal, Notre Dame, and San Antonio in North America, and in Nairobi, Kenya, Santiago, Chile, Port-au-Prince, Haiti, Dhaka, Bangladesh, and Bangalore, India.

The priests' Notre Dame province in the U. S. is responsible for the district of Chile and, together with the New Rochelle brothers' province, for Uganda, Kenya, and Tanzania. The Canadian priests' Montreal province is responsible for districts in Haiti and Brazil. The Bridgeport priests' province is responsible for the district of Peru. The Canadian brothers' province is responsible for the brothers' district in India. The brothers' province of Austin operates two colleges in Brazil.

Since its foundation, the congregation has furnished to the Church several members who were raised to episcopal rank, including Cardinal John Francis O'Hara, Archbishop of Philadelphia (1951–60). In April 2001 its members numbered 1,686 (986 priests, deacons, and seminarians and 700 brothers), including two archbishops and eight bishops, in 221 houses. Thirty percent of the members in 2001 were serving outside of North America and Europe.

Bibliography: CSC, Official Catholic Directory #0600 brothers, #0610 priests. E. and T. CATTA, *Basil Anthony Moreau,* tr. E. L. HESTON, 2 v. (Milwaukee 1956), lists sources and bibliography. T. CATTA, *Father Dujarié,* tr. E. L. HESTON (Milwaukee 1960), with bibliography. A. J. HOPE, *Notre Dame: One Hundred Years* (Notre Dame, IN 1943). P. ARMSTRONG, *A More Perfect Legacy* (Notre Dame, IN 1995). R. CLANCY, *The Congregation of Holy Cross in East Bengal, 1853–1953* (Washington 1953). M. R. O'CONNELL, *Edward Sorin* (Notre Dame, IN 2001). *Sainte-Croix au Canada* (St. Laurent, QC: 1947). D. SYIEMLIEH, *They Dared to Hope* (Bangalore, India 1998).

[E. L. HESTON/J. CONNELLY]

HOLY CROSS, CONGREGATION OF SISTERS OF THE

(CSC, Official Catholic Directory #1920, 1930); in 1841 Basil Anthony MOREAU founded at Le Mans, France, the MARIANITES OF THE HOLY CROSS, a female counterpart to his community of priests and brothers (*see* HOLY CROSS, CONGREGATION OF). Out of the missions of the sisters in the United States and Canada, the Congregation of Sisters of the Holy Cross emerged.

In 1843 four Marianite Sisters of the Holy Cross left France for the United States to join Father Edward SORIN, whom Moreau had sent to Indiana two years earlier. There, the sisters cared for the domestic service at the college (later University of Notre Dame) that Sorin had founded at South Bend. In addition, they opened their first school at Bertrand, Michigan, six miles north of Notre Dame. Their first pupils included Potawatomi Indians, deaf mutes, orphans, and neighboring children.

Additional sisters, trained by Mother Mary of Seven Dolors Gascoin, arrived from France and soon American girls also joined the community. One of the latter group, Eliza Gillespie, was sent to France for her novitiate. Upon her return to the United States, Mother Angela GILLESPIE greatly improved the congregation's educational program. In 1855 the community moved the convent, novitiate, and school to St. Mary's, Notre Dame, Indiana. Between 1855 and 1882, 45 schools were opened in the United States, and a curriculum of studies was organized and adapted to parochial and private schools.

With the outbreak of the Civil War the sisters responded to the government's call for nurses and were the first to serve on the hospital ship, *Red Rover,* plying the Mississippi, where fighting was heaviest. At the sacrifice of schools, which had to be closed temporarily in Washington, D.C., 80 members of the Holy Cross community staffed eight military hospitals in Illinois, Kentucky, Tennessee, Missouri, and the District of Columbia. This experience in hospital work later expanded into a large network of training schools and hospitals in the United States and clinics in foreign missions.

During the 1860s, communications with the motherhouse in France became increasingly difficult; accordingly, the government of the sisters was transferred from Moreau and the French motherhouse to Sorin and the province of Indiana. The sisters in France obtained papal approbation in 1869; those in the United States continued to live according to the rule given to them by Moreau. In 1882, with the permission of Bp. Joseph Dwenger of Fort Wayne, Indiana, they canonically elected Mother M. Augusta Anderson as superior general. Papal approbation of the U.S. Sisters of the Holy Cross was obtained in 1889.

Through the years, the community has exercised leadership in developing higher education for women. In the earliest curricula of what later became St. Mary's College, Notre Dame, Indiana, modern languages, artists-in-residence, and liberal and fine arts were integral. Following the establishment (1887) of the Catholic University of America, Washington, D.C., one of its early rectors, Bp. Thomas Shahan, organized and conducted summer schools at St. Mary's. In 1874 St. Catherine's, a Holy Cross school in Baltimore, held what was probably the first teacher-training institute for women under Catholic auspices. The establishment in 1944 of the Graduate School of Sacred Theology at St. Mary's, where lay and religious women can earn advanced degrees in sacred doctrine, was the work of Sister M. Madeleva Wolff, with the cooperation of eminent theologians.

When the Holy See assigned the missions in Bengal, India (1852), to the priests of Holy Cross, the sisters likewise became missionaries there. The American congregation has continued this work. In 1934 Rose Bernard Gehring, CSC, responding to episcopal and papal requests, organized a native sisterhood in Pakistan named the Associates of Mary, Queen of the Apostles. In 1947 the sisters opened a mission area in São Paulo, Brazil, where they conduct secondary schools and village mission stations. Graduates of St. Mary's College, Notre Dame, work as lay missionaries with the sisters in both Pakistan and Brazil.

[M. R. DAILY/EDS.]

HOLY CROSS, SISTERS OF MERCY OF THE

(SCSC, Official Catholic Directory #2630); Theodosius FLORENTINI, OFM Cap., founded a congregation in Switzerland in 1844 to give to the poor, the neglected, and the delinquent care and guidance based on Christian principles. The first three sisters undertook the teaching apostolate, and from this group there developed the Teaching Sisters of the Holy Cross of Menzingen, Switzerland. Another congregation developed under the direction of Sister Maria Theresia Scherer who went to Chur, Switzerland, in 1852 to direct a hospital and to open a novitiate. When Florentini established the generalate at Ingenbohl in 1856, Scherer became the first superior general of the Sisters of Mercy of the Holy Cross.

The congregation's first foreign mission, established in Bihar, India, in 1894, has extended its activities to Bengal and Madhya Pradesh. The sisters have assisted in founding two diocesan congregations and have also opened their own novitiate in India. The second mission field, Manchuria, had to be abandoned in 1950, but the missionaries returned to the Orient four years later to work in Taiwan. The community came to the United States in 1912 at the invitation of Bp. Vincent Wehrle of North Dakota, where the sisters opened a hospital in Dickinson. In 1923 Mother Aniceta Regli chose Merrill, Wisconsin, as the U.S. provincialate. In the United States, the sisters are engaged in academic education, hospitals, nursing, pastoral ministries, social outreach, parish ministries, retirement homes, campus ministry, and adult education.

[C. SCHNITZER]

HOLY FAMILY, CONGREGATION OF SISTERS OF THE

(SSF, Official Catholic Directory #1950), an African-American congregation of sisters who work among the poor and underprivileged. The congregation was founded at New Orleans, Louisiana, Nov. 21, 1842, by Henriette De Lisle and Juliette Gaudin, two freeborn black women, under the direction of Étienne Rousselon, vicar-general of the diocese, and with the assistance of Marie Jeanne Aliquot, a French immigrant who remained an auxiliary of the society until her death in 1863. A papal institute, its members take simple vows, engage in works of the apostolate, and follow the Rule of St. Augustine.

Prompted by the wretched condition of old, abandoned slaves and semiorphaned young children, the sisters began their work by caring for the abandoned and by teaching catechism to prepare children for the reception of the Sacraments. The needs were so great, however, that permanent institutions had to be provided. Within the first year of the congregation's existence, the sisters opened a home for the aged and a school, St. Mary's. Other institutions followed: in 1867, St. John Berchman's orphanage for girls; in 1882, St. Mary's boarding academy for girls, a secondary school; and in 1893, Lafon Home for orphan boys. Each of these was a first foundation for Black Catholics in the South. In subsequent years the scope of the sisters' work grew and now includes nursing, teaching, social work, vestment making, and the supplying of altar breads. The apostolic work of the society embraces the poor wherever they are found, but particularly in southern United States and in Central America. The sisters engage in a diversity of ministries, including education, daycare centers, parish administration, pastoral services, nursing, and care for the sick, aged and disabled. The motherhouse is in New Orleans, Louisiana.

[M. B. ADAMS/EDS.]

HOLY FAMILY, SISTERS OF THE

(SHF, Official Catholic Directory #1960), a pontifical congregation founded in 1872 by Elizabeth Armer (Mother M. Dolores) under the direction of Archbishop Joseph S. Alemany of San Francisco, California, to provide religious instruction for children unable to attend Catholic schools. The institute was awarded the papal decree of praise and approval in 1931, and final approbation in 1945. Steady growth prompted the transfer of the novitiate in 1949 to Mission San José, California. The Sisters are engaged in the ministries of education, catechetics, daycare centers, parish ministries, retreats, counseling,

home visitations and care of the developmentally disabled. The generalate is located in Mission San José, California.

Bibliography: D. J. KAVANAGH, *The Holy Family Sisters of San Francisco . . . 1872–1922* (San Francisco 1922). M. TERESITA, "Mother Dolores," *Review for Religious* 15 (September 1956) 238–46.

[M. T. BIHN/EDS.]

HOLY FAMILY, SONS OF THE

A congregation of priests and brothers whose official title is *Congregatio Filiorum Sacrae Familiae* (SF, Official Catholic Directory #0640). It was founded in 1864 by Father José Manyanet (d. 1901) in Tremp, Lerida, Spain, and was granted final approval by the Holy See in 1901. The purpose of the congregation is to promote devotion to the Holy Family and to foster Christian family life. This apostolate is accomplished through the education of youth and the organization of a family movement consisting of instruction in the faith and in the management of the ideal Catholic home. The early development of the congregation was slow and uncertain; political upheavals and persecutions, especially during the Spanish Civil War, brought the society close to extinction. Not until the reconstruction in Spain in the 1940s did the Sons of the Holy Family begin to prosper. Since then they have spread outside Spain and have founded new schools and institutions. By the 1960s they were well established as a teaching society in Spain, Italy, and Argentina.

The Sons of the Holy Family came as missionaries to the United States in 1920 and worked in the Diocese of Santa Fe, New Mexico, among the Spanish-speaking people of the Southwest. The generalate is located in Barcelona, Spain. The United States headquarters is located in Silver Spring, Maryland.

[L. HOFFMAN/EDS.]

HOLY FAMILY MISSIONARIES

Also known as the Congregation of Missionaries of the Holy Family (MSF, Official Catholic Directory #0630); a missionary society of papal right with simple vows, founded in 1895 at Grave, Netherlands, for the special purpose of fostering priestly vocations among the poor or those advanced in years. When the founder, Jean Baptiste BERTHIER (1840–1908), a La Salette missionary, submitted his proposal to Rome, Leo XIII gave his approval on Nov. 14, 1894. French anticlericalism, however, impelled Berthier to go to Holland, where, after obtaining the approbation of the bishop of s'Hertogenbosch, the congregation was established on Sept. 27, 1895, and 12 applicants were received in the dilapidated barracks of the former garrison of Grave. The first three members were ordained in 1905; at Berthier's death, Oct. 16, 1908, there were 25 priests, representing five nationalities.

In 1911 the first five missionaries were sent to Brazil, the same year Rome bestowed the decree of praise on the congregation which had spread to four countries. The war years brought severe losses to the society; 40 members were killed in World War I and more than 150 in World War II. Under the Nazi regime the society's schools were confiscated, requisitioned, or destroyed, and 50 of its Polish members were killed. The generalate is located in Rome. Its first foundation in the United States was made in 1924. Its United States provincialate is in San Antonio, Texas.

Bibliography: P. J. RAMERS, *Bonus Miles Christi Jesus: Johann Baptist Berthier* (Betzdorf 1931). F. NOLTE, *Historische Skizzen der Kongregation der Missionare von der Heiligen Familie,* 5 v. (Betzdorf 1931, Grave 1949–54).

[J. WAHLEN/EDS.]

HOLY FAMILY OF NAZARETH, SISTERS OF THE

The Congregation of the Sisters of the Holy Family of Nazareth (CSFN, Official Catholic Directory #1970) is an international apostolic congregation dedicated to the moral and spiritual renewal of family life that was founded in Rome in 1875 by Blessed Mary of Jesus the Good Shepherd, Frances Siedliska. Responding to the needs of the vast immigrant population in the United States, she arrived in Chicago with 11 sisters in 1885 to launch the first American province. By the time of her death in 1902, Blessed Frances Siedliska had established 29 foundations throughout Europe and the United States. The congregation has four provinces in the United States. Three provinces were formed in 1918: Sacred Heart Province (headquartered in Des Plaines, Ill.), Immaculate Conception Province (headquartered in Philadelphia) and Saint Joseph Province (headquartered in Pittsburgh, Pa.). The fourth province, the Blessed Frances Siedliska Province, headquartered in Grand Prairie, Texas, was established in 1993. The elected superior general governs the international congregation from the Generalate in Rome. Internationally, the congregation operates in Italy, France, Germany, England, Spain, Switzerland, Poland, Belarus, Lithuania, Russia, Ukraine, Israel, Australia, and the Philippines. Pope John Paul II beatified Blessed Frances Siedliska on April 23, 1989. On March 5, 2000, Pope John Paul II also beatified 11 sisters of the congre-

Mother Frances Siedliska, foundress of the Sisters of the Holy Family of Nazareth.

gation, the Martyrs of Nowogródek, who were summarily executed by Nazi soldiers on Aug. 1, 1943.

Bibliography: M. DECHANTAL, *Out of Nazareth: A Centenary of the Sisters of the Holy Family of Nazareth in Service of the Church* (New York 1974).

[L. V. MIKOLAJEK]

HOLY FAMILY OF VILLEFRANCHE SISTERS OF THE

A religious congregation with papal approbation whose motherhouse is in Villefranche, near Rodez, France. The institute was founded in 1816 by St. Émile de RODAT, with the assistance of Abbé Anton Marty, for the education of girls, the care of the sick, and other works of mercy. In addition to the French convents, the sisters have houses and missions in various countries in Europe and Latin America, where they teach in primary and secondary schools, run hospitals and clinics, and engage in nursing.

[A. J. ENNIS/EDS.]

HOLY GHOST FATHERS

(CSSP, Official Catholic Directory #0650); a congregation of priests and lay brothers; they are known also as Spiritans but the official title is the Congregation of the Holy Ghost and of the Immaculate Heart of Mary. Since 1855 the members have bound themselves by simple vows of poverty, chastity, and obedience. The purpose of the congregation, to bring "the Gospel everywhere, to undertake the most humble and laborious works for which it is difficult to find laborers," is fulfilled through teaching, social outreach, mission and evangelization.

Foundation. On the feast of Pentecost, May 27, 1703, Claude Francis Poullart des Places, formerly a lawyer, then a seminarian, founded in Paris a group that became known as the Seminary and the Congregation of the Holy Ghost. His intention was to provide the Church with priests at a time when adequate seminary training was the exception rather than the rule. Two years later he selected the best of his fellow students and shared with them the direction of the Seminary. In 1707 he accepted the first two as members of the new congregation. Although the founder died in 1709 at the age of 30, less than two years after his ordination, and his first two associates also died less than a year later, the organization survived.

Development. In 1734 the congregation obtained its first official approval by the Church and was legally recognized by the French government, a privilege granted to only a few societies of priests. The society became famous for its learning and integrity of doctrine; none of its members in France ever gave adherence to the Jansenists or took the schismatic constitutional oath of the clergy. It began to interest itself in missionary work, at first supplying candidates to the Paris Foreign Mission Society, but soon after also sending them directly to the missions and assuming charge of mission territories. In 1732 its priests made their first recorded entry into the New World missions in the person of Rev. François Frison de la Mothe of the Seminary of Quebec, Canada. Three years later they began to labor among the French settlers and Indians of Acadia, to whom they ministered during the years preceding the deportation of all Acadians from Nova Scotia and adjacent lands. Jean Louis Le Loutre, Father of the Acadians, and Pierre Maillard, Apostle of the Micmac Indians, did notable work among these people.

Both the Seminary and the Congregation of the Holy Ghost almost perished in the persecution resulting from the French Revolution of 1789. Although they were restored in 1805 in accord with the demand of Pius VII, recurrent persecution left them barely able to survive until the year 1848 when (Ven.) François LIBERMANN became superior general and infused both with new life. A Jewish convert, Libermann had established the Congregation of the Holy Heart of Mary in 1841 to bring the faith to Africa. The next year he sent the first group of his priests to work in the vicariate of the two Guineas, which stretched along 5,000 miles of Africa's West coast, and without limits to the interior. It had been entrusted by the Holy See to Bp. Edward Barron, former vicar-general of Philadelphia, PA (1842), but the death of nearly all missionaries soon after caused his withdrawal. Libermann then accepted full responsibility for the entire mission (1845). In the extreme north of the Guineas and in the islands of Mauritius and Reunion, Libermann's priests met missionaries sent by the Holy Ghost Fathers. In 1848, encouraged by the Holy See, the two congregations decided to merge. Giving preference to the older of the two, which alone was officially approved by Church and State, the Holy See suppressed Libermann's society, and its members entered the Congregation of the Holy Ghost. Elected its 11th superior general, Libermann so effectively reorganized the congregation that he is regarded as its second founder.

The congregation spread throughout Europe and the Americas, establishing educational and social works as well as seminaries for the training of priests to staff its missions in Africa, South America, the West Indies, and the islands of the Indian Ocean. As the vicariate of the two Guineas is called the "Mother of All Churches in West Africa," so the prefecture of Zanguebar is considered the "Mother of All Churches in East Africa." Founded in 1860, this mission stretched along 2,000 miles of coast and also without limits to the interior. Although charged with many works not specifically dedicated to Africa, the Spiritans have sent more missionaries to Africa than any other organization. Their most famous missionaries include Abp. Alexandre LE ROY of Gabon, Abp. Prosper Augouard of the Congo, Bp. Joseph Shanahan of Nigeria, Rev. Charles Duparquet of Angola, and Rev. Antoine Horner of East Africa.

U.S. Foundations. In 1783 when the Holy See was negotiating with Benjamin Franklin over the ecclesiastical organization of the states, there was question of entrusting the training of its clergy to the Holy Ghost Fathers. Nothing, however, came of this. It was only in 1794 or 1795 that the first Spiritan, John Moranvillé, landed in Norfolk, Va., a refugee from persecution in Guiana. A few years later be became pastor of St. Patrick's Church in Baltimore, Md. He is credited with being the founder of the first free school in Baltimore, and, together with Bp. John David of Bardstown, the creator of Catholic religious chant in the U.S. Although two other Spiritans joined him a few years later, their stay did not result in a permanent foundation. When the last of them died in 1839, he was not replaced.

The permanent establishment of the Holy Ghost Fathers in the U.S. dates from 1873. The previous year Otto von Bismarck had ordered them expelled from Germany under the pretext of their alleged "affiliation with the Jesuits." When their original plan to open a college in the Diocese of Covington, Ky., had to be abandoned, they accepted Abp. John B. Purcell's invitation to the Archdiocese of Cincinnati, Ohio. Soon after, however, they were forced to leave Ohio because the archbishop imposed conditions that made community life impossible. Under the leadership of Rev. Joseph Strub they then established themselves in Pennsylvania and Arkansas. Following the waves of European immigration, they opened parishes for French, German, Polish, Portuguese, and Spanish-speaking Catholics in Pennsylvania, Rhode Island, Michigan, Arkansas, and California. In addition, they founded missions for Blacks in the South. The Spiritans' most important educational institutions are Duquesne University, begun in 1878 by Strub.

Bibliography: H. J. KOREN, *The Spiritans: A History of the Congregation of the Holy Ghost* (Duquesne Studies, Spiritan Series 1; Pittsburgh 1958); *Knights or Knaves? A History of the Spiritan Missionaries in Acadia and North America 1732–1839* (Duquesne Studies, Spiritan Series 4; Pittsburgh 1962). C. F. POULLART DES PLACES, *Spiritual Writings,* ed. H. J. KOREN (Duquesne Studies, Spiritan Series 3; Pittsburgh 1959).

[H. J. KOREN/EDS.]

HOLY GRAIL, THE

The name of a legendary sacred vessel, variously identified with the chalice of the Eucharist or the dish of the paschal lamb, and the theme of a famous medieval cycle of romance. In the romances the conception of the Grail varies considerably; its nature is often but vaguely indicated, and in the case of Chrétien de Troyes's Perceval poem, it is left wholly unexplained. The meaning of the word has also been variously explained. The generally accepted meaning is that given by the Cistercian chronicler Helinandus (d. *c.* 1230), who *c.* 717 mentions a hermit's vision concerning the vessel used by Our Lord at the Last Supper, and about which the hermit wrote a Latin book called "Gradale." "Now in French," so Helinandus informs us, "*Gradalis* or *Gradale* means a dish [*scutella*], wide and somewhat deep, in which costly viands are wont to be served to the rich successively [*gradatim*], one morsel after another. In popular speech it is also called "*Graalz,*" because it is pleasing [*grata*] and acceptable to him eating therein" (PL 212:814).

The medieval Latin word *gradale* became in Old French *graal, greal,* or *greel,* whence English *grail.* Some scholars derive the word from *cratalis* (*crater,* a mixing bowl). It certainly means a dish; the derivation from *gradatim* or from *grata,* suggested by Helinandus, is fanciful. The explanation of *San greal* as *sang real* (kingly blood) was not current until the later Middle Ages. Other etymologies that have been advanced may be passed over as obsolete.

When the literary tradition concerning the Grail is examined, it is noticeable at the outset that the Grail legend is closely connected with that of Perceval as well as that of King Arthur. Yet all these legends were originally independent. The Perceval story may have a mythical origin, or it may be regarded as the tale of one who, though a simpleton (OF *nicelot*), nevertheless finally achieves great things. In all extant versions, the Perceval legend is a part of the Arthurian legend, and in almost all it is connected with the Grail. Reconstruction of the original Grail legend, accordingly, can be accomplished only by an analytical comparison of all extant versions—a task that has given rise to some of the most difficult problems in literary history.

The great body of the Grail romances developed between 1180 and 1240, and after the 13th century nothing essentially new was added. Most of these romances are in French, but there are versions in German, English, Norwegian, Italian, and Portuguese. These are of very unequal value as sources; some are mere translations or adaptations of French romances. All may be conveniently divided into two classes: those concerned chiefly with the quest of the Grail and with the adventures and personality of the hero of this quest; and those mainly concerned with the history of the sacred vessel itself. These two classes have been styled respectively the Quest and the Early History versions.

QUEST VERSIONS

Of the first class are the *Perceval,* or *Conte del Graal,* of Chrétien de Troyes and his continuators, a vast poetic compilation of some 60,000 verses, composed between 1180 and 1240, and the Middle High German epic poem *Parzival* of Wolfram von Eschenbach, written between 1205 and 1215, and based, according to Wolfram's statement, on the French poem of a certain "Kyot [Guiot] der Provenzâl," which, however, is not extant, if it ever existed. To these may be added the Welsh *Peredur* contained in the collection of tales called the *Mabinogion* (extant in MSS of the 13th century, though the material is certainly older), and the English poem *Sir Perceval,* of the 14th century. In these latter versions only the adventures of Perceval are related, no mention being made of the Grail.

Of the Early History versions, the oldest extant is the metrical *Joseph,* or *Roman de l'estoire dou Graal,* com-

Sir Percival and the Holy Grail, manuscript painting. (©Bettmann/CORBIS)

posed between 1170 and 1212 by Robert de Boron. The MS containing this text follows it with the first 502 verses of an unfinished *Merlin,* and many scholars think that Robert had composed a trilogy of Grail romances, the third being a version of the Quest by Perceval. There is a complete version comprising these three parts (and perhaps derived from Robert's metrical trilogy) in the so-called Didot MS (Paris, Bibliothèque Nationale, n.a.f. 4166) and in a MS in the Biblioteca Estense in Modena.

The most detailed history of the Grail is found in the *Grand Saint Graal,* also called *L'Estoire del Saint Graal,* a bulky French prose romance of the first half of the 13th century, where it says that Christ Himself presented to a pious hermit the book containing this history. This version is followed by a *Merlin* and a *Queste del Saint Graal:* it is well known to English readers because it was adapted almost in its entirety in Malory's *Morte d'Arthur.* The others are the so-called Didot *Perceval,* mentioned above, and the lengthy and rather prolix *Perlesvaus.*

The poem of Chrétien, regarded by many as the oldest known Grail romance, tells of Perceval's visit to the Grail castle, where he sees a *graal,* together with a bleeding lance and a silver plate, borne in by a damsel. The *graal* is a precious vessel set with jewels, and so resplendent as to eclipse the lights of the hall. Mindful of the teaching of his first instructor in knighthood who warned him against excessive speaking, Perceval does not ask the significance of what he sees, and thereby incurs guilt and later reproach.

Undoubtedly Chrétien meant to relate the hero's second visit to the castle when Perceval would have put the question and received the desired information. But the poet did not live to finish his story, and whether the explanation of the *graal* offered by his continuators is what Chrétien had in mind is doubtful. As it is, we are not informed by Chrétien what the *graal* signifies; in his version it has no explicit or even clearly implied religious character. In the Early History versions, however, it is invested with the greatest sanctity: it is the dish from which Christ ate the paschal lamb with his disciples and which passed into the possession of Joseph of Arimathea, to be used by him to gather the Precious Blood from Christ's body on the cross. It becomes identified also with the chalice of the Eucharist. The lance is identified as the one with which Longinus pierced Our Lord's side, and the silver plate becomes the paten covering the chalice. The quest in these versions assumes a most sacred character; the atmosphere of chivalric adventure in Chrétien's poem yields to a militant asceticism that insists not only on the purity of the quester, but also, in some versions (*Queste, Perlesvaus*), on his virginity. In the *Queste* and the *Grand Saint Graal,* moreover, the hero is not Perceval but the

maiden knight, Galaad. Other knights of the Round Table who participate in the quest achieve at best only a partial success.

EARLY HISTORY VERSIONS

In the Early History versions the Grail is intimately connected with the story of Joseph of Arimathea. When he is cast into prison Christ appears to him and gives him the sacred vessel through which he is miraculously sustained for 42 years, until liberated by Vespasian. The Grail is then brought to the West, to Britain, either by Joseph and Josephes, his son (*Grand Saint Graal*), or by Alain, one of his kin (Robert de Boron). Galaad (or Perceval) achieves the quest; after the death of its keeper the Grail vanishes. According to the version of the *Perlesvaus,* Perceval is removed, no one knows whither, by a ship with white sails marked by a red cross. In the Guiot-Wolfram version we meet with a conception of the Grail wholly different from that of the French romances. Wolfram conceives of it as a precious stone, *lapis exillis,* of special purity, possessing miraculous powers conferred upon it by a consecrated Host that a dove brings down from heaven and lays upon it each Good Friday, thus endowing it with the power to feed the whole brotherhood of the Grail. It is guarded in the splendid castle of Munsalvaesche (*mons salvationis or silvaticus?*) by a special order of knights, the Templeisen, chosen by the Host and nourished by its miraculous power.

The relationship of the Grail versions to each other, especially that of Chrétien to those of Robert de Boron and the *Queste,* is a matter of dispute, and their relative chronology is uncertain. But in all these versions the legend appears in an advanced state of development. Its preceding phases, however, are not attested by extant texts and can, therefore, only be the subject of conjecture.

OBSCURE ORIGINS

The origin of the legend is involved in obscurity, and scholars hold various views. An Oriental, a Celtic, and a purely Christian origin have been claimed. But the Oriental parallels, like the sun table of the Ethiopians, the Persian cup of Jamshīd, and the Hindu paradise, Cridavana, are not very convincing, and Wolfram's statement that Guiot's source was an Arabic manuscript of Toledo is open to grave doubt. The theory of a Celtic origin seems better founded. There are undoubtedly Celtic elements in the legend as we have it; the Perceval story is probably, and the Arthurian legend certainly, of Celtic origin, and both these legends are intimately connected with the quest story. Talismans, such as magic lances and food-giving vessels, figure prominently in early Celtic narratives of mythological origin. Some scholars hold that the *Peredur* (in the *Mabinogion*) version, with its simple story of vengeance by means of talismans and its lack of religious significance, would yield the version nearest to the original form of the Perceval legend. Back of the quest story would be some pre-Christian tale of a hero seeking to avenge the injury done to a kinsman. The religious element would then be secondary and would have come into the legend when the old vengeance tale was fused with the legend of Joseph of Arimathea, essentially a legend of the conversion of Britain.

Argument for Christian Origin. Those who maintain the theory of a purely Christian origin regard the religious element in the story as fundamental and trace the leading motifs to Christian ideas and conceptions. The apocryphal *Gospel of Nicodemus,* which was in vogue in the 12th century, particularly in Britain, tells how Joseph in prison was miraculously fed by Christ Himself. Additional traits were furnished by the *Vindicta Salvatoris,* the legendary account of the destruction of Jerusalem. Furthermore, Joseph was confused with the Jewish historian, Flavius JOSEPHUS, whose liberation by Titus is narrated by Suetonius. The food-producing properties of the vessel can be explained, without resorting to Celtic parallels, by the association of the Grail with the Eucharist, which gives spiritual nourishment to the faithful and in many saints' lives is said to have been their sole physical nourishment as well. According to this theory, the purely Christian legend that thus had arisen became the generally accepted version of the evangelization of Britain, and then developed on British soil, in Wales; this accounts for its undeniably Celtic stamp. In the 13th century, the Abbey of GLASTONBURY combined the story of Joseph of Arimathea with its own older version of the evangelization of Britain, and so became a powerful instrument in the propagation of the legend of Joseph's evangelization of England, which was accepted as historical fact for at least two centuries.

The fully developed Grail legend was later on still further connected with other legends, as in Wolfram's poem with that of Lohengrin, the swan knight, and also with that of PRESTER JOHN, the fabled Christian monarch of the East. Here also the story of Klinschor, the magician, was added. After the Renaissance the Grail legend, together with most medieval legends, fell into oblivion, from which it was rescued when the Romantic Movement began at the beginning of the 19th century. The most famous modern versions are Tennyson's ''Holy Grail'' in the *Idylls of the King* (1869), and Wagner's music drama, the festival play *Parsifal,* produced for the first time at Bayreuth in 1882.

Attitude of the Church. It would seem that a legend so distinctively Christian would find favor with the Church, but it did not. Excepting Helinandus, clerical writers do not mention the Grail (although the apocryphal Joseph of Arimathea and other legends were widely adopted), and the Church completely ignored it, for the legend contained elements the Church could not approve. Its sources are in survivals of pagan heathendom and in apocryphal, not canonical, scripture, and the claims of sanctity made for the Grail were refuted by their very extravagance. Moreover, the legend claimed for the Church in Britain an origin well-nigh as illustrious as that of the Church of Rome, and independent of Rome. It was thus calculated to encourage and to foster any separatist tendencies that might exist in Britain. The whole tradition concerning the Grail is of late origin and on many points at variance with historical truth.

Bibliography: Texts. CHRÉTIEN DE TROYES, *Der Percevalroman del Graal,* ed. A. HILKA (1932), v.5 of *Sämtliche Werke,* ed. W. FOERSTER, 5 v. (Halle 1884–1932); *Le Roman de Perceval,* ed. W. J. ROACH (Paris 1956; 2d ed. 1959); *The Story of the Grail,* tr. R. W. LINKER (Chapel Hill 1952). Perceval. *Continuations of the Old French Perceval,* ed. W. J. ROACH (Philadelphia 1949–); *The Didot Perceval according to Manuscripts of Modena and Paris,* ed. W. J. ROACH (Philadelphia 1941); *The Romance of Perceval in Prose: A Translation of the E Manuscript of the Didot Perceval,* tr. D. SKEELS (Seattle 1961). R. DE BORON, *Le Roman de l'estoire dou Grand,* ed. W. A. NITZE (Paris 1927). Perlesvaus. *Le Haut livre du graal,* ed. W. A. NITZE and T. A. JENKINS, 2 v. (Chicago 1932–37); *The High History of the Grail,* tr. S. EVANS (New York 1903). King Arthur. *L'Estoire del Saint Graal and les aventures ou la queste del Saint Graal,* v.1 and 6 of *The Vulgate Version of the Arthurian Romances,* ed. H. O. SOMMER, 8 v. (Washington 1908–16). *La Queste du Saint-Graal,* ed. A. PAUPHILET (Melun 1949). W. VON ESCHENBACH, ''Parzival,'' in v.1 of *Wolfram von Eschenbach,* ed. K. LACHMANN (7th ed. Berlin 1952); *Parzival,* tr. H. M. MUSTARD and C. E. PASSAGE, (pa. New York 1961). T. MALORY, ''The Tale of Sankgreal,'' *Works,* ed. E. VINAVER, 3 v. (Oxford 1947) v.2. ''Peredur,'' in *The Mabinogion,* tr. T. and G. JONES (New York 1949) 183–227. General Studies. R. S. LOOMIS, *The Grail: From Celtic Myth to Christian Symbol* (New York 1963), the best recent study. J. MARX, *La Légende arthurienne et le Graal* (Paris 1951), useful review and critical studies of the Grail texts with outlines of all the principal texts in an appendix. H. H. NEWSTEAD, *Bran the Blessed in Arthurian Romance* (New York 1939), the Welsh prototype of the Grail King in the various versions. Colloques internationaux du Centre National de la Recherche Scientifique 3: *Les Romans du Graal aux XIIe? et XIIIe siècles* (Paris 1956), discusses various aspects and problems of the legend. R. S. LOOMIS, ed., *Arthurian Literature in the Middle Ages* (Oxford 1959) general discussion of the various Grail texts.

[H. C. GARDINER; J. MISRAHI]

HOLY HEART OF MARY, SERVANTS OF THE

(SSCM, Official Catholic Directory #3520), a religious community of women that began in the middle of the 19th century when François Delaplace, a Holy Ghost Father, sought to gather abandoned children from the streets of Paris. In 1860 Jeanne Marie Moysan undertook to share his apostolate by directing an orphanage. After two years' preparation, she and others who followed her made private vows of poverty, chastity, and obedience. From this initial group the congregation gradually developed. The orphanage was only the first step in Delaplace's life work, namely, the founding and directing of a religious congregation that became engaged in various apostolic works in France and elsewhere. The community received final approval from the Holy See in 1932.

In 1889, at the invitation of the VIATORIANS, the sisters came to the United States to serve at St. Viator College, Bourbonnais, Illinois. Charged with the infirmary and supervision of meal preparation, laundry, and linen rooms, the sisters thus participated in the work of the Viatorian Fathers until their college closed in 1938. Members of the congregation are engaged in teaching in elementary and secondary schools, in nursing and nursing education, in parish ministries, and in social work. The general motherhouse is in Montreal, Quebec, Canada. The United States provincialate is in Kankakee, Illinois.

[M. A. DOHENY/EDS.]

HOLY HOUR

An hour of mental or vocal prayer spent in veneration of the sufferings of Jesus, particularly those He endured in Gethsemane, and in worship of the love whereby He was led to institute the Eucharist. If the hour is spent in a church, or a public or semipublic oratory, a plenary indulgence may be gained under the usual conditions. The Holy Hour can be made alone or in company with others. Public Holy Hour is commonly accompanied by exposition of the Blessed Sacrament to add solemnity to the devotion. As a private devotion the preferred hour is from 11 P.M. until midnight on Thursdays, or from 2 P.M. on Thursday until midnight of Friday, but it is a commendable practice at any time.

St. Margaret Mary ALACOQUE has written the story of its origin. In 1674, very probably on the first Friday of July, she wrote ". . . while the Blessed Sacrament was exposed, I felt drawn within myself by an extraordinary recollection of all my senses and powers. Jesus Christ presented Himself to me all resplendent with glory. . . .'Every week between Thursday and Friday, [He said] I will grant you to share in that mortal sadness which I chose to feel in the Garden of Olives. . . . You shall keep me company in the prayer I then offered to my Father. . . .'' Each week thereafter Margaret kept the Holy Hour.

In France the devotion was propagated by a Jesuit priest, Robert Debrosse, who in 1829 formed an association that became the Archconfraternity of the Holy Hour with its center at the Visitation Convent at Paray-le-Monial. In the U.S. a public Holy Hour often terminates a day of recollection or a retreat. Many parishes have one scheduled weekly.

Enriched with indulgences, the exercise is singularly effective for spiritual growth. Sin is presented from God's point of view and in its relation to the agony of Christ; the example of His heroic obedience is considered; the main message of the Sacred Heart is made evident: "Behold this Heart which has so loved men."

Bibliography: F. M. CATHERINET, *Ce qu'il faut savoir pour bien comprendre et bien faire l'Heure Sainte* (Paray-le-Monial 1932). K. RAHNER, *Heilige Stunde und Passionsandacht* (3d ed. Freiburg im Br. 1960).

[F. COSTA]

HOLY INFANT JESUS, SISTERS OF THE

Also known as Ladies Of St. Maur. The Sisters of the Holy Infant Jesus (*Soeurs du Saint Enfant Jésus de Saint-Maur,* HIJ), a congregation with papal approbation (1866), begun near Rouen, France, *c.* 1662 by (Blessed) Nicolas Barré, OMinim, for the education of poor girls. The sisters, who profess simple perpetual vows, are governed by a superior general who resides in Paris. The motherhouse is located on a street formerly called Saint-Maur; hence the title Ladies of St. Maur. Although engaged primarily as teachers in primary, secondary, and technical schools, they are active also in parish and social work, and child care institutions. The sisters are active in Europe and Asia.

[J. LE GRAND/EDS.]

HOLY LANCE

The spear that pierced Christ's side at His crucifixion. According to legend, the spear (*hasta,* ἔγχος) with which a Roman soldier pierced the side of Christ (Jn 19.34) was discovered by St. HELENA, at the time of the finding of the holy CROSS, in the early 4th century.

The presence of such a relic in Jerusalem is attested by numerous writers since the 6th century. When JERUSALEM was captured by the Persians in 614, the lance and other relics remained there, but the lance's point was broken off and given to the Patriarch Nicetas, who brought it to Constantinople, Oct. 28, 614. At some unknown date between 670 and 723 the lance was taken from Jerusalem to Constantinople. Both the shaft of the lance and its point remained at Constantinople after the pillage of the city in the Fourth Crusade, 1204 (*see* LATIN EMPIRE OF CONSTANTINOPLE). In 1241 a relic of the holy lance was sold by the Latin Emperor Baldwin II to LOUIS IX, King of France. Just what this relic was is uncertain. It remained in the Sainte-Chapelle at Paris until the French Revolution, when it was destroyed. The Constantinople lance was at Constantinople until 1492, when Sultan Bayazid II presented it to Pope INNOCENT VIII. It was then brought to Rome, where it still remains.

The holy lance now in the Weltliches Schatzkammer in Vienna is known as the lance of St. Maurice or Constantine's lance. Archeological evidence makes it certain, however, that this lance does not antedate the 8th or 9th century. Its history is attested by documentary evidence since the 10th century. It was used as a symbol of the imperial power, bestowed upon the Holy Roman Emperors at the time of their coronation. Another holy lance, that of Kraków, is apparently a facsimile of the Vienna lance and was presented by the German emperors to the Polish monarchs in the early 11th century.

Another holy lance was discovered at Antioch during the First Crusade by a Provençal peasant, Peter Bartholomew. The Antioch lance was in the possession of RAYMOND IV of Toulouse, until 1101, when it was lost during a battle in Asia Minor. From the early 13th century the Armenians have had a holy lance at Etchmiadzin. Its origin is unknown. It may be significant that this lance appeared in Armenia not long after the Antioch lance was lost, but it is impossible to prove that the two lances are identical.

See Also: RELICS.

Bibliography: BENEDICT XIV, *De servorum Dei beatificatione et beatorum canonizatione*, v.1–7 of *Opera omnia*, 17 v. (new ed. Prato 1839–47) 4:619–620, 625–626, 647–648, 695–697. F. D. DE MÉLY, *Exuviae sacrae constantinopolitanae . . . La sainte Lance . . .* (Paris 1904). S. RUNCIMAN, "The Holy Lance Found at Antioch," *Analecta Bollandiana* 68 (1950) 197–209. P. E. SCHRAMM, *Herrschaftszeichen und Staatssymbolik*, 3 v. (Schriften der Monumenta Germaniae historica 13; Stuttgart 1954–56) v.2. A. BÜHLER, "Die heilige Lanze," *Das Münster* 16 (1963) 85–116.

[J. A. BRUNDAGE]

HOLY NAME, DEVOTION TO THE

The early Christians had a special reverence for the name of Jesus. The Holy Name appears in the earliest manuscripts and monuments under the abbreviated form, IH, which are the first two letters, iota and eta, of the Greek ΙΗΣΟΥΣ. In the 2nd century the final sigma was added, thus making it IHΣ or IHS. This custom became universal by the 6th century. The same abbreviation is found inscribed on many liturgical vestments today.

The Fathers. There is also a high esteem for the Holy Name in the writings of the early Christian Fathers. Following the example of St. PAUL in his Epistle to the Romans, they often concluded their letters and homilies with a doxology in which mention is made of the name of Jesus. Perhaps the earliest example is the *Epistle of St. Clement to the Corinthians.* The *Shepherd of Hermas*, dating from the 2nd century, extols the great power of the Savior's Holy Name: "The Name of the Son of God is great and all-powerful: He it is Who sustains the entire world." St. Justin, in his *Dialogue with Trypho,* declares that while certain people blaspheme the name Jesus, the whole world, Greek and barbarian, offers prayer and thanksgiving to God the Creator in the name of the crucified Jesus. St. PETER CHRYSOLOGUS, who was much respected in a later period of Christianity, attributes miraculous powers to the Holy Name.

The Middle Ages. During the Middle Ages there was a steady growth in the devotion to the sacred humanity of Christ, and one of the chief aspects of this form of piety was the reverence for the name of the Savior. St. Anselm, archbishop of Canterbury from 1093 to 1109, wrote a *Prayer to the name of Jesus,* which became very popular. It is found in many manuscripts, and was included in numerous "books of hours" printed in the 15th and 16th centuries. St. BERNARD OF CLAIRVAUX, one of the greatest figures of the 12th century, devoted his *Fifteenth Sermon on the Canticle of Canticles* to the Holy Name. Commenting on the text: "your name is balm, poured forth," the saint selects three qualities of balm (it illumines, nourishes, and heals) and applies them to the Holy Name. Portions of this sermon form the second lessons of the present Office in honor of the Holy Name. The famous hymn, *Jesu dulcis memoria,* written by an unknown monk toward the end of the 12th century was inspired by St. Bernard and testifies to the effect his preaching had in spreading the devotion. St. FRANCIS OF ASSISI, St. Bonaventure, and the Order of Friars Minor contributed greatly in the extending of the cult. In 1268, St. Louis the King, who was a Franciscan tertiary, sought and obtained from CLEMENT IV an indulgence for anyone reciting the prayer: "Blessed forever be the sweet name of our Saviour, Jesus Christ, and that of the most glorious Virgin Mary, His Mother, Amen." The Second Council of Lyons, convened by GREGORY X in 1274, prescribed in canon 25 that the faithful should incline the head at the mention of the Holy Name, as a mark of reverence. Shortly after the council closed, the same pope addressed a letter to John of Vercelli, Master General of the Dominican Order, urging him to help spread the devotion to the Holy Name. The Dominican general acted at once, and informed all his provincials of the pope's wish and instructed them to take steps in fostering the devotion of the faithful by the preaching and teaching of the Friars. In the words of A. Cabassut, "This authoritative intervention only confirmed a devotion practiced in the order from its beginning."

In the 14th century three principal figures emerge as champions of the devotion. Richard Rolle of Hampole, an English hermit who received his theological training at Oxford and Paris, considered devotion to the Holy Name to be the base of the spiritual life, and the cornerstone of all Christian virtue. The results of his efforts were seen in the piety of the English monasteries. Bl. Henry Suso, the great Dominican mystic, drew the attention of the religious in Germany to the power and greatness of the name of Jesus. While these two men concentrated on the piety in the cloister, Bl. John Columbini of Siena preached the devotion to the masses in Italy. He noted with sadness that "the name of Jesus is dying." He urged his followers to correct this. "May your apostolate be directed to the praise of Jesus Christ, and may His Name never be distant from your hearts and mouths, even when you find yourselves occupied with exterior business."

SS. Bernardine and John Capistran. St. BERNARDINE of Siena, a Franciscan of the 15th century, added new momentum to the devotion. He was perhaps the most celebrated orator in Italy during his lifetime. In 1422, during a course of sermons at Venice, he launched a campaign whose aim was to revivify in the hearts of the faithful a love for, and a devotion to, the name of Jesus. At the conclusion of the sermons, the saint displayed before the throng a tablet bearing the Savior's name in letters of gold. The people responded with enthusiasm to St. Bernardine's theme and method. In their processions the faithful began to carry aloft the tablet bearing the inscription of the Holy Name. This form of adoration, however, met with disapproval in certain quarters and was considered to be nothing short of idolatry. Toward the end of the century, for example, the Dominican, Savonarola, fulminated against those who, treated such tablets as some sort of charm. Because of charges such as this, St. Bernardine, in his own lifetime, was summoned to the Papal Court in 1427 to render an explanation of his doctrine. MARTIN V listened to the saint expose his ideas concerning the cult of the Holy Name, and manifested wholehearted approval at once by requesting him to deliver some sermons in the Eternal City. In order to remove the occasion of any further misunderstanding, the pope ordered that in future processions the tablets bearing the inscription of the Savior's name should also carry an image of the crucifix. Hence today we sometimes see the symbol of the Holy Name and the crucifix together. Papal endorsement added to St. Bernardine's personal prestige

and authority, and consequently to the growing devotion to the Holy Name.

St. JOHN CAPISTRAN, a friend and follower of St. Bernardine of Siena, stressed the devotion in many sermons delivered in Italy, France, and Germany. In 1455 the pope asked St. John to help in the preaching of a crusade against the oncoming Turks. The saint complied at once. One day while celebrating Mass, St. John received the assurance that victory for the Christians was inevitable, and that it would come through the power of the Holy Name and the crucifix. As a result, St. John concentrated all the more on this theme in his preaching. The promised victory became a reality on July 14, 1456.

The work of men such as St. Bernardine and St. John had an unmistakable effect on Christian piety during the 15th century. Many Christians had the name of Jesus inscribed over the doorways of their houses. Letters and official documents frequently began with an invocation to the Holy Name. St. JOAN OF ARC, for example, headed all her letters in this way, and her standard also bore the names of Jesus and Mary. Her dying words were "Jesus, Jesus, Jesus." Fifteenth century Missals contain a votive Mass to the "most sweet name of Jesus." The official liturgy, however, contained no special feast in honor of the Holy Name. Bernardine of Busti, a noted Franciscan preacher, asked Sixtus IV, and later Innocent VIII, to institute a special feast. He composed an Office and sent it along with his request. Although Bernardine's efforts went unrewarded in his lifetime, Clement VII, in 1530, allowed the Order of Friars Minor to celebrate a feast in honor of the Holy Name each year on January 14. In 1721, Germany's Emperor Charles VI prevailed on INNOCENT XIII to extend the celebration of the feast to the universal Church. The time was set at first for the second Sunday after Epiphany. PIUS X moved it to the Sunday between January 1 and Epiphany Sunday, or to January 2, when no Sunday intervenes.

Bibliography: A. CABASSUT, "La Dévotion au Nom de Jésus dans l'Église d'Occident," *La Vie spirituelle* 86 (Paris 1952) 46–69.

[M. KELLEY/EDS.]

HOLY NAME, ICONOGRAPHY OF

In early Greek manuscripts of the New Testament the name of Jesus was written in the abbreviated form IC (IHCOYC). The abbreviation was considered not only a practical device but also a way of conveying the sacred character. In the Latin manuscripts of the 4th century, the Greek letters were retained for the name of Jesus: IHS. St. Bernardino of Siena (1380–1444) was responsible for

Child's stone sarcophagus, 4th century, decorated with two angels supporting a laurel wreath containing a Chi-Rho monogram of the name of Christ.

the devotion to the Holy Name, under the trigram IHS, made popular through his preaching and approved in 1432 by Eugene IV. In 1424 it was painted on the façade of S. Croce, Florence. The trigram on a flaming disc is represented in art as an attribute of St. Bernardino. Joan of Arc had it embroidered on her standard; later it was adopted by the Jesuit order as an abbreviation for *Iesus Hominum Salvator.* In the 17th century, the ceiling fresco "The Triumph of the Name of Jesus," showing the Holy Name adored by saints and angels, was painted in the Gesù Church, Rome, by G. B. Gaulli (Bacciccio).

The Chi-Rho monogram is formed of the first two letters in the Greek name of Christ (XPICTOC). There are many variations of this design, which is often represented with the addition of the first and last letters of the Greek alphabet, alpha (A) and omega (Ω). The monogram was of exceptional importance in early Christian art.

Bibliography: C. H. TURNER, "The *nomina sacra* in Early Latin Christian MSS," in *Miscellanea Francesco Ehrle,* 5 v. (*Studi et Testi* 37–41; 1924) 4:62–74. É. MÂLE, *L'Art religieux de la fin du XVIe siècle, du XVIIe siècle et du XVIIIe siècle* (2d ed. Paris 1951). D. FORSTNER, *Die Welt der Symbole* (Innsbruck 1961) 48–58. P. R. BIASIOTTO, *History of the Development of Devotion to the Holy Name* (St. Bonaventure, N.Y. 1943).

[J. U. MORRIS]

HOLY NAMES OF JESUS AND MARY, SISTERS OF THE

A religious congregation (SNJM, Official Catholic Directory #1990) canonically established at Longueuil, Quebec, Canada (1844), by Bp. Ignatius Bourget of Montreal for the Christian education of children and young girls. The institute was legally incorporated by the Canadian Parliament on March 17, 1845. The decree of praise was issued by Pope Pius IX, Feb. 27, 1863; temporary approval of the constitutions followed on Sept. 4, 1877, and definite approval on June 26, 1901.

The need for recruits for his diocese led Bourget to Marseílles, France, in 1841, where Bp. Charles Eugène de Mazenod offered him the services of his newly established OBLATES OF MARY IMMACULATE. Peter Telmon, OMI, was assigned to the parish of Beloeil, Canada. Two years later Telmon made an unsuccessful appeal for religious teachers to the Sisters of the Holy Names of Jesus and Mary of Marseilles. The idea then developed of establishing a new community. To Eulalie Durocher (1811–49), a young woman of Beloeil, was confided the task of adapting the rule of the Marseilles community to conditions in Canada. Melodie Dufresne and Henriette Cere joined her and for several months they lived as novices under the direction of Francis Allard, OMI. When Bourget decided they were ready for admission to religious profession and for the canonical erection of the institute, the double ceremony took place on Dec. 8, 1844. The bishop then organized the first government of the Sisters of the Holy Names by appointing Mother Marie Rose Durocher superior, novice mistress, and procurator; Sister M. Agnes Dufresne, assistant; and Sister M. Madeleine Cere, general directress of manual work.

The community soon attracted other young women and the work was expanded by the opening of schools in Beloeil (1846) and in St. Lin and St. Timothy (1848). When Mother Marie Rose died on Oct. 6, 1849, she was succeeded as superior general by Mother Veronica Davignon (1849–57). Her contribution was the consolidation of the work and the preparation of the sisters for the expansion that was to come under her successor, Mother Theresa Martin, who was superior general for a decade (1857–67).

Responding to the urgent appeal of a missionary in the U.S., Abp. Francis Norbert Blanchet of Oregon City, Mother Theresa selected 12 from among the 72 members of her community and sent them (1859) to the Pacific Coast. Others joined them in Oregon in 1863 and 1864. In 1865, in response to an invitation from Bp. John J. Conroy of Albany, N.Y., a convent and an academy were established there. About the same time, Bp. Augustine Verot of St. Augustine, Fla., applied to the motherhouse for sisters. Under Mother Mary Stanislaus (1867–77), fourth superior general, missions were founded in Florida and California, and in Manitoba, Canada. A school that was opened in Oakland, Calif. (1868), at the invitation of Abp. Joseph S. Alemany of San Francisco, became the center from which elementary and secondary schools were established throughout California.

During the 20th century foundations multiplied: elementary and secondary schools, normal schools and colleges. In 1931 a mission was established in Basutoland, South Africa. A school was established (1931) in Kagoshima, Japan, but extreme nationalistic feeling made it necessary to recall the sisters in 1940. A native Japanese community maintains the school at Kagoshima. Three sisters from the California Province went to Arequipa, Peru, on Dec. 27, 1961. The generalate in Longueuil, Quebec, Canada directs the work of the community.

There are four provinces in the U.S.: Oregon (estb. 1859), California (estb. 1868), New York (estb. 1865) and Washington (estb. 1962).

Bibliography: J. B. CODE, *Great American Foundresses* (New York 1929). E. T. DEHEY, *Religious Orders of Women in the U. S.* (Hammond, Ind. 1930). P. J. B. DUCHAUSSOIS, *Rose of Canada* (Montreal 1934). M. F. DUNN, *Gleanings of Fifty Years* (Portland, Ore. 1909). J. M. MELANCON, *Life of Mother Marie Rose* (Montreal 1930).

[L. M. LYONS/EDS.]

HOLY OILS

Three holy oils are used in the Church's worship today: chrism, a blessed mixture of olive oil and balm; oil of catechumens, blessed olive oil; and oil of the sick, also blessed olive oil. This article treats the following subjects: use of oil in the Bible, use of oil in the rites of Baptism and Confirmation, use of oil of the sick, and other uses of holy oils.

Use of Oil in the Bible. In biblical times, oil was a condiment (Nm 11.8), a fuel for lamps (Mt 25.1–9), and a healing agent for wounds (Lk 10.34; cf. also Is 1.6). Perhaps the most frequently mentioned use of oil in the Bible is that of anointing. Kings (e.g., 1 Sm 10.1; 16.1, 13), priests (e.g., Ex 29.7), and prophets (e.g., 1 Kgs 19.16) were anointed. According to the Council of Trent, Christ instituted the Sacrament of Anointing of the Sick that was promulgated by the Apostle James (Jas 5.14; cf. H. Denzinger, *Enchiridion symbolorum*, ed. A. Schönmetzer [Freiburg 1963] 1716). It was a mark of honor to anoint the head of a guest with oil (e.g., Lk 7.46). Anointing was a preparation for burial (Mk 16.1; Lk 23.56). Anointing with oil served also as a cosmetic to beautify and to prevent dessication of the skin (e.g., Ru 3.3; Jdt 10.3). Not only people were anointed; objects were as well. Jacob poured oil over the stone at Bethel as a kind of consecration (Gn 28.18); the tabernacle and its furniture were consecrated by anointing with oil (Ex 30.26–28); the shield of a warrior might be anointed (Is 21.5). Oil was also used in sacrifice (e.g., Ex 29.40; Nm 28.5). Finally, oil is used in certain figurative expressions to signify such things as abundance (Jl 2.24), soft words (e.g., Prv 5.3), joy (e.g., Is 61.3), brotherly unity (Ps 132.1–2), and the influence of the Holy Spirit (1 Jn 2.20, 27). Subsequently, the biblical use of oil influenced to a greater or lesser degree the Christian use of it. (*See* ANOINTING.)

Use of Oil in Baptism and Confirmation. The *Apostolic Tradition* (*c.* third century) speaks of an "oil of exorcism," with which the candidate was anointed before Baptism, and of an "oil of thanksgiving," with which he was anointed afterward (B. Botte, ed., *La tradition apostolique de saint Hippolyte: Essai de reconstitution* [*Liturgiegeschichtliche Quellen und Forschunger*, 1963] 21–22). Similarly, Tertullian (d. 230; *De Bapt.* 7), Cyprian (d. 258; *Epist.* 70.2), Cyril of Jerusalem (d. 386; *Catech.* 21.3), and Basil (d. 379; *On the Spirit* 27.66), among others, speak of anointing after Baptism. In the fourth-century *Euchologion* of Serapion (15–16) there are formulas for blessing the oils used in connection with Baptism; and there is a parallel passage in the *Apostolic Constitutions* (fourth century 7.42). In some cases, these anointings covered the whole body (cf. Pseudo-Dionysius, *De eccl. hier.* 2.3). Frequently the anointings conferred immediately after Baptism in the ancient Church were the Sacrament of Confirmation, which is the complement of Baptism. The oil employed in these early anointings was olive oil, the oil in common use. Possibly it was mixed with balm in some cases. Balm seems to have been used everywhere for chrism at least from the sixth century.

Oil of the Sick. There are few, if any, references to oil destined for the sick in the first two centuries of the Christian era. The reason is uncertain. The *Apostolic Tradition* contains a formula for blessing oil destined for the sick, but the document implies that the oil will be either tasted or applied to the body (5; Botte, 18). There are similar passages in the *Apostolic Constitutions* (8.29) and in the *Euchologion* of Serapion (5, 17). The Persian Aphraates (fourth century) speaks of an anointing of the sick with olive oil (*Demonstrationes* 23.3). However it is not always clear from these and other early testimonies whether such anointings of the sick are the Sacrament of Anointing of the Sick or only sacramentals [*See* ANOINTING OF THE SICK, I (THEOLOGY OF)]. An early reference (416) to the Anointing of the Sick is unquestionably the letter of Innocent I (401–417) to Decentius (Denzinger: 216).

Other Uses of Holy Oils. From the sixth century on, anointing gradually became an integral part of the coronation ceremony of Christian kings. It probably was suggested by the ancient Hebrew practice. In the Roman rite, a newly consecrated bishop was anointed upon the head with chrism. Amalarius of Metz (770?–850?) mentions an episcopal anointing in his *Liber officialis* (ed. J. Hanssens, 234). Historically, the hands of a newly ordained priest were anointed with the oil of catechumens. An early reference to this rite is found in the eighth-century *Missale Francorum* (ed. Mohlberg, 33). It seems that the anointing of bishop and priest was inspired by the kingly anointing. In the Eastern Churches, episcopal and sacerdotal anointings are almost unknown.

Bibliography: L. L. MITCHELL, *Baptismal anointing* (London 1966). G. AUSTIN, *Anointing with the Spirit: The Rite of Confirmation: The Use of Oil and Chrism* (New York 1985). G. AUSTIN, "Anointing with the Oil of Catechumens," in *Commentaries on the Rite of Christian Initiation of Adults* (Chicago 1988) 15–24. D. BOROBIO, "An Enquiry into Healing Anointing in the Early Church," in *Concilium* (1991/2) 37–49. M. DUDLEY, G. ROWELL, eds. *The Oil of Gladness: Anointing in the Christian Tradition* (Collegeville, Minn. 1993).

[E. J. GRATSCH/EDS.]

HOLY ORDERS

Order signifies a relation of many things in reference to one common beginning or end, and so arranged as to be mutually related. In ecclesiastical language, by a certain excellence the spiritual or sacred power that is conferred in the Church has been called "order" (Latin *ordo*, Greek τάξις or τάγμα). The Catechism of the Catholic Church explains that holy orders is the sacrament of apostolic ministry, i.e., "the sacrament through which the mission entrusted by Christ to his apostles continues to be exercised in the Church until the end of time" (CCC 1536). The term also signifies the sacred ordination or "to ordain," i.e., the external rite or ceremonial whereby a degree of power is imparted, called in Greek the extension or IMPOSITION OF HANDS (χειροτονία, χεροθεσία). There are three degrees of holy orders: episcopate, presbyterate and diaconate.

Institution by Christ

The Council of Trent clearly reaffirmed (H. Denzinger, *Enchiridion Symbolorum* 1766) the previous teaching of the Church that Holy Orders or sacred ordination by which sacred power is conferred as instituted by Christ is a true Sacrament of the New Covenant. The priesthood and the sacrifice of the Old Law especially prefigured the New Dispensation, as the Prophets had foretold. It has always been Catholic teaching, based upon the testimony of Scripture, apostolic tradition, and the unanimous agreement of the Fathers, that to the new sacrifice that Christ inaugurated He associated a new priesthood empowered to continue His own priesthood until the consummation of the world (Council of Trent; Denzinger 1740, 1764). That the Apostles were conscious of and exercised this power and that they ordained bishops, priests, and deacons by the sacramental rite of the imposition of hands and the invocation of the Holy Spirit, is shown in the Acts and the Epistles (e.g., Acts 6.6; 13.3; 1 Tm 4.14; 5.22; 2 Tm 1.6). The witness of tradition from the earliest documents offers explicit acknowledgment of a divinely constituted hierarchy of bishops, priests, and deacons, and by the 4th century there is found express mention of the grace of order as clearly distinct from the sacred power conferred.

Categories of Orders

Sacred Scripture mentions priests and deacons; the historical minor orders of subdeacon, acolyte, exorcist, lector, and porter, were known since the early Church. In the sacerdotal order the bishop, as successor of the Apostles, is superior to the priest and is the principal hierarch with powers not at all possessed or not ordinarily enjoyed by other orders.

Origin. *Bishop.* It is of faith that the episcopacy is divinely instituted, and immediately by Christ, according to the far more common theological teaching. The institution of the episcopacy as such, as an order distinct from the simple priesthood, cannot be established with certainty from the Scriptures alone without the witness of tradition. The Scriptural terminology is quite fluid and the later fixed usage regarding bishop, priest, deacon does not appear in the New Testament writings. The names πρεσβύτερος and ἐπίσκοπος (as well as *hegoumenos, praesidentes*) were often used synonymously. Some interpret them to mean simple priests only; others, bishops only; and others, simple priests and sometimes bishops. All, however, are under the direction of the Apostles.

From Scripture it is clear that Christ established a priesthood and in this sense certainly an episcopacy. There are indications that in the Scriptures some are singled out for powers and functions that are proper and exclusive to those specifically called bishops in later times. This is the more ancient and common teaching of theologians. It is an open theological question whether or not the episcopacy as distinguished from the priesthood is sacramental, the older opinion judging negatively, the later and now more common, affirmatively. Leo XIII wrote: "But the episcopacy undoubtedly by the institution of Christ pertains most truly to the Sacrament of Orders and constitutes the sacerdotium in the highest degree, which surely by the teaching of the holy Fathers and our liturgical customs is called the 'summum sacerdotium, sacri ministerii summa'" (*Apostolicae curae;* Denzinger 3317). This doctrine was taught also by Vatican Council II in practically the same words (*Const. on the Church* 20–21).

It would seem that those to whom the terms bishop and successor of the Apostles subsequently were exclusively applied were individuals in the Apostolic Church whom the Apostles associated with themselves or delegated to carry on the office of Apostle-successors, e.g., Timothy and Titus (and according to some, James of Jerusalem inasmuch as he was not James of Alpheus, one of the Twelve). The presbyters-bishops were dependent upon these Apostle-successors, as originally upon the Apostles themselves. In the tradition of the primitive Church the appellations of the incumbents of these successors evolved, although the hierarchical structure remained the same. Until the late 2d century, when the designation was clearly fixed, the term ἐπίσκοπος designated the presbyter, the presbyter-president of the college of presbyters, the bishop. *See* BISHOP (IN THE BIBLE); BISHOP (IN THE CHURCH); BISHOP (SACRAMENTAL THEOLOGY OF).

Priest. Since the Scriptural usage of the terms was not fixed, and since certainly not all termed ἐπίσκοποι were bishops, or all called πρεσβύτεροι priests, the meaning cannot be derived from the words themselves but rather from the contexts or from what was signified in the particular instances. Probably the one *sacerdotium* was being referred to, at one time in its fullness and at another in a lesser degree, i.e., in a higher or lower order.

Precision of terminology begins only in the 2d century, and then only in the letters of Ignatius of Antioch (*Ad Philadelphenses* 4; J. Quasten, *Monumenta eucharista et liturgica vetustissima* 335). By the end of the 3d century the name presbyter was specifically applied only to the second grade of the hierarchy, and thereafter the distinction was commonly employed. Only much later, after the 5th century, did the term "sacerdos" (which had applied to bishops, priests, and deacons) come to be restricted to the presbyters. *See* PRIESTHOOD IN CHRISTIAN TRADITION.

Deacon. The existence of the diaconate (διακονία, ministry) as a distinct hierarchical and sacramental order is found in Scripture (Phil 1.1; 1 Tm 3.8–13; Acts 6.1–6) and is confirmed by the witness of tradition [Justin, 1 *Apol.* 65; Ignatius of Antioch, *Ad Philadelphenses* 4 (Quasten 17, 335)], its full characteristics being clearly discussed by the 4th century. DEACONS are clearly distinguished from the laity and from the priests (simple or episcopal) to whom they are subordinate and ministering. Deacons have from the beginning been ordained by the imposition of the hand of the bishop with the invocation of the Holy Spirit.

It is more commonly held that the Apostles ordained the original seven deacons. Theologians today hold it to be certain that the diaconate is of divine institution and a sacramental order (Council of Trent; Denzinger 1765, 1776). The "serving at table" would include their assistance at the celebration of the Eucharist and its distribution, which was usually joined with the agape of the early Christians. Moreover, they preached and administered Baptism (Acts 6.8–15; 7.1–60; 8.5–13, 38).

Subdeacon. The origins of the historical subdiaconate are obscure and testimony concerning it, silent. The existence of the SUBDEACON in the 3d century is affirmed in the *Apostolic Tradition* and in the practice of the Roman and African churches. Only gradually did it grow in importance through the assumption of more sacred functions and of the law of celibacy, and through its increasing connection with and necessity for higher orders. By the close of the 12th century it was patently ranked in the West among the major orders. In the East the subdiaconate was certainly an institution by the 4th century, as mentioned in the Councils of Antioch (341) and Laodicea (*c.* 343–381), but it has never to this day been reckoned among the sacred or major orders. In the Latin Church, the order of subdeaconate was abolished by Pope Paul VI in his motu proprio, *Ministeria quaedam* (Aug. 15, 1972).

Acolyte. An historical order that was found only in the Western Church. In fact, it was hardly even noted in the Gallican-rite churches of the West (Gaul, Spain, Milan). Early evidence of it in Rome and in Africa is found in SS. Jerome, Augustine, and Cyprian, and Popes Siricius and Zosimus. The later influence of the Gallican upon the Roman liturgy lessened the position and functions of this office. However, with the lapse of the lectorship and office of exorcist from about the 6th to the 9th centuries, the ACOLYTE remained to assist at the altar and at priestly ministrations. By the 8th century the order had become the requisite step to the subdiaconate. In 1972, it was abolished by Pope Paul VI in his *motu proprio, Ministeria quaedam*, who created the ministry of acolyte in its place and opened it to the laity.

Lector. This is the most ancient order below the diaconate of which there is record; it is mentioned early in the 3d century by Tertullian, the *Apostolic Tradition,* and in about the middle of the next century by the *Didascalia Apostolorum.* The LECTOR was used very early in the Roman, Carthaginian, and Syriac churches. From about the 4th to the 10th centuries it lost a large portion of its prominence and functions. This was due to the practice of conferring ordinations that bypassed (*per saltum*) the lectorship and to the admission to this order of youngsters with the result that the function of singing was restricted to them and the other functions of the office assumed by older and higher clerics. In the Latin Church, Pope Paul VI abolished the minor order of lector in his *motu proprio Ministeria quaedam*, and replaced it with the ministry of reader, which is opened to laypeople.

Exorcist. Sepulchral inscriptions of the 3d and 4th centuries attest to the existence of the exorcist (*see* EXORCISM). The position of this order subsequently declined with the promotion of young men to the other clerical grades and due to instances in which adults were ordained by bypassing (*per saltum*) the order of exorcist. Likewise, with the lapse of the catechumenate during which period the exorcist had exercised his order, and with the assumption of these baptismal exorcisms by the acolytes and priests, the role of the exorcist was lessened. Its long presence in the Roman usage came with the influence of the Gallican practice. Pope Paul VI suppressed the minor order of the exorcist in 1972.

Porter. The order of PORTER seems not to have received much attention in the early Church because of its slight importance. At best it is mentioned only in passing in the early testimonies. Although Pelagius I referred to it in the 6th century as the beginning of the clerical state, it appears to have fallen into desuetude by the end of the 4th century, and its functions were exercised even by laymen. The survival of the porter in Gallican usage brought about its revival in the Roman practice around the 10th century. It survived in the Roman Rite until its abolition in 1972 by Pope Paul VI.

Tonsure. Clerical TONSURE was never considered an order but only a special rite of introduction into the ranks of the clergy. It appeared to have developed from the early Christian practice, with Semitic roots, of cutting the hair to symbolize humility. In relation to the clerical state it was also a sign of holiness. The rite, already indicated in the 6th century, was in stable use by the 8th century, as noted in the Gelasian and Gregorian Sacramentaries. From being a private ceremony in the beginning, it gradually assumed a public and official character. Initially it was connected with the ceremony of first ordination, but in the West certainly by the 12th century it had become a separate and distinct ceremony. The tonsured person was thus set apart from the laity, whether or not he thereafter received clerical orders. In the East tonsure was a less prominent rite and it seems probable that, as today, it was always joined to the reception of the lectorship or cantorship. In the Latin Church, Pope Paul VI abolished the tonsure in his 1972 motu proprio, *Ministeria quaedam.*

Deaconess. From the period of the public ministry of Our Lord and of the Apostles pious women had offered their service to the ministers of the Church in the form of works of charity and temporal aid. The office of DEACONESS in the Church developed in time, probably growing out of the system of organized widowhood in the early Church (about the 2d century). The institution of the deaconess arose in the East (about the 3d century) before appearing as such in the West (about the 5th century). With the rise of monastic houses for women and with the gradual discontinuance of the ceremony of Baptism by immersion in which the deaconess assisted the women candidates, the office of the deaconess correspondingly lapsed in the 7th century. Between the 10th and 12th centuries it disappeared in the West, although it survived somewhat longer in parts of the East.

Historical Division into Major and Minor Orders. In the Latin Church, historically the major orders comprised priesthood, diaconate, and subdiaconate; the minor orders were those of porter, lector, exorcist, and acolyte (Council of Trent; Denzinger 1765). First tonsure is not commonly listed among the orders, nor is the episcopacy, which was not considered an order adequately distinct from the priesthood; some, however, taking ''order'' in the wider sense, enumerate one or both. Before the 12th century the present distinction of major and minor orders was not clearly fixed. That the Latin Church, in particular the Roman Church, developed the minor orders early can be discerned from ancient documents. These orders may be distinguished from other offices and dignities by reason of their stable character and conferral by a sacred rite. The full list of orders below the diaconate was given by Pope Cornelius around 251 as existing in the Roman Church. By the end of the 12th century the subdiaconate had taken on such prominence that it was already classed among the major or sacred orders. The 1972 motu proprio of Pope Paul VI, *Ministeria quaedam,* abolished all the minor orders and the subdiaconate, thereby removing the distinction between minor and major orders.

In the Eastern Church the subdiaconate has always been held as a minor order, except for some few rites, notably the Armenians, who since the 11th century have followed the Latins. This is probably because the subdeacon does not minister at the altar nor come to it for the sacrifice nor touch the sacred vessels on the altar. The earliest mention of orders below the diaconate is to the lectorship and the subdiaconate; these two alone have been commonly maintained in the Eastern Church. More generally the office of cantor has been attached to the lectorship, although some would hold it to be an order. Others maintain that the lectorship or subdiaconate contains the order of porter, exorcist, and acolyte.

One or Many Sacraments. It is Catholic teaching that there are only seven Sacraments, no more or less, and that Holy Orders is one of them. Thus, regardless of the number of orders existing and accepted, they all together constitute but one Sacrament. The priesthood (with the episcopacy) and the diaconate at least are clearly sacramental as of divine institution, notwithstanding theological opinion respecting the other orders. The problem thus lies in the manner in which these orders are Sacraments and yet form but the one specific Sacrament of Holy Orders. Several solutions have been proposed.

The most common solution follows the view of St. Thomas (*Summa Theologiae,* Suppl. 37.1 ad 2) that considers this Sacrament in the manner of a potential or potestative whole, whereby the essence, power, and character of the Sacrament reside perfectly and fully in the priesthood and less completely in the diaconate (and, according to some, in the other orders). To consider this Sacrament as a universal whole would result in several specifically different Sacraments; to consider it as an integral whole would require the presence of all the orders at once.

Sacramental Rite

The conferral of the Sacrament of Holy Orders is through a sacred sign. Whether the entire sign or only its signification has been instituted by Christ depends upon whether the theory of the generic or specific institution of this Sacrament is supported. The opinion that Christ established only the signification of this Sacrament and left it to the Church to determine the material element that under a form or formula of words would convey this signification, or that He instituted an indeterminate material element or merely an imposition of hands and left the rest to the determination of the Church, is held by some. The more common opinion holds for a specific institution.

Matter and Form. In the churches of the Christian East, the orders have always been conferred by the imposition of hands and this was the one essential rite in the Latin Church before the 10th century. It seems to have been generally taught in the late Middle Ages and for a long time thereafter that the essential rite was the handing over of the instruments, although this does not disprove the continued existence of the rite of imposition of hands. The Decree for the Armenians of the Council of Florence cites the handing over of the instruments as the matter of the Sacrament in each order (Denzinger 1326), but the doctrinal value of this decree is disputed and some assert that it is not definitive but merely expository in that it states the common theology of the day in this question. It is more probable that the imposition was always the matter of this Sacrament and even by divine institution.

In his apostolic constitution *Sacramentum Ordinis* of Nov. 30, 1947, Pius XII declared that thenceforth the episcopacy, priesthood, and diaconate would be conferred in each instance by the one and only essential and valid rite, namely, the designated imposition of hands and the designated form, the consecratory Preface [*Acta Apostolicae Sedis* 40 (1948) 5–7].

Minister. It has always been Catholic teaching that the bishop is the ordinary minister of the Sacrament of Holy Orders by divine institution (Council of Trent; Denz 1768, 1777, CIC 1983, c. 1012). Scripture indicates only bishops as the ministers of sacred orders (Acts 6.6; 13.3; 1 Tm 4.14; 5.22; 2 Tm 1.6). This has been the traditional practice in the Church, as ancient liturgical and canonical writings testify.

Priest as Extraordinary Minister. The question has been long discussed whether a simple priest can be also an extraordinary minister of Holy Orders or whether the bishop is the exclusive minister by divine right. Contrary to the opinion of the canonists, the older theologians held that a simple priest could not by commission of the pope become the extraordinary minister of the major orders. They followed more or less this conclusion as stated by both St. Thomas and Duns Scotus, although for different reasons. It became commonly agreed that a properly commissioned priest could confer minor orders (this commission was often given by the pope) and even the subdiaconate (a practice in the Greek Church but not in the Latin).

With the coming to light of three papal bulls (Boniface IX, *Sacrae religionis,* Feb. 1, 1400; Martin V, *Gerentes ad vos,* Nov. 16, 1427; Innocent VIII, *Exposcit,* April 9, 1489), an increasing number of theologians to the present day have been maintaining, with varying degrees of theological probability and of certitude, that a simple priest can be commissioned by the pope to confer the diaconate and even the priesthood. The cited papal bulls seem to have granted to certain abbots (not in episcopal orders) the power to ordain their subjects to the diaconate. Dispute obtains regarding the force and meaning of these documents in view of the longstanding tradition in the Church and the widespread theological teaching regarding the bishop as the exclusive minister of the diaconate and the priesthood. The common teaching today rejects the opinion that a simple priest may act as extraordinary minister of these orders, although the opinion that he may must be considered as at least probable.

Worthiness and the Question of Reordination. For the valid administration of Holy Orders neither the presence of grace nor the state of grace is required in the minister (Council of Trent; Denzinger 1612, 1710), since the power of God and the merits of Christ and not the dispositions and merits of the minister confer this sacramental validity. But the sanctity and dignity of the Sacrament demands for its lawful and worthy administration that the minister be in the state of grace, free of ecclesiastical penalties, and observant of the requirements of law regarding the conferral of ordination.

The firm and explicit teaching of the Church regarding the relationship or dependence of the validity of a Sacrament upon the dispositions or condition of the minister and its common practice regarding REORDINATION was long in coming. The doubts and the subsequent controversies began with St. Cyprian in the 3d century in regard to the validity of Baptism administered by heretics. The dispute was extended during the Donatist heresy and schism to the validity of ordinations performed by those who were publicly unworthy. In subsequent centuries unworthiness tended to center especially around those in-

volved in concubinage or simony, or subjected to excommunication. Theologians disputed the question and many prelates, even some popes, practiced reordination in such cases. The definitive settlement of the controversy began with the efforts of Paschal II (Council of Guastalla, 1106; Denzinger 705) and of Innocent III (in the profession of faith required of the Waldensians in 1208; Denzinger 793) whereby the principle of the validity of the Sacraments independently of the dispositions of the minister was upheld. Thus the ancient practice and teaching of the Church was restored and became widely and permanently effective.

Intention. The Council of Trent, in harmony with previous papal statements, made it clear that in effecting and conferring the Sacraments the minister must have an intention at least of doing what the Church does (sess. 7, c.11; Denzinger 1624). Thus in conferring the Sacrament of Holy Orders the minister is a voluntary and vitally responsible agent of Christ in this action. He must have a deliberate intention formed at least in some general and implicit fashion, and this must truly bear upon the conferral by his action of what, by the institution of Christ, is a sacramental administration of Holy Orders. He thus intends to do at least what the Church does (which is a sacramental conferral). This is implicitly the very same intention of doing what Christ's Church herself does. Besides a defective matter or form, an intention which is defective also invalidates the Sacrament. Thus there must be on the part of the minister a serious will not merely to perform an external application of the matter and form but also to confer a rite that as a matter of fact is considered by the Church as sacred. The intention need not be actual but it must be at least virtual in order to bear upon the sacramental action at hand. A minister, otherwise qualified and applying valid matter and form, who has at least the above minimum qualities of intention, will validly confer Holy Orders. (*See* ANGLICAN ORDERS; APOSTOLICAE CURAE.)

Recipient. Just as for the minister, there are certain requirements that must be met by the ordinand. Some of these requirements pertain to validity, others to liceity.

Valid Reception. Only a baptized male with at least a habitual intention of receiving this Sacrament is a capable subject of valid ordination (CIC 1983, c. 1024). Only males can validly receive sacred ordination by divine law, and any prudent doubt, as in the case of the hermaphrodite or pseudohermaphrodite, must bar the candidate from ordination. Moreover, the Church has always understood and insisted upon as essential the reception of Baptism before allowing the reception of Holy Orders.

Essential to valid reception also is an internal intention or will of receiving this Sacrament, since no adult receives a Sacrament unwillingly. There must be a voluntary, positive act of the will and not a passive attitude to the reception. For the reception of a Sacrament a habitual intention suffices, although a virtual or actual intention is recommended as more fruitful. The recipient is in the condition of one receiving a gift and a benefit, and thus it suffices that the reception be voluntary, which is ensured by a habitual intention. However, for the reception of Holy Orders the habitual intention must be explicit to receive what *de facto* the Church and the minister intend to confer and thus to be received, namely, the Sacrament and its effect. The reason is that the intention must include an advertence to the clerical state and its obligations, since these are not practically contained implicitly in the habitual intention to live a Christian life. Only when such an explicit intention is present can the ordination of one asleep or unconscious, drunk, or insane be considered valid. Baptized infants are validly ordained, but may choose the clerical or lay state upon completion of their 16th year.

It is commonly taught that a candidate who deceitfully (*ficte*) receives Orders, i.e., inwardly dissenting or refusing, is invalidly ordained. However, a cleric who receives Orders under the influence of grave fear or deceit receives them validly; he is to be reduced to the lay state unless he has subsequently ratified the ordination upon the removal of the obstacle. The lawful intention required of a clerical vocation is considered below.

Lawful Reception. For the lawful reception of Holy Orders, i.e., that the candidate be considered qualified, other conditions are required by the Church and are comprised under the qualities of divine vocation, suitability, and freedom from canonical impediments.

Admission to Holy Orders is subject to the judgment and authority of the Church, to whom the Sacraments have been entrusted. The norms or requirements forming the basis of judgment are signs of the presence of a divine interior vocation, which they presuppose, guarantee, or recognize. Vocation to the clerical state, then, consists of the divine interior act of selection of and preparation of the candidate with suitable endowments of nature and grace for the worthy exercise of priestly duties. Together with this must be the call and acceptance of the Church through the bishop upon judgment of the suitability or worthiness of the candidate who gives evidence of an interior vocation. The principal signs of this clerical vocation are a right intention, probity of life, and suitability.

Besides the intention, which is necessary for the valid reception of the Sacrament, the candidate must have the right intention essential to a clerical vocation. It is his response to God's special grace and the primary sign of a divine vocation, namely, a free, firm, and constant supernatural motivation to procure the glory of God and the salvation of souls with the determination to go on for the priesthood.

The bishop should confer Sacred Orders only if he is morally certain of the canonical fitness of each candidate, i.e., of the presence of the qualities of mind and body, of nature and grace and proven virtue required and suited for bearing the burdens and fulfilling the tasks of the priesthood. The candidate must be sound physically and psychologically and possess the intellectual ability and knowledge set forth in the pertinent regulations of the Church and other competent authorities. The lawful reception of Orders demands outstanding and habitual goodness of life, especially perfect chastity. Solid possession of this latter virtue is an indispensable condition of a clerical vocation and its presence must be positively evident, profoundly appreciated, and zealously cherished and not merely assumed by reason of any absence of deviation.

The 1983 Code of Canon Law also prescribes minimum age requirements: "The presbyterate is not to be conferred except on those who have completed the 25th year of age and possess sufficient maturity; an interval of at least six months to be observed between the diaconate and the presbyterate. Those destined to the presbyterate are to be admitted to the order of deacon only after completing the twenty-third year of age" (CIC 1983, c.1031 §1). The interstices are to be observed, i.e., the fitting intervals laid down by law between the reception of one order and another, in order to provide a period of trial and preparation as well as the exercise of one order before promotion to the next.

The lawful reception of Holy Orders requires that the candidate have already received the Sacrament of Confirmation (CIC 1983, c.1024). Those who are bound to the divine ministry by ordination ought to be strong in the faith themselves and leaders of others in its witness and defense. Holy Orders fittingly complements the perfections of grace and the gifts of the Holy Spirit already received in the other Sacraments. Each order is to be received in its proper sequence and no intermediate order omitted *per saltum*.

A candidate for Holy Orders must be free of all canonical irregularities and impediments. Both are ecclesiastical disqualifications prohibiting primarily and directly the reception of orders and secondarily and indirectly their exercise. They do not invalidate but rather render unlawful the reception or exercise of orders, and are considered to bind gravely. An irregularity is of its nature perpetual, whether based upon a defect or a delict, and is removable only by dispensation. An impediment is temporary, the basis being considered to be lack of faith or of freedom or of good repute. The impediment may cease by dispensation, the lapse of time, or the removal of the cause. The purpose behind all these disqualifications is to safeguard the dignity of the clerical state and office, reverence and becomingness in the sacred ministry, and to avoid offense to the laity by reason of unfit ministers of the altar.

Canonical Procedures. Candidates for promotion to orders must possess testimonial letters giving proof of Baptism and Confirmation or of the last order received, of the prescribed studies completed, of good moral character, and of the absence of a canonical impediment.

Differing from the aforesaid are DIMISSORIAL LETTERS by which one bishop or superior releases his subject and sends him to another bishop with the faculty of receiving orders from him.

The names of candidates for individual sacred orders (with the exception of perpetually professed religious) should be announced publicly in their respective parish churches, unless the ordinary dispenses or makes other arrangements.

Fruitful Reception. As a Sacrament of the living, Holy Orders should be received in the state of grace. To receive in the state of sin an order that certainly has the dignity of a Sacrament would itself be a grave sin. In order to provide for better dispositions for the reception of orders, all candidates for any order are to make a spiritual retreat for at least five days in a place or manner determined by the ordinary (CIC 1983, c. 1039).

Effects

It is of faith that Sacraments confer grace; it is also a defined dogma that Holy Orders confers, in addition, an indelible character.

Sacramental Grace. "From the testimony of Scripture, apostolic tradition and the unanimous agreement of the Fathers it is clear that grace is conferred by sacred ordination" [Trent, sess. 23, ch. (Denz 1766); c.4 (Denz 1774)]. This grace is noted by the Apostle Paul in 1 Tm 4.14 and 2 Tm 1.6–7. It is not only sanctifying grace, which is common to all the Sacraments, but also sacramental grace, the particular effect of grace of this Sacrament of Holy Orders. This sacramental effect, whether it be, theologically speaking, in the nature of a right to the actual graces corresponding to the purpose of the Sacrament or a modality of habitual grace directing to the same goal, is specified by the end of the Sacrament. The Council of Florence (Decree for the Armenians) speaks of an "increase of grace so that one may be a suitable minister," and Pius XII of "the grace proper to this particular function and state of life" (*Mediator Dei* 42). To be a suitable minister implies all the virtues and supernatural helps attendant upon the proper and worthy exercise of liturgical functions, especially the Sacrifice of the Mass, and the duties respecting the sanctification, instruction, and direction of the faithful. In particular the form for the ordination of a deacon prays that the Holy Spirit might strengthen the candidate "with the sevenfold gift of grace to carry out faithfully the work of the ministry"; the form for the priesthood asks the Father Almighty to "renew within him the spirit of holiness so that he may hold the office of second rank which he has received from Thee, O God, and by the example of his life give a pattern of upright conduct"; the form for episcopal consecration beseeches, "give to thy priest the fullness of thy ministry, and sanctify with the dew of the heavenly anointing him who is adorned with the vesture of the highest dignity." The various virtues and leadership in holiness that the documents of tradition describe regarding the recipients of sacred ordination seem to be reduced to various aspects of charity, enlightenment, and service on the part of the bishop, priest, and deacon, respectively.

Character. The other and permanent effect of the Sacrament of Holy Orders is the spiritual and indelible character imprinted on the soul of the recipient of ordination, with the result that no valid order may be repeated or lost (Council of Trent; Denz 1767, 1774). Besides the nature and function common to the characters of Baptism and Confirmation, the character of Holy Orders has its proper and specific role, "shaping sacred ministers to the likeness of Christ the Priest, and enabling them to perform the lawful acts of religion by which men are sanctified and God duly glorified according to the divine ordinance" (Pius XII, *Mediator Dei* 42). It confers the power over the real body of Christ to consecrate, offer, and administer His Body and Blood, and the power over His Mystical Body to prepare the faithful, by the Sacraments and the preaching of the word, to be fit and worthy for the Sacrament of the Eucharist. This character is imprinted in each sacramental order, depending on the theological view held as to the sacramentality of the various orders. It is an active power whereby the recipient, according to his order, can accomplish in the name and person of Christ the sacramental rites destined for Christian worship and for the sanctification of the faithful, and by which also he is constituted a leader of the Christian community in liturgical functions. Theologians dispute whether this character is one, with many powers being, as it were, successively released or conferred, or many, either adequately or inadequately distinct among themselves, perfectly or imperfectly.

Bibliography: *De ordinatione episcopi, presbyterorum et diaconorum* (Vatican City 1990). A. STANTANTONI, *L'ordinazione episcopale: storia e teologia dei riti dell'ordinazione nelle antiche*

Regalia from the Holy Roman Empire. (©Ali Meyer/CORBIS)

liturgie dell'Occidente (Rome 1976). P.F. BRADSHAW, *Ordination Rites of the Ancient Churches of East and West* (New York 1990). J. PUGLISI, *The Process of Admission to Ordained Ministry: A Comparative Study*, 3 vols. (Collegeville, Minn. 1996–). A. LAMERI, *La traditio instrumentorum e delle insegne nei riti di ordinazione: studio storico-liturgico* (Rome 1998). J. S. H, GIBAUT, *The Cursus Honorum: A Study of the Origins and Evolution of Sequential Ordination* (New York 2000).

[N. HALLIGAN/EDS.]

HOLY ROMAN EMPIRE

The term "Holy Roman Empire" has been used to distinguish the Medieval German Empire from the Ancient Roman Empire and the Greek Roman (Byzantine) Empire in the East. The line of emperors in the Western provinces of the Roman Empire came to an end with the death of Romulus Augustulus in A.D. 476. An Eastern line of Roman emperors continued to rule in Greek Constantinople, and these emperors carried on the traditions of ancient Rome until the city was conquered by the Ottoman Turks in 1453. They called themselves "Roman," and they were Christian. Like the ancient Romans, they never called their empire "Holy." There was a long interregnum in the West from the death of Romulus Augustulus until Pope Leo III crowned Charles the Great (CHARLE-

MAGNE) emperor in Rome on Dec. 25, 800. Charles was the king of a Germanic tribe, the FRANKS. Although his new title may have been Roman, his lordship, customs, and concepts of kingship were thoroughly Germanic. In Roman terms he was emperor in name only. The best example of the new empire's Germanic roots is its inheritance laws. Following Germanic customary law, Charles and his successors conceived of their realm as their private, not public, property. When they died, they divided it among their male heirs. They could not imagine that an empire or a kingdom should be an inalienable, unified territory. This practice led to political instability and civil war and, in a short time, a fragmented empire.

After Charlemagne revived the title of emperor in the West, the title "Holy Roman Empire" evolved slowly. Charles had styled himself simply "emperor." In 982 Emperor OTTO II began to use the title "emperor Augustus of the Romans." The expansion of the title had political consequences. To validate their assumption of the title "Emperor of the Romans," the Ottonian emperors tried to extend their authority into Italy. They also created even more elevated titles for themselves. Otto III (983–1002) adopted Byzantine practices of calling himself "servant of Jesus Christ" and "servant of the apostles." This last title imitated the pope's "servant of the servants of God." Sacral kingship was a widespread notion in the early Middle Ages. Kings and emperors received the unction of consecrated oil at their coronations. It gave them a special liturgical and canonical status. No emperor could received major clerical orders, but he occupied a position above other laymen. The emperor was the Advocate and Defender of the Roman church (*advocatus et defensor romanae ecclesiae*) and was also responsible for establishing the City of God on earth and ruling it as the Son of the Church (*filius ecclesiae.*). The emperor was consequently the lord of Christendom, universal and omnicompetent, the terrestrial agent of the divine Emperor, God, to whom every faithful Christian (*fidelis*) owed obedience and faith (*fides*). It is not surprising then that the term "Holy Empire" was used in the letters of Emperor FREDERICK BARBAROSSA (ca. 1157) to describe the territory over which he ruled. If he were the divinely appointed ruler over all Christians, his realm could be justifiably described as holy. Finally, the entire title "Holy Roman Empire" was used for the first time in 1254. Ironically this title was not adopted until after the empire had begun its long decline in the later Middle Ages. When the eighteenth-century French philosopher Voltaire declared that the Holy Roman Empire was "neither holy, nor Roman, nor an empire" his epigram had more than a grain of historical truth.

Sacred imagery characterized the rhetoric of the Germanic empire and permeated the language of its documents. The chancellery of Frederick Barbarossa added "holy" to the title of his empire to signify that the empire was divinely ordained and worthy of sharing power and authority with the Roman Catholic Church in the Christian world. The emperor was God's representative on earth. Frederick also asserted that he was the "Lord of the world" (*Dominus mundi*) and held a higher office than all other kings. From the early Middle Ages, the Church had been called the "Holy Roman Church." Its title indicated that it represented in the divine order. Kingdoms were not normally labeled "holy." The use of the term "Holy Empire" is an important signpost for understanding the most significant conflict between Church and State in the Middle Ages.

During the high Middle Ages the Germanic empire and the Roman Catholic Church both claimed universal authority over Christendom. Each represented a model of rulership that mirrored the heavenly monarchy. Each represented the unity of Christendom. In the period from 900 to 1250, the "Holy Empire" vied with the "Holy Roman Church" to be the embodiment of Christian universal authority. In the beginning the empire and the Church were not equals. From the time of the first Christian emperor, Constantine, until the middle of the eleventh century, the emperors exercised considerable authority and power over bishops and their clergy. The Germanic emperors who succeeded Charlemagne and other secular princes appointed bishops, abbots, and clergy to ecclesiastical offices. They employed bishops as officials in the imperial courts. Occasionally they even deposed popes and selected their successors. The eleventh century, however, marked a fundamental change in the relationship between the Church and the Empire. Reformers within and outside the Church began to realize that secular lay princes should not exercise authority in ecclesiastical affairs. Pope NICHOLAS II (1058–1061) promulgated a decree that forbade the emperor from participating in the election of the pope in 1059, and Pope GREGORY VII (1073–1085) issued several decrees that forbade the emperor and lay princes from investing bishops with the symbols of their offices. Gregory made *Libertas ecclesiae*, Freedom of the Church, a principle of canon law and a maxim of ecclesiastical rhetoric. Gregory VII attacked the emperor's sacral, almost clerical, status and his position as the head of Christendom. By forbidding the emperor's investiture of bishops Gregory undermined imperial control of bishops. A long series of events marked the bitter conflict between the Roman church and the Germanic empire. Gregory excommunicated and then deposed Emperor Henry IV (1056–1106) in an unprecedented action. Henry retaliated by supporting an anti-pope, Clement III (1080–1100) militarily. Emperor Henry V (1106–1125) finally acknowledged the autonomy of the Church in the

Concordat of WORMS (September 1122), but that treaty with the papacy did not establish a completely independent Church. The empire was, however, considerably weakened. The emperor gave up his right to bestow the ring and episcopal staff (crozier) that were the symbols of spiritual authority in the Concordat. This was a significant step in recognizing the Church as a separate institution that was completely independent of imperial and lay control. The Concordat was binding only within the empire. It was a compromise that did not ultimately solve the problem of how the Church and the Empire would coexist in Christendom.

During the twelfth century the popes attempted to establish *Libertas ecclesiae*, which they interpreted as complete freedom from lay interference and control, as a fundamental principle of ecclesiastical government. The emperors, especially Frederick Barbarossa, refused to accept a Church that claimed superiority over them. Consequently, with the emperor's support there were many papal schisms within the Latin church. The emperors opposed papal claims of authority by supporting pro-imperial factions within the Church who elected anti-popes. These anti-popes recognized imperial prerogatives. The emperors' ecclesiastical policies put enormous strain on the stability of the Church. The twelfth-century emperors supported ten anti-popes. These "popes" reigned for a total of 41 years. Pope Alexander III's (1059–1081) agreement with the Emperor Frederick I Barbarossa in 1177 brought this long line of "imperial anti-popes" to an end and began a short period of reconciliation between the pope and the empire.

Pope Innocent III's (1198–1216) policies posed a new challenge to the relationship of the Sacerdotium (Church) and Regnum (State) that had been established in the twelfth century. Innocent had a high and exalted view of papal power. He claimed that the pope "has his authority because he does not exercise the office of man, but of the true God on earth." He also compared imperial power to the moon and papal power to the sun. The dignity of the empire came from the light that it received from the sun. Innocent clearly wished to place the office of the pope above the emperor's. The most difficult task Innocent faced in his first years as pope was the struggle between Otto of Brunswick and Philip of Hohenstaufen for the office of the emperor after the death of the Emperor Henry VI (1190–1197). The German princes had divided their votes between these two candidates for the imperial throne. Innocent had moved quickly to assert his authority to choose between them. This was an unprecedented exercise of papal jurisdiction over an imperial election. He established the right of the pope to choose one of the candidates as emperor in a decretal letter, Venerabilem, which quickly became part of canon law of the Church.

Innocent promulgated a number of decrees that in which he claimed papal authority over a number of secular matters. Papal claims of secular authority and power over the Papal States in Central Italy led to further conflicts with the Emperor FREDERICK II (1212–1250) during the thirteenth century. Innocent's successors, popes Gregory IX (1227–1241) and Innocent IV (1243–1254), carried on Innocent's campaign to establish the papacy as the highest tribunal of Christendom. Gregory and Innocent excommunicated Frederick II when he threatened papal authority and lordship in Italy. Finally Innocent IV convened a general council in the city of Lyon (1245). He summoned Frederick II to stand trial and charged Frederick with a variety of crimes. When the emperor refused to submit to the Council, Innocent excommunicated him and called upon the king of France to launch a crusade against him. Frederick died a few years later.

This last sorry spectacle was the final battle in the war to establish a single, universal authority in Christendom. The Holy Roman Church triumphed over the Holy Roman Empire. After the death of Frederick II and after the long interregnum that followed, the Holy Roman Empire was little more than one medieval kingdom among many. The interregnum was ended in 1273 by the election of Rudolph I of Hapsburg, and under his successors the Medieval Roman Empire grew even more limited in power and territory. The kings of the national monarchies adopted many imperial prerogatives formerly reserved for emperors. In the later Middle Ages some of these kings attempted to exercise lordship over the Church that had similarities to the authority claimed by the Germanic emperors before the Investiture Controversy. From 1438 the Holy Roman Empire came to be the virtual possession of the house of Hapsburg and so lingered on as a mere relic of its medieval greatness, until its final dissolution in 1806.

Bibliography: J. B. BRYCE, *The Holy Roman Empire* (New York 1919). J. W. THOMPSON, *Feudal Germany* (Chicago 1928). G. BARRACLOUGH, *The Origins of Modern Germany* (2d ed. Oxford 1957; pa. New York 1963). K. HAMPE, *Deutsche Kaisergeschichte in der Zeit der Salier und Staufer*, ed. F. BAETHGEN (10th ed. Heidelberg 1949). F. KEMPF, *Papsttum und Kaisertum bei Innocenz III.: Die geistigen und rechlichen Grundlagen seiner Thronstrietpolitik* (Miscellanea Historiae Pontificiae 58; Rome 1954). W. GOEZ, *Translatio imperii* (Tübingen 1958). G. TELLENBACH, *Church, State and Christian Society at the Time of the Investiture Contest*, tr. R. F. BENNETT (Oxford 1959). T. E. MOMMSEN and K. F. MORRISON, trs., *Imperial Lives and Letters of the Eleventh Century* (New York 1962). B. TIERNEY, *The Crisis of Church and State, 1050–1300* (Englewood Cliffs, New Jersey 1964, reprint Toronto 1994). R. MCKITTERICK, *The Frankish Kingdoms under the Carolingians, 751–987* (London-New York 1983). T. REUTER, *Germany in the Early Middle Ages 800–1056* (Longman History of Germany; London-New York 1991). H. FUHRMANN, *Germany in the High Middle Ages c. 1050–1200*, trans. T. REUTER (Cambridge Medieval Textbooks; Cambridge 1986). A. HAVERKAMP, *Medieval Germany 1056–1273*, trans. H. BRAUN and R. MORTIMER (2nd ed. Oxford 1988). D. ABULAFIA, *Frederick II: A Medieval Emperor* (London 1992). K. PENNINGTON, *The Prince and the Law: Sovereignty and Rights in the Western Legal Tradition* (Berkeley-Los Angeles-London 1993).

[K. PENNINGTON]

HOLY ROOD, ABBEY OF

Former royal monastery of the canons regular, adjoining Holyrood Palace, Edinburgh, Scotland. It was founded by DAVID I of Scotland *c.* 1128. Liberally endowed for the CANONS REGULAR OF ST. AUGUSTINE, it had close associations with the Scottish crown, being frequently used by the Stewarts as a royal residence. There James II was born in 1430 and married Mary of Gueldres in 1449, and there, too, James III and James IV were married in 1469 and 1503 respectively. Sacked and burned by the English in 1544 and 1547, and desecrated by the Reformers in 1559, the abbey fell into ruin, and while its chapel became the reformed parish church of the Canongate, the abbey lands were appropriated and created into a temporal lordship. Restored as a chapel royal by Charles I in 1633, and again by James II, the church was once more sacked in 1688, and later attempts to repair it were abandoned when its roof collapsed in 1768. It is now a ruin.

Bibliography: R. PITCAIRN, ed. *Chronicon coenobii Sanctae Crucis Edinburgensis* (Edinburgh 1828). C. INNES, ed. *Liber cartarum Sancte Crucis* (Edinburgh 1840). J. HARRISON, *The History of the Monastery of the Holy Rood* (London 1919). D. E. EASSON, *Medieval Religious Houses: Scotland* (London 1957) 75.

[L. MACFARLANE]

HOLY SEE

A term designating Rome as the bishopric of the pope. The word is derived from the Latin *sedes,* which denotes the seat or residence of the bishop: this is because the bishop's office is symbolized by the chair in which he presides over his people. The word see is accordingly applied to all bishoprics, although it was first used of the Churches founded by Apostles. They would be known further as apostolic or holy sees, in as much as it was the function of the Apostles to mediate Christ's holiness to their flocks. As the titles pope and apostolic see came to be used especially of the bishop of Rome and his see, so too the title holy see was restricted to Rome. In canonical and diplomatic language it now refers to Rome as the bishopric of the pope and to his Curia, the Roman Congregations, tribunals, and offices.

[B. FORSHAW]

HOLY SPIRIT, BAPTISM IN

Impetus to a greater appreciation of the role of the Holy Spirit in the Christian life has come through the CHARISMATIC RENEWAL. While better classified as a renewal *in* the Holy Spirit than a devotion *to* him, the movement stresses the experiential nature of faith and finds support in those Scripture passages that speak of the gift of the Holy Spirit.

Baptism in the Holy Spirit. Stress is laid on an initial experience popularly called the "baptism in the Holy Spirit," accompanied by the expectation of some charismatic manifestation, such as praying in tongues or prophecy. Precedents for this relationship between the Holy Spirit as Gift and the gifts of the Holy Spirit are seen especially in Acts. How the charisms and the Sacraments of Christian initiation are related is a matter of current theological discussion. In practice, the "baptism in the Holy Spirit" (also sometimes referred to as "infilling" or "release" of the Holy Spirit) is experienced as a new departure in the Christian life effected usually through prayer and the laying on of hands by other Christians. The central and unique characteristic of the charismatic movement is the relation perceived between this renewal in the Holy Spirit and the charisms. With the encouragement of Paul (1 Cor 14.1), the gifts are actively sought. Those listed in 1 Cor 12–14 are held to be available today, such as tongues, prophecy, healing, the word of knowledge, the word of wisdom (*see* CHARISMATIC PRAYER). Yielding to these gifts is seen as a way of cooperating with the renewing work of the Spirit.

Theological Explanations. Among the theological explanations of this relationship, there are those who would explain it as an unfolding of the sacramental grace particularly of Baptism and Confirmation. Note is taken of the fact that the reception of the Spirit in Acts is always accompanied by a charismatic manifestation. Others seek an understanding of the relationship in a more general theology of grace, for which the praying community as such would be sufficient ecclesial cause. In discussing the missions of the divine persons, specifically the sending of the Son and the Spirit into the soul of the Christian, St. Thomas Aquinas says that such a sending "is especially seen in that kind of increase of grace whereby a person moves forward into some new act or some new state of grace: as, for example, when a person moves forward into the grace of working miracles, or of prophecy, or out of the burning love of God offers his life as a martyr, or renounces all his possessions, or undertakes some other such heroic act" (*Summa theologiae* 1a, 43.6 ad 2). It is significant that the sending he speaks of is not the initial sending, but a subsequent "breakthrough" into a new experience of grace. It is further significant that the

examples Aquinas gives of such an *innovatio* or *profectus* are connected with charismatic manifestation. These two aspects correspond to the charismatic experience as it is described and lived today by many Christians. It further appears that the division of grace into sanctifying (*gratia gratum faciens*) and charismatic (*gratia gratis data*), which in the past often led to a disregard for the latter in favor of the former, should be made with great caution, since what is aimed at building up the Church will normally also be related to a personal growth in grace (ibid. 43.3 ad 4). To seek the gifts and to yield to them may thus be as important an exercise for spiritual growth as practices of asceticism. The gifts are, at any rate, calculated to expand the community's experience of God as gift.

Although the charisms are sought as particular manifestations of the Spirit, the charismatic movement has a strong Christocentric devotional base, so that the Holy Spirit appears more as a power moving the Church through his gifts than as an object of devotion in himself.

Bibliography: D. L. GELPI, *Charism and Sacrament: A Theology of Christian Conversion* (New York 1976). K. MCDONNELL, *The Holy Spirit and Power: The Catholic Charismatic Renewal* (New York 1975). G. T. MONTAGUE, *The Spirit and His Gifts* (New York 1974); *The Holy Spirit: Growth of a Biblical Tradition* (New York 1976). E. D. O'CONNOR, *Perspectives on Charismatic Renewal* (Notre Dame, Ind. 1975) extensive bibliography. L. J. SUENENS, *A New Pentecost?* (New York 1975); *Theological and Pastoral Orientations on the Catholic Charismatic Renewal* (Notre Dame, Ind. 1974). F. SULLIVAN, "The Baptism in the Holy Spirit and Christian Tradition." *New Covenant* 3 (May 1974) 30.

[G. T. MONTAGUE]

HOLY SPIRIT, DAUGHTERS OF THE

(D.H.S., Official Catholic Directory #0820), a pontifical institute founded on Dec. 8, 1706, when Marie Balavenne and Renée Burel made their religious profession in the chapel of Plérin, Brittany, France, and dedicated themselves to the care of the sick and the education of youth. The founder and director of the young community was a priest of Plérin, Jean Leuduger. The congregation continued to grow in the 18th century until the French Revolution, when it suffered the suppression and confiscation that was the common fate of all the religious orders. Some of the sisters carried on their work secretly until the congregation was reconstituted in 1800. After its reorganization, and official recognition by imperial decree on Dec. 10, 1810, a new era of development followed. When the mother-house at Plérin was no longer large enough, the sisters chose a new site in Saint-Brieuc, western France, in 1834.

The 20th century brought new problems. The series of laws directed in 1902 and 1903 against teaching congregations in France suppressed Catholic schools. Seven hundred Daughters of the Holy Ghost were expelled from their convents. Seeking a place to carry on their work, a group of six sisters arrived in the United States on Dec. 8, 1902. Others went to Belgium, Holland, and England. In these areas the 20th century has been one of steady advance for the congregation. In 1936 the community found a new field of endeavor in Manchuria. Although expulsion from Chinese territory brought the missionary labors of the sisters there to an abrupt close in 1951, new missions were begun in Africa and South America. In addition to teaching at all levels, the sisters also work in healthcare services, pastoral ministries, catechetics, nursing and care facilities for the aged. The provincial center in the United States is in Putnam, Connecticut.

[C. P. COMTOIS/EDS.]

HOLY SPIRIT, DEVOTION TO

In the Christian Era has its roots in the Old Testament, although among the Hebrews the Spirit (*ruah*, breath, wind) was regarded more as a manifestation of the divine presence and activity than as a divine person. The operations of the Spirit (1 Cor ch. 14) were not uncommon in the apostolic Church, but these provide no clear evidence of the recognition of the personal distinction of the Holy Spirit or of the tribute of a special devotion. By the mid-fourth century Catholic doctrine regarding the Holy Spirit was explained fully and clearly, but for long this resulted in no widespread popular devotion. Among the elite, however, devotion to the Holy Spirit, especially as Sanctifier, existed from early times. From the earliest Christian writers, both Greek and Latin, to the present, there is a rich and unbroken tradition of devotion to the Holy Spirit that is supported by Christian art and archeology, hymnology (e.g., *VENI SANCTE SPIRITUS, VENI CREATOR SPIRITUS*), and liturgy. In the Middle Ages popular devotion to the Holy Spirit was given an impetus with the rise of confraternities dedicated to Him, notably those connected with the Hospitalers of the Holy Spirit (see P. BRUNE, *Histoire de l'ordre Hospitalier du Saint-Esprit*, Paris 1892). In the 17th century there was a remarkable surge of popular devotion to the Holy Spirit (*see Dictionnaire de spiritualité ascétique et mystique. Doctrine et histoire*, ed. M. Viller et al. [Paris 1932–] 5: 1604–10), and in recent times the encyclicals of Leo XIII (*Provida Matris,* 1895, and *Divinum illud munus,* 1897) and of Plus XII (*Mystici Corporis,* 1948) have been effectual in promoting devotion to the Holy Spirit among the faithful.

Bibliography: H. B. SWETE, *The Holy Spirit in the New Testament* (London 1909); *The Holy Spirit in the Ancient Church* (London 1912). H. LECLERCQ, *Dictionnaire d'archéologie chrétienne et de liturgie,* ed. F. CABROL, H. LECLERCQ and H. I. MARROU (Paris 1907–53) 5.1:525–529. J. RUTHCÉ, *L'Élite et la dévotion au Saint-Esprit* (Gembloux 1926). F. SÜHLING, *Die Taube als religiöses Symbol im Christlichen Altertum* (Freiburg 1930). E. L. HESTON, *The Spiritual Life and the Role of the Holy Ghost in the Sanctification of the Soul as Described in the Works of Didymus of Alexandria* (St. Meinrad, Ind. 1938). P. GALTIER, *Le Saint-Esprit en nous d'après les Pères grecs* (Rome 1946). S. TROMP, *De Spiritu Sancto anima corporis, mystici,* 2 v. (Rome 1932). A. GARDEIL, *Le Saint-Esprit dans la vie chrétienne* (4th ed. Paris 1950). T. MAERTENS, *Le Souffle et l'Esprit de Dieu* (Paris 1955). J. ISAAC, *La Révélation progressive des personnes divines* (Paris 1960). G. LEFEBVRE, *L'Esprit de Dieu dans la sainte liturgie* (Paris 1958). F. VANDENBROUCKE, *Dictionnaire de spiritualité ascétique et mystique. Doctrine et histoire,* ed. M. VILLER et al. (Paris 1932–) 4.2:1316–18.

[M. F. LAUGHLIN]

HOLY SPIRIT, FRUITS OF

Those good affections listed by St. Paul as the achievement of man's spirit (Gal 5.22–23) in contrast to the ills inflicted on him by his flesh (Gal 5.19–21). As in many other places, Paul was speaking of the soul transformed by the Holy Spirit. Thus, some Fathers considered his enumeration a partial list of the many goods effected in the soul by the Holy Spirit's unity of action. St. Thomas Aquinas, influenced by the Fathers, attempted an adaptation of St. Paul's concept by fitting the fruits into his own theory of a supernatural organism. He considered man's supernatural life an organic synthesis, the interaction of whose parts influenced the maturation of the soul in grace. The gifts and infused virtues are bound together, some gifts serving the theological virtues, others directing the cardinal virtues. Into this spiritual composite, he fitted the fruits, attaching each to intense acts of virtues or gifts. Because of a sort of blessedness that comes to the soul from the intense activity of certain gifts, he called their fruits beatitudes. The good affections wrought in the soul by other intense acts of the gifts and of the virtues he called simply fruits. The virtue of faith perfected by the intellectual gifts results in a fruit, a kind of security, called faith, to which is attached a fruit called joy. Charity also produces joy, to which is added peace and the special fruit, charity (acts of). Counsel has no special fruit, since its end is action; yet acts of counsel have mercy and kindness attached. Piety's direct fruits are goodness and benignity; its indirect fruit, serenity. The fruits of fortitude are patience and long-suffering. FEAR OF THE LORD, through its direction of temperance, produces the fruits of chastity, modesty, continence. Pope Leo XIII, though not citing the specific relationship of acts and fruits, spoke of "those blessed fruits enumerated by the Apostle which the Spirit produces and shows forth in the just" (*Divinum illud munus*).

Bibliography: L. M. MARTÍNEZ, *The Sanctifier,* tr. M. AQUINAS (Paterson 1957). B. FROGET, *The Indwelling of the Holy Spirit in the*

"Virgin Mary and St. John Receiving the Seven Gifts of the Holy Spirit," Spanish Gothic Altarpiece. (©Andrea Jemolo/CORBIS)

Souls of the Just, tr. S. A. RAEMERS (Westminster, Md. 1950). LEO XIII, *Divinum illud munus* (encyclical, May 9, 1897), *Acta Sanctae Sedis* 29 (1896–97) 644–658, Eng. *The Great Encyclical Letters,* ed. J. J. WYNNE (New York 1903) 422–440, A. GARDEIL, *Dictionnaire de théologie catholique,* ed. A. VACANT et al., (Paris 1903—50) 6.1: 944–949.

[P. F. MULHERN]

HOLY SPIRIT, GIFTS OF

The source of the Church's teaching on the gifts of the Holy Spirit is the manifestation of the Holy Spirit in the OT and the NT, and in the life of the Church. The Spirit promised in Isaiah (11.1–3) manifested Himself at the Baptism of Jesus and communicated Himself to the Apostles at Pentecost. Thereafter He gave Himself to the Church, which lived under His continuing influence. The Church sees the gifts promised in Isaiah (six in the Hebrew, seven in the Septuagint) realized first in Christ and

then, by a participation in His plenitude, in itself, His body. As Vatican Council II has declared, it is in the souls of the faithful who make up this body that the Spirit gives His gifts for the welfare of the Church (see *Dogmatic Constitution on the Church* 7).

Teaching of the Fathers. Educated in the apostolic tradition, the early Fathers wrote of the Holy Spirit in the life of the Christian (*see* GOD [HOLY SPIRIT]). Most of them spoke of two stages, one the Christian life at its minimum, the other in which the Spirit dominates the soul under its constant motion. But the early Fathers did not speak clearly of seven special gifts distinct from the graces of the Holy Spirit in general and from the Pauline charisms.

The Greek Fathers, beginning with St. Clement, recalled Isaiah's list of gifts, but they did not confine themselves to precise numbers. It was enough for them that the Spirit poured out His riches on Christ, then on the

Church in its members. The Latin Fathers, however, cited the number and allegorized about it. St. Victorinus of Pettau (*In. Apoc.* 1) related the seven gifts to the seven spirits of the Apocalypse; St. Hilary (*In Mt.* 15.10) connected them with the seven loaves in the miracle of the bread and fishes; St. Augustine (*Serm.* 347) traced a parallel between the seven gifts and the beatitudes, and he saw in Isaiah's words a complete description of the Holy Spirit's work in the soul. St. Gregory the Great drew on Augustine especially (*Moralia* 2); he saw the gifts as special aids to the Christian in his war against evil. His writings furnished a foundation for the theology on the gifts to be developed in the Middle Ages.

Middle Ages. From Gregory in the 7th century to the 11th century, nothing was added to the literature on the gifts. In the 12th century, there came a renascence of interest attributable principally to the reading of SS. Augustine and Gregory. Inquiry began into questions that the Fathers had not asked: Are the gifts a species of VIRTUE, or are they quite distinct? What role do they play in the spiritual life? Why are there seven of them, and how are they classified? The answers to these questions were to have a profound effect on the theology of the spiritual life.

In the early 13th century, there was no precise terminology on the gifts, although much had been written on them. Some thought the gifts to be the source of the virtues; others saw them as effects. Most of the theologians, however, identified gifts and virtues. Then, in 1235, with the *Summa* of Philip the Chancellor (cf. *Recherches de théologie ancienne et médiévale* 1:76–82), a trend began toward viewing the gifts as distinct from and superior to the virtues. This became the classic teaching at the University of Paris, especially by the Franciscan and Dominican schools, and it was given its perfect expression by St. Thomas Aquinas (*Summa theologiae* 1a2ae 68.2).

Teaching of St. Thomas. Beginning, as was his way, with an existent reality, Aquinas reasoned to the soul's need for supernatural aids, superior to the virtues and by which the soul could become habitually pliable to the influence of the Holy Spirit. He saw that, despite the dignity given the soul by the theological virtues, because of the supernatural object (i.e., God Himself) to which they oriented it, the virtues do not give to the soul a perfection of action comparable to what it has in the natural order from the natural virtues. It became clear to him that a man with the supernatural virtues alone would be much less at home in the things of God than a man with the natural virtues was in the things of nature. For, as he said, "We know and love God imperfectly with the supernatural virtues" (*Summa theologiae* 1a2ae 68.2). In effect, if a man had only virtues, without the gifts, he would be less able to achieve supernatural perfection than to achieve natural perfection.

It was unthinkable to St. Thomas that God, who shared His inner life with man by grace, would provide for his needs less perfectly in the supernatural than in the natural order. Thus, he argued that with the life of grace God gives supplementary forces to the soul by which it can achieve the same level of performance supernaturally that it achieves naturally. Since our sanctification is appropriated to the Holy Spirit, St. Thomas concluded that the same Spirit meets this normal need of the soul by directing it supernaturally, much as human reason directs it in the purely natural order. This influence of the Holy Spirit intervenes in man's supernatural psychology, bestowing on it a capacity for action parallel to the perfect action achieved by the natural virtues. The modifications, or dispositions, or tendencies in the soul, that result from the action of the Holy Spirit are called His gifts: wisdom, understanding, knowledge, piety, fortitude, counsel, and fear of the Lord. Through these the Holy Spirit can direct the supernatural life of the soul much as human reason, through the virtues, directs the moral life of the soul.

Because the need of the soul was lasting, it was clear to St. Thomas that the entities by which the need was met were lasting too. Hence, though distinct from the virtues, the gifts were like the virtues in that they were habits. As habits, the gifts and the supernatural virtues have the same efficient cause, God, the author of the supernatural order. But the principal or motor cause is different: for the infused virtues, the immediate principle of action is human reason elevated by grace; for the gifts, the principle of action is the Holy Spirit. Through the gifts, He moves men as His immediate and direct instruments. Therein lies a pivotal distinction: the infused virtues can be used by their possessor at will, presuming the actual grace, which is never wanting; the gifts, however, are actuated not at the will of the possessor but only at the will of the Holy Spirit. Thus, although the practice of the virtues is said to prepare the soul for the activity of the gifts, this is only because virtuous actions remove the obstacles in men that impede the activity of the Holy Spirit. The gifts will not operate if there are obstacles, but they do not operate automatically when the obstacles are taken away. Their action depends on the Holy Spirit.

The gifts, then, differ from the virtues. In the use of the virtues, even the infused ones, the soul is fully active; it is capable of such fully supernatural action because it is supernaturalized in its being by habitual grace. Still, its actions are performed in a human mode. A person in sanctifying grace, for example, elicits an act of love of God at will; the soul is the motor cause. A soul under the motion of the gifts acts vitally, but seconding a divine motion. It is passive only to the divine agent; it executes what the Holy Spirit executes in it. The action of the gift is an activity received.

Moved by the direct and immediate action of the Holy Spirit, the gifts, as His instruments, are subordinate to the virtues, but only in that the purpose of the gifts is the perfection of the infused virtues. So the fruits of the Holy Spirit are actions of virtues that have been perfected by the gifts. More perfect than the fruits are the BEATITUDES, actions that flow from the gifts and the virtues working together; these are the highest actions of the soul on earth, an anticipation of eternal beatitude.

The teaching of St. Thomas on the gifts found favor because of its simplicity and its principles. But it has always met opposition, especially from the Scotists, who deny the distinction between the gifts and the virtues. Since the gifts are not distinct entities to these theologians, they make no attempt to fit them into the supernatural organism. Today St. Thomas's exposition is sometimes criticized as being dependent on an imperfect understanding of the famous text of Isaiah. However, although he, following the Fathers, took the exact number of the gifts from Isaiah, his teaching on the function of the gifts in the spiritual life flows from the principle, verified throughout the NT, that the souls of the just need the special help of the Holy Spirit. What he says about the gifts has been given much authority in modern times by the generous use of his concepts and language in the encyclical on the Holy Spirit, *Divinum illud munus* of LEO XIII.

Bibliography: LEO XIII, "Divinum illud munus" (encyclical, May 9, 1897) *Acta Sanctae Sedis* 29 (1896–97) 644–658, Eng. *Catholic Mind* 36 (May 8, 1938) 161–181. B. FROGET, *The Indwelling of the Holy Spirit in the Souls of the Just,* tr. S. A. RAEMERS (Westminster, Md. 1950). JOHN OF ST. THOMAS, *The Gifts of the Holy Ghost,* tr. W. D. HUGHES (New York 1951). J. DE GUIBERT, *The Theology of the Spiritual Life,* tr. P. BARRETT (New York 1953). A. GARDEIL, *Dictionnaire de théologie catholique,* ed. A. VACANT et al. (Paris 1903–50) 4.2:1728–81. R. CESSARIO, *Christian Faith and the Theological Life* (Washington, D.C. 1996). S. PINCKAERS, *The Sources of Christian Ethics,* tr. M. T. NOBLE (3d rev. ed.; Washington, D.C. 1995). THOMAS AQUINAS, *Summa theologiae* 1a2ae 68.2.

[P. F. MULHERN]

HOLY SPIRIT, ICONOGRAPHY OF

The third Person of the Holy TRINITY was represented in all periods of Christian art preeminently in the form of a snow-white dove. The use of the dove as a symbol of the Holy Spirit was formally approved by a local council of Constantinople in 536. In scenes of Pentecost, the Holy Spirit appears as described in Acts, in the form of fiery tongues descending on the Apostles. The additional symbolization of the Holy Spirit as a dove in Pentecost scenes, although not attested in the Biblical narrative, is supported by the anonymous *Liber de rebaptismate* (*Patrologia Latina*, ed. J. P. Migne [Paris 1878–90] 3:1203). The Holy Spirit has been represented anthropomorphically in painting and sculpture of the Holy Trinity, but this mode of representation declined after the Middle Ages and was ultimately declared unacceptable in a decree by Benedict XIV (Oct. 1, 1745).

The Holy Spirit is represented principally in three scenes from the New Testament: the Annunciation to the Blessed Virgin, the Baptism in the Jordan, and Pentecost. They occur then at the conception of Jesus Christ, at the beginning of His public life, and at His last manifestation in the cycle of the glorification, for it was He who promised that He would send the Holy Spirit.

Annunciation. In the Annunciation scene, the Virgin is present with the angel and the dove of the Holy Spirit. The dove is not found in all representations of the Annunciation, but it is present in the fully elaborated depictions. One may also find God the Father and an embryon or homunculus of Christ. The figure of the dove in its descent courses along golden rays of light proceeding from the mouth of God the Father on high. One may also mention at this point representations of Mary with the Holy Spirit present, which are not scenes of the Annunciation. In the "Virgin and Child with Angels, Prophets, and Symbols" by the early Netherlandish painter Provost (Hermitage, Leningrad), the dove of the Holy Spirit hovers over the Virgin with her crown in its claws.

Baptism of Christ. The three essential figures in representations of the Baptism of Christ are the Son, the Baptist, and the dove of the Holy Spirit, usually shown directly above the head of Christ. Sometimes at the top of the painting God the Father is also shown ruling over the scene that inaugurates the public life of Christ. According to Matthew, the Holy Spirit, at the moment of the Baptism, descended like a dove, but Luke avers that the Spirit descended indeed in the corporeal form of a dove. In the "Baptist" by Jan Joest (Church of St. Nicholas, Kalkar), the dove of the Holy Spirit is on a parallel with the head of St. John, with Christ in the center. Andrea Verrocchio (15th century) shows the dove issuing from the open hands of God, its beams forming a secondary radiance above the head of Christ and falling upon the lustral water in the scoop held above the head of Christ by St. John. Paintings of the Baptism of Christ, in their arrangement, frequently recall the vertical Trinities of the late Middle Ages and early Renaissance with God the Father uppermost, then the dove of the Holy Spirit, and Christ below.

Pentecost. The dove of the Holy Spirit occurs in representations of Pentecost, although its appearance is not

"The Baptism of Christ," panel of the *"Altarpiece of Jan de Trompes"* by Gerard David, depicting St. John the Baptist baptising Christ with God the Father and the Holy Spirit present above, 1505, in the Groeninge Museum, Bruges, Belgium. (©Francis G. Mayer/CORBIS)

mentioned in the Acts of the Apostles. In Acts the Holy Spirit manifests itself to the disciples of Christ under the form of tongues of fire that descend upon their heads. The dove entered artistic representations of Pentecost on the authority of the early anonymous *Liber de rebaptismate:* ''Et hominibus quidem Spiritus perseverat hodie invisibilis, . . . Sed in principio mysterii fidei et spiritalis Baptismatis hic idem Spiritus manifeste visus est et super discipulos insedisse quasi ignis: item, coelis apertis, descendisse super Dominum columbae similem'' (*Patrologia Latina,* 3:1203).

In one of the earliest representations of the Pentecost (sixth century, Gospel Book of Rabbula), the Holy Spirit is represented by tongues of fire alone descending upon the heads of the Apostles and the Virgin in their midst. However, the standard mode of representing the Holy Spirit in this scene is double, by the tongues of fire and by the dove (1403, fresco by Taddeo di Bartolo; Municipal Palace, Perugia). The flames may be represented directly on the heads of the participants in the Pentecost scene, as in the Gospel Book of Rabbula, or hovering a short distance above their heads, as in a late medieval painting of the Ulm school (Saint Bavo), or with the fiery tongues darting down upon their heads, as in a Pentecost painting by Rappaert (Bruges Museum). In a painting of deep agitation and physical movement, Titian combines the dove, streaming beams of light, and tongues of flame in a manneristic composition of the Pentecost (1543; S. Maria della Salute, Venice). The severely classical treatment of the same subject by Bordone (*c.* 1550; Brera Gallery, Milan) conceals the body of the dove of the Holy Spirit behind the central portion of a great classical arch showing only the lower limits of the burst of radiance behind the line of the stone archway that frames the scene.

Attribute of Saints. The dove appears as a source of inspiration to certain saints. It is an attribute of all those inspired by the Holy Spirit, notably the Evangelists and the Doctors of the Church. In Michael Pacher's ''The Four Latin Fathers'' (*c.* 1483; Pinakothek, Munich) a dove appears over each of the Doctors: Jerome, Augustine, Ambrose, and Gregory; Gregory bears his on the right shoulder. It is said in his *Life* by Paul the Deacon (ch. 28) that the dove of the Holy Spirit was seen repeatedly inspiring the author of the *Pastoral Care* and the *Great Morals.* Thus the dove appears in Carpaccio's ''Meditation on the Passion'' (Metropolitan Museum of Art, New York) perched on the sarcophagus throne on which Christ sits—meditated upon by St. Jerome and Job. (The *Great Morals* of St. Gregory was based on the Book of Job.) St. Basil is shown dictating under the inspiration of the Holy Spirit (*c.* 1656, painting by Francisco de Herrera, Louvre).

See Also: TRINITY, HOLY, ICONOGRAPHY OF.

''St. Gregory the Great and the Holy Spirit,'' detail of a 13th-century fresco at Subiaco, Italy.

Bibliography: W. STENGEL, *Das Taubensymbol des Heiligen Geistes* (Strasbourg 1904). W. F. STADELMAN, *Glories of the Holy Ghost* (Techny, Ill. 1919), 100 illus. H. KÜCHES, *Der Heilige Geist in der Kunst* (Knechtsteden 1923). K. KÜNSTLE, *Ikonographie der Christ-lichen Kunst,* 2 v. (Freiburg 1926–28) 1:221–239. F. SÜHLING, *Die Taube als religiöses Symbol im christlichen Altertum* (Freiburg 1930) 1–51. L. RÉAU, *Iconographie de l'art chrétien* (Paris 1955–59) 2.1:11–29. V. H. ELBERN, *Lexikon für Theologie und Kirche,* ed. J. HOFER and K. RAHNER (Freiberg 1957–65) 5:113–114.

[L. P. SIGER]

HOLY SPIRIT, ORDER OF THE

An order of HOSPITALLERS, founded *c.* 1180 in France by GUY DE MONTPELLIER. Through the patronage of INNOCENT III and later popes, the Order of the Holy Spirit rapidly became the vehicle of worldwide comprehensive social programs that lasted for more than 500 years. Before 1198 its chief center was the hospital of the Holy Spirit in Montpellier, which had eight affiliates, including two houses in Rome. Medically progressive in its care of the sick, it expanded Christian HOSPITALITY to embrace the works of mercy in general.

Within months of his accession in 1198, Innocent issued the brief *His praecipue,* recommending the order to all bishops of the world. In the briefs of July 1 and Nov. 25, 1198 (*Religiosam vitam*), Innocent moved to make the new order an instrument of his crusade on behalf of the suffering poor, which probably constitutes one of the grandest and least-heralded achievements of his pontificate. Of decisive importance is the bull *Inter opera pietatis* of June 19, 1204, which committed the newly built Roman hospital of the Holy Spirit near *S. Maria in Saxia* on the Tiber to the hospitallers of the Holy Spirit and united it with that of Montpellier under the spiritual administration of Guy. The church of *S. Maria in Saxia* stood near a ruinous complex of buildings that had once been a flourishing house of hospitality for English pilgrims, the *Schola Saxonum,* founded in the 8th century. Acquiring the site and properties of the *Schola Saxonum,* Innocent built the hospital of the Holy Spirit in Saxia, delivered it to the Order of the Holy Spirit, and made the entire project directly subject to the Holy See.

Probably from 1204 to 1208, when Guy is known to have lived in Rome, the ancient rule of the order took definitive shape. Both the brothers and the sisters observed the same rule and cared equally for the sick, the indigent, orphans, foundlings, unmarried mothers, the aged, the insane, and the homeless. To supplement the papal-guaranteed income and privileges, the Confraternity of the Holy Spirit enrolled laymen of every social rank. The members provided money and pledged themselves annually to some days of personal service.

By an amazing expansion, hospitals of the Holy Spirit and auxiliary associations, displaying the official device of the double cross surmounted by the dove, sprang up throughout Christendom as legal and spiritual affiliates of the Roman institute, sharing the latter's exemption from local ecclesiastical and civil authorities. The grand master or preceptor of the hospitallers exercised quasi-episcopal power over all affiliates, their workers, clients, and dependents, wherever they existed. There is written record of 1,240 affiliates throughout Europe, with 10 in Asia, Africa, and Latin America. Many others left no written trace.

After this prodigious early growth and expansion, periods of decadence set in. EUGENE IV, in 1444, noting that the ravages of war, negligent administration, absence of the papacy from Rome, and breakdown of religious life had practically destroyed Christian ''hospitality,'' undertook to reform the order, reestablish the confraternity, and personally assume the preceptorship. SIXTUS IV in 1477, as the order's second founder, tightened the administration and replaced the old buildings with splendid new constructions. Under LEO XII in 1826 reform again became urgent. His elaborate plan encountered the opposition of vested interests and died with him in 1829. Pius

IX's bull *Inter plurima* (July 1, 1847) suppressed the Order of the Holy Spirit. Causes of the collapse included the following: rivalry between Rome and Montpellier, admission of unsettled religious from other orders, civil wars, loss of religious dedication to the poor, greedy enjoyment of fat priorates, and parasitic exploitation of the order's handsome properties.

In its best days, the Order of the Holy Spirit and its affiliates embodied the spirit of Christian mercy on a vaster scale and with more creative adaptability than anything hitherto seen in Christendom. From the beginning, it courageously enlisted women religious as infirmarians; it maintained an incorruptible policy of gratuitous service; it spurred medical progress by its schools of anatomy, surgery, and pharmaceutics; it introduced an elaborate program of music therapy not only for mental patients but for all, including infants at feeding time. As an organization it passed from history, but as the spirit of humility serving Christ in the sick and poor it passed over into younger orders and lives on to this day.

See Also: HOSPITALS, HISTORY OF.

Bibliography: P. BRUNE, *Histoire de l'ordre hospitalier du Saint Esprit* (Paris 1892). A. CANEZZA, *Gli arcispedali di Roma nella vita cittadina, nella storia e nell'arte* (Rome 1933). O. DE ANGELIS, *L'arciospedale di Santo Spirito in Saxia nel passato e nel presente* (Rome 1952); *Regula sive statuta hospitalis Sancti Spiritus: La piu antica regola ospitaliera di Santo Spirito in Saxia* (Rome 1954); *L'ospedale apostolico di Santo Spirito in Saxia nella mente e nel cuore dei papi* (Rome 1956); *L'ospedale di Santo Spirito in Saxia e le sue filiali nel mondo* (Rome 1958). J. RATH, *Lexikon für Theologie und Kirche,* ed. J. HOFER and K. RAHNER (Freiburg 1957–65) 5:114–115.

[P. L. HUG]

HOLY SPIRIT, SISTERS OF THE

(SHS, Official Catholic Directory #2040), a diocesan congregation founded on April 25, 1913, at Donora, Pennsylvania, by J. F. Regis Canevin, Bishop of Pittsburgh (1904 to 1920). The community follows the Rule of St. Augustine. As the number of sisters increased, larger facilities were needed, and on Aug. 14, 1926, a new motherhouse and novitiate were dedicated in West View, Pittsburgh. The sisters are principally engaged in teaching, nursing, and care of children and the aged. The motherhouse is in Ross Township, Pittsburgh, Pennsylvania.

[M. E. KWIATKOWSKI/EDS.]

HOLY SPIRIT AND MARY IMMACULATE, SISTERS OF THE

The Sisters of the Holy Spirit and Mary Immaculate (S.H.Sp., Official Catholic Directory, #2050), a congregation with papal approbation (1939), was founded in 1893 in San Antonio, Texas, by Mrs. Margaret Mary Healy Murphy. After the death of her husband, Mrs. Murphy thought about several aspects of the apostolate to which she might devote the remaining years of her life. She was especially anxious to help educate black children. With ecclesiastical approval Mrs. Murphy and a small group of helpers took simple vows of poverty, chastity, and obedience. Mrs. Murphy, as Sister Margaret Mary, was elected first superior general, and governed the congregation until her death in 1907. Her charity, faith, and courage inspired her successors to continue her work; the sisters staffed parochial schools in Texas, Louisiana, and Mississippi. Their chief work is the education of youth, especially the poor and the marginalized. The sisters are also involved in pastoral ministry, youth ministry, retreats, catechetics and social services. The generalate is located in San Antonio, Texas.

[M. I. MCGANN/EDS.]

HOLY SPIRIT MISSIONARY SISTERS

A pontifical institute founded specifically for the propagation of the faith in the underdeveloped countries of the world. The congregation, whose official title is Missionary Sisters Servants of the Holy Spirit (SSPS, Official Catholic Directory #3530), was begun by Arnold JANSSEN, founder of the Society of the Divine Word, at Steyl, Holland, in 1889. Devotion to the Holy Spirit and zeal for the salvation of souls are the characteristics of this society, which undertakes educational, medical, and social work in predominantly non-Christian areas.

Their work in the U.S. began when Mother Leonarda Lentrup came from Holland in 1901 with four other sisters and established a motherhouse in Techny, Ill. The congregation has conducted retreat houses, taught in schools, and trained missionaries to send abroad. Mother Leonarda was a pioneer in the lay retreat movement; she opened her motherhouse to this apostolate from the beginning. In 1908 the community staffed an elementary school for African-Americans in Vicksburg, Miss., the first of a series of schools established in Arkansas and Mississippi. The sisters' first secondary school for blacks, Sacred Heart High School, began its work in Greenville, Miss., in 1920. Maurice Rousseve, Anthony Bourges, and Francis Wade, members of the Society of the Divine Word and three of the first five black priests to be ordained in the U.S., had attended this high school.

As early as 1910 the U.S. province had begun work in the foreign missions. In that year four sisters went to New Guinea. In the intervening years, sisters were sent to China, the Philippines, India, Africa, and Japan.

The generalate is in Rome; the U.S. headquarters is in Techny, Illinois.

[T. M. MCNEELY/EDS.]

HOLY SYNOD

The Russian Holy Synod was instituted by PETER I, the Great (Jan. 25, 1721) to govern the Orthodox Church of Russia in place of the patriarchate. It consisted of a college of bishops and monks under a lay procurator. Its full name was the Most Holy Directing Synod. It originated after Leibniz suggested to Peter that he should complete his reorganization of the state by creating an ecclesiastical college. Peter conceived the idea of establishing an ecclesiastical body that would be unable to impede his reforms; yet he declined to become himself a part of the general structure of the Russian Church. He wanted to be its patron, not its spiritual head. On one occasion, however, when the Russian bishops asked him to restore the patriarchate, he struck his breast and replied, "Here is your patriarch."

The Church-State relation was outlined in detail in the organization of the Holy Synod. It was impossible for the hierarchy to meddle in state affairs, but the Czar would not be able to treat the bishops as Ivan the Terrible (1533–84) had. The opposition of the Russian episcopate to Peter's reform looked to Patriarch Adrian for support, but that indecisive churchman suffered from poor health and offered only a tacit resistance. Adrian died in 1700, and the Moscow Patriarchate, which began in 1589, ceased to exist in 1721. Peter the Great prevented the appointment of a patriarch of Moscow by naming STEFAN, Bishop of Riasan, as keeper and administrator of the patriarchal see (October 1721). Stefan sided with the Czar in the beginning, but later, especially after the execution of Czarevich Alexej, he became an opponent of the change. Peter found a more willing collaborator in Feofan PROKOPOVICH, whose ideas were embodied in the Church Statute of 1721. Stefan, a former Jesuit novice and a pro-Catholic, provided the last serious opposition to the Holy Synod, but he capitulated eventually and cooperated as an appointed member of it.

The statute was more a political charter than an ecclesiastical one; it provided for the reorganization of Church administration and outlined an educational program. Stefan opposed Prokopovich's episcopal consecration and accused him of Calvinism. Prokopovich, in his treatise *The Right to the Monarch's Will,* delineated modern Western ideas on the absolute power of the ruler combined with Byzantine theocratic concepts. His *Ecclesiastical Regulation* applied to religion and the state and made the Church subject to the state's laws and ordinances.

Members of the Holy Synod were drawn from both the "white" (secular) and the "black" (monastic) clergy. By founding the Synod, Peter ended the "state within the state" by abolishing the patriarchate, which had come to rival the Czar. Originally there were to be 12 members, all appointed by the Czar. The Ukase of 1763 determined that there should be at least six ecclesiastical members. In accord with the Czar, Prokopovich elaborated the spiritual regulations and in 1721 solemnly opened the Holy Synod, where, in spite of the nominal presidency of Stefan, he himself governed and reformed the Russian Church. The members of the ecclesiastical college had to swear that they recognized "as supreme judge of this college, our most clement monarch of all Russia." By a decree of March 11, 1722, the Holy Synod was placed under the supervision of a lay chief procurator who was *de facto* the head of Church administration. During the reign of Peter the Great, the Synod retained, for the most part, its ecclesiastical character. After his death, however, this character was lost by degrees, and the Synod became a vast political bureaucracy. Under such rulers as Šakhovskij, Čhebyšeff, and Galycin, the Russian Church was mistreated and humiliated. In 1881 Konstantin Pobedonostsev was called to the government of the Synod; he was a man of great culture who wished to unite all the religions professed in Russia into the one Orthodox Church. The Statute of 1721 provided the Holy Synod with the "full" rights and powers of the patriarch in religious matters, but in ecclesiastical administration it became a bureaucratic department. The jurisdiction of the Holy Synod extended not only to all kinds of ecclesiastical questions but also to some that were purely secular. All processes for heresy and all matrimonial cases were brought before the Synod.

The patriarchs of Antioch and Jerusalem recognized the Holy Synod in 1723, but the liberal Russian clergy attacked both the Synod and the anticanonical constitution of the Church and demanded a reestablishment of the patriarchate. The government then proposed the convocation of a great national synod to restore the Church's liberties and to give it a new constitution, but this purpose was defeated by friction between the "white" and the "black" clergy and by the outbreak of the revolution. The Holy Synod survived until 1917, when the patriarchate was restored (November 5), with TIKHON as the first patriarch. On Jan. 23, 1918, a law of State-Church separation was promulgated. (*See* ORTHODOX CHURCHES).

Bibliography: A. M. AMMANN, *Storia della Chiesa Russa* (Turin 1948), Ger. tr. *Abriss der ostslawischen Kirchengeschichte* (Vienna 1950). T. V. BARSOV, *Sviatieiš Synod V jego prošlom* (Most Holy Synod and Its History) (St. Petersburg 1896). F. DVORNIK, *The Slavs in European History and Civilization* (New Brunswick, N.J. 1962) 556–. M. I. FLORINSKY, *Russia, A History and an Interpretation* (New York 1960). J. LEDIT, "Russie," *Dictionnaire de theologie catholique*, ed. A. VACANT et al. (Paris 1903–50) 14:324–333. A. PALMIERI, *La Chiesa Russa* (Florence 1908). J. SERECH, "Stephan Yavorsky and the Conflict of Ideologies in the Age of Peter I," *Slavonic and East European Review* 30 (1951) 40–62. P. V. VERKHOVSKOI, *Uchrezdenie dukhovnoi Kollegii i dukhovnii reglament* (Establishment of the Ecclesiastical College and the Ecclesiastical Regulation) (Warsaw 1916).

[J. PAPIN]

HOLY THURSDAY

The Thursday before Easter, and first day of the Easter Triduum has had several names in the course of time; all of them point to one or another aspect of the day's celebration. The official name, and at the same time probably the oldest, is *Feria Quinta in Coena Domini* (Thursday of the Lord's Supper), because it chiefly commemorates the institution of the Holy Eucharist. The same idea lies behind the charming and original name given it in the calendar of Polemius Silvius (fifth century), *natalis calicis* (birth of the chalice), also current in southern Gaul during the sixth and seventh centuries. The term *natale sacramenti* (birth of the Sacrament) is similar in meaning. In some places in the past, it was called *dies traditionis*, referring to the many *traditiones* (betrayal or handing over) that occurred on that day: the betrayal of Jesus by Judas, Jesus' handing over of himself for the salvation of humanity, and the giving of his body and blood in the Eucharist. English-speaking lands often call it Maundy Thursday, a corruption of the Latin word *mandatum*, used to describe the rite of washing of the feet associated with Holy Thursday for centuries. The Germans call it *Gründonnerstag (Grinenden, greinenden, weinenden*, weeping), which appears to be a reference to the reconciliation of the penitents that took place on this day for many centuries. The most popular name in all languages, however, is Holy Thursday.

Historical Background. The celebration of Holy Thursday is very ancient. Historically, the reconciliation of penitents took place on this day, to enable them to participate in the paschal feast. Traditionally, the holy oils were also consecrated on Thursday because they would be needed for the blessing of the baptismal water, and this was the last day that would be free for their consecration. Before the seventh century, however, they were consecrated during the East Vigil. The 1955 reforms of Pope Pius XII called for a special Mass of the Chrism, distinct from the solemn evening liturgy, to be celebrated in cathedrals in the morning. The prayers and the proper preface for the Mass of the Chrism were taken from the Gelasian Sacramentary, but new readings were provided.

It was altogether natural that there should be a special commemoration of the institution of the Eucharist on the day when this great event had taken place. Already in the fourth century it was known as *in coena Domini*, i.e., Thursday of the Lord's Supper. The custom of celebrating the Eucharist itself on the evening of Holy Thursday about the hour when it was instituted seems to have originated in Jerusalem.

The rite of WASHING OF THE FEET was originally a simple act of charity very common in the Church. It did not become a liturgical rite until about the seventh century. Its purpose is to manifest the charity and love that should motivate those who will be participating in the Lord's Supper.

The procession of the reserved sacrament to the altar of repose is the one modern survival of the earlier, more common practice of reserving consecrated hosts for Communion on those days when the Eucharist was not celebrated. Such aliturgical days occurred more frequently in earlier times. Originally, there was no special ceremony about it; as soon as Mass was over the deacon took the consecrated hosts in the pyx from the main altar and carried them to the sacristy where they were reserved until the next day. During the High Middle Ages this altogether practical procedure was transformed into an elaborate ritual. Once Good Friday had become the one day of the year when the Eucharist was not celebrated, reserving the Eucharist for Communion took place only once a year and became surrounded with greater ceremony. The first mention of a formal procession comes from the 11th century.

The stripping of the altars on Holy Thursday became a liturgical rite in the course of time. In reality it is a survival, on this one day of the year, of what was, for centuries, done every day after Mass; it was the practice to remove the altar cloths each day and put them on again the next. A simple everyday practice has thus been transformed into a religious rite.

Liturgical Structure. The present celebration of Mass of the Lord's Supper dates back from Pius XII's reforms of the Holy Week liturgy in 1955. His Holy Week Ordinal restored the Mass of the Last Supper to the evening hours. Normally, there is to be only one evening Mass in each parish and religious community; this is intended to emphasize the oneness of the Eucharistic celebration. The tabernacle is empty because all will receive Holy Communion from the bread and wine consecrated at this Eucharist. The washing of feet is placed within the Mass, instead of after Mass. After Mass the celebrant carries the ciborium containing the consecrated hosts for the communion service on Good Friday in solemn procession to the simply and soberly adorned repository. There, the Blessed Sacrament is reserved until the Communion service on the next day. Veneration of the Blessed Sacrament by the faithful is prescribed until midnight. After the Blessed Sacrament has been placed in the repository, the service concludes with the stripping of the altar.

Bibliography: W. J. O'SHEA, *The Meaning of Holy Week* (Collegeville, Minn. 1958). T. J. TALLEY, *The Origins of the Liturgical Year* (Collegeville 1991). A. J. MARTIMORT, ed. *The Church at Prayer IV: The Liturgy and Time* (Collegeville 1986). A. NOCENT, *The Liturgical Year* (Collegeville 1977). J. M. PIERCE, ''Holy Week and Easter in the Middle Ages,'' in *Passover and Easter: Origin and History to Modern Times*, eds. P. F. BRADSHAW and L. A. HOFFMAN (Notre Dame, Ind. 1999) 161–185. A. ADAM, *The Liturgical Year: Its History & Its Meaning after the Reform of the Liturgy* (New York 1981).

[W. J. O'SHEA/EDS.]

HOLY UNION SISTERS

Officially, the Religious of the Holy Union of the Sacred Hearts (SUSC, Official Catholic Directory #2070); a congregation of teaching sisters with papal approbation, dedicated to the Sacred Heart of Jesus and the Immaculate Heart of Mary. Father Jean Baptiste Debrabant (1801–1880) founded the community in Douai, France, in 1826 to provide the religious instruction that was urgently needed in the period following the French Revolution. The community received full canonical approbation from Rome in 1843. In 1902, under a law authorizing the expulsion of all teaching religious from French schools, the French government confiscated 70 convents and schools of the congregation between 1902 and 1904. The sisters took refuge in their already established convents in Kain, Belgium (1833); Bath, England (1857); Bannagher, Ireland (1853); the U.S. (1886); and Argentina (1888). Not until 1941 did the sisters reopen their French schools.

Although the chief work of the community has always been teaching, on three occasions the sisters have taken up special tasks at the request of the Holy See. From 1923 to 1934 they assisted the Jesuit Orientalist Michael d' HERBIGNY by taking charge of the Villa Albani in Rome, a home for refugee Russians under the special jurisdiction of Pius XI. In 1928 the pope asked the sisters to train in their novitiate, then in Rome, candidates for the Byzantine Congregation of Sisters of the Theotokos Pammakaristos (founded in 1921 by George Calavassy, then apostolic exarch of Constantinople). Then in 1941, at the suggestion of their cardinal protector, the sisters opened their convent, Villa Santa Teresa, as a hostel for college and university women studying in Rome.

The community came to the U.S. in 1886 when the Academy of Sacred Hearts, Fall River, MA, was opened by Mother Marie Helena (1849–1937). Mother Helena

"Semana Santa," or Holy Week celebrations, Seville, Spain, ca. 1900–1925. (©Scheufler Collection/CORBIS)

later became the first provincial superior in the United States. A novitiate was begun in Fall River in 1902. In the U.S., the congregation is divided into two separate provinces: Holy Union Fall River Province (headquartered in Fall River, MA) and Sacred Heart Province (headquartered in Groton, MA). Since 1958, the generalate is located in Rome.

Bibliography: A. CURTAYNE, *Jean Baptist Debrabant* (Paterson, NJ 1936). J. R. N. MAXWELL, *Fifty Golden Years* (Paterson, NJ 1963). A. DELPLANQUE, *Portrait de M. Debrabant, fondateur de la Sainte Union des Sacrés Coeurs* (Lille 1925).

[J. E. CREAMER/EDS.]

HOLY WEEK

Holy Week is the week immediately preceding Easter, the principal week of the liturgical year. Besides the name Holy Week, it is also called Major or Greater Week. In earlier centuries it was known as Passion Week because it commemorated the events of the Passion, as well as Paschal Week since in Christian antiquity the notion of Passion always included the resurrection. The AMBROSIAN RITE calls it "authentic week," which is also an allusion to the events celebrated during these days. Because public sinners were absolved of their sins on Holy Thursday, Holy Week was in some places "the week of remission." Less happy was the designation "painful week," which it was given in other parts of the Church because of the increased burden of penance and fasting during these days. More to the point is what the Eastern Christians still call it, "the Week of Salvation".

Although the first recorded reference to Holy Week is in St. Athanasius's *Festal Letters* announcing the date of Easter, the original nucleus of Holy Week was the annual celebration of the Paschal Feast, which was then (3rd century) a three–day (*triduum*) commemoration beginning on Friday and ending on the morning of Easter Sunday. Holy Thursday was added by at least the 4th century. The entire week was rounded out at some time in the 5th or 6th century. Many of the Holy Week observances as we know them came originally from Jerusalem and spread through the West.

In 1955, Pius XII restored Holy Week to the prominence it had had in the early church, a prominence it had largely lost through the accretions of extraneous rites and ceremonies over time. In effect, Holy Week was restored as the heart of the Church's year; through the rites of this week we relive the central elements of the paschal mystery. This pastoral consideration prompted Pius XII to insist on the active participation of the people in the Holy Week rites so that the whole Church is drawn into the celebration.

See Also: PALM SUNDAY; HOLY THURSDAY; GOOD FRIDAY; EASTER VIGIL.

Bibliography: M. TIERNEY, *Holy Week: A Commentary* (Dublin 1958). C. HOWELL, *Preparing for Easter* (rev. and enl. Collegeville, Minn. 1957). H. SCHMIDT, *Hebdomada Sancta,* 2 v. (Rome 1956–57). W. J. O'SHEA, *The Meaning of Holy Week* (Collegeville, Minn. 1958). T. J. TALLEY, *The Origins of the Liturgical Year* (Collegeville, 1991). A. J. MARTIMORT, ed., *The Church at Prayer IV: The Liturgy and Time* (Collegeville 1986). A. NOCENT, *The Liturgical Year* (Collegeville 1977). J. M. PIERCE, "Holy Week and Easter in the Middle Ages," in *Passover and Easter: Origin and History to Modern Times*, eds. P. F. BRADSHAW and L. A. HOFFMAN (South Bend, Ind. 1999) 161–185. A. ADAM, *The Liturgical Year: Its History & Its Meaning after the Reform of the Liturgy* (New York 1981).

[W. J. O'SHEA/EDS.]

HOLY YEAR

A year during which a solemn plenary indulgence is granted to the faithful under certain conditions. Holy Years are ordinary when they occur at regular intervals (every 25 years in modern times) and extraordinary when they are proclaimed for some very special reason, e.g., in 1933, to celebrate the anniversary of the Redemption.

In pre-Exilic Judaism every 50th year was a JUBILEE YEAR, or year of remission (Lev 25.25–54), in which debts were pardoned and slaves freed. After the Exile and until A.D. 70, the Jews continued to hold a sabbatical year in which debts of fellow Jews were remitted. The medieval popes came to apply such a custom spiritually, decreeing a Holy Year or Jubilee, beginning and ending with special sacred ceremonies, which was intended to improve the religious life of the faithful.

History. The first Holy Year in 1300 began on the evening of December 24–25 (the end of the old year and beginning of the new, by the reckoning of the Roman Curia), when large crowds visited St. Peter's basilica. Others continued to come on the following days, for a tradition had arisen that the first year of every century was especially propitious for gaining special indulgences. Though no written source could be located, Pope BONIFACE VIII issued the bull *Antiquorum habet* (February 22), which determined that every 100 years a universal jubilee should be celebrated. During the centenary year, under condition of contrition and confession, the faithful could gain a plenary indulgence by making visits to the basilicas of ST. PETER's and SAINT PAUL-OUTSIDE-THE-WALLS: 30 if they were Romans, otherwise 15. Immense crowds of pilgrims visited Rome in answer to this bull (engraved in marble and still found at the side of the Holy Door in St. Peter's). In 1342 CLEMENT VI decreed a jubilee every 50 years; hence the second Holy Year was in 1350. In 1389 URBAN VI reduced the time to 33 years (according to the belief that our Savior had lived that long) and proclaimed the third Holy Year for 1390. Two more basilicas were to be visited, St. John Lateran, and St. Mary Major. The fourth jubilee was the centenary year 1400, and the fifth was held in 1425 by MARTIN V, who preferred in those unsettled times to wait two years after the 33 years as determined by Urban VI had elapsed. In 1450, NICHOLAS V celebrated a jubilee and canonized the popular BERNARDINE OF SIENA. Finally, in 1470, PAUL II reduced the time to 25 years, so that the next Holy Year was in 1475, and up to our days this custom has remained. In 1500 ALEXANDER VI prescribed the ceremonies that are observed essentially even today: the pope opens the Holy Door of St. Peter's and appoints three cardinals to do the same in the other basilicas, using assigned rites and prayers. At the end of the Holy Year, the Porta Santa is again walled up.

Great pomp accompanied later jubilees, although the French invasion of Italy prevented its celebration in 1800. Though LEO XII in 1825 held another jubilee, political troubles prevented that of 1850. In 1875 Pius IX was a prisoner in the Vatican and felt obliged to celebrate the jubilee in a very restricted way. But LEO XIII renewed the solemnity in 1900, and PIUS XI proclaimed the ordinary Holy Year in 1925, and the extraordinary in 1933. The Holy Year of 2000, marking the transition to the third Christian millennium witnessed unprecedented crowds

Pope Boniface VIII blessing pilgrims during the Holy Year 1300; fresco in St. John Lateran, Rome, attributed to Giotto. (Alinari-Art Reference/Art Resource, NY)

visiting Rome and other designated shrines worldwide for the jubilee indulgence.

Requirements and Ceremonies. An ordinary Holy Year begins on December 24, with first vespers of Christmas. On this day, the Holy Doors of the four basilicas are simultaneously opened. Conditions for the jubilee indulgence include confession made especially for gaining the jubilee indulgence; communion, and visits to the four major basilicas, for those who are in Rome, but elsewhere, to churches designated by the local ordinary. Each papal document of proclamation specifies the exact conditions of the jubilee. Local ordinaries receive faculties to dispense from these conditions all those who are unable to fulfill them.

Bibliography: P. BREZZI, *Storia degli anni santi* (Milan 1949). R. FOREVILLE, ''L'idée de jubilé chez les théologiens et les canonistes (XIIᵉ–XIIIᵉ): avant l'institution du jubilé romain (1300),'' *Revue d'Histoire Ecclesiastique* 56 (1961) 401–423. F. FERRERO, ''Año Santo y moral: originalidad y perspectivas historicas de un gesto eclesial controvertido,'' *Studia Moralia* 11 (1973) 181–200. T. J. REESE, ''A Eucharistic Millennial Jubilee,'' *Worship* 69 (1995) 531–537.

[J. J. GAVIGAN/EDS.]

HOLYWOOD, CHRISTOPHER

Superior of the Jesuit mission in Ireland; b. Dublin, 1562; d. Dublin, Sept. 4, 1626. He was the elder son of Nicholas, Lord of Artane, County Dublin, and Elizabeth, daughter of John Plunket, third Baron Dunsany. He entered the novitiate at Verdun in 1584. After studies at the university of Pont-à-Mousson, he lectured on theology at Dôle and later at Padua. He was appointed superior of the Irish mission in 1598, but was arrested at Dover and detained in different prisons until May 1603. He was then transported to France, and eventually arrived in Ireland in March 1604. Although he suffered from poor health and impaired eyesight, his government of this Jesuit mission until his death fully justified his appointment. During his term of office the number of Jesuits in Ireland increased from 7 to 44, and residences were established by him in the principal towns of Leinster, Munster, and Connaght. He promoted the introduction and expansion of the Sodality of the Blessed Virgin, especially among the Anglo-Irish of the larger towns who were most exposed to the protestantizing influence of the government.

Holywood was the author of two important controversial works published at Antwerp, and before his death had just completed a treatise on the moral virtues.

Bibliography: J. MACERLEAN, "Superiors of the Irish Mission, 1598–1774," *Irish Jesuit Year Book* (Dublin 1929). E. HOGAN, *Ibernia Ignatiana* (Dublin 1880). C. SOMMERVOGEL et al., *Bibliothèque de la Compagnie de Jésus,* 11 v. (Brussels-Paris 1890–1932) 4:446–447.

[F. FINEGAN]

HOLZHAUSER, BARTHOLOMEW

Ecclesiastical writer, founder of Bartholomites; b. Langna, Bavaria, Aug. 24, 1613; d. Bingen, May 20, 1658. He was one of 11 children of an impoverished family. In 1639, after working his way through school, he was ordained at Ingolstadt. The next year, while exercising his priestly duties, he attended the university and earned a licentiate in theology and a doctorate in philosophy. He served as pastor in Tittmonig, Leukenthat, and Bingen on the Rhine.

At the university, the general laxity in morals and weakening of the faith caused by the THIRTY YEARS' WAR disturbed him, and he envisioned a congregation for diocesan priests whose objective would be the sanctification of its members in their missionary apostolate. Other than a promise of obedience to a superior no vows would be taken. Those members leading exemplary lives were to teach in seminaries or live by twos and threes as zealous leaders in parishes. He was unable to make a foundation in Eichstadt, but established one at Tittmonig, Bavaria, in the Archdiocese of Salzburg, under the title *Institutum Clericorum saecularium in communi viventium,* often referred to as the "United Brothers" or "Bartholomites." The latter term is not to be confused with the Armenian monks of the same title who sought refuge in Italy in the 13th century. In 1658 the request for papal approbation was denied; however, at the request of Emperor Leopold, the approval was given in 1680, twelve years after Holzhauser's death. The institute flourished in many countries, having at one time more than 1,500 members; many seminaries were entrusted to its members. However, the institute had many enemies who helped bring about its extinction in the late 18th century. The congregation was restored in France in the 19th century.

One of Holzhauser's important writings is *Constitutiones et exercitia spiritualia clericorum saecularium in communi viventium,* a constitution used in many seminaries in the 17th and 18th centuries, and as a handbook for education of the laity. His *Interpretatio Apocalypsis usque ad cap XV,* has as its central feature the familiar theme of the Middle Ages, that of JOACHIM OF FIORE, the seven ages of the Church. *De diversis orandi modis et de modo meditandi, De humilitate,* and *Epistola fundamentalis* are among his writings aimed to help clerical and laic spiritual development. A petition for Holzhauser's canonization was begun in Rome.

Bibliography: M. HEIMBUCHER, *Die Orden und Kongregationen der katholischen Kirche,* 2 v. (3d ed. Paderborn 1932–34) 2:595–598. H. HURTER, *Nomenclator literarius theologiae catholicae,* 5 v. in 6 (3d ed. Innsbruck 1903–13) 3:1039. M. J. HUFNAGEL, *Lexikon für Theologie und Kirche,* ed. J. HOFER and K. RAHNER, 10 v. (2d, new ed. Freiburg 1957–65) 2:7; 5:458.

[C. LYNCH]

HOMILETICS

Homiletics in its broadest sense may be defined as the theory of preaching, and as such it is a part of pastoral theology, coordinate with CATECHETICS and liturgy. The part of this theory that considers the Church's mission to preach, the role of preaching in the economy of salvation, the supernatural efficacy of preaching, and the relationships of preaching to Sacred Scripture, to the liturgy, and to the hierarchical powers of teaching, Orders, and jurisdiction is more commonly called the theology of preaching. In a restricted sense, however, in which it is also sometimes called sacred eloquence or sacred rhetoric, homiletics may be defined as the body of concepts and principles that govern effective preaching. In this sense it is concerned with both the matter and the form of the preacher's discourse. To the extent that it is concerned with the actual substance of what is to be preached, it is known as material homiletics. To the extent that it is concerned with the investigation, arrangement, and expression of ideas, it is formal homiletics. Both material and formal homiletics may be general or special. General homiletics is the body of concepts and principles that govern all effective preaching. Special homiletics is a more limited body of concepts and principles, applying only to the preaching of a particular area of doctrine or discipline, or to a particular type of audience, or in a particular situation. Special homiletics has not achieved any typical systematization or organization of its concepts and principles, and therefore a synopsis of its content is scarcely possible. It must treat, however, the specific problems of missions and retreats, religious conferences and recollections, cursillos, novenas, and other types of preaching beyond the usual preaching during the Mass, all of which have their own characteristics.

General homiletics, concerned with all effective preaching, draws its concepts and principles from reflection on the example of Jesus Christ and His Apostles and Christian preachers who have followed them down through the centuries. Counsels for the preparation and delivery of effective discourse derived in this way have been organized in many different systems by various authors in the long history of the theory of preaching *see* PREACHING, II (HOMILETIC THEORY). The most typical system over the centuries has employed the framework of the perennial rhetoric, with its fivefold process of invention, arrangement, style, memory, and delivery. Employment of this rhetorical canon as a form of organization, however, indicates that general homiletics depends on the perennial rhetoric not as its foundation, but rather as its framework. This relationship is analogous to that between Catholic theology and scholastic philosophy, which are sciences independent of each other and yet of the greatest mutual assistance.

A synopsis of the content of general homiletics may therefore be given under six headings. The first of these, an introductory tract, stands for preliminary discussion of the whole of preaching, such as the role of the preacher, his personal qualities, his duty to preach, his mandate from the Church, his habits of study and work. For this tract, *see* PREACHING, III (THEOLOGY OF). The other five, corresponding to the rhetorical canon, are concerned respectively with finding the ideas (invention); putting then into effective order (arrangement); expressing them in words and sentences (style); fixing them in mind (memory); and uttering them with effective voice and action (delivery).

Invention. This tract deals with finding what is to be preached. It explains the principles of searching out the

material, sifting it, rejecting what is less suitable, and finally selecting the ideas to be expressed. Important in this tract is the discussion of the psychological phenomena of the creative process in all its phases, to which the preacher, as any other creative worker, is subject. Principles are established for determining the preacher's theme in a given situation, such as the principles of adequate instruction, liturgical unity, and audience analysis. Methods of investigating the selected theme by reflection, discussion, and reading are expounded, with particular attention to the standard current reference works and available research tools. The various aims of preaching are then discussed: transcendent, generic, and specific. The ultimate or transcendent aim is the glory of God through the salvation of souls, from which it follows that preaching is a supernatural act and that all of its norms of effectiveness must not be literary or aesthetic, but functional and pragmatic. Moreover, since this aim is to be achieved through human cooperation with grace, which requires an act of will, Catholic preaching as a whole is persuasive and must lead ultimately to moral resolution and action. This, however, is not to say that every individual sermon must be persuasive. On the contrary, the intermediate or generic aims of preaching are traditionally to instruct, to affect, and to persuade, these three being English terms evolved from the *docere, delectare, movere* of St. Augustine after Cicero and Quintilian; and although they are seldom isolated from each other, each of the three aims suffices by itself for a single discourse. The specific or proximate aim of preaching is, finally, the particular good that the preacher intends to achieve in a given discourse.

In further discussion of the creative process a complete homiletic theory explains the *topoi*, otherwise known as "topics" or "commonplaces," after the τόποι and *loci communes* of the ancients. These are a list of general headings or concepts that the preacher will learn to check off in sorting out the ideas he has accumulated in his remote and proximate preparation for preaching on a given theme. Sometimes the *topoi* are broadly distinguished as instructive, affective, or persuasive, corresponding to the three generic aims served by the ideas to which each of the respective *topoi* are related.

The purpose of the instructive *topoi* is to provide the preacher with a checklist of headings that will help him to take inventory of the ideas he can use to instruct his listeners on a theme, such as definition, derivation, description, distinction, division, distribution, comparison, contrast, causality, quotations, statistics, probability, history, example, and analogy. Affective *topoi* provide the preacher with a checklist of clues to the inspiring aspects of a theme, such as size, power, magnificence, mystery, solemnity, terror, universality, antiquity, nostalgia, nobility, tenderness, and poignancy. Persuasive *topoi* are those aspects of his material that give the preacher the power to move his listeners to definite action. Any authentic series of motives or drives discovered in human psychology is a checklist of such *topoi*. One given by St. Thomas Aquinas consists of the 11 interrelated passions that he describes in the *Summa theologiae*. The doctrine of the *topoi*, long an integral part of homiletic theory, but often controversial and recently out of favor, is being revived by contemporary psychological investigation of the creative process.

Arrangement. The tract on arrangement is concerned with putting into the most effective sequence the thought that the preacher has chosen for expression. Its basic principle is that it is important to determine not only what is to be said in a given discourse but also in what order it is to be said, since each thought prepares the listeners either well or poorly for what follows. Principles of good arrangement are therefore concerned with the frame of mind and tone of feeling that listeners have at the outset, during the progress, and toward the conclusion of the discourse. Fundamental qualities to be observed in arrangement are: unity, the relation of ideas to each other and to the specific aim of the sermon; structure, the relationship among the major units of discourse; emergence, the clarity and force with which the essential message stands out from its background of supporting material; and progression, the forward movement of ideas that arouses, sustains, and finally satisfies the interest of the listeners. Basic also is the discussion of the laws of attention and interest and similar psychological factors.

Distinction may be made between static and dynamic arrangement: the former may be defined as a sequence characterized by neat divisions of material, well unified and structured, but in which the earlier part of the discourse does not set up psychological momentum to carry the interest forward; the latter may be defined as a sequence characterized by a kind of tension and involvement in the earlier parts that naturally drive the mind and emotions onward by setting up a need for satisfaction. Although the variety of sequences implementing these concepts and principles is unlimited, there are a number of formulas, or typical outlines, that historically and psychologically have proved themselves as basic plans of arrangement. From patristic and early medieval times there are the various forms of the HOMILY; from late medieval times there is the scholastic thesis and the simple syllogism; from the Renaissance tracts on ecclesiastical rhetoric there is the five- or six-part classical oration; from 17th-century France there is the Little Method of St. Vincent de Paul. All of these have had their vogue in the history of Christian preaching and are worthy of close study on the part of the student even in the 20th century. In addition, a number of formulas derived both from practical experience and from the psychological research of modern times can be brought forward as effective plans, such as those based on the problem-solution arrangement and the motivated sequence. These formulas serve in the creative process as *topoi* of arrangement, corresponding to the *topoi* of invention described above.

Style. The tract on style concerns the principles by which the actual words, phrases, and sentences are to be chosen for expressing the ideas already discovered and arranged. The general qualities of language, such as clearness, concreteness, emphasis, and coherence, are discussed. This tract deals also with the levels or types of style, of which three were distinguished by St. Augustine after Cicero and Quintilian and of which three may still be distinguished as corresponding to the generic aims of preaching, namely, the instructive style, the affective style, and the persuasive style. Avoiding any impression that style is concerned with literary ornament rather than with the functional effectiveness that is the touchstone of every other part of formal homiletic theory, the general features of each of these three styles and their relationship is described. A feature of all of them is the use of stylistic modes, a term that may be employed for the "tropes and figures" of earlier ecclesiastical rhetorics, standing for the rhetorical movement of phrases and sentences or even whole paragraphs, the same thought of which can be cast in a variety of stylistic modes, just as the same argument can be framed in a dozen different moods of syllogism. This part of the tract on style, almost entirely atrophied in contemporary manuals, must, like the *topoi*, be interpreted anew.

Memory and Delivery. The tracts on memory and delivery in general homiletics differ little, if at all, from the corresponding theory in secular rhetoric or public speaking. In these days, when discourses are commonly much shorter than in ancient times, the discussion of memory is limited almost entirely to a consideration of the comparative merits of preaching from manuscript, or from memory, or from nothing more than an outline firmly fixed in the mind. Which of these methods is best has been hotly debated since the time of St. Augustine. The merits of these various degrees of memorizing as against extemporizing may, however, be summed up in an explanation of an extempore-memoriter continuum to indicate the degree of memorizing as against extemporizing in any given type of preparation for preaching. What type is best in any instance will depend on the preacher's experience and aptitudes, the theme, the audience, and the circumstances.

The tract on delivery, finally, includes consideration of vocal variety and bodily action, elements so essential to effective preaching that they must be the object of extensive practice. Under the vocal aspect of delivery comes discussion of variety in the vocal elements of time, pitch, force, and quality. Under the bodily aspect comes discussion of covert and overt action, posture, and gesture.

For bibliography, *see* PREACHING, I (HISTORY OF).

[J. M. CONNORS]

HOMILETICS, TEACHING OF

After the Second Vatican Council II there were significant changes in the teaching of homiletics in Catholic seminaries. These changes were the result of a number of factors. Probably the most important one was the renewed emphasis on preaching within the Catholic Church. The Council's Decree on the Ministry and Life of Priests states that the proclamation of the Word of God through preaching is the most important duty of the priest (*Presbyterorum ordinis* 4). Contemporary theology of preaching views preaching not as a message about faith, but as the occasion *for an actual salvific meeting* between God and man. "In still another way yet more truly . . . (God) is present in the Church as she preaches, since the Gospel proclaimed is the Word of God, which is preached only in the name and by the authority of Christ and with his presence . . ." (Paul VI MystFid; *Acta Apostolicae Sedis* 57 [1965] 763).

A second factor was the general decline in the public's unquestioning acceptance of institutional authority. In the Church one of the results has been a more vocal laity who feel freer to criticize the quality of preaching and the qualifications of preachers. This has been accentuated by the ecumenical movement which has familiarized Catholic clergy and laity with the centrality of preaching in the Protestant tradition in contrast to its lack of emphasis in the Catholic tradition.

A third factor was a change in the field of speech education. Public speaking, which provided the traditional framework for instruction in homiletics, came to be situated within the broader context of communication so that public speaking is seen as but one form of public communication. Introductory speech courses address include approaches to intrapersonal, interpersonal, and mass communication.

Curricular Elements. Although there is no standard homiletics curriculum, there is a consensus that an effective program of instruction in homiletics must include the following elements.

The Person as Preacher. From both a theological and a communications viewpoint the preacher is central to the preaching task. The homily in essence must be a witness to a saving encounter between God and the preacher. Thus his spiritual life is an essential part of preaching. The preacher must learn to be honest about his own concerns, failures, and successes. This portion of the course must provide the seminarian with tools for self-analysis and a setting for rededication in faith.

Theology and Preaching. The preacher must understand the importance of preaching in God's salvific plan. Preaching is the normative link between God and man. He must be aware of the kerygmatic nature of preaching in which Christ actually meets men through the preaching event (Ebeling). In another vein, instruction in practical exegesis must be given in which a biblical passage is analyzed not only for its theological but also its "homiletic" content.

Preaching as Communication. An overview of research in communication is crucial for effective preaching. A course would cover such topics as speaker credibility, persuasion, attitudes, dissonance theories. A preacher must know his congregation. Thus he must be provided with proper tools for audience analysis. These include strategies for overcoming audience barriers to the message. According to communication theory this is one of the most neglected and most important areas of preaching.

Homily Preparation and Evaluation. The elements of the traditional speech course are still essential for the preacher. Its format can be based upon the classical rhetorical canons (invention, arrangement, style, memory, and delivery) or on other contemporary arrangements. The element of added importance today is a full treatment of homily evaluation through individual critiques, video and audio taping, and critique teams.

New Forms of Preaching. While instruction in special forms of preaching (retreats, cursillos, etc.) has been a peripheral part of the curriculum in homiletics, being introduced are such types of preaching as dialogue homilies (chancel and congregational), multi-media homilies, and the use of radio and television. While these forms will not replace the traditional preaching format, they remain important to the preacher.

See Also: PREACHING III (THEOLOGY OF).

Bibliography: G. EBELING, *Theology and Proclamation: Dialogue with Bultmann* (Philadelphia 1966). R. HOWE, *The Miracle of Dialogue* (New York 1963); *Partners in Preaching: Clergy and Laity in Dialogue* (New York 1967). J. JUNGMANN, *The Good News Yesterday and Today* (New York 1962). W. MALCOMSON, *The Preaching Event* (Philadelphia 1968). K. RAHNER, ed., *The Renewal of Preaching: Theory and Practice* (New York 1968). D. RANDOLPH, *The Renewal of Preaching: A New Homiletic Based on the New Hermeneutic* (Philadelphia 1969). W. THOMPSON and G. BEN-

NET, *Dialogue Preaching: The Shared Sermon* (Valley Forge 1969). G. ROXBURGH, ed., *Clergy in Communication*, 4 v. (Ottawa 1970). R. P. WAZNAK, *Sunday after Sunday: Preaching the Homily as Story* (New York 1983). G. S. SLOYAN, *Worshipful Preaching* (Philadelphia 1984). W. J. BURGHARDT, *Preaching: The Art and the Craft* (New York 1987).

[A. STEICHEN]

HOMILY

Derived from the Greek word *homilia* (verb form *homilein*) that means primarily a being together, communion, social intercourse; the parallel Latin word is *commercium*. Homily connotes the idea of a meeting of minds and hearts and so it very soon took on the meaning of familiar speech with someone, of conversation, and of familiar discourse with a gathering. These still remain the basic notes of a genuine homily: a familiar (in the sense of fatherly) conversation with a group of people.

History. Although the etymology is an aid to understanding what the homily essentially is, a familiar discourse, it does not really give the specific Christian meaning of the word. For that one must look to the history of preaching and the use of the term in Christian literature. There the homily is a familiar discourse made by a pastor of souls to the people confided to his care, a conversational discourse that is given during the liturgical action upon a text suggested by the liturgy. This is the character of the genuine homily from the time it makes its first appearance in the 2d-century description of the Mass given by St. Justin down through the golden age of the homily in the 4th and 5th centuries and well into medieval times. This form of preaching at once so pastoral and so biblical has been revived by the *Constitution on the Sacred Liturgy* of Vatican Council II.

Beginning. While the remote origin of the homily may have been the commentary on the Scriptures that were read in the synagogue service, the Christian form was something altogether new. The Scripture commentary that formed part of the synagogue service was more didactic and explanatory whereas the Christian homily appears more as an exhortation based upon the text, or an application of the text to Christian living. The homily described by Justin in his first *Apology* is certainly more than a mere exegesis of the text: "After the reading of the Scriptures the president of the brethren exhorts us (or verbally admonishes us) to the imitation of these good examples (things) in a speech" (1 *Apology* 67; J. Quasten, ed., *Monumenta eucharista et liturgica vetusstissima* 19).

Patristic Period. From the 3d century onward the homily took more definite shape and this type of preaching reached its fullest development in the homilies of the

Fathers of the Church, in both East and West. Normally the homily was given by the celebrant (who was usually the bishop) during the Eucharistic synaxis; in fact it was an almost indispensable part of Sunday worship. It consisted of an explanation and application of one or other of the texts read or sung in the liturgical assembly.

The great homilists among the Fathers were Origen, the Cappadocians, and John Chrysostom in the East, and Hippolytus, Ambrose, Augustine, Maximus of Turin, Zeno of Verona, and Leo the Great in the West. Origen himself shows that the homily is more than a mere commentary on the Scripture: "It is not a time to comment, but to edify the Church of God and to move inert and nonchalant hearers by the example of the saints and mystical explanations" (*Hom. in Gen.* 10.5; *Patrologia Graeca*, ed. J. P. Migne, 12:219). He was also the first to make the distinction between "logos" (sermo) and "homilia" (tractatus). The first was preaching in the style of the classical orations, while the homily was the form of preaching in which popular exegesis of Scripture was given.

Basil is remembered for his homilies on the Hexaemeron (six days of creation), on the Psalms, and on moral subjects. John Chrysostom commented upon Genesis, the Psalms, the Gospels of Matthew and John, the Acts of the Apostles, and the Epistles of Paul. In the West Hilary of Poitiers gave homilies on the Psalms. From Ambrose came homilies on the Hexaemeron, the Psalms, and the Gospel of Saint Luke. Augustine emerged as the greatest preacher among the Western Fathers. He commented in homilies upon the Sermon on the Mount, the Gospel of John, and the Psalms, as well as upon numerous other isolated passages in the Scriptures. Less well known, yet of considerable value, are the Biblical homilies of Peter Chrysologus, Maximus of Turin, Faustus of Rietz, and Caesarius of Arles. Gregory I kept up the patristic tradition of Biblical homilies.

Because the Scripture readings were, in due time, selected with a view to their appropriateness for the feast celebrated, the homily took on a new task, that of explaining the meaning of the feast. Consequently, many of the patristic collections of sermons center around the great feasts of the Church year. This is true both in the East and in the West. In the East John Chrysostom and the two Gregories are the most conspicuous. In the West Augustine is joined by Zeno of Verona and especially by Leo the Great. His sermons on the great feasts remain one of the best commentaries on the liturgical year.

The homilies spoken of up to this point were delivered by pastors to their flocks. They exemplify the principle that a true homily is a popular exposition and application of the Scriptures. There is another kind of homily however, delivered to a more select audience; this type had considerable influence on later spiritual writers. These were the monastic homilies, given to a community of monks by such leading writers as Jerome and Cassiodorus. Both of these men dealt with the Psalms in their homilies, but Jerome commented on the Gospels as well. Gregory the Great concentrated on the Book of Job, while the Venerable Bede dealt mostly with the Gospels. Some writers consider Bernard to be the last of the Fathers; in any case his sermons on the Church year and the Canticle of Canticles found many admirers and imitators.

In general one must say that the homilies of the Fathers from Origen to Bernard set the tradition for the homily for all time. For them the homily was essentially a popular exposition of the Scriptures read or sung in the liturgical assembly. The fact that they stayed close to the text and sought to make the Word of God the instrument for the spiritual formation of the faithful makes their approach valid in any age.

Medieval Period. The homilies of the Fathers set the tone for preaching right down to the 13th century. But with the coming of the friars the homily properly so-called declined, and it was replaced chiefly by the sermon, which developed more or less independently of the liturgical action.

The Council of Trent commanded pastors of souls to preach during Mass upon the text of the Mass, but it was not until the 19th century that the homily in the ancient patristic sense began to revive.

20th Century Developments. The 1917 Code of Canon Law enjoined the homily upon pastors of souls at the principal Mass on Sundays and feast days. But it was not until the LITURGICAL MOVEMENT began to take hold in Europe that the homily was revived in many places. It was the Second Vatican Council which gave the impetus needed for the restoration of the Homily to its privileged place within the Eucharist and, indeed, within the liturgies of all the Sacraments.

The *Constitution on the Sacred Liturgy* of Vatican Council II not only enjoined the homily upon those who have the care of souls but it also restated and amplified the traditional concept of what a homily is. Never before in any official document has there been so clear a statement of the nature and aim of the homily. The homily is "an exposition of the mysteries of faith and the guiding principles of the Christian life expounded from the sacred text read in the liturgy during the liturgical assembly" (52). It is "a proclamation of God's wonderful works in the history of salvation, the mystery of Christ ever made present and active within us, especially during the celebration of the sacred liturgy" (35). Consequently, the homily is "part of the liturgy itself" (52), "part of the

liturgical service" (35). To this end, the Constitution decreed: (1) "more ample, more varied and more suitable readings from Sacred Scripture," and (2) a sermon or homily drawing its content "mainly from scriptural and liturgical sources" and directed toward a deeper understanding of "the mystery of Christ ever made present and active in us," especially in the liturgical celebration itself (34).

United States Bishops on the Homily. The 1982 United States Bishops' document, *Fulfilled in Your Hearing: The Homily in the Sunday Assembly* unfolds and develops the theological principles and pastoral norms on the homily that were enunciated in the *Constitution on the Sacred Liturgy,* incorporating the "reading of the signs of the times" motif from the *Pastoral Constitution on the Church in the Modern World.* In doing so, it speaks of the homily as "a scriptural interpretation of human existence which enables a community to recognize God's active presence" (*Fulfilled in Your Hearing* 29). It reiterates the point that the homily does not primarily concern itself with a systematic theological understanding of the faith, because the liturgical gathering is not primarily an educational or catechetical assembly, but a worshiping assembly (*Fulfilled in Your Hearing* 17–18). The document defines the homilist as a "mediator of meaning" (*Fulfilled in Your Hearing* 7), who "does not so much attempt to explain the scriptures as to interpret the human situation through the Scriptures" (*Fulfilled in Your Hearing* 20). It explains that the preacher "represents this community voicing its concerns, by naming its demons, and thus enabling it to gain some understanding and control of the evil which afflicts it. He represents the Lord by offering the community another word, a word of healing and pardon, of acceptance and love" (*Fulfilled in Your Hearing* 7). Therefore, the primary responsibility of the homilist is not to explain but to interpret for the benefit of the liturgical assembly.

The Homily is conceived of not merely as a catechetical instruction located within the Eucharistic Liturgy; rather, it is conceived of primarily as a pastoral reflection on the mystery actually being celebrated in the liturgical event, an event which is a kind of peak moment in the ongoing mystery of the believer's new life in Christ. This same view of the importance and the chief function of the Homily has prevailed in the post-conciliar development of the other Sacraments; it is reflected in the postconciliar rituals for Baptism, Penance, Matrimony, and the Anointing of the Sick. The ritual for each of these Sacraments calls for a Homily following selected scriptural Readings, based on the Readings, and directed towards a greater understanding of, and therefore a greater participation in, the sacramental mystery itself. The new regime of the Sacraments, therefore, calls for the closest possible integration of the ministry of Word and Sacrament, in order to bring about a more perfect interiorization of the Christian mystery itself, a mystery revealed in the Word, symbolized in Sacrament, and lived out in the faith-life of a believer continually inspired and energized by Word and Sacrament.

Bibliography: E. ECHLIN, *Priest as Preacher* (Cork 1973). J. HOFINGER, *Evangelization and Catechesis* (New York 1976). BISHOPS' COMMITTEE ON PRIESTLY LIFE AND MINISTRY: N.C.C.B., *Fulfilled in Your Hearing: The Homily in the Sunday Assembly* (Washington, D.C. 1982). Y. BRILIOTH, *A Brief History of Preaching* (Philadelphia 1965). K. RAHNER, ed., *The Renewal of Preaching: Theory and Practice* (New York 1968). W. SKUDLAREK, *The Word in Worship: Preaching in a Liturgical Context* (Nashville 1981). T. K. CARROLL, *Preaching the Word* (Wilmington, Del. 1984). R. P. WAZNAK, *Sunday After Sunday: Preaching the Homily As Story* (New York 1983). R. P. WAZNAK, *Like Fresh Bread: Sunday Homilies in the Parish* (New York 1993). R. P. WAZNAK, *An Introduction to the Homily* (Collegeville, Minn. 1998). P. JANOWIAK, *The Holy Preaching: The Sacramentality of the Word in the Liturgical Assembly* (Collegeville, Minn. 2000).

[W. J. O'SHEA/T. D. ROVER/EDS.]

HOMINES INTELLIGENTIAE

Pseudomystic sect active in and around Brussels in late 14th and early 15th century. Aegidius Cantoris (Sanghers), an uneducated layman who was apparently influenced by the visionary and poetess Bl. HADEWIJCH and by Marie of Valenciennes, founded the sect, which was especially popular among women. The most notable convert was the Carmelite William of Hildernisse, who assumed leadership at the death of Aegidius and developed his ideas (*see* WILLIAMITES). The salient points of doctrine were pantheism; illuminism; belief in the age of the Holy Spirit and of spiritual freedom; sexual libertinism; contempt of good works; and rejection of the means of grace, of the priesthood, and of the Church. The sect was condemned by PETER OF AILLY in 1411 [E. Baluze, *Miscellanea* (Paris 1678) 2:277–297].

Bibliography: P. FRÉDÉRICQ, ed., *Corpus documentorum Inquisitionis haereticae pravitatis Neerlandicae,* 5 v. (Ghent 1889–1906) 1:267–279. H. C. LEA, *A History of the Inquisition of the Middle Ages,* 3 v. (New York 1958). F. VERNET, *Dictionnaire de theologie catholique,* ed. A. VACANT et al. (Paris 1903–50) 7:38–39.

[M. F. LAUGHLIN]

HOMINISATION

Hominisation is broadly understood as the process (and its implications) whereby a human being comes into existence. Three problematic aspects of the process can be specified: the biological, the medical/moral, and the theological. For the biologist, "hominisation (anthropogenesis) means the phylogenetic processes by which man has developed by continuous transformations from a presumed Primate group of the Tertiary era in his bodily characteristics and also in his psyche" (Overhage). The biologist recognizes, therefore, the close resemblance between man and the higher Primates, but also emphasizes that with the emergence of man there is a completely new type of organism, i.e., one endowed with speech, spiritual behavior, and the capacity to form a culture. Thus, although there are no unambiguous criteria for distinguishing man from lower animal organisms, and although substantial evidence for evolution from behavioral patterns common to all vertebrates clearly exists, all attempts to explain abstract thought by evolution remain unsuccessful. Discontinuity between animal and human behavior is acknowledged, and scientific research cannot yet give any definitive explanation of the evolutionary process leading to the appearance of man.

The term hominisation is also used in discussing the prenatal development of human beings, with obvious implications for the morality of abortion. Recent studies (Williams and Milhaven) have shown that Christian theology has varied considerably in its estimation of the moment when the fetus is endowed with a human soul (hominisation). The Church Fathers were divided on the issue, some holding that human life properly so-called was present at conception, while others decided upon hominisation at a later stage of fetal development. Thomas Aquinas's theory, defended today by Joseph Donceel both for its inherent worth and its appeal to the modern rejection of any soul-body dualism, supports delayed hominisation over immediate hominisation. According to Aquinas's hylomorphism, a substantial form—in this case a human soul—can exist only in matter developed sufficiently to receive it, i.e., only after several weeks of gestation. The more common Catholic teaching over at least the past two centuries, however, is that of immediate hominisation (Mangan). The absence of any qualitative difference in the human zygote from the time of conception to the time of birth is the central argument used for this position.

Theological reflection on hominisation deals especially with evolution and the place of man in the universe. Because any theological anthropology recognizes the radical difference between man and non-spiritual forms of life, it must hold for a definitive creative act in the evolutionary process whereby God brings man into being. Nor is this adequately conceived as an evolution of the human body and a special creative initiative by God in regard to the human soul. Since soul and body are not two autonomous entities but rather substantial principles of one individual being, "the spiritual soul which results from one direct creative act of God of necessity also signifies a transforming specification of the bodily component" (Rahner). This theory of moderate transformism seems to enjoy wide acceptance among Catholic theologians, especially insofar as it is compatible with biological theories of evolution, traditional teaching about the specific creation of man, and the eschatological dynamism whereby all existence tends toward spirit and spirit toward the one God (Teilhard de Chardin).

Bibliography: The March 1970 issue of *Theological Studies* (volume 31) is completely devoted to the problem of abortion and hominisation, and contains (among others) the articles by Williams, Donceel, Milhaven and Mangan referred to in the text of this article. P. OVERHAGE "Hominisation" in *Sacramentum Mundi* 2, 286–89. R. OVERMAN *Evolution and the Christian Doctrine of Creation* (Philadelphia 1967). K. RAHNER *Hominisation, The Evolutionary Origin of Man as a Theological Problem* (New York 1965). P. TEILHARD DE CHARDIN *The Phenomenon of Man* (New York 1959); *The Future of Man* (New York 1969).

[T. M. MCFADDEN]

HOMOOUSIOS

This article considers the history of the term (1) before Nicaea I, (2) at Nicaea I and afterward, and (3) in Christology.

Before Nicaea I. The word *homoousios* (ὁμοούσιος), traditionally translated into English by "consubstantial," (one in being) was an everyday word in the Greek language with the meaning "of the same kind of stuff as." It had been used technically, however, in the vocabulary of Gnosticism. Thus, in the system of VALENTINUS, Truth emanates from the substance of Mind and is consubstantial with it. Christian writers at Alexandria adopted the word to express the eternal origin of the Son from the Father. In explaining Heb 1.3 Origen wrote:

> Light without brightness is unthinkable. If that is true, there was never a time when the Son was not the Son. He will be . . . , as it were, the splendor of the unbegotten light. . . ..

> Thus Wisdom, too, since it proceeds from God, is generated out of the divine substance itself. Under the figure of a bodily outflow, nevertheless, it, too, is thus called "a sort of clean and pure outflow of omnipotent glory" (Wisd. 7, 25). Both these similes manifestly show the community of substance between Son and Father. For an outflow seems *homoousios,* i.e., of one substance with that body of which it is the outflow or exhalation. [*Fr. in Heb.* 24.359; J. Quasten, *Patrology* 2:78]

Homoousios had become so common a theological term by the middle of the 3rd century that one of the accu-

sations made against St. Dionysius the Great, Bishop of Alexandria, when he was denounced to the pope was that he refused to use the word *homoousios.* On the other hand, in Antioch a synod held in the year 267 to anathematize PAUL OF SAMOSATA expressly condemned the use of the word. This almost forgotten fact was made much of a century later by the enemies of Nicaea I. Since no writings of Paul of Samosata are extant, it can only be surmised what he meant by the term. Probably he was asserting what would be termed today a unity of Person or HYPOSTASIS between Father and Son. This hypothesis is consonant with Paul's known MONARCHIANISM. Another possibility is that in calling Father and Son consubstantial he was asserting their common origin from a third, preexisting substance. According to ARIUS this latter is what the Manichees meant by *homoousios,* and it was for this reason that Arius rejected the term.

In the West the equivalent term *consubstantialis* was already in use in the 3rd century. Tertullian spoke of the Trinity as a unity of substance (*Adv. Prax.* 12).

At Nicaea I and Afterward. The Council of NICAEA I (A.D. 325) in using *homoousios* intended (1) to exclude any imperfection from the Word and (2) to assert His full equality with the Father. Whether the Council intended to affirm the numerical identity of the substance of Father and Son is doubtful, since this question had not been raised by the Arians. Both before and after the Council *homoousios* was used of beings that are numerically distinct, as parents and children. ATHANASIUS spoke of Esau and Jacob as ὁμοούσιοι.

After Nicaea I *homoousios* became the touchstone of orthodoxy. Only after a long and bitter struggle did the formula of the Council find acceptance. At times during this period the term was abandoned, as in the third formula of the Synod of Sirmium, which was subscribed to by Pope LIBERIUS in 358. This did not always mean a compromise of principle with the Semi-Arians, however, because many churchmen, including Cyril of Jerusalem, adhered to the faith of Nicaea I but avoided using *homoousios* because of its Sabellian associations (*see* SABELLIANISM). Even Athanasius admitted:

> Those who accept everything else that was defined at Nicaea and doubt only about the "consubstantial" must not be treated as enemies . . . , but we discuss the matter with them as brothers who mean what we mean and dispute only about the word. [*De syn.* 41]

It is interesting that 60 years after Nicaea I the Council of Constantinople I avoided *homoousios* in its definition of the divinity of the Holy Spirit.

In Christology. In the Christological conflict of the early 5th century the term *homoousios* was of secondary importance. On the one hand, NESTORIUS denied that the consubstantial Word was born, suffered, or rose from the dead. On the other hand, EUTYCHES was reluctant to admit that Christ is consubstantial with mankind. When interrogated, he replied:

> I confess that the holy Virgin is consubstantial with us and that of her our God was incarnate.
>
> Since the Mother is consubstantial with us, then surely the Son is also?
>
> If you wish me to add that He who is of the Virgin is consubstantial with us, I will do so. . . . But I take the word consubstantial in such a way as not to deny that He is the Son of God. [*Acta conciliorum oecumenicorum* 2.1.1:135]

The Council of Chalcedon in its definition repeated the phrase of Nicaea I, "consubstantial with the Father," and added "consubstantial with us in his humanity" (H. Denziger, *Enchiridion symbolorum* 148).

See Also: ARIANISM; CONSUBSTANTIALITY; GENERATION OF THE WORD; LOGOS; TRINITY, HOLY, ARTICLES ON; WORD, THE.

Bibliography: A. GRILLMEIER, *Lexicon für Theologie und Kirche* (Freiburg 1957–66) 5:467–468. I. ORTIZ DE URBINA, *Nicée et Constantinople* (Paris 1963) 82–87. G. L. PRESTIGE, *God in Patristic Thought* (Society for Promoting Christian Knowledge; 1935; repr. 1959).

[J. M. CARMODY]

HOMOSEXUALITY

Homosexuality is a sustained condition or adaptation in which erotic fantasy, attraction and arousal is predominately directed toward one's own sex. The term "sustained" is used because confusion about one's sexual orientation is not unusual during adolescence. Although the Catholic Church recognizes that homosexual attraction is not chosen, and therefore the orientation in itself is not a sin (*Catechism of the Catholic Church* 2358), it has been the constant tradition in Church teaching, based on Scripture and natural law, that homosexual activity is morally wrong. This article expounds the basis for this judgment in terms of the Church's teaching on marriage, and its proper, virtuous expression of sexuality.

Scripture. Traditionally, six texts in Scripture have been accepted in Christian Churches as condemnations of homosexual behavior. Genesis (19.1–29) contains the story of Sodom and Gomorrah, destroyed by God for wickedness which included homosexual demands on Lot's guests. Leviticus forbids practices such as adultery and bestiality, and includes the prohibition: "You shall not lie with a male as with a woman; such a thing is an abomination" (18.20–23), a condemnation repeated in Lv 20.13. In the New Testament, St. Paul's Letter to the Romans cites indulgence in same-sex lust and the perverse actions of men with men, women with women, as deserving penalty (1.26ff). In the First Letter to the Corinthians Paul includes homosexual activity as one of the sins that bars inheritance of God's kingdom (6.9-11). The First Letter to Timothy also lists homosexual activity as an offense of the wicked and godless (1.8,11). Finally, the author of the Letter of Jude refers to Sodom and Gomorrah and surrounding towns which indulged in unnatural vice, with the admonition that their punishment is meant to dissuade us (1.6-8).

Beginning with Anglican author D. Sherwin Baily's 1955 book *Homosexuality and Western Christian Tradition,* a number of scholars and pro-gay apologists have reinterpreted the standard scriptural texts, thereby encouraging a revisionist theology which accepts homosexual activity as morally acceptable for homosexual persons. This interpretation stands against the constant teaching of the Church, dating from the Fathers of the early Christian centuries, affirmed by the major theological Doctors of the Middle Ages, and reaffirmed in current Catholic magisterial pronouncements.

These revisionist views take various forms, generally proposing that the scriptural texts were written in the setting of a different culture, and in times when the notion of differing sexual orientations was not known. Some maintain that the sin of the Sodomites was inhospitality rather than homosexual activity, or, while admitting that the Genesis story concerns homosexual activity, see its condemnation aimed at the violence of threatened homosexual rape. Others maintain that the text in Romans refers to homosexual actions by heterosexual persons, and that the strictures were against homosexual prostitution in a setting of orgiastic idolatry.

A simple reply to these views would be to note that nowhere in Scripture is homosexual genital behavior mentioned in a positive manner. More striking, in both Testaments one finds the over-arching affirmation of heterosexual marriage as a symbol of God's covenant relationship with his people and of the union of Christ with his spouse, the Church. The 1986 letter of the Congregation for the Doctrine of the Faith, *On the Pastoral Care of Homosexual Persons,* notes that God fashions mankind male and female, in his own image and likeness. Human beings therefore are nothing less than the work of God Himself; and in the complementarity of the sexes they are called to reflect the inner unity of the Creator. They do this in a striking way in their cooperation with Him in the transmission of life by a mutual donation of self to the other (6).

The *Catechism of the Catholic Church,* published in 1992, does not see ambiguity in the Scripture references to homosexual behavior. Citing four of the classic texts, it states: "Basing itself on Sacred Scripture, which presents homosexual acts as acts of grave depravity, tradition has always declared that 'homosexual acts are intrinsically disordered' . . . contrary to the natural law . . . (and) under no circumstances can they be approved" (2357).

The first chapter of Genesis contains the nucleus of the theology of marriage. "God created man in his image . . . male and female he created them, and blessed them saying 'be fertile and multiply'" (1.27). "That is why a man leaves his father and mother and clings to his wife, and the two of them become one" (2.24).

Morality. Catholic moral theology sees marriage in terms of two inseparable purposes. One purpose is procreation, to which homosexual acts are obviously closed. "God created man in his image; in the divine image he created him; male and female he created them. God blessed them, saying; 'Be fertile and multiply, fill the earth and subdue it'" (Gn 1.27f). The other purpose is the complementary union of the sexes. "This is why a man leaves his father and mother and clings to his wife and the two become one body" (Gn 2.24). The conjugal union is a symbol of the covenant relationship of God with his people, of Christ and the Church (Hos 2.21f; Is 54.10f.; Eph 5).

Sexuality in marriage is designed to be life-giving and love-giving, that is, open to children and establishing a permanent union of fidelity. The Second VATICAN COUNCIL brought into sharper focus the covenantal relationship of conjugal love, bringing it to equal emphasis with the begetting of children. This unitive relationship is of no less account than procreation (*Gaudium et spes* 50).

Magisterial Church teaching states that homosexual genital relations are objectively immoral because they "lack an essential and indispensable finality," namely, the procreative function of sexuality, the openness to new life (*Declaration on Certain Questions concerning Sexual Ethics* [Dec. 29, 1975] #8). Homosexual activity annuls the goals and meaning of the Creator's sexual design. Homosexual genital acts are not a truly physical or psychological union but an imitation of heterosexual intercourse. In marriage the psychological differences of the sexes sets the partners on an ongoing spousal journey toward a deeper, mutual understanding, thereby completing each other, with each partner called to transcend self through mutual self-donation. Homosexual acts join persons who are sexually and psychologically of the same gender, a sameness lacking the rich marital symbol of God's union with His people, Christ's union with His spouse, the Church.

Etiology. At the beginning of the third millennium the majority professional view is that homosexuality is inborn, immutable, and a normal variant of human sexuality. This is the stated position of the American Psychiatric Association, followed by the American Psychological Association, and other associations of various therapists such as social workers and marriage and family counselors, as well as the gay-lesbian activist organizations. These groups also emphasize that the origins of homosexual orientation are largely unknown.

However, acceptance of the inborn and immutable character of homosexual orientation has not gone unchallenged. Some members of the psychotherapeutic professions object that their professional organizations have taken a politically correct position rather than one based on scientific data, noting that the 1973 American Psychiatric Association's decision to remove homosexuality from the *Diagnostic and Statistical Manual of Mental Disorders* (3d ed.) was done in haste, bypassing ordinary decision-making channels, and under pressure from gay groups. The Catholic Medical Association, marshaling an impressive compendium of research, takes issue with the current prevalent professional position. The association does not accept that homosexuality is inborn, sees it as preventable, and treatable for those who are motivated (*Homosexuality and Hope,* 2000).

There is much yet to be learned about the origins and causes of homosexuality, and more is unknown than known. (It depends on one's perspective whether the glass is partly empty or partly full.) There is a considerable body of research literature regarding possible correlates of homosexual development. Since the 1973 decision of the APA the research findings and clinical insights regarding homosexuality of the prior 75 years have been largely ignored. in many scientific circles. Subsequent research is better known by the general public through limited exposure in the media rather than through critical assessment of the studies themselves. There is sufficient research on homosexuality for some therapists to have formulated theories of its development, and to have devised therapy aimed at conversion from homosexuality to heterosexuality for those who desire to attempt to make this change.

The development of sexuality, both physical and psychological, is an extremely complex process. Empirical research and accumulated clinical experience does allow the construction of a tentative outline of development, while acknowledging that more is still unknown about it than has been firmly established, and that subsequent research may modify or radically change present theories.

Physical sexual history begins at conception and continues in a definite sequential pattern until birth. There are three principal stages in uterine sexual development, namely, genetic sex, gonadal sex, and sexual differentiation in the brain. At conception, a person receives a sex chromosome, X or Y, from each parent. XX produces a female, XY a male. Though there are anomalies such as XXY, or XYY, these are rare. From conception on, a person is male or female in every body cell. However, genetic sex alone does not constitute or guarantee proper physical sexual development. In the seventh week of human foetal development rudimentary sexual tissues begin to differentiate into female or male genital organs. In males the Y chromosome produces a protein which coats the tissues otherwise programmed to become female sexual organs, and effects the formation of male sexual organs. This development establishes gonadal sex. In the second trimester testosterone, produced by the newly formed testes, masculinizes clusters of cells in the "old brain," the brain structures humans share with lower vertebrates. In the female, estrogen and progesterone from the ovaries feminize corresponding brain tissues. These parts of the brain influence traits such as aggressiveness and preference for rough and tumble play, typical of males, and tendencies to nurture and cyclic sexual arousal in females.

Genetic sex, gonadal sex, and "brain sex" are the components of physical sexuality, the development of which continues after birth, particularly in adolescence when hormone function brings increased sexual drive and promotes development of secondary sex characteristics, such as male musculature and female breasts. Some experiments with animals as well as anomalous development in humans suggest that occurrences in fetal development may make an individual more vulnerable to later environmental influences on psychosexuality after birth.

Mental sex, distinct from physical sex, is a postnatal development. Psychosexuality or sexualized consciousness is sexuality as it manifests itself in the mind. It is a pervasive and fundamental personality feature which includes three interwoven components. The first component is the basic conviction of being male or female. The second component, subtly different, is the sense of being masculine or feminine. The third component is an individual's erotic preference for male or female partners, or both. These components, variously labeled in the literature, are core gender identity, gender role identity, and psychosexual orientation.

Core gender identity is the recognition "I am male" or "I am female." It begins to crystallize in the second year of life as the infant undergoes psychological birth, which includes moving away from his or her symbiotic relationship with the mother, and acquiring a dawning sense of being a separate individual who is a boy, or a girl.

Gender role identity is the subtly different recognition, "I am masculine" or "I am feminine." The individual gradually attains the conviction that he or she matches or falls short of the gender role expectations of a particular family and social environment. Gender role identity may vary on a fairly wide spectrum without infringing on core gender identity or orientation. Conversely, depending on a family and/or peer environment, gender role identity may become infected with a sense of inadequacy which can have a damaging effect on proper psychosexual orientation.

The third eventual psychosexual component is orientation: preferential erotic attraction to members of the opposite sex, same sex, or both sexes in varied degree. This is the defining element of heterosexuality, homosexuality, bisexuality.

This simplified division of interwoven physical and psychological elements in human sexuality provides some appreciation of its complexity and indicates that it cannot be viewed as a unitary dimension of personality. Sigmund Freud noted that the physical and mental characteristics of sexuality, including orientation, may vary independently of one another "up to a certain point . . . and are met within different individuals in manifold permutations" (Freud, 1962). It is hardly possible that these components of sexuality culminating in orientation are the result of a single gene. In addition, Columbia University researchers Byne and Parsons, reviewing the biological evidence and theories of the origins of homosexuality, concluded that it is extremely unlikely that the gamut and plasticity of human sexual behavior can be reduced to factors as simple as prenatal hormone programming. The general opinion among scientists who consolidate the various studies is that genetic, hormonal, and constitutional factors may predispose to sexual orientation, but it is postnatal environmental and psycho-social history which are its predetermining factors (Bancroft 1994; Byne & Parsons 1993; Money 1993).

Current Research. The current font of research does not include any that establishes or even claims a purely genetic base for homosexual orientation. A well-publicized study of monozygotic (identical) male twins found that 52 percent of the twin brothers of declared homosexual men were also homosexually oriented. (Bailey & Pillard, 1991) This finding does point to some common, as yet unidentified inherited factors which have an etiological role. The study does not support the direct inheritance of homosexuality itself since roughly half the identical co-twins, who share the same genetic program, were not homosexual. Other studies of identical twins, one of whom is homosexual, produced similar results, all with a lower percentage of homosexual co-twins than the study cited above. A study of identical lesbian twins reared apart from childhood, showed no concordance for homosexual behavior. This suggests that homosexuality is more dependent on acquired and learned factors than on genetic influences among lesbians (Elke et al., 1986). Sexual orientation may be less hardwired among women than among men.

As for immutability, the fact of change of orientation is cogent proof against it. Some pro-gay apologists claim that the persons who testified that they had changed were not really homosexual in the first place, a seeming case of killing the messenger. Prior to the 1973 APA decision to normalize homosexuality, the most generally reported therapeutic success rate for homosexual individuals who desired to change to heterosexuality was about 33 percent. Some homosexual clients who had sought reorientation motivated by religious convictions, disillusionment with the gay lifestyle and/or a desire for marriage, did in fact move to predominant heterosexual orientation (Hadden 1958; Bieber 1962; Willis 1967; Hatterer 1970; Socarides 1978).

A 1998 survey by the National Association of Research and Therapy of Homosexuality reported that a third of 882 homosexual persons made the transition to exclusive or predominant heterosexual orientation through therapy and counseling. The study confirmed that homosexuality is subject to modification through therapy (Nicolosi et al. 2000). At the 2001 APA convention in New Orleans, Robert L. Spitzer, M.D., presented a two-year clinical interview: "200 Subjects Who Claim to Have Changed Their Sexual Orientation from Homosexual to Heterosexual." The 143 men and 57 women who claimed reorientation which had lasted at least five years were recruited through Narth, ex-gay ministries, and individual therapists. Though complete change was uncommon, Spitzer concluded, "Some highly motivated individuals through a variety of change efforts can make substantial changes in multiple indicators of sexual orientation and achieve good heterosexual function."

This study is significant for two reasons: its results and its principal researcher. Spitzer was at the forefront of the movement to delete homosexuality from the official psychiatric diagnostic manual in 1973. The current results are a reversal of his own previously held opinion on the immutability of homosexual orientation. The *Narth Bulletin* (Aug. 2001) quotes Spitzer: "Like most psychiatrists I thought that homosexual behavior could be resisted—but no one could really change their sexual orientation. I now believe that's untrue—some people can and do change." Spitzer cautions that this study does not

justify any coercion to change, but that individuals should have the right to explore their heterosexual potential.

Although the possibility of change through psychotherapy by some homosexual persons is definitely established, it is reckless to overplay it and arouse false hopes. The consistent figures on successful reorientation hover around 30 percent. Informed and experienced therapists are few. Commitment through the process is not easy. Over 40 percent drop out of the therapy which is long-term, minimally two years, and often requires considerable expense. Several Protestant groups, under the umbrella heading Exodus, stress religious motivation in working out of homosexuality to heterosexual orientation. Exodus, which relies on strong faith in the transforming power of Jesus Christ, sponsors more than 100 ministries in the United States, most of which are non professional counseling centers. The Mormon agency Evergreen also sponsors this work. Jonah is the Jewish counterpart.

As might be expected, conversion therapists do not accept homosexuality as a normal variant of human sexuality. Judgment on the outcomes of sexual development and of sexual behavior are regarded as evaluative judgments. Values, in this view, are outside the purview of science as science. Science tells us what *is,* ethics and religious morals state what *ought to be.* Conversion or reparative therapists do not hold that homosexuality is a mental illness but do consider it a developmental anomaly. Erik Erikson's socio-psychological theory of development outlines how excessive mistrust, self doubt, crippling guilt, inferiority feelings and the like are precipitates of dysfunctional family and other relationships. In parallel fashion some theorists see influences from difficult interpersonal situations as impinging on a vulnerable youngster, occasioning detachment from identification with the same-sex parent, and blocking the emergence of heterosexual orientation which they view as the proper development of the human person.

Ministry to Homosexual Persons. The Catholic Bishops of the United States have produced three documents regarding ministry to homosexual persons: *To Live in Christ Jesus* (1978); *Human Sexuality* (1991); and *Always Our Children* (rev. 1998), a pastoral message to the parents of homosexual children, with suggestions for pastoral ministers. All three documents emphasize that the homosexual condition itself is not sinful; it is discovered, not chosen by the individual. All three documents state categorically that homosexual persons are called to chastity as are unmarried heterosexual persons. They point out that prejudice, demeaning behavior, or derogatory humor aimed at persons with same-sex attractions is definitely not Christian and is indeed totally unjustified, a sin against charity. The documents call for the inclusion of homosexual persons in parish and other Church communities. The 1976 document states: "Some persons find themselves through no fault of their own to have a homosexual orientation. Homosexual persons like everyone else should not suffer from prejudice against basic human rights. They have a right to respect, friendship and justice. They should have an active role in the Christian Community . . . . The Christian community should provide them a special degree of pastoral understanding and care." *Always Our Children* continues: "We understand that having a homosexual orientation brings with it enough anxiety, pain, and issues related to self acceptance without society adding additional prejudicial treatment."

The pastoral minister, therefore, must be charitable, compassionate and sensitive. It is hard to realize adequately the anguish that an adolescent experiences, sometimes with thoughts of suicide, upon first realizing he or she is different from the greater society of which each desperately wants to be a participant. As homosexual individuals grow older they hear, all too often, the mocking of peers and contemptuous, disparaging epithets. Thus it should be no surprise that persons with same-sex attractions are easily vulnerable to self-hatred, depression, and ultimately considerable anger against the society, mentality, and institutions which they see as demeaning and rejecting. The pastoral minister must be able to understand and cope with the negativism that they themselves will sometimes meet, to respond to it charitably and prudently, rather than react in ways that will only aggravate smoldering resentments. On the other hand, pastoral ministers must take care that compassion does not draw them into condoning or indirectly enabling sinful behaviors by a silence presumed to be consent. This approach can lead to the homosexual person's devastating physical and spiritual harm. Besides a firm conviction of Church teaching, the pastoral minister needs some appreciation of the psychology of persons with same-sex attractions. He or she needs an ability prudently to deal with opposition, both from the persons they seek to serve, and those who consider themselves supportive to the homosexual community by rejecting Church teachings.

In 1980 Cardinal Terrence Cook of New York City asked Fr. John Harvey O.S.F.S. to begin a ministry to Catholic homosexual persons. Fr. Harvey's efforts led to Courage, a movement which has grown to over a hundred chapters in the United States, Canada, England, Ireland, Australia, and other countries. The goals of Courage are to provide persons with same-sex attractions with a program of deeper spiritual life in order to deal with sexual issues and temptations, to deal with the unique difficulties of homosexual orientation, and to develop fellowship among them for facing their problems with mutual support amid chaste friendship. While some clergy and pastoral ministers may put emphasis on the sixth commandment, Courage moves to intimacy with Jesus Christ as the most cogent force in fostering interior chastity. It does not promote reorientation, leaving the choice of that goal to the individual. Instead it focuses on the member's spiritual life. Pope John Paul II has called Courage "the work of God."

Another outreach to homosexual persons is the National Association of Catholic Diocesan Gay and Lesbian Ministries. Several dioceses have adopted its mission statement which calls for fostering ministry with lesbian and gay Catholics, their families and friends. The NACDGLM also encourages the participation of lesbian and gay Catholics within the Church. It stresses that it is not enough that they should not suffer prejudice against basic human rights but also should have an active role in the Christian community, a goal set by the bishops pastoral documents cited above.

In 1999, Cardinal Francis George, Archbishop of Chicago praised the outreach to homosexual persons as an important and necessary ministry. Addressing the annual meeting of NACDGLM he stressed that such ministry must make clear the purpose "to help those who identify themselves in their own hearts and also publically, as homosexuals, to live chastely with the respect and encouragement of the Church." Acknowledging that some may not share this purpose, he stressed the Paschal Mystery: "To deny that the power of God's grace enables homosexuals to live chastely is to deny, effectively, that Jesus has risen from the dead."

Bibliography: J. M. BAILEY and R. PILLARD, "A Genetic Study of Male Sexual Orientation," *Archives of General Psychiatry* 48 (1991)1089–96. J. BANCROFT, "Homosexual Orientation: The Search for a Biological Basis," *British Journal of Psychiatry* 164 (1994) 437–440. A. BUTLER, "Trends in Same-Gender Sexual Partners, 1988–1998," *Journal of Sexual Research* 37 (2000) 333–343. W. BYNE and B. PARSONS, "Human Sexual Orientation: The Biological Theories Reappraised," *Archives of General Psychiatry* 50 (1993) 228–239. E. ELKE, et al., "Homosexuality in Monozygotic Twins Reared Apart," *British Journal of Psychiatry* 148 (1986) 421–425. S. FREUD, *Collected Papers,* v. 2, tr. J. RIVIERE (New York 1962). F. GEORGE, "Address to the Annual Meeting of the National Association of Catholic Diocesan Gay and Lesbian Ministries," Chicago (Oct. 9, 1998). S. HADDEN, "Treatment of Homosexuality by Individual and Group Psychotherapy," *American Journal of Psychiatry* 142 (1958) 810–815. J. HARVEY, *The Truth about Homosexuality* (San Francisco 1995). L. J. HATTERER, *Changing Homosexuality in the Male* (New York 1970). Catholic Medical Association, *Homosexuality and Hope* (Pewaukee, Wis. 2000). A. KINSEY, et al., *Sexual Behavior in the Human Male* (Philadelphia 1948); *Sexual Behavior in the Human Female* (Philadelphia 1953). J. MONEY, "Sin, Sickness, or Status? Homosexual Gender Identity and Psychoneuroendocrinology," in *Psychological Perspectives in Lesbian and Gay Male Experiences,* ed. L. D. GARNETS and D. C. KIMMEL (New York 1993) 130–167. J. G. MUIR, "Homosexuals and the 10 Percent Fallacy," *Wall Street Journal* (March 31, 1993). J. NICOLOSI, et al., "Retrospective Self-reports of Changes in Homosexual Orientation: A Consumer Survey of Conversion Therapy Clients," *Psychological Reports* 86 (2000) 1071–1088. G. REMFEDI, et al., "Demography of Sexual Orientation in Adolescents," *Pediatrics* 89 (1992) 714–720. C. W. SOCARIDES, *Homosexuality* (New York 1978). R. L. SPITZER, "200 Subjects Who Claim to Have Changed Their Orientation from Homosexual to Heterosexual," presentation at the American Psychiatric Association annual convention, New Orleans (May 9, 2001). S. WILLIS, *Understanding and Counseling the Homosexual Male* (Boston 1967).

[J. KEEFE]

HOMOSEXUALS, PASTORAL CARE OF

A letter addressed to the worldwide Catholic episcopate by the Congregation for the Doctrine of the Faith (CDF), "On the Pastoral Care of Homosexual Persons" (Oct. 1, 1986), effectively confirmed the position of the United States National Conference of Catholic Bishops (NCCB) that homosexual persons are entitled to "a special degree of understanding and care" from the Christian community (pastoral letter, "To Live in Christ Jesus," Nov. 11, 1976).

The essential requisites of this special pastoral care, as indicated in the CDF letter and in previous statements of the Holy See and local/regional episcopates, can be discussed under the following headings: 1) a realistic and compassionate understanding of the homosexual orientation or condition; 2) the avoidance of permissive approaches to the moral evaluation of homosexual genital activity; and 3) positive initiatives to facilitate the harmonious integration of homosexual persons into the Christian community and wider society.

Homosexual orientation. In its earlier "Declaration on Certain Questions Concerning Sexual Ethics" (Dec. 29, 1975), CDF acknowledged the homosexual orientation as follows:

> A distinction is drawn, and it seems with some reason, between homosexuals whose tendency comes from a false education, from a lack of normal sexual development, from habit, from bad example, or from other similar causes, and is transitory or at least not incurable; and homosexuals who are definitively such because of some kind of innate instinct or a pathological constitution judged to be incurable (n. 8).

Consistent with this acknowledgment, the NCCB stated in 1976 that "some persons" discover that they have a homosexual orientation "through no fault of their

own," and the 1986 CDF letter reaffirms that this orientation, in and of itself, "is not a sin" (n. 3). On the contrary, it is sinful to subject anyone to opprobrium or discrimination on account of his/her sexual orientation [Washington State Catholic Conference, "The Prejudice Against Homosexuals and the Ministry of the Church" (April 28, 1983)]. Persons so oriented, "like everyone else, . . . have a right to respect, friendship and justice, . . . [and] should have an active role in the Christian community" (NCCB 1976). Moreover, especially where a homosexual orientation is perceived as unalterable so as to exclude all prospect of marriage, it is precisely this fact which gives the person a special claim on the Church's "pastoral understanding and care" (*ibid.*).

Considerable difficulties still beset efforts to reach a sound understanding of the homosexual orientation itself from an authentically Christian perspective. Behavioral and social scientists offer no clear or uniform account of this orientation in terms of its genesis, exclusivity, permanence or other related questions. Confronted with obscure data and often conflicting interpretations from within the scientific community, the Church disowns any pretense at "an exhaustive treatment" of the "complex" homosexual question, remaining open to enlightenment from the human sciences while confident of its own "more global vision . . . [of] the rich reality of the human person" (CDF 1986, n. 2).

In line with its mandate to uphold "the Catholic moral perspective" (*ibid.*), CDF indicates some concern lest a duly compassionate regard for persons with a homosexual orientation be misconstrued as license for the genital activity to which that orientation inclines. This is the evident sense of the Congregation's statement that the homosexual "inclination," understood as "a more or less strong tendency ordered toward an intrinsic moral evil"—i.e., seen under the precise aspect of an inclination toward sinful sexual acts—is itself "an objective disorder" (n. 3). Whatever legitimate difficulties may be raised concerning this last phrase, two points should be made clear: the phrase does not signify that the homosexual orientation itself is in any sense sinful (indeed, as noted above, the exact opposite is stated); and it refers only to "a particular inclination" toward sin inherent in the homosexual orientation, not globally to all aspects of the sexual affectivity of persons so oriented—nor, even less, to the overall personality or character of such persons.

Reactions to the 1986 CDF letter, however, indicated that pastors find it extremely difficult to dissuade homosexual people from the notion that the Church views them as fundamentally flawed persons on account of their sexual orientation. This misperception may reflect the proneness of many homosexual people to over-identify with their sexual orientation, viewing any criticism of any aspect of that orientation as a profound assault on their personal dignity. While such over-identification is surely inappropriate (CDF 1986, n. 16), it is often an understandable overreaction to the unjust rejection which these persons suffer [Bishop Francis Mugavero (Brooklyn), pastoral letter, "Sexuality: God's Gift" (Feb. 11, 1976)]. Hence the foremost pastoral imperative—even prior to offering moral instruction—is for the Church to convince homosexuals in practical terms that it accepts them fully as persons whom it is ready to serve with genuine love and respect.

Homosexual activity. Inasmuch as pastoral care must also include moral instruction, the magisterium adheres to the traditional Judeo-Christian teaching that "homosexual activity, . . . as distinguished from homosexual orientation, is morally wrong" (NCCB 1976). Pope John Paul II, confirming this stand in an address to the United States hierarchy (Chicago, Oct. 5, 1979), stressed the obligation of bishops to maintain this teaching as "compassionate pastors" and "not betray [any homosexual] brother or sister" by holding out "false hope" that the teaching could change. The 1986 CDF letter echoes this approach (n. 15).

By contrast with the 1975 CDF declaration and the earlier tradition centered on natural law reasoning with reference to the procreative meaning of sexuality, the 1986 letter articulates the Church's rejection of homosexual genital activity in terms of a theological anthropology emphasizing the unitive equally with the procreative dimension, as seen in the Genesis teaching on creation:

> God . . . fashions mankind male and female, in his own image and likeness. Human beings, . . . in the complementarity of the sexes, . . . are called to reflect the inner reality of the Creator. They do this in a striking way in their cooperation with Him in the transmission of life by a mutual donation of the self to the other. . . . Homosexual activity is not a complementary union, able to transmit life; and so it thwarts the call to a life of that form of self-giving which the Gospel says is the essence of Christian living (nn. 5–7).

Although the same CDF document (n. 6) also cites various other biblical texts which comment adversely on homosexual practices—the Sodom story (Gn 19), the Levitical condemnations (Lv 18:22; 20:13) and Pauline writings (Rom 1:26–27; 1 Cor 6:9; 1 Tm 1:10)—these references are preceded by a stipulation that the Church's position is not based "on isolated phrases for facile theological argument" (n. 5). In any case the relevance of this material is subordinate to that of the Genesis creation theology which provides "the basic plan for understanding

this entire discussion of homosexuality" (n. 6). Hence, in accord with sound theology as well as pastoral sensitivity, the presentation of the Church's moral teaching should avoid an exaggerated emphasis on the condemnation of homosexual activity (such as would result from simplistic Biblical proofing) but should concentrate on articulating the positive "spousal significance" of human sexuality as the basis for recognizing the deficiency of any genital activity that does not do full justice to that significance.

The Church's pastoral strategy is less developed as regards the positive guidance of those believers whose homosexual orientation precludes marriage—perhaps permanently, if this orientation resists change—and who meanwhile seem unprepared to live a celibate life. The dilemma of such persons is a very difficult one demanding special support and help from pastors and from the entire Christian community, instead of the contempt or rejection which has too often been the response.

The authoritative teaching (CDF 1975) indicates a general negative norm, *viz.*, that "no pastoral method can be employed which would give moral approval to these [homosexual] acts on the grounds that they would be consonant with the condition of such people," but positive alternatives remain unspecified. Some local and regional episcopates (England and Wales 1979; San Francisco 1983), without recognizing committed homosexual relationships as an acceptable equivalent of marriage or morally endorsing homogenital acts within such relationships, have suggested the appropriateness of welcoming homosexuals thus situated into the full sacramental life of the Church if their relationship is prudently deemed the only present alternative to the incomparably worse evil of promiscuity (a particularly acute danger in face of the AIDS peril), and if there is reasonable hope that through prayer and the support of the Sacraments they may progressively grow into chastity. This approach emphasizes the need to respect the believer's sincere and upright conscience, as well as the principle of gradualism as enunciated by John Paul II [*Familiaris consortio*, n. 34; confer, application to homosexuality by B. Kiely, *L'Osservatore Romano* (Nov. 14, 1986) n. 7].

Positive initiatives. The process of growth toward chastity itself requires support from pastors and the whole Church community. The Church cannot be effective in insisting upon rigorous moral standards for homosexual persons as regards chastity, or in discouraging their participation in permissive homophile communities, as long as it does not make wholesome friendship available to such persons within its own body. Ironically the deprivation of such friendship is itself a major provocation (often unconsciously) toward the very unchastity which the Church condemns; if the basic human need for companionship, affection and intimacy is not met in wholesome ways, its fulfillment will be sought in disordered ways including inappropriate sexual conduct. The 1986 CDF letter includes a guarded but unmistakably clear acknowledgment that all Catholics must take every reasonable opportunity to help their homosexual fellow believers replace their lonely isolation with healthy interpersonal relationships (n. 15).

The same document contains other noteworthy progressive elements, for example, the identification of "violent malice in speech or in action"—now often called homophobia—as a continuing evil which "deserves condemnation from the Church's pastors wherever it occurs," and likewise a strong affirmation that homosexual people share in "the intrinsic dignity of each person [which] must always be respected in word, in action and in law" (n. 10). Inclusion of the homosexual question in catechetical programs on sexuality is now encouraged, and particular concern is also to be shown for the families of homosexual persons (n. 17).

It is the responsibility of diocesan bishops, individually and/or in regional conference, to implement such initiatives according to conditions in their respective territories (CDF 1986, nn. 13, 15, 17). During the 1990s a growing number of United States dioceses developed programs of outreach and support for gay and lesbian Catholics; and the NCCB officially recognizes the National Association of Catholic Diocesan Lesbian and Gay Ministries (NACDLGM). In 1997 the NCCB Committee on Marriage and Family issued a warmly positive pastoral letter titled "Always Our Children" that was directed primarily to parents of homosexual persons but was also addressed to gay and lesbian Catholic themselves; it was slightly revised in 1998, following input from the CDF.

The tendency of the CDF has been to stress the cautionary points of its 1986 letter. In a June 1997 memorandum, the congregation again advised bishops to be wary of civil-rights initiatives regarding homosexual persons, even suggesting that some instances of social discrimination against these persons would not be unjust. In July 1999, after years of investigation by various church agencies, the CDF ordered Sr. Jeannine Gramick, SSND, and Father Robert Nugent, SDS, the co-founders of New Ways Ministry in the United States, to cease their nearly three decades of nationwide ministry to homosexual persons and their families; the two had not satisfied the congregation's demand for an "unequivocal" declaration of their "personal assent" to the condemnations articulated in its 1975 and 1986 documents with regard to homosexual activity. NCCB president Bishop Joseph Fiorenza (of Houston, Texas) sought at once to assure gay Catholics

and their families that the CDF action against Gramick and Nugent would not weaken the United States hierarchy's commitment to promote a caring and compassionate ministry to the homosexual community.

The Catechism of the Catholic Church reiterates that homosexual acts can "under no circumstances . . .be approved" (no. 2357), and adds that the homosexual orientation itself is "objectively disordered" (no. 2358, in the *editio typica*). The same text also states, however, that the number of homosexually oriented men and women "is not negligible," that these persons "must be accepted with respect, compassion and sensitivity," and that any sign of "unjust discrimination" against them should be avoided. Even the summons to chastity is couched in terms of a confident expectation that homosexual people are capable of "Christian perfection" (no. 2359).

In presenting the full range of church teaching as summarized in these Catechism references, the more benign and positive elements of this teaching (which are less well known) need to be better highlighted and more broadly applied in practice, whereas the more severe and cautionary elements should be treated as subordinate though not ignored. These latter actually indicate problems, which can be effectively addressed only by a full and unambiguous commitment of the Church to a multidimensional effort of positive pastoral support for homosexual persons. If the attraction of such persons to homophile movements opposed to Catholic moral teaching is cause for concern, it must also be admitted that such movements have provided at least a modicum of the needed personal acceptance and understanding, which homosexuals have not often found in the Church or elsewhere. Hence the Church must provide an alternative for these men and women that clearly offers a more adequate and genuine affirmation of their personal worth. In sum, the commitment to uphold authentic Christian standards of sexual morality must be seen as an integral part of wider pastoral efforts to promote charity and justice.

Bibliography: *Homosexuality and the Magisterium: Documents from the Vatican and the U.S. Bishops,* ed., J. GALLAGHER (Mt. Rainier, Md. 1986). UNITED STATES CATHOLIC CONFERENCE, *Human Sexuality: A Catholic Perspective for Education and Lifelong Learning* (Washington, D.C. 1990). L. S. CAHILL, *Sex, Gender, and Christian Ethics* (Cambridge 1996). *Sexual Orientation and Human Rights in American Religious Discourse,* eds., S. M. OLYAN, and M. C. NUSSBAUM (Oxford 1998).

[B. WILLIAMS]

HONDURAS, THE CATHOLIC CHURCH IN

A republic located in Central America, Honduras is bounded on the north by the Caribbean Sea, on the south-

Capital: Tegucigalpa.
Size: 43,277 sq. miles.
Population: 6,249,598 in 2000.
Languages: Spanish; Amerindian dialects are spoken in various regions.
Religions: 4,999,678 Catholics (80%), 1,249,920 Evangelical Protestants (20%); indigenous tribal religions are also practiced.
Archdiocese: Tegucigalpa, with suffragans Choluteca, Comayagua, Juticalpa, San Pedro Sula, Santa Rosa de Copán, and Trujillo.

east by Nicaragua, on the South by the Pacific Ocean, on the southwest by El Salvador, and on the west by Guatemala. A mountainous country, Honduras contains deposits of gold, silver, copper, lead, iron ore, and other minerals. The population is predominately mestizo, with a large minority population of Amerindians descended from the region's ancient Mayan tribes. The Honduran economy is primarily agricultural and produces the tropical export crops of cacao, sugar, coffee, and bananas; it also has great forest wealth, although increasing deforestation due to logging activity raised environmental concerns beginning in the 1990s.

Christopher Columbus disembarked on the coast of Honduras on Aug. 14, 1502, and colonization of the region was begun two decades later, when Francisco de las Casas, a lieutenant of Hernan Cortéz, founded the port city of Trujillo. During the colonial period Honduras was one of the provinces of the captaincy-general of Guatemala. These provinces declared their independence June 24, 1823, and Honduras joined the short-lived United Provinces of Central America. One of the presidents of the confederation was Francisco Morazán, a Honduran.

A bishopric was erected in the Honduras area in the 16th century, and the See of Comayagua was functioning at the time of independence. However, there was no bishop there from 1819 to 1842. The constitution of republican Honduras gave preferential treatment to Catholicism until 1880 when complete religious freedom was established.

Throughout the late 19th century and into the 20th Honduras was the scene of continuous political upheaval, often of a violent nature. Internal wars and military coups were overshadowed during World Wars I and II, when Hondurans fought against Germany. During the 1950s and 1960s border disputes with neighboring Nicaragua and El Salvador seemed to be resolved, and with U.S. support the government adopted a new constitution in 1982. Unfortunately, the border dispute with Nicaragua continued to threaten violence as late as 1999, in part due

to Honduras's use by guerilla fighters as a base during the Contra's war with the Nicaraguan government. A failing economy and increasing poverty was the result. By the late 1990s countries such as France came to the region's aid by agreeing to forgive its portion of the $4.3 million in assistance loans, and international aid arrived in the wake of the death and destruction caused by Hurricane Mitch in November 1998. Pope John Paul II was vocal in his encouragement of such efforts in the Honduras and neighboring countries, and he also engaged in efforts to mediate in Central America's political disputes.

Within this politically unstable region, a shortage of clergy was a continuing problem throughout the mid- to late 20th century. In 1964 there were fewer than 200 priests, half of them members of religious orders, although by 2000 that number had grown to 327 priests. Of the few secular clergy, about half were Hondurans; others traveled from Spain, Italy, and other Latin American countries. Regular clergy from Spain, the United States, Canada, and Italy included members of the Congregation of the Missions, Franciscans, Jesuits, the Society for Foreign Missions (Quebec), and Maryknoll. Franciscan Sisters, School Sisters of Notre Dame, and Sisters of Mercy conducted several primary and secondary schools throughout Honduras. The Honduran government continued its amicable relationship with the Church, funding the construction of a statue of Christ on a mountain overlooking Tegucigalpa in 1997. As the government moved from military to civilian control it also sought ways to involve members of the Catholic hierarchy in the transition as a way to establish confidence among Honduran citizens. In 1998 it authorized Solidarity Catholic, the first Church television network in Honduras. In a more controversial move, in 2000 the government ordered that the Bible be read in all Honduran schools, a measure even the Church opposed as unconstitutional. Into the 21st century the Church looked to address the problems of poverty, gang violence, threats to the family, and the growth of spiritual indifference.

The Honduran Catholic Church enthusiastically supported ecumenical outreach, and Archbishop Oscar Rodriguez Maradiaga of Tegucigalpa was given charge of interreligious relations in the country. The Archbishop also planned to create an interfaith library in the nation's capital that would be available to all. While ecumenicism was encouraged among recognized faiths, controversial groups, such as the Unification Church and certain evangelical Protestant sects, continued to be viewed with disfavor by the government. A Methodist population, established in Honduras in 1859, was one of the largest recognized minority religions; others included Central American Missions, Quaker, Seventh-Day Adventist, Moravian, Foursquare Gospel, Baptist, and Mormon.

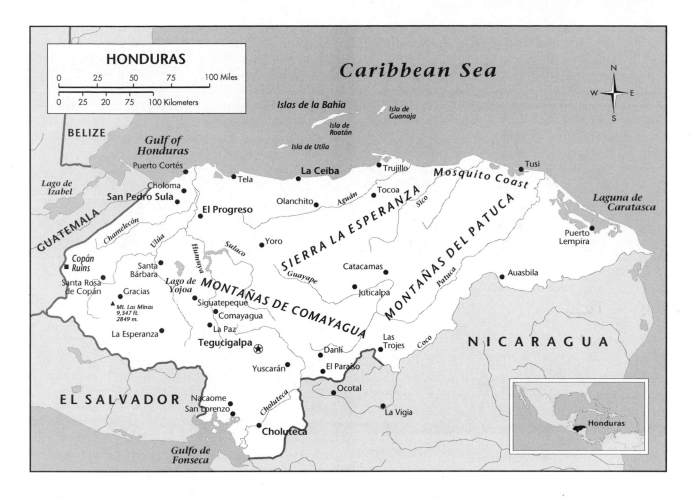

HONDURAS

Caribbean Sea

Bibliography: R. S. CHAMBERLAIN, *Conquest and Colonization of Honduras, 1502–1550* (Washington 1953). F. D. PARKER, *The Central American Republics* (New York 1964).

[J. HERRICK/EDS.]

HONG KONG, THE CATHOLIC CHURCH IN

Hong Kong is adjacent to Guangdong province in southeast China, 40 miles east of Macau. It includes Hong Kong Island, the Kowloon peninsula and adjoining New Territories, and a number of offshore islands. Long a target of Western colonization efforts, it was administered by Britain from 1842 until 1997, when it became a special administrative region of China. The population is 95 percent ethnic Chinese.

The Church in Colonial Hong Kong. Almost immediately after China ceded Hong Kong to Great Britain in 1842, Protestant chaplaincies were established to minister the British colonists and soldiers and to evangelize the Chinese people. Baptist, Congregationalist and Basel missionaries formed congregations, and as early as 1849

the Anglicans constructed St. John's Cathedral. Schools, charity centers, and dispensaries soon followed up. In 1887, the London Missionary Society opened the first Christian hospital.

In 1841, the Holy See made Hong Kong into a prefecture apostolic independent from the diocese of Macau. The following year, Catholic missionaries began to build their first church dedicated to the Immaculate Conception. The first Catholic school for Chinese boys opened in 1843. Missionaries societies and orders also cared for foundlings, the sick, and old people. The Paris Foreign Missions Society came in 1847 and the Foreign Missions of Milan (PIME) took over the charge of the prefecture in 1867. In 1874, Hong Kong became a vicariate apostolic.

After the First World War, Hong Kong, like the rest of China, experienced great turmoil. In the midst of the Sino-Japanese war (1937-1945) and as a consequence of the civil war between Communist and Nationalist forces, Hong Kong was flooded with refugees. During the Japanese occupation of Hong Kong (1941-1945), most foreign missionaries were forced to flee or were interned. The Chinese clergy, however, proved to be self-reliant

Church in Tegucigalpa, Honduras. (©The Purcell Team/CORBIS)

administratively, financially, and pastorally. In 1946, Hong Kong was elevated to a diocese, and its first bishop, Henricus Valtorta, was officially installed in 1948. The first Chinese Catholic bishop, Francis Hsu, was installed in 1969.

The Communist victory in 1949 was destined to make a notable impact on the ecclesiastical scene in Hong Kong. Refugees flowed from mainland China en masse in the 1950s and 1960s. As a result, emergency social work, temporary housing, and makeshift educational facilities were in great demand. The churches, Protestant and Catholic alike, rose to meet the challenge. They raised needed funds for relief services from abroad. They also set about opening much-needed regular schools and started educational services for children and young adults with learning disabilities and special needs.

The churches became pioneers in social services, sometimes encouraging the government to take on welfare programs, sometimes working with the government's social welfare department to provide social services. Caritas Centers, a network of social service centers organized by the Catholic Church with generous donations from abroad, became an important church-sponsored social service institution. The Protestant

counterpart, the Hong Kong Christian Service, operated some 50 social service centers offering a wide spectrum of services and was an equally important church-related organization. By the end of the 20th century, 40 percent of Hong Kong's schools and 60 percent of social welfare services were administered by Church affiliated institutions. With 20 percent of the hospitals under their administration, the Churches performed important and innovative medical services. But most of the grass-roots health care services for the sick poor were performed in their community clinics.

Post-Colonial Development. On July 1, 1997, Hong Kong ceased to be a British Crown colony and reverted to Chinese sovereignty as a Special Administrative Region of the People's Republic of China. Under the "one country, two systems" formula, and the Basic Law that serves as Hong Kong's unofficial constitution, freedom of religion was guaranteed to all Hong Kong residents.

The Catholic Church, with its 56 parishes, was the largest Christian denomination in Hong Kong. Although many Catholics emigrated to foreign countries just before and after the 1997 handover, their number was replaced by over 2,000 adult converts and over 2,000 children baptized each year. With the increasing number of Filipino migrant workers, mostly women serving as domestic helpers, Filipino Catholics numbered about one-third of Catholics in Hong Kong. John B. Wu Cheng-chung was installed bishop of the diocese in 1975 and made cardinal in 1988. Beginning in 1996 he was assisted by a coadjutor, Bishop Joseph Zen Ze-kiun and an auxiliary, Bishop John Tong Hon. The Hong Kong Catholic Church is still dependent on foreign mission clergy, with locally born clergy constituting only about 40 percent of the total Catholic clergy. Catholic schools, ranging from kindergarten to colleges and vocational schools, maintain a reputation for scholastic excellence. The Catholic Church also operates a healthcare network comprising six hospitals and numerous clinics, nursing homes, hospices and secondary care facilities.

The diocese supports two weekly newspapers. The Chinese-language *Kung Kao Po* was established in 1928; the *Sunday Examiner* began publication in English in 1946. In addition, two major Catholic journals are published in Hong Kong. Beginning in 1980 *Tripod* was published four times a year in Chinese and in English by the Holy Spirit Centre, focusing mainly on the Church in the Chinese mainland. It became a biannual in 2001. *Spirit* was established in 1989 as a quarterly review for Catholic theology and spirituality. The *Union of Catholic Asian News* (*UCA News*), has its headquarters and an office in Hong Kong. The Catholic Institute for Religion and Society runs workshops and publishes literature on the interaction of modern society and Christian living for Hong Kong people as well as those on the mainland.

Ecumenical Relations. Among the Protestants, the Baptists form the largest denomination, followed by the Lutherans, Adventists, Anglicans, Methodists, Pentecostal, the Christian and Missionary Alliance, and the Church of Christ in China. With their emphasis on youth work, many congregations contain a high proportion of young people. Protestant churches also operate three tertiary education institutions: Chung Chi College at the Chinese University of Hong Kong, Hong Kong Baptist University, and Lingnan University, as well as 13 theological colleges, seminaries and Bible institutes. Like the Catholic Church, they also have an extensive network of educational and healthcare facilities, with many kindergartens, elementary and high schools, hospitals, clinics and other medical facilities. The *Christian Weekly* and the *Christian Times* are the two principal vehicles for disseminating news of interest to Chinese Protestant communities.

Two ecumenical bodies facilitate cooperative work among the Protestant denominations. The Hong Kong Chinese Christian Churches Union, established in1915, has a membership of 275 congregations. It coordinates

---

Capital: Victoria
Size: 415.3 sq. miles.
Population: 6.87 million in 2000.
Languages: Chinese (Cantonese) and English are both official languages.
Religions: Some 90% of the population practices a mix of Taoism, Confucianism, and Buddhism. Christians comprise about 8% of the total population (Catholics, 5%; Protestants, 3%). There are also small Muslim, Jewish, and Sikh communities.
Diocese: Hong Kong.

---

evangelistic activities and encourages Christians to play an active part in the development of Hong Kong society through a wide range of auxiliaries agencies. Another interdenominational body, the Hong Kong Christian Council was organized in 1954 to promote unity of witness and outreach by the mainline Churches to the people of Hong Kong. It coordinates their social services and maintain relationships with churches in China and overseas. The Catholic Church has not entered into any formal ecumenical links with the Protestant Churches, but collaborates in the areas of social services and audio-visual communication. Few of the Protestant independent churches that have developed in recent years are ecumenical-minded.

The Protestant and Catholic churches of the Special Administrative Region of Hong Kong maintain close ties with their counterparts on mainland China and assist them in materials and other ways. They interact according to the principles of mutual respect and mutual assistance but do not interfere with each other.

Bibliography: S BLYTH and I. WOTHERSPOON, *Hong Kong Remembers* (Hong Kong 1996). *Catholic Hong Kong: A Hundred Years of Missionary Activity* (Hong Kong 1958). *Christianity Today Magazine* 1999-2000. *Hong Kong Catholic Church Directory*, published annually. *Hong Kong in a New Era: A Review of 1997* (Hong Kong 1998). "Hong Kong in Transition," *Tripod* March–April 1997. "Hong Kong: Between Optimism and Pessimism," *Tripod* May-June 1997. "Hong Kong: New Challenges and Identity," *Tripod* January-February 1997. C. K. LEE, *Studies in the History of the Church in Hong Kong* (in Chinese) (Hong Kong 1987). R. MALEK, ed. *Hong Kong, Kirche und Gesellschaft in Übergang: Materialen und Dokumente* (Sank Augustin, Germany 1997). *Papers of the International Conference on the Transition of HK-SARPRC. Held at Hong Kong Baptist University, The University of Hong Kong, and The Hong Kong University of Science & Technology, July 7–9, 1997. People's Republic of China Year Book*, published biennially. T. RYAN, *Catholic Guide to Hong Kong* (Hong Kong 1962). S. TICOZZI, *Historical Documents of the Hong Kong Catholic Church* (Hong Kong 1997).

[J.-P. WIEST]

HONOR

From the Latin *honor,* cognate to *honestas,* τὸ καλόν, τιμή, *honorabilis* and *honestus,* and by itself, without these fringe senses, a sufficiently ambiguous term. It signifies in an object a quality of being handsome, gracious, beautiful; a kind of embellishment of the good; a worth that is set off and exalted. Thus Aristotle, the Stoics, and the Fathers speak of an end as a *bonum honestum,* a value for its own sake and not because it is serviceable (*bonum utile*) or pleasurable (*bonum delectabile*). In the human subject it comes then to mean his response to such a special distinction, which is given glory and fame and held in respect and esteem. Thus one is said to do or pay honor to someone. Later this dignity may be assimilated; a personal sentiment of honor, a fine sense of what is due, may be cultivated and perhaps demand renown or at least some acknowledgement. So one gives his word of honor, and will neither brook offense nor bend to find recognition. It is an aristocratic and indeed, in the West, a soldierly notion, entering into the spirit and institutions of chivalry. It acquired a special Christian quality of gallantry and knightliness, which it still keeps, despite its sharing in the decay of chivalry into punctilio, mannerisms, and courtly sophistication. Since from the beginning honor seemed set on the glory of this world and later protested personal and independent values that were not the plain decencies of the common cardinal virtues or of humility, it is easy to see why Christian moralists have either neglected it for otherworldly categories, or have treated it as bound up with a pride of life that was either vain or at best to be suspected as a doubtful blessing. Nevertheless, it is clearly marked in a classical theology of the 13th century, where eschatological convictions, no less strong than any before or since, went with a welcome for what the Greco-Roman world respected and for the statesmanlike and military values that were forming a new civilization.

Honor enters into the *Summa theologiae* of St. Thomas at three points where he discusses the giving of honor, the striving for honor, and the feeling of honor.

The giving of honor. This is regarded as a matter of justice and specifically of that potential part of justice called RESPECT (*observantia*), a distinctive virtue, which, serving others because of the dignity of their office or character, finds its formal expression in the virtue of OBEDIENCE to a superior, extends also to the honoring of excellence, not only in inward appreciation, but also in outward signs. This is due and proper, and when accompanied by feelings of veneration for a person who is leader of a country, race, corps, or family group, is called dulia (δουλεία) or worship, as in England, where this is an honorific title for mayors and magistrates.

The striving for honor. This belongs to the cardinal virtue of fortitude and specifically to that potential part called greatheartedness, or high-mindedness (MAGNANIMITY), though another potential part called grandeur (MAGNIFICENCE) may also be engaged. There is bravery in not shirking the renown that is the proper consequence of great deeds and the splendor it is laudable that some works should possess, so long as this is not allowed to become inflated into a display of ostentation and pompousness (*Summa theologiae* 2a2ae, 129–135).

Feelings of honor. These are treated as an integral part of temperance. Aristotle and the Latin Stoics noted a certain fastidiousness (*verecundia*) in the life of virtue, a sensitiveness to what is shameful and disgraceful, which, though not itself a virtue, is a material condition of virtue. But more positive and to the point is the honorable quality (*honestas*) in virtue, in keeping with its dynamism as a disposition of the good to the best, a clean and candid beauty that relates honor to the virtue of temperance in particular and to all virtue in general (*Summa theologiae* 2a2ae, 144–145), so much so that a high-mettled and fine-tempered morality will act to others not merely according to the debt of strict justice (*debitum legale*), but also from its charge of honor (*debitum morale, ex honestate virtutis*). The obligation, though it cannot be enforced by law, is no less grave for the life of virtue.

Bibliography: K. E. LOGSTRUP, *Die Religion in Geschichte und Gegenwart* (3rd ed. Tübingen 1957–63) 2:339–341. H. REINER, *Die Ehre* (Darmstadt 1956).

[T. GILBY]

HONORATUS OF AMIENS, ST.

Bishop of Amiens; b. probably in Port-le-Grand; d. in the Diocese of Amiens, *c.* 600. According to the unreliable biography written not earlier than the late 11th century, Honoratus was a contemporary of Pope PELAGIUS II (579–590). His cult became widespread in France as a result of cures effected when his body was elevated in 1060. In 1204 Reynold Cherez and his wife placed the church they had built in Paris under his patronage, and a century later the charterhouse at Abbéville was dedicated to him. The famous Faubourg and Rue Saint-Honoré in Paris are named also for him. He is recognized as the patron of bakers and those who work with flour.

Feast: May 16.

Bibliography: *Bibliotheca hagiographica latina antiquae ct mediae aetatis,* 2 v. (Brussels 1898–1901; suppl. 1911) 1:3972–74. *Acta Sanctorum* May 3:609–613. L. DUCHESNE, *Fastes épiscopaux de l'ancienne Gaule,* 3 v. (2d. ed. Paris 1907–15) 3:125, 143. A. BUTLER, *The Lives of the Saints,* ed. H. THURSTON and D. ATTWATER, 4 v. (New York 1956) 2:330.

[C. R. BYERLY]

HONORATUS OF ARLES, ST.

Bishop, first abbot of Lérins; d. Arles, Jan. 14 or 15, probably 430. The anniversary *Sermon* preached at Arles by his successor, Hilary, notes that he was of a consular family but gives neither place nor date of birth. It records his baptism as an adolescent and subsequent embracing of monasticism with a brother Venantius and their friend (St.) Caprasius (d. 430), first at home, then at Marseilles (?), Greece (where Venantius died at Methoni), Italy, and eventually Lérins (modern Saint Honorat in the Bay of Cannes) on which island Honoratus established his renowned abbey (*c.* 410). Upon visiting his home (Toul?, Trier?), Honoratus induced Hilary, his kinsman and episcopal successor, to join him at Lérins. That Honoratus was a priest is certified by the anniversary *Sermon* (16) and by the writings of PAULINUS OF NOLA (*Epist.* 51).

From Lérins Honoratus was chosen bishop of Arles (*Serm.* 25, 28). Duchesne dates this 426 or 427, after the assassination of Bp. Patroclus. Chadwick more justly interposes Euladius between Patroclus and Honoratus, so that Honoratus's episcopate probably commenced in late 427 or early 428. He is the Arles prelate to whom Pope CELESTINE I refers (*Epist.* 4); his reputation is reflected in CASSIAN (*Coll.* 18). He died with Hilary at his side (*Serm.* 29), and was interred at Aliscamps in the now secularized church of his name on January 16.

Feast: Jan. 16.

Bibliography: S. CAVALLIN, *Vitae Sanctorum Honorati et Hilarii* (Lund 1952). HILARY OF ARLES, *Sermon,* tr. R. J. DEFERRARI, *The Fathers of the Church: A New Translation,* ed. R. J. DEFERRARI et al.15 (New York 1952) 355–394. F. BONNARD, *S. Honorat de Lérins* (Tours 1914). É. GRIFFE, *La Gaule chrétienne à l'époque romaine* (Paris 1947) 2:191–197. J. R. PALANQUE, ''Les Évêchés provençaux à l'époque romaine,'' *Provence historique* 1 (1951) 131–132. O. CHADWICK, ''Euladius of Arles,'' *Journal of Theological Studies* 46 (London 1945) 200–205. R. FERAUT, *La vida de Sant Honorat: légende en vers provençaux* (Geneva 1974).

[H. G. J. BECK]

HONORIUS I, POPE

Pontificate: Oct. 27, 625, to Oct. 12, 638. The *LIBER PONTIFICALIS* identifies Honorius as a native of the Campania and son of the consul Petronius. If his election as pope received the traditional imperial confirmation, it came not from the Byzantine Emperor himself, but from the exarch at Ravenna, as is known to have been the case in 686 (*Liber pontificalis*, ed. L. Duchesne [Paris 1886–92, 1958] n. 85).

West. Honorius was immediately involved with affairs in Italy. In 625 he demanded that Exarch Isaac

St. Honoratus of Arles, detail of a miniature in the Book of Hours of the Maréchal de Boucicaut, 14th century, in the Musée Jacquemart, Paris. The saint has been given the features of Honorat Durand, chaplain and confessor of the Maréchal.

(625–643) send to Rome for penance those bishops who had helped Arioald, Duke of Turin, to overthrow the Lombard King Adaloald (616–625). Then, two letters of June 10, 627, deal with the excesses of the Sardinian official Theodore, and two later ones commit the government of Naples to the notary Gaudiosus and the military captain Anatholius. Honorius's epitaph asserts that he ended the minor schism caused by Istria's refusal to accede to the condemnation of the THREE CHAPTERS pronounced in 553 by the Council of CONSTANTINOPLE II. The fact seems to be that on Feb. 18, 628, Honorius provided a Roman subdeacon, Primogenius, to Istria's See of Grado (which see Primogenius continued to hold as late as 642 or 649).

As for Spain, Honorius sent the deacon Turninus to the Council of TOLEDO VI (638) with instructions to urge the prelates to greater efforts in restraining the infidels. Caspar (2:671) holds that this letter referred to the Jewish question. In any event, the reply written by Bp. BRAULIO of Saragossa in the name of the whole synod (*Patrologia Latina*, ed. J. P. Migne [Paris 1878–90] 80:667–670) makes it clear that such a papal admonition was uncalled for. It is a fact, however, that the decrees of the Council

Pope Honorius I, detail of the 7th-century mosaic in the apse of the church of S. Agnese at Rome.

of Toledo VI (J. D. Mansi, *Sacrorum Conciliorum nova et amplissima collectio* [Graz 1960–] 10:663)—like those of the Council of Toledo IV in 663 (*Sacrorum Conciliorum nova et amplissima collectio* 10:633–35)—reveal a decidedly anti-Jewish attitude on the part of the Spanish hierarchy.

England's Venerable Bede (*Ecclesiastical History* 2.17–19) records Honorius's grant of the PALLIUM in 634 to Abp, HONORIUS OF CANTERBURY and Abp. PAULINUS OF YORK. However, the document by which Honorius is supposed to have bestowed primacy upon Canterbury (P. Jaffé, *Regesta pontificum romanorum ab condita ecclesia ad annum post Christum natum 1198,* ẹd. P. Ewald, [Graz 1956] 590–882 2021) is now considered a forgery [*Gregorianum* 12 (1931) 44–46]. Bede notes that the Pope appealed to Britain's Celtic Christians to abandon their non-Roman manner of calculating Easter. Honorius also sent Bishop Birinus to labor among the West Saxons (*Ecclesiastical History* 3.7).

Controversy over Monothelitism. More important, perhaps, than Honorius's involvement in the West was the role he played in the BYZANTINE CHURCH's vital controversy over MONOPHYSITISM, which by this time had also given rise to MONOTHELITISM. His actions in this affair occasioned violent debate over his orthodoxy, over papal INFALLIBILITY, and over the relationship of pope and council—issues that were contested down to VATICAN COUNCIL I.

In a letter of 634 (*Sacrorum Conciliorum nova et amplissima collectio* 11.529–37) Patriarch SERGIUS I OF CONSTANTINOPLE reported current developments to Honorius. At stake was an attempt to win Eastern Monophysites back to Catholic unity by means of a formula that stressed oneness of operation in Christ. A year earlier Patriarch Cyrus of Alexandria (630 or 631–643 or 644) had successfully reconciled dissidents in his patriarchate by professing "one theandric operation" in the Lord (*Sacrorum Conciliorum nova et amplissima collectio* 11:565d). However, the monk Sophronius, soon to be patriarch of Jerusalem (633 or 634–638) had adduced patristic evidence for two operations in Christ and had required Cyrus to promise that in the future he would speak neither of one nor of two operations. In his letter Sergius stated that he himself accepted the Catholic faith as expounded by Pope LEO I. He too had counseled Cyrus to refrain from speaking of operations, even though the patriarch's personal sympathies lay with a theology of a single operation, and he thought that mention of a double operation would only imply that Christ was in possession of two contrary wills, with the human will being set against the divine in undergoing the Passion. At the end, his letter sought the Pope's reaction.

Honorius's reply has been preserved in the Greek translation that was read at the Council of CONSTANTINOPLE III on March 22, 681 (*Sacrorum Conciliorum nova et amplissima collectio* 11:537–544; the Latin in *Patrologia Latina* 80:470–474 is probably a retranslation). The Pope fully supported the position that there be no further discussion of either one or two operations, preferring to leave such questions to grammarians. Rather, he urged concentration upon the one Christ who operates both in His divine and in His human nature. He cited the formula of the Council of CHALCEDON to the effect that the two natures are unconfusedly and immutably united, and from this unity Honorius deduced the presence of a single will in Christ since His human nature is uncorrupted and not subject to the law of the members to which Rom 7.23 refers. He interpreted Mk 14.36 ("Not my will . . .") as spoken for our instruction in accord with the "economy" of the assumed humanity and not as marking a will differing from that of the Father's will. By economy Honorius meant "a manner of speaking." This, indeed, appears to be Monothelitism and would exclude a true human will in Christ. However, Galtier (*Gregorianum* [Rome 1920–] 29:53–61) maintains that the Pope was actually positing a real human will in a real humanity, yet a will that is ever submissive to Christ's divine will.

Chapman (*Dublin Review* 139:129–134) has remarked that Honorius's reply to Sergius was a private communication and does not fall into the category of public papal definitions of faith guaranteed by infallibility. However, it is undeniable that Honorius did counsel not mentioning either one or two operations in Christ, thus at least placing the heretical assertion (one operation) on an equal plane with the orthodox expression (two operations).

This papal fault was compounded after Honorius received a synodical letter (*Sacrorum Conciliorum nova et amplissima collectio* 11:461–509) from Sophronius of Jerusalem that argued from the diversity of the divine and human natures to the distinction of operations in the Lord (*Sacrorum Conciliorum nova et amplissima collectio* 11:481–484), although it did not raise the question of the number of wills in Christ. A fragmentary notice (*Sacrorum Conciliorum nova et amplissima collectio* 11:580–581) to Sergius—Honorius's reply to Sophronius is lost—shows that the Pope was again intent upon terminating any discussion as to one or two operations and had received a pledge to this end from Sophronius. However, Honorius was quite insistent upon two integral natures in Christ, each operating in a manner proper to it in the one person of the Son of God. What is deplorable in Honorius's approach to the whole Monophysite controversy is not his theology, but his failure to realize that the new terms introduced into the discussion required official evaluation. Four years later (638) this line of thinking reached a natural conclusion with the appearance of Emperor HERACLIUS's *Ecthesis* (*Sacrorum Conciliorum nova et amplissima collectio* 10:992–997), that simply forbade reference to operations and confessed but a single will in Christ (*see* TYPOS).

Honorius's successor, Pope SEVERINUS, seems to have condemned Monothelitism (*Regesta pontificum romanorum ab condita ecclesia ad annum post Christum natum 1198,* 2039); and Pope JOHN IV, who assuredly anathematized the *Ecthesis* (*Sacrorum Conciliorum nova et amplissima collectio* 11:9), deplored the action of the new patriarch of Constantinople, PYRRHUS, when he cited Honorius's authority in favor of Monothelitism (*Sacrorum Conciliorum nova et amplissima collectio* 10:682–686). John's interpretation of his predecessor's mind is that Honorius's exclusion of two contrary wills in Christ is explicitly limited to the human nature; he was in no way envisioning a single will common to both the divinity and humanity. This is a valid observation as far as it goes, but it says nothing of Honorius's blindness in prohibiting discussion on the number of operations in Christ.

His Condemnation Evaluated. Honorius's stand became the subject of much criticism. In a disputation of

July 645 St. MAXIMUS THE CONFESSOR (d. 662) replied to the deposed Patriarch Pyrrhus that Honorius kept within the limits of the problem proposed to him and thus did not have to enter into the further question of the will inherent in the divine nature of Christ (*Patrologia Graeca* ed. J. P. Migne, [Paris 1857–66] 91:329b). However, subsequent developments, especially the Lateran Synod of 649 under Pope MARTIN I, which condemned Monothelitism and whose 18th canon named Patriarch Sergius a heretic, and the assembling of the sixth ecumenical council, CONSTANTINOPLE III (680–681), led inevitably to a reevaluation of Honorius's action. At Constantinople III, in the presence of papal legates who had delivered an important dogmatic letter from Pope AGATHO, Honorius was mentioned several times and his two letters to Sergius were read at the 12th and 13th sessions. At the 13th session (March 28, 681), Monothelites were condemned and expelled from the Church; these included Honorius "because . . . by his letter to Sergius he followed his opinion in all things and confirmed his wicked dogmas" (*Sacrorum Conciliorum nova et amplissima collectio* 11:556C). In the final session of Sept. 16, 681, Honorius was again listed among the heretics because he had followed in the footsteps of Sergius and Cyrus (*Sacrorum Conciliorum nova et amplissima collectio* 11:636; 656; 665). The council's letter to Pope Agatho, asking confirmation of the *Acta* and marked by recognition for Rome's magisterium (*Sacrorum Conciliorum nova et amplissima collectio* 11:684–88), also lists Honorius among the heretics, where, the council fathers said, he was placed in accord with Agatho's own letter.

Agatho, however, had died Jan. 10, 681, and it was his successor, Pope LEO II, who had to evaluate the *Acta.* In 682 Leo wrote to Emperor CONSTANTINE IV approving the council and condemning Honorius "qui hanc apostolicam ecclesiam non apostolice traditionis doctrina lustravit sed prophana pro traditione immaculatam fidem dari permittendo conatus est" (MS Vat. Reg. lat. 1040, fol. 84r; variant reading *Patrologia Latina* 96:408). In a similar letter to the bishops of Spain, Leo charged Honorius with negligence: "qui flammam heretici dogmatis, non ut decuit apostolicam auctoritatem, incipientem extinxit, sed negligendo confovit" (*Patrologia Latina* 96:414B). A third papal letter, to the Visigoth King Ervigius, states that Honorius allowed the unsullied standard of apostolic tradition inherited from his predecessors to be soiled: "qui . . . regulam quam a praedecessoribus suis accepit, maculari consensit" (*Patrologia Latina* 96:419D). It is in this sense of guilty negligence that the papacy ratified the condemnation of Honorius.

Honorius is credited with beautifying several Roman churches and with founding the monastery of SS. Andrew and Bartholomew in the vicinity of the Lateran.

Bibliography: *Liber pontificalis,* ed. L. DUCHESNE (Paris 1886–92, 1958) 1:323–327. *Patrologia Latina,* ed. J. P. MIGNE (Paris 1878–90) 80:469–484, P. JAFFÉ, *Regesta pontificum romanorum ab condita ecclesia ad annum post Christum natum 1198,* ed. S. LÖWENFELD et al. (Graz 1956) 1:223–226; 2:698. *Clavis Patrum latinorum,* ed. E. DEKKERS (Streenbrugge 1961) 1726–28. J. CHAPMAN, "The Condemnation of Pope Honorius," *Dublin Review* 139 (1906) 129–154; 140 (1907) 42–72. C. J. VON HEFELE, *Histoire des conciles d'après les documents originaux,* tr. and continued by H. LECLERECQ (Paris 1907–38) v.3. H. K. MANN, *The Lives of the Popes in the Early Middle Ages from 590 to 1304* (London 1902–32) 1:304–345. J. TIXERONT, *History of Dogmas,* tr. H. L. BRINCEAU, v.3 (2d ed. St. Louis 1926) 153–184. É. AMANN, *Dictionnaire de théologie catholique,* ed. A. VACANT et al., (Paris 1903—50) 7.1:93–132. *Dictionnaire de théologie catholique* Tables générales 2112–13. E. CASPAR, *Geschichte de Papsttums von den Aufängen bis zur Höhe der Weltherrschaft* (Tübingen 1930–33) 2:523–619. P. GALTIER, "La Première lettre du Pape Honorius," *Gregorianum* (Rome 1920–) 29 (1948), 42–61. F. X. SEPPELT, *Geschichte der Päpste vonden Anfängen bis zur Mitte des 20. Jh.* (Munich 1959) 2:47–58, 74–76, 428–429. R. BÄUMER, *Lexikon für Theologie und Kirche,* ed. J. HOFER and K. RAHNER (Freiberg 1957–65) 5:474–475. G. ROWEKAMP, *Lexikon der antiken christlichen Literatur* (Freiburg 1998). A. R. TERRERO, "El problema judio en la mente de tres importantes personajes del siglo VII: un papa, un Obispo español y un rey visigodo," *Espacio, Tiempo y Forma: Historia Antigua,* Serie II (Madrid 1993) 585–604. J. N. D. KELLY, *Oxford Dictionary of Popes* (New York 1986) 70–71.

[H. G. J. BECK]

HONORIUS II, POPE

Pontificate: Dec. 15, 1124 to Feb. 13 or 14, 1130; b. Lambert Scannabecchi, at Fagnano, near Imola, Italy, date unknown; d. Rome. Widely known for his learning, he entered papal service under URBAN II and was made a cardinal by PASCHAL II in 1117. His most important task as a papal diplomat was acting as CALLISTUS II's representative in the negotiations with Emperor HENRY V that culminated in the Concordat of Worms in 1122. His pontificate was concerned in large part with securing for the Church the rights promised by that concordat. Lambert's election as pope was marked by an outbreak of the feud between the PIERLEONI and the FRANGIPANI families, which divided the Roman nobility and interfered with the electoral process. The first CONCLAVE ended on Dec. 15, 1124, with the election of Honorius, supported by the Frangipani, and the election of an ANTIPOPE, Celestine II (Cardinal Teobaldo Buccapecci), supported by the Pierleoni. After it became clear that Honorius was supported by the *sanior pars* of the cardinals, Celestine lost his supporters and resigned. On December 21, Honorius also resigned, only to be reelected immediately by the assembled cardinals. With the death of Henry V in 1125, Honorius moved to consolidate the Church's position with regard to the empire by supporting the election of LOTHAIR III, count of Supplinburg, to succeed to the imperial throne rather than allow either of Henry's nephews, Frederick or Conrad of Hohenstaufen (later to rule as Conrad III), to assume power. When Conrad declared himself king in opposition to Lothair, Honorius excommunicated him, thus placing the papacy clearly on Lothair's side. Within the papal lands Honorius sought to pacify the rebellious Roman barons and to defend the duchy of Apulia from ROGER II of Sicily, but after failing to prevent Roger's seizure of the duchy, Honorius recognized his right to hold it in return for Roger's oath of fealty, thus paving the way for the creation of the Kingdom of the Two Sicilies. In addition to these political controversies, Honorius was mindful of the spirit of reform within the Church. In 1126 he confirmed the establishment of the PREMONSTRATENSIANS, who combined the active with the contemplative life, and in 1128 he approved the rule of the TEMPLARS, who had been founded to protect pilgrims in the Holy Land. Even as he lay dying, however, the two factions that disputed his election were gathering for the new election, which was to lead to a serious schism.

Bibliography: P. JAFFÉ, *Regesta pontificum romanorum ab condita ecclesia ad annum post Christum natum 1198,* ed. S. LÖWENFELD (Graz 1956) 1:823–839, 2:755. *Patrologia Latina,* ed. J. P. MIGNE (Paris 1878–90) 166:1217–1320. H. K. MANN, *The Lives of the Popes in the Early Middle Ages from 590 to 1304* (London 1902–32) 8:228–305. E. AMANN, *Dictionnaire de théologie catholique,* ed. A. VACANT et al. (Paris 1903–50) 7:132–135. A. FLICHE and V. MARTIN, *Histoire de l'église depuis les origines jusqu'à nos jours* (Paris 1935—) 9:43–53. H. W. KLEWITZ, *Reformpapsttum und Kardinalkolleg* (Darmstadt 1957). F. X. SEPPELT, *Geschichte der Päpste von den Anfängen bis zur Mitte des 20. Jh.* (Munich 1956) 3:165–171. H. SCHMIDINGER, *Lexikon für Theologie und Kirche,* ed. J. HOFER and K. RAHNER (Freiburg 1957–65) 5:476. U. R. BLUMENTHAL, "The Text of a Lost Letter of Pope Honorius II," *Bulletin of Medieval Cannon Law* (Berkeley, CA 1974) 64–66. F. GELDNER, "Kaiserin Mathilde, die deutsche Königswahl von 1125 und das Gegenkönigtum Konrads III," *Zeitschrift für Bayerische Landesgeschichte* (München 1977) 3–22. G. HAENDLER, "Zur Missionsreise des Bischofs Otto von Bamberg, 1128–1278," *Theologische Literaturzeitung* (Berlin 1981) 305–14. J. LECLERCQ, "La 'paternité' de S. Bernard et les débuts de l'Ordre cistercien," *Revue Bénédictine* (Maredsous, Belgium 1993) 445–81. F. V. LOMBARDI, "La bolla di papa Onorio II a Pietro vescovo di Montefeltro (anno 1125)," *Studi Montefeltrani* (1976) 57–99. G. J. SCHIRO, "The Career of Lamberto da Fagnano: Honorius II 1035?–1130 and the Gregorian Reform," *Dissertation Abstracts* (Ann Arbor, Mich. 1975/1976) 3913–14. R. SOMERVILLE, "Pope Honorius II, Conrad of Hohenstaufen, and Lothar III," *Archivum Historiae Pontificiae* (Roma 1972) 341–6. H. STOOB, "Zur Königswahl Lothars von Sächsen im Jahre 1125," *Festschrift für Walter Schlesinger, II* (Köln 1976) 438–61. J. N. D. KELLY, *Oxford Dictionary of Popes* (New York 1986) 165–66.

[J. M. MULDOON]

HONORIUS II, ANTIPOPE

Pontificate: Oct. 28, 1061 to May 31, 1064. Known as Peter Cadalus (also Cadalous), he was born 1009 or 1010 into a wealthy family near Verona. He was bursar for the bishop of Verona in the early 1040s and was made bishop of Parma in 1045. He died in 1071 or early 1072. In the midst of the Investiture Controversy, Peter was selected as antipope in a meeting of the royal court in Basle. He was supported by the Empress Agnes, regent for the young Henry IV (1056–1106); various Lombard bishops, under the leadership of GUIBERT OF RAVENNA (later anti-Pope CLEMENT III, 1080–1100); and members of the Roman nobility, who saw this as an opportunity to regain control of the papacy. Peter Cadalus was known as an opponent of the papal reformers and also of the Pataria, a revolutionary movement among the middle and lower classes that sought both sociopolitical reform (the overthrow of the ruling oligarchy) and ecclesiastical reforms (e.g., in 1057 they used arms in an effort to force priests to give up their concubines). His election was meant to challenge that of the reform party's pope, Alexander II (1061–73).

On April 14, 1062 Honorius defeated Alexander's forces and took up residence in Rome, but the city remained divided into warring camps. When Duke Godfrey the Bearded of Lorraine arrived in May with superior forces, he compelled both claimants to leave the city for their former dioceses. Meanwhile the German court would decide who was rightful pope. This left the matter in the hands of Anno, the archbishop of Cologne (1056–75) and new regent. Anno favored Alexander (as did the influential reformer Peter Damian) and the Synods of Augsburg (October 1062) and Rome (Christmas 1062) upheld his decision. Nevertheless, the two rivals excommunicated each other. In May 1063, Honorius again attacked Rome and seized St. Peter's and the Castel Sant' Angelo. While he occupied Sant' Angelo for several months, he was more prisoner than victor. Soon Alexander, with strong Norman support, forced Honorius to flee back to Parma. In May 1064, a synod of German and Italian bishops met at Mantua; it invited both claimants to attend. Honorius asked to preside over the synod and decided to stay away when his request was denied. For his part, Alexander went to Mantua and presided over the synod. His claim as pope was upheld, and Honorius was formally deposed with the agreement of the imperial court under the leadership of Anno of Cologne.

Afterward, Cadalus remained in his diocese and continued to be recognized as bishop of Parma, even though he never formally abandoned his claim to the Holy See. In 1065 and again in 1068 he hoped the German court would rule in his favor, but it never did. He died as bishop of Parma in late 1071 or very early in 1072.

Honorius III, detail from "St. Francis Preaching Before Honorius III" by Giotto. (©Elio Ciol/CORBIS)

Bibliography: L. DUCHESNE, ed. *Liber Pontificalis* (Paris 1886–92; repr. 1955–57) 2.281, 284, 336, 358–60. P. JAFFÉ, *Regesta pontificum Romanorum* (Leipzig 1885–88; repr. Graz 1956) 1.530, 566–94. PETER DAMIAN, Letters 81, 88, 89, and 112, *Die Briefe des Petrus Damiani*, K. REINDEL, ed., *Monumenta Germaniae historica, Briefe der deutschen Kaiserzeit* (Munich 1983ff); trans. O. BLUM, *The Letters of Peter Damian* (Washington, DC 1989ff). See especially REINDEL 2.534, nn. 23–25 on Cadalus' election. I. M. WATTERICH, *Pontificum Romanorum* (Leipzig; repr. Aalen 1862) 1.235–90. F. HERBERHOLD, "Die Angriffe des Cadalus von Parma (Gegenpapst Honorius II.) auf Rom in den Jahren 1062 und 1063," *Studia Gregoriana* 2 (1947) 477–503. F. BAIX, *Dictionnaire d'histoire et de géographie ecclésiastiques* (Paris 1949) 11.53–99. V. CAVALLARI, "Cadalo e gli Erzoni," *Studi Storici Veronesi Luigi Simeoni* 15 (1965) 59–170. T. SCHMIDT, *Alexander II (1061–1073) und die Römische Reformgruppe seiner Zeit* (Stuttgart 1972) 104–73 passim. W. ULLMANN, *A Short History of the Papacy in the Middle Ages* (London 1972). M. STOLLER, "Eight Anti-Gregorian Councils," *Annuarium historiae conciliorum* 17 (1985) 252–321. J. N. D. KELLY, *The Oxford Dictionary of Popes* (New York 1986) 153–54. T. STRUVE, "Kaisertum und Romgedanke in salischer Zeit," *Deutsches Archiv für Erforschung des Mittelalters* 44 (1988) 424–54. *Dictionnaire d'histoire et de géographie ecclésiastiques* (Paris 1993) 24.1050.

[P. M. SAVAGE]

HONORIUS III, POPE

Pontificate: July 18, 1216 to March 18, 1227. He was from Rome, and his original name was Cencius. According to a later tradition, which is without contemporary foundation, he was a member of the Savelli family. He was probably born in the 1150s. This date supports the view that he was elderly when elected pope. He had been a canon of Santa Maria Maggiore and chamberlain under Popes Clement III and Celestine III. He was named cardinal-deacon of S. Lucia in Orthea before March 4, 1193 and raised to cardinal priest of Saints John and Paul in early 1200 by Pope Innocent III. His most important achievement prior to his pontificate was his compilation of the *Liber Censuum Romane Ecclesie*, a work which provided a detailed statement of the rights and patrimony of the Apostolic See. He was clearly in the mainstream of twelfth-century popes, who worked to establish and strengthen the position of the papacy in Rome. There is some evidence that he did not agree fully with his predecessor, Innocent III, but his differences seem to have been partly a matter of style. He generally refrained from broad statements regarding papal policy toward secular rulers, though he vigorously defended the interests of the church. He seems, however, to have sought cooperation and worked to promote good relations with secular powers. Some historians have viewed this as a policy of weakness.

Innocent III had died at a critical moment, with the Fourth Lateran Council recently completed and a new crusade already in the late planning stages. This crusade had recruited the youthful and recently-elected emperor Frederick II, whom Innocent had supported for the crown. Since it was supposed to begin in 1217, Honorius quickly reaffirmed the date of departure and vigorously supported efforts to collect the crusade tax levied on the clergy at the Fourth Lateran Council, so that momentum would not slip away after Innocent's death. The difficulties, however, were considerable, since, among other factors, Frederick could not depart while his opponents were still in the field. The problem of the crusade would remain central to Honorius's pontificate.

In order to understand the political role of Honorius, it is essential to view it in relationship to his crusade policies. The conflict between the English and French monarchies required intensive negotiations, not only to resolve differences between these rulers but also to ensure the succession to the English throne for the nine-year-old Henry III. Innocent III had been quite unpopular at the French court, because of his support for Queen Ingeborg of Denmark, whom Philip II, Augustus, wanted to divorce. Honorius lost no time in trying to build better relations with Philip, while giving strong support to Henry against his barons and Philip's son, the later Louis VIII. In this case, the results of his irenic policy were a major success, as the large number of English participants in the Fifth Crusade bear witness. On the French side, he altered Innocent's belated efforts to heal the wounds caused by the Albigensian Crusade by lending his support to Louis VIII against the nobility of the Midi, thus promoting the interests of the French crown. Still, the monarchy remained less supportive of the crusade and more concerned with protecting its rights.

Many historians have had a negative view of his pontificate because of the failure of his efforts to induce Frederick II to go on crusade, and later the disastrous loss of Damietta in Egypt by the crusaders. What has not been sufficiently understood is the genuine commitment that Frederick himself made to the crusade, but it was complicated by the complexities of his position as emperor and king of Sicily. Impelled by an extremely strong sense of his rights, which was fed by his advisors, Frederick was unwilling to depart on a crusade until he had arranged settlements in Germany as well as Italy. The patience of Honorius, which he himself said had brought criticism down upon him, may have been excessive, but he was working against conditions that were most unfavorable.

Honorius worked hard to continue the reform program of the Fourth Lateran Council. He was especially concerned about the reform of preaching. Like his predecessor and almost unique among the popes of his time, he authored a collection of sermons *de tempore* and *de sanctis,* which he sent, so far as we know, to the Dominicans in the Bologna, the Cistercians at Citeaux, and the Archpriest of Santa Maria Maggiore, which contained his views on preaching. He was, in fact, vaguely critical of the sermons of his predecessor, a point made more specific by his direct revisions of some parts of Innocent's sermons. His letter accompanying the sermons, which he sent to the Dominicans in Bologna, is of especial value both for his recognition of the order and for his active role in promoting its work.

Honorius also played a significant role in the foundation of the Franciscans. Because of problems in earlier Franciscan historiography, his efforts on behalf of the order have been neglected. His letters, however, give witness to his support for St. Francis of Assisi, and it seems unlikely that Francis would have received papal recognition of his rule, *regula bullata* so quickly without that support, since some in the curia were critical of Francis. In spite of the opposition, on Nov. 29, 1223, Honorius issued the bull *Solet annuere,* which gave formal approval to Franciscan rule. Honorius worked closely with Hugolino, cardinal bishop of Ostia, a devoted supporter of Francis, whom he appointed as the first cardinal protector of the order, in taking concrete steps to protect the Franciscans and to encourage their spread. Perhaps even more than the Dominicans, the Franciscans were active in the reform of the laity and so transformed their role in the church. This culminated in papal recognition of their Third Order in 1289.

The promulgation of *Compilatio Quinta* (*Novae Causarum* May 2, 1226) places this pope in the forefront, along with his predecessor, in the effort to influence the direction of the teaching of canon law in the schools. That work had been going on for more than a half century. It was quite clear that the canon law was an effective instrument in many aspects of reform. Law as an instrument of papal policy thus received a further impetus from this pope.

Bibliography: H. SCHULZ, *Realencyklopädie für protestantische Theologie* eds., J. J. HERZOG and A. HAUCK 8:318–323, excellent for bibliography to 1900. F. GREGOROVIUS, *History of the City of Rome in the Middle Ages,* tr. A. HAMILTON, 8 v. in 13 (London 1894–1902) v.5.1. H. K. MANN, *The Lives of the Popes in the Early Middle Ages from 590 to 1304* (London 1902–32), 13:1–164. J. CLAUSEN, *Papst Honorius III* (Bonn 1895); H. X. ARQUILLIÈRE, *Dictionnaire de thélogie catholique,* ed. A. VACANT, et al. (Paris 1903–50), 7.1: 135–138. M. MICHAUD, *Dictionnaire de droit canonique,* ed. R. NAZ, 233–53. R. NAZ, *ibid.,* 1239–41. A. FLICHE and V. MARTIN, eds., *Historie de l'élise depuis les origines jusqu'à nos jours* (Paris 1935–), 10, 291–304. S. KUTTNER, *Repertorium der Kanonistik* (Rome 1931), 382–385. A. M. STICKLER, *Historia iuris canonici:* v. 1, *Historia fontium* (Turin 1950), 235–236. J. HALLER, *Das Papsttum* (2d. rev. ed. Stuttgart 1950–53), 4:1–46. F. X. SEPPELT, *Geschichte der Päpste von den Anfängen bis zur Mitte des 20. Jahrhunderts* (Munich 1956), 3:390–411. P. MIKAT, *Lexikon für Theologie und Kirke,* eds. J. HOFER and K. RAHNER (Freiburg 1957–65), 5: 476–477. J. SAYERS, *Papal Government and England during the Pontificate of Honorius III* (Cambridge 1984). W. MALECZEK, *Papst und Kardinalskolleg von 1191–1212* (Vienna 1984), 111–113. J. M. POWELL, *Anatomy of a Crusade, 1213–1221* (Philadelphia 1986).

[J. M. POWELL]

HONORIUS IV, POPE

Pontificate: April 2, 1285, to April 3, 1287; b. Jacobus (Giacomo) SAVELLI, Rome, 1210. Of aristocratic Roman lineage, his family supported the GUELF party. His granduncle was HONORIUS III, whose name he adopted upon his election to the Holy See. As a student at the University of Paris, he obtained a prebend and a canonry at the cathedral of Châlons sur Marne, to which was later added a benefice at the church of Bert in the diocese of Norwich. MARTIN IV nominated him cardinal-deacon of Santa Maria in Cosmedin (1261). In this new capacity, he served as papal prefect in Tuscany and captain of the apostolic army. In 1274 he participated in the Second Council of Lyons (*see* LYONS, COUNCILS OF). Giacomo was actively engaged in papal diplomacy, especially in the negotiations concerning Sicily, and was a member of the apostolic delegation that invested Charles of Anjou with the Sicilian crown (July 28, 1265). He also took part in the papal negotiations with the German king, Rudolf I of Habsburg, over his imperial coronation and his dealings with Charles of Anjou in Sicily (July 1276). The imminent death of Pope ADRIAN V, however, postponed the conclusion of the deliberations.

"Tomb monument of Pope Honorius IV" in the Church of S. Maria in Aracoeli, Rome, 14th century.

Only four days after the death of Martin IV, the cardinal of Santa Maria in Cosmedin was unanimously elected to the See of Peter in spite of his advanced age and deteriorated health (crippled by arthritis, he could neither stand nor walk). The conclave's speed, which was unprecedented in the history of the papacy, was meant to avoid both external, (i.e., Charles of Anjou's) interference and any prolonged interregnum in the face of the Sicilian crisis. As son of a prestigious Roman family, Honorius was auspiciously accepted in Rome, where he was crowned shortly afterwards (May 20)—a privilege that had been denied to his immediate predecessor. Elected senator for life, Honorius commissioned his brother Pandulf—having being elected himself the preceding summer as an annual senator of Rome—to restore order in the city. The pope further annulled the interdict placed upon Venice by Martin IV (March 16, 1286), and canceled anticlerical legislation in Florence and Bergamo. Honorius's conciliatory methods, together with his strong hand, brought about the pacification of Rome and the recognition of papal authority over an extensive territory, which included the Exarchate of Ravenna, the March of Ancona, the Duchy of Spoleto, the County of Bertinoro, the Mathildian lands, and the cities of Rimini, Pesaro, Fano, Sinigaglia, and Ancona (the Pentapolis). Once again, the pope was able to reside in Rome, where he built a magnificent palace on the Aventine.

A great supporter of the MENDICANT ORDERS, whose privileges he enlarged, Honorius IV promoted their members to the highest Church positions and entrusted them with the INQUISITION. He also confirmed the privileges of the CARMELITES and the AUGUSTINIAN hermits and improved the living conditions and privileges of the Williamites, an order founded by St. William of Aquitaine (d. 1156). On the other hand, he solemnly condemned the so-called APOSTOLICI or False Apostles (March 11, 1286). Established by Gerald Segarelli at Parma about 20 years earlier, the sect drew its inspiration from the Franciscan teaching on poverty, but in open defiance of ecclesiastical norms.

As a means of facilitating the union with the Eastern Church and the mission among the Muslims, Honorius encouraged the study of Oriental languages at Paris. On the other hand, the crusade announced by GREGORY X languished during his pontificate; the funds raised for the Holy Land were diverted to finance papal conflicts in Europe, especially in Aragon and Sicily, which he labeled a crusade.

Honorius's pontificate, indeed, was devoted to seeking a solution for the Kingdom of Sicily, where papal suzerainty had been seriously jeopardized as a result of the Sicilian Vespers (March 30, 1282). The brutal massacre of the French led to Charles of Anjou's loss of the kingdom, the crown of which was bestowed on Peter III of Aragon as Manfred's heir. Upon Honorius's accession to the papacy, the Sicilians cherished the hope that the pope would change the pro-French, Angevin policy fostered by Martin IV. Although the new pope was more conciliatory, he never renounced papal claims on the island, a policy that in actual practice meant the reestablishment of the House of Anjou. Still, aware of the oppressive rule of the Angevins and the many vicissitudes of the Sicilian people, the pope, as overlord, tried to pave the way for a more reliable and peaceful government, while giving all inhabitants the right of appeal to the Holy See. The 45 ordinances of the *Constitutio super ordinatione regni Siciliae* (Sept. 17, 1285) defined in detail the rights and limitations of royal administration vis-à-vis the local population, the clergy included. The constitution was a partial fulfillment of an earlier papal pledge to reestablish the laws of William II (d. 1189), whose reign was considered the golden age of Sicilian justice.

Still, beyond a benign policy in the long term, Honorius's most imperative ambition was to recover the kingdom as a papal fief for the Angevins. Under the influence of his family's links and the pro-French faction in the college, he pushed the policy of his predecessor, who had instigated an open conflict with King Peter III. The pope also rejected the mediation efforts of King Edward I of England. In order to force the withdrawal of the Aragonese from Sicily, Honorius called upon PHILIP III OF FRANCE to invade Aragon, while conferring upon the campaign all the spiritual and financial advantages of a crusade. Ravaged by disease, however, the French army was forced to withdraw, and both Philip and Peter died in the course of the year. Desolated by his allies' failure, and after a long captivity in Aragon, Charles of Anjou's son, Charles II of Salerno, renounced the Angevin claim to Sicily in return for his release (Feb. 27, 1287). Although Honorius refused to endorse the agreement—which actually meant the renunciation of papal control over the island—the kingdom of Sicily was lost to the Angevins. On the other hand, Honorius began negotiations with Peter's successor, Alfonso III of Aragon, but these did not bear fruit because of the pope's death.

With regard to the empire, as well, papal diplomacy did not encounter much success. Honorius reopened negotiations with the German king, Rudolf of Habsburg, in an attempt to bring about his coronation at Rome, an act that his predecessor had postponed time and again. The fixed date (Feb. 2, 1287), however, had to be postponed because of Rudolf's inability to make the *Romfahrt* owing to his own conflicts in Germany. A papal legate, Cardinal John of Tusculum, was sent to hasten the king's journey to Rome and to facilitate its implementation. The pope's envoy found a very obstructive audience at the Diet of Würzburg (March 16–18, 1287), with German prelates and princes uniting in an effort to safeguard their election prerogatives against any papal interference. The imperial coronation was postponed yet again, and never materialized. The question of whether this failure should be laid at the pope's door remains open to further research.

On the whole, Honorius's two-year pontificate, neither ambitious nor innovative, continued the aims and premises set by his predecessors.

Bibliography: *Les registres d'Honorius IV,* ed. M. PROU (Paris 1888). B. PAWLICKI, *Papst Honorius IV* (Münster 1896). E. JORDAN, *Les Origines de la domination angevine en Italie* (Paris 1909). S. RUNCIMAN, *The Sicilian Vespers* (Cambridge, Eng. 1958). J. R. EASTMAN, ''Relating Martin Luther to Giles of Rome: How to Proceed!'' *Medieval Perspectives* 8 (1993) 41–52. P. HERDE, ''I papai tra Gregori X e Celestino V: il papato e gli Angiò,'' *Storia della Chiesa,* ed. D. QUAGLIONI, v. 11 (San Paolo 1994) 23–91. T. GRAAFEN and V. M. PUNDT, ''Ein Appellationsverfähren an der päpstlichen Kurie gegen die Trierer Familie Systapp im 13. Jahrhundert,'' *Liber amicorum necnon et amicarum für Alfred Heit* (Trier 1996) 97–109.

[S. MENACHE]

HONORIUS, ROMAN EMPEROR

Honorius was Emperor in the West, 395 to 423; b. Constantinople, Sept. 9, 384; d. Ravenna, Aug. 15, 423. As a child Flavius Honorius accompanied his father THEODOSIUS I to Rome for his triumphal entry in 389, and was in Milan in 394 when he was proclaimed co-Emperor for the West. There with his brother Arcadius he witnessed the influence exercised by St. AMBROSE (d. 397) on both his father and Stilicho, the Vandal general who controlled the Roman military forces in Italy. Nothing is known of Honorius's formal education, but he seems never to have achieved the knowledge, energy, or resolution required of an efficient ruler. He succeeded Theodosius I as Emperor of the West (Jan. 17, 395) under the guidance of St. Ambrose and the guardianship of Stilicho, whose daughter Maria he married in 398. He journeyed to Ravenna, Brescia, Verona, Padua, and Altinum c. 399. During his early years the military and political difficulties of his reign were handled mainly by Stilicho.

One crisis followed another. Under Alaric, the Visigoths revolted, spreading death and desolation through Thrace and Macedonia and on the border of Italy until in 403 at Verona Alaric was defeated by Stilicho, but allowed to escape. In 405 Stilicho defeated the Ostrogoths and other tribes, but the defenses of the Rhine were weakened, so the Vandals, Suevians, and Alans were able to cross into Gaul. Constantine, a general in Britain, revolted, came to Gaul, and with the aid of his son Constans, who took control of Spain, ruled a strip of land from the Channel to the Mediterranean. Stilicho was accused of incompetence and treasonable plans and was put to death (408).

Alaric again invaded Italy. He besieged Rome three times. Finally in 410 he entered the city and allowed his followers to burn, pillage, and slay for three days, but neither the destruction nor the slayings were wholesale. Alaric carried off Galla Placidia, the sister of Honorius, and rich booty; however, he died at Cosenza on his way to Africa.

Constantius, Stilicho's successor as general, defeated Constantine at Arles (411). He also put down the revolt of Heraclian in Africa. Ataulf, the new leader of the Visigoths, supported Rome and ended the revolt of Jovinus in Gaul. He married Galla Placidia, but was forced down into Spain where he was assassinated. Wallia, a Gothic leader, finally came to terms with Rome. In return for the supply of corn, he agreed to return Galla Placidia and make war on the enemies of the empire who had been ravaging Spain. In pursuit of this policy he subjected the Alans, and in two years virtually wiped out the Siling Vandals. In 422 the Hasding Vandals and the Suevians went to Baetica, and the Visigoths got a perma-

Sardonyx cameo carved with image of Emperor Honorius and wife Maria, ca. 398.

nent home in Aquitania Secunda. Constantius married Galla Placidia and became coruler with Honorius.

Honorius issued laws to alleviate the burden of taxation in Italy and to attract cultivators to the waste lands. He said that whatever had been laid down by his predecessors in regard to the Church would continue. When the civil jurisdiction of bishops was found to interfere with their pastoral duties it was required that both litigants should agree to use the bishops' services, before he was approached. In 395 the laws against pagans and heretics were reaffirmed: no one was allowed to enter the temples to sacrifice, and pagan priests lost their last immunities. However, Honorius endeavored to safeguard the decorations of the public monuments and to save the temples for public use.

As a result of acts of terrorism by the Donatists, a decree of suppression, the first of many such decrees, was put out against them in 405. In similar circumstances Honorius proceeded against the Pelagians. After Telemachus had paid with his life for his protest against the sanguinary combats, they were abolished. In the double election of Pope BONIFACE I (418–422) and Eulalius, the government at first favored the latter, but later it was arranged that a synod should decide between them, and until then neither was to sojourn in Rome. But Eulalius returned and so disturbed the peace that Boniface was recognized. When Honorius was asked to keep the peace in the event of another double election, he answered that he would recognize only a morally unanimous choice.

Upon receiving an appeal from the exiled JOHN CHRYSOSTOM, Honorius urged Pope Innocent I to hold the synod in which it was decided that a council should be held at Thessalonica to judge his case. But when Honorius sent a delegation to the Eastern Emperor Arcadius with this decision, the Eastern envoys were arrested and the Western envoys were deported. In 421 Theodosius II issued an edict supporting the authority of the bishops of Illyricum as dependent on the Patriarchate of Constantinople. Pope Boniface objected and Honorius obtained its revocation. He was buried in Ravenna, where he had maintained his official residence since 404.

Bibliography: G. BÖING, *Lexikon für Theologie und Kirche*, ed. J. HOFER and K. RAHNER, 10 v. (2d, new ed. Freiburg 1957–65) 5:478. E. STEIN, *Histoire du Bas-Empire*, tr. J. R. PALANQUE, 2 v. in 3 (Paris 1949–59) 1:218–311. A. FLICHE and V. MARTIN eds., *Histoire de l'église depuis les origines jusqu'à nos jours* (Paris 1935–) v.4. W. GWATKIN et al., *Cambridge Medieval History*, 8 v. (London-New York 1911–36) v.1. E. DEMOUGEOT, *De l'unité à la division de l'Empire romain* (Paris 1951). F. LOT, *The End of the Ancient World and the Beginnings of the Middle Ages,* tr. P. and M. LEON (New York 1931; Torchbk 1961). O. SEECK, *Paulys Realenzyklopädie der klassischen Altertumswissenschaft*, ed. G. WISSOWA et al. 8.2 (1913) 2277–91.

[F. MEEHAN]

HONORIUS MAGISTER

Archdeacon of Richmond and outstanding canonist of the Anglo-Norman school of the late 12th century; date and place of birth unknown; d. Richmond, *c.* 1210–13. His scholastic career covered the period *c.* 1185 to 1195. He belonged to a group of English DECRETISTS active in Paris *c.* 1186 to 1190 (RICHARD DE MORES, the anonymous author of the *Summa Omnis qui iuste,* and others). During this time he wrote his only known work, the *Summa decretalium questionum.* It introduced a new didatic and literary method, soon to be imitated by others: a systematic treatise combined with the dialectical discussion and solution of problems of interpretation or, sometimes, of cases. Honorius's *Summa* grew out of a formal course given on Fridays (*questiones veneriales secundum mag. Honorium* in one MS); it is preserved in seven MSS, which is more than for any other work of the Anglo-Norman school of the time, indicating its success. Honorius taught at Oxford from 1192 (perhaps earlier) until 1195, when he entered the service of Abp. Geoffrey Plantagenet of York. In 1198 Geoffrey conferred the archdeaconry of Richmond upon Master Honorius, but the cathedral chapter of York sided with the king's candidate and refused his installation. This was the beginning of a lengthy and complex litigation, in the course of which Archbishop Geoffrey broke with Honorius; for a time two interlocking lawsuits were pending in Rome,

where from 1201 Honorius pleaded his case in person. On the main issue Pope INNOCENT III finally pronounced sentence in his favor (June 1, 1202). Soon thereafter Honorius became a member of the household of Abp. Hubert Walter of Canterbury, for whom he performed important services. After the archbishop's death he was one of the proctors for King John in Rome (1205) in the great Canterbury election case. But a few years later he was stripped of all his possessions and in prison for a debt of 300 marks he owed the crown from the years of his struggle for Richmond. His name occurs for the last time in the records of the exchequer by Michaelmas in 1210. He must have died between that date and 1213, when the first mention is made of his successor in the Archdeaconry of Richmond.

Bibliography: S. KUTTNER and E. RATHBONE,"Anglo-Norman Canonists of the 12th Century," *Traditio* 7 (1949–51) 304–316, 326, 344–347, full coverage of sources and bibliog. A. B. EMDEN, *A Biographical Register of the University of Oxford to A.D. 1500*, 3 v. (Oxford 1957–59) 2: 956–957; 3:xxix. *Bulletin of the Institute of Research and Study in Medieval Canon Law* in *Traditio* 11 (1955) 448.

[S. KUTTNER]

HONORIUS OF AUTUN

Writer; b. *c.* 1080 or 1090; d. *c.* 1156. Notwithstanding his traditional association with Autun, cumulative evidence indicates Regensburg as the main scene of his activity. Honorius has been identified as a monk of Regensburg who concealed his name from envious critics under the pseudonym *Augustodunensis,* "the hill (*dunum*) of Augustus," i.e., the site of a supposed victory of Charlemagne before Regensburg. He has been distinguished from Honorius "the solitary," and identified with Honorius, a priest of Autun, who later joined the Irish Benedictines at Regensburg.

His success as a Christian teacher is attested by the numerous manuscripts and early printings of his theological manual, the *Clarification (Elucidarium)*, as well as by medieval versions of it in French, Provençal, Italian, Old Norse, Swedish, Gaelic, English, and a German compilation of materials taken from the *Philosophia mundi* of WILLIAM OF CONCHES and from several of Honorius's works. Though devoted to tradition, Honorius was an original thinker. A zealous defender of the Real Presence and of moral standards for the clergy (see his *Offendiculum*), he claimed that a Sacrament confected by a priest of evil life is valid by the power of Christ but invalid should the priest be ex-communicated. The body of the Lord that an unworthy recipient of the Eucharist appears to receive is restored inviolate to the substance of Christ.

Honorius teaches that God is an invisible Spirit beyond the grasp of any creature, but He contains them all and is "the substance of all things" (Endres, 100). Everything created is good, and the term "good" is convertible with "substance" and "nature." Evil, less a nature than the perversion of nature, is the nothing opposed to substance. A freely corrupted will is no longer nature and is rightly termed "sin." The divine motive in tolerating evil in the universe is an aesthetic one: like an artist, God renders the just the more glorious with the contrast. In comparison with God, the created universe is, as it were, nothing—a kind of falsity in juxta-position to the Truth that is God. At best, the world is a shadow of God who is Life and Truth Itself.

About man he taught that the reprobate have been created for the sake of the elect. Both Scripture and reason show that the creation of man is more than a device to supply for fallen angels. If man had not been created for his own sake, his dignity would be less than that of a worm, whereas the glory of his combat gives him a dignity greater than that of angels. Freedom of choice is the power of guarding "rectitude of will for the sake of rectitude itself" (*Patrologia Latina*, ed. J. P. Migne, 217 v., indexes 4 v. (Paris 1878–90) 172:1200C). A captive now, man can neither desire nor move toward a good without the prior grace of God. Predestination is two-fold, to glory or to punishment, but it is prepared eternally according to the merits of each one. Not the fall, but the predestination of man to deification is the cause of the Incarnation, for sin can be the cause of nothing good. At death the mortal Body will be changed into a spiritual one and what is spiritual into deity, its own substance perduring.

The derivative quality of much of his material shows Honorius to be a valuable witness to the learning considered respectable by his contemporaries. At the same time, his use of dialectic to expound the faith, at once daring and awkward, makes him a modest collaborator with the great 12th-century theologians.

Bibliography: *Omnia opera: Patrologia Latina*, ed. J. P. MIGNE, 217 v., indexes 4 v. (Paris 1878–90) 172; the *Philosophia Mundi* (*Patrologia Latina* 172:39–102) belongs to William of Conches, while Honorius's *Cognitio vitae* is among the works of Augustine (*Patrologia Latina* 40:1003–32). Y. LEFÈVRE, *L'Elucidarium et les Lucidaires* (Bibliothèque des Ècoles Françaises d'Athènes et de Rome 180; Paris 1954). E. AMANN, *Dictionnaire de théologie catholique*, ed. A. VACANT et al., 15 v. (Paris 1903–50; Tables Générales 1951–) 7.1:139–158. J. A. ENDRES, *Honorius Augustodunensis* (Kempten 1906). E. M. SANFORD, "Honorius, Presbyter and Scholasticus," *Speculum* 23 (1948) 397–425. *Miscellanea Giovanni Mercati*, 6 v. (Rome 1946); *Studi e Testi* 121–126. 2:220–258. P. DELHAYE, *Catholicisme* 5:929–932. H. MENHARDT, "Der Nachlass des Honorius Augustodunensis," *Zeitschrift für deutsches Altertum und deutsche Literatur* 89 (1959) 23–69. P. ROUSSET, "À propos de l'Elucidarium d'Honorius Augustodunensis: Quelques problèmes d'histoire ecclésiastique," *Zeitschrift für schweizer Kirchengeschichte* 52 (1958) 223–230.

[E. A. SYNAN]

HONORIUS OF CANTERBURY, ST.

Archbishop, fifth successor of AUGUSTINE OF CANTERBURY; d. Sept. 30, 653. A disciple of Pope GREGORY THE GREAT at Rome, he may have been a member of Augustine's original mission to England. He was consecrated archbishop of Canterbury by the senior English bishop, PAULINUS OF YORK, at Lincoln, 627. When the death of King EDWIN OF NORTHUMBRIA (633) and the collapse of the new Northumbrian church under the pagan king, Penda, sent Paulinus into exile, he fled to Honorius under whom he served as bishop of Rochester. Honorius received the pallium from the pope in 634. Early in his career Honorius had a valuable assistant in a Burgundian bishop, Felix of Dunwich, whom he sent to evangelize the East Anglians. Honorius retained a special interest in this mission and when Felix died there after 17 years, Honorius found the East Anglians another bishop, Thomas. It was under Honorius that BIRINUS began the conversion of the West Saxons. Although the death of Edwin and the flight of Paulinus had seemed to mark the end of the infant Northumbrian church, in 635 King OSWALD seized power there and invited a Celtic monk, Aidan, from IONA to become bishop of the Northumbrians. This created a difficult situation; although Honorius had great respect for Aidan, he opposed his Celtic customs for observing Easter. The matter did not, however, come to a head until after Honorius's death (*see* WHITBY, ABBEY OF).

Feast: Sept. 30.

Bibliography: BEDE, *Ecclesiastical History* bks. 2 and 3. A. W. HADDAM and W. STUBBS, eds., *Councils and Ecclesiastical Documents Relating to Great Britain and Ireland*, 3 v. in 4 (Oxford 1869–78) 3:82–98. F. M. STENTON, *Anglo-Saxon England* (2d ed. Oxford 1947).

[E. JOHN]

HONTHEIM, JOHANN NIKOLAUS VON

Suffragan bishop of Trier and founder of FEBRONIANISM; b. Trier, Germany, Jan. 27, 1701; d. Montquintin, Luxembourg, Sept. 2, 1790. He studied jurisprudence and theology at Trier, Louvain (where he was acquainted with Zeger Bernhard van ESPEN), and Leiden. After extensive travels and a stay of three years in Rome, he obtained the degree of doctor of jurisprudence (1724) and was ordained (1728). He was a professor of the Pandects in Trier (1732–38), a chancery official of the bishop, and a parish priest at Koblenz (1739). He became the suffragan bishop of Trier (1748) and until 1778 was vicar-general for Trier and pro-chancellor of the university. In this capacity the learned and austere Hontheim became influential in the archdiocese. Already in his student days he had leaned toward GALLICANISM and had been interested in the union between Catholics and Protestants. In 1763 he published under the pseudonym Justinus Febronius the two-volume work *De statu ecclesiae et legitima potestate Romani Pontificis liber singularis ad reuniendos dissidentes in religione Christianos compositus.* The work, composed from Gallican, Jansenist, and Protestant sources, created such a stir that it soon appeared in German, French, and Italian translations. Its theses undermine papal authority: Christ transmitted the power of the keys to the faithful as a group (collectivity of the faithful) and only the execution of this power to the pope and the bishops. The pope has only a primacy of honor, not of jurisdiction, a primacy in the Church, not over the Church. At the same time Hontheim raises episcopal authority immoderately by maintaining, against historical truth, that in the course of history the popes, especially through the pseudo-Isidorian decretals (*see* FALSE DECRETALS), deprived the bishops of many rights conferred upon them by Christ Himself. Thus he denied supreme papal jurisdiction in favor of practically unlimited episcopal executive power. The bishops would still be in communion with the Holy See and were to report to Rome in important official matters, but they could appeal from a papal decision to a general council, since, according to Hontheim, only the collective Church is the real bearer of infallibility.

Significantly, Hontheim, having thus erected his episcopal system, turned to the secular princes and urged them to interfere, if necessary, with the internal affairs of the Church, even at the risk of a schism. His book was put on the Index by Clement XIII as early as Feb. 27, 1764. On May 21 of the same year the pope in a letter to the German bishops summoned them to suppress the work, whereupon Abp. Clement Wenceslaus of Trier and nine other bishops forbade it. Later Hontheim wrote a rejoinder to various refutations that appeared against his work, notably those by F. A. ZACCARIA and T. M. Mamacchi. Wenzel Anton von Kaunitz declared to Empress Maria Theresa that the doctrines of Hontheim were precisely those ''that are publicly taught at all Your Majesty's universities and are recognized as true and correct by the whole intelligent Catholic world, the only exception being the Roman curialists and their adherents.'' Later the author of the book, who long remained unknown, was identified, and summoned by Rome to retract. This he

did, but only half-heartedly, as appears clearly from his correspondence with Councilor Krufft, an administrative official in the state chancery in Vienna, and also from a commentary to his recantation, which he published in 1781. His real reconciliation with the Church took place only shortly before his death.

Bibliography: O. MEJER, *Febronius* (2d ed. Tübingen 1885). L. JUST, ed., *Der Wiederruf des Febronius in der Korrespondenz des Abbé F. H. Beck mit dem Wiener Nuntius G. Garampi* (Wiesbaden 1960). J. ZILLICH, *Febronius* (Halle 1906). E. WOLF, *Die Religion in Geschichte und Gegenwart*, 7 v. (3d ed. Tübingen 1957–65) 3:447–448. H. RAAB, *Lexikon für Theologie und Kirche*, ed. J. HOFER and K. RAHNER, 10 v. (2d, new ed. Freiburg 1957–65) 5:479–480. T. ORTOLAN, *Dictionnaire de théologie catholique*, ed. A. VACANT et al., 15 v. (Paris 1903–50; Tables Générales 1951–) 5.2:2115–24. Y. M. J. CONGAR, *Catholicisme* 5:933.

[F. MAASS]

HOOKER, RICHARD

Leading Anglican theologian; b. Heavitree, near Exeter, March 1554; d. Bishopsbourne, near Canterbury, Nov. 2, 1600. He early demonstrated academic ability and, with aid from Bishop J. JEWEL and others, attended Oxford, distinguishing himself in Hebrew, Greek, and music. After graduation he stayed on as tutor and fellow at Corpus Christi College. He was ordained in 1581 and attracted notice by disagreeing with Calvin, then at the height of his influence. As a result, Hooker became known as an opponent of the PURITAN party, which was trying to infiltrate the Church of England and abolish the episcopate and Prayer Book. In 1585 he was appointed master of the Temple by the archbishop of York.

The Temple Church became the scene of a celebrated theological controversy. Hooker preached for the Established Church and his rival for the mastership, the reader Walter Travers, spoke for the thoroughgoing Calvinists. When the controversy moved from sermons to a series of tracts, Hooker felt obliged to treat the matter at greater length and was given a quiet country parish in Boscombe and later another benefice in Bishopsbourne. During this period appeared five volumes of his famous work, *Of the Laws of Ecclesiastical Polity* (v. 1–4 in 1594, v. 5 in 1597). Volumes 6 and 8, suspected of revision by Hooker's widow and Puritans, appeared in 1648; volume 7, by Bishop John Gauden of Worcester, appeared in 1662. This work, which showed the way later followed by the CAROLINE DIVINES, became the quasi-official apologia of the Church of England and influenced almost every position within Anglicanism. Hooker's brilliant analysis of natural law has had a profound effect on subsequent political theorists. As a work of art, it stands as the first great original masterpiece of English prose.

The problem facing the Church of England was the claim of thoroughgoing Calvinists that the pattern of Geneva was the only legitimate one for a reformed church. Those who maintained this position held that only Presbyterian polity had the warrant of Scripture and that Anglican worship was vitiated by the ''dregs of Popery.'' The Puritans were encouraged in their hopes for further reform by the instability of the Anglican Church in its early years; they found much support for their position among those most influential in Church and State, that is, Leicester, Walsingham, and Archbishop Grindal.

Doctrinal Presuppositions. The ground taken by Hooker had previously been covered by Archbishop J. WHITGIFT, but less thoroughly, and from an essentially Calvinist position that prevented any critical examination of the Puritan presuppositions. The virtue of Hooker's work was that it moved the whole issue to the higher ground of general principles and worked out a rationale for the Elizabethan settlement.

While agreeing with the Calvinists that Scripture was the ultimate source of authority, Hooker maintained that it was not a complete body of positive law governing every aspect of the life of the church. In matters of polity or worship, he found the Bible often ambiguous or silent and insisted that patristic tradition must be consulted to clarify the situation. In those details where tradition was also ambiguous or silent, he was convinced that the common understanding of reasonable men could be relied upon; when conclusions were reached in this manner, he required no explicit scriptural authority, but held that it was sufficient that the results should not be contrary to the Bible. By means of this analysis, he justified episcopacy and the Book of Common Prayer as both reasonable in themselves and congruous with Holy Writ.

In the course of this argument, it was necessary for him to demonstrate the reliability of reason, and this he did by relating it to natural theology. In so doing, he rejected the Augustinianism, or VOLUNTARISM, prevalent in the churches of the Reformation and based his theories upon Thomas Aquinas and the scholastics. Thus he saw reason as grounded in God Himself, and he could look upon the episcopate as divinely ordered even if its origin were to be found in the Apostles or in the church as a whole. The church, he said, had made use of reason to develop her tradition, and the episcopacy was a providential element of the constitution of the church, not an element of divine law.

Church and State. Hooker showed some concern to maintain the integrity of the Church with respect to the State. He granted the Church a juridical autonomy to determine her rites and ceremonies, but not complete autonomy in her own sphere. He saw Church and State as

Richard Hooker, engraving by William Faithorne.

divinely ordered aspects of one society and united the two in an unstable equilibrium on the theories of MARSILIUS OF PADUA. The monarch, as head of the State, was head of the Church, though without any spiritual power. The exigencies of the Elizabethan establishment prevented the resolution of the problem in other ways that might have been more consistent with Hooker's earlier volumes and more congenial to him personally. He is credited with determining the Anglican *via media* between Calvin and Rome, as well as the cosmic orientation of Anglican theology. His denial of transubstantiation may be viewed as linked with his denial of complete autonomy for the Church.

Hooker restored the idea of natural law and sought to harmonize it (or reason) with revelation. The supernatural law of Holy Scripture, he said, is only part of God's law and requires knowledge of the natural law to be understood. He also sought to harmonize the two sources of the State: nature, (i.e., God); and the social compact (his notion of which is less individualistic than that of LOCKE). He rejects the theories of resistance and tyrannicide, emphasizing the divine origin of power more than its human origin.

Bibliography: *Works,* ed. R. W. CHURCH and F. PAGET, 3 v. (7th ed. Oxford 1888). L. S. THORNTON, *R. Hooker: A Study of His Theology* (London 1924). E. T. DAVIES, *The Political Ideas of R. Hooker* (London 1946). F. J. SHIRLEY, *R. Hooker and Contemporary Political Ideas* (London 1949). P. S. SCHÜTZ, *R. Hooker, der grundlegende Theologie des Anglikanismus* (Göttingen 1952). P. MUNZ, *The Place of Hooker in the History of Thought* (London 1952). J. S. MARSHALL, *Hooker's Theology of Common Prayer* (Sewanee 1956). A. PASSERIN D'ENTRÈVES, *Medieval Contribution to Political Thought* (New York 1959). Y. CONGAR, *Catholicisme* 5:935–937. G. HILLERDAL, *Reason and Revelation in R. Hooker* (Lund 1962).

[R. H. GREENFIELD]

HOOKER, THOMAS

Puritan clergyman, founder of Connecticut; b. probably at Marfield, Leicestershire, England, 1586; d. Hartford, Conn., July 7, 1647. He was a fellow (1609–18) of Emmanuel College, Cambridge University; rector (1620) of Esher in Surrey; and lecturer (1626) at St. Mary's, Chelmsford (Essex). His increasing reputation as a leader of the PURITANS finally caused William Laud, Archbishop of Canterbury, to retire him. To escape prosecution for his dissenting views, Hooker fled (1630) to Holland, where for two years he was minister of an English church at Delft, near Rotterdam. Meanwhile, a group of settlers from Chelmsford had settled in New England and they urged him to join them. He arrived in America on Sept. 4, 1633, and was chosen pastor of the church in Newton, Mass. Two years later, for reasons possibly more political than economic, he and his congregation applied for permission from the Massachusetts authorities to settle in Connecticut. When this was refused, they defied the magistrates, moving to Hartford, where Hooker was pastor until his death. Among all the New England ministers he was probably the best preacher, with a style filled with similes and examples. He believed in democracy and helped to draft the Fundamental Orders (1639), under which Connecticut was democratically governed.

In his sermon at the general court of Connecticut he declared that "the formation of all authority is laid . . . in the free consent of the people," His *Survey of the Summe of Church Discipline* (1648) held that since authority in both Church and State is founded on the consent of the people, a compact can be the basis for both ecclesiastical and civil government.

Bibliography: G. L. WALKER, *Thomas Hooker* (New York 1891). C. M. ANDREWS, *The Beginnings of Connecticut, 1632–1662* (New Haven 1934). P. G. MILLER, "Thomas Hooker and the Democracy of Early Connecticut," *The New England Quarterly* 4 (1931) 4:663–712.

[E. DELANEY]

HOPE

The supernatural, infused, theological virtue that makes it possible for the Christian to expect with confidence to attain eternal life. The theological development of the virtue of hope has been less marked and less fruitful than that of faith and charity, although hope is mentioned in the Scriptures hardly less frequently than are the other two theological virtues. Classical treatises on hope contrast in their brevity with those devoted to faith and charity, but since World War II, perhaps in consequence of the turmoil of the war, the subject has received more adequate treatment. For the most part, however, what is human and natural in the notion has received more stress than what is divine and supernatural; and it is with the latter aspect, or the virtue of hope strictly so-called, that the present article is concerned. It considers hope first in itself and then in relation to analogous or connected realities.

Christian Hope in Itself

The word "hope," in its biblical and theological usage, sometimes signifies the act of hope (e.g., Col 1.23; Heb 3.6); at other times, the virtue (1 Cor 13.13) or the motive [e.g., Ps 69(70).3, 5; Col 1.27; 1 Pt 1.21]; and at still other times, the object or thing hoped for (e.g., Rom 8.24; Gal 5.5), these different notions lending themselves readily to the metonymy so common in the Scriptures. Beneath this figurative language, however, are to be found the principles by which Christian hope is particularized and defined. Since hope as a virtue is an operative habit, it must be identified by the relation of its proper act to its proper object (see St. Thomas Aquinas, *Summa theologiae* 2a2ae, 4.1; *De Spe* 1; hereafter all citations with the author unnamed will be to the works of St. Thomas). This portion of the present article must therefore discuss the object, the subject, the acts, and the habit of hope.

Object of hope. The term object, with reference to hope, may mean either that which hope seeks to obtain or the objective basis for regarding that object as attainable. The first is called the material or terminative object; the second, the formal object or motive.

Material Object. Christians hope to obtain from God all that He has promised to give them and all that they ask from Him with respect to eternal life. This embraces two things, namely, the ultimate end itself and the means that lead to the ultimate end.

The good promised by God and sought of Him in the OT consisted for the most part in the natural and material good of earthly life, such as health, long life, and victory over enemies. But supernatural and spiritual good was also promised and asked for, such as the coming of the Messiah, forgiveness of sin, and the service and love of God and its full possession in the future life (see Van der Ploeg, 481–507). In the NT, however, the eternal and imperishable good of the future life is primarily what is promised and sought, with the temporal and perishable goods of this life relegated to a secondary place. One is to seek first the kingdom of God and His justice (Mt 6.19–20). The object of hope is the clear and intuitive vision of what is now the object of belief; it is the full possession of what faith presents and anticipates, the full development of that of which faith is the substance, or the foundation and beginning—the vision of God as He is in Himself (cf. Rom 8.24–25; Heb 11.1). If we had hope only for the things of this life, we would be of all men the most to be pitied (1 Cor 15.19). We hope then for entrance into God's rest (Heb 4.1–11), into the holies of heaven (Heb 10.19–23), the eternal dwelling (2 Cor 5.1, 8) that Christ has prepared for us (Jn 14.2; Phil 3.20–21).

Prayer is a manifestation and interpretation of hope. The material object of hope is nowhere more admirably expressed than in the ''Lord's Prayer,'' which, as St. Augustine declared, contains all that we should hope from God (*Enchir.* 114; *Patrologia Latina* 40:285). In this prayer the heavenly Father is asked to grant us eternal life (Thy kingdom come) and also the means necessary to attain it. The means are both positive and negative. Positive means of a spiritual kind are summed up in the doing of God's will, and temporal necessities to the end of eternal life are summed up comprehensively in the petition for our daily bread. Negatively, we stand in need of protection against the evils that could prevent the coming of the kingdom: the past evil we have done (forgive us our trespasses); the future evil we may do (lead us not into temptation); and the future evil of punishment we may have to suffer, especially the evil of eternal death (deliver us from evil).

The magisterium of the Church has also given expression to the object of hope. Since the object of hope is identified with the object of faith, inasmuch as faith is the substance of things hoped for, the evidence of things unseen (Heb 11.1), the articles of faith and the definitions of the Church with respect to the object of faith, also indicate the object of hope. We not only believe in, therefore, but we also hope for the resurrection of the body and life eternal [H. Denzinger, *Enchiridion symbolorum* (Freiburg 1963) 10–36, 72, 76, 150, 443]. The Council of Trent insisted that we should hope through the mercy of God for the pardon of our sins and the infusion of His grace, the final aim of which is eternal life (*ibid.* 1526–28). Those regenerated by Baptism should preserve the robe of grace clean and immaculate to present it before the tribunal of Christ to obtain eternal life (*ibid.*

Hope with the four Evangelists, Renaissance European Gold and Silverwork Reliquary. (© Elio Ciol/CORBIS)

1530–31). Those who persevere in good works, innocent or penitent, should consider eternal life as the greatest of the graces promised by God to His children (*ibid.* 1545–49).

The liturgy reinforces the same lesson, particularizing and interpreting in concrete form the good things for which we turn to God. Its incessant plea is that God grant us eternal life and deliver us from eternal death; and to that end it asks health of body, pardon of sins, fidelity to grace, and final perseverance. It contains petitions for every kind of good and for remedies against every kind of evil. In the Roman Missal there are Masses and prayers for peace; against war, illness and persecutions, drought and storms, the snares of the enemies of our souls; and for humility, purity, charity, and the other virtues necessary to our spiritual welfare. The litanies are rich in petitions for deliverance from every kind of evil of body or soul and for every kind of corporal and spiritual good. We beg God to deliver us from eternal damnation, from a sudden and unprovided death, from the occasions of sin, the attacks of the enemy, bad thoughts, ill will, every kind of uncleanness of body or soul, lightning, storms, earthquakes, plagues, hunger, and war. We ask Him to give and preserve for us the fruits of the earth, our homes and villages, our life and health and to bring about the propagation and increase of faith, and finally eternal happiness for each and every one.

The object of theological hope is thus the attainment of all true good and deliverance from all that is truly evil. This objective universality is characteristic of the theological virtues, which are primarily concerned with God but which, like God Himself, extend their radius of action and their dominion over everything. Thus faith is not concerned with God and divine things alone, but also with the whole of creation since it is God's handiwork. Charity does not consist in loving God only but extends its love also to ourselves, to our neighbors, and to all created things because they belong to God, being made in His image or committed to His service. In a similar way, hope not only aspires to the possession of God, but also reaches out to all the means of nature and of grace that lead to the possession of God and that free the soul from every temporal and eternal evil (see *In 3 Sent.* 26.2).

However, not all these things fall under hope in an equal way. There is a principal object, there are secondary objects, and there is an order between these. They pertain to hope analogically, the principal object being the supreme analogue and the other objects sharing in varying ways and degrees in its desirability.

Principal Terminative Object. The principal object of hope is the perfect and completely secure possession of God Himself for all eternity (Ps 72.25–28), the kingdom of God and His justice (Mt 6.33), the full possession of this kingdom (Mt 6.10; 25.34), the full vision of God as He is in Himself, so that He is seen face to face (1 Jn 3.2–3). In a word, it is eternal life, eternal happiness, as is stated in the symbols of faith and the definitions to which reference was made above.

That God Himself must be the principal object of hope is evident from the above-noted parallelism between faith and hope. We hope for a thing unseen, i.e., something that is now an object of belief (Rom 8.24–25). On the other hand, we believe what we hope for (Heb 11.1). Therefore what is now not seen, what is now invisible and inaccessible, but which we hope to see face to face in the future life, is the object both of faith and of hope—and that is God Himself as He is in Himself (Jn 1.18; 1 Jn 4.17; 1 Tm 1.17; 6.16; 1 Cor 13.2; 1 Jn 3.2–3).

The same truth is implied in the classification, based on the Scriptures and affirmed by the Fathers and theologians, of hope as a theological virtue. As such it must have God for its object, for it is by having God as its object that a theological virtue is distinguished from a moral virtue.

But further precision is necessary. God as eternal beatitude is the object of hope, but it remains to be determined whether the beatitude in question is to be understood in an objective, or a subjective (formal), or an integral sense—in other words, whether it is God, or the vision of Him, or both together for which we hope.

Some have held that the object of Christian hope is objective beatitude alone and that subjective or formal beatitude is necessary only as a condition *sine qua non.* This was the opinion of the Salmanticenses (*Cursus Theologicus,* "De spe" 1.1.4), but it is open to objection on the grounds that the object alone, without the possessive act, does not in fact beatify man. Eternal happiness is essentially something vital. It is eternal life, and this life for man does not exist in the object alone. Man's possession of it therefore must be something more than a mere condition of his beatitude.

Others, such as Durandus of Saint-Porçain, have held that the principal object of hope is only subjective beatitude, or the possessive act, although this demands and supposes the objective beatitude that is possessed. This view is unacceptable because man's formal beatitude is essentially something created and finite, since it is a vital act of man himself. If this were its principal object, hope would be a moral rather than a theological virtue.

A third position endeavors to synthesize these two extremes of opinion and sees the primary and principal object of Christian hope as including both the objective and the formal in a total or integral beatitude, an explanation that has been proposed in two forms. According to some—e.g., P. Lorca (*De spe* 2.7), G. Vázquez (In 1am2ae, 15.4), and F. Suárez (*De spe* 1.1.2, 4)— beatitude in both senses is equally contained, since formal beatitude is as essential as the objective to man's beatitude understood in an integral sense. Others—such as Cajetan (In 2a2ae, 17.2.1; 17.5.3–8) and John of St. Thomas (*Cursus Theologicus,* "De spe," 4.205)—held that beatitude in both senses pertains to the object of hope, but unequally and distinctly. Directly (*in recto*) the object of hope is objective beatitude; obliquely (*in obliquo*) it is subjective beatitude. Objective beatitude pertains to the object constitutively; subjective beatitude, connotatively. This explanation has the advantage of preserving the due subordination of the created to the uncreated and prevents a confusion of their relative value and importance. Moreover, it eliminates the possibility of seeing hope as a kind of amphibious or hybrid virtue, theological in reference to its uncreated object, but moral so far as its created object is concerned.

Object difficult of attainment. The attainment of the primary object of hope is extremely difficult and arduous for man, especially in his present state of fallen and weakened nature. Moreover, this difficulty amounts to sheer impossibility if one considers it only from the point of view of man's inherent and natural power. Between God as He is in Himself and the natural powers, cognitive and appetitive, not only of man but also of any intellectual creature created or creatable, there is a radical and insurmountable disproportion. God as He is in Himself infinitely transcends every creature. He is higher than the heavens (Jb 11.8; 32.12; Heb 7.26), greater than the heavens and the earth and all gods (Ps 46.3; 76.14; 94.3). His greatness is incomparable and inscrutable (Is 46.9; Ps 114.3; Jb 36.32). He is essential greatness (Ti 2.13; Lk 1.15, 32; Heb 4.14; 6.13). His name is the Most High (Ps 17.14; 49.14; Lk 1.32, 35, 76; 6.28). "Thou only art Most High," as the Church declares in the Gloria of the Mass. God inhabits a light that is inaccessible to us: no one has seen Him or can see Him (Jn 1.18; 1 Tm 6.16). Only God knows Himself intimately. No one knows the Son but the Father nor the Father but the Son, and he to whom He has revealed Himself (Mt 11.27; Lk 10.22; Jn 6.46). Basing itself on these testimonies, Vatican Council I therefore taught that the hidden mysteries of God, and a fortiori His intimate being in itself, are naturally inaccessible to all created intelligence, whether human or angelic, in regard to both its simple existence and its intimate nature (H. Denzinger, *Enchiridion symbolorum* [Freiburg 1963] 3016). Not even when aided by the supernatural light of faith and theological science is one capable of seeing God face to face.

This radical and connatural impossibility of seeing God is further complicated in man's present state because his natural powers of both body and soul are greatly diminished (*ibid.* 371, 385, 1511). In his body he is subject to suffering, disease, and finally death (*ibid.* 371, 385, 1511). His soul has lost its innocence and original justice; the light of his intelligence is darkened (*ibid.* 1616, 1644, 2756), his will is weakened (*ibid.* 371, 378, 383, 396, 633, 622, 1486, 1521), and he is inclined to sin by the disorderly impulses of concupiscence (*ibid.* 1515). Furthermore, the wounds and weaknesses inherited with original sin are variously aggravated in different individuals by their own personal sins. And in addition to all this, man is beset by enemies, temptations, and dangers on every side, as is repeatedly stated in the liturgy (see, for example, the Collects for the 4th Sunday after Epiphany, the 2d Sunday of Lent, and Monday of Holy Week). The primary object of hope is thus extremely difficult of attainment; moreover, it is impossible to attain if man's natural powers only are taken into account, for these, even if they were undamaged by sin, would be essentially inadequate

for the attainment of a goal infinitely beyond the grasp of any created power.

Secondary object of hope. Everything that one hopes from God in addition to the principal object will be either a means leading to the attainment of God or a consequential or complementary result of having attained God.

Means Leading to God. These include whatever really contributes to the attainment of eternal life. Some means are positive and include the gifts of nature and of grace that are to be used; others are negative and include protection against the evils or impediments that hinder or prevent the attainment of God. In summary and in condensed form, the necessary means are expressed, together with the primary object of hope, in the "Lord's Prayer," as was said above.

The positive means belong to two categories because gifts of nature as well as of grace are necessary. Grace supposes, elevates, and perfects nature (*Summa theologiae* 1a, 1.8 ad 2; 2.2 ad 1; 62.5; 1a2ae, 99.2 ad 1; 3a, 71.1 ad 1). Eternal life cannot be attained without good works (Mt 5.12; 16.27; Ti 2.12; 1 Cor 15.58). But good works are not performed without human acts, nor are the latter possible without nature and the human person. Moreover, by nature should be understood human nature, complete and perfect, composed of a rational soul and a body, with the operative faculties of the composite sound and developed, and its complement of intellectual and moral virtues. A sufficiency of material good is necessary to conserve and develop individual and social life in a manner worthy of a rational being. All this is contained in the petition: "Give us this day our daily bread" (Mt 6.11). Bread here is taken as representative of whatever is necessary to maintain life on earth. Not food only is needed, but many other things as well, such as clothing, shelter, health, employment, transportation, refreshment, relaxation, all of which can be understood as petitioned under the general heading of bread. Yet the wise man asks of God only what is necessary to live honestly (Prv 30.8). External corporal goods should always be considered according to their true worth in the designs of God. Essentially they are means, not ends; they represent useful, not absolute, values.

Moreover, gifts of nature, while necessary and useful, are neither sufficient in themselves nor proportionate to the supernatural end that is eternal life. Of themselves alone they cannot enable man to gain entry into the kingdom of heaven. This cannot be denied without falling into the naturalist heresy of Pelagianism or Semi-Pelagianism, later renewed by rationalism and semirationalism, and repeatedly condemned by the Church (cf. H. Denzinger, *Enchiridion symbolorum* 226–227; *In-*

diculus 243–245, 373–395, 3028, 3041, 2856, 2903–05, 2909). The ultimate end is essentially supernatural. Consequently, the natural powers and means of any nature, human or angelic, cannot suffice to attain it. Natural means, inadequate in themselves, can contribute only as conditions and as instruments and when used in perfect subordination to the proportionate and supernatural means.

The proportionate and supernatural means are all reducible to sanctifying grace, which includes all habitual grace, the Sacraments of the New Law (channels and instrumental causes of it), the infused theological and moral virtues, the gifts of the Holy Spirit, sufficient and efficacious actual graces, and merit.

These supernatural means operate directly toward the attainment of eternal life, each in its own way. Habitual grace is like an entitative habit deifying the soul; and it is the root, as it were, and remote principle of meritorious acts. The infused virtues and gifts of the Holy Spirit are the proximate principles from which these acts immediately flow. Actual graces put them in motion. Charity is the main principle, and the other virtues and gifts are secondary principles and subordinate to charity.

These means are condensed in the second petition of the "Lord's Prayer," that is, that we do God's will here on earth as it is done by the blessed in heaven. This conformity to the divine will is expressed in the elicited and commanded works of charity, which are precisely the works that are meritorious of eternal life.

Negative Means. These consist in the overcoming or avoiding of the evils or impediments that might hinder or prevent the attainment of eternal life. The negative means are parallel to the positive, because they remove or overcome obstacles opposed to the positive means. Some of the obstacles are hindrances to the supernatural means; others, to the natural means. The first are evils of fault; the second, evils of punishment. The evils of fault are past, present, and future sins, which stand opposed to grace and charity and therefore to salutary and meritorious action. The evils of punishment are the miseries, infirmities, and calamities of body and soul that may oppress a man and prevent his leading a life worthy of his rational nature. In the fifth petition of the "Lord's Prayer" we ask that the heavenly Father pardon our sins past and present; and in the sixth, that He permit us not to fall into temptation that will lead to future sin (Mt 6.12–13).

Complementary Result of Attaining God. The secondary object of hope also includes what will result from essential beatitude as its complement, i.e., all the gifts of nature and of grace that will result in the blessed in conse-

quence of their seeing God (for an account of these, *see* BEATIFIC VISION).

Principal motive of hope. The motive or formal object of hope is the real and objective foundation of one's hope, i.e., the objective basis for the expectation that one will be able to attain what is hoped for. It is that which makes the attainment of the object possible. As the motive is something essentially correlative and proportioned to the material object, Christian hope will have a primary and principal, and a secondary motive.

The chief motive and foundation of Christian hope is God, and God alone. This is an explicitly revealed truth, frequently repeated throughout the Old and New Testaments. There is nothing more insistently stated in the Psalms than that the Lord is our only hope, our refuge, our defense, our strength and counsel against every kind of enemy and difficulty (Ps 7.2; 15.1–2; 16.6–9; 32.20–22; 39.5; 61.2–10; 90.1–16; 145.2–6). In the NT it is also apparent that we must look to God alone for the realization of our hope—our liberation from all danger (2 Cor 1.9–10), the resurrection of our bodies (Acts 24.15), the salvation of our souls (1 Tm 4.10; 5.5). Therefore, God is called the God of hope (Rom 15.13); for He is the living God (1 Tm 4.10), who gives us eternal life (1 Jn 3.2–3).

It is true that Jesus Christ also is the foundation of our hope (1 Cor 15.19; Phil 2.19), and He is even called our hope (1 Tm 1.1). But, as St. Augustine observed, this is proper because of His divinity, not His humanity (*In psalm.* 145.9).

The magisterium of the Church also teaches that our hope is based on God. We hope to obtain from Him life eternal (H. Denzinger, *Enchiridion symbolorum* 72). We hope and trust in the mercy of God (*ibid.* 1525, 1676), in the help of God (*ibid.* 1541), in the promise of God (*ibid.* 1545), that He will Himself give us eternal life (*ibid.* 1545, 1576).

Theological reasoning confirms the same truth. Because Christian hope is a theological virtue properly and strictly speaking, just as are faith and charity (1 Cor 13.13; 1 Pt 1.21; 1 Jn 4.16; H. Denzinger, *Enchiridion symbolorum* 1001), it must have God alone as its principal terminative object and motive. Again, since the primary and principal object of Christian hope is essentially supernatural and as such beyond the acquisitive powers of all created and creatable nature, it is attainable per se only by God. He alone is naturally blessed.

However, there are in God many attributes and perfections that, although they are not really distinguished from His being, manifest His infinite riches and are the exemplar causes of created things of the natural and supernatural order. Theologians ask which of the divine attributes is the formal motive of hope. God is the formal motive of faith inasmuch as He is *Prima Veritas,* and of charity as *Prima Bonitas,* and similarly He ought to be the motive of hope by reason of one or another of His attributes. Scripture and the magisterium of the Church indicate some attributes of God as the formal foundation of our hope.

God's Love. God desires to and can save us; He wants to grant us the good of eternal life. This is apparent from the fact of creation, from Redemption, from our status as His children. If the Father so loved us, despite our being sinners and as such His enemies, that He delivered His only begotten Son to death on the cross that we might be reconciled with Him and to give us His grace, what will He not do for us after we have been converted into His friends and His children? He will certainly lead us to eternal life and provide us with every means of attaining salvation (Rom 5.8; Ti 3.4–7).

God's Promise. God has given His solemn word, promising under oath to give the inheritance to His sons, the brothers of Christ, who believe in Him and live without stain. In this promise He cannot fail, for He cannot lie (Heb 6.18) but rather is faithful and unable to disown Himself (Heb 11.11; 2 Tm 2.13). He is called faithful and true (Rv 19.11). Nor can He be prevented against His will from fulfilling His promise, for He is omnipotent and can realize all that He has promised (Rom 2.21). A hope, then, founded on the infallibility of the word of God and on His omnipotence to fulfill it ought to be strong and unshakable. It is a firm and secure anchor, because He who has given the promise is faithful (Heb 10.23).

God's Mercy. In other places the Scriptures declare that our hope depends on the infinite mercy of God, who loves us and has greater pity for us than an earthly father for his children. He knows our weakness and misery and has pity on us (Ps 102.13–14). He is patient, long-suffering, deeply compassionate, and merciful (Ps 102.2; 144.8; Sir 2.11–13), the very Father of mercies and God of all counsel (2 Cor 1.3). Numerous texts from both Old and New Testaments could be adduced to show the divine mercy represented as the basis of our hope.

God's Almighty Power. At other times, the Scriptures point to the omnipotence of God, or His omnipotent help, as the foundation of our hope. The basis of human hope is human power; of Christian hope, divine power. All human power is weak, uncertain, fragile, and inconsistent; and therefore human hope is uncertain and changing, and fails many times (1 Tm 6.17). But the power of God is absolute and irresistible, and Christian hope cannot come to nothing through a failure on the part of Him in whom we hope (Ps 21.6; 30.2; 70.1; Rom 5.4; Col 1.23; Heb 10.23).

The teaching of the Scriptures regarding the motive of hope has been summed up and proposed in precise terms by the magisterium of the Church (e.g., see H. Denzinger, *Enchiridion symbolorum* 1526, 1533, 1576, 1670, 1676, 1693, 1638, 1649, 1689, 1545). The liturgy gathers together the same doctrine and formulates it in numerous ways (see Ramirez, *La esencia,* 71–84).

For the more abstruse but less practical theological question as to which of the divine attributes is more formally and immediately the motive of hope, the reader is referred to various theological treatises on the subject (see, e.g., S. Harent, *Dictionnaire de théologie catholique,* ed. A. Vacant [Paris 1903–50] 5.632–644). Suffice it here to say that just as God is that for which we hope, so is He also in His goodness, love, mercy, fidelity, and almighty power, that on which we rely in daring to hope.

Secondary motives of hope. Besides the proper and principal motive, other things may serve as secondary and derivative motives, but only in relation to and dependently on the principal motive. This is as should be expected, for between the object and the motive of hope there is a proportion and exact correlation, as between the end and the agent. Therefore, since the principal terminative object of hope leaves room for secondary objects referring to it and ordered to it, we should expect that in addition to the uncreated source of grace that is the principal motive of hope, there should be secondary motives deriving from it. These are the created graces given by God and received by us, together with their instrumental and moral causes.

First among the secondary or created motives of hope is the habitual grace that deifies the soul, making the Christian a true child of God by adoption (1 Jn 3.1), heir of God and joint heir with Christ (Rom 8.17). Habitual sanctifying grace, whose formal and proper effect is divine affiliation, of itself gives the right to eternal life. One's merits and good works, which are the fruit of grace, constitute another secondary motive for hope. Thus St. Paul reminded the Corinthians that they should be abounding in the work of the Lord, knowing that their labor was not in vain (1 Cor 15.58; cf. Heb 10.32–36).

A third such motive is to be found in the created causes of grace, instrumental or ministerial, whether of the physical or moral order. First among these, and in a category apart, is the humanity of Christ. There is no salutary or meritorious act leading to eternal life that does not have this as its source, from the inexhaustible plenitude of which all our grace proceeds (Jn 1.16). Next come the Sacraments, which are instrumental causes of grace, producing their effect *ex opere operato* in all those who receive them with the proper dispositions.

The moral ministerial causes of grace are of two kinds. One is universal, having a part in the meriting and distribution of all grace. This is the Blessed Virgin Mary, spiritual mother of all and co-redemptress with Christ, who is believed to have merited congruously the graces that Christ merited condignly. Hence she is rightly called *omnipotentia supplex,* mother of our hope, and even, as in the *Salve Regina,* our hope. (Ramirez, *La esencia,* 92–100). Particular moral ministerial causes of grace are the merits and prayers of the angels and the saints in heaven and on earth, for all form one single Mystical Body, which is the Church, and are united one with the other in the Communion of Saints. Inasmuch as the unceasing prayer of a just man is of great avail and Christians are urged to pray for one another that they may be saved (Jas 5.16), such prayer is obviously a legitimate though secondary motive for hope.

Subject of hope. By the subject of hope is understood both the person who hopes (the subject *qui*) and the person for whom one hopes (the subject *cui*).

The Subject Who Hopes. The subject *qui* is necessarily a person in the strict sense, i.e., a rational intellectual substance, which is alone capable of the possession of God, the object of hope, in beatific vision. Irrational creatures are radically incapable of such happiness, and consequently also of its corresponding hope. Moreover, the subject of hope must be a *viator,* a wayfarer, or one journeying toward eternal life. Just as the obscure and imperfect knowledge of faith disappears at the journey's end when one enters upon the vision of God (1 Cor 12.9–12), so hope gives place to possession. "Hope that is seen is not hope. For how can a man hope for what he sees?" (Rom 8.24). Thus it was defined by Benedict XII that the vision of the divine essence and its enjoyment make void the acts of faith and hope in the blessed (H. Denzinger, *Enchiridion symbolorum* 1001). This definition applies to the *act* of hope, but it is the commoner opinion of theologians that the habit or virtue does not remain in the blessed, since such a habit would be superfluous, inasmuch as its act would be perpetually and intrinsically impossible. Theological hope does not remain in lost souls, for the object of hope must be seen as a future good possible of attainment. For the souls in purgatory, beatitude is still a future good that will be reached only through hardship and suffering, and hence it remains for them an object of hope.

One who has not yet attained to the vision of God cannot be the subject of hope without possessing Christian faith, for if one does not believe in the God of the Christians, he cannot hope in Him. Therefore St. Paul spoke of the heathens and gentiles as being without God and without hope (Eph 2.12; 1 Thes 4.13). The first step toward God must be by faith (Heb 11.6). Everyone who believes can and should have hope, but faith is possible without hope.

Christ, as man, was simultaneously wayfarer and blessed. But inasmuch as He enjoyed the beatific vision from the beginning, there was clearly no role in Him for either faith or hope understood as theological virtues. Yet Scripture expressly says that He hoped in the Father and trusted in Him (Ps 30.1, 7, 15; Heb 2.13), and theologians commonly teach that in some sense Christ did hope while He was on earth, not with theological hope, for this would have lacked in His case its proper and principal object, i.e., blessedness not actually possessed, but with a hope identifiable with confidence and security and reducible to the virtue of magnanimity (*Summa theologiae* 2a2ae, 129.6–7).

There is no role for hope in the angels or in the souls of the blessed with respect to the resurrection and the renovation of created nature. This they look to with simple desire and a secure and confident expectation.

Subject for Whom One Hopes. Does one hope only for oneself or for other men as well? Is hope a strictly personal expectation, or does it look to a social or communitarian good? This has been the subject of some controversy in the mid-20th century, some theologians making Christian hope primarily communitarian in character, others claiming the authority of St. Augustine, considering it something more purely personal and individual (Ramirez, *La esencia,* 128–129). However, in Christian tradition hope is, in fact, both personal and social, or communitarian.

It is personal inasmuch as each one hopes to attain his own happiness. He attains it by good works done in charity that are meritorious of eternal life, and these works or actions are properly personal: *actiones sunt suppositorum.* Moreover, the individual is saved individually. Scripture abounds in texts in which individual hope is mentioned. In the judgment, reward or punishment is meted out to each according to his personal deserts. The Apostle said, in the singular, "I have fought the good fight . . . . For the rest there is laid up for me a crown of justice, which the Lord, the just judge, will give me in that day" (2 Tm 4.6–8). According to the universal practice of Christians, each one asks for the salvation of his own soul, as did the good thief on the cross.

However, hope is also social and communitarian. Its terminative object is accessible, its motive available, to all alike. Moreover, its subject also is in a real sense a community, that is, the people of God, or the Mystical Body of Christ, which is the Church. All are one with Christ (Gal 2.28), members of the same body and united one with the other (1 Cor 12.26; Eph 4.16; Col 2.19), children of the same heavenly Father (Mt 22.9; Eph 4.6), brothers of the same firstborn Jesus Christ (Heb 2.11), and heirs of the same glory (Eph 4.4; 1 Pt 1.3–4). From this there spontaneously arises a common interest and a common longing for the good of the whole body and of each one of its members, an ardent desire and a firm hope of the salvation of the whole Christian family. This social character of Christian hope finds strong expression in the "Lord's Prayer," the best interpretation of our hope, in which the singular, which could suggest pure self-interest, is avoided and in its place the plural is used, thus invoking God's blessing on all alike.

Act of hope. There is a principal act of hope, which is one because the virtue and its corresponding object are one, and there are secondary acts that can be varied and multiple.

Principal Act. The proper and specific act of this virtue is to hope to attain eternal life by the help of God's grace. It is an act elicited from the will (since its object is goodness, indeed the Supreme Good) with respect to the supernatural end. Now the acts of the will with respect to the end are three: simple volition, intention, and fruition. The act of hope cannot be simple volition, because this prescinds from the presence or absence of its object, while the object of hope is the Supreme Good not yet possessed. Still less is it an act of fruition, for this supposes the good to be present and really possessed. Hope therefore must be an act of intention, an act intending the attainment of the Supreme Good through the use of the necessary and pertinent means.

It is an act having certain properties or characteristics, some by reason of its relation to the end (beatitude), others by reason of its relation to the means. With regard to the end, hope is the fixation of the intention upon God alone as one's ultimate goal. But, as was shown above, subjective beatitude, or the possession of God, is included in the total or integral beatitude for which one hopes and pertains connotatively to the primary and principal object of Christian hope. Hope therefore looks to God as possessable, and the love or desire that is characteristic of hope as such is of a concupiscent kind, as distinguished from the benevolent love of friendship. Our possession of God is an accident, an operation in us, a thing, not a person. Still it is a good that is loved or desired for those whom one loves with the love of friendship: God, to whom the greatest glory is given by the salvation of the blessed; oneself, for it is the highest perfection of which one is capable; one's neighbor, whose greatest good it also is. But while the note of concupiscence or interest characterizes the love of hope, this is not altogether lacking even in the benevolent love that is charity,

for in its secondary act charity is concerned with the good things desired for persons loved with the love of friendship. When formal beatitude is hoped for oneself, the divine is not ordered to the human or God to oneself, with perverse or egoistic love, as quietists and semiquietists maintained. On the contrary, the proper order of things to persons, of accidents to substances, and of everything created to the Creator is duly observed.

The other property of the act of hope in relation to integral beatitude is the lifting up of the will (*erectio animi*) to the level of God Himself. The will marshals its forces and dares to aspire to the achievement of the divine good despite the difficulties that lie in the way.

In relation to its formal motive, the act of hope is characterized by a quality of firmness and certainty that is unshakable and absolute, for nothing can be firmer or more certain than its motive. God has promised to give the needed help; He cannot be unfaithful to His word, and no obstacle can be too great for His omnipotence to overcome.

However, the certainty of inclination or intention that characterizes hope is not the certainty of faith or of knowledge, as some theologians have claimed (see Ramirez, *La esencia*, 224–253). It does not exclude but rather postulates a holy fear that one may not arrive at the goal of eternal life, not because God may fail to give the necessary help but because one's will to make use of that help may fail. The association of hope and fear is brought out in many passages of Scripture (e.g., Ps 39.4; Sir 2.9; Rom 11.20–23; 1 Cor 10.12; 1 Pt 5.8; Phil 2.12; Eph 6.10–17; 1 Cor 9.27; cf. H. Denzinger, *Enchiridion symbolorum* 1533, 1541). Both are necessary: hope without fear degenerates into presumption; fear without hope leads to despair.

In regard to the means, the act of hope is dynamic, energizing the will most efficaciously and putting right order in its relation to the means. Its dynamic potential is caused by the fact that it brings to bear on the whole of one's life and activity the powerful attractive influence of hope's end and object. The will, intent on this object, is prepared to move and to exploit all the energies of grace and nature at its command with an active power proportionate to the great attraction of its object. The propulsive force of the habit and act of hope is thus a power of infinite energy, for by hope one is in direct and immediate contact with the fount of all energy, God Himself, so that St. Bernard could truly say that God "makes omnipotent all those who hope in Him (*Sermo 83 in Cant.* 5; *Patrologia Latina* 183:1190).

The act of hope also results in a true evaluation of the means, causing them to be seen at their true worth, i.e., as means, not as ends, and to be valued in proportion to the importance of their function as means. No one can serve two masters (Mt 6.24). To one who enters upon the service of God through hope, all else becomes subordinate to that commitment.

Secondary Acts or Effects. Certain secondary acts follow upon the principal act of Christian hope. Since there are in a sense caused by the principal act, it is proper to speak of them simply as effects. Among these, two in particular deserve special mention: joy and patience.

Because the Christian is a child of God, an heir and coheir with Christ, in whom he has been incorporated by Baptism, he possesses a living (or lively) hope (1 Pt 1.3–5), indeed a certain hope of eternal life, guaranteed by God's own word (Heb 6.16–18). The prospect of seeing God and enjoying Him eternally invites the Christian to rejoice in hope (Rom 12.12). "Rejoice in the Lord always; again I say, rejoice. . . . The Lord is near" (Phil 4.4–5). Jesus Himself had declared that such joy is meet: "Rejoice and exult, because your reward is great in heaven" (Mt 5.12), where "your names are written" (Lk 10.20).

Along with joy Christians find in hope strength to endure patiently every trial. We shall be glorified with Christ if we suffer with Him (Rom 8.17). We shall not enter the kingdom of heaven except through tribulations (Acts 14.21). All who want to live piously in Christ Jesus will suffer persecution (2 Tm 3.12). But all this becomes endurable when compared with the glory that awaits us (2 Cor 4.7). And therefore can it be said: "We exult in tribulations, knowing that tribulation works out endurance, and endurance tried virtue, and tried virtue hope" (Rom 5.3–4).

Habit and virtue of hope. Christian hope is a VIRTUE, i.e., a good operative habit. Together faith, hope, and charity form a compact trilogy that abides throughout the Christian's life as his breastplate and the principle of his well-doing (1 Cor 13.13; 1 Thes 1.3; 5.8; Heb 10.38; 1 Jn 3.3, 16–18). They constitute a kind of second nature. The magisterium of the Church so understands it: God infuses them with His sanctifying grace, which does not belong to man simply by extrinsic denomination but is something real and inherent in those who receive it, so that they are not only called, but truly are, just (H. Denzinger, *Enchiridion symbolorum* 1530, 1561). The Catechism of the Council of Trent uses another equivalent formula: a divine quality inherent in the soul (2, *De sacramento baptismi,* 30). Vatican Council I expressly referred to faith as a virtue (*ibid.* 3008). With regard to hope and charity, Innocent III, the Council of Vienne, Benedict XII, and the practice of the Church in the processes of beatification and canonization take it for granted (*ibid.* 780, 904, 1001, 2021; cf. 1917 *Codex iuris canonici* c. 2104). Pius XII in the encyclical *Mystici Corporis* applied the term "virtue" to faith, hope, and charity [*Acta Apostolicae Sedis* 35 (1943) 227]. The dogmatic constitution *Benedictus Deus* of Benedict XII went so far as to determine the classification of these virtues and called them theological virtues (H. Denzinger, *Enchiridion symbolorum* 1001).

That hope is a theological virtue is evident from the fact that its object and motive are God Himself. God is the object sought, and it is on God that one depends immediately for the attainment of what he seeks. It is distinguished from the other two theological virtues by the power that it perfects, by the nature of its act, by its object, and by its motive. Thus it is distinguished from faith, which is of the intellect or mind, whereas hope is a perfection of the will (cf. Pius X, *Acerbo nimis;* Acta Pii X, 2.72). It is distinguished from both faith and charity by its proper act, which is one of intention or expectation, whereas the act of faith is one of assent; and that of charity, one of dilection. Although all the theological virtues have God for their object, still in the case of each of these virtues it is God considered under a distinct aspect. The object of faith is God under the aspect of Supreme Truth; both hope and charity view Him as the Supreme Good, yet with this difference: that charity looks to this goodness as it is in itself, whereas hope looks to it as something that we can possess. In their formal motive they also differ: faith depends on the truth of God; charity, on His essential goodness; hope, on the readiness of His almighty power to come to our assistance.

Hope and Related or Connected Realities

Since aspects of this subject are dealt with in separate articles (e.g., the sins opposed to hope, PRESUMPTION and despair, and the gift of FEAR that corresponds to hope), attention here can be confined to two matters, namely, hope and the other theological virtues, and the precepts of divine law with regard to hope.

Hope and the other theological virtues. Faith is the first step toward God, the cornerstone on which the whole edifice of the house of God is built (1 Cor 3.9; 1 Tm 1.4; cf. *Summa theologiae* 2a2ae, 161.5 ad 2). Faith gives to hope the divine plan that is to be followed: it makes known the end and the road that leads to it. Hope, then, necessarily supposes faith and goes a step further in the approach to God. Without faith there could be no hope (Eph 2.12; 1 Thes 4.13), but hope is nevertheless superior to faith (*De virt. card.* 30). But it is charity, the bond of perfection (Col 3.14), that completes the work and abides forever (1 Cor 13.8). Charity is the most perfect of the three (1 Cor 13.13): faith and hope put us in contact with

God as a means of raising ourselves up to Him, but it is charity that unites us to Him.

Hope is essentially an intermediary virtue between faith and charity: faith begins, hope follows, and charity concludes. Like every intermediary, it participates to an extent in both extremes. Hope can exist without charity, for charity is lost by mortal sin (H. Denzinger, *Enchiridion symbolorum* 1544), but not hope. Therefore, sinners can and ought to hope for the pardon of their sins and the salvation of their souls (*ibid.* 1526, 1678, 1690). But without faith, which is its root and foundation, hope collapses. Faith, on the contrary, can exist without hope (*Summa theologiae* 2a2ae, 20.2).

Precepts concerning hope. The precepts of divine law with regard to hope are primarily and directly concerned with acts of hope and the contrary acts of presumption and despair. These precepts are positive or affirmative if they prescribe acts of hope, negative if they prohibit acts of despair or presumption. What falls under precept is obligatory, and therefore something must be said about the necessity of hope.

Extreme and mitigated Protestant theology tends to deny the necessity of acts of hope for justification and salvation and prefers to regard such acts as sinful inasmuch as they are selfish and appear to ordain eternal happiness and the possession of God to an individual's own advantage, which would indeed be a true perversion of values. Thus the sinner who grieves for his sins because he fears losing happiness or tries to avoid sin in order to escape the punishment of hell is a hypocrite and sins the more for sorrowing for his sins or striving to avoid them for such a reason. The same could be said of the souls in purgatory who seek release from their punishment (propositions 6 and 39 of Luther, condemned by Leo X; H. Denzinger, *Enchiridion symbolorum* 1456, 1488). In this theory there is no middle ground between the perfect love of charity and the sinful love of concupiscence; and therefore, since the love characteristic of hope is not that of charity, hope must be sinful concupiscence and should be avoided by Christians, whether just or sinners, as sinful and as self-defeating.

The quietists and semiquietists denied the necessity of hope for just and perfect Christians, holding it to be essentially imperfect and mercenary and therefore incompatible with a state of perfection. They did not, like the Protestants, contend that hope is evil or sinful but only that it is imperfect, as is servile fear, i.e., something useful and perhaps necessary for slaves and sinners desiring to be freed from their evil state but improper in the just and children of God. The love of God to which more perfect souls attain is so pure that it admits of no mixture of self-interest and is even prepared to sacrifice all for the love of God, including happiness and the possession of God Himself. Such a doctrine was attributed to Meister Eckhart (proposition 10, condemned by John XXII; H. Denzinger, *Enchiridion symbolorum* 957), and it was taught by Molinos (propositions 7, 12, 13, condemned by Innocent XI; H. Denzinger, *ibid.* 2207, 2212–14). Fénelon questioned the utility of the acts of hope in the mystical states and taught that one could habitually abstain from such acts as imperfect and selfish (propositions 1, 2, 6, 8, 21, condemned by Innocent XII; *ibid.* 2351–52, 2356, 2358, 2371).

However, both positions are manifestly contrary to the doctrine of the Scriptures. It cannot be said that God has invited us to sin and to hypocrisy; yet, He has invited us repeatedly to abandon sin for fear of losing eternal life and incurring damnation. John the Baptist preached repentance that was necessary if men would flee the wrath to come (Mt 3.8; Lk 3.8). Jesus warned his hearers that unless they repented, they would perish (Lk 13.3, 5). And He also said: ''If thy right eye is an occasion of sin to thee, pluck it out and cast it from thee; for it is better for thee that one of thy members should perish than that thy whole body should be thrown into hell'' (Mt 5.29); ''Do not be afraid of those who kill the body, but cannot kill the soul. But rather be afraid of him who is able to destroy both soul and body in hell'' (Mt 10.28). Texts such as these are too well known to need multiplication here.

The Scriptures also teach us to do good in order to attain eternal blessedness. ''Do good to the just man and reward will be yours, if not from him, from the Lord'' (Sir 12.2). ''Everyone in a contest abstains from all things—and they indeed do receive a perishable crown, but we an imperishable'' (1 Cor 9.25). ''Whatever you do, work at it from the heart as for the Lord and not for men, knowing that from the Lord you will receive the inheritance as your reward'' (Col 3.23). ''Be steadfast and immovable, always abounding in the work of the Lord, knowing that your labor is not in vain in the Lord'' (1 Cor 15.58). ''Do not, therefore, lose your confidence, which has a great reward'' (Heb 10.35). ''Be thou faithful unto death, and I will give thee the crown of life'' (Rv 2.10). ''And everyone who has this hope in him makes himself holy, just as he is holy'' (1 Jn 3.3).

Still less is it true that the exercise of hope is incompatible with the state of mystical perfection at which saintly souls have arrived. The love of concupiscence that is in hope is not a mercenary love, although it is a love of the reward that God has promised. It does not exclude Him, but on the contrary includes Him and leads to the most intimate love of Him. ''Forgetting what is behind, I strain forward to what is before, I press on towards the goal, to the prize of God's heavenly call in Christ Jesus.

Let us then, as many as are perfect, be of this mind'' (Phil 3.13–14). Thus did Moses stand firm, ''looking to the reward'' (Heb 11.26).

In the processes of beatification and canonization an examination is made among other things of whether or not the servants of God exercised theological hope in a heroic degree (1917 *Codex iuris canonici* c. 2104), which proves that the exercise of this virtue is not only not incompatible with the most perfect sanctity but is demanded by it.

Hope is indeed necessary for justification and salvation. This necessity is to be understood as one of means, if it is a question of habitual hope, or the virtue of hope; for no one is saved if not in the state of grace, and no *viator* can be in the state of grace without faith, hope, and charity. Actual hope, or the act of hope, is also necessary for the justification of all adult sinners and for the salvation of all those adults who are in the state of grace, for no one is saved in fact without final perseverance, and this is obtained only by a special grace that does not fall under merit. This should be sought by fervent prayer, which prayer will necessarily be an interpretation and manifestation of hope and indeed an act of hope. Moreover, actual hope is necessary by a necessity of precept, for it has been required by God with the greatest insistence (Ps 4.6; 36.3; 61.9; Hos 12.6; 1 Tm 6.17; 1 Thes 5.8). It is, furthermore, a precept inculcated with great frequency in the command to pray. As a positive command, its fulfillment is always obligatory, but not at each moment. It is difficult to indicate the exact times when one is obliged to make such an act. Theologians agree that it obliges at the beginning of the fully conscious moral life and at the end of life and also at different times during the course of life (H. Denzinger, *Enchiridion symbolorum* 2021). It is necessary on certain specific occasions because of other precepts that cannot be fulfilled without it, such as the precept to pray, to receive the Sacraments, and to resist serious temptation against hope.

There is a negative precept forbidding acts directly opposed to hope, such as acts of despair and presumption. As negative, this precept obliges always and at every moment. It is less explicitly formulated in the Scriptures, its distinct mention being less necessary. The equivalent is contained in the positive precept regarding the act of hope: he who commands one to hope forbids one to despair or to presume.

Bibliography: R. BULTMANN and K. H. RENGSTORF, in G. KITTEL, *Theological Dictionary of the New Testament* (Grand Rapids, Mich. 1964—) 2:515–531. J. VAN DER PLOEG, ''L'Espérance dans l'A.T.,'' *Revue biblique* 61 (1954) 481–507. W. GROSSOUW, ''L'Espérance dans le N.T.,'' *ibid.* 508–532. J. M. BOVER, ''La esperanza en la Epístola a los Hebreos,'' *Gregorianum* 19 (1938) 110–120. T. DE ORBISO, ''Los motivos de la esperanza cristiana, según San Pablo,'' *Estudios biblicos* 4 (1945) 61–85, 197–210. F. ORTIZ DE URTARAN, ''Esperanza y caridad en el N.T.,'' *Scriptorium Victorense* 1 (1954) 1–50. C. SPICQ, *La Révélation de l'espérance dans le N.T.* (Paris 1931). L. FEDELE, ''La speranza cristiana nelle lettere di San Paolo,'' *Studi di scienze ecclesiastiche* 1 (1960) 19–68. S. PINKAERS, ''L'Espérance dans l'A.T. est-elle la même que la nôtre?'' *Nouvelle revue théologique* 77 (1955) 685–799; ''Les Origines de la définition de l'Espérance dans les Sentences de Pierre Lombard,'' *Recherches de théologie ancienne et médiévale* 22 (1955) 306–312; ''La Nature vertueuse de l'Espérance,'' *Revue thomiste* 58 (1958) 405–442, 623–644; ''Peut-on espérer pour les autres,'' *Mélanges de science religieuse* 16 (1959) 31–46. C. ZIMARA, *Das Wesen der Hoffnung in Nature und Übernatur* (Paderborn 1933). J. PIEPER, *Über die Hoffnung* (4th ed. Munich 1949). B. OLIVIER, ''Hope,'' *The Virtues and States of Life,* ed. A. M. HENRY (Theology Library 4; Chicago 1957) 63–125. A. M. CARRÉ, *Hope Or Despair,* tr. R. HAGUE (New York 1955). P. CHARLES, ''Spes Christi,'' *Nouvelle revue théologique* 61 (1934) 1008–21; 64 (1937) 1057–75. P. DELHAYE and J. BOULANGE, *Espérance et vie chrétienne* (Tournai 1958), v. 3 of *Rencontre de Dieu et de l'homme.* S. HARENT, *Dictionnaire de théologie catholique,* ed. A. VACANT et al. (Paris 1903–50) 5.1:605–676. P. LATIN ENTRALGO, *La espera y la esperanza* (Madrid 1956). G. MARCEL, *Homo Viator: Introduction to a Metaphysic of Hope,* tr. E. CRAUFURD (Chicago 1951). L. B. GILLON, ''Certitude de notre Espérance,'' *Revue thomiste* 45 (1939) 232–248. J. M. RAMIREZ, *De certitudine spei christianae* (Salamanca 1939); *De spei christianae fideique divinae mutua dependentia* (Fribourg 1940); *La esencia de la esperanza cristiana* (Madrid 1960). C. A. BERNARD, *Théologie de l'Espérance selon saint Thomas d'Aquin* (Paris 1961).

[S. M. RAMIREZ]

HOPE (IN THE BIBLE)

Hope is an analogical term that has many different meanings in the Bible. The Hebrew words most frequently translated into English by hope have the basic meanings to trust (*bṭḥ*), seek refuge (*ḥsh*), expect (*yḥl*), and wait for (*qwh* and *śbr*). Following the usage of the Greek OT (LXX), the biblical Greek of the NT uses ἐλπίς in much the same way as the OT, especially in theological contexts, in contrast to the classical Greek usage, which makes hope to be more neutral, i.e., an expectation for the future that may be either good or bad, dependent upon how a man acts at the present time. Biblical hope is much more of a confidence in God, who is uncontrollable by man but who has committed Himself to His COVENANT promises. For the biblical man God is the basis for any future hope, whereas to base one's expectations on anything less than God, be it human endeavor or magic, leads to frustration. Biblical hope is God-grounded, while the Greek ἐλπίς stands or falls on the character of men and how they act.

In the Old Testament. Confident reliance on God, eager longing for His fidelity to be manifested, patient bearing of present trials in view of God's promises of vindication, and taking refuge with God as one's rock or fortress to escape one's foes are all attitudes of OT hope. The object of such longing is not the future good, which may or may not be specified, so much as the person upon whom the realization of the future good depends, God who is full of loving covenantal loyalty (*ḥesed,* Ex 34.6 and parallels). God is the "Hope of Israel," its "savior in time of need" (Jer 14.8).

A graphic example of such confidence in YAHWEH is found in ch. 18 and 19 of 2 Kings. Hezekiah is classified as a king who above all others "trusted in the Lord" (18.5). He therefore fulfilled Isaiah's advice given to his father to trust not in foreign allies but in God alone who had made a covenant with the House of David (Is 7.10–16), but he had turned away from this advice by relying on Egypt, a reliance that led to the destruction of almost all his southern cities. Now Jerusalem itself was under siege, and, in a mocking speech, he was challenged to renew his trust in God (18.19–25) by an envoy of the king of Assyria, Sennacherib. Hezekiah's confident prayer that follows (19.15–19), Isaiah's oracle of deliverance for the holy remnant of Israel (19.20–34), and the destruction of Sennacherib's army (19.35–36) describe the ideal of Israelite hope in action; God is, indeed, Israel's "savior in time of need."

The quiet waiting for God, preached by Isaiah (Is 30.15) and so many other Prophets, eventually developed into a confident longing for deliverance not merely from present affliction but from all sorrow and pain in a new world (Is 11.6–9 and parallels; 25.9; 51.5–6; Jer 29.11; 31.16–17). There is nothing right in the world upon which one could rely for future happiness; but every faithful servant of Yahweh can cry out with Micah, "But as for me, I will look to the Lord, I will put my trust in God my savior; my God will hear me!" and, "I will arise" (Mi 7.7, 8).

In the New Testament. The patient yearning for the one who is to come to establish the new order continued to motivate the oppressed and poor servants of Yahweh (Zep 2.3; 3.11–20) until they recognized in Jesus "the consolation of Israel" (Lk 2.25), "the redemption of Jerusalem" (2.38), the revelation to the Gentiles and Israel's glory (2.32), and the Lord's gentle servant who was the hope of the Gentiles (Mt 12.21; 8.17). Their hope was for a moment shattered by His death (Lk 24.21), but it was revived in a way they had never dreamed by His Resurrection (24.25–35). Henceforth, the hope of the new Israel rested on Christ's Resurrection from the dead (Acts 23.6; 24.15; 26.6–7; 28.20), through which He had been proclaimed Lord and Christ (Acts 2.29–36), the giver of the promised Holy Spirit (1.4; 2.33, 38–39), and the only one "under heaven given to men by which we must be saved" (4.12). Even more concretely than in the OT, the

new Israel's hope was grounded on God's presence in its midst rather than on any expectation based on human striving (Mt 1.23; 28.20). God had proved His fidelity once for all. Now all men must respond by turning to Him and waiting for the return of His Son for the restoration of all things (Acts 3.19–26).

For Paul hope is intertwined with faith and love, not as if they were separate virtues, but as aspects of the activity of Jesus Christ in His faithful, giving them the power to perform arduous good works with constancy and steadfastness (1 Thes 1.3; 1 Cor 13.7, 13). Christian hope, which is Christ Himself (1 Tm 1.1), expects the ultimate glory destined for God's sons and is very much involved in the process of patient endurance that produces tried character and thereby even greater hope. The whole movement is based on the Father's love for mankind revealed in His Son's death and the pouring out of the Holy Spirit (Rom 5.1–9). All creation is concerned with this hope and it will not be confounded because it is embedded in God's and Christ's ardent loyalty (Rom 8.18–39). Revelation, a book that is full of hope without specifically mentioning it, ends with the cry of hope, "Amen! Come, Lord Jesus!" (Rv 22.20).

Bibliography: *Encyclopedic Dictionary of the Bible,* tr and adap. L. HARTMAN (New York 1963) 1024–27. P. S. MINEAR, *The Interpreters' Dictionary of the Bible,* ed. G. A. BUTTRICK (Nashville, Tenn. 1962) 2:640–643. J. DUPLACY, *Vocabulaire de Théologie biblique,* ed. X. LEON-DUFOUR (Paris 1962) 305–310. R. BULTMANN, *Theological Dictionary of the New Testament,* ed. G. KITTEL (Grand Rapids, Mich. 1964—) 2:517–523, 529–535. C. F. D. MOULE, *The Meaning of Hope* (Philadelphia, Pa. 1963).

[J. E. FALLON]

HOPE OF SALVATION (IN THE BIBLE)

This article concentrates on the evolution of Israel's yearning for a definitive deliverance from all its woes and the fulfillment of this hope for the new Israel, in the new order, free from sin and death and wrought by the victory of Jesus of Nazareth, the MESSIAH.

IN THE OLD TESTAMENT

Israelite ideas on salvation originated from the experiences of the chosen people during the EXODUS FROM EGYPT, the desert journey of the Israelites, and the constant wars waged against neighboring nations after they gained a foothold in Palestine. The earliest meanings given to words coming from the Hebrew root *yš'* centered on the idea of a military victory over Israel's enemies (Jgs 15.18; 1 Sm 11.13). Yahweh was, ultimately, the one who gave Israel its victories by raising up skilled military

"The Crucifixion." (©Hulton/Archive Photos)

chieftains called rescuers or saviors (Jgs 3.9, 15) and by His presence at Israelite battles in the ARK OF THE COVENANT. He became therefore the SAVIOR above all saviors who led the armies of Israel out of the slavery of Egypt into the promised land through, for the Israelites, His greatest work of salvation (Ex 14.30). By the divine ELECTION and the covenant the Israelites were assured that He would remain their deliverer from all foes as long as they continued faithful to His pact and to the demands handed down to them in the Mosaic Law, especially in the Ten Commandments. The basic notion of salvation as a victory over one's enemies perdured in Israelite history down to the day when, after the multiplication of the loaves, the Jewish crowd wanted to seize Jesus and make Him their king (Jn 6.15), but in the meantime it had taken on other meanings that are concerned with the end of history [see ESCHATOLOGY (IN THE BIBLE); DAY OF THE LORD] and MESSIANISM. The development of determinants of salvation, as it occurs in the course of SALVATION HISTORY, is a complex matter that demands a step-by-step examination, beginning with the pre-exilic Prophets followed by Second Isaiah, the restoration period, and the Psalms.

Preexilic Period. In what could be a somewhat old Israelite tradition, the antimonarchist account of the institution of the kingship (1 Sm ch. 8; 10.17–27; ch. 12), Samuel recalls to assembled Israel the mighty works of Yahweh, who had delivered the Israelites from all past evils (12.7–11), and claims that God, their savior, is now being rejected by their demands for a national king (10.17–19). The Prophets emphasized much the same message during the crisis of the last half of the eighth century, leading to the downfall of the Northern Kingdom, Samaria, and to the desolation and vassalage of Judah. Israel and Judah had defected from their only true King, Yahweh, refusing to put their hope for deliverance in Him alone (Is 2.6–22; 7.17–25; 8.5–8; 17.10; 30.15, cf. 7.9). In Isaiah's intention, the salvation that Israel rejected was more than merely deliverance from enemy empires; it was a holiness and justice coming from the Holy One of Israel Himself, a participation in His grandeur and an intimate knowledge of Him (Is 2.1–5; 4.2–3; 9.1–6; 11.1–9). The poem of Is 12.1–3 expresses beautifully this longing for a salvation that surpasses deliverance from political oppression. The Prophet Micah expressed a similar hope in Yahweh's salvation despite the universal rebellion against God that he saw all around him (Mi 7.1–7).

Among the Prophets of the eighth century, what the ordinary people longed for as a day of deliverance through Yahweh's power became a day of wrath, of dire punishment for the chosen people's defection from God (Am 5.18–20; Is 2.6–21; Mi 3.9–12; Hos 13.12–14.1).

Salvation would be granted only a few escapees, the remnant of Israel (Is 4.2–3; Am 3.12; 5.15; 9.8b–10). About a century later, the dreadful day of the Lord (Zep 1.14–18) is identified as a time when perhaps only the humble who observed God's commands would be sheltered from His anger; the hoped-for deliverance is no longer a rescue from oppressors, but from God Himself (2.3). This humble remnant, in contrast to the haughty rebels, "shall take refuge in the name of the Lord" and "shall do no wrong" but shall have a peaceful dwelling on the Lord's mountain (3.11–13). In this context, Yahweh is described as the mighty savior who will renew Zion "in his love" (3.14–18a), and, even if the following verses (18b–20) come from the period of the Exile, they are in the same tradition: Yahweh will "save the lame and assemble the outcasts" and "bring about their restoration." Jeremiah, with all his dire warnings, was in the same tradition. The salvation of Israel can come only from the Lord God (Jer 3.23); He alone is the champion who can save them (14.8–9). The deliverance for which Jeremiah hopes is not merely from the various tribulations afflicting the land; it is that of a new era when the people will be led by a new David whose symbolic name will be "The Lord our justice" (23.5–6). In fact, this deliverance will be a new covenant in which Yahweh's law will be written on the remnant's heart and their sins will be forgiven (31.31–34). The psalm of Habakkuk (ch. 3) recalls the tradition that God is a warrior-savior who, with all His cosmic power, will rescue His people from their foes; it adds very little to the evolution of the previous ideas about salvation, but it became an important antecedent and model for the apocalyptic traditions (see DANIEL, BOOK OF) and was popular in the QUMRAN COMMUNITY. Ezekiel does add something, however, to the idea of salvation, the regeneration of Israel by their deliverance from their sins of apostasy and from their impurities (Ez 37.23; 36.29).

Second Isaian (ch. 40–55; ch. 60–62). The themes of salvation, restoration, and creation are linked together in this masterpiece of consolation literature was intended to encourage the exiles who had returned to Yahweh during their banishment from the holy land. The JUSTICE OF GOD, His justification or vindication of His people, brings about their restoration and salvation (45.21). He is their only savior, and His acts of salvation establish the fact that He is the only God (43.3, 8–13). His present act of salvation is a more glorious deliverance than even that of the Exodus; it extends to wiping away and forgetting Israel's sins (43.16–28). It is a new creation (41.19–20). It is a gratuitous salvation, not merited in any way (55.1–3), a free and merciful act of God at the sight of which "all the trees of the countryside shall clap their hands." It has as its goal Yahweh's dominion (52.7), which will be over all the earth and not over Israel alone (45.22; 49.6). It is a glorious freedom for lowly prisoners who in their gleaming mantles will be "oaks of justice" reflecting the glory of Yahweh (61.1–3). God has clothed his faithful one "with a robe of salvation" and wrapped him "in a mantle of justice" (61.10). That the poetic raptures of Second Isaiah instilled hope for a deliverance from evil that exceeded the realities of the return from the Exile is obvious from the disenchantment of the refugees during the restoration period.

Restoration Period. Zechariah attempted to bolster the hopes of the few thousand who returned to Jerusalem in ruins (Zec 8.7–13). The Isaiah school also kept proclaiming that the Judeans' disappointment would soon be ended by a revelation of God's salvation and justice (Is 56.1); and if it was delayed (59.1), it was because of the people's sins (59.2–15a). Yet a redeemer would come for those who repented (59.15b–20). In fact, because of the poverty and frustration of this period, the Isaiah school began to envision salvation beyond the confines of this life, when those who lie in the dust would awake and sing (Is 25.6–9; 26.17–19).

The Psalms. As one would expect, the prayers of Israel gave poignant expression to their longing for salvation. In them, the ideas abound of military victory, reconstitution of the nation centered on a new Jerusalem, and violent vengeance against all their foes [Ps 75(76).8–11; Ps 117(118); 131(132).14–18]. Salvation became more personal [Ps 7; 53(54).3–5] and included freedom from illness (6.5) and any kind of distress [68(69).2–5]. This personal deliverance evoked a desire for rescue from personal sins and for a more holy way of life [49(50).22–23; 50(51).3–14]. The spiritual descendants of Jeremiah and Zephaniah developed the longing for salvation on behalf of the just, pious men whose only hope was in Yahweh and whose earthly existence was miserable. Their delight was in the Lord, and salvation could come only by being near to Him [Ps 15(16).7–11; 17(18).21–31; 24(25).4–7; 144(145).17–20].

IN THE NEW TESTAMENT

Rescue from evil through God's intervention into man's existence and human, experienced consciousness is proclaimed in the New Testament through the unthought-of newness of the mystery of Jesus from Nazareth, the Messiah and the completely dominating Lord of the process of salvation that is still being accomplished. What Jesus said and did and how He died and was raised from the dead form the inner reality of this mystery; and His chosen pupils' elaboration and their understanding of it under the guidance of the Holy Spirit of God, His Spirit, leads the men who wish to listen to them into the fullness of truth (Jn 16.13).

In the Life and Teaching of Jesus. The kingdom that Jesus proclaimed to be at hand is God's manifested conquest of all evil, i.e., disease, enmity, cosmic chaos, sin, and death through the salvific death and Resurrection of the SON OF MAN. He is the one who "took up our infirmities, and bore the burden of our ills" (Mt 8.17). This Palestinian peasant's power to cure the sick, to transcend such an adamant force as humanly devised social hatred and bring salvation to the hated dogs, the Gentiles (Mt 8.5–13; Mk 7.24–30; Lk 10.25–37), to command the sea to be calm (Mt 8.23–27), to conquer the power of evil spirits (8.28–34), to forgive sins while curing paralysis (9.1–8), and to raise men from the dead (9.18–26; Lk 7.11–17) resulted from His complete submission to the Father's will that the Son should die on behalf of all mankind so that man's sin could be taken away and he could enter into everlasting life, free from all evil (Jn 1.29; Mk 8.31–33; 9.29–31; 10.32–34, 42–45; 14.34–36). Jesus was completely innocent of any rebellion against God; yet He identified Himself by His baptism with the sinfulness of all mankind. He lined up with John the Baptist's repentant sinners, who were preparing themselves for the ultimate coming of God's kingdom by symbolically taking a bath as they confessed sorrow for their sins in view of the coming kingdom. Jesus came up out of the water, having fulfilled all justice; the heavens were opened; the Spirit came upon Him; and He was proclaimed by God to be His beloved Son, His unique Son, in whom He was pleased (Mt 3.1–17). This is the salvation preached and lived by Jesus the Messiah—God's pleasure with the new humanity created by Jesus' willed solidarity with man's sin, prefigured by His baptism and effected by His laying down His life for His sheep (Jn 10.11). The justice of God was thereby satisfied through His own gracious plan, and man was saved from the realm of sin, death, and the prince of this world (Jn 12.31–32). Jesus had lived up to His name; He had saved His people from sin (Mt 1.21).

In the Apostolic Preaching. The most difficult thing for the Disciples of Christ, so steeped in the Jewish tradition of a victorious Messiah-Savior, to understand was the death of Jesus on the cross. Yet this death was at the exact center of God's idea of salvation in contrast with the traditional Old Testament view. So it was that, after His Resurrection, Jesus had to teach them that the Messiah had to suffer before entering into His glory (Lk 24.25–27, 44–49). The doctrine of the cross, i.e., the mystery of the Messiah's death, revealed once for all God's power in saving men not from an external oppressor, but from themselves, from the slavery to sin within them (1 Cor 1.18). Salvation came from believing in the favor that Jesus won for man by His cross (Acts 2.37–41; 11.14; 15.1, 11). Jesus' own deliverance from death through the Resurrection the Father gave Him was merited by His submission and thus became the cause of eternal salvation for all who obey Him (Heb 5.7–10). The exaltation of Jesus proclaimed Him to be the all-powerful Lord of the universe (Phil 2.5–11) in whom everyone who wants to be saved must believe (Acts 16.17, 30–31; Rom 10.9–13). Because of the grace of justification that Christians already enjoyed, they were living a new life in Christ for God (Rom 6.1–11), but they still waited for the ultimate revelation of the glory of God's sons at the Lord's PAROUSIA (Rom 8.18–39). Then they would enjoy the salvation of living forever with Jesus in the kingdom of His Father (1 Thes 5.9–11; 1 Corinthians ch. 15). Every Christian was assured that he would be delivered from every evil and preserved for God's heavenly kingdom (2 Tm 4.18) because, once justified by Christ's death, he would be saved by the life that Christ lives now with His Father (Rom 5.9–10; Col 3.1–4). Indeed, "God our Savior . . . wishes all men to be saved and to come to the knowledge of the truth. For there is one God, and one Mediator between God and men, himself man, Christ Jesus, who gave himself a ransom for all, bearing witness in his own time" (1 Tm 2.4–6; Ti 3.3–7).

See Also: REDEMPTION (IN THE BIBLE); REBIRTH (IN THE BIBLE).

Bibliography: *Encyclopedic Dictionary of the Bible*, tr. and adap. by L. HARTMAN (New York 1963) 2101–07. A. RICHARDSON, *The Interpreteers' Dictionary of the Bible*, ed. G. A. BUTTRICK (Nashville 1962) 4:168–181. C. LESQUIVIT and P. GRELOT, *Vocabulaire de théologie biblique*, ed. X. LÉON-DUFOUR (Paris 1962) 987–994. F. BAMMEL et al., *Die Religion in Geschichte und Gegenwart* (Tübingen 1957–65) 2:584–590.

[J. E. FALLON]

HOPKINS, GERARD MANLEY

English poet; b. Stratford, Essex, July 28, 1844; d. Dublin, Ireland, June 8, 1889. Hopkins was the eldest of nine children in a comfortable family devoted to the Church of England. His father, Manley, headed a maritime-insurance firm and published two books of poetry and five of prose; his mother, Kate Smith, was a sensitive and accomplished Victorian woman. Both encouraged their children to develop their talents in drawing, painting, music, and writing.

Growing up in London's Hampstead, Hopkins entered the nearby Highgate School (also known as Sir Roger Cholmeley's School) in 1854, where he later boarded. Two early poems show talent: his prizewinning "The Escorial" (1860) manifests a painterly eye, vivid detail, and precise diction; "A Vision of the Mermaids" (1862) reflects the sensuous intensity of Keats.

In April 1863, Hopkins went up to Balliol College, Oxford, where he remained until June 1867, studying

Gerard Manley Hopkins.

Greek and Latin under Benjamin Jowett and Walter Pater, enjoying the stimulation of undergraduate life, and winning the highest honors. Skilled in drawing, he read John Ruskin and thought of becoming an artist. During summers he sketched, read, and traveled. At Oxford he developed a love of the Eucharist that enriched his whole life, and in the disputes between liberals and High-Church Anglicans he supported the Church party, following E. B. Pusey and H. P. Liddon and embracing a spirtuality that blended High-Church ritual and evangelical morality. His poems reflect his religious struggle ("Nondum"), his guilt ("Myself unholy"), his devotion to the Eucharist ("Barnfloor and Winepress"), and his distrust of the senses and the world ("Heaven-Haven," "The Habit of Perfection"). His dry humor appears in light poems and epigrams, and his "St. Dorothea (Lines for a picture)" (1868) foreshadows his distinctive "sprung rhythm." At Oxford he met Robert Bridges, later a physician and poet laureate, who became his dearest friend and lifetime correspondent.

Conversion and Vocation. Hopkins's religious quest brought him to the Roman Catholic Church, into which he was received on Oct. 21, 1866 by John Henry Newman, from whom he had sought advice. In 1868, while teaching at Newman's Oratory School, Birmingham, he decided to become a priest in the Society of

Jesus. He burned his poems before entering the Jesuits, but few if any were lost since his friends had copies. He entered the Jesuit novitiate at Roehampton, London, on Sept. 7, 1868, and took perpetual vows on Sept. 8, 1870. Studying philosophy at St. Mary's Hall near Stonyhurst College in rural Lancashire, he learned traditional Suarezian Thomism, but was more excited by his first reading of Duns Scotus whose concept of *haecceitas* (''thisness'') supported his already strong views on individuality and the self. In August 1873 he returned to Roehampton to teach literature to young Jesuits. A year later he began the study of theology at St. Beuno's College in North Wales, a beautiful land he loved and celebrated as ''wild Wales.''

The St. Beuno's Poems. As a Jesuit, Hopkins had written only a few poems in English and Latin: some Marian verses, an occasional presentation piece, the comic ''‘Consule Jones.’'' Then in December 1875, moved by the drowning of five nuns in a shipwreck in the Thames estuary, he began ''The Wreck of the Deutschland'' at the suggestion of his rector. His first great poem, it is recognized as one of the finest odes in English. Complex in thought and brilliant in imagery and metaphor, ''The Wreck'' (1875–76) is a grand meditation on God and the world, on suffering and redemption, and on God's dealings with Hopkins, with the shipwreck victims, and with England itself. In ''Part the First,'' the poet recalls a past religious struggle (his conversion or his decision to enter the Jesuits) with autobiographical accuracy and vivid imagery. ''Part the Second'' narrates the shipwreck, imagines one nun's vision of Christ, reflects on the nuns' deaths, begs for the redemption of Hopkin's ''ráre-dear Britain,'' and praises Christ as ''hero of us, high-priest, / Oür héart's charity's héarth's fíre, oür thóughts' chivalry's thróng's Lórd.''

Popular among his fellow Jesuits, Hopkins was considered a good moralist. In 1877 he wrote eleven sonnets which reflect his love of nature and God, his moral concerns, and his Jesuit spirituality. In ''God's Grandeur,'' the divine presence shines through nature with ''the dearest freshness'' even though humans disobey God and damage nature through industry and trade. In ''The Starlight Night,'' the sky's ''bright boroughs,'' ''circlecitadels,'' and ''elves' eyes'' are like the chinks of a barn-wall which offer glimpses of bright light within ''Christ and his mother and all his hallows.'' ''As kingfishers catch fire'' expresses both Hopkins's Jesuit spirituality and his Scotism: God is found in all things, ''each mortal thing'' proclaims its self, and ''the just man justices'' because (more than any actor can) ''Christ plays in ten thousand places / . . . / To the Father through the features of men's faces.'' Two poems mark springtime and summer's end (''Spring,'' ''Hurrahing in Harvest''),

and ''The Windhover'' celebrates a falcon's flight as grandly masterful when smooth yet even lovelier when triumphing over strong opposing winds; many commentators, citing the poem's subtitle ''to Christ Our Lord'' (added seven years later), find the falcon a symbol of Christ. Popular and original is ''Pied Beauty'' which glorifies God for creation's quirky individualities; it also initiates Hopkin's experiments with the sonnet form as he changes the traditional structure (the eight to six ratio of octave and sestet) into a ''curtal'' (curtailed) sonnet three-fourths the normal length (a 6 to 4 2/5 ratio). Hopkins's sonnets are normally in the Italian form, more difficult than the Shakespearean form because its octave's rhyme-scheme (abbaabba) twice demands four rhymes, a feat more difficult in English than in Italian with its similar word-endings.

Poems of the Middle Years. Hopkins remained at St. Beuno's for three years, until after his priestly ordination on Sept. 23, 1877. He had expected a fourth year of theology, but his third-year examination grade, though sufficient to pass, did not merit a fourth year (a Jesuit friend wrote that he gave Scotist answers instead of the Suarezian Thomism he was taught). From 1877 to 1881 he worked in Jesuit schools and parishes in England and Scotland, enduring (like other British Jesuits) frequent changes of place: teacher at Mount St. Mary's College, Chesterfield, (1877–78) and Stonyhurst College (1878); then parish curate at the Immaculate Conception (Farm Street), London (1878); St. Aloysius's, Oxford (1878–79); St. Joseph's, Bedford Leigh (1879); St. Francis Xavier's, Liverpool (1879–81); and St. Aloysius's, Glasgow (1881). No lover of cities, Hopkins was pained by the Liverpool and Glasgow slums, yet wrote fine poems during this period. From Mount St. Mary's came ''The Loss of the Eurydice,'' a second long shipwreck poem which recalls and prays for 300 young sailors drowned off the Isle of Wight. At Oxford he wrote ''Duns Scotus's Oxford,'' which celebrates the philosopher and the city he most loved; ''Binsey Poplars,'' which mourns the destruction of the nearby countryside; ''Henry Purcell,'' which honors his favorite composer; and (with original rhythm and rhyme) ''The Bugler's First Communion,'' which asks God to preserve a young soldier's ''breathing bloom of a chastity in mansex fine.'' His Liverpool months brought ''Felix Randal,'' which reflects on the death of a blacksmith under Hopkins's pastoral care, and the delicate ''Spring and Fall'' (perhaps his most approachable poem), which ponders the common mortality of nature and of a young girl. On a day's trip from Glasgow, the beauty and sound of a waterfall at ''Inversnaid'' evoked the cry, ''O let them be left, wildness and wet; / Long live the weeds and the wilderness yet.'' Hopkins, also a master of prose, wrote fine sermons during these years and began two important exchanges of letters: in 1878, a ten-year correspondence with Richard Watson Dixon, an Anglican vicar and poet, with whom he discussed poetry and religion, and in 1883, a five-year correspondence with the Catholic poet Coventry Patmore.

Hopkins spent 1881–82 at Roehampton for a peaceful (though apparently poemless) "tertianship," a final year of spiritual training during which he did a second 30-day retreat, delved into Jesuit history and spirituality, and began an unfinished commentary on the *Spiritual Exercises.* Sent afterwards to teach university-level students at Stonyhurst College, he was not heavily burdened, yet found his work tiring, suffered from melancholy, and worried that "there is no likelihood of my ever doing anything to last"—attitudes reflected in his sonnet "Ribblesdale." The Stonyhurst years also brought forth the musical "The Leaden Echo and the Golden Echo" and the lyrical "The Blessed Virgin compared to the Air we Breathe."

The Dublin Poems. Moving to Dublin in 1884 to teach Greek at the ailing Catholic University recently entrusted to the Jesuits, Hopkins found good friends, both Jesuit and lay, yet suffered from "nervous weakness," "fits of sadness," and "the melancholy I have all my life been subject to." He was troubled by headaches, aching eyes, separation from family and friends, Irish rancor against Britain, exhaustion from examination grading, and a sense that God was absent from him. A number of marvelous, searing sonnets of 1885(–86?) express his anguish, especially "To seem the stranger," "I wake and feel," "No worst," and "(Carrion Comfort)." Cries of deep pain ("I am gall, I am heartburn. God's most deep decree / Bitter would have me taste: my taste was me"), they are written in perfect sonnet form. Peace begins to return in "Patience, hard thing!" and "My own heart." Hopkins' poetic experiments continue in several "caudal" sonnets (sonnets with tails), especially the difficult "Harry Ploughman" and "Tom's Garland" (1887) and the exultant "That Nature is a Heraclitean Fire and of the comfort of the Resurrection" (1888), the latter a "sonnet" of 24 lines with its jubilant close, "In a flash, at a trumpet crash, / I am all at once what Christ is, since he was what I am, and / This Jack, joke, poor potsherd, patch, matchwood, immortal diamond, / Is immortal diamond."

Hopkins's last four poems (1888–89) return to traditional sonnet form and greater simplicity of language. "In honour of St. Alphonsus Rodriguez" recalls the poet's own suffering and "war within," while "The shepherd's brow" is an ironic self-portrait. With subtler irony, "Thou are indeed just, Lord" and "To R.B."

(Robert Bridges) are eloquent, perfect sonnets about Hopkins's inability to write sonnets: "Send my roots rain," "I want the one rapture of an inspiration." On June 8, 1889, six weeks before his 45th birthday, Gerard M. Hopkins, S.J., (as he signed himself) died, a victim of typhoid fever. He is buried in the Jesuit plot at Glasnevin Cemetery, Dublin.

Inscape, Instress, Sprung Rhythm. To express insights into poetry and reality, Hopkins developed three concepts now associated with his name. "Inscape," formed to imitate the word "landscape" and first used in 1868, means both the individual essence or uniqueness of a thing and its distinctive shape. "Instress" is the inner force which sustains a thing and its inner drive to express itself or be understood. "Sprung rhythm," first significantly used in "The Wreck of the Deutschland," "consists in scanning by accents or stresses alone, without any account of the number of syllables." A line leaps or "springs" from stress to stress, downplaying the intervening unstressed syllables which may be several or none. Sprung rhythm stands in contrast to the smooth-flowing "running rhythm" of the ten-syllable iambic-pentameter line or of any line which counts syllables and alternates stressed and unstressed syllables. Instead, sprung rhythm "feels" the timing, as in music, and fits in unstressed syllables (or even silences, like rests in music) according to the poet's ear or the subject of the line. The five-stress line "áll félled, félled, are áll félled" ("Binsey Poplars") catches in six syllables the harsh strokes of an axe felling aspens. Hopkins recognized that earlier poets had used such rhythm he cited Milton among others but held that none before him had used it as a structural principle throughout a poem. (The best treatment of sprung rhythm is in Stephenson, *What Sprung Rhythm Really Is.*)

Stature. A poet of nature, religion, and the self, Hopkins had an imagination that was inventive and leaping, reveling in physical images, rich sounds, and startling, self-crafted words. His poems were written to be "performed" rather than read. Yet Hopkins, conflicted about personal fame, published few poems during his lifetime. The first collection of his work, *Poems of Gerard Manley Hopkins,* did not appear until 1918, edited by his Oxford friend Robert Bridges (then poet laureate), to whom Hopkins had sent copies of most poems. An expanded second edition (also by Bridges) appeared in 1930 with an introduction by Charles Williams, and was praised by that era's New Critics for its textual richness and complexity. Hopkins's reputation grew gradually, but because of his limited experience and small output he was long deemed a minor Victorian poet inferior to Matthew Arnold, Robert Browning, and Alfred, Lord Tennyson. With Arnold's and Tennyson's reputations declining, Hopkins and Browning are recognized as the finest poets of Victorian England. In 1961, lines from "The Wreck of the Deutschland" were carved on a large wall at the United Nations' Palais des Nations in Geneva (the Lord Cecil Memorial), and on Dec. 8, 1975, a hundred years after the Deutschland's wreck, a memorial stone was dedicated to Hopkins in the Poets' Corner of Westminster Abbey. The 1989 centennial of his death brought celebrations throughout the world in books, journals, scholarly and popular essays, conferences, one-man plays, and exhibitions. Two journals are devoted to his work, *The Hopkins Quarterly* (Philadelphia) and *Hopkins Research* (Tokyo).

Bibliography: *The Poetical Works of Gerard Manley Hopkins,* ed. N. H. MACKENZIE (Oxford 1990). *The Oxford Authors: Gerard Manley Hopkins,* ed. C. PHILLIPS (Oxford 1986). *The Letters of Gerard Manley Hopkins to Robert Bridges,* ed. C. C. ABBOTT (London 1955). *The Correspondence of Gerard Manley Hopkins and Richard Watson Dixon,* ed. C. C. ABBOTT (London 1955). *Further Letters of Gerard Manley Hopkins,* ed. C. C. ABBOTT (2d ed. London 1956). *The Journals and Papers of Gerard Manley Hopkins,* ed. H. HOUSE (London 1959). *The Sermons and Devotional Writings of Gerard Manley Hopkins,* ed. C. DEVLIN, S.J. (London 1959). P. L. MARIANI, *A Commentary on the Complete Poems of Gerard Manley Hopkins* (Ithaca NY 1970). N. H. MACKENZIE, *A Reader's Guide to Gerard Manley Hopkins* (Ithaca NY 1981). E. STEPHENSON, *What Sprung Rhythm Really Is* (Alma ON 1987). T. DUNNE, *Gerard Manley Hopkins: A Comprehensive Bibliography* (Oxford 1976). N. WHITE, *Hopkins: A Literary Biography* (Oxford 1992).

[J. J. FEENEY]

HOREB, MOUNT

The "mountain of God" where Moses received the Law. It was called Horeb by the Elohist and the Deuteronomist, whereas the Yahwist and the Priestly Writers call it SINAI. Horeb (Heb. *ḥōrēb,* "dryness, desolation") is mentioned in Ex 3.1; 17.6; 33.6; Dt 1.2, 6, 19; 4.10, 15; 5.2; 9.8; 18.16; 29.1; 1 Kgs 8.9; 19.8; 2 Chr 5.10; Ps 105(106).19; Mal 3.22. Elsewhere the mountain is called Sinai. As early as St. Jerome (*De situ et nom. Hebr.*) Horeb was considered another name for Sinai. According to some scholars, Horeb was the name of the whole mountain range of which Sinai was one of the peaks. The term Horeb may have been substituted for the term Sinai because of the worship of the god Sin.

Bibliography: G. HÖLSCHER, "Sinai und Choreb," *Festschrift Rudolf Bultmann* (Stuttgart 1949) 127–132. M. NOTH, *Überlieferungsgeschichte des Pentateuch* (Stuttgart 1948) 150–155.

[C. MCGOUGH]

HORGAN, THADDEUS DANIEL

Franciscan, ecumenist, administrator, author; b. Jersey City, NJ, March 16, 1936; d. Waterbury, CT, April 19, 1990. Thaddeus Daniel Horgan entered the Atonement Friars of Graymoor in 1956 and was ordained a priest in 1963. After receiving the S.T.L. degree from the Catholic University of America in 1965, he pursued further studies at Columbia University and the Gregorian University. A prolific writer, he wrote and edited seven books and more than 150 articles and pamphlets on Catholic teachings, ecumenism, and Franciscan spirituality.

An energetic ecumenist, in 1968 Horgan established the Centro Pro Unione in Rome, an ecumenical library and conference center. He was director of this center until 1973, when he was elected to the general council of the Atonement Friars and had oversight responsibility for its ecumenical ministries. Horgan served in various capacities at the Graymoor Ecumenical Institute, where he participated in national and international ecumenical initiatives. He also filled editorial positions for *Ecumenical Trends*, a monthly ecumenical journal. Dedicated to both scholarly and grassroots ecumenism, he served in numerous organizations, including the Faith and Order Commission of the National Council of Churches of Christ, USA, and the North American Academy of Ecumenists. From 1988 until his death, he was associate director of the Bishops' Committee for Ecumenical and Interreligious Affairs of the National Conference of Catholic Bishops. This position brought him into direct involvement with the ecumenical bilateral dialogues in the United States.

In addition to his ecumenical work, Horgan was noted for his activity among Third Order Regular Franciscans. A member of the International Franciscan Commission from 1979 to 1982, he was an instrumental collaborator for the revised Rule of the Third Order Regular of Saint Francis that received papal approval in 1982. His pastoral ministry also included a three-year tenure as pastor in Jamaica, West Indies, from 1982 to 1985 at a covenanted Anglican/Roman Catholic parish where he combined daily parochial leadership and ecumenical life.

Bibliography: T. D. HORGAN, ed., *Walking Together: Roman Catholics and Ecumenism 25 Years After Vatican II* (Grand Rapids 1990).

[P. COGAN]

HORMISDAS, POPE, ST.

Pontificate: July 20, 514 to Aug. 6, 523. Pope Symmachus was succeeded by Hormisdas, archdeacon of the Roman Church, whose name points to a Persian or Eastern origin, possibly on the maternal side. The new pope's father was Justus; Hormisdas's son Silverius later became pope. Under Hormisdas hopes were raised for a settlement of the ACACIAN SCHISM. In a conciliatory gesture, Hormisdas received the remaining followers of Laurentius into communion. After consulting Theodoric, Arian Gothic king of Italy, Hormisdas dispatched an embassy consisting of Bp. ENNODIUS of Pavia and Bp. Fortunatus of Catina to Constantinople with precise instructions on how to act in reply to Emperor ANASTASIUS I's request for a council. The schism with the East was ultimately settled, four years later, in almost exact conformity with the terms laid down by Hormisdas in 515, and it was insisted that the council was to clearly recognize CHALCEDON and the Tome of Leo as the standard of orthodoxy; that the emperor's letter requesting the bishops' signatures must state this unequivocally; that the bishops must make a formal profession of orthodoxy in their churches and must condemn the Monophysite leaders by name; that, in the presence of witnesses, they must sign a formula or *libellus* containing a statement of the true faith drawn up by the papal notaries; and that the cases of exiled bishops must be examined afresh by the apostolic see, while those of bishops who were accused of persecuting the orthodox were to be reserved to the pope.

Hormisdas promised to come to Constantinople if his presence were needed but Emperor Anastasius I had overcome the immediate danger to his throne and began to temporize on the question of holding a council. He tried to stir up the Roman senate against Pope Hormisdas. New legates were sent to Constantinople, but they were dismissed after an attempt had been made to corrupt them. At this juncture, the emperor died and was succeeded by the Chalcedonian Prefect of the Praetorian Guard, a former peasant, JUSTIN I.

Aided by his nephew and mentor JUSTINIAN I, the new emperor at once took steps aimed at restoring Chalcedonian orthodoxy in the empire and invited the pope to send legates to end the schism. Hormisdas complied, designating two bishops, a priest, a deacon, a notary, and the skillful deacon DIOSCORUS (later pope) to represent him. The papal emissaries arrived at Constantinople on March 25, 519; they were greeted outside the city walls by Count Justinian and escorted with great pomp into the presence of the emperor, who received them surrounded by the senate and the four patriarchs of the East.

Since the legates had come only to receive signatures, they refused to enter into discussions. Three days later, Patriarch John II of Constantinople and all the bishops present in the capital, as well as the heads of monasteries, signed the papal statement of faith, and the names of Acacius, ZENO, and Anastasius I were stricken from the diptychs. The pope had not requested condemnation of the emperors, but Justin and Justinian decided to demean the reputations of their predecessors to strengthen their own positions. The legates remained in the East for a year and a half, collecting signatures and supervising the restoration of communion. Only in a few instances did they meet with effective resistance from churches that objected to the stringency of the demand regarding the removal of names from the diptychs. Justin and Justinian both appealed to the pope for a more lenient attitude, and Hormisdas agreed to allow the patriarch of Constantinople "to put on our person" and decide each case on its merits, informing the apostolic see of the results. But there were also setbacks. The emperor refused to agree to sending Eastern bishops to Rome for trial; he also denied Hormisdas' wish that Dioscorus be appointed Bishop of Alexandria.

The statement signed by the Eastern bishops is commonly known as the formula of Hormisdas and undoubtedly represents a great triumph for the Roman see, or rather, for the orthodoxy for which it so firmly stood. It is unquestionably the most pro-Roman, propapal statement ever signed by the Byzantine bishops. Some of them, doubtless, signed against their better judgment. The recognition of Roman claims implicit in some of the language, particularly the apparent identification of what is orthodox with what the Roman see has defined, and the equating of communion with that see with the Catholic Church, was probably going further than many would have preferred. However, when viewed in context, it is evident that the pro-Roman phraseology used was compatible with looser Byzantine notions about the hierarchy and the papal primacy, and there is danger in attempting to read too much into it as an acknowledgment of Roman claims. It must also be recognized that this triumph resulted almost completely from the desire of the emperor and his nephew to settle the schism not only because they were Chalcedonians but also because they considered that step to be a prerequisite to their intended extension of Byzantine power into Italy.

The text of the formula is extant in seven ancient versions that differ slightly one from another. The version that Pope Hormisdas sent to the bishops of Spain in 517 is probably the most authentic. The preface that Patriarch John II insisted on appending to the version he signed was designed to safeguard the rights of his see as defined by previous councils. Its acceptance by Rome implied at least tacit recognition of the Council of CONSTANTINOPLE I (381) as ecumenical, which Rome had hitherto always refused. It was not the intention of this preface to water down the language of the formula itself.

Before leaving Constantinople the papal legates were approached by the theopaschite monks from Little

Scythia, so called because they endeavored to reconcile the Monophysites by winning general acceptance for the formula: ''One of the Trinity suffered in the flesh.'' Undaunted by the refusal of the legates to approve the phrase since it had Monophysite associations, the monks came to Rome and besieged the pope with entreaties until he finally had them expelled from the city. To Emperor Justin, who had meanwhile taken up the phrase in the hopes of being able to reconcile the Severan Monophysites to Chalcedon, the pope wrote that the Council of Chalcedon and the Tome of Pope Leo were sufficient; he would neither approve nor disapprove the new formula, but he warned against its possible misinterpretation.

The death of King Thrasamund (523) brought an end to the persecution of the Church in the Vandal kingdom of North Africa, and the pope re-established contact with the African hierarchy. He also requested Dionysius Exiguus, a Scythian monk resident in Rome, to prepare a Latin translation of the canons of the Eastern churches. Pope Hormisdas was buried in the portico of St. Peter's. Over 100 of his letters are extant; most of them are preserved by the *Collectio Avellana* (*Corpus scriptorum ecclesiasticorum latinorum* 35).

Feast: Aug. 6.

Bibliography: *Clavis Patrum latinorum,* ed. E. DEKKERS (2d. ed. Streenbrugge 1961) 1683–1684. *Patrologia Latina,* ed. J. P. MIGNE (Paris 1878–90) 63:367–534. A. THIEL, ed., *Epistolae romanorum pontificum,* v.1 (Braunsberg 1868) 741–990. R. HAACKE, *Lexikon für Theologie und Kirche,* ed. J. HOFER and K. RAHNER, (2d, new ed. Freiburg 1957–65) 5:483–484. F. DVORNIK, *The Idea of Apostolicity in Byzantium and the Legend of the Apostle Andrew* (Cambridge, Mass. 1958). R. U. MONTINI, *Le tombe dei papi* (Paris 1957) 105–106. E. FERGUSON, ed., *Encyclopedia of Early Christianity* (New York 1997) 1:545. W. H. C. FREND, *Rise of the Monophysite Movement* (Cambridge 1972) 227–229. H. JEDIN, *History of the Church* (New York 1980) 2:435–437; 622–625. J. N. D. KELLY, *Oxford Dictionary of Popes* (New York 1986) 52–54. J. RICHARDS, *Popes and Papacy the Early Middle Ages* (London 1979) 100–109. S. RANALLI, ''L'epistolario di Papa Ormisda, nel quadro della letteratura latina cristiana del VI secolo,'' *Studi e Materiali di Storia delle Religioni* 19:19–54. S. RANALLI, L'opera del pontifice Ormisda nel panorama del monachesimo occidentale del VI secolo,'' *Rivista Cistercense* 12:3–20.

[J. CHAPIN]

HORNER, NICHOLAS, BL.

Lay martyr; b. at Grantley, Yorkshire, England; hanged, drawn, and quartered at Smithfield, London, d. March 4, 1590. Arrested in London on the charge of assisting Catholic priests, he was released after contracting blood poisoning that required the amputation of his leg. Charged a second time with assisting Bl. Christopher BALES, a seminary priest, he refused to conform reli-

giously in exchange for his life. On the eve of his execution, according to a letter from Horner's friend to St. Robert SOUTHWELL (dated March 18, 1590), he had a vision of a crown of glory hanging over his head, which filled him with courage to face the impending ordeal. He was beatified by Pope John Paul II on Nov. 22, 1987 with George Haydock and Companions.

Feast of the English Martyrs: May 4 (England).

See Also: ENGLAND, SCOTLAND AND WALES, MARTYRS OF.

Bibliography: R. CHALLONER, *Memoirs of Missionary Priests,* ed. J. H. POLLEN (rev. ed. London 1924), I, 166, 169, 218. J. MORRIS, ed., *The Troubles of Our Catholic Forefathers Related by Themselves* (London 1872–77), v. 3. J. H. POLLEN, *Acts of English Martyrs* (London 1891).

[K. I. RABENSTEIN]

HOROSCOPES

Originally the Greek word *horoskopos* denoted the point of the ecliptic rising at any given moment, that is, the intersection of the zodiac with the eastern horizon. Because of the great importance of this point in astrological forecasts, the term came to mean an entire prediction. Hence the ordinary sense of the word horoscope.

Astrological Backgrounds. Many peoples have believed that the heavenly bodies exert a preponderant influence over the world and its inhabitants and that man's fate, at least in part, is fixed in advance and can be predicted by carefully observing at the moment of birth or conception the positions of the sun and moon and the planets in relation to each other, to the signs of the zodiac, and to the eastern and western horizons and midheaven, the highest point of the ecliptic. On this foundation the pseudoscience of astrology was erected. It was a highly complicated and technical structure requiring considerable knowledge of mathematics and astronomy in its practitioners, who often differed from one another in the details and even in the fundamental assumptions of their profession.

Astrologers sometimes made predictions applying to cities, states, or entire regions of the earth. For this purpose the regions of the ancient world were apportioned among the signs of the zodiac according to various systems, of which Ptolemy's (*Tetrabiblos* 2.3) is the most elaborate. For instance, Britain was assigned to Aries. Eclipses, comets, and other phenomena occurring in Aries and observed in Britain would then be interpreted as applying to Britain.

Genethlialogy. The astrologer's highest knowledge was exhibited in genethlialogy, the art of prediction ap-

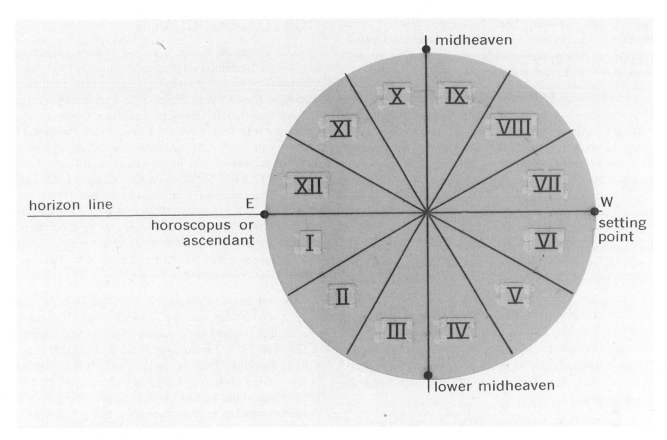

The twelve loci of the horoscope.

plied to an individual, based on the positions of the heavenly bodies at the moment of his birth. Each planet was believed to have its own nature and influence, which were nevertheless capable of great variation, just as the gods were variable and capricious.

Houses and Loci. Each planet had its day and night houses, or signs of the zodiac in which it was especially "at home," where its natural influence would be accentuated; its exaltation and depression, particular degrees of the ecliptic where its influence would be maximum or minimum; and its terms, a fixed section in each sign of the zodiac. For example, Mars had its day house in Scorpio and its night house in Aries; its exaltation at 28° in Capricorn and its depression at 28° in Cancer; and a term of a certain number of degrees, arranged on any of three systems, in each sign. In addition, each planet might affect various features of a man's life, depending on its location in one of the 12 loc. The significance of the loci was as follows: I, life, body, spirit or breath; II, livelihood, property, partnership, intercourse with women, business, profit from inheritance; III, brothers, living abroad, royalty, wealth, friends, relatives, slaves; IV, parents, spirits, life in the temple, repute, children; V, children, good fortune, friendship, accomplishments,

marriage; VI, slaves, bad fortune, illness, enmity, infirmity; VII, marriage; VIII, death, trial, penalty, loss, weakness; IX, travel, friendship, benefit from kings, revelations, manifestations of gods, soothsaying; X, careers and honors, accomplishment, reputation, children, wife; XI, "good daemon," friends, hopes, gifts, children, freed persons, accomplishment; and XII, "bad daemon," enmity, foreign country, slaves, illness, dangers, court trials, infirmity, death.

Aspects of the Planets. More important than the loci were the aspects of the planets, the angles at which they "looked at" one another and the earth, depending on their relative positions in the signs of the zodiac. Astrologers recognized conjunction of planets in the same sign and four aspects as especially important. (1) Opposition: this occurs when two planets are in opposite signs, as Aries and Libra. (2) Trine aspect: the 12 signs can be connected by threes to form equilateral triangles, such as Aries, Leo, and Sagittarius, so that planets in any two of such a set are in trine aspect. (3) Quartile aspect: similarly, the signs can be connected by fours to form squares, e.g., Aries, Cancer, Libra, Capricorn; planets in Aries and Cancer or in Aries and Capricorn are in quartile aspect. (4) Sextile Aspect: the 12 signs can be connected to form two different equilateral hexagons; thus, a planet in Aries is in sextile aspect to one in Gemini or Aquarius. Opposition was regularly, and quartile aspect generally, considered ill-omened; trine and sextile aspects, favorable.

Elaboration of Horoscopes and Their Wide Use. Horoscopes of a simple type have been found in great numbers in the "library" of the Assyrian king Assurbanipal (7th century B. C.) at Nineveh (now in the British Museum). Great elaboration became possible only when Babylonian doctrines were combined with Hellenistic Greek astronomy in Egypt, culminating in the astronomical works and extant handbook of astrology, the *Tetrabiblos,* of Claudius Ptolemaeus (2d century A.D.). Representative Roman works are the *Astronomica* of Manilius (fl. early 1st century A.D.) and the handbook by Vettius Valens (2d century A.D.). Horoscopes were widely used in the Green-Roman period by all classes, from the Roman emperor to the humblest slave. The curious hold that astrology had on men is well illustrated by the fact that Constantine, after his victory over Licinius, removed the sun-god Helios from his coins, but had an astrologer cast the horoscope of his new capital, Constantinople.

The Church Fathers opposed astrology, but it revived during the Byzantine renaissance of the 9th century, when Greek astrology was rediscovered along with astronomy. From then on astrology flourished and horoscopes were east although the Church officially was opposed. In the later Middle Ages the Universities of Padua, Bologna, and Paris (among others) provided expert instruction in casting horoscopes. Most of the leading astronomers of the age of the Renaissance and the Reformation, among them Tycho Brahe, Copernicus, Galileo, and Kepler, practiced astrology; and all the rulers of the time, including several popes, employed official astrologers at their courts. The art of casting horoscopes still flourishes, and this form of astrology continues to have a surprising number of adherents at all intellectual levels.

See Also: ASTRAL RELIGION; ASTROLOGY; MAGIC.

Bibliography: *Ptolemy, Tetrabiblos,* ed. F. E. ROBBINS, with Eng. tr. (Loeb Classical Library 1940). BOUCHÉ-LECLERCQ, *L'Astrologie grecque* (Paris 1899), still the best account of Greco-Roman techniques. F. W. BOLL, *Sternglaube und Sterndeutung,* 4th ed. W. GUNDEL (Leipzig 1931), brief on technique but excellent on history. O. NEUGEBAUER and H. B. VAN HOESEN, *Greek Horoscopes* (Philadelphia 1959), 1,099 Greek horoscopes with astronomical commentary, glossary of terms, and bibliography. J. H. CREHAN, "Astrology and Theology", H. F. DAVIS. et al., *A Catholic Dictionary of Theology* (London 1962–) 1:179–182.

[H. S. LONG]

HORTON, DOUGLAS

U.S. Protestant leader; b. Brooklyn, New York, July 27, 1891; d. Berlin, New Hampshire, Aug. 21, 1968. Horton graduated from Princeton University in 1912 and then studied at New College, Edinburgh; Mansfield College, Oxford; and the University of Tübingen, Germany. He received a B.D. from Hartford (Connecticut) Theological Seminary in 1915. After ordination as a Congregational minister the same year, he served as minister of First Church of Christ in Middletown, Connecticut (1915–25); Leyden Congregational Church in Brookline, Massachusetts (1925–31); and United Church of Hyde Park, Chicago (1931–38). He then became chief executive officer of the Congregational Christian Churches, serving until 1955 as minister and executive secretary of the denomination's General Council.

He led his denomination's representatives in the merger negotiations with the Evangelical and Reformed Church that resulted in formation of the United Church of Christ in 1957. The concept of the new church, along with its theology, structure, and program, was explained in *The United Church of Christ,* a book he published in 1962. Meanwhile, he had become dean of the Harvard Divinity School in 1955 and served in that position until 1959. He had also become prominent in the ecumenical movement, participating in the formation of the National and World Councils of Churches and holding important positions in both council, including chairmanship of the WCC's Faith and Order Commission (1957–63).

As an observer for the International Congregational Council he attended all four sessions of the Second Vatican Council and published four volumes of sympathetic diary reports. His publications included 14 books, the last being *Toward an Undivided Church* (1967). By translating Karl Barth's *Word of God and Word of Man* in 1928 he became one of the first to introduce the Barthian theology to the English-speaking world. In 1945 he married Mildred McAfee, president of Wellesley College from 1936 to 1949 and holder of other significant posts in church and public affairs.

Bibliography: D. HORTON, *The United Church of Christ* (New York 1962); *Vatican Diary,* 4 v. (Philadelphia 1964–66).

[T. EARLY]

HORTULUS ANIMAE

The Little Garden of the Soul, a type of devotional book of prayers, intended for the laity, that was widespread in Germany in the early 16th century. The *hortuli* are to be distinguished from the medieval Psalter, which contained Psalms and part of the liturgical Office, with perhaps a supplement of miscellaneous prayers. They were similar in general content and arrangement to many of the Latin *Horae,* or books of hours, or to the English primers, from which they developed; however, they were more popular in character. The *hortuli* contained the Little Office of Our Lady, extracts from the Gospel accounts of the Passion, the Penitential Psalms, and the Litany of the Saints, with a large selection of supplementary devotional matter. This material of private prayer had the tendency to increase in size and in extravagance. For example, promises of spurious indulgences and of complete forgiveness of sins became attached to many prayers. That these devotional books were very popular can be judged by the number of editions. Early copies *c.* 1500 had numerous woodcuts, sometimes by famous artists such as Hans Holbein. After the Reformation the Lutherans put out a modified version. The Council of Trent legislated against the accretions, the false promises of indulgences, and the incorrect versions of the Little Office of Our Lady. A bull of Pius V (March 11, 1571) demanded rigorous censorship of all editions. A modern "Garden of the Soul" is the book of prayers and instructions in the spiritual life written by Richard Challoner in 1740 and reprinted seven times by 1757.

See Also: PRAYER BOOKS.

Bibliography: H. THURSTON, "The Original *Garden of the Soul,*" *American Ecclesiastical Review* 26 (1902) 167–187. A. A. SCHMID and A. BOECKLER, in *Handbuch der Bibliothekswissenschaft,* ed. F. MILKAU, 3 v. (2d ed. Leipzig 1931–40) 1:121.

[M. M. BARRY]

HOSANNA

A liturgical exclamation derived through the Greek transcription ὡσαννά of the Aramaic term *hôša'-nā'* that represents the Hebrew term *hôšî'â-nnâ* meaning "Do save (us)!" It occurs in Ps 118.25 as a cry for continued help after victory and a joyous shout of homage to God. This Psalm is one of the Hallel Psalms (Psalms 113–118) that were recited especially at the Jewish feasts of PASSOVER, PENTECOST, BOOTHS (TABERNACLES), and the DEDICATION OF THE TEMPLE. The verse Ps 118.25 was sung during the octave of the feast of Booths once a day and seven times on the seventh day while the priests went in procession around the altar. During the procession on the seventh day, the people waved festive branches (*hōšannōt*) and sang hymns of praise with "Hosanna" as their refrain (Josephus, *Ant.* 3.10.4; 3 Maccabees 10.6–7). This spontaneous acclamation of joy and supplication was sung when Christ entered Jerusalem at His last Passover (Mt 21.9, 15; Mk 11.10; Jn 12.13). In the context here Hosanna expresses the messianic hopes of the people; it is the cry of welcome ("Blessed in the name of the Lord be he who come"—the standard Hebrew formula of welcome) to "the Son of David," i.e., the Messiah. At a very early date (Didache 10.6; *Const. Apost.* 8.13) the word Hosanna was incorporated in the Christian liturgy at the Sanctus of the Mass; later it was introduced into the Palm Sunday procession.

[M. R. E. MASTERMAN/EDS.]

HOSEA, BOOK OF

Hosea, whose name is an abbreviated form meaning "Yahweh is salvation," was one of the two Prophets from the Northern Kingdom who left us writings of their ministry.

The Prophet. Unlike Amos, his precedessor from the South, Hosea was probably an Ephraimite, for he frequently refers to this tribe and to sites in this geographical area. He possessed a perceptive mind and refined sensitivity and, like Jeremiah a century later, had to endure the personal agony of announcing the visitation of divine retribution upon his native land. Because of the many images drawn from agriculture and nature, it is likely that he came from a rural rather than an urban background. There is no evidence that he belonged to one of the prophetic guilds or was of priestly descent, though he is acquainted with both offices as well as with the political realities of his time. The opening verse places his ministry during the reigns of Jeroboam II (786–746 B.C.) to Hezekiah (715–687 B.C.), but this is a later Judean addition to the work intended to make Hosea a contemporary of Isaiah (Is 1.1). Internal evidence points to the last years of Jeroboam II as the beginning of his ministry, thus, *c.* 750 B.C. The turbulent years of the dynastic upheavals from 746–732 B.C. are alluded to (5.8–10; 7.3–7; 8.4), but the end of his ministry is a matter of conjecture. Since the fall of Samaria (721 B.C.) is nowhere mentioned, it is probable that Hosea did not live to see it. (For the social conditions and the political situation of this period, *see* ISRAEL, 3.)

Characteristics of the Book. Hosea stands at the head of the canon of the "Twelve Prophets" in the Hebrew and Greek Bibles. From a literary point of view, the work is a mélange of terse, originally independent oracles that contain warnings, threats, pleas for conversion, and a number of Messianic passages of hope for a happier future. Characteristic of the book is the abrupt alternation between the words of Yahweh and those of the prophet (4.10–15; 12.1–15). This is best explained as a conscious use of the disputation form (*rîb*) common in litigation before the elders at the gate of the city. The prophecy is rich in imagery redolent with the language of love; parallelism, play on words, alliteration, and repetition of a key idea are devices employed by Hosea to seize the attention of his hearers. Hosea's fragmented style, due in part to the poor condition of the text, raises many problems about the original order and sequence of his preaching. Various statements about Judah, at times interrupting the harmony of thought, are signs of a Judean redaction after the death of the Prophet (1.7; 5.5; 6.11; 12.1). These were probably interpolated to make the prophecy pertinent to readers of the South. There are also some other additions and glosses (e.g., 14.10) but the present form was perhaps fixed by the year 700 B.C. Scholars are generally agreed today upon the substantial genuineness of the work and attribute it to Hosea himself, though much was recorded and compiled by his disciples.

Contents. The prophecy falls into two unequal divisions: ch. 1–3 treat of the marriage of Hosea; ch. 4–14 are a collection of oracles that evince little logical organization or chronological continuity.

The celebrated marriage of the Prophet to Gomer is presented in an unusual fashion: in chapter one the episode is related biographically; in chapter three the Prophet speaks of it in a firsthand account; chapter two contains in oracular speech the divinely intended significance of the event. The juxtaposition of these forms in one literary unity is almost certainly artificial and the result of editing.

From the patristic age to modern times an allegorical interpretation of the marriage was in vogue. Since the 19th century, however, exegetes have tended to view the marriage as an historical reality that had symbolic meaning. An attempt at reconstruction is as follows: At the bidding of God, Hosea took to wife Gomer, who is called a harlot (1.2). After bearing Hosea several children, who by divine command received the ominous names: "Jezrael," "Unpitied," and "Not my People," she abandoned her husband and gave herself up to a life of adultery. The outraged anger of the Prophet is vanquished by the still more ardent love he feels for his perfidious spouse. At this point the seer is instructed to reclaim his erring wife; symbolism demands that the unnamed woman of ch. 3 be Gomer. Hosea ransomed her for the price of a slave and then imposed upon her a time of salutary chastisement before restoring her to full marital union. Aided by revelation Hosea understands that his unrequited love for Gomer and her wayward conduct are but a reflection of what Yahweh has experienced from faithless Israel (2.4–15).

In the second part of his prophecy (ch. 4–14), Hosea applies this symbolism to the concrete reality of his society in a series of severe denunciations of the immorality of the priests (4) and the princes (5) who bear a major share of guilt for the apostasy of the nation. He deplores Ephraim's ephemeral conversions to the Lord, which are likened to the passing of the morning dew (6). He warns of the folly of political alliances with Assyria and Egypt (7–8), as if these could deliver the land from the "day of the Lord" (9). Idolatry, a syncretism of Baalistic practices with the worship of Yahweh, is the crime of Ephraim (9), which merits utter destruction of king and people alike (10). Yet for all this, God's love for His son endures, and in ch. 11 Hosea rises to one of the most sublime expressions of Yahweh's tender concern for the chosen people. To this, Israel continually responds with rebelliousness (12–13). The prophecy closes with an impassioned plea for a sincere return to God with the assurance of His pardon and favor (14).

Theology. The prophet's chief complaint is the lack of knowledge of God in the land (4.1,6; 5.4; 6.6), which is practically synonymous with faithful obedience to the religion of Moses. No other prophet insists so poignantly upon the loyal devotedness (ḥesed) that binds Yahweh and Israel and that should inspire the Israelites in their dealings with each other. Hosea in his portrait of Yahweh as a God of love (2.21–25;11.1–4) approaches as close as anyone in the OT to the conception of the fourth Evangelist. The idolatrous Baal ritual he terms the whoredom of Israel. While the overall tone of the message is one of despair of salvaging the ancient alliance, there appear passages of hope for a new covenant (2.20–22) to be based on right, justice, love, and loyalty, which will bring about the reunion of all of the chosen people (2.2; 3.5). Hosea's grasp of Israel's past as a history of salvation, his insistence upon purity of worship and a morality in accord with the postulates of the Law certainly influenced the Deuteronomical writers. He was the first to conceive of the marriage image to describe the relation of Yahweh and his people, which became a classical figure in the writings of Isaiah, Jeremiah, Ezekiel, and St. Paul.

Bibliography: Commentaries A. VAN HOONACKER, *Les Douze Petits Prophètes* (*Études bibliques*; Paris 1908). W. R. HARPER, *Critical and Exegetical Commentary on Amos and Hosea* (*International Critical Commentary*, ed. S. R. DRIVER et al. New York 1905). H. W. WOLFF, *Dodekapropheton I: Hosea* (Biblischer Kommentar: Altes Testament 14; Neukirchen 1961). G. RINALDI, *I Profeti Minori II: Osea-Giole-Abia-Giona* (Turin 1960). A. DEISSLER, *Les Petits prophètes* (Osée; Bible Pirot-Clamer, 8.1; Paris 1961). Studies. A. GELIN, "Osée (Livre D')," *Dictionnaire de la Bible*, suppl. ed. L. PIROT, et al. (Paris 1928–) 6:926–940. H. H. ROWLEY, "Marriage of Hosea," *The Bulletin of the John Rylands Library* 39 (1956) 200–233. N. H. SNAITH, *Mercy and Sacrifice* (London 1953). J. L. MCKENZIE, "Divine Passion in Osee," *The Catholic Biblical Quarterly* 17 (1955) 287–299; "Knowledge of God in Hosea," *Journal of Biblical Literature* 74 (1955) 22–27. E. H. MALY, "Messianism in Osee," *The Catholic Biblical Quarterly*

19 (1957) 213–225. B. VAWTER, *Conscience of Israel* (New York 1961).

[J. K. SOLARI]

HOSIUS, STANISLAUS

Ecclesiologist and leading churchman during the Counter Reformation; b. Cracow, Poland, May 5, 1504; d. Rome, Aug. 5, 1579. He studied humanities at the Universities of Cracow and Padua and pursued law in Bologna. Paul III nominated him bishop of Culm in 1549; in 1551 he was transferred to the see of Ermland in East Prussia. He was the spirit behind the Catholic movement to stem the tide of Protestantism not only in his native land but throughout Europe. He combatted heresy; rallied wavering bishops, clergy, and princes to the cause of Catholicism; convoked synods; and opened schools and colleges for training future priests. His *Confessio Catholicae Fidei Christiana*—32 editions appeared during his lifetime—numerous polemical writings, and a constant flow of correspondence with leading personalities of the day gained him universal esteem and prestige. He came to be called the ''second Augustine'' and ''hammer of heretics.'' Paul IV called him to work in Rome; Pius IV sent him on diplomatic missions to Vienna with a view toward reopening the Council of Trent. He was created cardinal on Feb. 26, 1561, and appointed papal legate to preside at the Council. He is buried in Rome in the Church of S. Maria in Trastevere.

Bibliography: Complete bibliog. to 1937, J. SMOCZYNSKI, *Bibliographia Hosiana* (Pelplin 1937). A. HUMBERT, *Dictionnaire de théologie catholique*, ed. A. VACANT et al., 15 v. (Paris 1903–50; Tables Générales 1951–) 7.1: 178–190. G. M. GRABKA, *Cardinalis Hosii doctrina de corpore christi mystico* (Washington 1945); ''Cardinal Hosius and the Council of Trent,'' *Theological Studies* 7 (1946) 558–576. F. J. ZDRODOWSKI, *The Concept of Heresy According to Cardinal Hosius* (Washington 1947).

[G. M. GRABKA]

HOSPICE MOVEMENT

The modern hospice movement is a medically directed, nurse-coordinated program providing a continuum of home and inpatient care for the terminally ill and their families. The program affords palliative and supportive care to meet the special needs arising out of the physical, emotional, spiritual, social, and economic stresses that are experienced during the final stages of illness, and during dying and bereavement. An interdisciplinary team, under the direction of an autonomous hospice administration, provides the care.

In medieval times many hospices such as that connected with the monastery of St. Bernard in the Swiss Alps were established to care for sick travelers and indigent pilgrims. The modern movement, however, with its concern for the terminally ill, traces its origins to the 19th century. The Irish Sisters of Charity, inspired by the vision of their foundress, Sister Mary AIKENHEAD (d. 1858), a one-time coworker of Florence Nightingale, established Our Lady's Hospice at Harold's Cross, outside Dublin in 1879. Another of the early hospices, Sacred Heart Hospice, was founded by the Sisters of Charity in Australia in 1890. In the United States there were a few not-for-profit institutions such as Calvary Hospital in New York and Youville Hospital in Cambridge, Mass., that cared for dying patients who were indigent. About the turn of the century, two hospices in London, St. Luke's Home (1893) and St. Joseph's (1905), developed the groundwork for the holistic care that has become the hallmark of the modern movement.

The hospice movement, as it is known today, is associated with the names of Dame Cicely Saunders and Elizabeth Kübler-Ross. Dame Cicely worked at St. Joseph's until 1967 when, with an initial gift of £500 from a dying patient, she established St. Christopher's Hospice in Sydenham, just outside London. Dr. Saunders stated: ''the name hospice, 'a resting place for travelers or pilgrims,' was chosen because this will be something between a hospital and a home, with the skills of one and the hospitality, warmth and the time of the other.'' In 1963 Saunders lectured at Yale University; the audience included Florence Wald, who was to become a pioneer in the movement in the United States. Wald was a founder of the freestanding Connecticut Hospice in Cambridge, Mass., the first such agency in the United States.

The ground had been prepared for the hospice concept by *The Meaning of Death* (1959), a series of essays edited by Henry Fiefel, and similar works, but it was the publication of Kübler-Ross's *On Death and Dying* (1970) that proved the real catalyst to the acceptance and development of hospice care in the U.S. Acute-care hospitals have as their primary purpose the cure of sick patients and are not equipped to attend the wide range of stresses that concern the terminally ill. Until recently, medical and nursing schools seldom dealt with the many aspects of death and dying; physicians and nurses, trained to save lives, were not instructed on how to address the varied needs of dying patients and their families.

The hospice movement centers on the freestanding, autonomous agency that provides comprehensive home-care services as well as inpatient care. Most hospices also provide hospital back up. The treatment parameters have been broadened to include patients with any prognosis in need of symptom management.

Whatever the organizational basis, hospice care is provided by a physician-directed team that invariably includes a nurse and several if not all the following: a social worker, a pastoral counselor, a dietician, and volunteers to assist the patient and family with personal care and the chores of daily living. Despite the recognized need for a more humane and sensitive approach to palliative care, the hospice movement in the U.S. has not become more widespread because of financial, organizational, legal, and psychological obstacles. Major strides have been made in funding, with 95 percent of the daily sum covered by health care, the remaining five percent being obtained by volunteer hours.

The National Hospice Organization (NHO), established in 1978, has as its primary functions the promotion of hospice care, research, consultation, education and the advocacy of patients' interests, as well as those of their family and care givers. Presently, there are more than 3,000 organizations providing hospice interests. The NHO headquarters is located in Arlington, Va.

Bibliography: J. E. CIMINO, ''Palliative Care: Overview of the Major Hospice Movement—Some Issues and Some Answers,'' *Journal of Long-Term Home Health Care* 17 (Fall 1998).

[M. CRONIN-MARTHALER]

HOSPITALITY

Almost all of the religious traditions of the world regard hospitality as a universal value and obligation. In ancient Greek mythology, the gods sometimes appeared on Earth disguised as humans who rewarded humans who offered them hospitality. For example, by offering hospitality to Zeus and Hermes in their human form, Baucis and Philemon were saved from the flood. In the Hindu tradition, hospitality is one of the five obligatory offerings required of all Hindus. In Buddhism, offering hospitality to monks is regarded as a virtuous deed with favorable karmic consequences. In the Qur'ān, hospitality toward strangers and the unfortunate is one of the principal ethical duties of all Muslims. Islamic hospitality is patterned upon the hospitality that the inhabitants of Medina showered upon the prophet Muḥammad when he was fleeing from his enemies in Mecca. These ideals are also found in Jewish and Christian understandings of hospitality.

In the OT the patriarchs are cited as models (Gn 19.2; 24.17–33; 43.24, etc.) particularly since the visit of Yahweh to Abraham (Gn 18.2–8) left a religious mark upon Jewish hospitality that was further emphasized by Dt 10.18–19. In the NT hospitality is connected with the Christian's earthly condition as a pilgrim (Heb 11.13). It is a charism from heaven (1 Pt 4.9), assimilates man to angels (3 Jn 8), and was recommended by Christ (Lk

11.5–8; 14.12–15) who set an example (Mk 6.41–45; 8.6–9; Lk 22.27; Jn 13.1–17) and gave Himself to His guests (Mk 14.22). Hospitality is a function of charity (Lk 10.33–37) whose practice is decisive for eternal life, when the Son of Man comes in His glory (Mt 25.35–42). In a NT exhortation the guest is identified with Christ Himself (Mt 10.42; 25.35–44), and this explains the frequency with which it is mentioned (Acts 10.6; 10.23; 18.1–2; 21.16; 28.23; Rom 16.23; 1 Cor 16.19; Gal 4.14; 3 Jn 5, 9–10). However its practice was not without limitation since Christ Himself drew up rules for the Apostles (Mt 10.9–14; Mk 6.10–11) and Disciples (Lk 10.5–11) in accepting hospitality; and St. Paul cautioned the Thessalonians against vagabonds and those living in idleness (2 Th 3.6–15) or consorting with excommunicated Christians (1 Cor 5.11–12), while St. John outlawed the company of heretics (2 Jn 10).

In the post-Apostolic times, the letter of CLEMENT I of Rome (1 Clem. 1.2) praised Corinthian hospitality, and ARISTIDES credited all Christians with similar virtues (*Apol.* 15.7). Missionaries, bishops and priests visiting a neighborhood community, deacons serving as messengers, and simple Christians working in another village were given hospitality (Didache 11.1–10; 13.1–4; Hermas, *Shepherd* 8.10.3; 9.27.2). IGNATIUS OF ANTIOCH insisted on the presence of Christ in guests (*Ad Eph.* 6.1) and lauded hospitality as gratitude to Christ. ORIGEN devoted two homilies to hospitality (*In Gen. hom.* 4–5) and St. CYPRIAN appointed a priest to take over the care of poor foreigners during his absence (*Epist.* 7), while St. JOHN CHRYSOSTOM boasted that the community of Antioch took care of 3,000 widows, foreigners, and patients daily (*Hom. in Mt.* 66.3). By the 4th century special buildings (*xenodochia*) were constructed for the lodging of pilgrims and strangers, as well as for foundlings, orphans, aged people, and the sick. Most impressive was the village near Caesarea, founded by St. BASIL for such indigents (*Epist.* 94). Hospitality was a special duty of the bishop (*Didasc.* 2.58.6; Synod of Elvira, c.25; of Arles, c.9; of Antioch, c.9) who delegated this task often to the deacons or the DIACONIA. Gradually, hospitality became the duty of the monks and was subsequently incorporated in St. Benedict's Rule (ch. 53).

Bibliography: D. W. RIDDLE, ''Early Christian Hospitality,'' *Journal of Biblical Literature* 57 (1938) 141–154. J. MARTY, ''Sur le devoir chreátien de l'hospitaliteá aux trois premiers siècles,'' *Revue d'histoire et de philosophie religieuses* 19 (1939) 288–295. D. GORCE, *Les Voyages, l'hospitalité . . . dans le monde chrétien des IVe et Ve siècles* (Paris 1925). E. VON SEVERUS, *Fremde beherbergen* (Hamburg 1947). M. DHAVAMONY, ''Hindu Hospitality and Tolerance: Hindu Attitude to Foreigners, Strangers and Immigrants,'' *Studia Missionalia* 39 (1990) 303–320. D. B. GOWLER, ''Hospitality and Characterization in Luke 11:37–54: A Socio-Narratological Approach,'' *Semeia* 64 (1994) 213–251. J. KOENIG,

New Testament Hospitality: Partnership with Strangers as Promise and Mission (Philadelphia 1985).

[J. VAN PAASSEN]

HOSPITALLERS AND HOSPITAL SISTERS

These are general terms used to describe the various nursing orders whose chief duty was serving medieval hospitals.

Origins. Although by 800 every important city of the Muslim world had its medical hospitals with trained physicians and substantial endowments, western Europe did not come near to matching that achievement until about 1200. A distinction was drawn between the *hospice,* a house for permanent occupation by the poor, the insane, and the incurable, and the *hospital,* a place where the sick were temporarily accommodated for medical treatment, though the same foundation could be both hospice and hospital, and guests, especially pilgrims, were often cared for in both. In many instances the hospital developed from the hospice, and a majority of hospitals came to be administered by a community vowed to the religious life. Some were staffed only by men, others only by women, others still—e.g., scores of *Maisons-Dieu* and *Hôtels-Dieu* (*see* HÔTEL-DIEU DE PARIS)—by both sexes. Even the patients might be bound by a form of religious profession. A monastery could itself be a hospital, as were certain English GILBERTINE houses. Conversely, some hospitals developed into monasteries, and even lost their eleemosynary character. St. Bartholomew's, London, was both a monastery and a hospital, each division having its own organization, seals, and income. Many a hospital, without being integrated into a particular order, observed the Rule of St. AUGUSTINE (the most popular), or the BENEDICTINE RULE, or that of the FRANCISCANS, or the Knights Hospitallers of St. John of Jerusalem (*see* KNIGHTS OF MALTA). Even so, the diocesan bishop was often called upon to compile hospital statutes. During the 13th and 14th centuries in Germany and Italy the control of many of these independent hospitals passed to the municipalities. In every century the solicitude of the popes for the hospitallers expressed itself in innumerable bulls granting them chapels, cemeteries, exemptions, and indulgences. Lay patronage had a significant share in the distribution of wardenships, hospital offices, and corodies. The master was sometimes a layman, more often a religious; generally he lived in a separate house, and he might also be a physician. The professed brothers and sisters, who often paid entry fees, might live in a corody house and carry out only honorary duties; but for the most part they were nurses of the sick, and in the larger hospi-

Original of the "Agreement whereby the Knights Hospitallers of St. John of Jerusalem surrender to Richard of Ilchester, Bishop of Winchester, the charge and administration of the hospital of St. Cross without the walls of Winchester," dated at Dover, April 10, 1185. Attached at bottom are the seals of Roger des Moulins, Master of the Hospitallers, Bishop Richard, and Garnier de Nablus, prior of the order in England.

tals they were assisted in worship and work by clerks in minor orders and lay servants.

The Nursing Orders. The 11th and 12th centuries were an age of momentous increase in the number of hospitals. In medieval England, for instance, 980 hospitals have been identified, their number reaching its maximum in the 13th century, and diminishing after 1350. In every generation, old hospitals, usually un-endowed, disappeared and new ones were founded. The pattern was similar in all Catholic countries, and by the 14th century such great cities as Rome and Florence had 30 hospitals each. This hospital expansion must be associated with the development of orders specifically devoted to nursing, of which the history of the ANTONINES may be taken as characteristic. About 1100, a nobleman, Gaston de Dauphiné, founded the hospital of SAINT-ANTOINE-DE-VIENNOIS as a dependency of the monastery of the same name, establishing an almonry house with a separate hospital for poor persons suffering from the diseases (including erysipelas and ergotism) known collectively as "St. Anthony's Fire." During the 12th and 13th centuries Antonine hospitals were founded in most of the larger towns of France, Italy, Spain, and Germany and at Constantinople and Acre. The chief officers of the order and the heads of its houses were priests, though the majority of the members in the early years were lay brothers and lay sisters. In 1231 statutes were drawn up under papal supervision, and the order was freed from subjection to the Benedictines and put under the government of an elective master and an annual chapter-general of all the commanders. In 1247 the order adopted the Rule of St. Augustine, and in 1301 Pope BONIFACE VIII converted it to an order of Augustinian Canons and exempted it from episcopal jurisdiction. The Antonines wore a black habit with the blue St. Anthony's cross (the *tau*). Included among their patients were the sick of the papal household.

Mention should be made also of the work of the Order of the HOLY SPIRIT, founded at Montpellier in 1145, and confirmed by Pope INNOCENT III in 1198. By 1250 its houses were to be found in every important town in western Europe. The Order of St. William of the Desert (*see* SAINT-GUILHEM-DU-DÉSERT, ABBEY OF), the Knights of Malta, the BETHLEHEMITES, and the hospital sisters of the Order of St. Catherine all made significant contributions to the development of the movement. The influence of the MENDICANT orders is illustrated by the work of St. ELIZABETH OF HUNGARY, Landgravine of Thuringia, who, after founding a hospital with 28 beds near Eisenach in 1226, and attending 900 poor daily, became a Franciscan tertiary in 1228 and built a second hospital for the sick at Marburg; or by the hospital of POOR CLARES that her great-niece St. ELIZABETH OF PORTUGAL established at Coimbra.

From early in the 13th century the BEGUINES, an association of women in the Low Countries started by the priest Lambert le Bègue (d. 1177), frequently supported themselves by nursing the sick, especially at Liège, Malines, Brussels, Louvain, and Bruges. The Beguines were devoted to a life of religion and sometimes organized into semiconventual communities and later even into houses of Dominican, Franciscan, or Augustinian tertiaries. The similar male communities of Beghards, first appearing at Louvain in 1220, also nursed the sick, but hospital nursing was never the major preoccupation of the Beguines and Beghards. In contrast, the ALEXIAN BROTHERS, whose patron was St. Alexius of Edessa, arose in Malines in the early 15th century under the layman Tobias to succor plague victims and bury those who died (hence their other name of Cellites, from *cella,* a grave). The Alexians spread through Flanders, Brabant, and Germany; they are still active in hospital work today.

The Knights of St. John of Jerusalem (more widely known as the Knights of Malta) were founded not later than 1108 to nurse the sick and tend pilgrims in the Holy Land. They soon became a MILITARY ORDER, but they always laid special emphasis on medical work, founding and managing hundreds of hospitals and hospices in Catholic Europe and the Levant. Unlike their rivals, the TEMPLARS, they affiliated hospitaller sisters to their order, many of them with the duty of ministering to patients (chiefly women). Such were the Johannines St. Toscana at Verona (d. 1338) and St. Ubaldesca at Pisa (d. 1206). The order's principal hospital, at Jerusalem from 1108 to 1187, was governed under the rules drawn up by the Grand Masters Raymond du Puy (d. *c.* 1160) and Roger des Moulins (d. 1187) and accommodated 2,000 patients. In their later Convent (or headquarters) of Rhodes (1306–1523), the Knights of St. John sheltered pilgrims in the Hospice of St. Catherine and also built a commodious infirmary exclusively for the sick and wounded, which was administered by their *Hospitalarius* (always a French knight), two *prud'hommes,* and a lay staff of physicians (some of them Jews), surgeons, apothecaries, and male nurses. The infirmary in Malta, where the Convent was located from 1530 to 1798, was completed in 1578; it had a great ward 503 feet long, 35 feet wide, and 30 feet high, one of Europe's largest interiors, free from draughts and sun-glare, and equipped with the unusual luxury of 300 *single* beds. After Malta was lost, the order eventually reestablished its headquarters in Rome (1834), and its medical role has since then vastly expanded.

No medieval hospitallers had greater influence on medical progress than those who served leper-houses. In the ancient world there had been no consistent understanding of the spread of infection by contact. In the Middle Ages the group of diseases today termed leprosy was treated by regarding it as contagious (although not all such medieval diseases were properly leprosy) and sternly excluding it by confining all known lepers to leper-houses. Leprosy appeared in Catholic Europe about 500, reached its apogee in the 13th century, was in decline by 1350, and was extremely rare by 1500. The success of isolation (helped by leprosy's low infectivity) led to the realization that other diseases were infectious: e.g., erysipelas, scabies, conjunctivitis, phthisis, fevers with rashes, and bubonic plague; and medieval governments began to enforce rigorous measures against the spread of epidemics. The leper-house was a group of individual houses clustered around a chapel, standing well out of town in the open country, sometimes close to a healing spring, e.g., the famous wells at a house near Nantwich, England. The master would be a priest presiding over a community of nursing brothers and sisters, often 13 in number, who might well be lepers themselves, and who would include a *capellanus* and a clerk to collect rent and alms. Usually their patients were also regarded as brothers and sisters of the house. By the 13th century the comprehensive attack on leprosy had produced 2,000 leper-houses in France alone, and hundreds in every other country of Europe. Most houses were autonomous, not belonging to any congregation. A great house such as Saint-Lazare at Paris was dependent on the local bishop, though after 1200 many municipalities took over control of their lazar-houses. The HOSPITALLERS OF ST. LAZARUS, founded to treat leprosy in 12th-century Jerusalem, acquired many houses and endowments in the West, but their work is only part of a story that has been deemed "a great social and hygienic movement."

Hospital Facilities Hospitals other than leper-houses were usually located at a town, preferably on a site outside the walls to counter the spread of disease (e.g., S. Spirito, Florence), and if possible on a river bank (e.g., St. Francis, Prague). The early form was that of a church, with the aisled hall opening at the east end into a chapel. Later there was developed a plan resembling that of a monastery or college. King HENRY II of England built the hospital of Saint-Jean at Angers with three wings, and in many hospitals the hall ranged around three or four sides of a quadrangle. It must be emphasized, however, that most medieval hospitals had fewer than 30 beds, although every country had its great infirmaries. Margaret of Burgundy built one at Tonnerre with a hall 260 feet long, 60 feet wide; the main ward of S. Spirito, Rome, was 409 feet long, 40 feet wide, and that of the Holy Ghost, Lübeck, 300 feet long with 140 beds in four rows of cubicles. The lavishly staffed St. Leonard's, York, could accommodate 224 sick and poor. At Milan between 1445 and 1500 the Visconti and the SFORZA built the finest hospital of the Middle Ages. Toward the end of the period the great new foundations, such as Santa Cruz, Toledo (1504–14), were often given a cruciform plan, with four wards meeting at a central altar. An alternative, late-medieval design was the row of almshouses, each with its own fireplace and offices. The hospital hall or ward had a tiled floor and large windows, the lower parts of which could be opened, and it was sometimes divided into private cubicles, each patient being expected, if well enough, to join in evening prayers at his cubicle door.

Medical Knowledge of the Hospitallers. By 1200 the medieval hospitaller worked under physicians trained at Salerno, Montpellier, and other universities (compared with which the monastic orders contributed little to the progress of medical science). These men, though their pathology was still that of the four humors and their knowledge of drugs empirical, could refer to the *consilia* of such writers as Taddeo Alderotti (d. 1295) with their careful and perceptive descriptions of symptoms and treatments. There was, for example, a rich variety of mercurial recipes for the nurse to apply against a large group

of chronic skin infections, some probably syphilitic. Guglielmo di Saliceto (d. 1276) had challenged the Arab view that pus-formation was good for wounds and had recommended dressings to heal "by first intention," though his new principle was to be painfully slow in acceptance; he had also pointed to the connection between dropsy and nephritis, prescribing draughts of oxymel and barley water. The nurse needed an understanding of the use of traction in the treatment of fractures; of uroscopy; of the use of the instep of the naked foot as a clinical thermometer; and of the anesthetic sponge, impregnated with opium and mandragora, and soused in hot water, to produce fumes for the patient to inhale. The miniatures that illuminate some of the Salernitan codices show the wide range and enterprising techniques of medieval surgery. The hospitaller attended on operations for piles, fistula, stricture, nasal polyps, rupture, and cataract, as well as on venesection, cupping, and trephining. Thousands of foundation charters, statutes, and ordinances testify to the well-regulated character of medieval nursing: the prohibition on leaving the sick unattended, the confinement of the very sick to private wards (some Italian hospitals having separate wards— *pazzerie*—for the delirious), and the emphasis on the care of women in childbirth and for 3 weeks thereafter as a major duty. Above all, in hospitals following a rule, the canonical hours had to be strictly observed, and even patients were often enjoined, under vows, to perform their religious exercises.

See Also: HOSPITALS, HISTORY OF, 1.

Bibliography: P. HÉLYOT, *Histoire des ordres monastiques,* 8 v. (Paris 1714–19). M. A. NUTTING and L. L. DOCK, *A History of Nursing,* 4 v. (New York 1907–12). Knowles-Hadcock. W. G. WYLIE, *Hospitals: Their History, Organization, and Construction* (New York 1877). R. M. CLAY, *The Mediaeval Hospitals of England* (London 1909). R. GRAHAM, "The Order of St. Antoine de Viennois and Its English Commandery, St. Anthony's, Threadneedle Street," *Archaeological Journal* NS 34 (1927) 341–406. H. PIRENNE, *Histoire de Belgique,* v.1 (Brussels 1903) 337–340, for Beguines and Beghards. P. FERRAND, *Précis historique des Ordres de Saint-Lazare et de Saint-Maurice* (Lyons 1860). C. A. MERCIER, *Leper Houses and Mediaeval Hospitals* (London 1915). C. J. SINGER and E. A. UNDERWOOD, *A Short History of Medicine* (2d ed. New York 1962). A. CASTIGLIONI, *A History of Medicine,* ed. and tr. E. B. KRUMBHAAR (2d ed. New York 1947). F. H. GARRISON, *Introduction to the History of Medicine* (4th ed. Philadelphia 1929). L. THORNDIKE, *A History of Magic and Experimental Science,* 8 v. (New York 1923–58). v.1 and 2. L. C. MACKINNEY, *Early Medieval Medicine, with Special Reference to Paris and Chartres* (Baltimore 1937); *Medical Illustrations in Medieval Manuscripts* (Berkeley 1965). D. RIESMAN, *The Story of Medicine in the Middle Ages* (New York 1935). P. DIEPGEN, *Geschichte der Medizin,* 2 v. (Berlin 1949–55). K. SUDHOFF, ed., *Studien zur Geschichte der Medizin,* 23 v. (Leipzig 1907–37); *Beiträge zur Geschichte der Chirurgie im Mittelalter,* 2 v. (Leipzig 1914–18); *Aus der Frühgeschichte der syphilis* (Leipzig 1912). P. GIACOSA, ed., *Magistri Salernitani nondum editi* (Turin 1901), 1 v. and atlas. E. E. HUME, *Medical Work *of the Knights Hospitallers of St. John of Jerusalem* (Baltimore 1940).

[L. BUTLER]

HOSPITALLERS OF ST. JOHN OF GOD

(Official Catholic Directory #0670) A nursing order of brothers founded in Spain in 1537 by St. JOHN OF GOD, a Portuguese shepherd who became an apostle of charity among the sick and needy of Granada. Pius V, in 1572, 22 years after the founder's death, recognized the Hospitaller Order of St. John of God (OH), which had adopted the Rule of St. Augustine and a monastic habit of robe, cincture, scapular, and cowl. In addition to solemn vows of poverty, chastity, and obedience, the brothers take a vow of hospitality by which they bind themselves to work for the sick. The spirit of the order is summed up in its motto "Caritas," which denotes a striving after the love of God through a love of the sick, in each of whom the brothers see the person of Christ.

The order spread rapidly throughout Europe where some of its hospitals acquired renown because of the brothers' medical and surgical skill. Still more widespread was the rural hospital where the brother-infirmarian paid daily domiciliary visits to the sick, the brother-pharmacist grew herbs to treat diseases, and the brother-chaplain (some of the members become priests) cared for the spiritual needs of religious, patients, and peasants. In the 17th century nearly 70 such hospitals were established in South America, where by the example of their charity the brothers played a part in the conversion of the native Americans. In the 18th century the order had 300 hospitals in Europe and South America, staffed by 2,700 brothers.

The French Revolution (1789) and its aftermath proved calamitous to the order; the brothers were expelled from 40 hospitals. With the return of religious tolerance, however, the brothers opened new hospitals. Their history in the first half of the 20th century was marked by a wider diffusion throughout the world. The brothers arrived in the U.S. in 1941. The generalate is in Rome. The U.S. provincialate is in Los Angeles, CA.

Bibliography: N. MCMAHON, *The Story of the Hospitallers of St. John of God* (Westminster, Md. 1959).

[N. MCMAHON/EDS.]

HOSPITALLERS OF ST. JOHN OF GOD, MARTYRS OF THE, BB.

Also known as Blessed Braulio María Corres, Federico Rubio, and companions; d. 1936–37, Spain; beatified at Rome by John Paul II, Oct. 25, 1992.

The 71 Hospitallers of St. John of God assumed under this title died at various times and places during the infamous persecution of the Church during the Spanish Civil War. At the outbreak of violence, the prior general, Father Narcissus Durchschein, urged the brothers to continue their sacred duty to the sick, unless the civil authorities took over the work or "until such time as a *force majeure* obliges them to leave" (letter dated April 4, 1936). The martyrs were all brothers serving in different capacities, ranging in age from 18 to 75 years old, and were Spaniards except seven young Colombians.

Apostolic School of Talavera de la Reina. (d. July 25,1936, Toledo). The first four martyrs ran the order's new Juniorate (opened 1935) in Talavera near Toledo:

Federico Rubio Alvarez, baptized Carlos, brother and priest; b. 1862, Benavides, Léon.

Jerónimo Ochoa Urdangarín, brother; b. 1904, Goñi, Navarre.

Juan de la Cruz Delgado Pastor, baptized Eloy, brother; b. Dec. 10, 1914, Puebla de Alcocer, Badajoz.

Primo Martínez de S Vicente Castillo, superior; b. 1869, San Román de Campezo, Alaya.

At the outbreak of civil unrest, they sent their 22 youngest charges home. The brothers' house was searched twice for weapons (July 23 and 25, 1936). Following the second raid the brothers were arrested, interrogated, and taken to a site near the *Virgen del Prado,* where they were shot. All four were buried in a common grave in Talavera's cemetery, but reinterred in separate tombs (November 1936). On Nov. 22, 1946, their bodies were translated to Ciempozuelos (Madrid), where they were buried in the Pantheon Chapel (Jan. 14, 1937).

San Juan de Dios Sanitarium at Calafell. (d. July 30, 1936, Tarragona). About the same time as the house of the Hospitallers was searched in Toledo, the Communist authorities began harassing the brothers in Tarragona (July 23–29, 1936). On July 25, the militia took charge of the institute. They stripped the brothers of their habits and removed any sign of religion. The brothers continued their work for the next several days, while increasing the time spent in prayer. The brothers were provided documentation to travel to France, but warned that their safety could not be guaranteed. Nevertheless, 19 of the 27 Hospitallers left for Barcelona the morning of July 30. They were picked up by the militia en route. The truck stopped within the border of the Calafell District and four youths were removed from the group. A firing squad of 19 militiamen shot the others:

Antonio Llauradó Parisi, novice; b. June 13, 1920, Reus, Tarragona.

Antonio Sanchiz Silvestre, novice; b. Dec. 6, 1910, Villamarchante, Valencia.

Benito José Labre Mañoso González, baptized Arsenio, brother; July 19, 1879, Lomoviejo near Valladolid.

Braulio María Corres Díaz de Cerio, baptized Pablo, brother and priest; b. 1897, Torralba de Rio, Navarre.

Constancio Roca Huguet, baptized Saturnino, brother; b. Aug. 12, 1895, Sant Sadurni d'Anoia near Barcelona.

Domingo Pitarch Gurrea, novice; b. Feb. 12, 1909, Villareal, Castellón.

Enrique Beltrán Llorca, novice; b. Nov. 14, 1899, Villareal, Castellón.

Eusebio Forcades Ferraté, baptized Antonio, brother; b. September 28, Reus, Tarragona.

Ignacio Tejero Molina, novice; b. July 31, 1916, Monzalbarba near Zaragoza (shot the day before his twentieth birthday).

Julián Carrasquer Fos, baptized Miguel, superior; b. 1881, Sueca, Valencia.

Manuel Jiménez Salado, brother; b. Oct. 29, 1907, Jerez de la Frontera near Cadiz.

Manuel López Orbara, novice; b. Feb. 5, 1913, Puente de la Reina, Navarre.

Rafael Flamarique Salinas, novice; b. Oct. 24, 1903, Mendívil, Navarre.

Tomás Urdanoz Aldaz, novice; b. March 7, 1903, Echarri, Navarre.

Vicente de Paúl Canelles Vives, brother; b. June 25, 1894, Onda, Castellón.

Colombian Martyrs. (d. Aug. 9, 1936, Barcelona). These seven Colombians became the first of their homeland to be beatified. They were sent from the Colombian mission (opened 1920) to the San José Psychiatric Institute in Ciempozuelos (near Madrid) for training. When the Spanish brothers of the community were taken into custody on August 7, Br. Guillermo Llop arranged with the Colombian ambassador, Dr. Uribe Echeverry, for their safe passage and repatriation and with the Claretian Sisters for money to cover travel expenses. The seven

young brothers were taken off the train from Madrid to Barcelona, incarcerated overnight, and kept incommunicado with the embassy. Embassy officials found their bodies at the hospital mortuary the following morning, together with more than 100 others killed that day in Barcelona. The first Colombian *beati* are:

Arturo Ayala Niño, baptized Luis, brother; b. April 7, 1909, Paipa, Boyacá, Colombia. Brother Arturo joined the Hospitallers (1928) and joined the community at Ciempozuelos, Spain, in 1930.

Esteban Maya Gutiérrez, baptized Gabriel, brother; b. March 19, 1907, Pácora Calda, Antioquia, Colombia. In 1932 he joined the order, where he was known for his humility, intelligence, and obedience.

Eugenio Ramírez Salazar, baptized Alfonso Antonio, brother; b. Sept. 2, 1913, La Ceja, Antioquia, Colombia. He entered the order (1932), professed his vows (1935), then was transferred to Spain.

Gaspar Páez Perdomo, baptized Luis Modesto, brother; b. June 15, 1913, La Unión, Huila, Colombia. Shortly after joining the Hospitallers (1933) and professing his solemn vows, he was sent to Spain to finish his religious and professional formation.

Juan Bautista Velázquez Peláez, baptized Juan José, brother; b. July 9, 1909, Antioquía, Colombia. He was a teacher prior to joining (1932) the Hospitallers, who characterized him as joyful and pious. After traveling to Spain (1934), he lived with the communities at Córdoba, Granada, and Ciempozuelos.

Melquíades Ramírez Zuloaga, baptized Ramón, brother; b. Feb. 13, 1909, Sonsón, Antioquia, Colombia. Ramón entered the order at age 21. In April 1935 he traveled to Spain to complete his professional and religious formation at the community of Ciempozuelos, where he was known for his simplicity and patience.

Rubén de Jesús López Aguilar, brother; b. April 12, 1908, Concepción, Antioquia, Colombia. He was known for his spirit of prayer and obedience. During the armed conflict between Colombia and Peru (1933), he volunteered to work in the hospital at Pasto in the militarized zone. In 1936 he joined the community at Cimpozuelos, Spain.

Institute San José de Carabanchel Alto. (d. Sept. 1, 1936, Madrid). The isolated hospital for epileptics was relatively untouched by the violence of early July. On July 29, 1936, militia searched the institute for three hours and forbade the brothers to engage in any further "worship or religious expression." Undeterred, the brothers continued to pray together in secret for the next month. The mayor of Carbanchel arrived (August 29) with an armed escort, confiscated administrative records and money, and appropriated the hospital. Three days later (September 1) the brothers were herded into vehicles and taken to the ''Charco Cabrera,'' where they were executed for being the servants of God. The mortal remains of the following martyrs were solemnly translated, June 18, 1942, to the church crypt in the Institute of San José:

Benjamín Cobos Celada, baptized Alejandro, brother; b. July 9, 1887, Palencia.

Canuto Franco Gómez, baptized José, brother; b. Dec. 23, 1871, Aljucer, Murcia.

Carmelo Gil Arano, baptized Isidro, brother; b. May 15, 1879, Tudela, Navarre.

Cecilio López López, baptized Enrique, brother; b. June 25, 1901, Fondón, Almeria.

Cesáreo Niño Pérez, baptized Maríano, brother; b. Sept. 15, 1878, Torregutiérrez near Segovia.

Cosme Brun Arará, baptized Simon, brother; b. Nov. 12, 1894, Santa Coloma de Farners, Girona.

Cristino Roca Huguet, baptized Miguel, priest, director of the juniorate; b. June 6, 1899, Mollins de Rei, Barcelona.

Dositeo Rubio Alonso, baptized Guillermo, brother; b. Feb. 10, 1869, Madrigalejo near Burgos.

Eutimio Aramendía García, baptized Nicolás, assistant superior; b. Dec. 23, 1878, Oteiza de la Solanna, Navarre.

Faustino Villanueva Igual, baptized Antonio, brother; b. Jan. 23, 1913, Sarrión, Teruel.

Proceso Ruiz Cascales, baptized Joaquín, superior; b. Oct. 4, 1887, Beniel, Murcia.

Rufino Lasheras Aizcorbe, baptized Crescencio, brother; b. June 15, 1900, Arandigoyen, Navarre.

Martyrs at Barcelona. (d. 1936). The Hospitallers of St. John of God ran two institutions in Barcelona. All but one of the 52 brothers who staffed the Psychiatric Hospital of Our Lady of Monserrat of San Baudilio de Llobregat made it safely to Marseilles, France, after a period of physical and psychological harm.

Protasio Cubells Minguell (baptized Antonio, provincial councillor and secretary; b. 1880, Coll de Nargó near Lleida; d. Dec. 14, 1936) was arrested while giving music lessons to two children. His body was found in the street the next day.

The others martyred in Barcelona were attached to the Children's Hospital, whose institute was the resi-

dence of the Brother Provincial of Aragon. The 22 brothers were subjected to various threats and indignities, including the confiscation of the hospital and all its goods, July 20–26. The brothers scattered to find refuge in various parts of the city, but five were killed:

Acisclo Piña Piazuelo, baptized Joaquín, brother; b. 1878, Caspe, Zaragoza; d. Nov. 10, 1936. He was arrested in the home of his superior's relative on November 5 and killed with 40 other people after suffering in St. Elia Prison.

Francisco Javier Ponsa Casallach, brother; b. 1916, Moiá near Barcelona; d. Sept. 28, 1936. He was arrested at his family's country home (September 27), taken to San Feliu de Codinas, Barcelona, by truck, and shot.

Juan Antonio Burró Más, brother; b. June 28, 1914, Barcelona; d. Nov. 5, 1936. Although attached to the institute at Barcelona, Juan Antonio was completing his military service at the time of the revolution. He was betrayed as a brother and killed.

Juan Bautista Egozcuezábal Aldaz, brother; b. March 13, 1882, Nuin, Navarre; d. July 29, 1936. Juan Bautista was captured near Esplugas de Llobregat and shot. He died in the hospital the following day.

Pedro de Alcántara Villanueva Larráyoz, baptized Lorenzo, brother; b. 1881, Navarre; d. Sept. 11, 1936. He was arrested (September 4) with the family who gave him refuge.

Hospital of San Rafael. (d. Madrid). The 35-member community at San Rafael's were harassed from the middle of July 1936. The situation was made more difficult because the hospital depended on charity personally collected by the brothers, who could no longer walk safely through the streets. The hospital was confiscated by the government August 20 and the brothers force to leave by October 24. Although there were members of the community who were missing after 1939, only three were known to have been martyred:

Gonzalo Gonzalo Gonzalo, brother; b. Feb. 24, 1909, Conquezuela, Soria; d. Aug. 4, 1936. He was killed while dressed as a peasant to collect alms to support the hospital and institute.

Jacinto Hoyuelos Gonzalo, brother; b. Sept. 11, 1914, Matarrepudio near Santander; d. Sept. 19, 1936.

Nicéforo Salvador del Río, brother; b. Feb. 9, 1913, Villamorco near Palencia; d. Nov. 30, 1936.

Psychiatric Hospital of San José, Ciempozuelos. (Madrid). As in the other hospitals, the government took over the hospital (July 31, 1936) at Ciempozuelos (about 18 miles from Madrid), posted militiamen around the perimeter, removed all religious symbols, and suppressed worship. The brothers continued to nurse the sick and to gather early in the morning for worship. On August 7 each brother was searched, imprisoned, and told he would die the following day. Brother Guillermo Llop asked the chief of general security to spare the brothers. The chief responded by having all 53 religious taken to an underground prison for the night and transferred on August 9 to San Antonio Prison in the former Scolopian College on the Calle Hortaleza. They were temporarily separated on November 28 when 15 were assassinated; another six died on November 30, and the last, on February 11.

Angel Sastre Corporales, novice; b. Aug. 16, 1916, Vallaralbo del Vino near Zamora; d. Nov. 28, 1936.

Antonio Martínez Gil-Leonis, novice; b. Nov. 2, 1916, Montellano near Seville; d. Nov. 30, 1936.

Arturo Donoso Murillo, brother; b. March 31, 1917, Puebla de Alcocer near Badajoz; d. Nov. 30, 1936.

Clemente Díez Sahagún, brother; b. Nov. 23, 1861, Fuentes de Nava, Palencia; d. Nov. 28, 1936.

Diego de Cádiz García Molina, baptized Santiago, provincial secretary; b. Dec. 14, 1892, Moral de Calatrava near Ciudad Real; d. Nov. 30, 1936.

Eduardo Bautista Jiménez, brother; b. Jan. 5, 1885, La Gineta, Albacete; d. Nov. 28, 1936.

Flavio Argüeso González, baptized Atilano, brother; b. 1877, Mazuecos, Palencia; d. Dec. 12, 1936.

Francisco Arias Martín, priest, novice; b. April 26, 1884, Granada; d. Aug. 18, 1936.

Guillermo Llop Gayá, baptized Vicente, brother, superior; b. Nov. 10, 1880, Villareal, Castellón; d. Nov. 28, 1936. Brother Guillermo had a distinguished career among the Hospitallers. He entered the order in 1898. From 1912 to 1922 he served as novice master for the Roman province, where he tended the wounded during World War I, and later he became prior of the house at Frascati. He helped reinvigorate the order in Chile (1922–28). He returned to Spain in 1928 to serve as prior of community running the Psychiatric Hospital in Ciempozuelos near Madrid.

Hilario Delgado Vilchez, baptized Antonio, brother; b. April 18, 1918, Cañar near Granada; d. Nov. 28, 1936.

Isidoro Martínez Izquierdo, novice; b. April 9, 1918, Madrid; d. Nov. 28, 1936.

Jesús Gesta de Piquer, brother; b. Jan. 19, 1915, Madrid; d. Nov. 30, 1936.

José Mora Velasco, priest, postulant; b. Aug. 18, 1886, Córdoba; d. Nov. 28, 1936.

José Ruiz Cuesta, postulant; b. Nov. 6, 1907, Dílar near Granada; d. Nov. 28, 1936.

Juan Alcalde Alcalde, novice; b. Oct. 20, 1911, Zuzones near Burgos; d. Nov. 28, 1936.

Juan Jesús Adradas Gonzalo, baptized Maríano, priest and brother; b. Aug. 15, 1978, Conquezuela, Soria; d. Nov. 28, 1936.

Julián Plazaola Artola, brother; b. Sept. 12, 1915, San Sebastián, Guipúzcoa; d. Nov. 28, 1936.

Lázaro Mújica Goiburu, baptized Juan María, brother; b. April 5, 1867, Ideazábal, Guipúzcoa; d. Nov. 28, 1936.

Martiniano Meléndez Sánchez, baptized Antonio, brother; b. Jan. 15, 1878, Malaga, Costa del Sol; d. Nov. 28, 1936.

Miguel Rueda Mejías, baptized Francisco, brother; b. Jan. 19, 1902, Motril near Granada; d. Nov. 30, 1936.

Pedro de Alcántara Bernalte Calzado, novice; b. Aug. 4, 1910, Moral de Calatrava near Ciudad Real; d. Nov. 28, 1936.

Pedro María Alcalde Negredo, brother; b. Nov. 26, 1878, Ledesma near Soria; d. Nov. 28, 1936.

Román Touceda Fernández, baptized Rafael, assistant superior; b. Jan. 22, 1904, Madrid; d. Nov. 30, 1936.

Tobías Borrás Román, baptized Francisco, brother; b. April 14, 1861, San Jorge, Castellón; d. Feb. 11, 1937.

Feast: July 30 (Hospitallers).

Bibliography: V. CÁRCEL ORTÍ, *Martires españoles del siglo XX* (Madrid 1995). F. GÓMEZ CATÓN, *La Iglesia de los mártires en la provincia eclesiástica tarraconense* (Barcelona 1989). J. PÉREZ DE URBEL, *Catholic Martyrs of the Spanish Civil War*, tr. M. F. INGRAMS (Kansas City, Mo. 1993). *Acta Apostolicae Sedis*, no. 21 (1992) 1064.

[K. I. RABENSTEIN]

HOSPITALLERS OF ST. LAZARUS OF JERUSALEM

An order of knights and nurses following the Rule of St. AUGUSTINE, the Hospitallers of St. Lazarus of Jerusalem was founded *c.* 1120 in Jerusalem. Its functions were to operate hospitals, especially hospitals for lepers; to spread the faith; and to assist and protect pilgrims to the Holy Land. During the first century of its existence the order operated principally in the Holy Land. Following the drastic contraction of the Latin CRUSADER states there in the 13th century, the order transferred its activities to Europe (1253) and established houses in France, Italy, England, Scotland, Hungary, Germany, and Switzerland. During the 14th and 15th centuries the order fell into decay and in 1490 INNOCENT VIII decreed that it be united with the Order of the Hospitallers of St. John of Jerusalem (*see* KNIGHTS OF MALTA). The French knights of the Lazarite Order, however, opposed this union vigorously, and the Lazarites lived on as an independent order in France, subject to their own grand master at Boigny, near Orléans. Bowing to this opposition, LEO X restored the Lazarites as an independent order early in the 16th century. In 1572, under the Grand Master Gianetto Castiglione, a further attempt was made to suppress the Lazarites when GREGORY XIII ordered their union with the Order of St. Maurice and installed Duke Emmanuel Philibert of Savoy as grand master of the united orders. Once again the French Lazarites resisted and refused to accept the union. In 1608 King HENRY IV united the French Lazarites with the Knights of Our Lady of Mount Carmel. Both the French and Italian branches of the order were suppressed during the French Revolution, and the hospitals that they operated disappeared. The Hospitallers of St. Lazarus were revived in Italy in 1814 by Victor Emmanuel I and in France in 1830. The order survives now as a purely honorific organization.

See Also: HOSPITALLERS AND HOSPITAL SISTERS; HOSPITALS, HISTORY OF.

Bibliography: Sources. A. DE MARSY, "Fragments d'un cartulaire de l'ordre de S. Lazare en Terre Sainte," *Archives de l'orient latin* 2 (1884) 121–157. Literature. P. BERTRAND, *Histoire des chevaliers–hospitaliers de Saint–Lazare* (Paris 1932). M. HEIM-BUCHER, *Die Orden und Kongregationen der katholischen Kirche,* 2 v. (3d ed. Paderborn 1932–34) 1:612–613. E. NASALLI-ROCCA, "Gli ospedali italiani di S. Lazzaro o dei lebbrosi," *Zeitschrift der Savigny–Stiftung für Rechtsgeschichte, Kanonistische Abteilung* 27 (1938) 262–298. R. JANIN, *Lexikon für Theologie und Kirche*[2], ed. J. HOFER and K. RAHNER, 10 v. (2d, new ed. Freiburg 1957–65) 5:494.

[J. A. BRUNDAGE]

HOSPITALS, HISTORY OF

Hospital history in the Christian era is here discussed under three headings: (1) the Christian hospital to 1500; (2) the hospital from 1500 to the twentieth century; (3) the Catholic hospital in the twentieth century.

1. THE CHRISTIAN HOSPITAL TO 1500

The history of hospitals has been shaped by principles in accord with the teachings of Christ and the commandment of fraternal charity. The origin of the institutions of the early and late Middle Ages that we now call hospitals, was the hospice. The Christian virtue of hospitality (*hospitalitas*) had broad significance, its application extending to embrace various forms of assistance, both individual and collective, and to meet a diversity of needs. Hospices sheltered travelers, gave help to the poor, the sick, the aged, orphans, abandoned children, and widows.

Diaconia. The earliest forms of Christian "hospital" assistance, organized from the 2d to the 5th centuries around active ecclesiastical centers, had their origin and development in the diaconate. The deacon, collaborating with the presbyter and bishop, had the explicit duty of carrying out the functions of *hospitalitas*. His duty was to help needy brethren in the name of the Christian community. Around the *diaconia* a variety of activities, primarily eleemosynary in character, gradually developed into centers of operation, known variously as *xenodochia* (inns for travelers), *nosocomia* (infirmaries), *brephotrophia* (foundling homes), *orphanotrophia* (orphanages), *gerocomia* (homes for the aged).

Although permanent charitable institutions were not established until later, the Church early concerned herself with collective assistance as such, depending on individuals to perform this task. Since the functions of deacons included, among others, the providing of material aid to all in need (the indigent, the homeless, widows, orphans, etc.), they could not exclude the care of the sick grouped in institutions. Historians of the *diaconia* agree in attributing a medical function to deacons; in some instances their duties were those of hospital workers or nurses in the strict sense. The *diaconia* existed in every city, even in the smaller ones, and very often their names signified that they were hospitals. The *diaconiae* of Rome in the late Empire were situated usually in municipal buildings located on spacious and convenient sites in the busiest sections of the city.

Byzantine and Western Xenodochia and Hospitals. A specific form of assistance, developing directly from the ancient concept of hospitality, provided for individuals who were obliged to make long journeys for personal or commercial reasons, or in fulfillment of a public responsibility. These works of Christian fraternal charity were intended primarily to help pilgrims on long and dangerous journeys of a religious character to the great sanctuaries of the faith, such as Compostella, Rome, and Jerusalem (*see* PILGRIMAGES).

The *xenodochium* (from ξένος, stranger) was the first hospital institution attached to the *diaconia*. It was open to all in need of shelter, and was originally a hospice for travelers and pilgrims from distant places and in financial need. However, in most cases a change of emphasis gradually took place. Assistance to the sick took precedence over the provision of shelter that was limited by regula-

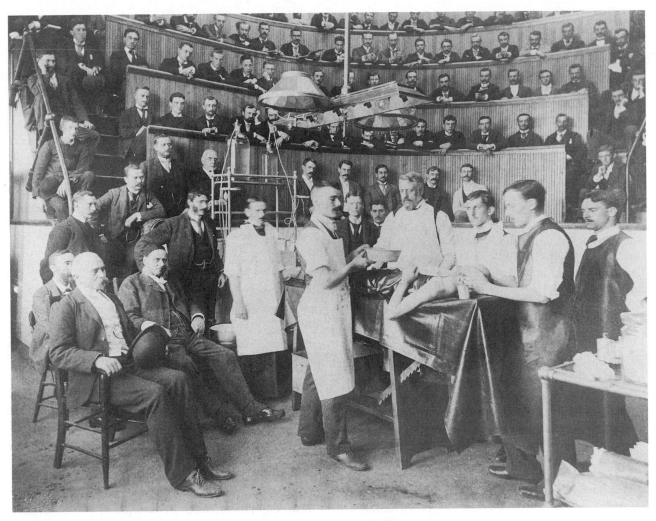

Early operative surgical procedure, Bellevue Medical Center, New York. (©Bettmann/CORBIS)

tion to three days. The name increasingly signified shelter for the sick and in time the *xenodochium* became synonymous with *hospitale.* Up to the 9th century in the West *xenodochium* was used in its Byzantine sense. The Latin word, *hospitale,* however, was gradually preferred, causing *xenodochium* to disappear by the 12th century.

Public assistance to the sick, already favored by the Church at the time of the institution of the diaconate, was subsequently encouraged by the directives of Emperor CONSTANTINE I, who arranged for the systematic erection of hospitals. Reflecting his actions and the approval of the Council of NICAEA (325), canon 75 of the pseudoapostolic *Canones Arabici Nicaeni* declared that in every city separate facilities were to be provided for pilgrims, the sick, and the poor.

Such were the origins of public hospitals, or rather of the institutions later to be called hospitals. As activities relating to the care and healing of the sick were extended

and improved, the other forms of welfare activity originally included were eliminated from them. The first historical records of institutions of this sort date from the 4th century. A large hospital, the *Basiliad,* erected by St. BASIL near Caesarea in Cappadocia *c.* 370, is described by Gregory Nazianzus; the hospital of the Roman matron, FABIOLA, and another erected by the patrician PAMMACHIUS at the mouth of the Tiber, are mentioned by JEROME and others. Subsequently many similar institutions were built with the encouragement of GREGORY THE GREAT and other popes. Along with *xenodochia* for pilgrims, hospitals for the sick were constructed in various dioceses. Antioch and Alexandria had them, and at Constantinople the earliest hospital activity was associated with JOHN CHRYSOSTOM.

In the West episcopal hospitals were built in Merovingian Gaul during the 6th and 7th centuries; the famous HÔTEL-DIEU DE PARIS, however, supposedly founded by St. LANDRY in 651, can be documented only as early as

829. The hospital of Milan, specializing in assistance to foundlings, was founded in the 8th century by the priest Dateo.

Henceforth hospitals were under the supervision of bishops and their organization varied with the needs of the times. At first they were situated in monasteries, but as they branched out into dioceses, they were located near city cathedrals and in rural parishes in outlying areas. In the cities organizations similar to those of the city hospitals were founded near the cathedral chapters and the houses of Canons Regular. Later both religious and private institutions were established by kings and lords.

These different types of hospital organization developed under specific juridical regulations that determined their essential characteristics. At first ecclesiastical authorities ruled in these juridical matters, as the civil authorities were later to do. The generosity of private donors, under the supervision of bishops, encouraged the steady growth of hospital institutes, a noble work that was to continue to the present time.

In the early period of Christianity, the East played an important part in the history of hospitals. The Eastern Church already had its own bureaucratic organization strongly bound up with the institutions of the Byzantine Empire. The hospital specialization of the East was of great interest, even though it was not adopted *in toto* by the West. It disappeared during the progressive decadence of the Byzantine Empire, and hospital organization declined also in the West during the age of the barbarian invasions.

Western Hospitals through the Carolingian Age. Nevertheless, the technical and juridical experience of the Late Empire and of the early Middle Ages bore fruit in later centuries, influencing the affirmation of the medieval world that substituted its own laws for those of the early Christian period. Byzantine juridical tradition, together with the intellectual legacy of the patristic age, both depending on fundamental Gospel principles, helped to mold the thought of the early Middle Ages. Ecclesiastical bodies, such as bishoprics, parishes, and monasteries, on which the society was built, were responsible for the founding and organizing of hospitals. The work represented a moral and juridical obligation in justice and charity. The bishop had the obligation of hospitality, which he fulfilled, not in his own person, but through his priests living in common as "canons regular" in cities and rural parishes. It was they who set up the basic jurisdictional church organization of the Middle Ages from the 4th century onward. They represented the community of the faithful in the earliest civic and religious centers scattered over the countryside—situated along the chief routes, near the centers of trade; in the vi-

cinity of castles, which were seats of government; and in mountain valleys.

In the 8th and 9th centuries, hospitality found expression not only in dioceses and parishes, but also in the monasteries, especially after the period of Benedictine reform. It was considered a fundamental obligation of the monks to exercise hospitality toward travelers. At first it was limited to pilgrims, but it gradually took on the more permanent aspect of hospitality to the sick and the disabled. The Benedictine interest in medicine, evident in the medical manuscripts preserved in their libraries, is perhaps best illustrated by the work of CONSTANTINE THE AFRICAN who provided Monte Cassino and the West with medical translations from Arabic and Greek.

Before the year 1000 an innovation had appeared with the founding of the first private lay hospitals. A few appeared at the peak of the Lombard era, but in the Frankish period their number increased rapidly. These foundations owed their existence primarily to feudal influences and to the Emperor who was the head of organized political society. There were also several imperial hospitals; accordingly, a considerable body of Carolingian legislation regarding hospitals is to be found in the CAPITULARIES.

From Feudal Times to the Age of Communes. In the period following the depression of the 9th and 10th centuries and the weakening of the imperial concept, a form of particularism, typical of the Middle Ages, developed in government and was reflected also in hospital structure. The influence of centralized civil legislation practically disappeared and no longer shaped hospital organization. However, hospitals continued to spring up in great numbers through the 11th and 12th centuries. During this time the canonical legislation of the Church exerted a growing and more exclusive influence. Typical were the "roadside" hospitals, "bridge" hospitals, "valley" hospitals in the Alps and Apennines, and "port" hospitals on the seacoasts.

But where and how did these hospitals come into being and in what form? An interesting phenomenon of this period was the development of what might be called the "hospital guild," the *universitas*. It had points in common with the more familiar *universitas* or guild, related to the institutions of Roman law. These new institutions were guilds of the sick and the well alike, organized confraternities of laymen, usually living under a religious rule, who dedicated themselves to the care of the sick. But the sick also were considered to be active members of the hospital community, and as such participated in the financial if not the disciplinary administration of the hospital, which was under the direction and government of the *magister*. This typical medieval hospital organization is of great interest because it provided the first and most unique forms of statutes, many of them worthy of careful study. For with the establishment of hospital guilds, there emerged a body of hospital law, regulated by Canon Law through decretals, to which were added the interpretations of jurists (*see* HOSPITALLERS AND HOSPITAL SISTERS).

By the 12th and 13th centuries towns and communes began to grow in size and power. The men of the communes gave an important place to hospitals in the texts of their statutes, but respected the form and structure of hospital guilds, which were at least semi-religious confraternities. It was inconceivable in the Middle Ages for any individual or collective work of charity to be excluded from the discipline of ecclesiastical authority. The communes intervened in political and social matters, however, and sought to assert their influence on these activities.

Meanwhile the generosity of private individuals toward hospitals continued to increase, especially in grants of real estate. Many persons, both men and women, also offered their services to hospitals as nurses, oblates, and lay brothers.

Hospitals of Military Religious Orders. A new development appeared in the rise of military religious orders whose private hospitals were forerunners of many present-day hospitals. The MILITARY ORDERS had gone to the Middle East during the CRUSADES, joining military action in defense of the Holy Land to medical care of the sick and wounded. Among them were the Knights Hospitaller of St. John, founded early in the 12th century (*see* KNIGHTS OF MALTA), the TEUTONIC KNIGHTS, and the HOSPITALLERS OF ST. LAZARUS. The last-named order, also founded in the 12th century, was dedicated specifically to the care of lepers, and had a history all its own. It was founded in the East, but eventually spread to Europe where it established many hospitals.

Another order of the same period, specifically dedicated to hospital work, was the Order of the HOLY SPIRIT, founded by GUY DE MONTPELLIER, propagated throughout Europe and established in Rome by INNOCENT III. A similar group with hospital statutes such as those of the Order of St. John had its seat at Altopascio in Tuscany. The military hospital orders of the Middle Ages disappeared after the loss of the Holy Land. Only one of these survived, the above mentioned Order of St. John, afterward known as the Knights of Rhodes and the Knights of Malta. It resumed its hospital activities in Cyprus, Rhodes, and Malta with the same spirit it had once displayed at Acre.

Rise of Large Hospitals. In the era of the city-states (*signorie*) of the Renaissance, hospital organization was again transformed. The change, which reached its height at the end of the 15th century, consisted in the centralization of hospitals and the suppression of a great number of small hospitals and infirmaries. The latter had been inspired by the spirit of charity—in itself a praiseworthy effort—but at the same time their proliferation reflected the anarchic and individualistic tendencies of the Middle Ages. There was a futile splintering of effort and initiative. Small hospitals existed often simply to provide sustenance to a few of the *fratres* of the surviving hospital confraternities, as well as to members of certain types of trade corporations. Some of the hospitals were convinced that they had established effective *universitates* attached to their own institutions, but many of them had meager resources and few beds.

The centralization of hospitals conformed to political trends of the modern state in the 15th century and to the spirit of the city-states and principalities. This phenomenon of consolidation is of historical and juridical interest for it represented the joining of the exercise of individual spiritual initiative with both traditional and newer forms of economic activity, involving all classes and social institutions, lay and ecclesiastic, individual and collective. Individual and concentric forces could not coalesce, however, without papal sanction and authorization. For ecclesiastical authority continued to have complete supervision and control over all such organizations. This principle had been affirmed in a famous decree of the Council of Vienne of 1311, issued by Pope CLEMENT V in the constitution *Quia contingit* (*Conciliorum oecumenicorum decreta* 350–352). Besides papal sanction, the new trend needed local episcopal authorization, and in the area of civil jurisdiction, the authorization of the lords (which was decisive), as well as that of the communes. Henceforth, however, the communes were completely under the control of the lords, and their influence diminished until it was absorbed by royal authority.

By the end of the 15th century large hospitals had been established in the major cities throughout Europe, especially in northern and central Italy. Milan provided a typical example of this trend with the foundation of a hospital sponsored by Duke Francesco Sforza. But in many other European cities there were similar and equally interesting examples of territorial and disciplinary centralization, and of administrative reform involving both ecclesiastical and lay institutions.

The foundation of large hospitals necessitated the construction of new unitary structures or the adapting of old buildings, usually monasteries, and a consequent modification of hospital architecture. Formerly, in the small hospitals there had been a rectangular ward with an altar in the rear, following ancient traditions of Roman and Byzantine architecture. An example of the new 15th-century hospital structure was the Hospital of the Holy Spirit in Rome, on which many subsequent institutions of the same order were modeled. The typical shape of the building was cruciform. The ward usually had four arms with the altar in the center for the celebration of divine services.

Critique of Medieval Hospital Effort. Given the great body of hospital sources still in part unedited, it is difficult to assess the number of hospitals erected in the lands of western Europe. If England in the 14th century could count 600 hospitals, large and small, serving a population of 3,750,000 (1347), the more populous and socially advanced countries of France, Germany, and Italy had many more. The quality of medical and nursing service and the efficiency of administration, however, are the other side of the coin. Until the end of the 14th century, hospitals in France—and presumably elsewhere—were without resident physicians and surgeons. Before that time when professional service was needed, the physician was called in and paid by the day or by the visit. Generally, hospital care included attention to both the temporal and the spiritual needs of the patient. The prevailing view that all medieval hospitals practiced "bed-crowding" needs some emendation. The practice was indeed widespread—in the interest of saving space. But in the larger and better organized hospitals, in addition to a number of oversized beds, accommodating three and four patients, there were always single beds for the serious cases. The latter were also assigned separate wards where special-duty nurses attended their needs day and night.

Upon arrival, the patient was bathed "head and foot"—a practice that perhaps had connotations more religious than sanitary. He was fed wholesome food of the same quality taken by the hospital personnel and, according to the statutes of many hospitals, at fixed times (11 A.M. and 6 P.M.)—before the attendant brothers or sisters had eaten. Medication and treatment tended to be stereotyped, consisting of syrups, herb drinks, bloodletting, and baths. The death rate in medieval hospitals was moderate. At Saint-Jean en l'Estrés in Arras, serving from 2,000 to 4,000 patients annually, the average number of deaths per year between 1307 and 1336 was 102.

The status of medieval hospital nursing was proportionate to the status of medicine in the same period. Yet the religious orientation of most hospital institutions, founded on the traditional virtue of hospitality, generally guaranteed a higher type of bedside service than might be expected. Especially after the development of religious hospital orders of women, living by a rule adapted from the Rule of ST. AUGUSTINE, the sick were treated as

"masters of the house." Abuses were, of course, recurrent; but episcopal supervision of both the finances and the internal deportment of the religious and lay personnel of the hospital was designed to reform any malpractice and restore the institute's original fervor.

The tendency for many medieval hospitals in the late Middle Ages, e.g., in France, to become secularized has been noted with some surprise. That this was the result of a growing antagonism between the lay and clerical world is an unwarranted conclusion. The development came about largely for financial reasons. Never affluent, the medieval hospital depended for its income on land (the original foundation and subsequent grants), on rents, *decima,* donations, annual fund-raising days (such as those approved by INNOCENT III for the hospital of the Holy Spirit in Rome), and by will and testament. Medical care in the Middle Ages, it should be noted, was free to the patient; the obligation for financing his recovery and his return to productive society was corporate. With the devastation of the Hundred Years' War and its concomitant impoverishment of many hospitals, the Church in France found it increasingly difficult to continue hospital service on the level demanded by the age. The depression of the 14th and 15th centuries increasingly led to urban, lay control of hospital administration and finance.

Bibliography: L. LE GRAND, ed., *Statuts d'Hôtels-Dieu et de léproseries* (Paris 1901). J. J. WALSH, *The Catholic Encyclopedia*, ed. C. G. HERBERMANN et al., 16 v. (New York 1907–14) 7:480–487. L. LALLEMAND, *Histoire de la charité*, 4 v. in 5 (Paris 1902–12). H. LECLERQ, *Dictionnaire d'archéologie chrétienne et de liturgie*, ed. F. CABROL, H. LECLERCQ, and H. I. MARROU, 15 v. (Paris 1907–53) 6.2:2748–70. R. M. CLAY, *The Mediaeval Hospitals of England* (London 1909). W. LIESE, *Geschichte der Caritas*, 2 v. (Freiburg 1922). S. REICKE, *Das deutsche Spital und sein Recht im Mittelalter* (Stuttgart 1932). G. E. GASK and J. TODD, "The Origin of Hospitals," *Science, Medicine, and History*, ed. E. A. UNDERWOOD, 2 v. (New York 1953) 1:122–130. E. NASALLI-ROCCA, *Il diritto ospedaliero nei suoi lineamenti storici* (Milan 1956). J. IMBERT, *Les Hôpitaux en droit canonique* (2d. ed Paris 1958). D. KNOWLES and R. N. HADCOCK, *Medieval Religious Houses: England and Wales* (New York 1953) 250–324. M. T. BASSEREAU, *Hôtels-Dieu, hospices, hôpitaux et infirmeries au moyen-âge* (Paris 1958). A. PAZZINI, *L'ospedale nei secoli* (Rome 1958). P. DE ANGELIS, *L'ospedale di Santo Spirito in Saxia e le sue filiali nel mondo* (Collana di studi storici sull' ospedale di Santo Spirito in Saxia e sugli ospedali romani; Rome 1958). B. TIERNEY, *Medieval Poor Law* (Berkeley 1959). *Atti del I e II congresso Italiano di storia ospitaliera* (Reggio Emilia 1957; Turin 1962). *Atti del I congresso europeo di storia ospitaliera* (Bologna 1962). U. CRAEMER, *Das Hospital als Bautyp des Mittelalters* (Cologne 1963).

[E. NASALLI-ROCCA]

2. 1500 TO PRESENT

With the dawn of the 16th century and of the modern era, new forms relating to a changing religious orientation developed in various countries. Ethical criteria and even the juridical organization that had governed the hospitals of Christian Europe in the Middle Ages underwent alteration. This transformation appeared in the change of concepts on which charitable institutions were founded, in the favoring of secularization, the dispersal of religious hospital institutes, and the intervention of absolute kings.

Prior to the Reformation provision for medical care was primarily a local responsibility, shared by the church and the town. The sick poor were cared for in the monasteries or in hospitals that were a combination almshouse, home for the aged, and shelter for the sick. Physicians and attendants were engaged by the community. With the advent of the Reformation and the rise of the absolutist state, management of hospital services became a municipal responsibility. The immediate cause of this transition was the confiscation of church property and revenues, but more remote factors had initiated the trend in this direction. The breakdown of the feudal system and the social unrest and economic changes following the Black Death in 1348–49 contributed to the decline of a rural economy in favor of growing urbanization. The decimation of the population by the plague created a premium on labor, and the availability of higher wages in the cities, combined with the rise of a mercantile class, attracted workers in large numbers.

Nevertheless, the hospitals of the Renaissance perpetuated in new forms a tradition that had already persisted more than 1,000 years. Nearly all modern hospitals, whether they were new or reformed or improved hospitals of former times, had their origins and inspiration in medieval hospitals. For whether medieval hospitals were founded to provide assistance of a general nature or specifically to provide collective care of the sick in the interests of society, they were imbued with the spirit of charity. Awareness of the essential need for fraternal collaboration by all who were united in faith in Christ was their foundation.

Evolution of the Function of Hospitals. The quality of hospital care during the 17th century was very poor. Hospitals were primarily almshouses, serving to isolate from the community those who were considered undesirable rather than providing medical treatment for the ill. However, a trend toward the study and teaching of medicine centered in the hospitals of this period was initiated in Holland with the introduction of bedside teaching in Leiden in 1626. Later in the century, under the leadership of Herman Boerhaave (1668–1738), a Dutch physician and professor of medicine at Leiden, this trend was consolidated and influenced other medical centers, especially in Edinburgh. Francis Bacon was one of its leading exponents in England, although the technique was not actually put into practice there until the 18th century. By the be-

ginning of the 18th century the character and concept of the hospital was becoming more socially constructive, and there was a growing emphasis on its function of treating illness.

The investigations published by John Howard (1726–90), a prison reformer, by James Lind (1716–94), a pioneer of naval hygiene in England, and by M. Tenon, a professor at the Royal Academy in Paris, revealed the deplorable conditions in hospitals of the period and instigated needed reforms. A brief summary of Tenon's findings gives some idea of the conditions, typical in varying degrees, of the hospitals of the period. The mortality rate for the Hôtel Dieu was 25 percent, and the figure included six to 12 percent of the physicians and attendants; mortality for obstetrical patients was one out of 15 and for births one out of 13. Diseases of the 2,500 to 3,000 patients included smallpox, measles, rabies, dysenteries, and fevers of all kinds. In addition there were accident, surgical, and obstetrical cases. Segregation was provided by one ward for smallpox, one for obstetrics, and two for accident and surgical cases; all other patients, including the insane, were grouped indiscriminately. Beds were 52 inches wide and accommodated four to six patients, ranging from convalescent to dying. Surgery was performed without anesthesia under restraint by strapping and powerful attendants. Wards were unheated (except by pails of live coals, a fire hazard) and unventilated, and sanitary facilities consisted of five seats over a sewer per 583 patients, plus a few commode chairs for the nonambulatory. All waste was disposed of in these same sewers.

At the beginning of the 18th century the involuntary hospital, supported by the community and designed for the curable poor, appeared in England and France. The municipal hospital administered by stewards appointed by the city council dates from the same period. Toward mid-18th century special hospitals for the treatment of specific illness, e.g., venereal (lock hospitals), smallpox, chest, eye, and orthopedic diseases, were developed, as well as lying-in and mental hospitals, lazarettos, and hospitals for incurables.

In the American colonies a hospital for sick soldiers was built on Manhattan Island in 1633, but it was not until mid-18th century that hospitals functioning without interruption from their foundation were established. The oldest of these hospitals is Philadelphia General, which evolved from a public almshouse for the infirm and insane. The first incorporated hospital for the cure of the physically and mentally ill, receiving its charter from the King of England in 1751, was the Pennsylvania Hospital in Philadelphia. It provided city physicians with a facility for treatment of private patients and was not charitable in purpose. It is the prototype of the modern voluntary, nonprofit hospital. The New York General Hospital and the New York Dispensary were founded in 1791; and Bellevue, which originated as an infirmary in the public workhouse (1736), became a general hospital in 1816. It established the first city ambulance service in the world in 1869. In Boston, the Massachusetts General and the MacLean Hospital for the Insane were founded in 1813, and by 1825 there were general hospitals in Baltimore, Maryland; Cincinnati, Ohio; and Savannah, Georgia. The American Medical Association (AMA) was founded in 1847.

Mental hospitals, as such, date their development from later in the 18th century. For centuries prior to that time, ignorance, superstition, and moral condemnation dominated the treatment of the insane. They were confined in jails, workhouses, and so-called madhouses for the protection of the community. More humane and enlightened treatment was initiated by Philippe Pinel (1745–1826) in France and by William Tuke (1732–1822) in England. Pinel, a physician to the Bicêtre in Paris, replaced brutality with humane treatment for the mentally ill male patients under his charge. Tuke, a Quaker merchant, interested the Society of Friends in founding the York Retreat in 1792 to replace the York Asylum (1777). The new institution incorporated a regimen of care for mental patients based on Christian principles and common sense. It represented a major influence in effecting reforms throughout Great Britian, the Continent, and the United States. The Friends' Asylum in Frankford, Pennsylvania (1817) and the Bloomingdale Asylum in New York (1821) were patterned after it. Dorothea Dix (1802–87), an American philanthropist and reformer, worked for legislation and the establishment of proper hospital facilities for the mentally ill in the United States and was instrumental in the founding of St. Elizabeth's Hospital, Washington, D.C. (1855). She was directly responsible for the foundation or enlargement of 30 other mental hospitals. By 1870 there were approximately 50 public and 16 private mental hospitals in the United States, having a total capacity of 17,000 patients. This trend implemented the scientific study of various mental illness.

The development of military hospitals is also of significance. With the rise of national states in the 15th and 16th centuries, a form of military hospital emerged. Queen Isabella is credited with maintaining a field hospital service, and in the late 16th century there were stationary military hospitals in England and in Pamplona, Spain. France and Prussia, however, gave the first real impetus to the development of military hospitals on a large scale. In the United States by the end of the 18th century, permanent army, navy, and marine general hospitals had been established; and in the 19th century station hospitals were attached to army posts. Hospitals for sick and wounded soldiers during the Civil War embodied principles later applied to postwar civilian hospitals and adapted by the Germans during the Franco-Prussian War. Base and evacuation hospital units, composed of medical and nursing teams from civilian hospitals, were introduced in World War I.

Modern Hospial Care. In the latter part of the 19th century there began to emerge a type of health facility that was to evolve into the highly scientific, well-managed, 20th-century hospital. Many forces were developing that would change the character of the hospital from a forbidding, infection-laden last resort for the indigent dying to a modern, aseptic institution in which emphasis was placed on curative procedures.

Under the influence of Florence Nightingale and certain religious congregations of women, nursing became an art dedicated to giving continuous care to sick beings. This influence of improved nursing brought order and cleanliness to hospital wards and provided a means of giving, on a continuing basis, the care the physician prescribed. The discovery and use of anesthesia made possible longer and more delicate surgical procedures. In 1847 Ignaz Philipp Semmelweis (1818–65) of Vienna demonstrated that infections were transmitted by personal carriers; a few years later Louis Pasteur (1822–95), by his discovery of the reproduction of bacteria, originated the modern science of bacteriology and the beginnings of the hospital clinical laboratory. At the end of the 19th century Joseph Lord Lister (1827–1912), carrying Pasteur's work further, proved that wound healing could be hastened by the use of antiseptics.

The acceptance and use of these discoveries by physicians and nurses practicing in the hospital gave the institution a completely new image. Thus began the institutional evolution that made the hospital an environment where advancements in medicine would be attracted. Medical students and young physicians were sent to the hospital for basic and advanced education. Formal nursing education first reached professional status in the hospital and the hospital school. Physicians and hospital officials, mobilizing all of these forces, translated them into better patient care. Improved procedures and standards of care attracted patients in numbers that required a rapid and continuing expansion in facilities and services up to and beyond the mid-20th century. The United Federal government constructed an elaborate system of hospitals for veterans of military service in addition to large numbers of general and special hospitals. There developed a widespread awareness of the important role of the hospital in the health of the people. All types of hospitals—governmental, voluntary, and religious—accepted responsibility for developing and giving the best possible care.

Bibliography: N. W. FAXON, *The Hospital in Contemporary Life* (Cambridge, England 1949). A. C. BACHMEYER and G. HARTMAN, eds., *The Hospital in Modern Society* (New York 1943). G. ROSEN, *Encyclopedia Americana* 14:427–433. J. J. WALSH, *The Catholic Encyclopedia*, ed. C. G. HERBERMANN et al., 16 v. (New York 1907–14) 7:480–488. C. U. LETOURNEAU, "A History of Hospitals," *Hospital Management* 87 (1959), March, April, May, June.

[A. B. MCPADDEN/J. FLANAGAN]

3. CATHOLIC HOSPITALS

Catholic health care began in America under the sponsorship of religious communities of women. As health services became institutionalized, the Catholic hospital evolved a parallel course with nonprofit, public, and investor owned institutions. Because Catholic health care institutions developed in concert with secular institutions, they are an integral part of the American health care establishment and share the concerns of other providers of health care. When the Catholic Hospital Association of the United States and Canada was organized in 1915, there were 541 Catholic hospitals in the United States. By 2001, Catholic hospitals were the largest group of not-for-profit hospitals, and accounted for 11 percent of all admissions to community hospitals.

After 1950 lay personnel began to take an increasingly important place in the operation and management of Catholic hospitals. Not only did they come to constitute the major part of the nursing and technical staff, but they held administrative positions as supervisors, department heads, accountants, purchasing agents, personnel directors, and assistant and associate administrators. By the late 1980s, lay administrators sat in board rooms of Catholic hospitals.

It became clear by the early years of the 20th century that the Catholic hospital could not concentrate on care of the indigent sick alone. Because the well-organized hospital had become the center for improved care, physicians tended to bring their patients to the hospital rather than to see them in their homes. Like other health care facilities Catholic hospitals found themselves assuming the responsibility of caring for patients who could pay for their care. Gradually all hospitals, including Catholic, were expected to serve the communities in which they were located by providing a level of care that reflected the advances in medicine, nursing, and paramedical services.

This acceptance of community responsibility necessitated a more complex administrative organization and forced the hospitals to conduct their activities in a more businesslike manner. General and financial administration became important functions in developing health services that were both apostolic and professional in nature.

Health Care Systems. The economic depression that began in 1929 sharply focused attention upon the difficulties many people had been experiencing in paying for hospital care. From this experience developed a program of prepaid hospital care: by paying regular monthly premiums individuals and families insured the payment of their basic hospital expenses in the event of illness. This program, known as the Blue Cross Plan, spread and a similar voluntary plan of prepaying doctor's bills, popularly known as the Blue Shield Plan, was developed. The success of these plans stimulated many commercial insurance companies to offer their own group health insurance programs.

In 1965 the federal government began funding health insurance for people over 65 years of age (Medicare) and supported health insurance for recipients of state welfare programs (Medicaid), making it the major health insurance agency in the country. In the nineties, Medicaid was separated from the welfare program and the state children's health insurance program (SCHIP) was added to make health insurance available to poor children whose mothers were not eligible for welfare.

Another force to be considered in the Catholic health care environment is the development of multi-institutional groups or systems, one or more hospitals owned, leased, or managed by a central organization. Although investor-owned systems dominate the multi-hospital establishment, local systems in the non-sectarian voluntary sector have joined together. There has also been system development under Catholic sponsorship. In 2001, there were 61 multi-hospital systems under Roman Catholic auspices. The Catholic systems are unique in that they offer a continuum of care which includes senior housing programs, adult day care, home health and hospice programs and community-based services, often linked to Catholic Charities. The emergence of the for profit hospital systems and the development of managed care as the dominant form of health insurance re-inforce competition, concern with return on equity, and innovative marketing and management techniques designed to attract cost-conscious physicians and insured patients to investor-owned and not-for-profit acute care hospitals.

Hospitals under Catholic sponsorship experience financially driven health care as a tension between mission and market. The awakened fiscal consciousness in all parts of the health community has stimulated mergers between Catholic and non-Catholic hospitals. Strengthening the essence and meaning of Catholic identity and sponsorship of hospitals is a continuing concern. In the years before the Second Vatican Council, Catholic hospitals were identified with the numbers of women and men religious in administrative and clinical positions. In 1965,

96.8 percent of administrators in Catholic hospitals were religious; by 1986, the figure was 38.9 percent, and the number continued to decline. It is no longer possible to explain the mission of Catholic hospitals by reference to the presence of religious sponsors in acute care hospitals.

The Catholic Mission. The charism that prompted attention to the sick as a work of mercy, the autonomy and decision making processes of the sponsoring religious communities, the age and declining numbers of religious women engaged in health ministry, and the growing secularization in the health care field threatens the continuation of large health care systems under Catholic auspices and Catholic influence in acute care. New structures, like the leadership development and mission integration programs that exist in Catholic systems and the revised ethical and religious directives for Catholic health care services, are being developed to present, monitor, and preserve the enactment of the Catholic health care ethic.

Bibliography: *Health and Health Care: A Pastoral Letter of the American Catholic Bishops* (Washington, D.C. 1981). ''Is Religion a Competitive Edge?'' *Hospitals* (April 20, 1987). R. A. MC-CORMICK, *Health and Medicine in the Catholic Tradition* (New York 1984). THE CATHOLIC HEALTH ASSOCIATION, *Annual Report* (St. Louis 2001–86); *No Room in the Market Place: The Health Care of the Poor* (St. Louis 1986).

[J. FLANAGAN/R. DONLEY]

HÖSS, CRESCENTIA, BL.

Eminent mystic of the Franciscan Third Order; b. Kaufbeuren, Bavaria, Oct. 20, 1682; d. there, April 5, 1744. From her childhood she showed unusual spiritual maturity and special regard for virginity. The benevolence of the Protestant burgomeister assisted her entrance into the Franciscan convent, frustrated earlier by her lack of the needed dowry. There she endured the severe trials that developed her religious perfection. During her appointment as mistress of novices and superior, her reputation for visions, ecstasy, prophecy, and the mystical suffering of the Passion, brought her into correspondence with ecclesiastics and many of the Catholic and Protestant laity. She was beatified by LEO XIII on October 7, 1900. In 1849, six sisters from Kaufbeuren came to Milwaukee, Wis., and founded the first community of the Franciscan Tertiaries in the U.S.

Feast: April 6 (formerly April 5).

Bibliography: R. PAZZELLI, *Il Terz'ordine regolore di S. Francesco* (Rome 1958). E. SCHLUND, *Zeitschrift für Aszese und Mystik* 2:295–319. A. M. MILLER, *Crescentia von Kaufbeuren; das Leben einer schwäbischen Mystikerin* (Augsburg 1968), extensive bibiliography. D. OTT, *Crescentia Höss v. Kaufbeuren in der Sicht*

ihrer Zeit, ed. J. GATZ (Landshut 1971). M. J. HEINRICHSPERGER, *Die Ältesten Quellen zum Leben der Schwester Crescentia Höss* (Landshut 1975), critical ed. F. BOESPFLUG, *Dieu dans l'art: Sollicitudini Nostrae de Benoît XIV et l'affaire Cresence de Kaufbeuren* (Paris 1984). R. GLÄSER, *Die selige Crescentia von Kaufbeuren: Leben, Worte, Schriften und Lehre* (St. Ottilien 1984). K. PÖRNBACHER, *Crescentia Höss von Kaufbeuren* (Weissenhorn 1993).

[V. PETRICCIONE]

HOSTIENSIS (HENRY OF SEGUSIO)

Hostiensis (Henry of Segusio, Enrico Bartolomei), cardinal and canonist whose writings exerted a great influence on Canon Law in the 13th century; b. Susa (Segusia, Diocese of Turin), *c.* 1200; d. Lyon, Oct. 25 or Nov. 6, 1271. He was not only one of the most famous DECRETALISTS, he proved himself also a capable diplomat. Hostiensis studied civil law in Bologna at the time of Sinibaldus de' Fieschi (later Pope Innocent IV), under Jacobus Balduinus and Homobono, and Canon Law under JAMES OF ALBENGA. Later he taught, perhaps at Bologna and certainly at Paris (1239). Before 1233 he became a cleric; he was appointed prior of Antibes (perhaps in 1234), and made frequent visits to England, where he gained the confidence of Henry III. When consecrated bishop of Sisteron (at the end of 1243), Hostiensis soon caught the eye of Innocent IV, and he was appointed archbishop of Embrun (about 1250). He was entrusted with a mission to Germany in support of William of Holland (1251–52) and with other legations, particularly that to Treviso against the ghibelline Ezzelino (1259). Named cardinal by Urban IV (1262), he continued to discharge numerous duties until the conclave of Viterbo, which he was compelled to abandon because of illness (June 1270).

Works. He began his *Summa* in 1239 in Paris; it was partially destroyed by a fire, but he continued and completed it in 1253 at Embrun. This monumental work, often called *Summa 'Copiosa,'* was inspired by the writings of Pillius (*De feudis*), but most of all by the works of Godfrey of Trani and of Azo, from which some passages were taken word for word. Nevertheless, the originality of the work cannot be doubted. If Hostiensis followed the decretals of GREGORY IX, he also added many new titles. He made a synthesis of Roman law and Canon Law and thus accomplished a summary of the *utrumque ius*. This treatise became the vade mecum of canonists until the 17th century.

The *Lectura in novellas Innocentii IV* followed the *Summa* almost immediately, but preceded the bull *Ad explicandos* (Sept. 9, 1253). It is a commentary on the decretals of the *Collectio I* and *II,* on five decretals from the *Collectio III* (28 s. 32, 40 s.), and on two *extravagantes* (see QUINQUE COMPILATIONES ANTIQUAE). Also to be noted are a short treatise on the framing of a decree concerning episcopal elections [cf. A. von Vretschko, *Ein Traktat d. Kard. H.* in *Deutsche Zeitschr. f. KR* 17 (1907) 73-] and the *Diamargariton* (MS 993 Leipzig University Library). The *Lectura in quinque libros decretalium,* like the *Summa,* goes back to the time of Hostiensis' teaching in Paris, and is thought to have been written at the request of Alexander IV. That it was completed is known from the author's testament (April 30, 1271). All the decretals are commented on, but some rather briefly. The spirit of this work appears to be somewhat different from that of the *Summa:* the author is more openly under the influence of theologians than previously (HUGH OF SAINT-CHER, ODO OF CHÂTEAUROUX). As a result Canon Law is often presented in opposition to Roman law; thus, the *aequitas canonica* is preferred to the *ius civile.* The importance of the commentary allowed the author to make more frequent references than in the *Summa* to canonists and civil jurists who had preceded him and to contemporaries such as BERNARD OF PARMA and Innocent IV. In it he criticized Innocent often and somewhat sharply for his devotion to Roman law and was at pains (10.3, 5, 33) to emphasize that the *Lectura* represents his own considered state of mind.

Principles. The chronicler Rolandino of Padua has underlined Hostiensis' profound knowledge of both canon and civil law, as well as his being *theologia scientia plenus.* This is apparent particularly in the *Lectura:* emphasis is put on *aequitas canonica,* on natural law, on good faith, on sin, but also on the power of the pope and on the power of bishops. Theological principles are given precedence over juridical concepts.

Natural law is divided into rational and common. The former must be respected by any positive law and by any institution. Its violation brings with it sin, and every effort must be made in order to avoid sin: in fact, the *periculum animae* is to be avoided before all. Many a time Hostiensis invoked this principle in order to reject a solution sponsored by some canonists. This recourse to the gospel also led him to emphasize equity, which he claimed should be invoked not only in the application or nonapplication of law, but also in its interpretation. In the same spirit, he admitted the binding force of natural obligations and of good faith, particularly in matters of prescription, except in respect to custom (because of its nature). This same approach is found again in connection with summary procedure and, above all, when he treats of the gospel condemnation of sin (*denunciatio evangelica*).

Hostiensis held for the plenitude of papal power. If he allowed that the civil and spiritual powers were com-

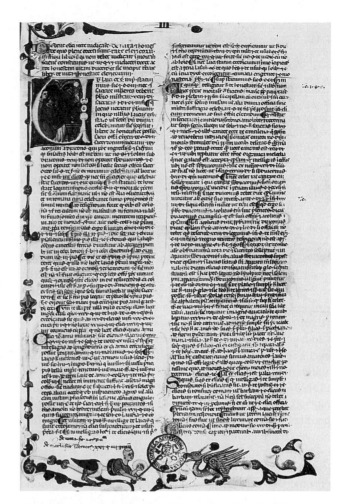

Manuscript opening page from "Summa Copiosa," 13th century, by Hostiensis.

pletely distinct, he recognized that the pope could intervene in an imperial vacancy, as well as when (*ratione peccati*) an imperial incumbent was disqualified because of sin (*a fortiori* in cases of a refusal to admit justice). For Hostiensis, this papal control of the *imperium* derived from the Church, which in turn had inherited it from the Roman Empire and from Christ.

The influences of Hostiensis' works, especially of the *Summa,* have been considerable, although the *Lectura* numbers fewer manuscripts and fewer editions than the *Summa.* However, unlike Innocent IV or the *glossa ordinaria,* Hostiensis was not held to possess the authority to offset a standard interpretation (*opinio communis*).

Bibliography: C. LEFEBVRE, *Dictionnaire de droit canonique,* ed. R. NAZ, 7 v. (Paris 1935–65) 5:1211–27, with complete bibliog.; "La Doctrine de l'Hostiensis sur la préférence à assurer en droit aux intérêts spirituels," *Ephemendes iuris canonici* 8 (1952) 24–44. N. DIDIER, "Henri de Suse en Angleterre (1236?–1244)," *Studi in onore di Vincenzo Arangio-Ruiz,* 4 v. (Naples 1952) 2:333–351. P. VACCARI, "Teologia e diritto canonico nel XII secolo,'' in *Scritti in onore di Contardo Ferrini*, 4 v. (Milan 1947–49) 1:418–428. G. SIMON, *La Conception du droit naturel chez un canoniste du XIIIe siècle, Henri de Suse, cardinal d'Hostie* (doctoral diss. unpub. Institut Catholique, Paris 1954). G. LE BRAS, ''Théologie et droit romain dans Henri de Suse,'' *Études historiques à la mémoire de Noël Didier* (Paris 1960) 195–204; et al., *Sources et théorie du droit au moyen-âge* (Paris 1964), *passim.* P. MICHAUD-QUANTIN, ''Commentaires sur les deux premiéres décrétales du recueil de Grégoire IX au XIIIe siècle,'' in *Die Metaphysik im Mittelalter*, ed. P. WILPERT (Miscellanea Mediaevalia 2; Berlin 1963) 103–109.

[C. LEFEBVRE]

HOTCHKIN, JOHN FRANCIS

Ecumenist, theologian, and priest; b. Mokena, Illinois, Feb. 3, 1935, d. Washington, D.C., June 24, 2001; son of John E. and Sarah (Cure) Hotchkin; ordained in Rome (July 12, 1959) for the Archdiocese of Chicago, Hotchkin served in two successive parish assignments in Chicago (1960–4). Albert Cardinal Meyer assigned him in 1964 for further studies in Rome during the Second Vatican Council when major shifts were occurring in Catholic thinking—on the nature of the church, the promotion of Christian unity, and relations with Jews and peoples of other Religions—that would shape the career of the future ecumenical leader. Hotchkin earned a doctorate in sacred theology with a specialization in ecumenical theology from the Pontifical Gregorian University (1966). He accepted an appointment to the U. S. Catholic bishops' conference and its Secretariat for Ecumenical and Interreligious Affairs (SEIA) beginning Jan. 1, 1967; in April 1971, he became SEIA Executive Director, a post he would hold until his death.

Hotchkin was a member of the U. S. Faith and Order Commission and other joint commissions co-sponsored by the National Council of Churches of Christ in the USA, and beginning in 1967 he served as a Catholic observer and consultant to the Consultation on Church Union, attending every plenary assembly from its inception. He received numerous appointments: observer to the fifth Assembly of the Lutheran World Federation (Evian, 1970); delegate to the first Assembly of the World Conference on Religion and Peace (Kyoto, 1970); consultor to the Pontifical Council for Promoting Christian Unity (1973), renewed every five years for the rest of his life; voting member, international Roman Catholic-Lutheran Commission (1973–84); observer to the fifth Assembly of the World Council of Churches (Nairobi, 1975), to the sixth assembly of the same body (Vancouver, 1983), and to the World Convocation on Justice, Peace, and the Integrity of Creation (Seoul, 1990); co-chairman of the Anglican-Roman Catholic Consultation on Women's Ordination (Versailles, 1978); consultor to

the Pontifical Council for Interreligious Dialogue (1985–90); and observer to the signing of the Joint Declaration on Justification by Faith (Augsburg, 1999).

Among his awards were: James Fitzgerald Award for Ecumenism (1990), National Association of Diocesan Ecumenical Officers; Patron of Christian Unity (1991), the Christian Church (Disciples of Christ); Joseph Cardinal Bernardin Laureate in Ecumenical and Interreligious Affairs (1997), Archdiocese of Chicago; and Paul Wattson Christian Unity Award (2000), Franciscan Friars of the Atonement.

Under his direction, ecumenical dialogues were initiated with the Oriental Orthodox Churches, the Polish National Catholic Church, the Christian Church (Disciples of Christ), and the Southern Baptist Convention. These and the already ongoing ecumenical dialogues produced dozens of reports during his tenure; among these, two were ostensibly significant in increasing reconciliation between Christian communities and the Catholic Church: the U. S. Lutheran-Catholic dialogue report, *Justification by Faith* (1983), and the Polish National Catholic-Roman Catholic report, *Journeying Together in Christ* (1990). In addition, he played a significant role in the preparation of two evaluations by the U. S. bishops' conference of international ecumenical documents that affected meaningfully the worldwide response to these documents: *The Final Report* (1981) of the Anglican-Roman Catholic International Commission and *Baptism, Eucharist and Ministry* (1982).

Finally, he often drew attention to *Facing Unity* (1984), a report of the international Roman Catholic-Lutheran Commission produced while he was a member, as an example of a new and third stage in the ecumenical movement that he termed ''phased reconciliation.'' While Executive Director, Hotchkin successfully added to the Secretariat expertise in the fields of interreligious relations and Eastern Christianity, expanding the staff from five to nine. In 2001, the BCEIA established a Subcommittee on Interreligious Dialogue. At the time of Hotchkin's death, there were nine Christian bi-lateral dialogues, two dialogues with Jewish groups, and three dialogues with Islamic groups—all benefitting from his guidance in varying degrees. Hotchkin was at the service of the whole conference of Catholic bishops whether offering insight on a particular case, updating progress on Christian unity, drafting reflections on a theological or pastoral question, or responding to ecumenical texts.

As a long-time participant in the ecumenical movement, Hotchkin was often requested to offer insights and observations on various aspects of the progress towards Christian unity. Numerous church leaders and ecumenical staff sought his counsel. In an address on the 1993 *Ec-*

umenical Directory to the National Association of Diocesan Ecumenical Officers, he reminded them that "the work of ecumenism is to remove all obstacles to that communion so this energy and life may flow forth with ever greater power and abundance" and thus "that is why ecumenism is not something extra or a specialty for a few; it is a constitutive element of our very lives as Christians" (Origins, 24, 3). In the Hecker Lecture for 1995, reviewing the ecumenical movement, he deduced that "what is developing among us is so far reaching and loaded with implications that it is hard to think it all through and see it whole." He cited Vatican II's Decree on Ecumenism, saying that indeed movement to restore unity "transcends human energies." In an address to the Mercersburg Society in 1998, he observed that "dialogue can only appear a magic sure-fire trick to those who have not tried it" and described how theological progress is experienced in dialogue: "At different points, after an arduous trek, I can almost name the day and the hour when a corner was turned, the key turned in the lock of a previously barred passageway." He noted that "at such moments a truly palpable sense of relief and lifting of the atmosphere." In his last published piece, an address to the Canon Law Society of America (2000), Hotchkin affirmed that there can be no real reconciliation without true repentance: "What we experience in our individual spiritual growth, Christian communities also will experience in their growth in unity." A few weeks later, when he received the Paul Wattson Award, he expressed the hope that Christians of the third millennium will be remembered as "those who worked and succeeded with the Lord's help to free themselves of splits and divisions and be blessed with reconciliation in the unity which will ever be Christ's will and prayer for us, that we may be one, as he and the Father are one, that this old world may believe. And have hope."

His published works included contributions to the New Catholic Encyclopedia and the New Dictionary of Sacramental Worship. His prominent essays and articles include: "Ministry – An Ecumenical Concern," The American Ecclesiastical Review 161 (1969) 386–95; "Ecumenism in the 1970s: Is There a New Direction?" CTSA Proceedings 31 (1976) 203–15; "Familiaris Consortio: New Light on Mixed Marriages," One in Christ 22 (1986) 73–9; "Bilaterals: Phasing into Unity?" Journal of Ecumenical Studies 23 (1986) 404–11; "Standards for Measuring Ecumenism's Course," Origins 20, 32 (Jan. 17, 1991) 509–14; "Directory for the Application of Principles and Norms on Ecumenism," Ecumenism 117 (March 1995) 4–12, appeared earlier in Origins 24, 3 (June 2, 1994): 23–8 ; "The Third Stage of Ecumenism," Occasional Paper, No. 45, Institute for Ecumenical and Cultural Research, Collegeville, MN (November 1995), appeared also in Origins 25, 21 (Nov. 9, 1995): 355–61; and "Canon Law and Ecumenism: Giving Shape to the Future," CLSA Proceeding 62 (2000) 1–16, appeared also in Origins 30, 19 (Oct. 19, 2000) 289–98.

[J. BORELLI]

HÔTEL-DIEU DE PARIS

Hospital located near Notre Dame cathedral in Paris. Having grown out of an early monastery that was transformed into a hospice for the poor in the 9th century, the Hôtel-Dieu was a dependency of the cathedral chapter of Notre Dame by 1006. It was called the Hôpital Notre Dame at that time, but during the 12th century it became known as the Maison-Dieu de Paris—the modern name of Hôtel-Dieu being a late medieval term. From the middle of the 12th century—when it seems to have begun accepting the sick of Paris rather than the poor—the Hôtel-Dieu was continually enriched by donations. During the 13th century the kings expanded the hospital on the land lying along the Seine between the cathedral and the Petit Pont: the hospital consisted of three large Gothic halls divided by rows of pillars. Vaults (the famous "cagnards") protected the building against floods. The oldest known rule for the hospital dates from this time (1217) and is attributed to the canon Stephen. It required a sick person to confess and receive Communion before being admitted; he was then brought to a bed and from then on the lay brothers and sisters serving the hospital were to treat him as master of the house. During the late 13th century, religious replaced the lay brothers and sisters. In 1352 King John the Good granted the Hôtel-Dieu the right to levy a tax on all seafood and other produce brought into Paris. At the same time the guilds were to provide the meals for the hospital on stated days. Louis XI provided a new building for the sick. Because of certain abuses, the Parlement of Paris in 1505 deprived the cathedral canons of the temporal administration of the hospital and entrusted it to eight townsmen. At the same time the Parlement requested the chapter to reform the religious men and women who staffed the hospital, but it was only under Prioress Geneviève (Soeur du Saint Nom de Jesus) Bouquet (d.1665) that the discipline of the hospital's AUGUSTINIAN NUNS (the male branch of the community having disappeared) was fully restored. Meanwhile, in an effort to relieve the shortage of beds and to isolate the plague victims, Francis I founded the Hôpital de la Charité. In 1530 the generosity of Cardinal A. Duprat provided for the building of the Salle du Légat. Under HENRY IV, when the hospital had 500 beds, the buildings were reinforced and the St. Thomas and St. Louis halls were remodeled: a several-storied structure replaced the ogival naves. Be-

"Exercice des Religieuses de l'hôtel Dieu de Paris a 5 heures et demy du matin," Paris. (©CORBIS)

ginning in 1626 the Pont-au-Double was built and surmounted by the Rosary House connecting the later St. Jacques and St. Charles halls, built along the left bank of the Seine. In 1634 St. VINCENT DE PAUL doubled the hospital's religious staff by introducing the Ladies of Charity. Despite the founding of the Hôpital Sainte-Anne for contagious cases and the Hôpital General, the old Hôtel-Dieu proved inadequate. In 1709, for example, some 6,000 patients were admitted while the hospital had been planned for only 2,000. During the night of Dec. 30–31, 1772, fire destroyed almost all the buildings along the right bank. In the new hospital, Louis XVI prescribed facilities for 3,000 patients, with a single bed for each, and with halls segregated according to sex and particular illnesses. During the French Revolution (1791) the hospitals of Paris were entrusted to a commission of five members, and the Hôtel-Dieu became the Grand Hospice d'Humanité. Rebuilt at the beginning of the 19th century and reserved for serious illnesses exclusively, the Hôtel-Dieu proved again to be too small. It was demolished under the Second Empire and rebuilt (1868–78), not at its previous location, but along the northern side of Notre-Dame Square, and the principal façade of the three buildings, which altogether occupy an area of about 5 acres, faces on the square itself. The Augustinian nuns who were expelled from the Hôtel-Dieu in 1907 went to the hospital of Notre-Dame-de-Bon-Secours, which was also in Paris.

Bibliography: F. DISSARD, *La Réforme des hôpitaux et maladreries au XVIIe siècle* (Paris 1938). P. VALLERY-RADOT, *Nos hôpitaux parisiens,* v.2: *Un siècle d'histoire hospitalière. . .* (Paris 1949). H. LEGIER-DESGRANGES, *Hospitaliers d'autrefois* (Paris 1952). E. WICKERSHEIMER, *Les Édifices hospitaliers à travers les âges* (Paris 1953). P. PARENT, *Vieux hôpitaux parisiens* (Paris 1943).

[J. DAOUST]

HOUBEN, CHARLES OF MOUNT ARGUS, BL.

Baptized Johannes Andreas, Passionist missionary priest; b. Dec. 11, 1821, Munstergeleen, the Netherlands; d. Jan. 5, 1893, Dublin, Ireland. The fourth of the 11 children of Peter Joseph and Elizabeth Houben, Johannes had difficulties with his studies, yet persevered and realized his religious vocation. While serving five years in the military reserves (1840–45), Houben worked in his uncle's mill. He entered the Passionist novitiate (1845), took his vows (1846) and the name Charles of St. Andrew, and was ordained (1850). Thereafter he worked among the poor and humble in England. In July 1857 he was assigned to the Mount Argus Retreat House, Dublin, Ireland, where he distinguished himself through his apos-

tolate as a confessor. He remained in Dublin the remainder of his life, except for a short return to England in 1866. Houben suffered patiently in his later years. Since 1949 his relics have been interred in the Passionist church at Mount Argus. Pope John Paul II praised Houben during his beatification ceremony (Oct. 16, 1988) for his ecumenical work and ministry of reconciliation.

Bibliography: P. F. SPENCER, *To Heal the Broken-Hearted* (Dublin 1988).

[K. I. RABENSTEIN]

HOUCK, GEORGE FRANCIS

Diocesan chancellor, author; b. Tiffin, Ohio, July 9, 1847; d. Lakewood, Ohio, March 26, 1916. He was the son of John and Odile (Fischer) Houck, both natives of Germany. He was educated in Ohio at Heidelberg College, Tiffin; Mount St. Mary's Seminary, Cincinnati; and St. Mary's Seminary, Cleveland. After his ordination on July 4, 1875, he was pastor of St. Joseph Church, Crestline, Ohio, until 1877, when he was appointed first chancellor of the Diocese of Cleveland and secretary to the bishop. While holding these offices under Bps. Richard Gilmour, Ignatius F. Horstmann, and John P. Farrelly, he also served (1877–94) as the first Catholic chaplain to the Cleveland Workhouse and as chaplain at St. Vincent Charity Hospital. He organized the diocesan system of burials in Catholic cemeteries and purchased the property for Calvary Cemetery, the largest in the diocese in 1900. Under Gilmour, he acted as spokesman for the diocese in refuting the violent anti-Catholic attacks that appeared in the *Cleveland Leader.* In 1905 he was made a domestic prelate, and in 1909 he resigned as chancellor and retired as chaplain to the convent of the Sisters of Charity of ST. AUGUSTINE.

Houck devoted much of his time in his early years to the organizational task of bringing order to a rapidly growing diocese. This work brought him into close contact with individual parish administrations and led to his exhaustive *History of the Catholic Church in Northern Ohio and the Diocese of Cleveland* (2 v. 1903).

[N. J. CALLAHAN]

HOUGHTON, JOHN, ST.

Carthusian martyr; b. Essex, England, ca. 1487; d. Tyburn (London), May 4, 1535. He received the LL.B. degree at Cambridge in 1506. To avoid the marriage planned by his parents, who were of minor gentry, he left home to live with a secular priest who trained him for ordination. In about 1514 he entered the London Charterhouse, then governed by the Irish Prior Tynbygh. There he served for seven years as sacristan, and for four years as procurator. In May 1531 he was elected prior of Beauvale in Nottinghamshire, but returned to London in November to succeed the deceased Prior Batemanson. In the next year he was chosen by the chapter general to be covisitator of the English province.

During his visitation of Mountgrace Priory in Yorkshire occurred an incident said to presage his future martyrdom. The traveling clothes of both visitators were left to dry, and Houghton's were found pecked and torn by birds, whereas his companion's were untouched. The details of his interior life and external administration attest to his reputation for holiness, austerity, zeal for the Divine Office, love of books, enlightened handling of his subjects. He is said to have had the gift of tears. His confessor was the martyr, Bl. William EXMEW.

In April 1534 Houghton with his procurator, Bl. Humphrey MIDDLEMORE, was imprisoned in the Tower for a month for refusing to swear to the Act of Succession, which denied the validity of HENRY VIII's marriage to CATHERINE OF ARAGON. They were persuaded to take the oath with the reservation "as far as it was lawful." On February 15, 1535, the king announced his title of supreme head of the English Church. After being advised by Father Fewterer, confessor general of the Bridgettines of Syon, that he must die rather than accept this title (advice that this counselor did not himself keep), Houghton convened his monks and warned them of the danger.

At the beginning of April, accompanied by St. Robert LAWRENCE and St. Augustine WEBSTER, priors of Beauvale and Axholme, he called upon Thomas Cromwell for a form of the oath that would be acceptable in conscience. Instead of being granted their request, they were imprisoned in the Tower together with St. Richard REYNOLDS, a Bridgettine of Syon. On April 20 they were examined by royal commissioners and sent to trial in Westminster Hall. They pleaded not guilty since they had not seditiously opposed the king's supremacy. A hesitant jury after two days and pressure from Cromwell found them guilty. On May 4, accompanied by Bl. John HAILE, the aged vicar of Isleworth, and seen from a window by Thomas MORE and his daughter, Margaret Roper, these protomartyrs were placed on hurdles, dragged to Tyburn, where they were hanged, cut down while alive, eviscerated, and quartered. As the executioner groped for his heart, Houghton was heard by a spectator, Anthony Rescius, OP, to say, "Good Jesu, what will ye do with my heart?" Houghton was canonized by Paul VI on October 25, 1970 as one of the Forty Martyrs of England and Wales.

Feast: Oct. 25 (Feast of the 40 Martyrs of England and Wales); May 4 (Feast of the English Martyrs in England).

Bibliography: Contemporary accounts by M. CHAUNCY, "De B.B. Martyribus Carthusiensibus in Anglia," ed. F. VAN ORTROY, *Analecta Bollandiana* 14 (1895) 268–283; "Martyrum Monachorum Carthusianorum in Anglia Passio minor," ed. F. VAN ORTROY, *ibid.*, 22 (1903) 51–78; *Passion and Martyrdom of the Holy English Carthusian Fathers*, tr. A. F. RADCLIFFE (New York 1936). L. HENDRIKS, *London Charterhouse, Its Monks and Its Martyrs* (London 1889). E. M. THOMPSON, *The Carthusian Order in England* (New York 1930). L. E. WHATMORE, *Blessed Carthusian Martyrs* (London 1962). *El Beato Juan Houghton, 1487-1535* (Madrid 1965).

[L. E. WHATMORE]

HOUSELANDER, FRANCES CARYLL

Writer and artist; b. Bath, England, Sept. 29, 1901; d. London, Oct. 12, 1954. Houselander was the younger daughter of Willmott and Gertrude Houselander. She was educated in a Jewish kindergarten, French and English convents, a state school, a Protestant private school, St. John's Wood Art School, and St. Martin's Art School. Although she was baptized in the Church of England, she became a Catholic at the age of six. She worked at various occupations: as a layout artist for an advertising firm; as a sculptor, carving crib figures and stations of the cross for an ecclesiastical decorator; as a house decorator; and as a book illustrator. During World War II she worked in the censorship office.

Houselander wrote and illustrated stories, verses, and articles for the *Messenger of the Sacred Heart,* the *Children's Messenger,* and the *Grail Magazine.* She also wrote powerful and original works of spirituality on the theme of the suffering Christ in man that became best sellers. From 1942, doctors sent both children and adult patients to her for therapy. The best authorities on Caryll Houselander are her own writings: *This War is the Passion* (1941), revised as *The Comforting of Christ* (1946); *The Reed of God* (1944); *The Flowering Tree* (1945); *The Dry Wood* (1947); *The Passion of the Infant Christ* (1949); *Guilt* (1951); *The Stations of the Cross* (1955); and *The Risen Christ* (1958). Her books of children's stories, collected and published posthumously, include *Inside the Ark* (1956), *Terrible Father Timson* (1957), and *Bird on the Wing* (1958).

Bibliography: F. C. HOUSELANDER, *A Rocking-Horse Catholic* (New York 1955), brief autobiog. M. WARD, *Caryll Houselander* (New York 1962), biog.

[E. FALLAUX]

HOUTIN, ALBERT

Historian of Biblical criticism and of the religious and moral crises at the time of Modernism; b. La Flèche, France, Oct. 4, 1867; d. Paris, July 28, 1926. He was ordained (1891) for the Angers diocese and taught at the minor seminary. He left his diocese (1901) because of difficulties with his bishop over research on local ecclesiastical history and went to Saint-Sulpice in Paris, where he was in touch with many of the chief figures in Modernism. His *La Question biblique chez les catholiques de France au XIXMe siècle* was placed on the Index (1903), a fate shared by four of his other books. About 1900 his faith began to deteriorate. By 1912 he put aside clerical garb and worked from 1913 on at the Musée pedagogique, whose director he became in 1919.

From a broad idea of the evolution of dogma he moved to a Christian theism akin to that of the Unitarians, then to a conviction that there is no revealed religion, and finally to a philosophy of distrust that considered religion as "humbug." As a "disabused Don Quixote" he looked continually in history for the "pious lie" and considered the Church as the personification of it. His ultimate position questioned the sincerity of all men, systems, and beliefs, a stance that he denied was misanthropic. Houtin had a strong, uncompromising mind, which was neither supple nor subtle. His narrowing of vision to a search for insincerity and fraud led many observers, including several figures in Modernism, simultaneously to prize certain facts that he had documented and to assail his evaluation as vitiated by his personal assessment of the presence of insincerity. His two volumes on *La Question biblique* and the *Histoire du modernisme catholique* (1913) are his best known works. The ceremonies at his funeral were civil only. His body was cremated.

Bibliography: A. HOUTIN, *Mon expérience*, 2 v. (Paris 1926–28). J. RIVIÈRE, *Le Modernisme dans l'Église* (Paris 1929). É. POULAT, *Histoire, dogme, et critique dans la crise moderniste* (Tournai 1962).

[J. J. HEANEY]

HOVDA, ROBERT W.

Priest, writer, editor, leader in the liturgical movement; b. Wisconsin, April 10, 1920; d. New York City, Feb. 5, 1992. Raised in Minnesota, Hovda discovered the social gospel in the Methodist youth movement. By the time he left high school he was a member of the Socialist party, and in college he discovered the connections being made between liturgy and social justice. As a conscientious objector during World War II he came to know the Catholic Worker movement; before the war ended he had entered the Roman Catholic Church and was attending the seminary in Collegeville, MN. Hovda was ordained for the Diocese of Fargo and served for ten years in North Dakota parishes.

Drawing on his pastoral experience and interest in the liturgical movement, he began publishing in *Amen, Commonweal, Worship,* and *Liturgical Arts.* Teaching and campus ministry followed. In 1965 Hovda began thirteen years as an editor at The Liturgical Conference in Washington, DC. The liturgical, social and ecumenical directions of the conference mirrored Hovda's own developing thought. His monthly essays, published in *Living Worship* and in several books, especially *Manual of Celebration* and *Strong, Loving and Wise,* were of critical importance to implementing the reforms of Vatican II. *Environment and Art in Catholic Worship,* a document of the Bishop's Committee on the Liturgy, was written largely by Hovda.

In the 1980s Hovda lived in New York City, doing parish work there and extensive speaking around the United States. He continued his writing in the "Amen Corner" for the journal *Worship.* Hovda was an outspoken advocate of the ordination of women, the rights of homosexuals, and a host of causes that flowed from his conviction that the exalted equality Christians are meant to experience at the eucharistic table is a model for their only politics, in church and out. Until his death, he continued to insist in every forum that the liturgy both inspires and expresses those apparent opposites, human freedom and human solidarity.

[G. HUCK]

HOWARD, FRANCIS WILLIAM

Bishop, educator; b. Columbus, Ohio, June 21, 1867; d. Covington, Ky., Jan. 18, 1944. He studied at the Seminary of Our Lady of Angels, Niagara, N.Y., and at Mt. St. Mary Seminary of the West, Cincinnati, Ohio. He was ordained by Bp. John Watterson, on June 16, 1891, at St. Joseph Cathedral, Columbus. From 1891 to 1895, Howard was stationed at Holy Trinity parish, Jackson, Ohio. After three years at Columbia University, New York City, and a year of study in Rome, he returned to Columbus, where he received assignments in educational work. In May 1905, he was appointed pastor of Holy Rosary parish in Columbus, holding this pastorate until his appointment as bishop of Covington, March 26, 1923. He was consecrated by Abp. Henry Moeller of Cincinnati at St. Mary's Cathedral, Covington, July 15, 1923.

As bishop, Howard continued to labor for Christian education. He established in his diocese special schools known as "Bishop's Schools," with a specially adapted classical curriculum. They were open to talented boys at the completion of the sixth grade. Howard was convinced that such schools would elevate contemporary standards of education, and he hoped they would be established in other dioceses. He enjoyed international recognition as an educator. Howard served the interests of the NATIONAL CATHOLIC EDUCATIONAL ASSOCIATION for more than 40 years as its first secretary general (1904–28), as its president (1929–35), and as chairman of its advisory board (1936–44). He always insisted that the association remain a voluntary organization and provide Catholic educators with a forum in which they could strengthen their agreements and debate their differences.

Bibliography: Archives, Diocese of Covington. P. E. RYAN, *History of the Diocese of Covington, Kentucky* (Covington 1954).

[P. E. RYAN]

HOWARD, PHILIP, ST.

Earl of Arundel and English martyr; b. Arundel House, London, June of 1557; d. Tower of London, Oct. 19, 1595. Philip was the eldest son of the fourth Duke of Norfolk by his first wife Anne Fitz-Alan Howard, daughter and heir of the Earl of Arundel, the premier earl of England. As Earl of Surrey, heir to the only dukedom in Tudor England, heir to the premier earldom and five baronies, Philip was born to the highest position in the land after the throne. Philip II, king of Spain, stood godfather at his christening. On the accession of Queen Elizabeth, Philip's father adopted the new religion and Philip was brought up a Protestant, with John Foxe, the Protestant martyrologist, as tutor (*see* FOXE'S BOOK OF MARTYRS). However, the Arundels were disgraced when the duke proposed marriage to the captive MARY STUART, QUEEN OF SCOTS. She would have been the duke's fourth wife. He was tried, found guilty of high treason, and executed Feb. 11, 1572, after appointing Lord Burghley as Philip's guardian.

Burghley sent Philip to Cambridge and then introduced him to the glittering court. Philip was married to his stepsister Anne Dacres, daughter of the duke's third wife. Philip, witty, handsome, and well-born, neglected his wife and won the favor of the queen.

In 1580, on the death of his grandfather, Philip became the Earl of Arundel and was reconciled with Anne. In 1581 he attended a dispute at court between the notorious prisoner Edmund CAMPION and Protestant theologians. Philip left convinced of the truth of Campion's mission, but he was still unable to sacrifice his gay life as a courtier and to face probable death as a Catholic. Meanwhile the queen became angered at Philip's devotion to his wife, who had become a Catholic.

In 1584 he was received into the Church by William WESTON, SJ. He attempted to leave England on April 14, 1585, but was betrayed and captured at sea. He was fined and sent to the Tower. He was never allowed to see Anne again or to see his son born after his imprisonment. In the Tower Philip grew in holiness, assisted by letters from Robert SOUTHWELL (later published as *The Epistle of Comfort*). Philip was tried in 1589 for allegedly having prayed for the success of the Armada. Although his accuser admitted the story was fabricated and many judges thought a prayer could not constitute treason, he was found guilty and sentenced to death. The queen stayed the execution expecting Philip to recant. After 11 years of imprisonment he died from the hardships.

Philip Howard, whose body is venerated in the Fitz-Alan Chapel, Arundel, was beatified by Pius XI on Dec. 15, 1929, and canonized by Paul VI on Oct. 25, 1970, as one of the Forty Martyrs of England and Wales.

Feast: Oct. 19; Oct. 25 (Feast of the Forty Martyrs of England and Wales); May 4 (Feast of the English Martyrs in England).

See Also: ENGLAND, SCOTLAND AND WALES, MARTYRS OF.

Bibliography: H. G. F. HOWARD, ed., *The Lives of Philip Howard and of Anne Dacres, His Wife* (London 1857). A. BUTLER, *The Lives of Saints*, ed. H. THURSTON and D. ATTWATER, 4 v., (New York, 1956) 4:152–154. M. WAUGH, *Blessed Philip Howard* (Postulation pamphlet; London 1961). *Publications of the Catholic Record Society*, v. 21 (1919) devoted to Philip Howard. M. CREIGHTON, in *The Dictionary of National Biography from the Earliest Times to 1900*, 63 v. (London 1885–1900; reprinted with corrections, 21 v., 1908–09, 1921–22, 1938; supplement 1901–) 10:52–54.

[G. FITZHERBERT]

HOWARD, PHILIP THOMAS

Cardinal–protector of England; b. Arundel House, London, Sept. 21, 1629; d. Rome, June 17, 1694. He was the great grandson and namesake of the Elizabethan martyr Philip HOWARD, Earl of Arundel, and the son of Henry Frederick Howard, third Earl of Arundel, and Elizabeth, daughter of Esmé Stuart, Lord d'Aubigny. Because of his Protestant grandfather, Thomas Earl of Arundel, some of his tutors were Protestant, but Philip's education was essentially Catholic. In 1640–41 he was at St. John's College, Cambridge, but after that was sent to Utrecht and then to Antwerp. Over the severe objections of his grandfather, he entered the Dominican Order at Cremona (1645), taking the religious name Thomas. The lengthy struggle between the youth and his grandfather was settled by Innocent X. The Pope decided after careful investigation that Howard's vocation was genuine and sent him to Naples for study (1646–50). From there Howard went to Rennes, Brittany, where he finished his studies and was ordained at 23, by a papal dispensation necessitated by his age.

He raised money (£1,600) in England (1655–57) to found an English friary at Bornhem, Flanders, whose first prior he became on Dec. 15, 1657. Prince Charles (later Charles II) sent him on a secret mission to England, where he was denounced by an informer and forced to flee in the suite of the Polish ambassador. Returning to England at the Restoration, he, engaged in furthering a Portuguese marriage for Charles II, to which he was a witness. He became Queen Catherine's first chaplain (1662) and her grand–almoner (1665) with an annual salary of £500, plus £500 for his table, and £100 for Her Majesty's oratory at Whitehall. He became entangled in the dispute among English Catholics concerning the appointment of a bishop or vicar–apostolic for England. In 1672 he resigned as grand–almoner and returned to Bornhem, where he was reappointed prior. Clement X created him bishop *in partibus* (1672) and cardinal priest (1675), attaching him thereafter to the papal Curia.

Titus Oates implicated him in the Popish Plot, but, although he was condemned for treason, he was in Rome and the sentence could not be executed. In 1679 he was created cardinal protector of England and Scotland, and was principal counselor to the Holy See in English affairs. Under his direction a series of new buildings was erected for the English College at Rome, including his own palace, completed in 1685. He himself lived as a simple friar in the convent of Santa Sabina. He viewed James II's policies with alarm and foresaw their unfortunate results. In the political atmosphere that prevailed after the REVOLUTION OF 1688, he was cut off from communication with England. He continued to live quietly in Rome until his death.

Bibliography: B. JARRETT, *Letters of Philip Cardinal Howard . . .* (London 1925). B. HEMPHILL, *The Early Vicars Apostolic of England, 1685–1750* (London 1954). A. WALZ, *I cardinali dominicani* (Rome 1940). C. F. R. PALMER, *The Life of Philip Thomas Howard, O.P., Cardinal of Norfolk . . .* (London 1867). M. V. HAY, *The Jesuits and the Popish Plot* (London 1934). G. ANSTRUTHER, ''Cardinal Howard and the English Court 1658–94,'' *Archivum Fratrum Praedicatorum* 28 (Rome 1958) 315–361. T. COOPER, *The Dictionary of National Biography from the Earliest Times to 1900* 10:54–57. J. GILLOW, *A Literary and Biographical History or Bibliographical Dictionary of the English Catholics from 1534 to the Present time* 3:442–451. A. SCHMITT, *Lexikon für Theologie und Kirche*² 5:498.

[H. S. REINMUTH, JR.]

Philip Thomas Howard, miniature painting on copper, 17th century.

HOWLETT, WILLIAM JOSEPH

Missionary, writer; b. Monroe County, N.Y., March 6, 1847; d. Loretto, Ky., Jan. 17, 1936. His parents, John and Ellen (Doyle) Howlett, came from Ireland to the U.S. by way of Canada. The family settled first in New York; they then moved to Michigan, and finally to Denver, Colo. In spite of his limited early education, Howlett entered St. Thomas's Seminary, Bardstown, Ky., and later continued his studies at the Sulpician seminary, Issy-sur-Seine, France, the Grand Seminary in Paris, and the University of Würzburg in Bavaria. He was ordained for the Diocese of Denver on June 11, 1876, by Cardinal Joseph H. Guibert, Archbishop of Paris. Howlett served in Denver for 36 years, first as a pioneer missionary, then as a pastor and builder of churches. During the last 23 years of his life, which he spent as chaplain at the motherhouse of the Sisters of Loretto in Loretto, Ky., he wrote works of biography and history, including an account of St. Thomas's Seminary in Bardstown and biographies of Bp. Joseph P. Macheboeuf of Denver and Charles Nerinckx, the Kentucky missionary. He published also brief lives of early Kentucky and Colorado priests and a number of historical articles.

[M. M. BARRETT]

HROZNATA, BL.

Crusader, monastic founder, and Premonstratensian canon; b. Tepl, Bohemia, *c.* 1170; d. Alt-Kinsburg, near Cheb, present-day Czechoslovakia, July 14, 1217. A descendant of the counts of Mielnic, as a young man he found a place at the court of Henry Bretislav (d. 1197), PRINCE-BISHOP of Prague. The sudden and tragic death of his wife and young son brought about a profound transformation in his life, leading him to join the Crusade of Emperor HENRY VI. When the expedition failed to get under way, Hroznata sought a dispensation from his crusading vow, which Pope CELESTINE III commuted into a vow to found a religious institute, and returned to Bohemia, where he tried to end the civil war that raged over the inheritance of Henry Bretislav. Before he had left on Crusade he had founded a monastery at TEPL and settled it with PREMONSTRATENSIANS from STRAHOV. After he returned he established a convent of nuns of the same order in his family castle at Choteschau. Hroznata himself entered Tepl, receiving the habit from INNOCENT III when he went to Rome in 1202 to seek confirmation of his foundations, and was placed in charge of the abbey's temporal affairs. A group of local nobles, envious of the house's growth and wishing to extort some of its revenues, seized the holy founder, who died of the maltreatment he received at their hands. Venerated as a martyr, he was buried at Tepl; his cult was approved by LEO XIII in 1897.

Feast: July 14.

Bibliography: J. LE PAIGE, *Bibliotheca praemonstratensis ordinis* (Paris 1633) 440–445. *Acta sanctorum* July 3:793–810. *Analecta ecclesiastica* 5 (1897) 452–453. I. VAN SPILBEECK, *Vie du bx. Hroznata, prince de Boheme* (Tamines, Belg. 1897). GEUDENS, *Life of Blessed Hrosnata* (Manchester 1899). *Todestage: Zum 700 jährigen, des seligen Hrozanta* (Marienbad 1917). N. BACKMUND, *Monasticon Praemonstratense* 1:315. F. PETIT, *La Spiritualité des Prémontrés aux XII e et XIIIe siècles* (Paris 1947), *passim*. A. BUTLER, *The Lives of the Saints* 3:102. A. K. HUBER, *Lexikon für Theologie und Kirche* 2 5:500–501. R. GAZEAU, *Catholicisme* 5:996.

[L. L. RUMMEL]

HUBERT, JEAN FRANÇOIS

Ninth bishop of Quebec, Canada; b. Quebec, Feb. 23, 1739; d. there, Oct. 17, 1797. He was the son of Jacques François, a baker, and Marie Louise (Maranda) Hubert. After studies at the Quebec seminary, he was ordained July 20, 1766, the first candidate to receive Holy Orders after the reestablishment of the episcopate under the English regime. He served as professor, procurator, and first Canadian superior of the seminary. In 1785 he went first to the Illinois and then to the Detroit missions.

A year later he was consecrated coadjutor of Quebec, with the title of bishop of Almyra, and he succeeded to the see in 1788. In 1797, a few months before he died, Hubert resigned his see, having distinguished himself by receiving several refugee priests of the French Revolution, by encouraging Catholic education, and by safeguarding against the threat of a nondenominational university in 1789.

Bibliography: H. TÊTU, *Les Évêques de Québec* (Quebec 1889). A. H. GOSSELIN, *L'Église du Canada après la conquête,* 2 v. (Quebec 1916–17) v.2. L. P. AUDET, *Le Système scolaire de la Province de Québec,* v.2 (Quebec 1951).

[H. PROVOST]

HUBERT OF MAASTRICHT, ST.

Bishop, count Palatine; b. *c.* 655; d. Tervueren, near Brussels, May 30, 727. Leaving the world, Hubert worked under St. LAMBERT OF MAASTRICHT. He succeeded Lambert as bishop of Tongres-Maastricht in 705 and is responsible for converting the last pagans of the Ardennes. In 717 or 718 he moved Lambert's remains and the episcopal seat to Liège. Hubert's own relics were transported to the Abbey of SAINT-HUBERT in the Ardennes in 825 but were lost during the Reformation. In the late Middle Ages he became the protector against mad dogs because of a miraculous stole supposedly given him by the Blessed Virgin. Hubert and St. Eustace—and many other saints—were supposed to have been converted by seeing a stag with a cross between its antlers, and hence they are patrons of hunters. Hubert's cult has been popular also with artists and noblemen. A confraternity, the two military orders of SAINT HUBERT, and the city of Liège claimed Hubert as patron.

Feast: Nov. 3.

Bibliography: *Acta Sanctorum* (Paris 1863–) Nov. 1:759–930. É. DE MOREAU, *Histoire de l'église en Belgique* (2d ed. Brussels 1945–) 53–70. L. HUYGHEBAERT, *S. Hubert, patron des chasseurs* (Antwerp 1927); *S. Hubert, patroon van de jagers* (Antwerp 1949). A. J. BARNOUW, *The Pageant of Netherlands History* (New York 1952) 10–11. A. BUTLER, *The Lives of the Saints,* ed. H. THURSTON and D. ATTWATER, 4 v. (New York 1956) 4:247–248. W. HILDEBRAND, *Sankt Hubertus und Sankt Eustachius* (Gräfelfing 1979). Centre Pierre-Joseph Redouté (Saint-Hubert, Belgium), *Le culte de saint Hubert en Namurois,* ed. A. DIERKENS and J. M. DUVOSQUEL (Brussels 1992). M. DENIS, *Maurice Denis: la légende de saint Hubert* (Paris 1999).

[R. BALCH]

HUBERT WALTER

Archbishop of Canterbury, chancellor of England; d. en route, Canterbury to Boxley, England, 1205. He was brought up in the household of his uncle, the great lawyer Ranulf de Glanville, and so was early prepared for the career of civil servant that he pursued with consummate skill. In 1186 he was appointed dean of YORK and in 1189, Bishop of SALISBURY. The following year he accompanied King RICHARD I and Abp. BALDWIN OF CANTERBURY on the Third CRUSADE where he distinguished himself by both his diplomatic ability and his practical care for the crusaders in distress. During the return journey to England he visited the imprisoned King Richard in Austria. Hubert was elected archbishop of CANTERBURY in 1193; the next year Richard appointed him justiciar of England. As justiciar in Richard's absence Hubert governed England, devising new forms of taxation, new methods of local government, and a superior system of governmental record-keeping. Then in 1198, when INNOCENT III renewed the ancient prohibition against priests holding secular office, Hubert resigned the justiciarship. But with the death of Richard the next year, he accepted the office of chancellor under King JOHN and exercised that office with great efficiency until his death. In the course of his unceasing public work, Hubert became embroiled in many quarrels, some with saintly antagonists such as Bp. HUGH OF LINCOLN, others with egotists such as GIRALDUS CAMBRENSIS, one with his own chapter at Christ Church, Canterbury. He incurred at times the wrath of kings and popes. As a result Hubert gained a somewhat justified reputation for being too worldly, though his foundation of PREMONSTRATENSIANS at West Dereham, his solicitude for WITHAM CHARTERHOUSE, and his concern for his cathedral at Canterbury betoken genuine piety.

Bibliography: K. NORGATE, *The Dictionary of National Biography from the Earliest Times to 1900*, 63 v. (London 1885–1900) 10:137–140. C. R. CHENEY, *From Becket to Langton* (Manchester 1956). F. L. CROSS, *The Oxford Dictionary of the Christian Church* (London 1957) 661.

[D. NICHOLL]

HUBMAIER, BALTHASAR

Anabaptist leader involved in the 16th-century Peasant War and key figure in the Moravian Anabaptist movement; b. Friedberg near Augsburg, after 1480?; d. Vienna, March 10, 1528. A priest and disciple of Johann Eck, Hubmaier followed his teacher from Freiburg to Ingolstadt (1512) where he served as professor and pastor. When called to the cathedral at Regensburg (1516), Hubmaier participated in the expulsion of the Jews and served as chaplain of the church, which replaced the razed synagogue. While pastor in Waldshut on the Rhine after 1521, Hubmaier read Luther and personally contacted Erasmus and Zwingli, supporting the latter in the Second Zurich

"The Conversion of St. Hubert."

Disputation (1523), but later joined the Anabaptist opposition. He was involved in the abortive revolt of the peasants and Waldshut against Austrian rule, and fled first to Zurich, and later to Nikolsburg, Moravia, where he led a large Anabaptist community. Arrested upon the request of the Austrian authorities, he was turned over to them and burned at the stake in Vienna. His work is distinguished from other Anabaptist writings by scholastic learning (e.g., *On Free Will* vs. Luther) and the acknowledgment of the legitimacy of government (e.g., *On The Sword* vs. absolute pacifists).

Bibliography: T. BERGSTEN, *Balthasar Hubmaier: Seine Stellung zu Reformation und Täufertum 1521–1528* (Kassel 1961). H. C. VEDDER, *Balthasar Hubmaier, the Leader of the Anabaptists* (New York 1905). G. H. WILLIAMS, ed.; *Spiritual and Anabaptist Writers* (Philadelphia 1957); *The Radical Reformation* (Philadelphia 1962). F. ZOEPFL, *Lexikon für Theologie und Kirche*, ed. J. HOFER and K. RAHNER, 10 v. (2d, new ed. Freiburg 1957–65) 5:503–504. R. DOLLINGER, *Die Religion in Geschichte und Gegenwart*, 7 v. (3d ed. Tübingen 1957–65) 3:464–465.

[G. W. FORELL]

HUC, ÉVARISTE RÉGIS

Missionary and traveler; b. Caylus, Tarn-et-Garonne, France, June 1, 1813; d. Paris, March 1860. He entered the Vincentians Sept. 5, 1836, and after being ordained in 1839, was sent to China. In Macau and then at a Christian mission in southern China he further prepared himself for missionary work and learned the Chinese language. For several years he labored at the Mission of the Valley of Black Waters about 300 miles north of Beijing within the newly created (1840) Vicariate of Tatary-Mongolia. There he studied the dialects and customs of the Tatars and translated various religious works.

In 1844 Huc and his fellow Vincentian Joseph Gabet (1808–53) were ordered by the Vicar Apostolic Martial Mouly to journey through Mongolia and Tibet in order to gain knowledge of the various peoples included in the vicariate. Dressed as lamas to escape attention, and with only a young Christian native, they set out in early August 1844 for Duolon in Inner Mongolia, where they obtained supplies and information for their further journey. They left there October 1 and proceeded westward, crossing the Huang-Ho and the Mu Us Desert to Dabsun-nor and Ninghsia. After reaching Gansu province, they were hospitably received at the large and famous Buddhist monastery of Kumbum. Remaining there for some months, they learned the Tibetan language, and Hue translated a small Tibetan work dealing with the 42 points of Buddha's instruction.

In October 1845 they joined at Qinghai the caravan of a Tibetan embassy returning from Beijing, and after much hardship crossing the snow-covered Bayan Kara and Tanggula Mountains, they entered Lhasa Jan. 29, 1846. There they enjoyed the favor of the Tibetan officials and began their apostolate. However, after about six weeks the enmity of the Chinese ambassador, Ki-Chan, forced their departure. At the end of September they arrived in Guangzhou, where Huc remained for nearly three years, but Gabet returned to Europe and later went to Rio de Janeiro. Huc returned to France in 1852 in shattered health and left the order in 1853.

Along with the many other writings of Huc and Gabet in the *Annales de la propagation de la foi* and the *Annales de la Congregation de la Mission,* Huc is renowned for *Souvenirs d'un voyage dans la Tartarie, le Thibet, et la Chine pendant les années 1844–46* (2 v. Paris 1850), which has gone through numerous editions and has been published in eight languages. He wrote also *L'Empire Chinois* (2 v. Paris 1854), which received recognition from the French Academy, and *Le Christianisme en Chine, en Tartarie, et au Thibet* (4 v. Paris 1857–58).

Bibliography: E. R. HUC, *Souvenirs of a Journey through Tartary, Tibet, and China during the Years 1844, 1845 and 1846,* tr. J. M. PLANCHET, 2 v. (Peking 1931); *High Road in Tartary,* ed. J. BEDIER (New York 1948); *Mémoires de la Congrégation de la Mission,* v.3 *La Chine* (Paris 1912) 407–. R. STREIT and J. DINDINGER, *Bibliotheca missionum* (Freiburg 1916–) 12:230–238. H. CORDIER, *The Catholic Encyclopedia,* ed. C. G. HERBERMANN et al., 16 v. (New York 1907–14; suppl. 1922) 7:510.

[J. C. WILLKE]

HUCBALD OF SAINT-AMAND

Benedictine poet, hagiographer, and theorist of GREGORIAN CHANT; b. *c.* 840; d. SAINT-AMAND, France, June 20, 930. He studied with his uncle Milo and HEIRIC OF AUXERRE before becoming director of schools at Saint-Amand. Hucbald's musical fame rests on the Offices he composed and his treatise *De institutione harmonica,* one of the first attempts to unite Greco-Boethian theories with chant practice and to find an accurate symbol for pitch notation [M. Gerbert, *Scriptores ecclesiastici de musica sacra potissimum,* 3 v. (Milan 1931) 1:104–121]. His poem in honor of Charles II the Bald, *Ecloga de calvis,* is a *tour de force,* using only words beginning with "c" [*Monumenta Germaniae Historica: Poetae* (Berlin 1826–) 4:265–271]. Lives of several saints [*Patrologia Latina,* ed. J. P. Migne, 217 v. indexes 4 v. (Paris 1878–90) 132:825–1050] may safely be attributed to him.

Bibliography: H. MÜLLER, *Hucbalds echte und unechte Schriften über Musik* (Leipzig 1884). L. VAN DER ESSEN, "Hucbald de Saint-Amand et sa place dans le mouvement hagiographique médiéval," *Revue d'histoire ecclésiastique* 12 (1923) 331–351; 522–552. R. G. WEAKLAND, "Hucbald as Musician and Theorist," *Musical Quarterly* 42 (New York 1956) 66–84. "The Compositions of Hucbald," *Études grégoriennes* 3 (1959) 155–162. Y. CHARTIER, "La *Musica* d'Hucbald de Saint-Amand: Introduction, établissement du texte, traduction et commentaire" (Ph.D. diss. University of Paris, 1972); *L'Œuvre musicale d'Hucbald de Saint-Amand: Les compositions et le traité de musique* (Quebec 1995). R. L. CROCKER, "Hucbald" in *The New Grove Dictionary of Music and Musicians,* v. 8, ed. S. SADIE (New York 1980) 758–759. D. M. RANDEL, ed., *The Harvard Biographical Dictionary of Music* (Cambridge 1996) 398. N. SLONIMSKY, ed. *Baker's Biographical Dictionary of Musicians,* (New York 1992) 808.

[R. G. WEAKLAND]

HUDDLESTON, JOHN

Benedictine monk; b. (place unknown) 1608; d. London, Sept. 22, 1698. The second son of Joseph of Farington Hall, near Preston, Lancashire, he is said to have served in the army of Charles I during the Civil Wars. He is considered to have been educated and ordained at Douay College, although his name is not found in the Douay lists. When he came to the English mission, he served first in Wensleydale, Yorkshire, and then at the home of Mr. Whitgrave at Moseley, Staffordshire. On

Sept. 3, 1651, CHARLES II was defeated by Cromwell at the Battle of Worcester, and fleeing in disguise he came to Moseley, where HUDDLESTON hid him in his own room for several days. Charles never forgot that Huddleston had saved his life, and when he returned to power he lodged him in the palace of Somerset House in London as chaplain to the Queen Mother, Henrietta Maria, and after her death in 1669 appointed him chaplain to Queen Catherine of Braganza. When Charles was on his death-bed, he was asked by his Catholic brother, the future James II, if he wanted a priest. Replying fervently that he did, the king was converted and received the Last Sacraments from Huddleston, who had been fetched secretly by a back stair to the bedroom, after the Protestant clergy had departed.

Bibliography: B. WELDON, *Chronological Notes* (London 1881). J. GILLOW, *A Literary and Biographical History or Bibliographical Dictionary of the English Catholics from 1534 to the Present time*, 5 v. (London-New York 1885–1902; repr. New York 1961) 3:463–465. H. FOLEY, *Records of the English Province of the Society of Jesus,* 7 v. (London 1877–82). J. S. CLARKE, *Life of James II,* 2 v. (London 1816).

[B. WHELAN]

HUDSON, DANIEL ELDRED

Editor; b. Nahant, Mass., Dec. 18, 1849; d. Notre Dame, Ind., Jan. 12, 1934. He was the son of Samuel Henry and Mary (Hawkes) Hudson. He received his early education in the public schools of Nahant and at Holy Cross College, Worcester, Mass. He entered the novitiate of the Congregation of Holy Cross at Notre Dame, March 7, 1871, and was professed March 19, 1872. He was ordained on June 4, 1875, and appointed editor of the *Ave Maria* that same year. This octavo weekly magazine, which became an important factor in the propagation of devotion to the Blessed Virgin, had begun publication at Notre Dame in May 1865 under the direction of Rev. Edward F. Sorin and his associates, Mother Angela Gillespie of the Sisters of Holy Cross and her brother, Rev. Neal Gillespie, CSC. Although other priests of the Holy Cross Congregation assisted Hudson, the magazine came to have a special tone that was attributed to him. Little that he wrote in *Ave Maria* was signed, but he was considered the author of its editorial comments during these years. Hudson did not hesitate to answer journalists who attacked the Church, and he had definite opinions on most of the religious problems of the day. He exerted a directing influence on the careers of Charles Warren Stoddard, Maurice Francis Egan, and Christian Reed (Frances Tiernan) and gave encouragement to many young Catholic writers. He retired in 1928 because of illness.

Daniel Eldred Hudson. (Ave Maria Press)

Bibliography: J. W. CAVANAUGH, *Ave Maria* NS 39 (Jan. 27–Feb. 17, 1934) 97–101, 135–140, 169–173, 201–205. J. J. WALSH, *Catholic World* 139 (April 1934) 31–39.

[T. T. MCAVOY]

HUELGAS DE BURGOS, ABBEY OF

Cistercian convent of the Blessed Virgin, BURGOS archdiocese, established and richly endowed on June 1, 1187, by Alfonso VIII of Castile as a burial place for his family. Huelgas became the head of the Cistercian convents in Castile and León, and in 1199 was affiliated with CÎTEAUX rather than with its own mother convent, that of Tulebras. It had civil jurisdiction over 64 villages. Not only was Huelgas exempt from episcopal jurisdiction but it exercised its own quasi-episcopal authority over convents, churches, and towns, conferring benefices, authorizing and restricting preaching, judging papal dispositions and matrimonial and civil cases, supervising charitable works and notaries, giving faculties to confessors, and even presiding over synods of abbesses of divers convents. Its abbesses were usually of royal blood, and many of the nuns were of the high nobility. In 1257 the number of noblewomen was restricted to 100. The abbey's spiritual jurisdiction was not granted by the pope but was based on immemorial custom. The bishops of Burgos and even the abbot of Cîteaux contested this jurisdiction, but Urban VIII confirmed it. In 1873 Huelgas, along with all other exempt jurisdictions in Spain, was suspended by Pius IX.

In 1590 the official term of the abbess, which had been perpetual, became triennial. Not all of the medieval building remains, but the architecture is noteworthy (Romanesque ogives, Mudéjar, ornate floral decorations). In 1808 the convent was looted by Napoleonic troops. Huelgas contains the Moorish banner captured at Las Navas de Tolosa in 1212, the cross of Rodrigo XIMÉNEZ, many documents, and a codex of medieval songs. Alfonso XI, Henry II, and John I were crowned there, and in 1938 the Nationalist government was sworn in at Las Huelgas. The Cisterian convent of Las Huelgas in Valladolid, founded in 1282 by Maria de Molina, was modeled on that at Burgos.

Bibliography: A. RODRÍGUEZ LÓPEZ, *El real monasterio de las Huelgas de Burgos,* 2 v. (Burgos 1907). M. GÓMEZ-MORENO, *El panteón real de las Huelgas de Burgos* (Madrid 1946). L. DE ECHEVERRÍA, ''En torno a la jurisdicción eclesiástica de la abadesa de las Huelgas,'' *Revista española de derecho canónico* 1 (1946) 219–233. J. M. ESCRIVÁ, *La abadesa de Las Huelgas* (Madrid 1944). *Enciclopedia de la Religión Católica,* ed. R. D. FERRERES et al., 7 v. (Barcelona 1950–56) 4:254–255.

[D. W. LOMAX]

HUET, PIERRE DANIEL

Theologian and philosopher, the last of the ''Christian skeptics'' following after M. E. de MONTAIGNE and P. CHARRON; b. Caen (Normandy), Feb. 8, 1630; d. Paris, Jan. 26, 1721. In 1670 Louis XIV appointed him Bossuet's assistant in teaching the Dauphin. Here he initiated the famous set of classical texts, *ad usum Delphini.* At court Huet became a priest, and was later appointed bishop of Soissons, which diocese he traded for Avranches. He retired in 1699 to a Jesuit establishment in Paris to which he had given his immense library (now in the Bibliothèque Nationale), and he remained there until his death.

His most important works were *Demonstratio Evangelica* (1679), which grew out of his conversations with Rabbi Menasseh ben Israel in Amsterdam; *Censura philosophiae cartesianae* (1689), a skeptical critique of Cartesianism; and the posthumous skeptical *Traité philosophique de la foiblesse de l'esprit humain,* written around 1692, first published in 1723. Huet's views combined thorough-going SKEPTICISM, LATITUDINARIANISM, probabilistic defenses of Christianity, empirical scientific researches, and advocacy of FIDEISM. He was considered

the most learned man of his age, and his erudite findings were used by Enlightenment figures to attack traditional religion.

Bibliography: P. D. HUET, *Traité philosophique de la foiblesse de l'esprit humain* (Amsterdam 1723), Eng. *A Philosophical Treatise concerning the Weakness of Human Understanding* (London 1725). C. J. C. BARTHOLOMÈSS, *Huet, évêque d'Avranches, ou le scepticisme théologique* (Paris 1850). L. TOLMER, ''Pierre-Daniel Huet: Humaniste-physicien,'' *Académie Nationale des Sciences, Arts et Belles-lettres de Caen. Mémoires* NS 11 (1949) 718.

[R. H. POPKIN]

HÜGEL, FRIEDRICH VON

Theologian, philosopher, writer; b. Florence, Italy, May 5, 1852; d. London, England, Jan. 27, 1925. Baron Carl von Hügel, his father, was of German origin and was serving as Austrian ambassador to Tuscany in 1852. Friedrich's mother, who was of Scottish origin, was a convert from Presbyterianism. Anatole, a younger brother, became well known as an anthropologist at Cambridge University. Educated by private tutors and given no formal university training, Friedrich was left deaf, nervous, and delicate in health by an attack of typhoid fever (1870). Raymond Hocking, a Dutch Dominican, exercised great influence over his early spiritual development. In 1873 Hügel married Lady Mary (Molly) Herbert, a convert from Anglicanism, and by her had three daughters. The couple dwelt in England from 1876, at Hampstead (1876–1903) and then in London at Kensington (1903–25).

Among Baron von Hügel's close friends were Wilfrid WARD and two French priests: Henri BREMOND and Henri Huvelin. Huvelin had great spiritual influence over Hügel and guided him in his attempt to overcome discouragement over ill health and a tendency to worry excessively. Under Huvelin's influence, Hügel came to distrust a type of SCHOLASTIC theology that resorted to syllogisms to answer current philosophical and scientific attacks on Catholicism. Encouraged by Louis DUCHESNE, the Baron studied the Church's historical foundations, utilizing his command over English, French, German, and Italian. After learning Hebrew he commented regularly on Biblical topics for the *Bulletin Critique,* edited by Duchesne. Hügel came early under the influence of the philosophers Rudolf Eucken, Maurice BLONDEL, and Lucien LABERTHONNIÈRE. Contact with Ernst TROELTSCH from 1902 confirmed Hügel in his conviction that religion begins with the otherness of reality originating in the transcendent God.

In 1897 Hügel contributed to the Catholic International Scientific Congress at Fribourg, Switzerland, a paper entitled "The Historical Method and the Documents of the Hexateuch." His first writing published in English was a privately-printed pamphlet on Biblical inspiration and inerrancy (1901). Hügel began in 1897 a lifelong friendship with George TYRRELL, who was later expelled from the Jesuits and excommunicated as a Modernist. After the Baron had introduced Father Tyrrell to the religious writings of Continental authors, the two men frequently discussed Biblical criticism and mysticism, Hügel's favorite topics. By 1901 Hügel was disturbed by the storm brewing over the head of another of his friends, Alfred LOISY, whose views on the Book of Genesis and on the Fourth Gospel were troubling the Holy Office. When Loisy's *L'Évangile et L'Église* appeared in 1902, Hügel praised it as an effective reply to Harnack's *Das Wesen des Christentums* (1900). He was more reserved in his praise for Loisy's *Autour d'un petit livre* (1903). Both of these books were placed on the Index in 1904. In 1904 von Hügel founded the London Society for the Study of Religion, a discussion group that developed into a notable society of Catholic scholars. Hügel was never condemned as a Modernist, but his admiration for and friendship with many Modernist leaders caused deep concern when Modernism was officially condemned in 1907.

Hügel's best book was *The Mystical Element of Religion as Studied in St. Catherine of Genoa and Her Friends* (1908). In *Eternal Life* (1912) he argued that eternal life is not restricted to the hereafter but is part of man's earthly existence. The first volume of his *Essays and Addresses on the Philosophy of Religion* appeared in 1921, and the second volume in 1926. Hügel was too ill to deliver the Gifford Lectures for 1924–25, but his incomplete manuscript was printed in 1931 as *The Reality of God.*

Bibliography: *Selected Letters, 1896–1924,* ed. with a memoir B. HOLLAND (New York 1928); *Letters to a Niece,* ed. G. GREEN (Chicago 1955). M. NÉDONCELLE, *Baron Friedrich von Hügel: A Study of His Life and Thought,* tr. M. VERNON (New York 1937). M. DE LA BEDOYÈRE, *The Life of Baron von Hügel* (New York 1952). R. MARLÉ, comp., *Au Coeur de la crise moderniste: Lettres de Maurice Blondel, Henri Bremond, Fr. von Hügel, Alfred Loisy* (Paris 1960). M. D. PETRE, *Von Hügel and Tyrrell* (New York 1938). J. STEINMANN, *Friedrich von Hügel* (Paris 1963).

[F. M. O'CONNOR]

HUGH BONNEVAUX, ST.

Cistercian monk, abbot of Bonnevaux in Dauphiné, France; b. Châteauneuf d'Isère, France, c. 1120; d. 1194. He was born into the family of the counts of Châteauneuf and was a nephew of St. HUGH OF GRENOBLE. About 1138 he entered the Cistercian Abbey of Miroir, near Louhans. When he became ill during his novitiate, he re-

ceived a letter of encouragement from St. BERNARD. He was sent to the Abbey of Léoncel, near Saint-Jean-en-Royans, where he became abbot in 1162. In 1166 he was elected abbot of Bonnevaux, the mother abbey, and founded three daughter abbeys: Sauveréal (1173), Valbenoîte (1184), and Valcroissant (1188). During the Octavian schism (*see* ANTIPOPE) his efforts led Emperor FREDERICK BARBAROSSA to recognize Pope ALEXANDER III (1177) by the Peace of Venice. Hugh's grave, defiled (1576) during the THIRTY YEARS' WAR, was recently discovered in the ruins of a small chapel built in his honor.

Feast: April 1 (Cistercians; Breviary of Valence since 1473 and in its Proper since 1884).

Bibliography: Sources. BERNARD OF CLAIRVAUX, Epistola 322; *Patrologia Latina,* ed. J. P. MIGNE 182:527–528. FREDERICK I BARBAROSSA in E. MARTÈNE and U. DURAND, *Thesaurus novus anecdotorum* (Paris 1717) 1: 585. ALEXANDER III, Epistola, *ibid.* 1:1847. U. CHEVALIER, *Cartulaire de l'abbaye N.-D. de Bonnevaux* (Grenoble 1889). M. A. DIMIER, *Cartulaire de l'abbaye N.-D. de Bonnevaux* (Tamié 1942). *S. Bernardi vita prima, Patrologia Latina,* ed. J. P. MIGNE 185–345. *Exordium magnum, ibid.* 1193–95. **Literature.** M. F. CHUZEL, *Histoire de l'abbaye de Bonnevaux* (Bourgoin 1932). M. A. DIMIER, *Saint Hugues de Bonnevaux* (Tamié 1942); "Un Office rimé de saint H. de B.," *Revue Bénédictine* 68 (1958) 265–280. M. B. BRARD, *Catholicisme* 5:1018–19.

[M. A. DIMIER]

HUGH OF AMIENS

Archbishop of Rouen; b. *c.* 1080; d. Rouen, Nov. 11, 1164. He was educated in the famous Cathedral School of Laon, and entered the monastic life at CLUNY. His administrative qualities marked him for rapid promotion and he was appointed prior of LEWES in 1123, then, at the instigation of Henry I of England, abbot of the new foundation at READING in 1125. He is said to have been a champion of the formal celebration of the Feast of the IMMACULATE CONCEPTION. He gave active support to the claims of Pope INNOCENT II against those of Anacletus II. He welcomed (May 9, 1131) Anacletus as his guest at Rouen, to which see he had been elevated Sept. 11, 1130. As a strict disciplinarian, Hugh came into conflict with certain abbots, notably Alan of Saint-Wandrille, who disputed his authority over them. He was much sought after as an arbitrator in both ecclesiastical and secular matters and enjoyed the support of Henry I, Stephen, and Henry II.

Hugh was the author of several exegetic and polemical writings. Notable are the seven books of *Dialogi,* dealing with God and His attributes, the creation, the fall of Satan and of man, free will, the Sacraments, and life eternal. He also wrote three books *Contra haereticos.* His views on the nonvalidity of the Sacraments administered by excommunicated priests caused some scandal, but he is one of the most redoubtable 12th-century champions of Church tradition. He was influenced by St. AUGUSTINE in the matter of grace and free will.

Bibliography: Works. *Patrologia Latina*, ed. J. P. MIGNE, 217 v., indexes 4 v. (Paris 1878–90) 192:1131–1352; *Epistolae, Patrologia Latina* 179: 665–666; 180:1617; 186:1399. E. VACANDARD, *Dictionnaire de théologie catholique*, ed. A. VACANT et al., 15 v. (Paris 1903–50; Tables Générales 1951–) 7.1:205–215. P. HÉBERT, "Hugues III d'Amiens," *Revue des questions historiques* 64 (1898) 325–371. J. B. HURRY, *In Honour of Hugh de Boves* (Reading, Eng. 1911). D. VAN DEN EYNDE, "Nouvelles précisions chronologiques sur quelques oeuvres théologiques du XIIᵉ siècle," *Franciscan Studies* 13 (1953) 71–118. F. LECOMTE, "Un Commentaire scripturaire du XIIᵉ s.: Le *Tractatus in Hexaemeron* de Hugues d'Amiens," *Archives d'histoire doctrinale et littéraire du moyen-âge* 33 (1958) 227–294. J. C. DIDIER, *Catholicisme* 5:1038–39.

[P. B. CORBETT]

HUGH OF BALMA

Carthusian mystical writer. Precise information regarding the dates or other circumstances of his birth and death is not available. It is known only that he was a Carthusian monk, and later prior of the Charterhouse of Meyriat. Sometime between 1246 and 1297 he wrote a work called *De theologia mystica*. This book has also been attributed to St. Bonaventure and printed in collections of his works under the title *Theologia mystica*. This is not to be confused with Bonaventure's *De triplici via*, of whose authenticity there is no question. Hugh's *De theologia mystica* was also sometimes known as *De triplici via*, and sometimes, from its first words, as *Viae Sion lugent*. This book was among the first to attempt a methodical description of the interior life according to the schema of the "three ways." In the purgative way the soul considers God's goodness in the mysteries of Creation and Redemption, and is cleansed of its sin by contrition. In the illuminative way, it meditates upon the Scriptures and becomes more enlightened and guided by grace. In the unitive way, it is closely united to God by the experience of divine wisdom in contemplation. In describing contemplation as a *cognitio Dei per ignorantiam*—a knowledge of God by unknowing—Hugh showed himself a disciple of Pseudo-Dionysius. He held that the affective union with God in which contemplation culminates confers a knowledge far more penetrating than intellect and reason can provide. Among the means of arriving at truly contemplative prayer, Hugh made much of the usefulness of "anagogic movements" of the soul, short upward movements of mind and heart, fervent aspirations that build up and maintain the desire of tending toward God. The analogy of this type of prayer with that of the *CLOUD OF UNKNOWING* is evident. It may also be compared with the Jesus-Prayer of Hesychasm in the Eastern Church, as this was described in the *Story of a Russian Pilgrim* [see B. du Moustier, "The Jesus-Prayer," *Cross and Crown* (September 1960) 301–312]. Through the *De triplici via* this simple way to unitive prayer seems to have influenced the teachings of Jean GERSON, DENIS THE CARTHUSIAN, HENRY OF HERP (HARPHIUS VAN ERP), BERNARDINO OF LAREDO, David Augustine BAKER, and many others. Most of these also show the influence of Hugh in other points of spiritual doctrine.

Bibliography: S. AUTORE, in *Dictionnaire de théologie catholique*, ed. A. VACANT et al., 15 v. (Paris 1903–50; Tables générales 1951–) 7.1:215–220. A. M. SOCHAY, *Catholicisme. Hier, aujourd'hui et demain*, ed. G. JACQUEMET (Paris 1947–) 5:1028–30. J. KRYNEN, "La Pratique et la théorie de l'amour sans connaissance dans le *Viae Sion lugent* d'Hugues de Balma," *Revue d'ascétique et de mystique* 49 (1964) 161–183.

[B. DU MOUSTIER]

HUGH OF CLUNY, ST.

Sixth abbot of CLUNY; b. Burgundy, 1024; d. Cluny, April 29, 1109. Hugh, son of Dalmace, Count of Semur and of Aremberge, was educated by Bp. Hugh of Auxerre. In 1038 he entered Cluny, then governed by Abbot ODILO. He was ordained in 1044, was named prior in 1048, and succeeded in ending a controversy between Emperor HENRY III and the Abbey of Payerne. On the death of Odilo, January 1049, Hugh was elected abbot of Cluny, receiving the abbatial blessing from Abp. Hugh of Besançon on Feb. 22, 1049. His 60 years as abbot were prodigiously fruitful and marked the apogee of Cluny (*see* CLUNIAC REFORM). Hugh took part in numerous councils and synods, such as those at the Lateran (1050, 1059, and 1080), Vienne (1060), and Plaisance and Clermont (1095). The popes entrusted him with important diplomatic missions to Hungary (1051) and Germany (1072); he was present at the encounter between Emperor HENRY IV and GREGORY VII at Canossa. Although the greatest expansion of Cluny had taken place before Hugh's abbacy, Cluny continued to found new monasteries and aggregate older ones during his term. Of particular interest is the founding of the first convent of Cluniac nuns at Marcigny in 1056. Hugh obtained papal confirmation of the temporal and spiritual privileges of his order. A former Cluniac monk, Pope URBAN II, returned to consecrate the main altar of the abbey church on Oct. 25, 1095. Despite intense activity in the service of his monks and of the Church, Hugh remained a man of prayer. His human qualities won him the friendship of the great and the confidence of men of lesser estate. His prudence and humaneness were noteworthy, especially in his rulings on liturgical celebrations and monastic discipline. Hugh was canonized by CALLISTUS II, Jan. 1, 1120.

Feast: April 29.

Bibliography: Sources. M. MARRIER and A. DUCHESNE, eds., *Bibliotheca cluniacensis* (Paris 1614; 1915) 413–472. *Patrologia Latina*, ed. J. P. MIGNE, 217 v. (Paris 1878–90) 159:857–984. A. BRUEL, ed., *Recueil des chartes de l'abbaye de Cluny*, 6 v. (Paris 1876–1903) 4:174–824; 5:1–230. **Literature.** A. L'HUILLIER, *Vie de saint Hugues* (Solesmes 1888). G. TELLENBACH, "Zum Wesen der Cluniacenser," *Saeculum* 9 (1958) 370–378. K. HALLINGER, "Klunys Bräuche zur Zeit Hugos des Grossen, 1049–1109," *Zeitschrift der Savigny-Stiftung für Rechtsgeschichte, Kanonistische Abteilung* 45 (1959) 99–140. H. DIENER, "Das Verhältnis Clunys zu den Bischöfen, vor allem in der Zeit seines Abtes Hugo, 1049–1109," in J. WOLLASCH et al., *Neue Forschungen über Cluny und die Cluniacenser*, ed. G. TELLENBACH (Freiburg 1959) 219–352. G. CANTARELLA and D. TUNIZ, eds., *Cluny e il suo abate Ugo: splendore e crisi di un grande ordine monastico* (Milan 1983).

[R. GRÉGOIRE]

HUGH OF DIE

Gregorian reformer, archbishop; called also Hugh of Romans; b. *c.* 1040; d. Susa, Italy, October 1106. He was ordained and served as precentor of the Cathedral of Lyons. He was consecrated bishop of Die in 1074 and was translated to the archbishopric of Lyons in 1082–83. From 1075 to 1087 he was papal legate in France and, in addition, from 1082–83 he was primate of the French Church. A stern and uncompromising advocate of Pope GREGORY VII's Church reforms, Hugh battled successfully with both the French hierarchy and the French monarchy to secure the objectives of the reform in France (*see* INVESTITURE STRUGGLE). After Gregory VII's death, Hugh criticized his successor, Pope VICTOR III, for compromising the principles of the GREGORIAN REFORM. As a result, Hugh was excommunicated at the Council of Benevento (Aug. 29, 1087). He was soon reconciled, however, and in 1094 Pope URBAN II restored him to the post of papal legate. In 1095–96 Hugh accompanied Urban on his tour through France. As a leading advocate of monastic reform, Hugh was an early patron and supporter of the CISTERCIANS, and became that order's first protector. In 1100 Hugh went on crusade to the Holy Land.

Bibliography: Sources. HUGH OF DIE, *Epistolae et privilegia*, M. BOUQUET, *Recueil de historiens des Gaules et de la France (Rerum gallicarum et francicarum scriptores)*, 24 v. (Paris 1738–1904) 14:776–797; *Patrologia Latina* 157:507–528. HUGH OF FLAVIGNY, *Chronicon, Monumenta Germaniae Historica: Scriptores* (Berlin 1826–) 8:280–503. **Literature.** F. LIEBERMANN, "Anselm von Canterbury und Hugo von Lyon," *Historische Aufsätze dem Andenken an Georg Waitz gewidmet* (Hanover 1886) 156–203. ABBÉ RONY, "Hugues de Romans: Légat pontifical," *Revue des questions historiques* 107 (1927) 287–303; "La Politique française de Grégoire VII: Conflit entre le pape et son légat," *ibid.* 109 (1928) 5–34; "La Légation d'Hugues . . . sous le pontificat d'Urbain II," *ibid.* 112 (1930) 124–147; "Élection de Victor III: Conflit entre le nouveau pape et Hugues . . . ," *Revue d'histoire de l'Église de France* 14 (1928) 145–160. T. SCHIEFFER, *Die päpstlichen Legaten in Frankreich vom Vertrage von Meersen (870) bis zum Schisma von 1130* (Berlin 1935). A. FLICHE and V. MARTIN eds., *Histoire de l'église depuis les origines jusqu'à nos jours* (Paris 1935–) v.8.

[J. A. BRUNDAGE]

HUGH OF DIGNE

Franciscan Provincial Minister in Provence and commentator on the Franciscan Rule; date of birth unknown; d. between 1254 and 1257. He was a native of Provence, the son of Berengar of Digne, a merchant, and Huguette of Barjols; St. DOUCELINE was his sister. Hugh was of dark complexion, and medium height; he had a powerful voice. He was an eccentric but influential figure among the Franciscans of southern France and was regarded by the FRANCISCAN SPIRITUALS as one of their forerunners. In his later years he lived at Hyères, where he preached to St. LOUIS IX, and where he was visited by the chronicler SALIMBENE, who gives a vivid account of his austerity, his freedom of speech in denouncing the inadequacies even of the papal Curia, and his devotion to poverty and to the doctrines of JOACHIM OF FIORE. Hugh inspired the formation of the Order of Friars of the Sack, and also of his sister's Order of Beguines, of which he was the spiritual director (*see* BEGUINES AND BEGHARDS). He wrote two treatises on poverty, *De finibus paupertatis* and *Tractatus de paupertate inter zelatorem paupertatis et inimicum domesticum,* and an elaborate exposition of the Rule (probably 1241–43), which was the first fully systematic commentary. In his zeal for poverty, his learning, and Joachism he resembled the later leaders of the Spirituals. His interpretation of poverty was strict, but by no means rigid or inflexible; and he took pains to defend by scholastic argument a fairly extensive use of books—without which his own range of learning would have been impossible.

Bibliography: HUGH OF DIGNE, *Expositio regulae*, in *Firmamenta trium ordinum* (Paris 1512; 2d ed. 1513) pt. 4: fol. 34 va-54 rb; also in 1st ed. *Monumenta ordinis minorum* (Salamanca 1506–11); *Tractatus de paupertate*, in *Firmamenta* (1512) fol. 105 ra-108 vb. N. MORIN, *Speculum minorum* (Rouen 1509). C. FLOROVSKY, "*De finibus paupertatis* auctore Hugone de Digna, O.F.M.," *Archivum Franciscanum historicum* 5 (1912) 277–290. SALIMBENE, *Cronica fratris Salimbene de Adam*, ed. O. HOLDER-EGGER in *Monumenta Germanica Scriptores* 32 (1905–13). J. POULENC, *Catholicisme* 5:1020–22. R. B. BROOKE, *Early Franciscan Government: Elias to Bonaventure* (Cambridge, Eng. 1959).

[R. B. BROOKE]

HUGH OF FLEURY

Historian, biographer; d. after 1118; not to be confused with Hugh of Fleury of Canterbury (d. 1124). Hugh was a Benedictine priest of Saint-Benoît-sur-Loire, who was known also as Hugh of Sainte-Marie. In 1109 he wrote a *Historia ecclesiastica* in four books, dedicated to Adela, Countess of Blois. In 1110 he reworked the *Historia* into six books, covering the period to 855. In about 1114, he wrote a chronicle of the kings of France, *Modernorum regum Francorum liber* (842–1108). Sometime after 1102, he wrote a *Tractatus de regia potestate et sacerdotali dignitate* in two books, addressed to HENRY I of England. This work presented Hugh's stand in the INVESTITURE struggle, restating the divine rights of both royal and ecclesiastical authority. Besides the *Vita sancti Sacerdotis,* a biography of Bishop Sacerdos of Limoges, several other works have been attributed to him, including the *De miraculis s. Benedicti.*

Bibliography: Works. *Monumenta Germaniae Historica*: Scriptores (Berlin 1826–) 9:237–395. *Patrologia Latina*, ed. J. P. MIGNE, 217 v., indexes 4 v. (Paris 1878–90) 163:821–830; *Monumenta Germaniae Historica*: Libelli de lite. (Berlin 1826–) 2:465–494; *Vita s. Sacerdotis, Acta Sanctorum* (Antwerp 1643– ; Venice 1734– ; Paris 1863–) May 2:15–23; *De miraculis s. Benedicti*, in *Les Miracles de S. Benoît*, ed. E. DE CERTAIN (Paris 1858) 357–371. Literature. M. MANITIUS, *Geschichte der lateinischen Literatur des Mittelalters*, 3 v. (Munich 1911–31) 3:518–521. A. WILMART, "L'Histoire ecclésiastique composée par Hugues de Fleury et ses destinataires," *Revue Bénédictine* 50 (1938) 293–305. Y. M. J. CONGAR, *Catholicisme* 5:1033.

[B. LACROIX]

HUGH OF FOSSE, BL.

First abbot general of the PREMONSTRATENSIANS; b. Fosses, near Namur, Belgium, probably 1093; d. Prémontré, Feb. 10, 1164. Chaplain of Bp. Burchard of Cambrai, he became the leading disciple of NORBERT OF XANTEN in 1119. Having been appointed Norbert's representative at PRÉMONTRÉ in 1126, he succeeded him as abbot in 1128. Hugh guided the rapid development of the order and formulated its first constitutions, which were in many ways similar to those of the CISTERCIANS. He drafted the first *Vita Norberti* and promulgated the ceremonial books of the order. It is not certain that he was the "Hugo Farsitus" who wrote *De miraculis b. Mariae Suessionensis* (c. 1135; *Patrologia Latina*, ed. J. P. Migne, 79: 1777–1800). His cult was approved in 1927; it is doubtful that the relics in the priory of Bois-Seigneur-Isaac are his.

Feast: Feb. 10.

Bibliography: *Acta Sanctorum* Feb. 2:378. H. LAMY, *Vie du B. Hugues . . .* (Charleroi 1925). F. PETIT, *La spiritualité des Pré-*

montrés (Paris 1947). P. F. LEFÈVRE, *L'Ordinaire de Prémontré* (Louvain 1941). J. DUBOIS, *Catholicisme* 5:1025–26.

[N. BACKMUND]

HUGH OF FOUILLOY

Prior, spiritual writer, CANON REGULAR OF ST. AUGUSTINE; b. Fouilloy, near Corbie and Amiens, between 1100 and 1110; d. Saint-Laurent-au-Bois, 1172–73. Probably a student at the Benedictine Abbey of CORBIE, he joined the nearby priory of Saint-Laurent-au-Bois in the period when it was not under Corbie but was held by Austin canons. In 1153 he became prior, four years after declining the more important priorship of Saint-Denis, Reims. Before the research of J. MABILLON his works were usually attributed to his famous contemporary, HUGH OF SAINT-VICTOR (d. 1141). Each of his four major spiritual treatises is built upon a sustained analogy; the religious cloister and the detached, recollected soul; medicines for physical illnesses and remedies for analogous sins; carnal marriage and spiritual marriage with Christ; and the hub, rim, and spokes of a wheel as the figure of the religious superior, community, and the various virtues or vices that may govern their relationship. These four are the *De claustro animae* (*Patrologia Latina*, ed. J. P. Migne 176:1017–1182), the *De medicina animae* (*Patrologia Latina* 176:1183–1202), the *De Nuptiis* (*Patrologia Latina* 176:1201–18), and the unpublished *De rota praelationis et de rota simulationis.* He wrote also the *De avibus ad Raynerum,* which is included as bk. 1, ch. 1 to 56 of the treatise *De bestiis* (*Patrologia Latina* 177:15–55). His *De pastoribus et ovibus* and his chartulary of Saint-Laurent are both unpublished.

Bibliography: J. MABILLON, *Annales Ordinis S. Benedicti*, 6 v. (Lucca 1739–45) 6:421–425, with his letter of refusal to Reims, repr. in *Patrologia Latina*, ed. J. P. MIGNE, 217 v., indexes 4 v. (Paris 1878–90) 196:1553–58. *Histoire littéraire de la France* (Paris 1814–1941) 13:492–507. M. MANITIUS, *Geschichte der lateinischen Literatur des Mittelalters*, 3 v. (Munich 1911–31) 3:226–228 H. PELTIER, "Hugues de Fouilloy, chanoine régulier de Saint-Laurent-au-Bois," *Revue du moyen-âge latin* 2 (1946) 25–44. J. C. DIDIER, *Catholicisme* 5:1033–34.

[W. E. WILKIE]

HUGH OF GRENOBLE, ST.

Bishop and reformer; b. Châteauneuf-d'Isère, Dauphiné, France, 1052; d. Grenoble, France, April 1, 1132. His father, Odilo, a military man, ended his days in a Carthusian monastery. Hugh's first ecclesiastical office was a canonry at the cathedral of Valence, an office he held although still a layman. His learning and other qualities so impressed Bp. HUGH OF DIE, who was papal legate and later to become archbishop of Lyons, that he took him into his service. In 1080, while at a synod at Lyons, Hugh, although only 27 and not yet ordained, was elected bishop of Grenoble, a see much in need of reform. Ordained immediately, Hugh went to Rome and received consecration from Pope GREGORY VII. His strenuous efforts at reform during an episcopate of 52 years were marked with success, although at times he thought himself a failure and repeatedly asked to be replaced. His friendship with BRUNO THE CARTHUSIAN and the monks of La Grande Chartreuse, to whom he gave land and a warm welcome in 1084, was a source of great comfort to him. He was canonized by INNOCENT II in 1134; his life was written by his contemporary, GUIGO I, prior of La Grande Chartreuse. His relics, preserved in the cathedral at Grenoble, were lost in the THIRTY YEARS' WAR.

Feast: April 1.

Bibliography: GUIGO I OF THE GRANDE CHARTREUSE, *Vie de saint Hugues,* tr. M. A. CHOMEL (Salzburg, Austria 1986). *Patrologia Latina,* ed. J. P. MIGNE, 217 v. (Paris 1878–90) 153:759–784. *Acta Sanctorum* April 1:36–46. *Bibliotheca hagiographica latina antiquae ct mediae aetatis,* 2 v. (Brussels 1898–1901; suppl. 1911) 1:4016. J. L. BAUDOT and L. CHAUSSIN, *Vies des saints et des bienheueux selon l'ordre du calendrier avec l'historique des fêtes* (Paris 1935–56) 4:18–24. F. L. CROSS, *The Oxford Dictionary of the Christian Church* (London 1957) 663. L. GAILLARD, *Catholicisme* 5:1022. A. BUTLER, *The Lives of the Saints,* ed. H. THURSTON and D. ATTWATER, 4 v. (New York 1956) 2:3–5.

[H. MACKINNON]

Seal of St. Hugh of Lincoln.

HUGH OF HONAU

Theologian of Alsace-Lorraine, author of two works in MS Cambridge Univ. Lib. Ii.4.27. The first is entitled *A Book Concerning Homousion and Homoeusion* (fols. 2–129) and aims mainly at the clarification of such concepts as substance, nature, person, essence, existence, divinity, and many others. The author offers a multitude of texts gathered from Greek and Latin writings, including Aristotle's *Physics*, in support of his views. The second work, *A Book Concerning the Difference between Nature and Person* (fols. 130–177), explains the meaning of Trinitarian terminology and contains translations from the Greek Fathers made by Hugh Etherian at Hugh of Honau's request. The date of the first work is uncertain; the second was completed about 1180.

Hugh of Honau, a canon regular, was a "schoolman" and a "deacon of the Sacred Palace" at the court of Frederick Barbarossa (1152–91). As Barbarossa's legate to Manuel I (1143–80), Hugh went to Constantinople twice. On his first mission, about 1171, he asked Hugh Etherian for translations of texts in which Greek Fathers speak of a distinction between nature and person in God. Hugh's teacher, GILBERT DE LA PORRÉE, had insisted on the necessity of making such a distinction, but his view had been criticized at Rheims (1148). Gilbert's followers, however, were anxious to prove that Greek Fathers had taught the same doctrine. Hugh received the evidence of this on his second mission to Constantinople in 1179.

Bibliography: Two letters to Hugh of Etherian ed. by A. DONDAINE, *Archives d'histoire doctrinale et littéraire du moyen-âge* 27 (1952) 128–131. V. LAURENT, *Catholicisme* 5:1034. N. M. HARING, "The *Liber de diversitate naturae et personae* by Hugh of Honau," ibid. 29 (1962) 120–216; "The *Liber de differentia naturae et personae* by Hugh Etherian and the Letters Addressed to Him by Peter of Vienna and Hugh of Honau," *Mediaeval Studies* 24 (1962) 16–19.

[N. M. HARING]

HUGH OF LINCOLN, ST.

Carthusian bishop; b. Avalon, France 1140; d. London, Nov. 16, 1200. He was educated by the Austin Canons of Villarbenoit and was professed there at an early age. Soon he joined La Grande Chartreuse, where he became procurator some years later, In 1179 he came to the notice of HENRY II, who made him prior of the languishing charterhouse at WITHAM, which Henry had founded in partial expiation for the murder of Thomas BECKET. In a short time Hugh built a church and monastery, and the community's fervor attracted many recruits. Hugh became bishop of Lincoln in 1186, at the instigation of Henry II and under obedience to the prior of the Grand Chartreuse. At Lincoln he proved himself a firm and resourceful defender of the Church's liberties, a zealous pastor and incorruptible judge, a contemplative whose prayer bore fruit in tireless action and devotion to others. He won the affection and respect of Henry II, RICHARD I, and JOHN, even when he opposed and rebuked them. Moreover, his charity was extended toward lepers, children, the Jews, etc. He spent one month every year with his community of Witham. He rebuilt Lincoln Cathedral and established a notable clerical school there. On occasion he served as royal ambassador and papal judge-delegate. His funeral, at which three kings and three bishops carried his coffin, is depicted in contemporary stained glass in the Dean's Eye of Lincoln Cathedral. Hugh was the first of the CARTHUSIANS to be canonized (1220), and Lincoln's principal saint throughout the Middle Ages. His most common iconographical attribute is his pet swan.

Feast: Nov. 17.

Bibliography: ADAM OF EYNSHAM, *The Life of St. Hugh of Lincoln,* eds. D. L. DOUIE and D. H. FARMER, 2 v. (New York 1961–62, repr. New York 1985). GIRALDUS CAMBRENSIS, *The life of St. Hugh of Avalon, Bishop of Lincoln,* ed. and tr. R. M. LOOMIS (New York 1985). *The Metrical Life of Saint Hugh of Lincoln,* tr. C. GARTON (Lincoln 1986), Latin and English. R. M. WOOLLEY, *St. Hugh of Lincoln* (London 1927). J. CLAYTON, *St. Hugh of Lincoln* (New York 1932). D. KNOWLES, *The Monastic Order in England, 943–1216* (2d ed. Cambridge, Eng. 1962) 375–391. A. BUTLER, *The Lives of the Saints,* ed. H. THURSTON and D. ATTWATER, 4 v. (New York 1956) 4:370–374. D. H. FARMER, ''The Canonization of St. Hugh of Lincoln,'' *Lincolnshire Archaeological Society of Reports and Papers* 6 (1956) 86–117; *Saint Hugh of Lincoln* (London 1985). H. MAYR-HARTING, ed., *St Hugh of Lincoln* (Oxford 1987), lectures delivered at Oxford and Lincoln to celebrate the eighth centenary of St Hugh's consecration as bishop of Lincoln.

[H. FARMER]

HUGH OF LINCOLN, ST.

Known also as Little St. Hugh to avoid confusion with Bp. St. HUGH OF LINCOLN; d. at Lincoln at the age of nine on Aug. 27, 1255. His death, believed to have followed scourging, crowning with thorns, and crucifixion, was allegedly the work of Koppin, a Lincoln Jew, who confessed under torture and was put to death along with 18 supposed accomplices. The other 74 accused were bailed out of prison by Franciscans who interceded for them and paid heavy fines. Hugh's body was thrown down a well and discovered later; it was translated to a shrine in the cathedral and was laid beside that of ROBERT GROSSETESTE. Modern historians, Christian and Jewish, have refuted general charges of such ritual murder by the Jews, and no single case of it has ever been proved. Such allegations were widely believed, however, in the Middle Ages; thus Chaucer's *Prioress's Tale* ends with an invocation to this saint (684–687):

> O yonge Hugh of Lincoln, slayn also With [by] cursed Jewes, as it is notable, For it is but a litel while ago, Preye eek [also] for us. . . .

Little Hugh's feast on Aug. 27 has been removed from the calendar of the Diocese of Nottingham, England, where it had been celebrated for centuries. His cultus was never officially recognized.

See Also: MEDIEVAL BOY MARTYRS.

Bibliography: *Acta sanctorum* July 6:494–495. A. BUTLER, *The Lives of the Saints* 3:421–422.

[H. FARMER]

HUGH OF NEWCASTLE (NOVOCASTRO)

Franciscan theologian, *Doctor scholasticus;* b. Newcastle, Durham (or Neufchâteau, Lorraine), *c.* 1280; d. Paris, after 1322. He studied at the University of Paris as a disciple of DUNS SCOTUS, and between 1307 and 1317 commented on the *Sentences* of PETER LOMBARD. He was a master of theology and doctor of both laws, exercising his regency *c.* 1322. Hugh attended the Franciscan general chapter in Perugia (1322), where, with WILLIAM OF AL-NWICK, he signed the declaration concerning the poverty controversy.

Only a few questions of his commentary on the *Sentences* have been edited: *Franziskanische Studien* (Müster-Werl 1914–) 20 (1933) 177–222; Studi Francescani 41 (1944) 126–47; *Recherches de théologie ancienne et médiévale* (Louvain 1929–) 18 (1951) 112–13; 21 (1954) 111; 22 (1955) 294–302; and *Mélanges J. de Ghellinck* (Gembloux 1951) 2:867–871. Hugh wrote also a series of *Quaestiones quodlibetales* (mentioned in his *In 2 sent.* 2.5; Cod. Vat. lat. 4871, fol. 25a), in addition to *De victoria Christi contra antichristum.* Certain other works whose authenticity is yet to be established, such as *De commercio indulgentiarum, Mariale,* and the *Collationes,* are also attributed to him.

Hugh is a faithful, though independent, follower of Duns Scotus, not infrequently developing his own points of view. His doctrine is presented clearly and precisely. In his discussions he often deals with Thomistic doctrines, which he frequently, but not invariably, rejects. Some names that repeatedly occur in Hugh's commentary are HENRY OF GHENT, DURANDUS of Saint-Pourçain, GODFREY OF FONTAINES, GILES OF ROME, and JAMES OF VITERBO.

During the 14th and 15th centuries Hugh enjoyed considerable fame among Franciscans. An unnamed 15th-century Franciscan of Greifswald remarked that "the *Doctor scholasticus,* Hugh of Novocastro, leads students marvelously from natural philosophy and metaphysics to growth in virtue; his discussion of predestination and divine foreknowledge in *In 1 sent.* pleased me very much when I read it" [F. Ehrie, *Die Ehrentitel der scholastischen Lehrer des Mittelalters* (Munich 1919) 47.10]. He was repeatedly quoted by Prosper of Reggie (fl. 1320), Alphonsus of Toledo (fl. 1345), John Bremer (fl. 1429), and WILLIAM OF VAUROUILLON.

In his question *De conceptione B. M. V.* he defends in a modest, fully impersonal way, the IMMACULATE CONCEPTION, relying principally on Duns Scotus and secondarily on St. BONAVENTURE and WILLIAM OF WARE. As a defender of the Immaculate Conception he influenced Bernard de Deo (fl. 1320), Thomas de Rossy (fl. 1373), and Andrew Novocastro (fl. 1387). He is quoted as one of the earliest defenders of this doctrine by Gerard Rondellus (fl. 1400), by Ludovicus a Turre (fl. 1485), and by Anthony de Cucharo (fl. 1507).

Bibliography: A. EMMEN, *Lexikon für Theologie und Kirche,* ed. J. HOFER and K. RAHNER, 10 v. (2d, new ed. Freiburg 1957–65) 5:515–516. J. H. SBARALEA, *Supplementum et castigatio ad scriptores trium ordinum S. Francisci a Waddingo,* 2 v. (Rome 1806; new ed. in 4 v. 1906–36) 1: 383. C. V. LANGLOIS, "Hugo de Novocastro," *Essays in Medieval History,* ed. A. G. LITTLE and F. M. POWICKE (Manchester 1925) 269–275; *Histoire littéraire de la France* (Paris 1814–1941) 36:342–349. E. AUWEILER, "De codice commentarii in IV librum sententiarum H. de N., OFM, Washingtonii servato," *Archivum Franciscanum historicum* 28 (1935) 570–573. F. STEGMÜLLER *Repertorium Commentariorum in Sententias Petri Lombardi* (Wurzburg 1947) 1:nos. 366, 366.1. V. HEYNCK, "Der Skotist H. de Novo Castro, OFM," *Franziskanische Studien* 43 (1961) 244–270.

[A. EMMEN]

HUGH OF REMIREMONT

Cardinal, known also as Hugo Candidus, early promoter and later adversary of the GREGORIAN REFORM; b. Lorraine, *c.* 1020; d. after 1098. He was called from his Abbey of REMIREMONT with the original group brought to Rome by Pope LEO IX and was created cardinal priest of S. Clemente in 1049. He next appeared in 1061 opposing the reform party and supporting Cadalus of Parma (d. after 1071), the antipope Honorius II. Soon disillusioned, he was absolved by Pope ALEXANDER II and made his legate to Spain in 1063; he subsequently convoked synods in Avignon (1063), Aragon (1065, 1067), Auch, Toulouse, Barcelona, and Gerona (1068). After an interval in Rome Hugh again returned to Spain in 1071 but conflict with CLUNY, whose hitherto exclusive interest in Spain was thus reduced, culminated in charges against Hugh at a Roman synod in February 1073. Hugh was exonerated, perhaps with the help of Hildebrand, in whose election as Pope GREGORY VII he had a leading part. His Spanish legation was renewed in 1073 (*Registrum* 1.6, 7). Thus under two popes Hugh zealously promoted the aims of the Holy See: moral reform, establishment of papal authority and liturgical uniformity, and reconquest of the Spanish Muslim dominions (*see* SPAIN, MEDIEVAL). In conformity with his instructions he made special efforts in the kingdom of Aragon to replace the MOZARABIC RITE with Roman usages. For reasons still obscure, from 1075 he definitively joined the anti-Gregorian party and took a decisive part in synods convoked by Emperor HENRY IV in Worms, January 1076, incurring excommunication the same year and deposition in 1078 (*Registrum* 5.14a). He was at Brixen in 1080, where he signed the decree deposing Gregory VII and supported GUIBERT OF RAVENNA (d. 1100) as the antipope Clement III. As Clement's legate in Germany he was excommunicated by the QUEDLINBURG Synod of 1085, and an attempt to win England to the anti-Gregorian party was thwarted by LANFRANC of Canterbury. At Rome in August 1098 he signed the proclamation of the schismatical cardinals against Pope URBAN II as bishop of Palestrina, a post Hugh had received some years before. The harm done by a quarter century of relentless schismatical activity overshadowed his earlier services for the reform.

Bibliography: Sources. BONIZO OF SUTRI, *Liber ad amicum, Monumenta Germaniae Historica: Libelli de lite.* (Berlin 1826–) 1:568–620. *Benonis aliorumque cardinalium schismaticorum contra Gregorium VII. et Urbanum II. scripta: Epist. IV, V, VIII, ibid.,* 2:403–405, 405–407, 408–416. **Literature.** A. FLICHE and V. MARTIN eds., *Histoire de l'église depuis les origines jusqu'à nos jours* (Paris 1935–) 8:36–37, 47–48, 53, 65, 90, 96, 133, 149. F. LERNER, *Kardinal Hugo Candidus* (*Historische Zeitschrift* Beiheft 22 (1931). G. B. BORINO, "Note gregoriane, 2: Quando il card. Ugo Candido e Guiberto arcivescovo di Ravenna furono insieme scomunicati," *Studi gregoriani,* ed. G. B. BORINO 4 (1952) 456–465. A. DUMAS, *Catholicisme* 5:1047–48. A. POSCH, *Lexikon für Theologie und Kirche,* ed. J. HOFER and K. RAHNER, 10 v. (2d, new ed. Freiburg 1957–65) 5:516.

[J. J. RYAN]

HUGH OF SAINT-CHER

Theologian and Biblical scholar; b. Saint-Cher, Dauphiné, France, *c.* 1200; d. Orvieto, Italy, March 19, 1263. He studied at the University of Paris and was already a doctor in law and a bachelor in theology when he entered the Dominican Order in 1225 at St. Jacques, Paris. Within a year he was elected provincial of France, but he continued his studies under ROLAND OF CREMONA, first Dominican master of sacred theology at the University of Paris. Relieved of provincial's duties in 1230, he taught theology and Sacred Scripture at the university. Again as provincial (1236–1244) he played an important part in Dominican affairs, particularly in the election of (St.) RAYMOND OF PEÑAFORT as master general, and served as the order's vicar-general in 1240 and 1241.

On May 28, 1244, he became the first Dominican cardinal, his titular church being S. Sabina. He participated in the 12th ecumenical council, held at Lyons, France (1245). By papal commission he reformed the Carmelite rule and liturgy (1247), a reform used again by (St.) John of the Cross and (St.) Teresa of Avila in the 16th century. While cardinal legate to Germany (1251–53), he sanctioned the institution at Liège of the feast of CORPUS CHRISTI, a feast extended through his urging to the universal Church by Urban IV in 1264.

Under Alexander IV he became embroiled in the acrid controversy at the University of Paris between the religious orders and the secular professors, and he was a member of the commission that condemned William of St. Amour's "Tract concerning the dangers of these latter days," a bitter tirade against the religious. Although he received power from Alexander IV in 1255 to revise the legislation of the Dominican Order, why he did not do so is not clear. Some suspect that HUMBERT OF ROMANS, then master general, was opposed to the revision. After his death Hugh was accorded the same Dominican suffrages that were extended to deceased master generals.

Although his interest also embraced theology, Hugh is particularly remembered for three Biblical works: a Latin Concordance of the Bible (1240), which served as a model, despite its crudities, for more elaborate subsequent attempts; the *Postillae* (exegetical notes on the whole Bible according to the literal and spiritual senses), which was reprinted many times up to the 17th century; and a Correctory of the Latin Vulgate, now extant only in MSS (a noble effort, but hardly adequate because of the primitive state of textual criticism).

Bibliography: J. QUÉTIF and J. ÉCHARD, *Scriptores Ordinis Praedicatorum* (New York 1959) 1:194–209, C. JERMAN, "Hugh of St. Cher," *Dominicana* 44 (1959) 338–347. E. FILTHAUT, *Lexikon für Theologie und Kirche,* ed. J. HOFER and K. RAHNER, 10 v. (2d, new ed. Freiburg 1957–65) 5:517–518.

[A. SMITH]

HUGH OF SAINT-VICTOR

Biblical interpreter, theologian and mystical writer; b. end 11th century; d. Paris, Feb. 11, 1141.

Life. Very little is known about Hugh's origin and early youth. He reveals but one detail about that period when he writes: "Since my childhood I have been an exile" (*Didasc.* 3:20). According to one tradition, founded partly on Victorine and partly on German sources, he was descended from the family of the counts of Blankenburg in Saxony and related to Reinhard, Bishop of Halberstadt. After joining the community of Canons Regular of St. Augustine at Hamersleven, he was sent abroad by the bishop. Traveling with his uncle, Archdeacon Hugh of Halberstadt, he first obtained relics of the martyr Victor at Marseilles, then went to Paris. There around 1115 they settled in the newly founded monastery of Saint-Victor. The Victorine necrology records a major gift to the abbey by Hugh's uncle. Another substantial tradition points to a non-Saxon origin. Robert of Torigny, writing about Hugh as early as 1154, calls him *Magister Lothariensis,* and two manuscripts from the end of the 12th century (Douai 361 and 362) put his birthplace in the region of Ypres in Flanders. The diversity of opinions originating from the disagreement of the sources has lasted for several centuries. Even modern scholars are divided on the matter: neither F. E. Croydon, who rejects, nor J. Taylor, who supports the traditional view was able to settle the question for lack of sufficient evidence. It may well be that some combination of the two traditions, such as Saxon birth coupled with formation in the Low Countries before coming to Saint-Victor, offers the most suitable solution barring further discoveries.

About Hugh's later life, there are reliable but meager records. From the mid-1120s until his death he was the leading master at the school of Saint-Victor. His signature appears on official acts in 1127, 1139, and again between 1133 and 1140. Only a few times did he leave the abbey, once to visit the papal court under Innocent II (1130–43), either in France or in Italy. He took no part in the condemnation of Abelard's errors at Sens, June 2 and 3, 1140. Canon Osbert, who was in charge of the infirmary at Saint-Victor, left a written account of Hugh's pious death (*Patrologia Latina* 175:161–163).

Doctrine. Although Hugh's merits as a scholar are well recognized, only in recent years, with the careful study of his works by Roger Baron, Heinrich Weisweiler, Ludwig Ott, Damien van den Eynde and others, has it been possible to be confident that his authentic works have been identified and spurious ones weeded out. Moreover, the careful work of van den Eynde now makes it possible to have a good sense of the sequence of Hugh's writings, something that is of great assistance in judging his mature thought. Among all the authors of the time, none dealt more thoroughly with a broad range of basic questions and topics such as: the method of reading and studying; the fundamental task of the trivium and the quadrivium; the distinction the "works of creation" (the natural order) and the "works of salvation" (the sacraments); the nature of philosophy, conceived as universal knowledge, and its division into "theoretical, practical, mechanical, and logical" parts; the classification, origin, and progress of all sciences; the primary importance of the literal sense for the interpretation of Scripture; the rules of exegesis; the creation of a "summa" of theological doctrine; and the formation of a body of literature directed toward instruction in the ascetic/contemplative life leading to what today is called mysticism.

As a philosophical thinker Hugh made only a limited contribution, but his effect on the study of the liberal arts and philosophy was exceptional. Except the *Epitome in philosophiam,* the treatise *De unione spiritus et corporis,* and the first half of the *Didascalicon* (critical ed. C. H. Buttimer, Washington 1939), none of his works is dedicated exclusively or even principally to philosophical matters. However, in his *Didascalicon: On the Study of Reading,* Hugh outlines a program of study for the pursuit of "Wisdom" embracing the parts of philosophy (Books 1–3) and the study of divine Scripture (Books 4–6). As a guide to subjects, a classification of the parts of philosophy, and a guide to reading, the *Didascalicon* exerted a long and deep influence on medieval intellectual culture. Hugh divides philosophy into four major categories of arts and disciplines: theoretical, practical, mechanical, and logical. For Hugh these are necessarily related to the "restoration of humanity" following the Fall, the primordial event which resulted in human ignorance, concupiscence and bodily weakness. The theoretical arts restore the loss of knowledge; the practical arts restore the loss of virtue, the mechanical arts ameliorate the weakness of body consequent on the Fall, while the logical arts insure clarity in pursuit of the others. The important place Hugh granted to the mechanical arts is striking. Integrated into this broader scheme are the seven "liberal arts" around which so much medieval philosophical learning was initially ordered. Hugh's concern with proper reading, the proper books to read, and the demeanor of the reader (see Book 3 of the *Didascalicon*) reflects the insights of a master teacher, the central figure in a major school founded in the early part of the 12th century by William of Champeaux. William, former chancellor of the cathedral school of Notre Dame, Paris, left his position at the cathedral school to establish a small religious community on the left bank of the Seine. That community grew into the major abbey and school of Saint-Victor, a community of Regular Canons. The Victorine school was open to "outsiders" during Hugh's lifetime and later. Connected with Hugh's concern with reading is the fact that the preface to his *Chronicon* is an important text teaching an "art of memory," one of the few between classical antiquity and the 13th century.

Exegesis. Hugh was an exegete, practical and theoretical; besides expounding many parts of the Bible, he was concerned with the method and rules of its interpretation. Beryl Smalley, who brought to scholarly attention Hugh's insistence on the fundamental role of history and the literal sense in Christian Biblical exegesis, rightly stressed the innovative aspect of this. Henri de Lubac considered Hugh to be merely a continuator of traditional 3- or 4-fold Biblical exegesis. While Hugh did follow tradition, his emphasis on history as the foundation of all Biblical study and interpretation (especially allegory and tropology) truly brought a new focus to the exegetical project. The *Didascalicon* (Books 4–6) offered an outline of an ideal syllabus of readings for scripture study (what Biblical books to read for "history," what for "allegory"), the distinction of the three senses (there called "disciplines" to be mastered in sequence by the student) of history, allegory, and tropology (using Gregory the Great's illustration of history as the foundation, allegory as the structure, and tropology as the beautiful coloring of a building), and general directions for the reader, cautions against error, and an affirmation of the place of a firm doctrinal foundation preceding allegorical exegesis. Nevertheless, it remained for another work to provide the true introduction to the craft of Biblical interpretation. Often relegated to a secondary place, Hugh's *De scripturis et scriptoribus sacris* is shown by its placement in manuscripts to be the work Hugh intended as an introduction to the practice of exegesis (the *Didascalicon* seems more like a handbook for a school master). In formal structure, and in the fact that in manuscripts it prefaces Hugh's literal notes on Genesis and other books of the Hebrew Bible, *De scripturis* is an *accessus ad auctores* text, modeled directly on the *accessus* form then widely used in the arts faculty for non-Biblical texts. It covers the usual topics: *titulus libri, nomen auctoris, materia libri, modus tractandi, ordo libri, utilitas, and cui parti philosophiae supponitur.* Hugh's extant works of Biblical exegesis are directed toward the literal sense of the Hebrew Bible. *Notulae (Adnotationes elucidatoriae)* exist for the Pentateuch, Judges, Ruth, Kings, and Lamentations, with commentary on diverse Psalm texts found as Book II of Hugh's *Miscellanea* printed in vol 177 of Migne. A brief summation of exegetical principles is found in the opening prologue to Hugh's *De sacramentis;* there he points out that the historical sense is served by the *trivium* (grammar, dialectic and rhetoric), while allegory and tropology are served by the *quadrivium* (arithmetic, music, geometry and astronomy) plus physics. His spiritual writings often draw directly on Biblical verses and images; see especially *De arca Noe morali* and *De vanitate mundi*, plus the *Libellus de formatione arche* (also known as *De arca Noe mystica*).

Theology. Hugh was one of the most creative and innovative theologians of the 12th century and deeply influenced succeeding generations through the creation of the first *summa* of theology in the Parisian schools and through his theological analysis and conclusions. His major work, *De sacramentis christianae fidei (On the Sacraments of the Christian Faith)* raises and answers essentially all significant theological questions, while keeping to what Hugh understood to be an historical and Biblical framework. Structuring his thought around the two great divine works, the work of creation (the natural world) and the work of restoration (Christ and all his sacraments, those that preceded and those that followed the Incarnation), Hugh utilized the *quaestio* form then becoming popular in the schools and in the work of Abelard for the purpose of exploring reflection on theological matters. He was indebted to William of Champeaux and Anselm of Laon, whose Biblical commentary and question tradition preceded his own work. Hugh was thought of in the middle ages as a "second Augustine." Bonaventure, who owed much to Hugh's influence in theology and spirituality, reflected the specialization of the 13th century when he noted that while individual patristic and contemporary writers were masters of the fields of rational thought (theology), preaching, and contemplation (here Richard of Saint-Victor figured), only one was master of all three: Hugh of Saint-Victor.

Hugh's theology follows the pattern of the historical economy of salvation, beginning with the Creation of the cosmos and the fall of the first humans, culminating in Christ's Incarnation, and ending with the consummation of all things. Deeply indebted, like most in his generation, to the thought of Augustine, Hugh made extensive use of the works of previous thinkers. He rarely cites his sources, hence his dependence is harder to note. The work of Weisweiler and Ott has, however, made quite clear his extensive citation and paraphrase of Augustine, Gregory the Great, Hilary of Poitiers, as well as texts from Ivo of Chartres and other more nearly contemporaries. His definition of faith as "a certainty about things absent, above opinion and below science," became classical throughout scholasticism. He contributed notably to the elaboration of the definition of a Sacrament in the strict sense of the term, considering extensively each that would become constitutive of the "seven sacraments." Moreover, he was the only theologian of his day who emphasized the role of absolution in Penance and associated divine grace with Matrimony, which he considered (as

did Bonaventure later) the sole sacrament established before the Fall. Thanks to his initiative, theology was enriched with two hitherto neglected treatises, one on the Church, the other on the Last Things. Although he wrote no separate treatise on ethics, the portion of *De sacramentis* devoted to that topic shows the clarity and breadth of his thought on such topics, with an emphasis on the analysis of the nature of love, and, in the case of marriage, an emphasis upon the vow between two persons, rather than consummation, as the essential element. Hugh commented on Eriugena's translation of the *Celestial Hierarchy* of Dionysius the Pseudo-Areopagite, thus introducing the thought of that enigmatic Eastern Christian writer of the 6th century to a wider audience. One also finds in Hugh's theology and especially his spirituality a distinctive Dionysian element, found particularly in Hugh's sense that the material world is a divinely meant "upward leading" guide for the spiritual quest.

Spirituality. Hugh's spiritual writings were part of the great upsurge in mystical and devotional writing fueled in part by the spirit of reform and regeneration that took root in the later 11th and early 12th century, producing the Cistercian Order, numerous wandering preachers, a renewal of the "apostolic life," and a greater concern with the systematic ordering of the spiritual life. Hugh shared the heritage of centuries of "monastic mysticism" (to use Bernard McGinn's phrase) with the Cistercians; he was also part of the new move to systematize thought in the schools and brought that spirit to his analysis of the mystical quest. Hugh's two major spiritual treatises, *De arca Noe morali* and *Libellus de formatione arche* (also known as *De arca Noe mystica*) utilize a drawing based on Christ seated in Majesty (based on Isaiah's vision recounted in Isaiah, 6) and incorporating a diagram of Noah's Ark to represent the line of history, the centrality of Christ, and the 12 stages of the mystic's quest. This drawing (described by Hugh but thus far not found in a realized form) functioned much like a device for focusing and meditation, as well as for spiritual transformation and the conveying of spiritual/theological teaching. Hugh also wrote other spiritual treatises: *De vanitate mundi* (which again uses vivid visual images and the image of the Ark as well), *De arrha anima (The Soul's betrothal gift*, which concerns with love relation between the soul and the divine), *De substantia dilectionis (On the substance of love)*, and others. Hugh presents the spiritual quest as a return from fallen humanity's scattered, diffuse, misdirected love of the material world to a unifying (and unified) love evoked by the Incarnate Christ, the divine Bridegroom, who has come to call humans back to reformation, transformation and experience of the divine presence. This return begins with the material reality of the world, which is a manifestation of God's creative power and functions as an initial "vehicle" of divine presence, moves through a deeper understanding of Scripture as the "new" voice of God which speaks to fallen humanity, and finally comes to an inward transformation (presented as a melting) which reforms human beings into the lost image of God.

Bibliography: Works. HUGH OF SAINT-VICTOR, *Omnia opera, Patrologia Latina,* ed. J. P. MIGNE, 217 v. (Paris 1878–90) 175–177. *Hugonis de Sancto Victore, Didascalicon: de studio legendi. A Critical Text,* ed. C. H. BUTTIMER (Washington, D.C. 1939). *The "Didascalicon" of Hugh of St. Victor: A Medieval Guide to the Arts,* tr. J. TAYLOR (New York 1961). *Hugh of Saint Victor on the Sacraments of the Christian Faith (De sacramentis),* tr. R. J. DEFERRARI (Cambridge 1951). *Hugh of Saint-Victor: Selected Spiritual Writings,* tr. A Religious of C.S.M.V. (London 1962). *L'Oeuvre de Hugues de Saint-Victor,* coll. "Sous la règle de Saint Augustin," dir. P. SICARD (Turnhout v. 1, 1997; v. 2, 2000). *Hugues de Saint-Victor et son École,* intr. and tr. P. SICARD (Turnhout 1991). *Textes Spirituels de Hugues de Saint-Victor,* tr. R. BARON (Tournai 1962). *Hugonis de Sancto Victore: Opera Propaedeutica. Practica geometriae, De grammatica, Epitome Dindimi in Philosophiam,* ed. R. BARON (Notre Dame 1966). R. BARON, "Hugues de Saint-Victor: Contribution à un nouvel examen de son oeuvre," *Traditio* 15 (1959) 223–297; "Études sur l'authenticité de l'oeuvre de Hugues de Saint-Victor d'apres les mss. Paris Maz., 717, BN 14506 et Douai 360–6," *Scriptorium* 10 (1956) 182–220. P. GAUTIER DALCHÉ, *La "Descriptio mappe mundi" de Hugues de Saint-Victor. Texte inédit avec introduction et commentaire* (Paris 1988). D. VAN DEN EYNDE, *Essai sur la succession et la date des écrits de Hugues de Saint-Victor* (Spicilegium Pontificii Athenaei Antonianum 13; Rome 1960). **General.** M. MANITIUS, *Geschichte der lateinischen Literatur des Mittelalters,* 3 v. (Munich 1911–31) 3:112–118. F. UEBERWEG, *Grundriss der Geschicte der Philosophie,* ed. K. PRAECHTER (Berlin 1923–28) 2:261–267. J. DE GHELLINCK, *Le Mouvement théologique du XIIᵉsiècle* (Bruges 1948). **Life.** F. E. CROYDON, "Notes on the Life of Hugh of St. Victor," *Journal of Theological Studies* 40 (London 1939) 232–253. R. BARON, "Notes biographiques sur Hugues de Saint-Victor," *Revue d'histoire ecclésiastique* 51 (Louvain 1956) 920–934. J. TAYLOR, *The Origin and Early Life of Hugh of St. Victor* (Notre Dame, Ind. 1957). **Exegesis.** B. SMALLEY, *The Study of the Bible in the Middle Ages* 3rd ed. (Oxford 1983), chap. 3. H. DE LUBAC, *Exégèse médiévale,* 2 v. (Paris 1959–64) 2.1:287–359. **Doctrine.** H. WEISWEILER, *Die Wirksamkeit der Sakramente nach Hugo von St. Victor* (Freiburg 1932); "Die Arbeitsmethode Hugos von St. Viktor. Ein Beitrag zum Entstehen seines Hauptwerke De sacramentis," *Scholastik* 20–24 (1949) 59–87, 232–267. L. OTT, "Untersuchungen zur theologischen Briefliteratur de Frühscholastik," *Beiträge zur Geschichte der Philosophie und Theologie des Mittelalters* 34.2 (Münster 1937) 126–347. D. LASI, *Hugonis de S. Victore theologia perfectiva* (Studia Antonia 7; Rome 1956). R. BARON, *Science et Sagesse chez Hugues de Saint-Victor* (Paris 1957). J. P. KLEINZ, *The Theory of Knowledge of Hugh of St. Victor* (CUA Philosophical Studies 87; Washington 1945). B. LACROIX, "Hugues de Saint-Victor et les conditions du savoir au moyen-âge," *An Etienne Gilson Tribute,* ed. C. J. O'NEIL (Milwaukee 1959). J. EHLERS, *Hugo von St. Viktor: Studien zum Geschichtsdenken und zur Geschichtsschreibung des 12. Jahrhunderts* (Wiesbaden 1973); "Arca significat ecclesiam: ein theologisches Weltmodell aus der ersten Hälfte des 12. Jahrhunderts," *Jahrbuch des Institutes für Frühmittelalterforschung der Universität Münster* 6 (Münster 1972) 121–187. I. ILLICH, *In the Vineyard of the Text: A Commentary to Hugh's Didascalicon* (Chicago and London 1993). A. M. LANDGRAF, *Introduction à la littérature théologique de la scolastique naissante* (Montréal 1973). A. M. PIAZZONI, ed. "Il De unione spiritus et corporis di Ugo di San Vittore," *Studi Medievali* 21 (1980) 861–888. R. ROQUES, "Connaissance de Dieu et théologie symbolique d'après l'In Hierarchiam coelestem sancti Dionysii de Hugues de Saint- Victor," in R. ROQUES, *Structures Théologiques de la Gnose à Richard de Saint-Victor. Essais et analyses critiques* (Paris 1962) 294–364. P. SICARD, *Diagrammes médiévaux et exégèse visuelle. Le "Libellus de formatione arche" de Hugues de Saint-Victor* Bibliotheca Victorina 4; Turnhout-Paris 1993). R. W. SOUTHERN, "Aspects of the European Tradition of Historical Writing, 2: Hugh of St. Victor and the Idea of Historical Development," *Transactions of the Royal Historical Society,* fifth series, v. 21 (London 1971). J. W. M. VAN ZWIETEN, *The Place and Significance of Literal Exegesis in Hugh of St Victor* (Ph.D. dissertation, University of Amsterdam, 1992). G. A. ZINN, "Hugh of St. Victor and the Art of Memory," *Viator* 5 (1974) 211–234; "Hugh of St Victor, Isaiah's Vision, and *De arca Noe,*" in *The Church and the Arts,* ed. D. WOOD (Oxford 1992); "Hugh of St. Victor's *De scripturis et scriptoribus sacris* as an Accessus Treatise for the Study of the Bible," *Traditio: Studies in Ancient and Medieval History, Thought, and Religion* 52 (1997) 111–134.

[G. A. ZINN/D. VAN DEN EYNDE]

HUGHES, ANGELA, MOTHER

Social worker, administrator; b. Annaloghan, County Tyrone, Ireland, *c.* 1806; d. New York City, Sept. 5, 1866. Ellen was the daughter of Patrick and Margaret (McKenna) Hughes. She immigrated to the U.S. in 1818 and lived with her family at Chambersburg, Pa. She attended St. Joseph Academy (now College), Emmitsburg, Md., where she entered the Sisters of Charity in 1825, receiving the name of Sister Mary Angela; she pronounced her vows in 1828. Between 1837 and 1846, she served in asylums for children in St. Louis, Mo.; Utica, N.Y.; and New York City.

Then in December 1846, at the first election of the New York community since it had separated from the Sisters of Charity at Emmitsburg, she was elected assistant to Mother General Elizabeth Boyle. In 1849 Sister Mary Angela founded the New York community's first mission and New York City's first Catholic hospital, St. Vincent's. In 1855 she was elected mother general. A year later she bought the Font Hill estate on the Hudson River and in 1859 the motherhouse was moved to this site from McGown's Pass (present Fifth Avenue and 107th Street), New York City. In the same year two branches of her community were established with independent motherhouses at Mt. St. Vincent, Halifax, Nova Scotia; and at Newark, N.J. During her two terms as general, 15 schools and convents were opened also. In 1861 Mother Angela returned to New York City as superior of St. Vincent's Hospital, where she died two years after the death of her brother, Abp. John J. Hughes, of New York.

John Joseph Hughes.

Bibliography: M. A. MCCANN, *History of Mother Seton's Daughters,* 3 v. (New York 1917–23). M. DE L. WALSH, *The Sisters of Charity of New York, 1809–1959,* 3 v. (New York 1960).

[M. L. FELL]

HUGHES, JOHN JOSEPH

First archbishop of New York; b. County Tyrone, Ireland, June 24, 1797; d. New York, N.Y., Jan. 3, 1864. John was the third of seven children of Patrick and Margaret (McKenna) Hughes, small farmers who avoided involvement in Ireland's political disturbances. John attended the local schools, and soon showed an interest in the priesthood. In 1816 the father and an older son immigrated to the U. S., sending for John the following year, and for the rest of the family in 1818. They settled in Chambersburg, Pennsylvania, where John worked in the quarries, at mending roads, and as a gardener. He made several applications for admission to Mt. St. Mary's Seminary, Emmitsburg, Md., only to learn that there was no room. When, however, Rev. John DUBOIS offered to take him as a gardener until a vacancy occurred, Hughes went to Mt. St. Mary's on Nov. 10, 1819, and a year later was received in the seminary. He was accepted by Bp. Henry CONWELL for the Diocese of PHILA-

DELPHIA, Pa., and ordained in St. Joseph's Church, Philadelphia, on Oct. 15, 1826; arrangements were made for him to continue his studies under Michael Hurley, OSA, who was assigned to St. Augustine's parish in that city.

Career in Philadelphia. When Hughes arrived, the trustees of St. Mary's Cathedral were in open conflict with Conwell as a result of the Hogan schism, which dated from 1821. After about a year at St. Augustine's, where he had a chance to watch developments at St. Mary's, Hughes spent a few weeks as pastor of Bedford, Pa.; he was then recalled to Philadelphia to become, successively, pastor at St. Joseph's (January 1827) and at St. Mary's (April 1827). When the trustees of St. Mary's refused to pay his salary, he returned in July to St. Joseph's, where he remained until St. John's Church was built and dedicated in April 1832. The new church had no lay incorporators and Hughes administered his parish with a firm hand.

Although highly successful in his pastoral activities, he attracted more attention by his controversial writings and speeches. His first published sermon, which enhanced his reputation as a preacher, was on Catholic EMANCIPATION, then recently granted in Ireland, and was dedicated to Daniel O'Connell, whom he greatly admired. Anti-Catholicism, then strong in Philadelphia, was expressed freely in sermons, lectures, and the bitterly polemical Protestant weeklies. There was no Catholic paper, since many Catholics, including Bp. Francis Kenrick, who had been appointed coadjutor with full jurisdiction in 1830, thought the best policy was to suffer in silence. Hughes, on the contrary, believed in a vigorous defense. He founded the *Catholic Herald,* a newspaper that he later turned over to the diocese. Earlier he had established a Catholic Tract Society to distribute free pamphlets. In 1830, using the pseudonym "Cranmer," he wrote letters to the *Protestant,* a New York weekly specializing in anti-Catholic propaganda. When, however, his wildly improbable accounts of Catholic plots and progress failed to strain the credulity of the editors and readers, he exposed the hoax. His best known controversy in Philadelphia was with Dr. John Breckinridge, a Presbyterian clergyman, with whom he debated in writing (1833) and orally (1835) on the Rule of Faith, and Catholicism as an obstacle to civil and religious liberty.

Hughes did not overestimate the value of controversy, but used it to make the enemies of the Church more cautious and to raise the morale of the sorely tried Catholic masses. His talents and his achievements attracted attention, and his promotion to the episcopate was generally expected. He had been recommended as coadjutor of Philadelphia by Conwell in 1829, and for Cincinnati in 1833. In 1836 the Holy See designated Hughes as coadjutor of Philadelphia and Kenrick as bishop of a new see to be erected at Pittsburgh, but Gregory XVI delayed formal approval. In 1837 when the Third Provincial Council of Baltimore asked that the division of Philadelphia be postponed, Hughes was preconized titular bishop of Basileopolis and coadjutor, with the right of succession, of New York. He was consecrated there on Jan. 7, 1838, in old St. Patrick's Cathedral.

New York. The diocese then consisted of all of New York State and about one-half of New Jersey, an area of about 55,000 square miles. Hughes found 22 churches, 10 of which had been erected in 1837, and 40 priests, to serve the needs of 200,000 Catholics, in a total population of about 2,700,000. The Emmitsburg Sisters of Charity were the only religious community in the diocese. Seven parochial schools, all in New York City, and four orphan asylums, two of which were in the city, made up the total of Catholic charitable and educational institutions. The population of the U.S. was increasing rapidly; in New York City the increase was five times the national rate. Moreover, the churches of the city were burdened with a heavy debt, $300,000. When, in January 1838, Dubois suffered a stroke, responsibilty for the diocese devolved upon Hughes, who was named apostolic administrator in August 1839 and succeeded to the see on Dec. 20, 1842. He became archbishop of New York on July 19, 1850, when it was made an archdiocese.

Hughes's authority was challenged in February 1839, when the cathedral trustees had a catechist appointed by Dubois ejected from the Sunday school by the police. A pastoral, written by Hughes and signed by Dubois, threatened the parishoners with an interdict unless they repudiated the trustees. This was done promptly, at a meeting summoned, addressed, and presided over, by Hughes. Except for the parish of St. Louis in Buffalo, where the trustees held out for years, New York had no further difficulty with TRUSTEEISM.

After a preliminary visitation of the diocese, Hughes went to Europe in October 1839, seeking aid in Paris, Rome, Munich, Vienna, and Dublin. On his return in 1840, he engaged in his greatest contest over the question of religion and the public schools. The Public School Society, a private organization, practically monopolized public funds for education in New York City from 1825 to 1840. Professedly nonsectarian, it provided religious training that was offensive to Catholics, who wanted state aid for denominational schools and a proportionate share of public funds. Governor William Seward agreed with the Catholics, but the city aldermen and the state legislature were hostile. The resultant controversy, which destroyed the Public School Society, led to two quite unexpected developments—the total secularization of U.S. public education on all levels, and the creation of the parochial school system in the U.S.

The growth of political nativism had led, in 1844, to the burning of Catholic churches and widespread riots in Philadelphia. Hughes's success in arousing his people to defend the churches against mob violence, while exhorting them to give no provocation, prevented similar disorders in New York. His firm stand on this and on the school question made him known throughout the country. Although attacked and misrepresented in the press, he was, nevertheless, highly respected in both Catholic and non-Catholic circles.

His achievements in the diocese included the erection of four new sees; the beginning of the new St. Patrick's Cathedral; the founding of a seminary, and of a college at Fordham, New York City, which he later transferred to the Jesuits; the introduction of many religions communities; and the development of charitable and educational works. He was instrumental in separating a group of Sisters of Charity from Emmitsburg, Md., thus founding the independent Mt. St. Vincent community in New York City.

National and International Affairs. Hughes was a vigorous defender of the temporal power of the pope, and sponsored more than one special collection to help Pius IX. He took a leading part in the founding of the North American College at Rome in 1859. Thoroughly unsympathetic to the abolitionist movement in the U.S., he believed that sudden emancipation would injure the slaves. He opposed plans to settle Irish immigrants on farm lands in the West, fearing they would be lost to the Church because of the shortage of priests. Although he endorsed Irish nationalism, he disapproved of risings that he thought could not succeed, and condemned Irish antislavery sentiment as an intrusion into U.S. politics. Because he was convinced of the basic harmony between American political institutions and Catholicism, he urged Catholic support of the U.S. Constitution and was friendly with officials of the national government. When President James Polk tried to send him to Mexico in 1847, he refused the mission because of its unofficial character. A visit to Europe in support of the Union, 1861–62, was undertaken at the request of President Lincoln and Secretary Seward. He was recommended to Rome for the red hat by Lincoln's government; when no action was taken, some believed the time was not ripe for an American cardinal, while others thought Hughes was not the best choice. His last public appearance was made in July 1863, at the request of New York Gov. Horatio Seymour, who was attempting to stop the draft riots that were then occurring in the City of New York.

Character and Personality. Archbishop Hughes was a born leader and fighter. Prompt and vigorous in action, and unyielding in conflict, he believed he had the duty and the ability to lead and defend his people, and to prove that American Catholics were not second-class citizens. If he was autocratic and at times fought harder than was necessary, he merely displayed the defects of his virtues.

Although Hughes became increasingly intolerant of disagreement, he nevertheless rendered valuable service to both Church and country. As his successor, Abp. John McCloskey, said: ". . . if ever there was a man who in the whole history and character of his life impressed upon us the sense and conviction that he had been raised up by God, was chosen as His instrument to do an appointed work . . . that man was Archbishop Hughes." Hughes died of Bright's disease, after a long illness, and was buried in the old cathedral. His remains were translated to the new St. Patrick's Cathedral in 1883.

Bibliography: *Complete Works,* comp. and ed. L. KEHOE, 2 v. (New York 1865). J. R. HASSARD, *Life of the Most Reverend John Hughes, D.D., First Archbishop of New York* (New York 1866). H. A. BRANN, *Most Reverend John Hughes: First Archbishop of New York* (2d ed. New York 1912). E. M. CONNORS, *Church-State Relationships in Education in the State of New York* (Washington 1951). F. D. COHALAN, *A Popular History of the Archdiocese of New York* (Yonkers, N.Y. 1983). R. SHAW, *Dagger John: The Unquiet Life and Times of Archbishop John Hughes of New York* (New York 1977).

[F. D. COHALAN]

HUGHES, PHILIP

Internationally recognized authority on Roman Catholic Church history; b. Manchester, England, May 11, 1895; d. South Bend, Indiana, Oct. 6, 1967. He was educated in Manchester at St. Bede's College, then at Ushaw seminary and the University of Louvain. This was followed by two years of research in Rome. Following ordination to the priesthood on Aug. 8, 1920, he spent seven years (1924–31) in parish work in the Diocese of Salford before becoming archivist of the Archdiocese of Westminster (1931–43). Poor health required him to relinquish this position but did not prevent him from continuing his research and writing. He became professor of Church history at the University of Notre Dame in 1955, where his courses, spiced with as much wit as learning, became favorites of the graduate students. Frail health forced him to give up regular teaching in 1963, at which point he became a scholar-in-residence.

Hughes's reputation as a scholar is based largely on two major works. The three-volume *History of the Church* (1933–47), which carried the story up to the beginnings of the Reformation, is a synthesis of the best scholarship of his generation on the subject. His most important study is the three-volume *History of the Reformation in England* (1951–54). Both works incorporated his penetrating insights and frank evaluations of crucial events and periods.

The range of his scholarship can be seen in such books as *The Catholic Question, 1688–1829* (1929), *St. John Fisher* (1935), and *The Life of Pius XI* (1937). A priest of deep faith, he wrote two books for the spiritual life of the faithful: *The Faith in Practice* (rev. ed. 1965) and *Meditations for Lent from St. Thomas Aquinas* (1938). He also wrote three books to help the general reader to understand the background of the Christian world he lived in: *A Popular History of the Church* (1938), *A Popular History of the Reformation* (1957), and *The Church in Crisis: A History of the General Councils, 325–1870* (1961).

Bibliography: *London Times* (Oct. 7, 1967). *Catholic Historical Review* 53 (1968) 703–704.

[J. A. CORBETT]

HUGO, CHARLES HYACINTHE

Norbertine (O Praem.) historiographer; b. St. Mihiel, France, Sept. 20, 1667; d. Étival Abbey, Aug. 2, 1739. He was professed at the Premonstratensian Abbey at Pont–Mousson Aug. 28, 1685, taking Louis as his religious name. He received a doctorate in theology from the University of Bourges (1691) and taught theology at the Abbeys of Jandeuvres (1691) and Étival (1693) until elected prior at Nancy (1700). He was named historiographer and councilor of state by Duke Leopold of Lorraine (1708).

Hugo's *Traité historique et critique sur l'origine et la généalogie de la maison de Lorraine* (1711) irked Louis XIV and was condemned by the Parliament of Paris Sept. 27, 1712. In 1710 he accepted his election as coadjutor abbot at Étival, having refused a similar post at the Abbey of Flambémont, which was held *in commendam* by Nicholas Brisacier, doctor of the Sorbonne. In the next year he received the title of abbot of Fontaine–André, a suppresed abbey in the Swiss canton of Neufchâtel. In 1722 he assumed full control of the Étival Abbey and began the coordination of his historical research.

The list of Hugo's works includes *Vie de St. Norbert, fondateur des Prémontrés* (1704), *Sacrae antiquitatis monumenta historica, dogmatica, diplomatica notis illustrata* (2 v. 1725–31), and *Sacri et canonici ordinis*

Praemonstratensis annales (2 v. 1734–36). In 1725 Hugo was in conflict with the bishop of Tours over his rights as *abbas nullius*. The bishop, who ignored the abbot's immunity, brought the affair to the general assembly of the clergy, which condemned Hugo. He was exiled to the Abbey of Rangeval (1726), but upon appeal to Rome was named bishop of Ptolemais *in partibus* (1728).

Bibliography: N. BACKMUND, *Monasticon Praemonstratense*, 3:68–71. A. L. GOOVAERTS, *Écrivains, artistes, et savants de l'ordre de Prémontré*, 4 v. (Brussels 1899–1920) 3:110–129. N. BACKMUND, *Lexikon für Theologie und Kirche*, 5:520. R. GAZEAU, *Catholicisme*, 5:1007–08.

[E. D. MCSHANE]

HUGOLINO OF GUALDO CATTANEO, BL.

Augustinian friar; b. Bevagna, Italy; d. Gualdo Cattaneo, Jan. 1, 1260. He accepted a former Benedictine monastery in Gualdo (Diocese of Spoleto) in 1258, becoming its first prior. At his death, his body was transferred to the parish church, SS. Anthony and Antonine, which on Sept. 2, 1262, was solemnly consecrated by the seven bishops of the district, who mentioned the relics of ''Hugolino'' in their letter of indulgence. Local veneration resulted in a penitential society that engaged in charitable work. His cult was approved Mar. 12, 1919. However, W. Hümpfner identifies this Augustinian as Hugolino Michaelis of Bevagna, a hermit who erected a monastery in 1340, followed the BENEDICTINE RULE, and was alive in 1393. In 1425 his monastery was given to the Olivetans of Foligno and in 1437 to the AUGUSTINIANS, who had been in Gualdo since 1363. He was venerated as an Augustinian saint by 1482.

Feast: Jan. 1 (formerly Jan. 3).

Bibliography: For the older viewpoint, *Analecta Augustiniana* 8 (1919) 49–51. W. HÜMPFNER, *Lexikon für Theologie und Kirche*, 10 v. (2d new ed. Freiburg 1957–65) 5:520–521.

[F. ROTH]

HUGOLINO OF ORVIETO

Augustinian friar and important representative of the Augustinian School; b. sometime after 1300, Orvieto, Italy; d. 1373, Aquapendente. Mentioned for the first time in 1334, he studied in Paris from 1335 to 1338. In 1347–1348 he gave his lectures on the Sentences in Paris and in 1352 was promoted to Master of Theology. He taught from 1357 to 1360 as head of his Order's house of studies in Perugia. From 1360 on he taught in Bologna

as a member of the theological faculty for which he wrote statutes. His ecclesiastical career began in 1368 with his election as prior general of the Augustinians. In 1370 he was consecrated bishop of Gallipoli in the Dardanelles. On Oct. 2, 1371 Pope Gregory XI named him Latin Patriarch of Constantinople and administrator of the diocese of Rimini.

Hugolino was a clear and sharp thinker who oriented his teachings on the Augustinian theology of grace, following closely both St. AUGUSTINE and GREGORY OF RIMINI. He drew only seldom on the work of Aristotle. The main idea of his theology is the living God *(deus vita).* His sacramental theology is based on his Christology. Foundations of his thought include the Augustinian doctrine of illumination, theological enlightenment *(lumen theologicum),* and the necessity of grace for every morally good act. He fought against Joachimite errors (Joachim of Fiore) regarding the doctrine of the Trinity. He was open to contemporary language theory, but tried to find his own way between realism and conceptualism. His Commentary on the Sentences exerted a decisive influence on the theological development of the late Middle Ages, and served as a foundation and preparation for other Commentaries on the Sentences, notably those of Konrad von Ebrach, Dionysius of Moden and Simon of Cremona. His work was used extensively by Johnnes Hiltalingen of Basel, Angelus of Dobeln, Johannes Zachariae and Augustinus Favaroni of Rome. His Commentaries continued to be influential at the universities of Paris, Bologna, and Vienna.

Bibliography: Works. W. ECKERMANN, ed., *Hugolini de Urbe Veteri OESA Commentarius in quatuor libros Sentnetiarum,* 4 vols. (Wurzburg 1980–88); *Zwei neuentdeckte theologihsce Principien Hugolins von Orvieto: Schwerpenkte und Wirkungen* (Wurzburg 1990), 43–83; *Der Physikkommentar Hugolins von Orvieto OESA: Ein Beitrag zur Erkenntnislehre des spatmittelalterlichen Augustinismus* (partial edition) (Berlin and New York 1972). **Literature.** V. MARCOLINO, ''Die Wirkung der Theologie Hugolins von Orvieto im Spatmittelalter,'' *Analecta Augustiniana* 56 (1993) 5–124. W. ECKERMANN and B. U. HUCKER, eds., *Hugolin von Orvieto, ein spatmittelalterlicher Augustinertheologe in seiner Zeit* (Cloppenburg 1992). W. ECKERMANN, ed., *Schwerpuntte und Wirkungen des Sentenzenkommentars Hugolins von Orvieto OESA* (Wurzburg 1990).

[W. ECKERMANN]

HUGON, ÉDOUARD

Theologian; b. Lafarre, France, Aug. 25, 1867; d. Rome, Feb. 7, 1929. He joined the Dominican Order in 1885 and was ordained in 1892. He taught philosophy and theology at Rosary Hill, New York, and at Poitiers, Angers, and Rijckholt. Hugon became one of the first professors at the Pontifical Institute Angelicum founded in 1909. His teaching and his written works won him the esteem of contemporary popes. Benedict XV made him a consulter on the Congregation for the Oriental Church on March 21, 1918, and Pius XI asked him to prepare a draft for the encyclical *Quas Primas* (1925) on the kingship of Christ.

Hugon's incisive teaching has been preserved in volumes often reprinted: *Logica* (Paris 1902), *Philosophia Naturalis* (Paris 1905), *Metaphysica* (Paris 1907), *Tractatus Theologici* (5 v. Paris 1920–27). As quasi–popular monographs he published *Le Mystère de la Rédemption* (Paris 1910), *Le Mystère de la Trinité* (Paris 1912), *Le Mystère de l'Incarnation* (Paris 1913), *La Sainte Eucharistie* (Paris, 7th ed. 1935), *Les Vingtquatre thèses thomistes* (Paris 8th ed. 1938). His work *Vierge–Prêtre* (Paris 1911) occasioned a lively reaction [cf. R. LAURENTIN, *Marie, l'Église et le Sacerdoce* (Paris 1952) 476–479]. He also made notable contributions to *La Vie Spirituelle*.

Bibliography: R. GARRIGOU–LAGRANGE, *Un Théologien apôtre: Le Père Maître Edouard Hugon* (Paris 1929). H. HUGON, *Le Père Hugon* (Paris 1930). Y. CONGAR, *Dictionnaire de théologie catholique*, Tables Générales 16.2:2123–24.

[A. DUVAL]

HUGUCCIO (HUGH OF PISA)

Classical canonist and the most famous of all decretists; b. Pisa, Italy, during the first half of the 12th century; d. Ferrara, Italy, April 30, 1210. His name appears under various forms: Hugo, Ugo, hugucio, huguccio, hugutio, uguicio, hugwiccio, ugwicio, oguicio, hugotio, and so on. His identifying initials in the glosses are: hug., ug., hu., hugu., h., N., yg., wig., gw., Gwi., and wiz. His Pisan origin is confirmed not only by a constant tradition but also by references found in his works. In fact, frequent allusions are made to the conditions existing in Pisa, while in the foreward of the *Liber derivationum* he calls himself *patria Pisanum* and, under the term *Pis/pisa*, clearly professes his origin from this city.

Indications obtained from his works show that Huguccio dedicated himself to profound studies of liberal arts. At the same time he devoted himself to the study of theology and especially of Canon Law in Bologna, where he also taught, counting among his disciples Lotharius of Segni, who later became Innocent III. On May 1, 1190, Clement III appointed him bishop of Ferrara. During this time the Roman pontiffs entrusted him with numerous assignments, references to which are to be found in the decretals of the pontiffs [*Corpus iuris canonici*, ed. A. Friedberg (Leipzig 1879–81) X 1.29.34; 3.41.8; 4.19.7; 5.39.43; 3.43.3].

His works are divided into three classes: grammatical, theological, and juridical. Among the grammatical works are the *Tractatus de dubio accentu* wherein the accent of composed terms is determined together with prosodic explanations. This work was composed before the *Liber derivationum* in which it is cited. The *Rosarium*, which deals with declination of verbs, was likewise written before the *Liber derivationum*, wherein it is quoted. In the *Summa artis grammaticae* the author reveals his juridical knowledge, and therefore the work appears to have been composed at a later date.

The *Liber derivationum,* however, assured Huguccio of philological and lexicographic fame. In alphabetical order it gives etymological explanations of words. This extensive work followed the pattern of similar publications by Osbern of Gloucester and Papia and for nearly two centuries was known throughout Europe, until it was superseded by the *Catholicon* of John de Balbis Januensis. Even today it holds its importance, and an edition is projected by the Istituto di Studi Romani in Rome. The date of composition of this work has always been attributed to the years of his episcopacy in Ferrara and more precisely to the period 1197 to 1201, when he was present in Nonantula. The work reveals a lack of perfection of that juridical thinking that he shows later, in his *Summa decretorum.*

Consequently, it must have preceded this last publication. In fact, Huguccio himself quotes the *Liber derivationum* in his *Hagiographia,* which appears together with the *Summa decreti* (manuscript Paris, Biblical naturalist, 14877, folio 127r). This later work, therefore, seems to be a product of his activities as a young student diligently and profoundly dedicated to the study of arts, as proved by his writings.

Three treatises give testimony of his theological studies. The above–mentioned *Hagiographia* constitutes a transition from grammatical works to theological ones. It is an etymological glossary of the names of the days of the week, of the months, and of the saints assigned to each day; it was composed before the *Summa decreti.* Huguccio's principal theological writings are the *Expositio symboli apostolorum*, containing numerous etymological explanations that confirm his broad grammatical knowledge, and the *Expositio dominicae orationis,* wherein are illustrated seven invocations, the seven Gifts of the Holy Spirit, seven Beatitudes, and compiled at an earlier date than that of the *Summa decreti.*

Huguccio's principal work, which reveal his exceptional qualities and profound culture, is the *Summa super decreta,* or *Summa super corpore decretorum,* which, according to the testimony of John of God, he wrote *ad instantiam discipulorum.* Huguccio's *Summa* excels as the most complete of all commentaries written on the Decree of Gratian and justly honors the author as the greatest of all DECRETISTS.

Origin. The *Summa* was for the most part published between the years 1188 and 1190. At a later date appeared *Causa I,* the *Tractatus de poenitentia* (33.3) and *Pars III* (*De consecratione*), *Causa* 23.1–4 ad 34. The continuation of this incomplete part was written by the Portuguese John of God about 1243. In certain manuscript codes these *Causae* (23–26) were replaced by other works of that time. The manuscript codes of the *Summa,* more or less complete, amount to more than 40. This *Summa* is a treatise *ad modum apparatuum;* that is, it explains in synthesis not only the matter and doctrine but also the legal text that is examined and interpreted exagetically and analytically.

Sources. The works and glosses that Huguccio consulted quoted implicitly or explicitly, analyzed, discussed, and followed in his writings, were almost all of his own time. With reference to Roman law, the great doctors Irnerius, Bulgarus, Martinus Gosia, Placentinus, Joannes Bassianus, and other legal experts were mentioned by name. Among the theologians, he quoted all those of greater fame, especially those of the school of Paris, such as Peter Lombard, P. Cantor, P. Comestor or Manducator, and Gilbertus Porretanus. In addition, he did not neglect mentioning the works of all preceding and contemporary canonists, not only of the school of Bologna, but almost in the same manner, of the Gallo–Rhine and Anglo–Norman schools as well. Among the scholars of Bologna, he quoted very frequently Gandulphus, Albert, Cardinalis, Bazianus, John of Faenza, Rufinus, Stephanus Tornacensis, Simon de Bisignano, Siccardus of Cremona. With reference to legal texts not contained in the Decree, he often cited the *Decretum* of BURCHARD, the *Canones Concilii Romani* (Lat. III from 1179), and the decretals of the Roman pontiffs, especially of Alexander III, up to Gregory VIII. Nevertheless, Huguccio did not make use of the *Compilatio prima antiqua.*

Importance. The *Summa* is not a mere compilation of glosses and doctrines, though as was then the custom Huguccio did report, even word for word, many passages from the works of others. It is rather a personal exposition, discussion, and elaboration by which Huguccio manifested his competent opinion, often with vivid expressions, and submitted the opinions of others to a sometimes meticulous analysis. At that time, when the classical juridical doctrine was being expounded by means of the teaching and legislation of the Roman pontiffs, his opinions played a most important role in this effort, though they were not always totally correct and definitive. Almost no subsequent author has disregarded

Huguccio's *Summa.* All have more or less depended on, mentioned, and quoted it. Owing to the fact that Huguccio's *Summa* touches on numerous other subjects, such as theology, Roman law, liturgy, historical happenings of his time, philology, and grammar, it is of utmost importance for sciences besides Canon Law. Furthermore, it is significant for the explication of the text of the Decree.

An edition of this vast work, now in preparation by a number of collaborators, will undoubtedly favor a more thorough inquiry.

Bibliography: J. F. VON SCHULTE, *Die Geschichte der Quellen und der Literatur des kanonischen Rechts,* 3 v. in 4 pts. (Stuttgart 1875–80) 1:156–170. S. KUTTNER, *Repertorium der Kanonistik* (Rome 1937) 155–160. S. KUTTNER, "Bernardus Compostellanus Antiquus," *Traditio,* 1 (1943) 283. A. VAN HOVE, *Commentarium Lovaniense in Codicem iuris canonici 1,* V. 1–5 (Mechlin 1928—) 1:419. G. CATALANO, "Contributo alla biografia di Uguccione da Pisa," *Diritto Ecclesiastico* 65 (1954) 3–67. G. LE BRAS, "Notes pour l'histoire littéraire du droit canon: Du nouveau sur Huguccio de Pise," *Revue de droit cannonique,* (Strasbourg 1951—), 5 (1955) 133–146. C. LEONARDI, "La vita e l'opera di Uguccione da Pisa decretista," *Studia Gratiana,* 4 (1956–57) 37–120. A. M. STICKLER, *Lexikon für Theologie und Kirche²,* ed. J. HOFER and K. RAHNER, 10 v. (2d, new ed. Freiburg 1957–65) 5:521–522. *Dictionnaire de droit canonique,* ed. R. NAZ, 7 v. (Paris 1935–65) 7:1355–62. J. ROMAN, "Summa d'Huguccio sur le Décret de Gratien d'après le Ms. 3891 de la Bibliothèque Nationale, Causa XXVII, q. II," *Nouvelle revue historique de droit français et étranger* (Paris 1877–1921) 27 (1903) 745–805. F. GILLMANN, "Die Abfassungszeit der Dekretsumme Huguccios," *Archiv für katholisches Kirchenrecht,* 94 (1914) 233–251, comment by F. HEYER, 513–514; "Paucapalea und Paleae bei Huguccio," *ibidem,* 88 (1908) 466–479. L. PROSDOCIMI, "La 'Summa decretorum' di Uguccione da Pisa: Studi preliminari per una edizione critica," *Studia Gratiana,* 3 (1955) 349–374; "I manoscritti della *Summa decretorum* di Uguccione da Pisa, I: Iter Germanicum," *ibidem,* 7 (1959) 251–272. A. M. STICKLER, "Problemi di ricerca e di edizione per Uguccione da Pisa e nella decretistica," *Actes du Congrès de droit canonique médiéval, 1958* (Louvain 1959) 111–122. *Bulletin of the Institute of Research and Study in Medieval Canon Law in Traditio* 11 (1955) 435, 441–444; 12 (1956) 559, 563; 13 (1957) 465, 469; 15 (1959) 450; 17 (1961) 534; 18 (1962) 449; 19 (1963) 511, for catalogs of modern manuscripts and editions in progress. V. ROSSI, "Per una edizione delle *Magnae derivationes* di Uguccione da Pisa," in *Atti del III congresso nazionale di Studi Romani,* 2 (Rome 1935) 42–46. A. MARIGO, *I codici manoscritti delle "Derivationes" di Uguccione Pisano* (Rome 1936). S. G. MERCATI, "Sul luogo e sulla data della composizione delle *Derivationes* di Uguccione da Pisa," *Aevum,* 33 (1959) 490–494.

[A. M. STICKLER]

HUGUENOTS

The nickname given to the French Protestants who followed the teachings of John CALVIN. During the wars of religion the term referred to a militant political party. The Huguenots were the most revolutionary of 16th-century Protestants.

Origin of the Term. The official name given to the Huguenots before the French Revolution was the "pseudo-reformed" (*les prétendus réformés*); after the revolution it was "French Protestants" or "Calvinists." The etymology of the term "Huguenot" is hazy. According to one view it may derive from the German *Eidgenossen* (confederates, conspirators), which in Geneva became *eiguenotz*—a popular term for those rebelling against authority. By coincidence the Genevan conspirators who revolted (*c.* 1520–24) against the Duke of Savoy and advocated union with the Swiss confederation were called "huguenots," after one of their leaders, Hugues Besançon, or Bezanson. According to another view the word *hugonot* was a local term, which in 1552 was used at Tours with reference to adherents of the reformed religion who gathered at night near the tower named after the legendary King Hugon. Still another legend has it that "King Hugon" was a nocturnal spirit in whose existence the inhabitants of Tours believed. Mockingly they called the Calvinists the disciples of Hugon or *huguenaux*. The term was in common use after the Conspiracy of Amboise, which occurred in 1560.

Doctrine and Organization. Both the doctrine and the organizational structure of Calvinism matured between 1510 and 1559. The pioneer brain of French reform was Jacques LEFÈVRE D'ÉTAPLES, the author of *Quincuplex Psalterium . . .* (1509) and of a Latin version of the Epistles of St. Paul (1512). In his commentary on the latter Lefèvre stated that the Scriptures are the chief authority in religious matters. After 1520 the writings of Luther gave the French reform movement a strong impulse. In 1535 appeared a revised version of Lefèvre's Bible by Pierre OLIVÉTAN; and in March 1536, Calvin's *Institutio Christianae Religionis* (*see* INSTITUTES OF CALVIN), the most systematic exposition of Protestant doctrine. The book taught glorification of and obedience to God as the chief ends of man. It served as a declaration of faith, a justification for the new doctrine, and a program for the new Protestant adherents. The *Institutes* won Calvin many followers and helped to establish his leadership of the reform at Geneva, when he went to live there in the same year. His reform program soon proved too extreme for the Genevans and he and his associate William Farel were expelled from the city in 1538. Despite these fits and starts, Calvin and Farel returned to Geneva in 1540 and began to mold the city into a disciplined outpost of their reformed teaching. Throughout the 1540s and 1550s they were able to wrest important powers from the town council, despite the frequent vocal opposition of some of the town's most prominent families. By the 1550s, most of the components of Geneva's theocracy were in place: Christian ministers and magistrates shared power in a consistory that met regularly to discipline moral infractions and to insure purity of teaching and uniformity of belief and practice. At the same time Geneva became an important missionary training ground for the movement. The town's population doubled, swelled by students, disciples, and Protestant refugees from throughout Europe. Eventually these missionaries would carry Calvinist teaching back to their homelands.

Persecution. From the onset of his work as a reformer, Calvin had longed for the conversion of France and his missionary efforts at Geneva cannot be understood outside of his attempt to establish a Protestant Church in his native land. As the movement grew in France, so did the monarchy's desire to destroy heresy. Francis I (1515–47), who at first assumed an ambivalent attitude, decided in favor of persecution and passed a series of edicts to that end (1539, 1540, 1542, 1543). In 1545 the Sorbonne published a list of 65 condemned books, which included the works of Calvin, Luther, and Melanchton. Toward the end of Francis' reign persecution was encouraged by both the king and the Paris *parlement* (the chief organ of justice). Between 1544 and 1547 many were martyred in Toulouse, Rouen, Grenoble, Bordeaux, and Paris. Provence became the scene of a large-scale massacre of the Vaudois Protestants in which 3,000 died. The effort of Henry II (1547–59) to systematize persecution consisted of appointing a special commission of the Paris *parlement* (*chambre ardente*) in 1547 to try heretics and of codifying in 1551 (Edict of Chateaubriand) all the previous enactments against them. But persecution proved ineffective. By 1555 Paris had its first Reformed church. In 1559 the first national synod, representing 72 churches, met at Saint-Germain and organized a National Evangelical Church. A confession of faith and disciplinary rules, as prescribed by Calvin, were drawn up (*See* CONFESSIONS OF FAITH PROTESTANT). Furthermore Calvin's compact organizational structure was adopted for the Church. The constitution prescribed the method of appointment of ministers and lay elders (grouped in the consistory), by whom each congregation was governed. Consistories were linked by the colloquy, or district assembly. Higher up the scale was the provincial synod; still higher was the national synod, consisting of two ministers and two elders for each province (*see* REFORMED CHURCHES).

Political Influence. After 1559 Calvinism came into the open, and for 70 years the Reformed Church played an important political role. Individual churches sought the protection of the nobility. The military and political organization of the party took shape. The leadership of the Huguenot organization was assumed by a president, known as the protector of the churches; the Huguenot system of laws extended to administration, justice, commerce, finance, and war. Military and ecclesiastical organization were closely related to each other. Thus, to conform with the military organization established in November, 1561 in the Provinces of Bordeaux and Toulouse, the congregation had its captain, the colloquy had its colonel, and the province had its general. After 1572 the religious elements in the Huguenot camp were dominated by the military and political factions; significantly, its religious organization was conducive to political separation. The final organizational structure did not come into being until 1611 (Assembly of Saumur).

During the short reign of Francis II (1559–60) persecution of the Huguenots was intensified by the Dukes of GUISE. *Chambres ardentes* were established under the local *parlements;* heresy was punishable by death, banishment, and confiscation. But the Huguenot ranks were strengthened by many nobles, like Admiral Gaspard de Coligny and the Dukes of Bourbon and CONDÉ, who became the party leader. (The Huguenot party remained mainly aristocratic until the end of the 16th century; then the character of its membership changed to include more ''popular'' elements, particularly middle-class townspeople.) The conspiracy of Amboise (1560), initiated by Louis I, Prince of Condé, against the Guises, ended in failure. Under Charles IX (1560–74) and the regency of the Queen Mother CATHERINE DE MÉDICIS, a policy of compromise and concession was sought (inspired by Chancellor Michel de l'Hôpital). At the States-General of the same year Coligny tried to promote a program including a national council under the king to settle religious matters. The results were the suspension of persecution and the convening of a special religious conference of all beliefs in 1561 (*see* POISSY, CONFERENCE OF). The chief spokesmen for the Catholics were Louis II de Guise, Cardinal de Lorraine, and for the Huguenots, Theodore BEZA. Other main participants included PETER MARTYR VERMIGLI and the Jesuit Diego LAÍNEZ. No agreement resulted from the debates. The next step was taken by the government: the edict of January 1562, was a measure of toleration introduced by de l'Hôpital. Its intention was to grant the Huguenots civic status and the right to worship outside the towns; the Huguenot nobles were given the privilege of organizing religious rites on their own estates. But the attempts of de l'Hôpital and Catherine to bring peace were ineffective. The Guises strongly opposed the policy of conciliation, and both sides prepared for war. The massacre of Vassy (March 1, 1562) began the THIRTY YEARS' WAR.

Wars of Religion. In the next two decades there were seven wars and the Massacre of ST. BARTHOLOMEW'S DAY (1572). Among the many leading Huguenots killed were Anthony de Navarre (first war), Louis I Condé (third war), and Coligny (St. Bartholomew); victims on the Catholic side were Marshal de St. André (first

war), Francis, Duke of Guise (first war), and Constable Anne de Montmorency (second war). During the second decade the Huguenot organization was so strengthened and unified that it resembled a state within the state. Wherever they held power, the Huguenots imposed a rigid rule, which demanded obedience to their code and included censorship and severe penalties. They cultivated their own way of life and educational institutions (e.g., five academies: Montauban, Saumur, Nîmes, Montpellier, Sedan). The Holy LEAGUE, which emerged in 1576 to meet the need for an alliance outside the monarchy and to make the COUNTER REFORMATION more effective, took the Huguenot organization as its pattern.

The Huguenots participated in the battle of ideas that accompanied the wars of religion; they were noted for vigorous political pamphleteering. Among the outstanding Huguenot books were: François Hotman's *Franco-Gallia* (1573), a defense of limited popular monarchy; *Vindiciae contra tyrannos* (1579), a classical work of the Huguenot monarchomach theory that justified the right to rebel against a tyrant; and *Mémoires de l'Estat de France,* edited by Simon Goulart (1576), a massive collection of materials relating to political theory.

The wars of religion were marked by an abundance of short-lived treaties and ineffective edicts. The so-called intervals of ''peace'' (Amboise, 1563; Longjumeau, 1568; Saint-Germain, 1570) were no more than truces. Measures intended to bring peace and order alternated with enactments revoking rights and privileges. The only measure of note (introduced before the Edict of NANTES) was the Edict of Beaulieu, or of ''Monsieur'' (1576), which was revived the following year, after the Peace of Bergerac, as the Edict of Poitiers. Although it brought no essential change, it implied broad religious liberty—a remarkable achievement but a compendium of edicts previously passed.

Edict of Nantes. The Edict of Nantes did not result from a true spirit of tolerance but from a number of political factors. These included the decline of the Guises; the rise to power of Henry de Navarre (a Huguenot who, upon the death of Francis, Duke of Alençon, Catherine's youngest son, became heir to the throne in 1854); and the growing influence of the *politiques* (include Navarre), who were anxious to end hostilities and put a stop to foreign influence.

Unlike its predecessors, the Edict of Nantes was to remain in effect, at least nominally, for 87 years. From the beginning, however, its fate was precarious. Despite genuine efforts to carry out its provisions, it was never applied in its entirely because French society was not ready to adopt its principles and was therefore unwilling to aid their application.

The relative sense of security enjoyed by the Huguenots ended with the assassination of HENRY IV in 1610. The reign of his son, Louis XIII (1610–43), saw the end of their political hopes. The Huguenot organization reached its peak at the Assembly of Saumur (1611), where final form was given to the representative system. In the religious sphere the existence of consistories, colloquies, and provincial and national synods was confirmed. In the political sphere, corresponding provincial councils, circles assemblies, and general assemblies were provided. The provincial councils, although known before Saumur, did not meet regularly before 1611; it was then that their continuous history began, to be interrupted after the fall of La Rochelle in 1629. Although not all the decisions made at Saumur were carried into full effect, the problem of extending political activities was taken up at La Rochelle in 1621. A provisional Protestant republic was then created, following the manifesto *Ordre et Réglement Général,* which gave a pattern for an autonomous organization. France was subdivided into eight departments, each to be headed by a governor general (*chef général*) concerned with justice, finances, and the militia. La Rochelle was given a supreme court with the powers of an emergency tribunal.

In 1615 three Huguenot provinces—Languedoc, Guigenne, and Poitou—rose under the leadership of Henry de Condé (the party's spokesman, although not a Huguenot) against the Regent Marie de' Médicis as a protest against her pro-Spanish policy. Henry, Duke of Rohan, the official protector of the Huguenots, also took up arms. Hostilities ended with the Treaty of Loudun (May 3, 1616), which extended for six years the use by the Huguenots of their strongholds (''places of surety'').

In 1620 another rising took place following restitution to the Catholic bishops of their property in Béarn after absorption of the latter by France. (Catholic worship was reintroduced to Béarn by Henry IV when he abjured Protestantism.) The revolt was led by Rohan and his brother Soubise. It ended with the Peace of Montpellier (Oct. 18, 1622), which confirmed the Edict of Nantes but forbade political assemblies without royal authorization and left the Huguenots only two ''places of surety'': La Rochelle and Montauban. Hostilities were started again in 1625 by Soubise, who first seized the Isle of Ré and then Oléron. Cardinal RICHELIEU brought the war to a temporary end in February 1626. He needed internal peace in order to set out on an expedition to deal with the Mantuan succession and undertook no action until 1627.

Policy of Richelieu. In 1627, in accordance with his design to destroy the Huguenot party—a matter of *raison d'état* since the Huguenots constituted a threat to the central government—Richelieu launched a full-scale assault against La Rochelle, defended by Jean Guiton who was ineffectively aided by the English. (There were abortive attempts by the fleet of George Villiers, the duke of Buckingham, to support the beseiged city.) Richelieu entered La Rochelle on Oct. 30, 1628; he then led his forces against Rohan, took Privas, and beseiged Alais. Rohan capitulated, and Richelieu dictated the terms of the Peace of Alais (June 1629). The Huguenots lost their ''places of surety'' and became politically subservient to the state. Although the Edict of Nantes was reaffirmed in the sense that their liberty of conscience was preserved, the Huguenot party was in reality doomed.

Until his death in 1643 Richelieu refrained from active oppression of the Huguenots and created a fairly strong impression of being tolerant—an impression that persisted during his lifetime because events moved against his proselytizing plans (comprised in the Plan Codur). Richelieu accepted toleration of the Huguenots as a temporary political expedient, even as he ultimately aimed to eliminate the Huguenot minority. Richelieu had destroyed the Huguenots politically, not in order to assure their survival in the religious sphere but in order to make their religious practice at a later stage difficult and, much later, impossible. His political will was executed with great accuracy. Jules MAZARIN entirely, and LOUIS XIV to a large degree, continued his policy. (The revocation of the Edict of Nantes probably reflected Richelieu's intentions quite accurately.)

Revocation of the Edict of Nantes. Persecution was begun again by Louis XIV (1661–1715) after Cardinal Mazarin's death (1661). The rights enjoyed by the Huguenots were gradually withdrawn; after 1680 the government resorted to brutal *dragonnades,* or quartering troops in Huguenot households, in order to force conversions. On Oct. 18, 1685, the Edict of Nantes was revoked, causing massive Huguenot emigration (between 200,000 and 300,000 left France). During Louis XIV's War of the Spanish Succession there was a Huguenot uprising in the Cevennes by the CAMISARDS (1702–04), led by Jean Cavalier. In 1724 the revocation of the Edict of Nantes was confirmed. The situation did not change until 1787, when by the Edict of Toleration partial equality of rights was reestablished (except the right to hold public office) and marriages and baptisms in the Protestant faith were declared valid. The Calvinists were granted full equality by the Napoleonic code.

Bibliography: General. J. VIÉNOT, *Histoire de la réforme française,* 2 v. (Paris 1926–34). E. LÉONARD, *Histoire générale du Protestantisme,* 2 v. (Paris 1961). R. STÉPHAN, *L'Epopée huguenote* (Paris 1945); *Histoire du Protestantisme français* (Paris 1961). A. J. GRANT, *The Huguenots* (London 1934). Calvin and Geneva. R. N. C. HUNT, *Calvin* (London 1933). A. BOSSERT, *Calvin* (Paris 1906). R. M. KINGDON, *Geneva and the Coming of the Wars of Religion in*

France (Geneva 1956). J. A. F. PUAUX and L. A. SABATIER, *Études sur la révocation de l'édit de Nantes* (Paris 1886). W. J. STANKIEWICZ, "The Edict of Nantes in the Light of Mediaeval Political Theory," *Proceedings of the Huguenot Society of London* 19 (1955) 82–91. Particular reigns. J. E. NEALE, *The Age of Catherine de Medici* (new ed. London 1957). L. ROMIER, *Catholiques et Huguenots à la cour de Charles IX* (Paris 1924). W. J. STANKIEWICZ, "The Huguenot Downfall: The Influence of Richelieu's Policy and Doctrine," *Proceedings of the American Philosophical Society* 99 (1955) 146–168. J. ORCIBAL, *Louis XIV et les Protestants* (Paris 1951). Problem of toleration. J. LECLER, *Toleration and the Reformation*, tr. T. L. WESTOW, 2 v. (New York 1960). A. J. GRANT, "The Problem of Religious Toleration in XVIth Century France," *Proceedings of the Huguenot Society of London* 13 (1923–29). W. J. STANKIEWICZ, "Intoleranz im Frankreich des XVI. Jahrhunderts," *Der Deutsche Hugenott* 23 (1959), tr. from the English by M. GOETZ; "Rationalismus gegen Thenlogic: der Bayle-Jurieu Streit ueber die Toleranz," *ibid.* 22 (1958), tr. from the English by M. GOETZ. R. H. BAINTON et al., *Castellioniana* (Leiden 1951). J. A. F. PUAUX, *Les Précurseurs français de la tolérance au XVIIe siècle* (Paris 1881). H. ROBINSON, *Bayle the Skeptic* (New York 1931). Political and social thought. E. ARMSTRONG, "The Political Theory of the Huguenots," *English Historical Review* 4 (1889) 13–40. J. E. ACTON, "The Protestant Theory of Persecution," *Essays on Freedom and Power* (Boston 1948). S. J. BRUTUS, *A Defence of Liberty against Tyrants*, tr. W. WALKER (London 1924), see introduction by H. J. LASKI. E. BARKER, "A Huguenot Theory of Politics: The *Vindiciae contra tyrannos*," in his *Church, State and Education* (pa. Ann Arbor 1957). W. F. CHURCH, *Constitutional Thought in Sixteenth-Century France* (Cambridge, MA 1941). G. J. WEILL, *Les Théories sur le pouvoir royal en France pendant les guerres de religion* (Paris 1892). J. A. F. PUAUX, *Les Défenseurs de la souveraineté du peuple sous le règne de Louis XIV* (Paris 1917). R. LUREAI, *Les Doctrines politiques de Jurieu, 1637–1713* (Bordeaux 1904). P. HAZARD, *The European Mind, 1680–1715*, tr. J. L. MAY (New York 1963). G. H. DODGE, *The Political Theory of the Huguenots of the Dispersion* (New York 1947). W. J. STANKIEWICZ, *Politics and Religion in Seventeenth-century France* (Berkeley 1960). P. BENEDICT, *The Huguenot Connection* (Philadelphia 1981). R. KINGDON, *Myths about the Saint Bartholomew's Day Massacre, 1472–1576* (Cambridge, MA 1988). R. MENTZER, *Blood and Belief* (West Lafayette, IN 1994). E. PERRY, *French Religious Controversy and the Revocation of the Edict of Nantes* (The Hague 1973).

[W. J. STANKIEWICZ]

HULL, ERNEST REGINALD

Author, editor, pioneer of the Catholic press in India; b. Sept. 9, 1863, Greenhays, Manchester, England; d. July 19, 1952, Roehampton, England. Converted from Aglicanism in 1882, he entered the Society of Jesus in 1886 and was engaged in literary work when a request came from India for an English Jesuit to edit the Bombay *Catholic Examiner,* a 53–year–old diocesan paper. He arrived in Bombay in 1902, and remained there until 1932, occupying the position of editor from Jan. 1, 1903 to Nov. 29, 1924. During his editorship, the papers rose from its former status of "a derelict" to become an important organ in the apostolate.

An index of Hull's writing from 1903 to 1930 contains 15,000 titles. Reprints of series originally written for the paper total 56, and cover character building, morals, culture, religion, science doctrine, controversy, and history (both English and Indian, ecclesiastical and secular). From 1924 to 1932 he was archivist and secretary to the archbishop of Bombay. On his return to England, he was editor of *Stella Maris* (1934–35), and wrote for various journals. Of his many book, the most influential was *Man's Great Concern: The Management of Life* (1918), which was adopted as a textbook in schools; translated into Hindi, Malayalam, Tamil, and Chinese; and ran into several editions.

[H. ROZARIO]

HUMAN ACT

An ACT that is performed only by a human being and thus is proper to MAN. Not every act that a human being does is a distinctively human act. Some acts that human beings do are performed also by animals, e.g., vegetative acts and acts of perception and of emotion. When a human being does such acts, they are called acts of man but not human acts. Acts of man, therefore, are acts shared in common by man and other animals, whereas human acts are proper to human beings. What makes an act performed by a human being distinctively a human act is that it is voluntary in character, that is, an act in some way under the control or direction of the will, which is proper to man. One can therefore identify the human act with the voluntary act. A voluntary act proceeds either from the will itself—for example, an act of love or of choice—or from some other human power that can in some way be moved by the will, whether an act of the intellect, of sense cognition, or of emotion; even an act of some bodily member as commanded by the will can be a voluntary act.

A moral analysis of the human act analyzes the human act in relation to the good that is sought and insofar as all acts are moved to their ends by the will. A psychological consideration of the human act distinguishes the internal and external principles of the human act, treats the notion of human freedom, and analyzes the human act into its component parts. This article deals with the human act primarily in its psychological aspect, which a moral analysis must presuppose.

INTERNAL PRINCIPLES OF HUMAN ACTS

The internal principles of human acts include the intellect, the will, and the sense appetites, and the habits—both virtues and vices—with which these powers, or faculties, are endowed (*see* FACULTIES OF THE SOUL).

Intellect. As a power of the human soul, the INTELLECT is the principle of all intellectual acts of knowing. The human intellect is either speculative or practical, a difference deriving from the end to which knowledge is ordered (*see* COGNITION SPECULATIVE-PRACTICAL). If the end in view is the consideration of truth itself, the intellect is speculative in its mode of knowing. Thus through acts of understanding and reasoning man arrives at scientific knowledge, when possible, or at something less than truth and certainty—opinion, for example. If the end in view is operation or action of some kind, then the intellect is practical in its knowing, as in the making of works of art or in judgments of prudence in regard to actions one is to perform. And just as in speculative knowing ordered to arriving at truth where there are FIRST PRINCIPLES grasped by the special habit of UNDERSTANDING, from which true and necessary conclusions follow, so in practical knowing there are the primary practical principles grasped by the special habit of SYNDERESIS, enabling man to know the common precepts in regard to good and evil action.

Will and Sense Appetites. The WILL, as intellectual APPETITE, is a power directed to some object under the aspect of universal GOOD. Because the good so understood is the object of the will, it moves the will as an end, and in this sense the will presupposes the intellect, which thus moves the will to its appropriate end; the intellect, in other words, moves the will as specifying the act of the will. The will, on the other hand, moves the intellect in the manner in which one thing moves another as an AGENT. Since each power is directed to a good suitable to it and since the object of the will is the universal good, the good of the intellect, to know the true, falls within the scope of the will. Although the will tends to objects as universal, it tends also to singular things existing outside the mind by tending to them under a universal aspect. One person loves another, for example, because of the latter's virtuous character, which is a good realized in this person. The desiring of a good in this way, and in general the desiring of an immaterial or spiritual good, distinguishes the will as rational appetite from sense appetite.

The sense appetite is related to sense cognition as the will is related to intellectual knowing, each appetite tending to a good as apprehended. But since sense cognition cannot apprehend the good as universal, the sense appetite cannot be directed to the common notion of the good. Hence the will and the sense appetite can be basically contrasted as desire for a universal good and desire for a particular good. There are two fundamentally different aspects of the particular good that differentiate the sense appetite, or EMOTION, into two main parts: the concupiscible and the irascible. The concupiscible appetite is concerned with a particular good as pleasing and suitable; the irascible appetite is concerned with repelling and combating harmful aspects of objects that prevent the attaining of a particular good.

Habit. In addition to the various human powers, habits are also internal principles of human acts. A HABIT can be understood initially as a disposing of a power to act in a determinate way. In virtue of the intellectual and appetitive powers man has, he is able to do a variety of acts, but without the disposing influence of habit upon his powers of acting, most of his distinctively human acts would be done haphazardly. A habit therefore develops and strengthens a human power, enabling the power to operate more effectively and with more facility.

Accordingly, a habit can be defined as a firm DISPOSITION of a power to act regularly in a determinate way. So understood, a habit is then seen to be a perfection. Man's powers of themselves are largely indeterminate with regard to their objects. The engendering of habits, acquired by repeated acts of a certain kind, dispose and determine powers more readily and more determinately to their objects. Hence a habit, far from being merely mechanical in operation and somehow alien to good human action, actually enters into the performing of human acts so intrinsically that it may be regarded as a second nature; habit makes its distinctive act a kind of natural act just as a power is the first source of a natural act. For this reason, in addition to a habit's producing uniformity in operation and enabling an act to be done more quickly and effectively, a habit makes human action pleasurable in operation. The meaning of habit as developed here restricts habit to the intellectual and appetitive human powers.

Virtue and Vice. The notion of habit as bettering human action is not in conflict with the division of habit into good and bad, that is, into VIRTUE and VICE. Any habit permits man to operate better than he otherwise would, but whether a habit is good or bad is a moral consideration, distinct from the psychological point showing how any habit develops a power more fully. In general terms, the distinction between virtue as a good habit and vice as a bad habit turns on whether the habit produces acts conducive to promoting man's moral good or evil. Acts of virtue are those that are suitable to human nature; that is, they are acts habitually performed according to the rule of reason. Acts of vice are opposed to human nature inasmuch as they are habitually opposed to the direction of reason.

Virtue may then be defined somewhat as St. Augustine phrased it: virtue is a good habit of the mind, by which one lives righteously and of which no one can make bad use. In a somewhat more specific way, virtue can be defined also as a habit inclining one to choose the relative mean between the extremes of excess and defect. Vice, as the contrary habit, would incline one to choose either of the extremes, both morally evil.

These definitions apply primarily to moral virtue, the primary meaning of virtue. However, human virtue is divided analogously into moral and intellectual. This division follows upon the fact that there are two principles of human action, the intellect and the appetite. Any virtue perfects one of these two powers. Good habits of thinking perfect the human intellect either in its speculative dimension with the intellectual virtues of understanding, science, and wisdom, or in its practical dimension with the virtues of art and prudence, although the latter virtue is also moral to the extent that it requires right appetite for its good operation. Good habits of desiring perfect the appetite, either the will by means of the cardinal virtue of justice or the sense appetite by means of the cardinal virtue of fortitude for the irascible appetite and temperance for the concupiscible appetite. The fourth cardinal virtue, prudence, as has been noted, is both intellectual and moral. There will be corresponding vices for each of these virtues by way of contrary habits.

In addition to moral and intellectual virtues, theological virtues also are principles of human acts. The need of such virtues for man arises from the fact that man's happiness, the goal of all his actions, is twofold: a happiness proportionate to human nature and obtainable by means of natural principles including the moral and intellectual virtues; a happiness surpassing human nature and obtainable by and through God's power alone. Since the natural virtues cannot suffice to direct man to supernatural happiness, man has need for additional principles of action in order to be directed to attaining supernatural happiness. Such principles are the theological virtues, which are infused by God, in which respect they are not wholly intrinsic principles of human action. These theological virtues are faith, hope, and charity.

EXTERNAL PRINCIPLES OF HUMAN ACTS

Among the internal principles of human acts, virtue is the primary means of directing man to the good of human happiness. Other means by which he is ordered to leading the good life are law and grace, both of which may be referred to as extrinsic principles of human action.

Law. As is evident from experience, the COMMON GOOD is the end or purpose of all LAW, and without an understanding of what the common good properly is, the nature and function of law in directing human acts cannot be appreciated. A common good is clearly distinct from a private good, the latter being the good of one person only, to the exclusion of its being possessed by any other.

A common good is distinct also from a collective good, which, though possessed by all of a group, is not really participated in by the members of the group; as divided up, a collective good becomes respectively private goods of the members, as in the manner in which a man's estate is divided up among his inheritors.

A true common good is universal, not singular or collective, and is distributive in character, being communicable to many without becoming anyone's private good. Moreover, each person participates in the whole common good, not merely in a part of it, nor can any one person possess it wholly. The distinctive common good to which human law is ordered is the civil, or political, common good of peace and order. Such direction of human acts by law is clearly indispensable for human development and perfection.

Civil Law. The classic definition of law is based on the foregoing notion of the common good: law is a certain ordination of reason for the common good, promulgated by one who has care of the community. This common definition of law applies proportionately or analogously to the different kinds of law. According to man's mode of knowing, civil, or human positive, law primarily realizes the common definition of law. Hence law is first understood to be an ordinance of reason by one who has authority to direct the political society and its members to the common civil good, a happiness consisting primarily in peace and order. Civil law directly concerns the external acts of human beings, presupposing the interior principles and acts. Although civil law therefore does not directly aim to make men virtuous in their actions, it does command certain acts that dispose men to become virtuous and forbid other acts that lead to vice and tend to make life in society impossible.

Natural Law. Every civil law, insofar as it aims at the common good and is accordingly a just law, carries an obligation to be obeyed. Yet this obligation rests on more than civil law itself. It derives from a law more fundamental than civil law and its political sanction, viz, what is called natural law. This is the "unwritten law" that, in its most common precepts, is fundamentally the same for all. The natural law expresses, in universal form primarily, the fundamental inclinations of human nature formulated by reason in a judgment naturally made, that is, with little or no discursive reasoning. Such law, then, is natural on two scores: (1) it is not law *made* by reason so much as *discovered* by reason; and (2) all men thus naturally know the most universal precepts expressed in natural law. Natural law, so understood, is clearly a fundamental principle for directing human acts. (*See* NATURAL LAW.)

Eternal Law. One other kind of law must still be mentioned: eternal law. It is even more fundamental than natural law, being the law in which even natural law participates. Eternal law refers to the idea of the government of things that exists in the mind of God; it is the plan of God's wisdom by which all action and motion of the universe is directed. It directs the universe as a whole to the common good of God Himself. This is not the law given through revelation (*see* LAW, DIVINE POSITIVE). The knowledge about eternal law can be arrived at by reason alone, though usually indirectly. Eternal law is therefore the ultimate source of all law and the ultimate directive principle of all acts and motions of creatures to their proper ends.

Grace. As a principle of human action, GRACE differs from virtue not only as an external principle differs from an internal one, but also in that grace is infused directly into the human soul itself, whereas virtue is realized in some power of the soul. Grace differs from law in that, though both are external principles, law directs man by instruction and command, whereas grace supernaturally elevates him so that he can participate in the divine life, receive assistance in doing so, and attain the happiness that is eternal life. Hence sanctifying or habitual grace is a supernatural quality of the soul by which man participates in the divine nature and is thereby enabled to perform acts meriting supernatural happiness. It is clear that such a principle directing human action is absolutely necessary for all human beings if they are to obtain eternal life.

HUMAN FREEDOM

A discussion of the internal and external principles of the human act is logically followed by a consideration of the human act itself. Prior to an analysis of the human act into its component parts, however, it is convenient to treat how and in what way the human act is free. At the beginning of this article, the human act was identified with the voluntary act, an act proceeding either immediately from the will or from some power or act in some way under the control and direction of the will. (For a consideration of the voluntary act especially in its moral dimension, *see* VOLUNTARITY.)

It is now necessary to distinguish between a voluntary act and a free act; for although every free act is necessarily a voluntary act, not every voluntary act is strictly a free act. A free act, most properly speaking, is an act of CHOICE. There are occasions, however, when it makes sense to say that man has no choice and that what he wills to do he must will to do. Such acts are voluntary in that they still proceed from the will as a principle, but they are not free, at least in the usual and proper sense of the term.

Freedom of Exercise. It must be recognized, however, that there are two types of free act, or two kinds of freedom. One type is freedom of exercise. This is the freedom of an agent to act or not to act in an absolute sense; freedom of exercise is thus said to be about contradictory alternatives. In any given situation, a man at all rational can will to act or not. This sort of freedom man as a voluntary agent always has; and as related to the interior act of willing or not willing, the voluntary act and the free act, for all practical purposes, are identifiable.

Freedom of Specification. The other type of freedom is freedom of specification. This is the sort of freedom one usually has in mind when he speaks of man as being a free agent and is what he means by the act of choice. This freedom arises not in terms of the agent as acting or not acting (which is freedom of exercise and is presupposed) but in terms of some object specifying the act to be done by the agent. Freedom of specification, in other words, is the choice of this alternative rather than that alternative or, to put it more precisely, the choice of this means in relation to a desired end. The free act as choice, therefore, is concerned with means properly, not with ends as ends. In this context, one can distinguish voluntary acts that are not free acts strictly. To will an end as an end is not a matter of choice but a matter of simple willing. An act of the will centering precisely on the means is the act of choice. This meaning of freedom, the freedom of specification exercised by choice, is the relevant meaning of human freedom in the discussion here. (*See* FREE WILL; FREEDOM.)

Limitations of Freedom. Many contemporary authors point out that to be fully human in its exercise, the will must be free both philosophically and psychologically. Philosophical freedom is the power, given certain prerequisites of knowledge and motivation, of saying yes or no freely to a proposed action or of choosing freely between two alternative courses. It means that at the time the choice was made, the person could have made the opposite choice even though with difficulty or repugnance. Psychological freedom is a freedom from obstacles and pressures that make the exercise of philosophical freedom difficult. Philosophical freedom is *freedom to determine* its own choices; psychological freedom is *freedom from the obstacles*, pressures, and impediments which make choices difficult. In the minds of some contemporaries, the classical tradition in moral theology seemed to take for granted the human person's freedom as a perfectly autonomous power of decision hindered in the exercise of its sovereignty only accidentally by factors that are rather exceptional. Contemporary authors seem to be less reluctant to admit that freedom of the will can be influenced only in exceptional cases. They tend to see human freedom as "freedom in situation" and they insist that the dialectic between freedom and determinism is essential for every human action.

Many contemporary moralists indicate the presence in all of the human person's actions of a determinism traceable to three sources—the biological, the social, and the psychological. They point out that recent discoveries of neurosurgery, endocrinology, and the use of drugs have demonstrated the influence of biological factors on the freedom of moral action. The pressure of society can also exert great influence on free activity and pressure groups and pressure factors have enormous determining potential in contemporary society. Finally, studies in depth psychology reveal constant neuroticizing factors under which many people live within the course of their growth and development as human beings.

ANALYSIS OF THE HUMAN ACT

The full grasp of what the free human act is and the role it plays in human action cannot be appreciated without an analysis of the whole human act as it is exercised in the concrete order, involving both the intellect and the will.

Component Parts. Presupposing what has been said about the internal and external principles of human action, one may distinguish the component parts or specific acts that make up the complex human act, which is always concerned in some way with ends and means. The list below analyzes the human act in terms of its various steps.

Intellect

Concerning the end
Apprehending an end
Judgment about an end
Concerning the means
Deliberating about means
Judgment about choice
Concerning execution
Command to execute choice
Judgment of end attained

Will

Concerning the end
Willing an end
Intending an end
Concerning the means
Consent to means
Choice of means
Concerning execution
Use of powers to execute
Enjoyment of end attained

This list outlines a fully conscious human action in dealing with a more or less complex practical situation. Not every human act man performs involves all these individual steps, but every human act in the practical order does involve seeking some end, a judgment and choice of means, and a consequent decision to attain to a desired end by carrying out the chosen course of action. It is well to bear in mind also that man does not always proceed in his human action in so orderly a way as the diagram list suggests. Often, indeed, particularly in difficult situations, he vacillates between one act on the part of the practical intellect and a corresponding act on the part of the will. But a knowledge of these various steps within the complex human act is helpful for successfully carrying out human decisions and choices; such knowledge is helpful also when one cannot resolve a practical problem, for he can, with reflection, ascertain where he is in the process and which step is holding him up or preventing him from attaining a resolution.

Interplay of Intellect and Will. The numbering of the steps, evenly divided between the intellect and the will, manifests the intimate connection between the intellect and the will in human action. On the one hand, the intellectual acts specify the acts of the will, for what one wills does depend on what he knows; on the other hand, each act of the will subsequently moves the intellect to a further act of knowing until the will is brought to some rest in an enjoyment of what was initially desired or, if unsuccessful, to a sorrow in not attaining what was initially desired. It should be noted that the human act is outlined here in terms of its intrinsic parts; the role of the emotions and other influences have also to be taken into account. Primarily, however, the human act is constituted of individual acts on the part of the intellect and the will.

This analysis of the human act enables one to understand human freedom better and to see, more precisely, what constitutes the free human act, which is usually spoken of as free will. One can now comprehend that actually a man's free act is a joint product of intellect and will. It is exercised principally, though not exclusively, in steps seven and eight of the list, the judgment on the part of the intellect that is inseparably allied with the choice of means. The connection between intellect and will is most intimate here. The intellect, in its practical judgment with regard to a means, is a determining cause of the will's choosing one object rather than another. But this is a determination coming from knowledge; and hence the will, in exercising the act of choice, is still choosing freely what is proposed on the part of the intellect. In a concrete instance facing man in knowing what he should do, his judgment of the choice is made and the will accordingly freely exercises its act of choice. This is positive freedom of specification: freely choosing to do what one knows one should do. Negative freedom consists in one's being able to reject what he knows he should do. What is involved here also is the judgment of CON-SCIENCE, which is still distinct from the practical judgment of the intellect in regard to choice. The latter judgment, as has been seen, is inseparably connected with appetite—with the will in its act of choice. The judgment of conscience, analytically prior to the practical judgment with reference to choice, is wholly an act of the intellect and thus apart from an actual choice to be made here and now; in an act of conscience one judges that an individual act is right to do as falling under a universal judgment or precept that acts of this kind should be done. It is a judgment of conscience, for example, that this debt should be paid, as falling under the universal judgment that debts should be paid. It is not yet the practical judgment with regard to choice and the ensuing act of choice, which takes place here and now, and where freedom of the human act is ultimately and principally located.

The foregoing discussion of the human act, starting with the internal and external principles and extending to the analysis of the human act into its component parts, is primarily psychological in character and treatment. A moral consideration of the human act, analyzing when and how acts are good or bad, presupposes this analysis (*see* MORALITY).

See Also: SIN.

Bibliography: ARISTOTLE, *Eth. Nic.* 1103a 12–1119b 19, 1138b 15–1145a 12. THOMAS AQUINAS 1a2ae, 6–21. J. A. OESTER-LE, *Ethics: The Introduction to Moral Science* (Englewood Cliffs, N.J. 1957) 45–100. M. V. MURRAY, *Problems in Ethics* (New York 1960) 72–106. V. J. BOURKE, *Ethics* (New York 1951) 57–120. J. FORD and G. KELLY, *Contemporary Moral Theology* 1 (Paramus, N.J. 1958) 174–312. J. FUCHS, *Human Values and Christian Morality*, tr. M. H. HEELAN (Dublin 1970), esp. "Basic Freedom and Morality," 92–111. E. MCDONAGH, "Towards a Christian Theology of Morality: The Moral Subject," *The Irish Theological Quarterly* 39 (1972) 3–22. L. MONDEN, *Sin, Liberty and Law* (New York 1965) 19–72. G. REGAN, *New Trends in Moral Theology* (New York 1971) 187–207.

[J. A. OESTERLE/J. A. O'DONOHOE]

HUMAN GENOME

A genome is an aspect of living organisms that enables them to pass on characteristics to the next generation. "Genome" specifies the totality of genes that make up the hereditary constitution of any particular organism. While each organism will have its own distinct set of genes (unless it is a twin), scientists seek to uncover the general attributes of the genomes of species as a whole. Thus, there are specialists studying the mouse genome, the frog genome, or the human genome. While this project lies within the field of organic science, much discussion has taken place over the social, ethical and economic implications of the study of the human genome. After giving a brief description of the Human Genome Project, this article will discuss the various issues raised, which

can be grouped as follows: (1) marketplace issues, including ownership of genetic knowledge or materials, and patenting; (2) genetic discrimination, which leads to questions about privacy, about health insurance, life insurance, and employment; (3) genetic testing, both adult testing and pre-natal screening; (4) genetic counseling and its new challenges; (5) eugenics and the use of gene selection for trait enhancement rather than treatment of disease; (6) gene therapy, both somatic cell therapy and germline therapy; (7) theological principles and questions of free will, determinism, and "playing God" and (8) cloning and embryo research.

The Human Genome Project. The Human Genome Project has been the collaborative work of many scientists and laboratories in the United States seeking to chart the DNA of the human genome. The idea of coordinating genetic research first surfaced in 1985 and 1986 from several directions, involving both the U.S. Dept. of Energy and the National Institutes of Health. By 1990 the U.S. Congress had allocated 3 to 5 billion dollars to be spent over 15 years in the quest to "map" and "sequence" the human genome. Similar work has been undertaken in other countries, coordinated by an international group, the Human Genome Organization (HUGO).

As the scope and funding of this project has been vast, so has its goal. The proteins needed to keep a human person functioning are coded in approximately 30,000 genes. These genes make up the "words" of the code, using four different nucleotides. Each nucleotide contain a nitrogenous base (Adenine, Cytosine, Guanine, or Thymine) attached to an outer structure of sugar and phosphate. These nucleotides pair up along the spiraled double helix: A with T and G with C. It is estimated that the human genome contains three billion of these base pairs. If one considers each base pair as a single "letter," creating the code book for the human genome is equivalent to decoding 13 complete sets of the *Encyclopedia Britannica.* Furthermore, such a code book is only useful if a "grammar" is developed by which one can "read" what has been gathered. So this massive project involves both finding what is there, in terms of strings of nucleotides, and interpreting what it means.

While the HGP is publicly funded, other private industry groups have been seeking to map the human genome on their own. In June of 2000, a joint announcement was made by the National Institutes of Health and Celera Genomics, a private corporation in Maryland, claiming that the human genome had now been mapped. While these two endeavors have taken different research strategies, and while significant gaps in information still exist, the work of the two groups together constitutes a significant advance in the goal of identifying all the genetic markers on the human genome.

Selected Issues.

Ownership. In the United States, the rise of new technologies, as a necessary side-product of research, as well as new forms of genetic material (cloned strings of base-pair sequences) has stirred up a significant controversy over the patenting of genetic materials and processes. U.S. patent law was derived as an incentive for private industry to engage in research and development, but has long since recognized that natural materials cannot be patented. In other words, the U.S. Patent and Trademark Office has functionally recognized a distinction between inventions and discoveries, refusing to patent the latter. Work in genetics has challenged this easy distinction. For example, in 1991 a California company, SyStemix, applied for a patent on a composition of stem cells developed out of bone-marrow stem cells, a biological product that could be useful in treating leukemia or AIDS. Both the process of production and the stem cell composition were patented. Since the particular stem cell composition does not exist in human bodies on its own, this is deemed an invention rather than a discovery.

The patenting issue raises broader questions about the commodification of genetic knowledge. This became evident early on in the U.S. program, when one of the researchers from the National Institutes of Health sought a patent for the gene sequences he had identified. A controversy arose over whether NIH ought to seek patents, something that James Watson—co-discoverer of DNA and head of the HGP at the time—vehemently opposed on the grounds that such action would hamper the free flow of information, on which scientific collegiality depends. The controversy had several results: James Watson resigned as director of the HGP, while NIH withdrew its patent applications. The questions of (1) whether genetic knowledge involving so-called inventions can/should be patented and (2) whether such patents should be granted to government agencies (and whose names will appear on them) remain highly contested (see Peters, 1997, 126ff).

Another set of ownership questions arises in light of the Human Genome Diversity Project (Peters, 1998). While its goal is admirable, seeking—through regional centers around the world—to advance the study of genetic diversity (and thereby offset the assumption that the "normal" genome is that of a Western Caucasian), the ethical and legal problems have mounted quickly. The project depends on the collection of vast numbers of DNA samples from widely diverse populations. The question of ownership rights over these samples is complicated by the fact that the Western notion of informed consent assumes an individualism with little salience in non-Western cultures. Further, who will benefit from the

Students pose with model of DNA molecule. (©James A. Sugar/ CORBIS)

knowledge gained by such samples? Are we once again facing a situation in which aboriginal and Third World peoples are exploited, for access to their DNA, so that the more prosperous might benefit? Finally, how can we deal with the normative judgments that come with potential discoveries for example, if it were to be disclosed that the gene for schizophrenia is more prevalent in Native Americans than in other populations? Will the quest for diversity turn into another excuse for racism?

Genetic Discrimination. Once tests or treatments for a certain genetic condition are available (and some are), will this information will be used to segregate the "normal" from the "diseased"? Advances in treatment of such things as growth hormone deficiency, using genetically engineered techniques, raise fears that those living with certain congenital conditions will be pushed more and more to the margins. Those living with deafness, dwarfism, and other conditions, already vulnerable to social disdain, may be made to feel even more isolated. In sum, will new developments in the treatment of genetic conditions exacerbate prejudice with regard to certain disabilities?

Genetic Testing. With tests for adult onset diseases such as Huntingdon's Chorea now available, the possibility of genetic discrimination is real. Debates in this area

Mary Pat Reeves-Daly, mapping human Y chromosome, as part of Human Genome Mapping Project. (Roger Ressmeyer/CORBIS)

revolve around concerns for confidentiality, employment, and life and health insurance. With the growing ability to determine which individuals carry which disease genes, efforts to ensure genetic privacy are increasing. There is particular concern that genetic information, in the hands of insurers or employers, will lead to discriminatory practice.

The insurance industry will change dramatically once genetic disease testing becomes routine. There are two approaches to risk classification and health insurance: the libertarian approach assumes that persons should pay premiums according to their risk classification, while the egalitarian view assumes that the risk burden should be borne by all, regardless of the personal probability of illness. As the ability to predict health risks based on genetic tests grows, these two approaches will come into conflict. The entire insurance industry, founded as it is on actuarial tables and calculations of

risk, will be challenged by new information about probabilities of future illness.

The possibility of being tested to see if one has a gene for a specific disease has been the most immediate practical result of the Human Genome Project. Yet the benefits of such testing are not so simple as they might seem. Not all genetic disorders arise from a single genetic mutation; some are multifactorial, meaning that they arise from the interaction of several genes, along with environmental factors. In these cases, as with breast cancer, heart disease, and diabetes, identifying genes simply indicates a propensity for a disease. Other cases are much more clear cut but nonetheless raise difficult questions. Huntingdon's disease is determined by a single genetic mutation: a person either does or does not have it, and one who does will get the disease. Having a relative who has had the disease is the indicator of risk. Whether an individual at risk wants to know for certain or not is a further question. In almost all cases, the technology for testing an individual's disease status has far outrun the development of treatments for a disease, putting many in the situation of having knowledge without effective options. Moreover, such genetic testing is almost never an individual matter: others who are at risk will be affected by the knowledge, either because they will be caretakers or because one person's status may have implications for their own. The potency of such genetic knowledge has led some to label this "toxic knowledge."

The genetic testing issues come to a head in the case of prenatal genetic testing. This can take the form of testing fetuses in the womb or of testing embryos in vitro, before implantation. The lack of effective treatment for most genetic diseases means that the point of genetic testing is simply to provide parents with the option of not having a certain child, either by abortion (in the case of fetal testing) or through discarding embryos before implantation. The Catholic position rejects both abortion and in vitro fertilization, raising the question of whether genetic screening (of all pregnant women) or genetic testing (of those shown to be at risk) is even desirable. Assumptions of "normality" versus "deformity," along with the presumption in favor of abortion for defective children, press the questions of genetic discrimination once again: to choose to have a child with a disability, even a fatal one, can put parents in a counter-cultural position.

Genetic Counseling. Genetic counseling is a relatively new profession, begun in order to explain genetic risks and probabilities to parents, usually those who already have one child suffering from a genetic disease. The rapid growth in genetic testing technology has created many new challenges for those in this profession. As genetic testing becomes more and more common, not only with regard to prospective parents but with persons tested for adult onset diseases, the engagement of the counselor in making normative judgments comes to the fore. Counselors are seeing the limitations of merely providing information, and are being pressed to help in decision-making and on-going support of families in crisis. The presumption of value neutrality on the part the genetic counselor is being questioned. Clergy and other pastoral counselors may have an important role to play in this area, though many, if not most, are poorly informed in basics of genetic medicine. Further, counselors themselves are raising concerns over genetic enhancement and the criteria for normalcy. What is the counselor to do, for example, if parents come seeking ways to ensure that they have a child who is tall, or bright, or, alternatively, deaf or dwarfed?

Eugenics. Another area of concern emerges: the question of eugenics and whether genetic technology ought to be used to engineer ideal traits in individuals or a more ideal population in general, or both. The notion that humans might enhance the gene pool through social policy and mating practices is an old one, with a very jaded history. Many discussions of genetic engineering move quickly to recounting the horrors of Nazi eugenic policies and the incipient racism of earlier eugenics movements. Nevertheless, dismissing eugenics as prejudicial requires further nuance with regard to the very category of "disease." Here the question is where and how to draw the line between genetic traits and genetic diseases, and which deserve medical treatment (Shinn 1996; Walters and Palmer 1997).

For example, if genetically altered hormones are available to help those with Growth Hormone Deficiency, what about their use in promoting tallness for those who wish it? If parents' hopes for their child include developing talents as a basketball player, why not use genetically engineered drugs to assist in this goal? These questions strike at the heart, not only of ideals about perfection and normality, but of the freedom of choice that grounds modern culture. If a couple wants to use genetic knowledge to enhance their child's biological makeup, and if they can afford to pay for the necessary procedures, what should prohibit them from doing so? Likewise, if parents want a child with certain characteristics, why not select among embryos screened for such characteristics in order to implant the desired ones in the mother's womb?

Such eugenics, whether based on individual choice or social policy, is rejected on several accounts from the Catholic perspective. First, modern genetics depends almost entirely on the conception of embryos outside the womb, in vitro, and the subsequent selective implantation of genetically preferred embryos in the mother. This technology was rejected by the encyclical *Donum vitae* in 1987 due to its violation of the marital act. Further, the commodification of children involved in such a eugenics mentality directly contradicts the Catholic notion that children are gifts, not products or achievements. Children, complete with their genetic assets and liabilities, are to be conceived through unitive marital acts and to be welcomed as gifts from God.

Genetic Therapy. Another complex result of the Human Genome Project lies in the area of genetic therapy. The first point to be made in this regard is the distinction between somatic cell therapy and germline therapy. Somatic cells include all the cells of the body, while germline cells are the reproductive cells, eggs and sperm as well as embryos. Gene therapy that targets somatic cells seeks to affect the symptoms of a disease, or alter the genetic composition of cells that are defective due to genetic disease. For example, cystic fibrosis arises from a defective gene that prevents liquid from being transported through cell membranes, resulting in mucous accumulation in the lungs. Attempts have been made to deliver aerosolized, normal genes to the lungs of affected patients in order to correct the deficiency. These kinds of treatments need to be repeated regularly and, even if the effectiveness of the technology improves dramatically, will have an impact only on the life of the individual patient. Germline therapy would involve altering the genes of the patient's egg or sperm (or an embryo conceived by the patient) so that his or her child would not be affected by the disease. What is distinctive about this latter kind of therapy, yet to be developed, is that it would have an impact on all future generations, not merely the affected individual (Walters and Palmer 1997).

Generally, the ethical concerns over somatic cell therapy remain simply those of any medical research: informed consent, assessment of risk, cost-benefit analysis, etc. These standard principles break down with germline therapy: the persons affected do not yet exist and cannot therefore provide informed consent, and the risks are hard to calculate since the effects of tampering with DNA may not appear for several generations. Further, the research itself cannot go forward without experimentation on human embryos. While those who do not hold that life begins at conception find such research not only acceptable but urgent, the Catholic insistence on the dignity of life from the moment of conception rejects all such research. Even if germline therapy could move beyond tampering with embryos in vitro (to altering ova and sperm), there still remains the concern over eugenics and discrimination: if we begin altering future generations in order to cure disease, what is to stop persons from using the same techniques to eliminate unwanted characteristics from the population? What will happen to the diversity of the gene pool?

Theological Principles. Implicit in many of the concerns about justice and social policy discussed above is the notion of the dignity of the human person and the preferential focus on the poor, the vulnerable, and the marginalized, including embryos. This applies to questions of global justice as well as issues of discrimination, access to health care, racist eugenics, and concerns for the unborn.

A related salient question with regard to the Human Genome Project has to do with theological anthropology and the divine. Just what does it mean to be human and how do new genetic knowledge and capabilities alter our view of the human-divine relationship? These questions have entered the literature as discussions of the ''gene myth'' and ''playing God'' (Peter 1997). Almost all

Christian theologians reject any absolute genetic determinism, harkening to the theological notion of humans as created *imago Dei*—in the image of God—with rationality and free will. Yet the limit of this freedom is highlighted by the oft-repeated insistence that humans must not try to usurp the role of God. Still, this latter injunction raises its own problems, since not intervening at all in the natural order is an utter impossibility. How far human agents can go in altering processes at the level of DNA remains a hotly disputed question.

The two sides of this conundrum are evident in the different models to which theological ethicists appeal. Those more in favor of pressing the edges of genetic therapies emphasize the duty toward alleviating suffering, and insist on modeling this work after Jesus as a divine healer. Those who want to be more cautious about advances in genetic research and treatment tend to focus more on natural law and the dangers of human hubris. Both streams of thought are present in the Roman Catholic tradition, with its legacy of works of mercy and medical missions as well as its adherence to a natural law theory that cautions against excessive intervention in nature.

Cloning. While not a direct result of the HGP, cloning nevertheless has yielded great debate in the past several years. The birth of Dolly, the cloned sheep, at the Roslin Institute in Scotland in the spring of 1997 brought the possibility of human cloning to the fore. This event elicited a wide range of perspectives, ethically, theologically, and denominationally (Cole-Turner 1998). Those who oppose human cloning most strongly identify themselves with either the Reformed tradition or the Roman Catholic tradition. Their arguments focus on the uniqueness and divinity of each individual, the reductionism and consumerism inherent in most bio-technologies, the disruption of family integrity, and the hubris of genetic manipulation.

For those who are not entirely opposed to human cloning, several themes appear repeatedly. Many question whether human cloning is even possible, given the technological and moral obstacles. It took 277 tries before Dolly was born. Of these, only 29 embryos survived beyond six days and 62 percent of fetuses implanted in ewes were lost by 14 days. In other words, the wastage in terms of human embryos would be extreme, not to mention the number of women needed to undergo implantation and pregnancy, with little hope of bringing a baby to term. Many believe that these facts alone will set sanctions against proceeding towards human cloning. Others believe that the technology already exists, and it is only a matter of time before it reaches the public domain.

The point most often made by those cautiously accepting of human cloning is that this reproductive process, in and of itself, will not destroy the unique identity of an individual. Genetic makeup is only a portion of individual identity, as is illustrated in the case of identical twins.

Other ethical concerns focus on the motives for creating a clone. Given other available procedures for dealing with infertility, the reasons for wanting a clone come down to the following: (1) to clone oneself or to create children with enhanced genetic capabilities; (2) to create a second child genetically identical to a first child who is terminally ill, in order to aid in treatment of the ill child; or (3) to create a replacement for a child who has died. None of these seem to be warranted, on the grounds that each motive makes of the clone an instrument used in fulfilling another's aspirations or needs. Since there is no way to obtain informed consent from the clone for such an instrumental birth, human cloning is rendered suspect.

Bibliography: A. R. CHAPMAN, *Unprecedented Choices: Religious Ethics at the Frontiers of Genetic Science* (Minneapolis 1999). R. COLE-TURNER, ed., *Human Cloning: Religious Responses* (Louisville 1997). M. JUNKER-KENNY and L. S. CAHILL, eds., *The Ethics of Genetic Engineering* (Maryknoll, NY 1998). J. F. KILNER, R. D. PENTZ, and F. E. YOUNG, eds., *Genetic Ethics: Do the Ends Justify the Genes?* (Grand Rapids, MI 1997). T. PETERS, *Playing God? Genetic Determinism and Human Freedom* (New York 1997). T. PETERS, ed., *Genetics: Issues of Social Justice* (Cleveland 1998). R. L. SHINN, *The New Genetics* (London 1996). L. WALTERS and J. G. PALMER, *The Ethics of Human Gene Therapy* (New York 1997). R. A. WILLER, ed., *Genetic Testing and Screening: Critical Engagement at the Intersection of Faith and Science* (Minneapolis 1998).

[C. S. W. CRYSDALE]

HUMAN RESPECT

Human respect is an excessive regard for the opinions or esteem of other men. The expression is not used by classical theologians, but it does signify a powerful influence in human affairs and one of which Christian moralists have not been unaware. Because honor or the recognition of a person's worth is so great a human good—the greatest of man's external goods (St. Thomas Aquinas, *Summa theologiae,* 2a2ae, 129.1)—men naturally strive for it. Theologians note the special virtue of MAGNANIMITY or greatness of soul that moderates one's undertaking works worthy of honor. Human respect, then, is not to be confused with magnanimity or with the reticence that prevents one from rashly divulging his inner secrets or hidden defects that would ruin his reputation. Since human respect is a kind of fear of the judgment of others, one acting from this motive lacks courage or fortitude, but as a vice human respect seems more directly opposed to magnanimity because it seeks honor rather than the works worthy of honor.

Concern for the opinion of others may lead one to act against moral principles and thus to do evil in order to gain the esteem of others. This obviously is morally wrong, for it involves an inversion of moral values, a preferring of human esteem to the virtuous good. If the matter is serious, the sin can be grave.

But the common human tendency to be concerned about the favorable opinion of others can be put to better use. If care is taken to associate with those who hold virtue in honor, the desire for the approval of others can encourage one to right living. This appears to be a matter of importance especially for adolescents, who are particularly concerned for the approval of others, since they are just becoming aware of their individuality and are searching for value and meaning in their lives.

If a morally good act is motivated purely, or at least principally, by human respect, it falls outside the order of merit. Such an act, performed not because of its intrinsic goodness or out of obedience to divine law, is not done, even virtually, for the love of God. However, such acts may have a certain utility insofar as they are at least an external fulfillment of the moral law and may lead to the formation of good habits.

Bibliography: C. DAMEN, in F. ROBERTI et al., *Dictionary of Moral Theology,* ed. P. PALAZZINI et al. from 2d Ital. ed. (Westminster, Md. 1962) 1310–11. N. JUNG, *Dictionnaire de théologie catholique,* ed. A. VACANT et al., 15 v. (Paris 1903–50; Tables générales 1951–) 13.2:2461–66.

[J. HENNESSEY]

HUMANAE VITAE

Encyclical letter of Pope PAUL VI, on the regulation of birth, issued July 29, 1968.

Background. In acknowledgment of a growing sentiment both within and outside the Church, John XXIII appointed a commission (March 1963) to restudy the morality of using anovulant pills as a precoital measure of birth prevention; such use had once been characterized by PIUS XII (1958) as a direct temporary sterilization and therefore as immoral. Paul VI twice reconstituted Pope John's commission and, in response to mounting public agitation, invited it to evaluate the Church's overall ban on contraception rather than simply the application of that ban to the anovulant pill.

The commission majority's report (June 1966) favored leaving the method of birth regulation to the consciences of individual married couples, provided that selfishness were excluded and the conjugal life taken as a whole were open to procreation. The pope, however, undertook an independent study and eventually, in *Humanae Vitae,* rejected the commission's recommendations for a relaxation of the Church's traditional teaching.

Doctrine. After reviewing the controversy that occasioned its issuance and reasserting the Church's competence to interpret the natural law, *Humanae Vitae* articulates fundamental principles concerning conjugal love and responsible parenthood. Conjugal love, like marriage itself, is described as a good instituted by God "to realize in mankind his design of love" and to enable spouses "to collaborate with God in the generation and education of new lives" (No. 8). Responsible parenthood involves understanding and respecting the biological laws "which are part of the human person," mastering instinct and passion by rational control, deciding prudently about family size in concrete circumstances, and adhering to "the objective moral order established by God" (10).

While he did not assign an order of priority between the procreative and unitive goods of marriage, Pope Paul did insist that both values taken together are essential to the integrity of the conjugal act. Accordingly, he reiterated the requirement of natural law that "each and every marriage act (*quilibet matrimonii usus*) must remain open to the transmission of life" (11). This entails rejection of the following birth control techniques: (1) direct abortion under all circumstances; (2) direct sterilization of either spouse, whether permanent or temporary; (3) any procedure "which, *either in anticipation of the conjugal act, or in its accomplishment, or in the development of its natural consequences, proposes, whether as an end or as a means, to render procreation impossible*" (14). The italicized words in the last quoted phrase refer to the anovulant pill.

In an apparent response to the papal commission's majority, Pope Paul emphasized that deliberate violence to the integrity of even a single conjugal act constitutes an evil which cannot be rectified either by a good ulterior motive or by other conjugal acts left open to procreation (14). The pope further sought to counter the consequentialist reasoning of contraception advocates by observing that contraception, in addition to its intrinsic evil, can have disastrous consequences, such as encouraging promiscuity and marital infidelity, degrading women into objects of sexual satisfaction, and furnishing unscrupulous governments with the means of violating the procreative freedom of their subjects (17).

While rejecting contraception, the pope reaffirmed the legitimacy of conjugal acts foreseen to be infecund

"for causes independent of the will of husband and wife" (11). It is therefore allowable to use therapeutic measures necessary for health which are not calculated to suppress procreation, even if an obstacle to procreation will arise as a side effect (15). Moreover, for "serious motives," spouses may regulate births by utilizing "the natural rhythms immanent in the generative functions" (16). Acknowledging that the observance of rhythm necessitates self-discipline and restraint, the pope affirmed that this can contribute significantly to developing the mutual unselfishness that is essential to a happy and stable marriage.

In the lengthy pastoral section that concludes *Humanae Vitae* (19–30), Pope Paul admonished public authorities to promote a social climate favorable to chastity and to refrain from either supporting or imposing unnatural birth-control techniques to solve demographic problems. Scientists are asked to search out a way of furnishing "a sufficiently secure basis" for birth regulation through the observance of rhythm (24). Married couples are exhorted to pursue the positive value of conjugal chastity aided by prayer and the Sacraments, without being discouraged by natural weakness. Priests and bishops, finally, are urged to propose the Pope's teaching faithfully and to encourage spouses to adhere to it.

Authority. The encyclical was released to the press by Msgr. (later Archbishop) Ferdinando Lambruschini, with the comment that the document did not propose its teaching as infallible and irreformable although it did reflect the serious judgment of the Church's highest magisterial authority. Barely a month later, writing to an assembly of German Catholics, Pope Paul himself expressed hope that "the lively debate aroused by our encyclical will lead to a better understanding of God's will" (*Acta Apostolicae Sedis* 60 [1968] 575). The authoritative status of *Humanae vitae* has itself become the subject of lively debate. Some scholars, notably John C. Ford and Germain Grisez, have argued that the teaching against contraception bespeaks a long unbroken tradition of the ordinary magisterium and, therefore, was already infallible before Pope Paul issued his encyclical (*Theological Studies* 39 [1978] 258–312). In 1984 Pope John Paul II claimed that this teaching "belongs not only to the natural moral law, but also to the *moral order revealed by God:* also from this point of view, it could not be different, but solely what is handed down by Tradition and the Magisterium and, in our days, the Encyclical *Humanae vitae* as a modern document of this Magisterium" (General Audience, July 18, 1984; *L'osservatore Romano* [Eng. ed.], July 23, 1984, 1; italics original). This papal statement, however, is not itself a definitive declaration; and the anti-contraception teaching is not included in a more recent list of moral and dogmatic teachings characterized by the Congregation for the Doctrine of the Faith as infallible even though not formally defined (*L'osservatore Romano,* June 30–July 1, 1998, 5). Theologians such as Francis A. Sullivan have meanwhile contested the arguments of Ford and Grisez (Sullivan, *Magisterium: Teaching Authority in the Catholic Church* [1983] 119–152). Grisez has published several additional articles replying to Sullivan and other critics, thus keeping ''the lively debate'' going in scholarly circles. Among Catholic believers generally, it is apparent that the teaching of *Humanae vitae* has not been effectively received or widely practiced. Many dioceses in the United States and elsewhere, however, refer married and engaged couples to the Natural Family Planning services which are increasingly available. Some proponents of the encyclical's teaching suggest hopefully that further advances in the development of reliable natural methods of monitoring fertility, combined with greater apprehensions about the safety of much contraceptive technology (including the anovulant pill), will eventually foster a more favorable climate for the wider reception of papal teaching about responsible birth regulation.

Bibliography: PAUL VI, *Humanae Vitae* (July 25, 1968), *Acta Apostolicae Sedis,* 60 (1968) 481–503; Eng. tr. *Humanae Vitae* (Washington, D.C. 1968), also *Pope Speaks* 13 (1968–69) 305–316 and *Catholic Mind* 66 (Sept. 1968) 35–48; address to obstetricans and gynecologists (Oct. 29, 1966), *Acta Apostolicae Sedis,* 58 (1966) 1166–70; Eng. tr. *Pope Speaks* 11 (1966) 401–402. *Human Life in Our Day,* pastoral letter of U.S. bishops (Washington, D.C. 1968). J. COSTANZO, ''Papal Magisterium, Natural Law and *Humanae Vitae,*'' *American Journal of Jurisprudence* 16 (1971) 259–289. C. CURRAN, ed., *Contraception: Authority and Dissent* (New York 1969). J.A. KOMONCHAK, ''*Humanae vitae* and its Reception: Ecclesiological Reflections,'' *Theological Studies* 39 (1978) 221–257. R.A. MCCORMICK, ''Notes on Moral Theology, 1978: *Humanae vitae* and the Magisterium,'' *Theological Studies* 40 (1979) 80–97. R. DENNEHY, ed., *Christian Married Love* (San Francisco, 1981). R. MALONE, ''*Humanae Vitae* Revisited,'' *Communio (US)* 15 (Winter 1988) 517–520. J.E. SMITH, *Humanae vitae: A Generation Later* (Washington, DC, 1991). C.E. CURRAN and R.A. MCCORMICK, eds., *Dialogue about Catholic Sexual Teaching* (New York 1993). P. BRISTOW, ''Dualism: The Obstacle to Understanding *Humanae Vitae,*'' *Downside Review* 113 (1995) 104–111. D. S. CRAWFORD, ''*Humanae Vitae* and the Perfection of Love,'' *Communio (US)* 25 (Fall 1998) 414–438.

[B. A. WILLIAMS]

HUMANI GENERIS

An encyclical issued by Pope PIUS XII on Aug. 12, 1950, to meet the thrust of the theological revival after World War II. At the end of that war the pent-up energies of Catholic scholars, together with the freedom to publish and exchange opinions, set in motion the theological revival sometimes labeled the ''new theology.'' The purpose of the encyclical was twofold: to correct certain extreme opinions held in some Catholic circles; and to restate those traditional Catholic teachings relative to the direction in which the postwar theological revival was heading.

The opening paragraphs of the encyclical catalogued extreme non-Christian philosophies of evolutionism, existentialism, and HISTORICISM as contributing to the spread of error. However, at the same time, it called for Catholic philosophers and theologians to study these philosophies for the purpose of combating them. The encyclical significantly stated that each of these philosophies contains a certain amount of truth, and that such study will lead Catholic scholars to a fruitful discussion and evaluation of philosophical and theological truths.

In the field of theology the encyclical specifically restated the condemnations of earlier pontiffs of merely relativistic conceptions of Catholic dogma. Such conceptions lead to the more dangerous error of neglect of the teaching authority of the Church. At this point the encyclicals themselves are spoken of as organs of the ordinary teaching (*magisterium*) of the Church.

In modern Biblical studies the encyclical condemned as specific errors the exegesis of Scripture that ignores or is opposed to the analogy of faith and the tradition of the Church and that which is marked by either ignorance or contempt for the literal meaning of the text in favor of a purely spiritual interpretation.

Theological reaffirmations of traditional Catholic teaching concerned the following: the demonstration of the existence of God, creation, predestination, the existence of ANGELS, the gratuity of the supernatural order, ORIGINAL SIN, the meaning of SIN, TRANSUBSTANTIATION, and membership in the Church, MYSTICAL BODY OF CHRIST. In philosophy, the encyclical reaffirmed the Church's approval of THOMISM according to the norms of Pope LEO XIII and Pope St. PIUS X.

Finally, the encyclical considered specific teachings derived from the ''positive sciences'' but more or less connected to the truths of the Christian religion. In the question of human evolution specific direction is given to continue present research and inquiry by specialists; in addition, two statements are made about problems related directly to evolution. The first concerns the evolution of the human body from preexisting and living matter, that is, that such an opinion is not as yet a certain conclusion from the facts and that revelation demands moderation and caution. The second concerns polygenism, and is to the effect that it cannot at the present time be taught by Catholics, for it is not yet apparent how polygenism is to be reconciled with the traditional teaching of the Church on original sin. Finally, in the sphere of historical study, the encyclical condemns those who empty the Genesis accounts in the OT of any historical sense. However, the history contained in those accounts is, according to the encyclical, to be determined by exegetes keeping in mind the process of inspiration, the popular intent of the documents, and the metaphorical nature of the language.

Humani generis did not stop the postwar theological revival, nor was it intended to do so; but it did serve to channel that revival toward constructive work, and to limit prudently certain areas of speculation. The ultimately prudential nature of the encyclical is evident in its refusal to name or censure specific persons or even titles of works, and in its evident awareness of and interest in modern thought.

The significance of *Humani generis* as regards to various theological topics has been discussed where pertinent in the respective related articles of this encyclopedia.

Bibliography: PIUS XII, "Humani generis" (Encyclical, 12 Aug. 1950) *ActApS* 42 (1950) 561–578, Eng. *Catholic Mind* 48 (Nov. 1950) 688–700. A. C. COTTER, *The Encyclical "Humani generis"* (Weston, Mass. 1951). S. TROMP, *Lexikon für Theologie und Kirche*, ed. J. HOFER and K. RAHNER (Freiburg 1957–65) 5:524–525. J. M. CONNOLLY, *Voices of France* (New York 1961). J. LEVIE, "L'Encyclique *Humani generis,*" *Nouvelle Revue théologique* 72 (1950) 785–793. F. TAYMÁNS, "L'Encyclique *Humani generis* et la théologie," *ibid.,* 73 (1951) 3–20. R. GUELLUY, "Les antécédents de l'encyclique Humani Generis dans les sanctions Romaines de 1942: Chenu, Charlier, Draguet," *Revue d'Histoire Ecclesiastique* 81 (1986) 421–97.

[J. M. CONNOLLY]

HUMANISM

The term humanism has a number of more or less distinct meanings, all referring to a world view in some way centered on man rather than on the suprahuman or the abstract. In its strictest sense, the word refers to a literary and intellectual movement, the "new learning," running from 14th-century Italy through Western culture generally into the 17th century or, more vaguely, even beyond, and marked by devotion to Greek and Latin classics as the central and highest expression of human values. The term has been extended to comparable movements in the Middle Ages, notably to the 12th-century educational reform typified by the ideals of JOHN OF SALISBURY (d. 1180) and to Carolingian scholarly activity centering around ALCUIN (*see* CAROLINGIAN RENAISSANCE). Humanism refers at times also to certain specific 20th-century developments. One of these early in the century, growing out of the work of William JAMES, John Dewey, and F. C. S. Schiller, envisioned joining scientif-

ic concerns with the "higher" life of the human spirit. A second was that of Irving Babbitt and Paul Elmer More, who reacted strongly against vocational specialization and scientism. Twentieth-century Neothomism, particularly as propounded by Jacques Maritain, has often viewed itself as a Christian humanism (*see* NEOSCHOLASTICISM AND NEOTHOMISM; HUMANISM, CHRISTIAN). More recently, Christian humanism has acquired further meanings, some of them associated with the views of Pierre TEILHARD DE CHARDIN, SJ (with whom, however, the term humanism itself found little favor). Taking mankind in a fuller cosmic setting, these later humanisms make much of the "hominization" of the globe, its increasing subjection to man, as the culmination of the cosmic evolutionary processes to which the Incarnation gives a new and final significance. On the other hand, an atheistic type of existentialism has been proposed by Jean Paul Sartre and others as a humanism, a view of life centered on man conceived of as creating himself for himself in his own system of values. The term secular HUMANISM is often used for this and various other systems of thought that propose purportedly integrated views of life which, often in a highly polemic spirit, exclude belief in the existence of God.

The present article is concerned with humanism in the strict sense. Often styled Renaissance humanism, this 14th-century movement is sometimes taken as coextensive with the Renaissance itself, and sometimes as a more specific manifestation. In its specific sense, Renaissance humanism is basically academic. Humanists as such were textual scholars and devisers of curricula—on the one hand the successors of the medieval scribes, that is, of the masters of the ars dictaminis, and on the other hand more or less professional educators. At the core of humanism lay the *studia humanitatis* of the Renaissance, a specific educational curriculum that stressed grammar, rhetoric, history, poetry, and ethics, all studied in classical texts, and competed as an educational alternative with the established scholasticism of the arts course or SCHOLASTIC "philosophy," which had stressed logic or dialectic and natural philosophy (something akin to modern "science," of which it was one of the seedbeds), with some token interest in ethics and metaphysics (*see* SCHOLASTICISM, 1). Attentive to man's life in the world as such rather than to abstractions, humanism encouraged music and the visual arts as well as the cultivation of manners and at times, especially in Italy, of athletic skills. As a concrete educational program, humanism incorporated various and even competing ideologies and resources; and, although it effected changes, its breaks with the immediate past were seldom clean. Scholastic dialectic and humanist rhetoric, for example, often clearly overlapped not only in matter but even in method: typical humanist rhe-

Cosimo de' Medici as patron of philosophers and artists, detail of a fresco by Giorgio Vasari in the Sala di Cosmo il Vecchio, Palazzo Vecchio, Florence.

Pietro Cardinal Bembo.

torical procedure was far more committed to logical formalism than what is generally considered RHETORIC today.

Humanism, even in the strict sense of an academic phenomenon, is connected with and often intimately dependent on political, intellectual, artistic, social, and other cultural developments. Thus interpretations of humanism have varied in accord with interpretations of the Renaissance itself. Since the Renaissance is handled in a separate article, the present article treats humanism chiefly in its academic aspects.

Beginnings. Humanism developed in an academic tradition that had never associated serious teaching with any language other than Latin, and it represents in great part a crisis within the use of that language.

Linguistic and Cultural Background. When, between the 6th century and the 9th, the modern romance languages were evolving out of Latin and new non-romance languages were flooding into the late Roman Empire, schools and learned circles in western Europe generally had continued to conduct their business as usual—that is, with Latin texts, which did not change as the spoken language did and had no competition since virtually nothing was written in the vernaculars.

At first there was relatively little difference between the Latin of the schools and that which was spoken, but, as the spoken language changed more and more, even speakers of languages developed out of Latin found it necessary to study Latin as more or less a foreign language in order to go to school. The problem of translating Latin texts into the hundreds of rapidly evolving and largely unwritten dialects was too vast to be seriously considered. These dialects did not even have words needed to express what was studied in school (grammatical terms, for example), so that classroom explanation itself had somehow to be couched in Latin. After antiquity the Latin used in learned circles changed somewhat, but negligibly. Medieval Latin added greatly to its vocabulary and devised or favored some few characteristic structures of its own, and some medieval users knew Latin better than others; but essentially the language remained Learned Latin, a written language modeled on the Latin of classical antiquity.

Humanism and the Middle Ages. The Middle Ages thus remained in contact to a degree with the ancient world and were consistently nourished by it directly or indirectly. In the early Middle Ages classical works that were directly utilized tended to be those serving in a utilitarian fashion the study of the Latin language and of rhetoric, but by the 11th and 12th centuries works of literary and scientific value were widely used. Ovid, Horace, Persius, Juvenal, and Terence were among the favorites, as well as the first two treatises of Aristotle's *Organon,* translated into Latin, of course, often from Arabic versions. Knowledge of Greek was exceedingly rare. In the mid-13th century even a scholar of the distinction of St. THOMAS AQUINAS could do without a personal mastery of Greek in explaining Greek authors themselves, relying on his younger Dominican brother, WILLIAM OF MOERBEKE, who had gone to Greece to learn the language, as his philological adviser.

As a continuation of the medieval dependence upon texts of classical antiquity, Renaissance humanism was thus not only nothing new but was rather one of the most typically medieval phenomena the Middle Ages produced. Humanism did, however, reorient and intensify devotion to antiquity, making of this devotion a symbol of something new, opposed to the cultural *status quo.* It is this reorientation and intensification that needs to be explained.

The Role of Petrarch. PETRARCH is generally identified as the first significant writer to evince the kind of enthusiasm for the ancients that was typical of Renaissance humanism. He was an enthusiast for literature as a manifestation and implement of the "good life," that is, of a self-conscious, urbane, moderately austere, but open and genial appreciation of the goods of the natural world, combined with a sense of the limitations of human existence, of the "tears of things." Thus viewed, this "good life" did not foster the other-worldly religious intensity of either a St. IGNATIUS LOYOLA or a Martin LUTHER, but as Petrarch viewed it, it was nevertheless Christian. Europe in places, notably in northern Italy, had reached a state of opulence (Florentine humanists were rather uniformly of the wealthy class), civic organization, and cultural self-confidence sufficient for Petrarch's type of enthusiasm to have appeal and to be indulged on a significantly wider scale than before. Petrarch and his circle found little to feed this love of literature and the good life in the world of scholasticism, whether "philosophy," medicine, law, or theology, but much to nourish it in classical antiquity.

Petrarch and later Renaissance humanists, however, appropriated classical writers quite selectively, apotheosizing only those who struck a responsive chord and downgrading those, largely technical or "abstract" writers such as Aristotle, who had chiefly interested the Middle Ages. The good life was served at best only to a limited extent by technical, abstract knowledge and utilitarian approaches to the natural world. Science, if indulged, was to be pursued in leisurely and genteel fashion. The master art for Petrarch was rhetoric, which had dominated liberal education in antiquity and which related to human action, not dialectic or logic, which had to do with technicalities and were at best a part of elementary education not worth the attention of mature men.

Petrarch's love of the classics was closely tied to Italian patriotism and to the feeling that the Rome of his day and that of the ancient Republic were one. He wrote a book (*De viris illustribus*) on the great men of the ancient Roman Republic, and here, as elsewhere, laid the ground for the cult of fame and glory and of gracefully competent and spectacular individual achievement, or *virtù*, which was to remain a noteworthy feature of Renaissance humanism. Under Cicero's influence, Petrarch had believed that Latin literature was far superior to Greek, but by 1342 he began to learn Greek; while he never became fully adept in the language, he prepared Italy for the reception of ancient Greek culture. Petrarch's devotion to the classics was crucial in arousing the interests of his compatriot Giovanni Boccaccio in ancient Latin literature.

Manuscripts and Libraries. Humanism fed on addiction to reading, grown notably stronger during the Middle Ages; the ancients had been more deeply committed to the spoken word both in educational procedure and in cultural life. Petrarch himself was a manuscript hunter and collector, as were Boccaccio and the chancellor at Florence, Coluccio SALUTATI. The age immediately following Petrarch's—that of POGGIO Bracciolini (1380–1459), Niccolo dei Niccoli (1363–1437), and NICHOLAS OF CUSA—was marked by the greatest discoveries of Latin manuscripts the West had ever seen.

Interest in texts bred interest in textual criticism, and the humanist drive toward textual accuracy manifested itself in efforts to get at the two principal substrata underlying Western Latin literary culture, namely, Greek and Hebrew. Humanist interest in Greek has sometimes been dated from the fall of Constantinople to the Ottoman Turks in 1453 and the consequent flight to the West of Greek Christians, who were fluent in classical Greek because their own vernacular Greek had kept close to the classical and because the study of classical Greek had remained the basic tradition in Eastern schools as had the study of Latin in the West. But it is certain that interest in Greek texts was growing massively in Italy long before 1453. The correspondence of the Camaldolese monk Ambrogio Traversari (1386–1439) lists acquisitions of Greek manuscripts sent by Giovanni Aurispa and Francesco Filelfo to Florence upon their return from the East in 1424 and 1427. The fall of Constantinople simply stimulated existing activities. The archbishop of Nicaea, Cardinal BESSARION, who adhered to Rome after the Council of FLORENCE (1438–45), put much of his energy into acquiring Greek manuscripts, and John (or Janus) Lascaris, one of the refugee Greek scholars, collected for the MEDICI, and brought back, over 200 Greek manuscripts at one time in 1492.

Hebrew manuscripts, extant in Europe through the Middle Ages but virtually ignored by medieval Christians, also began to make their way into Christian collections at this time, although to a limited degree. Giovanni PICO DELLA MIRANDOLA owned more than 100 Hebrew manuscripts, and Federigo, Duke of Urbino, had nearly as many.

Many of the great European libraries date from this period of manuscript collecting, when the VATICAN LIBRARY in particular began to acquire its preeminence under NICHOLAS V (1447–55), himself a copyist, manuscript collector, and patron of the arts.

Greek Revival, Florentine and Other Academies. In the humanists' self-conscious return to the past and their general expansion of intellectual horizons, Greek played the most significant linguistic role, with Rome, Venice, and Florence the chief centers of activity. Nicholas V patronized the great project of translating the principal Greek prose authors into Latin, carried forward by the Greek exiles Bessarion, George of TREBIZOND, known also as Trapezuntius, and Theodore of Gaza (c. 1400–75), as well as by Italian scholars such as Lorenzo VALLA,

Niccolo Perotti (1430–80), Poggio Bracciolini, and Guarino da Verona (1374–1460). The Venetian humanist printer Aldus MANUTIUS and the scholars he had gathered around him in the Venetian Academy undertook the printing of careful first editions of the Greek texts of many of the authors translated into Latin at Rome.

Florence a Center. Florence became especially important as a center of Platonic studies, which were undertaken largely by some of the most well-to-do among the citizenry. Manuel Chrysoloras, a Byzantine schoolmaster turned diplomat, had taught Greek at Florence and translated Plato's *Republic* at the beginning of the 15th century. Gemistos PLETHON, a native of Constantinople and teacher of Bessarion, as a representative of the Greek Church at the Council of Florence had fanned the interests of the Florentine Cosimo de' Medici in PLATONISM, and, with Theodore of Gaza on the opposite or Aristotelian side, had touched off the controversy between Platonists and Aristotelians that polarized much philosophical discussion for generations. Cosimo founded the Accademia Platonica of Florence, where scholars gathered to exchange ideas and thus cultivate the good life. The Accademia achieved its greatest fame under Lorenzo de' Medici, ''The Magnificent,'' who reigned from 1469 to 1492, the ''incarnation of the spirit of the Renaissance,'' politician, poet, patron of the arts, philosophy, and classical learning. This academy had counterparts in Naples and Rome. The Roman Academy flourished especially under LEO X (Giovanni de' Medici) from 1513 to 1521, with the future cardinals Pietro Bembo and Jacopo SADOLETO as members, together with Paolo Giovio (1483–1552) and Baldassare Castiglione.

Ficino and Pico della Mirandola. These academies, particularly that of Florence, gave humanists an interest in intellectual speculation largely missing among the early Greek immigrants, men who had often found a place in the Western intellectual world because they knew Greek rather than because they had serious intellectual interests. The center of the Florentine academy was Marsilio FICINO, who, when still a mere boy, had been selected by Cosimo to be educated in Greek. Ficino and Giovanni PICO DELLA MIRANDOLA, who together set the tone of the academy, depended more on the Neoplatonism of PLOTINUS and of PSEUDO-DIONYSIUS than on Plato himself for their deepest inspiration. Ficino's Platonic philosophy was based on the harmony he believed existed between Platonism and the Christian faith, and in its holistic approach resembled the thought of the early Fathers of the Church, particularly AUGUSTINE, rather than that of the scholastics, although Ficino perceived less of a gulf between Platonism and faith than had Augustine. Both philosophy and the Christian religion were for Ficino manifestations of the spiritual life, as the created worlds emanate from God in a descending hierarchical order. He emphasized the divine element in man and other created things, from literature to sexual love (aroused by beauty and terminating in the begetting of children), and put high value on many forms of ardor, such as the drives toward glory, honor, and patriotism. Ficino, a devout Christian ordained at the age of 40, was more tolerant of the material world than ancient pagan Greek thinkers had been: although the soul finds happiness only in God, it retains permanently its affinity to matter, so that the body itself must have its eternity.

Ficino's thought was complemented by that of Pico della Mirandola, whose view of man somewhat anticipated certain elements of 20th-century existentialism: man's distinctive humanness is due to his power of free choice. For Pico, however, this power of choice does not isolate man but rather enables him to share in the properties of all other beings. The holistic sense of actuality here evident appears also in Pico's other important idea of the unity of all philosophical thought, a unity that, as Paul Oskar Kristeller has explained, is not a blurred product of fuzzy syncretism or SKEPTICISM but is quite clear-cut: in various philosophers, Pico maintains, one can isolate specific instances of clearly articulated truths that bind the philosophers together despite varying admixtures of error. Even more than Ficino, Pico made use of the scholastic heritage, which he often defended against other humanists.

Ficino and Pico were typical in that they processed Greek thought somewhat in Western terms, for contact with that thought did not cure the Renaissance of its clearly Western bias, marked by a stress on sobriety and order, on dignity and a sometimes ponderous magnificence, rather than on Greek spontaneity, grace, and venturesomeness. The spirit of ancient Greece came more alive for the West only in the 19th century.

Although with Renaissance humanism ancient Greek literature entered into the mainstream of Western thought as never before, the end result of the humanist excursion into Greek as a language fell short of sanguine humanist ambitions. Under humanist encouragement, Greek was indeed added to the regular program of the best schools throughout Europe from the 15th century on, but it was regularly accorded only a fraction of the curricular time assigned to Latin. Greek never remotely approached Latin as a means of communication among educated men. But, scarce as they always remained, Western scholars who had truly mastered ancient Greek were still numerous enough during the Renaissance to have a tremendous effect on the intellectual life, as they always have had since.

Hebrew Revival. Hebrew, the third of the major ancient languages championed by humanists, never achieved more than a small fraction of the limited currency of Greek, despite the brave talk at institutions such as the Collegium Trilingue for Latin, Greek, and Hebrew founded in Louvain in 1517 by Jerome Busleiden. Yet the work of Renaissance Hebrew specialists was of major importance.

Italy and Spain were the first centers of Hebrew scholarship. In early 15th-century Italy, Ambrogio Traversari had studied Hebrew, and, under Nicholas V, Giannozzo Manetti was known as a Hebrew scholar and collector of Hebrew manuscripts. In Spain, where Jewish exegetical and mystical thought had developed greatly in the Middle Ages, often under the direct influence of ARABIAN PHILOSOPHY, the influence of both the Jewish CABALA and the TALMUD had begun to be felt in Christian thinking by the second half of the 15th century.

To Christian Neoplatonists, the Jewish works appeared often to provide welcome, because seemingly independent, confirmation of some of their own persuasions, particularly those regarding divine TRANSCENDENCE and the importance of love in the scheme of things. In fact, however, the Christian Neoplatonists were picking up in the Jewish works chiefly echoes of their own Neoplatonic sources, which had come into Jewish thinking through the Arabs.

Pico della Mirandola, the outstanding Hebrew scholar of his day, shows the influence of Jewish thought in much of his encyclopedic work. Following Pico's premature death, the greatest Hebraist of the age was the Alsatian Johann REUCHLIN, who began his study of Hebrew in Italy and published the first Hebrew grammar for Christians in 1506. He immediately became embroiled in the dispute over the activities of a converted Jew, Johannes PFEFFERKORN, who, under a mandate from the Emperor Maximilian, was supervising the destruction of those Jewish works he considered a danger to Christianity; according to his accusers, he was extorting bribes from wealthy Jews for immunity. As referee in the disputes swirling around Pfefferkorn, Reuchlin pleaded moderately for minimal destruction of dangerous books and for a positive approach by Christians to the study of Jewish literature. He was attacked by Pfefferkorn, who soon had the Dominicans of Cologne on his side, while champions of the new learning made common cause with Reuchlin. The controversy occasioned a major Latin satirical work, the anonymous *EPISTOLAE OBSCURORUM VIRORUM*, which attacked religious and scholarly obscurantism and helped discredit both the Church and older methods of teaching.

Textual Scholarship, Biblical and Other. The Reuchlin-Pfefferkorn controversy showed how central the question of textual scholarship had become to the in-

tellectual life of the age affected by humanist learning. Intent on matters of style, Petrarch and his successors had focused attention as never before on the exact way a document originally read. Resulting close textual study alerted thinking men to the temporal and geographical variations in human experience and expression, sowing the seeds not only of modern "scientific" history—political, intellectual, religious, and other—but also of modern linguistics, cultural anthropology, sociology, political science, comparative religion, and many other areas of study.

The work of Lorenzo Valla was both epoch-making and representative. He was able to show (1440) on stylistic grounds that the DONATION OF CONSTANTINE could not have been written at its supposed date but was in fact a Carolingian production. The demonstration had interesting implications, since it made law dependent on philology. Valla turned also to the textual study of the Scriptures; in his *Annotationes* he pointed out various errors and suspect translations in the Latin Vulgate by comparing it with Greek texts. ERASMUS, who found this work of Valla's unpublished and edited it in 1505, set himself the task of producing his own new Latin version of the New Testament, with a commentary (1516). Meanwhile, the University of Alcalá, founded (1508) by Cardinal Francisco XIMÉNEZ, was laboring on the Complutensian Polyglot Bible (the Latin for Alcalá is *Complutum*). This edition (completed 1522) ranged in parallel columns the Old and New Testaments in their original languages and the Vulgate version. However great the admirable industry devoted to this edition, the aims of Ximénez were less in accord with the ideals of modern scholarship than were the aims of Erasmus, whose critical attitude toward textual study represented the best in Renaissance tradition and was, indeed, in many ways far ahead of his own time. Ximénez presented the original texts as supports rather than sources of the Vulgate.

Humanism and Typography. Alphabetic typography, developed toward the middle of the 15th century when humanism was in full career, was intimately connected with the humanist desire for controlled texts. It resulted from the application of mechanical techniques (in which the Middle Ages, by and large, had advanced far beyond ancient Greece and Rome) and accumulated capital to scribal problems, manifesting that juncture of craftsmanship, business sense, and scholarly interests which is one marked feature of the humanist milieu. Although the first typographers were hardly working under direct humanist inspiration, the concurrence of the invention of printing with the peak of humanist activity is something more than a coincidence, for the drive toward alphabetic typography grew out of the general avidity for textual material that had been built up by the end of the Middle Ages, and which formed a seedbed for humanism itself.

Typography gave Renaissance humanistic scholarship much of its effectiveness. The effort put into textual scholarship could now be conserved with only negligible error instead of being dissipated by successive copyists. Moreover, information-retrieval techniques, such as indexing, eventually cut down on the time and effort consumed by massive memorization. The indexing of manuscripts had never been very inviting because each handmade copy would have to have its own specially made index, which was seldom worth the time required. Printing and indexing helped give special contours to humanist educational techniques. One of the humanists' most widespread methods of teaching classical literature and of doing their own writing was through use of indexed excerpts or *loci communes*.

The close alliance of humanist and typographic interests can be seen everywhere—from Venice, where the printer Aldus Manutius preempted the services of exiled Greek scholars, through Basel, Strasbourg, and Paris to London, where St. Thomas MORE's brother-in-law, John Rastell, was a printer. The plaque on Erasmus' tomb in Basel openly advertises the printer-publisher-humanist alliance: it was erected by the three great Basel printing firms of Johannes Amerbach, FROBEN, and Episcopius.

Humanist Methods of Study. These all cluster around the doctrine and practice of imitation of the classics.

Imitatio. This had roots in antiquity but became especially critical in humanist procedure because the humanists were training in a language no longer the vernacular it had been for Cicero's and Virgil's world (although humanists almost never discussed this obvious fact). Boys generally came to Latin in medieval and Renaissance times not with a limited vocabulary and limited modes of expression, as schoolchildren come to the study of their own languages today, but with no vocabulary at all, no ability to say anything. They had to be taught simultaneously even the most elementary Latin words and the proper way to use them. This meant for humanists the way classical writers had used them, particularly Cicero, whose usage was admired by everyone and proposed by some Ciceronian extremists, such as Cardinal Bembo, as practically the sole model for Latin style.

To foster imitation, humanists undertook among other things to cut up the entire corpus of classical Latin (and, less successfully, Greek) writings into excerpts. Of the hundreds of major collectors of classical phrases, turns of expression, and anecdotes, Erasmus was the most indefatigable and influential. As he read through the classics, he digested virtually the entire corpus into a series of anecdotes and phrases for classroom use in his *De copia verborum et rerum,* his *Adagia,* his *Apophthegmata,* and other works, which indexed the excerpts under appropriate headings; one could find exactly what classical writers had said about virtue, vice, death, learning, ignorance, and so on, including anecdotes ranged under such headings, and variant ways of expressing an idea.

In the *De copia,* for example, Erasmus listed over 400 different ways, each presumably found in a classical Latin writer, to say "has delighted" in the Latin equivalent of "Your letter has delighted me." Collecting and arranging excerpts under headings was essentially the same procedure used by the Middle Ages in compiling its florilegia of stories for preachers. The humanists, however, who scorned the medieval florilegia, generally cited their sources and kept the exact original expressions, for they were interested in manner as much as in matter. Schoolboys often translated the passages from the classics into the vernacular and then, with the original text removed, from the vernacular back into Latin. In the process, no direct attention at all was given to vernacular training.

This method crammed the minds of even very young boys with a mass of classical lore—mythological, historical, philosophical, medical, and much other—and it accounts in great part for what appears to be fantastically wide reading in such writers as Shakespeare. The method produced a Latin style close to, but not identical with, the classical. The difficulty with the method was its assumption, never fully articulated but still operative, that the total effect of a work of literature is the sum of separate impressions. Humanist literary criticism, like most previous criticism, was much more able to treat special rhetorical effects in separate passages than to deal with sophisticated questions of overall organization.

Relation to Oral Performance. It is becoming more and more apparent that the humanist approach to literature by excerpts to be stored on the page or in the mind and then retrieved as occasion offered and "rhapsodized" or "stitched together" to form a whole was a technique belonging more properly to oral performance than to literature or writing as such—the technique of tremendously skilled, generally illiterate verbalizing experts such as Homer. This is not to say that the approach did not help produce effective writers. If it did not place the value on "originality" that post-romantic writers did, neither did it value sheer plagiarism; one should have an abundant store (*copia*) of material so that one could weave together a whole never before put together quite this way. Not originality, but superlative skill, *virtù*, was of prime value. Pope's "What oft was thought but ne'er so well expressed" catches the feeling of the older tradition, which was essentially conservative, as oral performance or orally oriented performance must be.

The oral residue in the humanist mentality was heightened by the humanist revival of interest in rhetoric and in the classical ideal of the public speaker as the most fully or most liberally educated man. But the humanists were ambiguous on this point: when they said rhetoric or oratory they often meant writing. Erasmus' program was concerned essentially with written expression.

Humanism and Vernacular Languages. Although, as has been seen, humanism itself was directly concerned only with the "learned languages," Latin, Greek, and Hebrew, together with related tongues such as Arabic and "Chaldean" (now known as Aramaic), the effect of the movement on the vernacular languages was massive. Since the vernaculars as such were not taught in school, writers inevitably imported into the vernaculars the procedures, literary values, and even the vocabulary ("inkhorn terms") they learned studying Latin.

Imitations of the classical genres, such as epics, odes, satires, pastoral, stage plays, and orations (which often served the functions later to be fulfilled by the essay when this developed out of the collections of *loci communes*), proliferated in most European languages, and not the least in English. Translations of the classics supplied the needs of those who had not been to school (this included women generally, for schools had from antiquity been only for boys, so that girls could learn Latin only privately) or of the countless thousands who, despite 6, 8, or 10 years of Latin, had never acquired fluency in the language. Modern scholarship has made it evident, however, that Renaissance writers, like their successors, by no means always read, even in translations, the works they refer to or quote. They often knew classical works in snippets, acquired either in school or from the multitudinous books of reference compiled by humanist scholars. But in one way or another the classics were a massive presence. Virtually all Renaissance vernacular literature, except such popular non-academic forms as the ballad, show classical influence, many of them predominantly. By putting the classics in the mouths of educated persons generally, humanism thus enabled the vernaculars to mature quickly: they could borrow from the classics some of the sophistication they themselves lacked because, largely through the work of the humanists, the classical heritage had been made a permanent part of Western sensibility. Moreover, by intensifying study of language in the classics, humanism sensitized western European man to language generally and improved vernacular expression by raising vernacular ideals. Groups of vernacular writers, such as the 16th-century *Pléiade* in France or the group around the Countess of Pembroke, Sir Philip Sidney's sister, in England, undertook explicitly to raise the vernacular to the level of the classical languages. The vernaculars eventually became the real heirs of humanism, for the humanists' program deliberately to rehabilitate Latin was, in fact, advance notice of the effective demise of Latin as an academic *lingua franca*.

Humanism, Change, and History. One of the noteworthy features of humanism, as of the Renaissance itself, is its sense of involvement in change. Petrarch, Valla, Erasmus, and their circles were aware that they were doing something to make man's life-world different. With some exceptions, they were commonly inclined to think of the change they ambitioned as a revivification of the remote past, involving a repudiation of their immediate scholastic predecessors, particularly the logicians. But the very return to the past and the accumulation of knowledge implemented by printing produced a sense of historic distance, not so developed as that of 20th-century man, but far more active than that of the Middle Ages, which had been curiously insensitive to the reality of time.

The close textual scholarship fostered by humanism led inevitably to recognition that many dimensions of existence previously taken for granted as inalterable were not indeed so: conditions had been quite different in other ages. In historians such as Francesco Guicciardini, human motives and free decisions are seen as shaping man's life and history, and both history and biography are freed from the fatalistic and unconsciously pagan determinism so common in the Middle Ages. At that time the typical saint's life was a pastiche of predestinarian patterns, built around clear signs present from the moment of the saint's birth, or even before, showing that he was unerringly destined for sainthood, and minimizing the real decisions that actually structure any person's life. Direct personal accounts of historical developments, such as the *Memoirs* of Philippe de Comines, register the new outlook. They contrast with the older-style world chronicles that had lumped side-by-side contemporary and Biblical events in settings and costumes suggesting that they had all occurred simultaneously.

The humanist break with the immediate past in favor of antiquity was not always clear-cut. St. Thomas More's *Richard III* (1557), touching and full of human interest though it is, predestines its protagonist to villainy and mounts him on the cyclic wheel of Fortune, guaranteeing the fall of the mighty from high places in the style of medieval works *de casibus virorum illustrium*. More's *Utopia* (1516) is more typical of the Renaissance in its message, somewhat enigmatically delivered, that men can plan society to be different from the way it has been and different from the way it is.

Spread of Humanism. Outside Italy, humanism at first developed more rapidly in the territories of the Empire. They were relatively free of the nationalism growing in France, England, and Spain, where scholarly talent was often siphoned off into governmental work.

Germany. The community-minded German principalities often patronized humanists for their local schools. Moreover, the Empire, whose universities were newer than those of France, England, or Spain, was prone to accept Italian cultural leadership (and then, of course, to resent it) possibly more than the other countries. Shortly after the mid-15th century, humanist centers were to be found at Vienna, Hcidelberg, Wesel, and Emmerich. Rudolphus Agricola, a kind of minor Erasmus, played a major role in importing Italian humanism to German lands, and Conrad Celtis, who was crowned poet laureate by Frederick II in the late 1480s, in domesticating and disseminating it. Agricola's early education had been under the BRETHREN OF THE COMMON LIFE, who conducted a complex of humanist-oriented schools in the Low Countries. The brothers of this order can be credited also with some of the early training of the most universally influential and in many ways the greatest of all Renaissance humanists, Erasmus of Rotterdam.

France. French humanism, initiated when Jean de Montreuil (1354–1418) espoused the cause of Petrarch, was slow in really getting under way until the military expedition of Charles VIII in quest of the Kingdom of Naples in 1495 aroused enthusiasm for the Renaissance as a byproduct among French courtiers. The group of *professeurs royaux,* or regius professors, later known as the Collège de France, was founded in 1530 by Francis I, inspired by the Italian academies. Perhaps the most famous of these regius professors was their first "dean," the programmatically anti-Aristotelian Peter RAMUS (PIERRE DE LA RAMÉE). He was a polymath who had read exhaustively in the classics but notoriously lacked poetic sense; his passion for a supersimplified logical "method" nullified the original Petrarchan humanist program for gracious and technically uncomplicated academic living. Ramus's "method" was taken over throughout Europe, largely in Calvinist circles, where it fostered a perfunctory encyclopedism developed extensively among 3rd- and 4th-generation German humanists through the late 16th and 17th centuries. Humanism in countries adjacent to the Empire, such as the Scandinavian and Slavic countries, grew largely under German influence.

England. In England, Humphrey, Duke of Gloucester, was educated by Italian teachers and collected Renaissance manuscripts. Early English visitors to Renaissance Italy, such as Gloucester's younger contemporary John Tiptoft, Earl of Worcester, William Grey (d. 1478), and John Free (or Phreas), however, were to become servants of State or Church, with little time for spreading classical learning. The first noteworthy flowering of humanism in England occurred in the circle of the physician Thomas LINACRE, the Oxford dons William Grocyn and Hugh LATIMER, and William Lily, the first headmaster of St. Paul's School, founded under humanist inspiration by another of this group, John COLET, Dean of St. Paul's Cathedral. All these men were associated with the young Thomas More, later lord chancellor and finally martyr, and, with Erasmus, a frequent house guest of More's. Less closely involved with this group, but still a patron of the new learning and in particular of Erasmus, was More's fellow martyr under Henry VIII, John FISHER, Bishop of Rochester, canonized with More in 1935 (*see* MORE, SCHOOL OF).

Colet and More were the most interested in new ideas and in literary style, and it is significant that Erasmus' most subtle piece of writing was his *Encomium Moriae* (1511), a pun on More's name meaning simultaneously "The Praise of Folly" and "The Praise of More-ishness." The work caught the spirit of More's own bantering seriousness and advertised the fact that, although More was a competent scholar, his humanism transcended imitation of the classics to concern itself with social improvement, notably in his *Utopia.*

With few exceptions, English humanism did not succeed in producing classical scholars of the competence of those on the Continent. The chief literary monuments to humanism in the British Isles are in the vernacular literature, which shows the marks of the movement in style, literary genres, subject matter, literary theory, and criticism. Many Englishmen, such as Arthur Golding (1536?–1605?), Sir Thomas North (1535?–1601?), Philemon Holland (1552–1637), and George Chapman (1559?–1634?), produced English translations of classical Latin and Greek writings. The work of the mid-17th-century philosophers known as the CAMBRIDGE PLATONISTS—Ralph Cudworth, Henry More, John Smith, and Nathanael Culverwel—may be regarded as a late flowering of British humanism.

Humanism and Religion: Scholasticism, Reformation and Counter Reformation, Secularism. The relationship between humanism, the Protestant REFORMATION, and reform within the Catholic Church itself has always been a live question. The age of humanism coincided closely with the age of the Reformation. Humanism and Protestantism both sought a return to conditions reputed to have existed in the remote past and to have been "corrupted" in the intervening ages, and certain humanist preoccupations, such as textual criticism, were related closely to certain Protestant principles, such as the necessity of reading the Bible. Moreover, humanism tended to mingle a concern for the reform of society generally, including ecclesiastical institutions, with its concern for bettering the education of the members of society.

Early humanism in Italy, Spain, France, and England generally managed to effect changes within the existing intellectual and educational framework without physical or intellectual violence. The humanist temperament was in accord with St. Thomas Aquinas's teachings on the positive relationships obtaining between nature and grace (see GRACE AND NATURE). These relationships were worked out on various grounds by various humanists. Typical of Florence was the Neoplatonism of Ficino and Pico, mentioned above. In Spain, Cardinal Ximénez made specific provision for accord between the older scholasticism and the new learning as part of his reform program within the Church, which he brought under rather effective, and austere, secular control. France had as a typical figure Jacques LEFÈVRE D'ÉTAPLES, who mingled medieval Christian mysticism, textual work on the Scriptures, and a strong preference for Biblical over scholastic formulas with a professional interest in developing the technicalities of logic inherited from the Middle Ages. He appeared to the theology faculty at Paris to be aligned with Luther, and they therefore condemned him. But he repudiated the reformers and died in communion with Rome.

Humanists expressed divergent views regarding religious orders. The humanist authentication of the natural world led some, such as Valla, to condemn the taking of the vows of religion, which appeared to pass adverse judgment on the naturally good life, but other humanists, such as Coluccio Salutati, were more favorably disposed; indeed, some, such as the Carmelite Latin poet Bl. Giovanni Battista Spagnuoli (1447–1516), known as Mantuanus from his birthplace, were themselves members of religious orders. In his *Enchiridion Militis Christiani* (1504), Erasmus expressed the view that the value of monastic life depended on the suitability of the individual for it. The Society of Jesus, approved by Pope Paul III in 1540, can be seen as influenced in its Constitutions by the humanist spirit: its members bound themselves by the three vows of religion—poverty, chastity, and obedience—but they also retained contact with the secular world to a degree unusual among earlier religious orders.

Scholasticism. In England, the circle of St. Thomas More reveals some of the underlying issues between humanism and scholasticism. Although medieval scholasticism had been far from being purely, or even chiefly, a religious phenomenon, since it governed logic, natural philosophy (physics, meteorology, etc.), medicine, law, and other miscellaneous disciplines quite as much as or even more than it governed theology, the humanist attack on scholasticism did have a special religious relevance. The attack was commonly made not on scientific grounds—humanists had no logic or physics seriously competing with these scholastic disciplines—but in terms of value judgments: scholasticism was thorny, knotty, tortured, and generally repulsive to man as man.

The qualities that More objected to in scholastic logic were actually its technical virtues, the suppositional and other theories that carried medieval logic far beyond Aristotle toward modern quantified formal logic (see LOGIC, HISTORY OF). But technical virtues are not always humanly appealing. Insofar as scholasticism was used to purvey or explain religious truths, this kind of attack was particularly telling, for what is religion if it is not adapted to man and his real life-world? By contrast with technical scholastic treatments, John Colet's historical and humane approach to St. Paul in his sermons had tremendous religious immediacy. Still, the most virulent humanist attacks were directed not against scholastic theologians but against scholastic logicians such as PETER OF SPAIN. The great theologians, such as St. THOMAS AQUINAS and St. BONAVENTURE, were often not skilled in the technicalities of scholastic logic propounded by their contemporaries, and, as a matter of fact, Erasmus, with some warrant grouped Aquinas with the Fathers of the Church rather than with scholastic logicians.

Reformation and Counter Reformation. If the humanists' attacks on scholasticism had religious implications, the humanists themselves were assaulted by two kinds of religious zealots: first, by anti-Greek "Trojans" who were addicted to scholastic manipulation of abstract theological questions in a historical and philological vacuum, and, second, by pietists who maintained that humanist interest in the natural world was irreligious and that many humanist writers, particularly Italians, purveyed pagan immorality by teaching the classics. St. Thomas More indicted and convicted the "Trojans" of gross ignorance and of seeking to protect themselves by means of what today are called defense mechanisms. The pietists he found guilty of betraying the Catholic tradition that grace works with nature. He further pleaded that both types of accusers deny the patristic heritage and narrow the scope of Catholic teaching to their own forms of thought—indeed, that the scholastics make revelation itself worldly with their logic. Each side thus accused the other of secularism, and both with some warrant (see PIETISM).

In the Empire the struggle between advocates of the old order and the new took on particularly violent religious overtones, in part because the absence of a central secular authority left the Church the most obvious target for deep-seated resentments about the state of society at large. German humanism has been divided into three successive schools in terms of religious attitudes. The first group consisted of earlier, more scholastic humanists, such as Rudolphus Agricola and Alexander Hegius, who were loyal supporters of the Church.

A second, later group of humanists protested strongly against scholasticism and abuses in the Church, wishing to put humanism to the service of Church reform. Reuchlin belonged to this group, but Erasmus was its outstanding representative, proposing a *docta pietas* or educated piety as a pedagogical ideal. Like St. Ignatius Loyola and Luther, Erasmus advocated an interiorization of religious motivation, but his concern with corresponding religious institutions was minimal. To many Catholics Erasmus seemed to favor Luther; yet he was certainly a loyal Catholic, whose loyalty, however, did not lead him to countenance obscurantism, of which Catholic apologists were not always innocent. Even after Luther's break with Catholicism, Erasmus continued to speak his mind as pre-1517 critics of the Church had regularly done, never fully recognizing the fact that the Church was under siege and that what was once commendable frankness could now be taken as disloyalty. In this sense Erasmus was living in the past. In another sense he was far ahead of his age and his spirit more like that of later 20th-century Catholicism: he felt that the truth would not destroy anything in the Church worth saving and that Catholics generally should be able to live as he himself did, with some unresolved tensions concerning the relationship of ancient classical culture and Christianity. Erasmus has sometimes been taken to be a ''rationalist''; if this means that he believed in the powers of natural intelligence, he was. But in his truly profound *Encomium Moriae* (1509), written at More's instigation, he satirized those who would place reason above faith and, indeed, ultimately vindicated, above everything, the Christian folly of the cross. Erasmus ultimately repudiated Luther and Luther's break with Rome as spelling the ruin both of the Church and of humanistic studies. The future of reform and of true scholarship lay for him within the old unity.

Secularism. The third and later group of German humanists felt otherwise than Erasmus. These were avowedly Protestant humanists, typified by Ulrich von HUTTEN, one of the principal authors of the above-mentioned *Epistolae obscurorum virorum*. Hutten's protestations in favor of liberty were at best somewhat disorganized and at worst licentious, hardly representative of the best in Protestantism. Even among more devout reformers, however, the relationship of humanism to the Protestant spirit was uneasy. Luther's stress on the depravity of human nature appeared to rule out genuine humanism, and Protestant mobs sacked the studies of humanist scholars such as Conrath Muth (Mutianus Rufus, *c.* 1471–1526). But Luther's close associate Philipp MELANCHTHON was a great humanist scholar and educator and had hundreds of distinguished Protestant successors. Among Calvinists, humanism, often under Ramist influence, tended to run to encyclopedism. Encyclopedic humanism was strong in Lyons and Geneva, and up the Rhine valley from Leiden through Frankfort on the Main to Basel.

Results and Interpretations of Humanism. As a pedagogical program, humanism advanced classical scholarship and vastly improved critical and historical methods. In its sensitive concern with literature and history, it directed serious effort to the mature interpretation of concrete everyday human experience, which possessed great cultural, intellectual, and scientific potential, and about which scholasticism had been inarticulate. In the process, humanism opened the way to modern philology and to the vast fields of study which philology in turn has opened into, as mentioned above. The influence of humanism on painting, sculpture, architecture, and other arts is seen in the proliferation of classical themes and forms in these fields, where such themes and forms have not played out even today.

Insofar as it competed with scholasticism as a pedagogical program, humanism can hardly be said to have won any clear-cut victory. While humanist scholarship grew and while scholastic logic after about 1530 lost its medieval vigor and seriousness, which it never completely recovered, scholasticism continued through much or most of the 18th century to dominate school curricula in the West. Far from becoming the all-encompassing mature pursuit that Erasmus and other humanists wanted it to be, the humanist study of rhetoric, with which poetic was in effect more or less identified, remained virtually always a course to perfect the student in his early teens in the practical use of Latin so that he could go on to logic, philosophy, and, if he wished, medicine, law, or theology. Scholastic philosophy (including physics) commonly remained at the top of arts curricula. In Jesuit schools, for example, the student typically ceased studying literature as such around age 13: the ''humanities'' were basically an elementary school subject by today's standards (*see* RATIO STUDIORUM). Individual scholars might, of course, devote their whole lives to philology and its manifold derivatives. But the establishment of literature as such in the upper reaches of the curriculum hardly began before the mid-19th century and became widespread only in the 20th. In the extent, depth, and maturity of academic literary and cultural studies, humanism, for all its weaknesses, is in a far stronger condition today than ever, most notably in the U.S.

One of the results of humanism has been the widespread study of humanism itself as a historical phenomenon. Until recently, the accepted view, derivative from the work of Georg Voigt and Jakob Burckhardt in the 19th century, had seen humanism as a definitive break with the Middle Ages, antischolastic, antiauthoritarian, and even anti-Christian. This concept was modified when more detailed studies of medieval culture by Heinrich Thode, Charles Homer Haskins, Paul Renucci, and others revealed many elements of Renaissance humanism in the Middle Ages and much medievalism in the Renaissance. The concept of humanism as essentially and unequivocally pagan was quite completely discarded by the mid-20th century, but Giuseppe Toffanin's reduction of humanism to a body of appealing truths perennially accessible to natural reason and in incontestable accord with Christianity has not found wide acceptance. The relationship of humanism to religion and to the maturing knowledge of the natural world has come to be recognized as exceedingly complex, with humanists and anti-humanists on both Catholic and Protestant, religious and irreligious sides. Earlier views of humanism as favorable to modern science, based on the uninformed assumption of a simple opposition between medieval scholasticism and the modern mind, have been seriously modified as it has become apparent that the scholastic mind was often more scientific in tone, if not always in content or procedure, than the minds of typical humanists.

The relationship of humanism, an academic movement, to other cultural developments is still actively debated. In recent decades the work of Charles Trinkaus revived the notion that a Burckhardtian individualism was to be found in the texts of Renaissance humanists, but this humanism, he argued, was more religious and spiritual than Burckhardt had originally characterized it. By contrast Hans Baron labored to show how actively humanism was allied with civic life, stressing the movement's political impact in Florence and in subsequent centuries. Still others have viewed humanism as a basically conservative textual movement, often more antiquarian in its outlook than revolutionary in its impact. Clearly the last word about humanism has not been written. Most scholars continue to recognize a link between the movement and modern forms of education and consciousness, although they often disagree about the precise influence the movement has had on those phenomena.

Bibliography: H. BARON, *The Crisis of the Early Italian Renaissance,* 2 v. (Princeton 1955). R. R. BOLGAR, *The Classical Heritage and Its Beneficiaries* (Cambridge, England 1954). W. J. BOUSMA, *The Interpretation of Renaissance Humanism* (Washington 1959), pamphlet. J. C. BURCKHARDT, *Die Cultur der Renaissance in Italien: Ein Versuch,* 2 v. (Basel 1860), Eng. tr. available in many eds., e.g., *The Civilization of the Renaissance in Italy,* ed. H. HOLBORN, tr. S. G. MIDDLEMORE (New York 1954). D. BUSH, *The Renaissance and English Humanism* (Toronto 1939). E. GARIN, *L'educazione in Europa, 1400–1600* (Bari 1957). M. P. GILMORE, *The World of Humanism, 1453–1517* (New York 1952). E. H. HARBISON, *The Christian Scholar in the Age of the Reformation* (New York 1956). C. H. HASKINS, *The Renaissance of the Twelfth Century* (Cambridge, MA 1927). P. O. KRISTELLER, ''Studies on Renaissance Humanism during the Last Twenty Years,'' *Studies in the Renaissance* 9 (1962) 7–30. L. MARTINES, *The Social World of the Florentine Humanists, 1390–1460* (Princeton 1963). W. J. ONG, *Ramus: Method, and the Decay of Dialogue* (Cambridge, MA 1958). A. RENAUDET, *Humanisme et Renaissance* (Geneva 1958). P. RENUCCI, *L'aventure de l'humanisme européen au Moyen Age, IV e-XIV e siècle* (Paris 1953). J. E. SANDYS, *History of Classical Scholarship,* 3 v. (Cambridge, Eng.), v. 1 (3rd ed. 1921), v. 2, 3 (2d ed. 1906–08); repr. (New York 1958). H. THODE, *Franz von Assisi und die Anfänge der Kunst der Renaissance in Italien* (2d ed. Berlin 1904). G. TOFFANIN, *History of Humanism,* tr. E. GIANTURCO (New York 1954). B. L. ULLMAN, *Studies in the Italian Renaissance* (Rome 1955). G. VOIGT, *Die Wiederbelebung des classischen Alterthums,* ed. M. LEHNERDT, 2 v. (3d ed. Berlin 1893). A. GRAFTON, *Defenders of the Text* (Cambrige, MA 1991). D. KELLEY, *Renaissance Humanism* (Boston 1991). B. KOHL, *Renaissance Humanism, 1300–1550: a Bibliography* (New York 1985). C. TRINKAUS, *In Our Image and Likeness,* 2 vols. (Chicago 1970).

[W. J. ONG]

HUMANISM, CHRISTIAN

''Christian humanism'' means the view (and action based upon this view) that human culture and its tradition have value in the Christian life to the extent in which they are subordinated, in some way, to Christ's teaching, to what is preeminent in the tradition of the faith and consequently in the tradition of the Church. St. Justin seems to have been the first to offer a basic formulation of Christian humanism, for he held that Christ the Word had subordinated all culture to Himself (Apol. 1.46). Justin's position has been reflected in the Christian use of the doctrines of Plato and Aristotle, as well as in the Christian appraisal of such artifacts as the plays of Sophocles and ancient architectural masterpieces. According to Justin's formulation, Christian humanism avoids the errors of philistinism, which would leave the Christian in a vulgar condition during his earthly life, as well as the mistake of those who attach more importance to human culture than to the truths of the faith.

The need for a contemporary formulation of Christian humanism arose especially in the 1930s, when the Socialist Popular Front movement began to use the ideal of ''Socialist humanism.'' Christian thinkers like Jacques Maritain, F. Charmot, A. Rademacher and others thought out the conditions for Christian humanism. (See Maritain, *Humanisme intégral.*)

The Judeo-Christian revelation contains a virtual humanism with its notion of man as the image of God. St. Thomas Aquinas lays the basis for Christian humanism with his teaching that philosophy is distinct from theology, and that human reason has its own value and consistency apart from grace and must build the under-structure for the life of grace. The great medieval adage, "Grace does not destroy nature but perfects it," can be deemed a basic tenet of Christian humanism. The perfection of grace requires at least some perfection and balance in the human subject, and, in turn, it acts through that subject, drawing out latent powers and developing them.

According to Maritain, Christian humanism integrates all that is best in the humanist effort of the centuries. He admits that classical Renaissance humanism discovered the values of human liberty, but accuses it of being anthropocentric; man is turned in upon himself, cut off from God. The great intuition of Marxist humanism is to recognize that proletarian man has been estranged from his true nature by being dispossessed of property and subordinated to material, economic forces. Christian humanism is ultimately theocentric; man fully realizes himself only in right relation to God and must develop himself according to the exigencies of the actual supernatural order as the "new creature" of revelation (2 Cor 5.17; Gal 6.15).

Several recent writers, like Louis Bouyer, have observed that the cross must not be absent from Christian humanism. The Christian's true pathway of development is a dialectic from life through the death of the cross to higher life.

Bibliography: L. BOUYER, *Christian Humanism,* tr. A. V. LITTLEDALE (Westminster, Md. 1959). H. E. BRUNNER, *Christianity and Civilization,* 2 v. (New York 1948–49). F. HERMANS, *Histoire doctrinale de l'humanisme chrétien,* 4 v. (Tournai 1948). W. JAEGER, *Humanisme et théologie,* tr. H. D. SAFFREY (Paris 1956). L. LENHART, *Das Problem des Humanismus in der neuzeitlichen katholischen Theologie* (Mainz 1947). J. MARITAIN, *Du régime temporel et la liberté* (Paris 1933); *Freedom in the Modern World,* tr. R. O'SULLIVAN (London 1935); *Humanisme intégral* (Paris 1936); *True Humanism,* tr. M. R. ADAMSON (6th ed. New York 1954). F. MARTY, *La Perfection de l'homme selon s. Thomas d'Aquin (Analecta Gregoriana* 123; Rome 1962). C. MOELLER, *Humanisme et sainteté* (Tournai 1946). A. RADEMACHER, *Religion und Leben* (2d ed. Freiburg 1929); *Religion and Life* (Westminster, Md. 1962). J. SELLMAIR, *Humanitas Christiana: Geschichte des christlichen Humanismus* (Munich 1950). P. TILLICH, *Theology of Culture,* ed. R. C. KIMBALL (New York 1959).

[D. J. FORBES]

HUMANISM, DEVOUT

This expression, though used earlier, was given currency by H. Brémond, who employed it as the title of the first volume of his *Histoire littéraire du sentiment religieux en France* (11 v. Paris 1915–33). The movement was a conscious effort to wed humanism's favorable attitude toward the "goodness" of human nature to Christian teaching on original sin and predestination. The problem was to avoid both the rigorous views of human fallibility inherent in AUGUSTINIANISM (and much more in CALVINISM) and the canonization of human perfectibility espoused by PELAGIANISM and proclaimed by some of the more secular-minded humanists.

The movement's great theological proponent was L. LESSIUS, professor at the University of Louvain, who opposed the doctrines of M. BAIUS; Baius's teaching was condemned by Pope St. Pius V in 1567 [H. Denzinger, *Enchiridion symbolorum,* ed. A. Schönmetzer (32d ed. Freiburg 1963) 1901–80] and by Gregory XIII in 1579. Lessius's theological bases were welcomed and put into practical use especially by St. FRANCIS DE SALES in his *Introduction to the Devout Life* and *The Love of God.* Through him, perhaps more than through anyone else, humanism responded to the needs of the interior life and opened to all the principles and spirit of Christian humanism (Brémond, *op. cit.* 1:17). St. Jane Frances de CHANTAL, the disciple of St. Francis de Sales, was instrumental in the diffusion of devout humanism through her Visitation foundation. Others who popularized the movement were É. BINET and Jean Pierre Camus (1584–1652), Bishop of Belley.

The spirit of devout humanism is now part of the authentic humanism represented by such thinkers as J. Maritain, G. Marcel, Christopher Dawson, M. D'Arcy, John Courtney Murray, and many others, both Catholic and non-Catholic.

See Also: HUMANISM; HUMANISM, CHRISTIAN.

Bibliography: P. POURRAT, *Christian Spirituality,* tr. D. ATTWATER, v.4 (Westminster, Md. 1955) 1–30. G. JACQUEMET, *Catholicisme,* 5:1077–78.

[H. C. GARDINER]

HUMANISM, SECULAR

A humanism so-called to distinguish it from Christian or other theological humanisms. It may be defined as any philosophical, political, or cultural affirmation of man as the principal object of concern, to the exclusion of all religious or theological theses about his origin and destiny. Secular humanism, however, sometimes identifies itself as religious, as in the two significant humanist manifestoes. In 1933 a group of Unitarian ministers and educators published "The Humanist Manifesto," which affirmed the relevance of religion as a "shared quest for the good life'' and established social reform as one of the principal aims of religion. In 1953 the *Humanist* published ''A Humanist Manifesto,'' in which the authors refer to themselves as ''religious humanists.'' Their doctrine may be summarized as follows: (1) the universe is self-existing and not created; (2) man is part of nature and has evolved as part of a continuous process; (3) modern science provides the only acceptable description of the universe; (4) modern science excludes any supernatural explanation of the universe or of human values; and (5) the end of man's life is the complete realization of the human personality in this world. Although it is unequivocally secularist, this humanism is called religious because it offers a doctrine that claims the ultimacy of a religious truth. While secular humanism is generally associated with a definite ATHEISM, AGNOSTICISM, or SCIENTISM, attempts have been made to show that a secular humanism is completely compatible with belief in the supernatural. Pragmatism and NATURALISM, for example, strive for peaceful coexistence with religious doctrine.

Historical Origins. Secular humanism in its recent manifestations shares certain common characteristics with the teachings of Protagoras and other SOPHISTS. Protagoras's well-known dictum to the effect that ''man is the measure of all things, of those that are that they are, and of those that are not that they are not'' may have been intended to apply as well to individual men as to the community. It implies not a necessary hostility to the gods but rather a pragmatic neutrality. ''With regard to the gods, I cannot feel sure either that they are or that they are not, nor what they are like in figure; for there are many things that hinder sure knowledge, the obscurity of the subject and the shortness of human life.'' The Sophists, in true humanitarian spirit, espoused the cause of the defenseless and the less fortunate; in time, however, their efforts were strongly disparaged.

Renaissance humanism was generally Christian in its attitude, although it revived classical learning and the study of pagan sources that were in opposition to scholastic forms of thought. Paralleling its development, the physical sciences began to assume a new autonomy. NOMINALISM had already drawn into question the continuity and agreement between the eternal verities of philosophy and theology. The result was a reduction of natural philosophy to mathematical-scientific description and a reduction of theology to blind faith. The ENLIGHTENMENT of the 17th to the 19th centuries finally asserted the autonomy of reason as absolute ruler of man's life and supreme arbiter of truth (see RATIONALISM).

Jean Jacques ROUSSEAU gave impetus to the new humanism by seeking to explain the origin and destiny of man without reliance on theological sources. He argued

Julian Huxley.

that for man to be himself he must defy the institutions of Christian Europe, return as closely to natural simplicity as possible, and then reconstruct a new, democratic society that embodied the general will of all men. No longer, in his view, does man have to appeal to God for his sacredness; he is sacred in himself. Among other things, religion and philosophical reasoning have robbed man of his pristine innocence.

Auguste Comte argued in reverse, in the name of science, that the theological and metaphysical stages of human development were a result of primitive superstition and ignorance. The time had arrived, he claimed, when the ''positive'' stage—in which factual knowledge is gathered and interpreted scientifically—would show what men are and how they should live. The science of sociology was thus born and was destined to rival ethics and theology in their efforts to relate man to reality.

Feuerbach, Marx, and Engels. The new humanism had a theological beginning also in the works of Ludwig FEUERBACH, who was preoccupied with questions about the nature of theology, the relationship between man and God, and the mysteries of Christian faith and yet concluded by reducing theology to anthropology. Karl Barth suggests that this reduction was the logical outcome of the Protestant (and especially Lutheran) shift of interest from what God is in Himself to what He means for men [Introd. to L. Feuerbach, *The Essence of Christianity* (New York 1957) xix]. Feuerbach declares the purpose of his undertaking to be "to show that the antithesis of divine and human is altogether illusory, that it is nothing else than the antithesis between the human nature in general and the human individual; that, consequently, the object and contents of the Christian religion are altogether human" (*ibid.* 14). His humanism strongly emphasizes the intrapersonal "I" and "Thou" and the social aspect of salvation. "My fellow-man is *per se* the mediator between men and the sacred idea of the species. *Homo homini Deus est*" (*ibid.* 159). It is in Feuerbach particularly that one sees humanism raised to the level of a religion. "The beginning, middle and end of religion is man" (*ibid.* 184).

The dialectical MATERIALISM of K. MARX and F. ENGELS is an attempt to establish the theoretical foundations and practical implications of Feuerbach's humanism. All reality is explainable as matter. Even mind is only an outgrowth of matter. Moving in space and time, matter transforms itself by creating oppositions and by resolving them. Man, both ontologically and chronologically, is totally and exclusively a product of this process. His destiny is bound up in his understanding and control of the dialectics of matter, especially as these are realized in social forces. Communism represents itself as a totally materialistic, socialistic, and scientific humanism in which, in the words of N. LENIN, "every religious idea is an abomination." All morality derived from religion or from any other social institution must give way to an ethic based on the ever developing self-interest of man. To emphasize its humanistic superiority over Western Christendom, communist societies stress the importance of excellence in every endeavor, scientific, athletic, and cultural.

Empiricist Bias. In the English-speaking world secular humanism has been characterized by a strong empiricist bias expressed in the writings of F. C. S. Schiller (1864–1937), William JAMES, and John Dewey. In England Schiller described his brand of pragmatism as humanism in *Humanism, Philosophical Studies* (London 1903) and other works similarly titled. He revived the thought of Protagoras that man is the measure of reality and indeed the creator of the meaning of reality (*Plato or Protagoras?*, London 1908). While Schiller's humanism centered more on questions of logic and epistemology, James's thought had wider scope and currency because he dealt with man as a psychological and social whole and paid particular attention to religious faith. His humanism placed a high value on religion as an expression of the human will; for him, however, God shares fate and becoming with man. Dewey advanced the thesis of prag-

matism by accommodating it to the scientific and democratic ambitions of American society and, as a philosopher of education, profoundly influenced the development of humanism in the U.S. For him, there is no true religion with a fixed dogma and an ultimate end; there is only the adjective "religious," which applies to the search for a working truth that becomes instrumental in the endless pursuit of scientific meaning. His naturalism concedes no content to the supernatural, while his INSTRUMENTALISM has both personal and social implications, for it is proposed as the only way that man can achieve any measure of peace and happiness.

Although a radically scientific humanism tends to treat generalizations and spiritual concepts as meaningless because they are beyond the pragmatic test, still there are some authors—J. B. Conant, for one—who grant that such spiritual notions as generosity and kindness are valuable hypotheses capable of proving their worth for society (*Modern Science and Modern Man,* New York 1952). More representative of humanist thought based strictly upon scientific method, however, is the evolutionary humanism of Sir Julian Huxley (1887–1975). Huxley views man as a self-contained, self-sufficient entity and suggests that to know how man has evolved in the past and to contemplate with awe what he might yet make of his destiny is to be reverent and even religious. One of the major results of religious psychology, in his view, is "the realisation that God is one among several hypotheses to account for the phenomena of human destiny, and that it is now proving to be an inadequate hypothesis" (*Religion without Revelation,* New York 1927; pref. to rev. ed. 1957).

Aesthetic Humanism. There also exists what might be called an aesthetic humanism, which is embodied in the thought of Arthur SCHOPENHAUER and Rainer Maria Rilke. As the pragmatist proposes that human activity creates the scientific meaning of the world, Schopenhauer urges that music creates the meaning of the world as will and power. In his view, music transcends time and place and the natures of particular things and reveals the onward thrust of being itself. He does not hesitate to proclaim that in music "I recognize the highest objectification of the will once more, the rational life and aspiration of man" (*The World as Will and Idea,* London 1907). Rilke, a poet, speaks in obscurities but is nonetheless influential, especially in existentialist circles. For him, God is in the process of creating Himself, and the poet is an active and conscious partner in that struggle; God is in fact "a direction of the heart" who depends as much upon man for His fulfillment as man does upon himself. "Indeed man must transform and transfigure himself; and in transfiguring himself he will be the redeemer and transfigurer of all existence" (*Sonnets to Or-*

pheus, tr. J. B. Leishman, London 1936). Although art need not be didactic, mid-20th-century art has become consciously preoccupied with matters of "ultimate concern," as Paul Tillich expresses it. This follows logically from a secular humanism in which there is no place for theology and in which philosophy bemoans its own lack of content. When a foundation for ultimate meaning cannot be found apart from human SUBJECTIVITY, art must create an imaginative meaning for man. This was the poetic and humanistic ambition of Rilke; it remains the concern of contemporary artists generally.

Existentialism. In its philosophical and literary attitude, existentialism lays strong claim to being the secular humanism of the 20th century. Despite origins in the religious thought of S. A. KIERKEGAARD and the support of religious protagonists such as Gabriel Marcel, the existentialist thought of F. W. NIETZSCHE, Albert Camus, and Jean Paul Sartre has marked atheistic presuppositions. The humanism of other existentialists such as Martin Heidegger, Franz Kafka, Karl Jaspers, and Paul Tillich, although ambiguous in its evaluation of religion, is also partially reflected in the thought of Nietzsche, Camus, and Sartre. It was Nietzsche who celebrated the "death of God" and the apotheosis of man. The Superman is the one who rises above the distinction between good and evil, a distinction that is necessary only in the slave morality of those who cannot stand freedom. Nietzsche predicts no utopia, for there must always be slavery and war if there is to be heroism and superiority. Camus, a novelist, shares this characteristically sober view. In the *Myth of Sisyphus* (Paris 1943) he explains that man reaches heroic stature when he is conscious enough to accept the tragedy of fate. "There is no fate that cannot be surmounted by scorn." This tragic heroism "drives out of this world a god who had come into it with dissatisfaction and a preference for futile suffering. It makes of fate a human matter, which must be settled among men." Sartre, finally, gives full expression to the humanistic pretensions of existentialism in the essay *Existentialism and Humanism* (tr. P. Mairet, London 1948). Though Sartre has modified his view since its publication, this essay has become influential on all levels. In it he laments the impossibility of God, for without God all order and consequence disappear, leaving man with the freedom to create his own nature and thus with the total responsibility for his destiny. Man desires to be God, but cannot be God without self-contradiction. Hence his dictum, "man is a useless passion" [*Existentialism and Human Emotions* (New York 1957) 90].

In spite of Sartre's onetime espousal and subsequent disavowal of Marxism, there are definite points of agreement in the two systems as humanisms. Each accepts the definition of man as conditioned by the contingencies of history. Each makes man totally responsible for his own future and denies him any escape from responsibility through established moral systems. And each insists that activity takes precedence over speculative thought. Both the Marxist revolutionary and the existentialist must act in the face of opposition, in a dialectical situation. The result is not derived; it is created anew.

Other Directions. Under the influence of existentialism and PHENOMENOLOGY, the science of psychology has modified its earlier positivistic approach to man and is reconsidering such questions as freedom, responsibility, finality, conscience, and faith. Gordon Allport, Carl Rogers, and Abraham Maslow have criticized the methods of radical empiricism because they exclude from study any aspect of man that cannot be reduced to mechanistic principles. Similarly, the Freudian reduction of religious faith and conscience to blind drives for gratification has been seriously criticized, although it had constituted a basic theme in secular humanism until the middle of the 20th century.

In legal philosophy and politics, secular humanism continues to influence American society. Since the turn of the century such organizations as the American Secular Union have striven to effect a total separation of Church and State, especially in the area of education. The underlying philosophical supposition of this movement is that religious values are merely personal and should not be allowed to influence the laws and institutions of a democratic society. Much legal philosophy and jurisprudence is likewise under the influence of the pragmatic legal theory of Supreme Court justices such as O. W. HOLMES, who, rejecting all absolute moral standards, maintained that the "ought" of natural law can be expressed in the metaphor "a dog will fight for his bone."

Critique. Every form of humanism must be judged as a historical reaction to some dehumanization of philosophy, theology, or social life. When humanism is atheistic, it can survive only on the destruction of false images of God, themselves often the result of a prior disintegration in theology. When it is agnostic, it derives its vitality from some misrepresentation of the evidence for the existence and nature of God. Thus the Stoics reaffirmed man against the idealism of the Academy and the anthropomorphized gods of the state. Rousseau reacted against rationalism and a not-too-healthy Christianity. Feuerbach condemned the ego of I. Kant, the absolute identity of F. W. J. Schelling, and the absolute mind of G. W. F. Hegel. Communism stands in direct contradiction to the false alliance of Christian ethics and capitalist exploitation. Pragmatists and naturalists react against a disembodied supernaturalism, and existentialism rejects all pretense of finding meaning in idealist philosophies of history. In contrast to a totally atheistic secular humanism, there stands the humanism of reformed theology, as expressed by Karl Barth, who, even in his later writings, still claims "there is no humanism without the Gospel" [*The Faith of the Church* (New York 1958) 32]. The assumption here is that humanity has no meaning other than the meaning it receives from the divine history of redemption and that even with redemption humanity remains without inherent value.

Between a godless humanism and a hyper-Christian humanism, there stands the Christian humanism of the Aristotelian-Thomist tradition, which maintains that humanity, even damaged with sin, retains an essential meaning and value. Man is the image of God, not exclusively in grace, but "inasmuch as he too is the principle of his actions, as having free-will and control of his actions" (St. Thomas Aquinas, *Summa theologiae* 1a2ae, *prol.*). It is important to note that, whereas neither secular humanism nor hyper-Christian humanism can tolerate or assimilate each other, the Christian humanism of Aquinas can reconcile both. It can admit the measure of autonomy proper to man, as well as tolerate the ambiguities involved in the human struggle for knowledge and self-control. In its view, God is not the *primum cognitum* from which man discovers his own value. Rather God is discovered only as the term of a process that begins with man's self-understanding as part of a truly meaningful world. Yet THOMISM can admit, with equal simplicity, the transcendence of the supernatural order. Grace and redemption perfect nature and give it a meaning it could never achieve of its own power. Merely by being true to his nature man does not merit supernatural glorification; but by being untrue to his nature, he can jeopardize his supernatural destiny.

See Also: HUMANISM; HUMANISM, CHRISTIAN.

Bibliography: J. MARITAIN, *True Humanism*, tr. M. R. ADAMSON (6th ed. New York 1954). É. H. GILSON, *Elements of Christian Philosophy* (New York 1960). W. A. KAUFMANN, ed., *Existentialism from Dostoevsky to Sartre* (New York 1956). C. CARBONARA, *Enciclopedia filosofica*, 4 v. (Venice-Rome 1957) 4:1373–79. H. DE LUBAC, *The Drama of Atheist Humanism*, tr. E. M. RILEY (New York 1949). C. N. R. MCCOY, *The Structure of Political Thought* (New York 1963).

[W. P. HAAS]

HUMBELINE, BL.

Sister of BERNARD OF CLAIRVAUX; b. *c.* 1091; d. before 1136. Humbeline was married to a wealthy nobleman and lived a worldly life until a visit to her brothers at CLAIRVAUX. Her magnificent dress and splendid retinue caused Bernard to refuse to see her. She burst into tears, moaning, "I may indeed be a sinful woman, but it was for such as me that Christ died on the Cross and because I am so sinful that I seek and need the help of godly men." Bernard then urged her to shun the dictates of the world and follow the holy example of her mother, Bl. Alice. She thereafter lived a life of prayer and fasting and two years later, with her husband's consent, entered the Benedictine priory of Jully where she was prioress when she died in the presence of her surviving brothers.

Feast: Aug. 21 (formerly Feb. 12).

Bibliography: A. M. ZIMMERMANN, *Kalendarium Benedictinum: Die Heiligen und Seligen des Benediktinerorderns und seiner Zweige*, 4 v. (Metten 1933–38) 1:203–205. WILLIAM OF SAINT-THIERRY, *Vita prima sancti Bernardi, Patrologia Latina*, ed. J. P. MIGNE, 217 v. (Paris 1878–90) 185:244–245; Eng. *St. Bernard of Clairvaux*, tr. G. WEBB and A. WALKER (Westminster, Md. 1960) 51–52. M. RAYMOND, *The Family That Overtook Christ* (Boston 1986) 258–292.

[J. R. SOMMERFELDT]

HUMBERT OF MAROILLES, ST.

Benedictine abbot; b. Mezières-sur-Oise, beginning of the seventh century; d. Maroilles, March 25, *c.* 680. According to tradition, he became a monk and priest at Laon, from which he retired upon the death of his parents to claim an inheritance. Having made two pilgrimages to Rome, he became first abbot of Maroilles and, according to a later working of the legend, bishop. The document by which he ceded (675) his villa at Mezièressur-Oise to Maroilles has survived [J. M. Pardessus, *Diplomata* 2:155f; *Monumenta Germaniae Scriptores* 7:412]. His cult was already widespread in the Frankish kingdom in the eighth century.

Feast: March 25.

Bibliography: J. MABILLON, *Acta sanctorum ordinis S. Benedicti*, 9 v. (Paris 1668–1701; 2d ed. Venice 1733–40) 2:767–772. *Acta sanctorum Belgii selecta*, ed. J. H. GHESQUIÈRE et al., 6 v. (Brussels 1783–94) 4: 146. *Acta Sanctorum* March 3:557–565. J. L. BAUDOT and L. CHAUSSIN, *Vies des saints et des bienheueux selon l'ordre du calendrier avec l'historique des fêtes* (Paris 1935–56) 3:547–548. P. GAZEAU, *Catholicisme* 5:1088. A. M. ZIMMERMANN, *Kalendarium Benedictinum: Die Heiligen und Seligen des Benediktinerorderns und seiner Zweige*, 4 v. (Metten 1933–38) 1:370–372.

[B. F. SCHERER]

HUMBERT OF ROMANS

Fifth master general of the Order of Preachers; b. Roman, Diocese of Vienne, *c.* 1194; d. Valence, July 14, 1277 (also given as Jan. 15, 1274). Having graduated as master of arts at Paris, Humbert of Romans (de Romanis) became a Dominican in 1224. He was appointed professor of theology in 1226 and elected prior at Lyons in 1236, serving until 1239. In 1240 he was elected provincial of the Roman Dominican province and in 1244, of the French province. The 1254 general chapter at Budapest elected him master general. After nine years as general, he resigned in 1263, retiring to Valence where he devoted the remainder of his life to writing books that were the fruit of his experience as master general. These works still exercise an influence within the order. While he was general the order perfected itself liturgically, academically, and governmentally. The broad lines of administration that he laid down remained guiding principles for many of his successors.

In 1256, Humbert completed the revision of the Dominican liturgy, which had been started in 1244. He also consolidated the order's internal regime of studies and unified its ranks. During the conflict between the mendicant orders and the University of Paris in 1252, Humbert sponsored the creation of the office of procurator general to represent the order at the papal court, and with papal support, vindicated the position of the mendicant orders at the University. Humbert's ascetical works—*Epistola de tribus votis substantialibus religionis, Expositio Regulae B. Augustini, Expositio in Constitutiones* (a partial commentary), *De Officiis Ordinis, De Eruditione praedicatorum, De Dono timoris, De Praedicatione Crucis contra Saracenos*—as well as his encyclical letters to the order, did much to solidify and interpret the Dominican spirit and have always been highly regarded within the order.

Bibliography: F. HEINTKE, *Humbert von Romans* (Berlin 1933). J. QUÉTIF and J. ÉCHARD, *Scriptores Ordinis Praedicatorm,* 5 v. (Paris 1719–23) 1:141–148.

[C. LOZIER]

HUMBERT OF SILVA CANDIDA

Papal legate and adviser, canonist and publicist; b. Lorraine *c.* 1000; d. Rome, May 5, 1061. The events of his early years are unknown until 1015, when he entered MOYENMOUTIER as a novice. His studies centered on law and theology, and he became concerned with the problem of the temporal–spiritual relationship and with the EASTERN SCHISM. Humbert also learned Greek, which later proved useful in the dispute between Rome and Constantinople, 1053–54. His career from *c.* 1035 to 1049 cannot be delineated exactly, but two things seem certain: he became associated with Bruno of Toul (later Pope Leo IX), and he began his career as a writer, initially as a hagiographer.

Humbert's main period of influence was from 1050 to 1061, covering the reigns of four popes. Late in 1049 Leo IX brought Humbert to Rome and first created him archbishop of Sicily and later cardinal bishop of Silva Candida. His opposition to ecclesiastical abuses, together with Leo's reforming zeal, made Humbert an ideal instrument of reform. Already in 1050 he had condemned the heresiarch Berengarius of Tours. Humbert's subsequent activities marked him a legate, a theologian of the school of St. Cyprian, and a strong proponent of Roman primacy (*see* PRIMACY OF THE POPE).

As a legate he went to Benevento in 1051 to recover that city for the papal patrimony; and in 1054, on the mission to Constantinople, Humbert's correspondence leaves no doubt that his was an intransigent attitude. He began by hoping to win the Greek Emperor and Church over to the papacy; he ended by excommunicating the Patriarch MICHAEL CERULARIUS and alienating Greek sympathy. Meanwhile Leo IX had died, and the legates returned to Rome.

The cardinal continued as a papal adviser. He accompanied Victor II to Germany in 1056 and then went to Monte Cassino where he had his old colleague, Frederick of Lorraine, elected as abbot. Frederick presently became Pope Stephen IX (Aug. 5, 1057). This event promised an even greater degree of influence for Humbert. Stephen appointed him chancellor and librarian of the Roman Church, in which capacity he directed the papal chancery and helped to formulate policy. But Stephen died on March 29, 1058, and the papacy fell into schism.

Some historians, like A. Michel, have exaggerated Humbert's part in the subsequent pontificate of Nicholas II. Certainly he participated in formulating the Papal Election Decree (*see* POPES, ELECTION OF), in the Normanno–Papal alliance (1059), and in measures against simony. But Humbert's was not the only voice. Late in 1060 Humbert visited Moyenmoutier and then returned to Rome, where he died and was buried in the Lateran.

The question of Humbert's influence is integrally related to the problem of the authenticity of writings attributed to him. His main work was the *Libri tres adversus simoniacos* (1054–58); but Michel and others have attributed to him such other works as the vitae of Saints, HIDULF and Deodat of Moyenmoutier, Bruno's privileges, the *Pseudo-Wido,* works on the Greek Schism (1053–54), papal privileges (1051–61), the *Vita Leonis IX,* the Collection in 74 Titles (*see* CANONICAL COLLECTIONS BEFORE GRATIAN) and the 1059–60 synodal decrees at Rome. The authorship of these works can never be decisively proved, but certainly Humbert's ideology fits most of them. Moreover, Humbert's known works sufficiently indicate that he identified the problems and solutions commonly regarded as the GREGORIAN RE-

FORM, such as the separation of temporal and spiritual jurisdiction, and opposition to lay ownership of church property. At times Humbert's influence was disastrous, as in 1054. His theological extremism, rejecting the validity of heretical (and simoniacal) sacraments, brought him into unsuccessful conflict with PETER DAMIAN. With Damian and Hildebrand (*see* GREGORY VII) he ranks as one of the great churchmen of the 11th century.

Bibliography: Texts of *Pseudo-Wido* and *Libri tres adversus simoniacos, Monumenta Germaniae Historica, Libelli de lite* (Berlin 1826—) 1:5–7, 100–253. *Patrologia latina,* ed. J. P. MIGNE, 217 v., indexes 4 v. (Paris 1878–90) 143:929–1218. For a discussion of works, see articles by HALLER, MICHEL, PELSTER, TRITZ, ULLMANN, and KRAUSE, *Studi gregoriani,* ed. G. B. BORINO, 1–7 (Rome 1947–1960). A. MICHEL, *Humbert und Kerullarios,* 2 v. (Paderborn 1924–30); "Die folgenschweren Ideen des Kardinals Humbert," *Studi gregoriani,* ed. G. B. BORINO, 1 (1947) 65–92. J. J. RYAN, "Cardinal Humbert *De s. Romana ecclesia,*" *Mediaeval Studies,* 20 (1958) 206–238. J. GILCHRIST, "Cardinal Humbert of Silva–Candida (d. 1061)," *Annuale Mediaevale,* 3 (1962) 29–42; "Humbert of Silva-Candida and the Political Concept of Ecclesia . . . ," *Journal of Religious History* 2 (1962) 13–28.

[J. GILCHRIST]

HUME, DAVID

Scottish philosopher, political theorist, and historian; b. Edinburgh, April 26, 1711; d. there, Aug. 25, 1776. Little is known of his education, save that he completed it at Edinburgh University and that he spent much of his time even as a youth reading philosophy and classical literature. When he was 17 he tried to study law, but he eventually abandoned his efforts and entered a merchant's office in Bristol for a few months. However, his "passion for literature" made commerce as distasteful as the law, and in 1734 he went to France and settled at La Flèche to pursue his studies.

Works. In 1737 Hume returned to London with the completed MSS of *A Treatise of Human Nature,* which remains to this day the most widely read and warmly discussed study in classical British EMPIRICISM. He published the first two volumes anonymously in 1739 and the third volume in 1740; but to his intense disappointment they attracted little attention. The work, he said, "fell dead-born from the press." On returning to Scotland, Hume published two volumes of *Essays Moral and Political* (1741–42), which sold so well that he was encouraged to revise the *Treatise* and present its contents in a style better suited to the ordinary reader. In 1745 he applied unsuccessfully for the chair of ethics and pneumatic philosophy at Edinburgh University. In 1746 he went to France as secretary to Gen. J. St. Clair and in 1748 accompanied him to Vienna and Turin on a diplomatic mission, returning to England in 1749. In 1748 he published

a third volume of *Essays Moral and Political* and *Philosophical Essays concerning Human Understanding* (the revision of the first book of the *Treatise*), later known as *An Enquiry concerning the Human Understanding* from the title he gave the second edition (1751). In 1751 he published *An Enquiry concerning the Principles of Morals,* which was in effect a revision of book three of the *Treatise,* and also completed his *Political Discourses,* which added considerably to his fame at home and abroad. About this time he began work on the *Dialogues concerning Natural Religion,* which he revised many times but withheld from publication during his lifetime.

In 1751 he also became librarian to the Faculty of Advocates and, having access to a large collection of books, began writing the four volumes of his *History of England,* in which he worked his way back from the Revolution of 1688 to the invasion of Caesar. Hume wrote the greater part as an anti-Whig polemic, and it became the center of disputes between Whigs and Tories for several years. The *History* occupied him from 1754 to 1761, but he found time to publish *Four Dissertations* (1757) containing a revision of the second book of the *Treatise* (on the passions), and a natural history of religion, in which he tried to show that polytheism was the earlier and more natural form of religion than monotheism. In 1763 Hume went to Paris and served as secretary to the embassy. He was received with enthusiasm by the court and consorted with *les philosophes* of Encyclopedist circles in Paris. In 1766 he returned to London with J. J. ROUSSEAU, but they soon parted as the result of their famous quarrel. Hume stayed in London for two years as undersecretary of state, and in 1769 he returned to Edinburgh. When in 1775 his health began to fail, he wrote the well-known sketch of *My Own Life,* which his lifelong friend Adam SMITH published in 1777. His nephew published his *Dialogues concerning Natural Religion* in 1779 in accordance with his will.

Method. On the title page Hume described his *Treatise* as "an attempt to introduce the experimental method of reasoning into moral subjects." At the starting point of his philosophy is his complete SKEPTICISM about "the tedious lingring method, which we have hitherto followed," which made it necessary for him to reject all the uncritical convictions of common sense and the dogmatic assurance of philosophers concerning the existence or reality of unperceived and unperceivable metaphysical entities. As he explains in the introduction to the *Treatise,* Hume's ambition was to set all the sciences on the sure path to the conquest of truth by introducing two radical reforms.

First, he accepted the basic position of "some late philosophers in England, who have begun to put the science of man on a new footing,'' and took it to its logical conclusion by treating the science of man as ''the only solid foundation for the other sciences.'' All other sciences have a relation of some kind to man, the study of whose nature pertains to the philosopher. Hence Hume proposed ''to march up directly to the capital or center of these sciences, to human nature itself'' in the anticipation that ''from this station we may extend our conquests over all those sciences, which more intimately concern human life, and may afterwards proceed at leisure to discover more fully those, which are the objects of pure curiosity.'' Given a new science of man, Hume argued, '''tis impossible to tell what changes and improvements we might make in these sciences were we thoroughly acquainted with the extent and force of human understanding, and could explain the nature of the ideas we employ, and of the operations we perform in our reasonings.'' Thus by ''moral subjects'' Hume understood questions about the nature and limits of human understanding; the workings of the passions, feelings, and sentiments; the origins of belief; and the first principles of conduct.

Second, Hume proposed to apply Newton's method for the study of the physical world to the study of human nature, to the exclusion of any other method. He assumed without question that ''as the science of man is the only solid foundation for the other sciences, so the only solid foundation we can give to this science itself must be laid on experience and observation.'' EXPERIENCE is the one and only source of human knowledge, according to Hume, and ''a cautious observation of human life'' is the only possible method of constructing the science of man ''which will not be inferior in certainty, and will be much superior in utility to any other of human comprehension.'' Plainly, then, Hume was committed from the start to a conception of experience as purely sensible and to the postulate that the one ''true metaphysics'' is a phenomenalistic study of human life.

Empiricism. Hume called the contents of human experience ''perceptions'' and found that all man's perceptions are of two kinds, ''impressions'' and ''ideas.'' The difference between them is that impressions are given sensations that arise ''from unknown causes,'' whereas ideas are man's thoughts, i.e., fainter copies or images in the imagination or memory of the sensations he has experienced. Hume argued that ''every simple idea is derived from a corresponding impression,'' which is best understood by saying that ''every indefinable term can be explained *ostensively*, by indicating the sort of experience to which it refers'' (MacNabb, 30). Complex ideas are just those that can be analyzed into simple ideas or explained by a definition; ultimately, Hume insisted, all definitions must be reduced to certain simple indefinables,

David Hume.

whose meaning one must learn from ''simple impressions'' or ostensively.

Substance. On the basis of this doctrine that man's knowledge of things is solely of his impressions of sense, or of what can be pointed out empirically, Hume denied reality to any kind of SUBSTANCE, material (*Treatise*, 1.1.6) and immaterial in the case of persons (1.4.3, 5). What one calls substance is nothing more than a bundle of sense data one finds constantly associated with each other. There is no such reality as a permanent essence or structure proper to things. The self is just a flux of impressions, emotions, and feelings linked together in the unity of the person one observes in memory (1.4.6). One should not speak of a SELF but only of ideas attracting each other and becoming associated.

Causality. If Hume banished the idea of substance altogether, he transformed that of EFFICIENT CAUSALITY in accordance with the demands of his PHENOMENALISM. Hume held that causality involves a necessary relationship between the thing called a cause and its effects. But one has no sense impressions of a necessary link between a cause and its effects. What, then, is the origin of this idea of ''necessary connection''? Hume held that the constantly repeated conjunction of the same sense impressions in the same temporal sequence gives rise to the expectation that they will continue to be conjoined in the future, and thus to the idea of the imagination that they must be conjoined. There is nothing objectively or inherently necessary in the links observed between things (cf. 1.3.14–). Hume considered that the proposition "whatever has a beginning has also a cause of its existence" is neither intuitively nor demonstrably certain, for "as all distinct ideas are separable from each other, and as the ideas of cause and effect are evidently distinct, 'twill be easy for us to conceive any object to be non-existent this moment, and existent the next, without conjoining to it the distinct idea of a cause or productive principle. The separation, therefore, of the idea of cause from that of a beginning of existence, is certainly possible for the imagination; and consequently the actual separation of these objects is so far possible, that it implies no contradiction nor absurdity" (1.3.3)—an argument that simply assumes what it purports to prove, namely, that beginning to exist does not necessarily imply being caused.

God. Hume denied that one can establish the existence of God by a causal argument, for God and his relation to the universe lie beyond experience. He agreed, however, that one can postulate a cause or causes of the order exhibited in the universe on the probability that it bears a remote analogy to the human mind. But he denied that man can go any further. One cannot ascribe any attributes to a divine cause (*Dialogues,* ed. N. K. Smith, 227). [*See* MIRACLES (THEOLOGY OF).]

Critique. Hume's world was that of a radical skeptic, for "it is not a world of persons and things but one of transitory atomic events. The connection of these events is in principle wholly unpredictable. Terms like being, substance and cause become almost or entirely meaningless. There is no room in such a world for a metaphysic or general science of Being" [D. J. B. Hawkins, *Being and Becoming* (New York 1954) 23]. Hume neglected all the permanent or enduring data of experience; he denied any permanent structure inherent in things and reduced human experience to transitory impressions and images. He concentrated on the purely passive aspects of mental receptivity to the point of ignoring the activities of man's thinking life. Thus he reduces things to sensible impressions, mind to memory and imagination, and philosophy to empirical psychology. He is, however, the most ruthlessly consistent of the empiricists and remains to this day the guiding light of all empiricists in philosophy.

See Also: EMPIRICISM; PHILOSOPHY, HISTORY OF.

Bibliography: Works. *The Philosophical Works,* ed. T. H. GREEN and T. H. GROSE, 4 v. (London 1878); *A Treatise of Human Nature,* ed. L. A. SELBY-BIGGE (Oxford 1896); *Enquiries concerning the Human Understanding and Concerning the Principles of Morals,* ed. L. A. SELBY-BIGGE (2d ed. Oxford 1902; repr. 1951); *Dialogues concerning Natural Religion,* ed. N. K. SMITH (New York 1947), contains sketch of *My Own Life; Letters,* ed. J. Y. T. GREIG, 2 v. (Oxford 1932). Literature. A. CARLINI, *Enciclopedia filosofica* 2:1128–44. N. K. SMITH, *The Philosophy of David Hume* (London 1941). H. H. PRICE, *Hume's Theory of the External World* (Oxford 1940). R. W. CHURCH, *Hume's Theory of the Understanding* (Ithaca, N.Y. 1935). J. A. PASSMORE, *Hume's Intentions* (Cambridge, Eng. 1952). D. G. MACNABB, *David Hume: His Theory of Knowledge and Morality* (London 1951). M. O'DONNELL, "Hume's Approach to Causation," *Philosophical Studies* 10 (Maynooth 1960) 64–99. A. E. MICHOTTE, *La Perception de la causalité* (2d ed. Louvain 1954).

[E. A. SILLEM]

HUME, GEORGE BASIL

Cardinal Archbishop of Westminster, 1976–1999; b. Newcastle-upon-Tyne, England, 1923; novitiate at Ampleforth Abbey 1941; studied at Ampleforth, Oxford (history), and Fribourg University (theology); ordained priest 1950; elected *Magister Scholarum* for the English Benedictine Congregation 1957, 1961; Abbot of Ampleforth 1963–1976; appointed by Pope Paul VI to the Metropolitan See of Westminster on Feb. 17, 1976; created cardinal May 24, 976; d. Westminster, June 17, 1999.

Hume was widely regarded as the spiritual leader in Britain at the end of the twentieth century. Part of the legacy he left is the acceptance of the Roman Catholic Church as a native (and not foreign) Church, alongside the Established and Free Churches, thus signaling the demise of any lingering effects of the Penal Laws in Britain.

As abbot of a large monastery at the time of the Second Vatican Council and as archbishop of the premier see in Britain, he was able to maintain peace, stability, and unity within the communities he served. Hume could do this because he listened with great honesty and openness and recognized that whatever tensions there might be, all involved shared a common faith. The last talk he prepared on this theme, under the auspices of the Catholic Common Ground initiative, was called "One in Christ, Unity and Diversity in the Church Today."

His episcopate was marked by a number of significant events. Among these was the National Pastoral Congress (1980), which elicited *The Easter People,* the bishops' accompanying response. His tenure also saw the publication of *The Common Good,* which articulated Catholic social teaching for contemporary society (1996), and the publication of *One Bread, One Body* (1998), which set out teaching on the Eucharist. This latter document was to be useful in making decisions about the admission of non-Catholic Christians to communion, reconciliation, and the anointing of the sick.

Hume served the Church in England and the world in a number of roles. From 1979 to 1999 he was president of the Bishops' Conference of England and Wales. From 1979 to 1987 he served as president of the Council of European Bishops' Conferences, which was established to deal with social and ethical problems within the European Economic Community. He was also co-chair of the Council of European Churches (Orthodox, Reformed and Anglican Churches). He was a member of the Secretariat for Christian Unity, Congregation of Religious and Secular Institutes, Pontifical Commission for the Revision of the Code of Canon Law, and the Joint Commission set up by the Holy See and the Orthodox Church to promote theological dialogue between their Churches. He also attended the synods of bishops in 1977, 1980, 1983, 1987, 1990, 1994 (serving as relator general); and the Extraordinary Synod in 1985.

Ecumenism and Social Justice. Hume played an important role in ecumenism. He began to dialogue with the Orthodox while he was abbot of Ampleforth. Recognizing the special position of the Anglican communion in ecumenical affairs, he made particular efforts to ensure close and developing relationships with the Church of England. His first act as archbishop of Westminster was to lead a group of Benedictine monks to Westminster Abbey to sing Vespers there for the first time since the Reformation. Pope John Paul II's visit in 1982 was both a celebration for Catholics in Britain and an occasion of great ecumenical significance. During this visit the pope met Queen Elizabeth II at Buckingham Palace and the archbishop of Canterbury at the shrine of St. Thomas à Becket.

In 1987 at an important ecumenical gathering at which plans for new ecumenical instruments were being discussed, Hume urged Catholics to move from "cooperation to commitment" in the search for Christian unity. He subsequently became joint president both of Churches Together in England and of the Council of Churches for Britain and Ireland.

After the decision of the Church of England to ordain women as priests, large numbers of Anglican clergy petitioned to join the Catholic Church. Rome gave permission for married convert clergy, under certain conditions, to be ordained priests. In his most public initiative (encouraged by the Holy See), Hume managed to ensure that individuals whose conscience led them to the Catholic Church were duly welcomed, but without the cordial relationships with the Church of England being spoiled. At the same time Catholic sensitivities to the introduction of married clergy, and anxieties there might be over priestly celibacy were largely overcome.

A reconciler and bridge-builder, Hume did much to heal wounds between the Jewish and Catholic communities. He was active in promoting understanding with peo-

George Basil Cardinal Hume. (Catholic News Service)

ple of other faiths. He was with Pope John Paul II at the gathering of world religious leaders at Assisi to pray for peace (1986).

Hume was deeply committed to matters of justice. His initiative in highlighting certain serious miscarriages of justice in England led to the release of a number of prisoners and to a new system of investigation of such cases. By other initiatives he gave clear guidance on a wide variety of public moral and social issues: life issues, marriage and family life, global poverty and international debt, human rights, homelessness, refugees and asylum seekers, the arms trade and nuclear disarmament, homosexuality, and education. Hume was instrumental in mounting significant seminars in London that discussed topics like business and moral standards in post-communist Europe (1992), the arms trade (1995), and world debt (1996).

Two weeks prior to Hume's death Queen Elizabeth II presented him with the Order of Merit—awarded to individuals of exceptional merit, in the personal gift of the Queen. The Chief Rabbi in England (Dr. Jonathan Sacks) wrote of him in *The Times:* "He spoke of God in a secular age and was listened to. He articulated clear moral values and his words shone through the relativistic mist. He took principled political stands and was respected for it.

He showed that humility has a power and presence of its own.''

At the time of Cardinal Hume's death, Pope John Paul II commented on his devoted service, thanking God for ''having given the Church a shepherd of great spiritual and moral character, of sensitive and unflinching ecumenical commitment and firm leadership in helping people of all beliefs to face the challenges of the last part of this difficult century.''

George Basil Hume was an outstanding figure in the Catholic Church in the latter part of the twentieth century, with an influence far beyond his own country and his own family of faith. He was a leader, a profoundly spiritual, impressively intelligent, a man of great authority. His loyalty to the Church was complete and came from his childlike faith in Christ. Hume always kept in touch with his Benedictine roots; he was described as ''someone who turns strangers into friends.''

Bibliography: G. B. HUME, *Searching for God* (London 1977); *In Praise of Benedict* (London 1981); *To Be A Pilgrim* (London 1984), *Towards a Civilisation of Love* (London 1988); *Light in the Lord* (London 1991); *Remaking Europe: the Gospel in a Divided World* (London 1994); *Footprints of the Northern Saints* (London 1996); *Basil in Blunderland* (London 1997); *The Mystery of the Cross* (London 1998). *Mystery of the Incarnation* (London 1999). ''Basil Hume, Archbishop of Westminster'' in *Oremus* (Magazine of Westminster Cathedral, Special Edition, July 1999). Bishops' Conference of England and Wales. *Briefing* 29 (July 1999). C. BUTLER. *Basil Hume by His Friends* (1999). T. CASTLE, ed., *Basil Hume, A Portrait* (1986). P. STANFORD, *Cardinal Hume and the Changing Face of English Catholicism* (London 2000).

[D. KONSTANT]

HUMILIANA DE CIRCULUS, BL.

Franciscan tertiary; b. Florence, Italy, December 1219; d. there, May 19, 1246. Married at 16, she was freed by the death of her husband (*c.* 1241) from a difficult marriage patiently borne for five years. As the mother of two little girls, she was prevented from entering the POOR CLARES of Monticelli; instead she became a Franciscan tertiary, living a life of prayer and penance in a tower of her father's home, which she left only to attend church services and to help the poor. The recipient of notable graces, and impervious even to diabolical attacks, she was also a model of meekness and courage during her last illness. She was buried at the Franciscan Church of Santa Croce where her relics are kept in the Calderini chapel. Many miracles have been ascribed to her, some even in her lifetime. The first translation of her remains occurred in August 1246; the second, in November 1314. Her cult was confirmed by INNOCENT XII (1694).

Feast: May 19 (Florence); June 15 (Franciscans).

Bibliography: *Acta Sanctorum* May 4:384–418. F. CIONACCI, *Storia della beata Vmiliana de'Cerchi* (Florence 1682). C. VITUS, *Leggenda della beata Vmiliana de'Cerchi*, ed. D. MORENI (Florence 1827). Z. LAZZERI, *Studi francescani* 7 (1921) 196–206. LÉON DE CLARY, *Lives of the Saints and Blessed of the Three Orders of St. Francis*, 4 v. (Taunton, England 1885–87) 2:275–279. J. L. BAUDOT and L. CHAUSSIN, *Vies des saints et des bienheueux selon l'ordre du calendrier avec l'historique des fêtes*, ed. by The Benedictines of Paris, 12 v. (Paris 1935–56) 5:370–373. J. CAMBELL, *Lexikon für Theologie und Kirche*, ed. J. HOFER and K. RAHNER, 10 v. (2d, new ed. Freiburg 1957–65) 5:534.

[J. CAMBELL]

HUMILIATI

Members of a 12th-century lay-poverty movement, known also as Berettini, so-called because of their ash-gray garments of undyed (*berrettine, humile*) wool. They first appeared in Lombardy in the second half of the 12th century. Their origin is obscure, but seems to be connected with the then prevalent desire to return to the state of the primitive church. The theory that associates their origin with Emperor HENRY IV, or with St. BERNARD OF CLAIRVAUX and St. John Meda, is at best improbable. The Humiliati first lived as devout laymen (mostly members of the higher social levels) in the married state, or in double convents observing continence. Distinguished for their penitential austerity, they fasted frequently, spoke little, refused to bear arms, and preached publicly against heresy and abuses in the church. They observed personal and communal poverty, but as manual laborers rather than as mendicants, and became involved in the wool industry. The women cared for the sick poor, especially lepers, while the men devoted themselves to social and civic affairs, providing work for the unemployed, forming trade associations, and aiding the indigent. Though orthodox in intention, they were closely related to the PATARINES and other heretical penitential sects of the period. In the matter of apostolic preaching, they resembled the CATHARI; they also resembled the WALDENSES, but differed from them in their interpretation of evangelical poverty. When their attacks on the clergy became excessive, Pope ALEXANDER III forbade them to preach in public (1179), but they refused to obey. LUCIUS III excommunicated them together with the Waldenses in 1184. Many submitted, however, and in 1201 INNOCENT III reorganized them as a three-order institute: canons and sisters in solemn religious consecration living in double monasteries; continent laymen and laywomen; and married men and women living as secular tertiaries; the last group withdrew in 1272. The order grew rapidly in power and prestige, rendering distinguished service to the Church in the struggle against heresy and against the socioeconomic problems of the times. However, their association with the wool industry brought them wealth and rapid decline. Toward the end there were only 170 members for the 94 houses. When St. Charles BORROMEO undertook their reform, some of the members attempted to take his life; whereupon PIUS V suppressed the male branch of the order (1571).

Bibliography: G. TIRABOSCHI, *Vetera humiliatorum monumenta*, 3 v. (Milan 1766–68). L. ZANONI, *Gli umiliati nei loro rapporti con l'eresia, l'industria della lana ed i comuni nei secoli XII e XIII* (Milan 1911). J. B. PIERRON, *Die katholischen Armen* (Freiburg 1911). F. VAN DEN BORNE, *Die Anfänge des franziskanischen Dritten Ordens* (Münster 1925). F. VERNET, *Dictionnaire de théologie catholique*, ed. A. VACANT et al., 15 v. (Paris 1903–50) 7.1:311–321. P. GUERRINI, ''Gli umiliati a Brescia,'' *Miscellanea Pio Paschini*, 2 v. (Rome 1948–49) 1:187–214. A. MENS, *Lexikon für Theologie und Kirche*, ed. J. HOFER and K. RAHNER, 10 v. (2d. new ed. Freiburg 1957–65) 5:534–535. H. GRUNDMANN, *Religiöse Bewegungen im Mittelalter* (2d ed. Hildesheim 1961). M. H. VICAIRE, *Catholicisme* 5:1097–98.

[M. F. LAUGHLIN]

HUMILITY

The virtue by which a man attributes to God all the good he possesses. In this article humility is treated (1) as it appears in the Bible, (2) as it is considered by theology, and (3) as it is applied to practice.

In the Bible. According to the OT, man, created by God's love but preferring proud disobedience to filial dependence (Gn 2.17), broke the bonds with his Creator (Gn 3.22–24) and the harmony of creation (Romans ch. 1–2) by introducing sin and death into the world (Rom 5.12).

When God revealed his plan of salvation, the chosen people learned again its complete dependence on God in all things (Hos 13.9) by witnessing the powerful works of Yahweh (Dt 11.7) who created it as the PEOPLE OF GOD (Dt 32.6), fed its poverty in the desert (Ex ch. 16), and defended it in its helplessness (Ex ch. 14). It learned also its sinfulness and the mercy of Yahweh (Ps 78[77]) and underwent the purifying chastisement of the exile (Jer 16.12–13, 31; Ez 36.24–28). This humble attitude was expressed and fostered by the cult of praise, thanksgiving, and propitiation. The real people of God, then, was the small ''remnant'' of the ''poor of Yahweh'' (Zep 3.12–14), whose attitude was one of trustful and humble dependence (Jdt 9.11), filial fear (Prv 15.23; 22.4), faithful obedience (1 Mc 2.20–22), CONTRITION (Is 57.15; 66.2), poverty (Ps 9–10; 22[21]), MEEKNESS, and MODESTY (Nm 12.3).

In the NT, all these traits converge, through the humble handmaid of the Lord (Lk 1.38, 48), upon the real Servant of Yahweh (Isaiah ch. 42, 50; Lk 4.17–21; Is 61.1–2), the King meek and humble of heart (Zec 9.9; Mt 21.5; Zep 3.12; Mt 11.29), born as a child of men, Jesus. Being the Son of God, He came to obey (Jn 4.34), to save (Jn 3.17), to serve (Mt 20.28), and to accept the humiliation of the cross (Phil 2.8). Thus He revealed the humility of love: charity stooped down, renouncing all SELF-LOVE, so that nothing might hinder His communion with the little ones (Phil 2.2–8). He was the definitive image of humility (Jn 13.1–17).

His kingdom is to be received, not as a right, but as a gift (1 Cor 4.7), in the manner of a child (Mt 18.3–5). Hence the poor and the meek are blessed (Mt 5.3–5). The basic new law of love implies service (Eph 4.2; 1 Pt 3.8–9), but it implies also humble forgiveness (Lk 18.14).

Humility (ταπεινοφροσύνη) opens man to grace (1 Cor 15.10) and to divine secrets (Mt 11.25), makes him an instrument of salvation (1 Cor 1.25–31; 2 Cor 12–10), and will exalt the humble forever (Mt 23.12); while pride closes man to grace (1 Pt 5.5) and causes the horror of God (Lk 16.15) and His chastisements (Is 2.6–22; Mt 23.12).

In Theology. Humility is the moral VIRTUE by which the human will accepts readily the fact that all a person's good—nature and grace, being and action—is a gift of God's creative and salvific love, and by which one wants consequently to ''unself'' the self radically in thought, word, and deed, in order to be true to his (natural and supernatural) being. The opposite of humility is PRIDE, by which man thinks and wants to be independent of God (and of others) and, consequently, self-sufficient (in being), self-reliant (in action), and self-seeking (morally).

As any sin is fundamentally a form of pride and perverse self-love, so any good act of the just man is basically an act of love (charity), which is the fundamental driving force of his SELF-OBLATION to God and men. But because he is a creature, a redeemed sinner, and an adopted son, this love must be humble: it is totally received (Phil 2.13) and gratefully returned by a liberty that itself is made possible by the gratuitous help (*concursus*) of God. Humility is thus as essential for a man as is his creaturehood and adoptive sonship.

After the theological virtues (charity founded on faith and hope), which constitute the (supernatural) soul of our moral activity by immediately connecting us with God (Col 3.14), humility is the most important moral virtue since it regulates the whole of virtuous life by submitting it to the true order of being. It even affects charity, hope, and faith themselves insofar as these are the theological virtues of a created, adopted son; humility is their creaturely aspect. It is thus the foundation of all virtues

The Humility of the Publican and Haughtiness of the Pharisee, miniature illustrating the parable in the Gospel of Luke 18.9–14.

(see St. Augustine, *Serm.* 69, *Patrologia Latina* 38.441). It opens us to the gifts of the Father (1 Pt 5.5) by breaking open the closed and separate selfhood. While pride tends to make an absolute of man's littleness, humility opens it to the infinite by accepting its relativeness to God and to others. Hence the evangelical paradox: "Whoever exalts himself shall be humbled, and whoever humbles himself shall be exalted" (Mt 23.12). When the one who receives is nothing of himself, his independence from the source of being means self-destruction, and his dependence, self-fulfillment. Humility is the true greatness of a creature; it is liberation from its limited selfhood.

At a deeper level still, humility shares in Christ's filial humility. As God, the Son receives Himself totally from the Father, but is equal to Him in all things (Phil 2.6). As man, His sonship expresses itself in a total relativeness by which He voluntarily receives all from His Father (Jn 4.34; 5.30; 7.16; Lk 22.42), who is greater than He (Jn 14.28). The humility of Christ's members partici-

pates in this filial "receptiveness" and is an expression of their adoptive sonship. It has a trinitarian value. In Christ, one may speak of the humility of God. Some even see it as an attribute of the divinity, inclining God's love toward the littleness of his creatures (R. Guardini).

Besides, Christ, accepting the solidarity with man's sinfulness (2 Cor 5.21), was humiliated unto death in order to save his brethren (Phil 2.7–11). This humiliation of Christ is an exigency of His charity: His love does not suffer its self-surrender to be limited by any prerogative that could hamper communion. Superiority is service (Mt 20.25–28). Man's fraternal charity has the same exigency of humility.

In a classical Aristotelian context, St. Thomas Aquinas classified humility as a virtue moderating the irascible appetite in its tendency to excel, restraining it from presumption and thus balancing the effects of MAGNANIMITY, which stimulates reasonably the same appetite against DESPAIR (*Summa theologiae* 2a2ae, 161.1). As such humility is one kind of modesty that, in turn, is a potential part of the cardinal virtue of TEMPERANCE (*ibid.* 161.4). Essentially in the will, it presupposes as its rule a judgment of faith and reason about man's utter CONTINGENCY (*ibid.* 161.2). For St. Thomas, humility is more important than any moral virtue except (legal) JUSTICE; it is also second to the theological and intellectual virtues (*ibid.* 161.5). Evangelical humility is too rich and positive to be classified in any moral category.

In Practice. Humility has as its foundation the sincere acknowledgment of truth perceived clearly by faith. Humility indeed is truth: all good comes from God as its first cause. Only deficiencies belong to man. Hence a humble man can acknowledge the good in others and himself as it really is, i.e., as coming from God and not from self (Rom 12.3), and only the evil as his own work. Therefore, there is no room for vainglory, but only for gratitude and contrition, nor for presumption, but only for the duty of using the gifts with magnanimity; for the humble are God's fearless trustees (Lk 17.10). The "little way" of St. THÉRÈSE DE LISIEUX inspires both boldness and generosity. Humility does not abolish true self-respect, nor oblige anyone to say that God's gifts of nature and grace are greater in others than in himself, except to such extent as that may be true. But humility abhors envy of the gifts of others, or the attributing to self of superiority or talent as if these were not God-given. It genuinely rejoices in acknowledging the superiority of others when in fact they are superior. Moreover, as a remedy to the propensity to self-complacency and pride that are results of original sin, humility inclines a person to consider chiefly in others the good in which he himself is lacking, and in himself the defects others do not have (Phil 2.3). The saints excelled in this practice of humility, entertaining thereby a low estimate of themselves and positively choosing contempt with Christ. An excellent example of this is to be found in the third kind of humility described in the *Spiritual Exercises* of St. Ignatius of Loyola. Humiliation is the touchstone of humility. Only true humility can save a man from a false pride in his truly splendid achievements without at the same time discouraging his effort.

Bibliography: X. LÉON-DUFOUR, ed., *Vocabulaire de théologie biblique* (Paris 1962). E. HUGUENY, *Dictionnaire apologétique de la foi catholique,* ed. A. D'ALÈS, 4 v. (Paris 1911–22; Table analytique 1931) 2:519–528. G. JACQUEMET, *Catholicisme. Hier, aujourd'hui et demain,* ed. G. JACQUEMET (Paris 1947–) 5:1098–1103. B. HÄRING, *The Law of Christ,* tr. E. G. KAISER (Westminster, Md. 1961–) 1:546–557. FATHER CANICE, *Humility* (Westminster, Md. 1951). S. CARLSON, *The Virtue of Humility* (Dubuque 1952). A. TANQUEREY, *The Spiritual Life,* tr. H. BRANDERIS (2d ed. Tournai 1930; repr. Westminster, Md. 1945) 1127–53. N. KINSELLA, *Un-*

profitable Servants (Westminster, Md. 1960). H. VAN ZELLER, "Of Humility," *American Benedictine Review* 8 (1957) 324–349.

[G. GILLEMAN]

HUMILITY OF MARY, SISTERS OF THE

(HM, Official Catholic Directory 2110), or "Blue Nuns"; a pontifical institute that conducts schools, catechetical centers, and hospitals under two separate motherhouses, one at Villa Maria, Pennsylvania, and the other at Ottumwa, Iowa. The congregation was established in 1854 by John Joseph Begel, parish priest of the Diocese of Nancy. At the invitation of Bishop Amadeus Rappe of Cleveland, Ohio, the entire community immigrated to the United States in 1864, when an anticlerical French government frustrated its teaching apostolate. The foundress, Mother Magdalen Potiers, died before the voyage and the group of ten professed sisters and three orphans was under the leadership of Mother Anna Tabourat, the American foundress. After a brief stay in Louisville, Ohio, the sisters settled near New Bedford, Pennsylvania, on a large farm assigned to them by the bishop. Despite severe trials and hardships, the sisters learned the language and, within a few years, were conducting parochial schools in nearby towns. Mother Anna guided the sisters until 1883 when illness forced her resignation. Mother Patrick Ward, the first American-born general superior, was elected (1889) and served for 27 years. In 1870 four sisters were sent to the Diocese of St. Joseph, Missouri; 11 years later this group formed the nucleus for a separate Congregation of the Humility of Mary (CHM, Official Catholic Directory #2100) with its motherhouse located at Ottumwa, Iowa. In addition to their principal ministries of education, healthcare and catechetics, the sisters also operate extensive outreach programs to Native Americans, immigrant communities, the homeless and marginalized. The motherhouse is located in Villa Maria, Pennsylvania.

[M. K. FLANIGAN/EDS.]

HUMMEL, JOHANN NEPOMUK

Pianist and composer whose works were important sources of the romanticist idiom; b. Bratislava, Slovakia, Nov. 14, 1778; d. Weimar, Germany, Oct. 17, 1837. He studied under MOZART and Clementi and succeeded Franz Joseph HAYDN as Prince Esterházy's music director. After a productive period in Vienna, where he was BEETHOVEN's chief rival as pianist, he became *Kapellmeister* in Stuttgart in 1811, and in Weimar, 1819, whence he toured Europe as a piano virtuoso. His early compositions are often crude and derivative (especially from Mozart), but his later works, with their elaborate pianistic figurations and subtle harmonic sense, anticipate Chopin and the young SCHUMANN. His chamber music is melodious and well constructed, if not always profound. His church music is in the Viennese classical style of Mozart and Michael HAYDN. A *Graduale* and *Offertorium* are still performed in Austrian churches. Of his three Masses the B-flat is best known and typifies the "popular" church music of the early 19th century.

Bibliography: K. BENYOVSKY, *J. N. Hummel* (Bratislava 1934). D. HUME, *Grove's Dictionary of Music and Musicians*, ed. E. BLOM, 9 v. (5th ed. London 1954) 4:406–409. D. BROCK, "The Instrumental Music of Hummel" (Ph.D. diss. University of Sheffield 1976). J. R. KERSHAW, "The Solo Keyboard Works of J. N. Hummel" (Ph.D. diss. Balliol College, Oxford University 1976). D. M. RANDEL, ed., *The Harvard Biographical Dictionary of Music* (Cambridge 1996) 399–400. J. RICE, "The Musical Bee: References to Mozart and Cherubini in Hummel's 'New Year' Concerto," *Music and Letters* 77 (1996) 401–424. J. SACHS, *Kapellmeister Hummel in England and France* (Detroit 1977); "Johann Nepomuk Hummel" in *The New Grove Dictionary of Music and Musicians*, v. 8, ed. S. SADIE (New York 1980) 781–788. N. SLONIMSKY, ed. *Baker's Biographical Dictionary of Musicians* (New York 1992) 812.

[R. M. LONGYEAR]

HUMMEL, MARIA INNOCENTIA

Franciscan; b. Massing, Bavaria, 1909; d. Siessen, 1946. Berta Humel was the third of six children. She began her education in a local Catholic elementary school. At the age of 12, she enrolled in the Institute of English Sisters, a boarding school in Marienhoehe. There, she demonstrated an early artistic talent, especially in watercolor and pastels. From 1927, she attended the Academy of Applied Arts in Munich from which she graduated in 1931. The predominant theme in her art was children in a Bavarian rural and folk setting. After graduation, she entered the Convent of the Franciscan Sisters of Siessen, a community of 250 sisters with an apostolate of teaching. She took the name in religion of Sr. Maria Innocentia. During her novitiate, she designed vestments and altar clothes. Upon her profession she taught for a time at St. Anna, a school for girls in Saulgau. Her art was published in books and art cards where it caught the eye of Franz Goebel of Goebel Porzellenfabrik, the head of a porcelain company who was looking to establish a new line of porcelain figurines. Based on her watercolors of children in Bavarian folk settings, the line of "Hummel" figures was introduced in January 1935. They were immediately popular within Germany. During the occupation after May 1945, they were especially popular with GI's who brought them back to the U.S. Sr. Mary Innocentia died from tuberculosis at the young age of 37 in 1946. New figures are still being produced in Sr. Mary Innocentia's style after review by the Artistic Board of the Siessen Convent. The M. I. Hummel figures have achieved world renown and are widely collected.

[D. P. SHERIDAN]

HUNEGUNDIS, ST.

Virgin, monastic foundress (known also as Hunégonde); b. Lemblais (Picardy, France), first half of seventh century; d. Homblières, c. 690. She was compelled by her parents to marry, but simultaneously took a vow of virginity and promised to enter a convent. She persuaded her bridegroom to accompany her on a pilgrimage to Rome and there vowed perpetual virginity before the Pope St. VITALIAN and asked him for the veil. On her return to France she founded the monastery of Homblières near Saint-Quentin. She was widely venerated in the West Frankish kingdom as early as the ninth century.

Feast: Aug. 25.

Bibliography: *Acta Sanctorum* Aug. 5:223–240, *Vita* by BERENGAR OF HOMBLIÈRES. J. MABILLON, *Acta sanctorum ordinis S. Benedicti*, 9 v. (Paris 1668–1701; 2d ed. Venice 1733–40) 2:977–983; 5:216–224. M. MANITIUS, *Geschichte der lateinischen Literatur des Mittelalters*, 3 v. (Munich 1911–31) 2: 417–420. A. M. ZIMMERMANN, *Kalendarium Benedictinum: Die Heiligen und Seligen des Benediktinerorderns und seiner Zweige*, 4 v. (Metten 1933–38) 2:618, 620–. *The Book of Saints* (4th ed. New York 1947) 301. J. VAN DER STRAETEN, "S. Hunégonde d'Homblières," *Analecta Bollandiana* 72 (1954) 39–74. L. RÉAU, *Iconographie de l'art chrétien*, 6 v. (Paris 1955–59) 3.2:667.

[M. CSÁKY]

HUNFRIED, ST.

Benedictine abbot and bishop; d. Thérouanne, France, March 8, 870. Having become a monk at an early age, he was abbot of PRÜM on his election as bishop of Thérouanne (856). In 861 the NORMANS devastated Thérouanne. Discouraged by the disaster, Hunfried wished to return to Prüm but was dissuaded by Pope NICHOLAS I (*Monumenta Germaniae Epistolae* 6:613). Thérouanne was rebuilt, and Hunfried marked the restoration with the solemn celebration of the Feast of the ASSUMPTION in 862. He was abbot of SAINT-BERTIN (864–866) and assisted at a number of councils in France, including the Third Council of Soissons, September 866. Hunfried's relics were exhumed April 13, 1108, by Bp. John of Thérouanne. His head is venerated at Saint-Omer; in 1553 the rest of his relics were brought to Ypres, where they were burned by the anti-Spanish faction, the Geuzen, in 1563.

Feast: March 8.

Bibliography: *Acta Sanctorum* March 1:789–792. J. L. BAU-DOT and L. CHAUSSIN, *Vies des saints et des bienheueux selon l'ordre du calendrier avec l'historique des fêtes* (Paris 1935–56) 3:175–176. A. M. ZIMMERMANN, *Kalendarium Benedictinum: Die Heiligen und Seligen des Benediktinerorderns und seiner Zweige,* 4 v. (Metten 1933–38) 1:300–302.

[G. J. DONNELLY]

HUNGARY, THE CATHOLIC CHURCH IN

The Republic of Hungary is bordered on the north by Slovakia, on the northeast by Ukraine, on the east by Romania, on the south by Yugoslavia and Slovenia, on the west by Austria and on the northwest by Slovakia. Primarily consisting of flat or rolling plains rising to low mountains in the northwest, Hungary has a temperate climate, with humid winters. Natural resources in the region include bauxite, coal and natural gas; its fertile land produces such crops as wheat, corn, sunflower seeds, sugar beets and potatoes. Budapest, its capital city, is on the Danube River, which bisects Hungary from north to south.

Hungary became an independent kingdom in 1000. From 1526 to 1686 much of the country was under Turkish control. After that Hungary was ruled by the HAPSBURG HOUSE until 1918, when it became independent of Austria but lost most of its territory and population. In 1946 Hungary was proclaimed a republic. A Communistic People's Republic was proclaimed in 1949, and remained under Soviet control until 1991 despite an effort to break the Warsaw Pact in 1956. A member of NATO since 1999, Hungary was slated for inclusion in the European Union by 2000.

The following essay is in two parts. Part one discusses the history of the church through 1950; Part two discusses the Church under communism and into the 21st century.

Christian Origins

As part of the Roman Empire, the region comprised portions of the provinces of Pannonia and Dacia. Accounts of martyrdoms and remains of tombs, funeral chapels and churches attest to a thriving Christian community, with some groups surviving the barbarian migrations that accompanied the fall of the Empire. Sizable Christian communities may have lasted into the AVAR rule from 500–700, while Christian traditions may also have been inherited by the SLAVS and passed to the Hungarians (Magyars), who eventually subjugated and assimilated the people of the region.

> **Capital:** Budapest.
> **Size:** 35,919 sq. miles.
> **Population:** 10,138,845 in 2000.
> **Languages:** Hungarian.
> **Religions:** 6,833,580 Catholics (67.5%), 2,534,710 Protestants (25%), 770,555 without religious affiliation.

Conversion of Magyars. Even before invading Hungary the Hungarians had encountered Christianity. The Finno-Ugric Hungarian nomads of Eurasia's Great Steppes, composed of western and eastern Turki tribes, became a nation in the fifth century. They adopted the religion of the shamans, which was influenced by the religions of the East, and eventually came into contact with the BYZANTINE CHURCH and BYZANTINE CIVILIZATION. Many of their slaves were Christians. Christian missionaries visited them on several occasions. As allies of Byzantium the Hungarians entered the northwestern shores of the Black Sea. After being defeated by the Bulgarians, they moved into the Danube Basin and gradually spread throughout the Great Plain subjugating Slavonic, Bulgarian and Avar minority groups. For the next six decades their destructive raids into Western Europe reminded medieval chroniclers of the Huns. The tendency by tribal chiefs of making raids on their own authority tended to weaken the central power established by Árpád (d. 907), Hungary's national hero, who had led the Magyars into the Danube area *c.* 875. In 955 Emperor OTTO I annihilated the Magyars on the Lechfeld, near Augsburg.

Géza became the national leader (972–997), restored the central power, and recognized that some accommodation to Western Christianity was essential for the survival of his people, as it had been for the neighboring nomadic or seminomadic tribes. Géza, whose wife was the daughter of a tribal chief in Transylvania who had been converted to Byzantine Christianity, was baptized by St. ADALBERT OF PRAGUE (986). Thereafter he welcomed German missionaries from Passau and Regensburg. Adalbert, a supporter of the CLUNIAC REFORM, strengthened the faith of Géza's son Stephen (Istvan), who had been baptized as a child by Bishop PILGRIM OF PASSAU, and who was married to Blessed GISELA. As ruler (997–1038), St. STEPHEN I promoted the evangelization of Hungary by inviting German and Italian missionaries and the scholar St. GERARD OF CSANÁD. With the approval of Emperor Otto III, Pope Sylvester II crowned Stephen as first king of Hungary (1000). Stephen organized the Church in Hungary by creating the archdioceses of Esztergom and Kalocsa, eight dioceses and five Benedictine abbeys (notably PANNONHALMA). From his headquarters in Esztergom, the capital, Stephen organized the country politically as well. He defeated pagan tribes, re-

Archdioceses	Suffragans
Budapest-Esztergom	Györ, Székesfehérvár
Eger	Debrecen-Nyíregyháza, Vác
Kalocsa-Kecskemét	Pécs, Szeged-Csanád
Veszprém (1993)	Kaposvár, Szombathely

Pannonhalma is an abbey nullius, immediately subject to the Holy See, and a military ordinariate is also located in the country. The Hungarian Byzantine-rite has a metropolitan in Hajdúdorog and an apostolic exarchy at Miskolc. The Ruthenian-rite diocese of Munkács (Mukachevo; created 1771) is suffragan to Esztergom.

placed the tribal divisions by territorial counties and resisted the ecclesiastical influence of Byzantium, which remained strong. Stephen's religious accomplishments, which were not based on mere power politics, survived a pagan reaction after his death that was partly motivated by hostility to Western influences. Paganism gradually disappeared, only to reappear later with the arrival of the nomadic Cumans, belonging to the Turki peoples. Some of these pagan traditions were assimilated into Christian customs and folklore. In 1996 the relics of Stephen and Gisela were reunited in Veszprem to mark the 1,000th anniversary of their wedding, as well as the founding of the local diocese.

Árpáds. The Church and the Árpád dynasty were sources of strength to one another. The 40 or so Árpáds who became saints or blesseds indicate the genuine spirituality that characterized this dynasty, which played an important role in imbuing Hungary with the Christian spirit. At the same time the kings enjoyed the privileges of creating dioceses, naming bishops and supervising Church property. The archbishops of Esztergom, who became primates of Hungary, crowned the kings and exercised great authority. Together with the other bishops and the abbots, they were a potent political force. Until the battle of Mohács in 1526, prelates, especially along the frontiers, commanded the military forces against sporadic pagan invasions. Hierarchical influence served to curb abuses of royal power and anarchical tendencies of the nobles while fostering ties with Rome.

Hungary became a bulwark of Western Christianity against barbarian incursions from the east. As king (1077–95), St. LADISLAUS I (László) promoted the canonization of Stephen I and EMERIC (1083), defended Hungary's Christian culture against the pagan Cumans, conquered Croatia, and accepted the GREGORIAN REFORM. King Kálmán I (Coloman, 1095–1114), who con-

quered Dalmatia, completed the Christianization of Hungary, which served as an avenue for the armies of the CRUSADES on their route to the Holy Land. Kálmán's successors had to protect Hungarian independence against Byzantium. Géza II (1141–62) settled Catholic Germans (Saxons) in the southern passes of Transylvania. Under Béla III (1173–96) Cistercians spread rapidly in Hungary. King Andrew II (1205–35), father of St. ELIZABETH OF HUNGARY, headed an unsuccessful Crusade to Palestine (1217) and was constrained to sign the Golden Bull (1222), which became a charter of feudal privileges for the nobles. Devastating invasions by the MONGOLS from 1241–42 destroyed six dioceses and retarded Hungary's development but did not undermine the country's Christian foundation. Béla IV (1235–70) had three daughters renowned for sanctity: St. MARGARET OF HUNGARY, Blessed JOLENTA and Blessed Kinga. Following the Mongol raids Catholics emigrated from Germany and Bohemia, Orthodox from Romania and Ruthenia, and pagan Cumans from outside the frontiers. Cuman influence proved particularly harmful to the Church, especially under the half-Cuman King Ladislaus IV (1272–90), who in 1279 forcibly dissolved a synod in Buda presided over by a papal legate. With Andrew III (1290–1301) the Árpád dynasty became extinct.

Work of Religious Orders. Religious orders played an important role in Hungary's religious and cultural development. Following the Benedictines came the PREMONSTRATENSIANS (1130), the CISTERCIANS from France (1142) and CANONS REGULAR OF ST. AUGUSTINE (1198). The HERMITS OF ST. PAUL, founded in Hungary in 1250, spread to Italy, Germany, Austria, Poland, Lithuania and Sweden. The KNIGHTS OF MALTA, CARTHUSIANS, CARMELITES, FRANCISCANS, DOMINICANS, and TEUTONIC KNIGHTS also established houses in the country. Religious houses and churches became the centers around which new towns developed. Priests and religious, who served to maintain concord between the Hungarians and other ethnic groups in towns and villages, were responsible for erecting schools, hospitals, leprosaria and a variety of charitable institutions. Because Hungary possessed few institutions of higher learning until the 17th century, ecclesiastics and nobles attended the universities of Paris, Bologna and Padua. Later they studied at Vienna, Cracow and Charles University in Prague. The various religious orders introduced German, Italian and French influences. Priests who had been educated in Western European universities provided the officials in the royal chancery.

Franciscans and Dominicans took a leading role in fostering an intensive spiritual life among the laity. They were the first to distribute religious literature to lay persons and to groups of women dwelling in communities,

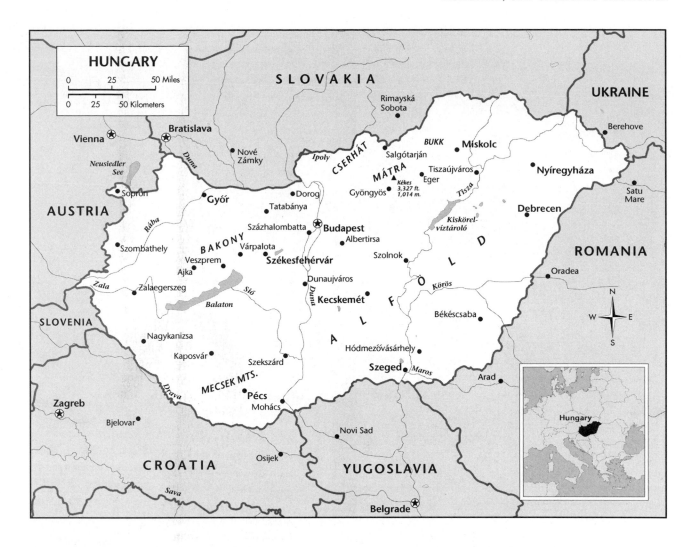

such as the BEGUINES. The Franciscans, who in 1232 established a separate Hungarian province with its center in Eger, had more than 50 houses by 1300. After the Mongol devastations the Franciscans were utilized by the kings to restore religious life. During the 14th century they evangelized the Mongols and Tatars in Russia, and also took the lead in opposing the heresy of the BOGOMILS, which infiltrated Hungary from the Balkans. Later the heretical influences of the WALDENSES and HUSSITES penetrated Hungary from the West and caused widespread social upheavals. Hussites, or Franciscans influenced by them, made the first translation of the Bible into Hungarian.

Growing Turkish Menace. The Neopolitan branch of the House of Anjou came into control of the Hungarian throne with Charles I (1308–42). Charles I of Anjou was aided by the papal embassy of Cardinal Gentilis in gaining the throne. The Anjou dynasty continued the close relationship with the Holy See that had characterized the rule of the Árpáds. Under Louis I, the Great (1342–82), who also governed Poland, both State and Church

reached their peak. Hungary's influence extended to Moldavia, Wallachia, Bosnia and Serbia. Louis I built churches and monasteries, filled church offices with competent ecclesiastics, and strove for the reunion of the Orthodox within his kingdom. He founded the first Hungarian university at Pécs in 1367. In his last years he confronted the threat of invasion by the OTTOMAN TURKS, who were followers of Islam. SIGISMUND (1387–1437), emperor in 1433, kept Hungary on the side of Rome during the WESTERN SCHISM; but he appropriated ecclesiastical funds for his own purposes, subjected papal documents to his royal *placet* (1404), and presumed to nominate bishops. After his disastrous defeat at Nicopolis in 1396 during his crusade against the Turks, Sigismund's authority in Hungary passed to the feudal nobility. From 1420 Hussite armies ravaged the country.

Ladislaus V (Ladislaus III of Poland) lost his life at Varna in 1444 doing battle against the Turks, whereupon John Hunyadi became governor of the kingdom. Hudyadi's leadership in the crusade against the Ottomans made him a national hero, supported as he was in his mili-

High altar in the interior of the Coronation Church of the Hungarian Kings, Budapest, designed by F. Schulek, 1898.

tary campaigns by the papal envoys Giuliano CESARINI and Juan de CARVAJAL. Hunyadi's greatest victory over the Turks came in 1456, two years after their conquest of Constantinople, at Belgrade, where St. JOHN Capistran urged on Christian troops by his preaching. Although the battle cost Hunyadi his life, it arrested the Turkish advance for 70 years.

Matthias Corvinus, Hunyadi's son, ruled from 1458 to 1490, the sole Hungarian to be king after the disappearance of the Árpáds. He continued the war against the Turks with little help from Western Christendom except from Rome. His conquests of Vienna in 1485 and other western territories were lost to Hungary after his death. The principality of Transylvania, established with the help of Paulite diplomat György MARTINUZZI, had to defend itself against both Hapsburgs and Turks. In his dealings with the Church Matthias Corvinus appropriated ecclesiastical revenues to his own use and appointed foreigners to Hungarian sees. Both he and his father promoted Renaissance humanism in Hungary, especially at the court in Buda. It was there that Matthias collected his famous library, the Bibliotheca Corvina. Although he founded the University of Bratislava (1465), he later neglected it as he did the University of Pécs.

1526 to 1918

Ladislaus II (1490–1516), king of Bohemia, proved to be a weak ruler in Hungary. A group of peasants protesting the Turks and organized by Tamás Bakócz, turned against the nobles; in 1514 the crusade was ruthlessly suppressed, and participants condemned to ''eternal servitude.'' Ladislaus's children entered into arranged marriages with members of the Hapsburg family. The codification of Hungarian customary law by Stephen Verböczi (1514) never received official approval, but it was regarded as authoritative until 1848. In 1526 Louis II (b. 1516) and most of the Hungarian bishops died in the defeat of the Hungarian army by the Turks at Mohács, whereupon central and southern Hungary were annexed to the Turkish empire for the next 150 years. In the struggle (1526–28) for the throne between Ferdinand I of Hapsburg and John Zápolya, ecclesiastical possessions were looted by both claimants. Western and northeastern Hungary were organized as a kingdom under the Hapsburg emperors and served as a bulwark for Catholicism. Transylvania, in the southeast, became a separate principality held by the Turks in vassalage but left semi-independent under Cardinal Martinuzzi.

The Protestant Reformation. It was while Hungary was weakened by Turkish conquerors from without and rent by political discord within, that the Protestant REFORMATION began to influence the region. Until 1526 LU-

The largest Roman Catholic Cathedral in Hungary, located in Esztergom; its dome is fashioned after Saint Peter's in Rome. (©Peter Wilson/CORBIS)

THERANISM was repressed; after that it made rapid progress, particularly in Transylvania, where it was welcomed by local Germans who had maintained contacts with Germany since the 12th century. CALVINISM entered later and found wide acceptance, particularly among the Magyars. SOCINIANISM won followers among the Szekels. By allying itself with anti-Hapsburg nationalism, Protestantism helped its cause. At the court of Louis II, many German nobles welcomed the new doctrines, which were at first promoted as internal reforms in the Church. When the Catholic bishops decreed stern measures against the religious innovators, many returned to their faith. In Transylvania, however, Protestantism was too powerful to be overcome by forceful measures, gaining in some towns the support of the majority of the citizenry. The religiously indifferent Emperor Maximilian II (1564–76), son of Ferdinand I, facilitated further progress of Protestantism; at the end of his reign there were about 900 Lutheran congregations and as many more Calvinist

Altar with Latin inscription in low relief on front, in cemetery chapel, Pécs, Hungary.

ones in the sections not subject to the Turks. About 90 percent of the population had gone over to Protestantism, mostly to Calvinism. Scarcely 300 Catholic priests and religious remained in the country.

Catholic Restoration. The COUNTER REFORMATION began in the second half of the 16th century and proved extremely successful. Emperor Rudolf II (1516–1608) and succeeding Hapsburg rulers gave it strong support. More important were the reforms undertaken in the Church, the improvement in the quality of the clergy by the introduction of SEMINARY EDUCATION, and closer contacts between clergy and laity, and the promotion of more fervent interior life. A key role was played by the JESUITS, who were welcomed into the royal territories by Miklós OLÁH (Olahus), archbishop of Esztergom, and into Transylvania by Stephen BÁTHORY, prince of Transylvania (1571–76) and king of Poland (1575–86). The Jesuit college in Nagyszombat (Trnava) developed into a university under the patronage of Péter PÁZMÁNY

(1570–1637), archbishop of Esztergom and the leading figure in the Catholic restoration. The Jesuit university eventually became the University of Budapest, while the German-Hungarian College in Rome, founded in 1578, was also very important for its work in training priests.

The majority of Hungarians in the sections ruled by the kings ultimately returned to the Church, and Lutheranism lost most of its following. However, the country remained permanently divided religiously. In Transylvania the Magyars adhered in large part to Calvinism, and became a Protestant bastion with close ties to the Netherlands and England. Transylvania granted religious liberty to all in 1557. Aiding the Protestant cause was the struggle led by Transylvanian rulers Stephen Bocskay (1557–1606), Gabor Bethlen (1580–1629) and Georg Rákóczi I (1591–1648) against the Hapsburgs, wherein national independence and defense of Protestantism went hand in hand. The Serbs and a large percentage of the country's Romanians retained their allegiance to the Or-

Interior and altar of parish church, designed by Mihaly Pollack in 1820, Theresa district, Budapest, Hungary.

thodox Church. Many Ukrainians (Ruthenians) did also, but a sizable minority later united with Rome after successful missionary work among them.

Little was recorded of Turkish Hungary during its 150 years of subjection to Muslim rule. Plague and starvation killed many of those who were not carried off into slavery, leaving surviving Magyars clustered in the towns for protection. Serbs and Romanians moved into the vacated countryside. While the Reformation did not concern the Turks directly, they showed less tolerance toward Catholics than toward Protestants. The Church survived mainly due to the work of the Franciscans, although the laity also did much to keep their faith alive by organizing pilgrimages to Marian shrines and by maintaining religious customs.

To defend the Hapsburg territories the government depended partly on Hungarians, and partly on foreign mercenaries, who tormented the peasants almost as much as the Turks did. The Holy League, formed in 1684 under the sponsorship of INNOCENT XI, joined Austria, Venice, and, for a short time, Poland against the Turks. Their armies, together with those of other Western powers, succeeded in liberating most of Turkish-occupied Hungary by 1700. Buas was regained in 1686. According to the Treaty of Karlowitz (1699) the Hapsburg emperor received all of Hungary (except the Banat of Temesvar). Hapsburg rule continued until 1918. Once Hungary was liberated the former ecclesiastical organization was reestablished.

The 18th Century and the Rise of Liberalism. Emperor from 1658 to 1735, Leopold I set out to crush Hungarian separatism and Protestantism. His policy of *cuius regio eius religio* caused the anti-Hapsburg movement to assume a predominantly Protestant tinge. Catholic Francis Rákóczi II (1676–1735) headed the struggle for Hungarian independence, his armies fighting under flags adorned with pictures of the Blessed Virgin. After Rákóczi's defeat in 1708 he went into exile. Transylvania joined the rest of Hungary in being incorporated into the Hapsburg Empire, and Charles VI, emperor from 1711 to 1740, repeopled devastated regions with foreign settlers, mostly Germans. He also granted full religious liberty to Protestants but required them to restore confiscated Catholic churches. Mixed marriages were permitted, with the provision that any children of such marriages be reared as Catholics. Charles created a seminary for each diocese and ordered that monastic revenues be diverted for their support.

Education continued under Church control during the reign of Charles VI, most prominently under the Jesuits, who ran about 40 schools by 1700. The Hermits of St. Paul, Benedictines, Cistercians, Premonstratensians

and PIARISTS became increasingly active in education from the late 17th century onward, the Piarists introducing the study of Hungarian history and literature, geography and natural science.

The reign of MARIA THERESA (1740–80) was characterized by attempts to dominate the Church in the name of enlightened humanism and state absolutism. The state established its own schools and exercised control over private ones. It sought further to supervise all religious life, Catholic or Protestant. JOSEPH II (1765–90) carried his mother's policies to their conclusion by suppressing most religious orders, cutting off much contact with Rome, and otherwise attempting to bend the Church to the will of the state while otherwise granting extensive liberties to Protestants. His system, dubbed JOSEPHINISM, remained influential within Hungarian political, intellectual and religious life until 1918, despite efforts of the Church to counter it.

Meanwhile, Cardinal Leopold Kollonitsch (1637–1707), archbishop of Esztergom, succeeded in reuniting with Rome more than 100,000 Romanian- and Ukrainian-rite schismatics in southeastern Hungary. To care for Romanian-rite Catholics in 1721 the diocese of Făgăras was erected, followed in 1777 by the diocese of Oradea Mare (Nagyvárad; both now in Romania). The diocese of Križevci was erected in 1777 for Byzantine-Rite Catholics (now in Yugoslavia), and the diocese of Munkács (Mukachevo), was created in 1771 for the Ruthenians. Five Latin-rite dioceses were created in 1776 and 1777: Beszterczebanya (Banská Bystrica, 1776), Rozsnyó (Rožnava, 1776) and Szepes (Spiš), all now in the Czech Republic; and Szombathely and Székesfehérvár, in western Hungary.

Although the ENLIGHTENMENT, patronized by Joseph II, increasingly influenced late 18th-century intellectual life more and more, most Hungarian intellectuals came from the religious orders and belonged to the Benedictines, Hermits of St. Paul, Piarists, and Jesuits. Abbot Ignác Martinovics headed the sole professedly revolutionary society upholding the ideals of the French Revolution.

The Rise of Nationalism: The 19th Century. Humanism and ever-increasing, anti-Hapsburg nationalism were dominant and closely connected trends in 19th-century Hungarian political and intellectual life. Magyar asserted itself as the official language, the condition of the serfs improved, greater liberty was granted, and a Hungarian assembly was established that was responsible only to the imperial parliament. An awakening Hungarian consciousness also aroused nationalist sentiments within those ethnic groups living within Hungary. As revolution swept over Europe in 1848, Metternich was driven from power. Lajos (Louis) Kossuth led an unsuccessful two-year struggle for independence that drew nobles and peasants together, but was unable to destroy the mutual hostilities of the national groups within the Hapsburg dominion. After the Russian army came to the aid of Austria, Hapsburg absolutism retrenched for another two decades. Among the many Catholic clerics who participated in this independence movement was Mihály Horváth (1809–78), bishop of Csanád and an outstanding historian who served in the short-lived cabinet as minister of worship and education. Following the Hungarian defeat, he and several other patriotic archbishops and bishops were removed from office and imprisoned or exiled.

After the revolution of 1848 political and intellectual life became completely secularized. Protestants, more active in the uprising, accommodated themselves more easily to the new developments and gained political power disproportionate to their numbers. It became increasingly difficult to differentiate creative intellectuals on the basis of their faith, as religious and metaphysical viewpoints faded into the background. By the time of the 1867 compromise agreement that granted Hungary extensive independence within the Hapsburg empire, scarcely any of the prominent statesmen or intellectuals owed their outlook to Catholic convictions; notable exceptions included distinguished statesman Count István Széchenyi (17911860), statesman, humanist and noveliest Baron József Eötvös (1813–71) and composer Franz LISZT.

The 20th Century. After 1867, religious literature, art, music and philosophy maintained an existence apart from the cultural mainstream. Still, the Catholic viewpoint became an important element of balance as Catholic priests produced important theological, historical and sociological studies. Nationalism, however, provided for many a substitute for religion. The rise of capitalism in Hungary also influenced the Church, which still owned much of its huge holdings from the past and was therefore forced into a defensive position politically and intellectually. In virtue of its rights of patronage, the government exercised great influence in episcopal nominations and selected as bishops men favorable to its policies. Baron Eötvös and other convinced Catholics among the ranks of statesmen, scholars, and writers considered it desirable for the Church to obtain independence of the State. The conference of bishops drafted a preliminary plan to this effect in 1869, but it did not receive the approval of Emperor Francis Joseph I. When the minister of worship and education kept deferring consideration of it, the bishops did not press the matter. Count Albert Apponyi (1846–1933), one of Hungary's leading statesmen at the turn of the 20th century, submitted a bill granting autonomy to the Church, but the military collapse of the Central

Powers and the onset of World War I shattered all hopes for its passage. The measure was eventually nacted after Hungary became independent but within the framework of an arrangement that made Catholicism the state religion.

Catholic Life. Religious statistics for 1914 indicated that in Hungary (including the autonomous areas of Croatia and Slovenia) Latin-rite Catholics constituted half the population, Catholics belonging to the Eastern Churches under ten percent, Orthodox 14.3 percent, and Calvinists, Lutherans and Jews comprising the remainder. Despite their majority, most people who identified themselves as Catholics retained their faith as something hallowed by tradition; Catholic beliefs did not guide their outlook and actions. Sunday Mass was esteemed as a social gathering. Very few Catholics went to confession except at the times of marriage and death. There existed a chasm between the hierarchy and the lower clergy and between priests and laity. Higher ecclesiastical positions signified primarily temporal dignity and power. Indicative of the close connection between the ecclesiastical and political spheres was the fact that János Czernoch (1852–1927) became archbishop of Esztergom and cardinal after serving for years in parliament as representative of the People's party and after promoting the Christian Socialist party, whose program was pseudo-social. The diminished numbers in religious orders provided an index of the decline in the spiritual life.

New Movements. To remedy these deficiences the Catholic Youth Association (1856) and the Altar Society (1859) were formed, largely on the initiative of the Piarists. *Alkotmány*, founded in 1896, was the first Catholic daily newspaper to enjoy an extended existence. Until its demise in 1919 it promoted the agenda of the People's party, a Catholic party whose program represented the ideals of the Catholic aristocracy and lower middle class.

Hungarian Catholics followed the example of the German Catholic *Katholikentage* by organizing annual gatherings and imitating several other initiatives before later gaining inspiration from French Catholicism. The Regnum Marianum, organized in 1903, became a flourishing spiritual center among Catholic students and *bourgeoisie* in Budapest. About this time Gyula Glattfelder, Bishop of Csanád, founded St. Emeric Catholic Youth Association and St. Emetic College, which provided a residence for Catholic university students. Worthy as these and later organizations were, they suffered from their obsessive opposition to LIBERALISM and freemasonry and from their failure to understand Hungary's social problems.

Catholic reform movements demonstrated a close connection between the strengthening of discipline within the religious orders and the deepening of popular religious life. As a result of improvements within the orders, the Benedictines, Carmelites, Capuchins, Dominicans and Jesuits increasingly engaged in apostolic endeavors. The leading pioneers of Catholic renewal before 1914 were Ottokár Prohászka (1858–1927) and Sándor Giesswein (1856–1923). As bishop of Székesfehérvár, Prohászka was the first to coordinate developments in the natural and social sciences and modern intellectual trends with the Catholic viewpoint, his aim to win the educated classes back to the Church. Giesswein, a prelate, sought to implement Catholic social principles, especially through movements for Catholic workers.

Since 1918

The collapse of the Austro-Hungarian Empire in 1918 ended Hungary's political connections with Austria. After the October Revolution (1918), an independent republic was proclaimed, but much of the region was occupied by the newly created states of the Little Entente. Since the governing classes were unconcerned with social problems, dissatisfaction was widespread and a chaotic situation developed that made possible a brief Communist takeover in 1919 under Béla Kun, the first dictatorship of the proletariat. Short as this regime was, its consequences were momentous.

Citing as their motivation the close relationship between the Church and the semifeudal landowners, the Communist government enacted severe antireligious legislation. Following the regime's military collapse under an attack from the armies of the Little Entente, the conservatives regained power and anti-semitism increased. A "white" terror then followed the "red" terror. While some priests and laymen believed the time propitious for the establishment of a political, social and cultural order based on Catholic principles, conservatives, led by Admiral Miklós (Nicholas) Horthy (1868–1957), nullified most of their proposals. In order to put into effect some of their program Catholic reform leaders had to make compromises. Horthy proclaimed Hungary a monarchy in 1920 and, in the absence of a king, ruled the country as regent. Jusztinian Serédi, an outstanding canon lawyer who collaborated with Cardinal Gasparri in the codification of the Code of Canon Law, was archbishop of Esztergom (1927–45). During these years as primate, his episcopate manifested the contradictory trends that characterized Hungarian life as a whole.

By the 1920 Treaty of Trianon, based on the principle of nationality, Hungary lost almost 75 percent of its territory and over half its 18 million inhabitants to the newly established states of Czechoslovakia, Romania, and Yugoslavia. As a result of the change, the percentage of Latin-rite Catholics and Calvinists increased, while that of Eastern-rite Catholics declined considerably and that of the Orthodox fell to negligible size.

Ecclesiastical organization underwent radical changes also. Five Latin-rite dioceses and two Eastern-rite sees passed to Czechoslovakia. Four Latin-rite dioceses and four Eastern Catholic sees became part of Romania. Three Latin sees, one Eastern see, and territory later formed into two apostolic administrations went to Yugoslavia. Italy acquired territory that later became a diocese. Only four sees in Hungary remained territorially intact. As reorganized at this time Hungary possessed three metropolitan sees and eight dioceses.

Catholic Activities to 1944. During his term as regent (1920–44), Horthy, a Calvinist, permitted the Church to realize partially its ambition of freedom from state supervision. In 1929 Horthy exercised the traditional governmental power of ecclesiastical patronage, at which time the Holy See admitted that the assent of the minister of worship and education, always a Catholic, was necessary for the nomination of bishops, chosen on the basis of recommendations by the conference of bishops. Despite such government intervention, the Church continued to control most elementary schools and a substantial minority of the secondary ones, while the state maintained all higher education. The government supported the Church's right to establish, administer and supervise schools and subsidized Church-affiliated schools with public funds. Seminaries enjoyed freedom from government interference.

Among those noted for their apostolic endeavors were the Jesuits Béla Bangha (1880–1940) and Ferenc Biró (1869–1938), who worked in Budapest to foster a Catholic press; Count Gusztáv Majláth, a bishop of Transylvania, who was known as "everybody's confessor," and Sándor SÍK, a Piarist priest, university professor and noted poet who was a leader in the Catholic Boy Scout movement and founder of the Young Hungarians, an organization for youthful intellectuals. Tihamér Tóth (1889–1940), bishop of Veszprém, was a noted preacher, writer, and an apostle of youth. The Catholic People's Alliance (Katolikus Népszövetseg) maintained a close relationship with the Catholic political parties and declined in importance with them.

Congregations of religious women were founded to engage in educational and charitable works. The Social Mission Sisters were started in 1908. From this institute developed the Sisters of Social Service, founded in 1923 by Margit Schlachta, and active in the U.S. since 1926. Osvát Oslay, OFM, founded the Sisters of the Poor. These and other religious congregations, in collaboration with lay Catholics, organized the Association of Catholic

Working Girls and Women and the Crusade of the Sacred Heart (Szivgárda), which became very popular among elementary school children. Ward College trained lay teachers of religion.

Jenő Kerkai, SJ, and other priests cooperated to organize the long-neglected rural youths and to instill in them a Catholic social spirit by means of retreats and "people's universities." To aid young urban workers, EMSZO (Egyházközségi Munkás Szakosztályok) and KIOE (Katolikus Iparos Ifjak Országos Egyesülete) were created in the 1930s. KALÁSZ (Katolikus Lányok Szövetkezete) sought to assist young women in country districts.

The Rising Tide of Fascism and Anti-Semitism. Late in the 1930s the Fascist states gained a steadily increasing influence in Hungary, particularly after the German annexation of Austria in 1938. As a result Hungary's fascist element became increasingly aggressive. Following the Munich Agreement in September of 1938, Hungary, supported by Germany and Italy, acquired southern Slovakia, then moved, with German backing, to occupy Carpathian Ukraine in March of 1939. When Germany, Italy and Japan concluded their three-power pact in September of 1940, the Hungarian government endorsed it.

Under pressure from German chancellor Adolf Hitler, in May of 1939 the Hungarian parliament passed drastic anti-Jewish laws, which rendered precarious the fate of Hungarian Jews, including many Christians of Jewish origin and many converts. Following the German occupation of Hungary in March of 1944, anti-Semitism was carried to extremes, as it was elsewhere under Nazi domination. Huge numbers of Jews were sent to extermination centers in Germany or Austria. Only a temporary halt in this program of genocide was effected by the strong resistance of the Hungarian populace, aided by Western European nations, the United States and particularly by the Holy See. Angelo Rotta, the papal nuncio, sent numerous protests against the deportations of Jews, organized the united remonstration of Western diplomats and gave papal safeguard to many Jews by letters of asylum and by homes rendered inviolable by Vatican protection. While many individual Christians helped the persecuted Jews, organized help only came from the Catholic and Protestant churches. Religious orders and congregations of men and women were especially active in this work, many, like as did Bishops József Mindszenty and Vilmos Apor and Archabbot Krizosztom Kelemen of Pannonhalma, endangering their own lives in the process. As a result the majority of the Jews in Budapest were spared.

The Church under Communism. After the collapse of Germany, Hungary was occupied by Soviet troops in late 1944. Some contacts with the West survived until 1948, sparking hope that the country would once again gain political and cultural independence. However, a totalitarian Communist regime remained in power until the early 1990s. By 1970 all the Church-related elementary schools and the 32 Church-related teacher's colleges existing in 1945 had disappeared. Church-related secondary schools dropped in number from 49 to eight, Catholic newspapers from 68 to four, Catholic publishers from 50 to two, and religious societies for lay Catholics from 4,000 to two.

Persecution. The Catholic Church ceased to be the state religion. Bishops, provincial superiors of religious orders and archabbots lost their membership in the upper house of parliament. In 1945 the government confiscated huge amounts of ecclesiastical possessions, depriving the Church of almost all its 1,225,000 acres of land. Despite the long-recognized need for land reform in the region, this action was not so much a reform as a confiscation intended to prepare the way for a collective farming system in which private property scarcely existed.

The government abolished also the parish assessments, resulting in a great decline in revenues and forcing the Church to depend more and more on government subsidies. The Communist regime used these subsidies as a means of intimidating the Church. Another part of the government program, which called for the confiscation of books from private and Church libraries, resulted in the sequestration or burning of a large percentage of the existing religious literature. Until 1957 it was forbidden to publish religious books, and from that date until the fall of communism this type of literature was given no space in Hungary's public libraries.

Under communism, many priests were deported or imprisoned, generally on the pretext that they were conspiring against the state. The same reason was used to justify the suppression of almost all Catholic organizations, particularly youth movements. The Soviet army of occupation put to death Bishop Vilmos Apor of Györ on March 30, 1945, while he was defending women against brutalities.

Mindszenty. József MINDSZENTY (1892–1975) led the Hungarian people in their steady opposition to communism. In the eyes of the masses he was the nation's leader. As pastor in a small town and as bishop of Veszprém (1944–45) he was very active in apostolic and social endeavors. In conjunction with several other bishops, he sought the cessation of useless blood shedding, causing fascist agents to imprison him. In 1945 he became archbishop of Esztergom, and in 1946 cardinal. As primate he composed the pastoral letters of the hierarchy revealing the details of religious persecution and decrying tyranny and atrocities, although Archbishop Gyula Czapik and other bishops preferred a more conciliatory attitude.

The year 1948, proclaimed by the cardinal as the Year of Our Lady, was marked by massive demonstrations in favor of religious and national freedom. To the Communists, Mindszenty's tremendous popularity was the main obstacle to their success. Annihilation of the Church's power and influence became their immediate objective. To attain it, and also to remove political rivals, they purged the Christian Democratic People's party, the Liberty party, and the Smallholders party, all of which favored the Church. Ferenc Nagy, prime minister and Monsignor Béla Varga, president of Parliament, went into exile. In December of 1948 Mindszenty was accused of subversion, treason, spying and currency manipulation and was arrested, tried, and condemned to death. After torture and drugs had extorted a confession of guilt from him, his statements were publicized during a showcase trial, and his sentence was commuted to life imprisonment.

Concurrent with Mindszenty's imprisonment, the anti-Catholic efforts of the government escalated. Leading Catholic priests and laymen were condemned. Arrests of many other outstanding priests followed. Almost all members of religious orders were imprisoned or deported. Compulsory religious instruction was abolished. All Catholic schools were closed, and their property was confiscated.

By means of intimidation the bench of bishops was constrained to sign an agreement with the government on Aug. 30, 1949 that assured the Church liberty and the ability to conduct its work. Six Catholic schools for boys and two for girls were returned. Except for the Benedictines, the Franciscans, the Piarists and the School Sisters of Szeged, all religious orders were suppressed, but deportations of religious ceased. The hierarchy recognized the existing regime and permitted priests to take an oath of loyalty to the government. The Church was obligated to support the economic goals of the regime and to condemn anti-Communist activities. The government, on its part, assured a meager financial subsidy to the Church. Despite this agreement, relations between the Church and the Hungarian government remained strained into the 1950s.

The Communist government now claimed the right to exercise the power formerly held by the minister of worship and education in the nomination of bishops. Through its Office of Church Affairs (1951), the government named and transferred pastors and supervised or otherwise controlled other Church business through its own "Progressive" Catholic church. In June of 1951

József Grösz, archbishop of Kalocsa, was sentenced to 15 years in prison after a forced confession of guilt. Mindszenty and Grösz were placed under house arrest in 1955. In 1956 Grösz was freed and permitted to assume leadership of the hierarchy; Cardinal Mindszenty was liberated by freedom fighters during the failed October Revolution against Soviet control led by Imre Nagy but, after the defeat of the national uprising, took refuge at the U.S. legation in Budapest, where he remained in permanent protest against the subjugation of the Catholic faith. Upon Pope Paul VI's emphatic request, Cardinal Mindszenty left for Rome in September of 1971 and later moved to Vienna. Until Mindszenty's death in 1975 the pope declared the primate's chair in Esztergom as vacant.

Bibliography: *Bibliographia hungariae*, ed. R. GRAGGER, 4 v. in 1 (Berlin 1923–39). L. BALICS, *The History of the Catholic Church in Hungary to c. 1300*, 3 v. (Budapest 1885–90) in Hung.; *The History of Christianity in the Area of Our Present Homeland until the Settling of the Hungarians* (Budapest 1901) in Hung. E. HORN, *Le Christianisme en Hongrie* (Paris 1906); *Organisation religieuse de la Hongrie* (Paris 1906). *Dictionnaire de théologie catholique*, ed. A. VACANT et al., 15 v. (Paris 1903–50) 7.1:41–61, 9.2:1566–71. C. WOLFSGRUBER, *Kirchengeschichte Österreichs-Ungarn* (Vienna 1909). T. NAGY, *History of Christianity in Hungary* (Budapest 1939), in Hung. B. HÓMAN and G. SZEKFÜ, *Hungarian History*, 5 v. (2d ed. Budapest 1935–36), in Hung. B. HÓMAN, *Geschichte des ungarischen Mittelalters*, 2 v. (Berlin 1940–43). J. CSUDAY, *Die Geschichte der Ungarn*, tr. M. DARVAI, 2 v. (2d ed. Berlin 1900). C. A. MACARTNEY, *Hungary* (London 1934); *Hungary: A Short History* (Chicago 1962); *The Magyars in the Ninth Century* (Cambridge, Eng. 1931); *A History of Hungary, 1929–1945*, 2 v. (New York 1956–57). D. G. KOSÁRY, *A History of Hungary* (Cleveland 1941). F. DVORNIK, *The Making of Central and Eastern Europe* (London 1949). L. FEKETEKÚTY, *Ungarn vom heiligen Stephan his Kardinal Mindszenty* (Zurich 1950). J. ZEILLER, *Les Origines chrétiennes dans les provinces danubiennes de l'Empire romain* (Bibliothéque des Écoles françaises d'Athènes et de Rome, fasc. 112; Paris 1918). H. LECLERCQ, "Pannonie," *Dictionnaire d'archéologie chrétienne et de liturgie*, eds., F. CABROL, H. LE CLERCQ and H. I. MARROU, 15 v. (Paris 1907–53) 13.1:1046–63. J. DEÉR, *Heathen Hungarians, Christian Hungarians* (Szeged 1934), in Hung. B. RÖSS, "Die Bekehrung der Ungarn," *Zeitschrift für Missionswissenschaft und Religionswissenschaft*, 24 (1934) 301–311. G. LÁSZLÓ, "Die Reiternomaden der Völkerwanderungszeit und das Christentum in Ungarn," *Zeitschrift für Kirchengeschicte*, 59 (1940) 125–146. A. LIPPOLD and E. KIRSTEN, "Donauprovinzen," *Reallexikon für Antike und Christentum*, ed. T. KLAUSER [Stuttgart 1941 (1950)–] 4:147–189. K. JUHÁSZ, *Das Tschanad-Temesvarer Bistum im frühen Mittelalter, 1030–1307* (Münster 1930); *Laien im Dienst der Seelsorge während der Türkenherrschaft in Ungarn* (Münster 1960). B. EBERL, *Die Ungarnschlacht auf dem Lechfeld (Gunzenlê) im Jahre 955* (Augsburg 1955). A. LEFAIVRE, *Les Magyars pendant la domination ottomane en Hongrie, 1526–1722*, 2 v. (Paris 1902). A. S. ATIYA, *The Crusade of Nicopolis* (London 1934). L. POLGÁR, *Bibliographia de historia Societatis Iesu in regnis olim corona hungarica unitis, 1560–1773* (Rome 1957). J. MISKOLCZY, *Ungarn in der Habsburger-Monarchie* (Vienna 1959). W. P. JUHÁSZ, "Social and Political Catholicism in Hungary," in *Church and Society*, ed. J. N. MOODY (New York 1953) 659–719; *Blueprint for a Red Generation* (New York 1952); *Hungarian Social Reader, 1945–1964* (Munich 1965). K. KIRALY, *The History of Attempts for* *a Catholic-Protestant Unity in Hungary* (New Brunswick, NJ 1965). *The Red and the Black: The Church in the Communist State* (New York 1953). A. GALTER, *The Red Book ! of the Persecuted Church* (Westminster, MD 1957), tr. from French. S. MIHALOVICS , *Mindszenty, Ungarn, Europa* (Karlsruhe 1949). G. N. SHUSTER, *Religion behind the Iron Curtain* (New York 1954). G. SZÉCHÉNYI, *Ungarn zwischen Rot und Rot* (Munich 1963). R. A. GRAHAM, *The Church of Silence* (New York 1955). J. S. SZABÓ, *Der Protestantis- mus in Ungarn* (Berlin 1927), tr. from Hung. W. TOTH, "Christian- ization of the Magyars," *Church History,* 11 (1942) 33–54; "Highlights of the Hungarian Reformation," *ibid.* 9 (1940) 141–156; "Trinitarianism versus Antitrinitarianism in the Hungari- an Reformation," *ibid.* 13 (1944) 255–268; "Stephan Kis of Sze- ged," *Archiv für Reformationsgeschichte,* 44 (1953) 86–181. *Bilan du Monde. Encyclopédie catholique du monde chrétien,* 2 v. (2d ed. Tournai 1964). 2:452–461. *Annuario Pontificio* has information on all diocese. *Katholikus szemle* (Rome 1936–). *Lexikon für Theolo- gie und Kirche¹,* ed. M. BUCHBERGER, 10 v. (Freiburg 1930–38) v.1, 10:383–389; v. 2, 10:488–494.

[W. JUHÁSZ]

The Church under Communism. The effects of decades of communist oppression were many. Beside the loss of political faith, the national traditions were being eliminated under far-reaching modernization policies. The agricultural sector was collectivized, and the peas- antry fled to the cities. The existing geographical and so- cial structure disintegrated. The totalitarian regime made the organization of a new social system difficult. Individ- ualism and atomization increased, as did social problems. The rate of suicides, divorces, abortions and alcoholism rose to among the highest in the world, while the life ex- pectancy of Hungarians began to drop markedly during the 1970s.

While in the official central government the role of the party and the ideology decreased, society began to be- come independent. In 1966 the government instituted economic reforms designed to overcome the inefficien- cies of central planning, increase productivity, make Hungary more competitive in world markets and create prosperity to ensure political stability. In contrast to the state-controlled economy, the home economy and moon- lighting became so dominant that it generated a greater part of the national product than did the state economy. Beside the centrally controlled press, a larger number of illegal samizdats appeared. In the state-supervised Church, there flourished an underground activity and so- cial groups. In short, the development of society out- smarted and undermined central control and supervision. Until the mid-1980s this was a spontaneous process; after that time there was a conscious pursuit to the regime. The political revolution of 1989 was successful in Hungary because it took place over an already existing market economy, on the initiatives of democratic institutions and on private enterprises.

Development of the Underground Church. While after the 1949 agreement between the bishops and the government the practice of religion was allowed in the churches, the state continued to prohibit congregational activity, all movements and organizations, public activity and religious presence in every day life. Religious in- struction became impossible, or was forced underground. As priests became the subject of surveillance due to their public profile, ties between the visible Church and the un- derground Church weakened, and the two levels began to develop independently of one another. In the end the underground sector disintegrated as well, since during the persecution everyone strove for the utmost secrecy.

On the underground, or unofficial level, the key questions for the Church were community building, reli- gious instruction, the fostering of spirituality, and the ac- quisition of a Christian culture. These goals were achieved primarily through the small communities and through camps camouflaged as tourist sites. All these were considered illegal by the state, or classified as con- spiracy against the state, and persecuted and punished ac- cordingly. In the 1970s the number of illegal Catholic communities was around 4,000, with an estimated mem- bership of 100,000. Apart from the Communist Party and the party-supervised unions, there was no other social movement comparable in size. While during the first two decades of Communism persecution was directed primar- ily towards priests and religious, from the 1960s increas- ingly the laity was targeted.

Between 1945 and 1964, 360 diocesan priests (out of a total of 3,600), 940 religious priests (out of 1,420), 200 religious brothers (out of 1,300) and 2,200 women religious (out of 10,000) were imprisoned or placed in concentration camps. Thirty-four priests were either exe- cuted or died in prison. The most common forms of per- secution against laypeople were loss or restrictions on jobs, prohibitions against higher education, and continual police surveillance; such persecutions often extended to other members of the family. Community-organizing ac- tivities resulted in imprisonment. Those arrested in these persecutions were gradually released during the 1970s; Pope Paul VI won the release of the last of the imprisoned priests in June of 1977 when he gave an audience to János Kádár, the secretary general of the Hungarian Commu- nist Party.

Both the Vatican and Hungarian bishops attempted to maintain religious life within the framework autho- rized by the state. Faced with the possibilities of leaving sees long vacant or having them filled by unworthy gov- ernment appointees, the Holy See signed an agreement with the Hungarian government on Sept. 30, 1964 where- by bishops appointed in accordance with the pact were required to take oaths of loyalty to the communist gov- ernment following their consecration. This agreement resulted in the appointment of five bishops; the state and the Vatican shared the appointment of future bishops. Further results included the opening of the Hungarian Pontifical Institute in Rome in 1965 and a pilgrim house in 1967; permission for a pilgrimage to Rome in 1972; and the opening of a Christian museum. Unfortunately, because the issue of the imprisoned priests and other Catholics was not addressed in this agreement, many Catholics felt betrayed and the Church began to lose parishioners.

The presence of Cardinal Mindszenty in Budapest had remained a constant irritant to the state, and his departure for Rome in 1971 at the urging of the pope did much to improve Hungarian-Vatican relations. György Lázár, the Hungarian prime minister, received an audience with Pope Paul VI in November of 1975, followed by a meeting between the pope and Communist Party general secretary János Kádár, two years later. In November of 1984 Pope John Paul II received the president of the Office of Church Affairs, which had been in charge of the church persecutions. In response, the state continued to loosen restrictions on Church activity. In 1978, it allowed lay people to register for theological studies and permitted Hans-Peter Kolvenbach, the superior general of the Society of Jesus, to visit his fellow Jesuits in Hungary in 1985, the latter move interpreted as an unspoken recognition of the Jesuit order, which had been suppressed in 1950.

The Fall of Communism. Because of the moderate economic programs of its communist leadership, Hungary experienced a smooth transition to capitalism and parliamentary democracy compared to many nations in the Soviet sphere. Social and political activism increased and by 1987 nationalist movements were active and Budapest-based intellectuals were increasing pressure for change. Numerous political parties came into being, their purpose to gain independence. In 1988 the constitution was revised to allow freedom of association and freedom of religion. The Soviet Union reduced its presence within Hungary, and withdrew its forces by June of 1991. A symbolic reburial in June of 1989 of executed October Revolution leader Imre Nagy and his associates, helped to give closure to those victimized during the tragedy of 1956.

On Oct. 18, 1989 a new constitution was promulgated and two days later the region became a democratic republic. The fall of Communism wrought a fundamental change in ecclesiastical policy, as well as social and political life. The new Hungarian government extended an invitation to Pope John Paul II to visit Hungary. The diplomatic ties that had been severed in 1945 were reestablished. The 1950 decree that had suppressed reli-

gious orders was repealed. Early in 1990 the Parliament passed a law guaranteeing freedom of conscience and religion. The Supreme Court nullified the 1948 verdict against Cardinal Mindszenty. Representatives of the state and the Church mutually declared void the 1950 agreement between the Hungarian Catholic Church and the state that had been forced by the Communist government. A Christian democratic coalition won the elections that were held in the spring of 1990. It was a free Hungary that received Pope John Paul II in August of 1991.

The Resurgence of the Church. Between 1945 and 1990 the nature of religion changed, moving from an integral part of Hungarian culture to an antiquated tradition out of touch with a society devoid of hope. Before the late 1950s most Hungarians attended church regularly, and all children were baptized. The failure of the October Revolution and the concurrent economic downturn marked a shift, and between 1960 and 1978 the percentage of children baptized fell to 69 percent, and Sunday church attendance fell from 70 to eight percent.

Despite the large scale de-Christianization of Hungarian society, the phenomenon of a religion based on personal conviction increased during the last two decades of the 20th century. As the public lost faith in the Communist regime during the 1980s, many reverted to their traditional faith and looked for solutions to the country's social and economic ills to the same Church-run institutions that had supported the social fabric through schools, hospitals and other social outreach programs in the past. The rural congregations of the past were replaced by an evolving urban-based faith that gained strength among the intellectuals, the young, and those in major cities. A surge in religiosity became apparent. Hungarian society, while becoming more independent economically and culturally, demonstrated that it had become independent ideologically as well. In 1986, 60 percent of the population considered themselves religious; by 1991, that figure had risen to 70 percent. In 1990 Hungary reestablished diplomatic relations with the Holy See, and three years later Pope John Paul II restructured the hierarchy to realign the diocese with territorial changes as well as the growing population.

During the 1990s the government enacted economic reforms and privatized many industries, also adopting a policy of fiscal austerity in 1995. In response to voters's demands for the inclusion of the churches in public affairs and the return of previous ecclesiastical institutions, a law was passed in 1990 that legalized religious institutions. However, three issues remained unresolved. The government declared the separation of church and state, but the meaning of the ''separation'' remained unclear. In addition, the legal status of the Churches was unclear.

Also, there was no mention of the return of Church property nationalized in the 1950s, nor of compensation for losses suffered due to persecution under the Communist era. Separation meant that the Church, plundered and ruined, was left on its own. During the debates that followed, a strong social polarization developed along religious lines, showing that communist indoctrination of anti-Church prejudice had been successful among some Hungarians. In 1991 a law was passed allowing partial compensation to the churches for property confiscated in the 1940s and 1950s, and for the restoration of property required for religious, educational, welfare, health and monastic purposes within ten years; due to financial difficulties, the law was amended in 1995. On June 20, 1997 the government and the Vatican concluded an agreement regulating state subsidies for Church-operated schools and hospitals, and setting up the restoration of former Church property. The 850 properties in state hands were scheduled to be returned between 1998 and 2010, while an additional 1,000 formerly church properties would be retained and compensated for by the state. Restitution for the over 600,000 Hungarian Jews killed during the Holocaust Parliament was also granted through the creation of a Hungarian Jewish Heritage Fund. The state also passed a law allowing citizens to allocate one percent of their personal income tax to the Church.

Into the 21st Century. The documents of Vatican II appeared in Hungarian only in 1975, and were of little relevance for a Church then attempting to survive in an oppressive environment. A defense against persecution at times led to a fundamentalist position that contravened the spirit of the Second Vatican Council. Any renewal, a dialogue with the rest of the world, or ecumenical cooperation occurred among the secular Christians and within the small, underground communities. The fall of communism resulted in a reappraisal of the Church; the recognition of its institutionalized, structured ecclesiastical order and its practical re-evaluation. During his trip to Hungary in September of 1996, Pope John Paul II encouraged Catholic leaders ''to promote unity among Christians,'' through ''engagement in dialogue, in listening, and in the advancement of those things which bring us together.''

The rebuilding of the Church would be a monumental challenge that would continue for many decades. By 2000 the religious orders were regaining their former strength, with over 60 female orders and 25 male religious orders in Hungary. The rebuilding of Catholic education institutions was underway, and by 2000 there were 50 nursery schools, 96 elementary schools, 50 secondary schools, 18 teacher-training colleges and several colleges directed by catholic communities or religious orders. The Catholic media also expanded. However, crime and an increasing indifference to religion on the part of many Hungarians was also noted, and during the 2001 ad limina visit from Hungary's bishops, the pope expressed his concern over the rising abortion rate in the country resulting from the availability of legal abortions. He encouraged the bishops to extend their ministries to younger generations, who had not grown up with faith, and establish a Catholic university in the country.

By 2000 there were 2,214 parishes tended by 2,000 diocesan and 505 religious priests. Other religious included approximately 160 brothers and 1,700 sisters, who were involved in education and other outreach programs. In 2000 a step toward resolution between Orthodox and Catholics in Hungary was made when the Patriarch of Constantinople recognized the Catholic saint King Stephen I, founder of Hungary in 1000, as an Orthodox saint; both faiths celebrated St. Stephen's day for the first time on Aug. 21, 2000, in a gathering in Budapest.

Bibliography: E. ANDRÁS and J. MOREL, *Kirche im Übergang. Die katholische Kirche Ungarns 1945–1982* (Wien 1982); *Hungarian Catholicism: A Handbook* (Wien 1983). I. ANDRÁS, ''L'Église de Hongrie,'' *Pro Mundi Vita Dossiers,* 2 (1984). P. G. BOZSOKY and L. LUKÁCS, *De l'oppression à la liberté.L'Église en Hongrie 1945–1992* (Paris 1993). A. MOLNÁR and M. TOMKA, ''Youth and Religion in Hungary,'' *Religion in Communist Lands,* 3 (1989) 209–229. M. TOMKA, ''Stages of Religious Change in Hungary,'' in *World Catholicism in Transition,* ed. T.M. GANNON (New York 1988) 169–183; *Religion und Kirche in Ungarn. Ergebnisse religionssoziologischer Forschung 1969–1988* (Wien 1990); ''Secularization or Anomy?'' *Social Compass,* 1 (1991) 93–102; ''Church and Religion in a Communist State 1945–1990,'' *New Hungarian Quarterly,* 121 (spring 1991) 59–69; ''Religion and Religiosity,'' in *Social Report,* ed. R. ANDORKA, T. KOLOSI and G. VUKOVICH (Budapest 1992) 379–393; ''Modernizzazione e Chiesa: l'esperienza dell'Ungheria comunista e postcomunista,'' in *La religione degli europei,* ed. D. HERVIEU-LÉGER, et al. (Torino 1992).

[M. TOMKA]

HUNS

Mongolians who invaded Europe via the Russian steppes during the 4th century A.D. and precipitated the Germanic invasions of the Roman world. Their identity and their reasons for migrating westward are undetermined. True nomads, grouped in many small tribes and clans without a central government, they advanced into Europe presumably after an ephemeral tribal coalition. Ammianus Marcellinus indicates that with their strange racial features, crude habits, expert horsemanship, swift movement, and short, powerful bow they had psychological and military advantages over more sedentary peoples. About 369 they swept along the conquered Alans as their unwilling allies. They decimated the Ostrogoths and occupied their land (370–375). For five decades they dominated East Central Europe as Germans fled from them

Attila ("King of the Huns"). (©Bettmann/CORBIS)

across the Rhine-Danube frontier. Little is known of their internal affairs. Loosely organized, they were ready to serve as mercenary troops for the Visigoths (Adrianople 378), Theodosius (388), Stilicho (406), or Aetius (425, 433–439). They raided the Balkans in 395, 408, and 422, but only after they had concentrated their forces under a centralized government could they threaten the Roman Empire. By 425 three brothers (Mundiuch, Octar, and Rua) ruled the Huns. When Rua died in 434 Attila and Bleda inherited the power of their uncles. Attila reigned alone after he murdered Bleda *c.* 445. The Huns crossed the Danube in raids (422, 441–443, 447) and exacted tribute from Byzantium (430, 435, 443, 448). The historian Priscus supplies valuable information about them in these years. When Marcian in 450 stopped the tribute, Attila for unknown reasons decided to undertake a western campaign. In early 451 the Huns and their Germanic allies crossed the Rhine to Metz and Orléans where they were stopped in June. Attila retreated to the "Mauriac Plain" near Troyes, where the Roman general Aetius attacked him. The battle was indecisive but Attila with-

drew and, as Aetius failed to exploit his advantage, descended into Italy in 452. Cities surrendered without resistance until food shortages, losses of troops, and an East Roman attack at his rear disposed Attila to heed the pleas of an embassy from Rome: Pope Leo I, the Prefect Trygetius, and the Consul Avienus. Attila returned to Hungary and died in 453. Quarrels among his sons permitted the Germans to rebel and shatter the Hun empire in a battle at the Nedao River in Pannonia *c.* 454. Thereafter Hunnish remnants entered the East and West Roman armies or wandered about the steppes as Kotrigurs, Onogundurs, and Utigurs. They probably merged with Bulgarians, Avars, and similar Mongol groups eventually.

Bibliography: E. A. THOMPSON, *A History of Attila and the Huns* (Oxford 1948). F. ALTHEIM, *Geschichte der Hunnen,* 5 v. (Berlin 1959–62). C. D. GORDON, *The Age of Attila* (Ann Arbor 1961).

[R. H. SCHMANDT]

HUNT, DUANE GARRISON

Bishop, preacher; b. Reynolds, Nebraska, Sept. 19, 1884; d. Salt Lake City, Utah, March 31, 1960. He was the son of Andrew Dixon and Dema (Garrison) Hunt, both Methodists. Hunt attended Cornell College, Mount Vernon, Iowa, and the State University of Iowa, Iowa City. While doing graduate work at the University of Chicago, he began to study the history of the Catholic Church, into which he was received in January 1913. He accepted a position on the faculty of the University of Utah, Salt Lake City, where further study in the field of religion led him to enter St. Patrick's Seminary, San Francisco, to prepare for the priesthood. He was ordained in 1920 by Joseph Glass, second bishop of Salt Lake City, and served in various parishes of that diocese. Its third bishop, John J. Mitty, appointed him vicar-general, a position he retained during Bishop James E. Kearney's administration (1932–37). When Kearney was transferred to the Rochester Diocese, Hunt was appointed fifth bishop of Salt Lake City and was consecrated on Oct. 28, 1937. In 1946 he was made an assistant at the pontifical throne.

Hunt was outstanding as a preacher and for many years conducted a popular radio program of Catholic information, which served to dissipate anti-Catholic prejudice and led many to enter the Church. He wrote *The People, the Clergy and the Church* (1936) and was editor of the *Intermountain Catholic* (1930–32).

[J. E. KEARNEY]

HUNT, THOMAS, BL.

Priest, martyr; *vere* Benstead; b. *c.* 1574 in Norfolk, England; d. *c.* July 11, 1600, hanged, drawn, and quartered at Lincoln. He studied at the English Colleges of Valladolid and Seville, Spain, where he was ordained (*c.* 1599). He was not in England long before he was arrested. Imprisoned at Wisbeach, Hunt escaped with five others and remained free for several months. He was with Bl. Thomas SPROTT at Saracen's Head Inn, Lincoln, when he was arrested a second time. They were convicted of treason for being priests. The two were beatified by Pope John Paul II on Nov. 22, 1987 with George Haydock and Companions.

Feast: Feb. 12; May 4 (Feast of the English Martyrs in England).

See Also: ENGLAND, SCOTLAND, AND WALES, MARTYRS OF.

Bibliography: R. CHALLONER, *Memoirs of Missionary Priests,* ed. J. H. POLLEN (rev. ed. London 1924). J. H. POLLEN, *Acts of English Martyrs* (London 1891).

[K. I. RABENSTEIN]

HUNT, THURSTAN, BL.

Priest, martyr; *alias* Greenlow; b. ca. 1555 at Carlton Hall (near Leeds), Yorkshire, England; hanged, drawn, and quartered ca. April 3, 1601 at Lancaster. The well-born Hunt was ordained (1585) at Rheims by Cardinal de Guise after he completed study there in 1584. Thereafter he worked in Lancashire, Yorkshire, and Cheshire for 15 years. On Sept. 30, 1600, he was captured near Preston by the authorities while trying to rescue Bl. Fr. Robert MIDDLETON as he was being taken to prison. They were imprisoned in London, but returned to Lancaster for sentencing and execution. Following their execution, their relics were eagerly gathered and venerated. Hunt's "haughty courage stout" was commemorated in a contemporary song. He was beatified by Pope John Paul II on Nov. 22, 1987 with George Haydock and Companions.

Feast: Feb. 12; May 4 (Feast of the English Martyrs in England).

See Also: ENGLAND, SCOTLAND, AND WALES, MARTYRS OF.

Bibliography: R. CHALLONER, *Memoirs of Missionary Priests,* ed. J. H. POLLEN (rev. ed. London 1924). J. H. POLLEN, *Acts of English Martyrs* (London 1891).

[K. I. RABENSTEIN]

HUNT, WALTER

Carmelite theologian; b. in the west of England, early 15th century; d. Oxford, England, Nov. 28, 1478. A member of the CARMELITES, he was by 1450 a doctor in theology from the University of OXFORD. He attended the Ecumenical Council of FLORENCE, during which he was presumably prominent in the doctrinal discussions with the Greeks. He wrote a work about this council and compiled its *acta,* but neither this work nor his other writings on a wide range of subjects are extant [for a list of his writings, some with *incipit*'s, see A. B. Emden, *A Biographical Register of the University of Oxford to A.D. 1500,* 3 v. (Oxford 1957–59) 2:986–987]. Hunt was a representative of the Oxford section of the English Carmelite province at a provincial meeting held in 1446 or 1447 concerning reform measures to be taken up at the general chapter of 1447. In 1450 he was a chaplain to Cardinal John KEMP, and despite his status as a friar he had dispensations for livings and held various benefices, canonries, and prebends. He was buried in the church of the Carmelite friary at Oxford.

Bibliography: J. BALE, *Scriptorum illustrium maioris Brytanniae, quam nunc Angliam et Scotiam vocant, catalogus,* 2 v. (Basel 1557–59), 1:615–616. C. DE VILLIERS, *Bibliotheca carmelitana,* ed. G. WESSELS, 2 v. in 1 (Rome 1927) 1:579–581. J. TAIT, *The Dictionary of National Biography From the Earliest Times to 1900,* 63 v. (London 1885–1900) 10:281.

[K. J. EGAN]

HUONDER, ANTON

Jesuit missiologist and ascetical writer, whose works were mainly concerned with the history, development, and peculiar problems of the various missionary fields; b. Chur, Switzerland, Dec. 25, 1858; d. Bonn, Germany, Aug. 23, 1926. He entered the Society of Jesus on Sept. 30, 1875, made his theological studies in Holland and England, and was ordained in 1889. He became a renowned preacher of the Spiritual Exercises of St. Ignatius, specializing in retreats to priests. He waged a constant battle against Europeanism in the missions, and was a contributor to and the vigorous director of the periodical *Die Katholischen Missionen.* He exercised a great and efficacious influence in his many writings on the development of the native clergy and the growth of missionary societies at home. His principal works began to be published in 1899 and extend through 1932. A three–volume work, *Die Mission auf der Kanzel und im Verein,* was published at Freiburg im Breisgau between 1912 and 1914. As an ascetical writer, he is best known for his series of meditations, *Zu Fuessen des Meisters,* in four volumes, and for his character study of St. Ignatius Loyola, published posthumously in 1932.

Bibliography: J. A. OTTO, *Lexikon für Theologie und Kirche*, ed. J. HOFER and K. RAHNER, 10 v. (2d, new ed. Freiburg 1957–65) 5:542.

[J. FLYNN]

HUREZI (HOREZI), ABBEY OF

In Moldavia, district of Vîlcea, built in 1690 by order of Prince John Constantin Brâncoveanu in the forest of Hurezi. Accomplished craftsmen, using the costliest material, worked on the abbey, which was built to commemorate Brâncoveanu's reign. It was the most important and representative Romanian monastery of its time, and was made stauropegial, i.e., subject directly to the patriarch of Constantinople. It comprises, besides the principal church, a chapel to the Virgin, several sketes (hermitages), and a hospital. Its beautiful arcades, graceful loggias, and intricate columns, as well as its windows and gates framed with floral designs, show the influence of Venice on Romanian religious art. The walls of the principal church are richly decorated with paintings representing religious subjects and also portraits of the founder, of his family and ancestry. This abbey once owned an excellent library and a rich treasure of sacred objects. At present it is inhabited by nuns.

Bibliography: N. IORGA, *Istoria bisericii românesti*, 2 v. (2d ed. Bucharest 1929–32); and G. BALS, *Histoire de l'art roumain ancien* (Paris 1922). *Enciclopedia României*, 4 v. (Bucharest 1936–43) 2:506.

[T. FOTITCH]

HURLEY, MICHAEL

Religious superior; b. perhaps in Ireland, *c.* 1780; d. Philadelphia, Pa., May 15, 1837. His father, Thomas, an Irish immigrant, settled the family in Philadelphia. In 1797 or 1798 Michael Hurley became the first American candidate for the Augustinian Order. He went to Italy for his clerical education, and was ordained in 1803. He returned to Philadelphia to assist the founder of St. Augustine's Church (1796), Rev. Thomas Matthew Carr. In 1805 Hurley went to help at St. Peter's Church in New York City, where he remained for two years. During that time he met Mrs. Elizabeth Bayley SETON and became her spiritual adviser and close friend. After returning to Philadelphia, Hurley became pastor of St. Augustine's (1820) and Augustinian superior in the U.S. (1826). As one of the promoters of the St. Joseph's Society for Catholic Orphans, he was instrumental in bringing the Sisters of Charity from Emmitsburg, Md., to Philadelphia for this work in 1814. He assisted Bp. Henry Conwell at the

public excommunication (1821) of the renegade priest William HOGAN. In 1832 he was acclaimed by Philadelphia city officials for his services during the cholera epidemic.

[A. J. ENNIS]

HURTADO, CASPAR

Jesuit theologian; b. Mondejar, New Castile, 1575; d. Alcalá, Aug. 5, 1646. He studied at the University of Alcalá de Henares, where he won high honors over many competitors in his doctoral examination. He was immediately appointed professor at the University, where he lectured with success until 1607. Then, at age 32, he resigned his chair to enter the Society of Jesus. He continued lecturing in theology, with brief stays at Murcia and Madrid. Subsequently, he went to Alcalá, where he taught for the remaining 30 years of his life. When he died, he was dean of the faculty. Hurtado's life was distinguished by learning and piety. A famous orator as well as a distinguished lecturer, he preached successfully before the Spanish Court. In his theological writings, noted for their concision and clarity, Hurtado was among the first to depart from the method of St. Thomas and to follow a system of his own. His principal works are: *De Eucharistia, sacrificio missae et ordine* (Alcalá 1620), *De matrimonio et censuris* (Alcalá 1627), *De incarnatione Verbi* (Alcalá 1628), *De Sacramentis in genere et in specie* (Alcalá 1628), *De beatitudine, de actibus humanis, bonitate et malitia, habitibus, virtutibus et peccatis* (Madrid 1632), *Disputationes de sacramentis et censuris* (Antwerp 1633), and *De Deo* (Madrid 1642).

Bibliography: C. SOMMERVOGEL, *Bibliothèque de la Compagnie de Jésus*, 11 v. (Brussels–Paris 1890–1932) 4:532–533. H. HURTER, *Nomenclator literarius theologiae catholicae*, 5 v. in 6 (3d ed. Innsbruck 1903–13) 3.922–923. J. SIMÓN-DÍAZ, *Historia del Colegio imperial de Madrid*, v.1 (Madrid 1952). J. URRIZA, *La preclara Facultad de Arte y Filosofía de la Universidad de Alcalá de Henares en el siglo de oro, 1509–1621* (Madrid 1941). N. ANTONIO, *Bibliotheca hispana sive Hispanorum*, 2 v. (Rome 1672). P. ALEGAMBA, *Bibliotheca scriptorum Societatis Jesu* (Antwerp 1643).

[J. E. KOEHLER]

HURTADO CRUCHAGA, ALBERTO, BL.

Jesuit priest; b. Jan. 22, 1901, Viña del Mar, Chile; d. Aug. 18, 1952, Santiago de Chile. Hurtado, known as "the Apostle of the Poor," experienced poverty himself following the death of his aristocratic father when he was four. While attending the Jesuit Colegio San Ignacio (1909–17) in Santiago, he spent his Sunday afternoons tending the city's poor. He postponed entering the Jesuit novitiate until Aug. 14, 1923, in order to support his family, complete his military service, and earn a law degree (August 1923) at the Catholic University of Santiago.

He entered the Jesuit novitiate at Chillán (1923–24) and Córdoba, Argentina (1925). After professing his first vows (Aug. 15, 1925), he continued his studies in the humanities, philosophy, and theology in Spain (1927–32), Ireland, and finally Belgium, where he was ordained at Louvain in 1933. After completing his final year of training at Drongen, he returned to Santiago de Chile (1936) to teach theology at the Colegio San Ignacio and pedagogy at Catholic University of Santiago.

As a frequent retreat master he affected the lives of many young men. He fostered more than 100 priestly vocations and led others to committed service as laymen. In 1941, he undertook the chaplaincy of Catholic Action's youth movement in Santiago, and later nationally. In 1944, the charismatic priest challenged female retreatants to assist the city's poor. Their response resulted in the founding of El Hogar de Cristo (Christ's Hearth), family-like housing first for homeless children, then for adults, that provided vocational training and/or rehabilitation.

In 1945–46, while studying sociology at the Catholic University of America and residing with the Jesuit community at Georgetown University, Washington, D.C., Fr. Hurtado visited Fr. Flanagan's Boys Town to adapt the concept to Chile. Returning to Chile he founded (1947) the Chilean Trade Union Association (ASICH) based on the social teachings of the Church. His last years were spent extending his work and the social teachings of the Church. He died in 1952 of pancreatic cancer.

His most famous composition is *Is Chile a Catholic country?* (Santiago 1941); however, between 1947 and 1950 he wrote on the Church's social teaching, including *Social Humanism, On Unions,* and *The Christian Social Order.* In 1951 he founded the journal *Mensaje (Messages)* to further explain magisterial teaching on social justice.

During the beatification ceremony, Oct. 16, 1994, Pope John Paul II praised him for his use of modern communications methods to spread the Gospel.

Feast: Aug. 18 (Jesuits).

Bibliography: *Alberto Hurtado: cómo lo vimos,* ed. H. M. BRUNET (Santiago, Chile 1994). *El padre Hurtado: quién fue?: qué haría hoy?* (Santiago, Chile 1994). *Padre Alberto Hurtado: ''contento, señor, contento,'' vida, obra y testimonios* (Santiago, Chile 1990). A. MAGNET, *El Padre Hurtado* (Santiago, Chile 1990). O. MARFÁN, *Alberto Hurtado: Cristo estaba en él* (Santiago, Chile 1993). L. E. MARIUS, *Mensaje y compromiso del Padre Alberto Hurtado* (Caracas 1994). J. L. RUIZ–TAGLE IBAÑEZ, *Alberto Hurtado: un hombre, un santo* (Santiago, Chile 1992). J. VADELL, *Bienaventurados los pobres* (Santiago, Chile 1978).

[K. I. RABENSTEIN]

HURTER, HUGO VON

Jesuit theologian and historian; b. Schaffhausen, Switzerland, Jan. 11, 1832; d. Innsbruck, Austria, Dec. 10, 1914. With training in historical method from his father, he became a Catholic in 1844 in Rome. He was ordained in 1855, received doctorates in philosophy and theology at the German college in Rome in 1856, and became a Jesuit in 1857. From 1858 to 1912 he taught dogmatic theology at the University of Innsbruck. His reputation rests on his works *Theologiae dogmaticae compendium* (3 v., 1876–78, 12th ed. 1909), an abridgment of the *Medulla theologiae dogmaticae* (1870, 8th ed. 1908), and especially *Nomenclator literarius theologiae catholicae* (3 v., 1871–86), an annotated catalogue of Catholic theologians from the Council of Trent to his day. The second edition of the *Nomenclator* (1891–92) includes the period 1109 to 1563, and the third edition (1903–13) begins with the Patristic period, and is indispensable for the study of the history of Catholic theology.

Hugo's father Frederick, b. Schaffhausen, March 19, 1787; d. Graz, Austria, Aug. 27, 1865; was a Protestant minister from 1808 to 1841. Through his sympathy with Catholicism, because of his attitude toward authority in an age of revolution, and perhaps through the influence of the ethos of Romanticism, he and his family were converted to the Church in 1844. He favored Metternich. In 1846 he was made a noble and historian of the court of Vienna. He wrote historical studies of Innocent III (4 v., 1834–42), Emperor Ferdinand II (11 v., 1850–64), and Wallenstein (1855, 1862), and several volumes of an autobiographical nature. A son, Henry, wrote his biography (2 v., Graz 1876–77).

Bibliography: J. M. HILLENKAMP, *P. Hurter, S.J.* (Innsbruck 1917). P. BERNARD, *Dictionnaire de théologie catholique,* ed. A. VACANT et al., 15 v. (Paris 1903–50) 7.1:332–333. F. LAKNER, ''Die Dogmatische Theologie an der Universität Innsbruck,'' *Zeitschrift für katholische Theologie* (Vienna 1877—) 80 (1958) 104, 111–113.

[F. X. MURPHY]

HUS, JOHN

Czech reformer; b. Husinec, southwest Bohemia, 1369?; d. Constance, July 6, 1415. In 1393 he received a B.A. and in 1396 an M.A. in Prague. He was ordained in 1400, and from 1402 he was the preacher at Bethlehem chapel, which had been founded in 1391 for sermons in the Czech language. He became a bachelor of theology in 1404 and taught philosophy and theology. At Bethlehem he followed the tradition of other reforming preachers, advocating reform in morals with great oratorical success. He wrote theological treatises, commentaries on Holy Scripture, various pieces on the spiritual life, and works of controversy in both Latin and Czech. Excommunicated in 1412, he left Prague to spare his fellow citizens the penalties of interdict. He was invited to the Council of CONSTANCE, where he was condemned to death in the absence of a supreme pontiff (JOHN XXIII had fled, GREGORY XII had abdicated, and BENEDICT XIII had refused to come to the council). Hus went to the stake on July 6, 1415. Under various headings the council condemned 30 propositions extracted from his works (H. Denzinger, *Enchiridion symbolorum,* [Freiburg 1963] 1201–1230).

The nineteenth century saw Hus mainly as a national hero. The historical pretext for this view was the fact that King WENCESLAUS IV in 1409 had altered the method of voting at the Charles University of Prague. To make sure that the university would support the reform-minded cardinals at the Council of PISA, who in turn would support his imperial title, Wenceslaus gave three votes to the Czech nation, which was well-disposed toward Pisa, but only one vote to the combined "foreign" nations (the Bavarian, Saxon, and Polish) who chose instead to remain faithful to Pope Gregory XII. Legend credits this victory of the Czechs over the Germans to Hus. In fact, the king had acted from purely political motives. Further, among the nations discriminated against, one, the Polish, was Slavic; while the Czech nation itself comprised a good percentage of Bohemians originally of German stock. The cleavage, then, did not have a national basis. Besides, at the moment Wenceslaus made his decision at Kutna Hora, Hus lay seriously ill in Prague. Moreover, the myth that Hus was a nationalist leader was strengthened by the fact that he was executed at Constance, despite the safe conduct that the Emperor SIGISMUND had rather unwisely granted.

There was in fact much rivalry in Prague between Czech and German masters in the early fifteenth century, but not on the basis of nationalism. Age divided them, the Czechs on the whole belonging to a younger generation. There were also doctrinal dissensions, for in philosophical matters the Czechs were usually adherents of REALISM, and the Germans of NOMINALISM. The Czechs on the whole favored reform, while the Germans, as holders of large benefices, were conservative. This explains their attitude in 1409. The Germans wanted the status quo, but the Czechs supported the accession of Wenceslaus at Pisa, because they looked forward to the end of the WESTERN SCHISM and to reform in the Church.

Influence of Wyclif. About 1400, the reformers in Bohemia came strongly under the influence of John WYCLIF. Quite early in the movement, Hus became the leader of the Wyclifite party and did not conceal his admiration for the Oxford master. He defended his books and copied him widely. But although Hus adopted Wyclif's ideals of reform, he avoided subscribing to his formal heresies. A fortiori, he knew nothing of *sola fides* or *sola scriptura,* or of the great theses of future Protestantism. Most of Wyclif's ideas were to be found in Hus, but in his writings they received a Catholic inflection. Hus insisted on the sacramental idea of the Eucharistic bread, without denying TRANSUBSTANTIATION. Basing himself on the doctrine of the Good Shepherd, he taught that a bishop was "true" in the sense of "good," only so far as he lived an evangelical life, but he did not deny the sacramental character of episcopal orders. He accepted a legal, empirical, and transitory Church, but believed in another Church whose character was changeless and eternal: the Church of the predestined, as he called it. He taught that a person was a worthy member of the Church on earth only so far as he gave indisputable signs of belonging to the heavenly Church. He did not attack indulgences, but was opposed to those granted by the antipope John XXIII, who had attached them to his "crusade" against Pope Gregory XII in Rome. The only real heresy in his teaching concerned the primacy of the Bishop of Rome. The latter appeared to him to go back to Jesus Christ, but not in the sense that he possessed a formal and necessary primacy of jurisdiction (*see* PAPACY). In addition he attributed this predominance of Rome, which was unknown in the Gospel, to the Emperor CONSTANTINE. He did not reject the idea of a pope, but accepted it only on condition that the pope's conduct marked him as a disciple of Jesus Christ.

Council of Constance. Hus' teaching alone does not account for his tragic end at CONSTANCE. Together with his compromise with Wyclifite doctrines, both his character and the provocative turn of his ideas against avarice and simony, and against the richly endowed prelates guilty of those vices, must all be borne in mind. He alienated the most influential of his earliest friends, both Czechs and reformers. These led a tireless cabal against him in Constance, where they found an audience that was only too attentive, in an assembly prejudiced by his reputation as a heretic—for which the Germans, who left Prague in 1409, were responsible. In the last analysis, the emergence of a Hus must be ascribed to the condition of Christianity after almost 40 years of schism. The degradation of authority, the perversion of institutions, the general state of corruption supported his protest.

Hus went voluntarily to the council. If he did not come to an understanding with his judges, it was primarily because he refused to renounce a body of heresies that he had either not taught at all or only to a slight degree. He was condemned because he lacked suppleness, and because he appeared before a tribunal that had already reached its verdict. Hus died pardoning his enemies, invoking the name of Jesus, and reciting the Credo.

See Also: HUSSITES.

Bibliography: Sources. *Historia et Monumenta Johannis Hus . . . ,* 2 v. (Nuremberg 1558). K. J. ERBEN, *Mistra Jana Husi Sebrané spisy české z nejstarších známých pramenů,* 3 v. (Prague 1865–68). For the many recent partial editions see below. **Literature.** J. SEDLÁK, *M. Jan Hus* (Prague 1915). V. NOVOTNÝ and V. KYBAL, *M. Jan Hus: Zivot a Učení,* 5 v. (Prague 1919–31). M. VISCHER, *Jan Hus: Aufruhr wider Papst und Reich* (Frankfurt an Main 1955). M. SPINKA, *John Hus and the Czech Reform* (Chicago 1941). F. G. HEYMANN, *John Žizka . . .* (Princeton 1955). P. DE VOOGHT, *L'Hérésie de Jean Huss* (Louvain 1960); *Hussiana* (Louvain 1960). M. SPINKA, *John Hus' Concept of the Church* (Princeton 1966).

[P. DE VOOGHT]

HUSSERL, EDMUND

Philosopher, founder and originator of the phenomenological movement in twentieth-century European thought; b. Prossnitz, Austria, April 8, 1859; d. Freiburg im Breisgau, April 27, 1938. Of Jewish background, Edmund Husserl was schooled early in Vienna and Olmütz. In 1897 he entered the University of Leipzig to study science, but he transferred in 1878 to Berlin and studied mathematics under Kronecker, Kummer, and Weierstrass. Returning to Vienna in 1881, he received his doctorate two years later for his dissertation (unpublished) on the calculus of variations. Here he fell under the strongest intellectual influence of his life, the teaching and the person of Franz BRENTANO.

Teaching. The first period of Husserl's philosophical career, the prephenomenological period, consists of the 15 years he spent as privatdocent at the University of Halle. During this time he was assistant to the psychologist Carl Stumpf and engaged in an intensive study of mathematics and logic. In *Philosophie der Arithmetik* (Halle 1891) Husserl proposed the thesis of PSYCHOLOGISM, namely, that the structure and principles of mathematics were reducible to psychic acts and the content of psychic acts.

The publication of *Logische Untersuchungen,* 2 v. (Halle 1900–01), won for Husserl the post of lecturer in philosophy at Göttingen, where he remained until 1916.

The first volume of this work gave public expression to Husserl's rejection of his earlier thesis of psychologism. The six studies of the second volume were preliminary studies in phenomenology concerned with the meaning of meaning and the theory of knowledge. His early lectures at Göttingen continued these interests in phenomenology. The five spring lectures of 1907 were published posthumously as *Die Idee der Phänomenologie.* In 1910 appeared the famous essay entitled ''Philosophie als strenge Wissenschaft,'' *Logos* (1910–11) 289–341, in which Husserl criticized both naturalism and the historicism of *Weltanschauung* philosophy in his attempt to establish philosophy as a strict science.

During the 15 Göttingen years, Husserl suffered from professional disappointments and from severe doubts over his vocation as a teacher and as a philosopher. His intense discussions attracted a small and devoted circle about him, the original Göttingen Circle, from which the Munich Circle of phenomenologists drew their ideas and enthusiasm. In 1913 Husserl collaborated with Max SCHELER in founding and editing the phenomenological journal *Jahrbuch für Philosophie und phänomenologische Forschung.* Part one of volume one was the first volume of Husserl's major work, commonly referred to as *Ideen I,* although he was never well enough satisfied with the two subsequent volumes to allow their publication in his lifetime. Here he worked out many of the detailed techniques of phenomenology. Phenomenological reduction (*epoché*) is achieved by ''bracketing off'' every irrelevant item in a given experience in order to gain direct intuition into the essence immediately given as the object of the experiencing act. In the truncated article on phenomenology in the *Encyclopaedia Brittanica* (14th ed. 1929), Husserl stated that the object of phenomenology must be to proceed from psychological descriptions of eidetic essences (first philosophy) to a transcendental phenomenology of total intentional subjectivity. Such a science of pure consciousness would be the pure phenomenology announced in the title of *Ideen I.*

In *Formale und transzendentale Logik* (Halle 1929) Husserl attempted to solve the problem of idealism through a careful phenomenological investigation of the mind's activity constituting its own ideating acts and the study of that constitution in the very moments of their genesis. Thus a ''genetic phenomenology'' was to lead to ''transcendental phenomenology,'' that is, one that would transcend the purely ideal limitation of the individual subject.

In February of 1929 Husserl delivered a series of lectures at the Sorbonne in Paris known as the *Méditations cartésiennes.* The chief purpose of these lectures was to escape from idealistic SOLIPSISM. In them Husserl maintained that the transcendental ego enters into partnership with an intersubjective community by "pairing" itself off against another ego; through empathetic understanding of the whole transcendental intersubjective community, the first ego is in community with the second.

After retirement in 1929, Husserl wrote *Die Krise der europäischen Wissenschaften und die transzendentale Phänomenologie;* here he worked out his notion of the *Lebenswelt,* the world of lived experience. Husserl's Jewish family background served as the grounds for political harassment during his last years, and so he withdrew quietly to a Benedictine monastery to be near a former student; there he died, silently aware of the transcendence of God.

Influence. It has been difficult to assign Husserl's significance in the phenomenological movement. He was slow to publish his own manuscripts—H. L. Van Breda has gathered all of Husserl's papers into the Husserlian Archives at the University of Louvain—and, at times, he openly rejected the work of his closest followers. The original circles of phenomenologists gathered in Munich and Göttingen were small, but the personnel carried out their projects with great enthusiasm and great scientific rigor. The original spirit and methodology of phenomenology remains strong in Continental thought, not only in philosophy, but also in literature, psychology, psychoanalysis, sociology, and theology.

See Also: PHENOMENOLOGY.

Bibliography: Works. *Gesammelte Werke (Husserliana)* (The Hague 1950–) v. 1, *Cartesianische Meditationen und Pariser Vorträge,* ed. S. STRASSER (1950); v. 2, *Die Idee der Phänomenologie,* ed. W. BIEMEL (1950); v. 3–5, *Ideen zu einer Reinen Phänomenologie und phänomenologischen Philosophie I–III,* ed. W. and M. BIEMEL (1950–52); v. 6, *Die Krise der europäischen Wissenschaften und die transzendentale Phänomenologie,* ed. W. BIEMEL (1954); v. 7–8, *Erste Philosophie (1923–24) I–II,* ed. R. BOEHM (1956–59); v. 9, *Phänomenologische Psychologie,* ed. W. BIEMEL (1962). Translations. *Cartesian Meditations,* tr. D. CAIRNS (The Hague 1960); *Ideas: General Introduction to Pure Phenomenology,* tr. W. R. BOYCE GIBSON (New York 1931; repr. 1962); "Philosophy as a Strict Science," tr. J. Q. LAUER, *Cross Currents* 6 (1956): 227–246. Literature. *Edmund Husserl, 1859–1959* (The Hague 1959), centenary commemoration. J. Q. LAUER, *The Triumph of Subjectivity* (New York 1958). H. SPIEGELBERG, *The Phenomenological Movement,* 2 v. (The Hague 1960). J. OESTERREICHER, "Edmund Husserl: Acolyte of Truth," *Walls Are Crumbling* (New York 1952) 49–97. M. FARBER, *The Foundations of Phenomenology* (Cambridge, Mass. 1943).

[E. W. RANLY]

HUSSITES

Even before John HUS, a Hussite spirit characterized the Czech reform movement whose origins go back to the rule of the archbishop of Prague, ERNEST OF PARDUBICE (1343–64). After the Hussite wars of the 15th century, the Hussite spirit persevered among the UTRAQUISTS (Calixtines) and in the communities of the BOHEMIAN BRETHREN. It left its imprint on the Protestant sects that entered Bohemia in the 16th century. After World War I, it prompted the foundation of a national Czechoslovak church which drew 300 priests and a million Catholics away from their allegiance to Rome (1920). It remains alive among non-Catholic Christian sects of present-day Czechoslovakia. Strictly speaking, however, the history of the Hussites in Bohemia is limited to the period between the death of Hus (1415) and the end of the Hussite wars (1436).

Pre-Hussites. There are several important figures in the pre-Hussite reform movement: Conrad of Waldhausen, summoned to Bohemia by Archbishop Ernest to assist attempts at reform (1360); JOHN MILÍČ, his successor, an ascetic visionary, originator of a program for the rehabilitation of reformed prostitutes, and the first of a line of reforming preachers reaching down to Hus; Matthias of Janov (d. 1393), a theologian of great originality whose work was a powerful attempt to restore a Biblical character to theology; Thomas of Štítné (d. 1409), a lay writer on spiritual matters who translated Christian teaching into vivid and familiar language, bringing it closer to the everyday life of the humblest man. These four spearheaded the reform. In their struggle against relaxed moral standards, they tried to lead Christians, especially the clergy, back to the way of Christ. They fought idolatry and the traffic in relics, the superstitious abuse of indulgences, pseudo pilgrimages to places made famous by "miracles" that were often only frauds, excessive veneration of images and statues, and pompous, expensive church ceremonies. The reformers, however, held the Sacrament of the Eucharist in great esteem and even encouraged frequent Communion, although they criticized all ritualistic and simoniacal administration of the Sacraments. They insisted on the need for preaching, appealing frequently to Scripture, which was the word of God to them.

About 1400, these tendencies became stronger and veered away from orthodoxy as the reformers adopted the teaching of John WYCLIF. However, the violent behavior of reformers like Hus, JEROME OF PRAGUE, James of Stříbro (Jacobellus), and Nicholas of Dresden led to a conservative reaction on the part of men like Stanislas of Znojmo and Stephen of Páleč, who were likewise reformers but who had come to the conclusion that Wyclif was a heretic. When this latter group rallied to the Church, the "Hussites" adopted a more demanding attitude, insisting on the poverty of the clergy and on the punishment of priests guilty of mortal sin. They also demanded that the word of God be preached freely. After the departure of Hus for the Council of CONSTANCE, Jacobellus at Prague inaugurated Communion under both species. Although the position of Hus on reform was less cogent than that of his friends, his death at the stake (1415) and the condemnation of Communion under both species at Constance infuriated the Czechs. These two events changed the reformers into real "Hussites." Their program was reduced to four points: the word of God should be preached freely by Christian priests, in the way that Christ had commanded; the Eucharist should be distributed under both species to all believing Christians; all who committed mortal sins should be punished, including priests; the clergy should renounce ownership of worldly goods in order to live and work according to the teaching of the Apostles.

Hussite Wars. Deaf to the remonstrances of MARTIN V and heedless of the threats of the Emperor SIGISMUND, the Hussites decided on armed resistance. Enrollment in the Hussite armies was furthered by religious motivation and also by merely temporal considerations; by the desire of the workers in the towns, especially in Prague, to wrest power from the patrician families; and by the urge of an impoverished nobility to enrich itself by seizing the possessions of the Church and by sharing in the spoils. Two crusades instigated by Martin V and a third by EUGENE IV (1431) failed to put down the Czechs. A military genius, John ŽIŽKA, had emerged from their ranks, and on his death (1421) a priest, Prokop the Great, succeeded, proving as invincible as his predecessor. It was a war marked both by acts of generosity and by atrocities. For 15 years Bohemia was ravaged. Žižka "punished one sacrilege by a thousand sacriliges." Sigismund likewise gave free rein to cruelty.

No army could conquer the Hussites, but internal dissensions did. The TABORITES, the Prague party, the Adamites, and the "Orphans" fought each other in the pauses in the war against Pope and Emperor. In 1434, the imperial troops, with the help of the Hussites from Prague, defeated the Taborite extremists at Lipany. Meanwhile, the Council of BASEL had invited the Hussites to discuss differences. After a preliminary meeting at Cheb (1432), the Council received a Hussite delegation with great ceremony in Basel itself (1433). They conferred together, and after much emendation four articles were accepted by both parties: the word of God was to be preached freely, but only by those who had received their mission from the Church; the use of the chalice was conceded to the laity, i.e., Communion under the species of wine was conceded, provided it was believed and taught that Christ was present wholly under either species; mortal sins, particularly those causing public scandal, were to be punished in conformity with divine and

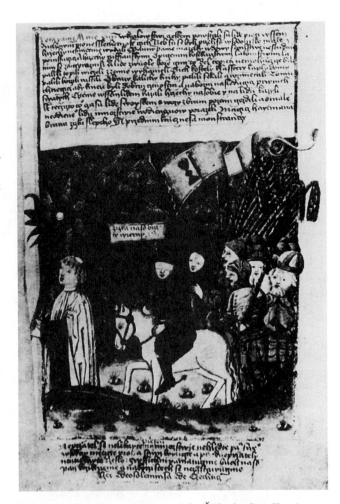

Manuscript illustration depicting John Žižka leading Hussite troops.

ecclesiastical laws, though only by legitimate authority; the Church had a right of ownership and so did the clergy, but they were obliged to administer and use their goods in an entirely just way. In 1436 these four articles, under the name of *Compacts,* were promulgated solemnly at Jihlava. On the same occasion the Czechs recognized Sigismund as their king. The status quo regarding Church property that had changed hands during the disturbances, as well as the churches taken over by the Calixtines, was accepted. Thus ended the Hussite wars. Of the Hussite movement, only the Catholic UTRAQUISTS remained, for whom the fundamental charter was provided by the *Compacts.* But the spirit of Hus was soon to revive through another great spiritual adventure, that of the Bohemian Brethren.

Bibliography: V. V. TOMEK, *Dějepis města Prahy* (Prague 1855–). C. J. VON HEFELE, *Histoire des conciles d'après les documents originaux,* tr. And continued by H. LECLERCQ, 10 v. in 19 (Paris 1907–38), 7. P. MONCELLE, *Dictionnaire de théologie catholique,* ed. A. VACANT, 15 v. (Paris 1903–50; Tables générales 1951–) 7.1:346–348. F. HREJSA, *Dějiny křesťanství v*

Bohemian martyr John Hus being burned at the stake, engraving. (Hulton-Getty/Tony Stone Images)

Československu (Prague 1950). F. G. HEYMAN, *John Žižka and the Hussite Revolution* (Princeton 1955). F. SEIBT, *Lexikon für Theologie und Kirche,* ed. J. HOFER and K. RAHNER, 10 v. (2d, new ed. Freiburg 1957–65); suppl., *Das ZweiteVatikanische Konzil: Dokumente und kommentare,* ed. H. S. BRECHTER et al., pt. 1 (1966) 5:546–549. P. DE VOOGHT, *L'Hérésie de Jean Huss* (Louvain 1960). F. BARTOS, *The Hussite Revolution, 1424–1437* (Boulder 1986). F. GRAUS, ''The Crisis of the Middle Ages and the Hussites,'' in S. OZMENT, ed. *The Reformation in Medieval Perspective* (Chicago 1971). H. KAMINSKY, *A History of the Hussite Revolution* (Boulder 1978). J. MACEK, *The Hussite Movement in Bohemia* (New York 1980).

[P. DE VOOGHT]

HUTTEN

A family of knights within the Holy Roman Empire, of whom the following are notable.

Ulrich von, Romantic imperialist German knight and militant humanist critic of the Church; b. Fortress Steck-elberg, April 21, 1488; d. Island of Ufenau, Lake Zurich, Aug. 29, 1523. Ulrich at age 11 was sent to the monastery at Fulda, but at 17 he fled; he subsequently studied at Cologne, Erfurt, and Frankfurt on the Oder, received an A.B. degree (September, 1506), and then traveled to Leipzig, Greifswald, and Rostock. He published *De arte versificandi* and the *Querelae,* blistering attacks on his former hosts, the Lötze family in Greifswald. As a member of the knightly class then rapidly losing status, Hutten looked back romantically to better days. In 1515 he addressed five orations against Duke Ulrich of Württemberg, who had murdered his cousin Hans. He studied law in Italy (1515–17) and grew increasingly critical of the Curia. He criticized current ecclesiastical abuses in a series of violent tracts, the *Vadiscus dialogus sive Trias Romana* (Roman Trinity), *Febris I, Febris II* (Fever I and II), *Inspicientes* (Spectators), and the *Nemo* (Nobody), playing up the themes of Italian exploitation of the Germans and corruption in the church. Together with Crotus

Rubeanus he published the *Epistolae obscurorum virorum,* ridiculing the scholastics of Cologne as obscurantists persecuting Reuchlin and the humanist defenders of Hebrew letters.

In 1517 he published an edition of Lorenzo Valla's *De donatione Constantini* intended to cast doubt on the legal foundation of papal temporal authority. Although Hutten did not really appreciate the deeper levels of Luther's theology, he wrote a series of polemical pamphlets in his support, the *Bulla Decimi Leonis contra errores Martini Lutheri,* in which he indicted the Pope as antichrist; the *Bullicida,* in which the papal bull, German liberty, Hutten, Franz von Sickingen, and other Germans carry on the dialogue; the *Monitor I* and *Praedones,* contrasting papal tyranny and Christian liberty; and a *Gesprächbüchlein* (Dialogue). He turned to the use of the vernacular in his first German tract, *A Remonstrance and a Warning against the Presumptuous, Unchristian Power of the Bishop of Rome and the Unspiritual Estate.* This was followed by *Invective against Aleander, Invective against the Luther-chewing Priests, Exhortation to Emperor Charles V, Litany to the Gemans,* and *Expostulatio.* Luther maintained a careful reserve, disapproving of Hutten's threats of force and resort to arms. Illness prevented Hutten from participating with Franz von Sickingen in the Knights' revolt (1522). He sought refuge with Erasmus in Basel (1522–23), but Erasmus had him driven away. Hutten avenged himself with an *Expostulatio cum Erasmo* (1523), to which Erasmus replied with his unworthy *Spongia adversus aspergines Hutteni.* Zwingli gave Hutten refuge and sent him for medical care to a pastor, Hans Klarer, of Ufenau, where he died of syphilis in poverty at the age of 35.

Moritz von, Bishop of Eichstätt; b. Arnstein, Nov. 26, 1503; d. Eichstätt, Dec. 6, 1552. He studied in Ingolstadt and became a canon in Eichstätt, 1512; canon in Würzburg, 1530; and provost of the cathedral in Würzburg, 1536. He became bishop of Eichstätt, 1539; he was personally above reproach and sought to reform the clergy of his diocese. He attended the Council of Trent, June 1543, presided at the Regensburg Colloquy, 1546, and held a diocesan synod, 1548.

Christoph Franz von, Prince-bishop of Würzburg; b. Jan. 19, 1673; d. Würzburg, March 25, 1729. Well educated, he promoted art and learning during his brief ecclesiastical career, during which he rose from dean of the cathedral to bishop.

Franz Christoph von, Bishop of Speyer; b. Wisenfeld, March 6, 1706; d. Bruchsal, April 20, 1770. He became bishop of Speyer on Nov. 14, 1743, and was created a cardinal on Nov. 23, 1761. An aristocratic ecclesiast, he patronized art and music, conducted a resplendent

Ulrich von Hutten.

court life, promoted education of laity and priests, constructed many churches and completed the castle at Bruchsal.

Bibliography: *Ulrici Hutteni Equitis Germani opera . . . ,* ed. E. BÖCKING, 7 v. (Leipzig 1859–70). H. HOLBORN, *Ulrich von Hutten and the German Reformation,* tr. R. H. BAINTON (New Haven 1937). D. F. STRAUSS, *Ulrich von Hutten,* 2 v. (Leipzig 1858). P. HELD, *Ulrich von Hutten: Seine religiös-geistige Auseinandersetzung mit Katholizismus, Humanismus, Reformation* (Leipzig 1928). L. FISCHER, ed., *Beiträge zur Geschichte der Renaissance und Reformation: J. Schlecht . . . als Festgabe* (Freising 1917), on Moritz. L. STAMER, *Kirchengeschichte der Pfalz* (Speyer 1959) 3.2:116–120, on Franz Christoph. F. ZOEPFL et al., *Lexikon für Theologie und Kirche,* ed. J. HOFER and K. RAHNER, 10 v. (2d, new ed. Freiburg 1957–65) 5:549–551. D. STRAUSS, *Ulrich von Hutten His Life and Time* (Reprint: New York 1974).

[L. W. SPITZ]

HUTTER, JAKOB

Anabaptist leader who organized orderly Christian communist communities that have survived to the present under the name Hutterites; b. Moos, South-Tyrol, date unknown; d. Innsbruck, Feb. 25, 1536. An itinerant hatmaker possessing only rudimentary formal education, Hutter early joined the Anabaptists, and he became the acknowledged leader of this movement in Tyrol after the execution of Georg Blaurock (1529). When it became known that Moravia offered a haven to religious nonconformists, Hutter tried to make it a refuge for his persecuted adherents. After initial conflicts with the existing ineffective leadership in Moravia, he reorganized some Anabaptist communities into collective farms (*Bruderhof* or *Haushaben*) in and around Auspitz, Moravia. The basic pattern developed by him at that time has been retained by his followers. As a result of renewed persecution, Hutter left again for Tyrol. He kept in touch with his Moravian followers by letters, which are his only genuine literary remains. Arrested in Clausen, Tyrol, in November 1535, he was taken to Innsbruck, where, after lengthy cross-examination and torture, he was condemned to death and burned at the stake.

Bibliography: H. FISCHER, *Jacob Huter* (Newton, KS 1956). R. FRIEDMANN, *Hutterite Studies* (Goshen, IN 1961). G. H. WILLIAMS, *The Radical Reformation* (Philadelphia 1962). K. ALGERMISSEN, *Lexikon für Theologie und Kirche*, ed. J. HOFER and K. RAHNER, 10 v. (2d, new ed. Freiburg 1957–65) 5:551. G. MECENSEFFY, *Die Religion in Geschichte und Gegenwart*, 7 v. (3d ed. Tübingen 1957–65) 3:495–496.

[G. W. FORELL]

HUTTERITES

The only pacifist ANABAPTIST sect practicing complete community of goods and the only communitarian lay group that has lasted more than 200 years. The Hutterian Brethren were founded in Moravia (1529–33) by the Tyrolean Jakob HUTTER, who was burned at the stake in Innsbruck in 1536.

Doctrine. Their Christocentric theology, derived primarily from the Synoptic Gospels, stresses several basic Anabaptist concepts: *Nachfolge Christi,* a voluntary obedience of the thorn-crowned Redeemer in a life of committed discipleship, sealed by the covenant of (adult) Baptism; and *Gelassenheit,* a serene ascetical submission to God's will. But to the Anabaptist social ideals of nonresistance, martyrdom, and a free congregational church, Hutter added a radical extension of *Gemeinschaft* as not only a loving brotherhood, ritually celebrated in the Lord's Supper, but as complete renunciation of all private property, selfless service of a community of God's chosen people (Acts 2.44–45; 4.32–35), and absolute separation from the world (2 Col 6.14–18). A corpus of traditional Hutterian doctrines was recorded in a rich collection of 16th and 17th century tracts, sermons, epistles, rules, hymns, and chronicles, which are still extant and often reread in hand-copied manuscripts.

Growth and Organization. Despite the loss of more than 2,000 martyrs in successive waves of persecution, missionaries active in all German lands sent streams of converts to establish numerous agricultural colonies in Moravia (1542–56) under the Vorsteher (bishop) Peter Riedemann and after 1546 also in Slovakia. At the peak of their "golden period" around 1585, about 25,000 brethren farmed 100 prosperous colonies on the estates of tolerant manorial lords. Turkish incursions, persecution under Cardinal Franz von Dietrichstein, and depredations during the Thirty Years' War drove them from Moravia in 1622. A colony of refugees flourished in Transylvania, but had to flee into the Ukraine (1767–70). Hundreds of "Habaner" colonists in Slovakia underwent forced conversions between 1759 and 1762 under the Empress Maria Theresa. Spiritual declines resulted in abandonment of missions after 1662 and of community of goods in 1685, 1695, and between 1819 and 1854. To avoid conscription (1874–77) the three colonies surviving in Russia migrated to the U.S., where in South Dakota they increased to 17 by 1913. Severe hardships suffered as German-language pacifists induced most Hutterites to move to Canada after 1917. In 1965 a total of 15,000 Hutterian Brethren were living in 150 colonies (four-fifths in Alberta, Manitoba, and Saskatchewan; one-fifth in South Dakota and Montana).

Now classed among MENNONITES, they have no central organization, but form three kinship branches. Each branch has a bishop, and its ministers meet at intervals. Each independent colony is governed by a minister, chosen by lot for life (subject to recall) from among a council of elders elected by adult males. Colonies have 60 to 150 members, farming from 4,000 to 12,000 acres under a business manager and assistant "bosses." Job assignments may be regularly rotated. Colonies buy coffee, salt, drygoods, leather, and machinery, and sell crops and cattle. Shoes, clothes, and furniture are homemade. Colonies pay taxes, refuse social security, but accept crop limitation payments.

Other Characteristics. Daily evening prayer hours and Sunday morning hymn-and-sermon services are held in the school. Families average six to ten children, who are taught in English until the age of 14 by teachers from outside, with religion classes in German under the minister. They live in two- to four-bedroom apartments or houses (without kitchen or dining room). While retaining their Old World costume, the Hutterites accept electricity, modern farm equipment, and trucks, but exclude radios, musical instruments, dancing, smoking, gambling, and motion pictures.

Hutterite children in Forest River Colony, Fordville, North Dakota. (©Kevin Fleming/CORBIS)

Psychological and sociological surveys have shown that despite inner tensions, most colonists have excellent mental health, well-balanced personalities, and remarkable peace of soul, with a deep Bible-based culture. Significant recent trends include moves toward more centralized authority, stress on education, participation in civic charities, and official agreements accepting dispersal patterns for daughter colonies which each existing colony must found every 15 to 20 years, owing to their record high 45.9 per 1,000 annual birth rate. M. Bach's novel *The Dream Gate* (Indianapolis 1949) and a 1963 National Film Board of Canada documentary depict life in modern Hutterite colonies.

The Society of Brothers. A modern branch of the sect was founded independently in Germany in 1922 by Dr. Eberhard Arnold (1883–1935), who was ordained in 1930 by Hutterite ministers in Canada. Its Bruderhof communities in Germany (1926–37), Lichtenstein (1934–38), and England (1936–40) moved to Paraguay during World War II (1940), and in 1954 to the U.S. Their three church communities in Rifton, NY; Norfolk, CT; and Farmington, PA, with a fourth in England, number 1,000 members engaged in education, publishing, and the manufacture of playthings. The Society of Brothers is not affiliated with the Hutterian Brethren; it practices community of goods with an open interest in current thought and problems.

Bibliography: *Die Lieder der Hutterischen Brüder,* ed. E. WALTER (Scottdale, PA 1914, 1953). A. J. F. ZIEGLSCHMID, ed., *Die älteste Chronik der Hutterischen Brüder* (Ithaca, NY 1943); *Das Klein-Geschichtsbuch der Hutterischen Brüder* (Philadelphia 1947). J. HORSCH, *The Hutterian Brethren, 1528–1931* (Goshen, IN 1931). R. FRIEDMANN, *Hutterite Studies,* ed. H. S. BENDER (Goshen, IN 1961), reprints of articles from *The Mennonite Encyclopedia.* J. A. HOSTETLER, *Education and Marginality in the Communal Society of the Hutterites* (University Park, PA 1965). "Arnold, Eberhard," in *The Mennonite Encyclopedia,* 4 v. (Scottdale, PA 1955–60) 1:162–164. "Society of Brothers," *ibid.* 4:426–427, cf. 976. *Eberhard Arnold* (Rifton, NY 1964). E. ARNOLD, *Torches Together: The Beginning and Early Years of the Bruderhof Communities,* tr. from Ger. (Rifton, NY 1964). P. J. KLASSEN, *The Economics of Anabaptism, 1525–1560* (The Hague 1964). P. RIEDEMANN, *Account of Our Religion, Doctrine and Faith,* tr. K. E. HASENBURG (London 1950). V. PETERS, *All Things Common: The Hutterites and Their Way of Life* (Minneapolis 1965). B. S. HOSTETLER and J. A. HOSTETLER, *The Hutterites in North America,* 3d. ed. (Orlando 1995).

[R. BROWN]

HYACINTH, ST.

Apostle of the Slavs, patron of Poland; b. Duchy of Oppeln, between Breslau and Cracow, Silesia, before 1200; d. Cracow, Aug. 15, 1257. His Polish name, Jacek, is a form of John; his family (Odrawaž) belonged to the nobility. He studied at the University of Cracow and perhaps also at Bologna. The traditional account of his entry into the Order of Preachers relates that he and Bl. Ceslaus (either his brother or his cousin) accompanied their uncle Ivo Odrawaž to Rome, where he was to be consecrated bishop of Cracow. There they witnessed St. DOMINIC's miraculous resuscitation of a young man who had been killed by a fall from his horse. Both Hyacinth and Ceslaus became DOMINICANS in Rome (c. 1217–18). The earliest biography of Hyacinth was written a century after his death by STANISLAUS OF CRACOW. Subsequent accounts are more like sagas than sober historical records. Although it is certain that during his time the Dominicans carried on extensive missionary activities, the exact details of Hyacinth's career have not been established. Tradition credits him with the founding of numerous convents (e.g., at Cracow, Danzig), and missionary journeys of thousands of miles on foot, preaching in many countries, including Lithuania, Bohemia, Denmark, Greece, Russia, Tatary, and Tibet, besides his native Poland. Among the miracles attributed to Hyacinth are the crossing of rivers dry-shod, restoration of sight to the blind, and the raising of the dead. Hyacinth was celebrated for his devotion to the Blessed Virgin; he died on the feast of the Assumption. He was canonized in 1594.

Feast: Aug. 17.

Bibliography: STANISLAUS OF CRACOW, *De vita et miraculis sancti Jacchonis (Hyacinthi) Ordinis Fratrum Praedicatorum* in *Monumenta Poloniae historica,* 6 v. (Lvov 1864–93) 4:818–903. *Année Dominicaine* (Lyons 1898) Aug. 2:613–646. B. ALTANER, *Die Dominikanermissionen des 13. Jh.* (Habelschwerdt 1924), best modern study. A. BUTLER, *The Lives of the Saints,* ed. H. THURSTON and D. ATTWATER, 4 v. (New York 1956) 3:338–339. R. J. LOENERTZ, "La Vie de S. Hyacinthe . . . ," *Archivum Fratrum Praedicatorum* 27 (1957) 5–38. M. F. WINDEATT, *Northern Lights: The Story of Saint Hyacinth of Poland and His Companions* (New York 1945).

[M. J. FINNEGAN]

HYDATIUS

Bishop of Chaves? (Portugal) and historian; b. Lemica, *c.* 395; d. Galicia?, after 468. As a child he visited the Levant. He was a priest in 416, bishop in 427, and legate to Aetius in 431. He opposed the misrule of the Sueves and the heresies of MANICHAEISM and PRISCILLIANISM (441–447). Hydatius seems to have annotated and kept

Bishop pronouncing a benediction, unfinished miniature from the "Benedictional of St. Ethelwold," written at Hyde Abbey, c. 965 (Add. MS 49598, fol.118v). Some scholars believe the bishop is St. Ethelwold.

up to date a list of consuls (*Fasti*) from 509 B.C. to A.D. 468 at the same time that he continued the chronicle of JEROME from 379 to 468. Dates in his chronicle are erratic, and signs and wonders become portentous; but he gives a valuable contemporary account of the barbarian invasions of Spain. After ISIDORE OF SEVILLE his work was neglected.

Bibliography: ISIDORE OF SEVILLE, *Vir. illus.,* ch. 9. *Monumenta Germaniae Historica, Auctores antiquissimi* (Berlin 1826—) 9:197–247, 11:3–36. O. SEECK, *Paulys Realencyklopädie der klassischen Altertumswissenschaft,* ed. G. WISSOWA et al. (Stuttgart 1893—) 9.1 (1914) 40–43. C. TORRES RODRÍGUEZ, "Hidacio, el primer cronista Español," *Revista de Archivos, Bibliotecas y Museos,* 62 (1956), 755–794. J. KRAUS, *Lexikon für Theologie und Kirche,* ed. J. HOFER and K. RAHNER, 10 v. (2d new ed. Freiburg 1957–65) 5:554. F. TOLLU, *Catholicisme,* 5:1170.

[E. P. COLBERT]

HYDE, ABBEY OF

Former Benedictine monastery, known also as New Minster, in the county of Hampshire, England, ancient see of WINCHESTER. In 901 King Edward the Elder, in

Pope Hyginus, effigy from 9th-century series of papal portraits in basilica of St. Paul at Rome, Italy.

fulfilment of the wishes of his father, ALFRED THE GREAT, established the New Minster in honor of the Holy Trinity, the Blessed Virgin, and St. Peter. Located at Winchester, it was the church where Alfred was buried. In 965 ETHEL-WOLD OF WINCHESTER replaced the secular canons with Benedictine monks from ABINGDON. The community moved from its original site close to Winchester cathedral to new buildings at Hyde in 1111. After destruction by fire during the Barons' War (1141) the monastery was rebuilt. It was famous for the production of fine liturgical and Biblical manuscripts, of which the *Benedictional of St. Ethelwold* is an excellent example. At the Dissolution in April 1538 the 21 monks of the community were pensioned and the buildings completely destroyed.

Bibliography: Hampshire Record Society, *Liber vitae: Register and Martyrology of New Minster and Hyde Abbey, Winchester,* ed. W. DE G. BIRCH (London 1892). *The Victoria History of the County of Hampshire and the Isle of Wight,* ed. H. A. DOUBLEDAY and W. PAGE, 5 v. (Westminster, Eng. 1900–12) v. 2. D. KNOWLES, *The Monastic Order in England, 943–1216* (2d ed. Cambridge, Eng. 1962). D. KNOWLES, *The Religious Orders in England,* 3 v. (Cambridge, Eng. 1948–60). D. KNOWLES and R. N. HADCOCK, *Medieval Religious Houses: England and Wales* (New York 1953).

[F. R. JOHNSTON]

HYGINUS, ST. POPE

Pontificate: 138 to 142 or 149. Eusebius dates his reign from 138, the year of Telesphorus's death, and indicates that Hyginus died in 142 (*Hist.* 4.10, 11; 5.6, 24).

The Liberian catalogue says he reigned 12 years. The *Liber pontificalis* fixes his term as four years and says he was a philosopher from Athens. Since Justin Martyr was a philosopher who joined the Roman church, the LP account is possibly true. There are no sources to support the report in the Roman MARTYROLOGY that he was a martyr. According to St. IRENAEUS (3.4) the Gnostic heretics VALENTINUS and Cerdo, predecessors of MARCION, came to Rome during his pontificate. Although nothing is known of their effects on the community, their presence proves that Rome was becoming a Christian intellectual center. Modern excavations do not confirm the statement in the *Liber pontificalis* that Hyginus was buried in the Vatican near St. Peter.

Feast: Jan. 11.

Bibliography: *Liber pontificalis,* ed. L. DUCHESNE (Paris 1886–92, 1958) 1:56–57, 131. É. AMANN, *Dictionnaire de théologie catholique.* ed. A. VACANT et al., (Paris 1903–50) 7.1:356–357. J. N. D.KELLY, *Oxford Dictionary of Popes* (New York 1986), 10. CH. BREURER-WINKLER, *Lexikon für Theologie und Kirche* (3d ed. Freiburg 1996).

[E. G. WELTIN]

HYLOMORPHISM

A term coined from the Greek words ὕλη (matter) and μορφή (form) and used to designate the Aristotelian-scholastic teaching that all natural or physical bodies are composed of matter and form as essential substantial principles. Apart from its philosophical importance, the doctrine has been used extensively by Catholic theologians to explain transubstantiation, the soul-body relationship, and various points of sacramental theology. This article sketches the salient features of the doctrine and then outlines its principal applications in Catholic theology.

Doctrine. Hylomorphism (sometimes spelled hylemorphism) is usually opposed to ATOMISM, which attempts to explain all natural changes and the properties of bodies in terms of atoms or some purely material principle, and to DYNAMISM, which attempts to explain similar phenomena in terms of energy or some purely formal principle. Hylomorphism, as opposed to such monistic doctrines, is dualistic in character. It maintains that the SUBSTANCE and activity of things found in the physical universe must ultimately be explained in terms of two principles, one material and the other formal, traditionally referred to as primary matter and substantial form, respectively. As coconstituting substantial principles, these are not to be confused with elements, which enter into the structure of compounds but are not their essential constitutives (*see* PRINCIPLE; ELEMENT). No inconsistency need be involved, however, in invoking both an essential composition and a structural composition in explaining the properties of bodies.

Primary matter, as the material principle, is undetermined, passive, and purely potential; the same in all bodies, it serves to explain such common features as extension, mass, and inertia. Substantial form, as the formal principle, is determining and actualizing; it accounts for the specific properties and characteristics that serve to differentiate one type of body from another. Primary matter and substantial form unite under the influence of their reciprocal CAUSALITY as intrinsic principles and go to make up secondary matter—a term used to designate a corporeal substance of some determined nature, such as marble. Secondary matter, in its turn, is regarded as the recipient of accidental forms, or accidents, that further modify the substance without changing its nature; an example of such further modification is the shape imposed on marble by a sculptor.

The existence and characteristics of primary matter and substantial form have been established traditionally by an analysis of the changes taking place in the order of nature, particularly those of the type recognizable as SUBSTANTIAL CHANGE. Other arguments in support of hylomorphic composition also have been proposed—some metaphysical, based on the application of the doctrine of potency and act to material substance; others logical, based on the analysis of modes of predication respecting subjects of change; and still others phenomenological, based on the classification of various opposed properties of bodies, such as their activity and passivity and their individuality and common essential characteristics.

When classical atomic theories of the mechanist and determinist type were in the greatest vogue among scientists, before the advent of quantum mechanics, some thinkers rejected hylomorphism as in conflict with reigning scientific theories and attempted to replace it by a more concordist doctrine referred to as HYLOSYSTEMISM. With the advent of quantum theory and the various philosophical interpretations placed on the uncertainty principle, however, together with developments in high-energy physics, particularly the discovery of large numbers of so-called elementary particles, hylomorphism has again found favor among scholastics interested in the philosophy of science and its problems. (For a fuller explanation and justification of hylomorphic doctrine, *see* MATTER AND FORM; MATTER; FORM.)

Applications. From the beginning of the 13th century on, with such thinkers as WILLIAM OF AUXERRE, PHILIP THE CHANCELLOR, and WILLIAM OF AUVERGNE, Aristotelian terminology worked its way gradually into theology. The climax of the Aristotelian development was reached in the teachings of ALBERT THE GREAT and of THOMAS AQUINAS during the high scholastic period, the latter in particular making extensive use of matter and form as well as the related doctrines of potency and act and of essence and existence in his theological elaborations. The Thomistic influence persists in Catholic theology to the present, and serves to explain much of its terminology. Yet the concepts of matter and form have not always been understood exactly as Aquinas proposed them, there being considerable controversy over such topics as the unity of substantial form in composites. Though agreeing on fundamental doctrines, the Franciscan school opposed Aquinas in a number of particulars, as did F. Suárez in a later thought context.

An important theological application of hylomorphism is in explaining what happens during the Eucharistic rite of transubstantiation. Medieval theologians regarded bread and wine as single substances composed of primary matter and substantial form. In their view, when the words of consecration are spoken, under God's action the single substance of bread is converted into the substance of Christ's Body in such a way that the substantial form of bread no longer remains; the primary matter is likewise changed, so that only the accidents of bread remain after the conversion has been effected (Thomas Aquinas, *Summa theologiae* 3a, 75.6–8). Modern Catholic theologians, making use of scientific analyses, no longer regard bread and wine as single substances but otherwise employ a similar conceptual framework when explaining the effects of consecration (*see* TRANSUBSTANTIATION).

Another theological application of hylomorphism is in explaining how the human soul is united to the body (*see* SOUL-BODY RELATIONSHIP), a teaching that has been further developed in conjunction with the doctrines of the HYPOSTATIC UNION and of the immortality of the human soul (*see* IMMORTALITY). The teaching on sanctifying GRACE as an accidental and supernatural form of the soul is also based on matter-form concepts. The same may be said in an analogous way for much of sacramental theology, where the notion of a matter and a form proper to each Sacrament has its historical origin in hylomorphism.

See Also: HYLOSYSTEMISM.

Bibliography: G. MEYER and E. GUTWENGER, *Lexikon für Theologie und Kirche*, ed. J. HOFER and K. RAHNER, 10 v. (2d, new ed. Freiburg 1957–65) 5:556–58 A. M. MOSCHETTI, *Enciclopedia filosofica*, 4 v. (Venice-Rome 1957) 2:1235–36. M. J. ADLER, ed., *The Great Ideas: A Syntopicon of Great Books of the Western World*, 2 v. (Chicago 1952) 1:526–542, 2:63–79. A. MICHEL, *Dictionnaire de théologie catholique*, ed. A. VACANT et al., 15 v. (Paris 1903–50) 10.1335–55.

[W. A. WALLACE]

HYLOSYSTEMISM

A philosophical theory proposed by Albert Mitterer (1877–1966) as an alternative to HYLOMORPHISM for explaining the substantial composition of inorganic bodies. Instead of regarding elements and compounds as composed of primary matter and substantial form, Mitterer sees them as composed of "hylons," or matter-particles (e.g., electrons, positrons, protons, and neutrons), that form a "hylomeric" (from the Greek ὕλη, matter, and μέρος, part or particle) system. Hylosystemism differs from hylomorphism in the following aspects: (1) it is pluralistic, as opposed to dualistic, in enumerating the essential constitutives of inorganic bodies; (2) it holds that the essential components of inorganic bodies are complete substances, as opposed to incomplete substantial principles; (3) it maintains a heterogeneity of structure within the inorganic body, as opposed to the homogeneous structure attributed to elements and compounds by medieval scholastics; and (4) it allows for empty space between hylons, as opposed to the continuity of matter usually associated with hylomorphic doctrine. Mitterer's ideas were popularized in the United States by C. N. Bittle (1884–1960) and enjoyed considerable vogue at a time when the Bohr-Rutherford model of the atom was regarded by scientists as an actual picture of matter's structure. They have not been generally adopted by scholastic philosophers, however, partly because of the naïve interpretation they place on hylomorphism, particularly by regarding it as irrevocably tied to the conceptual framework of medieval science, and partly because of the awkward dichotomy they introduce between explanations of substantial composition in the realm of the organic and in the realm of the inorganic.

See Also: MATTER AND FORM; ATOMISM.

Bibliography: A. MITTERER, *Wandel des Weltbildes von Thomas auf heute,* 3 v. (v.1 Innsbruck 1935; v. 2 Bressanone 1936; v. 3 Vienna 1947). C. N. BITTLE, *From Aether to Cosmos* (Milwaukee 1941). L. A. FOLEY, *Cosmology: Philosophical and Scientific* (Milwaukee 1962).

[W. A. WALLACE]

HYLOZOISM

Hylozoism, from the Greek ὕλη meaning matter, and ζωή meaning life, is the doctrine according to which all matter is animated, either in itself or as participating in the action of a superior principle, usually the WORLD SOUL (*anima mundi*).

Historical Origins. The term appears for the first time in the works of Ralph Cudworth (1617–88), one of the CAMBRIDGE PLATONISTS. Taken in its strict sense, it indicates a conception of matter that is different both from ANIMISM, the imaginary personification of nature in primitive races, and PANPSYCHISM, the theory that matter is not only alive but possesses some form of sensation or consciousness. This distinction is not clear in the early Greek philosophers, the first hylozoists recorded in history. Thales, for example, is reported by Aristotle as holding that water is the primary substrate (*Meta.* 983b 21), and that "all things are full of gods" (*Anim.* 411a 8). For Anaximander the universal material cause and animating principle is an infinite and indeterminate substance; while for Anaximenes it is air; and for Heraclitus it is fire.

Hylozoism acquires its distinct traits from Strato of Lampsacus, successor of Theophrastus as the head of the peripatetic school at Athens. While rejecting the mechanistic theory of the atomists, Strato retains their materialistic monism. He reduces all reality to matter and all vital and psychical activities to motion, thus making life a property of matter. Hylozoism is also the characteristic feature of the Stoic doctrine that the entire universe forms a unitary and living whole, in which all things are the determinate forms assumed by a divine primitive power. This power is described either as soul, mind, and reason, or as fire, ether, and pneuma, but in all cases it appears to be something material.

The Stoic concept of a world soul was taken over by the Neoplatonists and adapted to their system. For PLOTINUS and his followers the world soul is a spiritual principle emanating from the One, the supreme transcendent Being, through Intellect or *Nous*. Matter proceeds from the One inasmuch as it becomes a factor in the constitution of the phenomenal world, but in itself it forms the lowest level of being. As the principle of imperfection, limitation, and evil, it is like darkness compared to light; it is the antithesis of the One. Thus it is only in a qualified sense that Plotinus and the Neoplatonists can be called hylozoists.

Renaissance and Modern Times. The notion of an animated world gained wide acceptance among Renaissance philosophers, although it is difficult in specific cases to tell a hylozoist from a panpsychist. Paracelsus (1493–1541) conceived the world as animated by an immanent but unconscious vital principle, the *Archeus*. His disciple, J. B. van Helmont (1577–1644), called this principle *aura vitalis* and made it responsible for the formation of each individual organism and its different parts. Geronimo Cardano (1501–76) shared the belief in universal animation through the world soul, as did Giordano BRUNO after him. A somewhat different hylozoist theory was advanced by the Cambridge Platonists, Ralph Cudworth and Henry More, through their doctrine of "plastic nature," an incorporeal but unconscious substance that acts like an instrument of God in the production of natural events. The plastic nature exercises its power over matter by organizing it and directing all its motions and activities. Like an inferior soul, it does for nature as a whole roughly what the soul of a plant does for a plant.

Traces of hylozoism can be found in Spinoza's conception of reality, as well as in Leibniz's theory of monads. However it is with a group of 18th-century ENCYCLOPEDISTS, such as D. Diderot, P. J. G. Cabanis, and J. B. R. Robinet, that hylozoism comes again into prominence. Their dynamic-materialistic view of the world is in many respects similar to that of Strato. This same attitude toward the problem of matter and life can be observed in 19th-century philosophers who supported evolutionism. If matter is the only reality, as E. H. Haeckel maintained, and life comes from matter, then life must be contained virtually in matter as one of its essential properties. Hylozoism becomes for Haeckel a necessary postulate of his system.

Not all evolutionists would commit themselves to Haeckel's thoroughly materialistic view. Some, like B. SPINOZA, modified the very concept of matter and described both matter and mind as two distinct aspects of one and the same reality. For Herbert SPENCER (1820–1903) this reality is unknowable and different from matter and mind; for Gustav Fechner, Rudolph LOTZE, and William Wundt the reality is matter and mind, these two latter being nothing but its outer and its inner sides. In both views we are faced with a psychophysical parallelism that closely resembles panpsychism. The recent evolutionary theories of H. BERGSON and P. TEILHARD DE CHARDIN are also preeminently of a panpsychic nature.

Evaluation. Hylozoism fails to recognize the characteristic properties that distinguish living beings from brute matter. The differences between the two orders of being are so fundamental, especially when highly developed organisms are considered, that to confuse one with the other is to disregard completely the observational and experimental methods professed by scientists. To consider life derived from brute matter in virtue of some hidden and mysterious potentialities, without the action of an extrinsic agent, is also to violate the fundamental principle that no being can be the adequate cause of its own transition from potentiality to actuality. A being would give to itself what it does not have, or, which is equally contradictory, it would be in act and potency at one and the same time and in the same respect (*see* POTENCY AND ACT; EFFICIENT CAUSALITY). Hylozoism has, therefore, the support of neither science nor philosophy.

See Also: LIFE; MATTER; MECHANISM, BIOLOGICAL.

Bibliography: A. LALANDE, *Vocabulaire technique et critique de la philosophie* (8th ed., rev. and enl. Paris 1960). R. EISLER, *Wörterbuch der philosophischen Begriffe*, 3 v. (4th ed. Berlin 1927–30) 1:641–642. G. MARTANO, *Enciclopedia filosofica* (Venice-Rome) 2:1257–60. J. BURNET, *Early Greek Philosophy* (4th ed. New York 1957). J. CARLES, *Les Origines de la vie* (Paris 1950). G. MATISSE, *A la Source des phénomènes vitaux* (Paris 1951). J. M. DE CORRAL, *El Problema de las causas de la vida y las concepciones del mundo* (Madrid 1956).

[B. M. BONANSEA]

HYMNARY

The hymnary is the medieval liturgical book of the ROMAN RITE containing the hymns of the divine office arranged according to the days of the week and the feasts of the ecclesiastical year. Its contents, often appended to the Psalter or to the Antiphonary, were later incorporated into the medieval Roman BREVIARY.

Five extant manuscripts, representative of which is the Vatican Library's MS Vat. Reg. 11, preserve the oldest hymns in monastic usage, i.e., from the 6th century. St. BENEDICT (d. 543) gives directions for hymns in the BENEDICTINE RULE; CAESARIUS (d. 542) and AURELIAN (d. 551), bishops of Arles, name many of the hymns they prescribe for use in the canonical hours. In 1908 Clemens Blume, in comparing the rules of these successors of St. Benedict and collating the manuscripts, constructed the Old Cycle, or Old Hymnal, containing 34 hymns, which he believed comprised the original Benedictine hymnary. Although the majority of the hymns are anonymous, there are several, attributed to St. AMBROSE, that form the basis of all hymnaries in the Western Church.

In the 9th century a new cycle of monastic hymns appeared. Believed by Blume to be of Anglo-Irish origin in use in Britain since Gregory the Great, this later hymnal, which numbers 37 hymns (only seven repeated from the Old Cycle) gradually replaced the original throughout the Continent.

The Benedictine scholar André WILMART, reinterpreting Blume's conclusions in 1911, contended that the Old Cycle was only a Gallican hymnal, which fell into disuse during the Carolingian period, and that the later hymnal, for which Blume posited Anglo-Irish origin, was only the normal outgrowth of Benedictine practice as it evolved through the centuries. Wilmart's position seems justified by the progress of the BENEDICTINES during the CAROLINGIAN RENAISSANCE, when learning flourished with the expansion of monasteries, and ecclesiastical reform led to renewed interest in the liturgy and a revival in hymnology. Celtic, Byzantine, and Germanic influences impinged on the culture of this period between the 6th and 10th centuries in the Carolingian Empire, enriching and diversifying the new hymn cycles. By the 10th century, ten representative hymnals show 50 to 100 hymns, many of which are common to several hymnals. Writers of a few of these may be identified, e.g., Ambrose and his contemporary PRUDENTIUS.

The process of growth continued through the Middle Ages. Although a few hymns were added after the 16th century, the great body of Office hymns was in fact determined by 1100.

See Also: LITURGY OF THE HOURS.

Bibliography: C. BLUME, *Der Cursus S. Benedicti Nursini und die liturgischen Hymnen des 6–9 Jahrhunderts* (Leipzig 1908). *Analecta hymnica* (Leipzig 1886–1922) 51, introd. D. A. WILMART, ''Le Psautier de la Reine, N. XI, sa provenance et sa date,'' *Revue Bénédictine,* 28 (1911) 341–376. J. MEARNS, *Early Latin Hymnaries* (Cambridge, Eng. 1913). A. S. WALPOLE, *Early Latin Hymns* (Cambridge, Eng. 1922) xi–xxi. R. E. MESSENGER, ''Whence the Ninth Century Hymnal?'' *Transactions of the American Philological Association* 69 (1938) 446–464; *The Medieval Latin Hymn* (Washington 1953), valuable bibliog. and notes pp. 114–117. F. J. E. RABY, *A History of Christian–Latin Poetry* (2d ed. Oxford 1953) 36–41.

[M. I. J. ROUSSEAU/EDS.]

HYMNOLOGY

Hymnology is that discipline that is concerned with the historical and scientific study of the hymn, from both a textual and musical point of view. Hymns have been a part of Christian worship from its very beginnings. Originally the word seems to have been used to describe any song in praise of God—scriptural or not, stanzaic or free. Later it came to be applied in a more restrictive sense to any nonscriptural, religious poem in strophic form, usually in a regular meter, and set to a relatively simple melody. This entry restricts itself to the various forms of Christian hymnody as they evolved through the centuries to 1500, with emphasis on representative authors and texts, and points to some of the hymnographical problems in the field through the bibliography here cited.

Early Christian period. Christian worship first developed chiefly from patterns supplied by the traditions of the Temple and the Jewish synagogues. Thus the PSALMS and CANTICLES of the OT (as well as the NT MAGNIFICAT, NUNC DIMITTIS, BENEDICTUS) played an important role. In addition, the NT contains many passages that are regarded by scholars as echoes of early Christian hymns (among others, Phil 2.6–11; 1 Tm 3.16). In this connection reference can be made to St. Paul's words (Col 3.16) speaking of three categories of early Christian songs (among them hymns and psalms). With few exceptions, early Christian hymns did not survive because they were not written down and were often the

Manuscript folio, 8th or 9th century, hymns used in services of Greek Church.

product of sudden inspiration. They probably resembled Jewish psalms and canticles, using parallelism in structure, long enumerations of the attributes of the Deity, etc.

The transition to Greek hymnody was made by hymns composed by the Gnostics. Many texts scattered in apocryphal literature prove that GNOSTICISM made definite efforts to establish a new kind of hymnody, amalgamating early Christian and Hellenistic traditions; cf. the ''Naassene Psalm'' and the ''Valentinos Psalm''; a special place is occupied by the Odes of Solomon, which belong, perhaps, to the earliest strata. As a reaction to this tendency, a new Greek hymnody gradually emerged. To this group, besides the hymn attributed to CLEMENT OF ALEXANDRIA and the OXYRHYNCHUS hymn, belong also a Morning Hymn, a hymn of the APOSTOLIC CONSTITUTIONS (written before 150?), an Evening Hymn, the Hymn of Grace at meals, the Candle-light Hymn (Φῶς ἱλαρὸν), and others.

Syriac hymnody. This linguistic group was also affected by the propaganda of the heretics, the chief representatives of which were BARDESANES (BAR-DAISĀN) and his son Harmonius, against whose hymns the new orthodox hymns of St. EPHREM were directed. Two hymn categories are represented in Syriac hymnody: the Mêmrê, or "poetic speeches and expositions of Holy Scripture in a uniform meter, without strophic division," and the Madrashê, or songs and hymns of four to six lines and refrain. Of the latter, more than 60 are directed against the heretics; others celebrate Christian mysteries (the Incarnation), the faith, death, paradise, and similar topics. Many of these gained liturgical acceptance. By stressing apologetics, Ephrem laid the foundation of later Christian hymnody and also influenced its development in the West. He had various lesser followers: Cyrillonas (end of the 4th century), with hymns on the Crucifixion, Easter, and the Grain of Wheat; Balaeus (c. 430), creator of a new, "baleasic" form of pentasyllabic verse; and James of Sarough (d. 521), with Monophysite tendencies (*see* MONOPHYSITISM).

Greek and Byzantine hymnography. The growing influence of Hellenistic traditions roused opposition in monastic and ecclesiastical circles, and attempts were made to suppress all but hymns of scriptural character. This led to the destruction of many ancient texts and traditions; nevertheless a new hymnody emerged. At an early stage, a nonliturgical hymn poetry in the wider sense of the word was represented by METHODIUS OF OLYMPUS or Philippoi, GREGORY OF NAZIANZUS, SYNESIUS OF CYRENE, with anacreontic hymns. Metrophanes of Smyrna and ANATOLIUS, patriarch of Constantinople, also belong to this period. Synesius is particularly important since he attempted to insert Neoplatonic ideas into Christian hymns.

Three main poetic forms dominate Greek-Byzantine hymnody: the *troparion,* the *kontakion,* and the *kanon.* "The name troparion . . . was given to short prayers which, in the earliest stage of hymnography, were written in poetic prose and inserted after each verse of a psalm. In the 5th century, when the troparia were composed in strophic form and became longer, these . . . were sung only after the 3 to 6 last verses of a psalm" (Wellesz). A later development is the *kontakion,* associated with the names of Kyriakos and ROMANUS MELODUS. "The kontakion . . . consists of from 18 to 30 or even more stanzas, all structurally alike. The single stanza is called troparion; its length varies from 3 to 13 lines. All the troparia are composed on the pattern of a model stanza, the *hirmus* . . . . At the beginning of the kontakion stands a short troparion, metrically and melodically independent of it; this is the *prooemium . . .* or *kukulion*" (Wellesz). From the 7th century onward, the *kanon* was inserted into the liturgy. The *kanon* is a complex poetical form, built up of nine odes, each containing six to nine *troparia.* The odes of the *kanon* have praise character, based on the nine Canticles from Sacred Scripture. The *kontakion,* however, is a kind of poetic homily.

Nothing has been identified from the hymn production of the first Byzantine hymnodists, who are known only by name: the Orthodox Anthimus and the Monophysite Timocles, both living in the reign of the Emperor LEO I (452–474). Auxentius, poet of *troparia,* came from Syria to Constantinople during the reign of Theodosius II. His songs were inspired by Hebrew poetry, both in style and in form. Anastasius, Kyriakos, and Romanus Melodus were authors of *kontakia* and came to Byzantium during the reign of Anastasius I (491–518). Romanus learned much from St. Ephrem's Syriac hymns but followed another path in many ways. Because of their excellence, *kontakia* of these authors were in continuous use at the Imperial Palace in Constantinople until the 12th century.

One of the most famous Byzantine hymns is the AKATHISTOS, a Marian hymn that exercised great influence on both Western hymnody and Western theology from the 11th century onward. It, too, is attributed to Romanus as well as to Patriarch SERGIUS I; it is a panegyrical poem, associated with the successful defense of Constantinople against the AVARS. Its *prooemium* may have served as a model for the "hymn introductions" in the Irish *LIBER HYMNORUM.*

Traditionally, the *kanon* is said to have been invented by ANDREW OF CRETE; his technique owed much to that of Romanus. The monastery of St. Sabas near the Dead Sea became a center of *kanon* writers (Greek, Syrian, Armenian, and Coptic monks), led by JOHN DAMASCENE and his foster-brother, COSMAS THE MELODIAN, who lived during the first period of the iconoclastic controversy (*see* ICONOCLASM). The production of *kanons* later shifted to the monastery of STUDION, where Abbot THEODORE THE STUDITE excelled, following the tradition created by Romanus. These compositions, however, were no longer paraphrases of the Canticles. Contemporary and later hymnodists were Joseph of Thessalonica, Theodore's brother; the brothers THEOPHANES (c. 759–842) and Theodore; METHODIUS I, patriarch of Constantinople, mutilated by the iconoclasts; Joseph of Studion (c. 883); METROPHANES OF SMYRNA; and the nun Kasia (Ikassia), who lived during the middle of the 9th century. Emperors who wrote hymns were LEO VI (d. 917) and CONSTANTINE VII PORPHYROGENITUS (d. 959).

Near Rome a new center of hymnody was created at GROTTAFERRATA, founded by NILUS OF ROSSANO, himself a hymnodist, who was followed by his successor, Paulus, and a continuing line of poets: St. Bartholomew, Clement, Arsenius, Germanus, John, Joseph, Pancratius,

Procopius, Sophronius, and others. The last great hymn writer of the East was John Mauropus (d. 1060), metropolitan of Euchaita, the contemporary of Nicetas Serron (d. 1075). After the 11th century, Byzantine hymnody underwent a critical change; the immense number of hymns already introduced into the liturgy necessitated a limitation that slowed down further hymn production. Later Byzantine hymnography is represented by NICEPHORUS BLEMMYDES (d. 1272); Theodore I Lascaris, emperor of Nicaea (1204–22); John Vatatzes (d. 1222); GERMANUS II of Constantinople; Giobasus Vlachus (13th century); Athanasius the Younger, patriarch of Alexandria (d. *c.* 1315); GREGORY SINAITES; and Isidore Vouchiras, patriarch of Constantinople (d. 1349). The 13th and 14th centuries brought a new development in musical style, ornamented with extended *coloraturas;* among the masters of this period were John Glykys, Manual Chrysaphes, Theodulos Hieromonachus, John Koukouzeles, and John Lampadarius.

Armenian Hymnody. Among the Armenians hymnography flourished particularly in the period between the 12th and the 14th centuries. Representative Armenian hymnodists were NERSES GRATIOSUS (Snorhali; d. 1173); Nerses of Lambron (d. 1198), regarded as the second St. Paul; Chatshatur of Taraun (d. 1197); Wardan the Great (*c.* 1271); Wardan of Bardzrberd (d. *c.* 1310); John of Erznka or Erzingan (1250–1330); Constantine Srik; and the catholikos Constantine I (d. 1267).

Beginnings of western Latin hymnody. St. AMBROSE (d. 397), bishop of Milan, is regarded as the father of Latin hymnody. He had several minor predecessors. The African rhetor MARIUS VICTORINUS (*c.*360?) left three Trinitarian hymns of apologetic character, but they belong to the category of free compositions, influenced by scriptural and psalm traditions. Pope DAMASUS I, however, wrote only epigrams; no hymns can be attributed to him with certainty. The first Latin hymnodist in the traditional sense, so styled by St. Jerome and by Isidore of Seville, was St. HILARY OF POITIERS, who brought his inspiration to the West from his Eastern exile. His *Liber hymnorum* is lost, but in 1884 G. F. Gamurrini rediscovered three hymn fragments from this work. A fourth hymn, the *Hymnum dicat turba fratrum,* is ascribed to him by several MSS and by some recent scholars (S. Gaselee), but it may not be his. Two of Hilary's genuine hymn fragments are alphabetic poems. They contain many dogmatic elements, and the first of them can be regarded as a solemn declaration of faith against the Arians. The second is a symbolic representation of the rebirth of the soul in Baptism. The third treats of the Redemption, and there Christ is represented as the second Adam. None of Hilary's hymns had popular appeal, which may explain his failure as a hymnodist.

St. Ambrose and the Ambrosian school. Thus it fell to the lot of Ambrose of Milan to create a Western Latin hymnody. The occasion was the struggle against the Arians in 385 and 386, when Ambrose composed several hymns for the use of his congregation. They have a simple, popular form, are written in a uniform meter (the Ambrosian strophe: four-line iambic dimeters with irregular rhyme), and proclaim the orthodox doctrine of the Trinity. Nonetheless, they have an extremely high poetic value, never surpassed in the history of Western hymnody.

Only 14 pieces can be identified as genuine hymns of Ambrose. They serve partly for the Hours of the Divine Office, partly for the feasts of Christmas, Easter, and Epiphany; for the feasts of SS. Peter and Paul, St. John the Evangelist, St. Lawrence, SS. Gervase and Protase, and St. Agnes; and for the common of the martyrs. Four others, of which three are still used in revised form at Terce, Sext, and None, and one for the common of the virgins, cannot be attributed to him with certainty, but they belong to the Ambrosian (Milanese) tradition, together with some 41 other hymns recorded in relatively early MSS. In the AETERNE RERUM CONDITOR, a genuine hymn of Ambrose, the cock appears as the symbol of Christ. The hymn describes the awakening of the soul from the dangerous and deadly sleep of night. There, and in the *Splendor paternae gloriae,* Christ is the embodiment of light, the reflection of the Father's glory, the real Sun. He is also the eternal food and drink, by whom man becomes mystically intoxicated—an image borrowed from the writings of PHILO JUDAEUS. The Christmas hymn celebrates the mystery of the Incarnation, the Virgin Birth, and has a Mariological motif as well. The Epiphany hymn refers to four biblical miracles associated with the liturgy of the feast. The Peter and Paul hymn relates briefly their martyrdom and echoes the end of the Gospel of St. John. The Agnes hymn is a detailed narrative of her martyrdom, containing high praise of virginity. The AETERNA CHRISTI MUNERA recalls the memory of the cruel persecution of the Christians in terms borrowed from legend.

Some would call the Ambrosian hymns austere; but in fact they are well balanced, functional, and simple. "Dignity, directness, and evangelical fervor" prevail in them, and "the hymns of Ambrose reflect the mind of the great teacher of the Latin Church. Bred as a lawyer and man of affairs, with all the practical genius of the Roman . . . , Ambrose cared little for the speculations which exercised fascination over the Greek Fathers" (Raby). His hymns served well their congregational purpose and became, gems of the liturgy in the West. He was so cleverly imitated in the Milanese Church that it becomes difficult to reestablish the identity of several genuine hymns among their many imitations. In the 5th century the hymns of Ambrose spread throughout the Church, and they were accepted by the BENEDICTINE RULE for the monastic liturgy. The Ambrosian hymn formed the basis for CISTERCIAN liturgical reform in the late 11th and the early 12th centuries. St. AUGUSTINE and many others in successive generations bear witness to the greatness of Ambrosian hymnody.

Augustine himself did not imitate the Ambrosian hymns, but he wrote an alphabetic poem entitled the *Psalm Against the Donatists,* characterized by long lines with a kind of rhythmical structure, regarded by some as a precursor of later accentual poetry. It was also designed for congregational purposes and possesses a distinctly apologetic quality. Its Syriac and Punic heritage is beyond doubt; it may have been imitated by others, but the only surviving piece of its kind is a psalm by FULGENTIUS OF RUSPE.

Early Middle Ages. While Ambrose composed liturgical hymns for his congregation, his younger contemporary PRUDENTIUS was writing exquisite hymns for cultured Romans, who preferred the blending of classical literary taste and the Christian spirit. Prudentius created two collections of hymnological interest, the *Cathemerinon* and the *Peristephanon,* with 36 poems in all. The first shows occasional influence from Ambrose and contains hymns for the daily round as well as several for specific feasts. The second celebrates Spanish and Roman martyrs. Their inspiration is mainly literary, but one cannot ignore Prudentius's Christian fervor. Whereas Ambrose displays a striving for classical dignity, Prudentius betrays a romantic spirit and a rare literary talent. His poems are long and rich in imagery, but they are often rhetorical and dense. Although his hymns first served as literary readings, selections were later made from them and used as centos in the liturgy, mainly in Spain. A few (seven selections in all) are still in the Roman liturgy.

Little is known about 5th-century hymnody, except for a few names. PAULINUS OF NOLA and Paulinus of Pella (d. *c.* 459), the grandson of Ausonius, were chiefly religious poets but wrote no real hymns. The greatest hymnodist of the age was Sedulius (possibly an Italian), who wrote two poems, one of which, the *A solis ortus cardine,* is an alphabetic hymn on the life of Christ. Two extracts from it are still in the Roman Breviary, and its influence was very great throughout the Middle Ages. In this hymn much space is devoted to various biblical events, which are narrated in Ambrosian verses. Raby identified as north Italian several hymns of nonliturgical character that had hitherto been assigned to the early Spanish tradition: the *Obduxere polum nubila, Squalent arva soli, Saevus bella serit,* and *Tristes nunc populi,* which refer to the frequent incursions of the barbarians into Italy.

Quite different in character is the first St. Patrick hymn, the *Audite omnes amantes,* which may be a poem by St. Sechnall (Secundinus, d. *c.* 447). The hymn quotes from the Old Latin and not from the Vulgate version of the Bible; it is constructed of 23 alphabetic stanzas of four long lines each, accentual in type, without rhyme. Another piece, the famous Eucharistic hymn *Sancti venite,* is also ascribed to Sechnall, but probably without sufficient evidence. Of the hymns of Pope GELASIUS I little is known, but there is more solid support for the Gallican hymns that were used in religious houses of the 6th century or earlier. CAESARIUS OF ARLES and his successor, AURELIAN OF ARLES, list nine of these, in addition to several Ambrosian hymns. The Ambrosian form survives, but makes some concessions to the accentual rhythmical principle; assonance is sparsely used, as in several other contemporary poems. All the hymns in question served the daily liturgy. The cult of the saints is more strongly reflected in the hymnody of ENNODIUS, bishop of Pavia, a mediocre poet who wrote the first Marian hymn, the *Ut virginem fetam.* The attribution of the Peter and Paul hymn, the *Aurea luce et decore roseo,* to a certain Elpis, long assumed to be the wife of BOETHIUS, is certainly wrong; it is a fine Carolingian hymn (*see* DECORA LUX, AETERNITATIS; EGREGIE DOCTOR PAULE) and, in revised version, is in the Roman Breviary.

The most celebrated hymnodist of the 6th century was Venantius FORTUNATUS, an Italian priest, a favorite of the Austrasian court, who became bishop of Poitiers. He is best known for his hymns of the Holy Cross, the *PANGE LINGUA* and *VEXILLA REGIS* (also the *Crux benedicta nitet*), included in the liturgy of Passiontide. He was, moreover, the author of another hymn, the *Tempore florigero,* which became the model for numerous processional hymns in the Middle Ages of the type, *Salve festa dies.* Two further hymns, the *Agnoscat omne saeculum* and *QUEM TERRA, PONTUS, SIDERA,* were wrongly ascribed to him. King Chilperic of Neustria (d. 584) was another contemporary hymnodist (e.g. his Medard hymn). Liturgical MSS attribute the *Tellus ac aethra iubilent,* a hymn for the mandatum on Holy Thursday, to Bp. Flavius of Châlon-sur-Saône (d. 591). Its dramatic text recalls the biblical events on which the ceremony is based.

Seventh and Eighth Centuries. The authorship of GREGORY I (THE GREAT) in the field of hymnology has aroused much controversy. C. Blume ascribed 16 hymns to Gregory, but it cannot be proved that he is the author, even if most of them were written by the same hand. The Milanese poet Maximian (c. 600) composed hymns for use in the local liturgy, e.g., his Ambrose hymn,

Miraculum laudabile. An Irish hymn of the same period is the famous *Altus prosator,* an early medieval *Paradise Lost,* attributed to St. COLUMBA OF IONA. R. J. Hesbert assumes that the hymn of praise in honor of St. COLUMBAN OF LUXUEIL was written by another famous Irishman, St. GALL. Another Columban hymn, the *Nostris solemnis saeculis,* is a poem of JONAS OF BOBBIO. Here the legend of the saint is recounted and his miracles are praised.

No definite chronology can be given for the Spanish hymns of the period, listed by C. M. Diaz y Diaz. Many of them celebrate Apostles and Spanish saints; others were written for special occasions, e.g., the consecration of a church, a burial, a marriage, a war. A hymn honoring the Holy Cross, the *Ab ore verbum prolatum,* written in the meter of the *Pange lingua* of Venantius Fortunatus, may precede them in time. A. Baumstark assumes here Byzantine liturgical patterns. Another famous hymn of the period (7th century?) is the *URBS BEATA JERUSALEM,* which Diaz y Diaz assigns to Spain. It is a poetic vision of the heavenly Jerusalem, often imitated by later hymns. Among Spanish hymn writers are the following: ISIDORE OF SEVILLE, BRAULIO of Saragossa and his brother John, MAXIMUS OF SARAGOSSA, ILDEFONSUS OF TOLEDO, EUGENE II (III) OF TOLEDO, and Quiricus of Barcelona (d. 666). Among other works, there are Braulio's hymn honoring St. Aemilian (*O magna rerum Christe*) and two Eulalia hymns from Quiricus; only one hymn, the *Adsunt punicea floscula,* can be ascribed with certainty to Isidore. From Eugene several have survived, e.g., the *Inclitae parentis almae,* completed by the recent discovery of J. Leclercq. The author of the Saint-Denis hymn, the *Coeli cives adplaudite,* however, is neither Eugene of Deuil nor Eugene of Toledo, but HILDUIN OF SAINT-DENIS (first half of the 9th century).

The most important Irish monument of the period is the Antiphonary of Bangor (end of the 7th century), which also contains the *Hymnum dicat turba fratrum,* a Gallican hymn wrongly attributed to Hilary of Poitiers. It is difficult to date a peculiar Irish-Celtic hymn type called the *lorica* (breast-plate), displaying a mixture of Christian and pre-Christian Celtic beliefs. One of them, the *Suffragare trinitatis unitas,* is described as a *lorica* of GILDAS (*c.* 516–570), but without foundation. Another is the *Sancte sator suffragator,* imploring heavenly protection on the user (reciter) of the text.

Some 16 hymns represent the so-called Gallican liturgical tradition between 600 and 700 (cf. MS Vat. Reg. lat. XI, analyzed by A. WILMART). Many of them appear later in Spanish-Mozarabic and other local liturgies (cf. the *Hymnarium Moissiacense*). Anglo-Saxon hymnodists of the period include ALDHELM and the Venerable BEDE. At least 16 hymns are attributed to Bede, but many may

not be his. Among his genuine compositions is a hymn in honor of St. ETHELREDA, the *Alma Deus trinitas,* a laud of virginity, which he opposes to the heroic subjects celebrated by Virgil and Homer. Fortunately for the historian, Bede mentions a number of hymns in his other works, e.g., the St. Lupus hymn, *Trecassinorum antistitem.* He also refers to the *Apparebit repentina dies magna,* one of the precursors of the famed *Dies irae.* It is a poem containing a detailed description of the Last Judgment, based on scriptural background, and was once believed to be of the late classical period. K. Strecker sees in it reflections of the sermon tradition of St. Ephrem.

The 8th century produced another harvest of Spanish hymns, many of them composed in the territory occupied by the Arabs and therefore called MOZARABIC. Some are unusually long, such as the Christopher hymn, *0 beate mundi auctor,* based largely on the Oriental branch of the St. CHRISTOPHER legend. Two hymns can be attributed to Bp. Cixilanus of Toledo (d. 783): the *Exulta nimium turba* (on St. Thyrsus) and the *Urbis Romuleae iam toga* (on St. Torquatus). A St. James hymn (JAMES [SON OF ZEBEDEE]) in 12 strophes has an acrostic, indicating that it was composed during the reign of King Mauregato between 783 and 788. Many Irish-Latin hymns recorded in the Irish *Liber hymnorum* (MSS from the 11th century) are ascribed to persons living during the period: St. Ultan of Ardbreccan (d. 656); Colman MacMurchon, abbot of Maghbile (d. *c.* 731); Oengus MacTipraite (*c.* 741); Cuchuimne (*c.* 746); and St. Maolruain, abbot of Tallaght (d. 792). Among the saints celebrated in these hymns are BRIGID OF IRELAND, Kiaran of Cluain-Macnois, Michael, Peter, MARTIN OF TOURS, Aed MacBricc, and Andrew.

Carolingian period. The first stage of early Christian and medieval hymnography ends with a succession of Carolingian poets belonging to several generations. The earliest group lived as part of the entourage of CHARLEMAGNE and as members of his court were strongly influenced by classical literary traditions.

The Court Circle. PAUL THE DEACON (d. 799), who came from northern Italy, in addition to a St. Benedict hymn, the *Fratres alacri pectore,* was credited also with the authorship of the famous hymn in honor of St. John the Baptist, UT QUEANT LAXIS RESONARE FIBRIS. This view is no longer held; but this hymn, a masterpiece in its own right, is regarded as a product of the Carolingian era. The attribution to Paul of the Marian hymn *Quis possit amplo famine* is uncertain. His contemporary ALCUIN is the author of the St. Vedast hymn, *Christe, salvator hominis,* of the evening song *Luminis fons, lux et origo,* and the Holy Cross hymn *Crux decus es mundi.* Two hymns called the Rhythms of Gotha, written *c.* 800, belong to anonymous poets in Alcuin's circle. The first, a double alphabetic poem, *Altus auctor omnium,* was directed against the heresy of ADOPTIONISM. A large number of hymns is associated with the name of PAULINUS OF AQUILEIA, but his authorship is not quite clear. Of these, the Peter and Paul hymn *Felix per omnes* shows some affinity to that attributed to Elpis, and the two appear as an amalgam in the Roman Breviary. The hymn to St. Mark, the *Jam nunc per omne lux,* is clearly linked with Aquileia. His accentual hymn on the resurrection of Lazarus is unusually long. According to D. Norberg, the *Congregavit nos in unum,* a laud of fraternal charity that later became a part of the mandatum ceremony, is also the work of Paulinus. WALAFRID STRABO asserted that Paulinus wrote hymns for private Masses, a statement that some scholars interpret in favor of the early origin of the SEQUENCE. The Spaniard THEODULF OF ORLÉANS is the author of the processional hymn for Palm Sunday, the *GLORIA, LAUS ET HONOR.*

With this period are associated numerous Carolingian "rhythms," chiefly hymns without liturgical function, which closely adhere to the principles of accentual versification. Most of them are edited (in *Monumenta Germaniae Historica: Poetae* [Berlin 1826–]). No fixed chronology can be assigned to these works, but some of them go back to the Merovingian period. Several have eschatological character; others are Christmas and Marian hymns. One of them, the *Gratia excelso regi,* was written by a certain Gaidhaldus, a parish priest in Verona. Another, the unusual *Audiat coelum atque terra,* describing Christ's harrowing of hell, closely follows the story of the apocrypha. [*See* BIBLE] The Venetian bishop Christophorus (*c.* 800) is credited with the translation of a Marian hymn, the *Akathistos* (Meersseman). Among the anonymous hymns are two that are particularly beautiful: the *VENI CREATOR SPIRITUS*, a hymn of the Holy Spirit (*not* by Rabanus Maurus), and the famous Marian hymn *AVE MARIS STELLA*, a glorification of the Virgin Mary, who changed Eve's heritage. The hymn *Alleluia dulce carmen* refers to the symbolic liturgical ceremony of the time in which one bade farewell to the ALLELUIA during lent.

Later Carolingian period. An outstanding figure of the time was RABANUS MAURUS, archbishop of Mainz (d. 847), whom G. M. Dreves credited with some 27 hymns, most of which are of uncertain ascription and are even earlier than Rubanus. Walafrid Strabo (d. 849), a pupil of Rabanus, left many works, including several hymns and related types of poetry. His lengthy hymn on the THEBAN LEGION is particularly impressive, showing the influence of Prudentius. The renowned Lupus of Ferrières (d. after 862) was a gifted letter-writer, but the two Wigbert hymns associated with his name are somewhat less than outstanding. The deacon FLORUS OF LYONS, the adversary of the liturgist AMALARIUS of Metz, apart from

psalm paraphrases, left several hymns (Michael, John and Paul, etc.) and a *Laus cerei paschalis.* His hymns are dramatic and vivid, conjuring up great scenes and visions and contrasting Christianity and paganism.

The greatest hymnodist of the time was GOTTSCHALK OF ORBAIS (or Fulda), who was involved in the PREDESTINATION controversy and was excommunicated over that issue. His hymns are the moving expression of a soul seeing its own sinfulness and helplessness. Gottschalk left two series of hymns, the second of which was discovered by G. Morin and N. Fickermann. Eight of these are for the Hours of the Office; another is a "kind of personal litany full of melancholy but of considerable poetic power" (M. L. W. Laistner, *Thought and Letters in Western Europe,* A.D. *to 900* [New York 1957]). Five of the older series are personal confessions and prayers to Christ, and the sixth is a much-discussed poem in praise of the Trinity. Trust in the mercy of God is one of the dominating themes of these poems.

Abbot ERMENRICH OF PASSAU (ELLWANGEN), who also belonged to the circle of Rabanus, wrote a St. Sualo (Solus) hymn. Wandalbert of Prüm (d. *c.* 870) is known for his versified martyrology. His hymn of All Saints, the *Christe coelorum modulans caterva,* is not recorded in liturgical MSS. The *Unam duorum gloriam,* on SS. Chrysanthus and Daria, whose relics were translated to a church associated with Prüm, may also be by Wandalbert. BERTHARIUS of Monte Cassino wrote several hymns about which there is some confusion. Among the Spanish hymnodists of the Carolingian period were the martyr EULOGIUS and his friend Albar of Córdoba. According to B. Thorsberg, three hymns honoring SS. Euphemia, Dorothy, and Sebastian belong to Eulogius. Albar honored his friend in the acrostic poem *Almi nunc revehit.* He may have also written a hymn on St. Jerome, the *Christus est virtus,* and a nuptial hymn, *Tuba clarifica plebs.* HUCBALD OF SAINT-AMAND (d. 930), important for the history of early Offices, was the author of hymns (listed by R. Weakland), sequences, and poetic offices. Bishop Stephen of Liège is credited with the composition of the earliest Trinity Office. Abbot Gurdestin (Wurdestinus, d. 884) and the monk Clement (*c.* 870) represent the monastery of Landévennec with hymns and an Office of St. Winwaloe. The celebrated Irish poet Sedulius Scotus, living on the Continent, wrote three religious poems for the feast of the Resurrection and another praising the Irish victory over the Norsemen. His splendid Easter song, *Haec est alma dies almarum,* drew its inspiration partly from the work of Fortunatus. About 886 an unknown monk wrote two hymns in honor of St. Cornelius, and the 9th century also saw the birth of the *Caritas* songs, extolling fraternal charity in the monasteries.

Perhaps no monastery in the 9th century contributed more to the growth of hymnody than SANKT GALLEN. Three particular hymn types flourished there, the *versus,* the TROPE, and the Sequence. Three monks of the abbey wrote *versus* (processional hymns): Ratpert (d. 890), Hartmann the Younger (d. 925), and Waldram (c. 900). The authorship of Hartmann is doubted by some. Sankt Gallen produced also semiliturgical hymns of greeting (*susceptacula regum*) for members of royal families. A master, but not the inventor of the trope, was Tutilo, whose Christmas trope, *Hodie cantandus est,* has dramatic character.

Tropes are particularly important since they form the starting point for the development of the liturgical drama. The Sequence, on the other hand, is essentially a textual and musical trope attached to the Alleluia of the Mass. The first Sequence, as is now known, came from JUMIÈGES (Gimedia) to Sankt Gallen just after the middle of the 9th century. Its pattern was greatly developed and extended by NOTKER BALBULUS (d. 912), who wrote his first Sequences between 860 and 870; his *Liber ymnorum,* a generous selection of early Sequences, was edited by W. von den Steinen. In other monasteries, however, Sequences were composed before and simultaneously with Notker (e.g., the *Stans a longe*); there is also early evidence of them in a MS from Verona (before 900), at Toul, and soon afterward at the Abbey of St. Martial in Limoges. The Notkerian Sequence became the model for the German type, and that of Limoges served as an example for France. Notker wrote at least 40 Sequences and several tropes as well; his most important compositions are *Laudes Deo, Psallat ecclesia* and *Sancti Spiritus assit nobis* (to the Holy Spirit). His Peter and Paul Sequence, the *Petre, summe Christi pastor,* had widespread acceptance. In the early non-Notkerian Sequence tradition are a Swan-sequence, the *Clangam filii,* a lyrical allegory; the *Alleluia dic nobis,* a "sequence counterpart" of the farewell to the Alleluia; and a number of "double sequences" (called also *da capo* sequences), e.g., the *Dulce carmen et melodum* (a St. Maurice Sequence). The Notkerian and early French Sequences may be called "irregular"; after the 11th century the Sequence type becomes "regular," or normalized; those lying between may be regarded as transitional.

Tenth and eleventh centuries. The 10th century marks the extension of the hymn tradition. At the turn of the century lived such authors as Peter the Deacon of Naples (Barbara, Martin the Hermit, and Agnellus hymns) and EUGENIUS VULGARIUS (d. *c.* 928). Bishop RADBOD OF UTRECHT was credited with the Sequence *Ave summa praesulum* (about Martin of Tours), which is not his. However, he wrote an Office and a long hymn in honor of St. Martin. Other hymnologists include Abbot Pilgrim

of Bremati (Belegrimmus, early 10th century), the author of a Marian hymn, and ODO OF CLUNY (d. 943), with hymns about St. Martin of Tours. The first Mary Magdalen hymns, the *Jesu Christe, auctor vitae* and *Votiva cunctis orbita,* and one Sequence, the *Adest praecelsa,* are from the 10th century. Some uncertainty prevails about the identity of the poet Cosmas of Matera (or Cosmas of Japygas, 950 or early 11th century?). The Sequence *Gaude coelestis sponsa* was once wrongly attributed to the nun ROSWITHA OF GANDERSHEIM (P. von Winterfeld). EKKEHARD OF SANKT GALLEN (910–973) had six Sequences and one hymn; his Columbanus Sequence and that on the Trinity were composed *c.* 950; other hymnodists of Sanki Gallen were Notker Physicus (d. 975) and Ekkehard II (d. 990). In this period the early Sequence was gradually replaced by a new type, the Ottonian Sequence. Also at that time an anonymous poet of Reichenau (*c.* 1000) was the author of five Pentecost Sequences; the Office of St. Folcwin was written by FOLCWIN OF LOBBES (d. 990); Bishop Reginold of Eichstätt composed a multilingual (Latin, Greek, and Hebrew) "Sequence" of St. Willibald and several poetic Offices; and ADSO OF MONTIER-EN-DER (d. 998) wrote hymns not yet identified.

The English hymnodist Wulfstan of Winchester (d. 990), cantor of S. Swithun, wrote many hymns, Sequences, and tropes of local and English saints (Ethelwold, Swithun, Birinus, Augustine of Canterbury). He often followed patterns created by Bede. Two important MSS of the period are the Winchester tropes; and another liturgical book of hymnological interest is the *Hymnarium* of MOISSAC (i.e., Saint-Martin of Montauriol, *c.* 1000), with two series of hymns (about 140 items). The *Hymnarius Severinianus* is a Neapolitan hymn collection of liturgical poems used in southern Italy. In Spain many hymns are associated with the monastery of Silos. Several hymnodists of this period are Abbot Salvus Albeldensis, Orientius, Sarracinus, and Grimoaldus. The curious and dramatic processional *Sancta Maria quid est* was used in Rome about the turn of the millennium; Meersseman associates it with the name of Pope SYLVESTER II. It is difficult to date the strange hymn on the divine names, the *Deus pater piissime,* which probably originated in France under Irish influence and spread to the North. Other hymnodists *c.* 1000 are Abbot HERIGER OF LOBBES (d. 1007), author of a St. Ursmar hymn; Virus Felix Decanus, with a hymn to St. Genevieve; and the Anonymus Augiensis of Reichenau, author of three long, interesting hymns on the life of the Virgin Mary and the Holy Cross.

The greatest representative of the poetry of the cathedral schools is FULBERT OF CHARTRES (d. 1029). Some of his hymns have Oriental (Byzantine) inspiration and background (A. Baumstark), especially his hymn on the

Magi and his famous Easter hymn, *Chorus novae Jerusalem.* His hymn on peace, the *Sanctum simpliciter patrem cole,* betrays classical influences (Horace, Vergil, Juvenal), but basically it is an echo of the *Treuga Dei* movement of his age (*see* PEACE OF GOD). The morning song of Fleury, the *Phoebi claro nondum orto,* has bilingual features and is thought to have been influenced by Mithraic traditions.

Hymnodists of the 11th century are Adenulphus of Capua (d. 1058); Melus; Carus; Giraldus, a monk of Fleury; Frulandus of Murbach; Dietrich of St. Matthew in Trier; and above all, Adhémar of Chabannes (d. 1034), whose several Eparchius hymns have survived. The friends Meginfred of Magdeburg and Arnold of Vohberg (d. 1035) wrote St. Emmeram hymns. Bishop Heribert of Rothenburg (d. 1042) left a legacy of hymns in honor of the Holy Cross; of All Saints; and of SS. Willibald, Walburga, Stephen, and Lawrence. Mention should also be made of Olbert of Gembloux (d. 1048); Odoramnus of Sens (d. 1046), author of an Office (*c.* 1029) of SS. Savinian and Potentian; and BERNO OF REICHENAU, author of tropes, hymns, and Sequences. Wipo of Burgundy, the chaplain of Emperor Conrad II, was the author of the Easter Sequence *VICTIMAE PASCHALI LAUDES.* J. Handschin sees distinct apologetic tendencies in this beautiful Sequence of the transitional period. It was soon accepted by various liturgies and is still in use. ODILO OF CLUNY (d. 1048) composed, among other works, some eight Maiolus hymns. HERMANNUS CONTRACTUS of Reichenau was credited with the authorship of the Marian antiphons the *ALMA REDEMPTORIS MATER* and the *SALVE REGINA (MATER) MISERICORDIAE* . Others named as possible authors of these hymns are Adhémar of Puy and Peter of Compostella. Hermannus, moreover, composed several outstanding Sequences: the *Grates, honos* (Holy Cross), *Ave praeclara* (the Assumption), *Exsurgat almiphonus* (Mary Magdalen), *Benedictio trinae unitati* (Bl. Trinity), and an Office of St. Afra. Pope LEO IX (d. 1054) left an Office of St. Gregory the Great and several other poems.

Italian poets of the second half of the 11th century are Guaiferus, Amatus of Monte Cassino, Alberic of Monte Cassino, and Wido of Ivrea (d. 1075), who produced a number of hymns honoring Irish and other saints. Albertic has hymns on SS. Dominic of Sora and Scholastica, but he may also have been the author of many others (O. J. Blum). PETER DAMIAN, cardinal bishop of Ostia (d. 1072), was credited with many hymns, among them four eschatological poems. The beautiful *Quis est hic qui pulsat,* inspired by the Song of Songs does not belong among his poems. Alphanus of Salerno (d. 1085) composed more than 30 liturgical and nonliturgical hymns; some were elegant odes that are among his best. The *O ROMA NOBILIS,* a song on SS. Peter and Paul, is not a poem from

Verona but probably from southern Italy or Monte Cassino (B. Peebles). OTHLO OF SANKT EMMERAM (d. 1072) has two Easter hymns; Eusebius Bruno, bishop of Angers (d. 1081), with 11 hymns, and BERENGARIUS OF TOURS, with one, are all contemporary hymnodists. Gottschalk of Limburg, monk and imperial chaplain, is a master in Sequence composition (23 Sequences). The Christmas Sequence *Laetabundus,* one of the most frequently imitated of the time, is a lofty piece by an anonymous author. The first of the ''regular'' Sequences appear at the end of the 11th century; among them are many Marian Sequences and the famed *Verbum bonum et suave* for Christmas.

Twelfth century. ANSELM OF CANTERBURY was not a hymnodist, as Dreves had assumed. REGINALD OF CANTERBURY (d. 1109) wrote poems on St. Malchus, some of them possessing hymn characteristics. A typical expression of monastic mysticism is the long *Epithalamium Christi virginum* by a monk of HIRSAU (Peregrinus or Conrad of Hirsau?). Abbot THIOFRID OF ECHTERNACH (d. 1110) is the author of the Holy Cross hymn *Salve crux sancta* but not of the Willibrord Sequence *Willibrordi sancti.* Franciscus Camenus Perusinus (fl. 1098–1117?), a somewhat mysterious poet, composed a hymn in sapphics honoring Nicolas of Trani. A Spanish monk, Grimoald, wrote, among other works, three hymns on St. Felix. Some scholars have ascribed the hymn *Cives coelestis patriae* to ANSELM OF LAON (d. 1117) or to MARBOD OF RENNES (d. 1123), who has many other hymns, among them several on Mary Magdalen. HILDEBERT OF LAVARDIN (d. 1133), along with Marbod, is representative of the hymnography of the 12th-century Renaissance. His best-known hymn is the *Alpha et O, magne Deus,* a praise of the Trinity; his Christmas hymn, *Salve festa dies,* follows Fortunatus and echos Vergil's fourth *Eclogue.* Baudry of Bourgueil (d. 1130) is less important (hymns on Samson of Dol and on St. Catherine). GEOFFREY OF VENDÔME (d. 1132) wrote Marian hymns and several on Mary Magdalen. Reginaldus of Colle di Mezzo (d. 1165) is associated with hymns of St. Placid. ORDERICUS VITALIS, a historian, reworked several hymns written by Wulfstan, in addition to writing his own compositions.

Peter ABELARD, abbot of St. Gildas, was one of the most original and prolific hymnodists of the century with his *Hymnarius Paraclitensis* (133 hymns) and his series *Planctus.* By contrast BERNARD OF CLAIRVAUX wrote only two hymns, one on St. Victor, the other on Malachy of Armagh. The famous Jubilus, *Dulcis Jesu memoria,* later in the Roman Breviary ''reformed'' to *JESU, DULCIS MEMORIA,* is not Bernard's. It belongs to an English Cistercian at the end of the 12th century who was influenced by Bernard's ideas. Nicholas of Clairvaux (d. 1176) wrote some ten Sequences, only recently discovered.

Bishop Hatto of Troyes (d. 1145) may have been the author of one hynmn in the *Codex Calixtinus* (see below). BERNARD OF CLUNY (Morlas, d. 1140) wrote the poem *De contemptu mundi* and a long *Mariale,* which also contains the hymn OMNI DIE DIC MARIAE.

Other hymnodists of the period include Abbot Udalric of Maissach (d. 1150), PETER THE VENERABLE (d. 1156), and the Goliardic poet Hugh of Orleans or Primas (d. 1160), who is the author of the Holy Cross Sequence *Laudes crucis.* ADAM OF SAINT-VICTOR is credited with many regular Sequences, e.g., *Profitentes unitatem* and some 50 others. He uses many ideas borrowed from contemporary theology, biblical allusions, and legendary material and presents a highly developed system of symbolism (allegories, typology, etc.) well-established in homiletic and exegetic literature. In Adam's Sequences "the whole visible universe in its smallest details appeared . . . as fraught with a hidden meaning" (Raby). His Sequences were acclaimed and imitated as well as plagiarized. His melodies were composed not by him but by a fellow monk (H. Spanke). Another great poet is WALTER OF CHÂTILLON (d. 1180), author of many Christmas and Marian songs (nonliturgical and paraliturgical texts). The *Codex Calixtinus,* originally from the 1160s, is the chief monument of contemporary polyphonic music. Its St. James hymns (about 25) are ascribed in the MS to a variety of poets. The canonization of Charlemagne by the antipope Paschal III in 1165 brought about the composition of the famous Sequence *Urbs Aquensis, urbs regalis,* followed by many used in the Diocese of Aachen. Other hymnodists are the Englishman Osbert of Clare (d. 1160), with the first hymns of St. Anne; Bishop Adalbert III of Tournel (or of Mende, d. 1187), with 11 hymns on St. Privatus; and ECKBERT OF SCHÖNAU, belonging to the circle of German mystics. In the same group were St. HILDEGARDE OF BINGEN (d. 1179) and the Abbess HERRAD OF LANDSBERG (d. 1195), compiler of the *Hortus deliciarum.* Thomas BECKET, too, wrote a hymn on the joys of the Virgin. GODFREY OF SAINT-VICTOR (not Godfrey of Breteuil) is the author of the famous *Planctus ante nescia* (end of the 12th century). Contemporary poets are Stephen of Tournai (d. 1203), with hymns honoring St. GERARD OF SAUVE-MAJEURE; ALAN OF LILLE, one of the most outstanding poets and thinkers of the *fin du siècle,* with three hymns and a rather curious Christmas song about the failure of the arts, the *Exceptivam actionem*; and Guy of Bazoches (d. 1203), with a long series of hymns for friends and acquaintances. Mathieu, Cantor of Rievaulx, was identified by A. Wilmart as a hymnodist, a contemporary of the Cistercian Anonymus Noanus. The beginnings of Scandinavian hymnody are also associated with the 12th century.

Thirteenth century. After 1200 the Dominicans, Franciscans, and Cistercians created a new hymnody. ALEXANDER NECKHAM (d. 1217), abbot of Cirencester, was a schoolman, writing among other works Marian Sequences. Peter Corbeil (d. 1222, as bishops of Sens) compiled the texts of the Office of the FEAST OF FOOLS. The authorship of the Pentecost Sequence *VENI SANCTE SPIRITUS,* still used in the liturgy, is a debated subject; it is likely that the author was STEPHEN LANGTON, archbishop of Canterbury (d. 1228). The Cistercian Gosswin of Bossut (d. *c.* 1230) wrote hymns on St. Arnulf of Villers-en-Brabant. The most distinguished poet of the period is PHILIP, the chancellor of the University of Paris (d. 1236 or 1237), wrongly identified with PHILIP OF GRÈVE. His Mary Magdalen hymns and songs (conductus, motets, etc.) for Easter and Passiontide are unsurpassed. The Premonstratensian HERMAN JOSEPH (d. 1241) has the distinction of producing the first hymn of the Sacred Heart, the *Summi regis cor aveto.* Authors of hymns in honor of St. FRANCIS are Pope GREGORY IX (d. 1241), Thomas of Capua (d. 1243), and JULIAN OF SPEYER, author and composer of poetic Offices of great importance. THOMAS OF CELANO (d. 1250?) has been credited with three hymns, including the *DIES IRAE.* His authorship, however, cannot be proved, since the *Dies irae,* though it may be a Franciscan product, seems not to have been composed by Thomas. The first hymns for the feast of CORPUS CHRISTI were written by John of Mont-Cornillon (*c.* 1246). Arnulf of Louvain (d. 1248) is a hymnodist of the Cistercian Order; and Constantine of Medici, bishop of Orvieto (d. 1257), was the Dominican author of the Office of St. Dominic. Another Cistercian, Jean de Limoges (d. 1250 or after), wrote a hymn honoring St. Bernard. Three hymns on St. CLARE may be attributed to Pope ALEXANDER IV. THOMAS OF CANTIMPRÉ wrote a St. Jordan hymn; JAMES OF VORAGINE, author of the *Golden Legend,* supposedly composed several Syrus hymns.

Generally, St. THOMAS AQUINAS is credited with the Corpus Christi hymns, PANGE LINGUA, *SACRIS SOLEMNIIS,* and *VERBUM SUPERNUM PRODIENS,* and the Sequence *LAUDA SION SALVATOREM* ; but his authorship is difficult to prove. The *ADORO TE DEVOTE* is certainly not by him (Wilmart). BONAVENTURE (Cardinal John of Fidanza, d. 1274) is mentioned as the poet of the Holy Cross and of the *Laudismus de s. cruce,* but none of these can be surely ascribed to him. Two English poets are John of Garland (d. 1258) and Henry of Avranches; but the best English poet of the century may have been JOHN OF HOVEDEN (Howden, d. 1275), a representative of mystical poetry. Adam de la Bassée wrote poetic inserts for a dramatized form of Alan of Lille's *Anticl audianus,* and a Franciscan of high reputation, JOHN PECKHAM (Pecham), archbishop of Canterbury (1292), was the author of the long *Philo-*

mena and of a poetic Office of the Trinity with hymns. Spain is represented by another Franciscan, Gil de Zamora (*c.* 1300); the Milanese Origo Scaccabarozzi wrote a *Liber Hymnorum* for Milanese churches. Although the Franciscan JACOPONE DA TODI (Jacobus de Benedictis, d. 1306) is probably not the author of the Sequence *STABAT MATER*, it possesses a spirit common to his *Laude.* Scandinavian hymnodists are Ragvaldus I (1266) or Ragvaldus II (1321), the Dominican Jón Halldorsson (d. 1339?, author of a St. Torlach Office?), and Brynolf Algotsson (d. 1317, bishop of Skara), who wrote several hymns and other pieces.

Fourteenth and fifteenth centuries. Among the hymnodists of the 14th century are Frater Honofrius of Sulmona; William of Mandagout, bishop of Palestrina (d. 1321); Engelbert of Volkersdorf (d. 1331); the Cistercian Christian of Lilienfeld (d. before 1332), with some 150 hymns; the *plebanus* Jakob von Mühldorf (d. 1350); the English mystic and hermit Richard ROLLE DE HAMPOLE (d. 1349); Cardinal JAMES GAËTANI STEFANESCHI (d.1343); the Franciscan General Gerardus Odonis (d. 1349), with hymns for the feast of stigmatization of St. Francis; two Carthusians, Conrad of Gaming (d. 1360, called also Conrad of Haimburg) and Albert of Prague (d. 1386?); the Cistercian William de Deguilleville (d. after 1358); Johannes Decanus (*c.* 1360, in the Mosburg *Cantionale*); and a series of Scandinavian hymnodists associated with St. BRIDGET OF SWEDEN (Petrus Olavi, d. 1378; Birger Gregersson, d. 1383; NICHOLAS HERMANSSON, d. 1391) also Raymund delle Vigne (d. 1399); Archbishop Johannes de Jetzenstein (d. 1400) and Cardinal ADAM EASTON (d. 1397), hymnodists of the Visitation. Philippe de Mézières (Frater Rostagnus, d. 1405), too, belongs to this group, composing hymns for Mary's Presentation. About the turn of the century there were Peter of Candia, the antipope Alexander V (d. 1410); Lippold of Steinberg (d. 1415); Jean GERSON OF France (d. 1429), with hymns and poems on St. Joseph; and John HUS (1415). The monk Ronto, Dante's translator into Latin (d. 1443); Abbot Ulric of Stöcklin (d. 1443); Winand Ort von Steeg (d. 1447); and Johannes Hofmann, bishop of Meissen (d. 1451), belong to another generation. Two Dominicans are Petrus Ranzanus and Martialis Auribellus (*c.* 1455); John Benechini and John de Beka are less important. Pope PIUS II (Aeneas Silvius Piccolomini, d. 1464) is credited with hymns on St. Catherine of Siena. DENIS THE CARTHUSIAN (d. 1471) left more than 120 hymns written in the mystical spirit. The spirit of the DEVOTIO MODERNA is expressed in hymns by THOMAS À KEMPIS (d. 1471). Jerome of Wörth (Hieronymus de Werdea, d. 1475); Heinrich of Gundelfingen (d. 1490, hymns on St. NICHOLAS OF FLÜE); Arnoldus Heimerich (d. 1491); and the Carthusian Antonius de Lantsee (*c.* 1492) are representatives of late medieval hymnody. The Franciscan Jean Tisserand (d. 1494) wrote, among other works, the Easter song *O FILII ET FILIAE.* Among the last names to be mentioned are Johannes Mauburnus, abbot of Livry (d. 1503), and Granciscan Bernardino de' Busti (d. 1500).

There were many minor hymnodists in the period, but the new spirit was then represented by the humanists. The tradition of Western Latin hymnody, more than 1,000 years old, was interrupted by HUMANISM, by the REFORMATION; and by the COUNTER REFORMATION, which brought forth a new hymnody, only faintly resembling the old hymns and Sequences, written for use in dioceses and religious orders, which are still found in the Roman Breviary and in local liturgies. The systematic study of hymnody did not emerge until the 19th century. It began with the work of H. A. Daniel, J. Kehrein, F. J. Mone, G. Morel, G. Milchsack, R. C. Trench, J. M. Neale, R. Stevenson, W. H. Frere, G. E. Klemming, and mainly the two Jesuits G. M. Dreves and C. Blume.

Bibliography: A. THIERFELDER, *De Christianorum psalmis et hymnis usque ad Ambrosii tempora* (Leipzig 1868). J. B. PITRA, *Hymnographie de l'Église grecque* (Rome 1867). W. VON CHRIST and M. PARANIKAS, eds., *Anthologia Graeca carminum Christianorum* (Leipzig 1871). P. MAAS, *Frühbyzantinische Kirchenpoesie* (2d ed. Berlin 1931), cf. also G. CAMMELLI, ed., *Romano il melode* (Florence 1930). E. J. WELLESZ, "The Earliest Example of Christian Hymnody," *Classical Quarterly* 39 (1945) 34–45. H. FOLLIERI, *Initia hymnorum ecclesiae Graecae,* 4 v. (Studi e Testi 211–214; 1960–63), a complete list of Greek and Byzantine hymns known to date (a most important instrument of research and study). E. WELLESZ, *A History of Byzantine Music and Hymnography,* a summary of modern research with extensive bibliog. M. SIMONETTI, "Studi sull'innologia popolare cristiana dei primi secoli," *Atti dell'Accademia nazionale dei Lincei. Memorie Classe di scienze morali, storiche e filologiche,* Ser. 8, 6 (1952) fasc. 6. Texts. *Analecta hymnica* (Leipzig 1886–1922) is the largest single collection. W. BULST, ed., *Hymni Latini antiquissimi LXXV* (Heidelberg 1956), an excellent source for the earliest hymns, superseding in many ways A. S. WALPOLE, ed., *Early Latin Hymns* (Cambridge, Eng. 1922). Still indispensable are H. A. DANIEL, *Thesaurus hymnologicus,* 5 v. (Halle-Leipzig 1841–56). F. J. MONE, ed., *Lateinische Hymnen des Mittelalters,* 3 v. (Freiburg 1853–55). Repertory. U. CHEVALIER, *Repertorium hymnologicum* (Louvain-Brussels 1892–1921), with correction by C. BLUME, *Repertorium repertorii* (Leipzig 1901) and J. MEARNS, *Early Latin Hymnaries* (Cambridge 1913). Melodies. B. STÄBLEIN, ed., *Die mittelalterlichen Hymnenmelodien des Abendlandes* (Monumenta monodica medii aevi 1; Kassel 1956). B. RAJECZKY, *Melodiarium Hungariae medii aevi* (Budapest 1956—) v. 1. History. J.SZÖVÉRFFY, *Die Annalen der lateinischen Hymnendichtung,* 2 v. (Berlin 1964–65), the most detailed work at present. R. E. MESSENGER, *The Medieval Latin Hymn* (Washington, D.C. 1953), a good summary of all problems involved. F. J. E. RABY, *A History of Christian-Latin Poetry from the Beginnings to the Close of the Middle Ages* (2d ed. Oxford 1953); *A History of Secular Latin Poetry in the Middle Ages* (2d ed. Oxford 1957). H. LECLERCQ, *Dictionnaire d'archéologie chrétienne et de liturgie,* ed. F. CABROT, H. LECLERQ, and H. I. MARROU (Paris 1907–53) 6.2:2901–28. Roman liturgy. J. CONNELLY, *Hymns of the Roman Liturgy* (Westminster, Md. 1957). W. H. FRERE, *Historical*

Catholic priest at Saint Joseph's School leads the choir in a hymn during Sunday Mass, Singmari, India. (©Earl & Nazima Kowall/ CORBIS)

Edition of "Hymns Ancient and Modern" (London 1909). M. FROST, ed., *Historical Companion to "Hymns Ancient and Modern"* (London 1962). *The Hymnal 1940, Companion* (3d rev. ed., New York 1951). G. P. JACKSON, *Spiritual Folk Songs of Early America* (New York n.d.). H. A. L. JEFFERSON, *Hymns in Christian Worship* (London 1950). B. STÄBLEIN, "Hymnus," *Die Musik in Geschichte und Gegenwart* 6:987–1032. O. WESTENDORF, "The State of Catholic Hymnody," *The Hymn* 28 (1977) 54–60.

[J. SZÖVÉRFFY/R. B. HALLER/EDS.]

HYMNS AND HYMNALS, I: HISTORICAL DEVELOPMENTS

Until the Reformation, melodies of the Latin hymn predominated in Christian worship. The vernacular hymn has been used in worship since the Reformation in both the Catholic and the Protestant tradition. This article traces the history and development of Latin hymnody,

Catholic vernacular hymnody in Europe, Protestant hymnody in Europe since the Reformation, Protestant hymnody in the U.S., and Catholic vernacular hymnody in the U.S. until the Second Vatican Council. For developments after Vatican II, *see* HYMNS AND HYMNALS, II: VATICAN II AND BEYOND.

Latin Hymnody. The music of Latin hymnody may be divided into three periods: the formative phase from the 4th to the 8th century; the period of florescence in the Middle Ages, from the Carolingian period to the end of the Renaissance; and the decline during the baroque, classical, and romantic periods.

Earliest Western Hymnody. Although it is certain that the early Christians used Psalms, hymns, and spiritual songs (Col 3.16) derived from the Jewish worship in the synagogue, knowledge of the music of these hymns can be only conjectural. With regard to hymn melodies prior to the 9th century, the date of the first MSS with mu-

Latin hymnal. (©Ted Streshinsky/CORBIS)

sical notation, any assertion must be based on the deduction or assumption that the melodies are older than the MSS in which they are first recorded.

Perhaps the greatest, as well as the most popular, Christian hymn of all ages is the *TE DEUM.* Unlike other Office hymns, the *Te Deum* is written in rhythmic prose. Textually as well as musically it is composed of three distinct parts. The first, in praise of the Holy Trinity, consists of 15 verses with an alternation of two melodic elements, which are initially stated with the words *Te Dominum confitemur* and *Te aeternum Patrem.* The second part is in praise of Our Lord as Redeemer; thus, at the words *Tu Rex gloriae, Christe* appears a new melodic formula retained through verse 23 (the *Aeterna fac cum Sanctis*), which in earlier times marked the end of the hymn. The antiquity of the melodies of these first two sections cannot be doubted. The third part, of later accretion, consists of an old series of verses drawn from the Psalms [27 (28).9; 144 (145).2; 122 (123).3; 32 (33).22; 30 (31).2]. Since the Middle Ages the *Te Deum* has inspired a number of polyphonic and free compositions. It has also been frequently translated as a strophic vernacular hymn. Notable among these is the forceful version in English by the Paulist Clarence WALWORTH, ''Holy God, We Praise Thy Name,'' a translation of the German *Grosser Gott, wir loben Dich.* Both are commonly sung to a melody from *Allgemeines katholisches Gesangbuch* (Vienna 1774).

Influence of the Ambrosian Hymn. The strophic Latin hymn as it is known today came into being in the 4th cen-tury. It may safely be stated that important hymn writers of the period, such as St. Ambrose, Bishop of Milan (340–397), were acquainted with and influenced by the hymns of the Eastern Churches. From a textual point of view it is generally believed that the impetus occasioning early hymnody came as a result of the Arian heresy, whose proponents used popular songs to promulgate their false teaching. Responding in kind, Ambrose and his followers wrote and used hymns to stir up and inspire the faithful to withstand the Church's enemies. In view of the Arian heresy, it is understandable that the tradition of closing each hymn with a doxology was already firmly established in these earliest Latin hymns, for example in the following (from Ambrose, *Splendor Paternae gloriae*):

> Deo Patri sit gloria, Ejusque soli Filio,
>
> Cum Spiritu Paraclito, Nunc et per omne saeculum.

It can therefore be assumed that the text and the melodies of the Ambrosian hymns had immediate congregational appeal, for they were written with congregational participation in mind. First, they were written in simple Latin, which would have been readily understood by the common people, not in Greek, the language of the learned. Second, the hymns drew liberally from scriptural sources and stressed orthodox faith and pious living. Finally, the simple meter selected (iambic dimeter) could be rendered easily by a congregation and must have added to the hymns' effectiveness. Although St. HILARY OF POITIERS (*c.* 310–366) also wrote hymns against the Arians and earned for himself the title *Malleus Arianum* (hammer of the Arians), the authenticated fragments of his hymns never enjoyed the same kind of popularity because they lack congregational appeal.

The number of authentic Ambrosian hymns is still a matter of conjecture. (*See* HYMNOLOGY.) Not all are in liturgical use, but the following three were found in the Tridentine Roman Breviary: *Aeterna rerum conditor* (Sunday at Lauds), *Splendor paternae gloriae* (Monday at Lauds), and *Aeterna Christi munera* (Common of Apostles and Evangelists). Another authentic hymn from the pen of St. Ambrose is *Veni redemptor gentium.* Though not in Roman usage, it survived in the Sarum (*see* SARUM USE) and other rites. It is important because of its subsequent translation into German as *Nun komm der Heiden Heiland.* The tremendous influence of the Ambrosian hymns on the music of hymns in later centuries has been noted by M. Britt:

> The Breviary hymns written in iambics outnumber all other verse forms combined. Iambic meter has always been popular. It is closer to prose than any other kind of verse, and it thus gives a poet

an opportunity to give expression to his thoughts in a form which will appeal both to the learned and the unlearned. St. Ambrose understood this well, as did the long line of his imitators, many of whose hymns have found their way into the liturgy. [*The Hymns of the Breviary and Missal* (rev. ed. New York 1948) xxvii.]

Other Metrical Hymns. Another important hymn writer of the early period was Aurelius Clemens PRUDENTIUS (348–413). Seven of his hymns were used in the Tridentine Breviary. These, however, are all centos of hymns from his *Liber Cathemerinon,* a great poetic work containing hymns for the daily hours and feasts of the year. Of particular note are the cento *O sola magnarum urbium* (for Lauds on Epiphany and its octave) and the Christmas hymn *Corde natus ex parentis,* which has become very popular among English-speaking Christians because of John Mason Neale's translation, ''Of the Father's Love Begotten.'' It is unlikely that the present melodies for these hymns are as old as the texts. The same is true of the beautiful Christmas hymn *A solis ortus cardine* by Caelius Sedulius (fl.450), which has assured its author a place among the great hymn writers of antiquity. It is an alphabetic acrostic in which each strophe begins with successive letters of the Latin alphabet. In liturgical usage the hymn has been divided, the first part being used at Lauds from Christmas to the eve of the Epiphany, and the second for Matins and Vespers for Epiphany and its octave. The use of an acrostic points to an influence from Byzantium, where such acrostics are common. Also of note is Venantius FORTUNATUS (530–609), a native of Treviso who became bishop of Poitiers. His best-known hymns are *Vexilla Regis prodeunt* (traditionally sung for Vespers from Passion Sunday to the Wednesday of Holy Week) and *Pange, lingua, gloriosi Lauream,* which has a considerably wider usage. It is sung on Good Friday at the Veneration of the Cross. It has been said that Fortunatus as a poet is one of the last of the Latin classicists. The truth of this statement may be seen in the meter of the *Pange, lingua,* which is trochaic tetrameter instead of the popular iambic dimeter. Music historians have assumed that these hymns give some idea of the style of Gallican chant; they are among the few remnants that survived the Carolingian attempts at suppression of it.

Although Rome was slow to adopt the hymn, it became the task of the monasteries to preserve and further develop the hymnody of the Latin Church. The establishment of the canonical hours in the Benedictine Rule helped foster the use of hymns of the Ambrosian type along with the singing of the Psalter. Latin hymns gradually developed into cycles for the entire Church year. They commemorated the great feasts of the year, as well as the feasts of the saints. The pope and doctor of the Church whose name was given to the music of the Church in the West should certainly not be overlooked, even though scholars disagree on the number of hymns that might be attributed to him. As abbot of the Benedictine monastery of St. Andrew, which he founded in Rome, St. Gregory the Great (540–604) certainly must have had more than a passing interest in the Office hymn. At least fourteen hymns are attributed to him. Of these, mention should be made of *Nocte surgentes vigilemus omnes* (historically sung at Matins on the fourth and subsequent Sundays after Pentecost), its companion hymn *Ecce jam noctis tenuatur* (for Lauds during the same period), and the great hymn for Vespers on Sunday *Lucis Creator optime.* The melodies of these hymns were among the most popular in the Middle Ages. In popularity they rivaled only the *Veni, Creator Spiritus,* which is generally, but probably erroneously, ascribed to Rabanus Maurus (776–856). With perhaps the exception of the *Te Deum,* this hymn of invocation to the Holy Spirit has had wider use for liturgical and extraliturgical functions than any other.

Two hymns may serve as examples of a difficult musical problem upon which scholars are not in agreement: *Ut queant laxis* in Sapphic meter and *Gloria, laus et honor* in elegiac meter. There is disagreement concerning the relationship between the poetic meter of the text and the rhythm of the music in these and similar Carolingian attempts at classic meter. Most scholars fail to see how the metrics of the texts are reflected in the music. The *Ut queant laxis* (traditionally assigned to the Vespers of feast of the Nativity of St. John the Baptist) is attributed to Paul the Deacon (d. 799) of Monte Cassino; *Goria, laus et honor* (Palm Sunday processional hymn) is attributed to Theodulph, Bishop of Orleans (760–821). The former acquired great popularity in providing the basis for the system of solemnization because the first syllable of each line of the first stanza begins on successively rising pitches; *ut, re, mi, fa, sol, la.*

Hymn and Sequence. With the rise of the SEQUENCE the composition of new hymns seemed less necessary. In the Sequence the medieval composer found opportunity for emotional and musical expression and for experimentation with new meters and forms. It is not surprising that it is more and more difficult in the late Middle Ages to differentiate between hymns and Sequences. The great Sequence authors and writers in general were also the great hymn writers. They include Abelhard and Bernard of Clairvaux (1091–1153) who is credited with one of the most popular of hymns, *Jesu, dulcis memoria.* Thomas Aquinas (1227–74) contributed to the repertoire by writing hymns for the Office of Corpus Christi and the famous Sequence *Lauda, Sion, Salvatorem.* The music for these, and the famous Sequences of Adam of Saint-Victor

(d. 1192), was not newly composed, but the melodies were, almost without exception, adaptations of existing pieces. The distinction between Sequence and hymn eventually became one of function only.

Decline. From the 16th century onward, Latin hymnody was on the decline. One of the chief reasons advanced is the fact that Latin ceased to be a "mother tongue," even among religious orders. Another reason is that the Renaissance passion for classical purity overemphasized form to the detriment of thought and content. C. Blume depicted the situation in these words: "The humanists abominated the rhythmical poetry of the Middle Ages from an exaggerated enthusiasm for ancient classical forms and meters. Hymnody then received its death blow as, on the revision of the Breviary under Pope Urban VIII (1568–1644), the medieval rhythmical hymns were forced into more classical forms by means of so-called corrections." Hundreds of "corrections" were made by Urban and a commission of scholars appointed by him. Fortunately, the Breviaries of some monastic orders, e.g., the Benedictine, did not adopt the changes. Although the texts of some of the ancient hymns were changed, the melodies remained the same. In several chant MSS of the Renaissance the hymns are in measured notation; they were sung in a style different from that of the remaining chant repertory. Yet, even the period of decline of the Latin hymn, from the Renaissance to the present, is not completely devoid of pieces of poetic and musical inspiration. Notwithstanding the fact that it is not in liturgical usage, there is no hymn more beloved by all Christians than the Christmas *Adeste Fideles,* ascribed to John Francis Wade (1711–86). Father Charles Coffin (1676–1749), Rector of the University of Paris, was among those commissioned to revise the Paris Breviary of 1736. The revision included a number of his Latin hymns, of which two Advent hymns are remarkable: *Jordanis oras praevia* and *Instantis adventum Dei.*

Vernacular Hymnody. Medieval vernacular hymnody had its roots in the development of the TROPE and Sequence. The use of the vernacular was to serve as an aid in comprehending the Latin of the chant. Many of the Latin farced tropes were written to the various melodies of the Kyrie eleison. The hymns derived from this source were called *Kirleis* or *Leis.* A good example of this type of hymn is *Nun bitten wir den Heiligen Geist* (13th century) with its *kyrieleis* refrain. Another, from a later period, is the chorale *Kyrie, Gott Vater in Ewigkeit . . . Eleison eleison,* derived from the *Kyrie fons bonitatis.*

The vernacular hymns derived from the Sequences were called *Leich.* The following example will serve to show the relation between the vernacular strophe and the Latin Sequence from which it was derived:

Ave Maria Klarer Meerstern zum Licht der Heidenschaft aus Gottesgnaden aufgegangen.

Ave praeclara maris stella in lucem gentium Maria divinitus orta.

The 13th-century *Christ ist erstanden* is another example of a vernacular Sequence hymn. It is derived from the Easter Sequence *Victimae paschali laudes.* Both the *Leis* and the *Leich* are found in Germany as early as the 9th century.

The development of polyphony also gave impetus to the development of vernacular hymnody. The harmonic structure of the *laudi* (Italy), the *cantigas* (Spain), the *cantique* (France), and *Lieder* (Germany) was, however, more of a conservative type than that of the essentially intricate contrapuntal style of the Mass and motet of that era. Hymns of this type are found in the repertory of the trouvères and minnesingers alongside their secular airs.

Throughout this development vernacular hymns were restricted to extra-and nonliturgical devotions and functions, especially in France and Italy. In Germany, however, possibly because of the influence of the Lutheran vernacular service, vernacular hymns invaded the domain of the Catholic liturgy after the 16th century. By 1605 the *Cantual* of Mainz allowed the use of German hymns for the Proper of the Mass. Later in the same century this was expanded to include portions of the Ordinary. Such Masses were called *Singmessen.* The widespread use of chorales by the Lutherans in Germany precipitated a further demand for congregational singing among Catholics. In response to this need, the first Catholic hymnbook with German text appeared in Leipzig in 1537. This was Michael Vehe's *Ein New Gesangbuechlein geystlicher Lieder.* Other such collections appeared soon after, among them Johann Leisentritt's *Geistliche Lieder und Psalmen,* which went through three editions between 1567 and 1584. A 17th-century collection of importance was David Gregor Corner's *Gottweiher Gesangbuch* of 1625. Under the impact of the baroque concertato style, *Singmessen* were expanded to include the choir and instruments, as well as congregational singing. Ignaz Holzbauer (1711–83), for example, composed German Masses of this type. The *Singmesse* continued to find favor in Germany throughout the 18th century. Its popularity caused an ever-widening separation from the liturgy, and it became one of the objects of reform by the 19th-century CAECILIAN movement.

While the chief objective of the Caecilianverein was to raise the standards of German Catholic church music in general, it attempted also to restore order in the use of the vernacular hymn. There were two aspects to hymn reform. The first was the historic restriction of vernacular hymns to extraliturgical services and devotions. The second was the elimination of secular and rationalistic influences. The most lasting result of this reform was a renewed interest in the older Latin hymns.

Protestant Hymnody. Two distinct types of hymns developed at the time of the Reformation: the great body of German vernacular chorales fostered by the Lutheran reformers, and the French metrical Psalms developed by Calvin and his associates (*see* PSALTERS, METRICAL). The distinction between them is more than one of language. It is primarily one of divergent theological approaches to worship.

German Chants. Martin Luther's (1483–1546) practice was to retain all of the Catholic liturgy that in his opinion was not contrary to the Scriptures. This permitted retention of the Ordinary of the Mass together with its great repertory of music, whether chant or polyphony, as well as some of the musical Propers, the ancient pericopes, and many of the Collects. In the Calvinistic concept of worship, only what was specified in the Scriptures and was in use in the primitive Church could be used in worship—in other words, the Psalter, the Canticles, and the Decalogue. While the shape of the Lutheran liturgy retained most of the traditional musical elements of the Mass, these still had to be sung by trained choristers, and they were still in Latin. They were never discarded, and the excellent musical standards of the *Kantorei* have been maintained down to the present. It was necessary, however, to find suitable hymns for the congregation. As previously indicated, some popular German hymns were already in use, but the greater number of congregational hymns had to grow out of the experience and ability of the reformers.

In general, the chorale may be divided into four classes: (1) Hymns that were translated directly from Latin hymns and whose melodies were preserved with slight alterations, e.g., *Komm, Gott Schöpfer, Heiliger Geist,* translated from *Veni, Creator Spiritus; Christum wir sollen loben schon,* translated from Sedulius's *A solis ortus cardine.* (2) Vernacular hymns based on parts of the Latin Ordinary; Kyrie: *Kyrie, Gott Vater in Ewigkeit,* which makes use of the melody of the *Kyrie fons bonitatis* and is a partial translation by an unknown writer of the *fons bonitatis* trope; Gloria: *Allein Gott in der Höh' sei Ehr,* a metrical paraphrase of the Gloria by Nikolaus Decius (?–1541), who adapted the melody from that of the Paschal Gloria (see Mass I in the Liber Usualis); Credo: *Wir glauben all' en einen Gott,* a metrical paraphrase of the NICENE CREED by Luther, who adapted the melody from Credo IV; Sanctus: *Jesaia dem Propheten, das geschah'* (also called the German Sanctus), which paraphrases the vision of the Prophet Isaiah (Is 6.1–4) and was adapted by Luther from the melody of the Sanctus

of Mass XVII (Liber Usualis); Agnus: *O Lamm Gottes, unschuldig,* by Nikolaus Decius, who adapted the melody of the Agnus of Mass IX. (3) Metrical versions or paraphrases of Psalms and canticles; e.g., Psalm 129 (130) *De Profundis: Aus tiefer Noth* by Luther; the melody has a strong Phrygian character but cannot be traced to any Gregorian source; *Nunc Dimittis: Mit Fried' und Freud',* also by Luther; the melody is in the Dorian mode but it cannot be traced; *Te Deum: Herr, Gott, dich loben wir,* adapted by Luther from the ancient simple tone. (4) Hymns that are original in text and melody. These became more numerous with the passage of time and eventually formed the great bulk of the German chorale. Among the important hymn and tune writers were Paul Speratus, Johann Walter, Ludwig Helmbold, Nicholas Selnecker, Philipp Nicolai, Johann Franck, Paul Gerhardt, Johann Freylinghausen, and Erdmann Neumeister.

The chorale is of the greatest musical significance because of its use as a vehicle for choral and instrumental compositions. The climax of its importance is seen in the works of J. S. BACH. For him the chorale was at the very center of the Passions, the church cantatas, and the great part of his organ pieces.

French Psalters. English hymnody was in part influenced by the French metrical PSALTERS. John Calvin (1509–64), because he considered only the Scriptures suitable vehicles for congregational singing, literally fettered his followers to the Psalter for centuries. In 1538, during his exile in Strassburg, Calvin heard the congregational singing of Psalms and hymns in German, set to melodies by Matthias Greiter. The singing impressed him greatly, paving the way for a whole new series of French Psalters, beginning with the Strasbourg Psalter of 1539 and culminating in the first complete Geneva Psalter of 1562. The literary task of translation and versification was principally that of Clément Marot (c. 1497–1544) and, after his death, Théodore de Bèze (1519–1605), although Calvin supplied some of the earlier ones. The principal musical editor of these Psalters was Louis Bourgeois (c. 1510–61), who gave final form to approximately 85 melodies of the completed Psalter. While Calvin was opposed to polyphony, and insisted that the Psalms be sung in unison, nevertheless part settings using as many as six voices appeared in the hymns of Bourgeois himself. More important musically are those of Claude GOUDIMEL (?–1572).

English Hymns and Psalters. Pre-Reformation vernacular hymnody in England consisted mostly of spiritual folksongs and carols. In 1531 Miles Coverdale (1486–1569) attempted to introduce Lutheran chorales into England. His collection, *Goostly Psalmes and Spiritual Songes,* is generally regarded as the first English hymnbook. All but five of the hymns in this collection were translations from the German. In 1546 Henry VIII prohibited the use of this hymnal.

The most important aspect of Reformation hymnody in England was what Millar Patrick has called "the battle of the Psalters." Early English metrical Psalters, begun by Thomas Sternhold (1500–49) as an attempt to substitute pious and serious songs for the ribald ballads sung by his fellow courtiers, went through a series of turbulent editions. In 1549, the year of his death, Sternhold published 37 of his own Psalter translations. His work was continued by John Hopkins (d. 1570). With the accession of Queen Mary to the English throne, many of the English reformers took refuge in Geneva. As a result, there appeared in 1556 the first Anglo-Genevan Psalter (*One and Fiftie Psalmes of Davide in English Metre*), which contained 44 settings by Sternhold and Hopkins plus seven by William Whittingham, Calvin's brother-in-law. This Psalter, together with its second edition of 1558, shows the strong influence of the French Psalters, the melodies having been modeled on those of Bourgeois. After the death of Queen Mary, a first complete English Psalter was published by John Day in 1562, by coincidence the same year as the first complete French Psalter. Today this Psalter is known as the "Old Version." It remained in use until 1696, when the "New Version" of Nahum Tate and Nicholas Brady supplanted it. During the intervening century other attempts were made by John Playford, Francis Rous, and Thomas Ravenscroft to supplant the Old Version.

In Scotland, likewise, the Lutheran influence was short-lived with the return of John Knox from Geneva in 1559; he brought with him the Anglo-Genevan Psalter. A new version, based in part on the Anglo-Genevan Psalter, appeared as part of the *Book of Common Order* in 1564. Much of the work of revision and expansion was done by Robert Pont and John Craig. This was supplanted in 1650 by a final version.

While such men as George Wither (1588–1667), John Cosin (1594–1672), Thomas Ken (1627–1711), Richard Baxter (1615–91), and Joseph Addison (1672–1710) made some attempt to liberate English hymnody from the shackles of metrical psalmody, it was the work of Isaac Watts (1674–1748) that ushered in a new era of English hymns. What he first attempted to do is unfolded in the lengthy title of his 1719 publication, *The Psalms of David Imitated in the Language of the New Testament, and Apply'd to the Christian State and Worship.* From this "Christianization" of the Psalms it was just one step to the writing of new and thoroughly original Christian hymns. For this Watts justly deserves the title "Father of English Hymnody." Many of Watts's

hymns have become standard among English-speaking peoples of all denominations. Some of the best known are: "Our God, Our Help in Ages Past"; "Before Jehovah's Awful Throne"; "Jesus Shall Reign Where'er the Sun"; "Come, Holy Spirit, Heavenly Dove," and "Joy to the World! the Lord Is Come." The new burst of song attracted numerous other hymn writers in imitation, as St. Ambrose's hymns had centuries before. Among the imitators of Watts were Simon Browne (1680–1732) and Philip Doddridge (1702–51). Even as late as 1787, John Rippon (1751–1836) published what was intended to be an appendix to Watts's *Psalms and Hymns.*

Methodist Hymns. The next stage in the development of the English hymn paralleled the rise of Methodism. In 1735, through a chance meeting with a group of Moravians on their way to America on the same ship with him and his brother Charles, John WESLEY (1703–91) was introduced to the German pietistic hymns of Count von Zinzendorf and Johann Freylinghausen. Wesley's first hymnbook was printed in America in 1737. It also showed the extraordinary influence of Watts, since half of its 70 hymns were by him. Five more were Wesley's translations of German hymns, probably from the Zinzendorf *Herrnhut Gesangbuch.* Others were by his father and some by his brother Samuel, but none by Charles. His second hymnal appeared almost immediately after his return to England in 1738.

While Wesley gave the initial impetus to the early hymns of the Methodist Revival, he gradually turned this task over to his brother Charles. Of certain hymns it is difficult to ascertain which of the two is the author. It is said that Charles Wesley wrote some 6,500 hymns, many of which were intended only for the occasion or moment. Many, however, have passed into general Protestant usage and, judged by the highest standards, they are excellent hymns. Among them are the well-known Christmas and Easter hymns, "Hark, the Herald Angels Sing" and "Christ the Lord Is Risen Today." "O for a Thousand Tongues to Sing," "Jesus, Lover of my Soul," "Come, Thou Long-Expected Jesus," and "Christ, Whose Glory Fills the Skies" were composed by him also. Although John Wesley's greatest contribution to English hymnody consisted in masterful translations, especially of German hymns, he wrote also some excellent original hymns, "Jesus, Thy Boundless Love to Me" and "Thee Will I Love, My Strength, My Tower," among them.

Protestant Hymnody in the U.S. It would be difficult to divorce early American hymnody from that of England. Protestant hymnody in the U.S. also had its roots in metrical psalmody.

Early American Hymnody. The Puritans, both orthodox and separatist, brought with them their Psalters. The orthodox adhered to those of Sternhold and Hopkins, and the separatists kept the Ainsworth Psalter printed in Amsterdam in 1612. General dissatisfaction with all of these led to the publication of the first book of any kind printed in the U.S., the BAY PSALM BOOK (called also the New England Version) printed at Cambridge, Mass., by Stephen Day in 1640. It was not long, however, before the influence of Isaac Watts began to be felt in the New World. His *Psalms of David* appeared in Boston in 1729. This and the publication of his *Hymns* in 1739 were British imports. A distinctively American hymnody began only with the revision of Watts, attempted by Joel Barlow in 1786 and by Timothy Dwight in 1801. In the American spirit of independence, Dwight, who was president of Yale from 1795 to 1815, showed no inclination to be tied down to mere paraphrases of existent metrical Psalms. Typical of Dwight's hymns is "I Love Thy Kingdom, Lord."

At the same time, the impact of the Wesleys was felt by reason of their mission to the U.S. and the 1737 publication of John Wesley's hymns. From these facts alone it could be predicted that 18th- and 19th-century Protestant hymnody in America would become largely a matter of denominational development.

During the mid-19th century, the GOSPEL SONG took root in many parts of the U.S. While many had a part in its development, the gospel song is chiefly the work of Dwight L. Moody and Ira D. Sankey as part of their evangelistic campaigns, which penetrated even the British Isles. Such gems as "Let the Lower Lights Be Burning," "Almost Persuaded Now to Believe," and "I Love to Tell the Story" almost uprooted established hymnody, especially in the Methodist and Baptist Churches, and perhaps would have done so had the tide not been turned by the hymns that came out of England's Oxford Revival.

The Oxford Movement. The Oxford Revival in England was preceded by a rediscovery of the great Latin hymns of the Breviary. All who worship in the English language are indebted to John Mason Neale (1818–66) for his masterful translations, not only of many Latin, but also of many ancient Greek hymns. There is not a contemporary good Protestant hymnal that does not contain some of his translations. Many Catholic hymnals also include them. The list of his translations is too lengthy for enumeration. His "All Glory, Laud and Honor" was translated from Theodulph's *Gloria, laus et honor,* and "Come, Ye Faithful, Raise the Strain" was translated from John of Damascus' Ασωμεν, πάντες λαοί. Other translators were Edward Caswall (1814–78), Richard F. Littledale (1833–90), and John Brownlie (1859–1925), the last contributing English versions especially of Greek hymns. Because the Oxford Movement was a spiritual revival based on the liturgical life, it was bound to produce many good hymns and hymn writers. A compromise between the "high church" and evangelical schools had to be achieved. It came about with the publication of *Hymns Ancient and Modern, For Use in the Services of the Church* (1861). Sir Henry Baker (1821–77) was chairman of the commission that produced this most influential hymnal, which in little more than a century was disseminated in one edition or another to a total of almost 200 million copies. Sir Henry himself contributed what is possibly one of the most sublime hymns based on Psalm 22 (23), "The King of Love My Shepherd Is." Other significant contributors and their hymns were: John Keble (1792–1866), author of "Sun of My Soul"; William Chatterdon Dix (1823–98), writer of the joyful Epiphany hymn "As with Gladness Men of Old"; William Walsham How (1823–97), "For All the Saints Who from Their Labours Rest"; William Whiting (1825–78), "Eternal Father, Strong to Save"; and C. F. Alexander (1825–78), "I Bind unto Myself Today." Musically, too, *Hymns Ancient and Modern* produced excellent tunes that are still widely used. *Coronae, Diademata, St. Crispin, St. George's Windsor, Aurelia, St. Agnes,* and *Nicaea* are but a few of the most representative ones.

Influence of the Spiritual. Another important phase of 19th-century Protestant hymnody in America was the rise of the spiritual. Its development paralleled the increasing dissent from the established Protestant denominations at the time of the American Revolution and the establishment of splinter sects from these branches. The initial desire for religious freedom, which had motivated some of the early settlers (e.g., the Pilgrims), had slowly but surely crystallized itself into a new authoritarian establishment. The great mass of subsequent settlers chafed under this ecclesiastic authority. Hence at the dawn of the Revolution there was, in addition to a wish for political independence from the crown, a demand for renewed religious liberty as well. Shortly after the close of the War for Independence, itinerant preachers of Baptist and Methodist origin began evangelistic crusades throughout the states, especially in the rural areas. For their enthusiastic type of preaching and worship, the Psalters of the established churches were too staid and dull. Even the hymns of Watts and the Wesleys had to be recast to British and American popular folksongs. Among numerous collections of this type, a notable one was Jeremiah Ingall's *Christian Harmony,* published in 1805.

In time, even these spirituals proved to be too severe in style, and the texts and tunes were gradually lightened and simplified. This took place at the same time as the emergence of camp meeting revivals in the mid-19th century. Both were part of a missionary effort among the African Americans undertaken by Baptists and Methodists.

They, together with some Presbyterians, showed more of an interest in Christianizing the slaves than did the established denominations. A people for whom English was little more than a foreign language could hardly be expected to take to the severe hymnody of the established churches. Hence the spiritual folksongs of the Nonconformists appealed to the slaves, and over time they became a part of the African American musical idiom. An examination of numerous tunes and lyrics of Black Spirituals reveals a striking similarity to the spiritual folksongs of the camp meeting evangelists.

20th-century Protestant Hymnody. Accordingly, at the dawn of the 20th century, the hymnody of the established English-speaking Protestant denominations shows an understandable dichotomy. There are, on the one hand, the substantial hymnals containing metrical Psalms, the hymns of Watts and the Wesleys, Latin and Greek translations by Neale and others, and hymns drawn from *Hymns Ancient and Modern.* On the other hand, there are also hundreds of collections of gospel songs, spirituals, and so-called choruses. As a rule, the former were used at the regular services of worship, the latter at revivals and youth meetings.

Catholic Vernacular Hymnody in the U.S. Catholic vernacular hymnody in America in its incipient stages reflected the cosmopolitan quality characterized by the nation itself. Through the activities of the missionaries and early settlers, practically every European nation indirectly transplanted its own heritage of religious song to the young nation. The adoption of these hymns, or at least of their stylistic traits, is an integral part of the history of hymnody in America from the first years of colonization until the 20th century.

Missionary Efforts. Manuscripts found in the Franciscan missions of the southwestern U.S. contain a number of hymn tunes in the style of the Spanish folk hymn with texts in Spanish. The earliest published collection in America, however, the *Psalmodia Christiana* compiled by Fray Bernadino de Sahagun, consists of hymns in the language of the Aztecs sung to Native American melodies. The melodies, unfortunately, were never recorded. French Jesuit missionaries, active in eastern Canada and the northeastern U.S. at about the same period of the 17th century, adapted the Huron language to Gregorian chant melodies and to French *cantiques.* Many of these can be found in Catholic hymnals compiled for the Native Americans, the earliest of which dates from 1847. Because both melody and words were preserved, the Christmas hymn *Jesous Ahatonnia,* composed by Jean de Brebeuf, SJ, and adapted to a 16th-century Breton noel tune, may be considered the earliest of extant vernacular American hymns. (*See* LITURGICAL MUSIC, HISTORY OF.)

The hardships experienced by the early English colonists in the practice of their religion may account in part for the substantial lack of evidence concerning Catholic church music until the last quarter of the 18th century. It was not until 1787 that the first printed collection containing Catholic hymn tunes was published in the U.S. This *Compilation of the Litanies and Vespers Hymns and Anthems as They Are Sung in the Catholic Church* was published by John Aitken in Philadelphia and contains almost as much Anglican music as music for the Catholic service. The book is significant for its inclusion of traditional chant hymns and several German chorales.

19th-Century Hymnals. Catholic hymn publications in the 19th century include *Anthems, Hymns Usually Sung at the Catholick Church,* edited by Rev. John Cheverus at Boston in 1800; *Morning and Evening Service of the Catholic Church, Comprising a Choice Collection of Gregorian and Other Masses, Litanies, Psalms, Sacred Hymns, Anthems, Versicles and Motetts,* compiled by G. Garbett (New York 1840); and *Catholic Melodies,* edited by Rev. James Horner (Baltimore 1845). English influence in late 19th-century hymnals resulted in publications of poor taste, which often featured adaptations of secular music. The more unscrupulous compilers even adapted themes of popular instrumental and operatic music of famous composers such as Haydn, Mozart, Beethoven, and Mendelssohn. German Catholic immigrants of the mid-19th century were provided with a publication of the hymns they knew in the 1858 collection of B. H. F. Hellebusch entitled *Katholisches Gesang und Gebetbuch: Eine Auswahl der vorzüglichsten Chorüle und Kirchenlieder.* Unfortunately, many of the German Catholic chorales and folk hymns introduced in America through this publication were presented in the decadent rhythmic style then prevalent in Germany. Many other tunes of inferior quality also were included. A higher musical standard was maintained in other German Catholic hymn collections of the late 19th and early 20th centuries, and these became basic material for many subsequent Catholic hymnals with English texts, of which the following are representative: *Laudate pueri,* compiled by Sisters of Notre Dame (Cleveland, Ohio 1886, 1903); *Psallite,* compiled by Alexander Roesler, SJ (St. Louis 1901, 1909); *Laudate,* compiled by Rev. Joseph Hohe (Kansas City 1909); *Hosanna,* compiled by Ludwig Bonvin, SJ (St. Louis 1910); *Cantate,* compiled by John Singenberger (New York 1912); and *New Hymn Book for Church and School,* compiled by Hans Marx for the Chicago Archdiocese (New York 1917). Many of these hymnals represented the reforming efforts of members of the American Caecilian Society. Characteristic of the American-Caecilian style of hymn writing were the use of slightly florid rhythms within a common meter, and melodies of a diatonic nature with a judicious use of skips.

France and England exerted the second influence on 19th-century American Catholic hymnody. French borrowings were evident particularly in the *Catholic Youth's Hymnbook,* edited by the Brothers of the Christian Schools (Montreal 1871; New York 1885). Many of the tunes in the collection were French *cantique* tunes of a degenerate type; a few were representative of better French tradition; while a third group were original tunes in the style of the *cantique.* Many were traditionally associated with certain religious events and devotions. Mid-19th-century English tradition was superimposed on the French tradition in the following collections: *Laudis corona* (New York 1885) and *St. Basil's Hymnal* (Toronto 1889; 5th ed. New York 1896). These and others, such as *The Crown Hymnal* (Boston 1911), *De La Salle Hymnal* (New York 1913), *Gloria Hymnal* (New York 1933), and *American Catholic Hymnal* (New York 1913), reflected the traditions of the 19th century. Typical of the style of this tradition is the dancelike 3/4 and 6/8 meters with melodies of a triadic outline that feature also melodic intervals of a sixth. Harmonically, the progressions are frequently static or else chromatic.

The best traditions of Germany, France, and England were represented in the best Catholic hymnal published in America in the 19th century, namely, the *Roman Hymnal,* compiled and arranged by J. B. Young, SJ (New York 1884). This collection included many Gregorian chant melodies, as well as some original American tunes.

20th-Century Hymnals. Early 20th-century hymnals of a cosmopolitan character included *Hymns for the Ecclesiastical Year,* compiled by Alphonsus Dress (1908); *Parish Hymnal,* compiled by Joseph Otten (1915); and *Manual of Catholic Hymns,* compiled by B. Dieringer and J. Pierron (1916). Many English Catholic hymn tunes were contained in *Choir Manual,* compiled by G. Burton (1914); *A Treasury of Catholic Song,* compiled by Sidney Hurlbut (New York 1915); and *Standard Catholic Hymnal,* compiled by James A. Reilly (Boston 1921). Three hymnals in the early decades of the 20th century included traditional Protestant hymn tunes: *St. Mark's Hymnal* (1910), *Oregon Catholic Hymnal* (1912), and *St. Francis Hymnal and Choir Manual* (1912). A few other significant hymnals of the same period were *Holy Cross Hymnal* (1915) with original texts and music by Cardinal William O'Connell; *Catholic Education Series Hymnal,* compiled by Justine Ward (Washington 1918); *Catholic Hymns for the People,* edited by James M. Rakar (1919); and *Catholic Hymnal,* compiled by John G. Hacker, SJ (New York 1920). The *St. Gregory Hymnal and Catholic Choir Book,* edited by N. A. Montani, was the result of interest in the improvement of Catholic hymnody, an aim of the newly formed Society of St. Gregory. Slightly more than half the compositions included are original

American tunes, but German, Slovak, Gregorian chant hymns, English, Italian, and French tunes also were represented.

This same interest in the improvement of hymnody was evident in significant publications between 1920 and 1945: *St. Mary's Hymnal,* edited and compiled by C. A. Zittel (New York 1924); *St. Joseph Hymnal,* edited by Joseph Wolf (Chicago 1925); *Diocesan Hymnal,* compiled by Rt. Rev. Joseph SCHREMBS (New York 1928); *St. Caecilia Hymnal,* compiled and edited by J. Alfred Schehl (New York 1929); *Ave Maria Hymnal,* compiled and edited by Rev. Joseph Pierron (Milwaukee 1929); *Parochial Hymnal,* compiled and arranged by Rev. Carlo Rossini (New York 1936); *Mt. Mary Hymnal,* compiled by Sister M. Gisela, SSND (Boston 1938); *Saint Rose Hymnal,* compiled by the Sisters of St. Francis of Perpetual Adoration (Boston 1940); and *Laudate Hymnal and Choir Book,* originally compiled by Rev. Joseph Hohe and completely revised by Rev. Herman J. Koch and Rev. Andrew Green, OSB (Boston 1942). Notable hymnals in the 1940s and early 1950s included *St. Andrew Hymnal,* compiled by Philip Kreckel; *Official Holy Name Hymnal,* compiled by Rev. J. J. McLarney, OP; *Alverno Hymnal and Choir Book,* compiled by Sister M. Cherubim, OSF; *Gregorian Institute Hymnal, Catholic Hymns,* compiled by Rev. John C. Selner, SS; *Cantemus Domino,* by the Sisters of Marylhurst, Oregon; *Pius X Hymnal,* compiled and edited by the faculty of the Pius Tenth School of Liturgical Music; *Monastery Hymnal,* compiled and edited by Achille Bragers; *Mediator Dei Hymnal,* compiled and edited by Cyr de Brant (pseud. of V. J. Higgenson); and *The New Saint Basil Hymnal.*

[M. M. HUELLER/M. A. BICHSEL/E. J. SELHORST/EDS.]

HYMNS AND HYMNALS, II: VATICAN II AND BEYOND

The promulgation of the *Constitution on the Liturgy* (*Sacrosanctum Concilium* [*SC*]) on Dec. 4, 1963, profoundly affected the development and publication of hymnody and hymnals in the Roman Catholic Church in the United States. Responding to the Vatican Council II's call to promote the active participation of the assembly, composers, text writers, and publishers began researching traditional hymnody, revising and adapting Latin hymn tunes to vernacular languages, composing new texts and melodies, and adapting contemporary musical styles to church music from a variety of cultural contexts. This entry will provide a summary of what has been a complex development. Its primary focus is Roman Catholic hymns and hymnals in the United States since Vatican II. In addition, some general remarks will be made regarding trends and developments in some mainline Protestant churches.

The Introduction of the Vernacular. Permission to introduce the use of the vernacular in the liturgy was the catalyst for far-reaching changes in Roman Catholic hymnody. In the majority of parishes in the United States, this meant the introduction of English into the Eucharist, followed by Spanish and other ethnic languages. Although the liturgical reforms did result in some bitter divisions regarding the direction of church music, there was, in general, widespread enthusiasm for singing hymns and service music in the vernacular.

Nevertheless, in the late 1960s, there was little available repertoire for singing either the Propers or the Ordinary of the Mass in English. Hymnody available in the vernacular had been composed for popular devotions rather than for liturgical celebrations. Almost overnight, there was a demand for hymns in the vernacular that would promote the active participation of the assembly and appropriately serve the reformed liturgy of Paul VI. In an effort to preserve the rich heritage of church music, composers and translators set about the work of adapting traditional chants and translating the Latin texts. The results of early efforts were mixed. Some later efforts, notably the work of such arrangers and composers as Robert Batastini, David Hurd, and Paul Ford have been more musically and linguistically satisfying. Because vernacular hymnody had been an important component of Protestant worship since the Reformation, it was natural that Roman Catholics turned to Protestant resources for vernacular repertoire. Many Catholic hymnals incorporated a large percentage of original Protestant hymns in their early editions. Later editions continued to include Protestant hymnody, but often with new texts or translations. As part of the reform, the new emphasis on the centrality of Sacred Scripture encouraged composers to set scriptural texts. The biblical hymns and psalm settings of the French composer and liturgist, Lucien Deiss, and the Canadian composer, Stephen Somerville, helped to set the standard for new vernacular hymn texts.

Folk Music. In addition to the publication of traditional hymnody in the vernacular, a style of music developed that was commonly referred to as "folk." Within the Catholic context, these songs, inspired by the secular folk-music culture of the time, often included trite texts and simplistic music. Singing congregations were often led by self-taught amateur guitar players who could not read music. Folk music's major contribution to liturgical renewal was its success in coaxing congregations to sing. It also convinced Roman Catholics that contemporary cultural expressions could have a meaningful place in liturgical prayer.

The earliest "folk" or "guitar" hymnal was *Hymnal for Young Christians, Volume I: With Roman Catholic Mass Supplement,* published by F.E.L. Publications of Los Angeles in 1966. It included early folk hymns, e.g., "They'll Know We Are Christians" by Peter Scholtes, "Here We Are" and "Of My Hands" by Ray Repp, and "Sons of God" by James Thiem. Early folk groups used this hymnal, reprinted several times, well into the 1970s when it was eventually superseded by the "Glory & Praise" hymnals published by the North American Liturgy Resources in Phoenix.

Glory & Praise: Songs for the Worshiping Assembly, Volume 1 was published in 1977. This hymnal included 60 contemporary folk hymns and 20 pieces of service music. Settings of the lectionary psalms were not included. Two additional volumes were published in 1979 and 1982, respectively. *Glory & Praise: Comprehensive Edition,* published in 1987, added for the first time 50 traditional hymns to the usual repertoire of contemporary music. This edition was soon followed by *Glory & Praise: Volume 4* and *Glory & Praise: Classic Edition* in 1990. The 1998 edition was entitled *Glory & Praise: Second Edition,* published by Oregon Catholic Press.

In many ways, the history of the publication of the various editions of *Glory & Praise* provides a record of the development of folk music in the United States since the early days of the liturgical renewal. The more elementary guitar accompaniments of many of the early folk hymns were gradually replaced by accompaniments that required more guitar skill. Additional instrumental accompaniments, including parts for piano, woodwind, brass, string, and percussion were gradually included by many composers. Texts improved significantly, not only in the quality of the poetry and their use of Sacred Scripture, but also in their attention to inclusivity. Instead of serving as a "folk" resource exclusively, *Glory & Praise* eventually included a significant amount of traditional hymns and an expanded selection of higher quality service music.

G.I.A. Publications contributed to the development of "folk" hymnals in their publication of *Gather* in 1988. Contemporary composers who published in this hymnal include J. Michael Joncas, Marty Haugen, and David Haas. In addition to offering comtemporary hymns, the various editions of *Gather* include contemporary psalm settings, a more generous amount of service music, and settings for morning and evening prayer, all easily located through extensive indices.

Traditional Hymnal Development. Since the promulgation of *SC,* an unusually large number of hymnals—over 100 new and revised hymnals—have been published in the United States for use in Roman Catholic worship. The *People's Mass Book,* published in 1964 by World Library of Sacred Music in Cincinnati, was a post-conciliar version of the *People's Hymnal* originally published in 1955. This hymnal, probably the first major response to the renewal of Vatican II, included hymns, psalms, Mass settings, and Bible services to enable the active participation of the faithful as mandated by *SC.* It was particularly important because it included European music, especially from the Netherlands, Belgium, and France. It was through the *People's Mass Book* that most Catholics were first introduced to the biblical psalms and canticles of Lucien Deiss. The hymnal also helped to popularize several Protestant hymns among Roman Catholics, including such traditional hymns as "A Mighty Fortress" and "Lord, Who at Thy First Eucharist."

It was the hymnal entitled *Worship,* however, which eventually was to set a new standard for Roman Catholic hymnals, especially in its later editions. The first edition, published in 1971, printed 351 items, including extensive ecumenical hymnody, the Gelineau psalms, and such contemporary hymns as "I Am the Bread of Life" by Suzanne Toolan. A second edition, entitled *Worship II,* appeared in 1974. This hymnal set a new standard for Catholic hymn texts by its inclusion of such noted poets as Fred Pratt Green and Brian Wren. *Worship, Third Edition: Hymnal and Service Book for Roman Catholics,* was published in 1986. The arrangement of this hymnal by seasons, topics, and liturgical themes with its numerous and comprehensive indices, settings of morning and evening prayer, and other ritual music, again raised the standards that other publishers have since emulated. G.I.A.'s publication of *RitualSong* in the 1990s is an example of a trend toward the more comprehensive hymnal as opposed to the more specialized book. Whereas in the past, G.I.A. published *Worship* as its traditional hymnal and *Gather* as its more "folk" oriented hymnal, *RitualSong* and *Gather Comprehensive* are hymnals that contain both styles in significant proportions, including African American, Hispanic, and other ethnic entries from around the world.

While periodic worship aids, often referred to as missalettes, cannot properly be considered an example of hymnals, *Music Issue* and *Breaking Bread* by Oregon Catholic Press represent a new development for providing congregations with inexpensive, albeit disposable hymn books. These publications, issued annually, provide the publisher with the opportunity to update the collections more easily and more frequently. Generally, such annual hymnals do not provide the exhaustive indices of the more permanent hymnals. *We Celebrate* by World Library Publications, on the other hand, is an example of a softcover hymnal of a more permanent nature.

The traditional hymnal is becoming increasingly an expression of the global church. More and more hymnals, not only in the Roman Catholic tradition, but also various Protestant traditions, have begun to include not only traditional and contemporary African American and Hispanic music, but also Asian and African hymns. The Taizé music by Jacques Berthier and the music of the Iona Community by John Bell are also increasingly found in traditional hymnals.

Texts and Translations. Vernacular texts immediately after the council were often only partially successful as translations of Latin texts or attempts at contemporary expression. Gradually, the poetic quality of hymn texts improved and attentiveness to giving expression to a wider gamut of both Christian and human concerns became more evident. Increasingly, Scripture became a primary source of inspiration for text writers. Beginning in the late 1970s and early 1980s, inclusive language emerged as an important issue.

Hispanic Hymnals. The first Hispanic hymnal, *Cantemos al Senor: Himnos para Celebración Liturgica,* was published in the United States by Our Sunday Visitor in 1974. *Alleluya, Alabad al Señor,* edited by Elias Isla, followed in 1977. In addition to the Ordinary of the Mass and a format for morning and evening Prayer, this hymnal included hymns from 14 Spanish-speaking countries. Other hymnals followed in the 1980s, including *Canticos de Gracias y Alabanza* published in 1982 and *Flor y Canto* in 1989, both by Oregon Catholic Press.

African American Hymns and Hymnals. Beginning in the 1980s, both Roman Catholic and Protestant churches began including a significant number of African spirituals, hymns, and gospel songs in their principal hymnals. Some have also published separate African American hymnals. In 1981 the Church Hymnal Corporation published *Lift Every Voice and Sing: A Collection of Afro-American Spirituals and Other Songs* as a supplement to the hymnal of the Episcopal Church. In 1987 G.I.A. Publications published *Lead Me, Guide Me: The African-American Catholic Hymnal.* This hymnal, a response to the small, but growing black community within the Roman Catholic Church, features gospel songs, spirituals, African and Caribbean material, plus hymnody from Catholic, Protestant, and evangelical traditions. It also includes new compositions by such leading black composers as Edward Bonnemere, Leon Roberts, Grayson Warren Brown, and Clarence Rivers. In 1999 Augsburg Fortress Press published *This Far by Faith: An African American Resource for Worship.* This hymnal was a joint project of the Evangelical Lutheran Church in America and the Lutheran Church-Missouri Synod. Like the Episcopal hymnal, *Lift Every Voice and Sing,*

This Far by Faith can be considered a supplement to the *Lutheran Book of Worship.*

Protestant Hymnals. Enthusiasm for liturgical renewal generated by Vatican II spilled over into mainstream Protestant denominations. In the United States, Canada, and Great Britain most of the major denominations have published a new hymnal, sometimes even a revised edition, since the mid-1960s. Similar to the Roman Catholic hymnals, the Protestant hymnals offer a broad range of offerings, including psalmody, both metrical and responsorial; international hymnody, especially from non-European areas of the world, including Central and South America, Asia, and Africa; African American spirituals and gospel songs; music from the Taizé community; and new mainstream hymn writers from the United States, Canada, and Great Britain. The new hymnals have been designed to focus on the following: the celebration of the Christian year, the celebration of the Lord's Supper, the need for responsible stewardship of Earth's resources, a belief in the Church as an expression of the presence of Christ on Earth, the incorporation of more scripturally based hymn texts, and attentiveness—in varying ways—to inclusive language.

Divergent Efforts to Retrieve Traditional Catholic Hymnody. In the decades that have passed since 1963 when article 114 of *SC* stated that "the treasury of sacred music is to be preserved and fostered with great care," divergent views continue to critique the direction church music has taken. Some have worked to adapt the ancient treasury of sacred music to the requirements of the reformed liturgy. An example of this approach is Paul Ford's *By Flowing Waters* published by the Liturgical Press. Others have looked to contemporary musical vocabulary to discover a voice for worship. A great number of new hymnals include a generous number of selections that reflect this approach. Still others have maintained the "classicist" view that sees in the ancient treasures of chant, hymnody, and polyphony the only authentic means for worship. The *Adoramus Hymnal* embodies this approach.

Future Developments. Shortly after the close of Vatican Council II, there was much speculation regarding the potential for creating a national hymnal for the United States. Since then, there seems to be no evidence that such a hymnal is on the horizon. Using an official hymnal in the United States has not been mandated by the National Conference of Catholic Bishops. While some conversations have occurred among publishers and within the forum of the National Association of Pastoral Musicians regarding the feasibility of a national hymnal, no concrete steps have been taken to make this a reality.

Bibliography: C. M. HAWN, "A Survey of Trends in Recent Protestant Hymnals: African-American Spirituals, Hymns, and Gospel Songs," *Hymn* 43:1 (Jan. 1992) 21–28. C. M. HAWN, "A Survey of Trends in Recent Protestant Hymnals: Mainstream American, British, and Canadian Hymnody since 1960," *Hymn* 42:3 (July 1991) 17–25. F. A. PISCITELLI, "Thirty-five Years of Catholic Hymnals in the United States (1962–1997): A Chronological Listing," *Hymn* 49:4 (1998). J. M. KUBICKI, "The Role of Music as Ritual Symbol in Roman Catholic Liturgy," *Worship* 69 (1995) 427–446. G. BLACK, "Gather and Worship: One Concept in Two Books and Many Editions," *Hymn* 42 (1991) 12–15. E. FOLEY, "When American Roman Catholics Sing," *Worship* 63 (1989) 98–112. W. F. SMITH, "Lead Me, Guide Me: The African American Catholic Hymnal," *Hymn* 40 (1989) 13–15.

[J. M. KUBICKI]

HYPATIUS OF EPHESUS

Sixth-century bishop of Ephesus; d. after 536. Hypatius was one of the chief advisers for ecclesiastical affairs to the Byzantine Emperor JUSTINIAN I from 531 to 536. About 531 Justinian invited Monophysite leaders to Constantinople in order to persuade them to accept the Christological formula of the Council of CHALCEDON (451). First mentioned in 531, Hypatius spoke in 532 for the orthodox at a colloquy between orthodox and Monophysite bishops. Here Hypatius' Christology was that of a moderately strict Dyophysite: Jesus Christ is one of the Trinity not so much in His one person as by reason of His divine nature. Hypatius also denied the authenticity of the writings of PSEUDO-DIONYSIUS the Areopagite and the so-called Apollinarian frauds. Justinian sent him to Pope JOHN II in Rome in 533–534 to win papal approval of the Theopaschite formula "one of the Trinity suffered in the flesh." At the Council of Constantinople in 536, which banished the Monophysites, he played a role second only to that of the Patriarch Mennas. He is not heard of afterward.

Hypatius composed a work called *Various Questions,* a collection of replies to questions asked by one of his suffragan bishops. Only fragments remain, including his defense of icons in the church. He is perhaps the author also of a commentary on the Minor Prophets. In 1904 an inscription was found in Ephesus containing the promulgation of his directives to his diocese concerning the burial of the dead.

Bibliography: F. DIEKAMP, *Orientalia Christiana Analecta* 117 (1938) 109–153. C. MOELLER, in A. GRILLMEIER and H. BACHT, *Das Konzil von Chalkedon: Geschichte und Gegenwart,* 3 v. (Würzburg 1951–54) 1:661–662, 674–676. E. KITZINGER, "The Cult of Images before Iconoclasm," *Dumbarton Oaks Papers* 8 (1954) 137–139.

[D. B. EVANS]

HYPOCRISY

Form of SIMULATION or acted lie. Indeed, it is simulation at its worst, for it prostitutes works of VIRTUE to the ignoble ends of self-glorification or monetary gain or worse, and it lowers men's esteem for the life of the spirit. Our Lord uttered his severest rebukes against the Pharisees precisely for their hypocrisy (Mt 23.23), and one of His saddest complaints was against the hypocritical treachery of Judas: "Dost thou betray the Son of Man with a kiss?" (Lk 22.48).

In its strictest sense, hypocrisy is the simulation of one who wishes to seem, but not to be, virtuous. This is a serious sin since it shows indifference and contempt for virtue, while at the same time using it for base and selfish ends. This type of hypocrisy especially makes virtue appear mean and ugly. It discourages honest men from giving themselves to virtue and religion and provides the godless man with an excuse for avoiding them.

But hypocrisy is seldom realized in so serious a form. Far more common is the hypocrisy of the man who does have some appreciation for virtue and religion, and perhaps for this very reason simulates a degree of goodness or holiness beyond what is actually his. He does not think enough of virtue to expend the effort required to achieve it, but he does find it sufficiently worthwhile to pose as virtuous. Here the sin is mortal or venial according to one's motive. For example, to make a show of virtue in order to prepare the ground for an eventual seduction would be a mortal sin, while to do so out of mere vanity would rarely be more than a venial sin.

If an individual merely conceals his sin, even if this results in his being mistakenly regarded as good and holy, he is not on that account a hypocrite. Indeed, he ought to avoid the scandal that could easily be the consequence of imprudently advertising the sinful state of his own soul. As long as he does nothing to encourage belief in his supposed goodness or sanctity, he is not being hypocritical by simply remaining silent about his sin. Nor would it be hypocrisy for a person to show himself as having the virtue that he really has. On the contrary, though it is always wise and prudent for one not to wear his virtue on his sleeve, he lies who, being good and virtuous, openly claims or pretends to be vicious.

Bibliography: J. A. MCHUGH and C. J. CALLAN, *Moral Theology,* rev. E. P. FARRELL, 2 v. (New York 1958) 2:2405.

[S. F. PARMISANO]

HYPOSTASIS

The theological equivalence of hypostasis with person is the result of a long development. The original meaning of the Greek word was substructure, support. Then it came to mean something real and objective as opposed to a mere appearance or abstraction. In Scripture it usually means moral support, assurance, conviction, e.g., in Heb 11.1: "Now faith is the substance [ὑπόστασις; Vulgate: *substantia*] of things to be hoped for . . ." (cf. Heb 3.14; 2 Cor 9.4).

In patristic writings it was first used about the Trinity. Origen speaks of three hypostases in God—the Father, the Son, and the Holy Spirit. Dionysius of Alexandria, writing against Arius and Sabellius, says that there are three hypostases in the unity of the divine monarchy. Gradually hypostasis came to be distinguished from οὐσία (*ousia;* being, reality), which was reserved for what was common to the three Persons, the divine nature. In the Council of Nicaea I, nevertheless, *ousia* and hypostasis are still roughly equivalent: "If anyone says . . . that the Son of God is from a different hypostasis, or *ousia* [than the Father], . . . him the Catholic Church anathematizes" (H. Denzinger, *Enchiridion symbolorum* [Freiburg 1963] 126).

The translation of hypostasis into Latin by its literal equivalent, *substantia,* aroused in the West the suspicion that the Greeks were Arians or tritheists, while the translation of the Latin *persona* into the Greek πρόσωπον made the West sound Sabellian to the East. The good sense of men like Gregory of Nazianzus brought East and West to see that they held the same faith despite the different connotations of the terms in Greek and in Latin. The acceptance of the term "person" as orthodox in the East can be seen in a synodal letter of Eastern bishops to Pope Damasus in 382: "in three perfect hypostases, or three perfect Persons [πρόσωπα]."

Hypostasis played an important part in the Christological controversies of the 5th century. APOLLINARIS OF LAODICEA held that the human nature of Christ does not include a human soul. One of his arguments was that this would make Him two hypostases and therefore not really a unity. CYRIL OF ALEXANDRIA expressed the union of the human and the divine in Christ as a union in hypostasis (ἕνωσις καθ ὑποστασιν), a phrase that meant for him, as Galtier has shown, merely that the union is one in reality, not in mere appearance. Cyril did not distinguish between physis (φύσις) and hypostasis, and his terminology laid him open to the charge of MONOPHYSITISM. The distinction between the two terms was formulated by Pope LEO I as a unity in Person, or hypostasis, and a duality in nature, or *physis.* Chalcedon canonized the distinction as well as the equivalence of the respective Greek and Latin terms: "[T]he particular natures unite in the one person and one hypostasis" (H. Denzinger, *Enchiridion symbolorum* [Freiburg 1963] 302).

After Chalcedon the theologians' task was to convince the Monophysites that the decrees of Ephesus had not been abandoned and to explain the difference between person and nature. Boethius made clear that only a rational being could be a hypostasis: "We have found the definition of person, 'the individual substance of a rational nature.' Now by this definition we Latins have described what the Greeks call hypostasis" (*Tract. theol. quintus* 1.4). Leontius of Byzantium answered the Monophysite objection that nature without hypostasis is nothing, and hence one hypostasis in Christ means one nature, by saying that the human nature of Christ is "neither uncentered [*anhypostatos*] nor self-centered, but 'encentered' [*enhypostatos*] in God" (Hardy and Richardson, 375–376). Finally, John Damascene summed up the tradition of the earlier Fathers and further emphasized that hypostasis implies incommunicability (*De fide orthodoxa* 1.8; *Patrologia Graeca* [Paris 1857–66] 95:828) and that it signifies not what, but who.

Modern theological speculation on the HYPOSTATIC UNION has centered on the question of what the formal constituent of personality is and, more recently, on the relation between the human consciousness of Christ and the hypostasis of the Word.

See Also: JESUS CHRIST; TRINITY, HOLY; INCARNATION; INCOMMUNICABILITY; PERSON (IN PHILOSOPHY); PERSON (IN THEOLOGY); SUBSISTENCE; SUBSISTENCE (IN CHRISTOLOGY).

Bibliography: A. MICHEL, *Dictionnaire de théologie catholique,* ed. A. VACANT et al. (Paris 1903–50) 7.1:369–437. V. HAMP and H. DIEPEN, *Lexikon für Theologie und Kirche,* ed. J. HOFER and K. RAHNER (Freiburg 1957–65) 5:577–579. A. GRILLMEIER and H. BACHT, *Das Konzil von Chalkedon: Geschichte und Gegenwart* (Würzburg 1951–54). E. R. HARDY and C. C. RICHARDSON, eds., *Christology of the Later Fathers* (Philadelphia, Pa. 1954). P. GALTIER, "L'*Unio secundum hypostasim* chez s. Cyrille," *Gregorianum* 33 (1952) 351–398. M. NÉDONCELLE, "*Prosōpon et persona,*" *Revue des sciences religieuses* 22 (1948) 277–299. M. RICHARD, "L'Introduction du mot hypostasis dans la théologie de l'incarnation," *Mélanges de science religieuse* 2 (1945) 5–32; 243–270.

[J. M. CARMODY]

HYPOSTATIC UNION

The union in one PERSON, or HYPOSTASIS, of the divine and human natures. Jesus Christ is both God and man in virtue of the hypostatic union, a mystery of faith in the strict sense. "As God he was begotten of the substance of the Father before time; as man he was born in time of the substance of his mother. He is perfect God; and he is perfect man, with a rational soul and human flesh. He is equal to the Father in His divinity but He is inferior to the Father in his humanity. Although he is God and man, he is not two but one Christ. And he is one, not because his divinity was changed into flesh, but because His humanity was assumed to God. He is one, not at all because of a mingling of substances, but because he is one person" [the so-called Athanasian Creed; H. Denzinger, *Enchiridion symbolorum* 76; tr. J. F. Clarkson et al., *The Church Teaches* (St. Louis 1955) 5–6].

Biblical affirmations of the divinity and humanity of Christ were transformed into technical, theological expressions and (to some extent) explanations of the mystery when heresies began to pervert the true faith. Docetism, Arianism, and Apollinarianism attacked the true humanity of Christ; Arianism, rationalism, Modernism, the true divinity. In addition, NESTORIANISM, ADOPTIONISM, MONOPHYSITISM, and MONOTHELITISM erroneously understood the manner of the union between the divine and human natures. The evolution of the fixed technical terminology of the hypostatic union was gradual. The Council of CHALCEDON (451) established the usage whereby hypostasis means person and whereby *ousia* and *physis* mean substance and nature. A consideration of the Council of Nicaea I's use of hypostasis and *ousia* (Denzinger 126) will bring out the earlier (325) fluidity of terminology.

See Also: JESUS CHRIST, II (IN THEOLOGY); HYPOSTATIC UNION, GRACE OF; PERSON (IN PHILOSOPHY); PERSON (IN THEOLOGY); NATURE; JESUS CHRIST, ARTICLES ON.

Bibliography: A. MICHEL, *Dictionnaire de théologie catholique,* ed. A. VACANT et al. (Paris 1903–50) 7.1:437–568. M. SCHMAUS, *Lexikon für Theologie und Kirche,* ed. J. HOFER and K. RAHNER (Freiburg 1957–65) 5:579–583.

[E. A. WEIS]

HYPOSTATIC UNION, GRACE OF

The INCARNATION of the SON OF GOD is the supreme gift or GRACE of God to man. From the 12th century, theologians have designated this aspect of the hypostatic union as "the grace of union" (*gratia unionis*).

Historical. The New Testament frequently speaks of Christ as the manifestation or gift of God's graciousness toward sinful man, sometimes using the word χάρις (grace), e.g., Jn 1.14–17; Ti 2.11. For St. Augustine, the hypostatic union is the model of man's grace; just as Jesus did not merit to be the Christ, the unique and sinless Son of God, so men do not merit to be Christians, reborn, freed from sin (*Praed. sanct.* 15.30–31, *Patrologia Latina* 44:981–983; cf. *Enchir.* 36, *Patrologia Latina* 40:250). The Middle Ages in developing Augustine's teaching sought to safeguard the gratuity of the Incarnation without making Christ a merely adoptive son. Against Spanish ADOPTIONISM of the late 8th century, Alcuin (*Adv. haer. Felic.* 69; *Patrologia Latina* 101:116) insisted on distinguishing grace and adoption. In the 12th century, a frequent formula (attributed, without clear textual support, to both Ambrose and Augustine) was that the humanity or soul of Christ received by grace all that His divinity had by nature. Christ as man, though not an adoptive Son, was declared to be *Son by grace* and *Son by union,* in contrast with His being in His divinity *Son by nature.* Finally Peter Lombard (3 *Sent.* 10.2.67–69; Quaracchi 2.595–596) combined both expressions in the phrase "grace of union." Thirteenth-century theologians explored this *gratia unionis* and identified it variously as the Holy Spirit producing the union, as a created disposition for the union, as the hypostatic union itself, etc. St. Thomas Aquinas (*Comp. theol.* 214; cf. *Summa theologiae* 3a, 7, introd.; 8.5 ad 3) and others distinguished a threefold grace in Christ: grace of union, habitual grace, and grace of headship. In subsequent theology the grace of union was discussed primarily in connection with the substantial sanctity of Christ and was explained in accordance with various speculative theories of the hypostatic union. The two principal questions on which theologians continued to differ were the following: (1) Is the grace of union created or uncreated? (2) Does the grace of union sanctify the humanity of itself or only because it has habitual grace as consequence?

Systematic. The hypostatic union, as a gift proceeding from the gracious will of God communicating Himself substantially to man beyond the powers, exigencies, or merits of human nature, is the supreme grace. This grace of union may be termed uncreated or created accordingly as one regards the Divine Person of the WORD, who communicates Himself to His humanity, or the created reality of union in that humanity. Theologians commonly distinguish this substantial grace, which is identical with the hypostatic union, from Christ's habitual or sanctifying grace and His grace of headship, accidental graces that flow from the grace of union and are measured by it. Because of the grace of union, Christ's humanity is holy and sinless (*see* IMPECCABILITY OF CHRIST), and the man Christ is the natural, not adoptive, Son of God. It is ultimately because of the grace of union that His habitual grace and virtues have a quasi-infinite perfection, and His salvific actions are intrinsically apt to sanctify all mankind, whose grace is incarnational and filial because it participates in the grace of union through the mediation of Christ's habitual grace and virtues as informing His saving action.

Bibliography: A. MICHEL, *Dictionnaire de théologie catholique,* ed. A. VACANT et al. (Paris 1903–50) 7.1:437–568. A.

VUGTS, *La Grâce d'union d'après S. Thomas d'Aquin: Essai historique et doctrinal* (Tilburg 1946). J. ROHOF, *La Sainteté substantielle du Christ dans la théologie scolastique: Histoire du problème* (Fribourg 1952). se

[T. E. CLARKE]

HYSTERECTOMY

Hysterectomy is the surgical removal of the womb by an incision in the abdomen or through the vagina. A hysterectomy is called subtotal, supracervical, or supravaginal if the cervix (the neck of the womb) is left in place. It is called radical if the entire womb, fallopian tubes, and ovaries are removed.

As early as 1768 Cavalini had speculated on the feasibility of the surgical removal of the womb, and the first recorded hysterectomy was reported by G. Bixby in 1869. According to Bixby it was done by one H. R. Stover as an emergency procedure in the presence of massive hemorrhage subsequent to caesarean section. The patient died after 78 hours. During the next few years, E. Porro (for whom the caesarean hysterectomy is now named) conducted surgical experiments on rabbits; in 1876 he performed the first completely successful hysterectomy and recommended the procedure whenever caesarean section was to be done.

As surgical technique improved and hazards decreased, hysterectomy increased at such a rate that in 1946 Norman Miller, in his review of the procedure in the *American Journal of Obstetrics and Gynecology,* entitled his article: "Hysterectomy: Therapeutic Necessity or Surgical Racket?" [51 (1946) 804], and in 1956 Waverly R. Payne made unnecessary hysterectomy the subject of his presidential address to the South Atlantic Association of Obstetricians and Gynecologists [72 (1956) 1165]. This type of study may indicate a too free attitude on the part of some physicians in regard to hysterectomy, but it is much more indicative of the constant self-evaluation of the medical profession, with a view to the best welfare of the individual patient.

The principal moral considerations involved in the surgical removal of the womb arise from the fact that hysterectomy is an operation that seriously compromises the functional integrity of the body and results in the permanent loss of the reproductive function. When this is done simply as a contraceptive measure, it is recognized by the Church as humanly disordered and morally wrong. An example of this would be a hysterectomy performed because the abdomen is already open in the surgical treatment of some benign adnexal disease and the patient likewise wished to be rid of her childbearing potential [A.

D'Esposo, "Hysterectomy when the Uterus Is Grossly Normal," *American Journal of Obstetrics and Gynecology* 83 (1962) 113–122].

The moral questions concerned with hysterectomy can be conveniently divided into three categories. First there are those cases in which some pathology of the womb itself makes its continued presence in the body a threat to life or health independent of any future pregnancy. Such, for example, would be the presence of a malignant tumor, irreparable damage of the uterine wall, or placenta accreta in a pronounced degree. When this kind and degree of uterine pathology is verified, the principle of totality indicates the removal of the womb. The consequent loss of the reproductive function is acceptable and justified under the principle of DOUBLE EFFECT.

The second category of cases can be classified under the concept of functional compromise of the womb because of the impossibility of adequate and lasting surgical repair. These are cases in which the womb itself has become affected in a way that will (or may) demand a future hysterectomy, although at the present an inadequate sort of repair, consisting mainly in plication of the fascia and shortening of the relaxed ligaments, as well as a modification of the cervix, would be adequate. This would enable the woman to have another pregnancy or two, with delivery usually by caesarean section; eventually, however, a hysterectomy would likely be indicated. However, if the patient should prefer that the definitive surgery be done right away, instead of later, because she is not so anxious to increase her family as to be inclined to undergo this extra surgical procedure, there is no reason, from a moral viewpoint, why hysterectomy could not be done initially. Since under ordinary circumstances one is not obliged to take extraordinary measures to prolong one's life, she is certainly not obliged to take them to prolong her generative function.

In much the same way, if, after a varying number of caesarean sections, the obstetrician judges that the womb is beyond safe and adequate repair in regard to future childbearing, it can be removed as a damaged organ. Although some theologians have been disturbed by an apparent contraceptive dimension of this procedure (Zalba, 2:152, ad 4), still one must consider that the primary approach to the problem is in terms of the removal of a damaged organ of the body that can no longer function safely and may therefore be removed, despite the fact that its function is generative. This opinion favoring hysterectomy is sufficiently established to be followed safely (G. Kelly, "Notes on Moral Theology," 70–71). Moreover, a view that would permit tubal ligation in this particular case, as a measure of simply isolating the uterus instead of removing it, is being studied (from a moral viewpoint) by a number of theologians (*see* Tesson and Cardegna in bibliography).

Bibliography: G. A. KELLY, *Medico-Moral Problems* (St. Louis 1958); "Notes on Moral Theology, 1950," *Theological Studies* 12 (1951) 70–71. J. P. KENNY, *Principles of Medical Ethics* (2d ed. Westminster, Md. 1962). C. J. MCFADDEN *Medical Ethics* (5th ed. Philadelphia 1961). T. J. O'DONNELL, *Morals in Medicine* (2d ed. Westminster, Md. 1959). C. MCLANE et al., "Indications for Hysterectomy: A Panel Discussion," *American Journal of Obstetrics and Gynecology* 72 (1956) 534–533. M. ZALBA, *Theologiae moralis summa*, v. 2 (*Biblioteca de autores cristianos* 106; 2d ed. Madrid 1957) 152, ad 4. E. TESSON, "Discussion morale," *Cahiers Laennec* 24 (1964) 64–73. F. F. CARDEGNA, "Contraception, the Pill, and Responsible Parenthood," *Theological Studies* 25 (1964) 611–636, see esp. n. 21.

[T. J. O'DONNELL]

HYVERNAT, HENRI

Orientalist and professor; b. Loire, France, June 30, 1858; d. Washington, D.C., May 29, 1941. In 1877 Hyvernat began his studies for the priesthood at Issy and Paris. Fellow students who became his lifelong friends included M. J. LAGRANGE and P. BATIFFOL. Hyvernat, encouraged by the famous Abbé F. G. Vigouroux, made the Semitic languages, including Babylonian and Egyptian, his chosen field of study and began to prepare for a scientific career. After ordination in Lyons, France, on June 3, 1882, he was appointed chaplain at the French church of St. Louis in Rome. In 1885, with his degree of doctor of divinity from the Pontifical University, he was made professor of Assyriology and Egyptology at the Roman Seminary and interpreter of Oriental languages at the Congregation De Propaganda Fide.

In 1883 *Le Monde* published Hyvernat's study of the Assyrian monuments in the Vatican. In 1886–87 he published his *Actes des Martyrs de l'Egypte* (Coptic text with French translation), and in 1888 his *Album de paléographie Copte*.

In 1887 he accepted the offer of a professorship at The Catholic University of America that was to be established in Washington, D.C., in 1889. During the intervening year he undertook a scientific survey for the French government of the cuneiform inscriptions preserved in Armenia and Kurdistan. The account of the results and adventures of this survey appeared in book form in 1892 (*Du Caucase au golfe Persique*, with P. Müller-Simonis). Hyvernat assumed his duties at Catholic University on the day of its solemn opening in 1889 and he retained his professorship there for 52 years until his death.

Besides teaching, Hyvernat wrote articles on the Coptic versions of the Bible and other subjects related to

Egypt for Vigouroux's *Dictionnaire de la Bible* in 1895, for the *Jewish Encyclopedia* in 1901, and for the *Catholic Encyclopedia* in 1903. For the *Revue Biblique* he wrote his *Études sur les versions Coptes de la Bible* in 1896 and his *Petite introduction a l'étude de la Massore* between 1902 and 1904. In 1903 he collaborated with Dr. J. B. CHABOT in founding the *Corpus Scriptorum Christianorum Orientalium*, and he edited its volumes of the Coptic *Acta Martyrum.* In 1912 he was instrumental in having the *Corpus* enterprise tranferred to the joint ownership of the two Catholic Universities of Louvain and America.

While in Europe in 1910, Hyvernat became deeply interested in the unique collection of 50 ancient Coptic manuscripts discovered at Hamuli in Egypt. When this was purchased by J. P. Morgan of New York in 1911, Hyvernat obtained the commission to prepare a catalogue of the manuscripts, to have them taken to the Vatican Library Studios to be repaired, rebound, and photographed, and to have a photographic edition prepared for distribution to a list of great libraries. The work was completed in 1925.

While recovering from serious illness in 1927, Hyvernat began his work on a *Catalogue raisonné*, which was to fill ten or more volumes and serve as a *Summa* of all Coptic learning. This he completed in abbreviated form by 1932 and turned over to the Pierpont Morgan Library. To the Institute for Christian Oriental Research at the Catholic University of America, a project he had planned, he deeded his library and all his life's savings. In this way he secured for himself a share in the continuation by others of his long life's unfinished labors.

Bibliography: T. C. PETERSEN, "Professor Henry Hyvernat," *Catholic World* 153 (Sept. 1941) 653–666.

[T. C. PETERSEN]

I

IAM CHRISTUS ASTRA ASCENDERAT

Office hymn that was historically prescribed for Matins on the feast of Pentecost. It dates from the fourth or fifth century and some ascribe the hymn to St. AMBROSE. Others disagree, however, basing their opinion in part on metrical variations that are unusual in Ambrosian hymns. The hymn, in eight strophes, is a somewhat pedestrian metrical setting of Acts 2.1–16, describing the coming of the Holy Spirit upon the Apostles, the miracle of tongues, and St. Peter's response to the charge of drunkenness made by some of the mystified hearers. The meter is iambic dimeter.

Bibliography: *Analecta hymnica* 2:49; 51:98. J. JULIAN, ed., *A Dictionary of Hymnology* (New York 1957) 1:576. M. BRITT, ed., *The Hymns of the Breviary and Missal* (new ed. New York 1948). J. CONNELLY, *Hymns of the Roman Liturgy* (Westminster MD 1957) 108–109.

[J. P. MCCORMICK]

IAM SOL RECEDIT IGNEUS

Office hymn that was traditionally used at first Vespers of the Sundays after Epiphany and after Pentecost. With the variation of one word in the fourth line of the first stanza (*Infunde amorem cordibus* instead of *Infunde lumen cordibus*), it was also assigned for use at Vespers of Trinity Sunday. The original text began *O lux beata trinitas,/ Et principalis unitas.* The original hymn, written in iambic dimeter, is often ascribed to St. AMBROSE; he is actually cited as its author by Hincmar of Reims in a work of 857. However, more recent works on hymnology tend to refer to the authorship as unknown. Some would ascribe it to GREGORY THE GREAT; however, it may date only from the 9th century. The 1632 revision of the Roman Breviary abbreviated the hymn to two stanzas and a doxology.

Bibliography: *Analecta hymnica* 51:38. J. JULIAN, ed., *A Dictionary of Hymnology* (New York 1957) 1:842. M. BRITT, ed., *The Hymns of the Breviary and Missal* (new ed. New York 1948)

62–63, 164–165. J. CONNELLY, *Hymns of the Roman Liturgy* (Westminster MD 1957) 43. J. SZÖVÉRFFY, *Die Annalen der lateinischen Hymnendichtung* (Berlin 1964–65)1:142, 214.

[J. P. MCCORMICK]

IAM TOTO SUBITUS VESPER

Office hymn that was historically sung, first at Matins, subsequently at Vespers, on the feast of the Seven Sorrows of Our Lady. Its composition is ascribed to Callisto Palumbella, a bishop of the 18th century, who was a member of the SERVITES, and to whom the feast had been granted in 1688. The meter is minor asclepiadic in the first three lines of each strophe and glyconic in the fourth line. Within the space of its six stanzas the hymn details the sufferings of Christ upon the cross and stresses their effect on His Mother.

Bibliography: J. JULIAN, ed., *A Dictionary of Hymnology* (New York 1957) 1:578. M. BRITT, ed., *The Hymns of the Breviary and Missal* (new ed. New York 1948).

[J. P. MCCORMICK]

IAMBLICHUS

Neoplatonist philosopher; b. Chalcis in Coele Syria, *c.* A.D. 250; d. *c.* 325. He was a student of PORPHYRY, the successor of PLOTINUS, and later conducted his own school, possibly at Apamea. He is credited by his successors with important elaborations within the scheme of Neoplatonist emanation, with the promotion of theurgy and with the dethronement of the human soul from its Plotinian perpetual union with the intellect. Unfortunately, his commentaries upon various dialogues of PLATO have not survived, and one is left to conjecture what his system may have been from quotations and testimonies in later writers, especially PROCLUS and Damascius.

See Also: NEOPLATONISM.

Bibliography: His extant works form part of a Pythagorean collection: *De vita pythagorica,* ed. L. DEUBNER (Leipzig 1937);

Adhortatio ad philosophiam or *Protrepticus*, ed. H. PISTELLI (Leipzig 1888); *De communi mathematica scientia liber*, ed. N. FESTA (Leipzig 1891); *In Nicomachi arthmeticam introductionis liber*, ed. H. PISTELLI (Leipzig 1894); *Theologoumena arithmeticae*, ed. V. DE FALCO (Leipzig 1922), authorship disputed; *De mysteriis liber*, ed. G. PARTHEY (Berlin 1857), probably correctly attributed to Iamblichus. Grouped together with commentary are fragments of his lost treatise *De anima*, in *La Révélation d'Hermès Trismésiste*, ed. and tr. A. J. FESTUGIÈRE, 4 v. (Paris 1950–54) v.3. Lost are works on the gods and on the Chaldean oracles. G. FAGGIN, *Enciclopedia filosofica*, 4 v. (Venice–Rome 1957) 2:707–708. F. UEBERWEG. *Grundriss der Geschichte der Philosophie*, ed. K. PRAECHTER et al., 5 v. (12th ed. Berlin 1923–28) 1:612–618. P. MERLAN, *From Platonism to Neoplatonism* (2d ed. The Hague 1960). ARISTOTLE, *Protrepticus*, ed. I. DÜRING (Göteborg 1961).

[W. H. O'NEILL]

IBARRA Y GONZÁLEZ, RAMÓN

Mexican archbishop and educational reformer, first archbishop of Puebla; b. Olinalá, Guerrero, Mexico, Oct. 22, 1853; d. Mexico City, Feb. 1, 1917. Educated in Puebla and in Rome, he was personally presented with a special medal by Pope Leo XIII for his brilliant scholarship. After being ordained on Feb. 21, 1880, he returned to Mexico in 1883. In August 1889, he was chosen bishop of the Diocese of Chilapa. In 1902 he was transferred to the Diocese of Puebla, which became an archdiocese a year later by order of Pius X. Thus he was the last bishop and first archbishop of Puebla. At the time of his death he was in hiding because of religious persecutions: his flock dispersed, the clergy scattered in all directions, many of his works undone, the seminary and Catholic university that he founded destroyed.

A man both gentle and firm, he is remembered for his nobility and his many accomplishments. He was extremely active, talented, and highly creative, optimistic and generous by nature, and a tireless fighter in the cause of God. He founded 15 schools, a preparatory school, and a Catholic university that had six faculties. He was responsible for bringing into Mexico the Christian Brothers and the Teresians. The poorer classes owe to him the founding of two free hospitals, an asylum, a Catholic workers' circle, and a theater that he endowed. He improved the Palafoxiano Seminary, for which he obtained the privilege of offering academic degrees. He founded the Institute of Missionaries of Guadalupe especially for the Indian population and the Mexican Congregation of the Missionaries of the Holy Spirit. He also obtained pontifical approval for the order of the Religious of the Cross, and founded the Apostolic League of diocesan priests. He organized the First Catholic National Congress in 1903. He published a total of 17 pastoral letters, held four diocesan synods, and founded two Catholic chapters and a Catholic social action center.

Bibliography: O. MÁRQUEZ, *Monseñor Ibarra: Biografía del Excmo. Sr. Dr. y maestro D. Ramón Ibarra y González . . .* (Mexico City 1962).

[R. GUÍZAR DÍAZ]

IBN AL-'ASSĀL

Canon lawyer and chief of protocol to the Coptic Patriarch Cyril III (1235–43). Little else is known of his life and death. In preparation for the synod of 1239 he prepared a canonical collection known as the *Nomocanon* of Ibn al-'Assāl. It gives the civil and ecclesiastical law of the Monophysite Coptic Church and is noted for its orderliness and careful reproduction of sources. Manuscripts of the work can be found in the Vatican Library, the British Museum, and the Bibliothèque Nationale of Paris. Two editions in Arabic were published in Cairo in 1908 and 1927. The work is sometimes erroneously attributed to two younger brothers of the author.

Bibliography: S. JARGY, *Dictionnaire de droit canonique*, ed. R. NAZ, 7 v. (Paris 1935–65) 5:1237–42. J. M. WANSLEBEN, *Histoire de l'Église d'Alexandrie* (Paris 1677) 335.

[H. A. LARROQUE]

IBN 'ARABĪ

Muḥyī al-Dīn ibn 'Arabī, Islamic philosopher; b. Murcia, Spain, 1165; d. Damascus, 1240. Making use of the contribution of his predecessors in all branches of religious and philosophical science, and guided by his own unique spiritual experience, Ibn 'Arabī conceived a vast theosophical synthesis, monistic in inspiration, which he set forth in many writings. Although his work was severely criticized by orthodox SUNNITES, it had a decisive influence on the subsequent development of Muslim mysticism and of esoteric speculation in the East and the West, e.g., Dante.

Life. Ibn 'Arabī's family, of Arabic origin, had ties with SUFISM. When he was eight years old he was sent from his birthplace in southeastern Spain to Lisbon to study the QUR'ĀN and Muslim law. He then went to Seville, where he pursued his studies in the philosophical and religious sciences. His education kept pace with his initiation into the mystical life, which was greatly influenced by his filial friendship with two venerable Sufi women. On a journey to Cordova, his father, a friend of Averroës (ibn-Rushd), arranged an interview for his son with the famous philosopher, who was amazed at Ibn 'Arabī's genius.

In 1200, when he was 35, Ibn 'Arabī had a vision. Because of it, he left Spain permanently for the Orient in the hope of finding a more favorable reception for his symbolical exegesis. This was the beginning of an itinerant life that took him to Arabia, Egypt, Iraq, Syria, and Asia Minor, and continued until 1223, when he settled permanently in Damascus. There he spent the last 17 years of his life, working in tranquility. An encounter he had in Mecca in 1201, during his first sojourn there, influenced the orientation of his thought. The daughter of his host seemed to him the earthly manifestation of eternal Wisdom. She became for him what Beatrice would be for Dante later on.

Works. Ibn ʿArabī's writings, unequal in length, number in the hundreds. Three of them deserve to be mentioned as the foundation of his fame. His *Tarjumān al-ashwāq* (The Interpreter of Eager Desires) is a collection of love poems composed in honor of his Meccan Beatrice; it is dated 1215. At Aleppo a few months later, the author prepared an esoteric commentary on these poems. His *Futuḥāt al-makkiyah* (The Revelations Received at Mecca concerning the Knowledge of the Secrets of the King and of the Kingdom) constitutes a summa of mystical theosophy, at once theoretical and experimental, developed as inspiration dictated. The editing of these works, begun in 1230, was to occupy Ibn ʿArabī for many years. Finally, the *Fuṣuṣ al-Ḥikam* (The Gems of the Wisdoms of the Prophets, 1230) summed up the author's esoteric doctrine. It should be noted that the style of this last-named work is particularly difficult. It is marked by discontinuity, permutation of contrary and complementary terms, a taste for paradox, and fluctuation of a vocabulary borrowed from disparate sources. These qualities are a challenge not merely for the translation, but even for the comprehension of the author's thought.

Teaching. Ibn ʿArabī's doctrine, which is very complex, is never explained by him in systematic fashion. The terms "pantheism" and "existential monism," which are usually used to describe it, are equivocal and could mask its originality. H. Corbin rightly prefers the term *kathenotheism,* which means: the presence of the divine Being, total each time and in each being, an epiphanic form, in which it manifests itself as clothed with one or several of its Names.

"I was a hidden Treasure and I loved to be known. Therefore I created creatures so as to be known by them." Meditation on this ḥadīth brought Ibn ʿArabī to the conception of an eternal cosmogony, "a sequence of manifestations of being, by the intensification of a growing light, within the primordially undifferentiated Divine"; strictly, a succession of *tajalliyāt,* "theophanies" (Corbin, 88). The divine Essence conceals many attributes, designated by the divine Names, which have meaning only for beings that are its epiphanic forms. In a "compassionate sigh" for his unnamed Names, God conceives in Himself the latent individualities of these forms (archetypes, angels, Islamic Reality). These individualities are concretized in creatures, in which and through which God reveals Himself to Himself, contemplating Himself in them as in a mirror. Each divine Name is the Lord of the being that manifests it. Each being manifests the divine Essence only as particularized in its own particular lord; hence the diversity of individual vocations, as well as of religions. The Perfect Man, the final cause of creation, is the epiphany of the totality of the divine Names. To speak of union with God is a snare, presupposing an illusory duality. The good and heaven consist in consciously realizing ever more perfectly the epiphany of God in Himself and in creatures. Evil and hell consist in conferring an illusory autonomy upon created things. The Prophets, manifestations of the divine wisdoms, guide men toward Reality. Their messages, which are also epiphanic, are to be interpreted symbolically. Muhammed is the most perfect of the Prophets.

Bibliography: A. E. AFFIFI, *The Mystical Philosophy of Muḥyid Dín-Ibnul ʿArabī* (Cambridge, Eng. 1939). R. LANDAU, *The Philosophy of Ibn ʿArabī* (London 1959). M. ASÍN PALACIOS, *El-Islam cristianizado* (Madrid 1931), stresses the Christian influences. H. CORBIN, *L'Imagination créatrice dans le soufisme d'Ibn ʿArabī* (Paris 1958), stresses the Oriental esoteric influences.

[S. DE BEAURECUEIL]

IBN EZRA, ABRAHAM BEN MEÏR

Hebrew poet, hymnographer, philologist, grammarian, and commentator on the Bible; b. Toledo (Castile) or Tudela (Navarre), Spain, 1092; d. Calahorra (Logoño), Spain, Jan. 23, 1167. Known to the Christians of the Middle Ages as Ebenare and given the epithet of the Great Sage by his fellow Jews of Spain, Ibn Ezra was one of the most celebrated rabbis of the 12th century. He first settled in Cordova, but being of a restless nature and in quest of an encyclopedic knowledge, he became a wanderer in search of the Eternal. His footsteps can be traced on all the roads of Europe and Egypt; he visited Narbonne (1139), Rome (1140), Salerno, Mantua, and Lucca (1145), Verona (1146–47), Beziers and Rodez in southern France (1155–57), London (1158–59), and again Rome (1166). Shortly after his return to his native land, he died at the age of 75.

During his travels Ibn Ezra never ceased to compose his works. His writings are as varied and turbulent as his life and reflect his versatility and encyclopedic knowledge. His chief work is his commentary on the Bible (printed in RABBINICAL BIBLES), which treats of all the OT books except Chronicles; he issued several recensions of his commentary on the Pentateuch. He even availed himself of the cabalistic genre (*see* CABALA) in his works: *The Book of the Secrets of the Law* (an attempt to explain the mysteries of the Pentateuch); *The Mystery of the Form of the Letters; The Enigma of the Quiescent Letters;* and *The Book of the Name* (which treats of the sacred Tetragrammaton YHWH). To these must be added numerous poetic, philological, astronomical, and grammatical works, such as *The Book of the Balance of the Holy Tongue, The Book of Purity* (of language), *The Pure Lip,* and *The Speech of Nobility,* which explains the rare and difficult words of the Bible.

To be appreciated, Ibn Ezra must be seen in the setting of his own time. Contrary to the previous servile and punctilious rabbinical compilations of Palestine and Babylon, the period extending from the 10th to the 15th century ushered in a personal, conscientious, and deeper study of the word of God. Grammar and lexicography became the foundation of a saner and more open-minded exegesis. This became the golden age of Jewish exegesis, and the movement achieved its most brilliant triumphs in the West, especially in Moorish Spain. Ibn Ezra was one of the leaders of this movement. Prolific and marvelously learned, he gave, through his commentaries, added impulse to the Biblical studies of his coreligionists. His prodigious memory enabled him to propagate and popularize in Latin and Saxon lands the works of his illustrious Andalusian compatriots of the 10th and 11th centuries. His supple mind was able to digest them and to set them forth with great clarity.

In his commentary on the Bible he gave attention, first of all, to the grammatical sense of the words, and he then looked for the direct, literal interpretation. The allegorizing so dear to the rabbis and the futile fantasies of the cabalists are absent from this work. With the cabalists, however, he was acquainted, since in other works he developed them with great relish. But in his commentary his erudite and scientific mind showed the way to a group of enlightened men who sought to explain the Bible with the aid of reason and science. He offered for the first time the spectacle of the tension between faith and reason, between traditional piety and a critical approach. His exegetical work vacillated between these two poles just as he himself wandered from one country to the other. He had one fixed purpose—the faithful interpretation of the Bible—and one goal—to reveal to his coreligionists of France, Italy, and England the renaissance of the intellectual and scientific spirit of Jewish Spain. "He can be considered as the first Biblical critic who elevated exegesis to the level of a science" (I. Bloch and E. Levy). Spinoza has described him as having been "a man of free mind and of great erudition."

Ibn Ezra was the first to sense the problem of the different sources in the Pentateuch and the problem of Deutero-Isaia. He was the first to uphold the opinion that in order to cross the Red Sea the Israelites had availed themselves of a low tide and that they had crossed at the end of the gulf. In proposing such daring opinions he felt the necessity of veiling his thought in allusions and involved constructions.

Ordinarily, however, his style was correct, clear, supple, and elegant; his expression was vibrant and witty. Having succeeded in creating a style of remarkable precision, he bequeathed a prose without peer. He made it a point of honor to write in the purest Hebrew, although up to that time Arabic was the cultural bond of the Mediterranean world. Every Jewish writer who then wished to gain an audience with the mass of the people and ensure the diffusion of his ideas wrote in Arabic. Ibn Ezra broke the trend, and he succeeded remarkably well. "One can rightly say of him that he created Hebrew prose as a medium of scientific thought" (Cecil Roth). For this reason also he may be placed in the ranks of the best Hebrew poets and hymn writers, although his poetry is characterized, not by lyrical flights and soulful effusions, but by reflections, maxims, and moralizings. Richard SIMON declared that "his style approaches that of Sallust."

See Also: JEWISH PHILOSOPHY.

Bibliography: W. BACHER, *The Jewish Encyclopedia,* ed. J. SINGER, (New York 1901–06) 6:520–524. S. BERNFELD, *Encyclopaedia Judaica: Das Judentum in Geschichte und Gegenwart* (Berlin 1928–34) 8:326–341. C. LEVIAS, *Universal Jewish Encyclopedia,* (New York 1939–44) 5:523–525. J. CANTERA, *Lexikon für Theologie und Kirche,* ed. J. HOFER and K. RAHNER, 10 v. (2d, new ed. Freiburg 1957–65) [2] 1:60–61. D. ROSIN, "Die Religionsphilosophie Abraham Ibn Ezras," *Monatschrift für Geschichte und Wissenschaft des Judenthums* 42–43. D. HERZOG, "Bemerkungen zu Abraham Ibn Ezra dem Historiker," *ibid.* 81. R. LEVY, *Astrological Works of Abraham Ibn Ezra* (Baltimore 1927).

[A. BRUNOT]

IBN PAQŪDA

Jewish religious philosopher, active in the second half of the 11th century. Nothing is known of his life except that his full name was Baḥya ben Joseph ibn Paqūda (Pakūda) and that he was a *dayyan* (rabbinical judge) in Saragossa or Cordova in Muslim Spain. Besides writing a certain number of liturgical poems, he was the author of an important work in Arabic on Jewish ethics, *Al-hidâya ila farâ'iḍ al-qulub* (Introduction to the Duties of the Heart). Joseph Kimchi's Hebrew translation of the work has not been preserved, but the 12th-century Hebrew version of it by Judah IBN TIBBON under the title *Ḥovot ha-levavot* (Duties of the Heart) became very popular and has been preserved in many MSS. A critical edition of the Arabic text was published by A. S. Yahuda (Leyden 1912). Modern translations have appeared in German by E. Baumgarten (Hamburg 1922) and in French by A. Chouraqui (Paris n.d.), but the English translation by M. Hyamson (New York 1945) offers only the sixth, seventh, and eighth treatises.

Ibn Paqūda set himself the task of harmonizing seemingly incompatible values: soul and reason, faith and science, Hellenistic systems of wisdom and Judeo-Islamic religious practices, the external "duties of the members" and the interior "duties of the heart." To the revealed religion of the Bible and rabbinical tradition he brought the support of a rational theology concerning God, the soul, and the world in general. His doctrine has three aspects: the one God, the relationship between man and God, and the relationship between man and man. These are distributed through a "preliminary elevation" and through the "ten portals" through which the truly pious man must ascend to the divine union.

Although Ibn Paqūda insists on a negative theology—for while the God of the Bible is one, discursive human knowledge is necessarily multiple—he endeavors to give proof of God's existence in terms of a Neoplatonic dialectic that does not exclude traces of pseudo-Aristotelian texts.

The basic attitude of the believer must be one of abandonment to God's will, and his most serious obstacles are passion and pride. Therefore repentance and an effective return to God should be conspicuous among the "duties of the heart." The means thereto are examination of conscience, prayer, corporal works of mercy, purity of intention, and asceticism; but the goal of all should be the pure love of God and the union it effects. In language of distinguished poetic quality (even in translation) this Jewish sage praises the delights of mystical union. The product of the interaction of Judaism, Christianity, and Islam, Ibn Paqūda's religious philosophy breathes an ecumenical air that conforms to his idea of the theologian as one who would reconcile but not suppress conflicting claims. Although Ibn Paqūda remained scrupulously faithful to rabbinical Judaism, he was not blind to the spiritual values current outside the Synagogue in 11th-century Spain.

Bibliography: G. VAJDA, *La Théologie ascétique de Bahya Ibn Paquda* (Paris 1947); *Introduction À la pensée juive du moyen-âge* (Paris 1947). A. KAHLBERG, *Die Ethik des Bachja Ibn Pakuda* (Heidelberg 1914). M. SISTER, *Bachja-Studien* (Berlin 1936). M. RAFFAELLA DE SION, "Bahya Ibn Paḳuda: Tutor of Hearts," *The Bridge*, v.4 (New York 1959). J. CANTERA, *Lexikon für Theologie und Kirche*, ed. J. HOFER and K. RAHNER, 10 v. (2d, new ed. Freiburg 1957–65) 1:1180. J. GUTTMANN, *Universal Jewish Encyclopedia*, 10 v. (New York 1939–44) 2:34–35. *The Jewish Encyclopedia*, ed. J. SINGER, 13 v. (New York 1901–06) 2:447–454. *Encyclopaedia Judaica: Das Judentum in Geschichte und Gegenwart*, 10 v. (Berlin 1928–34) 8:358–368.

[M. R. NÔTRE]

IBN TIBBON

A famous Jewish family of Hebrew translators from the Arabic of philosophical, linguistic, and scientific treatises by Jewish and Arab scholars. It flourished in Provence (southern France) during the 12th and 13th centuries. The prodigious efforts of the members of this family made available to non-Arabic-speaking Jews (and through renditions of their translations, to non-Jews) works previously inaccessible and established Hebrew as a useful vehicle of scientific expression by embellishing the language with new words and an appropriate style. Among the more notable representatives of the family are Judah ben Saul, Samuel ben Judah, Moses ben Samuel, and Jacob ben Makhir.

Judah ben Saul. The family patriarch; b. Granada, Spain, *c.* 1120; d. Marseilles, France, *c.* 1190. He fled his birthplace in 1150 because of the Almohade persecution of the Jews and settled in Lunel, France, where he practiced medicine. The pioneer of Hebrew translators, he was especially suited for his avocation by virtue of a thorough knowledge of Arabic, a resourcefulness in adapting Hebrew to new and intricate terminology, and a very precise and pedantic approach to his work, the last characteristic a source of criticism for a style deemed overly literal. In the preface to his translation of IBN PAQŪDA's *Duties of the Heart,* he expressed some doubts concerning his Hebrew competence, excused his invention of new vocabulary, criticized those who failed to adhere to the original by interpolating their interpretations of the text, and recommended a literal rendering as the basis for an original revision. Among his other translations are Ibn Gabirol's (Avicebron's) *Improvement of the Moral Qualities,* Judah ben Samuel ha-Levi's Kuzari, SA'ADIA's *Beliefs and Opinions*, and the grammar and lexicon of Ibn Janah (Jonah Marinus). He appears to have composed a treatise on grammar and rhetoric and possibly a commentary on Proverbs ch. 31.

Judah ben Saul's character, outlook, and concerns are revealed in his ethical will, *A Father's Admonition,* in which he reproved and counseled his son, Samuel, regarding the latter's course and purpose in life. In the *Admonition* he extolled the usefulness and care of books, commended the pursuit of scientific studies (with emphasis on medicine), advised meticulousness in handwriting and language, and urged respect for the son's wife.

Samuel ben Judah. Physician and scholar; b. Lunel, France, *c.* 1150; d. Marseilles, France, *c.* 1230. Although the recipient of a very thorough education in medicine, Talmud, Arabic, and philosophy under the compulsive supervision of his father (whose material support he enjoyed), he early rebelled against his parent's overbearing control and influence. But following a period of independence marked by failure in various business ventures, he applied for Judah's help and resumed his studies, destined to excel the father, who had despaired of his son's chances for success.

Samuel's most notable accomplishment was the translation of the *Guide of the Perplexed* by MAIMONIDES, with whom he corresponded for advice on difficult passages. Very much influenced by the teachings of the great philosopher, he was attacked by the anti-Maimonists for contributing to the dissemination of the latter's rationalistic approach. He translated also Maimonides's treatise on resurrection, the introduction to the MISHNAH, and the commentary on its ethical tract, *PIRKE AVOTH*. Other translations include Ibn Ridwan's commentary on Galen's *Ars Parva,* works of Averroës, and the Arabic version of Aristotle's *Meteora.* Among his original works are philosophical commentaries on Genesis, Ecclesiastes, and the Song of Songs, which evidence a reliance on Maimonides's allegorical method. He also compiled glossaries of the philosophical terms and foreign words in the *Guide of the Perplexed.*

Moses ben Samuel. Prolific translator of Arabic versions of Greek works; b. Marseilles, France, *c.* 1240; d. there, *c.* 1283. He translated Euclid's *Elements,* ALFARABI's *Book of Principles,* Avicenna's digest of his *Canon of Medicine,* and Averroës's commentaries on Aristotle. He added to his father's translations of Maimonides's works with renditions of the *Book of the Commandments,* essays on logic, hygiene, and poisons, and the commentary on the Mishnah.

His original works include commentaries on the Canticle of Canticles and the Pentateuch, and *Sefer haPe'ah,* an allegorical interpretation of Haggadic (*see* HAGGADAH) portions of the TALMUD and Midrash (*see* MIDRASHIC LITERATURE) in which he polemicized against the Christian contention of anthropomorphism in these writings. He also wrote a commentary on Avicenna's *Canon.*

Jacob ben Makhir. Known also as Don Profiat Tibbon and Profatius Judaeus, physician, noted astronomer, and grandson of Samuel; b. Marseilles, France, *c.* 1230; d. Montpellier, France, *c.* 1312. He headed the medical school of the University of Montpellier and was a leader of the Jewish community. A strong exponent of scientific studies, he led the struggle against the anti-Maimonists who attempted, under the direction of Solomon ben Adret of Barcelona, to impose a ban on philosophical interpretation and speculation in Provence.

His translations include Euclid's *Elements* and *Data,* Averroës's *Compendium of Logic* and his commentaries on Aristotle, Costa ben Luka's treatise on the sphere, and Ibn al-Saffar's on the astrolabe. He composed astronomical tables and wrote a description of a new quadrant that he had devised, which came to be known as *Quadrans Judaicus.* Both works were rendered into Latin and quoted by Copernicus and Kepler.

Bibliography: M. SCHLOESSINGER et al., *The Jewish Encyclopedia,* ed. J. SINGER, 13 v. (New York 1901–06) 6:544–550. *Universal Jewish Encyclopedia,* 10 v. (New York 1939–44) 5:530–531. H. H. GRAETZ, *History of the Jews,* ed. and tr. B. LÖWY, 6 v. (Philadelphia 1945) 4:30–34, 40–42. I. ABRAHAMS, ed. and tr., *Hebrew Ethical Wills,* 2 v. (Philadelphia 1926; repr. 1948) 1:54–92.

[R. KRINSKY]

ICELAND, THE CATHOLIC CHURCH IN

Iceland is an island located in the North Atlantic between NORWAY and GREENLAND, touching the Arctic Circle. A volcanic island, Iceland is noted for its hot springs and other volcanic geological formations. It forms a tableland the average elevation of which varies from 2,000 to 3,000 feet and whose highest point is 6,952 feet. A large part of the interior of the island is uninhabitable, and the island contains no arable land. Iceland's capital city of Reykjavik is home to almost half the country's total population, the vast majority of which belong to the Evangelical Lutheran Church, the state church. Boasting one of the world's oldest parliaments, Iceland also has among the world's highest literacy and personal income levels.

As an island with few natural resources and no agriculture, Iceland has traditionally relied on the fishing industry to buoy its economy. An independent republic from 930 to 1262, it fell under the control of Norway, and then Denmark due to its reliance on imports of wood and agricultural products. Iceland has been an independent state since July of 1944.

Catholic Origins and Development. By the 8th century Irish hermits were already dwelling in Iceland. Between 870–930 settlers began immigrating to Iceland from Norway and that country's possessions in Ireland, Scotland and neighboring islands. Some of these settlers were Christians while others were pagans familiar with Christianity. Missionaries first came to Iceland at the end of the 10th century, bringing priests from abroad to convert the island's inhabitants. The first recorded missionary, Thorvaldur Kodransson brought the German bishop Fredrekur in 981, while in 996, the recently converted

King OLAF I TRYGGVESSØN of Norway sent Stefnir Thorgilsson over the sea to Iceland. While these early missionaries had some success, their methods were too violent and they were forced to leave the country. In 997 Olaf again attempted conversion through Thangbrand, a "belligerent man and a warrior, but a good priest and efficient," in the words of Snorri Sturluson in *Heimskringla*. While able to convert several chieftains, other disgruntled Icelandic chiefs eventually forced Thangbrand back to Norway, and his negative report to Olaf caused the king to threaten to kill every Icelander in Norway. It was only after the converted chiefs Gizurr Teitsson and Hjalti Skeggjason promised Olaf they would make open their conversion to the new faith that Christianity made rapid progress in Iceland.

In 1000 Christianity was officially accepted as the national faith by the Icelandic parliament—called the *Althing*. To keep good relations with Norway and to prevent warring between Christians and heathens, non-Christian leader Thorgeir Ljosvetningagodi proposed that the Christian law should serve the whole country, and this was accepted by all; mass baptisms were undertaken in one of the island's hot springs. By this time a few small Christian churches had been built on private lands. During the next 50 years a few priests and bishops moved to Iceland, and in 1056, Isleifur Gizurrarsson, was consecrated by ADALBERT OF BREMEN as bishop of Skalholt in southern Iceland.

Iselifur's son Gizurr, who succeeded him as bishop (1082–1118), built the cathedral of St. Peter in Skalholt and endowed it with his patrimony. The tithe was introduced in 1096. A second bishopric was founded at Holar in the north, where Jon helgi Ogmundarson, one of Isleifur's disciples, was its first bishop (1106–21). Church schools were founded with native and foreign teachers. Monasteries were established in the north, with Benedictines at Thingeyri (1133), Munkathvera (1155) and Modruvellir. In the south, Augustinian canons were installed at Thykkvabaer (1168), Flatey-Helgafell (1172) and Skriduklaustur. A convent was established at Kirkjubaer in the south in 1186 and at Reynistadir in the north in the 13th century.

The Church in Iceland was at first suffragan to Bremen-Hamburg, to Lund from 1104 and to Trondheim from 1152. THORLÁK THÓRHALLSSON, who became the first Augustinian abbot at Thykkvibaer, was elected bishop of Skaholt from 1178–93 and struggled to make the Church independent of the local government as well as the laity, many of whom had erected Church buildings on their property and now sought to gain from this arrangement. Thorlák became the patron saint of Iceland. Gudmundur godi, Bishop of Holar (1203–37), also had

Capital: Reykjavik.
Size: 39,758 sq. miles.
Population: 276,365 in 2000.
Languages: Icelandic.
Religions: 251,492 Lutherans (91%), 2,950 Catholics (1%), 8,291 other (3%), 13,632 without religious affiliation.
Diocese: Reykjavik.

difficulties, but there is no evidence that the INVESTITURE STRUGGLE reached Iceland, for the bishops were elected by the clergy and people and sent to the metropolitan to be consecrated. In Bishop Pall Jonssons' time (1195–1211) there were 220 small churches and 290 priests in the See of Skalholt alone. Between the 12th and the 18th century the total population was less than 100,000.

In the 13th century, the great century of the sagas, monks were active in cataloguing and translating Icelandic literature. Previously the libraries in the monasteries were much like those on the Continent, for Icelanders were in constant contact with Norway and some studied in Germany, France and England.

The fierce 13th-century struggles among the foremost families, combined with the continued economic dependence upon Norway for wood, grain and other necessities, drove Iceland into a union with Norway by 1264. Bishop Arni Thorlaksson (1269–98) fought against proprietary churches and in favor of clerical celibacy, but without significant success. In the 14th century bishops still had a high sense of duty. In the middle of the century, Brother Eysteinn Arngrimsson wrote *Lilja* ("The Lily"), a pearl of literature and theology. Then a great decline set in. Several foreigners were sent to Iceland as bishops.

Early in the 15th century the plague epidemic (1402–05) reached Iceland. A third of the population perished and few priests survived. Iceland, under the control of Denmark since 1380, was more isolated than ever; this attracted ecclesiastical adventurers. Foreign bishops such as Jon Gerreksson (1426–33) were sometimes corrupted by business or political interests and did harm, but others, such as Gotsveinn Comhaer, a Dutch Carthusian monk at Skalholt, were loved by their people. At the close of the century a new epidemic nearly as severe as the Black Death struck Iceland.

The 16th Century and Reformation. After the 15th century spiritual decline and economic misery set in; celibacy was less observed by priests and discipline in the monasteries was relaxed. The influence of the REFORMATION was felt via Denmark, prompting Bishops Jon Arason of Holar (1524–50) and Ogmundur Palsson, OSA

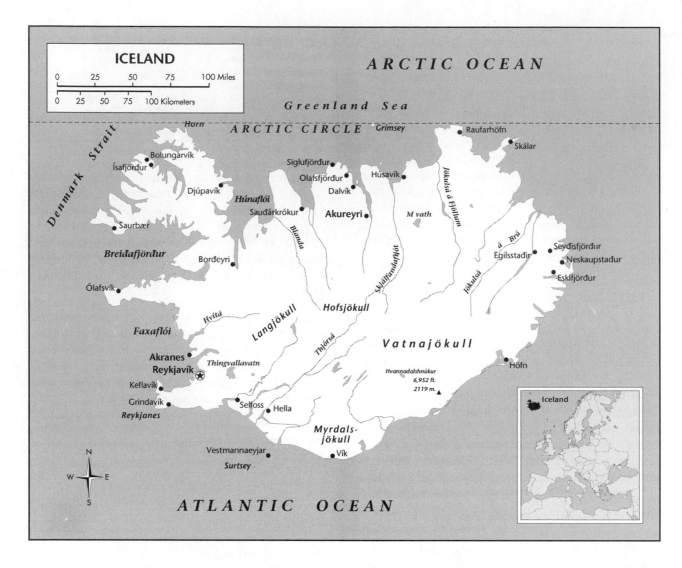

(1522–40), of Skalholt to unite in an effort to prevent it. However their efforts proved futile. Soon German merchants had introduced writings of the reformers. A priest named Jon Einarsson was accused of reformed preaching at Skalholt. Gizurr Einarsson, educated at the bishop's expense in Germany, became acquainted with the Reformation; together with Oddur Gottskalksson, son of Bishop Gottskalk Nikulasson and others, he worked to alienate people from the bishops.

The efforts of the Reformers proved successful. Christian III, the Lutheran king of Denmark, sent two warships to Iceland and with the help of Lutheran Gizurr Einarsson, abducted Iceland's aged and blind Bishop Ogmundur onboard one of these ships. The bishop later died, probably en route to Denmark, and Gizurr installed himself as the first Lutheran bishop at Ogmundur's former see at Skalholt.

The Reformation continued to be imposed upon the Icelanders between 1537 and 1552. Denmark's King Christian III claimed the property of the Church, much of which was destroyed. Monks were forced to leave their monasteries, with the consequence that the pillage of monastic libraries resulted in the loss of much valuable information about the Icelandic Middle Ages. Bishop Jon Arason, who continued his ministry in defiance of the orders of King Christian as well as the king of Iceland, held his see at Holar until he too was taken prisoner and beheaded with both his sons at Skalholt (1550), a martyr for his faith and his country.

The Church after the Reformation. The history of the Catholic Church in Iceland following the Reformation was closely associated with the history of the Lutheran Church in Denmark. The Catholic Church was now illegal, although the faithful continued to worship in secret gatherings. With relations with Rome and almost all of Europe now at an end, Iceland maintained a cultural exchange only with Denmark. Society remained static but stable: the king of Iceland provided good schools to replace those of the Church, while Oddur Gottskalksson translated the New Testament into Icelandic (printed 1540 in Roskilde, Denmark). Gudbrandur Thorlakson, Lutheran bishop of Holar (1571–1627), edited an Icelandic version of the entire Bible (1584), as well as translated and published many other devotional writings using the printing press brought to the county by Bishop Jon Arason.

In 1783 terrible earthquakes struck Iceland, destroying most of Skalholt. Two years later Reykjavik became the Lutheran bishopric for the south, spreading its influence to the whole island after Holar was suppressed in 1801.

When Denmark revised its constitution to include freedom of religion in the mid-1800s, a similar change in Iceland soon followed. Two Catholic chaplains administering to the spiritual needs of Iceland's French fishing fleet started missionary work in Iceland in 1857, and an increasingly liberal Icelandic government granted total freedom of religion in 1874. By 1900 secular priests had established a church and the Sisters of St. Joseph opened the kingdom's first hospital in Reykjavik under the vicar apostolic of Denmark. In 1903 the German MONTFORT FATHERS (SMM) arrived on the island.

Church Reasserts Itself in Twentieth Century. In 1923 Cardinal Willem van Rossum, prefect of Propaganda Fide, visited Iceland's Catholic minority and was welcomed by the Icelandic government. Van Rossum announced the creation of the Vicariate Apostolic of Iceland, and in 1929 Montfort priest Martin Meulenberg, (d. 1941) was ordained as bishop. The cathedral of Landakot was also constructed during this period; for many years it would be the largest church in Iceland.

A resurgence of interest in the Church continued prior to World War II, with literature reflecting aspects of the Catholic faith and the growth of the Catholic community. A Carmelite convent was opened in Hafnarfjördur, while schools and hospitals run by the Church sprang up in other communities. Jóhannes Gunnarsson, the first Icelandic bishop in three centuries, was ordained in 1943. Iceland became independent of Danish rule in 1944.

Reykjavik was made a diocese in the mid-1960s, and by 2000 Iceland had four centers of Catholicism—Reykjavik, Hafnarfjördur, Stykkisholmur and Akureyri—although the majority of the country's Catholic minority made their home in Reykjavik. While the Icelandic government financially supported the Lutheran Church as the state church, freedom of religion was guaranteed in the country's constitution and continued to be protected in full. In the 1990s a church registration and tax was imposed by the government, with a portion of the proceeds distributed to the Catholic Church.

By 2000 Iceland had 12 priests, 4 parishes, 9 churches and one school, the Lankdakot School located in Reykjavik, which provided religious instruction to over 160 students. Religious instruction was also provided by Iceland's public schools, although debate had risen by 2000 over whether such instruction should be ''Christian'' in nature or more inclusive of a variety of religions. In June 2000 Iceland celebrated its first millennium of Christianity by hosting a representative of Pope John Paul II at ecumenical festivals around the country.

Bibliography: Sources. *Diplomatarium Islandicum* (Copenhagen-Reykjavik 1857–), 16 v. to 1956. F. JÓNSSON (Johannaeus), *Historia ecclesiastica Islandiae*, 4 v. (Copenhagen 1772–78). ''Die Kirche in Island,'' v.2 of *Ekklesia,* ed. F. SIEGMEND-SCHULTZE (Leipzig 1937). Literature. B. THÓRDARSON, *Iceland Past and Present* (2d ed. New York 1945). H. P. BRIEM, *Iceland and the Icelanders* (New York 1945). J. C. F. HOOD, *Icelandic Church Saga* (London 1946). E. O. SVEINSSON, *Age of the Sturlungs: Icelandic Civilization in the 13th Century,* tr. J. S. HANNESSON (Ithaca, NY 1953). V. WASCHNITIUS, *Die Religion in Geschichte und Gegenwart³,* 7 v. (3d ed. Tübingen 1957–65) 3:932–935. W. GÖBELL, *Lexikon für Theologie und Kirche²,* eds., J. HOFER and K. RAHNER, 10 v. (2d, new ed. Freiburg 1957–65) 5:799–801. G. SCHWAIGER, *Die Reformation in den nordischen Ländern* (Munich 1962) 86–99, 165–166, bibliog. *Scandinavian Churches,* ed. L. S. HUNTER, (New York 1965). *Annuario Pontificio* (1965) 753.

[M. P. JAKOBSSON/EDS.]

ICHTHUS

The Greek word (IXΘΥΣ) for FISH was used in Christian antiquity as an acrostic formed by the initial letters of a primitive symbol of faith. When the word Savior (Σωτήρ) was added to the formula confessed by the Ethiopian eunuch whom Philip baptized (Acts 8.37), the acrostic was evident: Ἰησοῦς Χριστὸς Θεοῦ Υἱὸς Σωτήρ, Jesus Christ, Son of God, Savior. There are abundant monumental and literary witnesses to the popularity of the formula. Tertullian (*De Baptismo* 1) spoke of Christians as ''little fishes'' (*pisciculi*) like our ''IXΘΥΣ Jesus Christ.'' Application of the symbol to the Holy Eucharist is found in the inscriptions of ABERCIUS and PECTORIUS; Pectorius bound together his first five verses with the acrostic. Other Eucharistic associations are found in funeral inscriptions, where, in at least one case, the formula is found thus: IXΘΥΣ ΖΩΝΤΩΝ (the Fish of the living). The Christian Sibylline Oracles (bk. 8) make use of the acrostic for eschatological purposes.

See Also: ACROSTIC.

Bibliography: H. LECLERCQ, *Dictionnaire d'archéologie Chretiénne et de liturgie* (Paris 1907–53) 7.2:1990–2086. E. DIEZ,

Icon of Saint Anthony the Great, 17th century painting. (©Chris Hellier/CORBIS)

Reallexikon für Antike und Christentum, ed. T. KLAUSER (Stuttgart 1950–) 3:667–682. F. J. DÖLGER, ΙΧΘΥΣ, v.1 (Münster 1910) 8–15, 87–182; v.2 (1922) 454–574. Λ. C. RUSH, *Death and Burial in Christian Antiquity* (Washington 1941) 86–87.

[M. C. HILFERTY]

ICON

Icon, from the Greek *eikon* meaning image, is a word now generally applied to paintings of sacred subjects or scenes from sacred histories. As established in the Byzantine Orthodox Church icons were a liturgical art, theology in visible form. By presenting the physical appearance of a holy figure the icon itself became embued with the sanctity of its divine prototype, serving as an object of religious contemplation and as a conduit for the prayers of the faithful.

Tradition names the Evangelist Luke as the first icon painter and the Virgin and Child as the first subjects. Other icons were said to be *acheiropoietoi*, not made by human hand. One such icon is the Mandylion, a cloth believed to have been imprinted with the features of Christ. The origins of Christian icons and their veneration can be traced with surety only to the sixth century—the date

of the earliest surviving icons—but textual evidence documents their earlier use. Eusebius, the fourth-century bishop of Caesarea in Palestine, writes of having seen icons of Christ and his Apostles. He traces icon veneration back to "the ancients" who used icons in "their pagan customs," reflecting knowledge of Greco-Roman practices. SS. Basil the Great (*Patrologia Graeca*, ed J. P. Migne [Paris 1857–66] 31:489), Gregory of Nyssa (*Patrologia Graeca* 46:737) and Paulinus of Nola (*Patrologia Latina*, ed. J. P. Migne [Paris 1878–90] 61: 339) also record Christian veneration of icons in the fourth and fifth centuries.

By the seventh century icons permeated nearly every aspect of Byzantine life. Multiple icons were combined into an *iconostasis,* or icon-screen, which separated the sanctuary from the nave in Byzantine churches. Icons were hung on church walls for veneration by the faithful and were displayed in private homes. Monumental two-sided icons were processed through towns and villages and small icons were carried or worn by individuals. While the most familiar type of Byzantine icon is a painting executed in tempera on a wooden panel, icons were also made of mosaic tesserae (cubes), carved of marble, steatite or ivory and painted onto walls or the pages of illuminated manuscripts. Famous icons were copied on coins and lead seals or recreated in gold and jewels and worn as rings, necklaces and bracelets.

More than simply objects of religious contemplation, icons also protected believers, healed the sick, punished the wicked and ensured truthfulness. The Virgin, known in Byzantine theology as the *Theotokos* (Bearer of God), was the patron saint and traditional protector of Constantinople. An icon of the *Theotokos* was paraded on the walls of the city during periods of siege and was carried into battle at the head of the imperial army. Some icons wept, bled or worked miracles—the latter sometimes on a regular schedule, as is documented by accounts of what is called "the usual miracle," performed every Friday night by an icon of the *Theotokos* in the Blachernai church in Constantinople.

The power and prevalence of icons in Byzantine society provoked a theological debate in which the ability to represent the divine and the role of art in Christian worship were central issues. From 726–843 the Byzantine Empire was shattered by ICONOCLASM (image-breaking), during which icon veneration was forbidden, icon painters were persecuted, and icons were destroyed. While there are numerous documents describing events and defining the ideologies of the iconophiles (image-lovers) and iconoclasts (image-breakers), the very nature of the contest means that little in the way of religious art survives to us from before or during the time of the destruction of images.

Icons are not portraits in the modern sense—icon-painters did not strive for realism, for example—but served as visible symbols of their divine prototypes. In this sense they are one of the more conservative forms of art: by their very definition icons must provide a readily recognizable representation of a holy person or scene. Particular costumes, emblems, and attributes were developed to indicate specific categories of holy men and women. Prophets hold scrolls, indicative of the Old Testament, while Evangelists wear antique tunics and display their codices, the more modern book-form. Soldier saints wear military costumes and some are shown on horseback while monks wear habits and healing saints display medicines and surgical instruments. Handbooks created for Byzantine icon painters list the characteristic traits of each holy figure, including facial expressions, hair (or the lack thereof) and age. John the Baptist, for example, is depicted with the tattered garments, wind-blown hair, and gaunt face appropriate for a desert-dwelling ascetic. Church Fathers, such as John Chrysostom, are shown in venerable old age wearing the robes of their office.

While icon painters were required to faithfully replicate the traditionally-accepted physical attributes of their holy subjects, icons did not remain wholly static, but reflected doctrinal, societal, and artistic changes. Before Iconoclasm, most icons were painted in encaustic, using pigments suspended in a wax medium. This resulted in a soft, unfocused line. After Iconoclasm, encaustic was replaced by tempera, which dries to a matte finish and creates a sharp, clearly-defined line, allowing artists to achieve a new level of detail. The catalog of icon subjects was also expanded to include newly-recognized saints and martyrs, and there was an increase in the production of narrative icons, particularly scenes from the life of Christ and the *Theotokos*. Narrative and iconic subjects were also combined to create so-called biographical icons. These feature a central large icon of one saint enframed by a series of smaller scenes illustrating key events in the saint's life.

After Iconoclasm icons were also increasingly accompanied by inscriptions identifying the subject by name, category and/or type, further strengthening the link between the image and its prototype. These inscriptions reflect the development of different types of representations of one subject, particularly icons of Christ and the Theotokos. One famous type of Christ is the *Pantokrator,* or Ruler of All, which depicts Christ as a mature, bearded man in a frontal pose, raising his right hand in blessing and holding the Gospel Book in his left. The *Theotokos,* the most frequently depicted subject on surviving Byzantine icons, is represented by more icon types than are accorded to her son. Famous miracle-working icons of the

Our Lady of Perpetual Help, original icon preserved at Redemptorist Church of Sant' Alfonso, Rome.

Theotokos such as the *Hodegetria, Eleousa,* and *Kykkotissa* show her in different guises and were named for the shrines in which they were held. Icons such as these became the focus of pilgrimage, and pilgrims commissioned copies that were then disseminated throughout the Empire.

As the production and veneration of icons spread from Byzantium into other Orthodox cultures, new subjects and styles were introduced and established images were given new artistic interpretations. Icons of holy bishops produced in Russia show their subjects wearing the local liturgical garments and thus differ from those produced in Constantinople. Despite such differences, each icon presented a faithful replication of its subject for the contemplation of the believer. Today, the legacy of Byzantine icons is evident in the many parts of the world where icons remain a vital and integral part of spiritual life.

Bibliography: H. BELTING, *Likeness and Presence: A History of the Image before the Era of Art* (Chicago 1994); *The Image and its Public in the Middle Ages* (New York 1990); ''An Image and Its Function in the Liturgy: The Man of Sorrows in Byzantium,'' *Dumbarton Oaks Papers* 34–35 (1980-81): 1–16. M. CHATZIDAKIS, *Icons of Patmos: Questions of Byzantine and Post-Byzantine Painting* (Athens 1985). R. CORMACK, *Writing in Gold* (London 1985). G. DAGRON, ''Holy Images and Likeness,'' *Dumbarton Oaks Pa-*

Leo III, Byzantine Emperor, 717–741, who condemned the veneration of images in c. 724. (Archive Photos)

pers 45 (1991): 23–33. H.C. EVANS and W.D. WIXOM, *The Glory of Byzantium. Art and Culture of the Middle Byzantine Era, AD 845–1261* (New York 1997). A. GRABAR, *L'Iconoclasme byzantin: Le dossier archéologique* (Paris 1984). A. KARTSONIS, *Anastasis. The Making of an Image,* (Princeton 1986). E. KITZINGER, "Reflections on the Feast Cycle in Byzantine Art," *Cahiers archéologiques* 36 (1988): 51–73; "The Cult of Images in the Age before Iconoclasm," *Dumbarton Oaks Papers* 8 (1954): 81–150. H. MAGUIRE, *The Icons of Their Bodies. Saints and Their Images in Byzantium* (Princeton 1996). J. PELIKAN, *Imago Dei: The Byzantine Apologia for Icons* (Princeton 1990). R. OUSTERHOUT and L. BRUBAKER, *The Sacred Image East and West* (Chicago and Urbana, Illinois 1995). N. ŠEVCENKO, *The Life of St. Nicholas in Byzantine Art* (Turin 1983). A. M. TALBOT, *Byzantine Defenders of Images: Eight Lives in English Translation* (Washington D.C. 1998). M. VASSILAKI, ed. *Mother of God. Representations of the Virgin in Byzantine Art* (Milan 2000). K. WEITZMANN, *The Icon, Holy Images, Sixth to Fourteenth Century* (London 1978).

[L. JONES]

ICONOCLASM

A term meaning "image breaking," referring to extreme opposition to the representation of the human figure and the veneration of images, the two being held inseparable. Iconoclasm in its Christian context is especially associated with a period in the history of the Byzantine Empire that can be divided into three discernible phases; that of its emergence under emperors Leo (717–741) and CONSTANTINE V (741–775), and the iconoclast council of 754; its check at the second ecumenical council of Nicaea (787), and its restoration (815–842) and final extinction.

Emergence and Apogee. The exact origin of the movement is obscure. Iconoclasm was based on the First Commandment (Ex 20.4–5) and other biblical passages and iconoclasts were genuinely concerned that increasing devotion to icons would lead to idolatry. They accepted that only the Eucharist, church buildings and the sign of the cross were fully holy as they had been consecrated either by God directly or through a priest. Iconophiles referred to biblical passages that showed approval of images, and claimed that the Commandment was not intended for the Christians, but only for the Jews who were prone to idolatry. They argued that icons and relics were effective vehicles of the holy. Unease about the artistic depiction of sacred figures was present in early Christianity, and in the fourth century Eusebius, following Origen, had denied that Christ's image could be delineated. He in turn was followed later in the fourth century by Epiphanius of Salamis, who claimed that images in churches distracted Christians from the contemplation of purely spiritual matters. However, apart from a short-lived iconoclastic movement in Armenia in the late sixth and early seventh centuries, there was no further discussion of the issue until the eighth century.

In *c.* 724 two bishops of Asia Minor, Constantine of Nakoleia and Thomas of Claudiopolis, supported by Emperor Leo III and some of his advisers, condemned the veneration of images, citing traditional biblical prohibitions. They were opposed by Patriarch Germanus I, but in 726 the emperor publicly supported the new movement when he ordered the figure of Christ surmounting the Chalke palace gate to be taken down. Finally, pressing Germanus in a solemn audience to sign a decree against images of the saints, he in effect forced the patriarch to resign on Jan. 7, 730. The nature and exact wording of the decree are unknown as is its application. The ensuing destruction of icons, crosses, and storied reliquaries seems to have been concentrated primarily on movable objects that lent themselves to manifestations of devotion (kissing, surrounding with votive lamps, etc.). Destruction was neither general nor equally intense in all places. Leo's alleged hostility to the cult of the cross was a later invention; nor is there any proof that he was opposed per se to the cult of the saints or of relics. The chief opponents of Leo's policy were the monks and members of the civil service of Constantinople. Leo's repressive action against the opposition was limited to exile, confiscation, and at worst, mutilation. There is no certain proof of any martyrdom in this period: the *passio* of the Chalke martyrs is a worthless document, and the burning of the "university" library, together with its scholars, is a legend. The higher clergy submitted to the emperor, accepting the new Patriarch ANASTASIUS (730–741) while applying the imperial directives with greater or lesser zeal. Outside the capital JOHN DAMASCENE, spokesman for the patriarch of Jerusalem, wrote three defenses of sacred images, while the papacy, still politically subject to the Byzantine Empire, reacted vigorously against the imperial policy. Popes GREGORY II (715–731) and GREGORY III (731–741) wrote letters of protest, and the Roman synod of 731 expressed its opposition. Tension was further exacerbated by Leo's decision to remove Illyricum, Sicily and Calabria from the papal jurisdiction. This schism was to drive the papacy into the hand of the Franks.

Historians are divided as to Leo's basic motivation. At this time, there was little theological basis to support iconoclasm. Some claim the influence of Islamic culture; the emperor was aware of Islam's opposition to the human figure in art, and even though he did not imitate his contemporary Caliph Jazid's decree against images, he may have come under its influence. Moreover, in Asia Minor, which was then the main source of army recruits, there were many groups unfavorable to images (heretically or otherwise); the whole of Asia Minor in fact became the main enclave of iconoclasm and the army became its most fanatical agent. Others have suggested political motives, but the emperor's opposition to MONASTICISM was a result, not a cause, of iconoclasm, and there is no foundation for the contention that he had an economic goal in mind; that is, that non-compliance would lead to confiscation of monastic and ecclesiastical property. On theological grounds, it can be noted that Leo III's family came from a MONOPHYSITE region and that iconoclasm was seen by many as the logical, if extreme conclusion, to monophysite Christianity. However, the most likely reason was that iconoclasm, which began in the eighth century as a small movement, attracted imperial support at a time when Byzantium was suffering a series of disasters. In 726 there was a severe volcanic eruption at Thera, and territory had been lost to the Slavs, Avars and Arabs. The letters of the patriarch Germanos and the chronicles of Theophanes and Nikephorus give testimony to the hypothesis that Leo regarded these setbacks as a sign of God's displeasure at the veneration of images; the purity of Islamic worship which did not allow the depiction of holy images had led to a spectacular success.

Leo III's policy suffered from having no theoretical foundation in theology. To eliminate this handicap, his successor Emperor Constantine V Copronymos sought to have images condemned by the Church and to impose iconoclasm as a duty of conscience as well as the obliga-tion of a citizen. About 752 he elaborated an original theory of images, which he developed into treatises and which he—like his father—defended in public audiences. Two years later he had it ratified in a general council of the Byzantine episcopate held in the suburban palace of Hiereia from February 10 to August 8. Though 338 council fathers attended, the protagonists were three prelates of Asia Minor, in particular the Metropolitan, Theodosius Apsimar of Ephesus (the patriarchal see being vacant). The definition of iconoclasm prepared by this council—which was proclaimed "ecumenical"— has been preserved in the Acta of the seventh council (Nicaea II). The iconoclasts denounced all pictorial representations as idols, and declared that any such representation of Christ was false because it must necessarily either separate the two natures of Christ (which had been the error of Nestorius) and thus create a fourth member of the Trinity, or circumscribe the person of the Word who has no limits (the confusion of the divinity with humanity had been the error of the monophysites). The Eucharist was the only appropriate non-anthropomorphic image of Christ. The iconophiles argued that God had been uncircumscribable, but following the Incarnation when God had revealed Himself in the flesh, it was now possible to make a pictorial representation of Christ. To deny that Christ had assumed a circumscribable form would be to deny the Incarnation, the instrument of man's salvation. Iconoclasts rejected representations of saints for moral reasons; adoration of such images amounted to adoration of dead matter. Iconophiles countered that they adored not the materials, but the subjects represented in the images. The Council of Hiereia, however, did set strict bounds to any extension of its definitions to include a complete negation of the veneration of saints or relics. It based its definitions on Scripture and tradition and ended by anathematizing the Greek champions of images, namely, Germanus, John Damascene and George, a monk of Cyprus.

Artistically these decisions resulted in a substitution of secular decorations for biblical and hagiographic scenes and the replacement of monumental figures in apses by a cross. At first the authorities showed a certain moderation in effecting the anti-image decisions of the emperor and the council; violent repression of the opposition did not occur until a dozen years later. Then in 761 or 762 the monk ANDREW OF CRETE was executed, and in 756 persecution broke out in full force. A holy recluse, Stephen the Younger, promoted a movement hostile to the Council of Hiereia, some few miles out of Constantinople, and among his followers were many of the elite of Constantinople's society. Patriarch Constantine II himself (754–766) was lukewarm in applying the imperial edicts, and the emperor came more and more to suspect a cabal or even a plot. On Nov. 20, 765, Stephen was killed by the populace; shortly thereafter the emperor imposed a loyalty oath to promote the hostile imperial policy. On his return from the summer campaign of 766 he humiliated all monks by a grotesque parade in the hippodrome; he attacked members of his own entourage and high officials; and finally dismissed the patriarch and had him beheaded the next year. He followed this up by seizing any monastery where he encountered resistance. Simultaneously he placed loyal generals in key command of military areas in Asia Minor, the most famous of whom, Lachanodracon, distinguished himself in the region of Ephesus by dispersing the monks, giving them their choice between marriage, on the one hand, or mutilation and exile, on the other, and by confiscating monastic property. Iconoclasm had thus evolved by force of circumstances into a war on monasticism, although they were two distinct movements. It is not clear whether monks were targeted by Constantine because they resisted his imperial policy more robustly, or whether he saw them as a drain on manpower and economic resources. Emperor Constantine's enemies attributed to him attacks on Mary's divine maternity and on the intercession of the saints, but such accusations were undoubtedly biased and must be handled with caution. According to the *Life of St. Stephen the Younger,* Constantine replaced the pictures in the Church of the Virgin at Blachernae with mosaics of trees, birds and animals. However, images of Christ and saints remained in the St. Sophia until 768–769 when the patriarch Nicholas I (766–780) had them removed. From this period of persecution non-iconoclasts have preserved the names of four martyred monks who are commemorated in liturgical calendars on November 20 or 28: Peter, Stephen (the best known), Andrew and Paul. Eastern patriarchs outside Constantinople were deeply stirred by Constantine's persecutions, for they condemned the Council of Hiereia and advised Pope Paul I (757–767) of their condemnation; Pope Stephen III (IV) (768–772) convened a second Roman synod on the subject in 769.

Temporary Restoration of Images. The accession of Emperor Leo IV (775–780) marked a relaxation of iconoclastic policy that members of the bureaucracy had been waiting for and were able to exploit to the fullest when Empress Irene assumed the regency (780). Assisted by a high palace official, Tarasius, whom she made patriarch of Constantinople (784), she set to work forthwith preparing a reconciliation of the Eastern and Western Churches on the basis of ancient and common custom. The ecumenical Council of Nicaea II was announced and the pope sent two legates. The council convened on Aug. 1, 786, in Constantinople at the church of the Holy Apostles, but the imperial guard, in league with some bishops, dispersed the council fathers attending the first session.

Irene maneuvered skillfully to get her own men into the garrison, and the council convened a year later at Nicaea. It lasted 15 days (Sept. 24–Oct. 7, 787) and was entirely dominated by Patriarch Tarasius. As for what to do about the known iconoclasts among the council fathers, the council decided to admit the iconoclastic bishops en bloc after nine iconoclastic metropolitans and two archbishops of Asia Minor had abjured their heresy. The council decree of iconoclasm, generically and moderately phrased, defined the legitimacy, the excellence and the limitation of veneration or "relative" cult of images. Because of political circumstances the council's action was badly received by the Carolingian court in the West, and Pope ADRIAN I had to defend it in a letter to Charlemagne. There was even some dissatisfaction among Western iconophiles who opposed such a complete endorsement of the worship of icons; they believed that images should be used to educate Christians about the virtuous deeds of Christ and the saints. In Byzantium, however, the council ushered in a short period of tranquillity, which the orthodox turned to their profit: Irene showered the monks with endowments, Tarasius improved the standards of the upper clergy, THEODORE THE STUDITE began restoring monastic discipline. Thus the Eastern Church was better prepared for the second wave of iconoclasm.

Renewed Iconoclasm and Final Restoration of Images. The pressure to return to a policy of iconoclasm initially came from the army, who supported the rise of an Armenian governor of the Anatolikon thema to imperial power. Leo V the Armenian (813–820) dismissed Patriarch Nicephorus (806–815), used the Easter Synod of Hagia Sophia (815) to annul the decree of 787 and recognised the ecumenical status of the Council of Hiereia. But times had changed, and this synod made no mention of idolatry in connection with the veneration of images. Further, the enemies of images distinguished between devotional images and educational images and listed real abuses in their use. But orthodox Christians had enlightened spokesmen, such as Nicephorus and Theodore the Studite, and the bishops' opposition to iconoclasm was better organized. Both camps adopted a more refined dialectical technique, although in truth the theology of images did not become more profound. Persecution this time was less cruel. Emperor Michael II (820–829) was even tolerant of individuals. His son Theophilus (829–842), however, under the influence of his teacher, the future patriarch JOHN VII GRAMMATICUS (837–843), was more violent in his disapproval of images; Euthymius of Sardis was beaten to death (831); Theodore and Theophanes of Palestine were tattooed on their faces as foreign agitators. But a year after the death of Theophilus, regents Empress THEODORA (2) and Theocistus restored images. A hastily summoned synod, inspired by MET-

HODIUS, who had become patriarch (834–847), and by Hilarion, Symeon, and Joannicios, the grand survivors of 815 declared in favor of the ecumenical Council of Nicaea II. The churches under the patriarch of Constantinople still celebrate this event every year on the Feast of Orthodoxy, the first Sunday of Lent, by a triumphant procession of images and by the Synodicon of Orthodoxy. The decree of 843 was renewed by more solemn councils in 861, 867, 869, 879. Iconoclasm soon disappeared from Byzantine society though not from all individual consciences.

The policy of the iconoclastic emperors, despite the ruin and abuse it cost, make a positive contribution to the joint development of the Byzantine Church and State since it fostered an increase in the prestige of the patriarch through an awareness of dogmatic autonomy. Meanwhile, the victory of the orthodox brought with it a revival of sacred art, made icons more popular than ever, and entailed a concentration of religious feeling on the humanity of Christ. This long dispute, however, did little to advance theology or to enrich contemplative spirituality. The supporters of image worship seem indeed to have had scarcely any idea of the development of the image in the early Church, and, consequently, of the proper limits on the veneration of images.

Bibliography: Acta of the Synod of 754 and of the seventh ecumenical Council of Nicaea in J. D. MANSI, *Sacrorum Conciliorum nova et amplissima collectio* (Florence-Venice 1757–98) v.12–13. Synod of 815, ed. P.J. ALEXANDER, *Dumbarton Oaks Papers* 7 (1953). Writings of Germanus (*Patrologia Graeca* 98:77–80; 156–193), John Damascene (PG 94:1232–1420), Nicephorus (PG 100:169–850. *Life of Stephen the Younger* PG 100, (1069–1186). *Orations of Constantine V*, ed. G. OSTROGORSKY, *Studien zur Geschichte des byzantinischen Bilderstreites* (Amsterdam 1964). *The Chronicle of Theophanes Confessor,* tr. C. MANGO and R. SCOTT (Oxford 1997). *Chronicle of Patriarch Nicephorus,* ed. D. DE BOOR (Leipzig 1880). *Nicephoros, Patriarch of Constantinople: Short History,* ed. and tr. C. MANGO (Washington 1990). D.J. SAHAS ed., *Icon and Logos: Sources in Eighth-century Iconoclasm: An Annotated Translation of the Sixth Session of the Seventh Ecumenical Council* (Toronto 1986). M.V. ANASTOS, "Leo III's Edict against the images in the year 726–727 and Italo- Byzantine Relations between 726 and 730," *Byzantinische Forschungen* 3 (1968), 5–41. L. W. BARNARD, "Byzantium and Islam: The Interaction of Two Worlds in the Iconoclastic Era," *Byzantinoslavica* 36 (1975). L. BRUBAKER and J. HALDON, *Byzantium in the Iconoclast Era (c. 680–850): The Sources* (Aldershot 2000). A. BRYER and J. HERRIN, eds., *Iconoclasm* (Birmingham 1975). P. BROWN, "A Dark-Age Crisis: Aspects of the Iconoclast Controversy," *English Historical Review* 88 (1973) 1–34. R. CORMACK, *Writing in Gold* (London 1985). P. CRONE, "Islam, Judeo-Christianity and Byzantine Iconoclasm," *Jerusalem Studies in Arabic and Islam* 2 (1980) 59–95. S. GERO, *Byzantine Iconoclasm during the Reign of Leo III* (Louvain 1993). A. GRABAR, *L'iconoclasme byzantin: le dossier archéologique* (Paris 1984). J. HERRIN, "Women and the Faith in Icons in Early Christianity," in *Culture, Ideology and Politics,* ed. R. SAMUEL and G. STEDMAN JONES (London 1982) 56–83. J. HERRIN, *The Formation of Christendom* (Oxford 1987). G. R. D. KING, "Islam, Iconoclasm, and the Declaration of Doctrine," *Bulletin of the School of Oriental and African Studies* 48 (1985). J. MOORHEAD, "Iconoclasm, the Cross and the Imperial Image," *Byzantion* 55 (1985) 165–179. J. PELIKAN, *Imago Dei: The Byzantine Apologia for Icons* (Princeton 1990). P. SCHRINER, "Der byzantinische Bilderstreit; kritische Analyse der zeitgenössischen Meinungen und das Urteil der Nachwelt bis heute," *Settimane di Studio del Centro Italiano di Studi sull'-alto medioevo* 34.1 (1988) 319–407. D. STRATOUDAKI-WHITE, "The Patriarch Photois and the Conclusion of Iconoclasm," *Greek Orthodox Review* 44 (1999) 341–355. D. STEIN, *Der Beginn des byzantinischen Bilderstreites und seine Entwicklung* (Munich 1980). W. TREADGOLD, *The Byzantine Revival, 780–842* (Stanford, CA 1988). M. WHITTOW, *The Making of Orthodox Byzantium, 600–1025* (Basingstoke 1996).

[F. NICKS/J. GOUILLARD]

ICONOLOGY AND ICONOGRAPHY

The terms iconology and iconography are derived from the Greek word for image (εἰκών) combined with either the word for writing (γράφειν, to write, thus iconography) or with the word for reason and thought (λόγος, thus iconology). The two terms are closely connected and have often been used interchangeably. However, different meanings can be attributed to each term.

Iconography ordinarily refers to historical documentation through imagery. Portraiture is an important aspect of image documentation, and thus in archeological circles the term iconography is used to denote the study of historical portraiture, which by its nature is closely connected with numismatics. But to the art historian iconography generally refers to the description of an image or representation; the term is used either to describe an independent work of art or collectively to designate all the representations of a single subject matter.

For years the word was given the meaning more properly attributed to iconology, namely, the extended explanation of the deeper implications of the subject represented in a picture, sculpture, etc. For practical reasons, in order not to complicate matters further, some authors (e.g., J. J. M. Timmers) prefer to avoid the term iconology. At the end of the 16th century, Cesare Ripa, one of the first users of the term iconology, gave it a meaning completely different from the modern one. For Ripa iconology consisted of the description of the symbols and personifications used in emblems and allegories for the purpose of aiding artists.

Since the studies of Erwin Panofsky in 1930, iconology has come to mean the explanation of the work of art in its entire historical context as an unmistakable symptom of a specific situation in the history of culture and human ideology. The preparations for this explanation are then called pre-iconography, which is the determination of the primary, natural meaning of things; and iconography, which is the subsequent determination of their secondary conventional meaning as allegories (see the Panofsky schema below).

In 1952 Creighton Gilbert added yet another nuance to the meaning of the word iconology. According to him, iconology was not the actual investigation of the work of art but rather the result of this investigation. Hans Sedlmayr makes the distinction between *sachliche* and *methodische* iconology. Thus *sachliche* iconology refers to the "general meaning of an individual painting or of an artistic complex (church, palace, monument) as seen and explained with reference to the ideas which take shape in them." *Methodische* iconology, on the other hand, is the "integral iconography which accounts for the changes and development in the representations."

Each of the various definitions of iconography and iconology is only partially acceptable. And although reviewing the series of definitions clarifies the matter, in practice one cannot work simultaneously with all definitions. The discussion presented by G. H. Hoogewerff [*Ikonographie en Ikonologie . . .* (Gravenhage 1950)] provides clarification:

> *Iconography* amounts to a description of the works of art and a systematic division according to the subject matter represented. Its approach is descriptive, but when applying detailed observations it becomes analytical. It points out and determines existing differences. It is not its task to make any further distinctions. It is synoptical only insofar as it observes existing and always external connections between motifs. *Iconology*, on the other hand, consists of the investigation and explanation of the meaning of the representations. Its purpose is to explain as much as possible its meaning and essence. It uses pre-iconographical observation and from the results it not only tries to recognize as such the themes which are represented, but whenever feasible and in so far as possible, it tries to penetrate them. It does not decipher: it analyzes. Its method is truly synoptical and exegetical.

Hoogewerff further observes that outstanding iconographers have not limited themselves to describing and classifying images, but have in fact if not in name practiced iconology.

ICONOLOGY AND ICONOGRAPHY AS SCIENCES

It is noticeable that Hoogewerff in the explanation quoted above does not use the term "science," but other statements in the same work reveal that he considered both iconography and iconology to be sciences. If it is agreed that science is the systematically ordered integration of a specific knowledge and of the methods according to which this knowledge can be developed, then both iconography and iconology as described by Hoogewerff can be considered sciences and hence deserve the academic chairs that they have received. Nevertheless they remain subdivisions of art history and are related in a somewhat less immediate sense to the history of civilization.

The field of art cannot reject iconography or iconology under the pretext that they are concerned—and sometimes by preference—with objects that no longer, or do not yet, belong to the realm of art, such as a simple popular design or an artistically inferior but clearly legible copy. The latter are not goals in themselves, but merely instruments in reaching, not only precise accreditation, dating, localization, and stylistic classification, but especially a deep insight into the meaning and objective of true art works. Thus, they answer the common questions: why did the artist do this, what is he telling us consciously or unconsciously, to what does he want to move us, either consciously or unconsciously? These are questions that even the most abstract work of art cannot avoid. When iconography and iconology at times attempt to reply to these questions by means that lie outside the realm proper to art, then, *mutatis mutandis*, they act no differently than the science that examines the chemical formula of a specific paint, not as a phenomenon that has something to do with the essence of art, but simply in order to understand better and to enjoy the work of art in its totality.

Naturally, iconology and iconography demand a strict discipline of thought. This particularly applies to iconology, in which imagination and intuition play a role. If these are not constantly tested against the factual data, then it is only too easy to lose oneself in unscientific fantasy. Erwin Panofsky stressed this in both theory and practice.

HISTORICAL DEVELOPMENT

Iconography and iconology are relatively young sciences. The beginning of iconography can be traced to 16th-century works such as those of Achilles Statius [*Inlustrium virorum ut extant in Urbe expressi vultus* (Rome 1569)] from Portugal and Fulvius Ursinus [*Imagines et elogia virorum inlustrium et eruditorum. . .* (Rome 1570)] from Italy. Both were archeologists with particular interest in portraiture. Their work was followed by the *Iconographia* (1669) of G. A. Canini.

Preoccupation with this particular form of iconography was not widespread until the late 19th and early 20th centuries. Germany produced a number of scholars: J. J. Bernoulli [*Römische Ikonographie* (Stuttgart 1882–94) and *Griechische Ikonographie* (Munich 1901)], P. Arndt

[*Griechische und Römische Porträts* (Munich 1891)], and A. Hekler [*Die Bildnisskunst der Griechen und Römer* (Stuttgart 1912)]. Meanwhile, the kindred science of numismatics was pursued in France by H. Cohen (1808–80) and E. Babelon (1854–1924). In England from 1923 on, H. Mattingly, E. A. Sydenham, and C. H. V. Sutherland published standard works on these matters. Although their studies were oriented toward archeology, they made an important contribution to the development of iconography as an integral part of art history. Accordingly, a work of art was viewed not only from the standpoint of aesthetics, but also from that of history and of the work's didactic intent. This concurred with the then existing desire for a reclassification of collected material on the basis of concrete and objective characterizations.

Because of the lack of sufficient graphic material and photographic documentation, minute descriptions of the art works were required. At the same time, in connection with archeological research, attention was paid to the classification of works on the basis of subject matter. The first to use this iconographical method was Ph. de Caylus [*Recueil d'antiquités* . . . (Paris 1761–67)]. Johann J. Winckelmann [*Geschichte der Kunst des Altertums* (Dresden 1764)] strongly opposed him by stating that the artistic elements and style of a work of art are more important than its antiquarian and hermeneutic character. In spite of this E. Q. Visconti [*Iconographie ancienne* (Paris 1811–29)] and F. de Clarac [*Musée de sculpture antique et moderne* (Paris 1850–53)] continued to use the method of classification by subject. Scientific contributions were made by specialists in the restoring of objects (e.g., B. Cavaceppi, 1786). Iconographical investigations were linked also with the comparative philological investigations of relevant texts. In this respect J. Overbeck [*Gallerie heroischer Bildwerke der alten Kunst* (Brunswick 1853); *Griechische Kunstmythologie* (Leipzig 1871–89)], H. von Brunn [*Geschichte der griechischen Künstler* (1883–)], A. Furtwängler [*Die antiken Gemmen* (Berlin 1900)], and A. della Seta [*Il nudo nell'arte* (Rome 1930)] aided the advancement of iconography.

The Stimulus of Christian Art. Early Christian art lent itself to archeological iconography, since objects found did not have their own stylistic character but in primitive manner imitated the forms of their environment. Their specific value was derived from their content, which was related to religious beliefs and meanings. It is natural when investigating the content of Christian art to seek explanatory texts not only in the Bible and the Fathers, which are so important for early Christian art, but also in other valuable sources such as the medieval works of WALAFRID STRABO and Berchorius (*Reportorium morale*), liturgical writings such as the *Rationale* by Durandus, compilations of saints' lives such as *Legenda*

aurea by JAMES OF VORAGINE, and the *Speculum* of VINCENT OF BEAUVAIS.

Although religious art activity in the East was often controlled by *canones*, that of the West revealed a freedom and a progressive development.

Johannes Molanus (Jan Vermeulen) was one of the first Christian iconographers. His *De picturis et imaginibus sacris* (Louvain 1570) was written with the intention of prescribing to artists how they might correctly (in the spirit of the Counter Reformation) represent Biblical, hagiographical, liturgical, and other religious subjects. In this field he fulfilled the role that Cesare Ripa would later play in the field of secular art. According to present-day thinking, Molanus is somewhat rationalistic and does not leave much room for feeling or fantasy. This lack is understandable when judged against the background of the confusion of Christian iconography of the Middle Ages and the period of Mannerism. The same spirit is evident in the 1679 reformatory treatise of P. Rohr, *Pictor errans.*

The rediscovery of the catacombs was an important event in the development of Christian iconography. In 1578 the Spanish historian Alphonso Ciacconio (Chacón) chanced upon the Coemiterium Jordanorum on the Via Salaria. This stimulated Philips van Winghe from Louvain and Hendrik de Raeff from Delft to further research in the same century. However, systematic research was not started until 1593 by Antonio Bosio whose work *Roma subterranea* was published posthumously in Rome in 1632.

The *Legenda aurea* lost its supremacy when systematic work in hagiography was initiated by a group of Jesuits from the southern Netherlands, the so-called BOLLANDISTS; their work was realized in the continuing *Acta Sanctorum* (1643–).

French Studies. There was little advance during the period of the Enlightenment, but the beginning of the 19th century saw renewed interest in early Christian art. In France, under the influence of the Catholic "revival" of Chateaubriand and others, interest in early Christianity was initially apologetical and religious rather than directed to art history. Yet important works in iconography were published in time by J. Seroux d'Agincourt [*Histoire de l'art par les monuments* . . . (Paris 1810–33)] and A. N. Didron [*Iconographie chrétienne* (Paris 1843)]. The latter attained special fame by the publication in 1845 of the so-called "Painter's Book of Mount Athos," an 18th-century MS that leaned, however, on early Christian iconographical traditions. Then followed iconographic studies by C. Cahier and A. Martin, C. Rohault de Fleury [*Archéologie chretiénne: Les saints*. . . (Paris 1890–1900)], X. Barbier de Montault, E. Le Blant, and L. Bréhier. Next came the Byzantinists G. Millet, C. Diehl, and André Grabar. The *Dictionnaire d' archéologie chretiénne et de liturgie* by the Benedictines F. Cabrol and H. Leclerq, which appeared between 1907 and 1953 in 15 parts (30 volumes), constitutes the most valuable single source of iconographical data. With some reservation about incomplete documentation, the reference works of L. Réau are also an invaluable source. Emile Mâle has produced expert studies of iconography of religious art after the 12th century in France. His works [*L'art religieux du XIIIe siècle en france* (Paris 1898); *L'art religieux après le concile de Trente* (Paris 1932)] are still being reprinted. Canon V. Leroquais produced outstanding studies (1940–41) on the illuminated liturgical MSS, and P. Thoby has studied the development of the crucifix (1959).

Germanic and Central European Scholarship. The interaction between the religious thoughts expressed in the literary and plastic arts was indicated by A. Springer [*Ikonographische Studien* (Vienna 1860)] and F. Piper [*Mythologie und Symbolik der christlichen Kunst* (Weimar 1847–51)]. Important work was done also by F. F. Leitschuh and J. J. Tikkanen. The latter was a Finn who published in German and is known, among other things, for his intensive studies on Eastern and Western Psalters, particularly the Psalter of Utrecht (1900). Several decades later K. Künstle [*Ikonographie der christlichen Kunst* (Freiburg 1926–28)] and the Jesuits S. Beissel and J. Braun, hagiographer-liturgist, began to attract notice.

The works of F. X. Kraus, H. Detzel, and R. Garrucci [*Storia dell'arte cristiana* (Prato 1872–81)] can be viewed as an introduction to the publications of Joseph Wilpert [Die Malereien der Katakomben Roms (Freiburg 1903); *Die Römischen Mosaiken und Malereien. . .* (Freiburg 1916); *I sarcofagi cristiani antichi* (Rome 1929–36)], who at the same time continued to build on the extensive research performed by Giovanni B. de Rossi in the Roman catacombs and elsewhere [*La Roma sotterranea cristiana. . .* (Rome 1864–77); *Musaici cristiani e saggi dei pavimenti della chiesa di Roma anteriori al secolo XV* (Rome 1872–96)]. Victor Schultze turned in revolt against the religious and apologetical tendencies of this group, and Josef Strzygowski opposed their one-sided orientation in a study pointedly entitled *Orient oder Rom* (1901). However, in the long run his Oriental theories can be considered to be just as one-sided. Nearly the same point of view was adopted by Oscar Wulff, N. Kondakov from Russia, and L. H. Grondijs, professor of art history at the University of Utrecht.

Rafael Ligtenberg, OFM, who laid the foundation of iconographical-iconological studies in the Netherlands, was followed by Grondijs and G. J. Hoogewerff. Research was undertaken at the Catholic University of Nijmegen by J. J. M. Timmers [*Symboliek en iconografie der christelijke kunst* (Roermund-Maaseik 1947)], J. B. Knipping [*De iconografie van de contrareformatie in de Nederlanden* (Hilversum 1939–40)], and above all F. van der Meer.

American and English Work. There was much activity also in the English-speaking countries, by E. Baldwin Smith [*Early Christian Iconography . . .* (Princeton 1918)] and the excellent medievalist F. Wormwald. In 1947 Charles Rufus Morey founded the Department of Art and Archeology at Princeton University, Princeton, N.J.

He was instrumental in founding the *Index of Christian Art,* which initially contained entries only of early Christian art but now goes to 1400. Copies of this reference work (under continuing compilation) can be found in the Dumbarton Oaks Research Library and Collection in Washington, D.C., in the Pontificio Istituto di Archeologia Christiana in Rome, and since 1963 in the Rijksuniversiteit in Utrecht. Princeton has beautiful facsimile editions in this field, edited by E. T. DeWald, K. Weitzman, M. Avery, and others. O. M. Dalton and D. Talbot Rice are specialists of Byzantine art; Byzantine art scholarship is represented in the work also of Greek scholars such as F. Sotiriou and M. Chatzidakis.

Secular Iconography. Secular art, as well as Christian, attracted diligent iconographers. In France P. L. Duchartre, R. Saulnier, and P. Saintyves described imagery in popular art, which, in addition to devotional pilgrimage souvenirs, includes objects of everyday life, e.g., housewares, kitchen utensils, clothing.

In the Germanic and Scandinavian countries an interest developed in the original Germanic style and decoration motifs. It was expressed by F. Adama van Scheltema (1924), W. A. von Jenny (1933), and also Josef Strzygowski. Particular contributions to the iconography of secular art *qua talis* were made by R. van Marle [*Iconographie de l'art profane . . .* (The Hague 1931–32)] and Guy de Tervarent [*Attributs et symboles dans l'art profane, 1450–1600* (Geneva 1958–59)].

It was only natural that in this age of evolving cosmopolitanism, interest would extend beyond Europe. The art of India with its characteristic form and religious content was iconographically examined in the 19th century by J. Fergusson, J. Burgess, and Alfred Foucher [*Étude sat l'iconographie bouddhique de l'Inde* (Paris 1900–05)]. Studies in the 20th century were published by E. A. G. Rao, A. K. Coomaraswamy, J. N. Banerjea, and H. Zimmer. O. Sirèn and E. Chavannes delved into the

Buddhist art of China, while George Coedès, W. F. Stutterheim, R. von Heine-Geldern, and P. Mus pursued that of Indo-China and Indonesia. Giuseppe Tucci, Antoinette Gordon [*The Iconography of Tibetan Lamaism* (New York 1939)], and others examined iconographical phenomena in Central Asia. The art of Japan was treated by indigenous scholars, especially Anesaki and Ōmura Seigai. Ancient Judaic symbolism was extensively described by E. R. Goodenough [*Jewish Symbols in the Greco-Roman Period,* 11 v. (New York 1953–64)].

MODERN ICONOLOGY

As has already been explained, iconographical development was consistently and necessarily under the influence of what today would be called iconological research. To some extent this applies to each branch of art history, but most of all to the study of early Christian and Indian art works, which were closely linked with religious, social, and historical ideologies. However, not until the early 20th century, was iconology considered to be a discipline distinct from iconography. Until then the term iconography had been used as a label for both disciplines. The term iconology had quite a different meaning from that understood today when it was first used in 16th- and 17th-century handbooks on symbols, allegories, personifications, emblems, etc., as for instance, the handbooks of A. Alciati (1548), J. P. Valeriano (1556), and P. Picinelli (1695). Its initial designation has been discussed above in reference to the most famous of these handbooks, namely the *Iconologia* (Rome 1593) by Cesare Ripa. The same meaning as Ripa's can be found in J. Lacombe's *Dictionnaire iconologique* (Paris 1756), namely the description, for the convenience of artists, of symbols and personifications used in emblems and allegories.

Schools of Thought. Hippolyte Taine, in the mid-19th century, studied the relationships between art objects and the race and social class of their creators and the historical circumstances of their inception. Subsequently, E. Müntz [*L'Histoire de l'art pendant la Renaissance* (Paris 1889–95)] and others viewed iconographical matter more explicitly against the background of social, technical, and stylistic conventions.

In comparing the various schools of iconographical and iconological thought, one finds them classifiable according to the element of art that they considered primary. The positive-visual school emphasized stylistic qualities and reduced iconography to the realm of a secondary or auxiliary science. This was the viewpoint of L. Venturi [*Storia della critica dell'arte* (Rome 1945)]. Max Dvořák qualified that idea and formulated a doctrine that was acceptable to many scholars. Although he himself was a disciple of the classical visual school of A. Riegl,

he saw a connection between the artistic composition and the religious and philosophical content of a work of art. He predicted a shift to a method of iconographical interpretation that would be very searching. Similar statements were made by H. Tietze and P. Toesca.

The development of psychoanalysis at the beginning of the 20th century corroborated and directed the method of interpretation. It forced the analysis of art works to the deepest, even unconscious sources of their origin and the meanings connected therewith. S. Freud applied his system to iconographical interpretation and thereby made it available to the field that has come to be known as iconology. Pioneers of the modern science of iconology are Aby Warburg (*Nachleben der Antiken*), Fritz Saxl, and Erwin Panofsky.

Erwin Panofsky. Aby Warburg used the term iconology in its new meaning as early as 1907, as has been proven by recent research by W. S. Heckscher. Hoogewerff formulated his definition of this concept in 1928. He was followed by Panofsky, who in 1930 in his introduction to *Hercules am Scheidewege* set forth some basic principles of the new method. He further developed this in 1932 in the philosophical journal *Logos*. But it was especially in the introduction to his now famous *Studies in Iconology* (New York 1939) that he revealed himself the great theorist in this field. According to Panofsky, iconology is a method of interpretation that arises from synthesis rather than from analysis. For him, just as the correct identification of motifs is the prerequisite of correct iconographical analysis, so the correct analysis of images, stories, and allegories is the prerequisite of correct iconographical interpretation, unless it is a question of works of art from which the whole sphere of secondary or conventional subject matter is eliminated, as is the case in certain landscape, still life, and genre paintings, as well as in nonobjective art. The interpreter must possess practical experience (familiarity with objects and events) and he must have a knowledge of the history of styles (insight into the manner in which, under changing historical conditions, objects and events are expressed by forms). For further iconographical analysis he must have knowledge of literary sources and be familiar with the history of types and iconographical themes. Finally, for iconological interpretation, he will need to have the so-called "synthetic intuition" (familiarity with the basic drives of the human mind as well as deep understanding of the manner in which, under varying historical conditions, these basic drives are expressed by specific themes and concepts). This approach by Panofsky can be best understood through the outline he published originally in *Studies in Iconology.*

The objections that can be made against these theories, at least in their most extreme forms, have already been mentioned. The greatest difficulties lie in the art after the Renaissance. The medieval artist thought in symbols that in general were easily understood. But after the beginning of the 15th century, naturalistic realism, of which the new emphasis on perspective is an example, became dominant in art. At first, however, this realism was still in the service of a thousand years of Christian tradition. The result was a veiled symbolism in which it is often very difficult, if not impossible, to decide where the symbol begins and reality ends. This explains why Panofsky tempered his statements on works of the period.

The spreading of his ideas to England and to America resulted to a great extent from the transfer in 1933 of Kulturwissenschaftliche Bibliothek Warburg from Hamburg to London, where it is presently kept in the Warburg and Courtauld Institutes, as well as from the departure to the New World of several German iconologists, among whom were Aby Warburg and Panofsky himself. The Netherlands also felt the effects of his widening influence. In 1955 Utrecht instituted a chair of iconology and W. S. Heckscher placed an *Index Iconologicus* alongside the copy of the Princeton *Index of Christian Art*. H. van de Waal, an art historian from Leiden, applied iconological interpretation to the paintings of the Dutch school of the 16th and 17th centuries, which are usually considered to be purely realistic.

Finally, the iconological interpretation of architecture was pursued by E. Panofsky, E. Baldwin Smith, R. Wittkower, R. Krautheimer, H. Sedlmayr, and others. In 1956 A. Pigler analyzed baroque motifs, and the Zentral Institut für Kunstgeschichte in Munich construed an index of baroque ceiling decorations that are characterized by complicated types of iconographical programs.

For specific iconographic themes, *see* GOD THE FATHER, ICONOGRAPHY OF; TRINITY, HOLY, ICONOGRAPHY OF; HOLY SPIRIT, ICONOGRAPHY OF; JESUS CHRIST, ICONOGRAPHY OF; MARY BLESSED VIRGIN, ICONOGRAPHY OF; SAINTS, ICONOGRAPHY OF; EVANGELISTS, ICONOGRAPHY OF; SACRAMENTS, ICONOGRAPHY OF; ICON; etc. For problems related to the use of image in Christianity *see* IMAGES, VENERATION OF; ICONOCLASM.

Bibliography: M. DVOŘÁK, *Kunstgeschichte als Geistesgeschichte* (Munich 1924), posthumous. K. KÜNSTLE, *Ikonographie der christlichen Kunst,* 2 v. (Freiburg 1926–28). A. WARBURG, *Gesammelte Schriften* (Leipzig-Berlin 1932). R. VAN MARLE, *Iconographie de l'art profane au moyen-âge et à la Renaissance,* 2 v. (The Hague 1931–32). F. SAXL, *Classical Mythology in Mediaeval Art* (Metropolitan Museum Studies 4; New York 1933) 228–280. E. PANOFSKY, *Studies in Iconology* (New York 1939). J. B. KNIPPING, *De iconographie van de Contrareformatie in de Nederlanden,* 2 v. (Hilversum 1939–40). J. J. M. TIMMERS, *Symboliek en iconographie der Christelijke kunst* (Maaseik 1947). G. J. HOOGEWERFF, *Ikonographie en Ikonologie van de oude christelijke kunst* (The Hague 1950). D. T. RICE, *Byzantine Art* (Baltimore 1962). L. RÉAU, *Iconographie de l'art chrétien,* 6 v. (Paris 1955–59). W. S. HECKSCHER and K. A. WIRTH, "Emblem, Emblembuch," *Reallikon zur deutschen Kunstgeschichte,* ed. O. SCHMITT v.5 (Stuttgart 1959) 85–228. J. BIALOSTOCKI, *Encyclopedia of World Art* (New York 1959–) 7:769–785.

[J. H. A. ENGELBREGT]

IDA, BB.

Three CISTERCIAN nuns of this name in the 13th century.

Ida of Leeuw; b. Leeuw (Léau), Belgium; d. *c.* 1260. Sometime after 1216 she entered the convent of La Ramée in Brabant, where she became known for the mystical graces she received and for her love of learning. Her cult spread through Belgium in the 16th and 17th centuries.

Feast: Oct. 30.

Ida of Louvain; b. Louvain, Belgium, early 13th century; d. *c.* 1300. She entered the Abbey of Roosendael near Malines. Her biography attributed to a certain Hugh, her confessor, is of doubtful historical value but recounts that she received extraordinary mystical graces and was marked with the stigmata. Her relics were venerated in the church of the monastery until the advent of CALVINISM. CLEMENT XI established her feast for the Cistercians and BENEDICTINES in 1719.

Feast: April 13.

Ida of Nivelles; b. Nivelles, Belgium, *c.* 1190; d. Brabant, Belgium, Dec. 11, 1231. She entered Kerkhem Abbey near Louvain at the age of 16 and moved with her community to La Ramée in 1215. She meditated with special predilection upon the Passion of Christ and had particular devotion to the Blessed Sacrament. She had an apostolic outlook, offering her sufferings for harassed priests and religious. She was reputed to enjoy mystical favors, and she used her supernatural gifts to help others. Shortly before her 33d birthday she died after a long and harrowing illness. Her cult is one of long standing at the convent of La Ramée.

Feast: Dec. 12.

Bibliography: Ida of Leeuw, Bl., and Ida of Louvain, Bl. *Acta sanctorum* April 2:156–189, Oct. 13:100–124. A. M. ZIMMERMANN, *Kalendarium Benedictinum* 2:49–51; 3:235–236. K. SPAHR, *Lexikon für Theologie und Kirche* ²5:600. M. B. BRARD, *Catholicisme* 5:1172–73. *Bibliographica hagiographica latina* 4144–45. Ida of Nivelles, Bl. Vita, ed. C. HENRIQUEZ, *Quinque prudentes virgines* (Antwerp 1630) 199–297. *Bibliographica hagiographica latina* 4146–47. A. M. ZIMMERMANN, *Kalendarium Benedictinum* 3:421–422. M. B. BRARD, *Catholicisme* 5:1173. S. ROISIN, *L'Hagiographie cistercienne dans le diocèse de Liège au XIIIᵉ siècle* (Louvain 1947) 54–59.

[F. M. BEACH/C. SPAHR]

IDA OF BOULOGNE, BL.

Noblewoman; b. Bouillon, Belgium, *c.* 1040; d. April 13, 1113. Ida, daughter of Duke Godfrey II, of Lower Lorraine, and niece of Pope STEPHEN IX, married Eustace II, count of Boulogne, *c.* 1057. She was the mother of GODFREY OF BOUILLON and King BALDWIN OF JERUSALEM. A correspondent of ANSELM OF CANTERBURY, Ida practiced the highest Christian virtues. She built the church of Notre Dame of Boulogne, founded several monasteries, and was especially generous to SAINT-BERTIN and AFFLIGEM. She ceded her domains in Brabant to the convent of Nivelles. She was buried at the Abbey of SAINT-VAAST, where shortly after her death a monk of the abbey wrote her life. Her relics were brought to Paris in 1669 and transferred to Bayeux during the reign of Napoleon I, a small relic being given to Arras.

Feast: April 13 (Dioceses of Arras and Bayeux).

Bibliography: *Acta Sanctorum* April 2:139–150. *La Vie de la bienheureuse Ide,* tr. D. HAIGNERÉ (Boulogne 1852). A. LEROY, *Biographie nationale de Belgique,* 28 v. (Brussels 1866–1944) 10: 3–4. F. DUCATEL, *Vie de sainte Ide* (Brussels 1900). G. MARSOT, *Catholicisme* 5:1171–72. A. BUTLER, *The Lives of the Saints,* ed. H. THURSTON and D. ATTWATER, 4 v. (New York 1956) 2:85.

[É. BROUETTE]

IDA OF HERZFELD, ST.

Widow; d. Herzfeld, Sept. 4, 825, or possibly 813. Ida was the sister of Abbot ADALARD and of WALA. A descendant of Charles Martel and a member of the court of CHARLEMAGNE, she married Egbert, a Saxon duke, and was the mother of Bl. WARIN. As a widow she lived at Herzfeld, where she was distinguished for piety, penance, and charity, exercised especially at the church founded by Egbert and herself in Herzfeld (Diocese of Münster). Bishop Dodo (980) exhumed her remains. There are pilgrimages to her tomb, where she is invoked especially by expectant mothers. A monk of WERDEN, named Uffing, wrote her vita.

Feast: Sept. 4, Nov. 26.

Bibliography: *Acta Sanctorum* Sept. 2:255–270. *Monumenta Germaniae Scriptores* (Berlin 1825–) 2:569–576. I. HELLINGHAUS, *Die hl. Ida von Herzfeld* (Kaldenkirchen 1925). *Heilige Ida von Herzfeld: Festschrift zur tausendjährigen Wiederkehr ihrer Heiligsprechung,* ed. G. JÁSZAI (Munster 1980). G. MARSOT, *Catholicisme* 5:1172.

[G. J. DONNELLY]

IDA OF TOGGENBURG, BL.

Died between 1138 and 1410. Nothing is known of her except that she has been honored since before 1410 at the church of Fischingen, near Lake Constance in Switzerland. A biography of St. Ida dating from the late 15th century is a fictitious account based on an old legend. She was probably a recluse (*see* ANCHORITES) who lived near the Benedictine convent at Fischingen. Her cultus was confirmed in 1724.

Feast: Nov. 3.

Bibliography: *Acta Sanctorum* Nov. 2.1:102–125. L. KERN, *Die Ida von Toggenburg-Legende* (Frauenfeld 1928). J. L. BAUDOT and L. CHAUSSIN, *Vies des saints et des bienheureux selon l'ordre du calendrier avec l'historique des fêtes* 11:100–101. H. DELEHAYE, *Nova et vetera* 4 (1929) 359–365; *Subsidia hagiographica* 21 (1934) 38–40. I. LÜTHOLD-MINDER, *Heilige Idda von Toggenburg: Beschützerin der Armen, Kranken und Sterbenden* (Einsiedeln 1976). W. BÖHNE, *Lexikon für Theologie und Kirche,* 10 v. (2d, new ed. Freiburg 1957–65) 5:600.

[J. C. MOORE]

IDAHO, THE CATHOLIC CHURCH IN

The first Catholic influence within the territory of the present-day Diocese of Boise, which comprises the entire state of Idaho, came with French-Canadian fur trappers during the mid-18th and early 19th centuries. In the early 1800s, a band of Iroquois migrated from eastern Canada to Idaho, bringing with them the rudiments of the Catholic religion; they often spoke of the necessity of having "Black Robes" to teach them the way to Heaven. In spite of four journeys made by members of the Flathead and Nez Perce tribes to St. Louis, Missouri, to plead for a priest, none came until February 1840. At that time a Belgian Jesuit, Pierre Jean DE SMET, was appointed superior of the Rocky Mountains Mission. He celebrated the first Mass in Idaho on July 22, 1840, at Henrys Lake, near the western end of what is today Yellowstone Park.

The first Catholic Church in Idaho was built in 1843 by Father Nicholas Point, S.J., on the St. Joe River, near the present Idaho town of St. Maries. Though it was originally called Sacred Heart, it is popularly known as the Cataldo Mission, named after a much-loved Jesuit missionary, Father Joseph Cataldo. The church was opened for services in 1853 and is the oldest building still standing in Idaho. These early missionaries had some success in making converts among the various tribes of Native Americans. Nevertheless, after the discovery of gold in the Boise Basin caused an influx of prospectors and miners into the southern part of the state, the Catholic population became predominantly Irish, many of whom moved to Idaho from the exhausted gold mines of California.

On March 5, 1863, President Abraham Lincoln signed legislation creating the Territory of Idaho. Five years later, on March 3, 1868, Pope Pius IX declared

Roman Catholic Mission: before the mission's dedication in 1874, it was called the Slickpoo Mission, Near Culdesac, Idaho. (©Michael Lewis/CORBIS)

Idaho a vicariate apostolic, a jurisdiction that also included some parts of what are now Montana and Wyoming. The first vicar apostolic was Louis Aloysius Lootens, a Belgian and a priest of the Archdiocese of San Francisco. At the time, Catholics numbered a little over seven percent, or 1,500, of the state's population of about 20,000, many of whom left in the early 1870s with the end of the gold rush. Bishop Lootens resigned in 1875, and returned to Oregon, where he had previously served as a missionary. He died on Jan. 12, 1898. The vicariate was then placed under the administration of the archbishops of Oregon City (now Portland). A new vicar apostolic for Idaho, Alphonse Joseph Glorieux, also a Belgian, was not appointed until Oct. 7, 1884. On his arrival, he found that the entire vicariate consisted of only two secular priests, four Jesuits, eight nuns, and a widely scattered Catholic population of about 3,500 people.

By the time Glorieux was consecrated bishop in Baltimore in 1885, the territory of the vicariate had been re-structured by the Holy See to its present boundaries. He made Boise City his see city and established the parish church of St. John the Evangelist as his cathedral. In 1893, when the Catholic population had doubled to 7,000, Boise City was established as a diocese and Bishop Glorieux was appointed its first ordinary. The passage of the Homestead Act (1862) and similar laws, as well as the building of the transcontinental railroad, opened up vast tracts of former Native American lands to settlement. Many of these settlers were German Catholics from the Midwest, eager for religious training for their large farm families. Now with sufficient population, Idaho became the 43rd state to enter the Union, on July 3, 1890.

Bishop Glorieux's successor, Iowan Daniel Mary Gorman (1918–1927), presided over a time of rapid growth in the diocese. By the end of his nine-year tenure, the cathedral had been completed to its present size (1921), there were 32 more diocesan priests, and twice as many students in the parochial schools. The growth continued under the long episcopate of Bishop Edward J. Kelly (1928–1956), resulting in the building of 41 churches, and the construction or purchase of 26 rectories, 4 convents, and 10 additional schools. Those schools were staffed almost entirely by Benedictine Sisters, who established their motherhouse near Cottonwood in 1907. They staffed their first school at Genesee in 1896 and grew in numbers and influence until 1968, when they were teaching in 15 elementary schools. Membership in the order peaked in 1967, when they counted 183 Sisters. At the urging of Popes Pius XII and John XXIII, and after a year of intense preparation, Sisters from St. Gertrude's joined other Benedictines in 1963 in an educational mission venture at San Carlos, Bogotá, Colombia. They later worked at Colegio Santa María and at Colegio San Benito, where they also opened a dependent priory in order to foster local vocations. The final member of the order serving in Colombia returned to the States in 1989. During the mission period several priests of the diocese also served in Colombia.

One of the many outstanding members of the community was Sister M. Alfreda Elsensohn, O.S.B. (1897–1989), a noted natural scientist, historian, and writer. She published *Pioneer Days in Idaho County* (v. 1, 1947; v. 2, 1951), *Idaho Chinese Lore* (1970), and *Idaho County's Most Romantic Character: Polly Bemis* (1980). During her teaching career she cataloged the flora of the prairie and began a collection of natural science specimens and artifacts that is preserved at the Historical Museum at St. Gertrude's. She received the Governor's Award, a special recognition in the arts and humanities from then-Governor Don Samuelson, and membership in the American Association of Museums, the Idaho Writers League, the Idaho Academy of Science, the Northwest

Scientific Association, and the American Benedictine Academy.

During Kelly's episcopacy, hospitals and other buildings were erected or enlarged throughout the diocese, including a chancery office building in Boise. At the death of Kelly, who was the first native of the Pacific Northwest to be appointed a bishop, James J. Byrne, the auxiliary bishop of St. Paul, Minnesota, was named the ordinary (1956–62). In 1958 Bishop Byrne established a diocesan newspaper, the *Idaho Register*, which became the largest weekly in the state, with a circulation of 16,000. During his short administration the Catholic population increased to over 44,000.

The fifth bishop, Sylvester Treinen (1962–88), had been a priest of the Diocese of Bismarck, North Dakota. He attended three sessions of Vatican Council II and returned to Idaho, endeavoring to implement the decrees of the council there. Initiatives under his leadership included the establishment of a new Catholic Education Office, the Idaho Catholic Liturgical Commission, the Search Program for youth retreats, the Catholic Communication Center, and Catholic student centers at each of Idaho's three state universities. In 1978 the diocese acquired 15 acres near the western boundary of Boise for Nazareth Retreat Center, a place for spiritual growth and renewal. Bishop Treinen served as ordinary for 34 years, the longest episcopacy in the history of the diocese.

The sixth bishop of Boise, Tod David Brown, a Californian, was ordained and installed in 1989, remaining in the state until he was appointed the third bishop of Orange, California, in 1998. Bishop Brown presided over sweeping administrative and financial changes in the Diocese of Boise. His successor in 1999, the seventh bishop, was Michael P. Driscoll, also of California. His early efforts focused on a local response to "Our Hearts Were Burning within Us," a document from the U. S. Catholic Bishops calling for adult education, and on the formation of Catholic Charities in the diocese.

Religious Communities. Since its organization into a vicariate apostolic, several congregations of women and men religious have come to Idaho and have served its people in important ways, initially concentrating in education and health care ministries. The Holy Cross Sisters were the first to arrive, opening a school in Idaho City in 1868. Franciscan Sisters conducted St. Aloysius Academy in Lewiston from 1884 to 1887. They were followed by the Sisters of St. Joseph of Carondelet (1903), Immaculate Heart of Mary Sisters (1903), Benedictine Sisters (1904), Ursulines (1908), and the Sisters of Mercy (1916). In addition to the Jesuits, Salvatorian, Redemptorist, Marist, and Oblate of Mary Immaculate priests have served in Idaho over the years. Monks occupied St.

Priest and Native American woman, dancing outside Cataldo Mission, Idaho. (©Dean Conger/CORBIS)

Michael's Benedictine Monastery at Cottonwood from 1904 to 1924.

Thirteen different religious communities of women were represented at the beginning of the third millennium, working in a variety of ministries: education, migrant services, hospital chaplaincies, retreat work, parish work, and others. Only the Benedictine Monastery of St. Gertrude, with its 58 members, had a numerically large presence. They continued the Benedictine mission to transform the world through prayer, community, and service, and are especially active in retreat work.

Other groups represented at the end of the twentieth century were the Congregation of Sisters of the Holy Cross (5); Dominican Sisters of Edmonds, Washington (1); Dominican Sisters of Sinsinawa, Wisconsin (1); Franciscan Sisters of Perpetual Adoration (2); Franciscan Sisters of the Eucharist (7); Marymount Hermitage (2); Sisters of Providence (1); Sisters of St. Francis of Assisi (1); Sisters of St. Joseph of Carondelet (3); Sisters of the Holy Name (2); the Society of Sisters for the Church (1); and the Ursulines (5). At the same time, there were only 14 men religious, most of whom were members of the Benedictine Monastery of the Ascension in Jerome, founded in 1968.

Catholic Education. In 2000 the Church in Idaho was maintaining 13 Catholic grade schools, located in Coeur d'Alene, Grangeville, Lewiston, Moscow, Idaho Falls, Rupert, Twin Falls, Nampa, Pocatello, and Boise (4). They had a total enrollment of 2,478 students, and were staffed primarily by Catholic laywomen, and not by Sisters, as in previous years. The diocese operated a single Catholic high school, Bishop Kelly, in Boise, with an enrollment of 672. There were no Catholic colleges, but seven Catholic student centers were in operation for the benefit of college and university students throughout the state. Moreover, Catholic education was extended to over 7,000 grade school children, more than 3,000 high school students, and some 3,000 adults. The Rite of Christian Initiation for Adults had been firmly established throughout the diocese, and was the principal vehicle for the formation of new Catholics.

In 1996 the permanent diaconate program was begun. The first class of 17 candidates was ordained in 2001, and a new class was scheduled to begin later in the year. LIMEX, an extension program offering a master's degree in theology from Loyola University in New Orleans, and After-Renew programs were in operation at parish and deanery levels. Parish efforts at adult education were extensive, though local offerings were sometimes uneven. The diocese continued its leadership role in trying to overcome these types of inequities, especially through the use of the Instrument of Growth Survey.

The KNIGHTS OF COLUMBUS, CATHOLIC DAUGHTERS OF AMERICA, and the NATIONAL COUNCIL OF CATHOLIC WOMEN were the most prominent among the lay Catholic organizations in existence. These organizations performed many works of service in the diocese while building community with Catholics in other states and nations. Membership in many of these organizations declined in the 1990s in light of the changing nature of ministry in parishes and the nearly universal entry of women into the workplace.

Catholic Charities of Idaho, seeking to develop social services throughout the Diocese of Boise, was incorporated in 2000. Services have included individual, marriage, and family counseling; outreach and development assistance to the Hispanic population of Idaho; family and youth support services; advocacy for social justice; and consultation services in order to assist Catholic parishes to develop parish-based social ministries programs.

In the 2000 census, the population of Idaho was approximately 1,350,000, and the Catholic population had risen to somewhere between 10 and 11 percent, making it the state's second-largest religious group after the Church of Jesus Christ of Latter-day Saints, or Mormons.

Among Catholics, slightly fewer than 70 percent were Caucasian. Hispanics, a growing population, came to constitute the next-largest ethnic group in the state, particularly in south, where migrant laborers came to work in the irrigated agricultural industry and have remained. Hispanics comprised about 7 percent of the general population of the state and about 50 percent identified themselves as Catholics. Spanish Masses were being offered wherever the size of the Spanish-speaking population indicated they were needed. Other ethnic groups included the Basques, who emigrated early in the twentieth century mainly to work in the sheep industry, Native Americans, Southeast Asians, and a small number of African Americans.

The diocese, divided into six deaneries, includes 55 parishes, 32 chapels, and 24 stations, served by approximately 80 priests and 29 deacons. Fifteen seminarians were preparing for service in the Diocese of Boise in 2001. Despite the decline in farm and small-town populations in the north and north central deaneries due to the scaling back of resource-based industries such as mining and timber harvesting, major growth in the state has taken place in the south and southwestern parts of the state during the 1990s. As the possessor of the nation's fifth-fastest-growing economy, the state attracted young professionals to jobs in high-tech industries. Among other industries that contributed to the state's economy were agricultural processing, chiefly potatoes, and recreation.

Bibliography: C. BRADLEY and E. J. KELLY, *History of the Diocese of Boise, 1863–1952* (Boise, Idaho 1953). Z. CHEDSEY and C. FREI, *Idaho County Voices* (Grangeville, Idaho 1990). M. A. ELSENSOHN, *Pioneer Days in Idaho County,* v. 1 (Cottonwood, Idaho, 1978). M. L. NACHTSHEIM, *On the Way: The Journey of the Idaho Benedictine Sisters* (Cottonwood, Idaho 1997).

[C. J. FREI]

IDEA

Derived ultimately from the Greek verb ἰδεῖν, to see, to know; and proximately from the noun εἶδος, that which is seen, the form, shape, or figure (Lat. *species*). In current usage idea has acquired two meanings: (1) a conception or representation that is known; and (2) a pattern or plan according to which a thing is made.

Platonic Concept. The word idea has strong Platonic overtones, for it forms the keystone of Plato's philosophy. The poetic sage had been exposed to two apparently contradictory influences: HERACLITUS, who emphasized that the world was in a state of constant flux; and SOCRATES, who insisted that the goal of the philosopher's search was the attainment of fixed and eternal truth. The philosophy of PLATO may be called an attempt to counterbalance the teachings of Heraclitus and Socrates. Consequently, Plato held that determinate, universal knowledge could not be derived from the continually changing world of sense; at best one could derive only δόξα (opinion). Yet he experienced within himself an awareness of the fixed and the universal. ''When returning into herself [the soul] reflects, then she passes into the other world, a region of purity, and eternity, and immortality, and unchangeableness, which are her kindred, and with them she ever lives, when she is by herself and is not let or hindered; then she ceases from her erring ways, and being in communion with the unchanging is unchanging. And this state of the soul is called wisdom'' (*Phaedo* 79D).

Since Plato could not explain the origin of such experience from below, he tried to explain it from above, by positing a world of Ideas wherein man-himself, beauty-itself, health-itself existed as things. Each human soul had also previously existed in that blessed land, and had directly contemplated these Idea-things. After being imprisoned in the body, probably for some sin, on the occasion of sensing some object in the world below the soul recalls what it previously intuited in the world of Ideas (*Phaedrus* 249E).

Having thus arrived at the existence of a world of ideal types, and facing the fact that the perception of concrete things on earth at least occasioned the presence of certain thoughts in the mind, Plato posited some vague sort of influence of the archetypes on the corresponding imperfect reflections in the world of sense. ''As to the manner, I am uncertain, but I stoutly contend that by beauty all beautiful things become beautiful'' (*Phaedo* 100D).

Hence, through Plato, the word idea came to have two different but related meanings: (1) what the intellect knows; and (2) the pattern in imitation of which things come to be.

Reactions to Plato. Although ARISTOTLE was Plato's pupil, he was vigorously opposed to the notion of a world of Ideas. He regarded it as contradictory: a subsistent Idea would have to be simultaneously incommunicable (since it was singular) and communicable (since it was universal); it would have to be unchanging and changing. He stated summarily: ''The Forms we can dispense with, for they are mere sound without sense'' (*Anal. post.* 83a 33). Aristotle seldom, if ever, used the Platonic word ἰδέα; even when discussing Plato's theory he would use εἶδος (form). When speaking of human ''ideas,'' Aristotle preferred to use ὑπόληψις (conception) or παθήματα τῆς ψυχῆς (passions of the soul).

The Neoplatonists, seeing the difficulty in accepting a sphere of impersonal immaterial essences, interpreted

Aristotle and Plato in dialectical debate, from the Campanile del Duomo, Florence. (Art Resource)

the Platonic Ideas as thoughts of God and placed them in the Nous, the divine mind that emanates from the One. St. AUGUSTINE found this notion attractive for two reasons: it would avoid any contention that God had created unintelligently; and it would explain the fact that every man has some unchanging standards of beauty and truth. Hence Augustine posited exemplar ideas and eternal truths in the mind of God (*see* EXEMPLARISM). ''The ideas are certain archetypal forms or stable and immutable essences of things, which have not themselves been formed but, existing eternally and without change, are contained in the divine intelligence'' (*Divers. quaest.* 46.2). This doctrine forms the ultimate basis for his theory of knowledge based on ILLUMINATION. Augustine held that just as the sunlight makes corporeal things visible to the human eye, so a divine illumination makes the eternal truths visible to the human mind (*Trin.* 12.15.24).

Aquinas's Synthesis. St. THOMAS AQUINAS synthesized the opinions of the two most prominent ancients. He agreed with Aristotle that the world of Ideas is contradictory and that all universals are derived from sense data. Yet he agreed with Plato (through Augustine) that there are eternal exemplars according to which all things are made; but these he regarded not as subsistent entities, but as objects of divine thought. Hence, in Aquinas and his followers, idea is used to refer to three quite different but interrelated data: (1) divine ideas, the eternal exemplars; (2) human practical concepts, the mental plans of an artisan; and (3) human speculative concepts, the subjective means by which man knows the universal and the abstract.

Divine Ideas. First, idea refers primarily to the divine ideas, the notions in the divine mind according to which all things were created. It would be inaccurate to say that, for Aquinas, the Platonic world of Ideas was simply transplanted to the divine mind. The divine ideas are not individual things, they are objects known. For St. Thomas these exemplars do not exist in God formally as things, but merely eminently as objects known. Thus, he wrote: "But the divine essence comprehends within itself the nobilities of all beings, not indeed compositely, but . . . according to the mode of perfection. . . . The intellect of God, therefore, can comprehend in His essence that which is proper to each thing by understanding wherein the divine essence is being imitated and wherein each thing falls short of its perfection. Thus, by understanding His essence as imitable in the mode of life and not of knowledge, God has the proper form of a plant; and if He knows His essence as imitable in the mode of knowledge and not of intellect, God has the proper form of animal, and so forth" (*C. gent.* 1.54). Consequently, the plurality of divine ideas is in no way opposed to God's simplicity, for there is no multiplication of concepts as entities (formal concepts) but merely a multiplicity of objects known (objective concepts).

Practical Concepts. Second, by analogy the term idea has been properly applied to human practical concepts, the subjective exemplars according to which an artisan intends to produce something. Aquinas wrote of the human analogue to the divine ideas: "The likeness of a house preexists in the mind of the builder. And this may be called the idea of the house, since the builder intends to build his house like to the form conceived in his mind" (ST 1a, 15.1). The noted commentator JOHN OF ST. THOMAS took special pains to emphasize that such practical ideas must include not only the "whatness" of the thing, but also the practical plans for its production. He wrote: "For an idea it is required, not only that the thing be known absolutely in itself, but that it is formulated in considering the form as imitable in another, not by a natural propagation, but through an imitation directed by the intellect. [An idea] is a form as imitable, not by propagation, but by direction" (*Curs. phil.,* phil. nat. 1.11.3). The truth or goodness of the practical order consists in the conformity of the thing produced to the practical concept of the artisan. Thus a work of art is not called good to the degree that it perfectly represents a thing in nature, but

rather it is called good if it conforms to the artist's idea (cf. ST 1a2ae, 64.1; 2a2ae, 57.1 ad 2).

Speculative Concepts. Third, the term idea is most frequently but least precisely used for any notion or CONCEPT; as when one says, "My idea about democracy is . . . ." St. Thomas himself acknowledged that idea could signify either practical or speculative notions. He wrote: "The Greek word idea is in Latin *forma.* Hence by ideas are understood the forms of things, existing apart from the things themselves. Now the form of anything existing apart from the thing itself can be for one of two ends; either to be the type of that of which it is called the form, or to be the principle of knowledge of that thing, inasmuch as the forms of things knowable are said to be in him who knows them" (ST 1a, 15.1). Here again an important distinction must be made between the subjective means by which something is known and the object that is thus immanently attained. The commentators distinguished these two aspects of the concept or idea, calling the one the formal concept and the other the objective concept. John of St. Thomas explained: "The concept is not known as an object except reflexly, when the very entity of the concept itself is known . . . [and not when] only the object is known as constituted in its status as an object illumined and understood as an object . . . . For thus the mental word is not numerically identical with the internalized object, since a mental word is especially required for us, that the object be made spiritualized or illumined and formed in its status as an object, as a term intrinsically understood" (*Curs. phil.,* phil. nat. 1.11.3).

Interrelation. The synthesizing mind of Aquinas saw a close interrelation in these various usages of idea. The divine ideas were the originating exemplars, which, in creation, implanted faithful exemplifications of themselves in creatures. Creatures, thus realizing the divine ideas in their structure, could impress themselves on the human mind and thereby enable man to form speculative ideas from the created exemplifications by which he knew not only the created thing but also something of the Creator. In imitation of Him of whom he is an image, man the maker forms his own practical ideas, to some degree based on divine artifacts, which direct his production of human artifacts.

Modern Views. The clear-cut and cohesive development of the term idea from Plato through Aristotle and Augustine to Aquinas has not been continued in modern thought. René DESCARTES is commonly regarded as the father of modern philosophy, and he is the source of modern confusion about ideas. A classic example is to be found in his *Meditations on First Philosophy:* "And although it may be that one idea gives birth to another, this process cannot be carried back in an infinite series: we must eventually reach a first idea whose cause is, as it were, the archetype in which all the reality or perfection that is in the idea only objectively, or by representation, is contained formally or actually. Thus the natural light makes it evident to me that ideas are present in me like pictures or images which, although they may certainly fall short of the perfection of the things from which they are derived, can never contain anything greater or more perfect'' (*Med.* 3). Two things are especially noteworthy in Descartes's statement. First, he still maintains the original Platonic notion of external archetypes, regarding these as somehow in the mind of God and yet containing the perfections of creatures formally and actually. Second, he regards the human idea as the thing known, missing entirely its intentional function.

The English philosopher, John LOCKE, was vigorously opposed to Descartes's INNATISM, but he further accentuated the subjectivism implicit in Descartes. He ignored or rejected any divine exemplars influencing human conceptualization, even indirectly. But more clearly, he made the subjective modification, on whatever level, to be the object known. At the beginning of *An Essay Concerning Human Understanding* he stated that the word idea stands ''for whatsoever is the object of understanding when a man thinks. I have used it to express whatever is meant by phantasm, notion, species, or whatever it is which the mind can be employed about in thinking'' (Introd. sec. 8).

George BERKELEY accepted the Lockean interpretation of idea as something subjectively known, but went beyond Locke to hold what many regard as a type of subjective idealism. Berkeley maintained that there were only three existents: the Infinite Spirit, finite spirits, and their ideas. Hence Berkeley seems to have regarded ideas as purely subjective objects of thought without any counterpart in the world or in God. David HUME, in a sense, went even a step beyond Berkeley. For him there was no Infinite Spirit and no finite spirits; there were merely disembodied and desubjectivized ideas and sense impressions. Hume held only a difference of degree between impressions and ideas, the latter being merely faint copies of the former. He wrote in *An Inquiry Concerning Human Understanding*: ''By the term impression, then, I mean all our more lively perceptions, when we hear, see, or feel, or love, or hate, or desire, or will. And impressions are distinguished from ideas, which are less lively perceptions of which we are conscious when we reflect on any of those sensations or movements above mentioned'' (sec. 2).

Subjectivist Connotations. After Hume, the general significance of idea was well established as something purely subjective. While almost every dictionary in any modern language will give idea and concept as synonyms, philosophers are significantly more discriminate. The more subjectively inclined the philosopher, the more he tends to use idea; the more realistically inclined, the more he tends to use concept; the more undecided he is, the more he is inclined to use both indiscriminately, with a preference for a different word of his own choosing such as perception or intuition. As noted above, Descartes's subjectivist proclivities inclined to the use of idea; Berkeley's idealism and Hume's panphenomenalism are expressed in their exclusive use of idea. Significantly, the absolute idealist, G. W. F. HEGEL, called the manifestations of Reason idea; and A. SCHOPENHAUER entitled his main work *The World as Will and Idea.*

Realist Connotations. On the other hand, those who have some commitment to REALISM tend to use concept more frequently. Concept implies a passivity to an external force, as in animal and human conception. Thus Kant requires sense data for his a priori concepts to organize. The American pragmatists, who were not nearly so much concerned about ideogenesis as its practical effects, used both terms indiscriminately. William JAMES is typical: ''A glance at the history of the idea will show you still better what pragmatism means. . . . Our conception of these effects, whether immediate or remote, is then for us the whole conception of the object, so far as that conception has positive significance at all'' [*Pragmatism,* 7th ed. (New York 1960) 43]. As Gilbert Ryle has become less positivistic, he tends to use concept more frequently. For example, in his book—significantly entitled *The Concept of Mind*—Ryle used concept six times in a nine-sentence paragraph. To take a portion: ''It does not, of course, follow from its being a technical concept that it is an illegitimate or useless concept. 'Ionisation' and 'off-side' are technical concepts, but both are legitimate and useful. 'Phlogiston' and 'animal spirits' were technical concepts, though they have no utility'' (62).

Thus, it seems that idea is irrevocably a part of the vocabulary of mankind and that it will forever bear at least the overtones of its Platonic origins.

See Also: IDEALISM; PLATONISM; KNOWLEDGE, THEORIES OF.

Bibliography: F. C. COPLESTON, *History of Philosophy* (Westminster, Md. 1946–). W. D. ROSS, *Plato's Theory of Ideas* (Oxford 1951). N. GULLEY, *Plato's Theory of Knowledge* (New York 1962). A. E. TAYLOR, *Aristotle* (rev. ed. New York 1956). C. BOYER, *Christianisme et néo-platonisme dans la formation de saint Augustin* (Paris 1920). É. H. GILSON, *The Christian Philosophy of Saint Augustine,* tr. L. E. M. LYNCH (New York 1960); *The Spirit of Medieval Philosophy,* tr. A. H. C. DOWNES (New York 1940); *The Christian Philosophy of St. Thomas Aquinas,* tr. L. K. SHOOK (New York 1956). J. MARITAIN, *The Degrees of Knowledge,* tr. G. B. PHELAN et al. from 4th Fr. ed. (New York 1959). J. F. PEIFER, *The Concept in Thomism* (New York 1952). V. M. KUIPER, ''Pour ou contre l'idée-

Immanuel Kant. (©Archivo Iconografico, S.A./CORBIS)

objet,'' *Angelicum* 15 (1938) 121–138. R. GARRIGOU-LAGRANGE, *God: His Existence and His Nature,* tr. B. ROSE from 5th Fr. ed., 2 v. (St. Louis 1934–36). M. DE MUNNYNCK, ''Notes on Intuition,'' *Thomist* 1 (1939) 143–168. M. C. BEARDSLEY, ed., *The European Philosophers from Descartes to Nietzsche* (New York 1960). E. A. BURTT, ed., *The English Philosophers from Bacon to Mill* (New York 1939). W. BARRETT and H. D. AIKEN, eds., *Philosophy in the Twentieth Century,* 4 v. (New York 1962). G. RYLE, *The Concept of Mind* (New York 1949).

[J. F. PEIFER]

IDEALISM

In philosophy, the family of doctrines revolving around the contention that the OBJECT is dependent on, and constituted by, the experiencing SUBJECT. In objective idealism the relation of interdependence holds mutually between subject and object in experience; in subjective idealism the dependence is one-way, upon the subject. Idealism is opposed to MATERIALISM, denying that mind originates from or is reducible to matter. It is equally opposed to all types of REALISM holding that either the objects of experience, or at least noumenal things-in-themselves, exist apart from being experienced. Idealisms may be either rationalistic, as with Leibniz, or empiricistic, as with Berkeley. Historical examples of both pluralistic and monistic-pantheistic idealisms can be found, although the post-Kantian systems of absolute idealism are monistic.

This article is divided into three parts: the first surveys the development of idealism from its earliest origins to its classical statement by Hegel; the second concentrates on post-Hegelianism idealism in Europe; and the third, on post-Hegelian idealism in the United States.

Origins and Development

Idealism as above described strictly speaking is found only in modern philosophy, and pure examples of this position cannot be found in either ancient or medieval philosophy.

Ancient Thought. The famous remark of PARMENIDES in frg. 3 (H. Diels, *Die Fragmente der Vorsokratiker: Griechisch und Deutsch,* ed. W. Kranz) equating thinking and being has sometimes been understood as idealistic; but Parmenides seems rather to have meant by it that thought has to be explained in terms of being as its object rather than being by thought. The pre-Socratic philosophers seem to have been materialists. For the Sophists, the assertion that the object of perception exists only in relation to a perceiving subject led not to idealism but to SKEPTICISM, or to a pragmatic concern with the utility, rather than truth, of opinions.

Plato's famous theory of transcendent Ideas, or Forms, has often been denominated as idealism. Certainly PLATO is in agreement with modern idealists in holding, as he does in *Laws* (book 10), that soul is the eldest of all things and that the physical is the product of the spiritual. The order of nature is due to divine mind, as the Demiurge of the *Timaeus,* but there is an underived material principle, and the archetypal Ideas, or Forms, to which the Demiurge looks are not thoughts in any mind, as the *Parmenides* explicitly states. The Platonic Ideas are the ultimate objective realities apprehended by knowledge in the soul, which has for Plato an intermediate grade of reality between the Ideas and the changing sensibles.

Curiously it is in Aristotle rather than in Plato that a certain anticipation of modern idealistic doctrine is to be found. The being qua being of metaphysics is identified by Aristotle with the divine entities separated in existence and definition from matter and motion; and these entities in turn, with perfect intelligences, ''thinking upon thinking,'' in whom knowing subject and known object are identical. But such divine minds do not creatively produce lesser realities, nor are they even cognizant of them. No one is more uncompromisingly realistic than Aristotle in his account of physical nature and of human knowledge, and his theory has often been regarded, with some plausibility, as tending to naturalism.

PLOTINUS, and the Neoplatonic tradition, contributed perhaps more to the formation of modern idealism than any other ancient or medieval thinkers. The Aristotelian identification of contemplative mind and divine being was taken over, and an effort was made to account for soul and physical nature by a process of emanation out of divine mind, which precontains in a higher, more unified mode all that exists in exile here below. But divine mind itself, although inclusive of the fullness of being, was seen as derived from a higher principle that is not intelligence or being.

Medieval Thought. No medieval thinker can be regarded as an idealist in the modern sense, although there were developments in the Middle Ages that helped to prepare the ground. The Augustinian tradition of interiorism, with its insistence that the road to truth and being lies within, was one such development. Augustine's doctrines of the spiritual autonomy of the soul and the active production by the soul of its own sense data, on the occasion of bodily changes, were others. Avicenna's famous "floating man," who still knows himself and his own mental operations even though all channels of physical sensation are blocked off, epitomized a long tradition, opposed by THOMAS AQUINAS, that extended to Descartes. There is even a sense in which medieval "realism" concerning UNIVERSALS—as found in such thinkers as BOETHIUS, WILLIAM OF CHAMPEAUX, and DUNS SCOTUS, who attributed to physical objects the identical forms or essences found in abstract thought—constituted a remote preparation for modern idealism.

Lastly, there was a little-noted medieval background for the 17th-century assumption that man experiences only his own ideas—an assumption that came to be crucial for the subjective, empirical idealism of Berkeley. This was to be found in the "formal object" analysis of sensation, common to much medieval and late medieval SCHOLASTICISM. The ultimate "given" of sensation, for this theory, becomes a congeries of atomic colors, sounds, odors, tastes, and tactile sensations. Sensation experiences, in this view, only the sensible accidents, not substance or the "This man Callias" of Aristotle's account; and the intellectual inference to underlying realities was opened to the critical attacks later to be launched by the British empiricists. When such "data" (themselves the product of formal intellectual abstraction) were made into the direct objects of sensation, contrary to St. Thomas's injunction against making sensible species objects, the characteristic modern epistemological situation was produced—within which modern idealism came to flower. It is remarkable that SOLIPSISM seems to have become a serious philosophical problem only in the modern era.

Modern Thought. The egocentric predicament has typified most of modern philosophy since R. DESCARTES, for if one directly experiences only one's own ideas, problems of extramental reference and reality become crucial. The very existence of physical entities outside of and independent of mind thus became a significant question for modern philosophers.

Berkeley. G. BERKELEY initiated the empiricist variety of modern idealism by answering in the negative. J. LOCKE had made the famous distinction of primary and secondary qualities, the former being regarded as properties of physical substances, the latter being dismissed as subjective and relative. Berkeley was able to show that the so-called primary qualities are just as dependent on their being perceived as the secondary ones. As an empiricist, he held that all of man's knowledge is derived from the ideas of sense experience, and cannot reach to anything different from ideas, apart from minds in which ideas exist. The very being of ideas, for him, is their being experienced. Consequently, the very existence of independent material substances was denied; in this step Berkeley believed be had refuted not only materialism but also atheism and skepticism. Skepticism is overcome since man is certain of his own existence and of the ideas in his mind. The insuperable problems of representational theories of knowledge need not be faced, for there are no real physical entities beyond such ideas. Atheism is refuted by showing that it is impossible for the whole or any part of the visible world to exist without a mind. Since collections of ideas (trees, rocks, etc.) exist independently of human will, and appear in regular order, they are results of divine will, and exist in God's mind when not perceived by creatures.

Leibniz. In the works of G. W. LEIBNIZ, idealistic conclusions were reached by a purely rationalistic method. Taking as a premise that every complex is analyzable into simples, a proposition he considers self-evident, Leibniz shows that the simple units or monads of reality cannot be material, since everything material is infinitely divisible. Leibniz's system is summarized in his *Monadology* (1720).

Kant. While Berkeley had attempted to found idealism on empirical grounds, D. HUME held that the EMPIRICISM of ideas led rather to skepticism. The impact of Hume on the great German philosopher I. KANT led to the central crisis of modern philosophy. Kant saw that if a radical empiricism entails skepticism, a radical RATIONALISM in its turn leads to sterility. The empirical critique had made the supposed primary data of experience into a manifold of sense in itself unordered and unintelligible, incapable by itself of constituting scientifically knowable objects or even experiential objects. In the *Critique of Pure Reason* (1st ed. 1781; 2d ed. 1787), Kant maintains that the objective world of experience that founds mathematics and physics must be constituted by the organizing forms and categories of mind out of the materials of the sensuous manifold. Such a scientifically meaningful objective realm of experience is, however, only phenomenal, not noumenal. The mind determines only the forms in which things appear, but man's mentality is devoid of intellectual intuition and real "things-in-themselves" are unknowable to him. The attempt by pure reason to attain metaphysical knowledge is doomed to founder in illusion and antinomy. There is, however, a practical use of reason that establishes, over against deterministic physical nature, the spiritual world of moral duty and freedom. Confidence in the reality of this moral universe is an affair of faith, not of pure speculative reason.

Post-Kantian Idealism. Post-Kantian German philosophers sought to restore authentic metaphysical knowledge by insisting on the fact of intellectual INTUITION and by abandoning the unknowable Kantian *Ding ansich.* J. G. FICHTE thus sought to advance beyond Kant's transcendental idealism to a new form of subjective idealism. In particular, Fichte (and Schelling and Hegel after him) desired to overcome the Kantian dualisms: the form and matter of experience, physical necessity and spiritual freedom, theoretical and practical uses of reason, and phenomenal and noumenal worlds. To do so, they evolved a general idealistic premise that philosophy must begin with the unconditioned absolute met with in human CONSCIOUSNESS. For Fichte, this is the ego or SELF, and its unity is the ground of the systematic interconnection of the antithetic principles of experience. The entire body of knowledge is to be deduced starting with the first three principles that the self posits. In the thesis, the ego posits its own being; in the antithesis, the nonego is "op-posited" to the ego; in the synthesis within the absolute ego there is "op-posited" a divisible, finite nonego to the divisible, finite ego. "Being," for Fichte, is this self-positing process. The nonself is irreducible only from the point of view of the theoretical ego, but not in relation to the practical ego, which posits this barrier to force the theoretical ego to reflect back upon itself. The realms of morality and right are deduced from the infinite striving of the practical ego.

In the works of F. W. J. von SCHELLING, nature is given more than a moralistic significance in relation to the practical ego. The identical activity of the absolute is manifested unconsciously in nature and consciously in human mind. The absolute, which is the source of both, was originally conceived as a point of indifference, in which the oppositions characterizing finite perspectives

are overcome. Hegel's ridicule of this position forced Schelling to attempt to explain how such opposites can be radicated in God, or the ABSOLUTE, and distinctions borrowed from the theosophist J. BÖHME were employed.

Post-Kantian absolute idealism culminated in the great system of G. W. F. HEGEL. Absolute spirit is identified by Hegel with the concrete universal, the absolute concept whose self-development is traced through the dialectical phases of logic, philosophy of nature, and philosophy of spirit, and is finally consummated not in religion but in philosophical thought. The object in finite understanding is other than mind, but philosophic reason manifests their dialectical identity in the union of absolute mind. Schelling rejected Hegel's dialectic of absolute concept as neglecting the existential factor.

Post-Hegelian Idealism in Europe

Idealism, as described in the preceding section, continued as a living philosophical movement beyond Hegel into the 19th and 20th centuries although it was somewhat in eclipse by the middle of the 20th century. This part of the article considers post-Hegelian thinkers in Germany (Schopenhauer), England, France, and Italy.

Germany. The voluntaristic, pessimistic idealism of A. SCHOPENHAUER grew out of Kant more than Hegel, whose dialectic of rational concepts was rejected. A nonrational metaphysical intuition was sought to attain the noumenal order; this was identified with a blind, irrational will to live, a unitary principle manifesting itself in the pluralistic phenomena. As for Kant, objects of knowledge for Schopenhauer are phenomena constituted by forms organizing the inchoate sensuous manifold. But sufficient reason applies only to phenomena, not to the world as a whole or to its noumenal basis. There cannot be a plurality of things-in-themselves, since the forms of space and time that individuate objects apply only to phenomena. Human experiences of the self and of one's own body as striving expressions and manifestations of will and freedom, combined with an inference extended to all perceived objects, point to a unitary cosmic will. Although man's knowledge of this cosmic willl is interior and privileged it is known by him only through the form of time and, indirectly, in the acts of the body. In its own nature, the thing-in-itself, or will, is not a knowing subject, but is nonrational, even irrational, since that which is the ultimate ground of every kind of sufficient reason cannot be proportionate to any cognitive power. The will-to-live incarnates itself at every level of nature, according to Platonic ideas, but such archetypal patterns do not imply intelligent planning. The higher and lower levels of will's embodiment are incessantly at war, objectively manifesting will's own internal hostilities and essential need, deficiency, and consequent pain. This is the source of Schopenhauer's famous PESSIMISM. Schopenhauer considers three ways of escape from the egoism and hatred stemming from the will-to-live, viz, suicide, art, and morality. Suicide is futile, since it destroys not the will but only the phenomenal individual. Art, in contemplating disinterestedly the "Platonic Ideas," is only temporary release. Moral sympathy and renunciation in an ascetic denial of the will-to-live constitute the only cure. There is a final suggestion that perhaps such a renunciation might lead to a positive union with the thing-in-itself in a character transcending its aspect of pain-bearing will.

England. The definitive entrance of German idealism into England was signalized by the publication (1865) of J. H. Stirling's *Secret of Hegel.* Thomas Hill Green (1836–82) is the first important figure in the British idealistic school of the late 19th century. Green accepted the main tendencies of post-Kantian German idealism, and on this basis attacked the traditional British empirical and utilitarian positions, as well as the evolutionism of Herbert SPENCER. Man could not, according to Green, be a product of natural forces or a member of the phenomenal series since such a product could not know and explain himself, and thereby possess moral significance. It is the spiritual that produces the order and unity of nature, which is radicated finally in self-consciousness, an all-uniting consciousness that is eternal mind. Biological evolution itself, culminating in human mentality and self-consciousness, manifests the eternal, universal spirit. Human free activity is not in time and has no antecedents, just as self-consciousness has no origin. Human conduct, to be distinctively human, involves the conscious presentation of a want to a subject who identifies himself with it, transforming natural desire into will. Green's ethical theory is based on self-realization, the self being understood as the ideal self whose good includes the perfection of all rational agents.

The greatest of the English post-Hegelian idealists is F. H. BRADLEY, whose metaphysical masterwork is *Appearance and Reality* (London 1893). Bradley is not a Hegelian; he rejects the dialectical unfolding of the Idea. Rather, Bradley is a modern Eleatic, a disciple of Parmenides who employs, like his ancient predecessors, sharp dialectical instruments of refutation to convict the pluralistic phenomenal world of contradiction and unreality. The German realist J. F. Herbart also had held that nothing can be real that is contradictory, maintaining that reality must be an absolutely self-consistent system. Using this test, Herbart had found contradictions in such supposedly clear concepts as thing, change, becoming, matter, and self-consciousness. The Herbartian critique had been aimed at establishing the reality of many unchanging reals only externally related to each other. The

Bradleyan dialectic, more powerful and subtle than Herbart's, proposed to show the internal contradictions of all realistic or pluralistic hypotheses. As opposed to Hegel, the Absolute Reality that is a coherent whole is not identified with dialectical reason; reason itself, in its discursive movement, deals only with appearances and can never be consummated in a union of identity with the Absolute. Thinking is essentially relational. External relations, which make no difference to their terms, require in turn new relations to bond them with their terms and an infinite regression arises. Even internal relations, where the relations bite into the being of the terms, only import into the interior of such entities the same disjunction and residual externality. Reason, in its effort to judge truly that *A* is *B,* must expand *A* beyond its naked isolation (in which state it cannot be a subject of judgment at all, even of identical predication) until it becomes the totality of the real, which is "such that" the predicate *B* can be truly asserted of it. But reason can never achieve this final synthesis or reunion of concrete existence and separated abstract content. Even if, *per impossibile,* reason could complete its infinite task, it would not *be* the Absolute, although the Absolute is a unity of experience, a seamless whole beyond all disrupting relationships, which mysteriously includes reason and all else. Man's experience begins with an immediate unity of feeling that is below the level of rational analysis, although it is somehow pregnant with such structures and contrasts. It is by a remote analogy with this original felt unity that man forms his notion of the Absolute Reality. It is an experience having for its sole materials feeling, thought, and volition—there are no others—but uniting them in a harmonious whole above the relations of the many appearances dealt with by reason. Thought cannot give man any intuitive vision of this ultimate harmony of experience, nor does Bradley posit any mystical union with the Absolute.

Bernard Bosanquet (1848–1923), whose most important work is *The Principle of Individuality and Value* (London 1912), followed Bradley in many respects but was more akin to Hegel than his famous contemporary had been. As for Hegel, for Bosanquet the notion of the concrete universal, of a universal which determines its own particularization, is central. Individuality is a striving toward completion and fulfillment, and may be exemplified in a logical system, a work of art, the moral self, a social institution. In all cases the fulfillment of individuality is in the whole, so that the goal of knowledge, moral conduct, and artistic creation is always the Absolute. Reality and value are inseparably one. In the sphere of knowledge, truth is the ideal completed totality of the system of knowledge; thus Bosanquet affirms the characteristic idealistic theory of degrees of truth and reality and the coherence theory of truth. Ethically, the moral value of an action is judged by coherence with a more inclusive scheme, and ultimately with the Absolute itself. In art, the ideal of beauty is the harmony of the completed whole.

A more minor figure in post-Hegelian British idealism is John Ellis McTaggart (1866–1925), who did commentaries on Hegel's logic and dialectic and developed, in *The Nature of Existence* (2 v. Cambridge, Eng. 1921–27), a pluralistic, personalistic idealism more akin to that of the American personal idealists Bowne and Brightman than to that of Hegel. All beings are spiritual persons, including God, if He exists. Such a God, however, would be finite, and is not to be identified either with the infinite personal God of traditional Christianity or with the Absolute of Green, Bradley, and Bosanquet. Others who contributed to the development of British idealism are Edward Caird (1835–1908), who wrote *The Critical Philosophy of Kant* (2 v. Glasgow 1889); John Caird (1820–98); and the great Platonic scholar Alfred Edward Taylor (1869–1945), whose early work, the *Elements of Metaphysics* (London 1903), was heavily influenced by Bradley.

France. French idealism was less a development out of German and Hegelian idealism than was the case in England. Negatively, it developed as a reaction against the POSITIVISM of Auguste Comte. The activistic or dynamistic philosophy of MAINE DE BIRAN, which opposed positivism, became one of the native sources of French idealism. Maine de Biran organized his philosophy around the notion of the active force or effort of which one is conscious in overcoming obstacles, a concept having some kinship with Fichte's active ego that requires the nonego for its fulfillment. But Kant lay in back of the French idealistic development, as did native sources. C. B. Renouvier named his philosophy neocriticism to indicate its Kantian source. However, like McTaggart later in England and the American personalists, Renouvier moved beyond Kantian criticism to the construction of a pluralistic and personalistic idealistic metaphysics. The thing-in-itself was abandoned. Unlike Royce in America, Renouvier regarded actual infinity as self-contradictory, and his world is a finite sum of finite beings. Infinite transition is impossible, so that real discontinuity in nature must be admitted, and to Renouvier this provides an opening for uncaused beginnings and consequently for free will.

The emphasis on the reality of contingency and freedom is characteristic of French idealism. A. A. COURNOT, in terms of mathematical probability theory, had opposed the reigning dogma of the certitude and necessity of scientific laws, and with É. BOUTROUX this dogma received its definitive challenge in *The Contingency of the Laws of Nature* (1874, 4th ed. 1902, tr. F. Rothwell, London

1916). Real indeterminacy was taken as the foundation for freedom, and God was regarded as the maximal point in the hierarchy of beings in terms of freedom and indeterminacy.

One more figure in French idealism deserves mention. Alfred Jules Emile Fouillée (1838–1912) was not, to be sure, an idealist strictly speaking, since he sought to synthesize idealism and MATERIALISM in an evolutionistic and voluntaristic philosophy that makes mind and matter aspects of one and the same thing. Neverrtheless, for him only psychi phenomena are directly experienced by man, and consequently the primary analogate for man's understanding of reality must be active mind and its *idées-forces*.

Italy. Italian idealism derived from Hegel but chiefly from the historical side of HEGELIANISM, the Hegel of the *Phenomenology of Mind,* where the dialectical advance of the human spirit in history, art, religion, and philosophy is described. The absolutism of Hegel's thought, which made such a strong appeal in England, was regarded in Italy as static and alien to the dynamic, temporal, and progressive movement of the human spirit. It was the latter that B. CROCE understood as reality, rather than some transcendent absolute experience. Reality is focused on the present, and past and future are real only in relation to present experience. One of Croce's most influential contributions was in the area of AESTHETICS. Sense perception and artistic creation differ only in degree; intuition is creative of the data of both.

The other prominent modern Italian idealist was G. GENTILE, who, unlike Croce, made common cause with the fascism of his day. The dualisms engendered by the subject-object contrast are synthesized in the unity of self-consciousness, which is manifested at its peak in philosophy. Art is one-sidedly subjective, religion one-sidedly objective, but philosophy alone achieves perfect synthesis; it not merely knows reality, it *is* reality. But since philosophical reflection develops through history, philosophy is history.

Critique. From the point of view of Catholic Christian theism, two variants of modern idealism appear clearly unacceptable. The absolute MONISM of post-Kantian German idealism is certainly one. But even the pluralistic, personalistic idealisms cannot be reconciled with Christian theism if they are regarded as implying divine finitude.

Bibliography: J. D. COLLINS, *A History of Modern European Philosophy* (Milwaukee 1954). F. C. COPLESTON, *History of Philosophy* (Westminster, Md. 1946–), esp. v.7, *Fichte to Nietzsche* (1963). J. MARÉCHAL, *Le Point de départ de la métaphysique*, v.4 *Le Système idéaliste chez Kant et les postkantiens* (3d ed. Paris 1947). R. JOLIVET, *Les Sources de l'idéalisme* (Paris 1936). H. D.

GARDEIL, *Les Étages de la philosophie idéaliste* (Paris 1935). A. CARLINI, *Enciclopedia filosofica*, 4 v. (Venice-Rome 1957) 2:1189–1201. J. MÖLLER, *Lexikon für Theologie und Kirche*, ed. J. HOFER and K. RAHNER, 10 v. (2d, new ed. Freiburg 1957–65) 5:601–02. W. WIELAND, *Die Religion in Geschichte und Gegenwart*, 7 v. (3d ed. Tübingen 1957–65) 3:556–62. R. EISLER, *Wörterbuch der philosophischen Begriffe*, 3 v. (4th ed. Berlin 1927–30) 1:672–81.

[L. J. ESLICK]

American Idealism

Although American idealism reflects the many varieties of its British and German antecedents, most American idealists fall into one of two groups, personal or absolute. Personal idealists conceive reality as a self or as belonging to a self; they are indebted to Berkeley, whom they consider to have shown conclusively that matter does not exist, and are usually theistic. Absolute idealists, on the other hand, tend to be monistic and pantheistic; they hold that reality is included within one complete system, present to an all-comprehensive Mind called the ABSOLUTE. They believe that Berkeley went too far in denying the existence of matter altogether, although they credit him with rightly insisting that everything in reality is dependent on mind. They are convinced also that personal idealism places too much emphasis on the separateness of persons from one another and from God.

The history of idealism in America is largely a record of protest by religious-orientated thinkers against various forms of materialism, naturalism, and positivism that tend to deny the intelligible order of the universe and its dependence on mind. Most American idealists have been led to their position in search of a rational basis for morality and religion. This is true equally of the early idealists of New England, of the St. Louis Group, of B. P. Bowne and J. Royce, and most recently of Errol Harris.

Early Idealists. American idealism finds its earliest representatives in Jonathan EDWARDS and Samuel Johnson (1696–1772), both of Connecticut. Although Edwards is known primarily as a Calvinist theologian and preacher, he developed from a critical reading of Newton and Locke a personal idealism that was to parallel in many respects the work of Berkeley, although he was probably ignorant of the fact that the British philosopher had reached similar conclusions. Johnson, who was the founder and first president of King's College, was directly influenced by Berkeley, with whom he became personally acquainted during Berkeley's visit to America (1729–31). Johnson retained enough of his earlier acquaintance with scholasticism, however, to prevent him from accepting outright Berkeley's nominalism. Neither Johnson's idealism nor Edwards', however, were to make a permanent impression on American thought.

Idealism in the U.S. was to receive its major impetus through the efforts of a group of influential teachers and professional men who met regularly in St. Louis during the years immediately following the Civil War. This group met at first informally in the home of William Harris, the future U.S. commissioner of education, for the study of German philosophy. Later, owing to the influence of Henry Conrad Brockmeyer (1828–1906), it undertook the serious study of Hegel, methodically analyzing Brockmeyer's translation of one of Hegel's works. It eventually founded the *Journal of Speculative Philosophy,* the first philosophical periodical in the English language, in which it published translations and commentaries on German philosophy. Other members included G. H. Howison, Thomas Davidson, and Joseph Pulitzer. Bronson Alcott was so impressed with the St. Louis Hegelians, as they came to be known, that he resolved to make their Hegelianism known in the East, which he did by inviting various representatives of it to the Concord Summer School of Philosophy.

Howison and Bowne. George Holmes Howison (1834–1916), who later taught for man years at the University of California, Berkeley, became one of the better-known members of the St. Louis group. A personal idealist, he devoted much of his effort to combating the evolutionary agnosticism of Herbert Spencer. He also attacked the pantheistic and solipsistic tendencies of absolute idealism. He suggested that cosmic evolution, as a judgment about nature, is essentially a teleological idea. Science must rest upon the assumption of an all-pervading rationality in things. This implies, he thought, a self-conscious intelligence underlying, and responsible for the connectedness of, all phenomena.

The cause of personal idealism was simultaneously advanced, and perhaps with greater success because he was a more systematic thinker than Howison, by Borden Parker Bowne (1847–1910) of Boston University. In his major work, *Personalism* (New York 1908), Bowne discloses himself as at once indebted to and critical of Kant. He believed that Kant and his followers paid so much attention to the forms by which the mind organizes experience that they had all but forgotten the self whose characteristic activity is to know by means of the organization of experience. Bowne taught that man's cognitive powers are in general reliable. "Intelligence is simply a bottom fact which explains everything but accepts itself." Persons and the external world exist, but they exist as objectified or realized ideas. Bowne's epistemology is dualistic insofar as he holds that the idea and its object are numerically distinct. He accepts the Kantian distinction between the phenomenal and the noumenal, identifying the latter with the personal. A Supreme Person is the ground for both the system of nature and the community of persons. Bowne's personalism is also voluntaristic. To be is to act, and to act is to will. Attacking a mechanistic sense-bound naturalism on the one hand, Bowne criticizes an idealistic impersonalism on the other.

Royce and Others. Of American idealists, Josiah ROYCE is probably the most outstanding. His principal work, *The World and the Individual,* the Gifford lectures of 1899–1900 (2 v. New York 1900–01), earned him a lasting place in the history of American philosophy. In these lectures Royce argued that "the whole universe including the physical world is essentially one living thing, a mind, one great spirit." This conclusion, Royce believed, was not only in accord with the demands of reason but also with the facts of human experience and the assumptions of science. Since the universe is one great all-inclusive mind, the best method of acquiring an understanding of its nature is by an examination of one's own conscious experience. Just as the human mind is the sum total of fleeting conscious experience, so the Absolute is composed of all the conscious selves into which he has differentiated himself and whose conscious experiences are embraced in his own universal Mind. Royce believes it impossible to think of the world in a realistic or materialistic sense, as first having existence independent of human minds and later producing them. Like Howison and Bowne, he attacks materialistic conceptions of evolution. For Royce, the world and the mind are organically related; neither can be taken apart from the other; there can be no object without a subject that knows it.

The cause of idealism was advanced also by James E. Creighton (1861–1924), for many years the editor (from 1893 until his death) of the *Philosophical Review;* by W. E. Hocking (1873–1966), an absolute idealist; by E. S. BRIGHTMAN, whose idealism is best described as PERSONALISM; and most recently by E. E. Harris, who in his *Nature, Mind and Modern Science* (New York 1954), attempts to show that classical empiricism and LOGICAL POSITIVISM are dead ends, reopening the idealistic examination of evolution.

Although between 1875, and 1900 almost every professor of philosophy in the U.S. was an idealist, and idealists remained in the majority for a decade or two later, idealism could not maintain itself on the American scene. Bowne and Royce bequeathed to America a host of inspired religious teachers, ministers, and administrators; but their influence was to give way before the criticism of REALISM and naturalism. This trend from idealism to naturalism is strikingly reflected in the intellectual development of John Dewey as he moved from an early defense of idealism to an outright naturalism. In general, idealism came to be regarded as unscientific or as insufficiently imbued with the scientific spirit.

Critique. From the viewpoint of moderate realism, American idealism begins not with experience but with the problems bequeathed to it by the erroneous epistemologies of Locke and Hume, whose empiricism, in turn, has its origin in the exaggerated realism of Descartes. A moderate realism, offered as an alternative explanation, would insist that things exist independently of the human mind, which is capable of discovering not only their phenomenal but also their essential aspects. The intelligibility of the universe is accounted for in terms of a personal, creator God, distinct in essence from His creatures, who is at once their origin and their goal, as well as continually responsible for their existence.

See Also: TRANSCENDENTALISM.

Bibliography: C. M. PERRY, ed., *The St. Louis Movement in Philosophy* (Norman, Okla. 1931). W. G. MUELDER and L. SEARS, eds., *The Development of American Philosophy* (New York 1940). H. G. TOWNSEND, *Philosophical Ideas in the United States* (New York 1934).

[J. P. DOUGHERTY]

IDENTITY

A RELATION distinct from all others in its being the most fundamental both in thought and in reality. All others in one way or another are reducible to it. It is both mental and real. As mental it is the essential relation in JUDGMENT and in the PROPOSITION. When the subject and the predicate of the proposition are in no way different either in extension or in comprehension, then their identity makes the proposition a tautology. When both of these differ as aspects of one and the same reality, then the proposition is held to be formal. Many philosophers hold that only the latter is the valid type of proposition. If its real identity is substantial, then it points to the most fundamental ontological unity. Accidental identity according to quantity or form is less fundamental. The real existence of this relation is much disputed. In some schools of philosophy it is categorically denied.

The sort of pluralism implied by the logical atomism of B. RUSSELL is an example of this. For him, reality is an absolute plurality to which the relation of identity is brought by the mind. This alone creates the unity of experience. Other philosophers deny this. PARMENIDES thought that all being is identically one in number and that diversity is an illusion of the mind caused by sense knowledge. B. SPINOZA held the same doctrine, attributing the appearance of multiplicity to the fracturing effect of imagination exercised upon the continuum of sense experience. F. W. J. SCHELLING, G. W. F. HEGEL and F. H. BRADLEY taught a somewhat similar doctrine, holding that the beginning of experience is in an un-differentiated being, which is then rendered multiple and structured through the insertion of the relation of identity. Identity therefore was a relation immanent in being and in experience.

Many other philosophers, such as St. THOMAS AQUINAS, take a mediating position between these two extremes. They therefore admit of an ontological structure in things by reason of which they are partly diverse and partly identical. Things that are identical in form but different in number are thereby similar and come under one genus or species. The identity, in this case, is real since it has a real grounding. But it can also be purely mental, as happens when it binds together different concepts of one and the same thing. Modern mathematical logic has been much concerned with this relation, but less from the point of view of its nature than from the point of view of its application in particular cases.

See Also: IDENTITY, PRINCIPLE OF.

Bibliography: S. VANNI-ROVIGHI, *Enciclopedia filosofica* 2:1214–15. B. SPINOZA, *Ethics*, pt. 1, props. 18, 25, 28; pt. 2, definitions and prop. 10. G. W. LEIBNIZ, "Primae veritates," in his *Opuscules et fragments inédits de Leibniz*, ed. L. COUTURAT (Paris 1903) 518-. F. H. BRADLEY, *Essays on Truth and Reality* (Oxford 1914); *Appearance and Reality* (2d ed. London 1902). B. STEVENS, *The Identity Theory* (2d ed. London 1936). H. GLOCKNER, *Identität und Individualität* (Willhelmshaven 1952).

[K. A. WALL]

IDENTITY, PRINCIPLE OF

A principle asserting the unity, consistency, and stability of being, and commonly enumerated among the FIRST PRINCIPLES. In ONTOLOGY it is expressed: "Every being is determined in itself, is one with itself, and is consistent in itself"; in LOGIC: "What belongs to being must be predicated of it," or, "Whatever is true (e.g., a CONCEPT, a PROPOSITION, or a relationship) is, as such, absolutely and always true." Since the notion of identity is closely associated with that of UNITY, similar distinctions may be applied to both. Thus one may speak of an identity that is real or logical, physical or moral, and numerical or specific (cf. Aristotle, *Meta.* 1015b 17–1017a 7; St. Thomas Aquinas, *In 5 meta.,* 8–9; ST 1a, 11.1 ad 2).

Explanation. The principle of identity is itself an explication of the concept of BEING. Being denotes positiveness and determination; it also implies coherence and agreement with itself, without which the determination, and consequently being itself, would dissolve. Although explicitly concerned with the unity of being, the principle of identity also contains an implicit reference to the distinction and multiplicity of being.

The algebraic statement of the principle of identity, "A being is a being, or $A = A$," is somewhat tautological.

If the predicate in no way amplifies the subject, or does not fulfill the expectation of the copula, it would seem that no judgment has in reality been expressed. Thus the statement, "A man is a man," really says nothing; its predicate belies the promise of the verb "is." On the other hand, when the principle is expressed "A being is identical with itself, or is one and consistent in itself," the subject is determined as something underlying unity, and therefore the statement asserts something definite and positive.

Various Interpretations. As a metaphysical principle, the principle of identity has been variously interpreted, while as a logical principle it receives rather uniform interpretation. The statement, "A being is identical to itself and is one in itself," usually is interpreted as applying to being in a transcendental sense, that is, with a potential reference to all its possible concrete determinations, but without referring to any one thing in particular. Thus, identity and coherence with itself is said not merely of the one, eternal, and unchangeable Being, but rather of being as such, whether this be one or multiple. In its logical formulation, the principle of identity presupposes no precise concept of real being, and thus does not create serious theoretical disagreements.

Monistic Views. PARMENIDES presumed to deduce a sweeping theory of reality from the concept of being alone: "One must say and think that being exists" [H. Diels, *Die Fragmente der Vorsokratiker: Griechisch und Deutsch*, ed. W. Kranz, 3 v. (8th ed. Berlin 1956) frg 6]. "Being is without origin, is immortal, and is everything in itself. It was not, and it will not be, because it is complete in itself, one and continuous" (*ibid.* frgs 7–8). By reasoning analogous to this, the ancients thought that all reality could be resolved to one identity; the Epicureans and the Stoics understood this in a materialist, the Neoplatonists in a spiritualist sense. A like tendency is at the roots of the various forms of MONISM in modern thought—e.g., that of G. BRUNO, B. SPINOZA, and F. W. J. SCHELLING. Schelling's conception is in fact known as the "philosophy of identity," according to which the diversity and multiplicity manifest in the world is relative and phenomenal and does not mar the absolute unity that is the foundation of being.

Dualism and Multiplicity. A metaphysical DUALISM within being is, on the other hand, essential to Aristotelian and to Christian thought, with their accent on matter and form, participated and unparticipated being, and the unity and multiplicity of being. This dualism presents a fundamental problem: how to reconcile the multiplicity of entities with the concept of unity. In Christian thought, a solution is furnished in terms of the concept of PURE ACT, infinite and unparticipated in Itself, and at the same time the creative and exemplary principle of PARTICIPATION for individual and finite beings. The doctrine of ANALOGY is further proposed as a logical and metaphysical concept that is most useful for an objective understanding of being in its totality. As Aristotle has remarked, "There are many senses in which a thing may be said to be" (*Meta.* 1003a 33). The concept of being is formally one, but it is not univocal in its concrete manifestations, and therefore does not warrant an absolute resolution into uniform identity. On the contrary, it manifests an immanent tension, in a real as well as in a dialectical sense, toward an infinity of both determinations and forms.

Evaluation. No solution to the metaphysical problem of unity and multiplicity can be deduced simply from the principle of identity. It is impossible for the human mind to determine the absolute structure of being in general, or of concrete beings, by means of a purely transcendental deduction from the concept of being itself. The intellect does not grasp being in its original concreteness by intuition, but rather attains knowledge of being through abstract concepts based on EXPERIENCE. The basic problem of the unity or multiplicity of concrete being is intimately connected with the processes of analysis, interpretation, and deduction, whereby thought is brought to bear on experience.

With regard to its logical and metaphysical import, one may say that the principle of identity is of lesser significance than the principle of CONTRADICTION. Its chief contribution is that it accentuates the value of the positiveness that is essential to the concept of being. Because of this positiveness and consistency in itself, being contains, implicitly and virtually, infinite possibilities of differentiation and development. Given the fact of CREATION, since being is positive, it can (and perhaps must) set in motion, embrace, and stimulate the processes generating the diverse, the relative, and the contrary, all of which it potentially holds within itself. But these processes, which take place in reality and in history on so grand a scale, are determined by the principle of identity only so far as this in turn implies the principle of contradiction. The expansion of the principle of identity into the principle of contradiction is spontaneous and even necessary, since in its implication of diversity and distinction the very concept of identity becomes, at least indirectly, dialectical. For this reason, St. THOMAS AQUINAS, following Aristotle, accords a primacy among first principles to the principle of contradiction.

See Also: IDENTITY

Bibliography: L. FUETSCHER, "Die ersten Seins- und Denkprinzipien," *Philosophie und Grenzwissenschaft* 3:2–4 (1930). E. MEYERSON, *Identity and Reality,* tr. K. LOEWENBERG (New York 1930); "La Notion de l'identique," *Essais* (Paris 1936). J. MARÉCHAL, *Le Thomisme devant la philosophie critique* (2d ed.) 561–68, v.5 of *Le Point de départ de la métaphysique,* 5 v. (3d ed. Paris 1944–49). J. M. DE ESTRADA, "Reflexión acerca del principio de identidad," *Sapientia* 8 (1953) 276–82. S. VANNIROVIGHI, *Enciclopedia filosofica,* 4 v. (Venice-Rome 1957) 2:1215–19. R. EISLER, *Wörterbuch der philosophischen Begriffe,* 3 v. (4th ed. Berlin 1927–30) 1:700–13.

[U. VIGLINO]

IDESBALD, BL.

Cistercian abbot; b. Flanders, 1100; d. between Dunkirk and Nieuport, after July 22, 1167. Idesbald was probably a member of the higher nobility in the area of Furnes in Flanders. Some sources relate that he was married, but after a few years of married life, his wife died. After spending 30 years in public service, which culminated in a post at the court of the count of Flanders, Idesbald entered the Cistercian Abbey of LES DUNES. A few years later, he was elected the third abbot; he ruled the monastery for 20 years. His vigor in religion was matched by his energy in increasing the possessions of the monastery. At his death, he was interred in a lead sarcophagus, contrary to the custom of the order. His cultus was approved in 1894.

Feast: April 18.

Bibliography: *Acta Sanctorum,* Apr. 2:584–590. A. M. ZIMMERMANN, *Kalendarium Benedictinum: Die Heiligen und Seligen des Benediktinerordens und seiner Zweige* 2:69, 72. J. DE CUYPER, *Idesbald van der Gracht* (Bruges 1946). J. ARNOLD, *Idesbald, le phare du Westhoek* (Bruges 1969). S. LENSSEN, *Hagiologium cisterciense* 109–111.

[J. R. SOMMERFELDT]

IDLENESS, MORAL ASPECTS OF

Idleness is inactivity, although when applied to persons it is often understood less as a negation than as a misdirection of activity, as when a person busies himself with trivial or futile things and neglects what is serious and worthwhile. In contrast to terms sometimes taken as its synonyms—laziness, indolence, and slothfulness—it may or may not have moral connotations. The enforced idleness of workers in times of general unemployment, for example, is not a moral situation, so far, at least, as the workers are concerned. Idleness is the substantive of the adjective idle, which comes from the Middle English and Anglo Saxon *idel,* meaning vain or useless. This sense persists in the use of the adjectival form, but the current meaning of the substantive tends to emphasize the derived notion of inactivity, and it is often accompanied by the disparaging suggestion of culpable laziness. This trend to a moral sense brings the meaning of the word close to that of other terms more familiar in the Latin tradition—*otiositas, pigritia, segnities,* and *torpor.* However, because the meaning of these terms is only indifferently conveyed by the English "idleness," this word is not commonly used in manuals of asceticism, moral theology, or ethics. Laziness, or sloth in the sense of spiritual laziness, are the more common terms.

Idleness, even when voluntary, is not necessarily sinful. Eagerness to improve each shining hour can be excessive, for a man has need of rest and relaxation (*see* EUTRAPELIA). When in the overall picture too much time is given to relaxation, there is inevitably some fault because of the neglect both of duty and of the opportunity for good. Thus it is stated in the *Rule of St. Benedict,* "Idleness is an enemy of the soul" (ch. 48). The law of work is the law of man's nature as well as the law of God (Gn 2.15; 3.19). Created imperfect, man must use his faculties to develop them. Idleness is a threat to, if not a frustration of, this process. In this sense it is opposed to all virtue, rather than to any virtue in particular, and this perhaps explains why St. Thomas Aquinas treated it only in passing (*Summa theologiae* 1a2ae, 41.4; 44.4 ad 3), associating it with fear, and specifically the fear of the exertion that work would entail.

Since idleness is culpable because it involves the neglect of something obligatory, its specific nature and gravity as a sin depends on the character of the obligation that is left unfulfilled. Sometimes idleness is blameworthy because of its source, as when it comes from a disinterest in or distaste for the spiritual values that should arouse one to effort and activity (*see* ACEDIA). Finally, idleness can be culpable because it provides an occasion of sin, "for idleness is an apt teacher of mischief" (Sir 33.28). The specific malice in this case is indistinguishable from that of the mischief to which it generally leads.

Bibliography: E. VANSTEENBERGHE, *Dictionnaire de théologie catholique,* ed. A. VACANT et al. (Paris 1903–50) 11.2:2023–30.

[P. FITZGERALD]

IDOLATRY

The worship or paying of divine honors to a false god as represented by some image or idol in which he is believed to be present. Idolatry is an offense against the virtue of religion and a direct violation of the First Commandment. It is also opposed to charity and faith: to charity, because it would deprive God of the supreme sovereignty that is His; to faith, because it is a denial of the truth that faith professes. This opposition to faith is manifestly evident when the external act of idolatrous worship proceeds from an inner conviction, or opinion, or suspicion, that the idol is adorable, because such a state of mind is radically incompatible with faith in the one true God. But there is opposition to faith even if the act is only externally simulated in conformity to custom or law but without internal belief in the false divinity or desire to honor it, for it is a transgression of the precept of divine law obliging men to confess their faith externally and under no circumstances to deny it (Mt 10.32–33). How abhorrent even a pretense of idolatry is to the Christian conscience is apparent from the reaction of 3d-century Christians to the behavior of the so-called *libellatici,* i.e., those who purchased or secured in some other manner *libelli,* or certificates attesting that they had conformed to idolatrous religious tests required by an edict of Decius, even though they had not in fact done so.

Idolatry is not formally sinful on the part of those who are in inculpable ignorance of the true God and of the sham and falsity of the idol. It is, however, a misfortune and an evil, because the worshiper puts his trust in a lifeless idol from which no good can come [Ps 113B(115)] and accepts in some degree at least the perversion or distortion of values that it represents.

In modern times idolatry in any strict sense of the word is not a sin of frequent occurrence in the Western world, although it appears to have a place in the practices of DEVIL WORSHIP and SATANISM. For the most part, however, modern man's closest acquaintance with it is likely to be in its metaphorical form, i.e., the idolatry into which one falls when he attributes supreme value to something less than God and pursues it as his ultimate goal in life. Avarice in its grosser forms seems to invite this metaphor. It is the worshiping of a golden calf; thus Our Lord personified Mammon and represented it as a false god (Mt 6.24), and St. Paul spoke of covetousness as a serving of idols (Eph 5.5; Col 3.5).

Bibliography: THOMAS AQUINAS, ST 2a2ae, 94, 1–4. A. MICHEL, *Dictionnaire de théologie catholique,* ed. A. VACANT et al. (Paris 1903–50) 7:602–669.

[P. K. MEAGHER]

IDOLATRY (IN THE BIBLE)

In the OT, idolatry was strictly prohibited; Yahweh is represented as a "jealous God" who tolerates no other god or idol besides Him (Ex 20.3–6; Dt 5.7–10). However, the Israelites at various times in their history committed idolatry, worshiping Canaanitic and Mesopotamian deities (Nm 25.3; Jgs 2.12; 3.37; 1 Kgs 14.22–24; 2 Kgs

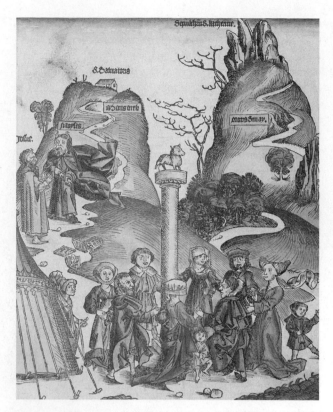

Israelites Worshiping the Golden Calf, from "Liber Chronicarum." (©Historical Picture Archive/CORBIS)

21.2–7; Hos 2.8–13; Am 8.14; Jer 2.23). Various deities, symbols, and images were worshiped, e.g., the Canaanite god BAAL (represented as a bull), the goddess ASTARTE, the stars, and the sun. After the division of Solomon's kingdom Jeroboam I sponsored idolatrous worship of the cities Dan and BETHEL (1 Kgs 12.29–33). Ahab, under the influence of Jezebel, established the cult of Baal in Samaria (1 Kgs 16.32; 2 Kgs ch. 10). Earlier the liberal policy of SOLOMON had encouraged the idolatrous cults introduced by his foreign wives into Judah (1 Kgs 11.1–12; 15.13). The later reforms of Kings Hezekiah (2 Kgs 18.4) and Josiah (2 Kings ch. 23) indicate to what extent idolatry had pervaded Jerusalem and even the Temple itself. But after the death of Josiah even grosser forms of idolatry were practiced (Ez 8.10, 14, 16; Is 65.2–7; 66.3, 17). The Israelite exiles, however, regarded the Babylonian cults with ridicule and supreme contempt (Is 40.18–26; 44.9–20; 46.1–2). The true worshiper of Yahweh always considered idolatry as infidelity or adultery (in symbolic language) against God (Hos 2.4–7; Jer 2.20–24); Yahweh alone is the one true God, and outside of Him there is no other (Dt 4.35; 1 Kgs 8.6–60; 2 Kgs 19.15; Jer 2.11; Is 41.29; 46.9). The Prophets often inveighed against Baal and other idols venerated by the Israelites (1 Kgs 18.27; Is 2.8; Ezekiel ch. 6). Amos (2.4) branded idols as "lies which lead men astray"; and Jere-

miah (2.5, 11; 5.7) called them "empty idols" and "nogods" (Wis 13.10–14.11; Bar ch. 6). According to Wis 14.15–21, idolatry is caused by images made in memory of the dead that in the course of time became objects of worship. Later Judaism regarded pagan deities not merely as nonentities or as dead but also as spirits or angels sent by God Himself to rule over pagan nations (Dt 32.8; Dn 10.20–21; 12.1; Enoch 89.59), or as demons and evil spirits (Dt 32.17; Bar 4.7; Enoch 19.1).

In the NT the same ideas prevail for the most part: idolatry refers to the worship of gods other than the one, true God, and the use of images is characteristic of the life of the heathen. Idols are viewed as nonentities and helpless (Acts 7.41; 15.20; Rom 2.22; 1 Cor 12.2; 2 Cor 6.16; 1 Thes 1.9; 1 Jn 5.21; Ap 9.20); they have no real existence (1 Cor 8.4; 10.19; Gal 4.8), and they are nothing more than the inventions of sinful men (Rom 1.23). Pagan worship is really paid to evil spirits (1 Cor 8.4–5; 10.19–21) and thereby viewed as a grave sin (1 Cor 5.10–11; Gal 5.20). The term idolatry is used also figuratively in the NT to signify the undue desire for wealth and created things instead of fidelity and devotion to God (Mt 6.24; Eph 5.5; Phil 3.19; Col 3.5).

Bibliography: M. REHM and J. SCHMID, *Lexikon für Theologie und Kirche*, ed. J. HOFER and K. RAHNER, 10 v (2nd, new ed. Freiburg 1957–65). 4:1146–49. K. KOCH, *Die Religion in Geschichte und Gegenwart*, 7 v. (3d ed. Tübingen 1957–65). 2:1680–82. A. GELIN, *Dictionnaire de la Bible*, suppl. ed., L. PIROT et al. (Paris 1928–). 4:169–187. *Encyclopedic Dictionary of the Bible*, tr. and adap. by L. HARTMAN (New York 1963). 1047–48. J. GRAY, G. A. BUTTRICK, ed., *The Interpreters' Dictionary of the Bible*, 4 v. (Nashville 1962). 2:675–678. F. BÜCHSEL, G. KITTEL, Theologisches Wörterbuch Zum Neuen Testament (Stuttgart 1935–). 2:373–377.

[C. H. PICKAR]

IDUBERGA, BL.

Widow; b. *c.* 592; d. Nivelles, May 8, 652. Iduberga (Ida or Itta) was the daughter of a count of Aquitaine, was married to Bl. Pepin of Landen, the mayor of the palace, and was the mother of SS. BEGGA and GERTRUDE OF NIVELLES. As a widow, she was advised by St. AMANDUS to found an abbey at Nivelles (Belgium). She dedicated herself and all her property to this monastery, whose first nuns came from Ireland. Five years before she died Iduberga arranged for her daughter Gertrude to succeed her as superior at Nivelles; she was buried in St. Peter's, Nivelles. Later her relics were placed in a reliquary that is carried in a procession each year with the relics of the other saints of Nivelles.

Feast: May 8.

Bibliography: Life. *Acta Sanctorum* March 2:594–600. *Monumenta Germaniae Scriptores rerum Merovingicarum* (Berlin

1825–) 2:447–474. Literature. B. DELANNE, *Histoire . . . Nivelles* (Nivelles, Belgium 1944). É. DE MOREAU, *Histoire de l'église en Belgique* (2d ed. Brussels 1945–) v.1. J. J. HOEBANX, *L'Abbaye de Nivelles . . .* (Brussels 1952). G. MARSOT, *Catholicisme* 5:1172–73.

[É. BROUETTE]

IGNATIAN SPIRITUALITY

The JESUITS have derived their spirituality from the experience of their founder, St. IGNATIUS OF LOYOLA, and from the spirit that he inculcated in his growing order. The writings that he left—his *Autobiography, SPIRITUAL EXERCISES, Letters, Spiritual Journal,* and *Constitutions*—give an idea of what these were, although he did not present them systematically or didactically. From this material it is evident that the principal features of Ignatian spirituality can be traced back to St. Ignatius' personal concept of God and to his concept of the behavior and the prayer life of the spiritual man.

Concept of God. After his interior transformation at Loyola, Ignatius remained at Manresa from March 1522 to February 1523. "At that time," as the *Autobiography* declares (n. 27), "God treated him exactly as a schoolmaster treats a child—He instructed him. This can be seen in the five points that follow." These five points describe the mystical knowledge he received about the Trinity, creation, Christ in the Eucharist, Jesus in His humanity, Our Lady, and finally, of all things seen in a new light (*Autobiography* 28–30). Thus God revealed Himself to Ignatius as the transcendent Trinity, which creates the world, sends the Son to it in the Eucharistic Sacrament, and brings all back to Itself through the mediation of Jesus and the Virgin, following a design that embraces all terrestrial reality in salvation.

These elements of Ignatian spirituality are expressed in the *Exercises* and perhaps more explicitly in the *Spiritual Journal.* He emphasizes in his "Contemplation to Attain the Love of God" (*Exercises* 230–237), which seems to be the goal of his *Exercises,* that it is God who gives blessings and Himself. It is He who lives in His creatures and works through them for us, He who is the source of all good things. It is He who moves the will and brings to one's mind what he ought to do (*ibid.* 180) by His love that descends from above (*ibid.* 184), for it has designs for us, a holy will (*ibid.* 1, 91, 135) that is dynamically made known in the inner recesses of our being.

Such a concept explains the titles that Ignatius easily gives to God, calling Him, for example, Creator, Goodness, and Providence. These terms had a very concrete sense for Ignatius. They imply a divine action exercised upon us and one that we can "feel." In the Trinity the

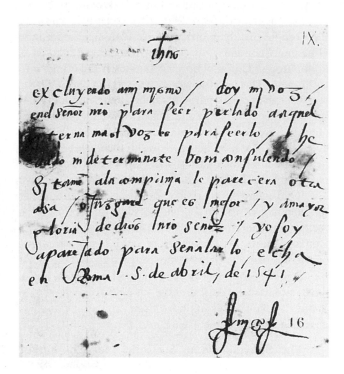

Autograph vote of St. Ignatius Loyola, April 5, 1541, for the election of preposito generale.

God of infinite fullness pours Himself forth in an unceasing creative act and in an operation that in us is light, incitement, and union. Ignatius' letters generally were concluded with some such expression as "I close asking that God will grant us grace to know His holy will and perfectly to do it." The will of God is a "divine motion" (*Monumenta historica Societatis Jesu* "Epistolae" [Rome 1932–] 7.465). "I hope in the Lord," he wrote, "that if my prayers win you any favor, it will be entirely from on high, descending from His infinite goodness" (*ibid.* 1.339). "May it be pleasing to His divine clemency to communicate Himself so intimately to you and to direct your house and all that is entrusted to your care with a providence so particular that it may be known in a tangible manner that it is His divine majesty that disposes and watches over all in this matter" (*ibid.* 3.14). In heaven "all our wickedness will be entirely consumed in the furnace of the everlasting love of God, our Creator and Lord, when our souls shall be completely penetrated and possessed by Him and our wills thus totally conformed to—or rather, transformed into—His will, which is rectitude and infinite goodness" (*ibid.* 1.627).

This divine influence passes through Christ. Jesus Christ is at the center of Ignatian spirituality. He is "the Creator who has stooped to become man" and who became "the eternal Lord of all things" (*Exercises* 53, 98); He calls us, and our whole destiny consists in knowing the Lord intimately in order to love Him more and follow Him more closely (*ibid.* 104). Thus the will of God is done through Christ, who incorporates it and brings it to fulfillment. Through the work done in Him (*ibid.* 95), the story of salvation is completed. During the year and a half between his ordination and his first Mass, Ignatius frequently asked Mary to "put him with her Son"; before celebrating Mass, he had a vision in the chapel of Storta near Rome in which Christ, carrying a cross and accompanied by His Father, said to him: "I want you to serve us." One enters the "Company of Jesus" to "fight under the standard of the Cross and to serve the one Lord as well as the Church, His Spouse, under the guidance of the Roman Pontiff, who takes the place of Christ on earth" (*Formula Instituti* 1). It is not surprising that the great majority of spiritual authors of the society in their works have emphasized assimilation to Christ, the Incarnate Word, or that the Jesuits have been ardent promoters of devotion to the Sacred Heart.

The Spiritual Man According to St. Ignatius. From this view of God, an idea of the behavior that befits a Christian is easily deduced. In the presence of the Divine Majesty who is the source of all good, man must respond with reverence and grateful attention. He should feel what Ignatius calls "loving humility" (*Spiritual Journal* March 30) and a eucharistic kind of gratitude that causes him to say: "You have given me all, I give it back to You, Lord" (*Exercises* 234). He is aware that priority in the spiritual life must be given to "the interior law of charity and love that the Holy Spirit writes and imprints in our hearts" (preamble to the *Constitutions*). That is to say, the creature is called upon to abandon itself to belong to its Creator (*Epistolae* 1.339), to become docile to the action of the Holy Spirit in it, to submit itself lovingly to the divine will. Because of this, Ignatius attached great importance to self-denial, spiritual DISCERNMENT, and obedience. One must be attentive in following the divine will in all decisions that he makes (*Constitutions* 3.1, 26); the examination of conscience, to which St. Ignatius held so strongly and which is the daily repetition of the "Contemplation to Attain the Love of God," is for the purpose of causing one to keep check upon the rightness of his dispositions.

However since one is engaged in work with Christ, one must have a spirituality that directs the heart, with Christ's, toward others, the Church, and the design of God that must be fulfilled here on earth. Ignatian spirituality is essentially apostolic, that is, concerned with the kingdom. Ignatius frequently used, especially in the *Constitutions*, the formula "to help one's neighbor"; his eternal King calls each in particular "to the conquest of the

world" (*Exercises* 95). Man is created to serve God and Christ in the enterprise of the salvation of mankind (*ibid.* 146). Reverence toward the God of majesty is expressed in the service of others accomplished under the impetus coming from this same God, who is at work on earth through Jesus Christ. For St. Ignatius, the glory of God always connotes an apostolic perspective, a reference to neighbor, to the "universal good"; a truly remarkable view of this is found in the *Spiritual Journal*. After his mystical insight into the divine essence, the Persons of the Trinity, the humanity of Christ, Ignatius was moved to a profound, reverential love for these great things and was also moved in an extraordinary manner by the Lord, to a similar loving reverence for creatures (*Spiritual Journal*, March 30). The whole *Ad amorem* of the *Exercises* is there; it is "to love and serve the divine majesty in all things" (*Exercises* 233). If this apostolic ideal in the society presupposes a magnanimous docility on the part of all, it nevertheless demands a strong cohesive bond tying Jesuits one to another: in his *Constitutions* Ignatius insists upon fraternal charity as well as upon obedience.

Ignatian Prayer. Faithful to the graces he had received, Ignatius placed the life of prayer more in work undertaken under the impulse of love than in the repose of contemplation. His Lord is a God of action, present in the world and in history; it is a duty of man to "seek God in all things," to "love Him in all His creatures" (*Constitutions* 3.1, 26), to "serve Him in all" (*Exercises* 233). Thus one ought to be, according to the formula of Ignatius' confidant, G. NADAL, a "contemplative in action." In union with God in every thing and activity, St. Ignatius saw an eminent form of prayer. He declared: "Occupations undertaken for His greater service and in conformity to His divine will interpreted through obedience, can be not only the equivalent of the union and recollection of uninterrupted contemplation, but even more acceptable to God, proceeding as they do from a more active and vigorous charity" (*Epistolae* 4.127).

That is not to say that he belittled prayer. He wanted novices to be taught "the way of praying and meditating" (*Constitutions* 3.1, 20), and although he generally dispensed his students from meditation, leaving them the Mass, two examinations of conscience a day, and vocal prayer (*ibid.* 4.4, 3), he wished for those religious who have arrived at the term of their formation that "there should be no other rule except the one that prudent charity would dictate" (*ibid.* 6.3, 1). He himself had recourse to long prayers as is revealed in his *Spiritual Journal*.

There was a tension in him between mental prayer and contemplative action. In his order this tension soon took on the form of a conflict between the contemplatives and those who held to practical prayer. In 1590 C. AC-QUAVIVA, then general of the society, ended the debate by determining that the daily prayer hour for all, instituted by Borgia, should remain in the rule, but that formed religious should not be forbidden to exceed that time, nor should those who had the grace be forbidden to practice higher forms of prayer provided these did not prove to be an obstacle to apostolic works. Forty years later M. VI-TELLESCHI approved the teaching of Louis LALLEMANT on contemplation.

Even if some Jesuits have shown opposition to mysticism, one could not fairly accuse the society itself of it. Ignatius was a mystic, as were several of his companions and first disciples, and in the long course of its history the society has given great spiritual writers to the Church. At the end of his book *An Ignatian Approach to Divine Union* (tr. H. L. Brozowski, Milwaukee 1956), Louis Peeters, SJ, names about 100 Jesuits who were mystical authors. It remains true, nevertheless, that the spirituality proper to St. Ignatius is complete "familiarity with God" that causes one to be a "united instrument" of God (*Constitutions* 10.2).

Conclusion. St. Ignatius, who so often received "visits from the Lord," always kept to himself his nostalgia for the luminous abysses of the Trinity; but he knew he had been chosen more to transmit the divine light than to enjoy it. God called him to the work of the redemption, to the service of the Lord in the establishment of the kingdom. Thus he chose to be a soldier under the standard of the cross. Above, and at the same time the source of both contemplation and action, there is "love" (*Exercises* 230). However, though loving action often demands that one renounce the pleasures of contemplation, these are not lost without compensation in the holy gifts and spiritual favors from the Lord (cf. *Epistolae* 2.236; *Exercises* 316). Such a spirituality reminds one of St. Paul, the apostle of the Gentiles, "urged by a love of Christ" and living in the intimacy of the Spirit.

Bibliography: Bibliographies. J. JUAMBELZ, *Bibliografía sobre la vida, obras y escritos de San Ignacio de Loyola 1900–1950* (Madrid 1956). E. F. SUTCLIFFE, *Bibliography of the English Province of the Society of Jesus* (London 1957). J. F. GILMONT and P. DAMAN, *Bibliographie Ignatienne 1894–1957* (Paris 1958). I. IPARRAGUIRRE, *Répertoire de spiritualité ignatienne de la mort de S. Ignace à celle du P. Aquaviva, 1556–1615* (Rome 1961). Writings of St. Ignatius. Spiritual Exercises, tr. L. J. PUHL (Westminster, Md. 1951); *Letters of St. Ignatius Loyola,* ed. and tr. W. J. YOUNG (Chicago 1959); *Constitutiones Societatis Iesu,* ed. A. CODINA (*Monumenta historica Societas Jesu*; Rome 1934–38); "Spiritual Journal of St. I. Loyola," tr. W. J. YOUNG, *Woodstock Letters* 87 (1958) 195–267; *St. Ignatius' Own Story as Told to Luis González de Cámara,* tr. W. J. YOUNG (Chicago 1956). Literature. P. DE CHASTONAY, *Les Constitutions de l'Ordre des Jésuites* (Paris 1941). J. F. CONWELL, *Contemplation in Action* (Spokane 1957). J. DANIÉLOU, "La Vision ignatienne du monde et de l'homme," *Revue d'ascétique at de mystique* 26 (1950) 5–17. J. DE GUIBERT, *The Jesuits: Their Spiritual Doctrine and Practice,* tr. W. J. YOUNG (Chicago 1964). J. A. HARDON, *All My Liberty: Theology of the Spiritual Exercises* (Westminster, Md. 1959). I. IPARRAGUIRRE, "Visión ignaciana de Dios," *Gregorianum* 37 (1956) 366–390. M. NICOLAU, *Jeronimo Nadal, S.J. 1507–1580: Sus obras y doctrinas espirituales* (Madrid 1949). L. PEETERS, *An Ignatian Approach to Divine Union,* tr. H. L. BROZOWSKI (Milwaukee 1956). E. PRZYWARA, *Majestas divina: Ignatianische Frömmigkeit* (Augsburg 1925); *Deus semper maior: Theologie der Exerzitien,* 3 v. (Freiburg 1938–40). H. RAHNER, *The Spirituality of St. Ignatius Loyola, An Account of Its Historical Development,* tr. F. J. SMITH (Westminster, Md. 1953). W. J. YOUNG, tr., *Finding God in All Things: Essays in Ignatian Spirituality, Selected from "Christus"* (Chicago 1958).

[J. LEWIS]

IGNATIUS, PATRIARCH OF CONSTANTINOPLE, ST.

Patriarchate, July 4, 847 to 858, and Nov. 23, 867 to Oct. 23, 877; b. *c.* 798; d. 877. He was the son of the Byzantine Emperor Michael I Rhangabe. When Michael was deposed in 813 by the iconoclastic Emperor LEO V, his sons, Nicetas, Theophylactus, and Stauracius, were castrated and with their whole family were obliged to take monastic vows. On becoming a monk, Nicetas took the name of Ignatius. He became abbot of three monasteries that he had founded in the Islands of the Princes. After the death of Patriarch METHODIUS I (847), who had condemned ICONOCLASM in 843, Empress Theodora (2) appointed Ignatius patriarch of Constantinople without convoking a local synod. She was motivated by fear of new conflicts between the zealot monks of STUDION, excommunicated by Methodius for their opposition to his ecclesiastical policy, and the liberals who recommended milder treatment of penitent iconoclasts. Ignatius reconciled the Studite monks with the Church, and while patriarch manifested himself in sympathy with the policy of the zealots. Because of this he was sharply criticized by the more liberal prelates, some of whose leaders he suspended in 853. They appealed from the judgment of their patriarch to Pope LEO IV, who asked Ignatius to send a representative to Rome to vindicate his action. Ignatius complied. But before Rome could make a decision on the appeal, Ignatius became involved in the conflict between Theodora and her brother Bardas, who had forced her to end her regency for Emperor MICHAEL III. When Theodora tried vainly to return to power, she was forced to join her daughters in their confinement in a monastery. Ignatius refused to bless their monastic garb and abdicated (858), on the advice of the bishops who feared a harmful conflict between the Church and the new regime. PHOTIUS was elected as his successor by a local synod and recognized as legitimate patriarch by all the bishops, even by the followers of Ignatius on his recommendation. However, about two months after the enthronement of Photius, the radical followers of Ignatius rejected the new patriarch and demanded the restoration of Ignatius. Their revolt seems to have been directed against the new government. The leaders of the revolt were arrested by the imperial police and condemned by a local synod, convoked by Photius; the regent Bardas imprisoned Ignatius and interned him in various places, ultimately on the island of Terebinthus. Bardas must have recognized, however, that Ignatius was not the initiator of the revolt, because in 860 he permitted him to live in Constantinople in the palace of Posis built by Ignatius' mother. At the request of Michael III and Photius, Pope NICHOLAS I sent two legates to Constantinople to investigate the legality of Photius' election. After learning of the circumstances leading to Ignatius' abdication and Photius' election, the legates confirmed (861) the decision of the synod of 858, which had declared the patriarchate of Ignatius illegitimate because he had not been elected by a local synod, and they confirmed his deposition. Ignatius also seems to have accepted the decision of the synod, declaring that he had not appealed to Rome and had no intention of doing so. However, some radical supporters of Ignatius, especially Abbot THEOGNOSTOS, took refuge in Rome and appealed to Pope Nicholas in the name of Ignatius. The pope disavowed the action of his legates and, won over by the radical Ignatians, excommunicated Photius in a Roman synod (863), calling on Michael III to reinstate Ignatius as legitimate patriarch. Four years later the new Emperor Basil I, after murdering Michael III, looked for support from the radical Ignatians and Rome. He therefore deposed Photius and reinstated Ignatius (Nov. 23, 867). The legates of Pope ADRIAN II obtained from the Council of CONSTANTINOPLE IV in 869–870 the confirmation of the decisions of the Roman synod, although the majority of the clergy remained faithful to the deposed Patriarch Photius. The reinstated Ignatius soon came into sharp conflict with Pope John VIII because he established a hierarchy in Bulgaria, which defected from Rome. And when he defended his action and the interests of his Church among the Bulgars, he was threatened with excommunication by Rome. When Photius was recalled from exile by Basil I, who confided to him the education of his sons, Ignatius became reconciled with Photius and took the initiative in calling for another council, which would confirm the pacification of his Church. But before the papal legates had reached Rome, Ignatius died and Photius recovered the see. Ignatius was canonized by Photius himself. The mosaic portrait of Ignatius recently discovered in the HAGIA SOPHIA was probably initiated by Photius.

Feast: Oct. 23.

Bibliography: NICETAS DAVID, *Life, Patrologia Graeca*, ed. J. P. MIGNE (Paris 1857–66) 105:487–574. J. D. MANSI, *Sacrorum Conciliorum nova et amplissima collectio,* 31 v. (Florence-Venice 1757–98); reprinted and continued by L. PETIT and J. B. MARTIN, 53 v. in 60 (Paris 1889–1927; repr. Graz 1960–) 16:209–550. *Synodicon vetus:* Monastery of Sinai, MS. Graecus Sinaiticus 482 (1117), fols. 364ff., for reconciliation and canonization. J. HERGENRÖTHER, *Photius, Patriarch von Konstantinopel,* 4 v. in 3 (Regensburg 1867–69) v.1, 2. J. B. BURY, *A History of the Eastern Roman Empire . . . A.D. 802–867* (London 1912). R. JANIN, *Dictionnaire de théologie catholique,* ed. A. VACANT, 15 v. (Paris 1903–50; Tables générales 1951–) 7.1:713–722. V. GRUMEL, *Les Regestes des actes du patriarcat de Constantinople* (Kadikoi-Bucharest 1932–) v.1, 2 (1936). V. GRUMEL, ''La Genèse du schisme photien,'' *Studi Bizantini* 5 (1939) 177–185; ''Le Schisme de Grégoire de Syracuse,'' *Échos d'Orient* 39 (1940–42) 257–267. P. STÉPHANOU, ''La Violation du compromis entre Photius et les ignatiens,'' *Orientalia Christiana periodica* 21 (1955) 291–307. F. DVORNIK, *The Photian Schism* (Cambridge, Eng. 1948); *The Patriarch Photius in the Light of Recent Research* (Munich 1958). R. J. H. JENKINS, ''A Note on Nicolas David Paphlago and the *Vita Constantini,*'' *Dumbarton Oaks Papers* (Cambridge, MA 1941–) 19 (1965).

[F. DVORNIK]

IGNATIUS OF ANTIOCH, ST.

Bishop, primitive Church theologian, and martyr; b. Syria; d. Rome *c.* 110. Ignatius is known primarily through seven epistles he wrote in the course of his journey from Antioch to Rome as a prisoner condemned to death for his faith during the reign of Trajan (98–117). Apparently of Syrian origin and a convert from paganism, he was one of the earliest bishops of Antioch, possibly the third (Eusebius, *Hist. Eccl.* 3.22). Ignatius was received with great honor at Smyrna by Bishop (St.) POLYCARP, and visited by representatives of nearby churches. From Smyrna he wrote letters to the churches at Ephesus, Magnesia, Tralles, and Rome. When taken to Troas, he wrote to the churches at Philadelphia and Smyrna, and to Polycarp. His journey then proceeded through Macedonia and Illyria to Dyrrachium, where he took a ship to Italy. His martyrdom in Rome is attested to by Polycarp, whose epistle to the Philippians appears to consist of two sections: chapters 13 and 14 are a note that accompanied a collection of the Ignatian epistles sent to Philippi soon after the visit of Ignatius; chapters 1 to 12 were written *c.* 130 or 140 when Ignatius' martyrdom had become a memory that was already cherished throughout the Church.

Referring to himself as Theophorus, the God-bearer (*Rom. praef.; Trall. praef.*), Ignatius addressed the various churches to thank them for the sympathy they had expressed regarding his fate; he then exhorted them to fidelity to God and obedience to their superiors, warning them against heretical doctrines, and providing them with the solid truths of the Christian faith. He pleaded with the Romans not to use political influence to prevent his martyrdom since he considered himself the "wheat of God; and I must be ground by the teeth of wild beasts, to become the pure bread of Christ" (*Rom.* 1.2; 2.1; 4.1).

Ignatius recognized the continuity of revelation between the Old and the New Testament, seeing God's providence as fulfilled in Jesus Christ "our only teacher, of Whom the prophets were disciples in the Spirit" (*Mag.* 9.1–2). He asserted unequivocally both the divinity and the humanity of Christ, the Savior: "the one and only physician, Who is both flesh and spiritual, born and unborn, God in man, true life in death, both of Mary and of God, first subject to suffering and then incapable of it, Jesus Christ our Lord" (*Eph.* 7.2). Against the heresy of DOCETISM, he insisted on the reality of Christ's human sufferings, and His Real Presence in the Eucharist, and His Resurrection in the flesh: "He is really of the line of David according to the flesh, and the Son of God by the will and power of God; was truly born of a Virgin; and baptized by John to comply with all justice" (*Smyr.* 1.1). The Docetists, he charged, "refrain from the Eucharist and prayer because they do not confess that the Eucharist is the Flesh of our Savior, Jesus Christ, Who suffered for our sins; and that the Father in his goodness raised up" (*Smyr.* 7.1).

Concerning the Church, Ignatius insisted upon its sacramental character and unity under the governance of the bishop. "Take care to use one Eucharist: for there is one flesh of our Lord Jesus Christ, and one cup in the union of His blood, and one altar, as there is one bishop, assisted by the presbytery and the deacons, my fellow servants" (*Phil.* 4). Insisting on the bishop's function, Ignatius described the bishop and priests as representing Christ and the Apostles; and warned that nothing should be done concerning the Church without the bishop; Eucharist, Baptism, the celebration of the agape were valid only when done with his approval. "Wherever the bishop is, there let the people be, for there is the Catholic church" (*Smyr.* 8.1–2). Despite his possible youth, the bishop "presides in the place of God; the presbyters function as the council of the apostles, and the deacons are entrusted with the ministry of Jesus Christ" (*Mag.* 6.1).

In regard to the daily life of the Christian, the Ignatian epistles display a different concern from that of the Epistles of St. Paul. Addressing an audience almost completely devoid of the Judaic preoccupation with justification by the Law, Ignatius dealt with the Hellenistic experience of the omnipresence of death and destruction, and the longing for an imperishable life. In opposition to the superstitions and false beliefs of his pagan fellow citizens, he focused attention on the "newness of eternal life in Christ," and urged on his Christian converts a complete transformation of mentality brought about by regeneration in Christ through Baptism.

The Christian, then, imitates God (*Trall.* 1.2; *Pol.* 1.3) and Christ in His Passion (*Rom.* 6.3); death in and with Christ will be the consummation of the union with God that he strives for in the practice of virtue, particularly in charity (*agape*), whereby he gives himself totally to the community (*Eph.* 10.1–3; 14.1–2; *Smyr.* 6.2–7). This becomes concrete in the care for the "widow and the orphan, the oppressed, the prisoner, as well as the freeman, the hungry and the thirsty" (*Smyr.* 6.2).

Concerning marriage, Christians have a right to enter the married state with the sanction of the bishop that it may be according to the Lord, and not for passion. Wives who love the Lord will be content with their husbands in body and in spirit; and husbands are to love their wives as Christ loves the Church. At the same time "if any man can remain continent to the honor of the flesh of the Lord, let him do so without boasting" (*Pol.* 5.1–2).

Writing to the Romans, Ignatius acknowledged that their Church "presides in the land of the Romans" and is worthy of God; of honor, blessing, praise, success, and holiness; and of presiding in love. He likewise acknowledged that he could not command them as did "Peter and Paul who were apostles." Despite considerable discussion and controversy over the significance of this deference and extensive praise, the letter cannot be used as witness to the primacy of the Roman See as such, since Ignatius' purpose was instead to persuade the Romans to do nothing to interfere with his martyrdom.

His literary style, while highly personal, reflects the Asianism then characteristic of the Hellenistic education he received. His doctrine is strongly Pauline, particulary in Christology and moral direction, but he exhibited also a close familiarity with the Johannine theology.

The manuscript tradition of these letters presented a long and a short recension, the former containing six spurious letters added by an interpolator in the fourth century. The authenticity of the original short recension is now fully vindicated.

Feast: Oct. 17 (formerly Feb. 1); Dec. 20 (Greek Church).

Bibliography: *Cartes*, tr. M. ESTRADÉ (Montserrat 1988). K. BIHLMEYER, ed., *Die Apostolischen Väter*, v.1 (2d ed. Tübingen 1956). M. P. BROWN, *The Authentic Writings of Ignatius: A Study of Linguistic Criteria* (Durham, N.C. 1963). K. LAKE, ed., *The Apostolic Fathers*, 2 v. (*Loeb Classical Library*; London–New York–Cambridge, Mass. 1912–13) v.1. T. LECHNER, *Ignatius adversus Valentinianos?: chronologische und theologiegeschichtliche Studien zu den Briefen des Ignatius von Antiochien* (Leiden 1999). J. RIUS–CAMPS, *The Four Authentic Letters of Ignatius, the*

Martyr (Rome 1980). W. R. SCHOEDEL, *A Commentary on the Letters of Ignatius of Antioch*, ed. H. KOESTER (Philadelphia 1985). C. UHRIG, *Sorge für die Einheit, über die nichts geht: zum episkopalen Selbstverständnis des Ignatius von Antiochien* (Altenberge 1998), bibliography. L. WEHR, *Arznei der Unsterblichkeit: die Eucharistie bei Ignatius von Antiochien und im Johannesevangelium* (Münster 1987), Eucharistic theology. C. T. BROWN, *The Gospel and Ignatius of Antioch* (New York 2000). J. KLEIST, ed. and tr., *Ancient Christian Writers* 1 (1946) 52–146. J. QUASTEN, *Patrology*, 3 v. (Westminster, Md. 1950–53) 1:63–76. J. LEBRETON, *Recherches de science religieuse* 15 (1925) 97–126, Trinity. J. JOUSSARD, *ibid.* 39 (1951–52) 361–367, martyr. J. H. CREHAN, *Studia patristica* v.1 (*Texte und Untersuchungen zur Geschichte der altchristlichen Literatur* 63; 1957) 23–32. L. CRISTIANI, *Revue d'ascétique et de mystique* 25 (1949) 109–116, mysticism. V. CORWIN, *St. Ignatius and Christianity in Antioch* (New Haven 1960). H. RIESENFELD, *Studia patristica*, v.4 (*Texte und Untersuchungen zur Geschichte der altchristlichen Literatur* 70; 1961) 312–322, theology. P. MEINHOLD, *Historisches Jahrbuch der Görres–Gesellschaft* 77 (1958) 50–62, ethics. K. P. WESCHE, "The Criterion of Orthodoxy and the Marks of Catholicity," *Pro Ecclesia* 3 (winter 1994): 89–109. A. BRENT, "History and Eschatological Mysticism in Ignatius of Antioch," *Ephemerides Theologicae Lovanienses* 65 no. 4 (1989): 309–329.

[F. X. MURPHY]

IGNATIUS OF LACONI, ST.

Lay brother; b. Laconi (Nuoro), Sardinia, Dec. 10, 1701; d. Cagliari, Sardinia, May 11, 1781. The second of seven children born to peasants Mattia and Anna Maria Peis was baptized Francis Ignatius Vincent. He was never taught to read or write, but from childhood he gave evidence of sanctity. On Nov. 10, 1721, he entered the Capuchin Order at Cagliari as a lay brother. For 60 years he edified his confreres and the people of Cagliari, where he served his Order as questor for alms, by his heroic austerity, humility, and charity, and the gift of miracles. Ignatius was beatified by PIUS XII, June 16, 1940, and later canonized by the same pontiff, Oct. 21, 1951.

Feast: May 11 (formerly May 12).

Bibliography: A. FIORENTINO, *Yours Is the Kingdom: The Life of St. Ignatius of Laconi*, ed. tr. C. FLORA and M. MOAKLER (Paterson, N.J. 1953). *Lexicon Capuccinum* (Rome 1951) 800–801.

[T. MACVICAR]

IGNATIUS OF LOYOLA, ST.

Founder and first general of the Society of Jesus; b. Casa Torre of Loyola, Azpeitia, province of Guipúzcoa, Spain, 1491; d. Rome, July 31, 1556. This last son of Beltrán Yáñez de Oñaz and María Sáenz de Licona was baptized Iñigo in the parish church of St. Sebastian. From 1537 on he used also the name Ignatius, particularly in official documents, because it was more universally known (Ribadeneyra). There is no justification for the family name Recalde, as formerly alleged. His boyhood was spent in the Casa Torre, and during his adolescent years (1506?–17), he was a page of Juan Velázquez de Cuéllar, alcalde of the fortress towns of Arévalo and Truxillo, and *ministro de Hacienda* (treasurer general) for Ferdinand the Catholic. Ignatius followed the court to Arévalo, Valladolid, Medina del Campo, Segovia, and Madrid; and when Velázquez lost the favor of the king, Ignatius was attached to the household of Antonio Manrique de Lara, Duke of Nájera and Viceroy of Navarre (1516). In his service he accomplished successful military assignments, including the defeat of the *Comuneros* of Guipúzcoa (a faction opposed to Emperor Charles V).

Conversion. When King Francis I of France sent troops into Spain to reestablish the claims of Jean d'Albret to the kingdom of Navarre, Ignatius, while defending the castle of Pamplona, was struck by a cannon shot that wounded one leg and broke the other (May 20, 1521). In the course of his convalescence at Loyola he learned of the heroism of sanctity by reading the *Vita Christi* of LUDOLPH OF SAXONY and the *Flos sanctorum* of JAMES OF VORAGINE, and he resolved to go to the Holy Land. He traveled first to Montserrat, where he made a night vigil before Our Lady (March 24–25, 1522) and received spiritual direction from the French Benedictine Jean Chanones. Before reaching Montserrat Ignatius vowed perpetual chastity and dedicated himself to a spiritual life. Then for 11 months he remained at nearby Manresa, residing for a time in a cell of the Dominican priory, administering to the sick at the Hospital of St. Lucy, and spending hours in penance and prayer in a cave. At this time he wrote in substance the SPIRITUAL EXERCISES, which he completed in Paris and Rome (1522–41). At Manresa he suffered from scruples, which gave way to spiritual revelations and the decisive illumination near the Cardoner River.

Ignatius left Manresa toward the end of February 1523, and after many delays landed at Jaffa on September 1, with a party of pilgrims. The hostility of the Turks prevented fulfillment of his original plan to remain in the Holy Land, so he returned to Europe and began a program of study at Barcelona (1524–26), Alcalá (1526–27), Salamanca (1527), and Paris (1528–35). During these 11 years he studied Latin, philosophy, and theology. Both at Alcalá and Salamanca he was suspected of being an ALUMBRADOS (ILLUMINATI) and was interrogated and imprisoned.

Ignatius obtained his master of arts degree at Paris in 1534, and on August 15 of that year, together with Peter FABER, Francis XAVIER, Diego LAÍNEZ, Alfonso SALMERÓN, Nicolás de BOBADILLA, and Simón Rodriguez, he vowed to live in poverty and chastity and to go to the Holy Land. It was determined that, if this journey became impossible, the group would offer itself to the apostolic service of the pope. The following year on the same day, he renewed the vows with three new companions, Paschase Broët, Jean Codure, and Claude LE JAY. When the war between Venice and the Turkish Empire prevented their pilgrimage, they placed themselves in the hands of Paul III (1538).

Foundation of the Society of Jesus. At this time Ignatius resolved to make their association permanent. After the encouragement of his vision at La Storta, a shrine nine miles from Rome (November 1537), in which he heard the words, "Ego vobis Romae propitius ero" ("I shall be favorable to you at Rome"), and after long deliberations with his followers, he drew up the five fundamental chapters of the rule for a new institute. The Society of Jesus was approved orally by Paul III at Tivoli (Sept. 3, 1539), and solemnly confirmed by him in the bull *Regimini militantis ecclesiae* (Sept. 27, 1540). During Lent 1541, Ignatius, against his desire, was elected general of the new society and on April 22, with his companions, went on pilgrimage to the seven stational basilicas of Rome and made solemn profession at St. Paul–Outside–the–Walls. While his companions were sent on missions by the pope, he remained in Rome to consolidate the society, direct the admission of new members, write the first two texts of the constitution (1547–49), and carry on an enormous correspondence (more than 6,000 letters are published). At the same time he founded and supported many apostolic projects for the moral renewal of the city—homes for orphans, for catechumens, and for penitent women (House of St. Martha). Through the influence of Francis BORGIA, Duke of Gandia, he obtained Paul III's approval of the *Spiritual Exercises* (July 31, 1548). JULIUS III, by the bull *Exposcit debitum* (July 21, 1550), reconfirmed the society and determined its internal structure, giving as its goal the defense and propagation of the faith. In February 1551 Ignatius founded the Roman College, intended as the prototype for the colleges of the society. By the next year it had 300 students. Although initially dedicated to the teaching of grammar and humanities, it offered classes in philosophy and theology in 1553. He also instituted the German College (1552) for the training of future apostles of Germany.

Constitutions. During his generalate, besides writing rules of conduct and instructions, such as the famed letter on obedience (1553), Ignatius spent years of thought and experimentation in determining the *Constitutions*. To his followers, designated canonically as Canons Regular, he gave distinctive characteristics that would have extensive effect in religious life in general. To as-

St. Ignatius of Loyola.

sure efficacy and mobility in the apostolate, he proposed obedience as the prominent virtue, renounced monastic choir, a fixed garb, and penances obligatory on all. Members of the society in any of its various grades must shun high ecclesiastical office unless ordered by the pope. Ignatius prolonged the novitiate to a period of two years, established simple vows that preceded the solemn profession, and a third probation after studies. He was inflexible in refusing the regular ministry of religious women, and excluded the foundation of any women's branch of the society, especially after the unsuccessful experiment in which, to please his benefactress, Isabel Roser, he allowed a group of religious women to place themselves under his obedience. He also replaced various types of capitular jurisdiction with a monarchical organization, in which the general, though aided by consultors and provincials, was elected for life and responsible only to the general congregation.

Ignatian Ideal. By those portions of his *Diario espiritual* that have been preserved (Feb. 2, 1544–Feb. 27, 1545), Ignatius is revealed as a true mystic. His spiritual life moved in an atmosphere that was particularly Trinitarian, Christological, and Eucharistic. To his devotion to the Trinity, Christ as Savior and prototype of perfection, and the Eucharistic life centered in the Mass, he added a great affection for Our Lady. His ideal was the greater promotion of God's glory (*ad majorem Dei gloriam*), and he saw this as the work of the society. To bring men to know their destiny and to teach them how to attain it is the apostolic ideal that guided his actions and his rules. All apostolic action must however be guided by true love of the Church and an unconditional obedience to the Vicar of Christ. For this end Ignatius imposed on all professed members a fourth solemn vow of obedience to the pope. His aspiration was to give the Church and the papacy the greatest possible service, and his direction of the society was based on this foundation.

Ignatius' emphasis upon obedience has often given a misguided impression of inflexibility and militaristic regime. The love from his subjects and the admiration of contemporaries for his genius in organization and profound understanding of personalities prove such a view unjustified. In 1551 he asked the fathers, assembled for the examination of the *Constitutions,* to be relieved of his office because of ill health, but was refused. He continued in power and at the end of his life declared that God had granted the three graces he most desired: the confirmation of the Society, the approval of the *Spiritual Exercises,* and the completion of the *Constitutions.* At his death, the Society had 1,000 members distributed throughout 100 houses in 12 provinces. Ignatius was beatified by Pope Paul V on July 27, 1609, and canonized by Paul's successor, Pope Gregory XV on March 12, 1622. Pope Pius XI in 1922 declared him patron of spiritual exercises and retreats.

Iconography. Besides the death mask (see illustration) and portraits taken from it, three paintings are considered authentic, those by Jacopino del Conte and Alonzo Sánchez Coello, and an anonymous portrait. Among numerous artistic representations are the statues by Juan Martínez Montañes, Gregorio Hernández, and Pierre le Gros. The last exists in a copy by Ludovisi in the church of the Gesù, Rome. There are paintings by Andreas Pozzo, SJ, in the church of S. Ignazio, Rome; by Juan Espinosa in the museum in Valencia; by Peter Paul Rubens, painted for the Jesuit church at Antwerp and now in the Hofmuseum, Vienna; and by Juan de las Roelas; and bas–reliefs by Allesandro Algardi and Renato Fremin.

Feast: July 31.

See Also: JESUITS.

Bibliography: *Obras completas,* ed. I. IPARRAGUIRRE and C. DE DALMASES (*Biblioteca de autores cristanos* 86; 2d ed. Madrid 1963). Extensive sources for his life and writings are found in the *Monumenta historica Societatis Jesu* (Madrid 1894– Rome 1932–). Autobiography, *ibid.* v.1, critical text; *St. Ignatius' Own Story as Told to Luis González de Cámara,* tr. W. J. YOUNG (Toronto 1956); *Cartes espirituals de S. Ignasi de Loyola,* ed. I. CASANOVAS,

2 v. (Barcelona 1936); *Lettres,* tr. G. DUMEIGE (Paris 1959); *Letters and Instructions,* ed. A. GOODIER, tr. D. F. O'LEARY, v.1 (St. Louis 1914); *Letters to Women,* ed. H. RAHNER, tr. K. POND and S. A. H. WEETMAN (New York 1960). Literature. J. BRODRICK, *Saint Ignatius Loyola: The Pilgrim Years* (New York 1956). P. DUDON, *St. Ignatius of Loyola,* tr. W. J. YOUNG (Milwaukee 1949). P. LETURIA, *Iñigo de Loyola,* tr. A. J. OWEN (Syracuse, N.Y. 1949). L. VON MATT and H. RAHNER, *St. Ignatius of Loyola: A Pictorial Biography,* tr. J. MURRAY (Chicago 1956). M. PURCELL, *The First Jesuit* (Westminster, Md. 1957). P. TACCHI–VENTURI, *Storia della Compagnia di Gesù in Italia* (2d ed. Rome 1950–51). R. GARCIA–VILLOSLADA, *Ignacio de Loyola, un español al servicio del pontificado* (Zaragoza 1956). J. DE GUIBERT, *The Jesuits: Their Spiritual Doctrine and Practice,* tr. W. J. YOUNG (Chicago 1964). A. M. ALAREDA, *Sant Ignasi a Montserrat* (Monserrat 1935). A. HUONDER, *Ignatius von Loyola: Beiträge zu seinem Charakterbild* (Cologne 1932). H. RAHNER, *The Spirituality of St. Ignatius Loyola,* tr. F. J. SMITH (Westminster, Md. 1953). J. F. GILMONT and P. DAMAN, *Bibliographie ignatienne 1894–1957* (Paris 1958). I. IPARRAGUIRRE, *Orientaciones bibliográficas sobre san Ignacio de Loyola* (2d ed. Rome 1965). J. F. CONWELL, *Impelling Spirit: Revisiting a Founding Experience: 1539, Ignatius Loyola and His Companions* (Chicago 1997). M. J. BUCKLEY, "Ecclesial Mysticism in the Spiritual Exercises of Ignatius," *Theological Studies* 56 (1995): 441–463. J. I. TELLECHEA IDIGORAS, *Ignatius of Loyola: The Pilgrim Saint,* trans. C. M. BUCKLEY (Chicago 1994). J. GIULIETTI, "Contemplative Hearts, Compassionate Hands: The Ignatian Vision of Justice," in *Let Justice Roll Down Like Waters,* ed. W. J. O'BRIEN (Washington, D.C. 1993), 1–17. P. CARAMAN, *Ignatius Loyola: A Biography of the Founder of the Jesuits* (San Francisco 1990). J. L. SEGUNDO, *The Christ of the Ignatian Exercises* (London 1987). A. RAVIER, *Ignatius of Loyola and the Founding of the Society of Jesus* (San Francisco 1987). F. WULF, *Ignatius of Loyola: His Personality and Spiritual Heritage, 1556–1956: Studies on the 400th Anniversary of His Death* (St. Louis 1977).

[C. DE DALMASES]

IGNORANCE

Lack of knowledge in someone capable of having such knowledge (St. Thomas Aquinas, *Summa theologiae* 1a, 101.1 ad 2; 1a2ae, 76.2; *De malo* 3.7). As a defect of KNOWLEDGE, ignorance resembles ERROR and nescience. However, ignorance denotes no cognitive activity, whereas error denotes cognitive activity of a kind that is either positively or negatively inadequate. Ignorance differs from nescience also in that ignorance is the lack of knowledge in someone who is by nature capable of having it; nescience is the absence of knowledge in someone not naturally capable of having it. Hence, one should attribute nescience rather than ignorance to infants.

Role in Knowledge. Ignorance can be privative or negative respectively, insofar as he who lacks knowledge can or cannot reasonably be expected to possess it. Thus ignorance of anatomy is negative ignorance for an engineer; it is privative ignorance for a medical doctor.

Unconscious, unrecognized ignorance is sterile—equivalent in effect to mere nescience. However, ignorance recognized as such ceases to be complete ignorance (cf. ST 1a2ae, 27.2 ad 1), and indeed plays a fundamental role in the acquisition of knowledge. WONDER is said to be the beginning of philosophizing, but wonder itself is founded on awareness of one's ignorance and the desire to be rid of it (*In 1 meta.* 3.55). One wonders and begins to investigate because he or she perceives some effect but is ignorant of its cause (ST 1a2ae, 3.8; 32.8). The wish to escape ignorance thus fosters a desire for the deeper and more ultimate understanding of things that constitute philosophy.

See Also: DOUBT; EPISTEMOLOGY.

Bibliography: L. M. RÉGIS, *Epistemology,* tr. I. C. BYRNE (New York 1959). R. GARRIGOU-LAGRANGE, *Beatitude,* tr. P. CUMMINS (St. Louis 1956). T. J. HIGGINS, *Man as Man* (rev. ed. Milwaukee 1958).

[J. B. NUGENT]

Moral Aspect. As it affects the morality of an action, ignorance can be defined as the lack of knowledge in a person with regard to the nature or moral quality of an act he or she is performing or proposes to perform.

Ignorance may be viewed under different aspects. As to its object or subject matter, it may be ignorance of law (*ignorantia iuris*) or ignorance of fact (*ignorantia facti*); that is, an agent may be ignorant of the existence of a law covering the matter in hand, or of the extension of the law to it; or he may be ignorant of some circumstance or condition of his action which would cause it to fall under a law that is known to exist.

Of more importance, however, is the distinction made on the basis of the subject's accountability for the ignorance. Ignorance is said to be invincible when it cannot be dispelled by the reasonable diligence a prudent man would be expected to exercise in a given situation—and situations vary according to circumstances of persons, places, etc. In the case of invincible ignorance, the agent is inculpably unaware of the nature of a situation or of the obligations it involves. Ignorance of this kind excuses from moral fault. It causes the act to be involuntary, at least as far as its objective moral character is concerned. What is unknown cannot be the object of volition.

Vincible ignorance, on the other hand, is that which could be dispelled by the application of reasonable diligence. Because the agent culpably neglects to make the effort necessary to become better informed, his ignorance is, in one degree or another, voluntary and imputable. The degree of imputability is measured by the extent of the agent's culpable negligence.

Authors distinguish between simply vincible ignorance, which exists when some, but insufficient, effort is made to be rid of it, and crass or supine ignorance, in which very little effort, if any at all, is made to dispel it. Ignorance is said to be affected or a studied ignorance when it is directly voluntary; a person prefers to remain in ignorance so as to be free from a sense of obligation. A wrong done out of simply vincible ignorance, or even of crass ignorance, is less imputable than if it were done with full knowledge, for the act is less voluntary.

Since affected ignorance is a species of vincible ignorance, directly willed and positively fostered, what is done through it remains entirely voluntary. This is a hypocritical type of ignorance and leaves the voluntariness of one's action almost untouched. It may indicate a certain respect for law that one should prefer to act without the consciousness that he is violating the law, and from that point of view, an act committed through affected ignorance is not quite as voluntary as the same act committed with full knowledge; however, this consideration is of small moment and the lessening of voluntariness in such a case is so slight as to be negligible.

St. Thomas distinguished between antecedent, consequent, and concomitant ignorance. His ''antecedent'' ignorance corresponds so closely with the ''invincible'' ignorance described above that it needs no special discussion here; the same is true of his ''consequent'' ignorance, which corresponds with what is today more commonly called ''vincible'' ignorance. His ''concomitant'' ignorance is that of an agent who does something he is not aware he is doing, and who yet would be quite willing to do the same thing even if he were not ignorant. For example, a man unwittingly insults another person whom he happens to dislike and would be only too happy to insult if an occasion presented itself. His act is not involuntary in the sense that it is opposed to his will; neither is it voluntary in this particular case because he does not know what he is doing. He acts, therefore, *with* ignorance but not *out of* ignorance. St. Thomas describes such an act as nonvoluntary. The external act is not imputable to the agent, but he is not free of fault because of his habitual malicious disposition toward his neighbor.

See Also: HUMAN ACT; VOLUNTARITY.

Bibliography: THOMAS AQUINAS, *Summa theologiae,* 1a 2ae, 6.8; 19.6; 76. B. H. MERKELBACH, *Summa theologiae moralis,* ed. P. L. GAUDÉ, 3 v. (Paris 1938) 1:80–83. H. NOLDIN, *Summa theologiae moralis,* ed. A. SCHMITT, 3 v. (Barcelona 1945) 1:48–50. H. DAVIS, *Moral and Pastoral Theology,* 4 v. (3d ed. New York 1938) 1:16–19. E. MANGENOT, *Dictionnaire de théologie catholique,* ed. A. VACANT et al., 15 v. (Paris 1903–50) 7.1:734–740.

[F. D. NEALY]

ILDEFONSUS OF TOLEDO, ST.

Bishop and writer; b. probably in Toledo, Spain, *c.* 610; d. Toledo, 667. Ildefonsus entered the monastery of Agalia near Toledo, became its abbot, and in 657 was chosen archbishop of Toledo. Nothing is known about his government of the archdiocese, and no national councils were held during his tenure; but he did play a part in the development of the MOZARABIC RITE.

Two of his letters and four of his writings are extant: *De viris illustribus* contains brief biographies of 14 men, all of whom had lived in Spain except GREGORY THE GREAT; *De cognitione baptismi* contains interesting information about the administration of Baptism in Visigothic Spain; *De progressu spiritualis deserti* traces the road by which the neophytes must travel in order to reach heaven; and his *De virginitate sanctae Mariae,* though neither original nor profound, is an excellent summary of what JEROME and earlier theologians had written. It deepened the devotion of the Spanish people, writers, and artists to the Blessed Virgin. A legend in which Mary is said to have placed a chasuble over Ildefonsus' shoulders was depicted by Spanish artists of the 17th and 18th centuries.

Feast: Jan. 23.

Bibliography: A. BRAEGELMANN, *The Life and Writings of St. Ildefonsus* (Washington 1942). M. SCHAPIRO, *The Parma Ildefonsus: A Romanesque Illuminated Manuscript from Cluny . . .* (New York 1964). E. FERNÁNDEZ-PRIETO DOMÍNGUEZ, *Actas de visitas reales y otras realizadas por acontecimientos extraordinarios a los cuerpos santos de San Ildefonso y San Atilano* (Zamora, Spain 1973). J. M. HORMAECHE BASAURI, *La pastoral de la iniciación cristiana en la España visigoda: estudio sobre el De cognitione baptismi de San Ildefonso de Toledo* (Toledo 1983). J. F. RIVERA RECIO, *San Ildefonso de Toledo: biografía, época y posteridad* (Madrid 1985). O. ENGELS, *Lexikon für Theologie und Kirche,* ed. J. HOFER and K. RAHNER, 10 v. (2d, new ed. Freiburg 1957–65) 5:622. A. BUTLER, *The Lives of the Saints,* ed. H. THURSTON and D. ATTWATER, 4 v. (New York 1956) 1:155–156.

[S. J. MCKENNA]

ILGA, BL.

Recluse; d. *c.* 1115. Ilga (Hilga, Helga) is said to have lived as a recluse in Schwarzenberg (in the forest of Bregenz). According to tradition she was the sister of Bl. Merbot and Bl. Diedo. Persons suffering from diseases of the eye used to visit a spring named for her. She has never been canonized.

Feast: June 8.

Bibliography: *Acta Sanctorum,* Sept. 3:890, n.8. A. MERCATI and A. PELZER, *Dizionario ecclesiastico* (Turin 1954–58) 2:387. L. WELTI, *Lexikon für Theologie und Kirche,* 10 v. (2d, new ed. Freiburg 1957–65) 5:6:23.

[M. J. FINNEGAN]

ILLIG, ALVIN ANTHONY

Paulist priest, evangelist, and founder of the Paulist National Catholic Evangelization Association; b. Los Angeles, California, Aug. 17, 1926; d. Washington, DC, Aug. 2, 1991. Alvin Illig, the third of four sons born to Joseph and Katherina Illig, entered the Paulist novitiate in 1945 and completed his studies at St. Paul's College in Washington, DC. He was ordained a priest by Bishop Fulton SHEEN on May 1, 1953 at the church of St. Paul the Apostle in New York City.

Illig was assigned to Paulist Press following his ordination, and served as an assistant editor of *Information* magazine. During his twenty years at the press, he was part of a team of young PAULISTS who transformed this pamphlet and tract house into one of the largest Catholic publishing houses in the United States. Illig's particular talent was marketing, and by the late 1960s he had created the American Library and Education Service Company (ALESCO) that distributed books and audio-visual materials to school libraries. When the program was criticized for making Catholic incursions into the American public school system, ALESCO was sold. Seeking a new challenge, Illig retired from publishing in 1973.

In January 1974 Illig went to Pascagaoula, MS, to devise a campaign of Catholic evangelization that involved radio ads, billboard space, telephone volunteers, and door-to-door visitations. In two months, his success led to a program called "We Care, We Share," that expanded the outreach campaign across the diocese of Natchez-Jackson. In 1975, Illig became Director of Evangelization for the Archdiocese of Washington. He established the Paulist National Catholic Evangelization Association in November 1977 and was simultaneously named the first Executive Director of the National Conference of Catholic Bishops' Committee on Evangelization.

Illig used his marketing and communication skills to promote Catholic evangelization and became a significant influence in the national Church's growing awareness of the unchurched and of inactive Catholics. He was an early and important influence in the development and dissemination of new forms and approaches to evangelization in the modern church. The American Bishops' National Plan for Evangelization, Go and Make Disciples, issued in November 1992, is dedicated to his memory.

Bibliography: D. R. HOGE, *Converts, Dropouts, and Returnees* (Washington 1981). A. A. ILLIG, *Evangelization Portraits* (Washington 1981). K. BOYACK, ed., *Catholic Evangelization Today* (New York 1987); *The New Evangelization* (New York 1992).

[P. ROBICHAUD]

ILLINOIS, CATHOLIC CHURCH IN

A north central state in the Great Prairie region of the U.S., admitted (1818) to the Union as the 21st state, Illinois is bordered on the north by Wisconsin, on the northeast by Lake Michigan, on the east by Indiana, on the southeast by the Wabash and Ohio Rivers, on the south by the Ohio River, and on the west by the Mississippi River. Springfield is the capital; the largest city is Chicago. In 2001 there were 3.8 million Catholics, about 32 percent of the total population (12.1 million) of the state. They are served by the Archdiocese of Chicago and five suffragan sees: Belleville (1887), Joliet (1919), Peoria (1877), Rockford (1908), and Springfield (established as diocese of Quincy, 1853).

Early History. The Illinois country was under the jurisdiction of the Quebec diocese from 1674 to 1784, during which period from 15,000 to 20,000 members of Native American tribes and eventually about 2,000 French trappers and settlers formed the Illinois mission field. Among the early Jesuits to serve the area were Jacques MARQUETTE, who accompanied the Louis Jolliet expedition (1673); Claude ALLOUEZ, who labored there for more than 11 years; and Jacques Gravier, Pierre Gabriel Marest, Jean Mermet, and Alexandre Guyenne. Other missionaries active in Illinois included the Seminary Priests of the Foreign Missions of Quebec and the Franciscans Zenobius Membré, Louis HENNEPIN, and Gabriel de la Ribourde. When the century-long struggle between England and France in the New World ended in French defeat (1763) and British occupancy of the Illinois country, there was a mass exodus of French Catholics to the Louisiana territory. Among the many priests who worked in Illinois from 1763 to 1843, when Chicago was made a diocese, were Sebastian MEURIN, SJ, the "patriot priest" Pierre GIBAULT, the Sulpician Gabriel RICHARD, and Donatien Olivier. Other itinerant priests who visited the area from time to time were Stephen Theodore BADIN, Elisha DURBIN, Charles Felix VAN QUICKENBORNE, SJ, Peter Doutreluingue, CM, John Francis Loisel, Vitalis Van Coostere, John Mary Irenaeus St. Cyr, Peter Paul LEFEVERE, John Blase Raho, CM, Aloysius Parodi, CM, and Patrick McCabe. Chicago was designated a metropolitan see in 1880, and its suffragans eventually included the Dioceses of Belleville, Joliet, Peoria, Rockford, and Springfield.

Diocesan Development. On Feb. 12, 1875, the Diocese of Peoria was created, embracing 23 counties in central Illinois; it now consists of 26. On Jan. 7, 1887, the 28 southernmost counties of the state were detached from the Diocese of Alton and formed into the Diocese of Belleville. The Diocese of Rockford was established on Sept. 23, 1908, for 11 counties of northwestern Illinois.

Archdiocese/Diocese	Year Created
Archdiocese of Chicago	1880
Diocese of Belleville	1887
Diocese of Joliet in Illinois	1949
Diocese of Peoria	1877
Diocese of Rockford	1908
Diocese of Springfield in Illinois	1853

Finally, the Diocese of Joliet came into being on Dec. 11, 1948, covering seven counties. Thus the see of Chicago was left with only two counties, Cook and Lake. Meanwhile, on Sept. 10, 1880, Chicago had been raised to metropolitan rank. The new ecclesiastical province was coterminous with the State of Illinois; the first archbishop, appointed on the same date, was Patrick Augustine Feehan, a native of Ireland and formerly Bishop of Nashville. The Ukrainian Catholic Diocese of St. Nicholas in Chicago was established in 1961; it comprises all the United States west of the western borders of Ohio, Kentucky, Tennessee, and Mississippi.

The first American-born bishop in Illinois was Thomas Foley, a native of Baltimore, who in 1869 was appointed coadjutor to the bishop of Chicago with right of succession, and apostolic administrator of the diocese (because of the insanity of Bishop James Duggan); he served in that office until he died in 1879. In 1924 George William Mundelein, Archbishop of Chicago, became the "First Cardinal of the West" (i.e., west of the Alleghenies). The first black to head a diocese in Illinois was Wilton D. Gregory, who was appointed to the See of Belleville in 1993 after having been an auxiliary to the Archbishop of Chicago for ten years.

Illinois was the scene of the labors of the first black American priest recognized as black, namely, Augustus Tolton. Born a slave of Catholic parents in Missouri in 1854, he was brought by his mother to Quincy during the Civil War and was tutored by a German priest and educated at Quincy College. He then studied at the Urban College of the Congregation de Propaganda Fide and was ordained in Rome in 1886. Having been accepted by the Diocese of Alton, he became pastor of a black church in Quincy, but because of opposition from the clergy and the paucity of black Catholics, in 1889 he was transferred at his request to Chicago, where he was appointed founding pastor of St. Monica's Parish. He died in 1897 and was buried in Quincy.

Education and Catholic Schools. Catholic schools at all levels have flourished in Illinois although the State Constitution of 1870 denies public funds to sectarian institutions. In 1889 the General Assembly, dominated by

Republicans, passed the Edwards Law, named after the superintendent of Public Instruction, Richard Edwards, which provided for compulsory school attendance and required that the elementary subjects be taught in the English language. Catholics and Lutherans protested vehemently against it, mainly because it vested undue power over parochial school in local school boards, which could determine whether private day schools satisfied the state requirements for instruction. This controversy should be viewed in the context of a national intensification of anti-Catholic feeling and the rise of the nativist American Protective Association, which was strong in Illinois. In a joint pastoral letter issued in September, 1892, the Catholic bishops of Illinois denounced the law as a violation of their constitutional rights and urged that it be repealed. After the Democrats won majorities in both houses of the General Assembly and the governorship in the November elections, the law was repealed. When the Illinois Federation of German Catholic Societies was organized in 1893, it established a Legislative Committee to scrutinize bills dealing with education; its members also testified frequently before the Education Committees of both the House and the Senate.

Following the chartering of the short-lived University of St. Mary of the Lake, 23 Catholic institutions of higher learning were founded in Illinois, ten of which survived into the 21st century, namely, St. Francis Xavier College for Women (now Saint Xavier University) in Chicago, founded by the Sisters of Mercy and chartered in 1847; Quincy College (now University), founded in 1860 by the Friars Minor (Diocese of Springfield); Loyola University Chicago (St. Ignatius College until 1909), founded in 1870 by the Jesuits; St. Procopius College (now Benedictine University), founded in 1887 by the Benedictine monks at Lisle (Diocese of Joliet); DePaul University, founded in 1898 by the Vincentian Fathers in Chicago; Barat College, founded in 1918 by the Religious of the Sacred Heart in Lake Forest (Archdiocese of Chicago); College (now University) of Illinois, St. Francis, chartered in 1920 and opened in 1925 by the Sisters of St. Francis of Mary Immaculate in Joliet; Rosary College (now Dominican University), founded in 1922 by the Dominican Sisters of Sinsinawa (Wisconsin) at River Forest (Archdiocese of Chicago); Springfield College in Illinois, founded in 1929 by the Ursuline Sisters; and Lewis College of Science and Technology (now Lewis University), founded in 1930 by the Brothers of the Christian Schools at Lockport (now Romeoville, Diocese of Joliet).

The only major seminary for diocesan students in the state, founded by Archbishop Mundelein, opened in 1921. The University of St. Mary of the Lake and Munde-lein Seminary, as it came to be called, was staffed by Jesuits of the Missouri Province who occupied the principal chairs in theology and philosophy and provided spiritual direction. By virtue of its 1844 charter from the State of Illinois, the University of St. Mary of the Lake was authorized to confer the bachelor of arts degree and the master of arts in religious studies. In 1929 the Sacred Congregation of Seminaries and Universities granted the theological faculty the power to confer a baccalaureate, license, and doctorate in Sacred Theology. At this time the seminary was also designated a provincial seminary and opened to students from other dioceses in Illinois. St. Mary of the Lake became the first American institution designated as a "pontifical faculty of theology" under the apostolic constitution *Deus Scientiarum Dominus* (1931). In 1970 the seminary became an associate member of the Association of Theological Schools and in 1972 a full member with the right to award the master of divinity degree and to have its other academic degrees recognized as accredited.

Catholic Conference of Illinois and the Historical Society. The Catholic Welfare Committee of Illinois, organized by the bishops in 1929 to give a unified and official expression of the positions of the Church on pending and proposed legislation, was superseded in July, 1969, by the Catholic Conference of Illinois. Under the leadership of John Cardinal Cody, Archbishop of Chicago, the Conference was formed originally to obtain from the state direct financial aid for Catholic schools. It is the agency that enables the six dioceses of the state to develop, coordinate, and implement interdiocesan programs and to cooperate with other religious bodies and with secular and governmental organizations in promoting the social and moral welfare of the people of Illinois. The Conference has its headquarters in Chicago and an office in Springfield. It is governed by a board of directors composed of the six diocesan bishops of the state, all auxiliary and retired bishops, one priest, one lay man, and one lay woman from each diocese, and four religious who are at-large members. The Archbishop of Chicago is ex officio chairman of the board.

The Illinois Catholic Historical Society was founded and incorporated in 1918, the centenary of statehood and the 75th anniversary of the erection of the See of Chicago. It was organized at Loyola University in Chicago under the guidance of Frederic Siedenburg, S.J., dean of the School of Sociology, who became first vice-president. The first president was the prominent layman, William J. Onahan. It published a quarterly, the *Illinois Catholic Historical Review* from July, 1918, to April, 1929. Articles and source materials on the colonial era predominated. Since the editors felt themselves hampered by the limitations imposed by the name of the state in the title of the journal, the name of the journal was changed to *Mid-America* beginning with the 12th volume in July, 1929, and the administration was taken over by Loyola University.

Bibliography: G. J. GARRAGHAN, *The Catholic Church in Chicago, 1673–1871* (Chicago 1921, reprinted Ann Arbor 1968). J. P. DONNELLY, *Jacques Marquette, S.J., 1637–1675* (Chicago 1968); *Pierre Gibault, Missionary, 1737–1802* (Chicago 1971). D. W. KUCERA, *Church-State Relationships in Education in Illinois* (Washington, D.C. 1955). H. C. KOENIG, *Caritas Christi Urget Nos: A History of the Offices, Agencies, and Institutions of the Archdiocese of Chicago,* 2 vols. (Chicago 1981). J. F. MCDERMOTT, *Old Cahokia: A Narrative and Documents Illustrating the First Century of Its History* (St. Louis 1949). R. R. MILLER, *That All May Be One: A History of the Rockford Diocese* (Rockford 1976). A. O'ROURKE, *The Good Work Begun: Centennial History of Peoria Diocese* (n.p. 1977).

[I. EVANS/R. TRISCO]

ILLTUD, ST.

One of the founders of Welsh monasticism; b. *c.* 450; d. *c.* 525. The earliest account of Illtud (Illtyd or Latin, *Iltutus*) is in the vita by St. SAMSON, written *c.* 610 in Brittany, where Illtud is said to have been a disciple of St. GERMAIN OF AUXERRE, who ordained him priest. Later he established a monastery and school in Wales (probably at Llantwit Major in Glamorgan), and many of the great Welsh saints (Paul Aurelian, GILDAS, Samson, and even DAVID) were said to have been his pupils. The earliest vita of Illtud himself dates from 1140 and links his name with King Arthur. He is honored in Welsh tradition for his great learning and for giving shape to the monastic movement of the sixth century. Many of the legends associated with him—angelic visitations, the taming of a stag, his being miraculously fed from heaven—are commonplaces of Celtic hagiography. But the account of his death in the vita of Samson seems to be an authentic picture of a saint of acknowledged holiness, surrounded by devoted disciples. On the evidence of a stone inscription at CALDEY Island, Illtud's monastery has sometimes been identified with that early Christian center; Breton tradition gives a prominent place to his work in that country, where he is said to have died, at Dol. We may suppose him to have been a man of learning, inheriting the Roman traditions of early Christianity in Britain, whose monastery was the training ground for the intense religious revival of sixth-century Wales.

Feast: Nov. 6 (Archdiocese of Cardiff and Brittany).

Bibliography: G. H. DOBLE, *Saint Iltut* (Cardiff 1944). A. W. WADE-EVANS, ed. and tr., *Vitae sanctorum britanniae et genealogiae* (Cardiff 1944), includes text of Latin life of St. Illtud.

[I. EVANS]

ILLUMINATION

Literally, the action of illuminating or the condition of being illuminated; in philosophy and theology, a special divine influence aiding man in obtaining certain, necessary, and universal knowledge. The latter notion is discussed here in its sources, in Augustinian thought, and in some later applications.

Sources. In ancient and medieval thought, light was considered ontologically as both a physical and a spiritual substance. On this basis a metaphysics of LIGHT developed; its offspring was a noetics of light called the theory of illumination. The premises for such a theory were found in the monistic system of emanation of PLOTINUS, who taught that the WORLD SOUL emanates from the One via the Nous. This world soul sends its rays and mirrors itself in bodies as the fourth hypostasis. Such illumination is a two-way process, however, for the rays reflected from the bodies return to the soul, to the Nous, to the One in a mystic ascent, and to a final reunion in which being and cognition are identical.

Plotinus's teaching was transmitted to the later Middle Ages through NEOPLATONISM. The Arabs generally adopted the theory, but brought into it Aristotelian notions. In this amalgam the *intellectus agens* of Aristotle was no longer an individual human possession, but one for the entire human species, identified with the tenth Cosmic Intelligence.

Augustine's Theory. St. AUGUSTINE utilized the doctrine of divine light in St. John's gospel to develop a theory of knowledge. Convinced of man's personal nature, Augustine was safe from Plotinus's monopsychism of the fourth hypostasis; human knowledge, for him, does not originate in an identity of man with the intelligible world, but rather in an encounter with this world without loss of personal uniqueness.

Augustine's theory of knowledge distinguishes an object, a subject, and a medium of knowledge. These three components are proportioned to, and cooperate with, one another in the noetic process. The objects are the material and immaterial things known. The knowledge of sensible things, as well as the knowledge of spiritual objects, can be obtained only under the influence of divine illumination. The senses draw the soul's attention to what is happening outside the soul, and their reports are judged in the divine light by the intellect. The true objects of knowledge are the eternal reasons, which rank higher than the created intellect, being contained in the divine intelligence. They constitute the intelligible world of truths hierarchically ordered to, and culminating in, eternal truth. By participation in these *rationes aeternae* a thing is what it is. Therefore, the human intellect can find these reasons in all things. It depends on these truths for its judgment and certainty.

The subject in this process of knowledge is the knowing intellect, man's soul. The soul is not the very nature of truth. Although "all men are lamps" (*In Ioann.* 23.3), they remain in darkness unless they are illuminated by the true Light. And while man, by virtue of his intellectual nature, corresponds to the intelligible truths in the divine light, the whole man (intellect and will) is required in knowing by divine illumination. The medium through which object and subject unite in knowledge is the divine light. God alone is the true light. It is He who enlightens and makes intelligible.

Later Developments. In the 13th century, because of contact with Arabian theories of knowledge and with translations of Aristotle's works (especially William of Moerbeke's), Augustine's theory of illumination—until then the only theory of knowledge for Christian thinkers—was gradually supplanted by the theory of ABSTRACTION. St. BONAVENTURE, however, while using the Aristotelian theory to explain sense knowledge, invoked divine illumination—i.e., direct action of the eternal reasons upon the intellect—as necessary for making infallible judgments.

St. THOMAS AQUINAS replaced divine illumination by the agent INTELLECT, a power created and given by God to man for the purpose of knowing and judging. Thus, for him, the illuminating factor is given in man's nature. In a "conversion to the phantasm" the agent intellect makes the noetic object appear in the human consciousness. But that which is seen (illuminated) is not the thing as such (a form in matter) but a form abstracted from matter, the universal abstracted from the particular, the intelligible species abstracted from the phantasm. "Therefore, we must say that our intellect understands material things by abstracting from the phantasms; and through material things thus considered we acquire some knowledge of immaterial things" (*Summa theologiae* 1a, 85.1).

A return to the illumination theory occurred in the 17th century with Nicolas MALEBRANCHE. He says in his answer to the first objection to the tenth of his *Éclaircissements sur les six livres de la Recherche de la Verité* (Paris 1678, 3:124): "Naturally, the mind is capable of movement in its ideas. . . . But it does not move itself, it does not enlighten itself; it is God who effects everything (*qui fait tout*) in the minds as well as in the bodies." This ontological premise led Malebranche directly to OCCASIONALISM, which holds that God establishes occasional causes in order to produce definite effects—such as the individual man's recognizing and knowing the here-and-now presented object.

A 20th-century controversy arose over interpretations of St. Augustine's illumination theory, with various scholars favoring the ontologistic, the historical, the concordant, and the existential schools respectively. Although many issues of Augustinian epistemology were thus clarified, there remained a shadow of opaqueness, for Augustine himself never completely elucidated the function of the divine light in the noetic realm.

See Also: ILLUMINISM; KNOWLEDGE, THEORIES OF

Bibliography: F. C. COPLESTON, *History of Philosophy* (Westminster, Md. 1946) v. 2, 4. S. VANNI-ROVIGHI, *Enciclopedia filosofica* 2:1237–41. J. AUER, *Lexikon für Theologie und Kirche*, ed. J. HOFER and K. RAHNER, 10 v. (2d new ed. Freiburg 1957–65) 5:624–625. É. H. GILSON and T. D. LANGAN, *Modern Philosophy: Descartes to Kant* (New York 1963). A. A. MAURER, *Medieval Philosophy* (New York 1962). K. RAHNER, *Geist in Welt* (2d ed. Munich 1957). J. RATZINGER, "Licht und Erleuchtung: Erwägungen zur Stellung und Entwicklung des Themas in der abendländischen Geistesgeschichte," *Studium generale* 13 (1960) 368–378. C. E. SCHÜTZINGER, *The German Controversy on St. Augustine's Illumination Theory* (New York 1960).

[C. E. SCHÜTZINGER]

ILLUMINISM

A term for any teaching concerning the ILLUMINATION of the human mind; it is attributed to enthusiasts of two distinct types: those who have the "light" as a direct communication from a higher source; and those who possess "enlightenment" as a result of a clarified and exalted condition of the human reason.

Direct Illumination. To the first class belong various religious sects who claimed direct enlightenment by God, chiefly the Gnostics, the Alumbrados of Spain, and the Illuminés of France. Historically first among these was GNOSTICISM, a generic name for a group of heretical religious movements that flourished during the early Christian centuries, all of whom commonly held that salvation comes through "enlightened knowledge," a knowledge that is secret and mysterious, based on direct revelation, and limited to a gifted elite.

Alumbrados. In 16th-century Spain, the adherents of illuminism were called Alumbrados. The name identifies a group of pseudo-mystic Spaniards who claimed to act always under illumination received directly and immediately from the Holy Spirit, and independently of the means of grace dispensed by the Church.

Illuminés. In 1623 there appeared in southern France what appeared to be a branch of the Alumbrados, under the name of *Illuminés*. The sect developed and gained proportion when it was joined in 1634 by Pierre Guérin, curé of Saint Georges de Roye. Under his strong influence, the group soon became known as the Guérinets. Both the Alumbrados and the Guérinets were suppressed by the middle of the 17th century.

In its broadest meaning, illuminism could further be applied to any and all groups or sects that claim the possession of an inner light by a select group of enlightened souls who have received the illumination as a revelation directly from God. Examples are the ROSICRUCIANS, who rose to public notice in 1537—a sect that combined enlightened possession of esoteric principles of religion with the mysteries of alchemy; the Molinists, founded by Miguel de MOLINOS in 1697; the French Martinists founded in 1754 by Martinez Pasqualis, as well as the Russian Martinists headed by Schwartz of Moscow about 1790. Both of these latter groups were cabalists and allegorists, and followers of the ideas of Jakob BÖHME and Emanuel SWEDENBORG (*see* CABALA).

Illumined Human Reason. Illuminism applies also, and more commonly, to those who possess enlightenment as a result of a clarified, purified, and exalted condition of the human reason. In this sense of the word, illuminism has two major historical applications, viz, the Enlightenment and the *Illuminati.*

The Enlightenment. First, both chronologically and influentially, is illuminism as referring to the intellectual and cultural movement more widely known as the ENLIGHTENMENT. Originating in England in 1688 at the close of the Glorious Revolution, it reached its violent climax in the French Revolution a century later. This illuminism enthroned reason and empowered it infallibly to judge, condemn, and banish all the nonreason of the past. Culture, religion, and government of the past was claimed to be unworthy of enlightened man and therefore had to be changed or abolished.

Such illuminism could neither exist, nor can it be understood, apart from the philosophical RATIONALISM, EMPIRICISM, and MECHANISM that preceded it, nor isolated from the social and political evils of the later 17th and 18th centuries, from the progress of science, nor from the spirit of independence and rebellion against TRADITION and AUTHORITY characteristic of Europeans since the 16th century. Philosophically it was an amalgam of empiricism, DEISM, rationalism, HEDONISM, UTILITARIANISM, RELATIVISM, antihistoricism, egoistic humanism, optimism, and a veneration of science—all springing from nature and converging toward naturalism, with its emphasis on natural rights, natural society, and natural religion.

Illuminati. Again, illuminism is identified with a group of Bavarian enthusiasts, known as the *Illuminati* (Perfectibilists or *Perfektibilisten*). Their main objective was to establish and propagate a new religion, and politically to establish a universal democratic republic that would follow the overthrow of existing government. The foundation of both was "enlightened reason," i.e., reason liberated from the dominating authority of Church and State. The group was founded by Adam Weishaupt on May 1, 1776. Weishaupt had been educated by the Jesuits, and became the first lay professor of Canon Law at the University of Ingolstadt.

Three factors in Weishaupt's background were manifest in his group: (1) his association and familiarity with Jesuit methods of education, organization, and discipline, although here he missed the essential point and actually made a caricature of Jesuit authority and obedience; (2) his association with, and knowledge of, FREEMASONRY, which he used as a prototype for the structure and model for the degrees and ceremonials of his organization; and (3) the rationalism, free thought, naturalism, anticlericalism, egotistic humanism, and antitraditionalism, characteristic of the Enlightenment, which he imbibed from his contemporaries. His great goal, viz, a world where all men would be free and happy, was to be achieved by the establishment of a secret and highly organized Order of Illuminati. Weishaupt considered this end desirable enough to justify any and every means in its attainment.

Illuminist Ethics. From the above, it is immediately evident that illuminism includes a wide range of ethical theories, from divine illumination and passivism, to hedonism, utilitarianism, naturalism, humanism, altruism; and of these latter, some atheistic, some deistic; some associated with rationalism as a basis, some with empiricism; some optimistic, some pessimistic, some even nihilistic.

A detailed critique of illuminist ethics would entail a critique of each of the above-mentioned ethical theories. However, in any and all of them, one or more of the following truths that are fundamental to a discussion of morality have been overlooked or denied: (1) Man has a rational nature; i.e., he is a PERSON endowed with reason and free will. Therefore, his moral judgments, like all other judgments, are either self-evident truths or are arrived at by reasoning; and he is personally responsible for his moral decisions and actions. (2) Man is saved by fulfilling his nature, i.e., by knowing and doing. Action without knowledge is unintelligent, and knowledge without action is sterile with regard to salvation. Salvation demands intelligence, faith, and good works. (3) By his nature, man is under moral OBLIGATION to obey the NATURAL LAW. Man possesses natural rights, but he also has moral duties. (4) Although God does act within man, He has ordained that this action be through the instrumentality of the Church, and that normally His interior guidance of a soul is conditioned by His exterior guidance through the Church established by Jesus Christ, His Son. Thus, He "enlightens" human minds to accept what the Church teaches; He moves human wills to execute what the Church advises and commands.

See Also: ENLIGHTENMENT, PHILOSOPHY OF; SYNDERESIS; KNOWLEDGE, THEORIES OF.

Bibliography: J. P. ARENDZEN, *The Catholic Encyclopedia,* ed. C. G. HERBERMANN et al., 16 v. (New York 1907–14) 6:592–02. F. H. KRUGER, *La Grande Encyclopédie* 20:573–74. A. SCHWARZ, E. HEGEL and L. SCHEFFCZYK, *Lexikon für Theologie und Kirche,* ed. J. HOFER and K. RAHNER, 10 v. (2d, new ed. Freiburg 1957–65) 1:1055–66. G. CAPONE BRAGA, *Enciclopedia filosofica,* 4 v. (Venice-Rome 1957) 2:1242–54. E. CASSIRER, *Die Philosophie der Aufklärung* (Tübingen 1932). G. BAREILLE, *Dictionnaire de théologie catholique,* ed. A. VACANT et al., 15 v. (Paris 1903–50) 7:756–66. J. ROBISON, *Proofs of a Conspiracy Against all the Governments of Europe Carried on in the Secret Meetings of Free Masons, Illuminati, and Reading Societies* (2d ed. London 1797). V. STAUFFER, *New England and the Bavarian Illuminati* (Studies in History, Economics and Public Law . . . Columbia University 82.1; New York 1918).

[M. W. HOLLENBACH]

ILLYRICUS, THOMAS

Theologian; b. Vrana (near Zadar in modern Yugoslavia), *c.* 1485; d. Menton, near Monaco, 1528. He entered the Franciscan Observants at Osimo, Italy, and preached throughout Italy, France, and Germany. Clement VII named him inquisitor general in Savoy. Besides his *Sermones* (2 v. Toulouse 1521), he wrote works against Protestantism, including *Libellus de potestate summi pontificis* (Turin 1523) and *In lutheranas haereses clypeus catholicae ecclesiae* (Turin 1524). In his teaching on the papacy, Illyricus held that ecumenical councils are superior to the Roman pontiff.

Bibliography: F. SCHUBERT, *Lexikon für Theologie und Kirche* 10:128–129.

[J. H. MILLER]

IMAGE OF GOD

Genesis teaches not only the EXEMPLARITY OF GOD relative to the created universe but also the correlative truth that man is the image of God (Gn 1.26). In fact, "image of God" is the theological definition of man that is the only basis for an authentic Christian anthropology.

It belongs to the nature of an image to imitate, in some manner and degree, the being and activity of the thing imaged. In classical theology, the relevant being and activity of God were regarded as those of a pure spirit knowing and loving itself. Therefore, of all the creatures of the material universe, man alone can be called the image of God, because man's soul and its faculties for knowing and loving are spiritual (St. Augustine, *Gen. ad litt.* 6, *Corpus scriptorum ecclesiasticorum latinorum,* 28.1:170–200; St. Thomas Aquinas, *Summa theologiae,* 1a, 93.2).

The image of God that is in man by reason of his intellectual nature can be perfected by the "image of re-creation" that is GRACE, and, finally, by the "image of glory" (St. Thomas, *Summa theologiae,* 1a, 93.4). But even the "perfect" image of glory will always be imperfect *as image.* This is because man can never achieve equality or identity of nature with God.

Only the Son is so perfect an image of His Father as to be equal to, and identical in nature with, Him. Hence it is that the WORD is called *the* image of God, while man is said to be created *to* that image. The preposition "to" implies the approach of the image which is distant from the exemplar (St. Thomas, *Summa theologiae,* 1a, 35.1, 2; 93.1, c. and ad 2). This "approach" of the image to the divine exemplar reveals the image as the dynamic source of man's striving toward "the mature measure of the fullness of Christ" (Eph 4.13) and of man's transformation "into his very image from glory to glory" (2 Cor 3.18).

See Also: CREATION; EXEMPLARISM; EXEMPLARY CAUSALITY; LOGOS; MAN, 3.

Bibliography: A. MICHEL, *Dictionnaire de théologie catholique,* ed. A. VACANT et al., 15 v. (Paris 1903–50; Tables générales 1951–) Tables générales 2:2181–86. H. GROSS et al., *Lexikon für Theologie und Kirche²,* ed. J. HOFER and K. RAHNER, 10 v. (2d, new ed. Freiburg 1957–65) 4:1087–92. H. LESÊTRE, *Dictionnaire de la Bible,* ed. F. VIGOUROUX, 5 v. (Paris 1895–1912) 3:843–844. H. CROUZEL, *Catholicisme* 5:1238–40. J. E. SULLIVAN, *The Image of God: The Doctrine of St. Augustine and Its Influence* (Dubuque 1963).

[C. J. CHERESO]

IMAGES, BIBLICAL PROHIBITION OF

Not only metal statues or plaques (Ex 34.17) or gold or silver images (Ex 20.23) representing pagan gods, but images of Yahweh were prohibited by the Mosaic Law (Ex 20.4–5; Dt 5.8–9; Lv 26.1). The OT offers several reasons for this prohibition; e.g., according to Dt 4.15–19 images of Yahweh were forbidden because on Mt. Sinai God did not permit the Israelites to see Him in any form or figure; in Is 40.18–26 the point is made that no image of a creature can depict Yahweh, the Creator of the universe. From various Biblical accounts it is evident that the true worship of God was devoid of images: the ARK OF THE COVENANT, the CHERUBIM above it, and the oxen that supported the bronze sea (1 Kgs 7.23-25) were never considered objects of worship by the Israelites. For a time the bronze serpent (Nm 21.8–9) was venerated with incense, but eventually it, too, was removed from the Temple (2 Kgs 18.4). All other objects, such as the Ephod and the Theraphim (teraphim), found in certain sanctuaries of God were never considered to be objects of divine worship in themselves.

Images, however, occurred in the illegitimate worship of Yahweh, e.g., in that of the Danites (Jgs 17.4–5, 13; 18.24, 30). Although the golden calves of King Jeroboam I of Israel served originally as pedestals upon which the invisible God Yahweh was enthroned, the Israelites later worshiped these as the God (or gods) who liberated them from Egypt (1 Kgs 12.28; Hos 8.5; 13.2; cf. Exodus ch. 32). Eventually Yahweh was reduced to the status of a nature god like BAAL, and these images were stigmatized as foreign gods [1 Kgs 14.9; Ps 105 (106).19–22; 2 Chr11.13–15; 13.8–11]. The deuteronomic reforms of King Josiah of Judah (2 Kgs 23.4–20) purified Israel of all form of idolatry, but illegitimate acts of worship continued until the Fall of Jerusalem (587 B.C.). After the Babylonian Exile images of Yahweh and of strange gods disappeared almost completely among the Jews (Josephus, *Ant.* 18.3.1; 6.2.8).

In the NT, too, the worship of alien gods and idols is prohibited (Acts 15.20, 29; 21.25; Rom 2.22; 1 Cor 5.10; 10.14, 28; 2 Cor 6.16; 1 Thes 1.9; Rev. 9.20). In Christian as in Jewish literature IDOLATRY is a common term of abuse for pagan worship, even though for the pagan the idol was often regarded merely as a symbol of a god and not the god itself and, therefore, not divine.

Bibliography: J. HASPECKER, *Lexikon für Theologie und Kirche*, J. HOFER and K. RAHNER, eds. (Freiburg 1957–65) 2:459–460. G. VON RAD and G. KITTEL, *Theologisches Wörterbuch zum Neuen Testament* (Stuttgart 1935) 2:378–386. B. GEMSER, *Die Religion in Geschichte und Gegenwart* (Tubingen 1957–65) 1:1271–73. J. B. FREY, "La Question des images chez les juifs a la lumière des récentes découvertes," *Biblica* 15 (1934) 265–300.

[C. H. PICKAR]

IMAGES, VENERATION OF

The phrase refers to those exterior acts of honor or reverence directed to God, the angels, or the saints through some artifact of the representative or symbolic arts. Veneration is a religious act, an act of WORSHIP; and images can include not only pictures, ICONS, statues, and symbols, but also ritual acts such as the Sign of the Cross,

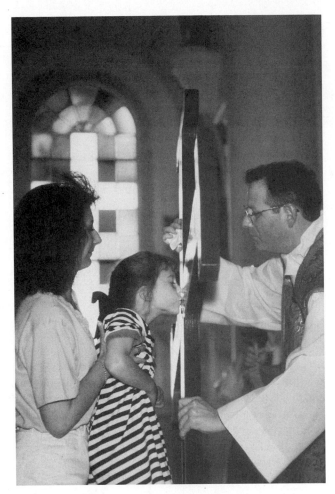

A young congregation member venerates the cross, St. Martin of Tours Catholic Church, St. Martinsville, Louisiana. (©Philip Gould/CORBIS)

the crowning of statues, processions of the cross, the Way of the Cross, and other symbolic acts of worship. The practice of veneration of images has a distinctive and continuous tradition in Christian history, with roots in the Old Covenant, and with natural counterparts in the religious practices of paganism. The doctrinal development is related to the history of religious practice. It is in this broad historical frame of reference from paganism to Christian renewal that the full meaning of the Catholic position on veneration of images can be understood. The following summary traces those parallel lines of development.

The veneration of images is natural to man. The religious practice of veneration of images is related to the natural inclination of man to express his thoughts and feelings in various forms of art. "It is natural for man to imitate" is axiomatic, and its correlative, "Man delights in imitation," assures the spontaneous practice of imitative arts, whether in image-making or in dramatic or ritual acts. Since man has always expressed his most profound thoughts, needs, and desires in art forms, it is normal that man's religious beliefs and sentiments should be channeled through every form of artistic expression. ART is rooted in human nature and sacred art is the expression of religious belief.

Images in Pagan Religions. The pagans employed art forms corresponding to and expressing their beliefs. Some pagans, awed by the phenomena of nature, worshiped the sun, the moon, etc. This worship was expressed in various art forms—ritual dances, offerings, incantations, and the like. These ritual acts themselves became sacred, honored, and venerable because of their association with the gods. Other pagans made use of totems in a form of animal worship. Often they made images of the sacred animals, which they sometimes believed to possess hidden powers and divine qualities worthy of adoration. However, it should be noted that not all paganism involved idol worship, for not every figure was an idol, but was sometimes an image representing or symbolizing a force or power considered to be divine. IDOLATRY is itself a degenerate form of paganism. This was the form of paganism practiced in the Gentile nations surrounding Israel: "They changed the glory of the incorruptible God into the likeness of the image of a corruptible man, and of birds, and of four-footed beasts, and of creeping things" (Rom 1.23). This fact has important bearing on the use of images in the worship of the Chosen People.

Images in the Old Testament. Consideration of the use of images in the Old Testament centers on two factors—the milieu of idolatrous polytheism in which the Old Covenant was established between the Chosen People and the one true God, and the conditions (the Commandments) of that covenant revealed by God. The First Commandment, a condition of the lasting covenant between Yahweh and the Israelites, was "Thou shalt not have strange gods before me. Thou shalt not make to thyself a graven thing, nor the likeness of any thing that is in heaven above, or in the earth below, nor of those things that are in the waters under the earth. Thou shalt not adore them, nor serve them" (Ex 20.3–5). The implication is clear: once God has revealed Himself as the one true God, then in distinction to the Gentiles, Israel was to worship the unseen God; Israel was to avoid paganism; thus, to attempt to represent the God of Israel in idols was an abominable practice in imitation of idolators, but it is not verified by fact that the Israelites understoon the Commandment to be an absolute prohibition of the use of an image in authentic worship of the true God. If "veneration of images" is understood in a broad sense to include not only "graven things," but ritual acts, symbolic representations, and sacred signs, the Old Testament is replete

with sensible representations of divine truth, and these representations were honored, reverenced, and venerated. Far from being condemned by God, the use of sensible material adorned by human art was directed by God, and demanded by Him as integral to the worship due Him. The ARK OF THE COVENANT, a sensible sign of the sacred covenant, was held in honor by the Jews; the temple itself was a sign of the presence of God. Although they were not idols to be adored, they were sacred signs to be reverenced and venerated. Even the use of carved images of creatures was generally not considered forbidden. Great carved figures of beasts (Ez 1.5; 10.20) stood over the Ark of the Covenant itself (Ex 25.18–22; 1 Kgs 6.23–28; 8.6–7). Examples of such images include fruits, flowers, trees, lions, bulls, and others too numerous to mention here (Nm 8.4; 1 Kgs 6.18; 7.36; 10.19–20).

During the Maccabean period, however, a strong reaction arose against the use of any kind of carved image of living creatures (Josephus, *Antiq. Jud.* 1.17. 6.2). It was unlawful to have images or pictures or any representation of a living thing in the temple (Josephus, *De bello Jud.* 1.1.33(4).2; cf. also Tacitus, *Hist.* 5.4). This severe interpretation of the law did not last. Although faithful Israelites always resisted idol worship, the use of images—pictures, symbols, carvings, etc.— continued and became very much a part of the culture of the Jews of the Diaspora.

There are a number of Jewish catacombs, cemeteries, and sarcophagi containing examples of pictures, wall and ceiling paintings, and carved figures of every kind of creature (cf. H. Leclercq, *Manuel d'archéologie chrétienne* 1.4:95–528). That such images had a place of honor can be surmised not only from the fact that they are associated with sacred rituals, but from their association with the very artifacts of worship (e.g., the figures supporting the seven-branched candlestick; see Leclercq, *op. cit.,* 522).

Although such usage does not throw much light on the kind or degree of veneration, or on the doctrinal basis of the practice, it reflects, at least, that these Jews did not consider the use of images—whether pictures or carvings of creatures—or sacred symbolics—whether in material artifacts or ritual acts—as forbidden in the worship of the true God. Further, such an understanding does give historical continuity to the development of Christian art and symbolics in the earliest days of Christianity.

Images in the New Testament. The use of images in early Christian worship cannot now be reasonably questioned in view of the modern discoveries of archeology. Although there were some who doubted the early Christians employed images in worship (e.g., Erasmus), it can no longer be doubted, for the Christian catacombs are veritable galleries of early Christian art. Scenes from the Old and New Testaments, the symbolism of palms, the vine, etc., the CHI-RHO monograms, and even mythological figures adorn the holy chambers of sacred worship and burial. Typical of Old Testament scenes are Daniel in the lion's den, Noah and the ark, and Moses striking the rock. From the New Testament there are the Nativity, the visit of the wise men, the baptism of Jesus, the raising of Lazarus, the marriage feast at Cana, and Christ teaching the Apostles. Examples of symbolism are a woman lifting her hands (symbolizing the Church) and harts drinking from a fountain (flowing from the symbolic Chi-Rho monogram). Among memorials are to be found the Cross, Christ the Good Shepherd, the Madonna, SS. Peter and Paul, and martyrs. (*See* BIBLE CYCLES IN ART; ART, EARLY CHRISTIAN)

Doctrine. Very little was written about the veneration of images during the early period of Christianity. In one sense, then, little is known about the doctrinal basis of veneration as practiced by Christians of that time. Yet the very number of images associated with worship, their location in places of honor, the absence of controversy about images at a time when much religious teaching was aimed at protecting the true faith in the face of public hostility, the casualness of the few references made to images (e.g., St. Ambrose, *Ep.* 2, *Patrologia Latina*, ed. J. P. Migne [Paris 1878–90] 17:821; St. Augustine, *Cons. Evang.*, *Patrologia Latina* 34:1049; Gregory of Tours, *Historia Francorum* 2.17, *Patrologia Latina* 71: 215) all testify to the perfect orthodoxy of their understanding of the use of images. In a sermon St. Basil (d. 379) suggested that painters gave St. Barlaam more honor by making pictures of him than Basil himself could do with words (*Or. in S. Barlaam, Patrologia Graeca.* ed J. P. Migne [Paris 1857–66] 31:488–489). This reveals what must have been the general attitude of early Christians to images. The paintings, etc. were an expression of their thoughts and feelings, and perhaps a better expression than words of the honor and reverence they felt for Christ, the Apostles, the martyrs, and the saints. Far from being an abuse of their faith and worship, the use of images was a spontaneous and reverent expression of their faith in the word of God and their love for Christ, His mother, His Apostles, and His Church. No more doctrinal justification or explanation was needed for a practice that was a simple, normal, instructive, and appealing expression of the true faith.

During the era of development of Christian art after Constantine, when Christians began to build basilicas adorned with mosaics, carvings, and statues, images were venerated with more elaborate ritual. Especially in the East, the means of showing respect and of honoring persons of high station (e.g., reverence to the empty throne as a symbol of civil authority) were employed in the rituals of religious reverence. Thus bows, kisses, incensing, and other ritual acts were used in reverence to images of Christ, the altar, the cross, etc. Such traditions of reverence became fixed ceremonials. Some of the practices spread to Rome and the West, but usually in less elaborate form.

Doctrinally, this era, from Constantine to the eighth century, evidenced no change from the earlier era of Christian worship; but ritually, the practices—now enjoyed in greater freedom, manifested more publicly, and exercised with more elaborate pageantry—were more susceptible to misunderstanding and abuse. That abuses did creep in, and that these did to some degree contributed to the Iconoclast persecutions (726) can hardly be doubted. The Iconoclasts, whether from a misunderstanding of orthodox practice, or from the existence of real abuses, or from political motives, made many charges of idolatry, superstition, and magic in the use of images. (*See* ICONOCLASM).

Nicaea II (787) was the result of the Iconoclast persecutions. The council, in its seventh session, clarified the confusion that had arisen over the ritual use of images in worship and, while correcting excesses, allowed wide range of practice according to the customs of various nations. The council distinguished adoration (λατρεία; in Latin, *latria*), which according to Catholic faith is due only to the divine nature, and the respect and worshipful honor (ἀσπασμὸν καὶ τιμητικὴν προσκύνησιν) given to Our Lady, angels, saints, and holy men. Further, the council made clear that the veneration of images is not directed to the image, but to the person worthy of honor. "For honor paid to an image passes on to its prototype; he who worships an image worships the reality of him who is painted in it" (H. Denzinger, *Enchiridion symbolorum*, ed. A. Schönmetzer [Freiburg 1963] 601). Thus the council defined the doctrinal basis for the pious custom of ancient times. The practice of early Christianity was to continue and be embellished according to the customs of the times, but now with the clear teaching of the Church to direct it and enable it to avoid the excesses of idolatry, superstition, and magic.

The practice of veneration of images, however, awaited the *Summa* of St. Thomas Aquinas to find its place within the total synthesis of Catholic doctrine and, consequently, to find its own fullest explanation. St. Thomas treats of two kinds of worship: *latria*, the adoration due to God alone, and *dulia*, the honor or homage due to distinguished persons. Adoration is an exterior act of the virtue of religion that is directed to God (*Summa theologiae* 2a2ae, 84.1–3). Honor or veneration is a part of the virtue of observance, which pays homage to those in a position of dignity. Thus, the adoration of God and homage to saints are distinct but complementary elements in worship. With regard to the use of images, St. Thomas placed the question within the broader context of sacred signs. He showed the difference between the sign as a thing in itself and the sign as referring to the thing signified. It is as a sign—a category that includes the Sacraments, sacred symbolics, ceremonial rites, etc.—that the use of images should be understood. "There is a twofold movement of the mind toward an image: one toward the image as a thing in itself; another toward the image insofar as it is a representation of something else. . . . Therefore, we must say that no reverence is shown to Christ's image as a thing—for instance, carved or painted wood. . . . It follows therefore that reverence should be shown to it insofar only as it is an image" (*Summa theologiae* 3a, 25.3). Since the worship given to an image reaches and terminates in the person represented, the same type of worship due the person can be rendered to the image as representing the person: the worship of *latria,* to Christ as the Divine Word; *dulia,* to the angels and saints.

Bibliography: H. LECLERCQ, *Manuel d' archéologie chrétienne depuis les origines jusqu'au VIIIe siècle,* 2 v. (Paris 1907). F. X. KRAUS, *Geschichte Handbuch der christlichen Archäologie* (Paderborn 1905). W. PALMER, *An Introduction to Early Christian Symbolism* (London 1885). J. P. REID, *Anatomy of Atheism* (Compact Studies; Washington 1965). D. ROVER, "Poetics of Maritain," *Texts and Studies* (Washington 1965) esp. 68–78. D. SABBATUCCI et al., *Encyclopedia of World Art* (New York 1959–) 4:364–382. M. ELAIDE et al., *ibid.* 382–420. L. RÉAU, *Iconographie de l'art Chrétien,* 6 v. (Paris 1955–59) 1:410–4:15.

[A. D. LEE]

IMAGINATION

From the Lat. *imaginatio* (Gr. φαντασία), the power or faculty of imagining, i.e., of representing in an image or PHANTASM, something past or absent or otherwise inaccessible to the external senses. This article discusses the notion from the viewpoint of Thomistic and modern psychology, with emphasis on the nature of the imagination, its use, and its control.

Thomistic Notion. According to St. Thomas Aquinas (*Summa theologiae* 1a, 78.4), the CENTRAL SENSE (*sensus communis*) forms images of sensible things, and the fantasy or imagination preserves them to be available when needed. The memorative power, by contrast, preserves former estimates of good and bad made by means of the ESTIMATIVE (COGITATIVE) power. Both imagination and memorative power are active as well as passive. They not only receive and preserve what has been experienced before but they also revive these experiences. The imagination revives sense images, whereas the memorative power revives former estimates of the way things affect one. When sense images are revived by the imagination, this can be done in exactly the same sequence and pattern as the original experience so that one reexperiences what has happened before, though it is *recognized as past* through the memorative power. Or, the imagination can recombine sense images in different patterns so that one can experience in imagination what has never been experienced in fact (e.g., a golden mountain).

St. Thomas's use of the term imagination covers what in modern times is called memory, but also what is called fantasy or imagination. And his term *memoria* or memorative power is hardly recognized in modern usage, largely because psychologists do not often engage in an exact analysis of psychological functions. It could be called "affective memory" because the revival of past estimates and the recognition of something as past is affective rather than cognitive in nature.

Uses of Imagination. Modern psychological notions of fantasy and imagination have been influenced by S. Freud's notion that the first psychological activity of the infant consists in fantasy images of wish-fulfilling objects. This "primary process" thinking, Freud says, is used even by the adult whenever wishes are not immediately gratified. But contrary to Freud, imagination is used not only for purposes of wish fulfillment but for almost every action of everyday life. Whenever a person has to do anything that is not strictly repetitive, he imagines what needs to be done and what are likely to be the consequences before he decides on action.

Imagination is used also to supplement memory. Bartlett has shown that a picture, a story, or an experience that cannot be remembered exactly is reproduced by filling in the memory gaps by imagination. When disease has made the recall of memories impossible, as, for instance, in Korsakoff psychosis, imagination takes over altogether and the patient confabulates instead of remembering. During sleep, sense experiences such as warmth, cold, and pressure cannot be identified because the recall of memories is blocked. Consequently, imagination weaves such experiences into dream sequences that may be bizarre and illogical because one cannot check dream imaginings against what he knows to be true, possible, or expedient.

Control of Imagination. Whether in waking life or in dreams, the imaginative process must be directed in some way. When awake and planning action, man directs imagination deliberately to explore various possibilities. In daydreams, he also directs and controls his imagination; but this time, to engage in imaginary actions that offer some emotional satisfaction (the conquering hero dream, or the suffering hero dream). This is the "wish fulfillment" through fantasy of which Freud speaks.

Nondeliberate Direction. In addition to such deliberate control of imagination, there are also imaginative processes that run their appointed course without deliberate direction. The DREAM is the best but not the only example. In writing a story, for instance, the decision to do so merely supplies the impulse to start imagining; it does not direct the creative process. Novelists often say that the story writes itself, that the characters develop a life of their own which unfolds in front of their eyes. And Arnold Schönberg tells how he wrote down the whole of his "String Quartet No. 2" as he heard it in imagination, without stopping or deliberating.

Still, there must be some direction in dreams as well as in products of artistic imagination. For imagination is a cognitive function and can only preserve and reproduce images; it cannot choose them any more than the eye can choose what it will see. Something else must guide the brush and sketch the outline: and that something can be only an appetitive tendency, either deliberate or emotional. This seems to be the will impulse when imagination is used for the purpose of daily life, and emotion when imagination is released from deliberate control (in dreams and stories). Since affective memory, in the modern sense, always accompanies imagination, the emotional attitudes a person has developed as a result of his life experiences are bound to affect and direct his creative efforts. A novelist recreates human life as he sees it and unwittingly passes judgment on his story characters and their actions in the way he lets them live and love, suffer and die.

Creativity. In present-day psychological writings, there is a reawakening of interest in "creativity," though the role of imagination in creative effort is almost forgotten. One reads, for instance, that creativity implies prelogical thought, an "appropriate selection and rejection of available connections" (Roe)—yet it is the hallmark of creative work that available connections are neglected and entirely new ones are hit upon. Surely, creativity implies imagination freed from deliberate control, imagination that is extraordinarily fertile and original. When a man's attitudes are so rigid that they prevent him from looking for the unexpected, the unconventional, his imagination remains fettered and never blossoms into creativity. (*See* CREATIVE IMAGINATION.)

As a human power, imagination is active whenever conditions are favorable. If man does not employ it deliberately, in planning, or creatively, in writing or artistic pursuits, it will call to mind spontaneous images that mirror his desires, emotions, and appetites. A man tormented by hate will be plagued by thoughts of revenge, the lover distracted by the image of his beloved. So also, sexual desire will inevitably arouse tempting images. Since all these images arouse action tendencies, this poses a moral problem (*see* THOUGHTS, MORALITY OF). To avoid taking delight in such unsought fantasies, imagination must be employed in other ways, in absorbing interests, stimulating work. To block fantasy by engaging in exhausting physical effort is rarely effective because imagination will flourish more luxuriantly during enforced rest.

See Also: SENSES; PHANTASM.

Bibliography: M. B. ARNOLD, *Story Sequence Analysis* (New York 1962); "The Internal Senses: Functions or Powers?," *The Thomist* 26 (1963) 15–34. J. A. GASSON, "The Internal Senses: Functions or Powers?" *ibid.* 1–14. H. RUGG, *Imagination* (New York 1963). A. ROE, "The Psychology of the Scientist," *Science* 134 (1961) 456–59. S. FREUD, *New Introductory Lectures on Psychoanalysis,* tr. W. J. H. SPROTT (New York 1933). F. C. BARTLETT, *Remembering* (New York 1932).

[M. B. ARNOLD]

IMĀM

Imām is a substantive from the Arabic verb *amma* meaning to precede, to lead; serving as an example or object of imitation, particularly in prayer. The substantive *imām* may designate a person, or an object serving as a model or guide. The Prophet Muhammad is the imām of the Muslim community. In this sense, the successor to the Prophet, the CALIPH, is the imām of his subjects. The "four imāms" are the founders and heads of the four principal schools of the SUNNITES. In the sense of religious leader, the term is also applied to the great jurisconsults and theologians of Islam, such as ALGAZEL (GHAZZĀLĪ, AL-) and Ibn Taimīya. In the sense of guide, imām is applied to the QU'RAN (sacred scripture of the Muslims) as the guide of the Muslims; it also designates the vulgate of the Qu'ran, the copying of which was ordered by the third caliph, 'Uthmān. In the Qu'ran itself, the term imām is used to designate the scripture of any people. The term was also used to designate the leader who guided travelers, or the driver of camels.

In Muslim constitutional law, the imām is the supreme head of the executive power (*see* ISLAMIC LAW). As such, "the Supreme Imām" (*al-imām al-a'ẓam*) is the title given to the caliph. The function itself is called "the imamate" (*al-imāma*) or "the supreme imamate" (*al-imāma al-'uẓmā*), a term that is synonymous with caliphate (*khilāfa*). The imām is also the person who leads the prayer, and *imāma* is the term applied to that function (originally, the caliph led the prayer). This is not necessarily an official function; any competent Muslim may lead the prayer, and as such would be the imām of the prayer.

Imām is also used by the SHĪ'ITES to designate a legitimate successor of the Caliph 'Alī. Shī'ites Imāms are believed by their followers (currently 9 percent of Islam) to be impeccable; in Shī'ites usage the term takes on mystical and eschatological overtones.

See Also: ISMAILITES.

[G. MAKDISI]

IMBERT, JOSEPH, BL.

Martyr, Jesuit priest, apostolic vicar for the Diocese of Moulins; b. ca. 1720; Marseille, France; d. June 9, 1794 on the *Deux–Associés.* Imbert entered the Jesuits at Avignon (1748), took his first vows (1750), and was ordained (1754). Thereafter he was a teacher at Châlons–sur–Saône, Besançon, and Grenoble until the Society of Jesus was suppressed (1762). He then placed himself under the authority of the bishop of Moulins and accepted parochial responsibilities. Instead of fleeing the country during the persecution, he continued to minister covertly until his bishop was expelled and Imbert appointed apostolic vicar for the diocese. He was arrested (1793) and imprisoned locally until his deportation in early 1794 with 24 diocesan priests. During their several–month journey to the prison ship at Rochefort to await deportation, Father Imbert wrote *The Priests' Marseillaise,* uplifting words to the national anthem of the French Revolution. He was beatified by John Paul II, Oct. 1, 1995, together with other martyrs of La Rochelle.

Feast: Jan. 19 (Jesuits).

See Also: ROCHEFORT SHIPS, MARTYRS OF, BB.

Bibliography: I. GOBRY, *Les martyrs de la Révolution française* (Paris 1989). J. N. TYLENDA, *Jesuit Saints & Martyrs,* 2d ed. (Chicago 1998): 165–167. *Acta Apostolicae Sedis* (1995): 923–926. *L'Osservatore Romano,* no. 40 (1995): 3–5; *Documentation Catholique* 19 (1995): 923–26.

[K. I. RABENSTEIN]

IMITATION OF CHRIST

One of the best-known classics of devotional literature. It is generally claimed to be the work, indeed the chief work, of THOMAS À KEMPIS, but it would be a more accurate expression of scholarly opinion to say simply that this book and the name of Thomas à Kempis are inseparably linked. It is a work that opens the way to an understanding of the spirit of the DEVOTIO MODERNA and of late medieval piety in general and is among the most widely read books in the whole of world literature. It has appeared in innumerable editions and has been translated into more than 50 different languages. This accounts for the great attention that has been given to the problem of its authorship—a problem that was first raised shortly after the death of Thomas à Kempis and is still discussed. The many editions and translations testify that the question of authorship has not detracted from the attention given to its content. On the contrary, the controversies about its origin appear to have stimulated an ever increasing interest in the *Imitation* itself, and the counsel of the author—"Ask not who said this, but give your attention to what is said; for men pass away, but the truth of the Lord abides forever"—has not been entirely unheeded. After reviewing the controversy about the authorship, Lucidius Verschueren, OFM, expressed satisfaction that not only was the *Imitation* being debated, but that its contents were being taken to heart.

Authorship. If anything is to be said about the origin, composition, sources, and inspiration of the *Imitation,* the problem of authorship must be faced. Among the first to discuss the question was Nicholas of Winghe, the earliest translator of the *Imitation,* who in 1548 published a Dutch version. (It can be safely assumed that the Latin text is to be considered the original.) Winghe opposed the claim that Jean GERSON, chancellor of the University of Paris, was the author. In this he was supported by Heribert Rosweydus, who in his *Vindiciae Kempenses* (1617) and later in his treatise *Certissima testimonia a quibus Thomas a Kempis asseritur auctor librorum de Imitatione Christi* concluded that the book was written by à Kempis. His argument was based on the testimony of John Busch, chronicler of Windesheim, and the abbot, TRITHEMIUS. Rosweydus's work was written in reaction to a claim to the authorship made on behalf of the Italian abbot, Giovanni Gersen, to whom the work was attributed in certain old Italian MSS of the *Imitation.*

From the beginning of the 17th century onward, there appeared a long succession of controversial works on the question of authorship, and even by 1965 the controversy was not completely settled. The discussion waxed keen during the 19th century, and as late as the end of the century various works were being published defending the authorship of Thomas à Kempis with sound arguments. The evangelical theologian Karl Hirsche, the Catholic theologian O. A. Spitzen, and J. B. Malou, Bishop of Ghent, defended the authorship of Thomas à Kempis vigorously and incisively. About the turn of the century a period of silence began, and it appeared as if the opinion in favor of Thomas à Kempis had become generally and firmly established. However, the authorship of Giovanni Gersen was still being advocated by P. E. Puyol, and that of Jean Gerson by J. B. Monneyeur.

More impressive, however, was the series of writings published after 1925 by J. van Ginneken, SJ, favoring the view that not Thomas à Kempis but Gerard GROOTE was author of the famous work. Van Ginneken's thesis was that Thomas à Kempis only formulated and edited posthumously the diary notes of Groote, and this version was later erroneously taken to be an original work of Thomas à Kempis himself. According to Van Ginneken, the original text existed before Thomas à Kempis came to work upon it. This idea was adopted and further developed by Fritz and Liselotte Kern, who tried to reconstruct the text that supposedly preceded that of Thomas à Kempis.

L. M. J. Delaissé brought the problem closer to a solution with his basic and detailed study *Le Manuscrit autographe de Thomas a Kempis (MS Bruxellensis 5855–5861) et l'Imitation de Jésus-Christ.* First, he rather satisfactorily ruled out the authorship of Giovanni Gersen and of Jean Gerson. Second, he convincingly proved that there never was a pre-Kempian text of the *Imitation* as a whole. On the basis of a profound archeological analysis of the Brussels manuscript, Delaissé showed it probable that Thomas à Kempis wrote 13 short and independent treatises (*libelli*) and brought them together in one and the same codex. Afterward he conscientiously and thoroughly rewrote the text of each of these treatises and, as it were, made them ready for the press. Therefore, this codex (*MS Bruxellensis* 5855–5861) is an autograph that makes it possible to bring the problem of the origin of the *Imitation* closer to solution. In it are found four treatises that came—at a time when printing was not in common use everywhere—to be copied together. They thus came to be considered as one coherent work to which the name *De Imitatione Christi* was given, drawn from the thought expressed in the first words of chapter one of the first treatise: "Qui sequitur me non ambulat in tenebris, dicit Dominus. Haec sunt verba Christi quibus ammonemur quatenus vitam eius et mores imitemur." When at a later date this collection of the four *libelli* came to be printed, the same tradition was adopted. Thus, not only the title of the book, but also the book itself in its familiar form does not date back to Thomas à Kempis; however, the four *libelli* are by his hand.

Sources. Thomas à Kempis drew from a number of sources. In the first place, he drew from the New Testament, as Gerard Groote had already commended: "Radix studii tui et speculum vitae sint primo evangelium Christi, quia ibi est vita Christi." Second, Thomas drew from the writings that were being read at the time in the circles of the Devotio Moderna and were therefore at his disposal. Enough is known about the copying of MSS done by the Brethren of the Common Life and the religious of the Windesheim Congregation to justify the assumption that a series of more or less complete manuscripts of devotional works were available to Thomas. Among these

Thomas à Kempis. (©Michael Nicholson/CORBIS)

were the *Collationes patrum* of John CASSIAN and the *Vitae patrum,* a collection of monastic biographies. Both works were very much read among the *devoti* (as is shown in the chronicle of the Augustinian chapter-house at Frenswegen). The study of these works had also been recommended by Gerard Groote. In the *Imitation,* Thomas mentions his sources only in a number of cases in which he deals with passages from the Bible, but through studies of certain sections it has been established that, besides the more than a thousand Biblical passages pointed out by M. J. Pohl, there are also indications of the influence of the great masters of the spiritual life upon Thomas in his writing of the *Imitation;* especially noticeable is that of St. Bernard of Clairvaux, whose sermons, and particularly his *Sermones in canticum,* were greatly esteemed by the *devoti.* In addition, some other writings, mistakenly attributed to St. Bernard, very probably exercised an influence on the *Imitation.* Among these were the *Speculum monachorum* (also called *Speculum Bernardi* or *Speculum peccatorum*), the *Meditationes,* and the *Epistola ad fratres de Monte Dei* of William of Saint-Thierry. All these works are recorded in biographies of *devoti* as being among their daily reading matter; for example, in the *Conclusa et proposita* of Gerard Groote and in the chronicle of Frenswegen. Furthermore, the *Speculum monachorum* of David of Augsburg and the *Scala paradisi* of John Climacus deserve mention. Both works were much read, often quoted, and parts of their text have found a place in various *rapiaria.* Of the older texts, the *Homiliae* of Gregory the Great and his *Moralia in Job* should receive particular mention.

The library of the brethren in Deventer undoubtedly included copies of these works, and considering the scriptorial activity of the *devoti,* which contributed much to the circulation of these works, one has the right to assume that they were also to be found at Mount St. Agnes, the monastery near Zwolle where Thomas wrote the *Imitation.* Among the works mentioned in the chronicle of the brethren's house at Emmerich as copied by the *devoti* at Deventer during Thomas's life were: the *Horologium aeternae sapientiae* of Henry Suso (which was much read and frequently quoted in the circle of the Devotio Moderna), the *Dialogus miraculorum* of Caesarius of Heisterbach, the *Vitae patrum,* the *Libellum de arte moriendi* (another name for the *Quattuor novissima* of Dionysius the Carthusian), *et multa huiusmodi quibus usque hodie layci nostri utuntur,* as the chronicle of Emmerich says. It is not likely that all these works were available to Thomas in their complete version. It is rather to be assumed that he partly used spiritual notebooks (or *rapiaria,* as they were called among the *devoti*) that included extensive quotations from these works. Thus, for example, the *Omnes, inquit, artes* of Florentius Radewijns was a *rapiarium* that belonged to the inventory of every house of the brethren and of the Augustinian house of Windesheim. The treatises of Gerard Zerbolt of Zutphen, equally familiar to Thomas, can also in part be traced back to this work. Finally, the affinity of the *Imitation* with the two works of Gerard Groote, the Dicta and the *Conclusa et proposita non vota,* should be noted.

As yet no systematic investigation has been undertaken to discover all the sources not mentioned by name in the *Imitation.* This would be no simple task, since Thomas, following the medieval manner of quoting, did not, in most cases, reproduce the exact text of the source. This style of quotation was used not because the writer wished to conceal his source, but because he had to use texts that had perhaps been altered or incorrectly quoted by other authors, or because he had made the original text his own by way of personal assimilation.

Content. It is impossible to summarize the contents of the *Imitation* in a few lines. The book shows that Thomas, like other *devoti,* was moved by a strong desire to serve and to imitate Christ. This ideal permeates all his thoughts and his whole life in all its manifestations. The *Imitation* has opened the way to a more personal and inner life of faith for many people, especially for those who want to renew their spiritual lives without contract-

ing permanent ties in a religious community. The *Imitation* was intended to strengthen them in their striving for communion with God and in their effort to prepare themselves for eternal life. The first book contains admonitions useful to the spiritual life and deals with the means of liberating oneself from worldly inclinations and of preparing for conversation with God. The second book contains an appeal and admonitions to promote the interior life that leads to conversation with God and the interior consolation of the third book, starting with the words: "audiam quid loquatur in me Dominus Deus." The fourth book urges the reader to receive Holy Communion in a devout manner. The *Imitation* has impressively summarized the religious attitude of the Devotio Moderna and given it its most representative expression. In this light it is possible to explain its impact upon later generations. The renewal in spiritual life brought about by the Devotio Moderna did not come from the introduction of new ideas opposed by the Church or contrary to its doctrine. On the contrary, the movement aimed at leading people closer to God within the Church. Although Protestants, as well as Catholics, have found inspiration in it, it is incorrect to speak of a unilateral continuity between the Devotio Moderna and Protestantism.

Bibliography: W. JAPPE ALBERTS, "Zur Historiographie der Devotio Moderna und ihrer Erforschung," in F. PETRI and W. JAPPE ALBERTS, *Gemeinsame Probleme deutsch-niederländischer Landes-und Volksforschung* (Groningen 1963) 144–171, discussion of much of the lit. on the *Imitatio. Thomae Hemerken a Kempis opera omnia,* ed. M. J. POHL, 7 v. (Freiburg 1902–22), v.2 contains the *Imitatio,* v.7:87–109 contains G. Groote, *Conclusa et proposita non vota.* S. AXTERS, *Geschiedenis van de Vroomheid in de Nederlanden,* 3 v. (Antwerp 1950–56), v.3 for *Devotio Moderna,* 3:170–198 on Thomas à Kempis, an excellent work; *The Spirituality of the Old Low Countries,* tr. D. ATTWATER (London 1954). R. R. POST, *Kerkgeschiedenis van Nederland in de Middeleeuwen,* 2 v. (Utrecht 1957) 1:367–414, a clear, orderly discussion of the spirituality and writings of the *Devotio Moderna.* A. HYMA, *The Brethren of Common Life* (Grand Rapids, Mich. 1950); Hyma's thesis that Gerard Zerbolt is the author of the first book of the *Imitatio* is rejected by several scholars, such as P. Grootens and B. Spaapen. See *Ons Geestelijk Erf* 25 (1951) 300; 28 (1954) 91. G. BONET-MAURY, *Quaeritur e quibus nederlandicis fontibus hauserit scriptor libri cui titulus est "De Imitatione Christi," 1384–1464* (Paris 1878). J. J. VAN GINNEKEN, *De navolging van Christus naar de oudsten teksten in de authentieke volgorde bewerkt* (Amsterdam 1944); Van Ginneken's ideas are disputed by many authors. L. M. J. DELAISSÉ, *Le Manuscrit autographe de Thomas à Kempis et "L'Imitation de Jésus-Christ": Examen archéologique et édition diplomatique du Bruxellensis 5855–61,* 2 v. (Brussels 1956), reviewed by R. POST, in *Bijdragen voor de geschiedenis der Nederlanden* 13 (1958) 59–62, and E. F. JACOB, *English Historical Review* 75 (1960) 302–303. M. VAN WOERKUM, "Het libellus *Omnes, inquit, artes* een rapiarium van Florentius Radewijns," *Ons Geestelijk Erf* 25 (1951) 113–158, 225–268, esp. important for the literary sources of the Imitatio. W. JAPPE ALBERT and A. L. HULSHOFF, *Het Frensweger handschrift betreffende de geschiedenis van de Moderne devotie*

(Groningen 1958), text of the chronicle of the Augustinian chapterhouse at Frenswegen, with extensive bibliog.

[W. JAPPE ALBERTS]

IMMA, BL.

Known also as Emma, Imina, Immina, Benedictine abbess; d. *c.* 750. According to a 12th-century life of St. BURCHARD, Bp. of Würzburg, she was the daughter of Hetan II, Duke of Thuringia, who built a church on the Burgberg (known later as Marienburg) that dominated the city of Würzburg. Here Imma established a Benedictine monastery that she later gave to Burchard in exchange for a location at Karlsburg-on-Main (Karlstadt) a few miles north. Her burial there is noted in a 9th-century martyrology. After the destruction of this house in 1236, her relics were transferred on October 27 of that year to the choir of the cathedral in Würzburg. Exhumed in 1700 to be placed in a new reliquary, they disappeared. The village of Himmelstadt (*Imminestat* given in 840 by Louis I the Pious to the bishopric of Würzburg) is named for Bl. Imma.

Feast: Nov. 25 or Dec. 10.

Bibliography: *Acta Santorum* Oct. 6:584–585. J. MABILLON, *Annales ordinis S. Benedicti*, 6 v. (Lucca 1739–45) 2:138–139. W. SCHATZ, *Lexikon für Theologie und Kirche*, ed. J. HOFER and K. RAHNER, 10 v. (2d, new ed. Freiburg 1957–65) 5:629.

[W. E. WILKIE]

IMMACULATE CONCEPTION

The term "Immaculate Conception" designates the belief that the Virgin Mary was free from ORIGINAL SIN from the very beginning of her life, i.e., from her conception. The rest of mankind inherits a human nature infected with sin, because of the Fall of ADAM, from whom the human race takes its origin. Each person is delivered from this original sin only by his adherence to Christ, the Redeemer. But Mary was, by a unique GRACE, preserved from ever contracting original sin; she inherited human nature in an untainted condition and hence is said to have been conceived immaculate. This privilege, designed to make her a suitable mother for Christ, was given her in view of His future merits.

The Church holds that the Immaculate Conception was included in the body of doctrine originally entrusted to the Apostles and transmitted by them to the Church (*see* DEPOSIT OF FAITH); otherwise it could not now be made a matter of faith. But this does not imply that the Apostles received an explicit instruction on the matter. If the doctrine of the Immaculate Conception was, in the beginning, only a hidden implication contained in other more express teachings, and destined to be perceived and brought out into the open only after the gospel had germinated in the Christian mind and brought forth fruit through centuries of meditation, this would suffice to make the Immaculate Conception part of the Apostolic teaching in the sense required by the Church.

Scriptural and Apostolic Teaching. Historical research indicates that such was, in fact, the case. For, in the first place, Scripture makes no direct reference to Mary's conception. Some hold that her absolute sinlessness is referred to in Gn 3.15: "I will put enmity between you and the woman, between your seed and her seed: he shall crush your head, and you shall lie in wait for his heel." Pope Pius IX cited this text as a prophecy of the Immaculate Conception (*Ineffabilis Deus, Acta Pii IX* 1.1:607). This text by itself, however, would hardly suffice to make the doctrine known. The Immaculate Conception needs to be established on some other basis, and then may be seen as included in the broad reference of Gn 3.15.

Much confusion has resulted from the fact that the second half of this verse was inaccurately translated in the Vulgate to read, "*She* shall crush your head." This translation, which has strongly affected the traditional representations of the Blessed Virgin, is today generally recognized to be a mistake for "it [or 'he,' i.e., the seed of the woman] shall crush," and consequently can no longer be cited in favor of the Immaculate Conception. (*See* PROTO-EVANGELIUM.)

The words of Gabriel, "Hail, full of grace" (Lk 1.28), have also been appealed to as a revelation of the Immaculate Conception, on the grounds that to be truly full of grace, Mary must have had it always. This interpretation, however, overlooks the fact that the Greek term κεχαριτωμένη is not nearly so explicit as the translation "full of grace" might suggest. It implies only that God's favor has been lavished on Mary, without defining the degree of grace.

But even though the Immaculate Conception is not taught explicitly in Scripture, the question must be considered whether it may not have belonged to the oral teaching of the Apostles and been recorded only later on. Historical evidence, however, is against such a supposition, as will be clear from the discussion that follows.

Explicit belief in the Immaculate Conception seems to have arisen in the Church as an application or specification of the general doctrine of Mary's holiness. Chapters 1 and 2 of Luke (confirmed by ch. 1 of Mt) represent Mary as an exceptionally holy person. They also seem to

"The Immaculate Conception," 14th- or 15th-century manuscript painting by a Flemish artist from "The Life of Our Lady." This drawing is one of the earliest representations of the Immaculate Conception in art.

relate her holiness to her being chosen as Christ's Mother: "thou hast found grace with God. And behold, thou shalt conceive" (Lk 1.30–31). It is clear that only a flawless holiness would be in any way proportionate to the sacredness of her office. To determine just how far such considerations can take one is a delicate task. They must be considered against the background of God's universal demand for holiness on the part of those who draw near to Him (see 1 Pt 1.16) and the thoroughly biblical doctrine that it is God who calls and fashions His saints according to His good pleasure (Rom ch. 8, 9). Mary's virginity, which must be viewed in a Christian perspective, and the miracle by which God preserved it, even when calling her to motherhood, are signs of the extraordinary way in which divine grace fitted her for her vocation. That these indications, taken together, imply an incomparable holiness in Mary that was not only actual at the moment of the ANNUNCIATION, but extended back to the very beginning of her life, is a judgment that the

Church has made—but only after the way had been prepared by centuries of reflection, clarification, and discussion. There were two phases to the historical process: first, development of an adequate appreciation of the immensity of Mary's holiness in general; second, realization that this holiness included her initial preservation from all taint of sin.

Early Development. The earliest Church Fathers regarded Mary as holy but not as absolutely sinless. Origen and some of his followers assumed that she had been imperfect like other human beings. But as time went on, the thought of her became more and more characterized in the mind of the Church by the note of holiness—a tendency that was powerfully stimulated in the East by the Council of EPHESUS (431), when it ratified her title MOTHER OF GOD. By the 8th century, belief that her holiness was both flawless and immense was firmly established throughout the Byzantine world. In the Latin West, the same development took place more slowly; but by 1099 St. Anselm was writing, "it was fitting that she be clothed with a purity so splendid that none greater under God could be conceived" (*De conceptu virginali* 18).

Such affirmations arose, not from a clear concept or definite thesis about the degree of her grace, but from an obscure yet powerful impulse of Christian hearts to attribute to her the greatest holiness and glory compatible with her status as a creature. This was not mere pious wishfulness, but the germination of the Gospel teaching in souls that had incarnated the truths of faith in their own lives, and now experienced the inherent demands of these truths in their own inclinations.

The further specification that Mary had never been tainted by sin, not even at the first moment of her existence, came to be affirmed quite spontaneously, as a natural part of this same development. The affirmation appears first in the East, without emphasis, in the course of general eulogies of the holiness of the Mother of God. Usually it is expressed only by vague and sometimes indirect references. There seems to have been little reflection upon the difficulty of reconciling such a teaching with the doctrine of original sin, and no great issue was ever made of the point. It is impossible to give a precise date when the belief was held as a matter of faith, but by the 8th or 9th century it seems to have been generally admitted. After the separation of the Eastern Church from Rome, the belief gradually languished (although it appeared as late as the 15th century, in George Scholarios [Gennadius II], d. *c.* 1472) and finally disappeared altogether from the Byzantine tradition, so that to the Greek Orthodox theologians of the 19th century, the doctrine of Pius IX appeared as an innovation.

Theological Objections in Medieval West. Meanwhile, however, the belief had been transplanted to the Western Church by means of a feast in honor of Mary's conception. This feast had originated before 700 (probably in the monasteries of Syria) and had since spread throughout the Byzantine world. It reached England—no one knows exactly how—around 1050, but was suppressed during the reform of the Anglo-Saxon Church under William the Conqueror (reign 1066–87). When it was revived in spite of some protests a few decades later (about 1125), an argument ensued, in which, for the first time, the character of Our Lady's conception became the direct subject of critical discussion. It was through this discussion that the idea of Mary's Immaculate Conception was gradually brought to general attention, clarified, and eventually accepted in the Church.

In the beginning, the argument bore directly on the question whether it was right to celebrate the new feast, and only incidentally on the question of Mary's sinlessness. (It must be kept in mind that the feast itself did not represent Mary's conception precisely as immaculate, but merely honored the event.) Gradually, however, the argument came to focus on the issue of an Immaculate Conception. The earliest extant defense of the feast, and also of belief in a sinless conception for Mary, is a charming and naive, yet substantial little treatise, *De conceptione B. Virginis Mariae,* composed (1123?, 1139?) by the English monk Eadmer (*Patrologia Latina,* ed. J. P. Migne, 271 v., indexes 4 v. [Paris 1878–90] 159:301–318; critical ed. H. Thurston and T. Slater [Freiburg im Breisgau 1904]). The classic condemnation of the feast (and of the belief) is a letter from St. Bernard of Clairvaux to the canons of the Cathedral at Lyons in 1140 or thereabouts (Letter 174, *Patrologia Latina* 182:332–336). Bernard argues that the Holy Spirit could not have been involved in anything so inherently evil as the conception of a child.

The scholastic theologians began to interest themselves seriously in the question at Paris about a third of the way through the 13th century. Their discussions were complicated by the biological notion, then prevalent, that the human soul is not infused into the fetus until 40 or 80 days after its conception. They were handicapped also by a lingering tendency to imagine original sin as a quality infecting the body even prior to the soul's advent. Hence, they posed the question in terms of three possibilities: whether the Blessed Virgin had been sanctified (and hence made free from original sin) before, after, or at the very instant of the infusion of the soul into her body.

At first, the theologians were practically unanimous in declaring that Mary could not have been sanctified until *after* the infusion of the soul into her body; hence they held that she must have been subject to original sin prior to that moment. The reasons for rejecting the possibility of an earlier sanctification were various, but the crucial one was thus formulated by St. Thomas: "If the soul of the Blessed Virgin had never been stained with the contagion of original sin, this would have detracted from Christ's dignity as the savior of all men" (*Summa theologiae* 3a, 27.2 ad 2). For she would not have needed the Redemption that Christ brings; hence He would not be, as Scripture says He is, the savior of all men (cf. 1 Tm 4.10). St. Thomas concludes: "The Blessed Virgin indeed contracted original sin, but was cleansed from it before her birth" (*ibid.*). For the view that St. Thomas did not intend to deny the Immaculate Conception as the Church defines it, see N. Del Prado, *Divus Thomas et bulla dogmatica "Ineffabilis Deus"* (Fribourg 1919); P. Lumbreras, "St. Thomas and the Immaculate Conception," *Homiletic and Pastoral Review* 24 (1924) 253–263.

The Paris theologians were not insensitive to the general inclination of Christendom to credit Mary with the greatest possible sanctity. On the contrary, they testified to it. St. Thomas declared that she enjoyed a fullness of grace surpassing any other under Christ (*Summa theologiae* 3a, 27.5), and others expressed similar views. All these theologians tended to reduce to the minimum the length of time during which they supposed Mary had been under the stain of original sin. But they hesitated to say that she had been completely exempted from sin for fear of jeopardizing another doctrine of the faith, the universality of the REDEMPTION.

Scotus's Solution, Spread of Explicit Acceptance. Acceptance of the doctrine of the Immaculate Conception in the Church came about, not as the result of any decisive demonstration, but in consequence of the elimination of the obstacle that was holding back the natural inclination of Christians to believe it. That is to say, the doctrine was shown not to be in contradiction with the doctrine of the universal Redemption. John DUNS SCOTUS (*c.* 1264–1308), a Franciscan from Oxford, was chiefly responsible for this. He argued that if Mary had been preserved from original sin, this would not have freed her from dependence on Christ's redemptive work; on the contrary, "Mary more than anyone else would have needed Christ as her Redeemer, since she would have contracted original sin . . . if the grace of the Mediator had not prevented this. Thus, as others needed Christ so that the sin already contracted should be remitted for them through His merit, so Mary had even greater need of a prevenient Mediator lest there be sin to be contracted and lest she contract it" (*In 3 sentences* 3.1, "Per illud patet" [Vivès 14:171]; cf. C. Balič, *I. D. Scoti theologiae marianae elementa* [Sibenik 1933] 35).

The intervention of Duns Scotus seems to have been the factor that turned the tide of theological opinion in favor of the belief. Not, of course, at once; a controversy was to rage for centuries over the matter, embittered by the fact that those who opposed the Immaculate Conception felt that the faith itself was at stake, while its defenders regarded it as a matter of loyal devotion to the Mother of God. But as generations reflected prayerfully on the question, the doctrine of the Immaculate Conception steadily gained adherents, as the position more in accord with the profound exigencies of the Christian faith. By the end of the 17th century, scarcely any question was raised about it anymore.

Meanwhile, the great Thomistic commentator, Cajetan (1469–1534), gave the discussion a new direction by asserting that the Immaculate Conception could be reconciled with the universal Redemption only on condition that one acknowledge in Mary a *debitum peccati,* that is, an inherent tendency toward original sin, although not its actuality. This would explain why she would have con-

tracted original sin had it not been for the intervention of grace (*De conceptione B. Mariae Virginis ad Leonem X* [*Opuscula omnia,* Venice 1580, 2.1:71–73]). This notion of a *debitum* in Mary has been variously interpreted and bitterly debated. Cajetan himself modified his first notion in his commentary on *Summa theologiae* 3a, 27.2, no. 7. The question whether a *debitum peccati* should be postulated in Our Lady remains today one of the principal points of theological controversy on the subject of the Immaculate Conception. See J. Bonnefoy, OFM, "La negacion del *debitum peccati* en Maria. Sintesis historica," *Verdad y Vita* 12 (1954) 103–171.

Popes and Dogmatic Definition. The popes at first, and for a long time, left the question of the Immaculate Conception, like so many other theological disagreements, open for free discussion. From time to time, however, the heat of the controversy obliged them to intervene in order to protect the peace of the Church. When this occurred, they tended to assume more and more decidedly the role of defenders of the belief against its attackers. Thus Sixtus IV, in 1482 and 1483, forbade the accusation of heresy to be used by either side in the dispute when it was being used chiefly by the opponents of the belief; he had given permission for a liturgical office of the Conception (1477 and 1480). This had the effect of reassuring proponents of the belief, and led to an outburst of artistic representations, above all in Spain, where the classical iconography of the Immaculate Conception became fixed during the 17th century (MURILLO [1617–82]).

During the 17th century, numerous requests for a favorable definition of the belief were firmly declined by the popes. Gregory XV declared, "The Holy Spirit, although besought by the most constant prayers, has not yet opened to His Church the secrets of this mystery" (see O'Connor, 306). After a peaceful 18th century, the 19th began with a new campaign of requests, as devotion to the belief continued to grow. This devotion was further stimulated by the MIRACULOUS MEDAL apparitions in Paris in 1830. The Sixth Provincial Council of Baltimore made the Immaculate Conception the patronal feast of the United States, 1846. POPE PIUS IX (1846–78), almost immediately after his election, undertook a series of acts in favor of the belief, and in 1854, after consultation with all the bishops of the Church as well as several theological committees, defined the dogma of faith: "the doctrine," he said, "which holds that the most Blessed Virgin Mary was preserved from all stain of original sin in the first instant of her Conception, by a singular grace and privilege of almighty God, in consideration of the merits of Jesus Christ, savior of the human race, has been revealed by God and must, therefore, firmly and constantly be believed by all the faithful" (H. Denzinger, *Enchi-*

ridion symbolorum, ed. A. Schönmetzer [32d ed. Freiburg 1963] 2803). The text of the definition was published and explained in the encyclical letter of that same year, *Ineffabilis Deus* (*Acta Pii IX* 1.1:616).

See Also: DOCTRINE, DEVELOPMENT OF; MARY, BLESSED VIRGIN, ARTICLES ON.

Bibliography: A. MICHEL, *Dictionnaire de théologie catholique,* ed. A. VACANT et al., 15 v. (Paris; Tables générales 1951–) 2:2193–2214. "Unbefleckte Emfängnis Mariä," *Lexikon für Theologie und Kirche,* ed. J. HOFER and K. RAHNER, 10 v. (2d, new ed. Freiburg 1957–65) v. 10. K. H. SCHELKLE and O. SEMMELROTH, H. FRIES, ed., *Handbuch theologischer Grundbegriffe,* 2 v. (Munich 1962–63) 2:111–122. CONGRESSO MARIOLOGICO INTERNATIONALE, *Virgo Immaculata: acta congressus mariologicimariani Romae anno 1954 celebrati,* ed. C. BALIČ, 18 v. (Rome 1955–56). M. JUGIE, *L'Immaculée conception dans l'Écriture Sainte et dans la tradition orientale* (Rome 1952). E. D. O'CONNOR, ed., *The Dogma of the Immaculate Conception* (Notre Dame, Ind. 1958). J. B. CAROL, *A History of the Controversy over the "debitum peccati"* (St. Bonaventure, N.Y. 1978).

[E. D. O'CONNOR]

IMMACULATE CONCEPTION, DAUGHTERS OF MARY OF THE

(D.M., Official Catholic Directory #0860), a congregation founded in New Britain, Conn., in 1904 by the Rev. Lucian Bojnowski. Wishing to help orphaned children and at the same time to commemorate in a special way the golden jubilee (1904) of the proclamation of the dogma of the Immaculate Conception, Bojnowski gathered together a group of devout sodalists of his parish and formed the nucleus of the community. The sisters adopted royal blue for the color of their habit and the miraculous medal as their official emblem. In 1939 the congregation was raised to the status of a pontifical institute. The sisters are concentrated in the Middle Atlantic states. The generalate is in New Britain, CT.

[M. L. PERZANOWSKI]

IMMACULATE CONCEPTION, MISSIONARY SISTERS OF THE

(SMIC, Official Catholic Directory #2760), a pontifical institute founded in Santarém, Brazil, in 1910 by Bp. Amandus Bahlmann, OFM (d. 1939). The congregation follows the rule of the Third Order Regular of St. Francis. Elizabeth Tombrock, a German schoolteacher who became Mother Maria Immaculata of Jesus, and four Conceptionist nuns exclaustrated by papal indult from Ajuda Convent in Rio de Janeiro, Brazil, made up the first community. Mother Immaculata, the first superior general,

died on April 23, 1938, in Allegany, N.Y., where the congregation had made its first U.S. foundation in 1922. The sisters staff schools, hospitals and other healthcare facilities, and centers for catechetical instruction and for social work. The generalate is in Paterson, NJ.

[J. B. CAROL]

IMMACULATE CONCEPTION BROTHERS

Or Maastricht Brothers (*Congregatio Fratrum Immaculatae Conceptionis,* FIC), a congregation founded at Maastricht, Netherlands, by Louis Rutten (1809–91), a secular priest, and Jacob Hoecken (1810–80), a layman. Papal approval came in 1848 and 1870. The brothers have taught in schools, cared for orphans, and nursed the sick. Missions were opened in South America, Africa and Asia. In all these missions the brothers teach boys, especially in secondary schools, and also direct training schools for teachers.

[W. UBACHS/EDS.]

IMMACULATE HEART OF MARY

Devotion to the Immaculate Heart of Mary has always been closely associated with devotion to the Sacred Heart of Jesus. It has, however, a distinct history, a distinct essential nature, and a distinct and specific purpose among spiritual devotions.

Since 1942, when PIUS XII solemnly consecrated the world to the Immaculate Heart of Mary, this devotion has been incorporated into the official liturgical worship of the Church. In 1944, to commemorate this special consecration, Pius XII extended the solemn feast to the universal Church, naming August 22 as the new feast date and giving it a proper liturgical formulary.

History. Devotion to the heart of the MOTHER OF GOD can be traced to the commentaries of the Fathers on the *Sponsa* of the Song of Songs. However, although the heart of Mary is twice mentioned in the Gospel of Luke, there is no indication of any truly significant devotion of this nature in the early centuries of Christian history. It was not until the 16th century, and notably in the 17th, under St. John Eudes, that there arose a widespread devotional practice honoring Mary's heart. In 1805, Pius VII granted general approbation for the celebration of a special feast by any diocese or religious institute that desired to adopt it.

In recent times, devotion to Our Lady of Fatima and new theological studies have brought the devotion into

The Immaculate Heart of Mary. (©Andrea Jemolo/CORBIS)

prominence, and the special recognition of Pius XII has established it as a singularly worthy form of consecration.

Meaning. The heart of Mary is the material object of this devotion, and it is from the material object that its title is derived. It is however, the formal object, namely, Mary's love, that gives the devotion its true meaning and significance.

All forms of Marian cult, of course, whether they look to some particular mystery in the life of Our Lady, or to some special attribute, have in common a single object—the person of Mary. Devotion to the heart of the Mother of God is most fitting, therefore, since veneration is directed toward an object that symbolizes and encompasses all the qualities that are predicated of her.

In a very real sense, the heart of the Virgin played an important role in her physical maternity and is associated directly with the affections of her maternal soul. The splendor of Mary's sanctity and the great mysteries of her life, especially that of the divine maternity, are closely related to her love, and since the word "heart" frequently has a symbolic or metaphorical meaning, devotion to the Immaculate Heart of Mary is properly understood to include and represent Mary's entire sanctity and inner life, along with her various gifts and perfections, all related intimately to her love.

The Church considers it fitting to approve for veneration objects that are sensible manifestations of spiritual truth, for man himself is composed of elements both sensible and spiritual. It is, therefore, appropriate that a physical element, such as Mary's heart, be chosen to objectify the great charity or love of the Mother of God.

Finally, in any Marian devotion a threefold homage is rendered to Mary. Honor is paid to her maternity, her sanctity, and her role in the redemptive mission of Christ, her Son. Since each of the three is inseparably associated with her love, and is thus truly reflected in her heart, the Church has further reason for fostering this devotion.

Beyond what it obviously incorporates and symbolizes, devotion to the Immaculate Heart has as a prime purpose the recognition of the special instrumentality of Mary in the bringing of souls to God. This is achieved in the practice of the devotion through two acts, themselves part of the devotion—the acts of consecration and reparation.

Since one is consecrated to Mary only because she is the Mother of God and closely associated through her Queenship with the Deity, such a consecration is always referred ultimately to God Himself. Proper foundation for a consecration to Mary, however, is to be sought in her dominion over and concern for her spiritual children.

This is typified in her Queenship, and the better this is understood, the more evident becomes the dignity of the act of consecration, and the more clear all that is implied in it. It is significant, therefore, that the opening words of the formula of consecration employed by Pius XII in the world consecration ceremonies of 1942 directly concern Mary's sovereignty and call upon her as "Queen."

A true and complete act of consecration is actually a state in which the faithful are totally and perpetually dedicated to the Heart of Mary, entrusting to her all that they have and are. For this reason the act of consecration constitutes a relationship that affords Our Lady complete veneration.

Because of the broad nature of its object—the entire sanctity and love of the Mother of God—and because of the ramifications and significance of an act of consecration, the devotion to the Immaculate Heart of Mary can be regarded as the synthesis of all Marian doctrine and devotion.

Bibliography: PIUS XII, "Regina del Santissimo Rosario" (Prayer, Oct. 31, 1942) *Acta Apostolicae Sedis* 34 (1942) 345–346, act of consecration to the Immaculate Heart. Office and Mass of the feast, with decree of promulgation and changes in rubrics, *ibid.* 37 (1945) 44–52. E. DUBLANCHY, *Dictionnaire de théologie catholique*, ed. A. VACANT et al. (Paris 1903–50) 3.1:351–354. J. EUDES, *The Admirable Heart of Mary,* tr. C. DI TARGIANI and R. HAUSER (New York 1948). T. M. SPARKS, *Summarium de cultu Cordis Immaculati Beatae Mariae Virginis* (Turin 1951). J. F. MURPHY, *Mary's Immaculate Heart* (Milwaukee 1951).

[J. F. MURPHY]

IMMACULATE HEART OF MARY, CONGREGATION OF THE (MISSIONHURST)

Also known as, Scheut Missionaries or Immaculate Heart Missioners or, in the U.S., Missionhurst Missioners. The *Congregatio Immaculati Cordis Mariae* (CICM, Official Catholic Directory #0860) is a mission society of priests and brothers founded by Theophile VERBIST at Scheut (Brussels, Belgium) in 1862. It was originally limited to recruiting Belgian and Dutch missionaries for China, but it became international in 1947 when members from other nationalities were accepted.

In 1865 Verbist, with three priests and one lay helper, left for the Apostolic Vicariate of Xiwanzi (Siwantze) in Inner Mongolia. Verbist died in China in 1868; his remains were transferred to Scheut in 1931. His followers were instrumental in improving social conditions for the native converts in Inner Mongolia (250,000 Catholics before World War II). The missionaries bought land, leased it to small farmers who formed Catholic towns, and introduced irrigation in the Province of Ning-hia. In 1931 the Scheut missionaries, through the efforts of Rev. Joseph Rutten, were instrumental in finding a vaccine against spotted typhoid, thus saving the lives of hundreds of Catholic missioners in China. Ten Scheut missionaries were victims of the Boxer uprising (1900). Another 16 met violent death at the hands of bandits, Communists, or Japanese troops. A total of 665 priests and two brothers served in six dioceses and one archdiocese of Inner Mongolia and northern China. The last foreign-born member of the congregation left China in November 1955.

The Scheut missionaries began mission work in the Congo in 1885; the first native priest was ordained in 1934, and the first native bishop was consecrated in 1959. A foundation was made in 1907 in the Philippine Islands, where the missionaries concentrated their efforts in Mountain Province, northern Luzon. Other foundations followed in Singapore (1932), Indonesia (1937), Japan (1947), Hong Kong (1949), Haiti (1953), Chile (founded 1953, terminated 1957), Taiwan (1954), Guatemala (1955), and the Dominican Republic (1958). In 1946 the first permanent establishment was made in the U.S.

Scheut missionaries are ordained for foreign mission. The generalate is in Rome; the U.S. provincialate is in Arlington, VA.

Bibliography: J. RUTTEN, *Les Missionnaires de Scheut et leur Fondateur* (Louvain 1930). V. RONDELEZ, *Scheut, Congregation missionnaire* (Brussels 1962).

[A. F. VERSTRAETE/EDS.]

IMMACULATE HEART OF MARY, SISTERS, SERVANTS OF THE

(IHM); founded in Monroe, MI in 1845 by Louis Florent Gillet and Theresa Maxis DUCHEMIN. To the original foundation in Monroe were added two independent congregations in Pennsylvania, one centered in Immaculata, and the other in Scranton. All three congregations engage in a variety of ministries evolving from their original focus on the works of education.

Gillet, a Redemptorist missionary from Belgium, established a mission in Monroe in 1843. Concerned about the evangelization of the French Canadian girls in the area, Gillet was eager to obtain the collaboration of bilingual sisters. He turned to a sister he had known in Baltimore, Theresa Maxis Duchemin.

Duchemin was a member of the Oblate Sisters of Providence, the first congregation of African American

sisters. She was one of the four founding members of the congregation, all women of Haitian ethnicity, and the first U.S.-born African American to become a woman religious. The congregation's original ministry was the education of Haitian immigrant children. As the number of Haitian children dwindled and the poor African Americans who attended could not afford to pay, the sisters turned to manual labor activities to support themselves. Archbishop Samuel Eccleston, who was not supportive of the congregation, ordered them to discontinue accepting new members.

Gillet had visited the Oblate convent during his trips to Baltimore, happy to minister to the French-speaking sisters. In 1845, he proposed that Duchemin assist him in founding a new congregation in Monroe to minister to the French-speaking girls. It seemed to Theresa that the Oblate congregation was fated to disband. She therefore accepted Gillet's invitation, traveled to Monroe, and on Nov. 10, 1845 initiated community life with two other sisters, Charlotte Shaaff (also from the Oblates) and Theresa Renault. Louis and Theresa provided an Alphonsian foundation for the congregation, adapting the Redemptorist rule to the circumstances of the new congregation of sisters. The school for girls opened in January 1846, initiating IHM ministry that has extended throughout the U.S. and to Latin America, the Middle East, and Africa.

After almost a decade of successful ministry and growth in Michigan, the congregation was caught up in difficulties arising between the bishop, Peter Paul Lefevere and the Redemptorist Fathers. The bishop's reaction was to strive to eradicate all Alphonsian influences on the IHM congregation. Theresa was eager to preserve the Alphonsian tradition to the congregation and recognized this was no longer possible in Monroe. She persuaded Bishop Lefevere to allow her to accept a mission in the diocese of Philadelphia, Pennsylvania, where the Redemptorist Saint John Neumann was bishop. Her efforts to move the entire congregation to Pennsylvania led the bishop to dismiss those sisters he deemed to be disloyal and to declare the two convents separate congregations as of 1859. The diocese of Scranton was created in northeastern Pennsylvania in 1868; in 1871 William O'Hara, the first bishop of Scranton, separated the sisters within his jurisdiction from the Philadelphia congregation, establishing the third independent congregation.

For the first one hundred years after the original foundation, each of the three IHM congregations focused its ministry of education. The endeavors extended from day nurseries and kindergartens to the three higher education institutions the congregations founded: Marygrove College in Detroit (1905), Marywood University in Scranton (1915), and Immaculata College (1920). During this period, some sisters engaged in social service and health care ministries, but the majority were in the education ministry.

The reforms of Vatican Council II brought numerous radical changes to the lives and ministries of the sisters. They responded to the Church's call to a more incarnationally centered and more scripturally based spirituality. They heeded the Council's urging to return to the roots of the foundation and to discern its charism and the vision of the founders. The Council's focus on individual personal dignity strengthened the sisters' commitment to personal responsibility and to supportive community. In striving to respond to the needs of God's people in contemporary times, the sisters engage in a wide range of health care, human service, educational, spiritual, and pastoral ministries. They understand their ministries as participation in the Church's mission of action on behalf of justice. Each congregation maintains a number of congregation-sponsored institutions and congregational commitments to parishes and schools. Many sisters are engaged in individual ministries within the Church and in the broader society.

The three IHM congregations, which number more than two thousand sisters, share planning on significant issues in the Tri-IHM Conference. In the late 20th century the Oblate Sisters of Providence joined with the IHM congregations in their deliberations, creating the Tri-IHM/Oblate Conference, thereby bringing the history of the four congregations full circle in the Providence of God.

Bibliography: Official Catholic Directory #2150; Official Catholic Directory #2170; Official Catholic Directory #2160. M. GANNON, ed., *Paths of Daring, Deeds of Hope: Letters by and about Mother Theresa Maxis Duchemin*, Sisters of IHM (Scranton, PA 1992). R. KELLY, *No Greater Service: The History of the Congregation of the Sisters, Servants of the Immaculate Heart of Mary* (Monroe, MI 1948). G. H. SHERWOOD, *The Oblates One Hundred and One Years* (New York 1931). SISTERS, SERVANTS OF THE IMMACULATE HEART OF MARY, MONROE, MICHIGAN, *Building Sisterhood: A Feminist History of the Sisters, Servants of the Immaculate Heart of Mary* (Syracuse 1997). *The Sisters of the IHM* (New York 1923).

[M. GANNON]

IMMACULATE HEART OF THE BLESSED VIRGIN MARY, SISTERS OF

(IHM, Official Catholic Directory #2930); a congregation with papal approbation whose official title is The California Institute of the Sisters of the Most Holy and Immaculate Heart of the Blessed Virgin Mary (IHM).

Motherhouse of the Sisters, Servants of the Immaculate Heart of Mary, Monroe, Michigan.

This community, which follows the Rule of St. Augustine, dates its foundation from April, 26, 1924, when what had formerly been a province connected with the original motherhouse in Gerona, Spain, became a pontifical institute in its own right. At that time there were 100 professed sisters, whose chief work was in Catholic education on the elementary, secondary, and college levels. The sisters staffed educational institutions in various parts of California, although most of their work was done in and around Los Angeles, where the motherhouse is located. As the community expanded during the next 40 years, schools and convents were erected in Texas and Arizona. Missionary work with the native children on government reservations in Canada was inaugurated in the 1940s.

Some 30 years after the break with the governing body in Spain, the members of the congregation voted to include hospital work as one of their specific aims. Subsequently they opened medical hospitals in Apple Valley (1956) and West Covina (1962), and a convalescent hospital in Salinas (1956), all in California. About the same time a retreat house for married couples was opened in Montecito, Calif.

Two sisters whose work was outstanding in the growth of the community were Mother Eucharia Harney, Superior general (1939–51), whose administration provided new vigor to the congregation; Mother Regina McPartlin, superior general (1951–63) who was responsible for the expansion of the apostolic work of the sisters. By the mid-1960s, there were 600 professed sisters, most of them engaged in teaching in 68 grammar schools, eleven high schools, and one college (the Immaculate Heart College), which was closed in 1980.

In response to the Second Vatican Council's call for renewal of religious life and under the leadership of Mother Humiliata (later President Anita Caspary) (1963–73), the IHM sisters entered a period of prayer and reflection culminating in a Chapter of Renewal in 1967. Specific aspects of the renewal led to disputes both within the community and between the IHM sisters and the local ordinary, Cardinal James Francis McIntyre. With no satisfactory resolution of the disputed issues, in 1969 more than 300 sisters voted to become a non-canonical community of religious persons, the Immaculate Heart Community. About 50 sisters chose to continue in the traditional, canonical structure, retaining the name Sisters of the Immaculate Heart.

At the beginning of the 21st century, the Immaculate Heart Community numbered about 175 members, single and married, female and male, from several Christian denominations. The members were involved in public and private education, law, social work, parish ministry, retreat work, and health care. The Sisters of the Immaculate Heart had about 20 members engaged in retreat work and education. Both groups maintained their headquarters in Los Angeles.

[M. SHARPLES/M. EGAN]

IMMANENCE

From the Latin *manere,* meaning to remain within as distinct from to go beyond or outside of; a term used generally to designate the self-sufficiency and interiority of being. Immanence is opposed to TRANSCENDENCE, although it is sometimes used as complementary to it. If it excludes transcendence, it ignores extrinsic causality and an external referent for knowledge; if it recognizes transcendence, it emphasizes the inner dynamism and self-perfecting character of being or the awareness of self in the knowing act.

History. When the problem of immanence presents itself in history, it is usually stated in relation to that of transcendence. Philosophers have sought to solve the problems raised by the notions of BEING and the SELF by alternately emphasizing immanence to the exclusion of transcendence or transcendence to the exclusion of immanence. The IMMANENTISM of the pre-Socratics and the Stoics, who posited the unfolding of the physical universe from a material principle, has thus been balanced by the TRANSCENDENTALISM of others, such as the Platonists and the Augustinians, who located the fullness of reality in the world of SPIRIT. Intermediate between these are philosophies such as those of SOCRATES, PLATO, ARISTOTLE, and St. THOMAS AQUINAS, which recognize the mutual complementarity of immanence and transcendence.

The earliest concept of immanence is that associated with units that are self-perfecting in their being and operation. The Greek naturalists saw the universe as composed of such units, which develop organically and possess within themselves their own perfective principle. Thus they tended to solve the problem of the one and the many in terms other than those of extrinsic causality. Concern with the living and self-sufficiency of the organism led to the immanentist philosophy of HYLOZOISM, formulated by the pre-Socratics and the Stoics and later developed more systematically by vitalists and creative evolutionists. A similar concern with animal life prompted the emergence of PANPSYCHISM, as exemplified in the philosophies of G. BRUNO, R. H. LOTZE, and E. H. Haeckel.

Aquinas's treatment of immanence associated it with the activity of the AGENT. He implicitly distinguished between transient activities, which pass outside the agent and produce an effect in the patient, and immanent activities, which remain within the agent and contribute to its own perfecting (*Summa theologiae* 1a, 18.3 ad 1); this distinction was made explicitly by later scholastics such as T. de Vio CAJETAN and JOHN OF ST. THOMAS. The scholastic tradition recognized also various degrees of immanent activity, which was associated with the degree of IMMATERIALITY on the part of the agent. The ultimate of interiority, autonomy, and independence was attributed to God—a type of immanence Aristotle earlier had seen in divinity when he described it as Thought Thinking Itself (*Meta.* 1074b 34).

The scholastic conception of immanence was gradually rejected with the development of modern philosophy. At one extreme, the mechanistic conception of the universe fostered by thinkers such as R. DESCARTES and I. Newton accented the determinism imposed on matter from without, with a consequent deemphasis on intrinsic principles of operation (*see* MECHANISM). At the other extreme, the monistic theory of cosmological immanence proposed by B. SPINOZA placed great stress on substance as embodying the principles of its own activity and development. It prepared the way for other monistic philosophies of an idealistic, materialistic, or pantheistic turn, all of which developed the concept of immanence in an absolute and exclusive sense; typical thinkers were J. G. FICHTE, F. W. J. SCHELLING, and G. W. F. HEGEL. In reaction to these extremes, existentialist and personalist philosophers have stressed the inadequacy of the concept of self and its perfecting without some acknowledgment of exteriority and dependence on others.

Kinds. The various meanings of immanence, usually discernible from the context in which the term is used, may be reduced to five, viz, cosmological, psychological, epistemological, ontological, and apologetical.

Cosmological Immanence. This type of immanence stresses the autodetermination and the self-sufficiency of the universe, and in so doing excludes the influence of a transcendent being. Evolution or an inner dynamism of some type is used to replace transcendent causality. God is either eliminated in favor of some type of energy principle, or the universe itself is absorbed in Absolute Substance (Spinoza) or Absolute Spirit (Hegel). Because of the monistic attitude it fosters, cosmological immanence is the key concept in philosophies of absolute immanentism, among which may be enumerated ATHEISM, evolutionism, MATERIALISM, vitalism, and secular HUMANISM.

Psychological Immanence. This term is used to describe the attributes of living and knowing beings whose activities originate within themselves and also are self-perfecting. It recognizes a distinction between such activities and those that pass outside the subject, otherwise known as transient actions. While stressing interiority in vital and cognitional activities, psychological immanence admits a plurality of entities in the universe and does not exclude transcendence, as does cosmological immanence. Usually psychological immanence is regarded as present in different types of being in varying degrees, ranging from the lowest level, that of vegetative life, to the highest level, that of pure spirit. When applied to God, psychological immanence takes on an absolute character in the sense that God's being is absolute perfection and His knowledge is all-embracing, uncaused, and immutable.

Epistemological Immanence. In some theories of knowledge the immanent activity involved in knowing is so stressed as to exclude everything extrinsic to the knowing subject. Insistence on immanence in this sense gives rise to theories variously designated as immanentism, SOLIPSISM, IDEALISM, PHENOMENALISM, and subjectivism. Their proponents affirm a principle of immanence, which they state in either absolute or relative fashion. The absolute principle of immanence maintains that anything beyond thought is unthinkable, that the human mind can know only what is already contained within it (E. LE ROY). According to this principle, it is impossible to know anything existing outside one's self in any way whatsoever. The relative principle of immanence maintains that man cannot know anything unless he has somehow an inward preparation or need, either intellectual or moral, to assimilate it to himself (M. BLONDEL). This principle is at the basis of the so-called method of immanence, whereby man prepares himself to enter into relation with the truth on the theory that nothing radically foreign to his thought can be assimilated by him.

In the Kantian theory of knowledge, immanence is used to designate what remains within the domain of ex-

perience. For I. KANT, the ''transcendental illusion'' consists in regarding principles of immanence as having transcendental applications, i.e., to conclude that what is valid within man's experience is valid also for the thing-in-itself.

Ontological Immanence. From the viewpoint of metaphysics, one meaning of ontological immanence is that everything is intrinsic to everything else, that all elements of the real rigorously imply all other elements and actually constitute only one reality. Carried to its logical extreme, such a concept of ontological immanence leads to PANTHEISM or PANENTHEISM. Another meaning of ontological immanence allows for God's presence within the world while maintaining His transcendence. God's relative immanence in the universe, in this understanding, is explained by the doctrine of the PARTICIPATION of being and by God's causal influence on creatures (*see* CASUALITY, DIVINE).

Apologetical Immanence. The term immanence is given prominence also by some apologetes who propose a method of immanence as the way to discover God from a study of man's consciousness. According to their method, the discovery of the insufficiency of the self and the obvious implications of human activity call man's attention to God as a transcendent Absolute Being without whom man cannot attain his fulfillment. There are various ways of proposing apologetical or religious immanentism, some of which are condemned by the Catholic Church. (*See* IMMANENCE APOLOGETICS.)

Critique. Immanence and transcendence are pivotal notions for explaining the relationships between the universe and God and between man and the universe. Thinkers through the ages have been tempted to choose between universe and God, and between self and nonself. Thus some have maintained that the universe alone exists and that there is no God, whereas others have made God or Spirit the supreme reality and the universe only a mode of the Divine Being; similarly, some center on the self to the exclusion of the nonself in their concern over the problem of knowledge. Too great a stress on immanence accents interiority and self-sufficiency, but it also impoverishes the universe and the self by closing both in upon themselves. The more balanced view of immanence accents its polarity with transcendence. While admitting the existence and reality of the universe, it affirms a transcendent God above and beyond the universe as its first cause and ultimate explanation. While admitting the immanence involved in knowledge, it admits the knower's ability to attain the universe, other selves, and ultimately God, and thus to transcend knowledge of self.

The extreme notions of absolute immanence proposed in the history of thought, when viewed comparatively, effectively counterbalance each other. Thus cosmological immanence, which stresses a universe without a transcending God, is at the opposite polarity from ontological immanence, which stresses the absolute being of God and underemphasizes His creatures. Similarly, epistemological immanence, which places such stress on the thinking subject as to neglect the object of his thought, is offset by apologetical immanence, which stresses to an extreme the insufficiency of the human person and his exigency for God as the Transcendent Being.

A correct understanding of the concepts of relative immanence and relative transcendence, on the other hand, provides a natural basis for man's appreciation of the supernatural order. These concepts need not entail the reduction of the supernatural to the natural or the identification of the order of grace with that of nature. Rather, they serve to focus man's attention on the means whereby he, through an appreciation of his own immanent activity, can rise to a knowledge of the entities that transcend his limited mode of being and are ultimately most meaningful for him.

See Also: GOD; KNOWLEDGE; INTENTIONALITY; MODERNISM.

Bibliography: J. DE TONQUÉDEC, *Immanence* (3d ed. Paris 1933); *Dictionnaire apologétique de la foi catholique* 2:579–612. A. and A. VALENSIN, *ibid.* 2:569–579, doctrine. H. LECLÈRE, *Catholicisme* 5:1295–1303. A. C. MCGIFFERT, *Encyclopedia of Religion and Ethics*, ed. J. HASTINGS 7:167–172. E. CORETH, *Lexikon für Theologie und Kirche,* 5:629–631. J. B. LOTZ, "Immanenz und Transzendenz," *Scholastik* 13 (1938) 1–21, 161–172. G. DI NAPOLI, *Enciclopedia filosofica* 2: 1277–80.

[B. A. GENDREAU]

IMMANENCE APOLOGETICS

Immanence here refers to relative IMMANENCE, not the philosophy of absolute immanence condemned by *Pascendi* (*Enchiridion symbolorum*[31] 2103, 2106) and *Humani generis* (*Enchiridion symbolorum* 3878, 3894). Absolute immanence rules out the possibility of anything transcendent or SUPERNATURAL. Relative immanence admits this possibility and provides a method for studying the steps of the approach to Christianity. Though it is used as apologetics for Christianity, it is properly an APOLOGETICS for the supernatural. Since it draws its arguments from a study of human actions, it might also be regarded as a philosophy of action.

Historical Background. St. Justin's apologetics recognized in man a germ of truth (λόγος σπερματικός) that finds its fulfillment only through union with Christ, *the* LOGOS. Apart from St. Augustine and a few other exceptions, apologists of succeeding ages have argued their

case with external proofs. The most important reemphasis of the internal or subjective arguments came from Cardinal V. DECHAMPS (1810–83). He wrote: "There are only two facts to verify, one is in you [the human heart], the other is outside you [the Church]. They search for each other to embrace each other, and of both of them you are the witness" (see *Dictionnaire apologétique de la foi catholique* 2:610). Though Cardinal Dechamps stressed the subjective aspect of apologetics, the scientific study and organization of this aspect of apologetics was the independent work of Maurice BLONDEL (1861–1949).

Absolute IMMANENTISM was the prevailing philosophy at the beginning of the 20th century. In reaction to it, Blondel's deeply Christian spirit led him to seek a solution to the apparent mutual exclusion of immanentism and Christianity. Immanentists held as valid only those truths coming from within. Their principle was: "Nothing can enter man which does not issue from him and correspond in some way to a need for expansion. Neither historic fact, nor traditional teaching, nor an extrinsic, superadded obligation is reckoned as truth for him and admissible as precept if it is not in some way autonomous or autochthonous" (*Lettre* 34). Traditional external apologetics was unacceptable unless its arguments corresponded to some need for expansion within man. Writing as a philosopher, Blondel attempted to show that such an inner need for Christianity existed. According to him, immanentism leads autonomously and spontaneously to a confrontation with Christianity.

Blondel's Method of Immanence. He accepts the immanentist's principle cited above as his point of departure. To discover man's inner needs referred to in this principle, he studies man's actions since they are the most perfect expression of the human personality. They involve the whole man; in them man commits himself in one way or another. Through a regressive analysis of man's actions, he comes to discern the fundamental needs and desires inspiring man's actions. Between man's WILL involved at this deep level (his implicit, or willing-will) and his will involved in his actions (his explicit, or willed-will) lies a conflict. His implicit will seeks one thing, but the explicit will acts otherwise; man's actions do not seem to be able to satisfy the demands of his inner will. A dialectic exists between the implicit will (*voluntas ut natura*) and the explicit will (*voluntas ut elicita*). Blondel's method of immanence seeks to equate these two wills: "equate within conscience itself what we seem to think, to wish and to do with what we really wish and think" (*Lettre* 39).

In reconciling these two wills, Blondel distinguishes three steps. First, it is through a manifestation of this inner will that the nonbeliever can come to see that Christian truth and life concern him. His awareness of these inner needs and demands leads him to recognize a twofold impossibility: (1) the impossibility of *not* recognizing the insufficiency of the natural order and of *not* experiencing a further need; and (2) the impossibility of finding within oneself the wherewithal to satisfy this religious need (*L'Action* 319). The discovery of these inner demands and the impossibility of satisfying them does not follow any set pattern but varies as forms of human activity vary. The general conclusion, however, is the same; namely, that the necessary condition for the perfection of human action is inaccessible to human action.

Confronted with this impossible situation, man passes on to the second and crucial step through his recognition and acceptance of a new affirmation, namely, that there is a unique necessary being (*unique nécessaire*). He affirms either that he himself is "god," his own master, the unique necessary being, or that this unique necessary being exists outside himself, the omnipotent God of the universe. To consider oneself as god is to revert back to the frustration of the first step. To acknowledge God exists, however, is to admit one's powerlessness; God is needed to satisfy the demands of the inner will. Here the supernatural is involved in a general, undetermined sense. In speaking of the absolute necessity of the supernatural in this sense, Blondel is referring to man's acknowledgment of his inevitable dependence on the Creator. Man sees he cannot enter into communion with God except by God's initiative and sovereign action. It is the creature's recognition of his need for his Creator. Even men unacquainted with Christianity admit this absolute need. It means opening oneself to the divine action, whatever it be. Many have failed to distinguish Blondel's general use of the term "supernatural" in this step and have rejected his method as denying the gratuity of the strictly supernatural (see Bouillard 86–131).

In the third step the interested nonbeliever studies the religions that would specify the notion of the generic supernatural idea referred to in step two. No sincere study could overlook the Christian explanation of the supernatural order. The dogmas of Christianity are considered as a hypothetical answer to man's needs. Neither the reality nor even the intrinsic possibility of this hypothesis is an issue at this point. The nonbeliever studies the correspondence of these hypothetical truths to his needs. If the Christian hypothesis is seen as the answer to those needs, Christianity then becomes a necessary hypothesis. If preaching effectively shows him that this hypothesis is a reality, he has a practical obligation to accept it. God's gift of FAITH, however, must intervene for the nonbeliever to be converted and receive the reality of Christian truth and life. In this third step, therefore, one sees the internal apologetics of relative immanentism join with the external apologetics of tradition to form an integral apologetics including both the subjective and objective aspects.

Appreciation of Immanence Apologetics. Blondel's writings on this subject have been a source of controversy since they first appeared. The two main charges brought against them are naturalism and FIDEISM. His supposed denial of the gratuity of the supernatural has already been treated. Despite numerous clarifications of his teachings, critics still disagree in their interpretation of his idea of the supernatural (cf. Bouillard, Duméry, and Nicolas for opposed interpretations). As regards fideism, some have thought that this method overstressed the study of action to the point of neglecting the role of the intellect. Blondel, however, notes the role of the intellect both in the theoretical considerations preceding action and in the practical or experimental knowledge associated with action. One of the main values of immanence apologetics is its reemphasis of subjective apologetics as part of an integral apologetics. In this respect it has helped to throw light on the question of miracles and the relation of faith and reason.

See Also: CONVERSION, III (PSYCHOLOGY OF); CONVERSION, II (THEOLOGY OF); MIRACLES (THEOLOGY OF); OBEDIENTIAL POTENCY; SUPERNATURAL EXISTENTIAL.

Bibliography: J. TRÜTSCH, *Lexikon für Theologie und Kirche,* ed. J. HOFER and K. RAHNER, 10 v. (2d, new ed. Freiburg 1957–65) 5:631–633. L. MAISONNEUVE, *Dictionnaire de théologie catholique,* ed. A. VACANT et al., 15 v. (Paris 1903–50; Tables générales 1951–) 1.2:1573–80. A. VALENSIN, *Dictionnaire apologétique de la foi catholique,* ed. A. D'ALÈS, 4 v. (Paris 1911–22; Table analytique 1931) 2:569–612. M. BLONDEL, *L'Action* (1893; Paris 1950); "Lettre sur les exigences de la pensée contemporaine en matière d'apologétique. . . (1896)," *Les Premiers écrits de Maurice Blondel* (Paris 1956). A. HAYEN, *Bibliographie Blondélienne, 1888–1951* (Brussels 1953). H. DUMÉRY, *Blondel et la religion: Essai critique sur la "Lettre" de 1896* (Paris 1954). D. GABOARDI, "Teologia fondamentale: Il metodo apologetico," *Problemi e orientamenti di teologia dommatica,* 2 v. (Milan 1957) 1:57–103. G. COLOMBO, "Il problema del soprannaturale negli ultimi clinquant'anni," *ibid.,* 2:547–563. R. AUBERT, *Le Problème de l'acte de foi* (3d ed. Louvain 1958) 265–392. J. SOMERVILLE, "Maurice Blondel, 1861–1949," *Thought* 36 (1961) 371–410. H. BOUILLARD, *Blondel et le Christianisme* (Paris 1961). J. H. NICOLAS, "Le Centenaire de Blondel," *Revue thomiste* 62 (1962) 432–444.

[R. X. REDMOND]

IMMANENTISM

A philosophical position maintaining that human experience is the only ultimate source of VERIFICATION. Absolute immanentism insists upon the self-sufficiency of man as the measure of all reality and defends its doctrine on the grounds that any supposed transcendence of reason would be, by definition, "beyond reason" and therefore beyond the scope of discourse or rational penetration.

Kinds. The various kinds of immanentism may be classified as metaphysical, existentialist, ethical, religious, and political.

Metaphysical immanentism restricts reality either to the data of human experience furnished by the senses, as in the EMPIRICISM of D. HUME and his positivist heirs, or to the data of human thought, as in subjective IDEALISM. Another instance is HISTORICISM, particularly as developed in the thought of W. DILTHEY and B. CROCE. This maintains that the only field of reference for all human knowledge and activity is history and that judgments must be verified historically or not at all.

Existentialist immanentism maintains that man encounters himself as "thrown" into a world to which all his acts are related intentionally. All significant action and thought grow out of the human situation in which man finds himself. It follows that any metaphysics of being implicates man as the articulation of being; this prevents any effective transcendence. (*See* EXISTENTIALISM.)

Ethical immanentism denies the possibility of an ethics formulated objectively and without immediate reference to the immanent or existential situation in which man finds himself. This position is related to SITUATIONAL ETHICS, which stresses the personal element in choice at the expense of universal moral principles.

Religious immanentism supposes the impossibility of distinguishing between religious experience and its object and teaches, as did W. JAMES, that belief must be measured by human response. MODERNISM, a heresy condemned by the Church, is related to this in attempting to reduce all dogmatic formulations to their subjective and historical antecedents.

Political immanentism reduces all reality to the state and denies man any transcendence of the political order. The doctrine is latent in the thought of J. BODIN and N. MACHIAVELLI, and explicitly stated by T. HOBBES. It is linked also with Hegel's insistence upon the state as the only synthesis capable of resolving the alienation and abstraction found in the individual (thesis) and his disappearance in communities such as the family (antithesis). This position is adopted, with some modifications, by Marxist communism.

Critique. Realist objections to immanentism have most cogency when couched in terms of an analysis of the concept of the immanent. Logically, the immanent

makes sense in terms of the non-immanent, or of that which transcends or falls outside the immanent; it follows that the very meaning of immanence implies its own limit, i.e., transcendence. Phenomenologically or experientially, cognitive, volitional, and emotive experiences reveal man's being as structurally related to something beyond itself, as having meaning in terms of the other, as being intentional or "toward the other," i.e., as transcending.

See Also: IMMANENCE; INTENTIONALITY; TRANSCENDENCE.

Bibliography: G. DI NAPOLI, *Enciclopedia filosofica* 2:1277–80 (Venice-Rome 1957). R. EISLER, *Wörterbuch der philosophischen Begriffe,* 1:718–721 (4th ed. Berlin 1927–30). P. FOULQUIÉ and R. SAINT-JEAN, *Dictionnaire de la langue philosophique* 348 (Paris 1962).

[F. D. WILHELMSEN]

IMMATERIALITY

The state of being or acting in independence of MATTER. The term is applied in an ontological sense to any SPIRIT, such as GOD, ANGELS, or the human soul (*see* SOUL, HUMAN). It is used also in an epistemological sense in scholastic discussions of knowledge and the knower, and it is this sense that is the concern of this article.

Matter and Knowledge. The things that are directly apprehended with the SENSES and the INTELLECT are things that exist in the external world and have their own natural being distinct from man's knowledge of them. They are sensibly various, extended, and multiple, in motion or at rest. Some are generated and come into being, whereas others become corrupted and cease to be. Such things are said to be material, that is, potential and capable of change. Although they actually exist, they are not completely actual, but include in their makeup something imperfect and passive, something potential and determinable, called matter. By reason of matter or the material principle in things, they are capable of becoming otherwise and even other than they are. Such things include also the formal determinations by which they are what and as they are, for instance, a red rose or a gold ring.

In their reflections on the mysteries of nature and knowledge, the early Greek philosophers assumed that only material things exist, and that both the knower and the things known are made of the same matter or material elements, which also constitute food and drink for the knower. These philosophers thought that like is known by like, namely, that man knows water in the outside world by water within himself, air by air, etc. Further reflection, however, on the order and harmony of the world convinced other thinkers that material things and material principles are not sufficient to account for nature and for knowledge. They decided that there must be something of a different kind, something simple and unmixed, indeed some divine intelligence that rules the world. In this intelligent principle man somehow participates by reason of his intellect, which is distinct from sense and much more perfect, because by intellect he knows not only sensible things but also relations and causes that are not sensible. Thus the problem of accounting for knowledge became more complex, and included not only the sensible and sense but also the intelligible and intellectual knowledge.

PLATO regarded sensible things as objects for opinion only, or likely interpretation, and maintained that the things known by intellect in a philosophical way are Forms or Ideas existing apart in a world of realities separated from sensible matter. Aristotle rejected this explanation as incomplete and unnatural, and held that even sensible things are intelligible. These things consist not merely of potential matter but also of sensible and intelligible forms or specifying principles by which they are what they are and as they are. Aristotle distinguished between the sensible in potency and the sensible in act. In the dark, something colored is sensible in potency, but in the light and with an eye present to see it, the colored thing is sensible in act. Likewise, he distinguished in the knower an organ and power for sensing that is sometimes merely in potency, that is, able to sense, and sometimes in the act of sensing. This occurs when the sensible is present and acting on the organ of sense. Indeed, the sensation is the very action of the sensible in the sense, and there are not two activities, but only one activity with two aspects. The very same action that proceeds actively from the sensible is received passively in and by the sense, but it is received by the sense according to its own manner of sensitivity, and this is the sensation itself. In view of this account, Aristotle did not simply concede that like is known by like, but maintained that the sensible thing acts upon the sense, and by its action makes the sense like itself, whereas the sense was previously in potency and unlike the sensible disposed for action.

Immateriality in Knowing. Considerations such as these lead to the question of what precisely is KNOWLEDGE, or what is a knower, and whether one can determine the different kinds and degrees of knowledge and knowers. One can proceed to solve these questions by reflecting on acts of knowing, and by contrasting the knower with the nonknower. A nonknower, such as a piece of wood or of wax, is limited to itself and within itself. It is a material thing that is distinct from all others. It has certain formal determinations of color, figure, etc., that are its own, not another's, and it is capable of receiving other determinations in a passive and subjective way, as its own and not another's. A knower, on the other hand, is a distinct individual; it is not limited to itself, or closed within itself, but is open to others.

Indeed, a knower is open to all the others that it can know, and thus it is not only itself but also in some manner it is everything that it can know. A knower is somehow able to transcend the real distinction between itself and the others that are found in the natural world, and somehow becomes and is the other that it knows. This it does by way of increase: remaining itself, it becomes also the other. It receives formal determinations not merely as its own, but also as the other's. Thus it receives not only in a subjective manner, as material things receive, but also in an objective or intentional manner. Hence the knower has a certain preeminence over the potentiality of matter, an amplitude of being and perfection, a removal of the limitations of matter that is manifested by the objective, intentional, or immaterial way by which it receives formal determinations in knowing. This fullness or perfection of being by which the knower can overcome its own material limitations and its distinction from other things, so that it can become and can be in an objective or intentional way everything it can know, is called immateriality, that is, removal from the limitations of matter and eminence over the potentiality of matter.

The immateriality of the knower can be appreciated through the contrast between eating and knowing. The organism draws its food from the environment and by the processes of digestion and assimilation makes the food become part of itself. The organism consists materially of what it eats, although it does not become like the food but changes the food into itself. On the other hand, the knower also draws its knowledge from the environment, but not in a material way. It does not materially change the things that it knows, nor does it take them into itself materially. Rather, it is the knower that becomes changed in acquiring knowledge, yet in such a way that, without ceasing to be what it was, it becomes assimilated to the thing known. The knower becomes and is the thing known in a way that transcends the distinctions between them and unites them in the most intimate union of all, that is, in a kind of identity, not material or subjective but objective and immaterial. This eminent perfection of the knower, its immateriality or fullness of being and perfection by which it transcends material things as such and is able to become and to be other than itself, extending to everything it can know, is what essentially constitutes a knower and knowledge itself. A knower has a double mode of being, and leads a double life. A knower is what it is in itself materially, and it is immaterially, objectively, or intentionally all that it knows or can know.

Degrees of Immateriality. By reflecting on knowledge and by comparing the self with other knowers, one can distinguish various kinds of knowledge and various degrees of immateriality in knowledge and knowers. Because of the peculiar identity between the knower and the things known that is established in and by the act of knowledge, the degree of immateriality in knowledge and in the knower is proportioned to the thing known, as such. From this point of view one can differentiate between sense knowledge and human intelligence or reason. Sense knowledge is dependent upon the presence and action of SENSIBLES on the senses, and is really the same as the action of the sensible in the sense. The sensible acts on the sense, not by means of its material being, but by means of a special quality, which is an active FORM in singular matter. The SENSATION, or act of sensing, is the action of the sensible through its special quality, by which the sense is assimilated to the sensible in act. When the sense is activated in this way, the knower receives an impression by which it is assimilated to the sensible and, by reason of its own immateriality, it becomes and is the sensible in act. This is the lowest degree of immateriality, according to which the knower is or can be immaterially or objectively identified with singular sensible things. Within this first degree of immateriality, however, many species of sense knowledge are found in man and other animals. These can be differentiated by their peculiar objects, and by the special ways in which various sensible things act on different sense organs, as the eye, the ear, the tongue, etc.

In addition to sense knowledge, man has intellectual knowledge of boundless scope. He understands not merely this or that in the particular case, but BEING in general, and also NONBEING, one and many in general, whole, and part in general. He understands not merely this or that natural body, but matter and body in general, plant or animal in general, man or human nature in general. The proper object of the human intellect is indeed something in the material world, but this man knows by intellect as universal, that is, as abstracted from singular matter. Thus the human knower enjoys a higher degree of immateriality, by which he becomes and is in an immaterial way not merely a singular material thing but something universal and transcendent or simply immaterial (*see* UNIVERSALS). Hence the human knower as intellective is simply immaterial, and the intellective power is anorganic or spiritual.

Above man as a knower are the angels and God. The angels are immaterial or spiritual creatures of limited being, and the proper objects of their knowledge are correspondingly immaterial. God is PURE ACT, immateriality without any limitation, and so he is knower in the highest degree, incomparably transcending created knowers. In God, being and knowing are one and the same, and so He is subsistent intellection or comprehensive knowledge of Himself.

See Also: IMMORTALITY; INTENTIONALITY; KNOWLEDGE, PROCESS OF; SPECIES, INTENTIONAL.

Bibliography: L. M. RÉGIS, *Epistemology*, tr. I. C. BYRNE (New York 1959) 157–252. J. OWENS, *An Elementary Christian Metaphysics* (Milwaukee 1963) 217–219. J. MARITAIN, *Distinguish to Unite, or The Degrees of Knowledge*, tr. G. B. PHELAN (New York 1959).

[W. H. KANE]

IMMORTALE DEI

Encyclical letter of Pope LEO XIII, issued Nov. 1, 1885; frequently entitled in English "The Christian Constitution of States," after a phrase from the final paragraph. It was one of a long series of letters that Leo wrote on the political order, whose declared aim was "to contrast with the lessons taught by Christ the novel theories now advanced touching the State" (par. 2). Scholars agree that it contains the most complete exposition and clarification of Leo's teaching on the problem of CHURCH AND STATE.

During the 19th century the concept of "the modern state" became widely accepted in many parts of Europe. "Liberal democracy" was the most common of the many terms used to describe it. It is a state governed by elected representatives of the people; maintaining neutrality on questions of religion, professing neither to support nor to suppress any particular creed or cult; considering public, nonreligious education to be the business of the state; recognizing as valid only those marriages which are contracted according to civil regulations; providing for divorce and the remarriage of divorced persons; sponsoring freedom of speech and press, completely rejecting government censorship. Many Catholics in Europe, especially in France, wondered whether a good Catholic could actively support the modern state. The encyclical set forth some broad principles to help Catholics answer the question; in addition, it included some particular directives relevant to the actual situation in France.

Unless studied in its proper context, and in the light of the full papal teaching on the political order, *Immortale Dei* can be easily misunderstood by present readers. The following generalizations indicate its contents: The Church is not opposed to the rightful aims of civil government. Any mode of government is legitimate as long as rulers govern with justice and for the common good. Since the authority of the state, like all authority, is from God, the state must acknowledge its indebtedness to God by professing religion and indeed the true religion, which is not hard to discover. God has established two powers: the ecclesiastical power set over divine things and the civil power set over human things. Since each of these two powers has authority over the same subjects, there should exist between them a certain orderly connection and collaboration; the contemporary doctrine that favors their separation is absurd. It must be remembered that the Church is the true and sole guardian of morals. Individual Catholics must cooperate with any form of government that is not obviously immoral. By thus restating traditional teaching and noting the legitimacy of differences among Catholics "in matters merely political" (par. 49), Leo made it clear that the Church was not opposed to the ascendant democracy, even though it deplored its tolerance or legalization of certain social evils.

Bibliography: *Acta Sanctorum Sedis* 18:161–180, has the official Latin text. E. T. GARGAN, ed., *Leo XIII and the Modern World* (New York 1961), includes bibliog. items.

[D. L. LOWERY]

IMMORTALITY

The doctrine that the human soul is immortal and will continue to exist after man's death and the dissolution of his body is one of the cornerstones of Christian philosophy and theology. Because of its importance, it is treated here from four different points of view: first the history of the problem in ancient and medieval thought is sketched; then a philosophical analysis is given that relates the doctrine to modern thought; thirdly, the place the teaching holds in the Bible is indicated; and finally revelational data pertinent to the doctrine are presented and analyzed.

1. History of the Problem

When the Apologists and early Fathers presented Christianity to the Greeks, the Last Judgment formed part of their message. Since this doctrine implied the survival and immortality of the soul, they appealed to the poets and philosophers and general tradition of Greek thought in support of belief in immortality. Later, the scholastics preferred to make use of Plato or principles from Aristotle.

Ancient Thought. Despite a generally materialist concept of soul, all ancient peoples seem to have had some belief that a part of man survives the death of the body and is subjected to reward or punishment in another world. An exception may be found in those pantheistic religions which taught an absorption at death, at least for the virtuous, into some higher entity—e.g., Brahmanism, DAOISM, perhaps ancient BUDDHISM, and certainly more

Angels carry the soul of Germanus, Bishop of Capua, to heaven in the view of St. Benedict and Servandus, illumination in an 11th-century manuscript of the life of St. Benedict

than one Greek tradition, as in Euripides. In Egypt, the myth of Osiris and the 42 judges, together with the care lavished upon the dead (because the survival depended on the preservation of the body); in Persia, the cult of Mithra as judge of the dead; and in Greece, the myths of Homer, such as the descent of Ulysses into Hades (*Odyssey* 11), ORPHISM and the cult of Dionysos, the theme of escape to the Isles of the Blessed, and the myths of transmigration related by Plato are all tenuous examples sometimes advanced of more positive beliefs. Yet one may reasonably doubt whether such traditions touched the daily lives of ordinary people. Immortality of fame or even of posterity seems to have been a more prevalent ideal (cf. Plato, *Symp.* 206E–209E).

It is rather in the philosophers that the Fathers found support for the message of Christianity. PYTHAGORAS and EMPEDOCLES, cited by Saint Justin (*Apol.* 1.18.5), both teach the survival and transmigration of the soul, which for them is made from heavenly particles of ether. Yet the doctrine is less philosophical than religious, and may have been borrowed from Orphism. The thought of SOCRATES, who left no writings, is probably that expressed in Plato's *Apology:* that some "divine element" in him makes him believe death is no evil; he hopes it is a good, though he has no proof of this.

Platonic doctrine, often cited by the Fathers, is clear-cut and positive. The soul, for PLATO a self-moving principle, is ungenerated and eternal; it has existed before the body, to which it is united by way of punishment for some fault, and will therefore survive it. To be without the body is indeed the natural and proper state of the soul, though Plato admits transmigrations and future unions should the soul not attain full purification in this life (*Phaedo* 81). A series of arguments is offered in the *Phaedo* based on reminiscence or recollection (*Phaedo* 72–77; *Meno* 81–86; *Theaet.* 150B–151D), the simplicity and spirituality of the soul, its likeness to the divine (*Phaedo* 78–80) and, by contrast, its loose union with the body (87B–88C), and its likeness to, and participation in, the Ideas (99D–105C), especially in the Idea of life (105D). Yet Plato himself, in accordance with his theory of knowledge (cf. *Tim.* 29C), seems to admit that these arguments give no more than a "likely account" because of "the greatness of the subject and the weakness of man" (*Phaedo* 107A). For Christian thinkers, Plato's position was sometimes considered dangerous, since it implied not only the preexistence of soul but also a certain divine character attaching to it.

The same must be said of the early Aristotelian teaching in *On Philosophy, Eudemus,* and other dialogues, since Aristotle first saw the soul as something divine, sojourning on earth and longing to return to its natural state of separate existence. When, however, he attained the maturity of his thought in the *De anima,* he had long since abandoned such Platonic dualism. As ENTELECHY of the body, the soul is distinguished from the body as act from potency. Aristotle concedes that "mind may be capable of existing apart, as what is eternal from what is corruptible" (413b 25–27); and in the *Metaphysics* he grants that "there is nothing to prevent some form surviving the union with the body; the soul, for example, may be of this sort, not all soul, but the reason" (1070a 25–28). In another text only the "active reason" is said to be immortal and eternal because it alone is by nature impassible and simple (*Anim.* 430a 20–25). Since this obscure passage has given rise to greatly divergent interpretations, one cannot conclude from it that Aristotle explicitly taught a personal immortality.

The explicit negation of immortality in the earthbound atomism of DEMOCRITUS is repeated by EPICURUS. Since for these thinkers the soul as well as the body is composed of atoms, it dissolves at death: "So death, the most terrifying of ills, is nothing for us: for as long as we exist, death is not with us; and when death comes, then we do not exist" (*Epist.* 3). Though, at the other extreme, STOICISM made the soul a spark from the Eternal Fire, a particle of God, and spoke of it as immortal, individual Stoics were never agreed whether the separated soul retained its own existence or was absorbed into the monistic Fire.

If Christianity roughly disposed of these philosophies (cf. Augustine, *Serm.* 150, *Patrologia Latina*, ed. J. P. Migne, 38:807–14), it found NEOPLATONISM more tempting. Yet it soon realized that the immortality proposed therein, though of a spiritual and intellective soul of "the same species as the gods" (Plotinus, *Enn.* 5.1.2), was not greatly different from that of Stoicism. Souls came from Soul, the third of Plotinus's divine hypostases, and yet were never quite separate from it. They would return to it after a good life on earth (*Enn.* 4.3.24) and make but one Soul, to the point of having no individual identity. Fundamental to such a doctrine, Augustine points out, is the argument that nothing can be immortal unless it has existed eternally (*Civ.* 10.31).

If Greek philosophy thus favors rather than denies immortality, it has no clear conception or proof of such a doctrine. Given indeed the whole framework of Greek thought on God and His relation to the world (as in Aristotle), a doctrine of personal immortality has relatively little meaning or importance to the Greek mind.

Patristic Teaching. Even when it used the dualistic language of the Greek world, patristic thought recognized that man is not a soul that has descended to the body as to an alien dwelling, but is a living whole created as such by God and called in body and soul to the resurrection and to eternal life (Pseudo-Justin, *De resurrectione* 8, *Patrologia Graeca*, ed. J. P. Migne, 6:1585). Yet some early Fathers were persuaded that the soul was mortal by nature but could become immortal by good works, or, as others preferred to stress, by union with the Spirit of God, a teaching they thought to find in Saint Paul. Thus, in writing that "immortality is not the consequence of nature, but the reward and prize of virtue," Lactantius (*Div. instit.* 7.5) repeats a thought expressed before him by Justin and Tatian. Yet these same Fathers claimed that the wicked are to live on, to receive "the punishment of death in immortality" (Tatian, *Discurs.* 13). Such imprecision was abolished by AUGUSTINE, with his distinction between physical and moral immortality (*Civ.* 13.2; *C. Maximin.* 2.12.2; *Serm.* 65 4–6).

Again, under the influence of the Jewish belief in Sheol, the parable of Dives and Lazarus, Christ's descent into hell, millenarianism, and sometimes in reaction to Gnosticism, most of the early Fathers posited a period of rest and even of "sleep" for souls between death and the general resurrection. The wicked, they generally admitted, were immediately subjected to some intermediate punishment; but of the just, only the martyrs were, according to IRENAEUS, TERTULLIAN, and even Augustine, admitted immediately to the beatific vision (cf. Augustine, *Retract.* 1.14, *Patrologia Latina* 32:606).

Very few Fathers attempt lengthy rational proofs for immortality. Tertullian suggests a reason from simplicity (*De anim.* 14); LACTANTIUS, from the moral order (*Div. instit.* 7.8–9). Augustine, who knew the *Phaedo* at least indirectly, preferred to formulate his own, from the indestructibility of truth (*Soliloq.* 2.19.33) and of the thinking subject (*Immort. anim.* 11.18). Neither proof is very convincing; both works show the incomplete development of his thought shortly after his conversion. His later works offer only one new argument, from incorporeality (*Gen. ad litt.* 7.28.43). More philosophical is Gregory of Nyssa's approach in *Macrinia,* a Christian adaptation of the *Phaedo,* where one finds a long proof based on the simplicity of the soul and the immateriality of its intellectual operations (*Patrologia Graeca* 46:44–49). NEMESIUS OF EMESA recalls that Plato and others offer many arguments, but they are difficult and obscure; man's assurance is rather from Sacred Writ (*De nat. homin.* 2, *Patrologia Graeca* 40:589). Saint Bonaventure repeats Nemesius's words almost literally (*Opera omnia* 6:37).

Scholasticism. Interest in a philosophical demonstration of immortality was awakened in 12th- and 13th-century SCHOLASTICISM by the *De immortalitate animae* of DOMINIC GUNDISALVI composed at Toledo after 1150. A century later the question became acute as scholastics recognized that Averroës and Moses MAIMONIDES denied personal immortality. Still later, the value of such philosophical proofs was subjected to much debate, which carried over into the Renaissance.

Besides theological arguments from the justice of God, Gundisalvi proposed a whole series of demonstrations *ex propriis,* from the proper nature, activities, properties, and relations of the soul. His arguments, many drawn from Avicenna, others based on Aristotelian principles of being, become almost standard among such scholastics as Robert of Melun, William of Auvergne, Alexander of Hales, Philip the Chancellor, and John of La Rochelle. Yet with the expansion of the university programs, the schoolmen began to develop more original arguments and to probe such questions as the status and activity of the separated soul. The proofs offered varied from theologian to theologian. Saint BONAVENTURE considered the final end of man the most apt means of establishing the doctrine (*Opera omnia* 2:460), a proof that is primarily theological. Saint THOMAS AQUINAS, improving considerably on the philosophical proofs of Gundisalvi, found immortality a consequence of the spirituality and substantiality of the soul. The intellectual operations prove the soul is a spiritual subsistent being, which is subject to no type of corruptibility. Only secondarily did Aquinas advance as a proof man's universal desire or appetite for immortality, or appeal to God's will not to take from things what is proper to their natures (*Summa*

theologiae 1a, 75.6; *De anim.* 14; *C. gent.* 2.55, 79). The metaphysical proofs were called into question by John DUNS SCOTUS; not indeed denied, any more than Scotus denied immortality itself, but not accepted as valid philosophical demonstrations; for immortality man has only probable reasons (*Opus Ox.* 4.43.2.46). Not all Scotists accepted this viewpoint; William of Alnwick directly attacked it as extreme [*Gregorianum* 30 (1949) 279–289]. The Latin Averroists, for quite other reasons, held that no rational proof was possible; their discussions filled the late Middle Ages at Bologna and Padua. The debate was renewed with Donato's translation (Venice 1495) of the first book of Alexander of Aphrodisias' *De anima* and the teachings of P. POMPONAZZI and others. Cardinal Tommaso de Vio CAJETAN was drawn into the question and led to change his opinion. If in his commentaries on Saint Thomas (1507) and Aristotle (1509) he was sure that immortality could be proved, by 1532 he had reached the conclusion that it was a matter of faith only, though supported by probable arguments. The controversy continued through much of the 16th century.

Bibliography: A. J. FESTUGIÈRE, *L'Idéal religieux des Grecs et l'Évangile* (Paris 1932). F. CUMONT, *Lux perpetua* (Paris 1949), to be read with caution. J. DANIÉLOU, *Message évangélique et culture hellénistique aux IIe et IIIe siècles* (Tournai 1961). M. SCHMAUS, "Die Unsterblichkeit der Seele und die Auferstehung des Leibes nach Bonaventura," *L'Homme et son destin, d'après les penseurs des moyen âge* (Congrès international de philosophie médiévale 1; Louvain 1960) 505–19. S. VANNI ROVIGHI, *L'immortalità dell'anima nei maestri francescani del secolo XIII* (Milan 1936). E. VERGA, "L'immortalità dell'anima nel pensiero del Card. Gaetano," *Rivista di filosofica neoscolastica* 27 supplement (1935) 21–46. R. M. MARTIN, "L'Immortalité de l'âme d'après Robert de Melun," *Revue néo-scolastique de philosophie* 36 (1934) 128–45.

[I. C. BRADY]

2. Philosophical Analysis

Immortality means immunity from death, or unceasing duration of life. It differs from ETERNITY in that the latter implies no beginning. Here it means that the human spiritual soul will endure forever, regardless of biological DEATH or subsequent resurrection of the body. It does not mean mere temporary revival after apparent death or continuation of some functions for a short time. Nor does it mean metaphorical immortality by continued existence in the memory of mankind or as a symbol. Lastly, it does not mean absorption into the eternal existence of God or transmigration into another being. Immortality means actual continued existence in one's own identity.

Arguments for Immortality. Three chief arguments are usually given for the immortality of the human soul: one from its nature, another from its unlimited spiritual capacities, and a third from the necessity of a future sanction for the moral order. Claims of contact with the spirits of the dead, through spiritualist mediums and the like, are, at best, evidence of some future life but not of strict immortality.

Nature of the Soul. Of its nature the human soul is incorruptible. Being simple, it lacks any spatial or constitutive parts into which it can break up. Being spiritual, at the death of the body it is not subject to corruption incidental to any intrinsic dependence on matter, for its spiritual operations of intellection and volition show it to have only extrinsic dependence on matter (*see* SOUL, HUMAN 4; SPIRIT). The only way it could cease to exist is by annihilation, the failure of God as First Cause to conserve it in being. But for God to annihilate what He has made immortal by nature would be inconsistent and unreasonable, a contradiction of His own design. Such an imperfection is impossible to God.

Capacities of the Soul. The argument for immortality from the soul's unlimited capacities is sometimes called the argument from desire; but one might desire many things and not get them, or one might not consciously desire immortality. It argues rather from the very nature of man's two highest powers to the conclusion that he is made to live forever, whether he desires it or not. The INTELLECT can know whatever is or can be, all that is intelligible. This unlimited capacity for truth sets up in man an insatiable curiosity. The WILL has a corresponding capacity for unlimited goodness. However much it may possess, it can always want further. True, one may rightly expect a reasonable amount of happiness in this life, but even those who claim to be quite content are capable of having much more.

Now these unlimited capacities of intellect and will can never be fully satisfied in this life, or with anything less than an eternity with God. Only when the intellect can explore the inexhaustible intelligibility of Infinite Truth will curiosity be sated. Only when the will possesses the infinite goodness and beauty of Goodness Itself will it rest content. But it is absurd that in a universe where other things reach their natural goals, for the most part and with admitted exceptions, only man should be necessarily and completely frustrated in achieving the end for which he was designed. If the human soul is not immortal, it means that no man achieves his end, that the entire species is aimed at a nonexistent goal.

It is true that some people may not attain God and thus may miss their end. This possibility is the inevitable consequence of free choice. But they do so by their own agency, not because their end was impossible of achievement.

Moral Sanctions. Lastly, one may infer the logical necessity of a life after death from the fact that people generally experience moral obligation and a sense of responsibility. The question is whether this widespread phenomenological fact has any validity if the soul is not immortal. In an orderly universe it is preposterous that disorder would reign only in the case of man. Yet one sees people trying to do what they think right, and receiving no reward in this life. Others, who commit crime, go unpunished; and still others are punished unjustly for crimes they did not commit. Moral values, a sense of obligation, and responsibility find no adequate sanction in this life. Unless there is a life after death in which wrongs will be righted and people receive what they deserve, the whole notion of obligation seems irrational.

Some scholastic philosophers claim that this last argument proves that there will be some future life, but not that it will last forever. Others disagree, for the reason that a sanction that is not everlasting is not adequate ultimately. If the good knew that heaven would eventually cease, they would be tempted to feel that a virtuous life is not worth the effort. Likewise, if the bad knew that they would be freed no matter what they did or how severe the punishment was, it would mean that in the end everybody would be the same; so the difference between moral and immoral would become zero eventually, and mere expediency would become at least as reasonable as obligation. Only immortality provides adequate sanction.

Conditions of Afterlife. It is argued that the existence of the immortal soul after death of the body would be meaningless because the soul would be without its proper operation, viz, perceptual knowing or understanding derived from sense. It is true that without some special supernatural aid the human intellect will be unable to know singular material objects or acquire further knowledge of the physical universe. But there seems to be no intrinsic impossibility of knowing spiritual realities, for they are intelligible and the intellect is spiritual. God, angels, one's own, and other human souls would thus be known without need of the senses. Again, habitual knowledge is stored in the intellect by way of HABIT. The use of this and the acquisition of other knowledge does seem to call for extra help on the part of God to substitute for the role played by sense knowledge when the soul is joined to matter. But although one does not know exactly how, there seems to be no absurdity in this possibility because matter has only an extrinsic and subordinate part in human intellection. Even God could not supply for sense if matter entered intrinsically and necessarily into the activity of the intellect. But since it does not, it seems legitimate to assume that He will somehow provide the necessary conditions for man's intellect to function (Saint Thomas Aquinas, *Summa theologiae* 1a, 75.6 ad 1–3; 89.1–8).

If its highest powers are satisfied, the soul's happiness will be essentially achieved. It will be too absorbed in enjoying God to be distracted by any desire for bodily pleasures, for God contains all such pleasures equivalently and to a supereminent degree. Failure to grasp the essential nature of the future life causes people to claim they do not desire heaven because they imagine it an eternity of harp playing, instead of the enjoyment of God as Infinite Truth and Goodness. Any other objects or persons or the lack thereof are so minor as to be negligible.

As to maintaining one's personal identity when the soul is no longer united with matter, a soul is not any human soul but is identifiable as the soul that united with matter to form this person in a certain place at a certain time. This is historically and irrevocably true. Even after separation by death, for all eternity the human soul retains this transcendental relation to the composite who was this man and no other. (*See* METEMPSYCHOSIS.)

See Also: SOUL, HUMAN, ORIGIN OF.

Bibliography: THOMAS AQUINAS, *Summa theologiae* 1, 75.2, 6; 89; 1a2ae, 85.6; *C. gent.* 2.55, 79–82; *De anim.* 14. M. J. ADLER, ed., *The Great Ideas: A Syntopicon of Great Books of the Western World*, 2 v. (Chicago 1952) 1:784–804. E. PEILLAUBE, *Dictionnaire de théologie catholique*, ed. A. VACANT et al., 15 v. (Paris 1903–50) 1.1:1021–41. M. T. COCONNIER, *Dictionnaire apologétique de la foi catholique*, ed. A. D'LÈS, 4 v. (Paris 1911–22) 1:86–107. A. VACANT, *Dictionnaire de la Bible*, ed. F. VIGOUROUX, 5 v. (Paris 1895–1912) 1:453–73. M. C. D'ARCY, *Death and Life* (London 1942). A. E. TAYLOR, *The Christian Hope of Immortality* (New York 1947); *Faith of a Moralist* (London 1951). M. MAHER, *Psychology* (9th ed. New York 1921) 525–44. J. E. ROYCE, *Man and His Nature* (New York 1961) 321–36. R. VERARDO, "Il problema dell'immortalità," *Sapienza* 2 (1949) 283–309, esp. 294. W. E. HOCKING, *The Meaning of Immortality in Human Experience* (New York 1957). R. A. FALCONER, *The Idea of Immortality and Western Civilization* (Cambridge, Massachusetts 1930). C. LAMONT, *The Illusion of Immortality* (3d ed. New York 1959), strong but often confused case against immortality. A. MONTAGU, *Immortality* (New York 1955), dismisses personal immortality as wishful thinking; takes advantage of the fact that scholastic arguments are sometimes poorly put.

[J. E. ROYCE]

3. In the Bible

When we speak of the immortality of the soul in the Bible, we must clearly distinguish between the general notion of survival after DEATH and the Platonic idea of specific survival of an immaterial principle after death.

Survival of Soul. The notion of the soul surviving after death is not readily discernible in the Bible. The concept of the human SOUL itself is not the same in the Old Testament as it is in Greek and modern philosophy, and the Hebrew OT has its own idea of a future life (*see* AFTERLIFE, 2). Immortality, ἀθανασία, has no Hebrew equivalent in the Masoretic Text and occurs only five times in the Septuagint (LXX), all in the Book of Wisdom. The adjective ἀθάνατος occurs once in Wisdom (1.15), where it modifies justice, and perhaps twice in Sirach. The substantive occurs only three times in the New Testament: 1 Timothy 6.16 speaks of the immortality of the Lord of lords; and 1 Corinthians 15.53–54 speak of mortal nature putting on immortality. The closely allied concept of incorruptibility, ἀφθαρσία, occurs a little more frequently in the Epistles of Paul (see 1 Cor 15.42, 50, 53, 54), but only twice in Wisdom (2.23; 6.19).

Moreover, although the LXX renders it as ψυχή, the Hebrews *nepeš* is a term of far greater extension than our "soul," signifying LIFE (Ex 21.23; Dt 19.21) and its various vital manifestations: breathing (Gn 35.18; Job 41.13), blood [Gn 9.4; Dt 12.23; Ps 140(141).8], desire (2 Sm 3.21; Prv 23.2). The soul in the Old Testament means not a part of MAN, but the whole man—man as a living being. Similarly, in the New Testament it signifies human life: the life of an individual, conscious subject (Mt 2.20; 6.25; Lk 12.22–23; 14.26; Jn 10.11, 15, 17; 13.37; Acts 27.10, 22; Phil 2.30; 1 Th 2.8). Consequently, for the Israelite, man dies when his *nepeš* leaves him (Gn 35.18; 2 Sm 1.9; 1 Kgs 17.21), and death is somehow a diminution of life, a loss of life. The New Testament remains faithful to this understanding of death (Mt 16.25; 20.28; 1 Jn 3.16). Hence, save for a few important examples (Wis; Mk 8.35; Mt 10.39; 16.25–26; Lk 9.24–25; Jn 12.25) where life is seen as a necessary condition for eternal blessings, the Bible does not speak of the survival of an immaterial soul. This is not surprising if one considers that categories of Greek philosophy are not likely to be found in a Semitic corpus of literature.

Survival after Death. A general notion of survival after death is found, however, both in the Old Testament and New Testament. In examining the evidence, a distinction between the fact of survival and its mode is useful. The fact, stated negatively, is that in neither Testament is death regarded as an absolute end to all life, as a total annihilation. Such passages as Gn 42.13; Job 7.21; Psalms 38(39).14; and Jeremiah 31.15 speak of "being no more" with regard to earthly existence, not existence as such. Survival after death is attested to in the Old Testament by the burial of the dead (Gn 23.1–20) and the desire to be buried with one's own (Gn 47.29–31; 49.29); especially by the belief in an abode for the dead (SHEOL, HADES, the "nether world") as in Numbers 16.30, 33; Job 7.9; 14.13; Psalms 29(30).4; Hosea 13.14; Isaiah 5.14; 14.9; by some prayers in the Psalter, which possibly indicate a desire for a vital afterlife [Ps 6; 7; 29(30).9–10; 87]; and by a growing sense of the divine justice that will punish the persecutor and crown with glory the works of the suffering just [Ps 9A.18,

19;15(16).10; especially the late wisdom Ps 33(34).20–23].

On the other hand, the mode of survival after death is extremely confused in its inception, but gains greater clarity with the approach to New Testament times, receiving in some quarters (e.g., the tenets of the Essenes as related by Flavius Josephus in *The Jewish War* 2.8) a formulation distinctly Hellenistic. The confusion is owing to the imperfect state of Biblical anthropology, to the lack of sufficient revelational data on the subject, and to the prevalent Hebrew mentality that regarded the permanence of the community as more fundamental than that of the individual. Hence, there is an ardent desire for progeny and a curse attached to sterility in Genesis 30.1; 1 Samuel 1.5; Isaiah 4.1; 47.9; Jeremiah 18.21; Hosea 9.12; and Luke 1.25. Moreover, the lot of the evil and the good who died remained for a long time in the Hebrew mind the same lot in Sheol (see Smith, ch. 3, 8).

A succession of national tragedies and the sufferings endured by the just on earth brought about a deeper reflection upon the specific lot of each individual after death. Here the wisdom of Israel's scribes achieved greater precision concerning the afterlife. It reached its apogee shortly before our era in the Book of Wisdom. Although Wisdom's formulation of the doctrine of immortality is still disputed by exegetes, it seems likely that "the whole Book has at its basis the conviction that the soul survives after death," while "the immortality of which the author speaks is never the immortality which the soul has of its very nature" (Weisengoff, 109–110).

Is the New Testament more explicit on the point? Recent exegetes [Cullmann, *Immortality of the Soul;* see J. Coppens in *Ephemerides theologicae Lovanienses* 33 (1957) 372–73; J. Levie in *Nouvelle revue théologique* 80 (1958) 537–38; and P. Benoit in *Revue biblique* 65 (1958) 147–48] have maintained that the New Testament does not teach the immortality of the soul in the Hellenistic sense of survival of an immaterial principle after death. This does not mean that the doctrine is denied there; but it does emphasize that the ultimate solution to the problem is to be found not so much in philosophical speculation as in the supernatural gift of the Resurrection.

Bibliography: G. KITTEL, *Theologisches Wörterbuch zum Neuen Testament* (Stuttgart 1935–) 2:844–53, 857–58; 3:7–21. *Encyclopedic Dictionary of the Bible,* tr. and adap. by L. HARTMAN (New York 1963), from A. VAN DEN BORN, *Bijbels Woordenboek* 508–10, 532–36, 1052–54, 1347–49, 2196, 2286–90. C. R. SMITH, *The Bible Doctrine of the Hereafter* (London 1958). J. P. WEISENGOFF, "Death and Immortality in the Book of Wisdom," *Catholic Biblical Quarterly* 3 (1941) 104–33. O. CULLMANN, *Immortality of the Soul or Resurrection of the Dead?* (New York 1958).

[S. B. MARROW]

4. Revelational Data

The immortality of the human soul is a truth that has always been asserted by professing Christians. It was taken for granted by both sides at the Reformation. As examples of this one can recall John Calvin's use of the arguments from moral consciousness and the way Saint Thomas More in his *Utopia* made public denial of this truth punishable by death. René Descartes illustrates how philosophers who are Christians have tried to find a place for immortality in their systems. It is because of this agreement that the official Church pronouncements are few.

A Theological Issue. Since the immortality of the soul is a truth that is to some extent attested by reason as well as by faith, Catholic apologists have always been ready to demonstrate the reasonableness of the teaching of revelation. But, valuable as these arguments have been, one must remember that for Catholic theology the immortality of the soul is not primarily a philosophical problem. The theologian must begin with the fact of man's restoration through Christ to a share in the divine life (*see* ELEVATION OF MAN). This is the "life everlasting" of the early creeds. God alone is truly immortal and incorruptible by nature; He is the eternal one who transcends the categories of space and time. But man is made in the image and likeness of God, and by the free gift of eternal life he finds his fulfillment in a sharing in the intimate life of God. The immortality of the soul is bound up with the immortality of God and the life of GRACE. Consequently in the first Christian writers one does not find arguments from reason concerning the immortality of the soul but rather the proclamation that God through Christ has called man to a life of HAPPINESS that will never end. It begins here in the new life one receives in Baptism, but it will reach its fulness only at the PAROUSIA, when the resurrection of the flesh takes place. The gaze of the early Fathers is fixed on entrance into the full possession of immortality so that the life everlasting is to be associated with the resurrection of the flesh; it concerns the destiny of the whole of man Sometimes this stress on the gratuitous nature of immortality and the desire to distinguish it from a merely natural quality of the soul led Christian writers to deny that the soul is immortal by nature. Irenaeus was so conscious of the supernatural life of the soul as union with God that he opposed the Gnostic idea of a natural immortality.

God's original plan was that this God-directed terrestrial life would prolong itself into eternity, but as a result of the sin of Adam this life was lost and death ensued. Death in the theological sense is the loss of this eternal life, of the sharing in the divine nature. This loss is manifested to man by the death of the body. This dissolution of man's being is but a symbol of his separation from God that is due to his sin. Saint Augustine develops this line of thought, and in this he is simply following the teaching of Saint John. But Christ conquered death insofar as He brought back to men true life, union with God in grace. The death of the body still remains for men, but now it no longer signifies their final separation from God. It is now the means of union with Him. It is the way to sanctification, since men have to follow Christ through death to resurrection. One dies only to rise with Christ. This changed attitude to death is seen in many of the early catacomb paintings in which the figures of Jonas, Daniel, and the children in the fiery furnace show one that death does not conflict with the hope of immortality.

Yet death of the body is an overwhelming fact of human experience, and despite the claims of spiritualism one has no sure sensible evidence of survival. One knows from faith that there is a life beyond the grave and knows further that this is a survival of the individual in the sense that there is a continuity between this life and the next. This is brought home by the Scripture teaching on RETRIBUTION. In the next life one will be rewarded or punished as he has lived in this life: Romans 2.7; Matthew 25.34–46. A just retribution demands the permanent existence of the subject. It was to safeguard this truth that the Church spoke out at the Fifth Lateran Council in 1513 (H. Denzinger, *Enchiridion symbolorum*, ed. A. Schönmetzer, 1440) and affirmed the survival of the individual soul. The teaching of Averroës that there is one common intellect for all mankind was thus rejected. It was not that the Church was particularly interested in Averroism as such, but only insofar as this doctrine endangered the idea of individual responsibility (*see* AVERROISM, LATIN).

Theology Looks at Rational Arguments. And so the theologian starts his reflections with what revelation teaches about man's share in the everlasting life of God that begins at Baptism and will continue into the next life. However, the Church has always insisted that reason has a contribution to make to the question of immortality. The apologists of the 2d and 3d centuries were quick to seize on those aspects of Greek thought that could be made to show that the Christian message was not at complete variance with man's desires and thoughts on this subject. Tertullian in his *De anima* gave a fairly full treatment of the soul, and Lactantius made use of some of the arguments of Plato and other pagan authors in favor of immortality. However, the use of reason in this matter can never be completely satisfactory, and many of the pagan philosophers held to a view of immortality that involved a preexistence of the soul, i.e., before this earthly life. Irenaeus was aware of this danger and distrusted the Gnostic's arguments from reason; but Origen, who was much more susceptible to rational argument, was led to

the opinion that souls did indeed preexist and were put into bodies as a punishment for sins committed in a previous life. This view was partly motivated by a desire to show that the sorrows of this life are not an argument against the justice of God. There was a reason for suffering. This idea of his met with general opposition. Methodius explicitly rejected it, and later, under Pope Vigilius in 543, this view of the Origenists was condemned (*Enchiridion symbolorum* 403). In the early 16th century when disputes arose in Italy concerning the true interpretation of Aristotle on the nature of the soul, the Fifth Lateran Council, already referred to, defended its immortality as not being contrary to reason and required teachers at universities to make clear to students of philosophy what the Christian view on this matter is (*Enchiridion symbolorum* 1440–41, but for full text see *Conciliorum oecumenicorum decreta* 581–82).

This of course does not rule out the view of those theologians who follow Duns Scotus and Cajetan and allow only a probable probative force to the arguments from reason when taken in isolation from the facts of revelation. In more recent years (1844) it has been stated against Bautain that reason can prove the immortality of the soul, although there has been no indication of what the actual proof is (*Enchiridion symbolorum* 2766). Nowadays this fact is taken for granted (cf. Pius XI, *Divini Redemptoris; Enchiridion symbolorum* 3771).

Immortality of the Damned. The problem of the eternity of Hell is also connected with the immortality of the soul. From time to time there has recurred the idea of a conditional immortality. That is, survival after death is conditional on conformity with God's law and wishes. Against the Gnostics Irenaeus said that the soul is not immortal by nature, but it can become immortal if it lives according to God's law. Arnobius the Elder also held this view; it implies that the damned are not in fact called to immortality. In their eagerness to point out the salvific significance of immortality, that it is a gratuitous gift and is intended to benefit man, some writers, such as Justin and Tatian, tended to favor the idea that the souls of the wicked died or were annihilated (thanatopsychism). They did not fully appreciate that the eternal death of which the Apocalypse speaks, i.e., being cut off from God forever, does involve some sort of immortality, although not the immortality intended by God. They did not pay sufficient attention to the fact that man's conduct here on earth decides his lot forever, not only in the sense that he can earn eternal reward but in the sense that he can also earn eternal damnation.

Intermediate State. Some of the most difficult problems from both the philosophical and theological viewpoints arise in connection with the intermediate state between death and final resurrection. The first-generation Christians faced the problem concerning the state of those who die when they began to recognize that the Parousia would be delayed. Saint Paul himself seems to have changed his emphasis. In the earlier Epistles, for example, Thessalonians, he looked forward to the Parousia, although he had already to meet the objection as to what happens to those who die before this event. But in his later writings he sees the probability of his own death before the Lord's coming, and he says something about those who are already dead. In Philippians 1.23–26 he tells of their union with Christ, a union much fuller than anything achieved on this earth, although it is not yet the glory of the resurrection. In the 14th century the discussions about the nature of the human soul led finally to the question concerning immediate retribution at death. John XXII in two sermons before he became pope expressed the view that no full reward or punishment would be given until the last day. The social character of retribution was uppermost in his mind, and perhaps the Aristotelian notion of man as a complete entity of body and soul and not a soul imprisoned in a body also created a difficulty in explaining the intermediate state. But in Benedict XII's constitution BENEDICTUS DEUS (Enchiridion symbolorum 1000–02) it is laid down that the BEATIFIC VISION is given before the resurrection and also eternal punishment. This doctrine about the particular judgment is repeated in the Council of Florence (Enchiridion symbolorum 1304–06).

But there still remains a difficulty in understanding this state. It is a greater one for those of an Aristotelian or Semitic turn of mind who consider man as being truly man only when he is body and soul, a totality. It is difficult to see how there can be a full reward if man is essentially incomplete and how the resurrection of the body can add something that is only accidental. The capabilities of the separated soul have exercised the ingenuity of Catholic thinkers, but perhaps there has been too much consideration of the problem in terms of the nature of the soul and not sufficient attention paid to the element of time. Death is a *transitus,* a going over, to a new order of reality; and man enters a world where the time differences are transcended. To speak of a resurrection in the future would not have the same connotations for the departed as it has for those here on earth.

This problem has become increasingly prominent as the tendency has been away from a Platonic view of the soul as being a complete entity in itself and toward a Semitic notion of man. This has brought a deeper appreciation of the resurrection of the body. But one must not see the resurrection of the body as a truth that is in opposition to the immortality of the soul. O. Cullmann revived the idea that at death the soul enters into a state of unconsciousness or sleep until the resurrection. This was rightly

criticized by Biblical scholars as being contrary to the teaching of the Gospel of Saint Luke and the Epistles of Saint Paul. The references to death as a sleep in early Church documents are not to be taken as a denial of consciousness beyond the grave, but as a natural metaphor for death. Moreover, the *Benedictus Deus* and Catholic teaching on PURGATORY rule out such a view. Likewise the view of J. Héring as to the possibility of reconciling a doctrine of reincarnation with that of the resurrection seems to be doomed to failure from a Catholic point of view, since the good and the wicked receive their final reward "soon after death" (Enchiridion symbolorum 1001–02).

See Also: DEATH (THEOLOGY OF); DESTINY, SUPERNATURAL; ESCHATOLOGY, ARTICLES ON; HEAVEN (THEOLOGY OF); HELL (THEOLOGY OF); JUDGMENT, DIVINE (IN THEOLOGY); MAN, 3; RESURRECTION OF CHRIST; RESURRECTION OF THE DEAD; SOUL, HUMAN, 5.

Bibliography: *Dictionnaire de théologie catholique, Tables générales,* ed. A. VACANT et al. (1951–) 2:2218–21. "Unsterblichkeit," *Lexikon für Theologie und Kirche,* ed. J. HOFER and K. RAHNER, 10 v. (2d new ed. Freiburg 1957–65) v.10. A. ETCHEVERY et al., *Catholicisme. Hier, aujourd'hui et demain,* ed. G. JACQUEMET (Paris 1947–) 5:1316–28. ἀθάνατος, ἀθανασία, ἄφθαρτος, ἀφθαρσία in G. W. H. LAMPE, ed., *A Patristic Greek Lexicon* (Oxford 1961–). "Unsterblichkeit," K. RAHNER and H. VORGRIMLER, *Kleines theologisches Wörterbuch* (Freiburg 1961). O. CULLMANN, *Immortality of the Soul or Resurrection of the Dead?* (New York 1958). C. DAVIS, *Theology for Today* (New York 1962). R. W. GLEASON, *The World to Come* (New York 1958). J. N. D. KELLY, *Early Christian Doctrines* (2d ed. New York 1960). G. PALA, *La risurrezione dei corpi nella teologia moderna* (Rome 1963). K. RAHNER, *On The Theology of Death,* tr. C. H. HENKEY (Quaestiones disputatae 2; New York 1961). M. SCHMAUS, *Katholische Dogmatik,* 5 v. in 8 (5th ed. Munch 1953–59) v.4.2. A. VONIER, *The Human Soul and Its Relations with Other Spirits* (3d ed. Saint Louis 1925; repr. London 1939). S. GAROFALO, "Sulla *eschatologia intermedia* in S. Paolo," *Gregorianum* 39 (1958) 335–52. É. H. GILSON, "Autour de Pomponazzi: Problématique de l'immortalité de l'âme en Italie au début du XVIe siècle," *Archives d'histoire doctrinale et littéraire du moyen-âge* 36 (1961) 163–279. J. HÉRING, "Entre la mort e la résurrection," *Revue d'histoire et de philosophie religieuses* 40 (1960) 338–48; "Eschatologie biblique et idéalisme platonicien" in *The Background of the New Testament and Its Eschatology: Studies in Honour of C. H. Dodd,* ed. W. D. DAVIES and D. DAUBE (Cambridge, Eng. 1956) 443–63. Y. B. TRÉMEL, "L'Homme entre la mort et la résurrection d'après le N.T.," *Lumière et vie* 24 (1955) 33–58.

[M. E. WILLIAMS]

IMMUTABILITY OF GOD

Immutability is the divine attribute whereby God is said to be completely changeless and unchangeable.

Biblical basis. The Old Testament reveals that God, through his immanent actions within time and history, is personal, knowing, and loving. Moreover, these same immanent divine acts reveal that God transcends all else that exists. As the One God, who is Savior, Creator, and Sanctifier, he is completely "other," and so cannot be numbered among all else that exists. Thus, God is present and active within the created order of time and history as the one who, as the "wholly other," transcends it. Unlike creatures, who change either through their own actions or by being acted upon, God transcends this changeable created order. He can neither change himself nor be changed by another and so He is immutable. Thus the Old Testament speaks of God as unchangeable. "Surely I the Lord do not change" (Mal 3:6); and the Psalmist echoes this, "Thou art unchanging" (Ps 101:27). With greater explicitness the author of the Letter of James in the New Testament writes of the "Father of lights with whom there is no change nor shadow of alteration" (Jas 1:17).

The Old Testament also speaks of God changing his mind. In Genesis, because of the wickedness of the human race, God is said to have been sorry that he had created humankind (Gn 6:6–7). In Exodus, Moses implored God "to change his mind" and so not bring disaster on his people; God heard Moses' prayer and so "changed his mind" (Ex 32:12–14). Moreover, at the repentance of the Ninevites God changed his mind and did not bring calamity upon them (Jon 3:10). Again, God hoped that his people would reform their lives so that he could change his mind concerning his threatened catastrophe (Jer 26:3). However, there are also passages where it is stated that God does not change his mind. Because he is not human or mortal, he will not change his mind (Nm 23:19). Because of his oath, he will not change his mind (Ps 110:4, 132:11). God will do what he has promised and so will not relent (Jer 4:28, Ez 24:14, Zec 8:14). In 1 Samuel 15 on the one hand God is said to regret and be sorry that he had made Saul king, and, on the other hand, it is said that: "Moreover the Glory of Israel will not recant or change his mind; for he is not a mortal, that he should change his mind." These seeming contradictions within God of changing and not changing his mind can be reconciled if one interprets those passages where God is said to change his mind as God expressing his unchanging nature. It is precisely because God is unchangeable in his love, mercy and compassion and yet equally adamant in his demand for goodness and justice that he is said to forgive the Ninevites or his people and regret that he had created humankind or appointed Saul king. As "wholly other" God does not change as to his perfect love, mercy and compassion or as to his unalterable demand for righteousness and holiness, but the manifestation of these unchanging divine attributes may find different expressions depending upon the changing human situation. The Old Testament thus testifies that

God is ethically immutable, that is, that he is unchanging in his love and justice. This ethical immutability would seem to demand an ontological immutability: that is, God can only be unchangeable in his love and justice if he ontologically immutably perfect. This is a philosophical issue the Bible does not address.

Christian tradition. The Fathers of the Church consistently taught that God is immutable. ATHENAGORAS stated that unlike the pagan gods, who are subject to time and so change, the true God is "immortal, and immovable, and unalterable" (*Leg. pro Christ.*, 22). Theophilus stated that God is without beginning because he is unbegotten and "he is unchangeable, because he is immortal" (*Ad Autol.* 1.4). For IRENAEUS God, unlike changing created beings, is "unchangeable Being" (*Adv. Haer.*, 2.34.2). Similar passages can be found in, for example, CLEMENT OF ALEXANDRIA (*Strom.* 2.11; 4.23; 6.7), Origen (*C. Cel.*, 1.21; 4.14; 6.62) and AUGUSTINE (*De. Trin.*, 3.2; 4.1; 5.5). In stating that God is immutable the Fathers were primarily denying of him anything that would place him within the changeable world of creation. Because God, unlike creatures, is perfectly good and loving, he cannot change. God's nature is unalterably perfect.

Scholastic theologians of the Middle Ages gave further philosophical depth to the notion of God's immutability. St. THOMAS AQUINAS offers three arguments, metaphysical in nature, that establish that God is immutable (*Summa theologiae*, 1.9.1). These are based upon understanding divinity as pure act, as simple and as omniperfect. All change is incompatible with these three concepts. First, anything that undergoes change must be able to change, that is, it must be in potency with regard to what it can actually become (*see* MOTION; BECOMING). Thus creatures, while they exist and so are in act, possess the potential to change either accidentally (i.e., acquire new actuality) or substantially (i.e., become something else). God, unlike creatures, is being itself (*ipsum esse*). His very nature is the act "to be," and so he is pure act (*actus purus*). Thus God possesses no interior potential to become more of what he is. All of his attributes are perfectly in act, and thus he is perfect wisdom in act, perfect love in act, perfect knowledge in act. To say then that God is immutable is to say that he does not undergo change, as do creatures and to accentuate that he is perfect in every way and that no change could make him more perfect. Second, Aquinas argues that since creatures are composite beings, they can undergo change and mutation, again either accidental or substantial (*see* MATTER AND FORM). However, God is perfectly simple, for he is simply pure being itself and thus is simply pure act; therefore he cannot undergo change. Third, following upon the first argument, Aquinas argues that change within creatures testifies that they are not perfect for through change they acquire new perfection. However, since God is pure act he possesses all goods perfectly and thus is in no need to change in order to actualize further perfection.

The Church's liturgical practice testifies to God's immutability. For example, in the Liturgy of the Hours the hymn for Prayer during the Day reads: "While all must change and know decay, You are unchanging, always new." The Church at the Council of NICAEA (425) solemnly condemned those who would hold that "the Son of God is subject to change and to alteration" (H. Denzinger, *Enchiridion symbolorum* 126). Other councils have also upheld God's immutability, especially Lateran IV (Denzinger 501) and Vatican I (Denzinger 3001).

The modern challenge to the doctrine of God's immutability is rooted in Hegelian philosophy, yet its most ardent proponents are found within process philosophy and theology, following the lead of A. N. Whitehead and C. Hartshorne (see, for example, J. B. Cobb, D. Griffin, N. Pittenger, S. Ogden). It is argued that an immutable God is static and inert and so incapable of having personal and loving relationships. To make God more active and relational it is proposed that God, as a member of the eternal cosmic process, changes as he interacts with the world and human beings and so develops and actualizes his own potential. Such a proposal for a mutable God makes him dependent upon the world for his existence. He is no longer wholly other than all else, and thus he is no longer the creator God who gives existence to all else. He merely becomes another acting member within the ever-changing process of finite reality, and as such is himself trapped within the vicissitudes and evils of human history, so undermining his transcendent ability to save.

Immutability of the Trinity. The Fathers and Scholastics almost exclusively focused their attention upon the immutability of God in so far as he is one. However, the one God is a trinity of persons, the Father, the Son and the Holy Spirit, immutable in themselves. Because the Father eternally begets the Son and spirates the Holy Spirit as his eternal love for the Son, he is immutably the Father. Equally the Son as eternally begotten and who eternally loves the Father in the Holy Spirit is immutably the Son. The Holy Spirit as the eternal love of the Father for the Son and the eternal love of the Son for the Father and who thus conforms the Father to be the loving Father for the Son and conforms the Son to be the loving Son for the Father is immutably the Holy Spirit. Neither the Father, nor the Son, nor the Holy Spirit can become more perfectly who they are for one another. They too are perfectly in act in relation to one another, and so subsist, that is, be who they are, only in their immutably perfect relationships with one another. These immutably perfect re-

lationships not only distinguish who they perfectly are, but also make them the one immutably perfect God. (*see* TRINITY, HOLY)

Some theologians, again often influenced by Hegelian or PROCESS PHILOSOPHY, argue that God becomes a trinity of persons through his interaction with the world and human history (see, for example, P. Fiddes, R. Jenson and J. Moltmann). The persons of the Trinity become who they are through their historical actions and thus the Trinity itself comes to be. The motivation for such a developmental view of the Trinity is to allow for greater salvific interaction and interplay between the divine and human persons, bringing about the mature evolution of both. However, only if God is an eternal Trinity of immutably (and so dynamically) mutually related persons can they act in time and history in such a manner as to bring others into their divine life and love. It is only because the Father is eternally the Father that he can send his eternal Son into the world as man so that through his salvific work the eternal Holy Spirit is able to transform human persons into the likeness of the Son and so become children of the Father.

Further issues. If God creates, does this not imply that he changes from being noncreator to being creator? It must be noted that if the act of creation is an act whereby something comes to be and so be actual, only a being who is BEING itself (*ipsum esse*) can create for it is the precisely existence (*esse*) that is needed in order for something to exist. Thus, when God creates, he creates by the immutably pure act that he is for no other act will do. While God, BEING PURE act, has no interior potential to be actualized, his being pure act gives him the potential to perform actions that only he can perform, such as to create out of nothing. The act of creation does not imply then a change in God for he acts by no other act than the immutably pure act that he is. The "change" that occurs at the "moment" of creation is entirely on the part of creatures, the transposition from nonexistence to existence. The term "creator" does not then imply a change in God but rather that since creatures have come to exist by the act of God, he is now newly called creator. The mystery of the Incarnation offers a somewhat similar problem. While the Son of God comes to be man at a certain moment in time, this "becoming" man does not imply a change in the eternal and immutable Son. The change that takes place is that within the womb of Mary the humanity comes to be and is united to the person of the Son by the power of the Holy Spirit in such a manner that the Son now exists as man. There is a change in that the Son now exists as man, but there is no change in so far as the Son exists as God. Equally, the Son of God as man experiences changes. He is born, hungers, thirsts, weeps, suffers and dies. It is truly the Son of God who is experiencing these changes, but he is experiencing these changes in so far as he truly exists as man for they are truly human experiences. As God, the Son remains immutable and impassible (*see* INCARNATION; IMPASSIBILITY OF GOD).

However, does not creation and incarnation imply an act of the will on the part of God, that is, he freely transposes himself from indetermination to determination and so changes? Within human beings free acts bring about change within the person freely acting. Human freedom is a power through which a person is capable of electing to act or not to act in a certain manner. The act of choice then involves the transition from possibility to actuality. However, freedom itself does not necessarily imply change. In God's case there is no previous state of indifference. He is eternally freely self-determined. He eternally wills what he wills for his will is commensurate with his nature as immutably pure act. The effects of what he wills may take place in time and history and so bring about changes, but his act of willing itself transcends time and history.

Bibliography: *Process Philosophy and Christian Thought*, eds., D. BROWN, R. JAMES, and G. REEVES (Indianapolis 1971). D. BURRELL, *Aquinas: God and Action* (Notre Dame 1979); ''Does Process Theology Rest on a Mistake?,'' *Theological Studies,* 43 (1982) 125–35; *Knowing the Unknowable God* (Notre Dame 1986). J. B. COBB, *A Christian Natural Theology* (London 1966). J. B. COBB and D. GRIFFIN, *Process Thought: An Introductory Exposition* (Philadelphia 1976). M. DODDS, *The Unchanging God of Love* (Fribourg 1985). P. FIDDES, *The Creative Suffering of God* (Oxford 1990); *Participating in God* (London 2000). C. HARTSHORNE, *The Divine Relativity* (New Haven 1948). W. HILL, ''Two Gods of Love: Aquinas and Whitehead,'' *Listening,* 14 (1979) 249–278; ''The Historicity of God,'' *Theological Studies,* 45 (1984) 320–33. H. KÜNG, *The Incarnation of God* (New York 1987). J. MOLTMANN, *The Crucified God* (London 1974); *The Trinity and Kingdom of God* (London 1981); *History and the Triune God* (London 1991). S. M. OGDEN, *The Reality of God* (New York 1971). N. PITTENGER, *God in Process* (London 1967). S. SIA, ''The Doctrine of God's Immutability: Introducing the Modern Debate,'' *New Blackfriars,* 68 (1987) 220–32. R. SWINBURNE, *The Coherence of Theism* (Oxford 1993). R. SWINBURNE, *The Christian God* (Oxford 1994). T. G. WEINANDY, *Does God Change?: The Word's Becoming in the Incarnation* (Petersham 1985); *Does God Suffer?* (Notre Dame 2000).

[T. G. WEINANDY]

IMPASSIBILITY OF GOD

Impassibility is that divine attribute whereby God is said not to experience inner emotional changes of state whether enacted freely from within or effected by his relationship to and interaction with human beings and the created order. More specifically, impassibility means that God does not experience suffering and pain, and thus does not have feelings that are analogous to human feelings. Divine impassibility follows upon His IMMUTABILITY, in that, since God is changeless and unchangeable, his inner emotional state cannot change from joy to sorrow or from delight to suffering.

Biblical basis. The Bible does not address the philosophical question of whether or not God is impassible. Nonetheless, divine impassibility is founded upon the same scriptural evidence as that of divine immutability. Summarily, God, within the Old Testament, reveals through his immanent actions within time and history that he is personal, knowing, and loving. He is the One God who is Savior, Creator, and Sanctifier. These immanent divine acts reveal that God transcends all else that exists. He is completely ''other,'' and so He cannot be numbered among all else that exists. Thus, God is present and active within the created order of time and history as the one who, as the ''Wholly Other,'' transcends it. Unlike creatures, whose emotional inner states change either through their own actions or by being acted upon, God as all perfect transcends this changeable created order. He neither can change his own inner emotional state nor can another effect a change in his inner emotional state, and thus He is impassible.

Within this Old Testament context God, nonetheless, is seen as displaying a variety of emotions. Due to his faithful love, God hears the cry of his enslaved people in Egypt and so ''suffers'' over their plight (Ex 2:23–25; 3:1–8, 15–17; Dt 4:37). Moreover, because of his love God equally grieves over the sinful disloyalty of his people and even becomes angry (Hos 11:1–4). Yet, his heart ''recoils'' within him and his compassion ''grows warm and tender,'' and thus he will not execute ''his fierce anger.'' The reason is, ''For I am God and not mortal; the Holy One in your midst and I will not come in wrath'' (Hos 11:8–9). While God's wrath rises in justice, it is always tempered by his forgiving, compassionate, and faithful love (Ex 32:11–14; 1 Sam 15:11). Within the Old Testament then God is seen as ''suffering'' with, or on behalf of, or because of his people, and so he grieves with or over them (Ps 78:40, 95:10–11). These various ''emotional'' states are said to cause God to ''repent'' or ''change his mind'' (Gn 6:6–7; Judg 2:18; 2 Sam 24:16; 1 Chr 21:15; Ps 106:45; Jer 18:8; Amos 7:3 & 6; Joel 2:13; Jon 3:19). In the end, God consistently acts with great compassion and mercy. ''For my thoughts are not your thoughts, nor are your ways my ways, says the Lord. For as the heavens are higher than the earth, so are my ways higher than your ways and my thought about your thoughts'' (Is 55:6–9).

The traditional defense for God's impassibility, in the light of such passages, was to argue that the Old Testament is using anthropomorphic language, and so cannot be taken literally. Therefore, God does not literally "groan," "suffer," or "grieve," nor does his heart "grow warm." However, while the Old Testament is undoubtedly using anthropomorphic language, it is nonetheless saying something that is actually true about God. Such passages can only rightfully be interpreted if one keeps in mind that they are predicated of the Wholly Other, "the Holy One in your midst." The very superlative, extravagant, and even excessive, expression of the love, the compassion, the forgiveness and, indeed, the anger, accentuates that the one who displays all of this intense passion is someone who transcends what is beyond the merely customary and human. The Lord is "God and not mortal." God is supremely passionate but his passion is that of the Wholly Other, and he is able to express such depth of passion only because he is the Wholly Other. Therefore, there is a legitimate literalness to what is said, but it is a literalness that must be interpreted from within the complete otherness of God, for this is the manner in which this passion is expressed. If God were not wholly other, he would not be able to be as passionate as He is. Moreover, the various passions that are predicated of God—affection, pity, mercy, compassion, forgiveness, anger, suffering—must be placed within the primary attribute of God's unchanging, faithful, and all-consuming love. Thus, to speak of God's grief or suffering over the plight of his people or over their own sin is not to denote an emotional change within God, but rather to accentuate his unchangeable and all-consuming love. Even God's anger is an expression of his unchanging love. Such references to God's emotional changes of state are not then expressions of God actually experiencing first pleasure and then sorrow, or joy and then suffering; rather, they express the reality of his unchanging love which is experienced differently depending upon historical situations and circumstances. God's unchanging love is experienced as grief or even anger in the face of sin. Because of his love God is said to be jealous at losing his people due to their sinful disloyalty. His love is experienced as forgiveness and mercy in the face of repentance. Because of God's unchanging love, it is said that he suffers at the plight of his people.

Christian tradition. While the Fathers of the Church inherit the term "impassibility" from Greek philosophy, they nonetheless interpret it, for the most part, from within the biblical understanding of God's transcendence. Because God differs from created reality, in that He is eternal and incorruptible, JUSTIN MARTYR professes that Christians dedicate themselves to the "impassible God" (*Apol.*, 1.13). Similarly, Irenaeus argues that because God as Creator is unchangeably perfect, He is impassible (*Ad. Haer.*, 2.12.1; 2.17.3, 8). Tertullian states that because God is eternal, and thus outside of time, He

does not change or suffer (*Ad. Mar.*, 1.3, 8). Yet, precisely because God is perfectly and unchangeably good, Tertullian holds that creatures experience this goodness in differing manners—anger toward sinners and mercy toward the repentant (*Ad. Mar.*, 2.13). Origen holds that one cannot interpret literally those passages which speak of God being subject to any humanlike emotion, for "God must be believed to be entirely without passion and destitute of all these emotions" (*De Prin.*, 2.4.4). Nonetheless, because the Father is moved by our sinful plight, Origen can also state that "the Father is not impassible" (*In Ezech. Hom.*, 6.6). God is impassible in the sense that He does not undergo emotional changes of state, but He is not impassible in the sense that He is devoid of passionate love. It is precisely because of His unchanging and abiding all consuming love that He comes to our aid. In attributing impassibility to God, then the Fathers of the Church are primarily denying of him anything that would place Him within the changeable created order, and thus, unlike human beings, He does not undergo emotional changes of state. Moreover, in their denial, they wish to enhance the absolute perfection of God's unchanging passionate love.

THOMAS AQUINAS discusses God's impassibility within the context of His will and love. He argues that God does not undergo passible emotional changes as do human beings. Human beings either tend toward a known good or attempt to avoid a known evil and in so tending or avoiding their sensitive (bodily) emotions and feelings are aroused, such as affection or fear. In contrast, God does not undergo this passible process. He neither possesses a body nor sensitive appetites, and "therefore, there is no passion in God" (*S.C.G.*, I.89.2; see also I.89.1–7). However, God does possess intellect and will, and being pure act, He knows and wills in the one act that He himself is (*Summa Theologiae*, I.14.1–4; I.19.1). Thus God loves not in the human sense of arousing affectionate feelings or passions, but in that His perfect love is eternally in act, and in this sense God loves without passion (*ibid.*, I.20.1.ad 1). However, God is passionate in the sense that His all-consuming and perfect love is fully in act, and so He can be said to be the most passionate of all beings. Moreover, because God's love is fully in act, unlike the love of human beings, all facets of his love are fully in act. His fully actualized love embraces goodness, kindness, mercy, compassion, justice, admonition, anger, correction, and so on. God need not undergo passible changes in order to lovingly reprimand the sinner or be lovingly merciful to the repentant. Thus God, within His fully actualized love, can even be said to grieve over sin, not in the sense that He undergoes an emotional change of state or experiences sorrow in the human sense of feeling bodily sadness, but because, in His love, He always is concerned with those He loves, even sinners. Moreover, God is merciful and compassionate, not in the sense that He "feels" pain or suffering, but in the sense that His perfect love embraces those who suffer. His mercy is primarily expressed by acting to alleviate the cause of the suffering, something that even compassionate human beings are often unable to do. For Aquinas God's omnipotence is ultimately expressed in His mercy, the alleviation of sin and death and in the outpouring of grace and the bestowal of eternal life (*ibid.*, II–II.30.4).

The persons of the Trinity are equally impassible, though this has not been developed within the Christian tradition. The persons of the Trinity subsist as who they are only in relation to one another. The Father subsists as Father in that through the procession of the fully actualized Spirit of love he begets the Son. The Son subsists as Son in that through the same procession of the fully actualized Spirit of love, He equally loves the Father. The Holy Spirit subsists as Holy Spirit in that through proceeding from the Father and the Son as their fully actualized love He conforms the Father to be the loving Father of the Son and conforms the Son to be the loving Son of the Father. Thus, the persons of the Trinity need not undergo passible emotional changes of state, for they eternally and perfectly express and enjoy the bliss of their mutual fully actualized love for one another. Equally then, it is the fully actualized persons of the Trinity who embrace human beings, through Their redemptive work, within Their fully actualized love.

Contemporary issues. From the later part of the nineteenth century to the present, many Christian theologians have come to deny that God is impassible by specifically asserting that God must suffer. There are three reasons for this radical shift: (1) The experience of immense suffering within the world, exemplified in the Holocaust and similar horrendous events, produces an ardent yearning for the consolation of knowing that God suffers in solidarity with those who unjustly suffer. Only in a suffering God does one truly find a loving and compassionate God. An impassible God, it is asserted, is aloof to human suffering and thus indifferent. (2) The Bible bears witness to a passible and so suffering God. As seen above God, within the Old Testament, is said to suffer with, on behalf of, and because of his people. Moreover, through the INCARNATION, the Son of God must not only suffer as man but also as God. This divine suffering within the Incarnation discloses that God has always suffered in solidarity with human suffering. Likewise in the crucifixion, the Son not only suffers the loss of his Father, but the Father equally suffers the loss of his Son. (3) PROCESS PHILOSOPHY, has fostered the notion that God's immanence within the world and its history demands that he changes and develops in relation to the world and its history. Thus he experiences time and changeable emotional states such as suffering.

In response to this denial of God's impassibility, a number of points can be made: (1) As seen above, to say that God is impassible is not a positive statement affirming that God is static, inert, and lifeless, and so aloof and indifferent. Rather it is a denial of those "human" characteristics that would make Him less than fully loving. (2) Moreover, God is impassible precisely because He need not undergo passible changes of state that would make him more loving. As PURE ACT God is pure and perfect love in act. (3) Because God, both in His unity and in His triunity, possesses all his attributes fully in act, He cannot suffer the loss of any these perfect goods and so He cannot experience the suffering due to their loss. (4) If God did suffer, not only would His love not be perfect, but His love would also not be entirely altruistic and beneficent in the face of human suffering. He would be acting so as to relieve His own suffering. (5) Equally, while God is immanent within the world, He is immanent as the one who is wholly other than the world. He acts immanently within time and history as the One who transcends time and history. Thus, while God is in the midst of evil, the evil of the created order does not reverberate back into His divine being and so cause Him to suffer. As Creator, He exists in a distinct ontological order from that of the created order. (6) If God did suffer, it would mean that He was a member of the created order and so He would not be the Creator and thus, as a suffering member of that order, would Himself need to be freed from evil. Thus those who espouse a suffering God by necessity advocate panentheism, as exemplified in process philosophy, that is, that while God is more than all else that is, He nonetheless embodies and so experiences all that is, including suffering. However, having placed God within the created order, He can no longer be its omnipotent Creator since He himself is now dependent upon the finite order for His own development and growth. (7) Moreover, God could no longer be the omnipotent God of mercy who could act so as to surmount the causes of suffering such as sin, death, and damnation.

Similarly, a number of points can be made with regard to the suffering of Jesus: (1) The Church's doctrinal understanding of the Incarnation demands that, since the divine Son of God actually existed as man, all human attributes could truly be predicated of Him. The Son of God as man hungered, cried, suffered, and died; however, within His divine nature He remained impassible. (2) The assertion that the Son of God, within His incarnate state, suffers as God robs the Incarnation of its authentic salvific value. What is important is that the Son of God experiences authentic human suffering in an authentic human manner and not that He experiences human suffering in a mitigated divine manner. It is the Son of God as man who offers His human life to the Father as a sacrifice for sin that is salvific. (3) Moreover, on the cross, the Son of God as man may humanly experience being forsaken by the Father, but He equally trusts that He is not so forsaken and that the Father will come to His aid (Ps 22). As God, though, He was not forsaken. Nor does the Father suffer the loss of his Son. To place the suffering of the cross as an experience within the Trinity itself deprives Christ's suffering of its authentic historical importance and human value, and instead places it within an ahistorical and ethereal divine realm where what is transpiring is more significant for the Trinity than for humankind. (4) While the Father may judge that the crucifixion of his Son is unjust, yet the New Testament testifies not to His suffering but to His pleasure in what his Son is doing on behalf of humankind in accordance with his will (Mt 20:28, Jn 15:13, Eph 5:2, 1 Jn 3:16). Such pleasure is radically and dramatically manifested in the Father raising his Son gloriously from the dead. (5) While Jesus, as the Son of God incarnate, is now gloriously risen from the dead, yet as head of His body, He continues to suffer in union with His body—the church. This is central to Paul's conversion experience. "Saul, Saul, why do you persecute me? . . . I am Jesus, whom you are persecuting" (Acts 9:4–5, see 1 Cor 12:26). Augustine exemplifies this tradition: "For whatever he has suffered we too have suffered with him, and what we suffer he too suffers with us. If the head suffers in any way, how can the hand assert that it does not suffer? If the hand suffers, how can the head say that it does not suffer? . . . and he is now ascended into heaven and is seated at the right hand of the Father, whatever his Church suffers by way of this life's tribulations, temptations, constrictions and deprivations, . . . this he also suffers" (*Enar. in Ps.*, 62.2). This is what brings true consolation to human beings in the midst of their suffering, not that God suffers in his divine nature, but that Christ, who has conquered all evil, continues to suffer in union with His body so as to assure that It too will triumph with him. "For as we share in Christ's sufferings, so through Christ we share abundantly in comfort too" (2 Cor 1:5; see Phil 3:10, Rom 8:17, 1 Pt 4:12, 1 Pt 5:1).

Bibliography: T. AQUINAS, *Summa Theologiae*, I.20; II–II.30; *Summa Contra Gentiles*, I.89–91. R. BAUCKHAM, "'Only the Suffering God Helps': Divine Passibility in Modern Theology," *Themelios* 9.3 (1984) 6–13. J. B. COBB and D. GRIFFIN, eds., *Process Thought: An Introductory Exposition* (Philadelphia 1976). R. CREEL, *Divine Impassibility* (Cambridge 1986). N. M. DE S. CAMERON, ed., *The Power and Weakness of God* (Edinburgh 1990). M. DODDS, *The Unchanging God of Love* (Fribourg 1985); "Thomas Aquinas, Human Suffering, and the Unchanging God of Love," *Theological Studies* 52 (1991) 330–44. P. FIDDES, *The Creative Suffering of God* (Oxford 1990); *Participating in God* (London 2000). T. E. FRETHEIM, *The Suffering of God: An Old Testament Perspective* (Philadelphia 1984). J. GALOT, *Dieu Souffre-t-il?* (Paris 1976). R. GOETZ, "The Suffering God: The Rise of a New Orthodoxy," *New Christian Century* 103/13 (1986) 385–89. G. HANRATTY, "Divine Immutability and Impassibility Revisited," in *At the Heart of the Real*, ed. F. O'ROURKE (Dublin 1992). A. HESCHEL, *The Prophets* (New York 1962). W. WILL, "Two Gods of Love: Aquinas and Whitehead," *Listening* 14 (1979) 249–265. JOHN PAUL II, *Salvifici Doloris* (1984). K. KITAMORI, *Theology of the Pain of God* (London 1966). J. LAMBRECHT and R. F. COLLINS, eds., *God and Human Suffering* (Louvain 1990). J. Y. LEE, *God Suffers for Us: A Systematic Inquiry into a Concept of Divine Passibility* (The Hague 1974). J. MOLTMANN, *The Crucified God* (London 1974). J. K. MOZLEY, *The Impassibility of God: A Survey of Christian Thought* (Cambridge 1926). M. SAROT, *God, Passibility and Corporeality* (Kampen 1992). T. G. WEINANDY, *Does God Suffer?* (Edinburgh 2000). H. ROBINSON WHEELER, *Suffering Human and Divine* (New York 1939).

[T. G. WEINANDY]

IMPECCABILITY

Impeccability is more than freedom from sin. It is the impossibility of sinning. It can be considered as intrinsic, springing from a being's nature, or extrinsic, resulting from special help. It can be absolute, without any conditions, or relative and conditioned. Both angels and men are, by nature, capable of sin [2 Pt 2.4; H. Denzinger, *Enchiridion symbolorum*, ed. A. Schönmetzer (32d ed. Freiburg 1963) 800; Rom 5.12; H. Denzinger, *ibid.*, 1511–12]. It is of faith that Christ, as man, was without sin (Jn 8.46; 14.30; H. Denzinger, *ibid.*, 434). Because of His fullness of grace, the beatific vision, and, especially, the hypostatic union, He could not sin. Faith teaches that Mary had the unique privilege of an immaculate conception and was free from all actual sin (H. Denzinger, *ibid.*, 2803). Some hold that St. Joseph also, at least after marriage, was free from all sin. The Apostles are considered to have been confirmed in grace after Pentecost (St. Thomas Aquinas, *De verit.* 24.9). Even the holy, however, do sin venially (Jas 3.2; 1 Jn 1.8). The blessed, being in eternal possession of their final end, will not and cannot sin (Jn 10.28; 1 Thes 4.17; H. Denzinger, *ibid.*, 1000). They are immediately united to the fullness of truth, goodness, and beauty. Theologians agree that beings could be created with the beatific vision and thus be impeccable, or they could be preserved by special grace. It is disputed, however, whether a creature could be impeccable by nature (intrinsically) either absolutely, and so incapable of sin against natural or supernatural law, or relatively, and so be impeccable with respect only to natural law. It is commonly held that absolute impeccability is impossible. All creatures "are changeable because they were made from nothing" (H. Denzinger, *ibid.*, 1333). The created will has rectitude of action only when "regulated according to the divine will" (St. Thomas Aquinas, *Summa theologiae*, 63.1, *C. gent.* 3.109). Most Thomists hold that it is possible for a creature to be relatively impeccable by nature and that the angels were in fact so created.

Bibliography: Commentaries on Thomas Aquinas, *Summa theologicae*, 1, esp. q. 63, by CAJETAN, SALMANTICENSES, JOHN OF ST. THOMAS, D. BÁÑEZ. J. CAPREOLUS, In Sent. 22. FERRARIENSIS, *In C. gent.* 3.109. DUNS SCOTUS, *In 2 sent.* 5.1. F. DE SUÁREZ, *De angelis* (Lyons 1620), bk. 3, ch. 7. E. HUGON, *Tractatus dogmaticus,* v.1 (11th ed. Paris 1933). P. RICHARD, *Dictionnaire de théologie catholique,* ed. A. VACANT et al., 15 v. (Paris 1903–50; Tables générales 1951–) 7.1:1265–80.

[P. J. KELLY]

IMPECCABILITY OF CHRIST

It is a defined dogma of faith that Jesus Christ in His humanity never committed a sin (Council of Florence, H. Denzinger, *Enchiridion symbolorum,* ed. A. Schönmetzer [32d ed. Freiburg 1963] 1347). He was sinless—He knew neither mortal nor venial sin, neither original nor personal sin. As the earlier Third Council of Constantinople also firmly had asserted, "Christ has two volitions or wills, and two natural operations, without division or change, without partition or commingling. And the two natural wills are not opposed (by no means!) as the godless heretics have said; but the human will is compliant, and not opposing or contrary; as a matter of fact it is even obedient to his divine and omnipotent will" (H. Denzinger, *Enchiridion symbolorum* 556; *The Church Teaches,* tr. J. F. Clarkson et al. [St. Louis 1955] 187).

The conciliar teaching is a careful reflection of the testimony of Sacred Scripture. "Which of you can convict me of sin?" (Jn 8.46). "I will no longer speak much with you, for the prince of the world is coming, and in me he has nothing" (Jn 14.30). Or, as the Epistle to the Hebrews affirms emphatically, "For it was fitting that we should have such a high priest, holy, innocent, undefiled, set apart from sinners" (7.26).

Although not defined, it is of Catholic faith that Jesus Christ was in His humanity not merely sinless but impeccable; that is, He could not sin; He did not have the power to sin. It is theologically certain (from the consensus of theologians) that such impeccability was antecedent and internal. By antecedent is meant that the impeccability of Christ was effected by the will of God before, so to speak, God consulted His own knowledge of the FUTURIBLES. By internal is designated that kind of impeccability that flows from the very ontological constitution of the creature, at least as an exigency of that constitution. That is, it is an impeccability that, if it is not effected by the very ontological constitution itself, is at least demanded by the ontological constitution.

Conciliar affirmations such as that of CONSTANTINO-PLE III cited above and equivalent ecclesiastical affirmations are the basis of the theological qualification "of Catholic faith" given to the fact of Christ's impeccability. The consensus of theologians concerning the antecedent, internal character is based on the facile reasoning that any sin of the human will of Christ would be attributable to the Second Person of the Blessed Trinity. Such an attribution is inconceivable and hence the firm note of "theologically certain."

As to how the impeccability is actually effected, that is, as to what psychic means are present in the humanity of Christ whereby impeccability is brought about, two principal schools of thought exist. Thomists hold that the impeccability is brought about by the beatific vision possessed by Christ from the first moment of His life. According to them, the beatific vision by itself always renders sin absolutely impossible. Scotists say otherwise. According to them the will remains free even though the intellect sees God face to face. God, however, knowing that no happiness can be perfect unless it is to endure forever, "prevents," in the radical sense of going before or guiding, the will so that it never interrupts its act of enjoying God, and as long as this act continues, sin is impossible. Theologians commonly differ from the Scotistic view, but the view may not be censured.

A theological question closely connected with the explanation of Christ's impeccability is the problem of the MANDATE.

See Also: JESUS CHRIST, ARTICLES ON.

Bibliography: *Dictionnaire de théologie catholique,* ed. A. VACANT et al., 15 v. (Paris 1903–50; Tables générales 1951–) Tables générales 2:2225–27. L. SCHEFFCZYK, "Unsündlichkeit Christi," *Lexikon für Theologie und Kirche,* ed. J. HOFER and K. RAHNER, 10 v. (2d, new ed. Freiburg 1957–65) 10:527–528. L. LERCHER, *Institutiones theologiae dogmaticae,* v. 3 (5th ed. Barcelona 1951). I. SOLANO, *Sacrae theologiae summa,* ed. FATHERS OF THE SOCIETY OF JESUS, PROFESSORS OF THE THEOLOGICAL FACULTIES IN SPAIN, 4 v. (4th ed. Madrid 1961) 3.1:329–369.

[E. A. WEIS]

IMPENETRABILITY

The impossibility of one body's receiving another within itself, or the impossibility of two bodies' occupying the same space at the same time. Impenetrability is not resistance, which seems to be an active quality; nor is penetration to be identified with absorption or similar phenomena, which are the result of the porous or reticular structure of matter. The fact of impenetrability is a datum of sensible experience.

The search for a causal explanation of impenetrability arises from the theological consideration of the GLORI-

FIED BODY of Christ, and from speculation about the glorified bodies of the blessed. Christ's emergence from the sealed tomb at the Resurrection and His entrance through the closed doors of the Upper Room represent suppressions of the natural impenetrability of bodies (*see* RESURRECTION OF CHRIST). Discussion of such miracles leads to an analysis of the nature and cause of impenetrability.

Two opposing solutions were offered in the Middle Ages. St. THOMAS AQUINAS sees impenetrability as an effect, in the order of formal causality, of the accident of QUANTITY. Bodies are numerically diverse by reason of their dimensions, dimensions follow on SITUATION (*situs*), and situation derives from quantity (*In Boeth. de Trin.* 4.3; *In 4 sent.* 44.2.2.2). In the terminology of later commentators, impenetrability is a secondary formal effect of the accident of quantity, something negative and arising from the relationship of a body to PLACE. John Duns Scotus holds that impenetrability is an active force, the result, in the order of efficient causality, of quantity (*In 4 sent.* 49.16).

Most 20th-century scholastics follow the solution of St. Thomas. Others, while not accepting Scotus's reasons, agree with him in assigning a positive, active nature to impenetrability. All concur that God can miraculously suppress impenetrability as an effect, while retaining intact the quantity that is its cause.

See Also: LOCATION (UBI); BILOCATION; EXTENSION.

Bibliography: J. GREDT, *Elementa Philosophiae Aristotelico–Thomisticae,* ed. E. ZENZEN, 2 v. (13th ed., rev. and augm. Freiburg 1961) 1:279–282. P. HOENEN, *Cosmologia* (5th ed. Rome 1956). A. TOGNOLO, *Enciclopedia filosofica,* 4 v. (Venice–Rome 1957) 2:1293–94.

[W. B. MAHONEY]

IMPENITENCE

The primary condition for the forgiveness of sin is the transgressor's heartfelt sorrow for his culpable act as an offense against God, together with his firm intention to sin no more and to make satisfactory amends so far as this is possible. Impenitence is the state of the sinner who either has not yet achieved this primary condition or, worse, is positively unwilling to achieve it. Thus there is the simple fact of impenitence and also a willful or directly voluntary impenitence which is itself a special sin.

The Council of Trent in 1551 expressly taught that REPENTANCE is necessary at all times for the remission of serious sin (*Enchiridion symbolorum,* 1676). Without sorrow for sin there is no forgiveness. Grief for sin, refor-

mation of life, and willingness to expiate form the object of manifold exhortations and warnings in both the Old and New Testaments. These are summarized in the words of Christ: ''Unless you do penance, you shall all likewise perish'' (Lk 13.5). Theologians agree that there is question here not only of God's positive command establishing penance as requisite for forgiveness but also of a real necessity of means, so that in the present order of providence God Himself cannot forgive sins unless there is real repentance.

Although any impenitence makes the forgiveness of sin impossible, there is a great difference between simple impenitence and willful impenitence or sinful obstinacy. A sinner is not obliged to repent immediately after his sinful act, and his nonrepentance does not necessarily imply a sin distinct from that of which he is already guilty. Unless there is a particular reason making repentance an urgent necessity, he may postpone his sorrow for some time without falling into the special sin of impenitence. Generally, however, a sinner cannot remain in the state of grave sin for long without falling into other sins, because deprived of sanctifying grace, he will lack the strength to resist them. It is impossible to determine the length of this time with mathematical precision. Differences in state of life, moral formation, and tenderness of conscience inevitably make the length of time different for each individual.

The special sin of impenitence consists in willing not to do penance and a resolution not to be converted to God. This voluntary impenitence will necessarily be only relative and incomplete on earth and will vary in individuals in degree of malice and formal guilt, but in any case it will constitute a dangerous predisposition to final impenitence.

Final, like temporary, impenitence may or may not be directly voluntary. Basically final impenitence means that death comes while one is in the state of mortal sin. Although every sinner is undoubtedly obliged to repent at least at the moment of death, it does not follow that all final impenitence is directly voluntary. A sinner may die without having done penance but without conscious rejection of a final grace of repentance. As a special sin, final impenitence includes an ultimate voluntary rejection of grace, aptly described as a sin against the Holy Spirit. This final impenitence may or may not be a sequel to voluntary temporary impenitence. The mystery of divine predestination is here much involved. In all cases, final impenitence on earth opens the way to the eternal impenitence of the damned.

See Also: REPENTANCE; CONTRITION

Bibliography: THOMAS AQUINAS, *Summa theologiae* 2a2ae, 14. P. RICHARD, *Dictionnaire de théologie catholique,* ed. A. VA-

CANT et al., 15 v. (Paris 1903–50; Tables générales 1951) 7:1280–85.

[J. F. RIGNEY]

IMPETUS

An anglicized Latin term from the Latin roots *in* and *petere,* meaning a thrust toward some goal, it was commonly used in classical, ecclesiastical, and scholastic Latin without the technical connotation it was to acquire in the 14th century. Hence, in Roman and Biblical literature it was used for military attacks, the force of a river's current, and human drives; it was almost synonymous with *nisus.* In the first quarter of the 14th century, however, the term acquired a technical, philosophical meaning that eventually was rendered as *impeto* and *momento* by GALILEO in the field of mechanics. The term lost much of its original scholastic significance in discussions of the ''quantity of motion'' by Galileo, R. DESCARTES, and G. W. LEIBNIZ. The last replaced it with the concept of force, *lebendige Kraft,* which is measured by MASS times velocity squared (mv^2). Here the term is considered in its technical scholastic context.

The origin of the notion was the Aristotelian problem of explaining violent, or compulsory, motion after the body was separated from the impelling agent. Natural motion springs spontaneously from NATURE (φύσις), an internal, innate principle of motion and rest motion of heavy bodies, but it cannot explain the unnatural motion of a heavy body upward. All unnatural, or violent, motions must be explained in terms of an extrinsic, alien mover; insofar as a thing is moved at all, it must be moved by something distinct from its own nature. PLATO suggested that the original mover also moves the medium, which continues to move the projectile by rushing behind and pushing it forward ἀντιπερίστασις (*Tim.* 80C). ARISTOTLE rejected this as insufficient and held that the original mover gives not only movement, but also the power of moving (δύναμις τοῦ κινεῖν) to the medium (*Phys.* 226b 27–267a 22; *Cael.* 301b 17–33). In this way the reality of nature was preserved and violent motion could continue as long as there was sufficient force in the medium to move the body. Aristotle argued further that if there were no medium, there could be no violent motion (*Phys.* 215a 1–18).

JOHN PHILOPONUS presented many commonsense objections to Aristotle's theory and concluded: ''It is necessary that a certain incorporeal motive power (κινητικήν τινὰ δύναμιν ἀσώματον) be given to the projectile in the act of throwing'' [*Commentaria in Aristotelem Graeca* 17 (Berlin 1888) 636–642]. He pointed out that the motive ''energy'' (ἐνέργεια) is only bor-

rowed and is decreased by the natural tendency of the body and the resistance of the medium. This new theory of an alien energy given to the body by the original mover was attacked by Simplicius (d. 549), who did not present the new view clearly and adequately. The scholastics did not have a Latin translation of Philoponus; thus it is doubtful that he played any role in the scholastic concept of impetus.

The scholastic theory seems to have been first suggested by Francis of Marchia. While discussing sacramental causality in his commentary on the *Sentences,* bk. 4, he used a concept of impetus to explain how both Sacraments and projectiles have a certain force resident within, by which something is produced. This *virtus derelicta in lapide a motore* is a ''certain extrinsic form'' that will in time diminish. JOHN BURIDAN, perhaps independently, reached the same conclusions in his *Quaestiones super lib. Physicorum,* 8.12, and *Quaestiones de caelo et mundo,* 2.12–13, 3.2. For him, the mover impresses a certain *impetus* on the body itself by which the body continues to move until overcome by air resistance and natural gravity. He insisted that impetus is ''violent and unnatural, since it is violently impressed by an extrinsic principle and foreign to the natural form.'' He even suggested impetus as a possible explanation for the perpetual rotation of celestial bodies, in which there is no resistance or fixed natural inclination. ALBERT OF SAXONY and MARSILIUS OF INGHEN promulgated the theory and continued to speak of impetus as an ''accidental and extrinsic force,'' thus preserving the Aristotelian notion of nature and violence. Later scholastics—such as Laurence Londorius, first rector of St. Andrew's; Agostino NIFO; Tommaso de Vio CAJETAN; Alessandro PICCOLOMINI; and J. C. Scaliger—interpreted Aristotle's words in a wide sense consistent with the theory of impetus. Thomists such as John CAPREOLUS and Domingo de SOTO claimed it as the ''opinion of St. Thomas.''

Some scholastic authors considered impetus to be a ''mover'' accompanying the body. However, if impetus were a true efficient cause of motion, then it would be philosophically impossible to distinguish projectiles from living things, which move themselves. Domingo de Soto argued against this misconception and explained that impetus is only an instrument of the AGENT who is the true efficient cause. He pointed out the analogy between impetus and nature. Both are formal principles of motion, not efficient causes; just as the cause of natural activity is the progenitor, not nature, so too the cause of violent motion is the agent, not impetus.

See Also: SCIENCE (IN THE MIDDLE AGES).

Bibliography: A. MAIER, *Enciclopedia filosofica* (Venice-Rome 1957) 2:1299–1301. J. A. WEISHEIPL, ''Natural and Compul-

tñu et preſentantibs eum. atqz dua̅
cibus duobus diaconilry uſqz ad
pbros. et antea letaim̅ encienfuły
duo preſbn̅ adduca̅nt eum uſqz
ad ſcam̅ poꝛtaſuas. et diaconus
diac. P oſtulat mater ccrlia.
ut ſupra in oꝛdinacoe̅ diaconi et
uſr ſe erigens in eenrgens ſi digꝰ
ſit. ul. aiir acnfinncibus eandem
dignuin et ultum ẽ di graciа.
epiis ſeeudo eum mitra dieat.

Pater nr̅. Et ne nos indueas in temptaconem. Saluos far ſeruos tuos.
D̅ne deus uirtutu couerte nos. Mitte eis auxilium de ſco̅: Et de ħ. I Don
mttes m iudiciu cu̅ ſeruis tuis. D̅ne exaudi oꝛonem meam. Et damoꝛ. Dominus
uobiſeum. Et eum ſpiritu tuo.
ctioues nr̅as q̅s d̅ne aſpirando preueni et adiuuando proſequere.ut aucr
tu uoſtra operaeio. et a te ſemper inapiat. et per te eepta fuiatur. Per
dominum.

Miniature from "Pontifical of Arles," depicting imposition of hands, 14th century

sory Motion," *The New Scholasticism* 29 (1955) 50–81; "The Principle *Omne quod movetur ab alio movetur* in Medieval Physics," *Isis* 56 (1965) 26–45. M. CLAGETT, *The Science of Mechanics in the Middle Ages* (Madison, Wis. 1959).

[J. A. WEISHEIPL]

IMPOSITION OF HANDS

The rite of imposing hands on the head of another is one of the most frequent in both Old and New Testaments and in Christian liturgy, although in very different circumstances and with different significations. The fundamental idea seems to be that of the transmission of some power or quality, in most cases beneficent and mainly by way of conferring a blessing.

Old Testament. In the books of the OT the rite occurs only once for the transmission of something not beneficent, namely, in putting on the SCAPEGOAT the iniquities, transgressions, and sins of Israel (Lv 16.21–22). The belief that sin, disease, and the like can be transferred to living creatures, beasts, or birds, and so be removed from man, finds some analogy in Lv 14.4–7 (cf. also Zec 5.5–10).

A beneficent use of the rite occurs in Gn 48.14, where it conveys the blessing of Jacob-Israel to the two sons of Joseph, Ephraim and Manasseh. The blessing imparted by the Patriarch is fecundity, so that the two blessed persons may grow into "numbers on the earth," "a multitude of nations."

A second beneficent use of the laying on of hands is present in the stories relating the installation of Joshua as successor to Moses. The tradition is not quite homogeneous. In Dt 34.9 the rite is attested, and Joshua's spirit of wisdom seems to be attributed to it. According to Nm 27.18–30, which is considered a younger tradition, Joshua already possessed this spirit of wisdom, and the rite seems to be used only for the solemn and public installation of Moses' successor. It appears to be more in conformity with the views of the OT that the gift of the Spirit was not bound to certain external rites (cf. Dt 31.14–15; Nm 11.25).

The rite appears as a purely indicative gesture in Lv 24.14 and Dn 13.34, as testimony against the presumed culprits.

Another use of the rite belonged to the offering of sacrifices. It was used in all sacrifices except the guilt offering, namely, the *'āšām* that was prescribed in the Levitical system for cases involving restitution (see, for the holocaust, or burnt offering, Lv 1.4; 8.18; Ex 29.15; Nm 8.12; for the peace offering, Lv 3.2, 8, 13; for the sin offering, Lv 4.4, 24, 29, 33; Ex 29.10; Nm 8.12; 2 Chr 29.23). There is much difference of opinion about the exact meaning of this rite in the sacrifice. Many hypotheses have been proposed: rite of liberation from slavery, of appropriation, of substitution. The texts do not provide sufficient information. The fundamental meaning seems to be an indicative gesture by which the offerer intends to make his own the sacrifice that the priests will present to God for him. The idea of substitution, which appears only very late in the OT, does not seem to have been present in the older period. The rite is said to have been present also in Mesopotamian rituals.

Sometimes it is supposed that laying on of hands was also part of the so-called ordination of the LEVITES (Nm 8.5–22). Though a laying on of hands is mentioned in the text, it does not indicate ordination. It is part of the text because the installation of the Levites is described as a sacrificial oblation, and all sacrificial offerings, with the exception of the guilt offering, included a laying on of hands.

Judaism. At the time of Christ, the documents of Judaism relate two additional applications of the old rite that are very important for understanding the rite in the NT. First, the rite was used for healing (see the Qumran document: N. Avigod and Y. Yadin, *A Genesis Apocryphon* [Jerusalem 1956] 20.22.29). Second, it was employed also in the Judaism of NT times as a ceremony for the installation of rabbinic teachers. (*See* RABBI.) According to the latest research (H. Mantel, "Ordination and Appointment in the Period of the Temple," *Harvard Theological Review* 57 [1964] 325–346), one must distinguish between the appointment of judges "to judge cases involving fines" (an appointment called *minnûi* and not involving the laying on of hands) and the giving of permission (*rešût*) to teach, involving in Palestine, even at the time of the temple and of Christ, the *semîkâ,* or imposition of hands.

If one looks for the fundamental symbolism of the rite, it must first be answered that it is quite a natural gesture. Reference should also be made to the Hebrew concept of man (see A. R. Johnson, *The Vitality of the Individual in the Thought of Ancient Israel* [Cardiff 1964]).The Israelites regarded man as a psychophysical unity. Hence the hand is not merely an instrument but is in some way an extension of the self, especially of its power. Hence the "hand of God" stands for the power of God. The "hand" becomes nearly equivalent to the personal pronoun, and in Is 45.12 it is used to emphasize this pronoun: "It was I, my hands."

New Testament. For his deeds of healing, Jesus made constant use of the rite. So did the Apostles. Mention of the gesture occurs in those texts that are called "summaries," covering in a concise manner the usual way of acting of Christ and his Apostles (Mk 6.5; 16.18; Lk 4.40; Acts 5.12; 9.17).

This use is illustrated by the above-mentioned texts of Qumran. The blessing of the children by Christ through the imposition of the hands (Mk 10.13–16; Mt 19.13–15; Lk 18.15–17) poses no problem, since this custom continues that of the OT and is attested for NT times (see E. Tisserant, *Ascension d'Isaïe* [Paris 1919]). A special mention is due the blessing of the Apostles by Christ in Lk 24.50, because this blessing follows closely the promise of the mission of the Holy Spirit and so seems to be in some relation with the apostolic rite of giving the Holy Spirit.

Apostolic Age. In addition to the practices already mentioned in biblical literature and continued by the Church, this period reveals two new Christian uses for the laying on of hands.

Rite of Ordination. Apparently, by way of analogy to the use of this rite in Jewish circles, laying on of hands was introduced for Christian ordination. If Acts 13.1–3 is of dubious interpretation (the ceremony may connote only a blessing), the testimony of Acts 6.1–6; 1 Tm 4.14; 5.22; 2 Tm 1.6 is perfectly clear. The ceremony was performed by Paul himself (2 Tm 1.6) or was to be performed by Timothy (1 Tm 5.22); the elders or PRESBYTERS collaborated in the rite (1 Tm 4.14). The ordination followed an election by the local church and was accompanied by prayer and a profession of faith on the part of those to be ordained.

A more complicated problem is whether those rites of ordination concern the various degrees of ecclesiastical ministry recognized by the Catholic Church. The ordination of Timothy by Paul was ordination to the ministry of bishop (2 Tm 1.6); the ordinations committed to Timothy (1 Tm 5.22) concerned the ministry of priests; and the ordination of the seven by the Apostles had to do with the ministry of deacons (Acts 6.1–6). Nevertheless, in the several texts that tell of the institution of presbyters (see Acts 14.22; Ti 1.5), it is difficult to determine whether the texts always meant priests or sometimes, only "older men" whose role was to preside over the local church as far as discipline was concerned. In the subapostolic age, the terms ἐπίσκοποι, πρεσβύτεροι, and διάκονοι, indicate without doubt three orders of a hierarchy, endowed not only with disciplinary power but also with a liturgical one. At that time, they were bishops, priests, and deacons in the strict sense of those words. St. Jerome, however, still seems to understand the πρεσβύτεροι of Acts 20.17 as *majores natu,* i.e., elders.

The laying on of hands was kept for ordination universally in the Church both East and West. There was even a tendency to extend the rite to the consecration of virgins (see R. Metz, *La Consécration des vierges dans l'Église romaine* [Paris 1954]), but this untraditional use of the rite was quickly dropped. In the ordination of priests, the *porrectio instrumentorum,* i.e., the delivery of the symbols and instruments of the priesthood, won great prestige in the course of time, but the apostolic constitution *Sacramentum ordinis* (1947) firmly reemphasized the imposition of hands with the accompanying prayer as the essential sacramental rite.

Rites of Initiation. The second new application of the rite in the apostolic age was for imparting the postbaptismal gift of the Holy Spirit. Apart from a rather ambiguous text in Heb 6.1–3, there are two major witnesses to this new sacramental ceremony, namely, Acts 8.8–25; 19.1–6. Apart from these three references, there is no other mention of this postbaptismal rite in the writings of the NT, and the Christian authors of the 2d century are almost silent about it.

This gives rise to several questions. Was the rite an ordinary or an extraordinary element of Christian initiation? Did the rite disappear under the influence of Pauline theology, which stressed already among the effects of baptism a giving of the Holy Spirit, and later under the influence of a new rite, the postbaptismal unction with chrism? If the rite was combined with baptism, did Christians continue to distinguish a twofold gift of the Holy Spirit and does the term *sphragis* signify the second one? What is the exact meaning of the postbaptismal gift of the Holy Spirit if such a gift is to be admitted?

A radical solution was adopted by some scholars who contend that in the beginning the gifts of baptism and of the laying on of hands (ἐπίθεσις τῶν χειρῶν, χειροθεσία) were distinguished as the baptism in water for the remission of sins and the baptism of the Holy Spirit for full aggregation to the people and the Church of God. Paul was the Christian theologian who united the two gifts and connected both with baptism. The Pauline conception won general support and became dominant in the 2d century. The combination persisted in the Greek Church, but the baptismal gift of the Holy Spirit was more specially attributed to a newly introduced baptismal rite, the unction with myron or chrism. In the Latin Church the two gifts continued to be clearly distinguished and the laying on of hands reappeared as a distinct, postbaptismal rite.

The author of the treatise *De rebaptismate* adopts a position that is very near to the so-called primitive, pre-Pauline doctrine. The heretics can confer baptism, but they cannot give the Holy Spirit with the laying on of hands. Cyprian denied the validity of either Sacrament when conferred by heretics. Stephen I considered both valid Sacraments, but in his milieu there was introduced an imposition of hands for the reconciliation of the heretics.

Some people regard the laying on of hands as the reconciliation of the penitents in 1 Tm 5.22, but without sufficient foundation (see P. Galtier, "La réconciliation des pécheurs dans la première épître à Timothée," *Recherches de science religieuse* 39 [1951] 317–320). The history of the rite of reconciliation in the first centuries is a complicated one (see A. Vacandard, *La Pénitence publique dans l'Église primitive* [2 v. Paris 1903]).

In the light of the documents still available, one can draw certain conclusions. In the very beginning there seems to have been a distinction between the gifts of baptism and the gift (which may be termed "pentecostal") of the Holy Spirit. This second gift was not always given in the same way. It appears that sometimes it was given without any rite; sometimes it was conferred by the laying on of hands; it is possible that it came to be imparted at the moment of baptism itself.

Paul seems to have conceived the initiation into Christianity as one complex thing. So the rite of laying on of hands is no longer explicitly mentioned, although it may have been practiced. Even if the rites were combined, Paul and those churches that followed him closely could still have distinguished the gifts to some extent and could have reserved, some scholars still maintain, the term *sphragis* (seal) to the special gift of the Holy Spirit. There is no doubt that later this term designated the postbaptismal gift.

Only if it is supposed that the Church was always mindful of this distinction can it be explained how the Greek Church introduced and put so much stress on the rite of anointing with chrism at the time of baptism. Although the postbaptismal laying on of hands is not frequently mentioned in the first centuries, there are some witnesses to it coming from the Church of Alexandria (SS. Athanasius, Cyril of Alexandria), and in some late Greek writers there is a tendency to return to the title of "laying on of hands" instead of "the chrism." There is, however, no reason to suppose that a notable change of practice was introduced (see the writings of Anastasius of Sinai, St. John Damascene, Oecumenius, Theophylactus), for the stress on the old terminology may be a result of their commenting on the Acts of the Apostles or the Epistle to the Hebrews. In sharp contrast with those of the Greek Church, the writers of the Latin Church gave much attention to the postbaptismal laying on of hands and distinguished more clearly between baptismal and postbaptismal gifts, although they did not succeed in proposing a clear and unanimously accepted view of the postbaptismal gift of the Holy Spirit.

Bibliography: J. COPPENS, *L'Imposition des mains et les rites connexes dans le Nouveau Testament et dans L'Église ancienne* (Paris 1925). N. ADLER, *Taufe und Handauflegung: Eine exegetisch-theologische Untersuchung von Apg 8, 14–17* (Münster 1951). E. LOHSE, *Die Ordination in Spätjudentum und im Neuen Testament* (Göttingen 1951). B. NEUNHEUSER, *Baptism and Confirmation,* tr. J. J. HUGHES (New York 1964). L. VISCHER, *La Confirmation au cours des siècles,* tr. J. CARRÈRE (Cahiers théologiques 44; Neufchâtel 1959). B. KLEINHEYER, *Die Priesterweihe im römischen Ritus* (Trier 1962). J. NEUMANN, *Die Spendung der Firmung in der Kirche des Abendlandes bis zum Ende des kirchlichen Altertums* (Mettingen 1963). On the terms *episcopos, presbyters, diaconos,* see M. GUERRA Y GOMEZ, *Diaconos helenicos y biblicos* (Burgos 1962); *Episcopos y presbyteros: Evolución semántica de los términos episcopos—presbyteros désde Homero hasta el siglo segundo después Jesucristo* (Burgos 1962). On the interpretation of *sphragis,* see J. YSEBAERT, *Greek Baptismal Terminology: Its Origin and Early Development* (Nijmegen 1962).

[J. COPPENS/EDS.]

IMPROPERIA

The reproaches directed against God's own people, and appearing as utterances of Jesus during the Adoration

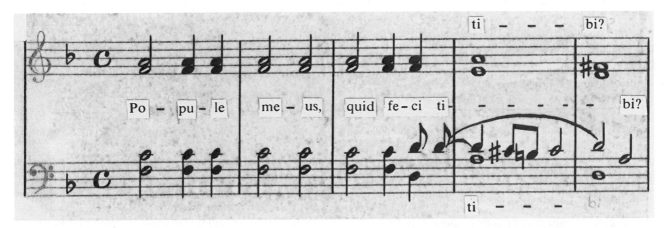

"Improperia," by Palestrina, liturgical sheet music.

of the Cross in the Roman liturgy of GOOD FRIDAY. The first part of the Improperia consists of three verses (*Popule meus, Quia eduxi te per desertum,* and *Quid ultra*), including the TRISAGION. This first part is found in the *Antiphonale Sylvanectense* (of Senlis; *c.* 880; ed. R. Hesbert, *Antiphonale missarum sextuplex* [Brussels 1935]) and in the *Pontificale Romano-Germanicum* (*c.* 950; ed. M. Hittorp, *De catholicae ecclesiae divinis officiis* [Cologne 1568]). The second part, which is not found until the 11th century, consists of nine verses, all of which begin with the word *Ego* (I). A Gallican origin has been claimed for the plain chant melodies (*see* GALLICAN CHANT).

Bibliography: H. A. SCHMIDT, *Hebdomada Sancta,* 2 v. (Rome 1956–57) 2:794–796. E. WERNER, "Zur Textgeschichte der Improperia," *Festschrift Bruno Stäblein,* ed. M. RUHNKE (Kassel 1967) 274–86. W. SCHÜTZ, "'Was habe ich dir getan, mein Volk?': die Wurzeln der Karfreitagsimproperien in der alten Kirche," *Jahrbuch für Liturgik und Hymnologie,* 13 (1968) 1–38. J. DRUMBL, "Die Improperien der lateinischen Liturgie," *Archiv für Liturgiewissenschaft,* 15 (1973) 68–100. M. MARX-WEBER, "Die Improperien im Repertoire der Cappella sistina," *Studien zur Musikgeschichte: eine Festschrift für Ludwig Finscher,* ed. A. LAUBENTHAL (Kassel 1995) 157–62.

[E. J. GRATSCH/L. J. WAGNER/EDS.]

IMPUTATION OF JUSTICE AND MERIT

The early reformers, founders of Protestantism, identified CONCUPISCENCE in fallen man with ORIGINAL SIN. Knowing as they did that the corruption of nature remains even in the justified, they refused to admit that in justification the believer undergoes any real ontological change such as takes place, according to Catholic doctrine, in the infusion of sanctifying GRACE and the theological VIRTUES. For that reason justice, or righteousness, is not intrinsic in the full sense of the word but rather extrinsic. The sinner, they said, is justified when God imputes to him the justice of Christ. Though his sins are forgiven when by faith he takes to himself the merits of Christ, still they are not really blotted out or extirpated from the soul but remain in it covered over by the merits of the Savior as long as this mortal life endures. It is thus that the justified man is at the same time just and sinful, *simul justus et peccator.*

Martin Luther at the height of his career commented on Gal 3.6: "Abraham believed God, and it was credited to him as justice." He wrote:

Christian righteousness is to be defined properly and accurately, namely, that it is a trust in the Son of God or a trust of the heart in God through Christ . . . two things make Christian righteousness perfect. The first is faith in the heart, which is a divinely granted gift and which formally believes in Christ; the second is that God reckons this imperfect faith as perfect righteousness for the sake of Christ His Son . . . . On account of faith in Christ God does not see the sin that still remains in me. For so long as I go on living in the flesh, there is certainly sin in me. But meanwhile Christ protects me under the shadow of His wings and spreads over me the wide heaven of the forgiveness of sins, under which I live in safety. This prevents God from seeing the sins that still cling to my flesh. My flesh distrusts God, is angry with Him, does not rejoice in Him, etc. But God overlooks these sins, and in His sight they are as though they were not sins. This is accompanied by imputation on account of the faith by which I begin to take hold of Christ; and on His account God reckons imperfect righteousness as perfect righteousness and sin as not sin even though it really is sin. [*Luther's Works,* ed. J. Pelikan, v.26 (St. Louis 1963) 231–232.]

But it should not be thought that Luther conceived of no internal change in the justification of the sinner. In the same commentary he writes:

> We become doers of the law and are accounted guilty of no transgression. How? First, through the forgiveness of sins and the imputation of righteousness on account of faith in Christ; secondly, through the gift and the Holy Spirit, who creates a new life and new impulses in us, so that we keep the Law also in a formal sense. Whatever is not kept is forgiven for the sake of Christ. Besides, whatever sin is left is not imputed to us. [*Op. cit.* 260.]

The great reformer, therefore, thought that the justified man received "new life" from the Spirit, but he never admitted an ontological sanctification and interior renovation in the sense of the Council of Trent.

John Calvin also taught the total depravity of fallen man, and justification by faith alone.

> The just man, excluded from the righteousness of works, apprehends by faith the justice of Christ, invested in which he appears in the sight of God not as a sinner but as a just man. Thus we simply explain justification to be an acceptance by which God receives us into His favor and esteems us as just persons; and we say that it consists in the remission of sins and the imputation of the justice of Christ. [*Inst. relig. chr.* 3.11.2.]

Luther was always adverse to the idea of personal MERIT on the part of man, not only before but also after justification. His disciple Philipp Melanchthon, however, admitted "spiritual and corporal rewards in this life and the next for the good works of those who were reconciled and pleased by their faith." By this, however, he did not mean to imply that the good works of the righteous really merit glory, for he added, "Our virtues are not the price of eternal life; this is surely given for the sake of the Mediator" (*Loci theologici* 9, *De bonis operibus; Corpus reformatorium* 21:778, 780).

The concept of imputation of merits comes out more clearly in Calvin.

> It is the teaching of Scripture that our good works are constantly bespattered with much uncleanness by which God is rightly offended and is angry with us . . . but because through His leniency He does not weigh them with all strictness, therefore He accepts them as though they were very pure. Hence, though these works are not worthy of it, He remunerates them with infinite benefits both of this life and the future life. [*Op. cit.* 3.15.4.]

In modern times Protestant theologians have tended to abandon the idea of imputation and to postulate a real internal renovation of the justified man. However, they do not generally concede the ontological change that is an essential part of Catholic doctrine.

See Also: JUSTIFICATION; CALVINISM; COLOGNE, SCHOOL OF; EXTRINSICISM; JUSTICE, DOUBLE; JUSTICE OF MEN; LUTHERANISM; PHILIPPISM; SYNERGISM.

Bibliography: *Dictionnaire de théologie catholique*, Tables générales 2:2790–93. H. VOLK, *Lexikon für Theologie und Kirche*, ed. J. HOFER and K. RAHNER, 10 v. (2d new ed. Freiburg1957–65) 5:641–642. L. BOUYER, *The Spirit and Forms of Protestantism*, tr. A. V. LITTLEDALE (Westminster, Md. 1956). H. KÜNG, *Justification: The Doctrine of Karl Barth and a Catholic Reflection*, tr. T. COLLINS et al. (New York 1964). J. LORTZ, *Die Reformation in Deutschland*, 2 v. (Freiburg 1940; 4th ed. 1962). J. H. NEWMAN, *Lectures on the Doctrine of Justification* (London 1838; New York 1900). *Histoire de l'église depuis les origines jusqu'à nos jours*, v.16.

[T. J. MOTHERWAY]

INCA RELIGION

Originating in the Peruvian highlands, the Incas were, by the time of the arrival of the Spaniards, the supreme rulers of a vast region that extended from Quito, Ecuador, to the Maule River in Chile. Their religion, an integral part of the empire, was established and supported by the state. In addition, the local people supported their own cults, whose shrines and priests were a part of the total religious complex and differed only in elaboration and formalization. Emphasis was placed mainly on ritual and organization rather than on mysticism and spirituality. The chief function of the religion was the increase or maintenance of the food supply and the cure of the sick. The concepts of sin and purification were vital. Sacrifice, although rarely of human beings, was an important part of almost every religious rite.

The Incas worshiped many supernatural beings of varying power and importance. The supreme deity was regarded as the creator, and adored under the name of Viracocha. However, he was little worshipped by the masses, since he had little to do with their destinies. The sun god, the servant of Viracocha, was believed to be the progenitor of the Inca dynasty. The Incas worshiped natural phenomena also, such as thunder, the moon, the earth, and the sea, as well as sacred places and beings called *huacas*. The priesthood, consisting of a graded hierarchy of which the head was generally a near relative of the emperor, was expected to participate in religious rites, make divinations, interpret oracles, offer sacrifices, pray for suppliants, and cure the sick. The major Inca religious ceremonies were annual religious holidays associated with stages in the agricultural year or with the calendar.

Bibliography: J. ROWE, "Inca Culture at the Time of the Spanish Conquest," *Handbook of South American Indians*, 2 v.

(Bureau of American Ethnology, Bull. 143, 1946) 2:293–314. J. A. MASON, *The Ancient Civilizations of Peru* (Baltimore 1961). J. A. VÁZQUEZ, "The Reconstruction of the Myth of Inkarri," *Latin American Indian Literatures Journal* 2:2 (1986) 92–109. D. A. BRADING, "The Incas and the Renaissance: The Royal Commentaries of Inca Garcilaso de la Vega," *Journal of Latin American Studies,* 18 (1986) 1–23. M. M. MARZAL, "Andean Religion at the Time of the Conquest," in *South and Meso–American Native Spirituality* (New York 1993) 86–115.

[J. RUBIN/EDS.]

INCANTATION

Incantation, the speaking or singing of words that are thought to have, by the mere fact of being said, power to work magic and produce the results desired. The practice is found universally from remote antiquity. In the *Odyssey,* reference is made to incantation's stopping the flow of blood, and working other wonders. There is evidence that in the early historical period of both Greece and Rome, people believed in the efficacy of incantation, but subsequently philosophers and lawgivers condemned it. In the Hellenistic period it had a considerable vogue, as is indicated by magical papyri, inscriptions, and literary works. Orpheus, the legendary singer, was a magician, as were also Musaeus and others. The best-known practitioner of the art in Greek literature was Medea, who was the daughter of the sun. In the magical papyri the incantations read almost like prayers, but these utterances were undoubtedly thought to have in themselves magical powers to accomplish results. Christianity from the beginning opposed this and other forms of magic.

See Also: MAGIC.

Bibliography: F. PHISTER, "Epode," *Paulys Realenzyklopädie der klassischen Altertumswissenschaft,* ed. G. WISSOWA et al. Supplement 4 (Stuttgart 1924) 323–343. K. PRÜMM, *Religionsgeschichtliches Handbuch für den Raum der altchristlichen Umwelt* (2d ed. Rome 1954) 366–371. S. THOMPSON, *Motif-Index of Folk-Literature,* 6 v. (rev. and enl. ed. Bloomington, Ind. 1955–58) v.5 index s.v. "Incantation."

[T. A. BRADY]

INCARNATE WORD, SISTERS OF CHARITY OF THE

The Congregation of the Sisters of Charity of the Incarnate Word (CCVI) was founded by Bp. Claude Marie Dubuis of Galveston, Tex., to exercise the spiritual and corporal works of mercy in that state, ravaged by the Civil War. In 1866 he went to Europe seeking help, especially for the many victims of yellow fever in his diocese. Unable to persuade any European community to sponsor a branch house in Texas, he secured three volunteers from among the sisters in the hospital of L'Antiquaille, Lyons, France, and with them he established a new congregation. Mother Angélique, superior of the Monastery of the Incarnate Word and Blessed Sacrament in Lyons, agreed to train these mission-minded French girls. From 1866 to 1869 she formed 19 young women for mission work in Texas. For their habit, she replaced the white garb worn in her own cloister by a black one, modified to fit the active apostolate. She gave them the rule of her order, recommending adaptation to the exigencies of missionary activity, and selected their title: Sisters of Charity of the Incarnate Word. In 1867 Dubuis requested the first three sisters who arrived in Galveston to found St. Mary's Infirmary, the first Catholic hospital in Texas. Two years later he sent three sisters to open Santa Rosa Infirmary in San Antonio. From these two independent centers, two distinct congregations evolved.

Sisters of Charity of the Incarnate Word, Houston. (Official Catholic Directory, #0470). This group developed from the foundation at St. Mary's Infirmary, Galveston. In July 1867, three months after the opening of the infirmary, an epidemic of yellow fever took the lives of more than 1,100 people in Galveston, among them Mother Blandine, one of the pioneers. The two remaining religious, Sisters Joseph and Ange, continued to care for the sick in their crowded and understaffed hospital, and also provided for the children orphaned by the epidemic. From 1867 until the opening of St. Mary's Orphanage in 1874, the children were cared for on hospital property. During the storm of 1900 in Galveston the congregation lost 10 sisters and 91 orphans. The constitutions of the congregation received the approbation of the Holy See in 1912. In 1904 the motherhouse and general administration was established at St. Mary's Infirmary, Galveston. Since 1928, however, the motherhouse and novitiate have been located at Villa de Matel, Houston, Tex.

Sisters of Charity of the Incarnate Word, San Antonio. (Official Catholic Directory #0460). This group began with the three sisters who founded Santa Rosa Infirmary in 1869. When they admitted their first postulants in 1870, Dubuis appointed Mother Madeleine as the first superior and Mother Pierre as novice mistress. Considered the foundresses of the congregation, these two pioneers gave, between them, more than 30 years of leadership to the community. Under their direction the new congregation rapidly expanded its work to meet contemporary needs. In 1874 Mother Pierre opened St. Joseph Orphanage and San Fernando parochial school, the first of many to be added in Texas in the succeeding decades. In 1881 the congregation became a chartered body under the laws of Texas, empowered to conduct nonprofit institutions and to grant diplomas. The work assumed national scope when, in 1889, Mother Pierre sent sisters north to staff the Missouri-Pacific Hospital in St. Louis, Mo. In the years that followed, schools and hospitals were opened throughout Missouri, and in Illinois, Oklahoma, and Louisiana. Simultaneously, the apostolate spread south beyond national boundaries as the sisters successively pioneered 17 foundations in Mexico, stretching from Oaxaca in the south to Chihuahua in the north. In 1910 the congregation received final papal approbation of their rule, based on that of St. Augustine. The general administration is located in the motherhouse in San Antonio.

Bibliography: M. H. FINCK, *The Congregation of the Sisters of Charity of the Incarnate Word of San Antonio, Texas* (Washington 1925). L. V. JACKS, *Claude Dubuis: Bishop of Galveston* (St. Louis 1947).

[M. L. HEGARTY/A. POWER/EDS.]

INCARNATE WORD AND BLESSED SACRAMENT, CONGREGATION OF

Official Catholic Directory #2200 (see also #2190 and #2205). The Order of the Incarnate Word and Blessed Sacrament was founded in seventeenth century France by Jeanne CHÉZARD DE MATEL as a contemplative cloistered Order. Teaching was an early and very important ministry with the students coming into the cloister for classes, but Mother de Matel does not describe the purpose of her Order in terms of any ministry. Rather, she describes it sometimes as "the extension of the Incarnation," sometimes as an Order through which the Incarnate Word would be introduced into the world once again." Ministry, especially the ministry of teaching, is an important means to achieve the ends of the Order. The structure of the Order was monastic with each monastery governmentally autonomous. The foundress did, however, urge her Sisters to foster a sisterly love between monasteries.

The Seventeenth Century

The first small community of three came together in great poverty in Roanne, France, on July 2, 1625. The group consisted of the foundress, Mother Jeanne Chézard de Matel (1596 to 1670), and two friends. Shortly thereafter, a fourth woman joined them, and with her arrival, teaching became a primary ministry of the incipient Institute. During the lifetime of the foundress, four Monasteries of the Incarnate Word and Blessed Sacrament were canonically erected in France: Avignon (1639), Grenoble (1643), Paris (1644), and Lyon (1655). Because of exterior interference, the Monastery of Paris was suppressed in 1672.

In prayer, Mother de Matel became convinced that the title of the new Institute should be "Incarnate Word," and this was the title that she requested for her Order. However, the Apostolic Bull of Erection for Lyon issued by Pope Urban VIII and dated May 21, 1633, gave as title "Incarnate Word and Blessed Sacrament." Mother de Matel, who said of herself that she "rejoiced in being a daughter of the Church," accepted this decision of the Church and used it interchangeably with the shorter title, "Incarnate Word." The Apostolic Bull also gave the Institute the Rule of Saint AUGUSTINE.

In July 1645, after Mother de Matel had founded three canonical Monasteries, she sought and received aggregation of the three existing Monasteries and all future houses of the Incarnate Word to the Order of Saint Augustine. This resulted in a spiritual union between the two Orders but preserved the autonomy of each.

In the late 1640's, Mother de Matel worked to establish a male branch of her Order, the Fathers of the Incarnate Word. Several priests worked with her on this project. However, the death of her advisor, Father Jean-Baptiste Carré, O.P., and other factors caused the project to fail at that time. It would be revived in the late twentieth century.

After the canonical establishment of the Monastery of Lyons in 1655, Mother de Matel worked to place on a firm footing and strengthen the spiritual life of all of her Monasteries. From 1662 until 1670, she lived in the Monastery of Paris, suffering much from a series of difficulties which beset that Monastery. Her death occurred in Paris on Sept. 11, 1670. Her heart was removed and sent as a precious relic to her beloved Monastery of Lyon. Then her mortal remains were interred in the crypt of the Monastery of Paris.

After the death of the foundress, the Monastery of Grenoble founded a daughter house in Sarrians in 1683. This community moved to Orange in 1687, then to Roquemaure in 1697. The Monastery of Lyon established a daughter house at Anduze in 1697.

The Eighteenth Century

In 1717, the Monastery of Grenoble was suppressed because of lack of vocations, but the Monasteries of Avignon and Lyon together with the second generation Monasteries of Roquemaure and Anduze continued to develop. Throughout the eighteenth century, vocations increased, and the various communities acquired additional property. But in 1790, the revolutionary government passed a decree suppressing all religious Institutes. This decree was not enforced in Lyon until 1792. On Sept. 29, 1792, when the Lyon Sisters refused to take the oath demanded by the state, they were expelled from their Monastery. Some returned to their families, others lived unobtrusively in small groups, one went into exile in Italy. All other Monasteries of the Incarnate Word and Blessed Sacrament were suppressed about the same time.

The Nineteenth Century

Europe. At the beginning of the nineteenth century, the Order of the Incarnate Word and Blessed Sacrament seemed to be dead. Most of the Sisters who had survived the Revolution were living quietly at home, alone, or in small groups, and most were advanced in years. But the flame of life had not gone out entirely from the Institute. Through the joint efforts of a French diocesan priest, Father Stephen Denis, and a member of the suppressed Monastery of Lyon, Mother Anne of the Holy Spirit Chinard-Durieux, the Institute was restored. In 1817, a group of religious women whom Father Denis had founded exchanged their original habit for the habit of Mother de Matel's community. At the same time, they accepted the Rule and Constitutions of the Sisters of the Incarnate Word. Twenty-five years after its suppression, the Order of the Incarnate Word and Blessed Sacrament was restored.

As many as nine new foundations were made directly from Azerables and one of these, the Monastery of Evaux, gave rise to two other non-cloistered Institutes. The first was a Second Order of the Incarnate Word founded in 1834. Later, the title of this Institute was changed to the Order of the Savior and of the Blessed Virgin. The second was an Institute of Hospital Sisters in 1846, founded to do works of charity such as visiting the sick in their own homes. The Monastery of Lyon was restored through the efforts of a diocesan priest of Lyon, Father Galtier, and a Sister, Rosalie Hiver. Rosalie was accepted as a postulant in the community of the Incarnate Word in Azerables on June 29, 1832. After she became a novice (at which time, she received the name of Sister Angelique of the Incarnation), she, a former Superior, and a postulant from Azerables went to Lyon to work toward the restoration of the Monastery there. On May 27, 1833, the chapel of the new Monastery was blessed, Mass was celebrated in it, and the cloister was established. Thus the Monastery of Lyon was formally re-established. In 1842, the Monastery of Lyon founded a daughter house, the Monastery of Belmont, which, in spite of great poverty and many difficulties, was in existence for 60 years.

The New World. In 1852, at the request of Bishop Odin, Bishop of the whole state of Texas, Mother Angelique Hiver of Lyon assigned four Sisters to make the first Incarnate Word foundation in the New World. Two were from the Monastery of Belmont: 23-year-old Sister Saint Claire Valentine, the founding Superior, and a lay Sister, Sister Dominique Ravier. The other two were from the Monastery of Lyon: Sister Saint-Ange Barre and Sister Saint-Ephrem. Satin. At the end of February 1853, in the border town of Brownsville, Texas, the first foundation in the New World was made. Just one week later, on March 7, 1853, the Sisters opened a school. In spite of great difficulties, the foundation flourished. In 1866, the Monastery of Brownsville established a daughter house in Victoria, Texas, and in 1871, Victoria and Brownsville cooperated in making a foundation in Corpus Christ, Texas. The Monastery of Victoria founded other daughter houses, among them the Monastery of Houston in 1873, Hallettsville in 1882, and Shiner in 1897. In 1898, Brownsville made a foundation in Rio Grande City, Texas, which lasted until the 1920s.

In 1866, at the request of Bishop Dubuis, second Bishop of Texas, the Monastery of Lyon gave preliminary formation to three women who would found a related Order to do the works of mercy in Texas, the Sisters of Charity of the Incarnate Word. After a very brief time in the Monastery of Lyon, the Sisters of Charity went to Galveston. From there the present Congregations grew and developed.

In 1894, the Monastery of Brownsville extended the international character of the Order by making a foundation in Mexico: San Juan Bautista in Tabasco, Mexico. In 1896, the Monastery of Corpus Christi made a foundation in Puebla, Mexico, which lasted until it was closed by religious persecution in 1929.

The Twentieth Century

France and Spain. In 1902, a leftist government came to power in France, and this led to a renewed attack on religion. As a result, some of the Incarnate Word communities, including the Monastery of Belmont, were dispersed. The community of the Incarnate Word of Lyon spent 25 years in exile in Fribourg, Switzerland. In the 1920s, they returned to Lyon, but had to leave again during the Second World War. When the war was over, the Sisters returned to Lyon and opened a boarding house for women. They also sent Sisters to Spain to open houses there. In the twentieth century, the other Incarnate Word foundations in France closed one by one. Now the only surviving French house is that of Lyon which continues to have Sisters in Spain. In 1970, this house was amalgamated with the Mexico City Generalate.

Mexico. In the twentieth century, the Monastery of Brownsville continued to make foundations in Mexico. In addition, the communities already in Mexico made further foundations. In 1903, a Monastery was established in Guadalajara by three French Sisters from the suppressed French Monastery of Belmont. About 1916, one of the three French Sisters made a foundation in Cuba which grew and developed until the Sisters were expelled in 1961 in the regime of Fidel Castro. In the early part of the century, the revolution in Mexico brought religious persecution and consequent suffering. For many years, there existed a pattern of expulsion of the Sisters from schools and convents, later return of their property, then a new wave of expulsion. The Sisters persevered throughout these difficult days and re-opened their schools whenever possible. By 1912, Mother Teresita Solis of Chilapa, Mexico, and Mother Stanislaus Dedieu of Brownsville, Texas, were dialoguing about the possibility of setting up a Generalate for the Order of the Incarnate Word and Blessed Sacrament—a radical change from the traditionally monastic structure of the Order. This did not happen in the lifetime of either of these Superiors. However, in 1929, Mother Concepción Solis of Mexico City set up the first Generalate in the Order, uniting in one Congregation three formerly autonomous Monasteries of the Incarnate Word—Chilapa, Matehuala, and Mexico City. The Motherhouse is in Mexico City. The decree of authorization from the Sacred Congregation for Religious is dated Feb. 28, 1929.

In addition to incorporating the European houses in France and Spain into its Generalate, the Mexico City Congregation opened many houses throughout Mexico and also in Guatemala, Argentina and Uruguay. In 1980, the Sisters of the Incarnate Word from Mexico City made the first Incarnate Word foundation in Africa — in Kenya where there are now native Kenyan Sisters. Most recently, they have opened missions in Tanzania.

In 1914, persecution caused the autonomous community of the Incarnate Word in Gomez Palacio in the state of Durango to go into exile. They went to Cuba where they stayed as refugees for many years. Eventually they were able to return to Gomez Palacio, but a new wave of persecution in 1926 caused those who were not Mexican citizens to leave Mexico again. These Sisters went first to Incarnate Word communities in Texas, then to Cleveland, Ohio, in the United States, where they made a foundation in 1927. The Cleveland Sisters are an Institute of diocesan right. They maintain a sisterly relationship with the Sisters from Gomez Palacio.

The United States in the United States, in the early part of the twentieth century, at the request of the Bishops of Texas, the Sisters of the Incarnate Word and Blessed Sacrament petitioned Rome for the abrogation of the cloister in order to better serve the Church in Texas. In 1915, the Monastery of Corpus Christi received permission from Rome for the abrogation of the cloister, and other Monasteries did likewise in the ensuing years.

In the 1930s, for vocational, financial or other reasons, two Generalates were formed in Texas, one with Motherhouse in Corpus Christi in 1932 and the other with Motherhouse in Victoria in 1939. Constitutions were rewritten which sought to preserve the ideals of Mother de Matel while providing for the new form of government. At this time, the monastic practice of having choir and lay Sisters ceased. All Congregations of the Incarnate Word now have only one class of religious.

In the twentieth century, Sisters of the Incarnate Word emphasized education and obtained academic degrees in a variety of fields. The number of Catholic schools increased as did the enrollment in individual schools and the workload of teaching Sisters. There was also an increase in vocations. These factors led to the erection of new convents and school buildings. In the 1950s, Pope Pius XII called for religious Institutes to update their life style and customs. This led to relatively minor changes in religious dress and customs just before the Second Vatican Council.

From 1965 to 1981, the Sisters of the Incarnate Word of Houston staffed a mission in Guatemala. In 1981, this mission was taken over by the Sisters of the Incarnate Word from Mexico City.

Worldwide Conciliar and Post-Conciliar Renewal. After the Second Vatican Council, about 1968, in response to directives from the Holy See, all the autonomous Congregations of the Incarnate Word held special renewal General Chapters. The decade of the 1970s and the early 1980s was a time of experimentation and renewal. In the experimental period, interim Constitutions were written and rewritten, but the new Constitutions were finalized and approved for each Congregation about the mid-1980s. The new Constitutions are couched in biblical terms and make a real effort to recapture the authentic vision of the foundress. They reemphasize the foundress' vision of "the extension of the Incarnation" as the primary end of the Order and broaden the understanding of ministry to enable Sisters to meet other needs of the Church.

In 1980, a series of International Reunions began in which all the Congregations share on the charism of the Order. The single Constitution that had spelled out the way of life of Sisters of the Incarnate Word everywhere for more than three hundred years was now replaced by individual Constitutions developed after the Second Vatican Council. To maintain unity of heart and to spell out together those basic points which are central to the charism of the Order, the representatives of each Congregation wrote a document called the Charter of Communion. It was agreed that this document would be placed with (but not as part of) the Constitutions of the various Congregations. One year later, on Dec. 22, 1981, this document was accepted and signed by the Superiors General of each Congregation.

Worldwide, autonomous Congregations of the Incarnate Word and Blessed Sacrament now number nine. There are four in the United States with Motherhouses in Cleveland, Ohio, and in Texas in Corpus Christi, Houston, and Victoria. In Mexico, there are five with Motherhouses in Mexico City, Mixcoac, Guadalajara, Gomez Palacio, and Tezuitldn. More than ever, representatives from the nine groups share in international and national meetings, and formation reunions. They work together to bring about the beatification of the foundress, Mother Chézard de Matel and to translate and make available her many writings in English and in Spanish. They have also cooperated in staffing mission houses. Nov. 5, 1995 began a Year of Jubilee for the worldwide Order in celebration of the 400' birthday of Mother de Matel on Nov. 6, 1996. The many activities of the year resulted in a new understanding and appreciation of the charism and spirit of the foundress and of the Order which she founded.

In the 1990s, there arose a new interest in establishing an Institute of Fathers of the Incarnate Word, a project dear to Mother de Matel's heart in the seventeenth century. This movement is still in its infancy but its growth is being fostered by more than one Incarnate Word Generalate.

In November 1994, Pope John Paul's Apostolic Letter, *Tertio Millennio Adveniente*, announced the Great Jubilee of the Incarnation to be celebrated in the Year 2000—a momentous event for Sisters of the Incarnate Word and Blessed Sacrament. As a result, the Sisters of the Incarnate Word and Blessed Sacrament are fully involved in preparing for and celebrating the 2000' anniversary of the Incarnation. The year 2000 also marks the 375th anniversary of the first beginnings of the Order in Roanne, France in 1625. At the beginning of the third millennium, the exterior milieu in which the Sisters of the Incarnate Word and Blessed Sacrament live is very different to that of the cloistered Sisters of the past. Interiorly, however, they strive to be ever faithful to the charism and spirituality entrusted to them by their seventeenth century foundress, Mother Jeanne Chézard de Matel.

Bibliography: J. CHÉZARD DE MATEL, *Autographic Life*, 1, 11, tr. SR. C. CASSO, IWBS (Rome 1993). *Positio for the Beatification and Canonization of the Servant of God, Jeanne Chézard de Matel*, 1, II (Rome 1987) tr. SR. C. CASSO, IWBS, 1989. T. DIAZ CONTI TENORIO, C.V.1. and S. E. MARES BANUELOS, C.V.I., *100 Años de-Anunciar la Encarnacion del Ferbo en Mexico* (Mexico 1994). MOTHER M. P. GUNNING, *To Texas with Love* (Corpus Christi, Texas 1971). SR. M. X. HOLWORTHY, *Diamonds for the King* (Corpus Christi, Texas 1945). J. M. LOZANO, *Jeanne Chézard de Matel and the Sisters of the Incarnate Word* (Chicago 1983). SR. S. MARBACH, IWBS, et al., *Extending the Incarnation into the Third Millennium* (Victoria, Texas 1998). SR. K. MCDONAGH, IWBS, *A Hundred Letters from the Correspondence of Mother Jeanne Chézard de Matel* (Corpus Christi, Texas 1994). MOTHER SAINT-PIERRE OF JESUS, *Life of the Reverend Mother Jeanne Chézard de Matel*, tr. H. CHURCHILL SEMPLE, S.J. (San Antonio, Texas 1922). **Unpublished Manuscripts.** *Annals of our Monastery of the Incarnate Word and Blessed Sacrament of Azerables, I, II*, anonymous English translation revised by SR. K. MCDONAGH (Corpus Christi, Texas 1991). *Annals of Lyon*, anonymous English translation. *Annals of the First Monastery of the Incarnate Word and Blessed Sacrament in America* (Brownsville, Texas 1890). J. DE JESUS DE BÉIY, *Memoirs, I, II, III*, tr. SR. N. BEGLEY, IWBS, and SR. K. MCDONAGH, IWBS (Corpus Christi, Texas 1992). C. L. CRISTIANI, *Historical-Critical Study of the Writings of Jeanne de Matel v. I, II and III*, tr. SR. C. CASSO, IWBS (Victoria, Texas 1981, 1996). *Biography of Father Antoine Galtier*, tr. SR. C. CASSO, IWBS (Victoria, Texas 1997). *Bodas de Oro de la Academia de Villa de Matel*, (Gomez Palacio, Durango 1906–56), tr. SR. S. PENA, IWBS, (Gomez Palacio, Mexico 1956). *First Convents of the Order of the Incarnate Word and Blessed Sacrament*, tr. SR. C. CASSO, IWBS (Victoria, Texas 1978). SR. M. GRACE, CVI, *The Incarnational Spirituality of Jeanne Chézard de Matel* (doctoral dissertation St. Louis University, 1991). SR. J. M. GUOKAS, CVI, *History of the Generalate of the Congregation of the Incarnate Word and Blessed Sacrament of Houston, Texas* (Houston, TX, 1994); *How We Live the Incarnation* (Houston, Texas, 1994). FR. HELYOT, "Le Verbe Incarné (Ordre de)" in *L'Encyclopedie Theologique XXIII*, ed. L'ABBÉ MIGNE (Paris 1850) tr. for private use by SR. K. MCDONAGH, IWBS (Rome 1984).

[K. MCDONAGH]

INCARNATION

The mystery of the Second Person of the Blessed Trinity's becoming man, the mystery of Jesus Christ's being God and man, the mystery of His being the God-Man. The word Incarnation (from the Latin *caro*, flesh) means the putting on or the taking on of flesh. "Καὶ ὁ λόγος σὰρξ ἐγένετο"—"And the Word was made flesh" (Jn 1.14). The word Incarnation may refer to the Word's becoming man; thus it would mean the operation by which the Triune God, forming a determined human nature in the womb of the Virgin, elevated it and efficiently united it to the Second Divine Person. The word *Incarnation* may also refer to the resultant union; thus it would mean the wondrous, singular, and eternally permanent union of the divine nature and the human nature in the one Person of the Word.

Scholastic theology considers the Incarnation in the following way. It first deals with the fact of the Incarnation, that is, that Jesus Christ had two natures, one divine, one human; it goes on to investigate the manner of this union; it then takes up the immediate consequences of the mystery: the holiness of Jesus, His knowledge, impeccability, power, His human limitations, divine sonship, mediatorship, as well as the adoration due Him, and the communication of idioms. All the above is the science of CHRISTOLOGY. Systematic theology then goes on to consider the work of Jesus Christ, His Redemption of man and how it was accomplished. This is the science of SOTERIOLOGY.

Mode of Union. How is the union of the two natures to be conceived? Under the guidance of the magisterium of the Church, theology rejects a moral or accidental union; it likewise rejects a union of coalescence, whereby the divine and human natures would merge into a divine-human nature. The union that it accepts is a hypostatic union, a union in Person. The Divine PERSON subsisting in the divine nature begins to subsist in a human nature. In its understanding of the terms nature and Person the magisterium of the Church does not canonize any purely scientific or purely philosophical definition of them, nor does it exclude such scientific or philosophical definitions. It is up to the theologians to reject definitions that are not in accord with the dogmas of the Church concerning this substantial union, that tend, on the one hand, to a Monophysitic, or Eutychian, understanding of the union, or, on the other hand, to a Nestorian understanding, both of which the Church has definitively rejected. The terminology of the Church itself, however, has undergone evolution.

There are, in Christ, consequently, two wills and two operations. Christ can act at the level of His divine nature, or He can act at the level of His human nature. This was denied by the Monothelites, who considered Christ to have only a divine will and only a divine operation. The impossibility of Christ's merit or satisfaction is a logical consequence of this heretical position. It is at this point that theology may aptly discuss the theandric acts of Christ.

It is of faith that the union of the human and divine natures in Christ, once effected, was never dissolved and will never be dissolved. The hypostatic union will endure forever.

Character of Union. Scholastic theology next takes up the question of the formal character (*ratio formalis*) of the HYPOSTATIC UNION, the ultimate human explanation of what is in fact a strict mystery. There have been, historically speaking, three stages in the doctrinal progress of this core area of Christology: (1) the scriptural (e.g., Phil 2.5–8); (2) the ecclesiastical, as formulated definitively by the Council of CHALCEDON; (3) and the theological. At the theological stage, theologians ask (relative to the specifics supplied by Chalcedon) such questions as *how* can one, perfect, integral human nature be joined to the divine? How can two things complete in themselves

become one being? Reflecting on the definitions of the Church, theologians see the opening to an explanation in the fact that *this* human nature lacks a human personality. Christology proceeds from there in its various theories of the *ratio formalis* presented by individual theologians and schools.

Consequences of Union. As for the consequences of the hypostatic union for the human nature of Christ, it is almost axiomatic to say that the human nature of Christ is ontologically and substantially holy by virtue of its intimate union with the Word. Sanctity in the divine nature is the very being of the divine nature insofar as it is the infinite good and the infinite love of the infinite good. Sanctity in creatures is a participation of the divine goodness; it is limited. According to most theologians, the human nature of Christ was sanctified by the grace of union directly and immediately. All theologians hold that Christ's humanity was sanctified by abundant sanctifying grace and the accompanying supernatural gifts; the gift of grace was in proportion to the magnitude of the gift of union—it was measureless in the sense that no one will ever receive more sanctifying grace.

Christ also had at every moment of His existence the beatific vision, and the support of magisterial affirmations in this regard has been greatly strengthened by the forthright statements of Pius XII's *Mystici corporis* (47, 76). Along with the knowledge of vision, Christ had infused knowledge and acquired knowledge. He was, moreover, impeccable, although it is of faith that He had the freedom requisite for meriting, and theologically certain that He had the freedom of active indifference. It is in this connection that the interesting theological problem of the mandate is discussed.

Although He possessed in His humanity the power of working miracles, Christ assumed with His humanity for the time before His death all and only those natural defects that are common to mankind and unblameworthy.

Regarding the consequences of the hypostatic union for the God-Man considered in His totality, theology affirms a true communication of idioms, that is, a manner of logical attribution, of predication, that is possible in speaking about Christ and that is entirely unique to Him. Designated according to one of His natures, He may have attributed to Himself predicates that are His because of His other nature.

Theology is careful to affirm that this man Jesus Christ is the natural Son of God, in no way His adoptive Son. It also says that even in His humanity He should be the recipient of the cult of absolute latria, that is, that His humanity is the object of adoration in the strictest sense.

In summary, theology says that because of the Incarnation, because Jesus Christ is who and what He is, He is the ontological mediator between God and men, perfectly suited to take up the work of moral mediation. This He did by all the salvific actions of His life, but especially by freely undergoing His Passion and suffering death on the cross.

See Also: JESUS CHRIST, ARTICLES ON; REDEMPTION, ARTICLES ON.

Bibliography: A. MICHEL, *Dictionnaire de théologie catholique,* ed. A. VACANT et al. (Paris 1903–50) 7.2:1445–1539. H. VORGRIMLER, *Lexikon für Theologie und Kirche,* ed. J. HOFER and K. RAHNER (Freiberg 1957–65) 5:678–679. F. MALMBERG, H. FRIES, ed., *Handbuch theologischer Grundbegriffe* (Munich 1962–63) 1:706–715. L. CERFAUX, *Christ in the Theology of St. Paul,* tr. G. WEBB and A. WALKER (New York 1959). J. DANIÉLOU, *Christ and Us,* tr. W. ROBERTS (New York 1961). H. M. DIEPEN, *La Théologie de l'Emmanuel: Les Lignes maîtresses d'une christologie* (Bruges 1960). F. X. DURRWELL, *The Resurrection: A Biblical Study,* tr. R. SHEED (New York 1960). J. GIBLET et al., *Lumière et vie* 7 (1958) 1–122. R. W. GLEASON, *Christ and the Christian* (New York 1959). L. DE GRANDMAISON, *Jesus Christ,* tr. B. WHELAN et al. (New York 1961). L. LERCHER, *Institutiones theologiae dogmaticae,* v.3 (5th ed. Barcelona 1951). S. LYONNET, *De peccato et redemptione* (Rome 1957–), 4 v. planned. *Son and Savior: The Divinity of Jesus Christ in the Scriptures,* tr. A. WHEATON (Baltimore 1960), symposium. L. RICHARD, *Le Mystère de la rédemption* (Tournai 1959). I. SOLANO, *Sacrae theologiae summa,* ed., Fathers of the Society of Jesus, Professors of the Theological Facullties in Spain (Madrid 1962) 3.1. B. M. XIBERTA Y ROQUETA, *Enchiridion de Verbo Incarnato* (Madrid 1957).

[E. A. WEIS]

INCARNATION, NECESSITY OF THE

Why the INCARNATION? What was the ultimate purpose of God taking on human nature? All theologians agree that Jesus Christ came primarily to save sinners. This is expressed in the earliest creeds: "Who for us men and for our salvation came down from heaven and was made flesh" (Nicene Creed). This creedal statement echoes the words of Christ Himself: ". . . the Son of Man has not come to be served but to serve, and to give his life as a ransom for many" (Mt 20.28). Paul puts it emphatically: "This saying is true and worthy of entire acceptance, that Jesus Christ came into the world to save sinners" (1 Tm 1.15).

The creedal statement gave rise to another question that theologians have discussed through the course of centuries: Did the Second Person of the Blessed Trinity have to become man or could satisfaction for sin have been made in another way? It is the classic question concerning the necessity of the Incarnation.

Anselm. Historians of dogma generally agree that St. ANSELM OF CANTERBURY was the first great systematic theologian who gave classic expression to the question in his *Cur Deus Homo.* In Anselm's framework, man was created in a state of justice by God, in order that enjoying God he might be happy. Created by God and remaining a creature of God, destined one day to take the place of the fallen angels of God, man owed *all* his service to God and was God's debtor for everything he could do or produce. Sin, Anselm went on, is simply nonpayment of this debt.

The effects of man's sin are that, though God's honor remains intact, man himself suffers consequences in the moral order that in turn have consequences in the physical order. Man must either suffer from God's eternal punishment or give God satisfaction—and this latter is the giving to God of what service he withheld along with something extra for the contumely. Man could not by himself give God this required satisfaction (1) because even his present service was owed, (2) because sin is an infinitely grave offense, (3) because he would have to conquer the devil, and (4) through one man justify others. "Nothing more just, nothing more impossible," as Boso, Anselm's partner in the *Cur Deus Homo* dialogue, commented succinctly.

Anselm went on to say that God's constancy to His own purpose required that He restore man by arranging for satisfaction to be given; and, taking the nature of sin and satisfaction to be as he described it, there was only one way—God had to become man. With the same "austere metaphysic" (J. Rivière's phrase) Anselm also reasoned to the necessity of Christ's death on the cross.

Thomistic and Scotistic Views. Anselm's basic reasoning was accepted by St. THOMAS AQUINAS as the ultimate motive for the Incarnation so that, had man not sinned, there would have been no Incarnation. Theologians in the Thomistic tradition hold that given God's decree requiring condign satisfaction from man for sin, it was necessary that one of the Persons of the Trinity become incarnate. For them Incarnation did not have an internal necessity, that is, of itself, or one consequent merely on the creation of the world, or one consequent on the Fall, or, finally, one consequent even on God's decree to restore man. The followers of DUNS SCOTUS, on the other hand, hold that the Incarnation was decreed by God even before the advent of sin. They proclaim that the Incarnation was from the first an integral part of the scheme of creation. Christ was to be the crown and glory of the Father's creation. Sin did not, then, occasion the Incarnation; it merely determined the manner. Christ, because of man's sin, would now come in a body that would suffer the Passion and death to redeem man. The Scotists argue that all men exist for Christ, not Christ because of them.

Thomists do not deny the primacy of Christ in creation and all the other benefits that have come from the

Incarnation. But they insist on the basically remedial purpose of His coming as the only adequate interpretation of the abundant scriptural passages attesting it. The Scotistic position has been that God could give a purely human person such gifts of grace that he would be able to give condign satisfaction for man's sin.

In the 14th century John WYCLIF, in accordance with a more general principle of necessity that he held, maintained that for the Incarnation there was an absolute necessity. Later philosophers like Leibniz, in accordance with the optimism that they maintained, and along with them some theologians, said that God either was forced by some internal necessity to create the best possible world (a world, therefore, in which the Divine Son would be incarnate) or was constrained by some kind of fittingness, once He had decreed the creation, to decree also the Incarnation.

The whole discussion of the necessity of the Incarnation has, historically, been intimately bound up with the theological notion of satisfaction. In the 20th-century renewal of Scripture studies and of Biblical theology, with keener interest in the nature of man's elevation and relationship to Christ, other elements of man's salvation are receiving more emphasis than previously. The discussion has broadened, with the consequence that theologians do not find the limited framework of satisfaction-necessity as useful as they once did. Nevertheless, as a concept solidly based on Scripture and as a word sanctified by conciliar usage (H. Denzinger, *Enchiridion Symbolorum* 1529), satisfaction will always be theologically illuminating.

See Also: REDEMPTION, ARTICLES ON.

Bibliography: J. F. BONNEFOY, "Il primato di Cristo nella teologia contemporanea," in *Problemi e Orientamenti di Teologia Dommatica.* (Milano, 1957). L. CERFAUX, *Christ in the Theology of St. Paul,* tr. G. WEBB and A. WALKER (New York 1959). L. LERCHER, *Institutiones theologiae dogmaticae,* v.3 (5th ed. Barcelona 1951). S. LYONNET, *Sin, Redemption and Sacrifice: A Biblical and Patristic Study* tr. L. SABOURIN (Rome 1970) I. SOLANO, *Sacrae theologiae summa,* ed. FATHERS OF THE SOCIETY OF JESUS, PROFESSORS OF THE THEOLOGICAL FACULTIES IN SPAIN (Madrid 1962) 3.1. B. M. XIBERTA Y ROQUETA, *Enchiridion de Verbo Incarnato* (Madrid 1957).

[E. A. WEIS/J. J. WALSH/EDS.]

INCENSE

Material that, when burned, produces a fragrant smoke. The term is applied also to the fragrant smoke. Various substances, such as aromatic wood, bark, seed, etc., but especially certain resins and gum resins, were used as incense in ancient times.

In the Bible. In the East the burning of incense as perfume was an ancient practice. From its use for secular purposes it was introduced into the religious worship of both the pagans and the Israelites, since it was a natural and beautiful symbol of prayer and sacrifice. But there was a difference between ordinary "profane" incense (Ex 30.9) and "sacred" incense that was used solely in Israelite worship. The latter was a finely ground powder (Lv 16.12) made up of a special blend, half frankincense (*lᵉbōnâ*) and half storax (*nātāp*), onycha (*šᵉḥelet*), and galbanum (*ḥelbᵉnâ*), to which salt was added as a preservative (Ex 30.34–38). When these resinous materials were burned they produced "fragrant smoke," which is the original meaning of the Hebrew word *qᵉṭōret*. However, the word came to be used much more often of the resins themselves.

When the legitimate worship of Yahweh is described in the OT and the verb *hiqṭîr* [to burn up (something) into fragrant smoke] is employed, the object of the verb is not necessarily incense. In fact, the common use of incense in the sacred rites was to burn it together with sacrificial victims, such as HOLOCAUSTS (Ex 29.18), the fat of other offerings (Ex 29.13), cereal offerings (Lv 6.8), and token offerings (Nm 5.26). It thus served as a secondary offering to Yahweh.

At times, however, incense was burned by itself as an independent offering in divine worship. In these cases it was consumed in the fire on a special altar, the altar of incense (Ex 30.1–10) or golden altar (Nm 4.11), or in a CENSER. (*See* ALTAR, 2.) Although this practice was carried on already in preexilic times, the references to it are mostly in postexilic documents, e.g., the so-called priestly code, which restricts this offering to the Aaronic priests (Nm 17.1–5).

In the NT the only reference to the burning of incense in the Temple worship is in Lk 1.8–12, where the Evangelist recounts the story of Zachary offering incense in the Temple and seeing the angel Gabriel at the right hand of the altar of incense. But in the heavenly liturgy of the Apocalypse "the golden bowls full of incense" symbolize "the prayers of the saints" (Rv 5.8; see also 8.3–4). In Ap 18.13 fragrant resins used as incense (θυμιάματα) are listed among the luxury imports of 1st-century Rome.

Bibliography: *Encyclopedic Dictionary of the Bible,* tr. and adap. by L. HARTMAN (New York 1963). 1056–57. R. DE VAUX *Ancient Israel, It's Life and Institutions,* tr. J. MCHUGH (New York 1961). 423, 430–432. B. KÖTTING, *Die Religion in Greschichte und Gegenwart,* 7 v. (3d ed. Tübingen 1957–65). 6:1571.

[J. J. MCGARRAGHY]

In Christian Liturgy. Incense was used copiously in pagan cult, and without it sacrifice was considered hardly complete. The emperor himself was often honored as a deity by means of incense. During persecutions Christians were frequently required to offer incense before an image of the emperor or a god as a test of their loyalty; those who did so were regarded as apostates by their fellow Christians. Although the use of incense was retained at funerals, since it had become a normal civil ceremony, protective in origin, Christianity rejected it as a form of worship because of antipathy toward paganism.

Once paganism had been vanquished, the Church slowly began to introduce the use of incense. The earliest witness in the East seems to have been Pseudo-Dionysius (*Eccl. hierarchia* 3.2; Quasten MonE 294), who reported that the bishop began the celebration of Mass with an incensation of altar and sanctuary. In the West, incense was first used by carrying it before the pope (Andrieu OR 2:82; cf. 88), for the pope was considered on a par with civil rulers who were so honored. An incensation of the oblation at Mass was first recorded in the 11th century (Bernold, *Micrologus* 9; PL 151:983). In time incense came to be used also in the Roman rite during Lauds and Vespers (8th century) and as a mark of respect for the altar, the ministers, and the faithful. In the 13th century, Innocent III saw an exorcistic significance in its use (*De sacro altaris mysterio* 2.17; PL 217:808). This notion can still be found in some blessings (e.g., when incense is blessed for use in the erection of a new cross: *Rituale Romanum* 9.9.14).

During the 17th and 18th centuries the natural materials burned as incense were replaced with substances borrowed from the perfume industry. But the fragrant resins prescribed for incense in Ex 30.34–35 (see above) are still the most satisfactory ingredients for liturgical use because the odor given off when they are burned is in no way reminiscent of the secular perfume industry. The resulting smoke is visible without excessive clouding.

Bibliography: E. G. ATCHLEY, *A History of the Use of Incense in Divine Worship* (New York 1909). E. FEHRENBACH, *Dictionnaire d'archéologie Chrétienne et de liturgie*, ed. F. CABROL, H. LECLERCQ, and H. I. MARROU, 15 v. (Paris 1907–53). 5.1:2–21. J. H. MILLER, *Fundamentals of the Liturgy* (Notre Dame, Ind. 1960). 203–204. P. MORRISROE, *The Catholic Encyclopedia*, ed. C. G. HERBERMANN et al, 16 v. (New York 1907–14). 7:716–717. O. BÖCHER, *Die Religion in Greschichte und Gegenwart*, 7 v. (3d ed. Tübingen 1957–65). 6:1571. K. HOFMANN, Lexikon für Theologie und Kirche, ed. M. BUCHBERGER, 10 v. (Freiburg 1930–38). 10:783–785.

[M. MCCANCE]

INCEST

Incest is a term derived from the Latin *incestus,* meaning unchaste, and applied to sexual relationship,

Archbishop Iakovos spreading incense during a special celebration at New York's Central Park. (Photograph by Mark Cardwell; Archive Photos)

complete or incomplete, between persons so related by blood or affinity that legal marriage cannot take place between them. In common with all other abuses of sex, it is an offense against the sixth commandment of God, but an added specific deformity exists in the case of incest by reason of the special affection and reverence that should exist between persons united in a close bond of family relationship.

Moral theology, for the most part, ignores the genetic considerations that are popularly thought to underlie the incest taboo. These, in any case, would be inapplicable to incest in which the relationship is one of affinity. St. Thomas finds three reasons why incest should be regarded as specially prohibited. (1) A violation of chastity committed between close relatives is contrary to the reverence owed in piety by the sinning parties to their parents or common ancestor. (2) The maintenance of chastity in family life requires that sexual intimacy between its members not united to each other by marriage should be made especially unthinkable in order that the close proximity in which they live should not provide too great an occasion for sin. (3) The special prohibition teaches people to take no sexual interest in those within the family circle, and this causes them to look outside of it for marriage partners. There is great advantage in this to those who marry, for marriage multiplies for them the number of those to whom they are amicably related, and it also helps build up a social unity between men on a broader basis than that of blood relationship.

The closer the relationship, the more grievous is the specific guilt of the sin of incest. Most grievous is incest of those related in the direct line, between parent and offspring. There is an essential indecency in such a case that is not found in transgressions involving other degrees of relationship. The prohibition of sexual union between those related by affinity is one of ecclesiastical law. One can also apply the term incest to the sin of people who are related by legal adoption, or who are spiritually related because of sponsorship in Baptism, and thus impeded from marriage. Strictly speaking, however, the term is used in this connection only by way of analogy. St. Thomas prefers to identify such sin between those spiritually related as sacrilege having the appearance of incest.

Bibliography: THOMAS AQUINAS, *Summa theologiae,* 2a2ae, 154.9. E. MANGENOT, *Dictionnaire de théologie catholique,* ed. A. VACANT et al., 15 v. (Paris 1903–50; Tables générales 1951–) 7.2:1539–55.

[L. G. MILLER]

INCEST (IN THE BIBLE)

The subject of incest in the Bible will be treated under three headings: incest in the patriarchal age, in the Mosaic Law, and in the New Testament.

Patriarchal Age. Instances are recorded during this period of intercourse between near relatives. Lot's daughters, motivated by a desire for children in a manless world, conceived Moab and Ammon by their father (Gn 19.30–38). The story, which is etiological in as far as it gives a folk etymology to the names of these peoples, was used to insult the Ammonites and Moabites because they refused to help Israel in time of need (Dt 23.3–5). Ruben was deprived of his birthright because of incest (Gn 35.22; 49.3–4). Judah had intercourse with Tamar, his daughter-in-law, but was not blamed for it, since he thereby raised up children for his dead sons. *See* LEVIRATE MARRIAGE (IN THE BIBLE).

Mosaic Law. God forbade the Israelites to imitate the incestuous customs of Egypt where marriage between

brothers and sisters was sometimes practiced (Lv 18.3, 6). The incestuous unions prohibited in the Law (some were legitimate at an earlier age in Israel) are those of son and mother, of a man with the wife of his father (Lv 18.8; Dt 27.20) and with the mother of his wife (Dt 27.23), of a man with his granddaughter or his wife's daughter or granddaughter (Lv 18.10, 17), of a man with his sister or half-sister (Lv 18.9; Dt 27.22; see, however, Gn 20.12), of a nephew with his aunt (Lv 18.12–14; cf. Ex 6.20), of a man with his daughter-in-law or with his sister-in-law (Lv 18.15, 16; 20.21); levirate marriage is an exception (Dt 25.5–10). Also forbidden was marriage to two sisters at the same time (Lv 18.18), although formerly it had been allowed (Gn 29.27–28). Penalties for incest were death (Lv 20.11–17), excommunication (Lv 18.29), and being cursed (Dt 27.20, 22–23), e.g., by being childless (Lv 20.21).

Other instances of incest are found in the Old Testament. Ammon, son of David, raped Tamar, his half-sister, for which Tamar's brother Absalom murdered him (2 Sm 13.1–32). Absalom committed incest with his father's concubines, to show that he now was king (2 Sm 16.21–22). David's son Adoniyah asked for Abishag, his father's concubine, a request that Solomon considered rebellion, although David had not "known" her (1 Kgs 2.13–23; 1.4). In Ez 22.10–11, among the crimes of Jerusalem, incest is listed (see also Am 2.7).

In the New Testament. There are only two instances of incest in the New Testament. Herod Antipas married Herodias, his niece, and the wife of his brother Philip who was still living. John the Baptist was imprisoned because of his condemnation of Herod for marrying his brother's wife (Mk 6.17–18).

In 1 Cor 5.1–12, St. Paul excommunicates and delivers to Satan a man sexually linked to his father's wife, no doubt his stepmother. Paul condemns such a sin as an "immorality . . . not found even among the Gentiles," and a corrupting influence on the sacred community. He also blames the Corinthian church for not having already excluded the man.

Neither in the Old Testament nor New Testament does incest seem to be condemned for eugenic reasons, although these may have been the basis for the moral prohibition.

Bibliography: H. LESÊTRE, *Dictionnaire de la Bible,* ed. F. VIGOUROUX, 5 v. (Paris 1895–1912) 3.1:864–867. W. CORSWANT, *A Dictionary of Life in Bible Times,* tr. A. HEATHCOTE (New York 1960) R. DE VAUX, *Ancient Israel, Its Life and Institutions,* tr. J. MCHUGH (New York 1961) 31 32, 42, 158–159.

[J. J. DAVIS]

INCOMMUNICABILITY

In scholastic philosophy and theology, incommunicability is that property which, together with SUBSISTENCE, characterizes the PERSON and, less properly, the irrational supposit; it indicates the person's individuality, distinctness, and independence.

Historical Aspects. The Vulgate of Wis 14.21 used *incommunicabile nomen* to designate what is the prerogative of God alone (cf. St. Augustine, *In evang. Ioh.* 79.2; *Corpus Christianorum. Series latina* 36:527). Boethius used *incommunicabilis proprietas* or *qualitas* of what is proper to a single individual (*Herm. sec.* 2; *Patrologia Latina*, ed. J. P. Migne (Paris 1878–90) 64:462–64; ed. C. Meiser, Lipsiae, 1877–80, 137–41). Fulgentius of Ruspe came closer to medieval speculations on personality when he said of the Trinity: ". . .se illa una veraque divinitas in singulis personis voluit *incommunicabiliter nominari* . . ." (*Epist.* 14.8; *Patrologia Latina* 65:399). But it was not till the Middle Ages that *incommunicabilitas* was used more technically and frequently for what is characteristic of the person. Boethius's definition of person as *naturae rationalis individua substantia* (C. *Eut.* 3, ed. H. Stewart and E. Rand, 84) was the basic point of departure. Richard of Saint-Victor sought to replace this formula as applied to God with *naturae divinae incommunicabilis exsistentia* (*De Trinitate* 4.21–24; ed. G. Salet, *Sources Chrétiennes*, ed. H. de Lubac et al. (Paris 1941–) 63:278–86; cf. pp. 487–89). Boethius's formula survived, however, although today it yields primacy to *distinctum subsistens in natura intellectuali* (St. Thomas, *In 1 sent.* 23.1.4). While *incommunicabilitas* did not appear in these two classic definitions, it was commonly used in their analysis, as the equivalent or refinement of *individua* and *distinctum*. In Alexander of Hales (*Summa theologiae* 3a; Quaracchi 4.2:78–79), followed by St. Bonaventure (In 3 sent. 5.2.2 ad 1; Quaracchi 3:133b), *incommunicabilitas* designated only one of three aspects of the individuality proper to the person. Such was not the case in St. Thomas's usage, which designated all three aspects as *incommunicabilitas* (*In 3 sent.* 5.2.1 ad 2); this usage has subsequently prevailed (see below).

Analysis. Each existent (*ens simpliciter*) as a unity is "undivided in itself, divided from every other." What this classic description seeks to convey is that every being as one: (1) is a totality, identical with itself, completely constituted in itself, an individual; and (2) precisely as such stands over against every other being. "Undivided in itself" regards the being's self-referent aspect, its self-identity, totality, completeness; "divided from every other" situates the being in the universe of distinct existents. The notion of *supposit* is a more technical designation of existent being in its unity. In the definition of the supposit as the distinct or incommunicable subsistent, subsistence represents the self-referent aspect of the supposit, while incommunicability represents its other-referent aspect. Following St. Thomas, scholastics speak of a threefold commonness or indistinctness as excluded from the supposit as incommunicable: (1) the commonness of a universal (for the supposit is subsistent, individual) or quasiuniversal (to allow for the commonness had by the divine NATURE in the TRINITY); (2) the commonness of a part (for the supposit is complete); (3) the commonness had by "assumption" by another supposit, as in the INCARNATION (see below). Incommunicability does not, however, exclude that the Divine Person of the Son draw His human nature to share in His divine subsistence.

Applications. (1) Irrational supposits possess incommunicability only by a very extended analogy, since their self-identity is minimal. (2) The human (and angelic) person, constituted as such because of its intellectuality and freedom exercised by a created ultimate subject of existence, is characterized by a lofty, though still imperfect, self-possession, and hence by incommunicability. The moral and juridical sacredness of the person has its roots in this ontological inviolability; it is because the person exists in itself and for itself that it cannot be treated as a mere means. (3) In the unique instance of the humanity of Christ, an individual created nature, rational and free, is not the ultimate subject of incommunicable existence; rather the WORD, divinely incommunicable from eternity, is now, in this individual assumed nature, humanly incommunicable. How a reality fully individual as nature can lack the individuality or incommunicability proper to person is the essential problem arising from the mystery of the Incarnation (*see* JESUS CHRIST IN THEOLOGY). (4) In the Trinity the divine nature, though subsistent, lacks strict incommunicability because of being common to the three Persons; the same is true of the subsistent relation of active SPIRATION, common to Father and Son. It is rather in the three Divine Persons, each a distinct, subsistent relation, that one finds the strict incommunicability of which there is question here (*see* RELATIONS, TRINITARIAN). From the Christological and Trinitarian applications it is clear that the philosophical analysis of incommunicability is strongly dependent on the two central Christian mysteries; it is doubtful, at the very least, that unaided reason would have perceived any distinction between the singularity or individuality of an existing nature and the further individuality or incommunicability that specifies the person.

Incommunicability and Personal Communication. Modern personalist and existentialist philosophy emphasizes interpersonal communication as essential to the person (*see* PERSONALISM; EXISTENTIALISM); man attains self-realization only in meaningful encounter with the other. Superficially this notion might seem to conflict with the notion of the person as incommunicable. In fact the two notions are not only compatible but require one another. Only as unique, distinct, and incommunicable can the person enter into a communion that is not a depersonalizing self-abdication; only as open to communion can the person retain a self-possession that is not solipsistic. The Trinitarian mystery, where each incommunicable Person is constituted by a distinct, subsistent relation, is for the Christian the model and guarantee of this necessary complementarity.

See Also: ASSUMPTUS-HOMO THEOLOGY; CONSUBSTANTIALITY; CREATED ACTUATION BY UNCREATED ACT; HOMOOUSIOS; HYPOSTASIS; KENOSIS; PERSON, DIVINE.

Bibliography: L. DE RAEYMAEKER, *The Philosophy of Being,* tr. E. H. ZIEGELMEYER (St. Louis 1954) 240–47. L. BILLOT, *De Verbo Incarnato* (9th ed. Rome 1949) 61–78; *De Deo uno et trino* (7th ed. Rome 1935) 460–74. A. MICHEL, *Dictionnaire de théologie catholique,* ed. A. VACANT et al., 15 v. (Paris 1903–50) 7.1:407–29.

[T. E. CLARKE]

INCORPORATION IN CHRIST

For St. Paul the essential eschatological reality is the risen Christ in His glorified Body (Col 2.17). In Biblical thought "body" stands for the whole human being in one's concrete reality as a living person. Sinful human beings are freed from "the body of sin" and "death" (Rom 6.6; 7.24) through the Lord Jesus, who in His own Body-person has destroyed the body of sin (Rom 8.3; 2 Cor 5.21; Col 1.22) and who, risen to new life in the Spirit (Rom 1.4), is in His "spiritual body" (1 Cor 15.44–49) the bearer of new life to human beings (Eph 2.5–6; 1 Cor 15.20–23; 45–49; Col 2.12–3.4; Rom 8.11). It is through Baptism in faith (Col 2.11–12; Rom 6.3–14; 1 Cor 12.13; Eph 5.26) that the sinner, delivered from his own sin-and-death body, is attached to Christ and to the work wrought by Christ in His own Body, and is made one Body with Christ living now as "spiritual body" and "life-giving Spirit" (1 Cor 15.44–45). It is into Christ's Body that Christians are incorporated as members and made His Church-Body; for once embodied into Christ, they become "fellow-members of the same body" (Eph 3.6) and "members of one another" (4.25).

According to Pius XII in the encyclical *MYSTICI CORPORIS,* incorporation into Christ is realized only in and through the Church, His social Body (see encycl., pars. 11, 40, 67, 73, 81). Christ's "social Body" (44, 51, 58, 67, etc.) is so "conjoined" (1, 5, 11, 55, 67, etc.) and so "made like" (46, 51, 54) to its Head, who shares with it His most "intimately personal goods" (53), that He is become a quasi-person sustaining His Church-Body (51–53, 56, 77). "The divine Savior with His social Body constitutes only one mystical person" (67; see 56, 78). At the same time, however, the social Body of the Church is itself personified, and given not a detached but a distinct collective existence (78, 53, 85, 5, 12, etc.). Vatican II's *Lumen Gentium* (7–8) continues the line of thought put forth in *Mystici Corporis,* though it broadens significantly the ecumenical outreach found already in that encyclical.

Baptism in water and the Spirit (18, 21, 26, 29) incorporates the whole human being into Christ in His social Body, qualifying the baptized to live in the total inward-outward life (60) of the company of those who in Christ's one Spirit (54–5) are one with Christ and with each other in faith, hope, and love (70–74).

The grace of incorporation invests the whole social Body, inwardly and outwardly (61, 68–69, 63), and all its single members similarly. It is an embodied grace.

Among the points elaborated by theologians are the following: (1) the precise nature of the Headship of Christ; (2) the role of Christ's Spirit—merely appropriated or also proper? (*see* APPROPRIATION)— in uniting the Body to the Head; (3) the grace of incorporation, as an inward-outward grace, sacramental and social; (4) the Eucharist and incorporation; (5) the nature of the unity—merely dynamic or also entitative?— between Head and Body; and (6) the meaning of incorporation in relation to the growing realization of the real though imperfect communion among various Christian denominations and the Catholic Church (*see* MEMBERSHIP IN THE CHURCH).

See Also: MYSTICAL BODY OF CHRIST.

Bibliography: R. SCHNACKENBURG, *Das Heilsgeschehen bei der Taufe nach dem Apostel Paulus* (Münchener theologische Studien 1; Munich 1950). A. WIKENHAUSER, *Pauline Mysticism,* tr. J. CUNNINGHAM (New York 1960). S. TROMP, *De Spiritu Christi Anima,* v.3 of *Corpus Christi Quod est Ecclesia,* 3 v. (Rome 1960). V. BRANICK, *The House Church in the Writings of Paul* (Wilmington, Del., 1989). M. ROOT and R. SAARINEN, eds., *Baptism and the Unity of the Church* (Geneva 1998).

[F. X. LAWLOR/D. M. DOYLE]

INCORPORATION INTO THE CHURCH (MEMBERSHIP)

In any contemporary discussion on "belonging to the Church" the first point to be stressed is that VATICAN COUNCIL II's *Dogmatic Constitution on the Church* (*Lumen gentium*) advisedly dropped the terms "member" and "membership." The first schema of the *Consti-*

tutio de Ecclesia had, in keeping with Pius XII's 1943 encyclical, *Mystici Corporis Christi,* employed the terms. But in its final form *Lumen gentium* used instead "incorporation," a notion at once more precise and more flexible. The deliberate substitution is clear from a comparison of *Lumen gentium,* art. 14 with the 1962 schema, art. 9, and the 1963 schema, art. 8. Likewise, the idea of *votum Ecclesiae* (intention of the Church— Abbott) did not keep the meaning given to it (in line with the thought of St. Robert Bellarmine) during the discussions of Vatican Council I (J. D. Mansi, *Sacrorum Conciliorum nova et amplissima collectio,* 31 v. [Florence-Venice 1757–98] reprinted and continued by L. Petit and J. B. Martin, 53 v. in 60 [Paris 1889–1927; repr. Graz 1960–] 53:311–312), in *Mystici Corporis Christi,* and in the Holy Office's letter to the archbishop of Boston regarding the "Feeney Case" (H. Denzinger, *Enchiridion symbolorum,* ed. A. Schönmetzer [32d ed. Freiburg 1963] 3870). The expression *votum Ecclesiae* retained that "classical" meaning only in the passage on catechumens (*Lumen gentium* 14.3). The application of *votum Ecclesiae* to non-Catholics reflects an entirely different viewpoint (*Lumen gentium* 15.2; 8.2—*ad unitatem catholicam impellunt,* "these elements or gifts properly belonging to the Church of Christ possess an inner dynamism toward Catholic unity"[Abbott]).

The setting aside of the idea of membership in favor of that of incorporation has called for the development of a carefully nuanced vocabulary, consistent with Vatican II ECCLESIOLOGY. With regard to Catholics, *Lumen gentium* uses "being incorporated" (*incorporatio*), qualifying the term with the adverb "fully" (*plene*) and emphasizing that full incorporation requires the presence of the Holy Spirit (*Lumen gentium* 14.2). For non-Catholics and catechumens, the constitution speaks of their being linked (*conjunctio*) to the Church, again carefully stressing the role of the Holy Spirit in each case (*Lumen gentium* 14.3; 15.2). As for non-Christians the constitution uses "being related" (*ordinantur*), a term that suggests a dynamic relationship, an orientation toward the Church (*Lumen gentium* 16). Every shade of difference in meaning among these terms is important. But the terms acquire their full force only in the light of the most authoritative commentaries on them, the Decree on Ecumenism and the Declaration on the Relationship of the Church to Non-Christian Religions. Then, supposing the nuances indicated, the richness of such expressions as the following becomes clear: "Churches and ecclesial communities" (*Unitatis redintegratio* 3.3; cf. *Lumen gentium* 15.1); "separated brethren" (brothers divided; *Unitatis redintegratio* 3.4); "separated Churches and ecclesial communities" (*Unitatis redintegratio* 3.4); "full communion"— "imperfect communion" (*ibid.* 3.1).

The Force of "Incorporation." Commentators on the conciliar texts have perhaps not paid enough attention to the fact that, although tightly linked, the terms "incorporation" (*Lumen gentium*) and *communio* (*Unitatis redintegratio*) are not synonymous. The main focus of "incorporation" is on individuals as such and although *Lumen gentium* (15) does make passing reference to the ecclesial standing of groups as such, that is not its primary emphasis. The main bearing of "communion," on the contrary, is on groups as such, in their relation to the Catholic Church and to each other. It is of some interest to point out that *Lumen gentium* (14.2; 14.1) uses the term *communio* to indicate union ("unity of communion"— Abbott) with the successor of St. Peter, but that in *Unitatis redintegratio* the term "communion" takes on the traditional sense of the *koinonia,* the fellowship, of the Churches (*Unitatis redintegratio* 3.4). In this respect, the Decree on Ecumenism is richer than the Constitution on the Church: it acknowledges a genuine salvific value in Churches and ecclesial communities as such (i.e., not merely in the ecclesial elements or vestiges existing in them).

Every ecclesial tradition affirms that incorporation in Christ involves a core element, known only by God, which consists in the presence within a person of the love of God poured forth by the Holy Spirit (Rom 5.5). This element is so important that without it there exists no full and complete incorporation, possessing every guarantee of authenticity (see *Lumen gentium* 14.2, a capital text on the point). This spiritual, interior incorporation often occurs before baptism (see St. Thomas Aquinas, *Summa theologiae* 3, 66.11 and 13 on baptism of desire and of blood) and at times even without any explicit knowledge of the mystery of Christ (*Lumen gentium* 16).

Here it should be stressed that when they speak formally of incorporation into the Church, most ecclesial traditions—even those that do not give prominence to the Sacraments—acknowledge that its accomplishment is normally through baptism. The gift of the Holy Spirit that is the inner mark of belonging to the Body of Christ is made ordinarily to those who seal their faith in Jesus Christ by baptism. Admittedly some Christian bodies born during or after the Reformation are silent on the point. The more ancient Christian traditions, however, are unanimous here, even though they may explain differently the connection between the sacramental rite and the inner incorporation or may not all recognize the validity of baptism administered in ways other than their own.

Every person baptized in a true BAPTISM belongs to the Body of Christ and therefore to the Church. One of the most important consequences of Vatican II ecclesiology is the break with Bellarmine's viewpoint, repeated in *Mystici Corporis Christi,* which in fact limited true belonging to the Church to those baptized within the Catholic community. For Vatican II every genuine baptism truly brings incorporation into Christ and the Church. Even though divided, the Church is single (*Unica Christi Ecclesia, Lumen gentium* 8.1) and baptism brings entrance into the single (though divided) Church. This is the profound implication of the expression "the one single Baptism of the one single Church." *Lumen gentium* refrains from stating that the Church is the Catholic Church; it chooses rather to affirm that the "Church subsists in the Catholic Church" (*subsistit in; Lumen gentium* 8). The precise reason of this choice is to give recognition to the presence of genuinely ecclesial elements in the non-Catholic bodies that the document, further on, designates as "Churches or ecclesial Communities." (The 1964 *schema* of the *Constitutio de Ecclesia* has this: *"loco 'est' 1.21, dicitur 'subsistit in' ut expressio melius concordet cum affirmatione de elementis ecclesialibus quae alibi adsunt."*) The implication is that in these "Churches and ecclesial Communities" the Church (the single Church) is present. Therefore those who by baptism belong to these bodies and within them live in faithfulness to the Spirit, relying on the elements of genuinely evangelical life they find there (*Lumen gentium* 8.2; 15.1 & 2; *Unitatis redintegratio* 3), by that same belonging also belong to the single Church.

Given the viewpoint of the conciliar documents (which in their own way mark a return to Thomas Aquinas's insistence on the interiority of incorporation into Christ—*Summa theologiae* 3a, 8.3), it is extremely important to keep in mind that belonging to the single Church comes about in and through belonging to the "Churches and ecclesial Communities." These bear within them elements of sanctification and of truth that make it possible for the baptized to live according to the Gospel. Therefore the value of each "Church or ecclesial Community" as such is not set aside—treated, that is, as meaningless or purely incidental. Moreover, the council refuses to conceive the incorporation as though it were an unmediated action of the Holy Spirit, between the Spirit and each individual alone. However far from being what the Catholic Church regards as the true form of the Church, every ecclesial community is the locus of a genuine incorporation into the single Church. Acknowledgment of that fact is an implication of the idea of "incomplete communion"; the accent falls on "communion," the noun, rather than on "incomplete," the adjective, and clearly the term "communion" should not be taken to mean anything other than the "communion" that incorporation in Christ brings about (see Bertrams; Hamer; Kasper; Lanne; McDonnell; McGovern).

Incorporation through baptism means, then, incorporation into the single Church. The Church, however, exists now as divided, disunited. *Lumen gentium* and the other conciliar documents that explicate its ecclesiology, affirm that incorporation, while real, does not have the same completeness in all Churches and ecclesial communities. The documents add that incorporation has this fullness only in the Catholic Church (*Lumen gentium* 8.2 [*subsistit* in passage]; *Unitatis redintegratio* 3.5). To illustrate let us give an image: a graft can be made onto a living body, yet for some reason not receive all the vigor and strength of the body because of some defect or lack in the way the grafting onto the whole organism is done. In the belief of the Catholic Church the baptized person fully (*plene*) incorporated into the Church is the one who shares truly in the Eucharist (i.e., as one having charity), within a community whose bishop, ordained in the apostolic succession, is in communion with the bishop of Rome (except for the last part the Catholic Church is at one with the Orthodox Churches in this understanding).

Two Views of the Church. To grasp the meaning of this Catholic position, it is important to recall the difference between two views of the Church, the "Catholic" view—that of Roman Catholics, the Orthodox, and some Anglicans—and the Protestant one. The Protestant view considers the Church essentially in its invisible reality (its res in the Scholastics' vocabulary). It looks immediately at what God works in the heart "of all who love the Lord Jesus Christ in sincerity and whose names are known only to God" (Moss 2, 41). Thus, the focus is on the effect of grace and the mysterious bond existing here and now between the glorified Christ and each sincere believer. Such a reading of the reality of the Church, therefore, centers on realized sanctification, that is on the invisible communion of all who are in grace. Outward signs—the Sacraments, the institutional Church—have a value of mere instrumentality, no more. All those who confess Christ—and thereby may *possibly* be sanctified—have the possibility of existing within the ecclesial plenitude to the degree that charity is alive in them. It is impossible, therefore, to take institutional elements as the index of degrees of ecclesiology.

The Catholic view is altogether different. The reality of the Church must be seen as consisting *at once and inseparably* of what Christ works here and now within the faithful and of the institutional elements established from the outset by the apostolic community, the interpreter of Christ's will. From the day of Christ's resurrection to the day of his second coming the Church, taken in its total reality, is the *Sacramentum salutis,* i.e., the expression of all that salvation implies—not only the inner presence of grace, but also the channels of grace. These instruments also are saving gifts of God and constitutives of the manifestation of his grace. The Church received its identity at once from its inner, mysterious reality (its *res*) and from the visible means (the *sacramentum*) of which it is the bearer. For the Church is, in the present world, the Body of Christ, to be seen always as tightly bound to the Jesus of the Incarnation—the eternal Son of the Father, but also the One Sent to give to human beings along with the event of salvation the means for entering into that salvation.

Full Incorporation. This makes clear the meaning of the important statement of the Constitution on the Church: "They are *fully* incorporated into the society of the Church who, possessing the Spirit of Christ, accept her *entire* system and all the means of salvation given to her" (*Lumen gentium* 14.2). Full incorporation comes about where the spiritual reality (the possession of the Spirit of Christ) and the entirety of visible, essential elements are present. To be joined only to the visible institution without charity is not to be "in the heart of the Church" (*ibid.*); to possess charity without holding fast to the outward, institutional, and essential elements is not to belong totally to the reality of the Sacrament that the Church is. The two aspects of incorporation into the Church, the spiritual and the visible, are, as it were, interfused. Among the factors that together give the Church its outward manifestation, the institutional aspect is inseparable from the communal profession of faith and from sharing in the Sacraments, above all in the Eucharistic *synaxis*. The Eucharist is the unifying center in which come together, within the *communio* of the Body of Christ, the communion of the profession of faith and the communion with the apostolic ministry, whose *centrum unitatis* is the bishop of Rome. Incorporation achieves in the Eucharist its full measure.

This understanding of the incorporation in Christ and the Church allows for breaking away from the Counter-Reformation positions maintaining that there is no genuine belonging to the Church other than within the Catholic community, bound fast to the pope (Bellarminus, *De conciliis* 3, 2 [ed. Fevre 1870] v. 2. 316–318). That conception remained in the thought of *Mystici Corporis*; use of the term "membership" made difficult any sort of nuancing. But thanks to its ecclesiology—prepared by the renewal of patristic studies and the ecumenical dialogue—Vatican II was able to affirm at the same time that Churches or ecclesial communities separated from the Catholic Church are part of the single Church, and that nevertheless incorporation in Christ and His Church possesses within the Catholic Church the fullness that it does not have elsewhere.

Bibliography: W. BERTRAMS, "De gradibus communionis in doctrina Concilii Vaticani II," *Gregorianum* 47 (1966) 286–305. Y.-M. CONGAR, "What Belonging to the Church Has Come to Mean," *Communio* 4 (1977) 146–160. J. HAMER, "La terminologie écclésiologique de Vatican II et les ministères protestants," *La Documentation Catholique* 53 (1971) 625–628. W. KASPER, "Der ekklesiologische Charakter der nichtkatholischen Kirchen," *Theologische Quartalschrift* 145 (1965) 42–62. E. LANNE, "Le Mystère de l'Église et de son unité," *Irénikon* 46 (1973) 298–342. K. MCDONNELL, "The Concept of Church in the Documents of Vatican II as Applied to Protestant Denominations," *Lutherans and Catholics in Dialogue—IV, Eucharist and Ministry* (Minneapolis 1970) 307–324. J. O. MCGOVERN, *The Church in the Churches* (Washington, D.C. 1968). C. B. MOSS, *What Do We Mean by Reunion* (London 1953).

[J. M. R. TILLARD/EDS.]

INCULTURATION, LITURGICAL

A hallmark of Pope JOHN PAUL II'S pontificate has been his extensive travels to the local churches on nearly every continent. Central to these visits are major liturgical celebrations that draw upon local culture to express the genius of the local churches. At the opening and closing of the special assemblies of the Synod of Bishops, the Eucharistic liturgies took up the particular cultural expressions, at the pope's expressed wishes (*Ecclesia in Africa*, no. 25). At the opening of the Holy Door to commence the Jubilee Year, African horns and signs of reverence from Asia and Oceania emphasized the universality of the salvation and the mission of the Church to the whole world.

Throughout the history of Christian worship, liturgy and culture have always been intricately entwined: the culture of a given group of people yielded great influence on the forms, symbols, language, time and place of their worship. With the documents of the Second VATICAN COUNCIL, the imperative of liturgical inculturation gained unparalleled impetus and theological articulation. This entry first takes up the issue of terminology surrounding the notion of liturgical inculturation. After considering historical evidence of the interaction of liturgy and culture, it presents the documents of Vatican II and the instruction on inculturation and liturgy. Then, it examines recent attempts at liturgical adaptation throughout the world.

Problem of Terminology. The term "inculturation" is an ambiguous neologism that arose in the 1960s. When one examines conciliar texts, one observes that the terms *aptatio* ("adaptation") and *accomodatio* ("accommodation") are used interchangeably to refer to the Church's task of *aggiornamento* and the whole process of liturgical change. After the council, the term *aptatio* came to refer to the task of the local bishops, part of the revitalization envisioned by the council, and *accomodatio* came to refer to the provisions in the typical editions of the Roman liturgical books for the minister to select alternatives in the local celebration of the liturgy.

Following A. Chupungco, adaptation is a culturally neutral term that refers to the Church's whole renewal. Different terms have been coined to speak of the methods of that renewal. The term "inculturation" was coined to refer to the need to keep the Christian message intact through the process of cultural exchange. In 1975 at the Thirty-second General Congregation of the Society of Jesus, the Latin word *inculturatio* was adopted in the discussions, probably the equivalent of the English "enculturation" (Roest-Crollius 1978). As A. Shorter explains, "enculturation" is a technical anthropological term for the socialization of a person, the way that the person is inserted into her or his culture (1988). "Inculturation" soon replaced "enculturation" in missiological, theological, and liturgical discourse and took on an entirely different meaning. Pope John Paul II introduced the term into Church documents in a 1979 address to the Pontifical Biblical Commission and later that year elaborated on it in *Catechesi tradendae,* no. 53.

In current liturgical discourse, the following principle terms are used to name the levels of interaction of liturgy and culture: acculturation, inculturation and creativity. The term "acculturation" refers to the interaction that ensues from the juxtaposition of two cultures (Shorter 1988; Chupungco 1989). Acculturation names the initial stage of the encounter of the Roman liturgy with the local culture. The liturgy of the Roman Latin typical editions is placed side by side with elements from the culture where they interact but neither the liturgy nor the culture is assimilated into the other. The initial interaction of the liturgy and the local culture could then lead to inculturation, that is, the liturgy is so inserted into the culture that it would absorb the genius of the culture and the culture would be affected by the liturgy. Yet, the liturgy would not become the culture nor the culture the liturgy; rather, both would undergo a process of internal transformation to shape something new (Chupungco 1993). Neither the liturgy nor the culture would lose their identities, but they would no longer be what they were before. The liturgy would be so inserted into the cultural frame that it might speak, sing and move according to the people's language, thought, rites, symbols, gestures and arts. Liturgy would thus ritualize according to the local cultural pattern. Some scholars go on to name a third phase, that of creativity. Here, the liturgical rites are fashioned independent of the Roman *ordo* and euchology. At this stage, the Christian faith might be embodied in the local culture in such a way that new forms of expressing it emerge and so enrich the Church universal. The task of inculturation is ongoing: in the process of mutual assimilation, dimensions of the culture will undergo transformation in light of the memories, values and hopes negotiated by the liturgy ordered in the typical editions

and by the proclamation of the Gospel. Likewise, the culture will more authentically embody the Christian faith.

Liturgy and Local Church in History. Christian WORSHIP has always interacted with cultures, adapting cultural elements, transforming them and even rejecting them. Christian worship originated in the culturally plural matrix of Palestinian Judaism, Hellenism and Roman imperialism. As Christianity quickly spread through the Mediterranean basin into Asia Minor, Africa and east to Syria, the regional styles of worship, already influenced by Jewish forms, developed according to the cultural genius of the local churches. The local churches of Alexandria, Antioch, Edessa, Milan, Jerusalem, Rome and Constantinople generated distinctive liturgical usages that could be classified as families of rites. The content and rhetoric of euchology, the anaphoral structure, the order of worship at eucharist and initiation, the times and seasons of prayer each varied according to the different churches.

The Roman rite itself bears the marks of cultural adaptation. While the locus of imperial power shifted to Constantinople, the influence of pagan Roman culture on Christian worship and ministry in the church at Rome was considerable. With the invasion of the northern peoples, Rome was obliged to open itself to their cultures. At the same time, the liturgy of Rome came to hold a preeminent, if not idealized, position namely other legitimate and integral usages in the northern territories. Roman liturgical books were exported to the Germanic and Gallican churches in the interest of unifying liturgical praxis. The editors charged with preparing the books found themselves confronted with the daunting task of conforming local usage to distinctly Roman practices that were celebrated in the geographical coordinates of the *Urbs* and suppressing that which did not conform. However, the hallmarks of Roman liturgy—its terse prayers, its sober ritual, and its juridical reserve—were foreign to the Germano-Gallican spirit. Thus, significant adaptations were required and the Franco-Germanic culture was intertwined with the Roman liturgy. The popes adopted this liturgy after systematic abbreviation, and it was passed throughout Europe.

Tridentine Uniformity. With the Council of TRENT, the liturgy of the Roman church became carefully regulated. The Missal of PIUS V (1570) was binding on all churches of the west except those that could trace their usages back two hundred years. The use of the vernacular, called for by the reformers, was rejected and the Latin language required. Trent sought to preserve and guarantee the venerable Roman tradition, as it was then perceived. The printing press made the dissemination of the uniform and codified liturgical books in Latin, or *edi-*

tiones typicae, facile. It is important to note that while the codified and uniform Roman liturgy became hegemonic, the relationship between cultic praxis of Christian faith and local culture survived and in many instances flourished on the "unofficial" level of popular devotions, pious practices, pilgrimages and the myriad local feasts and observances.

Missionary encounters with non-western European cultures prompted a reconsideration of the obligation to use the Tridentine forms. The CHINESE RITES CONTROVERSY (1603–1742), errupting around Matteo RICCI's (1552–1610) efforts of looking within the culture for authentic ways of expressing Christian faith, marks a significant point for the relationship of Roman liturgy and culture. Ricci made allowances for the Chinese Christians to participate in ancestral and Confucian rites. Rome became concerned and in 1742 definitively condemned these usages. The Chinese Rites controversy revealed two crucial developments: first, the imperative of discerning what is essential within the dominant sociocultural matrix and endeavoring to accommodate it in the Christian tradition. Second, it demonstrated how a thoroughly western, classicist perspective misapprehends the difference of an eastern approach to religion and culture (Luttio 1994).

In the nineteenth century, the issue of the relationship between local usages, the prevailing cultural scene and the codified Roman liturgy arose. In the instance of the revival of "neo-Gallican" usages in France, liturgists, like P. GUÉRANGER, argued that diversion from the pure Roman liturgy was aberrant and needed to be suppressed. The Roman liturgy, which had the approbation of papal authority, was a means to reckon with the prevailing cultural forces: nationalism, liberal bourgeois culture and the irrationality of romanticism. With the stirrings of the liturgical movement, the study of Christian liturgy and concern for participation in worship gave impetus to explore how to make the liturgy an authentic celebration of the people. The discussions at the Assisi Congress of Pastoral Liturgy in 1956 witnessed missionary interest in the relationship between liturgy and culture.

Vatican II. The interaction of the movements in the decades preceding prevailed upon the formulations of Vatican II. As K. RAHNER observed, Vatican II promised the actualization of the Church as a world Church, not a western European Church. The relationship between the Church and world is reciprocal: the Church acts on the world and the world on the Church. It is this spirit that permeates the documents of Vatican II. The first document issued by the council, *Sacrosanctum concilium* (SC), is a watershed moment for the relationship between liturgy and culture, but it must also be read in the context of later conciliar decrees.

Sacrosanctum concilium no. 21 states that there are both "unchangeable elements" and "elements subject to change" in the liturgy. Nos. 22–23 take up issues of authority and method. *Sacrosanctum concilium* posits the authority for change with the Apostolic See and local bishops and insists on the preservation of "sound tradition." Careful investigation through theological, historical and pastoral study must guide revision. Most significantly, if the good of the Church requires, "new forms adopted should in some way grow organically *(organice crescant)* from forms already existing" (no. 23). *Sacrosanctum concilium* nos. 37–40 have been called the "Magna Carta" of liturgical flexibility (Chupungco 1982). In this section, a Eurocentric perspective is attenuated: "Even in liturgy the Church has no wish to impose a rigid uniformity in matters which do not involve faith or the good of the whole community. Rather, she respects and fosters the spiritual adornments and gifts of the various races and peoples." In no. 38, given that "the substantial unity of the Roman rite is maintained," provision is made for legitimate local variations, and adaptations *(aptationes)* may be made even for the structuring of rites. No. 39 specifies that it is the task of the territorial ecclesiastical authority (that is, the bishops) and that the "limits of the typical editions of the liturgical books" are to be observed. However, no. 40 provides for an "even more radical adaptation *(profundior aptatio)*" that, developed by competent local authorities, will need the approbation of the Apostolic See.

These texts need to be read in light of other later conciliar documents. *Gaudium et spes* acknowledges the plurality of cultures (no. 53) and the fact that culture is a human product (no. 55). Most importantly, no. 58 states that the Church and the transmission of the Gospel are not tied exclusively to any one culture or any one way of life, but rather the Church can "enter into communion with various cultural modes, to her own enrichment and theirs, too." While Western culture has been the mediating form of evangelization, other cultures might be capable of handing on the Gospel as well. *Lumen gentium* no. 26 presents the understanding of the local realization of the universal Church. *Ad gentes* no. 15 calls for the assemblies of the faithful, "endowed with the riches of its own nation's culture," to be "deeply rooted in the people." No. 19 speaks of the phases of building a community of the faithful and no. 22 relates the nascent churches to the incarnation.

Recent Roman Documents. The *Catechism of the Catholic Church* (CCC) speaks of the context and need for inculturation, echoing contemporary theological and liturgical discourse on the relationship and between faith, liturgy and culture. The theme of diversity and the need for the Church to engage the variety of human cultures peppers the *Catechism of the Catholic Church*. For example, no. 814, in the context of Church unity, affirms that the Church "from the beginning" has been marked by "a great diversity," different gifts and "multiplicity of peoples and cultures." No. 1075 explains that the Church "aims to serve the whole Church in all the diversity of her rites and cultures." It acknowledges that sacramental signs and symbols are rooted in creation and human culture (no. 1145) and the Church is able to integrate "all the authentic riches of cultures" (no. 1202). "Liturgy requires," it emphasizes, "adaptation to the genius and culture of different people" (no. 1204). In its sensitivity to diversity, the *Catechism of the Catholic Church* states, "each Church proposes . . . according to its historic, social and cultural context, a language of prayer: words, melodies, gestures, iconography" (no. 2663). The need for critique and conversion is also noted (no. 1206; 2820).

In the midst of pastoral initiative and critical theological discourse, the Congregation for Divine Worship and the Discipline of the Sacraments issued the fourth instruction on the implementation of *Sacrosanctum Concilium,* "Inculturation of the Liturgy within the Roman Rite," (ILRR). The instruction sets down norms regarding the interpretation and implementation of *Sacrosanctum Concilium,* nos. 37–40. "Inculturation of the Liturgy within the Roman Rite," has five sections: an introduction with preliminary observations; part one on the process of inculturation throughout salvation history; part two, theological and ecclesiological bases and preliminary conditions for inculturation; part three, principles and practical norms with regard to the Roman rite; and part four, areas open to adaptation in the Roman rite.

In the introduction the document notes the use and meaning of the term "inculturation," explaining that it has a double movement of the Church's introducing the Gospel in the culture and at the same time assimilating the culture's values (no. 4). In number 7, "Inculturation of the Liturgy within the Roman Rite" acknowledges the coexistence of many cultures in the western churches of which the Church must take account, in addition to missionary churches on other continents. After discussing the encounter of Christian faith with various cultures, the instruction offers several theological and ecclesiological precepts concerning relationship between liturgy and the local churches. "Inculturation of the Liturgy within the Roman Rite" emphasizes the need for the proclamation of the scriptures in the local language as the first step of inculturation (no. 28). Only then, after study by scholars, by "wise people" who live the culture, and by pastors of the area, can any adaptations be made (no. 29–30). In

the third section "Inculturation of the Liturgy within the Roman Rite" explains that the governing principle of liturgical inculturation is the maintenance of "the substantial unity of the Roman rite. This is currently expressed in the typical editions of liturgical books published by the authority of the supreme pontiff and in the liturgical books approved by the Episcopal conferences for their areas and confirmed by the Apostolic See" (no. 36). It posits the authority for adaptations of the Roman rite first "to the Apostolic See, which exercises it through the Congregation for Divine Worship and Discipline of the Sacraments" (no. 37). In the fourth section, after elaborating areas for legitimate adaptation in the liturgy of the sacraments, blessings and liturgical year, "Inculturation of the Liturgy within the Roman Rite" lays down the procedure for the bishops' conferences to ask for the Apostolic See's approval. With regard to the "more profound adaptations" mentioned by *Sacrosanctum Concilium* no. 40, "Inculturation of the Liturgy within the Roman Rite" indicates that "adaptations of this kind do not envisage a transformation of the Roman rite" and "are made within the context of the Roman rite" (no. 63).

Contemporary Attempts. Since the promulgation of the typical editions of the Roman liturgical books, there have been several attempts at inculturating the Roman liturgy. India was one of the first countries to move on the program of cultural adaptation of the Roman liturgy. The task was daunting: India is an extremely culturally diverse country and Christians are a minority. As soon as 1965, a national liturgical center was set up. First, elements of Indian culture were juxtaposed with the Roman liturgical setting. Then, the liturgical books were not only translated into the vernacular, but new texts were composed. Third, non-Christian scriptures were introduced into the liturgy. On April 15, 1969 they enumerated twelve points of liturgical inculturation, concerning gestures and postures, forms of homage and objects and elements used in worship [see *Notitiae,* 5 (1969): 365–374]. Later, a new order for the Eucharist, new Eucharistic prayers and Catholic celebrations of Indian festivals were introduced. While only one revised Eucharistic prayer later received local approval, the task of liturgical adaptation continues, more so in the north than in the south. Also, it seems to be more evident on the "unofficial level" of popular devotion than in the official Latin rite liturgy (Chengalikavil 1993). Critical reflection by scholars and authorities continues.

The impetus toward indigenous liturgical expressions of the faith has marked the Catholic Church in Africa, Oceania and Asia. Relatively successful examples have taken place on an official level in the dioceses of the former Zaire, Malawi, Cameroon, Kenya and Ghana. In Polynesia, Melanesia and Oceania the local churches have sought to wed traditional island culture with liturgical celebration. Progress is also being made in the churches of Asia. Among liturgical scholars these local celebrations have raised questions concerning the methods and agency of the process of inculturation. Foreign authorities face thousands of cultures and languages and the fact that the very symbols of western Christian liturgy are foreign to non-western cultures. The people in the local churches, experts in their own culture, grapple with the forms and content of Christian faith. For example, debate has taken place with regard to the use of imported wheat bread and grape wine for the Eucharist in African and Asian cultures where rice, millet or palm wine are indigenous.

United States. The whole project of liturgical adaptation of the Roman liturgy heralded by the council touches not only Africa and Asia, but North and South America and Europe as well. With regard to contemporary western, Euro-American culture, some liturgists have questioned the premise of adapting the Roman liturgy to what they perceive as a dominant culture that cannot authentically incarnate the Christian gospel. Less pessimistic critics speak of the need to attenuate the counter-cultural notion of liturgy and stress the imperative of mutual interaction and critique so that the liturgy can most authentically express the given community's faith. In many ways, the liturgy is a cultural event because the liturgy is western European, so that the issues faced in Africa and Asia of foreign symbols, gestures and language are not so pronounced.

But many cultures make the face of the American church quite complex. Liturgical books have been translated into some of the Native American languages and Asian-American assemblies have begun to explore the question of the relationship between their cultures and liturgy. The question of inculturation is also alive for African-American and Hispanic assemblies and their desire to develop adequate forms for liturgical worship. Yet, even the terms "African-American," "Hispanic" or "Asian-American" cannot be used monolithically as if uniform African-American, Hispanic or Asian-American cultures existed. Hispanic liturgy is making great strides with regard to weaving the religious experience of Hispanic communities, popular religiosity and the liturgy. Hispanic liturgists have realized that it is through study of the particular values and practices of Hispanic pieties and popular devotions that the liturgy can be incarnated in the various assemblies. Hispanic composers have fashioned diverse liturgical music, and official liturgical texts have been translated into Spanish. The efforts of the Mexican American Cultural Center, the Hispanic subcommittee of the Bishops' Committee on the Liturgy and the Instituto de Liturgia Hispana have greatly aided the

assimilation of Hispanic culture and liturgy. Much work has also been done with regard to African-American communities. Through the publication of *In Spirit and Truth* (1987) and *Plenty Good Room* (1990), liturgical acculturation has taken root in most predominately African-American assemblies. These documents explore the ways that elements of the African-American religious experience and spirituality can be assimilated into the Roman Liturgy. The publication of *Lead Me, Guide Me* (Chicago 1987) offers a corpus of music for African-American Catholic assemblies.

The acculturation of Asian, Hispanic and African-American liturgy affords the Church in the United States a means of transforming its received notions of spirituality and worship. The work in these communities enables the rest of the Church to be aware of its own cultural patterns and see the Christian faith embodied in a plurality of ways. The mutual transformation enriches the Church's catholicity.

Conclusion. Consideration of historical and contemporary attempts at the program of liturgical adaptation demonstrate the importance of taking the concrete local culture and situation of the churches seriously. The process of liturgical inculturation presupposes a proclamation of the Gospel within the culture itself in order that the ritual celebration might be an authentic celebration of the people's paschal faith. Liturgical inculturation is a complex issue that raises serious theological, ecclesiological, hermeneutical and liturgical questions. Yet, it remains a pivotal issue as the Church enters the next millennium.

Bibliography: The literature on liturgical inculturation is extensive. The reader is directed to: S. A. STAUFFER, "Bibliography on Worship and Culture," in *Christian Worship: Unity and Cultural Diversity*, LWF Studies 1 (Geneva, 1996) 113–142. In particular the work of Anscar Chupungco figures prominently. A bibliography of his work can be found in *Liturgy for the New Millennium: A Commentary on the Revised Sacramentary. Essays in Honor of Anscar Chupungco*, ed., M. FRANCIS and K. PECKLERS (Collegeville, Minn., 2000), 165–168. Also see: S. BEVANS, *Models of Contextual Theology* (Maryknoll 1992). M. FRANCIS, *Shape a Circle Ever Wider: Liturgical Inculturation in the United States* (Chicago, Ill., 2000). D. POWER, "Liturgy and Culture Revisited," *Worship*, 69 (1995): 225–243. A. SHORTER, *Toward a Theology of Inculturation* (Maryknoll 1988). R. SCHREITER, *Constructing Local Theologies* (Maryknoll 1985); *The New Catholicity: Theology Between the Global and the Local* (Maryknoll 1997). A. PEREZ, "The History of Hispanic Liturgy since 1965" in *Hispanic Catholic Culture in the U.S.: Issues and Concerns*, ed. J. P. DOLAN and A. F. DECK (Notre Dame 1994) 360–408. Articles cited here include: L. CHENGALIKAVIL, "Indigenous Liturgy: An Indian Perspective," in *L'Adattamento culturale della liturgia: metodi e modelli*, ed. I. SCICOLONE, *Analecta Liturgica*, 19 (Rome 1993) 205–221. CONGREGATION FOR DIVINE WORSHIP AND DISCIPLINE OF THE SACRAMENTS, "De Liturgia romana et inculturatione. Instructio quarta ad exsecutionem Constitutionis Concilii Vaticani Secundi de Sacra Liturgia recte ordinandam (ad Const. art 37–40)," *Notitiae,* 30 (1994) 80–115. English trans. *Inculturation of the Liturgy within the Roman Rite* (Vatican City 1994). G. DE NAPOLI, "Inculturation as Communication," *Inculturation,* 9 (1987) 71–98. M. D. LUTTIO, "The Chinese Rites Controversy (1603–1742): A Diachronic and Synchronic Approach," *Worship,* 68 (1994) 290–312. K. RAHNER, "Toward a Fundamental Theological Interpretation of Vatican II," *Theological Studies,* 40 (1979) 44–56. A. ROEST-CROLLIUS, "What's So New About Inculturation? A Concept and its Implications," *Gregorianum,* 59 (1978) 721–738. *Lead Me, Guide Me: The African American Hymnal* (Chicago 1987). *In Spirit and Truth: Black Catholic Reflections on the Order of Mass,* The Secretariat of the Bishop's Committee on the Liturgy of the National Conference of Catholic Bishops (Washington DC 1987). *Plenty Good Room: The Spirit and Truth of African American Worship,* statement of the Black Liturgy Subcommittee of the Committee on the Liturgy of the National Conference of Catholic Bishops (Washington, D.C. 1990).

[R. E. MCCARRON]

INCULTURATION, THEOLOGY OF

The term "inculturation," as applied to Christianity, denotes the presentation and re-expression of the Gospel in forms and terms proper to a culture. It results in the creative reinterpretation of both, without being unfaithful to either. Evangelization respects culture as part of the human phenomenon and as a human right. The manipulation or oppression of culture is, therefore, an abuse. Culture is a coherent system of meanings embodied in images and symbols that enables the individual to relate cognitively, emotionally, and behaviorally to the world and to communicate this understanding to others. It is the prism through which a human society views the whole of its experience, domestic, political, social, economic, and political. Culture is learned by the human being through socialization and is developed throughout life. It gives identity to a human group and controls its perception of reality. For the purposes of theology, it is at once more positive and more precise than the term "context." Syncretism denotes an anomalous conflict of meaning when, in the process of evangelization, cultures "domesticate" the Gospel and distort its meaning. No culture is deemed to be unfailingly Christian, since inculturation is a constant call to conversion and renewal.

Evangelization must enter into dialogue with cultures if it is to produce any effect on human beings. Cultures are empirically diverse; therefore, evangelization leads to culturally diverse ways of living the Gospel. Inculturation, opposed to uniformity, demands the legitimization of diversity. There can be no monopoly of cultural forms in a truly Catholic communion. This is true in spite of the mutual influence of evangelizing and evangelized cultures ("interculturation") and of the accumulation by the Church of current, but contingent, cultural elements

as an inherited patrimony. Until the realization in the 20th century that culture is a plural phenomenon, the Church took it for granted that there was a single, universal culture of humanity, the perfection of which was deemed to be Christianity in its western, Latin form. No allowance was made for factors of cultural diversity in theological controversy, and the Church was unable to accommodate the initiatives of early Jesuit missionaries, such as Mateo RICCI, Roberto de NOBILI, and Pedro Paez, when they tried to evangelize foreign cultures from within. In the 20th century, particularly at the Second VATICAN COUNCIL, and in the subsequent assemblies of the SYNOD OF BISHOPS, cultural pluralism has been accepted, together with inculturation as a demand of evangelization. However, an influential minority in the Church still claims that western culture possesses a universal significance for evangelization, in spite of its technocratic nature, its secularizing influence, and its tendency to undermine the religious values of indigenous cultures.

Christological Basis for Inculturation. Among the Christological bases for inculturation, the doctrine of the world-seeding LOGOS as God's agent in creation goes back to JUSTIN MARTYR and the second century apologists, typified by CLEMENT OF ALEXANDRIA. It has reappeared in the missionary decree of the Second Vatican Council, *Ad gentes,* and in modern CREATION THEOLOGY. The Logos, the Divine Truth or Divine Reason, exists in disseminated form throughout creation, and every human tradition perceives it darkly, before it is enlightened for them by the proclamation of the Word incarnate. This proclamation does not outmode these traditions, but gladly recognizes the elements of truth they contain. Another Christological approach is the analogy with the incarnation of Jesus Christ and the parallel between his cultural education in Palestine and modern missionary evangelization. The parallel demonstrates that Christ is the subject of inculturation and that the incarnation inserted him into the intercultural dynamic of human history. However, it plays down the challenge that Christ offered to his own culture, and suggests that the Gospel, like the divine pre-existence, comes to a culture in a culturally disembodied form. The most fruitful Christological approach is to compare inculturation with the Paschal Mystery, to which it is linked causally as well as analogically. Through his passion, death and resurrection, Christ became universal Lord and made himself available to people of every culture. The Paschal Mystery also offers an analogy for the conversion of culture, which dies and rises under the impact of evangelization, thus becoming more authentic and more faithful to its underlying truth.

Ecclesiological Approaches to Inculturation. Ecclesiological approaches to inculturation include first the logic of the Church's universal mission. That mission is the continuation of the *missio Dei*, God's loving dialogue with the world, and the fulfilment of the great commandment of universal love that is logically prior to the great commission to teach all nations. This love is a perfect communion of differences and, therefore, liberating. In this area the theology of inculturation encounters the theology of liberation. The second ecclesiological basis of inculturation is the authentic tradition of the Church and the role of the Church's magisterium. The primary reality of the Church is local: the particular church and the socio-cultural region within which its witness takes place. Its primary task is to reconcile local culture to the Church's tradition, which is centered on the interpretation of the Christ event. This interpretation is based on a trajectory of meaning that ascends to the outlooks of the New Testament. Sacred tradition, with its growth of insight, passes organically from culture to culture and from clarity to clarity throughout history. Although the Bible occupies a privileged position in this tradition, together with the sacramental and hierarchical ministry that derives from the actions and commands of Christ witnessed by the New Testament, and although the meaning of faith-statements made by the Church's magisterium is not open to contradiction, all these can only be understood today with reference to their historical and cultural contexts. Reformulation in accordance with the Church's lived cultural plurality is strictly necessary, if they are to be taken seriously.

The concept of inculturation seems to carry certain consequences for the shape of the Church to come, among them the abandonment of a preference for western culture and a greater diversification in Christian life and practice. The fields of inculturation include: theology, catechesis, liturgy, religious life, marriage and family life, health and healing, secondary ecclesial ministries and structures. Inculturation would therefore assume a relative pluralism in all these fields. Since inculturation cannot be imposed, but depends on the experience and initiatives of the local community, the concept seems to envisage ecclesial structures that favor increased participation and collaboration.

Bibliography: M. AMALADOSS, *Beyond Inculturation: Can the Many Be One?* (Delhi 1998). D.S. AMALORPAVADASS, "Theological reflections on inculturation" *Studia Liturgica* 20 (1990) 36–54 (Pt. I) and 116–136 (Pt. II). G. A. ARBUCKLE, *Earthing the Gospel* (London 1990). M. DHAVAMONY, *Christian Theology of Inculturation* (Rome 1997). A. E. SHORTER, *Toward a Theology of Inculturation* (New York 1992); *Evangelization and Culture* (London 1994). P.C. PHAN, "Contemporary Theology and Inculturation in the United States," in *The Multicultural Church: A New Landscape in U.S. Theologies*, ed. W. CENKNER (New York 1996) 109–130. J.A. SCHERER & S.B. BEVANS, eds., *New Directions in Mission & Evangelization Vol 3: Faith and Culture* (Maryknoll 1999).

[A. E. SHORTER]

INDEFECTIBILITY

The Church of Christ is like the house built upon rock that is able to withstand the storm and tempest (Mt 16.18; cf. 7.24–27). This is because Christ will be with His Apostles all days even to the end of the world (Mt 28.20). Their faith will not fail, and the Holy Spirit has been sent to them to lead them to all truth and to abide with them for ever (Jn 14.16, 26). The Church will remain until the end of time.

This indefectibility is a basic teaching of Scripture and is bound up with the notion of the Church as the new People of God and the final covenant between God and man. This does not mean that there will be no falling away from the Church on the part of individual members or even sections of the community. History witnesses to HERESY and SCHISM. At times these have reached alarming proportions, as was the case with Arianism and at the time of the Reformation. But despite these disasters the Church of Christ continued in existence. The scandal was that its presence was rendered less obvious to the unbelieving world. Neither is one to understand indefectibility as eliminating accidental change and REFORM. The Church lives in the world, and there is always need to speak to men in their own language; hence ACCOMMODATION as well as the progress of dogma. There is also need to eliminate abuse, which comes from the fact that members of the Church remain men, fallible and weak. But there can be no wholesale departure from the teaching of Christ: however much the future is veiled one does know that on the last day it will be the same Church that is finally taken up to heaven by Christ.

Since the rock on which the Church is built is PETER, indefectibility concerns the successor of Peter in a special way. It is the same indefectibility as that of the Church, but it resides in a special way in his successor, the bishop of Rome.

See Also: MIRACLE, MORAL (THE CHURCH); CHURCH, ARTICLES ON.

Bibliography: Vatican II, *Dogmatic Constitution on the Church* 8, 9, 12; *Acta Apostolicae Sedis* 57 (1965) 11–14, 16–17; and *passim. Dictionnaire de théologie catholique,* ed. A. VACANT et al., 15 v. (Paris 1903–50; Tables générales 1951–), Tables générales 1:1116. I. SALAVERRI, *Sacrae theologiae summa,* ed. FATHERS OF THE SOCIETY OF JESUS, PROFESSORS OF THE THEOLOGICAL FACULTIES IN SPAIN, 4 v. (Madrid), v. 1 (5th ed. 1962), v. 2 (3d ed. 1958), v. 3 (4th ed. 1961), v. 4 (4th ed. 1962); *Bibliotheca de autores cristianos* 1.3:285–329.

[M. E. WILLIAMS]

INDEX OF PROHIBITED BOOKS

The Index of Prohibited Books, *Index Librorum Prohibitorum*, established in 1557 by Pope PAUL IV, was a list of books that Catholics were prohibited from reading on pain of excommunication. The books were prohibited because they contained material considered dangerous or contrary to faith or morals. The Index of Prohibited Books was increasingly problematic from the time of the Enlightenment. It was the source of much criticism of the Church, both from within and outside the Church, and was abolished by Pope PAUL VI in 1966 because it was considered to be contrary to the teaching of VATICAN II concerning freedom of inquiry (*Gaudium et spes*, 62: "let it be recognized that all the faithful, clerical and lay, possess a lawful freedom of inquiry and thought.").

History. The prohibition of books has a long history within the Church. The earliest instance is connected with the establishment of the canon of the Sacred Scriptures. The MURATORIAN CANON (c. A.D. 170) was an early determination of the authentic books of the New Testament that excluded others from liturgical usage. Theologically controversial books were also banned; for example, Pope Anastasius (d. 401) banned the works of ORIGEN. A decree issued by Pope Gelasius in 496 and published at a council in Rome has been called the first "Index of Prohibited Books." The GELASIAN DECREE is divided into three parts: a list of authentic scriptural books, a number of recommended readings, and a list of apocryphal and heretical books.

From the fifth to the sixteenth century there were many specific decrees condemning individual works. The following are offered by way of example: in 548 Pope Vigilius condemned the "Three Chapters"; in 589 the Council of Toledo condemned books on Arianism; in 649 Pope Martin I forbade the writings of the Monothelites; in 745 Pope Zacharius condemned the books of Adalbertus and Clement; and in 869 Pope Adrian II burned the works of Photius. From this time until the reign of Pope Paul IV many particular books were condemned. The works of Scotus Erugina were proscribed in 855, those of the Joachim of Fiora in 1215, of Peter Jean Olivi in 1328, of John Wyclif and John Hus in 1415 and 1418. The invention of the printing press intensified concern for the censorship and prohibition of dangerous books. In 1469 Pope Innocent VIII decreed that all books were to be submitted to the local Church authorities for examination before being issued for general reading. Pope Leo X decreed similarly in 1515.

The Council of TRENT (1545–63) elaborated upon and codified the regulations of the Church concerning books. In the fourth session (April 8, 1546) the council drew up a decree in which, besides establishing the Vulgate as the authentic Bible to be used in public discussion, sermons, and so on, they prescribed that no books should be printed on religious matters without the approbation of the ecclesiastical authorities.

In 1557 Pope Paul IV entrusted the Congregation of the INQUISITION with the task of drawing up a complete catalog of forbidden books. This general index was ready in the same year but did not meet with the pope's approval and was never published. The Congregation renewed its efforts and compiled a larger, more complete Index of Prohibited Books, which was published in January of 1559. This index of Pope Paul IV is the first general Roman Index ever published and the first list of forbidden books to carry the title "Index."

The widespread dissatisfaction among Catholic leaders with Paul IV's Index of Prohibited Books led the fathers of the Council of Trent to undertake its revision. The council was unable to accomplish this for lack of time and also because it would hinder Protestants from coming to the council. The revision of the index, therefore, was one of the council's projects left to the Holy See for completion. The council fathers appointed a commission to revise the index. The labors of the commission came to fruition after the close of the council and were ratified by Pope Pius IV with a papal brief (March 24, 1564). This work is known as either the Tridentine Index or the Index of Pope Pius IV. It consisted of a list of forbidden books and included ten general norms that would regulate the censorship and reading of future books. The first nine of these regulations concerned published works that were automatically forbidden because they dealt with false or heretical teaching. The final rule restated previous norms for the examination and censorship of a work by local authorities prior to its formal publication.

By order of Pope SIXTUS V, an amended index was prepared and printed in 1590. In it the Tridentine rules were replaced by 22 new ones. This index was never published, however, because Pope Sixtus died before he could approve it, and his successors did not promulgate it.

A new index was ordered by Pope CLEMENT VII; it was completed in 1596 and promulgated by his Bull *Sacrosanctum fidei.* Pope ALEXANDER VII published another edition of the Index of Prohibited Books on March 5, 1664. This was the first papal index to list all books and authors alphabetically. From this time until the mid-eighteenth century, little of note occurred in Church legislation on book censorship and prohibition. Many books, especially Jansenistic ones, were forbidden, for example, the *Provincial Letters* of Pascal. The indexes published during this period were only new editions of the Tridentine Index with the addition of books condemned since the preceding editions.

Sollicita ac Provida, a major document in the Church's legislation on forbidden books, was issued by Pope BENEDICT XIV on July 9, 1753. This constitution laid down detailed rules to be followed by the Congregation of the Holy Office and Index in the censorship and prohibition of books. Benedict XIV did not confine himself to laying down general rules; he also revised the index, freeing it from many typographical and other errors that had crept in over the centuries. On Dec. 23, 1757, he promulgated the revised index. From 1758 to 1897 all the indexes published were simply reprints of Benedict's edition, each adding works prohibited since the preceding edition.

Many of the fathers at the VATICAN COUNCIL I (1870) requested a revision of the entire index legislation. Unfortunately, the council adjourned before this matter could be discussed. Shortly thereafter, however, Pope LEO XIII took it upon himself to give the Church a new Index of Prohibited Books and legislation adapted to the changed and varied needs of the time. New general rules governing the censorship and prohibition of books were framed, and a revised and improved Index of Prohibited Books was published. The general norms were promulgated on Jan. 25, 1897, through the constitution *Officiorum ac Munerum*, and the new index was published through the brief *Romani Pontificis* on Sept. 17, 1900. The Leonine legislation on the censorship and prohibition of books suffered only slight changes as a result of the new general legislation of the 1917 Code of CANON LAW. Pope Leo's legislation was, in fact, embodied almost verbatim, though in a modified order, in canons 247.4, 1385 through 1405, and 2318 of the 1917 code.

The Index of Prohibited Books compiled by Leo XIII underwent several later editions, the latest being in 1948, by which time there were more than 5,000 titles on the index. It gradually became the policy of the Church to restrict the number of books explicitly condemned and to depend on the general principles regarding the prohibition of books to guide the faithful in this matter. The growing scandal of the Index of Prohibited Books is indicated by the breath and quality of the books and authors proscribed: Descartes, Pascal, Bacon, Becqnel, Voltaire, Gibbon, Renan, Lamenais, Hugo, Dumas père and fils, Comte, Zola, Loisy, Laberthonniere, Bergson, and Chenu. In the aftermath of the Modernist crisis, the bitter controversy that arose from the intensified effort to suppress open investigation and inquiry in theology, biblical studies, and philosophy drew attention to the appropriateness of the Index of Prohibited Books as part of the Church's apostolic mission within modernity. The use of, and the threat of the use of, the Index of Prohibited Books played a key role in the "silencing" of such theological figures as Marie-Dominique Chenu, Yves Congar, Henri de Lubac, Pierre Teilhard de Chardin, and Henri Bouillard that followed the publication of *Humani Generis* in 1950.

The Second Vatican Council reversed the "silencing" of these theologians. It is now known that Pope JOHN XXIII and Pope Paul VI were disturbed by the effort at theological retrogression. In 1959 Jean Steinmann's *La Vie de Jesus* had the dubious distinction of being the last work placed on the Index of Prohibited Books. As much later as spring of 1962, however, there was an attempt to place on the index Henri de Lubacs's *The Religious Thought of Teilhard*. Pope John XXIII personally vetoed this attempt.

The purpose and effectiveness of the Index of Prohibited Books was re-evaluated at the time of Vatican II as part of a review of the role of the Holy Office. Cardinal Frings, archbishop of Cologne, intervened eloquently in the aula of Saint Peter's, pleading for a reform of the Holy Office that would include the Index of Prohibited Books. For his written draft, Frings was assisted by Fr. Joseph Ratzinger. Finally, in 1966, Cardinal Alfredo Ottaviani, the head of the newly named Congregation of the Doctrine of the Faith, declared that there would be no more editions of the index; as such it remains only as a historical document.

Present Status. The 1983 Code of CANON LAW attempts to balance Vatican II's principle of freedom of inquiry (in *Gaudium et spes*, 62) and the Church's legitimate concern to protect its faithful from dangerous writings. Canons 822 to 832 in Book III of the 1983 Code (The Teaching Function of the Church, Title IV, Instruments of Social Communication and Books in Particular) deal with the prior censorship of a very narrow range of official or semi-official publications to which the *imprimatur* is now limited. These canons are subordinate to canons 211, and especially to 212, which states that "according to the knowledge, competence, and prestige which they possess, they [the faithful] have the right and at times the duty to manifest to the sacred pastors their opinion on matters which pertain to the good of the Church and to make their opinion known to the rest of the Christian faithful, without prejudice to the integrity of faith and morals, with reverence toward their pastors, and attentive to common advantage and the dignity of persons."

[D. DEE/D. P. SHERIDAN]

INDIA, CHRISTIANITY IN

After a brief overview of the history and culture of India, this entry surveys the history and present status of Christianity in that country, covering the three principal Christian communities: (1) the indigenous St. Thomas Christians, (2) the Latin Christians (Roman Catholics), and (3) the Protestant Christians.

Capital: New Delhi.
Size: 1,195,063 sq. miles.
Population: Over one billion in 2000. Indo-Aryans constitute approximately 70%, and Dravidians approx. 25%.
Languages: 325 spoken languages and 700 dialects; Hindi is the official national language, while English remains the second language recognized officially as the authoritative, legislative and juridical language. The Indian Constitution recognizes 18 regional languages: Assamese, Bengali, Gujarati, Hindi, Kannada, Kashmiri, Malayalam, Marathi, Oriya, Punjabi, Sanskrit, Tamil, Telugu, Urdu, Sindhi, Konkani, Manipuri and Nepali.
Religions: About 80% of Indians are adherents of Hinduism, 14% are Muslims, 2.5% are Christians, 2% Sikh, 0.7% are Buddhist, 0.5% are Jain, and 0.3% are tribal religionists, Baha'i, Ahmadiyyahs, Jews, and others. Roman Catholics constitute about 65% of Indian Christians, and slightly over 1% of India's total population. St. Thomas Christians (both Catholic and non-Catholic) comprise approximately 30% of Indian Christians, and slightly less than 1% of the population of India. The St. Thomas Christians are based mostly in Kerala, although there are growing diaspora communities in other parts of India. The remaining 5% of India's Christian population are mostly members of the two principal Protestant Churches–the Church of North India and the Church of South India, and the many small but active independent pentecostal churches. About 50% of Indian Christians belong to the lower classes, scheduled castes and scheduled tribes.

THE LAND, ITS PEOPLES AND RELIGIONS

Located in South Asia, the Indian subcontinent is surrounded by the Arabian Sea (west), the Bay of Bengal (east), the Indian Ocean (south) and the Himalayan mountains (north). It is home to the Indus Valley civilization (*c.* 2,500 B.C.), one of the oldest civilizations in the world. Aryan tribes from central Asia invaded the northwestern region of India around 1500 B.C., pushing the original inhabitants, the Dravidians, to the south. The invading Aryans and native Dravidians gradually intermingled, forming a composite culture and ethnicity. Arabs and Turkish Muslims came to India in the 8th and 12th century respectively. Muslim rulers governed a significant portion of India until the arrival of the European powers. Vasco da Gama led the first Portuguese expedition to India in 1498, paving the way for the colonization by the Portuguese, the Dutch, the French, and the British. The struggle for national independence gained momentum in the 20th century under the pacifist resistance movement of Mahatma Gandhi. The Indian subcontinent gained independence from Britain in 1947, but was partitioned into the secular nation of India and the Muslim nation of Pakistan. Present-day India is a federal republic with a Westminster-style parliamentary democracy within the British Commonwealth. The Indian Federation comprises 28 states and 6 union territories.

India is the birthplace of several world religions: HINDUISM, BUDDHISM, JAINISM and SIKHISM. It has welcomed other major religions, e.g., Christianity, Islam, Judaism and Zoroastrianism. Hinduism was originally the Vedic religion of the Aryans, but it absorbed many of the beliefs and practices of the native Dravidians. Buddhism and Jainism emerged in the 6th and 5th centuries B.C. respectively. Islam came to India with the Arab and Turkish invaders between the 8th and 12th centuries.

THE ST. THOMAS CHRISTIANS

This section describes the origins, history and present situation of the St. Thomas Christians in India, who trace the foundation of their community to St. THOMAS THE APOSTLE (Mar Thoma in Syriac).

Origins. According to an ancient South Indian oral tradition, St. Thomas, one of the 12 apostles, sailed to India and landed at Cranganore (Kodungalloor) on the coast of ancient Malabar (present-day Kerala) in the year 52 A.D. There he converted many high caste Hindus and established several Christian communities. He made his way to the Coromandel Coast on the eastern part of India and converted many before heading for China. After preaching the Gospel in China, he returned to Kerala and organized the Christian communities there and proceeded again to the Coromandel Coast where he was martyred. The Apostle of India was buried in Mylapore, close to Chennai (Madras). The early Christians built a pilgrimage shrine at his tomb.

No primary evidence of this ancient tradition exist today. Some scholars speculate that this ancient oral tradition was later recorded in the local languages and in Syriac, the ancient liturgical language of the Malabar Christians, before the manuscripts were lost or destroyed during the period of Portuguese rule. Some of these traditions are found in the ancient odes of Malabar, e.g., *Rabban Pattu, Veeradiyan Pattu,* and *Margam Kali Pattu.* The oldest written texts of these odes and other surviving accounts can only be traced back to the 17th century. The travel narratives of Cosmas Indicopleustes, an Egyptian who visited Arabia, East Africa and India around the year 530, as well as those of John of Monte Corvino (1292), and Jordan Catalani (1319) all record the mission of St. Thomas and early presence of Christians in India. The 16th and 17th century Portuguese documents are important sources of information on St. Thomas' mission to India, and the early history of the St. Thomas Christians. The Portuguese also visited the tomb of St. Thomas and made some excavations and recovered some relics in 1523.

Many church historians, including L. W. Brown, E. Tisserant, Placid Podipara, E. R. Hambye, and Mathias

Metropolitan Sees	Suffragans
Latin:	
Agra	Ajmer-Jaipur, Allahabad, Bareilly, Jhansi, Lucknow, Meerut, Udaipur, Varanasi
Bangalore	Belgaum, Bellary, Chikmagalur, Karwar, Mangalore, Mysore, Shimoga
Bhopal	Ambikapur, Gwalior, Indore, Jabalpur, Khandwa, Raigarh, Raipur
Bombay	Ahmedabad, Baroda, Nashik, Poona, Vasai
Calcutta	Asansol, Bagdogra, Baruipur, Darjeeling, Jalpaiguri, Krishnagar, Raiganj
Cuttack-Bhubaneswar	Balasore, Berhampur, Rourkela, Sambalpur
Delhi	Jammu-Srinangar, Jullundur, Simla and Chandigarh
Guwahati	Bongaigaon, Dibrugarh, Diphu, Tezpur
Hyderabad	Cuddapah, Eluru, Guntur, Khammam, Kurnool, Nalgonda, Nellore, Srikakulam, Vijayawada, Visakhapatnam, Warangal
Imphal	Kohima
Madras and Mylapore	Coimbatore, Ootacamund, Vellore
Madurai	Kottar, Palayamkottai, Sivagangai, Tiruchirapalli, Tuticorin
Nagpur	Amravati, Aurangabad
Patna	Bettiah, Bhagalpur, Muzaffarpur, Purnea
Pondicherry and Cuddalore	Dharmapuri, Kumbakonam, Salem, Tanjore
Ranchi	Daltonganj, Dumka, Gumla, Hazaribag, Jamshedpur, Khunti, Port Blair, Simdega
Shillong	Agartala, Aizawl, Tura
Verapoly	Alleppey, Calicut, Cochin, Kannur, Kottapuram, Neyyattinkara, Punalur, Quilon, Trivandrum of the Latins, Vijayapuram

Goa and Damão are directly subject to the Holy See.

Syro-Malabar suffragans of Latin Metropolitan Sees:

Archdioceses	Suffragans
Agra	Bijnor, Gorakhpur
Bhopal	Jagdalpur, Sagar, Satna, Ujjain
Bombay	Kalyan, Rajkot
Hyderabad	Adilabad
Nagpur	Chanda

Syro-Malabar Sees and Suffragans:

Archdioceses	Suffragans
Changanacherry	Kanjirapally, Kottayam, Palai, Thuckalay
Ernakulam-Angamaly	Kothamangalam
Tellicherry	Belthangady, Mananthavady, Thamarasserry
Trichur	Irinjalakuda, Palghat

The Syro-Malankara Metropolitan See of Trivandrum has suffragans Battery, Marthandom, and Tiruvalla.

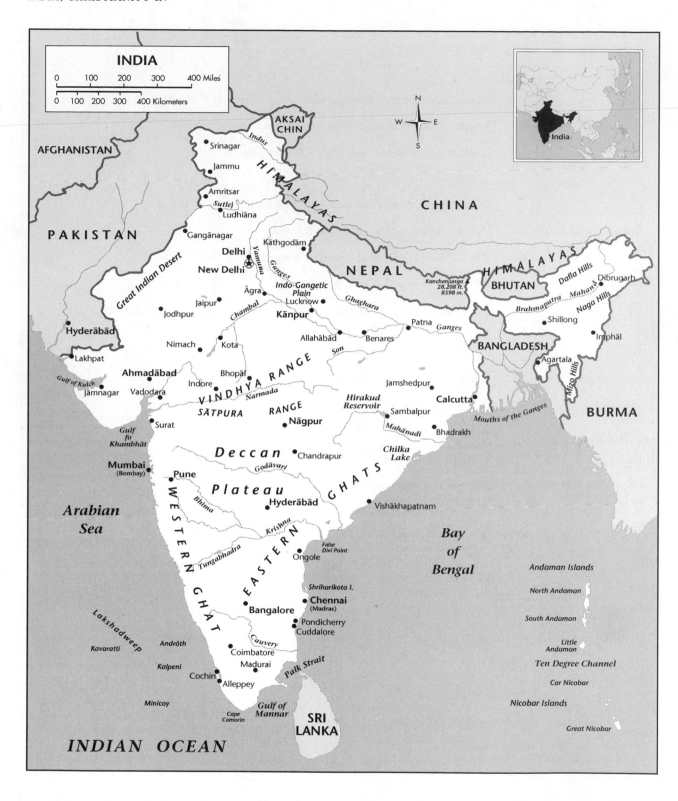

INDIA

0   100   200   300   400 Miles

0 100 200 300 400 Kilometers

AFGHANISTAN

AKSAI CHIN

• Srinagar

• Jammu

• Amritsar

Sutlej

• Ludhiāna

PAKISTAN

• Gangānagar

Delhi

New Delhi

CHINA

Indus

HIMALAYAS

Kāthgodām

NEPAL

HIMALAYAS

Kanchenjunga
28,208 ft.
8,598 m.

BHUTAN

Dafla Hills

Dibrugarh

Mahand.

Brahmaputra

Naga Hills

• Shillong

• Imphāl

Great Indian Desert

Yamuna

Ganges

Indo-Gangetic Plain

Āgra•

• Jaipur

• Jodhpur

• Nimach

• Kota

Lucknow•

Kānpur

Chambal

Ghaghara

Allahābād•

• Benares

• Patna

Ganges

BANGLADESH

Agartala

Mizo Hills

BURMA

Hyderābād

• Lakhpat

Gulf of Kutch

Jāmnagar

Ahmadābād

Vadodara•

• Indore

• Bhopāl

Son

• Jamshedpur

VINDHYA RANGE

Narmada

SĀTPURA   RANGE

• Nāgpur

Hirakud Reservoir

Sambalpur•

Mahānadi

Calcutta

• Bhadrakh

Mouths of the Ganges

• Surat

Gulf fo Khambhât

Deccan

• Chandrapur

Chilka Lake

Mumbai (Bombay)

Godāvari

• Pune

Plateau

Hyderābād

Bhima

GHATS

• Vishākhapatnam

Bay of Bengal

Arabian Sea

WESTERN GHAT

Krishna

EASTERN

Tungabhadrā

False Divi Point

• Ongole

Andaman Islands

North Andaman

South Andaman

Shriharikota I.

Chennai (Madras)

Bangalore

• Pondicherry
Cuddalore

Lakshadweep

Kavaratti

Andrôth

Cauvery

• Coimbatore

Little Andaman

Ten Degree Channel

Kalpeni

Madurai

Cochin•

• Alleppey

Palk Strait

Car Nicobar

Nicobar Islands

Minicoy

Cape Comorin

Gulf of Mannar

SRI LANKA

Great Nicobar

INDIAN OCEAN

Mundadan, point out that although the Malabar traditions are replete with the stories and legends from the Apocryphal Acts of Judas Thomas, St. Thomas's mission in south India is not only a possibility, it has a firm historical foundation on the basis of the unbroken South Indian Christian tradition, the sustained consciousness of the Malabar Christians of their apostolic origin, the presence of the tomb of St. Thomas in Mylapore and other associated monuments, and on the basis of references of early Christian witnesses.

Morning prayers at a village Catholic school, India. (©Liba Taylor/CORBIS)

The historical relationship between the St. Thomas Christians and the East Syrian (Chaldean) Church in Persia from the earliest times is based on two historical events. The first event was the arrival in Cranganore (Kodungalloor) of a group of East-Syrian Christians led by a certain Knai Thomman (Thomas Kinayi) around the fourth century. It remains unclear whether he was a merchant, a traveler or a pilgrim, whether he came to assist the St. Thomas Christians who were facing a leadership crisis, or whether he was leading a group of Christians who fled their homeland to escape from persecution. The second event was the arrival of another such group of Christians from Persia along with their two Church leaders, Mar Sapor and Mar Prot, around the 9th century.

Though various stories and traditions exist around these two events, a few points are undisputed. First, the Persian Christians brought new vigor, leadership, and a new liturgical tradition, i.e., the East Syrian (Chaldean) tradition to the fledging St. Thomas Christian communi-

ty. Second, the St. Thomas Christians warmly welcomed these Persian Christians and, according to the received tradition, the Kings of Kerala bestowed land and royal honors on them. Third, until the arrival of the Portuguese missionaries, the Persian Church exercised jurisdiction and oversight over the St. Thomas Christians. There is no evidence of any resistance or resentment against Persian ecclesiastical rule on the part of the St. Thomas Christians. On the contrary, during the Portuguese *padroado* rule (*see* PATRONATO REAL), the St. Thomas Christians appeared to yearn for Persian oversight. Fourth, there is an endogamous group among the St. Thomas Christians known as Southists (*Thekkumbhagar*) or the Knanaya community. Northists (*Vadakkumbhagar*) are said to be the ethnic St. Thomas Christian Indians, while the Southists are descendants of the emigrants from Persia led by Knai Thomman, who probably settled in the southern part of the Christian settlement.

The Church of Saint Sebastian, Kerala, southern India.
(©Charles & Josette Lenars/CORBIS)

Practices of the Early St. Thomas Christians. Much of what is known about the lifestyle and practices of the early St. Thomas Christians comes from written Portuguese accounts from the 16th to the 18th centuries, in addition to the living oral tradition that has been handed down through successive generations. From these sources, the following picture emerges: The St. Thomas Christians appeared to have their own unique lifestyle and practices from the earliest days. They were able to integrate their Christian faith to the wider socio-cultural customs and practices which they shared with their Hindu neighbors. Historically, the St. Thomas Christians enjoyed high social status and many social, political and royal privileges in Kerala along with their upper-caste Hindu counterparts. They followed the customs of the nobility such as feeding a newborn with powdered gold mixed with honey, teaching children to write the letters of the alphabet for the first time with rice, ceremonial baths and other purification rituals, the marriage ritual of tying the *tali* (a gold ornament in the Hindu style, but

with the marking of a cross on it) on the bride's neck and giving her a *mantrakodi* (bridal veil), as well as upper-caste funerary and death customs and rituals. During this period, the men of the St. Thomas Christian community pierced their ear-lobes, wore ornaments and styled their hair akin to the Hindus, but wore a cross on the tuft of hair. The St. Thomas Christians also practiced the rules of untouchability and pollution, with women living in separate quarters where they were specially protected. Churches were constructed according to the model of Hindu temples. While accepting and practicing Christian faith, they did not break away from their ancestral social-cultural traditions. Historians have described the pre-Portuguese St. Thomas Christians as "Hindu in culture, Christian in religion and Oriental in worship" *(Placid Podipara).*

Ecclesial structure and administration. The leadership and administration of the St. Thomas Christians combined East-Syrian ecclesial elements with indigenous Dravidian customs. The title of the Metropolitan was "Metropolitan and the Gate of All India," the word "gate" signifying sublime authority. The Metropolitans enjoyed quasi-Patriarchal authority. As Persian emissaries from the Chaldean Church, they were spiritual leaders who exercised the powers of holy orders, performing ordinations, blessings, and consecration of Churches as representatives of the Chaldean Patriarch. As the Metropolitans were foreigners who often did not speak the local dialects, the actual administration of the community lay in the hands of the archdeacon, who was always a native Dravidian. The position post of the archdeacon was also hereditary. Historically, the archdeacon was called the "Prince and Head of the Christian Community" and he was responsible for the whole community before the local king.

Another indigenous institution was the *yogam* or *malankara yogam,* which was the national assembly or synod of the whole Church and had the ultimate authority in dealing with all the matters of the Church. Lay and clerical representatives from all parishes were members of the *yogam*, presided over by the archdeacon. Similarly, all parishes had parish assemblies or *palliyogams,* which consisted of all the clergy and the heads of all of the families of the parish. The oldest priest in the parish presided over the *palliyogam*. The *palliyogam* has survived in present-day St. Thomas Christian communities. Both the *yogam* and *palliyogam* had real decision-making authority within the St. Thomas Christian community. On this basis, some historians regard the pre-Portuguese Church of St. Thomas in India as a Christian republic.

Christian-Hindu Relations. Before the arrival of the Portuguese missionaries, this ancient Church adopted

An inauguration service at St. George's Cathedral marking the formation of the South India United Church, Oct. 6, 1947. (©Hulton Getty/Liaison Agency)

a positive understanding of Hinduism, cultivating good relations with its Hindu neighbors in a spirit of communal harmony. The St. Thomas Christians held the view that "each one can be saved in his own law, all laws are right," the term "law" referring to other religions. The Synod of DIAMPER condemned this idea as one of the many egregious errors of St. Thomas Christians. The same synod also condemned another view held by the St. Thomas Christians that they were following "the Law of Thomas" whereas the Portuguese were following "the Law of Peter." What the St. Thomas Christians meant was not that they had two different faiths, but that each ecclesial community has its own ancient customs and sacred traditions which the other communities should respect. The Portuguese missionaries who came into contact with the St. Thomas Christians neither understood nor respected their customs and traditions. This resulted in conflict and schism within the St. Thomas Christian community.

The Advent of Portuguese Missionaries. India had some contacts with Latin Christianity in the 13th and 14th centuries through European travelers: JOHN OF MONTE CORVINO visited in 1292, and Jordan Catalani visited in 1319. However, Latin Christianity was established in India only with the arrival of the Portuguese in the 15th century. Vasco da Gama, the Portuguese navigator, landed in Kozhikode, South India, in 1498. The local St. Thomas Christians gave an enthusiastic welcome to the powerful Portuguese fleet and the *padroado* missionaries who accompanied them.

As Portuguese missionaries came in greater numbers, they began to interfere in the affairs of the St. Thomas Christians. Attempts to control and latinize them began mainly with the establishment of a seminary in Metropolitan See of Cranganore (Kodungalloor) around 1550 by the Franciscan friar Vicente de Lagos during the episcopacy of Bishop Mar Jacob. All those who were

Church of Our Lady of the Assumption, St. Xavier's College, Palayakottai, Tirunelveli-2, India.

trained in the seminary were formed in the Latin tradition and European cultural practices. With the death of Mar Jacob around 1552, Portuguese missionaries in collusion with the Portuguese political authorities began to block the arrival of Persian Metropolitans, seeking to bring the St. Thomas Christians completely under the jurisdiction of Portuguese Metropolitan of GOA. Occasionally, a few Persian bishops managed to undermine the Portuguese blockade: Mar Joseph and Mar Elias came in 1555, and Mar Abraham slipped into India on two occasions. In 1569 Mar Abraham took up residency in Angamaly, the metropolitan seat of the St. Thomas Christians, and ruled the St. Thomas Christians until his death in 1597. During his episcopacy, Jesuit missionaries introduced Latin ecclesial usages among the St. Thomas Christians, including priestly celibacy, confession before communion, burying the dead near the churches, and some feasts of the Latin calendar. In 1585, at the third Provincial Council of Goa, it was decreed that the Roman Pontifical and Sacramentary be translated into Syriac for the use of the St. Thomas Christians.

The death of Mar Abraham in 1597 marked a turning point in the history of the St. Thomas Christians. The Portuguese archbishop Alexis de Menezes of Goa arrived in Kerala, seeking to bring the St. Thomas Christians completely under the *padroado* jurisdiction. Mar Abraham had been already accused of heresy as he became estranged with the Jesuit missionaries. Archbishop Alexis de Menezes visited churches and ordained several priests in the Latin Rite. Despite fierce opposition from the archdeacon and the St. Thomas Christian community, Archbishop Menezes summoned a synod, which became known as the Synod of Diamper.

The Synod of Diamper. The Synod of Diamper was held in the parish church of Diamper (Udayamperoor) near Ernakulam, Kerala, in June of 1599. A total of 153 priests and 660 lay representatives attended the synod, as it was the custom of the *yogam* of the Malabar Church to include the laity. Many clergy refused to attend the synod as a mark of displeasure and protest against Menezes's interference. The official acts of the synod comprised the profession of faith and decrees on the sacraments, especially the Eucharist, corrections of "errors" in liturgical books, the reduction of the juridical status of the ancient metropolitan see of Angamaly to that of a Latin suffragan see under the *padroado* Metropolitan of Goa, and the expurgation of supposed errors in the customs and traditions of the St. Thomas Christians.

Menezes had prepared the decrees in Portuguese; they were translated into the vernacular and all attendees of the synod were forced to sign under duress and pain of excommunication. After the synod ended, Menezes stayed behind for several months, visiting parishes and implementing the synodal decrees. He also promulgated a decree that all who possessed Syriac books and manuscripts should hand over them to him on his visit under the threat of excommunication. Some of the books were corrected but many of them were burned by Menezes personally.

Many contemporary historians argue that the synod was invalid on the grounds that it was convoked without authority, it was not conducted in accordance with ecclesial canons, and it was never explicitly approved by Rome, which had merely authorized Archbishop Menezes to appoint a successor to Mar Abraham. Menezes never received authorization from Rome to convoke a synod to reform the ecclesial life and traditions of the St. Thomas Christians. The Portuguese Jesuit Francis Ros, Menezes's assistant who later became the first Latin bishop of Angamaly conceded that Menezes modified the synodal acts and unilaterally added new ones. In any event, the Synod of Diamper resulted in the latinization of the St. Thomas Christian communities. The synodal decrees condemned many of the ancient indigenous customs and traditions and latinized their Chaldean liturgy, prayers and devotions. It also resulted in the destruction of a significant number of valuable Syriac manuscripts and books on the suspicion of heresy. Historians are unanimous in concluding that the Synod of Diamper almost destroyed the identity of a unique and ancient church in India.

The Koonen Cross Oath. Resentment and violent reactions followed the Synod of Diamper. An outright rebellion occurred in 1653 during the episcopacy of the Jesuit archbishop of Goa, Francis Garcia. Bishop Attallah, a Syrian, was sent to Malabar by the Coptic Catholic Patriarch of Cairo at the request of the archdeacon of the St. Thomas Christians. Bishop Atallah reached Mylapore in 1653. But the Portuguese took him by force and shipped him to Goa. When the news spread that Atallah had arrived in the port city of Cochin on his way to Goa, many of the St. Thomas Christians gathered there. But they were denied permission to meet him, and a rumor soon spread that he had been drowned in the sea by the Portuguese. The angry and desperate Christians assembled before a cross (the "Koonen Cross") and swore that they would never submit to the authority of the Jesuit missionaries and never obey the archbishop of Goa. A few months later, many leading priests from among the St. Thomas Christians gathered at Alangad and consecrated Archdeacon Thomas as their bishop. This revolt of 1653 caused the tragic division among the St. Thomas Christians into two communities, those who maintained communion with bishop Garcia and the dissident group led by the archdeacon. Later in 1665 the dissident group received Mar Gregorios, a bishop from the Syrian (Jacobite) Patriarch of Antioch. As a result of their affiliation with the Syrian patriarchate, they became popularly known as the Jacobites.

Conflict and Confusion. Having realized the seriousness of the situation, the Congregation for the PROPAGATION OF FAITH sent several Discalced Carmelites, with Joseph Sebastiani as the Apostolic Commissary, to Malabar to study the situation. They arrived in Malabar in 1657 and returned to Rome in 1658, and Sebastiani came back to Malabar in 1661 as the Vicar Apostolic. In 1663 the Dutch captured the area and expelled Sebastiani. Before leaving, Sebastiani managed to consecrate a local Indian priest, Chandy Parampil (Alexander de Campo) as the Vicar Apostolic. Things were starting to look better for the St. Thomas Christians, when the death of bishop Chandy plunged the situation back to chaos. The long period of 200 years from the death of bishop Chandy in 1687 until the establishment of separate dioceses for the St. Thomas Christians in 1887 was one of utter confusion and conflict in the history of the St. Thomas Christians. During this period several heads of the Jacobite communities expressed interest in entering into a communion with the Church of Rome. But the *padroado* missionaries and the bishops vehemently opposed all such endeavors. Around 1773, Joseph Cariattil and Thomas Paremmakkal, two eminent priests and representatives of the St. Thomas Christian community, set out for Rome and Lisbon to inform Church authorities of the problems of their Church, to plead for steps to be taken toward the reunion of the Catholic and Jacobite wings of the St. Thomas Christians, and the restoration of the ancient Oriental ecclesial and liturgical traditions for the St. Thomas Christians. Their mission to Lisbon was somewhat successful. Cariattil was consecrated as the Archbishop of Cranganore (Kodungalloor) with the approval of Rome. The Congregation for the Propagation of the Faith vested Cariattil with the authority to receive Mar Thomas VI and the Jacobite community into communion with the Catholic Church. Upon returning, Archbishop Cariattil fell ill in Goa and died prematurely, scuttling all efforts at effecting a reunion.

Memoranda went to Rome and Lisbon from the St. Thomas Christians with repeated requests for their own bishops and permission to restore their ancient ecclesial and liturgical heritage. The most significant of these was the *Angamaly Padiyola* of 1787, drawn up by representatives from 84 St. Thomas Christian parishes and addressed to Rome, demanding their own bishops and listing the abuses of *padroado* clergy and foreign missionaries. But both the *padroado ecclesial* leadership and the Carmelite missionaries assigned to that region repeatedly overruled all their efforts to procure indigenous bishops or restore their ancient usages. Finally the St. Thomas Christians once again turned to the East Syrian Patriarchs for assistance. The Chaldean Catholic Patriarch Joseph Audo sent a bishop Thomas Rockos. Upon arrival in Cochin in 1861, he was ordered to leave immediately. He refused to do so, and was excommunicated by the Vicar Apostolic of Varapuzha. From 1861 until his return to Baghdad in 1862, his presence caused yet another schism. The same fate befell a second Catholic Chaldean bishop, Mar Elias Mellus, whom Patriarch Audo sent in 1874. As Rome took strong action against the patriarch, Mellus was recalled home. The Syrian Christians of the Assyrian Church of India, popularly known as the Surais, who are in communion with the ASSYRIAN CHURCH OF THE EAST, are the descendants of those St. Thomas Christians in the Trichur (Thrissur) region who broke away and rallied around Mar Mellus.

Restoration of Autonomy. The Chaldean Catholic Patriarch's interventions alerted Rome to the long-simmering dissatisfaction of the St. Thomas Christians. In 1887 Pope LEO XIII agreed to remove the St. Thomas Christians from the jurisdiction of the Latin bishops. Two Syro-Malabar vicariates in Trichur (Thrissur) and Kottayam were erected. To the disappointment of the St. Thomas Christians, the two vicars apostolic who were appointed—Adolf Medlycott and Charles Levigne—were foreigners. The struggles of the St. Thomas Christians for autonomy came to fruition in 1896, when Rome established three vicariates apostolic with local Indian bishops: Thrissur, with bishop John Menacherry, Ernakulam, with bishop Louis Pazheparampil, and Changanacherry with bishop Mathew Makil. In 1911, a fourth vicariate apostolic at Kottayam was erected for the endogamous Knanaya community.

Today, the St. Thomas Christians no longer form one church, but are found within the Catholic, Syrian Oriental Orthodox, East Syrian (Assyrian) and reformed traditions, in eight separate ecclesial entities:

1. The Syro-Malabar Catholic Church. The largest St. Thomas Christian community which is in communion with the Church of Rome, with an ecclesial heritage that combines aspects of Indian, Syrian and Latin Christian traditions and customs. It is based mainly in Kerala, India, but has large diasporic communities in India and throughout the world, especially in the United States. It has a flourishing church life, with many clerical and religious vocations, and numerous missionaries working in the Latin dioceses of India and other parts of the world,

especially in Africa, Europe and the Americas. In 1911 a new diocese was erected for the Knanaya community Kottayam. In 1923 Pope PIUS XI established a full-fledged Syro-Malabar hierarchy for the St. Thomas Christians. On Dec. 16, 1992, by the decree *Quae maiori,* Pope JOHN PAUL II elevated the Syro-Malabar Church to a *sui juris* Major Archiepiscopal Church. As a major archiepiscopal church, the *yogam* of the Syro-Malabar Church has full and independent powers in all matters including the election of its leader, the major archbishop, an appointment which merely requires papal confirmation. A petition is pending before the Holy See for the elevation of the Syro-Malabar Church to patriarchal status. For specific aspects of the history, present situation and liturgy of the Syro-Malabar Church *see* SYRO-MALABAR CHURCH and SYRO-MALABAR LITURGY.

2. The Malankara (Indian) Orthodox Syrian Church (Methran Kakshi).

3. The Syrian Orthodox Jacobite Church (Bava Kakshi). The descendants of the first wave of St. Thomas Christians who broke away as a result of the Koonen Cross Revolt of 1653. Subsequently, they accepted the oversight of the Syrian (Jacobite) Patriarch of Antioch who required that they embrace West Syrian (Antiochene) customs and usages. As a result of their allegiance to the Syrian Jacobite Patriarch of Antioch, they are popularly known as Jacobites. After a prolonged period of factional fighting, internal conflicts and lawsuits on the question of allegiance to the Syrian Patriarch and control of church property which had erupted at the beginning of the 20th century and went all the way to the Indian Supreme Court, the Jacobite community permanently splintered into two: the Syrian Orthodox Jacobite Church (Bava Kakshi, i.e., the patriarch's party) and the Malankara (Indian) Orthodox Syrian Church (Methran Kakshi, i.e., the bishop's party). Historically, the patriarch's party supported the attempts of the Syrian (Jacobite) Patriarch of Antioch to assert greater control over the Jacobite community, while the bishop's party pressed the case for autocephaly. Repeated attempts to effect a union between these two churches have been inconclusive.

4. The Syro-Malankara Catholic Church (Reeth Sabha). The Syro-Malankara Catholic Church was formed in 1930 when a faction of the Jacobite community led by Mar Ivanios and Theophilus entered into communion with the See of Rome. They continue to practice all the liturgical usages and ecclesial traditions of the West Syrian (Antiochene) Church. For specific aspects of its history, present situation and liturgy, *see* SYRO-MALANKARA CHURCH and SYRO-MALANKARA LITURGY.

5. The Assyrian Church of India (Surais). This is another group of St. Thomas Christians that has had an independent existence from the days of Mar Mellus, who managed to gather a small group of St. Thomas Christians in Trichur (Thrissur). In 1952, they received a bishop from the Assyrian Church of the East (Persian), thereby restoring ancient ties to the Persian Patriarch. Since 1968, all their bishops have been ethnic Indians.

6. *Malabar Independent Syrian Church of Thozhiyur.* A very small group of independent St. Thomas Christians found mainly in Thozhiyur (Thozhiyoor) or Anjur. In 1772, Bishop Mar Kurilose Kattumangatt fled to Thozhiyur with his supporters when his episcopal consecration by a foreign prelate was not approved by Mar Dionysius I of the Jacobite community. Although it has maintained a sister-church relationship with the Mar Thoma Syrian Church of Malabar (see below) since 1948, it has not accepted the reformed (evangelical) theology of the Mar Thoma Church. Since 1989, it has cultivated close ecumenical ties with, and extended intercommunion to the Anglican communion.

7. *The Mar Thoma Syrian Church of Malabar (Marthomites).* In the early 19th century, evangelical Anglican missionaries from the UK-based Church Missionary Society (CMS) came to the aid of the Jacobite community. Over time, the work of these missionaries led to conflicts, with detractors alleging that the Anglican missionaries wanted to implement a radical reform of ancient church traditions and practices. By the Synod of Mavelikkara in 1836, Metropolitan Chepat Mar Dionysius IV severed all the connections of the Jacobite community with the Anglican missionaries. However, a small reformist group led by Mar Abraham Malpan attempted to undertake radical reform within the Jacobite community. Excommunicated by Mar Dionysius, this reformist group reorganized itself as a distinct church that is the via media between the Oriental Orthodox and Reformed traditions. In full communion with the Church of South India since 1958, the Church of North India since 1972, and a full-fledged member of the worldwide Anglican communion, the Mar Thoma Church combines aspects of the St. Thomas Christian traditions and practices with the evangelical theology introduced by the CMS missionaries. The Mar Thoma Church believes that it is the true representative of the ancient Apostolic Church of St. Thomas and that the reform was only a purification of the Church.

8. *St. Thomas Evangelical Church of India.* This church originated as a splinter group from the Mar Thoma Church in 1961. Due to internal strife, members of this splinter group claimed that the evangelical principles of reform advocated by Mar Abraham Malpan could no longer be safeguarded in the Mar Thoma Church, and hence the need for a new Church.

LATIN CHRISTIANITY IN INDIA

Beginnings. The present Latin Christian (Roman Catholic) community in India had its origin in the work of the Portuguese *padroado* missionaries. The Franciscans comprised the first wave of missionaries. They arrived circa 1518 and worked in Goa, Bassein, Cochin, Quilon, and parts of Tamil Nadu, converting many Indians. Jesuit, Dominican and Augustinian missionaries followed the Franciscans, coming principally from Portugal, Spain and Italy. The early fruits of their labor resulted in the erection of the first Latin bishopric in Goa in 1534.

Around 1536, civil war broke out between the *paravas* (fisherfolk) and the Muslims in the Pearl Fishery coast region. The Portuguese came to the rescue of the *paravas,* resulting in a large number of *paravas* embracing Latin Christianity. The most successful missionary endeavor remains that of the Jesuit missionary St. Francis XAVIER, who arrived in Goa in 1542. Regarded as the "Apostle of Latin Christianity in India," Francis Xavier and his companions worked tirelessly in the regions of the Pearl Fishery coast, Coromandel coast, Goa, Bassein, and Bombay. He established seminaries in Quilon and Cochin and opened Jesuit houses in Cochin, Bassein, and Mylapore; schools were then opened in and around the main Portuguese settlements.

From the many Portuguese enclaves that dotted the coastal areas, the *padroado* missionaries gradually worked their way into the hinterland: Madurai (Robert De Nobili 1606), Trichinapoly, Dindigal, Tanjore, Hooghly, and parts of Bengal, Masulipatanam, Vizhakapatanam, and Golconda. At the invitation of the Moghul emperor Akbar, a few groups of Jesuits from Goa visited his court and were instrumental in establishing small Christian communities in Agra, Delhi, Lahore, Patna, Jaipur and Narwar. In 1558 Goa became an Archdiocese with Cochin and Melaka (in present-day Malaysia) as suffragans. Other suffragans were subsequently added: MACAU in China (1576), Funei in Japan (1588), Angamaly (1600, which was later moved to Kodungalloor in 1605), and Mylapore (1606). The Provincial Councils of Goa (1567, 1575, 1585, 1592, 1606 and 1894) played a significant role in the mission and life of the Latin Church during this period. The Portuguese crown and the rights given to them and their missionaries in Goa under the *padroado* system played a vital role in the success of the mission. The latter part of the 16th century witnessed the decline of the Portuguese mission in tandem with the decline of the Portuguese military power. The never-ending wars on land and sea between the Portuguese and the hostile Muslim rulers of India hindered the spread of the Gospel. The situation worsened in the 17th century when the rival Dutch and English colonial powers systematically wiped out the Portuguese presence, forcing the *padroado* missionaries to return to Portugal.

De Nobili and the Indian Rites Controversy. The 16th-century Portuguese missionary efforts succeeded only among the lower castes of the Hindu society. Following the same approach used in their Latin American mission colonies, the Portuguese missionaries required the newly baptized Indian neophytes to dress, eat, and behave like the Portuguese Christians, including taking Portuguese surnames. High caste Indians objected to these demands, labelling the neophytes "parangis" (detested foreigners) and treating them as outcasts. Realizing the need to attract the Brahmins, who comprised the high-caste Hindus, the Italian Jesuit missionary Robert de NOBILI established his mission in 1606 in Madurai, a Brahmin stronghold. De Nobili made a distinction between Christian faith and European civic and cultural customs. He himself adopted the customs of the Brahmins, dressed, behaved and lived like a Brahmin monk. De Nobili's approach was successful. He attracted many Brahmins of Madurai and its environs, and many embraced Christianity. But from the very beginning opinions regarding de Nobili's approach were sharply divided among Nobili's fellow Jesuits on one hand and the *padroado* authorities and Rome on the other. In many ways, de Nobili and his confrere in China, Matteo RICCI, were too advanced for their time. The debate continued for several years as opposition to de Nobili and his Jesuit colleagues mounted. Pope Benedict XIV, who had earlier condemned Ricci's Chinese approach in 1742, also condemned de Nobili's practices in 1744. As in China, missionaries to India were required to take an oath denouncing the practices that de Nobili had promoted. Such official disapproval negatively affected missionary outreach to high-caste Indians for a long time and led to the INDIAN RITES CONTROVERSY.

Tensions between Rome and Portugal. With the decline of Portuguese colonial power and its inability to protect its missionaries in the face of Dutch and English invaders, the Holy See began sending missionaries under the aegis of the Congregation for the Propagation of the Faith. Several vicariates apostolic were erected in India under the congregation: Bijapur (1637, which was shifted to Bombay in 1832), Verapoly (1659), Tibet-Hindustan (1808, later known as Agra), Calcutta, Madras, Colombo and Pondicherry (between 1834 and 1836). These vicariates were later divided, resulting in the creation of 14 new vicariates by 1882. These vicariates were normally outside the Portuguese territories, leading to a longstanding conflict and intense rivalry between the clergy of the *padroado* and the congregation. This conflict reached its climax during the Portuguese Revolution of 1834 with its resulting wave of anti-clericalism and severance of diplomatic relations with the Holy See. Responding to this crisis, in 1838 Pope GREGORY XVI withdrew Goa's jurisdiction over its suffragan sees of Cochin, Kodungalloor and Mylapore. This resulted in the so-called Goan or Indo-Portuguese Schism during which many *padroado* clergy disobeyed Rome. In 1886, a new concordat restored Goa's jurisdiction over Cochin and Mylapore. The Latin Catholic hierarchy for India and Ceylon (now Sri Lanka) was also established in 1886 with eight ecclesiastical provinces, with 19 dioceses and 3 vicariates as the suffragan. After India regained its independence in 1947, the Indian government signed a concordat limiting the *padroado* jurisdiction to the Portuguese territory. Finally, the occupation of Goa by the Indian Government in 1961 terminated practically the last remnant of the *padroado* system.

Tribal and Dalit Communities. Two great assets of Latin Christianity in India are the dynamic and flourishing tribal and dalit Christian communities. Many of these communities, except the early Tamil Christians, embraced Christianity in the 19th and 20th centuries. They are found mostly in Bihar, Orissa, Andhra and Tamil Nadu. Among them, the Bettiah community of the Bihar is one of the oldest. It originated as the Capuchin mission in Bihar in 1703. In 1745, the Capuchin missionaries came at the invitation of the king of Bettiah and established a Christian community. The Jesuit mission in Bengal penetrated Bihar and Orissa. In 1880s there was a mass movement of conversions in Chotanagpur (Jharkhand) due to the work of Belgian Jesuit missionaries, particularly of Constant Lievens in the district of Ranchi. Christian tribals in the northeast region of India are another strong force. The Portuguese Jesuit missionaries reached Assam in 1626, and the mission in Assam was under the Vicariate of Calcutta from its establishment in 1834. The mission in the northeast flourished due to the work of several missionary groups, namely, the PARIS FOREIGN MISSION SOCIETY (1850), the Foreign Mission Society of Milan (1870), the German SALVATORIANS (1890), the JESUITS (1915–1922), and from 1922 onwards, the SALESIANS. The Latin Christian mission among the tribals, the dalits, and the lower classes of India was pivotal in their increasing political awareness and willingness to fight for justice. This has threatened the status quo and the power of the upper-caste Hindus and the landlords, resulting in increasing opposition to Christian mission activities from the latter part of the 20th century.

PROTESTANT CHRISTIANITY IN INDIA

The Arrival of Protestant Missionaries. The first Protestant missionaries to India were two German Lutherans, Bartholomew Ziegenbalg and Henry Pleutschau, who were sent by King Frederick of Denmark in 1706. They landed in the Danish colony of Tranquebar, in the southeastern part of India. From Tranquebar, Protestant missionaries made their way to Madras, Trichy, Cuddalore, Tanjore and Tirunelveli. In 1806, the London Mission Society (LMS) of the Congregational Church sent a German Missionary, W. T. Ringeltaube, to work in the southern part of Travancore or South Kerala. Another pioneer was the English missionary of the Baptist Church, William Carey, who came to Calcutta in 1793 with Joshua Marshman and William Ward, settling in the Dutch colony of Serampore. The Serampore missionaries are well known for their educational, literary and social work. The Church Missionary Society (CMS) of the Anglicans began to send missionaries from 1813 onwards into the different parts of India. Benjamin Bailey, Henry Baker and Joseph Fenn were well-known CMS missionaries who worked in Kerala, especially for the reform of the Jacobite Christians. The Basel Missionary Society, an ecumenical endeavor among Lutherans, the Calvinists, and the Anglicans began to send missionaries to India from 1834 onwards. Hermann Gundert and Samuel Hebrich were two of their outstanding missionaries.

Growth of Protestant Religions. The northeast tribal region of India where the large majority is now Christian is the great success story of the Protestant missions. The British Baptists from Serampore reached northeast India in 1813. The American Baptists began their mission in Assam 1836. The Welsh Presbyterians started in Cherrapunji in 1841. Anglican missionaries of the SOCIETY FOR THE PROPAGATION OF THE GOSPEL (SPG) came in the 1870s. Lutherans started to work in Tezpur in 1860. American Presbyterians arrived in and around Allahabad in 1832. American Methodists came to Lucknow and Allahabad in 1857. German Lutherans started their mission in Chotanagpur in the 1840s. Beginning in the 20th century, many independent reformed, evangelical and pentecostal churches came to India, including the SEVENTH DAY ADVENTISTS, SALVATION ARMY, and the Disciples of Christ.

Ecumenism, Consolidation and Union. The 20th century also witnessed the great ecumenical movement among the Protestant Churches in India. Realizing the enormity of the scandal of a divided Christianity, the missionaries and leaders of the Indian churches realized that unity was essential for the success of evangelization, and that the Indian people should not be divided by denominations which had originated in Europe's fractured history. Motivated by this ecumenical spirit, four Protestant denominations in southern India—the Anglicans, the Presbyterians, the Congregational Churches and the Methodists—united to form the Church of South India (CSI) in 1947. The Church of South India has an episcopal system of governance as well as a common constitution and liturgy. In northern India, seven Protestant denominations—the Anglicans, the Presbyterians, the Congregational Churches, the Methodists, the Baptists, the Disciples of Christ, and the Brethren—united to form the Church of North India (CNI) in 1970. However, the powerful American Baptist Churches in the northeast and in Andhra, the American Methodist Churches in the north and south, and the Lutheran Churches in India did not join in the union. The Lutheran Churches in India have united under the umbrella of the United Evangelical Lutheran Churches in India.

Contributions. Protestant missionaries in India made tremendous contributions in the areas of education, health care, social transformation and literature. In the past, the Protestant Churches in India were conservative and remained visibly foreign as they were controlled by the overseas mission boards. During the latter part of the 20th century, most of the Protestant Churches in India became fully independent with their own personnel, structures and programs of inculturation.

PRESENT-DAY SITUATION OF CHRISTIANITY IN INDIA

Relations between Latin and Eastern Catholic Churches. The Catholic Church in India is a communion of three particular churches: (1) the Latin Church, (2) the Syro-Malabar Church, and (3) the Syro-Malankara Church. The Catholic Bishops Conference of India (CBCI) was established as the assembly of all the Catholic bishops of India in 1944. In view of the juridical status which VATICAN COUNCIL II gave to bishops conferences (*Christus Dominus,* 37), the CBCI revised its statutes in 1966 in accordance with the conciliar documents. With the promulgation of the new Codes of Canon Law for the Latins (1983) and the Orientals (1990), *sui juris* Catholic Churches are legally entitled to separate episcopal bodies and synods. In compliance with Pope John Paul II's 1987 letter to the Indian Catholic bishops, three separate episcopal bodies for the three particular Catholic Churches were created in 1988. However, the CBCI continues to exist and function as an umbrella organization for all three particular churches.

Relations between the three particular Catholic churches are by and large cordial, although two problematic areas remain. The first concerns the pastoral care of the emigrants from the Syro-Malabar and Syro-Malankara churches who are in the Latin territories. The directive of Vatican II that bishops and clergy from their own churches should be responsible for the pastoral care of these emigrants (*Christus Dominus,* 23) have not been implemented in India. Second, the two Oriental Catholic churches in India are restricted to their ancient historical territory of Kerala and cannot undertake evangelization in Latin territories outside that state. However, the Latin church is not bound to such jurisdictional limitation; Latin missionaries can work freely in Kerala. The Oriental churches resent this jurisdictional limitation and have petitioned to the Holy See for the freedom to undertake evangelization and pastoral care of emigrants outside of Kerala. As an interim solution, Rome entrusted recently created dioceses in central and north India to the Syro-Malabar Church. This does not fully satisfy the demands of the Oriental Catholic churches who are requesting removal of all restrictions on their evangelizing mission in India.

Protestant Christianity. The Protestant churches in India have a common ecumenical forum called the National Council of Churches in India (NCCI), which had its origin in 1914. The NCCI brings together most of the Protestant churches and organizations in India for mutual consultation, assistance and action in all matters related to the life and witness of the churches. Since 1979, its headquarters is located at Nagpur.

Ecumenical Ties. Although the three particular Catholic churches in India are not members of the NCCI, there is some collaboration between the NCCI and CBCI, especially on national and social issues. Together, they have organized common consultations and programs. After the year 2000, new initiatives were undertaken to explore the possibility for the Catholic Churches to join the NCCI or to create an alternative ecumenical structure that would encompass both the NCCI and CBCI. The Commission for Ecumenism of the CBCI contributed to the discussion with its *Guidelines for Ecumenism: Towards an Ecumenical Life-Style* (2000), which incorporates the doctrinal and theological insights of Vatican II and the Directory on Ecumenism.

Catholic Religious Orders and Congregations. Many European-based religious orders came and established communities in the different parts of India. The Franciscans, the Dominicans, the Jesuits, the Capuchins and the Carmelites were among the early wave, arriving in India during the Portuguese period. There are many indigenous Indian religious congregations, of which the first was the Carmelites of Mary Immaculate (CMI) founded by Kuriakose Elias CHAVARA in 1831. The two largest congregations for women are the Congregation of the Mother of Carmel (CMC), also founded by Chavara, and the Franciscan Clarist Congregation (FCC). Many of these religious congregations are engaged in education, running elementary and high schools, colleges, universities and theological institutes, technical schools and vocational institutes, and adult education and literacy

centers for women and other marginalized and underprivileged groups. Other religious orders operate healthcare facilities such as hospitals and clinics, orphanages, hospices, halfway houses and nursing homes, and media and communication.

Indian Christian Theological Trends. In Indian Christian theological thinking three different approaches or trends can be identified. The first is the classical philosophical-theological approach where attempts are made to articulate and interpret Christian faith in the classical Indian cultural, philosophical and religious categories of the *Vedas, Upanishads, Puranas* and their underlying philosophical systems. The second trend focuses on the socio-political realities and problems and responds to them in the light of the Gospel. The third trend is a spiritual-contemplative approach, which emphasizes the Indian spirituality and interiority. Indian theologians have tread new paths in the areas of christology, missiology, interreligious dialogue, and theology of religions. This has borne fruit in the articulation of christologies in the Vedanta and Advaita traditions, missiologies that are centered on the Kingdom of God, and theologies of religions which focus on the Harmony and Mystery of God. While many Indian theologians are gaining wide recognition for their insightful analyses and theological explorations, a few have become targets of criticism and even censure for the radical nature of their theologizing.

The Indian Christian Ashram movement and the emergence of numerous Dialogue Centers in the different parts of the country in the 20th century may be associated with the third trend, although not exclusively. The word "ashram" comes from the Sanskrit root "a + srama" which means total dedication, total pursuit, or ardent striving. The ashram is a place of work and pursuit, physical, mental and spiritual. It is a community of spiritual seekers who are gathered around an enlightened person known as a guru. Some of the pioneers of the Christian Ashram movement were S. Jesudasan (Thiruppattur), Murray Rogers (Bareilly), Monchanin and Bede Griffiths (Kulithalai), Francis Acharya (Kurisumala), Sr. Vandana (Rishikesh), and Amalorpavadass (Mysore).

Inculturation. Vatican II's call to all Christian communities to inculturate the faith in their actual sociocultural milieu (*Lumen Gentium* 10, *Ad Gentes* 22), and to enter into dialogue with people of all faiths (*Nostra Aetate*) encouraged the Indian Catholic bishops to explore new avenues of inculturation and dialogue. In 1969, Rome gave permission for Indian Catholics to adopt certain Indian cultural elements and ritual gestures in the celebration of the Eucharist in the "12-Point Statement." The Catholic bishops established the National Biblical, Catechetical, and Liturgical Center (NBCLC) in Bangalore to supervise and coordinate efforts at inculturation. Various attempts were made for the inculturation of liturgy and prayers at the National Center and at other theological centers like Dharmaram College, Bangalore, and at various Indian Christian Ashrams. An Indian Order of Mass and an Indian Anaphora were prepared by the NBCLC. The CBCI approved the Order of the Mass. The Indian Anaphora underwent several rounds of experimentation and revision before the Latin Bishops Conference (CCBI-Latin Rite) approved it in 1992 and forwarded it to the Holy See for approval.

Christian-Hindu Dialogue. Early Christian missionaries never had a genuine encounter with Hinduism and other Indian religions. What they did at the most was to translate the Christian faith into the various Indian languages. The emergence of a national consciousness and the cultural awakening as a result of the 19th-century Indian Renaissance movement led several missionaries and Indian Christian thinkers to engage in a serious dialogue with the Indian religions, cultures and philosophies, and to explore new paths of Indian theology. In 1875, K. M. Banerjee argued that Christianity, far from being a foreign religion, was the fulfillment of Hinduism (*Arian Witness* 8). For Brahmabandhav Upadhyaya (1861–1907), one could be Hindu and Christian at the same time, Hindu by cultural and religious traditions and Christian by faith in Christ. Sadhu Sunder Singh (1889–1929) was a great Christian mystic who eschewed all Christian denominations, proposing a Church of the sadhu ideal. Other pioneers of indigenous Christianity and Indian theology were K. C. Sen (1838–1884), who proposed the Navavidhan, the Church of New Dispensation; Nehemiah Goreh (1825–1895), who saw Hinduism as *preparatio evangelica*; A. J. Appasamy (1891–1976), who propounded the idea of Bhakti Marga and Yogic vision; P. Chenchaiah (1886–1959), who is known for his theology of New Creation; V. Chakkarai (1880–1958) who articulated an Indian Christology of the Spirit; and P. D. Devanandan (1901–1962) and M. M. Thomas (1916–1995) who both advocated a renewed Christian humanism in India and a servant church task with transforming the Indian society.

While most the pioneers of the 19th century were Protestants, some of the outstanding 20th-century theologians and thinkers were Catholics. Among them, Bede GRIFFITHS (1906–1993) held the idea of Christian Advaita; D.S. Amalorpavadass (1932–1990) emphasized a new evangelization and inculturation; Sebastian Kappen (1924–1993), articulated an Indian theology of liberation; Raimundo Panikkar (1918–) contributed to a cosmotheandric vision of reality, cross-cultural theologizing and to a theology of religions and dialogue; and Felix Wilfred and Michael Amaladoss (1936–), both of whom have articulated new theological paths for mission and liberation in India, inculturation, religious pluralism and interreligious dialogue.

THE IMPACT OF CHRISTIANITY ON INDIAN SOCIETY AND CULTURE

Some of the best dictionaries and grammars in many Indian languages were written by missionaries who were great scholars as well. Many Indian tribal languages were oral languages devoid of alphabets and script. It was the missionaries who mastered these languages and provided them script and grammar. The Serampore missionaries were well known for their study of tribal and popular cultures and languages, which became instrumental for their modernization and dynamic growth. Some of the best studies on Indian history, religions, philosophy, culture, art, architecture and music were written by the foreign missionaries.

It was the western education introduced by the Christian missionaries and later by the British administration that laid the foundation for the modern Indian society and culture. Alexander Duff, a Presbyterian pastor, was the first person to introduce the British system of higher education in India in 1835. Education was the basis for all the other changes. Modern scientific education gradually eliminated the superstitious and mythical worldviews and paved the way for rapid scientific, technological and material progress. It also resulted in new interpretations of the religious traditions, scriptures and myths. Through schools and colleges, Christian missionaries contributed substantially to the awakening of the Indian masses who were mostly uneducated, poor, exploited, and oppressed by the caste system. Opposition to the Christian mission in India in the latter part of the 20th and early 21st centuries came about not just because of religious differences, but also because the Christian missionaries' promotion of education threatened the economic, social and political power of the upper castes and the established dominant groups.

It was in constant encounter with Christianity that the Hindu Renaissance movement led by Ram Mohan Roy, Swami Vivekananda, Rabindranath Tagore, Mahatma Gandhi, and Radhakrishnan sought to integrate into Hinduism and Indian culture the values of human person, sound moral and ethical principles, community solidarity irrespective of caste and sex, a sense of history as a project for human action and creativity, and social transformation of Indian society to embrace the ideals of freedom, justice and equality. These Hindu reformers rejected the traditional understanding of human history in terms of inevitable fate or as the consequence of the past karma and condemned social evils like child marriage, sati (the custom of forcing widows to immolate themselves on the funeral pyre of their husbands) and the caste system as inhuman.

SAINTS AND SAGES

India is known as a land of Sages, Saints and Gurus. Sanyasa or religious life both in communities and as solitary monks is part of India's ancient tradition. Christian priestly and religious life is very much esteemed in India, and the Indian Church is blessed with an abundance of priestly and religious vocations. The saints and sages of the Indian churches are numerous, beginning with the Apostle St. Thomas and St. Francis Xavier. St. Gonsalo Garcia (1557–1597), born in Vasai, became a Franciscan and a missionary to Japan, where he was martyred in 1597. He was declared a saint in 1862 by Pius IX. St. John de Britto (1647–1693), born in Lisbon, became a Jesuit and went to India in 1673. He was martyred near Madurai, and was canonized by Pius XII in 1947. Kuriakose Elias Chavara, the founder of the Congregation of Mary Immaculate (CMI) for men and the Congregation of the Mother of Carmel (CMC) for women, was a Kerala native who became a great leader and reformer of the Syro-Malabar Church, a preacher, poet and educator. He was declared blessed in 1986 by John Paul II. Sister Alphonsa (1910–1946), born in Kerala, became a Franciscan Clarist nun but died young after a prolonged period of suffering and illness. She was beatified along with Kuriakose Elias Chavara by Pope John Paul II in 1986 during his visit to Kerala. Joseph Vaz (1651–1711), born in Goa, became a priest and went to Sri Lanka as a missionary and died there. He was beatified in 1997. Rudolf ACQUAVIVA (1550–1583), born in Italy, became a Jesuit priest, came to India in 1578, was invited as a scholar to the Mugal Emperor Akbar's court, was martyred in Goa along with four others, and was beatified in 1893.

Among those who were declared venerable are one bishop, two sisters and two priests: Bishop Hartmann Anastasius (1803–1866), Sr. Mary of the Passion (1839–1904), Sr. Mariam Thresia (1876–1926), Fr. Aurelian OCD (1887–1963), and Fr. Agnel D'Souza (1869–1927). There are many other clergy and religious whose sanctity have been publicly acclaimed, even if they have not been officially canonized or beatified: Bishop Melchior de Marion Bresillac (1813–1859), Sr. Mary Veronica (1823–1906), Fr. Mathew Kadalikkattil (1872–1935), Bishop Thomas Kurialacherry (1873–1925), Sr. Euphrasia CMC (1877–1952), Fr. Zacharias OCD (1887–1957), Fr. Augustine Thevarparampil (1891–1973), Bishop Stephen Fernando SDB (1895–1978), Fr. Francis Convertini SDB (1898–1976), Bishop Mathew Kavukatt (1904–1969), and the world-renowned MOTHER TERESA (1910–1997), the apostle of the poor and the unwanted. Three laymen were noted for their holiness: Devasagayam Pillai (1712–1752), Thommachan Puthenparampil (1836–1908) and Joseph Thamby (1882–1945).

It is not possible to list here all the names of the saints and sages from the other churches in India. Five holy metropolitans from the Syrian Orthodox churches may be mentioned: St. Baselius Yeldho (1593–1685), St. Ignatius Elias III (1867–1932), St. Mar Gregorios of Parumala (1848–1902), Sleeba Mar Osthathiose (1854–1930), and Mar Gregoriose Abdul Jaleel (d. 1681).

Bibliography: J. AERTHAYIL, *The Spiritual Heritage of St. Thomas Christians* (Bangalore 2001). D.S. AMALORPAVADASS, ed., *The Indian Church in the Struggle for a New Society* (Bangalore 1981). R. BOYD, *An Introduction to Indian Christian Theology* (Delhi 1991). L. BROWN, *The Indian Christians of St. Thomas* (Cambridge, England 1982). CBCI Commission for Ecumenism. *Guidelines for Ecumenism: Towards a New Ecumenical Lifestyle* (New Delhi 2000). CBCI Evaluation Committee. *CBCI Evaluation Report: The Catholic Bishops Conference of India—Retrospect and Prospectus* (New Delhi 1995). J.C. ENGLAND, *The Hidden History of Christianity in Asia* (Delhi 1996). *History of Christianity in India*, 5 v. (Bangalore 1982–97) K. KUNNUMPURAM, et al., eds., *The Church in India in Search of a New Identity* (Bangalore 1997). S.H. MOFFETT, *A History of Christianity in Asia*, v1, *Beginnings to 1500*, 2d rev. ed. (Maryknoll, NY 1998). A. MOOKENTHOTTAM, *Indian Theological Tendencies* (Frankfurt 1978). A. M. MUNDADAN, *Indian Christians: Search for Identity and Struggle for Autonomy* (Bangalore 1984); *Paths of Indian Theology* (Bangalore 1998). J. PANTHAPLAMTHOTTIYIL, ed., *Indian Christian Directory* (Kottayam 2000). K. PATHIL, *Indian Churches at the Crossroads* (Bangalore 1995). K. PATHIL, ed., *Mission in India Today: The Task of St. Thomas Christians* (Bangalore 1988); *Religious Pluralism: An Indian Christian Perspective* (Delhi 1991). T.V. PHILIP, *East of the Euphrates: Early Christianity in Asia* (Delhi 1998). P. PUTHANANGADY, ed., *Towards an Indian Theology of Liberation* (Bangalore 1986). J. PUTHENKALAM, and A. MAMPRA, *Sanctity in India* (Yercaud 2000). S. J. SAMARTHA, *One Christ, Many Religions: Towards a Revised Christology* (Maryknoll, NY 1994). J. THALIATH, *The Synod of Diamper* (Bangalore 1999). M. M. THOMAS, *The Acknowledged Christ of Indian Renaissance* (Madras 1976). B. VADAKKEKARA, *Origin of India's St. Thomas Christians: A Historiographical Critique* (Delhi 1995). G. VAN LEEUWEN, *Searching for an Indian Ecclesiology* (Bangalore 1984). F. WILFRED, *Beyond Settled Foundations: The Journey of Indian Theology* (Madras 1993).

[K. PATHIL]

INDIAN PHILOSOPHY

Philosophy in India consists not only in an understanding of the meaning of ultimate reality but also in the actual realization of this truth in one's life and conduct. Indian philosophy is concerned with what it considers the highest of human values, that is, the realization of liberation from the cycle of rebirths. The various philosophical *daranas* (visions of truth) are different paths that lead to the mystical life in order to bring about this liberation. Thus philosophy in India is an integral part of religion. The systems of Indian philosophy are classified into two groups: the orthodox (*astika*), which accepts the authority of the VEDAS, and the heterodox (*nāstika*), which does not. To the first group belong the six systems (see below), whereas the schools of the Cārvākas (materialists), the Buddhists, and the Jains belong to the heterodox group. Of the orthodox schools only the Vedānta survives in contemporary Indian philosophy.

HISTORICAL DEVELOPMENT

The essential growth of the philosophy of India occurred in four major phases known as the Vedic period, the Upanishads, the period of the Epic, and that of the six systems. After this, variations of the last of the six systems, the Vedānta, concludes the development.

Vedic Period (1500–1000 B.C.). The Vedas, the earliest source of Indian philosophy, inculcated a naturalistic polytheism and a sacrificial ritualism. Later hymns show the beginnings of a metaphysical quest for the One and Ultimate Reality. At first, the new names for the One Supreme, though more abstract, were still personal: Prajāpati, Viśvakarma, etc. In the Brāmaṇas a philosophical monism traced the world to a single dynamic and self-evolving primordial principal, *aditi,* (the Infinite), *kāla* (Time), and particularly *tat ekam* (That One).

Upanishads (700–600 B.C.). The prevailing view of the Upanishads alternated between an undefined pantheism and a pure monism. Brahman was considered the ultimate principle that spontaneously manifests itself as the Universe. This single reality was conceived to be spiritual in nature and all else was explained as existing in and through it. Ātman was regarded as the inner essence of man or the true self that knows but can never be known; although it can be intuitively realized, it cannot be made an object of thought. The identification of these two concepts of Ātman and Brahman constitutes the essential teaching of the Upanishads, represented by the expressions *Tat tvam asi* (That thou art) and *Aham Brahmāsmi* (I am Brahman). The spiritual and unitary character of this absolute reality is itself expressed as *saccidananda* (Being-Consciousness-Bliss). Several passages of the Upanishads teach that the world is but an appearance and that it has no actual place in ultimate reality; several others grant reality to the world, though not conceiving it as apart from Brahman. The goal of life is to overcome the congenital ignorance of the nature of true self and of the ultimate reality by attaining *jñāna* (full enlightenment); the enlightened state is called *mokṣa* (release), which consists of attaining one's true self-identity with Brahman.

Epic Period (200 B.C.–200 A.D.). In this period not only did the different currents of Vedic thought flourish but new and important schools of philosophy and religion, such as Jainism and Buddhism, emerged. The *Bha-gavad Gītā* (Song of the Adorable) is monotheistic; Kṛṣṇa, the eternal Lord, is a personal God. His transcendent personality commands the whole religious orientation of the poem, as does his universal immanence; on both of which are founded the doctrine of *avatāra* (incarnation) and the personal relations between Kṛṣṇa and his devotees. At the same time, the *Gītā*, heir to the Upanishads, reflected difficulty in reconciling theistic religion with philosophy; on this account it is semipantheistic.

Six Systems (A.D. 100–400). The six systems are comprised of (1) the Nyāya founded by Gotama; (2) the Vaieśeṣika, by Kanāda; (3) the Śāṅkhya, by Kapila; (4) the Yoga, by Pantañjali; (5) the Mīmāmsā by Jaimini; and (6) the Vedānta by Bādarāyaṇa.

Nyāya and Vaiśeṣika (A.D. 100–300). The Nyāya, an analytical inquiry into all the objects of human knowledge, uses the canons of formal logic. It accepts the metaphysics of the Vaiśeṣika (discrimination), which classifies the objects of experience under logical categories and attributes the origin of the world to atoms. This combined system is dualistic because it posits the existence of eternal atoms, together with eternal souls or with the Supreme Soul of the universe.

Śāṅkhya (A.D. 350). The Śāṅkhya (synthetic enumeration) is dualistic, for it argues that impure matter can never originate from pure spirit and that something cannot be produced from nothing. *Prakriti* is the original primordial *tattva* (eternally existing substance), which is made up of three constituent *guṇas* (qualities/principles): *sattva* (purity and goodness), *rajas* (activity and passion) and *tamas* (inertia and darkness). These make up the whole world of the senses, evolved from *prakriti* in varying proportions. In the case of man, they make him divine and noble, human and selfish, or bestial and ignorant, respectively, according to the predominance of the corresponding *guṇas*. The 24 entities (*tattvas*), all evolving from primordial *prakriti* as cream out of milk, are distinguished from a 25th, *puruṣa,* the spirit that is by itself destitute of the *guṇas* of *prakriti* but liable to be bound by them.

Prakriti evolves only for the sake of the *puruṣa* and comes into union with *puruṣa* like a crystal vase with a flower, entrapping the soul, which is ''spirit'' in its nature within the framework of the body, which is like material. This ''unnatural association'' of the soul with the body is the state of bondage in Śāṅkhya leading to the continued entrapment of soul in an apparently never ending cycle of birth-death-rebirth (*samsāra*). The goal of Śāṅkhya, like the other six systems of philosophy, is to gain freedom from *samsāra* and this consists in gaining the knowledge of the 24 principles of *prakriti,* and rightly discriminating the domains of puruṣa and prakriti, which are totally different from, and opposed to one another. It is through such discriminate knowledge that one attains the ultimate state of freedom (*mokṣa*).

Obviously, the pure Śāṅkhya is more atheistic than the pure Nyāya for if the creation produced by *prakriti* has an independent existence of its own, without any connection with the particular *puruṣa* to which it is joined, there can be no need of an intelligent creator of the world or even of a superintending power.

Yoga (A.D. *300).* The Yoga (union) aims at proposing the means by which the human soul may attain complete union with the universal soul. This union can be effected even in the body by the constant habit of keeping the mind in its unmodified state and by the practice of complete suppression of passions. The last condition of suppression of all action is to be achieved only by meditation on the supreme Being, who is a spirit unaffected by works, having for one of his appellations the mystical monosyllable "Om." Indeed, the repetition of "Om" is supposed to be efficacious in giving knowledge of the Supreme and in preventing obstacles to Yoga.

Mīmāmsā (A.D. *150–200).* The Mīmāmsā (reflection) attempts to solve the doubts regarding Vedic texts caused by the discordant explanations of opposite schools. Its topics are arranged according to particular categories such as authoritativeness, indirect precept, etc., and are treated according to a logical method. It does not deny a god, but the tendency of its teaching is to grant authority neither to reason nor to God. The Veda is practically the only God. The whole aim of philosophy is to know *dharma* (duty), which consists in the performance of the rites and sacrifices prescribed by the Veda without reference to the will of a personal God; *dharma* is itself regarded as the bestower of rewards.

Vedānta (A.D. *600–650).* The Vedānta (end of Veda) conforms more closely than any other system to the teachings of the Upanishads.

The short aphorisms of the Vedānta (*Vedānta Sūtra*) are unintelligible by themselves and for this reason have given rise to many different systems, both nondualistic and dualistic, that served to interpret its thought. We will look at the systems Śaṅkara, Rāmānuja, and Madhva, and the *bhedābheda* schools of Bhāskara and Nimbārka.

Advaita (A.D. *788–820).* The nature of Śaṅkara's *advaita* (nondualism) is stated in the well-known formula: *ekam evādvitiyam* (one essence alone, without a second). The idea of God is associated with the concept of personality, which implies limitation and consequently plurality. Thus Śaṅkara regards the Absolute as impersonal and without attributes. He makes a distinction between *nirguṇa* Brahman (Brahman without attributes) and

saguṇa Brahman (Brahman with attributes); these are not two Brahmans but the same reality from different points of view, the higher and the lower. In the *nirguṇa* Brahman there is no distinction between substance and attributes: *sat* (being), *cit* (consciousness) and *ānanda* (bliss) constitute the essence of the Absolute and are not its attributes. Their purpose is to indicate that Brahman is not the mutable world, which is ultimately non-real, inert, and of the nature of misery. Because the Absolute is not an object as opposed to a subject, the Upanishads characterize it as "not this, nor that." This does not mean that Brahman is nonbeing; it is the very essence of the knower, self-revealed and self-established.

Īsvaratva (the appearance of being God) is superimposed on Brahman by *māyā* and thus Brahman becomes *īsvara* (a personal God). *Māyā* is the principle of self-determination or cosmic illusion; it hides the real and manifests the non-real. It accounts for the conception of Brahman as the material as well as the efficient cause of the creation, the preservation and the destruction of the world. But Brahman's causality consists not in *parināma* (transformation), but in *vivarta* (transfiguration); Brahman is immutable and eternal and so cannot change itself into the world. It is through *māyā* which is his inscrutable power, that God becomes the cause of the world. The universe emerges from *īsvara* and exists within God.

The world of plurality then is the product of *māyā* or *avidyā* (ignorance). Hence the world is not nonexistent although it is not real. That is to say, the world is only empirically real, whereas Brahman is absolutely real and delusions and dreams are only apparently real. The delusion of taking for a snake what is only a rope is given as an example to illustrate world-appearance. Just as darkness leads one to suppose that a rope is a snake, *avidyā* is responsible for the superimposition of the world on Brahman. Deluded by the *avidyā* the *jīva* (individual soul) identifies itself with the mind-body composite and considers itself to belong to the world of rebirth. The truth, however, is that the soul is not different from Brahman. This is declared by the famous text: "That thou art." The souls seem to be many because of different adjuncts, such as the body and the senses. In reality they are one; Brahman and the souls appear different because of *avidyā*. When this is removed through *jñāna* (intuitive knowledge), the soul is freed from its individuality and realizes its Brahmanhood.

Coming after the time of Śaṅkara, the *Bhedābheda* ("Difference and non-difference") or *Dvaitādvaita* (Two and One) school of Bhāskara (*c.* ninth century) makes a transition from Śaṅkara's Advaita to Rāmānuja's Viśiṣtadvaita. Bhāskara was very critical of Śaṅkara's view that the manifold world is ultimately illusory (*māyā*). For Bhāskara it is the one ultimate reality (*Brahman*) that *becomes* many, and therefore, multiplicity is real. For Bhāskara, *Brahman* is on the one hand, "the unconditioned, beyond the categories of time, space and causality" and on the other, it is the same Brahman, by its infinite power finitises itself into three forms of *kāraṇa* (cause), *kārya* (effect) and *jīva* (Individual self). *Jīva*, a part (*aṁśa*) of Brahman is neither totally different from Brahman or is identical with Brahman. From Bhāskara's view, the *jīva* is the *aṁśa* or element of the absolute that subjects itself to metaphysical and moral imperfections (*upādhis*) and gets implicated in endless cycle of birth-death-rebirth. When it is free, it becomes one with Brahman. The finite self is atomic and monadic; it is a separate and "independent" being. In this state of separation it is subject to the law of *karma,* and when the association with karma is dissolved in the *mokṣa* (salvational) state the "separated self" is reunited with the "unconditional" Brahman.

The religious discipline for Bhāskara includes the coordination of knowledge and duty, *jñāna-karma-samuccaya.* Unlike Śaṅkara's Advaita, for *Bhedābheda,* the discipline of *karma* (*karmayoga*), which is performance of ritualistic duties, is not simply a preliminary step that can be dispensed with while practicing the discipline of knowledge (*jñānayoga*). In all stages of life, a person must perform the deeds enjoined by the scriptures. However, Bhāskara admits that simple performance of ritualistic duties cannot lead one to final liberation (*mokṣa*); it is knowledge combined with duties that can enable one to the realization of Brahman, where one realizes that he or she is indeed the *aṁśa,* or part of the Supreme reality.

The school of Nimbarka (11th–12th century), which also falls under the broad category of Dvaitādvaita (Bhedābheda) has been largely influential in the development of Bengal Vaiṣṇavism, with Caitanya as its leading figure. Nimbārka, like Bhāskara, was also critical of the Advaita vedānta of Śaṅkara. The Absolute, Brahman or Kṛṣṇa is Unity-in-difference. This Absolute manifests itself through the numberless *jīvas* and manifold material forms without losing itself in them. It is the very nature of Brahman to be different from and identical with the world of selves and matter at the same time. The individual selves are infinite in number and atomic in size. The "beginningless" association with karma provides these selves (*jīvas*) with bodies and traps them into a cycle of birth-death-rebirth (*samsāra*). Redemption is possible only through the grace of Kṛṣṇa. In the state of liberation (*mokṣa*) one realizes one's unity with Kṛṣṇa and abides in Kṛṣṇa as part of his energy.

The Vedāntic school of *Viśiṣṭādvaita* (Qualified non-dualism) is built on teachings of Rāmānuja (1050–1137), who was critical of Śaṅkara's non-dualistic understanding of the nature of Brahman, establishing that there are three eternal principles, *Brahman, ātman* and *prakṛti,* the Absolute, the principle of subjectivity (Self) and primal matter, respectively. These three principles are related to one another in the following manner: *ātman* and *prakṛti* are inseparably related to *Brahman* as its modes, as body and soul. Rāmānuja asserted that *ātman* and *prakṛti* constitute the body (*śarīra*) of *Brahman* (God/Viṣṇu), and *Brahman* in turn becomes their indweller (*śarīrin*). From the point of view of *Brahman* being the sole controlling principle, what is real is *One*; but from the fact there are three ontological principles (*tattvas*) this Oneness is *qualified,* and not *absolute* as in the case of Śaṅkara's nondualistic Vedānta. According to Rāmānuja, the world that we experience is not ultimately illusory (*māyā*). Creation is real; it is a process by which primal matter becomes the manifold universe, and *ātman* becomes the manifold *jīvas* (individual selves) with physical and subtle bodies. God is the instrumental cause for creation, although creation is not purposive in the sense that it is intended to accomplish anything. It is an expression of divine playfulness (*līlī*). In such a play, the *jīva* is invited to behold the glory of God and take part in divine play.

It is the failure of the individual to participate in this playful world with a playful frame of mind, that transforms the *līlī* world into *samsaric, karma*-bound world. In this "fallen state," the playful God assumes the role of a redeemer/savior. It is in this role that several of the divine manifestations take place including the ten major incarnations (*avatāras*), such as Rāmā and Kṛṣṇa. All these manifestations highlight "accessibility" (*saulabhya*) and closeness of the divine to the *jīvas* in bondage (*samsāra*), so that the *jīva* can benefit spiritually and be redeemed by the presence of the divine in the *samsaric* world. Redemption is to be gained through knowledge, the knowledge that the *jīva* truly belongs to God as his body (*śarīra*). This knowledge is to be gained by divine grace and through the practices of the disciplines (yoga) of *karma, jñana* and *bhakti,* action, knowledge, and devotion. Through disinterested action one's mind becomes purified; through knowledge, one realizes the nature of the self as different from the body; and through *bhakti* or loving devotion one realizes the relationship of the self with the divine, and the released soul enjoys the highest bliss in the presence of God, beholding and serving God.

Dvaita Madhva (1197–1276) provides a dualistic interpretation to the text of the *Brahmasūtras,* and hence his system of Vedānta is called Dvaita (Dualism). He reads the Upanisadic statement *tatvamasi* as *a-tvamasi,* "Thou are not That." He makes an absolute distinction between God, who is the only independent (*svatantra*) reality, and all other things, both animate and inanimate, which are dependent *(paratantra)* realities. God is omnipotent and transcendent and is the author of creation, maintenance and destruction of the cosmos. There are five-fold differences among these three principles, according to Madhva. Difference between God *(Brahman)* and souls *(jīvas),* between souls themselves, among inanimate objects *(prakṛti)* themselves, between inanimate objects and God, between inanimate matter and souls; all these differences are eternal. Since the distinction between God and the world is absolute and unqualified, for Madhva, the world is not the body of God. Therefore Madhava's Dvaita Vedānta is different from Śaṅkara and Rāmānuja, though it has many points common with Rāmānuja such as salvation through grace and equation of Brahman with Viṣṇu.

SYSTEMATIC NOTIONS

Basic Ideas. Recurrent themes in Indian philosophy deal with the soul, the matter of the universe, the union of body and soul, and the nature of God.

The *ātman* (soul) is eternal from the viewpoint of both its beginning and its end. It is of two kinds: the supreme universal Soul *(Brahman, Paramātman)* and the personal individual soul of living beings *(jīvātman).*

The matter or substance out of which the universe has been evolved is eternal. Evolution takes place from gross particles of matter, according to some materialists, or, as taught in the Vedānta, from the soul itself when this is overspread by *māyā.* This supposes the common doctrine of the Hindus that nothing can be produced out of nothing *(nāvastuno vastusiddhih).*

Although the soul is abstract knowledge, it can exercise thought, consciousness, sensation and volition only when connected with external objects of sensation, invested with some bodily form and joined to *manas* (mind). The union of soul and body is productive of bondage and, in the case of human souls, misery. All *karma,* whether good or bad, leads to bondage because it entails a consequence: good actions must be rewarded and bad ones punished. Souls have to transmigrate in order to work out the consequence of action. True knowledge of God and loving devotion to Him, obtained through His *prasāda* (grace), liberates the soul from this bondage.

The religious belief in many gods, reflected in the early Vedic hymns gives way to MONOTHEISM, with Prajāpati (Father-God) dominating all other gods. The theism of the epics *Mahābhārata* and *Rāmāyana* takes a more personal form in the conceptions of the two deities Śiva and Viṣṇu (Vishnu) as Supreme Gods, by the Śaiva and Vaiṣṇava communities respectively. Indian MONISM

traces the world not to a Creator but to a primordial principle that unfolds itself as the Universe in all its diversity. *Brahman* is the ultimate ground of all differentiated reality, identical with the *ātman* of every individual soul. Indian PANTHEISM conceives all existence as the parts of one Being who pervades the whole world, yet is not exhausted thereby.

Critique. As a system of religious thought and as an expression of faith and life in God, Hindu philosophy represents a high-water mark of India's deeply religious intuition. The way in which Hindu religion permeates one's entire life, as opposed to the idea that religion is a separate compartment occupying only a small portion thereof, is close to the Catholic ideal. The supreme transcendence and perfect simplicity of thc Absolute in Śaṅkara's philosophy, as well as the infinite lovableness and inexhaustible compassion of God in Rāmānuja's philosophy, are expressed in terms that are deeply moving for the Christian soul. The constant belief in the divine governance of the world and in the utter dependence of the "creature" on God is no less remarkable. The same may be said for the divine immanence and indwelling in all things. In this sense, Indian philosophy testifies to the untiring efforts by human beings to reach and worship the true God and to find rest in God alone.

See Also: BUDDHISM; HINDUISM; JAINISM; PANENTHEISM.

Bibliography: M. HIRIYANNA, *The Essentials of Indian Philosophy* (London 1949). S. CHATTERJEE and D. DATTA, *An Introduction to Indian Philosophy* (5th ed. Calcutta 1954). S. N. DASGUPTA, *A History of Indian Philosophy,* 5 v. (Cambridge, Eng. 1922–55). P. DEUSSEN, *The System of the Vedānta,* tr. C. JOHNSTON (Chicago 1912). K. K. KLOSTERMAIER, *A Survey of Hinduism,* 2d ed. (Albany 1994). V. S. GHATE, *The Vedanta* (Poona 1960). S. RADHAKRISHNAN, *Indian Philosophy* (London 1948). S. RADHAKRISHNAN and C. A. MOORE, *A Source Book in Indian Philosophy* (Princeton, NJ 1957). D. RIEPE, *The Philosophy of India and Its Impact on American Thought* (Springfield, IL 1970). P. T. RAJU, *The Philosophical Traditions of India* (London 1971).

[M. DHAVAMONY/K.R. SUNDARARAJAN]

INDIAN RITES CONTROVERSY

The term "Indian Rites" designates certain customs that Jesuit missionaries, notably Roberto de NOBILI and others, permitted to their neophytes in South India until their practice was forbidden by the Holy See. The region comprises the former kingdoms of Madura, Mysore, and the Carnatic.

Nobili's Approach to Inculturation. According to the missionary method in use in India in the sixteenth century, neophytes were expected to dress, eat, and behave as did their Portuguese colonists, and they were also required to take Portuguese surnames. These demands were considered intolerable by most Hindus, who termed the neophytes *parangis* (detested foreigners) and treated them as outcasts. At the beginning of the seventeenth century, Roberto de Nobili, SJ, introduced to the Madura mission a method of inculturation that had been successfully applied in China by the Italian Jesuit, Matteo RICCI, and encouraged by the Jesuit superior of the Far East Mission, Alessandro VALIGNANO. De Nobili's approach to inculturation, which then seemed radical and downright revolutionary, consisted in adapting Christianity to the Indian context by adopting indigenous rites and customs as far as possible without conceding any fundamental Christian truth or principle. Instead of forcing Indians to become Europeans, the missionaries would try to adjust their own way of life and preaching to existing Indian cultural heritage and social conventions.

Nobili took the saffron dress of a *sannyasi* (ascetic), lived and ate as an Indian, and studied the nondualistic Vedanta as a means of gaining entrance to the Brahmin intelligentsia in Madura, at whom his apostolate was aimed. After probing the history of Brahmin and Hindu practices, Nobili permitted his disciples and new converts the following usages that he considered primarily civil, not religious: (1) the *kudumi* (tuft), a distinctive sign of the Brahmin caste; (2) the thread, also a sign of the Brahmin caste; (3) the *santal* (mark on the brow); (4) the usual ablutions practiced by upper castes and virtually indispensable in a country with a climate as hot as India's.

Suspicion and Controversy. The Brahmins of Madura welcomed Nobili's method and under its conditions some became Christians. But Nobili's Portuguese colleagues were suspicious. They declared Nobili overtolerant, and apparently they feared that he was placing in jeopardy the Portuguese position as masters of India. Nobili defended himself by appealing to texts from St. Paul, St. Thomas Aquinas, and such later theologians as Juan Azor (1536–1603) and Domingo Bañez (1528–1604). At the bidding of Pope Paul V, Christopher de Sa, archbishop of Goa, summoned Nobili before the Inquisition of Goa. The archbishop, the Dominicans, the Franciscans, and the secular priests voted against Nobili, while the Inquisitor D'Almeida, Francisco Ros, SJ (archbishop of Cranganore), and all the Jesuits voted in his favor. Thus from the beginning there were sharply divided views. Nobili had made a distinction between religious rites and civil customs; he justified the latter where necessary by eliminating superstitious elements and directing the intention. For example, Indians often marked their brow with a mixture of ashes and sandal-paste; therefore, said Nobili, let us hallow this mixture with a Christian blessing and impose it not once a year, on Ash Wednesday,

but more frequently. His opponents argued that the Hindus were noted for their absence of logic. Therefore, in permitting them to retain certain rites one risked, despite all precautions, leaving them with the idea that Christianity did not exclude their earlier ways of religious thinking and behavior.

The dispute was submitted to Rome and to the grand inquisitor of Portugal. Martins de Mascarenhas (in 1621) and Gregory XV (in 1623, in his constitution *Romanae Sedis*) pronounced in favor of Nobili. For the moment, de Nobili's approach had triumphed and the Jesuits adopted it, dividing themselves into two groups: *sannyasis* to evangelize the higher castes and *pandara swamis* for the backward castes. In Madura, Mysore, and Trichinopoly good results were obtained; by 1704 the Christians of the Madura district numbered 90,000. In the course of the seventeenth and eighteenth centuries new concessions had been added to those originally adopted by Nobili.

In 1687 French Jesuits arrived to work alongside the Capuchins in the recently founded French colony of Pondicherry. They collaborated with Jesuits in Madura and created a special mission in the Carnatic following Nobili's method. Soon accusations against the Jesuits were being sent to Rome, and in order to uphold them the Capuchin François Marie de Tours returned there in 1703. He submitted 36 questions relating to the usages of the Indian Rites to the Congregation for the Propagation of the Faith.

Arrival of Charles de Tournon. Meanwhile Clement XI had appointed the Piedmontese prelate Charles Thomas Maillard de TOURNON as his *legatus a later* to examine the vexed question of Chinese rites, which was dividing not only missionaries but European thinkers (*see* CHINESE RITES CONTROVERSY). In view of the new complaints, he now instructed Tournon to interrupt his journey in order to examine the rites and customs of South India. Tournon, who knew neither Hindi nor the Portuguese language, and was forced to seek his information second hand, arrived in Pondicherry on Nov. 6, 1703, and remained until July of 1704. Sickness prevented him from visiting any part of the inland mission, but he gathered data on the usages in question, notably from the Jesuits Jean Bouchet (1655–1732) and Charles Bertoldi (1659–1720). On June 23, 1704, Tournon signed a decree condemning in 16 points several usages permitted to the Jesuits. His decree was confirmed by the Holy Office on Jan. 7, 1706, and at the same time a consultor was named to examine the question further. The Jesuits Boucher and Francisco Laynez (1656–1715), the former French, the latter Portuguese, came to Rome to defend their method in South India. In 1707 Laynez published *Defensio Indi-*

carum Missionum Madurensis to show that the missionaries had tolerated nothing superstitious, and he distributed copies in India after his appointment as bishop of Mylapore in 1708. By an *oraculum vivae vocis* granted to the procurator of the Madura mission, Clement XI declared the missionaries obliged to observe Tournon's decree "insofar as the Divine glory and the salvation of souls would permit." Appealing to this clause of the *oraculum,* the Jesuits continued to tolerate the usages condemned by Tournon. On Sept. 1, 1712, Clement renewed the Holy Office's decree of 1706, and in a brief of Sept. 17, 1712, reprimanded Laynez for failing to take action to carry out Tournon's decree. On July 24, 1715, the cardinal prefect of the Congregation for the Propagation of the Faith sent this brief and the decree of 1706 to Pondicherry, where they were promulgated on Jan. 11, 1716, Laynez having died meanwhile. In protest, the Jesuits sent Pierre Martin (1665–1716) and Broglia Brandolini (d. 1747) to Rome to secure further examination of the Indian Rites. Innocent XIII appointed a special Congregation for this purpose, with Prospero Lambertini, the future Pope Benedict XIV, as secretary. Brandolini published a justification of the rites, to which Luigi Lucino, OP, replied on behalf of the Holy Office.

The Oath of 16 Points. The special congregation's examination of the rites continued under Benedict XIII (1724–30) and Clement XII (1730–40). In a brief dated Dec. 12, 1727, Benedict XIII confirmed Tournon's decree. In 1733 the decisions of Tournon's decree, formulated in 16 points, were again examined by the Holy Office, and confirmed in 1734 by Clement XII's brief *Compertum exploratumque.* This, however, did not end the matter, for some missionaries tried to evade the injunctions of the brief. Finally with the bull *Omnium sollicitudinum* of Sept. 12, 1744, Benedict XIV decided the question of the Indian rites in accordance with the brief of 1734 and obliged all missionaries working in Madura, Mysore, and the Carnatic to swear a 16-point oath relating to the rites.

The oath bound the missionaries as follows: (1) They were obliged in the administration of Baptism to use sacramentals, notably saliva (which Hindus regarded with abhorrence) and insufflation; (2) a candidate for Baptism was obliged to take the name of a saint in the Roman Martyrology, and Indian names, formerly acceptable, were now forbidden; (3) in all ceremonies Latin or Latin translated into an Indian language was to be used; in the latter case exact equivalents must be found for the holy cross, saints, and holy things; (4) missionaries were obliged to baptize newborn babies with haste; (5) marriage before puberty was forbidden, as well as the custom whereby the bridegroom hangs on the bride's neck a nuptial jewel called *tali;* (6) Christian wives were forbidden to wear the *tali;* (7) Christians were forbidden to wear the girdle composed of 108 threads dyed red used by Hindus for hanging the *tali;* (8) the supposed "superstitious" ceremonies of Hindu marriages were forbidden, such as cutting the hair of bride and groom and use of the branch called *arasciomara;* (9) the matrimonial rite of breaking a coconut in order to foretell the future was prohibited; (10) it was the custom for South Indian women to remain at home during their menstrual periods until they had been ritually purified; henceforth Christian women were not to be kept from the Sacraments for this reason; (11) celebrations in honor of a young girl at her first menstruation were forbidden; (12) missionaries were commanded to administer the Sacraments to sick backward-caste Christians in their dwellings, publicly; (13) Christian singers and musicians were forbidden to take part in ceremonies in Hindu temples; (14) baths were permitted, provided they were not linked with superstition either in timing or in any other way; missionaries were allowed to wash only as a measure of hygiene, not with the intention of passing as *sannyasis* or Brahmins; (15) marking the brow with ashes of cow-dung or with red-and-white paste in accordance with Hindu customs was forbidden, and Christians were obliged to keep to the sign of the Cross and the use of palm ashes duly blessed; and (16) Christians were forbidden to read Hindu scriptures and other classical and devotional texts under penalty of excommunication.

All the Jesuits in the designated missions took the prescribed oath and observed its various points. They were, however, allowed to designate some missionaries for the exclusive service of the backward castes. This dispensation disappeared with the suppression of the Society of Jesus in 1773. Pius XII (1939–58) revisited the Indian rites controversy as part of an overall review of the Chinese rites controversy. On Dec. 8, 1939, the oath relating to Chinese rites was abolished and on April 9, 1940, the missionaries of India were dispensed from the oath relating to the Indian rites.

Bibliography: For bibliography: *see* NOBILI, ROBERTO DE.

[V. CRONIN/EDS.]

INDIANA, CATHOLIC CHURCH IN

A state in north central U.S., in the Middle West, bounded on the north by Lake Michigan and Michigan state, on the east by Ohio, on the south by the Ohio River, and on the west by Illinois and the Wabash River. The capital and largest city is Indianapolis. Agriculture predominates in the central part of the state, with some industries in its smaller cities. Since 1905, after U.S. Steel and other corporations built mills in and near Gary and East Chicago, the heaviest industries have centered in the northwestern counties. In 2001 Catholics were about 13 percent of the state's population—759,239 in a total population of 5,908,407. They were served by five dioceses that constituted the ecclesiastical province of Indianapolis, namely, the Archdiocese of Indianapolis, Fort Wayne-South Bend, Evansille, Lafayette, and Gary.

Archdiocese/Diocese	Year Created
Archdiocese of Indianapolis	1944
Diocese of Evansville	1944
Diocese of Fort Wayne-South Bend	1857
Diocese of Gary	1956
Diocese of Lafayette in Indiana	1944

History. It is not known just what tribes inhabited the region before the pioneer explorations, but shortly after the French explorers and missionaries reached the western Great Lakes, Algonquian tribes had moved south of the Great Lakes. From the northwest came the Miami, Potawatomi, Kickapoo, and Ouia; and from the east came remnants of the Delaware and Shawnee. During the French period (c. 1680–1763), water routes through the area connected French Canada with Louisiana, and centers for fur trading were established at Fort St. Joseph, Fort Wayne (then Fort Miami), and Ouiatenon, near the site of the present Lafayette; Vincennes, at the site of the present city of that name, was the most important center. By the Treaty of Paris of 1763, the region east of the Mississippi was ceded to England by France and was then ruled as part of Quebec under Gov. Thomas Gage. Although English traders and pioneers had begun to infiltrate the region, the inhabitants were predominantly French at the outbreak of the American Revolution. George Rogers Clark captured Vincennes assisted by Pierre GIBAULT, the Canadian missionary who served the Illinois missions. Indiana was part of the Northwest Territory established by the Ordinance of 1787. In the war of 1812 the power of the native tribes in the area was destroyed. After Ohio, Illinois, and Michigan were cut off as separate states, the territory of Indiana was reduced to its present dimensions and received into the Union as the 19th state on Dec. 11, 1816.

Missionary Activity. The northern region of what was to become the state of Indiana fell under the jurisdiction of the bishop of Quebec from 1674 to 1789. The earliest missionaries to travel to the area, visited near South Bend, on the St. Joseph River, in 1679, and was attended later by Jesuits from the old St. Joseph mission near what is now Niles, Michigan. After the suppression of the Society caused the Jesuits to withdrew from the missions along the St. Joseph River, priests based in Vincennes where the French had established a fort, visited the area, including Gibault, who signed the St. Joseph baptismal register; Louis Payet, who conducted Christmas services at Fort Miami in 1789; and Jean Rivet, who visited Indians in the area. After the American War of Independence, the state-to-be fell under the jurisdiction of Bishop John Carroll of Baltimore from 1789 until 1810 when the Diocese of Bardstown, Ky., was established. After 1808,

missionaries from Bardstown and Louisiana served Vincennes where John Leo Champomier, resident pastor from 1823 to 1831, constructed St. Francis Xavier Church, which became the cathedral when Vincennes was established as a diocese in 1834. It was there that Simon BRUTÉ, was installed as the first bishop, Nov. 5, 1834.

Diocese of Vincennes. Bruté's new diocese embraced all of Indiana and the eastern third of Illinois until the Diocese of Chicago was created in 1843. For his scattered flock he had only one church, an academy founded by the Sisters of Charity of Nazareth, Ky., and one priest. Although several missionaries were laboring in the diocese, only Simon Lalumière was permanently attached to it. After making a visitation of his diocese, Bruté went to Europe for aid and returned with 18 missionaries, including several Eudists. Before his death in 1839, Bruté established a college and seminary and continued the local academy, staffing it with the Sisters of Charity from Emmitsburg, Md.

Bishop Bruté was succeeded by his vicar-general, Celestine de la Hailandière, who was consecrated in Paris on Aug. 18, 1839. The new bishop returned to Vincennes with additional clerical recruits and the promise of foundations by the Sisters of Providence and the Congregation of Holy Cross, both of the Diocese of Le Mans, France. The sisters, under Mother Theodore GUERIN founded the convent of St. Mary-of-the-Woods, Ind., in 1840; opened an academy; and established a number of schools. The Eudists opened St. Gabriel College in Vincennes, and the seminary was reorganized and expanded. In 1844, Hailandière summoned the first diocesan synod. Despite his vigilance in checking tendencies toward TRUSTEEISM, he experienced many other difficulties, including that of Roman Weinzoepfel (a local aspect of American NATIVISM 1842–44), the departure of the Eudists, and the closing of their college. He resigned in 1847 and returned to France (where he died in 1882). His successor was also French-born, Stephen Bazin of Mobile, Ala., but his episcopate lasted less than a year (Oct. 24, 1847–April 23, 1848).

Bishop Bazin was succeeded in January 1849 by his vicar-general Maurice de St. Palais, who was a major fig-

Bell tower of the Basilica of the Sacred Heart, South Bend, Indiana. (©Layne Kennedy/CORBIS)

ure in the Church of Indiana for the next 28 years. During St. Palais' long tenure, the Catholic population, swelled by German immigrants, increased rapidly. St. Palais went to Europe (1851–52) and secured the establishment by the Benedictine Abbey of Maria Einsiedeln, Switzerland, of St. Meinrad (1854) in Spencer County, Ind., which became an independent abbey in 1870. The monks opened a college and seminary. In 1867 Benedictine sisters from Covington, Ky., established Immaculate Conception Convent and eventually an academy in nearby Ferdinand. Through the instrumentality of Francis Joseph Rudolf similar developments occurred in Oldenburg, Franklin County, where in 1851 Sister Teresa of Vienna founded a convent of Franciscan sisters who also opened an academy. In 1866, the Franciscan friars of the Cincinnati, Ohio, province took the first steps toward establishing a monastery that served as a house of studies until 1958, when the institution became a brothers' training school. In the same district, Brothers of Christian Instruction from France conducted St. Maurice Institute from 1857

to 1862. In Vincennes he established an orphanage for girls (1849) and one for boys (1850). In 1860 the latter was moved to Highland, Ind., and in 1876 the girls were sent to St. Ann Orphanage in Terre Haute, Ind. St. Charles Seminary, which the bishop reorganized in 1853, was abandoned, when in 1860 he sent the college students to St. Thomas, Ky., and in 1866, the seminarians to St. Meinrad.

In the period following the Civil War, large churches were erected in the growing cities, notably St. John in Indianapolis and Assumption in Evansville. In Indianapolis the Sisters of Providence, who had managed a hospital during the war, conducted St. John Infirmary for some time, while in Evansville, the Sisters of Charity of Emmitsburg opened St. Mary Hospital (1872). The Conventual Franciscans in 1872 were placed in charge of two parishes in Terre Haute where for a few years they conducted St. Bonaventure Lyceum. On property that they later acquired at Floyd Knobs in the southern part of the state, they established a training school for brothers and, in 1910, Mt. St. Francis College, a minor seminary. In 1873 the Little Sisters of the Poor and the Sisters of the Good Shepherd established their foundations, and in 1875 the Franciscan friars of the St. Louis Province established a monastery and Sacred Heart parish. Also in 1875 a diocesan weekly, the *Indiana Catholic and Record*, was begun.

Meanwhile, missionary activity in northern Indiana had begun in earnest with the arrival at St. Joseph mission of Father Stephen Theodore BADIN in September 1830. From there, Badin visited the Native Americans at Twin Lakes, near the present Plymouth, Ind., and the German and Irish Catholic workers on the canals between Fort Wayne and Terre Haute, Ind. On Feb. 2, 1833, Badin secured a charter for the St. Joseph Orphan Asylum from the Indiana state Legislature. In Kentucky he obtained two Sisters of Charity for this asylum, which he built in 1834 on the site of the future University of NOTRE DAME. The sisters did not stay long and the orphan asylum was soon abandoned. After 1839 St. Joseph mission was attended by priests from the Diocese of Detroit, Mich., until the arrival of Edward Sorin, CSC, who founded the University of Notre Dame on Nov. 26, 1842. The eastern part of the region was being cared for by Rev. Louis Mueller in Fort Wayne and the western part by Rev. Irenaeus Saint Cyr from Chicago. Augustus Martin and Claude François made Logansport the center of their missionary activity, with other missions established at Lagro, Peru, Lafayette, St. John's, and Huntington.

In 1857, in response to a petition of the first provincial council of Cincinnati (the Diocese of Vincennes since 1850 had been a suffragan see in the Province of

Cincinnati), the Diocese of Fort Wayne was erected, confining the Diocese of Vincennes to the southern half of the state. The first bishop of the new diocese, German-born John Henry Luers, was ordained in 1846 and did pastoral work in Cincinnati, Ohio, until his consecration on Jan. 10, 1858. Arriving in his diocese, the new bishop found 26 churches and 20 priests. The Catholics were mostly Irish laborers and some German immigrants who settled along the Indiana-Ohio state line. Notre Dame was a boarding school for boys and St. Mary's an academy for girls. Besides the priests, brothers, and sisters of Holy Cross at Notre Dame, there were the Sisters of Providence of Terre Haute, who conducted parish schools, and the Poor Handmaids of Jesus Christ, who immigrated from Germany to Hessen Cassel in 1863 and later went to Fort Wayne and Donaldson, conducting orphanages, hospitals, and schools.

Luers died suddenly on June 29, 1871, and was succeeded by Joseph DWENGER, CPPS, who was consecrated in Cincinnati on April 14, 1872. During his administration, he established a diocesan school board and added many parish schools. A new orphanage for boys was established near Lafayette in 1875 and one for girls in Fort Wayne in 1886. In 1891, at his invitation, the Fathers of the Precious Blood began St. Joseph's College near Rensselaer. Dwenger died on Jan. 22, 1893, and Bp. Joseph Rademacher of Nashville, Tenn., was transferred to Fort Wayne on July 13. His brief episcopate was characterized by an increase in the number of churches, missions, and schools. He also remodeled the cathedral before his health became impaired in 1898. His death on Jan. 12, 1900, ended a long illness during which his vicar-general, J. H. Guendling, was administrator of the diocese.

Move to Indianapolis. *Chatard.* In 1878 Francis Silas CHATARD was named as the successor of St. Palais, who died the previous year. Chatard established the episcopal residence in Indianapolis, while the cathedral and the title of the see were continued at Vincennes. Synods were held in 1878, 1880, 1886, and 1891. Although the bishop adopted a rather rigorous attitude toward secret societies, he encouraged Catholic societies of national character. A mutual insurance company for church property in the diocese was formed in 1883 and functioned until its liquidation in 1950. Chatard's most progressive efforts affected the clergy: he sent a number of seminarians to European institutions; established irremovable rectors, diocesan courts, and deanery conferences; ordered an annual collection for aged and infirm priests; encouraged a Clergy Relief Union, organized in 1894; and founded a St. Michael Society to ensure Masses for deceased clerics. He secured permission for the use in the diocese of the Calendar of the city of Rome, necessitating a special Ordo that developed into a Year Book.

In 1889, after a fire at St. Meinrad, the commercial department of the college was transferred to Jasper, where it became Jasper Academy (later in 1933 it was reestablished in Aurora, Ill., as Marmion Academy). In 1909 the high school and the college were distinctly separated at St. Mary-of-the-Woods. The Sisters of Charity of Emmitsburg founded St. Vincent Hospital, Indianapolis, in 1881, and the Poor Sisters of St. Francis Seraph of Perpetual Adoration from Lafayette opened hospitals in Terre Haute (1882), New Albany (1901), and Beech Grove (1913). In Evansville the Little Sisters of the Poor established a house in 1882 and the Poor Clares a convent in 1897.

By an Apostolic Brief dated March 28, 1898 the title of the diocese changed to Diocese of Indianapolis, making it the episcopal see. In 1906 SS. Peter and Paul Cathedral was built in Indianapolis, complete except for the façade, which was added in 1936.

Chartrand. Joseph Chartrand, who had been appointed coadjutor in 1910, succeeded to the see when Chatard died in 1918. The new bishop applied the decrees of Pius X regarding Holy Communion with enthusiasm and success and zealously promoted vocations to the priesthood. In 1921 the Daughters of Isabella opened St. Elizabeth Home in Indianapolis for working girls, and the Knights of Columbus of Indiana founded Gibault Home for delinquent boys near Terre Haute. Conducted at first by diocesan priests, this last institution was given to the charge of the Brothers of Holy Cross in 1934. In 1926 the Sisters of Providence opened Ladywood School in Indianapolis, which superseded the academy at St. Mary-of-the-Woods. Several high schools were built throughout the diocese, including Reitz Memorial High School, Evansville, and Cathedral High School, Indianapolis.

Margaret Mary Hospital, conducted by the Sisters of the Poor of St. Francis of Hartwell, Ohio, was opened in Batesville, Ind., in 1932. The Carmelite Monastery of the Resurrection, founded in New Albany, Ind., in 1922, was reestablished in Indianapolis in 1932, and members of this monastery founded the Carmel of St. Joseph in Terre Haute in 1947.

Noll. John Francis NOLL, then editor of the *Sunday Visitor* and pastor in Huntington, Ind., was consecrated by Cardinal G. W. Mundelein on June 30, 1925. Noll established seminary burses for the education of poor boys of the diocese; built a new orphanage for boys at Fort Wayne to replace St. Joseph Orphanage in Lafayette; created a diocesan Catholic Charities Board with centers in Fort Wayne, South Bend, Gary, and Hammond; and established a diocesan Council of Catholic Women and a Catholic Youth Organization. He set up Bishop Noll High School in Hammond and St. Joseph High School in

South Bend, and combined the high schools in Fort Wayne into one Central Catholic High School.

Noll was honored with the title of archbishop *ad personam* on Sept. 2, 1953, but suffered a stroke shortly after.

Pursley. Bishop Leo A. Pursley, who had been named auxiliary to Noll on July 22, 1950, became apostolic administrator of Fort Wayne on Feb. 21, 1955. After Noll's death on July 31, 1956, Pursley was appointed to the see and installed as its sixth bishop on Feb. 26, 1957.

Ritter. A native of New Albany, Ind., Joseph E. Ritter, was named auxiliary bishop in 1933 and upon Chartrand's death a year later succeeded him as ordinary. Ritter became the first archbishop of Indianapolis when, by decree of Pope Pius XII in December 1944, Indianapolis was made a metropolitan see.

Despite the economic depression of the 1930s, Ritter enlarged the diocesan curia, instituted three new deaneries, and created a number of new offices and committees, including a superintendent of schools, a Church music commission, and a rural life board, and reorganized Catholic Charities in the diocese. In 1934 the Jesuits established West Baden College for the scholastics of the Chicago province, and in 1937 the Franciscan Sisters of Oldenburg opened Marian College for Women in Indianapolis. Under Ritter's direction 14 new parishes and missions were established, but the action for which he gained national attention was the initiative he took in integrating the Catholic schools. In 1946 Ritter was transferred to the Archdiocese of St. Louis and named a cardinal in 1961.

The same decree that elevated Indianapolis to archbishopric status created the Dioceses of Evansville and Lafayette. To form the Diocese of Evansville 12 counties in the southwestern part of the state bordering on Illinois were carved out of the Archdiocese of Indianapolis. The first bishop, Henry J. Grimmelsman served until he retired in 1965 (he died June 26, 1972) and was succeeded by Bishop Paul F. Leibold (1966–1972). Four counties in the southern part of the Diocese of Fort Wayne were detached to form the Diocese of Lafayette. The first bishop, John G. Bennett who had been pastor in Garrett, Ind., was appointed the first bishop (1945–1957). A year before he died, Bishop John Carberry was appointed coadjutor with right of succession. Carberry was transferred to the diocese of Columbus (1965–1968) and later became cardinal and archbishop of St. Louis (he died June 17, 1998). In 1956 the western part of the Diocese of Fort Wayne was separated to form the new See of Gary, with Andrew G. Grutka as first bishop. Bishop Grutka retired in 1984 and was succeeded by the auxiliary bishop of Gr-

eensburg, Pa., Norbert F. Gaughan who retired in 1996. (Bishop Grutka died Nov. 11, 1993; Bishop Gaughan, Oct. 1, 1999.)

Catholic Institutions of Higher Education. Indiana is home to the University of Notre Dame du Lac (established, 1842, sponsored by the Congregation of the Holy Cross), the nation's premier Catholic university, and Saint-Mary-of-the-Woods College (established 1840, sponsored by the Sisters of Providence), the nation's oldest Catholic liberal arts college for women, and Saint Mary's College in Notre Dame (an all-women college sponsored by the Sisters of the Holy Cross, MADELEVA [Wolff], Mary). Other Catholic institutions of higher learning in the state include the University of Saint Francis in Fort Wayne (sponsored by the Sisters of St. Francis of Perpetual Adoration), Saint Joseph's College, Rensselaer (sponsored by the Society of the Precious Blood) and Marian College in Indianapolis (sponsored by the Sisters of the Third Order Regular of St. Francis).

Bibliography: H. A. ALERDING, *A History of the Catholic Church in the Diocese of Vincennes* (Indianapolis 1883). C. BLANCHARD, *History of the Catholic Church in Indiana,* 2 v. (Logansport, Ind. 1898). T. T. MCAVOY, *The Catholic Church in Indiana, 1789–1834* (New York 1940). J. H. SCHAUINGER, *Cathedrals in the Wilderness* (Milwaukee 1952). M. C. SCHROEDER, *The Catholic Church in the Diocese of Vincennes, 1847–1877* (Washington, D.C. 1946). J. P. DONNELLY, *Pierre Gibault, Missionary, 1737–1802* (Chicago 1971).

[T. T. MCAVOY/R. GORMAN/EDS.]

INDIANAPOLIS, ARCHDIOCESE OF

Established originally as the Diocese of Vincennes in 1834, the see was transferred to Indianapolis (*Indianapolitana*) in 1898 and became an archdiocese in 1944. In the year 2001 it comprised 38 counties and the township of Harrison, Spencer County (13,757 square miles), in the southern part of Indiana. There were 227,501 Catholics, about ten percent of the total population (2,359,104). The ecclesiastical Province of Indianapolis includes the other Indiana dioceses: Evansville, Fort Wayne-South Bend, Gary, and Lafayette.

From 1834, when Vincennes was established as a separate diocese, it was governed by the following prelates: Simon Gabriel Brute, S.S. 1834–d. 1839; Celestine de la Hailandiere, 1839–r. 1847 [d. France, 1882]; John S. Bazin, 1847–d. 1848; Maurice de St. Palais, 1849–d. 1877; Francis Silas Chatard, 1878–d. 1918; Joseph Chartrand, 1918–d. 1933; John Elmer Ritter, 1934–1946 [St Louis, d. 1967]; Paul G. Schulte, 1946–r. 1970 [d. Feb. 17, 1984]; George J. Biskup, 1970–r. 1979, [d. Oct. 17, 1979]; Edward O'Meara, 1979–1992; Daniel M. Buechlein, OSB, 1992—.

Diocese of Vincennes. French traders established a fort at Vincennes in 1752 and subsequently it became a the residence of French missionaries. In 1789, after the American Revolution it became part of the newly created Diocese of Baltimore. Later it was transferred to the see of Bardstown, Ky., when that diocese was established in 1808. John Leo Champomier, resident pastor from 1823 to 1831, constructed St. Francis Xavier Church, which became the cathedral when Vincennes was established as a diocese in 1834, and it was there that Simon BRUTÉ, was installed as the first bishop, Nov. 5, 1834. Work on the cathedral was completed in 1841.

In the beginning the Diocese of Vincennes included all of Indiana and, before Chicago was made a separate diocese in 1843, the eastern part of Illinois. Although several missionaries were laboring in the diocese, only one priest was permanently attached to it. Bruté made a trip to Europe where he was able to recruit 18 missionaries, including a number of Eudists that enabled him to establish a college and seminary. Bruté died June 26, 1839.

Hailandière. Celestine de la Hailandière, who had been vicar-general, succeeded Bruté as the second bishop of Vincennes. The apostolic brief that appointed Hailandière, gave him the option of establishing his residence either in Vincennes, Madison, Lafayette, or Indianapolis, but the See city was to remain Vincennes. He was consecrated in Paris on Aug. 18, 1839, returning to Vincennes with additional clerical help and promises by the Sisters of Providence and the Congregation of Holy Cross, both of the Diocese of Le Mans, France, to send sisters to Indiana. In 1844, Hailandière summoned a diocesan synod, and three years later in 1847, and returned to France (where he died in 1882).

St. Palais. The third bishop of Vincennes was Stephen Bazin of Mobile, Ala., but he died after less than a year in office (Oct. 24, 1847–April 23, 1848), and was succeeded by Maurice de St. Palais. At the time of his appointment in 1849, St. Palais, who had been vicar-general by Apostolic Brief, was allowed to establish the episcopal residence at Vincennes, Madison, or Indianapolis (Lafayette was not an option) as long the See city remained Vincennes. During St. Palais' long tenure (1849–1877) the Catholic population, swelled by German immigrants, increased rapidly. Early in his episcopate St. Palais went to Europe (1851–52) and secured an agreement by the Benedictine Abbey of Maria Einsiedeln, Switzerland, to establish a foundation at St. Meinrad (1854) in Spencer County. In 1867 Benedictine sisters from Covington, Ky., established Immaculate Conception Convent and later an academy in nearby Ferdinand.

When Cincinnati was elevated to the status of an archdiocese in 1850, Vincennes became a suffragan see in the newly constituted the Province of Cincinnati. In 1857, in response to a petition of the first provincial council of Cincinnati, the Holy See established the Diocese of Fort Wayne to include the counties across northern tier of the state, thereby, confining the Diocese of Vincennes to the southern part.

The period after the Civil War saw the growth of Terre Haute, Evansville, and Indianapolis. The Church of St. John was built in Indianapolis and the Church of the Assumption in Evansville. Railroads contributed to the development of Terre Haute where in 1872 the Conventual Franciscans were placed in charge of the parishes of St. Joseph and St. Benedict. Also in 1872 the Sisters of Charity of Emmitsburg opened St. Mary Hospital in Evansville (1872). The Sisters of Providence, who had managed a hospital during the war, conducted St. John Infirmary in Indianapolis, and in 1873 the Little Sisters of the Poor and the Sisters of the Good Shepherd established their foundations. In 1875 the Franciscan friars of the St. Louis Province established a monastery and Sacred Heart parish in Indianapolis. Also in 1875 a diocesan weekly, the *Indiana Catholic and Record*, was begun.

Chatard. When Francis Silas CHATARD, St. Palais' successor, was appointed the fifth bishop of Vincennes in 1878, he was directed to fix his episcopal residence in Indianapolis, while the cathedral and the title of the see continued at Vincennes. Later, by an Apostolic Brief dated March 28, 1898 the title of the diocese changed to Diocese of Indianapolis, making it the episcopal see. The same brief directed that St. Francis Xavier, the patron of the old cathedral in Vincennes, was to remain as the patron of the Diocese of Indianapolis. In 1906 SS. Peter and Paul Cathedral was built in Indianapolis, complete except for the façade, which was added in 1936.

During Chatard's tenure in office, diocesan synods were held in 1878, 1880, 1886, and 1891, and many of the measures affected the clergy. Chatard sent a number of seminarians to Europe for study, established irremovable rectors, diocesan courts, and deanery conferences; ordered an annual collection for aged and infirm priests; encouraged a Clergy Relief Union, organized in 1894; and founded a St. Michael Society to ensure Masses for deceased clerics. He secured permission for the use in the diocese of the Calendar of the city of Rome, necessitating a special Ordo that developed into a Year Book.

Chartrand. Chatard was bishop for four decades, but in 1910 Joseph Chartrand, was appointed coadjutor. Chartrand became Bishop of Indianapolis when Chatard died in 1918. Chartrand promulgated the decrees of Pius X regarding Holy Communion with enthusiasm and success. He was zealous in promoting vocations to the priesthood. In 1921 the Daughters of Isabella opened St.

Elizabeth Home in Indianapolis for working girls, and the Knights of Columbus of Indiana founded Gibault Home for delinquent boys near Terre Haute. Conducted at first by diocesan priests, this last institution was given to the charge of the Brothers of Holy Cross in 1934. In 1926 the Sisters of Providence opened Ladywood School in Indianapolis, which superseded the academy at St. Mary-of-the-Woods. Several high schools were built throughout the diocese, including Reitz Memorial High School, Evansville, and Cathedral High School, Indianapolis.

Margaret Mary Hospital, conducted by the Sisters of the Poor of St. Francis of Hartwell, Ohio, was opened in Batesville, Ind., in 1932. The Carmelite Monastery of the Resurrection, founded in New Albany, Ind., in 1922, was reestablished in Indianapolis in 1932, and members of this monastery founded the Carmel of St. Joseph in Terre Haute in 1947.

Ritter. New Albany-born Joseph E. Ritter, was named auxiliary bishop in Indianapolis and upon Chartrand's death a year later succeeded him as ordinary. Ritter became the first archbishop of Indianapolis when, by decree of Pope Pius XII in December 1944, Indianapolis was made a metropolitan see. Despite the economic depression of the 1930s, Ritter enlarged the diocesan curia, instituted three new deaneries, and several new offices and committees, including a superintendent of schools, a Church music commission, and a rural life board, and reorganized Catholic Charities in the diocese. He also established a number of new parishes and missions, but the action for which he gained national attention was the initiative he took in integrating the Catholic schools.

Schulte. When Ritter was transferred to the Archdiocese of St. Louis in 1946, he was succeeded by the Paul C. Schulte who had been Bishop of Leavenworth, Kansas. Among the most pressing local problems that Schulte faced was the rapid increase of population, largely an urban phenomenon, coupled with the growing need of vocations. In 1951, 11 priests of the archdiocese were in the armed forces. More than half of the new parishes he founded were located in Indianapolis and environs; he redrew parish lines, eliminating most of the national parishes; and directed that all parish records be microfilmed. Building plans included the erection and enlargement of schools, but the relative shortage of religious required the assistance of many lay teachers and the diocesan clergy. As a result, he supported the graduate education of clergy so that they could teach in the growing Catholic secondary schools.

Biskup. Archbishop Schulte attended the sessions of Vatican II and after the Council began implementing its directives. Reaching 80 in 1970, he resigned leaving the completion of the task to his successor Most Reverend George J. Biskup who had been appointed as coadjutor in 1967. Before coming to Indianapolis Biskup was auxiliary bishop in Des Moines after serving in the Congregation for Oriental Rites.

O'Meara. Archbishop Biskup resigned in March 1979 (he died a few months later, October 17) to be succeeded by Bishop Edward O'Meara, an auxiliary in St. Louis and, since 1967, National Director of the Society for the Propagation of the Faith. He remodeled Cathedral Grade School and turned it into the Catholic Center housing archdiocesan offices. Archbishop O'Meara gave priority to the development of priestly spirituality. He died Jan. 10, 1992.

Buechlein. The Most Reverend Daniel M. Buechlein, OSB, a monk of St. Meinrad Archabbey and rector of St. Meinrad School of Theology until he was consecrated bishop of Memphis, Tenn., in 1987, was installed as Archbishop of Indianapolis in July 1992. He immediately confronted the task of insuring the financial stability of the archdiocese, and finding a way to staff the parishes and schools in the face of the dwindling number of priests and religious. The first he accomplished by cutting staff and urging increased giving; there was no ready solution for the latter. He has continued the support and development of priestly spirituality and the continuing education of priestly spirituality and the continuing education of the clergy begun by his predecessors.

Bibliography: H. A. ALERDING, *A History of the Catholic Church in the Diocese of Vincennes* (Indianapolis 1883). C. BLANCHARD, *History of the Catholic Church in Indiana,* 2 v. (Logansport, Ind. 1898). T. T. MCAVOY, *The Catholic Church in Indiana, 1789–1834* (New York 1940). J. H. SCHAUINGER, *Cathedrals in the Wilderness* (Milwaukee 1952).

[R. GORMAN/EDS.]

INDICTION

A chronological term used to denote a measure of time, and, in the BYZANTINE CHURCH, a liturgical feast.

CHRONOLOGY.

The indiction (Lat. *indictio:* Gr. ἡ ἰνδικτιων, ἡ ἐπινέμησις) was a 15-year cycle or period used as a point of referral in determining the dates of acts, inscriptions, and chronicles. The word can refer either to the period itself or to the individual years of which it is composed, each one then designated by a number ranking it in the series. Each period forms an independent whole, not requiring a series number referring it to past series, except rarely, in several medieval charters.

The indiction was originally used to determine the land tax. The word came to denote a fiscal year when the annual tax was periodically fixed for a predetermined number of years. Its use in this context dates back to the time of DIOCLETIAN, who established an indiction of five years, beginning in 297–298, which was apparently concerned only with Egypt. Licinius later increased the indiction to 15 years, beginning in 312–313. First set up for Licinius's own eastern part of the empire, the indiction was later extended to the West. Indicating the year within a particular series quickly became a useful means of determining dates, even during the time when the five-year indiction was used. However, the 15-year series was regarded as much more convenient. St. ATHANASIUS used it in his festal letter, the first of which dates from 329 (indiction 2).

Several kinds of indictions were in use, distinguished from each other by the month of the year marking the beginning of the indictional year.

> 1. The Egyptian indiction was characterized by the dependence of its opening on the time of harvest, varying, from one year to another, between May and August.

> 2. The Byzantine indiction, known also as the Constantinopolitan or Constantinian indiction, was the only indiction used throughout the ROMAN EMPIRE, with the exception of Egypt. When this indiction was first instituted, the beginning of the indiction year fell on the day already designated the first day of the official year for the major part of the Orient since the time of AUGUSTUS, viz, September 23, the *Natalis Augusti*. It was later moved to September 1 during the latter half of the 5th century—most probably September 1, 462–463 (first year of the series). JUSTINIAN I made dating by indiction mandatory for all legal documents (CorpIurCivNov 47.2). The Byzantine indiction was used in the papal chancellery from the 5th century until 1087; it was used also in southern Italy in the states or principalities under Byzantine influence or control.

> 3. The Indiction of BEDE, called the Caesarean or Western indiction, was introduced by Bede, and began September 24.

> 4. The Papal indiction, appearing in the 11th century, began on December 25 and was in vogue up to the time of GREGORY XIII, when New Year's Day became January 1.

> 5. Local indictions were used at Genoa, Florence, Pisa, Siena, and Cologne.

To compute the Byzantine indiction for any year of the Christian era, the following rules apply: (1) for any date from January 1 to August 31, add 3 to the year date and divide by 15; the remainder is the year of the indic-

tion; if there is no remainder, the indiction is 15; (2) for any date from September 1 to December 31, add 4 instead of 3. Dates in the non-Byzantine indictions, which have different beginnings, can be computed in a similar manner.

THE FEAST OF THE INFLICTION.

September 23, the beginning of the indiction and the first day of the civil year, became also the first day of the ecclesiastical year. It was also the feast of the Conception of JOHN THE BAPTIST, chronologically the first of the evangelical mysteries. This feast was retained even after the indiction had been moved back to September 1. This new date, primarily the opening of the civil year, was given also a religious character by the celebration of a feast commemorating the first preaching of Christ, recalled in Lk 4.16–22. When this feast was instituted is not known, but it already existed in the 8th century (found in the so-called *Evangelary* of Theodosius and in the *Calendar* of Morcelli) and had by that time supplanted September 23 as the beginning of the ecclesiastical year. The latter date was still called νέον ἔτος (*novoe leto* among the Slavs) up to the 12th century in several MSS, even though by that time the year began on September 1. A sermon by Philip Kerameus (12th century) on the indiction is extant (*Patrologia Graeca* 132:136–161), and a miniature representing the Gospel scene is found in the menology of Basil II.

In Constantinople, the feast was celebrated at HAGIA SOPHIA and included a procession to the Form of Constantine where prayers and hymns were offered (ps. Codinus, 13th century, *Patrologia Graeca* 157:96). The actual form, established by Joachim III, was as follows: following the celebration of the liturgy in the patriarchal church, the patriarch and his metropolitans, members of the Holy Synod, were led into a great meeting hall. There, after appropriate prayers and liturgical hymns, the patriarch, having announced the year of the indiction and the world year according to the Byzantine era, gave general absolution to all the faithful of his patriarchate. He then signed the *praxis,* to which all the metropolitans added their signatures.

Bibliography: Chronology. L. IDELER, *Handbuch der mathematischen und technischen Chronologie*, 2 v. (Berlin 1825–26) 2:347–364. V. GARDTHAUSEN, *Griechische Palaeographie*, 2 v. (2d ed. Leipzig 1911–13) 2:454–467. F. K. GINZEL, *Handbuch der mathematischen und technischen Chronologie*, 3 v. (Leipzig 1906–14; repr. 1958) 3:148–155. *Paulys Realenzyklopädie der Klassischen Altertumswissenschaft* (Stuttgart 1893) 9.2 (1916) 1327–32. H. LECLERCQ, *Dictionnaire d'archéologie chrétienne et de liturgie* (Paris 1907–53) 7.1:530–535. G. MAY, *Lexikon für Theologie und Kirche*, J. HOFER and K. RAHNER, eds. (Freiburg 1957–65) 5:652–653. Various editions of Μήναιον (*Menaion*) under Sept. 1. Τυπικόν,

Typikon, (Athens 1862; Constantinople 1888). V. GRUMEL, *La Chronologie* (Paris 1958) 192–306.

[V. GRUMEL]

INDIFFERENT ACTS

The acts of a human being extend from hidden choices of the WILL to manifest physical operations. Of these acts some are completely involuntary since they are beyond the rational control of man. Acts such as digestion and respiration, for example, are not within the domain of choice, and accordingly they are morally indifferent. Many actions, however, are performed with conscious advertence and choice, and as a result man is responsible for them; the individual has it within his power to do them or omit them. Acts of the first kind are called acts of man; the latter, those with knowledge and from a deliberate will, are properly called HUMAN ACTS. With regard to the latter category, the question arises whether there can be a voluntary act that is morally indifferent, namely, an act that is neither morally good nor bad, an act that is therefore amoral.

Determinants of Morality. The morality of a human act is determined by three aspects of the action. First, there is the object about which the choice is concerned. This object, even when the choice remains purely internal, can be considered the substance of the act. Second, the circumstances of time, place, status of the person, means, and manner qualify the object of the act and are concomitant determinants of the morality of the act. Third, the circumstance of purpose or reason for the act deserves special attention because the end colors the entire choice as qualified by the other circumstances. For a human act to be morally good, all three of these moral determinants must be good; that is, they must conform to objective norms of morality. Subjectively, the individual must follow his certain conscience dictating that all three elements are moral. If any of the three moral determinants is evil, then the entire act is morally evil. To choose something good, but for an evil purpose, vitiates the entire act. To choose something good for a good purpose but at a wrong time can make the whole act evil.

Positions. The possibility of a morally indifferent act was sharply disputed by the theologians of the Middle Ages. Abelard proposed the extreme position that every human act is objectively indifferent, and only receives its goodness or sinfulness from the intention or purpose of the agent. This position, condemned by the Council of Sens, was strongly attacked by Peter Lombard, whose *Sentences* were a standard theological text for three centuries (see 2 *Sentences* 40). The notion that at least some acts possess an intrinsic goodness or badness was gener-

ally accepted by Catholic thinkers, who could reflect on the centuries-old aphorism of St. Jerome: "Continence is good, lust is evil; between the two, to walk is indifferent" (*Epist.* 112.16; *Corpus scriptorum ecclesiasticorum latinorum* 55.2:386). In succeeding centuries, however, many nominalists, and to some extent Scotus, tended toward EXTRINSICISM. For them, all or nearly all human acts are good or evil because of the positive will of God commanding or forbidding them rather than because of the nature of the acts themselves. This position, although it enjoyed favor at the end of the medieval period, attracts few today.

In the early Franciscan school the question of the moral quality of acts was not clearly distinguished from the problem of supernatural MERIT. Despite minor differences within the school, it held that some individual human acts are morally indifferent. St. Bonaventure, for example, held that some acts are positively ordered to God; others are not. The first are good; but not all of the second are evil. He insisted that there can be acts that are not made meritorious by charity, nor are they sinful, since they are not of obligation. With regard to these acts, God does not reward men, nor does He judge men to be sinners.

St. Thomas Aquinas commenting on Lombard (*In 2 sent.* 40) and even more explicitly in the *Summa theologiae* (1a2ae, 18.8–9) proposed the doctrine now commonly accepted by Catholic theologians. He distinguished between an act in its general nature—this kind of human activity, as praying, cursing, walking—and an act in the concrete conditions of its existence. In the first way, he remarks, an act can be indifferent, for some acts according to their nature neither imply something pertaining to the order of reason nor something contrary to this order. In the second sense, however, every human act is morally good or bad. Every individual deliberate act takes its goodness not only from the object, but also from the end or purpose of the agent and from the other circumstances. These individuating elements stand in the same relation to the object of the act as the individuating accidents to the essence of a thing. Thus even though the act considered in itself (i.e., from its object) is indifferent, it is either good or evil from the end and circumstances; for no act is performed except for some end or reason, and this is either good or evil. Hence no individual human act is indifferent. Note also that this morality belongs to the act precisely as human or ethical and does not, as such, express a relation to the SUPERNATURAL ORDER or to supernatural merit.

Two additional points should be noted. Does moral indifference constitute a distinct species of morality so that human acts are divided into three species: good, bad, and indifferent? Theologians are not in agreement. Many deny this and argue that moral indifference is not a true species of morality. This is the position of the Salmanticenses and J. Gonet among classic authors, A. Tanquerey and T. Bouquillon among more modern authors. Other theologians (e.g., John of St. Thomas, D. Prümmer, R. Garrigou-Lagrange) insist that moral indifference is a true, but incomplete, species of morality.

The second difficulty concerns the relation of moral acts to man's supernatural DESTINY. Although every individual human act is good or evil ethically, some may be, as it were, supernaturally indifferent. Some human actions can be ethically good but not supernaturally meritorious, nor even ordered to SALVATION; for they are the acts of one estranged from God by serious sin, and may even be done without actual grace. Aquinas reflects a common theological position when he teaches that these acts are not sinful, for man's nature is not so corrupted by sin that he is incapable of all good actions (cf. *Summa theologiae* 1a2ae, 85.2; 109.2). This same truth, that every act of the sinner is not a sin, has received confirmation from the teaching authority of the Church [H. Denzinger, *Enchiridion symbolorum,* ed. A. Schönmetzer, (32d ed. Freiburg 1963) 1481–82, 1539, 1557, 1575].

See Also: GOOD WORKS; MORALITY; SALUTARY ACTS.

Bibliography: THOMAS AQUINAS, *De malo* 2.5. SALMANTICENSES, *Cursus theologicus,* tr. 11, disp. 1, dub. 1, 2; tr. 11, disp. 7 (v. 6:53–62, 165–81). O. LOTTIN, *Psychologie et morale aux XIIe et XIIIe siècles,* 6 v. in 8 (Louvain 1942–60) 2:469–89. P. PALAZZINI, ed., *Dictionarium morale et canonicum,* v.2 (Vatican City 1965) 676–79.

[J. A. BURROUGHS; J. HENNESSEY]

INDIFFERENTISM

A doctrinal system that exalts the attitude (internal) that all philosophical opinions, all religions, and all ethical doctrines regarding life are equally true and valuable. Accordingly, no one religion contains certain truth. It differs from religious tolerance (in which a religion—considered false—is permitted to exist), from irreligion (in which all religions are judged to be false), from civil religious freedom of conscience (in which the state makes no judgment about the value of various forms of worship), and from religious neutrality (in which the state does not become involved in religious controversy). It also differs from practical religious indifference, which is the neglect of religious practice arising from contempt of religion or from psychological, sociological, and environmental factors. Syncretism, or the fusion of various creeds by surrendering certain dogmatic or moral teachings, is the outgrowth of religious indifferentism.

PIUS IX, in his *Syllabus of Errors,* condemned certain propositions under the heading of indifferentism, such as that man has a right to absolute freedom of religion and that one can come to salvation through any religion whatever. VATICAN COUNCIL II, employing a pastoral approach, reappraised the topics of *communicatio in sacris,* irreligious indifferentism, irenicism, and religious freedom.

Communicatio in sacris. This means common worship (*i.e.,* sharing in the official, public prayer of a Church). The Decree on Ecumenism replaced the strict attitude of Canon Law (*e.g.,* 1917 CIC cc. 732; 1258; 2319), which prohibited active participation on the grounds that other Christian communities lacked the character of a Church. Reversing this position, the Decree recommended a discriminating (not general) participation in the worship and Sacraments of other Churches (*Unitatis redintegratio* 8), particularly of the separated Eastern Churches (cf. *Orientalium Ecclesiarum* 26–29; Ecumenical Directory of the Secretariat for Unity, Part I, 39–54). The Decree provided two principles for avoiding religious indifferentism: first, liturgical worship and the Sacraments signify an already existing—even if not perfect—unity of the Church and thus general participation cannot be applied in most cases; second, as a means of grace for the faithful, liturgical worship and the Sacraments also contribute to the growth of unity.

Irreligious Indifferentism. Such indifferentism was divided into postulatory atheism of the West and atheistic communism of the East. The pastoral *Constitution on the Church in the Modern World* places atheism in its treatment on the question of man: that is, atheism is not considered from a metaphysical or epistemological perspective but is viewed in terms of an authentic desire for true humanism (*Gaudium et spes* 19–21). Postulatory atheism stresses the absence of God and the value of man alone on the existential level. Disregarding the economic and political aspects of atheistic communism of the East, the Decree refers to previous repudiations of communism; it then urges the Church to reflect on its own defective humanism and its role in the growth of Marxism. Irreligious indifferentism thus has its roots more in man's attempt to become truly human than in any positive act against God or religious institutions. Since Vatican II, LIBERATION THEOLOGY has attempted to develop humanistic principles (based on the dignity of man and his freedom as a Christian) that seek to avoid both postulatory atheism and atheistic communism (*see* ATHEISM).

Irenicism. As a conciliatory approach to doctrine, irenicism may be true or false. The Decree on Ecumenism rejects false irenicism, or the partial disclosure or diluting of tenets on either side of a dialogue to achieve peaceful union; it is contrary to the spirit of ecumenism and leads to mutual deception. On the contrary, the Decree encourages true irenicism, which avoids polemics, practices brotherly love, recognizes goodness and truth wherever found and emphasizes common aspects and presents Catholic doctrine more profoundly, more precisely, and more fully in a mutually understandable language (*Unitatis redintegratio* 11).

Religious Freedom. The *Declaration on Religious Freedom*, basing its position on the dignity of the human person (fully known only in the light of Revelation), insisted on two negatively stated rights: (1) no man may be compelled in the religious sphere to act in a manner contrary to his conscience; (2) within due limits no one may be prevented from acting in accordance with his conscience (*Dignitatis humanae* 2). The document considers only the moral dimensions of religious freedom—rights whose object is freedom from coercion but not the content of religious faith—and thus does not pass judgment on the problems of the true or the erroneous conscience. Regardless of former practices, a person today, whether believer or nonbeliever, has the right not to be prevented from practicing his religion, whether privately or publicly. Religious freedom thus leads to religious pluralism which, however, is not to be confused with religious indifference; religious pluralism is based on the right to profess and practice one's religion and makes no value judgment on truth and error; religious indifference, however, suggests that all religions equally possess truth and thus have equal value.

Bibliography: W. G. TOPMOELLER, *The Problem of Dogmatic Indifferentism according to John Henry Cardinal Newman* (Rome 1956). J. FEINER, "Decree on Ecumenism," Vorgrimler 2: 57–164. H. HOECK, "Decree on Eastern Catholic Churches," ibid. 1: 307–331. N. MOLINSKI, "Indifferentism," *Sacramentum Mundi* 3: 120–121, P. PAVAN, "Declaration on Human Freedom," Vorgrimler 4: 49–86. J. RATZINGER, "Pastoral Constitution on the Church in the Modern World," Part One, Introd. and ch. 1, "Dignity of the Human Person," ibid. 5: 115–163. Secretariat for Promoting Christian Unity, *Directorium. . .de re oecumenica, Pars 1, Acta Apostolicae Sedis* 59 (1967) 574–592, tr. *Directory for the Application of the Decisions of the Second Vatican Council concerning Ecumenical Matters*, Part I (USCC Publ. Office, Washington, D.C. 1967).

[T. F. MCMAHON/EDS.]

INDIVIDUALITY

An abstract word, individuality is a philosophical term for what constitutes the individual. Individual itself is the translation of the Greek term ἄτομον and designates what is not divided. In the strictest sense of the word, an individual is a being distinct from every other being and undivided in itself. It is, then, an ontological UNITY that is not identical with anything else.

Individual and Individuation. An individual is a concrete and substantial being. One cannot speak of an ACCIDENT, e.g., a color or a sound, as an individual. But man, this living man, is an individual, i.e., a BEING who subsists, who persists in existence by himself. An individual, then, is also a singular being, one among many, a being in a multitude or a SPECIES. It is not a species, not even the most determinate among all species; rather it is a being in which the species is fulfilled under a singular form by individuation.

This relation between the individual and the species gives rise to the logical intention associated with the term individual. Like the genus, the species is a being of reason, a being of second or logical intention. This logical intention presupposes a real intention that directly attains the thing formally called an individual, when focusing precisely on its inclusion in a species. (*See* INTENTIONALITY; LOGIC.)

The individual is therefore the singular, substantial, concrete being considered in its undivided unity and as separated from every other being. An angel is an individual, as also is a man, an animal, a particular plant, a concrete thing. The character of individual unity is easy to recognize in manifestly living things. On the borderline between the vegetal world and inorganic matter, individuality becomes more difficult to discern; yet molecules and atoms seem recognizable from their characteristics in some experimental situations as individual realities.

The notion of individuality transcends the world of matter. Within the material world, however, the individual comes to exist by a process known as individuation. Although there is much philosophical discussion about how individuation is accomplished, the most common answer proposes that, in material species, the specific form is individuated by reason of its relation to the matter that receives it. The latter, called primary matter, exists under conditions that imply an ordination to such or such a quantity, this quantity being what determines the individual material being when the substantial form is educed from the primary matter (*see* MATTER AND FORM; SUBSTANTIAL CHANGE). At least on the basis of a radical title, however, individuation does not result from quantity itself, even within material species. Corporeal substance is individuated and an individual by the mutual causality of the essential elements constituting a material being; the unity and individuality of this substance belong to the ontological order. Yet it is true that quantity, an accident, intervenes in individuation by an extrinsic title, and that the individuated substance is affected with a determinate quantity that makes it "one" in the order of number, i.e., in the world of numerical unities. In the human species, a man is one individual among many; but this man exists as an individual by reason of something other than mere quantitative unity.

The scholastic teaching on the human soul sheds light on this doctrine of the individuation of forms substantially united to this or that matter. Specifically identical, human souls exist only as this or that soul, i.e., as individuated in proportionate matter. Yet, when the human soul is separated from matter through death, it retains its character as a distinct soul, one in its essence and individualized by reason of the proportions that marked it. Obviously its individuality then does not essentially imply the presence of material quantity. (*See* SOUL, HUMAN.)

Meanings of Individuality. An ontological consideration of individuality is necessary to explain how individuality is common to both material and immaterial entities. One must first distinguish between individuality and individuation. Individuation is what results from the proportion between form and matter, and thus pertains to the physical order. Individuality, on the other hand, is what terminates an individual nature so that it receives existence for itself. Since this involves the consideration of the relation between an individual nature and its existence, abstracting from whether that nature is material or not, individuality pertains properly to the metaphysical or ontological order. (*See* INDIVIDUATION.)

In reference to man, the notion of individuality is closely related to that of PERSONALITY. An individual endowed with a rational nature is a person. [*See* PERSON (IN PHILOSOPHY).] The person is incommunicable, he is a whole within himself, by reason of his individuality. But the existing irrational individual is also incommunicable, with a similar type of individuality. To indicate the difference between the person and the irrational individual, the term personality is generally used to refer to the former, the term individuality to refer to the latter.

By reason of his rationality, however, the human person must be further considered under a moral aspect. Now this aspect is twofold, since the human person has one moral relation to his own perfection and another in his order to SOCIETY. Some authors use the term person to indicate the former aspect, the term individual to indicate the latter; and, consequently, they make corresponding moral predications respectively of personality and individuality. In this context they say that society is at the service of the person, although, considered as an individual, this same person is at the service of temporal society. They further claim that the individual (according to his moral definition) has only human values of the same order as those that belong to society, and that these values of the individual should be ordered to society as parts to a whole, while the person (again according to this moral definition), by reason of his value, transcends all properly so-called sociological values.

This position is presented here only to clarify a common moral usage of the term individuality. If individuality, in its moral sense, means the order of the individual human nature to society, then it implies the order of the individual's conduct to the COMMON GOOD of society. It does not signify, then, uniqueness in the sense of conduct that is completely dissonant from the order to the true social good. Nor does it signify originality in the current meaning of this word. However, in other contexts, it is possible to make a moral use of the term individuality in the pejorative sense of that which makes a person antisocial.

Multitude and Number. In the realm of separated forms, such as angels, individuation is accomplished without any relation to matter. The angel is this angel precisely as individuated by his form, by his very essence. (*See* ANGELS, 2.) Furthermore, as is commonly true in the realm of forms, even the least variation changes the species; thus the individual angel is a species to himself. The multitude of angels is composed of individuals who have nothing at all to do with matter or with number, in the quantitative sense of this term. By himself, by his being and definition, each angel is an individual or person. The term MULTITUDE designates the assembly, or, in a metaphorical sense, the great number of these angels.

If, however, one takes the word number in its proper meaning, it implies very many unities resulting from species and time. In this sense, number is a kind of QUANTITY, namely, discrete quantity. Each of the individuals included in this number, then, is deemed to belong to the realm of enumerable beings by its own quantity, which makes it numerically one, by reason of a certain homogeneity made visible by quantity and the accidents related to it.

See Also: INDIVIDUATION; PERSONALITY; UNITY.

Bibliography: J. MARITAIN, ''Personne et individu,'' *Acta Pontificiae Academiae Romanae S. Thomae Aquinatis* (1946); *The Person and the Common Good,* tr. J. J. FITZGERALD (New York 1947). A. WALTERS and K. O'HARA, *Persons and Personality* (New York 1953). T. HÉBERT, ''Notre connaissance intellectuelle du singulier matériel,'' *Laval Théologique et Philosophique* 5 (1949) 33–65. L. DE BROGLIE, ''Sur la complémentarité des idées d'individu et de système,'' *Dialectica* 2 (1948) 351–382. P. DESCOQS, ''Individu et personne,'' *Archivio di Filosofia* 8 (1938) 235–292. G. MORRA, *Enciclopedia filosofica,* 4 v. (Venice–Rome 1957) 2:1364–70. R. EISLER, *Wörterbuch der philosophischen Begriffe,* 3 v. (4th ed. Berlin 1927–30) 1:732–741.

[L. M. CORVEZ]

St. Thomas Aquinas. (Archive Photos)

INDIVIDUATION

The constitution of a being whereby it is "undivided in itself and divided from all other beings" (Thomas Aquinas, *Summa Theologiae* 3a, 77.2; 1a, 29.4) or the constitution of a being "in such manner that it is not, according to the *ratio* by which it is called 'one,' communicable to many as to inferiors that would be subject to it or would, according to that *ratio,* be many" (F. Suárez, *Disp. meta.* 5.1.2). This article presents a philosophical analysis of this notion as it has been developed in the scholastic tradition. It consists of the following: (1) a clarification of the term "individuation"; (2) a historical survey of ancient and medieval views concerning it; (3) a summary of the teaching found in the writings of Thomas Aquinas and some of the most important Thomistic commentators; (4) a summary of the teaching of John Duns Scotus; and (5) a summary of the teaching of Francisco Suárez. (For other meanings of individuation, *see* INDIVIDUALITY.).

Meaning of term. As is evident from the definitions cited above, two elements are involved in individuation, namely, indivision in self and DIVISION from every other individual. The negation of division involved in individuation is not, however, merely that which is found in UNITY in general. The negation of division proper to indi-viduation involves denial of division of an entity into many, each of which would be the same as the entire entity divided. Thus, the undividedness of the individual or of a singular unity involves incommunicability; that is, whatever is an individual cannot be common either in the sense of actually existing in various things or in the sense of being predicable of many in the same manner.

Individuation may be considered in three ways: metaphysically, physically, and logically. These three ways of viewing individuation are distinguished by JOHN OF ST. THOMAS in the following manner. Considered metaphysically, individuation means the last degree in the series of all predicaments or categories in the same way as the supreme GENUS means the first degree. This lowest degree is due to the ultimate difference by which a SPECIES is contracted to an individual. Considered physically, individuation means numerical unity, by means of which something is one in such manner that it is undivided in itself and divided from everything else. Considered logically, individuation means to be subjectable to all superior predicates and to be predicable of only one thing, that is, itself (*Curs. phil.* Nat. phil. 2.9.3).

The expression "principle of individuation" may be understood in various ways. The epistemological or manifestive principle of individuation is that by which one knows or recognizes an individual. This consists of the empirical signs of individuality, otherwise known as the individuating notes. The extrinsic principle of indi-viduation is the efficient cause that produces the individual. The intrinsic principle of individuation is whatever entity it is within the individual that accounts for the individual's being this individual and no other. This intrinsic principle may be viewed, moreover, either as a formal principle or as a radical or constitutive principle. Accordingly, it may refer to that which formally constitutes the intrinsic completeness and extrinsic definiteness of every individual being; or it may refer to that from which arises, or by which is constituted, this individual—undivided in itself, incommunicable, and separated from all others.

Also, the principle of individuation may be viewed with reference to either absolute or relative individuality. Individuality is regarded absolutely when a thing is considered merely in itself, with no advertence as to whether or not there are or can be other members in the same species. Thus, every being may be considered individual in the absolute sense. Individuality is regarded relatively when a thing is considered in relation to an actual or at least possible multitude of things of the same species. Hence, only being that does not exclude the possibility of a plurality of beings of the same species may be considered individual in the relative sense.

Ancient and medieval views. The solution to the problem of the principle of individuation has importance not only in itself, but also for its consequences in many fields, such as metaphysics, epistemology, psychology, ethics, and philosophy of value. Hence, as would be expected, philosophers in all ages have been interested in this problem. However, since various philosophers have adverted to different aspects of this problem and, further, have based their solutions on different metaphysical and epistemological principles, the solutions that have been proposed are numerous and widely diverse.

Aristotle. ARISTOTLE proposed MATTER as the principle of individuation (*Meta.* 1034a 5–8, 1074a 33). From his Platonic legacy, he accepted the principle that scientific knowledge is immutable and eternally valid knowledge and that, therefore, the object of such knowledge must also be immutable and eternal. Holding both that scientific knowledge is knowledge of the essences of things and that things receive their essences from their forms, Aristotle concluded that the forms of things cannot be the basis for the multiplicity and change connected with individuals. Every difference of form would effect a specific difference (*ibid.* 1058b 1–2). However, matter, which the individual includes in addition to its form, is apt to function as the basis for multiplicity and change, for matter is potential and undetermined. Thus, there is nothing on the part of matter that prohibits the connection of the same form with various parts of the matter and thereby a multiplicity of individuals originating as the result of the divisibility of matter.

Boethius, Gilbert, and the Arabs. BOETHIUS asserted that "numerical difference is caused by a variety of accidents" (*De Trin.* 1). Thus, instead of explaining the individuation of an essence by completely undetermined matter, Boethius taught that an essence is individualized in virtue of its being determined by place, time, and other accidents. GILBERT DE LA PORRÉE maintained that the individual is constituted of various forms that are not themselves singular; yet in each individual there is something unique. This uniqueness he explained as arising from the uniqueness of the collection of forms composing the individual. Thus, though the forms themselves are common, that is, shared by other individuals in the same species or genus, the particular combination of forms in the individual is never duplicated in any other being (*In librum de duabus naturis; Patrologia Latina* 64: 1372D). The Arabian philosophers, such as ALFARABI, AVICENNA, and AVERROËS, followed in general the Aristotelian doctrine that forms, universal in themselves, are individuated through matter.

Thirteenth- and fourteenth-century thinkers. Particularly during the thirteenth century there arose tremendous interest in the problem of individuation. In fact, solutions to this problem developed into programs distinctive of the various schools and consequently caused serious controversy. ROGER BACON placed great stress on the nobility and importance of the individual. In his youth, while lecturing on Aristotle's *Metaphysics* and writing his *Quaestiones,* Bacon did propose that individuation was derived principally from matter. In his later works, however, he presented an entirely different view, maintaining that there is no intrinsic cause of individuation since nothing can be added to a universal to make it an individual. It is God, he asserted, who causes individuals and therefore is ultimately responsible for individuation.

St. BONAVENTURE, following the teaching of ALEXANDER OF HALES, maintained that there is no form without matter. According to St. Bonaventure, however, matter may be either corporeal or spiritual, depending on the FORM it receives. Since matter is common to all beings, St. Bonaventure asserted that matter cannot be the source of individuation. Instead, he held that it is the union of the matter and form that is the true principle of individuation (*In 2 sent.* 3.1.2.3).

HENRY OF GHENT denied that individuality adds any real element to the existing specific ESSENCE. It is simply because individual things exist actually and extramentally that they differ from one another. Therefore, Henry asserted that individuation is explained by negation, namely, negation of intrinsic division and negation of identity with another being (*Quodl.* 5.8).

Most of the Franciscan thinkers of the thirteenth and fourteenth centuries, such as WILLIAM DE LA MARE, JOHN PECKHAM, Étienne TEMPIER, RICHARD OF MIDDLETON, and John Duns Scotus, rejected, at times quite forcefully, the theory of matter as the principle of individuation. There were also, of course, many defenders of the Aristotelian theory, among whom may be enumerated ALBERT THE GREAT, SIGER OF BRABANT, GILES OF ROME, and Thomas Aquinas.

For still other medieval philosophers, such as DURANDUS OF SAINT-POURÇAIN, PETER AUREOLI, HENRY OF HARCLAY, and WILLIAM OF OCKHAM, individuation presented no problem whatever. These philosophers, asserting that every being by reason of its actual existence is individual, found no meaning at all in the search for something whereby an extramental object is rendered individual.

Thomistic school. By far the most important of the defenders of the position that matter is the principle of individuation were St. THOMAS AQUINAS and his Dominican commentators, particularly Cajetan, John of St. Thomas, and Ferrariensis.

Aquinas's teaching. In accord with Aristotle, St. Thomas maintained that the form, which is the basis of the substantial essence, cannot be the basis of individuality; for form in itself is universal and can be received into one or more substrata. Also, accidents cannot account for individuality, for the individual belongs to the category of SUBSTANCE. Since the principle of individuation must then be substantial, but cannot be the form, which is a principle of specification, it follows that the principle of individuation must be matter. However, recognizing that primary matter, just as form, is by nature common and can be determined by many forms, St. Thomas introduced into his doctrine the notion of QUANTITY. He proposed signate matter, matter related to quantity, as the principle of individuation (*De ente* 2). (*See* MATTER AND FORM.)

This necessitated, however, an explanation of the precise relation of matter to quantity. In investigating the texts of St. Thomas with regard to this problem, one must consider these in their chronological order, for St. Thomas's thought on this subject underwent gradual evolution. In a very early work, influenced perhaps by Avicenna, he explained the diversity in matter by the *forma corporeitatis* (*In 1 sent.* 8.5.2). He quickly abandoned this position, however, and substituted in its place the notion of matter subject to indeterminate dimensions (*In Boeth. de Trin.* 4.2). Later, rejecting also this position, he maintained that matter with determined dimensions is the principle of individuation (*De nat. mat.* 3).

The individuation of human souls is explained by St. Thomas also by matter. He asserted that diversity and distinction of grades in souls is caused by diversity of bodies (*In 2 sent.* 3.2.2.3). Since the soul is according to its substance the form of a body, the soul necessarily retains its relation to the body, even after its separation from the body in death. It is by this relation to the body that St. Thomas explained the individuation of the separated soul. Further, since numerical difference comes about only by matter, it follows that where there is no matter beings cannot be multiplied within their kinds. Thus St. Thomas maintained that angels, in virtue of their having no matter, are infinite in the order of essence and therefore must differ specifically one from another (*De spir. creat.* 8).

Cajetan. Because St. Thomas did not clearly indicate in his writings the precise relation that matter bears to quantity in its role of principle of individuation, there arose considerable disagreement among his commentators. Tommaso de Vio CAJETAN, one of the principal interpreters of the thought of St. Thomas, rejected the opinion that the aggregate of matter and quantity is the principle of individuation. Rather, he maintained that matter itself is the proper root of individuation. In his commentary on *De ente et essentia* (5.37), Cajetan explained signed matter as matter capable of "this" quantity, so that it is not capable of "that." However, in his commentary on the *Summa Theologiae* (29.1), Cajetan modified his view slightly and explained signed matter as matter that is the source, the cause quasi-productive of the quantity. He argued that if quantity is able to accomplish its effect in things that receive it, surely the production of the same result should not be impossible to the fundamental source of quantity. Therefore, Cajetan asserted that matter is as capable as quantity of distinguishing numerically.

John of St. Thomas. John of St. Thomas held a similar opinion regarding the meaning of signed matter. He stated that the signation of matter is not accomplished by quantity as by an inherent form of matter affecting it, but by the intrinsic ordination of matter to quantity as to a dividing and separating form (*Curs. phil.* Phil. nat. 2.9.4). Just as matter implies an ordination to accidents as to dispositions by which the potentiality of matter is determined to this form rather than to that, so matter implies an ordination to quantity as to one of the dispositions. However, quantity has not only the function of informing the subject in which it is, thereby bestowing the formal effect of EXTENSION; but quantity is also related to its subject as dividing one part of matter from another part. Nonetheless, it is matter and not quantity that is the cause of incommunicability and substantial distinction.

Ferrariensis. An interpretation of signed matter that is very different from that presented by Cajetan and John of St. Thomas is found in the work of FERRARIENSIS (FRANCESCO SILVESTRI). According to him, signed matter is matter actually informed by quantity (Commentary on the *Contra Gentiles* 1.21). The fundamental reason on which he based his argument is that ACT is what distinguishes anything. Now signate matter is nothing other than matter so appropriated to a certain individual as to be capable of underlying that individual's quantity and no other. This appropriation, however, is either due to a form or not. If it is due to some form, either substantial or accidental, then the appropriated and signate matter does not imply only primary matter, but matter together with a form by which it is said to be appropriated and signate. If there is no form, then this situation must be reconciled with the fact that no potency whatever receives limitation and appropriation except by means of some act that it receives. Since primary matter is simply potency, it receives determination only from some form. Hence, if it is necessary that matter be signate in order that the form be individuated in virtue of this signation, then there must be in the matter some act that is really distinct from the matter.

Scotistic teaching. John Duns Scotus held that the principle of individuation must be a proper positive entity that is added to the nature and constitutes the individual. To determine the principle of individuation, Scotus considered two questions: (1) How is it that the individual is not divisible into subordinated parts? (2) How is it that the individual is really distinct from other individuals? His answer to the first question was based on the principle *unum et ens convertuntur.* He argued that an entity must correspond to every unity; and further, a different entity must correspond to a different unity. Since individuation is a special unity, there must be within the individual a corresponding entity. In answering the second question, Scotus asserted that the real distinction of individuals presupposes that there are contained in them realities that differ. Thus within the individual there must be, in addition to the common nature, a positive entity that corresponds to the singular unity and accounts for the distinctness of the individual. This positive entity, the *haecceitas,* which is formally distinct from the common nature, was likened by Scotus to the specific difference. He asserted that as the specific difference effects by its accession to the genus the indivisibility into further species and the distinctness of one species from all others, so the *haecceitas* effects by its accession to the species the indivisibility of the individual and the distinctness of one individual from all others (*Op. oxon.* 3.6.9).

Suárezian teaching. A position very different from both that of St. Thomas and that of Scotus is found in the work of Francisco SUÁREZ. Admitting nothing in reality that is not actually singular, Suárez found no need for a principle of individuation for an individual substance other than the entity of the substance itself. Thus he writes that "every entity is by itself the principle of its individuation" (*Disp. meta.* 5.6.1). Although Suárez admitted that individual unity does add something to the common nature, he insisted that what the individual unity adds is only mentally distinct from the nature (5.2.16). The individuation of all finite being, whether spiritual or material, is explained in the same way by Suárez. Further, with this explanation of individuation, it does not follow necessarily that purely spiritual creatures are specifically different; for similarity does not exclude distinctness.

See Also: ESSENCE.

Bibliography: J. R. ROSENBERG, *The Principle of Individuation: A Comparative Study of St. Thomas, Scotus and Suárez* (Washington 1950). A. GAZZANO, *Enciclopedia filosofica,* 4 v. (Venice-Rome 1957) 2:1360–1363. R. EISLER, *Wörterbuch der philosophischen Begriffe,* 3 v. (4th ed. Berlin 1927–30) 1:732–741. T. N. HARPER, *The Metaphysics of the School,* 3 v. (New York 1879–84; repr. New York 1940). H. MEYER, *The Philosophy of St. Thomas Aquinas,* tr. F. C. ECKHOFF (St. Louis 1948). G. M. MANSER, *Das Wesen des Thomismus* (Thomistische Studien 5; 3d ed. Fribourg 1949). J. ASSENMACHER, *Die Geschichte des Individuationsprinzips in der Scholastik* (Leipzig 1926). L. FUETSCHER, *Akt und Potenz* (Philosophie und Grenzwissenschaften 4.4–6; Innsbruck 1933) 168–243. R. MESSNER, ''Das Individuationsprinzip in skotistischer Schau,'' *Wissenschaft und Weisheit* 1 (1934) 8–27. JOHN OF ST. THOMAS, *Cursus philosophicus thomisticus,* ed. B. REISER, 3 v. (new ed. Turin 1930–37).

[J. R. ROSENBERG]

INDIVISIBLE

Literally, indivisible is that which cannot be divided. One may distinguish mathematical from physical indivisibles and their uses in philosophy and mathematics. Since DIVISION follows upon distinction, in turn dependent upon OPPOSITION, the term is understood with reference to material (quantitative) or to formal opposition. Material indivisibles are either absolute—points and numerical units; or relative—that which *de facto* is not divided or would be destroyed by division, e.g., an electron. Formally, indivisibles have, or are considered to have, simple intelligibility, e.g., a GENUS or a specific NATURE. Because a DEFINITION, being complex, cannot be formed of them, absolute formal indivisibles are often known only negatively or in relation to composites.

In the physical universe, perhaps exclusively, there are relative quantitative indivisibles. The discrete particles that, as a result of experimental and theoretical physics, are thought to constitute physical reality—e.g., atoms, subatomic particles, and photons—are destroyed when divided, although the matter-energy balance is thought to be preserved. Such indivisibles are not always individuals, though true individuals are always indivisibles.

Linear EXTENSION, along with MOTION and TIME, are considered instances of continua within which indivisibles are distinguished. The INSTANT of time and the moment of motion are compared analogously to the geometric point, and the question has been debated concerning their actual continuing and/or terminating function. Granted that they terminate, there is still question of their precise nature. The general view is that terminating indivisibles, e.g., points at the ends of lines, are positive and really but only modally distinct from that which they terminate. Concerning indivisibles in mathematics, *see* BOYER.

See Also: CONTINUUM.

Bibliography: J. GREDT, *Elementa philosophiae Aristotelico–Thomisticae,* ed. E. ZENZEN, 2 v. (13th ed. Freiburg 1961). R. P. PHILLIPS, *Modern Thomistic Philosophy,* 2 v. (Westminster, Md. 1934; repr. 1945). C. B. BOYER, *The History of the Calculus and Its Conceptual Development* (pa. New York 1959).

[C. F. WEIHER]

> **Capital:** Jakarta.
> **Size:** 779,675 sq. miles.
> **Population:** 228,437,870; the majority are Javanese, with significant communities of Sundanese, Madurese, Minang, Lampong, Macassarese, Banten, Bugese and others. There is a very small but economically significant Chinese community.
> **Languages:** Bahasa Indonesia (official), English, Dutch, local dialects, the most widely spoken of which is Javanese.
> **Religions:** Muslim 88%, Protestant 5%, Roman Catholic 3%, Hindu 2%, Buddhist 1%, other 1%.

INDONESIA, THE CATHOLIC CHURCH IN

The Republic of Indonesia is located in Southeast Asia, straddling the equator along 5,110 kilometers between the coast of Southeast Asia and Australia, extending from 6 to 11 degrees northern latitude and from 95 to 141 degrees eastern longitude. Indonesia is the world's largest archipelago comprising over 13,000 islands (6,000 inhabited). Previously known as the Dutch East Indies, Indonesia proclaimed its independence in 1945 and was acknowledged as an independent republic by international treaty in 1949. Indonesia is also the fourth most populous country in the world, with a population exceeding 225 million. The official motto, ''bhinneka tunggal ika'' (''unity in diversity''), reflects a nation with some 350 languages and over 30 major cultural domains.

Early Christian Missions. Archaeological excavations in the 1990s confirm seafarers' accounts of a Christian community at Baros on the west coast of northern Sumatra in the 7th century. There is evidence of small Christian communities in Southeast Sumatra and East Java during the 9th to the 13th centuries. Franciscans traveling to China also visited Indonesian ports. J. de Monte Corvino visited the east coast of Sumatra in 1291, Odoric of Pordenone spent some months in Sumatra, Java and Kalimantan (1312), and John de Marignolli also remained for a time in Palembang, Sumatra, in 1347. These small enclaves died out. Present day Christian churches date back to the early Catholic and Protestant missions of the 16th and 17th centuries and more particularly to the mission outreach of the 19th and 20th centuries.

Jesuit and Dominican Missions. The Portuguese sailed through Indonesian waters in 1511 seeking sandalwood from Timor and spices from the Moluccas. The first baptisms were carried out by a lay Portuguese trader, Gonzalo Veloso, in Mamuia, Halmahera in 1534. Catholic communities were established in the Moluccas, Amboina and Ternate. From 1546 to 1547, the Jesuit missionary St. Francis XAVIER spent 14 months in Indonesia, visiting North Sulawesi and Ternate Island and founding a minor seminary. From their base at Ternate, the Jesuits worked in the Moluccas and Sulawesi until the Dutch expelled them in 1605. In the 1550s, Joao Soares, a layman formed a Catholic mission in Nusa Tenggara (comprising Timor, Alor, Flores, and Solor islands). In 1562, the DOMINICANS from Malacca settled in Solor, the hub of the sandalwood trade, establishing a minor seminary in 1596. By 1599, there were more than 22,000 Catholics. As Dutch control expanded, the Dominicans moved from Solor to Larantuka in east Flores in 1613, then to Lifao c.1650 on the coast of west Timor, and finally to Dili on the coast of east Timor c.1771. At the beginning of the 17th century, there were some 50,000 Catholics in both the Moluccas and Nusa Tenggara.

From the 16th to the 18th centuries, the Portuguese directed their missions from Goa and Cochin in India, from Malacca on the Malay peninsula, and from Macao in China. Portuguese claim to east Nusa Tenggara was not made until 1702. Before that date, the Dominicans administered the territory, paying for military protection themselves. From 1581 to 1719, some 27 Dominicans were killed together with numerous Indonesian Catholics. Some were clearly martyrs for their faith (e.g., Agustinho da Magdalena, Joao Bautista and Simao de Madre Dos on Solor in 1621). Others were killed for commercial and political motives, because they were on the losing side of a trade war between the Catholic Portuguese and the Protestant Dutch, the latter supported by Muslim Sultanates such as that of Macassar. Often, the Dominicans led battles in Flores and Timor against the encroaching Dutch and Macassarese. In Aceh, on the northern tip of Sumatra, the Discalced Carmelites Bionysius and Redemptus were killed in 1638.

In 1605 the Dutch East India Company (VOC) suppressed the Catholic mission because of their support of Portuguese trading rivals. Defeated in war, many Catholics either converted to Protestantism (as in the Moluccas and Timor), or to Islam (as along the coast of Solor and Flores). In 1605, the first Protestant Church was established in Ambon. The Portuguese mission survived in east Timor and east Flores. However it was almost totally neglected during the 18th century. During this period, a fascinating symbiosis developed between local culture and popular Catholicism. Annual Holy Week Processions were organised by the Confreria Reinha Rosario, a group of powerful laymen in Larantuka who placed themselves under the protection of Renha Rosari, the Queen of the Rosary. These traditions maintained a Catholic identity until Dutch Catholic priests arrived in 1860. A Marian vision on the eve of a battle for Larantuka led to the defeat of a band of marauding Macassarese in 1641.

Missionary Revival. In 1800, the VOC was suppressed and Indonesia became a Dutch colony. In 1808 the first Dutch Catholic priests landed in Java to minister to Dutch expatriates, Eurasians and later the urban Chinese-Indonesians. In 1841 the Vicariate Apostolic of Batavia was erected for the whole archipelago. Dutch JESUITS arrived in 1858, and were gradually entrusted with the care of Catholics throughout the colony. Frequent conflicts erupted between the clergy and the colonial authorities because the Dutch governor general reserved to himself authority to appoint and transfer Protestant and Catholic clergy. Government regulations of 1853 (renewed in 1922)—the so-called "dubbele zending"—prohibited Protestant and Catholic missioners from working in the same district. Thus, Flores became Catholic and north Sumatra Protestant. As a result, even today, denominational allegiance largely follows ethnic and territorial lines. Missioners were also barred from regions considered strongly Muslim. Thus, there were no missions in west Java among the Sundanese and Banten people, or in Aceh on the north tip of Sumatra, or among the Malay and Lampong communities of Minangkabau in west Sumatra, or among the Macassarese and Bugese people of south Sulawesi, or indeed among the Hindus of Bali (where missioners first entered in the 1930s).

Francis van Lith SJ (1863–1926) came to Indonesia in 1896 and re-founded the Catholic Church in central Java among the indigenous population. The birth of the Catholic Church in Central Java can be dated to the baptism of four village heads on May 20, 1904, and more particularly to the baptism of 168 Javanese at the sacred spring of Sendangsono on December 15 by van Lith himself. Sendangsono eventually became the main pilgrimage centre for Javanese Catholics. F. van Lith lived in the villages, learned the Javanese language, and then established farming cooperatives. He founded a suburban high school at Muntilan and educated the first generation of Javanese clergy and nationalist politicians.

The 1859 Portuguese-Dutch treaty acceded Flores to the Dutch while the Portuguese retained the eastern half of Timor. A Dutch diocesan priest arrived in Flores a year later but was replaced by Jesuits in 1863. The latter began the long process of re-incorporating the popular Catholicism of Larantuka into the official Catholic Church. Growth was modest; by 1900 there were just 20,000 Catholics in east and central Flores. By 1914 the Jesuits had developed the two ancient Florenese communities of Larantuka and Sikka into flourishing congregations of about 30,000 adherents. In the 20th century, the Jesuits were complemented by other religious congregations— the CAPUCHINS in Kalimantan (1905) and Sumatra (1911), the Society of the Divine Word in Nusa Tenggara (1913), the Sacred Heart Missionaries in north Sulawesi

Metropolitan Sees	Suffragans
Ende	Denpasar, Larantuka, Ruteng
Jakarta	Bandung, Bogor
Kupang	Atambua, Weetebula
Medan	Padang, Palembang, Pangkal-Pinang, Sibolga, Tanjungkarang
Merauke	Agats, Jayapura, Manokwari-Sorong
Pontianak	Banjarmasin, Ketapang, Palangkaraya, Samarinda, Sanggau, Sintang
Semarang	Malang, Purwokerto, Surabaya
Ujung Pandang	Amboina, Manado

(1919). The Jesuits remained in central Java (from Yogyakarta to Semarang) and Batavia (present-day Jakarta). Most religious instruction in the villages was carried out by village catechists, the unsung heroes of the mass conversion of Flores from 1920 to 1950. In 1950 some 60 percent of Catholics lived in Nusa Tenggara; 50 years later, after growth elsewhere, over 30 percent still live in this region, the area with the most number of Catholics. In Central Java, Nusa Tengggara, the Moluccas and West Papua, missionary linguists wrote dictionaries and ethnologists recorded the cultures. A Catholic school system was established throughout the archipelago and all schools in Nusa Tenggara were entrusted to the church in 1913. Many of the first generation of national leaders were educated at these schools. Until Muslim revitalisation of the 1980s, many students became Christian while exposed to the dedication and example of teachers, both religious and lay. However, by the end of the 20th century, Catholic schools had largely lost this role and Muslims had developed their own educational system.

World War II. In March 1942 Japan invaded Indonesia and occupied the archipelago until August 1945. During this occupation most clergy were interned (the Germans in 1939, the Dutch in 1942). For both Catholics and Protestants the three-year occupation marked a short, sharp transition to adulthood. While the Protestant Churches already had indigenous elders and local synods in place, the Catholic Church was heavily dependent on European missionaries and its activities were severely inhibited when these missionaries were interned. During this period, village catechists and school teachers were entrusted with the running of parishes.

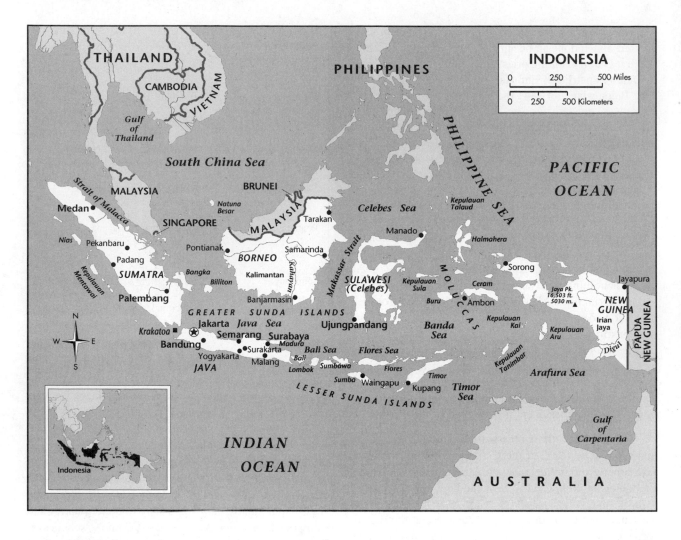

Independence. During the war of independence (1945–49), key nationalist figures were Christians: the Protestant Simatupang led the revolutionary army, the Catholic Adisucipto was in the top echelons of the air force while the provisional government was led for a time by the Protestant prime minister Sjarifoeddin. The Catholic Party was founded in 1923 and led for 32 years by Ignatius Josep Kasimo (1900–1986), a student of van Lith, with the firm support of the first Indonesian bishop, Albert Soegijapranata SJ of Semarang (1940–1963), another student of van Lith. Owing to the pivotal role of Catholics and Protestants during the independence struggle, both the Catholic and Protestant communities were accepted as an integral part of the independent state. The Catholic Church's slogan was ''Pro Ecclesia et Patria,'' ''100% Catholic, 100% Indonesian.'' The Indonesian hierarchy was established by JOHN XXIII in 1961. The first plenary session of the Indonesian hierarchy took place in 1964. Since 1970 the conference has met regularly once a year in Jakarta.

Vatican II. VATICAN COUNCIL II was a turning point for the Indonesian Catholic Church. The use of the vernacular in the Mass and the liturgical reforms were enthusiastically implemented. Liturgical texts were quickly translated into local languages, and liturgical INCULTURATION was promoted at the grassroots level in an ongoing effort to contextualize the Catholic Church in Indonesian soil. In 1974, the Catholic Church collaborated with Protestant churches to produce an ecumenical translation of the Bible in the national language, Bahasa Indonesia. The Indonesian Catholic Bishops' Conference enjoys good working relations with the Communion of Churches in Indonesia (PGI), an umbrella organization of 70 Protestant Churches in Indonesia that was founded in 1960.

Education and Media. The Catholic Church has enjoyed high prestige in the Indonesian society for its educational and social contributions. There are ten Catholic Universities in Jakarta, Bandung, Semarang, Yogyakarta, Surabaya and Malang (Java); in Medan (Sumatra); in Makassar (Sulawesi) and Kupang (Timor). Both Catholics and Protestants play an important role in the mass media. The Catholic-owned Kompas-Gramedia group publishes *Kompas,* the largest daily newspaper in Jakarta, in addition to producing books, journals and videos. The afternoon daily *Suara Pembaruan* is Protestant-owned, as is the English language *Jakarta Post.*

Continued Growth. The Indonesian Catholic Church has been blessed with many vocations. To accommodate them, there are nine major seminaries in Jakarta, Bandung, Yogyakarta and Malang (Java); Pematang Siantar (Sumatra), Manado (Sulawesi), Ledalero (Flores), Kupang (Timor) and Abepura (Papua). The national seminary is in Yogyakarta, while one of the largest seminaries in the world is that of Ledalero in Flores. Over 200 Indonesian DIVINE WORD missionaries are working in over 30 countries overseas. Locally, the continued heroic efforts of indigenous catechists and missionaries has resulted in a continuous growth, especially among the Dayaks (Kalimantan), Torajas (Sulawesi), Bataks (Sumatra) and Sumbanese (Sumba) as well as among the urban Chinese-Indonesians of Jakarta, Semarang and Surabaya. In 1923 the Catholic population came to just 275,000, half of whom were European or Eurasian. By 2000 the Catholic population had risen to almost 8 million.

The first National Catholic Congress was held in Yogyakarta in 1949 when bishops and lay people resolved to work for the newly independent state. Other lay-led National Congresses have been held in Semarang (1954) and Jakarta (1972, 1984, 1995). The 1984 Congress celebrated 450 years of the Catholic Church in Indonesia while the 1995 Congress celebrated the 50th anniversary of the Proclamation of Independence. A Jubilee Congress was held in Caringin-Bogor, west Java in 2000 on the theme "Empowerment of Base Communities in a New Indonesia."

Wanita Katolik, a member of the World Union for Catholic Women's Organisations was founded for women by Mrs. Suyadi Darmoseputro Sasraningrat in 1924. PMKRI, the Indonesian Catholic Student Association founded in 1947, has joined with other student movements, Protestant (GMKI - Student Christian Movement) and Muslim (HMI - Muslim Students of Indonesia), in the fight for political reform, justice and human rights. Emasculated during the Soeharto regime, PMKRI struggled to regain its historical charism in the years after Soeharto's downfall.

An Uncertain Future. Indonesia was a democracy from 1950 to 1959, when Soekarno, the founding president, declared a Guiding Democracy, the first step towards authoritarian rule. In 1965 a failed coup attempt destabilized the government and Soeharto, a general in

Church in old Batavia, Java, Indonesia. (©Bettmann/CORBIS)

the Indonesian army, was placed in control. The Soeharto dictatorship lasted for 32 years. In 1973 the government reduced the number of political parties to three, all of which were strictly government-controlled. Thus after 50 years the Catholic Party was dissolved. Nevertheless, Catholics were prominent in both Soeharto's economic think tank (CSIS) and in the cabinets of the 1970s and 1980s, in both financial and military portfolios. By 1997 systemic corruption and the centralization of both finance and political power was shaken by a monetary crisis. A popular student uprising forced Soeharto from power in May 1998. Many lay Catholics, supported by Catholic religious, were active in grassroots movements which led to the downfall of Soeharto. Inter-faith collaboration with Muslim activists, working for justice, democracy, and fact-finding on human rights abuses, augurs well for the future. However, the de facto collusion of many Catholics with the regime and the cooption of Catholic teachers and civil servants into Soeharto's Golkar Party has caused problems for the Church as an unstable Indonesia shuffles toward democracy. Regions that were exploited economically in the past have been either demanding independence (e.g, Aceh and Irian Jaya) or racked by interethnic and interreligious conflict (as in Ambon, where prolonged Christian-Muslism enmity shows no signs of abating). In the midst of social turmoil and religious ex-

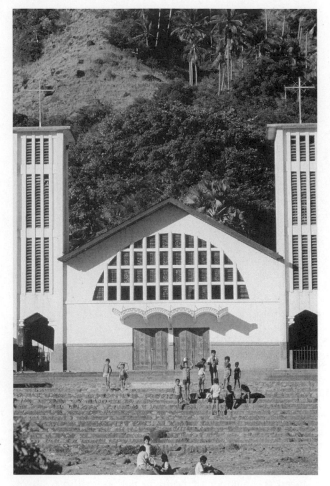

Catholic Church, Flores, Indonesia. (©Jeremy Horner/CORBIS)

tremism with no light at the end of the tunnel, Indonesian Catholics face the challenge of witnessing bravely to reconciliation and bridgebuilding.

Bibliography: J. BANK, *Katholieken en de Indonesische Revolutie* (Uitgeverij 1983), with extensive bibliography. TH. VAN DEN END and J. WEITJENS, *Ragi Carita: Sejarah Gereja di Indonesia (The Leaven of Love: History of the Church in Indonesia)* 2 v. (Jakarta 1993–1996). A. HEUKEN, SJ, *Ensiklopedi Gereja (Encyclopaedia of the Church)* 5 v. (Jakarta 1991–94). M. MUSKENS, ed., *Sejarah Gereja Katolik Indonesia (History of the Catholic Church in Indonesia)* 4 v. (Ende 1972–74) K. STEENBRINK, *Catholics in Indonesia, 1808–1942: A Documented History,* 2 v. (Leiden 2001–02), includes extensive primary sources.

[J. M. PRIOR]

INDRECHTACH, ST.

Martyr; d. 854. According to the Irish annals, he was an abbot of IONA who was martyred by Saxons while on his way to Rome. In the 12th century WILLIAM OF MALMESBURY wrote the life of a certain St. Indract (d. *c.*

710), the son of an Irish king, who was murdered along with some companions near Glastonbury while returning from Rome. J. F. Kenney is of the opinion that these two are to be identified. C. H. Slover, on the other hand, has rejected this opinion on the grounds that Indract was a secular prince whose relics were translated during the reign of INE, that he is not mentioned in the Irish MARTYROLOGIES, and that there is no Irish vita. Kenney was obviously aware of all these difficulties and rightly considered that they were not convincing, but even so his identification is a mere possibility, and the question still remains open. A marginal note in the *Martyrology of Tallaght* places the feast of Indract of Glastonbury on May 8.

Feast: Feb. 5.

Bibliography: Sources. For WILLIAM OF MALMESBURY'S vita (which has never been published) and the abridgement in the *Sanctilogium* of JOHN OF TYNEMOUTH, see J. F. KENNEY, *The Sources for the Early History of Ireland:* 446. For trs. of the vita, see G. H. DOBLE, *Saint Indract and Saint Dominic* (Cornish Saints Ser. 48; Long Compton 1944). C. PLATTS, "Martyrdom of St. Indract" in *Notes and Queries for Somerset and Dorset* 17 (1921–23) 17–23. **Literature.** J. F. KENNEY, *The Sources for the Early History of Ireland:* v.1, *Ecclesiastical* (New York 1929). C. H. SLOVER, "Glastonbury Abbey and the Fusing of English Literary Culture," *Speculum* 10 (1935) 147–160, esp. 152–153.

[C. MCGRATH]

INDUCTION

A method or activity by which one proceeds from observation to generalization. Although some regard it as the counterpart of DEDUCTION, it should more properly be seen as the counterpart of DEMONSTRATION, since its use leads to the acceptance of principles from which conclusions can be demonstrated. This article sketches the historical genesis of the notion and various views concerning the ground on which it is based.

Historical Genesis. Inductive method seems to have had its origin in the philosophizing of SOCRATES. "For two things may be fairly ascribed to Socrates: inductive arguments and universal definition, both of which are concerned with the starting point of science" (Aristotle, *Metaphysics* 1078b 27). In Western philosophy, this Socratic attribution is later confirmed by CICERO: "This form of argument which attains the desired proof by citing several parallels is called induction, in Greek ἐπαγωγή; Socrates frequently used this in his dialogue" (*Topica* 10.42; *Loeb Classical Library* 413).

For Aristotle, the sciences are distinguished by their methodological differences; thus the manner of demonstrating and the type of certitude in the speculative sciences are other than in the technical sciences (*De Partibus Animalium* 639b 30). Again, in the natural sciences a uniform method does not apply, since one must always seek whether demonstration or classification or some other procedure is best suited (*De Anima* 402a 11). Moreover, Aristotle forbids the transfer of a method from one science to another, for example, in proving geometrical truths by the methods of arithmetic (*Analytica Posteriora* 75a 38–75b 7). He further points out that the sciences are differentiated by their degree of exactness and that this degree depends on the object and the method chosen (*Ethica Nicomachea* 1094b 12, 23, 1098a 26; *Metaphysics* 982a 25, 1078a 9).

Inductive Procedure. Aristotle also distinguishes formally between two opposed procedures, the process *from* principles and the process *to* principles; in so doing, he recalls that Plato sought to determine which of the two is more advantageous (*Ethica Nicomachea* 1095a 30). In the *Republic* (510–511), Plato maintains that geometry and similar sciences start from accepted hypotheses and argue from these to conclusions, whereas dialectic first searches out the principles and then proceeds to conclusions. Just as Plato prefers the dialectical method, so too does Aristotle recommend the process leading from experience to principles, i.e., the process of generalization or ABSTRACTION by which man goes from what is more evident to him to what is more evident by nature (*Physica* 184a 17–21).

At a much later period in the history of philosophy, Francis BACON would wish to proceed from sensations to axioms (*Novum Organum* 1.19), and René DESCARTES would insist on beginning with objects that are "the easiest to know" (*Discourse* 2). Yet the naturalness of this procedure had long before been noted by Plato and Aristotle. All animals have sensations that, for some, are retained through memory; in man, memories form the basis of experience, and experience provides the basis of science (*Analytica Posteriora* 99b 15–100b 17; *Metaphysics* 980a 22–982a 1). Aristotle, however, insists on the experiential starting point more than does Plato. In the Aristotelian view, sciences, whether inductive or deductive, cannot overlook sensations (*Analytica Posteriora* 81a 37–81b 9); physicists, astronomers, and zoologists must reckon with phenomena (*De Partibus Animalium* 639a 2–642b 4; *Cael.* 306a 16). Aristotle is quick to blame those who, lacking sufficient experience, would explain nature (*De Generatione et Corruptione* 316a 5); even in morals, he says, one must begin with phenomena (*Ethica Nicomachea* 1145b 2). In some places he even indicates a preference for experience over reasoning. Speaking of the multiplication of bees, for example, he affirms that observation is more reliable than speculation (*Generatione Animalium* 760b 30); elsewhere he regards as

Scene of an angel appearing to the Virgin Mary, carved wooden church doors, Bali, Indonesia. The image has strong Indonesian motifs, including typically Indonesian clothing and jewelry. (©Lindsay Hebberd/CORBIS)

empty a general or logical explanation of the sterility of mules (*ibid.*, 747b 28; *De Generatione et Corruptione* 316a 10; *De Anima* 403a 29). For Aristotle, observation must be continuous and complete; he explains that if one, being on the Moon, would observe once that Earth faces the Sun and that an eclipse is taking place, he would not know its cause, but he would come to know it after numerous observations (*Analytica Posteriora* 87b 39–88a 4). On this score, he takes Democritus to task for his poor explanation of dentition based on limited observation of some animals alone (*De Generatione Animalium* 788b 9–19). Surely, the originality of Descartes is not to be found in this rule: "make everywhere divisions so complete and revisions so general [as to be] certain to omit nothing" (*Discourse* 2).

Nature of Induction. It is this method or procedure—from observation to generalization—that Aristotle usually calls induction. H. Maier has suggested that perhaps he is the first one to have used the word in this technical sense (*Die Syllogistik des Aristoteles* [3 v. Tübingen 1896–1900] 2.1:374). Aristotle specifies that the basis of induction is the resemblance or SIMILARITY among particular objects (*Topica* 108b 7; *De Rhetorica* 1356b 12). In relating induction to the syllogistic form, he also prescribes a completeness that includes all particular cases (*Analytica Priora* 68b 8–29). This prescription was challenged by Bacon (*Novum Organum* 1:105) and by all those who have failed to notice that the Aristotelian "particular" refers to the SPECIES and not to the individual. Other logicians have objected to Aristotle's limiting of induction to the observation of facts and his assigning of causal explanation to demonstration (*Analytica Posteriora* 92a 34). In fact, it seems that induction is justified by the very existence and recognition of causal relations (*see* CAUSALITY).

A variant of Aristotelian induction is the paradigm, or the exemplary model. As in induction, its basis is similarity or resemblance. But contrary to induction, it does not lead to the universal; rather, it concludes to the particular from the particular. The following is an example: If a war between two neighboring countries ends up as a liability for the aggressor, another war of the same type will likewise be fateful for the new assailant (*Analytica Priora* 68b 38–69a 19; *De Rhetorica* 1355b 26–1358a 35, 1393a 22–1394a 18). Example itself was considered by Aristotle as an instrument proper to rhetoric but improper to scientific logic (*Analytica Posteriora* 71a 1–10; *De Rhetorica* 1356b 5). Actually, it involves an analogical judgment (ἀναλογίζεσθαι) identical with that of induction.

Ground of Induction. The precise formulation of the ground of inductive reasoning has long been seen in the *regula philosophandi* of Sir Isaac Newton: "Effectuum generalium ejusdem generis eaedem sunt causae" (General effects of the same kind have the same causes). This ground, for Newton, is nothing more than an application of the principle of causality (*see* CAUSALITY, PRINCIPLE OF).

The attack on causality launched by David HUME is also an attack on induction or, at least, an attempt to seek its foundation elsewhere. Indeed the author of the *Treatise of Human Nature* and of the *Philosophical Essays* maintains that induction is based on habit or on a personal disposition that has nothing to do with truth or with the nature of things. "Having observed the constant relation between two things, for example heat with flame or solidity with weight, we are determined only by force of habit to conclude from the existence of one to the existence of the other. Otherwise, it is impossible to explain why we conclude from a thousand cases that which we could not conclude from a single case" (*Philosophical Essays* 5).

Yet another ground is proposed by Thomas REID and the SCOTTISH SCHOOL OF COMMON SENSE. "In the phenomena of nature, what is to be will probably be like to what has been in similar circumstances" (*Essays on the Intellectual Powers of the Human Mind,* 6, ch. 5, 12); this is to say that "nature is governed by invariable laws." For P. P. Royer-Collard (1763–1843), these laws are of two types, stable and general. Royer-Collard's first principle of induction is that "the universe is governed by stable laws," so that once known at one moment, they are known at all times. His second principle is that "the universe is governed by general laws," so that once known for a single case, they are alike for all cases. The later developments of Reid and of Royer-Collard seem reducible to a simpler Newtonian formulation: nature is governed by laws. The character of a law, or the sign that reveals its existence, is that it applies equally well to all cases covered by the law. Stated somewhat differently, the same cause, in the same circumstances, will produce the same effect. (*See* UNIFORMITY.)

Jean Nicod (1893–1924), basing his analysis on John Maynard Keynes's *Treatise on Probability* (1921), has come to the following conclusions: (1) induction by simple enumeration is a type of basic proof that cannot be dispensed with without resorting to sophistry; (2) this type of reasoning retains its value even without a prior postulate of determinism; (3) inductive proof can increase the probability of a hypothesis even if newly observed facts are merely repetitions without variation of facts already known; (4) if causes are eliminated as a ground of induction, the most that can be attained by this type of argument is a moderate degree of probability; and (5) it has yet to be demonstrated that inductive reasoning can raise the degree of probability of a law to that of absolute certitude (*Le Problème logique de l'induction,* Paris 1961).

Recent Theories. Recent attempts at solving the problem of induction have moved in two main directions. First, many thinkers basically accept Hume's criticism and take it as starting point in their investigation of the topic; they try to offer some kind of "vindication" or "validation" as a substitute for a definitive justification. Within this philosophical literature, induction has been examined mostly from a logical perspective; sometimes presumably an "exclusively" logical one. The post-Humean tendency has been to reduce the issue of induction to the process whereby a general proposition is obtained from several particular instances. There has also been a complementary effort to explain that process as the fulfillment of a psychological need of human beings. To date, these viewpoints sprung from a common source have been seen as different and very much unrelated.

Other authors, moving in the second direction, examine and reject the presuppositions on which Hume's famous attack is based. They prefer to unravel the confusions that cloud the issue. Noting that many of the approaches that accept Hume's criticism seem to presuppose some inductive procedures at any rate, they try to use the reduction *ad absurdum* against Hume's criticism. Hume's dilemma is thus interpreted as an indirect proof that the presuppositions on which it is based are at fault. In general, philosophers working along these lines find nothing wrong with a conclusion that in some way "says more than its premises." This approach has received some valuable support from nonpositivistic philosophers of science. William Kneale and Henry B. Veatch, among others, have criticized the attempt to reduce all necessity to logical necessity, a doctrine clearly formulated in Wittgenstein's *Tractatus* (6.37).

Other philosophical traditions have also tried to clarify the riddle of induction from their own viewpoints. Within a Thomistic framework, Lonergan has explained inductive conclusions as based on the principle that "similars are similarly understood" (*Insight: A Study of Human Understanding* 288). The real problem of induction is the problem of criteria of relevant similarity. There cannot be a difference in understanding the data unless there is a difference in the data themselves. In a further elaboration of Lonergan's theories, Philip McShane's *Randomness, Statistics and Emergence* provides an analysis of statistical science as a type of general knowledge of random aggregates.

Another group of philosophers has dealt with induction from a phenomenological perspective. Phenomenologists reject the empiricist principle upon which many of the investigations on induction depend: when such a principle is abandoned, it becomes questionable whether there still is a "problem of induction." The phenomenological notion of eidetic intuition is frequently mentioned in connection with induction, as the factor that guarantees the validity and certainty of inductive generalizations. In this sense, eidetic intuition is a necessary though not sufficient condition for the validity of inductive conclusions. Its peculiar role is to provide an insight into the contents of inductive generalizations, thereby providing the universality and necessity that cannot be found in simple repetition (cf. Joseph Kockelmans, *The World in Science and Philosophy* 123).

During the mid-20th century much thought was given to the origin and evolution of science. These investigations indirectly affected the discussions on induction, mostly in the sense of establishing the limits of its extent without, however, denying its existence as a valid way of knowledge. Thomas Kuhn's notion of paradigm (*The Structure of Scientific Revolutions,* Chicago 1962) and Norwood R. Hanson's analysis of seeing as "seeing that x" (*Patterns of Discovery*) emphasize the importance of formulating imaginative hypotheses in order to account for the facts that, for the most part, do not appear to be in a "pure" form, just ready for public inspection. The evolution and growth of science is not explained as a process of accumulation, but as dependent on the formulation, development, and eventual substitution of paradigms. Within the perspective of these approaches, induction may play a role in the origin of theories and may give some indications about their possible explanatory and predictive power. In this way, even though induction *does* exist, its role is by no means as decisive and primary as Baconian inductivism would want it to be.

As a result of long discussions on the topic, inductive inferences enjoyed an increasingly secure though less extended place in the world of science.

See Also: METHODOLOGY (PHILOSOPHY).

Bibliography: M. J. ADLER, ed., *The Great Ideas: A Syntopicon of Great Books of the Western World,* 2 v. (Chicago 1952); v. 2, 3 of *Great Books of the Western World* 1:805–815. R. EISLER, *Wörterbuch der philosophischen Begriffe,* 3 v. (4th ed. Berlin 1927–30) 1:741–745. R. HOUDE, "The Logic of Induction," *The Logic of Science,* ed. V. E. SMITH (New York 1963) 17–34. P. CONWAY, "Induction in Aristotle and St. Thomas," *Thomist* 22 (1959) 336–365. O. HAMELIN, *Le Système d'Aristote* (Paris 1920; 2d ed. 1931). For induction in the philosophy of science, see E. H. MADDEN, ed., *The Structure of Scientific Thought* (Boston 1960). For induction in comparative logic and Indian philosophy, see P. MASSON-OURSEL, *La Philosophie comparée* (Paris 1923). T. SHCHERBATSKY, *Buddhist Logic,* 2 v. (pa. New York 1962). P. EDWARDS, "Russell's Doubt about Induction," *Mind* 58 (1949) 141–163. I. P. CREED, "The Justification of the Habit of Induction," *Journal of Philosophy* 37 (1940) 85–97. F. L. WILL, "Is There a Problem of Induction?" *ibid.* 39 (1942) 505–513. W. H. V. READE, *The Problem of Inference* (Oxford 1938). A. J. AYER, *Language, Truth and Logic* (New York 1952). S. BARKER, *Induction and Hypothesis* (Ithaca, NY 1957). M. BLACK, *Problems of Analysis* (London 1954); "The Justification of Induction," *Language and Philosophy* (Ithaca, NY 1949). C. D. BROAD, *Induction, Probability and Causation* (Dordrecht, the Netherlands; New York 1968). M. BUNGE, *Causality* (Cleveland, New York 1963). R. CARNAP, *Foundation of Logic and Mathematics* (Chicago 1939). N. R. HANSON, *Patterns of Discovery* (Cambridge, Eng. 1965). R. HARRE, *Theories and Things* (London, New York 1961); *An Introduction to the Logic of the Sciences* (New York 1967); *The Principles of Scientific Thinking* (Chicago 1970). J. KATZ, *The Problem of Induction and Its Solution* (Chicago 1962). J. KOCKELMANS, *The World in Science and Philosophy* (Milwaukee 1969). J. KOCKELMANS and T. KISIEL, *Phenomenology and the Natural Sciences* (Evanston, IL 1970). W. KNEALE, *Probability and Induction* (Oxford 1949). H. E. KYBURG and E. NAGEL, eds., *Induction: Some Current Issues* (Middletown, CT 1963). C. I. LEWIS, *An Analysis of Knowledge and Valuation* (La Salle, IL 1946). B. LONERGAN, *Insight: A Study of Human Understanding* (New York 1957). E. H. MADDEN, ed., *The Structure of Scientific Thought* (Boston 1960). P. MCSHANE, *Randomness, Statistics, and Emergence* (Notre Dame 1970). J. PIAGET, *The Psychology of Intelligence* (New York 1950); *The Construction of Reality in the Child* (New

York 1954); *Genetic Epistemology* (New York 1970). K. R. POPPER, *The Logic of Scientific Discovery* (New York 1951); *Conjectures and Refutations* (London 1963). H. REICHENBACH, *Experience and Prediction* (Chicago 1938). D. WILLIAMS, *The Ground of Induction* (Cambridge, MA 1947).

[R. HOUDE/L. CAMACHO]

INDULGENCES

Actions accompanied by prayer that have been specified by the Church as an acceptable "remission before God" of the debt of "temporal punishment for sins" that remains due after forgiveness has been pronounced in the sacrament of penance (see *Codex iuris canonici*, c. 992). The practice of indulgences came to be fully developed by the eleventh century in the West. It has, however, a more remote historical origin in the system of confession and penance that was in use in the first centuries of the Church and its theological justification can find support in the New Testament.

Principle of Solidarity. On the basis of his experience of Christ St. PAUL was convinced that the members of his (mystical) Body are so closely related to one another that each contributes to the well-being of all, and especially of their ailing brothers and sisters. He so rejoiced in the sufferings that he bore for the Christians at Colossus that he formulated the paradox "What is lacking of the sufferings of Christ I fill up in my flesh for his body which is the Church" (Colonial 1:24). Nothing of course is missing in the salvific work of the Word Incarnate. Those, however, who by faith have been made part of his Body share in the mystery of salvation.

In keeping with this teaching CLEMENT OF ALEXANDRIA noted a traditional report that the Apostle John when he was in Ephesus not only made "supplications with a wealth of prayers" for the chief of a robber gang, but that he also "vied with him in protracted fasts" (*Quis dives salvetur* 42, *Die griechischen christlichen Schriftsteller der ersten drei Jahrhunderte*, 190). In the ensuing centuries the social character of public penance gave evidence that penitents were not left to their own resources for expiation of their public sins. The local Church in which they confessed their sin and waited for the bishop to pronounce their reconciliation with the community contributed to this. Tertullian underlined this corporate character of penance: "The body cannot rejoice over the misery of one of its members; rather the whole body must suffer and work together for a cure" (De Paenitentia 10.5, *Florilegium Patristicum*, 10:25). Special efficacy in this process came to be attached to the intercession of martyrs who had survived their torture during the persecutions. For the weak who had apostasized under threat,

a martyr's letter of recommendation could in some Churches win a more speedy reconciliation and, in consequence, a shortening of their assigned time of penance. Thus, even when he denounced abuses of the "martyr's privilege," St. CYPRIAN did not wish to abolish the privilege altogether (Letter 15.4, *Corpus scriptorum ecclesiasticorum latinorum* 3:516). At the close of the fifth century, CAESARIUS OF ARLES (d. 542) acknowledged the validity of vicarious satisfaction when he described repentant sinners asking for the prayers of the community in the ritual of public penance: "I believe that, before the number of his sins, he (the sinner) sees that he cannot by himself suffice for such grave evils; and so he wishes to seek the assistance of the whole people" (Sermon 261, *Patrologia Latina*, 39:2227). While the term indulgentia existed in Roman civil law, the Church used the words redemptio and remissio to designate the shortening of the time of penance between the absolution of a grave sin and the readmission of a penitent to communion.

Commutations of Penance. Taking the monastic practice of taxing faults against the Rule with specific penances as its model, the Celtic Church in the British Isles adopted a principle of strict correspondence between a specific sin and the appropriate penance. Each sin was assigned a penitential tariff that was specified in handbooks used by confessors. When the Anglo-Saxon Church in Britain inherited this system, however, it tended, following the practice of the archbishop of Canterbury Theodore (d. 690), to assign such long penances for grave public sins that many a penitent died before the penance could be fulfilled. It was to meet this problem that subsequent generations modified the system. The heavy penances prescribed in penitential books could then be replaced, in part or in whole, by prayers and other pious works, such as fasting or almsgiving. To the extent that these commutations relaxed penances that would otherwise have been imposed by the confessor, they functioned as indulgences in the broad sense of the term. They were substitute penances rather than conditions for gaining an indulgence in the later meaning of the term.

Absolution Grants. Beginning in the ninth century popes and bishops frequently concluded their letters with a petition (suffragium) asking God through the intercession of Christ and the saints to absolve the sinner of all remaining penalties due to sin. At times this prayer was made in favor of the deceased as well as the living. Confessors began to add a similar prayer to the formula of sacramental reconciliation. Although this has been called an absolution grant, it was not a remission of debt in the strict sense since it was offered per *modum suffragii*, and therefore with no guarantee that the temporal punishment due to sin was actually canceled by God. Though they frequently invoked the power of the keys and were often introduced by the affirmative formula "I absolve," these prayers remained too indefinite or general to be regarded as indulgence grants in the strict sense. They did not promise a relaxation or easing of the penance imposed by the confessor or a remission of the temporal debt due to sin that was to be paid in this life or in purgatory.

Indulgence Grants. Indulgence grants in the strict sense first appeared in southern France in the early eleventh century. They were closely related to penances imposed by confessors in the sacrament of reconciliation. Thus according to the indulgence granted to those who would contribute to the support of the monastic church of San Pedro de Portella in Spain (1035), a penance of three days of fasting during Lent could be reduced to two. In this case the support of a monastic church was a condition for gaining a relaxation of penance. In the course of time other occasions were introduced for gaining similar indulgences, such as contributions to the building or upkeep of churches, schools, hospitals and bridges. Pilgrims praying at the great shrines of Christendom, particularly ST. PETER in Rome, SANTIAGO DE COMPOSTELLA and JERUSALEM, could gain indulgences attached to each specific pilgrimage. In 1300, the first proclamation of a Jubilee year by Boniface VIII included the promulgation of indulgences for the pilgrims who went to Rome and also of substitute indulgences for those who for a good reason were unable to travel that far. Since that time all Jubilee years, including the Great Jubilee of the year 2000, have included the proclamation of specific indulgences that pilgrims could obtain by meeting the conditions specified in the relevant decree. Before Paul VI's reform the indulgence grants symbolized their effectiveness in terms of time—days, months, years—a practice that originated in a perceived analogy with the reduction of the long penances that used to be given for serious crimes in the sacrament of reconciliation.

Crusade Indulgences. In 1095 at the Council of CLERMONT, held under the auspices of URBAN II, the following canon was enacted: "Whoever from devotion alone, and not for the purpose of gaining honors and wealth, shall set out for the liberation of the Church of God at Jerusalem, that journey will be reckoned in place of all penance" (*Sacrorum Conciliorum nova et amplissima collectio,* 20:816). This indulgence was granted to those who had already confessed their sins, a condition that recurred in every indulgence grant of the medieval period. The crusades, which entailed the possibility of giving up one's life in combat for the faith and the Church, provided the context for the idea of a *plenary indulgence,* an indulgence that abolishes the entire penalty due to sin. It presupposes perfect charity in the recipient. In the course of time the crusade indulgence was extended to others than the crusaders, notably to all who con-tributed to the support of the crusades against the Moors in Spain, the Albigensians in Southern France and the Turks when their political and military pressure on Europe was believed to threaten the very existence of the Church.

The indulgence of the Portiuncula, granted by HONORIUS III at the request of FRANCIS OF ASSISI to those who, properly disposed, prayed at the chapel that he and his first followers had restored, was the first plenary indulgence that could be gained outside of the crusades.

Theology of Indulgences. That the bishops and the pope are able to grant indulgences to the faithful needed to be supported theologically. The theology of indulgences, however, came to be elaborated more than a century after the practice was well established. There was in fact considerable resistance. Abelard denied that such a power existed. Neither PETER LOMBARD in the *Sentences,* nor Gratian in the *Decretum,* mentioned the topic. It was HUGH OF SAINT-CHER who first based indulgences on the Church's "treasury" of the merits that have been stored up by Christ, the Blessed Virgin Mary and the saints. This insight reflected the principle of Christian solidarity in the MYSTICAL BODY OF CHRIST; and it implied a notion of vicarious satisfaction, which the great scholastics developed in the thirteenth century.

Both BONAVENTURE and THOMAS AQUINAS understood an indulgence to be the payment (solutio) or commutation (commutatio) of a debt rather than a remission of it. Bonaventure based his conclusions on the necessity of justice, for God is no less just than merciful. The penance for sin that is assigned in the sacrament should be both satisfactory to God in justice and medicinal for the repenting sinner. The penitent must shoulder medicinal punishment personally. Expiatory punishment, however, can also be assumed by another person on the basis of his "union of charity" with the penitent. In order to be acceptable in justice, however, vicarious satisfaction should be greater than the penance that is incumbent on the guilty person (CS IV, d. 20, p. 2, q. 1).

Thomas based vicarious satisfaction and indulgences more directly on the power of the keys entrusted to Peter in Matthew 16:19. He also found them justified by "the unity of the Mystical Body" (STh III suppl., q. 25, a. 1). Thanks to this unity the merit that has been accumulated by Christ and his saints can be applied to the members of the Body who are properly disposed. This merit far exceeds what would be needed for the expiation of all pains due to sin, Christ's merit alone being "infinitely higher than the efficacy of the sacraments." With Pope CLEMENT VI the Jubilee bull of 1343, *Unigenitus Dei Filius,* explicitly included the justification of an indulgence as a vicarious satisfaction that is made possible by "the Church's treasury" (DS 1025 1027).

Indulgences For The Dead. Devotion to the Holy Souls was developed largely under the influence of the monastery of CLUNY. The rapid spread of this devotion provided the occasion for the promulgation of indulgences applicable to the souls in purgatory. SIXTUS IV did this for the first time in the form of a plenary indulgence, in 1476. In the bull *Salvator noster* (*Enchiridion symbolorum,* 1398), Sixtus specified that this indulgence is applicable by way of petition (per modum suffragii). By excluding the way of absolution, Sixtus IV implied that there is no guarantee that the power of the keys has any effect beyond the present life. This view remained standard in regard to indulgences offered for the dead. It was confirmed in the nineteenth century when the Congregation on Indulgences and Holy Relics stated, on July 28, 1840, that the efficacy of a plenary indulgence attached to a privileged altar "corresponds to the good pleasure and acceptance of the divine mercy" (DS 2750). In other words, the indulgence offered for the dead is not a sentence of absolution pronounced by the Church; it is a prayer for a repenting sinner.

Abuses. The popularity of indulgences contributed no small part to the welfare of medieval society. Thanks to indulgences in the form of material and monetary gifts, great cathedrals and monastic establishments were built and kept in repair, schools and universities were founded and endowed, hospitals were maintained and bridges were built. And there were spiritual effects that cannot be measured. Not only were the people reminded of their solidarity with the whole family of God which is the Church, triumphant as well as militant, but the preaching of an indulgence was often the occasion of spiritual revivals when preachers exhorted the faithful to true repentance and confession.

In spite of this, abuses in the granting and preaching of indulgences were not slow to appear. Bishops multiplied indulgences, and preachers exaggerated their efficacy. When indulgences were granted for monetary gifts, as for the upkeep of churches or the building of new ones, the collectors (quaestores) often received more money than was due, thus paying themselves for their work. In addition, not all the money was used for the purpose for which the indulgence was preached. Already in 1215 the Fourth Lateran Council condemned "abuses in the granting of indulgences" (*Sacrorum Conciliorum nova et amplissima collectio,* 22:1050–56; DS 819). Moreover, there occasionally spread among the people rumors of indulgences that were entirely spurious. Such abuses and the "trafficking" in indulgences multiplied in the late Middle ages and above all during the Renaissance. In 1515 Emperor CHARLES V obtained from Pope LEO X a plenary indulgence for those who would contribute to the repair of the dikes in the Netherlands. In 1517 King Francis I of France was granted a similar indulgence for financing a crusade that he had no intention of launching.

The Reformation. In 1517 it was precisely the scandal associated in Germany with the preaching of an indulgence offered for the rebuilding of St. Peter's at the Vatican that led the Augustinian friar Martin LUTHER to criticize the actual preaching of indulgences and eventually to reject the underlying doctrine. He took issue with the preaching in the Ninety-Five Theses that he made public at Wittenberg in 1517. In these theses, however, Luther formulated what seem to be contradictory propositions. On the one hand he declared: "The treasury of indulgences is most acceptable, for it makes the last to be first" (thesis 64), and also: "Let him be anathema and accursed who denies the apostolic character of indulgences" (thesis 71). On the other hand he asserted: "The pope has neither the will nor the power to remit any penalties beyond those imposed either at his own discretion or by canon law" (thesis 5), and also: "The true treasure of the Church is the holy gospel of the glory and grace of God" (thesis 62). The commentary that Luther sent to the archbishop of Mainz on Oct. 31, 1517 (*Disputatio pro declaratione virtutis indulgentiarum*) was in fact moderate. It admitted the basic principles of a temporal penalty due to sin, of purgatory, and of the treasury of the Church. It also drew attention to the greater importance of interior conversion than of the remission of exterior penalties; and it inferred from the traditional teaching that an indulgence applied to the dead by way of petition is logically no more than a prayer. Only later, as he reflected on the implications of justification by faith alone without the works of the Law and as he gave up any hope of seeing the papacy reform itself did Luther reach the conclusion that indulgences are incompatible with the total trust in divine forgiveness *propter Christum,* "for the sake of Christ," that is essential to the Christian faith.

The Counter-Reformation. In the decree *Cum postquam* (Nov. 9, 1519), Pope Leo X condemned Luther's doctrine on indulgences. In the bull *Exsurge Domine* (June 15, 1520) he condemned Luther himself. While he regretted that abuses had occurred in the preaching of indulgences, Leo reaffirmed that the temporal penalty due to sin can be partially or fully remitted, in this world or the next, by application of the merits accumulated in the treasury of the Church by Christ and the saints. CLEMENT VII, however, took account of criticisms and attached no specific monetary contribution to the Jubilee indulgence of 1525. Few pilgrims, in fact, made the journey, partly because the streets of Rome were troubled by a violent conflict between the COLONNA and ORSINI families and partly because of the brewing struggle between the pope and the emperor, which brought about the sack of Rome in 1527. In 1550 JULIUS III restored the solemnity of the Jubilee celebration, but few pilgrims came. In 1563 a short decree of the last session of the Council of TRENT endorsed the right of the Church to grant indulgences (COD 772–773). In the same decree the council deplored the abuses that had taken place and ordered the bishops to correct them and to fight the superstitious use of indulgences. In 1567, however, PIUS V found that the TRIDENTINE regulations had so far been ineffective, and he abrogated "every indulgence . . . which contains in any way whatsoever permission to make collections" (*Bullarium Romanum,* 7:536). Furthermore, *The Catechism of the Council of Trent,* edited under Pius V, did not mention indulgences in its long chapter on the sacrament of penance, even though it explained that the Lord does not always remove "the remains of sin and the pain, measured in terms of time, that is due to sins" (*The Catechism of the Council of Trent,* p. 2, c. 5, n. 65), and it also affirmed such solidarity of all in the communion of saints that "the tasks (*officia*) of satisfaction are common among us" (n. 76). The theologians of the COUNTER-REFORMATION, however, generally defended the doctrine and practice of indulgences as being both traditional and pastorally useful. PETER CANISIUS related the indulgences to the action of the Holy Spirit. In his commentary of the Tertia pars of the Summa theologica (Disp. 49 57) SUAREZ saw them as rooted in the infinite redemptive merits of Christ.

In order to keep a tighter control on the use of indulgences, CLEMENT IX in 1669 entrusted their supervision to a new dicastery, the Congregation for Indulgences and Relics. In 1908 Pius X abolished this Congregation and assigned the regulation of indulgences to the Holy Office. From time to time a *Raccolta,* or *Enchiridion indulgentiarum: Normae et concessiones,* is published in the Vatican by the Apostolic Penitentiary; it contains the authentic list of currently available indulgences with the relevant conditions.

Paul VI. On July 24, 1963 Pope PAUL VI instructed Cardinal Fernando Cento to form a commission of *periti* that would recommend a new approach to indulgences. The ensuing study *Positio de sacrarum indulgentiarum recognitione* was presented to the council fathers of Vatican II on Nov. 9, 1965, shortly before the end of the last session. The bishops were invited to send their remarks to the commission. Having received a number of comments, and taking account of the beginning of ecumenical dialogues with the Churches of the Reformation, the pope issued the apostolic constitution *Indulgentiarum doctrina* (Jan. 1, 1967). In this document four short chapters explain the doctrine, and a fifth enunciates twenty practical norms. Paul VI recalls that true teaching is done through "pastoral practice" as well as "doctrinal documents," that both as "disobedience to divine law" and as "con-

tempt for the friendship of God" sin deserves punishment, that the full remission of sins therefore includes the restoration of friendship with God through forgiveness and the repair, through expiation, of the damage done by sin to "the universal order" of creation. Forgiveness is received sacramentally. Expiation takes place in purgatory unless it has already been done in this life (Ch. 1, nn. 1–3). The expiation of the temporal penalty due to sin is precisely the domain of indulgences.

Ch. 2, nn. 4–5, describes the "solidarity" that unites all the faithful in Christ, the communion of saints and "the supernatural unity of the Mystical Body of Christ." As a result of this unity one may say that, "as it were, a single mystical person is formed." In the process "an abundant exchange" takes place among all the faithful, whether these be in heaven, in purgatory, or on earth. Ch. 3, n. 6, evokes the "very ancient usage" of praying for sinners, the traditional practice of penance and the belief that satisfaction for sin is done by "the entire Church united to Christ" rather than by individual believers. It was in this spirit that bishops eventually "permitted canonical penances to be replaced by easier works." In ch. 4 Paul VI esteems that the usage of indulgences, when it came, was under the inspiration of the Holy Spirit and constituted a "progression" in doctrine and discipline rather than a "change" (n. 7). As the Council of Trent maintained that indulgences are "salutary for the Christian people" (n. 8), likewise the faithful today are invited to "ponder and meditate" on the benefits that can accrue from them to "all Christian society" (n. 9). Indulgences contribute to the Church's holiness (n. 10). They confirm "the preeminence of charity in Christian life" inasmuch as they require "a sincere conversion of mentality (metanoia)" (n. 11).

The norms present three notable aspects. First, partial indulgences are no longer to be assessed in function of time (days, months, years). Instead, the value of an indulgence depends on "the action itself of the faithful who perform a work to which an indulgence is attached" (n. 12). Two elements specify the value of such an action, "the charity of the one performing the act" and "the degree to which the act itself is performed in a more perfect way." Second, in keeping with this principle, Paul VI further defines a partial indulgence as "a remission of punishment through the intervention of the Church," that equals the value of the action as performed by the person (norm n. 5). In other words, as it grants an indulgence the Church promises to match the "merit" that accrues to the person who seeks the indulgence and performs the required work. Third, it follows that indulgences are not tied to places or objects but to actions that are performed "at least with a contrite heart" (n. 5). Regarding plenary indulgences, their number is reduced considerably, and the customary conditions are maintained: sacramental confession, Eucharistic communion and prayer for the intentions of the Supreme Pontiff (n. 7). Furthermore, they presuppose that "all attachment to sin, even to venial sin, be absent," that is, perfect charity. Following upon this reform of the theory and practice of indulgences, the Apostolic Penitentiary issued an *Enchiridion indulgentiarum* on June 28, 1969. Much shorter than the previous Raccolta (1957), it emphasized the prayers and dispositions of the faithful who seek an indulgence (*opus operantis*) rather than the works of piety (visits to churches with recitation of assigned prayers) for which the indulgence is granted (*opus operatum*).

The implementation of Paul VI's constitution was confirmed in the Code of CANON LAW of 1983, cc. 992 997, which replaced the provisions of the code of 1917, cc. 911 936. The canonical definition is the following:

> Indulgentia est remissio coram Deo poenae temporalis pro peccatis, ad culpam quod attinet jam deletis, quam christifidelis, apte dispositus et certis ac definitis condicionibus, consequitur ope Ecclesiae quae, ut ministra redemptionis, thesaurum satisfactionum Christi et sanctorum auctoritative dispensat et applicat (Can. 992). (An indulgence is a remission before God of the temporal pain due to sins that have already been forgiven as to guilt, which a Christian faithful, properly disposed and under clear and definite conditions, performs by virtue of the Church, which, as minister of Redemption, authoritatively dispenses and applies the treasure of the sactisfactions of Christ and the saints.)

The first part of the definition (to "jam deletis") is taken from the code of 1917, Can. 911. The second part differs in emphasis. The code of 1917 cited "the treasure of the Church" as the source of indulgences, the "ecclesiastical authority" as the agent, "the living" and "the dead" as the addressees, "absolution" and "prayer" (*suffragium*) as the respective "modes" or forms of the grant. By contrast, the code of 1983 emphasizes the connection of indulgence with the role of the Church in applying the fruits of Redemption to the faithful. The description implies four doctrinal propositions: (1) the Church is minister of Redemption; (2) sin has two consequences, moral guilt and a debt of temporal punishment proportional to the gravity of the sin; (3) forgiveness effaces moral guilt but not temporal punishment; (4) the temporal punishment can be partially or fully remitted through the Church's recourse to the satisfactions of Christ and the saints.

The Catechism of the Catholic Church, published in 1992 under JOHN PAUL II includes a moderate treatment of the question of indulgences in the context of the Communion of Saints (nn. 1471 1479), along the lines of Paul VI's *Indulgentiarum doctrina.* In keeping with the traditional recurrence of Holy Years the preparation for the third millennium after Christ occasioned the promulgation of a Jubilee for the year 2000. The bull of indiction of the Great Jubilee, *Incarnationis mysterium,* issued Nov. 29, 1999, included a summary of the doctrine on indulgences of Paul VI (nn. 9 10). An appendix contained a decree of the Apostolic Penitentiary on the indulgences of the year 2000. In keeping with these decrees the Apostolic Penitentiary issued an updated and much abridged version of *Enchiridion indulgentiarum: Normae et concessiones* (Vatican City 1999). In the meantime, however, the extremely sensitive nature of the question of indulgences in the contemporary ecumenical context was underlined by the decision of the World Alliance of Reformed Churches to withdraw its fraternal delegate from the Central Committee for the Great Jubilee 2000 (letter to Cardinal Cassidy, March 8, 1999), precisely because of the discussion of "the controversial concept of indulgences" in *Incarnationis mysterium.*

Remaining Questions. After VATICAN COUNCIL II a number of theologians reflected on the tradition regarding indulgences, notably Karl RAHNER [Theological Investigations 10 (1973)] and Charles JOURNET [*Nova et vetera* (April–June 1966)]. They generally wished to emphasize the inner dispositions of the recipient of the indulgence more than had been done in the past. Two orientations may be discerned in their writings. First, there is a greater insistence than in the past on *modus suffragii,* that is, on the Church's prayer as constituting the essence of the indulgence. Second, there is also a desire to maintain the authority and jurisdiction of the Church and the successor of Peter in the process of sanctification. The very fact that indulgences have remained unknown in the penitential practice of the Oriental Churches as was stressed by the response of Patriarch Maximos to the *Positio,* raises questions as to their necessity and their origin. They are clearly not a necessary part of authentic Christian life.

Given the fact that the beginning of the third millennium coincides with a general interest in problems that relate to the inculturation of the gospel in many lands, peoples, languages and cultures, one may expect a further reappraisal of the advisability of the practice of indulgences in the future. The ecumenical context of the twenty-first century, and notably the growing relations between Catholics and Orthodox and the dialogues that have been engaged since 1965 between Catholics and the major Churches issued from the Reformation, call for such a reappraisal. However, not one of the bilateral dialogues has so far taken indulgences (or purgatory) as a topic of discussion. Until this happens it is hardly possible to assess the ecumenical impact, if any, of the reform initiated by Paul VI, whose lasting merit it is to have perceived the necessity of a reform in the Catholic practice of indulgences.

Bibliography: N. PAULUS, *Geschichte des Ablasses im Mittelalter*, 3 vol. (Paderborn 1922/23); *Indulgences as a Social Factor in the Middle Ages* (New York 1922). J. E. CAMPBELL, *Indulgences. The Ordinary Power of Prelates Inferior to the Pope to Grant Indulgences: An Historical Synopsis and a Canonical Commentary* (Ottawa 1953). W. HERBST, *Indulgences* (Milwaukee 1955). B. POSCHMANN, *Penance and the Anointing of the Sick* (New York 1964). J. WICKS, "Martin Luther's Treaty on Indulgences," *Theological Studies*, 8 (1967): 481–510. E. M. JUNG-INGLESSIS, *The Holy Year in Rome: Past and Present* (Vatican City 1997). B. DE MARGERIE, *Le mystere des indulgences* (Paris 1998). PONTIFICAL COUNCIL FOR PROMOTING CHRISTIAN UNITY, "The Ecumenical Problem of Indulgences" [Information Bulletin, n.102 (1999/IV), p. 241–245]. *Codex iuris canonici* (Rome 1918; repr. Graz 1955). *Florilegium Patristicum*, ed. J. ZELLINGER et al., (Bonn 1904—). *Die griechischen christlichen Schriftsteller der ersten drei Jahrhunderte* (Leipzig 1897—). *Corpus scriptorum ecclesiasticorum latinorum* (Vienna 1866—). *Patrologia Latina*, ed. J. P. MIGNE, 217 v., indexes 4 v. (Paris 1878–90). J. D. MANSI, *Sacrorum Conciliorum nova et amplissima collectio*, 31 v. (Florence-Venice 1757–98). H. DENZINGER, *Enchiridion symbolorum*, ed. A. SCHÖNMETZER (32d ed. Freiburg 1963). *Bullarium Romanum* (Magnum) ed. H. MAINARDI and C. COCQUELINES, 18 folio v. (Rome 1733–62). *The Catechism of the Council of Trent* (The Roman Catechism), tr. J. A. MCHUGH and C. A. CALLAN (New York 1923).

[P. F. PALMER/G. A. TAVARD]

INDWELLING, DIVINE

In the commonly accepted meaning of the phrase, the divine indwelling designates the special permanent presence of God in the just, a presence different from God's OMNIPRESENCE by virtue of creation. The revealed doctrine on the life of GRACE, as attested in Scripture and the Fathers of the Church, states the fact of this special presence without explaining how it takes place. Theology endeavors to explain the manner of this presence.

Revealed Doctrine

We shall first of all briefly state the fact of the divine indwelling as taught in Sacred Scripture, the Fathers, and the documents of the Church.

Holy Scripture. We see, with Y. M. J. Congar (*The Mystery of the Temple*), the mystery of the divine indwelling gradually revealed in the message of SALVATION and of the economy of God's presence with His chosen people, first in the Old and then in the New Testament; it evolves from an external and social presence with the community to an interior and personal presence with each one. In the Old Testament Yahweh's dwelling with His people, both before and after the building of the Temple, is but a figure of the divine indwelling in the just.

In the New Testament the fulfillment of the messianic times, the same presence of God among the people of God is realized in a new way with the very coming of Christ and the advent of the kingdom of God (Mt 3.2; 4.17), and after Christ's glorification, with the sending of the Spirit, who dwells in His Church (1 Cor 3.16; 2 Cor 6.16). Already here there is a difference: Christ insists on the interiority of the kingdom of God (ch. 5 and 6 of Matthew) and on the newly revealed communion with the Father, Son, and Holy Spirit (Mt 23.9; Lk 10.22) begun in Baptism (cf. Mt 28.19). He promises His permanent presence in the Church (cf. Mt 28.20). This interiorization of God's presence leads up to the mystery of the divine indwelling in each of Christ's followers. St. John is explicit on this new communion with the Father, Son, and Holy Spirit: "If anyone love me . . . we [the Father and I] will come to him and make our abode with him" (Jn 14.23), and "the Advocate, the Holy Spirit . . . the Father will send in my name" (Jn 14.26; cf. 1 Jn 1.3; 2.23; 3.24). St. Paul speaks of the proper role of each of the three Persons in the sanctification of Christ's members: We are "sons of God [the Father]," by the "Spirit of God" who "dwells" in us, the "Spirit of Christ" by which Christ is "in" us and we are His, having received the "spirit of adoption as sons, by virtue of which we cry: 'Abba! Father!'" (cf. Rom 8.9–16; also 1 Cor 3.16; 6.19; 8.6; Gal 2.20; Phil 1.21; Eph 3.14–19). Hence, as F. Prat explains, there originates a relation of sonship with the Father, of consecration to the Holy Spirit, of mystical identity with Jesus Christ. Thus the New Testament states the fact of the special presence of God and the special role of the three Divine Persons with or in the just.

Fathers of the Church. The Fathers echo the Biblical message about God-in-us. The Greek Fathers are even more explicit on Uncreated Grace, or God dwelling in us, than on created grace. By indwelling in us the Spirit or the Word or the Trinity divinizes us. These Fathers draw a proof for the divinity of the Spirit or the Word from the fact that, by dwelling in us, they divinize us. Thus, after SS. Athanasius and Basil, St. Cyril of Alexandria says of the Spirit, ". . . we already have God dwelling in us permanently . . ." (*In Ioan. com.* 1.9; *Patrologia Graeca*, ed. J. P. Migne 73:157). Of the Word St. Athanasius says, "We are made sons and gods because of the Word we have in us" (*Adv. Arian.* 3.25; *Patrologia Graeca*, 26:376). St. John Chrysostom says of the indwelling Trinity, "Where one Person of the Trinity is present, there is the whole Trinity" (*In ep. ad Rom.* 13.8; *Patrologia Graeca*, 60:519). As St. Cyril of Alexandria specifies, "from the Father who through the Son causes the Holy Spirit to dwell in them" (*In Ioan. com.* 11.10; *Patrologia Graeca*, 74:540), such is the order of our sanctification. The Spirit sanctifies us by imprinting the seal of the Son and so making us sons of the Father.

With the Latin Fathers the teaching on the divine indwelling is less explicit and frequent; they speak more of created grace, more of the renewal of our being by grace, than of the divine presence. Yet they also witness to the faith in this mystery; thus Tertullian; thus also St. Hilary, who says, ''We are all spiritual, if the Spirit of God is in us. But the Spirit of God is also the Spirit of Christ'' (*De Trin.* 8.21; *Patrologia Latina,* ed. J. P. Migne 10:252); thus above all St. Augustine, the Latin Doctor on the Trinity (*Trin.* 15.17–19; *Patrologia Latina,* 42:1079–87).

The mystery of the divine indwelling, in the mind of the Fathers, pertains to the message of salvation.

Church Documents. Actually, the doctrine was never called into question within the Church, and so there is only passing reference to it in the documents on divine grace. At the time of Pelagianism (*see* PELAGIUS AND PELAGIANISM) and SEMI-PELAGIANISM, there is such a mention of the guidance and infusion of the Holy Spirit (H. Denzinger, *Enchiridion symolorum,* ed. A. Schönmetzer [32d ed. Freiburg 1963] 243, 376). The Council of Trent, in its teaching on justification, stressed the objective change worked in us by grace, i.e., the reality of created grace; yet it did not omit to mention our anointing by the Holy Spirit (*Enchiridion symolorum* 1529), our insertion into Christ (*Enchiridion symolorum,* 1530), the intervention of the three Persons in our sanctification (*Enchiridion symbolorum,* 1525, 1529–31). At the beginning of the 20th century, Leo XIII illustrated the divine indwelling in his encyclical *DIVINUM ILLUD MUNUS* on the gifts of the Holy Spirit (cf. *Enchiridion symbolorum,* 3329–31). Pius XII, later, in *MYSTICI CORPORIS* spoke of the Holy Spirit as the SOUL OF THE CHURCH (*Enchiridion symbolorum,* 3807) and of His indwelling in each soul in grace (*Enchiridion symbolorum,* 3814–15).

Theology of the Divine Indwelling

We may next take up the twofold theological problem concerning the manner of the divine presence by grace and the special relationships to the Divine Persons that originate in the divine indwelling.

Manner of the Divine Presence. The first theological question about the divine indwelling is this: in what way does this presence differ from God's omnipresence in all things, not excluding sinners? Various explanations were and are proposed. Some theologians appeal to divine EFFICIENT CAUSALITY: God is present in the just because He produces grace (G. Vázquez). This presence is in addition to His omnipresence (John of St. Thomas, R. Garrigou-Lagrange, H. Lange); or, as P. Galtier explains, it is a special presence because God produces grace by a special efficiency proper to grace. Others speak of EXEMPLARY CAUSALITY: grace makes us like unto God, wheth-

er under the aspect of deity (Garrigou-Lagrange), or that of Trinity (Galtier), or that of the divine nature as principle of divine activity (Galtier). Such explanations apparently fail to show what is specific to the presence of divine indwelling; they merely assert it. Efficient causality as such does not entail any other presence of God than that belonging to the order of creation. If this efficiency is said to be special, it should be shown what is special in it. As for exemplary causality, this entails a likeness with the exemplar; it does not involve the presence of the exemplar, unless again it be special EXEMPLARITY OF GOD.

St. Thomas. The explanation of St. Thomas Aquinas is well known (*Summa theologiae* 1a, 43.3): God is in the just ''as the known is in the knower and the loved in the lover.'' Various commentators have tried to show how here a real and not only ''intentional'' presence is involved (*see* INTENTIONALITY): not only an IMAGE OF GOD or imprint of God, but God Himself is in the just soul. Knowledge and love, in the context, do not mean only *acts,* for God's presence persists in the absence of acts; it ought to mean habitual knowledge and love and to result from the habitual principles of that knowledge and love. Why do these principles (FAITH and CHARITY, and the gifts of the Holy Spirit) bring about a new presence of God? Because they are principles not of *any* knowledge and love, but of a special, namely, SUPERNATURAL and theological, knowledge and love. This ''special'' requires further explanation.

De la Taille. This explanation may be derived from the divine causality that is proper to the SUPERNATURAL ORDER, such as is suggested in M. DE LA TAILLE's concept of the supernatural. What is proper to supernatural reality is God's self-gift: the Uncreated Act actuating, or communicating Himself as act to, the OBEDIENTIAL potency of spiritual creatures. Every spirit is open to the Infinite; not that he could of himself ''conquer'' the Infinite, but he can ''receive'' Him as the Act of his potency, if and when the Infinite deigns to give Himself. In so doing, God is not changed; all the change or newness is on the side of the creature, namely, the created actuation, or created grace. This is a link of immediate union with God, for it is what makes God's self-gift real. Thus grace, of its very essence, involves a new presence of God such as is nowhere found in the order of nature. This presence by actuation or self-communication of the Act has been called by some (e.g., K. Rahner) ''quasi-formal'' causality; the phrase means that God unites Himself to the soul after the manner of a form uniting itself to matter, although not in a univocal but in an analogical way (''quasi''): God cannot be the form of any creature but only (in the supernatural order) its quasi-form, changing the soul, but without in any way being affected Himself or entering into composition with the soul. In this context, the divine indwelling is not just one of the formal effects of sanctifying grace: Uncreated Grace and created grace are correlatives, two inseparable aspects of grace-life.

This idea of the divine indwelling is apt to show why the habitual presence of God as "the known is in the knower and the loved in the lover" is a real presence of God: God's self-gift, permanent as the gift of grace to which it is correlated, constitutes the presence. This presence is real or ontological, yet refers to the intentional order: it enables the just to know and love God in Himself, as personal, and definitely as tripersonal. Thus the divine indwelling originates a new relationship to the Trinity (*see* CREATED ACTUATION BY UNCREATED ACT).

Trinitarian Relationship. Here the theological question is the following: is our new relationship particular or proper to each of the Divine Persons, or is it the same for the three and diversified only by APPROPRIATION or by a (legitimate and significant) way of speaking? The reason for asking the question lies in the traditional teaching based on the councils [cf. Lateran IV (*Enchiridion symbolorum,* 800) and Florence (*Enchiridion symbolorum,* 1330)], and recalled by Pius XII: in all things where divine efficient causality is concerned, its effect must be said to be common to the three Persons, and not proper to any one of them, because of their unity in nature (*Enchiridion symbolorum,* 3814). None of them has a separate or distinct efficient causality. It may be that Holy Scripture seems to assign to each of the three Persons a distinct role in our sanctification or in the indwelling. This, however, cannot be an efficient causality.

More Common Teaching. The difficulty has been solved by theologians mainly in two ways. The more common teaching of the School, with St. Thomas (*Summa theologiae* 3a, 23.2), explains our relationships to the three Divine Persons by appropriation. That relationship, it is said, is one and the same, common to the three, because it refers to divine efficient causality; and the one effect of this causality is created grace: one foundation for our relationship to the Triune God. But because of the resemblance between some aspect of grace and a Person's proper way of existing within the Trinity, grace may be "attributed" to one Person (though it be the effect of the three as one God). Thus grace and the indwelling being the effect of God's love can be ascribed in a special way to the Holy Spirit, whose procession and manner of existing in the Trinity are by way of love. Accordingly, in this explanation, there are no proper or distinct relationships of the just souls to each of the Divine Persons except in our subjective or psychological approach to each of them. This approach is different for the

Father, whose adopted sons we are, for the Son, our elder Brother, and for the Holy Spirit, our indwelling Guest. In reality, none of the three does anything that is not done equally by or conjointly with the other two.

Proprium Theory. In recent years the appropriation theory has been losing ground: it apparently minimizes the sayings of Holy Scripture and, some say, savors nominalism. Another, more recent explanation, the *proprium* theory, is being proposed and spreading. It may point to antecedents in D. Petau, T. de Régnon, M. Scheeben, G. Waffelaert, who, however, may exaggerate by, as it were, restricting the indwelling to the Holy Spirit alone. Today the *proprium* theory seeks to assign to each of the three Persons a proper manner of indwelling. It distinguishes in the divine indwelling two really distinct aspects (the distinction is evident in the theory of De la Taille): an aspect of efficient causality, i.e., the production of created grace (or of the created actuation), which is common to the three Persons (cf. *Enchiridion symbolorum,* 3814), and the aspect of union or the relationship proper, which as such does not "produce" a created effect, since it only "unites" the just souls with the Triune God. This union being immediate, i.e., with God as personal (and not merely as Creator and Lord), is tripersonal, i.e., diversified for each of the three Persons. (Perhaps the distinction is implied in, certainly it is allowed by, the *quatenus* of the text of Pius XII, *Enchiridion symbolorum,* 3814.) It is so independently of our subjective approach. This distinction between efficiency and union is a prerequisite for the possibility of proper or distinct relationships to each of the Divine Persons: these would be unthinkable if the divine indwelling meant only divine efficient causality. In the *proprium* theory, the diversity in our attitude toward the Father, the Son, and the Holy Spirit is based on the ontological reality of the triune relationship that objectively brings us face to face (in the darkness of faith) with Father, Son, and Holy Spirit. The foundation of this triune relationship, both threefold and one, is one, the created grace, whose function is to draw us into a personal relationship with God as personal or as three Persons. Thus the divine indwelling relates or unites us in a real manner with each of the Persons; it includes a triune relationship, because it means personal presence of the tripersonal God. The divine indwelling is Trinitarian.

This second approach, more realistic and closer to scriptural and patristic teaching, seems to be gaining in appeal in our day. However, it is well to note that in the appropriation theory also, the doctrine of the divine indwelling means the presence in us of the three Divine Persons. Whichever way one conceives theologically the mystery of God-in-us, as a doctrine of the faith it is meant to have a bearing on the Christian life. Nor should the appropriation theory be said to impair the vital import of the doctrine—perhaps it shows deeper reverence for the mystery. It remains true, however, that a more real theology of the divine indwelling holds a greater appeal to the contemporary mind.

Practical Considerations

We may finally indicate briefly the spiritual (or pastoral) and ecumenical import of the doctrine.

Spiritual Theology. The doctrine and theology of the divine indwelling bring out the exalting and personal aspect of the life of grace. The change worked in us by God's transforming presence, for all its importance as the condition of the reality of that presence, is incomparably less important than the divine indwelling itself. This stands out better still when, as suggested above, God's presence in us is conceived, not as a formal effect, but as the constituent of the state of grace. What the divine indwelling means for the pastoral teaching on grace may be best exemplified in the message of the apostle of the divine indwelling, ELIZABETH OF THE TRINITY. Her *Reminiscences* (Westminster, MD 1952) are an object lesson in living by the mystery of the indwelling Trinity. Her message also points to the personal and Trinitarian aspect of the life of grace. The awareness of the indwelling Guests makes for a fruitful living by the life of grace. Here a theology of our relationships with the Divine Persons built on the *proprium* theory enhances the vital significance of the doctrine of divine indwelling.

Ecumenical Implications. The doctrine on the divine indwelling, when placed at the heart of our teaching on the life of grace, is apt to reveal a kinship with Oriental theology, heir to the tradition of the Greek Fathers, which the Latin stress on created grace may well have obscured. By stressing Uncreated Grace or the indwelling Spirit or Trinity, the more or less dimmed unity in doctrine, if not in theology, between the separated East and ourselves may be brought to the light of day. On the other hand, for the Christians of the Protestant communities, the personal relationships with Father, Son, and Holy Spirit, which the doctrine on the divine indwelling involves, should place in proper focus the ontological reality of grace—a stumbling block for them because it is "unscriptural." With them we may agree to say that it is our personal relationship with the Divine Persons that comes first, indeed, that it is the all of the life of grace, created grace being necessary only for these relations to be real.

See Also: GRACE, ARTICLES ON; GRACE, CREATED AND UNCREATED; HOLY SPIRIT, GIFTS OF; PRESENCE OF GOD, PRACTICE OF; JESUS CHRIST (IN THEOLOGY).

Bibliography: A. MICHEL, *Dictionnaire de théologie catholique*, ed. A. VACANT, 15 v. (Paris 1903–50; Tables générales 1951–) 15.2:1841–55. H. SCHAUF, *Lexikon für Theologie und Kirche*, ed. J. HOFER and K. RAHNER, 10 v. (2d, new ed. Freiburg 1957–65) 3:769–772. J. AUER, H. FRIES, ed., *Handbuch theologischer Grundbegriffe*, 2 v. (Munich 1962–63) 1:548–562. Y. M. J. CONGAR, *The Mystery of the Temple*, tr. R. F. TREVETT (Westminster, MD 1962). F. L. B. CUNNINGHAM, *The Indwelling of the Trinity* (Dubuque 1955). P. GALTIER, *L'Habitation en nous des trois personnes divines* (rev. ed. Rome 1949). L. CIAPPI, "The Presence, Mission, and Indwelling of the Divine Persons in the Just," *Thomist* 17 (1954) 131–144. P. DE LETTER, "Sanctifying Grace and Our Union with the Holy Trinity," *Theological Studies* 13 (1952) 33–58; 14 (1953) 242–272, current theology; 19 (1958) 1–31, incorporation and inhabitation; 24 (1963) 402–422, God's self-gift.

[P. DE LETTER]

INDY, VINCENT D'

Romanticist composer, teacher, writer; b. Paris, March 27, 1851; d. Paris, Dec. 2, 1931. D'Indy (christened Paul Marie Théodore Vincent) was reared and dominated by a music-loving grandmother; he received most of his musical instruction privately before studying under C. FRANCK at the Paris Conservatory, where he later taught. In 1896 he devoted his fortune to founding, with Bordes and F. Guilmant, the (Paris) SCHOLA CANTORUM (now the École César Franck), whose curriculum was mainly based on the best Catholic church music of all periods. D'Indy's chief literary works are biographies of Franck (1906) and BEETHOVEN (1911) and the five-volume *Cours de composition musicale* (1903, 1909, 1933), a rigorous course that is valuable despite its musicological inexactnesses. Although he was active in virtually every musical form, he is best known today for his orchestral works, especially the early *Symphony on a French Mountain Air* and the *Istar* variations. As a faithful Catholic, he wrote much organ and sacred choral music, his most monumental being the opera *La Légende de Saint Christophe* (1918), for which he also wrote the libretto. From both musical and textual standpoints it is an extremely moving work; because of its staging difficulties it is most effective in concert performance. His mature music is characterized by luxuriant harmony, counterpoint, and instrumentation, a craftsmanship that is often intricate but seldom unclear, and melodic ideas informed by plainchant and French folk song. As conductor (chiefly of his own works), d'Indy visited Russia, Spain, and the U.S. His valorous record in the Franco-Prussian War later brought him the appointment of Commander of the Legion of Honor by the French government.

Bibliography: N. DEMUTH, *Vincent d'Indy* (London 1951). L. VALLAS, *Vincent d'Indy*, 2 v. (Paris 1946–50); *Grove's Dictionary of Music and Musicians*, ed. E. BLOM, 9 v. (5th ed. London 1954) 4:467–477. G. FERCHAULT, *Die Musik in Geschichte und Gegenwart*, ed. F. BLUME (Kassel-Basel 1949–) 6:1199–1210. T. DAVIDI-

AN, "Debussy, d'Indy, and the Société Nationale," *Journal of Musicological Research,* 11 (1991) 285–301. W. E. GRIM, "(Paul-Marie-Théodore-) Vincent d'Indy," in *International Dictionary of Opera,* ed. C. S. LARUE, 2 v. (Detroit 1993) 343–344. S. KEYM, "'L'unité dans la variété': Vincent d'Indy und das zyklische Prinzip," *Musiktheorie,* 13 (1998) 223–241. R. ORLEDGE, "(Paul Marie Théodore) Vincent d'Indy," in *The New Grove Dictionary of Music and Musicians,* ed. S. SADIE, v. 9 (New York 1980) 220–225. N. SLONIMSKY, ed., *Baker's Biographical Dictionary of Musicians* (8th ed. New York 1992) 823–825.

[R. M. LONGYEAR]

INE, KING OF WESSEX

Reigned 688 to 726. He succeeded a distant cousin, Ceadwalla, on the latter's abdication and retirement to Rome. His own father was still living and apparently enjoyed some authority in the kingdom; Ine, however, had the title of king and the chief authority. He was the first West Saxon king to issue a written code of law. He was following Kentish example here but his laws show some original features. They are preserved only because ALFRED, his more famous descendant, quoted them extensively in his own code. The laws show great respect for the Church. Slaves may not work on Sundays, and the payment of church dues is enforced. The position of Ine's conquered Welsh subjects was fixed, by contemporary standards, in very lenient terms. The association of the great Abbey of GLASTONBURY and the West Saxon royal house began probably in this period. After a long reign Ine abdicated and went on pilgrimage to Rome. He is said to have founded the first English school in that city.

Bibliography: F. LIEBERMANN, ed., *Die Gesetze der Angelsachsen,* 3 v. (Halle 1898–1916; reprint 1960) 3:63–82. *Acta Santorum* Feb. 1:913 923. F. M. STENTON, *Anglo-Saxon England* (2d ed. Oxford 1947). R. GAZEAU, *Catholicisme* 5:1636–37.

[E. JOHN]

INEFFABILITY OF GOD

The ineffability of God designates his incomprehensibility. While human beings can come to some knowledge of God through reason and even more so through God's revelation, yet he continues to be incomprehensible.

Biblical Basis. Through his immanent actions within the world of time and history God reveals that he is completely other than the created order and so transcends it. As such God reveals himself as an ineffable mystery. God is known as the one who cannot be known. The name he gives to Moses, "I Am Who Am" (Ex 3:14), is a revelation, but it is also ineffable and incomprehensible. God "dwells in unapproachable light, whom no man has every seen or can see" (1 Tm 16). The ineffable mystery of God is testified in the prohibition against making images of him (Ex 20:4, Acts 17:29). Nonetheless, the marvels of creation manifest the unspeakable and ineffable grandeur of God (Job 38, Wis 13, Rom 1:19–20). When we speak about God "though we speak much we cannot reach the end, and the sum of our words is 'He is the All'" (Sir 43:27). The Psalmist declares that the mystery of how God knows is "too wonderful for me; it is high, I cannot attain it" (Ps 138/139:6). "His understanding is unsearchable" (Is 40:28). Before the mystery of God praise is the only proper response. "O the depth of the riches and wisdom and knowledge of God! How unsearchable are his judgements and how inscrutable his ways! For who has known the mind of the Lord, who has been his counselor?" (Rom 11:33–34). God is an ineffable mystery, yet that mystery is made known, though not comprehended, through God's actions, especially through the Incarnation of the Son (Jn 1:18; Mt 11:27). While the mystery of God remains, humankind comes to know the mystery of God by faith through the light of the Holy Spirit (Jn 14:26; 1 Cor 1:11–16).

Christian Tradition. Clement of Alexandria stated that we may advance in our understanding of God, yet "knowing not what he is, but what he is not" (*Strom.,* 5.73.5). Against the Eunomians, who held that the very nature of God could be known, Gregory of Nyssa wrote that our inability to give expression to the nature of God, "while it reflects upon the poverty of our own nature, affords an evidence of God's glory, teaching us as it does, in the words of the Apostle, that the only name naturally appropriate to God is to believe him to be 'above every name.' That he transcends every effort of thought, and is far beyond any circumscribing by a name, constitutes a proof to man of his ineffable majesty" (*C. Eun.* 2). Augustine echoes this (*In Ev. Joh.,*13.5; *Serm.* 117.5). Dionysius is the first to use the term "apophatic [negating] theology" as opposed to "cataphatic [affirming] theology" (*Mystical Theology* 3). All images and concepts of God are rejected and the soul enters into "the darkness with the Ineffable" (*ibid.*). This is why Christian mystics, especially within the Orthodox tradition, often speak of entering into the darkness of God's ineffable light. Aquinas teaches that "we cannot know what God is, but rather what he is not" and therefore "we have no means for considering how God is, but rather how he is not" (*Summa theologiae* I.3. preface). Thus we predicate of God such attributes as being infinite (not finite), immutable (does not change), impassible (does not possess emotional changes of state). Nonetheless, Aquinas, somewhat in contrast to the Eastern tradition, allowed that, founded upon human experience, we can truly affirm, by way of analogy, positive perfections to God such as being omniscient, good, wise, and loving. However, since these attributes concur with God's simple essence as being itself (*ipsum esse*) and so pure act (*actus purus*), we do not comprehend what it means for God to possess all knowledge fully in act or to be possess perfect love fully in act. For Aquinas, even in heaven, when we see the very essence of God, we will not comprehend him (*Summa theologiae* I, 12, 7).

The ineffability of God pertains to man's inability to comprehend him not only by reason alone, but also by revelation. The more God reveals himself (and so the more we come to know him) the more ineffable he becomes (and so the less we actually comprehend him). For example, God has revealed himself to be a trinity of persons. We know that God is the mystery of the Trinity, but we cannot comprehend the mystery of the Trinity. As Aquinas intimated above, in the beatific vision we will see clearly the mystery of the Trinity in all its glory, but in that vision we will simultaneously become aware of the complete ineffability of that mystery. Lateran Council IV expressly stated that God is ineffable [H. Denzinger, *Enchiridion symbolorum*, ed. A. Schönmetzer (32d ed. Freiburg 1963) 800; cf. 3001].

Some contemporary theologians have argued on the basis of God's ineffability that all that is said of God is relative to our historical and cultural symbolic understanding and expression. Appealing to the notion of apophatic theology, they maintain that the Church's teachings concerning such doctrines as the Trinity or the Incarnation are not objectively true statements about what God has revealed but symbolic approximations, and so can be changed. Such an approach misconstrues apophatic theology and the nature of God's ineffability. It is one thing to say that God is ineffable and it is another thing to say that we do not know the manner in which he is ineffable. The doctrines of the faith, such as that God is a trinity of persons or that Jesus is the Son of God existing as man, define what the ineffable mysteries of God and his actions are and so protect them from fully rational comprehension.

See Also: GOD, INTUITION OF; INFINITY OF GOD.

Bibliography: T. AQUINAS, *Summa theologiae*, I, 12–13. D. BURRELL, *Knowing the Unknowable God* (Notre Dame 1986). B. DAVIES, *The Thought of Thomas Aquinas* (Oxford 1992). R. HAIGHT, *Jesus Symbol of God* (Maryknoll, N.Y. 1999). C. M. LACUGNA, *God for Us* (San Francisco 1992). A. LOUTH, *Denys the Areopagite* (London 1989). E. L. MASCALL, *Existence and Analogy* (London 1966). JOHN PAUL II, *Fides et ratio* (1998). J. PIEPER, *The Silence of St. Thomas* (London 1957). *Pseudo-Dionysius: The Complete Works*, trans. C. LUIBHEID and P. ROREM (New York 1987). D. TURNER, *The Darkness of God: Negativity in Christian Mysticism* (Cambridge 1995). T. J. VAN BAVEL, ''God in between Affirmation and Negation according to Augustine,'' *Collectanea Augustiniana*, v. 2, eds. J. T. LIENHARD, E. C. MULLER, and R. J. TESKE (New York 1993) 73–97.

[T. G. WEINANDY]

INERRANCY, BIBLICAL

If God is the author of Sacred Scripture, the truth of Scripture follows as a necessary consequence. Since all the judgments of the sacred writers are fortified by the divine light, they must necessarily be clothed with divine truth.

Inerrancy of Scripture. Negatively, this quality of Scripture is known as inerrancy. The inerrancy of Scripture has been the constant teaching of the Fathers, theologians, and recent popes in their encyclicals on Biblical studies (Leo XIII, *Enchiridion biblicum* 124–131; Benedict XV, *Enchiridion biblicum* 453–461; Pius XII, *Enchiridion biblicum* 560). It is nonetheless obvious that many Biblical statements are simply not true when judged according to modern knowledge of science and history. The Earth is not stationary (cf. Eccl 1.4); Darius the Mede did not succeed Belsassar (cf. Dn 5.30–6.1). Even in religious matters, the Old Testament testifies to an imperfect knowledge of morality and life after death (cf. Dt 24.1; Ps 6.6). LEO XIII, appealing to St. Augustine, explained that it was not the purpose of the Biblical writers to teach us the intimate nature of the physical universe, for this knowledge was in no way profitable for salvation. Consequently, they spoke of the physical universe as it appeared to their senses, according to the custom of their day (*Enchiridion biblicum* 120–121). The pope asserted also that similar principles might be applied to matters of history (*Enchiridion biblicum* 1123).

Following the directive of Leo XIII, some exegetes hastily sought to resolve particular difficulties by proposing theories that postulated implicit citations not approved by the author, history according to appearances, and a relative character for Biblical truth. These solutions failed to go to the root of the problem of Biblical inerrancy and hence occasioned new interventions of the magisterium. The truths of history are more intimately associated with our salvation than are the truths of science. The historical truth of Israel's history and of the life of Christ are an integral part of God's supernatural revelation. There is no doubt that the sacred writers have used sources without citing them, but it must be presumed that they have made this material their own, unless the contrary is quite clearly demonstrated (decree of the Pontifical Biblical Commission, Feb. 13, 1905; *Enchiridion biblicum* 160; on the force of such decrees. (*See* PONTIFICAL BIBLICAL COMMISSION).

Similarly, all narrative is not necessarily historical, but if a historical event is an integral part of the author's argument, it must correspond in substance to the facts; nonetheless, it may be presented according to those forms in which ancient peoples remembered their past (decree of the Pontifical Biblical Commission, June 23, 1905; *Enchiridion biblicum* 161; Benedict XV, *Spiritus Paraclitus Enchiridion biblicum* 456; Pius XII, *Divino afflante Spiritu, Enchiridion biblicum* 559). Moreover, profane matters are certainly treated in the Bible in the light of their religious significance, but positive affirmations in their regard cannot be excluded from the privilege of Biblical inerrancy. Nor is Biblical truth simply relative to its time and culture; its expression is conditioned by the culture of the time, but whatever is affirmed is thereby clothed with the truth of God (*see SPIRITUS PARACLITUS Enchiridion biblicum* 454–455).

The total truth of the Scriptures can be appreciated only by trying to recapture the mind of the Biblical writers and to see the relationship of each part of Scripture to the whole. We must know the intention of the sacred author and the literary form that he is using if we are to determine what he intended to teach and what role he assigned to the various elements in his writing. This basic principle of all literary criticism is valid also for Sacred Scripture, once we recognize that God in His condescension deigned to entrust His revelation to the frail vessel of human language. When PIUS XII encouraged Catholic scholars to investigate Biblical literary genres or forms, he assured us that no ancient mode of expression need be excluded from the Scriptures, provided it does not contradict the holiness and truth of God (*Enchiridion biblicum* 559). These literary forms may be determined only by a careful and comparative study of ancient Near Eastern literature.

The investigation of literary forms has already provided a solution for many difficulties of the past, e.g., those connected with the PRIMEVAL AGE IN THE BIBLE and with the books of JUDITH and JONAH, but such studies alone will not remove all obscurities from the message of Scripture. For besides being far removed from us in time and culture, the sacred writers are trying to express in human language the fruit of their own personal encounter with God and the mystery of His saving plan, or to record what others have taught them of this ineffable mystery. Their affirmations are true insofar as they affirm; but they may also hesitate, grope, doubt, opine, or suspend judgment entirely (decree of the Pontifical Biblical Commission, June 18, 1915; *Enchiridion biblicum* 415). They may reflect the common opinions of their day without making them the object of their teaching. The exegete must, as a consequence, be sensitive to these varying degrees of human assertion and to the common psychology of human communication, if he is to evaluate correctly the teaching purpose of the sacred writers and to avoid taxing them with error in matters that are not the object of their teaching. (*See* FORM CRITICISM, BIBLICAL; MIDRASH).

Role of Scripture in the Church. Inerrancy, however, is not the only consequence of Biblical inspiration. Preoccupation with the so-called "Biblical question" has led to the neglect of other aspects of the Bible's role in the life of the Church. Theologians are now beginning to look more closely at these other effects of Biblical inspiration. In the first place, the Bible provides the Church with a written record of God's self-manifestation to men, which is itself a history of divine pedagogy. God did not reveal Himself completely in the beginning; He adapted His revelation to the cultural and religious condition of the men He visited; He tolerated their moral imperfections until such a time as He was able to educate their consciences; He led men by historical and moral experience to realize their need of His saving grace, which was fully revealed in Jesus Christ. The Apostles in turn used this record of Old Testament revelation to explain the full significance of the mystery of Christ. The knowledge of this divine pedagogy is itself a revelation of the mercy and gentleness of God from which the Church may profit.

Secondly, the Bible contains so manifold an expression of the word of God that all Christians may find in its pages spiritual nourishment adapted to their needs. In the Bible the chosen mediators of God's revelation teach us little by little what they have learned of the mystery of God. The written word of God thus mediates to us the personal experience of the Prophets and Apostles. Through them we may come in contact with God Himself. A privileged place of this mediation is the Church's liturgy of the word.

Finally, the Church is committed to continuing the work of Christ in the world. She must, therefore, preserve, explain, and safeguard the faith of the Apostles, for they were the privileged witnesses of the mystery of Christ. In the New Testament the Church finds the written record of Apostolic faith to which she always refers in fulfilling her divine mission. These other finalities of Sacred Scripture are the object of modern Biblical study. The Scriptures are not simply a code of dogmatic truths, but an integral part of God's self-communication to men. This self-communication was complete in the living person of Jesus Christ; it will be complete for the individual only in the beatific vision.

Bibliography: J. T. FORESTELL, "The Limitation of Inerrancy," *Catholic Biblical Quarterly* 20 (1958) 9–18.

[J. T. FORESTELL]

INFALLIBILITY

The term "infallibility" means an incapability of error or erring. While in an absolute sense, infallibility belongs to God alone, in a derivative sense, infallibility can be viewed as a gift of the Holy Spirit assisting the post-apostolic Church in knowing and teaching Christ's revelation without error. This divine assistance is indicated in the New Testament by Christ's promise to send the Spirit to lead His disciples to all truth and to enable them to remain in the truth. Infallibility is more than a simple, *de facto* absence of ERROR. It is a positive perfection, ruling out the possibility of error and entailing necessarily a central fidelity to the Christian revelation in the doctrine taught and accepted by the Church.

Infallibility is to be distinguished from both revelation, God's communication to man, and scriptural inspiration, God's guidance of the writers of the Bible. Like the term "inerrancy," which indicates that the scriptures teach "firmly, faithfully, and without error that truth which God wanted put into the sacred writings for the sake of our salvation" (Vatican II, *Constitution on Revelation* 11), "infallibility" indicates that the Church continues to believe and teach without error those truths that are necessary for salvation.

Doctrinal Formulation. While the Church from its beginning has been characterized by a continual concern for the truth of the Gospel, the relationship between revelatory truth and ecclesial teaching has been formulated in various ways depending on particular historical circumstances and theological perspectives. While the term infallibility first emerged in medieval theology, Christians eventually ascribed some type of infallibility to the Church, though with considerable divergence about its implications and implementation.

A definite teaching on the "infallible magisterium of the Roman Pontiff" was formulated by VATICAN COUNCIL I (*Pastor Aeternus,* July 18, 1870): "The Roman Pontiff, when he speaks *ex cathedra,* that is, when discharging the office of pastor and teacher of all Christians, and defines with his supreme apostolic authority a doctrine concerning faith or morals that is to be held by the universal Church, through the divine assistance promised him in St. Peter, exercises that infallibility which the divine Redeemer wished to endow his Church for defining doctrine concerning faith or morals" (H. Denzinger, *Enchiridion Symbolorum* 3074). Given the complexity of this statement, it is not surprising that considerable misunderstanding occurs in its interpretation, particularly concerning the following: (1) The Council, while speaking of doctrinal infallibility as an endowment of the Church, did not explain the meaning of infallibility nor indicate whether there are other types of infallibility (e.g.,

infallibility in believing, as well as in teaching). (2) The Council did not state that "the pope is infallible," rather that the pope "exercises" infallibility. Thus infallibility is not a personal quality, but an ecclesial endowment which the pope on specific occasions exercises on behalf of and in communion with the Church. In addition, Vatican I left undecided the question whether others in the Church can also exercise infallibility. (3) The "object" of such an exercise of infallibility was ambiguously described as "doctrine that is to be held," thus leaving open to further consideration what can or cannot be defined. While theologians generally agree that revelatory truths are a "primary object" of infallibility, there is considerable difference of opinion regarding the inclusion of "secondary objects" (matters of natural law, canonizations, etc.) under the aegis of infallibility.

Finally, the Council concluded that such "definitions of the Roman Pontiff are, of themselves, not by the consent of the Church, irreformable." This rejected the position adopted at a 1682 assembly of French bishops, the so-called Gallican Articles which postulated further appeal or ratification in order for definitions to be binding. Definitions, then, are "irreformable" in a juridical sense, but are not said to be "infallible" (in a philosophical sense), as if they were absolutely incapable of further development.

The topic of infallibility reappeared in VATICAN II's *Lumen gentium* (Nov. 21, 1964), which emphasized that the exercise of infallibility must be "in accord with revelation" and "extends as far as the deposit of revelation extends" (25). While reiterating Vatican I's teaching on the papal exercise of infallibility, Vatican II taught that "the infallibility promised to the Church also resides in the body of bishops." This episcopal exercise of infallibility may assume two possible forms: (1) when the bishops are "gathered together in an ecumenical council" or (2) "even when they are dispersed around the world, provided that while maintaining the bond of unity among themselves and with Peter's successor, and while teaching authentically on a matter of faith or morals, they concur in a single viewpoint as the one which must be held conclusively" (25).

The Object of Infallibility. The object of infallibility is limited, according to Vatican II, to those truths which form a part of the deposit of faith (LG 25). In a generic sense, the object of infallibility may be said to include doctrines of "faith and morals," a traditional couplet that was first used in a major Church document by the Council of TRENT.

Studies of the word "morals," or *mores* in Latin, show that at the Council of Trent the word was employed in both a moral and a religious sense, that is, to refer to teachings about how people should conduct their relationships with one another (*mores*, in the plural, was regularly used in this instance) and to refer to teachings about religious practices and ceremonial rites (*mos*, in the singular, used typically in this sense). Thus at Trent, *disciplina morum* included more than teaching about morals; it included as well matters of custom and ecclesiastical and liturgical discipline.

When at the First Vatican Council the bishops attempted to define papal infallibility in matters of "faith and morals," they encountered considerable difficulty in agreeing on what precisely was to be included in "morals." At the Council, Bishop GASSER explained, in the name of the Deputation of the Faith, that infallibility had both a direct and an indirect object: the direct object included those truths which are revealed, and the indirect object those which are not directly revealed but which are necessarily connected to revelation. Some bishops, however, wanted to broaden the secondary object to include "those things connected with the deposit of revelation." The bishops finally agreed, however, to a more restricted view, concluding that the secondary object included only those truths *necessarily* connected to revelation. They never reached agreement, however, as to just which truths were necessarily connected.

The Second Vatican Council did not attempt any clarification of the content of the secondary object of infallibility, except to say that infallibility "extends as far as the deposit of revelation extends" (LG 25). The Congregation for the Doctrine of the Faith's *Mysterium ecclesiae* (1973) restated the secondary object of infallibility in slightly different terms: "things without which the deposit cannot be properly safeguarded and explained." This teaching is echoed in the *Catechism of the Catholic Church* (2035).

The Subject of Infallibility. *The Church.* An unflawed Christian faith is an unfailing dowry of "those who are one family in the faith" (Gal 6.10), i.e., the whole Church, comprising all the faithful, lay and clerical alike, who constitute one Body in their one faith (see Eph 4.4–5). This unerring faith of the believing Church (see Mt 16.18b; Jn 14.16–17) is a basic created bond (see Denzinger 871) of the true and indissoluble community of life between the Lord Christ and His bride the Church (see Denzinger 3020). The Church returns a luminous pledge of faith and fidelity to Christ, "the holy one and true" (Rv 3.7), "full of grace and of truth" (Jn 1.14), who has "made known everything which I have heard from my Father" (Jn 15.15). The whole Church of all time is the destined hearer of the Word and of His message, the appointed bearer in the sanctity of its heart of the mystery of Christ's KINGDOM, the steadfast confessor

of the truth of Christ's mystery. The Church's faith is a total faith, i.e., one destined under the Spirit to an ever true realization, homogeneous to its apostolic origin (see Acts 2.42) and open to its final fullness (see Eph 4.13), precisely because the Spirit of Christ always holds the Church's faith in an integral fidelity to Christ. This indefectible faith is an incarnational grace, inward-outward in its radical purity, held holily in the heart and confessed unswervingly on the tongue (see Rom 10.10). It is an infallibility of sanctity in life, proper to the Church as the COMMUNION OF THE SAINTS, distinct from and served by the infallibility of the hierarchical ministry of teaching.

If the individual believer is to keep his faith from being adulterated by "strange varieties of teaching" (Heb 13.9), he must live his faith as a true part of the whole company of believers; his faith must be congruent with the faith of the Church. But the sense of faith of the whole Church infallibly adheres to the integral Christian revelation because the Spirit of Truth, residing in the heartland of the holy believers, moves the whole Church to a discerning obedience of faith in the apostolic revelation infallibly presented by those whom Christ has appointed to be His authoritative WITNESSES and to whom He has pledged the aid of His Spirit to fulfill their teaching mission. Christ's Spirit, the only interior teacher mandated by Christ to guide the whole Church, ensures the vital correspondence between the infallible communication of the message by the Church's TEACHING AUTHORITY and the infallible adherence to it on the side of the whole Christian people.

The welcome acceptance that the believing Church gives to the faith taught by those accredited as the successors of the APOSTLES is not to be misconstrued as a monotonous repetition or a mechanical playback of what has been received. "The eyes of the heart illumined" (Eph 1.18) by faith vitally penetrate into and assimilate the riches of the apostolic message and transpose them into gestures of prayer, worship, and Christian living. The teaching Church is critically regulative of the sense of faith of the whole Church; it directs, fosters, and finally sanctions the consensus in faith of the whole Church. Whenever there is a maturation of faith in the total mind of the Church, it is always under the prime tutelage, interior and exterior, of the Spirit, and under the ministerial leadership in the sociojuridic sphere of the teaching Church.

The College of Bishops. When the corporate episcopate defines a doctrine, it can in practice follow two procedures, not essentially different one from another. (1) It can act solemnly in ecumenical councils: Denzinger 2923; *Lumen gentium* 25, 22 [*Acta Apostolicae Sedis* 57 (1965) 29–31, 25–27]. Or (2) it can also act with what

Vatican I called its "ordinary and universal magisterium": Denzinger 3011; see Denzinger 2879; *Lumen gentium* 25.2 [*Acta Apostolicae Sedis* 57 (1965) 30]. In ecumenical councils the episcopal college, or a competent representation of it, is assembled in one place for common counsel and for joint decision; hence its collegial act of teaching acquires an especial clarity and efficacy. In their ordinary and universal magisterium, however, the same bishops, without coming together in one assembly, and with each remaining at his post, exercise consciously a collegial act of teaching, definitively setting forth some doctrine for the absolute acceptance of the entire Church. In practice it is not always easy to ascertain whether or not the magisterium in a given case is exercising its infallibility through this second procedure. In both procedures, however, the episcopal body stands fundamentally in the same vicarial relation to Christ, in the same ministerial service of Christ's revealed word in His Body the Church, and under the same protecting aid of Christ's Spirit. There can be no supreme collegial act of teaching, and hence no infallibility, unless the pope, the head of the college, contributes his specific role to the collegial act; see *Lumen gentium* 22.2 [*Acta Apostolicae Sedis* 57 (1965) 26]; "Nota explicativa praevia" 3–4 (*ibid.* 74–75); *Codex iuris canonical* c. 227.

The Pope. The Church's teaching office finds a special and eminent realization in the mission of the Roman pontiff, "true Vicar of Christ and head of the whole Church and father and teacher of all Christians" (Denzinger 3059). When the Roman pontiff, "in discharge of his office as shepherd and teacher of all Christians, in accord with his supreme apostolic authority, defines a doctrine concerning faith or morals to be held by the whole Church" (Denzinger 3074), he teaches infallibly by reason of the Spirit's aid proper to his special role as "the center of ecclesiastical unity (V. Gasser; Mansi 52:1213B). In order to give further precision to the ambit of papal infallibility—over and beyond affirming generically that its competence extends to "doctrine concerning faith and morals"—Vatican I compared the infallibility of the pope with that of the Church, understanding thereby that the scope of papal infallibility is exactly the same as that of the corporate episcopate in its definitions (see V. Gasser; Mansi 52:1225D–28A).

In its concern to dissipate any residue of doctrinal GALLICANISM, Vatican I decisively rejected any effort to make the collaboration or consent of the episcopate (or of the whole Church) an indispensable juridic condition either of the pope's infallibility (see V. Gasser; Mansi 52:1208C; 1317A–B) or of the pertinent information needed by the pope in order prudently to go forward to a definition (see V. Gasser; Mansi 52: 1217B–C). Nonetheless the Council did not look on the pope in the exercise of his infallible magisterium as withdrawn from the common life either of the episcopate or of the whole Church (see V. Gasser; Mansi 52:1213B–14A; 1228C). The pope's juridic autonomy does not entail discommunity or isolation; his juridic independence is never a solitary independence. He always acts as part of the Body, in the sense that he acts from within a metajuridic community of life, based on the fact that the Spirit assures a continuum of faith both lived and taught between the Roman pontiff and his fellow believers in the Church and his fellow bishops in the episcopate. This community of living faith is a fundamental Christian reality, always there and always to be there, incapable of any fundamental dislocation, even though the precisions of the object of faith that the pope is privileged to make are not always at the moment of definition explicitly shared by many members of that community. This symbiosis of faith is a great datum of Church life about which the Roman pontiff, while remaining juridically independent in his plenary act of definition, cannot be incurious as an irrelevancy, but which he must acknowledge and honor as capable under the Spirit of significantly enriching the religious worth of his act of definition.

In a similar way the pope should be duly attentive to the common mission that as chief bishop he has with the rest of the bishops, particularly in the matter of faith. The episcopate is an indispensable part of the Church's life and order, not obtrusive or competitive, but complementary and contributory, capable of giving a measure of light and strength, not available elsewhere, to the total religious excellence of the pope's act of definition, even though not constituting an essential component of the papal pronouncement as infallible. It remains within the pope's discretion how and in what measure to use these helps that the Church's communion of life affords him in the discharge of his office.

Contemporary Discussions. In the decade or so following Vatican II, three studies prompted special interest in the debate on papal infallibility in the U.S.: Hans KÜNG's *Infallible? An Inquiry* (New York 1971), Brian Tierney's *The Origins of Papal Infallibility: 1150–1350* (New York 1972), and August Hasler's *Pius IX (1846–1878), päpstliche Unfehlbarkeit und 1 Vatikanisches Konzil: Dogmatisierung und Durchsetzung ether Ideologie* (Stuttgart 1977).

Küng argued that indefectibility rather than infallibility is sufficient for the life of the Church; that is, the whole Church will continue to abide in the truth of Christ despite the errors contained in the official teachings of popes and councils. According to Küng, there have been too many errors in papal teaching—the most recent being the papal teaching on birth control, *Humanae vitae*—to allow for a doctrine of papal infallibility, a doctrine which mistakenly presumes that it is possible to formulate propositions that are a priori infallible.

Critics of Küng have pointed out numerous historical errors in his study, not the least of which is his assumption that *Humanae vitae* is an infallible teaching. Moreover, many critics have noted that although indefectibility assures that the Church will exist until the end of time, it alone does not assure that the Church will have the capacity to witness to the truth of the gospel message. Finally, most critics agree that Küng is mistaken to identify infallibility with propositions, which are a priori infallible. The infallibility of popes and councils is based upon the infallibility which, as Vatican I states explicitly, the Lord intended the Church to have, and in that sense is actually a posteriori rather than a priori.

Küng welcomed Brian Tierney's 1972 study on the origins of papal infallibility as an important contribution that filled in gaps in his own argument. Tierney, a historian of medieval canon law, argued that before the 14th century no one defended a doctrine of papal infallibility. Before that time, canonists argued, sometimes in extravagant terms, for papal sovereignty, but never for papal infallibility. Popes, they taught, could be either sovereign, that is, free to revoke the decrees of their predecessors, or infallible, that is, capable of making irrevocable decrees and therefore binding on their successors; they could not be both. For Tierney, papal infallibility consists in the power to create new non-Scriptural articles of faith.

Where then did the modern doctrine of papal infallibility come from? Tierney explained that it can be found first in the writings of the enigmatic Franciscan theologian PETER JOHN OLIVI (d. 1298) who in 1280 wrote up a question about the infallibility of the pope. Olivi was interested in investing the pope with the authority to make irrevocable decisions precisely in order to protect the particular notion of poverty approved in 1277 by Pope Nicholas III which was dear to the Spiritual Franciscans, but still under attack by the rest of the Order. In 1323, relying on his canonical sovereignty and, says Tierney, rejecting any notion of the irrevocability of papal decrees, Pope John XXII condemned that doctrine of poverty and revoked the decree (*Exiit*) of Nicholas III. Shortly thereafter, however, John began to defend himself against charges of heresy by claiming that he had not revoked a decree of faith and morals. John's claim, according to Tierney, left the door open to the idea that a pope could in such matters make irrevocable decisions. Papal theologians soon rushed through that open door and created the modern idea of papal infallibility to strengthen the hand of the pope against conciliarists. Tierney concluded that papal infallibility does not belong to the "ancient and constant faith of the Church," but is rather "the sudden creation . . . of a novel doctrine at the end of the 13th century" (273).

Tierney's study forced theologians to take the history of the doctrine more seriously. Tierney criticizes the idea of papal infallibility defended today by ecumenically minded theologians as "Pickwickian," that is, one so highly qualified that it ends up unreal in any practical and meaningful sense. Most scholars recognize that Tierney correctly located in the late 13th and early 14th centuries the first discussions of papal infallibility. Many, however, have criticized his work for overstating the opposition between SOVEREIGNTY and infallibility, for not attending to the relationship between ecclesial infallibility and papal infallibility, and for overlooking the ways in which many of the elements of doctrine were present earlier than 1300, as, for example, may be found, in Yves CONGAR's judgment, in the writings of Thomas Aquinas. Finally, it has been pointed out that throughout his study, Tierney writes a history of a highly ultramontane idea of papal infallibility, that is, one that emphasizes the power of the pope to define apart from the faith of the Church and without grounding in Scripture. Tierney responded to the criticisms of his work and the discussion continues.

The bitterest attack on the validity of papal infallibility was launched by August Hasler who from 1966 to 1971 worked for the Vatican Secretariat of Christian Unity. His two-volume work, published in 1977, was followed in 1979 by a shorter English version under the title of *How the Pope Became Infallible: Pius IX and the Politics of Persuasion* (New York 1981). Hans Küng contributed a provocative introduction to the English version. Hasler contended that the standard histories of Vatican I were written from the viewpoint of the "victors," those who supported the definition. Hasler's intention was to write a more comprehensive history of the Council, one that featured the viewpoint of the minority.

Hasler divides his work into two sections. The first section deals with history, which, in his opinion, shows clearly that the only reason for the passage of the definition of papal infallibility was Pius IX's manipulation and intimidation of minority bishops before, during, and after the Council. Moreover, according to Hasler, Pius was the victim of epilepsy, given to supernatural visions, and chronically manifested psychological imbalances. So much did Pius IX control the proceedings of the Council that, in Hasler's view, the Council lacked due freedom and therefore was not valid. In the second section of the book, the theological argument, Hasler could find no Biblical or theological basis for the doctrine, and concluded that the definition dethroned history by ideology.

Most critics appreciate the extensive new material which Hasler provides, such as the private notes of Archbishop Darboy of Paris and of Bishop Maret, rector of the Sorbonne. But his orchestration of his sources betrays a double standard: he subjects to relentless criticism those who supported the definition, often ascribing to them the worst of motives, including psychopathology, and presents without any critical comment the views of those who opposed the definition. As one Vatican I scholar put it, "Hasler's presentation is repeatedly flawed by partisan allegation, unsubstantiated conjecture, and biased analysis" (J. T. Ford). Küng, Tierney and Hasler, have each been criticized in different degrees for over-stating the intent and extent of the definition formulated at the First Vatican Council; and for denying, a priori, a legitimate development of the doctrine through history.

Bibliography: M. J. SCHEEBEN, "Theologische Erkenntnislehre," in *Handbuch der katholischen Dogmatik,* v.1 (2d ed. Freiburg 1948) pars. 11–14, p. 80–108. C. DILLENSCHNEIDER, *Le Sens de la foi et la progrès dogmatique du mystère marial* (Rome 1954). O. ROUSSEAU et al., *L'Infaillibilité de l'Église* (Chevetogne 1963). G. THILS, *L'Infaillibilité du peuple chrétien "in credendo"* (Louvain 1963); "L'Infaillibitité de l'Église *in credendo* et *in docendo,*" *Salesianum* 24 (1962) 298–336. M. GOULDER et al., *Infallibility in the Church* (London 1968). E. CASTELLI, ed., *L'infaillibilité* (Paris 1970). H. KÜNG, *Infallible? An Inquiry* (Garden City, N.Y. 1971). J. KIRVAN, ed., *The Infallibility Debate* (New York; Paramus, N.J.; Toronto 1971). J. FORD, "Infallibility—From Vatican I to the Present," *Journal of Ecumenical Studies* 8 (1971) 768–791. E. SCHILLEBEECKX and B. VAN IERSEL, eds., "Truth and Certainty," *Concilium* 83 (New York 1973). G. THILS, *L'infaillibilité pontificale* (Gembloux 1969). U. BETTI, *La Costituzione Dommatica "Pastor Aeternus" del Concilio Vaticano I* (Rome 1961). P. CHIRICO, *Infallibility: The Crossroads of Doctrine* (1985). J. L. HEFT, *John XXII and Papal Teaching Authority* (1986). U. HORST, *Unfehlbarkeit und Geschichte* (Mainz 1982). G. LINDBECK, *The Nature of Doctrine* (Westminster Press 1984). J. MAHONEY, *The Making of Moral Theology* (Oxford 1987). F. SULLIVAN, *Magisterium* (Mahwah, N.J. 1983). R. R. GAILLARDETZ, *Witnesses to the Faith: Community, Infallibility, and the Ordinary Magisterium of Bishops* (New York 1992).

[F. X. LAWLOR/J. T. FORD/J. L. HEFT]

INFANCY NARRATIVES

Term applied to the accounts of the birth and early life of Jesus as given in Mt 1.1–2.23 and Lk 1.5–2.52.

Composition and Themes. Although infancy narratives open two of our gospels, biblical criticism assigns them last in the order of composition. The passion story was composed first, reflecting the community's effort to make sense of the crucifixion of their Messiah. Next were added accounts of Jesus' ministry, and only afterwards did the infancy accounts evolve, answering to human curiosity about Jesus' origins.

A comparison with Mark, which was composed first gospel of the four gospels, illustrates the theological sig-

nificance of this compositional chronology. Mark's gospel, which lacks an infancy narrative, begins with Jesus' baptism. Although the holy spirit designates Jesus as the "beloved son" sent to preach a "baptism of repentance and forgiveness of sins" (Mk 1.4, 11), it is not until the crucifixion that people unequivocally recognize and acknowledge Jesus' divine stature; a Gentile centurion announces "Truly this man was the son of God" (15.39).

By contrast, the infancy narratives take for granted Jesus' divine and Messianic stature. Matthew's geneaology titles Jesus "Messiah" (Mt 1.16); an angel announces to Joseph that Jesus will be a savior who embodies the divine presence (Mt 1.21, 23). The ensuing episodes amount to a gospel in miniature that epitomizes the evangelist's christology and anticipates Jesus' double-edged destiny. Gentiles will honor Jesus' divinity and status as Davidic Messiah, just as the magi, in the infancy narrative, worship him at birth. The religious leaders of his day will persecute him and plot his death, just as the Jewish ruler Herod does at the start of Jesus' life.

Luke's infancy account also announces Jesus' divinity and his saving role in history. Like Matthew, who represents Jesus as the fulfillment of Old Testament scripture and Jewish hopes, Luke highlights the continuity of the Christian gospel with Judaism. The literary design of Luke's account draws a parallel between John the Baptist's story and that of Jesus. John the Baptist may be viewed as a transitional figure between the story of Israel and the story of Jesus (R. Brown, H. Conzelmann's). Zechariah and Elizabeth (the parents of John the Baptist), and Anna and Simeon (prophetic models of Jewish piety), set the stage for the savior's arrival. Jesus' Davidic stature (Lk 1.32; 2:11), together with his destiny as one who will incur opposition (Lk 2.34), are equally clear. Distinctively Lukan themes appear in this narrative, particularly his accent on social justice and the vindication of the oppressed (see, e.g., the Magnificat Lk 1.46–56).

Literary Relationship. Points of agreement between the two accounts must be balanced against their divergences in order to ascertain their literary relationship. The hypothesis that Matthew and Luke drew independently from oral tradition accounts better for the commonalities between the two accounts than does the hypothesis of direct dependence. The points of agreement include some of the principal characters, the Davidic descent and conception of Jesus by the holy spirit, the angelic annunciation, Jesus' birthplace at Bethlehem and residence in Nazareth, and the dating of his birth to the reign of Herod the Great.

While both accounts are concerned with showing the fulfillment of Old Testament prophecies in the Christ event, Matthew does so principally by explicit formulaic scriptural citations, which punctuate his infancy story five times (1.22–23; 2.5b–6, 15b, 17–18, 23b), whereas Luke's weaves single words or phrases from the Old Testament into his sentences (e.g., Lk 1.35, where the Greek verb ἐπισκιάζω (overshadow) is the same as that used in the Septuagint translation of Ex 40.35: ''the cloud overshadowed it [the TENT OF MEETING].'' One may detect Luke's theological emphases by such linguistic clues.

The divergences between the two accounts are obvious, including differences beween their genealogies, and in overall plot and themes. Matthew 2, including the visit of the magi, the star, and Herod's plot, is not found in Luke, while most of Luke 1–2, including the birth of John the Baptist, the canticles, the shepherds, and the presentation of Jesus at the Temple, are not found in Matthew. These differences often remain obscure to popular audiences who are accustomed to seasonal adaptations and liturgical recreations of the Christmas story that harmonize the two accounts.

Matthew's Structure. A number of different proposals have been suggested for the structure of Matthew's account. K. Stendahl divides the story into four parts (1.1–17, 18–25; 2.1–12, 13–23), dealing respectively with the questions of who Jesus is, how he came to be, where he was born, and whence his destiny. Others organize the story with reference to three dreams of Joseph that occur 1.18–25, 2.13–15, and 2.19–23. A structure that comprises a genealogy (1.1–17), followed by three episodes (1.18–25; 2.1–12; 2.13–2) is presented here and focuses on Exodus themes in Matthew's account.

The genealogy shows Jesus' descent from Abraham and David and form a unit with the second episode, demonstrating that the promises of God to Abraham and David are fulfilled in Jesus, the Messiah. Although He is born of a virgin, Jesus belongs to the family of David, since Joseph is a ''son of David'' and (1.20) has accepted Mary, Jesus' mother, as his wife.

The second episode (2.1–12) shows that the Gentiles, represented by the magi, have sought out and done homage to the Messiah of Israel, whereas His own people (Herod, ''all Jerusalem,'' the high priests, and the Scribes) have been disturbed by the news of His birth (2.3) and have either ignored or sought to kill Him (*See* MAGI).

Jesus the New Israel. A Jesus-Israel typology is the dominant theme of the following section (2.13–23); Jesus is presented as the true Israel who goes down to Egypt like the ancient people of God and is brought out of Egypt in a new Exodus (2.15). The words of Jer 31.15 that are cited in Mt 2.18 belong to a context that deals with the

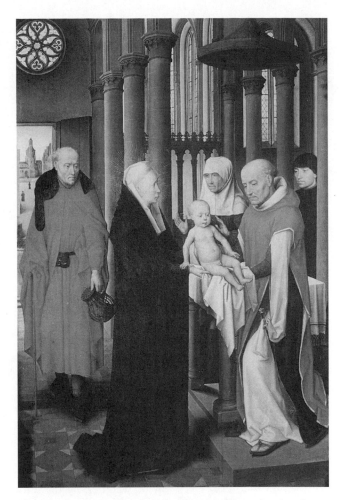

''Purification in the Temple,'' by Hans Memling, showing the Virgin presenting the Christ Child to a priest inside a Gothic church, c. 1470. (©Francis G. Mayer/CORBIS)

Exile and the return of Israel and Judah. Through the application of that text to Herod's slaughter of the children of Bethlehem, that massacre is seen not merely as an attempt to destroy the Messiah, but as the concomitant of the exile of Jesus, the new Israel. The midrashic account of the persecution of Jacob-Israel by Laban, because of which the patriarch was compelled (''by the word of God'') to take refuge in Egypt, may have been influential in the formation of Matthew's narrative. That MIDRASH, based on Dt 26.5–8, is found in the Passover HAGGADAH, the liturgy for the eve of Passover, and probably dates from the second century B.C. Its use in Matthew suggests the Passover celebration of the Jewish Christians as the *Sitz im Leben* (life situation) of this episode. It is possible that the magi episode was originally not concerned with those that follow, and it may even be the conflation of two distinct stories, but in the arrangement of Matthew, the magi's inquiry (2.2) is the point of departure for the entire flight and massacre complex; consequently, the Jesus-

Israel theme dominates the narrative as a whole, although it is not present in the first episode 1.18–25.

Jesus the New Moses. A Jesus-Moses typology also can be discerned, although it is subordinate. The clearest indication is in Mt 2.20, where Herod's death is announced to Joseph in terms that are taken from Ex 4.19. There Moses is told to go back to Egypt "for all the men who sought your life are dead"; in Matthew, Joseph is told that "those who sought the child's life are dead." The plural in Matthew is explicable only because the verse is a free quotation of Ex 4.19. There are also similarities to midrashic stories about the birth of Moses. The two points of closest correspondence are (1) the dream in which Amram, Moses' father, is told what his unborn child's mission will be (cf. Mt 1.20–21) and (2) the terror of the Egyptians at the prediction of Moses' birth (cf. Mt 2.3). Although the rabbinic sources containing the Moses legend are relatively late, most of its elements are found in Josephus, which shows that the possible influence of the legend on Matthew cannot be excluded on chronological grounds.

Luke's Account. Luke's narrative draws a parallel between the infancy of John the Baptist and that of Jesus, in which are noted similarities such as Gabriel's announcement to Zachary and to Mary, Zachary's canticle and Mary's, and also striking contrasts, e.g. while the Baptist, like other great Biblical figures, is born of a previously sterile woman (e.g. Sarah, Hannah), Jesus is born to a virgin who conceives out of wedlock by the holy spirit. Luke's design illustrates his theology of salvation history whereby Jesus stands as a prophet at once continuous and discontinuous with the prophets of Israel.

Fulfillment of the Old Testament. In a different manner from Matthew, Luke presents the Christ-event as the fulfillment of the Old Testament. The Baptist is the new Elijah, the precursor of the DAY OF THE LORD, who is to prepare the people for the coming of Yahweh (Lk 1.16; cf. Mal 3.1, 23); Jesus is the Messiah of Israel who will receive the throne of David his father (Lk 1.32–33). By anticipation, the newborn child is announced as Lord and Messiah (2.11), although those titles belong to Jesus properly only when He is raised from the dead (Acts 2.36). The prediction in Dn 9.21–24 of the eschatological consecration of the "most holy" and that in Mal 3.1 of Yahweh's coming to the Temple have influenced Luke's narrative. The angel Gabriel, who appears in the Old Testament only in Dn 8.16 and 9.21, is the one who announces ("at the hour of the incense offering"; cf. Dn 9.22) the conception of the Baptist and, later, that of Jesus (*see* GABRIEL, ARCHANGEL).

Jesus' coming to the Temple, where He is acknowledged by Simeon as the "glory" of Israel, is the sign that the final age has been inaugurated; in Him the eschatological dwelling of God in the midst of His people is accomplished. Other Old Testament texts to which it has been suggested that Luke alludes are: So 3.14–17 (Lk 1.28–33), 2 Sm 6.2–11, 16 (Lk 1.39–44, 56), Ex 40.35 (Lk 1.35), and Mi 4.7–10; 5.1–5 (Luke ch. 2 *passim*). The MAGNIFICAT (Lk 1.46–55) and the BENEDICTUS (1.68–79) are filled with Old Testament citations and are the most striking examples of the so-called anthological composition that is common to the rest of the narrative. The annunciations to Zachary and Mary (*see* ANNUNCIATION) correspond to the format of similar Old Testament announcements (cf. Gn ch. 17–18; Jgs 6.11–23); Mary's pondering and keeping "all these things" in her heart (Lk 2.19, 51) has its parallel in Gn 37.11 and Dn 7.28. The presence of these Old Testament references may be questioned in particular cases. Some that have been suggested give the appearance of being too subtle to be probable, but in estimating the probability account must be taken both of Luke's allusive method of citation and of the fact that he does not use the Old Testament in the manner of a scientific exegete.

See Also: LUKE, GOSPEL ACCORDING TO; MATTHEW, GOSPEL ACCORDING TO.

Bibliography: P. BENOIT, "L'Enfance de Jean-Baptiste selon Luc I," *New Testament Studies* 3 (1956–57) 169–194. R. BLOCH, *Dictionnaire de la Bible,* suppl. ed. L. PIROT, et al. (Paris 1928–) 5: 1263–81. M. M. BOURKE, "The Literary Genus of Matthew 1–2," *The Catholic Biblical Quarterly* 22 (1960) 160–175. E. BURROWS, *The Gospel of the Infancy and Other Biblical Essays* (The Bellarmine Ser. 6; London 1940) 1–58. D. DAUBE, "The Earliest Structure of the Gospels," *New Testament Studies* 5 (1958–59) 174–187. W. D. DAVIES, *The Setting of the Sermon on the Mount* (Cambridge, Eng. 1964) 61–83. R. LAURENTIN, *Structure et théologie de Luc I–II* (Études bibliques Paris 1957). S. MUÑOZ IGLESIAS, "El Evangelio de la infancia en San Lucas y las infancias de los héros bíblicos," *Estudios biblicos* 16 (1957) 329–382; "El género literario del Evangelio de la infancia en San Mateo," *ibid.* 17 (1958) 243–273. J. RACETTE, "L'Évangile de l'enfance selon saint Matthieu," *Sciences ecclésiastiques* 9 (1957) 77–85. W. L. KNOX, *The Sources of the Synoptic Gospels,* ed. H. CHADWICK, 2 v. (Cambridge, Eng. 1953–57) 2:39–44, 121–128. K. STENDAHL, "Quis et Unde? An Analysis of Matthew 1–2" *Judentum, Urchristentum, Kirche,* ed. W. ELTESTER (Berlin 1960) 94–105. A. VÖGTLE, "Die Genealogie Mt 1.2–16 und die matthäische Kindheitsgeschichte," *Biblische Zeitschrift* 8 (1964) 45–58, 239–262; 9 (1965) 32–49; *Lexikon für Theologie und Kirche,* ed. J. HOFER and K. RAHNER (Freiberg 1957–65) 6:162–163. P. WINTER, "Some Observations on the Language in the Birth and Infancy Stories of the Third Gospel," *New Testament Studies* 1 (1954–55) 111–121; "The Cultural Background of the Narrative in Luke I–II," *Jewish Quarterly Review* 45 (1954–55) 159–167, 230–242. R. E. BROWN, *The Birth of the Messiah* (Garden City, NY 1977).

[M. M. BOURKE/M. STEVENSON]

INFANT JESUS OF PRAGUE

A statue of the Christ Child King that has been preserved since 1628 in the church of Our Lady of Victory in Prague. Carved of wood and covered with wax, it stands 18 inches in height and rests on a broad pedestal. Its left hand encircles a miniature globe surmounted by a cross, and its right hand is extended in the manner of pontifical blessing. The figure appears to represent in symbolical synthesis the idea of the Kingship of Christ and that of the Holy Childhood. The origin of the figure is shrouded in legend. It was brought from Spain to Prague in the 16th century, and in 1628 was presented to the Discalced Carmelites. It became an object of popular devotion that received ecclesiastical approval through its coronation by the bishop of Prague on April 4, 1655, and through generous grants of indulgences.

Bibliography: EMMERICH OF ST. STEPHEN, *Great and Little One of Prague,* ed. L. NEMEC (Philadelphia 1959). A. M. MEYER, *The Infant King* (St. Meinrad, Ind. 1951). L. NEMEC, *The Infant of Prague: The Story of the Holy Image and the History of the Devotion.* (New York 1958).

[L. NEMEC]

INFIDEL

In the strict sense, not including apostates from the faith and those who have lost the faith either through formal heresy or in any other way, one who does not have true faith in the Christian revelation; this may be either through his own fault, because he formally refused to accept the faith when offered, or without any fault of his own, merely because he never sufficiently heard of the gospel. In the first case he is called a positive infidel, who gravely sinned when refusing the faith. In the second, he is called a negative infidel, who never rejected the faith but happens not to have the faith because he was never given the opportunity to accept it. It may also be that one who knew about the faith and came to doubt about his own religious conviction neglected further inquiry and through guilty neglect failed to come to the faith: such a one is at times called a privative infidel. In all three cases there is question of unbaptized persons.

It may happen, however, that negative infidels come to have, not without the help of GRACE, implicit FAITH in (Christian) revelation. Such will be the case of an unbaptized person who, following his conscience in all that he knows to be the will of God in his regard, comes to have the implicit desire of Baptism (baptism of desire). For one to have the implicit desire of Baptism and through it to live a life of grace, an act of charity, or love of God above all things, is necessary, and this is not possible without (SUPERNATURAL) faith in God. Such a person, baptized in desire, is no longer an infidel in the eyes of God while continuing to be so reckoned in the eyes of men. Another example of negative infidel in appearance only is that of an unbaptized person who, when offered the interior grace of faith, assents and believes in God but does not follow His will in all things, e.g., does not give up an immoral way of life. Such a half-hearted response to the grace of faith is insufficient for him to have the (implicit) desire of Baptism and receive the life of grace; but according to some theological opinion it may be sufficient for him to be given the habit of faith. Such a negative infidel would be an unbaptized but believing sinner.

Negative infidels who have a ''natural belief'' in God and were never given the grace of faith or never heard of the gospel may, theoretically speaking, be living a naturally good life or, more likely, a life of alternating sin and repentance. But contemporary theological understanding of God's universal salvific will holds that sooner or later, if not permanently, they are offered the grace of faith and are faced with the alternative of saying yes or no to God and Christ. If they say yes, they are no longer infidels except in appearance; if they say no, they become positive infidels, or sinners.

The case of atheists who reject all belief in God is different from that of infidels; they not only are without divine faith, but also without natural belief in God.

See Also: FAITHFUL.

Bibliography: S. HARENT, *Dictionnaire de théologie catholique,* ed. A. VACANT et al., 15 v. (Paris 1903–50; Tables générales 1951) 7.2:1726–1930. N. KRAUTWIG, *Lexikon für Theologie und Kirche,* ed. J. HOFER and K. RAHNER, 10 v. (2d new ed. Freiburg 1957–65) 4:930–931. H. BACHT, *ibid.* 949–951. S. PINCKAERS, *Catholicisme* 5:1587–88.

[P. DE LETTER]

INFINITY

Infinity is derived etymologically from the Latin, *infinitas,* which is a combination of *in* (meaning not) and *finis* (meaning end, boundary, limit, termination, etc.). In general, the word signifies the state or condition arising from an entity's not having some sort of end, limit, termination, or determining factor. It is predicated both of extramental, actually existing things (such as God, the visible universe, and matter) and of intramental entities (such as logical concepts and mathematical constructs). The condition it signifies in these can connote either perfection or imperfection, depending upon whether the termination, which is thereby stated to be absent, is itself a perfection and whether the entity in question should possess it. For example, when predicated of God, infinity denotes perfection. This is so because it reveals the absence in God of matter and of other intrinsic factors suggesting mere POTENCY, as well as the absence of extrinsic limits such as time, place, or comprehension by a created intellect—all of which can be linked with imperfection and none of which is proper to God. On the other hand, when applied to MATTER, infinity signifies a state of indigence, since it manifests that matter of itself lacks FORM and ACT; these are perfective factors that matter must receive if it is to exist within the real universe, and is to be even indirectly intelligible and describable.

This article traces the history of the concept of infinity, which falls into five main sections: (1) that of the ancient Greeks, (2) Neoplatonism, (3) that of the Fathers of the Church, (4) medieval scholasticism, and (5) the period since 1600. The following account treats the first two periods as representative of Greek and Neoplatonic thought, and the last three as representative of Christian and modern thought.

Greek and Neoplatonic Thought

The first period begins in ancient Greece with Anaximander of Miletus (*c.* 610–546 B.C.), who affirmed that "the first principle of existing things is the unlimited" (*Fragment* 1). It is "eternal and ageless" (*Frag.* 2), "deathless and indestructible" (*Frag.* 3), and, most likely, is some basic natural body that is unlimited because quantitatively inexhaustible. The Pythagoreans, as Aristotle reports (*Meta.* 987a 15–19), "thought that finitude and infinity were not attributes of certain other things, e.g., of fire or earth or anything else of this kind, but that infinity itself and unity itself were the substance of the things of which they are predicated." Under their influence PLATO also made infinity one of the constitutive factors of reality: "All things that are ever said to be consist [so the men of old say] of a one and a many, and have in their nature a conjunction of Limit and Unlimitedness" (*Philebus* 16C; also see 23C). But Aristotle dominates this first period, as well as most subsequent periods, with respect to quantitative infinity. (*See* GREEK PHILOSOPHY.)

Aristotelian Teaching. According to ARISTOTLE (see *Phys.* 202b 30-208a 27), QUANTITY, MOTION, and TIME are all infinite (*apeiron* or, less frequently, *aoriston*), but infinity (*apeiria* or *aoristia*) belongs to the last two only because of their relationship with the former: motion is infinite if the magnitude covered is somehow infinite, and time is so only as a measure of an infinite motion. What, then, is *apeiria* as found in quantity? Basically it has to do with certain conditions of a line.

Quantitative Infinity. Let *AO* be an actual line of definite length. Point *A* terminates it at the beginning and

point *O* at the end; thus, such a line is finite. Because of its definite dimensions, it can be measured, known, and described. Accordingly, its status of finiteness makes it knowable and describable. In it, extension is related to the terminating points in somewhat the same way as matter with respect to form; and it is itself a composite, so to speak, of matter and form (*see* MATTER AND FORM). Since perfection and actuality, no less than intelligibility, arise from the presence of form, *AO* is not only knowable but is perfect and actual as well. Consequently, the condition of finiteness in *AO* arises from its possession of definite dimensions and is aligned with perfection, actuality, and knowledge.

But how is *AO* infinite? If *AO* is finite inasmuch as it has definite dimensions because of its initial and final terminating points, it is infinite inasmuch as it can be conceived without one or other of those terminations. Thus *AO* is infinite with respect to increase, since no matter what its actual length may be, one can always imagine it as without its final point and thus as extending further. (The same applies to number, which is similarly infinite, since no matter what actual sum is suggested, one can always think of a larger one). *AO* is also infinite with respect to decrease under certain conditions. Thus, no matter how small it actually becomes by its initial point's receding toward its final one, one can always conceive it as smaller, provided that the recession through subtraction of parts takes place according to a fixed ratio. Thus, let *AO* be divided at *B, C, D,* etc., so that *AB* = ½ *AO*, *BC* = ½ *BO*, *CD* = ½ *CO*, and so on. The subtraction of *AB, BC,* etc., from *AO* can go on forever, and some of *AO* will always be left. No matter how small the remaining part becomes, one can conceive of it as still smaller because it, too, is similarly divisible. Consequently, *AO* is infinite with respect to decrease, when viewed without the initial point it actually has.

Characteristics. What are the characteristics of such infinity? Finitude is, as previously seen, linked with intelligibility, actuality, and perfection, because extension in a finite line is related to its terminal points (and consequent definite dimensions) as matter to form. On the other hand, a line is infinite when its extension is viewed as lacking either its initial or final points and, thus, infinity indicates that a line in such a condition is like matter without form. But form is the source of knowableness, actuality, and perfection. Accordingly, infinity is linked with a state of unintelligibility, mere potentiality, and imperfection. An infinite line, precisely as infinite, is unknowable because it lacks definite dimensions and thus cannot be measured or described. Its infinity, however, is merely a potential condition: every line is actually finite because of its definite length, though it can be considered as subjected to an endless process of addition or of division because of the very nature of quantity, just as primary matter can receive an endless series of substantial forms. An infinite line is imperfect because it is viewed as lacking the determinate dimensions it should and actually does have.

Imperfection of the Infinite. Aristotle frequently stresses this characteristic of imperfection. What is infinite, he explains in an important passage (*Phys.* 206b 32-207a 2), "turns out to be the contrary of what it is said to be. It is not what has nothing outside it that is infinite, but what always has something outside it." Why so? Because in quantity there is always some part beyond the point one has reached in dividing it, or in building it up by addition. Quantity is infinite because one can always take a part outside what has already been taken. Since, then, that which is infinite always has something outside and beyond, there is always something absent or lacking from it. Thus it is not complete or perfect. In fact, infinity itself is, Aristotle concludes, the very PRIVATION of wholeness and perfection, the subject of which is the sensible continuum (*ibid.,* 207b 35-208a 4).

Implications. For Aristotle, then, infinity basically is associated with quantity and is synonymous with imperfection. This synonymity has two important consequences. The Greek philosopher cannot predicate it directly of God Himself (for him, the First Mover and primal Separate Intelligence) but only of His power, and this through an extrinsic predication. That is, His power is so perfect as to be the cause of an infinite effect, viz, the endlessly recurring circular motion of the heavenly bodies through an infinity of time; it is this alone to which infinity directly belongs and through which divine power receives the predication (*Meta.* 1073a 6–10). Secondly, the material universe cannot be actually infinite in extent, nor is it merely one of an infinite number of universes, since such sorts of actual infinities are contradictory and impossible. Moreover, it is finite in virtue of the fact that as "uni-verse" it is whole, all-inclusive, complete, and perfect; and whatever is whole, complete, and perfect has an end, which is its limit and termination (*Phys.* 207a).

Neoplatonism and Plotinus. The second period in the history of infinity, that of NEOPLATONISM, was initiated by PLOTINUS (204–270 A.D.). As Aristotle had done before him, Plotinus affirmed that the power of God (the One-Good, the highest hypostasis) is infinite. "He who is capable of making all things, what greatness would He have? He is infinite and, if so, would have no physical magnitude. . . . The Principle would be great in this sense that nothing is more powerful than He or even equally so" (*Enn.* 6.7.32.14). "The One is the greatest of all things not in physical magnitude but in power, for that which is without extension is great through

power. . . . We must also insist that It is not infinite as though intraversable either in extension or in number but by the unboundedness of Its power" (6.9.6.1–13; also see 2.4.5.17–20; 5.5.10.20–24). This affirmation is apparently made through extrinsic denomination: the divine power is so great as to be the source of infinite effects—material existents that are infinitely numerous because they ceaselessly deploy in endlessly recurring world-cycles (5.7.1.9–27; 5.7.3.15; 6.2.22.11).

Infinity as Perfection. Unlike Aristotle, though, Plotinus developed a theory of infinity that is synonymous with perfection and that is applicable to God Himself. This theory rests on the insight that form and BEING are determining and terminating factors wherever found (5.1.7.19–26). If something is without form and being, then it is without their determination and, thus, is indeterminate or infinite. If it should possess them but does not, that status of indetermination is coterminous with imperfection. Thus, matter of itself is below form and entity and, accordingly, is indeterminate and simultaneously imperfect (1.8.4.14; 2.4.6.17; 2.4.10.1; 2.4.13.26; 2.4.15.16). On the other hand (and of this Aristotle shows no explicit awareness), God rises above the being and form proper only to lower levels of reality, viz, the intelligible, psychical, and sensible universes, and thereby also transcends any formal determination. By this TRANSCENDENCE He is infinite, and such infinity is aligned with absolute perfection and actual excellence. "Do not remark that [the Good] *is* in such and such a way because such language would determine It and make It become a particular thing. He who beholds It cannot say that It either is or is not such and such, for thereby he would say that It is one of those beings which can rightly be termed such and such, whereas It really is other than all such beings. Having seen that It is indeterminate, he can enumerate all the beings which come after It and then say that It is nothing of all of them but that It is Total Power which is really master of Itself" (6.8.9.37; see also 6.7.17.12–18; 5.1.7.19–26; 5.5.6.1–15; 5.5.11.16–37).

Infinity and Nonbeing. In thus showing that infinity can be coextensive with perfection and thereby predicable of the divine reality itself, Plotinus made a major contribution to the development of the concept of infinity. But one must remember that this predication is only implicit in Plotinus's text. He explicitly links infinity with NONBEING: the One is stated to be infinite because It transcends being and form. Granted that this infinity of nonbeing can imply that the One Itself is infinite, still this is only an implication.

Christian and Modern Thought

The third period in the history of infinity is occupied by the Fathers of the Church—SS. Hilary of Poitiers and

Augustine in the West; Clement of Alexandria, John Chrysostom, Gregory of Nazianzus, Gregory of Nyssa, Pseudo-Dionysius, and John Damascene in the East. These were all influenced by Sacred Scripture, as well as by Neoplatonism.

Scriptural Teaching. The Bible has only a few and (at best) indirect texts on infinity itself. An example would be the Vulgate's Ps 144.3: "Magnus Dominus et laudabilis nimis et magnitudinis eius non est finis" (the last clause is even less strong in modern translation: ". . . neque explorari potest magnitudo eius"). Still the Scriptures emphasize the awesome power of God (e.g., Gn 17.1; Ps 33.9; Ps 135.6; Jn 1.3), His eternity (Dt 32.40; Gn 21.33), His omnipresence (Dt 4.39; Ps 139.7–12) coupled with transcendence of any definite place (1 Kgs 8.27; Jb 11.8; Bar 3.25), His otherness from all else (Is 46.9), and the inability of any created intellect to know Him adequately (Rom 11.33; Eph 3.8). The result was that Latin and Greek Fathers of the Church speak of God as infinite in the sense that He is all-powerful, eternal, immense, incomprehensible, and, when under the influence also of Neoplatonism, nonbeing.

Latin and Greek Fathers. St. AUGUSTINE offers an example of the teaching of the Latin Fathers: "It is evident that the orderly disposition of the universe comes about through a mind [God], and that it can appropriately be called infinite, not in spatial relations, but in power which cannot be understood by human thought. . . . That which is incorporeal . . . can be called both complete and infinite: complete because of its wholeness, infinite because it is not confined by spatial boundaries" (*Epist. 118,* Fathers of Church ed., 284–285). Again: "What is in your mind and heart when you think of a certain substance which is living, perpetual, omnipotent, infinite, everywhere present, everywhere complete, nowhere enclosed? When you think of That, you have a conception of God in your heart" (*In evang. Ioh.* 1.8 see also *Nat. boni* 3).

St. JOHN DAMASCENE similarly speaks for the Greek Fathers: "[God] is not to be found among beings—not that He is not but, rather, because He is above all beings and even above being itself. For if knowledge has beings as its objects, then what transcends knowledge also transcends essence and, conversely, what is beyond essence also is beyond knowledge. Therefore, the Divinity is both infinite and incomprehensible, and this alone is comprehensible about Him—His very infinity and incomprehensibility" (*De fide orth.* 1.4). "We believe in one God: one principle, without beginning, uncreated, unbegotten, indestructible and immortal, eternal, unlimited, uncircumscribed, unbounded, infinite in power, simple, uncompounded, incorporeal" (*ibid.* 1.8). "Of all the

names given to God, the more proper one seems to be that of *He Who is . . . .* For, like some infinite and indeterminate sea of essence, He has and contains in Himself all beings" (*ibid* 1.9).

Another author deeply influenced by the Old Testament (in the Septuagint version), who antedates the Fathers and, for that matter, Plotinus too, is PHILO JUDAEUS of Alexandria, the Jewish theologian and philosopher. For him God is infinite in a threefold way: as incomprehensible, since we can know that He exists but not what He is; as omnipotent, since God freely created the world out of nothing; and as all-good, since He is freely and lovingly provident even over individuals (see H. A. Wolfson, *Religious Philosophy* [Cambridge, Mass. 1961] 5–11).

Medieval Scholasticism. The fourth period is that of medieval SCHOLASTICISM. Although JOHN SCOTUS ERIGENA held a doctrine on divine infinity that seems almost wholly Neoplatonic (see *De divisione naturae*, 1.56; *Patrologia Latina* 122; 499D), still from the 10th to the middle of the 13th century Christian authors appear to pay little or no attention to divine infinity. Generally, the term fails even to be listed by theologians among the divine attributes (for example, the Abelardian *Ysagoge in theologiam*, Robert of Melun's *Sententiae*, Stephen Langton's *Commentarius in sententias*, Peter of Poitier's *Sententiae*). Occasionally, infinity is applied to divine power or is made synonymous with eternity or with God's incomprehensibility (e.g., Peter of Lombard's *Libri IV sententiarum*, Hugh of Saint-Victor's *De sacramentis christianae fidei*, Hugh of Saint-Cher's *In sententiarum*, Alexander of Hales's *Glossa in sent.*, Albert the Great's *In sent.*). But nowhere is it itself discussed at any length.

Bonaventure and Aquinas. After this period of silence, though, the topic is given explicit and detailed attention by Christian authors, two of whom made important contributions to its development and whose position still influences many contemporary scholastics— SS. BONAVENTURE (see his *In 1 sent.* 19.2.3 ad 4; 43.1.1 and ad 3; 43.1.2, written *c.* 1250) and THOMAS AQUINAS (see his *In 1 sent.*, 43.1.1; written *c.* 1254; ST 1a, 7.1–2, written *c.* 1267). Their contribution directly concerns divine infinity, for with their contemporaries they accepted Aristotle's conception of quantitative infinity with reference to lines and numbers and, moreover, agreed that the world is finite in extent and is numerically one. But they broke with Aristotle by predicating infinity of God Himself, as Plotinus also had. Yet their position significantly differs from the Neoplatonist's because it rests upon an obviously different metaphysics.

Aquinas—whose doctrine is considered here for the sake of convenience, although in this matter Bonaventure's position does not differ from Thomas's and, in fact, chronologically anticipates it—agreed with Plotinus that forms, and, in general, every sort of act, are determining factors for whatever receives them. Accordingly, a recipient such as matter is indeterminate and infinite (and also imperfect) when considered in itself and as lacking form. But in contrast to Plotinus, Thomas taught also that matter and all other types of potencies are not mere negations, privations, or mental constructs, but are genuinely real and actually existing components within existents, and cause their own sort of determination. Accordingly, a subsistent form or act is without the limiting determination of matter or of potency and, thus, is infinite and infinitely perfect.

Infinity of God. God is such an existent. The divine essence contains no matter or potentiality of any sort and, as such, is totally free from their limitations. Consequently, infinity is a perfection of His very being (*see* PERFECTION, ONTOLOGICAL). Whereas each creature is a FINITE BEING because it is a composite of act(s) received and determined by potency, God is infinite Being because He is an entirely subsistent, PURE ACT and so without any recipient potency. Perfect Being because He is subsistent existence, God is infinite Being as free from the limiting determination of matter and all potency. (*See* INFINITY OF GOD.)

Such a clearly presented and solidly established doctrine was one force that helped focus the attention of Thomas's and Bonaventure's contemporaries and their successors upon infinity as an important topic for discussion. Few if any subsequent scholastic philosophers or theologians failed to investigate "Whether infinity may be attributed as a perfection to the divine being itself," and to give basically the same answer (on DUNS SCOTUS, see Bettoni, 132–159).

Modern Thinkers. Non-scholastic authors in the fifth period, which begins toward the end of the 16th century and continues to the present day, are greatly concerned with infinity too, but the doctrines they elaborate differ greatly from those of preceding eras. With regard to divine infinity they begin with a doctrine that is much the same in content as that of their scholastic predecessors, differing mainly in terminology. For example, R. DESCARTES thought that only God should be called "infinite," whereas quantitative items should be termed "indefinite" (see *Reply to Obj. 1*, Haldane-Ross transl., 2:17; *Principles of Philosophy*, 1.24, 26, 27, 1:229–230).

God and Infinity. B. SPINOZA, however, introduced quite a different doctrine, which was demanded by his MONISM (and, one may add, retained without radical modification by G. W. F. HEGEL and subsequent monists). Only God is truly real, individual things being mere modes or manifestations of the divine substance. Precisely as individual, as determinate, as this, as finite, they are unreal, since individuality and finitude are mere negations. But God *is* infinity because He is total reality and sheer affirmation: ("By God I understand Being absolutely infinite. . . . To the essence of that which is absolutely infinite pertains whatever expresses essence and involves no negation" (*Ethics,* 1.6, ed. J. Wild, 94–95).

In an effort to safeguard the reality of individual things while simultaneously retaining God, some subsequent philosophers went to the opposite extreme and made God finite—J. S. MILL, W. JAMES, A. N. WHITEHEAD (see Collins, 285–324).

Revolution in Cosmology. The main difference between this period and earlier ones, however, is seen in its cosmology. The Aristotelian notion of the universe as finite in extent and numerically one has been replaced, mainly through the discovery and use of the telescope, by a quite divergent conception. For example, the galaxy seen in the Milky Way, of which the solar system is a tiny part, is simply one among almost innumerable other galaxies. Add this to the fact that the galaxies seem to be receding from one another at enormous speeds, and the inference can easily be drawn that the UNIVERSE is somehow infinite in extent.

Such a doctrine was anticipated by Giordano BRUNO and others. Their theorizing has usually been accompanied by a tendency to speak of divine infinity in terms of OMNIPRESENCE and immensity. God is infinite insofar as He is everywhere present in this infinite universe, which in no way limits, contains, or terminates Him. Unfortunately, in the minds of some, divine infinity is so closely aligned with the infinity of absolute space as almost to seem identical (*see* PANTHEISM; PANENTHEISM).

Modern Mathematics. Coupled with this new cosmology is modern mathematics, including non-Euclidean geometry, which was initiated in the 17th century and came to offer a new approach to mathematical infinity. As developed by Georg CANTOR, this approach begins with such theorems as, "There are as many negative integers as there are positive integers; there are as many points on a line segment one unit in length as on a line segment two units long . . . , etc." It terminates by defining an infinite set as one that has this property: a proper subset of the set can be put into 1-to-1 reciprocal correspondence with the whole set. In brief, a set is infinite if a part of the set is equal to the whole (see Hausmann, 76–89).

Where previously it was assumed that the essence of mathematical infinity lay in quantity and variability, now the concepts of order and multiplicity are regarded as basic. Cantor marked the change by introducing the concept of transfinite numbers. What is a transfinite number? "In general, if we consider any class of sets of elements which are such that they can be put into a one-to-one reciprocal correspondence, we define the property common to every member of the class to be the cardinal number of each set in the class. If we now consider the class of all infinite sets which can be put into a one-to-one reciprocal correspondence, we may define that property of this class to be a transfinite cardinal number" (*ibid.*, 86).

Concluding Summary. Throughout its history infinity has been predicated mainly of quantitative items and of God; in each case it has undergone an evolution of meaning.

With respect to quantity that evolution was postponed until the most recent period. Before that Aristotle's conception held sway. Yet even now his conception is not entirely set aside. True enough, mathematical infinity is newly conceived and interpreted, and the common consensus is that the universe is not the simply bounded system it once was conceived to be. But when one says that the material world is infinite in extent, does he not mean that no matter how large it now actually is, it can still be conceived as (and perhaps will expand to be) of greater extent? If so, this meaning of infinity is still basically Aristotelian.

The evolution with respect to the infinity of God suffered no postponement. Lacking an explicit basis in Sacred Scripture, and linked with imperfection by the ancient Greeks, infinity was first predicated of God only through extrinsic denomination, viz, His power was regarded as infinite because it was capable of producing an infinite number of effects. Plotinus severed this link with imperfection, and infinity became a divine attribute, although explicitly aligned with nonbeing. Utilizing a different metaphysics, Bonaventure and Thomas Aquinas identified infinity with subsistent and all-perfect being. Resorting to a still different metaphysics, Spinoza and other monists made infinity synonymous with reality itself, and tended to reduce all existents other than God to nonentities. In reaction, still others pretended to save individual things by reducing God to their finite and imperfect level.

Bibliography: L. SWEENEY, "Infinity in Plotinus," *Gregorianum* 38 (1957) 515–535, 713–732; "Divine Infinity: 1150–1250," *The Modern Schoolman* 35 (1957–58) 38–51; "Another Interpretation of *Enneads,* VI, 7, 32," *ibid.* 38 (1960–61) 289–303; "L'Infini quantitatif chez Aristote," *Revue philsophique de Louvain* 58 (1960) 504–528; "Some Mediaeval Opponents of Divine Infinity," *Mediaeval Studies* 19 (1957) 233–245; "Lombard, Augustine and Infinity," *Manuscripta* 2 (1958) 24–40. J. D. COLLINS, *God in Modern Philosophy* (Chicago 1959) 285–324. E. BETTONI, *Duns Scotus: The Basic Principles of His Philosophy,* tr. and ed. B. BONANSEA (Washington 1961) 132–159. C. VOLLERT, "Origin and Age of the Universe Appraised by Science," *Theological Studies* 18 (1957) 137–168. B. A. HAUSMANN, *From an Ivory Tower: A Discussion of Philosophical Problems Originating in Modern Mathematics* (Milwaukee 1960) 76–89. G. GAMOW, *One, Two, Three . . . Infinity* (rev. ed. New York 1961). G. CANTOR, *Contributions to the Founding of the Theory of Transfinite Numbers,* tr. P. E. B. JOURDAIN (La Salle, Ill. 1941). A. KOYRÉ, *From the Closed World to the Infinite Universe* (Baltimore 1957).

[L. SWEENEY]

INFINITY OF GOD

The infinity of God has to do with God's perfection. The primary notion of God's infinity is that of denying that which would place him within the finite realm and so make him less than perfect. To say that God is infinite is simply to say that he is not finite. More positively God's infinity enhances those attributes which denote his perfection, such as, He is infinite in goodness, infinite in power, infinite in wisdom and love. There are no limits, bounds, or constraints, whether external or internal, imposed on his perfect being.

Biblical Basis. There is no explicit biblical teaching on God's infinity. However, it is implied within some of the other attributes predicated of God within the Bible. From the beauty, greatness, and power seen within the created order "comes a corresponding perception of their Creator" (Wis 13:3–5). God "knows all that may be known . . . no thought escapes him. He is from everlasting to everlasting. Nothing can be added or taken away . . . Though we speak much we cannot reach the end, and the sum of our words is: 'He is the all'" (Sir 42:15–43:35). God's "greatness is unsearchable" (Ps 144–145:3). There is none like God for he orders all time from beginning to end (Is 46:9–10). God is "exalted in his power" (Jb 36:22). God alone possesses immortality and exists in unapproachable light (1 Tm 6:15). It is in the perception of the grandeur and glory of God's perfection that his infinity is discerned.

Christian Tradition. While some Greek philosophical schools, such as the Stoics, conceived matter to be infinite, Christian theologians consistently attributed infinity to God in the absolute sense. The universe may be relatively infinite in that we do not know its bounds, limits, and ends nor do we know the infinite array of all that it contains, yet it is finite in that it was created and so is bound by time, space, and its own limited finite ability to be actualized (Thomas Aquinas, *Summa theologiae,* I.7.2–4). However, as Creator, God is not a member of the finite created order, and so is wholly other than all else. Therefore, God does not belong to any finite genus, that is, he cannot be named within or numbered among any genus of the created order and therefore does not partake of the limitations of that order (*Summa theologiae*, I.3.5). As God he belongs to an entirely different ontological order and as such is absolutely infinite. Moreover, Aquinas argues that because God's very nature is to be (*ipsum esse*) and so pure act (*actus purus*) he is absolutely "infinite and perfect" in that all the attributes that are predicated of him are fully and perfectly in act and thus infinitely in act (*Summa theologiae*, I.7.1). For example, because God is infinite as pure act "it is necessary that the active power of God should be infinite . . . Whence, since the divine essence, through which God acts, is infinite it follows that his power likewise is infinite" (*Summa theologiae*, I.25.2). All of God's perfections then are infinite in that they possess no limitations as in creatures but are fully and perfectly actualized within his divine being.

Theologians have treated the infinity of God, both philosophically and theologically, primarily from within his being the one God. However, the Trinity is equally infinite since the one God is a trinity of persons. The persons are infinite in their giving of themselves entirely to one another for they subsist only in relation to one another. They are all also infinitely perfect in their love, goodness, wisdom, power, and knowledge. The Father is infinitely perfect, the Son is infinitely perfect, the Holy Spirit is infinitely perfect, but there are not three separate infinite perfections but one infinite perfection that each person wholly and completely possesses in accordance with that person's distinct subjectivity. The Father possesses the one infinite perfection as Father, the Son as Son, and the Holy Spirit as Holy Spirit (Augustine, *De Trin.* 7; *Summa theologiae*, I.39). The Church has consistently taught that God as a trinity of persons is infinite in their various perfections: *Quicumque* (H. Denzinger, *Enchiridion Symbolorum* [Freiburg 1963] 75), the Nicene Creed (*Denz.*, 125–6), Lateran IV (*ibid.*, 800), Vatican I (*ibid.*, 3001).

Bibliography: T. AQUINAS, *Summa Theologiae* I.7. A. H. ARMSTRONG and R. A. MARKUS, "God's Transcendence and Infinity," in *Christian Faith and Greek Philosophy* (London 1960) 8–15. L. SWEENEY, *Divine Infinity in Greek and Medieval Thought* (New York 1992).

[T. G. WEINANDY]

INFRALAPSARIANS (SUBLAPSARIANS)

From Lat. *infra,* within, and *lapsus,* fall, originally 16th century Calvinists who held that God permitted the Fall of Adam and then elected some men out of the mass of the fallen to be saved and rejected others, leaving them to the just consequences of their sins. The Infralapsarians

opposed those Calvinists who held a SUPRALAPSARIAN view of predestination. Both parties claimed John CALVIN as favoring their view. Although some statements of Calvin, especially in his work *De aeterna predestinatione Dei* (1551), seem to indicate a Supralapsarian doctrine, the Genevan Reformer was neither Supralapsarian nor Infralapsarian. His desire was to place emphasis on the election or reprobation of man by divine decree, not to indicate when it was done. The view of the Infralapsarians concerned the order of God's decrees. They held that first God created man, then He permitted the Fall, and only then He elected some of the fallen to be saved, "passing over" (*Westminster Confession,* 1648) the others. God then provided a redeemer for the elect and, finally, sent the Holy Spirit to bring redemption to them. Infralapsarianism was condemned by the Dutch Synod of Dort (1618–19), but the triumph of the Supralapsarian view was short-lived; today no Reformed Church holds it, although a number teach Infralapsarianism.

See Also: CALVINISM; CONFESSIONS OF FAITH, PROTESTANT; PREDESTINATION (IN NON-CATHOLIC THEOLOGY).

[R. MATZERATH]

INGE, HUGH

Archbishop of Dublin and chancellor of Ireland; b. Shepton Mallet, Somerset, England, date unknown; d. Dublin, Aug. 3, 1528. He appears in history first as a scholar in Winchester (1480), and he became a fellow of New College, Oxford (1484), after which he went to the Continent to take his degree. He served in the Diocese of Bath and Wells, and visited Rome with his bishop in 1504 on a mission for Henry VIII. His appointments include the prebendaries of Cudworth (1501) and of East Harptree (1503), succentor of Wells Cathedral (1503), and vicar of West Zoyland (1508) and of Doulting (1509). He also held benefices in the Dioceses of Worcester and Lincoln. Inge attracted Cardinal Thomas WOLSEY's attention as a possibly tractable agent, and through Wolsey's influence, without which he would have had "small comfort in this world," he became bishop of Meath (1512). In 1520 he gave the archdeaconry of Meath to the king's physician. Dissatisfied, he had appealed to Wolsey, asking that he not be cast aside, and he was rewarded with the chancellorship in 1522 and the See of Dublin in the same year. He pursued Wolsey's policy of hostility to Gerald, Earl of Kildare; he was credited with a reputation for justice and probity, and the rebuilding of St. Sepulchre's, the archbishop's residence. He died of the sweating sickness.

Bibliography: B. H. BLACKER, *The Dictionary of National Biography from the Earliest Times to 1900* 10:431–432 F. E. BALL,

William Ralph Inge, portrait by A. Norris. (National Portrait Gallery, London)

The Judges in Ireland, 2 v. (London 1926) 1:194–195, *passim.* J. D'ALTON, *The Memoirs of the Archbishops of Dublin* (Dublin 1838) 182–184.

[J. J. MEAGHER]

INGE, WILLIAM RALPH

Anglican clergyman and author; b. Crayke, Yorkshire, England, June 6, 1860; d. Wallingford, Berkshire, England, Feb. 26, 1954. Educated at Eton and King's College, Cambridge, he became assistant master at Eton (1884), fellow at King's College (1886), fellow and tutor at Hertford College, Oxford (1889), vicar of All Saints', Knights-bridge (1905), and Lady Margaret Professor of Divinity at Cambridge (1907). When he was dean of St. Paul's, London (1911–34), his criticisms of the spirit of secular optimism earned him the sobriquet "The Gloomy Dean." He was named knight commander of the Victorian Order in 1930.

Inge's advocacy of Christian PLATONISM, with its tradition of "mysticism based on a foundation of reason," found expression in many widely read works, among them *Christian Mysticism* (1899), *Faith and Knowledge* (1905), *Personal Idealism and Mysticism* (1907), *Studies of English Mystics* (1906), *Faith and Its Psychology* (1919), *The Philosophy of Plotinus* (1918), and *The Platonic Tradition in English Religious Thought* (1926).

His critical treatments of contemporary thought include major works such as *God and the Astronomers* (1933). Two series of *Outspoken Essays* (1919, 1922) deal with a variety of subjects. *Christian Ethics and Modern Problems* (1930) is an examination of 20th-century personal and social morality. Inge's provocative views and brilliance of style made him one of the outstanding clerical and literary figures of his day.

Bibliography: A. FOX, *Dean Inge* (London 1960). R. M. HELM, *The Gloomy Dean: The Thought of William Ralph Inge* (Winston-Salem, NC 1962).

[R. M. HELM]

INGENUIN, ST.

Bishop; also known as Genuinus or Geminus; d. *c.* 605. PAUL THE DEACON in his *History of the Langobards* (3.26) mentions Ingenuin as partaking in the pseudosynod of Maran (Patriarchate of AQUILEIA) and he criticizes him sharply for defending in that synod (590) the schismatic position in the THREE CHAPTERS controversy. In 591 Ingenuin subscribed to the schismatic letter to Emperor MAURICE; there is ample evidence of his later conversion, however. In the 10th century the See of Säben was transferred to Brixen. The relics of Ingenuin were likewise transferred from Säben to Brixen, but at a later time.

Feast: Feb. 5.

Bibliography: *Acta Sanctorum* Feb. 1:675–681. J. KRÖSS, *Die Heiligen und Seligen Tirols* (Austria Sancta 1; Vienna 1910) 67–78. R. HEUBERGER, in *Festschrift Albert Brackmann* (Weimar 1931) 17–39.

[W. A. JURGENS]

INGLEBY, FRANCIS, BL.

Priest, martyr; b. ca. 1551 at Ripley, Yorkshire, England; hanged, drawn, and quartered June 3, 1586 (old calendar) at York. The fourth son of Sir William Ingleby and his wife Lady Anne Malory, Ingleby studied at Brasenose College, Oxford (before 1565), and was a student of the Inner Temple in 1576. He began seminary studies at Rheims in 1582 and was ordained priest at Laon in 1583. About three months later he left France to join the English Mission, where he labored in Yorkshire until he was arrested in the spring of 1586. Upon hearing his sentence of execution, Ingleby exclaimed, "Credo videre bona Domini in terra viventium" ("I believe that I shall see the goodness of the Lord in the land of the living."). He was one of the priests to whom St. Margaret CLITHEROW offered refuge in her home. He was beatified by Pope John Paul II on Nov. 22, 1987 with George Haydock and Companions.

Feast of the English Martyrs: May 4 (England).

See Also: ENGLAND, SCOTLAND, AND WALES, MARTYRS OF.

Bibliography: R. CHALLONER, *Memoirs of Missionary Priests,* ed. J. H. POLLEN (rev. ed. London 1924). J. H. POLLEN, *Acts of English Martyrs* (London 1891).

[K. I. RABENSTEIN]

INGLIS, CHARLES

Anglican bishop; b. Glencolumbkille, Donegal, Ireland, 1734; d. Nova Scotia, Canada, Feb. 24, 1816. After being educated in Ireland, he came to the U.S. in 1757 to teach at a church school in Lancaster, Pa. The following year he went to London, where he was ordained and assigned to a missionary post at Dover, Del. In 1765 Inglis became assistant rector at Trinity Church in New York City. During the Revolutionary War, his church was burned and his congregation scattered after he refused to omit the prayer for the king from his services. He left for Nova Scotia with other Loyalists, and in 1787 he was consecrated as the first Anglican bishop in Canada. With his see at Halifax, Nova Scotia, his diocese comprised all eastern Canada and the island of Bermuda. As bishop, he founded (1789) King's College, Windsor, Nova Scotia, one of the first English colleges in Canada.

Bibliography: J. C. H. MOCKRIDGE, *Bishops of the Church of England in Canada and Newfoundland* (Toronto 1896). O. W. ROWLEY, *Anglican Episcopate of Canada and Newfoundland* (Milwaukee 1928).

[F. REED]

INGRAM, JOHN, BL.

Priest, martyr; b. Stoke Edith, Herefordshire, England, 1565; d. hanged, drawn, and quartered at Gatehead, Newcastle-on-Tyne, July 26, 1594. John, probably the son of Anthony Ingram of Wolford (Warwickshire) and Lady Dorothy Hungerford, was educated first in Worcestershire, then at the New College (Oxford), English College (Rheims), Jesuit College (Pont-a-Mousson), and English College (Rome). He was ordained in Rome (1589) before entering the mission field in Scot-

land (1592) where he was frequently in the company of Lords Huntly, Angus, and Erroll, the abbot of Dumbries, and Sir Walter Lindsay of Balgavies. Following his arrest on the Tyne, Nov. 25, 1593, Fr. Ingram was imprisoned successively at Berwick, Durgam, York, and in the Tower of London, where he was tortured. During his imprisonment he wrote twenty Latin epigrams which have survived. Later he was again sent north to prisons at York, Newcastle, and Durham. He was tried at Durham with St. John BOSTE and Bl. George Swallowell, a converted minister. Ingram was found guilty of having been ordained abroad under 27 Eliz. c. 2, although there was no evidence that he had ever exercised his priestly faculties in England. It appears that an unnamed Scotsman vainly offered the English Government a thousand crowns for his life. Ingram was beatified by Pius XI on Dec. 15, 1929.

Feast of the English Martyrs: May 4 (England).

See Also: ENGLAND, SCOTLAND, AND WALES, MARTYRS OF.

Bibliography: R. CHALLONER, *Memoirs of Missionary Priests,* ed. J. H. POLLEN (rev. ed. London 1924; repr. Farnborough 1969). J. H. POLLEN, *Acts of English Martyrs* (London 1891).

[K. I. RABENSTEIN]

INHERITANCE (IN THE BIBLE)

The juridical notion of inheritance or heritage, designating the transmission or possession of goods not acquired personally but given by a previous possessor, is attested in the Bible rather frequently in its literal sense; but since it naturally lends itself to express the idea of the gratuitous gift of salvation, its theological usage in a figurative sense in the Bible is still more abundantly documented and more important. This article, after treating of the terminology, will first consider inheritance in the literal sense, and then in the figurative sense, and this for both the OT and the NT.

Terminology. The principal Hebrew equivalents for the English words, inherit, inheritance, heritage, and heir, are based on the verbal roots *yrš, nḥl,* and *ḥlq,* to which may be added the nouns *gôrāl* (lot), *ḥebel* (allotted portion), and perhaps also *segullâ* (private fortune). The root *yrš,* which occurs about 256 times in the Masoretic Text (MT), denotes specifically succession in possession, whether by conquest or by inheritance, and it is used almost always of immovables, such as a country, city, or house. The root *nḥl,* which is used about 282 times in the MT, designates precisely possession held by title of patrimony and is employed almost always of immovables. The root *ḥlq* refers to a heritage as a portion of a larger unit.

This orientation of the Hebrew roots toward the sense of stable possession forced the Septuagint translators at times to use Greek words in a sense broader than they had in the classical language. In adopting the Greek words κληρονομέω, (inherit), κληρονόμος (heir), and κληρονομία (inheritance, heritage) to express the notions contained in the Hebrew terms, the translators often went beyond the classical meaning of transmission of property by last will and testament or by other legal disposition and gave the Greek terms the meaning of stable, lasting possession. The same extension of sense is found in the NT also.

Literal Sense. In Israel the transmission of patrimonial goods was fixed by custom or by law; it was not determined by last will and testament (2 Sm 17.23; 2 Kgs 20.1; Sir 14.15). There are but few passages in the Bible that treat directly of the laws of inheritance (Dt 21.15–17; Nm 27.1–11; 36.6–9). It is known, however, from these and other passages, that the oldest son had a right to a double share of his father's possessions (Dt 21.17; see also Lk 15.12), that the sons of so-called concubines (*see* CONCUBINE [IN THE BIBLE]) received no inheritance, unless they were adopted as sons of full right (Gn 25.5–6), and that illegitimate sons were excluded from the inheritance (Jgs 11.1–2). Daughters did not inherit, unless there were no male heirs and the daughters married within the same clan (Nm 27.1–8; 36.1–9). A widow did not inherit; she could, however, be the guardian of her deceased husband's property until their sons came to full age (Ru 4.9; 2 Kgs 8.3–6); if she had no male descendant, the property of her deceased husband passed to his brothers or nearest male relatives, and she returned to her father's house (Gn 38.11; Lv 22.13), or she remained attached to her husband's family by a LEVIRATE MARRIAGE (Dt 25.5–10; Ru 2.20; 3.12). Toward the end of the OT period, however, a childless widow could apparently inherit the property of her deceased husband (Jdt 8.7).

Theological Usage in the Old Testament. Near the beginning of the Pentateuch, in the account of God's promise to Abraham (Genesis 15), the concept of inheritance already appears four times (in v. 3, 4, 7, and 8). This promise of a future inheritance was the point of departure for a line of theological thought continuing to the NT (Gn 12.7; 13.14–17; 15.18; 24.7; 26.3–5). The same promise of a land to be received as an inheritance is found in the ancient Mosaic traditions concerning the COVENANT (Ex 3.8, 17; 23.20–33); in later texts this possession is regarded as a fulfillment of the promise made to Abraham (Ex 6.8; 13.5; 32.13).

Canaan, the Inheritance of the Tribes of Israel. After the Exodus of the Israelites from Egypt, the land of Canaan was considered their inheritance (Gn 48.6; Nm 26.52–56; 33.50–54; 34.14–18). Deuteronomy returns time and time again to this idea (Dt 1.7, 8, 21, 35, 38; 2.12, 29; 3.18, 20, 28; etc.). If Israel succeeded in gaining possession (yrš) of the Promised Land, it was only because this land had been given to it as a patrimony (năḥālâ) by Yahweh (Jos 1.6; 3.10; 13.1, 7). The same idea recurs in the books of Samuel, Kings, Ezra, Nehemiah, and Chronicles (e.g., 1 Kgs 8.36; 9.7; 2 Kgs 21.8; Neh 9.8, 15, 23, 35, 36; 1 Chr 28.8; etc.), and the same is true of the Psalms (Ps 36[37].18; 46[47].5; 68[69].37; 104[105].11; 134[135].12; 135[136].21–22). In certain passages the land of Canaan is called ''Yahweh's heritage'' (1 Sm 26.19; 2 Sm 21.3; 1 Kgs 8.36).

Israel, Yahweh's Heritage. At the same time, however, Israel is regarded as the heritage of Yahweh (2 Sm 14.16; 20:19; 1 Sm 10.1; Dt 4.20; 9.26, 29; 1 Kgs 8.51, 53; 2 Kgs 21.14), and in the Oracles of Moses this assigning of Israel to Yahweh is said to go back to an early division of the various peoples among ''the sons of God'': ''The Most High assigned the nations their heritage . . . after the number of the sons of God, while the Lord's own portion was Jacob, His hereditary share was Israel'' (Dt 32.8–9; see also Ex 34.9). Thus, the fact that Yahweh holds Israel as His heritage implies that He governs it, not through any intermediary, such as an angel, but personally, by dwelling in the midst of His people (Ex 33.14–16).

In the Prophets. The inheritance idea plays practically no role in the Prophets of the 8th and 7th centuries B.C. (Amos, Hosea, Isaiah, Micah). With Jeremiah, however, it again becomes a central idea: the gift of the Promised Land as Israel's inheritance constitutes, with the Exodus, the preamble to the covenant and forms the basis for the expectation that Yahweh would be faithful to Israel (Jer 3.19; 7.7; 11.4–5; 12.7–10; etc.). Similar ideas are found in Ezekiel (Ez 33.24; 35.15; 37.25; 38.16; 47.14), Deutero-Isaiah (Is 47.6; 49.8), Trito-Isaiah (Is 60.21; 63.17), and Zechariah (Zec 2.16; 8.12). In the last two of these the perspective of the heritage has already become eschatological.

Development of the Concept. In the course of the OT the inheritance theology evolved in such a way that gradually the two originally distinct concepts of Canaan as Israel's heritage and Israel as Yahweh's heritage were integrated into each other, the former concept gradually disappearing in the latter. This was in germ in the theology of the covenant (Dt 4.25–28; 28.15–68; 29.21–27; see also Ex 19.5; Dt 7.6; 14.2; 26.18), and Israel would always be Yahweh's heritage, even in the state of the faithful ''remnant'' (Dt 30.5). When the Exile would have made the hopes of a terrestrial heritage unrealizable, the inheritance concept would be taken up in more universalist terms (Is 57.13; 60.21; 65.8–9; Ps 36[37].9, 11, 18, 22, 29, 34).

In the Maccabean period the inheritance concept became eschatological and personal (Wis 3.14; 5.5; 2 Mc 7.36; see also Dn 12.13). In this spiritualization of the inheritance concept the importance of a certain Israelite institution should be pointed out: the special situation of the tribe of Levi, whose heritage was Yahweh Himself (Dt 18.1–2; Nm 18.20; Jos 13.14, 33; 18.7; Ez 44.28). This situation was gradually transformed into a purely spiritual and personal hope (Ps 15[16].5–6; 72[73].25–26).

Theological Usage in the New Testament. The inheritance concept is developed theologically in the NT along two lines of thought: eschatological hope, and the fulfillment of the inheritance promises in Christ.

Eschatological Hope. As in Judaism of the last few pre-Christian centuries, so also in the NT the hope of the inheritances is transformed to an eschatological plane (Mk 10.17 and parallels; Mt 5.5; 25.34; 1 Cor 6.9–10; 15.50; Gal 5.21; Eph 5.5). In this perspective the possession of the KINGDOM OF GOD is now the inheritance of the believers (Rom 4.13–16; Eph 1.18; Heb 9.15; 1 Pt 1.4), of which the pledge is given with the Holy Spirit received in baptism (Eph 1.14).

Fulfillment of the Inheritance Promises in Christ. In the NT the promises of the inheritance made to Abraham are considered as fulfilled in Christ. This line of thought is well expressed in the parable of the vine dressers (Mk 12.1–12 and parallels). Christ is the heir who inherits the vineyard of Israel (Is 5.1–7) and who therefore receives the inheritance promised to Abraham (Gal 3.15–18), and this promised inheritance He shares with the believers (Gal 3.29) in the Church (Eph 3.6).

The inheritance concept has thus attained its full development: starting with the promise of a land in which Israel could live here on Earth, it now designates the blessings of salvation, the sharing in the divine sonship in the kingdom of the Father (Mt 25.34).

Bibliography: R. DE VAUX, *Ancient Israel, Its Life and Institutions,* tr. J. MCHUGH (New York 1961) 53–55. *Encyclopedic Dictionary of the Bible,* tr. and adap. by L. HARTMAN (New York 1963), from A. VAN DEN BORN, *Bijbels Woordenboek* 1062–64. W. FOERSTER and G. KITTEL, *Theologisches Wörterbuch zum Neuen Testament* (Stuttgart 1935–) 3:757–786. F. MUSSNER, *Lexikon für Theologie und Kirche,* ed. J. HOFER and K. RAHNER, 10 v. (2d, new ed. Freiburg 1957–65) 3:962–963. P. KOSCHAKER, *Reallexikon der Vorgeschichte,* ed. M. EBERT 15 v. (Berlin 1924–32) 3:114–119. X. LÉON-DUFOUR, ed., *Vocabulaire de théologie biblique* (Paris 1962) 435–439. J. B. BAUER, ed., *Bibeltheologisches Wörterbuch,* 2 v. (2d ed. Graz 1962) 1:267–272. J. HEMPEL, *Das Ethos des Alten Testaments (Beihefte zur Zeitschrift für die Alttestamentliche Wissenschaft* 67; Berlin 1938) 71–72, 119–120. F. DREYFUS, ''Le Thème de l'héritage dans l'Ancien Testament,'' *Revue des sciences philosophiques et théologiques* 42 (1958) 3–49. H. WILDBERGER, *Jahwehs Eigentumsvolk* (Zurich 1960).

[J. HARVEY]

INJURY, MORAL

As understood in moral theology, injury is a violation of right, or an act opposed to the virtue of justice. This was the earliest sense of the term, and in ordinary usage this sense is still discernible, although the word is used often in reference to harm suffered without injustice, such as might be sustained in an accident. The word, in its verbal form, may be used in an active sense to signify the doing of a wrong to another; as a substantive it is more commonly applied in the correlative passive sense to signify the result of such an act, i.e., the harm suffered by the person wronged. If the injustice is intended, the injury is said to be formal; if it is done without advertence or intent, it is merely material and is not sinful unless the lack of advertence is itself culpable. An injury is direct if it is intended as such; it is indirect if it is not intended but is forseen as a consequence of something one does intend. It may be inflicted by a positive act, such as theft, or by the omission of an act one is bound to perform. A further precision is made by moralists who distinguish injustice as injurious, and injustice as injurious and damaging. Any violation of justice is injurious, but it is also damaging if the victim sustains loss (damnum, or damage) on its account. The obligation to RESTITUTION in the strict sense of the word arises from injuries of the latter kind.

There are as many kinds of injury as there are species of injustice. Since injustice is *ex genere suo* gravely sinful, every act that is injurious in the proper sense is a mortal sin unless one or another of the conditions necessary for full subjective responsibility is wanting, or unless the harm done is too small to be taken seriously.

It is a rule of law that no injury is done to one who consents to the transgression of his right: *scienti et consentienti non fit iniuria et dolus (Liber Sextus,* rule 27). In such a case one cedes his right. However, this rule is applicable only if the party consenting is free to yield his right, which is not the case, for example, in a sin of adultery with a woman whose husband does not object, or in the taking of the life of another who wants to be released from the burden of living. The rule supposes also that the consent of the one whose right is violated is given freely, i.e., that he does not yield his right under the influence of error, fraud, fear, or violence.

The injustices done to those who, following the counsel of Christ (Mt 5.40), offer no resistance to evil, or who long for martyrdom, or rejoice over the injuries done to them (Heb 10.34) are in no way condoned by the willingness of the victims to submit to unjust treatment. The intention of the victims is not precisely to surrender their rights to the unjust, or to approve the wickedness, but to bear the trial patiently for the sake of Christ.

The sinful gravity of an injury is measured not only by the seriousness of the actual injustice that is done, but also by the harm to the social order, for the peace and security of the community may be threatened by an injury done to a private individual who feels little loss at the violation of his right. Nevertheless, the degree of the victim's unwillingness to suffer the injury should in some cases be taken into consideration, because if it can be assumed that he is not seriously unwilling and would not urge his strict right, the act would not be a grave violation of justice, on the principle *consentienti non fit iniuria*. But, on the other hand, a marked and emphatic unwillingness of a person to have his right disregarded in some trifling matter by which he happens to set great store would not aggravate a petty injustice to the extent of making it a grave sin against justice, for his excessive unwillingness would be unreasonable. Still, though a venial sin from the point of view of justice, such an act could involve a grave transgression of the law of charity.

Bibliography: THOMAS AQUINAS, *Summa theologiae* 2a2ae 72:1–4. ALPHONSUS LIGUORI, *Theologia moralis,* ed. L. GAUDÉ, 4 v. (new ed. Rome 1905–12; repr. 1953) 3:966, 984–990. A. THOUVENIN, *Dictionnaire de théologie catholique*, ed. A. VACANT et al., 15 v. (Paris 1903–50; Tables générales 1951) 7.2:1936–39. J. A. MCHUGH and C. J. CALLAN, *Moral Theology,* 2 v. (New York 1930) 2:46–50. H. DAVIS, *Moral and Pastoral Theology,* rev. and enl. ed. by L. W. GEDDES (New York 1958) 2:265–268.

[P. K. MEAGHER]

INNATISM

Innatism teaches that man is born with ideas. It is a psychological explanation of the origin of human thought, not to be confused with IDEALISM, which contends that thought generates its own content. Historically, innatism has taken two main forms, the Platonic and the Cartesian.

Plato's innatism is a psychological corollary to his theory of being and knowledge. Influenced by Parmenides's insistence that the mind knows being and that being as such precludes change, PLATO denied that the mind could abstract meaning from the material world experienced by the senses. Pure meaning, for him, was expressed in the judgment of identity (*A* is *A*), and this kind of judgment looked directly to the intelligible content that the mind found within itself. Man's advance from ignorance to knowledge was not the fruit of experience but of remembrance. It followed from this that the soul had lived in the world of forms before it was united to the body.

The innatism proposed by R. DESCARTES was less central to his philosophy; some Cartesians, such as L.

BRUNSCHVICG, maintain that Descartes's doctrine could have prescinded from it. The Cartesian clear and distinct idea is not measured by reality but is reality's measure. Things are true to the extent to which they conform to the idea expressing their nature. The mind must purge itself of the disturbing influence of the imagination and of the senses, draw within itself, and thus—by a supreme effort of concentration—intuit ideas that are reducible to their clearest and most distinct components. Once convinced that the mind does, in fact, possess an intuitive knowledge of clear and distinct ideas by withdrawing from experience, Descartes was forced to reject Aristotle's notion of ABSTRACTION and to conclude that human ideas are born with man.

A realist and Aristotelian theory of knowledge objects to innatism because the doctrine is based on an a priori metaphysics rather than on an analysis of human experience. Factually, men learn through experience. Intelligibility is first grasped in sensible "examples" (to use St. Thomas Aquinas's word) presented to the mind by way of experience. Distilling meanings from the material instances in which they are found, the intelligence predicates such meanings of things. The human INTELLECT thus depends upon sensation in two ways: (1) it abstracts meaning from things, and (2) reflecting upon the sensorial context in which these things are presented to it, it refers this meaning to the things themselves in judgment. Moreover, a phenomenological study of knowledge reveals no data supporting the innatist contention that man is born with ideas.

In some psychological and psychiatric theories, especially those of S. FREUD and C. G. JUNG, innatism can mean that man's sensorial equipment is predisposed at birth—through racial, biological, historical, and other circumstances—to a subsequent determination of his intellectual life. A similar kind of innatism is advocated by St. THOMAS AQUINAS, who taught that man's intellectual capacity and, to an extent, his achievement, is dependent upon the sensorial equipment with which he is born.

See Also: KNOWLEDGE, THEORIES OF; IDEA; ONTOLOGISM.

Bibliography: A. CARLINI, *Enciclopedia filosofica,* 4 v. (Venice–Rome 1957) 2:1422–28. P. FOULQUIÉ and R. SAINT-JEAN, *Ci-tionnaire de la langue philosophique* (Paris 1962) 364. R. EISLER, *Wörterbuch der philosophischen Begriffe,* 3 v. (4th ed. Berlin 1927–30) 1:49–51.

[F. D. WILHELMSEN]

INNITZER, THEODOR

Cardinal archbishop of Vienna; b. Vejprty (Weipert), Bohemia, Dec. 25, 1875; d. Vienna, Oct. 9, 1955. Theodor, son of a lacemaker, studied at Vienna and was ordained in 1902. From 1913 until 1932 he was professor of the New Testament at the University of Vienna and general secretary of a Catholic cultural society, the Leo-Gesellschaft. In the Schober cabinet (1929–30) he served as minister of social welfare. He became archbishop of Vienna (Sept. 20, 1932) and cardinal (March 1933). Innitzer was a strong supporter of the authoritarian regime of Engelbert Dollfuss and Kurt von Schuschnigg. He and the other Austrian bishops declared their support for the Anschluss in the faint hope of preserving Austria's Church liberties and tradition. Pope Pius XI and the German hierarchy did not approve of this optimistic policy, which was soon rendered meaningless by the Nazi refusal to honor agreements and by the attack on the archiepiscopal palace by members of Nazi youth organizations (Oct. 8, 1938). Promises made by Hitler to Innitzer in the course of two interviews were intended merely to win Catholic support in the plebiscite. In his last years Innitzer devoted himself to rebuilding the Church in Austria, especially to restoring the *Stefansdom,* damaged in the last days of World War II. He also remained more aloof from Austrian politics. Long a pioneer in providing advanced theological training for the laity, he established for this purpose the Vienna Catholic Academy (1945). Innitzer was outstanding for his love of his fellow men and for his awareness of social problems. Much less impressive was his political sense, which had developed in the tradition of JOSEPHINISM and under the influence of German national feeling in Bohemia.

Bibliography: *Geschichte der Republik Österreich,* ed. H. BENEDIKT (Munich 1954). J. WODKA, *Kirche in Österreich* (Vienna 1959). J. KOSNETTER, *Theodor Kardinal Innitzer zum Gedächtnis* (Vienna 1957); *Lexikon für Theologie und Kirche* 5:685.

[W. B. SLOTTMAN]

INNOCENT, ST.

Bishop of Tortona *c.* 322–350; d. 350. Although his vita is legendary, Innocent did exist and fragments of the legend are true. His family lived in Tortona in northern Italy, and were, by imperial license, exempt from persecution. However, when his father and mother died, Innocent was summoned to court. He refused to sacrifice to the gods, was tortured, and was condemned to burn at the stake. The night before his execution he dreamed that his father directed him to go to Rome; waking, he found his guards asleep and succeeded in making his escape. In Rome, he was received by Pope MILTIADES, and later he was raised to the diaconate by Pope SYLVESTER. Sent to Tortona as bishop, for 28 years he zealously spread the faith and built many churches.

Feast: April 17.

Pope Innocent I, effigy from 9th-century series of papal portraits, formerly at the basilica of St. Paul, Rome, Italy.

Bibliography: A. BUTLER, *The Lives of the Saints,* ed. H. THURSTON and D. ATTWATER, 4 v. (New York 1956) 2:113. *Acta Sanctorum* April 2:478–482. F. SAVIO, *Analecta Bollandiana* 15 (1896) 377–384.

[E. D. CARTER]

INNOCENT I, POPE, ST.

Pontificate: Dec. 22, 401 to March 12, 417. Innocent was most probably a Roman deacon, who succeeded ANASTASIUS I in December 401. In 410 he undertook a journey to Ravenna to arrange a truce between the Emperor HONORIUS and Alaric the Goth, and was therefore absent from Rome when the city was taken and pillaged by the Gothic king (August 24). He returned to Rome in 412, subsequently died there, and was buried like Anastasius in the cemetery called Ad Ursum Pileatum.

Correspondence. Of the correspondence of Innocent, 36 letters are preserved in the ancient canonical collections. Disregarding chronology, the letters can be classified according to the three areas in which Innocent tried to exercise his authority.

To Western Bishops. In writing to Victricius of Rouen (*Epist.* 2), EXUPERIUS OF TOULOUSE (*Epist.* 6), and the bishops of the Council of Toledo in 400 (*Epist.* 3), Innocent settled their questions regarding discipline and the liturgy. In his letter to Decentius of Gubbio (*Epist.* 25, March 19, 411) he deals with the Canon of the Roman Mass and speaks of Confirmation as reserved to bishops only, of Penance, and of Extreme Unction. On several occasions, Innocent reiterated the prohibition against marriage for bishops, priests, and deacons and the obligation of continence for those already married before entering the clergy; and he sanctioned the vow of chastity for consecrated virgins (*Epist.* 2). The letter to Exuperius contains also a list of the canon of the Bible and excludes several apocryphal books.

Innocent frequently asserted the authority of the Apostolic See, stating (rather ahistorically) that as all the Western churches owed their origin to Peter and to his successors in the See at Rome, it is according to Roman usage that liturgical worship should be observed everywhere (*Epist.* 25.1.2). Citing the erroneous canons of Nicaea and Sardica, he ruled that ecclesiastical affairs should be adjudicated by the provincial bishops, "without prejudice, however, to the Roman church, respect for which should, in all cases, be maintained," and to which major problems should be submitted (*Epist.* 2.5, 6).

To Eastern Bishops. Innocent formalized the policy of popes Siricius and Anastasius I entrusting to Anysius of Thessalonica surveillance over the churches in Eastern Illyricum and, probably following the civil practice of instituting imperial vicars, made Rufus, the successor to Anysius, his vicar for the ten provinces in the civil dioceses of Macedonia and Dacia. Innocent's primary intention was to curtail the claims of the patriarchate of Constantinople which, with the encouragement of the Eastern emperor, was attempting to extend its jurisdiction in that direction.

He likewise intervened in the difficulties that followed the deposition of St. JOHN CHRYSOSTOM at the Synod of the OAK in 403. After he had been informed of the matter by THEOPHILUS OF ALEXANDRIA and by John himself, he refused to exclude John from communion with Rome since the matter had not been decided by a legitimately constituted council in conformity with the canons of Nicaea (*Epist.* 5). He wrote several letters of encouragement to John, refused to recognize Arsacius as John's successor and finally, after John's death in exile, broke communion with Theophilus of Alexandria and the Eastern bishops who had removed John's name from the Diptychs. Communion with Antioch was restored in 414 when its bishop, Alexander, received from the pope an assurance concerning the ancient rights of his see; and an end was put to the MELETIAN SCHISM. Only after the death of Innocent was full communion with the East restored (*Epist.* 19, 20).

To African Bishops. Innocent intervened in the dispute over Pelagianism (*see* PELAGIUS AND PELAGIANISM). Pelagius had been condemned originally by a Council of Carthage in 411, but had received a pardon at a synod at

Diospolis in Palestine in 415. Following this action, councils in Carthage and Milevis reaffirmed the excommunication of 411 and forwarded their decisions to Rome in 416 (*Epist.* 26, 27). Five bishops, including Aurelius of Carthage and St. AUGUSTINE, sent a Pelagian dossier to the pope (*Epist.* 28), demanding the intervention of the Apostolic See and requesting the pope to summon Pelagius to Rome and anathematize his errors. They asked Innocent if "their small stream of doctrine flowed from the same source" as his own (*Epist.* 28.17).

Innocent replied to these letters on Jan. 27, 417 (*Epist.* 29, 30, 31) and boldly thanked the Africans for referring the matter to him, which they had not done. He denounced perverse doctrines concerning grace but did not condemn anyone or disavow the Council of Diospolis, fearing to create conflict between the African and Palestinian bishops. On receipt of these letters Augustine pronounced the famous words: "On this matter two councils have been sent to the Apostolic See and rescripts have been received in reply. The case is closed (*causa finita est*)—would that the error were likewise ended" (Sept. 23, 417; *Serm.* 131.10). Yet Innocent had little impact on the government's treatment of Donatism in Africa, which was probably for the best since no transmarine emperor or bishop ever understood Donatism.

Roman Primacy. In these matters Innocent consciously conducted himself with the authority of a successor of St. Peter. The African bishops acknowledged this fact in principle, declaring that they understood "what was due to the Apostolic See; since at Rome, it was desirable to follow the Apostle from whom the episcopate stemmed and obey the authority which was attached to his name." They agreed that while questions could be solved in distant provinces, it was not necessary to reach a decision before referring matters to the Holy See; and that a just decision should be confirmed by its authority in order that other churches might learn from it how to conduct themselves (*Epist.* 29.1). Innocent concurred, advising them that "Each time a problem has to do with a question of doctrine I consider that the bishops, our brothers, should refer it to Peter, the founder of the episcopate, to provide for the common good of all the churches throughout the whole world" (*Epist.* 30.2).

The authority of the bishop of Rome is that of the Apostle Peter himself, who was, in Christ, the first (*exordium*) of the Apostles and in the episcopate. The pope is to be referred to "as the head and the summit of the episcopate." Innocent thus attempts one of the first treatises on the Roman primacy. In this role, he played a decisive part in the Apostolic See's understanding of itself.

Feast: July 28.

Bibliography: *Patrologia Latina*, ed. J. P. MIGNE (Paris 1878–90) 20:457–640. P. JAFFÉ, *Regesta pontificum romanorum ab*

condita ecclesia ad annum post Christum natum 1198, ed. S. LÖWENFELD et al., 2 v. (2d ed. Leipzig 1881–88, repr. Graz 1956) 44–49. *Collectio Avellana,* ed. O. GUENTHER, 2 v. (Corpus scriptorum ecclesiasticorum latinorum 35; 1895–98). *Liber pontificalis,* ed. L. DUCHESNE, 1:220–224 (Paris 1886–92). É. AMANN, *Dictionnaire de théologie catholique,* ed. A. VACANT et al., 15 v. (Paris 1903–50; Tables générales 1951–) 7.2:1940–50. B. CAPELLE, ''Innocent Iᵉʳ et le canon de la messe,'' *Recherches de théologie ancienne et médiévale* 19: 5–16. A. DIBERARDINO, *Patrology* (Westminster, Md. 1986), 4:582–584. E. FERGUSON, ed., *Encyclopedia of Early Christianity* (New York 1997) 1:573–574. H. JEDIN, *History of the Church* (New York 1980) 2:256–259. J. N. D. KELLY, *Oxford History of Popes* (New York 1986) 37–38. J. MERDINGER, *Rome and the African Church* (New Haven 1997) 88–110. C. PIETRI, *Roma Christiana* (Rome 1976) 1166–1201. O. WERMLINGER, *Rom und Pelagius* (Stuttgart 1975). R. AUBERT, *Dictionnaire d'histoire et de géographie ecclésiastiques,* 25 (Paris 1995). C. H. PIETRI, ''L'aristocratie chrétienne entre Jean de Constantinople et Augustin d'Hippone,'' *Christiana Respublica. Éléments d'une enquête sur le christianisme antique* (Rome 1997) 789–305. G. SCHWAIGER, *Lexikon für Theologie und Kirche* (3d ed. Freiburg 1996).

[P. T. CAMELOT]

INNOCENT II, POPE

Pontificate: Feb. 14, 1130 to Sept. 24, 1143. Born Gregory Parareschi, Rome. As cardinal deacon of Sant'Angelo, he was one of three, including Cardinal Lambert, bishop of Ostia, who preceded him as Pope Honorius II, who negotiated the Concordat of WORMS in 1122, which brought an end to the Investiture Controversy. However, Worms was not without controversy itself. At the papal election of 1124, the papal chancellor, Cardinal Aimeric, played a leading role in securing the election of Cardinal Lambert as HONORIUS II. When Honorius died in 1130, he moved quickly, along with his FRANGIPANI supporters in Rome, to ensure the election of Cardinal Gregory. In doing so, he ignored the commission that had been established after the election of 1124 to prevent internal divisions from breaking out. A slight minority of the cardinals, which included six of the seven cardinal bishops, chose Gregory, while a small majority favored Cardinal Peter Pierleone, member of a distinguished Roman family and a strong supporter of the papal reform movement, as ANACLETUS II. Since numerical majority was not a determining factor in medieval electoral decisions, but had to be balanced by such considerations as the weightiness and merit of each side, the decision as to which candidate was pope remained unclear in the minds of many.

Behind this disputed election lay important differences within the reform party. Disappointment over the compromises made at Worms to secure an agreement was important, but so, too, was the reversal of the papal alli-

Pope Innocent II and St. Lawrence, detail of the 12th-century mosaic in the apse of the Basilica of S. Maria in Trastevere, Rome.

ance with the NORMANS. Perhaps even more important was the worry shared by both sides as to the future security of the patrimony of St. Peter, viewed as the guarantee of papal liberty. The party of Aimeric should not, therefore, be regarded as villains, nor should the party of Peter be labeled as extremists. How to protect the settlement reached at Worms was a divisive question, but it was more a strategic one than a matter of principle. As one might suspect, support for Peter was chiefly in Italy, while Innocent received the support of northern European reformers such as NORBERT OF XANTEN, SUGER OF ST. DENIS, PETER OF CLUNY, and BERNARD OF CLAIRVAUX. Since Archbishop Walter of Ravenna and the Pisans cast in their lot on his side, he clearly had the support of the emperor. Anacletus turned to the Normans in the person of Roger II, count of Sicily and duke of Apulia, whose quest for a royal title he recognized. This act, sometimes viewed as a crass bid for support, conferred legitimacy on his major supporter, raising him to the level of those secular rulers who embraced Innocent II. Bernard of Clairvaux was only one voice, although certainly among the most influential, among those who criticized the alliance with Roger II, the tyrant king, and used his crimes to attack Anacletus.

This support was not enough. Deserted by the Frangipani and facing the opposition of the Romans, Innocent had to flee Rome and seek refuge in Pisa. He was not crowned until 1133, when the emperor, Lothar, led Innocent back to Rome, but he was unable to keep him there. Lothar returned in 1136, but was unable to restore Innocent. In fact, he and Innocent quarreled, as he began to reassert imperial claims in northern Italy. The fragility of the papal position was revealed when Anacletus II died on Jan. 25, 1138 and Roger II recognized his successor, Victor IV. Although Victor soon made peace with Innocent, Roger II remained in the field. When Innocent led an army, composed in part of disaffected Normans, against him, he captured the pope, and in a scene reminiscent of Pope Leo IX and Robert Guiscard, negotiated an agreement that recognized him as king with the marvelously ambiguous title, "Rex Sicilie, ducatus Apulie, et Principatus Capue." It was interpreted by the papacy as confining the monarchy to Sicily, and by Roger and his successors as confirming their royal rule in southern Italy as well.

Innocent's major achievement was the Second LATERAN COUNCIL, which marked the end of the schism, but also reconfirmed his commitment to reform. The issues that had brought about the schism, however, remained alive, even as the circumstances changed, to create an aura of ambivalence in the relations between the papacy and secular powers.

Bibliography: L. DUCHESNE, ed., *Liber Pontificalis* (Paris 1886–92) 2:379–85. L. JAFFÉ, *Regesta pontificum romanorum ab condita ecclesia ad annum post Christum natum 1198* (Leipzig 1881–88) 1:840–911; *Patrologia Latina* 179:21–732. F. J. SCHMALE, *Studien zum Schisma des Jahres 1130* (Cologne 1961). H. W. KLEWITZ, "Das Ende des Reformpapsttums," *Deutsches Archiv für Erforschung des Mittelalters* 3 (1939) 371–412. E. MÜHLBACHER, *Die streitige Papstwahl des Jahres 1130* (Innsbruck 1876). P. F. PALUMBO, *Lo scisma del MCXXX* (Rome 1942). E. VACANDARD, *Dictionnaire d'histoire et géographie ecclésiastiques*, ed. A. BAURILLART et al. (Paris 1912—) 2:1408–1419. H. V. WHITE, *The Conflict of Papal Leadership Ideals from Gregory VII to Bernard of Clairvaux with Special reference to the Schism of 1130* (Ph.D. Diss., U. of Mich., Ann Arbor 1957). J. R. SOMMERFELDT, *Consistency of Thought in the works of Bernard of Clairvaux* (Ph.D. Diss., U. of Mich., Ann Arbor 1960). C. MORRIS, *The Papal Monarchy: The Western Church from 1050 to 1250* (Oxford 1989) 182–185. W. MALECZEK, "Das Kardinalskollegium unter Innocenz II und Anacletus II", *Archivum historiae pontificiae* 19, 1981, 27–78. T. REUTER, "Zur Anerkennung Papst Innocenz II" *Deutsches Archiv für Erforschung des Mittelalters* 39 (1983) 395–416. D. MATTHEW, *The Norman Kingdom of Sicily* (Cambridge 1992) 34–54. W. MALECZEK, *Lexikon des Mittelalters* 5:433–4.

[J. M. POWELL]

INNOCENT III, POPE

Pontificate: Jan. 8, 1198 to July 16, 1216; b. Lothar, son of Transmundus, of the family of the Lombard counts of Segni, and Clarissa, from the Roman family of Scotti (or Scorta), probably about 1160 or 1161. d. Perugia. He pursued his studies in Rome, Paris, and Bologna. In Rome, he studied at the monastery of St. Andrew with Peter Ismael, whom he later named bishop of Sutri. In Paris, his teacher was Peter of Corbeil, whom he designated bishop of Cambrai and later as archbishop of Sens. Although there is a tradition that he studied with the canonist, Hugucccio, in Bologna and later appointed him bishop of Ferrara, there is no contemporary evidence to support this view. In fact, the failure of the author of the *Gesta Innocentii III*, a contemporary, to mention Huguccio is sufficient to raise doubt since he mentions both Peters as teachers of the pope.

Prior to his election, Lothar wrote a number of treatises, the most popular of which was the *De miseria humane conditionis* (On the Misery of the Human Condition), which was widely circulated throughout the Middle Ages. Although modern scholars have often been dismissive of the work, it belonged to a genre that touched deep chords in an age when human suffering was commonplace. He also authored the *De missarum mysteriis* (1195), and the *De quadripartita specie nuptiarum* prior to his election. These works were important in gaining him the respect of his fellow cardinals. The author of the *Gesta,* possibly the canonist and later cardinal Petrus Beneventanus, singled out the *oposcula,* which he drafted and dictated at various times, as evidence that he surpassed his contemporaries both in philosophy and theology. Recent scholarship has suggested that Innocent's theological work is fundamental to the understanding of his pontificate.

Innocent's pontificate came at a critical moment in the history of the Western Church and of western European societies. Indeed, his personal name as well as his papal designation reminded his contemporaries of the internal conflicts of the 1120s and 1130s in the college of cardinals and the alliance of Pope Innocent II with the Emperor Lothar III. Politically, his reign was marked by consolidation at all levels from communes and counties to grand estates and kingdoms. The European economy was creating new forms of wealth from industry and trade. Europeans were also more conscious of the world beyond their own. The crusades had captured widespread attention with their aim of recovering the Holy Places in the East from Muslims. At the same time, higher education, literature, art, and religious life were all helping in the creation of a pan-European culture. Innocent himself was a product of this changing society. He was elected pope on Jan. 8, 1198, the same day that Celestine III died, and was ordained to the priesthood on Feb. 21, 1198. He was consecrated bishop and crowned as pope on the following day.

His pontificate reflects the manner in which this changing background helped to shape his policies. It may be conveniently divided into two periods, with the dividing point sometime around 1209 or 1210. In the first period, the influence of the schools seems to have been paramount. The pope not only presented his arguments in strong scholastic terms, as is evidenced in the decretal *Per venerabilem,* for example, but he embraced such reform groups as the HUMILIATI, the Order of the Holy Spirit, the TRINITARIANS, and finally, the followers of St. FRANCIS and St. DOMINIC. He canonized St. Homobonus, the humble tailor of Cremona, who had devoted himself to the poor and who, in his close ties to the clergy, represented a kind of counter image to Peter Waldo (Valdes), of Lyons, the founder of the Waldensians. To this period, also, belonged his bitterest disappointment: the failure of the Fourth Crusade. Although he had decreed a tax of a fortieth on all ecclesiastics to support the crusade, he had left its organization and direction in the hands of secular leaders like Boniface of Montferrat and the Venetian Doge. Its diversion, first against the Dalmatian city of Zara, claimed by the Venetians, and then against Constantinople, to restore the deposed Byzantine emperor, Isaac II and his son, Alexis IV, ran counter not merely to the principle that the crusades should not attack Christians, but also to the pope's goal that the Byzantine Emperor, Alexis III, brother of the deposed emperor, might be persuaded to participate in the crusade in a significant way.

To this period also belonged the disputed imperial election following the death of Henry VI in 1197. Ever since the eleventh century, the papacy had pursued a complex relationship with the German king-emperors. Although historians, as well as some contemporaries, have tended to personalize the grounds for disagreement in particular rulers, especially in the Hohenstaufen house in the twelfth and thirteenth centuries, in fact, the seeds of most of the disagreement reached back much further. They were based on such factors as imperial interests in Italy and the growing concern of the reform papacy in the second half of the eleventh century that the papacy would become merely an office of State. Increasingly, the popes wanted a territorial jurisdiction that would protect the Patrimony of St. Peter, on which the Roman Church largely depended for economic support. Innocent found himself at a point where the disputed imperial election provided an opportunity to get better terms from the new Emperor. Yet he was reluctant to interfere directly. He took the position that the pope, who crowned the emper-

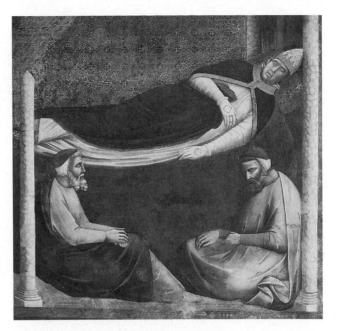

"The Dream of Pope Innocent III," detail from the fresco cycle on the Life of St. Francis of Assisi by Giotto, 1297–1299. (©Elio Ciol/CORBIS)

or, could judge the merits of the candidates. He vacillated between Philip of Swabia and Otto of Brunswick, only fully supporting the latter after Philip's assassination in a private quarrel in 1208.

At the same time, he pursued an aggressive policy of strengthening the papal position in central Italy. He appointed rectors throughout the area and often used members of his own family to create a network of local powers that would support the papacy. He especially worked to strengthen his position in Rome, which had long been a thorn in the side of papal policy. When the Emperor Otto began to push an aggressive imperial agenda in central Italy and the Kingdom of Sicily, Innocent, who was the guardian of Frederick, the son of Henry VI and Constance, opposed him. By 1212, he had joined Philip II Augustus of France in supporting the young Frederick for the German kingship and the imperial throne.

This early period was also marked by the manner in which Innocent attempted to define his views in his important decretals. Many of these found a place in *Compilatio tertia,* which was compiled by Petrus Beneventanus, a member of his curial family, and approved by the pope for use by the law professors in Bologna. It was the first time that a pope took a direct role in the compilation of canon law, and his example would be followed by his successors, Honorius III and Gregory IX. The latter promulgated the *Liber extra* which was compiled by Raymond of Peñafort in 1234, and which became the foundation of Canon Law in the Latin Church along with the *Decretum* of Gratian. Innocent's decretals (judicial decisions) reveal that he was decisive, but cautious. In ecclesiastical matters, he promoted the interests of the papacy over the that of the local church, using the famous Leonine term *plenitudo potestatis* (fullness of power) with reference to the papal role in the church, while the local bishops had merely a *partem sollicitudinis* (a sharing in the care of churches).

In secular affairs, Innocent's views were much more complex, depending on the particular circumstances with which he was dealing. Thus, in *Per venerabilem* (1202), Innocent refused to legitimate the sons of Count William of Montpellier so that they could enter the ranks of the clergy, but he defended the power of the pope to legitimize in the secular field. He argued that he would not use this power where there was a superior secular power with that same authority. He was, however, claiming a superior jurisdiction for the papacy. That Innocent was essentially asserting the position of Pope Gelasius I, though in rather extravagant language, is shown by the argument he advanced in *Novit ille* (1204). It was addressed to the French bishops and defended the right of the pope to act in a secular dispute where sin was involved (*ratione peccati*). It clearly followed the Gelasian principle that bishops are superior to secular rulers because they are responsible to God for the souls of kings. In *Venerabilem* (1202) and *Solitae* (late 1200 or early 1201), it is impossible to separate secular from ecclesiastic concerns.

There is no doubt, however, that these decretals helped to create an image of the papacy moving strongly into the secular sphere. But historians have become increasingly reluctant to view Innocent III as ambitious to wield temporal power. Indeed, there is a kind of ambivalence that separates Innocent from some of his successors, notably Innocent IV. Recent scholarship has put much more emphasis on the pastoral and theological aspects of Innocent's pontificate. Indeed, theological imagery is central in his writings, not merely in the *opuscula* and sermons but in his letters as well. In dealing with heresy, the decretal *Vergentis* (1200), promulgated against heretics in Viterbo at the beginning of his pontificate, taken by itself, creates a somewhat false impression of the manner in which Innocent dealt with heresy. His approach was more pastoral than juridical. Taken together, the efforts of these years provided a foundational experience for the efforts of the pope during the second part of his pontificate.

Two endeavors denote the character of this second period. They are summarized by Innocent himself under the terms reform and crusade. The first culminated in the Fourth LATERAN COUNCIL, and the second in the planning and preparations for the Fifth CRUSADE. But much re-

mained unresolved from the previous period, and both France and England occupied a great deal of his time, In England he was involved in the conflict over the election of the archbishop of Canterbury. In France he refused to allow Philip II Augustus to reject Ingeborg of Denmark as his wife and queen and to marry Agnes of Meran, whose father had supported Philip of Swabia. Ultimately, the resolution of conflicts between France and England also threatened his plan for the crusade. Yet, the assassination in 1208 of the papal legate, Peter of Castelnau, who was directing missionary efforts against the Cathars in the Midi, triggered his summons of military support against them, the Albigensian Crusade.

The Fourth Lateran Council was the greatest achievement of Innocent's pontificate. It brought together more than 400 bishops as well as some representatives from the East and as many more abbots from the West. The agenda, based at least in part on responses from local churches, attempted a major overhaul of numerous aspects of religious practice, from annual confession to preaching. The doctrinal decrees condemned the views of Aimery of Bene and David of Dinant, as well as the position of Joachim of Fiore on the Trinity. It also accepted the term *transubstantiation* to describe the change that occurred in the consecration of bread and wine in the mass. It prohibited the proliferation of new religious rules and forbade the clergy's participation in the judicial ordeal. In *Ad liberandam*, appended to the seventy constitutions approved by the council and pope, the council wrote a detailed plan for the newly summoned crusade, responding to many of the criticisms and failings aimed at previous crusades. Among the most controversial of the decrees was that requiring a distinctive mode of dress by Jews and Saracens and restricting their external activities during the Christian observances of Lent and Easter. As Robert Chazan has observed, these measures resulted in an intensification of traditional anxiety among the Jews. The decrees of the Fourth Lateran Council were not merely the product of Innocent III's will, nor were the decisions of the council that touched secular affairs always in line with his desires. The French bishops, who probably played the most active role in the council, opposed the pope's position regarding a settlement in the Midi. Innocent favored the rights of the count of Toulouse against Simon de Montfort, the leader of the Albigensian Crusade. In fact, recent scholarship has shown that Innocent compromised on other issues, such as the prohibition of new religious rules, most probably to secure support for his plan for the crusade, especially the tax on the clergy. Rather than viewing the Fourth Lateran Council as the culmination of Innocent' pontificate, though it did in fact turn out that way, it would probably be more accurate to see it as his plan for the future of the church. It combined much of the new spirit of reform with practical measures to meet problems, but it also left many issues, such as the relationship between Christians and non-Christians, in a largely unsatisfactory state from the point of view of all parties.

What especially marked the pontificate of Innocent III was his willingness to deal with the most difficult issues. Though some of his decisions have struck many as too rigid, a careful reading of his letters reveals that even in his strongest decretals, he tempered firmness with a willingness to act as a good shepherd. Indeed, the author of the *Gesta* makes this point on numerous occasions but never more forcefully than in the case of the attempted self-promotion of the bishop of Würzburg. Innocent exercised both patience and mercy in his role as judge. If history has not attached the word "great" to Innocent, it may well be a result of the complexity of the problems that he faced and that he himself recognized it in his dealing with the world.

Bibliography: *Patrologia Latina* v. 214–217; *Die Register Papst Innocenz III* (Graz, 1965–). *De Miseria Condicionis Humanae* (Athens, Ga. 1978). *De quadripartita specie nuptiarum* in *Patrologia Latina*; *De missarum mysteriis* in *Patrologia Latina*; *Regestum super negotio Romani imperii*, ed. F. KEMPF (Miscellanea historiae pontificiae 12; Rome 1947). C. R. CHENEY and W. H. SEMPLE, eds., *Selected Letters of Pope Innocent III concerning England* (New York 1953). H. TILLMANN, *Pope Innocent III* (Amsterdam 1980; tr. from the German edition, Bonn 1954). D. WALEY, *The Papal State in the Thirteenth Century* (London 1961). J. M. POWELL, *Innocent III: Vicar of Christ or Lord of the World?* (Boston 1961; revised and enlarged edition, Washington, D.C. 1994). C. R. CHENEY, *Innocent III and England* (Stuttgart 1976). M. LAUFS, *Politik und Recht bei Innocenz III* (Cologne 1980). W. IMKAMP, *Das Kirchenbild Innocenz III* (Stuttgart 1983). K. PENNINGTON, *Pope and Bishops: The Papal Monarchy in the Twelfth and Thirteenth Centuries* (Philadelphia 1984). J. M. POWELL, *Anatomy of a Crusade* (Philadelphia 1986). R. FOREVILLE, *Innocent III et la France* (Stuttgart 1992). M. MACCCARONE, *Nuovi studi su Innocenzo III* ed. R. LAMBERTINI (Rome 1995). C. EGGER, "Papst Innocenz als Theologe. Beiträge zur Kenntnis seines Denkens im Rahmen der Frühscholastik," *Archium historiae pontificiae* 30:55–123. W. P. MÜLLER, *Huguccio: The Life, Works, and Thought of a Twelfth Century Jurist* (Washington, D. C. 1994). B. BOLTON, *Studies on Papal Authority and Pastoral Care* (Aldershot 1995). *Pope Innocent III and His World*, ed. J. C. MOORE (Aldershot 1999).

[J. M. POWELL]

INNOCENT III, ANTIPOPE

Pontificate: Sept. 29, 1179 to Jan. 1180. Known as Lando of Sezze (also Landus Sitinus), he was born into a Lombard family and became cardinal deacon of St. Angelo under antipope VICTOR IV (1159–64), the first of three imperial antipopes backed by FREDERICK I BARBAROSSA (1152–90) during the schism of 1159–78 (cf. Paschal III, 1164–68 and Callistus III, 1168–78). Lando was proclaimed antipope and took the name Innocent III some 13 months after Callistus had submitted to Pope Alexander III (1159–81). Since he was elected by only a few schismatic cardinals, and without the consent of the emperor, his reign is generally not considered so much a part of the schism as an anomalous episode following it.

Prominent among Innocent's supporters were relatives of Victor IV, including the latter's brother, a knight who provided protection for Innocent in a fortified castle near Palombara. Alexander sent Cardinal Hugo of the powerful and wealthy Pierleoni family to negotiate with the knight, who exchanged Innocent for a handsome fee. The antipope was seized and imprisoned in the Holy Trinity monastery at La Cava (near Salerno), a favored place in which to confine 12th-century antipopes (cf. Theodoric, 1100, and Gregory VII 1118–21). It is assumed that he remained there until his death, but no more is known of him.

Bibliography: L. DUCHESNE, ed. *Liber Pontificalis* (Paris 1886–92; repr. 1955–57) 2.450. P. JAFFÉ, *Regesta pontificum Romanorum* (Leipzig 1885–88; repr. Graz 1956) 2.431. F. X. SEPPELT, *Geschichte der Päpste von den Anfängen bis zur Mitte des zwanzigsten Jahrhunderts* (Munich 1954–59) 3.272, 608ff. J. N. D. KELLY, *The Oxford Dictionary of Popes* (New York, 1986) 180. C. MORRIS, *The Papal Monarchy: The Western Church from 1050–1250* (Oxford 1989). G. SCHWAIGER, *Lexikon des Mittelalters* (Munich 1991) 5.434. R. AUBERT, *Dictionnaire d'histoire et de géographie ecclésiastiques* (Paris 1995) 25.1259.

[P. M. SAVAGE]

INNOCENT IV, POPE

Pontificate: June 25, 1243 to Dec. 7, 1254; b. Sinibaldo dei Fieschi in Genoa, *c.* 1200; d. Naples. He was born into one of the most powerful noble families in northwestern Italy. His father Hugh, Count of Lavagna, was the first to carry the name Fieschi, which was bestowed on him because he held the imperial office that controlled the fiscal affairs of the emperor. Pope Adrian V was Sinibaldo's nephew and had exercised much influence in the Roman curia before he became pope (Cardinal Ottobono Fieschi). Innocent studied law at Parma where Obizo, his uncle, was bishop. Obizo made his nephew a canon in the cathedral chapter of Parma. By 1213 he was in Bologna where he continued his studies. He is called a master *(magister)* and a papal subdeacon in a letter of Pope Honorius III of 1223. The title would indicate that he had earned a degree in law. There is no evidence that Sinibaldo taught at Bologna, but a short teaching career cannot be completely excluded. His expansive commentary on the *Decretals of Gregory IX* (see below) might have begun as lectures in Bologna. He left the schools permanently in 1226 when he became an auditor of the

Tomb of Pope Innocent IV, by Tommaso Malvito. (©Archivo Iconografico, S.A./CORBIS)

papal Curia. When Ugolino of Ostia was elected pope and took the name Gregory IX, the new pope recognized Sinibaldo's talents. He appointed him vice chancellor of the Roman church in 1227 and immediately elevated him to the cardinalate as cardinal priest of San Lorenzo in Lucina. In 1234 Gregory appointed him the governor of the March, a region of the Papal States. Since he continued to sign many papal letters with the other cardinals, he must have remained in Rome during most of his governorship.

The relationship between the pope and the Emperor FREDERICK II deteriorated dramatically during the time that Innocent worked in the Curia. From 1238 Frederick began to claim sovereignty over central Italy and Rome itself. Gregory called a general council to meet in Rome. Its purpose was to deal with the emperor and arrange a peace. Any chance of reconciliation between Gregory and the Frederick was dealt a severe blow when on May 3, 1241 Frederick captured a large number of prelates, including two cardinals, sailing from Genoa to Rome to participate in a council. Afterwards the emperor held them captive on the island of Giglio off the coast of Tuscany. When Gregory died in August 1241, the College of Cardinals elected a new pope immediately, but the ailing pope, Celestine IV, died after a pontificate of only 15

days. The political situation was perilous. Not only was Emperor Frederick excommunicated, but the two cardinals were still imperial prisoners, and the college of cardinals itself was deeply divided over how to deal with the emperor. A vacancy of almost 18 months ensued. Finally in June 1243 the cardinals elected Sinibaldo pope. He took the name Innocent IV.

Although Sinibaldo's decision to name himself after the most dominating pope of the thirteenth century (Innocent III) might have given Frederick pause, the emperor greeted Innocent's election with enthusiasm. He immediately began negotiations to conclude peace with the Roman church. A treaty was drafted in 1244 in which Frederick agreed to abandon the Papal States. Frederick and Innocent met in the Lateran Palace during Holy Week to confirm the agreement publicly. Innocent, however, did not trust the emperor and fled Italy to Lyon, a French city just within the borders of the empire. He never returned to Italy until after Frederick's death.

The First Ecumenical Council of Lyon 1245. When Innocent arrived in LYON he called for a general council. Lyon was subject to the Empire. Nonetheless, Innocent was secure there and could deal with Frederick without being threatened by his military power. He depended upon King Louis IX of France to protect him. The prelates of the northern European countries would have free entry into the city without the danger of imperial capture or detention. The council was convoked on June 26, 1245 and remained convened until July 17. One hundred and fifty prelates came from France, Italy, and Spain. The Latin emperor of Constantinople and other laymen were also in attendance. In his opening sermon Innocent announced an agenda that went far beyond his conflict with the emperor. He described the vices of the clergy in detail and spoke of the "insolence of the Muslims." The dangerous situation in the Eastern Mediterranean concerned him. He lamented the schism with the Greek Church in the East and the successes of the Greek schismatics who were intent on regaining control of Constantinople. He noted ferocity of the Tatars in Eastern Europe. Finally he expressed his grief that the emperor was a persecutor of the church.

The political situation in Eastern Europe and Asia had concerned Innocent for some time. He viewed the expansion of the Mongol empire and the invasion of Eastern Europe by the Tartars with interest and misgiving. In April 1245 the pope sent Giovanni Da Pian Del Carpini on an extraordinary mission. He was to travel into the Mongol empire and seek out the great khan. Carpini's long journey was the first papal attempt to contact distant non-Christian rulers and fit in well with Innocent's convictions. In his great legal commentary he had established that the pope had jurisdiction over non-Christians and could punish them for violating the law of nature. He also believed that if non-Christians did not permit Christian missionaries into their lands and permitted them to preach, the pope could call for a just war against them. Innocent established the intellectual framework for Christian missionary efforts for centuries to come.

When Innocent convened the Council, he also summoned Frederick II to stand trial, although he had excommunicated him once again just before the Council opened. The emperor did not attend but sent his legate Thaddeus of Suessa. The Council charged Frederick with a variety of crimes. Thaddeus put up an effective defense of his lord but could not prevent the Council from deposing the emperor. Innocent called upon the German princes to elect a new emperor and some of them responded by electing Henry Raspe, Landgrave of Thuringia. Unfortunately, Henry died on Feb. 17, 1247. The princes then selected William, the Count of Holland in his place. King LOUIS IX of France tried to mediate this scandalous spectacle, but Innocent responded by renewing Frederick's excommunication in April 1248. This unseemly and disastrous situation was resolved on Dec. 13, 1250 when Frederick died. Innocent was able to reassert papal authority in central Italy. Although he died before he could bestow the crown of the Kingdom of Sicily on a secular ruler who would not endanger the Papal States, his successors negotiated with many different candidates. Finally Pope URBAN IV (1261–1264) granted the crown to the brother of Louis IX of France, Charles of Anjou. The French ruled southern Italy until the fifteenth century. Never again did the empire seriously threaten the papacy and papal power in central Italy. The ultimate result was the political fragmentation of central and southern Europe that would last until the nineteenth century.

In spite of Innocent's announced agenda for reform, the Council of Lyon enacted no major legislation that dealt with the pastoral life of the church or the reform of the clergy. For the first time in the conciliar history of the medieval Christian church, political affairs completely overwhelmed spiritual concerns. The new canons did contain much that was important for the regulation of the church's judicial system. Innocent immediately published the 22 conciliar canons promulgated at Lyon on Aug. 25, 1245 and sent them to the schools in Bologna and Paris. He expanded this small collection of canons in 1246 and further in 1253 with other decretals. The last version of the collection was known as the Novels (*Novellae*). All these canons and decretals dealt with legal procedure and ecclesiastical administration.

Jurist Innocent was one of the most influential jurists of the Middle Ages. He wrote a massive commentary on the Decretals of Gregory IX, *Commentaria super libros quinque decretalium,* that was cited by every jurist from his immediate contemporaries to Hugo Grotius in the seventeenth century. He probably began writing his commentary long before he became pope and continued revising it up to the time of his death. He also wrote a commentary on the constitutions of the First Council of Lyon and on the additional decretals that were added to the constitutions in 1246 and 1253. The work was widely distributed in manuscripts and printed in a number of editions between 1477 and 1570.

Innocent emphasized papal authority and power in his commentary. His great predecessor, Pope Innocent III, had established the foundations of papal authority within the church and over secular affairs. Innocent IV expanded and refined Innocent III's legislation in significant ways. He claimed that the pope could choose between two imperial candidates, could depose the emperor (a power he exercised at Lyon), and could exercise imperial jurisdiction when the imperial throne was vacant. Although he granted non-Christian princes the right to hold legitimate political power, he tempered that right by asserting that they must permit Christian missionaries to preach in their realms (see above). In his commentary on the bull of deposition that he had promulgated at the Council of Lyon (*Ad apostolicae dignitatis apicem Liber sextus* 2.14.2), Innocent made remarkable claims for papal authority. The pope did not need the council to make the deposition of the emperor valid, because only the pope, not the council, has fullness of power. Innocent asserted that Christ had the power and authority to depose or condemn emperors by natural right (*ius naturale*). He concluded that the pope had the same authority since he held the office of the vicar of Christ, and it would be absurd if after the death of St. Peter human beings were left without the governance of one person (*regimen unius personae*). Few popes in the Middle Ages made a more powerful argument for the legitimacy and justness of papal monarchy.

Bibliography: Sources. INNOCENT IV, *Commentaria super libros quinque decretalium* (Frankfurt 1570; repr. Frankfurt 1968); *Les Registres d'Innocent IV,* ed. É BERGER, 4 v. (Paris 1884–1920). N. P. TANNER, S.J. ed. and trans., "First Council of Lyons—1245," *Decrees of the Ecumenical Councils* (Washington, D.C. 1990): 275–301 [English and Latin Text]. A selection of Innocent's letters can be found in *Monumenta Germaniae Historica,* Epistolae, saeculi XIII, ed. K. RODENBERG, v.2, 3 (Berlin 1826–). NICHOLAS DE CALVI [CARBIO or CURBIO], *Vita Innocentii,* L. A. MURATORI, *Rerum italicarum scriptores, 500–1500* (Milan 1723–51) 3.1:592–592. F. PAGNOTTI, ed., "Vita Innocentiii IV scripta a Fr. Nicolao de Carbio," *Archivio della Società romana di storia patria* 21:76–120. "Vita Innocentiii IV scripta a fr. Nicolao de Carbio," ed. A. MELLONI, *Innocenzo IV* (see below): 259–293. **Literature.** J. A. CANTINI and C. LEFEBVRE, *Dictionnaire de droit canonique,* ed. R. NAZ, 7 v. (Paris 1935–65) 7:1029–62. É. BERGER, *St. Louis et In-*

nocent IV (Paris 1893). M. PACAUT, "L'Autorité pontificale selon Innocent IV," *Moyen âge* 66:85–119. J. A. CANTINI, "De autonomia judicis saecularis et de Romani Pontificis plenitudine potestatis in temporalibus secundum Innocentium IV," *Salesianum* 23: 407–480. D. P. WALEY, *The Papal State in the Thirteenth Century* (New York 1961). J. A. WATT, *The Theory of Papal Monarchy in the Thirteenth Century: The Contribution of the Canonists* (London 1965). V. PIERGIOVANNI, "Sinibaldo Fieschi decretista," *Annali della Facoltà di Giurisprudenza dell'Università di Genova* 6: 415–442 and reprinted in *Studia Gratiana* 14 (1969) 125–154. B. Z. KEDAR, *Crusade and Mission: European Approaches toward the Muslims* (Princeton 1984). M. BERTRAM, "Angebliche Originale des Dekretalenapparats Innocenz IV.," *Proceedings of the Sixth International Congress of Medieval Canon Law, Berkeley* (Monumenta iuris canonici, Series C, 7) 41–47. E. VODOLA, *Dictionary of the Middle Ages* 6 (New York 1985): 465–467. .D. ABULAFIA, *Frederick II : A Medieval Emperor* (London 1988). A. MELLONI, *Innocenzo IV: La concezione e l'esperienza della cristianità come regimen unius personae* (Testi e ricerche di scienze religiose, 4). O. CAPITANI, "Problemi di giurisdizione nella ecclesiologia di Innocenzo IV nel conflitto con Federico II," *Friedrich II: Tagung des Deutschen Historischen Instituts in Rom im Gedenkjahr 1994*, eds. A. ESCH and N. KAMP (Tübingen 1996) 150–1162. M. BERTRAM, "Gregorio IX, Innocenzo IV e Federico II: Tre legislatori a confronto," *. . . colendo iustitiam et iura condendo . . . Federico III legislatore del Regno di Sicilia nell'Europa del Duecento: Per una storia comparata delle codificazione europee*, ed. A. Romano (Atti di convegni, 1; Rome 1997) 11–28. M. BERTRAM, "Zweivorläufige Textstufen des Dekretalenapparats Papst Innocenz IV," *Juristische Buchproduktion im Mittelalter*, ed. V. COLLI (Frankfurt am Main 2001).

[K. PENNINGTON]

INNOCENT V, POPE, BL.

Pontificate: Jan. 21 to June 22, 1276; b. Peter of Tarentaise, in Tarentaise (probably the one in Savoy or, less likely, the one near Lyons), *c.* 1224. Peter entered the DOMINICANS *c.* 1240, became master in theology at Paris in 1259, and taught there from 1259 to 1264, and from 1267 to 1269. He wrote a widely used commentary on the *SENTENCES,* scriptural commentaries, several treatises, questions, and sermons. In 1259 he helped prepare statutes organizing Dominican studies. Twice provincial of France (1264–67, 1269–72), he became archbishop of Lyons in 1272 and cardinal bishop of Ostia in 1273. Prominent at the Second Council of LYONS (1274), where he also furthered union with the Greeks (*see* EASTERN SCHISM), he became a leading candidate for the papacy, but as pope his favoring Charles of Anjou made relations with Emperor MICHAEL VIII PALAEOLOGUS of Byzantium difficult; it also hindered reorganization of the Crusades and added to tensions with Rudolph I of Hapsburg. Innocent had some political success in pacifying northern Italian cities and in aiding peace between Charles and Genoa. In 1898 Leo XIII approved the veneration long paid this devoted master and administrator. He was beatified on Mar. 13, 1898.

Feast: June 22.

Bibliography: H. K. MANN, *The Lives of the Popes in the Early Middle Ages from 590 to 1304* (London 1902–32) 16:1–22. *Beatus Innocentus PP. V (Petrus de Tarantasia O.P.): Studia et documenta* (Rome 1943), writings studied by H. D. SIMONIN, 163–335. M. H. LAURENT, *Le Bx. Innocent V (Pierre de Tarentaise) et son temps* (*Studi e Testi* 129; 1947), writings studied by L. B. GILLON, 361–390. F. X. SEPPELT, *Geschichte der Päpste von den Anfängen bis zur Mitte des 20. Jh.* (Munich 1956) 3:535–537, 620. P. A. AMARGIER, *Catholicisme* 5:166:1–64. R. C. DALE, ed., *Medieval Latin Texts on the Eternity of the World* (Leiden 1991). A. FRANCHI, "Innocenzo V et la 'questione dei mendicanti,' *L'Osservatore Romano* (Vatican City 1976) 6. A.P. FRUTAZ, "Maestro di teologia difeso da s. Tommaso, arcivescovo, cardinale, papa: Innocenzo V" *L'Osservatore Romano* (Vatican City 1976) 6. J. GARDENER, "The Tomb of Cardinal Annibaldi by Arnolfo di Cambio," *Burlington Magazine* (London 1972), 136–141. H. RIGUET, *Printemps en Chré, l'aventure spirituelle de Saint-Pierre de Tarentaise* (Tamié 1967). L. VONES, *Lexikon für Theologie und Kirche* 5 (3d ed. Freiburg 1996). J. N. D. KELLY, *Oxford Dictionary of Popes* (New York 1986) 198.

[W. H. PRINCIPE]

INNOCENT VI, POPE

Pontificate: Dec. 18, 1352 to Sept. 12, 1362; b. Stephen Aubert, date uncertain; d. Avignon. A professor of civil law at Toulouse, he became bishop of Noyons in 1338, of Clermont in 1340, and was made cardinal in 1342. In the conclave in Avignon the cardinals agreed that whoever was elected should divide the papal authority and revenues with the College of Cardinals. In 1353 Innocent declared the preelection CAPITULATIONS invalid. He corrected numerous abuses in the Papal Curia, condemned plurality of benefices, and ordered all prelates who had no business at Avignon to return to their benefices. He was unable to restrain the cruelties of Pedro I of Castile or to restore peace between Aragon and Castile; but in 1360 he effected the Peace of Brétigny between England and France. When Charles IV published his Golden Bull, Innocent did not protest against its disregard of papal rights. Using the military skill of Cardinal Gil ALBORNOS, he defeated the usurpers who had seized the STATES OF THE CHURCH. A Greek proposal for reunion of the Churches ended when it became clear that Innocent could not raise an army to fight the Turks. Though tainted with NEPOTISM and enfeebled by old age, Innocent was otherwise a good pope. The religious decline throughout Europe was not his fault; it had begun a century earlier and was aggravated by the Hundred Years' War and the Black Death. Despite his rigid economies, the war to regain the Papal States bankrupted him. In desperation, he increased the taxation of various countries, thereby provoking greater hostility against the papacy. Death thwarted his plan to return to Rome;

he was buried in the Charterhouse of Villeneuve—les–Avignon, built by him.

Bibliography: INNOCENT VI, *Lettres,* ed. E. DÉPREZ (Paris 1909). *Liber pontificalis,* ed. L. DUCHESNE (Paris 1886–92) 2:492–493. É. BALUZE, and *Vitae paparum Avenionensium,* ed. G. MOLLAT, 4 v. (Paris 1914–27) 1:309–348; 2:433–491. L. PASTOR, *The History of the Popes from the Close of the Middle Ages* (London-St. Louis 1938–61) 1:93–95, 283. G. MOLLAT, *The Popes at Avignon,* tr. J. LOVE (New York 1963) 44–51, 119–142, 152–154; *Dictionnaire de théologie catholique,* ed. A. VACANT et al. (Paris 1903–50) 7: 1997–2001; G. SCHWAIGER, *Lexikon für Theologie und Kirche,* ed. J. HOFER and K. RAHNER (Freiburg 1957–65) 5:690–691. M. J. HAREN, "Bishop Gynwell of Lincoln, Two Avignonese Statues and Archbishop FrizRalph of Armagh's Suit at the Roman Curia Against the Friars," *Archivum Historiae Pontificiae* (Rome 1993) 275–92. H. HOLD, "Leben in einer Welt der Ansehens: Das spämittelalterliche Pontifikalien–Rect der Klosterneuburger Pröpste," *Jahrbuch des Stiftes Klostenburg* (1997) 57–65. M. JONES, *Recueil des Actes de Charles de Blois et Jeanne de Penthièvre, duc et duchese de Bretagne (1341–1364), suivi des Actes de Jeanne de Penthièvre (1364–1384)* (Rennes 1996). F. KERN, "Karls IV. 'Kaiserlager' von Rom," in *Historische Aufsätze Karl Zeumer zum sechzigsten Geburtstag al Festgabe dargebracht von Freuden und Schüer* (Frankfurt 1987) 385–95. F. LOPES, *Chronique du roi D. Pedro I.* (Paris 1985). A. MATTONE and R. MAZEIKA, "Some Remarks upon Acta Innocentii PP.VI," *Archivum Historicum Societatis Iesu* (1985) 367–72. J. N. D. KELLY, *Oxford Dictionary of Popes* (New York 1986) 221.

[W. R. BONNIWELL]

"Pope Innocent V," 13th-century sculpture located in the Basilica of St. John Lateran, Rome. (Alinari-Art Reference/Art Resource, NY)

INNOCENT VII, POPE

Ponitficate: Oct. 17, 1404 to Nov. 6, 1406; b. Cosimo de' Migliorati, Sulmona, ltaly, *c.* 1336; d. Rome. After juridical studies at Bologna under Giovanni di Lignano he was professor of law at Perugia and Padua. He was sent by URBAN VI to England where he acted as papal collector for ten years. In 1387 he was made archbishop of Ravenna, was transferred to Bologna in 1389, and in the same year was created cardinal; in 1390 he was appointed legate for northern Italy. Upon his election as pope he was confronted with a Church rent by the WESTERN SCHISM. With the other cardinals in conclave he had made a pre-election promise to resign, if necessary, to restore unity to the Church (*see* CAPITULATIONS). In trying to keep his promise he made overtures to Benedict XIII and summoned a council. However, the obstinacy of Benedict, the rebellion of the Romans against his nephew Ludovico, and the pope's subsequent flight, the invasion of the Papal States by King Ladislaus of Naples, and above all, the shortness of Innocent's reign frustrated all his efforts. Upon his return to Rome (March 1406), he planned the reorganization of the University of Rome but was interrupted by death.

Bibliography: *Liber pontificalis,* ed. L. DUCHESNE 2:508–510, 531–533, 552–554. L. A. MURATORI, *Rerum italicarum scriptores,* 500–1500 3.2:832–835. H. DENIFLE, *Die Universitäten des Mittelalters bis 1400* (Berlin 1885). L. PASTOR, *The History of the Popes from the Close of the Middle Ages* (London-St. Louis 1938–61) 1:165–166, 169–171. E. VANSTEENBERGHE, *Dictionnaire de théologie catholique,* ed. A. VACANT et al. (Paris 1903–50) 14.1:1468–92. F. X. SEPPELT, *Geschichte der Päpste von den Anfängen bis zur Mitte des 20. Jh.* (Munich 1957) 4:480–484. J. GROHE, *Lexikon für Theologie und Kirche* (3d ed. Freiburg 1996). H. HEIMPEL, *Studien zur Kirchen—und Reichsreform des 15. Jahrhunderts. II.: Zu zwei Kirchenreform—Trakaten des beginnenden 15. Jahrhunderts* (Heidleberg 1974). M. MAILLARD-LUYPAERT, *Lettres d'Innocent VII (1404–1406).* (Brussels-Rome 1987). J. N. D. KELLY, *Oxford Dictionary of Popes* (New York 1986) 234.

[W. R. BONNIWELL]

INNOCENT VIII, POPE

Pontificate: Aug. 29, 1484 to July 25, 1492; b. Giovanni Battista Cibo, Genoa, 1432; d. Rome. After a profligate youth at the Neapolitan court, where he fathered

Pope Innocent VIII. (©Bettmann/CORBIS)

Bajazet II (d. 1512), who in 1492 presented him with the HOLY LANCE.

In 1486 Innocent censured the theses of PICO DELLA MIRANDOLA; tried repeatedly but ineffectually to improve ecclesiastical morals; condemned WITCHCRAFT which was spreading in Germany (*Summis desiderantes,* 1484); and punished with death two ecclesiastics who had forged and sold papal documents—one of which permitted Norwegian priests to say Mass without using wine. Innocent's vacillations and incompetence nullified his efforts at reform. When dying, he implored the cardinals to elect as successor a pope better than himself—a plea that proved as futile as his reign.

Bibliography: L. PASTOR, *The History of the Popes from the Close of the Middle Ages* (London-St. Louis 1938–61) 5:229–357; 375–378. E. ARMSTRONG and L. THORNDIKE, *Cambridge Medieval History* (London-New York 1911–36) 8:197–200, 685–686. F. A. GREGOROVIUS, *Geschichte der Stadt Rom,* ed. W. KAMPF, 3 v. (Tübingen 1953–57). P. PASCHINI, *Roma nel Rinascimento* (Bologna 1940). F. X. SEPPELT, *Geschichte der Päpste von den Anfängen bis zur Mitte des 20. Jh.* (Munich 1957) 4:369–376. F. MERZBACHER, *Lexikon für Theologie und Kirche,* ed. J. HOFER and K. RAHNER (Freiburg 1957–65) 5:692. O. BALDACCI, *Roma e Cristoforo Colombo* (Firenze 1992). C. COLOMBO, *Relazioni e lettere sul secondo, terzo e quarto viaggio* (Roma 1992). C. S. L. DAVIES, ''Bishop John Morton, the Holy See, and the Accession of Henry VII,'' *The English Historical Review* (1987) 2–30. R. MARINO, ''Cristoforo Colombo e Innocenzo VIII,'' in *Actas del Simposio Internacional. La evangelizatiòn del Nuevo Mundo* (Roma 1992) 299–307. G. RACHET, *Catherine Sforza. La dame de Forli* (Paris 1987). E. SORDINI, ''Barnadino da Feltre a Trevi per la riforma socio-religiosa dei costumi (1487),'' *Bollettino Storico di Foligno* 10 (Foligno 1986) 167–90. J. N. D. KELLY, *Oxford Dictionary of Popes* (New York 1986) 251.

[W. R. BONNIWELL]

three illegitimate children, he reformed and entered the priesthood. He studied at Rome and Padua. His affability won him many friends and led to his becoming bishop of Savona (1467); in 1472 he was transferred to Molfetta. Through the influence of Cardinal Giuliano Della Rovere (JULIUS II), whom he ardently admired, he was made cardinal in 1473. When SIXTUS IV died, Della Rovere, aware that he himself would not be elected, chose his weak-willed admirer as a candidate and by shameless bribery effected Cibo's election. The moral and political disorders of the time called for a pontiff of character and ability; Innocent possessed neither. A tool of Della Rovere, he was constantly embroiled in disputes and wars with various Italian states, especially Naples. The wars plunged the papacy into debt; to raise money, Innocent created numerous new posts, which he sold to the highest bidders. Hoping to check threatened Turkish attacks, he assembled Christian princes to discuss a crusade; nothing came of the meeting (1490). However, after the fall of Granada he secured some concessions from the Sultan

INNOCENT IX, POPE

Pontificate: Oct. 29 to Dec. 30, 1591; b. Giovanni Antonio Fachinetti, Bologna, Italy, July 20, 1519. His Veronese family had transferred to Bologna. There he studied law, and after receiving his doctorate at 25 went to Rome in the service of Cardinal Alessandro FARNESE. He represented Farnese at Avignon for four years, and later served as governor of Parma. PAUL IV made him refendary of the Segnatura di Grazia e Giustizia. In 1560 Pius IV made him bishop of Nicastro, and as bishop he took an active part in the Council of Trent in 1562. PIUS V made him nuncio to Venice in 1566, and he continued to hold that post under Gregory XIII until 1575. At Venice he was instrumental in the formation of the league against the Turks, which he led to the naval victory at Lepanto (1571). For health reasons, he resigned his diocese in 1575 and was named patriarch of Jerusalem by Gregory XIII, Nov. 12, 1576. He was employed by Gregory in the Consulta, Inquisition, and the Segnatura and on Dec. 12, 1583, was named by the same pope, Cardinal of the Four Crowned Martyrs. During the reign of the infirm Gregory XIV much of the burden of government fell upon him. Upon the death of Gregory XIV he was elected as a stop-gap pope, a choice that was expected because he had been a popular candidate at the previous conclave and because of his favor with the Spanish party, which procured his election. Realizing his indebtedness to PHILIP II, he supported Spain against Henry IV of France.

Innocent was active in repressing bandits in the vicinity of Rome, in improving the morals of the city, in regulating the course of the Tiber and the sanitation of the Borgo, in restoring the port of Ancona, and in completing the dome of St. Peter's. He gave his attention to the reform of the clergy and the manner of papal elections. On Nov. 4, 1591, he confirmed the bull of Pius V forbidding the sale of ecclesiastical property, imposing severe penalties for violations. One of his most important works was the distribution of responsibility within the Secretariate of State, dividing the work into three sections: one for France and Poland, one for Italy and Spain, and one for Germany. He established the German Congregation, and intended to revive the economic system of Sixtus V, being concerned with an orderly administration of finance. He appointed his great-nephew, Antonio Fachinetti to the Sacred College, in accordance with custom, and shortly afterward (Dec. 18, 1591) he fell ill but nevertheless made the pilgrimage to the Seven Churches, which gave him a cold and made him take to bed. On Dec. 29, 1591, he made his nephew Cesare Fachinetti general of the Church and commander in chief of the fleet. He died the next day after receiving the Last Sacraments. Considered an authority on Plato and Aristotle, and he wrote a work on the ''Politics,'' and a treatise on ethics, and one against Macchiavelli, none of which have been published. He was justly esteemed for his piety and knowledge of public affairs. The Romans venerated him as a saint.

Bibliography: A. CICCARELLI, ''Vita Innocentii IX,'' in B. Sacchi de Platina, *Historia . . . de vitis Pontificum Romanorum* (Cologne 1626). P. PECCHIAI, *Roma nel Cinquecento* (Bologna 1948). L. PASTOR, *The History of the Popes from the Close of the Middle Ages* (London–St. Louis 1938–61) 22:409–427 and *passim.* G. SCHWAIGER, *Lexikon für Theologie und Kirche,* ed. J. HOFER and K. RAHNER, 10 v. (2d, new ed. Freiburg 1957–65) 5:692, bibliog. M.R. O'CONNELL, *The Counter Reformation, 1559–1610* (New York 1974). J. DULUMEAU, *Catholicism between Luther and Voltaire* (London 1977).

[R. L. FOLEY]

Pope Innocent X. (Archive Photos)

INNOCENT X, POPE

Pontificate: Sept. 15, 1644, to Jan. 1, 1655; b. Giovanni Battista Pamfili, Rome, March 7, 1572; d. Rome. His family, originally from Gubbio, had been settled in Rome from the fifteenth century. His uncle, Girolamo, helped him with his education, and he earned a doctorate in both civil and Canon Law at the University of Rome. In 1597 he was ordained. Entering the papal service, he became a consistorial advocate (1601); and on the elevation of his uncle to the cardinalate, he succeeded him as auditor of the rota. For 25 years Pamfili efficiently carried out his work at this court. He was made nuncio to Naples and then sent to France and Spain as assistant to Urban VIII's nephew, Francesco. Urban then made Pamfili nuncio to Spain and titular patriarch of Antioch.

Although of 72 when elected, Innocent was in good health. He needed all his vigor because his pontificate was troubled by several crises. The dreary Thirty Years' War finally dragged to a conclusion in 1648, but the peace of Westphalia was far from pleasing to the Pope. Through his nuncio, Fabio Chigi (later ALEXANDER VII), Innocent protested against the injustices done to Catholics.

During the 1640s Ireland was engaged in a struggle for basic rights and Innocent sent help to the embattled

Gaels. His nuncio, Battista Rinuccini, was a clearsighted statesman who did his best to unravel the tangled situation in Ireland and unite the Catholics against the common foe. That he ultimately failed was the fault of neither Pope nor nuncio.

Nearer home Innocent maintained a cautious attitude on the troubles caused by Massaniello's rebellion in Naples. He also showed prudence in the vexing problem of Portuguese independence. Innocent was generous to the Venetians, who were engaged in a desperate struggle to defend Crete from the Ottoman Turks.

Innocent had to face not only external enemies of Catholicism, like the English, the Swedes and the Turks, but also the recalcitrant Jansenists, who were even more vexing. In 1642 Urban VIII had condemned *AUGUSTINUS,* the masterpiece of Cornelius Otto JANSEN, but the Jansenists ignored the condemnation and continued to make headway, especially in France. Cornet, a syndic of the University of Paris, extracted five propositions from the *Augustinus* and a number of French bishops sent them to Rome for condenmation. Since other French bishops pleaded against a condemnation, Innocent did not act hastily. He turned the matter over to a congregation of cardinals and gave this congregation a group of experts. This group included most of the best theologians available and represented quite diverse schools of theology and different religious orders. There was ample time and opportunity for study and for dialogue before this matter was settled. Indeed the Pope took a great deal of interest in the work of the congregation and urged it on. It is to Innocent's credit that at last, after two years, the congregation finished its work. The Pope then condemned the five propositions on June 9, 1653.

Innocent handled a dispute between Juan Palafox y Mendoza, Bishop of la Puebla de los Angeles in Mexico, and the Jesuits with his customary prudence. He suppressed a number of monasteries and religious communities in Italy that had so declined in numbers as to be unable to continue the work for which they had been founded. At the same time he strongly supported the missions in non-Christian countries and bolstered the Congregation of Propaganda. He proclaimed the jubilee of 1650 and had the satisfaction of seeing it to a successful conclusion.

Innocent was a man of piety, prudence, and moderation. But he was overly fond of his relatives. He raised two of his nephews to the purple and showered favors on other relatives. Of all his family members, the most dominant was a woman, Donna Olimpia, the wife of the Pope's deceased older brother, Pamfilio. Olimpia had great influence with the aged Pontiff. Aspirants for papal favors were quick to recognize this; and Olimpia, who

was as greedy as she was powerful, exploited her position. Although she fell into eclipse in 1650, two years later she was back in favor and she continued to exercise undue influence over Innocent until his death. Innocent's nepotism did not interfere with his charity. He was good to his people and helped them, especially during the bad years (1646–47) when flood and famine afflicted the Papal States. He can be considered a pioneer in a movement toward a better prison system. He reorganized the prisons of the Papal States and for the first time installed the cell system. After his death Innocent's body was treated shabbily. Olimpia refused to pay for solemn obsequies, and the body was kept a few days in the sacristy of St. Peter's and then buried quite simply.

Bibliography: L. PASTOR, *The History of the Popes from the Close of the Middle Ages,* (London–St. Louis 1938–61) v. 30. N. J. ABERCROMBIE, *The Origins of Jansenism* (Oxford 1936). I. CIAMPI, *Innocenzo X Pamfili e la sua corte* (Rome 1878). H. COVILLE, *Étude sur Mazarin et ses démêlés avec le pape Innocent X, 1644–1648* (Paris 1914). J. ORCIBAL, *Les Origines du jansénisme,* 5 v. (Louvain 1947–62). B. SUTTER, *Lexikon für Theologie und Kirche,* ed. J. HOFER and K. RAHNER, 10 v. (2d, new ed. Freiburg 1957–65) 5:692–693. J. PAQUIER, *Dictionnaire de théologie catholique,* ed. A. VACANT et al., 15 v. (Paris 1903–50; Tables générales 1951–) 7.2:2005–06. F. MASTROIANNI, *Inchiesta di Innocenzo X sui conventi cappuccini italiani* (Rome 1985). M. CALVESI, et al. *Innocenzo X. Arte e potere a Roma nell'eta barocca* (Rome 1990).

[J. S. BRUSHER]

INNOCENT XI, POPE, BL.

Pontificate: Sept. 21, 1676, to Aug. 12, 1689; b. Benedetto Odescalchi, Como, May 19, 1611. The scion of an ancient Lombard family with a reputation for piety, he received his early education at the Jesuit college in Como. At 15 he became an apprentice in the family bank in Genoa. He attended first the University of Rome followed by the University of Naples, where he obtained a doctorate in civil and Canon Law in 1639. Less than a year later, on the advice of Cardinal de la Cueva, he received the tonsure with the intention of fulfilling his inclination to prayer, study, and works of charity. He was appointed apostolic prothonotary by Pope Urban VIII and sent as financial commissary to the province of the Marches. During the conclave following the death of Pope Urban, he acted as governor of Macerata. He was named cardinal in 1645 by Innocent X, but not at the recommendation of Donna Olimpia Maidalchini as has been alleged. In 1648 he was cardinal legate to Ferrara, where his great charity won him the title "Father of the Poor." Two years later he was ordained to the priesthood (1650) and consecrated bishop of Novara in 1651. In 1656 he resigned his see and returned to Rome to work in the Curia. Although he was favored in the conclave of 1670, the influence of Louis XIV delayed his election until the next conclave in 1676. He assumed the name Innocent in memory of Innocent X, who had made him a cardinal.

Before accepting the tiara, Innocent requested the cardinals to approve the "Summary Agreement" consisting of 12 articles of ecclesiastical reform. This formed his program of action to achieve three objectives: the completion of the work of the Council of TRENT, the defense of the freedom and rights of the Church, and the assurance of the safety of Christian Europe against the Muslim Turks. From 1683 to 1689 he inspired a long and eventually successful campaign against the Turks.

In defense of ecclesiastical liberty Innocent's greatest and constant struggle was against the absolutist pretensions of Louis XIV of France. The king was encouraged by professors of the Sorbonne and personal advisers to claim the right to the revenues of vacant benefices and the control of appointment to future offices in Languedoc, Provence, Dauphiné, and Guyenne. Because a decision of the Council of Lyons (1274) and a concordat between the pope and the French king restricted such extension of the *régale* (royal right to revenues of vacant sees), Innocent resisted. Louis called an ASSEMBLY OF THE FRENCH CLERGY, which adopted the celebrated four Gallican articles on March 19, 1682 (*see* GALLICANISM). In a rescript (April 11, 1682) Innocent denounced these articles and refused papal approval to all episcopal candidates who had participated in the assembly. In 1685, as a move of conciliation, Louis revoked the Edict of NANTES, but the inhuman persecution of Protestants that followed brought expressions of disapproval from the Pope and a continued firm stand on the *régale*. Further conflict came from the papal decree of May 7, 1685, denying the widely abused "privilege of diplomatic residence," which offered haven to criminals in Rome as long as they remained within the neighborhood of the French embassy. Innocent refused to receive the new French ambassador, the Marquis de Lavardin, who insisted on this right and with a small military force took possession of his palace. Innocent in turn placed the French church of St. Louis in Rome under interdict on Dec. 24, 1687. Relations were again strained the next year when Innocent appointed Joseph Clement to the archiepiscopal and electoral see of Cologne over Cardinal Wilhelm FÜRSTENBERG, the candidate of Louis. In retaliation, the king seized the papal territory of Avignon, imprisoned the papal nuncio, and threatened a general council.

Innocent worked tirelessly to unite the Christian princes, both Catholic and Protestant, against the growing threat of Turkish invasion. The victory of the forces of Emperor Leopold, King JOHN III SOBIESKI OF POLAND, and Duke Charles of Lorraine on Sept. 11, 1683, which destroyed Turkish hopes at the gates of Vienna, was attributed, even at the time, to the prayers and great financial help of the pope.

During his pontificate Innocent issued decrees on frequent Communion (Feb. 12, 1679), confession (Nov. 18, 1682), and aspects of morality (March 4, 1679; June 26, 1680; and Aug. 28, 1687). In these later decrees he condemned LAXISM in moral theology and defended the PROBABILIORISM of Thyrsus Gonzalez, SJ, thus giving rise to a controversy whether the pope was condemning PROBABILISM. He also condemned the extension of human slavery (March 20, 1686) and the doctrines of Miguel de MOLINOS (Nov. 20, 1687). (*See* QUIETISM).

Immediately following Innocent's 13-year pontificate steps were taken toward his beatification, but the process was suspended by Benedict XIV in 1744 through pressure from the French court. The cause was again encouraged in 1889 and 1895 by Leo XIII, in 1934 by Pius XI, and effectively in 1942 by Pius XII, who beatified Innocent XI in October 1956.

Feast: Aug. 13.

Bibliography: J. J. BERTHIER, ed. *Innocentii PP. XI epistolae ad principes,* 2 v. (Rome 1891–95). F. DE BOJANI, *Innocent XI: sa correspondance avec ses nonces, 1676–84,* 3 v. (Rome 1910–12). *Bullarium Romanum* (Magnum), ed. H. MAINARDI and C. COCQUELINES, 18 folio v. (Rome 1733–62) v.19. L. PASTOR, *The History of the Popes from the Close of the Middle Ages* (London–St. Louis 1938–61) 32:1–524. F. X. SEPPELT, *Geschichte der Päpste von den Anfängen bis zur Mitte des 20 Jh.,* (Leipzig 1931–41) 5.2:346–371, 534–537. C. MICCINELLI, *Il grande Pontefice Innocenzo XI* (Rome 1956). G. PAPASOGLI, *Il beato Innocenzo XI* (2d ed. Como 1957); last two works contain fine bibliographies. W. DE VRIES, "Der selige Papst Innozenz XI und die Christen des Nahen Ostens," *Orientalia Christiana periodica* 23 (Rome 1957) 33–57. D. W. R. BAHLMANN, *The Moral Revolution of 1688* (New Haven 1957). J. PAQUIER, *Dictionnaire de théologie catholique,* ed. A. VACANT et al., 15 v. (Paris 1903–50; Tables générales 1951–) 7.2: 2006–13. J. ORCIBAL, *Louis XIV contre Innocent XI* (Paris 1949). L. O'BRIEN, *Innocent XI and the Revocation of the Edict of Nantes* (Berkeley 1930). S. MONTI, *Bibliografia di Papa Innocenzo XI . . . fino al 1927,* ed. M. ZECCHINELLI (Como 1957). G. SCHWAIGER, *Lexikon für Theologie und Kirche,* ed. J. HOFER and K. RAHNER, 10 v. (2d, new ed. Freiburg 1957–65) 5:693–695. E. DE SYRMIA, *At the Head of Nations* (New York 1978). R. J. MARAS, *Innocent XI: Pope of Christian Unity* (Notre Dame 1984). I. MARZOLA, *Pastorale liturgica di b. Innocenzo XI,* (Rovigo 1973). P. GINI, ed., *Epistolario Innoceniano* (Como 1977).

[S. V. RAMGE]

INNOCENT XII, POPE

Pontificate: July 12, 1691, to Sept. 27, 1700; b. Antonio Pignatelli, near Spinazzola (Puglia), Italy, March 13, 1615. This Neapolitan noble studied at the Collegio Romano, entered the Roman Curia under Urban VIII, and

Monument of Pope Innocent XII, with Innocent XII seated between Charity and Faith, by the 18th-century Florentine sculptor Filippo Valle, in the basilica of St. Peter, Vatican City. (Alinari-Art Reference/Art Resource, NY)

was appointed vice-legate of Urbino. Innocent X nominated him Inquisitor to Malta (1646–49). He served as governor of Viterbo, nuncio to Tuscany (1652), to Poland (1660), and to Vienna (1668). He fell into disfavor with Clement X, who removed him from Rome by giving him the bishopric of Lecce. He was recalled to Rome (1673) and named secretary of the Congregation of Bishops and Regulars, and then maestro di camera. Pope Innocent XI created him a cardinal (September 1, 1681), bishop of Faenza, legate of Bologna, and archbishop of Naples (1687). He was elected to the papacy as a compromise candidate on July 12, 1691. This exceptionally holy and charitable priest developed the Hospital of St. Michele for poor youths, opened the Lateran Palace to the unemployed, curtailed the sale of offices, and reduced court expenses. He reorganized the administration in the Curia Innocenziana. By the *Romanum decet pontificem* (June 22, 1692) he forbade NEPOTISM, decreeing that only one of the pope's relatives should be eligible for the cardinalate. He founded the Congregation for the Discipline and Reform of Regulars (1694). He also prohibited the electoral chapters in Germany from nominating to bishoprics and monasteries (1695). Innocent likewise promoted the development of the Propaganda in America, Persia, and China.

Innocent avoided a schism with the Gallican Church by inducing Louis XIV to revoke "THE DECLARATION OF THE FRENCH CLERGY," which obliged the bishops to sign the Four Gallican Articles. The bishops sent letters of retraction. Concerning JANSENISM, he prohibited the bishops' adding to the formulary of ALEXANDER VII, which he reconfirmed, and forbade the discussion of the Five Propositions. The question of French QUIETISM was decided by Innocent's *Cum alias* (1699), which condemned the 23 propositions contained in Fénelon's *Maximes.*

Through Innocent, Louis XIV placed in the Peace of Ryswick (1697) the clause that in all the restored countries the Catholic religion was to remain in the state in which it was found at the moment of the signing. Innocent approved the first constitution of the King of Spain, and his preference for Philip of Anjou as heir to the Spanish throne helped bring about the war of the Spanish succession.

Bibliography: INNOCENT XII, *Collectio Bullarum . . .* (Rome 1697). L. PASTOR, *The History of the Popes from the Close of the Middle Ages,* (London–St. Louis 1938–61) 32:414, 526, 563, 567–573. J. PAQUIER, *Dictionnaire de théologie catholique,* ed. A. VACANT et al., 15 v. (Paris 1903–50; Tables générales 1951–) 7.2: 2013–15. G. SCHWAIGER, *Lexikon für Theologie und Kirche,* ed. J. HOFER and K. RAHNER, 10 v. (2d, new ed. Freiburg 1957–65) 5:695. B. PELLEGRINO, *Reforme, religione, e politica durante il pontificato di Innocenzo XII,* (Galatina 1994). M. FATICA, "La reclusione dei poveri a Roma durante il pontificato di Innocenzo XII (1692–1700)," *Ricerche per la stroria religiosa di Roma* 3 (1979) 133–80. A. D. WRIGHT, *The Early Modern Papacy: From the Council of Trent to the French Revolution, 1564–1789* (London 2000).

[I. J. CALICCHIO]

INNOCENT XIII, POPE

Pontificate: May 8, 1721, to March 7, 1724; b. Michelangelo de' Conti, Poli, Papal States, May 13, 1655. Son of the Duke of Poli, his family was illustrious for its three thirteenth-century popes: Innocent III, Gregory IX, and Alexander IV. Michelangelo studied first at Ancona, then with the Jesuits at Rome. He chose the Church for his career and rose steadily in the papal service. He became a monsignor under Alexander VIII and was appointed governor of three Papal States in succession: Ascoli, Frosinone, and Viterbo. In 1695 Innocent XII sent him as nuncio to Switzerland and made him titular archbishop of Tarsus. Three years later he went as internuncio to Lisbon, where he remained until 1710. Clement XI raised him to the purple in 1706 as cardinal-priest of Santi Quirico e Giulitta. He became bishop of Osimo (1709–12), and then of Viterbo (1712–19), which he relinquished because of ill health. In the conclave that followed the death of Clement XI (1721), the early favorite was Clement's secretary of state, Cardinal Fabrizio Paolucci, but when his election seemed near, he was excluded by the veto of Emperor Charles VI. The vote then swung to Conti (May 8, 1721), who was noted for his prudence and diplomacy. His missions to Switzerland and Portugal had not caused him to fall into the bad graces of any of the great powers. He assumed the name of Innocent in memory of Innocent III, from whose family he descended.

Innocent XIII met the stubborn Jansenists with firmness, insisting on submission to Clement XI's constitution *UNIGENITUS* (1713). He also took a firm stand in the vexed controversy over the so-called Chinese rites and forbade the Jesuits to receive novices if within three years they did not satisfy him as to their obedience. Innocent also set up a commission to study ecclesiastical problems in Spain caused by the upheaval of the Spanish Succession War. He recognized James as king of England, promising subsidies contingent upon the re-establishment of Roman Catholicism in England.

Bibliography: L. PASTOR, *The History of the Popes from the Close of the Middle Ages* (London–St. Louis 1938–61) 34:1–97. A. F. ARTAUD DE MONTOR, *The Lives and Times of the Popes,* 10 v. (New York 1910–11) 6.1:218–229. *Bullarium Romanum* (Magnum), ed. H. MAINARDI and C. COCQUELINES, 18 folio v. (Rome 1733–62) 21:867–958. M. MAYER, *Die Papstwahl Innocenz XIII* (Vienna 1874). J. PAQUIER, *Dictionnaire de théologie catholique,* ed. A. VACANT et al., 15 v. (Paris 1903–50; Tables générales 1951–) 7.2:2015–16. G. SCHWAIGER, *Lexikon für Theologie und Kirche,* ed. J. HOFER and K. RAHNER, 10 v. (2d, new ed. Freiburg 1957–65) 2 5:695–696. H. GROSS, *Rome in the Age of the Enlightenment* (Cambridge 1990). J. DULUMEAU, *Catholicism between Luther and Voltaire* (London 1977).

[J. S. BRUSHER]

INNOCENT OF LE MANS, ST.

Bishop; b. second half of the fifth century; d. MONTE CASSINO, Italy, March 30, 542. He was consecrated bishop of Le Mans, France, in 496, three years after the death of his predecessor, Principius. He completed and dedicated the cathedral at Le Mans and was active in the foundation of monasteries and convents. He worked to introduce BENEDICTINE monks into his diocese, and to this end he made his last journey to Monte Cassino, the motherhouse of the order. Innocent was present at the synods of Orléans (533 and 541), and at the latter session he was the fourth to subscribe to the decrees. After his death there was a 15-year vacancy in the bishopric before DOMNOLUS, abbot of Saint-Laurent, Paris (d. 581), was nominated by King Clotaire I (d. 561). Innocent was buried

The martyrdom of the Holy Innocents, detail of mid 5th-century mosaic on the arch of the apse of the basilica of S. Maria Maggiore, Rome.

beside his predecessors in his cathedral, and as his cult became popular quite early, his relics were enshrined during the eighth century.

Feast: March 30; June 19 (episcopal consecration).

Bibliography: *Gallia Christiana,* v.1–13 (Paris 1715–85), v.14–16 (Paris 1856–65) 14:338, 418, 542. L. DUCHESNE, *Fastes épiscopaux de l'ancienne Gaule,* 3 v. (2d. ed. Paris 1907–15) 2:337. *Acta Sanctorum* June 4:712–719. *Monumenta Germaniae Concilia* (Berlin 1825–) 65, 97. E. GRIFFE, *Catholicisme* 5:1673.

[B. J. COMASKEY]

INNOCENTS, HOLY

The baby boys of BETHLEHEM who were put to death by King HEROD the Great after the Magi's visit to the Infant Jesus (Mt 2:16–18). Study of the Innocents has often been more poetical and imaginative than factual. The interest of the past has been chiefly to amass greater detail about the Innocents. Attempts have been made to date the episode accurately, but these have been of little value, since the date of Christ's birth is itself a matter of speculation. Various efforts have been made, based on the probable population of Bethlehem at Our Lord's birth, to determine the number of children involved. Estimates range from 10 or 12 (A. Bisping, P. Shegg) to an obviously exaggerated 64,000 (Syrian Liturgy) to a fantastic 144,000 (based on Rv 14:1–5, part of the Epistle of their feast).

The slaughter described in Mt 2:16–18 is not mentioned in any other source; it is notably absent in the works of Josephus. D. F. STRAUSS and other scholars have, therefore, questioned the historicity of the episode. The argument from silence is, at best, unconvincing. The very character of Herod suggests a reason for the silence. In the records of a king responsible for many deaths, including those of his beloved wife and his own sons, the slaughter of the Innocents (if estimates are kept within reason) would be relatively insignificant.

On the other hand, attempts, such as E. Stauffer's, to prove the historicity of the event are likewise unconvincing. A growing number of modern scholars question the historical character of the Innocents' story because of its relation to such midrashic elements as the star of Bethlehem and the Magi [see MAGI]. If, for example, one considers the visit of the Magi a legendary amplification, one would almost be forced to judge the story of the Innocents in the same way.

Modern scholars are inclined to regard the entire INFANCY GOSPEL as a literary form related to MIDRASH. Emphasis is placed, not so much on the isolated individual elements, as on their theological significance in the Christ story. It seems strongly probable that Matthew wished to present three basic themes in his Infancy narrative: Jesus is the new Moses; Jesus is true wisdom; Jesus is the new Israel. The last theme seems dominant. If this is true, a striking case can be made that, in the story of the Innocents, Matthew has been inspired by a midrash on Dt 26:5–8. According to the midrash, Laban the Aramaean sought to destroy Jacob (Israel) and his entire family; this attempt was later considered an effort to prevent the coming of the Messiah. Herod the Idumean, in his slaughter of the Innocents, represents Laban's oppression of Jacob-Israel and renews the attempt to prevent the coming of the Messiah. This comparison of Laban and Herod that is brought about by attributing to Herod a slaughter of the Innocents invites a comparison between Christ and Jacob. Implicitly, Christ is presented as the new Jacob-Israel, the bearer of messianic hope. Once the Jesus-Israel theme is established, Jacob's wife Rachel becomes an apt mourner and serves to underline the comparison once again. Especially is this true when one realizes that the prophecy of Jeremiah (Jer 31:15) to which Matthew refers opens with reference to the tragedy of the Exile (originally that of the Northern Kingdom and then extended to that of the Southern Kingdom) but continues with a description of restoration that is realized fully only in the coming of the Messiah. Seen in this setting, the episode of the Innocents, whether historical or not, contributes to the unfolding of the Jesus-Israel theme and helps one understand the role of Jesus, the new Israel, who will definitively establish the new people of God.

The Feast of the Holy Innocents was celebrated in the West as early as the 5th century. It was placed on December 28 in order to bring it close to Christmas. In Christian iconography the earliest representatives of the massacre of the Holy Innocents date from the 5th century, such as on the mosaic arch in the basilica of Santa Maria Maggiore, Rome, and on an ivory Gospel cover now in the cathedral of Milan. In the Middle Ages representations of the scene were common, especially as miniatures in illuminated Gospels.

Bibliography: M. M. BOURKE, "The Literary Genus of Matthew 1–2," *The Catholic Biblical Quarterly* 22 (1960) 160–175. D. DAUBE, "The Earliest Structure of the Gospels," *New Testament Studies* 5 (1958–59) 174–187. A. DURAND, *The Gospel according to Matthew* (Milwaukee 1957) 18–20. U. HOLZMEISTER, "Quot pueros urbis Bethlehem Herodes rex occiderit," *Verbum Domini* 15 (1935) 373–379. J. MICHL, *Lexicon für Theologie und Kirche,* (Freiburg, 1957–66) 2:313. K. HOFMANN, *Lexicon für Theologie und Kirche,* (Freiburg, 1930–38) 10:415–416. F. G. HOLWECK, CE 7:419. L. RÉAU, *Iconographie de l'art chrétien* (Paris 1955–59) 2.2:267–270.

[E. J. JOYCE]

INNOCENZO OF BERZO, BL.

Italian Capuchin priest; b. Niardo, near Brescia, March 19, 1844; d. Bergamo, March 3, 1890. When Pietro Scalvinoni, his father, died a month after the birth of the boy, Francesca, his mother, moved to Berzo and there raised her only child. After studying at the diocesan seminary in Brescia, Giovanni (his name in baptism) was ordained (1867). He worked as assistant to the pastor of Berzo and then as vice rector of the Brescia seminary, where the seminarians referred to him as "the saint." In 1874 he joined the Capuchins and took the name Innocenzo (see FRANCISCANS, CAPUCHIN). He pronounced his final vows (1878) and was appointed assistant master of novices. His remaining years were devoted also to preaching and hearing confessions. Soon after his death, his remains were transferred by popular request to Berzo. He was beatified Nov. 12, 1961.

Feast: March 3.

Bibliography: G. DA NADRO, *L'Ombra sua torna* (2d ed. Milan 1950). *Lexicon Capuccinum* (Rome 1951) 820. *Acta Apostolicae Sedis* 53 (1961) 803–808. B. BURKEY, "In Silence and Shadows," *The Cord* 12 (1962) 200–207.

[T. MACVICAR]

Galileo Galilei before the Inquisition, painting by Robert-Fleury. (©Bettmann/CORBIS)

INQUISITION

A form of legal procedure best known for its adoption by papally appointed inquisitors "of heretical depravity" in the thirteenth century and institutionalized in Spain and elsewhere in the late fifteenth and sixteenth centuries. Much caricatured and misrepresented between the sixteenth and the twenty-first centuries.

The Origins: The Problem of Clerical Discipline. Originally *inquisitio* was a form of legal procedure in classical Roman law in which a single magistrate supervised an entire case, from investigation to judgment. The procedure increased in use during the later Roman empire, when the law, both civil and criminal, became largely administrative, although it fell into disuse in the early folk-kingdoms and the Carolingian empire between the fourth and ninth centuries, when other legal procedures, notably those of accusation, denunciation, and ordeal, were more commonly used, except for some matters that touched directly the ruler's person and property.

In a decretal letter, *Licet Heli*, of Dec. 10, 1199, however, INNOCENT III (1198–1216) addressed the problems of both clerical misbehavior and prelatal negligence in imposing discipline on criminous clerks, "against whom, so that notorious excesses shall cease, there are three kinds of procedure possible: accusation, denunciation, and inquisition about them." Accusation was the older procedure, also grounded in Roman law and therefore ancient, but it required that an accuser willing to lay a formal charge, pay the court expenses, and risk a penalty if the accusation failed. Denunciation was justified by the exegesis of Mt 18:15–17, which required first, fraternal admonition and was aimed primarily at the rehabilitation of the offender rather than punishment. Inquisition, initially only into the reputation of the suspect and the degree of notoriety of the offense, proved to be more efficient and controllable than either of these procedures and was now added to denunciation when the offense was so notorious that it created a scandal in the Christian com-

Tribunal of the Inquisition. (©Archivo Iconografico, S.A./CORBIS)

munity. Notoriety of the offense and the reputation of the accused were widely discussed by twelfth-century jurists, and several argued that under such circumstances ecclesiastical judges might dispense with formal procedural rules of written charges and taking evidence, although jurists also tended to restrict the number of offenses that could be classed as notorious. In identifying inquisition as a legitimate procedure in cases of notoriety, Innocent III cited God's response to the outcry against Sodom and Gomorrah in Gn 18:21: "*I must go down and see whether they have done altogether according to the outcry that has come to me; and if not, I will know,*" and Lk 16:1–7, the case of the rich man who heard that his steward had squandered his property and demanded an accounting. Any prelate, Innocent says, who hears a public outcry or repeated complaints about a clerical offender, "*ought to go and see, that is, send and inquire, whether the outcry indicates the truth.*" That is, all prelates have the right and responsibility to conduct an inquiry into charges of clerical misconduct within their jurisdictions that come to their attention.

Innocent III was acutely sensitive to the responsibilities of prelates, and in a slightly earlier letter to the archbishop of Naples and the papal legate Cinthio he had also cited the biblical case of the priest Eli (1 Sm 1, 3–4, 18) who refused to restrain his sons from wrongdoing and suffered the wrath of God because of it. Episcopal responsibilities included formal visitations of institutions within their dioceses, and Innocent reminded them that they could use inquisition *ex officio*. In canon 8, *Qualiter et quando*, of the Fourth LATERAN COUNCIL of 1215, Innocent went further. He identified *inquisitio* as the standard procedure for use in ecclesiastical courts. He supported canon 8 with two further canons. In canon 18, Innocent prohibited clergy from participating in ordeals, and in canon 38 he required ecclesiastical judges to keep a scribe whose written record of every trial could be accurately reviewed upon appeal. In effect, by introducing, then standardizing inquisitorial procedure in criminal cases involving clergy, Innocent III had begun a revolution in criminal legal procedure that later went far beyond the disciplining of criminous clergy.

The problem of clerical misconduct was one of the main themes of the vast movement for ecclesiastical reform associated with the name of GREGORY VII in the late eleventh century. In an attempt to distinguish clerical from lay status and prevent the pollution of clerical status, the reformers prohibited clergy from marrying or engaging in sexual activity (Nicolaitism) and from accepting any ecclesiastical office from a layman (Simony). Through the twelfth century, clerical discipline for these and other offenses remained prominent on the agenda of popes, reform-minded prelates, and church councils. Innocent's rulings between 1199 and 1215 offered an efficient and authoritative legal procedure that could be controlled by appellate review and thus reflect juridically the ecclesiological hierarchy in the Church.

Inquisitorial Procedure in Canon Law. Innocent's rulings in these matters extended far beyond the immediate recipients of his letters and judicial decisions. In 1210 Innocent instructed PETRUS BENEVENTANUS to make a selection of the decretal letters of the first 12 years of his pontificate, the *Compilatio Tertia*, which was to be sent to the masters and students of the law school at BOLOGNA and taught as canon law for all of Christendom.

The classical age of canon law had begun (as is now known) with the two successive versions of the *Concordance of discordant canons*, or *Decretum*, attributed to Master GRATIAN and taught and commented on at Bologna, then in Paris, the Rhineland, and England since shortly after the middle of the twelfth century. The *Decretum* was supplemented by two informal collections of papal letters subsequent to Gratian, the *Brevarium extravagantium*, or *Compilatio prima*, by BERNARD OF PAVIA, topically divided into five books and each book subdivided into titles and chapters—the standard form for subsequent collections of canon law—and a later collection called the *Compilatio secunda*.

After the *Compilatio tertia* two later informal collections circulated until the authoritative *Liber Extra* issued by GREGORY IX (1227–1241) in 1234 made obsolete all five collections subsequent to Gratian. Book V of the *Liber Extra* was devoted to crimes and procedures against their perpetrators, and it is from there that Innocent III's reforms were taught, commented upon, and learned by canon lawyers.

The Problem of Heterodoxy. By the early twelfth century the Latin Christian Church had constructed a firm basis for the definition of orthodox belief, based on an increasingly standardized interpretation of scripture, the concept of authoritative apostolic tradition handed down through bishops, councils, and popes, and a standardized creed. The laws of the Christian Roman emperors included sanctions against heterodox beliefs and those who held them. Writings by the Church Fathers, particularly St. Augustine and Isidore of Seville, described and catalogued early heretical movements, and these were read for centuries and recapitulated in the popular *Sermons on the Song of Songs* by St. Bernard of Clairvaux in the early twelfth century. Until the eleventh century, however, debates concerning heretical beliefs were usually conducted among the learned.

Ecclesiastical reformers in the later eleventh century defined SIMONY as a HERESY, and twelfth-century churchmen used the term to designate other dissenting movements as well, followers of popular teachers whose doctrines were perceived to deviate from the more and more sharply defined content of orthodoxy. By the early thirteenth century the definition attributed to ROBERT GROSSETESTE, bishop of Lincoln, may serve as a working definition: "Heresy is an opinion chosen by human faculties, contrary to Holy Scripture, openly taught, and pertinaciously defended." That is, heresy was heteodox religious doctrine discovered by purely human error, contrary to orthodox authoritative teaching, but also openly taught (not secretly held) and persisted in after authoritative correction (and therefore pertinacious, a willful and public denial of the teaching authority of the Church). In the thirteenth century heresy was also described by churchmen as contumacious—openly contemptuous of ecclesiastical authority.

Responses to Heresy: *Persuasio* **and** *Coercitio.* Some eleventh and twelfth-century churchmen advocated patient, instructive toleration of heterodox belief. Others urged extensive magisterial preaching to teach people true doctrine. This pastoral effort continued during the pontificate of Innocent III and led to Innocent's approval of a number of formerly dissenting evangelical groups, notably the HUMILIATI, and his approval of the new MENDICANT ORDERS, the DOMINICANS and FRANCISCANS. Individual twelfth-century bishops, lacking a reliable, authoritative guide in law, usually resorted to the excommunication and exile of convicted heretics. In some eleventh- and twelfth-century instances local mob rule, possibly influenced by local authorities, took justice into its own hands. Gratian included a number of authoritative earlier texts on heresy in the second part of his *Decretum*, but it took several decades for a consistent corpus of teaching doctrine to be assembled and deployed throughout Europe.

Several twelfth-century church councils also issued legislation concerning heresy. The Second LATERAN COUNCIL of 1139 required secular rulers to prosecute heresy. Pope ALEXANDER III (1159–1181) was also vigorous in his attempts to impose suitable penalties for heresy. The Third Lateran Council of 1179 identified several heretical groups by name and urged the use of excommunication and denial of Christian burial to those found to be heretics. At the same time, bishops were also urged to use synodal witnesses, men of good local reputation who could issue a *denunciatio* of suspected heretics without incurring the liabilities of formal accusers. In 1184 Pope

LUCIUS III (1181–1185) issued the decretal letter *Ad abolendam*, which condemned the "insolence" of heretics and "their attempts to promote falsehood." Here are the grounds for the second part of Grosseteste's definition—public teaching and contumacious refusal to be taught and corrected. Lucius also insisted upon two annual episcopal visitations to any part of a diocese where heresy has been reported and that lay authorities are required to cooperate with ecclesiastical authorities.

In 1199 Innocent III issued the decretal *Vergentis in senium*, which incorporated much of *Ad abolendam*, but also identified heresy with the doctrine of treason in Roman law. If treason against the Roman emperor were such a great crime, argued Innocent, how much greater a crime was treason to God? In the decretal *Cum ex officii nostri* of 1207, Innocent stated that convicted heretics should be turned over to secular authority for punishment, that their property should be confiscated and sold, their houses should be levelled to the ground, and that even sympathizers of heretics should be fined one-fourth of their property.

In 1208, following the murder of the papal legate PETER OF CASTELNAU, Innocent launched his next response to the dangers of heresy in a local population, when he invoked the recently-formulated doctrine of crusade privileges and commissioned an army to extirpate heresy in southern France—the so-called Albigensian Crusade (1208–1229).

The Council of Toulouse in 1229 and the rulers of France and Sicily in the next few years urged the active seeking out and punishing of heretics by royal officials. Roffredus Beneventanus, a jurist in the service of Frederick II of Sicily, argued that inquisitorial procedure had been invented in classical Roman law and therefore could be employed by secular, especially imperial, courts. *The Constitutions of Melfi*, issued by Frederick II in 1231, also vigorously attacked the treason of heretics and established inquisition as an extraordinary procedure to be used in the detection of serious crimes, although for heresy the judges must be churchmen. From here, such doctrines also were adopted by the increasingly independent city-republics of northern Italy and in other territories and eventually established as part of the Romano-Canonical procedures of *ius commune* throughout continental Europe.

In inquisitorial procedure, jurists stated that the bad reputation of the accused acted in place of the formal accuser, that the accused could be legally summoned and questioned under oath, and the testimony of sworn witnesses as to both reputation and fact was acceptable against him. Normally the accused had the right to know the names of witnesses against him, but as early as 1229 the fear of local reprisals led a judge to conceal the names of witnesses, a procedure that survived in many inquisitorial courts that tried heresy.

The system of acceptable proofs in the *ius commune* procedure required either the identical testimony of two eyewitnesses or confession in order to convict. Without either of these, the judge had only partial evidence, no amount of which was sufficient to convict. Such evidence, however, could be weighed as *indicia* of different degrees of value, and when the judge was convinced that the *indicia* indicated guilt, he could order that the accused be tortured, but only to secure a confession. With the adoption of inquisitorial procedure in secular courts, torture also was adopted, along with rules of evidence and due process. In 1252 Pope INNOCENT IV (1243–1254) issued the decretal *Ad extirpanda*, which classified heretics as thieves of spiritual things and murderers of the soul, and he authorized secular courts in Italy to employ judicial torture in order to secure confessions in heresy trials, just as they already could in other criminal cases.

Inquisitors of Heretical Depravity. One of the most important institutional products of the late eleventh-century movement of ecclesiastical reform was the increasing office of the papal judge-delegate, a clerical official who was given papal authority to decide a particular case, work for a particular period of time, or in a specific area. Papal judges-delegate might also in some cases commission judges sub-delegate. The institution took some of the burdens of litigation off the shoulders of the Pope, while making it clear that the judge-delegate's jurisdiction was papally authorized. Between 1227 and 1233 GREGORY IX (1227–1241) appointed judges-delegate the Rhineland and in Burgundy whose irregular and uncontrolled activities brought heavy criticism. In 1231 Gregory reissued much earlier legislation against heretics and laid down the rule that repentant heretics were to be imprisoned for life, while unrepentant heretics were to be turned over to the secular arm for capital punishment. Gregory also charged specific judges-delegate to preach in areas where heresy was known to exist, inquire and discover heretics, their helpers, and defenders, and either reconcile them with the Church or turn them over to the secular arm for secular punishment. Gregory also indicated that other members of the mendicant orders were not to participate in these activities, since they were specialized and required particular skills.

In 1233 Gregory took a further step. He established papal judges-delegate in southern France in the wake of the recent crusade, pointing out to local bishops that the Dominicans appointed were to supplement the bishops' own inquiries. Eventually, inquisitors in particular places assumed more and more of this formerly episcopal function. By 1235 the procedures in inquisitions of heretical depravity in southern France began to be regularized: inquisitors delivered a public sermon and call for confessions, established a ''period of grace'' in which voluntary confessions would receive lighter penalties, and the names of suspected heretics would be gathered. Testimony, confessions, and sentences were recorded in special registers. Although local resistance to these procedures delayed the development of the process, the growing papal concerns and increasing cooperation of secular authorities continued to develop what has been called a unique ''technology of power.''

The most extensive inquisitorial investigation of heretical depravity occurred in the area around Toulouse during two hundred and one days between May 1245 and August 1246, when two inquisitors interrogated 5471 men and women and issued two hundred and seven sentences against convicted heretics, of which 23 consisted of perpetual imprisonment and 184 required the convicted to wear distinctive yellow crosses on their clothing. The sentences included no confiscation of property, nor was anyone sentenced to death. The inquisitors at Toulouse also produced a specialized manual of instruction for other inquisitors in 1248 or 1249, the first example of what became an important genre of legal literature. The manual gave sample forms of the citation of witnesses, the period of grace, formulas for interrogation, forms of summons, and instructions for reconciliation and punishment. By 1250 the office of inquisitor of heretical depravity was becoming a specialized function, especially among trained members of the mendicant Orders whose work distinguished them from other members of the Orders. The development of punitive and penitential imprisonment was an innovation of the inquisitors, the ancestor of the modern prison system, since it was taken up at the end of the thirteenth century by a number of Italian city-republics and later spread to northern Europe.

During the fourteenth and fifteenth centuries, both the inquisitorial judicial procedure and the appointment of inquisitors of heretical depravity spread rapidly, as learned Romano-canon law, the *ius commune*, spread northward in Europe, and popes (and occasionally bishops) undertook inquisitions against heresy in different parts of Christendom. One of the best-known instances was the episcopal inquisition carried out by Jacques Fournier, bishop of Pamiers (1318–1325). Inquisitorial archives provided a record and a history of heresy in particular places; manuals for inquisitors grew more specialized and longer, from the manual by Bernard Gui in 1324 to the immense manual, the *Directorium Inquisitorum* of Nicholau Eymeric in 1376, the first manual to be printed and the most influential inquisitor's manual in history. Popes and other authorities insisted that inquisitors of he-

retical depravity observe due process, allow all legal defenses, withhold the names of witnesses only when revealing them would place the witnesses in real danger, and permit legal counsel except in the cases of convicted heretics. Appeals were allowed. But testimony was also accepted from witnesses who would be otherwise disqualified, a practice that was also followed in secular courts for so-called excepted crimes, particularly treason. And a number of inquisitorial tribunals dealing with heresy tended increasingly to require that the defendant know something about the law, because the judge recognized no obligation to inform defendants of their rights. The trial of Joan of Arc in 1431 is the best known example of a (in this case highly irregular and politically dominated) court violating generally recognized inquisitorial procedures. In Joan's second inquisitorial trial, that of 1456, which followed proper inquisitorial procedures, the earlier verdict was reversed.

The Inquisitions of Spain and Portugal. Inquisitors of heretical depravity technically had little jurisdiction over Jews and Muslims, except in cases where members of these groups had converted to Christianity and then returned to their original faiths and in a few other instances, mostly concerning their relations with Christians. In the Iberian Peninsula, however, a series of pogroms beginning in 1391 had led to an extraordinary number of Jewish conversions to Christianity and to the creation of a group of converted Jews known as *conversos* or New Christians, *nuevos cristianos*. The prominence of *conversos* in fifteenth-century Iberian society, with increasing anti-semitism, led Isabella of Castile and Ferdinand of Aragon to request from the Pope the establishment of an inquisitorial tribunal in Spain. The bull of Sixtus IV (1471–1484), issued in November 1478, permitted the Crown to appoint two inquisitors, primarily to deal with the problem of relapsed *conversos*. In 1482 another bull permitted the appointment of a further seven inquisitors, among whom was Tomás de TORQUEMADA, a diligent, but hardly fanatic inquisitor. Ferdinand and Isabella had already established four Councils of State as institutional branches of royal government, and in 1483 they established a fifth: *Consejo de la Suprema y General Inquisición,* ''The Council of the Supreme and General Inquisition,'' the first institutional inquisition, with Torquemada as President, and later with the title Inquisitor-General.

From 1478 to 1530, and again from 1650 to 1720, the Spanish Inquisition concentrated on the problem of Judaizing. Between 1530 to 1650, however, it focused more on other problems: some aspects of Erasmian humanism in religious matters, deviations in piety among the *alumbrados*, and PROTESTANTISM, which it and others characterized as a form of heresy, in this case, *Luteranis-*

mo. It also dealt with other issues of disciplining the clergy, particularly that of sexual solicitation in the confessional.

The Council of the Supreme and General Inquisition developed its institutional form and its procedures early and maintained them until its abolition in 1834. It consisted of an Inquisitor-General and an unspecified number of other members. By the mid-sixteenth century it assumed operational and jurisdictional authority over all inquisitorial tribunals, requiring regular reports from them and periodically inspecting and supervising their activities. By the early seventeenth century there were nearly 20 regional tribunals directed by the *Suprema* as well as a group of tribunals in the Spanish Americas. Each of these operated according to the written instructions, *Instrucciones*, issued by the *Suprema*, the first of which was issued by Torquemada in 1484 and later supplemented by his successors. Each tribunal was to consist of two inquisitors, a legal adviser, a constable, and a *fiscal*, or prosecutor. Tribunals also had a network of familiars, privileged lay assistants who provided general staff support.

The bureaucratic features of the system governed by the *Suprema* were the systematic recruitment, appointment, and replacement of officials, the powerful and regular structure of command and supervision, the issuing of operational instructions enhanced by periodic visitations and reports from below, the preservation, use, and continuous supplementation of archives, the establishment of clearly defined rank and status, and internal financial management.

The procedures followed by the tribunals were essentially continuations of those developed from the late thirteenth century on. The general sermon, the period of grace, the collection of names and evidence during the period of grace, and the recording and summarizing of information. Such evidence was then assessed by one or more theological consultants. When an indictment was forthcoming, the prosecutor drew up charges, issued an arrest warrant, and took the accused into custody. At that moment, the accused's goods were sequestered, inventoried, and from that point until conviction or acquittal maintained by officers of the Inquisition. The accused was imprisoned until the hearing was completed. Inquisition officials were permitted to use most of the criminal procedures of the *ius commune*, including torture, although records indicate that torture was used far less than in comparable secular jurisdictions. Meticulous records were kept of all procedures, and these vast archives constitute a remarkable body of sources for both inquisitorial and social history.

At the end of all hearings, the local tribunal, with theological advisers and a representative of the bishop, decided upon guilt or innocence in a group of cases. During the seventeenth century the *Suprema* itself took over this task. The sentences were read publicly at a ceremony known as the *auto-de-fé*, "the Act of Faith," which consisted of processions of penitents, including the names of those posthumously condemned, public prayers, and sermons. These elaborate ceremonies were intended to serve as a means of reinforcing the faith of the public as much as a means of celebrating the repentance of those who had confessed and the condemnation of those who had not. The *auto-de-fé* is comparable to other manifestations of public ritual in early modern Europe. In the case of those convicted of capital offenses, the *Suprema* was obliged to turn them over to the secular arm for execution.

Antisemitic sentiments increased in Portugal during the late fifteenth and early sixteenth centuries, particularly following the large influx of Spanish *conversos* who left Spain after 1478 to 1483 and after the expulsion of all unbaptized Jews from Spain in 1492. In 1496 King João II ordered the expulsion of all Jews from Portugal and a year later commanded the forced conversion of all who remained. Thus, the absence of an unconverted Jewish community living side by side with *cristãos novos* made the Portuguese situation different from that of Spain between 1391 and 1492. But the rulers of Portugal eventually did request a local inquisition, and between 1534 and 1540 an Inquisition similar to that of Spain was established, although the Portuguese Inquisition continued to concern itself more with Judaizing than did the Spanish. In 1561 the Portuguese Inquisition established a tribunal at Goa, in India, parallel to the Spanish tribunals in Mexico, Lima, Cartagena, and Manila.

The Inquisitions of Spain and Portugal survived, but in much weakened form, until the nineteenth century. The Spanish Inquisition was finally abolished by the regent Maria Cristina, acting in the name of the Infanta Isabella II in July 1834. The Portuguese Inquisition was abolished in 1821.

The Inquisitions in Italy and Northern Europe. In 1542 Pope Paul III (1534–1549) established an institutional Inquisition in Rome with six inquisitors general for the Papal States and other parts of Italy, but claiming powers over all of Europe. When Sixtus V (1585–1590) restructured papal government into 15 secretariats, or congregations, in 1588, the Roman Inquisition was erected into one of these, the *Congregation of the Holy Roman and Universal Inquisition*, or Holy Office. The Roman Inquisition also established bodies of instructions for subordinate tribunals and extensive archives, most of which have been scattered or lost. The chief focus for the Roman Inquisition was originally Protestantism, although by the seventeenth century most trials were held for problems of clerical discipline and superstitious magic. Both the Spanish and Roman Inquisitions were the first institutional tribunals to express great scepticism about the problem of diabolical witchcraft, which troubled many other tribunals, ecclesiastical and lay, during the late sixteenth and seventeenth centuries. The occasions for sentencing in the procedure of the Roman Inquisition were secret—there were no Roman equivalents of the Spanish *auto-de-fé*. The powers of the Roman Inquisition were also limited by local control and resistance. The city of Lucca never admitted its officials, and in other territories, notably Genoa, Savoy, and Tuscany, city and territorial governments insisted on some degree of lay intervention. In 1908, Pius X changed the name of the institution to the *Congregation of the Holy Office*, merging its function with that of the *Congregation of the Index*, which had been established in 1571. In 1965 Paul VI changed the name once again to *The Sacred Congregation for the Doctrine of the Faith*, its present name, and in 1966 abolished the Index entirely.

In 1547 the government of Venice, which had included very stringent laws against heresy in its municipal legal code, instituted a tribunal, initially composed entirely of laymen, the *Tre Savii sopra eresia*, "The Three Wise Magistrates Concerned with Heresy," although by 1551 these lay officials were reduced to the role of consulting officials and witnesses, while the real work was done under a clerical Inquisitor-General. By the mid-sixteenth century the once-independent Venetian Inquisition was consulting regularly and cooperatively with the Roman Inquisition, as the trial records of Giordano BRUNO in 1600 and Galileo GALILEI in 1633 indicate. The Inquisition of Venice was abolished when Napoleon conquered the city in 1797. As governments became increasingly secularized and nonconfessionally based in the eighteenth and nineteenth centuries, the various surviving inquisitorial tribunals lost public power and legitimacy and functioned only internally in Roman Catholic affairs.

Myths of the Inquisition. The secrecy and power of inquisitorial tribunals had always generated criticism and opposition since the thirteenth century, most spectacularly in the case of the fourteenth-century Franciscan, Bernard Délicieux. But the great confessional divisions of the sixteenth century and later generated for the first time a mythology of the *Inquisition*, initially in Protestant histories of the Church and Protestant martyrologies, and then in the Low Countries, in the sixteenth century ruled by Spain, which resisted the importing of the Spanish Inquisition into their region. As Low Country political resistance to Spain was drawn during the Dutch Revolt after 1566 to the general conflict between Protestantism and Catholicism, anti-Spanish propaganda promulgated what was later called "The Black Legend," a polemical demonization of Spain that identified the Inquisition with the most hated features of Roman Catholicism and Spanish autocracy.

During the debates on religious toleration of the sixteenth and seventeenth centuries the inquisitions became popular targets as examples of religious fanaticism, most impressively in the great *History of the Inquisition* by the Dutch theologian Philip van Limborch (1633–1712), the original recipient of John Locke's *Letter on Toleration*. In the eighteenth century, enlightenment critics, most conspicuously Voltaire, satirized the inquisitions, and the Italian penal reformer Cesare Beccaria denounced them in his widely circulating treatise *On Crimes and Punishments*. The Gothic novel in the late eighteenth and early nineteenth centuries often used on imaginary inquisitorial settings and characters like the fantastic institution described in Edgar Allan Poe's "The Pit and the Pendulum," and by other writers of imaginative and polemical fiction. With the proliferation of illustrated books, both official and imaginary pictorial representations of scenes of inquisitorial torture, imprisonment, and executions appeared more and more frequently, sometimes in great art like that of Goya, but more often in crude or satirical book-illustrations. During the nineteenth and twentieth centuries the topic attracted great a number of great musical and literary artists—Schiller, Verdi, Dostoievsky, and Stefan Andres. Only in the late nineteenth century, with the imposition of modern standards of scholarship, did a reliable and document-based history of the Inquisition become possible. It has attracted historians ever since.

The modern historian John Lukacs once observed that "The purpose of history is the reduction of untruth." The problem of dismantling the long and often firmly-held mythology of the Inquisition is a case in point.

Bibliography: E. PETERS, *Inquisition* (New York 1988). E. VAN DER VEKENÉ, *Bibliotheca Bibliographica Historiae Sanctae Inquisitionis* 2 v. (Vaduz, 1982–83). W. TRUSEN, "Der Inquisitionsprozess. Seine historischen Grundlagen und frühen Formen," *Zeitschrift der Savigny-Stiftung für Rechtsgeschichte. Kanonistische Abteilung* 105 (1988) 168–230; "Das Verbot der Gottesurteile und der Inquisitionsprozess. Zum Wandel des Strafverfahrens unter dem Einfluss des gelehrten Rechts im Spätmittelalter," *Sozialer Wandel im Mittelalter. Wahrnehmungsformen, Erklärungsmuster, Regelungsmechanismen*, ed. J. MIETHKE and K. SCHREINER (Sigmagingen: Jan Thorbecke Verlag, 1994) 235–247. M. BELLOMO, *The Common Legal Past of Europe 1000–1800* (Washington, D.C.: The Catholic University of America Press, 1995). R. KIECKHEFER, "The Office of Inquisition and Medieval Heresy: The Transition from Personal to Institutional Jurisdiction," *Journal of Ecclesiastical History* 46 (1995) 36–61. R. FRAHER, "IV Lateran's Revolution in Criminal Procedure: The Birth of *Inquisitio*, the End of Ordeals, and Innocent III's Vision of Ecclesiastical Politics," *Studia in Honorem Eminentissimi Cardinalis*, A. M. STICKLER, ed. R. I. CARD, *Castillo Lara* (Rome: Las 1992) 97–111. W. L. WAKEFIELD, *Heresy, Crusade, and Inquisition in Southern France, 1100–1250* (Berkeley and Los Angeles 1974).

H. MAISONNEUVE, *Études sur les origines de l'inquisition* (Paris 1960). E. PETERS, *Heresy and Authority in Medieval Europe* (Philadelphia 1980). M. ZERNER, ed., *Inventer l'hérésie? Discours polémiques e pouvoirs avant l'Inquisition* (Nice 1998). M. G. PEGG, *The Corruption of Angels: The Great Inquisition of 1246–1246* (Princeton 2001). J. B. GIVEN, *Inquisition and Medieval Society: Power, Discipline, and Resistance in Languedoc* (Ithaca and London 1997). R. KIECKHEFER, *Repression of Heresy in Medieval Germany* (Philadelphia 1979). A. PATSCHOVSKY, *Die Anfänge einer ständigen Inquisition in Böhmen* (Berlin-New York: De Gruyter 1975). A. DONDAINE, *Les hérésies et l'Inquisition, XIIe-XIIIe siècles*, ed. Y. DOSSAT (Aldershot 1990), especially "Le manuel de l'inquisiteur (1230–1330)," II. A. FRIEDLANDER, *The Hammer of Inquisitors: Brother Bernard Délicieux and the Struggle Against the Inquisition in Fourteenth-Century France* (Leiden-Boston-Cologne 2000). *Bernard Gui et son monde, Cahiers de Fanjeaux* 16 (Toulouse 1981). H. ANSKAR KELLY, *Inquisitions and Other Trial Procedures in the Medieval West* (Aldershot-Brookfield 2001). H. C. LEA, *A History of the Inquisition of the Middle Ages,* 3 v. (New York 1888). R. I. MOORE, *The Formation of a Persecuting Society: Power and Deviance in Western Europe, 950–1250* (Oxford 1987). *Historia de la Inquisición en España y América*, ed. J. PÉREZ VILLANUEVA and B. ESCANDELL BONET, 3 v. (Madrid 1984–2000). J. EDWARDS, *The Spanish Inquisition* (Charleston 1999). M. ESCAMILLA-COLIN, *Crimes et chatiments dans l'Espagne inquisitoriale*, 2 v. (Paris 1992). S. HALICZER, *Inquisition and Society in the Kingdom of Valencia 1478–1834* (Berkeley-Los Angeles-Oxford 1990). H. C. LEA, *A History of the Inquisition of Spain*, 4 v. (New York 1906–1907). H. KAMEN, *The Spanish Inquisition: A Historical Revision* (New Haven and London 1998). A. ALCALÁ, ed., *The Spanish Inquisition and the Inquisitorial Mind* (New York 1987). M. E. PERRY and A. J. CRUZ, ed., *Cultural Encounters: The Impact of the Inquisition in Spain and the New World* (Berkeley and Los Angeles 1991). G. HENNINGSEN, *The Witches' Advocate: Basque Witchcraft and the Spanish Inquisition* (Reno 1980). *L'Inquisition de Goa*, ed. C. AMIEL and A. LIMA (Paris 1997). A. J. SARAIVA, *The Marrano Factory: The Portuguese Inquisition and Its New Christians, 1536–1765*, trans. H. P. SALOMON and I. S. D. SASSOON (Boston-Leiden-Cologne 2001). H. C. LEA, *A History of the Inquisition of Spain*, v. 3: 239–290. F. M. GILABERT, *La abolición de la Inquisición en España* (Pamplona 1975). *The Inquisition in Early Modern Europe: Studies on Sources and Methods*, ed. G. HENNINGSEN and J. TEDSECHI, with C. AMIEL (Dekalb, Illinois 1986). F. BETHENCOURT, *L'Inquisition à l'époque moderne: Espagne, Portugal, Italie Xve–XIX siècle* (Paris 1995). J. TEDESCHI, *The Prosecution of Heresy: Collected Studies on the Inquisition in Early Modern Italy* (Binghamton 1991). B. PULLAN, *The Jews of Europe and the Inquisition of Venice, 1550–1670* (Oxford 1983). G. DALL'OLIO, *Eretici e Inquisitori nella Bologna del Cinquecento* (Bologna 1999).

[E. PETERS]

INSIGHT

The term is used improperly by some (e.g., W. Köhler) for animal "solutions" to animal "problems" but has acquired a technical meaning, corresponding to its ordinary use for acumen or INTELLIGENCE, in the works of B. J. F. Lonergan. For him, it is the specifically human act of UNDERSTANDING. It is limited: "By insight we have not meant a pure understanding but an understand-ing of something" (*Insight* 343); and this limitation derives from presentations, or images, or experience (again a technical word for the materials to be understood, *ibid.* 357), which determine a specific object for human understanding. Thus one does not speak of divine insight, though one may speak of divine understanding.

The chief value of the word lies in the fact that it expresses the act of understanding familiar to everyone, without carrying the philosophical connotations of the term INTUITION. It also indicates the direct relationship of human understanding to materials to be understood, in contrast to the REFLECTION that is involved in judging. But "sight" is used only analogously of intellectual operations, which are properly to be studied in themselves (St. Thomas Aquinas, *Summa theologiae,* 1a, 88.2 ad 3). Since intuitionist philosophers may read their peculiar meanings into "insight" and justify them by its root meaning, it seems better to give preference to the term understanding, whose root meaning is more obscure and requires one to attend to the actual meaning assigned by the user.

See Also: UNDERSTANDING (INTELLECTUS); APPREHENSION, SIMPLE.

Bibliography: B. J. F. LONERGAN, "The Concept of *Verbum* in the Writings of St. Thomas Aquinas," *Theological Studies* 7 (1946) 349–392; 8 (1947) 35–79, 404–444; 10 (1949) 3–40, 359–393; *Insight: A Study of Human Understanding* (New York 1957). W. KÖHLER, *The Mentality of Apes,* tr. E. WINTER from 2d ed. (New York repr. 1959).

[F. E. CROWE]

INSPIRATION, BIBLICAL

By inspiration of the Bible is meant a unique divine influence in virtue of which the people responsible for the OT and NT were so moved and enlightened by God that their work may truly be called the Word of God. It has been the constant belief of the people of God both before and after the time of Christ that their Sacred Scriptures have been divinely inspired. Testimony to this fact, together with information concerning the nature of the inspired character of the Scriptures, is found in the OT, in Jewish writers, in the NT, as well as in the tradition of the Church.

Existence of Inspiration. *Old Testament and Jewish Writers.* Toward the end of the 2nd century B.C., the translator of Sirach recognized the normative character of the Law, the Prophets, and other writings for the Jewish people (Foreword to Sirach; see also 1 Mc 1:9–60; 7:16–17; 12.9; 2 Mc 2:13; Dan 9:2). The prophetic origin of this literature accounted for its authority. Moses and the great prophets of Israel were themselves conscious of speaking to the people in the name of God Himself (e.g., Ex 4:15–16; 19:7–8; Jer 1:9; 20.7–9; Ez 38:.1). The phenomenon of prophecy was attributed to the spirit of God that filled the prophet (Nm 11:25–26; 1 Sm 10:6; Hos 9:7). Occasional mention is made of the same spirit of God at work in the priest (2 Chr 24:20) and the psalmist (2 Sm 23:2).

The Prophets of Israel were primarily moved by God to speak the word of God to their contemporaries. Others recorded their words at a later date. Some prophetic oracles, however, were originally given in writing (Hb 2:2; Is 30:8); Jeremia was instructed to record all his oracles for posterity (Jer 30.1–3; 36.1–3). At the time of Christ the Jews sought the word of the Lord in this threefold collection of the Law, the Prophets, and the Writings (cf. Jn 5:39; 10:35). The rabbis so venerated the letter of the text that they saw a divine meaning in the very flourishes of the script (cf. Mt 5:18).

In the Diaspora the Jewish philosopher Philo wrote of the inspired character of the Hebrew Scriptures in their Greek translation. He explained the phenomenon of inspiration in terms of Greek religious ecstasy: the prophet was deprived of personal consciousness and possessed by God whenever he spoke or wrote (ἐνθουσιασμός: Quis rerum divinarum heres 53.265; *Loeb Classical Library* 4.418). According to the Jewish historian Flavius Josephus, the prophets wrote by inspiration received from God (κατά τὴν ἐπίπνοιαν τὴν ἀπὸ τοῦ: Contra Apionem 1.7.37; *Loeb Classical Library* 1.179). The Jews were more concerned with the divine character and authority of their sacred writings than with their human origins.

New Testament. The countless NT references and allusions to the Jewish Scriptures testify to the veneration that Christ and the apostles had for the Law, the Prophets, and the other writings (Lk 24:27, 44; Acts 3:22; 4:25; 28.25; Gal 3:8; Mk 7:10, 13; 12:36). In fact, the person, work, and teaching of Christ are presented in the NT as the supreme fulfillment of all that is written in the OT (Heb 1:1–2; Mt 5:17–19; 1 Cor 15:3–4; Rom 3:21, 31).

In 2 Pt 1:19–21 the OT prophetic texts are clearly attributed to the special influence of the Holy Spirit. To confirm the confidence that may be placed in OT prophecy, the author says that ''no prophecy of Scripture is made by private interpretation. For not by human will was prophecy brought at any time; rather, holy men of God spoke as they were moved [φερόμενοι] by the Holy Spirit.'' The permanent value of the OT is insisted on in 2 Tm 3:15–16 by explaining that ''all Scripture is inspired by God [θεόπνευστος] and useful for teaching, for reproving, for correcting, for instructing in justice; that

the man of God may be perfect, equipped for every good work.'' For these reasons the OT was retained as authoritative and useful in the Church (1 Cor 10:11).

Among the NT writings the Book of Revelation testifies to its own divine origin (1:1–3), and in 2 Pt 3:16 the epistles of Paul are treated as Scripture. Moreover, the Apostles claim for themselves and their teaching an authority superior to their predecessors (2 Cor 3:7–8; Eph 3:5; Col 1:26; 1 Thes 2:13; 2 Thes 2:15).

Church Tradition. By the middle of the 2nd Christian century there is evidence that the NT writings were being treated on a par with the OT [Justin Martyr, Apologia 1.66, 67; Dialogues c. Trypho 119; Irenaeus, Adv. Haer. 3.1.1–2; Theophilus of Antioch, Ad Autolycum 3.12; Hippolytus, In Cant. 2.8 (XI); Muratorian Fragment, *Enchiridion biblicum* 1–7].

Christian antiquity, in its prayer, preaching, and theological writing, universally recognized that the writings of the OT and NT were the work of the Holy Spirit and were all equally the word of God. It was the unanimous teaching of the Fathers that the Sacred Scriptures were free from error and from all contradiction. Even though other ecclesiastical writers were considered to be inspired by God (Clement of Rome says this of himself, 1 Clem 63.2; Gregory Nazianzus, of Basil, In Hex. Proem., *Patrologia Graeca* 44:61; Augustine, of Jerome, Epist. 82.2; Gregory the Great, of himself, In I Reg. Proem. 5, *Patrologia Latina* 79:21), the canonical Scriptures were always considered to be in a class apart. Athenagoras (c. 177) spoke of the prophets as the *organa* or instruments of God, writing in ecstasy as the flutes of the Holy Spirit (*Legatio pro Christianis* 7, 9). About A.D. 250 the *Cohortatio ad Graecos* (8) called them the harps or lyres of the Holy Spirit (see also Theophilus of Antioch, *Ad Autolycum* 2.9; Hippolytus, *De Antichristo* 2). The metaphor of the musical instrument is common among the Fathers but tends to minimize the role of the human author. Nevertheless, at the time of the Montanist heresy, Catholic writers rejected the notion that the sacred writers wrote in ecstasy, deprived of their senses and intellectual awareness (see Epiphanius, Adv. Haer. 48; Jerome, In Is. Prol., *Corpus Christianorum* 73.2–3; In Nah. et Hab. Prol., *Patrologia Latina* 25:1232, 1274).

The Fathers inherited from the rabbis the notion of divine dictation (ὑπαγορεύειν, dictare; see John Chrysostom, *In illud: Salutate Priscillam et Aquilam*, *Patrologia Graeca* 51: 187; Augustine, *Cons. Evang.* 1.35, 54), but it must be remembered that, when used by the magisterium, this Latin word has a wider sense than mechanical and verbal dictation. It expresses origin, causality, and responsibility; the Council of Trent used it of oral traditions (*Enchiridion biblicum* 57). It remains true, however, that the Fathers investigated primarily the divine meaning of the Scriptures in the full light of Christian faith, and little attention was actually paid to a historical investigation of the human writer's work (see Gregory the Great, *Moralia in Job Praef.* 1.2, *Patrologia Latina* 75:517). Indeed, the tools for such a study were lacking to the Fathers. At the same time, however, men such as the Antiochenes, Jerome, and Augustine, recognized the importance of investigating the character, style, and work of the human writers (Jerome, *In Am. Prol.*, *Patrologia Latina* 25:990; Augustine, *In evang. Ioh.* 1.1; *Civ.* 17.6.2; *Cons. Evang.* 2.12.27–29). Augustine (*Doctr. christ.* 2.5) wrote: "In reading it [i.e., Sacred Scripture], men are desirous only of discovering the thoughts and intentions of those by whom it was written. Through these in turn they discover the will of God, according to which we believe such men spoke" (*The Fathers of the Church: A New Translation* 4.64). Again in Epist. 82. 1.3: "If I do find anything in these books which seems contrary to truth, I decide that either the text is corrupt, or the translator did not follow what was really said, or that I failed to understand it" (*The Fathers of the Church: A New Translation* 9.392).

Although the Fathers treated the Scriptures as letters addressed by God to his people (John Chrysostom, *In Gn. Hom.* 2.2, *Patrologia Graeca* 53:28; Augustine, *In psalm.* 90 serm. 2.1), the term *auctor* (author) is not explicitly applied to God until the time of Gregory the Great (*Moralia in Job Praef.* 1.2, *Patrologia Latina* 75:517). In defending the faith against Marcion, the Gnostics, and the Manichees, Catholic writers and the magisterium insisted that one and the same God was at the origin of both the OT and the NT. In this context the Latin word *auctor* may simply mean principle or originator of both dispensations, although literary authorship cannot be excluded. The *Statuta Ecclesiae Antiqua* (*c.* 600) refer to God as "the author [*auctor*] of the OT and the NT, i.e., of the Law and the Prophets and [the writings of] the Apostles" (*Enchiridion biblicum* 30). The *Decree for the Jacobites* issued at the Council of Florence (1441) suggests literary authorship more explicitly: "The holy Roman Church acknowledges [*profitetur*] one and the same God as author of the OT and the NT, i.e., of the Law and the Prophets and the Gospel, because the holy men of both Testaments, whose books it receives and venerates, spoke under the inspiration of the same Holy Spirit" (*Enchiridion biblicum* 47). The same formula appears in the teaching of the Council of Trent (1546), although the Council itself was concerned primarily with maintaining equal reverence and authority (*pari pietatis affectu ac reverentia*) for oral traditions, in view of Protestant insistence on Scripture alone (*Enchiridion biblicum* 57). [*See* TRADITION (IN THEOLOGY).]

Providentissimus Deus. In the 18th and 19th centuries, with the rise of rationalism and positivism, the inspiration and divine authority of Sacred Scripture were seriously questioned. Textual, literary, and historical criticism discovered many imperfections, apparent errors, and seeming contradictions in the sacred texts. The human origins of the Bible appeared to be irreconcilable with divine inspiration. Outside the Church the notion of inspiration was reduced to religious and poetic genius. Within the Church some Catholics taught that the Church made certain books into Sacred Scripture by giving her approval to outstanding human works (D. Haneberg). Others taught that God merely protected the human authors from error in matters of faith and morals (M. Jahn). Vatican Council I (1870) defended the traditional teaching against contemporary errors by a solemn and infallible expression of Catholic faith: "The Church holds them [the books of the OT and the NT] as sacred and canonical, not because, having been composed by human industry alone, they were afterwards approved by her authority; nor only because they contain revelation without error; but because, having been written under the inspiration of the Holy Spirit, they have God as their author and, as such, have been handed over to the Church" (*Enchiridion biblicum* 77).

In view of new attempts to restrict unduly Biblical inspiration and inerrancy, Leo XIII, in his encyclical *Providentissimus Deus* (1893), repeated the teaching of Trent and Vatican Council I, and further explained the Catholic doctrine of inspiration: "Hence, because the Holy Spirit employed men as His instruments, we cannot therefore say that it was these inspired instruments who, perchance, have fallen into error, and not the primary Author. For, by supernatural power, He so moved and impelled them to write—He was so present to them—that the things that He ordered, and those only, they, first, rightly understood, then willed faithfully to write down, and finally expressed in apt words and with infallible truth. Otherwise it could not be said that He was the author of the entire Scripture" (*Enchiridion biblicum* 125). It is therefore of divine and Catholic faith that the entire extent of Scripture is inspired by God in such a way that He may be truly called its author.

Leo XIII, reflecting Christian tradition, spoke of the sacred writers as instruments of the Holy Spirit. It is necessary to conceive this divine and human cooperation in such a way as to preserve the free and responsible character of the human author, for modern study has made us acutely aware of the complex historical process that produced the literature of the Bible. The inspiration of the Bible must, however, be seen as one aspect of that divine providence which is leading men to salvation through Jesus Christ. God's supernatural revelation took place in the history of Israel and in the life of Christ before it was recorded in the pages of Scripture. The Bible then is the record of a progressive revelation, written according to the modes of writing prevalent in the ancient Near East at the time. Consequently, it is the fruit of a long oral and written tradition in which early texts were reinterpreted, glossed, and reorganized before reaching the state in which we read them today. Many have played a role in this process, but the work of all had a common social character; it was ordered to the service of a religious community. The prophets and the Apostles were the spiritual guides of Israel and the early Church, but they did not always write. Others recorded their teaching for posterity or sought to inculcate it by a literary presentation peculiar to themselves (see Lk 1.1–4; 2 Mc 2.27–32; 15.39). By His special providence God guided this entire process, whether it involved action, speech, or writing. Such divine guidance may fittingly be called inspiration, since inspiration is simply any impulse brought to bear upon an intelligent creature from without (see *Summa theologiae* 1a2ae, 68.1).

Human Authors as God's Instruments. The inspiration by which God moves his free creatures is distinguished according to the various effects produced. Biblical inspiration produces a book of which God is the author. In order to provide the Church with Sacred Scripture, the Holy Spirit elevated all the human activity required for its production in such a way that the books produced were entirely the work of God, the principal cause, and entirely the work of the human authors as instrumental causes (*Contra gentiles* 3.70). The notion of an instrumental cause is a fruitful one, provided it is not applied too rigidly to the inspired authors. St. Thomas developed the notion in treating the Sacraments (*Summa theologiae* 3a, 62.1 ad 2). An instrument, such as a saw or a trumpet, cannot produce any effect unless it is used by a carpenter or a musician. When so used, it produces an effect proper to its own nature; a saw is designed to cut wood, a trumpet to make music. The effect, however, surpasses the proper causality of the instrument even though the latter receives and conditions the action of the principal agent.

On occasion St. Thomas spoke of the prophet or sacred writer as an instrument (e.g., *Summa theologiae* 2a2ae, 173.4; 172.4 ad 1; In Heb. 11.1.7; Quodl. 7.6.1 ad 5). These, however, were free instruments and responsible agents. They understood what they had to speak or write and went about their work as conscious and free authors, working according to the methods proper to their own culture. Their work surpasses their human powers only insofar as it has divine authority and efficacy, and insofar as they may not have fully understood all that God intended in the events of which they treated and in the

words they used. They are at the same time true authors in their own right, even though they act only when moved by the Holy Spirit. Only in this wider sense (see De ver. 24.1 ad 5) may we speak of the sacred writers as instruments of the Holy Spirit. It is not necessary that they be conscious of this divine activity, but it seems fitting that they be consciously aware of undertaking a work of religious significance for the people of God. The manner in which God efficaciously moves a free agent, respecting his liberty and proper mode of action, is treated in the theology of GRACE.

The intellect plays a central role in any truly human work. St. Thomas's study of prophetic revelation (*Summa theologiae* 2a2ae, 171–174) contains valuable principles for Biblical inspiration when wisely and prudently applied. By the natural light of the human intellect a man judges the ideas or species that have been received through the channels of the senses, the imagination, and the agent intellect. In prophetic revelation God may disclose new ideas or species to the mind of the prophet by direct action upon the senses or the imagination, or by reordering existing ideas or species in an original way, or by direct action upon the intellect. When such action is accompanied by an infusion of the divine light, thereby ensuring the truth of the human judgment, one may speak of revelation in the strict sense; for God has disclosed to men truths that surpass their natural powers of reason or which they are naturally unable to attain in their peculiar circumstances. But God may also be satisfied to fortify the judgment of the prophet concerning truths that he has acquired in a normal human manner from tradition, instruction, experience, or investigation. St. Thomas considered this case as an imperfect mode of prophetic revelation (*Summa theologiae* 2a2ae, 173.2; 175.2 ad 4); some writers prefer to call it inspiration without revelation. The important consequence of this distinction is the realization that everything in Sacred Scripture need not be directly revealed by God, but everything in Scripture is inspired inasmuch as the judgment of the sacred writers is always fortified with the divine light. [*See* REVELATION, CONCEPT OF (IN THE BIBLE)].

St. Thomas was interested primarily in the communication of divine truth to the prophet's intellect and in the action of God upon his speculative judgments. To communicate this truth to others in speech or writing necessitates many practical judgments if the message is to be suitably presented and to achieve the desired result in the audience for which it is intended. A speaker or writer does not merely instruct the intellect; he may also want to act upon the emotions and move the will to conviction, repentance, enthusiasm, or action (see 2 Tm 3.15–16). These practical judgments also benefit from the charism of inspiration, but now the proper effect of inspiration is to assure the most suitable execution of the desired purpose in view of the peculiar circumstances of both the author and his audience. Formal truth and error are no longer at stake, for these are the concern only of the speculative judgment. Hence, in order to evaluate the truth of Scripture, one must consider the purpose of the whole work, the specific intention of the author concerned, and his method of composition. One must allow for the total psychology of human authors in the ancient Near East. If God has chosen to speak to us through such instruments, His intention can be discovered only by the investigating of the intentions of these human authors. In his encyclical *Divino afflante Spiritu* (1943) Pius XII invited Catholic exegetes to this study (*Enchiridion biblicum* 557–560).

Analogous Notion of Inspiration. Biblical inspiration, however, is not restricted to the illumination of the intellect; it elevates all the faculties of the sacred authors for the limited work they have to perform. Such an analogous notion of inspiration is supple enough to embrace all those who contributed in any way to giving the Bible in its present form to the Church. It may also be extended to the Septuagint translators, if it can be established that their work positively contributed to the progress of revelation [see P. Auvray, "Comment se pose le probléme de l'inspiration des Septante," *Revue biblique* 59 (1952) 321–336]. The suppleness of this concept may also resolve the problem of verbal inspiration. No one today would hold that God dictated the words of Scripture in an audible manner to the ear of the sacred writer. Cardinal Franzelin taught that God could be the author of Sacred Scripture provided He inspired all the ideas, but the choice of words could be left to the human authors. This theory applied a human notion of authorship univocally to God and violated the psychological integrity of the human instrument; for in man ideas are inseparable from the words in which they are expressed. A proper application of the notion of an instrument to a free agent and the analogous notion of inspiration suffice to explain how God may be considered responsible even for the words without violating the personal integrity and human freedom of the instruments He uses. In this way God may truly, though analogously, be called the author of the entire Bible.

Second Vatican Council. The Second Vatican Council while drafting the text of its *Dogmatic Constitution on Divine Revelation* (*Dei Verbum*) spent a good deal of time on the subject of inspiration. The Constitution's third chapter, "The Divine Inspiration and the Interpretation of Sacred Scripture," was clearly intended to reaffirm the Church's traditional position. It cited the classic texts, taking special care to include 2 Tm 3:16–17 so that there could be no mistake as to how the council fathers understood biblical inspiration and what they considered its purpose to be. The *Catechism of the Catholic Church*, quoting the third chapter of the Constitution verbatim and at length, recapitulates the Church's traditional teaching:

> Since therefore all that the inspired authors or sacred writers affirm should be regarded as affirmed by the Holy Spirit, we must acknowledge that the books of Scripture firmly, faithfully, and without error teach that truth which God, for the sake of our salvation, wished to see confided to the Sacred Scriptures (par. 107).

This quotation from the Constitution on Divine Revelation corresponds to the view of Christians of many traditions who regard 2 Tm 3:16–17 and 2 Pt 1:19–21 as the key texts in providing a correct understanding of biblical inspiration.

Bibliography: G. COURTADE, *Dictionnaire de la Bible*, suppl. ed. L. PIROT et. al. 4:482–559, with bibliog. **Historical.** G. M. PERRELLA, "La nozione dell'ispirazione scritturale secondo i primitivi documenti cristiani," *Angelicum* 20 (1943) 32–52. A. BEA, "Deus auctor sacrae scripturae: Herkunft und Bedeutung der Formel," *Angelicum* 20 (1943) 16–31. N. I. WEYNS, "De notione inspirationis biblicae iuxta Concilium Vaticanum," ibid. 30 (1953) 315–336. **Theological.** P. SYNAVE and P. BENOIT, Prophecy and Inspiration, tr. A. DULLES and T. L. SHERIDAN (New York 1961). A. ROBERT and A. TRICOT, *Guide to the Bible*, tr. E. P. ARBEZ and M. P. MCGUIRE 1:9–59. P. BENOIT, "Les Analogies de l'inspiration," *Sacra Pagina*, ed. J. COPPENS et al., 2 v. (Gembleux 1959) 1:86–99. "Révélation et inspiration," *Revue biblique* 70 (1963) 321–370. A. DESROCHES, *Jugement pratique et jugement spéculatif chez l'écrivain inspiré* (Ottawa 1958). J. T. FORESTELL, "The Limitation of Inerrancy," *The Catholic Biblical Quarterly* 20 (1958) 9–18. R. A. F. MACKENZIE, "Some Problems in the Field of Inspiration," ibid. 1–8. J. L. MCKENZIE, "The Social Character of Inspiration," ibid. 24 (1962) 115–124. K. RAHNER, *Inspiration in the Bible*, tr. C. H. HENKEY (Quaestiones disputatae 1; New York 1961). D. M. STANLEY, "The Concept of Biblical Inspiration," *Catholic Theological Society of America. Proceedings* 13 (1958) 65–95. P. GRELOT, "Études sur la théologie du Livre Saint," *Nouvelle revue théologique* 85 (1963) 785–806, 897–925; "L'inspiration scripturaire," *Recherches de science religieuse* 51 (1963) 337–382. D. M. BEEGLE, *The Inspiration of Scripture* (Philadelphia 1963). P. J. ACHTEMEIER, *The Inspiration of Scripture: Problems and Proposals* (Philadelphia, 1980). R. F. COLLINS, "Inspiration" in *The New Jerusalem Biblical Commentary*, (Englewood Cliffs, NJ: Prentice Hall, 1990), pp.1023–1033.

[J. T. FORESTELL/EDS]

INSTANT

Instant, the indivisible formal factor in TIME that measures SUBSTANTIAL change. The partless instant continues and divides the parts of time; were it divisible into sub-instants, no distinction could be made between past and future. Moreover, because no two instants can be continuous or contiguous, a stretch of time must intervene between them. Yet the instant is in and of time: in time, as its term and measure; of time, since pluralized instants furnish its number. Furthermore, only the instant can measure substantial change. If substantial change occurred in a span of time, either primary matter devoid of act would actually exist for an interval, or an individual would be both dead and alive at one and the same time. At the limiting instant a thing is neither dying nor living—it has ceased to exist. Yet the instant of corruption is the starting-point for a new existent, since primary matter is never unactualized (*see* MATTER AND FORM). In other words, there is no last instant of LIFE, and there is no next instant following the instant of DEATH, for between any two instants another instant is discernible. Thus as the limit of time, the instant measures substantial change, for a durationless change demands the durationless point of time.

[J. M. QUINN]

INSTINCT

Descriptive Analysis. The term instinct has been used, both in the scholastic philosophical tradition and by some scientific students of animal behavior, to refer to certain complex animal behavior patterns, e.g., hunting, nest building, and the tending of offspring. In these and similar examples, the complexity of the action is thought to exceed that of a direct stimulus-response or sensation-appetition sequence, but to fall short of intelligent or rational foresight and planning. Rough criteria are as follows: instinctive behavior involves the entire organism, not merely an isolated receptor-effector mechanism; it is exhibited with some uniformity by all members of a species (or specific subgroup, e.g., worker bees), and its appearance may be distinctive of the species or group; its performance depends on the appropriate physical maturation, but does not require mimicry, trial-and-error activities, or other forms of learning. Such behavior is almost always adaptive, i.e., of positive advantage to the survival of the individual or its species.

Although these criteria have a rough value, their scientific precision and significance have been seriously questioned. To say that certain behavior patterns are unlearned, species-specific, and adaptive does not distinguish them from the more inclusive metabolic processes. To say that a behavior pattern is innate is to ignore the biological theory that genes, not characters, are transmitted from one generation to the next. The development of an organism's anatomic, metabolic, and behavioral traits involves the interaction of its genetic constitution and its environment; consequently, the distinction of innate and learned behavior patterns is softened to the point that some authors speak of genetically controlled propensities

to learn rather than of innate behavior patterns. The prominent borderline phenomenon of "imprinting" is of similar significance. Imprinting is the tendency, e.g., of young birds, for a short, definite interval after hatching, to accept and follow a diverse variety of parent substitutes. Such performances are on the border between learning processes more extended in time and purely innate behavior.

Relation to *Vis Aestimativa*. In the philosophy of Saint THOMAS AQUINAS, the ESTIMATIVE POWER (*vis aestimativa*) is one of four interior sensory powers necessary for the life of a perfect animal. The others are the IMAGINATION, the CENTRAL SENSE, and the memory. Although references such as those to a "perfect" animal seem to give this position a deductive or rationalist tone, relevant factual materials are available for its inductive support: (1) The external sensation of at least some animals is quite like that of men. (2) Animals act with respect to objects that are neither gratifying nor unpleasant to the external senses, e.g., sight, touch, and smell. Birds are said to choose nesting materials that, though not attractive to sight or touch, are appropriate for nest construction, so that the choice serves the survival of that species of birds. (3) Such activities, as exhibited by the members of a particular species, exhibit a degree of uniformity. (4) But they also exhibit some plasticity or variability and are not altogether stereotyped. Consequently, what needs explanation is the order or pattern of the sequence of actions and not any mechanical repetition of identical behavioral elements. (5) The performance of these activities is likely to vary with the seasons and with the organic condition of the animal; it is not an automatic response to an external stimulus.

The interpretive principles employed in the analysis of these data include the following theses: (1) One knows, by observation and analogy, that such behavior flows from KNOWLEDGE and APPETITE. (2) In cases in which such behavior cannot be explained by the knowledge gained through the external senses, one may rightly infer the appropriate interior sense. (*See* SENSES.)

The various data are consequently explained by the existence of a distinct internal sense power (the estimative) capable of apprehending the concrete usefulness of particular sequences of actions. The power is said to be innately determined (diversely within various species) to recognize certain organism-environment groupings as desirable and others as undesirable. Inasmuch as the proper object of this sense power is the total organism-environment grouping, both plasticity and uniformity are accounted for. Similarly included within this proper object is the contemporary state of the organism itself, so that the dependence of instinctive activity upon seasonal and individual variations in metabolic state also is explained.

Critical Evaluation. The explanatory value of such statements as "the bird returned to its nest because of its homing instinct" and "the sheep flees the wolf because its estimative power is innately determined to recognize that particular organism-environment grouping as undesirable" have been called into question by students of scientific methodology. One important objection is that such explanations are really uninformative tautologies, i.e., they simply reformulate the data they pretend to explain. What is a homing instinct? If the philosopher can give no other answer than "the power by which the bird returns to its nest," the criticism seems accurate.

Another way of putting this criticism is to ask for some additional means of confirming the presence of a "homing instinct," or an "estimative power." Philosophers who hold a generally Thomistic position tend to reply with a negative argument, viz, one showing that instinctive behavior cannot be explained in terms of tropisms or reflexes and thus must be accounted for by the estimative power or some analogue for it. The formal requirements for an argument of this sort are impressive; e.g., it must be shown that the alternatives considered exhaust all possible alternatives. Argumentative rigor of this level has not actually been sought in past discussions of this topic. However, a number of interesting points have been made in illustration of weaknesses of any "mechanistic" explanation of animal behavior: (1) Reflex behavior lacks spontaneity or autonomy; it is controlled by outside stimuli. Reflex action exhibits a mechanical, off-on, relation to outside stimulation, rather than the dependence on internal events characteristic of instinctive behavior. (2) Reflex action is stereotyped or invariable in form, and so incapable of explaining the adaptive plasticity of instinctive behavior. Reflex behavior shows no tendency to improve with repeated performance as do many forms of animal behavior. From this sort of evidence it is argued that animal behavior cannot be explained in terms of a concatenation of neuromuscular reflexes and therefore must be explained in terms of some cognitive or conscious awareness of the form and purpose of the animal's activity, by the animal itself.

This last sort of argument seems to assume, however, that mechanistic theories are themselves invariable in form. In the third quarter of the 20th century, neurologists are not limited to summing the consequences of simple reflex acts, but have demonstrated a variety of facilitating, inhibiting, and correlating neural mechanisms whose activities, in ensemble, are not stereotyped and stimulus bound. At the same time, mechanism of a rigid and parochial sort is nowhere regarded as a philosophically viable explanation of animal behavior. Empiricist schools, which may be the nearest living relatives of past mechanist schools, are in fact critical of mechanism's pretensions completely and dogmatically to solve the problems of animal behavior.

Perhaps the most commendable aspect of the Thomistic explanation of instinctive activity in terms of the functioning of an estimative power is its emphasis on the really novel complexity of the phenomena in question. Instinctive behavior is not a topic on which one expects much illumination from any form of MONISM or exaggerated DUALISM. It is not a topic that is emphasized in the philosophies of atomists or Cartesians. Its appearance among the problems considered in the Thomistic theory of knowledge is a tribute to the complexity and richness of this theory, which permits cross-level, nuanced analyses where simple reductionist alternatives would seem to ignore relevant detail and significant form.

See Also: INTELLIGENCE.

Bibliography: R. G. BUSNEL, ed., *Acoustic Behavior of Animals* (New York 1963). J. F. DONCEEL, *Philosophical Psychology* (2d ed. New York 1961). J. J. DREHER and W. E. EVANS, "Cetacean Communication" in *Marine Bio-Acoustics,* ed. W. N. TAVOLGA (New York 1964). G. P. KLUBERTANZ, *The Discursive Power* (Saint Louis 1952). W. KÖHLER, *The Mentality of Apes,* tr. E. WINTER from 2d ed. (New York 1926; repr. 1959). A. PORTMANN, *Animals as Social Beings,* tr. O. COBURN (New York 1961). A. ROE and G. G. SIMPSON, eds., *Behavior and Evolution* (New Haven 1958). E. WASMANN, *Instinct and Intelligence in the Animal Kingdom,* tr. from 2d. ed. (Saint Louis 1903).

[A. E. MANIER]

INSTITUTES OF CALVIN

The major theological treatise of John CALVIN and the most important exposition of the doctrines of early Protestantism, the first draft of which appeared in 1536 and the final, definitive form in 1559. Calvin called his *Institutes of the Christian Religion* "a summary of the principal truths of the Christian religion." The original version, written in Latin in 1534 or early 1535 (*Institutio religionis Christianae*), was constantly revised and enlarged during Calvin's life. Latin editions appeared in 1539, 1543, 1550, and 1559 and French translations by Calvin were published in 1541, 1545, 1551, and 1560. The first printing of the *Institutes* was done in March 1536 at Basel, where Calvin had taken refuge after his flight from France. Prefaced by a dedicatory letter to Francis I, King of France, whom Calvin bids to respect the new doctrines, it consists of six chapters and follows the order of Martin Luther's *Der grosse Catechismus* (1529). The first four chapters treat the Ten Commandments, the Creed, the Lord's Prayer, and the Sacraments of Baptism and the Eucharist. The fifth chapter discusses and rejects the other Sacraments, and the sixth chapter deals with Christian liberty.

The second edition, published in Strassburg in 1539, during Calvin's temporary banishment from Geneva, is three times as large and has more coherent and systematic organization. It contains an extended statement of his doctrine of predestination, a tenet whose elaboration was influenced by the Strassburg reformer Martin BUCER. This edition, translated by Calvin into French and published in Geneva in 1541, is an important landmark in French literary style as well as French religious thought. The final revision of 1559, followed by a French translation in 1560, is five times the size of the original draft, with 80 chapters, divided into four books. It is the expression of Calvin's mature Biblical theology presented under four main headings (corresponding to the four books): (1) the knowledge of God the Creator, (2) the knowledge of God the Redeemer in Christ, (3) the way in which we receive the grace of Christ, (4) the external means or aids. The famous statement on eternal election, or predestination, is found in bk. 3, ch. 21.

The *Institutes* remains a theological masterpiece, the *summa* of Reformed Protestantism and the most important single work of the Reformers. The final edition was soon translated into most of the languages of Europe. A Dutch version appeared in 1560, the first English translation in 1561, and a German version at Heidelberg in 1572. (*See* CALVINISM; PREDESTINATION.)

Bibliography: J. CALVIN, *Institutes of the Christian Religion,* ed. J. T. MCNEILL, tr. F. L. BATTLES, 2 v. (Philadelphia 1960), the best English ed.; *Ioannis Calvini opera selecta,* ed. P. BARTH and W. NIESEL, 5 v. (Munich 1926–36), contains critical eds. of the 1536 and 1559 Latin text.

[J. C. OLIN]

INSTRUMENTAL CAUSALITY

Instrumental causality in the wide acceptation of the term signifies any type of causal subordination. More properly it applies to a special type of efficient cause that is itself moved and elevated by the power of a principal efficient cause to produce an effect proportionate to the nature and power of the principal cause. This article considers briefly the various types of instrument to which this causality is ascribed and then examines the notion of efficient instrumentality, the nature of instrumental power, and the proper action of the instrument. It concludes with a discussion of an important application of instrumental causality in the area of sacramental theology and a brief summary.

Kinds of Instrument. In a general way instrumental causality can be applied to any series of causes wherein one is subordinated to another. This usage includes the subordination that exists between the motion of God as primary principal cause and man as secondary principal cause in human actions. Although a secondary principal cause must be moved from first to second act in order to operate, the motion of God is only a CONDITION for the operation of man and not its formal constitutive, as it is in the stricter meaning of instrumental causality.

In a more limited sense, the term instrumental cause is applied to three particular types of instrumental causality, designated as moral, logical, and efficient.

Moral Instrument. A moral instrument is whatever moves a principal efficient cause by way of inducement, as a consciously sought END. The classical example of such causality is paper currency, which, though it has no intrinsic value itself, has, by the decree of the treasury, an extrinsic value. This value, itself presupposed to any financial transaction, gives the currency the status of an instrumental cause.

Logical Instrument. The logical instrument is the SIGN, and, as such, leads the one observing it to a knowledge of the object for which the sign stands, as in the case of a traffic signal. The sign consequently exercises the same type of causality as any other knowable object, namely, that of an extrinsic formal cause.

Efficient Instrument. An efficient instrument is that from which an effect flows by reason of the subordination of the instrument to a principal efficient cause, to which the instrument ministers and by which it is moved. An example would be the use of a pencil to write. Since this type of instrument exercises its ministerial activity through activity or motion, it alone can be properly termed an efficient instrument.

Notion of Efficient Instrumentality. An efficient instrument attains an effect beyond its own power. Whether the instrumental cause attains to the ultimate perfection of the form produced by the principal agent, or only disposes the appropriate matter for the reception of the form, the efficient instrument acts beyond its proper power. If the instrument did not attain an effect beyond this power, the effect could be attributed to the instrument as to a principal cause, and movement from another cause would not be required to produce the effect.

Yet this aspect of instrumentality does not furnish an adequate basis for distinguishing an instrumental cause from a principal cause. There are cases where the principal agent attains an effect beyond its proper nature without being an efficient instrument. Man, for example, is the principal agent in the production of supernatural acts, and yet these acts proceed from divinely infused virtues. The fact that an instrument attains an effect superior to its own nature, while a necessary condition of true instrumentality, is not its essential characteristic.

To understand the formal constitutive of efficient instrumentality, one must focus on the fact that an instrument, properly so called, performs a function to which it is directed by the principal cause while itself not possessing the permanent or proper power to perform that function. For this reason an instrument is most accurately defined as an agent that is moved and elevated by the action of the principal efficient cause to produce an effect that is proper to the nature and power of the principal cause. The formal aspect of instrumental causality consists in its operating precisely as moved by the principal agent. It is this dependence of the instrument on the principal cause that is emphasized in the definition proposed by St. THOMAS AQUINAS: "The precise formality of an instrument, insofar as it is an instrument, is that it moves precisely as already moved" (*C. gent.* 2.21).

Instrumental Power. From this concept of instrumental causality it follows that the instrument receives, after the manner of a MOTION, a power derived from the principal cause. This transiently received power enables the instrument to attain the effect of the principal cause, which itself exceeds, of course, the natural power of the instrument.

The instrumental power received from the principal agent is a transitory entity that begins and ends with the action for which it is given, and is received intrinsically by the instrument it perfects. Being thus intrinsically received, the power affects the nature of the instrument; and so it is said to be a physical entity, as opposed to a moral entity that acts from without. Further, such a physical power, being essentially a transitory and passing assistance communicated to the instrument by the principal cause to effect an action, is called a motion; since it is presupposed to the action of the instrument, it is also called a premotion (*see* PREMOTION, PHYSICAL).

The general doctrine of Thomists is that the ability of the instrument to be used by a principal efficient cause is a passive obediential POTENCY, i.e., that it does not consist in a positive ordination of the instrument to the effect of the principal cause, but only in a nonrepugnance to its use by the principal cause. As opposed to this, F. Suárez teaches (*Disp. meta.* 42.4.9) that there is an active obediential potency in such an instrument. This active potency places the instrument in first act with respect to the effect of a principal agent, and does so in such a way that the instrument remains in potency to the effect whether it is in use or not.

For true instrumental subordination it is necessary that the instrumental activity depend upon the activity of the principal cause, and that the action of the principal cause be received intrinsically into the instrument and so influence its action from within. In contradistinction to coordinated causes, each of which is responsible for part of the effect, both the principal and instrumental cause are responsible for the entire effect.

Proper Action of the Instrument. It is essential also that the instrument retain its proper power in its subordination to the principal cause, for otherwise it would cease to be an instrument, and become a mere medium for the passage of the power of the principal cause. Creatures use instruments because they need their help. A sculptor is incapable of producing a statue in marble unless he employs instruments that assist him in overcoming the resistant quality of the marble. "Because an instrument is not sought for its own sake but for the sake of the end, it is a better instrument not for being larger, but for being more adapted to the end" (St. Thomas, ST 2a3ae, 188.7 ad 1). Even in cases where God uses an instrument to produce a supernatural effect, as in the Sacraments, the instrument has its own proper activity. All that is required of the instrument used by God is that it limit in some way His mode of operation. God adapts His activity to the operation of the created instrument for the production of an effect, while not being limited, in attaining that effect, by the particular form of the instrument. He can use any instrument to attain any effect, so long as this use does not involve a contradiction.

The proper action of the instrumental form produces a MODE in the effect produced. An efficient instrument employed by a created agent limits the efficiency of such an agent to the proper operation of the instrumental form. An artist cannot produce violin music on a piano. In receiving the influx of the principal agent, the instrument exercises a determining causality upon the principal agent, placing a commensuration to its own form in the power it receives from the agent. The modification produced necessarily varies according to the form of the instrument. Since the mode reflects such modifications placed on the principal efficient cause, different instruments produce different modes in the ensuing effects, and these modes are commensurate with the corresponding instrumental forms.

Instrumental Causality in Theology. This notion of instrumental causality has a particular application in the doctrine of theologians who attribute a true instrumentality to the sacred humanity of Christ and to the Sacraments. The basic problem posed by those objecting to the predication of true efficient instrumentality in these cases is one of explaining how a supernatural power can inhere in a corporeal instrument. Theologians who hold for true instrumentality reply that this objection can be answered in terms of the transient nature of the instrumental power. To understand transient to mean merely of short duration is, for them, to consider only an accidental consideration; the power should rather be conceived as transient and incomplete by reason of the special task it accomplishes. A permanent and complete power constitutes a subject as a principal agent, whereas a transient and incomplete power subordinates one subject to another, the one serving the other in the attainment of its effect. Such a transient power, even though ordained to a supernatural effect, can be subjected in a corporeal instrument, not absolutely, but only insofar as that instrument is capable of being used by a spiritual power for the attainment of a spiritual effect.

Created instruments used by God in the production of supernatural effects, while diversifying the mode of His action through their proper operations and thus fulfilling the essential conditions for true efficient instrumentality, are not capable of producing in the supernatural effect any mode that is commensurate to their natural form. God is not limited by their proper operation, and furthermore there is no proportion between the natural form of such an instrument and the effect produced through its ministerial activity. If, then, there is to be an instrument that introduces a mode in a supernatural effect, the form of that instrument must be proportioned to the effect. Since the supernatural effect can be produced only by a supernatural agent, the form of the instrument proportioned to such an effect must likewise be received from a supernatural agent. And if the created instrument must modify not only the divine activity by its proper operation, but also the divine power communicated to it to make the effect produced commensurate with the signification imposed by the divine agent, it is necessary that the form of the instrument itself be supernatural.

It is in this way, according to many theologians, that the Sacraments differ from other forms of divine activity. In confecting the sacramental artifact, Christ gave these unique instruments a supernatural signification that bears a true proportion to the effect produced through their instrumentality. And in employing various Sacraments to sanctify men, God has freely limited His power to that signification.

Summary. An instrument is thus an efficient cause that is moved and elevated by the power of the principal agent to produce an effect proper to the power of the principal cause. It differs from the principal cause in that its effect is of an order higher than itself; that it operates by the power of another. According to Thomistic doctrine the instrumental power is a transient physical premotion. Through its proper operation an instrument used by a created principal cause produces in the effect some modality commensurate to this operation. While creatural instruments require a proper action that is accommodated to the effect produced, this is not so when God uses instruments for certain effects. Only when such instruments have a supernatural form do they produce in the effect a modality that is proper to the instrument itself.

See Also: CAUSALITY; CAUSALITY, DIVINE; EFFICIENT CAUSALITY; INSPIRATION, BIBLICAL.

Bibliography: R. P. PHILLIPS, *Modern Thomistic Philosophy,* 2 v. (Westminster, Md. 1934; reprint 1946). R. R. MASTERSON, "Sacramental Graces: Modes of Sanctifying Grace," *Thomist* 18 (1955) 311–372. J. GREDT, *Elementa philosophiae Aristotelico-Thomisticae,* ed. E. ZENZEN, 2 v. (13th ed. Freiburg 1961). F. X. MARQUART, *Elementa philosophiae,* 3 v. in 4 (Paris 1937–38). JOHN OF ST. THOMAS, *Cursus philosophicus thomisticus,* ed. B. REISER, 3 v. (Turin 1930–37).

[R. R. MASTERSON]

INSTRUMENTALISM

Instrumentalism is the name given to the pragmatic philosophy of John DEWEY. In his book *The Quest for Certainty* (New York 1929) Dewey defines his system thus: "the essence of pragmatic instrumentalism is to conceive of *both* knowledge and practice as means of making goods—excellencies of all kinds—secure in experienced existence" (37 n.). The instrumental character of knowledge is clearly indicated in Dewey's earlier work *How We Think* (Boston 1910), where he teaches that thinking is stimulated by a problem presented to a man by his environment. In Dewey's terms, an indeterminate situation becomes problematic and creates a search for some solution that will solve the problem and resolve the situation. The problematic situation instills a "felt need" into the troubled human being. As a result hypothetical solutions are proposed and tested.

By reflective intelligence the individual tries to search for solutions that have worked in the past and may work in the present. According to Dewey, one of the advantages of intellectual knowledge is that solutions proposed in the past may be applied to a present problem, and either be improved upon or rejected before being tried out in actual experience. On this account his system is sometimes called experimentalism. It is true that he considered the scientific method to be a paradigm for philosophers. He did not, however, hold that any inquiry should be judged by being stretched on the Procrustean bed of the positive sciences.

Dewey is obviously concerned with the adaptability of traditional solutions to current problems. He warns, however, that so far as any problem is really new it cannot be seen as a mere repetition of something previous.

Therefore the old solution must be adjusted to meet the demands of the new situation. Traditional theory is then always in tension with precisely those novel problems that were not known as problems when it itself was being formed. Dewey recognizes that the only intellectual equipment available for solving a new problem is knowledge already possessed, and he is convinced that one must make the most of the past solution in the present need. But to the extent that the past solution is inadequate it must be modified. One must, therefore, be always ready to add new truths to the tradition already possessed.

An important feature of Dewey's instrumentalism is his conviction of the reality of novelty and his appreciation of the risks involved in the interaction of an organism with its environment. This dialectic of interaction between developing man and reality in process shows the influence of G. W. F. HEGEL. Reflective intelligence seeks to avoid the risks or gain the rewards in the indeterminate situation. Out of the opposition of the felt need and the reflection of the thinker comes a new solution.

Another aspect of Dewey's instrumentalism is his theory of the "warranted assertion." Whereas William JAMES is content to grant truth to assertions that, when acted upon, make a difference to the individual, Dewey demands that a true statement be warranted by evidence that can be "public" in some suitable way. He is more interested in the problems of men than in those of any one man. In his instrumentalism he seems to focus on human problems in economics, art, ethics, education, and politics, all of which have a direct urgency and relevance for the present situation.

Dewey's instrumentalism is a useful account of practical knowledge. Like the other pragmatists, he overstresses the role of practical knowledge in human living and leaves little room for contemplation. As a system of practical philosophy his instrumentalism has far greater coherence than that of James, though it leaves room for less objectivity than the pragmaticism of Peirce.

See Also: PRAGMATISM; NATURALISM.

Bibliography: P. A. SCHILPP, ed., *The Philosophy of John Dewey* (Evanston 1939). M. G. WHITE, *The Origin of Dewey's Instrumentalism* (New York 1943). N. J. FLECKENSTEIN, *A Critique of John Dewey's Theory of the Nature and the Knowledge of Reality in the Light of the Principles of Thomism* (Washington 1954). J. A. MANN, "The Role of Reflective Intelligence According to the American Pragmatists," *American Catholic Philosophical Association. Proceedings of the Annual Meeting* 35 (1961) 117–124.

[J. A. MANN]

INSULT

Insult, or railing (*convicium*), as a sin refers to an offense, contrary to both charity and commutative justice, against the honor and dignity of another. It is closely related to CONTUMELY, or reviling, and to upbraiding or taunting speech (*improperium*). Many theologians (e.g., Cajetan, Soto, Sylvius) held that these pertain to the same species of sin, since all put dishonor and indignity into social relations that should be ruled by friendship and fairness. As Aquinas noted (*Summa theologiae*, 2a2ae 72.1 ad 3), the terms insult (*convicium*) and upbraiding (*improperium*) are frequently used interchangeably.

Insult may, however, be distinguished from contumely. Contumely refers to words and gestures of reproach for some moral defect involving sinfulness or guilt, whereas insult refers generically to all defects whether they are moral faults or not. To dishonor another by speaking spitefully to him of some physical defect, such as lameness or blindness, would be insult but not contumely. To dishonor him by calling him a drunkard or a thief would be both insult and contumely.

Although of its nature grave because it strikes at the decencies of human association, the sin of insult allows for slightness of matter. Insulting speech for correction or punishment may frequently not be seriously sinful, and allowances have to be made for a sort of insulting humor that is well accepted and may be used sometimes without any moral fault. However, great discretion should be employed when one is using terms that could dishonor another, even if dishonor is not intended.

The intention to dishonor need not always be explicit for the sin of insult. If one sufficiently perceives that his words or actions will have this effect, even though they are prompted by hatred, anger, envy, etc., rather than the deliberate will to dishonor the other, then the sin of insult is present.

The unfair treatment of minority groups frequently involves the sin of insult. The denial of civil rights by public authority can be an offense against distributive justice if it introduces disorder in the equitable sharing of the goods and honors of the community. But the offenses of private citizens against the dignity of someone because of racial differences, national origin, etc., are opposed to commutative justice and to charity as well, for everyone has rights to the honor and signs of respect commonly extended in the community. Since the motive for the offensive conduct is some natural quality (e.g., race, national origin) rather than a moral defect, such an offense would be insult rather than contumely in its narrower sense.

Bibliography: THOMAS AQUINAS, *Summa theologiae*, 2a2ae, 72, esp. art. 1 ad 3. P. PALAZZINI, ed., *Dictionarium morale et canonicum*, v. 1 (Vatican City 1962) 956–961.

[J. HENNESSEY]

INTEGRALISM

This term, which is sometimes used in a broad, vaguely defined sense, refers here to a tendency and also to a movement that arose about the time of the papal condemnation of Modernism (1907). *Intégrisme* developed an organization, secret in many of its operations, in order to carry out PIUS X's recommendations for vigilance against doctrinal deviations. Both the mentality and the methods of the "integral Catholics" were themselves the objects of widespread criticism.

Leo XIII's encyclical AETERNI PATRIS (1879) gave a strong impulse to a Catholic scholarly revival, but conservatives began before long to express alarm at some of the results of this activity. At the International Congress of Catholic Scholars in Brussels (1894) Maurice d' Hulst, a rector of the Institut Catholique in Paris, warned of a tendency among some Catholics who feared that employment of new scientific methods might endanger their faith and who reacted by casting suspicions of heterodoxy on those who differed with their outlook, even in matters that did not involve faith. He urged that scholars not be denounced as long as they were sincerely pursuing scientific knowledge about questions on which the Church had not decided authoritatively. During the controversy in the French Catholic press over AMERICANISM at the close of the 19th century, Abbé Charles Maignen and other conservative theologians attacked men whom they believed to be minimizing Catholic teachings.

Development of Integralism. After the condemnation of Modernism, the integralism that had appeared on occasion as a tendency gained a permanent organization. In his encyclical *Pascendi* (1907), Pius X urged bishops to supervise closely seminary teaching and writings by priests and to establish in each diocese vigilance committees. In 1910 the pope imposed an oath against Modernism (*see* MODERNISM, OATH AGAINST). Vigilance was needed in this tense period, but the type of vigilance exercised by integralists was often excessive and indefensible. In their zeal to defend the faith in all its purity, the integralists caused unnecessarily bitter polemics among Catholics, injured the reputations of orthodox Catholic scholars, and hampered the progress of Catholic scholarship.

Among the best-known integralists was the Italian priest and publicist Umberto BENIGNI, who in 1909 founded the sodalitium pianum, the principal organization engaged in anti-Modernist activities throughout Europe. The Sodalitium, or Sapinière, adopted the Modernist practices of using secrecy, pseudonyms, and codes. In France, which was the chief center of Modernism, the Sapinière was particularly strong. It numbered among its most eager workers priests who had led the op-

position to Americanism, such as Maignen, Canon H. Delassus, and two former Jesuits, Bernard Gaudeau, who edited *La Foi Catholique* in Toulouse, and J. Fontaine, his collaborator. Other priests who cooperated with Benigni were Paul Boulin, who edited *Vigie* under the pseudonym Roger Duguet; Monsignors Jouin and Delmont, Jacques Rocafort; the Eudist Father Le Doré; the Capuchin Father Pie de Langogne; and the Assumptionist Fathers Salvien and Ricard. Active in Rome was the Capuchin Father Le Floch, who was superior of the French seminary in Rome and a consultor of several Roman congregations. He, as well as other French integralists, supported ACTION FRANÇAISE, which used these zealots for political purposes. Emmanuel Barbier, a skillful controversialist, was one of the more accomplished theologians in this group that numbered few outstanding theologians. After leaving the Jesuits, Barbier published two attacks on Leo XIII's policies in France that were placed on the Index in 1908. As an integralist he was one of the most active in denunciations. Cardinal BILLOT was not an integralist, but he used his influence in Rome to help this group. Cardinal MERRY DEL VAL, the conservative secretary of state, was an acquaintance of Benigni. Pius X was aware of the existence of the Sodalitium but did not know the full extent of its operations or methods.

Because of the secrecy surrounding the Sodalitium, much remains unknown concerning its membership, aims, and methods. Great resentment was roused by its use of anonymous attacks on specific persons and by its common tactic of basing accusations on extracts from writings or talks, sometimes cited inaccurately or out of context to give them an unorthodox significance. Proponents of Catholic liberalism, social Catholicism, Christian democracy, and ecumenism were among those upon whom aspersions of heresy were cast. Accusations were disseminated through a European network of Catholic newspapers and periodicals to bring them to the attention of ecclesiastical authorities. Although these accusations did not always result in condemnations, they did envelop many distinguished scholars in an atmosphere of suspicion.

Among the objects of integralist attacks in France were Cardinal AMETTE of Paris; Archbishop MIGNOT, who had been deceived by LOISY; Bishop Chapon of Nice; Bishop Dadolle of Dijon; and Bishop du Vauroux of Agen. BAUDRILLART, GOYAU, De GRANDMAISON, LAGRANGE, and SERTILLANGES were among the most prominent scholars whose orthodoxy was attacked. Integralist pressures were believed responsible for the condemnation of Louis DUCHESNE's *Histoire ancienne de l'Église* (3 v. 1906–10), which was placed on the Index (Jan. 22, 1912) after the appearance of its Italian translation. The resignations of Ferdinand Prat in 1907 from an enlarged

Pontifical Biblical Commission and of Pierre BATIFFOL in 1908 as rector of the Institut Catholique of Toulouse were credited also to integralist influences. The same forces assailed the Catholic leaders in social reform, Léon HARMEL and Albert de Mun, Semaines Sociales de France and similar associations, Catholic youth organizations, and the Jesuit periodicals *Études* and *Action Populaire.*

Outside of France, Cardinals Ferrari of Milan, MERCIER of Mechelin, PIFFL of Vienna, and Von Rossum of the Roman Curia were denounced, as were many bishops. The Dominicans of the University of Fribourg, Switzerland, and some Jesuits connected with the periodicals *La Civiltà Cattolica* and *Stimmen aus Maria Laach* (later *Stimmen der Zeit*) suffered bitter denunciations. In Germany much of the integralist animosity was aimed at the section of the CENTER PARTY that favored social reforms.

Reaction against Integralism. Protests against the integralists were made during Pius X's pontificate, notably by Cardinal Ferrari and Bishop Cazzani in Italy and by *Stimmen aus Maria Laach* and the *Kölnische Volkszeitung* in Germany. In 1914 De Grandmaison deplored in *Études* (138:5–25, 272–273, 494–497) the integralist custom of dismissing their critics as "enemies of God, hypocrites, and false brethren" and of attempting to discredit loyal Catholics by associating them with known Modernists. After Pius X's death, Mignot addressed to the papal secretary of state a memoir on the integralist campaign in which he warned against hidden powers that acted irresponsibly, clandestinely, calumniously, and without hierarchical supervision. Mignot deplored the resultant disaffection, discouragement, and even retirement from intellectual pursuits of Catholic scholars. Meanwhile Cardinal Merry del Val had caused Benigni's *La Correspondance de Rome* to be suppressed. Benedict XV's first encyclical, *Ad beatissimi Apostolorum* (Nov. 1, 1914), pleaded for an end to dissensions among Catholics. It declared that in matters that the Church left open to discussion, moderation should reign and not unbased suspicions about the orthodoxy of opponents. The pope also pointed out that it was neither right nor fitting for Catholic writers to usurp the functions of the ecclesiastical magisterium. The pope further noted that the term "Catholic" does not require the qualification integral, but he did not mention the integralists specifically. The Sodalitium Pianum disbanded for a while after Pius X's death, but then it renewed its operations until in 1921 the Holy See suppressed it permanently.

Integralism was intellectually and tactically dangerous to the Church. It threatened to substitute routine for genuine tradition and to hamper the development of Catholic thought by refusing to disengage living tradi-

tions from attitudes or procedures dictated by the needs of the moment. With their connections in high ecclesiastical circles, the integralists attempted to safeguard Catholics by enclosing them in a ghetto inaccessible to the outside world, where a few would make all decisions and the mass of the faithful would do no more than comply with them.

Organized integralism disappeared, possibly not completely, with the dissolution of the Sodalitium, but the integralist mentality still exists.

Bibliography: N. FONTAINE, *Saint-Siège: Action française et catholiques intégraux* (Paris 1928). J. BRUGERETTE, *Le Prêtre français et la société contemporaine,* 3 v. (Paris 1933–38). E. SUHARD, *Growth or Decline? The Church Today,* tr. from Fr. by J. A. CORBETT (South Bend, Ind. 1948). A. DANSETTE, *Religious History of Modern France,* tr. J. DINGLE, 2 v. (New York 1961), v. 2. Y. M. J. CONGAR, *Vraie et fausse réforme dans l'Église* (Paris 1950). "Qu'est-ce que l'Intégrisme?," *La Vie intellectuelle et la revue des jeunes* 24 (1952) 136–152. R. DULAC, "Éloge de l'Intégrisme," *Pensée catholique* 21 (1952) 7–35; 23 (1954), for documents. R. BERTRAND-SERRET, "'L'Intégrisme' étudié dans un esprit non partisan," *ibid.* 39 (1955) 22–49; 40 (1955) 51–92. L. DAVALLON, "'La Sapinière' ou brève histoire de l'organisation intégriste," *Chronique sociale de France* 3 (May 1955) 241–261. P. BOULIN, *La Critique du Libéralisme religieux, politique, social,* 4 v. (Paris 1909–10), by a leading integralist. E. BARBIER, *Histoire du catholicisme libéral et du catholicisme social en France,* 5 v. (Bordeaux 1923), by a leading integralist. C. LEDRÉ, *Catholicisme. Hier, aujourd'hui et demain,* ed. G. JACQUEMET (Paris 1947–) 5:1822–34. O. B. ROEGELE, *Staatslexikon,* ed. Görres-Gesellschaft, 8 v. (6th, new and enl. ed. Freiburg 1957–63) 4:338–341. A. MICHEL, *Dictionnaire de théologie catholique,* ed. A. VACANT et al., 15 v. (Paris 1903–50; Tables générales 1951–) Tables générales 2294–2303. O. VON NELL-BREUNING, *Lexikon für Theologie und Kirche,* ed. J. HOFER and K. RAHNER, 10 v. (2d, new ed. Freiburg 1957–65) 5:717–718.

[G. J. O'BRIEN]

INTEGRITY, GIFT OF

Throughout its history the teaching Church has maintained that Adam and Eve were created not in a state of pure nature but rather were richly endowed with free gifts from God, among which was sanctifying GRACE. Possession of a nature fully in tune with the perfection of its grace could be had only were there to be granted an exemption from the inherent weaknesses of human nature. Such exemption was the "negative" side of a preternatural harmony between nature and supernature and has been called the gift of integrity.

Generally the gift of integrity is said to be immunity from CONCUPISCENCE, where concupiscence means an appetite for a sensible good contrary to the dictates of reason. This may cause confusion in the face of the modern understanding of concupiscence as the natural, indeliberate desire arising in the sense faculty when confronted with its object. Integrity simply is the subjection of body to soul and lower powers to reason.

Such a harmonious unity could not come from man's natural principles, for the objects of his powers being varied and disparate, it is natural that what is pleasing to one faculty may be opposed to the perfection of the whole man. Reason, having only political control over the sense appetite, would sometimes be uppermost; at other times the sense appetites would be. Hence, in the primeval state God bestowed a perfect order of subjection.

Not created in a state of pure nature, man was not endowed with just natural rectitude. He was predestined to a SUPERNATURAL end, a destiny attainable only by means of a gift utterly surpassing all exigencies and powers of nature (see DESTINY, SUPERNATURAL). This gift was sanctifying grace, and the common teaching of theologians, following St. Thomas Aquinas, is that Adam was created in sanctifying grace. Yet, if the body and the sensible nature were to be left in their own natural condition, they would (as seen previously) be a hindrance, in some sense, to the principal activity of the soul. Because of his composite nature, man could be gifted with another supernatural help, viz, the proper subjection of his powers one to the other.

Given to Adam as head of the human race, sanctifying grace, integrity, and the other gifts would have been the treasure of all men born of his seed. In committing ORIGINAL SIN, Adam lost grace and integrity both for himself and his posterity. In the present state, because of the redemptive sacrifice of the God-Man, Christ, man may again be granted sanctifying grace, but now only as a personal gift and without integrity. The latter will be perfectly restored only at the resurrection of the body although, as grace and the infused virtues grow during life, along with their corresponding natural virtues, the power of man's rectified will gains more and more control over the disordered powers, which gradually lose their harming effects.

See Also: ELEVATION OF MAN; ORIGINAL JUSTICE; PRETERNATURAL; PURE NATURE, STATE OF.

Bibliography: A. THOUVENIN, *Dictionnaire de théologie catholique,* ed. A. VACANT et al., 15 v. (Paris 1903–50; Tables générales 1951) 7.2:1939–40, 2266. A. MICHEL, *Dictionnaire de théologie catholique,* ed. A. VACANT et al., 15 v. (Paris 1903–50; Tables générales 1951) 8.2:2027–28. J. B. METZ, *Lexikon für Theologie und Kirche,* ed. J. HOFER and K. RAHNER, 10 v. (2d new ed. Freiburg 1957–65) 5:718–720. H. FRIES, ed., *Handbuch theologischer Grundbegriffe,* 2 v. (Munich 1962-63) 1:843–851. T. AQUINAS, *Comp. theol.* tr. C. VOLLERT (St. Louis 1947) 192, 195–196, 198–200, 226–227, 236, 239, 241; *Summa theologiae* 1a, 61, 94–95, 97, 100; 1a2ae, 17, 91, 81–82; 3a, 68–69. R. GARRIGOU-LAGRANGE, *Grace* (St. Louis 1952) 20–33. J. TIXERONT, *History of Dogmas,* tr. from 5th Fr. ed. H. L. B. 3 v. (St. Louis 1910–16). W. A. VAN ROO, *Grace and Original Justice according to St. Thomas* (*Analecta Gregoriana* 75; Rome 1955) 7–89, 140–147, 202. P. DE LETTER, "If Adam Had Not Sinned," *Irish Theological Quarterly* 28 (1961) 115–125; "The Reparation of Our Fallen Nature," *Thomist* 23 (1960) 564–583. E. V. MCCLEAR, "The Fall of Man and Original Sin in the Theology of Gregory of Nyssa," *Theological Studies* 9 (1948) 175–212. J. F. SWEENEY, "Recent Developments in Dogmatic Theology," *Theological Studies* 17 (1956) 368–413. C. VOLLERT, "The Two Senses of Original Justice in Medieval Theology," *Theological Studies* 5 (1944) 3–23.

[M. M. SCHANEN]

INTELLECT

The intellect is an immaterial or spiritual cognitive faculty. A faculty is that by means of which man performs mental or conscious operations, and a cognitive faculty is concerned with the mental operation of knowing (see FACULTIES OF THE SOUL). Immaterial or spiritual signifies something not intrinsically dependent on matter, not requiring matter as an auxiliary cause for its existence or for its operation. Vision requires material organs, the eyes, as an auxiliary cause; without them the soul cannot see. Thinking does not require a material cause, but is caused directly by the soul, through the intellect. And since thinking is an immaterial or spiritual operation, the faculty by means of which it occurs, the intellect, is itself immaterial. (See IMMATERIALITY.)

Intellect is sometimes considered to be synonymous with INTELLIGENCE. Yet it is better to distinguish between the two. The term "intelligence" is being used more and more to designate the mind of animals, in addition to that of man. Since the animal mind is a material power, intrinsically dependent on matter, it is essentially different from the human intellect.

Existence of the intellect. No one denies that man knows. But some philosophers—usually materialists, sensists, or positivists—deny that man possesses immaterial knowledge that is essentially different from SENSE KNOWLEDGE. Hence they deny also the existence of the intellect as defined above. Their principal argument invokes the fact that the human brain is required for thinking, since any serious impairment of man's brain makes thought impossible. This fact is undeniable and shows that the brain is somehow involved in thought. But Thomists maintain that the brain is a necessary CONDITION, not a cause, of thinking. A necessary condition is one that enables a cause to produce its effect, without actually contributing toward the production itself. A cause, on the other hand, contributes in a positive manner toward the production of the effect. For example, electricity is the cause of light in a bulb, while closure of the switch is a necessary condition (see CAUSALITY).

Brain and Immateriality. That the brain is not a cause of thinking can be explained through the principle: As a being acts, so it is (*agere sequitur esse*). The brain is a material substance, concrete, visible, tangible, singular, extended, existing in space and time, contingent, and not necessary; its effects must exhibit these characteristics also. And indeed, a brain tumor and a brain wave do. But man's intellectual operations show different characteristics. His ideas are universal, not limited to space and time, not extended, not concrete. Many of man's judgments are necessary, true at all times, in all places, in all circumstances; for example, whatever is, is; everything that comes to be has a cause; two plus two make four. Even ordinary judgments contain an element of necessity. Thus, if one says "It is raining," this proposition is not itself necessary; but, having affirmed that it is raining, he also has implicitly affirmed: "If it is raining, it cannot be not raining." The universality of man's ideas and the necessity (at least hypothetical) of his judgments cannot derive from a material organ such as the brain. They require a power that is, to some extent, beyond time and space, free from the contingency of matter. This immaterial, spiritual power is called the intellect.

Another proof for the immateriality of the intellect is derived from man's capability for REFLECTION. When man knows, he also knows that he knows. In his awareness of being aware, subject and object coincide. This cannot occur in a purely material being. The luminous self-presence of man's act of reflection is thus proof that he possesses an immaterial, spiritual power of thinking.

Image and Concept. A source of objection against this doctrine is the confusion that frequently arises between image and CONCEPT. This received classical expression from George BERKELEY: "Whether others have this wonderful faculty of abstracting their ideas, they best can tell; for myself, I find indeed I have a faculty of imagining, or representing to myself, the ideas of those particular things I have perceived . . . whatever hand or eye I imagine, it must have some particular shape and colour. Likewise, the idea of man that I frame to myself must be either of a white, or a black, or a tawny, a straight or a crooked, a tall or a low, or a middle-sized man" (*Principles of Human Knowledge,* Introd., § 10). Bishop Berkeley here confuses the image with the IDEA. It is true that every man one imagines must be a determinate individual, but it is not true that every man one thinks of must be such. This is apparent in the quotation itself, where mention is made of "whatever hand or eye." These words have meaning—some thought or concept corresponds to them in the objector's mind—yet they apply to all possible hands and eyes, each of which must indeed have "some particular shape and colour," without the intellect's making explicit reference to such shape and color.

Object of the intellect. To know a faculty well one must know its OBJECT, what it can know, and from what point of view it knows. This requires that the material and formal objects of the human intellect be ascertained. A further distinction has traditionally been made between its proper and adequate objects. The proper object of the intellect refers to the things it knows naturally and easily—the material objects in man's environment: other men, animals, plants, houses, and the like. Accordingly, the proper material object of man's intellect comprises all objects that can be perceived by the senses. The senses, however, perceive the color, sound, shape, distance, and the like, of these objects, while the intellect recognizes them for what they are. The eyes note the color of a dog and the ears hear its bark, but the intellect knows that this is a living being, an animal, a dog. This "whatness" or QUIDDITY of material objects is the proper formal object of the human intellect.

Being and Truth. Yet the scope of the human intellect extends beyond the realm of material objects. The fact that one speaks of material objects implies that he knows of other objects that are not material. What is required in any object, in order for it to be knowable by the human intellect, is that it be, or, at least, that it be able to be. Hence the total or adequate object of the intellect is BEING in all its extension, whether material or immaterial. Now the intellect knows such being from the viewpoint of its TRUTH or intelligibility. Accordingly, while the adequate material object of the intellect is being, its adequate formal object is truth or intelligibility.

Of every reality man knows he can affirm that it is. Yet, although being is its object, what his intellect continually meets is not being, but rather beings. In other words, in the repeated affirmation, "This is, that is," the predicate "is" happens always to be too wide for the subject to which it is applied. This explains why man continues to look for new things to know. No object of experience fills the full capacity of his intellect. Man is always in search of an object that will entirely exhaust his power of affirmation. He strives, albeit unconsciously, for the knowledge of a reality of which he can simply say: This *is,* without any restriction or limitation. In other words, his intellect strives toward knowledge of the unlimited being, of God.

Knowledge of God. Left to his own devices, however, man can reach only a deficient and imperfect knowledge of God. He knows Him, through analogy with creatures, as the all-perfect came that must possess eminently all perfections found in finite realities. This analogical, inadequate knowledge of God is the highest knowledge of Him that reason can offer to man.

Revelation, however, promises infinitely more—a knowledge of God as He is in Himself, in His inner essence, in the ineffable mystery of His triune inner life. Such knowledge is clearly beyond the powers, and even beyond the expectations, of the human intellect. It requires a transformation of that intellect, raising it above its natural state and supernaturalizing it. Sanctifying GRACE produces this transformation. It gives to the baptized person the supernatural gift of faith, which is the power of knowing, although darkly, God as He is in Himself. In the elect, during the next life, this gift of faith gives way to the BEATIFIC VISION; as St. THOMAS AQUINAS explains it, the human intellect sees the divine essence "through the divine essence itself; so that in this vision the divine essence is both that which is seen and that by means of which it is seen" (*C. gent.* 3.51).

Operation of the intellect. Since the intellect is an immaterial faculty, it cannot be influenced directly by material reality. The problem arises then as to how intellectual knowledge originates in man. One answer is that, as material objects affect the sense organs, so sense knowledge influences the intellect. But this answer implies that the intellect is a material power. The senses can be influenced by extramental reality because, like that reality, they are material. But how can the intellect, an immaterial power, be influenced by the senses and receive from them a material content?

The intellect, of course, may be influenced by immaterial causes. This is why some have held that its ideas come directly from God; such, with various modifications, was the teaching of PLATO, St. AUGUSTINE, DESCARTES, and MALEBRANCHE. But this theory contradicts human experience and leads to consequences that are inacceptable (*see* KNOWLEDGE, THEORIES OF).

If ideas cannot come from the senses and do not come directly from God, the intellect must receive them from itself. The intellect, therefore, acts upon itself and receives from itself. Thus we distinguish in it two faculties, an agent intellect and a passive or possible intellect. The agent intellect impresses ideas upon the possible intellect.

Agent intellect. Where does the agent intellect find these ideas? St. Thomas holds that it derives them from sense experience. The agent intellect actively abstracts the species from the PHANTASM and impresses it upon the possible intellect (*see* ABSTRACTION; SPECIES, INTENTIONAL). Phantasms are the highest products of the combined senses. In modern terminology they correspond to perceptions, or images; as material forms of knowledge, they represent single, concrete, material objects.

The passage from this concrete, singular phantasm to the abstract, universal concept is sometimes explained as follows: Viewing the phantasm of a particular tree, the intellect leaves aside all the individualizing, concrete features (e.g., the tree's size and color) and considers only the general, universal features. But how can the agent intellect distinguish between general and individual features, keeping the former and dropping the latter, unless it knows all of them? This seems to suppose that the intellect directly knows the material phantasm, a position that Thomists generally deny. Again, how can a material phantasm affect an immaterial intellect? It is often maintained that the agent intellect, acting as the principal efficient cause, uses the phantasm as an instrumental cause to impress the abstracted universal idea upon the possible intellect (*see* INSTRUMENTAL CAUSALITY). But it would seem that a material tool can produce only material effects, even when used by an immaterial agent. How then can it affect an immaterial reality?

An alternative, and possibly more acceptable, explanation of ideogenesis focuses on Aquinas's teaching that man never uses ideas without turning to the corresponding phantasm. Man knows ideas (or rather, what they represent) only in the phantasm. This seems to imply no actual extraction of the idea from the phantasm. Otherwise it would be difficult to see why, once man has separated the two, he cannot use the idea independently of the phantasm.

The substantial unity of man, in fact, implies not only the unity of body and soul but also that of sense and intellect (*see* SOUL-BODY RELATIONSHIP). As the soul is to the body, so the intellect is to the senses. The soul does not hover over the body, but rather is in the body. Likewise the intellect does not stand above the senses; it is in them. To speak of a "passage" from sense to intellectual knowledge is to fall into Cartesian DUALISM and admit that both the body and the soul have their own representations of the object. Actually there is only one knowing subject, composed of both body and soul. As the body never acts without being animated by the soul, so the senses never act without being animated by the intellect. This means that the intellect is already at work in the formation of the phantasm (*see* COGITATIVE POWER). It animates the formation of the phantasm, and this activity produces the universal idea. The impressed species of the intellect is this dynamic relationship between the intellect and the phantasm.

Expressed species. The agent intellect is like a powerful searchlight, of which St. Thomas says that it is always "in act." By itself it does not give knowledge. As soon as sense knowledge crosses its beam, however, the corresponding idea is generated. In this sense the phantasm is truly an instrumental cause—it gives the light of the intellect something to illuminate.

When an object comes within reach of the agent intellect, that object is seen as something, a being, a reality.

The intellect then consciously expresses the relation it has attained unconsciously in the impressed species. This is the expressed species, the WORD, the *verbum*. In such an expressed species the object is grasped intellectually. Most Thomists hold that this expressed species is the CONCEPT, attained by simple APPREHENSION. Others maintain that it is an ''affirmed concept,'' a concept embedded in a JUDGMENT, although often only an elementary judgment. According to this view, being is given in judgments, possibles in concepts. Hence the expressed species of the intellect, through which man gets his first intellectual contact with reality, is the elementary judgment that the intellect utters to itself (thus, the word) whenever it knows reality.

Acts of the Intellect. The first two acts of the intellect have already been mentioned, that is, simple apprehension and judgment. Once man possesses a certain number of concepts and judgments, he can then explicitly compare them, discover their relationships, derive one from the other, associate them with each other, and the like. This work constitutes the third act of the intellect, known as REASONING.

In explaining how knowledge perfects the knower, St. Thomas notes: ''. . . knowing beings are distinguished from non-knowing beings in that the latter possess only their own form; whereas the knowing being is naturally adapted to have also the form of some other thing, for the species of the thing known is in the knower'' (*Summa theologiae* 1a, 14.1). As explained above, this does not mean that the species is a self-sufficient picture of the object, for St. Thomas also teaches that man cannot know the object without reverting to the phantasm (*Summa theologiae* 1a, 84.7). Yet knowing things means to some extent becoming these things, since man has in him, for every object he knows, a phantasm and a species, the latter being understood as a dynamic relation of the intellect to the former. By animating the phantasm of the object, the intellect intentionally becomes that object. In this sense, the acts of conceiving and of judging perfect the human intellect.

In addition, reasoning perfects the intellect in other ways. First, by discovering connections between realities, it makes man aware of the structure, the order, and the harmony of the universe. This allows him also to direct his activities in the right way, according to the order of importance of goals and purposes. Again, having detected an underlying order and hierarchy in the universe, he discovers also its basic orientation and finality, and thus is led to acknowledge its Designer and Creator.

Differences in intellectual ability. The nature and operation of the human intellect has been the main concern here. Above the human intellect there are, however, higher and more perfect intellects. From revelation one knows of the existence of angels (*see* ANGELS, 2. THEOLOGY OF). Philosophically these are conceived to be pure forms, in no way dependent on matter (although they do have some relationship to the material universe). They are, therefore, basically intellects and wills. Whatever they know has been communicated to them at their creation. Angels know through infused species, which, coming directly from the Maker of all, give them certain and clear knowledge of reality. Thus their knowledge is more perfect than man's. Since angels differ from each other in ontological PERFECTION, each constituting an original, unique grade of being, their intellects too differ in acuity, penetration, and extension of knowledge.

Above all created intellects stands the Uncreated Intellect, God. God does not ''have'' an intellect. He ''is'' Intellect, as He is every other pure perfection substantially. As the Self-Subsistent Intellect, God knows Himself perfectly and comprehensively. He also knows in Himself, as they are in themselves, all existing and possible creatures.

Differences in intellectual abilities among men seem to be due not to the spiritual intellect itself, but to its relation to the body. Hence they are differences of intelligence, more than of intellect.

See Also: KNOWLEDGE, PROCESS OF; UNDERSTANDING (INTELLECTUS); INTUITION.

Bibliography: THOMAS AQUINAS, *Summa Theologiae* 1a, 14, 79, 84–87. J. F. DONCEEL, *Philosophical Psychology* (2d ed., rev. and enl. New York 1961). R. E. BRENNAN, *Thomistic Psychology* (New York 1952). B. LONERGAN, *Insight: A Study of Human Understanding* (New York 1957). J. MARITAIN, *Distinguish to Unite, or the Degrees of Knowledge,* tr. G. B. PHELAN from 4th French ed. (New York 1959). A. MARC, *Psychologie réflexive* (Brussels 1948). J. MARÉCHAL, *Le Point de départ de la métaphysique,* 5 v. (2d ed. Paris 1949). K. RAHNER, *Geist in Welt* (2d ed. Munich 1957).

[J. F. DONCEEL]

INTELLECT, UNITY OF

Is there one intellect for all men, or does each man have his own intellect? This problem involves two questions often discussed by Christians of the Middle Ages: (1) Is the agent intellect one for all men? (2) Is the possible intellect, as well as the agent intellect, one for all men? (*See* INTELLECT.) Of the two questions, the second presented the more serious difficulty and was the subject of a vigorous polemic in the 13th century. The meaning and implications of both questions can best be understood in the light of their historical background.

History of the problem. The story begins with Aristotle's *De anima.* Noting that in nature as a whole we find

"Triumph of St Thomas Aquinas over Averroes," fresco by Francesco Traini in the Church of Santa Caterina, Pisa, Italy.

two factors, a potential factor and an active one, ARISTOTLE says that "these distinct elements must likewise be found within the soul" (430a, 13). He then continues:

> And in fact mind as we have described it is what it is by virtue of becoming all things, while there is another which is what it is by virtue of making all things. . . . Mind in this sense is separable, impassible, unmixed, since it is in its essential nature activity. . . . When mind is set free from its present conditions it appears as just what it is and nothing more; this alone, is immortal and eternal. . . . While mind in this sense is impassible, mind as passive is destructible, and without it nothing thinks. [430a, 14–25.]

The fact that Aristotle distinguished an active intellect that makes things actually intelligible from a passive intellect that receives these intelligibles was clear, but precisely what he held about the natures of these intellects and their relationship to man was not. Although these words were to be examined and reexamined and compared with other of his statements, commentators could not agree on what he really meant. The reference to active mind as separable, impassible, unmixed, immortal and eternal, for example, gave rise to the question: Is active mind a power of the human soul or a substance separate and distinct from man?

Among the Greek commentators, Theophrastus (c. 370–285 B.C.) and Themistius (c. A.D. 387) interpreted Aristotle as holding that both active and passive intellects were parts or powers of each human soul. But Alexander of Aphrodisias (c. A.D. 200), though placing the passive or material intellect within the individual soul, which was for him perishable, taught that the active intellect is a separately existing divine intelligence.

Among Arabian thinkers, too, the active or agent intellect was held to be a separated substance and one for all men. For AVICENNA (980–1037), the last of the separate spiritual intelligences emanating from the one necessary Being was the agent intellect or Intelligence (*Meta.* 9.4). From this intellect, intelligible forms or species were infused into possible intellects belonging to individual human souls. Each human soul had to consider and compare the images coming to it from the senses. These movements prepared it to receive from the separated agent intellect an "abstraction," which in this context meant an emanation of intelligible forms. But the intelligibles so received were not retained. Each time a man wished to have intellectual knowledge, his soul again had to be united with the separate agent intellect (*De anima* 5.5–6).

For Avicenna, although there was one agent intellect for all men, each man had his own possible intellect. But for AVERROËS (1126–98), the individual man had neither; the possible as well as the agent intellect was a separated substance and one for all men. Reacting against the materialism of Alexander of Aphrodisias, Averroës held that the possible or "material" intellect must be a simple, impassible, separated substance dwelling wholly apart from matter. This was necessary to insure its power of knowing universals (*In 3 anim.* comm. 4,5,19,32). But since this view left the individual without a spiritual intellect, Averroës still had to explain how man can have intellectual knowledge. Therefore man's highest powers, the cogitative power, imagination, and memory, were given the task of preparing sensory data for the separated intellects to utilize (*ibid.,* comm. 6,20,33). The separated agent intellect then makes actually intelligible the intelligible species potentially present within the phantasms provided by these powers. The separated possible intellect can thereupon be actuated and become the subject in which knowledge exists (*ibid.,* comm. 4,5,18). Unless such data were provided by man, the separated possible intellect would know nothing (*ibid.,* comm. 33). Because of man's indispensable role in this process, he himself somehow shares in intellectual knowledge.

This may not completely explain how the individual man knows. But Averroës could not concede that the intellect was "numbered to the number of individuals," and still have that intellect sufficiently free of matter to preserve its power of knowing. He had no awareness of a spiritual intellective soul that could be the form of a body without being itself immersed in matter (*see* SOUL, HUMAN).

Christian thought. These views that gradually became known to the Christians of western Europe as the works of Aristotle, accompanied by commentaries of Arabian thinkers, became available in Latin translation during the 12th and 13th centuries. While Aristotle's logical works had previously been known and admired, Christians now had access to his other treatises, including that on the soul. Avicenna's *De anima* and Averroës' *Commentary* were also available as aids in understanding his complex thought.

This new literature was viewed by some authorities as a possible source of error. In 1210 the provincial council of Paris prohibited the teaching of Aristotle's works on natural philosophy or their commentaries. In 1215 the statutes of the University of Paris promulgated by ROBERT OF COURÇON, the papal legate, forbade the reading of the physical and metaphysical treatises of Aristotle and expositions based on them (*Chartularium universitatis Parisiensis,* 1:70, 78–79). But the prohibitions were not effective.

Avicenna's doctrine of a separated agent intellect had already been accepted, in a modified form, by a 12th century Christian, DOMINIC GUNDISALVI. He, ROGER BACON (b. *c.* 1214) and JOHN PECKHAM (d. 1292) all identified this agent intelligence with the Christian God. Étienne Gilson has seen in the work of these and others a fusion of the Avicennian doctrine on the agent intellect with an Augustinian doctrine of ILLUMINATION (Gilson, ''Pourquoi saint Thomas a critiqué saint Augustin,'' *Archives d'histoire doctrinale et littéraire du moyen-âge,* 1:5–127).

The unity of the agent intellect in the human species met further opposition in the 13th century. Along with the unity of the possible intellect, it was included in the condemnation of 1270 whereby Étienne TEMPIER, Bishop of Paris, anathematized 13 propositions bearing the stamp of Arabian authorship, and again in the list of 219 propositions condemned in 1277 (*Chartularium universitatis Parisiensis,* 1:486–487, 543–548).

It was also opposed in the writings of St. THOMAS AQUINAS (1225–74). According to St. Thomas, Aristotle taught that the agent intellect was not a separate substance but a power of the human soul with the function of making the potentially intelligible natures of sensible things actually intelligible, by abstracting them from individual matter (*C. gent.* 2.78). This view is confirmed, for St. Thomas, by man's experience in abstracting universal forms from their particular conditions. If the power that is the principle of this action were not something within man's soul, human nature would be a deficient nature, lacking the principle of an activity proper to it (*C. gent.* 2.76; ST 1a, 79.4; *In 2 sent.* 17.2.1; *De anim.* 5; *In 3 de anim.* 10.734). Wishing to save the efficacy of secondary causes, St. Thomas held that a being cannot be incapable of accomplishing an operation proper to its nature. Yet this need not rule out the dependence of man's intellectual soul upon a higher cause. ''The separate intellect, according to the teaching of our faith, is God Himself. . . . Therefore the human soul derives its intellectual light from Him,'' St. Thomas said. He went on: ''That true light illumines as a universal cause, from which the human soul derives a particular power'' (ST 1a, 79.4 and ad 1). There may then be some reason for holding that there is one agent intellect for all men, when this is understood not as a denial but as an explanation of the personal agent intellect that each man possesses. But, in St. Thomas's view, to say that the *possible* intellect is one for all men is wholly inadmissible (*De anim.* 5; *De unit. intell.* 4).

Before the emergence of a definite Averroistic school, St. ALBERT THE GREAT (*c.* 1200–80) had already dealt with this doctrine at the request of Pope Alexander IV. In 1256, in his *De unitate intellectus contra Averroem,* he presented 30 arguments for the unity of the human intellect and 36 arguments against it.

But the Averroist movement grew in strength (*see* AVERROISM, LATIN). As more Christian thinkers read Aristotle and Averroës in Latin translation, the Philosopher and philosophy were seen through the works of the Commentator. These Latin Averroists regarded the doctrine of one possible intellect for all men as a necessary conclusion of human reason, although as Christians they refrained from saying that this doctrine was true. Without explicitly teaching a theory of double truth, such a leading Averroist as SIGER OF BRABANT (fl. 1277) nevertheless conveyed the impression of a conflict between faith and reason. For those concerned with the unity of Christian wisdom, this challenge could not be ignored (*see* DOUBLE TRUTH, THEORY OF).

St. BONAVENTURE (1221–74) referred to the doctrine of one possible intellect for the whole human race as being against the Christian religion, against right reason and against sensible experience (*In 2 sent.* 18.2.1). The same doctrine was censured in the condemnations of 1270 and 1277. It was listed as an error by GILES OF ROME (*c.* 1247–1316, *Errores philosophorum,* c.4) and opposed in a treatise he wrote on the problem (*De plurificatione intellectus possibilis*).

Thomistic doctrine. The most thorough philosophical examination and refutation of the Averroist doctrine of the possible intellect was made by St. Thomas Aquinas. He discussed it in many places and composed the polemical treatise, *De unitate intellectus contra Averroistas,* specifically to deal with this problem. Written in 1270 against the Paris Averroists and especially against Siger of Brabant, it may have been an answer to a work of Siger's that is no longer extant but is known to us through the *Quodlibeta* of JOHN BACONTHORP, a 14th century Carmelite.

St. Thomas regards it as evident that Averroës' view of one possible and one agent intellect for all men is contrary to the truth of Christian faith. Since this would leave man without any incorruptible part of the soul, there could be no personal immortality and thus no reward and punishment in the afterlife. He concentrates on showing that the position of the Averroists is against both Aristotle and sound philosophy. On neither ground can they maintain that the possible intellect is (1) a substance separate in its being from man, or (2) one for all men (*De unit. intell.* proem.).

St. Thomas analyzes the relevant and often ambiguous texts of Aristotle and also cites the Greek and Arabian peripatetics, to show that all support the view that each man has his own possible intellect. His arguments include stress on the fact that ''this individual man knows'' and that Averroës' doctrine, which treats man as an object of knowledge for the separated possible intellect, fails to explain this. Man's proper operation as man is to understand. Therefore the principle that gives him his specific nature, the principle by which he understands, must be his own and not a separated substance (*ibid.* 3).

St. Thomas also deals with the chief difficulty of the Averroists. They thought that if the intellect is a power of a soul that is itself the substantial form of a body, then it would become immersed in matter and so be incapable of intellectual knowledge. St. Thomas answered that a proper understanding of the relation of the human soul to the matter it informs removes this difficulty. The human soul is not a material form existing with only the being of the composite; rather, it exists with its own being, and through that being the composite exists. Since this form is a substance communicating its being to matter, nothing prevents it from having an immaterial operation or power (*ibid.* 1.3).

For St. Thomas this error on the intellect pointed to an even greater error on the relation of faith and reason (*see* FAITH AND REASON). He was deeply disturbed that anyone could say: "By reason I necessarily conclude that the intellect is one in number, but I firmly hold the opposite by faith." Such a person, Siger for example, seemed to imply that faith is concerned with what is false and impossible (*ibid.* 5). Departing from his usual dispassionate style, St. Thomas concludes his treatise with a challenge to his adversary: "Let him not speak in corners nor before boys who do not know how to judge of such difficult matters, but let him write an answer to this if he dares. He will find not only me, least of all, but many others who are zealous for truth, through whom his error may be resisted or his ignorance remedied" (*ibid.* 5).

Because of the difficulty of establishing the authenticity and chronology of writings attributed to Siger of Brabant, it cannot be said for certain that this challenge was accepted by Siger. He may have replied in *De intellectu,* a treatise mentioned by JOHN OF JANDUN (d. 1328) and Agostino NIFO (1473– *c.* 1538). His *De anima intellectiva* seems to reflect a knowledge of some of St. Thomas's comments, and its doctrine of the intellective soul as united to the body "intrinsically" for its operation may represent a change or clarification of an earlier position (*De anim. intell.* 3). But unless the authenticity of such a work as the *Quaestiones in libros Aristotelis de anima* can be established, it cannot be said that Siger was converted to a Thomistic position.

The controversy over the intellect was to continue into the 16th century. Pietro POMPONAZZI (d. 1525), like John of Jandun before him, did not doubt that St. Thomas's conclusions were in agreement with faith, but could not see them as philosophical conclusions in accord with Aristotle's position. Those who identified philosophy with the historical Aristotle were thus reluctant to accept an Aristotle transformed by the creative insight of St. Thomas. Yet, regardless of such interpretations, there is no dearth of philosophical argument in support of the conclusion that each man has his own possible, as well as his own agent, intellect.

See Also: ARISTOTELIANISM; SCHOLASTICISM; THOMISM; ARABIAN PHILOSOPHY; ABSTRACTION; ILLUMINATION; NEOPLATONISM.

Bibliography: E. GILSON, *History of Christian Philosophy,* 181–225, 387–410. F. VAN STEENBERGHEN, *Aristotle in the West,* tr., L. JOHNSTON (Louvain 1955). P. F. MANDONNET, *Siger de Brabant et L'averroisme latin au XIII ͤ siècle,* 2 v. (2d ed. Louvain 1908–11). É. H. GILSON, "Les Sources gréco-arabes de l'Augustinisme avicennisant," *Archives d'histoire doctrinale et littéraire du moyen-âge,* 4 (1929–30) 5–149. *Chartularium universitatis Parisiensis,* ed., D. DENIFLE and E. CHATELAIN, 4 v. (Paris 1889–97).

[B. H. ZEDLER]

INTELLECTUAL LIFE

The intellectual life of man may be considered from the point of view of revelation or of reason. The first way is proper to THEOLOGY and the second to PHILOSOPHY. In the theological approach there are some practical applications that are not found in the merely speculative approach of philosophy. Though the two approaches are formally distinct, it is impossible to grasp satisfactorily the significance of the intellectual life without both the planes on which man lives, the SUPERNATURAL as well as the natural, being considered. Thus it is impossible to separate in fact a theological from a philosophical study of the intellectual life.

Early Greek Views on the Intellectual Life. Contrary to a view that is often held, the early Greeks were not merely investigators of nature but were also theologians. In their philosophizing about nature the most important consideration for them was the attainment of WISDOM. By attaining wisdom man was thought to participate in the divine life. The search for wisdom, therefore, was more than an investigation of nature—it was a way of life. It was the only way of life according to which man could be defined properly, since the goal or perfection of human existence consisted in the possession of wisdom.

Most of the pre-Socratic philosophers, even those thought to be materialists, made a sharp distinction between the kind of knowledge most easily reached by man, namely, that of sense experience, and the kind of knowledge esteemed by them as a participation in divine wisdom. Contrary to the view of F. Engels in his reference to the pre-Socratics as forerunners of dialectical materialism (*Herr Eugen Dühring's Revolution in Science,* tr. E. Burns [New York 1939] 26–27), these philosophers were deeply concerned with theological as well as philosophical questions. For example, there are in Heraclitus, whose philosophy Engels regarded as the most perfect primitive expression of the dialectics of nature, various phraseologies, admittedly metaphorical, that are consistent with the Christian notion of the LOGOS. Against the teaching of Xenophanes and Pythagoras, who had separated God from the universe of men, animals, plants, and inanimate things, Heraclitus affirmed the identity of the divinity with all that is. Though his thought appears pantheistic because of the kinds of metaphor he employs, he differentiated divinity (the pure form of Fire) from all those things that originated in divinity, which constitute the world of phenomena. He taught that the Logos (Mind) is prior to the downward movement of Fire. The Logos is present in all things, but most of all in man. Man should transcend the phenomena in order to seek wisdom (ἐπιστήμη), which is the knowledge of the eternal Logos. Logos is the purpose that steers all things. It is the Law (νόμος) with which man must agree. A person who wishes to speak with intelligence must base his knowledge on the eternal law that is common to all (K. Freeman, *Ancilla to the Pre-Socratic Philosophers* [Oxford 1948] 24).

In Parmenides is found the same teaching, with even greater stress on the priority of wisdom over sensory experience. Anaxagoras was, according to Aristotle, one of the greatest of philosophers because he pointed out the role that the divine Mind (νοῦς) played in the formation of the variety of things found in nature. Mind is infinite and self-ruling and mixed with no other thing; it is alone by itself. It has complete understanding of everything. All things are ruled by Mind, for it was Mind that took command of the universal revolution by which all things were, are now, and will come into existence (Freeman, 84–85).

The primacy of the intellectual life emerges most clearly in the philosophy of Plato and Aristotle. Their notions of the intellectual life are far more advanced than those of the pre-Socratics. The whole thrust of Aristotle's *Metaphysics* and of his *Politics,* etc., was toward the best life, the contemplative life; see, for instance, *Eth. Nic.* 1141a 20 and *Meta.* 1072b 14. In Plato and Aristotle the metaphysics of knowledge has been freed from the limitations of language of the earlier philosophers. According to Plato and Aristotle, the greatest perfection that man can reach on Earth is the possession of TRUTH, for in this he is assimilated to divinity (see C. N. R. McCoy, "The Political Life and the Contemplative Life," *The Structure of Political Thought* [New York 1963] 46–51).

Revelation and the Logos. However remarkable were the insights of the early Greeks into the nature of God and however great their esteem for the intellectual life, it was only a dim vision of the intellectual life of God. Through revelation man was permitted to peer into the transcendent intellectual life of the Triune God. As St. Thomas Aquinas pointed out in the beginning of his *Summa theologiae,* it was necessary that there be in addition to the light of human reason a special light of revelation about the existence and nature of God. The most intelligent men could achieve only the faintest knowledge of God through the use of reason, and even that struggle was marred by a great number of errors and carried through by very few men. The natural knowledge about God gained through speculation on natural causes is always cast in a negative mode, since the infinite perfection of God is the obverse of the limited perfections found in natural things. Without obtaining a direct knowledge of God, it was possible for man to rise to an essentially higher level of knowledge through revelation. The essence of knowledge through divine revelation is FAITH, the culmination of which for those who are both believers and doers of the word is the BEATIFIC VISION of God. This will be the absolute goal of man's intellectual life.

The doctrine of the Logos is found in the very earliest of Christian writings and is continued throughout the writings of the Fathers and Doctors of the Church. The Logos is the Second Person of the Holy Trinity. He is generated eternally in the understanding of the Father. The Logos is in turn, according to the prologue of St. John's Gospel, the intellectual life Who enlightens every man who comes into the world. All of creation is through the Logos, but in particular the creation of man, who is made to the image of the Trinity (*see* IMAGE OF GOD). Man alone, among visible creatures, has an intellect by which he can be identified in thought and be united in love with God (*see* MAN, 2, 3).

Considered in its totality, revelation through the Logos consists not only in the direct words that were spoken by Christ, the Word incarnate, during His lifetime on Earth, but also in the revelation made to man before the Incarnation and in the continuing unfolding of the meaning of the revealed truth through the magisterium of the Church.

The truth conferred through revelation was meant to be more than a mere speculative understanding of the nature of God—it was to be the practical basis for worship. In both the Old and New Testaments the notion of wisdom meant more than what is considered liberal or speculative knowledge, for as St. Paul told the early Christians, faith without charity and good works is useless. (*See* WISDOM [IN THE BIBLE].)

Anti-Intellectual Tendencies in the Church. Unfortunately, it has been greatly due to an exaggerated stress on the salvific aspect of revealed truth that from time to time in the history of the Church there have been anti-intellectual movements. The pragmatic view of revealed knowledge led to a disdain for all knowledge of the natural order that did not bear immediately on salvation. Frequently natural knowledge was held to be not only useless but in opposition to the pure teachings of Christ. The basis of this error was a failure to see the unity of all truth in the Logos. Taken out of context, the words of St. Paul might give credence to this view: "For it is written, 'I will destroy the wisdom of the wise, and the prudence of the prudent I will reject'" (1 Cor 1.19). Particularly in the 17th and 18th centuries, certain writers of ascetical works, who had fallen under the influence of Jansenism, were very influential in the formation of an anti-intellectual movement in the Church; this anti-intellectualism, in one form or another, lasted until the mid-20th century.

Renewal of a Christian Intellectualism. Beginning in the late 19th century and growing rapidly in the 20th century was a countermovement in the Church toward the notion of an integral Christian intellectual life. Catholic scholars began to be accepted as peers in the centers of learning. Such men as Pope Leo XIII, Cardinal J. H. Newman, and Cardinal D. Mercier in the 19th century preceded the numerous Catholic intellectuals in the 20th century. Among them, to name some, were A. G. Sertillanges, P. Rousselot, G. K. Chesterton, and H. Belloc; and more recently, Pius XI, Pius XII, É. H. Gilson, J. Maritain, Cardinal E. Suhard, and P. Teilhard de Chardin.

Through the prodding of these men and others like them a new interest in the intellectual life was aroused among Catholics. The relationship of nature and grace came into better perspective (*see* GRACE AND NATURE). The obligation of all Christians to participate in and to contribute to the common fund of human knowledge was more widely acknowledged. As Cardinal Newman had said earlier in his *University Sermons,* the time had come to see that the pursuit of intellectual excellence is not the undoing of man's nature but the natural preparation for a higher life of grace.

See Also: FAITH AND REASON.

Bibliography: P. TEILHARD DE CHARDIN, *The Divine Milieu,* tr. B. WALL et al. (New York 1960). É. H. GILSON, *Christianity and Philosophy,* tr. R. MACDONALD (New York 1939). J. H. NEWMAN, *The Scope and Nature of University Education* (pa. New York 1958). P. ROUSSELOT, *The Intellectualism of Saint Thomas,* tr. J. E. O'MAHONY (New York 1935). A G SERTILLANGES, *The Intellectual Life,* tr. M. RYAN (Westminster, Md. 1956).

[H. R. REITH]

INTELLECTUALISM

The term intellectualism generally designates a philosophical or theological system in which INTELLECT or conceptualization is accorded primacy, as opposed to will or affectivity. It is sometimes used in a context of SCHOLASTICISM to characterize the Thomistic synthesis as differing from that of the Franciscan and Augustinian schools. It is also applied in a pejorative sense, mainly by modern thinkers, to those philosophies that stress abstract generalization and rationalism to the exclusion of subjective and existential concerns. The following is a brief historical survey of various nuances in this usage.

GREEK PHILOSOPHY is intellectualist in the sense that it teaches that the idea specifies and determines action. SOCRATES and PLATO seem not to have believed in freedom, inasmuch as some of their followers taught that, since every moral fault results from an error, no one does evil voluntarily. Such intellectualism similarly inspires the philosophy of ARISTOTLE. All reality is intelligible, and this tenet refers to the phenomena of nature as well as to ideas in the mind. Science is placed well above the useful because it has value in and of itself. Understanding is so sovereign that one cannot possibly remove oneself from its jurisdiction. Even a universal doubt implies certitude; every denial implies an affirmation. One can criticize reason only by reason. Even the person who pretends to do without it has recourse to it; even one who scorns it gives it homage. The most important thing, then, is to think and to think well.

Somewhat the same, intellectualism is characteristic of St. THOMAS AQUINAS. Faithful to Aristotle's tradition, he improves it by indicating that God is not only necessity, but also freedom; not only thought, but also love. This is one of the ways whereby he avoids rationalism and, while stressing the primary of the intellect, also teaches the ontological importance of the will, freedom, and mysticism.

Traces of this intellectualism are encountered also in the modern era. In the 17th century, philosophers are concerned especially about the truth and the means of attaining it. Some have recourse to a method of observation, others to a metaphysical method. As usually employed, however, both of these methods are ultimately reducible to the mathematical method, which, used in the context of physics, can possibly claim a necessity that, in fact, nature does not have. From this there arises a twofold intellectualistic current: that of EMPIRICISM, which becomes POSITIVISM in the 19th century—it is represented by F. BACON, J. LOCKE, D. HUME, A. COMTE, and H. SPENCER. The second is that of the IDEALISM—of R. DESCARTES, N. MALEBRANCHE, B. SPINOZA, G. W. LEIBNIZ, J. G. FICHTE, F. SCHELLING, and G. W. F. HEGEL. For both groups, man's value and power are specified by his non-subjective or objective knowledge, a necessitating knowledge that, by reason of inflexibility in method, suppresses freedom in almost every case.

What should one say in criticism of intellectualism? It is difficult not to recognize its importance and value. Blind action is impotent; a life whose meaning is not perceived becomes evil. The sage who discovers the laws of nature is a great benefactor, and He who reveals God to us is the Savior. But intellectualism exposes one to the danger of RATIONALISM and determinism; being is not only necessary and intelligible, but also dynamic. If thought is sovereign because it is immanent and can think itself, the will, too, can will itself and is, thereby, autonomous and free. One is first in the order of truth, the other in the order of the good; their correlation produces their mutual value.

See Also: EXISTENTIALISM; IRRATIONALISM; VOLUNTARISM.

Bibliography: J. W. MILLER, *The Structure of Aristotelian Logic* (London 1938). P. ROUSSELOT, *The Intellectualism of Saint Thomas,* tr. J. E. O'MAHONY (New York 1935). A. G. SERTILLANGES, *St. Thomas Aquinas and His Work,* tr. G. ANSTRUTHER (London 1933; repr. 1957). J. LAPORTE, *Le Rationalisme de Descartes* (Paris 1945). V. MATHIEU, *Enciclopedia filosofica* 2:1457–60 (Venice-Rome 1957). R. EISLER, *Wörterbuch der philsophischen Begriffe,* 1:759 (4th ed. Berlin 1927–30).

[P. ORTEGAT]

INTELLIGIBILITY, PRINCIPLE OF

An immediate and necessary judgment or law, commonly enumerated among the FIRST PRINCIPLES, asserting that everything that is, in so far as it is, is intelligible; or that every being is capable of justifying itself, of explaining itself to the INTELLECT, of answering the question "Why?" The conviction that there *is* an answer to be known inspires the attempt to know. When, for example, one asks why stones sink while logs float, the asking implies that reality provides a knowable answer, even though this is not yet known. Such a conviction is an implicit acknowledgment of the principle of intelligibility.

Justification. Since the principle of intelligibility is a first principle, and hence cannot be deduced, it follows that it cannot be directly proved. Therefore the only justification this principle admits of is indirect, that is, by showing that the principle cannot be denied without contradiction.

If one could deny that being is intelligible, this negation would be a judgment, which one would intend to elicit as true. However, intending to elicit a judgment as true, one intends to exclude unconditionally its contradictory assertion. Hence one can intend to elicit a judgment as true only insofar as the act of judging affirms an objective norm, the norm of being, as justifying the unconditional exclusion of the contradictory judgment, that is, insofar as one affirms being itself as justifying the judgment one elicits.

One could, therefore, deny that being is intelligible only dependently on affirming being itself as justifying this judgment of the intellect. However, being as justifying the judgment is being as intelligible, since it is being as that to which the intellect is conformed. Hence one could deny that being is intelligible only dependently on affirming that being is intelligible. This means that the negation of the intelligibility of being contradicts and eliminates itself; or that the denial of the principle of intelligibility is impossible.

It is to be noted, however, that the contradiction does not appear by an inspection or analysis of the terms of the negation, as it does, for example, in the negation that a circle is round. Rather the contradiction is between the act itself of denying and the content denied. Hence, the necessity of the principle of intelligibility is not merely a necessity of idea, but is one of act, of being: the necessity is not merely logical, but it is primarily ontological.

Application. The principle of intelligibility implicitly affirms that every being, even before it is known, conforms to the exigencies or laws of the intellect. This principle, then, affirming that being is necessarily intelligible and cannot be absurd, affirms that the act of being is intelligibility, or affirmability, outside of which there is no intelligibility. Hence the act of being is the fullness of intelligibility (*see* BEING; EXISTENCE). Everything, therefore, is intelligible insofar as it is or verifies the act of being (St. THOMAS AQUINAS, *Summa theologiae* 1a, 16.3). Its act of being is its own light (*In lib. de caus.* 6), and by its act of being, it is synthesized with the totality of intelligibility. Hence, everything that is must be fully intelligible by reason of the act of being. It follows, therefore, that only that being that is fully identified with the act of being and hence is unlimited act of being, namely, GOD, is of Himself fully intelligible or is pure affirmability.

Every other being is of itself intelligible only in the measure in which it has the act of being, in the measure of its inadequate identity with the act of being. The measure in which it has the act of being is its ESSENCE. The properties of that being are intelligible by its essence. However, its essence itself is not intelligible by itself, but by the act of being. Since it is inadequately identified with the act of being, it has the act of being limitedly. The mind is therefore referred beyond this being itself for the complement of its intelligibility. Of itself alone such a being is not fully intelligible or affirmable, yet the conditions of full intelligibility by which it is affirmable must be given in being. This is to say that its intelligibility is completed by its relation to the cause of its being, God. It is not fully intelligible by the act of being precisely as found in this being, but rather as dependent upon the subsisting act of being. In this way the principle of intelligibility, when applied to finite being, evolves into another principle, namely, the principle of CAUSALITY.

Although God, the finally implied justification of the principle of intelligibility, is of Himself the most intelligible, He is not so for man, who first finds intelligibility in material reality. Hence the fullness of intelligibility affirmed in the principle of intelligibility remains beyond the grasp of the human intellect. However, the principle of intelligibility affirms a coherent totality of intelligibility, and urges man on in his quest for an ordered, unified explanation of the endless multiplicity and facets of the universe. It guides and governs his search for TRUTH and his rejection of ERROR, since it enables him to know that whatever is opposed to the intelligible is impossible and absurd.

See Also: KNOWLEDGE; FALSITY; ABSURDITY

Bibliography: R. GARRIGOU-LAGRANGE, *God: His Existence and His Nature,* tr. B. ROSE, 2 v. (5th ed. St. Louis 1934–36) 1:15–25. J. MARITAIN, *A Preface to Metaphysics: Seven Lectures on Being* (New York 1939). J. OWENS, "The Intelligibility of Being," Gregorianum 36 (1955) 169–193.

[F. P. O'FARRELL]

INTENTION, PURITY OF

Freedom from the mixture of less worthy with good intention in the performance of a good act. Such a mixture of motivation occurs when a man performs an act that is good, and his predominant reason for doing it is good and has of itself force enough to account for his acting, if he is influenced in the same act by a secondary motive or motives of a venially sinful kind. In any other case— if the act is evil in itself, or if the discreditable motive is predominant, or if it is gravely sinful—one would not speak of a mixture of good and bad motives, for the total motivation of the act would be substantially corrupt. The existence of a secondary and accessory motive of a venially sinful kind detracts from the excellence of what one does and makes the act partially evil; this becomes, in effect, a virtually multiple act: a good act insofar as it is directed to a good end; an evil act insofar as its motive is unworthy.

This kind of mixture of motivation is not uncommon in human life, and a person seriously intent upon growing in holiness will be concerned to free himself from the influence of less worthy motives. This is applicable not merely to a spiritual elite but to all Christians, for no one should set limits beyond which his charity should not aspire. Thus it seems objectionable to distinguish, as did Henry of Herp, between a right intention, which is appropriate to ordinary Christians, who in the substance of their actions and the general purposes of their hearts desire and seek God's glory yet mix in less worthy designs that debase the spiritual value of what they do, and a pure intention, which is without such mixture of motive. A person with a right intention as described by Herp compromises in his heart between the love of God and one kind or another of self-love, and it seems a misuse of language to call such an intention right.

Purity of intention is sometimes identified with charity; it is active and fervent charity directing all that one does and suffers to the love and glory of God (D. A. Baker, *Holy Wisdom* 2.2.4). It is a proximate disposition to interior prayer, for it signifies an indivision and cleanness of heart—the clean heart being the undivided heart, as St. Augustine observed in commenting on the beatitudes—and it is the clean of heart who see God (Mt 5.8).

The want of purity of intention is sometimes hidden by self-deception, as when one averts his attention from the self-love that he permits to move him. Purity of intention, however, is not rendered impossible by urges or impulses rooted in the unconscious, for these are not motives in the sense understood in moral and ascetical theology (*see* MOTIVE, UNCONSCIOUS).

See Also: SIMPLICITY, VIRTUE OF; PERFECTION, SPIRITUAL; CHARITY.

Bibliography: See ch. 6 in Matthew. B. H. MERKELBACH, *Summa theologiae moralis* (Paris 1949) 1:148–151. H. DAVIS, *Moral and Pastoral Theology* (New York 1958) 1:57–60. A. THOUVENIN, *Dictionnaire de théologie catholique,* ed. A. VACANT et al. (Paris 1903–50) 7:2267–80. R. BARON, *Catholicisme* 5:1863–65.

[P. K. MEAGHER]

INTENTIONALITY

A term, modern in coinage but medieval in inspiration, used by Franz BRENTANO to designate what he took to be the distinctive feature of mental, as contrasted with physical, phenomena—the feature, namely, of being of or about an OBJECT. An IDEA, for example, would not be an idea unless it were an idea of something. And the same goes, Brentano thought, not merely for concepts, images, sensations, etc., but also for feelings and emotions, hopes, fears, desires, etc. Although intentionality is thus comparatively recent as a technical term in philosophy, its manifest derivation is from the ancient scholastic term *intentio*. Indeed, the sense of both terms is suggested by their etymology, which refers to something that by its very nature tends toward, or is aimed at, something else. As St. THOMAS AQUINAS defines it: "intention, as the name itself indicates, means to tend toward something" (*Summa theologiae* 1a2ae, 12.1).

So understood, there is no reason why intentionality should not be manifested in any number of different contexts or domains: in that of ethics, insofar as moral agents intend or mean to do what they do; in that of logic or epistemology, insofar as images and concepts are necessarily always images and concepts of something, and statements, propositions and arguments are always about something; and despite Brentano, even in the physical realm, insofar as active potencies in things may be considered as tendencies toward something, or the causes of things as tending toward their effects.

The ordinary, as contrasted with the technical, use of intention is confined almost exclusively to ethical contexts. "Sir, hell is paved with good intentions!" Dr. Johnson remarked. And somewhat more technically, St. Thomas seems to understand an intention as any conscious aiming at a goal or an end (confer, ST 1a2ae, 12).

Avicenna and the Scholastics. In its less common logical use, the term *intentio* became current in scholastic philosophy after the translation of the works of AVICENNA into Latin (see Kneale, 229–230; Spiegelberg, "Begriff," 77). ARISTOTLE in both the *De anima* and the *De interpretatione* had sought to explain cognition in terms of the reception of forms into the soul. Such forms—as, for example, the form of yellow or that of horse—once they were received into the soul, could then function as meanings or notions of yellow or of horse. The form in the soul, that is to say, was simply a meaning or a cognition or an intention of the same form in reality. Indeed, it was Avicenna's Arabic term for such meanings and intentions that came to be tendered in Latin as *intentio*.

A further development, again traceable to Avicenna, was the distinction between first and second intentions. For even supposing that the forms received in the soul, for example, yellow and horse, are, as forms, indistinguishable from the forms of yellow or of horse as existing in things in the real world, still the conditions and circumstances of their existence in the soul are different from what they are in reality. As a CONCEPT in the mind, yellow can be a predicate of a proposition, a species of a genus, a universal, a middle term of a syllogism, etc.; but as it exists in particular things, yellow is certainly not a predicate or a middle term or a species of a genus or even a universal (though this last exclusion was hotly and variously debated between nominalists and realists).

Moreover, it was considerations of just this sort that provided the scholastics with the means for distinguishing LOGIC from other disciplines. For in sciences other than logic the concern is presumably with the natures and characters of things in the real world. Hence the intentions used in these sciences will be intentions such as yellow and horse, which signify or intend yellow and horse as real properties of real things. In logic, on the other hand, the concern is not with understanding the real world, but rather with understanding the logical means and instruments of such understanding. Hence the intentions used in logic will not be intentions of such things as yellow and horse, but rather intentions of intentions, or second intentions—that is, such intentions as *yellow* and *horse,* insofar as these function as subjects or predicates, as genera or species, as terms in a syllogism and generally as logical devices employed in acts of knowing. (For a comparison and contrast of this medieval conception of logic in terms of second intentions with the modern conception of logic in terms of so-called logical forms and formal truths, see Veatch).

However, it is not just the logician who concerns himself with forms in the soul; in addition, the very fact that such forms come to be or exist in the soul means that they become proper objects of investigation for both PSYCHOLOGY and what, in modern philosophy, has come to be known as EPISTEMOLOGY. Thus, for example, when the form yellow is received in a physical or material object, the object itself becomes yellow; however, when such a form is received intentionally in the soul, the soul does not become yellow. What, then, is the status and condition of such a form as it exists intentionally?

Thomas Aquinas. According to St. Thomas, such an intentionally received FORM is an intelligible *species,* in that through it the real form is rendered, as it were, perspicuous (*see* SPECIES, INTENTIONAL). So also, the form that is intentionally received may be considered to be a *similitudo* of the real form existing in the world. At the same time, this Thomistic doctrine of the likeness of the form in the soul to the form in the real world must not be construed in the manner of the various copy theories of modern epistemology.

For one thing, even if the form in the soul be a *similitudo,* or copy, of the form in reality, still, in the act of cognition, the human being does not first come to know the copy (the form in the soul) and then somehow infer the original (the form in reality). Rather it is *through* the intentionally received form, as a *similitudo* or an *intentio* of the real form, that the latter comes to be known. As St. Thomas put it, the likeness or the intelligible species in the intellect is the *id quo,* not the *id quod,* of knowledge (ST 1a, 85.2).

For another thing, St. Thomas, at least in one of his earlier works, the *De ente et essentia,* worked out an account of forms or essences of things according to which the form in the soul, in at least one fundamental respect (namely, formally or essentially, though not numerically), is the very form that is in things. This is possible, St. Thomas holds, because a form or an ESSENCE, or that in virtue of which things are what they are, is in and of itself neither universal and so a product of ABSTRACTION (as it is when it is a species or an intention in the intellect) nor particular and individual (as it is when existing in many different individual things in the real world). Consequently, when one says, "Peter is a man," Peter is certainly an individual, and the predicate concept "man" is certainly a universal. Yet in saying that what Peter is is a man, one is not saying that he is a universal. True, one *uses* the universal concept of intention in the intellect in order to know what Peter is; but *what* one thus comes to know him to be is not anything universal.

And so likewise, in saying of Peter just what he, the individual, is, one does not thereby restrict his human nature or essence, or what he is, to Peter alone. On the contrary, it is still through and only through a universal predicate concept—that is, through an intention or likeness or species in the soul, which is nonetheless universal—that one comes to know what Peter, the individual, is. In other words, in saying that what Peter is, is a man, one no more turns human nature into an individual than he turns Peter into a universal.

And all this is made possible by the fact that what Peter is, and more generally the forms or essences through which things are what they are, are in themselves neither universal nor particular, neither one nor many. So it is that the same form, which happens to be a universal intention or likeness or species of man in the mind, can come to be recognized as being the very form or essence of Peter in the real world, as being what the individual Peter is, in short.

Ockham. It is hardly surprising that both before and after St. Thomas, and in both scholastic and modern philosophy, the very puzzling notion of the form in the soul, of the form as an *intentio* or *similitudo* or *species* of the real form, should have occasioned no little discussion. WILLIAM OF OCKHAM, for example, seems to have moved from an earlier position in which he regarded forms existing intentionally in the soul as in some sense fictive or "objective" beings, to a position in which he repudiated all such purely intentional beings, or beings that exist as mere objects before the mind and that function simply as means through which real forms come to be known. Instead, his final doctrine seems to have been that the psychological act of understanding itself suffices for a direct and immediate signifying or intending of the real forms in things (see Boehner, 146–147).

Brentano, Meinong, and Husserl. In contrast, in modern times and with respect to much the same issue, Brentano seems to have taken a stand that could be interpreted as almost the opposite of that of Ockham. Impressed as all modern thinkers have been by epistemological problems, Brentano—if one were to formulate his position not in his own, but in scholastic, terms—insists that there are intentions in the soul and that all intentions are necessarily intentions of objects. But such objects of intentions, considered as such, are not the real forms of things, but only forms in the mind. Or, put in another way, every intention has an object, but considered simply as an object of an intention, such an object does not have to be anything extramental. Accordingly, Brentano can speak of "the intentional (and also mental) inexistence (*Inexistenz*) of an object (*Gegenstand*), and what we could call, although in not entirely unambiguous terms, the reference to a content, a direction upon an object (by which we are not to understand a reality in this case), or an immanent objectivity" (*Psychologie vom empirischen Standpunkt;* see Chisholm, 50).

This same stress upon the merely objective being of intentions is found in both A. Meinong and E. HUSSERL. Meinong, indeed, proliferates a vast realm of such objects of intention, peopling it with golden mountains, round squares, et al. And Husserl, in order to bring his method of phenomenological description properly to bear on the objects of intentions, insists that one must, as he puts it, simply "bracket" the question of the existence or nonexistence of such objects in the real world. Nevertheless, with Husserl there does seem to be a marked shift in emphasis from what one finds in Brentano. Rather than with the object of intention and the peculiar kind of existence or "inexistence" that such objects have, Husserl occupied himself more with intentional acts and with how such acts do not merely aim at their objects, but actually bring about the construction and constitution of their objects (see Spiegelberg, "Begriff," 81–32, 87–89).

Comparisons. But how are these more modern views regarding intentionality to be compared with St. Thomas's? Clearly, a comparison with Husserl is rendered difficult, if not impossible, to the extent that Husserl tends to regard intentional acts of the mind, such as thinking and perceiving, as actually constituting and building up their objects. Such a way of conceiving intentionality is so radically at variance with St. Thomas's basic REALISM, and is so thoroughly Kantian and post-Kantian in its inspiration, that one can scarcely imagine how St. Thomas might make rejoinder of it, short of a rebuttal of the entire *Critique of Pure Reason.*

On the other hand, with Brentano, one might imagine that, from St. Thomas's point of view, he is to be commended for insisting that in knowledge there is something on the order of a form actually present in the soul. Yet, at the same time, St. Thomas would surely insist that by making this received form the actual object of the *intentio*, Brentano and his followers had in effect confused the *id quo* of intentional reference with the *id quod*.

To be sure, St. Thomas seems not to have concerned himself particularly with the sort of epistemological consideration that is paramount with thinkers such as Brentano and Meinong. This is the consideration that the mere fact that one has intentions, and that intentions must and do have objects, does not as such give any warrant for inferring that such objects of intentions are either the same as, or similar to, objects existing in the real world. Nevertheless, St. Thomas's comparative indifference to this sort of epistemological problem may not have been a result of mere inadvertence. Instead, it needs always to be remembered that for him such things as forms or natures or essences are not, as such, either universal or particular, either mental or physical, either immanent or transcendent. Hence why suppose that, such forms or essences being upon occasion objects of intentions, they may therefore be no more than "immanent objects" and may possibly enjoy no more than an "intentional inexistence"? To suppose this would surely be, from St. Thomas's point of view, to create a problem where no problem exists. For on his account, a nature or form, even when it is a received form, does not have what the phenomenologists would call immanence attaching to it as an essential feature. But if the form be not essentially immanent, then the problem of its transcendence is not a problem, or at least is not the same problem as it was for Brentano and Meinong.

See Also: KNOWLEDGE; KNOWLEDGE, PROCESS OF; KNOWLEDGE, THEORIES OF; IMMATERIALITY.

Bibliography: H. B. VEATCH, *Intentional Logic* (New Haven 1952). W. and M. KNEALE, *The Development of Logic* (Oxford 1962), ch. IV, sec. 3. P. BOEHNER, *Collected Articles on Ockham,* ed., E. M. BUYTAERT (St. Bonaventure, N.Y. 1958). E. A. MOODY, *The Logic of William of Ockham* (New York 1935). H. SPIEGELBERG, *The Phenomenological Movement,* 2 v. (The Hague 1960); "Der Begriff der Intentionalität in der Scholastik, bei Brentano und bei Husserl," *Philosophische Hefte,* ed., M. BECK, 5 v. (Berlin 1928–36) 5:72–91. *Realism and the Background of Phenomenology,* ed., R. M. CHISHOLM, (Glentoe, Ill. 1961).

[H. B. VEATCH]

INTERCESSION

Derived from the Latin *inter* (between) and *cedere* (to go or pass), intercession is the act of reconciling the differences between two parties. This article considers: (1) the theological notion of intercession; (2) the intercession of Christ; (3) the intercession of Our Lady, the angels, and saints; and (4) the intercession of a wayfarer.

Theological Notion. From the theological viewpoint, intercession is the act of pleading by one who in God's sight has a right to do so in order to obtain mercy for one in need. In this definition the term "pleading" is used because intercession is a species of prayer—in the strict sense of the word, excluding adoration, thanksgiving, and propitiation. Prayer so considered is the act of the practical intellect seeking divine benefits (cf. St. Thomas, *Summa theologiae* 2a2ae, 83). Intercession, however, differs from all other species of prayer because the benefit sought is for another. Further, the intercessor must have standing before God, just as defense attorneys must have standing before the court in which they are pleading. The intercessor is taking the position of an advocate for another with God and consequently must have some claim upon the divine benefaction. Christ's right to plead is based on the Hypostatic Union and His Sacrifice on the cross; Mary's right is that of the divine maternity and her association with Christ's sacrifice; the angels and saints have a basis in their participation in the divine life through the beatific vision; a wayfarer can intercede by reason of his FRIENDSHIP with God produced by sanctifying grace and charity. The definition's "one in need" should not be restricted to those in mortal sin, for those in the state of grace need divine mercy since they bear the effects of original sin and forgiven actual sins, and are capable of future sins.

Intercession of Christ. Christ's intercession is part of His MEDIATION. First, the Scriptures explicitly affirm that Christ actually prays for us in heaven (Rom 8.34; Heb 7.25; Jn 2.1). Second, Christ acts as intercessor according to His human nature, for only thus can He stand between God and man.

Intercession of Mary, the Angels, and Saints. A Catholic may entertain no doubts about the fact of their intercession, since the Council of Trent clearly defined this dogma—"the saints, reigning together with Christ, offer their prayers to God for men" (*Enchiridion symbolorum* 1821). Further, this dogma is contained in both the Old and New Testaments (2 Mc 15.11–16; Tb 12.12; Rv 5.8, 8.3). Our Lady's intercession differs from that of the angels and saints because the basis of her intercession, besides her participation in glory, is the divine maternity and her unique cooperation in Christ's sacrifice; moreover, the result of her pleading brings all graces to all men—a point affirmed by many modern popes.

About the nature of the intercession of the blessed two questions arise: (1) How do they know man's needs?

and (2) Are their requests always fulfilled? The angels know man's needs through concepts infused in their minds by God and through the supernatural gift of the beatific vision, in which they see the divine decrees dealing with man. The blessed souls have no natural means of knowing those still *in via* (until the general resurrection), but as in the case of the angels they have knowledge through the beatific vision. In regard to the second question, it can be affirmed that their prayers are always fulfilled in this sense: knowing perfectly the divine decrees, they never request that which God does not intend to give, since their wills always conform to the divine will.

Intercession of Wayfarers. Those in this life are able to pray for others and, indeed, are obliged to do so because of fraternal charity. Although one is not obliged to pray explicitly for a particular individual, unless he is in extreme spiritual need, one may never exclude anyone from his prayers for all. It is useless to pray for the damned in hell and unnecessary to pray for the blessed in heaven. All others, those in the state of grace or not, should be the object of prayer.

Some Christians may object to the doctrine here described, because they see in it a diminution of Christ's mediation. Uneasiness about the doctrine, however, can result from a failure to appreciate a fundamental principle of the divine governance: in the execution of the divine providence God makes use of creatures to produce desired effects. This notion permeates the Scriptures: the role of the Jewish race before the Messiah's coming, Christ's redemptive activity, the Apostles' mission, the writings of the Evangelists, each is an application of the principle. In the same vein the blessed in heaven have a role to play in the sanctification of men; they participate in the divine causality through their intercession. Catholic doctrine in this matter does not diminish the role of Christ the Mediator, for the prayers of each member of His Mystical Body are channeled through the Head.

See Also: SAINTS, INTERCESSION OF.

Bibliography: F. L. B. CUNNINGHAM, *The Christian Life* (Dubuque, Iowa 1959). J. DOUILLET, *What Is a Saint?*, tr. D. ATTWATER (New York 1958). THOMAS AQUINAS, *Summa theologiae* 3a Suppl., 72. R. GUARDINI, *Prayer in Practice*, tr. PRINCE LEOPOLD OF LOEWENSTEIN-WERTHEIM (New York 1957) 184–199. J. DE BACIOCCHI, *Catholicisme. Hier, aujourd'hui et demain*, ed. G. JACQUEMET (Paris 1947–) 5:1870–73. P. SÉJOURNÉ, *Dictionnaire de théologie catholique*, ed. A. VACANT et al., 15 v. (Paris 1903–50; Tables générales 1951–) 14.1:870–978.

[P. J. MAHONEY]

INTERIMS

The doctrinal formulas agreed upon by a commission of theologians and adopted as a temporary (*ad interim*) solution for the religious disunity within the Empire of Charles V.

REGENSBURG (1541)

This enactment resulted from the failure of the Diet of Regensburg, which had opened on April 7, 1541, with high hopes of a religious settlement. From April 27 to May 22 an imperial committee of three Catholics (Johann ECK, Julius von PFLUG, and Johann Gropper) and three Protestants (Philipp MELANCHTHON, Martin BUCER, and Johannes Pistorius) deliberated on a schema drawn up probably by Gropper. In spite of genuine effort to reach unanimity and the conciliatory manner of the papal legate, Gasparo CONTARINI, the conference collapsed. This was attributable to the political interests of Johann Friedrich of Saxony and Francis I, King of France, who feared the power of a united Hapsburg Empire, and also to the influence of the conservative Lutheran Nikolaus von AMSDORF, who opposed any acceptance of transubstantiation or auricular confession. As a result, the Interim of Regensburg was published on July 29, 1541, postponing religious settlement until the next diet, suspending juridical processes in religious matters, forbidding Protestants to widen their political influence, upholding the provisions of the Peace of Nuremberg (1532) and the Confession of AUGSBURG (1530), and exhorting ecclesiastical reforms. It legislated further, on the one hand, that monasteries and prelates who had accepted the Confession of Augsburg were not to be deprived of their property; nor, on the other hand, were Protestants to force Catholic subjects to embrace their faith.

AUGSBURG (1548)

This Interim of 26 chapters appeared at the end of the Diet of Augsburg, June 30, 1548, and was called ''A Declaration of His Imperial Majesty on how things are to be managed in the Holy Roman Empire, touching the question of religion, until the General Council can be held.'' Johann von Pflug, Michael Helding, suffragan bishop of Mainz, Eberhard Billick, Pedro de Soto, and Johannes Agricola worked out a formula that phrased Catholic theology in terms as indefinite as possible, often employing Protestant modes of expression, and conceded Communion under both species as well as permission for married Protestant clergy to retain their wives. Though looked upon by Charles as an ingenious solution, it pleased few others. Elector Joachim of Brandenburg (called ''Father of the Interim''), Margrave Albrecht of Brandenburg-Culmbach, and the Elector of Mainz accepted it; but the princes of other Catholic Estates, even after assurance that the Interim was directed to the Protestants, submitted without enthusiasm. It was not endorsed by Paul III until August 1549. Among the Protestants who opposed it were Duke Johann Frederich of Saxony,

Margrave Hans von Cüstrin, Count Palatine Wolfgang Johann Zweibrücken, Duke Ulrich of Württenburg, Elector Maurice of Saxony, and Landgrave Philip of Hesse, who as a captive of Charles later signed it to hasten his release. The center of Protestant opposition was Magdeburg, where Matthias FLACIUS ILLYRICUS and Nikolaus von Amsdorf fought its adoption (see GNESIOLUTHERANISM). In general the Catholic clergy refused to become Interim priests and distribute the Sacrament under both species; the Protestant clergy looked upon the formula as "revived papistry." A Frankfort delegate to the Diet reported that the Interim was regarded as *interitum* (disaster).

LEIPZIG (1548)

In an attempt to make the reintroduction of Catholic ceremonial acceptable to Protestants, Maurice of Saxony, Melanchthon, and George III of Anhalt-Dessau met at Alt-Zella in November 1548. There a new document was drawn up, declaring that Catholic ceremonials, images of saints, etc., were neither good nor bad but indifferent things (*adiaphora*) and therefore not in opposition to Scripture. This was accepted by Saxony at the Diet of Leipzig in December, but elsewhere it led to renewed controversy.

See Also: PHILIPPISM; CRYPTO-CALVINISM; CONFESSIONS OF FAITH, PROTESTANT.

Bibliography: B. J. KIDD, ed., *Documents Illustrative of the Continental Reformation* (Oxford 1911) 340–346 (on Regensberg), 359–362 (on Augsburg). P. SCHAFF, *Bibliotheca symbolica ecclesiae universalis: The Creeds of Christendom,* 3 v. (6th ed. New York 1919) v.3. Janssen-Pastor 6:395–420. H. HOLBORN, *A History of Modern Germany,* 3 v. (New York 1959) v.1 *The Reformation.* K. BRANDI, *The Emperor Charles V: The Growth and Destiny of a Man and of a World Empire,* tr. C. V. WEDGWOOD (New York 1939). L. PASTOR, *The History of the Popes from the Close of the Middle Ages* (London-St. Louis 1938–61) 12:409–439.

[E. D. MC SHANE]

INTERNATIONAL CATHOLIC DEAF ASSOCIATION

The International Catholic Deaf Association (ICDA) was founded in 1949 in Toronto, Canada, by deaf people from Buffalo, Detroit, and Toronto at the first Congress of the Catholic Deaf. They worked with ten priests to lay plans for an international organization. James Cardinal McGuigan, then archbishop of Toronto, gave the project his approval. From these initial efforts came the ICDA. It has constituent memberships in the United States, France, Ireland, and elsewhere. The United States affiliate began in 1987 at Hartford, Connecticut, but officers were not elected until 1989 at the business convention in

Portland, Oregon. A constitution was adopted for the United States in July 1991, in Cleveland, Ohio.

The purpose of the ICDA is to promote cultural, spiritual, and social union among deaf and hard-of-hearing Catholics through the teachings and principles of the Catholic faith. The ICDA engages in work relative to the educational, social, and moral advancement of deaf people and acts as a means for public advocacy on behalf of the deaf. Since 1986, the ICDA has had biennial "Workshop Conventions" to further the deaf apostolate. These have been designed to incorporate more fully those deaf people called to ministry and leadership in various ecclesial contexts.

The membership of the ICDA-U.S. comprises local chapters and individual members. Each chapter is self-governing and operates under the constitution and by-laws of the ICDA-U.S. In 2001 there were 108 local chapters scattered among six regions. ICDA-U.S. is governed by the membership and a six-member elected Board of Directors consisting of the President, Vice-President, Secretary, Treasurer, Chaplain, and immediate Past President. With the possible exception of the Chaplain, all officers are deaf. The worldwide organization has an official English publication, *The Deaf Catholic*. Membership in the ICDA-U.S. is open to all Catholic deaf people and to hearing people who are interested in working with deaf Catholics.

Bibliography: The DeSales Project Report, *Eye Centered: A Study of the Spirituality of Deaf People with Implications for Pastoral Ministry* (Silver Spring, Maryland 1992). C. PADDEN and T. HUMPHRIES, *Deaf in America: Voices from a Culture* (Cambridge, Massachusetts 1988). An uncatalogued archive of materials related to the deaf, including the ICDA and its United States affiliate, is located at the College of the Holy Cross in Worcester, Massachusetts.

[P. J. HAYES]

INTERNATIONAL CATHOLIC MIGRATION COMMISSION

In response to the need for coordination of Catholic migration and refugee services on a worldwide basis, the International Catholic Migration Commission (ICMC) was established in 1951 with headquarters in Geneva. The lessons of the Second World War with respect to displaced persons and later the mass migrations in Eastern Europe beginning in 1949, prompted Catholic laity and clergy from Germany, Italy, and the United States to form the ICMC. Then Substitute Secretary of State, Archbishop Montini (the future Pope Paul VI), and Cardinal Joseph Frings of Germany, were instrumental in the foundation. The following year, Pope Pius XII, in his Apostolic Constitution *Exsul familia*, focused the attention of Catholics on the needs of migrants and refugees, and formally introduced the ICMC to the world. The first president of the ICMC was Mr. James J. Norris (1907 to 1976) of the National Catholic Welfare Conference's office of War Relief Services. He served as president for 23 years and retired in 1976.

Throughout the 1960s, the ICMC worked primarily in Europe, but by mid-decade their presence could be found in 42 countries worldwide. Much of this work involved the dispensing of loans to facilitate the movement of immigrants. These funds benefited over 40,000 from 1952 to 1962. By the early 1970s, the migration phenomenon had become more complex and international, where warring parties often made national borders arbitrary and aid to the displaced that much more difficult. The end of the war in Vietnam, the attempted genocide in Cambodia, and other hot spots forced the ICMC to begin resettlement work in Southeast Asia, among other places. With forced migration come the related problems of health, hunger, human smuggling, and often the peculiar horror of "ethnic cleansing." By the end of 1977, the ICMC had granted travel loans in the amount of approximately 50 million dollars, helping hundreds of thousands to find a country of permanent resettlement.

In 1999, the ICMC provided services to over 100,000 people, including protection for 63,000 of the most vulnerable refugees (elderly, widowed, mentally and physically disabled) in 11 countries. It also helped 2,600 refugees in Bosnia and Kosovo, primarily women and internally displaced people, move towards economic self-sufficiency through microcredit loans. About 42,000 were resettled in the United States that year. Wherever possible, the ICMC works in partnership with the local Church. In 2001, ICMC had around 30 international and almost 400 national staff members who work in 21 countries on all continents. It is also one of the chief collaborators in the Holy See's World Day of Migration, which calls attention to the needs of those affected by migration issues. It cooperates with the Pontifical Council for the Pastoral Care of Migrants and Itinerant Peoples. The ICMC was actively involved in the World Conference against Racism, Racial Discrimination, Xenophobia and Related Intolerance (WCAR) in Durban, South Africa (2001), precisely because of the impact of racism on refugees.

The ICMC cooperates especially with two intergovernmental organizations, the Office of the United Nations High Commissioner for Refugees (UNHCR) and the Intergovernmental Committee for European Migration (ICEM) and claims consultative status with the Council of Europe and, since 1952, the UN Economic and Social Council. Funding comes through a combination of grants from the United States government and the United Nations organization, among other sources.

Membership of the ICMC is open to all Catholic national episcopal conferences and their relevant organizations working with migrant and refugee populations. In 2001 the ICMC had 95 members and affiliate members from 82 countries. The ICMC is made up of a Council, Governing Committee, and General Secretariat. Council members are nominees of Catholic bishops conferences and national Catholic organizations working with refugees and migrants. The whole Council elects the President of the Commission, subject to approval of the Holy See, who convenes and chairs both the Council and Governing Committee meetings. Voting for the other members of the 12-person Governing Committee is regionally based. The ICMC Council meets once a year to determine the priorities of the organization. Every three years the Council elects the President and other officers of the Governing Committee.

Bibliography: The papers of James J. Norris are archived at the University of Notre Dame. The ICMC's 50-year history was in press in 2001.

[P. J. HAYES]

INTERNATIONAL CATHOLIC STEWARDSHIP COUNCIL

The International Catholic Stewardship Council (ICSC) had its origin in a 1962 meeting in St. Louis, organized by Reverend Paul Kaletta, of diocesan directors of development on their concerns. The group first called itself the National Association Council of Diocesan Financing, then the National Council of Diocesan Support Programs, then the National Catholic Stewardship Council (NCSC), and adopted the present name in 1999. The formulation of a constitution and by–laws and the election of the first officers occurred in 1967. The episcopal moderators have been Bishops Albert Zuroweste (Belleville) 1967 to 1974, from 1971 to 1974, co-moderator with Edward E. Swanstrom (auxiliary, New York); and William G. Connare (Greenburg) 1974 to the present. Reverend Robert Deming (Kansas City-St. Joseph) was first executive secretary and the Kansas City chancery the first, temporary headquarters. Father Kaletta (d. 1974) served as the Council's first chairman.

Early progress included the Publications Committee's *Parish Stewardship Educational Program*, known as the "red kit" because of its red cover. It furnished parishes with a variety of instructional materials on stewardship including a three-weekend stewardship program whereby parishioners received a biblical and spiritual concept of stewardship (first week), introduction of stewardship of time and talent (second week—after which they were invited to carry out an apostolate of their choice), and to stewardship of money (third week—after which they were asked to sign a pledge to contribute a certain amount of money to their church each week).

During his chairmanship of the NCSC, 1972 to 1974, Monsignor Charles Grahmann (San Antonio) became aware of three needs: (1) to expand the NCSC operation by giving more emphasis to stewardship of time and talent; (2) to move the office to Washington, D.C. in order to form a relationship with the USCC-NCCB; and (3) to find a full-time executive director to carry out the Executive Board's policies in a professional manner. At the tenth annual conference in Tucson in October 1973, participants voted to support all three areas.

On Feb. 4, 1974, Francis A. Novak, CSSR, then engaged in stewardship work in the Diocese of Grand Rapids, was elected NCSC's first full-time executive director. His mandate was to develop catechetical and pastoral programs on the total concept of stewardship.

In 1975, the NCSC published its first major program, *Stewardship of Money, A Manual for Parishes*, as an answer to requests from Ordinaries, development directors, pastors, and lay persons on parish and pastoral councils for assistance to solve parochial and diocesan fund-raising problems. It used the biblical teaching of returning to God a proportion of his material gifts, together with Vatican II's doctrine of co-responsibility, to explore the deeper meaning of the gifts of Eucharist. NCSC's second major program was published in 1976, *Stewardship of Time and Talent, A Parish Manual for Lay Ministries*. It fostered the development of lay ministries using some of the theological insights on ministry emerging from Vatican II. It has participated in the development of the NCCB *Principles and Guidelines for Fund Raising* (1977).

The ICSC is a member organization covering 18 regions throughout the world, with most found in North America, including all 13 United States episcopal regions. It serves arch-dioceses, parishes, professional firms, religious congregations, and Catholic associations through its seminars, publications, and annual conference. A number of committees attend to the mission of the ICSC, including those that focus on economic concerns, parish stewardship education, diocesan programs, and communications. Its primary concern continues to be to promote a biblical concept of Christian stewardship in which generosity of time, talent, and treasure are construed as God-given gifts. Its mission is to foster an environment in which stewardship is understood, accepted, and practiced throughout the Catholic Church. The Council promotes the concept that stewardship is not simply an appeal for funds; it is a way of life. ICSC publishes a journal, *Resource*, and facilitates a bilingual diocesan and parish exchange program on various facets of stewardship. ICSC has also sponsored the Comprehensive Diocesan Development Survey, an instrument that reports and analyzes information on annual appeal programs provided by arch/diocesan offices of stewardship and development. The Center of Applied Research in the Apostolate (CARA) conducts the research and writes the report for ICSC, which has been prepared almost yearly since 1992.

ICSC has hosted two international, multilingual Stewardship Seminars, held in Rome in 1973 and 1998. The First Annual Institute for Stewardship and Development, which provided a comprehensive introduction to the basic principles and techniques of stewardship and development, was held in Marriottsville, Maryland in 1993. Subsequent institutes have been held in Danville, California, and Mundelein, Illinois. ICSC's Board of Directors accepted a proposal in October 1993 from The National Planned Giving Institute at the College of William and Mary in Williamsburg, Virginia, to train diocesan executives and others in the area of planned giving.

Bibliography: NCSC Publications: *Stewardship of Time and Talent, A Parish Manual for Lay Ministries* (1976); *Stewardship of Money, A Manual for Parishes* (1975); *Money as an Offertory Gift* (1977); *Stewardship: Symbolic Presence of the Christ Event for the Church Today* (1976). M. R. MADDEN, *Gladly Will I Spend and Be Spent: A Brief History of the National Catholic Stewardship Council, 1962–1997* (Washington, D.C. 1998); NCCB, *Stewarship: A Disciples Response* (Washington, D.C., 1992); *Resource* (1993–), ICSC, *Stewardship and Development Guidelines for a Diocesan Office* (Washington, D.C., n.d).

[P. J. HAYES]

INTERNATIONAL COMMISSION ON ENGLISH IN THE LITURGY (ICEL)

In 1962 during the first session of Vatican Council II, a small group of English and American bishops, realizing that the use of the vernacular in the liturgy was about to be sanctioned to some degree, informally discussed the possibility of providing common texts for all English-speaking Catholics. Further discussion of this possibility continued among a widening group of English-speaking bishops during 1963. In October of that year bishops representing ten episcopal conferences met in the English College at Rome under the chairmanship of Archbishop Francis Grimshaw of England to lay plans for the work of the International Commission on English in the Liturgy (ICEL). The following conferences were represented at that meeting: Australia, Canada, England and Wales, India, Ireland, New Zealand, Pakistan, Scotland, South Africa, and the United States. In 1967 an 11th member, the conference of bishops of the Philippines, joined the original group. In addition to the member conferences there are also 15 associate-member conferences of ICEL.

Founding of ICEL. The International Commission on English in the Liturgy originating in Rome at the heart of the Council was the first response of a number of conferences sharing the same language to the directive of the Constitution on the Sacred Liturgy: "it is for the competent territorial ecclesiastical authority . . . , to decide whether, and to what extent, the vernacular is to be used. Their decrees are to be approved, that is, confirmed, by the APOSTOLIC SEE. And whenever it seems called for, this authority is to consult with bishops of neighboring regions that have the same language (*Sacrosanctum Concilium* 36.3)." The Council's wish that countries sharing the same language should work together was more forcefully underscored in a letter dated Oct. 16, 1964 of Cardinal Giacomo Lercaro, president of the Consilium for the Implementation of the Constitution on the Sacred Liturgy, to the presidents of conferences of bishops. In that letter Cardinal Lercaro stated that international commissions should be established by conferences of bishops sharing the same language to make one text for all. The pioneering work of ICEL became the inspiration for the several other language commissions which were established at the direction of the HOLY SEE.

In 1964 the bishops of ICEL prepared a formal mandate for the work to be undertaken as a common effort. This mandate, already anticipating the creation of a committee of experts to oversee the ICEL program, was addressed to the International Advisory Committee on English in the Liturgy. The mandate was submitted to each of the constituent conferences of bishops and was ratified by all of them in 1964. A formal constitution was adopted in the same year. The principal element in the constitution was the structured plan to relate the International Episcopal Committee on English in the Liturgy and the International Advisory Committee on English in the Liturgy as two distinct entities within the single organizations.

It was also in 1964 that the bishops of ICEL invited various experts, priests and lay people, to join them in their deliberations as they began to make definite plans towards the production of English vernacular texts which, it was hoped, would be acceptable to each of the member conferences. These experts who constituted the original advisory committee met for the first time in London during January 1965 and again, with the bishops, in Rome in November 1965. They represented the various

specializations which would be necessary in developing a vernacular liturgy: liturgists, classical scholars, patrologists, English scholars, musicians. At a later stage biblical experts were also consulted. The work of ICEL was depended heavily on the talents of numerous English-speaking people, representative of these several areas of scholarship. It was the function of the advisory committee to oversee the work of ICEL and to advise the bishops after a careful review of the proposed translations and projects.

Structure and Work. The episcopal board (originally, committee) is the governing body of ICEL. Each conference designates one bishop as its representative on the board. All projects and translations, having been endorsed by the advisory committee, must be submitted to the episcopal board for final approval. When a text has been approved by a two-thirds majority vote of the episcopal board it is then submitted to the separate conferences for the vote of their individual members. In addition to presenting the texts to their conferences, the members of the Episcopal Board regularly report to their conferences on the continuing work of ICEL as well as on proposals for future work. The 11 members of the Episcopal Board also serve as the board of trustees of the civil corporation, the International Committee on English in the Liturgy, Inc., which was established under Canadian law in 1967 to protect the copyright of the ICEL texts.

The daily activities of ICEL are carried on through a secretariat which was established in Washington, D.C. in 1965. The work of the secretariat is directed by an executive secretary who is immediately responsible to the advisory committee and ultimately to the episcopal board.

The episcopal board and advisory committee issued two booklets, *English for the Mass* (1966) and *English for the Mass: Part II* (1967), which gave various sample translations of the Order of the Mass and the proper parts of the Mass. In order to assist them in the pioneering work of translating the Latin liturgy into English, the bishops and specialists invited comments from "all who are interested in the liturgy, not only Roman Catholics, but also members of other Christian bodies."

The first liturgical text issued by ICEL was the translation of the Roman Canon (Eucharistic Prayer I) which was presented to the conferences of bishops in 1967. This work was the product of many draft proposals and careful deliberation by the advisory committee and episcopal board. In the process of reaching the final draft hundreds of consultants, specialists in the various disciplines represented on the Advisory Committee, were asked to submit comments. In addition, all of the bishops of the English-speaking world were invited to give their comments after studying the draft. Since ICEL's beginnings consultation has played a major part in the ICEL process. The generous participation of these many bishops, priests, religious, and lay people served to make the work more representative of the individual conferences and has ensured that the texts will be acceptable in each of the separate countries. The publication of the Roman Canon has been followed by 21 translations of the rites revised at the direction of Vatican II. Although each of these works involved wide consultation and the reworking of a number of drafts, the texts which stand out, in terms of the magnitude of work involved, as the principal accomplishments of ICEL are the *Roman Missal* (1974) and *The Liturgy of the Hours* (1975–76). For all of these translations, ICEL adopted the norms of translation set down in the *Instruction on Translation of Liturgical Texts (Comme le prévoit)* issued by the Consilium for the Implementation of the Constitution on the Sacred Liturgy (*Notitiae* 5 [1969] 3–12).

With major portions of its work of translation completed, ICEL implemented the second phase of its program. This second phase, endorsed by its episcopal board, was primarily directed to three general services: (1) the provision of music for the revised rites; (2) the provision of original texts, composed in the vernacular, in accord with the norms laid down in the revised Roman books; and (3) the reordering of the revised Roman books to make them more pastorally effective for the celebration of the rites in the English-speaking countries. The work of providing commentaries on the individual rites and other pastoral aids was also begun by ICEL as part of the second phase of its program. The procedure that ICEL adopted was as follows. First, the advisory committee determined which rites needed to be revised and what prayers were needed to supplement the *editio typica*. Next it assigned the task of revision to four standing subcommittees: (1) translation and revision, (2) original texts, (3) presentation of texts (layout/rubrics), and (4) music. The advisory committee was responsible for reviewing the work of these four subcommittees, before forwarding the final text to the Episcopal Board for its vote.

In the 1990s, the Congregation for Divine Worship and the Discipline of the Sacraments (CDWDS) adopted a critical stance toward ICEL, expressing its strong disapproval over several of ICEL's translation projects, especially the inclusive psalter project, ICEL's proposed translation of the second edition of Rite of Ordination (1992) and the proposed revision of the Sacramentary. This tension culminated in the demand of Cardinal Jorge Medina, Prefect of CDWDS, in 1999 that ICEL reorganize its structure and place itself under the direct control of the CDWDS.

As a result of this restructuring, the four standing subcommittees and advisory committee ceased to exist on Jan. 1, 2001. They were replaced by a consultants' committee, chaired by the chairman of the episcopal board (or his designate). As part of the restructuring, the actual work of preparing texts for the English-speaking world would now fall on an ad hoc committee appointed for each project by the episcopal board. Under the proposed new constitution of ICEL which is awaiting the approval of Rome, all draft translations were to be presented to the various bishop conferences in a three-column format comprising 1) the Latin text, 2) a literal translation and 3) the text as intended for proclamation. Once the bishop conferences approve the texts, they were to be submitted to the CDWDS for its *recognitio*.

Bibliography: J. M. KEMPER, *Behind the Text: A Study of the Principles and Procedures of Translation, Adaptation, and Composition of Original Texts by the International Commission on English in the Liturgy* (Ph.D. dissertation, University of Notre Dame, 1992). J. R. PAGE, "ICEL through Twenty-five Years," in *Disciples at the Crossroads*, ed. E. BERNSTEIN (Collegeville, Minn 1993) 63–80. J. R. PAGE, "ICEL, 1966–1989: Weaving the Words of Our Common Christian Prayer," in *Shaping English Liturgy*, eds. P.C. FINN and J.M. SCHELLMAN (Washington, D.C. 1990) 473–489. G. B. HARRISON and P. JONES, "Personal Reminiscences of the Early Years of ICEL," ibid., 461–472. F. R. MCMANUS, "ICEL: The First Years," *ibid.*, 433–459. A. TEGELS, "On Englishing the Liturgy," *Worship* 58 (1984) 441–445. M. COLLINS, "Glorious Praise: the ICEL Liturgical Psalter," *Worship* 66 (1992) 290–310. N. MITCHELL, "The ICEL Psalter," *Worship* 69 (1995) 361–370, 447–456, 556–565 (3 pts.). G. OSTDIEK, "Crafting English Prayer Texts: The ICEL Revision of the Sacramentary," *Studia Liturgica* 26:1 (1996) 128–139.

[J. R. PAGE/EDS.]

INTERNATIONAL CONSULTATION ON ENGLISH TEXTS (ICET)

Established in 1969, ICET was an independent, ecumenical organization distinct from the Roman Catholic body, INTERNATIONAL COMMISSION ON ENGLISH IN THE LITURGY (ICEL) which sought to produce common liturgical texts for ecumenical use. The need for ICET arose from two causes. First, the Roman Catholic Church, putting its liturgies officially into English for the first time, did not feel bound by the texts of the Anglican BOOK OF COMMON PRAYER, which other non–Anglican churches had largely followed. Second, the churches which had long used these Anglican texts, felt the need to modernize them. It seemed sensible that the churches should collaborate for parts of the liturgy they have in common.

In 1970, ICET published *Prayers We Have in Common,* containing texts in two categories. Category A consists of the Lord's Prayer, the Apostles' and Nicene

Creeds, the Gloria (Glory to God), the Sanctus (Holy, Holy, Holy), and the Glory Be to the Father. These texts had been under discussion for some considerable time, and the ICET had reached agreement about them. They were therefore presented to the churches for adoption. Category B comprises the experimental texts for the Sursum Corda (Preface Dialogue), the Agnus Dei (Lamb of God), and the Te Deum. Both sets of texts had brief explanatory commentaries. In 1971 the booklet appeared in an enlarged and revised edition. All the texts were now in one category. The only major changes were to items formerly in Category B, with corresponding changes in the commentary. The Lukan canticles (Magnificat, Benedictus, and Nunc Dimittis) were added. The American edition (1972) further altered two lines in the Te Deum. In 1974, ICET met again, to consider what improvements had been suggested by the actual use of the texts. The result of this meeting was a second revised edition of *Prayers We Have in Common* in 1975, which now included the *kyrie eleison* (Lord Have Mercy), and a new commentary on changes necessary in musical settings. The commentary, though containing much of its original material, defended the changes made in the 1975 edition. Most of the major churches adopted ICET's recommendations, with the exception of the Lord's Prayer, on which it is difficult to reach agreement.

Its work completed, ICET was disbanded in 1975, shortly after the publication of *Prayers We Have in Common*. In 1985, a successor organization, the ENGLISH LANGUAGE LITURGICAL CONSULTATION (ELLC) was established.

Bibliography: ICET, *Prayers We Have In Common* (London and Philadelphia 1970; enlarged and rev. ed. London 1971, Philadelphia 1972, 2nd rev. ed. London and Philadelphia 1975). M. A. O'CONNOR, *The NPM Reference for Prayers We Have in Common: A Catalog, Collection, and Evaluation of the ICET Texts* (Washington, D.C. 1990). H. R. ALLEN, JR., "Common Texts Revisited," *Worship* 60 (1986) 172–175.

[A.R. GEORGE/EDS.]

INTERNATIONAL COUNCIL FOR CATECHESIS (COINCAT)

The International Council for Catechesis (COINCAT) was established by Pope PAUL VI on June 7, 1973 as a consultative body within the Congregation for the Clergy. The general purpose of COINCAT as explained in the *Annuario Pontificio* is "to study the more important catechetical themes for the service of the Apostolic See and the episcopal conferences and to present proposals and suggestions." Specifically, it investigates concrete themes and important catechetical problems for the universal Church, suggesting solutions and proposals for pastoral action; it provides information on the necessity of catechesis and new approaches being taken in various parts of the world; and it facilitates the exchange of catechetical experiences between the Holy See and the diverse areas in the Church and among the members themselves.

Since its inception COINCAT has provided valuable service both to the Apostolic See and episcopal conferences, especially through its biannual plenary sessions. In the past it has studied such issues as catechesis as an ecclesial act (1976), the settings for catechesis (1977), catechesis and youth (1978), the formation of catechists for the 1980s (1979), catechesis and reconciliation (1983), adult catechesis in the Christian community (1988), catechesis for life in a pluralistic and secularized world (1990), and inculturation of faith and the language of catechesis (1992). The 1988 session resulted in the publication of *Adult Catechesis in the Christian Community*, a document that became a landmark within the body of the Holy See's catechetical works.

From the beginning COINCAT has been an international group. The first 24 permanent members appointed for five-year terms in 1976 included the patriarch of the Melkites and archbishops, bishops, priests, sisters, and lay people from Asia, Europe, Africa, Australia, and North, Central, and South America. Among the initial appointees were two from the United States, Bishop John B. McDowell of Pittsburgh and Sister Maria de la Cruz Aymes of San Francisco. McDowell was succeeded by Msgr. Wilfrid H. Paradis, then of the United States Catholic Conference Department of Education, who in turn was succeeded by Msgr. Francis Kelly of the National Catholic Education Association. Sister Maria de la Cruz was reappointed twice and for a time served as president of COINCAT. By 1992 the membership had grown to 30.

In 1994 the International Council was reorganized. The cardinal prefect of the Congregation for the Clergy became the president, and the secretary of the congregation served as vice-president. The number of permanent members, appointed to six-year terms, was set at ten. The new structure allows for the appointment of *periti* whose areas of expertise are suited to a particular project. These *periti* further enhance COINCAT's international character and competence. The newly constituted COINCAT met for the first time in Rome in September of 1994. The members and *periti* formulated general principles and drew up an outline for the revised edition of the *General Directory for Catechesis* published in 1997.

Bibliography: *Annuario Pontificio per l'Anno 2000* (Vatican City 2000). W. H. PARADIS, "Report on the Fifth Meeting of the International Catechetical Council, Rome, April 11–17, 1983," *The Living Light* 20 (1984) 159–70.

[J. POLLARD]

INTERNATIONAL MISSIONARY COUNCIL

The Council, established in 1921, was the cooperative missionary organization of Protestant churches through which the missionary movement found ecumenical expression. In 1961, it merged with the WORLD COUNCIL OF CHURCHES (WCC), becoming the Division of World Mission and Evangelism (DWME) of the WCC. In 1971, the DWME became known as the Commission on World Mission and Evangelism (CWME). This entry describes the historical development, influence, and main emphases of the International Missionary Council from 1921–1961.

The International Missionary Council (IMC) early became a focus of the emerging ECUMENICAL MOVEMENT. From 1939 its association with the WCC, while that council was in process of formation, continued to be close until 1961, when the IMC became the DWME. The World Missionary Conference in Edinburgh (1910), at which delegates from the churches studied the central place of missions in the life of the church, laid the foundation of missionary cooperation on which the IMC was formed. The process continued as the membership of the council increased with the formation of new national and regional councils in Asia, Africa, and Latin America. These in turn were recognized as the bodies representing the churches of their areas. Two main principles governed the council's work: (1) the only bodies entitled to determine policy were the churches themselves and their mission boards; (2) the successful working of the IMC was dependent on God's gift of fellowship and the desire to cooperate.

Through study, consultation, and programs of mutual assistance, the council served its member bodies. Questions were considered as they arose. Missionary freedom, general and theological education, opium addiction, labor, slavery, racial discrimination, the church in rural and industrial society, home and family life, and literature were the main emphases. IMC officers, staff, and committees consulted, stimulated, and advised an increasing number of local and regional church bodies. German missions, "orphaned" by World War II, were enabled to continue their work through extensive interchurch aid. At the meeting in Ghana (1958) a theological education fund was established, providing substantial aid for buildings, faculties, and libraries of institutions in which churches were united in training for the ministry.

While the council adhered to the principle that no decision would be taken on ecclesiastical or doctrinal questions in which the member bodies differed among themselves, it concentrated attention on the Christian message for evangelism. The meeting at Jerusalem (1928) made the message its first consideration, especially in relation to modern secularism. At the Madras meeting (1938) the study of the message in a non-Christian world influenced missionary thinking and evoked intensive discussion for years after the meeting. Evangelism was ever a central concern as the council focused attention on the Christian witness in the world. At Whitby, Ontario (1947), the IMC set itself to discover the relevance of the Gospel to the world recovering from war and to call the faith again to its central task of evangelism. Church union movements among the younger churches were inspired by concern for evangelism as the churches sought for a united Christian witness. At the IMC meeting in Willingen, Germany (1952), delegates of younger churches stated their belief in church unity as an essential condition of effective witness and advance. Parallel with the decision of the IMC and the WCC to integrate, the two councils assisted in the formation of regional councils in Asia and Africa.

Bibliography: INTERNATIONAL MISSIONARY COUNCIL, *The Jerusalem Meeting of the International Missionary Council*, 8 v. (New York 1928); *The Madras Series*, 7 v. (New York 1939). W. R. HOGG, *Ecumenical Foundations* (New York 1952). *The International Review of Missions* (Edinburgh 1912–).

[R. W. SCOTT/EDS.]

INTERNATIONAL THEOLOGICAL COMMISSION

Pope PAUL VI, in response to a recommendation made during VATICAN COUNCIL II and the specific proposal of the 1967 SYNOD OF BISHOPS, established the International Theological Commission, April 28, 1969 (*Acta Apostolicae Sedis* 61 [1969] 431–432; cf. 713–716). The function of the ITC is "to study doctrinal questions of major importance in order to offer advisory assistance to the Holy See and, in particular, the Congregation for the Doctrine of the Faith" (Statutes, ibid. 540–541). It has only a consultative and not a deliberative voice in the functioning of the ordinary magisterium of the Church.

Format. The commission consists of 30 members chosen by the pope from names recommended by the cardinal prefect of the Congregation for the Doctrine of the Faith after consultation with the national episcopal conferences. The members, representing various nations and diverse schools of theology, are chosen for their proficiency in one or another of the theological disciplines and for their fidelity to the magisterium. The initial appointment is for five years and may be renewed for another quinquennium. The cardinal prefect of the CDF presides over the commission and is assisted in the administration by a secretary general.

When the commission was first established in 1969, it had among its members many of the most prestigious Catholic theologians of the time. Several had been *periti* at the Second Vatican Council: Hans Urs von BALTHASAR, Louis Bouyer, Yves CONGAR, O.P., Philippe Delhaye, André Feuillet, P.S.S., Henri de LUBAC, S.J., Gerard Philips, Karl RAHNER, S.J., Joseph Ratzinger, and Rudolf Schnackenburg. The English-speaking theological community was represented by Barnabas AHERN, C.P., Walter Burghhardt, S.J., and Bernard LONERGAN, S.J. Several of these were reappointed for the second quinquennium (1974), and they were joined by Edouard Hamel, S.J., and Jean-Marie TILLARD, O.P., of Canada, and John Mahoney, S.J., from Great Britain. Half the appointees named to the commission in 1980 by Pope John Paul II were holdovers; new members included Michael Ledwith of Ireland, Carl PETER of the U.S., Walter Principe, C.S.B., of Canada, John Thornhill, S.M., of Australia, and Christophe von Schönborn of Switzerland.

In 1986 a new term of the commission began. Among the members were the distinguished theologians Hans Urs von Balthasar and Georges Cottier, O.P., of Switzerland, Giuseppe Colombo (Italy), Jean Corbon (Lebanon), Philippe Delhaye and Jan Walgrave, O.P., of Belgium, and Joachim Gnilka and Walter Kasper of West Germany. At the time of their appointment in 1986, Bonaventura Kloppenburg, O.F.M. (Brazil), and Franc Perko (Yugoslavia) were auxiliary bishops. The English-speaking world was represented by John Finnis of England, Gilles Langevin of Canada, Michael Ledwith of Ireland, Carl Peter and William May of the U.S., Francis Moloney, S.D.B., of Australia, and Felix Wilfred of India. Professors Finnis (Oxford University) and May (The Catholic University of America) were the first laymen to be appointed to the commission. By the end of the quinquennium in 1991 several members had been named diocesan bishops and were no longer eligible to serve on the commission, whose function is to offer informed advice to the magisterium. By reason of their position as residential bishops Walter Kasper, André-Jean Léonard (who had been appointed to the commission to replace the deceased Walgrave), Jorge Medina Estevez of Chile, a member from the beginning, and Franc Perko belonged to the magisterium.

Among internationally significant theologians appointed to the commission in 1992, Colombo, Corbon,

and Gnilka continued to give their prestigious service. They were joined by Joseph Doré, S.S. (France), Adolphe Gesché (Belgium), Hermann Pottmeyer (Germany), and Max Thurian (Switzerland-Italy). Langevin, Ledwith, May, and Moloney, joined by Avery Dulles, S.J., of the U.S., Charles Acton of England, Sebastian Karotemprel, S.D.B., of India, Joseph Osei-Bonsu of Ghana, represented the English-speaking theological community. A longstanding member of the Commission, Christoph von Schönborn, O.P., and three first-time members, Joseph Doré, S.S., Norbert Strotmann Hoppe, M.S.C. (Peru), and Joseph Osei-Bonsu were appointed bishops during the course of the quinquennium. Professor Gösta Hallonsten of Sweden was a new lay member of the commission, replacing Professor Finnis. During the course of the quinquennium, Max Thurian passed away and was not replaced.

Appointees in 1997 for a new quinquennium included holdovers Pottmeyer and Gesché, as well as three-termers Francis Moloney, S.D.B., Jean-Louis Bruguès, O.P., and Henrique Noronha Galvão. They were joined by new members: Roland Minnerath (France), Bruno Forte (Italy), Gerhard Müller (Germany), and several lesser known theologians. The Anglophone world was represented by Charles ACTON (England), Christopher Begg (USA), Joseph Di Noia, OP (USA), George Karakunnel (India), Sebastian Karotemprel, S.D.B. (India), Thomas Norris (Ireland), Anthony Ojo (Nigeria), and Luis Tagle (Philippines). An obvious effort was made to internationalize the commission further with appointment Tanios Bou Mansour, O.L.M., of Lebanon, Fadel Sidarouss, S.J., of Egypt, and Rafael Salzar Cardenas, M.Sp.S., of Mexico. The increased internationalization of the commission has had the unintended result of a diminution of the representation of the European centers of theological learning and to some extent a lessening of the expertise of the group as a whole. It has also made communication more difficult, especially in the subcommissions where instantaneous translation is not generally available.

In the first 30 years the commission had only two presidents. Cardinal Franjo Seper, prefect of the Congregation for the Doctrine of the Faith during the latter part of Pope Paul VI's pontificate, presided 1969–81. Cardinal Josef Ratzinger became president in 1981 when Pope John Paul II appointed him as prefect of the CDF. Monsignor Philippe Delhaye of Belgium served as secretary general of the commission from 1972 until ill health forced him to resign in 1989. Cardinal Ratzinger appointed Georges Cottier, O.P., of Switzerland to replace him in 1990.

Procedures and Themes. The commission begins each quinquennium with a wide-ranging discussion of a number of theological issues that the members regard as worthy of the Holy See's attention. The themes that are chosen for examination become the focal points of the commission in the following four years. In its early years the commission examined and published documents dealing with sacerdotal ministry (1971); the unity of faith and theological pluralism (1972); the apostolicity of the Church and apostolic succession (1973); criteria for the knowledge of Christian morality (1974); the relation between the magisterium and theologians (1975); Christian salvation and human progress (1976); and the sacrament of marriage (1977). These were followed by published statements dealing with the selected questions in christology (1979); theology, christology, and anthropology (1981); reconciliation and penance (1982); and the dignity and rights of the human person (1983). In commemoration of the 20th anniversary of the close of Vatican II, the commission published a document on selected items in ecclesiology (1984); and in 1985, it published a commentary on four propositions dealing with Jesus' self-consciousness and His awareness of His mission.

The four themes selected by the commission for study during the quinquennium beginning in 1986 were: faith and inculturation; interpretation of dogma; fundamental moral theology; and current questions in eschatology. The commission established in 1992 devoted itself to an examination of contemporary soteriology; Christianity in relation to other religions; a contemporary presentation of the mystery of God; and the Eucharist. The commission established in 1997 directed its attention to the Church and the sins of the past; the permanent diaconate; the inculturation of revelation; and the theology of creation.

The procedures of the commission follow a routine. After the selection of the themes to be studied during the quinquennium, the president of the ITC appoints subcommissions to examine them and draft a working paper, the *instrumentum laboris,* that serves as the basis for discussion and debate by the commission as a whole. When the members agree upon and approve a final text, the document is submitted to a plenary session of the commission for formal approval. The Congregation for the Doctrine of the Faith receives the finished documents, and decides how best to use the work of the Theological Commission. Some documents have been used as a resource for the CDF and others have been published. The commission's study that resulted in the document *Memory and Reconciliation: The Church and the Sins of the Past* (2000) took on a particular significance. On the Second Sunday of Lent 2000, Pope John Paul II made the presentation of the document a highlight with his own memorable comments at an event marking the celebration of the Jubilee Year.

Bibliography: International Theological Commission, *International Theological Commission: Texts and Documents 1969–1985,* ed. M. SHARKEY, (San Francisco 1989). A collection of the Commission's documents from 1985–1996, most of which have appeared in a number of languages in various international scholarly journals, is in preparation.

[B. M. AHERN/W. E. MAY/F. J. MOLONEY]

INTERNATIONAL UNION OF SUPERIORS GENERAL (WOMEN)

The International Union of Superiors General (UISG) is an organization of pontifical right, established by the Congregation for Religious on Dec. 8, 1965 to respond to Vatican Council II, *Perfectae caritatis* 23, and to efforts of superiors general of women's congregations to create an association for mutual collaboration, sharing, and support, centered in Rome but with two-way communication with religious sisters throughout the world. UISG aims to foster at the international level the continuous renewal of the life and mission of religious sisters in the Church through their superiors general by research and reflection, by collaboration with the Congregation for Religious and Secular Institutes (SCRSI), by representation on ecclesial and international bodies, and by appropriate communication and evaluation. It represents approximately 2,400 superiors general of women's congregations of apostolic life. Since the first general assembly in 1967 (statutes revised 1973), the UISG has operated through triennial assemblies of approximately 100 locally elected delegates across the world, annual meetings of an intercontinental council of 28 members (19 elected by the assembly, 9 appointed by the SCRSI), regular meetings of an executive committee of eight based in Rome, and a permanent secretariat. It is juridically recognized by the Italian state (Decree 1296. Dec. 10, 1971).

The Union sponsors annual international meetings in Rome. It participates in many ecclesial initiatives involving women religious and is their representative on the Council for Relations with the SCRSI. In a style that is prayerful, effective and sisterly, UISG tries to combine three main thrusts of service: primarily, up-to-date world awareness, through its councillors, of trends in the evolution of sisters' religious life; conjointly, reflection on these through permanent or *ad hoc* commissions, larger meetings, and a quarterly bulletin; complementarily, enrichment of input through relations with ecclesial and national bodies and with national conferences of religious. It maintains ongoing collaboration with the Union of Superiors General (Men).

Bibliography: UISG, *Bulletin* 30 (1973) 29.

[M. LINSCOTT]

INTERVENTION, DIVINE

The activity of God in a miraculous event. This does not mean that He enters a place in which He was absent, for He is always present in the whole of creation. A universe of self-sufficient laws being violated by an external, intervening power is, therefore, a mistaken conception of miracles.

Better understanding of scientific law and increased understanding of scriptural and patristic notions of miracle clarifies the meaning of divine intervention. God, whose presence makes possible the continuing miracle of CREATION, at times produces in a religious context an extraordinary event that acts as a sign inviting belief. To admit a Sovereign Creator is to admit the possibility of such intervention, although determining where it has actually occurred requires careful investigation pursued in a spirit of openness.

See Also: MIRACLES (IN THE BIBLE); MIRACLES (THEOLOGY OF).

[G. MORAN]

INTORCETTA, PROSPERO

Jesuit missionary in China; b. Piazza, Sicily, Aug. 28, 1625; d. Hangchow, Oct. 3, 1696. He arrived in China in 1657. His work in Kiangsi was interrupted by persecution. He was arrested in 1665, sent to Peking and then to Canton. In 1670 a Jesuit took his place in prison, and he left for Rome in 1672 to defend the Jesuits in the CHINESE RITES CONTROVERSY. He returned to China in 1674 and was appointed visitor to the missions of China and Japan (1676–84). In 1679 and in 1688 he experienced persecution. He translated the *Exercises of St. Ignatius* and the *Rules of the Society of Jesus* into Chinese. With several other Jesuits he published in Latin one of the first Western studies of Confucius' life and thought. His main work, on Chinese politics and ethics (Goa 1667), is in Chinese and Latin.

Bibliography: L. PFISTER, *Notices biographiques et bibliographiques,* 2 v. (Shanghai 1932–34). A. MERCATI and A. PELZER, *Dizionario ecclesiastico* 2:461. J. SCHÜTTE, *Lexikon für Theologie und Kirche* 5:737.

[B. LAHIFF]

INTROIT

The word "Introit," which comes from *introitus,* "entrance," designates the ANTIPHON, with Psalm or Psalm verse, and (usually) the doxology, "Glory be to the Father . . .," that was historically sung at the beginning of the Roman Rite of the Mass.

Extant evidence from the writings of the Church Fathers suggests the absence of an entrance chant at the beginning of the Eucharist in the first 500 years. References by both St John Chrysostom (*In epistolam ad Colossos*, Homily 3:4) and St. Augustine (*De civitate Dei*, 20:8) point to a Eucharist that began immediately with the readings after a brief salutation from the celebrant. Indeed, Augustine described a crowded Easter Sunday morning Eucharist as follows: "I greeted the throng, and when all had become silent there was solemn reading from the Holy Scriptures." It is not possible to date precisely when the Introit chant was first used in the Church of Rome. An earlier hypothesis that a passage in the *Liber pontificalis* describing the introduction by Pope Celestine I (d. 432) described an antiphonal Introit psalm "Constituit ut psalmi David CL ante sacrificium psalli antiphanatim ex omnibus, quod ante non fiebat, nisi tantum epistula beati Pauli recitabatur et sanctum Evangelium," is untenable. Recently scholarship has established that the phrase "antiphanatim ex omnibus" was inserted in the second quarter of the 6th century to reflect the then practice, and it referred to the responsorial psalm (Gradual) rather than to the Introit.

In all likelihood, the Introit came into use with the rise of stational liturgy, as witnessed in the 7th-century *Ordo Romanus I* (M. Andrieu, *Les "Ordines Romani" du haut moyen-âge* [Rome 1938–41] 2:83). The Introit emerged as a processional chant to accompany the movement of the papal entourage from the sacristy (located near the street entrance) to the altar. The psalmody, performed antiphonally (by alternating choirs), soon came to be introduced by a suitable verse, called Antiphon, which eventually proved to be the most enduring factor. For the psalmody, although originally important (as can be gauged by the richness of the chant and by the choice of a Psalm whose meaning is made clear only when the whole is sung), generally lost its significance due to the shortening of the psalm in monastic circles (where the clergy had already assembled for Terce) or where the procession was discarded (when the sacristy was relocated near the sanctuary). But the Antiphon, in turn, became more prominent. In the medieval period, the entire Mass formulary, and frequently the day itself, received its name from the first word(s) of the Introit antiphon, e.g., *Requiem, Rorate, Gaudete, Quasimodo.*

The antiphonal nature of the Introit was well suited as a musical accompaniment to the entrance procession making its way to the stational church for the Eucharist. The older manuscripts of the Mass chants indicated the use of an Antiphon, usually an appropriate verse of the Psalm being sung, but sometimes from another part of the Bible (e.g., *Populus Sion,* from Is), or even a free creation

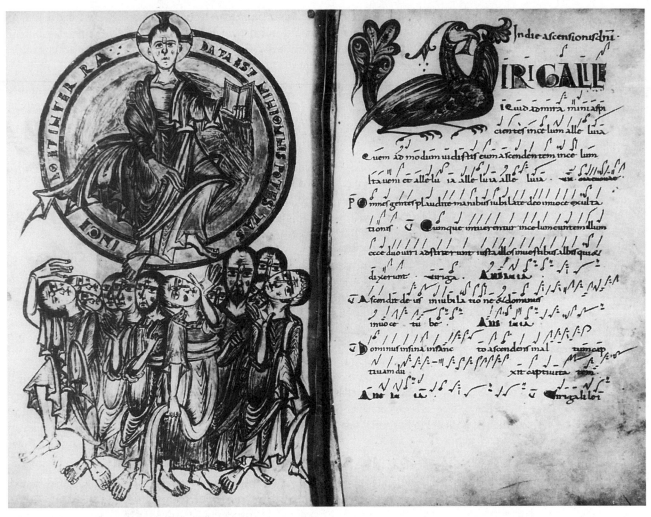

Words and musical notes of Introit for Feast of Ascension, Italian, ca. 1309.

(e.g., *Gaudeamus* for St. Agatha; or Sedulius's *Salve, sancta parens* for Masses of the Blessed Virgin).

In Carolingian times the Antiphon was often repeated after each verse of the Psalm (perhaps a Frankish usage), or a second verse from another Psalm was sung (a phenomenon that has puzzled researchers). Later the psalmody was reduced to one verse, or the chant was lengthened by repeating the antiphon before the Doxology. Already in the 8th century the psalmody was so curtailed that by the medieval period, eventually only one verse (plus the Doxology) remained.

Bibliography: J. A. JUNGMANN, *The Mass of the Roman Rite,* tr. F. A. BRUNNER, 2 v. (New York 1951–55) 1:320–333. W. APEL, *Gregorian Chant* (Bloomington, Ind. 1958). T. MATHEWS, "An Early Roman Chancel Arrangement and Its Liturgical Significance," *Rivista di archeologia cristiana,* xxxviii (1962) 71–95. A. ZWINGGI, "Der Wortgottesdienst bei Augustinus," *Liturgisches Jahrbuch* 20 (1970) 92–113, 129–40, 250–53. T. CONNOLLY, "Introits and Archetypes: Some Archaisms of the Old Roman Chant," *Journal of the American Musicological Society* 25 (1972) 157–74. H. VAN DER WERF, *The Emergence of Gregorian Chant: A Comparative Study of Ambrosian, Roman, and Gregorian Chant* (Rochester, NY 1983). A. CHAVASSE, "Cantatorium et antiphonale missarum," *Ecclesia orans* 1 (1984) 15–55. P. JEFFERY, "The Introduction of Psalmody into the Roman Mass by Pope Celestine I, 422–32," *Archiv für Liturgiewissenschaft* 26 (1984) 147–65. J. BALDOVIN, *The Urban Character of Christian Worship: The Origins, Development, and Meaning of Stational Liturgy* (Rome 1987). D. HILEY, *Western Plainchant: A Handbook* (Oxford, 1993). J. W. MCKINNON, "Antoine Chavasse and the Dating of Early Chant," *Plainsong and Medieval Music* 1 (1992) 123–47.

[F. A. BRUNNER/EDS.]

INTROSPECTION

The careful observation of one's CONSCIOUSNESS to ascertain its states and activities. It is one of the methods used in the science of psychology to study the facts of psychic life. Such facts can be studied from different points of view and are accessible to different methods of investigation. But of all methods, introspection alone is capable of reaching psychic facts in their immanent character. Without it, the psychologist would know psychic life only analogically—through relationships between mental states and their bodily resonances—much as a blind man might be said to know colors. Yet introspection as a method also has its limitations, and for this reason is not relied upon exclusively by most contemporary psychologists.

Uses. Some kind of introspection has always been used in psychological investigation. ARISTOTLE, regarded by many as the founder of psychology, dealt mainly with sensory perceptions, images, dreams, intellectual operations, and affective states. The first of these, for instance the perception of colors or of tones, would be impossible without the direct experience of certain sensitive qualities, e.g., the blue of the sky and the tone of a flute. It was precisely by means of such introspection that Aristotle collected the extensive material on which his psychology was based. Yet, for him, introspection was not a method for solving psychological problems, but rather a technique for acquiring psychical facts. E. B. Titchener has referred to this as an "information introspection," a type of introspection that has always been used in human medicine. The veterinarian, lacking this, is comparatively handicapped, for his patients are not able to tell him when they feel sick, where they feel pain, etc.

MAINE DE BIRAN in France and the British associationists made extensive use of introspection in their psychological investigations. Their method, however, was logical rather than observational (*see* ASSOCIATIONISM). Careful observation of consciousness was first developed in the 19th century by W. Wundt, who may rightly be considered the founder of modern psychology. Titchener, one of his disciples, brought the Wundtian tradition to the U.S.

For Wundt, the principal aim of psychology was to analyze the contents of mind. This analysis was to be effected not by ordinary reflection, but in a systematic, objective, and fully scientific manner. Because such a task was difficult, Wundtian introspectionists were given considerable laboratory training in special methods of observation. The subject matter studied by this "trained introspection" included sensations, images, and feelings. The introspectionist had to describe accurately what these looked like and how they were interrelated or combined; because of this Wundt's psychology was sometimes referred to as mental chemistry.

According to Wundt, the higher mental processes, thinking and willing, could not be studied by introspection because they were too abstract, the attention paid to them could hardly be controlled, the conditions under which they appeared could not be varied easily, and they could not be repeated. But many psychologists, among them several of Wundt's disciples, did not accept these strictures.

Oswald Külpe, for example, presented a "stimulus word" to his subjects with instructions to respond verbally to what the association of ideas suggested, and then to report what went through their minds while performing this intellectual operation. Again, he asked them to make judgments, e.g., determining which of two weights was the heavier, and then to give full introspective reports of the process. Others who did active work in this field include: R. S. Woodworth, K. Marbe, N. Ach, K. Bühler, K. Koffka, J. Lindworsky, and A. Willwoll.

Such introspective methods have considerably enriched man's knowledge of mental life, and many of their results have been incorporated into contemporary psychology. They furnish information not only about sensations, images, and feelings, but also to some degree about the higher psychic functions such as understanding, abstraction, reasoning, judgment, and choice.

Limitations. Yet introspective methods were vigorously attacked by many psychologists, particularly those with materialistic tendencies, and also Gestalt psychologists, psychoanalysts, and behaviorists. While some of their objections expressed simple prejudices, others had a real foundation in fact.

The limitations of introspective analysis as a "subjective" technique were brought out in the controversy among introspectionists on the theory of imageless thought. Observers trained by Wundt and Titchener found sensations in their thoughts, or, at least, images of sensations; subjects working in the laboratories of Külpe, Binet, and Woodworth, on the other hand, asserted that their thought was not made up of images or sensations, although they admitted that these accompanied thought processes.

Again, introspective methods have intrinsic limitations. They cannot be applied to children, to psychotics, or to animals. In addition, the question of unconscious or automatic psychic processes cannot be answered by introspection. The same applies to feelings, for as soon as one fixes his attention on these in order to observe them carefully, they lose their natural character or even disappear completely.

For these reasons, the exclusive use of introspectionist methods has long been abandoned by psychologists in favor of the more "objective" methods. Yet subjective and objective methods, when properly used, are complementary and capable of supplying useful information for psychological analysis.

Bibliography: P. SIWEK, *Experimental Psychology* (New York 1959). J. P. CHAPLIN and T. S. KRAWIEC, *Systems and Theories of Psychology* (New York 1960). T. G. ANDREWS, ed., *Methods of Psychology* (New York 1948). E. G. BORING, "A History of Introspection," *Psychological Bulletin* 50 (1953) 169–186; *A History of Experimental Psychology* (2d ed. New York 1950). A. GEMELLI and G. ZUNINI, *Introduzione alla psicologia* (4th ed. Milan 1954).

[P. SIWEK]

INTUITION

In common use, intuition may mean something like an intellectual counterpart of instinct (feminine intuition); in philosophy it can mean an immediate grasp by intelligence without conscious reasoning (*intellectus* as opposed to *ratio*); but in the strict sense it means an intellectual apprehension of reality in an act corresponding to ocular vision, so that man *sees* reality spiritually as he sees colors sensitively.

Historical Conspectus. The debate whether the human mind has the power of intuition is a modern one, but a few samples of relevant doctrine may be noted in earlier times. PLATO mentions souls carried to the summit of the celestial world and on the back of the heavens contemplating with the gods what is outside, namely, true being, the colorless, shapeless, intangible essences visible only to the mind (*Phaedrus* 247). Among Platonists the Christian form of this doctrine in St. AUGUSTINE is noteworthy: the Platonic ideas reside as *rationes aeternae* in the mind of God; man contemplates them in the exercise of his higher reason and finds in the *incommutabilis veritas* the source, measure, and guarantee of all his particular truth (various references with THOMAS AQUINAS's commentary in *Summa theologiae* la, 84.5; *C. gent.* 3.47).

Thomistic Teaching. Discussion of St. Thomas Aquinas must consider his use of the term intuit and the implications of his general cognitional theory. *Intueri* is used for God's "view" of the whole course of time at once (*Summa theologiae* la, 14.9; 86.4; etc.), for the simple act of *intellectus* in contrast to the discourse of *ratio* (*Summa theologiae* la, 59.1 ad 1), for the artist's inspection of the model from which he works (*Summa theologiae* la, 44.3), etc. Applied to intellectual operations it does not seem to have a technical sense, but merely to be a metaphor; thus St. Thomas compares God's view of all time to that which a man on a height has of the whole road (*Summa theologiae* la, 14.13 ad 3) and associates *intueri* with *inspicere* (*Summa theologiae* la, 19.5; 44.3; 58.3), which is clearly only a metaphor for intellectual grasp. His general cognitional theory is consonant. The natural object of intellect is indeed *ens* (*C. gent.* 2.83), but the way man knows being does not suggest a spiritual "vision" of an object confronting intellect; rather, the emphasis on ABSTRACTION for grasp of QUIDDITY [B. Lonergan, *Theological Studies* 10 (1949) 13–28], the doctrine of REFLECTION on sense for knowledge of the material singular (*ibid.* 20–22, 28–35), the campaign against Platonic views of knowing (confrontation=*contactus; ibid.* 359–360), and the roundabout way the human soul comes to know itself [*ibid.* 8 (1947) 62], all suggest just the opposite. However, later scholastics clearly teach an intuitive intellectual cognition of material and singular existents [S. DAY, *Intuitive Cognition. . .*, St. Bonaventure, N.Y. 1947, on DUNS SCOTUS and WILLIAM OF OCKHAM; H. Guthrie, *American Catholic Philosophical Asssociation. Proceedings of the Annual Meeting* 14 (1938) 144–151, on St. BONAVENTURE].

Modern Theories. The modern period can be summed up as the affirmation of intuition by R. DESCARTES, the denial of it by I. KANT, and subsequent efforts to overcome Kant either in his principles or in his facts.

Descartes reduces all certain knowledge to two sources, intuition and DEDUCTION, with the former primary, for deduction is valid only when it is a chain of successive intuitions. Intuition is "the undoubting conception of a pure and attentive mind," e.g., of the fact that I exist or that a triangle is bounded by three lines only (*Regulae,* 3). In proper evidence, the object is simple and is known without falsity; one can compound simple natures, but then error is possible (*ibid.* 12). For a century, views on intuition followed in the wake of Descartes (with varying degrees of departure: e.g., B. SPINOZA regards intuition of the divine attributes as a source for understanding modal realities, and J. LOCKE denies that intuition of self has a privileged position), but Kant started a new trend.

For Kant, intuition means immediate, direct reference to the proper object (*Critique of Pure Reason, A* 19, B 33); in man it is found in sense alone (*ibid.*), though in God it may be intellectual (*ibid.* B 145). Sensibility and understanding are both necessary to knowledge: "The understanding can intuit nothing, the senses can think nothing. Only through their union can knowledge arise" (*ibid. A* 51, B 75). Kant's successors find in his doctrine elements to support the very intuition he denied (apperception of self, the categorical imperative). For J. G. FICHTE there is immediate consciousness of one's act and of what one does. In the realm of the subject, various attempts are made to reach the ABSOLUTE by way of intuitive immediacy, moral in Fichte, aesthetic in F. W. J. SCHELLING, rational in G. W. F. HEGEL. A. SCHOPENHAUER makes understanding intuitive in contrast to abstractive reason and asserts a metaphysical intuition of the noumenal SELF as a striving agent. As the 20th century began, E. HUSSERL defended an intuition of essences that are given to essential vision as the individual object is given to individual vision, and H. BERGSON makes much of the contrast between practical, analytic intelligence and a speculative, metaphysical intuition whose primary object is duration.

Recent Scholasticism. The prominence given intuition in these philosophies led inevitably to a reexamination of Thomist doctrine; and since St. Thomas did not treat the question explicitly, the result has been a great divergence as different writers develop his principles in different ways (see G. Van Riet, *L'Épistémologie thomiste,* Louvain 1946). There is disagreement on the word itself, whether to give it a broad sense and extend its use to wide areas of human cognition or to give it a strict sense and severely limit its use, whether to accept the Kantian definition as does A. Lalande's *Vocabulaire . . . de la Philosophie* (8th ed. Paris 1960) or to reinterpret the word on Thomist principles. Those who admit intuition divide in various ways. Some hold that it regards the simple APPREHENSION of essences; abstract and universal, it includes being, but not the singular concrete existent reached only indirectly by reflection. Others say this does not meet the problem; there must be an intuition of the concrete existent in its very act of EXISTENCE, and this intuition in turn is abstractive for some, concrete for others. (Abstractive intuition, at first sight seemingly a contradiction in terms, is explained as only analogous to the abstraction of essences.) Another division regards the material objects of the alleged intuition; some give a privileged role to the ego and its acts, others extend intuition to external objects in the human world. [Some articles appearing after Van Riet's book: J. H. Nicolas, *Revue thomiste* 47 (1947) 113–134; F. Grégoire, *Revue philisophique de Louvain* 44 (1946) 401–415; N. Balthasar, *ibid.* 47 (1949) 351–365; R. Allers, *Franciscan Studies* 8 (1948) 47–68; N. Losskii, *Review of Metaphysics* 2 (June 1949) 47–96; J. Caussiman, *Revue de métaphysique et de morale* 55 (1950) 392–407; L. Geiger, *Revue des sciences philosophiques et théologiques* 34 (1950) 315–357; G. Esser, *The American Catholic Philosophical Associations. Proceedings of the Annual Meeting* 31 (1957) 165–177; B. Lonergan, *ibid.* 32 (1958) 71–81, *Gregorianum* 44 (1963) 307–318; G. McCool, *Thought* 37 (1962) 57–73.]

Systematic Analysis. The position of this article is that intuition, understood as a "look" corresponding to sensitive confrontation, is found in neither man's understanding of quiddity nor his knowledge of the existent. It is not even useful as an analogy for the direct relationship to data found in understanding of quiddity (as "insight" may be), for it is too loaded with philosophical connotations. In any case, one is not at the mercy of ANALOGY here, but may study the activity of understanding in itself (cf. *Summa theologiae* la, 88.2 ad 3), when it turns out to be no more a looking at data than is the WONDER that it answers. Neither is man's judgment of the real existent based on intuition. The flat assertion of such an intuition is not enough, nor is the argument that it is necessary if one is to save metaphysical REALISM, nor has the analogy of a sensitive look any scientific validity in determining the nature of human JUDGMENT (in fact, it is doubly misleading here where activity is reflective); the proper procedure is rather to study the process of judgment in itself and learn what actually happens there.

Newman's View. Pioneering work in this field was done by J. H. NEWMAN in his *An Essay in Aid of a Grammar of Assent* (London 1930). What struck Newman was the unconditional character of judgment (assent); his problem was to discover how one reaches this absolute in concrete judgments, and his solution was described in the pages devoted to what he called the illative sense and to its processes. It reaches the unconditional neither by intuitions nor by inference from invincible syllogisms, but "by objections overcome, by adverse theories neutralized, by difficulties gradually clearing up . . . , by all these ways, and many others," as a polygon tends to coincidence with a circle as its sides increase in number and diminish in length (320–321).

Lonergan's Development. Newman's path was followed by B. Lonergan [*Insight: A Study of Human Understanding* (New York 1957)], with such advances as these. First, Lonergan defines the structure of human cognition, which has three levels determined by the two basic questions, *quid sit* and *an sit. Quid sit* effects the ascent from data to understanding (a step as necessary for "internal" data of consciousness as for "external"); *an sit* effects the emergence of truth and of knowledge of the real from mere ideas or argument (a step as valid for "external" data as for "internal"). Second, he generalizes; the question *an sit* discloses the essentially hypothetical character of understanding: not only Newman's inference, but every human idea is, as such, just a possible explanation. Further, since every true judgment is about the really existent, an operation like that of the illative sense is always called for in the reduction to ultimates. Every act of human understanding must be rendered invulnerable for the absolute of judgment, errors excluded, imagined elements sifted from sensed, implications noted and checked experimentally, and the various conditions reflectively studied, until one reaches the virtually unconditioned ("virtually proved," Newman said, p. 323, but his technical term was "proved *interpretative*"). Third, Lonergan takes up the question of immediacy. Intellect in man is by nature an anticipation of being, an orientation to being through the structured series, inquiry (*quid*), understanding, reflection (*an*), the act of judgment in which he knows the real; and this orientation assures immediacy. The relationship of man's cognitional activities to real objects "is immediate in the intention of being; it is mediate . . . in understanding and thought and judgment, because these activities stand to the originating intention of being as answers stand to questions" [*Continuum* 2 (1964) 540].

This view of judgment squares with scientific procedures in which hypotheses are verified not by an intuition of being, but by a checking process and experiment. It is in harmony with the familiar facts that man judges as readily of the existence of God, of the guilt of the accused, and of the events of last year, as he does of the reality of objects present to sense; that he makes mistakes about present objects as well as about absent; that philosophers have difficulty assigning the foundations not only of man's judgments about God, but of all his judgments. The view has anticipations at least in the Thomist statements that assent does not mean "the movement of the intellect to the thing, but rather to its conception of the thing . . . , to which the intellect assents when it judges the conception to be true" (*De malo* 6.1 ad 14), and that man's knowledge of God's existence is just his knowledge of the truth of the proposition that God is (*Summa theologiae* la, 3.4 ad 2). Such a doctrine offers nothing, of course, to those who wish to prove *that* man knows, and the infinite versatility of the reflective power it finds basic lacks the apparent solidity of a "look" or a premise, but it accords well with the self-correcting process by which Newman held man does in fact learn (*Grammar* 377).

See Also: TRUTH; UNDERSTANDING (INTELLECTUS).

Bibliography: P. ORTEGAT, *Religion et intuition*, 2 v. (Gembloux 1948). B. AYBAR, *El realismo intuitivo* (Tucumán, Argen. 1954). A. MASULLO, *Intuizione e discorso* (Naples 1955). P. MASLOW, *Intuition versus Intellect* (Valley Stream, N.Y. 1957). A. J. BAHM, *Types of Intuition* (Albuquerque 1961). M. A. BUNGE, *Intuition and Science* (pa. Englewood Cliffs, N.J. 1962).

[F. E. CROWE]

INVESTITURE

Investiture (Lat. *vestitura, investitura*; Fr. *investiture*; Germ. *Lehnung*) is a ceremony comprising the symbolic surrender of the fief by the lord to his vassal. Its effect was to put the vassal in possession of his fief (*see* FEUDALISM). The *Libri feudorum* (2.2, pref.) call investiture in the strict sense possession or taking possession, i.e., the physical assumption of ownership of the fief (cf. *investitura* in the sense of *possessio* in *Leges Langobar-*

King Dagobert investing St. Omer with crozier, 10th century.

dorum 2.52.17). The *Libri* consider the use of the word *investitura,* as designating a symbolic transfer of the right to the fief, to be an impermissible extension of the meaning. But this second sense of the word is the more usual in the Middle Ages.

Investiture must be distinguished from homage (*homagium, hominium*), by which the vassal declared himself to be the "man" of his overlord. He thereby assumed the responsibility of furnishing him with the services, especially military and court service, incurred as a result of the ownership of a fief. Homage, like fidelity (*fidelitas*), but in a stricter fashion, created a personal bond between vassal and lord. Investiture was concerned with the "material" aspect of the feudal contract, but obviously there was a close tie between the two concepts, and it is debated whether the personal relationship (homage) took precedence over the material relationship (freehold contract) or vice versa.

Investiture normally followed the rendering of homage (except in Italy, cf. *Libri feudorum,* 2.4), since the feudal lord did not hand over the fief until the vassal had acknowledged himself to be his man. Originally the personal engagement (homage) and the handing over of the fief (investiture) were not connected. There were vassals without a fief and fiefs granted to men who were not vassals. But by the 13th century the bond between homage and investiture was normal, and homage was sworn in order to obtain a fief (*Établissements de Saint Louis,* ed. Viollet 2:19).

The origin of the investiture ritual must be sought in the procedures for transfer of goods practiced in the Frankish period. The new owner was given possession by having placed in his hands an object symbolic of the real estate to be transferred (a clod of earth, a branch of a tree, a stalk of grain, a knife, a staff, or a glove). The symbols used for investiture were quite varied (C. Du Cange, *Glossarium ad scriptores mediae et infimae latinitatis,* ed. L. Favre, 4:410–18, *s.v. investitura,* shows 98 of them in the charters of the 11th and 12th centuries). The most frequent were the rod or staff, the glove, the ring, the sword, and the oriflamme (M. Bloch, *op. cit.,* 1:267 and plate V). For ecclesiastical fiefs, feudal lords used the cross and ring, symbols of episcopal or abbatial authority; the use of these symbols gave rise to violent conflicts (*see* INVESTITURE STRUGGLE).

Investiture took place in the presence of two witnesses drawn for the most part from among the peers of the new vassal. It was accompanied by the payment of a fee to the suzerain: the seisin fee, or the chamberlain fee paid to the chamberlain if the suzerain were a great feudal lord [cf. its limitation by Philip the Bold in the Ordinance of Aug. 1272 (Isambert, *Recueil des anciennes lois* 2:648; Loysel, *Institutes coutumières,* 4:3, 11)].

The new vassal could not take possession of his fief before the investiture on pain of forfeiture (Beaumanoir, *Coutumes de Beauvaisis,* ed. Salmon, nos 861 and 1398). After the investiture ceremony, an official document known as an enfeoffment or an instrument of enfeoffment was drawn up. This document was given to the vassal and served him as proof of possession. In time the drawing up and handing over of this document replaced the symbolic investiture.

Bibliography: M. BLOCH, *Feudal Society,* tr. L. A. MANYON (Chicago 1961). C. E. PERRIN, ''La Société féodale,'' *Revue historique* 194 (1944) 23–41, 114–131. F. L. GANSHOF, *Qu'est-ce que la féodalité* (3d ed. Brussels 1957); *Feudalism,* tr. P. GRIERSON (New York 1952). H. MITTEIS, *Lehnrecht und Staatsgewalt* (Weimar 1933; new ed. Darmstadt 1958). R. BOUTRUCHE, *Seigneurie et féodalité* (Paris 1959–). For further bibliography, see INVESTITURE STRUGGLE.

[J. GAUDEMET]

INVESTITURE STRUGGLE

The conflict in which the Church, during the second half of the 11th and the first decades of the 12th century, opposed the power of lay feudal lords. It was settled in principle by the Concordat of WORMS (1122), but the long struggle between the PAPACY and the HOLY ROMAN EMPIRE down to the middle of the 13th century was in fact its continuation.

The Issue. The investiture struggle originated in the dispute occasioned by the manner in which bishops were granted possession of ecclesiastical property by their overlords (*see* FEUDALISM). Being a feudal lord himself, the bishop received his temporal property by investiture, but the symbols used for this investiture, the crosier and ring, were equivocal. They could be understood to represent also the prelate's power of jurisdiction. While it was legitimate for the overlord to confer the temporalities (the fief) upon his vassal, the bishop, the Church could not admit the lord's pretensions to confer ecclesiastical power, the *potestas jurisdictionis.* A clear distinction between the two powers and an exact interpretation of the meaning of the symbols should have sufficed to avert any difficulties. In France IVO OF CHARTRES had contributed to a calmer climate by just such precise distinctions and interpretations; but in the Empire juridical controversy was the pretext for a political conflict of the gravest sort.

During the first half of the 11th century, princes and fedual lords had, in fact, laid hands upon bishoprics, abbeys, local churches, and ecclesiastical revenues. By appropriating to themselves the revenues derived from land and TITHES and by the appointment of bishops and pastors, they had become the masters of the Church. The 10th-century papacy (JOHN X) had tolerated such lay pretensions, and at the beginning of the 11th century THIETMAR OF MERSEBURG justified royal interference by pointing out that the sovereign was God's representative on earth (*Chron.* 1:26). At about the same time, however, the CLUNIAC reformers were planning to free the Church from the tutelage of the laity, and their ideas were adopted in Rome after the middle of the 11th century. The Roman See itself had been freed from lay ascendancy as a result of the Election decree of 1059, and the papacy under GREGORY VII (1073–85) reacted vigorously. The Roman synod of February 1075 forbade clerics to receive investiture from the hands of a layman. This head-on counterthrust against practices that were abuses unleashed the struggle, which would vary in intensity according to country.

The conflict assumed little importance in Italy, except insofar as some bishops involved themselves in the struggle between pope and emperor. In England and Germany, it was of immediate interest to the ruling houses, which, having generously endowed their bishoprics, had every intention of continuing to control the recruiting of the episcopate. In France also, the king was engaged in the struggle, but the problem was of equal concern for many feudal lords having bishops as vassals.

The Policy of Gregory VII. The Gregorian reformers had denounced lay investiture as a usurpation. For HUMBERT OF SILVA CANDIDA (*Adversus simoniacos* 1057 or 1058; *Monumenta Germaniae Historica, Libelli de lite* 1), it was the "episcopal function" that was conferred by ring and staff, and such an investiture could not possibly be performed by laymen. It seemed also that the reform of the clergy, the struggle against SIMONY and clerical immorality begun in the middle of the 11th century, could succeed in reaching its goal only if the recruiting of the clergy were removed from the control of the laity. NICHOLAS II, in the Roman synod of April 1059, had forbidden "any cleric to receive in any way a church from the hands of laymen" (can. 6). This was, indeed, an early condemnation of lay investiture, but it was couched in very general terms, and no sanctions were attached. In the first years of his pontificate (1073–74), Gregory VII attacked only simony and clerical marriage (Nicolaitism). He put no bar on lay investitures either in France or in the Empire. But when his measures against clerical incontinence proved ineffective, Gregory VII proceeded in the Council of Rome of February 1075 to condemn lay investiture. The exact wording of the 1075 Decree is not known. The text advanced by Hugh of Flavigny (*Monumenta Germaniae Historica: Scriptores* 8:412) is too similar to that of the decree on investiture promulgated at the Council of 1080 to warrant much credence (*Histoire de l'église depuis les origines jusqu'à nos jours,* ed. A. Fliche and V. Martin). A letter of the pope to HUGH OF DIE (May 12, 1077) alluded to the 1075 decree: the intention was to repeat and render more precise canon 6 of the Lateran Synod of 1059 and to forbid bishops to receive their charges from the hands of laymen. But this text is also vague. Although it forbade laymen to presume to grant episcopal jurisdiction, it is questionable whether the pope did not tolerate the conferring by the lay feudal lord of the temporalities of the bishopric [on the immediacy with which this text was published, cf. G. B. Borino, *Studi gregoriani* 6 (1959–61) 329–348]. The ban on lay investiture in these general and therefore imprecise terms was renewed at the Roman synods of Nov. 19, 1078, and the spring of 1080. But the pope remained ready for compromise. The essential thing for him was to have higher clergy of quality. Wherever the prince was selecting good bishops, as in England and Normandy, the pope did not interfere. Consequently, there was no investiture struggle, properly speaking, either in England or in Spain.

In France, the decree, published after some hesitation and delay, was not strictly applied. Gregory was especially desirous of ending the traffic in bishoprics by which PHILIP I was giving a scandalous example. Hugh of Die, the papal legate, was ruthless with simonists, but tolerated lay intervention when it favored neither simony nor clerical marriage.

In the Empire, bishoprics were in the hands of HENRY IV. The king's appointment of an archbishop for Milan, followed by his selection of mediocre candidates for Bamberg, Fermo, Spoleto, and Cologne (1075), provoked an explosion. But, in condemning the lay investiture of bishops, Gregory VII, as the successor of Peter, included a claim to a general supervision of the rule of princes. "In Germany, the investiture struggle was to be nothing more than one aspect of the struggle between the *Sacerdotium* and the *Imperium*" (Fliche). In an assembly held at Worms (Jan. 14, 1076), the German episcopate backed Henry, attacked Gregory VII, and refused any longer to consider him Pope. Gregory's reply was Henry's excommunication (Feb. 14, 1076). Abandoned by a part of the episcopate and threatened with condemnation by an assembly convoked at Augsburg, at which the pope was to preside on Feb. 2, 1077, Henry submitted at Canossa (Jan. 25–28, 1077). But the conflict soon broke out again. Henry was once more excommunicated at the council of March 7, 1080; his subjects were absolved from their oath of fidelity; and Gregory recognized Rudolph of Swabia as king. Henry convened an assembly at Brixen (June 25, 1080) that in turn deposed Gregory and elected in his stead Abp. GUIBERT OF RAVENNA who took the name of Clement III. The antipope, however, was not recognized by any country in Christendom, and Henry tried to impose him upon Rome by force of arms. Gregory VII was expelled from Rome, went into exile (1084), and died May 25, 1085.

Doctrinal Approaches. Doctrinal controversies concerning investiture were not, at the time of Gregory VII, as prominent as the political struggle itself. Rare indeed were the authors who would grapple with the problem, whether to support the king (letter of WENRICH OF TRIER, November 1080; the anonymous *De investitura regali collectanea*), or expound the papal thesis [*Liber ad Gebehardum*, of MANEGOLD OF LAUTENBACH (1084); *Monumenta Germaniae Historica, Libelli de lite* 1]. A compromise had to be found. It was outlined, from a doctrinal point of view, by Guido of Ferrara [*De scismate Hildebrando* (1086); *Monumenta Germaniae Historica, Libelli de lite* 1], who distinguished between the spiritual and the secular functions of the bishop. As a man of God, the bishop is the subject of the pope, but as the tenant of temporal goods, he is subject to lay power. Guido granted further that the prince might nominate the bishop. Forgeries of almost contemporary date were used to back up this claim. Thus the distinction between the two aspects of a bishop had not as yet provided an acceptable solution of the conflict. It was, nevertheless, the formula that, 30 years later, would make it possible to resolve the dilemma.

Under Urban II. After the pontificate of VICTOR III, URBAN II (1088–99) did not become master of Rome until 1094. The antipope Clement III returned to Ravenna and no longer challenged the authority of the legitimate pope. Urban's policy was flexible, and he sought to reestablish peace through indulgence and by making use of the theory of dispensation from the canons that the contemporary BERNOLD OF CONSTANCE was developing in his *De excommunicatis vitandis.* Such conciliatory policy ran counter to the theories expounded by Cardinal Deusdedit (*see* DEUSDEDIT, COLLECTION OF), who was most anxious to root out lay investiture. His doctrinal position as well as the excesses of such rulers as WILLIAM II OF ENGLAND and Philip I in France led the Pope to assert anew the Gregorian doctrine [Councils of Piacenza and Clermont (1095), Nimes (1096), Bari (1098)]. Not only was lay investiture forbidden (Clermont can. 15–16), but so also was—and this was something new—any oath of loyalty by a bishop to a layman (*ibid.* can. 17). With the stiffening of the papal stand, concomitant though it was with the first attempts of Ivo of Chartres to find a solution of the conflict, the investiture struggle erupted more violently than ever. In France and England, however, a way to peace was to be found by Ivo and Hugh of Fleury, each taking a slightly different approach, but both operating via a more exact analysis of investiture and a sharp and clear distinction between the grant of ecclesiastical jurisdiction and the concession of temporal holdings. Hugh likewise permitted ''investiture with things secular'' by the lay lord, but even though a protagonist of the royal prerogative, he reserved to the archbishop the granting of ring and crosier.

The English Settlement. In England, LANFRANC OF CANTERBURY and the ANONYMOUS OF YORK (at least in the *De Romano pontifice, c.* 1104) likewise limited lay investiture to the granting ''of power over the people and of the ownership of things temporal.'' Shortly after, negotiations were initiated between HENRY I and ANSELM OF CANTERBURY. They led to an accord (1107) that eliminated lay investiture with ring and staff but admitted that the bishop owed the oath of vassalage to his suzerain in return for his fiefs. This meant sanctioning the theories of Hugh of Fleury; and the pope, who had been party to this compromise, showed himself less intransigent than the Councils of Clermont (1095) or Rome (1099) that had formally forbidden bishops to take the feudal oath. Consequently, there were scarcely any difficulties between the Holy See and Henry I (1100–35).

The French Solution. In France, the difficulties created by the designation of Stephen of Garland to Beauvais (1100) envenomed still further the conflict between Philip I and the papacy caused by the king's illicit relations with Bertrada de Montfort. However, in 1104, the sovereign was absolved from his excommunication, and the Beauvais affair was ably settled by the intervention of Ivo of Chartres. PASCHAL II, who had hoped for an accord with France, negotiated a settlement of the investiture question in 1107. Unfortunately, neither the form that the settlement took nor its precise terms are known. Canon 1 of the Council of Troyes (May 1107) formally forbade the investiture of a bishop, and during the reign of LOUIS VI, bishops were not invested by the King, although they did swear fealty to him. Here again, without benefit of an actual concordat, the ideas of Ivo of Chartres triumphed.

Germany in the Early 12th Century. Only in Germany, under Henry IV (d. 1106) and his successor HENRY V, who was determined to safeguard his right of investiture, did the struggle become violent. Veritable war ensued, with the king proceeding to the appointment of bishops and the pope again forbidding lay investure (Lateran Council, 1100). The opposing themes were the object of two important treatises: the *Tractatus de investitura episcoporum* (1109; *Monumenta Germaniae Historica, Libelli de lite* 2), written by a cleric of Liège at the request of Henry V, and the *Liber de anulo et baculo* by Rangerius of Lucca (1100; *ibid.*). However, a radical solution was suggested by the legates of Paschal II, who, in order to outlaw lay investiture, declared that the pope was ready to abandon in the name of the bishops all their temporal holdings. This solution was the *Concordate of Sutri* (1111; *Monumenta Germaniae Historica: Constitutiones* 1:140). But Henry V made its implementation contingent upon ratification by the German Episcopate. As was expected, the bishops, whom the concordate exposed to the risk of losing their fortune, refused to ratify. But Paschal II, prisoner of Henry V and as such, subjected to grave pressure, was constrained to grant the king the investiture of bishops and abbots, provided their election had not been simoniacal (April 1111). His promise (*Monumenta Germaniae Historica: Constitutiones* 1:144), extorted by violence, was not considered binding by the Italian and French clergy. A Council held in the Lateran (March 1112) annulled the *privilegium* extorted by Henry V and restored the Gregorian principles. Without submitting to the urgings of those prelates who were pressing him to break with Henry V and to excommunicate him, Paschal II reaffirmed the condemnation of lay investiture during the last years of his pontificate. At his death (1118), Henry V set up the antipope Gregory VIII to oppose GELASIUS II, chosen by the cardinals and the Roman clergy. The conflict broke out again. Gelasius excommunicated the Emperor and his antipope. But the pope wanted peace and knew that it would come only through arbitration. He hoped, perhaps, that Louis VI would provide mediation, but Gelasius died at Cluny

(Jan. 29, 1119) on his way to meet the king at Vézelay. His successor, Guy of Vienne, who took the name CALLISTUS II, showed himself an intransigent adversary of lay investiture, even though he was a relative of the emperor. But he wanted peace and sought the path of compromise in the doctrines of Chartres whose success he assured. He thus showed himself more moderate than his former partner in intransigence, GEOFFREY OF VENDÔME, who in 1118–19 published his *Tractatus de ordinatione episcoporum et de investitura laicorum*. Geoffrey held investiture to be a ''sacrament'' and declared that receiving it from lay hands meant ''casting that which is holy to the dogs.''

Concordat of Worms. In 1119, Callistus II commissioned the abbot of Cluny and WILLIAM OF CHAMPEAUX, Bishop of Chalons, two Frenchmen who were familiar with the compromise solution that had been adopted in France, to explain its advantages to Henry V (Strasbourg colloquy). After fruitless negotiation at Mouzon (October 1119), an accord was reached that was articulated in two declarations comprising the Concordat of WORMS (Sept. 23, 1122; *Monumenta Germaniae Historica: Constitutiones* 1:159). The emperor renounced investiture with ring and staff and guaranteed freedom of elections. The pope consented to elections held ''in the presence of the emperor'' and to his granting the regalia to the newly elected prelate by investiture with the scepter. Thus the Chartres distinction between the spiritual and the temporal in the bishopric, complemented by the distinction of dual investiture, by ring and staff for the spiritual, and by scepter for the temporal—a distinction clearly made by an anonymous French treatise, the *Defensio Paschalis papae*, c. 1122, (*Monumenta Germaniae Historica, Libelli de lite*)—finally triumphed in the Empire as it had 15 years previously in England and France.

Bibliography: E. BERNHEIM, *Quellen zur Geschichte des Investiturstreites*, 2 v. (Leipzig 1913). Z. N. BROOKE, *The English Church and the Papacy from the Conquest to the Reign of John* (Cambridge 1931); *Lay Investiture and Its Relation to the Conflict of Empire and Papacy* (London 1940). G. TELLENBACH, *Church, State, and Christian Society at the Time of the Investiture Contest*, tr. R. F. BENNETT (Oxford 1959). A. FLICHE, *La Querelle des Investitures* (Paris 1946); ''Grégoire VII à Canossa, a-t-il réintégré Henri IV dans sa fonction royale?'' *Studi gregoriani* (1947) 373–386. A. BRACKMANN, ''Gregor VII und die kirchliche Reformbewegung in Deutschland,'' *ibid.* 2 (1947) 7–30. A. GWYNN, ''Gregory VII and the Irish Church,'' *ibid.* 3 (1948) 105–128. H. L. MIKOLETZKY, ''Bemerkungen zu einer Vorgeschichte des Investiturstreites,'' *ibid.* 3 (1948) 233–285. G. B. BORINO, ''L'investitura laica dal decreto di Nicolò II al decreto di Gregorio VII,'' *ibid.* 5 (1956) 345–359. H. X. ARQUILLIÈRE,'' Le Sens juridique de l'absolution de Canossa,'' *Actes du Congrès de droit canonique* (Paris 1950) 157–164. A. BECKER, *Studien zum Investiturproblem in Frankreich* (Saarbrücken 1955). N. F. CANTOR, *Church, Kingship, and Lay Investiture in England, 1089–1135* (Princeton 1958). H. HOFFMANN, ''Ivo von Chartres und die Lösung des Investiturproblems,'' *Deutsches Archiv für Erforschung des Mittelalters* 15 (1959) 393–440. H. G. KRAUSE, *Das Papstwahldekret von 1059 und seine Rolle im Investiturstreit* (Studi gregoriani 7; 1960). A. HOFMEISTER, *Das Wormser Konkordat. Zum Streit um seine Bedeutung, mit einer textkritischen Beilage*, new edition with foreword by R. SCHMIDT (Darmstadt 1962). T. SCHIEFFER, ''Cluny et la querelle des Investitures,'' *Revue historique* 225 (1961) 47–72. R. SPRANDEL, *Ivo von Chartres* (Stuttgart 1962). J. FLECKENSTEIN, ed., *Investiturstreit und Reichsverfassung* (Sigmaringen 1973). R. SCHIEFFER, *Die Entstehung des päpstlichen Investiturverbots für den deutschen König*, (Stuttgart 1981). U.-R. BLUMENTHAL, *The Investiture Controversy: Church and Monarchy from the Ninth to the Twelfth Century* (Philadelphia 1988). H. E. J. COWDREY, *Pope Gregory VII, 1073–1085* (Oxford 1998).

[J. GAUDEMET]

INVOLUNTARITY

Involuntarity is the privation of VOLUNTARITY; a characteristic of acts performed through ignorance of the circumstances or under compulsion. The voluntary act is one performed with an adequate knowledge of the circumstances and without external restraint or force. Any deficiency in the relevant knowledge, any compulsion from outside forces, thus deprives an act of its voluntarity.

The act done under compulsion may be defined as one whose source is outside the agent and to which the agent contributes nothing. One who is seized and borne away against his wishes, who is compelled to go where his captors take him, is not held responsible for such activity. Acts done in FEAR present more difficulties. The captain who, out of fear of sinking, orders his cargo to be thrown overboard cannot be said to be doing what he wants to do, at least not without qualification. He certainly does not want to lose his cargo. He does, however, want to save ship, self, and crew; and if the jettisoning of the cargo is the sole means of securing the ship, then in these precise circumstances he does voluntarily jettison his cargo. ARISTOTLE speaks of such acts as mixing voluntarity and involuntarity; he suggests that, considered concretely, acts done out of fear are voluntary. [*See* FORCE AND MORAL RESPONSIBILITY; FORCE AND FEAR (CANNON LAW)].

Not every IGNORANCE deprives an act of its voluntarity. St. THOMAS AQUINAS distinguishes three kinds of ignorance: concomitant, consequent, and antecedent (*Summa theologiae*, 1a2ae, 6.8). (1) Concomitant ignorance does not necessarily render an act involuntary, as in the case of a man who wants to kill his enemy and does kill him while mistakenly thinking he is shooting a bear. Since the result, when he discovers it, does not go contrary to his desires, he can hardly be said to have acted involuntarily. (2) One can desire ignorance in order to es-

Iona Abbey. (©Kevin Schafer/CORBIS)

cape responsibility. For example, one who has difficulty with purity may choose not to inform himself of his obligations lest the knowledge hamper his activities. So too one whose disordered appetites prevent him from thinking of what he knows he should do ignores the moral dimensions of his situation. In both these cases, ignorance is consequent upon freedom and does not make the acts done in such ignorance involuntary. (3) The kind of ignorance that makes acts involuntary is antecedent and innocent; when one is unaware, for example, that his target is not an enemy but a comrade. A sign that he has acted contrary to his wishes is the sorrow and anguish that follow upon the shock of recognition.

(For bibliog. *see* VOLUNTARITY; HUMAN ACT.)

[R. M. MCINERNY]

IONA (HY), ABBEY OF

Former monastery on the island of Iona, part of the Inner Hebrides, Argyllshire, Scotland (Latin, *Insula Iova,*

of which Iona is a misreading). This Celtic island monastery, which was founded in 563 by COLUMBA OF IONA and was ruled by priest-abbots, was the most distinguished center of Irish religious life up to the end of the 7th century. Its phenomenal growth was attributable in part to the fact that Columba and his successors (usually his kinsmen) were closely related to Irish kings. Iona was regarded as the head of the Irish Church and of the Christian Scots in North Britain. From it the Picts received the faith and Columba's successors converted the English of Northumbria (*c.* 637) in less than half a century. Controversy about the acceptance of Roman customs after the decision of Whitby in 664 split its monks and precipitated its decline. However, until the Scandinavian raids of the 9th century (*see* NORMANS), Iona remained the primatial church in the *paruchia* (which consisted of at least 42 churches in Ireland and 57 in Scotland). Then the primacy passed to abbots in Ireland, usually to KELLS. Iona had a brief period of resurgence *c.* 844, when Kenneth mac Alpin succeeded to the Pictish throne. There were CULDEES at Iona in the 12th century, and it remained Celtic to *c.* 1204, when the BENEDICTINES took over. Iona was dissolved and dismantled during the Reformation in Scotland.

Bibliography: *Adamnan's Life of Columba,* ed. and tr. A. O. and M. O. ANDERSON (New York 1962). A. O. ANDERSON, ed. and tr., *Early Sources of Scottish History, A.D. 500–1286,* 2 v. (Edinburgh 1922) 1:17–71. W. REEVES, ed., *The Life of St. Columba . . . by Adamnan* (Dublin 1857). A. BELLESHEIM, *History of the Catholic Church of Scotland,* tr. D. O. HUNTER-BLAIR, 4 v. (Edinburgh 1887–90) 1:55–148. R. A. S. MACALISTER, "An Inventory of the Ancient Monuments . . . of Iona," in *Proceedings of the Society of Antiquaries of Scotland* 48 (1913–14) 421–430. H. LECLERCQ, *Dictionnaire d'archéologie chrétienne et de liturgie,* ed. F. CABROL, H. LECLERCQ, and H. I. MARROU, 15 v. (Paris 1907–53) 7.2:1425–61. J. F. KENNEY, *The Sources for the Early History of Ireland:* v.1, *Ecclesiastical* (New York 1929) 1:422–448, 629–630. A. K. PORTER, *The Crosses and Culture of Ireland* (New Haven 1931) 38–62. W. BONSER, *An Anglo-Saxon and Celtic Bibliography, 450–1087,* 2 v. (Berkeley 1957). F. L. CROSS, *The Oxford Dictionary of the Christian Church* (London 1957) 699–700. D. E. EASSON, *Medieval Religious Houses: Scotland* (London 1957).

[C. MCGRATH]

IOWA, CATHOLIC CHURCH IN

Located in the north central part of the U.S., Iowa is bounded on the north by Minnesota, on the east by Wisconsin and Illinois, on the south by Missouri, and on the west by Nebraska and South Dakota. The Mississippi River forms the east border; the Missouri and Big Sioux the west. It was the 29th state admitted to the Union (Dec. 28, 1846). Des Moines is its capital and largest city. The Catholic population was 526,635 in 2001, about 19 percent of the total population of 2.7 million.

History. Half a dozen prehistoric cultures preceded the score of tribes that are connected with Iowa history since the coming of European settlers. The later tribes included three linguistic stocks: Iroquoian, Algonquian, and Dakotan or Siouan (to which the Ioways belonged). As far as is known, the first whites to see Iowa were the French, specifically the men of the Jolliet-Marquette expedition, who went down the Mississippi in 1673. More than a century passed with only occasional visits from trappers, explorers, and the military before Julien Dubuque (d. 1810) from French Canada made the first settlement (1788) in the area that bears his name. When Napoleon sold Louisiana to the United States in 1803, Iowa became a part of the United States but was not organized as a separate Iowa Territory until 1838. In 1846 a constitution set the boundaries, and in the same year Iowa became the 29th state. The capital, originally at Iowa City, was moved to Des Moines (1857).

When the Black Hawk purchase (1832) opened eastern Iowa for claims, the movement of settlers began and with it the establishment of the Catholic Church in Iowa. The first missionary was C. F. VAN QUICKENBORNE, SJ, in southeast Iowa (1832). Others followed quickly, the most famous being S. MAZZUCHELLI, OP, who, in the years after 1835, helped to found most of the early churches from Dubuque south to the Missouri border (*see* DAVENPORT, DIOCESE OF). Church foundations in central and western Iowa were delayed until after 1850; in 1860 the only places in western Iowa with permanent pastors were Des Moines, Council Bluffs, and Fort Dodge.

In 1837 Mathias LORAS became bishop of the new Diocese of Dubuque, an area that included all of Iowa and reached north to Canada. Eventually, three more dioceses were created in Iowa, and in 1893 Dubuque became an archbishopric. The present Province of Dubuque is coextensive with the state of Iowa. The suffragans include the Dioceses of Davenport, established (1881) in the southern half of the state; Sioux City, formed (1902) from the western part of the Dubuque archdiocese; and Des Moines, fashioned (1911) from the western part of the Davenport diocese. In 1986 the Roman Catholic Bishops of the four dioceses established the Iowa Catholic Conference that enables them to collaborate in matters of interdiocesan and statewide interest. It is structured to include representation of the clergy, religious, and laity. Its headquarters are located in Des Moines.

Beginning with the *Western Star* of Dubuque in 1858, Iowa has had a number of Catholic papers, owned and edited by laymen, including the *Daily American Tribune* of Dubuque (1920–42). In 2001 each diocese owned its own weekly diocesan paper: the Dubuque *Witness* (1921), the Davenport *Catholic Messenger* (1882), the

Archdiocese/Diocese	Year Created
Archdiocese of Dubuque	1893
Diocese of Davenport	1881
Diocese of Des Moines	1911
Diocese of Sioux City	1902

Sioux City *Globe* (1949), and the Des Moines *Catholic Mirror* (formerly, *Catholic Messenger*, 1937).

Immigrant Ancestry. Although the earliest European influences in what became the state of Iowa were decidedly Catholic—French Jesuit missionaries, adventurers and trappers—Catholics have been a minority since the state was admitted to the Union in 1846. Iowa's early Catholic population included Irish and German immigrants in northeastern Iowa, in and around the city of Dubuque, seat of the first bishop, Mathias Loras, who himself was a French immigrant.

Settlers from Europe and other American states in the nineteenth century increased the state's Catholic population, but their numbers were dwarfed by Protestant migrants from both the North and South in the U.S. and by German and Scandinavian immigrants. German Catholics settled as farmers and helped to establish numerous parishes in rural Iowa. One of the most prominent outposts of rural German Catholics, was Carroll County in west central Iowa, named for Charles Carroll, the only Catholic to sign the Declaration of Independence. In addition to their presence in Dubuque, Davenport, Sioux City, and other urban areas, rural Iowa was also home to many Catholics of Irish ancestry. Emmetsburg, in northwest Iowa's Palo Alto County, was named for the Irish patriot Robert Emmet. Other ethnic groups that were well represented among Iowa's Catholic population were the Bohemians and Czechs, who migrated in the late nineteenth century to Cedar Rapids and Iowa City in eastern Iowa.

In the realm of public affairs and politics, Catholic voters in Iowa had long been identified with the Democratic Party, dating back to the period before the Civil War. As with Catholics in other states, their partisan allegiances was in part a result of their sense of themselves as a distinct cultural minority was vulnerable to the ambitions of a Protestant majority determined to define moral behavior and social values for all. During the Civil War, Dennis Mahoney of Dubuque, a Democratic politician and newspaper editor who was also one of the state's most prominent Catholics, was arrested and imprisoned for his criticism of the Lincoln Administration. Although many Iowa Catholics were less than enthusiastic, at least initially, about the prospect of fighting a war to free the

St. Ambrose Cathedral, Des Moines, Iowa. (©Richard Cummins/CORBIS)

slaves, many Iowa Catholics did serve in the U.S. army and Bishop Clement Smyth of Dubuque was a strong and outspoken supporter of the cause of the union.

Nativist Opposition. Iowa Catholics were the target of prejudice and nativism that flared up from time to time. In the 1880s, a group of Iowans, led by Henry F. Bowers, established the American Protective Association in Clinton. The men had become alarmed when a local Catholic priest had apparently tried to influence the votes of his parishioners in an election, although local political and economic factors also played a role in the APA's origins. The group distributed its own newspaper, named the *Menace*, as it tried to revive long held suspicions that Catholics could not be considered fully American because of their religious connections to Rome. The APA was an active organization for nearly a decade, as it sponsored lectures by former priests and nuns, or those claiming to be such, who described the horrors of life inside church and convent walls. One APA speaker incited a crowd in Keokuk, Iowa, to violence in 1892, although no

one was killed in the chaos. Several Iowa Catholics were outspoken critics of the APA, notably Father Joseph Nugent of Des Moines.

The KU KLUX KLAN, an important cultural force in the Midwest in the 1920s, was active in Davenport and Des Moines, among other cities in Iowa. In rural areas of the state, the Klan succeeded in pressuring local school boards not to hire Catholic teachers in the public schools. When Al Smith ran for President in 1928, the first Catholic to be nominated by a major party, he was the target of anti-Catholic rhetoric and imagery, including materials published in some of the state's leading newspapers. John F. Kennedy did not meet with the same overt religious hostility in 1960 that Smith had in 1928. This apparent increase in tolerance can be attributed in part to the way Catholics proved themselves loyal patriots in World War II. One prominent example that gained a good deal of notoriety, both locally and nationally, was the heroism of the five Sullivan brothers, scions of a Catholic family from Waterloo, Iowa, who lost their lives when their ship, the *USS Juneau*, was sunk in the Pacific in 1942.

Social Activism. In contrast to the nineteenth century when the Catholic Church in the United States remained silent on major socio-economic issues such as slavery, in the twentieth century Catholics, both clergy and laity, began to move into the public sphere and engage pressing issues. The National Catholic Rural Life Conference, founded in 1923, moved its headquarters to Des Moines in 1941. The conference has sought to strengthen the presence of the Catholic Church in the countryside. The NCRLC has become a vocal advocate for family farmers and a critic of economic conditions and practices that have forced many people in Iowa and other farming states off the land. The Catholic Church has had a high profile in many parts of rural Iowa. One Catholic community that was recognized for the strong faith of its parishioners and the distinctive gothic architecture of their parish church is in rural Dyersville, Dubuque County. In 1956 Pope Pius XII elevated the church of St. Francis to the rank of a Minor Basilica,

In the 1950s a group of socially concerned Catholics formed the Davenport League for Social Justice. It worked to counter racial discrimination and to make affordable housing accessible to the poor. In the early 1960s, the Quad Cities—Davenport and Bettendorf in Iowa, Moline and Rock Island in Illinois—were home to a Catholic Interracial Conference. The Conference undertook a study of racially based discrimination and organized civil rights rallies. In 1982 Catholic Worker houses were established in Waterloo and Cedar Rapids. Their ministry to the urban poor is modeled on the work done by Dorothy DAY at the original Catholic Workers House in New York City.

Early in the 1970s Catholics, both clergy and laity, were active in successfully lobbying the Iowa legislature against changing state laws prohibiting abortion. After the Supreme Court handed down the *Roe vs. Wade* decision in 1973 that essentially legalized abortion across the United States, Iowa Catholics became increasingly active in the Pro-life movement. Priests have spoken firmly against the practice of abortion from the pulpit, and priests and laity alike have joined in prayer meetings and Pro-life rallies demonstrating against abortion. One political consequence of the Church's stance on the abortion issue was that monolithic Catholic support for the Democratic Party in Iowa began to break up in the final decades of the twentieth century. The change in Iowa politics was reflected in the election of the state's first Catholic governor, Republican Terry Branstad, in 1982. After serving for four terms (sixteen years), Branstad was succeeded in the governor's office by another Catholic, Democrat Tom Vilsack.

Changing Patterns. The Catholic population of Iowa, long identified with German, Irish, Czech, and Bohemian immigrants and their descendants, became more diversified in the final decades of the twentieth century. Hispanic communities, largely consisting of Mexicans, established themselves in towns such as Columbus Junction, West Liberty and Muscatine, Storm Lake and Marshalltown, among others. Much of this migration was driven by economic factors, as these immigrants, most of whom are Catholic, came to Iowa in search of work in meatpacking plants and related industries. In addition, since the 1970s, there have been significant influxes of Vietnamese Catholic immigrants to cities such as Des Moines and Iowa City.

In October of 1979, Iowa garnered international attention when Pope John Paul II visited the state. Although Iowa had a lower percentage of Catholics in its population than did neighboring states, the Pope wanted to visit a rural setting and emphasize the important values involved in stewardship over the land and the connections between rural people and God. While in Iowa, John Paul II celebrated an outdoor Mass at Living History Farm Site near Des Moines, drawing a crowd estimated at 350,000, the biggest crowd to gather for any event in the state's history. The pontiff also visited St. Patrick's Church, a rural parish near Cumming in central Iowa, as he emphasized the theme of the taking proper care of the land as "God's stewards" in a place where agriculture loomed so large in Iowans understanding of their state's history and culture. The Pope's visit was named by readers of the *Des Moines Register*, the state's most influential newspaper, as the most important event in Iowa's history.

Capital: Teheran.
Size: 636,372 sq. miles.
Population: 65,619,636 in 2000.
Languages: Farsi (Persian); Turkic, Kurdish, Luri, Balochi, Arabic, and Turkish are spoken in various regions.
Religions: Shi'a Muslim 58,401,476 (89%), Sunni Muslim 6,561,900 (10 %), Jewish 196,859 (.3%), Catholic (various rites) 393,714 (.6 %), Baha'i and Zoroastrian 65,687 (.1%).

Bibliography: W. J. PETERSEN, *The Story of Iowa,* 4 v. (New York 1952); comp., *Iowa History Reference Guide* (Iowa City 1942; repr. 1952). C. COLE, *Iowa Through the Years* (Iowa City 1940). J. F. KEMPKER, *History of the Catholic Church in Iowa* (Iowa City 1887). M. M. HOFFMANN, ed., *Centennial History of the Archdiocese of Dubuque* (Dubuque 1938). M. K. GALLAGHER, ed., *Seed/ Harvest: A History of the Archdiocese of Dubuque.* (Dubque 1987). M. M. SCHMIDT, *Seasons of Growth: History of the Diocese of Davenport, 1881–1981* (Davenport, Iowa 1981).

[R. J. WELCH/J. K. DUNCAN]

IRAN, THE CATHOLIC CHURCH IN

Located on a plateau in western Asia, Iran is bordered on the north by the Caspian Sea, Armenia, Azerbaijan, and Turkmenistan, on the east by Afghanistan and Pakistan, on the south by the Persian Gulf and the Gulf of Oman, and on the west by Iraq and Turkey. Although rich in petroleum, natural gas, and other minerals, Iran is plagued by droughts, floods, and dust storms, and its climate combines with its rugged terrain to leave only 30 percent of the country available for farming. While sales of oil and other raw materials have created wealth within the country, half Iran's population live below the poverty line. An Islamic republic since 1979, Iran was known as PERSIA until 1935.

Three branches of the Catholic Church operate within Iran. CHALDEAN rite Catholics belong to the Archdiocese of Urmya, whose suffragan see, Salmas (erected in 1847), is united to it *ad personam,* an archeparchy located at Ahwaz, and an eparchy, or diocese, at Ispahan. The LATIN RITE Church has an archdiocese located in Ispahan, immediately subject to the Holy See. The Armenian Rite Church has an eparchy created in 1850 and located, as well, in Ispahan.

Early Church History. As a part of what then constituted Asia Minor, Persia fell under the domination of Alexander the Great in 327 B.C. Coming from a tradition of pantheism established within their own culture and influenced by the Hellenic traditions promoted under Alexander, few Persians were attracted to Christianity. Although by the end of the 1st century the earliest Chris-

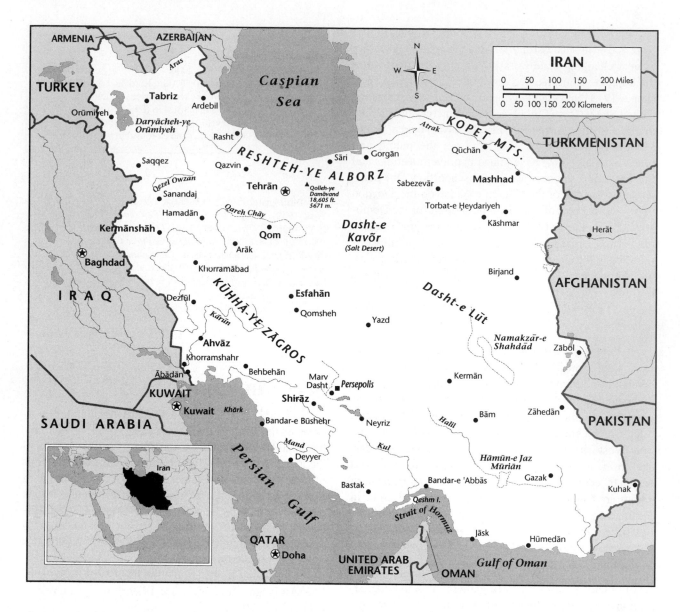

tian communities outside the Roman Empire were located in Persia, Christianity was still primarily the religion of minority ethnic groups, predominately Syrians. Because of its presentation as a universal cult demanding adherence, the new religion quickly encountered opposition from the official pagan cult. When Constantine I became Roman emperor early in the 4th century, he had a vision of a flaming cross; realizing this to be a Christian symbol, he was prompted to extend special privileges to the growing number of Christians living in his vast empire. Such preferential treatment by a neighboring Roman ruler caused Persian authorities to question the loyalty of Persian Christians. This nascent discrimination—a result of the continuing political hostility between Greeks and Romans—led to the long series of bloody persecutions begun in 340 under Shapur II (309–379). By the end of Shapur's reign, the Church in Persia was almost wholly

cut off from Western contacts and developed in its own fashion. In 424 the Synod of Markabta effectively declared its autonomy. Late in the 5th century, while Zoroastrianism had established itself as the state religion, NESTORIANISM became predominant among Persia's Christians. After the Arab invasion in 642 Islam was adopted by most of the populace. After this point Christians declined in numbers, although they engaged in missionary activity during the Middle Ages and even flourished for a time after the Mongol invasion (1220).

Catholic missionaries from the West labored in Persia with only slight success following the Middle Ages. Dominicans were active from the 14th to the 18th century. Augustianians, Carmelites, Capuchins, and Jesuits arrived in the 17th century; Vincentians, in 1839. The most sizeable increment to Christianity in Persia came from the immigration of Armenians, followers of MONOPHY-SITISM, especially at the beginning of the 17th century, when large numbers of them were deported from their homeland. Armenian Rite Monophysites continued to constitute the largest group of Christians in Iran through the 20th century. While religious liberty was granted in 1834, Christians were massacred in Persia as late as 1918.

The Church under Islamic Fundamentalism. By the mid-1960s there were 28,000 Latin rite Catholics, 100,000 Armenian Catholics, and 13,000 Chaldean Catholics present in Iran. The Holy See maintained an internuncio at Teheran, and Iran had an ambassador at the Vatican. However, Catholics still represented only a small segment of Iran's population, and the rise of Muslim activism in the coming years would mark them more strongly as outcasts within Iranian society.

In 1979 increasing political instability—the result of rising interference by Western businesses eager to profit from the nation's vast oil reserves—forced Iran's ruling shah into exile. On April 1, 1979, shortly after imposing martial law, Islamic fundamentalist Ruhollah Khomeini (1900–89) pronounced Iran an Islamic republic and began enforcement of strict Islamic traditions. Together with Zoroastrians and Jews, Christians were recognized as a ''minority religion'' under the new Iranian constitution of 1980; they were ''free to act within their own canon'' in religious matters, were extended protection of life and property, and were allowed representation in the republic's new parliament. However, the activities of non-Farsi-speaking religions such as Armenian Catholics were deemed ''detrimental to the fundamental health of Islam'' and as such were singled out for discriminatory treatment, including the prohibition of the importation of bibles into Iran. Over 70 Catholic missionaries left the country following the government's nationalization of church-run organizations, and the ability of Catholics to travel across Iran's borders was closely monitored.

While the government has become slightly more accepting of Western traditions since Khomeini's death in 1989, Iran continues to be plagued by religious intolerance, particularly against followers of the outlawed Baha'i faith, who were declared to have committed ''crimes against God.'' Iran's actions against religious minorities prompted statements of concern from the U.S. State Department as late as 2000. In addition, in March 1999 Pope John Paul II received Iranian President Mohammed Khatami at the Vatican to discuss means of improving relations between Muslims and Christians.

Bibliography: D. ATTWATER, *The Christian Churches of the East,* 2 v. (rev. ed. Milwaukee 1961–62). R. ETTELDORF, *The Catholic Church in the Middle East* (New York 1959). N. R. KEDDIE, *Iran: Religion, Politics, and Society,* (London 1990). R. MAYER and W. DE VRIES, *Lexicon für Theologie und Kirche,* ed. J. HOFER and K. RAHNER (Freiburg 1957–65) 8:283–287. *Bilan du Monde. Encyclopédie catholique du monde chrétien,* 2 v. (2d ed. Tournai 1964) 2:490–495.

[T. P. JOYCE/EDS.]

Capital: Baghdad.
Size: 252,116 sq. miles.
Population: 22,675,620 in 2000.
Languages: Arabic, Kurdish, Assyrian, Armenian.
Religions: 470,000 Catholics (2%), 7,811,320 Sunni Muslims (34%), 14,060,300 Shi'a Muslims (62%), 334,000 Protestants (2%).
Ecclesiastical organizations: Iraq has a Latin-rite archdiocese in Baghdad, but Eastern Catholic churches predominate. The Chaldean Catholic Church had a patriarchate at Babylon with suffragans Alquoch, Amadiyah, Aqra, Baghdad, (the patriarchal see), Sulaimaniya, and Zakho; an archdiocese at Kirkul, and archeparchies at Arbil, Basra, and Mosul. The Armenian Catholic Church has an archeparchy at Baghdad. The Syrian Catholic Church has archeparchies at Baghdad and Mosul.

IRAQ, THE CATHOLIC CHURCH IN

The Republic of Iraq, located in the Middle East, is bordered by on the north by Turkey, on the east by Iran, on the southeast by Kuwait, on the south and southwest by Saudi Arabia, and on the west by Jordan and Syria. Predominately a desert, the region rises to mountains and desert plateau in the north and falls to grassy wetlands in the south. The Tigris and Euphrates rivers cross the region from north to south, although the water, highly saline, is no natural aid to agriculture. Winters are mild, with melting snows causing flooding in the south, while summers are hot and dry. Sandstorms and dust storms are common in the central region. The greater part of Iraq's economy is derived from its petroleum reserves, while other natural resources include natural gas, phosphates and sulphur. Agriculture, which employs most of the nation's work force, includes such crops as wheat, barley, rice, dates, cotton, vegetables and livestock.

The heart of Iraq, the ''cradle of civilization,'' is the Tigris-Euphrates basin, ancient MESOPOTAMIA, which was ruled successively by Babylonians, Assyrians, Achaemenid Persians, Seleucid Greeks, Parthian and Sassanid Persians, Arabs, Mongols, Safawid Persians and Ottoman Turks. A British mandate from 1920 to 1932 and a constitutional monarchy beginning in 1921, Iraq became a republic in 1958 under a series of military governments. In July of 1979 Saddam Hussein gained control, and began a series of aggressive maneuvers in the

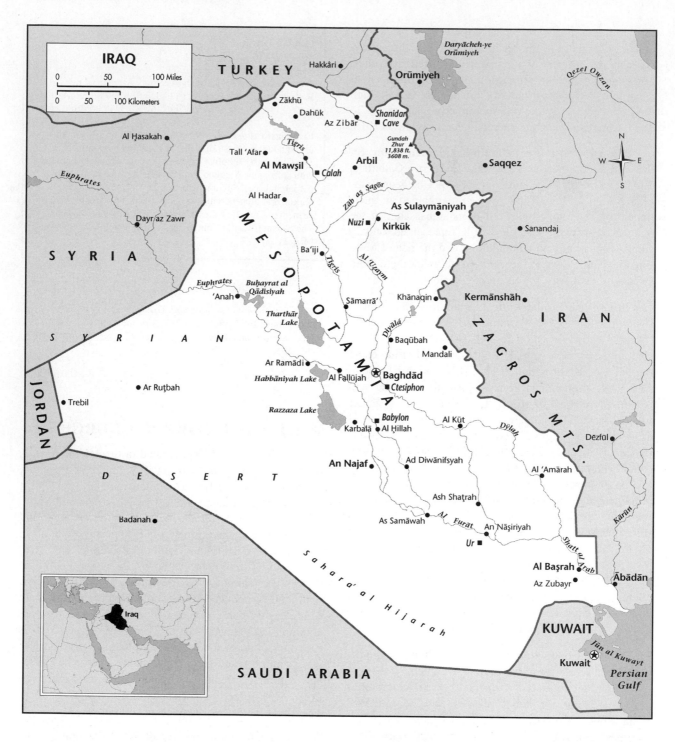

Middle East that ultimately resulted in the involvement of U.S. troops to repel Iraq's invasion of neighboring Kuwait in 1991. Hussein's acquisition of long-range missiles and his support of terrorist activities caused him to remain a threat to world peace. An international trade embargo was levied against the region in 1991, although an oil-for-food program initiated by the United Nations in 1996 helped to counter the economic hardship to the region's civilian population.

History. Iraq was invaded by Arab forces in the 7th century, and was incorporated as part of the Ottoman Empire in 1534. Islam remained the predominate influence, despite the occupation of British forces during World War I. A British-backed monarchy lasted from 1921 to 1958, during which time Catholic and other Christian faiths gained strength in the region. Although Islam was the state religion, religious liberty was guaranteed by the constitution of 1921 and maintained by the monarchy.

Iraqi Christians during New Year's Day Mass, Boutros Church, Baghdad. (©AP/Wide World Photos)

Most Iraqi Catholics were of the Chaldean RITE, while non-Catholic Christian communities included GREEK OR-THODOX, JACOBITES, NESTORIANS and Protestants. The majority of Catholics lived in the north of Iraq, as well as in Baghdad. Reflective of the concerns of the period, a Chaldean synod of 1957 dealt with administration, discipline, liturgy and Catholic Action. Iraq established diplomatic relations with the Holy See in 1966.

The monarchy of King Faisal I fell in 1958, and a coup ten years later brought a militaristic government to power. Quashing sporadic struggles for independence by the region's Kurdish population in the north teamed with the government's ongoing repression of Iraq's Shi'a Muslim leadership and militaristic foreign policy to create a climate of intolerance, the government acted against criticism of its policies by outspoken religious leaders and others. Sunni Muslims, although a minority of the population, continued to act as the country's elite, with an influential role in both government and business.

Their brutal repressions against Shi'a Muslims, as well as against other faiths, resulted in violence to both Church members and Church property. Assyrian Catholics came under increasing fire during the late 1980s when the government suspected them of aiding Kurdish rebels in the north, and in 1988 many Assyrian churches were destroyed by the military. In addition, increasing Islamic fundamentalism during the 1990s resulted in a number of incidences of mob violence against Catholics and other Christians living in the north. Neither the Chaldean nor the Syrian rites were recognized by the government as religions, although they were known to be the descendants of Iraq's first Christian communities, their services performed in the Syriac language.

Into the 21st Century. By 2000 there were 82 parishes of various Catholic rites, tended by a total of 104 diocesan and 26 religious priests. Other religious in the country included approximately 20 brothers and 350 sisters, many of whom tended to the humanitarian concerns of the region. Chaldean Patriarch Raphael I. Bidawid and his bishops in particular used their influence as the largest Catholic community—Chaldeans numbered approximately 400,000 by 2000— to loudly protest both the continued international embargo of the country and the repeated bombings by U.S. troops from 1998 through 2000. Church leaders claimed that the true victims were the poor and infirm, as well as the very young. Pope John Paul II also spoke out forcefully and repeatedly against the embargo as a cause of poverty, disease and death. The pope's advocacy of peace and his public statements, such as his entreaty in April of 2001 that "innocent people should not be made to pay the consequences of a destructive war whose effects are still being felt by those who are weakest and most vulnerable" earned him the thanks of Sadam Hussein as well as the acknowledgment of U.N. Secretary General Kofi Annan. In 1996 a U.S. Catholic group called Voices in the Wilderness defied a ban against travel to Iraq and began a continued program of bringing medicine and other aid to the region. A proposed visit to Iraq by Pope John Paul II in December of 1999 was ultimately suspended following concerns about the mixed impact the pontiff's visit would have.

Bibliography: *Église vivante*, 5–16 (1953–64). *Bilan du Monde*, 2: 486–490. *Oriente Cattolico*.

[J. A. DEVENNY/EDS.]

IRELAND, CHURCH OF

The Anglican church in Ireland, in communion with the Church of England, claims succession from the Roman Catholic Church established in Ireland in the 5th century by St. PATRICK and others. Henry VIII demanded from his subjects in Ireland, as he had from those in England, the recognition of himself as supreme head of the Church, and by parliamentary enactments he declared illegal the jurisdiction of the pope (1536). These changes were made possible through the reconquest of the English Pale in Ireland after the Geraldine rebellion (1534). The same changes were formally accepted by the clergy in this area but they obstructed George BROWN, who was nominated by Henry VIII as archbishop of Dublin. Contacts were maintained with the Holy See in the Gaelic independent lordships. The Anglo-Irish showed greater hostility toward Protestantism under Edward VI and quickly reverted to Catholicism under Mary I. As in England, the church was reconciled to Rome by Cardinal Reginald Pole. Accordingly only those clergy who had married were deprived, and Protestantism was permitted privately to the few English officials.

Elizabeth I to the 19th Century. The Elizabethan religious settlement finally handed over the fabric of the church to the Protestant clergy, who, however, lost the great majority of the people to the Counter Reformation missionaries. Adam Loftus, as archbishop of Dublin, maintained a more puritanical movement than would be permitted in England by Queen ELIZABETH I. As first provost of Trinity College, Dublin, he imported Cambridge Puritan divines. A more Calvinistic element became strengthened by the Scottish infiltration into early 17th-century Ulster. Substantial endowments were given to the church in the plantations. Under Charles I's viceroy, Thomas Wentworth, Earl of Strafford, working with the Laudian Bp. John Bramhall of Derry, pressure was imposed on landed proprietors to increase diocesan and parochial property while Calvinistic tendencies, particularly in the north, were discouraged. Ulster Scots sympathized with the anti-Laudian Bishop's War in Scotland (1638). After the Irish Catholics rebelled in 1641, the Church of Ireland lost ground. It was treated as disestablished by Oliver Cromwell, and the victorious parliamentarians, who substituted independent Congregationalism, tolerated PRESBYTERIANISM but persecuted Episcopalianism (ANGLICANISM) as well as Catholicism. After the restoration of Charles II, this reestablished church, while secure in the support of the army and the landed classes, had only one-eleventh of the population of 1,100,000 (there being twice as many Presbyterians) and did not improve its situation further despite penal laws against Catholic and Protestant conformists (*see* SCOTLAND, CHURCH OF).

Few Episcopalians (Anglicans) favored James II, but after the war in Ireland, only a small minority led by Charles Lesley refused to abjure the exiled monarch and became known as nonjurors. The declaration against transubstantiation, imposed on officeholders after 1689, strengthened the Calvinistic trend of Anglicanism. Presbyterianism, however, did not improve its public situation after the revolution, unlike that in Scotland, where it replaced Episcopalianism as the established Christian denomination. Thus the Irish Protestant episcopal clergy such as Archbishop William King of Dublin and Dean Jonathan Swift, while mainly Tories in church questions, were Whigs in other political issues. Their secular influence was maintained throughout the 18th century by the promotion to the highest church offices of Englishmen such as Primates Hugh Boulter and George Stone; but their useful government contacts were counterbalanced by the increasing resentment of Irish-born clerics who helped to foster colonial antipathy to British paternalism in administration and trade. Only a small fraction favored the United Irish revolutionary movement at the end of the century, and with the rise of the Presbyterian and Catholic middle classes to challenge their monopoly of power, the Episcopalians came to regard as a protection the act of union which amalgamated the Anglican churches as well as the parliaments (1801).

Catholic Emancipation. Catholic emancipation (1829) inaugurated the breakdown of Protestant ascendancy that attempted to arrest its own decline by improved relations with the Presbyterians, led by Henry Cooke; by a more aggressive missionary policy among impoverished Catholics; and by a more exact insistence on its rights to tithes from all occupiers of agricultural lands without reference to their religion. The OXFORD MOVEMENT had few Irish supporters except for people like William Maziere BRADY. The repeal of the union movement had even fewer, so that when disestablishment was urged it gained the support of many nationalists. Although the majority of the clergy opposed William Gladstone's Act of Disestablishment (1869–71), the establishment of the Church Representative Body and the organization of an annual synod in which a majority of participants were lay proved highly successful. Inevitably, as most of the Catholic clergy supported the home rule movement, the Protestants generally were among the Unionists. Episcopalian clergy were prominently identified with the Covenant against home rule in 1912, but since 1920, though not supporting political moves to end Irish partition, the Church of Ireland, like the Presbyterian and Catholic churches, continues to stress the essential national character of its organization. While their numbers in the Republic of Ireland are small—being less than 5 percent of the whole—in Northern Ireland, where 60 percent of the population is Protestant, they claim nearly 30 percent.

Bibliography: *Catalogue of Manuscripts in Possession of the Representative Church Body* (Dublin 1938). W. M. BRADY, *The Irish Reformation, or the Alleged Conversion of the Irish Bishops at the Accession of Queen Elizabeth* (London 1866). *Journal of the Session of the General Synod of the Church of Ireland* (1870–). R. D. EDWARDS, *Church and State in Tudor Ireland* (London 1935). T. J. JOHNSTON et al., *A History of the Church of Ireland* (Dublin 1953). H. J. LAWLOR, *The Reformation and the Irish Episcopate* (2d ed. London 1932). W. D. KILLEN, *Ecclesiastical History of Ireland,* 2 v. (London 1875). R. MANT, *History of the Church of Ireland, from the Reformation to the Union of the Churches of England and Ireland, 1801,* 2 v. (London 1840). W. A. PHILLIPS, ed., *History of the Church of Ireland,* 3 v. (London 1933–34). J. S. REID, *History of the Presbyterian Church in Ireland,* ed. W. D. KILLEN, 3 v. (Belfast 1867). J. H. TODD, *St. Patrick, Apostle of Ireland* (Dublin 1864).

[R. D. EDWARDS/EDS.]

IRELAND, JOHN

First archbishop of St. Paul, Minn.; b. Burnchurch, County Kilkenny, Ireland, exact date unknown, but baptismal date is Sept. 11, 1838; d. St. Paul, Sept. 25, 1918. His parents, Richard and Judith (Naughton) Ireland, im-

John Ireland.

migrated with their six children to the U.S. (1848), settling in Burlington, Vt. In 1851 they moved to Chicago, Ill., and a year later to the frontier town of St. Paul, Minnesota Territory.

Early Career

Joseph Cretin, first bishop of St. Paul, selected Ireland to study for the priesthood (1853) and enrolled him in his own alma mater in France, the preparatory seminary of Meximieux in the Diocese of Belley. Ireland completed the course in classics (1857) with academic honors in several fields, especially in French and in oratory. His exceptional fluency in French was a valuable asset in his later career. After theological studies at the French Marist seminary at Montbel, near Toulon, he was ordained (Dec. 22, 1861) in St. Paul by Cretin's successor, Bp. Thomas Langdon Grace, and served for a few months as a curate in the cathedral parish. Ireland then joined the Fifth Minnesota Infantry Regiment as its chaplain, serving with distinction until his uncertain health and his bishop's need for his services forced his resignation on March 19, 1863. Despite the brevity of his Civil War career, Ireland savored all his life the taste of action he had had at the Battle of Corinth, and he always maintained close bonds with other veterans of the Grand Army of the Republic.

In 1867 Ireland was appointed rector of St. Paul's Cathedral. He represented Bishop Grace at Vatican Council I (1869–70), although he could neither speak nor vote at the Council sessions. When Pius IX named Ireland titular bishop of Maronea and vicar apostolic of Nebraska (April 12, 1875), Grace went immediately to Rome and successfully petitioned the pope to revoke the appointment so that Ireland might continue to work for the Church in Minnesota. Later the same year, Pius IX confirmed Ireland's titular bishopric and appointed him coadjutor, with the right of succession, to the bishop of St. Paul; Ireland was consecrated by Grace on Dec. 21, 1875.

As an ardent spokesman for the Catholic Total Abstinence Society, Ireland was featured regularly at their meetings, and he soon earned a leading place in that movement as well as a wider, even national, reputation as an orator of force and eloquence. Disturbed by reports that Catholic immigrants in eastern cities were suffering from social and economic handicaps, he organized and directed in Minnesota (1876–81) the most successful rural colonization program ever sponsored by the Catholic Church in the U.S. (*see* IRISH CATHOLIC COLONIZATION ASSOCIATION OF THE U.S.). Working with the western railroads and with the state government, he brought more than 4,000 Catholic families from the slums of eastern urban areas and settled them on more than 400,000 acres of farmland in western Minnesota.

Ordinary of St. Paul

On July 31, 1884, ill health led Grace to resign as bishop of St. Paul in favor of his coadjutor. Two years later, at the Provincial Council of Milwaukee, Ireland joined the other bishops of the province in petitioning the Holy See to erect a new archdiocese west of Milwaukee to accommodate the growth of the Church in that region. On May 4, 1888, St. Paul was raised to the rank of an archdiocese, and Ireland was named its first archbishop. The next year five new dioceses (Winona, Duluth, and St. Cloud in Minnesota and Sioux Falls and Jamestown in Dakota Territory) were established and attached as suffragan sees to the new Archdiocese of St. Paul. The proliferation of dioceses in the Northwest prompted the *New York Times* to speculate that "another cardinal's hat was soon to be bestowed by Pope Leo on an American prelate . . . John Ireland," a rumor that was to follow the archbishop for the rest of his life.

At the Third Plenary Council of Baltimore (1884) Ireland delivered his famous address, "The Catholic Church and Civil Society," which remains the most eloquent statement of his lifelong concern to encourage mutual understanding and respect between the Catholic Church and the pluralistic democratic society of the U.S. The thesis of this address has since been often cited as a fundamental tenet of the progressive position in Church-State discussions. In ringing phrases Ireland confronted his fellow bishops with the challenge: "I do not, I think, mistake my fellow countrymen when I ascribe to them on the occasion of the Plenary Council holding session in Baltimore the wish that a statement be made as to the attitude of the Catholic Church in her teachings and in her history toward civil society and, in a special manner, toward the form of civil society which obtains in the United States of America."

In spite of growing administrative burdens, Ireland retained a scholarly interest and discipline throughout his life. He wrote regularly for learned reviews. His collected essays, significantly entitled *The Church and Modern Society* (1896), present his thoughtful and literate statement of the problems that confront the Church in a pluralistic and democratic society.

Ireland's last great project was the construction of a new cathedral commensurate with the growth and dignity of his archdiocese. Nine years (1906–15) were required for the work, and the result was the present Cathedral of St. Paul, recognized as one of the most impressive church buildings in North America.

Church Leader

In the last decade of the 19th century, Ireland joined Cardinal James GIBBONS as an acknowledged leader of the American hierarchy. On questions of national and ecclesiastical policy, the archbishop was an eloquent speaker and a tireless writer. His forthright positions on questions of the day often drew him into controversy with Church and State leaders who did not share his views, and he was often criticized by two opposite groups for precisely opposite reasons. Many of his fellow Catholics, especially in France, considered him too American and not sufficiently Catholic; it was chiefly French journalists and theologians who accused him of the "heresy of AMERICANISM." At the other end of the spectrum, some of his own countrymen who did not share his faith accused him of being too Catholic and not sufficiently American. In 1892 Ireland was commissioned to represent the Holy See in France when Leo XIII sought to convince the French hierarchy and Catholic lay leaders that the future of the Church lay with the people and not with the restoration of the monarchy. On the occasion of his public address to an elite Parisian audience on June 18, 1892, Ireland's elegant French, his tactful diplomacy, and his command of his subject won new respect in France for the position advocated by the Pope, a position Ireland considered to be best exemplified by the successful record of the Catholic Church in the U.S.

Immigrant Problem

In the years of the great Atlantic migration, Ireland was anxious that Catholic settlers in America should give generous and patriotic allegiance to their adopted land. He often spoke on patriotism and urged his people to accept the ways and the language of their new country. In this effort he earned the opposition of a zealous and religious German lay leader, Peter Paul CAHENSLY, who protested to Leo XIII that the insistence on "Americanizing" the immigrants was resulting in mass defections of German-born Catholics from the American Church. The solution proposed by Cahensly was the establishment of dioceses in the U.S. staffed exclusively by German bishops and priests. Whatever the justice of Cahensly's complaints against the Irish-dominated clergy, it is clear that the creation of German-speaking enclaves would have seriously impaired the unity of the Church in the U.S. Thanks largely to the promptings of Gibbons and Ireland, Leo XIII refused to support Cahensly.

Education

In the history of American education Ireland is often cited for his design of the so-called FARIBAULT SCHOOL PLAN, which he inaugurated in the Minnesota cities of Faribault and Stillwater. Under this plan the parochial school could be rented to the local public school board for use during the school day but retained as a center for religious instruction before and after the public school hours. His American critics charged him with violating the principle of separation of Church and State and also accused him of weakening the strong position of Catholic education recommended by the Third Plenary Council of Baltimore. So heated did the controversy on this subject become that the archbishop felt it necessary to go to Rome to explain his position. Investigation revealed that the plan he advocated was already operating successfully in ten American dioceses. Rome decided to allow the program to continue, but criticism of it did not subside. It is noteworthy that the Faribault Plan bears striking resemblance to the Shared Time plan, which has since been advanced by Catholic and public school administrators in many American communities.

When the hierarchy of the U.S. decided at the Third Plenary Council of Baltimore (1884) to establish a Catholic university for the U.S., Bps. John Lancaster SPALDING

of Peoria, Ill., and John Joseph KEANE of Richmond, Va., became the leaders in subsequent efforts to build and staff the institution that eventually came to be called The CATHOLIC UNIVERSITY OF AMERICA, Washington, D.C. In their zealous efforts to this end Spalding and Keane were ably assisted by Ireland, who was convinced that such a national Catholic center was both necessary and possible. Approval of the Holy See for this new institution was finally granted on Easter Sunday, April 10, 1887, largely through the persuasive efforts of Ireland and Keane, who had gone to Rome in 1886 as the representatives of the American hierarchy to seek such approval. Throughout his life Ireland retained a strong active interest in the Catholic University.

In his own archdiocese his efforts on behalf of Catholic education were equally vigorous. In 1885 he founded the College of St. Thomas. In 1894 he opened the St. Paul Seminary, built and endowed by James J. Hill, the famous empire builder. Ireland personally supervised the selection of a distinguished faculty for the new seminary, as well as the selection of its library collection. In his private letters, Ireland often recorded his conviction that a holy and learned clergy was essential for the advance of the Church. This explains his tireless efforts to secure for his seminary the best faculty he could assemble from Europe and the U.S. A corollary of his interest in priests was his strong desire to create new dioceses in the upper Middle West and to recommend holy and able priests as bishops in these new jurisdictions. Still unsurpassed in American history is the event of May 19, 1910, when Ireland acted as the chief consecrator for six bishops in the chapel of the St. Paul Seminary.

Labor and Racial Questions

The closing decades of the 19th century marked the difficult beginnings of the American labor movement. One prominent association of workmen was known as the KNIGHTS OF LABOR. In 1884, at the request of the archbishop of Quebec, the Holy See included the Knights among those conspiratorial and ritualistic secret societies prohibited to Catholics. At first most American prelates, aware that Catholics counted heavily in the leadership and the rank and file of the Knights of Labor and convinced that the condemnation was ill-advised, took the position that the decision applied to Canada and not the U.S. Then, foreseeing a possibly disastrous alienation of Catholic workingmen, the archbishops of the U.S., at their meeting in October 1886, decided to try to secure from the Holy See a formal statement of toleration of the Knights. This delicate mission was entrusted to Ireland, who was in Rome on other business. The outcome of the negotiations remained uncertain until a memorial, drawn up and signed by Cardinal Gibbons, was presented Feb.

20, 1887 by Ireland to the prefect of the Congregazione de Propaganda Fide and was favorably received. There is little doubt that Ireland had much to do with the framing of this decisive document and therefore deserves to share with Gibbons the credit for this vitally important step in the Catholic Church's largely successful efforts to retain the allegiance of the laboring class in the U.S. Writing in the *North American Review* of October 1901, Ireland gave a definitive statement of his views of the rights of labor to organize for its own protection at the same time that he reminded labor of the corresponding rights of management and of owners of private property.

On the subject of racial equality, Ireland was consistent and unequivocal. In 1890 he stated:

> There is but one solution of the problem, and it is to obliterate absolutely all color line. . . . Open up to the Negro as to the white man, the political offices of the country, making but one test, that of mental and moral fitness. Throw down at once the barriers which close out the Negro merely on account of his color from hotel, theater, and railway carriage. Meet your Negro brother as your equal at banquets and in social gatherings. Give him, in one word, and in full meaning of the terms, equal rights and equal privileges, political, civil, and social. . . . I know no color line, I will acknowledge none. . . . The time is not distant when Americans and Christians will wonder that there ever was a race prejudice.

Other Contributions

Although Ireland's allegiance to the Republican party and his defense of its policies on occasion drew criticism, the results also earned him the friendship and favor of many political leaders. In 1898 the Holy See asked him to intercede with Pres. William McKinley to try to avert the impending Spanish-American War. Although his diplomatic negotiations with McKinley were not successful, Ireland was recognized both by Rome and by the president as the spokesman for the Church in these discussions. At the end of the war the archbishop was appointed by Pres. Theodore Roosevelt to serve on the commission that negotiated between the U.S. and the Vatican a settlement for the friars' lands in the Philippine Islands. Among the many occasions on both sides of the Atlantic, when Ireland's presence added prestige to an already important event, was that of May 8, 1899, when, as the official guest of the French government, he preached the sermon in the cathedral of Orléans honoring the 470th anniversary of the raising of the siege of that city by St. JOAN OF ARC. A year later he returned to France at the request of President McKinley and presented to the French people, in the name of the U.S., a statue of the Marquis de Lafayette. In return Ireland was invested with the Cross of the Legion of Honor.

Although Ireland's vigorous administration of the affairs of the Church earned for him many critics at home and abroad, a careful review of his pronouncements on such varied topics as nationalism, education, race relations, labor, science, technology, temperance, the missions, Church and State, liberal arts, patriotism, international affairs, citizenship, and social work lead to the conclusion that events subsequent to his death have for the most part confirmed his opinions and validated his predictions. Moreover, his courageous and farsighted leadership in the metropolitan Province of St. Paul helped to make it a recognized center of Catholic culture and influence.

Bibliography: J. IRELAND, "The Catholic Church and the Saloon," *North American Review* 159 (1894) 498–505; "Personal Liberty and Labor Strikes," *ibid.* 173 (1901) 445–453. J. H. MOYNIHAN, *The Life of Archbishop John Ireland* (New York 1953). T. O'GORMAN, "The Educational Policy of Archbishop Ireland," *Educational Review* 3 (1892) 462–471. J. P. SHANNON, "Archbishop Ireland's Experiences as a Civil War Chaplain," *American Catholic Historical Review* 39 (1953) 298–305; *Catholic Colonization on the Western Frontier* (New Haven 1957). T. T. MCAVOY, "Americanism, Fact and Fiction," *American Catholic Historical Review* 31 (1945) 133–153. J. M. REARDON, *The Catholic Church in the Diocese of St. Paul* (St. Paul 1952). F. J. ZWIERLEIN, *Life and Letters of Bishop McQuaid*, 3 v. (Rochester 1925–27). P. H. AHERN, *The Catholic University of America, 1887–1896* (Washington 1949). C. J. BARRY, *The Catholic Church and German Americans* (Milwaukee 1953). H. J. BROWNE, *The Catholic Church and the Knights of Labor* (Studies in American Church History 38; Washington 1949). J. T. ELLIS, *The Life of James Cardinal Gibbons* 2 v. (Milwaukee 1952). J. IRELAND, *The Church and Modern Society* (St. Paul 1896).

[J. P. SHANNON]

IRELAND, JOHN, BL.

Priest, martyr; hanged, drawn, and quartered at Tyburn (London), March 7, 1544. Little is known of this seminary priest. He was chaplain of the Roper Chantry annexed to St. Dunstan's, in Canterbury (1535–36) before becoming vicar of Eltham, Kent, and thus the parish priest of St. Thomas More's daughter Margaret Roper of West Hall. For refusing to acknowledge the royal supremacy in spiritual matters, Ireland was indicted (Feb. 15, 1543) with BB. John LARKE, German GARDINER, and John HEYWOOD (who recanted on the hurdle). The bodies of the martyrs were buried under the gallows. Ireland was beatified by Pope Leo XIII on Dec. 9, 1886.

Feast of the English Martyrs: May 4 (England)

See Also: ENGLAND, SCOTLAND, AND WALES, MARTYRS OF.

Bibliography: R. CHALLONER, *Memoirs of Missionary Priests*, ed. J. H. POLLEN (rev. ed. London 1924; repr. Farnborough 1969). J. H. POLLEN, *Acts of English Martyrs* (London 1891).

[K. I. RABENSTEIN]

IRELAND, SERAPHINE, MOTHER

Religious superior, educator; b. Kilkenny, Ireland, July 1842; d. St. Paul, Minn., June 20, 1930. Ellen came with her parents to Minnesota at the age of ten and was educated at St. Joseph's Academy, St. Paul, Minn. She entered the novitiate of the Sisters of St. Joseph in 1858, taking the name Sister Seraphine. She acquired teaching and administrative experience in elementary and secondary schools, and profited vicariously from the broad American and European experiences of her brother, Abp. John IRELAND of St. Paul. She was named provincial superior in 1882, at which time her order numbered 116 sisters in eight educational and nursing institutions in and near the Twin Cities. Mother Seraphine prepared novices to qualify as teachers and nurses in accredited schools and hospitals. From 1887 to 1904, she devoted her efforts to securing staff, endowment, and buildings for the College of St. Catherine in St. Paul. When she retired in 1921, the St. Paul Province extended into North and South Dakota and contained 913 sisters, five hospitals, two orphanages, an infant's home, 45 parochial grade schools, 15 high schools, and a college.

See Also: MCHUGH, ANTONIA, SISTER.

[A. GLEASON]

IRELAND, THE CATHOLIC CHURCH IN

The Republic of Ireland (Eire) encompasses five-sixths of the island of Ireland. It is located west of Great Britain, from which it is separated by the North Channel, the Irish Sea and St. George's Channel. Under English control for centuries, the island was split into two political divisions during the early 20th century. Following a rebellion that resulted in the severing of political ties to Great Britain, the Republic of Ireland achieved political independence in 1949. The six counties in the north of the island were established as Northern Ireland in 1920 and are now a part of the United Kingdom and Northern Ireland. Comprising a rolling plain rising to low mountains and dotted with numerous lakes, Ireland has a number of good harbors. Formerly an agricultural economy, Ireland's exports of machinery and other equipment, computers, pharmaceuticals and animal products accounted for most of its gross domestic product by 2000. Ireland is a member of the European Monetary Union.

Capital: Dublin.
Size: 26,600 sq. miles.
Population: 3,797,255 in 2000.
Languages: English; Gaelic is spoken along the western coast.
Religions: 3,455,504 Roman Catholics (91%), 75,945 Anglicans (Church of Ireland; 2%), 221,560 other (6%), 41,250 without religious affiliation.

The Republic of Ireland is divided into 26 counties, with six additional counties in Northern Ireland.

The article that follows is divided into two parts. Part I is concerned primarily with the growth and development of the Catholic Church in the island, beginning with its Christianization in the 5th century, while part II covers the Church in the Republic of Ireland. For information on the Church in Northern Ireland, *see* NORTHERN IRELAND, THE CATHOLIC CHURCH IN.

EARLY CHURCH IN IRELAND

Goidelic Celts occupied the island of Ireland as early as the 6th century B.C. They were eventually joined by Bretonnic Celts and Picts. Remaining beyond the borders of the vast Roman Empire, Ireland had established trade connections with Roman-occupied Britain and Gaul. By the 5th century A.D. missionaries entered Ireland, among them PATRICK, son of Calpurnius, who evangelized the north and west in the mid-5th century. Paganism still survived among ruling families, particularly in the south, into the 7th century.

Development of Monasticism and Missionary Activity. Early missionaries established an episcopal system, but the rapid emergence of monastic centers of learning led to the subordination of the bishops in a monastic system, dominated by great rival foundations. Gaelic expansion to the Scottish highlands led Irish Christians to the same area. Among them was St. Columcille (Columba) from whose foundation at Iona, missionaries converted the Picts of Scotland and the Anglo-Saxons in northern England. Conflict with Roman missionaries over such peculiarities of Christian tradition, as the date of Easter and the tonsure, culminated at Whitby (664). While the Irish missionaries were expelled from Northumbria after Whitby, their greatest achievement in the history of Christianity was the conversion of the Picts and the inauguration of the mission to the Anglo-Saxons, whose bad relations with British Christianity are noted by the Venerable Bede, who also acknowledges a lasting tribute to the work of the Irish, and to the value of their schools (*see* MONASTICISM, EARLY IRISH).

Meanwhile other missionaries from Ireland entered the former Roman Empire to the west. St. COLUMBAN es-

Archdioceses	Suffragans
Armagh	Ardagh, Clogher, Derry, Down and Connor, Dromore, Kilmore, Meath, Raphoe
Cashel	Cloyne, Cork and Ross, Kerry, Killaloe, Limerick, Waterford and Lismore
Dublin	Ferns, Kildare and Leighlin, Ossory
Tuam	Achonry, Clonfert, Elphin, Galway and Kilmacduagh, Killala

The Archdiocese of Armagh, which covers the north and west regions of the island, oversees all of Northern Ireland.

tablished foundations at Luxeuil (590) and Bobbio, and helped introduce the PENITENTIALS and the system of frequent private confessions. However Irish Catholics' insistence on monastic immunity from episcopal jurisdiction led to the same struggle between Celtic and Roman traditions that had been addressed at Whitby, and it again brought about their eclipse. By the mid-8th century the victory of the Roman tradition in Ireland was complete.

Unification and the Viking Invasion. The emergence of the Uí Néill high kings coincided with the unification of the allied groupings of minor kingdoms (*mór thuaithe*). While there was no absolute central monarchy, the Uí Néill maintained a northern hegemony for some five centuries before power passed to Munster and then to Connaught. The first Scandinavian raids in the late 8th century led to the emergence of more warlike rulers who were able to resist the Viking invaders.

The Viking incursions resulted in the decline of monasticism, as many church buildings were robbed of their treasures. By the 10th century, the Scandinavians had settled along the coast, and organized trading communities linked to their northern homelands and to other Scandinavian communities in Britain. Although by the early 11th century a Danish dynasty dominated England, similar efforts failed in Ireland. After the Battle of Clontarf (1014) saw victory at the hands of high king Brian Boru, the Scandinavian communities of Dublin, Waterford, Cork and Limerick were made subordinate to their neighboring Irish rulers. While many Scandinavians had by now converted to Christianity, they snubbed their Irish neighbors by sending their higher clergy to the archbishop of Canterbury for consecration.

Repeated threats from Viking invaders prompted a reorganization of the monasteries to preserve them from attack, conserve their resources and increase their prestige. In such fashion the influence of ARMAGH, Derry, Kildare and Clonmacnoise increased. However, a rivalry eventually developed that led to political strife: by the 11th century many of these communities were dominated by lay heads, recognized as the successors (*comharbai*), or coarbs, of the founders. Bishops were maintained by the Church for the purposes of ordaining clergy but remained subordinate to the coarbs. Attempts to reform this system occurred intermittently but had little success at first, as they concentrated on poverty and austerity in rivalry with the rich and powerful institutions of the old regime. By the 11th century a move to reestablish episcopal jurisdiction had gathered some force. Associated with the political centralization policy of the O'Briens and the Uí Néill of the north, it resulted in an alliance between St. MALACHY and the reformed Cistercians of Clairvaux, particularly with St. BERNARD. While Malachy tried to break the control of the hereditary Uí Sinaich family of Armagh, his efforts proved unsuccessful; however his enterprise succeeded in the next generation.

For over a century following Clontarf, provincial kings tried to dominate Ireland, and ecclesiastical synods were held. A synod at Rath Breasail (1111) sought to divide the country between the metropolitans of Armagh and Cashel until the Synod of Kells (1154) gave an additional archbishopric to Tuam and to Dublin, in the chief Hiberno-Scandinavian community in the east.

Norman Conquest to the Death of Henry VIII: 1172–1547. The succession of the Plantagenet Angevin dynasty to the Norman kingdom of England in 1154, extended its king's ambitions to Wales, Scotland and Ireland. In 1166 high king Rory O'Conor (1116?–98) ejected Dermot MacMurrough from his Leinster Kingdom, who sought the support of several Cambro-Norman lords and knights to support him in returning to Ireland. English King HENRY II, encouraged by Pope ADRIAN IV (Nicholas Breakspear; the only English pope) to secure the rights of the Church in Ireland, supported MacMurrough in the invasion of Leinster and Meath, and then visited Ireland in 1171 to secure his power there. Henry confirmed Richard de Clare, second Earl of Pembroke and Strigul (known as Strongbow; d. 1176), as lord of Leinster and Hugh de Lacy (d. 1186) as lord of Meath, while retaining Dublin and the other Scandinavian towns in his own control. Most of the independent Irish kings accepted Henry II as lord of Ireland, as did Rory O'Conor who by the Treaty of Windsor in 1175, restricted his own claims to Connaught and to preeminence over Irish kings outside the Anglo-Norman lands of southeast Ireland given him by Henry.

Ecclesiastically the new Angevin Lord of Ireland was reinforced by letters from Pope ALEXANDER III, Adrian IV's successor, to Henry, to the clergy and to the lords and people of Ireland, according full papal recognition of Henry's new leadership. Ecclesiastical pronouncements attributed the invasion to divine displeasure with the Irish, for purchasing slaves from the English. Thereafter the chief ecclesiastics in the east of Ireland followed the Anglo-Norman custom of church contributions made by payment of tithes, although in the rest of Ireland the older system of voluntary gifts reinforced the wealth secured from ecclesiastical lands.

The Anglo-Norman conquest failed to extend over the whole country and Gaelic influence remained, mainly in the northwest, the west and the southwest. By the late 13th century independent Irish kingships were controlled by the families of O'Neill and O'Donnell, O'Conor, O'Brien, MacCarthy and MacMurrough. An ethnic war soon waged with the realization that the Anglo-Norman colony of the east had not merely been arrested but was shrinking into decay. After the assertion of Scottish independence by Robert Bruce (1274–1329) at the Battle of Bannockburn, his brother Edward invaded Ireland and, until his defeat and death in 1318, devastated the greater part of the English colony from the northeast to the southwest. Thereafter, a policy of sharp separation was adopted by the leading Anglo-Norman lords, and the Pale—an area around Dublin formally ruled by England—was formally established.

Within Irish parliaments Anglo-Norman institutions had been established on a small scale, and futile attempts were made to both exclude persons of Irish race and assuage conflicts between recently arrived and already-established English immigrants. To the Church this meant dealing with two wholly dissimilar ways of life. Within the English Pale conditions were similar to those in contemporary England and France: under the administration of bishoprics dispensed by the English king as rewards for faithful service a parochial system existed, while military orders such as the Templars were located at strategic points in Ireland to restrict attempts at Gaelic ascendancy. While some degree of civilized life was possible within walled towns, military conditions prevailed in the Gaelic spheres. The poorer civilization that inevitably resulted required a different kind of Church participation. Indeed, the glory of the Island of Saints and Scholars had ended.

During the 15th century the English Pale shrank to a small area, nowhere more than 30 miles distant from Dublin. Great Anglo-Irish lordships existed, notably the Fitzgeralds of Kildare, the Butlers of Kilkenny, the Talbots of Wexford, the Fitzgeralds of Desmond and the Burkes of Connaught. Between these lords a perennial condition of war existed. No longer a war of English ver-

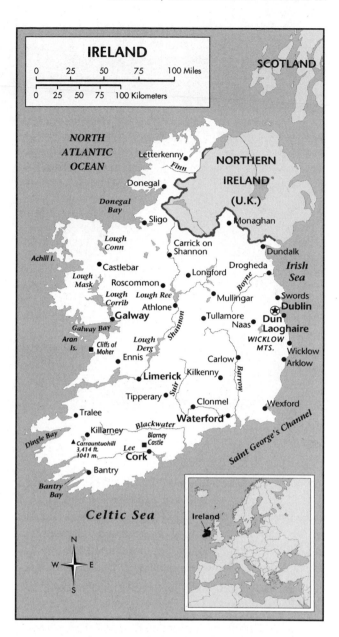

sus Irish, it now became a struggle for high kingship and culminated in the hegemony of the Earls of Kildare, who dominated the Pale and were made the English king's lieutenants. This situation prevailed until 1534, when HENRY VIII broke with Rome and was obliged to enter Ireland to defeat a Fitzgerald crusade against him.

Coming of the Reformation. In contrast to England, where papal power had long been under monarchic control, the appointments of the Holy See in Ireland were regarded with reverence. In part the papacy acted as umpire in the strife between Gaelic and Anglo-Norman administration, and it also aided in the Gaelic takeover of decayed English areas as immigrant populations dwindled. While the English government occasionally en-

Children making their First Communion, Ireland. (©Annie Griffiths Belt/CORBIS)

forced statutes of PROVISORS and *PRAEMUNIRE*, these proved unsuccessful for most purposes, and by the time of Henry VIII's break with Rome the influence wielded by the Holy See was not easily eradicated. Despite this loyalty, after Henry conquered the Kildare lordship and reestablished his power in Dublin, he was able to nominally enforce recognition of his claim to be head of the church.

At the Dublin Parliament of 1536–37, Henry's viceroy Lord Leonard Grey spearheaded the extinction of the Kildare order and abolished Papal authority. The claim of Henry VIII as head of the church was then asserted, as well as the English king's right to regulate and confiscate monasteries. This proved disastrous. While the diocesan clergy in the now-enlarged Pale acquiesced, other regular clergy withdrew to the independent Gaelic areas, which maintained contact with Rome. This tradition made it impossible to secure the same State dominance over the Church that was achieved in England. The conquest of Ireland continued to involve Tudor monarchs through the 16th century. While the Tudors eradicated the independent lordships, a tradition of resistance in Church matters was established; the forces of the Counter-Reformation secured sufficient foothold to enable the

Irish to build an effective independent Catholic Church in the succeeding centuries.

As early as 1538 Irish resistance made pessimists of Henry VIII's reformers in Ireland, such as George Brown, Archbishop of Dublin and Edward Staples, Bishop of Meath. At first they credited such resistance to the alleged treason of Lord Leonard Grey, but Grey's removal (1540) and execution changed nothing. His successor, Sir Anthony St. Leger, accelerated the dissolution of the monasteries within the Pale and used confiscated monastic wealth to enlarge his administration. In 1542, under St. Leger's influence, Henry VIII was made King of Ireland, abandoning the title "Dominus Hiberniae" as being tainted with Papal concessions. Throughout the country a policy of surrender and regrant was instituted, whereby various lords were induced to submit to the king, to secure from him the conversion of their elective chieftainships into hereditary peerages, and, theoretically, to extend Anglicanism. Bishops were similarly dealt with. The policy of surrender and regrant, which abandoned Irish Law in favor of English Common Law, was paralleled by the episcopal surrender of papal bulls and the regrant of their offices to the bishops under English law from the new Supreme Head. While Henry lived there was thus a nominal consent to his pretensions, the more distant from Dublin, the more nominal: but even within the Pale Church policy was subordinated to State necessity in marked contrast to contemporary England. Ultimately, ecclesiastical faculties were delegated to a commission [*see* REFORMATION, PROTESTANT (IN BRITISH ISLES)].

Under Edward VI many of the extreme penalties of Henry VIII were repealed, although his administration of Ireland was severe. Just as England took up arms against Scotland to compel the Scots to agree to the marriage of their queen with the English boy king, so the military policy of intimidating the Irish chiefs and extending royal authority, particularly in the Counties of Leix and Offaly, was carried out. The religious changes occurring in England—the abrogation of the Mass and the substitution of a communion service as incorporated in the Book of Common Prayer—were extended to Ireland, but reactions in the Pale against reformers preaching against transubstantiation made it clear that England would have to proceed slowly to gain even a nominal acquiescence. The Second Prayer Book, incorporating the Ordinal for consecrating clergy without making them sacrificial priests, was not specifically extended to Ireland.

On the accession of the Catholic Mary I (*see* MARY TUDOR, QUEEN OF ENGLAND), the speed with which the Mass was restored illustrated how even in the most English areas, Protestantism had gained no foothold. At the cost of good relations, the Protectorate had successfully intimidated the more independent Irish lords from becoming involved in the war with Scotland and France. Efforts to secure an Irish alliance with England's enemies also proved abortive: even the papal agents could not remain in Ireland due to lack of support and the fear that Dublin's military might strike down the northern chiefs among whom the papal negotiators had taken refuge.

Mary's reign exposed the similarity between the methods of each of the Tudor sovereigns in Ireland, Catholic and Protestant alike. In dealing with Parliament, coercive methods were used to secure an acquiescent majority. A policy of colonizing the midlands was planned and given statutory approval. King's County and Queen's County were established in place of Offaly and Leix in honor of Mary and her husband PHILIP II of Spain, and the independent Irish were driven from these areas as a prelude to the plantation which commenced under Elizabeth I. As in England, Cardinal Reginald POLE issued a bull of reconciliation with the Holy See that was incorporated in an act of parliament, reestablishing papal jurisdiction and guaranteeing absolution for the alienation of Church lands. While there was no persecution of Protestants in Ireland, the Tudor Irish continued to subordinate Church interests to those of the English State; specific key Englishmen were given immunity from persecution and granted permission to hold services in their homes.

On the accession of the Protestant ELIZABETH I those same officials who had presided over Parliament under Mary returned to the policy of Edward VI and the Book of Common Prayer. As before, there was no nationwide enforcement of the new law. A few bishops near Dublin were compelled to acquiesce, and two who refused were deposed. For the rest, the queen was careful to avoid any situation that might fuel a conspiracy appealing to the Catholic population. Such a policy was successful; no general rebellion broke out until the end of Elizabeth's reign, even though she was excommunicated (1570) by PIUS V in 1570. Papal efforts to maintain an Armagh archbishop and a nuncio were thwarted by the arrest and incarceration of Richard Creagh (1525?–85) and David Wolfe (d. 1578?) whom the pope appointed to these offices. They were not proceeded against to the point of execution, and ultimately they both escaped from prison, though Creagh was rearrested and died in the Tower of London.

During the mid-1500s various unsuccessful efforts were made to interest France and Spain, as well as the papacy, in a Catholic rebellion in Ireland, and Pope GREGORY XIII finally decided to sanction such an expedition. It secured little support from Spain and none elsewhere. En-

Muiredach's Cross, 10th century, Monasterboice, County Louth, Ireland. Each panel depicts a biblical story, and was intended to educate a largely illiterate public. (©Michael St. Maur Sheil/ CORBIS)

glish influence in Ireland was sufficiently strong to intimidate sympathizers and by 1583 the movement had collapsed. Elizabeth commenced the second plantation scheme on the extensive Munster lands, thus transferring a substantial number of titles to English colonists, who failed, however, to bring over a sufficient number of supporters to alter the complexion of the southern population as a whole.

In the last decade of Elizabeth's reign, a formidable rebellion by Hugh O'Neill (1550?–1616) and Hugh Roe O'DONNELL (1571?–1602) secured substantial support from the Church. For the first time it was openly involved in the struggle against Elizabeth in Ireland, perhaps in consequence of the 1584 execution under martial law of Archbishop Dermot O'HURLEY, whose arrest soon after his return from Rome did not reveal his complicity in any anti-English conspiracy. Northern bishops supported the rebels, even going so far as to operate the decrees of the Council of Trent. In this situation, Elizabeth was obliged to acquiesce in the direction of her viceroy to terminate Catholic persecution. Spain intervened momentarily but unsuccessfully, and in 1601 Elizabeth's forces defeated the Irish outside Kinsale, which was then occupied by

The Archbishop of Tuam celebrates High Mass on a mountaintop, County Mayo, Ireland, 1947. (©Hulton-Deutsch Collection/ CORBIS)

Don Juan del Aquila. In 1603, during the last days of Tudor reign, the war ended, and James VI, on his accession as James I, agreed to pardon and ennoble the leading Irish rebels.

The Rise of the Stuarts. The accession of the Stuarts in 1603 created serious problems in integration and ultimately led to civil war in the three kingdoms (1638–53). James I, was easily intimidated by his English ministers, despite his goodwill toward certain Irish lords; successive viceroys in Ireland reestablished the colonial and Protestant policies of Elizabeth. The Ulster chiefs, fearful of being imprisoned for conspiracy, fled to mainland Europe, and a project for colonizing six of the Ulster counties was approved and carried out. The only successful colonization project, this effort involved the lowland Scots and border English, who, by the end of the 1600s, had transformed the greater part of the northern province into Presbyterian and Anglican communities. Simulta-

neously, power passed finally from the old English and Irish upper classes to new colonists and landowners who secured grants on successive confiscations under James I, Oliver CROMWELL and William III. In addition, considerable property changed hands through the effect of economic erosion, as a more primitive order of society gave way before the more expansive demands of a more sophisticated society. Only in religious matters were the Stuarts obviously unsuccessful. Gaelic culture and traditional English medieval patterns were subordinated to the more cosmopolitan Protestant society, but the mass of the people continued to give allegiance to the Holy See. Ecclesiastics such as the Protestant archbishop Adam Loftus were great believers in coercion and, after the accession of James I, the justification for such a policy was reiterated. Government, however, was slightly unnerved at the restoration of Catholic worship in many of the Anglo-Irish towns on Elizabeth's death and, while this was abrogated, there was slowness to go with the ecclesiastics along the lines of coercion. With the Guy Fawkes conspiracy in England, a renewal of coercion was approved, but the policy of expelling the Catholic clergy and compelling local officials to conform did not prove successful. By the end of James' reign the government reluctantly agreed to informal toleration.

Era of Political Upheaval: 1600–1660. The reign of Charles I witnessed a great increase in power among the new colonists, and paralleling this, the Catholic Church was able to build itself up extensively throughout the country. Imitating the Scots, who took up arms against attempts to extend Anglicanism over their Calvinistic kingdom, Catholic Ireland attempted unsuccessfully to take over the whole kingdom and reestablish its religion. After the English Parliament and the king became involved in war, many Anglo-Irish attempted to reconcile with their monarch by allowing him to use their resources against Dublin. The Catholics in support of war were divided; centuries of history made it clear that a papal policy denying the legitimacy of English Protestant monarchical rule would find no success. The split was revealed after Irish and Anglo-Irish were brought together in a quasi-parliament at Kilkenny. Successive papal representatives Pier Francesco SCARAMPI and Giovanni Battista RINUCCINI (1592–1653) attempted to secure royal acquiescence in the public restoration of Catholicism. While initial negotiations were not ratified, a later peace secured ratification despite the continued opposition of Rinuccini, who ultimately withdrew in protest on the eve of Cromwell's conquest. The nuncio's own explanation was that the Anglo-Irish feared losing estates founded on the plunder of the monasteries as well as a Gaelic Irish resurgence.

The defeat and execution of the king at Cromwell's hands led all opponents of Parliamentarianism to combine in Ireland in support of his son CHARLES II, though almost inevitably this committed Charles to incompatible Calvinist concessions in Scotland and Catholic concessions in Ireland. The Cromwellian war in Ireland led to the defeat of the Royalist allies. There were no pitched battles, except the Battle of Baggot Rath (Rathmines) in 1649. A number of towns were stormed, including Drogheda and Wexford, and the garrisons put to the sword, together with any clergy found in the fortresses. The excuse was that these had been involved in the massacre of innocent Protestants in 1641 or subsequently. Strategically, these methods prompted surrenders at a number of other points, but the war as a whole did not end until 1653, after Cromwell had been replaced by his son-in-law Henry Ireton (1611–51) and after an Irish army led by Bishop Heber McMahon had been defeated in the north.

St. Patrick's Cathedral, built between 1838 and 1873, modernized by Liam McCormick in 1981. (©Michael St. Maur Sheil/CORBIS)

The civil war in Ireland was followed by a decree of the Commonwealth classifying the people of Ireland into categories determined by their relative disloyalty to the state. In the first category, certain specified persons were guilty of treason and declared to have forfeited their lives and property. All Catholics were to lose their lands, but those proving constant good affection to England would be permitted to enjoy property valued at two-thirds of what they had held previously. Catholics, however, would be permitted to hold land only in Connaught; land in the three remaining provinces was divided among loyal Protestants, land speculators who had advanced money to the government to fund the Irish war, and soldiers to whom the Parliamentarians owed wages. So far as the rest of the Catholics were concerned, if they could prove their non-involvement both in the murder of Protestants and of taking up arms against the Parliamentarians, they could remain in Ireland. Those implicated in the murder of Protestants were in danger of being executed. Those who fought the Parliamentarians were permitted to transport themselves beyond the seas. All Catholic clergy were deemed to be enemies of the state and, by a special indulgence, if not convicted of complicity in the Protestant massacres, might be transported abroad.

During the seven-year period before the restoration of the Stuart monarchy, no toleration was accorded to the Catholic clergy. The saying of Mass became a treasonable offense, according to the oppressive measures Parliamentarians extended to Irish Catholicism. In reality, however, after the war few of the clergy suffered an extreme penalty for celebrating their priestly functions, although many suffered imprisonment, deportation to the West Indies, or exile to the European mainland. So far as the Catholic laity was concerned, the Elizabethan recusancy penalties against those failing to attend Protestant Sunday services were not enforced. In fact, the Commonwealth prohibited interfering with any man's conscience, except where idolatry was concerned, and by 1658 reports indicated an increase in instances where Catholics met for religious purposes. Despite such personal freedoms, the organization of the Church was severely obstructed: few among the regular or higher clergy dared to remain within Ireland.

The Restoration and Further War: 1660–91. After the Restoration Charles II became king, and the Anglican Church, which had been dispossessed, came back. Concessions were made to Catholicism due to the private toleration accorded by the new king, though such toleration was contrary to current laws regarding religious. While Catholics were rarely persecuted for the exercise of their religion, some higher clergy were not permitted to return. An attempt was made to allow innocent Catholics to make a remonstrance or declaration of loyalty to the king, denying absolutely the right to withdraw allegiance in terms regarded as offensive by the Holy See. This remonstrance originated with Peter · WALSH (1618?–88), a Franciscan who secured the patronage of Irish nobleman James Ormonde, and whose opponents were exposed to persecution and banishment while Ormonde ruled Ireland. General conditions, however, were not unsatisfactory, and the Treaty of Limerick (1691) attempted to secure for Catholics the same immunities they had enjoyed under Charles II. So far as political power and landed property were concerned, however, Catholics were reduced to a very insignificant position. In any attempt to reverse this situation Protestants unified in opposition, and Cromwellian supporters finally forced Ormonde into abandoning the restoration of Catholics loyal to Charles II, and into passing the Act of Explanation to provide a legislative bar to them in the future. In the 1670s secret negotiations with LOUIS XIV provided Charles with adequate means to maintain himself without the Parliament, while also enabling him to issue a Declaration of Indulgence for Catholics and Dissenters. The resulting outcry in England caused the indulgence to be withdrawn. At the end of the decade, the allegations of Titus Oates (1649–1705) regarding a Catholic plot (*see*

OATES PLOT) to bring in a French army of occupation resulted in the judicial murder of Oliver PLUNKET, Archbishop of ARMAGH on July 1, 1681, the death of Peter Talbot, Archbishop of DUBLIN while in prison and the execution of several others on perjured testimony. The Church again became dislocated, but reestablished its position through royal connivance in the last years of Charles' reign.

Under JAMES II Catholicism obtained great favors and the Church's position improved. An attempt was made to financially endow the Catholic hierarchy by keeping a number of Protestant bishoprics unfilled. Official positions became open to Catholics, particularly in the army. The land question was again under consideration. Many Protestants fled to England in fear of their Catholic neighbors. But an alliance of Anglicans and Nonconformists invited James's son-in-law, William III of Orange, to "restore order," and James fled to France (1688). James was then invited to Ireland, where the Catholic Richard Talbot (1630–91), first Earl of Tyrconnell, had been appointed viceroy; in 1689 a Parliament in Dublin attainted absentee Protestant landowners, decreed the restoration of deprived Catholics, asserted the independence of Ireland from English Parliamentary legislation and affirmed a general toleration in religion.

James, however, failed to win the support of more than a handful of Irish Anglicans, and when his troops were excluded from Ulster towns he was unable to storm them. On the arrival of William III's army they rallied to his standard. William defeated James at the Battle of the Boyne, and thereafter James retired to France, while a Franco-Irish army waged a series of pitched battles before being advised to surrender following a campaign lasting more than two years. Unlike Cromwell, William III was prepared to make some Catholic concessions if only to end the war in Ireland and allow him to concentrate on his main objective: Louis XIV on the European mainland. In the articles agreed upon at Galway and Limerick (1691) Catholics willing to accept William's regime were guaranteed their lands, but provisions to tolerate Catholicism were not ratified by subsequent Irish Parliaments, from which Catholics were excluded by an act of the English Parliament.

The position of the clergy was somewhat different. The Holy See had accorded James II the right to nominate the higher prelates, a right indirectly accorded to his brother Charles II on at least one occasion. As James II still claimed to be king, and set up his court at St. Germains in France, he continued to exercise these claims, which the Church continued to accord to him. Catholic Europe recognized the exiled Stuarts until the death (1766) of "James III."

Irish Catholic clergy hoped, in the event of a second Stuart Restoration, to get back to the situation visualized in Rinuccini's time. At the same time the Catholic clergy sympathized with the Anglican doctrine of divine hereditary right. Certainly the refusal to take an oath in Ireland, abjuring the Stuarts, affected the vast majority of priests tolerated by Penal Statute, while only a small minority of Irish Anglicans became nonjurors. This was the Protestant justification for the later Penal Laws against the Catholic clergy, just as the laws against the laity were justified by fear that they would become strong enough to secure or compel the restoration of their forfeited lands.

1691–1848. From the English standpoint, after the Glorious Revolution of 1688, a fear existed that the Protestants in Ireland might become too independent. The same restrictions were put on the Irish Parliament's powers as were imposed upon colonial legislatures in the New World. In place was the same discrimination against Ireland in commercial export rivalry with Britain as existed in the colonies. In consolation for these restrictions, Irish Protestants were permitted to pass statutes discriminating against Catholics. Beginning with the war between William III and Louis XIV and extending until the end of the reign of George I in 1727, a series of acts were passed bringing Irish laws into line with British anti-Catholic legislation. Acts against the clergy decreed the banishment of all regulars and prelates. Parochial clergy, restricted to one per parish, were obliged to swear allegiance to the Protestant sovereign. When the oath of abjuration was imposed in 1709, the system broke down, as only some 30 out of more than 1,000 obeyed the law. The extreme penalties could no longer be applied, as Protestant sovereigns were constantly pressured by their Catholic allies, such as the Holy Roman Emperor. Returned exiled clergy, therefore, might be imprisoned but were not executed.

A declaration against transubstantiation imposed on all office holders proved to be effective in excluding the Catholic laity from political power. Similar restrictions were employed by municipal corporations and by professional guilds. Succession to Catholic estates operated under a discriminatory law that directed their division between all male children (gavelkind). Social discrimination deprived Catholics of the right to carry swords customarily conceded to all gentlemen. In local areas levies were imposed on Catholics to pay damages for Catholic invading forces in time of war. By the end of the 18th century, Catholic land holdings, which had dropped to 15 percent by 1704, had fallen to about eight percent. Although few nonpropertied people conformed to the Established Church, some 4,000 upper-class Catholics conformed during the century.

During the 18th century the Church was severely handicapped in its organization. By 1750, however, imprisonment of clergy was a thing of the past. In 1745, despite the Stuart invasion of Scotland, Philip Dormer Stanhope (1694–1773), fourth Earl of Chesterfield and Lord Lieutenant of Ireland, refused to close the Catholic chapels. He insisted that there was no danger from the Irish clergy and that the only dangerous papist in the kingdom was the reigning beauty Miss Eleanor Ambrose (1720?–1818). Catholic lay addresses of loyalty were privately accepted by the Hanoverians throughout the reign of George II (1727–60). After the accession of George III, the Dublin clergy offered prayers for the Hanoverian royal family, and the first steps to repeal the penal laws were taken in the 1770s.

By the time George III took the throne Parliamentary opposition to self-government had increased. The Protestant ascendancy organized volunteer corps to maintain order and defend England against possible invasion from France, since most regular troops were in service in North America. Among the Protestants seeking self-government there were few supporters of Catholic relief; Henry Grattan (1746–1820) was noteworthy. Government supported relief bills to remind Irish Protestants of their continued dependence upon England, if only due to the growing strength of Catholicism. By 1782, however, Protestant support of further concessions for Catholics had increased, and when the volunteers took up the question of reform, they were induced to pass resolutions favoring further Catholic relief.

The outbreak of the French Revolution revived the question of Parliamentary reform, and the Catholic Committee, which had played a substantial part in securing the first relief acts, demonstrated some sympathy toward the reformers. The bishops, however, largely influenced by the few upper-class Catholics, discouraged any alliance; ultimately French Revolutionary excesses led the bishops to accept government patronage for the establishment of Maynooth and even created some favor for the Union in 1800. The condemnation of the United Irishmen's Rebellion in 1798 was very general among the bishops, most of whom were prepared to accept the situation of a second-class establishment if the right to sit in Parliament were conceded to the Catholic laity at the time of the Union. However, democratic developments under Daniel O'CONNELL led bishops to reconsider a close association with the Protestant British government. A rising tide of nationalism opposed such an association, and the Irish hierarchy ultimately realigned its attitudes with the climate of Irish national opinion. When EMANCIPATION was finally conceded in 1829, several bishops resented the inflated property-ownership qualification imposed on those Catholics wishing to exercise the voting franchise.

Rising poverty among many rural Irish Catholics became an issue during the early 1800s, and in a property-dominated legislature, agricultural poverty was inconsequential. At the other end of the scale, Catholic wealth overall was increasing due to the rise in Irish exports and the superior initiative and resourcefulness of Catholic merchants. After the Battle of Waterloo in 1815, agricultural rents began to fall; nevertheless there was a substantial degree of church building in the years following Catholic emancipation (1829). From 1824, with the establishment of the Protestant New Light (New Reformation) movement, relations between Anglican and Catholic churches began to deteriorate. Protests from the farming community against tithe payments to the Protestant established clergy gained a sympathetic ear from Catholic clergy.

Break with Vatican over Education Question. A nondenominational primary school system was organized under a national education board set up in 1830 that included Archbishop Daniel MURRAY of Dublin among its members. The Protestant Episcopalian clergy resented this, since they considered education endowed by the state to be a monopoly of the Established Church. The Archbishop of Tuam, John MACHALE, broke with the board's policy of subsidizing schools, contending that the government connived to send Protestant missions to the pauper Catholics at Killala, and set about organizing Catholic schools with the help of teaching brothers.

The education question became the most significant issue for Church-State relations during the next 75 years. MacHale's objections to the primary school system secured an increasing number of supporters among the bishops, as the National Education Board weakened before a Presbyterian onslaught that secured the exclusion of Catholic priests from schools under Presbyterian management. Moreover, in the west of Ireland, the Protestant missionary activities were sufficiently successful among the poverty-stricken Killala peasants to make MacHale suspicious of all Protestant-dominated organizations, and ultimately of the government. On the other hand, Murray believed it to be in the Church's interest to cooperate with the government; he took an active part in the activities of the National Education Board whose policy, he felt satisfied, did not favor proselytism. Most bishops initially agreed with Murray, who resented MacHale's attacks upon the Board and stated that the Tuam prelate did not object until after the Board rejected the application for recognition of a school under MacHale's own patronage. However, MacHale gradually won over a number of bishops to his viewpoint, particularly after the refusal of the Board to dismiss a Connaught teacher who had become a Protestant. Both sides appealed to Rome, which after lengthy consideration recommended that bishops settle the matter individually. But Rome's simultaneous condemnation of clerical interference in politics aggravated the situation.

The MacHale party justified its adherence to Repeal of the Union on the basis of religion rather than politics, holding that British treachery in failing to implement Catholic emancipation fully necessitated its action. The people, alienated from the colonial ascendancy, had turned to it for leadership. O'Connell's organization of the Repeal movement in the last days of the government of William Lamb, led Viscount Melbourne (1779–1848) to incorporate inducements to the clergy, particularly to MacHale as the most popular ecclesiastic in Ireland. It is a moot point whether O'Connell could have revived general interest in Repeal had it not been for MacHale.

With the return of Sir Robert Peel (1788–1850) and the Tory party to power in 1841, the cold war condition worsened. While Melbourne had resented the Repeal movement, the Tories were determined to defeat it. For ten years Peel had quietly resisted the extremists in his own party who loudly advocated repeal of the emancipation and parliamentary reform acts. Now in office, he felt strong enough not merely to ignore these extremists. Repealers would not be countenanced; while the O'Connellites continued to cite Tory bigotry in confirmation of their oft-expressed fear of a renewal of Protestant tyranny, Peel set out to develop a Catholic policy that would divert the clergy from O'Connell.

Peel proposed to increase the endowment of Maynooth, provide a public organization for Catholic charities, and establish a system of university colleges for the education of the middle classes. While Murray considered this satisfactory evidence that the government could be trusted, MacHale condemned the successive Parliamentary measures introduced to implement this policy (except for the increased endowment of Maynooth) and described the Tory policy as a conspiracy to enslave and destroy the Church. He won the support of the majority of the bishops on the Colleges bill, and the result of his appeal to Rome was that for the next 60 years nondenominational education in Ireland was linked with the Anglican system of Trinity College, Dublin, in condemnation by the Church.

The Land League and the Rise of Irish Nationalism. A new era began in Ireland after the appointment of Paul Cullen as archbishop and apostolic delegate in 1849. The 1848 rebellion of the Young Irelanders had proved abortive, largely because of the catastrophe of the great famine (1845–50) but also through the discouragement of the clergy. Cullen, having experienced revolution in Rome, was determined to oppose it in Ireland and endeavored to keep the clergy out of politics. Economic issues dominated the famine-haunted people, and the next national party was organized for Tenant Right. Its failure in the early 1850s was attributed by its supporters to Cullen; they overlooked their own inability to provide leadership like O'Connell's or to resist the attractiveness of office under favorable British governments.

The Irish hierarchy's organization of a Catholic university attracted considerable attention during this same period, particularly through the appointment of John Henry NEWMAN as rector (1854–58) and the publication of his lectures on the idea of a university in Dublin. However, the Catholic University, like the Tenant Right movement, failed through public apathy and ecclesiastical dissensions and Newman soon retired. MacHale's interest weakened as Cullen's power grew, and denominationalism was accepted by the state in primary education about 1860. Disillusioned by British government partiality toward the Piedmontese attack on the Papal States, Cullen meanwhile revised his views on staying out of politics. The 1860s saw a revival of international interest in military activity in the wake of the Crimean War and the unification of Italy. The U.S. Civil War had involved many Irish exiles, who thereafter turned their minds toward supporting the Fenian movement for establishing an Irish Republic. Under Cullen's influence this movement and its organization, the Irish Republican Brotherhood, were condemned by Rome, although some clerics continued to give it secret support. Cullen organized the National Association to pressure Parliament to improve the middle class tenantry, secure disestablishment of the Protestant Episcopalian Church and win government endowment for an acceptable university system. He deserted Benjamin Disraeli (1804–81) and the Conservative party for W. E. GLADSTONE (1809–98) and the Liberals. The Liberals successfully negotiated the first two points in the program but failed on the third; they blamed Cullen and the Irish hierarchy for allegedly misleading them on the minimum requirements for Catholic recognition. The defeat of Gladstone (1874) by Irish votes permanently weakened the clergy's influence in politics. While Cullen disapproved of the Home Rule movement inaugurated by Isaac Butt (1813–79) to secure self-government for Ireland through a Parliament subordinate to that of the United Kingdom, he failed to prevent Butt's heading a party of some 60 of the 105 members representing Ireland at Westminster. Constitutional Fenians reinforced Butt. Cullen's National Association withered despite the efforts to revive the memory of O'Connell as a Catholic leader, which only resulted in the substantial diminution of O'Connell's stature in nationalist recollection. Butt was successful in only one measure—the reorganization of the Peel university plan into Royal University Act which permitted indirect endowment of Catholic university colleges and the conceding of university degrees by examination and without attendance. It was a disappointing achievement. The bishops closed the Catholic University and transferred the buildings to University College, Dublin, under the supervision of the Society of Jesus (1880). It was reconstituted as a chartered state college in 1911.

Butt's failure to secure Home Rule weakened that movement seriously. After the threatened famine of 1879, the position of the tenantry again dominated Ireland. Parnell, leader of the Land League, secured clerical support in the south and west against Cullen's successor in Dublin. In the election of 1880 advocates of Home Rule opposed one another on the land issue, with Parnell gaining a decided majority following. The following year Gladstone, having replaced Disraeli in 1880, introduced a new Land Act which only secured endorsement by the House of Lords through the intimidating tactics of Parnell's Land League. The revival of the Home Rule movement, supported by an increasing nationalist element (formerly Fenian) and by Irish- and other Americans, created serious difficulties in England. Efforts were made to renew diplomatic pressures in Rome. Ecclesiastical condemnations of political extremism and of a land policy aiming at the destruction of landlordism (partly accentuated by Irish ecclesiastical investment in land) widened the breach between nationalism and Catholicism. Even Home Rule was in danger of condemnation but for the conversion of Gladstone and the majority of the Liberal party; anti-Irish sentiment in England defeated the prime minister's first Home Rule Bill (1886) and led to his replacement for virtually 20 years by a Unionist government dominated by the Tories.

The Unionist experiment, "Kill Home Rule by kindness," was a repetition of the anti-Repeal policy of the 1840s. As on that occasion, a group of Irish bishops led by William WALSH of Dublin indicated their acquiescence in the government policy of improving the Catholic position with regard to education. On this, however, Walsh was quickly disillusioned, and the question was not settled until the Liberals passed the Irish Universities Act in 1908. Other Unionist aspects of Irish policy were more successful. Buying out the landlord interests in the Land Purchase Acts settled what was probably the second most contended issue in Victorian Ireland. The Local Government Act of 1898 permitted democracy to operate at county level and swept away most of the remaining local political powers of the landlords. The Unionists were nonetheless unsuccessful in reducing the Irish desire for self-government.

During the brief restoration of Liberal government (1892–95) Gladstone again failed with his second Home

Rule Bill. Meanwhile Parnell had died; his party was divided, and the bishops were somewhat uncertain of their position after the reactions to clerical interference in his fall. Thereafter the hierarchy largely withdrew from politics, and the nationalist-leaning Irish Parliamentary party's influence declined. Irish attention was beginning to be attracted by more radical forms of nationalism, in part a reaction to the British imperialism of the Boer War years (1899–1902). After the Unionist electoral defeat in 1906, Protestant Ulster's organization against Home Rule developed. By 1912 Ireland was divided on the issue, largely on a sectarian basis, with Anglicans and Presbyterians overwhelmingly pro-Unionist. The third Home Rule Bill (1912–14) was passed after the veto power of the House of Lords had been virtually abrogated.

The Easter Rebellion. The provisions of the 1914 Home Rule Bill were suspended as a consequence of the outbreak of World War I, but they foreshadowed the partition of Ireland into two separate political areas. In a sense, this had already been foreshadowed in the academic sphere by the provisions of the University Act establishing the Queen's University of Belfast separately from the National University of Ireland, whose constituent colleges lay in the three southern provinces. Only in the field of political labor did there appear to be substantial unity in the prewar years, and even here, the covenant against Home Rule broke down the good relations of a few years earlier.

At the outbreak of war, both the nationalist Irish Parliamentary party, led by John E. Redmond (1856–1918), and the Irish Unionist Party, led by Sir Edward Carson (1854–1935), pledged their support in the struggle against German imperialism. On this issue, nationalist opinion in Ireland was divided. A minority, holding that Redmond had abandoned the traditional Irish national position, organized themselves into the Irish Volunteers and split from Redmond's National Volunteers, many of whom joined the British Army against Germany. Carson and other Irish Unionists joined the war cabinet. Irish nationalist opinion of the moderates resented the decision of Secretary for War Herbert Earl Kitchener (1850–1916) to deny separate organization for Irish troops. A minority of the Irish Volunteers, in contact with U.S. and German sympathizers, rebelled in 1916. This second, or rather third, attempt to establish an Irish Republic was quickly defeated. One of the most conservative bishops, Edward Thomas O'Dwyer (1842–1917) of Limerick, expressed the general resentment at British severity after the rebellion.

Public opinion quickly moved toward the Republican party (Sinn Féin); the hierarchy identified itself with this feeling in 1918 in the expression of disapproval of the proposed conscription of Irishmen to fight in the war. At the general election after the Armistice, Sinn Féin won an overwhelming victory, except in the northeast. The members decided not to enter the United Kingdom Parliament and established themselves as an Irish unicameral legislature (Dáil Éireann) in Dublin in early 1919.

During the next two years a state of war developed between the Republicans and the British government, which made unsuccessful efforts to induce the bishops to condemn the insurgents. A Government of Ireland Act was passed in 1920, under which the six northeastern counties were established as Northern Ireland, with a subordinate legislature under the United Kingdom.

Bibliography: Bibliographies. J. CARTY, *Bibliography of Irish History, 1870–1921*, 2 v. (Dublin 1936–40). *Bibliography of British History: Tudor Period, 1485–1603*, ed. C. READ (2d ed. Oxford 1959). *Bibliography of British History: Stuart Period, 1603–1714*, ed. O. DAVIES (Oxford 1928). *Bibliography of British History: The 18th Century, 1714–1789*, eds., S. M. PARGELLIS and D. J. MEDLEY (Oxford 1951). A. R. EAGER, *A Guide to Irish Bibliographical Material* (London 1964). *Irish Historical Studies* (Dublin 1938—) has annual bibliogs. Literature. *Ireland: A Documentary Record*, ed. J. CARTY, 3 v. (v.1–2 3d v.3 2d ed.; Dublin 1957–58). A. BELLESHEIM, *Geschichte der katholischen Kirche in Irland*, 3 v. (Mainz 1890–91). *History of the Church of Ireland*, ed. W. A. PHILLIPS, 3 v (London 1933–34). T. J. JOHNSTON et al., *A History of the Church of Ireland* (Dublin 1953). W. DELIUS, *Geschichte der irischen Kirche* (Munich 1954). L. BIELER, *Ireland, Harbinger of the Middle Ages* (New York 1963). E. CURTIS, *A History of Ireland* (6th ed. London 1950). M. T. HAYDEN and G. MOONAN, *A Short History of the Irish People*, 2 v. (Dublin 1960). R. D. EDWARDS, *Church and State in Tudor Ireland* (New York 1935). M. V. RONAN, *The Reformation in Dublin, 1536–1558* (New York 1926); *The Reformation in Ireland under Elizabeth, 1558–1580* (New York 1930). T. L. COONAN, *The Irish Catholic Confederacy and the Puritan Revolution* (New York 1954). J. G. SIMMS, *The Williamite Confiscation in Ireland, 1690–1703* (London 1956). J. C. BECKETT, *Protestant Dissent in Ireland, 1687–1780* (London 1948). W. E. H. LECKY, *A History of Ireland in the 18th Century*, 5 v. (new ed. New York 1893). P. S. O'HEGARTY, *A History of Ireland under the Union, 1801–1922* (London 1952). D. R. GWYNN, *The Struggle for Catholic Emancipation, 1750–1829* (New York 1928); *The History of Partition 1912–1925* (Dublin 1950). J. A. REYNOLDS, *The Catholic Emancipation Crisis in Ireland, 1823–1829* (New Haven 1954). J. F. BRODERICK, *The Holy See and the Irish Movement for the Repeal of the Union with England, 1829–1847* (*Analecta Gregoriana*, 55; 1951). F. MCGRATH, *Newman's University: Idea and Reality* (New York 1951). D. MCARDLE, *The Irish Republic: A Documented Chronicle of the Anglo-Irish Conflict and the Partitioning of Ireland* (4th ed. Dublin 1951). E. R. NORMAN, *The Catholic Church in Ireland in the Age of Rebellion, 1859–1873* (Ithaca, NY 1965). *Handbook of British Chronology*, eds., F. M. POWICKE and E. B. FRYDE (2d ed. London 1961). R. N. HADCOCK, *Map of Monastic Ireland* (Dublin 1959). *Bilan du Monde*, 2:495–512. *Irish Catholic Directory* (Dublin) annual. K. B. NOWLAN, *The Politics of Repeal: A Study in the Relations between Great Britain and Ireland, 1841–1850* (Toronto 1964). *Annuario Pontificio* has data on all dioceses.

[R. D. EDWARDS]

THE CHURCH IN THE REPUBLIC OF IRELAND

After 1921 Ireland remained partitioned into two political entities. Northern Ireland was now a partially self-governing area within the United Kingdom, with a local parliament exercising limited jurisdiction. The remainder of the country attained its independence as the Irish Free State, a Commonwealth dominion, in 1922. The Free State gradually relinquished Commonwealth associations, abandoning the name "Free State" in 1937, and in 1949 left the Commonwealth to become the Republic of Ireland.

Establishes Commonwealth Government. A Republican majority, led by Sinn Fein activist Éamon De Valera (1882–1975), established the Fianna Fáil party in 1926, and became the main opposition party in 1927. In 1931 the minority Republican party Saor Éire was condemned by the hierarchy in what was regarded as a move against Fianna Fáil. In the following year, however, De Valera became head of the government, holding office for the next 16 years.

A new constitution enacted in 1938 maintained the independence of the country but permitted external association with the king of Great Britain as head of the British Commonwealth. The constitution admitted that civil authority comes from God, the form of government being decided by the people. It maintained the parliamentary system set up under the Irish Free State Act, recognized the special position of the Catholic Church as the Church of the majority of the people and established religious toleration for Anglicans, Presbyterians and other denominations.

The neutrality of the Republic of Ireland during World War II accentuated the resentment respecting the partition of the island. While a small minority remained hopeful that a German victory would result in the reunification of Ireland, most people thought otherwise. The attitude of the state was one of benevolent neutrality toward the Atlantic powers, particularly after the entry of the United States against the Axis Powers. While some communications were established between extremist Republican organizations and Germany, any plans for a German invasion proved abortive. Maria Duce, a small extremist Catholic element under the leadership of Denis Fahey, CSSp, favored Germany, largely because of suspicions of the alliance with Russia and because of objections to Zionism. It also organized a campaign against article 44 of the Constitution, which affirmed toleration for Jews and Protestants.

At the end of World War II Ireland was temporarily excluded from the United Nations, partly because of its wartime neutrality and partly because of Soviet resentment at Ireland's refusal to exchange diplomatic missions. Following the proclamation of the state as the Republic of Ireland in 1949 relations with Britain deteriorated; the British Labour government gave guarantees not to end formal Partition without the approval of Northern Ireland.

The Costello government collided with vested interests when it introduced a moderate form of the legislation of the British welfare state, and its subsequent defeat was in part attributed to what was generally regarded, notably by De Valera and his followers, as unwarrantable clerical interference. On its return to power in 1951 Fianna Fáil introduced a revised Health Act that secured many of the benefits of the earlier act but avoided ecclesiastical consultation.

Ireland Enters International Sphere. After 1955 Ireland took an increasing part in external affairs. Its historic opposition to imperialism led to requests for the loan of Irish troops by the United Nations, particularly in Lebanon, the Congo and Cyprus. In regard to the Cold War with Communist Europe, Ireland remained closer to the position of the United States than to that of Great Britain. The 1960s and 1970s brought about marked changes in Irish society and in the life of the Irish Church. The protectionist policies of the government gave way to free trade with Britain in the 1960s and with the European Economic Community in 1973. A growth in industry and skilled service jobs resulted in a decline in agriculture and an increased level of urbanization. By the 1980s one third of the people lived in the greater Dublin area.

Neither the Catholic Church nor the major Protestant churches, organized on an all-Ireland basis, took account of partition in their administrative structures. In both the Catholic and Church of Ireland (Anglican) churches, Armagh remained the primatial see of all Ireland, having been founded by Saint Patrick. After Vatican II the hierarchy adopted the modern form of an episcopal conference, consisting of all the bishops of Ireland, including coadjutors and auxiliaries as well as diocesan bishops, under the ex-officio presidency of the archbishop of Armagh. This represented little change from the existing structures for consultation, and joint action evolved from the principles formulated by the Synod of Thurles (1850).

Effects of Vatican II. The bishops who returned from the Second Vatican Council found an Ireland alerted to Church affairs in a manner never known in the past. The traditional loyalty of Irish Catholics to their faith was as strong as ever, but to this was now added an awareness of change: new emphases in doctrine, in the perception of other churches and in attitudes towards the laity. The people had acquired this conciliar vision partly through homilies and widely reported public lectures sponsored by the religious orders and partly from the secular press, radio and television, that by the final session of the Council were carrying extended daily reports from their own correspondents sent to cover developments in Rome first hand. The result was an emerging recognition of the Church as a human as well as a divine institution in which conflicts of opinion and personality played a part, in which teaching was arrived at through an exhaustively argued variety of viewpoints, and in which the exercise of authority was viewed as a service rather than as an imposition of legalistic dictates. The concern of some bishops that this novel image of the Church would distress Catholics imbued with an older ethos was reflected in the message of Archbishop John Charles MCQUAID (d. April 7, 1973) of Dublin at the conclusion of the Council in which he promised his people that "no change will worry the tranquility of your Christian lives." Such reassurance was in fact unnecessary. Although conciliar change provoked little resistance or disparagement at first, the Irish thought of change as a phenomenon to be initiated by authority, a service to be provided by an authority now perceived to be service-oriented.

The first result of authority-led reform was the enthusiastic acceptance of a revised liturgy following extensive pastoral preparation; another was in the field of ecumenism as Anglican, Presbyterian and Methodist believers joined Catholics in praying together for Christian unity. Annual ecumenical conferences were organized in County Louth, at Greenhills and another—specifically for theologians and church leaders—at Ballymascanlon, that built on the annual ecumenical conference hosted by the Benedictines of Glenstal Abbey, County Limerick, since the early 1960s. Of more immediate interest to most Catholics, and widely welcomed, was the lifting of prohibitions against attendance at Protestant weddings, funerals and worship services. The "ban" forbidding Catholics to attend Trinity College, Dublin, because of the allegedly Protestant character of Dublin University was rescinded in 1970. In that same year the enthusiasm of Jesuit scholar Michael Hurley resulted in the establishment of the Irish School of Ecumenics, where postgraduate students from all Christian traditions studied theology and related subjects and participated in one another's pastorate.

Led by the Archbishop of Armagh, William Cardinal CONWAY, ecumenical themes and the concept of a servant-church took root among Irish Catholics in the immediate postconciliar years without engendering antagonism or serious division. The responsibility of the local church toward the universal Church prompted the dispatch of Irish diocesan priests to assist the hard-pressed clergy in Peru and other parts of Latin America. Religious orders adopted new objectives in line with the conciliar spirit, often choosing an OPTION FOR THE POOR such

as setting up schools for the children of nomadic "itinerants" (the scrap-dealing "travellers" who wandered the roads of Ireland). In the early 1970s the Conference of Major Religious Superiors drew on the insights of the individual orders to create "Focus for Action," a program ensuring that the religious remained the most dynamic element within the Irish Church despite a chronic lack of vocations. Vocations to the priesthood in Ireland fell from 1,375 in 1965 to 322 in 1989. By 2000 the number of Masses were reduced due to a shortage of priests and the Holy Ghost Fathers were forced to relinquish management of their schools to secular educators due to a lack of religious. Catholic leaders predicted that the Irish Church would soon require priests from South America and Africa to immigrate as missionaries to the British Isles.

Encouraged by these developments, a thinking laity had begun to emerge, the leaders of which spoke from their own experience about subjects of social and moral significance. Intellectual Catholic journals had a much greater influence than their relatively small circulations would suggest since they addressed themselves to an audience that was theologically aware and conciliar by inclination, including the religious correspondents of the secular media.

Educational Reform. The postconciliar era also saw extensive State-initiated changes in the Irish educational system, despite the fact that the Catholic Church controlled a large number of schools in the Republic. Prior to Vatican II primary or first-level schools—called national schools—received most of their funding, including teacher's salaries, from the Ministry of Education. While the Ministry prescribed the basic curriculum, national schools were effectively denominational due to their management by local Catholic parish priests or Protestant pastors. Most second-level schools, on the other hand, were run by religious orders and charged whatever tuition was required to cover costs not able to be borne by the orders. Paralleling these Church schools were vocational schools owned and run by the state that provided technical, practical or commercial curriculums. The system favored the higher economic classes of Irish society, as the laboring classes could little afford to send their children to second-level schools.

During the mid-1960s government set about improving the opportunities for access to education and at the same time expanding the curriculum. In some cases it meant merging smaller schools within the same community into larger units to achieve the benefits of pooled resources. The state also combined secondary and vocational schools into "comprehensive schools" that taught the humanities, sciences and technical subjects. In

1966 the state assumed the total cost of secondary school administration in return for the abolition of fees, and by the end of the decade most Church-run schools elected to enter the "state scheme" on this basis. Despite the state's involvement, the religious remained at the heart of the system. In 1973 the Church leadership endorsed the state initiatives, and encouraged the continued cooperation and mergers between local schools. In 2000 the Ministry of Education continued to fund all schools, regardless of religious affiliation.

The reform of education continued with much analysis and a sometimes heated exchange of viewpoints on the content of the curriculum, on class sizes, on the career prospects for lay teachers in Church schools. By the 1980s questions involving career prospects were beginning to resolve themselves as the vocations crisis meant that fewer priests, brothers and sisters were available for teaching. By the end of the decade lay staff predominated in all schools, and the appointment of lay principals (headmasters or headmistresses) was increasingly becoming the norm. As trustees, the religious continued to wield control through the management boards but their position was becoming precarious with the hardening of proposals for the state to assume ownership of the schools for which it was bearing the cost. With the bishops, both Anglican and Catholic, opposed to relinquishing ownership, the debate continued.

The Church was also central to some of the radical reforms of third-level education undertaken in the postconciliar years. Its removal of the prohibition on Catholics attending Trinity College, Dublin, resulted in a major influx of Catholic students to that ancient institution, the establishment of a Catholic chaplaincy, and the provision of daily Mass in the college chapel. By the 1980s most Trinity College students were either Catholics or of Catholic background. The university's divinity school, which had been Anglican, became an interdenominational department of Hebrew, biblical and theological studies in 1980. Other universities in Ireland burgeoned in the decades after 1965, and two new universities were founded in the Republic in 1989: the University of Limerick and Dublin City University.

Missionary Efforts. Vatican II's emphasis on respect for local culture and the promotion of indigenous clergy and sisterhoods coincided with the attainment of independence by Third World countries and the fall-off in Irish vocations. Missionary work took on a new character in response to these stimuli. Long-established missionary activity in Africa and Asia by Irish religious had ensured that several generations of Irish Catholics were informed about the work of evangelization, education and medical help. The participation of lay helpers now became a characteristic of most missions, with doctors, nurses and other qualified personnel volunteering for a term of service in association with the missionaries. The principal concentration of Irish endeavor shifted to the relief of famine caused by drought, warfare or destitution. Special agencies were founded, including Trócaire (an Irish word meaning "mercy"), set up by the bishops in 1973. Together with some Irish secular agencies, these organizations became globally respected both for their provision of immediate assistance to the starving and their encouragement of improved methods of husbandry to prevent famine in the future.

Church Addresses Poverty. Through their Justice and Peace Commission, pastoral letters and other statements, Irish bishops took a leading role in protesting against an economic system that failed to address the problem of poverty in Ireland. They pointed to deficiencies in political planning, the criteria of the EUROPEAN UNION, and relations between workers and employers that contributed to what they saw as major injustices in Irish society, the greatest of which they identified as an unnecessarily high level of unemployment. An even more trenchant and sustained campaign for radical change was mounted by the Conference of Religious of Ireland (CRI), which presented plans, analyses, submissions and protests urging the government to break out of traditional patterns of economic thinking. During the 1990s the CRI became one of the more influential voices affecting the forward planning of successive administrations, and saw some of its proposals being accepted. Following the presidential elections two years later, the Conference again spoke out, noting that "Decisions taken in the past 20 years have resulted in the emergence of a two-tier society" wherein 34 percent of Irish lived below the poverty line. Showing similar resolve, a 1994 initiative by the government to encourage employment in the depressed regions of western Ireland was a direct result of the efforts of local bishops.

Social welfare agencies promoted through Church effort included the Catholic Communications Institute of Ireland, which advised bishops on media matters and maintained a number of book stores, a publishing firm (Veritas Publications), and a video production unit. CURA, an advice and counseling service for women with unwanted pregnancies, operated a confidential telephone contact system throughout the country. The Catholic Marriage Advisory Council provided a confidential service, operated by trained personnel, to help sustain and enrich marriage and family relationships.

Modern Church Confronts Social Issues. In Ireland as elsewhere, the first severe jolt for the postconciliar Church came with the publication of the encyclical

HUMANAE VITAE in 1968. While the condemnation of artificial birth control drew protests from a number of the newly articulate laity, Irish bishops stressed the obligation on Catholics to make "a religious submission of mind and will" to authentic papal teaching. Although controversy continued, because the sale of contraceptives was prohibited by civil law in Ireland, the crisis did not at first assume the same proportions as it did elsewhere. However, when the government proposed to modify the legal restriction against contraceptives, the church-state clash that followed revealed a major cleavage within the local church. While bishops accepted legislative authority to determine civil law, they added that the introduction of contraception would undermine the common good and would ultimately lead to the advocacy of abortion. Contraception was finally legalized in the 1980s, in careful stages by a parliament as cautious as the people it represented, and, prophetically, by 1999 a referendum was requested on the legalization of abortion.

The early stages of the contraception controversy coincided with a noticeable alienation of young people from the Church, an increase in resignations from the ministry, a sharp decrease in vocations and a growing criticism of Church affairs by the media. Corresponding to these negative factors was a new fervor among traditionalists opposed to innovative thinking and to all efforts aimed at persuading the Church to conform its teaching to meet and serve the needs of contemporary society.

Unique to this set of common circumstances among Irish Catholics was that polarization occurred within a community shaped by the Catholic ethos. Most advocates of social change were themselves practicing Catholics: theologians such as Maynooth professor Enda McDonagh and the Augustinian Gabriel Daly, and the political observers Garret FitzGerald (soon to be prime minister) and Mary Robinson (later to be president of Ireland). Historian Margaret MacCurtain, OP, and anti-poverty campaigner Stanislaus Kennedy, were religious sisters. Some liberals became antagonistic to the Church itself, certain extremists even resorted to antagonistic rhetoric that further hardened the traditionalist resistance to change. In general the greater part of the criticism directed against conservative Church attitudes in Ireland came from believing Catholics.

Genuine concerns existed over the encroachment of materialism to the detriment of the Christian family and the destruction of religious values and traditions. This stance, reflected by Pope John Paul II's address during a pastoral visit to Ireland in 1979, inspired the formation of lay groups dedicated to the defense of the family. Seeing their Church in jeopardy, groups formed to battle parliament's "liberalizing" civil legislation regarding abortion and divorce. Successful in the referendum on divorce in 1983 and the referendum on abortion in 1986, these groups eventually found their positions undermined. With regard to abortion, a clause banning the constitution from addressing abortion was so convoluted that the Supreme Court found that it actually permitted abortion in certain cases. Meanwhile, in 1993 a law was passed that provided an end-run around the abortion controversy by allowing Irish women to obtain abortions by traveling to Great Britain, where they were legal. And a campaign to scuttle a proposal to facilitate the introduction of divorce left many separated couples in a legal limbo; when the proposal was revived, it was passed and divorce became legal in February of 1997. Meanwhile, government legislation began to erode the traditional arena of the church. Passage of the Family Law Act of 1995 compromised canon law by raising the minimum age for marriage from 14 to 18. Church leaders protested the new law as a breach of human rights and a breach of the Church's right to determine the requirements of the holy state of matrimony.

The charge that the Catholic Church determined the laws of the Republic could not readily be countered as long as statute and constitutional law on matters of morality conspicuously conformed to Catholic teaching. The attitude of the bishops, who equated this conformity with the common good regardless of the wishes of citizens who disagreed with the Church, was felt by some to be at variance with the Vatican Council's advocacy of ecumenism and religious freedom. The hierarchical backing given to conservatives in the abortion and divorce controversies further exacerbated Liberal Catholic distress. The perceived non-concilar stance of the Holy See on internal issues—clerical celibacy, the position of women within the Church and the disciplining of theologians—also increased the progressive discontent and deepened the gulf between Irish Catholic factions. Opinion surveys in the 1990s showed substantial support in Ireland not only for the ordination of women but also for the abolition of compulsory priestly celibacy. A consequent concern throughout this period was the appointment of bishops, which in the case of some nominations to prominent Irish dioceses undoubtedly ignored the wishes of the local church.

Overt factionalism surfaced in 1994 when it came to light that the Irish Church had harbored the same problems related to pedophiliac and homosexual clergy, and to priests in illicit relationships with women, that assailed the Church elsewhere in the world. While slow to criticize the human weaknesses exposed in a succession of scandals, Irish Catholics expressed shock over the incompetence of Church authorities in dealing with the problems, especially in the case of clerics accused of pedophilia.

Situation in Northern Ireland. The "Troubles"—the guerilla-style violence in Northern Ireland that characterized that region throughout the second half of the 20th century—posed serious questions for the Church throughout the entire island. While society in the Republic was homogenous—there was little ethnic diversity and 91 percent of the population identified itself as Roman Catholic in 2000—loyalties to nationalist (Republican) or unionist causes sometimes influenced political attitudes and affiliations. This was not the case in the north, however. There only one third of the population identified itself as Catholic, and this minority looked forward to the eventual reunification of the island. The Protestant majority, with political and cultural ties to Great Britain, viewed their Catholics neighbors with suspicion. A local parliament with powers delegated from the British parliament had allowed Northern Ireland to enjoy what was effectively single-party rule until 1972 when that parliament was abolished.

In 1968 police violence in responding to activities of a group fighting discrimination against Catholics in housing, employment and electoral practices rekindled hostilities between the two factions. Over the next few years the conflict hardened into deadly guerrilla warfare as the nationalist Irish Republican Army (IRA)—a body illegal in the Republic as well as in the North—directed violent attacks on extremist groups on the loyalist side. Members of the British army, the police and many innocent civilians died in the bombings, shootings and other acts of violence that followed.

The dilemma for Church authorities was that while they shared the grievance of the Catholic people with regard to civil rights issues, they could not approve the violent tactics of the IRA. Northern bishops led by Armagh's Cardinal Conway vehemently denounced the violence. While they spoke for most of their fellow Catholics they alienated some who saw the IRA as protectors. They also upset others who, while disapproving of the IRA, also disliked their Church's giving comfort to unionists. And when the bishops condemned loyalist and military excesses pro-British commentators saw them as Janus-faced. Conway and his supporters resisted demands to excommunicate members of the IRA as they realized such an exercise would be pointless: Irish nationalists traditionally distinguished between their faith and their Church, believing that the Church in these circumstances acted out of its own interest rather than from ethical considerations. The bishops did, however, forbid the use of military symbolism within church buildings during the funerals of IRA members. Cardinal Conway's succes-

sors, Cardinals Tomás Ó Fiaich and Cahal Daly, reiterated the condemnations of all violence, including that from the nationalist side, and increasingly joined with Protestant church leaders to plead for peace, but with little evident effect.

While individual Catholic leaders rallied many to the cause of peace, the hierarchy took a much more subtle position. The Northern tensions were rooted in an historic antipathy between Catholics and Protestants, making ecumenical approaches obvious. However, a virtual halt in ecumenical progress accompanied the polarization of opinion among Catholics in the Republic. No Irish enthusiasm was officially voiced for the active pursuit of Anglican-Roman Catholic reunion. In the North, where thoughtful people felt that a major contribution towards the long-term elimination of communal tension could be made by the education of Catholic and Protestant children together in the same schools, official Catholic support was withheld. A few "integrated" schools of this kind were founded but without overt Church approval. In fairness to the Catholic authorities, it must be added that Protestant approval was equally difficult to generate.

The Downing Street Declaration, a joint statement outlining a proposed peace process made by Irish Prime Minister John Bruton and British Prime Minister John Major in December of 1993, led to an IRA and loyalist cease fire the following year. While hostilities erupted again in 1996, they were reduced to intermittent flare-ups as negotiations continued. On Good Friday, 1998, a peace settlement was reached by the IRA and loyalist factions that would create a 108-seat Assembly in Northern Ireland capable of protecting the political rights of the region's Catholic minority. While voters in both sections of the island approved the proposal, by 2001 it had yet to be implemented. Blessing the agreement, Pope John Paul II saw it as an affirmation that a "new era of hope" had begun for the region.

Bibliography: J. B. BELL, *The Irish Troubles: A Generation of Violence 1967–1992* (Dublin 1993). J. COONEY, *The Crozier and the Dail: Church and State 1922–1986* (Cork 1986). J. DUNN, *No Lions in the Hierarchy* (Dublin 1994). *Freedom to Hope: The Catholic Church in Ireland 20 Years after Vatican II*, eds., A. FALCONER, E. MCDONAGH and S. MACRÉAMOINN (Dublin 1985). B. FARRELL, *De Valera: His Constitution and Ours* (Dublin 1988). G. FITZGERALD, *All in a Life: An Autobiography* (Dublin 1992). M. FOGARTY, L. RYAN and J. LEE, *Irish Values and Attitudes: The Irish Report of the European Value Systems Study* (Dublin 1984). P. HANNON, *Church, State, Morality, and Law* (Dublin 1992). T. HESKETH, *The Second Partitioning of Ireland: The Abortion Referendum of 1983* (Dublin 1990). J. HICKEY, *Religion and the Northern Ireland Problem* (Dublin 1984). *Beyond Tolerance*, ed. M. HURLEY (London 1975). IRISH EPISCOPAL CONFERENCE, *Justice, Love, and Peace: Pastoral Letters of the Irish Bishops 1969–1979* (Dublin 1979); *Love Is for Life* (Dublin 1985); *Work Is the Key: Toward an Economy That Needs Everyone* (Dublin 1992); *The Pope in Ireland: Ad-*

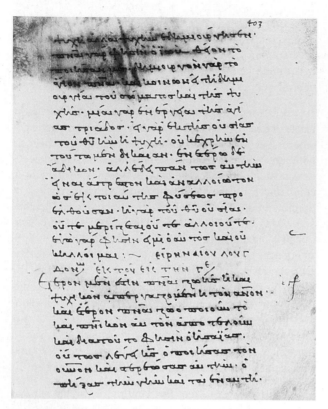

Manuscript folio from "Adversus haereses," 10th century, by St. Irenaeus (Cod. Vat. Grec. 423, fol. 403), from Biblioteca Apostolica Vaticana.

dresses and Homilies (Dublin 1979). D. KEOGH, Twentieth-Century Ireland: Nation and State (Dublin 1994). P. KIRBY, Is Irish Catholicism Dying? (Cork 1984). D. A. LANE, Foundations for a Social Theology (Dublin 1984). J. LEE, Ireland 1912–1985: Politics and Society (Cambridge 1989). Women in Irish Society: The Historical Dimension, eds., M. MACCURTAIN and D. Ó CORRÁIN (Dublin 1978). E. MCDONAGH, The Making of Disciples (Dublin 1982); Between Chaos and the New Creation (Dublin 1986); Irish Challenges to Theology (Dublin 1986). G. MCELROY, The Catholic Church and Northern Ireland Crisis 1968–1986 (Dublin 1991). K. MCNAMARA, Pluralism (Dublin 1986). J. NEWMAN, Ireland Must Choose (Dublin 1983). Values and Social Change in Ireland, ed. C. T. WHELAN (Dublin 1994). J. WHYTE, Church and State in Modern Ireland 1923–1979 (Dublin 1984); Interpreting Northern Ireland (Oxford 1990).

[L. MCREDMOND/EDS.]

IRENAEUS, ST.

Early Church Father and perhaps a martyr; b. Asia Minor *c.* 140–160; d. Lyons? *c.* 202. Although of crucial importance in the development of the Church's theology, Irenaeus presents problems of considerable difficulty in regard to details of his life, writings, and teaching.

Life. Irenaeus, a disciple of St. POLYCARP of Smyrna, migrated to Gaul, where he became a presbyter of the Church of Lyons during the reign of Marcus Aurelius. During the Montanist (*see* MONTANISM) controversy he was sent as an envoy to Rome by the Church of Lyons and upon his return was chosen to succeed the martyr Pothinus as bishop. In this capacity he strenuously opposed the teachings of GNOSTICISM and in the EASTER CONTROVERSY advised Pope VICTOR I to preserve peace with the churches of Asia Minor.

Christianity was most probably brought to many parts of eastern Gaul by Irenaeus. Of the last years of his life practically nothing is known and only in the late 6th century does GREGORY OF TOURS (*Hist. Francorum* 1.27) refer to Irenaeus as a martyr.

Writings. Only two complete works of Irenaeus, originally written in Greek, are extant.

The Detection and Overthrow of the False Gnosis. In five books, usually cited as *Adversus haereses,* this work is preserved in a Latin translation made probably *c.* 200. Fragments of the original Greek are found in the writings of HIPPOLYTUS OF ROME, EUSEBIUS OF CAESAREA, EPIPHANIUS, and THEODORET OF CYR; in *catenae;* and in papyri. Books 4 and 5 are also extant in an Armenian translation, and 23 fragments are found in Syriac. Book 1 deals chiefly with the detection of the false Gnosis and serves as a valuable history of Gnosticism. The next three books contain the refutation of Gnostic teachings with arguments drawn from reason (book 2), from the teaching and tradition of the Apostles (book 3), and from the sayings of the Lord (book 4). Book 5 treats of the "last things," especially the resurrection of the body, and concludes with some remarks on MILLENARIANISM.

Demonstration of the Apostolic Teaching. Until 1904, when a complete Armenian translation of the *Demonstration* (Ἐπίδειξις) was discovered, it was known only through a reference in Eusebius (*Hist. Eccl.* 5.26). The treatise is an apologetic work dealing with fundamental Christian teachings and presents the prophecies of the Old Testament as proofs for the truth of Christian revelation.

Other Writings. Excerpts from the letter to Victor I relative to the Easter controversy are quoted by Eusebius (*ibid.,* 5.23.3; 5.24.11–17). There is also a Syriac fragment of another letter to the same pope. The four fragments of letters published by C. M. Pfaff have been shown to be forgeries.

Known only through notices in Eusebius are: (1) a letter to Irenaeus's friend Florinus, *On the Sole Sovereignty,* or *That God Is Not the Author of Evil,* and a treatise written for the same friend, *On the Ogdoad* (Eusebius, 5.20.1); (2) a letter to Blastus, *On Schism* (Eusebius, *ibid.*); (3) a work titled *Concerning Knowledge*

(Eusebius, 5.26). Without giving a specific title, Eusebius also mentions a small book of various discourses.

Teaching. In opposition to Gnostic dualism Irenaeus teaches that there is but one God, who is the creator of the world and the father of Jesus Christ; one divine economy of salvation; and one revelation. He develops the Pauline doctrine of the ἀνακεφαλαίωσις, or RECAPITULATION IN CHRIST of all things: Christ as the new Adam renews all creation and leads it back to its author through the Incarnation and the Redemption. Mary, the Mother of God, is the new Eve. Visible creation is good, not evil, and the body will rise again. The Eucharist is both a Sacrament containing the real body of Christ and the true sacrifice of the New Law. As a witness to Apostolic tradition and a champion of the inspiration of both the OT and the NT, Irenaeus is one of the most important writers of the early Church.

Potentior Principalitas. One of the most frequently quoted passages of Irenaeus is a statement in *Adv. haer.* 3.3.3: "Ad hanc enim ecclesiam, propter potentiorem [potioriem] principalitatem, necesse est omnem convenire ecclesiam-hoc est eos qui sunt undique fideles-in qua semper ab his qui sunt undique conservata est ea quae est ab apostolis traditio." There is no settled translation of this passage and the difficulties are compounded by the lack of the original Greek text. Some think that the translation should read: "For with this Church on account of its more effective leadership every Church must agree, that is, the faithful throughout the world, in which the apostolic tradition has always been preserved by the [faithful] everywhere."

Some scholars take "this Church" to mean the Church of Rome. Nautin's philological study of the text, however, indicates that this meaning is not certain and suggests that the phrase refers to the universal Church. K. Baus thinks that the church referred to is any Church founded by an apostle in which the Apostolic tradition is preserved by an unbroken succession of bishops teaching the same doctrine.

The meaning of *potentior [potior] principalitas* is likewise disputed. Some translate it as "more effective leadership," "superior origin," "priority of time," with reference either to the Church of Rome or to any Apostolic Church. Others, however, maintain that the words do not refer to any Church, but to the unique social and political importance of the city of Rome.

Most probably the words *necesse est convenire*—"must agree with"—are not to be understood as a juridical obligation, because the context does not deal with the ecclesiastical constitution. Irenaeus rejects the Gnostic teachings because they are completely at variance with the teaching of any Apostolic Church; apostolicity is a proof of orthodoxy of doctrine.

On the basis of studies in early Christian Latin, C. Mohrmann suggests that *ab his qui sunt undique* contains the idea of a comparison and consequently the translation should read: "in this Church [its identity cannot be established beyond all doubt] the Apostolic tradition has always been preserved *and better than* in other Churches formed by the faithful living in all parts of the world."

In spite of uncertainties as to the correct translation of the passage, one point seems clear from the context: Irenaeus is primarily concerned with establishing the correct teaching handed down from the Twelve Apostles.

Irenaeus was buried in the crypt of St. John (now St.-Irenée) in Lyons, which was destroyed by Calvinists in 1562.

Feast: June 28 (West); Aug. 23 (East).

Bibliography: *Acta Sanctorum* June 5:335–49. F. L. BATTLES, ed., *Irenaeus, against Heresies . . .* (Allison Park, Pa. 1993). F. VERNET, *Dictionnaire de théologie catholique,* ed. A. VACANT et al., 15 v. (Paris 1903–50; Tables générales 1951–) 7.2:2394–2533. P. T. CAMELOT, *Lexikon für Theologie und Kirche,* ed. J. HOFER and K. RAHNER, 10 v. (2d, new ed. Freiburg 1957–65) 3:773–775. B. ALTANER, *Patrology,* tr. H. GRAEF from 5th German ed. (New York 1960) 150–158. J. QUASTEN, *Patrology,* 4 v. (Westminster, Md. 1950–86) 1:287–313. G. WINGREN, *Man and the Incarnation,* tr. R. MACKENZIE (Philadelphia 1959). C. MOHRMANN, *Vigiliae christianae* 3 (1949) 57–61. P. NAUTIN, *Revue de l'histoire des religions* 151 (1957) 37–78. R. P. C. HANSON, "Potentiorem principalitatem in Irenaeus," *Studia Patristica* (Texte und Untersuchungen zur Geschichte der altchristlichen Literatur 78; Berlin 1961) 366–369. K. BAUS and H. JEDIN, *Handbuch der Kirchengeschichte,* 6 v. (Freiburg 1962–): v. 1, K. BAUS, ed., *Von der Urgemeinde zur frühchristlichen Grosskirche,* with "Einleitung zur Kirchengeschichte" by H. JEDIN; Eng. tr. from 3d, rev. ed., H. JEDIN and J. DOLAN, eds., *Handbook of Church History* (New York 1965): v. 1, *From the Apostolic Community to Constantine,* tr. K. BAUS, with a "General Introduction to Church History" by H. JEDIN 1:399–400. R. and B. HEMMERDINGER, "Trois nouveaux fragments grecs del'*Adversus haereses* de saint Irenée," *Zeitschrift für die neutestamentliche Wissenschaft und die Kunde der älteren Kirche* 53 (1962) 252–255. H. LASSIAT, *Promotion de l'homme en Jésus-Christ: d'après Irénée de Lyon, témoin de la tradition des apôtres* (Paris 1974); *L'Actualité de la catéchèse apostolique* (Saint-Vincent-sur-Jabron 1979). M. BALWIERZ, *The Holy Spirit and the Church as a Subject of Evangelization according to St. Irenaeus* (Warsaw 1985). L. MENVIELLE, *Marie, mère de vie: approche du mystère marial à partir d'Irénée de Lyon* (Venasque 1986). A. ORBE, *Parábolas evangélicas en San Ireneo,* 2 v. (Madrid 1972); *Espiritualidad de San Ireneo* (Rome 1989). M. J. OLSON, *Irenaeus, the Valentinian Gnostics, and the Kingdom of God* (Lewiston, N.Y. 1992). M. HAUKE, *Heilsverlust in Adam: Stationen griechischer Erbsündenlehre: Irenäus, Origenes, Kappadozier* (Paderborn 1993). T. L. TIESSEN, *Irenaeus on the Salvation of the Unevangelized* (Metuchen, N.J. 1993). D. MINNS, *Irenaeus* (London 1994). R. M. GRANT, *Irenaeus of Lyons* (London 1997). M. A. DONOVANN, *One Right Reading? A Guide to Irenaeus* (Collegeville, Minn. 1997). T. SCHERRER, *La gloire de Dieu dans l'oeuvre de Saint Irénée* (Rome 1997). D. J.

BINGHAM, *Irenaeus' Use of Matthew's Gospel in* Adversus haereses (Leuven 1998). J. BEHR, *Asceticism and Anthropology in Irenaeus and Clement* (Oxford 2000). D. WANKE, *Das Kreuz Christi bei Irenäus von Lyon* (Berlin 2000), extensive bibliography.

[H. DRESSLER]

IRENE, BYZANTINE EMPRESS

Coregnant 780–797, sole ruler from 797 to Oct. 31, 802; b. Athens, *c.* 752; d. Lesbos, Aug. 9, 803. Although married to Leo IV, "the Khazar," one of the more moderate iconoclastic emperors, Irene herself strongly supported the veneration of images. At Leo's death she became regent and coruler with her ten-year-old son, Constantine VI, and from this date moved with caution to reverse the iconoclastic policies of the late Emperor's Isaurian administration. In 784 she replaced Patriarch PAUL IV with the moderate, politic TARASIUS, and in 787 the seventh Ecumenical Council met in NICAEA (II) under her auspices to condemn ICONOCLASM. Tarasius was the author of the decree proclaiming the efficacy of icon veneration. In 790 Irene failed in her attempt to remove Constantine, and, opposed by the higher levels of the bureaucracy and by the Asiatic regiments of the army, she herself was briefly removed from power. She regained her position as coruler in 792. In 797, aided by the antagonism Constantine had aroused through his tyrannical pretensions and poor military leadership, she finally overthrew her son and had him blinded and deposed.

The chief event affecting the Eastern Empire during her reign was the coronation of CHARLEMAGNE in Rome in 800. Although Irene and the anti-iconoclastic party had effected a *rapprochement* with ADRIAN I in the period of the Council, the creation of a second empire completely confounded the political ideals of the Byzantines. Irene was willing to compromise with the Frankish ruler and may even have offered herself in marriage to him to reunite the two worlds. But official Byzantine recognition of Charlemagne (as Emperor, but not as Emperor of the Romans) did not come until 814.

As emperor (i.e., *Basileus,* for *Basilissa* or Empress was not a recognized title at this time), Irene was not effective. She was unable to halt the incursions of the Bulgars, and her generous financial policies, especially friendly to monastic establishments, resulted in a severe loss of revenue. She was deposed in 802 by a conspiracy of high palace officials, one of whom succeeded her as Nicephorus I. Irene is venerated as a saint in the Eastern Church.

Feast: Aug. 9.

Bibliography: F. DÖLGER, *Corpus der griechischen Urkunden des Mittelalters und der neueren Zeit* 1:335–360. G. OSTROGORSKY, *History of the Byzantine State,* 156–165.

[D. A. MILLER]

IRENE OF PORTUGAL, ST.

Date and place of birth and death unknown; listed in the Antiphonary of León (10th? century) as *virgo in Scallabi Castro.* In vitae (all after 1100), notably in Breviaries of Braga and Évora, she is described as a beautiful nun of noble birth in THOMAR(?). After dissuading a noble from his desire, she had to reject her spiritual director, who, in revenge, gave her a potion that made her appear pregnant. The jealous noble had her murdered. Her body floated down the Nabão and the Zêzere to be miraculously entombed in a pool at Scallabis on the Tagus in 653. The town of Scallabis, it is said, then changed its name to Santarem (Santa Irene, Ira, Eriã). Irene was added to the Roman martyrology in 1586.

Feast: Oct. 20.

Bibliography: H. FLÓREZ et al., *España sagrada,* 54 v. (Madrid 1747–1957) 14:389–391. B. DE GAIFFIER, *Analecta Bollandiana* 57 (1939) 440; 58 (1940) 85; 66 (1948) 307.

[E. P. COLBERT]

IRENICISM

A term used to describe peaceful or conciliatory means in dealing with Church matters, particularly in the field of Christian unity, as distinct from polemics or controversy. It does not imply a dilution or diminution of the truth in order to secure a solution to thorny problems. The Decree on Ecumenism of Vatican II warned that "Nothing is so foreign to the spirit of ecumenism as a false conciliatory approach [irenicism] which harms the purity of Catholic doctrine and obscures its assured genuine meaning" (*UR* 11). At the same time, "the manner and order in which Catholic belief is expressed should in no way become an obstacle to dialogue with our brethren" (ibid.).

A true irenicism involves kindness and respect for the attitude and opinion of others who are not members of the Church and seeks to create a spirit of mutual understanding, but in no way does it attempt to compromise with truth or charity. It seeks to promote the principles of unity in the spirit of the Good Shepherd.

See Also: INDIFFERENTISM; ECUMENICAL MOVEMENT; TRIUMPHALISM.

Bibliography: B. LAMBERT, *Le Problème oecuménique,* 2 v. (Paris 1961). G. THILS, *Histoire doctrinale du mouvement oecu-*

ménique (Louvain 1955). M. J. LE GUILLOU, *Mission et Unité,* 2 v. (Paris 1960). C. J. DUMONT, *Les Voices de l'unité chrétienne* (Paris 1954).

[T. CRANNY/EDS.]

IRISH CATHOLIC COLONIZATION ASSOCIATION OF THE U.S.

Originated at a meeting in Chicago, Ill., on Jan. 20, 1879, when William J. Onahan, acting for the principal organizations then promoting Irish colonization, planned a national conference for March 17. Despite earlier colonization projects, conditions among the Irish in crowded eastern cities continued to be distressing from moral, political, and economic viewpoints. Attempts for a national society had proved unproductive in 1856, 1869, and 1873; yet Bp. John Ireland's flourishing Irish Catholic settlements of the late 1870s in Minnesota made him, along with Dillon O'Brien, the greatest colonizing layman in Minnesota, think the time was opportune to try again.

Ireland could count on support from Bps. John Lancaster Spalding, of Peoria, and James O'Connor, of Omaha, who was then negotiating with the Burlington-Missouri Railroad for land for a Catholic colony. At the organization meeting on April 18, 1879, Spalding was elected president of the board of directors (a position he held through 1891), consisting of 13 laymen and six bishops. The association was legally incorporated under Illinois law as a stock company with capital of $100,000 in shares of $100 each. Their aim was to assist people who had saved $250 to $300, which, with association help, would enable a family to become established. They judged it unwise to settle absolute destitutes and discouraged further emigration from Ireland. From June 1879, Ireland and Spalding gave numerous lectures throughout eastern dioceses, including mass meetings in Cooper Union, New York City. Despite outward public approval and assurance that this was a safe business venture, less than $10,000 was subscribed. Even after a second strenuous lecture campaign, only $83,000 was actually paid in.

The association bought 10,000 acres of railroad land in Nobles County, Minn., and 25,000 in Greeley County, Nebr., to sell at $1.25 to $5.00 per acre. The price was advanced 25 percent an acre over purchase in order to erect a church, rectory, school, and immigrant depot for the temporary convenience of settlers. Since Bp. Edward Fitzgerald of Little Rock, Ark., had several flourishing colonies, an association committee in 1881 "reserved" lands along the railroad there for eight years; but few Irish families came. Perhaps this was due to lack of assis-

Brother M. P. Riordan, second superior general of the Irish Christian Brothers.

tance from association funds or antipathy to Negro labor there. When the lease expired the Arkansas venture was closed. In 1884 the association was able to establish a helpful immigration bureau at Castle Garden, New York City. As soon as prosperity was assured for its colonies in Minnesota and Nebraska, the association began redemption at par of its stock and in 1891 closed all accounts.

Bibliography: M. E. HENTHORNE, *The Irish Catholic Colonization Association of the United States* (Champaign 1932). J. P. SHANNON, *Catholic Colonization on the Western Frontier* (New Haven 1957). J. L. SPALDING, *The Religious Mission of the Irish People and Catholic Colonization* (New York 1880).

[M. G. KELLY]

IRISH CHRISTIAN BROTHERS

Irish Christian Brothers is the popular name for the Congregation of Christian Brothers, also known as Christian Brothers Institute (CFC), a teaching congregation founded in 1802 in Waterford, Ireland, by Edmund Ignatius RICE, a merchant of that city.

The need to educate the youth of his native land, where religious persecution had reduced the majority of

Catholics to poverty and ignorance, led Rice to dispose of his prosperous business affairs. In 1802, he began to instruct the neglected youth of Waterford; others joined him, the work prospered, and schools were opened in neighboring towns. In August 1808, with six companions, Rice made his vows and received the name Brother Ignatius. When papal approval was granted in 1820, Brother Rice was elected the first superior general.

The spread of the congregation to distant countries was occasioned largely by the need of Irish-born prelates for help in educating the youth of their dioceses. Four brothers were sent to Australia in 1868. In 1876, the brothers were sent to Newfoundland, Canada. The congregation was introduced to the British colony of Gibraltar in 1877 and soon enjoyed a respected place in an education system long dominated by "regimental" academies and non-Catholic schools. In 1886 at the request of the Holy See, schools were opened in India. In 1906 Msgr. James W. Power invited the brothers to open a school at All Saints parish, New York City. This was the cradle of the North American province, which, with the incorporation of the Newfoundland schools, was formally established in 1916. The generalate is in Rome.

[J. H. VAUGHAN/EDS.]

IRISH COLLEGES ON THE CONTINENT

On the eve of the Reformation the clergy of Ireland were ill-equipped to meet the coming onslaught on the traditional faith. Two centuries earlier the University of St. Patrick's, Dublin, authorized by Clement V, proved to be stillborn. There was thus no *studium generale* in the country to maintain a good academic standard in the education of ecclesiastics whose training, acquired in the monasteries of the older religious orders or in a few cathedral schools, was adapted solely to the pastoral ministry among a people whose beliefs had hitherto been unchallenged. The authorization, accorded in 1564 by the Holy See to Archbishop Creagh of Armagh and David Woulfe, the papal commissary, to found a *studium generale* arrived too late. The Act of Supremacy and Uniformity was already in force in Ireland, and the Catholic faith was already in jeopardy.

Contemporary sources for the history of the period portray an Ireland that was likely to be susceptible to Protestantism. The Irish hierarchy had shown itself, with very few exceptions, weak and temporizing. Indeed the first ray of hope that worthy men would be appointed to rule the dioceses of the country appeared only after 1564 when the Holy See began to act on the recommendations

furnished by the papal commissary. And though the problem of manning Irish parishes with worthy clergy was pressing, there was to be no solution of this problem for another generation. It was the good fortune of the Catholic Church in Ireland to have enjoyed borrowed years until the first priests from the seminaries abroad returned to fortify their people against error. The early Elizabethan Protestant clergy in Ireland were themselves badly instructed and more anxious to possess parish revenues than to spread their doctrines, while their hierarchy steered an uncertain course between Anglicanism and Calvinism. Also Trinity College, Dublin, which was intended to be an intellectual center for the education of Irish Protestant clergy, was not established until the year before the opening of the Irish College, Salamanca. It was fortunate for the Church that the older religious orders, especially the Franciscans, were at home to man vacant parishes until the return of the first priests who had attended the Irish Colleges.

For more than 40 years before the establishment of the first Irish College abroad, Irish students for the priesthood were already an accepted phenomenon in the university centers of Flanders, Spain, Portugal, Italy, and France. There is no way of knowing, however, how many of these students returned as missionary priests to Ireland. There was, as yet, no organization to canalize for the spiritual benefit of Ireland what was evidently a fair potential source of priestly vocations.

To a few secular priests and Jesuits is due the credit for acting solely on their own individual initiative in bringing into being the Irish Colleges whose *raison d'être* was to educate Irishmen in the spirit of the Tridentine decrees for missionary service throughout Ireland.

THE IBERIAN PENINSULA

Salamanca College opened its doors in 1592 because of the efforts of a secular priest, Thomas WHITE, who for some years had been supporting a few poor Irish students out of his own means. He was eventually able to gain the approval and financial support of Philip II for the continuance of his work. Shortly after he became rector, White became a Jesuit. He devoted the rest of his life to the education of Irish clerical students. His collaborator at Salamanca and elsewhere was Richard Conway, a Jesuit. In 1593 another Irish Jesuit, John Howling, opened the Irish College of Lisbon.

The number of students rarely exceeded ten in each of these colleges; yet within 25 years Lisbon alone had sent forth 124 priests. Later establishments were the Irish Colleges of Compostella and Seville, founded by secular priests but subsequently entrusted to the Jesuits. The college at Compostella was ancillary to that of Salamanca, the former providing courses in arts and philosophy, the latter in theology. These peninsular foundations passed under the government of the secular clergy after the banishment of the Jesuits from Spain and Portugal. The Irish College of Salamanca continued to function until it was closed in 1955 by the Irish hierarchy.

FLANDERS

Christopher Cusack, another zealous and resourceful secular priest, long at work among Irish students, was enabled, by help from the Spanish Crown, to establish four centers for the education of Irish missionary priests. These were the Pastoral College (1594) of DOUAI with, later, the ancillary colleges of Antwerp, Tournai, and Lille. The last, due to the help of the Capuchin, Francis Nugent, became virtually a juvenate for the Capuchin order. The Pastoral College of Douai admitted lay as well as clerical students in its earlier years. By 1613, 148 Irish priests had been ordained from Douai.

Apparently, the only college founded through the initiative of a member of the Irish hierarchy was the Pastoral College of LOUVAIN established in 1623 by Urban VIII at the instance of Eugene MacMahon, Archbishop of Dublin. The College was affiliated with the University, which, since 1548, had witnessed the enrollment of Irish students in ever increasing numbers. The most notable of Irish alumni of the University was Dermot O'HURLEY, the martyred Archbishop of Cashel. All these Irish Colleges in the Low Countries disappeared in the troubled years of the French Revolution.

FRANCE

The Irish College in Paris does not seem to have been formally established until 1605, but its first rector, John Lee, a secular priest long settled in Paris, had already been engaged in seeking alms for the support of Irish students of the university. This college became numerically the largest of all the Irish seminaries and, when the National Seminary of Maynooth was founded, was training 180 students. It is still an Irish seminary, entrusted by the Irish hierarchy since 1858 to the supervision of the Irish Vincentians, but in recent years it has been on loan for the education of refugee clerical students from Poland.

In 1603 another Irish secular priest Dermot MacCarthy, founded the Irish College of Bordeaux for the education of priests for the south of Ireland. This seminary was later named the Collège de Ste. Anne la Royale to commemorate its chief benefactress Anne of Austria. In its early years it housed only about a dozen students, but at the time of the French Revolution it counted 40. The Irish College of Toulouse, also later named Collège de Ste. Anne la Royale, was established by MacCarthy in 1611 to meet the demands for admission at Bordeaux. Ancil-

lary centers to Bordeaux and Toulouse were also set up by MacCarthy. After 1654 the Irish students at Bordeaux and Toulouse were automatically granted French citizenship, and after ordination many settled permanently in France.

The Irish College of Nantes was founded during the Titus Oates Plot, and eventually became the second largest of all the Irish Colleges, with its enrollment of 80. It had its own professorial staff unlike the other Irish seminaries whose students attended lectures either in the universities or at Jesuit establishments. The Irish Colleges of Bordeaux, Toulouse, and Nantes lasted until the French Revolution.

The Irish College of Poitiers was never a seminary but rather a Jesuit boarding school for Irish boys, founded in 1674 through the munificence of Catherine, wife of Charles II. The College maintained its lay character to the end, although five burses for the education of students for the priesthood were available in the College in the 1730s. On the suppression of the Society of Jesus in France in 1762 these burses were acquired by the Irish College in Paris. What was saved from the royal foundation by the Jesuits helped later to purchase Clongowes Wood when the Society was restored.

ITALY

Although one of the smallest of the Irish seminaries in exile, the Irish College in Rome, the *Collegium Episcoporum,* became one of the most celebrated. It owed its existence to the munificence of Cardinal Ludovico Ludovisi (1595–1632), Protector of Ireland. By 1625 a small group of Irish students was being supported by the Cardinal at the English College, which was under Jesuit management. However, disputes between the Irish and English students necessitated the withdrawal of the former for whom Luke Wadding, the celebrated Franciscan, found a home near St. Isidore's. Thus the Irish College came into being on Jan. 1, 1628. Its first rector was a secular priest, and the students attended lectures in St. Isidore's with the young Franciscan scholastics. The government of the College was under the supervision of the Franciscan Order. Cardinal Ludovisi continued to support the students, but in his will, drawn up 16 months later, he entrusted the College to the Jesuits. This was disputed after his death, but a decree of the Rota in 1635 upheld the Cardinal's will.

The Irish College remained under the supervision of the Jesuits until 1772 when it was transferred to the management of the secular clergy. Suppressed by Napoleon in 1798, the College was restored in 1826. St. Oliver PLUNKET was an alumnus of this college.

IRISH HOUSES OF RELIGIOUS ORDERS

The most notable Irish houses of the religious orders abroad were those of the Franciscans at Louvain (1606), Prague (1629), and St. Isidore's, Rome (1625); of the Dominicans at Lisbon (1615), Louvain (1624), and San Clemente, Rome (1677); and of the Capuchins at Charleville (1615). The Franciscan College of St. Anthony and the Dominican College of Holy Cross were both affiliated to the University of Louvain. Both were closed and their property sequestrated in 1796. St. Anthony's was celebrated as the home of John Colgan, the hagiographer, and the collaborators of Michael O'Clery, compiler of the *Annals of the Four Masters*. The buildings of St. Anthony's were recovered by the Irish Franciscans in 1925, and serve once again as an Irish Franciscan house of studies. St. Isidore's and San Clemente in Rome are still held by the Franciscans and Dominicans respectively. The Irish Dominicans still serve the Church of Corpo Santo, Lisbon, on the site of the College, which was closed early in the 19th century.

It is universally admitted that the Irish Colleges in Europe were eminently successful in arresting the onrush of the Protestant Reformation in Ireland and in maintaining the Irish people in their allegiance to Rome. But the success of these colleges was conceived, born, and nurtured in trials and difficulties. There was the ever-present problem of finance. The income from foundations decreased alarmingly with the passing years and the declining value of money. The fact that many students after ordination chose to remain in Europe throws into greater relief the heroism of the majority who preferred to return and labor among their oppressed countrymen. The charge that too many students joined religious orders need not give rise to complaint. The religious orders were not permitted to maintain novitiates in Ireland, and it was inevitable that some students should choose the religious life abroad. In any event these Irishmen returned in due course to work in the Irish mission. The authorities in the Colleges had the ever-present problem of guarding their students against the pervasive doctrines of Jansenism and Gallicanism and, later, the arid philosophy of the 18th century. But it was Ireland's fortune that her priests brought back from the Irish Colleges what was best and most ennobling of European thought. Through these colleges Ireland maintained her place in the living stream of Catholic culture.

Bibliography: *Archivum Hibernicum,* Toulouse, 1 (1912) 122–147; Salamanca, 2 (1913) 1–36; 3 (1914) 87–112; 4 (1915) 1–58; 6 (1917) 1–26. Prague, 9 (1942) 173–294. Douai, 10 (1943) 163–210. Boulay, 11 (1944) 118–153. Douai and Antwerp, 13 (1947) 45–66. Low Countries, 14 (1949) 66–91. Bordeaux, 15 (1950) 92–141, Low Countries, 16 (1951) 1–39. Louvain, *ibid.* 40–61. San Clemente, Rome, 18 (1955) 145–149. Seville, 24 (1961) 103–147. J. MACERLEAN, "Richard Conway, S.J., 1573–1626," serialized in *Irish Monthly* 51–52 (1923–24). J. O'HEYN, *The Irish Dominicans of the Seventeenth Century,* tr. and ed. A. COLEMAN (Dundalk, Ire. 1902). P. BOYLE, *The Irish College in Paris from 1578 to 1901* (New York 1901).

[F. FINEGAN]

IRISH CONFESSORS AND MARTYRS

The history of the penal laws against Catholicism in Ireland may be said to date from 1536 when the parliament at Dublin, under pressure from HENRY VIII, passed legislation recognizing him as supreme head of the Church and, among other measures, ordered the suppression of the monasteries. In the following year the same parliament enacted further legislation, particularly an act that required an oath of clerics, degree candidates, and public officials stating they would "utterly renounce, refuse, relinquish, and forsake the Bishop of Rome and his authority, power, and jurisdiction." Such an oath, of course, was incompatible with membership in the Catholic Church. Contumacy, or the repeated refusal to take the oath when offered, could be punished by death. It became treasonable for the clergy and holders of public office to recognize the supremacy of the pope in spiritual matters.

Under Henry VIII. It has been much debated whether during the remainder of Henry's reign there was a religious persecution in Ireland, whether anyone suffered loss of fortune or liberty or life solely for acknowledging papal jurisdiction. The *Annals of the Four Masters,* under the year 1537, have the following well-known entry:

> They [i.e., the English schismatics] broke down the monasteries and sold their roofs and bells, so that from Aran of the Saints to the Iccian Sea [the English Channel] there was not one monastery that was not broken and shattered with the exception of a few in Ireland, of which the English took no notice or heed. They afterwards burned the images shrines and relics of the Saints of Ireland and England; they likewise burned the celebrated image of Mary at Trim, which was used to perform wonders and miracles, which used to heal the blind, the deaf and the crippled, and persons affected with all kinds of diseases; and [they also burned] the Staff of Jesus, which was in Dublin performing miracles from the time of St Patrick down to that time, and had been in the hands of Christ while he was among men. They also appointed archbishops and sub-bishops for themselves; and, though great was the persecution of the Roman emperors against the Church, scarcely had there ever come so great a persecution from Rome as this; so that it is impossible to narrate or tell its description, unless it should be narrated by one who saw it.

From the foregoing account it is evident that the religious susceptibilities of Catholic Ireland were deeply outraged by the destruction of the monasteries and the profanation of long-venerated relics. And it can be safely surmised that the destruction of the monasteries caused great suffering, hardship, and social dislocation for expelled religious and for the country as well. The monasteries were not simply abodes of study and prayer of the religious. They were schools, hospitals, and inns for wayfarers in remote areas. But the *Four Masters,* neither in the entry for 1537 nor in those for the rest of Henry's reign, makes any mention of persons who suffered imprisonment, loss of fortune, or death for refusing to recognize the royal supremacy.

The legislative machinery for persecution was certainly set in position by Henry and his subservient parliament in Dublin, but historical research has not hitherto established that such machinery was actually set in motion. It should be remembered that, at that time, the king's writ affected only one-third of Irish territory and that the old English settlers of the Pale and adjoining districts, whom Henry needed desperately to win over to his policy of conquest, proved thoroughly hostile to his religious innovation and unmistakably loyal to traditional obedience to Rome.

With the exception of the Spanish Trinitarian Domingo Lopez, historians of the penal times in Ireland have not attempted to portray the so-called Henrician persecution. Lopez's book, a laudatory account of the Trinitarian Order in the British Isles (Madrid 1714), has long been rejected by historians. According to Lopez, some 200 Trinitarians were put to death in Ireland during the period from 1539 to 1550, under circumstances of such publicity and revolting cruelty as could never have escaped the notice of the earlier Catholic annalists. In his earlier researches on the history of the religious persecutions in Ireland, Cardinal Moran all too uncritically accepted for truth the mischievous inventions of Lopez. But it is noteworthy that the cause of the Irish Trinitarians fabricated by Lopez was not submitted to Rome in 1907 when the causes of the Irish martyrs and confessors were forwarded by the Irish hierarchy for examination.

So far, only two causes of the Henrician period in Ireland are under consideration at the Holy See: (1) Ven. John Travers, Chancellor of St. Patrick's, Dublin, executed in 1535, during the rebellion of Silken Thomas. His cause has been presented with those of the English martyrs because it was believed, until recent times, that he was executed in London and not, as in fact he was, at Oxmanstown, Dublin. (2) The guardian and community of the Franciscan convent, Monaghan, beheaded by English soldiers in 1540. Their cause is discussed in the list below under the year 1589.

Under Edward VI. The Council of Regency, who were the real rulers during the reign of Henry's son and successor EDWARD VI, altered still further the doctrinal structure of the Church in England by superimposing Protestant doctrines on the schism of Henry. The Mass was rejected and the number of sacraments reduced from seven to two. Orders were transmitted to Ireland to conduct all future services as laid down in the Book of Common Prayer. Most of those in Ireland who had embraced Henry's schism—their numbers were quite insignificant—rejected outright the doctrinal errors being exported from England. For the next six years the Mass continued to be celebrated openly in the wide territories of the Irish chiefs. In the Pale and some towns of the English settlers a few priests preached the royal supremacy but otherwise continued in the old faith. Edward's successor, Mary Tudor, reconciled her dominions to the traditional obedience to the Apostolic See.

Under Elizabeth I. In 1560 Elizabeth exacted from the parliament at Dublin the enactment of legislation which reasserted the royal supremacy as claimed by Henry VIII. In addition, an Act of Uniformity was passed that obliged Irish Catholics to assist, under penalty of a fine, at the new heretical worship on Sundays and holy days.

ELIZABETH possessed little genuinely religious zeal, but she was anxious for the Protestantizing of Ireland as part of her plan to extirpate any national identity that the country had. Ireland, she decided, was to become English, culturally as well as politically subjugated to her own kingdom. After a generation of English control, the change in religion would be complete. So the religious legislation was not strictly enforced against the laity throughout her reign. Officials were advised not to provoke the resentment of the old English settlers, for without their good will it would have been almost impossible for her to maintain any grip on Ireland. That the Act of Uniformity stood little chance of being obeyed may be gauged from the fact that, even at the end of Elizabeth's reign, many officeholders had been able to discharge their duties without having taken the supremacy oath. By 1603 four-fifths of the peerage of Ireland were still Catholic.

After Elizabeth's excommunication (1570), the persecution of the faith in Ireland, which continued to the end of the reign, was directly aimed against the clergy. Many priests and bishops suffered the extreme penalty, yet the laity are also represented in the roll of honor for the period from 1572 to 1600. The martyrs and confessors who suffered at this time may be enumerated: eight bishops; 18 secular priests; 45 priests, lay brothers, and scholastics of the religious orders; and 26 lay persons, including one woman.

Under James I. The accession of JAMES I in 1603 bolstered the hopes of Catholic Ireland. In many of the populous centers public worship of the Church was once more set up but the Acts of Supremacy and Uniformity remained on the Statute Books. Throughout James's reign, the anti-Catholic laws were not strictly enforced against the laity but were sporadically set in motion, with considerable severity, against the clergy. King James was personally not inclined to enforce edicts against the priests, but the sovereign of England had really ceased to be the effectual master in his own house. For reasons of state, therefore, he had from time to time to order proclamations to be issued from Dublin Castle for the banishment of bishops and priests. But officials were instructed at the same time that while the priests, when discovered, might be transported, they should not be sought out or hunted down. The number of the clergy and laity who suffered during this reign amounts to hardly a quarter of the victims of Elizabeth: one bishop; six secular priests; nine religious; and seven laymen.

Under Charles I. Although some 34 persons died in prison or on the scaffold during the reign of Charles I, it should be noted that they were victims not of Charles himself but of the Parliamentarians. Early in the reign, Charles, a convinced Protestant, refused any relaxation of the Act of Uniformity but through "graces" granted in exchange for large monetary contributions to the royal treasury replaced the oath required by the Act of Supremacy with an oath of simple allegiance to the crown. This royal indulgence, as well as another concerning fixity of land tenure for those with undisturbed occupancy of 60 years, was purely unofficial and therefore revocable at the royal will. Officially the Acts of Supremacy and Uniformity remained the law of the land.

Under the Commonwealth. The persecution of the Church in Ireland under the Commonwealth (1649–60) far surpassed in ferocity that of Elizabethan days. In four years the number of its victims almost equaled that of Elizabeth's entire reign. Catholic worship was effectively outlawed. Apart from the clergy who suffered the extreme penalty, many died of hardship at home or on the high seas while being transported to exile or slavery to which they were condemned in the West Indies or American colonies. Countless thousands of nameless Catholic children and young people kidnaped throughout the Cromwellian regime for slave labor in the above-mentioned places were among the victims.

Restoration to 1714. From the Restoration (1660) to the death of Queen Anne (1714) no one, with the exception of St. Oliver PLUNKETT, was executed for the faith, but this period can point to its list of notable confessors.

Sources. While some information concerning the Irish martyrs and confessors is forthcoming from the State Papers, naturally distorted by the English anti-Catholic viewpoint, the main source of knowledge of the sufferers for the faith is derived from the various "martyrologies" drawn up from 1590 to 1629 and from 1659 to 1669. The Irish Jesuit John Howling (1539–99), founder of the Irish College in Lisbon, is the pioneer writer in this genre of history. His treatise compiled about 1590 was added to successively by Bl. Bp. Cornelius O'DEVANY (1611), Bp. David Rothe (1619), and two priests from Cork but living on the Continent, John Coppinger (1620) and John Molan (1629). At the end of the Commonwealth era, the Franciscan, Maurice Morison, published *Threnodia-Hiberno-Catholica,* and a decade later his colleague, Antony Bruodin, published *Propugnaculum* at Prague. Both Franciscan writers had had the experience of the mission in Ireland before they retired to the Continent. Bruodin, however, is not always to be regarded as a critical authority, perhaps because of the remoteness of his later place of residence.

The above-mentioned sources for the martyrology of Ireland during the penal times (1535–1714) are further amplified by the archives of various religious orders. A fairly full list of published works and MS sources is in the introduction to Father Denis Murphy's well-known work *Our Martyrs.*

The active persecution of the Catholic religion in Ireland ended with the death of Anne, although most of the penal laws remained unrepealed until the end of the 18th century. Throughout the century an appeal to Rome for recognition with public cult of the heroism of the Irish martyrs was thought inopportune. Indeed, until Catholic Emancipation in 1829, any move on the part of the Holy See to beatify the Irish who had suffered for the Catholic religion could have had only the result of inviting further penal legislation against the already heavily oppressed Catholics in Ireland.

Nearly a generation elapsed after Catholic EMANCIPATION before anything was done to revive interest in the cause of the Irish sufferers for the faith. However, Ireland, from 1830 to 1860 had many and immediate preoccupations: the Tithe War, the Repeal campaign of O'Connell and Young Ireland, the Great Famine, and the resulting exhaustion of the country in the 1850s. Also, throughout this period Catholic Ireland, after the disappearance of penal disabilities, was faced with the heavy task of building churches and schools.

Submission of Causes. The year 1861 saw the remote beginnings of the movement to present the cause of the Irish martyrs at Rome. In that year Dr. Moran (later cardinal) published his life of St. Oliver Plunket, a work designed to advance the cause of the martyr archbishop of Armagh. A few years later O'Reilly's *Memorials of Those Who Suffered for the Catholic Faith in Ireland* appeared. This work especially, together with Moran's reissue of the works of Bishop Rothe, focused attention widely on the desirability of submitting the cause of the Irish martyrs to the judgment of the Holy See. The Irish hierarchy soon afterward commissioned Denís Murphy, SJ, to prepare the necessary evidence for the *processus ordinarius informativus;* the result of his research, *Our Martyrs,* appeared posthumously in 1896. At the request of the Irish hierarchy, the archbishop of Dublin undertook the investigation of all the causes from every diocese in Ireland. The tribunal of investigation presided over by Abp. William Walsh held many sessions from 1903 to 1907. Its dossier, when dispatched to Rome on 16 March 1915, comprised some 292 causes (a few of them multiple). Of these, 11 were later rejected at Rome (mainly cases of confused identity) and 22 were deferred (for want of clearer evidence to show that imprisonment or death was inflicted principally for the profession of the faith) and are not included in the following lists. The lists reproduce those appearing in the *Irish Ecclesiastical Record,* 1918 (312–321), but, in some instances, changes with regard to year of death or other particulars established or cogently indicated by later research have been made.

Within the 20th century several Irishmen were raised to the honors of the altar. Only Oliver Plunket, beatified by Benedict XV, has been canonized (Oct. 17, 1975 by Paul VI). In 1929 Pope Pius XI beatified John Roche, John Cornelius (O'Mahony), John Carey, Patrick Salmon, and Ralph Corby with some of the English martyrs because they worked and were martyred in England.

A representative group of seventeen, known as Dermot O'Hurley and 16 Companions, were beatified Sept. 27, 1992 by Pope John Paul II. Blesseds in this group are indicated below by a †.

Chronological List of Confessors and Martyrs. This list covers the periods from Henry VIII to the death of Elizabeth I (1534–1603), the reign of James I (1603–25), the reign of Charles I, the Parlimentarians (1625–49), the Commonwealth (1649–60), and the Restoration to the death of Queen Anne (1660–1714).

> 1572 Edmund O'DONNELL (Daniel), Jesuit, first definitely recorded sufferer for the faith in Ireland under Elizabeth I; hanged, drawn, and quartered, Cork, October 25.
>
> 1575 Conor Macuarta (MacCourt), Rory MacConnell, and Fergal Ward, guardian, Franciscans; put to death at Armagh (*c.* 1575).

1576 Edmund Fitzsimon, Donough O'Rourke, and John O'Lochran, Franciscans; hanged at Down (*c.* 1576).

1577 William WALSH, bishop of Meath; d. in exile, Alcala. Thady O'Daly, Franciscan; hanged at Limerick. John O'Dowd, Franciscan of Moyne convent; put to death (or 1579).

1579 Bl. †Patrick O'HEALY, Franciscan, bishop of Mayo; hanged, Killmallock. Bl. †Cornelius O'Rourke, Franciscan; suffered with Bishop O'Healy. Abbot and brethren of Manisternenay, County Limerick, Cistercians; slain (probably 1579).

1580 Eugene Cronin, secular priest; executed, Dublin. Laurence O'Moore, secular priest; executed, Smerwick. John Kieran, of Tuam, Premonstratensian; hanged. Gelasius O'Cullenan, Cistercian, abbot of Boyle; hanged, Dublin. Daniel O'Neilan, Franciscan; slain at Youghal. William Walsh (Willick, etc.) and Oliver Plunket, laymen; executed with O'Moore.

1581 Richard French, secular priest; d. in prison, Wexford. Nicholas Fitzgerald, Cistercian; hanged, Dublin. Daniel (David) Sutton, his brother John, Robert Sherlock, Robert Fitzgerald, and William Wogan, laymen; executed, Dublin, May 26. Bl. †Matthew Lamport (Lambert), of Wexford, layman; arrested for harboring a Jesuit priest, hanged, July 5. [Lamport is sometimes described as a parish priest (pastor) of the Dublin Diocese, but was more probably a baker (pistor).] The "Wexford Martyrs": Bl. †Robert Meyler (Myler), Bl. †Edward Cheevers, John O'Lahy, and Bl. †Patrick Canavan (Cavanagh), all of Wexford, laymen and sailors; hanged for conveying priests and laymen to safety in France, July 5. Patrick Hayes, of Wexford, layman; d. on release from prison, Dublin. Maurice EUSTACE, nobleman and Jesuit novice in Flanders; hanged. Walter Aylmer and Thomas Eustace, with his son Christopher and brother Walter, laymen; hanged, Dublin.

1582 Aeneas Penny, secular priest; slain, Killagh. Philip O'Shea (O'Lea), Maurice O'Scanlon, and Daniel O'Hanrahan, Franciscans; slain at Lislactin. Charles MacGoran, Rory O'Donnellan, Peter O'Quillan, Patrick O'Kenna, James (John) Pillan, and Rory O'Hanlon, Franciscans; d. in prison, Dublin (*c.* 1582). Phelim O'Hara, Franciscan lay brother; strangled before the altar, Moyne convent (or 1578). Henry Delahoyde, Franciscan lay brother; said to have suffered with O'Hara. Thady O'Meran, Franciscan, guardian of Enniscorthy; d. under torture.

1584 Bl. † Dermot O'HURLEY, bishop of Cashel; tortured and hanged, Dublin. John O'Grady, secular priest; executed. Prior and brethren of Graiguenamanagh, Cistercians; slain. John O'Daly, Franciscan; d. under torture. Thady Clancy, of Ballyrobert, layman; beheaded, Limerick. Bl. † Eleonora Birmingham Ball, laywoman, only recorded woman sufferer for the faith in the Henrician and Elizabethan period; d. in prison, Dublin, July 5.

1585 Bl. †Maurice MacKenraghty (O'Kenraghty), secular priest; hanged, Clonmel, April 20. Patrick O'Connor and Malachy O'Kelly, Cistercians of the monastery of Boyle; hanged and quartered.

1586 Richard Creagh, bishop of Armagh; d. Tower of London. Donough O'Hurley, Franciscan, sacristan of Muckross convent; d. under torture.

1587 Maurice O'Brien, bishop of Emly; d. in prison, Dublin. John Cornelius, Franciscan of Askeaton convent; killed by English soldiers.

1588 Dermot O'Mulroney, Franciscan, guardian at Galbally, and two others, probably lay brothers; beheaded (or 1570; Rothe lists O'Mulroney among those who suffered in or after 1607). John O'Molloy, Cornelius O'Dogherty, and Geoffrey O'Farrell, Franciscans; hanged at Abbeyleix. Thady O'Boyle, Franciscan, guardian at Donegal convent; killed by English soldiers. Peter Meyler, layman; executed, Galway or Wexford, on his return from Spain.

1589 Patrick O'Brady (or Ward), Franciscan, guardian of Monaghan convent, and brethren; beheaded. [This is one of the most controverted of all the causes of the Irish martyrs. The *Annals of Lough Cé,* the *Annals of Connaught,* and the *Four Masters* all mention the massacre of the Monaghan community as of 1540. It is very unlikely that the alleged occurrence of 1589 could have escaped the notice of Howling, O'Devany, and Rothe. The last in his early priestly life was intimately associated with the neighboring (to Monaghan) Archdiocese of Armagh. The *Four Masters,* written some 15 years after the first mention by Coppinger and Ward of this 1589 massacre, make no allusion to it. No annalist could have failed to draw attention to a double massacre, i.e., in 1540 and 1589. The date 1540 vouched for by the Four Masters, who were Franciscans, seems to be the only acceptable one. There is the important consideration also that in that year the English forces penetrated to O'Neill's territory after their victorious rout of the Irish troops at Bellahoe.]

1590 Matthew O'Leyn, Franciscan, of Kilcrea convent, Muskerry; killed by English soldiers. Christopher Roche, of Wexford, layman; executed, London.

1591 Terence Magennis, Loughlin Mac O'Cagha, and Manus O'Fury, Franciscans; d. in prison. Michael Fitzsimon, of Fingall, layman; put to death.

1593 Edmund MacGauran, bishop of Armagh; slain at Tulsk.

1594 Andrew Stritch, secular priest; d. in prison, Dublin (*c.* 1594).

1596 Bernard Moriarty, secular priest, vicar-general; d. in prison, Dublin.

1597 John Stephens, secular priest, County Wicklow; hanged. Walter Fernan, secular priest, Diocese of Leighlin; d. under torture, Dublin.

1599 George Power, secular priest, vicar-general of Ossory; d. in prison, Dublin.

1600 John Walsh, secular priest, vicar-general of Dublin; d. in prison, Chester. Nicholas Young, of Trim, secular priest; d. in prison, Dublin. Thomas MacGreith (MacGrath), layman; beheaded.

1601 Redmund Gallagher, bishop of Derry; slain. Daniel Moloney, secular priest, vicar-general of Killaloe; d. under torture, Dublin. Donough Cronin, secular priest, cleric; hanged, Cork. John O'Kelly, of Connaught, secular priest; d. in prison, Dublin. Brian Murchertagh, secular priest, archdeacon of Clonfert; d. in prison, Dublin. Donough O'Falvey, secular priest; hanged, Cork.

1602 Bl. †Dominic COLLINS, Jesuit lay brother; hanged, Cork, October 31.

1603 Eugene MacEgan, bishop of Ross; slain. Patrick Browne, convert, alderman of Dublin; d. after suffering in prison (*c.* 1603).

The communities at Coleraine (21 members) and Derry (32 members), Dominicans; put to death at an unknown date in the reign of Elizabeth I.

1606 Bernard O'Carolan, secular priest, Diocese of Leighlin; hanged, Dublin. Eugene O'Gallagher, abbot of Assaroe, Donegal, and Bernard O'Treivir, Cistercians; slain by English soldiers. John Burke, lord of Brittas, layman; hanged, Limerick.

1607 John O'Luin (O'Lynn), Dominican; hanged.

1608 Donough O'Luin (O'Lynn), Dominican, prior of Derry convent, brother of John O'Luin (1607); hanged.

1609 Donough MacCreid, secular priest; hanged, Coleraine.

1610 John Lune (Lyng), of Wexford, secular priest; hanged.

1612 Bl. †Cornelius O'DEVANEY, bishop of Down and Connor; hanged, Dublin, February 1. Bl. †Patrick O'Loughran (O'Loughbrain, O'Lochran), secular priest from County Tyrone (some mention him as a Franciscan); hanged with Bishop O'Devaney.

1614 William MacGollen (Mac Giolla Choinne), of Coleraine, Dominican; d. of ill treatment by heretics.

1615 Laughlin O'Laverty, secular priest; hanged, Derry. Brian O'Neill, Art O'Neill, Rory O'Kane, Godfrey O'Kane, and Alexander MacSorley, laymen; hanged with O'Laverty, Derry.

1617 Thomas FitzGerald, Franciscan, commissary and visitator of the Irish province; d. in prison, Dublin. John Honan (MacConnan), of Connaught, Franciscan; hanged, Dublin (or 1618).

1618 Patrick O'Deery, secular priest; hanged, Derry.

1620 James Eustace, Cistercian; killed.

1621 Bl. † Francis Taylor (Tailler), mayor of Dublin, died of wounds from torture, January 30.

1622 John O'Cathan, Franciscan of Buttevant convent; d. in prison, Limerick.

1628 Edmund Dungan, bishop of Down and Connor; d. in prison, Dublin.

1642 Philip Cleray, of Raphoe(?), secular priest; slain. Malachy Shiel, Cistercian; hanged, Newry. Bl. † Peter Higgins (O'Higgin), Dominican, prior of Naas; hanged, Dublin, March 24. Cormac MacEgan, Dominican lay brother; hanged. Raymond Keogh, Dominican of Roscommon priory; hanged (or 1643). Stephen Petit, Dominican, sub-prior, Mullingar; shot (c. 1642). Hilary Conroy, Franciscan of Elphin convent; hanged Castlecoote. Fulgentius Jordan, Augustinian; hanged. Friar Thomas, Carmelite; hanged, Drogheda. Friar Angelus, Carmelite; killed, Drogheda.

1643 Edmund Mulligan, Cistercian; killed by soldiers, near Clones. Francis O'Mahony, Franciscan, guardian at Cork; hanged, before July 17. Peter, Carmelite lay brother; hanged, Dublin.

1644 Cornelius O'Connor and Eugene O'Daly, Trinitarians, returning from France; drowned at sea by Puritans. Hugh MacMahon, Ulster noble, layman; executed, Tyburn, November 22.

1645 Malachy O'Queely, archbishop of Tuam; killed by Parliamentarians, near Sligo. Augustine O'Higgin and Tadhg O'Connell, Augustinians; killed with O'Queely, October 26. Henry White, secular priest, aged 80; hanged, Racconnell, West-meath. Christopher Dunlevy, Franciscan; d. Newgate, London. Conor Maguire, baron of Enniskillen, layman; hanged, drawn, and quartered, Tyburn, February 20.

1647 Theobald Stapleton, secular priest, chancellor of church of Cashel, Theobald (misnamed Edward) Stapleton, and Thomas Morrissey, secular priests, vicars choral; killed in Cashel massacre,

September 13. Richard Barry, Dominican, prior; killed in Cashel massacre. John O'Flaverty, Dominican; killed, Coleraine. Richard Butler, Franciscan, and James Saul, lay brother; killed in Cashel massacre. William Hickey, Franciscan of Adare convent; slain. Nicholas Wogan, Franciscan; hanged, Dublin. William Boyton, Jesuit; killed in Cashel massacre. Elizabeth Kearney and Margaret of Cashel, laywomen; killed in Cashel massacre.

1648 Gerald Fitzgibbon, Dominican cleric and David Fox, lay brother; killed at Kilmallock. Donall O'Neaghtan, Dominican lay brother, Roscommon priory; killed. James Reilly, Dominican priest and poet; killed, near Clonmel.

1649 Thomas Bath, secular priest; killed in Drogheda massacre. John Bath, Jesuit; killed with his brother Thomas in Drogheda massacre. Dominic Dillon and Richard Oveton, Dominicans; killed in Drogheda massacre. Peter Costelloe, Dominican, of Straid; killed. Brian O'Gormley, Franciscan; hanged, Drogheda. Richard Synnot, John Esmond, Paul Synnot, Raymond Stafford, and Peter Stafford, Franciscans, and James Cheevers and Joseph Rochford, lay brothers; killed in Wexford massacre, October 11. Eugene O'Teevan (O'Leman), Franciscan; killed in Donegal convent (or 1650). Peter Taaffe, Augustinian; killed; in Drogheda massacre. Robert Netterville, Jesuit; killed in Drogheda.

1650 Ever (Heber) MACMAHON, bishop of Clogher; hanged, Enniskillen, September 17. Boetius Egan, Franciscan, bishop of Ross; hanged, Carrigadrohid. Francis FitzGerald, Franciscan; d. in prison, Cork (c. 1650). Anthony Hussey, Franciscan; hanged, Mullingar. Neilan Loughran, Franciscan; killed, Ulster (after 1650).

1651 Bl. †Terence Albert O'Brien, Dominican, bishop of Emly; hanged after siege of Limerick, October 31. Roger Normoyle (Ormilius), secular priest, of Brentire, County Clare; hanged. Hugh Carrighy, secular priest; hanged with Normoyle, 12 October. Myler MacGrath, Dominican; hanged, Clonmel. Laurence and Bernard O'Farrell, Dominicans; killed, Longford. Ambrose Aeneas O'Cahill, Dominican; killed, Cork. Edmund O'Beirne, Dominican; hanged, Jamestown. James Woulfe, Dominican; hanged after siege of Limerick. Gerard Dillon, Dominican; d. in prison, York. James Moran and Donough Niger, Dominican lay brothers; killed. William O'Connor, Dominican; killed, Clonmel. Thomas O'Higgin, Dominican; hanged, Clonmel. John O'Cullen, Dominican of Athenry convent; hanged, Limerick. Denis O'Neilan, Franciscan; hanged, Inchicronan. Tadhg O'Caraghy, Franciscan; hanged, Ennis. Jeremiah MacInerny and Daniel MacClanchy, Franciscan lay brothers; hanged, Quin. Roger MacNamara, Franciscan; killed, near Quin. Anthony O'Bruadair, Franciscan cleric; hanged, Turlevachan, County Galway. Donough Serenen, Augustinian, hanged. Raymond O'Malley and Thomas Tully, Augustinians, and Thomas Deir, lay brother; hanged (or 1652). Dominic Fanning, alderman and or of Limerick; Daniel O'Higgin, physician; Thomas Stritch, a former mayor; Major General Patrick Purcell; Geoffrey Galway, Member of Parliament for Limerick in 1634; Geoffrey Barron, nephew of Luke Wadding, OFM, and a member of the Supreme Council and agent of the Irish Confederation to France; all laymen; hanged after siege of Limerick, October 29–30. Donough O'Brien, nobleman, layman; burned alive by Parliamentarians, County Clare. James, Bernard, and Daniel O'Brien (brothers), laymen; hanged, Nenagh. Louis O'Ferral, layman; d. in prison, Athlone.

1652 Brian Fitzpatrick, secular priest, of Ossory; suffered for the faith. Philip Flatisbury, Franciscan; hanged, New Ross. Francis O'Sullivan, Franciscan provincial; shot, near Derrynane, June 23. Anthony O'Feral, Franciscan; killed, County Roscommon. Eugene O'Cahan, Franciscan, guardian of Askeaton; hanged, County Cork. John Ferall, Franciscan; killed. Bonaventure de Burgo, Franciscan; hanged. Walter Walsh, Franciscan; d. in prison, Dublin. Donough O'Kennedy, Augustinian; hanged. Tadhg O'Connor-Sligo, layman; hanged, Boyle. John O'Connor-Kerry, layman; hanged, Tralee. Bernard MacBriody, layman; hanged. Edward Butler, layman, son of Lord Mount-Garret; hanged, Dublin. Brigid D'Arcy, wife of Florence Fitzpatrick, laywoman; burned at stake, October, according to the more authoritative account of Ludlow. (She was victim of mendacious depositions taken in connection with the supposed Ulster massacre, 1641.)

1653 Daniel Delaney, secular priest, of Arklow; hanged, Gorey. Daniel O'Brien, secular priest, dean of Ferns; suffered with Delaney. Luke Bergin, Cistercian, of Baltinglass; hanged with Delaney and O'Brien. David Roche, Dominican, of Glenworth; d. in captivity, St. Kitt's. Brian O'Kelly, Dominican lay brother; hanged, Galway. Tadhg Moriarty, Dominican, prior of Tralee; hanged, Killarney. Hugh MacGoill, Dominican; executed, Waterford. Bl. † John Kearney, Franciscan; hanged, Clonmel, May 13. Theobald de Burgo, third viscount Mayo, layman; shot, Galway. Sir Phelim O'Neill, layman; hanged, drawn, and quartered, Dublin. Honoria Magan and Honoria de Burgo, Dominican tertiaries; d. of hardships while in flight from Puritan soldiers.

1654 Bl. †William TIRRY, Augustinian; hanged, Clonmel, May 12.

1655 William Lynch, Dominican, of Straid; hanged (before 1655).

1656 Fiacre Tobin, Capuchin; d. in captivity, Kinsale.

1659 Hugh MacKeon, Franciscan; d. on release from jail (after 1659).

1661 Brian Mac Giolla Choinne, Franciscan; d. in captivity(?), Galway.

1669 Raymond O'Moore, Dominican; d. in prison, Dublin.

1680 Peter Talbot, archbishop of Dublin; d. in prison (*see* TALBOT, PETER AND RICHARD).

1686 Felix O'Connor, Dominican; d. Sligo jail(?), c. 1686.

1703 John Keating, Dominican; d. in prison, Dublin.

1704 Clement MacColgan, Dominican; d. in Derry jail.

1707 Daniel MacDonnell, Dominican; d. Galway jail.

1708 Felix MacDonnell, Dominican; d. in prison, Dublin.

1710 John Baptist Dowdall, Capuchin, d. in prison, London.

1711 Father O'Hegarty (baptismal name unknown), secular priest; killed, according to tradition, by heretics, near Buncrana.

1713 Dominic Egan, Dominican; d. in prison.

Bibliography: D. MURPHY, *Our Martyrs* (Dublin 1896) excellent bibliog. xxiii–xxviii; there has been no major work on the subject since the publication of Father Murphy's book. Congregatio Sacrorum Rituum, *Positio super introductione causae . . . pro fide, uti fertur in Hibernia interfectorum* (Rome 1914). R. BAGWELL, *Dictionary of National Biography,* 14:773–74. BOURCHIER, *De Martyrio Fratrum Ord. Min.* (Ingolstadt 1583). W. M. BRADY, *The Episcopal Succession in England, Scotland, and Ireland, A.D. 1400 to 1875,* 3 v. (Rome 1876–77). A. BRUODIN, *Propugnaculum Catholicæ Veritatis* (Prague 1669). T. DE BURGO, *Hibernia Dominicana* (Cologne 1762). J. S. CRONE, *Concise Dictionary of Irish Biography,* rev. ed. (Dublin 1937). M. R. D'ARCY, *The Saints of Ireland* (St. Paul, Minn. 1985), 190–209. M. J. DORCY, *Saint Dominic's Family* (Dubuque, Iowa 1964), 412–14. J. T. GILBERT, *Dictionary of National Biography,* 14:864–65. GONZAGA, *De Origine Seraphic Religionis* (Rome 1587). M. B. HACKETT, "The Tirry Documents in the Augustinian General Archives," *Archivium Hibernicum* 20 (1957): 98–122. M. J. HYNES, *The Mission of Rinuccini . . .* (Dublin 1932). W. J. LOCKINGTON, *The Soul of Ireland* (New York 1920), 123–36. F. X. MARTIN, "The Tirry Documents in the Archives of France, Paris," *Archivium Hibernicum* 20 (1957): 69–97. M. MCALEESE, *The Irish Martyrs* (Ravensgate 1995). S. MCMANUS, *Story of the Irish Race* (New York 1944). H. P. MONTAGUE, *The Saints and Martyrs of Ireland* (Gerrards Cross, Ireland 1981):

78–88. CARDINAL MORAN, *Spicilegium Ossoriense* (Dublin 1874). S. Ó MURTHUILE, *A Martyred Archbishop of Cashel* (Dublin 1935). J. O'HEYN and A. COLEMAN, *Irish Dominicans of the 17th Century* (Dundalh 1902). M. O'REILLY, *Memorials of Those Who Suffered for the Catholic Faith* (London 1868); *Memoires of the Irish Martyrs* (New York 1869). O'SULLEVAN BEARR, *Patriciana Decas* (Madrid 1629). A. F. POLLARD, *Dictionary of National Biography,* 14:959. J. N. TYLENDA, *Jesuit Saints & Martyrs* (Chicago 1998) 357–59. A. J. WEBB, *Compendium of Irish Biography* (Dublin 1878).

[F. FINEGAN]

IRISH CROSSES

The sculptured standing stones and crosses of Early Christian Ireland form an impressive archeological and art-historical corpus. Some 50 survive from the period up to about A.D. 800. No single sequence of development stands out. Types are too varied, and contributing influences—from the eastern Mediterranean, Gaul, Pictish Scotland, and elsewhere in the British Isles—are too diverse and persistent. The earliest examples are rough stones incised with simple crosses and Celtic ornament in the primitive but elastic curvilinear style of the initials of the Cathach of St. Columba and date probably from the end of the 6th century. Examples are the Reask and Kilfountain pillars (both County Kerry). The simple 7-foot-high stele at Kilnasaggart (County Armagh) has a long-stemmed cross incised above, a longish Latin text in uneven rounded script incised in the middle, and an equal-armed cross with double-spiraled ends within a circle incised below. It can be dated around A.D. 700 by its inscription. In the 8th and 9th centuries more sophisticated monuments appeared. One type, paralleled in the Pictish areas of Scotland, is the tall slab, usually sculptured on both faces, with large interlace-filled crosses and animal or hunting scenes, or riding figures. Examples are the Carndonagh and Fahan Mura crosses (both County Donegal), and the panels from Banagher and CLONMACNOIS (both County Offaly). A Pictish-looking hunting scene occurs on the cross at Baelin (Westmeath). The high cross first appears in the late 8th century. Typically, it has a four-sided vertical shaft rising from a pyramidal base with a distinctive ringhead and a heavy stone circle, like a halo, surrounding the intersection of arms and vertical shaft. One of the finest, at Moone (County Kildare), is an elegant granite monument, over 16 feet high. It is carved with scenes that include the Twelve Apostles, the Flight into Egypt, the Crucifixion, the Temptation of St. Anthony, St. Paul and St. Anthony in the desert, the Three Hebrews in the Fiery Furnace, and a scene perhaps representing Christ in Majesty. The style is clear and assured, but the figures are no more than flat, doll-like narrative symbols. The styles of the figure carving vary, but

Muiredach's Cross, Monasterboice. (©Michael St. Maur Sheil/ CORBIS)

a flat profile rendering is usual. Stone-carving seems to have continued relatively unchanged through the period of Viking raids and settlement. A fine group of great crosses of the 10th century employs a wide range of scriptural subjects, as well as animal and other themes; a chief example is the Cross of Muiredach, nearly 18 feet high, at Monasterboice (County Louth). Another late group of 12th-century date shows large-scale figures of bishops and crucifixions. The crosses were set up as preaching stations in the countryside and were also regularly erected in and around monasteries. A monastic plan drawn in the Book of Mulling shows no less than ten.

Bibliography: H. S. CRAWFORD, *Handbook of Carved Ornament from Irish Monuments of the Christian Period* (Dublin 1926). A. K. PORTER, *The Crosses and Culture of Ireland* (New Haven 1931). E. H. L. SEXTON, *A Descriptive and Bibliograpical List of Irish Figure Sculpture of the Early Christian Period* (Portland, ME 1947). M. and L. DE PAOR, *Early Christian Ireland* (2d ed. New York 1960). F. HENRY, *La Sculpture Irlandaise,* 2 v. (Paris 1933);

Irish Art in the Early Christian Period (to 800 A.D.) (Ithaca, N.Y. 1965).

[R. L. S. BRUCE-MITFORD]

IRMENGARD, BL.

Abbess; b. Munich, Germany, c. 832; d. Chiemsee, July 16, 866. She was the granddaughter of Louis I the Pious, and the daughter of Louis the German and Hemma. Her father appointed her as abbess first of the Benedictine convent of Buchau and later of the royal Abbey of Chiemsee in Upper Bavaria. In the practice of the monastic life, Irmengard was a model of virtue and an example of penance. Her life was devoted to the care of the women under her tutelage. She was buried in the monastery church at Chiemsee. In 1004, Gerhard of Seeon wrote her epitaph (*Monumenta Germaniae Historica: Poetae* 5:327). Her cult was confirmed in 1928.

Feast: July 16 or 17.

Bibliography: *Acta Apostolicae Sedis* 21 (1929) 24–26. A. BUTLER, *The Lives of the Saints* 3:119. R. BAUERREISS, *Lexikon für Theologie und Kirche*, 10 v. (2d, new ed. Freiburg 1957–65) 5:758. R. GAZEAU, *Catholicisme* 6:100.

[A. CABANISS]

IRMGARDIS OF COLOGNE, ST.

Countess of Aspel; d. last quarter of the 11th century. Irmgardis expended her inheritance in founding churches, a cloister, and charitable institutions. According to a highly legendary vita, she resided as an ANCHORITE at Süchteln, where a chapel erected to her honor has stood since c. 1500. She moved to Cologne, where she lived the rest of her life, dedicating herself to works of charity. Three times she went on pilgrimage to Rome, and during the last she died. Her body was returned to Cologne, where it rests in a stone sarcophagus (dating from the first half of the 14th century) in the chapel of St. Agnes of the Cologne cathedral. The historical personality of Irmgardis is disputed. According to Oediger, Irmentrud of Aspel and Irmgardis of Cologne are the same person, to be distinguished from Irmgardis of Süchteln. Others claim that Irmgardis of Süchteln is Irmgardis of Cologne, a daughter of Irmentrud.

Feast: Sept. 4.

Bibliography: *Acta Sanctorum* Sept. 2:270–278. *Die Regesten der Erzbischöfe von Köln im Mittelalter*, ed. F. W. OEDIGER (Bonn 1954–) 1:1047, 1188. *Lexikon der deutschen Helligen. . .*, ed. J. TORSY (Cologne 1959) 254.

[C. R. BYERLY]

IRMHART, ÖSER

Theologian; d. Augsburg, latter half of the 14th century. After studying law in Bologna (1335), he became pastor in Sankt Marein (southern Steiermark), Austria, and (c. 1340) in Strassgang near Graz. In 1358 he was promoted to a canonry at Augsburg Cathedral. He translated the works of the Spanish Dominican ALFONSUS BONIHOMINIS into Latin (1339). He also translated from Arabic into German a treatise concerning the true Messiah and His Second Coming, the work of Rabbi Samuel, a convert from Judaism who had lived in Morocco in the mid-11th century. Approximately 30 manuscripts of the works of Irmhart, mostly those from around the middle of the 15th century, are extant.

Bibliography: W. STAMMLER, *Die deutsche Literatur des Mittelalters*, 1:671–673. H. MASCHEK, ''Zur deutschen & Übersetzungsliteratur des 14. Jahrhunderts,'' *Beiträge zur Geschichte der deutschen Sprache und Literatur* 60 (1936) 320–325 F. ZOEPFL, *Lexikon für Theologie und Kirche* 5:758.

[M. CSÁKY]

IRMINA, ST.

Benedictine abbess; d. Dec. 24, 710. Irmina's biography, written by THIOFRID OF ECHTERNACH 400 years after her death is today recognized as unreliable. He depicts her as the daughter of Dagobert I and affianced to a Count Herman, who was killed before their wedding day. Irmina is believed to be the foundress of the monastery of Öhren (*ad Horreum*) at TRIER, which she ruled as abbess in the last years of her life. A great benefactress of Irish and English monks, Irmina donated to WILLIBRORD and his monks the land for their monastery at ECHTERNACH. Despite Thiofrid's account, she may have been the mother of St. ADELA. Irmina was adopted as the patroness of the Diocese of Trier in the 14th century.

Feast: Dec. 30.

Bibliography: A. PONCELET, ''De fontibus vitae sanctae Irminae,'' *Analecta Bollandiana* 8 (1889) 285–286. M. WERNER, *Adelsfamilien im Umkreis der frühen Karolinger: die Verwandtschaft Irminas von Oeren und Adelas von Pfalzel* (Sigmaringen 1982). A. M. ZIMMERMANN, *Kalendarium Benedictinum: Die Heiligen und Seligen des Benediktinerorderns und seiner Zweige*, 4 v. (Metten 1933–38) 3: 450–452. A. HAUCK, *Kirchengeschichte Deutschlands*, 5 v. (9th ed. Berlin-Leipzig 1958) 1:280, n. 1. J. L. BAUDOT and L. CHAUSSIN, *Vies des saints et des bienheueux selon l'ordre du calendrier avec l'historique des fêtes* (Paris 1935–56) 12:638–639.

[L. MEAGHER]

IRNERIUS

(Or Guarnerius), jurist and founder of a school of glossators; b. Bologna, c. 1050; d. there, c. 1130. Little is known about this famous jurist's life and works. At the turn of the century his influence on medieval jurisprudence received attention justly deserved. At about age 20 he taught didactics and rhetoric at Bologna; and, encouraged by Countess Matilda of Tuscany, he devoted himself to the study of jurisprudence, principally through private studies. In 1084 he founded a school of jurisprudence at Bologna that gave great impulse to juridical studies throughout Europe. He was the first to introduce marginal glosses to expound Roman law, a custom that many followed. He defended the rights of Henry V in a papal election and the election of antipope Gregory VIII. Most of his works are not extant. His principal work, *Summa codicis,* is the first medieval system of Roman jurisprudence. This work was edited by Fitting (Berlin 1894). *Quaestiones de juris subtilitatibus* is generally ascribed to him. It, too, was edited by Fitting (Berlin 1894).

Bibliography: E. BESTA, *L'opera d'Irnerio: Contributo alla storia del diritto italiano,* 2 v. (Turin 1896). H. H. FITTING, *Die Anfänge der Rechtsschule zu Bologna* (Berlin 1888); "Die Summa Codicis und die Quaestiones des I.," *Zeitschrift der Savigny-Stiftung für Rechtsgeschichte, Romanistische Abteilung* 17 (1896) 1–96. F. K. V. SAVIGNY, *Geschichte des römischen Rechts im Mittelalter* 4:9–67, 447–470. F. SCHUPFER, *La scuola di Roma e la questione irneriana* (Rome 1898). F. PATETTA, *La Summa Codicis e la quaestiones falsamente attribite ad Irnerio* (Turin 1897). L. CHIAPPELLI, "I. secondo la nuova critica storica," *Rivista storica italiana* 11 (1894) 607–628. *Ius romanum medii aevi* (Milan 1961–) pt. 1. A. BERGER, *Encyclopedic Dictionary of Roman Law* (Trans. Amer. Philos. Soc. NS 43.2; Philadelphia 1953) 516. H. KANTOROWICZ and W. W. BUCKLAND, *Studies in the Glossators of the Roman Law* (Cambridge, Eng. 1938).

[T. D. DOUGHERTY]

IRRATIONALISM

An emphasis or overemphasis on that which is either opposed or alien to reason or on that which transcends reason. As a mental attitude, irrationalism distrusts reason and relies for certitude on feelings, emotions, instinct, intuition, will, desires, and experience. The basis of irrationalism is something encountered in experience that is refractory to logical reasoning and scientific systematization. Particular kinds of irrationalism are determined by their object, by the limitations of the knowing subject, and especially by what is meant by the term reason (Lat. *ratio*).

Kinds. In traditional terminology, reason or *ratio* may refer to the basis either of knowledge or of being, or it may refer to an intellectual process known as REASONING. When used in the first sense, its negative, the irrational, is the ontological abysmal; in the second sense, the irrational is the transintelligible that transcends and lies beyond rational knowability. The rational is thus not identical with the logical, nor the irrational with the alogical. The logical sphere is indeed the most rational, but since some regions of the real are transintelligible, the logical, too, can embrace elements that are irrational, for example, the concept of irrational number in mathematics. To the extent that the rational is characterized by its intelligibility and logical structure, the irrational can occur either as the transintelligible, as the alogical irrational, or as a combination of both—the "eminent irrational" of Nicolai Hartmann.

Philosophical irrationalism is based on the principle that being presents its paradoxes to understanding, that it has limitations for possible objectification, beyond which it becomes unintelligible for the knowing subject. The adherents of philosophical irrationalism maintain that it is impossible to comprehend the essence of individuals or of the world; that the world's origin, etc., will always remain a mystery. Thus any philosophy dealing with such objects must be ultimately irrational.

The irrational element is in the foreground also in the history of MYSTICISM. Mysticism does not attempt to penetrate mysteries by reason. It accepts the transintelligibility of its object and at the same time admits the limitations of the human subject. Although some mystics' profound knowledge made them utter *Cognosco unum Deo,* thus stating their version of the Credo, their insight resulted from experience rather than from reasoning—from intuition, ecstatic vision and the *amor dei intellectualis* rather than from ratiocination. Theirs was an *intellectio sine comprehensione.*

Early Forms. The history of philosophical irrationalism began with the history of ideas. Early Greek thinkers encountered the problem of the irrational in dealing with MATTER, for matter is knowable only through form. SOCRATES spoke of the mysterious δαιμόνιον, the nonobjectifiable remnant of the irrational in man that can occur at any moment in life; it does not give clarity, and does not speak as the Logos does. This Socratic teaching was directed against Protagoras, who held that "man is the measure of all things," a criterion purely subjective, hence to a marked degree irrational.

PARMENIDES and the Stoics shunned the irrational, but Poseidonius (*c.* 135–50 B.C.), himself a Stoic, reacted against their theory and admitted irrational elements. He spoke of an unconscious region in the soul and held that not all psychic events, experiences, and functions are rational. The great variety and complexity of the affective life in man seemed to him incomprehensible; such irrational forces and functions he regarded as rooted in man's nature. PLOTINUS saw in his highest form a transintelligibility that reaches beyond objectivity and subjectivity; in his view a finite spirit is not able to apprehend the living unity of the One.

The Aristotelian influence on St. THOMAS AQUINAS manifested itself in a negative attitude toward the irrational; the unformed and the unlimited, for Aquinas, belong in the realm of mere potency. The human soul, in contrast to the soul of the animals, is rational even in its hidden vital functions. "The sensible soul in man is not irrational; it is at once sensible and rational" (*De anim.* 9 ad 15).

Reaction to Rationalism. The period of the EN-LIGHTENMENT, characterized by efforts to proclaim reason the absolute ruler of man, was initiated in Germany by G. W. LEIBNIZ and reached its peak in the *Critiques* of I. KANT. Such radical RATIONALISM gave rise to strong opposition. In Kant's own system the avenues to God are open only to faith. The thing-in-itself is unknowable; PHENOMENA alone reveal it. Later some of the phenomena—human emotions, desires and experiences, historical events, the essence and the importance of the individual, religious belief and its impact on reason—became objects of doubt. The neglect of such aspects of reality provoked a strong reaction from the metacriticism of Hamann and Jacobi, from Herder and from their followers.

J. G. HAMANN (1730–88) emphasized feeling, experience, and faith. Reason had caused the Kantian split of knowledge into sensuality and intellectuality; but such disunity is not seen in the real order, where all opposites coincide. Consequently, truth is found in man's experience of reality rather than in speculative analysis. The firm conviction of the subject suffices as the criterion of truth.

J. G. HERDER (1744–1803) saw all of creation in a state of strife as well as in continuous renaissance and increasing harmony. Reason is the aggregate of the educative process of the human race. There is no "pure" reason; it is the same soul that "thinks and wills, that understands and senses, that reasons and wants."

F. H. JACOBI (1743–1819) defied the systematic philosophical thinking of Kant and defended the right of faith and its simultaneously given certainty. He distinguished between the knowing of the intellect and the immediate insight of faith. The proper essence of man is spirit, present in man's deepest consciousness. Analogously, God is present in the heart of man. For Jacobi the strength of the impressions of sensible, relative beings is greatly surpassed by those of the immaterial, absolute object. "But whenever I want to express what I know through the heart, the divine light extinguishes."

Reaction to Idealism. The absolute IDEALISM of G. W. F. HEGEL, in which "the world spirit carries on a conversation with itself in pure philosophy," provoked another irrationalist trend as represented in the teachings of Schopenhauer, Maine de Biran, and Kierkegaard.

A. SCHOPENHAUER (1788–1860) took the "experience of the will as experience of the world." Man's will awakens to self-consciousness; this is transformed into the idea that it is everlasting desire. The will is the world will; since this is blind, the whole world becomes irrational.

MAINE DE BIRAN (1766–1824) concentrated on an analysis of thinking and knowing. He maintained that the primary evidence of consciousness is the voluntary effort of the will and the resistance it encounters. In this resistance, the SELF experiences its limitations and thereby comes to an awareness of the irrational.

S. A. KIERKEGAARD (1813–55) opposed speculative philosophy and abstract thought, especially that of Hegel. He taught that all existence is in process, but that only individuals exist. Hence cognition can aim to know the individual only in his temporary setting; thought must originate in the nucleus of personality. Mathematical, speculative and historical reasoning do not show such a capability. Existence is always unfinished; therefore, existential thinking can never be systematized. Man has to face the paradoxes of the irrational, but he strives with great passion, nonetheless, to discover something that thought cannot think.

Later Variations. In addition to these reactions to rationalism and idealism, other forms of irrationalism manifested themselves in the 19th and 20th centuries. Among these, mention should be made of evolutionary historicism, individualism, philosophies of life and spirit and metaphysical irrationalism, as well as of existentialism.

Evolutionary Historicism. Evolutionary HISTORI-CISM considers understanding possible only from the viewpoint of historical existence. Historicity is the determining trait of the real, appearing as the highest level of the union of idea and extramental reality. Both idealism and irrationalism contribute to this current, developed by W. Dilthey, E. TROELTSCH, G. Misch; B. Groethuysen, E. Spranger, M. Frischeisen-Köhler, H. Freyer and E. Rothacker.

Individualism. Individualism places stress upon the particular and the unique. Some of its forms are the aesthetic, cultural and humanitarian individualism taught by F. SCHLEGEL and F. D. E. SCHLEIERMACHER; the enthusiastic individualism of Shaftesbury (1671–1713) that led to the individualism of genius, with the irrational factor explaining the uniqueness of effects; and finally, the dynamism of the period of *Sturm und Drang* (c. 1760–85) in the German cultural movement.

Philosophies of Life and Spirit. F. W. NIETZSCHE and H. BERGSON are exponents of LIFE PHILOSOPHIES that place emphasis on vital process, experience and intuition. Bergson sees the innermost metaphysical unity of the world, of man and of life in terms of his distinction between *entendement* (understanding) and *conscience* (awareness). Categorizing the intellect, in his view, falsifies insight; thus, to understand the inner unity of reality of life, intellection must be cut off. The intellect does not see the true world, but grasps only the material and the spatial—the world in its decay. Hence, the intellect deceives; that reality is life and movement is grasped by intuition alone.

B. CROCE, combining Vico's and Hegel's philosophies of the spirit, aimed at a cosmopolitical theory. He elevated aesthetical experience to the basic function of the spirit, and joined historicism with aestheticism to give new scope to irrationalist insights. Following Croce, G. GENTILE offered a theory of actual idealism that considered the individual as endowed with ineffable properties traceable to spontaneity and activity in vital and spiritual realms (*see* SPIRIT, MODERN PHILOSOPHIES OF).

Metaphysical Irrationalism. Metaphysical irrationalism maintains that some areas of reality remain inaccessible to reason. Knowledge in its essence, progress, and goal is rational; but it results from an "irrational given" that directs the process of rationalization and constantly limits it, especially in the realm of value, NOUMENA and eschatological truth. The perception of the irrational given in its manifoldness and transintelligibility may be called "irrational knowledge," in the terminology of R. Müller-Freienfels (1882–1949). As soon as order, coherence, meaning and significance touch the "web," logos is present. The criterion of the rationality of the real is then precisely that reality is (or becomes) ordered, coherent, meaningful, and purposive.

Nicolai HARTMANN (1882–1950) considered the irrational to be transintelligible, the APORIA in the classical Greek sense. Although the irrational exists for man, nothing irrational exists as such. The transintelligible realm, with its perennial questions, is the true field of metaphysics; it proves inexhaustible. Dealing with these problems, human reason discovers its own limits, thereby demonstrating that the world is not adapted to man's cognitive endowment. The latter, however, is adaptable to the world, and must be so—for noetic orientation is one of man's vital functions.

Existentialism. The existentialists (for example, M. Heidegger, K. Jaspers, and J. P. Sartre) returned in some form to Protagoras's SUBJECTIVISM; the understanding and interpreting of existence and existents is relative to man, who is again "the measure of all things." Jaspers speaks of "philosophical faith" that obtains access to God, whereas Max SCHELER assigns to religious knowledge a special domain that is inaccessible to philosophical reasoning.

Somewhat related is the *sensus numinis* of Rudolf OTTO, a feeling or experience of something mysterious and holy. It is the *mysterium tremendum* that lies beyond reason, beyond the good and the beautiful and is the object of the *sensus numinis;* this a priori category signifies an absolutely unique state of mind, that of the genuinely religious person experiencing the bliss of heaven (*see* EXISTENTIALISM; PHENOMENOLOGY).

Influence. The rationalism of the 18th and 19th centuries found its countermovements in the irrational trends of PIETISM, spiritual positivism, SENTIMENTALISM and ROMANTICISM. It was opposed by the metacriticism of Jacobi and Hamann, and by the different kinds of mysticism and occultism. Their influence, although strong, was not strong enough to overcome rationalism. Thus the modern era remains rationalist in inspiration; the purest form of this is science and the latter's application in technology and education. Rationalism rather than irrationalism will dominate Western culture as long as science influences education, public life, its economy and politics, its progress and movements and branches out into all the cells of its modern society.

See Also: ABSURDITY; NONBEING; PESSIMISM.

Bibliography: J. D. COLLINS, *A History of Modern European Philosophy* (Milwaukee 1954). J. HIRSCHBERGER, *The History of Philosophy,* tr., A. N. FUERST, 2 v. (Milwaukee 1958–59). F. C. COPLESTON, *History of Philosophy* (Westminster, Md 1946–). R. EISLER, *Wörterbuch der philosophischen Begriffe,* 3 v. (4th ed. Berlin 1927–30) 1:780–783. R. CRAWSHAY-WILLIAMS, *The Comforts of Unreason* (London 1947). H. LÄUBIN, *Studien zum Irrationalitätsproblem* (Halle 1941). R. MÜLLER-FREIENFELS, *Irrationalismus* (Leipzig 1922); *Metaphysik des Irrationalen* (Leipzig 1927). J. VÖLKELT, "Der Begriff des Irrationalen," *Jahrbuch der Schopenhauer-Gesellschaft,* 8 (1919) 55–93. N. HARTMANN, *Grundzüge einer Metaphysik der Erkenntnis* (4th ed. Berlin 1949).

[C. E. SCHÜTZINGER]

IRVING, EDWARD

Founder of the CATHOLIC APOSTOLIC CHURCH; b. Annan, Scotland, Aug. 4, 1792; d. Glasgow, Dec. 7, 1834. After receiving his M.A. in 1809 from Edinburgh University, he taught school at Haddington while studying Presbyterian theology part time. In 1819 he became assistant at St. John's parish, Glasgow, and in 1822 he accepted a call to London's Caledonian Chapel. His dramatic sermons filled the chapel, and later a new church was built for him in Regent Square. Several sources molded Irving's theology: the views of Samuel Taylor COLERIDGE on the Holy Spirit and the restoration of "apostolic gifts,'' as well as the writings of Lacunza, a Spanish ex-Jesuit, directed him toward MILLENARIANISM, and Irving joined the Albury Circle, which stressed the signs of Christ's Second Coming. When the Presbyterian General Assembly censured his writings on Christ's human nature, Irving and his followers prayed for the gifts of the Holy Spirit, which they claimed soon appeared. In 1832 Irving was dismissed by the London presbytery, but he established another congregation. The following year he was unfrocked by the Annan presbytery, but his congregation readmitted him as a deacon, lowest order in the emerging Catholic Apostolic Church. He died disillusioned with that group's hierarchy. Five volumes of his *Collected Writings* appeared from 1864 to 1865.

Bibliography: A. L. DRUMMOND, *Edward Irving and His Circle* (London 1937), T. CARLYLE, *Reminiscences,* ed. C. E. NORTON (New York 1932).

[E. E. BEAUREGARD]

ISAAC BEN ABRAHAM

Eminent Karaite physician, apologist, and polemical writer, and powerful opponent and disputant of the doctrines and dogmas of Christianity whose work in defense of Judaism titled *Ḥizzuk Emunah* (Strengthening of the Faith) gave rise to violent controversies within Christian circles; b. Troki, Province of Vilna, Lithuania, 1533; d. Troki, 1594 (or 8 years earlier in both cases; see Mann, 726, 1475). From the name of his native town he is commonly known as Troki.

As a student of the Karaite Ḥazzan and Ḥakham Zephaniah ben Mordecai, he became highly competent in Biblical studies and Hebrew literature. For his knowledge of Polish and Latin he was indebted to Christian scholars. Through them he gained access to the Christian community and was able to count Christians of all faiths and sects among his closest associates. Soon Troki found himself enveloped in religious controversy and challenged to participate in heated debates. He therefore studied Christian theology in general and read the NT extensively. He became familiar with the religious writings of his contemporaries and with the tenets of the various Christian sects. Troki felt that he must make manifest the truths of Israel's faith. In the preface to his famous apology he stated:

> I refer my coreligionist to the attentive perusal of *Ḥizzuk Emunah,* wherein he will find an ample supply of arguments and proofs in favor and support of our venerable creed. . . . I have endeavored to arraign before the tribunal of common sense the assertions made by Christians which tend to throw discredit on the truths of the Jewish Faith. For this purpose, I found it advisable to subdivide this work into two parts. The first portion is devoted to an examination of the objections raised by Christians against our religion, and to the proofs cited by them for the corroboration of their own doctrines. The refutation I have given it is, in many cases, based on the contradictory nature of their own statements. The second portion comprises a careful review and refutation of the glaring inconsistencies that are discoverable in the New Testament.

Death had summoned Troki before the completion of his work. On his deathbed, however, he had commissioned his favorite disciple, Joseph ben Mordecai Malinovski, to supply the missing preface and index and prepare the work for publication. Spanish authors of a previous period (e.g., Profiat DURAN) had contributed equally significant books in defense of Judaism, but none could compare with the extensive popularity of the *Ḥizzuk Emunah.* For years it remained in manuscript, and interested readers and copyists felt inclined to modify, amplify, or change the text in accordance with their own views and beliefs. One such corrupted manuscript that had been written by a rabbinite who had substituted Talmudical concepts for Troki's philosophical arguments came into the possession of the Hebraist Johann Christoph Wagenseil (1633–1705). Wagenseil published it (Altdorf 1681) with a Latin translation under the startling title of *Tela Ignea Satanae* (The Fiery Darts of Satan). Thus he helped to publicize it and to propagate its contents, although this may not have been his desire; and the extensive and violent refutations that he had supplied with his edition served only to fan the flames of controversy and cause passionate debates among Christians. Eventually, the free-thinkers and anticlerical philosophers of the 18th century quoted freely from Troki's writings in their campaign against Christianity. To VOLTAIRE, for example, the *Ḥizzuk* was ''a masterpiece in the treatment of its subject.'' In addition to Wagenseil's Latin edition, the book was translated into Judeo-German (Amsterdam 1717), into English by Moses Mocatta (London 1851), and into German by David Deutsch (Sohran 1865, 2d ed. Breslau 1873).

Bibliography: J. MANN, *Texts and Studies in Jewish History and Literature,* v.2 (Philadelphia 1935) 714–720, 726, 1475. I. BROYDÉ, *The Jewish Encyclopedia,* ed. J. SINGER, 13 v. (New York 1901–06) 12:265–266. L. NEMOY, *Universal Jewish Encyclopedia,* 10 v. (New York 1939–44) 10:311. S. M. DUBNOW, *Weltgeschichte des jüdischen Volkes,* 10 v. (Berlin 1925–29). A. M. GOLDBERG, *Lexikon für Theologie und Kirche,* ed. J. HOFER and K. RAHNER, 10 v. (2d, new ed. Freiburg 1957–65) 5:773.

[N. J. COHEN]

ISAAC ISRAELI

Son of Solomon, Jewish physician and philosopher, also known as Isaac Judaeus; d. *c.* 932. Isaac was a native of Egypt who emigrated to Qayrawān (in modern Tunisia) about 907 and became a physician to the Fatimid Caliph 'Ubayd Allah al-Mahdi. According to some authorities he died shortly before 932, but other accounts (of doubtful authority) imply that he was alive at later dates. His medical treatises, e.g., the *Book of Fevers,* the *Book of Urine,* the *Book of Foodstuffs and Drugs,* all written in Arabic, were long considered classics, and translated into Hebrew and Latin, giving their author fame among Muslims, Jews, and Christians. His medical reputation was somewhat overshadowed in the West by his Latin translator, CONSTANTINE THE AFRICAN. Constantine's work, completed by 1087, best described as a paraphrase of Isaac's writings, received wide currency in medieval schools of medicine, as attested by surviving MSS.

As a philosopher, Isaac's inspiration was mainly Neoplatonic. The writings of the Muslim philosopher al-KINDĪ ABŪ YŪSUF and a Neoplatonic treatise ascribed to Aristotle (Ibn Hasday's *Neoplatonist*) were the main influences on his philosophy. His writings in this field assumed the form of short treatises in Arabic: the *Book of Definitions* (Latin translation by Gerard of Cremona, two Hebrew translations); the *Book of Substances,* extant in fragmentary form; the *Book on Spirit and Soul,* in which Neoplatonic psychology is given Biblical foundation; a text known as *Chapter on the Elements* (in Hebrew translation only); and a somewhat longer treatise, *Book of the Elements* (extant in a Latin version by Gerard of Cremona, and two Hebrew versions). Whereas among the Muslim philosophers Israeli had no influence, his work seems to have been generally known among the Jewish Neoplatonists of Spain, although a more strictly Aristotelian philosopher of the rank of MAIMONIDES had naturally little sympathy with Israeli's somewhat primitive Neoplatonism. The texts available in Latin were used by schoolmen such as DOMINIC GUNDISALVI, ALBERT THE GREAT, and THOMAS AQUINAS.

Bibliography: *Omnia Opera Ysaac* (Lyons 1515). M. STEINSCHNEIDER, *Die hebräischen Übersetzungen des Mittelalters* (Berlin 1893); *Die arabische Literatur der Juden* (Frankfurt A. M. 1902). C. BROCKELMANN, *Geschichte der arabischen Literatur,* 3 v. (Leiden 1937–42). G. SARTON, *Introduction to the History of Science* (Baltimore 1927–48) v.1. A. ALTMANN and S. M. STERN, *Isaac Israeli: A Neoplatonic Philosopher of the Early Tenth Century* (London 1958). J. SCHMID, *Lexikon für Theologie und Kirche,* ed. J. HOFER and K. RAHNER (Freiberg 1957–65) 5:773.

[S. M. STERN]

ISAAC OF MONTE LUCO, ST.

Also known as Isaac of Spoleto, hermit; d. after mid-sixth century. He was a native of Syria who fled the Monophysite persecution and became a recluse for about 50 years in the caves of Monte Luco outside Spoleto, Italy. He was much honored by the Spoletans, in whose behalf he reputedly worked certain wonders. After spending some years in the eremitical life, he had a vision of Our Lady, who bade him to gather followers and to train them in asceticism. He never actually founded a monastery, but directed a kind of LAURA, or colony of hermits. Little is known of him except from the third book of the Dialogues (3.14) of St. GREGORY THE GREAT (*Patrologia Latina,* ed. J. P. Migne 77:244–248).

Feast: April 11; April 15 (Spoleto).

Bibliography: *Acta Sanctorum* April 2:27–30, contains also the pertinent section from *Gregorianum, Dialogi. Bibliotheca hagiographica latina antiquae et mediae aetatis,* 2 v. (Brussels 1898–1901; suppl. 1911) 1:4475.

[W. A. JURGENS]

ISAAC OF STELLA

Cistercian abbot, philosopher, theologian; b. England *c.* 1100; d. Étoile (Stella), near Chauvigny *c.* 1169. Isaac provides many details of his life in his works [*Patrologia Latina,* ed. J. P. Migne, 217 v. (Paris 1878–90) 194:1689–1893]. It is likely he began his ecclesiastical career in the curia of Theobald of Canterbury, and he probably studied theology at Paris (cf. *Sermon* 48; 1853D). A love of solitude (*Sermon* 14; 1737B) drew him to Cîteaux, where he may have been received in 1145. Isaac was probably already a priest, for in 1147 he was chosen abbot of Stella, an abbey that had joined the Cistercian reform, under Pontigny, only two years before. Many of Isaac's sermons or conferences as abbot contain references to a sojourn on a solitary island, Ré, about two miles from La Rochelle, where he had led a group of hardy monks to establish a new foundation. The most striking of his sermons is a series given at Ré during the week of Sexagesima. In them Isaac sought to provide better spiritual food for Lent by setting before his monks a course of theology comparable to the *Proslogion* of St. Anselm of Canterbury and deeply influenced by St. Augustine and Pseudo-Dionysius. For Isaac, monastic life was based on the Incarnation, the KENOSIS, the Mystical Body, Divine Sonship—themes to which he constantly returns.

In 1162 Isaac wrote his epistle on the soul at the request of ALCHER OF CLAIRVAUX (*Patrologia Latina,* 194:1875–90). This work was indirectly influential through its use in the famous *De spiritu et anima* (*Patrologia Latina,* 40:779–832), once attributed to Augustine but now considered, without great reason, as the work of Alcher. The epistle follows the Cistercian tradition, wherein a writer usually accompanied his spiritual works with a tract on man or the soul to provide the psychological basis for his mysticism. Isaac situates the soul midway between God and corporeal things in the hierarchy of being. He treats of the simplicity of the soul and the relation of the soul to its powers; enumerates the five cognitive powers as sense, imagination, reason, intellect, and intelligence; and explains their use as steps to wisdom (*Patrologia Latina,* 194: 1880B; cf. *Sermon 4,* 1702A). He also considers the union of soul and body, and says it takes place in the imagination, the *phantasticum animae* (*Patrologia Latina,* 194: 1881C) (*see* SOUL, HUMAN).

Isaac may also have written commentaries on Ruth and on the Canticle of Canticles, but the only other published work is the *De officio missae,* written about 1167 [*Patrologia Latina,* 194:1889–93; *Recherches de théologie ancienne et médiévale* 4 (1932) 135–37].

Bibliography: F. P. BLIEMETZRIEDER, "Isaak von Stella. I: Beiträge zur Lebensbeschreibung," *Jahrbuch für Philosophie und spekulative Theologie* 18 (1904) 1–34, and "Isaac de Stella: Sa spéculation théologique," *Recherches de théologie ancienne et médiévale* 4 (1932) 134–159. L. BOUYER, *The Cistercian Heritage,* tr. E. A. LIVINGSTONE (Westminster, Md. 1958). G. B. BURCH, *Early Medieval Philosophy* (New York 1951). B. MCGINN, *Golden Chain: A Study in the Theological Anthropology of Isaac of Stella* (Washington, D.C. 1972).

[I. C. BRADY]

ISAAC THE GOOD OF LANGRES, ST.

Bishop; b. first half of the ninth century; d. Langres, France, 880. Isaac was a contemporary of Charles the Bald (840–877), who assigned to him the reconstruction of the monastery of Saint-Bénigne in Dijon, which the Normans had destroyed. Charles gave Isaac the right to mint coins for Dijon and Langres. Isaac took part in the Councils of Soissons and TROYES. He composed a collection of diocesan statutes in 11 titles (*Canones seu selecta capitula*), taken from the capitulary of BENEDICT THE LEVITE. Isaac was bishop of Langres from 859 until his death. He is interred in Saint-Bénigne.

Feast: July 18.

Bibliography: *Patrologia Latina,* ed. J. P. MIGNE, 217 v. (Paris 1878–90) 124:1075–1110. J. D. MANSI, *Sacrorum Conciliorum nova et amplissima collectio,* 31 v. (Florence-Venice 1757–98); reprinted and continued by L. PETIT and J. B. MARTIN, 53 v. in 60 (Paris 1889–1927; repr. Graz 1960–) 17B:1233–82. *Histoire Littéraire de la France* (Paris 1733–68) 5:528–. P. FOURNIER

and G. LEBRAS, *Histoire des collections canoniques en occident depuis les fausses décrétales jusqu'au Décret de Gratien,* 2 v. (Paris 1931–32) 1:206. A. VAN HOVE, *Commentarium Lovaniense in Codicem iuris canonici 1,* v.1–5 (Mechlin 1928–); v.1, Prolegomena (2d ed. 1945) 1:185. A. WERMINGHOFF, "Verzeichnis der Akten fränkischer Synoden von 843–918," *Neues Archiv der Gesellschaft für ältere deutsche Geschichtskunde* 26 (1900) 670.

[M. CSÁKY]

ISAAC THE GREAT, ARMENIAN CATHOLICOS, ST.

C. 388 to 439; b. Cappadocia, c. 345; d. Belrotzatz, Sept. 7, 439. The son of NERSES THE GREAT (d. 373) and a relative of GREGORY THE ILLUMINATOR, Isaac was educated in the Hellenistic culture at Caesarea in Cappadocia and at Constantinople. He married and had a daughter named Sahaganush, whose son became the military captain Vardan Mamikonian. Isaac embraced the religious life, probably after the death of his wife, became catholicos of Armenia, and gave great impulse to the development of monasticism in that country. He turned the patriarchal palace into a monastery and is said to have frequently retired to a wilderness with his disciples to spend time in solitary prayer. He set about reforming clerical discipline and selected as his auxiliary bishop the monk MESROP MASHTOTZ (391), who is alleged to have aided him in the formation of a native liturgy and ritual, as well as in the translation of the Scriptures into Armenian (435–436).

In a synod, apparently at Ashtishat in 435, Isaac condemned as heretical the teaching of THEODORE OF MOPSUESTIA and Diodore of Tarsus. Despite his sympathy for the Hellenistic culture of the West, Isaac managed to get along with the Persian rulers of Armenia and won many privileges for his Catholic subjects. He resigned his see rather than become involved in the political activities of the Armenian princes (428 to 432). Tradition credits him (probably unjustifiably) with the composition of the liturgical hymns for Thursday and Friday of Holy Week, the translation of the Pentateuch and Isaiah, and the formation of ecclesiastical canons, as well as an epistolary exchange with the Byzantine Emperor and the patriarch of Constantinople. He was buried at Ashtishat. Three of his letters are preserved in Moses of Khoren, *History of Armenia Major* (3.57); other letters, ed. J. Izmiveantz, *Book of Letters* (Tiflis, 1901), in Armenian.

Feast: Thursday after the third Sunday after Assumption; in Orthodox church, Sept. 9; Nov. 25 (St. Sahak).

Bibliography: MOÏSE DE KHOREN, *Histoire de l'Arménie,* tr. V. LANGLOIS (Paris 1869) 153, 160–173. R. GROUSSET, *Histoire de l'Arménie* (Paris 1947) 171. J. DE MORGAN, *Histoire du peuple ar-*

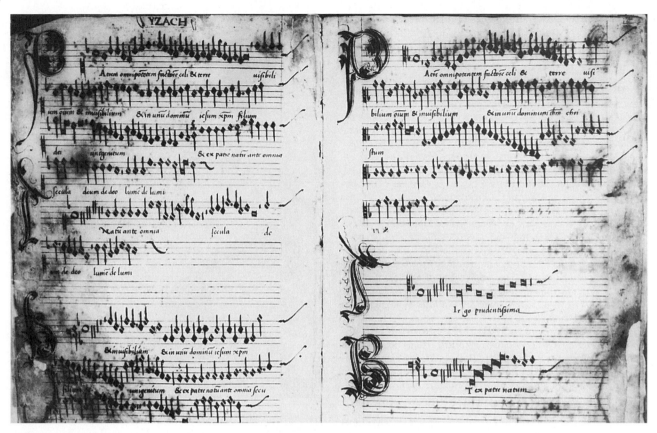

"Virgo Prudentissima," two folios from manuscript by Heinrich Isaak (Magliab, XIX, 58-11.1232, fols. 1 v. and 2 r.).

ménien (Paris 1919) 175, 312. O. BARDENHEWER, *Geschichte der altkirchlichen Literatur,* 5:195–197. B. ALTANER, *Patrology,* 409–410. V. INGLISIAN, *Lexikon für Theologie und Kirche,* 5:774; A. GRILLMEIER and H. BACHT, *Das Konzil von Chalkedon: Geschichte und Gegenwart,* 2:361–417. F. L. CROSS, *The Oxford Dictionary of the Christian Church,* 703. S. LYONNET, *Recherches de science réligieuse,* 25 (1935) 170–187; *Les Origines de la version arménienne de la Bible et le Diatessaron* (Rome 1950). A. VÖÖBUS, *Recherches de science réligieuse,* (1950) 581–586. C. TOUMANOFF, *Traditio* 10 (1954) 109–189.

[N. M. SETIAN]

ISAAK, HEINRICH

International polyphonic composer, b. Brabant, North Flanders *c.* 1450; d. Florence, Italy, 1517. Isaak is generally recognized to be of Netherlandish origin, although earlier biographers held him to be German or even Bohemian. His lineage is attested by the typically Flemish style of his sacred music, but even more irrefutably by his self-designation as *filius Ugonis de Flandria* in his will. Nothing is known of his early years; he first emerged in 1484 as a guest at the Innsbruck court, possibly while en route to Florence for service at the court of Lorenzo de' Medici ("the Magnificent"). His departure

from Flanders at about this time was perhaps occasioned by the dispersion of the Burgundian musical establishment, following the death of Mary of Burgundy in 1482. Since Archduke Maximilian (later Holy Roman Emperor) resided in Flanders for some 12 years after his marriage to Mary of Burgundy in 1477, he undoubtedly knew Isaak's talents; this accounts for Isaak's quick employment by the emperor in 1494, while encamped before Pisa, after the death of Lorenzo. Isaak remained nominally in the emperor's service until his death, although he was apparently permitted to spend long periods away from court. New evidence from Italian documents would indicate that he spent most of his time after 1508 in Italy (see D'Accone in bibliography).

Isaak was a skilled and versatile composer, equally at home with sacred and secular music. Undoubtedly his *magnum opus* was the unfinished *Choralis Constantinus,* which was planned to furnish polyphonic settings of certain items of the Proper of the Mass for the entire liturgical year. These were designed for *alternatim* performance, since only alternate lines or verses were composed. The MS was completed and prepared for publication (3 v. Nürnberg 1550–55) by his greatest student, Ludwig SENFL, who did not see his task fulfilled, since he died in 1543. An important feature of the *Choralis Constantinus* is the polyphonic setting of 47 sequences, which makes this the most comprehensive single source for the early 16th-century sequence-motet.

Bibliography: Works. *Choralis Constantinus, Book I*, ed. E. BEZECNY and W. RABL (Denkmäler der Tonkunst in Österreich 10; Graz 1959), *Book II*, ed. A. VON WEBERN (*ibid.*, 32; 1959), *Book III*, ed. L. E. CUYLER (Ann Arbor 1950); *Weltliche Werke*, ed. J. WOLF (Denkmäler der Tonkunst in Österreich 28; Graz 1959); *Five Polyphonic Masses*, ed. L. E. CUYLER (Ann Arbor 1956). Literature. P. BLASCHKE, "H. Isaak's *Choralis Constantinus*," *Kirchenmusikalisches Jahrbuch,* 26 (1931) 32–50. L. E. CUYLER, "The Sequences of Isaac's *Choralis Constantinus*," *Journal of the American Musicological Society* 3 (1950) 3–16. F. A. D'ACCONE, "H. Isaac in Florence: New and Unpublished Documents," *Musical Quarterly* 49 (1963) 464–483. G. REESE, *Music in the Renaissance* (rev. ed. New York 1959). E. C. KEMPSON, *The Motets of Henricus Isaac (c. 1450–1517), Transmission, Structure and Function* (Ph.D. diss. King's College, University of London 1998). E. LERNER, "*Choralis Constantinus* van Heinrich Isaac," *Musica Antiqua* 14 (1997) 117–125. J. A. OWENS, "An Isaac Autograph," in *Music in the German Renaissance: Sources, Styles, and Contexts*, ed. J. KMETZ (Cambridge, Eng. 1994) 27–53. D. M. RANDEL, ed., *The Harvard Biographical Dictionary of Music* (Cambridge, Mass. 1996) 407–408. N. SLONIMSKY, ed., *Baker's Biographical Dictionary of Musicians* (8th ed. New York 1992) 828. M. STAEHELIN, "Heinrich Isaac," in *The New Grove Dictionary of Music and Musicians*, ed. S. SADIE, v. 9 (New York 1980) 329–337.

[L. E. CUYLER]

Isabella I, Queen of Castile, engraving. (Archive Photos/Popperfoto)

ISABELLA I, QUEEN OF CASTILE

Reigned Dec. 11, 1474, to Nov. 26, 1504; b. Madrigal, Spain, April 22, 1451; d. Medina del Campo. She was devoted to the religious and political unity of Spain, the modern history of which begins with her reign. Daughter of John II of Castile, she gained the throne after the death of her brother Henry IV (1454–74) and united Castile with Aragon when Ferdinand V, whom she had married in 1469, succeeded to the throne of Aragon in 1479. Together the *reyes católicos* suppressed civil war and banditry; reformed the law, the judiciary, and the administration; encouraged sheepbreeding and trade; built a regular army; reconquered Granada (1481–92); and strengthened the monarchy vis-à-vis the nobles, the cities, and the Church. They thus acquired the right to administer the MILITARY ORDERS of CALATRAVA (1487), Santiago (1493), and Alcántara (1494); and to appoint all prelates in Granada (1486) and, in practice, all bishops in Spain. They chose excellent men, such as XIMÉNEZ DE CISNEROS and F. de Talavera. They reformed the secular and regular clergy, anticipating the COUNTER REFORMATION, and founded universities to encourage the revival of learning. In 1480 the INQUISITION was established for all of Spain, and under Tomás de TORQUEMADA (1483–98) it investigated MARRANOS, whose conversion to Christianity was suspect. In 1492 Jews were required to become Christian or leave Castile and Aragon, and in 1502 Moslems had to make the same choice. Isabella personally commissioned COLUMBUS's voyages and the settlement and evangelization of America. Of her five children, Joan the Mad, her successor, was the mother of CHARLES V, and Catherine married HENRY VIII OF ENGLAND. Isabella is buried in Granada.

Bibliography: W. T. WALSH, *Isabella of Spain* (New York 1930). H. DEL PULGAR, *Crónica de los reyes católicos,* ed. J. DE MATA CARRIAZO, 2 v. (Madrid 1943). B. LLORCA, *La Inquisición en España* (3d ed. Barcelona 1954). T. DE AZCONA, *La eclección y reforma del episcopado español en tiempo de los reyes católicos* (Madrid 1960). R. GARCÍA Y GARCÍA DE CASTRO, *Virtudes de la Reina Católica* (Madrid 1961). T. MILLER, *The Castles and the Crown* (New York 1963). J. H. ELLIOTT, *Imperial Spain, 1469–1716* (London 1963). T. DE AZCONA, *Isabel la Católica* (Madrid 1964).

[D. W. LOMAX]

ISABELLE OF FRANCE, BL.

Daughter of Louis VIII and Blanche of Castile, sister of LOUIS IX; b. March 1225; d. Longchamp (Paris), Feb. 23, 1270. Among her suitors, all of whom she rejected, was Conrad, son and heir to Frederick II; notwithstanding

INNOCENT IV's insistence, she resisted the political advantage of this marriage. Eventually the pope praised her decision. Throughout her life she exhibited a constant concern for charitable and hospital work that was channeled increasingly by her fondness for the Friars Minor. Innocent IV allowed Isabelle to retain Franciscans as her special confessors, and with the king's support she founded a convent for the POOR CLARES at Longchamps in Paris, which opened in 1260. Although she led a penitential life, she refused to become abbess of the convent or even to take vows. Her continued interest in this convent was reflected in its constitution; the rule she drafted with the advice of five Franciscan theologians was approved by ALEXANDER IV on February 10, 1259; a mitigated revision was submitted to URBAN IV and approved July 27, 1263. The sisters were called *Sorores minores inclusae*. Agnes of Harcourt, third abbess of Longchamps (d. 1289), composed Isabelle's vita in French; it was later put into Latin. Isabelle's cultus was approved in 1521 by LEO X.

Feast: Feb. 26 (formerly June 8).

Bibliography: B. GRATIEN, *Histoire de la fondation et de l'évolution de l'Ordre des Frères Mineurs au XIIIe siècle* (Paris 1928) 609–617. A. GARREAU, *Bse. Isabelle de France, soeur de Saint-Louis* (Paris 1955). AGNES OF HARCOURT, *Vita b. Elisabethae seu Isabellae, Acta Sanctorum* August 6 (1863) 798–808; cf. *Commentarius praevius, ibid.* 787–798.

[E. W. MCDONNELL]

ISAIAH

Isaiah (Heb. *y^{e}ša'-yahu*, "Yahweh is salvation" or "salvation of Yahweh") was born probably *c.* 760 B.C. His father's name, Amos, (Amoz, Heb. *'āmôṣ*) was not the same name as that of the Prophet Amos (Heb. *'āmôs*). Isaiah's birthplace is unknown. Since he appears only in Jerusalem and all his authentic oracles have a Jerusalem background, presumably he spent his entire career in that city. He was called to the prophetic office in the year King Uzziah of Judah died (*c.* 742 B.C.; Is 6.1). His easy access to the court as adviser to kings may suggest noble birth; his majestic poetic oracles reveal a man of profound intelligence, great literary genius, and broad education. He was married (Is 8.3, where he calls his wife "the prophetess") and had at least two sons, both of whom bore prophetic names (7.3; 8.3). His career covered half a century (*c.* 742 to *c.* 688) under Kings Jotham, Ahaz, and HEZEKIAH (1.1). He was a contemporary of the Prophets HOSEA, AMOS, and MICAH.

Isaiah was active in Jerusalem during a critical period of Israelite history, when Judah was in serious danger of becoming involved in the anti-Assyrian intrigues of

The prophet Isaiah holding a scroll on which is written his prophecy, "The Virgin shall be with Child, and bear a Son. . ." (Is 7.14), in the basilica of S. Maria in Trastevere, Rome.

the Syro-Ephraimite coalition (735–734; Is 7.1–25) that occasioned the Assyrian conquest of Damascus (732) and Samaria (722), when Sargon II captured Azotus (712–711; Is 20.1), and when Sennacherib besieged Jerusalem (701 and perhaps again *c.* 689; Is 36.1–37, 38).

Isaiah, who was an energetic leader in the cause of the Holy One of Israel (a favorite Isaian title), urged total confidence in the strength of Yahweh (Is 36.1), in opposition to religiously compromising and useless alliances with pagan nations (14.24–19.25). His inspired guidance in the political, religious, and social life in Jerusalem won him later acclaim (Sir 48.22). Vacillating Judah was suffering a growing moral decay, a sinful lack of faith; luxury, greed, oppression of the poor were rampant (1.4–8; 3.1; 5.8); the court and the leaders, even the priests, were filled with bribery, injustice, and graft (10.1)—sins "covered up" by a temple worship, grandiose, lavish, and scandalously insincere (1.10–17). All this the Prophet courageously and vividly (20.1) denounced, often alone. He was apparently most active and influential under Hezekiah, and he was largely responsible for the religious reform, all too short-lived, initiated by this good king (2 Kings ch. 18–20; 2 Chronicles ch. 29–31).

Overwhelmed by the majesty of God in his inaugural vision (Is 6.1), Isaiah preached the awesome transcendence of the God of Israel. His oracles show a profound concept of the one true God, the holy, powerful, mighty divine King, which is set forth in clear, concise, and majestic language, vivid imagery, and religious grandeur. He had a deep consciousness of the national sin (6.8–13); divine justice is inescapable. God punishes and destroys His enemies, even beloved Israel if necessary (3.1). Assyria is the rod of God's anger (10.5). Yet, Isaiah preached also a message of hope and promise. God will forgive, protect, and love Israel, if only His people remain faithful. Isaiah's visions presented the horizon of the glorious, ideal king and kingdom (ch. 9–11) that the Lord God would raise up for the faithful remnant of His people (10.20). The Prophet reaffirmed the promise to David (11.6), which afforded the messianic hope a classical prophetic form. His great message was that the Lord God alone is Israel's salvation: trust in Him alone. Yet Isaiah's hope was repeatedly frustrated during his day (22.1–4; 6.9–13).

The Prophet gathered disciples (8.16), who collected his oracles and presumably continued his work, perhaps in a so-called school of Isaiah that endured for a long time. His literary genius may have given a classic form to an Isaiahan-type of prophetic oracle (much like a "Davidic" psalm or a "Mosaic" law) that continued to be preached and composed for a long time; hence the late editing of the extremely diverse book that bears his name. (The biblical concept of "author" is much broader than the modern one).

Nothing is known of his career after 701 (or 689). A highly questionable and late tradition holds that he was martyred by being sawed asunder at the time of King Manasseh of Judah (c. 687 to c. 642). He is mentioned in the Roman Martyrology on July 6.

According to 2 Chr 26.22, Isaiah wrote also a history of the reign of Uzziah, of which nothing more is known. (The writing of royal annals was traditionally attributed to prophets). Several works among the Apocrypha are referred to him: the (Jewish) *Martyrium Isaiae*, the (Christian) *Ascensio Isaiae*, and the *Visio Isaiae* (a Christian addition to the *Martyrium*).

Christian iconography includes several scenes connected with the canonical Book of Isaiah and the apocryphal works attributed to him, such as his vision of the Seraphim (Is 6.1–31), the miracles he worked for King Hezekiah (the cure of the king and the receding shadow of the sun: 38.1–8), and the Prophet's martyrdom. The 2d-century fresco in the catacomb of Priscilla at Rome showing a man holding a scroll and standing beside a seated woman with a baby in her lap is commonly, though not with certainty, explained as Isaiah proclaiming his prophecy that "the virgin shall be with child, and bear a son, and shall name him Emmanuel" (7.14).

Bibliography: J. BRIGHT, *A History of Israel* (Philadelphia 1959) 251–287. B. VAWTER, *The Conscience of Israel* (New York 1961) 162–207. C. STUHLMUELLER, *The Prophets and the Word of God* (Notre Dame 1964) 139–202. F. L. MORIARTY, *Introducing the Old Testament* (Milwaukee 1960) 120–138. N. W. PORTEOUS, *Die Religion in Geschichte und Gegenwart*, (Tübingen 1957–65) 3:600–601. *Encyclopedic Dictionary of the Bible*, tr. and adap. by L. HARTMAN (New York 1963) 1074–77. For additional bibliography, *see* ISAIAH, BOOK OF. Iconography. L. RÉAU, *Iconographie de l'art chrétien* (Paris 1955–59) 2.1:365–369. E. LUCCHESI-PALLI, *Lexikon für Theologie und Kirche*, ed. J. HOFER and K. RAHNER (Freiburg 1957–65) 5:782. A. SCHOORS, "Historical Information in Isaiah 1–39," in *Studies in the Book of Isaiah*, ed. J. VAN RUITEN and M. VERVENNE (BETL 132; Leuven 1997) 73–93. J. JENSEN, "Weal and Woe in Isaiah: Consistency and Continuity," *Catholic Biblical Quarterly* 43 (1981) 167–87.

[W. HILL]

ISAIAH, BOOK OF

The first of the Major Prophets in the canon of the OT. It bears the name of the great Prophet Isaiah of the 8th century B.C., whose oracles occupy most of the first half of the book. The longest and greatest of the prophetic books, it contains the sublime prophetic message embracing the progress of God's plan for salvation from the middle of the monarchical period of Judah (c. 750 B.C.) to the postexilic restoration (c. 500 B.C.). It is characterized by its profound religious teaching as well as its elegant literary style, perhaps the best in the OT. After certain general remarks about the book as a whole, this article presents a separate analysis of each of its main parts.

GENERAL REMARKS

Because of the rather complicated nature of this long book, some preliminary remarks about its contents, multiple authorship, and text will prove useful.

Contents. The Book of Isaiah is neither a continuous narrative nor a literary unit, but an amalgam of religious literature of various genres and a collection of prophetic oracles from several historical periods. There is some prose (ch. 36–39), but the book is made up mainly of poems of varying length. They range from short proverb-like statements (29.9–10) to rather lengthy poems of several stanzas each (e.g., 9.7–10.4), which contain summaries of the prophetic message in poetry of various types, such as lyric and hymn (11.1–9; 42.10–25), allegory (5.1–7), parable (28.23–29), diatribe (48.1–11), satire (14.1–23; 47.1–15), lament (53.1–9), and psalm (12.1–6). These poems deal with a variety of subjects, including religious (40.12–31), political (19.1–5), and social life (13.1–26); personal moral conduct (5.8–25); autobiography (6.1–13); threats and warnings (28.1–22); promises and assurances (35.1–10); meditation and prayer (51.1–16; 60.7–19); and thanksgiving, praise, and worship (54.1–17; 60.1–22). The book thus preserves in a rich variety of form the sublime message of Isaiah, his disciples, and later prophets in an attractive, vivid, and highly imaginative style.

Multiple authorship. Although the book was always known under the title of Isaiah, despite the absence of any reference to him in its second section (ch. 40–66), it gives evidence of containing originally independent oracle collections (1.1; 2.1; 5.8; oracles against the nations, 13.1; book of consolation, 40.1) and suggests several hands in compilation (8.16). The interposition of a prose narrative (ch. 36–39) between two large poetic sections that are thematically and literarily diverse also implies a certain amount of collecting and compiling in the composition of the book.

Until the 19th century, the Prophet Isaiah was accepted uncritically as the author of the entire book for problems of literary form and composition are of rather recent interest in biblical science. Yet the second section (ch. 40–66), which is addressed to the exiles in Babylon or to those who returned from the Exile, has always been recognized as fundamentally different from the first section (ch. 1–39). Modern critical studies initiated by J. G. Eichhorn (d. 1827) and B. Duhm (d. 1928) gradually revealed the true nature of the book. It is a rich composite of poetic oracles composed over a long period of time (from *c.* 740 to *c.* 300 B.C.) by various authors (prophets and preachers) centered on the core message of the great Prophet Isaiah. Such a process of composition and editing is now known to be quite usual in gathering biblical literature, as, for example, in the PENTATEUCH, the Book of PSALMS, and even to some extent the Gospel according to St. JOHN.

Though admittedly it is difficult to say exactly how the book reached its present form, a plausible explanation is this: the Prophet Isaiah preached from 740 to 690; his message was preserved in poetic oracles gathered by his disciples (Is 8.16), who continued to preach the message and compose oracles, adding them to the original ones of Isaiah. This so-called school of Isaiah continued even after the destruction of Jerusalem (587 B.C.) and during the Exile. During the Babylonian Exile there arose a great

(now anonymous) poet-prophet, a genius in his own right (now called Deutero-Isaiah or Second Isaiah) who continued Isaiah's message in the magnificent poems of ch. 40 to 55, developing it and applying it to the situation of the Exile and the return (537 B.C.). He was followed by another or other great literary prophets, also anonymous (now called Trito-Isaiah or Third Isaiah), during the restoration in Jerusalem (520 B.C.), who composed further oracles that developed the message in light of the rebuilding of Jerusalem and the Temple, stressing further aspects of God's message that had become clear in the new situation of Israel. Some scholars such as J. Bright, hold that Third Isaiah was written by the same author who wrote Second Isaiah, but in the rebuilt Jerusalem. Finally, at some time between 400 and 200 B.C., when the biblical books in general were being edited into their present form (it is impossible at present to be more specific), these various collections of the Isaiah message and school, with some late APOCALYPTIC additions (ch. 24–27; ch. 34–35), were gathered together on one scroll for careful and safe preservation. Perhaps by this time the School of Isaiah was dying out; indeed, the office of prophet seems to have disappeared after *c.* 400 B.C. until the coming of John the Baptist. Sirach (190 B.C.) knew the book in something like its present form (see Sir 48.22–25), and the NT authors cite all sections of the book as Isaiah. (The citing of OT books in the NT follows popular acceptance at the time and does not involve settlement of any questions of authorship.) Isaiah proper is sometimes called Proto-Isaiah, to distinguish him from Deutero-Isaiah and Trito-Isaiah.

The theory just outlined on the composition of the book can be found with various specific refinements in the studies of S. Mowinckel, A. Bentzen, A. Condamin, P. Auvray and J. Steinmann, A. Feuillet, A. Gelin, and others, and it is widely accepted, though some few critics, Protestant and Jewish as well as Catholic, still defend the unity of authorship by Isaiah for the entire book. Nor does it contradict the carefully worded decree of the PONTIFICAL BIBLICAL COMMISSION of June 29, 1908, warning against hasty, ill-founded theories that were then inadequately substantiated. Since then scientific study, supported by growing literary and archeological evidence from ancient times, has made the theory of the multiple authorship of the book into a carefully considered, well-substantiated understanding of its true nature. Evidence will be indicated in the survey of the book below.

Text. The present text of the book, formerly based on medieval MSS of the accepted Masoretic text (MT) has been remarkably supported by the discovery in 1947 among the Qumran DEAD SEA SCROLLS of two scrolls of Isaiah, one complete (1QIsᵃ) and one almost complete (1QIsᵇ), along with many fragments of the book from about the 1st century B.C. Textual corruptions, however, are apparent from the comparison of the Qumran scrolls with the MT and the Septuagint (LXX) and from the comparison of the Qumran scrolls with each other; these are sufficiently diverse to suggest different textual traditions. Yet the overall text is in a good state of preservation. Translation is at times uncertain because of the involved Hebrew poetry, the 400-year span of language represented, and limitations of present knowledge of Hebrew. Moreover, the exact delimitation of the various poetic oracles is often uncertain, and at least in ch. 1 to 35 the oracles are not in chronological order. Thus variations will be found in the arrangement of the book, in the dating of some oracles, and in the translation of some passages.

For best understanding of the book, an edition that prints the poetry in poetic form and separates the individual poems (even though this is at times somewhat uncertain), preferably with explanatory titles, should be used, such as is done in volume four (Paterson, N.J. 1961) of the four-volume Confraternity of Christian Doctrine translation of the OT, in the Revised Standard Version, the Smith-Goodspeed Bible (Chicago 1951), the French *Bible de Jerusalem* (Paris 1951), and others.

ANALYSIS

The book divides itself easily into four main sections approximately dated as follows: (1) ch. 1 to 35, oracles connected chiefly with the pre-exilic preaching of (Proto-) Isaiah (740–690); (2) ch. 36 to 39, a historical appendix (705–690); (3) ch. 40 to 55 (Deutero-Isaiah), oracles of the Exile (550–538); and (4) ch. 56 to 66 (Trito-Isaiah), oracles of the restoration (520–500). For practical reasons, Deutero-Isaiah and Trito-Isaiah are treated here together.

Proto-Isaiah. According to the first verse of the book (a late editorial addition), the oracles of ch. 1 to 35 were delivered during the reigns of Uzziah (783–742), Jotham (750–735), Ahaz (735–715), and Hezekiah (715–687) in Judah probably between 740 and 690 B.C.

Historical Background. It was a critical period in the history of Israel. Assyria dominated the Near East, but the subdued nations were restless. King Achaz of Judah found himself under pressure from the anti-Assyrian forces with whom he did not sympathize. Syria and Israel (Ephraim) attacked Judah (735–734) to force her cooperation against Assyria. In spite of Isaiah's opposition (Is 7.1), Ahaz appealed to Assyria for aid, which he received at heavy cost of tribute and religious compromise. Later the Assyrians under Sargon II marched with devastation, destroying Damascus (Syria) in 732; Samaria and the Northern Kingdom (Israel) in 722; Ashdod and the Phi-

listine-Egyptian coalition in 711. Judah, sorely pressed, barely escaped. Under Hezekiah, who steered a perilous course of neutrality, comparative peace prevailed in Judah, though heavy tribute was paid to Assyria. Encouraged by Isaiah, Hezekiah undertook a rather extensive religious reform, which re-established the covenant and purified the worship of Yahweh. During this time Isaiah's preaching changed from the threats and warnings of the earlier period to the optimistic oracles of deliverance and blessing, partially, no doubt, in praise of the good efforts of Hezekiah, who became the historical figure behind the messianic imagery and expectation (ch. 9; ch. 11–12; ch. 32–33). The reform was short lived; when Sargon II was murdered in 705, the subject peoples again rebelled. Hezekiah resisted for a time, again no doubt influenced by Isaiah, but eventually he gave in to pressure from Merodach-Baladan of Babylon (ch. 39) and from Egypt and revolted. The result was almost complete disaster: in 701 the new king of Assyria, Sennacherib, devastated Judah and besieged Jerusalem (ch. 36). After this event, nothing further is heard of Isaiah. It is against this historical background that ch. 1 to 35 should be read.

Analysis of Chapters 1 to 35. Though the oracles in ch. 1 to 35 are not always in chronological order, most of them are authentic oracles of Proto-Isaiah. Chapters 1 to 12 are Isaiahan oracles concerning Judah and Jerusalem, mostly from the period of the Syro-Ephraimite war (735–734) in the reign of Ahaz. After an introduction (Is 1.1–8) there are various oracles on the moral degeneration of the people and their religious hypocrisy, with warnings of punishment and destruction (1.9–5.30), including the beautiful parable of the desolate vineyard of Israel (5.1–7).

Chapters 6 to 12 form the so-called Book of EMMANUEL, which begins with the autobiographical oracle of Isaiah's vision and call (6.1–13) and continues with the Emmanuel oracles delivered to Ahaz assuring deliverance from the Syro-Ephraim coalition (7.1–8.20). The oracle of the Prince of Peace (9.1–6), the warning drawn from the fall of Damascus and Israel (9.7–20), the condemnation of social injustice (10.1–4), and the designation of Assyria as the rod of God's anger (10.5–34) are followed by the optimistic view of the rule of Emmanuel and the eventual reunion of all Israel (11.1–6). The collection ends with a joyful psalm of thanksgiving (12.1–6).

Chapters 13 to 23 collect the oracles against the nations (God's judgment will fall upon them also) mostly from Isaiah, though some of them, especially those against Babylon (ch. 13; ch. 14; ch. 21) are probably of later (exilic) origin. Chapters 24 to 27 contain the late so-called Apocalypse of Isaiah (see below), logically placed here to show, following the judgment of the individual nations, the inevitable universal judgment and triumph of Yahweh and of His plan.

Chapters 28 to 33 contain Isaiahan oracles of various dates developing the theme of Yahweh's vengeance on Judah and Israel, with flashes of promise and hope of eventual restoration. Here, also, some of the oracles (29.17–24; ch. 33) may be of later date. Chapters 34 to 35 contain the late so-called Little Apocalypse of Isaiah (see below).

Doctrine of Proto-Isaiah. The dominant theme of ch. 1 to 35 is that of warning and threats of punishment against Judah and Jerusalem, especially for their infidelity to Yahweh and His covenant. Such infidelity led to the destruction of Samaria; Judah herself awaits a similar fate if there is no reform. The Holy One of Israel is a just God who punishes the misdeeds and crimes with which Judah is filled. He is Lord of all—not a mere nationalist god—before whom all men, Judah included, are unworthy to appear. He is powerful and majestic; His people must offer him profound reverence. He is holy and perfect; His people must be holy for Yahweh is holy. God's work in history, shown in His covenant with Israel, will eventually be accomplished even though His own people, Judah, becomes an obstacle. Unless there is repentance, change of ways, restoration of the covenant in sincerity and justice, even Judah must suffer the fate of all God's enemies. God's people must have faith; they must trust in His promises and have confidence in His holy will, which involves an orientation toward God of all aspects of man's existence. Without such faith there can be no stability.

Still, there is hope. Israel is the chosen of God. Yet not all will participate in God's plan. Isaiah is the great prophet of the Remnant of Israel—a small, distinctive group in the general body of Israel that will remain faithful, and through it God will fulfill His promise. (The so-called remnant theology receives greater refinement in ch. 40 to 66, where the returning exiles are regarded as the remnant.) Yahweh's promise is sure, and Isaiah is filled with an optimistic picture of the future of Emmanuel, the Prince of Peace, who will reign from Jerusalem, but only after the threats and warnings have been carried out. It is possible (according to Gelin) that the group of disciples who carried on Isaiah's work thought of themselves as this remnant keeping alive Israel's hope in Yahweh.

Historical appendix. Chapters 36 to 39 contain a historical appendix duplicating 2 Kgs 18.23–20.19, but also containing several Isaiahan oracles together with some biographical material and background detail. It has something of an apologetic aim: history bears out Isaiah's warnings. The events are not in chronological order: the embassy from Merodach-Baladan occurred most likely before the invasion of Sennacherib. Many (e.g., W. F. Albright, J. Bright, and E. Dhorme) think that the mention in Is 37.9 of Tharaca (Terhakah), who became king of Ethiopia in 690, and the repetitions and confusion of details indicate that there is a conflation in the biblical account of two Assyrian campaigns, one in 701 and one in 690. If so, Isaiah's ministry extended to the latter date.

Deutero-Isaiah and Trito-Isaiah. Beginning with ch. 40, the Book of Isaiah is transformed. Isaiah is never mentioned. The dominant theme is consolation, encouragement, hope, and promise of restoration. Jerusalem (Is 52.2, 9; 62.1–4) and the Temple (63.18; 64.10) are in ruins; the people are in Babylon, but deliverance is at hand. The situation is obviously that of the Exile. CYRUS, king of Persia (550–530 B.C.), who allowed the Jews to return to Judah in 538 B.C., is mentioned by name (44.28; 45.1) as the deliverer raised up by Yahweh. The oracles are now long, meditative, discourse-type poems, lyrical and sustained in mood, that stress not so much moral instruction as a profound religious reflection on God, His nature, His attributes, and a theological explanation of the destruction of Jerusalem and the Temple in light of God's plan for His people. The theme of forgiveness of sin replaces that of punishment; hope of restoration, that of destruction. There are marked changes in language and style and a more varied and technical vocabulary; the Hebrew is a later Hebrew. No longer is there the narrow vision of Judah and Jerusalem, but the broad vision of the nations and a universalism that would be strange in the first part of the book.

All these factors make it abundantly clear that ch. 40 to 66 contain the exilic and postexilic preaching of a prophet (or prophets) who, continuing the work and message of Isaiah and the Isaiahan school, spoke to the exiles (ch. 40–55) and to the first returnees to Jerusalem (ch. 56–66) in the spirit and tone of EZEKIEL, Zechariah, MALACHI, and HAGGAI. Babylon, not Assyria, is now the enemy. There is a remarkable polemic against idolatry and the pagan gods that seems to presuppose the Jewish people living in the midst of paganism and far from Jerusalem and its Temple. The authors (or author) of these poems remain anonymous; one can designate them only as Second and Third Isaiah.

Message of Faith and Hope. The year 587 marked an applling catastrophe for Israel: Jerusalem and the Temple were destroyed by the Babylonians; all Judah was a shambles, and the chief people were deported to Babylon. Yet Israel, unlike countless other nations similarly destroyed, in spite of its poor, desperate situation, did endure—a testimony to the divine mercy and the indestructibility of the divine plan. Even in exile Israel kept alive its faith, its law, and its identity because of the work of such men as Deutero-Isaiah. He offered a theological explanation for the national disaster and kept alive the spark of hope. Yahweh's righteous judgment was purifying Israel; it was not a contradiction but a vindication of Israel's historic faith. The prophet preached also of the inevitable, glorious triumph of Yahweh and the resurrection of Israel. It was this faith and hope that enabled Israel to survive, and Isaiah ch. 40 to 66 is a testament of such faith. Moreover, the original message of Proto-Isaiah was now more pertinent and meaningful than ever. His warnings had been realized and his message vindicated. Hence, the original oracles were studied and gathered religiously during the Exile, and the message was carried on in the preaching of his disciples. It is against this background that ch. 40 to 55 should be read.

Analysis of Deutero-Isaiah. The so-called Isaiahan Book of Consolation (ch. 40–55) includes a brief introduction (40.1–11), the body of the work setting forth the promise of release (40.12–55.9), and a conclusion of joy and thanks for the release and return (55.10–13). The first part (ch. 40–48) is centered on the exiles in Babylon; the second (ch. 49–55) on Zion (Jerusalem) and its impending restoration. In Deutero-Isaiah are the five famous songs of the SUFFERING SERVANT, 42.1–4; 49.1–6; 50.5–9; 52.13–53.12; 51.9–16. God, the creator (40.12–31) and liberator (41.1–29) of Zion is a gracious and loving savior. The period of trial is over; redemption is a reality (43.1–44.5); Yahweh has triumphed over the false gods, who are no-gods (44.6–23; 46.1–13). Cyrus is the Lord's anointed, freeing His people for a new exodus to the promised land (44.24–45.25). Proud Babylon has fallen ignominiously, an event described with masterful irony (47.1–15; c.f. 13.1–14.23; 21.1–10); the exiles can now rejoice in clear assurance of salvation (48.1–21).

Shifting his vision to Zion soon to be restored, the author proclaims that Israel's sins have been expiated (49.1–50.11); the Lord's goodness to Abraham and to Moses and to His people is re-established (51.1–16), as the cup of wrath is removed (51.17–23), and Zion rejoices at being reinhabited by the chosen remnant of God's people (52.1–12). The hope of the new Zion is brilliantly described (54.1–55.9).

Analysis of Trito-Isaiah. The scene shifts to Jerusalem. Hope of the restoration had been bright; but the actuality of the return and the first few years (538–500 B.C.) was bleak, difficult, and bitterly disappointing. Trito-Isaiah (Isaiah ch. 56–66) continued to speak of lofty hopes, but they were still in the future. Courage, determination, energetic building, unremitting toil, and prayer for Zion were the program of the present. The returnees were suffering the inevitable birth pangs of the new creation about to appear (65.17–25). Severe opposition to the restoration came even in Jerusalem itself from the doubters (59.9–11), from economic tensions, from the people who had remained behind and had now developed a somewhat syncretistic religion (57.3–10; 65.1–7), and from the callousness of some people behind a façade of piety (58.1–12; 59.1–8). The question of unity or religious separation between the returnees and those who had remained was perplexing (65.8–16; 66.15–17). Failure to make progress on the reconstruction of the Temple—not completed for some 20 years after the return—was no trivial thing; as a focal point, the Temple was desperately needed. Chapters 56 to 66 should be read in connection with the Books of EZRA and NEHEMIAH and the postexilic Prophets Haggai, Zechariah, and Malachi.

In such a situation, Trito-Isaiah (Isaiah ch. 56–66) speaks to the first returnees to Jerusalem. The Mosaic Law is being re-established and the Sabbath restored (56.1–8). The leaders must be purified and the faithless people restored to faith (56.9–57.13) in spite of the discouraging situation. Yahweh alone is His people's comfort (57.14–21). Fasting, reparation, and good works must characterize the new spiritual people, the returnees (58.1–14). Let them confess their sins and proceed with confidence to the task at hand, for Zion is restored (59.1–21). In a magnificent piece of poetry, the prophet describes the glory Yahweh has planned for His restored people when salvation for all men will come forth from Zion, the new bride and spouse of Yahweh, the Holy One of Israel (60.1–62.12). God's favor is returned; the necessary punishment is expiated; the good and the bad will be separated, and true worship will be re-established in the Lord's Temple (63.1–66.6). Mother Zion, the new Jerusalem, will rejoice as all nations gather to celebrate and enjoy the salvation of the Lord that will endure forever.

Isaiahan Apocalypse and Little Apocalypse. Here a word should be added on ch. 24 to 27, known as the Apocalypse of Isaiah, and ch. 34 to 35, the so-called Little Apocalypse. These chapters are more in the style of Second and Third Isaiah rather than that of Proto-Isaiah. They contain, moreover, the world vision and the literary characteristics of the apocalyptic form of literature of the late postexilic age. Yahweh will execute His vengeance on the rebellious and stubborn nations in the great DAY OF THE LORD, which will bring an eschatological judgment on the whole world and a definitive establishment of God's kingdom. Yahweh's victory will be final, over all celestial and terrestrial forces; salvation and the ultimate reassembly of Judah in the circumstance of a universal catastrophe will be effected; finally, there will be the resurrection of the pious ones and the triumph—re-echoing like a refrain—of the city of God over the city of evil. These are standard apocalyptic themes in the manner of the Books of DANIEL and Zechariah and other apocalyptic books and probably are to be dated around *c.* 300 B.C., which would thus make them the latest parts of the book and of the Isaiahan message.

Universal Redemption. Besides the doctrinal points mentioned in the analyses, the great theme of Isaiah ch. 40 to 66 is that of universal redemption. Israel is a nation and a people with a world mission, a nation founded on Abraham, Moses, and David, but with a vocation to bring the redemption and salvation of Yahweh to all mankind. Showing the divine control of history, the prophet preaches of the power of righteous suffering (cf. Job) and the role of Israel as witness and mediator between Yahweh and the nations of the world, a witness to the one true God who redeems and intends all men to share in His plan.

Yahweh, the Holy One of Israel, is Lord of all. Explicit and dynamic monotheism is nowhere more vigorously stated. Yahweh's cry, "I am God; there is no other!" (45.22) is the constant refrain, accompanied by a strong ironic and satiric polemic against idolatry. Yahweh is the God of all nations; there can be no other allegiance, not only for Israel, but for all nations. The creative and salvific activities of Yahweh are made clear: the creation of the world and the destiny of Israel are the two great divine works (cf. Gn ch. 1–11, where there is a development of the same themes, which probably attained their present form about the same time). The prophet daringly glimpses the day when all the nations will share the faith of Israel. He opens vistas unimagined by any previous prophet. The re-establishment of God's people is the beginning of the conversion of the nations.

Such universalism is not, indeed, that of Jesus or St. Paul, for it regards salvation as dependent upon Israel and under its dominance. But never was it so markedly clear that the covenant is for the service of all men. The theological development of Isaiah ch. 40 to 66 is remarkable; it is the climax of OT prophecy and epitomizes the whole prophetic tradition. The Israel that bears this vocation is not the great nation ruled by King David, but defined in religious terms, it is the "remnant"—the "poor" (*'ănāwîm*) of Yahweh—who have remained faithful despite crushing obstacles and have been constant in suffering; those who keep the Law in their hearts, who serve Yahweh and Him alone and hope only in Him (cf. the Sermon on the Mount), the race of Israel-Jacob in its full religious sense (cf. Gal and Rom). It is an Israel transformed through which Yahweh will re-enter the promised land and return to Jerusalem as king. This accomplishment is such that all the nations will be converted and incorporate themselves into the people of God.

Salvation will be marked by pardon of sin, of which the return from exile is the sign. It is a redemption: Yahweh is the *gō'ēn* (redeemer) in His land, its capital, and its reconstructed Temple; He will reign and begin building the New Israel and the New Jerusalem that are the objects of His promise. It will be a new alliance of peace and knowledge of the one true God served by all the nations. Christian faith has seen the vivid realization of these glorious promises and of the vocation of Israel in the establishment of God's reign through Jesus Christ and His Church; this is one reason why Isaiah ch. 40 to 66 is often quoted and alluded to in the NT.

Bibliography: Commentaries. B. DUHM, 4 v. (Göttingen 1892; 4th ed. 1922). K. MARTI (Tübingen 1900). A. CONDAMIN (Paris 1905). J. SKINNER, 2 v. (Cambridge, Eng. 1918; 2d ed. 1925). J. KNABENBAUER and F. ZORELL, 2 v. (Paris 1922–23). F. FELDMANN, 2 v. (Münster 1925–26). E. KÖNIG (Gütersloh 1926). A. VAN HOONACKER (Bruges 1932). J. FISCHER, 2 v. (Bonn 1937–39). H. W. HERTZBERG, 2 v. (Leipzig 1936–39). E. J. KISSANE, 2 v. (Dublin 1941–43; v. 1 repr. 1960). G. GIROTTI (Turin 1942). A. BENTZEN, 2 v. (Copenhagen 1943–44). P. AUVRAY and J. STEINMANN (2d ed. 1955). R. B. Y. SCOTT, *The Interpreter's Bible* 5, ed. G. A. BUTTRICK (New York 1956). V. HERNTRICH (Göttingen 1957). J. ZIEGLER (Würzburg 1958). A. PENNA (Turin 1958). G. B. GRAY, *Isaiah ch. 1–27* (London 1912; International Critical Commentary, Edinburgh–New York 1947). O. PROCKSCH, *Isaiah Ch. 1–39* (Leipzig 1930). K. F. R. BUDDE, *Isaiah ch. 40–66* (Tübingen 1909). C. C. TORREY, *Isaiah ch. 40–66* (International Critical Commentary; Edinburgh–New York 1928). P. VOLZ, *Isaiah Ch. 40–66* (Leipzig 1932). **Studies.** A. FEUILLET, *Dictionnaire de la Bible,* suppl. ed. L. PIROT (Paris 1928–) 4:647–729. *Encyclopedic Dictionary of the Bible* (New York 1963) 1077–84. J. ZIEGLER, *Lexikon für Theologie und Kirche,* ed. J. HOFER and K. RAHNER 5:779–782. O. KAISER, *Die Religion in Geschichte und Gegenwart* (Tübingen 1957–65) 3:601–611. J. STEINMANN, *Le Prophète Isaïe: Sa vie, son oeuvre et son temps* (2d ed. Paris 1955). J. H. EATON, "The Origin of the Book of Isaiahh," *Vetus Testamentum* 9 (1959) 138–157. R. T. MURPHY, "Second Isaiahs," *Catholic Bible Quarterly* 9 (1947) 170–178, 262–274. W. BRUEGGEMANN, *Isaiah 1–39* (Westminster Bible Companion; Louisville 1998). C. C. BROYLES and C. A. EVANS, eds., *Writing and Reading the Scroll of Isaiah: Studies on an Interpretive Tradition* (Vetus Testamentum Sup 70, 1 and 2; Formation and Interpretation of Old Testament Literature 1, 1 and 2; Leiden 1997). J. JENSEN, *Isaiah 1–39* (Old Testament Message 8; Wilmington, Del. 1984).

[W. HILL]

ISAIAS BONER OF CRACOW, BL.

Augustinian friar; b. Cracow, Poland, *c.* 1400; d. there, Feb. 8, 1471. Having joined the AUGUSTINIANS at Kazimiertz in Poland, he was sent in 1419 to study at the University of Padua, where he taught in the order's house of studies after 1422 and was appointed lector in theology in 1424. In 1438 he served as visitor of his province in Poland, and in May 1452 he presided at Regensburg as vicar general over the chapter of the Bavarian province. Meanwhile he had enrolled in 1443 at the University of Cracow, and he taught there as master of theology in

1460 as well as in 1463. He is thought to have written a commentary on the *Sentences*. His sincere piety, great love of neighbor, life of mortification, zeal for souls, and reputed miracles won him popular veneration even during his lifetime. Pope URBAN VIII authorized the transfer of his body to a distinct chapel, and at that time work began toward his formal beatification, which has not been realized. He is honored with the title "blessed" in Augustinian MARTYROLOGIES.

Feast: Feb. 8.

Bibliography: *Acta Sanctorum* February 2:213–217. F. JAROSZEWICZ, *Matka Świętych Polska* (Cracow 1767; repr. in 4 pts. Poznań 1893) 1:143–147. A. ZAHORSKA, *Ilustrowane Żywoty Świętych Polskich* (Potulice, Poland 1937) 232–242. T. GIEMMA, in *Polski słownik: biograficzny*, v.2 (Cracow 1936) 296. A. BUTLER, *The Lives of the Saints,* ed. H. THURSTON and D. ATTWATER, 4 v. (New York 1956) 1:282–283. J. L. BAUDOT and L. CHAUSSIN, *Vies des saints et des bienheueux selon l'ordre du calendrier avec l'historique des fêtes,* ed. by The Benedictines of Paris, 12 v. (Paris 1935–56) 2:194. M. T. DISDIER, *Dictionnaire d'histoire et de géographie ecclésiastiques,* ed. A. BAUDRILLART (Paris 1912–) 9:841. W. HÜMPFNER, *Lexikon für Theologie und Kirche,* ed. J. HOFER and K. RAHNER, 10 v. (2d, new ed. Freiburg 1957–65) 5:782.

[L. SIEKANIEC]

ISFRIED, ST.

Premonstratensian bishop; d. 1204, probably June 15. He was canon of Cappenberg and from 1159 provost of Jerichow; he was consecrated bishop of Ratzeburg (Regensburg, Germany) in 1180. Isfried, the "soul" of the PREMONSTRATENSIANS in North Germany, worked tirelessly for the consolidation of his own recently erected diocese and for the Christianization and German colonization of all the lands east of the Elbe. To the west his influence was felt as far away as FLOREFFE. He was Henry the Lion's confessor and attended him on his deathbed. He practiced heroic patience and self-denial, and miracles were credited to him within his lifetime. He is traditionally venerated in the Diocese of Osnabrück, and his cult was papally approved for the Premonstratensian Order *c.* 1725.

Feast: June 15.

Bibliography: *Acta Sanctorum* June 3:564–565. *Monumenta Germaniae Scriptores* (Berlin 1825–) 12:519; 16:231, 348, 354, 625; 21:131, 241. G. M. C. MASCH, *Geschichte des Bisthums Ratzeburg* (Lübeck 1835). F. WINTER, *Die Prämonstratenser des 12. Jahrhunderts u. ihre Bedeutung für das nordöstliche Deutschland* (Berlin 1865). P. GAMS, *Series epicoporum ecclisiae catholicae* (Regensburg 1873) 304. C. EUBEL et al., *Hierarchia Catholica medii (et recentioris) aevi:* v.1, 1198–1431 (2d ed. Münster 1913) 1:414. A. L. GOOVAERTS, *Écrivains, artistes, et savants de l'ordre de Prémontré,* 4 v. (Brussels 1899–1920) v.4.2. A. ZAK, "Episcopatus ordinis Praemonstratensis," *Analecta Praemonstratensia* 4

(1928) 406–413. G. WENTZ, ed., *Das Bistum Havelberg Germania Sacra* 1.2 (Berlin 1933) 201. N. BACKMUND, *Monasticon Praemonstratense,* 3 v. (Straubing 1949–56) 1:226, 242.

[J. J. JOHN]

ĪSHŌʻDĀD OF MERV

Nestorian bishop and outstanding exegete. Beyond the facts that he was born at Marū or Merv (Merw) in Khurasan (northeastern Persia) and that he became bishop of Ḥĕdhatha on the Tigris, practically nothing is known of his life. That he was active around the middle of the 9th century is known from the statements of the Arab historians Māri ibn Sulaymān and ʻAmr ibn Mattā, who report that at the death of Catholicos Abraham II, on Sept. 16, 850 (or 852 according to ʻAmr ibn Mattā), Īshōʻdād, as the most famous sage of the time, was proposed to Caliph Mutawakkil (847–861) as the best candidate for the patriarchal see. However, because of the machinations of the influential physician BUKHTĪSHŪʻ IBN JIBRĪL (d. 870), he lost the election in favor of Theodosius, Bishop of ʻAnbar.

Fortunately, the exegetical works of Īshōʼdād have been preserved. He shows in them that he was a continuer of the great reform movement that was initiated in the 6th century by Ḥanānā of Ḥĕdhayabh and lasted into the 9th century. In his exegesis Īshōʼdād endeavored to join the allegorical method of the Monophysite (Jacobite) school with the historical-grammatical method of THEODORE OF MOPSUESTIA, which was followed by the Nestorians. This explains why his works were well received and preserved by the Monophysite exegetes of the Middle Ages. In all his commentaries on the books of the OT and the NT, he used the form of questions and answers.

Bibliography: G. DIETTRICH, *Išoʼdadhs Stellung in der Auslegungsgeschichte des Alten Testaments (Beihefte zur Zeitschrift für die Alttestamentliche Wissenschaft* 6; 1902). J. M. VOSTÉ and C. VAN DEN EYNDE, *Commentaire d'Išoʼdad de Merv sur l'ancien testament,* 1, *Genèse* [*Corpus scriptorum Christianorum orientalium* 126 (text), 156 (tr.); 1950, 1955], 2, *Exode-Deutéronome* [*ibid.* 176 (text), 179 (tr.); 1958]. E. HAMMERSCHMIDT, *Lexikon für Theologie und Kirche* 5: 783–784.

[J. M. SOLA-SOLE]

ISIDORE OF KIEV

Humanist, Greek cardinal, and promoter of union of Florence; b. Monembasia, Greece, *c.* 1385; d. Rome, May 27, 1464. After being educated in Constantinople, Isidore became a monk in Monembasia and later abbot of the convent of Demetrius, Constantinople. Sent as envoy of the Emperor John VIII to the Council of Basel in 1434 to arrange for a council of union, he returned to Constantinople in the summer of 1435, and in 1436 was consecrated metropolitan of Kiev and all Russia. He arrived in Moscow on April 2, 1437, and almost immediately started on his way to the Council of Ferrara-Florence. He reached Ferrara only in mid-August 1438 and was elected one of the six Greek spokesmen in the Council. He had little occasion to speak, though he was throughout a force for union. In the months after the dogmatic sessions of March 1439 he was particularly active with BESSARION and others, and he had the confidence of both Emperor and Pope. He signed the decree of union, acting also as procurator for Antioch, and was nominated Apostolic Legate on August 17 for the Russias, and created cardinal on December 18. He issued an encyclical from Buda stressing the equality of the Churches; he was at first well received in Kiev and promulgated the union in Moscow (March 1441), but he was imprisoned on a charge of heresy by the Great Prince. Having escaped and been reimprisoned in Tver, he spent a year in Galizia, working for union; he then returned to Italy. After serving as legate on a mission to Greece (1444–48), he went to Constantinople in 1452 as papal legate and promulgated (Dec. 12) the union of Florence. He was wounded in the fall of the city and taken prisoner, but he escaped. Invested with the temporalities of the Latin patriarchate of Constantinople in 1452, he was appointed Greek patriarch on April 20, 1459, after resigning all his offices except the bishopric of Moscow (1458).

He was a notable humanist, interested in philosophy, mathematics, astronomy, and other branches of learning. Of his writings there remain a discourse in reply to Cardinal Cesarini at Basel, the unfinished drafts of several speeches prepared at Florence, a valuable report on the Eastern Church of *c.* 1448, and a treatise on the Procession of the Holy Spirit, as well as letters in Greek and Latin; the first of these items and many of the letters have been published.

Bibliography: G. MERCATI, *Scritti d'Isidoro il cardinale ruteno* (*Studi e Testi* 46; 1926). G. HOFMANN, "Quellen zu Isidor von Kiew," *Orientalia Christiana periodica* 18 (1952) 143–157. A. ZIEGLER, *Die Union des Konzils von Florenz in der russischen Kirche* (Würzburg 1938). J. GILL, "Isidore, Metropolitan of Kiev," *Personalities of the Council of Florence* (New York 1964) 65–78.

[J. GILL]

ISIDORE OF PELUSIUM, ST.

Monk and theologian; b. probably Alexandria, *c.* 360; d. *c.* 435–49. Ephraem of Antioch cites Alexandria as the birthplace of Isidore (*Patrologia Graeca,* ed. J. P. Migne 103:964) and indicates that he received a solid theological formation. He became a monk, retiring to a monastery on a hill not far from Pelusium, Egypt. FACUNDUS OF HERMIANE calls him a priest (*Patrologia Latina,* J. P. Migne 67:573–574; cf. *Synodicon, Patrologia Graeca* 84:587). Isidore took part in the ecclesiastical controversies of the early fifth century; he supported JOHN CHRYSOSTOM and insisted that his name be restored to the DIPTYCHS. He cautioned CYRIL OF ALEXANDRIA to moderation in dealing with Nestorius, telling him explicitly not to imitate the harsh example of his uncle Theophilus (*Epist.* 1.310).

Some 2,000 letters of Isidore have been preserved in five books. Usually brief but conforming to the epistolary fashion of the age, they reveal the author's literary formation and his ability to cite Homer, Demosthenes, PLATO, and ARISTOTLE, as well as the early Fathers of the Church, such as CLEMENT OF ALEXANDRIA. Of John Chrysostom he said, "If Saint Paul had desired to supply his own interpretation, he could not have done otherwise than this celebrated master of the Attic language" (*Epist.* 5.32). He cautioned against the abuses connected with the allegorical methods of Alexandrian exegesis and favored the Antiochene approach in theology. He refused to see a reference to Christ in every sentence of the Old Testament and maintained that while it was both historical and prophetic, it was necessary to distinguish carefully between the literal and the typical senses in interpreting that document (*Epist.* 2.95; 4.203).

Isidore followed the teaching of ATHANASIUS OF ALEXANDRIA in Christology and taught that Christ was "of two natures" in the Incarnation (*Epist.* 1.323). He repudiated a mixture or indwelling of one nature in the other (*Epist.* 4.99) and appears to have anticipated the terminology of CHALCEDON. He held that the Holy Spirit was consubstantial with the Father and the Son (*Epist.* 1.109). In the moral and ascetical sphere Isidore advised that entrance to the kingdom of God is based upon poverty and abstinence (*Epist.* 1.129), but that these virtues required the keeping of the Commandments (1.287) and the practice of a spiritual outlook on the things of the world (1.162). Virginity is better than marriage (4.192), but unavailing if practiced without humility (1.286). Among the recipients of his letters was the Emperor Theodosius II, whom he advised against allowing imperial officials to interfere in matters of faith (1.311).

The Migne edition of the letters in five books is arbitrary but based on an old tradition. Forty-nine of the letters were translated into Latin by the deacon Rusticus and appended to the acts of the Council of EPHESUS. Two lost works are mentioned: *Against the Greeks* and *On the Non-Existence of Fate.*

Feast: Feb. 4.

St. Isidore of Seville. (Archive Photos)

Bibliography: *Lettres,* ed. and tr. P. EVIEUX (Paris 1997–) *Patrologia Graeca,* ed. J. P. MIGNE (Paris 1857–66) v.78. C. H. TURNER, *Journal of Theological Studies* 6 (1905) 70–85. K. LAKE, *ibid.* 270–282. P. EVIEUX, *Isidore de Péluse* (Paris 1995). A. MOREL, *Synodicon adversus Tragoediam Irenaei,* ed. R. AIGRAIN (Paris 1911). E. SCHWARTZ, *Acta conciliorum oecumenicorum* (Berlin 1914–) 1.4:9–25. G. BAREILLE, *Dictionnaire de théologie catholique,* ed. A. VACANT, 15 v. (Paris 1903–50; Tables Générales 1951–) 8.1:84–98. B. ALTANER, *Patrology,* tr. H. GRAEF from the 5th German ed. (New York 1960) 308–309. J. QUASTEN, *Patrology,* 3 v. (Westminster, MD 1950–) 3:180–185. A. SCHMID, *Die Christologie Isidors von Pelusium* (Fribourg 1948). P. T. CAMELOT, *Catholicisme* 6:153–154. M. SMITH, *Harvard Theological Review* 47 (1954) 205–210, Manuscripts.

[F. X. MURPHY]

ISIDORE OF SEVILLE, ST.

Archbishop, theologian, encyclopedist, and Doctor of the Church; b. Spain, *c.* 560; d. Seville, April 4, 636.

Reckoned as the last of the Latin Fathers, Isidore of Seville was one of the most influential Church Fathers in the West from the early Middle Ages well into the modern period. His fame derived not only from encyclopedic works such as the *Etymologiae* and *De Natura Rerum,* but also from his synthesis of patristic and classical thought, his exegetical and devotional writings, his collections of Church Councils and Canons, his theories of kingship, and his historical writings.

Apart from a brief notice in Braulio of Saragossa's additions to *De Viris Illustribus* (*Patrologia Latina,* ed. J. P. Migne [Paris 1878–90] 81:15–17), no contemporary biography of Isidore has survived, and Isidore is known principally through his written works, through his letters, and through his reported actions at Spanish church councils. Isidore and his family were displaced Hispano-Romans who migrated from Carthagena in southeastern Spain to Seville sometime around 560, either fleeing the constant warfare between Byzantines and Goths that characterized the province of Carthaginensis, or perhaps forcibly resettled there by the Goths. Isidore may have been born after the family migration. Although the fate of his father, Severianus, is unknown, Isidore's brothers LEANDER and Fulgentius, as well as his sister Faustina, all entered the Church. His mother, whose name appears to have been Turtur, may also have entered the Church in her later years. The youngest of four children, Isidore was raised and educated by his elder brother Leander (*c.* 540–600), who was Archbishop of Seville (584–600). Isidore was well-versed in the Latin fathers, particularly Ambrose of Milan, Athanasius, Augustine of Hippo, Caesarius of Arles, Fulgentius of Ruspe, Gregory the Great, Jerome, John Chrysostom, and many other Gallic and North African writers. Isidore's knowledge of classical authors was also extensive, although in some cases through late antique anthologies, commentaries, and scholia. He appears to have had some knowledge of the Mishna or other rabbinic writings. Isidore's ancient fame as a master of the Greek and Hebrew languages has been called into question by modern scholars, and his knowledge of the Greek fathers stems largely from Latin translations.

Isidore succeeded his brother Leander as Archbishop of Seville, probably in the year 600, and had an episcopate of some 36 years, during which time he was one of the most prominent intellectual and spiritual leaders of the realm. His promotion of scholarship and education had long-reaching consequences for the realm, and the results of these endeavors have been termed an "Isidorian" or Visigothic Renaissance. He was confidant and advisor, although not always successfully, to several Visigothic kings, including Sisebut (612–620), Suinthila (621–631), and Sisenand (631–636). He was present in Toledo at the court of King Gundemar in 610, and assisted in transferring the metropolitan see of Carthaginensis from Cartagena to Toledo. In addition to his activities as archbishop of Seville, Isidore participated in several provincial and kingdom-wide Church councils between 610 and 633. He played a prominent role in the second council of Seville (619), where his summation of the Catholic faith so impressed contemporaries that it was included in the canons of the council (ibid. 84:593–608). Isidore's greatest conciliar imprint, however, was in 633 at the fourth council of TOLEDO, over which he presided. The canons of this famous and influential council (ibid. 84:363–390) reveal his influence at almost every turn. Sensing the approach of death in 636, Isidore resigned his episcopal office and performed public penance for his sins. He was canonized in 1589, and declared a Doctor of the Church in 1722.

When one considers the entire corpus of Isidore's writings, more than 20 books composed between 598 and 633, his earliest works tend to be very straightforward lexical or expository texts, whereas his later and more analytical or encyclopedic writings are characterized by an increasing complexity of thought, subtlety of meaning, and clarity of expression. Yet throughout his writings, several larger themes emerge, topics of such importance that Isidore frequently returns to them. These themes include the Church, the monarchy, heresy, the Jews, scriptural exegesis, and history.

Isidore worked to establish and maintain a strong and centralized church in the Visigothic realm, to preserve and transmit the treasury of faith, to promote Catholic orthodoxy, to refute heresy and religious error, and to facilitate cure of souls. In both his writings and his actions at regional and kingdom-wide synods and Church councils he promoted liturgical uniformity, monastic discipline, and the maintenance of diocesan schools. His *De Ecclesticis Officiis* (ibid. 83:736–826) takes a descriptive approach to the offices of the church, as well as the proper functions of clerics, and to various aspects of the liturgical year. This text may have been intended as a guide to uniformity of practice throughout the Visigothic realm. In his *Regula Monachorum* (ibid. 83:867–894) Isidore takes a regulative approach, establishing norms of discipline and practice for communities of religious, suggesting a regimen that is considerably less harsh than either the Benedictine or Columban rules. The precise nature of his many liturgical writings is difficult to ascertain because they have been incorporated anonymously into the great collection of Spanish liturgical texts known as the *Liturgica Mozarabica* (ibid. 85, 86), whose basic structure has been traditionally attributed to Isidore. Through the canons of the fourth council of Toledo (ibid. 84:593–608), especially canons 2 through 56, Isidore extended his legislative approach to ecclesiastical discipline and liturgical practice throughout the entire Gothic realm, stressing not only discipline but also the importance of learning and of uniform liturgical practice. Always emphasizing that the Church in Spain was a true and faithful successor to the Church of the great councils, Isidore assembled a great collection of Greek, African, Gallic and Spanish church councils, canons, and creeds, a collection known to us in its later form as the HISPANA (ibid. 84:93–626), which made available to Isidore's contemporaries and successors the canonical heritage of the universal Church.

Isidore supported a strong and centralized monarchy in the Visigothic realm to protect the Church, to control the violence endemic to the society, and to enhance the stability of the realm. He emphasized a kingdom-wide unity of purpose, but celebrated the uniqueness and primacy of the Visigoths as a ruling and military elite. Kings, he believed, had a responsibility to provide justice in the realm, to be exemplars of piety and mercy, and to promote an environment that would facilitate cure of souls. He insisted that kings would have to render an account to God for how well they ruled their realms. Although Isidore wrote much concerning kingship and governance in his *Sententiae* (ibid. 83:718–723) and *Etymologiae* (ibid. 82:341–345), his best known writings on monarchy appear in canon 75 of the fourth council of Toledo (ibid. 84:383–386), where Isidore emphasized the obligation of the king to rule well, and asserted the obligation of the king's subjects to be obedient to him as "the Lord's anointed one." Less is known about Isidore's attitude towards caesaropapism in the Gothic realm. The Visigothic kingdom was the most romanized of the seventh-century barbarian kingdoms, and the Visigothic kings thought of themselves as the head of the Church in their realms, much as had Roman Emperors such as Constantine, Justinian, and Heraclius. Recent scholarship has suggested that Isidore and his fellow Spanish and Gallic bishops were often expected to submit to royal authority as functionaries of the Visigothic realm, and that they may have acted with great hesitation on such troublesome issues such as anti-Jewish legislation and other affairs of state.

Isidore was an active opponent of the Arian, Macedonian, and Acephalite heresies throughout his lifetime, and in many of his exegetical and theological writings he asserted positions that implicitly refuted these heresies. His *De Haeresibus* (*Patrologiae cursus completus, series latina;* ed. A. Hamman 4.2, 1815–1820) and the sections on heresy in the *Etymologiae* (*Patrologia Latina* 82:296–305) are descriptive rather than analytical, but at the second council of Seville in 619 Isidore actively and analytically refuted an Acephalite heretic through an extensive combination of scriptural exegesis and citations of the Church Fathers, references to Church councils and appeals to the Christian tradition. Additionally, he thought heresy and heresiarchs sufficiently important to the historical record that he listed them in his historical chronicles in much the same spirit that he mentioned other enemies and persecutors of the Church.

Several of Isidore's writings, especially *De Fide Catholica Adversus Judaeos* (ibid. 83:449–538), reflected Isidore's interest in refuting rabbinic calumnies against Christianity, but Isidore opposed the increasingly harsh anti-Jewish legislation that characterized the Visigothic realm. He denounced forced conversions under Sisebut (ibid. 83:1073), and in the canons of the fourth council of Toledo again condemned forced baptisms (ibid. 84:379–380). Although Isidore's stern counsel seems to have restrained the rising tide of anti-Jewish actions and legislation in the Visigothic realm, following his death in 636 the Visigothic kings imposed an increasingly harsh regimen on their non-Christian subjects.

Scriptural exegesis is an important foundation of Isidore's epistemology, and most of his writings are characterized by extensive references to the Bible. His exegetical works are numerous, and include introductions to individual books of scripture (ibid. 83:155–180), a commentary on Isaiah (*Patrologiae cursus completus, series latina;* 4.2,1822–1839), as well as extensive allegorical and typological exegesis in *Quaestiones in Vetus Testamentum* (*Patrologia Latina* 83:207–424), in *Allegoriae Quaedam Sacrae Scripturae* (ibid. 83:97–130), and in *Liber Numerorum* (ibid. 83:179–200). In *Synonyma* (ibid. 83:825–868), a devotional work, Isidore demonstrates how reason can lead the despairing sinner to hope for divine pardon, and then he guides the remorseful soul through an intense and elaborate series of penitential devotions. These devotions make extensive use of synonyms and parallelisms in ways that allow the penitent sinner thoroughly to examine his conscience, to confess his sins, and to seek reconciliation with God.

Incorporating both sacred and secular events, Isidore's historical *Chronicon* (ibid. 83:1017–1058), emphasizes the rise and fall of empires and the course of God's revelations to and interactions with mankind from the creation through the early seventh century, but it also emphasizes innovations in thought and letters, as well as other contributions to the liberal arts. In his *Historia Regibus Gothorum* (ibid. 83:1057–1082), Isidore examines the origin and history of the Goths from their supposed Biblical origins through the early seventh century, incorporating them into the narrative salvation history. Isidore described the Goths as a great and noble people who had been poisoned by the Arian heresy and driven from their homeland centuries earlier, yet God brought a remnant of them to Spain, where they finally converted to the true Catholic faith under the guidance of Isidore's elder brother Leander, and where as kings of Spain the Goths had become the defenders of God's holy and Catholic Church in the uttermost west of Christendom. This Isidorian theme of Spain and its Catholic kings being the great champions and defenders of Catholic orthodoxy exercised a profound influence on Spanish historiography from the early Middle Ages to the present day.

Isidore was best known to medieval scholars as an encyclopedist, and he composed several works that were encyclopedic in nature. His *De Natura Rerum* (ibid. 83:963–1018) was composed at the request of King Sisebut, and focused on a great variety of terrestrial and celestial phenomena. Topical in organization, it deals with subjects as diverse as solar eclipses, the movements of the stars, and the course of the Nile River. His *Sententiae* (ibid. 83:537–738), the first medieval "book of sentences," presents a summary of patristic teachings on theological, moral, and social topics, and draws extensively on the writings of Gregory the Great and Augustine of Hippo. Also organized topically, the first book focuses on theological and dogmatic issues, the second book on ethical and moral problems, and the third book is concerned with the challenges and norms of maintaining the right social order in a Christian society. One of his earliest writings, *De Differentiis* (ibid. 83:1–98), reflects Isidore's lifelong interest in linguistic theory. More lexical than encyclopedic, this work presents topically organized list of words, defines them in terms of their meaning and their etymology, and relates them to their homonyms, synonyms, and antonyms.

The 20-volume *Etymologiae* (ibid. 82:73–928) was his most substantial and influential work. It remained the most comprehensive and important encyclopedia in the west until the publication of Diderot's Encyclopedia in the eighteenth century, and over 1,000 medieval and early modern manuscripts of the *Etymologiae* have survived. Organized topically, the encyclopedia presents descriptive and occasionally analytical accounts concerning thousands of sacred and secular topics, including cautious but open treatment of topics condemned by other Christian writers. Individual items are frequently explained in terms of their etymological origins, reflecting Isidore's belief that to understand the origins of a word is to understand its broader meaning and its relationship to other words. The *Etymologiae* took years of effort on Isidore's part, and his friends occasionally complained to him that he was taking far too long to complete it, demanding of him "render what you owe." The work is organized into 20 volumes, and each volume itself is hierarchically organized, wherein topics that are related to one another are gathered together in individual chapters. Other early medieval writers such as Nennius may have lamented that they had "made a heap" of all that was before them, but Isidore took what was before him and preserved it in an organized, topical, and hierarchical fashion, noting the connections between words and ideas as well as words and physical realities. Some recent scholars have over-enthusiastically referred to the *Etymologiae* as a "database," and it is perhaps Isidore's organized approach to the preservation and presentation of information, with its emphasis on hierarchical structure and the inter-relatedness of knowledge, that has inspired Isidore's popular veneration in the twenty-first century as the unofficial patron saint of computers and the Internet.

Feast: April 4.

Bibliography: Editions and Translations: *Sancti Isidori Hispalensis Opera Omnia,* ed. FAUSTINO ARÉVALO, 7 vols. (Rome 1797–1803), reprinted in *Patrologia Latina,* ed. J. P. MIGNE, vols. 81–84 (Paris 1850–62). *De Differentiis, Liber I,* ed. and tr. into Spanish, C. CODOÑER. *Isidoro de Sevilla, Diferencias Libro I,* Auteurs Latins du Moyen Âge (Paris 1992). *De Ecclesiasticiis Officiis,* ed. C. M. LAWSON, Corpus Christianorum Series Latina. Vol. 113 (Turnholt 1989). *Etymologiarum sive Originum Libri xx,* ed. W. M. LINDSAY. *Isidori Hispalensis episcopi etymologiarum sive originum libri xx,* 2 vols., Oxford Classical Texts (Oxford 1911). *De Haeresibus,* ed. A. C. VEGA. *S. Isidori Hispalensis Episcopi, De Haeresibus liber,* Scriptores Ecclesiastici Hispano-Latini Veteris et Medii Aevi, vol. 5 (Madrid 1940). Reprinted in *Patrologiae cursus completus, series latina;* ed. A. HAMMAN 4.2, 1815–1820. *Historia Regibus Gothorum, Sueborum, et Wandalorum,* ed. and tr. into Spanish, C. RODRIGUEZ ALONSO. *Las Historias de los Godos, Vandalos, Y Suevos de Isidore de Sevilla: Estudio, Edición Crítica Y Traducción,* Fuentes Y Estudios de Historia Leonesa, No. 13. (León: 1975). *History of the Kings of the Goths,* tr. K. B. WOLF. *Conquerors and Chroniclers of Early Medieval Spain,* translated Texts for Historians, vol. 9, 81–110 (Liverpool 1990). *The Letters of St. Isidore of Seville,* ed. and tr., G. FORD JR., (Amsterdam 1970). *The Medical Writings: An English Translation with an Introduction and Commentary,* tr. W. D. SHARPE, *Transactions of the American Philosophical Society,* New Series, vol. 54, Pt. 2 (1964), 1–75. *De Natura Rerum,* ed. and tr. into French, J. FONTAINE. *Isidore de Seville: Traité de la Nature,* Bibliothèque de L'École des Hautes Études Hispaniques. Fascicule XXVIII (Bordeaux 1960). *De Ortu et Obitu Patrum,* ed. and tr. into Spanish, C. CHAPARRO GÓMEZ, Auteurs Latins du Moyen Âge (Paris 1985). "The Rule of Isidore," tr., A. W. GODFREY, *Monastic Studies* 18 (1988), 7–29. *De Viris Illustribus,* ed. C. CODOÑER MERINO, *El "De Viris Illustribus" de Isidoro de Sevilla: Estudio Y Edicion Critica* (Salamanca 1964). *Sententiae,* ed. P. CAZIER, Corpus Christianorum Series Latina, vol. 111 (Turnholt 1998). *Versus,* ed. J. M. SÁNCHEZ MARTÍN, Corpus Christianorum Series Latina, vol. 113a (Turnholt 2000). Studies: J. FONTAINE, *Isidore de Séville et la culture classique dans l'Espagne wisigothique,* 3 v. (Paris 1959, 1983); *Isidore de Séville, Genèse et originalité de la culture hispanique au tempt des Wisigoths* (Turnhout 2000). P. CAZIER, "Isidore de Séville et la naissance de l'Espagne Catholique," *Théologie Historique* 96 (1994). P. J. MULLINS, *The Spiritual Life According to St. Isidore of Seville* (Washington, D.C. 1940). R. L. STOCKING, *Bishops, Councils, and Consensus in the Visigothic Kingdom, 589–633* (Ann Arbor 2000).

[J. T. CROUCH]

ISIDORE THE FARMER, ST.

Patron of Madrid and of farmers; b. Madrid, 1070; d. there May 15, 1130. Isidore entered the service of the wealthy Juan de Vergas, in whose employ he spent the remainder of his life. Isidore's wife, a saint also, María de la Cabeza (Torribia) (d. *c.* 1175; feast: Sept. 9), bore him one son who died at an early age. Isidore won the respect and admiration of all, especially his employer, by reason of his unusually devout life. Miracles were associated with him even during his lifetime, e.g., angels doing his farmwork when he lingered overlong in the local church. After his death his reputation for sanctity grew, culminating in his canonization on March 12, 1622, by Pope GREGORY XV. His tomb is in the church of St. Andrew, Madrid. Isidore is also the patron of the U.S. National Catholic Rural Life Conference.

Feast: May 15.

Bibliography: *Acta Sanctorum* May 3:509–546. Z. GARCÍA-VILLADA, "San Isidro Labrador en la historia y en la literatura," *Razón y Fe* 62 (1922) 36–46, 167–176, 323–335, 454–468. F. MORENO CHICARRO, *San Isidro Labrador* (Madrid 1992), extensive bibliography. A. BUTLER, *The Lives of the Saints,* ed. H. THURSTON and D. ATTWATER, 4 v. (New York 1956) 2:323–324.

[A. O'MALLEY]

ISIS AND OSIRIS

Egyptian god and goddess whose cult goes back to the 2d millennium B.C. and was adopted, with some modifications, by the Greeks after the conquest of Alexander the Great. The chief Greek innovation was the introduction of the god Sarapis, or Serapis, into the worship of Isis. The cult spread throughout the Mediterranean world, and along with the cults of Cybele and Mithras, it became one of the most common and popular pagan religions in the early centuries of the Christian era. The Egyptian god Horus often appears in the cult, frequently as the pudgy child Harpocrates and sometimes the hawk-headed Egyptian deity, Anubis, as well. The mysteries of Isis are described in Apuleius's *The Golden Ass,* and in Plutarch's *Concerning Isis and Osiris.* Both Isis and Sarapis are heralded in several long hymns, usually called aretalogies because they extol the wondrous powers and miracles of these divinities. Many of their temples are known in both East and West, the best preserved being those that have been excavated at Delos in the Aegean and at Pompeii in Italy.

Bibliography: T. A. BRADY, 308–309, 459–460, 793. J. G. MILNE, 6:374–384.

[T. A. BRADY]

Isis Omnia of Egypt, illustration. (Archive Photos)

ISLAM

The religion that God set forth for Abraham, Moses, Jesus, and MUHAMMAD proclaimed by the latter in Arabia in the 7th century, which enjoys the allegiance of approximately 1.2 billion persons, about one-sixth of the total estimated population of Earth. The name Islam, invariably preferred by its adherents to Muhammadanism (one of the archaic Western designations for the religion), is an Arabic word signifying "surrender," and its believers call themselves Muslims, "those who have surrendered to God." The world's Muslims are centered chiefly in the northern and eastern parts of Africa and the western and southern parts of Asia. The largest national representations are those of Pakistan and Indonesia, but Islam's traditional cultural centers have been the Arab world and Iran. Considered the fastest-growing religion in the world, Islam is expanding southward in both East and West Africa, as well as in the West, notably in the United States, where, ever since the conversion of the son of the founder of the Black Muslims to Sunnite Islam in the 1970s, the majority of African American Muslims have been "orthodox" Muslims. The subject will be treated in five parts: the origins of Islam; the Islamic creed; "The Five Pillars" and Islamic religious practice; Islamic law, theology, and mysticism; and modern trends in Islam.

Origins of Islam. Islam can never be disengaged from the life of the man Muhammad. Born at MECCA in Arabia about A.D. 570, he belonged to a cadet branch of the Quraysh tribe, then prominent in Mecca, and in young manhood married the widow of a wealthy merchant. When he was about 40, he began to make a series of remarkable claims. He maintained that he was the bearer of a "recitation" (Arabic QUR'ĀN) transmitted to him by the Angel Gabriel and "the Spirit." This Qur'ān, he claimed, was the final redaction of what *Allāh,* "the God of Abraham, Ismael, Isaac, and Jacob, and the Tribes [of Israel] . . . and Jesus" (Qur'ān 2.136) wished to communicate to the human race. It carried in itself, as he was ultimately compelled to insist, the power of invalidating the former Scriptures whenever they disagreed with it, although he readily allowed that those Scriptures (presumably including the whole of the Bible) represented divine revelation "in its original form" no less than the Qur'ān. He further regarded himself as a prophet, indeed as the last of the series of prophets or "messengers" whom God had sent to restore the purity of His religion; for not only had it been deformed by Jews and Christians, in his view, but it had also remained unknown to others, notably the Arabs. These claims enjoyed no striking success at Mecca, though Muhammad steadily enlisted small numbers. In 622 he and his followers fled to MEDINA, a city some distance north of Mecca, an "emigration" (Arabic *HIJRA*), from which Muslims date their era. At Medina, Muhammad added to the number of his followers and welded them together into a vital community and a military power, which was nearly ready, at the time of his death in 632, to extend itself by rapid conquests to mastery over much of Asia and Africa.

Various questions concerning Islam's origins and, more particularly, concerning the sources of the material contained in the Qur'ān, arise naturally. The orthodox Muslim position is a flat denial that such sources could possibly exist. The Muslims do not deny that Muhammad knew Jews and Christians; what they deny is that Muhammad was, in any sense, the author of the Qur'ān. Although God's revelations through Muhammad are considered the ultimate authority in Islam, Muhammad's deeds and sayings (collected in the bulky Islamic traditions or Hadīth literature) are considered to exemplify the ideal way of life for the Muslim. There are variations in orthodox Muslim thought as to how the balance should be drawn between patterning one's life after Muhammad and following one's own interpretation of Qur'ānic injunctions. Many Muslims do not deny that there were slight variants in the earliest versions of the Qur'ān or that the arrangement of the chapters according to length is an arbitrary one, but they hold that the present form, which was soon established, corresponds to a heavenly archetype of "the Book." The Islamic concept of revelation is thus considerably more rigid than is the Catholic, the Protestant Christian, or even the orthodox Jewish; for it excludes the notion of human, though divinely inspired, authorship of Scripture.

Jewish and Christian Influence. Non-Muslim scholarship has taken a different view of the matter. It has nearly always held that the major influences on Muhammad must have been principally, but not exclusively, Jewish and Christian, and that those influences were colored by Muhammad's own character and made over to conform to aspects and needs of the pre-Islamic Arabian mind. Within this broad framework, however, opinions have clashed. The prize dissertations of Abraham Geiger, the Jewish reformist, stimulated much of the modern scholarly discussion; in it he argued for a dominant Jewish influence on the Qur'ān. An opposing view, holding that influence to have been chiefly Gnostic, won the powerful support of Julius Wellhausen. The latter view was followed by many scholars until more recent studies, for example those by Charles Torrey and Abraham Katsh, persuasively argued again for a greater Jewish influence. It must also be noted that at the beginning of the 21st century, greater attention was paid to Muhammad's reactions to the traditional religions of South Arabia.

Although pre-Islamic Arabia was still distinctly pagan and, by comparison to Mediterranean lands, relatively uncivilized, it harbored numerous Jews and Christians. There is no difficulty in accounting for the presence of Christians there (*see* ARABIA, 5) or in explaining why those Christians tended to be Nestorians. The foremost Christian community was Najrān, under the Nestorian influence of the king of Hira. There were Jewish trading settlements at Teima, Khaybar, Medina, and cities farther south. They are occasionally mentioned in rabbinical literature and may have dated back to the 7th century B.C. There is evidence, too, of considerable numbers of Jewish proselytes among the Arabs. They do not appear to have possessed any higher learning, however, and it has been suggested that they had been affected by forms of heterodox thought in which both Christian and pagan notions had been incorporated.

Development of Muhammad's Ideas. For those coming from a scholarly tradition that puts a heavy emphasis upon the written word, it is difficult to sift the Qur'ān and the tradition literature for historical information. It is certain that as a boy and young man Muhammad knew, and was on friendly terms with, both Jews and Christians. He is reported to have heard the bishop of Najrān preach and to have met on a caravan a monk "well versed in the knowledge of the Christians" (Ibn-Ishāq, *Sīrat Rasūl Allāh* [*The Life of Mohammad*], tr. A. Guillaume [London 1955] 79–81). (*See* BAHIRA LEGEND.) The first encouragement he received after his prophetic call, if one excepts that of his wife, came from her cousin Waraqah, "who had become a Christian and read the scriptures and learned from those that followed the Torah and the Gospel" (*ibid.* 107). At the same time he was familiar with various classes of Jewish scholars, whom he could name accurately, and there is reason to believe that many Jews, expecting the imminent advent of a messiah in Arabia, showed special interest in him. Finally, he was associated with a mysterious group that called itself the Hanifs (Arabic *hunafā'*, "the pure ones"), whose members, disgusted with idol worship, favored a monotheism incorporating elements from both Judaism and Christianity.

After Muhammad began his preaching, he had constant and close contacts with Jews and Christians, but it is hard to say whether or in what manner he profited by them. His adversaries, among whom were many Jews and Christians, watched eagerly for indications of fraud; and Muhammad was able successfully to assume a remarkably self-assured attitude toward any accusations of that sort. In the early Meccan period, to be sure, he was given to appealing, though somewhat vaguely, to Jewish and Christian authority for his teachings on the unity of God and on divine judgment: "All this is written in earlier scriptures, the scriptures of Abraham and Moses" (Qur'ān 87.18). The only respect in which he then admitted differing from those Scriptures was that his own revelation was in the Arabic language: "Before [the Qur'ān] the Book of Moses was revealed, a guide and a blessing to all men. This book confirms it. It is revealed in the Arabic tongue" (Qur'ān 46.12). The late Meccan and early Medinese periods saw the greatest readiness on Muhammad's part to absorb Jewish elements into Islam, for at that time his special aim was to win Jewish converts, especially among the Jews of Medina.

Changed Attitude toward Jews and Christians. For a time Muhammad went out of his way to model Islam on the Bible, but later he assumed a sharply different attitude. That attitude stemmed, one suspects, from the unwillingness of Jews and Christians to accept his teaching. The Qur'ānic chapters of that later period clearly demonstrate Muhammad's wish to disassociate Islam from Jewish and Christian "orthodoxy" and to establish the supremacy of his own religion by vigorous disputation and the use of force. Unsuccessful in his attempt to convince the Jews and Christians, he began to attack them intellectually and physically. Only the Jews offered organized opposition. In the beginning they seem to have provided Islam with a number of false disciples. Nevertheless, they were incapable of prolonged or effective resistance to the growing Islamic power, and within a few years Khaybar and the other Jewish colonies in North Arabia had been vanquished.

Very probably Muḥammad had heard improvised translations of the Jewish and Christian Scriptures. It is quite possible, too, that information concerning one group may have come from the other and that wherever Scripture is misrepresented or distorted, Muḥammad followed homiletical embellishments. Julian Obermann summed up the problem of Islamic origins very well:

> What with the vast overlapping of Jewish and Christian lore, especially in the period and area involved [the general impression of greater Jewish influence on Islam], may be illusory or at least inexact, unless it be borne out by detailed evidence for each element under discussion. Obviously, Old Testament and even rabbinical materials might have been transmitted to Arabia by Christian channels; while seemingly New Testament matter might easily have been derived from rabbinical homilies. Indeed, the situation is of a kind that in a considerable number of instances we can go only as far as to demonstrate a given element in Islam as of Judaeo-Christian origin, but no further. (*The Arab Heritage,* ed. N. A. Faris [New York 1963] 59–60)

Islamic Creed. Islam has carefully maintained its distinction between faith (*imān*) and practice (*'ibādāt* or *iḥsān*). Faith, usually defined as "assent to that which comes from God, and confession to it," has been formulated in a creed considerably more complicated than the *shahādah,* the simple profession of faith: "There is no god but God [*Allāh*], and Muḥammad is His messenger." There are six classic articles in the otherwise varying Muslim creeds: concerning God, angels, the Holy Scriptures, prophets and "messengers," resurrection and judgment, and predestination. Muḥammad's monotheism began, no doubt, as a rejection of paganism; yet it was highly positive. It was, as he never ceased repeating, the monotheism of Israel. The God of Islam was Yahweh, without those truths about Him revealed by Christ. It is fairly certain that there were various interpretations of the Trinity in various Christian circles during Muḥammad's lifetime, some of which may have included the Virgin Mary. The Qur'ān denies the Incarnation: "God is one, eternal. He did not beget and was not begotten" (Qur'ān 112.3). For Muḥammad there was no redeemer, no need for redemption, no original sin. Otherwise Allah is invested with nearly the same general attributes of Yahweh. The angels and archangels, even to their names, are those

of the Bible. Satan also figures, as do the "genies" (Arabic *jinn*) and other spirits similar to but not precisely identical with lesser devils.

The references to earlier Scriptures in the Qur'ān are sufficiently vague to render their exact identification difficult. Only a few OT books are mentioned by name, and the Gospel (in the singular) is treated as though it were a book revealed to Christ. At first Muḥammad appealed to the authority of these books to uphold his own prophethood and religion, but later seemed to suggest that they had been hopelessly corrupted and falsified. Muslims have never felt obliged, therefore, to justify the inconsistencies and discrepancies (which exist in considerable numbers) between the Qur'ān and the earlier Scriptures in the forms in which they have come down to us. There is only one indisputable quotation from the Bible in the Qur'ān (that of Ps 36 [37].29 in 21.105), but scores of OT stories are repeated, in the main accurately, with many reminiscences of their Hebrew wording. There are also Talmudic stories, such as the lowing of Aaron's calf (7.146) and Abraham's trial by fire, a rabbinic play on Ur and the Hebrew *'ûr,* "fire" (21.68–70).

Muslims also distinguish prophets from "messengers"; the latter are believed to be holy men sent by God to teach specific peoples. Muḥammad is thus regarded both as the "seal" of the prophets and as the messenger to the Arabs. The Qur'ān mentions 8 messengers and 24 prophets, 4 of them Arabs and the rest Hebrews. The prophets include most of the major figures in the early history of the Hebrews, but exclude Isaiah, Jeremiah, Ezekiel, and all of the minor prophets but Jonah. Despite the honor in which Abraham is held, the predominant figure in the Qur'ān is Moses. If one follows Theodor Nöldeke's chronology of the chapters, Moses is mentioned more than 100 times in the chapters from the Meccan period alone. The angels refer to the Qur'ān in one passage as "a Scripture revealed since the time of Moses, confirming previous Scriptures" (46.30).

Christ, by contrast, is mentioned in only two chapters of the Meccan period, and references to Him throughout the Qur'ān are sparse. Many of Christ's utterances as found in the canonical Gospels and elsewhere in the New Testament are not mentioned in the Qur'ān, and those that are mentioned frequently deviate from the text of the NT. Christ appears as a messenger born (by Virgin Birth) of the Virgin Mary. Indeed, he is often referred to as the "Son of Mary." Some of the stories of His infancy, such as His speaking in the cradle (19.30–34; 5.109) and fashioning a live bird out of clay (3.43; 5.110), echo apocryphal writings known to have existed in Coptic, Syriac, and even Arabic versions. Muḥammad granted that Christ worked miracles, but denied that He was crucified.

That position, commonly taken by some Gnostics and Docetists, was expressed in the Qur'ān: "They [the Jews] declared: 'We have put to death the Messiah Jesus, the son of Mary, the apostle of Allāh.' They did not kill him, nor did they crucify him, but they thought they did" (4.156). It has been argued from what is missing in the Qur'ānic narratives that much of Muḥammad's information about Christ must have come from Jewish informants. It is a widespread later Islamic belief, still current and not without Qur'ānic support, that Christ will return at the end of the world to slay the Antichrist. He is often called the "Word" of God and His "Spirit" in the Qur'ān, and "Messiah" is usually added to His name.

The Qur'ān bears strong witness to the resurrection of the flesh and the Last Judgment. Only heaven and hell are everlasting, although it appears that hell serves as a kind of purgatory for some Muslims and that Muḥammad (and, according to some theologians, other prophets as well) has intercessory powers with God for them. The Islamic belief in predestination is not as rigid as some commentators have made it to be. It has always been a live issue in Islamic theology, and the matter of working out an acceptable formulation has been left to the devices of the exegete and the ordinary believer. The Qur'ān says, for example, "God causes whom He wills to err, and whom He wills He guides; and you shall assuredly be called to account for your doings" (16.93).

The "Five Pillars" and Islamic Religious Practice. By the time of its conquests outside Arabia, Islam regarded itself as a universal religion for all mankind; so there has never been any perfect ethnic or linguistic tie among Muslims, though Arabic (in a special way, over a wider area and for a longer time), Persian, Turkish, and Urdu have come to be the principal languages of its expression. Islamic practice is a complex realm, ranging from the obligatory Five Pillars through the "necessary but not obligatory" on to the "voluntary" acts of the Muslim. The Five Pillars are as follows: the profession of faith in Islam, prayer, fasting, almsgiving, and pilgrimage.

Orthodoxy. The profession of faith consists of the simple statement: "There is no god but God, and Muḥammad is His messenger." The believing recitation of this formula, preferably before witnesses, is sufficient in itself to make one a Muslim. Islam has no church, no priesthood, no sacramental system, and almost no liturgy. The pattern of belief and practice of the SUNNITES enjoys the adherence of all but a small percentage of Muslims. The SHĪ'ITES comprise the second-largest grouping of Muslims. Deriving from the political "partisans" of 'ALĪ and his heirs, they have developed distinct doctrinal, legal and ritualistic features. Sectarianism in Islam has never had quite the same connotations as heresy in the Christian church, allowing for the acceptance of numerous religio-legal entities within the community of Islam.

Prayer. One of the most attractive aspects of Islam for the Christian is its steadfast devotion to prayer. There is a set form of ritual prayer, prefaced by ablutions and accompanied by "bowings" (Arabic *rak'ah*), for the five daily prayers prescribed by Islamic tradition and law. Muslims are called to public prayer by the muezzin (Arabic *mu'adhdhin*) from the minaret of a MOSQUE. Many Muslims pray in the mosque only at noon on Fridays, when there is a sermon (Arabic *khuṭba*), although more devout believers may perform all of the prescribed prayers there. Formal prayer must be performed facing toward Mecca. There is a tradition also of private and contemplative prayer, largely associated with SUFISM.

Fasting. Muslims are obliged to fast during the entire month of RAMADAN, which, because of the lunar reckoning from the Hijra, may fall at any time of the year. It is a total fast, but only from daybreak to sunset. It is a community exercise. Those who are ill or on a journey during that time are exempted from it, but must fast an equal number of days later on. Muslim spiritual writers such as al-Ghazzālī emphasize that Ramadan implies more than mere fasting and is a time for repentance and drawing the heart nearer to God. Voluntary fasting during other times of the year, especially in expiation for sins, is recommended and practiced.

Almsgiving. Muslims are enjoined also to give alms (Arabic *zakāt*). In the early days of Islam free-will offerings were regarded as satisfying this obligation. Later, however, a formal tax of one-tenth or one-fifth of the income (according to circumstances) was imposed upon Muslims. A contribution of one-fortieth of the income was considered adequate by many later legists. In modern times almsgiving has generally reverted to a matter of free-will offerings. The Qur'ān distinguished the worthy objects of free-will offerings (relatives, orphans, travelers, and the poor; 2.211) from those upon whom the revenue of *zakāt* was to be expended (slaves and prisoners, debtors, tax collectors, those to be conciliated by the Islamic community, and those fighting in a holy war; 9.60).

Pilgrimage to Mecca. The fifth of the Five Pillars is the pilgrimage to Mecca (Arabic *ḤAJJ*). Every Muslim is expected to journey there once in his lifetime if he possesses the means. There are two types of pilgrimage: the lesser pilgrimage, which can be performed at any time of the year with an abbreviated ritual, and the greater pilgrimage, which must be performed on specific days during the month of Dhū al-Ḥijjah. When the pilgrim dons his simple white robes and enters into the state of *iḥrām,* he must abstain from all violence, sensual pleasures, and adornment for the duration of the pilgrimage. When he reaches Mecca, he goes immediately to the Ka'bah, the black-draped cuboidal "holy house" in the central square. This is the shrine, important in pre-Islamic religion, that Muslims believe was built in its original form by Abraham. It was only fairly late in his career that Muḥammad unequivocally incorporated the shrine and pilgrimage into Islam. The first Muslims had prayed facing Jerusalem. After kissing the Black Stone, the Muslim circumambulates the Ka'bah, marches seven times between the hills of al-Safā and al-Marwah, and then journeys the 14 miles to Mount 'Arafāt for the ceremony of *wuqūf*, "standing before God," for which lengthy prayers are prescribed. On the return to Mecca he prays at Muzdalifah, casts stones at certain pillars believed to represent the sites of temptations of Ismael, and offers a blood sacrifice commemorating Abraham's sacrifice in Gn 22.13. After ceremonial tonsure and a second circumambulation of the Ka'bah, the pilgrimage proper is ended, although most pilgrims go on to Medina to visit Muḥammad's grave and other sites associated with his life.

Other Religious Customs. According to some Muslim opinion, the *jihād*, or holy war, is to be considered a sixth "pillar" of Islam. This obligation was formulated in quite general terms in the Qur'ān 2.190, 193: "Fight in the way of God against those who fight against you, but do not commit aggression. . . . Fight against them until sedition is no more and allegiance is rendered to God alone; but if they make an end, then no aggression save against the evildoers." Although holy war has lost much of its persuasive force after the period of Islamic expansion (the consensus amongst orthodox Muslims has been that holy war should not be waged when it appeared as though the Muslims might lose), there have been modern attempts to revive it, especially amongst "radical" groups as a means of protesting Western, particularly American, global hegemony.

Besides these major matters of practice, the Qur'ān and Islamic tradition have supplied many others. Circumcision, for instance, is universally practiced among Muslims as a matter of religious observance, although the Qur'ān does not mention it. Wine, pork, gambling, and usury are forbidden. So, too, strictly speaking, are the making of images, the veneration of saints, and the use of devotional objects. Since the Qur'ān envisioned a close-knit community of true believers, it also contained many regulations concerning guardianship, dowries, divorce, and inheritance, as well as a complete punitive system against theft, fraud, perjury, and murder.

Festivals. Muslims celebrate many festivals. The most popular of them are the greater and lesser festivals that mark the end of Ramadan, the month of fasting. The greater festival, begun while fellow Muslims are sacrificing animals on the way back to Mecca, is celebrated with somewhat less enthusiasm than the lesser festival, which begins as soon as the new moon is visible after Ramadan. On that occasion there is great feasting and cheer, with exchanging of gifts. Paradoxically, it is also a favorite occasion for visiting the graves of one's departed relatives and friends. The birthday of Muḥammad (Arabic *mawlid al-nabī*) is marked with some solemnity, though rather less than one might have expected. Among the Shī'ites, the largest minority sect, the 10th day of the month of Muḥarram is the principal festival of the year. Shī'ism added two significant items to the Sunnite creed: first, a belief in a continuing divine "manifestation," particularly valuable with respect to Qur'ānic interpretation, in the descendants of 'Ali; second, a veneration for "the passion," for voluntary and innocent self-sacrifice to the point of martyrdom by the merits of which believers attain salvation and eternal life. These items, whose Christian parallels are obvious, are united in the liturgy of the 10th of Muḥarram, when Shī'ites commemorate the death of 'Ali's son Ḥusayn on Oct. 10, 680. Ḥusayn was killed in a skirmish between government troops and a small body of sympathetic supporters who were accompanying him to al-Kūfah in Iraq, where he intended to organize a revolt against the UMAYYAD caliphs of Damascus. The fate of Ḥusayn became a prototype and pattern for Shī'ite martyrdom and a symbol of the Shī'ite cause. In areas where Shī'ites are in a majority or at least represented in considerable numbers, this anniversary is preceded by nine days of rigorous religious discipline and culminates in a wild procession through the streets in which a catafalque for Ḥusayn is accompanied by horses, blood-smeared attendants, and numbers of naked young men flagellating themselves with chains and swords. The veneration of 'Ali and his sons has extended, it is interesting to note, to many of the Sunnite Muslims.

Islamic Law, Theology, and Mysticism. Islam is nothing if not the religion of the Qur'ān. The Qur'ān is believed by Muslims to constitute God's final and consequently singular revelation to mankind. There has never been any universally or even widely accepted ultimate authority in Islam except the Qur'ān. Questions of its interpretation have always been, therefore, of fundamental and crucial importance. Necessarily the Qur'ān had to be supplemented in several ways. It was supplemented first of all by the custom (Arabic *sunnah*, hence the name Sunnite) of Muḥammad himself, established principally by means of the tradition literature concerning him and his companions, based in turn upon chains of more or less authentic transmitting authorities (Arabic *isnād*), subsequently evaluated by an intricately developed science. It was obvious that traditions often conflicted; a man named Ibn-abī-al-'Awja was executed in al-Kūfah in 772 after confessing that he had forged several thousand traditions complete with chains of authority that would be regarded as genuine.

Law. The weakness of this supplement soon became obvious and a more efficacious supplement, designed to counteract that weakness and to serve the needs of a rapidly expanding state, was provided by the employment of certain principles, such as consensus of opinion (*ijma'*), analogical deduction (*qiyās*), independent reasoning (*ijtihād*), and private opinion (*ra'y*) in the creation of an Islamic law (*see* ISLAMIC LAW). Four recognized schools of legal interpretation (Arabic *sharī'ah*), namely the Hanafite, Malikite, Shafi'ite, and Hanbalite schools, all eponymous, were inaugurated during the 8th and 9th centuries and have remained in force until modern times. Today, while the impact of the *sharī'ah* has been abridged by the encroachment of modern civil law in certain areas of jurisprudence, there is at the same time a revival of the strict interpretation of the sharī'ah in many parts of the Islamic world. Throughout the medieval and early modern periods, however, owing to the virtually unique identification of the religion of Islam with the government of any Islamic state, the sharī'ah totally regulated the lives of Muslims. It extended to almost every detail of private life, comprehending all its religious, social, political, and domestic behavior. The offices of *qāḍi* (judge), *mufti* (legal expert), and *'ālim* (lawyer, though very often used simply for "learned man") rose to and maintained for many centuries positions that were of capital importance in Islamic life. In those places of the world where extensive Islamification of society is being attempted (such as the Sudan and Indonesia), as well as in those countries where the ruling factions have appropriated Islamic terminology to shore up their regimes (such as Saudi Arabia and Afghanistan), the sharī'ah and the concomitant penal code (e.g., the amputation of the hand of the thief) is the law of the land.

Systematic Theology. Distinct from the sciences of the traditions and of legal interpretation, systematic theology (*see* KALĀM) began later in the 9th century, partially in response to quarrels between the traditionalists and the incipient legists and to the influx of late Hellenistic philosophical notions, but most evidently in opposition to a group of rationalistic Muslims in Basra and Baghdad called the MU'TAZILITES. This group asserted a series of unpopular positions on current issues such as the "creation" of the Qur'ān, the unity and justice of God, the nature of salvation, and free will. Although their aim seems to have been to protect Islamic dogma from what they regarded as corruptions to which it was open, they made use of a naive and rudimentary philosophical pro-

cedure that associated them with the target of their own attacks. When they converted the caliph al-Ma'mūn to their viewpoints and instituted an inquisition (Arabic *miḥnah*), they generated a serious ideological crisis within the Islamic community and a powerful reaction that began with the apostasy of Abū al-Hasan 'Alī al-ASH'ARĪ (873?–935). Al-Ash'arī, concerned mainly with the preservation of the pure transcendence of God, disenchanted with his Mu'tazilite masters, and influenced by the thinking of Ibn-Hanbal, the founder of the legal school already mentioned, set about systematically to refute the Mu'tazilite propositions. Few of his works have survived; but from those that have, it is clear that he himself so far advanced the methodology of treatment of these questions that his enduring reputation as the founder of Islamic theology and symbol of its orthodoxy appears justified. He was responsible for the disengagement of philosophy from this realm, enabling Islamic philosophers to go their independent ways, and for the close connection that developed between theology and the legal schools of the *sharī'ah.*

Al-Ash'arī was the founder of the most influential school of Islamic theology; yet Ash'arism differs considerably from the teaching of al-Ash'arī himself. In the immediately succeeding centuries the work of al-Baqillani, al-Juwayni, and others continued and advanced the science. Later al-Ghazzālī, al-Rāzi, al-Ījī, and al-Jurjāni let their thought be formed by it. Eventually, however, it came to an intellectual standstill in stereotyped manuals for students. Its commanding position was not, of course, achieved at once. Its choice as an official system of the Seljuk sultanate and, later, of the Ottoman sultanate was doubtless instrumental toward that end. Still, it must be recognized that in the earlier period Ash'arism had a powerful rival in the school of al-Maturidi of Samarqand. The basic impulses of the two schools seem to have been very similar and the differences between them relatively slight. Maturidism died out for reasons principally political. At any rate, by the 12th century the most potent challenges to Islamic theology were those emanating from outside the discipline, from the philosophers, notably Ibn Sīnā (AVICENNA), and from the Sufis.

Mysticism. Sufism (Arabic *ṣūf,* "wool") is the name ascribed in general to the entire ascetical and mystical movement within Islam, as well as to its manifestations in the eremetical and regular religious life from the 8th century to the present. Questions concerning the origins of Sufism remain extremely difficult to solve, and there are still some matters on which scholarly opinion has differed with unusual sharpness. Louis Massignon sought to prove that the origins of Sufism lie wholly within the Islamic tradition of the Qur'ān and the *sunnah,* despite the surface facts that the Qur'ān says little that could be interpreted as a justification for the ascetic life as lived and loved by the Sufis and that the *ḥadīth* literature contains a number of explicit injunctions against it, for example: "There is to be no monasticism in Islam." Other scholars have adduced origins in the remnants of Christian asceticism within Islam after its conquests, in Zoroastrianism (*see* ZOROASTER [ZARATHUSHTRA]), and even in direct and indirect Hindu and Buddhist influences, although these scholars have fallen to quarreling among themselves. In any case, it cannot be denied that from the 8th century onward there was an increasingly influential movement, to be classified in the realm of popular religion, which produced more and more individuals willing to retire from the world in order to pursue an ascetic and contemplative life. That they may have done so partly in response to social and political instabilities and current theological controversies pales before the simple fact that they did so and, in doing so, greatly affected the course of Islamic intellectual history. The convention of periodizing the history of Sufism is largely the result of Sufi hagiography itself. Certainly there were early Muslim ascetics, many of them with Shī'ite leanings, who eventually grouped themselves together, were nourished by an esoteric reading of the Qur'ān and later by the writings of such mystics as al-Rabā'ah and al-Ḥallāj, and who, increasingly as the decades wore on, sought a communal life based on common conviction and intention.

Influence of Ghazzālī. From the ranks of the early Sufis came popular preachers and original thinkers who firmly founded Sufism and so disturbed the orthodox legal-theological institution of Islam that they were regarded not only as disruptive, but as bad Muslims. Into this situation was born, in the 11th century, Abū-Ḥāmid al-Ghazzālī (*see* ALGAZEL [GHAZZĀLĪ, AL-]). Influenced by Sufism in his youth, he nevertheless turned to the traditional sciences and to philosophy in his education and brilliant academic career. This prize student of al-Juwayni soon became a leading professor in Baghdad. As suddenly as he turned against philosophy because of the works of Avicenna, which he refuted in a book entitled *The Incoherence of Philosophy,* he turned against the whole orthodox system and toward Sufism. He resigned his professorship at Baghdad and began a radical reconsideration of Islam that resulted in the nearest thing to a reformation that Islam has ever experienced. By combining and indeed harmonizing the Islam of the Qur'ān, the theologians, the legists, and the Sufis against the philosophers, he created, in his greatest work, *The Revivification of Religious Sciences,* a sensitive, well-structured, and comprehensive *summa* of Islamic religious thought. His achievements, like al-Ash'arī's, became an integral part of Islamic orthodoxy and transformed it by opening an entire new universe of thought. Through al-Ghazzālī's

reforming efforts *kalām* gained a new vision and Sufism a new respectability. For many centuries philosophical, theological, and mystical writings in Islam bore the stamp of al-Ghazzālī's thought.

The directions and extent of the development of that thought cannot be said to have fulfilled the plan or spirit of al-Ghazzālī himself. The marriage of Sufism with *kalām* was intellectual rather than practical. In practice the two went their separate ways. Philosophy, as has been noted above, had always gone its separate way. As a result, there was never again to be such a unified system of Islam as al-Ghazzālī's, though each of the areas of thought mentioned deepened as a consequence of his system. Sufism, in particular, enjoyed an immense popularity during the succeeding centuries. As its theory continued to develop, however, a multiplicity of religious folk practices and heterodox notions were kneaded into it. The speculative aspects of later Sufism were combined in a new eclectic system by IBN 'ARABĪ of Murcia (d. Damascus, 1240), who turned the movement in a more pantheistic direction and toward closer circles of initiates. The loose mosque communities of early Sufism gave way to larger confraternities and finally to religious orders (*see* ISLAMIC CONFRATERNITIES), Elements of the monastic, the eremetical, and the mendicant states were combined in various proportions in these orders. Normally, however, a postulant came to a monastery, became a novice, led a communal life under the direction of a *shaykh* or *pīr,* whose position was either elective or hereditary. Later he might go out preaching or on to another community, but the characteristic ritual of *dhikr* and his manner of life readily identified him as a Sufi (Arabic *faqīr,* Persian *darvīsh*).

One of the greatest of the Sufi summarizers was Jalāl al-Dīn al-Rūmī, whose monumental *Masnavi* did more than other such compilations to inspire later Sufism and arrest its decline. Decline it did, however. The number of orders multiplied; observance was lax; and finally there was little left in the numerous popular lodges and clubs to suggest the grand origins of Sufism. Although Sufism still exists and is very influential on the modern frontiers of Islam, it enjoys nothing like its former glory.

Philosophy, too, responded to al-Ghazzālī's challenge. Al-Rāzī (RHAZES) speaking for himself, set the field on a more clearly rationalistic basis in vindication of Ibn Sīnā. It was in Muslim Spain, however, shrinking in the face of the Christian *Reconquista,* which had begun in the 11th century, that the last truly great philosophical work was done in Islam. There, in the Almohad court of Abū-Ya'qūb Yūsuf, Abū Bakr ibn Ṭufail wrote his *Ḥayy ibn-Yaqẓān,* a philosophical romance owing a great deal both to Neoplatonic compendia and to Sufism. There, too, one of the greatest Islamic philosophers, Ibn Rushd (AVERROËS), received his training. Rising quite literally to al-Ghazzālī's challenge in his work *The Incoherence of the Incoherence [of Philosophy]*, he rose to it even more profoundly and immortally in his series of commentaries upon the works of Aristotle, works that were very soon, in translation, to find a more appreciative audience in the new universities of Christian Europe and to influence very substantially the development of SCHOLASTICISM.

Islamic theology, on the other hand, grew more and more implacably hostile to what it regarded as the continuing innovations of Sufism and philosophy. As it did so, it strengthened its ties to the *sharī'ah*. In the work of Ibn-Taymīyah (1263–1328) the orthodox reaction was confidently and powerfully asserted in a return to fundamentalism. Thereafter, until modern times, the traditional disciplines and fundamental doctrines and principles of Islam engaged the energies of the orthodox thinkers completely. Though recent scholarship has discovered enough independent thought on the part of some Muslims to force a revision of the notion that the whole of the Ottoman period was one of intellectual sterility, it remains true that a basic unquestioning orthodoxy held the Islamic community fast together in a rigid system for centuries.

Modern Trends in Islam. The modern Muslim is true to these beliefs and practices and to this intellectual tradition, in his fashion. However thick may be the gloss of elements of "folk" Islam, the basic items in the creed and the Five Pillars are common, with only the slightest modifications, to all Muslims. In recent times there have been such stirrings within Islam, in response to various challenges from within and without, that the modern Muslim is by no means as fully complacent about the omniresponsive nature of his religion as his ancestors were. Few modern Muslims remain unaffected, in fact, by one or another of the more recent trends in Islam.

It is significant that the first impulse toward radical change in modern times came from Arabia. The low ebb to which Islam had sunk in the Arabian Peninsula by the 17th century, which apparently was virtually a return to primitive religion, gave rise to the movement called Wahhābism, founded by Muḥammad 'Abd-al-Wahhāb (1703–92), calling for a return to Islam's first principles and attacking laxity of morals and those innovations attributable, over the centuries, to Sufism and philosophy. It championed the severe Hanbalite legal code and the uncompromising interpretations of Ibn-Taymīyah. Having enjoyed the patronage of the Saudi tribal chieftains, whose descendants came to power over the entire peninsula after World War I, Wahhābism is now general within the kingdom of Saudi Arabia. It was followed by a daring

vindication of al-Ghazzālī by a Yemenite scholar, Muḥammad al-Murtaḍā (d. 1790). The introduction of Arabic printing into Egypt in 1828 led to the wide dissemination of standard theological works and evoked new controversy and thought. In northwest Africa Ahmad al-Tijāni founded in 1781 a new Sufi order. Later a new type of reforming congregation was organized along Sufi lines by Aḥmad ibn-Idrīs (d. 1837), whose disciples went on to establish other congregations in Libya and East Africa. A more revolutionary group was that of the al-MAHDĪ (Muḥammad Aḥmad; 1844–85) in the Sudan.

All of these movements, true to the inherent identification of the two within Islam, had political as well as religious aspects and goals. After Napoleon's invasion of Egypt and the subjection of various portions of the Islamic world to non-Muslim colonial powers, the issues were sharpened. The differences separating Muslims were stressed, in an attempt to unite them under a caliphate in defense of Islam. Such a pan-Islamism was advocated by Jamāl-al-Dīn al-Afghāni (1839–97), who traveled widely throughout the eastern Islamic countries propagating his theories and influencing other movements. He inspired revolutions in Egypt and Iran and laid the basis for more recent popular movements combining Islamic fundamentalism with a political program. The uncompromising attitude of the Muslim Brotherhood, for example, retained many of al-Afghāni's ideas. A different movement, a syncretism not unlike or unrelated to Unitarianism and the Ramakrishna mission in Hinduism, led the Bābis and Bahais out of Islam completely (*see* BABISM; BAHA'ISM). An apostolic group of a related tenor, called the AḤMADIYYAH, is viewed with considerable suspicion by both Sunnite and Shī'ite Muslims.

One of al-Afghāni's disciples, the Egyptian *shaykh* Muhammad 'Abduh (1849–1905), instituted a more interesting though ultimately less influential line of thought by separating the political from the religious side of the question. 'Abduh was the first great Islamic modernist, a man of enormous ability who attempted to reformulate Islamic doctrine in the light of advances, especially in the sciences, achieved in the West, confident that his efforts would only confirm the truth of Islam. The scene of his work was al-Azhar in Cairo, and it was published in the traditional form of a commentary on the Qur'ān. As carried on by his pupil Rashīd Ridā (1865–1935), however, the attempt came some way back toward Ibn-Taymīyah and a new doctrinal rigidity. More successful, perhaps, was the effort of the Indian Muslim Muḥammad Iqbāl (1876–1938), whose attempts at harmonizing Islam with the thought of Western writers on philosophy and mysticism, in his poetry and a prose work entitled *The Recon-*

struction of Religious Thought in Islam, closely resemble that of al-Ghazzālī.

The role of Islam in recent history has been such as to mingle and cloud such elements. Modernization, in particular industrialization, has started in the Muslim world with such force and momentum that nothing could possibly remove its effects or call a halt to it. Basic religious and social institutions are changing. Increased mobility, opportunities for livelihood, education, and political responsibility have accelerated the process. What further forms Islam's response to them might take is unclear. Certainly the secularism of Turkey and some of the Arab countries has not met with wide acceptance, but there is still little clarification of issues among modern Muslims. Israel's expansion beyond its 1948 borders resulted in an Islamic "revival," with many Muslim Palestinians returning to traditional religious practices. Various "radical" groups in the Middle East and elsewhere that have advocated violence as a legitimate means of overthrowing illegitimate political leaders, or subverting an undesirable social order, have a strong religious rhetoric. Especially since the fall of the Berlin Wall, certain elements in the Islamic world have increasingly seen the West, especially the United States, as a threat to Islamic society and traditional values. It remains to be seen how the relationship between Islam and the West, and Islam and Christianity will be negotiated in the 21st century.

Bibliography: D. B. MACDONALD, *The Development of Muslim Theology, Jurisprudence and Constitutional Theory* (New York 1903). T. W. ARNOLD and A. GUILLAUME, eds., *The Legacy of Islam* (Oxford 1931). A. GUILLAUME, *Islam* (Baltimore 1954). A. J. WENSINCK, *The Muslim Creed* (New York 1932). J. W. SWEETMAN, *Islam and Christian Theology* (London 1945). H. A. R. GIBB, *Modern Trends in Islam* (Chicago 1947). H. A. R. GIBB and J. H. KRAMERS, eds., *The Shorter Encyclopedia of Islam* (Leiden 1953). W. C. SMITH, *Islam in Modern History* (Princeton 1957). J. KRITZECK and R. B. WINDER, eds., *The World of Islam* (New York 1960). J. A. WILLIAMS, *Islam* (New York 1961). J. BURTON, *The Collection of the Quran* (Cambridge 1977). J. VAN ESS, *Theologie und Gesellschaft im 2. und 3. Jahrhundert Hidschra. Eine Geschichte des religiosen Denkens imfruhen Islam,* 6 v. (Berlin, New York 1991–97). W. A. GRAHAM, *Beyond the Written Word: Oral Aspects of Scripture in the History of Religion* (New York 1989). G. R. HAWTING, *The Idea of Idolatry and the Emergence of Islam: From Polemic to History* (Cambridge 1999). J. HOROVITZ, *Koranische Untersuchungen* (Berlin, Leipzig 1926). T. NOLDEKE, *Geschichte des Qorans,* new ed. by F. SCHWALLY, G. BERGSTRASSER, and O. PRETZL, 3 v. (Leipzig 1909–38). R. PARET, *Der Koran. Ubersetzung* (Stuttgart 1962). A. RIPPIN, ed., *Approaches to the History of the Interpretation of the Quran* (Oxford 1988).

[J. KRITZECK/C. WILDE]

ISLAMIC ART

Islam, among the world's major religions, is usually thought to have avoided significant aesthetic expressions of its major spiritual tenets. One will not find in Islamic art the artistic equivalents of Gothic cathedrals with their sophisticated reflection of Thomist thought, of Byzantine icons with their spiritual effectiveness, or of Buddhist sculptures with their involved iconographic programs and their pietistic quietness. And yet the artistic creation of Islamic civilization could not, any more than the creation of any culture, escape the needs and ideals of its faith. In this context of the relationship of the faith of ISLAM to Islamic art a brief presentation will be made here of the monuments that were erected between the 7th and the 17th centuries in the vast area that stretches from the Atlantic Ocean to the Gulf of Bengal. Since it will not be possible to mention either all monuments or all problems, this article will concentrate on three topics: it will first define the features of the faith that had a direct influence on the arts, then proceed to explain the major elements of Islamic religious architecture, and finally show that the faith had an influence on representational and decorative arts as well.

The Faith of Islam and Art. There is, first of all, one major area in which the faith of Islam requires some sort of monumental expression. This is the MOSQUE, from Arabic *masjid,* "a place to prostrate one's self [in front of God]," as in prayer. In a strict sense, the individual act of prayer, the main purely religious obligation of the Muslim, could be accomplished any place. But Islam is also a communitarian social order and, at least once a week, prayer is meant to be a congregational experience as well as a private one: "O ye who believe, when the call is heard for the Friday prayer, haste unto remembrance of God and leave your trading" (Qur'ān 62.9). In the early years of the Muslim community the private house of the Prophet in MEDINA (a simple courtyard with rows of columns on its southern and northern sides and private rooms to the east) became almost accidentally the place of gathering of the small band of faithful, and it was only later that it acquired the sacred value of being the first mosque. As the Muslim world grew and conquered, the mosque maintained its function as the place where the community assembled, learned, fulfilled some of its financial obligations, and proclaimed its allegiance to temporal rulers.

Liturgy and the Mosque. The mosque, in short, meant to serve all activities of the community, thereby emphasizing the key Muslim point of the inseparability of social order from allegiance to certain beliefs. Its main physical requirement was space, as large a space as would accommodate the body of believers available in any one community. From the very beginning it acquired three further needs: an orientation (the *qiblah*), since prayer is to be directed toward MECCA, the first and unique sanctuary of God; a device for calling the faithful, eventually to become, in most instances, the tall tower known as the minaret; and a place of honor for the IMĀM, or leader of prayer, usually the head of the Muslim community or his representative; it was a sort of throne, known as the *minbar,* and it is only little by little that it has become the multistepped structure found today in most mosques. Some place for ablutions must have been available, but it played no known part in early architecture. In the 7th and 8th centuries two other features were added: the *miḥrab* (a concave niche in the back of the mosque, usually supposed to indicate the direction of prayer, but more likely to have been originally a memorial to the place where the Prophet stood when leading prayers); and, in some mosques only, a *maqsūrah,* a screen identifying the place of the prince. Space commensurate to the population, plus orientation, minaret, *minbar, miḥrab,* and, secondarily, a place for ablutions and a *maqsūrah* were then the major features that, to speak liturgically, identified the purposes and requirements of the main Islamic religious building and the only ones needed almost at the very beginning of the new faith.

Islam and Images. The second area of Islam's impact on the arts concerns the representational arts. It is usually assumed that, from the very beginning, Islam asserted its opposition to any kind of representation of living forms. This is simply not so, and the whole problem can best be understood if put into its proper historical context. In 7th century Arabia, images of any kind played a very minor part in the life and culture of either nomads or city dwellers. In the Qur'ān there is no statement opposing or justifying images. The only references, in fact, to any kind of representation are either to prohibited idols (e.g., 6.75) or to one case of a miracle attributed to Jesus (3.49). However, two basic thoughts run throughout the Qur'ān: the absolute opposition to idolatry, and the total power of a single God (for instance, 39.62–63 or the celebrated passage, 2.255). After the conquest of Christian and other lands, Muslims with these ideas encountered a world in which holy images played a considerable part and in which the great crisis of iconoclasm and of the place of holy images within the faith was already brewing (to explode a century later). The Muslims clearly interpreted Christian, and later Buddhist, views on images as idolatry and as challenges to God's exclusive power; and since their lack of artistic background did not permit them to develop alternate ideas, they little by little formulated a theory of opposition to images in general because of the character of images in the 7th and 8th centuries in Christianity. In its extreme and absolute form, this antagonism was limited to religious circles only and there were several degrees of it, the most moderate of which merely prohibited the representation of God. But the general mood

Sculptured colonette of the Qutab Minar. (©Arthur Théuerart/ CORBIS)

of orthodox Islam remained throughout one of reluctance to deal with images for fear of their magical powers and, as a result, Muslim secular art tended to be most inventive in the formation of a characteristically Islamic imagery.

Architectural Development of the Mosque. The first four or five centuries of Islamic history were characterized by the creation in every Muslim city of large congregational mosques.

Regional Styles. Their type varied from province to province according to local circumstances and architectural traditions. In Syria the mosque of Damascus used the ancient Roman temple area and classical or Byzantine columns for an original composition of a courtyard surrounded by porticoes, with a three-aisled portico indicating the direction of prayer. In Iraq, Egypt, and the Muslim West the same basic plan was modified by the transformation of the *qiblah* area into a vast hypostyle hall of columns or piers. The most superb remaining in-

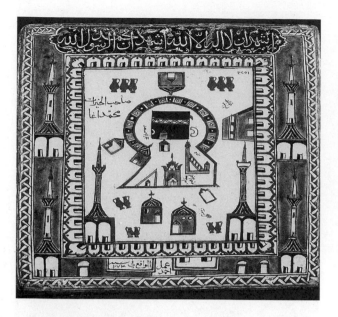

Islamic Ceramic with the tomb of Muḥammad. (©Archive Iconografico, S.A./CORBIS)

stance of this type is the mosque of CÓRDOBA, where the double tier of arches introduced a particularly original solution to the problem of light in a large hall (*see* UMAYYADS). A different solution was eventually found in Iran, where there had not been a major columnar tradition. The solution, as seen in Isfahan, was to keep the courtyard but to surround it with a screen of high vaults and arcades behind which vaults and domes covered variable interior arrangements. After the conquest of Constantinople in 1453, a highly original, centrally planned mosque evolved from the indigenous Christian tradition. In all instances the most significant feature was that local and extremely diverse architectural techniques were modified into new compositions, which succeeded in providing the main need of the Islamic mosque: large space. In almost all instances the court framed by covered halls remained as a constant memory of the Prophet's house in Medina.

Mosque and Palace. While the single large mosque remained for centuries the characteristic example of religious architecture in Islam, it was not the only one, and it underwent many internal changes. The history and significance of other architectural types as well as of changes within the mosque are complex matters, whose details are often still improperly investigated; only two points of wider interest will be considered here. The first is that the architecture of the mosque was constantly influenced by the architecture of the palace, about which, unfortunately, very little is known, except in the palaces of the first two Muslim centuries and in the Alhambra, at Granada, of the 14th Christian century. Yet it seems

clear that the slow development in mosque architecture of wide central naves, of domes in front of *miḥrabs,* and of outer monumental gates was a direct result of the taste created by princes in their palaces.

Special-Purpose Mosques; Endowed Institutions. The other change that occurred within Islamic religious architecture is perhaps of greater interest to the study of religious architectures in general. Although none of its basic tenets were modified, Islam as a whole changed considerably over the centuries. As its cities grew and its social order became more complex, the religious institution also developed in intricacy. Large congregational mosques still fulfilled their purpose as the main magnets of a city's life, but the very rich or groups of people tied together by a variety of bonds (guilds, tribal or family allegiances, city quarters) began to prefer to worship in smaller, less crowded surroundings. Many smaller mosques were therefore created, often on the same plans as the large ones but more intimate in character, like small havens of peace in the crowded and turbulent cities.

Another phenomenon of medieval Islam was the growth of heresies; to counter them the various orthodox princes instituted from the 11th century on a sort of educational institution, the *madrasah,* where principles of orthodox theology and jurisprudence were taught. Several types existed, but at its most monumental, as in the case of the *madrasah* of Sultan Hassan in Cairo (14th century), it had a large central court with several vaulted halls opening on it and quarters for students between these large halls. The tomb of the founder was often added to the composition.

Related to the *madrasah* were the *ribat* and the *khanqah,* institutions of uncertain origins that were the Muslim equivalents of the monastic orders of Christianity. All these institutions, to which must be added the more purely philanthropic hospitals, were usually founded by princes or wealthy merchants, who endowed them by developing business enterprises, hostelries, baths, warehouses, and bazaars, whose revenues were exclusively earmarked for holy institutions and therefore inalienable. Thus from about 1100 the whole Muslim world became literally covered with a large number of closely related philanthropic, religious, and business enterprises, whose remains can still be found in Cairo or Aleppo or Jerusalem. All of them received a monumentality commensurate with the wealth and prestige of the endowers; and all of them tended to use approximately the same basic forms: high gates, open courts, long vaulted halls, domed tomb chambers. Although comparable institutions existed in other systems of faith as well, it is peculiar to Islam that, quite early in the Middle Ages, they were all executed in monumental form.

Memorial Edifices. A phenomenon related to the preceding one is that of the monumental mausoleum. Early Islam was quite opposed to any form of visible commemoration of the dead. The earliest known memorial building, the Dome of the Rock in Jerusalem, did not acquire its precise memorial quality of a monument to the Ascension of the Prophet until later. But in the 10th century two separate movements became strong enough to initiate a complete reversal of earlier practices. One was purely secular and involved attempts by princes to proclaim their glory or that of their dynasties beyond death. The other was religious; the main Muslim heterodoxy, Shi'ism (*see* SHĪ'ITES), laid particular stress on the descendants of the Prophet and appealed to emotional and personal aspects of early Islamic history rather than to the strict and rather dry legalism of orthodoxy. This was often achieved by building up the sacred *martyria* to 'Alī, Husayn, and other descendants of the Prophet. As an answer to this development, the orthodox began to develop cults of holy men, from ancient Hebrew Prophets to contemporary heroes. Mystical orders also worshipped by the tombs of their founders. Thus the Muslim world became covered with mausoleums, from humble ones dedicated to obscure saints to the magically secular Taj Mahal. Their shapes varied considerably, but almost all of them were variants on the traditional classical mausoleum, i.e., the central plan, circle, square, polygon, always covered with a dome. These domes became characteristic focal points for popular piety or mere illustrations of princely vanity. As monuments of architecture such buildings as those of the Cairo cemeteries, of the Shah Sindah in Samarkand, and of Agra in India are among the most impressive creations of Islamic art and, together with the congregational mosques and the monuments of philanthropy, best identify the various facets of Muslim religious feeling.

Architecture and Decoration. It would not be proper to omit, in a discussion of Islamic architecture, those elements of construction or decoration that have given it its originality. From Spain to India, vaults and domes were the characteristic parts of construction on which most effort was exercised. The problem was to build high domes and vaults that would still manage to create wide interior spaces and to give light. Although solutions were numerous, it is in Ottoman architecture in Turkey that the most superb engineering effects were achieved, while Spain and Iran provided the most impressively original effects, in which decoration—stucco compositions of various three-dimensional shapes known as *muqarnas* or stalactites, and colored tiles—played a notable part. And, in a sense, the ultimate quality of Islamic architecture resides in the stunning fashion in which a wide variety of decorative devices tending to cover the totality of the wall struck

Thirteenth-century Islamic Candlestick. (©Archive Iconografico, S.A./CORBIS)

a generally successful balance with more properly architectural values of mass and spaces. Neither the specific aesthetic characteristics of these developments nor their historical contexts have yet been sufficiently studied to hazard a judgment on the causes of this phenomenon. And yet, as one contemplates the brilliant domes and minarets of Isfahan or the intensely logical mosques of Istanbul or the rich and solid monuments of Cairo, they express varying aspects of the Muslim faith: its order, its total involvement of all human activities, and the colorful poetry of its emotional fringes.

Decorative and Pictorial Art. The main emphasis of this article has been architecture, because in this, quite clearly, an art was created that was closely bound to the Islamic faith. But this is not to say that the faith of Islam did not affect, positively or negatively, other aspects of artistic creation. Three points of particular significance are here considered.

First, there is no doubt that the great development of calligraphy was related to Muslim veneration of the holy text of the Qur'ān. Qur'ānic passages served the purpose of images in Christian art in identifying and explaining the purpose of monuments. But the importance of this veneration of writing went much beyond this simple level. The smallest object or the largest building acquired

The Dome of the Rock, Jerusalem. (©Christine Osborne/CORBIS)

a decoration of letters, words, or quotations and formulas that gave them quality. It is for this reason that the calligrapher became the artist par excellence, so that even today his product is prized much above that of any other creator. It is curious to note that the first purely Islamic development of a new artistic form, that of a magnificent ceramic in the 9th century in eastern Iran, uses beautiful writing as its most characteristic decorative effect, although the content of the inscriptions is only remotely connected with the faith as such.

A second impact of the faith is perhaps more debatable but should be mentioned because it has often been discussed. It has always been agreed that some of the most typical values of Islamic art were decorative. One of the peculiarities of this decoration was that it usually abandoned natural elements and, instead, broke up visible forms and recombined them according to new and different abstract patterns. It has been suggested that this characteristic derived from an attempt to reflect the Muslim theological position that creation is a continuous divine miracle, whose individual elements are not automatically in the same relationship to each other. The artist, in other words, felt free to recompose the atoms of the universe and to create new and unknown shapes.

Finally, while it is clear that the main source of inspiration of Islamic painting—in books or on ceramics—was secular, certain peculiarities of iconography and style may be related to the mystical ideas of late medieval Islam. Thus, for instance, it can be argued that the tendency of Persian painters after the 14th century to create artificial settings in which man and nature seem to blend in superb masses of color reflected the pantheistic tendencies of some mystical groups that saw all things as equal symbols of the divine. It has also been argued that many images, especially those of love, had in fact a possible esoteric meaning, since love, like banqueting or drinking, particularly favorite subjects for representations, could be interpreted symbolically as well as literally.

Taj Mahal, Agra, India. (Archive Photos)

All these points still deserve considerable investigation, and it would be hazardous to accept them entirely at face value. They would, however, illustrate a fact of importance: beneath its superficial veneer of glamour and brilliance, Islamic art did try to reflect the more profound aspects of the faith of Islam. It was hampered, no doubt, by the fact that official orthodoxy was reluctant to rely on artistic creation for the expression of its beliefs; but the faith played too important a part in the lives of men not to have influenced their arts.

Bibliography: K. A. C. CRESWELL, *Early Muslim Architecture,* 2 v. (Oxford 1932–41); *A Short Account of Early Muslim Architecture* (Baltimore 1958); *Muslim Architecture of Egypt,* 2 v. (Oxford 1952–59). A. U. POPE and P. ACKERMAN, eds., *A Survey of Persian Art,* 7 v. (New York 1939), uneven. B. GRAY *Persian Painting* (New York 1961). R. ETTINGHAUSEN, *Arab Painting* (New York 1962). Articles in *Ars Islamica* and *Ars Orientalis.* For relations between art and faith see L. MASSIGNON, "Les Méthodes de réalisation artistique des peuples de l'Islam," *Syria* 2: 47–53 and B. FARÈS, *Essai sur l'esprit de la décoration islamique* (Cairo 1952). R. H. PINDER-WILSON, ed., *Studies in Islamic Art* (London 1985). O. GRABAR, *The Formation of Islamic Art* (New Haven, CT 1987). A. KHATIBI and M. SIJELMASSI, *The Splendor of Islamic Calligraphy* (New York 1996). K. OTTO-DORN, *The Art and Architecture of the Islamic World* (Berkeley 1996). R. IRWIN, *Islamic Art in Context: Art, Architecture, and the Literary World* (New York 1997). R. HILLENBRAND, *Islamic Art and Architecture* (New York 1999). J. BLOOM, *Early Islamic Art and Architecture* (Burlington, VT 2000). O. GRABAR and C. ROBINSON, *Islamic Art and Arabic Literature: Textuality and Visuality in the Islamic World* (Princeton NJ 2000). R. ETTINGHAUSEN, O. GRABAR and M. JENKINS, *The Art and Architecture of Islam 650–1250* (New Haven, CT 2001). Y. TABBAA, *The Transformation of Islamic Art during the Sunni Revival* (Seattle 2001).

[O. GRABAR]

ISLAMIC CONFRATERNITIES

Islamic organizations that have some similarities with religious orders in Christianity. Since the 12th century more than 30 such Muslim confraternities, often with widespread influence, have risen and fallen in ISLAM, from the Qādiri fraternal order, named after a Persian mystić, 'Abd-al-Qādir al-Jīlāni, who died in Baghdad in 1166, to the Sanūsi order, founded in 1837 by an Algerian warrior shaykh, al-Sanūsi. Members of these confraternities are commonly known as DERVISHES. Normally an applicant or novice (*murīd*) enters upon an initial stage (*'ahd,* covenant), passes through a course of instruction and discipline (*tarīqah,* path), and is then advanced into various stations (*maqāmāt*) of the spiritual life.

Practices and Beliefs. In these the fraternal orders differ widely. The members of an early and still popular one, al-Rifā'i, named after an Iraqi mystic Aḥmad al-Rifā'i (d. 1183), are commonly known as howling dervishes. They are distinguished by ability to perform strange feats, such as swallowing live coals and glass, holding red-hot irons, or passing knives through their bodies. Another fraternal order, al-Mawlawi, founded by a Persian, Jalāl al-Dīn al-Rūmi (d. 1273 in Qūniyah, Konieh), is commonly known as the whirling dervishes, because of the movements they practice to stimulate ecstasy. Their ritual includes music—frowned on by Islam—and monotonous chants, with a slow whirling circular movement while the arms are extended and eyes closed. The dance ends in the fall of one after the other of the exhausted participants.

All orders join in a common ritual, *dhikr* ("remembering," mentioning God's name, Qur'ān 33.41), which constitutes the main devotional exercise in the fraternities' quarters. The worshipers sit on the floor with legs folded in the Oriental pattern, turn their faces toward Mecca, close their eyes, and repeat the word Allah or such formulas as *lā ilāha illa Hū* (no God but He), while moving their heads from right to left. The *dhikr* is the only elaborate ritual in Islam.

The dervish orders' quarters (*takīyah, zāwiyah*) are often called monasteries but in their social and educational functions they correspond more nearly to Protestant places of worship. In fact the corporate bodies behind them may be said to have assumed the position of the separate church organizations in Protestant Christendom. In addition to the few regular members, cloistered or wandering, the orders have numerous laymen attached to them. These continue to live in the world, observe daily prayers, and occasionally attend the *dhikr* ceremony. They are comparable to Franciscan and Dominican tertiaries. In pre-Kemalist Turkey most men had some such affiliation with one order or another. The most popular and influential of these was the Bektāshi, dating from the early 16th century and once connected with the redoubtable Janissaries. Bektāshis share excessive SHĪ'ITE reverence for 'ALĪ ('ALĪ IBN ABĪ TĀLIB) and manifest Christian theological influence. A Bektāshi branch, termed Qalandari, enjoins a life of unceasing wandering. Another dervish order called Khalwīyah (seclusion practitioners) requires of all members a stated period of retreat, with fasting to the utmost capacity of the individual and continuous repetition of religious formulas.

Position within Islam. It is clear from the above that dervish fraternities have developed practices in violation of the spirit and letter of Islam. A tradition ascribes to Muḥammad the saying, "No *rahbānīyah* (monasticism) in Islam." Ṣūfī orders, as a rule, exalt their respective founders and surround them with halos of sanctity. (*See*

ṢŪFĪSM.) Miracles (*karāmāt*) are often ascribed even to the successive superiors. This power was denied Muḥammad himself in the Qur'ān. Despite orthodox Islam's disapproval, orders have always flourished. They seemed to fill the gap between the finite worshiper and the infinite worshiped. The great theologian ALGAZEL (Ghazzāli, al-, d. 1111), who himself practiced for a time Ṣūfīn wandering in quest of spiritual satisfaction, contributed to making mysticism palatable. But those extremists who ended in pantheism or antinomianism were accorded no toleration. A Persian mystic, al-Hallāj, who went so far as to declare, "I am the Truth," was in 922 flogged, exposed on a gibbet, decapitated, and burned by an 'Abbāsid inquisition. To the Ṣūfīs al-Hallāj became the first great martyr.

Besides introducing a form of monasticism and a ritual, dervish orders have contributed and popularized the cult of saints. Their sainthood did not preclude women. Female hagiology is headed by Rābi'ah al-'Adawīyah (d. 801) of Basra, who lived a life of celibacy, asceticism, and otherworldliness, instructing and guiding disciples in the "mystic way." When the Prophet appeared in a dream and asked her whether she loved him, her reply was: "My love of God has so possessed me that no place remains for hating ought or loving any save Him." Dervishes were evidently also responsible for introducing, or at least diffusing, the rosary beads (*subḥah*) as an instrument of Muslim devotion. They borrowed them from Eastern Christians, who had received them from Hindu sources. Only the austere WAHHĀBIS today reject the beads, as they do the cult of saints.

A fundamental difference between Ṣūfī and Christian monastic organizations stems from the fact that Islam, according to the learned system, is a lay religion, with no centralized authority, no hierarchy, no sacraments, no apostolic succession. This fact accounts for the self-development of the dervish orders, each in its own way, ending in a state bordering on chaos. It makes of the *ulema,* especially among the Sunnites, nothing but men learned in theology and canon law.

Bibliography: R. A. NICHOLSON, *Studies in Islamic Mysticism* (Cambridge, Eng. 1921). M. SMITH, comp., *Readings from the Mystics of Islām* (London 1950). D. B. MACDONALD, *Development of Muslim Theology, Jurisprudence and Constitutional Theory* (New York 1903). H. LAMMENS, *Islām: Beliefs and Institutions,* tr. E. D. ROSS (London 1929), ch. 6. C. H. A. FIELD, *Mystics and Saints of Islam* (London 1910). A. J. ARBERRY, *Ṣūfīsm: An Account of the Mystics of Islam* (New York 1952).

[P.K. HITTI/EDS.]

ISLAMIC LAW

Islamic law is designated in Arabic by the term *sharī'a,* the original sense of which is a place resorted to for drinking, and by extension, a way of conduct leading to eternal life. ISLAM is a lay theocracy. God is head of the Islamic community. God alone legislates, and His will is carried out by the community of believers. The law is what God has made known to the community of believers through revelation to the Prophets (among whom are Moses and Jesus), the last of whom is MUḤAMMAD, "seal of the Prophets." The prophets are the obedient instruments of the revelation, passing it on intact to the believing community. In its broadest sense, the law encompasses articles of belief, regulating man's relation to God (religion), as well as rights and obligations regulating man's relation to his fellow man (law). Thus religion and law, in the modern sense of the words, are found included, though distinct one from the other, under God's law.

Foundations of the Law. The law is found in scripture and tradition; i.e., in the QUR'ĀN, which is the sacred book of Islam, and in the Tradition of the Prophet Muḥammad. God's revelation ceased with the death of the Prophet. The Qur'ān was soon thereafter committed to writing and the traditions were codified. The science of jurisprudence (*fiqh*) came into being, including the auxiliary sciences of the Qur'ān and of tradition.

A Muslim submits to the law as a precept of faith (the literal meaning of *Islām* is "submission"); in so doing he fulfills his duty toward God. He also obeys the law as a social duty imposed by God, and in so doing he fulfills his duty toward man. Disobedience to the law is a sin committed against God, not only an infringement of the legal order.

While the Qur'ān contains the stories of many biblical prophets, Islam considers both Judaism and Christianity as suffering from their followers' having tampered with the divine revelations they received through the Prophets. The purest form of the divine revelation is to be found in its last manifestation through Muḥammad. God's creation is to be enjoyed by man, whose weakness is taken into consideration by the law. Man is not to be burdened beyond his capacity. The fundamental rule of law is liberty (*al-aṣl fī 'lumūr al-ibāḥa*).

Liberty is the starting point of the law. This is illustrated by the five categories under which the actions and omissions of men are classified: (1) obligatory, (2) recommended, (3) permissible, (4) disapproved, (5) forbidden. Between the absolutes of obligatory and forbidden, there are three categories under which actions and omissions may be classified in order to lessen the rigor of the law. All of the schools of law agree as to the definition of each of these categories but differ greatly as to the classification of actions and omissions therein. The tendency, however, of the four orthodox schools of law

which have survived to the present day is to make frequent use of the three intermediate categories. The Ẓāhirite school, no longer in existence, gave more leeway to the absolutes, going against the spirit of the law. But liberty cannot be absolute, lest it destroy itself. So the function of the law is to set limits on this liberty so as to guide it towards the benefit of the individual and society. Good and evil are defined by the law, that is, by God. It is divine voluntarism that characterizes Islamic law; there is no question of natural law as a "supreme reason existing in God," inscribed in the very nature of things. In Islam, there is no question of positive law subordinating itself to divine law and respecting its dictates; they are both the same: Islamic positive law is a divine positive law.

Sources of the Law. To scripture and tradition, the doctors of the law add two more sources: the consensus of the community (*ijmā'*) and the analogical method (*qiyās*); this was called for by the developing needs of the community as it expanded after the great conquests following the death of Muḥammad.

The Qur'ān is believed to be the uncreated word of God as it was literally revealed to Muḥammad in MECCA and MEDINA, the two holy cities of Islam. It is the most important single document for the study of Islam, not only in the fields of religion and law, but also in those of language and literature. The Sunna of the Prophet Muḥammad are his words, actions and tacit approval retained in the memory of his companions and later fixed in writing. The vehicle of the Sunna is the *ḥadīth* (tradition), which is composed of two parts: (1) a chain of transmission (*isnād*) containing the names of persons who transmitted the text of the tradition and upon whom rests its authenticity, and (2) the text (*matn*) itself, usually a terse statement. [*See* ISLAMIC TRADITIONS (HADITH)]. The importance of the Sunna gave rise to the science of tradition (transmission of traditions, their falsification, criticism, codification, and commentaries). The authority of the consensus (*ijmā'*) of the community of believers is based on the Qur'ān (4:115; 2:137; 3:98; 4:85); and it in turn guarantees the authenticity of the other sources.

The consensus, like the Sunna, appears under three forms: word, action, and tacit approval. This source is an extremely important one in the history of jurisprudence. It made possible the adoption and the elimination, as the need arose, of many elements of various provenance (Greek, Roman, Jewish, Persian, and Arab) in Islamic law. The fourth source, analogy, differs from the three cited above in that, unlike them, it is not in any way infallible. This source gave rise to bitter struggles in the Islamic community before it became adopted. The one school of law that failed to adopt it, the Ẓāhirite school, ceased to exist as a juridical school in the Middle Ages. Other schools, characterized by staunch traditionalism, accept the analogical method in the legal realm, but oppose this rational element in theology on the basis that the Sacred Book does not omit anything that must be known for salvation. Besides these four principal sources of the law, juridical methodology has recourse to subsidiary principles as developed by the various schools of law.

Science of Jurisprudence. Knowledge of scripture and tradition, highly desirable in itself, was not sufficient in order to arrive at a knowledge of the law. The law was not plainly written in the sacred texts, but had to be arrived at by painstaking study. This gave rise to the science of jurisprudence (*fiqh*) and to the science of the principles of jurisprudence (*uṣūl al-fiqh*).

The principal figure in the development of the law was the jurisconsult or interpreter of the law (*faqīh*). The study of the law became the most respected of all endeavors, assuming a position commensurate with its object: it enabled the community to fulfill the divine precept (Qur'ān 3:106) that it "promote the good and repress evil." Endowed chairs in the colleges (*madrasa*) in the 11th century were given to professors of jurisprudence (*mudarris*) and scholarships, including room and board, were given to students of the law (*mutafaqqiha*). *Fiqh* had first developed in close connection with the study of the Qur'ān and tradition; by now, it had become an independent study, the pursuit of which led to important official positions in the state. There being no clergy in Islam, the jurisconsult took on the highly important position of minister and interpreter of the law. By exerting himself to the utmost degree (*ijtihād*) to arrive at a legal decision in a case or concerning a rule of law, he was considered to be a *mujtahid*, capable of making his own decisions, as opposed to a *muqallid* who practiced *taqlīd*, that is, the imitation or following of the decision of another.

Not all jurisconsults were capable of the same degree of *ijtihād,* and they were ranked accordingly. As for the layman, he was understandably an "imitator." For the solution of a legal problem or a clarification of some point of law, anyone could approach a jurisconsult for a legal opinion, or *fatwā,* and the jurisconsult acting in this capacity is referred to as a *muftī.* Many of these legal opinions were collected and published under the designation of *Fatāwā* (pl. of *fatwā*). These legal sources contain a mine of information on the actual social, political, and religious life of their respective periods, for they dealt with questions that arose out of the need of the times, rather than with theoretical problems.

Law Books and Modern Practice. In time there came into being an extremely rich literature in the field of law, the Islamic science par excellence. The flourishing of this literature took place under the 'ABBĀSIDS (750–1258). Soon books on the law became standardized as to their content. These works are divided into two parts: the first dealing with ritual duties, i.e., the believer's relations with God; and the second, with prescriptions concerning the believer's relations with his fellow man. The ritual duties are five in number: ritual purity, prayer, alms, fasting, and pilgrimage. These are called the "pillars of faith." The other parts of the book include prescriptions concerning marriage, inheritance, contracts, and public and penal law.

In modern times, however, Islamic law is no longer operative in all of these fields in many Islamic countries. Its influence is limited to the spheres of dogma and ritual, and to the field of law concerning personal status, in the life of the Muslim family as well as in the relation of Muslims with non-Muslims (*see* DHIMMI). Certain Islamic states have adopted European civil codes, now operative side by side with Islamic law, each in its own sphere of action; but there have also been extreme solutions attempted. On the one hand, Turkey has abolished the caliphate and the whole notion of the Muslim community. On the other, Saudi Arabia under the WAHHĀBIS has maintained Islamic law as the only law of the land. The moderate solution between these two extremes has been to adopt Western-inspired or Western-derived codes of law except in matters of personal status. It was in Egypt that the modernist movement (*Salafīya*) took place, which advocated the maintenance of the supremacy of Islamic law, but urged a new era of interpretation (*ijtihād*) capable of meeting the changing needs of the community. This movement drew its inspiration from the Ḥanbalite school of law, especially from its foremost representative Ibn Taimīya (d. 1328).

By the end of the third century after the HIJRA (9th century) several schools of law had developed, of which four orthodox schools remain to this day. They are named after their founders as follows: the Ḥanafite school (named after Abū Ḥanīfa, d. 767), the Mālikite (Mālik, d. 795), the Shāfi'ite (Shāfi'ī, d. 820) and the Ḥanbalite (Ibn Ḥanbal, d. 855). All these schools (which are neither sects nor rites) are orthodox (SUNNITES) distinguishing themselves from the sectarian SHĪ'ITES, whom they consider to be heterodox. They represent 90 percent of Islam (as against 9 percent for the Shī'ite and one percent for the Khārijites, other heterodox sects whose origins date from a few decades after the death of Muḥammad).

Their geographical distribution is as follows: (1) Ḥanafites: Tatarstan, North Caucasus and Daghestan, Georgia and Kinghizia, China (Gansu, Kunming), India, Afghanistan, Turkey, Iraq, Syria, Jordan, Egypt, Libya, Eritrea, Ethiopia, Albania, Yugoslavia, Bulgaria, Greece, and Romania; (2) Mālikites: Saudi Arabia, Oman, and Qatar, Iraq, Syria, Algeria, Tunisia, Morocco, Libya, Sudan, Togo, Chad, and Ethiopia; (3) Shāfiʿites: Saudi Arabia, Yemen, Azerbaijan, China (Xinjiang), Indonesia, Malaysia, Singapore, Thailand, Pakistan, India, Turkey, Iraq, Syria, Jordan, Chad, Madagascar, Tanzania, Somalia, Ethiopia; (4) Ḥanbalites: Saudi Arabia, Oman, Trucial Oman, Iraq, Jordan, and Egypt.

Bibliography: D. SANTILLANA, *Istituzioni di diritto Musulmano Malikita,* 2 v. (Rome 1926–33) 1:1–119; "Law and Society," in *The Legacy of Islam,* ed. T. W. ARNOLD (Oxford 1931). H. LAOUST, *Essai sur les doctrines sociales et politiques de Takī-d-Dīn Aḥad b. Taimīya* (Cairo 1939). J. SCHACHT, *Origins of Muhammadan Jurisprudence* (Oxford 1950). L. MASSIGNON, ed., *Annuaire du monde Musulman* (Paris 1955). J. N. D. ANDERSON, *Islamic Law in the Modern World* (New York 1959), and the bibliographies cited in these works.

[G. MAKDISI/EDS.]

ISLAMIC TRADITIONS (ḤADĪTH)

Ḥadīth, the general term for news or narrative, has a technical religious meaning for Muslims, usually rendered by "tradition." More accurately it signifies either an account of a saying or action of Muḥammad or his early companions handed down by a chain of competent relators, or the total collection of these narrations found in the six canonical books of the Sunni Orthodox (*see* SUNNITES). The relation and criticism of these traditions is called *'ilm 'an-hadith* (the science of tradition).

Nature and Importance. These traditions, containing legal, ritual, religious, or moral matter, are cast in a particular form comprising a chain of relators ideally extending back unbroken to the Prophet Muḥammad and referred to as the *isnād* (support); the content of the tradition is called the *matn* (text).

The normative value of hadith for the Muslim is derived from the fact that it contains, though not exclusively, the *sunna* (practice) of the Prophet. In pre-Islamic Arabia the *sunna* of the ancestors set the pattern for society. Muḥammad, breaking from the tradition, established a new *sunna*. But in the early development of ISLAM the *sunna* followed was that of the community comprising the teaching and prescriptions of Muḥammad along with local customs and adaptations.

Given the basic Muslim outlook that man's incapacity requires revelations through the prophets, it was natural that religious logic should halt this rather free development of Muslim society and recast it on a religious base. This attitude appeared in two forms and gave rise to a wealth of traditions attributed to the Prophet and his companions. First, the pious opposition to the UMAY-

YADS (661–750) based its objections on the practice of the early community. This in turn prompted some traditions in support of the ruling faction and others justifying a middle position. Secondly, the divergences in the schools of law in Iraq, Syria, and Medina, stemming from local customs and personal opinions, caused some friction. Medina, as the center of Muḥammad's activity and the capital of the first four CALIPHS, made claims to traditional practice that finally crystallized in al-Shāfiʿī (d. 820). He established the *sunna* of the Prophet, not the *sunna* of the community or the living tradition of the law schools, as the primary source of law alongside the QURʾĀN.

The emphasis on tradition, spurred by these conflicts, and the political concern that the ʿABBĀSIDS (750–1258) professed for religion and law had produced many traditions of a conflicting nature. Further, al-Shāfiʿī's insistence on traditions going back to the Prophet forced traditionalists to lengthen their chain of authorities and to put the traditions on the lips of the Prophet. Inventions were patent and recognized as such; the discrimination of the orthodox community was never dormant.

Authoritative Collections. In the 3d Islamic century, the appearance of the two *Ṣaḥīḥ's* (the "correct" ones) by al-Bukhārī (d. 870) and Muslim (d. 875) marked the culmination of the critical religious spirit and established the foundation of the science of tradition. The title of the two collections, "The Sound Traditions," indicated their critical nature. It is related that al-Bukhārī chose less than 3,000 traditions out of some 600,000. Traditions were now criticized mainly on the basis of their *isnād*. To pass criticism, all the relators of the tradition had to be reliable witnesses extending back in an unbroken chain to the companions of the Prophet. In addition, the *isnād* had to have internal consistency, that is, the possibility of any one relator's having heard the tradition from his predecessor had to be established. This criteriology has been criticized as formalistic, since the concentration on the *isnād* led to the acceptance of traditions whose *matn* were in clear conflict. However, the consensus of the community was instrumental both in establishing the reliability of the witnesses and in allowing otherwise weakly supported traditions to be accepted; thus the apparent formalism was tempered.

The two *Ṣaḥīḥ's* were early accepted as authoritative precisely because they reflected this consensus. Four other collections were ultimately received as canonical. They are referred to as the four *Sunan* of Abū Dāwūd (d. 888), al-Tirmidhī (d. 892), Ibn Māja (d. 896) and al-Nasāʾī (d. 915). In these a more liberal critique led to the acceptance of many traditions discarded by the two *Ṣaḥīḥ's*.

The studied criticism of hadith gave rise to the genre of biographical literature known as the *Book of Classes* (*Kitāb al-ṭabaqāt*). From these works came a detailed classification of men in technical terminology, indicating their reliability, and a parallel technical classification of traditions. The custom of traveling to hear and collect traditions died out only slowly, but the six canonical books remained at the base of the later collections, abridgments, and commentaries.

The SHĪʿITES have their separate collections of traditions in which ALI, Muḥammad's son-in-law and cousin, is the main focus of attention.

Bibliography: A. GUILLAUME, *The Traditions of Islam: An Introduction to the Study of Hadith Literature* (Oxford 1924). I. GOLDZIHER, *Muhammadanische Studien* (Halle 1888) v.2., Fr. tr. by L. BERCHER, *Études sur la tradition Islamique* (Paris 1952). J. SCHACHT, *Origins of Muhammadan Jurisprudence* (Oxford 1953). H. A. R. GIBB, *Mohammedanism* (2d ed. New York 1962). O. HOUDAS and W. MARÇAIS, *Les Traditions Islamiques*, 4 v. (Paris 1903–14). M. MUHAMMAD ALI, *A Manual of Hadith* (Lahore 1958). M. IBN ʿABD ALLĀH, *Mischat al-Masabih, Or a Collection of the Most Authentic Traditions Regarding the Actions and Sayings of Muhammed*, tr. A. N. MATTHEWS, 2 v. (Calcutta 1809–10).

[J. J. DONOHUE/EDS.]

ISMĀʿĪLĪS

Ismāʿīlīs, also known as *Ismāʿīliyya*, is an Islamic sect, comprised of many subsects, and commonly identified with SHĪʿITE Islam. Ismāʿīl, the son of Jaʿfar al-Ṣādiq, the sixth Shīʿite IMĀM, died before his father in about 762. Upon the latter's death one group of Shīʿites refused allegiance to his son Mūsā and chose instead Ismāʿīl's son Muḥammad as imam. After Muḥammad's death a further split divided the Ismāʿīlīs. Some accepted the belief that this Muḥammad had been the last imam who would return to the earth at the end of the world; this group came to be known as the "Seveners" (*sabʿiyya*, i.e., those accepting only seven imams, in later distinction to the "Twelver" or *ithnā ʿashariyya*, i.e., those Shīʿa Muslims whose line of imams ended with the 12th in succession from Ali through Mūsā). It was this group that established the Qarmatian Empire of Arabia toward the end of the 9th century. The Sevener Qarmatians proper disappeared after about two centuries. The other group, which came to be known as the Fatimids (after Fāṭimah, Muḥammad's daughter and Ali's wife), chose a son of Muhammad ibn Ismāʿīl as imam and accepted the imamate of his successors. Parties of both of these groups, Qarmatians and Fatimids, were also called Baṭinites and Taʿlimites.

The Fatimid Ismāʿīli movement gained a considerable following throughout the Islamic world and organized itself according to a secret discipline. From 902 to 904 an unsuccessful attempt was made to conquer Syria. The imam ʿUbaydullāh (known as al-MAHDĪ) fled to North Africa to lead a far more rewarding campaign. Within 70 years the Fatimids ruled, from the newly founded capital city of Cairo, an empire that included most of Muslim Africa and Palestine. The body of the population was not converted to Ismailism, however, and rivalries within the ruling group led to schisms and the gradual diminishing of Fatimid power. The first important schism was that of the Ḥākimiyyah or DRUZES, who worshipped Caliph al-Ḥākim (d. 1021), who was responsible for the destruction of the Holy SEPULCHER.

Thereafter the Ismāʿīlīs remained split between the so-called Musta'li and Nizari branches. The Musta'lis were for a long time centered in Yemen, but enjoyed such missionary successes in India that their headquarters were transferred there in the 17th century. There they subdivided into the Da'ūdis and the Sulaymānis, the latter a Yemenite party. The NIZĀRĪS, who have had a more illustrious history, later split into two subsects, the Qāsim-shahis, who survive in large numbers under the leadership of the Aga Khan, and the Muḥammad-shahis, who became almost extinct in the 17th century. The majority of the Muḥammad-shahis, mostly Syrians, subsequently united with the Qāsim-shahis. Nizari Ismailism has prospered especially in Persia, India, and (owing to the migrations from India) East Africa. Missionaries from Persia had already opened centers in India in the 14th century. They presented an Ismaili doctrine, tinged with SUFISM, that showed itself willing to absorb Hindu elements. The vitality of the Khoja Ismāʿīlīs in India is a noteworthy result of that initiative.

It is exceedingly difficult to form a complete and coherent picture of Ismaili doctrine. For the earlier period of Ismaili history the sources of information on doctrine are few; for the later periods they are ambiguous and polemical. Ismailism seems always to have insisted upon the transmission of an esoteric knowledge centered mainly but not exclusively upon a hidden or "inner" meaning (Arabic *bâtin*) of the QURʾAN. The guidance of the imams, for all the difference of opinion on their identity, was regarded as essential since, even in its less extreme manifestations, Ismailism generally accorded them semidivine reverence. The imams were in fact at the pinnacle of a hierarchy of "emanations" of God, the structural theory for which, it is widely supposed, was derived principally from Neoplatonic works. The Ismaili *Epistles* (ed. K. Al-Zirikili, Cairo 1928) of the *Ikhwān al-Ṣafā* (Brethren of Purity) demonstrate how great was Ismailism's debt to Neoplatonism and remain one of the chief sources of modern knowledge of Ismaili doctrine.

Bibliography: S. M. STERN, *Studies in Early Isma'ilism* (Leiden 1983). A. MEHERALLY, *Understanding Ismailism: A unique Tariqah of Islam* (Burnaby, B.C., Canada 1988). F. DAFTARY, *The Isma'ilis: Their History and Doctrines* (Cambridge, Eng. 1990). F. DAFTARY, *Mediaeval Isma'ili History and Thought* (Cambridge, Eng. 1996). F. DAFTARY, *A Short History of the Ismailis: Traditions of a Muslim Community* (Edinburgh 1998).

[J. KRITZECK/EDS.]

ISNARD OF CHIAMPO, BL.

Preacher, spiritual director; b. Chiampo (Vicenza, Italy); d. Pavia, Mar. 19, 1244. Isnard was perhaps of the noble Nardi family. He received the Dominican habit from St. DOMINIC c. 1219 at Bologna or Padua and studied at Bologna and Milan. He founded the Pavia priory (1231) at the church of S. Maria di Nazareth. As prior at Pavia until his death, Isnard became noted as a preacher and director of souls, winning many from vice and heresy. Contemporaries esteemed him for his power of miracles, spirit of prayer and penance, fidelity to the rule, and constant study of the sacred sciences. Isnard, whose body lies in SS. Gervase and Protase, Pavia, was venerated immediately upon his death. His cult was approved in 1912 (decree published in 1919).

Feast: March 22.

Bibliography: *Analecta Sacri Ordinis Praedicatorum* 6 (1908) 650–651, 652; 10 (1911–12) 722; 11 (1913–14) 294, 475–477; 14 (1919) 81–85; 14 (1920) 6–11, 65. R. MAIOCCHI, *Il b. Isnardo da Vicenza* (2d ed. Foligno 1920). J. L. BAUDOT and L. CHAUSSIN, *Vies des saints et des bienheureux selon l'ordre du calendrier avec l'historique des fêtes* 13:31–32. A. DUVAL, *Catholicisme* 6:187–188.

[W. A. HINNEBUSCH]

ISORÉ, REMI, ST.

Martyr, Jesuit priest; b. Jan. 22, 1852, Bambeque, northern France; d. July 19, 1900, Wuyi, Hopeh (Hebei) Province, China. Remi (Remigius) Isoré was the eldest child of an elementary school teacher and his wife who produced another priest and a daughter who joined the Daughters of Charity of St. Vincent de Paul. Remi began studying Latin in childhood in preparation for the priesthood, then entered the minor seminary at 13 and the diocesan seminary at Cambrai (1871). Before being ordained, he taught elementary school at Roubaix. In the meantime he felt drawn to the Society of Jesus and entered the novitiate at Saint-Acheul, Nov. 20, 1875.

After his novitiate (1876) and before being sent to China, Isoré taught secondary school and studied Theology in Jersey. He had asked to be sent to Zambia, but accepted the opportunity to evangelize in China, arriving in Xian in 1882. He spent the next year studying Chinese, completed his theological studies, and was ordained in Xian cathedral on July 31, 1886 together with León Ignace Mangin. His assignments in China were varied: He was teacher at Zhangjiazhuang (Wei County, Zhili District, Tianjin), dean of Guangpingfu, and then parish priest of Zhoujiazhuang.

On June 18, 1900, Fr. Isoré arrived in Wuyi after a retreat to visit Fr. Modeste ANDLAUER. The Boxers had already arrived at the village to obtain the release of some of their fellows who had been imprisoned the previous winter. They delayed their departure upon hearing that a foreign priest was resident.

Realizing that probable martyrdom was at hand, the priests spent that night in prayer. About six o'clock PM the following afternoon the Boxers broke into the chapel where the priests were praying. The two were stabbed with swords and lances before being decapitated. Their heads were posted at the village gate as a warning to others. They were beatified by Pius XII (April 17, 1956) and canonized (Oct. 1, 2000) by Pope John Paul II with Augustine Zhao Rong and companions.

Feast: July 20; Feb. 4 (Jesuits).

Bibliography: P. X. MERTENS, *Du sang chrétien sur le fleuve jaune. Actes de martyrs dans la Chine contemporaine* (Paris 1937). J. SIMON, *Sous le sabre des Boxers* (Lille 1955). C. TESTORE, *Sangue e palme sul fiume giallo. I beati martiri cinesi nella persecuzione della Boxe Celi Sud–Est, 1900* (Rome 1955). J. N. TYLENDA, *Jesuit Saints & Martyrs* (Chicago 1998), 173–75. *L'Osservatore Romano*, Eng. Ed. 40 (2000): 1–2, 10.

[K. I. RABENSTEIN]

ISRAEL

The Biblical name of the people of God and of its eponymous ancestor who was also called Jacob. By way of introduction, this article first explains the origin, meaning, and usage of the name; then in the following sections it treats of the religion of ancient Israel and the biblical history of Israel. For information on the Catholic Church in the modern state of Israel, see the separate essay following.

1. Introduction

The Bible insists that the name Israel was conferred on the Patriarch JACOB by God, yet there are divergent accounts of its bestowal on him and various theories regarding its meaning. Besides being used to designate the Patriarch, it is more frequently employed as a collective title for his blood or spiritual descendants, the "children of Israel," the "house of Israel."

Satellite image of Sea of Galilee, Israel. (©CORBIS)

Origin and Meaning of the Name. There were two different traditions in Israel regarding the origin of its name. That they were ancient can be seen in the fact that they are already combined in Hosea 12.4–5. According to one account (Gn 32.22–31) the name Israel was bestowed on Jacob at Phanuel, near the Jaboc, east of the Jordan; according to the other account (Gn 35.9–15) God changed Jacob's name to Israel after the Patriarch had left Phanuel and returned to BETHEL. The first account ventures a folk etymology, whereas the second offers no conjecture on the origin or meaning of the name. The first account is boldly anthropomorphic; it depicts Jacob wrestling with God or the ANGEL OF THE LORD and stresses the Patriarch's victory (as also in Hos 12.5).

Traditionally this mysterious passage has been interpreted as signifying the conversion of Jacob, a spiritual victory over his natural tendency to self-reliance rooted in his native cunning and great strength (cf. Gn 29.2–3, 10), and the birth of his trust in God, grounded in the omniscience and omnipotence of God. It has been suggested that Israelite tradition used a pre-Israelite myth of a struggle between a river spirit and a man to dramatize the inner conflict that raged within the Patriarch. Although there is little probability to this theory, inspiration would not forbid the use or adaptation of such a pagan myth to dramatize the interior struggle between exuberant self-reliance and humble, trustful submission to God's plan, a contest between a man who represents his nation and God.

The actual derivation and meaning of *yiśrā'ēl* (Israel) is still uncertain. It is clear that the name is theophoric,

a compound of a verb and the proper noun *'ēl* [*See* EL (GOD)]. If the verbal component is the root *śry,* the name means "God contends," or perhaps (from a related root) "God is strong, sovereign, He rules." If the verbal root is *śrr* or *yśr* (both of which occur in Arabic but not in Hebrew), the name would mean, respectively, "God shines forth" or "God heals."

Use of the Name. The name Israel is often used as a mere substitute for the personal name Jacob. It is frequent also in the phrase, "the sons [or children] of Israel" (*benê yiśrā'ēl*), which is used of the immediate sons of Jacob in Ex 1.1, but which, along with such terms as the "seed of Israel," the "house of Israel," and the "assembly of Israel," is used very frequently of the more distant descendants of Jacob also.

The name Israel (alone) is applied to the immediate family of Jacob in Gn 34.7. Prior to the secession of the northern tribes and again after the restoration of the people of the southern kingdom, Israel designated the entire people of God. But during the period of the existence of the Northern Kingdom, Israel signified that kingdom in contradistinction to the Southern Kingdom, which was called Judah. In postexilic times, Israel was occasionally used to designate the laity in contrast to the priests, the levitical orders, and the Temple servants (1 Chr 9.2; Ezr 6.16; Neh 11.3). As used by St. Paul, the term is complex. It may signify the elect of the new dispensation, the "Israel of God" (Gal 6.19), or the unconverted Jews, "Israel according to the flesh" (1 Cor 10.18).

Bibliography: R. DE VAUX, *Dictionnaire de la Bible,* suppl. ed. L. PIROT, et al. (Paris 1928–) 4:730–31. *Encyclopedia Dictionary of the Bible,* tr. and adap. by L. HARTMAN (New York 1963), from A. VAN DEN BORN, *Bijbels Woordenboek* 1086–87.

[J. A. PIERCE]

2. Religion of Ancient Israel

An investigation will be made here of Israel's convictions and practice with respect to God. Of the many possible approaches to this consideration, this section will adopt the historical. Accordingly, Israelite religion will first be seen as it is described in the earliest literary sources that treat it as a contemporary phenomenon. Second, an examination will be made of the formative history of this religion according to the available sources. In turn, its subsequent development within Israelite history will be pursued; and finally, with a consideration of the influence of the Exile, the changes effected in the emergence of JUDAISM will be noted.

Early Israelite Religion. As can be seen in the references of the classical PROPHETS of the 8th century B.C., the external forms of Israelite worship differed little from

Natural hot pool at base of Mount Gilboa, Israel. (©Hanan Isachar/CORBIS)

the native Canaanite forms from which they had doubtless been principally drawn. Animal sacrifice was normative (Is 1.11; Am 5.4); there was also the offering of incense and cereal sacrifices (Is 1.13; Am 5.22). Festivals were kept at ancient shrines such as Gialgal and Bethel (Hos 4.15; Am 4.4; 5.4–5) on the occasion of Sabbaths, feast days, and new moons (Is 1.13–14; Hos 2.13; Am 8.4–5). Tithes were paid for the support of these sanctuaries (Am 5.4), and sacred banquets were eaten there (Am 2.8).

The motivation of this cult, however, differed sharply from that of the natural religions of the Gentiles, whose cult practices reflected and sought to control the annual cycle of nature and its seasons. Israel's God could not be controlled; rather, it was He who controlled the destiny of all peoples (Am 1.3–2.6; 9.7) as Creator of all things (Am 4.13; 5.8–9; 9.5–6) and as present, not immanent, in nature as its Lord and Master (Am 9.2–4). This God had revealed Himself and His moral will to Israel through His saving deeds (literally "justices": Mi 6.5). He revealed Himself as a loving God by calling Israel out of the slavery of Egypt (Hos 11.5; Am 3.1) and by settling it in the land of Canaan; this, the donation of the land of promise as Israel's inheritance, rather than the chthonic deities of paganism, was the source of the fertility of the soil (Hos 2.10; Am 2.9–10), which in turn was subject to YAHWEH's continual historical intervention (Am 4.6–10). Above all, Yahweh had given to Israel the gift of Himself, a continuing closeness revealed through prophecy (Hos 6.5; Am 2.11), whereby He might be known as He is, a God of righteousness and justice and love (Hos 2.20–21; 4.1–2) who truly spoke to Israel. True Israelite religion, therefore, was to "know" this God by living His law (*torah,* "instruction") as He had made it known in salvation history (Hos 4.6). Yahweh's holiness was thus a constant challenge to the emulation of His people; His kingship implied a way of life to be pursued and a constant rebuke to moral shortcomings (Is 6.5).

City of Hebron and pools, 1870. (©Hulton-Deutsch Collection/CORBIS)

The prophetic minimizing of the cultic expression of religion never (even in Am 5.25–27) amounted to an outright rejection of it in principle, but displayed a concern for the distinctively moral and social character of Israelite religion (Hos 6.6). The Prophets rebuked the priesthood, not for offering sacrifice, but for dereliction in their duty to inculcate Yahweh's moral torah (Hos 4.4–6; 5.1–2; Mi 3.11). Without this, no cult could ever be truly Israelite, directed to the God who had gratuitously chosen Israel to this end. It then became no different from the Gentile rites that it resembled and, in popular practice, all too frequently imitated: sacrifice on high places and under sacred trees (Is 1.29; Hos 4.13), the use of idols [Is 2.8; Hos 2.15; 8.5; 10.5; Mi 1.7; *see* IDOLATRY (IN THE BIBLE)], fertility rites (Hos 2.7; 3.1; 4.14; 7.14), DIVINATION (Is 2.6; Hos 4.12; Mi 3.5–8), and the like.

The "ethical monotheism" of the Prophets of the 8th century was no new discovery of theirs superimposed on a folk religion of ritual and sacrifice. It was, rather, the most primitive tradition of Israelite religion, a tradition, however, that had become clouded through lack of instruction and guidance on the part of Israel's civil and religious leadership (Is 1.26; 5.13; 10.1; Hos 4.4–6). The election by Yahweh (*see* ELECTION, DIVINE), in which Israel so passionately believed and which it could abuse as a false guarantee of security, was accepted by the Prophets implicitly; they found in it all the moral imperatives that they preached (Am 3.2). The moral God of the Prophets was the Yahweh of Israel's cult, whose living presence ISAIAH experienced in the Jerusalem Temple (Is 6.1–13). Prophetic teaching nowhere opposes any of the priestly torah of the Mosaic Law; Hos 4.1–6 implies a systematic summary of the moral code like that of the Decalogue, and Hos 8.12 refers even to a written torah (*see* COMMANDMENTS, TEN).

Formative History of Israelite Religion. The Prophets themselves ascribe the origins of Israelite religion to the Mosaic age and make frequent reference to

Mount Herman and the town of Metulla, Israel. (©Shai Ginott/CORBIS)

the Exodus traditions (Hos 9.10; 11.1, 5; Am 2.9–11; 3.1; 4.10). They presume a knowledge of the kerygmatic interpretation (*see* KERYGMA) of Israel's history that both the PENTATEUCH and the DEUTERONOMISTS record.

Covenant Relationship. The basis of this traditional faith was Israel's experience of divine election and covenant. *See* COVENANT (IN THE BIBLE). Contrary to the Canaanite conception of covenant (see Jgs 8.33; 9.46: cult in exchange for the protection of a chosen deity) and to the patriarchal conception faithfully represented by Gns 28.20–22, the Mosaic covenant signified an act of grace by which Yahweh chose Israel out of love (Dt 7.7–8), imposing on it a law of reciprocal love (Dt 6.5) as the condition of His continued protection and beneficence (Dt 7.9–16). Though it is the Deuteronomic theologians, following the Prophets, who have evolved the theological language of the covenant, the distinctive concept itself (law founded on history; covenant an act of beneficence; reciprocal fealty) has been convincingly related, in the studies of G. Mendenhall (and after him W. Baltzer, W. Beyerlin), to the treaty forms of the ancient Near East current in the time of MOSES. The covenant explains Israelite Law, but the covenant relation itself is less legal than familial; its guiding norm is not legal justice but recipro-

cal loyalty (*ḥesed,* "steadfast love," *pietas:* the norm of the brotherbond between David and Jonathan, 1 Sm 20.8; see also 18.3). Through the covenant, Israel was constituted Yahweh's family (Am 3.1); Yahweh became the father (Dt 32.6; Hos 11.1; Jer 3.19) of many brethren. Hence the duty of loving God above all (Dt 6.5) is only the vertical dimension of a covenant love that is familial: "You shall love your neighbor as yourself" (Lv 19.18). The prescriptions of the Law spelled out the obligations of *ḥesed* to God and neighbor (see Hos 6.6; 3.4, where "knowledge of God" and "fidelity" parallel *ḥesed;* see also Mi 6.8). Yahweh is the "faithful God who keeps covenant and *ḥesed* with those who love him and keep his commandments" (Dt 7.8).

Mosaic Law. The Law of Moses, as presented in the kerygma, has the formality of covenant duty and disregards specific origins or earlier intents of the individual prescriptions. The ancient feasts and observances of the past, whatever their original meaning, have been related to the covenantal history of Israel. Similarly, the ancient dietary customs and purificatory practices have been interpreted as outward manifestations of the holiness that must characterize a people consecrated to God. It would be impossible to isolate the oldest Mosaic nucleus of the

Solomon. (©Archive Photos)

Law from the unities discernible in the Pentateuch and Deuteronomy, since all of these presuppose progressive development and more recent formulation and collection. The form-critical studies of the Mosaic Law by A. Alt and M. Noth, among others, however, have perhaps made a more decisive contribution toward establishing its earliest dimensions. Israel's apodictic Law is substantially without parallel in the ancient Near East. This distinctively Israelitic form itself argues for the prophetic origin (and succession; see Dt 18.15–18) that Biblical tradition ascribes to Moses (Ex 33.7–11; etc.). The casuistic law, which had its origin in judicial decisions, often parallels other ancient Near Eastern law codes; however, this is the result of an independent application of common legal principles that owes little if anything to the influence of the legislations of the more advanced cultures that surrounded Israel (*see* LAW, ANCIENT NEAR-EASTERN; LAW, MOSAIC; HOLINESS, LAW OF).

Israel, the Product of its Religion. It is less correct to say that Israelite religion came out of Israel than that Israel itself was the product of its religion. It was a common religion with its central sanctuary at SHECHEM (possibly a proto-Israelite center from patriarchal times; see Gn 34; 48.22; Jos 24) or Shiloh (1 Sm 1.3; Jer 7.12) that provided the first unity of the federation of tribes whose historical and ethnic complexity can still be perceived be-

hind the traditions that have combined to make up the united history of Israel. Acceptance of the common covenant-God in rites such as the one described in Joshua 24.1–28 continually introduced new elements into the religious federation and assured the preservation and recasting of the Mosaic traditions. Israel's wars were religious wars, as is attested alike by the historical narratives and the ancient poetry preserved in them (e.g., Gn 49.22–26; Ex 15.21; Dt 33.26–29; Jgs 5.1–31). Israel's religion, with its unique conception of God and His relation to man, made this people unassimilable to either Canaanite or Philistine, and thus eventually brought it to nationhood. Even then, the constitutive influence of its religion continued to prevent Israel from ever becoming in reality "like all the nations" (1 Sm 8.5).

Relationship to Patriarchal Religion. The relation of Mosaic Yahwism to the religion of the Patriarchs is not easy to determine (*see* PATRIARCHS, BIBLICAL). While the patriarchal stories preserved in the Pentateuch have retained a remarkably accurate historical contact with the social and cultural milieu they presuppose, their continuity is artificial; popular tradition had inevitably assimilated patriarchal theology to that of the later Israel. The Prophets knew the patriarchal stories (see Is 1.10; Hos 11.8; 12.2–14; Am 5.11), but they made no effort to find Israelite origins in the Patriarchs; for them, as for the Deuteronomic historians, Israel's history began with the Mosaic age. The Pentateuchal traditions, however, saw in the patriarchal history partly a remote preparation for the Mosaic covenant, partly an additional proof of Yahweh's goodness in giving Israel a land in which its earliest ancestors had dwelt merely as pilgrims and strangers (Gn 23.3; etc.). The tradition of the patriarchal "covenant" [in reality, as represented in Gn 15.7–11, 17–21 (J), etc., an unconditioned promise on the part of God] has not been simply imagined after the analogy of the covenant of Sinai. It is a distinct tradition whose omission by the preexilic Prophets may well have been calculated; with its character of unconditioned promise it was hardly the emphasis needed in dealing with a people all too prone to take election for granted and to ignore covenant duties. Historically, covenant with the tribal God, "the God of the Fathers" (cf. God of Abraham, God of Isaac: Gn 28.13; 31.53; Shield of Abraham: Gn 15.1; Mighty One of Jacob, Shepherd, Rock of Israel; Gn 49.24; etc.), corresponds to the cultural background predicated of the Patriarchs; and their worship of the Deity under the name of EL (El Shaddai: Gn 17.1; 35.11, etc.; El Elyon: Gn 14.19–20; El Bethel: Gn 35.7; El Ro'i: Gn 16.13; El Olam: Gn 21.33; etc.) authentically reflects the Canaan of patriarchal times, as has been confirmed by the Ugaritic tablets, which contain some of the same titles (*see* UGARIT; UGARITIC-CANAANITE RELIGION). Though Isra-

Tel Aviv. (©Annie Griffiths Belt/CORBIS)

elite religion and Law have their proper beginnings with Moses, there must have been some real continuity with the patriarchal religion. A new religious movement rarely emerges that has not taken account of and built on prior beliefs.

Subsequent Development. The religion of Israel that began in historical events was also strongly affected by them in its subsequent development. There was a progressive revelation and an unfolding of doctrine that produced various theologies.

In the Period of the Kingdom. With the coming of Israel to nationhood and its adoption of kingship, the equilibrium between religion and people was disturbed and new postures were called forth. The covenant idea itself with its law was now challenged by the existence of a state possessed of a royal bureaucracy and ruled by kingly decrees; in any case, some of the ancient law was now manifestly inadequate in the face of changes that time had brought in culture and polity. Israelite religion responded to this threat to its existence through prophecy, which not only spoke with its own voice, but also influenced other currents of religious thought that offered partly alternative responses. The mixed reaction to monarchy discernible in the source material of the book of

Samuel [1 Sm 8.4–22; 10.17–24; 12.1–25 with 9.1–10.16; *see* SAMUEL, BOOK(S) OF] found echoes throughout Israelite history (contrast the idealized picture of the age of the Judges in the book of Ruth with the pro-monarchical supplement to the book of Judges in Judges ch. 17–21; *see* JUDGES, BOOK OF; RUTH, BOOK OF). On both sides the reaction was a religious one: on the one hand a reluctance to abandon a distinctive theocratic polity and to incur the concomitant danger of assimilation to the ways of "all the nations" from which Israel had been called, and on the other a discernment of Yahweh's guiding hand and will in the inevitable course of human events, a progressivism equally clear in the Israelitic tradition.

Work of the Prophets. Prophecy with its living word of God provided a religious direction for monarchic Israel that is unparalleled in any other ancient people and maintained the covenant ideal imperturbably in the face of institutions that should otherwise have brought about its eventual extinction. It remained always, however, a religious force that adopted no programmatic approach to Israelite society. It stood aloof from such reactionary movements as that of the Rechabites (see 2 Kgs 10.15–16; Jer 35.1–19); its frequent evocation of the

Pope John Paul II stands at Western Wall, Judaism's holiest site in Jerusalem's Old City on final day of pilgrimage to Holy Land. (AP/Wide World Photos)

(partly idealized) nomadic past (Jer 2.2–3; Hos 2.16; etc.) was not to support a movement of return to a more primitive economy, but like the prophetic references to paradisaic peace (Is 11.6–9; Hos 2.20), it held up the image of a vanished age of Israelitic purity (Jer 2.21; Hos 2.17; Am 6.25; a viewpoint not shared by Ezekiel ch. 16 and 20). Prophecy was always harsh in its criticism of the monarchy, but it did not seek its abolition. In general, prophetic religion was indifferent, even serenely indifferent, to human institutions and spoke beyond these institutions to the popular conscience.

Development of Older Laws. Another manifestation of the vitality of Israelite religion can be seen in the development and adaptation of its legal tradition. The Deuteronomic law code (Dt 12–26), which also shows evidence of prophetic influence, was elaborated probably in a circle of Levitical priests (a Deuteronomic term) and probably in northern Israel sometime before the capture

of Samaria by the Assyrians in 721 B.C. It is in part a recasting of earlier laws (cf. Ex 21.2–11 with Dt 15.12–18) and in part legislation peculiar to itself; the latter too, however, may contain ancient legal formulations. It is noteworthy for its law of the single sanctuary (Dt 12.13–14), supporting the ancient amphictyonic principle, a law that influenced the reforms of the Judahite Kings Hezekiah (2 Kgs 18.3–7) and especially Josiah (2 Kgs 22.3–23.27; the "book of the law" featured in this narrative is usually taken to have been Deuteronomy). Deuteronomy's humanitarian tone and provisions (e.g., Dt 14.27–29; 15.7–11) and its theme of covenant love as the spirit of observance of law thoroughly wedded the best in the prophetic and the legal traditions and also inspired the postexilic Deuteronomic history with its prophetic judgment on Israel's history under the covenant and the kings. A parallel legal development was the legislation of the Pentateuchal Priestly writers, which was codified and elaborated during the Exile by a school of

A model of the Temple of Jerusalem, as it appeared in the time of Herod the Great, part of a model of Jerusalem at the Holyland Hotel, in Jerusalem. (©Richard T. Nowitz/CORBIS)

Sadocite priests that had some relationship to the prophetic activity of EZEKIEL. Like the Deuteronomic, this priestly school also redacted the Mosaic traditions of the covenantal history and brought the Pentateuch to substantially its final form.

Influence of the Liturgy. Another dimension of priestly religion in which many Israelites found their most satisfying relation to God and to one another was the liturgy. The truly spiritual and productive influence of the liturgy is reflected in many ancient Psalms (*see* PSALMS, BOOK OF), and modern scholarship tends to detect liturgical influence in many other parts of the Old Testament, including the prophetical (Is 6.1–4; Hab 2.20; Zep 1.7; Zec 2.17). The liturgy became one of the mainstays of the postexilic religion. It obviously meant much to Ezekiel and the postexilic Prophets. It was central in the thought of the Biblical CHRONICLER, and for a pious Jew such as the late writer Ben Sirach (*see* SIRACH, BOOK

OF), it concretized all of Israel's religious heritage (Sirach 45.23–25; 50.1–21).

Development of Eschatological Ideas. Israelite religion likewise developed with respect to its doctrine on the destiny of the nation. Doubtless an eschatology of some kind was a part of Israelite religion from the beginning [*see* ESCHATOLOGY (IN THE BIBLE)]; election itself, when taken in the context of a total divine purpose (cf. Am 3.7), implies an eschatological idea. The cult undoubtedly made its contribution to the development of the idea, dwelling on such themes as that of the glorification of Jerusalem [Is 2.2–3; 4.2–6; Mi 4.1–4; Ps 47(48).2–4] and the universal kingship of Yahweh [Ps 92(93); 96(97); 98(99); etc.]. The early Prophets actually exploited this eschatological idea when they insisted that Israel stood under the coming judgment of God. However, whereas the preexilic Prophets had to oppose an uncritical expectation of divine intervention for good, the

Prophets of the Exile and postexilic period could indulge Israel's hopes of salvation, especially in view of the doctrine of redemption through suffering, first enunciated by preexilic Prophets (e.g., Hos 2.16–22) and applied to the exilic situation especially by Deutero-Isaiah (Is ch. 41–55; *see* ISAIAH, BOOK OF). Never, however, did prophetic eschatology become an unqualified assurance of salvation as it did in some of the post-Biblical apocalyptic writings. The restoration of Israel would still be a deed of God's grace, done for His own name's sake (Ez 36.32). By it Israel would be made a sign to the nations (Ez 34.29–31; 37.28) and a means whereby they might find the God of their own salvation (Is 45.6, 14; 49.22–23).

Development of Royal Messianism. One aspect of this salvation expectation, though by no means its only or exclusive aspect, is the Old Testament doctrine of royal MESSIANISM, the belief that Yahweh's universal domination would be effected through a Davidic king, the Lord's anointed (Heb. *māšîaḥ*; Aramaic *mešîḥā*; hence English Messiah). This belief, rising from the promise given to David through prophecy [2 Sm 7.4–16; Ps 88(89).3–5, 19–37], strongly influenced the authors of the royal Psalms [Ps 2; 71(72); 88(89); 109(110)] and some of the Prophets, notably Isaiah (Is 7.10–17; 9.2–7, etc.; see also such passages as Mi 4.14–5.3 and the additions to Hos 3.5; Am 9.11–12; etc.). It affected in varying degrees the thinking also of the Deuteronomic writers, the Chronicler, and other theologians of the Old Testament. It may be questioned whether in any part of the Old Testament the concept of a Messiah ever became, as it did in later Judaism, applied to a once-for-all ideal king in the pattern of David; generally speaking, the messianic hope of the Old Testament is fixed on the promise of the perpetuity of a dynasty. After the Exile royal messianism inspired the thoughts of the Prophets Haggai (Hg 2.21–23) and Zechariah (Zec 6.9–14), but with the passing away of the monarchy and the increasing authority of the high priesthood, it tended to disappear, though it was later revived in Judaism under apocalyptic influence. The same apocalyptic influence contributed to a rethinking of eschatology, placing it in an end time beyond history and reinterpreting in these terms other soteriological figures such as the Servant of Yahweh (*see* SUFFERING SERVANT, SONGS OF THE) and the SON OF MAN.

Postexilic Judaism. The Babylonian Exile was the final formative event of magnitude in the history of pre-Christian Israel. Not only did it shatter the unity of land, people, and religion that had characterized the preexilic faith; it also altered the direction of personal religion by focusing attention on new unities that had to be as operative outside Palestine as within the land of promise. Though exilic Prophets had looked for a restoration of Israel and Judah as a single nation (Ez 37.15–23, etc.), this

hope was never realized as a political fact; nor did the exiles who returned from Babylon (probably relatively few in number) assimilate with the remnants of the Israelite population that had not passed through the experience of the Exile (Ezr 4.1–5). The Israelite religion that reemerged in Palestine was that which had been formed by Judahite exiles in Babylonia. It became the normative, shared by the far greater number of Jews who henceforth would make up the DIASPORA.

Development of Personal Religion. This religion evidenced a new personalism, dictated by the changed conditions of the Exile and its aftermath, and already anticipated by JEREMIAH (Jer 31.29–30) and Ezekiel (Ez 18.2–30). It is not true that personal religion had been impossible before the Exile or that the individual had simply been submerged in the people; the evidence of innumerable Psalms and other records of personal piety (e.g., the "confessions" of Jer 11.18–12.6; 15.10–21, etc.) disproves this. Nevertheless, the new emphases in Judaism gave rise to a different kind of personal religion. The SYNAGOGUE replaced the TEMPLE for the great majority of Jews; assemblies for the reading of the Law with instruction by the scribe [*see* SCRIBES (IN THE BIBLE)], and the later RABBI, like that described in Nehemiah chapter 9, became the norm of Jewish observance rather than the cultic rites that could be attended by the few in Jerusalem. The prophetic doctrine of the remnant of Israel, the true Israel of faith that was expected to be the residue of Yahweh's destructive judgment (Is 1.24–27; 10.17–23), such as Jeremiah had hoped to find in the return from the Exile (Jer 24.1–7), was now applied to the postexilic community by Trito-Isaiah (Is ch. 56–66) and the other postexilic Prophets to distinguish the faithful from the faithless by the standard of obedience to the Law. The faithful were seen as the *'ănāwîm* of the Prophets, that is, the "poor," the "humble," originally the economically dispossessed, who could rely on Yahweh alone (Am 2.6–7, etc.), now simply those who were wholeheartedly devoted to Yahweh as evidenced by their adherence to His Law, and thus separated from the unrighteous who ignored the Law (the "fools" of the later Wisdom literature) [*See* WISDOM (IN THE BIBLE)].

Emphasis on the Law. The disappearance of prophecy contributed to the establishment of the Law as God's final and definitive revelation to Israel. As time drew on, the lack of prophecy was still keenly felt, but more and more the era of revelation was recognized as closed, and the reappearance of prophecy itself was expected merely as a means of solving problems of interpretation of law and custom (1 Mc 4.46). The covenant norm of *ḥesed* itself became synonymous with obedience to the Law; hence the HASIDAEANS (Hebrew *ḥăsîdîm,* the pious), the strict observers of the Law (1 Mc 2.42), who were the forerunners of the PHARISEES (the separated). As the late Biblical literature can testify, this legal religion could be a truly spiritual experience far removed from a soulless legalism.

Development of Doctrine. The tradition of Judaism, like that of the earlier Israel, laid far greater stress on moral performance and ethical conviction than on doctrinal formulation. It was a religion lived in the heart rather than the head, a fact not always appreciated by Christians, who are apt to find its attitude to doctrine vague and inadequate. Faith was first and foremost a complete reliance on God rather than the source of specific affirmations about the divine nature. Nevertheless, doctrine also developed in the postexilic Judaism. The Pharisees maintained a progressive attitude toward both law and doctrine, mitigating and adjusting the former in consideration of changed conditions and supplying for inadequacies in the latter, even with the help of non-Israelite forms of thought. Thus by recourse to the Greek idea of the immortality of the soul, an attempt is made in Wis 3.1–9 to solve the problem of the future life, which was never really faced before in the Old Testament, and a parallel solution is offered in 2 Mc 12.39–45 by testifying to a developing doctrine of personal resurrection (an idea foreshadowed in Ez 37.1–14 and Dn 12.1–3). The book of Daniel likewise shows the increasing interest of postexilic Judaism in angels and the spirit world (*see* ANGELS, 1). These works are Pharisaical in spirit; by contrast, the Sadducean Sirach (*see* SADDUCEES) ignores all such ideas and is content to stand on the earlier content of Old Testament revelation (Sir 24.23–29). Characteristically, too, it is in Wis 13.1–9; 14.12–21 that such doctrinal themes are continued and developed as the "theoretical" monotheism of the Deutero-Isaiah (Is 44.9–20, etc.), which considerably influenced the doctrine of the Priestly creation narrative (Gn 1.1–2.4a).

Development of Wisdom Literature. The Wisdom literature, which in substance is postexilic, is instructive in showing how varied were the currents of Jewish thought and in warning against a tendency to oversimplify the complex vitality of Judaism as it extended down into New Testament times. The Wisdom literature, moreover, is a valuable source of information on the religion of Israel as a way of life lived by its contemporaries. Laws that may be harsh in formulation may also be mild as interpreted in life. A wife who, theoretically, was the chattel of her husband might also be, in reality, his cherished partner in life (Prv 31.10–31; Eccl 9.9; Sir 26.1–4, 13–18; etc.). From this literature and from the entire Old Testament as the record of Israel's religion, there emerges a history of faith and progress that is Israel's heritage to the New Testament and to the world. Not chiefly in its inadequacies, but rather in its ability to provide a fruitful and positive interpretation of life, has the religion of Israel found a fulfillment in the New Testament.

See Also: FEASTS, RELIGIOUS; GOD; PROPHETISM (IN THE BIBLE); SACRIFICE, III (IN ISRAEL); WORSHIP (IN THE BIBLE)

Bibliography: R. DE VAUX, *Ancient Israel, Its Life and Institutions,* tr. J. MCHUGH (New York 1961), especially 271–517. J. P. E. PEDERSEN, *Israel: Its Life and Culture,* 4 v. in 2 (New York 1926–40; repr. 1959). W. F. ALBRIGHT, *Archaeology and the Religion of Israel* (Baltimore 1946; 4th ed. 1956); *From the Stone Age to Christianity* (2d ed. New York 1957). W. EICHRODT, *Theology of the Old Testament,* tr. J. A. BAKER (London 1961) v.1. G. VON RAD, *Old Testament Theology,* tr. D. M. G. STALKER, 2 v. (New York 1962–) v.1. G. E. MENDENHALL, "Covenant Forms in Israelite Tradition," *The Biblical Archaeologist* 17 (1954) 50–76. A. ALT, "Die Ursprünge des israelitischen Rechts," *Kleine Schriften zur Geschichte des Volkes Israel* (Munich 1953–) 1:278–332; "Der Gott der Väter," *ibid.* 1:1–78. M. NOTH, *Die Gesetze im Pentateuch* (Halle 1940). S. O. MOWINCKEL, *The Psalms in Israel's Worship,* tr. D. R. AP-THOMAS, 2 v. (Nashville 1962). J. W. GASPAR, *Social Ideas in the Wisdom Literature of the Old Testament* (Washington 1947).

[B. VAWTER]

3. History of Israel

Israel as a nation with its own government and its own territory is considered to have existed from *c.* 1200 B.C. to A.D. 70. The brief historical summation that follows will cover this period, although, at the beginning, some historical evaluation of the Israelite traditions that extended Israel's history back to its origins in Abraham's migration into Palestine (*c.* 19th century B.C.) must be given also. After the formative periods of the Exodus from Egypt and the conquest and settlement of the land of Canaan, Israel's history may be reviewed during the following main periods: the united monarchy (*c.* 1000 to *c.* 922 B.C.), the separate kingdoms of Israel and Judah (*c.* 922 to 587), and the postexilic period (538 B.C. to A.D. 70).

EMERGENCE OF ISRAEL

The ancient oral and liturgical traditions of the Israelite people were the foundations upon which they built the theologically centered summation of their origins, as it is now extant in the first seven books of the Bible. It was a popular, religious summation, not a history of Israel's origin in the modern sense. It was a unique type of literature that combined authentic, historical memories with profound theological insights into God's activity in bringing Israel into existence, an activity not subject to the historian's judgment. It was therefore SALVATION HISTORY (*HEILSGESCHICHTE*). Recent archeological discoveries have established, however, that the theological interpretation found in this sacred history did not nullify a basically accurate sketch of the Patriarchal age, the period of the Exodus from Egypt, and the settlement of the Israelite tribes in PALESTINE.

Patriarchal Age. The Book of GENESIS relates episodes from the lives of the three Patriarchs, ABRAHAM, ISAAC, and JACOB, the ancestors from whom the Israelites and some of their neighboring nations originated. At the beginning of the 20th century, historical critics had almost completely discounted that any authentic historical memories were reported in these Patriarchal narratives. They held that the earliest document, the YAHWIST, at the basis of these narratives, was not written down until almost 1,000 years after the events it described. It could not have given any accurate account of the events through which the Patriarchs lived and by which the Israelite people were formed and their faith awakened.

Such a negative attitude has recently been shown to have been wholly erroneous. An extensive comparison between names in Genesis and Northern Mesopotamian names, now known from extra-Biblical sources of the 1st half of the 2d millennium B.C., has established that the names Abraham, Isaac, Jacob, Haran, Nahor, Serug, Benjamin, etc., were common, or of a common form, during the general period ascribed by Genesis to the Patriarch's wanderings and in the general area whence Abraham and his seminomadic group migrated, a fact not true of the later period in Palestine when the Yahwistic traditions were definitively written down. The Genesis description of Patriarchal life and wanderings, including the places where they temporarily settled on the central Palestinian ridge, fits accurately into what is now known about the tribes of ass nomads, which were in the process of becoming sedentary during the major part of the 2d millennium B.C. Even journeys of such nomads to Egypt and their quasi settlement there on the fringe of the "sown" are well exemplified during this period from non-Biblical sources. Finally, many of the customs and institutions found in Genesis are now known not to have been those of Israel and JUDAH in the later monarchical period but ones found in sources from the mid-2d millennium B.C. from Nuzi and Mari, sources that were themselves records of more ancient customs that were prevalent in the general northern Mesopotamian region.

The honest historian should therefore conclude that Israel's remembrances of its origins, although not to be classified as history by intent and plan, were nevertheless rooted in history. Israel's traditions evoked a response of faith from those who believed in the God who chose the Patriarchs, which is not contradicted by what is now known of Near-Eastern history during the Middle Bronze (c. 2250 to c. 1500 B.C.) and Late Bronze Ages (c. 1500 to c. 1200 B.C.).

The Exodus. Israel's remembrance of its originally happy and then bitter sojourn in Egypt was so strong that it could not possibly have been legend. There would have been no reason to emphasize an inglorious period of servitude in a saga of a nation's origins. Probably not all the tribes descended to Egypt or remained there for such a long period as is ordinarily thought. The Rachel tribes, Joseph and BENJAMIN, elements of the Levi tribe, and sections of Judah and SIMEON, probably entered Egypt during the Hyksos period and dwelt for a long period on the northeastern fringe of the Egyptian Delta, "in the land of Gesen." There they were able to continue their traditional raising of sheep and goats (Gn 47.3–4).

Once this minority group began to be numerous and after Egyptian nationalism had reasserted itself against the Hyksos dynasty, as happens so often in human history, the nationalists began to persecute and enslave the growing minority group and eventually forced them to leave. The memory of this escape from Egyptian oppression remained throughout Israelite history the foremost example of God's saving protection for Israel, a theological conception that goes beyond mere human history [see EXODUS, BOOK OF].

Desert Wandering. The exact details of the desert journey of the Israelites and its stages have been lost in the liturgical and religious accounts of God's great saving act found in the Bible. The ancient traditional site of Mt. HOREB or SINAI has recently been called into doubt, so that some scholars map out a completely different route than the commonly accepted one; but the reasons for identifying Mt. Sinai with a mountain in the southern part of the Sinai peninsula still remain credible. The quasi settlement of the exiting Israelite tribes around Kadesh in southern Palestine is of more certain historicity. Here the nomadic tribes took a long step forward in their process of settlement. They learned more advanced social customs from the Madianites (Exodus ch. 18) and made some attempts to move more deeply into the ridge land of Palestine from the south, joining forces with neighboring tribes such as the sons of Caleb and the Kenites. Their experience with Yahweh at the time of their pilgrimage to Sinai became, however, the central magnet, the centripetal force, that made tribes of varying background cling together until they finally established a theocratic nation.

This process was directed by God's spokesmen and representatives, such as MOSES, JOSHUA (Son of Nun), the JUDGES, and King DAVID. Recently, historical criticism has returned to a more positive view concerning the historicity of Moses and has rescued him from being a legendary figure. There are no strong reasons for doubting that he was the leader of the Exodus, the organizer of Israel's basic religio-civil laws, and the inspired teacher of their faith.

Date of Exodus. When the formative egress from Egypt took place is still a disputed question. The arguments for dating the Exodus in the 15th century B.C. are being more and more discounted, while those indicating the 13th century are gaining probability and adherents. Some of the reasons for the latter theory are: the pharaohs of the Nineteenth Dynasty (13th century B.C.) resided in the Delta, where they carried on extensive building programs (cf. Ex 1.11–14); the kingdoms of the EDOMITES, MOABITES, and Ammonites are now known not to have existed before the 13th century, yet Israel's journey in the Transjordan supposes their existence; archeology shows a distinct retrogression in arts and crafts in Palestine at the beginning of the iron age in the last half of the 13th century, which would indicate the displacement of a higher civilization by nomadic tribes, such as were the Israelites; excavations at Bethel and Lachish date a destruction of these cities in the last half of the 13th century, and, finally, the STELE of Mer-ne-Ptah (1223 to 1211 B.C.) names Israel as a defeated foe but classifies them as a people and not as a country, i.e., they were not yet sedentary. The Exodus took place, then, about the mid-13th century B.C. during the latter part of the reign of Ramses II.

The Conquest and Settlement. The Book of JOSHUA simplified drastically the details of Israel's complex and slow conquest and settlement of the land later known by its name. The Book of JUDGES indicates that the tribes of Judah and Simeon, along with allied, non-Israelite tribes, gradually conquered southern Palestine from the south and perhaps also from the east, over a rather long period that was not completed until David took JERUSALEM and some upland Philistine cities in the beginning of the 10th century B.C. The Book of NUMBERS and the Book of JOSHUA recount that the main body of the Rachel tribes led by Moses and Joshua followed the Transjordanian pastoral route past Edom, Moab, and Ammon to penetrate Palestine from the east through the valley of the JORDAN, a constant gateway throughout history to Palestinian agricultural regions for invading Bedouin.

Time of Joshua. Although religious tradition attributed to the great hero Joshua, the successor of Moses as God's charismatic leader, many of Israel's victories that were not his or that took place after his time, he still remains the predominant leader in the conquest of central Palestine and not a mere creation of etiological legends [*see* ETIOLOGY (IN THE BIBLE)]. An initial victory at JERICHO followed by that at Bethel would have opened up for the Israelite tribes the main central ridge, which was sparsely settled at this time by seminomadic tribes similar, and probably related, to the main body of the Israelites. Other Israelite tribes, of long residence in the pastoral regions of northern Palestine, would have joined with their brothers, just arrived from the desert and their experience with Yahweh, to form at Shechem a greater Israelite federation by the acceptance of the Sinaitic covenant. This seems to be the historical background of Joshua's renewal of the covenant with Yahweh described in Jos 8.30–35 and chapter 24. Such a strong federation of nomadic tribes would have led some smaller enclaves, such as the Horites of Gibeon, to join with them in peaceful alliance (Joshua chapter 9), while the Canaanite city-states became alarmed and tried unsuccessfully to impede the growth of the Israelite federation at the battles of Gibeon (Joshua chapter 10) and the waters of Merom (Joshua chapter 11). Yet, at Joshua's death the Israelite amphictyony had really gained a strong foothold only in the hill region of Palestine. Much remained to be conquered from the three centers of strength, Judah and Simeon in the south, the Joseph tribes in the central region on both sides of the Jordan, and the northern tribes in Galilee. These Israelite islands were cut off from each other by Canaanite strongholds, such as Jerusalem and Beth-Shan, along with other cities of the Plain of Jezreel. Another, and eventually more serious, obstacle to Israelite expansion than the Canaanite population was the PHILISTINES, who had settled along the southern and central Palestinian coast shortly after the Israelites had established control of their pastures and vineyards located in the highlands.

Time of the Judges. The period that followed the original partial conquest saw Israel fighting constantly, now in one region, now in another, to maintain and expand its hold on the hill territory against three archenemies, the settled Canaanites, the aggressive and iron-armed Philistines, and the raiding camel nomads, called Madianites and Amalekites, who envied Israel's advance toward better food and stability. The repeated battles for existence brought leaders to the fore, who throughout the 12th and 11th centuries B.C. were scarcely able to maintain Israel's hold on the land given to it by Yahweh but who gradually strengthened Israel's sense of national unity. The main victory was the one at Taanach, by which control of the valley of Jezreel was won and a bridge was formed uniting the Joseph tribes with those of Galilee. Judah and Simeon remained in a somewhat cut-off position in the south, a division that was one of the causes for the later schism between the kingdoms of Israel and Judah. Near the end of this period of the Judges the Philistines won a great victory over Israel at Aphek (*c.* 1050). The central symbol of Israel's religious and national unity, the ARK OF THE COVENANT, was captured, and its sanctuary at Shiloh was destroyed. The Israelites had come to a crossroads: to maintain their very existence they had to have a central leader around whom all the tribes could rally against the Philistines. Israel had to have a king.

UNITED MONARCHY

The forces threatening Israel's existence led to a popular demand for a *nāgîd*, a martial, charismatic leader who would direct Israel's army against its foes. This desire was reluctantly implemented by SAMUEL when he anointed Saul as *nāgîd* (*c.* 1020 B.C.) and eventually led to the union of all the Israelite tribes under one *melek*, king, during the reigns of kings David and SOLOMON.

Institution. Two varying accounts of the institution of the monarchy are juxtaposed in the First Book of SAMUEL. The first account (1 Sm 9.1–10.16; 11.1–15) describes how Yahweh Himself guided the secret election of Saul as king of Israel, how Saul defeated the Ammonites, and how the people acclaimed him as king. The other account (1 Sm 8.1–22; 10.17–27; 12.1–25) shows Samuel first resisting the popular demand for a king and acceding to it only because of a divine command (8.7, 22). After Saul's election by lot, Samuel proclaimed the dire consequences of government by a human king (8.11–18) and in a menacing farewell discourse gave up his judgeship in the very act of exercising his role as prophet, i.e., spokesman for God (ch. 12). Both traditions are ancient, and from different points of view (to which all history is invariably subject in varying degrees) they transmit the essential facts—the need for centralized political and military control to defend against outside pressure and a nostalgic reluctance to give up the freedom of amphictyonic rule with its closer, more intimate ties with the ultimate *nāgîd*, God.

The type of kingship Saul exercised very likely resembled that of the kings of the recently established kingdoms of Ammon, Moab, and Edom rather than the allied tyrannies of the Philistines and the princelings of the Canaanite city-states. It was a national monarchy joining together under one warlord previously federated tribes. Much of the king's hold over these clans depended upon his success in battle and his loyalty to the basic religious elan that united Israel's disparate tribal loyalties. Thus, after Saul's initial victories over the Ammonites, the Amalekites, and the Philistines in the hill country and his repulse of Philistine attempts to invade Israelite highland strongholds via the narrow valleys leading eastward from the coast, he inevitably lost popular favor for his dynasty by the disastrous confrontation of Philistine chariots on the plain below Mt. Gilboa *c.* 1000 B.C. There he and his oldest sons died. Israel's collapse before Philistia seemed irremediable. Only another *nāgîd*, wiser and more popular than Saul, more loyal to the Yahwistic religion, and better versed in Philistine warfare could save Israel. Such a man was already upon the scene, and he gradually won over to himself the loyalty of all Israel—David, son of Jesse, of the tribe of Judah.

Reign of David. The ancient traditions recount the rise of David (r. *c.* 1000–*c.* 961) to prominence as a valiant warrior in Saul's militia, the jealousy of Saul that eventually led to David's life as the exiled leader of an outlaw band, and David's adventures as the prince of Ziklag in the employ of the Philistine ruler of Gath. These traditions have the form of popular sagas and are of different and variant origin, but they agree essentially in their picture of David as a very talented warrior and troubadour who could so charm the populace as to create violent jealousy in the unstable Saul. The loyalty he inspired in his small band of marauders and his partial friendship with certain Philistines gave him freedom to develop his power in the south, where he protected the established towns by his raids against pillaging nomads.

After Saul's death, David reigned as king in Hebron for about seven years and emerged, after Abner and Ishbaal were killed, as the only hero who could possibly save Israel from Philistine oppression. When the elders of the northern tribes had submitted to him and accepted him as the king of Israel, he wisely moved the capital to JERUSALEM, which had been conquered by his own army of loyal mercenaries, was not connected with tribal traditions, and was centrally located on the border between the southern and northern tribes. It became his own city, David's city, and he soon made it the central sanctuary for all Israel by bringing to it the ark of the covenant. He thus established a strong focus of unity for the northern and southern elements of Israel, although his reign always remained a divided one. He was separately the king of Israel (the north) and the king of Judah (the south) but never the king of a completely unified nation that had loyalties only to him.

By his victories over the Philistines, of which very little is known, and by his subjection of the Ammonites, Moabites, Edomites, and ARAMAEANS of central Syria and the Damascus area, David secured Israel from all its surrounding enemies. He thereby established a small empire whose extent was never matched under any other Israelite king. He organized the liturgy around the ark by favoring the survivors of the high-priestly clan of ELI, which Saul had almost exterminated.

One problem he never solved was the dynastic succession to his throne. His sons were at odds with him and each other. Absalom rebelled against him with the aid of some of David's formerly strongest supporters and of the Benjaminites who were in favor of Saul's line. After this revolt was suppressed by his loyal mercenaries, David had to deal with another rebellion by the Benjaminites. When he was near death, his oldest remaining son, Adonijah, attempted to overthrow his favored son Solomon by claiming the kingship. David was finally forced to have Solomon anointed king while he was still alive.

The history of David in the Bible is mainly that of Jerusalem and his own family's vicissitudes. It is not a chronicle of his political and military achievements. But from the point of view of salvation history it laid down a theme that would be almost as strong throughout the remainder of Israelite history as the original Mosaic covenant and legislation, God's new covenant with Zion and the Davidic dynasty. Henceforth Yahweh would never completely desert Jerusalem or David's house. He would correct and punish, but He would never entirely reject His chosen and anointed leader, His MESSIAH. This theme was to control the national perspectives and hopes of Israel especially after the absorption of the northern tribes by Assyria in the last quarter of the 8th century.

Reign of Solomon. The successes of David were consolidated and organized by Solomon (*c.* 961–*c.* 922 B.C.), who was fortunate to reign in a period when the great powers, Egypt and Assyria, were at their weakest, when the Sidonians were interested in maritime expansion and trade, and when the Aramaeans had not completely recovered from David's victories. Solomon and his kingdom were thus at peace, a peace ensured by the chariot army and garrisons that he established at great expense throughout his kingdom, of which the excavations at Megiddo have provided noteworthy evidence. He freely engaged in all kinds of commercial endeavors with the surrounding countries, allying himself with Hiram of Tyre in the production of metals and other trade and taking advantage of and exploiting the newly established camel trade over the vast wastelands of Arabia.

His building program included, besides the Jerusalem temple and royal palace, many fortified cities such as Gezer and Hazor, a fact confirmed by recent excavations. The PHOENICIANS aided him with artisans and material, but the main body of his workers were enslaved Canaanites and other neighboring peoples, and even Israelites themselves were drafted into forced labor battalions in alarming numbers.

Solomon continued his father's attempts to break down tribal barriers in order to concentrate Israel around the throne. Twelve governmental units were established over which the king appointed prefects whose main duty was to collect enough tribute from each unit to provide for the royal court for a month each year. From even a rough estimate of this tribute the magnitude of Solomon's court and the terrible burden of taxation on the people are clearly apparent. The seeds of rebellion had been sown by such extravagance and economic imbalance.

Yet the 70 years during which David and Solomon ruled the united kingdoms were prosperous and fruitful for the Israelite people. They increased immensely, perhaps even doubled in the period. New towns and cities were founded. Arts and crafts were perfected. Literacy and literature became no longer an extreme rarity relegated only to a few scribes. The HEBREW LANGUAGE, so glorious already in its oral transmission, entered its golden age as a written language in both prose and poetry. The economic oppression and draining of the still tribally oriented people, especially of the north, however, were factors too explosive to allow for a peaceful transmission of power to the next Davidic king. Add to the burden of maintaining the royal court the weakening of the pristine, centralizing Yahwism by syncretistic religious practices encouraged by Solomon's foreign harem and by his commerce with neighboring nations and one can easily see why the northerners shouted in the adamant face of Rehoboam, King of Judah (*c.* 922–*c.* 915), "What portion have we in David?" (1 Kgs 12.16).

ISRAEL AND JUDAH

Jeroboam I, King of Israel (*c.* 922–*c.* 901), led the northern tribes into a political and religious schism that lasted until the Assyrian destruction and colonization of the Northern Kingdom in the last quarter of the 8th century. After that, for another century and a half, the less important Southern Kingdom (Judah) carried on Israelite history until its destruction by the Babylonians in 587 B.C.

The Separate Kingdoms. Under the influence of PROPHETISM (1 Kgs 12.21–24), hostilities between the two kingdoms were kept minimal, but Israel's enemies, especially the resurgent Egypt and Aram (Damascus), took military advantage of the breakup of the Solomonic empire. Early in Rehoboam's reign Shishak I, the founder of the 22nd Egyptian Dynasty (*c.* 935–*c.* 725), drastically reduced Judah's boundaries to its highland region and levied a heavy tribute that emptied Jerusalem's coffers. He must also have secured freedom for his commercial enterprises along the caravan route that led through Israel's western territory. (A stele of Shishak has been unearthed at Mageddo, the city guarding the main north-south caravan route over Mt. CARMEL.) Hostilities between Israel and Judah continued during the short reign of Rehoboam's son Abijah (*c.* 915–*c.* 913). In the reign of Asa, King of Judah (*c.* 913–*c.* 873), Baasha (*c.* 900–*c.* 877) of Israel conquered Rama in a part of Benjamin previously occupied by Judah as a buffer region just north of Jerusalem and caused Asa to appeal to Damascus for aid. Henceforth Israel would have to contend constantly with Damascene incursions in Galilee and Gilead.

The Northern Kingdom in the meantime had already given evidence of a problem that would sap its strength throughout its existence—its dynastic instability. Baasha had usurped the throne by murdering Jeroboam's son Nadab in the second year of his reign (*c.* 901–*c.* 900); but Baasa's dynasty lasted only into the second year of the reign of his son Elah (*c.* 877–*c.* 876), who was murdered by Zimri. Zimri in turn was killed within a week. A civil war then broke out in Israel, and only after four years did one of the strongest of Israel's kings, Omri, secure his throne (1 Kgs 16.22).

Omri. King Omri (*c.* 876–*c.* 869) changed Israel's capital from Tirzah to the city of Samaria, thus orientating his economic outlook toward the prosperous land of the Phoenicians. He cemented relations with Phoenicia by marrying his son Ahab to a Sidonian, Princess Jezebel, and thereby gained an important ally against the continuing harassment of the Aramaeans. In Transjordan Omri retook Medeba and won tribute from the Moabites, as attested by the MESHA INSCRIPTION. He made such an impact among the neighboring nations by strengthening Israel that even after his dynasty's violent end the Assyrians continued to refer to Israel as the House of Omri.

Ahab. Omri's son Ahab (*c.* 869–*c.* 850) continued to follow a policy of useful alliances by concluding a pact with Asa's son Jehoshaphat of Judah (*c.* 873–*c.* 849) and by the marriage of his daughter (or sister) Athalia to Jehoshaphat's son Jehoram (r. *c.* 849–*c.* 842). Continued commercial ties with Phoenicia aided the economy, and the Moabite tribute remained a source of income. Only the Damascenes caused trouble, but they were eventually defeated by Ahab near the Sea of Galilee (1 Kgs 20.22–34). An alliance was made between the two states to confront the Assyrian advance under Shalmaneser III into Syria. At the battle of Karkor (853 B.C.) Shalmaneser won a victory against a coalition of 11 kings, among whom were numbered those of Israel and Damascus; but it was so indecisive that he withdrew to Assyria. After the Assyrian threat was over, Israel, in league with Judah, again tried to win back from Damascus the former Israelite territory around Ramoth in Gilead, but it was defeated when Ahab was killed in battle.

The gravest threat to Yahwism arose at this time as a consequence of Jezebel's propaganda for Baal worship. The details of prophetic reaction to the resulting syncretism are found in the sagas of ELIJAH and ELISHA recorded in the Books of KINGS.

Ahab's son Joram of Israel (*c.* 849–*c.* 842), brother and successor of the short-lived Ahaziah (*c.* 850–*c.* 849), allied his kingdom with Judah and Edom in an attempt to reconquer the rebellious King Mesha of Moab, but the coalition, after an initial victory, was repelled, and Moab remained independent. Relations with the Aramaeans remained fluid: Israel was allied with them against the threat of Assyria, but whenever the Assyrians retreated, the two countries renewed their rivalry. Judah during this period was very much involved with Israel's campaigns and lost control of much of its southern sphere of influence after the disastrous defeat by Mesha.

Jehu Dynasty. The Omri dynasty and its Queen Mother Jezebel, an ardent devotee of Baal, were slaughtered by a military uprising led by a certain Jehu (2 Kgs 9.1–10.11) and abetted by Elisha and his brother Prophets, who were reacting to the favoritism shown to Baal worship under the Omrides. Jehu (*c.* 842–*c.* 815) became the founder of the last strong dynasty of Israel. He tried, it seems, to destroy the Davidic dynasty and take control of Judah, for, when he wiped out the Omrides, he killed also Jehoshaphat's grandson Ahaziah, who was king of Judah for only one year (*c.* 842). But he never succeeded in this, either because soon after his usurpation he was hardpressed by Hazael of Damascus (2 Kgs 10.32–33), who conquered Transjordan as far as the Arnon, or because Athalia, the Queen Mother of Ahaziah of Judah, quickly seized power by murdering all his sons except an infant one. The pressure from Damascus became even more intense under Jehu's son Joahaz (*c.* 815–*c.* 801), and Israel lost much of its territory and most of its army (2 Kgs 13.7). However, Damascus' strength was greatly curtailed by an Assyrian siege of that city in 802, and Joahaz's son Jehoash (*c.* 801–*c.* 786) was able to win back the Israelite territories taken by Hazael, a reconquest brought to completion under Jehoash's son, the great King Jeroboam II (2 Kgs 14.25–27).

Jehoash and Amaziah of Judah. In Judah, after Athalia's short reign (*c.* 842–*c.* 837), the only remaining son of Ahaziah, Jehoash, enjoyed a long but rather disastrous rule (*c.* 837–*c.* 800), which was plagued by Aramaean invasions and was ended by his assassination when he was still in his forties. He fostered, however, a popular reaction to the Baal worship that had been introduced in Jerusalem by Athalia. He reformed the appropriation of temple revenues to insure that the priests would not become rich to the detriment of the necessary repairs of the temple's buildings and furniture (2 Kgs 12.5–17).

The son of Jehoash of Judah, Amaziah (*c.* 800–*c.* 783), began his reign well by a victory over the Edomites, which reopened for him the lucrative commerce with ARABIA; but he antagonized Jehoash of Israel, who conquered the Judean army at Beth-Shemesh and sacked Jerusalem, thus disturbing the long peace between the fraternal kingdoms. The crisis led to Amaziah's murder, the result of a palace rebellion (2 Kgs 14.19).

Jeroboam II of Israel and Azariah of Judah. A period of peaceful prosperity followed for both kingdoms during the long reigns of Jeroboam II (*c.* 786–*c.* 746) in Israel and of Azariah (known also as Ozia or Uzziah; *c.* 783–*c.* 742) in Judah. Since Damascus and Assyria were impotent at the time, Jeroboam was able to regain the fullest expanse of Israel and to enrich his country by commercial enterprises. Not all the populace benefited by this prosperity; the Books of AMOS and HOSEA bear witness to the extravagant luxury of the rich and the miserable poverty of the poor during Jeroboam's rule.

The prosperity in Judah was more evenly distributed but not so equitably as to prevent the recriminations against the rich, as described in the Books of ISAIAH and MICAH, dating from shortly after this period. Azariah continued his father's policy of controlling and exploiting the southern caravan routes from Arabia and may even have dominated the commercial routes passing through Philistia (2 Chr 26.6–8). After having become a leper (2 Kgs 15.5) he ruled for eight years (*c.* 750–*c.* 742) through his son Joatham (who reigned *c.* 750–*c.* 735) before he died. Extra-Biblical evidence (see J.B. Pritchard, *Ancient Near Eastern Texts Relating to the Old Testament*, 282–83) attests that a Syrian coalition was led by Azariah (*c.* 743) against the reawakening power of Assyria under Tilglath-Pileser III. The Jehu dynasty had passed from history with the assassination of Jeroboam's son Zechariah (*c.* 746–*c.* 745) by the usurper Shallum only six months after he had ascended the throne. Assyria was on the march, and the whole Palestinian and Syrian coastland was threatened.

The Fall of Samaria. Tiglath-Pileser III (called also Pul, the name he took when he became King of Babylon), by victories over Urartu, had freed his armies for campaigns in Syria. Menahem of Israel (*c.* 745–*c.* 738), who had killed Shallum a month after the latter's seizure of the throne, was forced to pay tribute to Tiglath-Pileser in 738.

Aramaean-Israelite Revolt. After Menahem's son Pekahiah (*c.* 738–*c.* 737) was killed by an anti-Assyrian faction led by Pekah (*c.* 737–*c.* 732), it was not long before Pul reacted to the Israelite revolt that, in the meantime, Pekah had strengthened by making an alliance with Rezin, King of Damascus. While Israel and Damascus were trying to force Judah, now ruled by Ahaz (*c.* 735–*c.* 715), into their anti-Assyrian coalition by threatening to replace him by Ben Tabeel, the Assyrians were busy in the north, giving the final blows to Urartu. It was in these circumstances (*c.* 735) that the Prophet Isaiah encouraged Ahaz to trust in Yahweh alone (Is 7.1–16), but Ahaz appealed to Tiglath-Pileser for help and sent him a vassal's tribute. In 734 the Assyrians marched on Philistia to cut off any aid that might come to the coalition from Egypt, conquering a good part of Galilee as they passed through it. They then turned on Damascus, took it in 732, and in the same thrust captured Israel's possessions in the Transjordan. The kingdom of Israel was thus reduced to the small highland area around Samaria, while a large part of the Israelite population of the occupied territories was deported and their land given to colonists from other regions of the Assyrian Empire. The Assyrians had found a practical plan for deterring the repetition of a vassal's rebellion [*see* DEPORTATION (IN THE BIBLE).]

Last Days of Samaria. Israel's misfortune led to another palace revolution. Hosea assassinated Pekah, quickly sent tribute to the Assyrians, and was thus allowed to reign (*c.* 732–724) as a vassal king over a very reduced kingdom. Ahaz made his vassalage official by submitting to the Assyrians at Damascus and thus rendered any move that Judah might attempt against Assyria an act of rebellion. At the same time the Assyrian religious cult was forced upon Judah, and Yahwism was endangered (2 Kgs 16.3–4, 10–18).

The next Assyrian King, Shalmaneser V, in the course of a campaign against Tyre (725), invaded Samaria and laid siege to its capital. King Hosea, who had vainly hoped to receive military aid from the King of Sais in the Egyptian Delta and had refused to give his annual tax to Assyria, was taken prisoner by Shalmaneser. But the city of Samaria withstood the siege for almost three years. A few months before Shalmaneser died (Dec. 721) it fell to the Assyrians and was destroyed. Sargon II of Assyria, who boasted of this conquest in his inscriptions because it took place in his accession year, deported most of the remaining inhabitants of the Northern Kingdom to northern Mesopotamia. Thus Israel disappeared from history. Its deported people lost their identity in foreign lands. The people who remained in the land were mixed with the new colonists, and many of them succumbed to the new religions formed by the amalgamation of various pagan creeds with an already watered-down Yahwism. Those who remained true to Yahweh were the ancestors of the later SAMARITANS. The history of the Israelite people and their religion was henceforth to continue in Judah alone.

Judah until Its Fall. Since the invasion of Judah by Sennacherib, King of Assyria, is certainly to be dated in 701, and since it occurred in the 14th year of Ahaz's son Hezekiah, King of Judah (2 Kgs 18.13), the date *c.* 715 for the beginning of Hezekiah's reign seems better than that indicated by the synchronism afforded by 2 Kgs 18.1–2, 9–10. Hezekiah had a long reign (until *c.* 687) in a period that saw the greatest extent (even into Egypt) of the Assyrian empire. That the tiny kingdom of Judah was not completely absorbed by the mammoth empire, as Israel had been absorbed, remains one of history's tantalizing problems. Sacred history has given an answer that transcends the historian's purview: Judah was saved because of a religious and, hence, also a national revival that procured for it Yahweh's protection. Whatever his judgment of this theological interpretation, the historian must admit that Judah could not have had a national renewal without a preceding religious renewal.

Hezekiah. During the first half of Hezekiah's reign the times were generally propitious for his reform. Assyria had temporary troubles at home, and except for the campaign of the Assyrian army against Ashdod in 712 (Is 20.1), Palestine was left in peace until Sennacherib's invasion of Judah in 701. The reform, which wiped away the Assyrian cultic importations, was motivated by the pure Yahwism preached by Isaiah and Micah. It then, apparently for the first time, attempted to destroy all local sanctuaries, even those dedicated to Yahweh, and to make the temple in Jerusalem the sole focus of the orthodox cult. The vital school of religious thinkers behind the attempt, probably never successful in Hezekiah's reign, remained dormant under the long and idolatrous reign of the weak Manasseh, to reappear in its full vigor under King Josiah of Judah.

The campaign of Sennacherib (705–683) as recounted in the Bible may be a telescoping to two separate Assyrian expeditions, one in 701, the other quite some time later. This would explain the appearance on the scene of the Egyptian King Taharqo (the Theraca of 2 Kgs 19.9), who did not begin his reign until *c.* 685. Another possible explanation is that in 701, after Sennacherib had quickly reduced to rubble most of Judah and while he was just about to crush some stubborn fortified cities (Lachish and Libna) more essential to his coastal campaign than Jerusalem, an Egyptian army, anachronistically said to have been under the command of Taharqo (who was only nine years old at the time), advanced from the south. It was in these circumstances that a plague broke out in the Assyrian army, and Sennacherib was forced to return home, leaving Judah devastated and Jerusalem "like a shed in a melon patch" (Is 1.8). The silence in the Assyrian royal records about such a setback is understandable, given the general success of the campaign and the relative unimportance of Jerusalem as an obstacle to an Assyrian invasion of Egypt.

Manasseh, Amon, and Josiah. Under Hezekiah's son Manasseh (*c.* 687–*c.* 642) a ravaged Judah returned to its vassal status, paying tribute to Esarhaddon in 673 and to Ashurbanipal in 668. The religious reform was suppressed and God's spokesmen, the Prophets, lay hidden. The next king, Amon (*c.* 642–*c.* 640), was murdered by his own officials, but another group started a counterrevolution and gained control of the small kingdom for Amon's son JOSIAH when he was still a boy. Josiah reigned (*c.* 640–609) until his tragic death in the battle of Mageddo, when he vainly tried to prevent the Egyptian army under Neco from invading Syria.

Under Josiah a religious reform, with which the Bible is almost exclusively concerned, accompanied and abetted a national resurgence that was possible because of Assyria's entrance into a fatal decline. As the Judean political and military reorganization progressed, the reform expelled from the land all foreign influences, religious and cultural. The discovery in Josiah's 18th year of at least the legislative parts of the Book of DEUTERONOMY (2 Kgs 22.3–23.24) gave added impetus and purpose to the renewal and led to the suppression of local sanctuaries and the concentration of priests in Jerusalem. Although the reform was shortlived, it expressed a religious fervor that was to survive the ruin of Jerusalem and the Exile and be developed and formulated in the homiletical sections of Deuteronomy and the doctrines of the Book of JEREMIAH.

When the cities of Asshur and NINEVEH were destroyed in quick succession (614 and 612) by the MEDES and CHALDEANS, the Judeans rejoiced to see their old archenemy Assyria humbled. Josiah was so eager to hasten the total destruction of the remaining Assyrian forces that he tried to impede the Egyptian pharaoh Neco from marching to their aid, and he was killed in 609 at the pass of Mageddo (2 Kgs 23.29–30).

Last Kings of Judah. After the death of Josiah the anti-Egyptian faction in Judah set his second-oldest son Shallum on the throne under the name of Jehoahaz. But after a reign of only threee months he was deposed by the Egyptians and taken a prisoner into Egypt.

The Egyptians then installed, as their puppet king of Judah, Josiah's oldest son Eliakim, who took the throne name of Jehoiakim. Despite the enormous tribute that Judah had to pay Pharaoh Neco, Jehoiakim received no substantial military aid from Egypt when the Chaldean King of Babylon, NEBUCHADNEZZAR, invaded Palestine in 603, and he was forced to become a vassal of Babylon. But three years later, egged on by Egypt, he threw off the Babylonian yoke. In 598 Nebuchadnezzar set out to punish his rebellious vassal in Judah. Jehoiakim, however, died on Dec. 8, 598 B.C., shortly before the Babylonian army encamped before Jerusalem.

As the only way to save the city, his son and successor, Jehoiachin, known previously as Conia, after a reign of only three months and ten days, offered himself, his family, his whole court, and most of the nobles as prisoners (March 16, 597 B.C.). This was the first deportation of Judeans to Babylon.

On the shaky throne of Jerusalem Nebuchadnezzar set Jehoiakim's younger brother Mattaniah, who took the throne name of Zedekiah. Although his nephew Jehoiachin received a somewhat liberal captivity in Babylon, so that he survived to carry on the Davidic line, Zedekiah ultimately brought a tragic end both to himself and to his kingdom. Against the pleadings of Jeremiah, who continually counseled him to submit to Babylon, Zedekiah followed the popular, stubborn nationalism in more than once seeking help from Egypt to start a rebellion. In 589 Nebuchadnezzar marched. He laid siege to Jerusalem in January 588, sent detachments to storm other Judean strongholds, and at the approach of the Egyptian king Apries (588–568) stirred up the false hopes of the fanatic defenders by sending most of his sieging forces against the Egyptians. But Egypt proved false once more: they withdrew across the sands, and Jerusalem remained alone the focus of Babylonian fury. In August 587 a breach was made from the north, and Zedekiah fled southward down the Kidron Valley; but he was captured, blinded, and imprisoned. Jerusalem was laid waste by fire, and most of the people of Judah who escaped the sword were deported as slaves.

With their temple destroyed, their last two kings held captive, their towns and country smoldering ruins, the people of God bitterly faced exile and oblivion. Yahweh had rejected His own. Yet already in Babylon a man of visions, EZEKIEL, had seen God's glory coming from His Temple to hover over His faithful and purified remnant, to give them new hope, and to lead them back to their home.

POSTEXILIC PERIOD

With the reduction of the kingdom of Judah to a province of the Babylonian empire, the history of what was left of God's holy people Israel reached a crisis. A thorough break with Israel's past, spelling the end of the theocratic amphictyony and monarchy, was mysteriously and sacrally changed into a renewal of the past and a resurgence of the sole rule of the one God over the Judean remnant of Israel. This dynamic rejuvenation germinated among the higher classes of the people who had been deported to Babylon, and it kept on developing after its most fervent devotees had returned to Palestine. During the Persian period it emerged as the social reality now known as Judaism, a reality so durable that it was to defy every attempt to exterminate it in the periods of Greek and Roman hegemony and, in fact, in every period up to the present day.

The Exile. First of all, it is clear that much of Judah's population remained in Palestine even after a third deportation in 582, but they were a disheartened lot, leaderless, harassed by the Edomites who occupied southern Judah, still plagued by religious syncretism, and only capable of lamenting bitterly over the ruins of Jerusalem. The sole hopeful note in their situation was that Babylon had not mongrelized them by settling foreign colonists in their midst, as Assyria had done to Samaria. However, the future of Yahwism rested rather with those exiles in Babylon who would rather have forgotten their right hand than

Jerusalem and all it meant for them [Ps 136(137).5]. In a quite liberal captivity the deportees kept a semblance of their traditional social structure ruled by the elders, priests, and Levites. Even more importantly, however, their Prophets were allowed free reign to preach their gospel of a new Israel, a new Jerusalem, and a new covenant and law written in the hearts of Yahweh's people (Ez 36.26–27; Is ch. 40–55). The religious revival borrowed almost nothing from the Babylonian culture and cult. It was a revival that defies rational explanation. God had chastized His people, had led them out into the desert again, had spoken tenderly to them through His Prophets (Hos 2.16), and had raised up for them a new school of holy men, the SCRIBES, who kept rehearsing for them the sacred lessons of their past. When CYRUS, King of Persia, gave the most enthusiastic of them leave to go to Palestine in 538, it was truly "a holy nation" and "a kingdom of priests" (Ex 19.6) who lifted their packs and followed the Lord Himself as He led them toward ZION.

Persian Period. The literary and chronological problems arising from the disarranged and lacunary sources for this era (*see* EZRA, BOOK OF; NEHEMIAH, BOOK OF) make it difficult to give an accurate account of its various phases. The summary that follows, therefore, claims merely plausibility for the sequence of events and their dates.

Restoration of the Temple. The exiles did not return in one great caravan; they kept coming back after 538 in separate groups and at various times. Sheshbazzar, apparently a son of Jehoiachin, the king of Judah who had been deported in 598, led the first group. Their hopes of rebuilding the temple were soon frustrated by the necessity of providing food and lodging for themselves in a depopulated and desolate land and by the opposition of the Samaritans, who considered Jerusalem under their control. The first resettlers succeeded only in leveling the temple area and arranging the foundations of the temple.

Another Davidic prince, Zerubbabel, succeeded where his uncle had failed. Encouraged by the prophetic utterances recorded in the Books of HAGGAI and Zechariah and, perhaps, by the loosening of Persian control of Palestine while the king of Persia, DARIUS I, was securing his throne, the Judeans, under the leadership of Zerubbabel and the high priest Joshua, son of Josedec, began again in 520 to rebuild the temple. Against the Samaritans' objections, they were allowed, by an appeal to the original edict of Cyrus, to continue until they completed the reconstruction in 515. It was more than 20 years since the first group of the deported had returned. The glorious hopes of Deutero-Isaiah (Is ch. 40–55) had not materialized, but at least the temple had been restored. More than half a century would pass before a new religious reform led by EZRA would pave the way for a political renewal under NEHEMIAH that would culminate in the rebuilding of Jerusalem's walls.

Reform of Ezra. According to the literary analysis of R. de Vaux (*Dictionnaire de la Bible*, suppl. ed. L. Pirot et al., 4:764–65), the collation or telescoping of Ezra's record of his religious reform with Nehemiah's memoirs by the Chronicler (who was not Ezra) is the basis for the confusion presently recognized in the Books of Ezra and Nehemiah. (For opposing opinions, see A. van Hoonacker and W. F. Albright in bibliography.) This opinion holds that in the 7th year of Artaxerxes I (458), Ezra, a secretary in charge of Jewish affairs in the Persian court, came, armed with a royal decree, to reorganize the Judean community in accordance with the law of Israel's God, in which he was an expert. He read the Law of Moses (not the whole PENTATEUCH, of course, but more than just the Priestly code) to the assembled people, which they accepted by celebrating the rites of the feast of BOOTHS (Tabernacles). The law thus became the official constitution for the hieratic society. The outcome of Ezra's severe strictures on marriages with non-Jews is unknown, for his report ends abruptly. These strictures certainly caused a great commotion among the faithful and in all probability were not very effective, as is evidenced by Nehemiah's grappling with the same problem. Ezra's commission was temporary, and he probably returned to his duties in Babylon when it expired.

Reform of Nehemiah. Ezra's religious reform gave birth to a national resurgence that had as its primary object the rebuilding of Jerusalem's fortified walls. A first attempt was thwarted by the Samaritans (Ez 4.8–22), who, by going beyond Artaxerxes' command that the work of fortification should merely be interrupted until a further decision be made, destroyed what had been accomplished (Neh 1.3; 2.3). Nehemiah, a high official in the Persian court, heard of these events and won from Artaxerxes a commission to repair Jerusalem's battlements. Soon after he arrived in Judea (445), he received a further commission as temporary governor of the Judean enclave (Neh 5.14). He stood firm against the threats and connivances of the Samaritans and their Judean collaborators and completed the basic fortifications within a few months. He then proceeded to populate the city (Neh 11.1) and regulate its social institutions (Neh ch. 5). He returned to the Persian court in 433 but was again present in Judea some years later, when he was forced to reconfirm his reform by having the community solemnly accept the obligations of God's law (Neh ch. 10).

After Nehemiah's time until the Greek conquest, i.e., for about a century (until 333), hardly anything is known of the Judean ethnarchy. Thanks to the reforms of Ezra and Nehemiah, Judea had become a land ruled by its own sacred law and thus enjoyed a certain autonomy and even the power to coin its own money.

The Greek Period. Before the victory of Alexander the Great at Issus (333), Greek influences had already spread into Palestine, but soon after it the whole of the Near East began to take on a Hellenistic appearance.

Domination by the Ptolemies. After the confusion following Alexander's death, Judea became a liberally controlled border land of the kingdom of the Ptolemies until they lost control of Palestine in 198 at the battle of Paneion. Under this rule during the 3d century B.C. the Jewish DIASPORA grew, especially in ALEXANDRIA, to whose Greek-speaking Jews the translation of the Hebrew Bible called the SEPTUAGINT is usually attributed. In Palestine Jerusalem was allowed to retain its ethnarchic autonomy throughout the conflicts between the Seleucid Dynasty and the Ptolemies, which are alluded to in Daniel ch. 11. When Antiochus III finally succeeded in winning control of Palestine it was not long before the relatively peaceful existence in Jerusalem was disturbed by Seleucus IV and his brother ANTIOCHUS IV EPIPHANES.

Maccabean Period. The history of the MACCABEES recorded in the Books of the Maccabees recounts the direst threat to the existence of God's people since the Babylonian deportation. Antiochus IV attempted to strengthen his hold on Palestine by destroying the core of Jewish unity, dedication to Yahweh's laws, by a thorough process of Hellenization. He attacked Judaism by forbidding the practice of fundamental Jewish customs, such as their DIETARY LAWS and CIRCUMCISION, and by forcing them to idolatry.

The reaction was noble in its loyalty to Yahweh and its fierce bravery. Judas Maccabee led a guerrilla war that succeeded in repelling the Greek forces sent against his rebellion and in gaining enough victories to cleanse and rededicate the temple in 165 B.C., which had been desecrated by Antiochus in 168. After the death of Judas, his brothers Jonathan and Simon continued hostilities against the Seleucids, who were involved in a dynastic struggle. By playing one claimant for the Antiochean throne against the other, the Judean leaders were successful in winning Jewish independence. The HASMONAEANS (the dynasty begun by Simon's son, John Hyrcanus) thenceforth ruled in Jerusalem until the Romans conquered Palestine.

The Roman Period. The Jewish sects of PHARISEES and SADDUCEES, as well as the ESSENES and the QUMRAN COMMUNITY, originated in the troubled Maccabean period and continued their bitter rivalry during the 1st century B.C. It was a land divided and ravaged by civil war between the two claimants to the royal high-priesthood of the Hasmonaean dynasty, Aristobulus and Hyrcanus, supported, respectively, by the Sadducees and the Pharisees, that the Roman General Pompey found when he marched on Jerusalem in 63. He demanded tribute from Judea and took from the rule of Hyrcanus, whom he allowed to serve as high priest, all the coastland conquered by the Hasmonaeans. An Idumean, Antipater, who had been continually aiding Hyrcanus's cause, during the civil wars that followed Caesar's rise to power and his assassination was quite adroit at staying in the favor of whoever gained control of the Roman Empire. His son HEROD THE GREAT finally succeeded in having the Roman Senate recognize him as King of Judea. In 37 Herod laid siege and took Jerusalem with Roman aid, killed Antigonus, the last Hasmonaean, and began his long rule, which was to last until 4 B.C.

Herod, like his father, cleverly changed policies to fit the changes in Roman politics. After the battle of Actium (31 B.C.) he submitted to Augustus and won a good deal of independence for the internal control of his kingdom, which was expanded to almost the extent it had under the most powerful Hasmonaean, Alexander Jannaeus. Of all his building programs, that of the reconstruction of the temple was the most important in Jewish eyes; but this half-Jew never won the support of his people, because of his fostering of emperor worship, his cruelty to his own family, and the opposition of the Pharisees.

After his death the Romans disregarded his disposition of his kingdom by dividing it between three of his sons, the Tetrarchs HEROD ANTIPAS, Archelaus, and Philip. In A.D. 6 Archelaus was deposed by the Romans on a complaint from the Jews, and the regions of Judea, Samaria, and Idumea were placed under the direct control of Roman procurators except for the period from 41 to 44, when Herod Agrippa (*see* AGRIPPA I AND II) was allowed an internal control of Samaria and Judea. The increasing tyranny of the procurators, e.g., of Pontius PILATE, despite the benign rule of Porcius FESTUS, finally led to a Jewish rebellion in 66. It was put down with merciless efficiency in the campaigns of Vespasian and Titus between 67 and 70. Jerusalem with its holy temple was captured and destroyed in April of the year 70, and thus the political history of Israel ended. Its sacred history continued in that of Christianity and in the post-Biblical history of the JEWS.

Bibliography: R. DE VAUX, *Dictionnaire de la Bible*, suppl. ed. L. PIROT, et al. (Paris 1928–) 4:729–77; "Les Patriarches hébreux et l'histoire," *Revue biblique* 72 (1965) 5–28. R. DE VAUX, *Ancient Israel, Its Life and Institutions*, tr. J. MCHUGH (New York 1961) F. SCHMIDTKE, *Lexikon für theologie*, ed. J. HOFER and K. RAHNER, 10 v. (2d, new ed. Freiburg 1957–65) 5:803–09. A. ALT and E. KUTSCH, *Die Religion in Geschichte und Gegenwart*, 7 v. (3d ed. Tübingen 1957–65) 3:936–44. W. F. ALBRIGHT, *From the Stone Age to Christianity* (2d ed. Baltimore 1957); *Archaeology and the Religion of Israel* (Baltimore 1946; 4th ed. 1956); *The Biblical Period from Abraham to Ezra* (New York 1963). M. NOTH, *The History of Israel*, tr. P. R. ACKROYD (2d ed. New York 1960). A. VAN HOONACKER, "La Succession chronologique: Néhémie-Esdras," *Revue biblique* 32 (1923) 481–94; 33 (1924) 33–64. J. BRIGHT, *A History of Israel* (Philadelphia 1959). F. F. BRUCE, *Israel and the Nations: From the Exodus to the Fall of the Second Temple* (Grand Rapids 1963). L. JOHNSTON, *A History of Israel* (New York 1964). W. FOERSTER, *From the Exile to Christ: A Historical Introduction to Palestinian Judaism*, tr. G. E. HARRIS (Philadelphia 1964).

[J. E. FALLON/ L. F. HARTMAN]

ISRAEL (STATE), THE CATHOLIC CHURCH IN

The modern independent republic of Israel occupies GALILEE, the Plain of Esdraelon, the Mount CARMEL range, the coastal plain and the Shephelah (the foothills of ancient Juda) from Carmel south to the Gaza Strip, including a "corridor" to Jerusalem, and finally the Negeb reaching south to a point at the northern end of the Gulf of Aqaba. It is, therefore, an irregular, generally narrow strip about 265 miles in length with disproportionately long borders—590 miles on land and 158 on water. It is bordered on the north by Lebanon, on the northeast by Syria and the Israeli-occupied Golan Heights, on the east by Jordan, and on the southwest by the Gaza Strip and the Sinai Desert of Egypt. Modern Israel includes but little of the heartland of ancient Israel—the highlands of Samaria and Judea. The region is predominately desert in the south, rising to mountains in the central region and low plains along the coast. Natural resources include copper, phosphates, bromide, clay, sulphur, manganese, and small natural gas and petroleum reserves. Agricultural products consist of citrus, vegetables, and cotton, as well as livestock and dairy.

History. The State of Israel grew out of the Zionist concept of a Jewish National Home. The Balfour Declaration of Nov. 2, 1917 established a Jewish national homeland in Palestine, which home was secured by the attribution to Great Britain of the Mandate on Palestine dated July 22, 1922. The working of the mandate—and the increase in the area's Jewish population—was increasingly hindered by the continuous friction between Arabs and Jews. Major riots occurred in 1921, 1929, and 1936, and in 1937 the Peel Commission recommended dividing the region into Arab and Jewish states. Matters came to a head after World War II, when the British refused to allow the immigration to Palestine of many thousands of Jews who had been victims of the Nazi persecution. Finally, Great Britain resigned her mandate,

Capital: Jerusalem; Tel Aviv is recognized by some nations.
Size: 7,993 sq. miles.
Population: 5,842,455 in 2000.
Languages: Hebrew, Arabic, English.
Religions: 117,000 Catholics (2%), 818,050 Muslims (14%),
116,580 Protestants (2%), 4,790,825 Jews (82%).
Ecclesiastical divisions: the Melkite Greek Catholic Church
in Israel has a patriarchal exarchate in Jerusalem and an
archeparchy in Akka; the Latin Catholic Church has a
patriarchate in Jerusalem; and the Maronite Catholic Church
has an archeparchy in Haifa (created 1996).

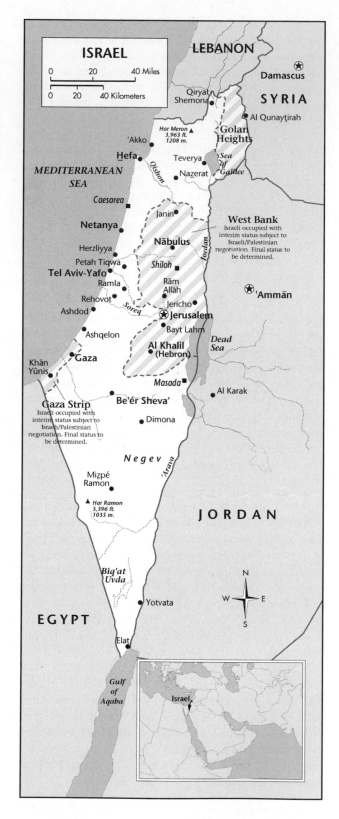

and the Second General Assembly of the United Nations
(UN) recommended the partitioning of Palestine into
Jewish and Arab states and the creation of a separate enclave embracing Jerusalem and its surroundings under
UN supervision. The Arabs rejected outright the Nov. 29,
1947 UN resolution, and the mandatory administration
refused to allow the special commission charged with its
implementation to come to Palestine. On May 14, 1948,
the day before the mandate was to expire, the Jewish National Council and the General Zionist Council at Tel
Aviv proclaimed establishment of a Jewish state, to be
called Israel. A provisional government was set up and
promptly recognized by the United States, the USSR, and
a score of other nations. Israel was admitted to the UN
on May 11, 1949.

While the Arab-Jewish war had actually started
many months before the proclamation of Israel's independence, only ''irregulars'' were engaged in warfare.
Now the troops of five Arab countries—Lebanon, Syria,
Transjordan, Iraq, and Egypt—invaded the region that
had previously been under British mandate. After four
weeks of fighting, the invaders were defeated, and Israel
succeeded in occupying a larger part of Palestine than
that stipulated by the UN partition plan. Active hostilities
continued until early 1949. Following protracted negotiations held in Rhodes that spring and summer, armistice
agreements were signed between Israel and the Arab
countries (except Iraq and Saudi Arabia) that fixed the
provisional boundaries of the State of Israel according to
the territory held at the end of the hostilities. Jerusalem
was divided into two parts: the Old City under Jordan's
rule, and the New City under Israeli administration. In
1950 Jerusalem was proclaimed the capital of Israel. On
Oct. 29, 1956, Israel launched the so-called Sinai Campaign and occupied the Sinai Desert and the Gaza Strip
in what became known as the Suez War. In compliance
with the resolutions of the UN General Assembly, Israel
later withdrew its contingents from the occupied areas.

Successive wars with its Arab neighbors occurred in
1967 and again in 1973, during which time further territories were occupied by Israeli troops, among them the
Sinai desert, the Golan Heights, and the West Bank. Despite granting Palestinians autonomy in the Gaza Strip

and areas of the West Bank after 1993, disputes with Palestinian leaders continued the fighting into 2000. Some West Bank territories were re-occupied by Israeli troops in 2001 in response to continued Palestinian insurrection.

Religion. Israel's Proclamation of Independence guarantees social and political equality as well as freedom of religion, language, education, and culture to all its citizens. The proclamation also promises that it will safeguard the holy places of all faiths within its domain. The most important of the Christian holy places in Israel are the CENACLE and the Church of the Dormition of the Virgin on ''Mount Zion'' (southwest of the walls of Old Jerusalem), the traditional home of Elizabeth and Zechariah in Ain Karim, and the sanctuaries in NAZARETH and on the shore of the Lake of Tiberias in Galilee. Although a secular democracy in principle, Israel maintains the Ottoman provision, according to which matters of personal status—marriage, divorce, alimony, maintenance, succession, etc.—are under the exclusive, or in some cases, concurrent jurisdiction of the religious courts of the recognized communities. These communities are the Muslim, with a special privileged status inherited from Ottoman times; the Jewish, whose prerogatives were precisely defined by the Rabbinical-Courts-Jurisdiction Law of 1953; the Christian communities; and the Druze community, which obtained legal status in 1957. According to the Day-of-Rest Ordinance of 1948, the official holidays were the Sabbath and the Jewish holy days, but non-Jews had the right to observe their own holy days.

Throughout much of Israel's history, the Vatican has worked toward an international recognition of Jerusalem as a sacred spot for all three of the world's major faiths, and has noted that despite the importance of other locations in Israel, Jerusalem remains of primary significance. Concerned that the historic and religious integrity of the city be preserved, Pope John Paul II, Latin Patriarch Michel Sabbah, and leaders of the other Catholic churches joined in encouraging all involved political leaders to work for the establishment of Jerusalem as a politically neutral, international city, its holy places open to Christians, Jews, and Muslims alike. However, by 1997 Israeli Prime Minister Benjamin Netanyahu was adamant that Jerusalem stay united; freedom of travel to the city's sacred sites would be allowed, but a united Jerusalem would not be relinquished, even in the pursuit of peace. Although not acknowledged by many world powers, Israel proclaimed Jerusalem as its capital; Palestinians also intended the eastern half of the city for their capital. Incidents such as damage to a 5th-century Christian church in eastern Jerusalem caused by a bulldozer during Israeli efforts, in 1997, to construct a new housing project exacerbated the problem and heightened the Vatican's concern.

Plains of Esdraelon and Hills of Galilee, mid 20th century, Israel. (©Hulton-Deutsch Collection/CORBIS)

By 2000, among the three Catholic rites—Latin, Greek MELKITE, and MARONITE—there were 97 parishes tended by 76 diocesan and 308 religious priests. Other religious included 160 brothers and 1,050 sisters. The Greek Orthodox Church also had communities of believers in the country, led by a patriarch in Jerusalem, and its ownership of large amounts of land in Jerusalem gave it some influence over the Israeli government. In 1994 full diplomatic relations were established between Israel and the Holy See, reflecting an improvement in the relationship between the two faiths. In an agreement ratified by the Knesset, the Catholic Church gained full legal status in 1997, its many entities gaining juridical status under Israeli law for the first time. In 1998 a Vatican study of the Holocaust was released that detailed the mistaken anti-Semitism existing in aspects of the Church's teachings as well as the moral failures of some Catholics, during the persecution of the Jews by the Nazis during World War II, either to prevent the genocide or to speak out more forcefully against it. This public atonement for past failings on the part of the Church was appreciated by many Jews, particularly Israeli Prime Minister Ariel Sharon, who in 2001 credited the pope with leading all Christians in working against hatred and violence in the region.

In March 2000 Pope John Paul II made an historic journey to the Holy Land that was supported by the Israeli government and which, as part of the Jubilee 2000 celebrations, served as a pilgrimage to rediscover the roots of the Bible. Calling his trip "a return to the origins, the roots of the faith and of the Church," the pope began his journey at Mount Nebo, moving from there to the Jordan River, Bethlehem, and Calvary, while also visiting a Palestinian refugee camp located near the city of the Nativity.

Bibliography: D. PERETZ, *Israel and the Palestine Arabs* (Washington, DC 1958). J. B. GLUBB, *A Soldier with the Arabs* (New York 1957). W. EYTAN, *The First Ten Years: A Diplomatic History of Israel* (New York 1958). R. PATAI, *Israel between East and West* (Philadelphia 1953). D. BEN-GURION, *Rebirth and Destiny of Israel,* ed. and tr. M. NUROCK (New York 1954). C. WEIZMANN, *Trial and Error* (New York 1949). G. E. IRANI, *The Papacy and the Middle East: The Role of the Holy See in the Arab- Israeli Conflict, 1962–1984* (Notre Dame, IN 1996). L. ROKACH, *The Catholic Church and the Question of Palestine* (Atlantic Highlands, NJ 1987). A. J. KENNY, *Catholics, Jews, and the State of Israel* (Mahwah, NY 1993). A. KREUTZ, *Vatican Policy on the Palestinian-Israeli Conflict* (Westport, CT 1990). J. RATZINGER, *Many Religions, One Covenant: Israel, the Church, and the World* (San Francisco 1999). *Bilan du Monde Encyclopédie catholique du monde chrétien,* 2 v. (2d ed. Tournai 1964). 2:504–511.

[M. J. STIASSNY/EDS.]

ISTE CONFESSOR DOMINI COLENTES

Office hymn that was traditionally sung at Vespers and Matins in the Common of confessors, bishops, and non-bishops. It is written in four-line stanzas, three sapphics and one adonic. It is of unknown authorship and is found in many MSS dating back to the tenth century, although it is conjectured to have been composed in the eighth century or earlier. The hymn extols the virtues of the saint, recounts cures wrought through his intercession, and asks for his continued assistance. The text was altered considerably in the Roman Breviary of 1632, only four lines remaining unchanged.

Bibliography: *Analecta hymnica* 51:134–135, text. J. CONNELLY, ed. and tr., *Hymns of the Roman Liturgy* (Westminster, Md. 1957), tr. and commentary. G. M. DREVES, *Ein Jahrtausend lateinischer Hymnendichtung,* 2 v. (Leipzig 1909). F. J. E. RABY, *A History of Christian-Latin Poetry from the Beginnings to the Close of the Middle Ages* (Oxford 1953).

[M. A. MALONE]

ITA OF KILLEEDY, ST.

Also known as Deidre, Ida, Mcda, Mida, or Ytha of Killeedy (from "Cell Ite" meaning Church of Ita); called also Clúain Credail, virgin, patron of the Úi Chonaill Gabra (a people inhabiting the western part of the plain of Limerick); b. Drum, County Waterford; d. 570 or 577. According to her genealogies (apparently later than the *Lives*), Ita was the daughter of Cenn-fáelad of the Déissi. Although the four accounts of her life probably go back to a very early original, no satisfactory information can be gleaned from them until they are critically examined and interpreted. The annals state that the Corcu Óche were defeated through her prayers in 553. Dedications in Cornwall and reference to her in a poem of ALCUIN show that her fame extended far beyond the plain of Limerick. The beautiful poem *Ísucán* ("Jesukin") traditionally attributed to her was rather inspired by her legend *c.* 900.

Feast: Jan. 15.

Bibliography: Sources. *Annals of Inisfallen,* ed. and tr. SEÁN MAC AIRT (Dublin 1951), under years 553, 570, with additions from the legend of Brendan of Clonfert. **Genealogies.** *Analecta Bollandiana* 46 (1928) 121. M. Ó. CLÉRIGH, *Genealogiae regum et sanctorum Hiberniae,* ed. P. WALSH (Archivium Hibernicum 5; Dublin 1918). C. PLUMMER, comp., *Vitae sanctorum Hiberniae,* 2 v. (Oxford 1910) 1:1xxii, n.6. G. MURPHY, ed., *Early Irish Lyrics: Eighth to Twelfth Century* (Oxford 1956) 26–29, 183–184, "Ísucán." **Literature.** J. F. KENNEY, *The Sources for the Early History of Ireland: v.1, Ecclesiastical* (New York 1929) 389–390, 779. A. BUTLER, *The Lives of the Saints,* ed. H. THURSTON and D. ATTWATER, 4 v. (New York 1956) 1:96–97.

[C. MCGRATH]

ITALO-ALBANIAN CATHOLIC CHURCH (EASTERN CATHOLIC)

The Italo-Albanian Catholic Church comprises the faithful of the Albanian colonies in Italy, grouped into the Eparchies of Lungro (Cosenza) and Piana degli Albanesi (Palermo). This is a remnant of a once widespread Italo-Greek Church throughout southern Italy, with numerous parish churches and Greek monasteries, formed from the refugees from the Byzantine Empire when it fell under Turkish domination in 1453.

At the end of the 20th century, the only remaining example of the once vibrant Italo-Greek Church was the Basilian monastery of GROTTAFERRATA, founded by Saint Nilo of Rossano in 1004, on the slopes of the Tusculan hills within the boundaries of the suburban Diocese of Frascati. The Holy See, after providing for the restoration of the ancient ecclesial and liturgical traditions of this Church in all its purity at the monastery, elevated it with the constitution *Pervetustum Cryptaeferratae Coenobium* (Sept. 26, 1937) to the rank of an exarchate, equivalent to a Latin territorial abbacy. However, in the pontifical documents and in ancient and modern accounts, no distinction is made between Italo-Greeks and Italo-Albanians.

Immigration to Italy. The first Albanian immigrations into Italy have not been precisely dated. The only certainty is that relatively large groups landed on the Italian shores between the middle of the 15th century and the 18th century. There were various reasons for the Albanian migrations, but two were particularly important: military service and the danger of falling under Turkish oppression.

In 1468 the Albanian hero Giorgio Castriota, known as Skanderbeg, died in Alessio. Later, Krujë, the stronghold of Albanian resistance against the repeated attacks of the Ottoman army, fell. These two losses extinguished the Albanians' hope of liberty and of reconquest. In the hope of fleeing Turkish oppression, many families preferred exile and migrated to the Italian peninsula.

It is impossible to determine the number of immigrations or the size of each group of immigrants. All we know is that the refugees settled in uninhabited areas or abandoned villages of Apulia, Abbruzzi e Molise, Lucania, Calabria, and Sicily. Historians do not agree as to the number of the Italo-Albanian colonies. Some put the figure at 62, others at 82, and still more recent estimates have gone as high as 120. This last figure seems closest to the truth inasmuch as it is confirmed by the most recent studies of the archives.

Most of the Albanians who sought refuge in Italy belonged to the Albanian Orthodox Church, as the great majority of them came from the south-central regions of Albania. Thus the Italo-Greek Church, already in complete decline, was restored to vigor by the new refugees from Albania.

Conflicting Jurisdiction. The presence of the Albanian Orthodox Christians on Italian soil, however, brought new difficulties concerning their relations with the local bishops and with the Latin population in the surrounding areas or in the same localities. These problems related to the provision of means for training the clergy who were to look after the needs of the Albanians according to the traditions and usages of the Christian East.

Evidently, when the Albanians settled in Latin territory, they automatically came under the jurisdiction of the Latin ordinaries. However, the latter were unacquainted with Greek ecclesial and liturgical traditions and did not hide a certain aversion and condescension toward them. For their part the Albanians, attached as they were to their Byzantine traditions and customs, had no intention of submitting to Latin practices that were alien to their own. Hence they more readily turned to prelates of their own Church.

The popes of the first half of the 16th century intervened several times in favor of the Italo-Greeks. The Al-banians benefited thereby, since they shared a common tradition with the Italo-Greeks and thus tended to be identified with them.

In his brief of May 18, 1521, Leo X ruled that the Greek liturgical rite was to be freely professed among the Latins; he conceded that the Greek prelates could celebrate pontifical functions in the Latin dioceses and commanded each Latin bishop to appoint a Greek vicar for the Greek faithful of his diocese; in areas where there were two bishops, a Greek and a Latin, each one was to exercise jurisdiction over the faithful according to their ecclesial traditions.

In the constitution of Dec. 23, 1534, Paul III confirmed all the concessions of Leo X and recognized as legitimate the ecclesial, disciplinary, liturgical customs of the Italo-Greek Catholic Church, e.g., the Byzantine formula of Baptism, the marriage of the clergy before receiving sacred orders, their wearing of beards, and the administration of triple sacraments of baptism, chrismation and the Eucharist to newly baptized infants. Two years later the same pontiff permitted Josaphat Lampos, Metropolitan of Rhodes who had taken refuge in Italy, to exercise jurisdiction over his Greek faithful residing on the peninsula.

In 1553 Julius III confirmed the same faculties for Italy and Sicily for Pafnuzio, who was consecrated archbishop of Agrigento by Prochoro, Archbishop of Ochrida. Other refugee bishops from the Eastern regions exercised an occasional ministry, administering the Sacraments and especially advancing candidates of the Greek Church to holy orders.

While the Catholic faith of many Greek prelates may have been open to question, the Italo-Albanians, confident in the possession of privileges granted them by the Roman pontiffs, addressed themselves in good faith to Bishops of the Albanian Orthodox Church for sacred ordinations, since they had no ordaining Byzantine Catholic bishop.

The occasional interference of the Greek prelates in the Italo-Albanian colonies and probably the aspirations of the latter to have their own bishop appeared to the ordinaries of the place as seriously prejudicial to their own jurisdictional powers. Thus the ancient aversion and distrust between Greeks and Latins soon revived. Appeals were made to the Holy See accusing the Italo-Albanians of heresies, errors, and lack of discipline. It was said that they did not admit the existence of purgatory or the primacy of the Roman pontiff, that they did not observe the feasts of the Blessed Virgin Mary, of the Holy Apostles, and of the other saints of the Roman Church; that they administered Communion to infants, etc.

The accusations so alarmed Pope Pius IV that he issued the constitution *Romanus Pontifex* (Feb. 16, 1564) revoking all concessions and privileges granted by his predecessors and subjecting all Greek institutions, clerics and faithful to the full and exclusive jurisdiction of the Latin ordinaries. Consequently, the authority to supervise Byzantine churches, to regulate the divine worship, and to administer the Sacraments devolved upon Latin bishops. These regulations notwithstanding, the pope declared that he did not intend to encourage the faithful to abandon their Byzantine heritage, not even when they were forbidden by their own Latin ordinaries or others from professing their rite freely.

But while this was the will of the Holy See, the bishops did not hold the same views. Therefore the Italo-Albanian Church, deprived of its own hierarchy, without its own seminary in which to educate new recruits for holy orders, unappreciated and misunderstood by the Latin prelates and clerics, lapsed into a decline in discipline and in the observance of its rite.

Attempts at Reform. Meanwhile the pastoral visitations, which became more frequent in accordance with the decrees of the Council of Trent, had turned the attention of the authorities to the Italo-Albanians. In answer to continued requests by the interested ordinaries, the Holy See entrusted the solution of these questions to a commission, which met in 1593. The results of its labors were summarized in the *Instructio super ritibus Italo-graecorum* transmitted by Clement VIII on Aug. 31, 1595, to the Latin bishops in whose territory resided the Italo-Albanians.

The Clementine instruction eliminated some of the more obvious abuses and established an ordaining bishop for the Greeks in Rome; unfortunately, it banned or modified several legitimate customs and traditions of the Greek church. Besides, it let it be known that its restrictive regulations were based on doubts regarding the orthodoxy of the Italo-Albanians, and it consequently gave a place of preeminence to the Latin rite.

The most significant regulations were: priests of the Byzantine rite were forbidden to administer Confirmation after Baptism, the use of the portable altar was recommended, and the use of antimensium tolerated. The indicative Latin form was to be used in sacramental formulae, rather than the indirect Byzantine form. A Latin husband did not have to observe the Greek rite of his wife; and a Latin wife did not have to observe the Greek rite of her husband. A Greek wife was encouraged to observe the rite of her Latin husband; the children followed the father's rite unless the Latin mother insisted otherwise. The use of meat was allowed on Saturday, and it was also permissible not to fast on the Saturdays of Lent.

It was stressed that it would be best if the Greeks were induced, without constraint, to observe the fasts and vigils of the Latin Church. In addition, they were required to observe the days of obligation of the Latin Church, and follow the Latin liturgical calendar.

The consequences of the Clementine regulations were highly detrimental to the Italo-Albanian community. Individuals, family groups, and entire regions turned to the Latin Church under duress from Latin prelates. The causes were varied, but the most compelling reason was to avoid finding themselves in a position of inferiority or ridicule, because they were Byzantines. Another contributing factor was the lack of Italo-Albanian clergy to replace those who died. The vacant posts were ultimately occupied by the Latin clergy, who looked upon the traditions and customs of Byzantine Christianity with disdain.

Growth in Calabria. To curb the fearful decline into extinction, to which the Italo-Albanian Church was headed, the Congregation for the Propagation of the Faith, toward the end of 1625, began to consider the erection of an Italo-Albanian seminary at Reggio Calabria. Difficulties of every sort, raised by the civil and ecclesiastical authorities of the locality, delayed its realization for another century.

Finally, in 1732, Clement XII erected a seminary for the Italo-Albanians of the Kingdom of Naples at San Benedetto Ullano (Cosenza) and named it Collegio Corsini after his own ancestral name. In 1735 the pope named the ordaining bishop for the Italo-Albanians to the presidency of the college. However, mistrust still prevailed. The territorial jurisdiction of the new prelate was circumscribed by the walls of the college, extending neither to the ecclesiastics nor to the Italo-Albanian faithful. He was permitted to visit the Italo-Albanian churches only with the previous permission of the Latin ordinaries, who retained the authority to have the wishes of the Albanian bishop executed at their own discretion.

The series of ordaining bishops began with Felice Samuele Rodotà (1735–40); nine others succeeded practically without interruption until 1912. With a few laudable exceptions these prelates generally took little interest in the seminary and practically none at all in the Albanian colonies.

The pope had a twofold purpose in conferring the presidency of Collegio Corsini upon a bishop: (1) to take away from the Latin bishops the formation of the Italo-Albanian clergy, so that the latter might be educated according to Byzantine tradition, and (2) to give the Latin bishops an auxiliary for the government of the Albanian parishes within their boundaries. Unfortunately, the pope's expectations were frustrated either by the incompetence of men, by the defects of the institutions and the lack of support by suspicious Latin prelates.

The Collegio Corsini was opposed first of all by the episcopal curia of Bisignano. In 1794, since the building was no longer adequate, it was transferred to San Demetrio Corone (Cosenza), on the site of the Basilian monastery of Saint Adrian. The college had a brief moment of splendor, but the incompetence of some of the presidents and poor administration caused its decline, until finally, following the political events of 1860, it became the property of the Italian state.

On the one hand, the ordaining bishops were never looked upon favorably by the Latin prelates, and consequently were never given the authority and jurisdiction over the Italo-Albanian faithful that Clement XII had envisaged. On the other hand, it must be admitted that not all the blame lay with intransigent Latin bishops. The Italo-Albanian bishops themselves did not always prove themselves equal to the mission entrusted to them.

Sicily. Things were not much better in Sicily. Here too the Albanian colonies were threatened with decline. A holy priest, Father Giorgio Guzzetta (1682–1756), an Italo-Albanian from Piana and member of the Congregation of the Oratory, founded a house of the Oratory in his own region, where he gathered together some celibate Byzantine priests. Within a short time they were able to open a school for young boys. In 1734, as had happened in Calabria, an Italo-Albanian seminary was opened near the Greek parish of Saint Nicholas in order to assure the colonies the supply of Byzantine clergy. The institution proved very valuable to the colonies and proved itself a vital cultural center. Father Guzzetta was anxious also to obtain an ordaining bishop for the Albanians of Sicily and to this end initiated proceedings with the competent authorities. In 1784 Pius VI satisfied this noble aspiration by promulgating the bull *Commissa nobis.*

Papal Intervention. The initiatives taken both in Calabria and Sicily, while very good, never settled the Italo-Albanian problems in a definitive way. Moreover, the legislative intervention of Benedict XIV in *Etsi pastoralis* did not attain its purpose because it was not free from defects, including the failure to understand the mentality of the Italo-Albanians.

In the above-mentioned bull, published on May 26, 1742, Benedict XIV reworked the earlier legislation for the Italo-Albanians and presented a new and very precise statute whose purpose was to eliminate all jurisdictional controversies between Italo-Albanians and Latins arising from shared ecclesial jurisdiction, which in practice meant that legitimate Byzantine traditions and usages were overwhelmed by Latin ones.

The fundamental principle underlying the Benedictine constitution was the superiority of the Latin rite, as the rite of the Holy Roman Church, the mother and teacher of all the Churches. There was greater reason for this superiority in Italian regions where the Albanians were subject to Latin bishops. In the light of this principle, *Etsi pastoralis* not only maintained the restrictive regulations of the Clementine instruction, but introduced a few more restrictive regulations. It called for the continued use of the FILIOQUE in the recitation of the Creed wherever it was already in use, and in certain instances it imposed the use of the filioque where it was not used. Communion under both species was restricted to places where it was still the custom, but the Latin faithful attending the Eucharist at Italo-Albanian Churches were forbidden to receive Communion in the form of leavened bread. The Greek faithful were permitted to receive Communion in the form of unleavened bread where there was no Greek parish. They were authorized to erect altars or chapels in addition to the main altar, so that Mass could be celebrated in either the Latin or the Greek rite. It prohibited the return to the Greek rite without special authorization of the Holy See of anyone who had received the simple tonsure or other minor orders in the Latin rite without apostolic dispensation, etc.

It was certainly not the intention of Benedict XIV to harm the Italo-Albanian Church in Italy. On the contrary, he expressly declared that he wanted to preserve it, enjoined the Latin ordinaries and clergy not to oppose it, and finally urged the Italo-Albanians to be faithful to their own legitimate traditions and customs. However, an eventual rigorous application of any of the regulations could not have failed to produce deleterious effects. Sometimes this proved to be true, and conflict between the Latin hierarchy and the Italo-Albanian faithful revived. It was due to the tenaciousness of the Italo-Albanians and to the unsuccessful exequatur of the Neapolitan government for Sicily that the decisions of the constitution did not have more harmful effects for the wider Italo-Albanian community in Italy.

In the second half of the 19th century a new attitude developed, resulting from a better understanding of the problems involved. *Etsi pastoralis* was supplemented by the constitution *Orientalium dignitas* of 1894, in which Leo XIII recognized the equality and dignity of the Italo-Albanian Church. From that time until the present there has been an uninterrupted succession of pontifical interventions to safeguard its legitimate traditions, laws and liturgical rites.

Organization and Structure. As presently constituted, the Italo-Albanian Catholic Church comprises two eparchies of equal rank and dignity. The eparchy of Lun-

Capital: Rome.
Size: 116,313 sq. miles.
Population: 57,634,327 in 2000.
Languages: Italian; German, French, and Slovene are spoken in some regions.
Religions: 85% Catholic, with relatively small populations of Muslims (1,000,000), Protestants (400,000), and Jews (30,000).

gro (in Calabria) was created on Feb. 13, 1919, by the constitution *Catholici fideles*. It covers all of southern Italy and includes 27 parishes, having jurisdiction over the Italo-Albanian Church in continental Italy. The eparchy of Piana degli Albanesi, was created by the constitution *Apostolica sedes* of Oct. 26, 1937. It covers the island of Sicily and includes 15 parishes, including the five Albanian colonies of Sicily: Piana degli Albanesi, Mezzoiuso, Palazzo Adriano, Contessa Entellina, and Santa Cristina Gela.

Bibliography: E. BENEDETTI, "La S. Congregazione di Propaganda Fide e gli Italo-greci del Regno di Napoli," *Roma e l'Oriente* 17 (1919) 52–61; 18 (1919) 37–52; 19 (1920) 56–69; 20 (1921) 91–99. A. FORTESCUE, *The Uniate Eastern Churches: The Byzantine Rite in Italy, Sicily, Syria and Egypt*, ed. G. D. SMITH, (New York 1923). C. GATTI and C. KOROLEVSKIJ, *Il rito bizantino e le Chiese bizantine*, v.1 of *I riti e le Chiese orientali* (Genova 1942). *Oriente Cattolico: Cenni storici e statistiche* (Vatican City 1962). D. ZANGARI, *Le colonie italo albanesi di Calabria: Storia e demografia secoli XV–XIX* (Naples 1941). R. ROBERSON, *The Eastern Christian Churches: A Brief Survey* (6th ed. Rome 1999).

[M. PETTA/EDS.]

ITALY, THE CATHOLIC CHURCH IN

Located in southern Europe, the Italian Republic is a peninsular region, bordered on the north by Switzerland and Austria, on the northeast by Slovakia, on the east by the Adriatic Sea, on the south by the Ionian Sea, on the west by the Mediterranean Sea and on the northwest by France. Several islands, among them Sicily, Sardinia, Elba, Capri and Ischia, are scattered along its long coast. The region is traversed by the Apennines mountain range, and mountains also form its northern boundaries. Moving southward from greater Europe, the mountains level to a great plain cut by the Po River as well as several large lakes. The southern part of the country is hot and dry, while an alpine climate characterizes the far north. Natural resources include mercury, marble, some natural gas and petroleum and coal; agricultural products consist of fruits, vegetables, grapes, potatoes, sugar beets, soybeans, grains and olives.

The area that comprises the modern state of Italy never formed a political unit during the first 15 centuries of Christianity, and for many centuries the region was ruled by petty states. Napoleon formed the Kingdom of Italy in 1805, and by 1870 the region had attained its modern political boundaries. Following World War I, the fascist leader Benito Mussolini seized control, and the region entered World War II as an ally of Germany. In 1946 it became a republic, and joined NATO as a charter member in 1949. Italy has been a major force in the political and economic unification of Europe as part of the European Economic Community (EEC) and adopted the euro in 1999. Northern Italy is more industrialized, and hence more affluent, than the agricultural south, which is troubled by organized crime, corruption and unemployment, which reached 20 percent by 2000.

The following essay is divided into three parts: the beginnings of Christianity to 1500, from 1500 to 1789 and from 1789 to the present.

EARLY HISTORY TO 1500

Christianity penetrated Italy soon after the death of Christ. A Christian community existed in Rome before the middle of the 1st century and served as the principal center for the dissemination of the new faith in Italy under the ROMAN EMPIRE. Christianity faced greater obstacles in Italy than in lands to the east, for in the West both the government and the aristocracy, wedded to the state religion as part of the Roman way of life, regarded it as a debased superstition. The rural classes clung to local cults, some of which would survive as late as the 6th century, and the Oriental mystery religions rivaled Christianity in attractive power among those who sought spiritual salvation.

The primary area of diffusion for Christianity during the first two centuries was central and southern Italy, where it was irradiated from Rome and from other towns that had Eastern connections and contained Greek, Jewish or Syrian colonies. In Rome itself the Christian Church was for several generations an immigrant church, composed largely of people from the Greek-speaking Levant. In fact, Greek was the official language of the Church in Rome until the end of the 2d century, when Latin members gained predominance and the Latin language replaced Greek [*see* LATIN (IN THE CHURCH)]. While by 250 the Roman community probably exceeded 25,000 members, outside the city Christian communities were small. In northern Italy, as distinguished from peninsular Italy, Christianity spread much more slowly.

During the first two centuries Italian Christians encountered sporadic attacks from hostile Jews and pagans, but the Roman government was generally tolerant. The

Metropolitan Sees	Suffragan Sees
Ecclesiastical Region of Abruzzi-Molise	
Campobasso-Bouiano	Isérnia-Venafroi, Termoli-Larino, Trivento
Chieto-Vaso	*Lanciano-Ortonay
L' Aquila	Avezzano, Sulmona-Valva
Pescara-Penne	Teramo-Atri
Ecclesiastical Region of Basilicata	
Potenza-Muro Lucano-Marisco Nuovo	*Acerenza, *Matera-Irsinaans, Melfi-Rapolla-Venosa, Tricarico, Tursi-Lagonegro
Ecclesistical Region of Calabria	
Catanzaro-Squillace	*Crotone-Santa Severina, Lamezia Terme
Cosenza Bisignano	Cassano all'Jonio, *Rossano-Cariati, San Marco Argentano-Scalea
Reggio Calabria-Bova	Locri-Gerace, Mileto-Nicotera-Tropea, Oppido Mamertina-Palmi
Ecclesiastical Region of Campania	
Benevento	Ariano Irpino-Lacedonia, Avellino, Cerreto Sannita-Telese-Sant'Agata de' Goti, *Angelo dei Lombardi-Conza-Nusco-Bisaccia
Napoli	Acerra, Alife-Caiazzo, Averso, Ischia, Nola, Pozzuoli, Sessa Arunca, Teano-Calvi, *Caserta, *Sorrento-Castellamare di Stabia
Salerno-Campagna-Acerno	Nocera Inferiore-Sarno, Teggiano-Policastro, Vallo della Lucania, *Amalfi-Cava de' Tirreni
Ecclesiastical Region of Emilia-Romagna	
Bologna	Faenza-Modigliana, Imola, *Ferrara-Comacchio
Modena-Nonantola	Carpi, Fidenza, Parma, Piacenza-Bobbio, Reggio Emilia-Guastalla
Ravenna-Cervia	Cesena-Sarsina, Forlì-Bertinoro, Rimini, San Marino-Montefeltro
Ecclesiastical Region of Latium	
Roma	Suburbicarian Churches: Frascati, Ostia, Palestrina, Porto-Santa Rufina, Sabina-Poggio Mirteto, Velletri-Segni
	Immediatly subject to the Holy See: *Gaeta, Anagni-Alatri, Civita Castellana, Civitavecchia-Tarquinia, Frosinone-Veroli-Ferentino, Latina-Terracina-Sezze-Priverno, Rieti, Sora-Aquino-Pontecorvo, Tivoli, Viterbo
Ecclesiastical Region of Liguria	
Genova	Albenga-Imperia, Chiavari, La Spezia-Sarzana-Brugnato, Savona-Noli, Tortona, Ventimiglia-San Remo
Ecclesiastical Region of Lombardy	
Milan	Bergamo, Brescia, Como, Crema, Cremona, Lodi, Mantova, Pavia, Vigenvano
Ecclesiastical Region of the Marches	
Ancona-Osimo	Fabriano-Matelica, Jesi, Senigallia
Fermo	Ascoli Piceno, *Camerino-San Severino Marche, Macerata-Tolentino-Recanati-Cingoli-Treia, San Benedetto del Tronto-Ripatransone-Montalto
Pesaro	Fano-Fossombrone-Cagli-Pergola, *Urbino-Urbania-Sant'Angelo in Vado
Ecclesiastical Region of Piedmont	
Torino	Acqui, Alba, Aosta, Asti, Cuneo, Fossano, Ivrea, Mondovì, Pinerolo, Saluzzo, Susa
Vercelli	Alessandria, Biella, Casale Monferrato, Novara

earliest known persecution by the government—in Rome after the great fire in 64—was only temporary. From that time on the profession of Christianity was a criminal offense, the definition and prosecution of which was left to the magistrates. Not until the 3d century were persecutions instituted by the emperors. Then in the throes of a military crisis, the government tried to rally its subjects by demanding loyalty tests in the form of general sacri-

Metropolitan Sees	Suffragan Sees
Ecclesiastical Region of Puglia	
Bari-Bitonto	Altamura-Gravina-Aquaviva delle Fonti, Andria, Conversano-Monopoli, Molfetta-Ruvo-Giovinazzo-Terlizzi, *Trani-Barletta-Bisceglie
Foggia-Bovino	Cerignola-Ascoli Satriano, Lucera-Troia, San Severo, *Manfredonia-Vieste
Lecce	Nardò-Gallipoli, Ugento-Santa Maria de Leuca, *Brindisi-Ostunia, *Otranto
Taranto	Castellaneta, Oria
Ecclesiastical Region of Sardinia	
Cagliari	Iglesias, Lanusei, Nuoro
Oristano	Ales-Terralba
Sassari	Alghero-Bosa, Ozieri, Tempio-Ampurias
Ecclesiastical Region of Sicily	
Agrigento	Caltanissetta, Piazza Armerina
Catania	Acireale, Caltagirone
Messina-Lipari-Santa Lucia	
del Mela	Nicosia, Patti
Palermo	Cefalù, Mazara del Vallo, *Monreale, Trapani
Siracusa	Noto, Ragusa
Ecclesiastical Region of Tuscany	
Firenze	Arezzo-Cortonoa-Sansepolcro, Fiesoel, Pistoia, Prato, San Miniato
Pisa	Livorni, Massa Carrara-Pontremoli, Pescia, Volterra
Siena-Colle di Val d'Elsa-	Grosseto, Massa Marittima-Piombion, Montepulciano-Chiusi-Pienza, Pitigliano-Sovana-Orbetello
Montalcino	
Lucca	
Ecclesiastical Region of Triveneto	
Gorizia	Trieste
Trento	Bolzano-Bressanone
Udine	
Veneto (patriarchate)	Adria-Rovigo, Belluno-Feltre, Chioggia, Concordia-Pordenone, Padova, Treviso, Verona, Vicenza, Vittorio Veneto
Ecclesiastical Region of Umbria	
Perugia-Città delle Pieve	Assisi-Nocera Umbra-Gualdo Tadino, Città di Castello, Foligno, Gubbio
Immediately subject to the	
Holy See:	*Spoleto-Norcia, Orvieto-Todi, Terni-Nardi-Amelia

*Suffragan archdiocese

The pope is the bishop of Rome. There are seven territorial abbeys in Italy and three prelatures, as well as a military ordinariate. The Italo-Albanian Church has eparchies at Lungro and at Piana on the island of Sicily, as well as a territorial abbey in Italy.

fices to the gods on behalf of the emperor. The refusal of Christians to comply led to a succession of empire-wide persecutions, the most violent being those under Emperors DECIUS (250–251), VALERIAN (257–259) and DIOCLETIAN (303–304). The Roman Church, as the leading Christian community in the West, suffered severely; a list of martyrs from the 5th century records 275 martyrs for peninsular Italy and the islands (Sicily, Sardinia, and Corsica) and 30 for northern Italy. The failure of Diocletian's persecution prompted Emperor GALERIUS to issue an edict of toleration in 311. The more inclusive policy of toleration agreed upon by Emperor CONSTANTINE I and Licinius at Milan in 312 and generalized throughout the empire in 313 established the Peace of the Church [see MILAN, EDICT (AGREEMENT) OF]. Christianity now entered upon a period of rapid growth.

Creation of the Diocese. By the end of the 2d century the main outlines of episcopal diocesan organization in peninsular Italy had been clearly drawn, although in the north only three dioceses—Milan, AQUILEIA and RAVENNA—have been dated before 314, although others

such as Parenzo (modern Poreč, Yugoslavia), Verona and Brescia may also have originated earlier. Because the northern bishoprics were much larger than those of central and southern Italy, when Italy's diocesan organization had been largely mapped out, *c.* 600, there were only 53 bishoprics in the entire north as contrasted with at least 197 in the south and center. The bishop of Rome was the metropolitan for peninsular Italy, but three metropolitan jurisdictions had been established in the north by the 5th century: Milan for Liguria, Aquileia for Venetia and Istria, and Ravenna for Emilia.

In accordance with ancient custom, Italian bishops were elected by the clergy and people of their dioceses, the rank and file of the laity participating through acclamation. In the disorders caused by the decay of the empire in the West and the influx of the Barbarian Nations, the bishops assumed a position of leadership in their region. They protected people against the barbarians, organized public services to aid the poor and helped ransom captives. Many public functions passed into their hands, and in 554 the Pragmatic Sanction issued by Emperor JUS-

"St. Justina" from "High Altar of St. Anthony" by Donatello, Basilica of Sant'Antonio, Padua, Italy. (©Elio Ciol/CORBIS)

TINIAN I legalized the governmental functions that the Italian bishops had assumed.

Italy's ecclesiastical organization was finished by the 8th century. With rural parishes now in existence, Christianity ceased to be primarily a city religion. The first parishes formed part of a closely regulated hierarchical structure subject to the bishops as their founders.

The Early Middle Ages: 500–1000. The main challenge of the medieval Church was to incorporate barbarian immigrants into the existing Church structure. The establishment of Germanic kingdoms in Italy during the 5th and 6th centuries created a heretical Arian church (*see* ARIANISM) alongside the older Catholic organization. Arian Ostrogoth king THEODORIC THE GREAT (493–526) regarded his rule as a continuation of the Roman Empire; he allowed the existing Catholic establishment to remain, thus causing a belated flowering of Romano-Christian literature through such Christian scholars as BOETHIUS, CASSIODORUS and ENNODIUS of Pavia. Under his successors the Gothic power in Italy was destroyed by Emperor Justinian in a long and devastating war (535–554). This Byzantine restoration proved ephemeral, however, for in 568 Italy was invaded by the Germanic LOMBARDS. Recent converts to Arianism, the Lombards treated Italians and their clergy harshly, destroying or exiling much of the Catholic hierarchy. They established a kingdom in northern Italy with its capital at Pavia, to which were connected the Lombard duchies of Spoleto and Benevento. The Duchy of Rome, including part of Tuscany and the Exarchate of Ravenna, together with the Duchy of Naples, the extreme south and Sicily, remained Byzantine.

Relations between the papacy and the Lombards improved under Lombard Queen Theudelinda. An anti-Catholic reaction followed, but in the course of the 7th century both the monarchy and people embraced Catholicism. Even after conversion the Lombard kings did not collaborate closely with the Church, nor did they include churchmen in their government. Furthermore, faced by the possibility of another Byzantine reconquest, the Lombards continually encroached upon the Exarchate of Ravenna and threatened Rome. The Byzantine government, absorbed in problems in the East, did not furnish adequate military protection, making the papacy under Gregory I and his successors the effective leaders of the Italo-Romans against any extension of Lombard power into the south.

The 8th century witnessed the culmination of long-standing tensions between the PAPACY and the Byzantine emperors (*see* BYZANTINE CHURCH), regarded as "Caesaropapists" who claimed the right to ratify papal elections and to intervene in doctrinal matters. Emperor Justinian had compelled Pope VIGILIUS to sanction the condemnation of the THREE CHAPTERS by the fifth ecumenical council, CONSTANTINOPLE II (553), thus precipitating a schism in Italy, where the measure was deemed heretical. Emperors HERACLIUS in 638 and CONSTANS II in 648 supported the heresy of MONOTHELITISM and Constans arrested and exiled Pope MARTIN I to the Crimea when he condemned the imperial decree *TYPOS*. The Isaurian emperors of the 8th century espoused ICONOCLASM, driving thousands of Greek monks to southern Italy and Rome. Popes GREGORY II (715–731) and GREGORY III (731–741) opposed the iconoclastic decrees of Emperor LEO III, who retaliated by confiscating papal estates in Calabria and Sicily. When Gregory III called a synod in Rome (731) that excluded image-breakers from the Church, he was supported by the people of central Italy.

The crisis came in 751, when Lombard King Aistulf captured Ravenna and threatened the Duchy of Rome. Byzantine military power in central Italy collapsed, and without protection against the Lombards the papacy turned to the rising power of the FRANKS in the north. In 754 Pope STEPHEN II crossed the Alps and made a personal appeal to Frankish King PEPIN III the Short, conferring upon him and his sons the title of PATRICIUS ROMANORUM, which carried the responsibility of defending Rome. In campaigns in 754–755 and 756 Pepin regained the territory of the exarchate, which he conferred upon the papacy, thus creating the STATES OF THE CHURCH.

The Franco-papal alliance was consummated in the reign of Pepin's son CHARLEMAGNE. In 774 he intervened

The courtyard of the Strozzi Palace in Florence, Italy, 1489–1497. (Alinari-Art Reference/Art Resource, NY)

in Italy on an appeal from Pope ADRIAN I (772–795) against Lombard King DESIDERIUS. Defeating and dethroning Desiderius, Charlemagne conquered the Lombard kingdom and assumed the title of King of the Lombards, bestowing it upon his infant son in 781. His coronation as Roman emperor by Pope LEO III in 800 gave a firm basis to Carolingian protection of the Church and at the same time permanently liberated the papacy from Byzantine control. For the next five centuries the destinies of Italy were bound up with the Carolingian kings and their successors in Germany.

Carolingian Italy. The Frankish semitheocratic conception of royal power was now transplanted to Italy, where it transformed Church-State relations. The assembly at Pavia came to include bishops as well as lay magnates. The royal right to confirm any episcopal election in the Lombard kingdom was established, together with the principle that a bishopric was in part a royal office involving obligations to the State, and that the bishop-elect must be the king's faithful servitor (*fidelis*). By the Roman edict of 824, LOTHAIR I, co-emperor with Louis I the Pious, affirmed the right of the emperor to confirm papal elections as well.

Various Frankish reforms were also introduced by the Carolingians, such as the civil enforcement of ecclesiastical TITHES and their assignment to the parish churches. Some Italian bishops voluntarily adopted for their cathedral clergy the communal life that CHRODEGANG OF METZ had designed for his episcopal family and that had become the norm in Frankish cathedrals. A general capitulary issued by Louis the Pious in 817 made the Benedictine Rule binding upon all monasteries in his empire and demanded the observance of the *vita canonica* by all cathedral chapters.

Although by no means fruitless, these reforms would be largely negated by the growth of FEUDALISM, which together with a new wave of invasions contributed to the

Christ crowning one of the Norman kings of Sicily (William II), 12th-century mosaic at Monreale, Sicily, Italy.

An art exhibition entitled "Michelangelo's Youth," Palazzo Vecchio, Florence, Italy, October 7, 1999. (AP/Wide World Photos)

collapse of the empire after 850. Many bishoprics and abbeys benefited from royal grants of immunity, which freed them from the authority of local state officials and in their more positive form granted the churches judicial and taxing powers over their tenants and serfs. During the course of the 9th century the more destructive aspects of feudalism became visible. Bishops acquired bodies of vassals in order to fulfill their obligations to the State, and carved benefices for these vassals out of church property. By the close of the century even parish churches and tithes were being infeudated in this manner.

The Kingdom of Italy: 889–962. Family feuds and internecine wars caused the demise of the Carolingian Empire. In 888, following the deposition of Emperor Charles III the Fat, Italy was detached from the empire and formed a separate kingdom, but it was a kingdom devoid of national character. The large number of Frankish and Alemannian soldiers and officials who had immigrated to Italy during the 9th century had often been appointed counts, and some of them had become founders of principalities in Italy. The struggles of the kings of Italy from 889 to 962 were mere contests for personal power. Furthermore, the region's growing anarchy was intensified by Muslim and Hungarian invasions. Saracens con-

quered Sicily in the 9th century, and southern Italy was also threatened. A Saracen attack on the suburbs of Rome in 843 later prompted Pope LEO IV to build the Leonine Wall, and under his leadership the maritime towns of Naples, Gaeta and Amalfi combined their navies and inflicted a crushing defeat on the Saracens off Ostia (849). Emperor Louis II (d. 875) devoted his life to campaigning against the Saracens in the south. The Hungarian invasions (*c.* 899–950), reaching as far south as Otranto, were equally devastating. Without a central government capable of defending the country, Italy became increasingly fragmented and feudalized as bishops and abbots as well as lay magnates built castles or strengthened existing walls.

By the end of the 9th century the papacy had become an almost purely local institution, the tool of Roman factions who dominated the elections (*see* CRESCENTII; TUSCULANI). Attempts on the part of individual popes to secure foreign protection or to carry out needed reforms produced no lasting results, and the north Italian episcopate was increasingly immersed in political struggles. As royal nominees, the bishops were in effect assimilated to the status of royal vassals, although a few prelates, such as RATHERIUS of Verona and ATTO of Vercelli, still demanded the enforcement of canonical rules.

Pope John Paul II, under canopy, during the beatification ceremony of three Servants of God, St. Peter's Square, Vatican City. In the background hang tapestries of the beatified: Bishop Giovanni Battista Scalabrini (l), Bishop Vilmos Apor, and Sister Dorotea Chayez (r). (AP/Wide World Photos)

The Ottonian Period: German Intervention and Rule. The intervention of German King OTTO I (936–973) in Italian politics and his assumption of the Lombard crown in 951 after defeating King Berengar II meant that there was once again a strong Germanic power in Italy. In 962 Otto intervened in Rome to protect Pope JOHN XII against the continued encroachments of Berengar and was crowned Roman emperor by the pope, thus reviving the empire of Charlemagne and establishing the personal union between Germany and Italy later known as the HOLY ROMAN EMPIRE.

Under Otto I, Italy was annexed to the German monarchy. The Ottonian (or Saxon) emperors used the Church as their principal instrument of government. Royal control of episcopal elections, already practiced in northern Italy, was now extended to the Romano-Ravennate territory. Otto forced Roman electors to recognize his right of approval and to choose two successive popes of his designation. He regularly nominated aristocratic bishops to Italian sees; some he made counts as well, thus conveying to them full political as well as spiritual authority over their cities and districts; from all he demanded the customary feudal services, including the furnishing of military contingents to his army. Similar measures were applied to the great Benedictine abbeys.

The reign of Emperor OTTO II (973–983) witnessed the growing power of the lesser feudatories (*secundi milites* or vavasors), many of whom were Church vassals. The emperor's efforts were devoted to resisting the Saracens, who defeated him at Cortona in 982.

The spiritual climate changed radically under Emperor OTTO III (983–1002). Influenced by Byzantine ideas, Otto wished to make Rome the capital of a Christian Roman Empire, a universal state ruled by an emperor who as "servant of the apostles" exercised priestly functions. Otto's ideals were shared and probably in part inspired by his teacher Gerbert of Aurillac, successively abbot of Bobbio, archbishop of Ravenna, and finally pope SYLVESTER II (999–1003). Otto was aided also by LEO of Vercelli, who received from him a strategic bishopric in northern Italy. Practical statesmen, these men realized that their goals could be realized only through German power and Church personnel. Unlike his predecessors, Otto appointed German bishops to Italian sees. In granting central Italian territory to the pope, he reserved rights

Pazzi Chapel, courtyard of Sant Croce, 1429, designed by Filippo Burnelleschi, Florence, Italy. (©Angelo Hornak/CORBIS)

assuring a firm line of military communication between Ravenna and Rome. He supported the pope in the program of practical Church reform suggested by Gerbert's experience at Bobbio. An imperial edict of 998 limited all leases of church property to the lifetime of the conceding bishop or abbot, thus striking a blow at the *secundi milites.* Otto's premature death was followed by an uprising of the *secundi milites* under Arduin of Ivrea, who briefly held the crown of Italy before being defeated by Emperor HENRY II of Germany with the help of Leo of Vercelli, a loyal "bishop of the empire." The last of the Saxon emperors, Henry presided in 1022 at a reforming council at Pavia that condemned marriage of the clergy (*see* CELIBACY, CLERICAL HISTORY OF).

Revolution and the Cluniac Reform: 1000–1300. The middle centuries of the medieval period witnessed a religious revolution that began in the monasteries but was soon communicated to all classes of society. The CLUNIAC REFORM movement gained ground late in the 10th century, and many monasteries came under its influence. But the strongest impulse to reform came from Italian eremitical monasticism, represented by the three very different figures of ROMUALD from Ravenna, JOHN GUALBERT and PETER DAMIAN. Romuald founded groups of hermit communities at CAMALDOLI and elsewhere, from which he preached against the abuse of SIMONY. John Gualbert (d. 1073), while a young monk at San Miniato, went into the streets of Florence to incite the people against simoniac churchmen, and after becoming abbot of VALLOMBROSA in 1039 he mobilized his monks to campaign throughout Tuscany against simony and clerical concubinage. The noblest representative of monastic reform was Peter Damian (1007–72), who taught that the monastic ideal should be the model for all Christians and urged the secular clergy also to adopt the common life (*vita communis*). This early phase of the reforming movement, stressing the moral regeneration of the clergy, was favored by the second Franconian emper-

Pulpit in the cathedral at Ravello, Italy, by Niccolò di Bartolommeo da Foggia, signed and dated 1272. (Alinari-Art Reference/Art Resource, NY)

or, HENRY III (1039–56), under whom imperial power over the papacy reached its height. Between 1046 and 1054, when he set aside three rival popes, Henry designated four German popes, of whom the third in succession, LEO IX (1048–1054), assumed the leadership of the reform movement.

The 1054 marriage of Beatrice of Tuscany with Duke Godfrey of Lorraine created a strong power in central Italy that supported the reforming cause via Florence. The Lotharingian bishop of Florence was elected by the reformers in 1058 and installed in Rome by Godfrey of Lorraine as Pope NICHOLAS II (1058–61). The Roman synod held by Nicholas in 1059 called for the moral reformation of the clergy, condemned simony, and, by a significant innovation set forth in the PAPAL ELECTION DECREE (1059), vested control of papal elections in the cardinals with only a vague reference to the right of the young Henry IV.

The influence Hildebrand exercised even before he became pope was especially evident from 1057 to 1059. Northern resentment against the clergy had by then erupted into violence, particularly in the Lombard towns. In Milan in 1057 Hildebrand gave encouragement and support to the leaders of the PATARINES, a revolutionary religious group that demanded "free elections" of bishops and repudiated the married clergy. The wrath of the *pattari* (ragpickers, peddlers) was directed against the upper clergy of Milan, connected by marriage and economic interests with the lay aristocracy. In 1059 the archbishop of Milan was forced to submit to the papal legate and accept the decrees of the Roman synod.

When Hildebrand became pope as GREGORY VII (1073–85), measures were taken against the married clergy, but the focus of the GREGORIAN REFORM was on lay INVESTITURE. Prohibited by a Roman synodal decree of 1075, lay investiture had come to represent the close symbiosis of Church and State that had destroyed the autonomy of the Church and caused the moral evils by which she was afflicted. Emperor HENRY IV's defiance of the decree of 1075, his insistence upon appointing his own candidate to the See of Milan and the candidate being invested with the ring and the staff precipitated the INVESTITURE STRUGGLE, which divided Italy for half a century. The Concordat of WORMS (1122) ended the investiture struggle by providing that the consecration of a newly elected bishop or abbot must precede his investiture with temporalities by the emperor. A victory for the Church through its reestablishment of the principle of canonical election, this was in reality a victory for the towns which had bargained with the contending parties in order to establish their own independence under elected consuls.

Southern Italy and Sicily: The Norman Kingdom. The south did not form part of the Carolingian Empire and therefore pursued an entirely different course of development from that of northern and central Italy. Disputed in the early Middle Ages between Lombards and Byzantines, ravaged by Saracen invasions and raids, the south had become a political vacuum that was conquered by Norman adventurers in the 11th century. Relations between the NORMANS and the papacy were at first hostile, but Pope Nicholas II recognized the Norman conquest as an accomplished fact and conceded Apulia, Calabria and Sicily as a fief to the Norman freebooter ROBERT GUISCARD in 1059. Robert rescued Gregory VII when Henry IV captured Rome in 1081, and Gregory died in exile at Salerno in the Norman kingdom. In 1091 Count ROGER OF Sicily, Guiscard's brother, completed the 30-year conquest of SICILY from the Muslims and in 1098 he received from Pope URBAN II a hereditary papal legateship over Sicily, later called the *MONARCHIA SICULA*, which gave him control over the religious establishment of the island. The Norman rulers favored the introduction of Latin monasticism into their dominions as a means of consolidating their power. While the Greek rite and Muslim religious practices were tolerated, most members of these groups gradually passed over to the Latin rite. The Norman monarchy attained its height under King Roger II of Sicily (1130–54), under whom Sicily and the mainland of southern Italy were united.

The Hohenstaufen Emperors. During the investiture struggle many imperial rights (REGALIA) had been taken over by the emergent communes in Italy. Hohenstaufen Emperor FREDERICK I BARBAROSSA (1152–90) determined to make imperial power preeminent in Italy. At the same time his exalted conception of his position involved him in a series of ideological conflicts with the papacy. Attempting to force his direct administration upon the north Italian communes, he met the military re-

Cathedral in Syracuse, Italy. (©Eye Ubiquitous/CORBIS)

sistance of the LOMBARD LEAGUE in alliance with Pope ALEXANDER III. In the fifth of six campaigns in Italy, Frederick was defeated by the League at Legnano (1176). Reconciled with the pope at Venice a year later, he concluded the Peace of Constance (1183), conceeding the communes *de facto* self-government but reserving extensive rights of overlordship. The marriage of his son and successor, Emperor HENRY VI (1190–97), with Constance of Sicily and his assumption of the Norman crown at Palermo (1194) created a Hohenstaufen empire in Italy that encircled the Papal States and again threatened the communes. A new crisis was averted only by Henry's death and the division of his empire between his brother, Philip of Swabia, and his infant son by Constance, Emperor FREDERICK II (1212–50), who ruled over only the *Regno* (southern Italy and Sicily) until his coronation as emperor in 1220.

In the papacy-empire conflict both sides drew ideological support from a revival of legal studies that was centered at the University of BOLOGNA. In the 12th century the renewed study of canon law succeeded in translating papal authority into legal terms. The Gregorian reformers had initially promoted such study, and *c.* 1140 at Bologna the Camaldolese monk Gratian published his magisterial *Decretum* (see GRATIAN, DECRETUM OF), which succeeded in placing canon law on a scientific basis. After 1150 the principles of the *Decretum* were applied and expanded by a succession of canonist popes, including Alexander III and INNOCENT III. By Innocent's time the structure of the Church had become monarchical and bureaucratic, operating through a staff of trained law-

The cathedral of Fermo, Italy, begun in the 13th century. The bell tower was restored in 1430 and completed in 1731. (Alinari-Art Reference/Art Resource, NY)

yers in the papal curia. Meanwhile, on the imperial side there was a similar but slower development. In 1158, for example, at the Diet of Roncaglia, Frederick I appealed to Bolognese experts in civil or Roman law to define the *regalia*. In 1224 Frederick II founded the University of Naples for the special purpose of providing himself with lawyers, and he consciously imitated the Code of Justinian in his Constitutions of Melfi, which he promulgated in 1231 as a code of law for the Regno.

Under Frederick II the triangular struggle between papacy, Hohenstaufens and communes was renewed with unprecedented bitterness (*see* GUELFS AND GHIBELLINES). After establishing a bureaucratic secular state in the Regno, Frederick directed his activities toward two goals: the unification of Italy and its reentrance into the Holy Roman Empire. To achieve this policy he would have to crush the northern communes and reannex the Papal States. He defeated the army of the Lombard League at Cortenuova in 1237, though resistance continued, led by popes GREGORY IX (1227–41) and INNOCENT IV (1243–54). Innocent excommunicated and deposed Frederick at the Council of LYONS I (1245) and finally proclaimed a crusade against him. Frederick's fortunes subsequently crumbled, but the outcome of the struggle was still in doubt at his death in 1250.

The struggle continued against Frederick's heirs in Italy, namely Conrad IV, who died prematurely in 1254 and Manfred, who ruled as regent in southern Italy and from 1258 as king of Sicily and Naples. In 1263 the French Pope URBAN IV offered the crown of the Regno to the French Prince Charles of Anjou. Charles's army defeated and killed Manfred at Benevento (1266), and Charles established Angevin rule in Naples and Sicily, also receiving the title of imperial vicar in Tuscany, from Pope Clement IV. The support given by several popes to the Angevin domination aroused suspicion among the other powers of Europe, and the expulsion of the French from Sicily in 1282 by the popular uprising known as the Sicilian Vespers was a mortal blow to papal prestige.

The terms ''Guelfs'' and ''Ghibellines'' originated in the course of these struggles between the popes and Hohenstaufens to describe the adherents of papacy and empire, respectively. However, without entirely losing their original significance, these names soon tended to become masks for the internal conflicts of the communes and petty despots who were now the real powers in Italy.

The Communes and the Church. In the era of the Crusades (*c.* 1100–1300) the Italian maritime republics of Venice, Genoa and Pisa and the great inland cities of Lombardy and Tuscany were at the forefront of economic advances taking place in western Europe. The expansion of trade and industry was most marked in the larger centers, but it affected all Italy to some extent, leading to a more diversified social structure and conflicts of interest among the various groups.

During most of the 12th century the communes were governed by oligarchies composed of landowners and more prosperous merchants with the communal governments quietly absorbing most of the political powers formerly exercised by the bishops. Toward the end of the century guilds of artisans and small merchants began to gain power, and during the 13th century a federation of guilds and other local groups took over the government in many towns. In this period of middle-class rule there were open conflicts between Church and State (represented by the communes) caused by the efforts of the communal governments to curtail or abolish clerical privileges and immunities and to subject the clergy to municipal taxation and the jurisdiction of the municipal courts. The wealth and the worldly lives of the cathedral clergy were constant targets of criticism. The outbursts of anticlericalism that manifested themselves during these jurisdictional struggles were nourished by the religious unrest that flourished especially among the poorer classes of the population.

Heresy and Evangelical Movements. Heresy began to spread in Italy in the 11th century. About 1030 Monforte in Piedmont is known to have harbored an organized community of CATHARI, which was forcibly repressed by the local authorities. Temporarily extinguished, or perhaps absorbed by the PATARINES, Catharism revived after 1150, and a Catharistic church was organized in the north with branches in many Lombard towns (including Milan, Brescia, Verona and Vicenza) and in Florence. Moreover, Catharism was only one stream in a proliferation of heresies, e.g., the followers of ARNOLD of Brescia, the WALDENSES and the Poor Men of Lombardy, all difficult to distinguish clearly because the name "Patarene" (*Patarinus,* originally meaning a member of the Patarines) was often applied indiscriminately to any heretic. In 1184 Pope LUCIUS III and Frederick Barbarossa published an edict at Verona establishing an INQUISITION against Italian heretics, but it failed to accomplish its purpose. Cathari were widespread and held municipal offices in some towns. In 1215 Milan was known to be a "sink of heretics," and in 1250 there were still six Catharistic churches in Verona.

Side by side with the heresies, various evangelical movements arose, their followers drawing inspiration from the apostolic age of the Church and exalting poverty as a Christian ideal. This POVERTY MOVEMENT drew most of its adherents from the poorer urban classes, such as the wool workers of Lombardy who formed a sect called the HUMILIATI whose members accepted and idealized poverty as an ennobling virtue. The cult of poverty, central to such extremist movements, may have been, in part, a protest by the urban poor against a rudimentary capitalism, but in the spiritual climate of the 12th century the religious motive of the movement must be considered to have been the dominant one.

Monasticism and the Mendicant Orders. In the 4th century, monasticism entered Italy from the East (*see* MONASTICISM, 1). The ascetic life was preached and practiced in Rome by ATHANASIUS (*c.* 340) and by JEROME (*c.* 375–385). Both AMBROSE (d. 397) and EUSEBIUS OF VERCELLI (d. 371) lent their support to monastic institutions. But the most decisive influence came from St. BENEDICT (d. 543), first at SUBIACO and later at MONTE CASSINO, where he formulated the famous rule for a monastic community for his disciples (*c.* 529–534). The BENEDICTINE RULE provided a model not only for the spiritual life but also for the economic organization of all the great Benedictine monasteries [FARFA, NONANTOLA, Novalesa, LA CAVA (Saints Trinità) and others] that were founded in Italy after the 7th century. In Apulia *c.* 540 CASSIODORUS founded two monasteries at Vivarium, where Roman classical culture was fused with the monastic life. GREGORY I the Great, a disciple of Benedict, founded six monasteries on his Sicilian estates (*c.* 576) and another in Rome on the Caelian, from which he was drawn by

"Madonna and Child" by Giovanni Battista Tiepolo, 18th century. (©Burstein Collection/CORBIS)

popular acclamation to become pope (590). A little later, the Irish monk COLUMBAN, in flight from Gaul, was received in Italy by the Lombard King Agilulf, an Arian, and his Catholic wife, Theudelinda, and in 614 established the Abbey of BOBBIO in the Apennines. Sometimes called the Monte Cassino of the north, Bobbio was a center for the evangelization of northwestern Italy. Like other Celtic monasteries it soon adopted the Benedictine Rule.

By the Middle Ages, traditional monasticism could no longer provide leadership for the spiritual crisis facing the urban communities. The newly founded CISTERCIANS began to expand throughout Italy after 1120, but their basic ideal called for withdrawal from society. The most influential of the Cistercians was the Calabrian Abbot JOACHIM of Fiore (d. 1202), who prophesied the coming of a new age to be heralded by the arrival of mendicant monks.

The ascetic spirit of monasticism was transformed and given social direction by the MENDICANT ORDERS, the Franciscans and Dominicans, early in the 13th century. The DOMINICANS, or Preaching Friars, recognized by Pope Innocent III in 1206, established their headquarters in Bologna, but the decisive influence lay with the FRANCISCANS. FRANCIS OF ASSISI (1182–1226) and his Friars

A Florentine-made silver and gilt silver chalice that was a gift from the Catholic people of Leopoli, Poland, to Pius IX in 1869. (©David Lees/CORBIS)

Minor were the bearers of a spiritual revolution that had far-reaching effects on Italian civilization. The Franciscan ideal incorporated the spiritual aspirations of the earlier evangelical movements—the appealing concept of the apostolic life and the cult of poverty—but with the imprint of Francis's creative personality. The early Franciscans were a highly mobile group, replacing the hermit preachers and the wandering evangelists and addressing their message to town-dwellers. Their success was immediate and overwhelming; they filled the gap between the secular clergy and the people and guided back to the Church many who would have drifted into heresy. The controversy over the holding of property by the order, which divided the Franciscans into Conventual FRANCISCANS and FRANCISCAN SPIRITUALS, and the emergence of the dissident heretical FRATICELLI, active chiefly in southern Italy, disrupted the unity of the order but did not really prevent the Franciscans from fulfilling their mission. By 1250 heresy in Italy had begun to diminish. Less than 100 years later it had become virtually extinct. The Franciscans, furthermore, brought a more personal religion to many who had never known it before, and through the Tertiaries, or Third Order, permitted laymen to share their ideal.

The Later Middle Ages: 1300–1500. The years coinciding with the lifetime of DANTE ALIGHIERI (1265–1321) constituted the close of the Middle Ages as a distinct cultural epoch. In the next two centuries medieval ideas and institutions merged imperceptibly with those of the Italian Renaissance.

After 1300 northern and central Italy still formed part of the Holy Roman Empire, but except for the futile expedition of Emperor HENRY VII (1310–13), the emperors made no attempt to assert effective control. In the south Pope BONIFACE VIII and Charles II of Anjou finally ended the 20-year war of the Sicilian Vespers in 1302, by recognizing a prince of the house of Aragon as ruler of Sicily. The Guelf-Ghibelline wars raging in northern Italy after the death of Emperor Frederick II had favored the rise of military leaders who seized every opportunity to establish themselves as city tyrants (*signori*). In the 14th century the more ruthless of these tyrants expanded their states through consolidation and conquest. Of the dozen or more principalities into which Italy was eventually divided, the most important were the Duchy of Milan, the republics of Venice and Florence, the States of the Church and the kingdom of Naples, all of whose shifting alliances and alignments in the 15th century were aimed at maintaining a balance of power.

For the papacy the later Middle Ages was a period of humiliation and division, as its very identification with Rome was broken during the 70-plus years of the AVIGNON PAPACY in France, and its prestige was shattered by the WESTERN SCHISM. The long residence of the popes at AVIGNON (1309–78) was due in part to the anarchical conditions that made Rome unsafe and the Papal States almost ungovernable, and the new fiscal system of the Avignon papacy was developed to meet the needs not only of an expensive court but also to restore the pope's authority over the Papal States. Papal taxation came to rest very heavily upon the churches and monasteries, and papal control over the episcopate was tightened by increased use of reservations. Yet the economic condition of the Church in Italy steadily deteriorated. The northern Church had been impoverished by 1500 largely as a result of the passage of its property into the hands of land speculators and tenants whose rents had remained stationary despite general inflation. Nevertheless the great prelates, in true Renaissance style, carried out expensive building and artistic programs.

Historians no longer regard the Italian Renaissance as predominantly pagan and antireligious in character, although these elements certainly did exist within its structure. The 14th century especially was a great age of religion; the plague epidemics at mid-century were followed by a wave of religious feeling among all classes that was vividly reflected in the art of the time. Great religious leaders of the period included the Dominican James Passavanti (d. 1357) of S. Maria Novella in Florence, John dalle Celle of Vallombrosa (d. 1394–1400), JOHN COLOMBINI, the founder of a new lay congregation, the JESUATI and CATHERINE OF SIENA, a Dominican tertiary. In 1334 Franciscan Spiritual John della Valle founded the

"Virgin and Child with Saints" by Titian. (©Archivo Iconografico, S.A./CORBIS.)

order of the Osservanti, or Observant Franciscans. In the following century ANTONINUS of Florence and BERNARDINE OF SIENA, vicar-general of the Observants, preached to rapt crowds. The SAVONAROLA episode is well known. The Florentine humanists of the Medici circle had a form of religion in NEOPLATONISM, by no means incompatible with the Christian tradition. Other noteworthy religious aspects of the Renaissance would include the turbulence of the Western Schism, the union of the Byzantine and Roman Churches temporarily achieved at the Council of FLORENCE in 1439, and the reorganization of the Italian BENEDICTINES into the Congregation of Santa Giustina of Padua by Pope EUGENE IV in 1432–35. Furthermore, accounts of the secular activities of the Renaissance popes as rulers of an Italian state, and of their patronage of humanists and artists do not constitute a full history of the Church; coexisting with the secular mood and style of the Renaissance was a profound religious consciousness. But any tendency toward the needed religious reformation in the 15th century was thwarted by the prevailing political disunity and lack of leadership. The French invasion of 1494 plunged Italy into an era of protracted warfare as a battleground for the monarchies of France and Spain. The seat of the most advanced civilization in Europe,

Italy entered the modern age without having established her national identity.

Bibliography: G. FORCHIELLI, *La pieve rurale* (Rome 1931). C. E. BOYD, *Tithes and Parishes in Medieval Italy* (Ithaca, NY 1952). *Storia di Milano* (Milan 1953–) v.1–8. G. PENCO, *Storia del monachesimo in Italia dalle origini alla fine del medio evo* (Rome 1961). W. ULLMANN, *The Growth of Papal Government in the Middle Ages* (2d ed. New York 1962). G. LA PIANA, *Foreign Groups in Rome during the First Centuries of the Empire* (Cambridge, MA 1928). F. LANZONI, *Le diocesi d'Italia dalle origini dal principio del secolo VII,* 2 v. (2d ed. Faenza 1927). S. MOCHI-ONORY, *Vescovi e città* (Bologna 1933). O. BERTOLINI, *Roma di fronte a Bisanzio e ai Longobardi* (Bologna 1941). T. HODGKIN, *Italy and Her Invaders,* 8 v. in 9 (Oxford 1892–99). C. G. MOR, *L'età feudale,* 2 v. (Milan 1952–53). C. MAGNI, *Ricerche sopra le elezioni episcopali in Italia durante l'alto medio evo* (Rome 1928). *Studi gregoriani,* ed. G. B. BORINO (Rome 1947–). C. VÌOLANTE, *La pataria milanese e la riforma ecclesiastica* (Rome 1955–) v.1 *Le premesse, 1054–1057.* L. T. WHITE, *Latin Monasticism in Norman Sicily* (Cambridge, MA 1938). L. SALVATORELLI, *L'Italia comunale* (Milan 1940). É. JORDAN, *L'Allemagne et l'Italie aux XIIe et XIIIe siècles* (Paris 1939). S. RUNCIMAN, *The Sicilian Vespers* (Cambridge, Eng. 1958). É. DELARUELLE et al., "Movimenti religiosi popolari ed eresie del medioevo," *Relazioni del X congresso internazionale di scienze storiche,* v.3 (Florence 1955) 307–541. A. DONDAINE, "La Hiérarchie cathare en Italie," *Archivum Fratrum Praedicatorum,* 20 (1950) 234–324. H. GRUNDMANN, *Religiöse Bewegungen im Mittelalter* (2d ed. Hildesheim 1961). E. S. DAVISON, *Forerunners of Saint Francis and Other Studies,* ed. G. R. B. RICHARDS (Boston

Church of San Sepolcro, Santo Stefano Complex, Bologna, Italy.
(©Vanni Archive/CORBIS)

1927). A. FRUGONI, *Arnoldo da Brescia nelle fonti del secolo XII* (Rome 1954). P. SABATIER, *Vie de Saint François d'Assise* (édition définitive; Paris 1931), Eng. tr. of 1st ed., *The Life of Saint Francis of Assisi* (New York 1920). GRATIEN DE PARIS (E. BADIN) *Histoire de la fondation et de l'évolution de l'Ordre des Frères Mineurs au XIIIe siècle* (Paris 1928). D. L. DOUIE, *The Nature and the Effect of the Heresy of the Fraticelli* (Manchester, Eng. 1932). E. R. LABANDE, *L'Italie de la Renaissance: Duecento, Trecento, Quattrocento: Évolution d'une société* (Paris 1954). G. MOLLAT, *The Popes at Avignon, 1305–1378,* tr. J. LOVE (New York 1963). C. ANGELERI, *Il problema religioso del Rinascimento* (Florence 1952). C. CIPOLLA, ''Une Crise ignoré. Comment s'est perdue la propriété ecclésiastique dans l'Italie du nord entre le XIe et le XVIe siècle,'' *Annales: Économies, sociétés, civilizations,* 2 (1947) 317–327. R. FAWTIER, *Saint Catherine de Sienne* (Paris 1921). R. RIDOLFI, *Life of Girolamo Savonarola,* tr. C. GRAYSON (New York 1959).

[C. E. BOYD]

1500 TO 1789

In the second half of the 15th century Italy was at the height of the RENAISSANCE and of her economic and commercial prosperity. While culturally she was exercising a profound influence on all of Western Europe, politically she was on the eve of disaster, and her regions—the major states of Venice, Milan, Florence, the STATES OF THE CHURCH and the kingdom of Naples, as well as the minor states of Ferrara, Mantua, Modena and Savoy—could hardly be less united. The city-states prided themselves on their individuality and independence, engaged in petty wars and played the dangerous game of balance of power politics, a game that inevitably led to appeals for help to outsiders only too willing to intervene. Even after the first great invasion, the Italian city-states could not perceive that the sun of their independence had set. For several centuries they were to become the victims of the rival political ambitions of powerful French, Spanish and Austrian monarchs.

The French in Italy: 1494–1559. In 1492 Florence and Naples made a secret alliance to attack Milan. As their intentions gradually became known, Ludovico SFORZA, Regent of Milan, who was faced with internal opposition to his rule, appealed to Charles VIII, King of France (1483–98). The young French ruler, motivated by a desire to enforce the Angevin claim on Naples, decided against his advisers to aid Ludovico, and he invaded Italy in 1494. Florence at first offered no resistance, then expelled Piero de' MEDICI for his support of the French king. Shortly thereafter, Charles entered Florence and was hailed as SAVONAROLA's man sent by God to regenerate Italy. From this time to 1512, Florence was practically a vassal state of France.

Early in 1495 Charles arrived at Rome, where he received permission to pass through papal territory on his march south. Alfonso of Naples could offer no effective opposition, and Charles entered the city on Feb. 22, 1495. The fury of the sacking of those areas that resisted and the redistribution of lands and offices to Frenchmen alienated support for Charles. Revolts broke out even before he was forced to leave Naples to meet the coalition—consisting of Milan, Venice, Emperor Maximilian, Pope ALEXANDER VI and Ferdinand V of Aragon, king of Castile—that had been rapidly formed against him. The army of the coalition, under the command of Francesco GONZAGA, fought well against Charles at the battle of Fornova (July 6, 1495) and captured his baggage train, but could not cut off his northward march and return to France. Naples recovered its independence, and the French lost practically all that they had won. However, the inclusion of Emperor Maximilian and King Ferdinand of Aragon in the coalition against the French was a clear sign that henceforth outsiders were going to play a decisive role in Italian affairs.

King Louis XII (1498–1515) of the house of Valois pressed the French claim to Milan, and the Venetians promised their support provided that they would get Cremona. Louis invaded Italy and pushed into Milan on Sept. 14, 1499. Regent Ludovico Sforza, who had escaped to Germany, returned the next year with an army of German mercenaries and drove out the French. But his forces disintegrated, the French reentered Milan, and Ludovico spent his remaining years as a prisoner in France.

By the Treaty of Granada (Nov. 11, 1500), Ferdinand of Aragon supported the French claim to Naples with the understanding that the French and Spaniards would divide that kingdom between them. In 1501–02, the allies took over Naples and then fell out over the division of the spoils. Spanish victories over the French at Cerignola in April of 1503 and at Garigliano eight months later were decisive, and the former kingdom of Naples became a Spanish possession. As the Spanish already had Sicily, they now became masters of southern Italy.

In December of 1508 a new coalition, the League of Cambrai, was formed to seize the mainland possessions of Venice. The original coalition of Louis XII and Emperor Maximilian was soon joined by Ferdinand of Aragon and Pope JULIUS II. Following the defeat of the Venetians at the battle of Agnadello in May 1509, there was a division of Venetian possessions between France and its allies. However, the Venetians soon recovered Padua, and Vicenza revolted against Maximilian. Julius II (1503–13) then decided to abandon the League of Cambrai and join the Venetians with the double purpose of driving the French from Italy and strengthening his own political position in the peninsula. In 1512 Ferdinand of Aragon, King HENRY VIII of England, Emperor Maximilian and the Swiss Confederation all joined the coalition against France, which suffered a heavy defeat at Novara the next year. The peace that followed, however, could hardly be more than temporary.

The new French king, Francis I (1515–47), resolved to invade Italy in force. He formed an alliance with Henry VIII of England and Venice against Emperor Maximilian (d. 1519), Pope LEO X (1513–21), Ferdinand of Aragon (d. 1516), Milan (under the restored Maximilian Sforza), Florence (under the restored Lorenzo de' Medici) and the Swiss Confederation. The French won a great victory at Marignano in a two-day battle in September 1516 that marked the end of the Swiss venture in Italian politics and also the end of the legend of the invincibility of the Swiss infantry. They recovered Milan, and the peace that followed favored their position in Italy, but again peace was to be of very short duration.

European politics entered a new epoch in 1516 with the accession of Charles I as king of Spain; three years later he became CHARLES V, Holy Roman Emperor, as successor to Emperor Maximilian and heir of the vast HAPSBURG dominions. It was inevitable that the rivalry between the Valois and Hapsburgs should have an Italian phase—and an important one.

Pope LEO X and Henry VIII supported Charles V against Francis I. In 1522 the French lost Milan, Parma, Piacenza and Genoa, but, returning in force in 1524, they recaptured Milan. On Feb. 24, 1525 the Spanish army under the command of Duke Charles de Bourbon (who had entered the Spanish service) and the Marquis de Pescara inflicted an overwhelming defeat on Francis I at Pavia. The French king was captured and taken as a prisoner to Madrid. Despite the Treaty of Madrid (January 1526) in which, among other things, he agreed to abandon all claims to Italy, Francis formed a new coalition, the League of Cognac, against Charles V a few months later. This coalition included Pope CLEMENT VII (1523–34), Milan, Venice and Florence. The pope's involvement in the League of Cognac, which failed to have any success, led to the terrible sack of Rome by the Spanish and German mercenaries of Emperor Charles in May of 1527. Clement himself for a time was a virtual prisoner in the CASTEL SANT' ANGELO. By the 1529 Treaty of Barcelona the emperor agreed that the Papal States should be restored to the pope and that the Medici should again rule Florence. Shortly thereafter the Treaty of Cambrai held that France again give up her claims to Italy, Venice had to return her conquests, Francesco Sforza received Milan and Alessandro de' Medici was confirmed as hereditary ruler for life. Charles V was solemnly crowned by the pope as emperor and king of Italy on Feb. 23, 1530.

A French invasion of Italy following the death of Sforza (1535) had very limited success, although the French captured Turin and retained two-thirds of Piedmont. By the Treaty of Crépy in September 1544, however, Piedmont and Savoy were returned to the Duke of Savoy, their traditional ruler. In 1556 Pope PAUL IV (1555–59), who wished to free Naples from Spanish rule, formed an alliance with King Henry II of France (1547–59), but the French had to withdraw from Italy after their defeat at Saint-Quentin in northern France in August 1557 by the Spanish under Philip II's general, Duke Emmanuel Philibert of Savoy. By the Treaty of Cateau-Cambrésis (1559), France agreed to give up all possessions in the peninsula except Turin, Saluzzo and Pinerolo. The new significance of Savoy at this time was reflected in the marriage of Duke Emmanuel Philibert to Margaret, the daughter of Francis I, in 1559.

A Disunited Italy: 1559–1701. By the mid-16th century large areas of Italy were directly under foreign control; states that had enjoyed nominal independence were reduced to a passive role in European politics, their fortunes often determined by battles fought by armies of great foreign powers on battlefields outside of Italy. Italy no longer played a major role in European trade and commerce, although the 18th century would see a resurgence of Italian intellectual life and achievement. The largest state in Italy during this period was that ruled by the popes; of the other states, which were at least nominally independent, the most important were Venice, Genoa and Savoy.

With the loss of most of her Far Eastern trade to the Portuguese, Dutch and English, Venice began a slow but steady decline. While domestically she adopted a policy of peace and neutrality, she continued to fight the OTTOMAN TURKS for her possessions in the eastern Mediterranean. Despite the brave defense of Famagusta on CYPRUS by Venetian Governor Marcantonio Bragadino, the city surrendered on Aug. 6, 1571, and Cyprus was lost. In violation of the terms of capitulation, Bragadino was flayed alive, his stuffed skin sent as a trophy to Constantinople. Two months later the Venetians had a major share in the great Christian naval victory over the Turks at LEPANTO. Further naval victories were won against them in the Candian War (1645–69). However, after a long and heroic defense of Candia (Herakleion), Francesco MOROSINI had to surrender both fortress and city, and the whole island of Candia (Crete) was lost. In 1684 Venice joined Austria and Poland in the Holy League against the Turks, and Morosini conquered the Peloponnesus (Morea, 1685–87). The Treaty of Karlowitz (Jan. 26, 1699) allowed Venice to keep the Morea, but the Turks recovered the area in 1716.

The Genoese Republic, likewise in decline, was constantly in fear of losing its independence to Savoy, France or Austria. Florence likewise declined rapidly. Cosimo de' Medici I (1519–74) became duke of Florence in 1537, and with the seizure and incorporation of Siena (1555), grand duke of Tuscany (1569). He was an energetic ruler, but absolutely ruthless and without scruple in attaining his ends—a living example of Machiavelli's *Prince*. The successors of Cosimo I, with the exception of Ferdinando I (1589–1609), were all relatively weak rulers, the line becoming extinct with Gian Gastone (1723–37). During this whole century and a half Naples and Milan were under Spanish rule.

With his reinstatement, Duke Emmanuel Philibert of Savoy (d. 1580) reorganized his duchy and made it into a prosperous and powerful state. His son and successor, Charles Emmanuel I (1580–1630), by his over ambitious attempts to seize territory and by his involvement in struggles with the French and Spanish, all but lost the duchy in his last years and left his territories in poor economic condition. His son Victor Amadeus I (1630–37), was able to recover most of his lost possessions through his wife, Christina, a daughter of King HENRY IV of France. Charles's second son and successor, Charles Emmanuel II (1638–75), was only a small child, and his mother, Christina, assumed the regency. A civil war broke out in Savoy in which Spain and France were invited to support the respective factions and in which Savoy

suffered severely from the fighting in its territory, but Charles Emmanuel succeeded in taking over the government personally in 1648, although Christina continued to have a strong influence over his policy until her death in 1663. It was under his rule that harsh measures, including numerous executions, were taken against the WALDENSES; this occasioned vehement protests in Protestant Europe—as expressed, for example, in Milton's famous Sonnet 18, "On the Late Massacre in Piedmont."

Charles Emmanuel was succeeded by his son Victor Amadeus II (1675–1730), who because of his age could not assume control of the state until 1684. Meantime his mother, the ambitious Jeanne de Savoie-Nemours, was regent. He married Anne, daughter of Philip of Orléans and niece of King LOUIS XIV of France. Under pressure of the latter, he renewed the persecution of the Waldenses (1685). When Louis demanded that he surrender Turin and Verona, however, Victor joined the coalition of Austria, Spain and Venice against him (1690), but six years later, with some justification, he deserted his allies and made a peace with Louis that was confirmed a year later by the Treaty of Ryswick (Sept. 30, 1697).

The War of the Spanish Succession to Napoleon: 1701–96. The Wars of Succession produced major changes in foreign domination in Italy, and in the fortunes of the independent Italian states. Politically, there was no essential change in the Papal States, but on the religious side this was a difficult period in the internal history of the Church (*see* STATES OF THE CHURCH; JANSENISM; JOSEPHINISM; ENLIGHTENMENT; and the individual articles on the popes of this period).

Savoy. In keeping with his policy of supporting Louis XIV, Victor Amadeus, at the outbreak of the War of the Spanish Succession (1701–13), permitted the French to seize Milan and Mantua. But two years later, irked by the insolent attitude of Louis XIV toward him, Victor joined the Grand Alliance (1703). The French invaded Savoy, but the great general of the imperial forces, Prince Eugene of Savoy, drove them out in 1705 and again in 1706. Savoy and the imperial forces occupied Milan (Sept. 24, 1706), bringing the war in Italy to an end. By the Treaty of Utrecht (April 11, 1713), Victor Amadeus received Sicily and took the royal title. Following the seizure of Sicily and Sardinia by King Philip V of Spain (1717–18), a new peace was made whereby Victor Amadeus gave Sicily to Austria and received Sardinia in exchange, assuming the title king of Sardinia. His successor, Charles Emmanuel III (1730–73), joined France and Spain against Austria in the War of the Polish Succession (1733–38). The Austrians were not driven out of Italy, but his own possessions were left intact by the Treaty of Vienna (1735). In the War of the Austrian Succession (1740–48), however, he supported Maria Theresa of Austria, and by the Treaty of Aix-la-Chapelle (Oct. 1748) he received as his reward a part of the Duchy of Milan. Victor Amadeus III (1773–96), a very conservative ruler, supported Austria against France in 1792 in spite of the French promise of Lombardy, but with the coming of Napoleon in 1796, independent action on his part quickly ended.

Naples and Venice. By the Peace of Utrecht, Sicily passed from the Spanish to Victor Amadeus II of Savoy, then back to Spain (1718), and, two years later, to Austria. Following the War of the Polish Succession, Naples and Sicily were given to the Spanish Bourbons (1735). Don Carlos, son of Philip V of Spain, took over Naples and Sicily as Charles IV (1735–59), assuming the title of King of the Two Sicilies in 1738. With the help of the Tuscan Bernardo TANUCCI, he carried through a reorganization of his government in the spirit of the Enlightenment. Conflict with the Church over secularization of CHURCH property was settled by the Concordat of 1741 with Pope BENEDICT XIV. On his abdication to become Charles III of Spain (1759–88), Don Carlos was succeeded by his third son, Ferdinand I (1759–1825). Tanucci served as regent until Ferdinand attained his majority (1767). In the following year Ferdinand married the dominating Maria Carolina, daughter of Maria Theresa of Austria. Under her influence and that of the Englishman Sir John Acton, who replaced Tanucci after Tanucci's dismissal in 1771, as chief adviser, Ferdinand was led to adopt a pro-Austrian policy. The 18th century was a golden age of artistic and intellectual activity at Naples.

The Venetians, by the Treaty of Passarowitz (July 1718), lost the Morea, their last possession in the eastern Mediterranean, and they were left with only their possessions on the Dalmatian coast. The continuance of their archaic aristocratic constitution reflected their political stagnation. In the arts, however, Venice remained one of the chief centers of Europe.

Other States. Mantua became a part of the Duchy of Milan after the death of the last Gonzaga (1701), and, by the Treaty of Utrecht (1713), Milan itself passed to the Hapsburgs. Following the death of the last FARNESE (1731), Parma and Piacenza were given to Don Carlos, son of Philip V of Spain, and passed back and forth from Spanish to Hapsburg control twice more before the coming of Napoleon. Genoa succeeded in maintaining its independence, although it was gravely threatened in the War of the Austrian Succession. Genoa asked France for aid in quelling the revolt of Corsica, which began in 1730, and eventually ceded the island to the French (1768). After the death of Gian Gastone, the last Medici (1737), Tuscany passed to Francis of Lorraine, the hus-

band of Maria Theresa of Austria. He gave up his ancestral Duchy of Lorraine to become grand duke of Tuscany. After his election as Francis I, Holy Roman Emperor (1745–65), his second son, Leopold I (1745–65), was made administrator and then, after his father's death, grand duke of Tuscany.

Under Austrian administration in the last half of the 18th century, Lombardy and Tuscany enjoyed a period of peace and prosperity and benefited from numerous reforms in agriculture, taxation, criminal law and education. However, in these areas, as in Savoy and elsewhere in Italy outside the Papal States, abolition of clerical privileges, suppression of monasteries, and secularization of other forms of Church property all revealed the spread of Enlightenment policy and its influence on government, especially after Emperor JOSEPH II (1780–90) replaced Maria Theresa on the throne of Austria. The ideas of the French philosophers also were spreading in Italy, and a national patriotism distinct from the local patriotism of the past was beginning to develop.

Bibliography: E. ROTA, *Le origini del Risorgimento, 1700–1800,* 2 v. (2d ed. Milan 1948). N. VALERI, *L'Italia nell'età dei principati, dal 1343 al 1516* (Milan 1949). R. AUBENAS and R. RICHARD, *L'Église et la renaissance, 1449–1517* (*Histoire de l'église depuis les origines jusqu'à nos jours,* eds., A. FLICHE and V. MARTIN, 15; 1951). H. S. LUCAS, *The Renaissance and the Reformation* (2d ed. New York 1960). A. VISCONTI, *L'Italia nell'epoca della controriforma dal 1516 al 1713,* rev. F. CURATO (Milan 1958).

[M. R. P. MCGUIRE]

MODERN ITALY: 1789 TO THE PRESENT

By 1789, when the FRENCH REVOLUTION began, the ENLIGHTENMENT had infiltrated from France into Italy by means of Freemasonry, whose lodges, during the first French domination of the peninsula (1796–99), were converted into Jacobin clubs favorable to the overthrow of the absolute regimes in the several Italian states and to the establishment of republics. The Church underwent a severe structural crisis during these years because many of its economic privileges were abolished, much of its property was seized, and its religious orders were suppressed. Fortunately the labors of St. ALPHONSUS DE LIGUORI, the *Amicizie Cristiane* of Nikolaus Diessbach, SJ (1732–98), Pio LANTERI and the St. Thomas academies checked JANSENISM, which seemed on the point of making greater advances, thanks to the Synod of PISTOIA convoked by Scipione de' RICCI. A reaction (Sept. 1798–Oct. 1799) caused anti-French uprisings, the most energetic being that of the SANFEDISTS led by Cardinal Fabrizio RUFFO. The second period of French domination (1800–14) saw groups of patriots, who favored conciliating Jacobinism with Catholicism, support of the first Italian republic, and also witnessed the negotiations for the

Italian concordat of 1803, modeled on the French CON-CORDAT OF 1801. Among the most important consequences of the French rule were the capture and exile of PIUS VI and PIUS VII and the suppression of the papal temporal power with the seizure of the STATES OF THE CHURCH (1797, 1808).

The Fall of Napoleon: 1815 to 1915. The Congress of VIENNA returned Italy substantially to the political conditions of the *ancien régime*. Papal temporal power and the Church's rights and privileges were restored, thanks to the diplomatic accomplishments of Cardinal Ercole CONSALVI. The Austrian HAPSBURGS, the real masters of the peninsula until the accession of NAPOLEON III (1852), smothered with bloodshed every ideal of constitutional and national liberty; they were faithful disciples of the jurisdictional principles of JOSEPHINISM and utilized for political purposes whatever benefits they conceded to the Church. To attenuate the results of the union of throne and altar, popes from Pius VII to Pius IX promoted with scant success a policy of concordats. Between 1818 and 1855 they concluded agreements with the Kingdom of the Two Sicilies (1818, 1834), the Kingdom of Sardinia (1836), the Duchy of Lucca (1841, 1846, 1856), the Grand Duchy of Tuscany (1848, 1851) and Austria (1855).

In this milieu developed the RISORGIMENTO, a movement working toward liberty, political independence and unity. It utilized the CARBONARI and other secret societies that organized revolutions (1820–21, 1830–31) to cast aside the yoke of absolutism and special privilege. Austria came to the rescue of the absolutist Italian states in the severe repressions of these revolts. Thereby it began the long catalogue of patriotic martyrs that included Silvio Pellico (1789–1854), Federico Confalonieri (1785–1846) and other citizens whose sentiments were sincerely Christian. Giuseppe Mazzini, a theist and a convinced patriot, joined the revolutionary movement and organized Young Italy, whose radical program for uniting Italy as a republic aimed to destroy the union of throne and altar as a preliminary to the liberation of all oppressed peoples.

In opposition to Mazzinian extremism Vincenzo GIOBERTI, Cesare Balbo, Massimo Taparelli d'Azeglio and others promoted NEO-GUELFISM, and advocated a federation of Italian states under a monarch and reforms enacted in legal fashion on state initiative, thus exalting the fatherland and religion as inseparable. For some time in 1848 this program appeared to unite all the patriotic groups whose common goal was independence and war against Austria. But the allocation of PIUS IX (Apr. 29, 1848) and the diplomatic and military failures of Piedmont ruined the neo-Guelf projects, causing a break in

patriotic ranks over politics that had profound repercussions on the religious level. The Piedmontese champions of LIBERALISM, with Camillo Benso di CAVOUR at their head, now took charge of the national movement. Capitalizing on the antagonisms between European governments and aided by Giuseppe GARIBALDI and other patriots, annexations and plebiscites, they gradually succeeded in proclaiming a unified kingdom of Italy with a constitutional monarch under the house of Savoy (March 14, 1861). Rome was declared the capital and actually became so in the autumn of 1870 after its capture.

While VATICAN COUNCIL I (1869–70) defined the papal spiritual prerogatives of primacy and infallibility, the final loss of the States of the Church at this time terminated effectively the pope's political power. Pius IX sent the ZOUAVES to battle the Piedmontese troops in a vain attempt to defend Rome. When the Italian government proposed the Law of GUARANTEES (1871) as its solution of the ROMAN QUESTION, the pope rejected it as a unilateral agreement that failed to ensure independence for the pope as pastor of the universal Church. The pope also appealed to all Catholics not to recognize the new state of Italy. Successive Italian governments, whether rightist (to 1876) or leftist (1876–1914), refused to recognize a territorial political sovereignty of the Holy See within the confines of the Kingdom of Italy. Although Italy spurned such examples of 18th-century jurisdictionalism as the *MONARCHIA SICULA* and the exequatur and *placet*, it introduced separatism by a series of laws injurious to the Church's rights and privileges. In the economic area these enactments decreed seizures and taxation of ecclesiastical properties and secularizations of charitable organizations; in the jurisdictional field, the abrogation of concordats, dissolution of religious orders, abolition of the privilege of the forum, introduction of obligatory military service by clerics, prohibition of religious instruction in schools, suppression of theological faculties in state universities (1873) and inauguration of civil marriages. Influencing public opinion, the state tolerated and even urged attacks against religion and propaganda hostile to the papacy and the clergy (*see* ANTICLERICALISM). On the institutional level the government secularized education and public institutions and favored the views of the extreme left and of the Freemasons, especially in the schools and in the army.

Religious Congregations. In the face of the radical subversiveness of the 19th century, the Church demonstrated its vitality by resisting corrosive elements of a structural and doctrinal type, and by making adjustments to the changed situation. During the Risorgimento the two most outstanding developments in the Church were the remarkable growth of religious congregations and the development of the modern Catholic movement. More than 300 religious congregations of women were founded in Italy between 1815 and 1915, besides many institutes for men. Like the vast majority of modern congregations, most of these dedicated themselves to the active apostolate through education, charitable and social services or missionary endeavors. The most phenomenal growth was experienced by the SALESIANS, founded by St. John BOSCO, and the SALESIAN SISTERS, started by him in conjunction with St. Maria MAZZARELLO; together these two groups spread throughout the world.

Church Enters Social Sphere. Catholics were eager to end the strained relations between Church and State, but not all agreed on the same solution. Conciliation was favored by Gino Capponi, the writer; Cesare Cantù, the historian; Niccolò Tommaseo, the patriot; Giacomo Zanella, the poet; Antonio ROSMINI-SERBATI, the philosopher; Massimo d'Azeglio, the statesman; and above all by Luigi TOSTI, OSB, Cardinal Alfonso CAPECELATRO and Bishop Geremia BONOMELLI. To others conciliation seemed inopportune; they demanded the restoration of all the Church's rights and privileges, including the return of the papal temporal power.

A third group abided by the view of Pius IX, who was influenced by Cardinal Giacomo ANTONELLI and who condemned the usurpations as iniquitous. This group created organizations that rejected the political unification of Italy and the selection of Rome as capital. They also advocated active and passive abstention from parliamentary life. To these ends Giambattista Casoni (d. 1919) started an association for the defense of the Church (1865) in Bologna. Mario Fani (1845–69) and Giovanni Acquaderni (1838–1922) created the Society of Italian Catholic Youth (1867).

In conjunction with Giovanni Battista Paganuzzi (1841–1923), Acquaderni stabilized in 1875 the Opera dei Congressi e dei Comitati Cattolici in Italia as a lay association in order that Catholic laymen might combat the dechristianizing work of agnostics. The Opera dei Congressi, the principal organization of Italian Catholics, became also a hierarchal association because its Catholic leaders repulsed all democratic principles, and a papal one, since it was in the service of the Holy See. On religious questions the Opera was intransigent, in conformity with the rigid interpretations of *QUANTA CURA* and the *SYLLABUS OF ERRORS* (1864). In political matters also its outlook shared the intransigence of the Holy See as expressed in the *NON EXPEDIT* policy. The Opera dei Congressi promoted, among other things, national, regional and diocesan congresses, action committees, aggressive journals, protest petitions, pilgrimages to Rome and festivals in honor of the pope. The purpose behind these measures was to keep Catholics continually aware of the Roman Question.

Within the Catholic movement one group formulated its static intransigent outlook in the phrase, *Nè eletti nè elettori* (neither elected nor electors); another group coined the more dynamic but yet intransigent motto, *Preparazione nell' astensione* (preparation by abstention). Some Catholics urged their coreligionists to resist the state until it collapsed. Giuseppe TONIOLO and others preferred to exert their influence in the fields of education, public opinion, labor and provincial and communal administration. With others, Toniolo originated the Catholic social movement, resulting in the Union for Social Studies and the *Rivista internazionale di scienze sociali e affini.* Catholics in this circle accepted Thomistic ideas concerning property and the state as expressed by the Jesuits Carlo Curci (d. 1891), Matteo LIBERATORE and Luigi Taparelli d'Azeglio. Besides reforms in the corporative sense previous to *Rerum novarum* (1891), they developed a program of democratic syndicalism. In addition they established numerous economic institutions, such as Catholic banks, credit unions and cooperatives, as well as social and charitable associations. Their interest in education moved the intransigent Catholics to hold meetings and circulate petitions to limit the secularizing process in the school and to promote Catholic schools on the parochial and diocesan levels. In 1921 they saw the opening of a Catholic university in Milan. A federation of educational institutions dependent on ecclesiastical authority was created in 1945 to coordinate the work of Italy's Catholic schools. Sacred Heart University in Milan and the Pontifical Salesian Athenaeum became centers of Catholic thought.

MODERNISM had one of its main centers in Italy early in the 20th century. Political Modernism, led by Romola MURRI, organized the Lega democratica nazionale. Theological Modernism, whose chief representatives were Ernesto BUONAIUTI and Salvatore Minocchi (d. 1943), caused a check in the development of the democratic movement by eliciting the condemnations of Modernism by Pius X and the disciplinary action taken against high ecclesiastics such as Cardinals Andrea Ferrari of Milan, Pietro Maffi of Pisa and Giacomo della Chiesa of Bologna (later Pope Benedict XV). Pius X disbanded the Opera dei Congressi in 1904 and reorganized the Catholic social movement along the lines of the German Volksverein. Christian syndicalism revived on a nationwide scale in 1918 under the leadership of Achille Grande, Luigi STURZO and the Partito Popolare Italiano (1919). The Gentilone Pact (1913) provided Catholic conservatives and clerical moderates with a basic charter politically and socially; it also signified the triumph of the ideas of men such as Toniolo over those of Murri.

Upheavals of the 20th Century. During World War I the understanding between Church and State culminated in the Unione Sacra (1916), whereby the government instituted military chaplains and abandoned anticlerical polemics, while the hierarchy appealed for solidarity behind the endangered fatherland. After 1918, Catholic forces, organized in party and in syndicate, could not create an alternative of the right or left to the classes then directing the nation's life. Fascism ended all democratic liberties (1922–26), but it made peace with the Church and papacy in the LATERAN PACTS (1929), which established Catholicism as the state religion, and in later agreements (1931, 1939). Benito Mussolini, the *Duce* of Italy until 1943, conceded privileges and favors to the Church in order to have its leaders support his dictatorial and imperialistic policies, although among the laity dissension arose over problems of liberty and racism. After Mussolini's downfall in 1943 many Catholics participated in the resistance movement in committees of liberation and joined the Christian Democratic Party. Among these was Father Giuseppe Dossetti (d. 1996), who would serve in the country's first national assembly before going on to found the Small Family of the Annunciation in 1954.

In 1946 Italy, defeated in World War II, became a republic. Its new constitution, dated Jan. 1, 1948, declared that Church-State relations would continue to be regulated by the Lateran Pacts, which could be modified only by bilateral agreements. The Christian Democratic Party, which headed the new government, attempted reconstruction and education of the masses while battling political parties and syndicates ranging from the extreme right (Movimento Sociale Italiano) to the Communist extreme left. Under the new constitution, the state was prohibited from funding private schools. After the death of Alcide De GASPERI (1958) there arose the problem of agreements with leftist and rightist groups (*dirigismo* or *liberalismo*) to obtain agrarian, fiscal, and social reforms. The more liberal of these parties were increasingly influential during the 1970s and 1980s.

Influenced by the increasingly liberalized morals of the 20th century, Italians began to stray from Church doctrine in the late 20th century. 1971 saw the legalization of divorce. In 1978 the government passed legislation legalizing abortion, and a Church-led referendum on the new law three years later was unsuccessful in its efforts to preserve the sanctity of human life. Concerns over declining enrollments at Church-run schools became cause for concern beginning in the 1960s; by 2000 Catholic schools educated approximately a third of all Italian children, despite the government's repeated unwillingness to extend subsidies to parents.

In part because of the influence of a radicalized liberal party within the government, the role of the Church in the 1980s and 1990s became increasingly subdued relative to its former influential position within both society and politics. In 1984, while preserving the recognition of the state of Vatican City as an independent, sovereign entity extended under the Lateran Pacts, a secularized Italy and the Vatican updated several provisions of the 1929 accords, diminishing a number of privileges formerly granted to the church and ending the status of Roman Catholicism as the religion of the Italian state. Under an *intesa*, the state extended certain financial and other privileges to not just the Catholic Church but to each of Italy's recognized faiths, although it remained unwilling to help fund parochial education. The increasing secularization of the country resulted in the demand for the removal of crucifixes and other symbols that had been displayed in courtrooms, government offices and other public places for many years.

Into the 21st Century. By 2000 there were 25,806 parishes tended by 36,566 diocesan and 18,930 religions priests. Other religious included 4,100 brothers and 115,775 sisters. In response to the Church's shifting demographic, a new seminary, opened in September of 1999 in Salerno, was intended in part to provide a new home for some of the country's aging priests. Despite the many social, educational and humanitarian efforts that continued to occupy Church members, calls for drug legalization, euthanasia and stem cell research required vigilance and outspokenness on the part of Italian bishops, as well as the pope. Church leaders also aggressively spoke out against agitation on the part of the Lombard League for the secession of Northern Italy as a consequence of discontent over increasing crime and corruption in the south, as well as the economic burden caused by the influx of illegal immigrants such as Muslim refugees from Albania and North Africa. A push by the European Parliament to grant homosexual couples the same legal rights as married heterosexual couples sparked a vigorous opposition by Church leaders, who also viewed the steadily declining birthrate in Italy with alarm. The Church was more successful in its efforts to curtail artificial insemination, after a 1999 law banned cloning and restricted previously unconstrained fertility procedures in the country.

Bibliography: J. LEFLON, *La Crise révolutionnaire, 1789–1846* (*Histoire de l'église depuis les origines jusqu'à nos jours,* eds., A. FLICHE and V. MARTIN, 20; 1949). R. AUBERT, *Le Pontificat de Pie IX, 1846–1878* (*Histoire de l'église depuis les origines jusqu'à nos jours,* eds., A. FLICHE and V. MARTIN, 21; 2d ed. 1964). K. BHILMEYER and H. TÜCHLE, *Kirchengeschichte,* 3 v. G. F. H. and J. BERKELEY, *Italy in the Making, 1815–1848,* 3 v. (Cambridge, Eng. 1932–40). S. JACINI, *La politica ecclesiastica italiana da Villafranca a Porta Pia* (Bari 1938). R. ALBRECHT-CARRIÉ, *Italy from Napoleon to Mussolini* (New York 1950). D. MACK SMITH, *Italy: A Modern History* (Ann Arbor 1959). S. W. HALPERIN, *Italy and the Vatican at War* (Chicago 1939). K. S. LATOURETTE, *Christianity in a Revolutionary Age: A History of Christianity in the Nineteenth* and Twentieth Centuries, 5 v. (New York 1958–62) v.1, 2, 4. G. MOLLAT, La Question romaine de Pie VI à Pie IX (2d ed. Paris 1932). A. C. JEMOLO, Chiesa e stato in Italia negli ultimi cento anni (Turin 1948); Church and State in Italy, 1850–1950, tr. from Italian by D. MOORE (Oxford 1960). G. SPADOLINI, L'opposizione cattolica da Porta Pia al '98 (4th ed. Florence 1961). F. FONZI, I cattolici e la società italiana dopo l'unità (2d ed. Rome 1960). E. ROTA "Gli svolgimenti storici di due forze costruttive: Liberalismo e nazionalità," in Questioni di storia contemporanea, v.2 (Milan 1955). P. SCOPPOLA, Dal neoguelfismo alla Democrazia cristiana (Rome 1958). R. F. ESPOSITO, La massoneria e l'Italia dal 1800 ai nostri giorni (2d ed. Rome 1959). Chiesa e stato nell'ottocento: Miscellanea in onore di P. Pirri, ed. R. AUBERT et al., 2 v. (Padua 1962). G. DE ROSA, Storia del movimento cattolico in Italia (Bari 1966) v.2. F. MAGRI, La democrazia cristiana in Italia, 2 v. (Rome 1956). A. GAMBASIN, Il movimento sociale nell'opera dei congressi cattolici in Italia, 1874–1904 (Rome 1958). T. ORTOLAN, Dictionnaire de théologie catholique, ed. A. VACANT et al., 15 v. (Paris 1903–50) 8.1:118–242. A. PIOLANTI, Dictionnaire de théologie catholique, ed. A. VACANT et al., 15 v. (Paris 1903–50) Tables générales 2338–67. J. MICHL et al., Lexikon für Theologie und Kirche², eds., J. HOFER and K. RAHNER, 10 v. (2d, new ed. Freiburg 1957–65) 5:811–821. Bilan du Monde. Encyclopédie catholique du monde chrétien, 2 v. (2d ed. Tournai 1964). 2: 511–531. Annuario Pontificio has annual data on all dioceses. Rivista di storia della Chiesa in Italia has full annual bibliog.

[A. GAMBASIN/EDS.]

ITE, MISSA EST

The concluding formula of dismissal in the Latin Mass (see ROMAN RITE). Although mentioned for the first time in the Ordo Romanus I (PL 78:948), it presumably belonged to the most ancient Latin Mass of Rome. Similar dismissal calls were already customary in old Roman assembly practice: Ilicet (ire licet, it is permitted to leave; see Vergil, Aeneid 6.23; Dölger, 123): Discedite Quirites (depart, Roman citizens; Dölger, 122). Ite, missa est has the meaning "Go, it is the dismissal," to which the assembly responds Deo gratias, "Thanks be to God."

The Ite, missa est is used at all Latin Masses except the evening Mass of Holy Thursday, other Masses followed by a procession, and Masses for the Dead (see REQUIEM MASS; for its medieval liturgical use, see BENEDICAMUS DOMINO). The dismissal was to be proclaimed by the deacon in the name of the bishop (or celebrant), in a loud voice, and sung to a melody, probably similar to the one given for Mass XV (see Dölger, 119). Since Vatican Council II the concluding formula of dismissal in vernacular Masses in the English-speaking countries is "The Mass is ended; go in peace."

Bibliography: F. J. DÖLGER, in Antike und Christentum 6 (1940) 81–132. Graduale Romanum (New York 1961). J. A. JUNGMANN, The Mass of the Roman Rite, tr. F. A. BRUNNER, 2 v. (New York 1951–55) v.2. C. MOHRMANN, "Missa," Vigilae Christianae 12 (1958) 67–92. W. APEL, Gregorian Chant (Bloomington IN 1958).

[C. KELLY]

ITINERARIA

Ancient, mainly Roman descriptions of travel routes, usually with distances in Roman miles, and later, Gallic leagues, with indications of relay posts (mutationes) and hostels (stationes; mansiones). Under Caesar Augustus, in preparation for the census of the whole world mentioned by Luke (2.1–4), geographical maps and charts were prepared, giving the divisions of the Roman provinces, the regions of Italy, the principal roads connecting Rome with all the cities of the empire, the posting-stations, main inhabitations, and peoples. These charts served as a basis for the famous Orbis pictus of Agrippa, a map of the Roman world depicted in colors on a large rectangular portico by Agrippa's sister Paulla (Pliny, Hist. nat. 3.3.14). Suetonius speaks of maps used in school and by the military (Domitian 10); and AMBROSE of Milan says that a soldier sent on a journey followed the itinerarium given him by the emperor (Comm. ad Ps. 118), while Eumenius of Autun refers to the children in school becoming familiar with the whole world (omnes terras et cuncta maria) through the maps on the walls (Orat. pro restaur. scholis 20). Traces of these early maps are preserved in the so-called Tabula Peutingeriana, a 12-page, parchment manuscript containing colored maps of the entire Roman Empire. This document was copied in 1265 by a monk of Colmar (Annal. Colmar. 1.1); it was rediscovered in 1494 by C. Meissel, who willed it to his friend Conrad Peutinger of Würzburg; and it is known under the latter's name.

The Peutinger Table gives evidence of at least six revisions, beginning with the Orbis pictus of Agrippa. In the 4th century in particular, the routes, main cities of Rome, Constantinople, and Antioch, as imperial residences, were given greater relief; there is evidence of additions in accord with the so-called Theodosian Tables of 425 and the conquests of JUSTINIAN I (527–565). Travelers in the empire had little difficulty obtaining maps and understanding routes and distances from the public monuments in the greater cities.

For the older Roman itineraria, the four silver vases discovered at Vicarello, near Lake Bracciano, some 20 miles north of Rome, give the route from Cadiz, Spain, to Rome with the names of the stationes and distances between them in Roman miles; the vases apparently date from the reign of Trajan (98–117). At Autun and Alichamp in France and at Tongres in Belgium, fragments of stone wall maps have been discovered, as well as parts of monuments on which were engraved the routes and distances between, for example, Tongres and seven main cities in the empire, following seven different roadways. Fragments of similar travel guides are found in many excavation sites.

Palestinian Pilgrimages. The route of a pilgrimage to Palestine made in 333 is described in the *Itinerarium Burdigalense* by the so-called Pilgrim of Bordeaux, who departed from that city (*ubi est fluvius Garonna*), crossed southern Gaul, the Alps, northern Italy, Pannonia, Thrace, stopped briefly at Constantinople, then continued through Asia Minor and Syria to arrive at Beirut. He continued down the coast of Phoenicia, passing Sidon, Sarepta, and Caesarea in Palestine, and turned east at Mt. Sinai to visit all the sites mentioned in the Bible on the way to Jerusalem and its environs. He records the distances between these sites and includes a description of the monuments or their biblical significance. His return journey took him through Macedonia to Italy and the close of his journey at Milan.

The *Peregrinatio ad loca sancta* of Aetheria was written *c.* 400. It describes the journey of a woman of the upper class who visited the monks in Egypt, the Holy places in Palestine, and Mesopotamia, and who returned to Constantinople by way of Tarsus, Seleucia, and Chalcedon. She used the *cursus publicus* or imperial post facilities on the main routes of the empire; she traveled mostly by horse or mule and received protection of the military in places infested by armed thieves. She stopped frequently at the *xenodochia,* or hostels, connected with the monasteries. The first part of the MS is missing; it begins with a description of Mt. Sinai, details of the liturgical services in Jerusalem, and of her excursions to the land of Job (Idumea) and to Mt. Nebo. Most of the biblical information regarding the monuments is taken from the Bible and the *Onomasticon* of EUSEBIUS OF CAESAREA as edited and revised by St. JEROME. The latter provides further Palestinian information in several letters describing the travels of St. Paula (*Epist.* 46 and 108), in letters to Dardanus (*Epist.* 129), to Paulinus (58), Sabinianus (147), and in his commentary on Ezekiel (47.15–20). A compilation of information taken from Jerome and Flavius Josephus was made *c.* 450 and has been preserved under the name of Eucherius of Lyons. The *Itinerarium de situ terrae sanctae* of the archdeacon Theodosius, written *c.* 525, and the *Breviarius de Hierosolyma,* written toward the end of the 5th century, are further examples of this travel literature as guides through the Holy Land.

The so-called *Itinerarium Antonini* describes the route from Milan, through Bergamo, Verona, Aquileia, Smyrna, Constantinople, Ancyra, Antioch, and Caesarea, to Jerusalem, and gives the distances and stations in a manner similar to that of the *Itinerarium Burdigalense.* The original document, now called the Anonymous of Piacenza, was the subject of several forgeries and legendary interpolations. In 670 ADAMNAN OF IONA wrote down the recital of the pilgrimage to the Holy Lands made by the Gallic Bishop Arculf, who had been shipwrecked on the west coast of Britain. The account is interesting for its reflections on the situation after the Arab conquest of Palestine. The *De locis sanctis* of BEDE is a compilation based largely on the work of Adamnan, while the recollections of St. WILLIBALD, nephew of St. Boniface, were written down by a nun of the monastery of Heidenheim (*c.* 727). A *Commemoratorium de casis Dei* was composed *c.* 808; the Frankish monk Bernard wrote an *Itinerarium trium monachorum* (*c.* 870), in which he notes the use of the holy fire in the Holy Saturday liturgy in Jerusalem.

In the Orient, the retired merchant Cosmas Indicopleustes wrote his *Christianikē topographia* (*c.* 550). He was probably a Nestorian who had traveled to East Africa and across Asia to Ceylon before settling as a monk in Alexandria; his work, which furnished much geographical and cultural information, opposed the biblical to the Ptolemaic conception of the universe. An Armenian *Rituale* and a Georgian calendar of the 7th century describe the processions to the various monuments in the Holy Land; and *c.* 660 an Armenian pilgrim wrote a *Description of the Holy Places.* The Greek monk Epiphanios Hagiopolites wrote his *Hodoiporikon* (*c.* 786), or traveler's guide, to Jerusalem and Palestine.

Rome. Caesar Augustus had a map of Rome engraved on the portico of the Campus Martius; in 177 Marcus Aurelius ordered a description of the city's monuments prepared in connection with the establishment of impost controls. Under Septimius Severus a *Forma urbis Romae* was prepared. Polemeus Silvius wrote *Quae sint Romae, c.* 449, and dedicated it to EUCHERIUS OF LYONS. It provides for pilgrims a description of the monuments dedicated to the Christian martyrs, and lists the hills, valleys, bridges, baths, and buildings of the Eternal City. The Syriac *Breviarium* of ZACHARY THE RHETOR (*c.* 540) is a compilation made from the *Notitia urbis Romae* with special attention to the monuments of the martyrs; it indicates that before 540 there existed a *Notitia regionum urbis* in which Rome's churches were described, along with their burial places.

For the pilgrims of the 7th to the 9th century, four Roman *itineraria* were in existence. The *Notitia ecclesiarum orbis Romae,* called the Salzburg Itinerary, dates from the reign of Pope HONORIUS I (625–638). The Vienna Itinerary, or the *De locis sanctis martyrum quae sunt foris civitatem Romae,* gives the locations of the bodies of the martyrs in the churches of Rome and appears to have been compiled under PELAGIUS II and revised under Honorius I. The Itinerary of William of Malmesbury, inserted in his *Gesta regum Anglorum,* describes the basilicas and suburban cemeteries before the translations of relics in the 8th century. The Itinerary of Einsiedeln was written by a monk who copied many of the pagan and Christian inscriptions and gave a description of the monuments and the ceremonies of Holy Week. The most exact of these itineraries—that of Salzburg—gives the location of the remains of the martyrs with considerable exactitude, describing them as "in the open," "on the ground," "in a crypt," "on the right [or left] side of the church," "near the entrance," etc. Finally, the *Mirabilia urbis Romae* (*c.* 11th century) is a compilation following in good part the *Liber pontificalis.*

Bibliography: H. LECLERCQ, *Dictionnaire d'archéologie chrétienne et de liturgie,* ed. F. CABROL, H. LECLERCQ, and H. I. MARROU, 15 v. (Paris 1907–53) 7.2:1841–1922; 14.1:65–176. H. LAHRKAMP, *Lexikon für Theologie und Kirche,* ed. J. HOFER and K. RAHNER, 10 v. (2d, new ed. Freiburg 1957–65) 5:822–824. E. DEKKERS, ed., *Clavis Patrum latinorum* (2d ed. Streenbrugge 1961) 519–522. *Corpus Christianorum. Series latina* 175 (1961). P. GEYER, ed., *Itinera Hierosolymitana saeculi IV–VIII* (*Corpus scriptorum ecclesiasticorum latinorum* 39; 1898). O. CUNTZ, ed., *Itineraria Romana I* (Leipzig 1929). A. BAUMSTARK, *Abendländische Palästinapilger des 1. Jahrtausends und ihre Berichte* (Cologne 1906). T. TOBLER and A. MOLINIER, eds., *Itinera Hierosolymitana et descriptiones Terra Sanctae bellis sacris anteriora,* 2 pts. (Geneva 1877–79). A. MOLINIER and C. KOHLER, *Itinerum bellis sacris anteriorum series chronologica* (Geneva 1885). *Palestine Pilgrims Text Society* (London 1896–97). K. MILLER, *Itineraria romana* (Stuttgart 1916). B. KÖTTING, *Peregrinatio religiosa* (Münster 1950). F. STUMMER (*Florilegium Patristicum,* ed. J. ZELLINGER et al. 41; 1935), Jerome. H. PÉTRÉ, ed. and tr., *Éthérie: Journal de voyage* (*Sources Chrétiennes* 21; 1948). M. ANASTOS, *Dumbarton Oaks Papers,* Harvard Univ. 3 (1946) 73–80, *Cosmas Indicopleustes.*

[J. HAMROGUE]

ITURRATE ZUBERO, DOMINGO, BL.

Known in religion as Dominic of the Most Holy Sacrament, Trinitarian priest; b. May 11, 1901, Dima (Basque region), Spain; d. April 8, 1927, Belmonte, Spain. Domingo evidenced a religious vocation from an early age, joined the Trinitarians, and was ordained a priest. During his short life, he became known for the devotion with which he celebrated Mass and for his obedience. John Paul II praised Domingo, saying: "He strove to live according to two central principles of the spirituality of his order: the mystery of the Holy Trinity and the work of the Redemption, which lead to a life of intense charity" (beatification homily, Oct. 30, 1983).

Feast: April 7.

Bibliography: *L'Osservatore Romano,* English edition, no. 46 (1983): 6–7.

[K. I. RABENSTEIN]

IUS PUBLICUM

Ius publicum are treatises on the "public law" of the Church have traditionally been divided into *ius publicum internum,* and *externum.* The former denotes that describe the internal constitution, structures, procedures, and power of the Church. The *NCE* treats these topics *passim* in articles pertinent to the Code of Canon Law and under such headings as Roman Curia, Pontifical Councils, and Synods. *Ius publicum externum* is the study of the external relationships between the Church and the civil legal systems which the Church encounters throughout the world.

See Also: CHURCH AND STATE (CANON LAW)

Bibliography: F. M. CAPPELLO, *Summa Iuris Publici Ecclesiastici* (Rome 1928). M. C. A CORONATA, *Ius Publicum Ecclesiasticum* (Turin 1948). A. OTTAVIANI, *Institutiones Iuris Publici Ecclesiastici,* 2 v. (Vatican City 1947–1948). A. OTTAVIANI, *Compendium Iuris Publici Ecclesiastici* (Vatican City 1954). F. M. MARCHESI, *Summula Iuris Publici Ecclesiastici* (Naples 1960). J. C. MURRAY, *We Hold These Truths: Catholic Reflections on the American Proposition* (New York 1960); *The Problem of Religious Freedom* (Westminster, Md. 1965). P. PAVAN, *Libertá religiosa e pubblici poteri* (Milan 1965). Vatican II, declaration *Dignitatis humanae* (Dec. 7, 1965). C. CARDIA, *Il governo della Chiesa* (Bologna 1984). Pertinent topics are also treated in the standard commentaries, e.g. J. P. BEAL et al., *New Commentary on the Code of Canon Law* (New York 2000); and L. CHIAPPETTA, *Il Codice di Diritto Canonico: Commento giuridico–pastorale* (Rome 1996).

[J. STAAB]

IVANIOS, MAR (GIVERGIS THOMAS PANIKERVIRTIS)

Malankar rite archbishop, leader in reunion efforts; b. Mavelikkara, Kerala, India, Sept. 18, 1882; d. Trivandrum, India, July 15, 1953. Ivanios, member of a leading Syrian family belonging to the dissident group in the MALANKAR rite, received his early education in Protestant and government schools. After studies in the seminary at Kottayam he was ordained deacon in 1898 and priest in 1909. He was the first Kerala cleric to graduate from Madras Christian College, where he obtained an M.A. in economics (1906). In 1908 he was named principal of a school in Kottayam. He was instrumental in establishing the autonomy of the Syro-Jacobite Church in India under a catholicos (1911–12). From 1913 to 1919 he was professor of Syriac and political economy at Serampore College, a Protestant institution near Calcutta. In 1919 he founded and acted as superior of the Order of the Imitation of Christ, the first religious communities in his Church for men and women. The MALINES CONVERSATIONS led him to inquire about reunion with Rome. As bishop (1925) with the name Mar Ivanios, and as metropolitan (1928), he received the approval of other Syrian Jacobite leaders to continue his correspondence with Rome. In 1930 Mar Ivanios entered into union with Rome, along with his suffragan, Mar Theophilos, the members of his religious communities, and a few laymen. As archbishop of Trivandrum (1932–53), a see belonging to the Malankar rite, he strove for reunion with other Christians and was zealous in erecting churches and schools throughout his jurisdiction. In 1950 he established a university college. He traveled widely in Europe, Australia, Canada, and the U.S., and published many periodical articles and booklets in English and Malayalam on the liturgy of his rite and on the Syriac language.

Bibliography: M. GIBBONS, *Mar Ivanios* (Dublin 1962). E. TISSERANT, *Eastern Christianity in India,* tr. E. R. HAMBYE (Westminster, Md. 1957) 157–162; *Dictionnaire de théologie catholique* 14.2:3143–49.

[E. R. HAMBYE]

Levi Silliman Ives.

IVES, LEVI SILLIMAN

Episcopal bishop, founder of the New York Catholic Protectory; b. Meriden, Conn., Sept. 16, 1797; d. New York City, Oct. 13, 1867. He was reared in Turin, N.Y., where he attended Lowville Academy, leaving to serve briefly in the War of 1812. After ill health interrupted his studies for the Presbyterian ministry at Hamilton College, Clinton, N.Y., he became an Episcopalian (1819) and studied theology in New York under Bp. John H. Hobart, former pastor and close friend of Mother Elizabeth Seton. He married Hobart's daughter, Rebecca, in 1822, and was ordained the following year. Ives advanced rapidly and, after serving at many parishes in Pennsylvania and New York, he became the first Episcopalian bishop of North Carolina (1831). Slavery was a vital issue in his episcopate, for he defended the institution as a field for Christian paternalism and wrote a catechism for the slaves. The Oxford Movement was also of concern and English Tractarian writings on Protestant origins and the early Church impressed Ives. At Valle Crucis, N.C., he founded the Brotherhood of the Holy Cross (1845), whose members were accused of adhering to monastic vows, auricular confession, the Real Presence, and other Catholic practices. After many diocesan quarrels he was arraigned in 1848 by an Episcopalian convention, which accepted his written assurances of his orthodoxy and dissolved the brotherhood. Ives soon regretted his recantation and issued a pastoral letter reaffirming his ideas. He was increasingly drawn to the Catholic Church by its means for achieving personal sanctity and its attachment to the poor in the U.S., and he finally journeyed to Rome and made a formal submission to Pius IX on Christmas Day 1852. Shortly after this his wife entered the Church. The story of his conversion was told in his *Trials of a Mind in its Progress to Catholicism* (1853).

Ives's return to New York in 1854 as a Catholic layman posed a problem for the American hierarchy. Since Rome directed that provision be made in such cases, a convert's fund was first attempted and then part-time lecturing in rhetoric was secured for him in New York City at St. Joseph's Seminary, St. John's College, and several convents. Eventually, Ives found a career for himself in Catholic charities. As president of New York's Superior Council, he urged the St. Vincent de Paul Society to expand its growing lay apostolate beyond parish activities to national organization. Ives had long opposed the system that sent destitute children to western farms or to state institutions essentially Protestant in character, and in 1863 he organized the New York Catholic Protectory and became its first president. He persuaded the Christian Brothers and the Sisters of Charity to join his venture and obtained public financial support for the protectory. His cottage in Manhattanville became a favorite meeting place for converts and a popular Catholic cultural center in New York.

Bibliography: J. O'GRADY, *Levi Silliman Ives* (New York 1933).

[E. F. LEONARD]

IVO, ST.

Legendary bishop and missionary to Britain in the sixth or seventh century. Goscelin (11th century) wrote his life, based on an account by Andrew Withman, abbot of RAMSEY, who collected his information on pilgrimage to Jerusalem. According to Goscelin, Ivo left his native Persia; visited Rome and Gaul; and proceeded to Britain, where with three companions he successfully preached the Christian faith and settled finally at Slepe, Huntingdonshire. Lack of documentation has caused some authorities to conclude that the story is a fabrication by Ramsey monks. Ivo's supposed relics were discovered (1001) at the present location of St. Ives, Huntingdonshire, where a priory dependent on Ramsey was established, the relics being translated to Ramsey itself. Ivo is unconnected with St. Ives, Cornwall.

Feast: April 24.

Bibliography: *Acta Sanctorum* June 2:284–289. T. D. HARDY, *Descriptive Catalogue of Materials Relating to the History of Great Britain and Ireland*, 3 v. in 4 (*Rerum Brittanicarum medii aevi scriptores* 26; 1862–71) 1.1:184–186. C. HOLE, *A Dictionary of Christian Biography*, ed. W. SMITH and H. WACE, 4 v. (London 1877–87) 3:324–325. G. H. DOBLE, "St. Ivo, Bishop and Confessor, Patron of the Town of St. Ives," *Laudate* 12 (1934) 149–156.

[R. W. HAYS]

IVO HÉLORY, ST.

Priest and lawyer; b. Kermartin, near Tréguier, France, Oct. 17, 1253; d. Trédrez, France, May 19, 1303. On completion of his theology and law studies, he became officialis of Rennes in 1280 and of Tréguier in 1284, rector of Trédrez in 1284, and, finally, curé of Louannec *c.* 1292. He resigned these offices in 1297–98 and retired to his native region, where he led a life of austerity and devoted himself to works of charity. To provide legal aid for the poor he created confraternities that have spread over France, Belgium, and Brazil and also to Rome. Proceedings for his canonization were opened in 1330, and he was canonized in 1347. His cult spread rapidly in Brittany, of which he is the second patron, and although his tomb was destroyed in the French Revolution, it was restored in 1890. He is the patron also of lawyers and of the University of Nantes. Each year on his feast day the famous pilgrimage procession of St. Ivo is held at Tréguier.

Feast: May 19.

Bibliography: *Acta Sanctorum* May 4:538–614. A. DE LA BORDERIE, *Les Monuments originaux et l'histoire de saint Yves* (Saint Brieuc 1885). A. DESJARDINS, *St. Yves avocat des pauvres et patron des avocats* (Paris 1897). U. CHEVALIER, *Répertoire des sources historiques du moyen–âge. Biobibliographie*, 2 v. (2d. ed. Paris 1905–07) 1:2291–92. B. POCQUET DU HAUT-JUSSÉ, *La Compagnie de St-Yves des Bretons à Rome* (Rome 1919). C. DE LA RONCIERE, *St. Yves* (5th ed. Paris 1925). A. MASSERON, *St. Yves* (Paris 1952). P. LA HAYE, *Saint Yves de Tréguier* (Châteaulin 1973). F. SEMUR, *Yves de Kermartin: magistrat et avocat du XIIIe siècle* (Bannalec, France 1983). A. RIECK, *Der Heilige Ivo von Hélory: advocatus pauperum und Patron der Juristen* (Frankfurt am Main 1998). A. BUTLER, *The Lives of the Saints*, ed. H. THURSTON and D. ATTWATER, 4 v. (New York 1956) 2:351–353. *Bibliotheca hagiographica latina antiquae et mediae aetatis*, 2 v. (Brussels 1898–1901; suppl. 1911) 4625–37.

[É. BROUETTE]

IVO OF CHARTRES, ST.

Bishop; b. Chartres, France, *c.* 1040; d. there Dec. 23, 1115. Ivo studied at Paris, then at the Abbey of Bec in Normandy. As a priest he was attached to the church of Nesle in Picardy, and later became provost of the monastery of Canons Regular of Saint-Quentin at Beauvais. He finally became bishop of Chartres, which see he occupied from November 1090 until his death. He traveled widely in France to attend numerous councils. His writings include 291 letters, 25 sermons, and two canonical collections (*see* IVO OF CHARTRES, COLLECTION OF).

He was a remarkable writer for his era, well informed on the scientific renaissance then in progress and imbued with ideals of friendship, humanity, and mercy. As a theologian, he contributed to the fixing of the number of Sacraments at seven. His reservations on the subject of the Crusades and his use of exclusively religious sanctions manifested his totally spiritual conception of the Church.

In his conflicts with secular rulers and in the INVESTITURE STRUGGLE, he defended the freedom of the bishop and protected the monasteries of monks and clerics regular, but he did not favor exemption or the centralization typified by papal legates. With a view to the reform of the Church, he brought about acceptance of the distinction between the election of bishops, which was to be free and clerical, and their investiture by the prince, which was to take place only afterward and to be of limited significance. This moderate reforming tendency bore fruit in the Concordat of Worms in 1122.

Feast: May 23.

Bibliography: IVO OF CHARTRES, *Patrologia Latina*, ed. J. P. MIGNE, 217 v. (Paris 1878–90) 162:11–296 (letters), 506–610 (sermons); *Correspondance 1090–1098,* ed. and tr. J. LECLERCQ (Paris 1949) contains letters 1–70. *The Miracles of Saint James,* tr. from *Liber sancti Jacobi,* tr. T. F. COFFEY, L. K. DAVIDSON and M. DUNN (New York 1996). R. SPRANDEL, *Ivo von Chartres und seine Stellung in der Kirchengeschichte* (Stuttgart 1962). F. LOT and R. FAWTIER, eds., *Histoire des institutions françaises au moyen âge* (Paris 1957–). M. GRANDJEAN, *Laïcs dans l'Eglise* (Paris 1994).

[J. LECLERCQ]

IVO OF CHARTRES, COLLECTION OF

Three canonical collections are attributed to Ivo of Chartres: the *Tripartita,* the *Decretum,* and the *Panormia.* There is considerable doubt about the sources, the dates, and the circumstances of the editing of these collections. These questions will be resolved definitively only when critical editions of these writings can be made and when the minor collections and the florilegia of the 11th century are better known.

As its name indicates, the *Tripartita* is composed of three parts. The first two parts, Collection A, are a group of 655 fragments of decretals, real or false, from Clement I to Urban II (Part 1), and 789 conciliar canons or patristic texts (Part 2). The third part, Collection B, is an abridgment in 29 titles (861 fragments) of the *Decretum* of Ivo. The *Tripartita* is unedited.

The *Decretum* (*Patrologia Latina* 161:59–1022) is a compilation of 3,760 chapters divided into 17 parts. Its immediate sources are: the *Decretum* of BURCHARD, taken over almost entirely; Collection A of the *Tripartita;* and a compilation of decretals related to the *Britannica* and, probably, to the Gregorian and French florilegia (schools of Laon, Bec, and Chartres). The composition of the collection leaves much to be desired: the series are transcribed without order or repeated; there are mistakes in the inscriptions. Theological questions form a great part of the work: I *Pars,* faith, Baptism, and Confirmation; II *Pars,* Eucharist; XVII *Pars,* theological virtues, and the four last things. One may also find in it almost 250 texts of *Corpus iuris civilis, Codex Iustinianus,* and 150 taken from authentic or apocryphal Carolingian legislation. Being too voluminous and inconvenient for a reference work, the *Decretum* was not very successful (list of MSS in Fournier-LeBras 2:67), but various abridgments were made of it until the 13th century.

The *Panormia* (*Patrologia Latina* 161:1045–1344) or *Pannormia* (collection of all the laws) contains 1038 chapters divided into eight books. 920 texts come from Ivo's own *Decretum;* the others are borrowed from the Collection of SEVENTY-FOUR TITLES, from Collection A of the *Tripartita,* and from a collection of decretals similar to the *Britannica.* The success of the *Panormia,* attested by the numerous preserved MSS of this collection, is due to its incontestable qualities of brevity, order, and the legal precision of the summaries (Gratian copied them by the hundred). In fact the work offers ''a compendious encyclopedia of Canon Law at the end of the 11th century'' (Fournier-LeBras 2:99).

If one accepts the conclusions of P. Fournier, one will have to admit that the three collections were composed in a fairly brief lapse of time (1093–95) by a group of copyists working under the direction of Ivo of Chartres, with the encouragement of Pope Urban II (*Ep.* 2, *Patrologia Latina* 162:13). Collection A of the *Tripartita* must have been prepared in 1093–94 from documents brought back from Rome (where Ivo had gone in 1090 and 1093), combined with traditional French Canon Law. The *Decretum* would date from 1094, as would the *Tripartita,* completed by the addition of Collection B; the *Panormia,* from 1095. The legal science displayed in the Summaries in the *Panormia,* the care taken in distinguishing the exact nature of juridical rules (precept, counsel, unchangeable and contingent laws), the space given to exemption, the rules given for reconciling conflicting texts (inspired partly by the works of BERNOLD OF CONSTANCE), reveal the guiding hand of the great canonist Ivo himself. The same tendencies run through the *Prologus* (*Patrologia Latina* 161:47–60 and 1041–46), of which it is difficult to say whether it was intended for the *Decretum* or the *Panormia.*

Bibliography: P. FOURNIER and G. LEBRAS, *Histoire des collections canoniques en occident depuis les fausses décrétales jusqu'au Décret de Gratien,* 2:55–114 (Paris 1931–32). É AMANN and L. GUIZARD, *Dictionnaire de théologie catholique* 15.2:3625–40 (Paris 1903–50). A. VAN HOVE, *Commentarium Lovaniense in Codicem iuris canonici 1* (Mechlin 1928) 1:331–332. IVO OF CHARTRES, *Correspondance,* ed. and tr. J. LECLERCQ (Les Classiques de l'histoire de France au moyen âge 22; Paris 1949) vii–xli. P. FOURNIER, ''Les Collections canoniques attribuées â Yves de Chartres,'' *Bibliothèque de l'École des Chartes* 57 (1896) 645–698; 58 (1897) 26–77, 293–326, 410–444, 624–676. J. DE GHELLINCK, *Le Mouvement théologique du XXIe siècle* (2nd ed. Bruges 1948) 445–459. C. MUNIER, *Les Sources patristiques du droit de l'église du VIIIe au XIIIe siècle* (Strasbourg 1957).

[C. MUNIER]

IVORY COAST, THE CATHOLIC CHURCH IN

Located in West Africa, Ivory Coast, or Republic of Côte d'Ivoire, is bordered on the south by the Atlantic Ocean, on the east by Ghana, on the north by Mali and

Capital: Yamoussoukro; Abidjan is the political center.
Size: 124,550 sq. miles.
Population: 15,980,950 in 2000.
Languages: French; numerous native dialects are spoken in various regions.
Religions: 2,237,350 Catholics (14%), 9,588,570 Muslims (60%), 1,438,285 Protestants (9%), 2,716,745 practice indigenous faiths (17%).

Archdioceses	Suffragans
Abidjan	Grand-Bassam, Yopougon
Bouaké	Abengourou, Bondoukou, Yamoussoukro
Gagnoa	Daloa , Man, San Pedro-en-Côte d'Ivoire
Korhogo	Katiola, Odienné

Burkina Faso, and on the west by Liberia and Guinea. With its coastline bordered by lagoons, the region rises to plains before ascending to a plateau region inland. Hills in the west and northwest are crowned by Mt. Nimba, the highest peak. Rivers include the Bandama, Sassandra and upper tributaries of the Niger and Volta. The world's largest producer of coffee and cocoa beans, the region's agricultural products also include corn, pineapples and rubber, while among its natural resources are industrial diamonds, petroleum, manganese, cobalt, iron and copper. Once containing the largest forests in West Africa, deforestation by the timber industry is now a problem in most Ivorian woodlands. Tropical along the coast, the climate becomes semi-arid farther inland, and the rainy season occurs in the fall.

A former territory of French West Africa, Ivory Coast became an independent republic in the French Community in 1960. The population includes 60 native Ivory Coast ethnic groups, and at least as many foreign ethnic groups, with the Muslim population living predominately in the north and Christians residing in the south. Despite the discovery of offshore petroleum reserves, Ivory Coast relies on agriculture, which employs almost 70 percent of the population. The average life expectancy for an Ivorian is 45.5 years, in part due to AIDS, while less than half of all the country's adults can read.

History. Capuchins arrived in the region in 1637, a century after the Portuguese and other Europeans had established a flourishing slave trade along the coast. In 1701 a Dominican was appointed the first prefect apostolic of the Prefecture of the Guinea Coast. From 1842–45 the French signed treaties with the Agni and several other native tribes living along the coast, and four years after a battle with the king of the Mandingo tribe in 1889 Ivory Coast became a French colony. While the first priests of the Congregation of the Holy Heart of Mary arrived in the region as early as 1844, systematic evangelization did not begin until 1895 when the Prefecture Apostolic of the Ivory Coast was created, and missionaries from the Society of African Missions came. Growth of the mission was slow until 1918, but quite rapid thereafter, and a number of Catholic schools were established. The hierarchy was established in 1955, when the Archdiocese of Abidjan

was created and made a metropolitan see for the country. The first African priest was ordained in 1934. Bernard Yago (d. 1998), the first native bishop in Ivory Coast, was ordained on May 8, 1960 as the archbishop of Abidjan, and was named a cardinal in 1983. In subsequent years, all new bishops were chosen from among the native population. When the last French bishop retired in 1975, the episcopacy of Ivory Coast became entirely indigenous.

The Modern Church. A territory of France after 1946, Ivory Coast gained autonomous status within the French Community in 1958, and declared its independence on Aug. 7, 1960. The new government permitted freedom of religion under its constitution, and traditionally favored the Church despite Catholicism's status as a minority faith. Félix Houphouët-Boigny (1905–93), a Catholic who led the independence movement, ruled as head of state in a one-party system until 1990, when a multiparty government system was introduced. Government funding of a cathedral in Abidjan—as well as a huge cathedral in Yamoussoukro, the birthplace of Houphouët-Boigny—sparked such ire within the Muslim community that the government extended similar support to other faiths. Interfaith relations were promoted by the government, which noted religious holidays and appeared at celebrations of all the country's major faiths. Although a military coup overthrew the existing government in December of 1999, the country returned to democratic elections in October of 2000.

The reforms following the Second Vatican Council in 1962–65 were well received in the region. While missionaries had previously rejected all local musical instruments that brought indigenous African religions to mind, following the council the Church encouraged the use of traditional African music and musical instruments in the liturgy. Many priests, catechists and lay people took up composing music using local tunes with lyrics either in French or in the local language. Traditional rites were introduced with numerous explanations that ensured their comprehension, although it was sometimes difficult to find gestures or symbolic objects common to all ethnic

groups. In many dioceses the pastoral ministry began to focus on base communities that met regularly. The CHARISMATIC RENEWAL experienced rapid growth throughout the country. The Catholic Institute of West Africa opened a section for the formation of lay people that became a great success. Catholic radio stations in the dioceses of Grand-Bassam and Man attracted a wide audience, and in the early 1990s stations were also established in Abidjan and Yamoussoukro.

The Jesuit-run African Institute for Economic and Social Development (INADES) was located in Abidjan, and its library was considered among the most modern on the African Continent. There also existed a major seminary for theology, although it was considered too small to respond to the number of those seeking admission. The Benedictine monastery founded at Bouaké in 1959 was affiliated with Toumliline in Morocco. In 1990 the cathedral in Yamoussoukro became the largest religious structure on the continent. Controversial, it was consecrated during a visit by Pope John Paul II only after the Church also agreed to build a hospital and youth center nearby.

Even after gaining its independence at mid-century, Ivory Coast retained strong ties with France, and these ties allowed it to maintain stable economic policies, encourage foreign investment and become one of the most prosperous state in west Africa. Still, this prosperity was relative; while Ivory Coast required financial aid from industrialized nations, a liberal debt repayment plan allowed the government to keep current on loan payments similar to those crippling the economies of many of its neighbors. The country's relative prosperity did not prevent it from experiencing outbreaks of ethnic violence by the late 1990s, particularly in the wake of a heated election in October of 2000. Fortunately, an increasingly politicized Church leadership was willing to mediate the contested returns, although a temporary military government ultimately supplanted both Christian and Muslim candidates.

By 2000 Ivory Coast had 243 parishes, tended by 418 secular and 267 religious priests. Other religious included 248 brothers and 901 sisters who worked diligently on behalf of the Church, and oversaw the country's 279 primary and 41 secondary schools. Among the goals of the Church was finding a way to bring Christianity into dialogue with the African culture and traditions, as well as with followers of Islam, a majority subject to some discrimination by a more educated Christian elite. Religious conversion between Catholic and Muslim were discouraged out of respect for Islamic laws, and leaders of the two faiths continued to work together to avoid religious conflict. In 2000 both Abidjan Archbishop Agre and Muslim leaders encouraged their followers to aid efforts to rebuild churches and mosques destroyed during an outbreak of violence following the fall elections. Relations between Catholics and other faiths remained on good terms, and regular ecumenical meetings were held with Methodist leaders.

Bibliography: R. J. MUDT *Historical Dictionary of Côte d'Ivoire* (Metuchen, NJ 1995). *Bilan du Monde,* 2 (1964) 290–293. *Annuario Pontificio* has annual data on all dioceses.

[J. HUCHET/P. TRICHET/EDS.]

J

JABLONSKA, BERNARDINA, BL.

Known in religion as Maria Bernardina; virgin, co-foundress of the Congregation of the Sisters of the Third Order of St. Francis of Assisi, Servants of the Poor (Albertines); b. Aug. 5, 1878, Pizuny-Lukawica, Poland; d. Sept. 23, 1940, Krakow.

Bernardina, the fourth child of the landed farmers Gregory Jablonski and Maria Romanow, received her education from private tutors and from books borrowed from her pastor's library. When she was eight years old she met and was impressed by Saint Albert Chmielowski. She assuaged her sorrow at her mother's death in 1893 by turning increasingly to prayer. On Sept. 13, 1896, she left home to begin her postulancy in the new congregation being founded by Chmielowski despite her father's opposition and without the approval of her pastor. The following year she was among the first seven Albertine sisters to receive the habit. Her initial decade of religious life was spent doing household chores and tending the sick, as her faith grew. In 1907, Chmielowski named her superior, a position she maintained until her death. Together with Saint Albert, she founded hospices for those who were sick and homeless as a result of war. Bernardina is remembered not only for her charity, but also for the way in which she helped the suffering regain their human dignity.

Mother Maria Bernardina was declared venerable on Dec. 17, 1996. On March 8, 1997, a miracle attributed to her intercession was approved, leading to her beatification by John Paul II, June 6, 1997, at Wielka Krokiew Arena, Zakopane, Poland. Patron of the poor and handicapped.

Feast: Sept. 23.

Bibliography: *L'Osservatore Romano*, 25 (1997): 6–7.

[K. I. RABENSTEIN]

JACKSON, DIOCESE OF

The diocese of Jackson (*Dioecesis Jacksoniensis*), Mississippi was established July 28, 1837 as the Diocese of Natchez. In 1957, the name was changed to Natchez-Jackson, and finally in 1977 to Jackson. It is a suffragan see of the metropolitan see of New Orleana. From the time it was first erected in 1837 until 1977 when the Diocese of Biloxi was established, the territory of Natchez-Jackson was coextensive with the state of Mississippi, an area of 46,340 square miles.

The first bishop, John Joseph Chanche, arrived in Natchez May 18, 1841, and found only two priests and no churches within his vast jurisdiction. Natchez, Vicksburg, and some places along the Gulf Coast had small groups of Catholics, with a few more scattered throughout the state, but numbers of them had not seen a priest for many years. Chanche, traveling throughout his diocese by stagecoach, river steamer, and any other means available at that time, worked vigorously for 11 years. By the time of his death, July 22, 1852, the basic structure of the fine Gothic cathedral had been completed in Natchez, and churches had been erected in nine other places; there were ten priests, a girls' orphanage, and plans for several other churches. His successor, James O. Van de Velde, SJ, arrived Nov. 23, 1853, but about two years later an accident led to his death on Nov. 13, 1855.

The third bishop, William H. ELDER, arrived on May 30, 1857, to direct the see, which, despite the paucity in numbers and the poverty of the Catholics, made heartening progress in the years following the Civil War. When in 1880 Elder was transferred to Cincinnati, Ohio, as coadjutor archbishop, the diocese had 19 priests, 48 churches, 15 parochial schools, and a Catholic population of 12,500. During the episcopate of Francis Janssens, who was consecrated for Natchez May 1, 1881, St. Mary's Cathedral, Natchez, was completed and solemnly consecrated on Sept. 19, 1886; missionary work among the African Americans and Native Americans in the state was advanced; and the number of Catholics had increased to

15,000, with 30 priests, 60 churches, and 26 parochial schools to care for their needs. When Janssens was transferred to New Orleans in 1888, Thomas Heslin was consecrated fifth bishop on June 18, 1889, and served until his death Feb. 22, 1911. His administration was characterized by slow but healthy growth. The sixth bishop was John E. Gunn, SM (1911–24), an eloquent speaker and effective administrator, who directed the establishment of nine new parishes and many mission chapels throughout the state.

On Oct. 15, 1924, Richard Oliver Gerow was consecrated seventh bishop of Natchez. A steady growth has marked his administration, during which the number of parishes has doubled and the number of priests more than doubled, while three Catholic hospitals, a monastery of cloistered Carmelite nuns, a lay retreat house, and a seminary of the Oblates of Mary Immaculate have been established, and other religious works inaugurated. In 1948 new chancery offices at Jackson, including administrative offices and bishop's residence, were completed and on July 22 of that year the bishop transferred his residence from Natchez to Jackson. The name of the diocese was changed to Natchez-Jackson on March 7, 1957 and St. Peter's Church in Jackson was named as cocathedral. By the time of Bishop Gerow's retirement in 1964, the diocese numbered 88 parishes, 190 priests, 52 brothers, and more than 400 sisters. There were 48 elementary schools, 26 high schools, three hospitals, two schools for nurses, and two orphanages under Catholic auspices.

Gerow was succeeded by his auxiliary bishop, Joseph B. Brunini, in 1966. A native of Vicksburg, Brunini was educated at the North American College in Rome and also received a doctorate in canon law from the Catholic University of America. In many respects he was both a visionary and activist. It was during his time and at his urging that the division of the diocese into the diocese of Jackson and the diocese of Biloxi took place in 1977. Brunini led the Mississippi Catholic Church through a number of rather difficult crises, including the integration of the Catholic school system, the implementation of Vatican II changes, and the creation of the Mississippi Religious Leadership Conference. He also led the diocese into unchartered waters when he delved into the political-social programs of the 1960s and 1970s. Under his direction, the Mississippi Catholic Church participated in federal programs designed to help the elderly and lower income groups. Finally, he encouraged the Church to reach out to their fellow Christians in Mississippi through specifically Catholic endeavors such as Catholic hospitals, Catholic charities, and Catholic education.

Brunini was succeeded by his Auxiliary Bishop, William R. Houck. A native of Birmingham, Alabama, Houck had advanced through the educational system before coming to Mississippi in 1979. In 1984, he assumed the administration of the diocese of Jackson and began to focus on evangelization, planning, the empowering of the laity, and the ever-growing role of women in the Catholic Church. In 2001, Houck submitted his letter of retirement to Rome, and subsequently he was appointed as the new director of the American Catholic Church Extension Society.

Over the years the diocese of Jackson, blessed with far-sighted leaders, experienced consistent growth and adjusted well to its Protestant environment, and by the end of the 20th century Catholicism is generally well regarded in Mississippi. The diocese has 74 parishes, 29 missions, nearly 100 religious and diocesan priests, 12 brothers, 240 sisters, and 47,873 Catholics out of a total state population of nearly two million people.

Bibliography: R. O. GEROW, *Catholicity in Mississippi* (Natchez 1939). M. V. NAMORATO, *The Catholic Church in Mississippi, 1911-1984* (Westport, CT, 1998).

[R. O. GEROW/M. V. NAMORATO]

JACOB, PATRIARCH

Jacob (Heb. *ya'ăqōb*, meaning uncertain), also known as Israel, son of Isaac and twin of Esau. By popular etymology his name was associated with the Hebrew word *'āqēb*, ''heel'' (Gn 25.26) and the denominative verb *'āqab*, ''to trip someone by seizing his heel, to supplant'' (Gn 27.36 and Hos 12.4). Either the sacred writer did not know the true derivation and meaning of the name, or he deliberately set it aside to highlight the fact that, because of divine election, Jacob, and through him, the Israelites, were destined to supplant Esau, and his progeny, the Edomites. It is probable that the name Jacob was originally an abbreviated form of a theophoric name such as *ya'ăqōb-'el* (M. Noth, *Personennamen* 179, 197, associates it with the South-Arabic root *'qb* and suggests the meaning ''God protects'').

Ostensibly the biblical narratives concerning Jacob appear as straightforward records of the personal exploits of Israel's progenitor. Yet closer scrutiny reveals that these narratives are, in reality, quite complex. They are skillfully edited accounts of traditional material to teach the significance of the patriarch's life both in relation to God's salvific plan and the character of the chosen people. Archeological data has demonstrated the genuine historical milieu of these narratives, and we are assured that the sacred writers did not arbitrarily create these stories. Yet the narratives are given a function beyond that of mere biography. They are deliberately didactic and succinctly evaluate national tendencies observed in the nation's progenitor, e.g., Jacob's cunning, occasionally rather unscrupulous, and his ready recourse to physical strength are portrayed as national traits that tend to hinder the divine plan of salvation and lead to the brink of disaster. Consider, for example, Jacob's fraudulent acquisition of the blessing reserved to the firstborn and the consequent threat to his, and the nation's, life. There can be no doubt that the author intends to censure these national traits and appeal for a humble faith and compliance to the divine plan. At times the narrative presages what has come to pass at the time of the actual editing of the narratives. Thus, Israel supplanted Edom at the time of the establishment of the Davidic empire, yet the very name, Jacob, is interpreted in terms of this supplanting, and the early narratives highlight its initial steps. Again, the flight of Jacob to Padan-Aram is reinterpreted (Gn 27.46–28.5) to emphasize the patriarch's concern for racial purity and depict him as an initiator of the later policy against mixed marriages.

One should be mindful, therefore, of the didactic rather than strictly biographical bent of the narratives. Some of the main religious themes of the Jacob stories are as follows: the cultural and religious differences and the hostile relations between the two nations, Edom and Israel (Gn 25.27–34); Jacob's fraudulent acquisition of the blessing-of-the-firstborn (Gn 27.1–46) and, by contrast, God's free choice of unworthy Israel as His instrument for the establishment of His kingdom (Gn 27.46–28.22); the conversion of Jacob, and the imposition of the name ISRAEL (Gn 32.22–33); the establishment in SHECHEM (Gn 33.18–20); the pact between the Israelites and the AMORRITES, and the later conquest of Sichem by the Israelites, thus giving Israel a right to the Holy Land (Gn 34.1–31; 48.21–22); the cleansing of the nation from paganism and the renewal of the divine pledge of election (Gn 35.1–15).

Bibliography: *Encyclopedic Dictionary of the Bible*, tr. and adap. by L. HARTMAN (New York 1963) 1094–95. M. NOTH, *Überlieferungsgeschichte des Pentateuch* (Stuttgart 1948) 86–111.

[J. A. PIERCE]

JACOB OF SARUG (SERUGH)

Bishop of the Syrian Church; b. *c.* 451; d. Nov. 29, 521. James was born in the village of Kurtam on the Euphrates, probably in the district of Sarug. When he was about 15 to 22 years old he received his theological schooling at the Persian School of Edessa, then under the influence of the Nestorian doctors, DIODORE, THEODORE, and THEODORET. In one of his letters, James avers that even as a student and on his own initiative he had de-

nounced them as heretics. He lived most of his life in a monastery in Haura in Sarug where, at least by 502 or 503, he had been appointed *periodeutes,* or ecclesiastical visitor, of the district. In 519, then more than 67 years old, he was consecrated bishop of Batnan, an important commercial city and capital of the district of Serugh. He died at the age of 70 and is revered as a saint and doctor of the Syrian Church. The JACOBITES honor him on November 29, June 29, and July 29; the MARONITES, on January 27 and April 5; and the ARMENIANS, on September 25.

Writings. James was a very prolific poet, and while his compatriots honored him with the title "Flute of the Holy Spirit and Harp of the Orthodox Church," most Westerners find his style repetitious and tedious. He is primarily known for his metrical homilies (*memre*), written in verses of two lines of 12 syllables each (4 + 4 + 4). According to Bar Hebraeus, these numbered 760 (James of Edessa says 763), and more than 70 scribes worked for a year in transcribing them. About 300 homilies have survived. Between 1905 and 1910, Paul Bedjan edited and published in five volumes 195 of these homilies. Among his prose works are six homilies (*turgame*) and 43 letters. The letters were edited and published by G. Olinder in 1937. Various liturgical works have been attributed to James (hymns, anaphoras, and an *ordo* for Baptism and Confirmation), but their authenticity is problematical.

Theology. Perhaps the most frequently studied aspect of James's thought has been his orthodoxy. In 1716, E. Renaudot, in his *Liturgiarum orientalium collectio,* accused James of being a Monophysite. Three years later, J. S. Assemani began publishing his monumental *Bibliotheca orientalis* in which he argues strongly for the orthodoxy of James. With the publication in 1876 of several key letters, P. Martin seemed to many to have settled the issue: James was a Monophysite. Subsequent defenders of his orthodoxy tend to take one of two approaches: (1) to admit that he was a Monophysite through most of his life but that he died reconciled with the orthodox Church (e.g., Matagne); or (2) to attack the authenticity of Martin's letters, adding arguments of a historical nature. P. Peeters is an impassioned protagonist of this position. P. Krüger has questioned James' orthodoxy; and T. Jansma, in three masterful articles, has proved conclusively that James was a Monophysite of the Severian school and remained so all his life.

James was not a controversialist and took virtually no part in the theological disputes of his day; the only polemic he shows is directed precisely against those who were engaged in heated theological polemics. In this he is very much in the tradition of EPHREM, who argued so strongly *adversus scrutatores* and their "poison, Greek wisdom." Also like Ephrem, James presents his theology in and through his poetry. His thought circles around, looking first at one facet, then at another of the mystery he is contemplating. At times his symbols combine contradictory elements which suggest things that cannot be fully said and which cannot be neatly systematized in conceptual language.

The subjects treated by James cover a wide spectrum, with most of his themes being drawn from the Bible (e.g., Old Testament—the Hexaemeron, the Patriarchs, Moses, Elijah, and so on; New Testament—the Incarnation of Jesus, His parables and miracles, His Passion, death, Resurrection, Ascension, etc.). He discusses virtues and vices, the last things, the Sacraments of Baptism and Eucharist, consolation for the bereaved, etc. F. Graffin notes three themes especially frequent in James: (1) a delight in finding figures, "types," of Christ in the lives and deeds of the Patriarchs; (2) the theme of the Church as the Bride of Christ, a subject treated often and with great devotion and lyricism; and (3) the pressing invitation to his hearers to consider the Scriptures and the mysteries of the faith with great love and a true childlike spirit, as opposed to the so-called wise men who examine them minutely and argue about them. James' spirituality is animated by charity, simplicity and poverty, and his homilies bear eloquent testimony to their author's ardent pastoral zeal and dedication to the spiritual growth of his people.

Bibliography: A. BAUMSTARK, *Geschichte der syrischen Literatur* (Bonn 1922, repr. 1968) 148–158. F. GRAFFIN, "Recherches sur le thème de l'église-épouse dans les liturgies et la littérature patristique de langue syriaque," *L'orient syrien* 3 (1958) 315–336; "L'homélie de Jacques de Saroug: De visione Jacobi in Bethel," *L'orient syrien* 5 (1960) 225–246; "Thème de la perle dans un lettre de Jacques de Saroug," *L'orient syrien* 12 (1967) 355–370; "Jacques de Saroug," *Dictionnaire de Spiritualite,* T. 8 unbd. fascicle LII–LIII (Paris 1972) 56–60, with extensive bibliography. T. JANSMA, "L'Hexaemeron de Jacques de Saroug," *L'orient syrien* 4 (1959) 3–14, 129–162, 253–284; "The Credo of James of Sarug: A Return to Nicea and Constantinople," *Nederlandsch Archief voor Kerkgeschiedenis* 44 (1960) 18–36; "Die Christologie Jakobs von Serugh und ihre Abhängigkeit von der alexandrinischen Theologie und von der Frömmigkeit Ephraems des Syrers," *Muséon* 78 (1965) 5–46; "Encore le Crédo de Jacques de Saroug," *L'orient syrien* 10 (1965) 75–88, 193–236, 331–370, 474–510. E. KHALIFÉ-HACHEM, "Homélie métrique de Jacques de Saroug sur l'amour," *Parole de l'orient* 1 (1970) 281–299. H. MATAGNE, *Acta sanctorum Octobris Bollandiana* 12 (Brussels 1884) 824–831, 927–929. J. VAN DER PLOEG, "Une homélie de Jacques de Saroug sur la reception de la sainte communion," *Mélange Eugene Tisserant* 3 (*Studi e Testi* 233) 395–418.

[M. GUINAN]

JACOBAZZI, DOMENICO

Cardinal and canonist; b. Rome, Italy, *c.* 1444; d. Rome, 1527. He became a consistorial lawyer at Rome in 1486 after studies in Roman and Canon Law at the University of BOLOGNA. In 1493 he became an auditor of the Roman Rota, of which he became dean in 1506. He was named *vicarius urbis* and bishop of Nocera dei Pagani in 1511 and a cardinal in 1517. His comprehensive work *De concilio* was written mainly during the Fifth LATERAN COUNCIL and published posthumously at Rome in 1538. Jacobazzi, a stanch defender of the papacy who held that the pope was not subordinate to a council or its decrees, nevertheless represented the view that in a state of emergency a council could be summoned without papal approval if the pope refused a formal request to convene one (*see* CONCILIARISM).

Bibliography: Sources. *De concilio,* repr. in MANSI *Sacrorum Conciliorum nova et amplissima collectio: Introductio:* 1–580. Literature. J. KLOTZNER, *Kardinal Dominikus Jacobazzi und sein Konzilswerk* (Rome 1948). H. JEDIN, *History of the Council of Trent* v.1 (St. Louis 1957–60), *passim.* R. GILLET, *Dictionnaire de droit canonique,* ed. R. NAZ, 7 v. (Paris 1935–65) 6:75–77. R. BÄUMER, *Lexikon für Theologie und Kirche,* ed. J. HOFER and K. RAHNER, 10 v. (2d, new ed. Freiburg 1957–65) 5:831.

[W. S. BARRON]

JACOBI, FRIEDRICH HEINRICH

German philosopher of faith and feeling; b. Düsseldorf, Jan. 25, 1743; d. Munich, March 10, 1819, where he had become president of the Bavarian Academy of Science. Influenced by J. J. ROUSSEAU and Lord Shaftesbury, Jacobi opposed the RATIONALISM of the ENLIGHTENMENT. He was closely associated with many significant men of his day, among them Goethe; J. K. Lavater; C. M. Wieland; M. Claudius; the later bishop of Regensburg, J. M. Sailer; Prince A. von Gallitzin; and especially J. G. HERDER and J. G. HAMANN, who exerted a strong influence over him. Jacobi made a sharp distinction between knowledge and faith. Under the influence of I. Kant, he had come to regard the thing-in-itself as unknowable; consequently, knowledge leads ultimately to nihilism. It leads also to atheism in that the comprehension of the Absolute and of metaphysical principles is equally impossible. To him, B. Spinoza's philosophy was a case in point. He also criticized the notion of the thing-in-itself in Kant's philosophy, remarking that without this supposition one could not enter into Kant's system and with it one could not remain there. He charged J. G. FICHTE and F. W. J. SCHELLING with being Spinoza in reverse. Jacobi himself built his thesis upon faith. For him the organ of faith is reason, which allows man to perceive the outer world as well as beauty and moral good, even the divine. The true essence of man consists in his spiritual nature, which stems immediately from God and finds its fullest expression in the heart. Jacobi thus termed himself "a heathen in the understanding and a Christian in feeling." He accepted the great truths of Christianity—God, freedom, and immortality—but he was of the opinion that these could not be conceptualized. Yet Christianity embraces more truths than Jacobi would admit, and if those truths he did admit were accessible only to the heart, they would be purely subjective. Jacobi exerted considerable influence over J. C. F. Schiller, the romantics, F. D. E. SCHLEIERMACHER, and the Catholic school at Tübingen.

Bibliography: Works. *Gesamtausgabe,* 6 v. (Leipzig 1812–25). New critical ed. by the Bavarian Academy in preparation. *Über die Lehre des Spinoza in Briefen an den Herrn M. Mendelssohn* (Breslau 1785; enl. ed. 1789). *D. Hume über den Glauben, oder Idealismus und Realismus* (Breslau 1787). *Sendschreiben an Fichte* (Hamburg 1799). *Über dan Unternehmen des Kritizismus, die Vernunft zu Verstande zu bringen* (Hamburg 1801). *Von den göttlichen Dingen* (Leipzig 1811). O. BOLLNOW, *Die Lebensphilosophie F. H. Jacobis* (Stuttgart 1933). A. HEBEISEN, *F. H. Jacobi: Seine Auseinandersetzung mit Spinoza* (Bern 1960). R. KNOLL, *J. G. Hamann and F. H. Jacobi* (Heidelberg 1963).

[J. HIRSCHBERGER]

JACOBINA OF PISA, BL.

Dominican tertiary; b. Pisa, *c.* 1280; d. Pisa, *c.* 1370. Her ancestry and early life are unknown. At about 20, she made a happy marriage with Peter Cascina, member of a prominent Pisan family. When he died (before 1366), Jacobina distributed her wealth to the poor and joined the Sisters of the Order of Penance of St. Dominic (Third Order). As prioress (from 1368) of the sisters attached to the Dominican priory of S. Caterina in Pisa, she was noted for fidelity to her religious life, prudent direction of the sisters, and tender care for the poor and sick. Jacobina was buried in the church of S. Chiara in Pisa, and her relics have been lost or indistinguishably mixed with others. Her cult has not been officially recognized but is immemorial.

Bibliography: S. BARSOTTI, *Un nuovo fiore domenicano, la Beata Jacopina da Pisa* (Pisa 1904), pamphlet, rev. in *Année Dominicaine,* Dec. 1 (Lyons 1909) 264–268.

[R. M. BEISSEL]

JACOBINI, LUDOVICO

Cardinal, secretary of state; b. Genzano (Latium), Italy, Jan. 6, 1832; d. Rome, Feb. 28, 1887. He came from a well-to-do family and pursued seminary studies at Al-

bano and Rome. Entering the service of the Roman Curia, he worked in the Congregation of Extraordinary Ecclesiastical Affairs. Pius IX named him secretary for Oriental affairs in the Congregation for the PROPAGATION OF THE FAITH. At VATICAN COUNCIL I his post as undersecretary gained him a remarkable knowledge of bishops throughout the world. Consecrated titular archbishop of Thessalonica, he became nuncio to Vienna (March 24, 1874). Relations between Austria-Hungary and the Church were then strained, since the government had in 1870 denounced the concordat and had attempted by three laws voted in 1874 to submit the Church to State tutelage. In this difficult situation the new nuncio displayed outstanding diplomatic qualities. Jacobini also searched for a *modus vivendi* to end the KULTURKAMPF, meeting with Bismarck in 1879.

Raised to the cardinalate (Sept. 19, 1879), he became secretary of state (Dec. 16, 1880) to LEO XIII and retained the post until death. In the secretariate of state his perseverance and sound knowledge of issues impelled him to a definitive settlement of the differences between the Holy See and Germany. One of his most important statements was his note (April 13, 1885) to the nuncio at Madrid, RAMPOLLA. In it Jacobini contradicted a journalist, Ramon Nocedal, who attributed to bishops an authority superior to that of nuncios, claimed to be merely diplomats. His note affirmed the right of nuncios, as delegates of the Holy See, to intervene in diocesan affairs.

Bibliography: E. SODERINI, *Il pontificato di Leone XIII,* 3 v. (Milan 1932–33); tr. B. B. CARTER, v.1 *The Pontificate of Leo XIII* (London 1934), v.2 *Leo XIII, Italy and France* (1935), v.3 not tr. F. ENGEL-JANOSI, *Österreich und der Vatikan, 1846–1918,* 2 v. (Graz 1958–60) v.1.

[J. M. MAYEUR]

JACOBIS, GIUSTINO DE, ST.

Missionary bishop in ETHIOPIA; b. San Fele, Lucania, Italy, Oct. 9, 1800; d. Aligadé, Ethiopia, July 31, 1860. Reared in Naples, he entered the VINCENTIANS (1818) and was ordained (1824). He engaged in mission preaching and was superior of various Vincentian communities in central Italy. In 1839 he became prefect apostolic of his congregation's mission in Ethiopia and resided at Adau. At first contemptuously called "the Frank" by the Monophysite Copts, he later came to be respected and affectionately known as "Abuna Yacob" (Father James). In 1841 the Copts induced him to accompany a mission to the Monophysite patriarch of Alexandria seeking the election of an Ethiopian metropolitan. His presence disturbed the patriarch, but de Jacobis persuaded one of the party, GHEBRE MICHAEL, to continue to

Rome and to visit Pope GREGORY XVI. In 1844 de Jacobis received Ghebre Michael into the Catholic Church and with his assistance established a seminary at Guala (1845). De Jacobis built a Catholic center on the Red Sea island of Massawa, where he was consecrated bishop by Guglielmo MASSAJA (1848). In 1855 he was imprisoned by the usurper Theodor and then banished. He spent the rest of his life ministering along the Red Sea coast. For befriending a French diplomatic mission he was again imprisoned in 1860. He was released, but the hardship of his captivity had worn him out, and he died while returning to his mission at Halai in Eritrea. He was beatified May 14, 1939 by Pius XII and canonized October 26, 1975 by Paul VI.

Feast: July 31.

Bibliography: A. DEVIN, *L'Abyssinie et son apôtre* (Paris 1866). S. ARATA, *Vita del B. Giustino de Jacobis* (Rome 1939). E. LUCATELLO, *L'abuna Yaqob Mariàm* (Rome 1975). K. O'MAHONEY, *''The ebullient phoenix'': A History of the Vicariate of Abyssinia, 1839–1860,* 2 v. (Asmara, Ethiopia 1982–7). J. L. BAUDOT and L. CHAUSSIN, *Vies des saints et des bienhereux selon l'ordre du calendrier avec l'historique des fêtes* (Paris 1935–56) 7:770–774. A. BUTLER, *The Lives of the Saints,* ed. H. THURSTON and D. ATTWATER (New York 1956) 3:230–235.

[T. P. JOYCE]

JACOBITES (ENGLISH)

Adherents to the movement (Jacobitism) for the restoration of the Stuart dynasty following the flight of JAMES II after the fateful REVOLUTION OF 1688. Until his death (1701) James maintained the leadership of the movement principally from Saint-Germainen-Laye, France.

Stuart Pretenders. After James's death three descendants upheld their claim to rule England, Scotland, and Ireland; two actively, one passively. The first was *James Francis Edward Stuart,* "The Old Pretender" (b. London, June 20, 1688; d. Rome, Jan. 1, 1766). He was the son of James II by his second wife, Mary of Modena. He succeeded his father at age 13 and was recognized by France, Spain, and the papacy as legitimate ruler. For nearly four decades he actively sought to regain the Stuart inheritance, especially in 1708 when an invasion of Scotland with 5,000 French troops was foiled by severe storms and the English fleet, and in 1715 when he tried almost unaided to raise the Scots. For all practical purposes the leadership of the movement devolved in the 1740s upon his elder son by his wife Clementina Sobieska, *Charles Edward Stuart,* "The Young Pretender" (b. Rome, Dec. 31, 1720; d. there, Jan. 1, 1788). His active leadership was confined to the early 1740s and culminated in the disastrous defeat at Culloden (1746).

Subsequently he lived in exile chiefly in Italy. It is noteworthy that even the papacy did not recognize his claim to the throne upon his father's death in 1766. The last male Stuart pretender was his younger brother, *Henry Stuart,* Cardinal of York (b. Rome, March 6, 1725; d. Frascati, Italy, July 13, 1807). He was never active in prosecuting his own claims; neither was he officially recognized anywhere as king in succession to Charles. Any practical chance of his becoming king was eliminated by his position successively as priest, bishop, and finally cardinal. In his declining years he was a pensioner of George III and obviously no threat to the ruling Hanoverians. With his death the Stuart claim came to an end as a movement of historical interest.

Any discussion of Jacobitism is complicated by the separate national bases of the movement—English, Scottish, and Irish—and by the disparate characteristics of its supporters. In Ireland the movement was of least importance once James II had been defeated in the Battle of the Boyne (July 12, 1690) and most of his principal supporters had come to terms with William III by the Treaty of Limerick (Oct. 13, 1691). After that time the Stuarts had little support from the predominantly Protestant ruling class, while the support of the vast majority of Roman Catholic Irish was of no practical significance. What meaningful aid there was came largely from Irish refugees who enlisted in the French army.

Sources of Support. In England assistance came from diverse and uncoordinated sources: Tories who believed in strict hereditary succession unalterable by parliament; the nonjuring clergy of the Church of England who believed in nonresistance to divinely ordained royal authority as defined by hereditary succession (*see* NONJURORS, ENGLISH); and the small minority of Roman Catholics. The first two groups predicated their allegiance on recognition by the Stuarts of the established Church, its property, universities and schools, and generally favored position; indeed many would support the Stuarts only if they renounced their Roman Catholicism, persistent adherence to which cost many English, though few Scottish or Irish supporters.

Scotland, especially the Highland clans, formed the strongest and most persistent base for Stuart claims. The Stuarts were in origin a Scottish dynasty and thus had a strong claim on traditional loyalty and sentiments. The clergy of the Anglican Church of Scotland supported the Stuarts much more strongly than did their English coreligionists because they were a minority group whom the Stuarts would support together with Roman Catholics against the dominant Presbyterian Kirk. The largely Catholic Highlanders opposed the tendency toward encroachment on their economic and social customs, against the centralizing tendencies of the late 17th- and early 18th-century English governments.

In general Jacobitism may be divided chronologically, 1688 to 1715 and 1715 to 1746. In the first period there was some chance for Stuart reestablishment, especially from 1706 to 1714, based partly upon internal adherents in England and Scotland, partly on foreign arms, chiefly from France. During this time many Tory politicians, such as Bolingbroke, and the nonjuring Anglican clergy favored a Stuart restoration when Queen Anne should die, rather than import the foreign Hanoverian dynasty. After 1714, however, leadership in England was lacking, especially after 1722 when the leading Jacobite, Bishop Atterbury, was exiled to France. After the successful advent of the Hanoverians, the death of LOUIS XIV (1715), and the failure of the abortive revolt of 1715 (the '15) the Old and Young Pretenders were heavily dependent on foreign assistance to initiate invasions, which clearly would have to receive greatest military strength from Scotland. Thus Stuart fortunes fluctuated wildly as the diplomatic situation in Europe changed. During the ascendency of Sir Robert Walpole in England and of Cardinal Fleury in France, roughly 1721 to 1742, the Jacobites had little hope of success since both men were committed to peace. Efforts to secure arms and money from Spain, Sweden, the papacy, and even Russia were largely unavailing.

Revolt and Defeat. Once England was at war with Spain (1739), later joined by France during the War of the Austrian Succession, large-scale support was again possible, but it gave the impression of imposing foreign rule, especially in England where France was the age-old enemy. In contrast France was Scotland's traditional ally (the Auld Alliance). The collapse of Jacobitism came after the Young Pretender's attempt to raise revolts in Scotland and England in 1745 to 1746 (the '45). In July 1745 Charles sailed to Scotland, where he received substantial, although not universal allegiance from the Highland clans, and also from the Lowlands, especially Edinburgh. In the fall he moved into northwest England and so toward London. Except for a few recruits in Lancashire, however, no Englishmen flocked to his standard, and at Derby, Dec. 5 to 6, 1745, the Young Pretender's military advisers forced a retreat since their men faced combat with overwhelming English armies. During the winter the Scots retreated through the Lowlands and up the east coast. Finally at Culloden, April 16, 1746, the Scottish Highlanders were slaughtered by the Hanoverian armies, which gave no quarter. After incredible hardships and romantic adventures in the western Highlands and Hebrides, Charles escaped in September to France. The Highlands were conquered by the building of military roads, through merciless devastation of the countryside,

and the brutal handling and transportation of Scottish prisoners; the Stuarts' last manpower reserve was eliminated. Charles ended his days an alcoholic; his younger brother, Henry, was never a serious threat to George III. Perhaps the final touch was the Prince Regent's commissioning of Canova in 1819 to design a fine marble monument in St. Peter's, Rome, to the three pretenders. The Hanoverians could afford to be generous; their enemies had long since been vanquished.

Bibliography: C. A. PETRIE, *The Jacobite Movement: The First Phase, 1688–1716* (London 1948). C. A. PETRIE, *The Jacobite Movement: The Last Phase, 1716–1807* (London 1950). *Britain after the Glorious Revolution*, ed. G. HOLMES (New York 1969). B. LENMAN, *The Jacobite Risings in Britain, 1689–1746* (London 1980). F. J. MCLYNN, *The Jacobites* (London 1985). P. KLEBER MONOD, *Jacobitism and the English People, 1688–1788* (Cambridge Eng. 1989). D. SZECHI, *The Jacobites, Britain and Europe, 1688–1788* (Manchester, Eng. 1994).

[H. S. REINMUTH, JR.]

JACOBITES (SYRIAN)

The title Jacobite, which appears after A.D. 575, comes from the name of James BARADAI, who organized a faction within the Syrian Orthodox Church. Consecrated bishop of Edessa (543) by the exiled patriarch of Alexandria at the instigation of Empress Theodora (1) and the Ghassanid Prince Harith, James Baradai ordained 30 bishops and thousands of priests and deacons during frequent trips through the Orient from Persia to Egypt.

The Syrian Jacobites trace their lineage to Sergius of Antioch (558–561), although the actual schism that gave rise to the name occurred during the patriarchate of Paul the Black (d. 581) and was healed after his death with the election of his successor, Peter of Callinicum (581–591). The name Jacobite was applied by the Byzantine Orthodox to differentiate the non–Chalcedonian Syrian Oriental Orthodox Church, which is not in communion with either Constantinople or Rome. Outstanding churchmen were Denis of Tellmahrē, James of Edessa, Michael of Antioch, and Gregorius ibn al–'Ibrī.

The Jacobites played an important role during the occupation of Syria by the Arabs, whom they received as liberators from the yoke of Byzantium. During the dynasty of the 'ABBĀSIDS, they were held in great esteem at the court of BAGHDAD.

While the Jacobite patriarch was never able to establish a firm residence in Antioch, he had his see successively in various monasteries and exercised jurisdiction over the churches located in the Sassanid Empire of Persia through a primate called Maphriān, who was a sort of universal delegate of the patriarch. In the 12th century the

Jacobite patriarchate numbered 2 million faithful with 20 metropolitans and 103 eparchs, or bishops, in Syria, Mesopotamia, and Cyprus. Internal problems, including a schism (1364–94), gradually weakened the church's membership and integrity, and by the 17th century it was reduced to 20 bishoprics. Since 1293 the Jacobite Patriarch of Antioch has taken the name of Ignatius on election.

Bibliography: C. L. SPIESSENS, "Les Patriarches d'Antioche," *L'Orient syrien* 7 (1962) 389–434. *Oriente Cattolico: Cenni storici e statistiche* (Vatican City 1962). R. ROBERSON, *The Eastern Christian Churches: A Brief Survey* (Rome 1999).

[E. EL HAYEK/EDS.]

JACOPONE DA TODI

Franciscan mystic and poet; b. Todi, Umbria, *c.*1230; d. *c.*1306. The available data on Jacopone's life are unreliable. He did pursue legal studies, probably at the University of Bologna, and exercised the profession of notary and legal procurator in Todi, the town of his birth. The hagiographic tradition surrounding him speaks of the tragic death of his wife, Vanna di Bernardino di Guidone, as the result of her fall from a balcony in a mansion where she was attending a party. Jacopone, who wasn't at the party, discovered his wife wearing a penitential hair shirt under her robes. This traumatic event provoked a psychological and spiritual crisis in Jacopone.

For some ten years (1268–1278), he lived the life of a wandering penitent or "bizzocone," as he refers to himself in one of his lauds. In 1278, he was admitted to the Order of the Friars Minor. He remained a lay brother and quickly became a zealous member of the Spiritual party. Regarded by many as its poet, he expounded the radical views of the FRANCISCAN SPIRITUALS and excoriated what he saw as the laxity of the Community faction for their mitigation of the early Franciscan ideal of total poverty.

In 1294, at the beginning of the pontificate of CELESTINE V, he addressed one of his lauds to the former hermit warning him of the perils of his office. A few months after his election Celestine resigned and Jacopone, among others, highly suspected that his successor, BONIFACE VIII, had a hand in his demise. Boniface represented everything that Jacopone, who had known him in his youth, abhorred. Because of his intrigues and corruption, he conceived him, in one of his lauds, as "a new Lucifer on the papal throne." Along with the Colonna Cardinals and others opponents of Boniface, Jacopone, in May 1297, signed the Longhezzo Manifesto declaring Boniface's election illegitimate. Boniface retaliated by declaring the rebels excommunicated and defeating them in a battle over the town of Palestrina in 1298. Jacopone was tried and jailed in the cellar of a friary, possibly in Todi. During his five years imprisonment, Jacopone softened his view on Boniface and, in one of his lauds, begged him to at least to be absolved from his excommunication if not released from his imprisonment.

Jacopone had to wait for the election of BENEDICT XI in 1303 before being granted freedom and readmitted to communion in the church. Aged and tired, he lived out his last years in the convent of S. Lorenzo of Colazzone, near a Poor Clare monastery, between Perugia and Todi, where he died on Christmas night in 1306. Popularly venerated as "Blessed" and "Saint," he is inscribed in the Franciscan martyrology. His cult, however, has never been officially confirmed by the Church.

Jacopone was the most famous and prolific known writer of the medieval literary genre known as the *lauda*. These *lauda* were written in the Umbrian dialect and often in ballad form. They were meant to stir up popular penitential devotion. Contemporary criticism maintains that ninety or so of Jacopone's lauds are authentic. Interweaving poetry, politics, and mysticism, they astonish in their range and complexity of tone and message. For Jacopone, life "is an unremitting battle" and in his *laudarium* he wages a fierce assault on the "counterfeit" self, the compromises and hypocrisy that he perceives in himself, in the nascent Franciscan brotherhood, and in the church leaders of his time. Jacopone is considered the most powerful religious poet in Italy before Dante's time. He is among the first to express God's presence in poetic form and a vernacular one at that. Jacopone's mysticism belongs in the fool of God tradition, but his lauds reveal an extensive theological culture, especially of the writings of St. Bonaventure. It is in singing the supremacy of sacred over profane love that his poetry is the most enchanting. "Totally annihilated," the soul, under Jacopone's pen, soars to the highest stages of divine union, "one without division." In the boldness with which he expresses his mystical experience, he ranks among the greatest medieval mystics, alongside ANGELA OF FOLIGNO, his contemporary and a twin soul, the Beguines, HADEWIJCH, Marguerite Porete, and MECHTHILD OF MAGDEBURG.

Aside from his lauds, Jacopone is also credited with a mystical tract entitled *Tractatus utilissimus* and various *Dicta*, or sayings. Even if it resembles in some respects Jacopone's widely acclaimed "Donna del Paradiso," his authorship of the *Stabat Mater,* one of the most famous Christian hymns, still has not been fully established.

Bibliography: F. MANCINI, ed., *Laude* (Bari 1974). E. MEMESTÒ, *Atti del Convegno Storico Iacoponico* (Florence 1981). S. and

E. HUGHES, *Jacoponi da Todi, The Lauds* (New York 1982). E. UNDERHILL, *Jacopone da Todi: Poet and Mystic, 1228–1306* (London 1919). G. T. PECK, *The Fool of God—Jacopone da Todi* (Tuscaloosa, AL 1980). B. MCGINN, *The Flowering of Mysticism: Men and Women in the New Mysticism (1200–1350)*, vol. III of the *Presence of God: A History of Western Mysticism* (New York, 1998), 125–131. V. L. KATAINEN, "Jacopone da Todi, Poet and Mystic: A Review of the History of Criticism," *Mystics Quarterly* 22 (1996): 46–57.

[P. LACHANCE]

JACQUES DE MOLAY

The last grand master of the TEMPLARS; b. Molay (Haute-Saône), France, between 1243 and 1254; d. Paris, March 19, 1314. About 1265 he entered the order of Knights Templars at Beaune. Hardly anything is known about his life prior to his promotion to the rank of grand master in 1298. In 1307 he was called to France by CLEMENT V, who had decided to unite the Templars and the KNIGHTS OF MALTA under a common authority. Molay rejected this project, which he believed would be detrimental to the property and independence of his order. He obtained permission from Pope Clement V to conduct a study of the order's moral condition, but it is not known whether this study was made. It seems probable that Clement, by so acting, attempted to prevent King PHILIP IV the Fair's resolve to arrest De Molay, to institute proceedings against the order, and to seize its wealth. The menace became real on Sept. 22, 1307, when Nogaret, an enemy of the Templars, was put in charge of the royal chancellery. Lulled into a false sense of security, Molay was arrested on Oct. 13, 1307. During the trial, presided over by William of Paris, the inquisitor and confessor of the king, the grand master pleaded guilty and, in his own name and that of his confreres, begged those present to obtain for him papal absolution and royal pardon. He soon retracted, however, and at a national council assembled in Tours (May 1308) the Templars were condemned and declared deserving of death. Despite a rather weak intervention by Pope Clement V, whom the king visited in Poitiers, the trial reopened in Paris, on Aug. 8, 1309. The case dragged on, and five years later, on March 19, 1314, a commission of cardinals delivered the sentence of life imprisonment. At this point, Jacques de Molay again retracted violently. That same evening, without further reference to the commission, the king had him burned as a relapsed heretic together with his codefendant, William of Charni, on a small island near the Île-de-la-Cîté. A violent man of little culture and subtlety, Jacques de Molay was overcome by events in the ruthless struggle of the French crown against the Catholic Church. Present evidence leaves no doubt that he was innocent of the charges brought against him.

Bibliography: P. DUGUEYST, *Essai sur J. de Molay* (Paris 1906). P. VIOLET, *Les Interrogatoires de Molay* (Paris 1909). A. TRUNZ, *Zur Geschichte des letzten Templermeisters* (Freiburg 1920). W. SCHWARZ, "Die Schuld des Jakob von Molay, des letzten Grossmeisters der Templer," *Die Welt als Geschichte* 17 (1957) 259–277. A. POSCH, *Lexicon für Theologie und Kirche*, 10 v. (Freiburg 1957–65) 5:843–844. G. BORDONOVE, *Les Templiers* (Paris 1963).

[É. BROUETTE]

JACQUES DE VITRY

Historian, crusade preacher, hagiographer, bishop of Acre (1216–28), and cardinal bishop of Tusculum (1228); b. Reims region, *c.* 1170; d. Rome, 1240. Jacques studied at Paris and, as a canon regular, developed an abiding interest in the feminine religious movement that centered around MARY OF OIGNIES (d. 1213) in the Diocese of Liège. His *Vita Mariae Oigniacensis* (*Acta Sanctorum*, June 5:542–572) defines the prototype of the BEGUINES. In 1216 he secured papal recognition for them. In 1213 Jacques de Vitry preached against the ALBIGENSES. In seven extant letters [R. B. C. Huygens, *Lettres de J. de V.* (Leiden 1960)] that date from 1216 to 1221, he left an account of the Fifth CRUSADE. He was back in the West by 1225, and in his last years he associated with Pope GREGORY IX. His works offer invaluable insight into the contemporary scene. The first part of his *Historia orientalis et occidentalis* [ed. F. Moschus (Douai 1597)] describes conditions in the East, but it shows the influence of WILLIAM OF TYRE. The second part presents the monastic and quasi-monastic movements of Belgium and Italy, together with vignettes of John of Nivelles, FULK OF NEUILLY, and PETER CANTOR. In particular the Beguines, HUMILIATI, and FRANCISCANS, with their emphasis on the *vita apostolica* and the primitive Church, appealed to him. If clerical delinquency and worldliness caused concern, this multiplicity of religious life provided the answer to internal decay and the threat of sectarianism. As *sermones ad status,* his *Sermones vulgares* (Paris, Bib. Nat. lat. 1759) are a substantial contribution to estates literature, for several lay callings as well as the secular clergy and monastic orders are addressed. These sermons are seeded with *exempla* (*see* EXEMPLUM) derived from both literary sources and personal experience, a preaching style that he popularized. Two other collections of sermons include *Sermones feriales et communes* [the *exempla,* ed. J. Greven (Heidelberg 1914)] and *Sermones in epistolas et evangelia dominicalia* (Antwerp 1575).

See Also: PREACHING (HISTORY OF); LAITY IN THE MIDDLE AGES.

Bibliography: JACQUES DE VITRY, *The Exempla, or Illustrative Sermons from the Sermones Vulgares,* ed. T. F. CRANE (London

1890). P. FUNK, *Jakob von Vitry: Leben und Werke* (Leipzig 1909). D. BIRCH, "Jacques de Vitry and the Ideology of the Middle Ages" in *Pilgrimage Explored* (Woodbridge 1999). J. HAMMESSE et al., eds., *Medieval Sermons and Society: Cloister, City, University—Proceedings of the International Symposia at Kalamazoo and New York* (Louvain 1998).

[E. W. MCDONNELL]

JADOT, JEAN

Belgian prelate, papal diplomat; b. Brussels, Nov. 23, 1909; the eldest of eight children of Lambert and Gabrielle (Flanneau) Jadot. Educated in London, Brussels, Paris, and Louvain, Jadot was ordained a priest for the diocese of Malines on Feb. 11, 1934 and was assigned to the large urban parish of St. Gertrude in Etterbeek.

During World War II, Jadot dedicated his efforts to the pastoral care of youth as chaplain to an independent Catholic youth organization. In March 1945 he became a military chaplain at the state infantry school and later at the Royal Military School. In 1952 Jadot became chief chaplain for the 25,000 public forces in the Belgian Congo. In 1960 he was called back to his native Belgium to become the national director of the Pontifical Missionary Works. This missionary role gave him personal exposure to the Church throughout the world, particularly in Asia, which served him well when in 1967 he was appointed to the reorganized Congregation for the Evangelization of Peoples (formerly the Congregation for Propagation of the Faith).

Diplomatic Career. Pope Paul VI brought Jadot, at the age of 59, into the diplomatic service of the Holy See. On May 1, 1968, Jadot was ordained a bishop in his parish church of Chant d'Oiseau in Brussels and was named titular archbishop of Zuri. His first diplomatic appointment was as apostolic delegate to Thailand, which included his representing the Holy See in Laos, Malaysia, and Singapore. His zest for interdisciplinary dialogue as a university student was rekindled by the challenge to engage Buddhist and other non-Christian religious communities.

After three years in Asia, Pope Paul VI appointed him pro-nuncio to Cameroon in West Africa and at the same time he served as pro-nuncio to Gabon and as apostolic delegate to Equatorial Guinea.

In the spring of 1973, Pope Paul VI appointed him apostolic delegate in the United States. His views on the need to prepare for a Church with declining numbers of priests, on racism, and on the role of Catholic laity in society received wide attention. Although formal diplomatic relations had not yet been established between the Holy See and the American government, Jadot's duties in Washington included his serving on behalf of the Vatican as permanent observer to the Organization of American States. In 1979 Jadot accompanied Pope John Paul II on his first pastoral visit to the United States. In June 1980, John Paul II named him pro-president of the Secretariat for Non-Christians. This appointment to the Roman Curia crowned Jean Jadot's more than fifty years of service to the Church. Upon retirement he returned to Brussels.

Bibliography: M. DELLICOUR, *Un Prêtre Diplomate, 50 Ans au service de l'Eglise. Entretiens avec Michel Dellicour* (Paris and Louvain-la-Neuve 1992). For extracts of Jadot's letters and talks, see L. BOUYER, *Dom Lambert Beauduin: un homme de l'Eglise* (Tournai 1964). G. A. KELLY, *The Battle for the American Church* (Garden City NY 1979). S. QUITSLUND, *Beauduin: A Prophet Vindicated* (New York 1973).

[L. PURCELL]

JADWIGA OF POLAND, ST.

Duchess of Silesia; b. Andechs, Bavaria, Germany, *c.* 1174; d. convent of Trzebnica, Wroclaw Province, Poland, Oct. 15, 1243. The daughter of Berthold IV, Count of Andechs, she was educated at the monastery of Kitzingen and (*c.* 1186) married Henry I, who in 1202 became duke of Silesia. Hedwig played an influential part in governmental administration, displaying prudence, fortitude, and piety, and she strove particularly to keep peace between the nobles within her area of influence. Founding new monasteries and supporting old ones, she introduced the MENDICANT orders, the FRANCISCANS and the DOMINICANS, into her realm. By her encouragement, her husband founded (1202) the first convent for religious women in Silesia, that of the CISTERCIANS at Trzebnica. After the birth of their seventh child in 1208, the couple took a vow of chastity before the bishop of Wroclaw. In the war over the possession of Kraków in 1229, Henry I of Silesia defeated Conrad of Masovia but was captured by surprise while at a church service. Hedwig, hastening to the rescue, made such an impression on Conrad that he released her husband after some concessions. After her husband's death (1238), Hedwig retired to the convent at Trzebnica, but did not become a nun so that she could retain her right over her possessions for distribution to charities. She was buried in the church attached to this convent. A woman of piety and gentleness, she practiced mortification and had a rich interior life; she was considered a saint during her lifetime. Pope CLEMENT IV canonized her in 1267, and in 1706 her feast was added to the general calendar of the Latin rite. She is honored as the patroness of Silesia.

Feast: Oct. 16 (formerly Oct. 17).

Bibliography: *Acta Sanctorum* Oct. 8:198–270. *Bibliotheca hagiographica latina antiquae ct mediae aetatis,* 2 v. (Brussels 1898–1901; suppl. 1911) 3766–68. *Der Hedwigs-Codex von 1353: Sammlung Ludwig,* ed. W. BRAUNFELS, tr. P. MORAW, 2 v. (Berlin 1972). *Heilige Hedwig,* ed. M. KACZMAREK, tr. J. RETZ (Berlin 1995), papers from the conference "Die heilige Hedwig: die Rolle der Frau in der Kirche im Mittelalter und Heute," Trzebnica, Poland, June 1993. G. BAZIN, *Sainte Hedwige, sa vie et ses oeuvres* (Paris 1895). E. GRUNEWALD and N. GUSSONE, *Das Bild der heiligen Hedwig in Mittelalter und Neuzeit* (Munich 1996). O. HABSBURG, *Die heilige Hedwig von Schlesien und unsere Zeit* (Vienna 1975). W. NIGG, *Hedwig von Schlesien* (Würzburg 1991); *Die Heiligen kommen wieder: Leitbilder christl. Existenz* (Freiburg im Breisgau 1973). *Podreczna encyklopedia Kościelna,* v.17 (Warsaw 1909) 261–262. G. PRESSLER, *Die Holzschnitte der deutschen Hedwigslegende (Breslau 1504)* (Hürtgenwald 1997). É. PROMNITZ, *Hedwig die Heilige, Gräfin von Andechs-Diessen* (Breslau 1926). A. ZAHORSKA, *Ilustrowane Żywoty Świetych Polskich* (Potulice 1937) 93–102. A. M. ZIMMERMANN, *Kalendarium Benedictinum: Die Heiligen und Seligen des Benediktinerorderns und seiner Zweige,* 4 v. (Metten 1933–38) 3:192–195. J. L. BAUDOT and L. CHAUSSIN, *Vies des saints et des bienheueux selon l'ordre du calendrier avec l'historique des fêtes,* ed. by The Benedictines of Paris, 12 v. (Paris 1935–56) 10:532–537. A. BUTLER, *The Lives of the Saints,* ed. H. THURSTON and D. ATTWATER, 4 v. (New York 1956) 4:124–125. M. BRARD, *Catholicisme* 5:559.

[L. SIEKANIEC]

JAEGEN, JEROME

German layman and mystical writer; b. Trier, Aug. 23, 1841; d. there, Jan. 26, 1919. In his youth he studied at Berlin and became an engineer. However, his long career in the business world was that of the director of a bank. He served also as deputy in the Prussian *Landtag* from 1899 until his retirement in 1906. Along with his business and political activities, he was very active in assisting various Catholic institutions and projects.

His writings on the spiritual life were the fruit of his own continual devotion and personal dedication to the Christian ideal and his experience of the high degrees of mystical union. He directed his writing largely to lay people and sought to refute the common assumption that the achicvement of Christian perfection is incompatible with an active life in the world. He saw perfection to consist in love of God and abandonment to the divine will and believed that mystical union is the harmonious conclusion of the achievement of Christian virtue. Furthermore, he warned against various delusions associated with mysticism, such as false visions, and held that ecstasy is not a necessary phenomenon in any stage of the mystical life. His works have been widely read and have gone through repeated editions. They include *Der Kampf um die Krone* (Dülmen 1883; also pub. as *Der Kampf um das höchste Gut,* Trier 1903) and *Das mystische Gnadenleben* (Trier 1911). The process for Jaegen's canonization was introduced in 1939.

St. Jadwiga, fragment of a carved and polychromed wood predella, c. 1492, in the church at Schweidnitz, Germany. (Marburg-Art Reference, Art Resource, NY)

Bibliography: J. JAEGEN, *Das mystische Gnadenleben,* ed. and annot. I. BACKES (Heidelberg 1949). E. MOSSMAIER, *Hieronymus Jaegen* (Paderborn 1959).

[J. C. WILLKE]

JAEGER, LORENZ

German Cardinal, archbishop, and ecumenist; b. Halle, Sept. 23, 1892; d. Paderborn, Apr. 2, 1975. An ordinary soldier during World War I, Jaeger was ordained to the priesthood in 1922. After 19 years in teaching and other pastoral ministries, he was ordained bishop of Paderborn in 1941. In the consistory of Feb. 22, 1965, he became a cardinal.

Especially interested in ecumenism, Cardinal Jaeger, along with Cardinal BEA, was influential in the establishment of the SECRETARIAT FOR PROMOTING CHRISTIAN UNITY. He was also a member of the Preparatory Commission for VATICAN COUNCIL II and a frequent intervener in conciliar discussions. Earlier (Jan. 18, 1957) in his own diocese, he founded the "Johann-Adam-Möhler-Institut für Konfessions and Diasporakunde" (the Johann Adam Möhler Institute), one of the world's foremost centers for ecumenical study, research, and publication. Its quarterly journal, *Catholica*, is one of the most authoritative in the Roman Catholic-Protestant (especially Lutheran and Calvanist) theological dialogue.

The institute's goals reflect Cardinal Jaeger's own interests and activities: scholarly research and description of the doctrine, worship, and life of those Christian churches separated from Rome, especially the Reformation Confessional Churches; the presentation of the Catholic faith in its fullness as the response to the questions posed by the Reformation; and the sharing of the results of these scholarly investigations with those engaged in other pastoral activity.

In addition to his episcopal and ecumenical activities, he was also a general spokesman for the German hierarchy on a wide range of other subjects, especially on pastoral care, on the status of women in civil and ecclesial society, on students, and on intellectuals. He played a significant role in the reconstruction of the German Church and nation after World War II. Jaeger's ecumenical outlook and insight are well illustrated in his pre-Vatican II *The Ecumenical Council, the Church and Christendom*, tr. A. V. Littledale (New York 1961) and his commentary on Vatican II's decree on ecumenism, *A Stand On Ecumenism: The Council's Decree*, tr. H. Graef (New York 1965).

[R. KRESS]

JAGIEŁŁO (WŁADYSŁAW II)

King of Poland and grand duke of Lithuania; b. *c.* 1350; d. Grodno, June 1, 1434. At his death (1377), Olgierd, the grand duke of Lithuania, left the supreme authority to his son Jagiełło. His power threatened from within by his convert cousin Witold and from without by hostile neighbors, Jagiełło accepted Polish plans to marry the young Jadwiga of Anjou, technically the "king" of Poland since Oct. 15, 1384. On Aug. 14, 1385 he signed a charter in which he promised, in order to receive Jadwiga as wife and the Polish crown, to convert to Catholicism along with the whole of Lithuania. He was baptized on Feb. 15, 1386 under the name of Władysław II. On February 18 he married Jadwiga, who gave up her original fiancé for the sake of bringing the whole nation to Catholicism. On March 4 he was crowned head of the kingdom of Poland that then included Lithuania and Ru-

thenia. Jagiełło returned to Lithuania in February 1387 to introduce the Catholic faith there officially and to see to the establishment of the bishopric of VILNA. Jadwiga died in 1399, but none of Jagiełło's three subsequent wives could obliterate her influence on Jagiełło. The next year, according to their plans, the University of Cracow was resuscitated and expanded. The TEUTONIC KNIGHTS challenged the sincerity of the Lithuanians' conversion and kept up their inroads, until finally on July 15, 1410, at the Battle of Grunwald, Jagiełło's forces broke the power and prestige of the order. The Polish kingdom gained much respect at the Council of CONSTANCE when the Poles arrived with Catholic delegates from hitherto pagan Lithuania and Samogitia, together with the Ruthenians headed by the metropolitan of Kiev. On Oct. 2, 1413 the Poles and Lithuanians signed the Union of Horodlo, which was uniquely and mystically Christian in that the elite of the two nations agreed to form a single, united family on the basis of the "Mystery of Charity," which the Polish nobility composing the document stressed as the fundamental element of public life. After Witold's death in 1430, relations between Poland and Lithuania deteriorated into a minor civil war. Jagiełło left two sons, Władysław III and Casimir, both of whom eventually came to the throne. Through the conversion of Lithuania, he was of outstanding service to the Church, and his reign saw Poland rise to the rank of a great power.

Bibliography: *Podręczna encyklopedia Kościelna*, v.17 (Warsaw 1909) 265–269. C. KELLOGG, *Jadwiga, Poland's Great Queen* (New York 1931). L. KOLANKOWSKI, *Polska Jagiellonów: Dzieje polityczne* (Lvov 1936). O. HALECKI, *A History of Poland* (3d ed. New York 1961). *The Cambridge History of Poland*, ed. W. F. REDDAWAY et al., 2 v. (Cambridge, Eng. 1941–50) 1:161, 195–234.

[L. SIEKANIEC]

JAINISM

Jainism is one of the religions born of the spiritual ferment that took place in India in the 6th century B.C. Its founder, Vardhamāna, called Mahāvīra (the Great Hero), a contemporary of the Buddha, was born *c.* 540 B.C. Like the Buddha he came of a princely family in the region of the Ganges valley and at 30 renounced his wife and family to lead the life of an ascetic. After 12 years he is said to have attained enlightenment or perfection (*kevala*) and to have become a "conqueror" (*jina*), from which his followers took the name of Jainism, the religion of the conquerors. At the beginning of his ascetic life Mahāvīra joined a group of ascetics called nirgranthas (free from bonds), who claimed that they had been founded by a certain Pārśva 250 years before. In the course of time Pārśva came to be regarded as the 23d Tīrthaṅkara (ford-maker) of the Jain religion and Mahāvīra as the 24th and last

Tīrthaṅkara, much as the Buddha came to be regarded as the last in a succession of Buddhas. Thus the Jain religion is considered to be of immemorial antiquity and in fact to be eternal.

Mahāvīra. He taught for 30 years in the region of the Ganges valley and was patronized by the same kings who patronized the Buddha. In the course of time he gained a large following, which he organized into a community of monks and lay followers. He died at 72 (*c.* 468 B.C.) of self-starvation, soon after the Buddha. He lived a life of extreme asceticism, going from place to place, begging his bread, and subjecting his body to every hardship. At first he wore only one garment, which he never changed, but after a short time he discarded even this and went about for the rest of his life completely naked. This custom also became the rule for his disciples and led in time to a marked division among them. For two centuries they remained a small community of monks and laymen. However, according to an ancient tradition, the first Mauryan emperor, Chandragupta (*c.* 317–293 B.C.), was a patron of Jainism and became a Jain monk at the end of his life.

At the end of Chandragupta's reign there occurred a famine, which led many of the Jain monks to leave the Ganges valley and migrate to the Deccan. This was the occasion of the great division among the Jains. The leader of the community that moved south, Bhadrabāhu, insisted on retaining the custom of complete nudity, but the community that remained in the north adopted a white garment, from which they came to be known as Sśvetāmbaras (white–clad); those who kept the ancient rule were known as Digambaras (space–clad). Unfortunately, as a result of this division, the sacred teachings of the Jains, which had been handed down by word of mouth until that time, were lost. It was said that Bhadrabāhu was the last to know them accurately. At his death an attempt was made to reconstruct the canon at a great council held by the Sśvetāmbaras at Pātaliputra, in which the ancient texts, known as *Pūrvas* (former texts), were replaced by 11 (originally 12) Angas or "sections." To these, other writings were added at a later date until the canon was finally completed at a council which was convened at Valabhī in Kāthiāwār sometime during the 5th century A.D.

Doctrine. Unlike Buddhism, Jainism underwent very little development in doctrine, and its basic teachings reflect the ideas of a very early period, probably that of Mahāvīra himself. Like Buddhism, Jainism is regarded by Hindus as one of the "unorthodox" (*nāstika*) doctrines and is atheistic in the sense that it gives no place to any God. It holds that the universe is eternal and is governed by a universal law. It is composed of a multi-

Adinath Temple, a large Jain temple in Ranakpur in northen India. (©Ric Ergenbright/CORBIS)

tude of souls (*jīvas*) that exist not only in living things but also in all the elements—earth, air, fire, and water. There is an infinite number of such souls in the universe, all of which are essentially equal, being by nature bright and pure, and enjoying perfect knowledge and bliss. Differences in souls are due to the adherence of matter, which is in its essence of a subtle nature, invisible to the human eye. It is this invisible matter that constitutes KARMA. Every action produces karma of some sort, although actions of a selfish nature produce more than others, and thus the soul by its actions becomes bound by matter and is involved in endless transmigration.

The purpose of life, according to Jain belief, is to rid the soul of this accumulation of karma and to prevent it from acquiring more, until it becomes perfectly purified and attains to liberation (*moksha*), after which it returns to its original state of pure knowledge and bliss. This purification of the soul can be accomplished only by means of rigid asceticism, i.e., by the restraint of all action, so that it is only monks who can be saved. The monks practiced fasting, even to the extent of starving themselves to death like Mahāvīra himself. They exposed themselves to the heat of the sun in summer and to the cold in winter. Nakedness was considered as essential to the abandonment of all worldly ties. Even in modern times Jainism remains extremely ascetic in character, and although nudity is no longer practiced as a rule even by the Digambaras, it is still regarded as a necessary step on the path to final release.

Monastic Life. The Jain monks took five vows, abjuring killing, stealing, lying, sexual intercourse, and property. However, it is the practice of nonviolence (*ahimsā*) that remains their most distinguishing characteristic. Every act of violence, even unintentional, is considered to cause an influx of karma. Eating meat was therefore forbidden to both monks and laymen. Even insect life might not be destroyed, so that a veil was used to cover the mouth lest living things in the air should enter it, and drinking water was carefully strained. The profession of agriculture was also forbidden, since it involved the destruction of plant life and of living things in the soil. As a result, the Jains have become a predominantly merchant community.

The strict rules of Jainism were to be followed only by the monks, but the lay followers were encouraged to observe them as far as possible and, if possible, to spend some time in a monastery. The Jains adopted religious customs of the Hindus—the rites of birth, marriage, and death—and worshipped the Tīrthaṅkaras in temples with offerings of flowers, fruit, and incense. Even some of the gods of the Hindus found their way into the temples of the Jains.

Cultural Significance. In spite of the archaic character of its doctrine, Jainism has survived to the present day. The Digambaras are found mostly in Mysore, where there is a famous temple at Śravana–Belgola with a statue of a naked Tīrthaṅkara 60 feet high. The Śśvetāmbaras are found in Gujarāt and Rājasthān, where they form a wealthy merchant community. There is no doubt that in the early centuries the Jains did much to spread the culture of the north in south India and were an influential community rivaling the Buddhists. One of their more attractive, and rather surprising, characteristics is that they took an active interest in secular literature and knowledge. Besides developing their own distinctive philosophy, they wrote treatises on politics and mathematics and produced some remarkable poets. But they are remembered especially for their preservation of ancient texts, both secular and religious, which they copied as an act of religious merit. Thus, in spite of the austerity of their doctrine, they have preserved a tradition of humanism, and it should not be forgotten that it was the example of

holy Jain monks in his native Gujarāt that was one of the major influences on Mahatma Gandhi's philosophy of non–violence.

See Also: HINDUISM.

Bibliography: C. RÉGAMEY, in F. KÖNIG, ed. *Christus und die Religionen der Erde: Handbuch der Religionsgeschichte,* 3 v. (2d ed. Vienna 1961) 3:209–220. H. JACOBI, in J. HASTINGS, ed., *Encyclopedia of Religion and Ethics,* 13 v. (Edinburgh 1908–27) 7:465–474. J. FINEGAN, *The Archeology of World Religions* (Princeton 1952) 182–233. H. VON GLASENAPP, *Der Jainismus* (Kultur und Weltanschauung 1; Berlin 1925). W. T. DE BARY, ed., *Sources of Indian Tradition* (Records of Civilization: Sources and Studies 56; New York 1958) A. L. BASHAM, *The Wonder That Was India: A Survey of the Culture of the Indian Sub–Continent before the Coming of the Muslims* (London 1954). H. JACOBI, tr., *Guina Sûtras* (Sacred Books of the East, v.22 and 45; Oxford 1884–95). J. JAINĪ, *Outlines of Jainism,* ed. F. W. THOMAS (London 1940).

[B. GRIFFITHS]

JAMAICA, THE CATHOLIC CHURCH IN

Located in the Caribbean Sea, south of Cuba, the West Indian island of Jamaica is a mountainous land edged by a narrow coastal plain. Its highest point, Blue Mt. Peak, located at the island's east stands at 7,388 ft. The climate is tropical, ranging to more temperate in the island's interior, and hurricanes are commonplace from July to November. Natural resources include bauxite, gypsum and limestone, while agricultural crops consist of sugarcane, banana, coffee, citrus fruits and vegetables.

A Spanish possession until the mid-17th century, Jamaica was under the control of the British as a colony until 1958. A flourishing slave trade existed at Port Royal until an earthquake demolished that city; Kingston became the capital and center for commerce in 1692. In 1958 Jamaica became a territory of the West Indies Federation and was granted independence four years later as part of the British Commonwealth. Ethnically, 90 percent of Jamaicans are of African heritage, with small groups of East Indians, Chinese and Europeans.

Early History. The region was originally inhabited by the Sub-Tainos, or Arawak people, aborigines who migrated from northern Venezuela by A.D. 700. As was the case with so many native cultures, these people would be all but exterminated with the introduction of European diseases, alcohol and violence. On May 5, 1494, Christopher Columbus anchored at St. Ann's Bay on his way to what is now known as Rio Bueno, and named the island Santiago. Mass was probably first celebrated by Columbus's chaplain, a Mercedarian priest, at Puerto Bueno between May 6 and May 9, 1494. In November of 1509,

Spanish colonization began with the founding of New Seville. Although it is probable that a missionary accompanied the first colonizers, it is certain that Franciscans were in Jamaica by 1512, establishing themselves in New Seville and later in Santiago de la Vega, where they built a monastery and a church dedicated to St. James. By 1514 colonists numbered 500. The *repartimiento* system was instituted by royal decree on July 26, 1515. Christian influence spread along the coast wherever Spaniards settled to carve out plantations or cattle ranches. Too poor to support a bishop, Jamaica was given an abbot *nullius* diocesis as ordinary with episcopal jurisdiction, suffragan to the archbishop of Santo Domingo and later to the bishop of Cuba.

New Seville remained the capital until 1534, when it was moved to the south side of the island and renamed Santiago de la Vega (now Spanish Town). Dominican missionaries, under the leadership of Miguel Ramírez, OP (1527–35), constructed a church under the patronage of Our Lady of Perpetual Help and a monastery dedicated to St. Dominic in Santiago de la Vega sometime after 1534. Franciscans and Dominicans labored there until British forces captured Jamaica on May 10, 1655.

From the advent of Cromwellian forces in 1655 to James II, Jamaica became a base for pirates; slaves were imported from Africa to work the flourishing sugar cane plantations and the Church was proscribed. James II appointed Thomas Churchill as chaplain to his majesty's subjects. Churchill arrived in January of 1687 (O.S.; 1688 N.S.), remained until August and established four parishes, out of which two are known: Spanish Town and Port Royal. During Churchill's pastorate the question of jurisdiction was raised by James Castillo, a Spanish layman, who claimed that Churchill had no faculties to work in Jamaica because ecclesiastically the island was still under the bishop of Cuba. This controversy terminated upon the accession to the English throne of William and Mary, when again the Church was proscribed.

Revival of Catholicism. In 1792 Spanish merchants residing in Kingston petitioned the government for a priest. Their petition was granted and the vicar apostolic of the London District, under whose jurisdiction the colony fell, sent Anthony Quigly, a Recollect. Quigly served in Kingston among the resident Spaniards and a few English Catholics, and in 1793 French refugees from Haiti augmented the tiny congregation. Upon Quigly's death in 1799 William LeCun, OP, a Haitian refugee, became pastor. At LeCun's death in 1807, the congregation was left without a single priest in all of Jamaica. Don Carlos Esteiro, a layman, persuaded Augustinian missionary Juan Jacinto Rodriquez de Araújo to emigrate from Veracruz, Mexico, whereupon he acted as pastor from 1808

Capital: Kingston.
Size: 4,471 sq. miles.
Population: 2,652,685 in 2000.
Languages: English, Creole.
Religions: 114,065 Catholics (4.3%), 4,200 Muslims (.1%), 1,618,140 Protestants (61%), 8,000 Hindus (.3%), 908,280 practice indigenous faiths or are involved in spiritual cults.
Archdiocese: Kingston, with suffragans Mandeville and Montego Bay.

to 1824. In 1820 Benito Fernández, OFM, a refugee from New Granada, sought asylum in Jamaica and, when Araújo departed for Lisbon in 1824, he was chosen pastor. In order to remain in the colony, Fernández was granted release from his religious vows in August of 1828.

On Jan. 10, 1837, Jamaica, which had by now been transferred from London to the jurisdiction of Trinidad, was raised to the status of a separate vicariate and Fernández was appointed the first vicar apostolic, with his area of influence comprising of Jamaica, British Honduras and the Bahamas. In 1838, during Fernández' pastorate, slavery was finally abolished from the island, allowing many Africans who had fled to the hills to enter Jamaican society. Unsatisfactory emigré priests, one of whom eventually created a schism, led Fernández to petition the Holy See for religious missionaries. Two Jesuits, William Cotham, an Englishman, and James E. Dupeyron, a Frenchman, arrived in December of 1837. Upon Fernández' death, Dupeyron became vicar apostolic, and the colony became a mission of the English Province of the Society of Jesus. For 22 years Dupeyron visited Catholics scattered throughout the island several times a year. Previous to this the Church had confined her activity to the Kingston area owing to a scarcity of priests.

In 1861 J. Sidney Woollett, SJ, replaced Dupeyron as missionary to the interior and in 1870 he acquired a residence near Montego Bay. Woollett served the Catholics of the interior for 33 years. Three other well-known missionaries labored in Jamaica at this time: Joseph Dupont, in whose memory a monument was erected in Kingston's public square (the Parade), in appreciation of 40 years of service to the needy of every creed; Frederick Hathaway, SJ, a convert who spent much of his missionary life teaching native children the elements of reading and writing; and Manuel Ignacio El Santa Cruz y Loydi, a secular priest of Carlist War fame, who spent 14 years in the difficult missions of the mountains. Three American missionaries were also notable: Joseph F. Ford, SJ, who pioneered in the rural areas; M. Oliver Semmes, SJ, whose work among the needy for more than 30 years identified the Church with the poor; and Leo T. Butler, SJ, who worked for 40 years in the field of education and in the conversion of the Chinese.

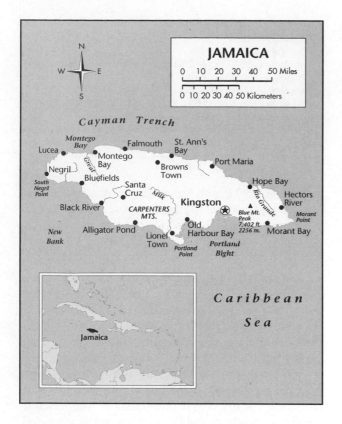

The Modern Church. On Feb. 29, 1956, the vicariate of Jamaica became the diocese of Kingston, and Vicar Apostolic John J. McEleney, SJ, became the first bishop. At this point the Church became involved with a number of social programs. A diocesan seminary, with excellent courses in the humanities and philosophy, was opened to foster vocations among native Jamaicans. Charitable Institutions included "Alpha," named for the Kingston estate where Jessie Ripoll opened an orphanage in 1880. Beginning with only one child, by the mid-20th century this institution was home to over 400 children and was staffed by the Sisters of Mercy. The St. Vincent de Paul society, established in 1904, funded the Ozanam Home for the Aged. The Holy Trinity Cathedral Mens' Sodality began the island's first credit union in 1941, and the movement quickly spread to hundreds of credit unions, which built on the solid foundation of an intensive educational program in the principles and technique of operation. Kingston was made an archdiocese in 1967.

Jamaica remained an English possession until Aug. 6, 1962, when it became independent within the framework of the Commonwealth of Nations. Unfortunately, the region's economy suffered under the new socialist government, sparking violence as the tourist traffic it relied on lessened. The 1980s ushered in a conservative government, but social instability continued. By the 1990s the island's continued economic woes sparked out-

breaks of violence, particularly during the 1994 elections. The continued violence and corruption prompted Church leaders to speak out against government economic policies that contained cutbacks in social services. The Church also attempted to increase food production by encouraging the use of government land for agriculture. Pope John Paul II visited the island in 1993.

Into the 21st Century. By 2000 there were 79 parishes tended by 55 diocesan and 45 religious priests. Other religious included approximately 12 brothers and 190 sisters, many of whom administered the island's 50 primary and 20 secondary schools. The Church remained one of several minority churches in a predominately Protestant country that featured a proliferation of small sects. Relations among all faiths were amicable. In 1999 Jamaica's bishops held a day of repentance on October 17, to publicly apologize for the Church's toleration of slavery during the 16th and 17th century.

Bibliography: F. MORALES PADRON, *Jamaica española* (Seville 1952). *Catholic Directory of the British Caribbean* (Kingston, Jamaica 1958–).

[F. J. OSBORNE/EDS.]

JAMES (SON OF ALPHAEUS), ST.

One of the 12 Apostles. In all four lists of the Apostles (Mt 10.3; Mk 3.18; Lk 6.15; and Acts 1.13) he is mentioned in ninth place, before Thaddeus in Matthew and Mark, before Simon in Luke and Acts. An ancient tradition has identified this James with James the Less of Mk 15.40; 16.1; Mt 27.56; Lk 24.10. Thus the title ὁ μικρός (the less; literally, the little one) came to be transferred to James of Alphaeus. It should be noted that the expression ὁ μικρός refers either to size or to age rather than to relative importance.

Tradition has also continued the process of identification by making "Mary [the mother] of James" the same as "Mary [the wife] of Cleopas" in Jn 19.25. The difficulty arising from the identification of Alphaeus and Cleopas is ordinarily answered by saying that they are equivalents of the same Aramaic name or that they are simply two names belonging to the same person. In this case James of Alphaeus would be James the brother (i.e., relative) of the Lord, for Mary of Clopas is called the sister (relative) of Mary the mother of Jesus in Jn 19.25. This series of identifications has remained the more widespread opinion among Catholics.

However, a number of recent scholars prefer to stress the fact that the New Testament maintains a distinction between the Apostles and the brethren of the Lord (Mk 6.3; Mt 13.55). James the brother of the Lord is mentioned in Gal 1.19 and is to be identified with James of Jerusalem (Acts 12.17; 15.13; 21.18; Gal 2.9, 12; 1 Cor 15.7). According to the Gospels, the TWELVE had already been chosen when Jesus' brethren manifested their unbelief (Mk 3.21; Jn 7.3); in Mk 6.3 the latter were still living in Nazareth. In Acts 1.14 and 1 Cor 15.7 a distinction is drawn between the Twelve and the brethren.

The passage in Gal 2.9, where Paul lists "James and Cephas and John" as pillars of the Church, can be understood in the light of Gal 1.19; the Greek εἰ μή, which the Vulgate translates as nisi, can have also the adversative meaning of "but only." Given the position of James of Jerusalem in the early Church, he would not have had to be an Apostle in order to be considered a "pillar."

Both Flavius Josephus (Ant. 20.9.1) and Hegesippus (in Eusebius, Ecclesiastical History 2.23) tell of the martyrdom of James of Jerusalem, and thus perhaps of James of Alphaeus. According to Josephus he was stoned to death in A.D. 62; according to Hegesippus he was cast from the pinnacle of the Temple, c. A.D. 66, and when the fall did not kill him, he was clubbed to death. The canonical Epistle of James is to be attributed to James the brother of the Lord, whether or not he is identified with James of Alphaeus.

In the Byzantine rite, James of Jerusalem and James of Alphaeus have separate feasts: October 23 and 9 respectively. In the Roman rite they have long (but not always) been identified; the feast of St. James (along with St. Philip) occurs on May 1. It is common to both the Gelasian and the Gregorian Sacramentaries and can be traced back to c. A.D. 563. In ecclesiastical art St. James is represented with a club or a heavy staff, the instrument of his martyrdom.

Bibliography: H. LECLERCQ, Dictionnaire d'archéologie chrétienne et de liturgie. ed. F. CABROL, H. LECLERCQ and H. I. MARROU (Paris 1907–53) 7.2:2109–16. J. BONSIRVEN, Dictionnaire de la Bible, suppl. ed. L. PIROT, et al. (Paris 1928–) 4:783–795. F. MAIER, "Zur Apostolizität des Jakobus und Judas," Biblische Zeitschrift 4 (1906) 164–191, 255–266. A. MALVY, "S. Jacques de Jérusalem était-il un des douze?" Recherches de science religieuse 9 (1918) 122–131. F. HAASE, "Apostel und Evangelisten in den orientalischen Überlieferungen," Neutestamentliche Abhandlungen 9 (1922) 267–271. S. LYONNET, "Témoignages de S. Jean Chrysostome et de S. Jérome sur Jacques le frère du Seigneur," Recherches de science religieuse 29 (1939) 335–351. L. CERFAUX, La Communauté apostolique (3d ed. Paris 1956) 90–99. A. CHARUE, Les Épîtres catholiques in La Sainte Bible, ed. L. PIROT and A. CLAMER, 12 v. (Paris 1935–61) 12:381–392.

[J. A. LEFRANÇOIS]

JAMES (SON OF ZEBEDEE), ST.

One of the 12 Apostles and the brother of the Apostle John (Mt 10.3; Mk 3.18; Lk 6.15; Acts 1.13; 12.2). His Greek name, Ἰάκωβος, represents the Hebrew ya'ăqōb (Jacob). Originally he was a fisherman of Galilee, and the narrative of his and John's call to the apostleship indicates that the family must have been fairly well-to-do when it mentions hired men working along with them (Mt 4.21; Mk 1.19–20; Lk 5.10). James of Zebedee is commonly called "the Greater," as opposed to James of Alphaeus, traditionally known as James the Less, but the New Testament does not give him this title. [See JAMES (SON OF ALPHAEUS), ST.] By comparing Mt 27.56 with Mk 15.40 it is deduced that the mother of James and John was Salome (Mt 20.20–21). In Mk 3.17 these two Apostles are given the name Boanerges (Βοανηργές), which the same verse translates as "sons of thunder." Whatever its precise meaning, the translation given may be explained by the impetuosity shown by these two brothers toward a certain Samaritan town (Lk 9.54). Along with Peter and John, James was a member of the special group of three mentioned in Mk 5.37; 13.3; Mt 17.1; 26.37. He was the first of the Apostles to die for Christ, being beheaded under Herod Agrippa in 44 (Acts 12. 1–2).

This might indicate that James was exceptionally active in Jerusalem. Tradition places James's journey to Spain sometime between the death of Jesus and the martyrdom of James, but the reality of such a visit is opposed to St. Paul's words in Rom 15.20–24. The apocryphal Greek Acts of James cannot be traced back earlier than the eighth century. The genuineness of the relics at SANTIAGO DE COMPOSTELA, his famous shrine in Spain, is seriously disputed despite the fact that Pope Leo XIII referred to them as authentic in his bull Omnipotens Deus in 1884. In ecclesiastical art he is ordinarily represented carrying a pilgrim's bell.

Feast: July 25 (Roman rite); April 30 (Byzantine rite).

Bibliography: V. ERMONI, Dictionnaire de la Bible, ed. F. VIGOUROUX (Paris 1895–1912) 3.2:1082–84. H. LECLERCQ, Dictionnaire d'archéologie chrétienne et de liturgie. ed. F. CABROL, H. LECLERCQ and H. I. MARROU (Paris 1907–53) 5.1:412–417; 7.2:2089–2109. A. WIKENHAUSER, Lexikon für Theologie und Kirche, ed. J. HOFER and K. RAHNER (Freiberg 1957–65) 5:833–834. F. HAASE, Apostel und Evangelisten in den orientalischen Ueberlieferungen (Neutestamentliche Abhandlungen 9; Münster 1922). P. JOÜON, "Notes de philologie évangélique," Recherches de science religieuse 15 (1925) 438–441.

[J. A. LEFRANÇOIS]

JAMES, EPISTLE OF

Place in the Canon. The epistle of James is one of a number of writings from the first two centuries attributed to James, the brother of Jesus. See also the Protevan-

Manuscript page, beginning of Epistle of St. James, written in North of France ca. 1200.

gelium of James and the Nag Hammadi *Apocryphon of James*, the first and second *Apocalypse of James*. Because of the popularity of the name in the first century, a few modern scholars questions this assumption. Recognition of authorship by James underlies the acceptance of the epistle into the canon. Evidence of its use is late and ambiguous. The first probable quotation (Jas 2.23) is by Irenaeus (AH 4.16.2) around A.D. 180. Circa 250 ORIGEN quotes from the epistle as if from scripture (*Commentary on John* fragment 6). Eusebius (HE 2.23.24–25) refers to James as the first of the General (Catholic) epistles, recognizing its questionable authenticity because "few of the ancients quote it." It is not included in the canonical list of the Council of NICAEA in 325. Nevertheless, Athenasius lists it amongst canonical works in his 39th Festal letter (A.D. 367). His judgement was adopted in the West by Jerome and Augustine and from that time its canonical place was secure.

Date and Authorship. James' canonical status was tied to its recognition as an epistle of the brother of the

Lord. This position is defended by modern commentators (J. B. Mayor; J. B. Adamson; R. Bauckham) who argue that it emanates from the Jerusalem church before the death of James in A.D. 62. Other scholars recognise a duality in the epistle. There is evidence of a Palestinian socio-economic context (the problem of poverty and wealth) and significant contact with the teaching of Jesus in the sermon on the mount (Mt 5–7). The epistle also has an orientation to the diaspora (1.1) and a somewhat more polished use of Greek than might be expected from James and his Jewish mission in Jerusalem. This suggests the epistle was developed on the basis of tradition from James by a Jewish believer in the diaspora some time after the destruction of Jerusalem (R. P. Martin; P. Davids; J. Painter). A third group of scholars sees the epistle as pseudonymous and coming from the late first, or second century. Though without connection to James, the epistle was perhaps based on a earlier Palestinian tradition (M. Dibelius). In time the epistle came to be understood as addressed to the church in every place by James. In this way it entered the canon.

James and Jesus. Studies have shown a relationship between James and the teaching of Jesus through tradition unique to Mattthew (M) and shared with Luke in the form found in Matthew (Q^M), especially in the sermon on the mount. The teaching about the benevolence of God in creation (Mt 5.45; 6.26–32 and Jas 1.17) is linked to the demand for greater righteousness in law observance (Mt 5.17–48 and Jas 1.25; 2.8–12; 4.11). Both Matthew and James show a concentration on the inner moral demand of the law. The unique connection between the prohibition of oaths in Jas 5.12 and Mt 5.33–37 provides a basis for recognising more links between the teaching of Jesus in Matthew and the ethical teaching of James.

James and Paul. The teaching about faith and works in Jas 2.14–26 resonates with the theme in Paul, especially in Rom 3–4. James' use of Gn 15.6 (in 2.23) seems to presuppose its use by Paul (Rom 4.3, 9, 22; Gal 3.6). Paul exploits the wording of Genesis which says that Abraham *believed* God, and it was reckoned to him for righteousness. James makes no use of the text, arguing that a person is justified by works as well as faith, not *by faith only* (2.24), denying the efficacy of faith *apart from works* (2.18, 26). Paul argues that a person is justified by faith *apart from works* of the law (Rom 3.28; 4.6). While Paul recognises the necessity of faith working through love, he rejects the notion that a person is justified by any work. The argument of James is directed against the language of Paul, but without actually addressing Paul's point of view. James, affirming the graciousness of God in creation (1.17), does not feature the distinctive nature of grace in justification that is found in Paul.

Jewish Wisdom and Paranesis. It is a mistake to see James as a mere moralist. His call to moral action arises from his understanding of God who is without partiality. Love for ones neighbour has a cutting edge in relation to the rich and on behalf of the poor (Jas 2.5). In James' Jewish wisdom, tradition overlaps with Hellenistic paranesis. A major theme concerns control of the tongue, a theme common in Jewish wisdom (Jas 1.26; 3.5–8; Ps 34.13; 39.1). Affirming God's goodness (1.16–18), James attributes sin to human passion (1.12–15).

Bibliography: J. B. ADAMSON, *James: The Man and His Message* (Grand Rapids 1989). W. R. BAKER, *Personal Speech: Ethics in the Epistle of James* (Wissenschaftliche Untersuchungen zum Neuen Testament 2/68; Tübingen 1995). R. BAUCKHAM, *James* (London 1999). M. DIBELIUS, *A Commentary on the Epistle of James,* rev. H. GREEVEN, tr. M. A. WILLIAMS, ed. H. KÖSTER (Philadelphia 1976). J. H. ELLIOTT, "The Epistle of James in Rhetorical and Social Scientific Perspective: Holiness—Wholeness and Patterns of Replication," *Biblical Theology Bulletin* 23 (1993) 71–81. D. E. GOWAN, "Wisdom and Endurance in James," *Horizons in Biblical Theology* 15 (1993) 145–53. P. J. HARTIN, *James and the Q Sayings of Jesus* (Sheffield 1991). L. T. JOHNSON, *The Letter of James* (New York 1995). "The Letter of James" in *New Interpreters Bible,* v. 12 (Nashville 1998) 177–225. R. P. MARTIN, *James* (Waco 1988). J. PAINTER, *Just James: The Brother of Jesus in History and Tradition* (Colombia, SC 1997), especially 234–269. W. H. WACHOB, *The Voice of Jesus in the Social Rhetoric of James* (Cambridge, Eng. 2000).

[J. PAINTER]

JAMES, WILLIAM

American psychologist and philosopher; b. New York, N.Y., Jan. 11, 1842; d. Chocorua, N.Y., Aug. 26, 1910. He was the oldest of five children—his brother Henry, the novelist, was the most celebrated. His father was independently wealthy, and James's early education was provided by numerous private schools in America and Europe. His higher formal education began in 1861 at the Lawrence Scientific School. Two years later he entered the Harvard Medical School, and he received his medical degree in 1869. For the next several years, he served as an instructor in anatomy and physiology at Harvard. In 1876 he was attracted to the study of psychology and shortly thereafter was appointed assistant professor of psychology. By 1880 his interests had shifted to philosophy; in 1885 he was appointed professor of philosophy at Harvard, a position he held until his retirement in 1907.

Teaching. James, an original thinker and a brilliant writer, exerted a striking influence on contemporary philosophy as a whole. His interest in psychology resulted in his adoption of radical empiricism, which in turn led to PRAGMATISM and his characteristic analysis of religious experience.

William James. (Archive Photos)

Psychology. In *The Principles of Psychology* (2 v. New York 1890), James argued that CONSCIOUSNESS is a stream, rather than a set of states, of human "impressions," or of isolated sensations. In a word, he rejected the older mechanical and associationist psychology for a dynamic and functional psychology; with this he also abandoned the traditional dualism of mind and body, of "thought and thing." Mind as substance he rejected for the notion of mind or consciousness as activity, regarding such activity as a means of adaptation to the environment by the individual.

Radical Empiricism. This stems partly from revolutionary changes in psychology, partly from James's reaction to traditional EMPIRICISM, particularly its determinism. James was influenced by the argument of C. S. PEIRCE that experience is not necessarily continuous, that a genuine empiricism may reveal novelties in a continuously changing process. He was moved also by C. B. Renouvier's argument that freedom is revealed in empiricism. In *The Will to Believe* (New York 1897), James argued that the question of freedom is not to be decided on intellectual grounds, but by man's actions and beliefs and by what difference his decision will mean to him as an individual. James's belief in an empiricism divorced from much of its intellectual background was reinforced by the influence of H. BERGSON, particularly by the latter's contention that experience is one and that any attempt to conceptualize it distorts its true meaning. Finally, James rejected the monism of IDEALISM with its determinism and its conception of a "block universe" devoid of all novelty and chance. He held that external relations are real because they are experienced relations, relations that connect human experiences. F. H. Bradley's defense of the intellectualistic logic of internal relations he regarded as weird. In consequence, he vindicated a pluralistic universe, that "concatenated unity," which he maintained is rooted in a radical empiricism than in logic (*A Pluralistic Universe,* New York 1909).

Pragmatism. Although he attacked an excessive intellectualism, James did not deny the value of intellectual activity provided it was correctly guided. Conceptualization often falsifies reality, but concepts and ideas can be highly useful in the practical sense when they are grounded upon experience. James rejected both the correspondence and coherence theories of TRUTH and held that truth was pragmatic, that the true is that which is the practical and the best (*Pragmatism,* New York 1907). Truth is utilitarian; man's ideas are true insofar as they are useful and practical in resolving his problems. For James, truth is something relative, expedient, useful, and practical. James not only applied these criteria of truth to metaphysical problems, but he was also greatly concerned to show how such a pragmatic conception of truth could be used to justify religious ideas and confirm religious experience. For James, a religious belief is to be judged not on intellectual grounds but on the concrete differences it makes in the life of the individual. Modifying Pascal's wager, he declared there is no problem of an intellectual proof for the existence of God. the problem for the individual is this: if the question of God's existence is a real possibility to him, a "live hypothesis," as James termed it, then it is necessary for him to go beyond any purely intellectual evidence and decide for himself whether he should believe in God. He cannot suspend judgment; agnosticism is untenable, for it means one acts as though God does not exist. The issue is one of an existential decision, rather than a summing up of evidence, which James held can never be completely summed up.

Religious Experience. In *The Varieties of Religious Experience* (New York 1902), James was convinced that there is an empiricial confirmation for the religious hypothesis. The religious experience and the needs of the individual demand an immediate answer to the question of God's existence. Such a requirement can be met only by a decision that stems from the "passional nature" of the individual—a decision that comes from the heart than the intellect. James's own views on religion were undoubtedly influenced by his father, who was extremely critical of the clergy but who in later life was strongly attracted to Swedenborgianism. Although James rejected all traditional religious beliefs, he felt that man's religious experience brought him in relation to a higher spiritual aspect of the universe. Such a higher or wider reality is a "something" greater than man. It may be identified with a finite God.

Influence and Critique. Although Peirce was the true founder of pragmatism, the name has been most often associated with James, for it was he who gave currency and popularity to many of its basic features and particularly to his own version of pragmatic truth. The influence of James was partly because of his person—he was a brilliant teacher and lecturer—and partly because his philosophy seemed to reflect so well the American culture and its tendency to determine truth and values by an appeal to the practical and the experiential. The philosophy of James had a considerable vogue down to the 1930s, but has since then been in large part absorbed by LOGICAL POSITIVISM and naturalism. As a philosophy its most serious deficiencies are its anti-intellectualism, its RELATIVISM, its appeal to the expedient in ethics, and its justification of religious belief solely upon the value of such beliefs to the individual.

See Also: RELIGION, PHILOSOPHY OF; VOLUNTARISM.

Bibliography: A. STOPPER, *Enciclopedia filosofica,* 4 v. (Venice- Rome 1957) 2:1604–1611. R. B. PERRY, *The Thought and Character of William James,* 2 v. (Boston 1935). P. R. ANDERSON and M. H. FISCH, *Philosophy in America from the Puritans to James* (New York 1939). B. BLANSHARD and H. W. SCHNEIDER, eds., *In Commemoration of William James, 1842–1942* (New York 1942). M. C. OTTO et al., *William James, the Man and the Thinker* (Madison 1942). H. V. KNOX, *The Philosophy of William James* (New York 1914).

[J. A. MOURANT]

JAMES II, KING OF ARAGON

Reigned 1291 to Nov. 2, 1327, king also of Sicily from 1286; b. 1267; d. Barcelona. James II "the Just" continued the expansionist policies of his predecessors (James I of Aragon, Peter III of Aragon). He invaded Castile, meanwhile annexing much of its Kingdom of Murcia (1291–1301); he seized Gibraltar briefly during a crusade against Granada (1309); conquered Sardinia against Pisan-Genoese resistance (1323–24); connived at the Catalan Company's seizure of Byzantine territory;

held Moslem Tunis, Bugia, and Tlemecen as tributaries; and secured a protectorate over Christians in the Holy Land. A poet and literary patron, he also founded the University of Lérida (1300), replaced the suppressed TEMPLARS with his KNIGHTS OF MONTESA (1317), and gained a specifically ''Aragonese'' metropolitanate. After surrendering Sicily to Anjou-papacy disposition (Anagni treaty, 1295), he connived at its retention by his brother Frederick III. Pope BONIFACE VIII slyly appointed James captain general of the Church, using as bait Corsica and Sardinia. But Ghibelline champion James merely waged a pseudowar against GUELF champion Frederick, thus marking the last phase of the Sicilian Vespers War (1297–1302).

Bibliography: *The Chronicle of Muntaner,* tr. A. GOODENOUGH, 2 v. (London 1920–1921). J. E. MARTÍNEZ FERRANDO, *Jaime II de Aragón, su vida familiar,* 2 v. (Barcelona 1948); *Els descendents de Pere el Gran* (Barcelona 1954). R. I. BURNS, ''The Catalan Company and the European Powers,'' *Speculum* 29 (1954) 751–771. V. SALAVERT Y ROCA, *Cerdeña y la expansión mediterránea de la Corona de Aragón, 1297–1314,* 2 v. (Madrid 1956). S. RUNCIMAN, *The Sicilian Vespers* (Cambridge, Eng. 1958).

[R. I. BURNS]

JAMES I, KING OF ENGLAND

Reigned March 24, 1603 to March 27, 1625, of the royal house of Stuart, son of MARY STUART, QUEEN OF SCOTS, and her second husband, Henry, Lord Darnley; b. Edinburgh Castle, June 19, 1556; d. Theobalds, England. As a result of his Catholic mother's enforced abdication and imprisonment in England, he was crowned James VI of Scotland while still a child, on July 29, 1567. During his minority James was a pawn trapped in the power struggle among the Scottish nobility. He was raised a Presbyterian, and his education was particularly entrusted to George Buchanan, the noted Scottish humanist. James proved to be a precocious scholar and rapidly developed a command of Latin, French, and English. In constant personal danger, James was forced to thread a difficult course among various rival groups. He maintained a precarious balance between English, French, Catholic, and Presbyterian factions. James protested to Queen ELIZABETH I when his mother was sentenced to death, but the execution of Mary in 1587 caused him no personal loss, for he then became the logical heir to the throne of England. On Aug. 20, 1589, James married Anne, second daughter of Frederick II of Denmark. She later proved an embarrassment to James because of her conversion to Catholicism.

Upon the death of Elizabeth, James was proclaimed King of England. Here he found himself caught in a struggle between Anglican, Puritan, and Catholic fac-

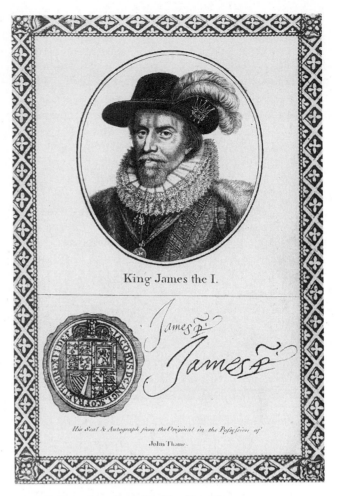

King James the I.

His Seal & Autograph from the Original in the Possession of John Thane.

James I, King of England. (Archive Photos)

tions. James became a firm supporter of the Church of England and fought off all attempts by the Puritans to purge it of popish practices. He also tended to take a more tolerant attitude toward Catholicism. He felt sympathy toward the Catholic laity, but remained hostile toward the clergy, especially the Jesuits. This sympathy, plus his correspondence with the papacy, led English Catholics to believe that he would grant toleration. His failure to act resulted in a conspiracy to blow up Parliament. The Gunpowder Plot was discovered in November 1605. James retaliated with harsh action against the Catholic clergy and complicated his position with his English subjects and with the papacy by his advocacy of divine right kingship. This involved him in a pamphlet war with Cardinal Robert BELLARMINE and developed in Parliament a suspicion of all his motives and actions that lasted throughout his reign. The divine right theory led him into conflict with his chief justice, the great advocate of the common law, Sir Edward Coke. His conflicts with Parliament were accentuated by his inability to judge men. James allowed himself to be guided by incompetent and self-seeking fa-

James II, King of England.

vorites, such as Robert Carr, Earl of Somerset, and George Villiers, Duke of Buckingham.

On the whole James pursued a policy of peace and sought the friendship of Spain, which only antagonized his Protestant subjects. In his later years James gave himself up to personal comforts and an excessive fondness for his favorite Buckingham.

Bibliography: J. P. KENYON, *Stuart England* (Hammondsworth, Eng. 1985). C. RUSSELL, *Parliaments and English Politics, 1621–1629* (Oxford 1979). B. COWARD, *The Stuart Age* (London 1980). D. HIRST, *Authority and Conflict: England 1603–1658* (London 1986). M. LEE, *Great Britain's Solomon: James I and VI in His Three Kingdoms* (Urbana Ill. 1990). D. N. BERGERSON, *Royal Family, Royal Lovers: King James of England and Scotland* (Columbia Mo. 1991).

[A. M. SCHLEICH]

JAMES II, KING OF ENGLAND

B. London, Oct. 14, 1633; d. St. Germain, France, Sept. 6, 1701. James, second son of Charles I and the French princess Henrietta Maria, was baptized a Protestant; he spent most of the Civil War in Oxford as duke of york. The fall of Oxford in 1646 placed him in the hands of the parliamentary forces, from which he escaped to France in April 1648. He served with distinction and bravery in the French army under Turenne and later in the Spanish army. When the Restoration placed his brother Charles II on the English throne, James returned to England with him.

Two daughters, Mary and Anne, were born of his marriage to Anne Hyde; both were brought up Protestants. Despite valuable service as lord admiral, James's popularity declined rapidly because of his Catholic leanings. His unannounced but rumored conversion to Catholicism sometime after 1668, followed by his marriage to a Catholic, Mary of Modena, in 1672, offended the religious sensibilities of the English people. Charles's attempt to ameliorate the position of Catholics in 1672 was successfully opposed by Parliament, which followed up its advantage with passage of the Test Act of 1673, barring Catholics from positions of trust and specifically forcing James to retire from all his offices. In the aftermath of the fictional Popish Plot of Titus Oates, anti-Catholicism flared up, and resulted in serious attempts to exclude James from the line of succession by law. These attempts were thwarted only by Charles's skillful maneuvering. The last years of his reign were marked by a vigorous royal counterattack that assured James's peaceful accession at Charles's death (Feb. 6, 1685).

The primary issue of the reign of James II was religion, but with pronounced constitutional overtones. James's attempts to obtain equality for his fellow Catholics and ultimately to effect the conversion of England led Protestants to fear for their religious liberty. Through his dispensing power he permitted Catholics to serve in offices forbidden them by law. Through his supremacy in the Church he attempted to soften Anglican hostility toward Catholicism and to intrude those with Catholic sympathies into ecclesiastical offices. He attempted also to arrange the election to Parliament of those who would vote with him on the religious issue. Anglicans soon began to realize that the privileged position of their Church was in danger. In addition, many Dissenters, to whom freedom of public worship was offered in 1687, were suspicious of James's motives and ultimate intentions. His policies were opposed also by moderate Catholics who feared that anything more than mere toleration was foredoomed and would only make their position worse.

Rejecting the counsel of moderation, he surrounded himself with extremists like the Jesuit Edward Petre and time-servers like the Earl of Sunderland. Thus deprived of realistic advice, he maneuvered himself into a position where opponents of his religious, political, and foreign policies were able to join forces to overthrow him.

The early summer of 1688 brought three events that, taken together, meant the end for James. He completed the alienation of the traditionally royalist Church of England by ordering the reading in all parishes of the second Declaration of Indulgence, which suspended the penal laws and the Test Acts. Seven bishops who petitioned the crown on the point were tried and acquitted. At the same time, the queen gave birth to a son, who superseded James's Protestant daughter Mary as next in line to the throne, thereby making likely the establishment of a Catholic dynasty. Many who had been willing to accept the Catholic James pending the succession of the Protestant Mary had now to reassess their position. Finally, seven leaders of the opposition wrote to Mary's husband, William of Orange (who himself was vitally concerned with English affairs), inviting his intervention. The upshot of the letter was the ''Glorious Revolution'' and James's subsequent flight to France on Dec. 23, 1688.

The rest of his life was anticlimactic. An attempt to conquer Ireland led to his defeat at the Battle of the Boyne, July 11, 1690. Henceforth he lived peacefully and, although earlier a man of loose morals, he won for himself a reputation for holiness.

Bibliography: F. C. TURNER, *James II* (London 1950). J. MILLER, *James II: A Study in Kingship* (London 1978). M. ASHLEY, *James II* (London 1978). J. P. KENYON, *Stuart England* (London 1978). T. HARRIS, *Politics under the Later Stuarts: Party Conflict in a Divided Society 1660–1715* (London 1993). M. MULLET, *James II and English Politics, 1678–1688* (London 1994). J. MILLER, *James II* (New Haven, Conn. 2000).

[E. F. WALL]

JAMES CINTI DE CERQUETO, BL.

AUGUSTINIAN hermit and ascetic; baptized Giacomo Cinti; b. Cerqueto near Perugia, Italy, at the close of the 13th century; d. Perugia, Apr. 17, 1367. He was noted for his exemplary life of virtue; many miracles were attributed to him, e.g., frogs ceased croaking when he preached outdoors. His relics have been venerated for centuries at Perugia, and his remains were enshrined by Horatius, bishop of Perugia, in 1754. His cult was first publicly approved in 1895 by LEO XIII. The fact that the Augustinians are sometimes permitted to wear white habits is attributed to his prayers.

Feast: Apr. 17.

Bibliography: *Analecta ecclesiastica* 3 (1895) 253–254. A. ROTELLI, *Il beato Giacomo da Cerqueto* (Perugia 1895). F. VON S. DOYÉ, *Heilige und Selige der römisch-katholischen Kirche*, 2 v. (Leipzig 1930) 1:542. A. BUTLER, *The Lives of the Saints* (New York 1956) 2:117. W. HÜMPFNER, *Lexikon für Theologie und Kirche*, 10 v. (2d, new ed. Freiburg 1957–65) 5:838.

[K. NOLAN]

JAMES DE BENEFACTIS, BL.

Giacomo Benefatti, bishop, preacher; b. Mantua, Italy, mid-13th century; d. there Nov. 19, *c.* 1328–38. He entered the Dominicans at an early age and became famous as a preacher. He was an advisor and secretary to the Dominican Pope BENEDICT XI, who appointed him bishop of Mantua in *c.* 1304. He defended the faith against heresy and schism, and for his solicitous care of his flock earned the title Father of the Poor. His cult was approved by PIUS IX in 1859.

Feast: Nov. 26.

Bibliography: A. TOURON, *Histoire des hommes illustres de l'ordre de S. Dominique*, 6 v. (Paris 1743–49) 2:134. L. JADIN, *Dictionnaire d'histoire et de géographie ecclésiastiques* 7:1293–94. A. WALZ, *Compendium historiae Ordinis Praedicatorum* (new ed. Rome 1948) 203. G. GIERATHS, *Lexikon für Theologie und Kirche*, 10 v. (2d, new ed. Freiburg 1957–65) 5:837. A. AMARGIER, *Catholicisme* 6:267. I. TAURISANO, *Catalogus hagiographicus ordinis praedicatorum* 28.

[J. D. CAMPBELL]

JAMES GAETANI STEFANESCHI

Cardinal; b. Rome, *c.* 1270; d. Avignon, France, June 23, 1343. A member of the influential GAETANI FAMILY, he studied and later taught at the University of Paris. He was obliged to Pope CELESTINE V for his promotion to the office of auditor at the apostolic palace and to BONIFACE VIII for the cardinalate, with the title of San Giorgio in Velabro (Dec. 17, 1295). At the time of the Anagni outrage he remained close to the pope, and during the conclave assembled at Perugia in 1305, he was among the adversaries of the candidacy of Bertrand de Got, the future CLEMENT V, participating in his election only by way of accession. When action was brought against the memory of Boniface, he acted as the pope's defender, despite the protests of Guillaume de Nogaret. A convinced Ghibelline (*see* GUELFS AND GHIBELLINES), he constantly demonstrated his opposition to the line of political action followed by Clement V and JOHN XXII in Italy. Deprived of any influence because of his intransigence, he devoted himself to the production of a number of important liturgical and historical works. His *Opus metricum,* a rather obscure poem [ed. F. X. Seppelt, *Monumenta Coelestiniana* (Paderborn 1921) 1–146], is divided into three parts: a life of Celestine V, composed before Dec. 17, 1295; an account of the election and coronation of Boniface VIII, completed after 1300; and an account of Celestine's canonization, written in 1314 and 1315. The cardinal revised the entire work and added a gloss and a dedication to the CELESTINES dated Jan. 28, 1319. His *Liber de centesimo seu jubileo anno* [ed. D. Quattrocchi, *Bessarione* 7 (1900)

299–317] concerned the JUBILEE YEAR. A Roman ceremonial by Stefaneschi (MS 1706 of the Bibliothèque d'Avignon) represents the first redaction in which notes during the pontificate of Clement V and John XXII, not transcribed after 1328, are collected. It is an important source for the study of the papal court in the period, but has been printed only in part. Stefaneschi wrote also a life of St. George the martyr (Capitular Archives of St. Peter's, Rome, MS 129C), and an account of a miracle that took place at Avignon in 1320 (in MS Paris, B.N. lat. 5931, fol. 95–102).

Bibliography: Works. *Opus metricum, Acta Sanctorum* May 4:437–484. *De centesimo anno seu jubileo liber,* tr. into Italian by A. FRUGONI, *Il libro del guibileo del cardinale Stefaneschi* (Brescia 1950). Extracts from the Roman ceremonial in F. EHRLE, "Zur Geschichte des päpstlichen Hofceremoniells im 14. Jahrhundert," H. DENIFLE and F. EHRLE, eds., *Archiv für Literatur- und Kirchengeschichte des Mittelalters* 5 (1889) 565–602. E. MÜLLER, *Das Konzil von Vienne* (Münster 1931) 671–678. L. H. LABANDE, "Le Cérémonial romain de Jacques Cajétan," *Bibliothèque de l'École des Chartes* 54 (1893) 45–74. G. MOLLAT, "Miscellanea Avenionensia," *Mélanges d'archéologie et d'histoire* 44 (1927) 1–5. J. MABILLON, *Museum italicum,* 2 v. (Paris 1687) 2:241–443. Literature. I. HÖSL, *Kardinal Jacobus Gaietani Stefaneschi: Ein Beitrag zur Literaturund Kirchengeschichte des beginnenden 14. Jahrhundert* (Berlin 1908). *Histoire Littéraire de la France* 34 (1914) 61. R. MORGHEN, "Il cardinale Jacopo Gaetano Stefaneschi e l'edizione del suo *Opus marticum,*" *Bullettino dell'Istituto storico Italiano e Archivio Muratoriano* 46 (1930) 1–35. M. ANDRIEU, "L'Ordinaire de la chapelle papale et le cardinal Jacques Stefaneschi," *Ephemerides liturgicae* 39 (1925) 230–260. A. FRUGONI, "La figura e l'opera del cardinale Jacopo Stefaneschi . . . ," *Atti dell'Accademia nazionale dei Lincei,* 8th ser., 5 (1950) 397–424.

[G. MOLLAT]

JAMES GRIESINGER OF ULM, BL.

Dominican artist also known as James (Jakob) of Ulm; b. Ulm, Germany, 1407; d. Bologna, Oct. 11, 1491. He went to Rome when 24, served in the army of Alphonse of Aragon, and then became steward to a wealthy Italian jurist. When 34, he became a Dominican lay brother at Bologna. There he turned his talents to glass painting, an art he must have acquired before entering the Order. Manuscripts tell of his holiness but not of his artistic activities. Proof of his artistry is found in the works of his pupils, especially Fra Anastasio of Como and Fra Ambrogino of Soncino, and in S. Petronio in Bologna. Soon after his death the people of Bologna invoked him as the patron of glass painters and glaziers. In 1825, LEO XII officially confirmed his cult.

Feast: Oct. 11.

Bibliography: *Acta Sanctorum* Oct. 5:790–803. I. TAURISANO, *Catalogus hagiographicus ordinis praedictorum* (Rome 1918) 46–47. J. L. BAUDOT and L. CHAUSSIN, *Vies des saints et des bienheueux selon l'ordre du calendrier avec l'historique des fêtes* (Paris 1935–56) 10:368–372. J. WILMS, *Lay Brother, Artist and Saint,* tr. M. FULGENCE (London 1957).

[L. M. SCHIER]

JAMES OF ALBENGA

Decretalist; b. about 1190 in Albenga, Italy, where he appears as early as 1210 as an advocate; time and place of his death are unknown. HOSTIENSIS (Henry of Segusio) and Peter of Sampson were among his students when he was teaching in Bologna between 1220 and 1230. He composed glosses on the decretum of GRATIAN (contained in the Manuscript Vatican lat. 1367) and supplementary glosses on Tancred's disquisition to *Compilatio Prima,* and the famous commentary disquisition to the *Compilatio Quinta.* He was provost in his native city of Albenga. After Abbas Antiquus (BERNARD OF MONTMIRAT) he held an archdeaconry, but resigned during a vacancy of the bishopric of Albenga in the hope of becoming bishop of his native city. The hope was never fulfilled. William DURANTI the Elder's note that James had been bishop of Faenza, since it has not been authenticated by a single witness, could be an error on Duranti's part.

Bibliography: J. F. V. SCHULTE, *Die Geschichte der Quellen und der Literatur des kanonischen Rechts* 1:205–207. S. KUTTNER, *Repertorium der Kanonistik* 76, 383–385. S. KUTTNER, "Bernardus Compostellanus antiquus," *Traditio* 1 (1943) 335. J. LIPS and H. WAGNON, *Dictionnaire de droit canonique* 6:77–78.

[R. WEIGAND]

JAMES OF BEVAGNA, BL.

Dominican preacher, founder, miracle worker also known as Giacomo (James) Bianconi of Mevania; b. Bevagna (Mevania), Umbria, Italy, March 7, 1220; d. Bevagna, Aug. 22, 1301. At 16, moved by the Lenten preaching of two DOMINICANS, he joined the order at Spoleto. He studied philosophy and theology and was ordained at Perugia. When assigned to preaching, he worked against Nicolaitanism (the defense of a married clergy); he confronted the heresiarch Ortinelli and succeeded in banning the heresy from Umbria. He founded the Dominican priory of St. George in his native Bevagna and directed the establishment of a convent of Benedictine nuns. Noteworthy in his life was the reputed vision accorded him while praying before a crucifix. Fearing the loss of his soul, he was comforted when he was bathed in the blood that spurted from the side of Christ. Warned by a vision on August 15, 1301, he prepared himself for death, which occurred eight days later. His intact remains are at Bevagna. BONIFACE IX sanctioned his cult on Jan. 7, 1400. PIUS V began a formal process that continued under PAUL V. In a bull of April 13, 1610, James is referred to as a saint. CLEMENT X authorized his feast on March 6, 1674.

Feast: Aug. 23.

Bibliography: I. TAURISANO, *Catalogus hagiographicus ordinis praedicatorum* (Rome 1918) 23. *Année Dominicaine* 23 v. (Lyons 1883–1909) August 2:779. *Acta Sanctorum* August 4:719–737. A. BUTLER, *The Lives of the Saints,* ed. H. THURSTON and D. ATTWATER, 4 v. (New York 1956) 3:390–391.

[B. CAVANAUGH]

JAMES OF CERTALDO, BL.

Camaldolese monk and parish priest; b. Certaldo, near Florence, Italy; d. Apr. 13, 1292. James (Giacomo) Guidi was the son of a knight of Volterra. He became a CAMALDOLESE in 1230 at the Abbey of San Giusto at Volterra, where his relics still remain. Having twice refused to accept the office of abbot, James reluctantly acquiesced on a third occasion, but shortly thereafter he resigned this office to return to his work as parish priest at the monastery church. He served in this capacity for 40 years with a reputation as a great pastor of souls. His father and two brothers became lay brothers at San Giusto.

Feast: Apr. 13.

Bibliography: *Acta Sanctorum* Apr. 2:153–156. A. M. ZIMMERMANN, *Lexikon für Theologie und Kirche,* 10 v. (2d, new ed. Freiburg 1957–65) 5:838 *Kalendarium Benedictinum: Die Heiligen und Seligen des Benediktinerorderns und seiner Zweige* 2:50, 52.

[K. J. EGAN]

JAMES OF METZ

Dominican theologian; fl. 1295–1309. Little is known with certainty about him. He is listed in the Stams Catalogue (1315) as author of a commentary on the *Sentences.* Presumably he belonged to the priory at Metz in the province of France. At Paris he lectured on the *Sentences* two times, but without becoming a master. The two versions of his commentary have been identified by J. Koch, who showed that the first exists as a *reportatio,* and that the second is a repetition with additional questions. Dating the second between 1295 and 1303, Koch maintained that he must have been the teacher of DURANDUS OF SAINT-POURÇAIN. R. Martin and P. Glorieux reject this in favor of a later dating (1308–09), in which case he could have been a disciple of Durandus. He was

more restrained and cautious than Durandus, although many of their minor arguments are identical. Some debatable views were attacked by HARVEY NEDELLEC in his *Correctorium fr. Jacobi,* composed after 1302. James maintained a real distinction between nature and Persons in the Trinity; this view, defended by Durandus, was declared heretical by a theological commission of the Dominican Order in 1314.

James presented the arguments against the real distinction of ESSENCE AND EXISTENCE without replying to them; he identified mental concepts with the human act of thinking, and followed PETER OF AUVERGNE on INDIVIDUATION by "this" form. On all other important points in scholastic philosophy he followed THOMAS AQUINAS, whom he calls "our Doctor." Although he did not always adhere to the teaching of Aquinas, he was neither anti-Thomist nor nominalist (*see* THOMISM).

Bibliography: É. H. GILSON, *A History of Christian Philosophy in the Middle Ages* (New York 1955) 773–774. J. KOCH, "Jakob von Metz, OP, der Lehrer des Durandus de S. Porciano, OP," *Archives d'histoire doctrinale et littéraire du moyen-âge* 4 (1929) 169–232. R. M. MARTIN, *La Controverse sur le péché originel au début du XIV e siècle* (Louvain 1930) 185–208.

[J. A. WEISHEIPL]

JAMES OF THE MARCHES, ST.

Papal nuncio, early leader of the Franciscan Observants; baptized Giacomo Gangala; also known as James (Giacomo) della Marca; b. Monteprandone, in the March of Ancona, 1393; d. Naples, Nov. 28, 1476. He was reared by a priest uncle at Offida, studied the humanities at Ascoli, and took civil and canon law at the University of Perugia. He was frequently sent on various missions in the interest of the Church and the Franciscan Order: in 1430 he went to Bohemia against the HUSSITES; in 1432 the Minister General William of Casale sent him to Bosnia to combat the BOGOMILS; and he was inquisitor against the FRATICELLI in 1441. He went back to Bosnia and Dalmatia in 1452, and replaced JOHN CAPISTRAN as nuncio to Hungary in 1456. With BERNARDINE OF SIENA and Capistran, James worked tirelessly throughout his life for the success of the Church and the Franciscan Order. These three "pillars of the Observance" (*see* FRANCISCANS) came together in a historic meeting near Lake Trasimeno in May 1444, shortly before Bernardine's death. James's efforts to effect Bernardine's canonization met with success on Pentecost 1450. James received two saintly disciples into the order: Bernardine of Fossa in 1445 and BERNARDINE OF FELTRE in 1456. James failed in his efforts to implement CALLISTUS III's *Bulla concordiae* (Feb. 2, 1456), designed to unite the

St. James of the Marches, painting by Carlo Crivelli, 1477, in the Picture Gallery of the Vatican in Rome.

Franciscan Conventuals and the Observants. In 1458 James returned to Italy and spent the rest of his life evangelizing Italian towns and establishing the MONTES PIETATIS In 1472 SIXTUS IV sent him to Naples to preach reform. James, whose body rests in S. Maria Nuova in Naples, was beatified in 1624 and canonized in 1726. His writings are largely unedited or lost.

Feast: Nov. 28.

Bibliography: *San Giacomo della Marca nell'Europa del '400,* International conference, September 7–10, 1994, ed. S. BRACCI (Padua 1997). A. GATTUCCI, ''Frate Giacomo della Marca bibliofilo e un episodo librario del 1450,'' in: *Miscellanea Augusto Campana, Mediaevalia e Umanistica,* 44–45 (Padua, 1981), 313–353. M. SGATTONI, *La vita di S. Giacomo della Marca per fra' Venanzio da Fabriano* (Zara 1940). D. LASIČ, *De vita et operibus S. Iacobi de Marchia: studium et recensio quorundam textuum* (Ancona 1974), includes text of ''Miracula facta virtute sacri nominis Jesu.'' A. GHINATO, ''Apostolato religioso e sociale di S. Giacomo della Marca in Terni,'' *Archivum Franciscanum historicum,* 49 (Quaracchi-Florence 1956) 106–142, 352–390. S. CANDELA, *S. Giacomo della Marca nel V centenario della morte* (Naples 1976);

S. Giacomo della Marca e Santa Maria la Nova di Napoli (Naples 1972). D. CAPONE, *Iconografia di s. Giacomo della Marca nell'ambiente napoletano lungo i secoli* (Naples 1976); ed., *S. Giacomo della Marca nel rotolo remissoriale della sua beatificazione* (Naples 1972).

[F. ETZKORN]

JAMES OF VITERBO, BL.

Italian Augustinian theologian, known by the scholastic titles of *Doctor gratiosus, Doctor inventivus,* and *Doctor speculativus;* b. Viterbo, *c.* 1255; d. Naples, 1308. A member of the Capocci family, he joined the Hermits of St. Augustine when he was very young (*c.* 1270), and he acquired the elements of learning at the order's house in Viterbo. From 1275 to 1282 he studied philosophy and theology in Paris. After a few years in Italy, where he had various administrative responsibilities, he was again sent to Paris, this time to enroll in the university and to succeed GILES OF ROME, the order's first master in theology. In May 1288 James had the title of bachelor. In April 1293 he became a master and succeeded Giles as regent master from 1293 to 1300. During his first years of teaching he held quodlibetal discussions and many *quaestiones disputatae,* notably 32 *De praedicamentis in divinis;* seven *De verbo;* 50 *De Spiritu Sancto; De animatione caelorum;* and *De angelorum compositione.* Directed by the general chapter of Siena in 1295 to devote himself especially to the study of Sacred Scripture, he composed commentaries on Matthew, Luke, and Paul that are now lost. Returning to Italy as definitor to the general chapter of Naples in 1300, he was put in charge of the *studium generale* founded in that city. Between March and September 1302, he composed and dedicated to the pope the earliest known treatise on the Church, *De regimine Christiano.* On Sept. 3, 1302, BONIFACE VIII created him bishop of Benevento; and on Dec. 12, 1303, he appointed him archbishop of Naples. At the height of the struggle between Boniface VIII and PHILIP IV, King of France, James strongly defended the rights of the Holy See, keeping always on a theological level. As archbishop he was actively engaged in the reconstruction of his cathedral. He was beatified on June 4, 1914.

Bibliography: P. GLORIEUX, *Répertoire des maîtres en théologie de Paris au XIII siècle* (Paris 1933–34) 2:309–312. D. GUTIÉRREZ, ''De B. Jacobi Viterbiensis vita, operibus et doctrina theologica,'' *Analecta Augustiniana* (Rome 1939). P. GLORIEUX, *La Littérature quodlibétique* (Kain 1925) 1:214–217. T. OSBORNE, ''James of Viterbo's Rejection of Giles of Rome's Arguments for the Natural Love of God over Self,'' *Augustiniana* 49 (1999) 235–249. M. GOSSIAUX, ''James of Viterbo on the Relationship between Essence and Existence,'' *Augustiniana* 49 (1999) 73–107. E. YPMA, ed. ''Jac. De Viterbo, Quaestiones de divinis praedicamentis,'' *Augustiniana* 46 (1996) 339–369, 48 (1998) 131–163, 49 (1999) 323–366.

[P. GLORIEUX]

JAMES OF VORAGINE, BL.

Dominican archbishop, chronicler; b. Varazze, Italy, *c.* 1230; d. Genoa, July 13–14, 1298. After joining the DOMINICANS in 1244, he completed all ranks of the *ratio studiorum* by 1264. As provincial of Lombardy (1267–77, 1281–86) he traveled extensively in Italy and bordering countries to attend the annual provincial chapters and the triennial general chapters. Named archbishop of Genoa by NICHOLAS IV, he governed that see from 1292 until his death, devoted to pastoral care and clerical reform, to his writings, and to the restoration of peace between the GUELFS and Ghibellines.

The *Legenda aurea* [*Legenda sanctorum,* ed. T. Graesse (Dresden, Leipzig 1846); tr. G. Ryan and H. Ripperger (New York 1941)], because of its wide circulation during the later Middle Ages, is James's best-known work. Although not a critical hagiographical piece, it was a stimulus for religious devotion in an age desirous of miracles. Its chief source is probably the *Liber epilogorum in gesta sanctorum* of BARTHOLOMEW OF TRENT [*Mitteilungen des Instituts für österreichische Geschichtforschung* 65 (1957) 376–377], the oldest manuscript in Einsiedeln (1288), first printed in 1470. In his *Chronicon Januense* [ed. G. Monleone, *Jacopo da Varagine e la sua cronaca di Genova* (Rome 1941) 2:404–405], James lists as his own the following additional works: *Sermones de omnibus sanctis, Sermones de omnibus evangeliis quae in singulis feriis in Quadragesima leguntur, Sermones de omnibus evangeliis dominicalibus,* the *Mariale,* and the *Chronica.* Varying in importance are 11 other works that may be considered authentic.

His cult in Varazze and throughout Liguria, uninterrupted since the time of his death, was confirmed by PIUS VII in 1816.

Feast: July 13.

Bibliography: JAMES OF VORAGINE, *Tractatus de libris a beato Augustino episcopo editis,* ed. M. J. A. MCCORMICK (Washington 1964); *Die altokzitanische Version B der "Legenda aurea,"* ed. M. TAUSEND (Tübingen 1995). G. FARRIS, ed., *Significati spirituali nei "Sermones" di Jacopo da Varazze* (Savona 1996, rev. 1998). J. QUÉTIF and J. ÉCHARD, *Scriptores Ordinis Praedictorum,* 5 v. (Paris 1719–23) 1.1:454–459. G. AIRALDI, *Jacopo da Varagine: tra santi e mercanti* (Milan 1988). V. PELAZZA, *Vita del beato Giacomo da Varazze* (Genoa 1867). M. WARESQUIEL, *Le Bienheureux Jacques de Voragine* (Paris 1902). I. PASOTTI, *Il beato Giacomo da Varazze* (Cogoleto 1974). E. C. RICHARDSON, *Materials for a Life of Jacopo da Varagine* (New York 1935), lacks bibliog. J. BAUDOT, *Dictionnaire de théologie catholique,* ed. A. VACANT, 15 v. (Paris

1903–50; Tables Générales 1951–) 8.1:309–313. P. LORENZIN, *Mariologia Iacobi a Varagine, O.P.* (Rome 1951). P. MALLONE, *Predicatori e frescanti: Jacopo da Varagine e la pitturaligure- piemontese del Quattrocento* (n.s. 1999), iconography.

[M. J. A. MCCORMICK]

JAMES SALOMONIUS, BL.

Dominican, known also as James of Venice; b. Venice, Italy, 1231; d. there May 31, 1314. His parents were Adam and Marchinina of the patrician Salomonius family. After his father's death and his mother's profession as a Cistercian nun, he was reared by his grandmother. At 17 he joined the DOMINICANS in the priory of SS. John and Paul, Venice, after distributing his patrimony to the poor. As his reputation for holiness grew, people became importunate, and at 21 he was sent to Forlì, but even there a grille had to be erected around his Mass-altar to restrain the devout. Except for periods when he was subprior at Faënza, San Severino, and Ravenna, he remained at Forlì until his death at 83 from a heart attack while in choir. A recollected and prayerful religious of a happy disposition, admired and respected by his brethren and by laymen alike, he showed a solicitous care for the poor, which won for him the title of ''father of the poor.'' He inspired men by his words and is said to have worked miracles. His cult, tacitly approved by JOHN XXII, was formally approved by CLEMENT VII, June 26, 1526; the observance of his feast was extended to the whole Dominican Order by GREGORY XI, 1622.

Feast: May 31 or June 5.

Bibliography: J. L. BAUDOT and L. CHAUSSIN, *Vies des saints et des bienheueux selon l'ordre du calendrier avec l'historique des fêtes,* ed. by The Benedictines of Paris, 12 v. (Paris 1935–56) 1:763. *Acta Sanctorum* May 7:450–456. *Année Dominicaine,* May 2 (Lyons 1891) 815–824. *Analecta Bollandiana* 12:367–370. *Archivum Fratrum Praedicatorum* 10 (1940) 109. C. DESMOND, *Blessed James Salomoni; Patron of Cancer Patients, Apostle of the Afflicted* (Boston 1971).

[B. CAVANAUGH]

JAMET, PIERRE-FRANÇOIS, BL.

Priest, b. Sept. 13, 1762, Fresnes, France; d. Jan. 12, 1845, Caen, France. Following Jamet's ordination (1787), he was assigned as chaplain to the Sisters of the Good Savior. He was forced into hiding in order to continue his ministry after refusing to take the oath of allegiance to civil authorities that was demanded by the revolutionaries. During this period, he wrote a sign-language dictionary for the deaf-mutes under his care. After the French Revolution, Jamet restored and expand-

Leoš Janáček. (©Bettmann/CORBIS)

ed the Good Saviors, continued to devote himself to the care of the mentally and physically disabled, and served as rector of Caen University (1822–30). He was beatified by John Paul II, May 10, 1987. Patron of the deaf.

Feast: May 7.

Bibliography: G. A. SIMON, *Une belle figure de prêtre et d'homme d'oeuvres a la fin du XVIIIe et au commencement du XIXe siecle. L'abbe Pierre-Francois Jamet, second fondateur de l'Institut du Bon-Sauveur, recteur de l'Academie de Caen* (Caen 1935). *Acta Apostolicae Sedis* (1987): 690. *L'Osservatore Romano*, English edition, 21 (1987): 18–19.

[K. I. RABENSTEIN]

JANÁČEK, LEOŠ

Composer, teacher, folk-music scholar; b. Hukvaldy, Moravia, Czechoslovakia, July 3, 1854; d. Moravská Ostravá, Aug. 12, 1928. His early education was with the Augustinian Friars of Old Brno Monastery, where he studied with Pavel Křížkovský whom he later succeeded as choirmaster. Despite extreme poverty, he studied further in Prague, Leipzig, and Vienna. After a brief period on the Teachers' Training Institute faculty in Brno, he founded the Brno Organ School in 1881 and taught there until its nationalization in 1920; thereafter he taught a master class at the state conservatory in Prague. He also conducted the Czech Philharmonic (1881–88). Janáček's music is nationalistic and individual, based upon old Slavonic modes and the speech rhythms of the Moravian peasant. His *Glagolitic Mass* (1926) for solos, mixed choir, and organ was written "to portray faith in the certainty of the nation . . . on the basis of moral strength which takes God for witness." Other important works include the operas *Jenufa, Kát'a Kabanová,* and *The Makropulos Secret;* a *Concertino* for piano and chamber orchestra; the song cycle *The Diary of One Who Vanished; a Sinfonietta;* the rhapsody *Taras Bulba* for orchestra; and many choral writings and folk-music transcriptions.

Bibliography: *Leoš Janáček: Letters and Reminiscences,* ed. S. BOHUMÍR, tr. G. THOMPSON (Prague 1955). M. BROD, *Leoš Janáček: Leben und Werk* (rev. and enl. Vienna 1956). H. HOLLANDER, *Leoš Janáček: His Life and Work,* tr. P. HAMBURGER (New York 1963). N. SLONIMSKY, ed., *Baker's Biographical Dictionary of Musicians* (5th ed. New York 1958) 773–774. Z. BLAZEK, "Polyphonie und Rhythmik in Janáceks Musiktheorie," *Sborník Prací Filosofické Fakulty Brnenské University* 4 (1969) 107–116. M. BECKERMAN, *Janácek as Theorist* (Hillsboro 1994). S. B. DORSEY, "Janácek's *Cunning Little Vixen,*" *Opera Journal* 29/4 (1996) 28–41. L. JANÁCEK, *Intimate Letters: Leoš Janáček to Kamila Stösslová,* ed. and tr. J. TYRRELL (Boston 1994); *Janácek's Uncollected Essays on Music,* ed. and tr. M. ZEMANOVÁ (London 1989). G. MARTIN, "There's More to Janácek than *Jenufa* and *The Makropulos Case,*" *World of Opera* 1/2 (1978) 1–18. F. PULCINI, *Janácek: vita, opere, scritti* (Florence 1993). B. STEDRON, "Precursors of Janácek's Opera *Její pastorkyna (Jenufa),*" *Sborník Prací Filosofické Fakulty Brnenské University* 3 (1968) 43–74. J. VYSLOUZIL, "Leoš Janácek und Wien," *Studien zur Musikwissenschaft* 41 (1992) 257–285.

[H. STEVENS]

JANEQUIN, CLÉMENT

Renaissance composer who developed the polyphonic chanson; b. Châtellerault, France, *c.* 1480; d. Paris, *c.* 1560. During his productive career he lived in or near Bordeaux to *c.* 1531; Angers, to *c.* 1548; and Paris, from 1549; and at various times he held posts as *curé,* canon, and chaplain at Angers cathedral and the chapel of Francis of Guise. He also attended universities at Angers and Paris as an adult. He was a singer and choral director at Angers cathedral *c.* 1534, honorary singer to Francis I, 1531, and singer and official composer to Henry II from 1555. His musical works include two Masses, one motet, one motet-book (lost), one Italian madrigal, French psalms, spiritual songs, and some 286 surviving chansons of immense popularity (several quoted in *fricassées*). Janequin is best known for his programmatic chansons with their lively syllabic declamation and onomatopoeia, but he excelled also in more lyrical types and occasionally experimented with chromaticism.

Bibliography: F. LESURE and P. ROUDIÉ, "La Jeunesse bordelaise de Clément Janequin," *Revue de musicologie* 49 (Paris 1963) 172–183. F. LESURE, *Die Musik in Geschichte und Gegenwart,* ed. F. BLUME (Kassel-Basel 1949–) 6:1695–1701. J. LEVRON, *Clément Janequin* (Grenoble 1948). D. HEARTZ, "Les Goûts réunis . . . ," *Chanson and Madrigal, 1480–1530,* ed. J. HAAR (Cambridge, Mass. 1964) 88–138. *Histoire de la musique,* ed. ROLAND-MANUEL, v.1 (Paris 1960–63). G. REESE, *Music in the Renaissance* (rev. ed. New York 1959). A complete edition of the chansons of Janequin is being prepared by T. MERRITT and F. LESURE. H. BROWN, "Clément Janequin" *New Grove Dictionary of Music and Musicians,* 9, ed. S. SADIE (New York 1980) 491–495. J.-P. OUVRARD, "Du narratif dans la polyphonie au 16th siècle, *Martin menoit son pourceau au marché*: Clément Marot, Clément Janequin, Claudin de Sermisy," *Analyse Musicale* 9 (1987), 11–16. D. M. RANDEL, ed., *Harvard Biographical Dictionary of Music* 416 (Cambridge 1996). N. SLONIMSKY, ed., *Baker's Biographical Dictionary of Musicians,* 8th ed. (New York 1992) 842–843.

[I. CAZEAUX]

JANSEN, CORNELIUS (THE ELDER)

Bishop and exegete; b. Hulst, Flanders, 1510; d. Ghent, April 11, 1576. After his studies at Ghent and Louvain (S.T.L. 1534), he taught Sacred Scripture at the Premonstratensian Abbey of Tongerloo until 1542. After some pastoral activity, he was appointed dean of the school of theology at Louvain (1560). In 1563 he attended the last sessions of the Council of Trent as university delegate of PHILIP II, King of Spain. He became bishop of Ghent (1568) at the command of Pope St. PIUS V and carried out the Tridentine decrees with the greatest exactness. His commentaries on the Scriptures, in which he insisted on the primacy of the literal over the so-called mystical sense, made him one of the most distinguished Catholic exegetes of the 16th century. Most valuable were his works on the Gospels, the *Concordia evangelica* (1549) and the *Commentarius in concordiam et totam historiam evangelicam* (1572). Among his other works were *Commentarius in Proverbia Solomonis* (1567), *Commentarius in Ecclesiasticum* (1569), *Commetarius in omnes Psalmos Davidicos* (1569), and *Annotationes in librum Sapientia* (1577). All were published at Louvain.

Bibliography: L. WILLAERT, *Lexikon für Theologie und Kirche,* ed. J. HOFER and K. RAHNER, 10 v. (2d, new ed. Freiburg 1957–65) 5:869. P. SCHLAGER, *The Catholic Encyclopedia,* ed. C. G. HERBERMANN, 16 v. (New York 1907–14; suppl. 1922) 8:284.

[J. J. MAHONEY]

JANSEN, CORNELIUS OTTO (JANSENIUS)

Flemish theologian noted for having given rise to the Jansenist controversies; b. at Accoi, near Leerdam, in

Cornelius (the Elder) Jansen, engraving from "Illustrium Galliae Belgicae."

southern Holland, Nov. 3, 1585; d. at Ypres, May 6, 1638. He belonged to a poor but solidly Catholic family; with the assistance of various protectors, it was possible for him to pursue his studies at Culenbourg, Utrecht, and the University of Louvain, where he was an outstanding student. After receiving his bachelor of theology degree in 1609, he went to Paris, for reasons of health, to continue his studies. There he met Jean DUVERGIER DE HAURANNE (1581–1643), future Abbot of Saint-Cyran, who was also a former student at Louvain. They formed a very close friendship and lived together almost continuously either in Paris or more often on the Duvergier estate at Camps-de-Prats near Bayonne. There they read in common the extensive works of the Fathers of the Church and the schoolmen, but without special attention to the question of grace. In the meantime, while staying at Pays-Bas, Jansen was ordained on Sept. 20, 1614. He received his doctorate in theology in October of 1617 and shortly afterward was named director of the Sainte-Pulchérie Seminary at Louvain and professor of exegesis at the university. There around 1619, in an atmosphere still strongly imbued with the ideas of BAIUS, he began to become interested in the problems of grace. He soon discovered the importance of St. Augustine's ideas, decided to devote himself to their defense, and toward the end of 1621 found a strong ally in the person of Saint-Cyran. He

Cornelius Otto Jansen (Jansenius). (Archive Photos)

became associated also with the Franciscan Florent Conry (Conrius), who held views similar to his own. He then decided to undertake the writing of an enormous work in which he would present the ideas of St. Augustine on grace in a systematic and continuous synthesis. After a meeting with Saint-Cyran at Péronne on May 10, 1623, he outlined the project and began to collate the documentation. His university duties, however, interrupted this work. In July of 1624 he went to Spain as a deputy for his colleagues to defend the privileges of the University of Louvain against the Jesuits, who wished to have the right of teaching those working for academic degrees. Jansen was successful at the court of Madrid. He also succeeded in winning the support of the universities of Alcalá and Salamanca. On his return to Louvain in May of 1625, he received warm congratulations from his colleagues and then proceeded to Paris to stay with Saint-Cyran until April of 1626. In May new complications in the affairs of the university obliged him to return to Madrid, where he took advantage of the occasion to circulate again among the Spanish universities and organize the re-

sistance against what he considered the encroachments of the Jesuits. He returned to Louvain in April of 1627. In October of 1628, on the occasion of the reform of the Benedictines of Afflighem, he openly but prudently manifested his Augustinianism in delivering his famous *Discours de la réformation de l'homme intérieur.* In 1630 he was appointed to the regius chair of Sacred Scripture. In the 145 lessons he gave annually, he commented on the Pentateuch, Proverbs, some other passages from the Old Testament, and on the Gospels. His commentaries, which were published after his death, show a profound concern for literal exegesis, a relative discretion in the use of allegory, and at the same time a very extensive knowledge of patristics. On controversial questions, especially on those concerning grace, he was extremely prudent. In 1635 he distinguished himself in his resistance to the invasion of Louvain by French troops. He subsequently exposed to ridicule the politics of Cardinal Richelieu and his alliances with the Protestants by publishing his *Mars gallicus,* a heavy and virulent pamphlet that had considerable success and earned him the hatred of the cardinal-statesman. Beginning in 1630, he engaged in polemics against the Protestants and published his *Alexipharmacon* against the Protestant ministers of Bois-le-Duc. In August of 1635 he was named rector of the University of Louvain, a post in which he proved to be extremely active, particularly in establishing the library and the archives. However, his personal affairs, as well as those of his office, necessitated long sojourns in Brussels. In October of 1635 he was appointed to the See of Ypres, and he was consecrated at Brussels on Oct. 28, 1636. He was a very zealous bishop and a competent administrator, succeeding even in maintaining good relations with the Jesuits despite his previous hostility. Amidst these duties he did not forget his great work, which he had begun to write toward the end of 1627 and which he entitled simply *AUGUSTINUS* to emphasize his fidelity to the Doctor of Grace. Despite several interruptions, the work was sufficiently advanced at the beginning of Jansen's episcopate for him to think of having it printed under his supervision in his own palace. For some time already he had foreseen the controversies that it would engender, and he had sought supporters especially among the French and Belgian Oratorians and the Dominicans. Aided by his chaplain, Reginald Lamée, he terminated the retouching of the text in April of 1638. A few days later, a victim of the plague, he died quietly, leaving the remembrance of a pious and austere priest deeply attached to the Church, an indefatigable worker with a penetrating intelligence and a tenacious and somewhat cold character, but endowed with a highly professional sense of duty.

See Also: JANSENISM.

Bibliography: J. CARREYRE, *Dictionnaire de théologie catholique,* 15 v. (Paris 1903–50) 8.1:319–330. L. WILLAERT, *Lex-*

ikon für Theologie und Kirche, 10 v. (Freiburg 1957–65) 5:869–870. J. ORCIBAL, *Correspondance de Jansénius,* v. 1 of *Les Origines du jansénisme* (Paris 1947); *Jansénius* (Paris 1989).

[L. J. COGNET]

JANSENISM

A religious movement, named after Cornelius JANSEN, bishop of Ypres (1585–1638) which began in Spanish Flanders and in France as a reaction to MOLINISM. In their struggle to assert and defend their positions, its members exerted a deep influence over church, society, and politics until the end of the 18th century. The generic term suggests an ideological homogeneity that never existed. The movement developed and attempted to impose an extreme Augustinian conception of man's relationship with God; it attacked and was resisted by a more humanistic school fostered by the Society of Jesus, which continued the optimism of the Renaissance. The opposition between the two visions became a war between two parties, Jansenism and "anti-Jansenism," waged not only theologicallly, but also politically. In this dramatic process the features of a Jansenist mentality developed. Its characteristics and influence were constantly modeled and remodeled by its conflictual history.

History

Origins. Cornelius Jansen's *AUGUSTINUS* (published 1640), reflected a desire by Louvain University professors to counter Molinist theology with a decisive exposition of the teaching of Saint AUGUSTINE, the "Doctor of Grace," on matters that had not been resolved by the Church Magisterium. Though some of its positions could appear close to those of another Augustinian from Louvain, Michel de Bai (BAIUS), who had been censured in 1567 by Pius V, it soon was acknowledged as the most representative work of positive theology on the matter of grace, and for that reason its publication signaled the beginning of anti-Jansenist offensive.

In France. Reprinted in Paris (1641) and Rouen (1643), the work was well received in French religious circles for its strict Augustinianism and its appeal to patristic authority alone. A friend of Jansen, Jean DUVERGIER DE HAURANNE, abbot of Saint-Cyran, was instrumental in influencing post-Tridentine renewal with his insistence upon the model of the early Church. Under his spiritual direction, the Abbey of PORT-ROYAL, reformed by Angélique Arnauld, had become both a workshop and a showcase of this enterprise, attracting influential members of the nobility and the bourgeoisie; later a group of laymen, the *solitaires,* lived next to the

Tower of Jansenius, Louvain, Belgium.

nuns. In his defense of the rights of bishops to control religious communities (*Petrus Aurelius*) Saint-Cyran antagonized regulars; his attacks on moral laxism displeased members of the secular clergy as well, including Cardinal Richelieu. This religious opposition became political with the *Parti dévot*'s resistence to Richelieu's alliance with Protestant countries.

First condemnations. *Augustinus* was opposed in Louvain by members of the Society of Jesus, who had their students attack it in theological defenses, but both the book and Jesuit theses were condemned by the Holy Office (1641) for renewing controversies on GRACE (*de auxiliis*), twice forbidden by popes. Dated 1642, but only published in 1643, the bull *In Eminenti* developed this condemnation, albeit in general terms. As this decision could be interpreted as a Roman rebuttal of Augustinian theology, the University of Louvain sent a deputation to inquire about its precise meaning; it was given reassurance to the contrary by the pope himself.

In France, where since 1638 Saint-Cyran had been imprisoned upon Richelieu's orders, *Augustinus* was at-

Mother Catherine Agnès Arnauld (Mother Agnès de Saint-Paul) and Sister Catherine of St. Susan (daughter of the artist), votive painting by Philippe de Champaigne, 1662. The family Arnauld was instrumental in the creation of the Jansenist Party of 17th-century France.

tacked by Isaac HABERT, the official theologian of the diocese, in three sermons preached at Notre Dame of Paris (1642–1643). He was acting on the Cardinal Richelieu's command. Antoine ARNAULD, a disciple of Saint-Cyran, replied in 1644 with a defense of Jansenius, a polemical work, as well as solid evidence of historical scholarship. He also expanded the controversy on more practical planes by attacking the Jesuits on their laxism concerning the reception of the Eucharist (*Fréquente communion,* 1642) and moral theology (*Théologie morale des Jésuites,* 1643). At that time the Port-Royal group was perceived to be supporters of the *Fronde,* the upheaveal against monarchical absolutism. To weaken them, Richelieu's successor, Cardinal Mazarin, supported by the queen regent, Ann of Austria, wanted a stronger papal condemnation. The occasion was seized when students of the Faculty of Theology of Paris defended as orthodox some of the very same theses that Jesuit students had ear-

lier denounced as Calvinist. The *Syndic,* or moderator of the Faculty, requested a formal condemnation of these seven "propositions" (July 1649), but he was unsuccessful, as was an attempt to obtain a condemnation from the General Assembly of the French Clergy (1650). However, Habert, now bishop of Vabres, was as a member of this assembly able to collect 85 episcopal signatures to a letter asking for papal intervention on the first "Five propositions" of the Sorbonne. As this referral to the Holy See intended to involve the Church's highest authority in the dispute, both French Jansenists and Anti-Jansenists sent agents to defend their positions. The bull *CUM OCCASIONE* (May 31, 1653, H. Denzinger, *Enchiridion symbolorum* [Freiburg 1962] 2001–2007) condemned the five propositions, but it was not sufficient to put an end to the controversy for it did not explicitly denote their origin and only disapproved of Jansenius's work in general.

Conflicts. Against an anti-Jansenist claim that in censuring the five propositions the pope had condemned Jansenius's synthesis and even disapproved of Augustinian theology, A. Arnauld disputed the presence of the propositions in *Augustinus*: only the first one could be found *verbatim* and in a context that supported its orthodoxy. Following a classical theological distinction, he asserted his obedience to the *droit* (the Calvinist doctrine the pope intended to condemn) and his rejection of the *fait* (the presence in the book of the said propositions). In so doing he manifested a spirit of resistance and division that countered the Church's desire to settle the matter once and for all. The French bishops added to the papal condemnation an oath or formulary that linked explicitly the five propositions and *Augustinus*. This was Mazarin's way of obtaining Rome's goodwill and fighting those he considered to be the supporters of his enemy the *frondeur* Cardinal de Retz. Arnauld's appeal to public opinion in defending his interpretation of *Cum Occasione* caused the Faculty of Theology to censure (January 1656) and expel him with a significant number of fellow theologians. Another familiar of Port-Royal, Blaise PASCAL, was more successful in his *Provincial Letters* (1656–1657), which vindicated Arnauld's position and attacked laxist morality.

The escalation of pronouncements that followed showed that in the mind of the new pope matters of ecclesiastical obedience were as primordial as questions of orthodoxy. In AD SANCTAM BEATI PETRI SEDEM (October 1656, H. Denzinger, *Enchiridion symbolorum* [Freiburg 1963] 2010–2012, sometimes indicated as *Ad Sacram*), Alexander VII intended to clarify the matter by specifying the presence of the propositions in the book and his predecessors's intention to condemn them "in the sense of Jansenius." He later followed the French bishops' oath requirement by prescribing his own formulary, in *REGIMINIS APOSTOLICI* (February 1665, H. Denzinger, *Enchiridion symbolorum* [Freiburg 1963] 2020).

Regiminis Apostolici added a level of complications to the already intricate question of Jansenism. In the pope's words, the Church had the ability to rule on a "fact," both the material presence of the propositions and their meaning as intended by the author. This claim bore on another intense debate taking place in France at the time, on the relationship between the spiritual and secular powers. In this instance, recourse to the Roman pontiff not only backed Ultramontanism in its assertion of the supremacy of the pope, it also demanded an acceptance of his infallibility that extended to "dogmatic facts," such as the presence of the propositions in *Augustinus*. The assertion at the Sorbonne of such theories (1663) started a wave of Gallicanism that had little to do with the writings of Jansenius. It emboldened a resistance

to the formulary that was endorsed by several pro-Jansenist bishops and prompted a settlement of the vexing formulary issue, by the agreement of a clause of conscience that allowed "respectful silence," that is private dissent on the fact. This "Peace of the Church" was authorized by Clement IX (Jan. 14, 1669).

By that time the movement had acquired its distinctive features, above all its individualism. In their insistence on defending what they considered to be the objective truth, most of the French Augustinians separated themselves from their more moderate associates in the Catholic Renewal; they also incurred Roman suspicion for their disobedience and government resentment for their political maneuvering, which at times threatened the unity of the kingdom. In their fight against laxist morality, they received the support of secular clergy but the success of their appeal to public opinion (Pascal's *Provincial Letters*) was a double-edged sword since it confirmed the existence of a "Jansenist party." In the same manner, this crusade, though moderately endorsed by Rome, was perceived there as dangerous because of its fierce opposition to religious orders and its occasional association with the secular power of the Parlements.

Truce. The "Peace of the Church" was a temporary but momentous respite. It allowed the Port-Royal circle to extend its influence through publishing, especially in biblical, patristic, liturgical, and historical studies; in a move to assert their orthodoxy, they also took an important part in the controversy with Protestants (*Perpétuité de la foi*, 1672). The campaign against laxism was carried on, receiving noticeable Roman support in 1679 (Condemnation of 65 propositions, H. Denzinger, *Enchiridion symbolorum* [Freiburg 1963] 2101–2167) and in 1690 (Condemnation of "philosophical sin," H. Denzinger, *Enchiridion symbolorum* [Freiburg 1963] 2291); it expanded to Jesuit missionary methods, a prelude to the Chinese Rites controversy. The adversaries of the Jansenists were not idle in their efforts to counter and disparage them. Louis XIV was alerted to their spirit of independence by their lack of support in his conflict with Innocent XI (1675). By 1679, only the nuns were allowed to remain at Port-Royal. Arnauld chose to go into exile; in 1685 his disciple P. QUESNEL joined him in Brussels—a perilous choice, for in that city since 1678 a "secret congregation against Jansenism" had been busy preparing a new offensive. They secured Roman censure of an important number of rigorist propositions (1690, H. Denzinger, *Enchiridion symbolorum* [Freiburg 1963] 2301–2332). They also initiated attacks against Quesnel's *Réflexions morales sur le Nouveau Testament*.

The Crisis of *Unigenitus*. Despite papal support for the "politics of silence," reiterated by Innocent XII in a brief to the Belgian bishops (1694), the conflict was bound to ignite. It was stirred up by the publication (1702) of a *Cas of conscience,* submitted to the Faculty of Theology of Paris. Forty doctors had approved a text that not only supported "respectful silence" on the "fact" but also exposed Jansenist positions on religious practice: Confession, Communion, Bible in the vernacular, restrained Marian devotion. The arrest of Quesnel in May of 1703 gave ample evidence of the activity, even in Rome, of a Jansenist network, a blatant breach of the "Peace of the Church." At Louis XIV's insistence, Clement XI promulgated an apostolic constitution, *Vineam Domini* (1705, H. Denzinger, *Enchiridion symbolorum* [Freiburg 1963] 2390), which contented itself with renewing former condemnations without taking into account the transformation of the movement. In its publication in France, the bull was accompanied by an affirmation of episcopal authority to resolve dogmatic issues in conjunction with the pope, an action that signaled an alliance between Jansenist doctrine and Gallican ecclesiology. Another apostolic constitution, the bull UNIGENITUS (1713, D.S. 2400–2502), also requested by the French king, aimed at a comprehensive condemnation of Jansenism. It censured with general qualifications 101 excerpts from Quesnel's *Réflexions morales.* A minority of French bishops, headed by Cardinal de NOAILLES, objected to this approach and asked for a revision of the document before its official publication in the kingdom. Their resistance infuriated the old king, who practically forsook his Gallican principles in order to squelch it, but he died a few days before the national council that was to convict them (1715). Political necessity forced his nephew, the Regent Philip of Orléans, to secure support of these very opponents. Emboldened by this situation, some extremists decided to appeal to a future general council against *Unigenitus* (1717), whereas the more moderate worked unsuccessfully on a official interpretation that would make it acceptable. In reaction, a new papal bull, *Pastoralis Officii* (1718), forbade any "explanation" of *Unigenitus* and declared the appellants excluded from his communion.

Despite the limited areas of resistance and the low numbers of opponents, *Unigenitus* generated a crisis that was to have ripple effects over the evolution of the post-Tridentine Church. The ill-fated papal constitution became exemplary of a type of Catholicism that was rejected for both its authoritarianism and its doctrinal deficiencies. This rejection also took political tones, due to the involment of the secular power in the conflict.

The Politics of Jansenism. When the impossibility of a resolution became evident, the French ministry under Cardinal Fleury took drastic steps: exile, imprisonment of the major opponents, even the impeachment of Bishop

Soanen by the Provincial Synod of Embrun (1727). In 1730 *Unigenitus* was registered as the law of the land. In 1749, the archbishop of Paris, Christophe de Beaumont, decided to deny the sacraments (and therefore Christian burial) to those who did not assent to the bull. These measures contributed to a weakening and dispersion of the Jansenists. An important group decided to yield, in order to maintain their original goal of Christian excellence. Between Jansenists and anti-Jansenists, they constituted an influential "Third Party." Many continued in their opposition: they appealed to public opinion and sought support from the lawyers of the Parlements. Inevitably, some became more extreme: the miracles of Saint-Médard cemetery and the *Convulsionaries* (1730–1760) manifested the spiritual confusion of many, whereas the biblical "figuratism" of Duguet and d'Ettemare expressed the complete disillusion of a few.

Theological and political resistance was not entirely unsuccessful. In 1748, Benedict XIV reaffirmed the "liberty of schools" between Molinism, THOMISM, and AUGUSTINIANISM. In 1754, after a serious conflict with the Parlements, Louis XV forbade any public controversy on *Unigenitus,* later obtaining papal support of that position (*Ex omnibus christiani orbis regionibus* 1756). The expulsion of the Jesuits from France (1761–64), and the suppression of the Society of Jesuits in 1773, were perceived as a victory of the Jansenists. It certainly manifested the influence of the movement, diffused through innumerable pamphlets, books, and the clandestine newsletter, the *Nouvelles ecclésiastiques* (1728–1803), to the major posts of "Catholic Enlightenment."

European Jansenism. Schism was not avoided in the Netherlands, where local tensions with Rome resulted in the election, and consecration by a French Jansenist, of the first bishop of the Old Catholic Church (1723). About the same time, in Mediterranean and Middle European countries, many of the Jansenist themes appeared in various expressions of the "Catholic Enlightenment" that developed under the protection of the States. Though opposed to the *Philosophes,* they favored a critical renewal of Christianity based on the early church model. As they found most of their inspiration in the writings of the Port-Royal circle, they revived the entire movement by developing an international network dedicated to this internal reform. The decrees of the Synod of PISTOIA (1786) are representative of this perspective, condemned by Pius VI in AUCTOREM FIDEI (1794, H. Denzinger, *Enchiridion symbolorum* [Freiburg 1963] 2600–2700).

Jansenism and Revolution. Transfering to the State the principles they advocated in the church, members of the Jansenist party were influential in the opposition to absolutism that prepared the way for the French Revolution. They were also involved in the first stages of the revolution, but they disagreed on the issue of the CIVIL CONSTITUTION OF THE CLERGY. Very few actually adhered to the Constitutional church, but as its leaders, especially Bishop Henri Grégoire, came to see themselves as the heirs of Port-Royal; they manifested in the early 19th century what can be seen as the last coherent form of Jansenism.

Jansenist Mentality

As a movement, Jansenism defies a compact definition because of a conflict-filled history that spans two centuries of major change in European society. A "Jansenist mentality" that unites the different forms of Jansenism might more easily be described. It is a combination of three elements: theological, social, and political.

Theological. The theological specificity of Jansenism has its origin with a rigid Augustinian interpretation of the relation between nature and grace. The five propositions condemned by Innocent X mark the limits of its orthodoxy. As a part of the French Catholic renewal, it soon took a practical expression: to the "humanistic conception" of Molinism was opposed a high ideal of personal holiness. Based on Scripture, sacraments, and a strict morality, a more personal and truthful piety was to improve society at large. The pastoral efforts of bishops and clergy associated with the movement show abundantly the importance of biblical rediscovery, and of liturgical participation supporting an authentic spirituality.

This "archaic Jansenism" flourished in the "frontiers of Catholicism," possibly emulating Protestantism. Its development was thwarted by its sacramental and moral rigorism, but also by an association of "patristic fundamentalism" with a static ecclesiology, incapable of accepting the post-Tridentine structure of the Church. The difficulties it encountered created an irresolvable opposition with the Magisterium of the Church, accentuating a form of individualism inherent to any reform movement. Hence a notable drift towards Gallican Episcopalism, and later Richerist Presbyterianism.

Social. The participation of the nobility and lower classes in the movement was limited, but it appears that especially in times of crisis the Jansenist cause received the support of an "old-style middle class," the "bourgeoisie de Robe." This may have a practical explanation: they had the education and time to be engaged in theological reflection. This explanation has been combined with a sociological interpretation: some members of this bourgeoisie expressed in their involvement with Jansenism the difficulties they experienced as a class in exerting political influence. Some found motivations for a spiritual

withdrawal, a complete "refusal of the world" (*Jansénisme extramondain*); others for a total resistance, religious and political (*Jansénisme intramondain*). This thesis has the merit of pointing to the social composition of the movement and its varying attitudes toward society. It does not offer a satisfactory interpretation of a centrist position more concerned with the religious reform of society, principally through education, social action, and political involvement. If Jansenist exaltation of the right of conscience represented values attractive to the bourgeois ideal in earlier times, Jansenist morality with its rejection of temporal achievement and its opposition to usury explains the disaffection of 18th-century bourgeoisie.

Political. The political ideal of Jansenius and of his disciples was that of a Catholic monarch supporting the interests of the Church. Their resolved attachment to this theory and criticism of the emerging modern State accounts for their alienation from public authorities, and the persecution they often had to endure. These difficulties stirred up a spirit of resistance that combined a "mentality of opposition" with a dynamic defense of their ideas. They looked for support in the higher circles of the State and the Church, established a network of influence, relentlessly attacked their adversaries, and constantly sought public support through pamphleteering. This activism enriched and nuanced their "political theology," which followed the religious evolution of the movement, but because of their theological perception of the monarchy, they never envisioned in the State the democratic polity they advocated in the Church. Jansenism's democratic influence on society is indirect and unintentional, the result of a resistance movement mentality and a participatory ecclesiology.

Jansenism cannot simply be reduced to a reactionary struggle over ideals of Church, State, and society. It was an authentic spiritual movement that exceedingly rationalized its experience and obstinately defended its conclusions. In doing so it limited the function and authority of the Church, a flaw that its enemies were keen to stress and use against it. Subsequent resistance amply supported the accusation, prompting condemnation of a notion of spiritual renewal and ecclesiastical reform that might have been condoned in a different context. Despite the diversity of the movement, one element kept it together: an elitist and intellectual conception of the relationship between God and man and a deep commitment to vindicate it. Paradoxically, it can therefore be said that by their conduct the Jansenists hindered the very process of renewal that they so tenaciously espoused.

Bibliography: E. APPOLIS, *Entre Jansénistes et Zelanti: Le Tiers Parti catholique au XVIIIe siècle* (Paris 1960). C. A. BOLTON, *Church Reform in 18th-Century Italy (The Synod of Pistoia, 1786)*

(The Hague 1969). L. CEYSSENS, "Les cinq propositions de Jansenius à Rome," *Jansenistica minora* XI; L. CEYSSENS and J. A. G. TANS, *Autour de l'Unigenitus* (Louvain 1987). P. CHAUNU, "Jansénisme et frontières de catholicité (XVIIᵉ et XVIIIᵉ siècles) *Revue historique* 227 (1962) 115–138. R. M. GOLDEN ed., *Church and Society under the Bourbon Kings* (Lawrence 1982). L. KOLAKOWSKI, *God Owes Us Nothing* (Chicago 1995). E. KOVACS, ed., *Katholische Aufklärung und Josephinismus* (Vienna 1977). B. R. KREISER, *Miracles, Convulsions and Ecclesiastical Politics in Early Eighteenth-Century Paris* (Princeton, N.J. 1978): H. DE LUBAC, *Augustinianism and Modern Theology* (London 1969). C. L. MAIRE, "Port-Royal: The Jansenist Schism," in P. NORA, ed., *Realms of Memory: The Construction of the French Past*, v. 1 (New York 1996) 301–351. B. NEVEU, *L'erreur et son juge*. B. PLONGERON, "Recherches sur l'Aufklärung catholique en Europe occidentale (1770–1830)," *Revue d'histoire moderne et contemporaine* 16 (1969) 555–605. J. L. QUANTIN, *Le Catholicisme classique et les Pères de l'Église* (Paris 1999). M. ROSA, ed., *Cattolicesimu e lumi nel settecento italiano* (Rome 1981). A. SEDGWICK, *Jansenism in Seventeenth-Century France* (Charlottesville 1977). J. SAUGNIEUX, *Le Jansénisme espagnol du XVIIIᵉ siècle: Ses composantes et ses sources* (Oviedo 1975). P. STELLA, *Studi sul Giansenismo* (Bari 1972). R. TAVENEAUX, *Jansénisme et politique* (Paris 1965). D. VAN KLEY, *The Jansenists and the Expulsion of the Jesuits from France, 1757–1765* (New Haven, Conn. 1975); *The Religious Origins of the French Revolution* (New Haven–London 1996). F. E. WEAVER, "The Neo-Gallican Liturgies Revisited," *Studia liturgica* 16 (1986–87) 54–72.

[J. M. GRES-GAYER]

JANSENISTIC PIETY

Though the strong divergent personalities of the Jansenist movement somewhat prevent identifying a clear and homogeneous spirituality, there are enough theoretical and practical elements to define a Jansenist type of piety. It would be irrelevant to find it in AUGUSTINUS, a purely theological book, but the Augustinian vision of the relation between God and man that it presents is certainly a key to understanding Jansenist spirituality. It was inspired by an abhorrence of MOLINISM, that is, a perspective that allowed for some human participation in the process of salvation. For the Jansenists, it was essential to stress God's transcendence and omnipotence in order to establish with him a proper relationship based on love. They saw the discernment of God's will in one's life mainly as a prayerful process, checked and guided by spiritual direction. What is particular to the movement may be the importance given to a knowledge of God acquired through meditation on Scripture and liturgy, the ordinary ways through which God inspires and communicates with the faithful. Consonant is the notion of "vocation" shared with the French school of SPIRITUALITY at large. Jansenist followers believed that every individual is called by God to a particular state of life and given the grace to live in it. This is clear in the case of religious or priestly vocations but is also applied to secular conditions

as well. In accord with the accent put on divine transcendence is the Jansenists' attraction to manifestations of the supernatural, in the form of signs and miracles.

The Jansenists have been decried for their rigorism in moral and sacramental life. Their moral rigorism was at times more pronounced, because of their opposition to Jesuit laxism, or due to the austerity of some, but it was not a distinct feature, being shared by the elite of the Catholic renewal since the times of Charles Borromeo. The sacramental practice of encouraging a delay of absolution and infrequent reception of the Eucharist, was likewise not simply limited to the PORT-ROYAL circle, but reflected a common conception of the sacraments as means of grace that had to be taken very seriously. By insisting on the necessity of preparation for—and cooperation in—the saving encounter with God, these authors, in continuity with the teaching of the early church, saw the sacraments as the "seal," the strengthening of a process of purification begun though prayer and mortification. This explains why the group was so keen on liturgical participation and reform, advocating the use of translations and revision of the ancient rituals (neo–Gallican liturgies). In their desire to maintain a Christocentric spirituality, many Jansenists were critical of extreme Marian devotions, and fought against the new devotion to the Sacred Heart of Jesus. In this they showed themselves in total disagreement with the type of popular spirituality successfully developed by the Society of Jesus.

All these features classically presented as typical of "Jansenism" were more representative of an intellectual, abstract, and rather haughty conception that did not respond to the needs of post–Tridentine Catholicism. It has been noted that the Jansenists did not involve themselves in any missionary action, preferring to focus on the communication of their ideas and perspectives. This attitude is indicative of what may be the main characteristic (and flaw) of the movement: their defective conception of the church. This is amply demonstrated first with C. Jansenius himself, preparing his *Augustinus* against a Roman ban; it was continued by successive resistance to papal and episcopal condemnations, and many instances of impertinence. The penitential practice of the Jansenists—rejection of attrition (allowed by Trent), placing of satisfaction (penance) before absolution—also suggests a sacramental theology that minimizes the mediation of the church.

In theory the type of ecclesiology exposed by the French Jansenists and their disciples was of the Gallican form, but more of a Richerist type than the classical episcopalism of the 1682 Articles. They saw the Church more as a community of believers sharing the same sacraments than a hierarchical and social structure, stressing therefore the "mysterial aspect" against the jurisdictional. As a consequence they recognized more the role of the laity, offering men and women a more active participation in the life of the church. This fit well with the spirituality of "vocation," mentioned above, and attracted a motivated elite. This defective ecclesiology, theoretical and above all practical, explains why from an early stage Rome saw the movement as a dangerous sect, disobedience being perceived as a sign of heterodoxy, and condemned it without nuances. The bull *UNIGENITUS* complicated the issues, as it seemed to condemn perfectly orthodox positions. Only *AUCTOREM FIDEI* would clarify the situation, though it created an image of "Jansenism" that was more abstract than real. The unfortunate result would be that many elements of Jansenist life and spirituality that were a part of the larger post–Tridentine renewal were suspected of Jansenism and too easily discarded.

Bibliography: R. A. KNOX, *Enthusiasm* (New York 1950; repr. 1961). E. DUBOIS, "Jansenism," in C. JONES, G. WAINWRIGHT, and E. YARNOLD, eds., *The Study of Spirituality* (New York and Oxford 1986) 396–408. L. DUPRÉ, "Jansenism and Quietism," in L. DUPRÉ and D. E. SALIERS, *Christian Spirituality: Post Reformation and Modern* (New York 1989) 121–142. M. DE CERTEAU, "De Saint–Cyran au Jansénisme: Conversion et Réforme," *Christus* 10 (1963), 399–414. L. MEZZADRI, *La Spiritualità cristiana nell'età moderna* (Rome 1987) 176–193. J. ORCIBAL, *Saint Cyran et le Jansénisme* (Paris 1961). L. COGNET, "La direction de conscience a Port–Royal," *Vie spirituelle*, Supplément 7 (1955) 289–305. "La dévotion mariale à Port–Royal," in *Maria: Études sur la Sainte Vierge*, ed. H. DU MANOIR (Paris 1950) III, 119–151; "Les Jansénistes et le Sacré–Cœur," *Le Cœur, Études Carmélitaines* (Paris 1950) 234–253. R. TAVENEAUX, *La vie quotidienne des Jansénistes aux XVIIe et XVIIIe siècle* (Paris 1973). *Jansénisme et réforme catholique* (Paris 1992). L. J. WANG, "A Controversial Treatise: Baillet's *De la Dévotion à la Sainte Vierge*," *Harvard Theological Review* 51 (1958) 263–274. N. D. KURLAND, "Antoine Arnauld's First Controversy: *De la Fréquente Communion*," in *The Dawn of Modern Studies*, ed. K. A. STRAND, (1962) 239–251. F. E. WEAVER, "Jansenist Bishops and Liturgical–Social Reforms," in R. M. GOLDEN, ed., *Church, State, and Society under the Bourbon Kings of France* (Lawrence, KS 1982); "Erudition, Spirituality, and Women: The Jansenist Contribution," in *Women in Reformation and Counter Reformation Europe*, ed. S. MARSHALL (1989) 189–206. J. M. GRES–GAYER, "The Bull Unigenitus: A Fresh Look at the Issues," *Theological Studies*, 49 (1988) 259–282; "L'idée d'Église des Jansénistes," *Port–Royal et les Protestants* (Paris 1998) 35–56. J. L. QUANTIN, *Le rigorisme* (Paris 2001).

[J. M. GRES–GAYER]

JANSSEN, ARNOLD, BL.

Religious founder; b. Goch, in the Rhineland, Germany, November 5, 1837; d. Steyl, Netherlands, January 15, 1909. After passing a state examination to teach natural sciences in the secondary schools in Bonn (1859), he studied for the priesthood in Münster and was ordained

(1861). For the next 12 years he taught science in a secondary school in Bocholt. From 1867 he was also diocesan director of the Apostleship of Prayer, which he promoted throughout Germany by publishing a periodical and distributing free leaflets. After relinquishing his teaching duties (1873), he devoted himself to propagating devotion to the Sacred Heart and interest in the missions. With four companions he opened a house to train German priests for foreign mission work. Because of the Kulturkampf the site selected for this house was in the Netherlands at Steyl, near the German border. Janssen's original plan of a missionary society of priests whose members would not take religious vows crystallized into the Society of the Divine Word, a congregation of priests and lay brothers with simple vows. The brothers operated the presses in his large printing establishment at Steyl. During Janssen's term as the first superior general, the institute grew rapidly and spread to the U.S. and to several other countries. In 1889 Janssen founded the Holy Spirit Missionary Sisters to educate girls in mission territories. He founded the cloistered Sisters Servants of the Holy Ghost of Perpetual Adoration, dedicated to perpetual adoration in order to aid by their prayers his missions and missionaries. The Roman decree introducing Janssen's cause for beatification was issued in 1942. He was beatified on Oct. 19, 1975 by Paul VI.

Feast: Jan. 15.

Bibliography: *Briefe in die Vereinigten Staaten von Amerika* (Nettetal 1994); *Briefe nach Neuguinea und Australien* (Nettetal 1996); *Briefe nach Südamerika* (Nettetal 1989–1993); *Mit dem Segen der Kirche: Briefe an Arnold Janssen* (St. Augustin, Steyler Mission, 1975); *P. Arnold Janssen und P. Josef Freinademetz: Briefwechsel 1904–1907: Korresponde[n]z zwischen zwei Seligen*, ed. R. HARTWICH (St. Augustin 1978). J. ALT, *Arnold Janssen: Lebensweg und Lebenswerk des Steyler Ordensgründers* (Nettetal 1999). J. A. BAUER, *Das Presseapostolat Arnold Janssens* (Nettetal 1989). H. DRENKELFORT, *Pater Arnold Janssen SVD* (Sankt Augustin 1975). H. FISCHER, *Arnold Janssen: Gründer des Steyler Missionswerkes* (Steyl 1919), Eng. *Life of Arnold Janssen*, tr. F. M. LYNK (Techny, Ill. 1925); *Vater Arnolds Getreuen* (Steyl 1925), Eng. *Father Arnold Janssen, a Modern Pioneer in Mission Work*, tr. and abr. S. KASBAUER, *Ein Mensch unter Gottes Meissel* (2d ed. Steyl 1959). F. M. LYNK (London 1934); *Tempel Gottes seid ihr!* (Steyl 1932).

[V. J. FECHER]

JANSSENS, ALOYSIUS

Theologian; b. Zele, Belgium, 1887; d. Louvain, 1941. A member of the Congregation of the Immaculate Heart of Mary, better known as the Scheut Fathers, he studied at the Schola Maior of the Jesuits and at the University of Louvain. Though he greatly profited by being in this scientific environment, he was nonetheless basically a self-educated man. Unable to go to the foreign missions for reasons of health, he was named professor of dogmatic theology for his religious community. His desire to keep his missionary fathers in the current of a living dogmatic theology led to a collection of dogmatic and apologetic treatises in Flemish, and he personally edited 17 of the 28 volumes that make up the series. These works go beyond mere popularization; they combine pedagogical clarity with the results of the research in Biblical and positive theology before 1940. Janssen's own research on the Assumption is still useful. He brought to bear on speculative questions a sound judgment and power of penetration. One of his chief merits was that he created a theological vocabulary in Flemish, at his time practically nonexistent. His works on Anglicanism, particularly on Cardinal Newman, encouraged a broader Catholic ecumenism. He was one of the founding members of the first Mariological society begun in 1931 at Tongerloo, Belgium, which by 1963 had published 20 volumes of proceedings. He was for his country the promoter of a theological renewal at once serious and apostolic.

Bibliography: A. VAN HOVE, *Ephemerides theologicae Lovanienses* (1941) 279–293. G. PHILIPS, *Enciclopedia cattolica* 7:565–566.

[G. PHILIPS]

JANSSENS, LOUIS

Professor of moral theology; b. July 23, 1908, Olen, Belgium; d. Leuven, Dec. 19, 2001. At the encouragement of the local parish priest, young Janssens left the Flemish village in which he was reared for Herentals, a Walloon village where he attended high school. After studying at the major seminary, Janssens was ordained a priest of the diocese of Mechelen on Feb. 11, 1934. Janssens completed the S.T.D. degree at the Catholic University of Leuven, and in 1939 he was awarded the degree of Magister in Sacra Theologia.

Janssens' earlier work was in the field of patrology. His doctoral thesis was devoted to CYRIL OF ALEXANDRIA's understanding of divine sonship (grace). He had published articles on GREGORY OF NYSSA (1936, under the pen name O. Van den Bergen) and Cyril (1938). Janssens' magisterial thesis, "Personne et société: théories actuelles et essai doctrinal," marked a clear turning point in Janssens' career. It was inspired by his ordinary, Cardinal Van Roey, who wanted the young scholar to study and respond to the depersonalizing social theories of the 1930s. Janssens' teaching career began at Mechelen's Seminary of St. Joseph in 1939, but Janssens was almost immediately called upon to teach a course in social phi-

losophy at Leuven. After lecturing at the university in the area of fundamental dogma, he turned to moral theology, the subject that would occupy his interest until his (mandatory) retirement in 1978.

Throughout his academic career, the human person was a focal point of his interest. For Janssens, the norm of morality is the human person in itself and its relationships (God, others, the world). His contemporary CHRISTIAN ANTHROPOLOGY focused on the intentionality, the interiority, the physicality, the uniqueness, and the historicity of the human person. These themes appear in *Personalisme en democratisering* (1957, 1965) and "Personalist Morals" [Louvain Studies (1970)]. For several years he lectured on conjugal morality, a topic to which he devoted a number of essays in local pastoral journals. The development of the birth control pill led him to publish a major article in the *Ephemerides theologicae lovanienses* (1963), in which he held that the use of the pill in conjugal relationships was licit insofar as its use basically respected the nature and structure of the conjugal act. Janssens' position was widely discussed and supported by theologians in the years preceding the issuance of Paul VI's HUMANAE VITAE (1968).

Ever the personalist, Janssens devoted much of his later publication to matters of fundamental moral theology. Chief among his interests was the matter of "ontic good and evil," i.e., pre-moral values and disvalues, and the importance of PROPORTIONALITY in determining the moral rightness of human conduct. Using Aquinas as a source and his own personalism as a frame of reference, Janssens proposed that it was the end that is primary in moral evaluation. Appropriate means are to be chosen with regard to their relationship to that end. Not content merely with theory, Janssens used these insights of fundamental moral theology to advance the discussion of such issues as artificial insemination and organ transplantation. His views received wide circulation. Although Janssens was not cited by name in John Paul II's VERITATIS SPLENDOR (1993), the papal encyclical appears to have taken issue with some of Janssens' theory. In "Teleology and Proportionality: Thoughts about the Encyclical *Veritatis Splendor*," (1995) Janssens offered his personal reflections on the papal text.

While most of Janssens' writings appeared in Dutch journals, he published a number of significant English-language articles in *Louvain Studies*. He wrote few books, but one of them, *Liberté de conscience et liberté religieuse* (1964) was an important component of the dialogue that led to Vatican Council II's *Dignitatis humanae*.

Bibliography: D. L. CHRISTIE, "Adequately Considered: An American Perspective on Louis Janssens' Personalist Morals,"

Louvain Theological and Pastoral Monographs 4 (Louvain and Grand Rapids 1990). L. JANSSENS, "Teleology and Proportionality: Thoughts about the Encyclical *Veritatis Splendor*," in *The Splendor of Accuracy,* ed. J. JANS and J. SELLING (Grand Rapids 1995). J. A. SELLING, ed., *Personalist Morals* (Leuven 1988).

[R. F. COLLINS]

JANSSOONE, FRÉDÉRIC CORNIL, BL.

Franciscan missionary; b. Nov. 19, 1838, Ghyvelde (near Dunkirk), Flanders, Belgium; d. Aug. 4, 1916, Montréal, Québec, Canada. Although Frédéric was the youngest of 13 children from a wealthy farm family, he had to quit school to help his mother after his father's death (*c.* 1848). He soon discovered that his love for others made him a great salesman—this talent later served him well as a preacher. After his mother's death in 1861, he discerned his vocation. He entered the Franciscan novitiate (June 1864), was ordained (Aug. 17, 1870), served as a military chaplain during the Franco-Prussian War (1870–71), and was custodian for a time at the Bordeaux monastery. In 1876 he was sent to the Holy Land, where he raised funds to maintain two ancient churches, built a new one at Bethlehem, and revived the custom of pilgrims praying the Stations of the Cross in the streets of Jerusalem. He traveled to Canada (1881–82) to collect alms for the Holy Land and returned there six years later (1888). The rest of his life was spent preaching, evangelizing, and establishing the Canadian province of the Franciscans from his base at the shrine of Our Lady of Cap-de-la-Madeleine. Janssoone also composed about 30 popular monographs, most of which are spiritual descriptions of the Holy Land and hagiography. His deep spirituality and ministerial zeal drew many through him to Christ. He was beatified by John Paul II, Sept. 25, 1988.

Feast: Aug. 5.

Bibliography: Works: *Vie de saint François d' Assise* (Montréal 1894); *Vie de notre Seigneur Jésus-Christ, écrite avec les paroles mêmes des quatre évangélistes* (Québec 1894); *La bonne sainte Anne. Sa vie, ses miracles, ses sanctuaires* (Montréal 1896); *Saint Joseph. Sa vie, son culte* (Québec 1902); *Le ciel, séjour des élus* (Montréal 1912). *The Life and Spirituality of Good Father Frederic Janssoone in His Own Words,* ed. R. LÉGARÉ, tr. R. BROWN (Quebec 1973). Literature: O. LAMONTAGNE, *Un témoin de l'autre monde: le père Frédéric dans l'intimité* (Trois-Rivières, Québec 1960). R. LÉGARÉ, *An Apostle of Two Worlds,* tr. R. BROWN (Chicago 1958), tr. of *Un apôtre des deux mondes: le père Frédéric Janssoone* (Montréal 1953); *Un grand serviteur de la Terre Sainte, le père Frédéric Janssoone* (Trois Rivières, Québec 1965); *Le bon père Frédéric,* with C. BAILLARGEON (Montreal 1988). H. LEMAY, *Bibliographie et iconographie du Serviteur de Dieu le R. P. Frédéric Janssoone* (Québec 1932). J.-F. MOTTE, *Frédéric Janssoone de Ghyvelde: franciscain apôtre du Christ en trois continents* (Paris 1988). T. F. MURPHY, *Our Lady's Herald. A Short Account of the Life of Father Frederick Janssoone* (Trois Rivières 1965). *Acta Apostolicae Sedis,* 32 (1940) 516ff.

[K. I. RABENSTEIN]

JANUARIUS, ST.

Martyr of Benevento, well known because of the liquefaction of a phial of his blood in the Cathedral of Naples; Januarius (or Gennaro) is believed to have been martyred in the DIOCLETIAN persecution of 305. Nothing is known of his life although a legendary *passio* narrates that after being thrown to the bears (*ad ursas*) in the amphitheater of Pozzuoli, he was decapitated together with the deacons Sossus, Festus, and Proculus, and Desiderius the lector. Januarius is mentioned by GREGORY OF TOURS and by BEDE. His remains are said to have been brought to Naples by Bishop John and placed in the catacomb of Capodimonte. In 831, they were translated to Benevento; in 1154, to Montevirgine; and in 1497, returned to Naples. The *passio* was translated into Greek in the 10th or 11th century, thus entering the *Synaxary of Constantinople.*

A dark mass that half fills a hermetically sealed four-inch glass container, and is preserved in a double reliquary in the Naples cathedral as the blood of St. Januarius, liquefies 18 times during the year: (1) on the Saturday before the first Sunday in May and the eight following days; (2) on the feast of St. Januarius, and during the octave; and (3) on December 16. This phenomenon goes back to the 14th century when it was mentioned in the chronicle of an unknown Sicilian in 1389 (published by G. de Blasiis, Naples 1887), although tradition connects it with a certain Eusebia, who had allegedly collected the blood after the martyrdom and given the reliquary to the bishop of Naples on the Via Antoniana during the transfer of the body from Pozzuoli to the catacomb. The ceremony accompanying the liquefaction is performed by holding the reliquary close to the altar on which is located what is believed to be the martyr's head. While the people pray, often tumultuously, the priest turns the reliquary up and down in the full sight of the onlookers until the liquefaction takes place. He then announces, "The miracle has happened," and the *Te Deum* is chanted by the people and clergy.

Various thermal experiments as well as spectroscopic analysis have been applied to the contents of the reliquary; but the phenomenon eludes natural explanation. There are, however, similar miraculous claims made for the blood of SS. JOHN THE BAPTIST, STEPHEN the protomartyr, Pantaleon, Patricia, NICHOLAS OF TOLENTINO, and ALOYSIUS GONZAGA—nearly all in the neighborhood of Naples.

St. Januarius in an attitude of prayer, a 4th-century fresco in the catacomb of St. Januarius, Naples.

St. Januarius is the patron of Naples, and a vast folklore is connected with his cult. The earliest representation of the saint exists in a catacomb on Capodimonte, where he is depicted praying between two dead persons, and clothed in tunic, pallium, and sandals, and with a nimbus, the Constantinian monogram, the Alpha and Omega, and an inscription. (*See* CHI-RHO.) Many churches were erected in his honor and decorated with a bust or pictures of the saint.

Feast: Sept. 19.

Bibliography: P. FRANCHI DE' CAVALIERI, "S. Gennaro vescovo e martire," *Note agiografiche* 3 (Studi e Testi 24; 1912). H. DELEHAYE, *Les Origines du culte des martyrs* (2d ed., Brussels 1933) 24–49. G. B. ALFANO and A. AMITRANO, *Il miraculo di S. Gennaro* (Naples 1950) with bibliog. A. CASERTA, *Storia e scienca di fronte al miracolo di s. Gennaro* (2d ed. Naples 1972). V. PALIOTTI, *San Gennaro: storia di un culto, di un mito, dell'anima di un popolo* (Milan 1983). M. L. STRANIERO, *Indagine su san Gennaro: miracoli, fede, scienza* (Milan 1991). ARCHDIOCESE OF NAPLES, *San Gennaro: tra fede, arte e mito* (Pozzuoli, Italy 1997).

[E. G. RYAN]

JAPAN, MARTYRS OF

This account of the martyrs of Japan is presented in five parts: (1) the reasons for the persecution of Christians, (2) the external course of the persecutions, (3) the spirit of martyrdom in the early Japanese Church, (4) individual martyrdoms (the 26 holy and the 205 blessed martyrs), and (5) the number of martyrs.

Reasons for the Persecution of Christians

The resistance to Christianity in Japan and the harassment of Christians that ended frequently in martyrdom is derived from the following principal causes.

Memorial to the 26 Holy Martyrs at the Church of San Philippo, Nagsaki, Japan. (©Ric Ergenbright/CORBIS)

Religious Opposition. The primary roots of the persecutions are found in religious opposition. Ignorance and erroneous interpretation of Christian doctrine, which had been discussed ever since the arrival of St. Francis XAVIER (Aug. 15, 1549), might well have occasioned distrust, since the notions of Christianity were so new in this world of quite different religious and cultural traditions. The Christian movement in Japan had, after some years, advanced rapidly, aided by an increased number of European missionaries, their native assistants, and Japanese lay apostles, including in the course of time several specially zealous and influential feudal lords. Over against this minority stood the powerful world of Japanese BUDDHISM, rooted for centuries in the traditions of the people and nurtured by a considerable social, literary, and artistic culture; Buddhism's countless shrines covered the entire country, and its intellectual centers were famous Temple Universities whose prelates were often scions of the noblest families. SHINTOISM also influenced the people, partly as it was permeated and absorbed by Buddhism. But with the forward thrust of the Christian idea, a more or less palpable decline of the Buddhist and Shintoist religions began in various regions. The withdrawal of prominent members and often of quite large groups of the temple communities involved a loss of prestige and

financial weakening. It is no wonder, accordingly, that the success of Christian missionary work aroused resentment on the part of the Buddhists and Shintoists. Since the bonzes in many localities had a strong influence on the provincial lords of the feudal states, the city governors, and the fortress captains, disapproval, if not open hostility, was to be expected from the authorities. The greater the success of Christianity, the more easily could the opposition be kindled into actual persecution.

Missionary Methods. Not infrequently anti-Christian feeling was deepened by the methods of the missionaries. They made efforts to win the favor of the provincial lords and wherever possible to convert them. They had great success in 1563 when the feudal lord of Ōmura and several respected noblemen in central Japan joined the Church. Soon other lords followed their example. Convinced that a durable Christianity could be guaranteed only if the entire fief became Christian, the missionaries began from 1574 to pressure the convert feudal lords (when the lords did not decide on the same course of action as a result of their own zeal) to open the path to complete conversion; the principle invoked was that of *cujus regio, ejus religio,* a principle often employed in Europe and not unknown in Japan in the dealings of the various sects with one another. Often the action was limited to inducing the population to take catechetical instruction, with no compulsory baptism being practiced. In other cases, everyone was faced with the decision of becoming a Christian or emigrating from the fief. This pressure was extended to include even the Buddhist bonzes, many of whom accepted baptism. The temples were either converted into Christian churches or destroyed, and the statues of the Buddhist and Shintoist shrines were burned (often as firewood in the mission stations), together with their sacred writings. Japanese chronicles of the period relate instances of bonzes fleeing with great difficulty into another feudal state, taking with them the secretly abducted religious pictures of their temple. It is not hard to imagine the motivation of their activity in their new home: to the extent of their influence, they became dangerous opponents of Christianity.

Domestic Political Tensions. With the growth of Christian influence and the almost simultaneous increase in the power of the Japanese central government, domestic political tensions came to the fore. At the outset of the mass conversion movement (from 1574) there was still some prospect of pushing Christianity to a complete triumph by the forcible methods mentioned above. The central government in the provinces around Kyōto was so weakened that, at least in distant Kyūshū, there was scarcely anything to be feared from it. And Oda Nobunaga (1534 to 1582), was so fiercely opposed to the bonzes that he openly favored the Jesuits. He was assassinated (June 1582) before any change of mind on his part could become disastrous for the missionaries. His successor, Toyotomi Hideyoshi (1536 to 1598), found a substantially different situation. More feudal lords had adhered to the Christian faith; among them was Ōtomo Yoshishige in Kyūshū, one of the greatest and, indeed, a few years earlier, the most important public figure in the Saikoku (southwest). In central Japan likewise the number and quality of the highly placed Christians was growing and the gifted, idealistic Justus Takayama Ukon was one of the most admirable. Toyotomi Hideyoshi, however, was not so completely opposed to the Buddhist circles as his predecessor had been. He had, indeed, to fight against the Sōhei (monk soldiers), and he knew how to keep the truculent bonzes drastically in check; but he also sought to win the good will of the monks: he allowed the rebuilding of the temples that Oda Nobunaga had destroyed, had a gigantic statue of Buddha erected in Kyōto (1586 to 1589), and gave the monks other proofs of his benevolence. Initially he seemed not unkindly disposed toward the Christian missionaries; indeed, the expressions of his favor mounted to an unexpected climax in the campaign in Kyūshū in 1587. But in Kyūshū the questions posed by the intensive Christian propaganda did not escape Hideyoshi's attention: Why were the Christians destroying the temples, which were an ornament of the country and objects of veneration to the Japanese as monuments of religious tradition and culture? How could there be effected a reconciliation of the Buddhist monks, who were so deeply disturbed by the development of the religious situation in Kūshū? But above all, the ruler believed he foresaw the possibility of severe domestic and political complications in a progressive Christianization of the country. He became convinced that all Christians, even the Christian feudal lords, had an inner unity that gave them solidarity; that the lords were submissive to the highly educated and intelligent missionaries; and that the effort of the missionaries was to convert not only the simple people but preferably and precisely the ruling circles. Hideyoshi compared the Christian missions with the Ikkō sects, whose head, the ''bonze of Osaka,'' i.e., the chief of the fortified temple of Ishiyama-Honganji in Osaka, had been able for many years to defy Oda Nobunaga and still represented a latent danger for Hideyoshi. But whereas the Ikkō-shū had contented himself with winning over the agrarian population, the Christians were aiming at the aristocracy. Hideyoshi prided himself on having been the first to recognize the great danger, and to free himself from the deceptive brilliance of the missionaries' well-chosen words. To what extent he was afraid on principle of a possible alliance among the Christian feudal lords, and to what extent he had knowledge of such an alliance actively developing in the plans of Gaspar Coelho, the imprudent major superior of the Jesuits, and the Church in Japan, it is difficult to say. Coelho tried this policy with little success and less wisdom and in the process had a thorough falling out with the two Christian feudal Lords of Arima and Ōura.

Fear of Foreign Invaders. The extent to which motives of foreign policy played a part even as early as the outbreak of the persecution (1587) is not clear. Hideyoshi laid greater stress on the inner unity of the Japanese Christians among themselves than on their connection with any foreign power. It is certain, however, that Coelho had asked for Spanish soldiers and ammunition from Manila quite some time before 1587; he probably wanted these primarily to secure the Christian position in Kyūshū. Alessandro VALIGNANO, then Jesuit provincial of India, had resolutely rejected this initiative. After the Decree of Exile (1587), Coelho again revived his plan, summoned a consultation on Feb. 11, 1589, in Takaku (Arima), and approved the dispatch of Melchior de Mora to Valignano in Macau or, in the event of Valignano's absence, to the Philippines. Mora was to ask for Spanish soldiers from the Philippines. Valignano at once hushed the matter up and in 1590 took Mora back with him to Japan. Coelho died in that year and with him the plan. It is conceivable that his intentions were known not at all or only vaguely to the Japanese central authorities despite their intelligence service. But the distrust of foreigners grew more acute in those years. European globes and world maps were known in Japan, and the Spanish conquests, not only in South America but particularly in the nearby Philippines, with whom direct contacts were becoming more frequent, aroused fears. When in October 1596 the San Felipe was forced to make port in Urado (Tosa, Shikoku), her pilot pointed to the map of the world and made the famous declaration, obviously in the belief that this would terrify the Japanese, that the missionaries would come first and then the king would send soldiers and so conquer country after country. There is scarcely sufficient reason to doubt this statement, although it is possible that it was used by the Japanese authorities more as a pretext than as a justification for requisitioning the cargo of the San Felipe and for condemning to death the Spanish Franciscans of Tosa who had intervened to save the vessel. Still, the threat from abroad remained operative, now latent, now overt, until the end of the early Japanese Church. The Europeans themselves imprudently gave the threat new strength. Sebastián Vizcaino, the famous explorer, boasted in dispatches to the Spanish king that he had sounded and surveyed the northeast coast of Japan in 1611 to 1612 with permission of the Japanese. This may have been cartographically and nautically worthwhile; but it provided the enemies of the Christians at court the opportunity of raising anew the question of the foreign connections of the Japanese Christians.

Lack of Unity among Europeans in Japan. Both the domestic and the foreign policy motives of the persecution were kept alive and heightened by the lack of unity, indeed hostility, between the various European groups in Japan: between the Portuguese, who had reached Japan via Goa-Malacca-Macau, and the Spaniards, who had come via New Spain and Manila; further and still more deep-seated, between the Nambanjin (the Southern Barbarians, i.e., the Iberians coming from Macau and Manila) and the *Kōmōjin* (the Redheads, i.e., the blond Englishmen and Dutchmen).

The Attitude of Christians toward the Japanese State and Its Laws. Whether in Japan, Macao, Manila, or elsewhere abroad, the Christian attitude toward the state and its laws gave rise to serious complications. Culpable conduct by individuals or groups was blamed by the Japanese authorities on the Christian religion as such. Scandals in the lives of the European merchants in Japan and the alleged kidnaping of Japanese for slavery were instances of such behavior. A total break in relations almost resulted from clashes in Macau between Japanese and Portuguese; for example, the disturbances set off by the Japanese passengers of two Go-shuin-sen (Red-Seal Ships) of the lord of Arima in Macau in 1608, which led to the Japanese attack (Jan. 6, 1610) against the *Nossa Senhora da Graça* in the harbor of Nagasaki. The quarrel (1611 to 1612) between two influential Christians, the lord of Arima (John Arima) and Paul Okamoto Daihachi, secretary at court, brought to light illegal operations on the part of both and resulted in their condemnation, thereby severely damaging the prestige of Christianity. In November 1613 several criminals, a Christian among them, were put to death near Miyako (Kyōto); there were Christians among the crowd of spectators who knelt at the moment of execution to pray for the dying Christian. This was interpreted by the pagans as an act of worship of the criminal. When the incident was reported to the authorities, Tokugawa Iyeyasu dismissed 14 Christian officials from court and deprived them of office. This example was quickly imitated by many feudal lords. The uneasiness of the court was augmented by reports of the rekindling of the Christian movement in Arima. Iyeyasu decreed unconditional banishment for the missionaries from the Gokinai (Central Japan) in February 1614 and from the whole of Japan in November 1614.

In later years, unlawful acts had an important influence on the vehemence of the persecution. The Dominican Diego Collado, for example, rescued a confrere from the Hirado prison only to have him again apprehended by pursuers in a boat, while Collado escaped into the neighboring forest. This infraction of Japanese justice caused a vehement outbreak of cruelty against the missionaries then under arrest. Again, Paulo dos Santos defied a Japanese ban by sending merchandise from Macau to Japan in 1632 in order to contribute by the proceeds to the support of the missionaries living clandestinely in Japan. In 1634 he wrote about it (this, too, was against the law) to a friend in Japan. His letter was confiscated and both the Portuguese who had the letter with him and the Japanese to whom it was addressed were publicly burned. Similar incidents increased the tensions between Japan and Macao. The Shimabara uprising of 1637 to 1638, a social revolt that rapidly assumed a religious character, resulted in the final break with the Portuguese: Macau, the last base of the Japanese mission, was eliminated in 1639.

These examples highlight the motives that impelled the Japanese rulers in the 16th and 17th centuries to disapprove of Christianity and to engage in a bloody persecution. The Japanese course of action is understandable, but even when all the circumstances are recognized and admitted, the government cannot be absolved of responsibility for its attitudes and methods.

External Course of the Persecutions

Though there was local molestation of Christians from the beginning of the Japanese mission, the first general persecution broke unexpectedly, like a hurricane. On the night of July 24 to July 25, 1587, Toyotomi Hideyoshi decreed the dismissal of the Christian general and feudal lord Justus Takayama Ukon and sent a moderately worded complaint to the Jesuit vice provincial, communicating to him on the same evening the measures taken against Ukon.

Toyotomi Hideyoshi's Decree of Banishment (1587). On July 25, 1587, Hideyoshi decreed that the missionaries could no longer remain in Japan because they were destroyers of the temples and preachers of a "diabolical" law. They were to leave within 20 days. The Portuguese merchants were still allowed unhindered access to Japan for trading purposes, so long as they observed Japanese laws. The decree could not be implemented in this form because there was no ship leaving Japan for Macau that soon. Hideyoshi's order did, however, have immediate serious consequences for the Church in Japan. A new piece of property in Hakata just given to the Church by Hideyoshi himself was lost; the port of Nagasaki, which for some years had been administered by the Church, was taken away from her jurisdiction, together with the smaller neighbor port of Mogi and the holdings in Urakami; and Hideyoshi levied an oppressive fine on the townsmen of Nagasaki. The church movables were for the most part successfully secured in Hirado, however, before Hideyoshi's men reached Nagasaki. These soldiers were willing to accept bribes to leave the churches in the city untouched and simply to close the main entrances. For the rest, they contented themselves with tearing down the city walls. The fortresses in the Christian fiefs of Ōmura and Arima also had to be dismantled. Later, Hideyoshi sent word that the fathers could remain in Japan until the next monsoon and the sailing of the China boat of the Portuguese, but meanwhile they must assemble on the Hirado Islands to await departure.

All the houses in central Japan, as well as the new foundations in southwest Hondo (Shimonoseki, Yamaguchi) and on Shikoku (in Dōgo, Iyo) were vacated. Most of the fathers in Kyūshū also came to Hirado. There in a consultation it was decided that all missionaries (with the exception of a few sick priests and some scholastics who could travel to Macau for ordination) were to remain in Japan and be secretly accommodated in the Christian fiefs. Soon after the persecution edict, Hideyoshi returned to central Japan; the decision taken at Hirado was forthwith carried out. In February 1588, shortly before the sailing for Macau, Capt. Domingos Monteiro sent Francisco Garcés to Hideyoshi with the message that not all the fathers had found accommodation on the boat and that the others would have to sail next year. Hideyoshi gave the order to destroy the Jesuit houses in Miyako, Osaka, and Sakai and many churches in the regions of Takatsuki (Settsu), Akashi (Harima), and Gifu (Mino). He threatened to kill all the missionaries who had remained behind. The *Nao* ran into port in Japan on Aug. 17, 1588. Captain Jeronymo Pereira sent the Portuguese Manoel Lopez to the court to take reassuring news to Hideyoshi (now Kambaku, a court title assumed in 1585) about the departure of the fathers. Hideyoshi appeared satisfied, but it was the general opinion that he knew they were still secretly in Japan. He gave permission for the fathers to accompany the Portuguese on the voyage from Macau to Japan so long as they departed again by the same ship; this was considered a further sign of relaxation of tensions.

Embassy of Alessandro Valignano (1590). After the audience, the Kambaku was notified that the ambassador of the viceroy of the Indies was waiting in Macau to come to Japan and pay his respects. Letters patent were made out that authorized the journey with the next ship. The announcement of this embassy had a further moderating effect on the ruler. The ambassador, Visitator Alessandro Valignano, SJ, arrived on July 21, 1590. On March 3, 1591, the memorable audience with Hideyoshi took place; it was as solemn as it was friendly. Although Valignano could not even bring up the question of the restitution of the fathers' former status, he indirectly achieved what he desired, for Hideyoshi permitted, indeed demanded, that ten fathers remain in Nagasaki as hostages until an answer had arrived from the viceroy of the Indies. This could be interpreted as a permission for all the Jesuits to remain in Japan, if they respected the Japanese mentality, accommodated their activities to the actual state of affairs, and did not irritate the ruler by any open protest against the persecution laws.

New Measures and the First Executions (1597). Even before the departure of the ambassador from Japan, the large church in Nagasaki was destroyed about August 1592; but it was established that this did not involve any new enmity toward Christianity; rather, Hideyoshi's minister simply wanted the valuable materials of the church for building operations in Nagoya (Hizen). The Korean War (1592 to 1598), which brought Hideyoshi several times to Kyūshū, made caution especially necessary. But basically a lively missionary activity still continued. It was only toward the end of his reign that the Taiko (court title Hideyoshi assumed in 1592) took sharper measures again, not against Christianity as such, but only against the monks who came from the Philippines. The open evangelization of the Spanish Franciscans, who were unfamiliar with the mentality and state of affairs in the country, their open intervention in favor of a Spanish ship, the *San Felipe*, stranded in Tosa, and the unfortunate expression of the pilot that was interpreted to mean that the Spaniards had come to conquer Japan, combined to create a new crisis. Hideyoshi condemned 26 Christians to death, among them six Franciscans, three Japanese Jesuits, and 17 Japanese laymen. Their deaths occurred on Feb. 5, 1597, on the Nishizaka, Nagasaki. Although the growing anti-Christian measures had not initially been directed against the Jesuits from Portugal, it soon caused them concern. Terazawa Hirotaka, Shimano-kami, Governor of Nagasaki, on receipt of a letter of Hideyoshi, forced the dissolution of the college and seminary and demanded a list of all Jesuits in order to dispatch them, with few exceptions, to Macau. He was given a list containing 25 names, primarily fathers and brothers who were known to him already. By Feb. 17, 1598, more than 130 churches had been burned in the Christian territories of Arima and Ōmura. The ship that sailed in February 1598 from Nagasaki to Macau took three Fathers, eight Irmãos, and seven or eight Dōjuku (lay acolytes or catechists). The death of Toyotomi Hideyoshi in September 1598 temporarily put an end to the persecution of Christians.

Policies of Tokugawa Iyeyasu. Although the Taikō had attempted to assure the succession of his son Toyotomi Hideyori, who was still a minor, by a most meticulously regulated regency government, civil war broke out. It ended in favor of Tokugawa Iyeyasu at the Battle of Sekigahara (Oct. 21, 1600). Christian lords in the armies that had taken the field against the victor expected his hostility. He vacillated for a time, but then yielded to the pressure of the Catholic feudal lords of Arima and Ōmura and allowed the free practice of the Christian religion. This made the period from 1601 to 1612 the golden age of Christianity in old Japan. Grim shadows, however, fell across these years. One of the saddest events was the banishment of Christians from the fief of Ōmura at the end of February 1606. From the year 1612 on, the Church in Japan rushed toward catastrophe. The lawsuit between John Arima and Paul Okamoto Daihachi and the family quarrel between the former and his son Michael Saemonnosuke (who, despite his valid marriage, had married again, this time to a great-granddaughter of Iyeyasu) led not only to the condemnation of both plaintiff and defendant but also to the persecution of the Church in the fief of Arima, since Michael had accommodated to the court line out of political interests. On June 13, 1612, all missionaries were banished from his territories (four Jesuit fathers secretly remained behind), and all subjects were ordered to renounce Christianity. But the massive resistance of the Catholic population forced the feudal lord to allow them to live according to their Christian faith.

Expulsion of All Missionaries (1614). The incident of November 1613 in the neighborhood of Miyako, where the Christians knelt during the execution of a crim-

inal, and a new wave of Christian religious enthusiasm in Arima were the first smoldering sparks of what was soon a conflagration. At the end of 1613 the Christians of the city of Miyako (Kyōto) were registered. On Feb. 14, 1614, the order went out to the missionaries to leave the Gokinai and retire to Nagasaki. Some managed to remain secretly in central Japan; the others took ship in Osaka on Feb. 25, 1614, and reached Nagasaki on March 11. In the autumn of 1614 the missionaries were definitively banished from Japan. At the beginning of November, four ships filled with missionaries left Nagasaki, three of them bound for Macau and the fourth for Manila. Only a small number succeeded in remaining behind. All religious houses were confiscated; many churches were at once destroyed or profaned; the others were shut down. This was the beginning of the suppression of the Japanese Church.

In the quarter century (1614 to 1639) before the sealing off of the country (Sakoku), the situation of the Church worsened. The year following the banishment (1615) was not so critical for the Church because attention was diverted by the domestic political struggle. The Osaka winter campaign (late 1614 and early 1615) had only effected an apparent reconciliation between the Tokugawas and the Toyotomis. The summer campaign (May and June 1615) ended with the fall of Osaka and the death of Toyotomi Hideyori, son and heir of Hideyoshi. Many Christian samurais and rōnins fought for Hideyori, their insignia and banners visible far and wide. At the fall of the fortress of Osaka, at least seven missionaries (two Jesuits, three monks, and two secular priests) were within its walls. Understandably this did not make Tokugawa Iyeyasu kindly disposed to the Christians. Yet comparative peace prevailed until the death of Iyeyasu (June 1, 1616).

The Ban of Tokugawa Hidetada (1616). Tokugawa Hidetada, Iyeyasu's successor, followed a decidedly anti-Christian policy. On Oct. 1, 1616, he published a new ban. When Bartholomew of Ōmura [grandson of the Christian *tono* (feudal lord) of the same name who had died in 1587] made his visit to the court at the Japanese New Year, he was instructed to search out Jesuits in Nagasaki and send them to Macau. That same year four European and several Japanese missionaries were put to death. The strife between the Christians Anthony Murayama Tōan and John Heizō at the beginning of 1618 occasioned new stringent measures, especially in Nagasaki. The apostate Murayama made accusations at court against the Jesuits still in Japan and against Heizō as favoring them. Heizō won the case, became head of the Otona of Nagasaki, and in November 1618, together with the governor of Nagasaki, Hasegawa Gonroku, he returned to the port city. Both had the strictest instructions to search out Jesuit priests. The grimmest threats against any householder sheltering the missionaries and against his entire family and street, together with rich rewards for informers, made the missionaries' situation in Nagasaki impossible; many were discovered and imprisoned. The imprudent and unsuccessful attempt to rescue a Dominican from prison in Hirado caused an outbreak of fury and cruelty on the part of Hidetada. He ordered to be burned alive not only the two monks in prison in Hirado and the captain who had brought them from Manila to Japan, but also all the missionaries hitherto incarcerated together with their hosts; Hidetada ordered also the beheading of the wives and sons (of whatever age) of the hosts, all Christians of that street with their wives and sons, and all the sailors and passengers of that ship. Even the wives and sons of the martyrs of the past three years were to be put to the sword, although there had previously been no talk of their punishment.

National Isolation under Shōgun Iyemitsu. If the missionaries still operating in Japan had hoped that the transition of power from Tokugawa Hidetada to his son Iyemitsu (1623) would bring moderation, they were bitterly disappointed. His long reign (1623 to 1651) meant for the Japanese Church a total severing of all contact with the outside world and a complete annihilation within Japan. Iyemitsu confirmed the anti-Christian laws. Searches for hidden missionaries were constantly intensified; the precautionary measures against any penetration of new missionaries from abroad became more meticulous and rigorous. The coasts were patrolled and the trading ships from Macau were searched thoroughly on arrival; even correspondence with priests abroad was forbidden under pain of death. The methods of torture became steadily more cruel; they were used not just to punish the "guilty" and terrorize the remaining faithful, but also to effect their apostasy.

A number of missionaries died from the exertions of their secret and harassed apostolate; most, however, fell sooner or later into the hands of the bailiffs. A long series of martyrdoms of priests and laymen fills the next years of the dying Church in Japan; but side by side with the heroic martyrs in the Japanese Church were many defectors from the faith, not only among the mass of Christians but even among their spiritual leaders (Christovão Ferreira and others).

The Shimabara Uprising. Year by year, the situation of Christians in Japan and communication with the centers in Macau and Manila became more unreliable. The total collapse of the Church in Japan was finally sealed by the Shimabara uprising (1637 to 1638). It originated as an act of desperation by the socially and economically oppressed agrarian population in Amakusa and

nearby Takaku (Shimabara Peninsula), but in these territories, which had once been entirely Christian, it soon grew into a religious movement. The rebels named as their leader Masuda Shirō (better known as Amakusa Shirō), the 18-year-old son of a Christian samurai. But the real leadership lay in all probability with a few retired but capable military men. The rebels were defeated in Amakusa (January 1638) but retreated to neighboring Takaku, where they seized the abandoned fortress of Hara (Arima). The government sent against them an army estimated at 100,000 men. The besieged in Hara-jō numbered perhaps 37,000 (men, women, and children). The fortress fell in mid-April 1638 when supplies of ammunition and food failed. All were put to death. The government troops had suffered severe losses during the siege, perhaps 13,000 men. The protracted uprising and the poor spirit of the government troops made a deep impression at court, so that plans that had been made for the conquest of Manila were dropped.

Last Contacts. The fear that the rebellion might have been fomented from abroad led to a complete cordoning off of the country. When the Portuguese ships made their usual call in 1639, the ban signed by the Rōjū (shogunal council of state) on Aug. 4, 1639, was laid before them. It forbade them under pain of death ever to return to Japan. When the city of Macau in 1640 sent an embassy to Japan to restore the old ties, the captain, passengers, and all but 13 sailors were killed. From 1640 an office of investigation in Yedo (Tokyo) directed the supervision of entry into the country, and it became impossible for any missionaries to penetrate clandestinely into Japan. The two groups of Jesuits making the crossing to Japan in 1642 (under the leadership of the Visitator Antonio RUBINO) and in 1643 (under the command of Pedro Marquez) were at once spotted and arrested. The Portuguese embassy that came to Nagasaki in 1647 in order to begin new negotiations in the name of a Portugal that had again become independent under King John IV was allowed to return to Macau but without obtaining any concessions. A similar reception awaited the Portuguese who in 1685 brought back a group of Japanese who had been driven off their course and aground at Macau. The last European missionary to enter Japan, the Sicilian secular priest Giovanni Battista Sidotti, was arrested soon after he landed (October 1708) and brought first to Nagasaki and then to Yedo (Tokyo), where he was kept in prison in the Kirishitan-Yashiki until his death in December 1715.

Spirit of Martyrdom in the Early Japanese Church

The religious life of the Japanese Christians and missionaries was extraordinarily deep and solid. From the beginning, Xavier and his confreres roused in their Japanese converts a spirit that could endure every test. The missionaries taught them profoundest reverence for the majesty of God, a resolute shunning of sin, a high esteem for the Redemption, and a fervent love for the crucified Savior. Appealing to the realization, so native to the Japanese, of the transience of terrestrial things and the scorn of death, characteristic of the samurai of the feudal period who were accustomed to battles as a daily fare, they awakened in the Christians the love for an eternal heaven to which martyrdom provided sure and instant access.

Symbolism of the Cross. In many Christian communities high wooden crosses were erected, which Christians visited singly or in groups, privately or in public procession. The cross as symbol of victory and devotion shone on the armor, helmets, and banners of the soldiers; silver or gold pectoral crosses were worn by distinguished Christians of both sexes; the crosses that gleamed on the roofs or towers of the churches could be seen for miles around, such as the gilt crosses on the roof of the Nambanjin in Kyōto. Sermons on the Passion of Christ were preached in honor of the holy cross on ferial days of Lent; the Blessed Sacrament was reserved in a richly ornamented "holy sepulchre"; the liturgical unveiling and veneration of the cross was practiced with utmost solemnity; and a sermon on the Passion and the reading of the Passion narrative translated into Japanese introduced the mysteries of these holy days. Often also a procession was organized in which persons carrying the instruments of the Passion engaged in a pious "dialogue" with the suffering Savior. The text of the Gospel Harmony of the Passion narrative had been translated into Japanese early (it is mentioned in the *History of Japan* by Luís Fróis as early as 1552, again in 1563, 1566, etc.); later (at the latest by 1607) it was disseminated in printed form. Also read on such occasions were Japanese versions of the meditations on the Passion by the Dominican LOUIS OF GRANADA. Many Japanese lives of saints and martyrs were available for imitation; these circulated originally in manuscript form but were printed as *Sanctos no Gosagveo* as early as 1591. The idea of the world to come and of eternity were instilled into the Christians likewise by the special solemnity of the burial services and Masses for the dead. It can be said in general that wherever the Christians could be trained sufficiently in the truths of the faith, the remote preparation for persecution and even for martyrdom was thorough and profound.

Inspiration for Heroism. A more proximate preparation was given the Christians as the persecution became more general and threatening. When Toyotomi Hideyoshi suddenly declared war on the Christian faith in 1587, the missionaries distributed in the Gokinai an instruction on how to behave during the persecution. The Jesuit vice provincial Pedro Gomez composed a little work on martyrdom when a new persecution flared up in 1596 to 1597; the main ideas of this work he had already expounded in 1593 to 1594 in the *Compendium Catholicae veritatis* (a theology textbook for the Japanese Irmãos). The *Exhortation to Martyrdom* (*Maruchirio no susume*) was written perhaps in 1615, the *Instruction on Martyrdom* (*Maruchirio no kokoroe*) still later (1622?). Reports on individual martyrdoms were composed in the vernacular and served to stiffen the courage of the Christians.

Especially in the first decade of the last great persecution (1614 to 1623) there were often thousands and at times tens of thousands of the faithful present at the death of the martyrs, whose example inflamed rather than diminished the fortitude of the survivors. The lay organizations founded by the orders in Japan were a forceful factor in the defense of the faith, especially from the time of the persecution in Arima (1612), when thousands of members of the "Congregations of Martyrs" swore to offer their possessions and their lives rather than waver in the faith. When their hour of martyrdom arrived, they left their families, friends, or fellow prisoners, and wherever possible donned festive attire. If permitted, they proceeded to the place of martyrdom praying together, singing psalms and sacred hymns, each encouraging the other until their heads fell under the sword or the flames and smoke choked off their voices. That tens of thousands made this highest sacrifice for the love of Christ is one of the glories of the early Japanese Church. It is sad, however, that for reasons humanly understandable, many fell away, at least outwardly, when pressure demanded the final commitment.

Individual Martyrdoms (The Canonized and Beatified)

The inner worth of the sacrifice made by each individual martyr is known in all its depths only to God. But in the long series of the martyrdoms, certain ones stand out especially because of the personality and number of the martyrs, of their manifest heroism, of the participation of enormous crowds, and of their subsequent beatification or canonization. Here are listed in chronological order the martyrdoms of those already beatified or canonized. Since there are often defects in the transcription of the names, especially of the Japanese names, even in the official ecclesiastical documents, the original MSS reports have been consulted. Even so, it should be noted that definitive judgment cannot be attained in all cases. This does not affect the identity of the martyrs, which is clarified in the ecclesiastical proceedings, where, however, many divergencies in the transcription of the names likewise appear. In this list the Christian names of the Japanese have been anglicized.

The 26 Holy Martyrs. These were crucified in Nagasaki on Feb. 5, 1597, and are the only ones so far canonized—*Six Franciscans:* Pedro Bautista, Spanish commissary of the friars; Martín de la Ascención Aguirre and Francisco Blanco, Spanish priests; Felipe de Jesús de las Casas, Mexican cleric, not yet ordained; Francisco de San Miguel, Spanish lay brother; and Gonzalo García, lay brother, born in Baçaim, India; *Three Jesuits:* Paul Miki, eminent Japanese preacher; John Soan de Gotō, Japanese, accepted as a member of the society shortly before death; Diogo Kisai (Kizayemon), Japanese catechist, accepted as a member of the society shortly before martyrdom; *17 Japanese laymen:* Leo Karasumaru (from Owari), baptized eight years earlier by the Jesuits, chief lay preacher of the Franciscans; Paul Ibaraki, brother of the preceding and a member of the Franciscan parish, baptized by Jesuits; Louis Ibaraki, Franciscan Dōjuku, 12 years old, nephew of the two preceding; Paul Suzuki (from Owari), 34 years old, baptized by the Jesuits 13 years earlier and one of the finest of the Franciscan preachers; Thomas Dangi (from Ise), baptized by Jesuits, Franciscan preacher; Anthony (from Nagasaki, father Chinese), Dōjuku of the Franciscans, 13 years old, baptized as an infant by the Jesuits; Gabriel (from Ise), Dōjuku of the Franciscans, 19 years old, his father was a porter with the Franciscans; Ventura (from Miyako), baptized as a child by the Jesuits, he fell away from the faith as a boy because of his father's death and became a bonze, but was instructed by the Franciscans and accepted as Dōjuku; Francis (from Miyako), physician and a Christian of one year, baptized by Franciscans; Leo Kinuya (from Miyako), 28-year-old carpenter [sources list him variously as Quinoya Leon and Quimiya Joan (Lúis Fróis), Quimiya João (Pedro Gomez), Quizuya Joannes (*Proc. Remiss. Mexico City*), Quizuja Joannes (*Acta. Can., An tuto . . .*), Guzaya Joannes (*Proc. Remiss. Puebla de los Angeles, Mexico*), and Guizaya Joannes (*Proc. Remiss. Japon.*)]; Matthias, converted (by the Franciscans) shortly before martyrdom, but not on the list of the condemned; when the others were arrested, the Franciscans' cook, named Matthias, was absent, and this Matthias offered himself in the cook's stead; Peter Sukejirō, long before baptized by the Jesuits, was sent by the Jesuit priest Organtino Soldo-Gnecchi to help the prisoners and was himself arrested (*adauctus*); Francis, carpenter, baptized by Franciscans, came to watch the death of the martyrs, was arrested and slain with them (*adauctus*); Cosmas Takeya (from Owari), baptized by Jesuits, preacher of Franciscans in Osaka; Michael Kosaki (from Ise), porter of Franciscans in Osaka; Thomas, son of the preceding, 16-year-old

Dōjuku of the Franciscans in Osaka; and Joachim Sakakibara (from Osaka), 40 years old, baptized shortly before by the Franciscans, cook for Franciscans in Osaka. These 26 martyrs were beatified on Sept. 14, 1627, by Urban VIII and solemnly canonized by Pius IX on June 8, 1862 (feast, Feb. 3).

The 205 Blessed Martyrs. This summary account of the martyrdoms follows (with Boero) the lists attached to the acts of the proceedings (numbers in brackets are the total for each day):

May 22, 1617, in Ōmura [2]: João Bapt. Machado, Jesuit priest; Pedro de la Asunción, Franciscan priest; both beheaded.

June 1, 1617, in Ōmura [3]: Alonso Navarete, Dominican priest; Hernando de San José, Augustinian priest; Leo Tanaka, catechist of the Jesuits; all beheaded.

Oct. 1, 1617, in Nagasaki [2]: Caspar Hikojirō, housekeeper of the martyr Alonso Navarete (d. June 1, 1617); Andrew Yoshida, former pupil in the seminary and housekeeper of the martyr Hernando de San José (d. June 1, 1617); both beheaded.

Aug. 16, 1618, in Miyako [1]: Juan de Santa Marta, Franciscan priest, taken prisoner in 1615 in Ōmura; beheaded.

March 19 (May, according to Boero), 1619, in Ōmura [1]: Juan de S. Domingo, Dominican priest; died in prison.

Nov. 18, 1619, in Nagasaki [5]: Leonard Kimura, Jesuit lay brother; Domingos Jorge, Portuguese housekeeper of the martyr Carlo Spinola (d. Sept. 10, 1622); Andrew Murayama Tokuan, Japanese; John Yoshida Shoun, Japanese (from Kami); Cosmas Takeya Sozaburō, Korean; all burned alive.

Nov. 27, 1619, in Nagasaki [11]: Thomas Kiuni Koteda, descendant of Anthony Koteda, who went into voluntary exile for the sake of the faith in 1599 together with his whole family and many vassals from the Hirado Islands; Anthony Kimura, relative of the martyr Leonard Kimura (d. Nov. 18, 1619); Leo Nakanishi; Alexis Nakamura; Michael (Tashita?) Sakaguchi; John Iwanaga; Bartholomew Seki; Matthias Nakano; Matthias Kozaka?; Romanus Motoyama (Matsuoka, Miōta?); John Motoyama; all beheaded.

Night of Jan. 6 to Jan. 7, 1620, in Omura (Suzuta) [1]: Ambrosio Fernandes, Portuguese Jesuit lay brother, arrested together with Carlo Spinola on Dec. 13, 1618; died in prison.

May 27 (not 22), 1620, in Nagasaki [1]: Matthias, Japanese servant of the Jesuit provincial, refused to reveal the whereabouts of the missionaries even under cruel torture; died in prison.

Aug. 16, 1620, in Kokura [5]: Simon Kiyota Bokusai, Kambō (catechist); Magdalena, his wife; Thomas Gengorō; Mary, his wife; James Bunzo, his son; the last three in the service of Simon Kiyota Bokusai; all crucified.

Aug. 10, 1622, on Ikinoshima (Hirado) Island [1]: Augustine Ota, Jesuit Kambō of the martyr Camillo Costanzo (d. Sept. 15, 1622), and received into the society on the day before his martyrdom; beheaded.

Aug. 19, 1622, in Nagasaki [15]: Luis Flores, Dominican priest; Pedro de Zuniga, Augustinian priest; Joachim Hirayama Diaz, captain of the ship that had brought the priests from the Philippines to Japan; all burned to death; John Soyemon and Leo Sukuyemon, ship's officers; Michael Diaz Hori; Anthony Yamada; Thomas Koyanagi; James Denji; Mark Shinyemon; Lawrence Rokusuke (Rokuyemon?); Paul Sankichi; John Matashichi; John Yago; Bartholomew Mohyōye, merchant passengers; all 12 beheaded.

Sept. 10, 1622, in Nagasaki [52]: the "Great Martyrdom" in which 23 were burned alive and 29 beheaded; those burned were eight Jesuits: Carlo Spinola, Italian priest, and Sebastian Kimura, Japanese priest, and the following Japanese Irmâos, received into the society in prison: Gonzales Fusai, Anthony Kiuni, Peter Sampo, Michael Sato, Thomas Akahoshi, and Louis Kawara; six Dominicans: Francisco de Morales, Spanish priest; Alonso de Mena, Spanish priest; Angelo Ferrer Orsucci, Italian priest; Joseph de S. Jacinto, Spanish priest; Jacinto Orfanel, Aragonese priest; Alexis, scholastic; three Franciscans: Pedro de Ávila, Castilian priest; Ricardo de Santa Anna, Belgian priest; Vincent de S. José, lay brother; Leo de Satsuma, catechist; five housekeepers of the missionaries: Anthony Sanga (from Sanga, Kawachi), nephew of one of the finest Christian feudal lords of the Gokinai, Paul Sanga Sampaku (Anthony had belonged to the society for a time and left for reasons of health); Anthony, a Korean catechist and housekeeper of the martyr Sebastian Kimura; Paul Tanaka, host of Joseph de S. Jacinto; Paul Nagaishi, Japanese; and Luzia de Freitas, wife of a Portuguese and hostess of Ricardo de Santa Anna. Before the above 23 were burned to death, the following 29 were beheaded before their eyes: Thomas del S. Rosario and Domingos del S. Rosario (thus he is listed in the proceedings and in Boero, though in the original *Annua* he is called João), both of them Dominicans; John (do) Chugoku, Jesuit; five relatives of the martyrs of Nov. 18, 1619: Isabel Fernandez, wife of the martyr Domingos Jorge and her four-year-old son Ignacio; Maria, wife of the martyr Andrew Murayama Tokuan; Mary, wife of the martyr John

Yoshida Shoun; Ines, wife of the Korean martyr Cosmas Takeya Sozaburō; Dominic Nakano, 19-year-old son of the martyr Matthias Nakano (d. Nov. 27, 1619); the original *Annua* lists also a five-year-old Peter Motoyama, son of the martyr John Motoyama (d. Nov. 27, 1619), but he is missing from the list of the beatified; seven relatives of those burned alive on Sept. 10, 1622: Magdalene, wife of Anthony Sanga; Maria, wife of Paul Tanaka; Maria, wife of the Korean Anthony, with her two sons, John, 12 years old, and Peter, three years old; Thecla, wife of Paul Nagaishi, with her son Peter, seven years old.

Eight male and five female martyrs were put to death because of their relationship to other condemned martyrs: Bartholomew Kawano Shichiyemon; Dominic Yamada and his wife, Clara (thus he appears in the proceedings and in the list of Boero; Garcia Garcés indicates only that Clara was the wife of a martyr; her name is not in the original *Annua*); Damian Yamichi Tanda with his son Michael, five years old; the 70-year-old Thomas Shikirō; Clement Ono with his son Anthony, three years old; Rufus Ishimoto; Apollonia, widow, aunt of the martyr Caspar Koteda, who was put to death on Sept. 11, 1622; Catherine, widow; Mary (or Marina) Tanaura, widow; Dominica Ogata, widow. The group originally numbered 25, but three freed themselves from the bonds, which had purposely been tied loosely to encourage apostasy: two allegedly in order to escape the fire and be beheaded, but according to the original *Annua* they would have denied the faith to save their lives; they were twice thrown back into the fire where they perished. Some doubt persisted concerning the third (Paul Nagaishi), but it was finally shown that he had freed himself only for a short time to encourage the other two in their faith; he is thus the only one of the three counted among the beatified. The witnesses in the proceedings, moreover, disagreed concerning the total number; some reports have 23 burned to death and 30 beheaded (apart from the two who fled the fire).

Sept. 11, 1622, in Nagasaki [3]: Caspar Koteda, catechist of the martyr Camillo Costanzo (d. Sept. 15, 1622); Francisco, the 12-year-old son of the martyr Cosmas Takeya Sozaburō (d. Nov. 18, 1619) and of his wife, Ines (beheaded Sept. 10, 1622); Peter, the seven-year-old son of the martyr Bartholomew Kawano Shichiyemon (d. Sept. 10, 1622); all beheaded.

Sept. 12, 1622, near Ōmura [6]: three Dominicans: Thomas del Espiritu Santo Zumarraga, priest, and the Irmãos Mancio de S. Thomas Shibata and Dominic Magoshichi de Hyūga, received into the order in prison; three Franciscans: Apollinar Franco, priest, and the Irmãos Francisco de S. Buenaventura and Pedro de S. Clara, clothed with the habit of the order in prison; all burned to death. With these suffered several others on which, however, no juridical records were available; only the above were beatified.

Sept. 15, 1622, in Tabira, at the strait between Hirado and Kyūshū [1]: Camillo Costanzo, Jesuit priest, burned to death.

Oct. 2, 1622, in Nagasaki [4]: Louis Yakichi, who had attempted to rescue the Dominican priest Luís Flores from the Hirado prison, burned alive; his wife, Lucy, and his two sons, Andrew, eight years old, and Francis, four years old, beheaded.

Nov. 1, 1622, in Shimabara [4]: Pedro Paulo Navarro, Jesuit priest, and the two Irmãos Peter Onizuka and Denis Fujishima (received into the society while in prison); also Clement Kyūyemon, a married layman in the service of the Jesuits.

Dec. 4, 1623, in Tōkyō [3]: 50 were burned alive for the faith, but for want of juridical evidence concerning the others only three have as yet been beatified: Francisco Galvez, Spanish Franciscan priest; Jeronymo de Angelis, Sicilian Jesuit priest; and Simon Yempo, Japanese Jesuit.

Feb. 22, 1624, in Sendai [1]: Diogo Carvalho, Portugese Jesuit priest, exposed to a slow death in the icy water of a river.

Aug. 25, 1624, in Hokonohara (Ōmura) [5]: Miguel Carvalho, Portuguese Jesuit priest; Pedro Vasquez, Spanish Dominican priest; Luis Sotelo, Spanish Franciscan priest; Louis Sasada, Japanese Franciscan priest; Louis Baba, Japanese Third Order Franciscan; all burned alive.

Nov. 15, 1624, in Nagasaki [1]: Gajo, Korean catechist, burned alive together with the Japanese layman James Koichi (thus far only Gajo has been beatified).

June 20, 1626, in Nagasaki [9]: Francisco Pacheco, Portuguese Jesuit provincial; Balthasar de Torres, Spanish Jesuit priest; Giovanni Battista Zola, Italian Jesuit priest; Peter Rinsei, Japanese; Michael Tozo, Japanese; Vicente Kahyōye Caum, Korean; Paul Shinsuke, Japanese; John Kisaku, Japanese; Caspar Sadamatsu, Japanese. Of the six who were not priests, Caspar Sadamatsu had been a Jesuit lay brother for 42 years; the other five were received into the society shortly before their martyrdom; all were burned to death.

July 12, 1626, in Nagasaki [8]: this group originally had nine, but Mancio Araki Kyūzaburō died in prison; the others in the group were his brother Matthias Araki Hyōzaemon; their cousin Peter Araki Chōbyōye and his wife, Susanna; John

Tanaka and his wife, Catherine; John Onizuka Naizen and his wife, Monica, together with their seven-year-old son, Louis. The women and boy were beheaded; the men were burned alive; they were housekeepers of the priests in Takaku.

July 29, 1627, in Ōmura [3]: three Dominicans and nine lay people (four men and five women) were burned to death; one woman and two small children were beheaded. Of these, three have been beatified: Luis Beltrán, Dominican priest, and Mancio de la Cruz and Pedro de S. Maria, lay brothers received into the Dominican Order before martyrdom.

Aug. 16, 1627, in Nagasaki [15]: 18 Christians were put to death, some by fire, others by the sword. Of these 15 have been beatified: Francisco de S. Maria, Spanish Franciscan priest; Bartholomeo Laruel, Mexican Franciscan lay brother; Anthony de S. Francisco, Japanese Franciscan lay brother (these last two admitted to the order before their death); also the housekeepers of the missionaries, Caspar Vas, Japanese; Francis Kuhyōye, Japanese; Magdalene Kiyota, a relative of the Ōtomos of Bungo; another Japanese woman named Frances; Francis (Leo?) Kurobyōye, Japanese; Caius Jinyemon, Korean?; Thomas Jinyemonō, Japanese; Luke Kiyemon, Japanese; Michael Kizaiyemon, Japanese; Louis Matsuo, Japanese; Martin Gomez, Japanese; Mary, Japanese.

Sept. 7, 1627, in Nagasaki [3]: Thomas Tsūji, Jesuit priest, his housekeeper Louis Maki, and the latter's adopted son John; all burned alive.

Sept. 8, 1628, in Nagasaki [22]: of the 11 burned alive, three were Dominicans: Domingos Castellet, priest; Thomas de S. Jacinto, lay brother; Antonio de S. Domingos, lay brother; two Franciscans: Antonio de S. Buenaventura, priest; and Domingos de S. Francisco (or de Nagasaki); six lay people: Luisa, the 80-year-old housekeeper of Domingos Castellet; Michael Yamada: John Tomachi; John Imamura; Paul Aibara Sōdai (Sandaya); Matheus Alvarez. The other 11 were beheaded: four sons of John Tomachi, Dominic, 16 years old, Michael, 13 years old, Thomas, ten years old, and Paul, seven years old; also Lawrence, three-year-old son of Michael Yamada; Romanus and Leo, sons of Paul Aibara; Louis Nihachi with his two sons, Francis, five years old, and Dominic, two years old; James Hayashi; the housekeeper Thomas (mentioned in Cardim) is not in the list of the beatified (Boero).

Sept. 16, 1628, in Nagasaki [3]: the Japanese laymen Dominic Shobyōye, Michael Himonoya, and the latter's son Paul; all beheaded.

Dec. 25, 1628 [1]: Michael Nakashima, Jesuit, admitted to the order before his martyrdom, died on Unzen Mountain.

Sept. 28, 1630, in Nagasaki [6]: John Mutsunoō Chōzaburō; Peter Sawaguchi Kūhyōye (Pedro de la Madre de Dios); Lawrence Kaida Hachizō (Lorenzo de S. Nicola); Mancio Yukimoto Ichizayemon (Mancio de Jesus Maria); Michael Ichinose Sukizayemon; Thomas Terai Kahyōye; all were fellow workers of the Augustinians and members of their third order. These were all beheaded. Numerous others were martyred in 1630 but are not yet beatified.

Sept. 3, 1632, in Nagasaki [6]: Bartholomeo Guttierez, Mexican Augustinian priest; Vicent Carvalho, Portuguese Augustinian priest; Francisco de Jesús, Spanish Augustinian priest; Anthony Ishida-Pinto, Japanese Jesuit priest; Jerome de la Cruz Iyo (called de Torres by Boero), Japanese secular priest; Gabriel de S. Magdalena, Franciscan lay brother; all buried alive.

The 205 martyrs were beatified by Pope Pius IX in the brief of May 7, 1867 (feast, June 1 and Sept. 10).

This list of the 26 canonized and 205 beatified martyrs accounts for only a small group among thousands. Testimony has been taken on still others (but few in comparison to the total number), and even apostolic proceedings have been instituted, but none have been concluded. Originals or copies of these testimonies lie today in the archives in Rome, Madrid, Lisbon, and elsewhere. But juridical testimony is lacking in respect of the vast majority of those who, it seems, must also be called martyrs; their heroic deaths are known from annual letters, reports, etc. An unknown number of others have not even been given this purely historical recognition, and their number will probably never be known for certain.

Number of Martyrs in Japan

Only those who have been forcibly put to death for the sake of the faith are here called "martyrs." (The final judgment on this fact is, of course, the right of the Church.)

Earliest Catalogues. The number of the Japanese martyrs was a subject of study as early as the 1620s and 1630s. At that time Fathers Pedro Morejón and António Francisco Cardim, both active in the diocesan proceedings of the cause of the Japanese martyrs, compiled in the Jesuit College in Macau *Martyr Lists* based on the materials of the archives of the Jesuit Japanese province and giving the date, place, and manner of the martyrdom; this was thus a calculation of the number of the martyrs of Japan based on as accurate a foundation as possible. By Nov. 10, 1625, Morejón had already finished the list of the martyrs of the period from 1614 to 1624 and reached a figure of 550 (letter to the assistant N. Mascarenhas). On May 10, 1631, he wrote to Father Virgilio Cepari that the catalogue of martyrs already included almost 1,200 names. Morejón's work was continued by Cardim. In his report of May 24, 1646, on the Japanese province of the Jesuits, which he compiled in Rome, he was able to report from a thorough study that the number of martyrs in Japan had grown to 1,600 during four general persecutions up to the year 1640. Cardim published his catalogue in Rome in the same year.

More Recent Investigations. Masaharu Anesaki, the Salesian Mario Marega, and others have discovered that many more Christians died for the faith in the subsequent decades of the 17th century. Likewise the lists of Morejón and Cardim have been checked and expanded by L. Pagès, L. Delplace, SJ, M. Anesaki, and J. Laures, SJ. Laures concluded (June 1951) that 3,171 were actually executed while 874 perished in prison or while fleeing the bailiffs, etc. "Thus, 4,045 Christians would have become martyrs in the true sense of the word, for the sake of Christ." And here the ones who were slaughtered during the Shimabara uprising, especially upon the conquest of Hara-jō, are not included. Laures, who estimated their number at 35,000, stated that they could have saved themselves by renouncing the faith. He added: "It is simply impossible to procure even approximately accurate statistics on the positively endless number of those who were robbed of their possessions, driven out of house and home, thrown into prison, tortured in all conceivable manners to make them apostasize, or exiled from their country for the sake of Christ."

The total given by the authors mentioned, including J. Laures, can hardly be the final number. A careful examination of the European sources preserved indicates occasionally that there are gaps in knowledge of the martyrs. From the 1630s, the decline in the number of missionaries and the greater intensity of the persecution necessarily made it increasingly difficult for the Europeans to get exact information. The Japanese sources, which are now gradually becoming available, reveal a similar difficulty. Certainly the persecutions after 1640 put heavy pressure on many more thousands, perhaps tens of thousands. However, how many persons included in these numbers can be designated as martyrs in the strict sense of the term is very difficult to determine, especially since in legal action against simple folk the trial was short and aroused little notice. One of the best informed scholars on the question, Hubert Cieslik, SJ, is inclined to the view that some thousands can be added with confidence to the number of martyrs established above (however, their names are unknown). The number that the Japanese scholar Arai Hakuseki mentioned in passing in a memo-

> **Location:** East Asia, between the North Pacific Ocean and the Sea of Japan, east of the Korean Peninsula.
> **Capital:** Tokyo.
> **Size:** 143,619 sq. miles.
> **Population:** 126.5 million. The people are racially homogeneous, except for small communities of ethnic Koreans and Chinese.
> **Religions:** More than three-quarters of the population observe both Shinto and Buddhism. Taoism, shamanism and new religious movements (e.g., Soka Gakkai, Rissho Kosei-kai, Tenrikyo and Konkokyo) attract a small but significant number of adherents. The Christian community is very small, comprising less than 1% of the total population.

randum to the government *c.* 1710, namely, that 230,000 Christians died for their faith, has no satisfactory foundation, at least in the concept of martyrs as it has been defined above.

Bibliography: Though this presentation is based largely upon manuscripts of the 16th and 17th centuries, the following were used repeatedly for comparison: For the causes, course of the persecutions, and the psychological attitude of the Japanese toward martyrdom, L. FRÓIS (Froes), *Die Geschichte Japans, 1549–78,* tr. G. SCHURHAMMER and E. A. VORETZSCH (Leipzig 1926); *Segunda parte da Historia de Japan, 1578–82,* ed. J. A. ABRANCHES PINTO and Y. OKAMOTO (Tokyo 1938); *Relación, del Martirio . . . , 1597,* ed. R. GALDOS (Rome 1935); *Kulturgegensätze Europa-Japan, 1585,* ed. and tr. J. F. SCHÜTTE (Tokyo 1955). D. BARTOLI, *Dell'istoria della Compagnie di Gesù l'Asia,* 3 v. (Rome 1653–63). C. R. BOXER, *The Christian Century in Japan, 1549–1650* (Berkeley 1951), bibliography. J. LAURES, *Geschichte der katholischen Kirche in Japan* (Kaldenkirchen 1956). Lists. A. F. CARDIM, *Fasciculus e Iapponicis floribus, suo adhuc madentibus sanguine,* 2 parts (Rome 1646); *Catalogus regularium et secularium, qui Iapponiae regnis a fundata ubi a S. Francisco Xaverio, gentis apostolo, ecclesia, ab ethnicis in odium Christianae fidei sub quatuor tyrannis violenta morte sublati sunt* (Rome 1646); *Mors felicissima quatuor legatorum Lusitanorum et sociorum, quos Iapponiae Imperator occidit in odium christianae religionis* (Rome 1646). L. PAGÈS, *op. cit.* L. C. PROFILLET, *Le Martyrologe de l'Église du Japon, 1549–1649,* 3 v. (Paris 1895–97). M. ANESAKI, *A Concordance to the History of Kirishitan Missions: Catholic Missions in Japan in the 16th and 17th Centuries* (Tokyo 1930). For the number of martyrs, J. LAURES, "Die Zahl der Christen und Martyrer im alten Japan," in *Monumenta Nipponica* 7 (1951) 84–101. J. R. DE MEDINA, *El martirologio del Japón, 1558–1873* (Rome 1999). P. HUMBERTCLAUDE, *Guillaume Courtet: Dominicain français, martyr au Japon (1590–1637)* (Paris 1981).

[J. F. SCHÜTTE]

JAPAN, THE CATHOLIC CHURCH IN

Christianity first came to Japan in the mid-16th century. The history of Christianity in Japan is closely connected with the history of Japan's relations with the West.

Although the population of Christians remained small at the beginning of the 21st century, Christian churches continued to play a significant role in shaping the Japanese society through their higher educational institutions, medical institutions and public think-tanks.

Background. The Japanese islands were partially unified in the early 3rd century A.D. under Queen Himiko who pacified the warring ruling clans, set up her court at Yamatai and, relying on her religious powers as priestess, ruled over a confederation of more than 30 states. Subsequent contacts with China and Korea led to the Japanese adopting Chinese culture, writing, art and Confucianism. Complete political unification was achieved around the beginning of the 5th century A.D. under the Yamato rulers. With the achievement of political unification, Japanese civilization grew in stature and power from its center, first at Nara in the 8th century A.D., and then at Heian (modern Kyoto) from the latter part of the 8th century onwards. From the late 12th century until the mid-19th century, Japan was ruled by various military rulers who imposed varying degrees of isolationism. This self-imposed isolationism was broken in the 19th century by Commodore Perry, ushering in a new wave of modernization. In their determination to place Japan on par with the European colonial powers, the Japanese ruling elite embarked on a disastrous path of military expansion in Asia, leading to confrontation with the United States and its allies and to defeat in World War II. In the ensuing period, the Japanese people rebuilt their society and achieved spectacular economic growth, vaulting their nation to the forefront of the global economy.

Japanese Religion. The primitive religion of Japan, Shintō, the "Way of the Gods"(in Japanese, *Kami*), originated as a form of nature worship which deified the forces of nature and fostered ancestor worship. The Shintoism described in the early Japanese historical works, *Kojiki* (A.D. 712), *Nihon Shoki* (720), and others, had as its central theme the myth of the sun goddess Amaterasu, who was worshiped also as the ancestral mother of the imperial family. This ancestral connection resulted in Shintoism's continuing link with the national emperor worship (in Japanese, *Tennō*). Confucianism was introduced from China and exercised a significant influence on Japanese culture in tandem with native ancestor worship and national emperor worship. Buddhism was introduced from China by way of Korea in the 6th century A.D., and owed its rapid success to imperial patronage, the allure of monastic life and its unlimited adaptability, which made possible not only its assimilation to Japanese folkways, but also its syncretistic combination with Shintoism. Within Buddhism, the Amida (Pure Land), Nichiren (Lotus Sutra) and the many schools of Zen Buddhism captured Japanese popular imagination. The vitality of Nichiren Buddhism, an entirely indigenous Japanese Buddhist school, inspired many Japanese new religious movements in the twentieth century (e.g., *Soka Gakkai* and *Rissho Kosei-kai*).

HISTORY OF THE CATHOLIC CHURCH IN JAPAN

Origins. After the Portuguese opened trade relations with Japan (1543), St. FRANCIS XAVIER met three Japanese at Malacca (December 1547). Six months later they were received into the Church as the first converts. Accompanied by them and by Father Cosme de Torres and Brother John Fernandez, both Jesuits, Francis Xavier landed in Kagoshima in the southern part of Kyushu Island (Aug. 15, 1549). Because neither the Emperor nor the Ashikaga shogunate possessed real control of the country, the first missionaries had to rely on the consent of the local lords to begin their apostolate. During his stay in Japan (1549-51) Xavier founded communities in Kagoshima, Hirado, Yamaguchi, and Funai (Oita) with a total of about 800 Catholics. Assured of protection for the missionaries by Otomo Yoshishige, the most influential daimio in Kyushu, Xavier departed from Japan (November 1551).

Early Successes. His successor, Torres, directed activities until 1570, during a period of recurring civil war. Lack of priests, opposition from Buddhist bonzes, and imprudent zeal of some missionaries and new converts greatly hampered Christian progress during these years. Brother Luis d'Almeida, a very capable physician and merchant from Lisbon, who had joined the Jesuits in Japan in 1556, made a significant contribution to the expansion of Christianity in southern Japan by dedicating his fortune to establish a foundling home (1556) and a hospital (1557) in Funai, and by founding the missions in Omura, on the Shimabara Peninsula, on Goto and Amakusa Islands (1562-70), and in Nagasaki. In Kyushu many converts were from the lower class, but in central Japan Father Vilela and Brother Lourenço, joined later by Father Luis Frois, converted many noblemen. Kyoto, Sakai, and Iimori became the first Christian centers there.

When Torres died (October 1570), Japan had about 30,000 Christians. Under his strong-willed successor Francisco Cabral, SJ (1570–81), the converts included the feudal lords of Arima and Amakusa, and Otomo Sorin of Bungo and about 100,000 in Kyushu. The Lord of Omura had been baptized in 1563. After 1568 the missionaries in central Japan enjoyed the protection of Oda Nobunaga, the pioneer of the movement that led to the restoration of a strong central government in a united Japanese Empire. After moving his headquarters from Gifu to Azuchi, Nobunaga gave the Jesuits a property near his new castle. Nearby, Father Organtino dedicated the

Metropolitan Sees	Suffragans
Nagasaki	Fukuoka, Kagoshima, Naha, Oita
Osaka	Hiroshima, Kyoto, Nagoya, Takamatsu
Tokyo	Niigata, Sapporo, Sendai, Urawa, Yokohama
Apostolic Prefecture:	Karafuto

newly constructed church to Our Lady of the Assumption (Nambanji) in Kyoto (Aug. 15, 1577) and also constructed a seminary and another church.

During the last three years of Nobunaga's reign (1579–82), Alessandro VALIGNANO made his first official visit to Japan as Jesuit visitor general. In lower Kyushu he received a rather poor impression. Several lords had become Christians from self-interest and had compelled their vassals to follow their example without sufficient preparation. Mass conversions in Arima were followed by mass desertions because of the attitude of the local lord. After visiting nearly all Christian centers and interviewing missionaries, catechists, and many Christians, Valignano reorganized the Japanese mission. To remedy the scarcity of missionaries, Valignano founded a novitiate and a college for the spiritual and scientific training of young Jesuits and also two seminaries for the education of boys desiring to become priests or catechists. He ordered European missionaries to study the Japanese language more thoroughly and to adapt themselves to Japanese ways. Since Cabral, the superior of the mission, opposed these changes, Valignano removed him from office (1581) and appointed in his place Gaspar Coelho, who became the first Jesuit vice provincial of Japan. A few months before leaving Japan, Valignano conceived the plan of taking along with him some young Japanese nobles as envoys from the Christian daimios of Bungo, Arima, and Omura, to the pope and the king of Spain. By means of this embassy Valignano hoped to arouse more European interest in Japan and to obtain material support for the Church there. He wanted also to give the young Japanese an opportunity to contact European culture. The envoys left Japan (Feb. 20, 1582), accompanied by Valignano as far as India, and by Father Diogo Mesquita from there to Rome and then back to Japan (1582–90). At the end of Valignano's first visitation Japan had about 150,000 Christians, two-thirds of whom lived in Kyushu.

After Nobunaga's assassination (1582), his most capable general, Toyotomi Hideyoshi (generally known by his title Taikosama), son of a woodcutter, inherited his master's territories and carried on the work of unifying

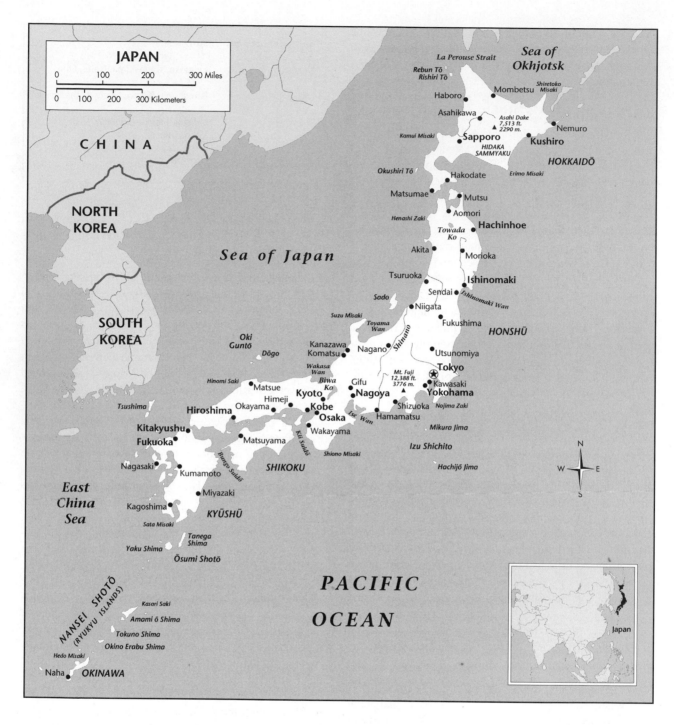

the country. Like Nobunaga, Hideyoshi was an enemy of the militant bonzes and for some years showed a rather favorable attitude toward Christianity. When the powerful anti-Christian Shimazu from southern Kyushu were on the point of subduing to their rule the entire island of Kyushu (1586–87), Hideyoshi acceded to the requests of the Otomo and Father Coelho by coming to their rescue with an army of 200,000. In Hideyoshi's service were Konishi Yukinaga and his father Ryusa, Takayama Ukon, Kuroda Yoshitaka, and other fervent Catholics. Through their efforts new churches were erected in Osaka, Sakai, Takatsuki, and Akashi. After Hideyoshi subdued Kyushu, he bestowed half of its fiefs on Christian lords.

The First Great Persecution. It was at this time that the first severe blow struck the Church and its 200,000 members. At the instigation of the former bonze Seyakuin Senso, a personal foe of Takayama Ukon and a bitter enemy of Christianity, Hideyoshi sent Ukon into exile and published a decree ordering the missionaries to leave Japan within 20 days (July 24, 1587). The real reasons for Hideyoshi's change of attitude are still imperfectly known. Most likely he was deeply offended by Coelho's refusal to deliver to him a well-armed ship, by the refusal of the Portuguese captain to bring his ship to Hakata, and by the refusal of other Christians to sacrifice their faith in exchange for Hideyoshi's favor. Most of the missionaries assembled in the port of Hirado, but others went into hiding. Since Hideyoshi did not enforce his decree for long, almost all the missionaries remained in Japan, under the protection of the Christian lords of Kyushu.

Before news of Hideyoshi's anti-Christian edict reached Europe, Pope Sixtus V created (Feb. 19, 1588) the Diocese of Funai (Oita), the first see in Japan. About the same time Valignano, accompanied by the four returning Japanese envoys, revisited Japan (1590–92). This time he came as ambassador of the Portuguese viceroy of India. Valignano and his entourage were received in audience by Hideyoshi (March 3, 1591). Although Valignano could not persuade Hideyoshi to abrogate his edict, he was allowed to move freely about Japan and received permission for ten priests to stay in Nagasaki.

In 1592 Juan Cobo, OP, arrived from Manila as an envoy of the governor of the Philippines. After Cobo's tragic death (1592), four Spanish Franciscans came to Japan from the Philippines on an embassy (1593). When they completed their business, they did not return home but remained in Japan and evangelized openly in Kyoto, Osaka, and Nagasaki. Two Franciscans and two Augustinians had visited Japan for two months in 1584 while on their way from Manila to China.

When the Spanish vessel *San Felipe* was stranded at Urado in Shikoku (Oct. 19, 1596), it started a fresh outbreak of Hideyoshi's anti-Christian animus. At his order the ship's rich cargo was confiscated and 26 Christians (six Franciscans, three Jesuits, and 17 Japanese lay persons) were put to death in Nagasaki on Feb. 5, 1597. These martyrs were canonized in 1862 (see JAPAN, MARTYRS OF). About that time most of the Christian lords were participating in the Korean war (1592–98), which ended soon after Hideyoshi's death (Sept. 16, 1598). For more than a year during this war Gregorio de Cespedes, SJ, and a Japanese Jesuit lay brother resided in Korea to minister to the Japanese Christian soldiers. During the years of restricted toleration (1587–98) the number of Christians came to exceed 300,000. Among the converts in central Japan (1595–96) were two sons of Maeda Munehisa, the governor of Kyoto; Oda Hidenobu, a grandson of Nobunaga; Hosokawa Okimoto; Kyogoku Takatomo; and Akashi Kamon. From 1598 to 1603

Roman Catholic Church, Nagasaki, Japan. (©Bettmann/CORBIS)

Valignano visited Japan for the third time, bringing with him Bp. Luis Cerqueira, SJ, the sole bishop who was permitted to reside in Nagasaki. He resided there until his death (Feb. 20, 1614). His predecessor, Bp. Pedro Martins (d. February 1598), had to leave Japan a few months after his arrival (1596) because of the new outbreak of persecution. Between the time of Hideyoshi's death and the outbreak of civil war (October 1600) many churches were rebuilt and more than 70,000 converts were won. When Konishi Yukinaga leagued with the enemy during the civil war, Tokugawa Ieyasu became enraged against Christianity. Konishi, the most influential Christian daimio, was put to death. Fortunately the Christian daimios Kuroda Yoshitaka and his son Nagamasa supported Ieyasu. This, coupled with the decided attitude of other Christian lords and an eagerness to continue trade with the Portuguese and Spaniards, made Ieyasu refrain from more hostile acts against Christianity.

The 17th-Century Suppression of Christianity. Ieyasu's somewhat tolerant attitude during the first decade of his rule permitted the Church to make notable progress. In 1601 the churches of Nagasaki, Kyoto, and Osaka were granted legal recognition. The Franciscans were allowed to build churches in Yedo (1599) and in Uraga (1608). The missionary personnel was greatly aug-

Peter Tatsuo Doi, who became the first Japanese cardinal in 1960. (©David Lees/CORBIS)

mented. By 1614 there were 140 Jesuits, 26 Franciscans, nine Dominicans, four Augustinians, and more than 400,000 Christians. From 1601 Nagasaki was the seat of the bishop and had a Jesuit college and novitiate, a seminary to train diocesan clergy, a printing press, and an academy of fine arts for the formation of painters and engravers; it became the most important Christian center. In 1611 Nagasaki had 11 churches and 40,000 Catholics. Between 1601 and 1614 Bishop Cerqueira ordained 15 Japanese priests (seven diocesan and eight Jesuits). Nevertheless, the Japanese Church's growth was greatly hampered by Ieyasu's anti-Christian edicts. Early in his reign he issued a decree forbidding all daimios and nobles to embrace Christianity. Christian lords were often urged to renounce their faith. As a result no mass conversions occurred after 1600, and many Christian lords abandoned their faith. For example, So Yoshitomo, Lord of Tsushima did so in 1600; Omura Yoshiaki, Mori Takamasa, and Goto Sumiharu, in 1606; and Arima Naozumi, in 1612 after his father's scandalous behavior in a bribery affair with Okamoto Daihachi, the Christian secretary of Ieyasu's minister Honda Masazumi. By that time Ieyasu, an ardent devotee of Buddhism since childhood, had become violently hostile to Christianity. Suden, a Zen priest; Hyashi Razan, a Confucian, Hasegawa Sahyoe, the governor of Nagasaki; and William Adams, an En-

glish sea pilot influenced this attitude; they were advisers of Ieyasu and bitter enemies of the missionaries. Another factor in Ieyasu's change of outlook was that by 1613 the prospects for expanded trade with the Spanish, Dutch, and English competitors had improved, and the activity of the Japanese fleet engaged in catching red seals had increased. These developments greatly reduced the importance of the Portuguese trade. Particularly injurious was the influence of William Adams, who in 1612 replaced João Rodriguez, SJ, as Ieyasu's commercial adviser. In this function he gave sinister interpretations to current events, such as the survey of the east coast by Vizcaino with the support of the daimio Date Masamune. Furthermore, an antigovernment conspiracy was discovered about the time that Masamune sent Hasekura Tsunenaga (Rokuemon) and Father Luis Sotelo with 150 Japanese as envoys to the king of Spain and the pope (1613–20).

The persecution edict of Jan. 27, 1614, manifested the intent of the Tokugawa regime to unify Japan by giving strong support to the national religions of Buddhism and Shintoism. The revival of Shintoism was inspired by the renaissance of Confucianism, which began *c.* 1600. The result of the edict was that all churches and missionary centers were destroyed within a year. More than 90 missionaries, together with Takayama Ukon, John Naito, and other leading Christians, had to leave Japan for Macau in China and Manila (November 1614); but at least 37 priests remained in the country to care for the faithful. After Ieyasu's death (April 17, 1616), the persecution grew in violence under his son Hidetada (1605–23); it reached its peak during the reign of Iemitsu (1623–51). To avoid depopulating entire districts, the persecutors resorted to increasingly cruel punishments, so that Christians would apostatize rather than face the horrors involved in martyrdom. It has been estimated that more than 4,000 Christians sacrificed their lives for their faith during this persecution.

This total does not include any of the 35,000 victims of the Shimabara rebellion (1637–38), which was caused by the intolerable fiscal exploitation of the poor peasants in the Shimabara Peninsula by Matsukura Shigeharu. This uprising developed later into a religious war and incited the Tokugawa government to sever all commercial relations with the Portuguese (July 5, 1639). The Dutch came to be the only Europeans allowed to have a factory on Deshima in Nagasaki. When a group of 74 Portuguese from Macau came to Nagasaki in 1640 in a last effort to reopen trade relations, 61 of them were put to death. The survivors were forced to witness the execution of their companions before being sent back to Macau with the warning that "Even if King Felipe himself, or even the God of the Christians, or the great Buddha contravened this prohibition, they shall pay for it with their heads!"

The last missionaries to Japan came in 1642 and 1643; they were quickly arrested, tortured, and executed. It was not until 1708 that another priest came. When Giovanni Sidotti, an Italian secular priest, landed at Yakushima (1708) he was arrested, imprisoned in Yedo, and interrogated by the famous Confucian scholar and statesman Arai Hakuseki (1657–1725). After converting his guard, Sidotti was thrown into an underground cell, where he died from starvation (Nov. 15, 1715).

Mid-19th Century Revival. For about two centuries the Church in Japan was cut off from contacts with the outside world. In 1844 Father Theodore Forcade, of the Paris Foreign Mission Society (MEP), disembarked at Naha in the Ryukyu Islands. He remained there until 1846 without being able to proceed farther. Not until Commodore Matthew Perry of the U.S. Navy induced (1853–54) Japan to open its doors to foreigners was it possible for another Paris Foreign Mission priest, Louis Théodore Furet to accompany a French commandant to Japan as an interpreter for a short while in 1855. After the United States, England, Russia, and France had concluded commercial treaties with Japan (1858–59), Paris Foreign Mission priests received permission to dwell in Yokohama (1859), Hakodate (1859), and Nagasaki (1863). It was in Nagasaki that Bernard Petitjean, MEP discovered (on March 17, 1865) a group of descendants of 17th-century Christians who had preserved their faith for two centuries in secret, despite persecutions and lack of priests. Later discoveries revealed that there were more than 15,000 such Christians in Kyushu. As the result of a new outbreak of persecution (1867–73) more than 4,000 Nagasaki Catholics were exiled. Many of them died from starvation and other forms of mistreatment.

Religious freedom was granted tentatively in 1873. The Meiji constitution of Feb. 11, 1889 gave a permanent guarantee of this liberty. This changed atmosphere permitted the bishops of Japan and Korea to hold in Nagasaki their first synod (March 1890). In 1890 the first regional seminary for Japan was established in Nagasaki. By 1894, 23 Japanese had been ordained there. In 1891 Pope Leo XIII established the Japanese hierarchy. The Archdiocese of Tokyo became the metropolitan see, with Hakodate, Osaka, and Nagasaki as suffragans. Previous to this, the single vicariate apostolic for all of Japan, created March 27, 1846, had been divided in 1876 into a northern and southern vicariate. The Vicariate of Central Japan was created in 1888. The Prefecture Apostolic of Karafuto was created in 1938. Tokyo was the scene of both the second (1895) and third (1924) synods of Japanese bishops. In 1925 a second regional seminary was opened in Tokyo. In 1946 the Jesuits assumed charge of it and subsequently incorporated it into the Catholic Sophia University.

Church of San Philippo at Nagasaki, Japan. The church stands near the site where 26 Christians, Japanese and Portuguese, were crucified after the outlawing of Christianity in Japan in the late 16th century. (©Ric Ergenbright/CORBIS)

The Paris Foreign Mission Society pioneered the 19th-century apostolate in Japan. Next to arrive were the Sisters of St. Maur who came in 1873. The coming of other religious congregations of women since 1877 has permitted the inauguration of numerous educational and social welfare activities. Until 1899 foreign missionaries were allowed into the interior of Japan under close supervision that required them to possess special passports. They were forbidden also to possess any residence and property outside the foreign concessions. These restrictions disappeared in 1899 when the whole of Japan was opened to foreigners. To provide adequate missionary personnel, the Congregation for the Propagation of the Faith in 1904 invited other religious institutes to send members to Japan. In reply the Marianists, whose educational work in Japan started in 1888, dispatched more members; so did the Trappists, whose first arrival was in 1896. Dominicans came in 1905; and the Society of the Divine Word in 1907. The Franciscans returned in 1906 and the Jesuits in 1908. The Paris Foreign Mission Society (MEP), which in Japan as elsewhere was always specially intent on training candidates for the priesthood, sent ten Japanese seminarians to Penang, Malaysia, in 1868 at the outbreak of persecution. Once persecution had ceased, they returned to Japan. The first three Japanese priests were ordained in 1882.

The Japanese mission undertook an educational apostolate early. After the Meiji restoration, however, the field of elementary education became more and more a government monopoly and the Church concentrated on Catholic secondary schools. The Marianists opened (1888) the first middle school for boys. Various religious orders opened secondary schools for girls from 1900 onwards. The first Catholic University (Sophia) was started in 1913 in Tokyo by the Jesuits, who were entrusted with this task by Pope Pius X. Catholic charitable works aroused admiration among non-Christians, particularly the care of the plague-stricken during the cholera epidemics of 1886 and 1890, the housing of abandoned girls, and the direction of leprosaria.

The imperial rescript on education (Oct. 30, 1890) imposed on all the cult of the imperial ancestors as a sacred duty of the Japanese people. After the outbreak of hostilities with China (1894) the influence of the militarist party, anti-Christian campaigns by intellectuals, such as Inoue Tetsujiro (1855–1944) and others set up new barriers against the progress of Christianity. The prospects for Christianity became even less enviable after the outbreak of the Manchurian war (1931), when Shintoism was identified with patriotism. The very existence of Catholic schools and, with them, the existence of the Church itself, was seriously menaced in 1932. A new threat came in 1939 with the promulgation of the Religious Organization Bill, which aimed to place all religious personnel and activities under close government control. The resignation of all foreign ordinaries and their replacement by Japanese bishops saved the Catholic Church in Japan from further government interference. During World War II most foreign priests were repatriated; many churches, convents, and schools were destroyed, and 13,097 Catholics, including 15 priests, lost their lives.

Rebuilding. The new democratic constitution (Nov. 3, 1946) imposed by the United States on Japan guaranteed complete freedom of religion to all. As the Catholic population increased, new dioceses were erected. Nagasaki, which had been a diocese since 1891, became in 1959 an archdiocese and metropolitan see, with Fukuoka, Hiroshima, and Kagoshima as suffragans, to which was added Oita in 1961. The apostolic delegation, established in 1919, was elevated to the status of internunciature on April 28, 1952.

THE CATHOLIC CHURCH IN JAPAN SINCE VATICAN II

The Impact of Vatican II. The Second Vatican Council brought about major changes in the practices and attitudes of Japanese Catholics. The change that had the greatest ramifications was the introduction of Japanese language and artistic forms in the liturgy. George Hirschboeck, MM, director of the Catechetical Center in Kyoto, was among the first to apply the insights of Vatican II in the Japanese Church. His team of catechists, trained at the Jesuit East Asian Pastoral Institute in Manila, produced literature and sponsored workshops on the new directions of the Church in mission. Kakichi Kadowaki, SJ, East-West Religious Research director at Sophia University, promoted Japanese art forms that combined Buddhist tradition, Zen practice, and Christian prayer. Father Kadowaki also produced ancient Noh drama with Christian themes in Japan and Europe. From the 1970s onwards, the Japanese Church became a sending Church. A Japanese lay mission organization was formed under Bishop Fumio Hamao, with members in the Philippines, Cambodia, and Indonesia. Japanese missioners, clerical, religious, and lay, went abroad to serve the Church in 47 countries in Africa, Southeast Asia, South America, and Oceania.

National Incentive Congresses. The desire to make the Christian presence more widely felt in Japanese society took new directions after Pope John Paul II's visit to Japan in 1981. The pope inspired a strong sense of Catholic identity and emphasized the responsibility of the local church for evangelization. This prompted the Japanese Bishops' Conference in June 1984 to publish a statement, "Basic Policies and Priorities of the Catholic Church in Japan." This paved the way for the first National Incentive Congress on Evangelization (NICE), Nov. 20–23, 1987, which brought together bishops, clergy, religious, and laity in Kyoto. Working on the theme of "Building an Open Church," the congress produced two important initiatives: to bring the light of the Gospel to social issues, and to build programs for lifelong growth in faith. One result was the establishment of a Japan Catholic Research and Training Center in Nagoya. A decade later, NICE II met in Nagasaki, Oct. 21–24, 1993, with the theme "to look for the ideal way of evangelization through the reality of the family."

Educational Ministry. The Christian contribution to the educational world of Japan is well-known and documented. Protestant missionaries founded the universities of Rikkyo (St. Paul), Aoyama, and Doshisha. The Jesuits operate Sophia University in Tokyo, while the Divine Word Society operates Nanzan University in Nagoya. Religious communities of women have operated distinguished colleges for girls, such as Sacred Heart, Shirayuri, and Futaba in the Tokyo area. In the Kyoto Diocese, Notre Dame Women's College was established by the School Sisters of Notre Dame from St. Louis in 1961. The chaos of 1969, when university administrators battled rioting students, resulted in the Japanese Ministry of Education taking control of university education. In the ensuing reorganization, all church-run universities and colleges lost their independence and autonomy. In return, the government subsidizes the operating costs of private universities and colleges.

Justice and Peace. One of the early results of Vatican II was the establishment of the Justice and Peace Office of the Bishops' Conference. Bishop Nobuo Soma took over this responsibility in the mid-1970s and built a very influential force for Christian justice in Asia. In the 1970s, the Japanese Justice and Peace Office brought to world attention the repression and exploitation of the Church in the Philippines during the Marcos era. In the early 1980s, it publicized the oppression endured by the South Korean Church under the military dictatorship, and appealed to the United Nations on behalf of the people of East Timor in their struggle for freedom. After Pope John Paul II's visit to Hiroshima and his worldwide "Peace Appeal" in February 1981, the Japanese Bishops' Conference issued a statement titled "Peace and the Japanese Catholic Church Today," which emphasized the importance of peace education and the participation of the whole Church in peace making. Episcopal concern led the Church to work with other Japanese religious leaders for world peace.

Subsequent Catholic justice and peace efforts have targeted two areas of discrimination within Japan: the Burakumin problem ("the Fourth Class") and Korean residents in Japan. The Kyoto Justice and Peace Council brought the issue of the Burakumin to its national gathering in 1978. Members of the Burakumin, a segregated community easily identified by their registration papers, were objects of prejudice in marriage arrangements and employment. In December 1987 the Catholic Church dropped the requirement that those seeking marriage provide copies of their family registries. The situation of Korean residents predated World War II. Korean laborers were seized, brought to Japan and forced to work in industrial plants. After the war many Koreans remained in Japan, forming a minority community of some 700,000 in 1993. Initially, as aliens, they had to be fingerprinted and were frequently discriminated against. In February 1984 the Episcopal Commission for Social Activities petitioned the Prime Minister, the Justice Minister, and the Home Affairs Minister to repeal the fingerprinting requirement of the Alien Registration Law. Father Edouard Brzostowski, a missionary, dramatized the issue in Octo-

ber 1984 by refusing to be fingerprinted, and other foreign missioners did likewise. Active awareness movements led to the revision of the fingerprinting law in 1987. Second and third generation Koreans born in Japan no longer needed to be fingerprinted, but other aliens were still required to be fingerprinted upon arrival in Japan.

Interfaith Dialogue Another area where the influence of Vatican II has been felt is the relationship of the Church to non-Christian religions. Jesuit pioneers Heinrich Dumoulin and Enomiya Lasalle had introduced Zen and its prayer forms to the Japanese Church and seminarians in the 1950s and 1960s. After the Council Dominican Shigeto Oshida established a rural farm where he conducted Bible studies and reflection groups in a Japanese Zen pattern. Xaverian Franco Sottocornola set up Seimeizan in Kumamoto in 1987 as an inter-religious dialogue temple where Buddhist and Christian traditions meet in mutual respect. In 1979 Jan Van Bragt, CICM, organized an ongoing exchange of Buddhist and Christian monks. Four years later, 17 European monks visited Kyoto to experience the Buddhist monastic life. August 1987 witnessed a gathering of world religious leaders for a Religions Peace Meeting at the Japanese Buddhist center on Mt. Hiei, above Kyoto.

A certain ambivalence, however, marks the attitude of the average Japanese Catholic towards interreligious dialogue. At one level, it seems to have made little practical difference in their faith. Like most other Japanese, Catholics regard multiple religious affiliation as normal. It is common practice in Japan for a person to be taken to a Shinto shrine as a baby, to celebrate a Christian wedding, and to have a Buddhist funeral. On another level, Japanese Catholics recognize the spiritual implications of cooperating with leaders of other religions in peace movements, social concerns, and environmental issues.

Ecumenical Relations and Cooperation. Although Dutch and British Protestants had commercial relations with Japan from about 1600, they did not inaugurate mission activities until 1859. Among the first arrivals were the American Episcopalian Channing M. Williams (1859) and the Presbyterians Hepburn (1861), Werbeck (1861), and Thompson (1863). Protestants completed the translation into Japanese of the New Testament (1880) and of the Old Testament (1887). As early as 1877 several Protestant groups started to merge into one association. Since 1890 this association has been called Nippon Kirisuto Kyôkai (Church of Christ in Japan). The Russian Orthodox Church was introduced in Japan in 1861 by Ivan Kasotkin (Nicolai), who was subsequently canonized in 1970 for his role in establishing Orthodox Christianity in Japan. Constituting less than one percent of the population, Catholics, Orthodox and Protestants find themselves a minority in the Japanese world. They have combined efforts in justice and peace activity, social programs, and prayer meetings. Activists in both communities find a mutual understanding and purpose in confronting public issues, and charismatics from both traditions find it congenial to pray together. One great achievement of the Japanese ecumenical movement is the common Bible translation of 1987 that forms the basis of worship for both Catholics and Protestants.

Bibliography: J. LAURES, *Kirishitan Bunko* (Tokyo 1957); *The Catholic Church in Japan: A Short History* (Rutland, Vt. 1954). A. EBIZAWA, *Christianity in Japan* (Tokyo 1960). J. JENNES, *History of the Catholic Church in Japan, 1549–1873* (Tokyo 1959). J. L. VAN HECKEN, *The Catholic Church in Japan since 1859*, tr. J. VAN HOYDONCK (Tokyo 1963). R. HAMMER, *Japan's Religious Torment* (London 1961). CATHOLIC CENTRAL COMMITTEE, *Cathopedia '92* (Tokyo 1992). R. H. DRUMMOND, *History of Christianity in Japan* (Grand Rapids 1971). Y. KUMAZAWA and D. SWAIN, *Christianity in Japan, 1971–90* (Tokyo 1991). P. F. O'DONOGHUE, *Japanese Catholics* (Tokyo 1985). J. M. PHILLIPS, *From the Rising of the Sun: Christians and Society in Contemporary Japan* (New York 1981). D. REID, *New Wine: The Cultural Shaping of Japanese Christianity* (Nagoya 1991). J. J. SPAE, *Japanese Religiosity* (Tokyo 1971); *Christianity Encounters Japan* (Tokyo 1968); *Christian Corridors to Japan* (Tokyo 1965). M. SUZUKI, *Japan Catholic History* (Tokyo 1993).

[A. SCHWADE/P. F. O'DONOGHUE/EDS.]

JARICOT, PAULINE

Foundress of the Society for the Propagation of the Faith; b. Lyons, France, July 22, 1799; d. Lyons, Jan. 9, 1862. On Christmas Day 1816 she took a perpetual vow of virginity. At the age of 17 she founded the Union of Prayers in Reparation to the Sacred Heart, an organization of servant girls. It was among them that she first solicited contributions for the foreign missions. In 1820 she formed an Association to Aid the Society of Foreign Missions of Paris, and in 1826 the Association of the Living Rosary. Each member was assigned a certain decade to say daily. This association also spread good books and distributed articles of piety. She founded the Loretta, a home for working girls, promoted the Association of the Holy Childhood, and engaged in other apostolic works for women of all classes.

Her main preoccupation, however, was to help the foreign missions through the alms and prayers of the faithful. In 1822 Angelo Inglesi, Vicar-General of New Orleans, came to Lyons to raise funds for his mission. He gathered a group of 12 laymen into an association. Because of Pauline Jaricot's success in such work, this association joined with her existing group to form the Society for the Propagation of the Faith (May 3, 1822). Pauline

Marie Jaricot is recognized as the foundress. At the time it was called also the Missionary Society of Lyons or the St. Francis Xavier Society. There was much discussion of the fund-raising technique. Pauline's, a simple system through which a promoter found ten persons to contribute a cent a week and who turned these funds over to another person in charge of ten promoters, and so on, was adopted. In 1822 the society collected more than $4,000.

The cause of her canonization was introduced in 1930. On Feb. 25, 1963, the Congregation of Rites declared that she had practiced virtue to a heroic degree.

Bibliography: J. MAURIN, *Pauline Marie Jaricot . . .*, tr. E. SHEPPARD (New York 1906). D. LATHOUD, *Marie-Pauline Jaricot*, 2 v. (Paris 1937). J. JOLINON, *Pauline Jaricot* (Paris 1956). K. BURTON, *Difficult Star: The Life of Pauline Jaricot* (New York 1947). M. CRISTIANI, *Marie-Pauline Jaricot* (Paris 1961). J. SERVEL, ed., *Un Autre visage: Textes inédits de Pauline Jaricot* (Lyons 1961). G. GORÉE, *Pauline Jaricot, une laïque engagée* (Paris 1962).

[J. A. MCCOY]

JARRETT, BEDE

Dominican preacher, historian, and spiritual writer; b. Greenwich, England, Aug. 22, 1881; d. London, March 17, 1934. The son of Col. H. S. and Agnes (née Beaufort) Jarrett, he was named Cyril at Baptism. After studying at Stonyhurst he entered the Dominicans at Woodchester in 1898 and was given the name Bede at his reception of the habit. He made his philosophical and theological studies at Woodchester and Hawkesyard. In 1904 he was the first Dominican in modern times to be sent to the University of Oxford, where he read history and took his degree in 1907. The following year he spent in Louvain, where he received his lectorate in theology. He was thereupon assigned to parish work in London. He was made prior of the London house of his order in 1914 and was elected provincial of the province of England in 1916, in which office he served for 16 years. During his provincialate Jarrett opened a study house for Dominicans at Oxford in 1921; it became a priory in 1929. He established a house at Edinburgh in 1931, transferred the school for boys to Laxton in 1924, and extended the work of the English Dominicans to South Africa in 1917. He helped the congregations of English Dominican Sisters in effecting their amalgamation. Despite his involvement in administration, he managed to find time for scholarly work and spiritual writing. At the expiration of his provincialate, Jarrett became the second prior of the house he had established at Oxford. He had a remarkable genius for friendship, was a man of vision and an exemplary Dominican—many have said that his *St. Dominic* (London 1924) was an unconscious self-portrait—who profoundly influenced all who knew him. Among his other works, all published in London, were: *Medieval Socialism* (1913), *St. Antonino and Medieval Economics* (1914), *Social Theories of the Middle Ages* (1926), *A History of Europe* (1929), *The Emperor Charles IV* (posthumous, 1935), *Religious Life* (1920), *The English Dominicans* (1921), *Meditations for Layfolk* (1915), *Living Temples* (1919), *The Space of Life Between* (1930), *The House of Gold* (1931), and *No Abiding City* (1934).

Bibliography: K. WYKEHAM-GEORGE and G. MATHEW, *Bede Jarrett* (London 1952). W. GUMBLEY, *Obituary Notices of the English Dominicans from 1555 to 1952* (London 1955).

[S. BULLOUGH]

JARRIGE, CATHERINE, BL.

Also known as Catinon Menette, lay Dominican tertiary; b. Oct. 4, 1754, Doumis near Cantal and Mauriac, Diocese of Saint-Flour, France; d. July 4, 1836, Mauriac, France. The youngest of seven children in a poor family, Catinon Menette ("Catherine the Little Nun") entered domestic service at age nine. About 1774, she moved to Mauriac, became a DOMINICAN tertiary, and rearranged her priorities so that she could live the Rule of the *menettes* in its entirety. By this time she was employed as a lace-maker to rent the garret room she shared with her sister. In her free time Catherine responded to the needs of the less fortunate, often by begging on their behalf. During the FRENCH REVOLUTION, she established and supplied a covert network of safe houses to protect refugee priests and deliver them to safety. Though she was arrested several times, the authorities were never able to convict her of any offense. Following the Reign of Terror, Catherine continued her charity, assisted in repairing the hospital, supervised the renovation of her parish church, and urged the lapsed to return to the Church. Her cause for beatification was not opened until 1929. She was declared venerable in 1953 and a miracle attributed to her intercession was approved June 25, 1996, which opened the way for her beatification by John Paul II, Nov. 24, 1996.

Feast: July 4.

Bibliography: M. C. DE GANAY, *La Menette des prêtres, Catherine Jarrige* (S. Maximin, France 1923). V. MARMOITON, *La vie héroïque de Catherine Jarrige* (Toulouse 1956). J. B. SERRES, *Catherine Jarrige, dite Catinon Menette* (Paris 1864, 3d ed. 1910). *L'Osservatore Romano*, Eng. ed. 48 (1996): 1–3.

[K. I. RABENSTEIN]

JARROW, ABBEY OF

Former English Benedictine monastery in Northumbria, England, on the Tyne River, in the present town of

Bede Jarrett.

Jarrow, six miles east of Newcastle upon Tyne. Dedicated to St. Paul, Jarrow was settled by CEOLFRID in 681 with 22 monks, almost eight years after its founder, Abbot BENEDICT BISCOP, had founded its sister abbey of WEARMOUTH (dedicated to St. Peter), about six miles to the southeast. Following customs based on the BENEDICTINE RULE, the two monasteries, both established on land presented by King Egfrid of Northumbria, comprised a joint foundation. These two abbeys were usually ruled by the same abbot; Ceolfrid eventually succeeded Benedict Biscop as the second abbot. It was at Jarrow that Venerable BEDE spent his life. Many of the community died of the plague in 686, and the abbey was sacked by the Norse (794), by the Danes (867–870), and by King William I the Conqueror (1069). Walcher, bishop of Durham, restored Jarrow in 1072. In 1083 both Jarrow and Wearmouth were reduced to the status of cells of DURHAM; both were dissolved in 1536 under King HENRY VIII. Jarrow was an important center of civilization and learning. Its SCRIPTORIUM may have produced the *Codex Amia-*

tinus of the Vulgate; its library seems also to have had the Itala version of the Bible.

Bibliography: "Historia abbatum auctore Baeda" and "Historia abbatum auctore anonymo" (used by Bede), ed. C. PLUMMER, in *Baedae opera historica*, 2 v. (Oxford 1896) 1:364–404. W. DUGDALE, *Monasticon Anglicanum* (London 1655–73) 1:501–503. H. LECLERCQ, *Dictionnaire d'archéologie chrétienne et de liturgie* (Paris 1907–53) 7:2163–64. D. KNOWLES and R. N. HADCOCK, *Medieval Religious Houses: England and Wales* (New York 1953). J. GODFREY, *The Church in Anglo-Saxon England* (Cambridge, Eng. 1962).

[C. MCGRATH]

JASHAR (YASHAR), BOOK OF

One of the last compositions of the Jewish haggadic literature, pretending to be the book of this name (now lost) that is mentioned in Jos 10.13 and 2 Sm 1.18 (the latter passage is misunderstood in the Vulgate and Douay Version). It is written in good Hebrew and covers the period from Adam to the Judges (*see* HAGGADAH; MIDRASHIC LITERATURE). Most of the work is concerned with the pre-Mosaic era, a fifth of it with the Mosaic period, and only three pages with later history. In elaborating on the Biblical themes, the author introduces entire sections, which he inserts between the Biblical texts. For example, he invents a long explanation of Cain's murder of Abel, and he adds a lengthy genealogy of Noah's descendants. Abraham's life is narrated in an elaborate manner, including an apparition of a star to him, and other details such as his two visits to his son Ishmael. Many other similar legends are thus added to various parts of the Biblical text.

This haggadic retelling of the Biblical story contains, no doubt, many ancient elements, but no critical or literary study of it has yet been made. There are interesting parallels between it and the writings of Flavius JOSEPHUS and PHILO JUDAEUS, which it would be most useful to examine scientifically (*see* JOSIPPON). The author's acquaintance with Italian place names, such as Tuscany, Lombardy, and the Tiber, indicates Italian origin; Arabic names also point to southern Italy, which was strongly influenced by Arabic culture in the 11th-century.

Bibliography: M. SELIGSOHN, *The Jewish Encyclopedia*, ed. J. SINGER (New York 1901–06) 7:74. S. OSCHER, *ibid.* 12:588–589.

[A. BRUNOT]

JASOV, ABBEY OF

Premonstratensian monastery, located near Košice in Slovakia. It was founded *c.* 1220, but the Tatars destroyed the buildings and reduced the archives to ashes. King Bela IV (d. 1270) rebuilt and enlarged it. From 1436 to 1591 Jasov was besieged by the Turks; after 1552 it was held by commendatory abbots and no canons lived there. From 1614 to 1650 it was the seat of the cathedral chapter of Eger. The PREMONSTRATENSIANS repossessed it in 1697 and under Abbot Andraeas Sauberer (1745–70) it was restored and proclaimed independent of Klosterbruck. Joseph II suppressed the abbey on March 26, 1787, but 25 years later it was reestablished. Jasov controlled the Institute Norbertinum in Budapest and conducted gymnasia in Leles, Great Varadin, Košice, and Rožňava. In 1922 Jasov became an abbey *nullius* with eight incorporated parishes. In 1924 Jasov opened a gymnasium with a resident community in Gödöllö, and in 1935 a gymnasium was added to the community in Košice. After World War II Jasov's possessions were confiscated by the government, and when the religious orders were suppressed Jasov became a concentration camp for religious women. On April 14, 1950, Premonstratensians, Jesuits, and other religious men from Slovakia replaced the sisters in the camp.

Bibliography: *Schematismus ven. cleri admin. apost. Cass. Satmar.* (Košice 1948) 63. *Schematismus ven. cleri dioec. Cassoviensis* (Košice 1943) 32. *Katolické Slovensko* (Trnava 1933) 179–181. V. WAGNER, *Dejiny výtvarného umenia na Slovensku* (Trnava 1930) 172–173. *Acta Apostolicae Sedis* 14 (1922) 582–584. A. Y. ZAK, *Contributions to the 800th Anniversary of the Premonst. Order* (Rožňava 1920), in Hung. N. BACKMUND, *Monasticon Praemonstratense, I–III* 1:445–448.

[J. PAPIN]

JASPERS, KARL

Philosopher; b. Feb. 23, 1883, Oldenburg, Germany; d. Feb. 25, 1969, Basel. Jaspers established himself as one of the leading existentialists of his time, although he himself did not accept the label existentialist. He followed his father into the study of law (1901), received his doctorate in medicine (1909) and married Gertrud Mayer in 1910. He worked as a scientific assistant in a psychiatric clinic, where he applied the methods of phenomenology to clinical psychiatry. He became a lecturer in psychology in 1913, and there began his transition from psychology to philosophy. He obtained his first post as lecturer in philosophy in 1916 at Heidelberg. In 1921 he was named professor of philosophy at Heidelberg. During this time he developed a friendship with Martin HEIDEGGER, which ended because of their differences over the growth of the Nazi party. He remained at Heidelberg until 1937, when the Nazis forced him to resign. He was reinstated in 1945, where he worked to rebuild the university and urged a national acknowledgment of guilt for the horrors of Naziism. Disappointed with the response he received, in 1948 he moved to Switzerland and became a professor at the University of Basel. He advocated a political unity to the world wherein various entities could live together in peace. His disapproval of the manner in which German democracy was developing after the war caused him to surrender his passport in 1967 and apply for Swiss citizenship.

Thought. When a student once asked him by what label he would like to be known, he retorted: "by that of a philosopher." For Jaspers philosophy was philosophizing and arose out of the philosopher's own life situation. Philosophy is not a body of knowledge accessible to consciousness in general, but rather a thoroughly personal struggle to understand life and by that activity to rise above objective knowledge (*Dasein*) to Being-for-oneself, where a person is conscious of the limits of science and of his basic freedom as a responsibility. To exist authentically, one must also accept his individual and collective past—his historicity—and make his free decisions with this in mind. Furthermore, communication with other unique existences of the present and of the past is a condition of self-fulfillment, a requirement of the good life.

Jaspers's special contribution to modern philosophy is his analysis of the critical fringes of human existence, what he calls the "limit-situation" (*Grenz-situation*). Limit situations, such as the death of another and one's own projected death, suffering, conflict, failure, and guilt lead the self to the edge of TRANSCENDENCE. As the objective world falls to pieces, personal existence is in a position to hear the voice of transcendence. At this level, FAITH becomes operative. Faith must not be considered a sure, objective, and communicable conquest of reason. Philosophy can only point to an experience of God; each person is left to himself for the last step. Being-for-oneself brings with it access to this intuitive cognition, a type of experience not to be equated with traditional mysticism. For Jaspers, contact with transcendence comes in rare high moments through reading "ciphers." Myths, religions, and philosophies are commentaries on the original ciphers: nature, history, and personal existence. None of these reveal a definitive truth about transcendence. On the other hand, they are the means through which one must acquire his personal convictions about the ultimate meaning of life.

In describing the limit-situation Jaspers tells us that every human being faces two unsettling experiences. First are the antinomies. These refer to the irreducibility of life to thought. The constructs of reason are always a distortion of the particularity and progressive character of truth. Second are the experiences constituting the limit-situation proper. These are the experiences on the boundary of our empirical existence (freedom, suffering, death, guilt). Here we become aware of the limits of objective thought.

Limit-situations can be resolved only by experience, not thought, because they involve contradictory poles (freedom-destiny, good-evil, life-death). Human existence is suspended between the law of the day and the passion of the night (i.e., between objective thought and existential aspirations). It is in the acceptance of this tension that the subject transcends mysticism and positivism and finds his salvation.

Bibliography: Main works. *Allgemeine Psychopathologie* (Berlin 1948). *Psychologie der Weltanschauungen* (Berlin 1925). *Philosophie*, 3 v. (Berlin 1956). Works in English. *Man in the Modern Age*, tr. E. and C. PAUL (London 1951). *Reason and Existenz*, tr. W. EARLE (New York 1955). *The Perennial Scope of Philosophy*, tr. R. MANHEIM (New York 1949). *The Origin and Goal of History*, tr. M. BULLOCK (New Haven 1953). "On My Philosophy," tr. F. KAUFMANN, *Existentialism from Dostoevsky to Sartre*, ed. W. KAUFMANN (New York 1956) 131–158. Literature. P. A. SCHILPP, ed., *The Philosophy of Karl Jaspers* (New York 1957). B. WELTE, *La Foi philosophique chez Jaspers et saint Thomas d'Aquin*, tr. M. ZEMB (Paris 1958). P. RICOEUR, *Gabriel Marcel et Karl Jaspers: Philosophie du mystère et philosophie du paradoxe* (Paris 1948). K. PIPER, ed., *Karl Jaspers' Wirk und Wirkung* (Munich 1963). C. WALLRAFF, *Karl Jaspers: An Introduction to His Philosophy* (Princeton 1970). J. F. KANE, *Pluralism and Truth in Religion: Karl Jaspers on Existential Truth* (Chico, CA 1981). L. H. EHRLICH, *Karl Jaspers: Philosophy as Faith* (Amherst 1975).

[J. K. LUOMA/L. A. BLAIN/EDS.]

JAVELLI, GIOVANNI CRISOSTOMO

Dominican philosopher and theologian; b. Casale, Italy, *c.* 1470; d. Bologna, *c.* 1538. He studied in Bologna, became bachelor of theology in 1513 and master in 1515, and was regent of studies from 1518 to 1521. His university career was confined entirely to Bologna in an era when the intellectual life of his order was directed by T. de Vio CAJETAN. Javelli studied under Cajetan and was a colleague of FERRARIENSIS. Preferring the contemplative life of study and writing, Javelli wrote extensive commentaries on the works of Plato and of Aristotle and numerous treatises in theology. His philosophical works seek to defend the interpretation of Aristotle as found in St. Thomas Aquinas and to reject Averroism. They have been published under the general title *Totius rationalis, naturalis, divinae, et moralis philosophiae compendium* (Lyons 1567–80; Venice 1577). In 1611 he wrote a commentary on the *prima pars* of Aquinas's *Summa theologiae* (Mainz and Venice 1612), to which he added a treatise on the Trinity and one on predestination and reprobation. In order to avoid the errors of M. LUTHER,

Javelli took a position that seems to depart from the accepted Thomistic doctrine; it is regarded by Quétif and Échard as semi-Pelagianism or at least Molinism. Javelli took an active part in the controversies over the rationalistic Aristotelianism of Pietro POMPONAZZI OF PADUA, at the latter's request. He refuted the errors of Pomponazzi's *De immortalitate animae* (1516) in a work entitled *Solutiones rationum animae mortalium probantium* (Bologna 1519). It was subsequently published by Pomponazzi with his own work (1525) and is reported to have saved Pomponazzi from more solemn condemnation at the hands of the inquisitor Jean de Torfani.

See Also: THOMISM, SCHOLASTICISM.

Bibliography: J. QUÉTIF and J. ECHARD, *Scriptores Ordinis Praedicatorum* 2.1:104–105. G. GIERATHS, *Lexikon für Theologie und Kirche* 5:885. *Enciclopedia Universal Ilustrada Europa-Americana* 28:2611–12. M. D. CHENU, *Dictionnaire de théologie catholique* 8.1:535–537. L. CARDIN, *Enciclopedia filosofica* 2:1620. H. HURTER *Nomenclator literarius theolgiae catholicae* 2:1209–1212. C. GIACON, *La seconda scolastica*, 3 v. (Milan 1944–51) 1:87–90.

[F. J. ROENSCH]

JAVOUHEY, ANNE MARIE, BL.

Religious foundress; b. Jallanges (Côte-d'Or), Burgundy, France, Nov. 10, 1779; d. Paris, July 15, 1851. She was fifth of the ten children of a prosperous farmer. During the French Revolution she helped her family house many nonjuring priests, one of whom, Abbé Ballanche, encouraged her religious vocation. She spent a few months in the novitiate of the Sisters of Charity of St. Joan Antida at Besançon (1800) and in that of the Trappistines near Riédra, Switzerland (1803). In 1806 Anne and her three sisters started a school and an Association of St. Joseph in Chalon-sur-Saône after PIUS VII had approved their plans when he passed through the town (1805). In 1807 Anne founded the Sisters of St. Joseph of Cluny (*see* ST. JOSEPH SISTERS) to conduct schools and orphanages and to aid the sick and aged. She became superior general and pronounced her vows, together with her three sisters and five others. Soon the congregation spread to mission territories. In reply to a request from the local governor, four sisters went to the island of Réunion (then called Bourbon), to the east of Africa (1817). After starting houses in France, Anne went to Senegal, where she inaugurated a project, later abandoned, of sending Senegalese boys to France to prepare for the priesthood. At the invitation of the British government, she set up hospitals in Gambia and Sierra Leone. In 1828 she went to French Guiana, where she achieved her most remarkable success by establishing a self-supporting colony for enfranchised slaves. Visits to her foundations within France and outside it caused her to travel very frequently. She had to suffer the opposition of colonial officials. The bishop of Autun, in whose diocese the motherhouse was at first located, and other French bishops sought to remake the constitutions and to direct the work of the congregation. Because of her differences with the bishop of Autun, the local clergy in Guiana denied her the Sacraments for 20 months. After 1843 she directed the institute from Paris, where the motherhouse was established permanently in 1848. At her death the congregation had 118 houses, 700 sisters in France, and 300 more in Africa, India (from 1827), Tahiti (1844), and South America. Anne Javouhey was beatified Oct. 15, 1950.

Feast: July 15.

Bibliography: *Lettres*, ed. J. HÉBERT and M. C. DE SEGONZAC (Paris 1994). C. C. MARTINDALE, *Life of Mère Anne-Marie Javouhey* (London 1953). G. D. KITTLER, *The Woman God Loved* (Garden City, N.Y. 1959). J. L. BAUDOT and L. CHAUSSIN, *Vies des saints et des bienheueux selon l'ordre du calendrier avec l'historique des fêtes* (Paris 1935–56) 13:142–162. B. A. MOORE, *A Little Good* (Melbourne 1982). J. CRAMBLIT, *Blessed Anne Marie Javouhey* (Northfield, Ill. 1995). J. LIBIS, *Folies douces: approches de la peinture de Marie Javouhey* (Mâcon 1995).

[C. E. MAGUIRE]

JEALOUSY

An intolerance, accompanied generally by some measure of emotional disturbance, of another's possession of a good that one wishes to belong exclusively to himself. It expresses itself often in suspicion, anger, hurt feelings, depression, etc., and sometimes issues in thoughts, words, or deeds contrary to justice and charity. In ordinary speech as well as in theological literature it is not always clearly distinguished from ENVY, although better usage favors taking envy to mean any coveting for oneself of a good possessed by another, and jealousy the desire for the exclusive possession of something.

St. Paul lists jealousy under the 15 works of the flesh (Gal 5.19–21) and under the 11 acts unworthy of a Christian (2 Cor 12.20–21). In these lists St. Paul piles up synonyms as is his custom, and his vocabulary is identical with that of the Stoics. Through St. Gregory the Great the capital sins of the Stoics were introduced into Christian terminology. Jealousy seems to be what St. Gregory meant by the fourth species of pride, whereby one is led to cherish the idea that he is the sole possessor of a given type of excellence. In the *Summa Theologiae* St. Thomas Aquinas seems to make jealousy synonymous with envy, in which form it appears as a capital sin, but it is doubtful that he had in mind jealousy used in the same sense as here defined.

The word jealousy is sometimes used without pejorative connotation, as in Ex 20.5: "For I, the Lord, your God, am a jealous God, . . ." The desire for the exclusive possession of something is not necessarily unreasonable, for one's right to such possession may be well founded, and its vindication is not sinful if it is accomplished in an ordinate manner. But when the claim to exclusive right is unjustified, or when its vindication involves violations of charity or justice, it is more or less gravely sinful, depending upon the harm that is done.

Exaggerated jealousy in the form of suspicion and resentment are symptoms often associated with such pathological states as melancholy, paranoia, and alcoholism. In such instances it can be assumed that what appears to be jealousy has no moral significance or that its moral quality is greatly attenuated. This is true also of the apparent jealousy found in the senile who suffer from cerebral arteriosclerosis.

Bibliography: F. ROBERTI et al., *Dictionary of Moral Theology,* ed. P. PALAZZINI et al., tr. H. J. YANNONE et al., from 2d Ital. ed. (Westminster, MD 1962). THOMAS AQUINAS, *Summa Theologiae* 1a2ae, 28.4; 2a2ae 36.4, 162.4.

[W. HERBST]

JEALOUSY OF GOD

The usual contemporary connotation of jealousy does not apply to God, that is, he is not neurotically suspicious or envious. Normally, one does not speak of righteous jealousy as one does of righteous anger. Nonetheless, the Bible does speak of the jealousy of God. "I the Lord your God am a jealous God" (Ex 20:5, also 34:14, Dt 4:24, 5:9, 6:15; Jos 24:19, Na 1:2). God is jealous for his holy name (Ez 39:25). The Lord becomes jealous for his land (Jl 2:18). He is jealous for Jerusalem and Zion (Zech 1:14, 8:2). God is stirred to jealousy by the worship of false gods (Dt 32:21, Ps 77–78:58). The Psalmist is concerned about how long God's jealous wrath will burn against them (Ps 78–79:5). God threatens that because of the Israelite's sin his jealousy will depart from them (Ez 16:42). God will set his hot jealousy against the nations who have plundered Israel (Ez 36:5–6). In God's jealous wrath all nations shall be consumed (Zeph 1:18, 3:8). Paul warns the Corinthians not to provoke the Lord to jealousy (1 Cor 10:22).

God, as the one true God, will not tolerate the worship of any false gods. He is rightly jealous, in the sense of protective, of his holy and righteous name and will not allow it to be profaned. God is also jealous in his love of his people. He has made a special covenant with his people and so he has bound himself to them with a special love. This love is like that between a husband and wife. "I will betroth you to me forever; I will betroth you to me in righteousness and in justice, in steadfast love, and in mercy. I will betroth you to me in faithfulness" (Hos 2:19–20). Because of this spousal love, God is jealous both in his protection and care of his people and their land, and he is also jealous in his demand that they remain faithful to him. Thus God jealously guards his people from the sin and evil of the pagan nations, and his jealous wrath can strike against them. Yet, God's jealous wrath can equally turn against his own people when they break the covenant and become unfaithful. Sin provokes the jealousy of God because, in sin, one has turned in false love to something other than God. Thus the greatest threat against his people is for God to revoke his jealousy, for to do so would mean that he would revoke his singular love for them. God wishes to call his people back precisely because he jealous. In his jealous love he does not want to lose his people.

Bibliography: J. J. SCULLION, "God," *The Anchor Bible Dictionary,* v. 2, ed. D. N. FREEDMAN (New York 1992) 1041–48.

[T. G. WEINANDY]

JEANNE MARIE DE MAILLÉ, BL.

Franciscan tertiary, mystic, and recluse; b. Roche-Saint-Quentin, near Tours, France, 1332; d. Tours, Mar. 28, 1414. Of noble birth, she was married at 16 to Robert de Sillé, with whom she maintained a virginal relationship. After his death (1362), dispossessed by the Sillé family, she returned to Tours, where in a little dwelling adjacent to the church of St. MARTIN she spent her days in prayer and good works. Later she became a recluse in a solitude near Cléry. Around 1377 she entered the Third Order of St. Francis at Tours. Her confessor, Martin de Boisgaultier, the guardian of the Franciscan community at Tours, was her first biographer. She prayed unceasingly for the end of the WESTERN SCHISM and sought to reform the morals of the French court of Charles VI and Isabelle. PIUS IX approved her cult in 1871.

Feast: Nov. 6.

Bibliography: *Acta Sanctorum* Mar. 3:733–762. J. BARBIER, *Jeanne-Marie de Maillé* (Vendée 1993). M. DE CRISENOY, *Bienheureuse Jeanne-Marie de Maillé* (Paris 1948).

[F. ETZKORN]

JEDBURGH, MONASTERY OF

Abbey of Canons Regular of St. Augustine, Roxburghshire, Diocese of Saint Andrews, Scotland.

Founded *c.* 1138 by DAVID I of Scotland with the help of Bp. John of Glasgow, the priory of St. Mary was built high on the banks of the Jed. It appears to have been raised to the status of an abbey before 1152. Its large and architecturally imaginative church was completed before 1250, but being near the English frontier it suffered heavily in the Anglo-Scottish wars (1297–1300) and again in the 15th and 16th centuries, being almost destroyed by the English in 1545. Finally suppressed in 1559, it was erected into a temporal lordship for Alexander Home in 1606. Partially used as a reformed church until the 19th century, the abbey is now an imposing ruin.

Bibliography: C. INNES, ed., *Origines parochiales Scotiae,* 2 v. (Bannatyne Club; Edinburgh 1850–55) v. 1. Royal Commission on the Ancient and Historical Monuments and Constructions of Scotland, *An Inventory of the Ancient and Historical Monuments of Roxburghshire,* 2 v. (Edinburgh 1956) v. 1. D. E. EASSON, *Medieval Religious Houses: Scotland* (London 1957) 77.

[L. MACFARLANE]

JEDIN, HUBERT

Church historian; b. June 17, 1900, Grossbriesen, near Breslau, Upper-Silesia; d. July 16, 1980, Bonn, West Germany. Jedin was ordained a diocesan priest on March 2, 1924. On Sept. 1, 1933 his academic authorization was removed by the German authorities because of his "non-Aryan" background. In 1936 he was named archivist of the archdiocese of Breslau. Since his mother was of Jewish ancestry, the Gestapo arrested Father Jedin in 1938, but he was released and left Germany on Nov. 1, 1939. He spent 1939 to 1949 in Rome researching the history of the Council of TRENT concerning which he became the acknowledged expert. In 1951 PIUS XII had offered him the post of Vice-prefect of the VATICAN LIBRARY, but he declined, preferring to succeed Wilhelm Neuss in the chair of Church history in Bonn, where he taught from 1949 to 1965.

After the 1959 announcement by Pope JOHN XXIII that an ecumenical council would be convoked, Jedin quickly published his *Ecumenical Councils of the Catholic Church: An Historical Outline* (Eng. trans. 1960) and then in 1964 his *Crisis and Closure of the Council of Trent* (Eng. trans. 1967). These were prepared for students of ecclesiastical history who needed perspective on the nature of an "ecumenical council" in the Catholic Church. Jedin also served as a peritus at the council. In 1970 Pope PAUL VI had offered him the position of Prefect of the Vatican Library, but he declined on the grounds of advancing age and infirmity. Poor health during the 1970s slowed his progress, but in the end none of his projected works were left incomplete.

Jedin's study of Trent resulted in the publication of a variety of works: four volumes of *The History of the Council of Trent* (two of which have appeared in English); *Papal Legate at the Council of Trent: Cardinal Seripando* (1937; Eng. trans. 1947); monographs on Tommaso Campeggio (1958), Carlo Borromeo (1971), and Cardinal Caesar Baronius (1978); and a longer book dealt with the closing of Trent, *Krisis und Abschluss des Trienter Konzils 1562–63* (1964). Jedin was also a generalist. He launched the massive ten-volume series *History of the Church* (Handbuch der Kirchengeschichte), intended as a text for students. It appeared in seven languages nearly simultaneously with the German. The tenth volume was finally translated into English in 1981, one year after Jedin's death. He also supervised the cartographic church history, *Atlas zur Kirchengeschichte. Die christlichen Kirchen in Geschichte und Gegenwart,* published in Germany in 1970.

The autobiographical book, *Lebensbericht: Mit einem Dokumentenanhang,* appeared posthumously in 1984 and was reprinted in 1988. It was not the first effort of this kind since his early youth had already been presented as "Eine Jugend in Schlesien, 1900–1925," and published in 1979 in the *Archiv für schlesische Kirchengeschichte.* The *Lebensbericht* outlines his professional career. It included the Memorandum he communicated in 1968 to the West German bishops after the annual "Katholikentag" held at Essen which seemed, to Jedin, to promote opposition to *Humanae vitae.* He drew upon his knowledge of Trent and the Reformation process to point out to the bishops a similar process underway in the postconciliar church. In a public controversy with Archbishop Annibale Bugnini in 1969 he published a criticism of the reform process in *L'Osservatore Romano.* However, these were rare interventions from a man who was a retiring and pure scholar.

Bibliography: H. JEDIN, *Kirche des Glaubens, Kirche der Geschichte: Ausgewählte Aufsätze und Vorträge,* 2 vols. (Fribourg-en-Br.-Bâle-Vienne 1966). Bibliography by R. SAMULSKI and G. BUTTERINI in *Jahrbuch des italienisch-deutschen historischen Instituts in Trient* 6 (1980) 287–367. J. KÖHLER, "Hubert Jedin, Schlesien und die schlesische Kirchengeschichte," *Archiv für schlesische Kirchengeschichte* 39 (1981): 12–19; "Geschichte des Konzils von Trient (1950–1975) ein Jahrhundertwerk oder der Abgesang einer kirchenhistorischen Methode," *Archiv für schlesische Kirchengeschichte* 55 (1997): 93–118.

[B. VAN HOVE]

JEHOVAH

False form of the divine name Yahweh. The name Jehovah first appeared in manuscripts in the 13th century A.D., but had probably been in use for some time. The form arose from a misunderstanding of the precautions taken by pious Jewish scribes to prevent the profanation of the divine name. About the 3d century B.C., the practice arose of reading the word ADONAI "Lord" or ELOHIM "God" instead of YAHWEH. After the invention of vowel signs, the vowels of the word Adonai were written beneath the consonants of the sacred name YHWH. With the passage of time the correct pronunciation of Yahweh was forgotten. The hybrid form of Jehovah, resulting from reading the consonants of Yahweh with the vowels of Adonai, the first "a" being changed to a short "e," became widespread in English-speaking circles because of its use in Ex 6.3 of the King James Version. In modern versions either Lord in capital letters or Yahweh is used for the sacred Tetragrammeton.

Bibliography: *Encyclopedic Dictionary of the Bible*, tr. and adap. by L. HARTMAN (New York 1963) 1109–10. P. JOÜON, *Grammaire de l'hébreu biblique* (2d ed. Rome 1947).

[R. T. A. MURPHY]

JEHOVAH'S WITNESSES

A sect, originally called Russellites, founded in the early 1870s by Charles Taze RUSSELL. In 1931 the title Jehovah's Witnesses was proclaimed by Joseph F. RUTHERFORD, the second president of their legal corporation, the Watch Tower Bible and Tract Society, at their convention in Columbus, Ohio.

"Judge" Rutherford introduced important changes in the Witnesses' creed and transformed the congregational structure of the sect as it was under "Pastor" Russell into a rigid theocracy. The third leader, "Brother" Nathan H. Knorr, gradually replaced the offensive convert-making tactics of the Rutherford era by suave manners that have gained the Witnesses their current reputation as one of the best-behaved groups in the world. In legal battles that they have often carried to the highest courts of many free countries—and by appealing to freedom of speech and religion—they have acquired the right to exercise their proselytism without interference. They hold that other religions and worldly power are the devil's instruments in keeping people away from the Truth.

Doctrine. According to Witness doctrine, there is but one God, and since 1931 they have insisted that He should be called Jehovah (Ex 3.15; Is 42.8). They condemn the Trinity as pagan idolatry and accordingly deny Christ's divinity.

They consider Jesus as the greatest of Jehovah's Witnesses, "a god" (so they translate John 1.1), inferior to no one but to Jehovah. Before existing as a human being,

he was a spirit creature called the Logos, or Word, or Michael the Archangel. He died as a man and was raised as an immortal spirit Son. His Passion and death were the price he paid to regain for humanity the right to live eternally on earth. Indeed, the "great multitude" (Rev 7.9) of true Witnesses hope in an earthly Paradise; only 144,000 faithful (Rev 7.4; 14.1, 4) may enjoy heavenly glory with Christ. The wicked will undergo complete destruction.

Russell had announced that Armageddon—the final clash between the forces of good and evil—could not happen later than 1914. From 1920 on Rutherford proclaimed that "millions now living will never die"; he also expected the princes of old, Abraham, Isaac, and the others, to come back to life by 1925 as rulers over the New World. The Watch Tower Society of the mid-20th century no longer specified an exact date; but it repeated that "this generation will by no means pass away until all things occur" (Lk 21.32). Thus, Witnesses are deeply convinced that the end of the world will come within a very few years. This vivid belief appears to be the strongest driving force behind their indefatigable zeal.

Way of Life. The fundamental obligation of each member of the sect is to give witness to Jehovah by announcing His approaching Kingdom. He may do this by door-to-door calling, by meeting with others for home Bible studies, or by standing at street corners to display Watch Tower literature. Preaching the good news is the only means of salvation. Baptism—which Witnesses practice by immersion and usually in mass demonstrations—is in no way a Sacrament but only the exterior symbol of their dedication to the service of Jehovah God.

Jehovah's Witnesses have attracted publicity by refusing blood transfusions even when it meant death to themselves or to their children. Except for birth control, which they leave to the couple's own decision, their conjugal and sexual morality is quite rigid. They abide by taboos such as those against smoking and the celebration of any kind of feast.

They regard the Bible as their only source of belief and rule of conduct, but the Witnesses' Bible aids are apparently used more abundantly than the Bible itself. They are allowed no other books than the Bible and the society's own publications, which includes its own translation of the Bible with an impressive critical apparatus. The work is excellent except when scientific knowledge comes into conflict with the accepted doctrines of the movement. In their so-called *New World Translation,* the term *Kyrios* is rendered Jehovah instead of Lord everywhere in the New Testament (237 times) except at Philippians 2.11, where St. Paul refers the word to Christ. In their book Jesus' words at the Last Supper become:

''Take, eat. This means my body'' (Mt 26.26). And they add but one word to the phrases of Col 1.16–17: ''By means of him [Christ Jesus] all *other* things were created in the heavens and upon the earth. . . . All *other* things have been created through him and for him. Also he is before all *other* things and by means of him all *other* things were made to exist.''

The rate of growth of the movement reached a peak in the late 1930s, when membership increased almost 25 percent annually: from 1938 to 1942 it grew from less than 50,000 to more than 100,000. Since then, growth has slowed somewhat.

Bibliography: Sources. Watch Tower Bible and Tract Society, *New World Translation of the Holy Scriptures* (rev. ed. Brooklyn 1961); *Let God Be True* (rev. ed. Brooklyn 1952), 18,900,000 copies in 54 languages; *From Paradise Lost to Paradise Regained* (Brooklyn 1958). *Yearbook of Jehovah's Witnesses* (1926–). *The Watchtower* (1879–), pub. semimonthly or monthly in 68 languages; *Awake!* (Brooklyn 1919–), pub. semi-monthly or monthly in 26 languages. Literature. H. H. STROUP, *The Jehovah's Witnesses* (New York 1945). W. J. WHALEN, *Armageddon Around the Corner: A Report on Jehovah's Witnesses* (New York 1962). G. HÉBERT, *Les Témoins de Jéhovah: Essai critique d'histoire et de doctrine* (Montréal 1960).

[G. HÉBERT/EDS.]

JENINGEN, PHILIPP, VEN.

Preacher of missions; b. Eichstätt, Bavaria, Jan. 5, 1642; d. Ellwangen, Swabia, Feb. 8, 1704. He entered the Society of Jesus at Landsberg, Jan. 19, 1663, and completed his studies at Ingolstadt in 1672. After his ordination on June 6 of that year, he asked to join the foreign missionary field but was refused because of poor health. He taught at the Gymnasium at Middelheim and Dillingen, and came to Ellwangen in 1680, where he won renown as a preacher. His missions throughout the Dioceses of Augsburg, Eichstätt, and Würzburg, his zeal and mystical gifts, and his devotion to the Blessed Virgin earned him the title ''Apostle of the Ries.'' He directed the construction of the shrine of Our Lady of Scönenberg, a popular place of pilgrimage and a fine example of baroque architectural style. The cause of his beatification was introduced on March 23, 1945.

Bibliography: A. HÖSS, *P. Philipp Jeningen, S.J.: Ein Volksmissionar und Mystiker des 17 Jahrhunderts* (3d ed. Ellwangen 1948). *Acta Apostolicae Sedis* 37 (1945) 221–223. L. KOCH, *Jesuiten-Lexikon: Die Gesellschaft Jesu einst und jetzt* 913–914.

[E. D. MCSHANE]

JEREMIAH

Jeremiah was born at Anathoth, a few miles northeast of Jerusalem, *c.* 650 B.C. At the time of his vocation in 627, he was a young man of a priestly class that had been excluded from the Temple cult (1 Kgs 2.26–35). During his ministry that lasted until after 587, he was a witness to one of the most troubled periods in the Near East.

When Ashurbanipal died *c.* 633, Assyria's power declined, leaving Josiah free to begin *c.* 621 a religious reform of JUDAH that also extended to the land once ruled by the Northern Kingdom of Israel (2 Kgs 22–23). Jeremiah, who had already severely attacked the Judeans' crimes (Jer 2–6), must have approved of this reform for he seems not to have preached again until Josiah's death in 609.

In Jehoiakim's reign idolatry revived and Jeremiah again began to condemn infidelity to God and hypocritical worship, at the same time opposing any alliance with Egypt against Babylon. His preaching caused him repeated persecution, but his warnings proved accurate when Joakim's policy led to the first capture of Jerusalem in 597. Judah's last king, Zedekiah, powerless before the political forces at work, followed the priests and false prophets in affirming the Egyptian alliance. Jeremiah strongly objected, proclaiming that Judah must be subjected to Babylon, but to no avail. As a result Jerusalem was destroyed completely in 587 and the Prophet was persecuted anew (Jer 37–38). After his release from detention, he joined the governor, Gedaliah, at Mizpah until Gedaliah's assassination. He then was forced by fugitives to go to Egypt, and witnessed the people's new apostasy before he died there. Thus, his whole life was one of suffering and frustration (Jer 40–44).

By attributing LAMENTATIONS to him, tradition has wrongly classified him as a lachrymose prophet, whereas his faith in God and his own mission strengthened his sensitive nature and made him ''a fortified city'' (Jer 1.18). Although he loved his people, he did not fail in his duty as God's spokesman but condemned them again and again. The conflict between his love and the harshness of his vocation caused the interior crises described in his ''Confessions.'' He was the only prophet to reveal his interior life.

The summation of his message is that the COVENANT promises will be realized only if people and leaders are faithful to the covenant's moral force. The new modality Jeremiah gives to this fidelity is found in each one's personal commitment and man's interior validation of external religion. Cult is vain when not inspired by the heart's religion that comes from love, justice, and faith (Jer 7.1–28).

In early Christian art Jeremiah was practically ignored compared to the three other major Prophets, especially Daniel. In the 6th century his images began to appear in basilicas—St. Ambrose, Milan, and St. Vitalis, Ravenna—and later in miniatures of manuscripts—Syriac codex 341 (National Library, Paris; 7th or 8th century) and a Greek manuscript of Cosmas Indicopleustes (Vatican 699; 8th or 9th century). Henceforth, his images proliferated in all media. Michelangelo's painting of him in the Sistine Chapel is the most famous.

Bibliography: J. SKINNER, *Prophecy and Religion* (Cambridge, Eng. 1922). A. C. WELCH, *Jeremiah, His Time and His Work* (Oxford 1928; reprint 1951). J. MUILENBURG, *The Interpreters' Dictionary of the Bible*, ed. G. A. BUTTRICK (Nashville 1962) 2:823–835. L. G. PERDUE, et al., *A Prophet to the Nations* (Winona Lake, 1984).

[G. COUTURIER]

JEREMIAH, BOOK OF

The contents, structure and composition, and theology of the Book of Jeremiah are discussed here.

Contents

Jeremiah can be divided into five parts according to each section's general theme. These include oracles against Judah and Jerusalem, oracles against the Nations, prophecy of Israel's and Judah's salvation, the story of the persecution of Jeremiah, and an appendix concerning the end of the Kingdom of Judah.

Oracles against Juda and Jerusalem (1.1–25.13b). With rare exceptions the oracles collected in the section are attacks against the political and religious errors of the chosen people; the collection probably dates from the first edition of the book by Baruch (ch. 36). The heading (1.1–3) is an editorial composition that shows an unawareness of the prophet's role in the events at Mizpah and Egypt (ch. 40–44). The vocation account (1.4–19) assumes two forms: a dialogue with Yahweh (1.4–10, 17–19) and visions (1.11–16). The prophet's predestination and God's help in the accomplishment of his mission, which will be mainly for condemnation, are especially emphasized.

The following chapters (2–6) contain Jeremiah's first warnings under Josiah, but before the Deuteronomic reform of 621 B.C. In the form of a trial, Jeremiah reproaches JUDAH for its foreign alliances and its idolatry, which break the Sinaitic covenant (ch. 2). *See* COVENANT (IN THE BIBLE). He then makes an urgent appeal for conversion (3.1–4.4), but this is humanly impossible; God is going to accomplish it through His mercy. The poem recalls Osee's preaching: Israel's alliance with Yahweh is the result of love by divine covenant.

The religious apostasy will be punished by an invasion coming from the north; the scourge is described in a long and vividly colored poem (4.5–6.30).

The "lion" from the north used to be identified with Assyria, or Babylon, but since B. Duhm's *Das Buch Jeremiah erklärt* (Tübingen 1901), the Scythians have attracted exegetes' attention. According to Herodotus the Scythians invaded Palestine between 630 and 625 B.C., but since such an invasion is not otherwise assured, it is more probable that Jeremiah had no particular people in mind when he composed his poem. His faith in God's justice assured him that a war would correct Judah's crimes; this is why he used such general terms in describing the scourge.

On the whole, ch. 7 to 20 date from the reign of Johoiakim: Josiah's reform had failed, and Jeremiah had to combat infidelities of all kinds. The "Temple Sermon" (7.1–8.3) attacks the superficiality of the cult, since cult could be a guaranty of salvation only if it were a genuine expression of interior religious values. Jeremiah, like the other prophets, does not reject the cult in itself, but only the legalistic counterfeits employed in carrying it out. Circumcision is criticized for the same reason (9.24–25). His plea for the covenant (11.1–14) is still a much-discussed problem, Jeremiah's attitude toward Josia's reform being one of its elements. The discourse is probably authentic and clearly shows that the prophet supported Josiah's policy. Under Johoiakim, however, he became painfully aware of the reform's failure.

During Johoiakim's reign, Jeremiah's severe warnings led to repeated persecutions of him. The interior crises that resulted are described in his "Confessions" (11.18–12.6; 15.10–21; 17.14–18; 18.18–23; 20.7–18). His faith in God and in his mission conquered these temptations to abandon his task.

The prophet proposes the same severe judgment in parabolic sermons (13.1–14; 18.1–12) and by symbolic, prophetic actions (19.1–20.6); in fact his life itself assumed a prophetic character (16.1–18).

The last part of this section (ch. 21–24) dates on the whole from the reign of Sedecia. It begins with the king's consulting of the prophet during the siege of the city in 588 B.C. (21.1–10). Then various oracles condemning the last kings of Judah are collected (21.11–23.8), except the one concerning the "future King" that belongs to the theme of royal, Davidic MESSIANISM (23.1–8). Oracles against false prophets follow (23.9–40) and are of interest because they raise the question of the true nature of PROPHETISM in Israel. Jeremiah here contrasts the traits of true prophecy with those of professional prophets who flatter the sinful people and play on their hopeful imaginations. The last discourse (25.1–13b) is a heavily glossed summation of Jeremiah's activity up to the year 605-604.

Oracles against Nations (25.13c–38; ch. 46–51). This second section presents great divergences between the Masoretic Text (MT) and the Septuagint (LXX). In the Greek, the oracles are placed immediately after the oracles against Juda, as in the works of other prophets. Most exegetes consider this to be the primitive order of the book. It is difficult to find a reason why the Hebrew transferred them to the end (ch. 46–51). The order of the oracles is different also in the two traditions: the LXX follows a logical order according to the historical importance of the nations while the MT adopts a geographical order going from south to north and from west to east. Finally, the section's authenticity is greatly disputed; some expositors have rejected it completely as a later addition (Duhm, Smend, Stade, etc.); others now hold it authentic but replete with additions. The long poem against Babylon (50.1–51.58) was undoubtedly composed later than Jeremiah.

The judgment of the nations (25.13c–38) is a summation of all this type of preaching: the theme of "the cup of divine wrath," symbolizing God's vengeance against the neighboring countries that had dealt harshly with the Chosen People, is the burden of the text. Israel's God, then, is the master of all nations and of history.

Israel's, Judah's Salvation (ch. 26–35). Jeremiah's mission was not only to destroy a present evil, but also to build up a promising future (1.10). Persecuted for his initial severe message (ch. 26), he attacks the groundless hope of escape proclaimed by the professional prophets (ch. 27–29). Judah's restoration can be secured only by its subjection to Babylon. The prophet graphically plays out this drama by a symbolic act (ch. 27), then envisions an exile of undetermined duration (70 years: 29,10; 25.11). Next, in exquisite poems that come very likely from the first years of his ministry, he proclaims the return of the northern kingdom, Israel: once its purification has been achieved, its return will be a new Exodus (30.1–31.22). Short oracles follow in which Juda also shares in this rebirth (31.23–40).

The oracle of the New Alliance is especially important (31.31–34). It is the same as the covenant of Sinai, yet it is new because it reaches into the depths of man's heart and can never be broken. Its fulfillment is accomplished in Christ's coming (Lk 22.20; 1 Cor 11.25; Heb 8.8–12).

Finally, oracles concerning Judah's future were pronounced during the last siege of Jerusalem (ch. 32–33); but the glorious future is possible only if Judah remains faithful (ch. 34–35).

Jeremiah's Passion (ch. 36–45). In style and subject this section forms a homogeneous whole, the work of one author, Baruch. He tells the story of the persecutions his master suffered, especially at the king's court during the last storming of Jerusalem (588-587 B.C.) and during the few months following its fall. The narration is a precious source for reconstructing the history of these troubled years. One must wait for the New Testament to see such detailed biographical narrations. An oracle in favor of Baruch completes this section (ch. 45).

Appendix (ch. 52). This chapter reproduces, with some variants, 2 Kgs 24.18–25.30 that relates the destruction of Juda. Obvioussly the addition's purpose is to illustrate the fulfillment of the prophet's message. The list of deportees in vv. 28–30 is a unique source that can hardly be questioned. A third deportation in 582-581 is recorded here, and according to Josephus (*Ant. Jud.* 10.181–182) might have coincided with an anti-Babylonian rebellion of Transjordanian states.

Structure and Composition

Even a cursory analysis of the book reveals that its production was quite complicated. There are numerous doublets (6.12–15 and 8.10–12; 10.12–16 and 51.15–19; 16.14–15 and 23.7–8; 17.3–4 and 15.13–14; 23.19–20 and 30.23–24; 30.10–11 and 46.27–28; 49.19–21 and 50.44–46). Also, the Greek text is an eighth shorter than the Hebrew, suggesting that the work underwent several redactions.

Literary Forms. With S. Mowinckel [*Zur Komposition des Buches Jeremiah* (Kristiania 1914)] one can distinguish three principal literary forms or sources: poetic oracles (1–25; 30–31; 46–51), biographical stories (26–29; 36–45), and deuteronomist sermons (7.1–8.3; 11.1–14; 16.1–13; 17.19–27; 18.1–12; 19.1–20.6; 21.1–10; 22.1–5; 25.1–13b; 32.1–2, 6–16, 24–44; 34–35). The authenticity of the first source is no longer disputed, while the second source is attributed to Baruch. The origin of the deuteronomist discourses is still debated; some label them pure deuteronomic interpolations, while others consider them later editions of Jeremian sermons in the style and spirit of Deuteronomy. It is probable that they have a style quite common in Juda during the seventh and sixth centuries (W. O. E. Oesterley and T. H. Robinson) and connected with liturgical assemblies (A. Weiser). Deuteronomy and these sermons are two different examples of the style. For this reason one may legitimately reject as unauthentic only the following passages: 3.14–18; 9.11–15; 10.1–16; 12.14–17; 16.19–21; 17.5–11, 19–27; 22.8–9; 23.19–20, 33–40; 31.38–40; 32.17–25, 29–41; 50.1–51.58; 52.

Compilation of Sources. Chapter 36 relates the story of the book's first editions; in 605 Jeremiah dictated his threats against Judah and Jerusalem to Baruch. They are found generally in ch. 1 to 25. Other partial compilations can be traced, such as discourses attacking kings and prophets (21–23), symbolic actions (18–20), Jeremiah's confessions scattered through the book's first section, salvation oracles for Israel (30–31) and Judah (32–35), Baruch's biographical accounts (36–45), and oracles against the nations (46–51). The book's present form must have been fixed sometime after the Exile [*see* E. Podechard, "Le Livre de Jérémie" *Revue biblique* 37 (1928) 181–97; O. Eissfeldt, *Einleitung in das AT³* (Tübingen 1964) 471–92].

Theology

Jeremiah's theological contribution was not original; he did not advance much beyond his predecessors, but his different approach to sin and conversion is worthy of note.

Sin. Jeremiah proposed traditional themes with an original insistence by emphasizing the interior spirit that should vivify religious life. Thus, God's knowledge of man reaches into the depths of his thoughts and heart (1.5–10; 11.20; 12.3; 17.16; 18.23); correspondingly, man's knowledge of God must spring from the heart (31.31–34). As a consequence, more than any other prophet, Jeremiah delved deeply into the problem of sin. He saw it as a refusal to know God (2.6–8), an apostasy (2.11–12), an ungrateful desertion of God (2.17–19,32; 3.21). Sin is an unnatural perversion (2.11, 21). Its universality in Juda led the prophet to describe it as almost an innate quality in man (13.23) although there is no clear idea yet of ORIGINAL SIN.

Conversion. In contrast, Jeremiah greatly developed the idea of conversion, which he believed impossible for man left to himself. Conversion could be accomplished only if God changed man's heart (3.1–4.4). In this connection his Messianism remained within the perspectives of the Davidic dynasty that must endure, but the future king would reign with justice according to the terms of the covenant (23.5–6; cf. Is 9.5–6; 11.1–4). His eschatology also remained within the normal sequence of history; the world would not end, but a new epoch coinciding with the return from the Exile would begin (23.1–8; 30.10–21; 31.10–14, 23–25; etc.) and would be marked by the conclusion of the New Alliance (31.31–34).

See Also: JEREMIAH; LAMENTATIONS, BOOK OF; JEREMIAH, LETTER OF; BARUCH, BOOK OF.

Bibliography: P. VOLZ, *Der Prophet Jeremia* (2d ed. Leipzig 1928). F. NÖTSCHER, *Das Buch Jeremias* (Bonn 1934). A. GELIN, *Dictionnaire de la Bible,* suppl. ed. L. PIROT, et al. (Paris 1928–) 4:857–889. A. WEISER, *Das Buch der Propheten Jeremia,* 2 v. (Göttingen 1952–55). A. PENNA, *Geremia* (Turin 1954). W. RUDOLPH, *Jeremiah* (2d ed. Tübingen 1958). J. PATERSON, "Jeremiah," *Peake's Commentary on the Bible,* ed. M. BLACK and H. H. ROWLEY (London 1962) 465–489. G. P. COUTURIER, *The New Jerome Bible Commentary* (Englewood Cliffs, N.J. 1990) 265–297. L. BOADT, *Jeremiah 1–25/26–52,* 2 v. (Wilmington 1982). E. W. NICHOLSON, *Jeremiah 1–25/26–52,* 2 v. (Cambridge 1973, 1975).

[G. COUTURIER]

JEREMIAH, LETTER OF

A paraenetic composition of the Hellenistic period directed to the Jewish exiles in Babylon urging them to repudiate Babylonian idolatry because the idols are not gods. In the Septuagint (LXX) the letter is found as an independent unit between Lamentations and Ezekiel, but in the Vulgate it is reckoned as ch. 6 of Baruch. It was formerly thought to be an original Greek composition, written at Alexandria against Egyptian idolatry, since its oldest preserved form is the Greek of the LXX; but internal evidence has now made it certain that it was written originally in Hebrew and most likely in Babylonia, since it is Babylonian idolatry that it condemns.

In subject matter the author, without much logical sequence or literary skill, treats of various aspects of the impotence of idols, thus demonstrating the folly of idol worship.

The author cannot be Jeremiah because, among other reasons, he speaks of the "seven generations" of the Exile, which, if taken literally, would date the work to *c.* 300 B.C. It is apparently a late and poor imitation, in synagogue-homily fashion, of the authentic letter of Jeremiah (Jer 29.1–28), with much borrowing from Jeremiah's polemic against idols (Jer 10.3–16). Arguments against idolatry have also been taken from Isaiah ch. 40 to 55, especially Is 44.9–20. The letter shows considerable knowledge of Babylonian religion.

Bibliography: A. ROBERT, *Dictionnaire de la Bible,* suppl. ed. L. PIROT, et al. (Paris 1928–) 4:849–857. C. J. BALL, "Epistle of Jeremy," *The Apocrypha and Pseudoepigrapha of the Old Testament in English,* ed. R. H. CHARLES et al., 2v. (Oxford 1913) 1:596–611. A. PENNA, "Geremia," *La Sacra Bibbia,* ed. S. GAROFALO, 3 v. (Rome 1954) 2:745–749.

[L. A. IRANYI]

JERICHO

In the Bible, Jericho is chiefly famous as the first city captured by the Israelites at the time of the conquest of Palestine during the last quarter of the 13th century (1220–1200) B.C. Two Old traditions that center around the Benjaminite sanctuary at Gilgal are intertwined in the story of Jericho's fall before Joshua's army (Jos 4.13–6.26). The narrative receives some epic coloring and establishes a parallel with the Exodus from Egypt. It could well be that the Jericho of Joshua's day was little more than a strong fort [see JOSHUA, SON OF NUN]. In Old Testament times Jericho does not appear again as an important town, although it is occasionally mentioned.

Several incidents in our Lord's life are associated with Jericho. The JORDAN ford where He was baptized is not far from the town (Mt 3.5–6). Jericho also figures in the stories of Bartimaeus (Mk 10.46) and of Zacchaeus (Lk 19.1), and in the parables of the gold pieces (Lk 19.11) and of the good Samaritan (Lk 10.30). Jericho is called the "city of palm trees" in Dt 34.3; Jgs 1.16; 3.13. The root meaning of the word Jericho, however, is perhaps connected with *yrḥ,* "moon," i.e., sanctuary of the moon-god.

Site. Jericho is situated about six miles north of the north end of the Dead Sea and five miles west of the Jordan River. It is the earth's lowest town, lying some 825 feet below sea level. Jerusalem is about 17 miles northeast and some 3,200 feet above Jericho's mounds.

Jericho has a series of sites, for the location of the city has changed after sieges, earthquakes, and other catastrophes. Modern Jericho, the small Arab town of er-Rīḥā, was also the Jericho at the time of the Crusaders. It is now a thriving municipality and, with its orange and banana groves, a fruitful cultivation center, but has little to interest the Bible student.

Tell es-Sulṭān, one mile northwest of er-Rīḥā, is the site of Old Testament Jericho. The large (six-acre) tell is adjacent to 'Ain es-Sulṭān, a copious water supply still known as the fountain of Elisha (2 Kgs 2.19–22) and fertilizing a rich oasis in the dry 14-mile wide plain of the Jordan Valley.

Square in the path of any invader of the hill country from the southern portion of the Jordan Valley, Jericho was a city of great strategic importance, a key defense position for the western section of the plain. In the background the hills of the western highlands rise sharply, the 1,500-foot ridge called the Mount of Temptation hardly one mile away. These are the hills where Joshua's spies hid (Jos 2.22). Forbidding as they appear, they are actually cut by hidden wadies giving access to the interior plateau of Palestine. Jericho thus controlled the access to the hill country from Transjordan.

Archeology of Old Testament Jericho. During the first part of the 20th century three major archeological expeditions investigated Tell es-Sulṭān. The latest (1952–58) and most important was conducted by Miss Kathleen M. Kenyon, director of the British school of ar-

cheology in Jerusalem. The work of the excavators has shown that Jericho was founded in the latter part of the New Stone Age (*c.* 7800 B.C.) before the invention of pottery. Jericho is thus the oldest settlement yet found in the Near East and an important element in the history of civilization.

Miss Kenyon's most remarkable find was a group of seven portrait skulls. These are actual human skulls on which the features of the face have been modeled in plaster. The eyes were inset with shells with slits representing the pupils. The heads have an astonishingly lifelike appearance and are perhaps the portraits of important leaders or venerated ancestors. They must be placed among the earliest examples of human art, being clay modeled portrait busts of individuals who died 7,000 years ago.

The most surprising result of Miss Kenyon's work has been the discovery that virtually nothing remains of the site from the late Bronze period (1500–1200 B.C.), which includes Joshua's time. The mound has suffered such extensive denudation of its upper strata through erosion and human depradations that almost all remains later than the third millennium have disappeared from its top. The two walls that preceding archeologists believed were ruins dating back to Joshua's time are now known to date back to the third millennium and to represent only two of some 15 different walls of that age. There is, however, evidence at BETHEL, Lachish, Debir, and Hazor of their destruction during the 13th century B.C., which agrees with the hypothesis that the Israelite conquest was in progress at that time.

Beneath the mud houses and tents of the large Arab refugee camp that is now north of the old Jericho mound lies the ancient cemetery area. A number of Middle-Bronze-Age (2000–1500) tombs were explored, some of them dating back to the 17th century B.C. Some of the objects placed with the deceased are in an amazing state of preservation and offer good evidence for the culture of these people living at the time of the Biblical patriarchs. Of particular interest are some human skulls 3,500 years old, with the desiccated brain shriveled to the size of a walnut, but with all its convolutions still plainly to be seen.

Archeology of New Testament Jericho. The Jericho of New Testament times (Tulūl Abū'l-'Alāyiq), through which our Lord often passed en route to Jerusalem, is situated about two miles south of Old Testament Jericho and one mile west of the modern town. Much of it was built by Herod the Great who died here in 4 B.C. The mound is located at the entry of Wadi Qelt into the Jordan Valley. The presence of an abundant waterway from the wadi along with the amenities of the winter climate made it a favored spot. It was a magnificent Roman-style city with pools, villas, a hippodrome, and a theater. Parts of an elaborate building with a great terrace-façade in Roman style *opus reticulatum* were excavated and may be Herod's palace. This particular type of construction, made by setting small square pyramidal stones into plaster, gives the appearance of a net (hence its name) and is characteristically Roman of that period. It bears witness to the international culture that was then Palestine's.

Bibliography: L. HENNEQUIN, *Dictionnaire de la Bible,* suppl. ed. L. PIROT, et al. (Paris 1928–) 3:410–414. K. M. KENYON and D. TUSHINGHAM, ''Jericho Gives up Its Secrets,'' *National Geographic* 104 (1953) 853–870. K. M. KENYON, ''Ancient Jericho . . . ,'' *Scientific American* 190 (1954) 76–83; *Digging up Jericho* (New York 1958). R. NORTH, ''Les Murs de Jericho,'' *Bible et Terre Sainte* no. 14 (1958) 10–17. J. B. PRITCHARD et al., *The Excavation of Herodian Jericho (1951)* (*Annual of the American Schools of Oriental Research,* 32–33; 1958).

[E. LUSSIER]

Woodcut of St. Jerome.

JEROME, ST.

Church Father, Scripture scholar, Doctor of the Church; b. Stridon, extreme (modern) northeast Italy, *c.* 345; d. Bethlehem, Palestine, 419–420.

Life, Literary Career, Character. Jerome was born Sophronius Eusebius, of Christian parents at Stridon ''on the confines of Dalmatia and Pannonia'' (*De vir. ill.* 135). At 12 he was sent to Rome with Bonosus to study grammar, rhetoric, and the liberal arts under the famed grammarian Donatus. There he met RUFINUS OF AQUILEIA and the patrician (St.) PAMMACHIUS, and there he was baptized at 19. He journeyed through Gaul, stopped at Treves (Trier, Germany) where he became acquainted with monasticism, copied HILARY OF POITIERS's *De Synodis* and *De Psalmis,* and then joined a choir of ascetics (Jerome, *Chron.* 329), including Rufinus and CHROMATIUS, in Aquileia under Bishop Valerian (*c.* 370). In 372 he suddenly left on ''an uncertain journey through Thrace, Bithynia, Pontus, Galicia, and Cilicia,'' settling finally in the home of Evagrius of Antioch (*Epist.* 3:3). He retired for two years to the desert of Chalcis, near Aleppo, where he fell sick and had his famous dream in which he was accused of being a ''Ciceronian not a Christian'' (*Epist.* 22:30), and perfected his Greek and studied Hebrew (*homo trilinguis: Contra Ruf.* 3:6).

Literary Career. Disturbed by the MELETIAN SCHISM in Antioch, Jerome wrote to Pope DAMASUS I concerning the Trinitarian terminology (*Epist.* 15, 16) and on return to Antioch began his literary career with his legendary life of Paul the Hermit (*c.* 377). He attended lectures of APOLLINARIS OF LAODICEA on Scripture and was ordained a priest (379) without pastoral obligation, by the Rome-recognized Paulinus of Antioch. In 380 he journeyed to Constantinople to consult with GREGORY OF NAZIANZUS, GREGORY OF NYSSA, and AMPHILOCHIUS OF ICONIUM, and to read ORIGEN. He translated the *World Chronicle* of EUSEBIUS OF CAESAREA (SALAMIS) as well as some of the homilies of Origen.

In 382 Jerome traveled to Rome with Paulinus of Antioch and EPIPHANIUS OF SALAMIS and became secretary to Pope Damasus I. He entered the ascetical life of the city, serving as spiritual pedagogue and director to a group of noble women on the Aventine: MARCELLA, her widowed mother, Albina, and sister, Asella; PAULA and her daughters Blesilla and EUSTOCHIUM; and Marcellina, Felicitas, Furia, Lea, FABIOLA, and Principia. He made a collation of Origen's *Hexapla* with Aquila's version of the Old Testament and prepared a correction of the *Old Versions (Itala) of the Gospels and Psalms* for Damasus. He also wrote the *Refutation of Helvidius,* to prove the perpetual virginity of the Blessed Virgin Mary; his *Dialogus contra Luciferianos,* concerned with the validity of heretical baptism and priestly and episcopal orders; and he prepared a translation of the tables of concordance of Eusebius of Caesarea.

His strictures on the laxity of the Roman clergy and married Christians and the accusation that his harsh ascetical advice caused the death of St. Blesilla destroyed his hope (*Epist.* 45:3) of succeeding Damasus (d. December 384), and he departed from Ostia for Palestine with his brother Paulinian and some monks (August 385).

Jerome visited Crete and Antioch, then with St. Paula and a group of Roman women toured the desert of Egypt and Palestine, talking with the hermits and making copious geographical and hagiographical notes. He settled in Bethlehem (386) where Paula built a double MONASTERY. He then entered cordial relations with a similar establishment under Rufinus and MELANIA THE ELDER in Jerusalem and embarked upon his scriptural exegesis. By way of cenobitical propaganda Jerome wrote his *Life of Hilarion, Life of the Monk Malchus, Two Books against Jovinian* in defense of virginity, and the *De viris illustribus* (393–395), a list of 135 authors from Peter to himself, including Philo, Josephus, and the heretics Tatian, Bardesanes, and Novatian for their influence on Christian authors. It was the first literary history, or attempt to dignify Christians as men of letters.

Quarrel over Origen. When Atarbius, an emissary of Epiphanius of Constantia, stirred anti-Origenistic propaganda in Palestine (395), Jerome forsook allegiance to Origen's teaching, while Rufinus remained loyal. There ensued a quarrel in which Bishop JOHN OF JERUSALEM took part with Rufinus and deprived Jerome and his monastery of spiritual assistance. Jerome attacked John in his *Contra Johannem Hierosolymitanum.* The quarrel was pacified at Easter 397, and Rufinus left for Italy; but it was renewed when Jerome's friends in Rome, particularly SS. Marcella and Eusebius of Cremona, complained that Rufinus had translated Origen's *Peri Archon* using Jerome's fame as guarantor. Rufinus replied to a warning from Jerome with his *Apology against Jerome;* Jerome answered him in two books before seeing the full text, rebutting Rufinus's reply with a third book. AUGUSTINE deplored this quarrel between former friends (*Epist.* 73:6–10), but Jerome continued the attack until Rufinus's death in Sicily (410), which Jerome announced with "Now that the scorpion lies buried in Tinacria . . ." (Jerome, *Praef. ad Ezech.*).

Of Jerome's correspondence, 117 letters remain; many among them are eulogies on Blesilla, Paula, Eustochium, Fabiola, Marcella, Nepotian, and Nebridius. Others reflect his interests in education; asceticism, history, and doctrine. He exchanged 19 letters with Augustine (*Florilegium Patristicum* 22) and several with PAULINUS OF NOLA (*Epist.* 53) and the virgin DEMETRIAS, and he made literal translations of Origen's *Peri Archon,* the festal letters of THEOPHILUS OF ALEXANDRIA, the anti-Origenistic writings of EPIPHANIUS, the tract on the Holy Spirit of DIDYMUS THE BLIND, and ascetical works of PA-

CHOMIUS, Theodore, and Orsisius. He opened a school for boys at Bethlehem, gave spiritual and scriptural homilies to the monks and nuns, wrote refutations of the antiascetical doctrines of Vigilantius and the Pelagians, and continued the immense work of his Scripture translations and studies. His monastery gave hospitality to the refugees from the sack of Rome and the Vandal invasions (410–412), and was burned by marauders (416). Following his death, his bones were deposited in the grotto at Bethlehem, then reportedly transferred to the crypt of St. Mary Major in Rome.

Probably the most learned man of the age, Jerome had an exceptionally fine classic style, but could adapt himself to the popular Latin of the day. Jerome was sensitive and suspicious of ascetical and theological rivals; his indulgences of his strong likes and dislikes, both literary and personal, betray his complicated character. Irascible in temperament, he used sarcasm, irony, and invective that reflect the hyperbole of the literary tradition of his age, as do his attitude toward women and extremes in asceticism. His personality cannot be readily subjected to modern psychiatric investigation because there is a problem with his literary sources, since much of his learned lore was taken bodily from Suetonius, Josephus, Porphyry, and Theophrastus.

Scripture Scholar. He was an exegete rather than a theologian; his first scriptural composition was an allegorical commentary on the Prophet Abdias, which he later deprecated as juvenile (*Pref. in lib. Job*).

Influence of Origen. At Constantinople (380–382) he translated 14 of Origen's homilies on Jeremiah, 14 on Ezekiel, eight on Isaiah, and two on the Song of Songs. He published his own treatise on Isaiah's vision of the Seraphim (Is. 6:1–8:cf. *Epist.* 18), in which he rejected Origen's explanation of the two Seraphim as signifying God the Son and the Holy Spirit (*Epist.* 84:3).

During his stay in Rome (382–385), he produced letters dealing with individual Hebrew words untranslated in the Latin version of the Scriptures, e.g., Hosanna (*Epist.* 20), alleluia, amen, and Maran Atha (*Epist.* 26) and with the Alphabetic Psalms (*Epist.* 30) and criticized the commentary of Reticius of Autun on the Song of Songs (*Epist.* 37). He revised the Old Latin version of the New Testament based on an excellent text of the original Greek Gospels, and made a new version of the Psalter from the Septuagint.

In Bethlehem (386–390) he started a new version of the Old Testament based on Origen's *Hexapla,* of which only the so-called Gallican Psalter has been preserved. For Paula's nuns he translated 39 homilies of Origen on St. Luke and composed his own commentaries on Philemon, Galatians, Ephesians, and Titus (386–387). His commentary on Ecclesiastes was the first Latin work to take cognizance of the Hebrew text (389), and a short while later he wrote the *Liber Hebraicarum quaestionum in Genesim,* based partially on current Hebrew exegesis (pref.) and published his book on Hebrew names, drawing heavily on Philo and Origen, and a book on Biblical place names, adapted from Eusebius's *Onomasticon* but corrected by Jerome's own information.

The Hebrew Bible. He published (391–406) a new translation of all the books of the Hebrew Bible, a commentary on the 12 minor Prophets, a series of notes on St. Matthew's Gospel for Eusebius of Cremona, and the *Commentarioli in Psalmos* (402). Two essays, one on the study of Scripture for Paulinus of Nola (*Epist.* 53), and one on translation (*Epist.* 57), are invaluable for an insight into Jerome's mind in approaching the understanding of the Word of God. He wrote a number of brief explanations of various scriptural problems in letters to friends and petitioners.

During the last 15 years of his life Jerome concentrated on his exegetical masterpieces, the *Opus prophetale,* as he calls it, with his commentaries on Daniel (407), Isaiah (408–410), Ezekiel (410–415), and Jeremiah (ch. 1–32:415–419) and a few minor tracts, closing with an exposition of Psalm 89 (*Epist.* 140), in which he dilates on the sorrows of "decrepit old age."

Jerome brought to his exegesis an enormous erudition beginning with his knowledge of the classics and amplified with a close attention to Hebrew tradition and an on-site appreciation of the milieu in which the Scriptures were composed. He had an original mind and excellent human intuition. He employed a well-defined hermeneutical method, borrowing what was good from all three traditions of exegesis, the Alexandrian, Antiochene, and Rabbinical, and while his earlier works abound in allegorical interpretation, his later demonstrate a well-balanced utilization of the best thought then available for "giving my Latin readers the hidden treasures of Hebrew erudition" in keeping with the true meaning of the Scriptures.

Vir Ecclesiasticus. Proud of his orthodoxy as a *vir ecclesiasticus,* he was gentle and kind with his close associates in the ascetical life, though unmerciful toward his enemies. His scriptural exegesis and historical information in his adaptation of Eusebius's *Chronicle* made him a founder of the Middle Ages, where he is frequently depicted with a lion for a companion in study. A favorite of Renaissance scholars for the elegance of his Latin style, his strong invective, and breadth of knowledge, he is frequently depicted in an act of supine penance, or with a cardinal's hat (Germany). Various nations including Spain have claimed him as a native.

He has been considered a Father of the Church since the eighth century. The Council of TRENT spoke of Jerome as the *Doctor maximus in sacris scripturis explanandis,* and modern exegesis—from the *Spiritus Paraclitus* of Benedict XV (*Acta Apostolicae Sedis* 12:385–420) and the *Divino afflante Spiritu* (Sept. 30, 1943) of PIUS XII to more recent exegetical progress—has found him an indispensable witness to the mind of the Church in dealing with the Word of God.

Feast: Sept. 30.

Bibliography: *Opera Omnia,* 9 v. *Patrologia Latina,* ed. J. P. MIGNE, 271 v., indexes 4 v. (Paris 1878–90) 22–30; *Opera,* ed. J. HILBERG and S. REITER, 4 v. (Corpus scriptorum ecclesiasticorum latinorum 54–56, 59; Vienna 1910–13); ed. P. LAGARDE et al., 2 v. (Corpus Christianorum. Series latina 72, 78; Turnhout, Belg. 1958–59); *Sur Jonas,* ed. and tr. P. ANTIN (Sources Chrétiennes, ed. H. DE LUBAC et al. 43; Paris 1956). *The Correspondence (394–419), between Jerome and Augustine of Hippo,* tr. C. WHITE (Lewiston, N.Y. 1990); *Curiosissimus excerptor: gli "Additamenta" di Girolamo ai "Chronica" di Eusebio,* ed. G. BRUGNOLI (Pisa 1995); *Epistula di misser sanctu Iheronimu ad Eustochiu,* ed. F. SALMERI (Palermo 1999). Literature. P. T. CAMELOT, *Lexikon für Theologie und Kirche,* ed. J. HOFER and K. RAHNER, 10 v. (2d, new ed. Freiburg 1957–65) suppl., *Das Zweite Vatikanische Konzil: Dokumente und Kommentare,* ed. H. S. BRECHTER et al., pt. 1 (1966) 5:326—329. H. LIETZMANN, *Paulys Realenzyklopädie der klassischen Altertumswissenschaft,* ed. G. WISSOWA et al. 8.2 (1913) 1565–81. J. FORGET, *Dictionnaire de théologie catholique,* ed. A. VACANT et al., 15 v. (Paris 1903–50; Tables générales 1951–) 8.1:894–983. *Dictionnaire de théologie catholique,* ed. A. VACANT et al., 15 v. (Paris 1903–50; Tables générales 1951–), Tables générales, 2:2498–2505. B. ALTANER, *Patrology,* tr. H. GRAEF from 5th German ed. (New York 1960) 462–476. F. CAVALLERA, *Saint Jérôme,* 2 v. (Spicilegium sacrum Lovaniense 1, 2; Louvain 1922); *Dictionnaire de la Bible,* suppl. ed. L. PIRTO et al. (Paris 1928–) 4:889–897. A. PENNA, *S. Gerolamo* (Turin 1949); *Principi e carattere dell' esegesi di S. Gerolamo* (Rome 1950). I. D'IVRAY [J. FAHMY-BEY], *Saint Jérôme et les dames de l'Aventin* (Paris 1938). P. ANTIN, *Essai sur saint Jérôme* (Paris 1951); "Les Idées morales de S. Jérôme," *Mélanges de science religieuse* 14 (1957) 135–150. F. X. MURPHY, ed., *A Monument to Saint Jerome* (New York 1952). H. HAGENDAHL, *Latin Fathers and the Classics* (Göteborg 1958). R. and M. PERNOUD, *Saint Jerome,* tr. R. SHEED (New York 1962); *Saint Jérôme: père de la Bible* (Monaco 1996). J. N. D. KELLY, *Jerome: His Life, Writings, and Controversies* (London 1975). H. FRIEDMANN, *A Bestiary for Saint Jerome* (Washington 1980). V. LARBAUD, *An Homage to Jerome: Patron Saint of Translators,* tr. J.-P. DE CHEZET (Marlboro, Vt. 1984). B. RIDDERBOS, *Saint and Symbol: Images of Saint Jerome in Early Italian Art,* tr. P. DE WAARD-DEKKING (Groningen 1984). M. HODGES, *St. Jerome and the Lion* (New York 1991). D. ERASMUS, *Patristic Scholarship,* ed. and tr. J. F. BRADY and J. C. OLIN (Toronto 1992), v. 61; *Vita di San Girolamo,* ed. and tr. A. MORISI GUERRA (L'Aquila 1988). D. BROWN, *Vir Trilinguis: A Study in the Biblical Exegesis of Saint Jerome* (Kampen, the Netherlands 1992). C. KRUMEICH, *Hieronymus und die christlichen feminae clarissimae* (Bonn 1993). P. LARDET, *L'apologie de Jérôme contre Rufin* (Leiden 1993). A. KAMESAR, *Jerome, Greek Scholarship, and the Hebrew Bible* (Oxford 1993). L. MIRRI, *La dolcezza nella lotta: donne e ascesi secondo Girolamo* (Magnano 1996). H. LOCHER, *Domenico Ghirlandaio, Hieronymus im Gehäuser* (Frankfurt am Main 1999). P. P. VERGERIO, *Pierpaolo*

Vergerio the Elder and Saint Jerome, tr. J. M. MCMANAMON (Tempe, Ariz. 1999). M. LUTHER, *Annotierungen zu den Werken des Hieronymus,* ed. M. BRECHT and C. PETERS (Cologne 2000). D. F. HEIMANN, "Christian Humanism in the Fourth Century: Saint Jerome," in *The Endless Fountain,* ed. M. MORFORD (Columbus, Ohio 1972), 58–126.

[F. X. MURPHY]

JEROME OF PRAGUE

Pre-Hussite; b. Prague, *c.* 1365; d. Constance, May 30, 1416. He studied at Prague, Paris, and then Oxford, where he copied John WYCLIF's theological treatises *Dialogue* and *Trialogue,* which he brought back to Prague (1401). On his return Jerome (Jeromyn) became a zealous propagator of Wyclif's doctrine in Prague, where he was on the university faculty. He was an active participant in the disputes at the University of Prague and played a special part in the Kutná Hora decree of 1409 (*see* HUS, JOHN). Through his traveling and eloquence he left his imprint on Paris, Heidelberg, Cologne, and Vienna; but the Wyclifite doctrine he propounded forced him to flee from city to city; e.g., in 1410 he had to flee the Inquisition in Vienna. Because of his renown and learning, King Ladislaus II JAGIEŁŁO of Poland employed him (1413) to organize the University of Cracow; but because of his dissemination of Wyclifite doctrine during his travels with Prince Vytautas, the Polish bishops turned against him. In April 1415 Jerome secretly went to the Council of CONSTANCE in a vain attempt to defend his friend Hus. On the way home he himself was arrested and brought back before the Council. On Sept. 23, 1415, he signed a retraction of the condemned articles of Wyclif and HUS. However, Michael de Causis and Stephen of Páleč declared his recantation ambiguous. On the last of his three appearances before the council (May 26, 1416) he withdrew his earlier retraction. He was proclaimed a relapsed heretic, and as such he was condemned and burned at the stake. Hussites venerate him as a reformer and martyr. He is remembered for his preaching more than for his writing (ed. *Fontes rerum Austriacarum* 6:112–128).

Bibliography: L. HELLER, *Hieronymus von Prag* (Lübeck 1835). J. PUTNY, *Mistr Jeronym Pražský* (Prague 1916). R. R. BETTS, "J. of P.," *Univ. of Birmingham Historical Journal* 1 (1947) 51–91. P. BERNARD, "J. of P., Austria and the Hussites," *Church History* 27 (1958) 3–22. L. R. LOOMIS, tr., *The Council of Constance,* ed. J. H. MUNDY and K. M. WOODY (New York 1961). P. DE VOOGHT, *Catholicisme* 6:706–707.

[J. PAPIN]

JERON (HIERON), ST.

Priest and missionary to the Frisians; a.k.a. Hieron or Iero; martyred by the Northmen, 856? Differing traditions place his birth in Egmond, Holland, England, or Scotland. When brought before a tribal assembly and sharply questioned, Jeron bore eloquent witness in the best tradition of the Roman martyrs, quoting fluently from the Scriptures. He was then tortured and slain. The saint's head is at Noordwijk, the scene of his martyrdom. Other relics are at St. Adalbert's monastery in Egmond. In the late Middle Ages, and again recently, his cult has been popular in Holland and miracles have been attributed to him.

Feast: Aug. 17; Aug. 18 (Diocese of Haarlem).

Bibliography: *Acta Sanctorum* Aug. 3:475–479. O. OPPERMAN, *Fontes egmundenses* (Utrecht 1933) 181–307. A. M. ZIMMERMANN, *Kalendarium Benedictinum: Die Heiligen und Seligen des Benediktinerorderns und seiner Zweige,* 4 v. (Metten 1933–38) 2:591. H. J. A. COPPENS, Algemeen *Overzicht der Kerkgeschiedenis van Noord-Nederland* (2d ed. Utrecht 1902) 96–97.

[R. BALCH]

JERUSALEM

Principal city of PALESTINE, capital of modern Israel, and the "Holy City" of Jews, Christians, and Muslims. Its history is of universal interest, not only in the Biblical period, but also in the Christian Era.

Biblical Jerusalem

Jerusalem's name, topography and water supply, archeological excavations, history, and fortifications are questions of particular concern to students of Sacred Scripture.

Name. The original Hebrew name of the city, *yᵉrûšālēm,* has been tendentiously vocalized in the Massoretic Text (MT) to the dual form of *yᵉrûšalaim* or (five times) *yᵉrûšālayim,* perhaps to indicate the two hills to which it spread, or to show its importance as the capital. The earlier, correct form, *yᵉrûšālēm,* is still shown in the Aramaic sections of the MT (Dn 5.2, 3; Ezr 4.12; 5.2, 15), and this is the pronunciation presupposed by the spelling *yrwšlm* of the Elephantine papyri. Both forms, *yrwšlm* and *yrwšlym,* are used indiscriminately on the shekels and half shekels of the First Revolt and in the DEAD SEA SCROLLS. In the Septuagint (LXX), Ἰερουσαλήμ prevails in the protocanonical books, Ἱεροσόλυμα in the deuterocanonical books. In the NT, the more common form is Ἰερουσαλήμ. In the so-called Execration Texts, the Egyptians of the 19th century B.C. wrote the name of the city as *'wš'mm* (for *rwšlm*). In the Amarna Letters of the 14th century B.C., the name is spelled in cuneiform as *Urušalim,* and in the Akkadian inscriptions of the Assyrians and Babylonians (middle of the 1st millennium B.C.)

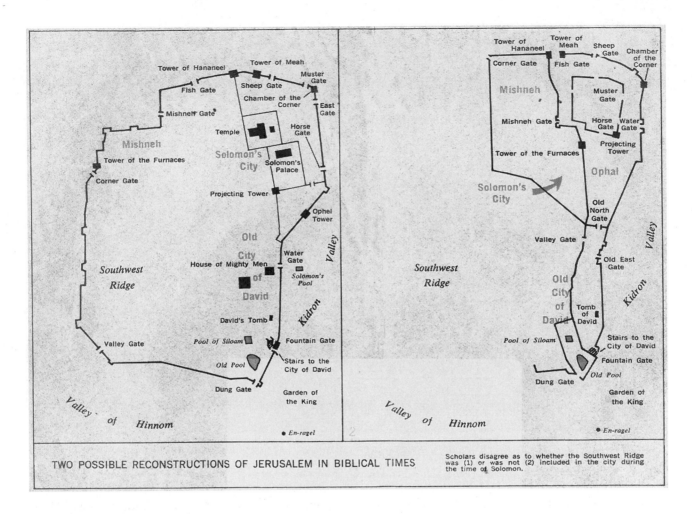

TWO POSSIBLE RECONSTRUCTIONS OF JERUSALEM IN BIBLICAL TIMES

Scholars disagree as to whether the Southwest Ridge was (1) or was not (2) included in the city during the time of Solomon.

the ordinary spelling is *Uršalimmu*. In 1962 there was found in a cave about five miles south of Jerusalem an inscription of the 8th century B.C., written in ancient Hebrew (or Phoenician) script, with the oldest known form of the name *yršlm*. The folk etymologies that connect *šālēm* with Hebrew *šālôm*, ''peace'' (already witnessed to in Heb 7.2) and explain the meaning of the city's name as ''city of peace,'' ''vision of peace,'' or ''possession of peace'' are of no scientific value. The probable meaning is Foundation (*yᵉrû* from the *yrw*, ''to found'') of (the god) Shalem. This god (*šālēm*) is a well-known deity of the Semitic pantheon, and his birth is recounted in the texts of UGARIT. Perhaps the word Salem (*šālēm*) in Genesis 14.18 originally had nothing to do with Jerusalem; but apparently it was later understood as a synonym for Jerusalem, for it is so used in Ps 75(76).3. Before David's capture of the city, the dominant clan among its mixed inhabitants was the Jebusites (*yᵉbûsî*: Jos 15.8; 18.28), and so it was also known at that time as Jebus (*yᵉbûs*: Jgs 19.10–11; 1 Chr 11.4–5). At present, its official name is Yerushalayim in the State of Israel, and El-Quds (''the holiness,'' i.e., holy place; cf. ''the holy city'' in Is 52.1;

Mt 4.5; 27.53; Rv 11.2) in the Hashemite Kingdom of Jordan.

Topography and Water Supply. Jerusalem is situated at 35°14' east longitude and 31°46' north latitude (about the same latitude as El Paso, Tex.), near the water divide on the central limestone plateau of Palestine, 32 miles east of the Mediterranean Sea and 14 miles west of the northern end of the Dead Sea. It has the general form of an inclined plain, somewhat wider and higher in the north than in the south, and surrounded on the east, south, and west by valleys that give it the appearance of a promontory. Actually, the city spreads over two hills that are separated by a valley running down from north to south, from the present Damascus Gate to the Pool of Siloam. In Roman times this was known as the Tyropoeon Valley or Valley of the Cheesemakers (τυροποιῶν); the present Arabic-speaking inhabitants call it simply el-Wād (the valley). The two hills are more noticeable at the southern end of the valley, where they face each other on the east and west outside the south wall of the present ''Old City.'' The western hill is higher (*c.* 2,525 feet above sea level) and broader than the eastern hill and is divided by

Greek Orthodox priests outside the Church of the Holy Sepulchre, constructed c. 12th Century, Jerusalem. (©Paul A. Souders/ CORBIS)

a slight east-west depression into the higher land at Herod's Gate (near Calvary) in the north and the higher land at the Cenacle (Christian Sion) in the south. The valley that skirts it at the west and south was known in Biblical times as the Valley of (the sons of) Hinnom, in Hebrew, *gê' (beͤnê) hinnôm,* whence the word GEHENNA; it is now called Wadi er-Rabābi. The eastern hill is less high (*c.* 2,425 feet above sea level) and less wide. Two slight depressions divide it into three elevations, decreasing in height from north to south: Bezetha, the Temple area (identified in post-exilic times with the Mount Moria of Abraham's sacrifice: cf. 2 Chr with Gn 22.2), and Ophel (Neh 3.26), now called edh-Dhahūra. On the east the Biblical valley of the Kidron, now called Wadi en-Nār, separates the eastern hill of Jerusalem from the MOUNT OF OLIVES and its southern extension, the so-called Mount of Scandal (or Offense: cf. 2 Kgs 23.13), now called Jebel Baṭn el-Hawa.

On the western side of the Kidron Valley, at the foot of Ophel, is the strong, intermittent spring of water known in OT times as Gihon (1 Kgs 1.33), now called in Arabic 'Ain Umm ed-Derej (Spring of the Mother of the Steps), from the double flight of 32 steps by which one now descends to the spring, or, especially by the

Christians, 'Ain Sitti Maryam (Spring of Lady Mary) from the traditional tomb of the Blessed Virgin Mary further up the Kidron Valley. This copious, perennial source of water is the primary reason why the hill of Ophel, just above it, has been settled by men ever since prehistoric times. In the archeological explorations around this spring that were begun by C. Warren in 1867 and resumed by the Parker Mission between 1909 and 1914, there was discovered a shaft tunnel by which the spring could be reached from within the ancient city. This tunnel is apparently the *ṣinnôr* (poorly translated as "gutter" in the Douay Version) by which Joab gained access to the city when he captured it for David (2 Sm 5.8). At the time of King Ahaz (*c.* 735–715) there were two pools or reservoirs at the southern end of Ophel, each of which received its water from Gihon through a conduit (*teͤ'ālâ*) constructed along the base of the hill. Isaiah speaks of this water as "the waters of Siloam" (Is 8.6), the Hebrew word *šīlōaḥ,* "the sending," being another term for conduit. The two reservoirs at the southern end of Ophel, one of which was on somewhat higher ground than the other, were known simply as "the Upper Pool" (*habbeͤrēkâ ha'elyônâ:* Is 7.3; 36.2) and "the Lower Pool" (*habbeͤrēkâ hattahtônâ.* Is 22.9). Since the Gihon spring and the conduits that brought its water to these pools lay exposed to besieging enemies, King Hezekiah (*c.* 715–687), in preparing for Sennacherib's siege (701 B.C.), had a tunnel cut under Ophel connecting Gihon with the "old" Upper Pool, "the Pool of Siloam" (Jn 9.7, 11), which he renovated (Is 22.9–11; 2 Kgs 20.20; Sir 48.17). He could thus block up and conceal the outside entrance to Gihon and discontinue the use of the exposed conduits. The Siloe (Siloam) tunnel (*c.* 600 yards long), a remarkably skillful work of engineering for that time (*see* SILOAM INSCRIPTION), still brings the water from 'Ain Sitti Maryam to the Pool of Siloe, now called Birket Silwān. The old Lower Pool, at present silted up and used as a vegetable garden, is now called Birket el-Ḥamra.

A little to the southeast of Ophel, at the juncture of the Kidron and the Hinnom valleys, is a poorer spring, En-ragel (Jos 15.7; 18.16; 2 Sm 17.17; 1 Kgs 1.9). With the present silting up of the valley, it is now considerably below the surface; its modern Arabic name is Bir Ayyub, "Job's Well." It is often considered, though not with certainty, the same as the *'ên hattannîn* [Dragon's(?) Well] of Nehemiah 2.13. The Pool of BETHESDA near the Sheepgate in Jerusalem (Jn 5.2) has been discovered and excavated near the Church of St. Ann.

No doubt, many houses in Jerusalem had their own cisterns for the storage of rain water (2 Kgs 18.31; Prv 5.15), and probably there were public cisterns also (cf. 2 Sm 23.15; 2 Chr 26.10). Modern Jerusalem has several public cisterns, such as Birket Ḥammam el-Baṭrak, Birket es-Sultān, Birket Mamilla, and Birket Sitti Maryam. The main water supply for modern Arab Jerusalem comes from the strong springs and reservoir in Wadi el-Fāra (Biblical Parah: Jos 18.23; Jer 13.4–7), about ten miles northeast of the city. Water for Israeli Jerusalem is pumped up from the reservoir fed by the powerful spring of Rās el-'Ain near ancient Antipatris.

Archeological Excavations. The archeology of Jerusalem presents special difficulties both because the city has often suffered violent destruction and because a large part of the ancient city, at least as it was at the time of Christ, is still thickly settled. Almost all the archeological excavations have been to the south of the southern wall of present-day Jerusalem. Fortunately, this thinly settled section contains the oldest part of ancient Jerusalem. A brief summary is given here in chronological order of the chief archeological explorations of the city.

Older Explorations. From 1867 to 1870 C. Warren explored the land below the southeast corner of the Ḥaram esh-Sherīf (area of Herod's Temple) and discovered the ancient well now known as Warren's Well. From 1880 to 1881 G. Schick and H. Guthe made soundings along the eastern base of Ophel from Birket el-Ḥamra to

Pope Paul VI celebrating Mass at the Holy Selpulcher during his January 1964 pilgrimage to the Holy Land. He was the first pope since St. Peter to set foot into the Holy City.

'Ain Sitti Maryam. From 1894 to 1897 F. I. Bliss and A. C. Dickie explored the Wadi er-Rabābi and excavated at the eastern side of Birket el-Ḥamra and among the ruins of a Byzantine church at the north of the Pool of Siloam.

Between 1904 and 1914 the Parker Mission made further explorations of the various tunnels and conduits connected with the Gihon Spring. At the same time L. H. Vincent published studies of the blind tunnels, Warren's Well, the second conduit, and Hezekiah's tunnel. In 1913 and 1914 and again in 1923 and 1924, R. W. Weil made methodical excavations in the southern part of edh-Dhahūra, where he discovered many ancient tombs, including the so-called royal necropolis, as well as important sections of ancient city-walls and the remnant of a large tower, which he identified with "the Tower of Siloam" of Luke 13.4. From 1923 to 1925 R. A. S. Macalister and G. Duncan made excavations at the northern end of Ophel, where they believed they discovered the northern limit of the Canaanite city with its moat that ran in an east-west direction across the hill and with its complicated system of city walls. Within the city an outcropping of rock was described as an altar. On the eastern edge of the hill, above the Gihon Spring, a well-preserved section of the city wall was dated to the Jebusite period, and the

King Jehu of Israel paying homage to King Salmanasar (Shalmaneser) III of Assyria (859–825 B.C.), detail of the black obelisk of Salmanasar III.

adjoining tower to the period of David or Solomon. In 1927 J. W. Crowfoot discovered, in a deep excavation in the Tyropoeon Valley, remnants of a large city gate that gave access to the western side of the original city. It was built in the Bronze Age and continued in use until the Hellenistic period. From 1925 to 1927 E. L. Sukenik and L. A. Mayer studied the groups of stone blocks left in a line at intervals some distance to the north of the present northern wall of Jerusalem, and they attributed them to the so-called Third Wall of the city. Between 1934 and 1940 and in 1947, C. N. Johns identified the remnants of Hellenistic and Herodian constructions in the Citadel (the so-called Tower of David) near the Jaffa Gate. In 1940 R. W. Hamilton made a sounding at the Damascus Gate and studied part of the Turkish wall.

From 1961 to 1963, K. Kenyon of the British School of Archeology and Père R. de Vaux of the École Biblique undertook a series of excavations at various points around the city, in order to check, according to the strict methods of modern scientific archeology, the findings of the earlier explorations of Jerusalem's system of defenses. A long trench that was dug in 1961 from the foot of the wall on top of Ophel that Macalister had discovered in 1925 down to the Gihon Spring showed that the

so-called "fine example of Canaanite wall" rested on houses that had been built in the 8th century B.C., and that the so-called Davidic-Solomonic tower was really a construction of the 2nd century B.C. Along the trench there were found remnants of houses from the Early Bronze Age (3rd millennium B.C.) and Iron Age II (900–600 B.C.) and, at 50 yards above the spring, part of a massive wall ascribed to the 18th century B.C. In 1961 and 1962 these dates were fully confirmed, and the massive wall of the 18th century B.C. was shown to have formed the eastern limit of the Canaanite city. The city that David captured from the Jebusites was not limited to the top of the hill of Ophel, as was previously thought, but it spread out over the steep eastern side of the hill, and so it remained until it was completely destroyed by NEBUCHADNEZZAR in 587 B.C. When Nehemiah rebuilt the walls of Jerusalem in the second half of the 5th century B.C., he did not follow the line of the ancient eastern wall, but built a new wall on top of the hill, as can be seen from the position of the pottery from the Persian period.

It was along this new wall of Nehemiah's that Jonathan, *c.* 143 B.C. (1 Mc 12.37), built the fortress tower that had formerly been attributed to Solomon. Likewise, the soundings made at the southern and western parts of

Ophel showed that the walls that Bliss and Guthe had ascribed to the time of the kings of Judah were really only of the 1st century B.C. Although the findings of this most recent archeological campaign at Jerusalem are not definitive, and further campaigns are announced, it can now be stated with certainty that both in the pre-exilic period and in the first few centuries of the post-exilic period the city was situated on the eastern hill, that is, between the Kidron Valley and the Tyropoeon Valley; the city gate in the Tyropoeon Valley that Crowfoot discovered in 1927 should have, even then, made this certain.

Biblical History of Jerusalem. This can be conveniently divided into three periods: (1) from earliest settlements to David's capture of the city (c. 3000–1000 B.C.); from David's conquest to the Babylonian destruction of the city (1000–587); from Nehemiah's rebuilding of the city to its destruction by the Romans in A.D. 70.

From Earliest Settlement to David's Conquest. Aborigines lived at various periods of the Paleolithic and Neolithic ages in caves near the Gihon Spring until they were supplanted by people possessing a higher culture and acquainted with the use of bronze. These people who invaded Palestine in the course of the 4th millennium B.C. the OT calls Canaanites—a term to be understood more in a geographic than in an ethnologic or linguistic sense (*see* CANAAN AND CANAANITES). The numerous samples of pottery dating from the end of the Chalcolithic Age to the end of the Early Bronze Age that the Parker Mission gathered from the caves on Ophel give concrete evidence of a primitive urban nucleus on this hill during the 3rd millennium B.C.

The Amorrite clan of Jebusites, who understood the importance of the Gihon Spring, settled on the hill above the spring, and to the natural defenses of the steep hill they added a strong encircling stone wall. In the center of their settlement they built for their king a fortress "palace" (no doubt of very modest proportions), which was known by the indigenous name of ZION (*ṣîyôn*), and to ensure their water supply in case of siege, they dug a secret shaft tunnel (*ṣinnôr*) that gave them access from within the city to the Gihon Spring. According to a Jewish tradition that was already known to Josephus (*Ant.* 1.10.2), it was in this city that Melchisedec, a priest of EL ELYON (the Most High God), ruled as king at the time when Abraham lived a seminomadic life in Palestine (Gn 14.17). Having come under Egyptian domination after the conquest of Palestine by Thutmose III (c. 1490–1436 B.C.), the mixed population of Jebusite Urušalim ("Your father was an Amorrite and your mother a Hittite": Ez 16.3) was governed as vassals of Pharaoh. At that time, it seems, members of a military caste were installed there, as can be deduced from a tomb, discovered in 1954 on

the Mount of Olives, that contained much pottery of the Middle and Late Bronze Age and Egyptian imports, such as alabaster vessels, seals, scarabs, and weapons. Even the city's ruler with the partly Hurrian name of 'Abdi(Putu-) Ḥepa sent a message (as known from the Amarna Letters) from his lofty fortress city asking Pharaoh to defend his *Bît Šulmān* (capital) from the attacks of the HABIRU (Habiri) marauders. At the time of the Israelite invasion under JOSHUA, the city's King Adonizedek made himself head of a league of neighboring Amorrite kings in an effort to withstand and stop the invasion at Gibeon (Jos 10.1–6). Although captured and put to death by Joshua (Jos 10.23–26), Adonizedek left his city so strongly fortified that it was able to hold out against the Israelite invaders for more than two centuries (Jgs 1.21; 19.10–12).

From David's Conquest to Babylonian Destruction. After David had reigned for seven years at Hebron, he finally succeeded in capturing Jerusalem, which he forthwith made the political and religious center of his kingdom. David's general Joab apparently caught the Jebusite garrison by surprise when he led his men up the secret shaft tunnel (the *ṣinnôr*) that connected the Gihon Spring with the center of the city (2 Sm 5.6–8;1 Chr 11.4–6). The first care of the conqueror was to repair the walls of the city and, with the help of workmen sent by the King of Tyre, to build a new palace for himself on the acropolis of Zion, which, because he had captured it, became his personal property, "the City of David" (2 Sm 5.9, 11). Later, he brought the ark of the covenant from Cariath-Jarim into Zion and installed it in its sacred tent on his acropolis; thus Jerusalem became the religious as well as the political center of the country.

David's son Solomon (c. 961–922), however, brought even more importance and splendor to the city by erecting, with the aid of skilled craftsmen sent by King Hiram of Tyre, a magnificent TEMPLE on the hill just to the north of the City of David (1 Kgs 5.1–6.38). The altar of holocaust in front (to the east) of the Temple was probably a little to the south of the sacred rock that is now in the center of the Muslim "Dome of the Rock" (the so-called Mosque of Omar; see B. Bagatti, *Biblica* 46:428–444). Although this "house of Yahweh," the abode of the ark of the covenant, was surrounded by an inner and an outer courtyard (1 Kgs 6.36; Jer 36.10), these open spaces should not be thought of as occupying the vast space that is now the Haram esh-Sherīf. The latter does indeed correspond quite well with the courts of Herod's Temple, which were designed to hold immense crowds of pilgrims. But Solomon's temple, like the later sanctuary of Yahweh in the Northern Kingdom, was primarily the king's private chapel (cf. Am 7.13). To the south of the Temple and its courts were the royal palaces and government buildings (1 Kgs 7.1–12). But later constructions and destructions have apparently removed all traces of these buildings, so that their exact location (in part probably where the modern Mosque el-Aqṣa stands) is now unknown. Likewise uncertain is the nature of the Millo (literally "filling") that Solomon made (1 Kgs 9.15–24; 11.27); probably it was a retaining wall with fill built to protect a weak section of the city wall between the City of David and the Temple area.

With the death of Solomon the city's growth was checked by the secession of the ten northern tribes of Israel, and Jerusalem remained henceforth the capital of merely the two tribes of Judah and Benjamin, ever more and more weakened by raids and invasions from without and by dissensions within. In the 5th year of Rehoboam's reign (c. 917 B.C.) King Shishak of Egypt invaded Palestine, captured Jerusalem, and pillaged its temple and royal palace (1 Kgs 14.25–26). About the year 897 B.C., King Asa of Judah impoverished the city in order to purchase the help of Ben-hadad of Syria against King Baasha of Israel (1 Kgs 15.18; 2 Chr 16.2–3). Toward the end of the 9th century B.C. King Joash had to pay immense tribute to Hazael of Damascus to have this Syrian king raise his siege of Jerusalem (2 Kgs 12.17–18). About the year 783 B.C., after Joash of Israel defeated Amaziah of Judah at the battle of Beth-Shemesh, the penalty that Jerusalem had to pay was not only a large indemnity from the Temple and palace treasures, but also the destruction of the northern wall of the city from the Ephraim Gate to the Corner Gate—a stretch of 600 feet (2 Kgs 14.13–14). Amaziah's successor, Uzziah, evidently repaired this damage, for he built fortified towers at the Corner Gate, the Valley Gate, and the Angle (2 Chr 26.9). The earthquake that occurred in the reign of Uzziah (Am 1.1; Zec 14.5) probably did much damage in the city, for his successor, Jotham (regent 750–742, king 742–735), had to repair the wall of Ophel (2 Kgs 15.35; 2 Chr 27.2–3). King Ahaz (735–715) again impoverished the city by paying a heavy tribute to the Assyrians for their help against Damascus (2 Kgs 16.5–9).

After the fall of Samaria in 721 B.C., Jerusalem probably received many refugees from the north. This growth in the city's population may be the reason why a section of Jerusalem was later known as the *mišneh,* "Second Ward" (2 Kgs 22.14; Zep 1.10). The work of King Hezekiah (715–687) in strengthening the defenses of the city under the threat of Sennacherib's siege, especially his construction of the tunnel under the hill of Ophel, to bring the water from the Gihon Spring into the Pool of Siloam, has been mentioned above. His successor, King Manasseh (687–642), made extensive repairs and new constructions in Jerusalem's defenses—"an outer wall for the City of David west of Gihon in the valley, and for the entrance of the Fish Gate, and around Ophel" (2 Chr 33.14). But all these measures proved useless against the battering rams of the Babylonians who besieged the city from Jan. 15, 588, until they captured it on July 30, 587. Its walls, its temple, and its houses were all completely demolished; its inhabitants were all either killed, enslaved, or deported into exile (2 Kgs 25.1–21).

From Nehemiah to Titus. After Cyrus issued his edict in favor of the Jews in 538 B.C., the people of the former Kingdom of Judah (or Jews, as they were now called) began to return in small groups to Palestine, and Jerusalem slowly revived. On the site of the ruined Temple of Solomon, Sheshbazzar began the building of a new Temple shortly after 538 B.C. (Ezr 5.16), but it was not until 515 B.C. that the Davidic prince Zerubbabel and the high priest Joshua were able to finish and dedicate it (Ezr 6.15). The city walls, however, still lay in ruins until NEHEMIAH had new ones built, at least in some places on new lines, in 439 B.C. (Neh 2.11–6.15). Yet during the Persian period (538–333 B.C.) the city, under the rule of the Persian governors and the Jewish high priests, was apparently slow in recovering its former glory.

With the conquest of Palestine by Alexander the Great in 331 B.C., Jerusalem passed to the dominion of Greek rulers, first of the Ptolemies of Egypt, and then (after 198 B.C.) of the Seleucids of Syria. During this Hellenistic period (331–63) the city grew greatly in size and population, spreading out to the north and west over an area that had not formed part of the older town. In 168 B.C. King ANTIOCHUS IV EPIPHANES of Syria pillaged the city and profaned its Temple (1 Mc 1.20–58). To keep control of the city, the Syrians built a strong citadel known as the Acra (1 Mc 3.45; 4.41; 6.18, etc.); it is uncertain whether it was situated on the southeast hill (Ophel) or on the southwest hill (the new part of the town). The strong Maccabean reaction, however, prevented the complete Hellenization of the city. After three years of hard fighting, Judas Maccabee recovered and purified the Temple (in 164 B.C.), which, in the language of that time, was spoken of as Mount Zion. Simon, the leader of the Maccabean party from 142 to 135 B.C., strengthened the fortifications of the city and finally succeeded in driving the Syrians from the Acra (1 Mc 13.49). During the following years of the Hasmonaean rulers, Jerusalem "the holy" (as it was called on the coins of the period) enjoyed a period of great prosperity, which was not greatly disturbed until the civil war that broke out in 69 B.C. between the Hasmonaean brothers Aristobulus II and Hyrcanus II and eventually led to Roman intervention. In 63 B.C. Pompey made Jerusalem tributary to Rome.

After HEROD THE GREAT, with the approval of Caesar Augustus, installed himself as king in Jerusalem in 37

B.C., this monarch embellished the city with many buildings in the Greco-Roman style: an agora, a theater, a gymnasium, and a hippodrome. On the western hill, near the present Jaffa Gate, he built a large fortress palace, which was protected by three towers, named respectively Hippicus after a friend of his, Phasael in memory of his older brother, and Mariamne in honor of his beloved Hasmonaean wife whom he had put to death. On the eastern hill, northwest of the Temple, there had been a fortress (bîrâ) at least from the time of Nehemiah (Neh 2.8), which served as the headquarters of the Persian governor (Neh 7.2). Known as the Baris, it was repaired by the Hasmonaeans (Josephus, *Ant.* 15.11.4; 18.4.3). Herod rebuilt it and named it the Antonia in honor of the Roman triumvir Mark Anthony. Under the Roman procurators of Palestine it served as the barrack for the Roman soldiers who policed the city, and it may well have been the PRAETORIUM where Pilate condemned Jesus to death. The chief marvel, however, of Herod's building activity in Jerusalem was the Temple, which he completely rebuilt on a much grander scale than before and with surrounding courtyards, the present Ḥaram esh-Sherîf, more than twice their former size. This is the Temple mentioned so often in the NT. Part of the immense retaining wall for the southwestern part of its enclosure, now known as the Wailing Wall, is the best-preserved example of Herodian construction in the city.

In A.D. 66 the Jewish revolt against Rome broke out and ended in A.D. 70 with the destruction of the city and its Temple by the Romans under Titus. After the suppression of the revolt of BAR KOKHBA in A.D. 135, Emperor Hadrian had the city completely rebuilt on the Roman plan and renamed Colonia Aelia Capitolina. The position of the city walls and the plan of its streets, with the main north-south avenue running from the Damascus Gate to the so-called Dung Gate and the transverse east-west avenue running from the Jaffa Gate to the Temple area, have been essentially preserved in the present "Old City" of Jerusalem.

Fortifications. The sparse and incidental topographical references to the walls and gates of Jerusalem that are given in 2 Samuel 5.9; 1 Kings 9.15; 2 Kings 14.13; 2 Chronicles 26.9; 27.3; 33.14, as well as the more detailed account of Nehemiah's nocturnal inspection of the city walls (Neh 2.11–15), his rebuilding of them (Neh 3.1–32), and the procession at their dedication (Neh 12.27–39), do not give sufficiently consistent data for delineating the extent of the city in either the pre-exilic or the early postexilic period.

According to Josephus. Flavius Josephus (*Bell. Jud.* 5.4.2) gives a rather elaborate account of the defenses of the city at the time of the Roman siege of A.D. 68–70. But this is not easy to follow, and its author was evidently mistaken in thinking that two of the walls of the city of his time were the same as those of earlier periods. The city that he knew certainly extended over the western as well as the eastern hill. It was protected by three walls, which he calls simply the First, the Second, and the Third Wall. Only the First Wall, however, made a complete circuit; the Second and the Third Wall were constructions added successively at the northern limits of the city.

The First Wall, Josephus says, was the most ancient, having been built by David and Solomon and their successors. In the north it ran east from the Hippicus Tower (El Qala'ah or the Citadel of the present day) to the west side of the Temple area, probably in the vicinity of the Bāb es-Silsileh (Gate of the Chain) entrance to the Ḥaram esh-Sherîf; on the west and the south it ran from the Hippicus Tower south along the western and southern edge of the western hill, above the Wadi er-Rabābi, till it met the eastern wall a little south of the Pool of Siloe; on the east it ran north from the latter point along the eastern edge of the Ophel Hill till it came to the southeast corner of the Temple area. The Second Wall, according to Josephus, began at the Gennath Gate (unidentified, but probably just to the east of the Hippicus Tower) in the First Wall and, enclosing the northern part of the city, ended at the Antonia.

Despite the statement of Josephus, no part of his First Wall was built by David. The Jebusite city that David captured and named the City of David was solely the eastern hill, between the Kidron and the Tyropoeon valleys, but also including the eastern slope of this hill and thus extending east of the First Wall of Josephus, which was at the top of this hill. Solomon built his Temple and palaces on the hillock to the north of this hill. The Millo of Solomon by which "he closed the breach of the City of David" (1 Kgs 11.27) may have been the "filling" used in the intervening space, but this is uncertain. Although the city evidently grew somewhat under the later kings of Judah, as evidenced by the mention of the Mishneh of "Second Ward" (apparently a new addition to the city), and also by the references to the walls that these kings built or rebuilt (the Hebrew verb *bānâ* having both meanings), the extent of the city that the Babylonians destroyed has been a much disputed question, depending mostly on the interpretation of the data supplied by Nehemiah.

According to L. H. Vincent. The most ardent defender of the opinion that Josephus's First Wall represented the city wall at the time of the last kings of Judah has been L. H. Vincent. According to this eminent archeologist the northern section of the First Wall had a gate, at about halfway along its course, called the Ephraim Gate, because the road from it led northward to the region of Ephraim (the Northern Kingdom of Israel), and about 200 yards to the west of this, at the place where Herod later built the Hippicus Tower, was the Corner Gate (cf. 2 Kgs 14.13). The wall on the western and southern edge of the western hill was the same as this section of Josephus's First Wall; at a point shortly after it bent to the east was the Valley Gate (2 Chr 26.9; Neh 2.13, 15), which opened on the Hinnom Valley, and 500 yards to the east of this gate (Neh 3.13) was the Dung Gate (Neh 2.13; 3.14; 12.31), which would thus be at the southeast corner of the wall. A short distance northward, up the Kidron Valley, was the Fountain Gate (Neh 2.14), near the Pool of Siloe and the stairs up to the City of David (3.15). Further up the Kidron Valley was the Water Gate (3.26; 8.1, 3; 12.37), near the Gihon Spring, followed by the Horse Gate (3.28; Jer 31.40), near the southeast corner of the Temple area, and the Muster Gate (Neh 3.31), corresponding to the modern (walled-up) Golden Gate.

To the north of the northern section of this First Wall, according to Vincent, was the Mishneh or Second Ward (2 Kgs 22.14; Zep 1.10), and to protect this suburb, Hezekiah built the "outer wall" (2 Chr 32.5), which was the same as Josephus's Second Wall. Along this wall, from east to west, were the following gates and towers: the Sheep Gate (Neh 3.1–32; 12.39; cf. Jn 5.2), north of the Temple area; the Tower of the Hundred (Neh 3.1; 12.39) and the Tower of Hananeel (*ḥănan'ēl:* 3.1; 12.39; Jer 31.38; Zec 14.10), at the northwest of the Temple area; the Fish Gate (Neh 3.3; 12.39; 2 Chr 33.14; Zep 1.10), in the upper Tyropoeon Valley; the Old Gate (Neh 3.6; 12.39); the Ephraim Gate (Neh 8.16; 12.39), which received its name from the Ephraim Gate in the First Wall whose place it took, and of which Vincent believed he found remnants under the modern Russian Hospice near the Basilica of the Holy SEPULCHER; and finally the Tower of the Ovens (Neh 3.11; 12.38), at the Corner Gate (2 Kgs 14.13; Jer 31.38) in the northwestern corner of the city.

According to More Recent Archeologists. Although this plan of the walls and towers of Jerusalem at the time of Nehemiah as drawn up by Vincent was reproduced in various maps of the city printed during the first half of the 20th century and still has its supporters, it is now rejected by several leading archeologists, who argue from the almost complete lack of pottery earlier than the Hellenistic age on the western hill of Jerusalem that the city of the pre-exilic and early postexilic periods did not extend over nearly so vast an area. The city gate that J. W. Crowfoot discovered in 1927 in the Tyropoeon Valley and showed to have been in use from the Bronze Age to the Greco-Roman period seems to clinch the argument that in the Persian period (the time of Nehemiah) Jerusa-

lem was still limited to the eastern hill, even though at the time of its destruction by the Babylonians it may well have extended further to the north and west of the Temple area than it did at the time of David and Solomon.

On the map of the city as drawn by M. Avi-Yonah, who is representative of the more recent opinion, the gates and towers are distributed as follows. In the north wall, from east to west: the Sheep Gate, which is the same as the Benjamin Gate (Jer 20.2; 37.13; 38.7; Zec 14.10); the Tower of the Hundred, protecting the eastern side of the Fish Gate; the Fish Gate, which is the same as the Ephraim Gate, located on the eastern slope of the northwestern hill; the Tower of Hananeel, protecting the western side of the Fish Gate and forming the northwestern corner of the city. In the west wall: the Mishneh Gate, which gave access to the northwestern part of the city known as the Mishneh or Second Ward; the Broad Wall (Neh 3.8; 12.38), which first turned east down the slope of the northwestern hill, then south in the Tyropoeon Valley; the Valley Gate, which gave access from the Tyropoeon Valley into the City of David. At the southern point of the city, where the western wall turned eastward to meet the eastern wall, the Fountain Gate (Neh 2.14; 3.15; 12.37), in which were "the stairs [stone steps] of the City of David" (Neh 12.37). Outside the southwest end of this wall there was another wall, the Outer Wall that King Hezekiah had built to protect the two pools that were supplied with water from his newly dug tunnel (2 Chr 32.2–5). This wall, or at least its eastern section, is called "the Wall of the Pool of Siloam at the King's Garden" in Nehemiah 3.15. At the southwestern corner of this Outer Wall was the Dung Gate, known also as "the Gate between the Two Walls" (2 Kgs 25.4; Jer 39.4). The eastern wall of the city would be the same as that described above. This hypothetical reconstruction of the wall of Jerusalem as it was at the time of Nehemiah has the advantage of being in agreement with the findings of archeology. All of its details, however, are not certain, particularly in regard to the distance between the various gates of the city.

The Third Wall. According to Josephus, the Third Wall of Jerusalem was begun by King Herod Agrippa I (d. A.D. 44), who laid immense stones for its foundation, but was obliged by the Emperor Claudius to desist from finishing it. It was hurriedly completed at the outbreak of the Jewish revolt in A.D. 66. Agrippa had planned this wall as a defense for the suburbs north of the city, which till then had been defenseless. Josephus says that this Third Wall began in the west at the Hippicus Tower of Herod the Great and first ran north for the distance of about 400 yards to a large tower called Psephinus; from here it turned to the east, passing south of the Tomb of Queen Helena of Adiabene (now commonly known as the Tomb of the Kings); on reaching a point north of the eastern wall of the city, it turned south to join this wall.

Formerly this Third Wall was regarded as on the same line as the present north wall of the Old City. Although the present walls of the Old City of Jerusalem date, in their actual condition, only from the reign of the Turkish Sultan Suleiman I the Magnificent (1520–66), at several places along its north wall there are stones near or under the ground that apparently come from the 1st century. Therefore, many scholars, especially Vincent, regarded this as marking the line of what Josephus calls the Third Wall.

But in 1925–27 and again in 1940 remnants of a city wall were found considerably to the north of the present wall. A large stone of this wall can be seen a little to the south of the American Consulate in Jordan, and other sections were discovered to the east of this, on the property of the American School of Oriental Research. Although Vincent protested to the end that this was hurriedly built by the Jews in the revolt of Bar Kokhba [see his article, "Jerusalem," *Dictionnaire de la Bible*, 4 (1949) 923–926], most archeologists now hold that this wall fits so well with the description that Josephus gives of the wall that Agrippa began that it cannot be other than the so-called Third Wall. In any case, the identification of this wall does not concern the question of the authenticity of the traditional site of Calvary—which was "outside the gate" (Heb 13.12). The Church of the Holy Sepulcher is a little to the north of the line of the Second Wall, and the Third Wall was not yet built at the time of the death of Jesus. The line of the present north wall of the city most likely does not antedate the 2nd century, the ancient 1st-century stones in its base having been probably reused from the destroyed walls of Herod's city when the Emperor Hadrian had the city rebuilt as Aelia Capitolina.

Christian Jerusalem

The history of Jerusalem in the Christian Era will be treated here in connection with that of the Greek (Orthodox) patriarchate. After that, something will be said of the other Christian patriarchates of the city.

Greek Patriarchate. The present Greek Orthodox patriarch of Jerusalem is, ecclesiastically speaking, the lineal descendant of the Apostle, St. James the Less, the first Bishop of Jerusalem. Historically, the history of this patriarchate, like that of the city itself in the Christian Era, falls into four main periods: (1) the Roman-Byzantine period, from the 1st century to the Muslim conquest of the city in A.D. 638; (2) the Arab period, from the Muslim conquest to the capture of the city by the Crusaders in 1099; (3) the period of the Latin Kingdom of Jerusalem till the loss of the city in 1187; (4) the Turkish

and modern period from the end of the 12th century to the present.

From the 1st Century to the Muslim Conquest. In Acts, the Apostle St. JAMES THE LESS acts as head of the first Christian community in Jerusalem, and so he has been traditionally reckoned as its first bishop. According to Eusebius (*Ecclesiastical History* 2.23), when James died a martyr in A.D. 63, he was succeeded by St. SIMON THE APOSTLE, who survived the Roman destruction of the city in A.D. 70 and died a martyr in 107 (*ibid.* 3.32). Eusebius gives a surprisingly long list of 13 successive bishops of Jerusalem between the death of St. Simon in 107 and the second Roman destruction of the city at the end of the Bar Kokhba revolt in 135. All of these were Judaeo-Christians. But from Mark of Caesarea (135–136) on, all the bishops of the rebuilt city (Aelia Capitolina) were of non-Jewish origin.

When the hierarchical structure of the whole Church was more highly developed in the 2nd century, Jerusalem, then mostly a pagan city, did not receive the position that might have been expected for it as the mother cell of Christianity. It was merely a suffragan see of the metropolitan see of Caesarea Maritima, itself under the patriarch of Antioch in Syria. Yet, after peace was restored to the Church by Constantine the Great in 312, Jerusalem soon acquired great importance because of the Basilica of the Holy Sepulcher and the other famous churches that this emperor and his wife, St. HELENA, built in or near the city; this led to a large influx of pilgrims and to the erection of many monasteries in or near Jerusalem. At the Council of Nicaea (325) Bishop Marcarius obtained for his see (still called Aelia) an honorary precedence immediately after the patriarchates of Rome, Alexandria, and Antioch, though still subject jurisdictionally to the metropolitan see of Caesarea Maritima—an anomalous situation that later led to much friction, particularly at the time of the celebrated bishop, St. Cyril of Jerusalem (352–386), in his disputes with the Arians.

Bishop Juvenal of Jerusalem (422–458), a clever, unscrupulous politician, succeeded in getting at the Council of Chalcedon (451) what he had failed to obtain at the Council of Ephesus (431)—the elevation of his see to a genuine patriarchate, independent of Antioch, with a territory south from Lebanon to Arabia embracing three metropolitan and 56 suffragan sees. The Empress Eudocia, wife of Theodosius II (408–450), and the Emperor Justinian I (527–565) contributed to the development of the city by building churches, monasteries, and public edifices, the magnificence of which can be seen in the mosaic map of Medaba. Throughout the Monophysite conflict the patriarchate of Jerusalem remained orthodox, thanks especially to the efforts of the monk St. Sabas (d. 532).

But there were sufficient Monophysites in Palestine for the Monophysite (Jacobite) patriarch of Antioch to appoint Severus Bishop of Jerusalem in 597, and from him is derived the line of Jacobite bishops of Jerusalem down to the present.

In 614 Christian Jerusalem suffered a dreadful disaster: the city was taken by the Persians, who destroyed most of its churches and monasteries, including the Basilica of the Holy Sepulcher, massacred thousands of its inhabitants, deported the Patriarch Zacharias to Persia, and took as booty the great relic of the holy cross. Yet, even before the Emperor Heraclius in 629 brought back the relic of the holy cross in triumph, the monk Modestus had begun a reconstruction of the Basilica of the Holy Sepulcher, though on a somewhat smaller scale than the Constantine Basilica. Some further reconstruction of the devastated churches continued until 636, when the Byzantine period of Jerusalem came to an end with the capture of the city by the Arabs under Caliph Umar.

From Muslim Conquest to Crusades (638–1099). After the city was besieged for four months, the Patriarch St. Sophronius (634–644) wisely capitulated to the Muslims on fair and honorable terms. For the next three centuries Christians and Muslims lived together in fairly friendly fashion in Jerusalem. With the aid of Byzantine architects and artists, Caliph 'Abd al-Malik (684–705) built on the site of Solomon's Temple the lovely Dome of the Rock (Qubbet es-Sahra), popularly known as the Mosque of Umar. From the death of Sophronius to the appointment of John IV (705–735) the patriarchal See of Jerusalem was vacant, being administered by vicars responsible to Constantinople or Rome. In 800 the Patriarch George (796–807) sent a delegation to Charlemagne to obtain his aid for the Holy Places, and in the same year Hārūn al-Rashīd sent Charlemagne the keys of the Basilica of the Holy Sepulcher as a sign of entrusting to him the protection of this sanctuary. But in 1010 the Fatimid Caliph al-Ḥākim leveled to the ground, not only the basilica, but the Holy Sepulcher itself. After negotiations between the Byzantine emperors and later caliphs, the rebuilding of the edifice on the lines of Modestus's structure was completed in 1048. With the restorations made by the Crusaders, this is still essentially the present basilica. In 1072 the Muslim SELJUKS took Jerusalem and closed its gates to Christian pilgrims. The resulting wave of indignation that swept Europe was the main cause of the Crusades.

Latin Kingdom of Jerusalem (1099–1187). After the capture of Jerusalem by the Crusaders on July 15, 1099, the first Christian ruler of Jerusalem, GODFREY OF BOUILLON, was satisfied with the title of *Defensor Hierosolymitanae Ecclesiae.* But after his death on July 18, 1100, his brother Baldwin I, who succeeded him, took the title of King of Jerusalem (1100–18). The Crusaders won more and more land in the Near East, and the kingdom continued to grow in territory under Baldwin II (1118–31) and Fulk (1131–43), until it reached its maximum extension for a time under Baldwin III (1143–62). Its internal unity, however, was unstable, and its borders insecure on both the north and the south. The kingdom was set up on a feudal basis, and its powerful feudal lords greatly limited the power of the king. Although it had a standing army, the need for a continuous influx of new men and supplies greatly handicapped the government.

In less than a century the Holy City again fell into the hands of the Muslims. Weakened by internal quarrels and lacking the men and means to withstand the almost continuous border raids of the Arabs, the Kingdom of Jerusalem suffered a disastrous defeat in the Battle of the Horns of Hattin, near Tiberias in Galilee, on July 4–5, 1187, at the hands of Muslims under the leadership of SALADIN, head of the Seljukian Turks. Guy of Lusignac, King of Jerusalem, was taken prisoner and later purchased his liberty by surrendering Ascalon. On Oct. 2, 1187, Jerusalem capitulated to the Seljuks. A few Christian strongholds in the Near East held out for another century, until the last of them, Saint-Jean d'Acre (Accho), the capital of the 13th-century nominal Kings of Jerusalem, fell before the onslaughts of the Mamelukes on May 29, 1291. The empty title of "King of Jerusalem" continued to be borne by various European princes almost to the end of the 19th century. For the later history of the Christian knights in the Near East, *see* CRUSADES.

Turkish and Modern Periods. When the Crusaders captured Jerusalem in 1099, its Greek Orthodox patriarch seems to have fled to Cyprus. Since at that time the Greek Church was not in union with the Latin Church, the next Greek patriarchs of Jerusalem lived at Constantinople until the Muslim reconquest of the Holy City. Thereafter, they have lived at or near Jerusalem. At the Second Council of Lyons (1274) the Greek patriarch of Jerusalem was opposed to union with Rome. At the Council of Florence the representative of the Jerusalem patriarchate signed the decree of union, but in 1443 the patriarch himself rejected it. In 1672 the learned Patriarch Dositheus (1669–1707) convoked the Synod of Jerusalem. At this synod, which was, in a general way, the Eastern equivalent of the Council of Trent, the bishops of the Greek Orthodox Church ably defended it against the inroads that Protestantism had been making even in the East.

The political history of Jerusalem after the Crusades follows the general course of the history of surrounding Muslim states. After the hegemony in the Near East passed from the Seljukian Turks to the Mamelukes of

Egypt and from them to the OTTOMAN TURKS of Asia Minor; Palestine was incorporated into the Ottoman Empire in 1516 by the Sultan Selim I (1512–20). Muḥammad II (1415–81), the conqueror of Constantinople, had already declared the Greek patriarch of Constantinople religious and civil head of all Christians in the Ottoman Empire. Although in theory the patriarchate of Jerusalem was not under the ecclesiastical jurisdiction of the patriarchate of Constantinople, in practice during the period of Turkish domination the patriarchs of Jerusalem were subservient to the patriarchs of Constantinople, and all of them during this time were Greeks and favored the Greek clergy against the native, Arabic-speaking Orthodox Christians. The 16th century saw the establishment of the Fraternity of the Holy Sepulcher, an organization of the Greek Orthodox clergy that had a monopoly of the high ecclesiastical offices and all the revenues of the sacred places in charge of the Greek patriarchate. This led to discontent and, in 1852, to open revolt of the native Orthodox Christians against the Fraternity of the Holy Sepulcher. The new regulations that were drawn up in 1875 for the election of the patriarch of Jerusalem still favored the Greeks. After the revolt of the Young Turks in 1908, the native Orthodox of Palestine renewed their demands for the abolition of the privileges of the Greeks. When the Patriarch Damian signified his willingness to make some concessions to the Arabic Christians, he was deposed by the Synod and only after some time restored to his office. The Mixed Council that was created never functioned and was abolished at the outbreak of World War I.

In the British campaign against Turkey in World War I, the British General Allenby, advancing from Egypt, entered Jerusalem on Dec. 11, 1917, and the centuries-old Turkish rule over the city came to an end. At the Treaty of Versailles, Palestine was made a British Mandate, and a High Commission was appointed to govern the country. A commission set up by the mandatory power acknowledged the just claims of the Arabic Christians, and in 1938 a new ecclesiastical constitution supplanting the one of 1875 was published. After the end of the British Mandate, the Hashemite Kingdom of Jordan, which retained control of the "Old City" of Jerusalem (within the walls), took up the question and in 1957 published a statute that was very favorable to the Arabic Christians. In 1958 a somewhat less radical statute was enacted, by which the Orthodox Church of Jerusalem is still governed. It ordains that the patriarch and his suffragan bishops must be citizens of Jordan and must know how to speak and write Arabic. A Council of Arabic Orthodox Christians is in charge of the finances, the schools, and the charitable works of the patriarchate.

But British Mandate did not bring peace to the region. Local Arabs were apprehensive at growing Jewish immigration and feared their aspirations. There had been a marked increase in terrorism and civil war when the Mandate ended on May 14, 1948, and all British troops departed. An inconclusive battle for Jerusalem immediately ensued, and the city remained partitioned between 1948 and 1967. Israel controlled the western suburbs, and Jordan held the Old City and the northern suburbs. After the Six Day War in 1967 Israel took control of the city and claimed that its sovereignty over the whole capital was non-negotiable. This claim was unacceptable to the local Arab population, and as of 2001 no accommodation had been reached. In his Christmas message of 1999, Patriarch Michael Sabbah stated: "The basis for any solution is sharing and equality for its citizens with their rights and duties so that no one is superior to anyone else, and no one subject to another or in need of protection from others. All are equal, and all are equally protected by the laws. Claiming exclusive rights or pretending to offer protectionism for others is a fundamental obstacle to peace."

Latin Patriarchate. When the Crusaders took Jerusalem in 1099, an ecclesiastical organization modeled on that of the West was set up in Palestine, with Latin-rite archbishops, bishops, and parish priests. Since the Greek patriarch was no longer in the country, a Latin Rite patriarchate of Jerusalem was established. Arnulf, chaplain of the Norman Crusaders, was elected, with doubtful legality, as the first patriarch, but because of his disreputable life, he was soon set aside in favor of Dagobert, Archbishop of Pisa (1100–07), who was followed in turn by seven other patriarchs residing in the city. During the near century of Crusader rule in Palestine the orders of the Knights TEMPLARS and the KNIGHTS OF ST. JOHN were powerful factors in the religious life of the land. Numerous castles and churches were built or restored in the Romanesque style, including the Church of the Holy Sepulcher, which, despite its present mutilated condition, is still basically a Crusader monument.

When Jerusalem was retaken by the Muslims in 1187, the Latin Patriarch Heraclius (1180–91) took refuge with the Latin King of Jerusalem at Accho. His eight successors resided here until Accho fell to the Muslims in 1291. Thereafter the line was continued by merely titular patriarchs who lived in Rome, with St. Laurence-outside-the-Walls as their patriarchal basilica, until Pius IX restored the real Latin patriarchate in Jerusalem in 1847.

With the disappearance of the Latin hierarchy in Palestine in the 13th century, the task of preserving the Catholic faith and guarding the Holy Places fell almost entirely upon the Franciscans, who constituted the Custody of the Holy Land. Thanks to their heroism in the face of untold hardships, the rights of the Latin Church at the principal shrines of the Holy Land have been saved through the centuries. However, in the 19th century, with the Turks becoming somewhat more tolerant and more and more European Catholics visiting the Holy Land and even residing there, Rome decided that it was time to re-establish a Latin hierarchy in Palestine. The new line of Latin patriarchs of Jerusalem were all Italians with the exception of Michael Sabbah, who is an Arab: G. Valerga (1847–72), V. Bracco (1872–89), L. Piavi (1889–1905), P. Camassei (1906–19), L. Barlassina (1920–47), A. Gori (1947-70), G. Beltritti (1970-88), M. Sabbah (1988–).

In 2001 there were 165,00 Christians out of a population of 8.7 million in the Patriarchate of Jerusalem, which comprises Israel proper and territories. There continued to be a dramatic drop in the Christian population, which began in the 1900s, when Christians represented 13 percent of the total population. By 1948 only seven percent of the population was Christian, and by 2001, only two percent. In Jerusalem itself by 2001 the total population of Christians was under 10,000 out of a total of 600,000. There were 3,500 Roman Catholics, and Melkites, 3,000 Greek Orthodox, 1,000 Armenian Orthodox, 1,000 Protestants, and 200 Coptic Orthodox. In Bethlehem the total population of Christians was 10,000 out of population of 72,000. Only 4,000 were Roman Catholics.

Between 1948 and 2001, 234,000 Christians left the Holy Land. The growth rate of Christians resident there is expected to decline to zero by 2020. In 1995 the Franciscan Custody, which has been ministering to the Christian population of the Holy Land since 1218, established the Holy Land Foundation to ameliorate the situation. Headquartered in both Washington, D.C. and Jerusalem, it provides incentives for young Christians to remain in their homeland. These include scholarships, employment opportunities, and housing.

Bibliography: On Biblical Jerusalem. General. J. SIMONS, *Jerusalem in the O.T.* (Leiden 1952). L. H. VINCENT and A. M. STÈVE, *Jérusalem de l'Ancien Testament,* 3 v. in 2 (Paris 1954–56). H. GEVA, ed., *Ancient Jerusalem: Excavations, 1993-1999* (Jerusalem 2000), On the topography and history. J. GERMER-DURAND, *Topographie de l'ancien Jerusalem des origines à Titus* (Paris 1912). G. DALMAN, *Jerusalem und seine Gelände* (Gütersloh 1930). J. JEREMIAS, *Jerusalem zur Zeit Jesu* (Göttingen 1958). K. GALLING, *Biblisches Reallexicon* (Tübingen 1937) 297–305. Excavations. C. W. WILSON and C. WARREN, *The Recovery of Jerusalem* (London 1871). C. WARREN, *Underground Jerusalem* (London 1876). F. J. BLISS and A. C. DICKIE, *Excavations at Jerusalem 1894–97* (London 1898). L. H. VINCENT, *Underground Jerusalem: Discovery on the Hill of Ophel, 1909–11* (London 1911); *Jérusalem: Recherches de topographie, d'archéologie et d'histoire,* 2 v. in 4 (Paris 1912–26) v.1. *Antique.* R. WEILL, *La Cité de David . . . Campagne, 1913–14* (Paris 1920). R. S. MACALISTER and J. G. DUNCAN, *Excavations on the Hill of Ophel, Jerusalem, 1923–25* (*Palestine Exploration Fund Annual* 4; 1926). J. W. CROWFOOT and G. M. FITZGERALD, *Excavations in the Tyropoeon Valley, 1927* (*ibid.* 5; 1929). C. N. JOHNS, "Recent Excavations at the Citadel," *Palestine Exploration Quarterly* (1940) 36–58; "The Citadel of Jerusalem," *Quarterly of the Department of Antiquities in Palestine* 14 (1950) 121–190. R. W. HAMILTON, "Excavations against the North Wall of Jerusalem," *ibid.* 10 (1940) 1–53. K. M. KENYON, "Excavations in Jerusalem," *Palestine Exploration Quarterly* 95 (1963) 7–21. The walls. L. H. VINCENT, "Jerusalem," *Dictionnaire de la Bible,* ed. L. PIROT, et al. (Paris 1928–) (1949) 4:897–966; *Revue biblique* 36 (1927) 516–548; 37 (1928) 80–100, 321–339; 54 (1947) 90–126. M. BURROWS, *Annual of the American Schools of Oriental Research* 14 (1933–34) 115–140; *The Bulletin of the American Schools of Oriental Research* 64 (1937) 11–64. M. AVI-YONAH, *Israel Exploration Journal* 4 (1954) 239–248. W. F. ALBRIGHT, *The Bulletin of the American Schools of Oriental Research* 81 (1941) 6–10. C. S. FISCHER, *ibid.* 83 (1941) 4–7. S. SALLER, *The Excavations at Dominus Flevit, v.2: The Jebusite Burial Place* (Jerusalem 1954). In the Christian Era. M. LE QUIEN, *Oriens Christianus,* 3 v. (Paris 1740; repr. Graz 1958) 3:101–528. T. E. DOWLING, *The Orthodox Greek Patriarchate of Jerusalem* (3d ed. rev. and enl. New York 1913). K. PIEPER, *Die Kirche Palästinas bis zum Jahre 135 . . .* (Cologne 1938). H. MUSSET, *Histoire du christianisme spécialement en Orient,* 2 v. (Harissa, Lebanon 1948). G. BATEH, *Les Chrétiens de Palestine sous la domination ottomane* (Jerusalem 1963). P. MEDIEBELLE, *La Diocesi del Patriarcato latino di Gerusalemme* (Jerusalem 1963). B. BAGATTI, *L'Église de la circoncision* (Jerusalem 1965). F. E. PETERS, *Jerusalem: The Holy City in the Eyes of Chroniclers, Visitors, Pilgrims, and Prophets from the Days of Abraham to the Beginnings of Modern Times* (Princeton 1985). J. J. MOSCROP, *Measuring Jerusalem: The Palestine Exploration Fund and British Interests in the Holy Land* (London and New York 2000). A. J. BOAS, *Jerusalem in the Time of the Crusades* (Great Britain 2001). M. SICKER, *Between Rome and Jerusalem: 300 Years of Roman Judaean Relations* (Westport, Conn. 2001). B. WASSERSTEIN, *Divided Jerusalem: The Struggle for the Holy City* (New Haven, Conn.: 2001). M. BIDDLE, *The Church of the Holy Sepulchre* (New York 2002). M. DUMPER, *The Politics of Sacred Space: The Old City of Jerusalem in the Middle East Conflict* (Boulder, Colo. 2002).

[D. BALDI/P. VASKO/B. SABELLA]

JERUSALEM, COUNCIL OF

Name given to the meeting described in Acts 15.1 to 15.35, which determined that Gentile Christians were not bound by the Mosaic Law. Acceptance of the date *c.* A.D. 50 is based on the fact that Gallio, to whose tribunal in Corinth Paul was summoned during his second missionary journey (Acts 18.12–17), was proconsul of Achaia in A.D. 51 to 53. If the Council was held, as Acts implies, shortly before that journey started, it must be dated *c.* 50.

Occasion. According to Acts 15.1, the meeting was occasioned by the arrival at Antioch of Judaic Christians from Jerusalem who insisted that Gentiles must observe the Mosaic Law. A vigorous controversy ensued, and Paul and Barnabas, with some others, were sent to Jerusalem to present the issue to the Apostles and other leaders. The question was settled after the defense of Gentile freedom from the Law was made by Peter, Barnabas, and Paul. James's confirmation of the defense made this view unanimous. The importance of James with regard to this question stemmed from three factors. He was "the brother of the Lord" (Gal 1.19), one of Jesus's relatives. He was also the head of the Jerusalem Church since Peter's departure (Acts 12.17). Finally, he was a devout observer of the Mosaic Law, a man to whom the most fanatically Jewish of the Christians would listen with respect. The Council did not consider, much less decide, the question of the binding force of the Law on Judaic Christians.

The main source of information about the Council is Acts 15. It is possible that Gal 2.1 to 2.10 describes the same meeting from a different viewpoint. However, the identification of Acts 15 with Galatians is disputed (*see* GALATIANS, EPISTLE TO THE).

The Speeches. Two speeches, those of Peter and James, are given in detail in Acts 15. The comments of Barnabas and Paul are simply summarized. One problem here, not yet solved with any unanimity, concerns the unity of events in 15.1 to 15.29. Some scholars maintain that, while there is basic unity, vv. 4 to 5 describe a preliminary meeting, vv. 6 to 21 a formal one among the officials, vv. 22 to 29 a final public session. Others call vv. 1 to 29 a composite, a literary summary of decisions made by the Church with regard to two different but related questions. The first concerned the necessity of the Mosaic Law for Gentile Christians; the second centered around the practical demands to be made on the Gentiles for the furtherance of peaceful common life with the Judaic Christians.

Peter claimed the Gentiles were not bound by the Law. He argued from fact—from the witness of the Holy Spirit who descended upon uncircumcised Gentiles (Cornelius and his household) even as He had upon the Apostles. Peter's final words, "We are saved through the grace of the Lord Jesus, just as they are," stated a principle from which would follow the freeing of even Judaic Christians from the Law.

Barnabas and Paul also appealed to the evidence of divine approval implied by the miracles God had worked among the pagans. They must surely have described the miracles at Iconium (Acts 14.3) and Lystra (Acts 14.9). The order of the names, "Barnabbas and Paul," indicate Luke's historical accuracy, for at Jerusalem Barnabas would have precedence over Paul.

James's speech (vv. 13–18), exclusive of the decree, viewed the acceptance of Gentiles into the Church as a fulfillment of Am 9.11 to 9.12. The crucial part of the citation is: "That the rest of mankind may seek after the Lord, and all the nations upon whom my name is in-

voked" (Acts 15.17). Such is the text found in the Septuagint, the Greek version of the OT. James, however, would most likely have quoted from the Hebrew, which reads: "That they may conquer what is left of Edom and all the nations that shall bear my name." The difference makes it appear that the reconstruction of the speech is somewhat artificial. Either James's words have been made more pertinent by recourse to the Greek version of Amos or this part of James's speech owes as much to Luke, or his source, as to James himself.

The Decree and Its Meaning. The decree is listed three times in Acts: fully in vv. 19 to 20 and vv. 28 to 29 and partially in vv. 21, 25. Its all-important point was the freedom of Gentile Christians from the Law. The formula, "For the Holy Spirit and we have decided" (15.28), states the Apostles' conviction that important Church decisions were assisted by the Holy Spirit.

The secondary element in the decree was an injunction to the Gentile Christians in Antioch, Syria, and Cilicia intended to make communal life between them and the Judaic Christians less difficult. There are variants in the text at this point, but it is certain that the so-called Eastern text, "to abstain from anything that has been contaminated by idols and from immorality and from anything strangled and from blood," is correct. The partaking of food offered to idols would imply a participation in pagan cults. The eating of meat from which the blood had not been properly drained would have offended the Judaic Christians, since for the Jews blood was the symbol of life and hence something which pertained to the divine (*see* BLOOD, RELIGIOUS SIGNIFICANCE OF). The "immorality" mentioned probably means marriage within forbidden degrees of kinship. This interpretation is based on the striking similarity between these conciliar injunctions and those of Lv 17 to 18.

In conclusion, the total decree of the Council was a compromise. It must be interpreted according to its historical setting. The main point was the exemption of Gentiles from the Law. The rest of the injunctions were given in the interest of peaceful unity and were applied only in localities where many Judaic Christians were to be found. Outside of Acts no mention is made of them; Paul never refers to them (cf. 1 Cor 8.1–10.30) in his Epistles, an indication that they were only of local and temporary importance.

Bibliography: J. GEWEISS, *Lexikon für Theologie und Kirche*, ed. J. HOFER and K. RAHNER, 10 v. (2d, new ed. Freiburg 1957–65) 1:742, 754–55. A. LEMONNYER, *Dictionnaire de la Bible*, suppl. ed. L. PIROT et al. (Paris 1928–) 113–20. L. MARCHAL, *Dictionnaire de théologie catholique*, ed. A. VACANT et al., 15 v. (Paris 1903–50) 8.2:1682–85. H. WAITZ, "Das Problem des sog. Aposteldekrets," *Zeitschrift für Kirchengeschicte* 55 (1936) 227–63. J. R. PORTER, "The 'Apostolic Decree' and Paul's Second Visit to Jerusalem,"

Journal of Theological Studies 47 (1946) 169–74. M. DIBELIUS, ''Das Apostelkonzil,'' *Theologische Literaturzeitung* 72 (1947) 193–98. J. DUPONT, ''Pierre et Paul à Antioch et à Jérusalem,'' *Recherches de science religieuse* 45 (1957) 42–60, 225–39; ''λαὸς ἐξ ἐθνῶν,'' *New Testament Studies* 3 (1956) 47–50. N. A. DAHL, ''A People for His Name,'' *New Testament Studies* 4 (1958) 319–27. C. N. JEFFORD, ''Tradition and Witness in Antioch: Acts 15 and Didache 6,'' *Perspectives in Religious Studies* 19 (1992) 409–19. J. A. WOOD, ''The Ethics of the Jerusalem Council,'' in *With Steadfast Purpose* (Waco, Tex. 1990) 239–58. O. KALU, ''Luke and the Gentile Mission: A Study on Acts 15,'' *American Journal of Biblical Studies* 1 (1986): 59–65. P. J. ACHTEMEIER, ''An Elusive Unity: Paul, Acts, and the Early Church,'' *Catholic Biblical Quarterly* 48 (1986) 1–26. F. F. BRUCE, ''The Church of Jerusalem in the Acts of the Apostles,'' *Bulletin of the John Rylands University Library of Manchester* 67 (1985) 641–61. C. K. BARRETT, ''Apostles in Council and in Conflict: [Acts 15; Gal 2],'' *Australian Biblical Review* 31 (1983) 14–32. P.-H. MENOUD, ''Justification by Faith according to the Book of Acts,'' *Jesus Christ and the Faith: A Collection of Studies* (Pittsburgh 1978) 202–27. G. ZUNTZ, ''An Analysis of the Report about the 'Apostolic Council,''' *Opuscula selecta: Classica, Hellenistica, Christiana* (Manchester, England 1972) 216–51.

[N. M. FLANAGAN]

JERUSALEM, KINGDOM OF

One of the states founded by the Crusaders in the Holy Land (1099–1291).

History. After the capture of Jerusalem, July 15, 1099, the barons and prelates constituting the ruling council of the First CRUSADE made GODFREY OF BOUILLON protector of the Holy Sepulcher with the rank of *advocatus:* the overlordship of the Holy City was to belong to the church of the Holy Sepulcher. But Godfrey's brother BALDWIN had himself crowned king (*rex Jerusalem Latinorum*) in 1100, brushing aside the claims of the patriarch to suzerainty.

The state thus founded survived because the crusaders seized the coastal towns (e.g., Tyre in 1124). Ascalon, the key to Egypt, fell to the crusaders in 1153 and served as base for the campaigns of King Amaury in that country. In the north TANCRED had founded the principality of Galilee and envisaged the conquest of Damascus; but his kingdom extended no further north than the headwaters of the Jordan and eastward to Paneas (Caesarea Philippi). In the south Baldwin I had occupied Transjordania and Arabia Petraea. Numerous fortresses were built to assure the defense of these frontiers and domestic security.

The kingdom of Jerusalem survived the loss even of Jerusalem and the conquests of SALADIN (1187). The later crusades enabled it to retake little by little the areas lost, and the treaties negotiated with the Muslims in 1229 and 1241 restored to it the Jordan River as a boundary, except in Samaria. The Muslim reconquest began with the recapture of Jerusalem (1244) and ended with the fall of Acre (1291).

Feudal Monarchy. Succession was not by election as has been said; it was hereditary and went to the heirs of Godfrey. His brother Baldwin I took the crown after Godfrey's death and transmitted it to his cousin Baldwin II. The eldest daughter of Baldwin II brought it to her husband Fulk of Anjou, then to his sons, Baldwin III and Amaury. The son of Amaury, Baldwin IV, a leper, named as successor Baldwin V, his sister Sybil's son. At Baldwin V's death, Sybil took the crown for herself and her husband, Guy of Lusignan, despite the opposition of Raymond III of Tripoli. And on Sybil's death the succession passed to her sister Isabel and her successive husbands, Conrad of Montferrat, Henry of Champagne, and Aimery of Lusignan. Conrad's daughter Mary married John of Brienne; their daughter was the wife of Emperor FREDERICK II and bore him a son Conrad. But a coup d'état led by the Ibelin family, which had already taken Acre from the king in 1232, postponed the recognition of Conrad as king (1243). The regency was entrusted to Mary's sister, Alice of Champagne, then to her descendants, the kings of Cyprus, who did not assume the royal title till 1268 and were to continue to call themselves kings of Jerusalem after 1291.

The monarchy had by then fallen under the control of the great noble families who expressed in the *Assizes of Jerusalem* their conception of a monarchy limited in the exercise of its power by the application of the feudal right and above all by the *Assise de la ligéce,* which permitted the vassals to league themselves against a despotic king. But this would be the outcome of a long evolution: the monarchy was much more powerful in the 12th century.

The Church of the Holy Land. The Latin Church took root in the kingdom of Jerusalem as it had in the other crusader states: bishops, archbishops, and the Latin patriarch installed themselves in the ancient Greek sees that were vacant. But the main emphasis was on the holy places: an archbishop was installed in Nazareth, bishops in Bethlehem and Hebron. To assure adequate service of the sanctuaries, canons were established in the Holy Sepulcher, in the *Templum Domini;* Benedictines at Josaphat and Thabor. And as pilgrims were arriving in great numbers from East and West, the hospital of St. John under the Hospitallers (*see* KNIGHTS OF MALTA), until then a simple dependency of the monastery of St. Mary of the Latins, was enlarged and developed to care for the sick, while the Knights TEMPLARS associated themselves with this venture as escort for the pilgrims. The two orders finally adopted analogous rules, were given the custody of castles, and became powers restive under the authority of king and patriarch. Frederick II tried to impart importance to the TEUTONIC KNIGHTS on whom he was counting for support.

Other religious orders were established in the Holy Land: the DOMINICANS of Jerusalem, notably, between 1229 and 1244, established relations with the Oriental Churches and tried to convert the Muslims by preaching. The Latins had not in fact tried to convert the Muslims forcibly and had likewise respected the religious liberty of their Christian subjects.

Trade. Because of the influx of pilgrims, the ports of the kingdom were frequented by Italian ships. The trading cities of Italy had received quarters in the ports that they had helped to conquer, and these became centers of active trading that sent the products of the Orient to French Syria, which thus could compete with Egypt. Acre and Tyre were, together with Tripoli, the principal trading centers. The Italian cities incidentally ended by exercising what amounted to a protectorate over the towns of the Kingdom of Jerusalem, and their quarrels contributed to create a climate of anarchy, which was one of the causes of the decline of this kingdom.

See Also: CRUSADERS' STATES.

Bibliography: W. VON HEYD, *Histoire du commerce du Levant au Moyen-Âge,* tr. F. RAYNAUD, 2 v. (Leipzig 1885–86; repr. Amsterdam 1959). R. ROEHRICHT, *Geschichte des Königreichs Jerusalem* (Innsbruck 1898). J. L. LA MONTE, *Feudal Monarchy in the Latin Kingdom of Jerusalem* (Cambridge, Mass. 1932). D. C. MUNRO, *The Kingdom of the Crusaders* (New York 1935). M. W. BALDWIN, *Raymond III of Tripolis and the Fall of Jerusalem* (Princeton 1936). PHILIPPE OF NOVARA, *The Wars of Frederick II against the Ibelins in Syria and Cyprus,* ed. and tr. J. L. LA MONTE and M. J. HUBERT (New York 1936). W. HOTZELT, *Kirchengeschichte Palästinas im Zeitalter der Kreuzzüge,* v. 3 of *Kirchengeschichte Palästinas* (Cologne 1940). J. RICHARD, *Le Royaume latin de Jérusalem* (Paris 1953). H. E. MAYER, *Bibliographie zur Geschichte der Kreuzzüge* (Hanover 1960).

[J. RICHARD]

JERUSALEM, PATRIARCHATE OF

Upon the destruction of Jerusalem by Titus in 70 A.D., Caesarea of Palestine became the capital of the civil province and the ecclesiastical center for Palestine with Jerusalem as a suffragan see. At the end of the fourth century, however, the bishops of Jerusalem began to assert their authority and desire for autonomy. At the Council of CHALCEDON (451) Bishop Juvenal obtained autonomy and jurisdiction over 58 bishoprics that formerly belonged to the Patriarchate of Antioch. Thus the Patriarchate of Jerusalem was given fifth place of honor after Rome, Constantinople, Alexandria, and Antioch.

From the Fourth to the End of the 12th Century. Under the Byzantine emperors, Palestine enjoyed a period of prosperity from the fourth to the seventh century. The Holy Places were covered with magnificent basilicas and chapels. Pilgrims from the Christian world flocked to this land, and the desert of Judea between Jerusalem and the Dead Sea became a *thebaïd* of monasteries. Palestinian monasticism, together with the theology based on Origen's celebrated school of Caesarea, became renowned.

The Islamic Persians invaded Palestine in 614, and in 637 the Arabs destroyed the shrines and oppressed the Christians, coercing many to embrace Islam. With the conquest of the Holy Land by the Crusaders in 1099 (*see* CRUSADES) and the establishment of a Latin kingdom in Jerusalem (1099–1187) liberty was returned to the Christians, but the Byzantines were subjected to a Latin hierarchy. The Orthodox Patriarch of Jerusalem took residence in Constantinople, and the Ecumenical Patriarch of Constantinople imposed his jurisdiction on the Patriarchate of Jerusalem. When Constantinople and Rome excommunicated each other in the schism of 1054, the patriarch of Jerusalem, residing under the roof of the Ecumenical Patriarch, supported him in his dispute with the papal legates.

From the End of the 12th Century to 1965. The Latin kingdom in Jerusalem dissolved in 1187, and the Orthodox Patriarchs gradually returned to their ancient patriarchal see from their exile in Constantinople. The struggle that ensued for the return of the Holy Places to the Jerusalem patriarch's authority lasted until the 19th century. The Greek Orthodox obtained control of the major portion of the Basilica of the Holy Sepulcher, half of Mt. Calvary, the main upper portion of the Basilica of the Nativity at Bethlehem, and the Tomb of Our Lady at Gethsemane.

A temporary reunion was effected between the patriarchs of Jerusalem, Antioch, Alexandria, and Rome following the Council of FLORENCE (1439), but lacking support among the faithful, did not survive long. An Eastern Catholic church never developed in the Jerusalem patriarchate. Melkite Catholics from Syria and Lebanon moved into this patriarchate, and in 1838 the Melkite Catholic Patriarch of Antioch, MAXIMOS III MAZLŪM, was given the title of Patriarch of Jerusalem and Alexandria with jurisdiction over all Melkite Catholics residing in these two patriarchates.

The Orthodox Patriarch of Jerusalem governs the patriarchate from Jerusalem with the members of his Holy Synod. The Melkite Catholic Patriarch also holds the title of Patriarch of Jerusalem (his formal title is ''Melkite Greek Catholic Patriarch of Antioch and All the East, of Alexandria and of Jerusalem''). Besides the Greek Orthodox and Melkite Catholic patriarchs, there is also a Latin Patriarch of Jerusalem. The Latin patriarchate was established in the Holy Land in 1099, when the Latin

The ruins of Jervaulx Abbey. (©Patrick Ward/CORBIS)

Akarius Fitzbardolph and Alan, Earl of Richmond, were the original patrons. Since the records have perished, little is known of its internal history. It made no foundations but was economically powerful, being specially noted for horses and sheep. Yet it was reduced to 16 monks and two lay brothers in 1381. It incorporated two churches, Aysgarth and Anderby, and got the privilege of miter in 1409. In 1535 one of the monks, George Lazenby, refused to take the Oath of Supremacy under King HENRY VIII and was executed. Two others, R. Hartlepoole and J. Stainton, were active in the PILGRIMAGE OF GRACE (1537), in which the last abbot, Adam Sedbergh, was unwillingly involved and was executed May 20, 1537; another monk died in prison. The abbey was declared forfeit (its revenue was £234), and none of the 26 monks received a pension. The buildings were dismantled in 1538. Today the ruins are scheduled for protection as an ancient monument although they are owned privately.

Bibliography: J. M. CANIVEZ, ed., *Statuta capitulorum generalium ordinis cisterciensis,* 8 v. (Louvain 1933–41) v.1–5. *Letters and Papers, Foreign and Domestic, of the Reign of Henry VIII . . . ,* 21 v. (London 1862–1907) v.12–13, ed. J. GAIRDNER, under Jervaulx, Sedbergh. W. DUGDALE, *Monasticon Anglicanum* (London 1655–73); best ed. by J. CALEY et al. (1817–30) 5:567–582, gives sources now lost. L. JANAUSCHEK, *Origines Cistercienses,* v.1 (Vienna 1877) 119–120. J. R. WALBRAN and J. T. FOWLER, eds., *Memorials of the Abbey of St. Mary of Fountains,* 3 v. (Surtees Society 42, 67, 130; Newcastle 1863–78) 1:268–274. L. H. COTTINEAU, *Répertoire topobibliographique des abbayes et prieurés,* 2 v. (Mâcon 1935–39) 1:1483. *The Victoria History of the County of York,* ed. W. PAGE, 4 v. and index (London 1907–13) 3:138–142, best modern account. L. E. WHATMORE, "George Lazenby, Monk of Jervaulx: A Forgotten Martyr?," *Downside Review* 60 (1942) 325–328. D. KNOWLES and R. N. HADCOCK, *Medieval Religious Houses: England and Wales* (New York 1953) 110.

[J. O'DEA]

Crusaders set up a kingdom under King Baldwin. It fell into long disuse, but was restored in 1847 to administer to the Latin Catholics, mostly of foreign background, found in the Holy Lands. The Latin patriarch resides in Jerusalem.

Bibliography: D. ATTWATER, *The Christian Churches of the East,* 2 v. (rev. ed. Milwaukee 1961–62). J. W. PARKES, *A History of Palestine from 135 A.D. to Modern Times* (New York 1949). R. ROBERSON, *The Eastern Christian Churches: A Brief Survey,* 6th ed (Rome 1999).

[G. A. MALONEY/EDS.]

JERVAULX, ABBEY OF

Former CISTERCIAN monastery near East Witton, York, England, Diocese of York (Latin, *Jorevallis,* from Jore or Eure Valley). Founded in 1150 from Byland Abbey in North Yorkshire, a daughterhouse of SAVIGNY, it was originally located at Fors but moved 16 miles east to Jervaulx in 1156. John de Kinstun was the first abbot;

JESU, CORONA VIRGINUM

The office hymn that was historically used at Vespers and Lauds of the Common of Virgins. It is in iambic dimeter and was composed probably by St. AMBROSE, although the tendency toward rhyme and the use of four stanzas instead of his customary eight make some scholars doubt Ambrose's authorship. The first three stanzas, based on Is 28.5, Sg 2.16, and Rv 14.4, respectively, are in praise of Christ, the heavenly bridegroom, rather than of the virgins who follow Him. The hymn concludes with a prayer directed to Christ for a life free of the wounds of sin.

Bibliography: *Analecta hymnica* 50:20–21, text. J. CONNELLY, ed. and tr., *Hymns of the Roman Liturgy* (Westminster, Md. 1957), translation and commentary. A. S. WALPOLE, ed., *Early Latin Hymns* (Cambridge, Eng. 1922). F. J. E. RABY, *A History of Chris-*

tian-Latin Poetry from the Beginnings to the Close of the Middle Ages (Oxford 1953).

[M. A. MALONE]

JESU, DULCIS MEMORIA

One of the best-known medieval Latin hymns. Originally, this hymn (beginning with the words *Dulcis Jesu memoria*) had 42 stanzas, each of four rhyming lines. A. Wilmart collected some 90 manuscripts showing divergent texts, and altogether they contain, among other things, 18 completely new, additional verses and 25 stanzas with major modifications, along with 19 doxologies. There were several major adaptations of the hymn as well as a number of medieval translations into vernacular languages. Originally a nonliturgical hymn, it gradually gained acceptance in local liturgies before it was introduced into the medieval Roman liturgy. In the late Middle Ages the original hymn was ascribed to Bernard of Clairvaux, but in fact the author was an anonymous English Cistercian who lived at the close of the 12th century. However, Gilson found clear evidence of the influence of the mystical writings of Bernard on this hymn. Post-Reformation liturgists made many arbitrary changes of dubious value in the verses of the original hymn and their order was greatly changed. The hymn achieves its best effect in its original version with eight divisions; see the reconstructed hymn by A. Wilmart [*Ephemerides Liturgicae* 57 (1943) 3–285]. Representative of the new spirit of medieval mysticism, this hymn was alien to the traditions of Ambrosian hymnody and thus marked a turning point in the history of early Cistercian hymnography. It may also be regarded as an excellent expression of early Gothic religious feelings, although it differs greatly from most of the contemporary regular sequences of Adam of Saint-Victor, and others. In a certain sense, this hymn was already ushering in the subjective-personal spirit of Franciscan poetry that culminated in the rich poesy of the Passion in the 13th century and afterward.

Bibliography: É. H. GILSON, "Sur le *Jesu Dulcis Memoria*," *Speculum* 3 (1928) 322–334; *Les Idées et les lettres* (Paris 1932) 39–57. F. J. E. RABY, *A History of Christian-Latin Poetry from the Beginnings to the Close of the Middle Ages* (Oxford 1953) 329–330. J. SZÖVÉRFFY, *Die Annalen der lateinischen Hymnendichtung* (Berlin 1964–65) 2:79–. H. LAUSBERG, *Der Hymnus Jesu dulcis memoria* (Munich 1965). J. CONNELLY, *Hymns of the Roman Liturgy* (Westminster MD 1957) 62–63, 219.

[J. SZÖVÉRFFY]

JESU, REDEMPTOR OMNIUM

Office hymn that was historically sung at Lauds in the Common of a confessor bishop. Although not attri-
buted directly to St. AMBROSE, it is one of the many hymns written in imitation of him designated as "Ambrosian" using the iambic dimeter. Its date of composition is usually assigned to the eighth century. Addressing Jesus as "the crown of bishops," it recalls the anniversary of the saint's entrance into glory, contrasting the fleeting joys of time with those of eternity. It concludes with a prayer for a like reward and, through the saint's intercession, for forgiveness of sin.

Bibliography: *Analecta hymnica* 51:133, text. J. CONNELLY, ed. and tr., *Hymns of the Roman Liturgy* (Westminster, Md. 1957), translation and commentary. J. JULIAN, ed., *A Dictionary of Hymnology* (rev. ed. London 1925). F. J. E. RABY, *A History of Christian-Latin Poetry from the Beginnings to the Close of the Middle Ages* (Oxford 1953).

[M. A. MALONE]

JESUATI

Originally a lay congregation; founded in Siena, Italy, by Bl. JOHN COLOMBINI about 1366. After his conversion Colombini, together with his disciples, lived on alms, cared for the plague stricken, and buried the dead. Colombini, accused of FRATICELLI errors, sought papal approbation to clear his order from this charge. After an investigation, Urban V approved the congregation in 1367. In the same year Colombini died, and Francesco Di Mino Vincenti assumed direction of the congregation. The Jesuati spread to many Italian cities, and in 1425 settled in Toulouse, France. At first they followed the Benedictine rule, but in 1426 Bl. John of Tossignano composed their constitutions based on the rule of St. Augustine. Their particular dedication was to the spiritual works of mercy, especially the care of the sick, and their piety was rigorously penitential. Their frequent ejaculatory mention of the name of Jesus led to their being called Jesuati. In 1499, by permission of Alexander VI, they were called Apostolic Clerics of St. Jerome after their special patron. Paul V in 1606 and 1611 granted permission for some of their members to pursue higher studies and be ordained. Finally, because they had departed from their early fervor and because of their small numbers, the Jesuati were suppressed by Clement IX in the bull *Romanus Pontifex* of Dec. 6, 1668.

About 1367, Catherine, Colombini's cousin, established the Poor Jesuatesses of the Visitation of the B.V.M., a contemplative order following the rule of St. Augustine; it survived in Italy until 1872.

Bibliography: *Acta Sanctorum* (Paris 1863—) July 7:344–408. P. MORIGIA, *Historia degli huomini illustri . . . che furono giesuati* (Venice 1604). M. HEIMBUCHER, *Die Orden und Kongregation der katholischen Kirche* (Paderborn 1932–34)

1:596–598. G. MORONI, *Dizionario de erudizione storico-ecclesiastica* (Venice 1840–61) 30:108–110.

[M. G. MCNEIL]

JESUIT RELATIONS

Relations des Jésuites was the name given to the annual report of the Mission of New France addressed by the superior of Quebec, Canada, to the provincial of Paris, who had it printed for public circulation.

Editions. The first *Relation* was that of 1632; the last, that of 1672. Thus the original collection is composed of 41 small volumes, duodecimo. Complete collections are rare today; there is one at Laval University, Quebec, and another at the John Carter Brown Library, Providence, R.I.

In 1858 the Canadian government had the full text of all the *Relations* from 1632 to 1673 printed in three octavo volumes. Also included was the *Relation* of Rev. Pierre Biard of the Acadian mission (1616) as well as the letter (1626) sent by Rev. Charles Lalemant from Quebec to his brother Jérôme. The text of the Quebec edition was not annotated, but the third volume contained an alphabetical index, incomplete but quite useful.

In Cleveland, Ohio, in 1896 Reuben Gold Thwaites began the publication of the vast collection, *The Jesuit Relations and Allied Documents,* in 73 volumes, which carry an English translation on the pages facing the original Latin or French. The Thwaites edition is superior to the Quebec edition because (1) it contains the *Relations* of 1673 to 1679, drafted in the 17th century by Rev. Claude DABLON, but published after the Quebec edition under the title of *Unpublished Relations* (*Relations inédites*); (2) its *Allied Documents,* the first of which is dated 1611 and the last dated 1791, provide a better understanding of the missionary work of the Jesuits in North America; and (3) its bibliographical notes, as well as its scholarly notes and detailed index, make it an important research tool.

Authors and contents. The Jesuit superior in Quebec was responsible for each *Relation,* and more often than not he drafted it himself. Among those who held this office were Paul Le Jeune, Barthélémy Vimont, Jérôme Lalemant, Paul Rageneau, François Le Mercier, and Claude Dablon, all of whom were eye-witnesses to the events that took place in the Quebec area. For the rest, they relied on the official reports addressed to them by their widely scattered missionaries.

The *Relations* are a source of information on the religion, the morals, the mechanics of government, and the tactics of warfare among the Native American nations of North America during the 17th century. Through these reports the forward movement of the Church through the vast forests of the country may be traced and an insight gained into the qualities of the colonists newly arrived from France. The *Relations* provide an account of the progress of the French colonies at Quebec, Trois-Rivières, and Montreal, as well as of the labors, sufferings, and successes of the missionaries throughout the region, especially in Huronia. They are an important source of information concerning the lives and deaths of the Jesuit martyrs.

Significance and value. As a means of arousing interest in France in the ministry of the Jesuits in America, the *Relations* were notably successful. They were, especially during their first years, an excellent medium of publicity, and they helped to populate New France by their descriptions of the beauty of the country, the fertility of the soil, the richness of its natural resources, and the peace and good fortune to be obtained by its inhabitants. They evoked fervent prayers, generous alms, and apostolic vocations. They were responsible for the origin of institutions that, 300 years later, were still serving the Church in Canada. It was in answer to an appeal of the *Relations* that the Ursulines and the Hospitalières disembarked at Quebec in 1639—the first time in the history of the Church that women's institutions were consecrated to a missionary ministry in a distant country. The *Relations* also exercised considerable influence in the founding of Montreal; its founder, M. Jérôme Le Royer de La Dauversière; its first governor, M. de Maisonneuve; and its first lay hospital nurse, Jeanne Mance, were all readers of the *Relations.*

The *Relations* should not be evaluated as a continuous history of the French colony or of the missionary work among the natives. The Jesuits were not and did not pretend to be formal and scientific historiographers. But if the *Relations* do not tell the whole story, they are worthy of belief in what they do recount. A specialist in the historical beginnings of the United States, Edmund Bailey O'Callaghan, wrote of them in 1847: "No historian can do a complete research job on the first settlements of this country without being acquainted with them, and those who pretend to be capable of doing this without having studied them in advance only give proof of their incapacity for this type of work."

Bibliography: E. B. O'CALLAGHAN, *Jesuit Relations. Discoveries and Other Occurrences in Canada and the Northern and Western States of the Union* (New York 1847), French tr. by F. MARTIN (Montreal 1850). J. C. MCCOY, *Jesuit Relations, 1632–1673* (Paris 1937), a bibliog. *Jesuit Relations and Allied Documents,* ed. R. G. THWAITES, 73 v. (Cleveland, Ohio 1896–1901; New York

1959—) 1:37–44, gen. intro. L. POULIOT, *Étude sur les Relations des Jésuites de la Nouvelle-France (1632–1672)* (Montreal 1940).

[L. POULIOT]

JESUITS

The Society of Jesus (SJ, Official Catholic Directory #0690) is a religious order of priests and brothers, popularly known as Jesuits, a name that was originally derisory. The order grew out of the activity of its founder, St. IGNATIUS OF LOYOLA, and six companions who at Montmartre in Paris on Aug. 15, 1534, bound themselves by vows to poverty, chastity, and apostolic labors in the Holy Land or, if this latter plan did not prove feasible, as it did not, to any apostolic endeavor enjoined by the pope. Canonical establishment of the order came on Sept. 27, 1540, when Pope Paul III, in *Regimini militantis Ecclesiae,* approved the first outline of the order's makeup (*Prima formula instituti*), authorized the framing of detailed constitutions, and limited to 60 the number of members. This last restriction was withdrawn four years later.

Purpose. The purpose of the society is the salvation and perfection of individual Jesuits and of the human race. Jesuit organization, manner of life, and ministries are all directed to fulfill this twofold aim. Official directives in these matters are contained in a body of writings known collectively as the Institute (*Institutum*). They comprise chiefly pertinent papal documents; the Jesuit constitutions and *Spiritual Exercises,* both composed by Ignatius; the rules and statutes of general congregations; instructions of superiors general; the *Epitome instituti;* and the Ratio Studiorum, or plan of studies. There are no secret regulations. The so-called *MONITA SECRETA* is a 17th-century forgery.

Government. Supreme authority, subject always to the pope, is vested in a general congregation. It alone possesses full legislative power, the capacity to enact permanent statutes on matters of greater moment, to alter or abrogate parts of the constitutions, or to make new decrees equal in force with the constitutions. Membership in this body is limited to the superior general, vicar-general, all assistants and provincials, two electors chosen from each province by a provincial congregation, and procurators from independent vice provinces and missions. Meetings are not held at regular intervals. A congregation must be convened for the election of a superior general. This accounts for 25 of the 31 meetings that took place between 1558 and 1965. It is otherwise permissible to convene sessions to handle questions of grave importance.

A superior general is at the head of the highly centralized, day-by-day government of the entire order. The

Ignatius Loyola, engraving by H. Adlard, 1870.

sole elected superior, he is selected for life by a general congregation, which also has power, never exercised to date, to remove him for serious causes. His authority, defined in the constitutions, is very extensive. It includes the right to admit or dismiss members, to make final decisions on all concerns of the entire order, and to appoint and remove all superiors. Terms of office for superiors are not fixed, but normally they last about six years. Frequent official correspondence keeps the superior general fully informed of Jesuit activities everywhere. His residence, together with that of his curia, is in Rome. The first superior general was Ignatius.

For administrative purposes, the order is divided into provinces, with a provincial at the head of each province. Groups of provinces in turn are formed into assistancies. Each assistancy is represented by an assistant, an official chosen normally by a general congregation, who dwells with the superior general and serves him in an advisory capacity.

Membership. Members are either priests, candidates preparing for the priesthood, or brothers whose assignments comprise a very wide variety of ministries. Upon entrance into the order, all spend two full years of spiritual training in a novitiate as novices, preceded in the case of brothers by a six-month postulancy. At the end

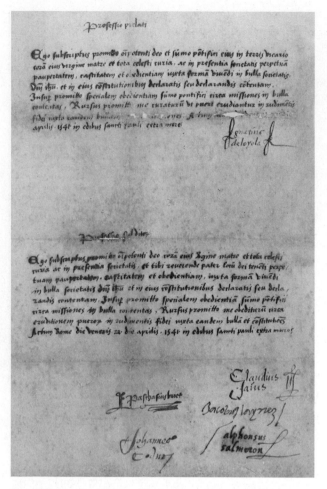

The Religious Profession of St. Ignatius of Loyola with his signature below it. At the bottom of the same page, the profession of his five companions with their attesting signatures, Rome, 1541.

of the novitiate, all take simple, perpetual, public vows of poverty, chastity, and obedience.

Those continuing for ordination, called approved scholastics, devote several more years to intellectual and spiritual formation in Jesuit houses of study. The duration varies according to individual academic backgrounds. Normally the course of studies involves two years of liberal disciplines; then ten years are devoted mainly to philosophy. This is followed by a few years of practical experience as teachers or prefects, a period that is called regency. Four years of theological studies ensue, with ordination to the priesthood at the close of the third year. Many also dedicate further years at universities to gain higher academic degrees in specialized branches of ecclesiastical or secular learning. Another year of spiritual formation, tertianship, completes the training.

Subsequently, priests receive their final grade, either as formed spiritual coadjutors, or as professed of solemn vows. At this time, the former take final simple vows of religion. The latter take these three vows of religion as solemn vows. To them they add a fourth solemn vow of special obedience to the pope in regard to accepting missions, as well as five simple vows obligating them never to seek or allow any mitigation in the vow of poverty; never to solicit or receive any ecclesiastical dignity outside the order unless directed under obedience to do so; and never to try, even indirectly, to win any dignity within the society. Solemn religious profession with only three vows occurs occasionally for special reasons. Only the solemnly professed may hold certain higher posts, such as superior general or provincial. But no special privileges attach to the profession. Duties of religious observance and external manner of living are similar to those of spiritual coadjutors. Brothers are assigned their final grade as formed temporal coadjutors after at least ten years in religion; and, since 1958, a tertianship of at least three months is required.

Distinctive features. In its structure, the society borrowed much from older orders, while introducing several original features, some of which have found their way into more recent congregations. These include high centralization of authority; life tenure of the head of the order; probation lasting several years preceding final vows; gradation of members; prohibition against preferments in the Church; private instead of choral recitation of the Divine Office; absence of regular penances or fasts obligatory on all; wearing of a religious habit that is not distinctive, but modeled on that of the secular clergy in each region; lack of a second, female branch; absence of a Third Order. Owing to the nature of his foundation, Ignatius particularly stressed the virtue of obedience. Expressions of his, characterizing obedience as blind, like that of a cadaver, or an old man's staff, were not coined by him; they are figurative phrases handed down from ancient monastic traditions, and they should be interpreted in that light. Jesuit obedience is not military but religious.

Jesuits were not the first religious to distinguish themselves as teachers, but theirs were the first constitutions to enjoin general educational work as a regular task. Another innovation of Ignatius was the extension of ministries, excluding secular businesses and political involvements, to embrace all types of apostolic endeavors in all parts of the world, as long as they tend to the greater glory of God. The order's motto is A.M.D.G. (*AD MAJOREM DEI GLORIAM*).

Objections to one or another of these innovations were early voiced by other religious orders and by a few 16th-century popes: Paul IV, Pius V, Sixtus V, and Clement VIII. But they proved temporary. The constitutions also survived intact, concerted attempts by certain Jesuits to alter them substantially, especially during the administration of Claudius ACQUAVIVA (1581–1615), whose handling of this severe internal crisis ranks him as one of the order's greatest superiors general.

IGNATIAN SPRIRITUALITY, rooted in the *SPIRITUAL EXERCISES*, has ever been that of the society, and it has had a profound effect on the development of modern spirituality (*see* SPIRITUALITY, CHRISTIAN, HISTORY OF).

History from Foundation to Suppression (1540–1773)

The growth of the Society of Jesus was continuous. During the first century, the increase was particularly rapid, totaling about 938 members in 1556 when Ignatius died; 3,500 in 1565; and 15,544 in 1626. A complete enumeration still available for 1710 shows a moderate increment over nearly a century to 19,998. In 1749, the last year previous to 1773 for which full information is extant, the total was 22,589 (11,293 being priests).

The society quickly won renown and maintained until 1773 a unique position. Its first century was far more abundant in men eminent for sanctity and learning, and more striking in its accomplishments in spreading the faith. Above all, this COUNTER REFORMATION era is memorable for the society's extremely prominent role in revivifying Catholicism spiritually and intellectually, stemming the advances of a hitherto victorious Protestantism, and even regaining vast regions lost to heresy or seriously threatened by it in the Low Countries, France, and Central and Eastern Europe. Ignatius did not, however, found the order specifically to counteract Protestantism. With the close of the Reformation period around mid-17th century, the same opportunities for accomplishment were not available. Yet the maintaining, and gradual extending, of previous gains in Europe and in the missions provided a formidable, if less spectacular, record during the society's second century. These were the decades, too, when Jesuits took the lead in combating JANSENISM. From about the mid-18th century, the order was under heavy attack, battling for its existence. So diversified was the Jesuit apostolate, so widely spread over the globe, so intricately interwoven into the fabric of ecclesiastical and secular history that it defies brief summation.

Education. Almost from the start, education turned out to be the society's principal work. Originally Ignatius did not envision such concentration in this area, but the needs of the time, the urging of popes, bishops, and laymen, reoriented his views. While he was superior general, the society became decisively committed to education, which by 1556 engaged three-fourths of available personnel (excluding brothers and those in training) in 46 colleges. In 1579 there were 144 colleges; in 1626, 444 colleges, 56 seminaries, and 44 houses of training for Jesuits; in 1749, 669 colleges, 176 seminaries, and 61 houses of study for Jesuits. Colleges provided education mostly on the secondary level. But in 1749, 24 universities were wholly or partly under Jesuit control.

Uniform norms for organization, methods, and subjects in all Jesuit schools were set forth in the RATIO STUDIORUM (1599). Stress was on the humanities. Students were drawn from all classes, from royalty to the sons of the poor. Tuition was not charged. Few were exclusively boarding schools. Only one school in four in 1749 accepted any boarders. Complete enrollment statistics are no longer extant; but the highest figures per year may well have attained 200,000. Clerical training also became largely a Jesuit responsibility. The best-known of these seminaries, and the most outstanding of all Jesuit educational institutions, was the Roman College. Begun in 1551 and since the time of Gregory XIII known also as the Gregorian University, it was the first modern seminary, and it served as a model for succeeding ones. Largely by means of these schools for laity and clergy, the order accomplished what it did during the Counter Reformation. Their academic repute caused Jesuits to be known as "the schoolmasters of Europe."

Scholarship. The promotion of sciences and letters by scholarly investigation and writings was diligently cultivated. Urgently needed, it was an efficacious apostolate. As a result, many branches of ecclesiastical and profane learning were advanced. The number of both writers and writings was very large. Quantity was greater in the latter 17th century and thenceforth, but superior talent was more evident in the earlier period.

Theological Disciplines. Theology and philosophy were the subjects most assiduously pursued. In the remarkable 16th-century revival of theology, subsequent to the pre-Reformation decline, Jesuits supplied much of the impetus. As a rule, they adhered to THOMISM, while showing a certain eclecticism. Unlike students of medieval SCHOLASTICISM, more intent on speculation, they attended also to positive theology and to a historical approach appropriate in refuting the new heresies. Controversies perforce engaged much of their energy, especially with the Protestants during the 16th century, and with the Jansenists thereafter. They crossed swords with Dominican and other Catholic theologians on erudite questions concerning divine grace, free will, and predestination in the celebrated dispute over Molinism. (*See* THEOLOGY, HISTORY OF.)

Leading theologians, whose fame often extended to other pursuits, included two 16th-century doctors of the

Church: St. Peter CANISIUS, noted for his catechisms; and St. Robert BELLARMINE, a celebrated controversialist. Francisco SUÁREZ remains the order's outstanding theologian and philosopher. Luis de Molina developed the system known as MOLINISM. Denis PÉTAU (PETAVIUS) founded the study of the history of dogmas and produced important works on patristics and chronology, as well as positive and polemical theology. Others of special merit were Francisco de TOLEDO, GREGORY OF VALENCIA, Gabriel VÁZQUEZ, Leonard LESSIUS, Adam TANNER, Juan de RIPALDA, and Jakob GRETSER.

Jesuits were preeminent in the development of moral theology into a separate discipline in the 16th century. They provided many, if not most, of the leading moralists up to 1773. Most conspicuous were the contributions of Paulus LAYMAN, Cardinal Juan de LUGO, and Hermann BUSENBAUM. During the 17th and 18th centuries long, bitter conflicts raged among rival systems of moral theology, ranging from RIGORISM to LAXISM. Almost all Jesuits upheld PROBABILISM, which is still taught in the Church. For this they were vilified as laxists by Jansenist rigorists, most notoriously by Blaise PASCAL in his *Provincial Letters*. When Tirso González, superior general (1687–1705), championed PROBABILIORISM he precipitated a crisis within the order. In the allied field of canon law, the writings of Franz SCHMALZGRUEBER were of enduring value. (*see* MORAL THEOLOGY, HISTORY OF; MORALITY, SYSTEMS OF). In scriptural scholarship, the most illustrious figures were Johannes MALDONATUS, Francisco de Ribera, and Cornelius a LAPIDE.

Among authors in ascetical theology, the following composed works still honored as classics: Alfonso RODRÍGUEZ, Diego ÁLVAREZ DE PAZ, Luis de LA PUENTE, Jeremias DREXEL, Nicholas LANCICIUS, Jean SAINT JURÉ, Jacques Nouet (1605–80), Nikolaus Avancini (1611–86), Giovanni SCARAMELLI, and Jean GROU.

Other Disciplines. Historical studies, especially ecclesiastical ones, list important Jesuit contributions. Several publications of patristic, conciliar, and hagiographic sources were permanent in value. Both Petavius and Jacques SIRMOND edited writings of the ancient Fathers. During the 17th and 18th centuries Philippe LABBE, Jean HARDOUIN, and Joseph Hartzheim printed collections of the councils. Pietro PALLAVICINO is noted as a historian of the Council of Trent. Most famous of all is the *Acta Sanctorum,* a vast collection of hagiographical source materials in 67 folio volumes, edited critically with commentaries by a small group called BOLLANDISTS. The work, conceived by Heribert Rosweyde (1569–1629) and developed by Jean van Bolland (1596–1665), first editor, has been carried out by succeeding generations of Belgian Jesuits and is still in the process of being published.

Although philosophy did not enjoy the resurgence that favored theology, Jesuit theologians were also masters of philosophy. The principal theologians, above all Suárez, were eminent in philosophy. The publications consisted largely of manuals, as well as commentaries on Aristotle, whom the Jesuits admired most among philosophers.

Other sciences vitally interested the Jesuits, who contributed much to them. Among the exact sciences, mathematics, physics, and astronomy were cultivated. Athanasius KIRCHER and Ruggiero Boscovich were the best-known mathematicians. Christopher CLAVIUS was celebrated as an astronomer. Missionaries were responsible for many original contributions in natural history; in geography, as explorers and cartographers; and in linguistics, as compilers of the first grammars and dictionaries in numerous primitive languages. Knowledge of distant lands, along with enthusiasm for the missions, were widely disseminated in Europe by accounts of the missionaries. Best remembered of this type of writing are the *JESUIT RELATIONS,* composed by French Jesuits in North America, which is still esteemed as a historical source and widely read in the original French or in English translation.

Art. In the development of art, Jesuits have been significant not so much for creating new forms as for advancing those currently in vogue. The so-called Jesuit style in church architecture is not distinct from baroque art. In Rome the Gesù, a church of the society, was artistically influential as the model for numerous other edifices built by the order.

Pastoral ministries. These exhibited wide diversity. Preaching, much neglected before the Council of Trent, occupied a foremost place. Among the famous pulpit orators in Italy were Diego LAÍNEZ, superior general succeeding St. Ignatius and eminent theologian, Francisco de Toledo, and Paolo SEGNERI; in Portugal and Brazil, Antônio VIEIRA, celebrated also as a missionary and diplomat; in Poland, Piotr SKARGA, whose writings are classics in his native tongue; and in France, Louis BOURDALOUE, a preacher at the court of Louis XIV for 34 years. Domestic missions were zealously promoted. In this labor excelled St. John Francis REGIS, FRANCIS OF GERONIMO and Bl. Antonio Baldinucci in Italy, and the martyr St. Andrew BOBOLA in Poland. Presenting retreats to clergy and laity, following the *Spiritual Exercises* of St. Ignatius, have ever been a favored apostolate.

Sodalities of the Blessed Mother (Marian Congregations) with spiritual and practical aims progressed under Jesuit impetus. Originating in the Roman College (1563), they sprang up wherever Jesuits were located, enrolling hundreds of thousands of men as sodalists. Devotion to the Sacred Heart has been prominent in the society, which has since the 17th century taken the lead in popularizing it. Restoration of discipline in religious houses was frequently entrusted to the order, especially during the 16th century. Jesuits displayed commendable zeal and courage in caring for the sick and plague-stricken, and in aiding and instructing the poor. Chaplaincies in the military services, galleys, and prisons have been accepted from the beginning.

Royal confessors. As ministers of the Sacraments, Jesuits undertook no task more memorable or controverted than that of confessors at courts and in noble houses. They became royal confessors reluctantly; yet, they came largely to monopolize these positions. Thus, they acted as royal confessors to all French kings for two centuries, from Henry III to Louis XV; to all German emperors after the early 17th century; to all dukes of Bavaria after 1579; to most rulers of Poland and Portugal; to the Spanish kings during the 18th century; to James II of England; and to many ruling or princely families throughout Europe. The post was both confidential and influential, since the director of the royal conscience might frequently be consulted and heeded above all others in ecclesiastical, political, and economic affairs. Almost without exception, these confessors were above reproach. Multifarious charges against them, springing from jealousy, were unsubstantiated or wild exaggerations. Among the most famed were the French royal confessors Pierre COTON, Nicholas Caussin, and especially François de LA CHAIZE, guide to Louis XIV's conscience for 34 years. Another noted confessor was Wilhelm LAMORMAINI.

Jesuits in Protestant countries. Strenuous efforts were expended to instruct and strengthen loyal Catholics and to win back those who had forsaken the traditional faith in regions such as the British Isles, Holland, Scandinavia, and parts of Germany, where governments supported Protestantism. Extreme hardships, discouragements, and dangers were the lot of those dedicated to this apostolate. Official opposition forced operations into secrecy. Detection meant torture, prison, exile, or death. Bitter hostility was almost unremitting in the British Isles. To prepare priests for this work, Jesuits directed seminaries on the Continent. In Rome they guided the English, Irish, and Scots Colleges; other colleges were located at Douai in France, and at Salamanca and Madrid in Spain.

In England the work of the society began in 1580 with the arrival of St. Edmund CAMPION, Robert PERSONS, and ten others. By 1623 this mission numbered 213 Jesuits, and it was established as a province. Its highest total was 374 in 1636. In 1773 it comprised 274, about half of whom resided within England. During the 18th century, about 100 Jesuits held chaplaincies in families of the Catholic gentry. Difficulties multiplied because of unjustified attempts to implicate Jesuits in the Gunpowder Plot (1605) and the OATES PLOT (1679), and because of differences with the secular clergy. Seventy or so sacrificed their lives during the 16th and 17th centuries. Of these, 26 have been beatified as martyrs, including Edmund Campion and Robert SOUTHWELL, who is also famous for his poetry (*See* ENGLAND, SCOTLAND, AND WALES, MARTYRS OF). In Scotland, despite severe persecution, a restricted number of Jesuits toiled, notably, St. John OGILVIE, who was martyred in 1615.

In Ireland, where the population remained overwhelmingly Catholic, English rulers persecuted the Church as they did in England. Jesuit efforts were confined largely to the Pale. There they preached, celebrated the Sacraments, and conducted schools in hiding, or occasionally in the open, when circumstances permitted. Irish Jesuits could also be found on the Continent, especially as teachers in the Irish colleges there. Their numbers attained a peak in the early 17th century, when there were 42 in Ireland and 40 on the Continent. In 1773 there were 24 in Ireland.

Missions. This apostolate has always been highly esteemed and has engaged more men than any other work, save education. In its constitutions, the order is designated as a missionary society. The Jesuit vocation requires a willingness to travel to various places and to dwell in any part of the world where there is hope for the salvation of souls. Ignatius was vitally interested in the conversion of the unbeliever. External circumstances alone prevented him and his first companions from devoting their lives completely after 1534 to evangelizing the Holy Land. Within months of the order's founding, Ignatius dispatched his ablest disciple, St. Francis XAVIER, with three companions to the East. When Ignatius died in 1556, his followers were already spreading the Gospel in Africa, Asia, and the New World.

Subsequent to the epochal discoveries of the 15th and early 16th centuries, and the resultant acquisition of vast overseas dominions by Catholic Spain, Portugal, and France, came an unequaled expenditure of efforts to convert the native populations. The Society of Jesus was born too late to share in the inauguration of this movement. In its early years, however, the society joined its predecessors in the field, principally the Franciscans, Dominicans, and Augustinians. In time, it surpassed them all in mission personnel and territory. Jesuit missionariess numbered 3,276, one-seventh of the whole order, in 1749. They could be found widely dispersed over five continents, although in 1749 more than nine out of were harvesting the claims of Spain and Portugal to natives in Asia and the New World.

The society's framework, with its centralization of authority and mobility of personnel, proved to be admirably adapted to these demands. As missionaries, Jesuits displayed marked organizational talent, zeal, daring, and persistence. They were not deterred by difficulties created by travel, climate, barbarous living conditions, loneliness, or opposition from both pagan natives and greedy, ruthless Europeans. Would-be missionaries received special training, for example, at the college of Coimbra, whence proceeded most of the over 1,700 Portuguese missionaries during two centuries. Abroad they were expected to master native dialects and to adapt their approach to local cultures and traditions, whether primitive or advanced, in order to allay prejudices and to inculturate the Christ Gospel in its new local setting. This practice of inculturation, so beneficial in many respects, involved the order in conflict over the CHINESE RITES CONTROVERSY and the INDIAN RITES CONTROVERSY, the longest, most acrimonious, and injurious in mission history. By no means could all attention be devoted to indigenous populations. Pastoral ministries among European settlers demanded much of the missionaries' attention, as did the conducting of schools. Sons of colonists or of natives were attending in mid-18th century 115 colleges and 23 seminaries in Spanish and Portuguese possessions alone.

Africa. In Africa, where mission penetration before the 19th century was comparatively slight, Jesuits labored in the Portuguese settlements along the west and east coasts, in the Congo, and on the island of Madagascar. Francis Xavier, on his way to the Orient, was the first missionary. In Africa, as in the New World, Jesuits sought to protect the natives against the notorious slave traders. They also came early to the north coast of the continent, to Morocco and Egypt. Ignatius himself dispatched the first group to Ethiopia.

Asia. This part of the world was much more intensively and extensively evangelized. Jesuits penetrated Asia Minor, the Near East, Persia, Tibet, Ceylon, Burma, the Malay Peninsula, Siam, Indochina (notably Alexandre de RHODES), and the islands of the East Indies. Their main efforts, however, were directed to India, China, Japan, and the Philippines. The first to reach the Far East was Francis Xavier, whose 12 years of organizing, preaching, and baptizing perhaps 30,000 people from India to Japan, ended with his death in 1552. One of the greatest missionaries since St. Paul, he was designated by Pope Pius XI as Patron of All Missions.

In India, Jesuits worked not only along the coast, but soon penetrated the interior. Particularly memorable was the mission inaugurated by Bl. Rudolf ACQUAVIVA and three companions in 1579 in the dominions of Akbar the Great Mogul. During the next two centuries 100 more Jesuits toiled there. In Madura, Robert de NOBILI, "Apostle of the Brahmins," began in 1606 a famous and important mission, using new methods of inculturation.

In China, Jesuit mission efforts began three decades after the death of Francis Xavier (1552) on the island of Sancian, off the China coast. During the next two centuries, a total of 456 Jesuits composed the most numerous and prominent of all mission groups. They became famed for their methods, devised by Alessandro VALIGNANO and Matteo RICCI. These were intended to inculturate the Catholic religion, insofar as possible, to Chinese traditions and manners and to attract educated, influential Chinese, who would in turn facilitate mass conversions among the populace. The huge population, the high culture regarded by Chinese as superior to European, the independence of the country, and the lack of political and commercial aids elsewhere available to missionaries combined to urge a novel approach. To impress the Chinese with Western culture and knowledge, especially of a scientific and technical kind, several leading Jesuit scientists gained a welcome at the imperial court, notably the astronomers Matteo Ricci, Johann Adam SCHALL VON BELL, and Ferdinand Verbiest. The vernacular was utilized in the liturgy. Chinese terms for the divinity were retained. Temporary permission was granted to converts to continue ancient, beloved practices honoring their ancestors and the sage CONFUCIUS. Western religion thereby became more palatable. But to some members of other missionary orders, and to powerful circles in the Roman Curia, it seemed rather to be undergoing a process of corruption. The resultant Chinese rites controversy, intensified by national and interorder rivalries, dragged out for more than a century to a final papal settlement (1742) that was unfavorable to the Jesuits. This dispute, along with government persecution, gravely injured the youthful Chinese Church.

Japan received its first Jesuit missionary in the person of Francis Xavier, who may have converted as many as 700 people. Until 1593 Jesuits alone staffed this mission. Development was rapid until 1614. At that time Catholics numbered about 300,000, and missionaries, 150, over three-fourths being Jesuits. Thereafter persecutions, particularly severe from 1614 to 1651, destroyed the Church almost entirely. Missionaries were banished or put to death. Jesuit martyrs totaled 111. For the coming two centuries Japan closed itself to the Gospel (*see* JAPAN, MARTYRS OF).

The Philippines, which fell to Spanish control, were the sole Asiatic region gained in large percentage to the faith. From 1581 Jesuits joined other orders in propagating Catholicism. Each order came to have its assigned sector. Spain's expulsion of the society from her colonies in 1767 affected 158 Jesuits in the Philippines and in the Mariana and Caroline Islands, and it deprived about 200,000 Catholics, a fifth of the total, of their ministries.

South America. The Western Hemisphere, more so than Asia, attracted Jesuit missionaries. Indeed, it engaged four out of five of them in 1749 (590 in Portuguese Brazil, 2,075 in Spanish possessions, 104 in French claims, less than a score in the English colonies). They were spread from Canada southward, on the mainland and in the adjoining islands of the West Indies. Preponderantly they dwelt south of the Rio Grande River, an area that was by far the most fruitful area of conversions anywhere (*see* MISSION IN COLONIAL AMERICA).

Brazil saw the first Jesuits in the New World when Manuel de NOBREGA arrived with five companions in 1549. By 1597 the total number of missionaries had risen to 120. The Society of Jesus continued to be the most numerous and prominent of the orders. Its labor of converting and educating the natives and the imported African slaves proved to be very rewarding. Many priests here, as elsewhere, also ministered to the Europeans. Many others staffed the schools which, begun in 1556, increased to nine colleges and a seminary two centuries later, thus constituting the Jesuits as the country's principal educators. In the evolution of a distinctive Brazilian culture and nation, the Jesuits played a major role, more prominent than in any other land. José de ANCHIETA, "Apostle of Brazil," whose work lasted 44 years until his death in 1597, was the most outstanding missionary, along with Antônio Vieira (1608–97), who was also remarkable as a preacher, writer, and defender of the oppressed.

Spanish territories embraced almost all of South America outside of Brazil, Central America, Mexico, large areas in the present United States., and a large segment of the West Indies. The first permanent Jesuit missions were in Peru (1567) and Mexico (1572). From there missionaries gradually radiated throughout these vast regions, as their numbers grew to 908 in 1615 and 1,768 in 1710. Schools appeared in Lima and Mexico City soon after the Jesuits' arrival. Under Jesuit control in Spanish America in mid-18th century were two universities, 79 colleges, and 16 seminaries. Apostolic endeavors among the natives were very successful. None, however, are better known than the REDUCTIONS. These were separate village communities of Catholic natives, under the spiritual, social, economic, and political direction of the missionaries, which were set up with the approval of the government. The aim was to convert and civilize the native tribes and to protect them from exploitation and vice. Jesuits did not originate or monopolize this system. Yet the

chief reductions lay in Spanish America under control of the Jesuits, who conducted about 100 of them, beginning early in the 17th century. Best known were those in the Jesuit province of Paraguay, which extended into modern Argentina, Bolivia, Uruguay, and Brazil. Here the 30 or so reductions among the Guaranis were the most notable. The Guarani population fluctuated widely, but it exceeded 140,000 in 1731. During a century and a half of operation, the Guarani reductions alone brought about the baptism of more than 700,000 people.

North America. North America occupied, during the course of two centuries, about 3,500 Jesuits (329 in French, 144 in British, and the rest in Spanish territories). The last mentioned were under the jurisdiction of the Mexican province, which included New Spain, reaching southward to Guatemala, and northward to encompass enormous, if imprecisely defined, sections of the present-day United States. The Mexican province, the largest and most important outside of Europe, listed 272 members in 1600, and 572 in 1749, most of whom were stationed mostly. In the latter year, there were 23 colleges and eight seminaries for Europeans, creoles, and natives. Under Jesuit charge was much of the public instruction in New Spain, which was culturally the most advanced of Spain's overseas dominions. Work among the native tribes began in 1591 and slowly moved into northwest Mexico, and Lower California (from 1683), regions where Jesuits were, until their suppression, almost the sole missionaries, as well as the first explorers and pioneers of civilization. They are credited with baptizing about two million people. They also organized the natives into communities similar to those in Paraguay. In 1767 there were 122 Jesuits supervising about 100 mission stations, with 122,000 natives.

Within the limits of the present United States, the first Jesuit mission (1566–72) was a short-lived one on the southeastern seaboard, between the states of Florida and Virginia, an area that the Spaniards called Florida. In all, 12 Jesuits came, together with seven or eight young catechists who were destined for the order. Their reception was extremely hostile. Pedro Martínez, leader of the first group of three, was tomahawked on the island of Cumberland, off of the Georgia coast, within a few weeks of landing. He became the first Jesuit martyr in the United States and in all of Spanish America. After his successor, Juan Segura, along with seven companions, met the same fate in 1571 in the neighborhood of Chesapeake Bay, the decimated mission withdrew to Mexico the following year.

In the southwest a permanent foothold was gained. The one responsible was Eusebio KINO, whose extensive journeys in the Pimería Alta region between 1687 and

1711 brought him to southern Arizona, where he established San Xavier del Bac and other missions.

In the immense French possessions of New France and Louisiana (in Canada and the United States), French Jesuits began their apostolate in 1611, when Enemond Massé and Pierre Biard came to Acadia, and to the Abenaki natives in Maine. Their numbers were never large, totaling only 51 in mid-18th century; but their zeal was extraordinary. The Jesuit school, started in Quebec in 1635 and developed into a classical college, initiated the educational system of French Canada. A considerable portion of the missionaries always resided in the French settlements as educators and pastors. Greater fame has attached to the Canadian mission that extended westward beyond the Great Lakes, and eastward into New York and northern New England. Jesuits were almost the sole missionaries in this arduous task, whose visible fruits were in no way commensurate with the heroic efforts expended, owing to the primitive savagery of the tribes, and the sparsity and nomadic character of the population. From Canada the mission moved southward along the Mississippi Valley to the Gulf of Mexico. The missionaries won renown also as explorers, especially Jacques MARQUETTE, who accompanied Joliet in the exploration of the Mississippi River in 1673. Martyrs numbered 22. Of these, eight, who were put to death by the Iroquois (1642–49), were canonized in 1930. Known as the NORTH AMERICAN MARTYRS, they include St. Isaac Jogues, slain with two companions near Auriesville, N.Y., and St. Jean de Brébeuf, slaughtered with four companions in Canada.

In the British possessions along the East Coast, during the entire Colonial period, pastoral care of the Catholics was consigned almost entirely to Jesuits of the English province. In 1634 Andrew WHITE and John Gravener (or Altham) arrived in Maryland with the first settlers. In numbers the missionariess varied from one to 23 (in 1771). Catholics represented about one percent of the colonists, totaling perhaps 25,000 on the eve of the American Revolution. Jesuit ministries were nearly all confined perforce to their coreligionists in Maryland and Pennsylvania, with some evangelizing among the native peoples.

Suppression and Restoration (1773–1814)

Supreme tragedy struck the order while it was in full vigor and free from evidence of internal corporate decadence. It occurred because of the concerted efforts of disparate groups in Catholic countries in Europe, whose numbers, strength, and determination increased with the passing decades of the 18th century.

The size, prestige, and educational and scholarly status of the society had aroused widespread jealousy. Its central involvement in great controversies, notably the *De auxiliis* theological dispute, and the conflict over rites in the missions, had bequeathed a heritage of resentment (*see* CONGREGATIO DE AUXILIIS). Its unwavering championship of Rome drew the ire of the partisans of GALLICANISM and monarchical absolutism. As a result, influential circles of Catholic laity and clergy, including segments of religious orders, the hierarchy, and the Roman Curia, sought at least to humiliate or weaken the order. Consciously or unconsciously, however, these served the ends of the bitterest foes bent on the order's ruin.

Chief among its foes were proponents of JANSENISM, whose heresy had met its greatest opposition from the Jesuits. Even more important were the radical devotees of the rationalistic ENLIGHTENMENT, who attacked the Jesuits as a step toward their ultimate objective of abolishing all religious orders, the papacy, and finally the Church itself. Promoting these aims were richly talented and influential writers, such as Voltaire, Rousseau, and other "philosophers" among the ENCYCLOPEDISTS, the followers of Freemasonry, and high-placed government officials. Along with direct action there was devised a long campaign of calumnies, false rumors, distorted manipulation of incidents, which were all intended to undermine the society's reputation by ascribing to it nefarious doctrines, purposes, and practices. The advisability of doing away with the order became a major issue in the Church and in European politics from about the middle of the 18th century.

Partial suppression. Preparing the way for complete suppression was a series of expulsions from Latin countries and their colonies between 1759 and 1768. Portugal seized the initiative, due mainly to the machinations of its powerful, ruthless minister of state, POMBAL, a disciple of the Enlightenment. By royal decree in 1759 the society's properties were ordered confiscated, and its members were expelled from the Portuguese homeland and overseas possessions, unless they abandoned their vocation. This the vast majority of the more than 1,700 affected religious refused to do. Brutality characterized the expulsion. Thus about 1,100 were unceremoniously dumped penniless on the shores of the States of the Church. Some 250 more were cast into dungeons, many to perish from mistreatment.

France, headquarters of the Enlightenment, Gallicanism, and Jansenism, abounded with enemies of the order. They also included the Parlement; Mme. Pompadour, the royal mistress; and Étienne François de Choiseul, minister of state and patron of the "philosophers." In their schemings, they made capital of the unfortunate LA VALETTE case in the Jesuit mission in Martinique. Finally they demolished the resistance of King Louis XV. In 1764 the society was declared an illegal body in France and its colonies, but the over 3,500 Jesuits involved were not exiled.

Spain and its territories, impelled by a few influential civil officials, in 1767 confiscated the order's properties and expelled more than 5,100 of its members with great cruelty. The same year another region ruled by the Spanish Bourbons, the Kingdom of the Two Sicilies, took a similar action against more than 1,400 Jesuits. In the next year, the Duchy of Parma, likewise under Spanish Bourbon representatives, summarily banished another 170 or so Jesuits.

Complete suppression. With half the order affected by these expulsions, the Bourbon courts turned to Rome to legislate the entire order out of existence. Clement XIII (1758–69) resisted and spoke out in defense of the persecuted body. In the conclave following this pontiff's death, the fate of the Jesuits was the dominating issue. Foes determined to secure a pope favorable to their views. Cardinal Giovanni Ganganelli, their choice, emerged as Clement XIV, although there is no proof of an explicit bargain struck to win the tiara. For four years the pope kept deferring a decision in the face of steadily mounting pressure and threats of schism. Then, in the brief *Dominus ac Redemptor* (July 21, 1773), in virtue of his supreme apostolic authority, he decreed complete dissolution. As reasons the document cited the need to restore peace within the Church, the inability of the society under the circumstances to provide the usefulness for which it came into being, and other unspecified considerations, which Clement XIV said were ''suggested to Us by the principles of prudence and which We retain concealed in Our breast.'' No condemnation of the Ignatian constitutions appeared, nor were there charges against the orthodoxy or personal conduct of individual members.

To the Church as a whole this papal act came as a severe blow; to Catholic education and missions, it was a crippling one. To the order it came as a death sentence and was accepted with obedience. Lorenzo RICCI, the superior general, was imprisoned in Rome until his death in 1775. Very many priests carried on their sacerdotal functions as part of the secular clergy. In good part German and Austrian Jesuits were not obliged to desert their educational or scholarly pursuits; they frequently continued to dwell together in communities. Some were raised to the hierarchy, such as John CARROLL, archbishop of Baltimore and first member of the hierarchy in the United States. Twenty-three, martyred during the French Revolution, were beatified in 1927. A few joined the Society of the SACRED HEART OF JESUS, which was founded in 1794; or the PACCANARISTS, which began in 1797. Both were congregations modeled on the Society of Jesus and dedicated to strive for its revival.

History from 1814 to the Twenty-first Century

Restoration. The suppression was never put fully into effect. The order was not completely extinguished; a small remnant endured from 1773 to 1814. Unwittingly, the dismemberment of Poland proved to be the society's salvation, for the Partition of Poland in 1772 brought 201 Polish Jesuits under the scepter of the schismatic Russian Empress CATHERINE II. To take effect, Clement XIV's brief had to be officially promulgated locally. Catherine II never permitted this in Russian dominions, because of her esteem for Jesuits as teachers and her resolve to keep alive their schools. In White Russia Jesuits lawfully prolonged their corporate existence and even perpetuated themselves by accepting novices, with the approval of Pius VI and Pius VII. At the time of the restoration, this group had 337 members. In Prussia, Frederick II did not allow the brief of suppression to take full effect until 1780. Pius VII canonically restored the order in the Kingdom of the Two Sicilies in 1804. By 1814 membership there had attained 199. Pius VII also permitted those of the old society in Europe, England, and the United States to affiliate with their brethren in White Russia. The pope awaited a favorable political climate before proceeding further. This came about with the downfall of Napoleon and the release of Pius VII from captivity in France. Soon thereafter, on Aug. 7, 1814, appeared the apostolic constitution *Sollicitudo omnium ecclesiarum,* revoking the brief of suppression and completely restoring the order. Since its restoration, the Society of Jesus has fashioned a unique history, in the service of the Roman Catholic Church, which can be reviewed by way of the Jesuits who have been responsible for its leadership. By focusing upon their administrations over almost two centuries, it is possible to trace in broad outline the history of the Jesuits since their restoration.

Tadeusz Brzozowski. First among the leaders was Tadeusz Brzozowski (1749–1820), a Pole, who was elected general of the Society of Jesus on Aug. 7, 1814, and who governed the Jesuit Order until Feb. 5, 1820. Since 1812 there had been growing tensions between the Jesuits and the Russian Tsar over Brzozowski's desire to leave Russia for Rome. Shortly after Brzozowski's death, Tsar Alexander I expelled 350 Jesuits from his empire on March 13, 1820.

Elsewhere the restoration of the Jesuits met with various reactions as veterans of the old Society of Jesus assumed leadership roles. On the Italian peninsula, where St. Joseph PIGNATELLI (1737–1811) had labored for its restoration while preserving the archives of the old Jesuit

Order, its members faced severe challenges as its individual states began the march toward nationhood. In Spain, within a year of the restoration, at least 120 Jesuits, mostly priests, accepted King Ferdinand VII's invitation to return to take over the Imperial College. In France, Pierre-Joseph Picot de Clorivière (1735–1820), who had witnessed the horrors of the French Revolution that took the lives of 25 former Jesuits, assumed leadership; in Belgium, Henri Fonteye (1746–1816) opened a novitiate; and, in Ireland, Peter Kenney (1779–1841) founded a school, Clongowes Wood College. In Mexico, which was emerging as a new nation, 20 Jesuits directed two seminaries and four colleges before they were forced into exile in 1821.

In the United States, Brzozowski's tenure was marked by the return of the Jesuits to Maryland with Robert Molyneaux (1738–1808) as the superior and with Giovanni A. Grassi (1775–1849) becoming, on March 1, 1815, the first president of a Catholic university in that nation, when President James Madison signed a bill recognizing Georgetown as a university. The Jesuits in Maryland had become diocesan priests during the suppression and recited their vows as members of the Society of Jesus upon its restoration. On May 6, 1816, in an exchange of letters between two former American Presidents, John Adams wrote to Thomas Jefferson: ''I do not like the resurrection of the Jesuits.'' Fortunately, the Jesuits in the United States had the staunch support of former Jesuit John Carroll (1736–1815), founder of Georgetown and archbishop of Baltimore. In 1825, the Jesuits took over St. Louis University, a diocesan institution that was established in 1818.

Luigi Fortis. To succeed Brzozowski, the society elected Luigi Fortis (1748–1829), a native of Verona, as superior general on Oct. 18, 1820. He continued in office until Jan. 27, 1829 and focused on the growth of the order. The Twentieth General Congregation, which had elected him, approved of all the laws and rules of the old Society of Jesus in its determination to preserve the true Jesuit character in the formation of its members. While the same congregation had mandated the updating of the *Ratio Studiorum*, other problems prevented Fortis from implementing the recommendations that a special commission had made with respect to teaching subjects more relevant to the times. Nevertheless, in pursuit of education, the Jesuits had the consolation of returning to operate the old Roman College in 1824.

During the tenure of Fortis, the English Jesuits encountered opposition in 1819 from the civil authority until the pope made it clear in 1829 that they had been validly restored. The Polish Jesuits, who had been forced out of White Russia in 1820, founded colleges in Krakow, Lemberg, and Tarnopol, and they established *Przeglad Powszcheny*, their special review. In Spain, where revolution broke out, 25 Jesuits lost their lives in the early 1820s, forcing the other Jesuits to leave the country until they could return in 1823. By 1826, the Spanish Jesuits, operating schools and residences, saw their number grow to 350 members over the next 12 years. In 1826, when the Jesuits were involved in ten educational institutions, hostility against the Society of Jesus in France rose to such an extent as to prohibit the Jesuits from teaching by 1829. In this year, after 70 years of absence, the Society of Jesus returned to Portugal under a handful of French Jesuits.

Jan Roothan. Jan ROOTHAN (1785–1853), a native of Amsterdam, became the third Jesuit general of the restored Society of Jesus with his election on July 9, 1829. In office until May 8, 1853, he was a strong advocate of the value of Jesuit spirituality and of the expansion of the Society of Jesus overseas. His vision brought Belgian Jesuits to Africa, French Jesuits to China, German Jesuits to India, and Italian Jesuits to Bangalore, India.

In Europe, moreover, where Roothan had split the Jesuits into a Belgian and a Dutch province, he had to cope with the continuing expulsions of Jesuits. Having visited his men in Belgium, Germany, Ireland, the Netherlands, and Sicily, he witnessed the challenges facing the Society of Jesus, encouraging the members not to lose hope. In Madrid, after 15 of the fathers were slaughtered on June 17, 1834, the Jesuits were driven out of Spain in 1835. In France, in 1843, Jules Michelet published his diatribe, *Les Jésuites*, before François Guizot, a Protestant, dispersed the Jesuits. In 1847, during the *Sonderbund* war, the Jesuits were expelled from Switzerland while anti-clericals forced about 275 Jesuits out of Germany. And, in 1848, the year of Vincenzo Gioberti's attack on the Jesuits with his *Il Gesuita Moderno*, revolutionary disturbances forced the Jesuit general himself to flee Rome in disguise.

On the intellectual front, *La CIVILTÀ CATTOLICA*, a journal dealing with religion in society approved by Pope Pius IX, published its first issue during April of 1850. The first of a number of journals of opinion that the Jesuits founded in various countries, it reflected their outlook as upholders of a stable social order in their support of conservative regimes. The latter had been the victors at the Congress of Vienna (1815) in restoring Europe after the final defeat of Napoleon Bonaparte, who was no friend of the Jesuits on the international scene.

In the fast-developing United States, there was sizable growth in colleges and universities during Roothan's years. New Jesuit educational institutions were founded in such cities as Mobile, Ala., in 1830; Cincinnati, Ohio, in 1831; Bronx, N.Y., in 1841; Worcester, Mass., in 1843; Santa Clara, Calif., and Philadelphia, Pa., in 1851, and Baltimore, Md., in 1852. By updating the *Ratio Studiorum* in 1832, Roothan had brought the work of Father Fortis to completion.

Furthermore, in Latin America, Roothan saw his men return to such countries as Argentina, Brazil, Chile, and New Granada (it became Colombia in 1886). But there were setbacks. Ecuador banished the Jesuits in 1830; Brazil, under Don Pedro, expelled them in 1834; and similar turmoil in Argentina resulted in Jesuits moving into Paraguay and Venezuela in 1842, and into Chile in 1843. Likewise, when troubles hit New Granada, the Jesuits moved into Ecuador again in 1850.

Pieter Beckx. Pieter Beckx (1795–1887), a Belgian, was Roothan's successor as superior general from July 2, 1853 to March 4, 1887. As the streak of expulsions of Jesuits in various countries continued, Beckx sought to keep the Jesuits together pastorally when their religious lives were being affected by frequent banishments. In 1861, the Society of Jesus helped to spread devotion to the Sacred Heart by initiating the Apostleship of Prayer. In Spain, where the Jesuits had returned and grown into a province of 860 members, Beckx divided the country into two provinces in 1863, before another revolution expelled the Jesuits for almost a decade in 1868.

In France, where Gustave Xavier Lacroix de Ravignan (1795–1858) was a renowned orator and author, the Jesuits founded in 1856 *Études*, a journal of history, philosophy, and theology. Tragically, during the violence of the Commune of Paris, in May of 1871, a number of Jesuits were executed by the Communists. However, once calm had returned them to their country, the French Jesuits were operating about 30 colleges and six seminaries by 1880. Then the anticlerical government sent the Jesuits into exile once more after the passage of the decree by Minister of Public Instruction Jules Ferry. In both Spain and France, the Jesuits would return but not for very long after these troubles, thereby underscoring the frequency with which European nations were banishing the members of the Society of Jesus during the 19th century. Despite such turmoil, there was a hopeful sign when ten Spanish Jesuits arrived in the Philippine Islands on April 14, 1859, thereby paving the way for a university at the Ateneo de Manila, from which would come the renowned Jesuit historian Horacio De La Costa (1916–1977).

In Europe there were further troubles. In Italy, the proclamation of a united country in 1860 led to the banishment of the Jesuits. Ten years later, during the invasion of Rome in 1870, the forces of King Victor Emmanuel plundered the Jesuit properties. Eventually, in 1873, Father Beckx was forced to move his headquarters to Fiesole, taking with him those segments of the Jesuit archives that the Italian government did not confiscate. In Germany, starting in 1872, the *Kulturkampf* was being implemented, when Dr. Adalbert Falk, not unlike Ferry in France, pursued a course that forbade the Jesuits, opponents of the Bismarckian supremacy of the State over the Church, to teach, thus forcing 550 of them into exile.

In the face of these difficulties, the embattled papacy signaled its appreciation for the loyalty of the society. Pope Pius IX elevated the Jesuit Johann B. Franzelin (1816–1886), a papal theologian in 1876, in the wake of VATICAN COUNCIL I. The latter had come to depend on the Jesuits as his allies in fighting the revolutionary ideas of the age, especially by defending his *Syllabus of Errors* (1864). The Jesuit Superior General came to be popularly known as the "black pope" because of the power of the Jesuits during the papacy of Pius IX. While the Jesuits were gaining enemies in Europe as they followed a line of thinking which even John Henry NEWMAN considered to be too conservative, they were gaining friends in America. However, there were problems for the Jesuits even in the United States, as the tarring and feathering by Know-Nothings of the Jesuit John Bapst (1815–1887), a Swiss refugee, in Ellsworth, Maine, on the night of Oct. 14, 1854, had earlier demonstrated.

Nevertheless, the distresses in Europe during the years of Father Beckx were counterbalanced by the successes in the new world. In the United States during his tenure, University of San Francisco (1855), Boston College (1863), Canisius College (1870), Loyola University of Chicago (1870), St. Peter's College (1872), Regis University (1877), University of Detroit Mercy (1877), Creighton University (1878), and Marquette University (1881) were founded. Some of these institutions were in regions where banished European Jesuits were working. In 1854, the Rocky Mountain Mission, which Father Pierre DE SMET (1801–1873), the first Jesuit among the Native Americans since the suppression, had established in 1840, and California were placed under the Jesuits of the Province of Turin. In 1869, the Sante Fe Mission became the work of the Neapolitan Province; the German Jesuits were given responsibility for the Buffalo Mission; and Woodstock College, the Jesuit house of studies in Maryland, opened with Italian Jesuits in charge. Meanwhile, in 1863, De Smet distinguished himself as a mediator between the Native Americans and Washington.

In Latin America, the fortunes of the Jesuits were not those of the Jesuits in Europe. In Mexico, where the Jesuits had been banned in 1821, they returned in 1853, only to be banned again in 1855, restored again in 1863, and banned again in 1873. The same rotating doors of banishment were true for Jesuits in Guatemala in 1871, in San Salvador in 1872, in Nicaragua in 1881, and in New Granada in 1859 and 1875.

Anton Anderledy. To succeed Beckx, the Jesuits chose Anton Anderledy (1819–1892), a Swiss Jesuit, who served first as his vicar (1883–1887) and then as general (1887–1892) of the Society of Jesus. Pope Leo XIII, having expressed his sorrow for the sufferings of the Jesuits in France, reaffirmed the documents of his predecessors supporting the Society of Jesus and, on Jan. 15, 1888, canonized Alfonso Rodriguez, John Berchmans, and Peter Claver as saints of the Society of Jesus. The pope supported the work of the Jesuits at *La Civiltà Cattolica* and brought them together at the Gregorian University to advance the thought of St. Thomas Aquinas. In June of 1889 came the death of Gerard Manley HOPKINS (1844–1889), the English Jesuit who is honored as a poet in Westminster Abbey.

During Anderledy's tenure, troubles with the civil authorities continued. Even though Germany revoked the Falk Laws in 1886, the Jesuits did not return there until after World War I. In France, after their expulsion again in 1880, they were able to return for about a decade in 1890. With the Italian political situation still very unpredictable, Anderledy continued to maintain the Jesuit headquarters at Fiesole.

Upon the direction of Pope Leo XIII, moreover, the Jesuits by means of both *La Civiltà Cattolica* and of the Gregorian University helped to bring about a renewal in theology and philosophy based on the teachings of St. Thomas Aquinas. This resurgence of neo-scholastic thought reached into the new Jesuit institutions like John Carroll University (1886), Gonzaga University (1887), University of Scranton (1888), and Seattle University (1890) that came into being in the United States. For his part in the revival of St. Thomas, Leo XIII raised the Jesuit Camillo Mazzella (1833–1900), who had been the first prefect of studies at Woodstock College in Maryland, to the rank of cardinal in 1886.

Luis Martín. To succeed Anderledy, Luis Martín (1846–1906) was elected the general of the Jesuits at Loyola in his native Spain on Oct. 2, 1892, and he continued in office until his death on April 18, 1906. During his years, the Jesuits returned to Egypt and Madagascar, and moved into the Belgian Congo. As French republicans prepared more legislation against the religious orders, the Jesuits came under attack for being on the side of those who had accused Alfred Dreyfus of spying in 1894. Expelled from France in 1902 and again in 1904, the Jesuits were forced to leave behind 28 educational institutions after the passage of civil laws aimed at the destruction of their work. In the face of such challenges, Jesuits like

Henri Leroy (1847–1917) and Gustave Desbuquois (1869–1959) sought to compensate for the lack of the influence of religion in French society. They brought about *Action Populaire*, a center of social studies to make sure that Christian principles were available to help solve France's social problems.

As general, Martin's most significant contribution was his effort to preserve the history of the Jesuit Order. Having directed the provincials of the various provinces around the world to assign Jesuits to record the history of the Society of Jesus, the superior general devoted himself to gathering in Rome the important documents on its history, thereby bringing about the *Monumenta Historica Societatis Iesu*, a vast collection of sources relating to the origins and history of the religious order that he governed. To write this history, Martin set up in 1894 the *College of Writers* for Jesuits.

Franz Xavier Wernz. Upon the death of Father Martin, Franz Xavier Wernz (1842–1914), a German, was elected general on Sept. 8, 1906, and he served until Aug. 19, 1914, as the Society of Jesus continued to face severe challenges on both the secular and religious fronts. With the overthrow of Manuel II, the Jesuits were again banished from Portugal in 1910. On the intellectual front, the turmoil raised by George TYRRELL (1861–1909), who had been dismissed from the society in 1906, contributed to the controversy over Modernism with the publication of his work, *Christianity at the Crossroads* (1909). Wernz, a canon lawyer, had become involved in the debate when he attacked the roots of Modernism, of which he had himself been suspected. In the United States, *America*, a journal of opinion, in which American Jesuits would voice their views on religion and society, was founded in 1909.

One of those involved in the controversy over Modernism in 1912 was the French theologian Léonce de GRANDMAISON (1868–1927). Among his pupils at Hastings was Pierre TEILARD DE CHARDIN (1881–1955), who took up the study of paleontology. This Jesuit later helped to shape the ideas that would influence the Catholic Church in a liberal direction with the advent of the Second Vatican Council, when the Jesuits would be distinguished once more for intellectual leadership.

Much was accomplished in the spread of the Jesuits under Wernz. New Jesuit houses of studies and colleges were established inside and outside of Europe. The dispersed German Jesuits had established their theologate at Valkenburg while the Austrian Jesuits were able to accommodate some 300 Jesuit students of theology in their center at Innsbruck. Similar developments were taking place in Krakow, Louvain, and Toledo, thereby indicating the deepening strength of the Jesuit Order. Then it had a handful of provinces in North America and missionaries stationed in such disparate areas as Albania, Armenia, Australia, Denmark, Egypt, the Greek Islands, Indonesia, Sweden, and Syria. Given the rising importance of overseas missions, where in Calcutta, 130,000 were converted to Catholicism and another 12,000 in China, Father Wernz realized the need to preserve the historical record of their missions and established the *Monumenta Missionica* for the Jesuits.

The foundation of the PONTIFICAL BIBLICAL INSTITUTE in Rome in 1909, the opening of Sophia University in Tokyo under the leadership of the German Jesuit Hermann A. Hoffmann (1864–1937) in 1913, the establishment in the United States of new Jesuit institutions like Rockhurst College (1910), Loyola Marymount (1911), and Loyola University of New Orleans (1912), underscored the diversity in education of the Society of Jesus, which was also active in Argentina, Brazil, and Mexico. In these countries, as in Canada and the United States, and even Ireland, the rapid growth of the worldwide Society of Jesus forced the Jesuits to explore further expansion plans. In Mexico, where the revolution began in 1910, the Jesuits had to flee from a movement that would make martyrs of a small number of them before the third decade of the twentieth century ended.

Wladimir Ledochowski. Upon the death of Wernz, Wladimir LEDOCHOWSKI (1866–1942), a Polish noble, was elected Jesuit superior general and began a tenure that lasted from Feb. 11, 1915, to Dec. 13, 1942. Having served as a young page in the court of the Hapsburgs at Vienna, he had imbibed the Catholic monarchical ideas that were totally against the spirit of the age in which he lived. With the outbreak of World War I, Ledochowski faced a crisis that enveloped at least 2,000 of his own men. Of the 855 Jesuits involved in the French army and navy, including the 165 who perished, they won a total of 1,056 decorations. In 1915, Pierre ROUSSELOT (1878–1915) was killed in action; in 1916, Teilhard de Chardin was writing in the trenches and working as a stretcher-bearer while earning the *Croix de Guerre* and the *Legion d'Honneur*; Joseph de GUIBERT (1877–1942), the expert on Jesuit spirituality, served as a chaplain; and, in 1917, Henri de LUBAC (1896–1991) was seriously wounded in the fighting. In addition to the French, other Jesuits were involved from Austria (82), Belgium (165), Canada (4), England (83), Germany (376), Ireland (30), and the United States (50).

Ledochowski, who had to leave Italy during the war because he was a citizen of the Austro-Hungarian Empire, governed the Jesuit Order from Schloss Zizers in Switzerland, where the Jesuits once operated three schools. Upon his return to Rome after the war, he had

to bring about the reorganization of provinces in accord with the political realities of Europe and to bring the laws of the Society of Jesus in accord with 1917 Code of Canon Law. It was a time when statistics for 1920 showed that the Jesuits numbered 17,245 members, spread over 25 provinces throughout the world, compared to 600 at the time of the restoration. In the Twenty-Seventh General Congregation in 1923, everything was adapted to a rigid legal framework. Meanwhile, the thinking of German Jesuits on religion and society was reflected in a journal like *Stimmen der Zeit,* which dated from 1915.

The fact that the Russian Revolution had broken out in 1917 created more problems for the Roman Catholic Church and the Jesuits. At Ledochowski's urging, the Holy See entrusted the apostolate for Russia to the Society of Jesus, including the operation of the *Russicum* in Rome. Edmund A. WALSH (1885–1956), the Jesuit who headed the Papal Relief Mission during the Russian famine (1922–24) was later chosen by Ledochowski to lead the fight against communism. Michel d' HERBINGNY (1880–1957), another Jesuit, was sent by the pope to Moscow to consecrate quietly three bishops after he had himself been secretly ordained for this mission in Berlin. These and other efforts did not bear much fruit, except to lead to the martyrdom of a large number of the faithful.

Likewise, in coping with the attacks on the church in Mexico and in Spain, the results were costly. Blessed Miguel Augustin PRO JUAREZ (1891–1927) had fled Mexico to continue his studies for the priesthood and was later was given permission to return to his native country in July of 1926, only to be captured and executed 16 months later. In Spain, the civil war there was responsible for some 6,800 killed due to hatred of the faith, among them at least 120 Jesuits, of which 11 have been beatified.

Moreover, Ledochowski, who had a sense of history, was very pleased with the canonizations of such Jesuit luminaries before the suppression as Peter Canisius (1925) and of Robert Bellarmine and the NORTH AMERICAN MARTYRS (1930). That same year, with his dream of a new Jesuit headquarters in Rome realized, he founded on February 11 the *Institutum Historicum Societatis Iesu,* which continues to publish its findings twice a year in the *Archivum Historicum.* Having done all that after the 1929 settlement of the Roman Question between Pope PIUS XI and Benito Mussolini, all the documents of the Society of Jesus were moved to the archives at the new headquarters. During these years, the Jesuits and the Holy See had Pietro Tacchi Venturi (1861–1956), the eminent Jesuit historian, act as the intermediary of the Catholic Church with the Italian government.

In coping with the challenges rising from the political, economic, and social crises of the depression years, the Society of Jesus under Ledochowski was very much at the service of the papacy. This was particularly true of Oswald von Nell-Breuning (1890–1991), a disciple of Heinrich Pesch (1854–1926), the Jesuit social philosopher. With the help of another Jesuit, Gustav GUNDLACH (1892–1963), Nell-Breuning became the main architect of *QUADRAGESIMO ANNO* (1931), an encyclical designed to meet the problems of society, especially with its emphasis on the principle of SUBSIDIARITY. Its ideas influenced social legislation in the United States and Europe, with the rise of the Christian Democrats after World War II. At the same time, the Society of Jesus was stressing the importance of the social apostolate as the Twenty-Eighth General Congregation had decreed in 1938. American Jesuits like John LAFARGE (1880–1963), Leo C. Brown (1900–1978), and Louis J. TWOMEY (1905–1969) were deeply involved in spreading the papal teachings on social justice in a nation in which the Jesuits founded still another educational institution with Fairfield University in 1942.

Meanwhile, the rise of Nazism, coming as it did in the wake of the problems with Russia, Mexico, and Spain, would capture much of Father Ledochowski's attention, especially after the invasion of Poland in 1939. Having taken precautions to continue the government of the Society of Jesus, he had the general congregation, on the eve of World War II, appoint Maurice Schurmans (1901–1970), a Belgian Jesuit, to be his vicar. With Italy in the war, Ledochowski, in a generous delegation of power for one who had issued directives to Jesuits on such minute details as the care of one's hair, gave some regional assistants the necessary authority to make decisions with respect to their areas of jurisdiction when it involved seeking approval from Rome. In the case of the American assistant Zachaeus Maher (1882–1963), Ledochowski had a Jesuit who unhesitatingly took up his responsibilities until 1946, when he was replaced by Vincent McCormick (1886–1963), a confidant of Pope Pius XII.

An astute observer of contemporary events, Ledochowski had sensed the problems facing the Jesuits in Germany as early as February of 1934. Remaining in Rome, he led the battle against Nazism through the Jesuits who operated Vatican Radio. Although the Jesuit general has been blamed by some scholars for sidetracking the encyclical that Pope Pius XI, before his death, was about to publish against anti-Semitism, Ledochowski cannot be regarded as in any way sympathetic to the Nazis. His strong and steady hand was firmly behind Vatican Radio's transmissions, which inspired hope for many peoples oppressed by the Nazis, including the Jews. With respect to the latter, Tacchi Venturi, whose name is as venerated in Rome as much as that of Felice

M. Capello (1879–1962), the popular confessor, and Riccardo Lombardi (1908–1979), the founder of the Movement for the Better World and famed preacher, used his quiet diplomacy with Italy to help save many of them from the Holocaust.

That almost 150 Jesuits, among them the German Alfred Delp (1907–1945) and the Frenchmen Victor Dillard (1897–1945) and Yves de MONTCHEUIL (1900–1944), perished as victims of the Nazis as they defended the rights of others, some even risking their lives to save Jews, stands as a tribute of the resistance that Ledochowski led against the Nazis who went so far as to outlaw the Jesuits. Among the prisoners who survived was the famous English writer and preacher Cyril Charles MARTINDALE (1879–1963) and Blessed Rupert MAYER (1876–1945), the Munich preacher who had earned the Iron Cross in World War I and boldly opposed the Nazis. Martindale, like Jesuits Martin C. D'ARCY (1888–1976) and Frederick COPLESTON (1907–1994) after him, had an impact on religion and culture outside of his native England.

Interim vicars general. Between Ledochowski's death and the election of John Baptist Janssens (1889–1964) in 1946, due to the situation of World War II, which prevented a meeting a general congregation, Alessio A. Magni (1872–1944), an Italian, and Norbert de Boynes (1870–1954), a Frenchman, served as vicars general of the society. While Magni's tenure was a relatively quiet one, de Boynes sought to tone down what Vatican Radio was doing in resisting the Nazis. In fact, before assuming office as vicar, he did not hesitate to tell the French, as Ledochowski's assistant in 1941, that they should fall in line behind the government of Vichy under Marshall Philippe Pétain, who had restored the Society of Jesus in France. This did not go over well with Jesuits like Henri de Lubac and others in the resistance movement, who were openly opposed to such collaboration.

John Baptist Janssens. On Sept. 6, 1946, the Jesuits elected John Baptist Janssens, a Belgian, who served as their superior general until Oct. 5, 1964. Recognized as a "Righteous Among the Nations" by Yad Vashem, he had helped to save Jews in Brussels during the war. However, with the end of World War II, the world had changed and the Catholic Church faced a new threat from Russia's dominance over Eastern Europe where, since 1944, the Society of Jesus saw its work severely restricted, if not entirely banished.

Perceptive and realistic, Janssens encouraged the Jesuits to keep pace with the changes that industry, science, technology, and war had brought about in human society. All this came from a man who appeared quite isolated from the developments of the modern world and whose failing health required him to appoint the Jesuit John L. Swain (1907–1987) as his vicar in 1960. During Janssens' tenure, the American Jesuits established two more colleges: LeMoyne (1946) and Wheeling (1954).

At the same time, Janssens left his mark by his own concern for the social apostolate and the missions. In itself, the latter was a reflection of Father Janssens' zeal, which was confirmed at the meeting of the Second Vatican Council by at least some 40 Jesuit bishops, who were pictured in Rome with Augustin Cardinal Bea (1881–1968). As for the goals of the social apostolate, the activities of Bl. Alberto Hurtado Cruchaga (1901–1952) in Santiago, Chile, in caring for the homeless, and the work of Jerome D'Souza (1897–1977), a Jesuit from India, in establishing a social institute in his native land at Janssens's suggestion, stand as good examples.

The society suffered a setback among its scholars during Janssens' time. Biblical experts like Stanislas LYONNET (1902–1986), Luis Alonso Schökel (1920–1998), and Maximilian Zerwick (1901–1975), and such theologians as Henri de Lubac (1896–1991) and John Courtney MURRAY (1904–1967) were silenced. They would be vindicated later by Pope John XXIII during the Second Vatican Council, when many of their ideas became the foundation for the Second Vatican Council. In particular, those biblical scholars had put into practice the words of Pius XII's *Divino afflante Spiritu* (1943) about Catholic scholars approaching the biblical texts critically and historically. That restoration, it should be noted, came about due to the intervention of Cardinal Augustin BEA, who was influential in the composition of *Divino afflante Spiritu*.

Janssens' years were also marked by much suffering because of the communist regimes that established themselves in Eastern Europe and in China. In Eastern Europe, Walter J. Ciszek (1904–1984) had gone through the gulag after one of his Jesuit associates, Jerzy Moskwa (1910–1941), had perished. One of the more distinguished Jesuits among many behind the Iron Curtain, where at least 20 were killed, was Jan Korec (b. 1924), now cardinal, who kept the underground church alive in Czechoslovakia. Behind China's Bamboo Curtain, where at least 15 Jesuits have been killed, Dominic Tang Yee Ming (1908–1995), archbishop of Canton; Paul Li Zhenrong (1919–1992), bishop of Cangzhou; and priests like Francis Chu (1913–1983) and Xavier Cai (1907–1997) were some of members of the Society of Jesus who suffered for their loyalty to the Holy See in the land where the name of the Jesuit Matteo Ricci (1552–1610) is still revered 300 years after his arrival in Bejing.

Pedro Arrupe. Pedro ARRUPE (1907–1991) succeeded Janssens on May 22, 1965. The first Basque since St. Ignatius to head the Jesuit Order, his life was affected by two decisive world events before his election as superior general. One was the expulsion on June 23, 1932 of the Society of Jesus from Spain on the eve of the Spanish Civil War, sending him as a Jesuit scholastic into exile in Belgium. The other was the explosion of the atomic bomb on Hiroshima on Aug. 6, 1945, when he was the master of novices on the outskirts of that city, where he turned the Jesuit novitiate into a hospital.

At the time of the Second Vatican Council, the Society of Jesus numbered some 36,000 members, with more than 8,000 of them in the United States, including 6,000 of them who were laboring as missionaries around the world and operating an educational complex of some 4,000 schools (more than half in elementary education, with at least 800 in secondary education and 750 in higher education). Among the outstanding Jesuits who served in various capacities at the council were Karl RAHNER (1904–1984), John Courtney MURRAY (1904–1967), and Bernard LONERGAN (1904–1984). With such capable minds, including Jean DANIELOU (1907–1974) and Josef A. JUNGMANN (1889–1975), in 1963 Pope Paul VI assigned the Jesuits the task of putting together the documents relating to the actions of Pope Pius XII during Holocaust and, in 1965, the mission of confronting atheism in the aftermath of the Second Vatican Council.

As superior general, Arrupe endeavored to reshape the Society of Jesus in accordance with the documents of the Second Vatican Council. This was done by holding a second session of the Thirty-First General Congregation between Sept. 8 and Nov. 17, 1966, to take care of the issues that were not resolved in the first session. Subsequently, he convened the Thirty-Second General Congregation between Dec. 2, 1974, and March 7, 1975. Renewal and reform came at a cost. The number of Jesuits declined from 36,038 members when Arrupe was elected to 25,952 when he left office.

Father Arrupe brought the Society of Jesus to an agonizing reappraisal of itself and espoused the Church's teaching at Medellin, Columbia in 1968, with its emphasis on the preferential option for the poor. As the numbers of departure of Jesuits from the society increased and vocations declined, dissatisfaction with the superior general grew. A group of Spanish Jesuits petitioned Pope Paul VI that they be removed from Arrupe's authority. The very conservative views of those Jesuits and the Basque identity of the Jesuit superior general, who was perhaps even a nationalist spirit, in a country where Spanish far outnumber the Basques in the society, helped fuel their request.

Although Pope Paul VI was aware of the challenges confronting the superior general, as he indicated in the concerns that he had voiced in addressing the Jesuits at the closing of their general congregation on Nov. 17, 1966, he refused, especially since there was no reason to doubt the dedication and loyalty of Arrupe to the Holy See, as was evident when later the Jesuit General called for "unswerving and decisive loyalty" in the wake of *Humanae Vitae* (1968), the controversial encyclical on birth control. While staunch conservatives within the order were disgruntled with the changes wrought by the Second Vatican Council and were inclined to blame Arrupe for the crisis within the Society of Jesus, there was more to it than that.

During that time, although the Jesuits witnessed an increase in the number of local-born Jesuits in the Third World, especially in parts of Africa and Asia, this increase was dwarfed by a huge decline in numbers in Europe and North America. In the United States, the numbers declined from 8,400 to less than 5,000. This decline was due to a number of factors, including changes in traditional practices. No less a Jesuit than Carlo M. Martini (b. 1927), later cardinal archbishop of Milan, pointed out in preparation for the opening of the Thirty-Second General Congregation in 1974 that a number of Jesuits, at least in Europe, had already abandoned such practices as daily Mass, the examination of conscience, and the annual eight-day retreat. Then, in the work of the congregation, Arrupe ran into resistance from Paul VI when changes regarding the fourth vow of obedience to the pope were discussed.

In that same period, the colleges and the universities in the United States were becoming separately incorporated from the Jesuits communities. That development came under the leadership of Paul C. REINERT (1910–2001), Jesuit president of St. Louis University. In adapting these educational institutions to the realities of American society, many Jesuits were defensive in believing that the Society of Jesus was abandoning its legacy in having the religious community recognized in civil law as separate from the educational institution. In view of the decline in vocations to the Society of Jesus, the move in that direction can be regarded as beneficial, especially in providing the financial means to support these Jesuit colleges and universities.

Furthermore, there was the confusion that arose from priests becoming involved in politics, usually regarded as reserved for the laity in the United States. While the Jesuit John J. McLaughlin (b. 1927), a speechwriter at the White House, was defending Richard M. Nixon and his Watergate crimes, Robert F. Drinan (b. 1920), another Jesuit, was bringing articles of impeachment against the President in the United States House of Representatives. At the same time, another Jesuit, Daniel J. Berrigan (b.

1921), made headlines in protesting against Nixon's foreign policy. When Drinan's position in Congress became a subject of controversy with the Holy See, he showed true Jesuit obedience early in 1981 by stepping down from his elected office, in which he had served for ten years, once Pope John Paul II had urged this.

Undeterred, Arrupe moved to implement the decrees of the Second Vatican Council on religious life. To this end, he sought to recapture the original charism of St. Ignatius so as to enable the Society of Jesus to adjust to the contemporary world. This was evident when the Thirty-Second General Congregation stated that the basic challenge for Jesuits was engagement in "the struggle for faith and the struggle for justice that the same faith requires," and at least 40 Jesuits in the Third World have borne witness with their own lives to what this idea of a Jesuit means today. Among those who reflected this by their martyrdom were Rutilio Grande (1928–1977) in El Salvador, John Conway (1920–1977) and Christopher Shepherd-Smith (1943–1977) in Rhodesia (now Zimbabwe), João B. Penido Burnier (1917–1976) in Brazil, and Tarcisius Dewanto (1965–1999) and Karl Albrecht Karim Arbie (1929–1999) in East Timor in September of 1999.

As John Paul II succeeded to the papacy, the tensions between the Vatican and the Jesuits increased until Aug. 7, 1981, when Arrupe was afflicted with by a disabling stroke. Given Arrupe's frail health and the difficult situation in which the Jesuits found themselves with respect to the papacy, Pope John Paul II appointed Paolo Dezza (1901–1999) as the pontifical delegate to govern the Society of Jesus from Oct. 5, 1981 to Sept. 13, 1983. In this way, the pope sidetracked the possibility of Vincent T. O'Keefe, a highly respected American Jesuit, whom Arrupe had appointed as his temporary vicar, from becoming the next superior general. For two years, Dezza held the Society of Jesus together, despite the hostile reaction that the papal intervention had caused among some members within the society. For this, he was duly rewarded when Pope John Paul II named him as a cardinal in 1991.

Peter-Hans Kolvenbach. Subsequently, when the pope found that the time was suitable, the Jesuits gathered in Rome to elect a superior general to succeed Arrupe, who resigned on Sept. 3, 1983. On the following September 13, the Jesuits elected Peter-Hans Kolvenbach (b. 1928), a native of Holland, to take over the leadership of the Jesuit Order. His tenure has been marked by improvement in relations with the pope, by the opening up of the dialogue with the religions of the non-Christian world, and by the strengthening of the Society of Jesus in Eastern Europe after the fall of communism.

At the same time, Father Kolvenbach's government of the society has been noteworthy in a number of other ways. While the tragic murder by the military in El Salvador of six Jesuits and their two helpers on Nov. 16, 1989 stands out, there was of importance as well the Thirty-Fourth General Congregation of the Society of Jesus, from Jan. 5 to March 22, 1995. Although it dealt in part with the updating of the Jesuit Order in accord with the new code of Canon Law published in 1983, among its decisions was a positive stand on the rights of women, which made news.

Nevertheless, though the relationship between the Jesuits and the Vatican has improved, Kolvenbach's years have forced the Society of Jesus to face up to its traditional role in higher education as more Jesuits were becoming involved in other apostolates, including in the United States the increasing number of "Nativity Schools" that the Jesuits have started to educate inner-city youth in their later elementary grades. While some alumni found that Jesuit institutions in higher education have been losing their Catholic character, others maintain that these institutions are more truly Catholic than they have been in the past, especially in teaching their students to have a deep concern for justice in society. Such a debate was not unrelated to the Vatican's attempt to exercise some control over Catholic colleges and universities. This was explicitly stated when Pope John Paul II issued on Aug. 15, 1990 *Ex Corde Ecclesiae*, a document that has occasioned discussions about academic freedom within Jesuit institutions themselves.

The attitude of the papacy toward the Society of Jesus has been a significant development during Kolvenbach's tenure. An indication of this where John Paul II really stands can be derived from the way that the pope has increased the number of Jesuit saints and blessed and the number of Jesuit cardinals. Of the 28 Jesuits who have been raised to the rank of cardinal in the past, John Paul II has created 12 of them, a number that surpasses what any of his predecessors have done. The pope has shown similar affection for the Society of Jesus in having raised some 24 Jesuits to the ranks of the beatified and about half that number to the ranks of the canonized.

When the Jesuits celebrated the 500th anniversary of the birth of their founder in 1991, the Society of Jesus had endured many changes, many of which came during the period since the restoration of the Society of Jesus in 1814. That the Jesuit Order has survived the many challenges that it faced from its enemies and from the changes within its company is due in part to the leadership of those who have been elected Jesuit superior general. There is reason for optimism. By the year 2000 the Jesuits numbered at least 21,000 members, with its largest segments in India (3,559), the United States (3,495), and Spain (1,774). Laboring in 112 nations throughout the world, the Society of Jesus, which has almost 50 canonized saints and about 150 blessed in its history, is still involved in many apostolates, especially in schools, colleges, and universities, where it continues to form men and women for others.

Bibliography: W. V. BANGERT, *A History of the Society of Jesus* (2d edition; St. Louis, Mo. 1986). M. BARTHEL, *The Jesuits,* tr. Mark Howson (New York 1987). J. A. CASCIOTTI, *Supplementum Catalogorum Societatis Iesu 2002* (Rome 2001). F. R. DUMAS, *Grandeur et Misère des Jésuites* (Paris 1963). J. A. FITZMYER, "A Recent Roman Scriptural Controversy," *Theological Studies* 22 (1961) 426–444. C. HOLLIS, *The Jesuits* (New York 1968). J. LACOUTURE, *Jesuits,* tr. Jeremy Leggatt (Washington, D.C. 1995). V. A. LAPOMARDA, *The Jesuits and the Third Reich* (Lewiston, N.Y. 1989). W. LEDOCHOWSKI, *Selected Writings of Father Ledochowski* (Chicago, Ill. 1945). J. F. MACDONNELL, *Companions of Jesuits* (Fairfield, Conn., 1995). P. MCDONOUGH, *Men Astutely Trained* (New York 1992). P. MCDONOUGH and E. C. BIANCHI, *Passionate Uncertainty: Inside the American Jesuits* (Berkeley, Calif. 2002). R. MENDIZÁBAL, N. R. VERÁSTEGUÎ, and C. J. JACKSON, *Catalogus Defunctorum,* 3 v. (Rome 1972–2000). J. W. O'MALLEY, G. A. BAILEY, S. J. HARRIS, and T. F. KENNEDY, *The Jesuits* (Toronto, Canada 1999). W. J. O'MALLEY, *The Voice of Blood* (Maryknoll, N.Y. 1980). J. W. PADBERG, ed., *The Constitutions of the Society of Jesus and Their Complementary Norms* (St. Louis, Mo. 1996). M. R. TRIPOLE, ed., *Jesuit Education 21* (Philadelphia, Pa. 2000). J. N. TYLENDA, *Jesuit Saints & Martyrs* (2d ed Chicago, Ill. 1998). J. M. DE VERA, ed., *Jesuits, Yearbook of the Society of Jesus, 2000* (Rome 1999).

[J. F. BRODERICK/V. A. LAPOMARDA]

JESUS (THE NAME)

In English the name Jesus is a transliteration of the Latin form *Iesus,* which represents the Greek form Ἰησοῦς of the Hebrew name *yēšûa'*. The latter is a late form, by vowel dissimilation, of the name *yôšûa',* itself a contracted form of *yᵉhôšûa',* "Yahweh is salvation." This was the name of Moses' successor, JOSHUA, son of Nun. Both because of the fame of this early hero of Israel and because of the meaning of the name, many men both in the Old Testament and in the New Testament bore the name of Joshua or Jesus. The Septuagint generally uses the Greek form Ἰησοῦς where the Hebrew text has the form *yôšûa'* or *yᵉhôšûa'*. So also the New Testament, in referring to Joshua, son of Nun, calls him Jesus (Acts 7.45; Heb 4.8). An allusion is made in Mt 1.21 to the meaning of the name ("Yahweh is salvation"): Joseph is told by the angel of the Lord to name the child born of Mary's virginal conception "Jesus, for he shall save his people from their sins."

Bibliography: *Encyclopedic Dictionary of the Bible,* tr. and adap. by L. HARTMAN (New York 1963), from A. VAN DEN BORN, *Bijbels Woordenboek* 1141–42. L. W. FOESTER, G. KITTEL, *Theologisches Wörterbuch zum Neuen Testament* 3:284–94.

[L. F. HARTMAN]

"The Transfiguration," Christ in glory flanked by Old Testament figures, Moses (holding tablets of the Law) and Elijah, appearing in an opening in the clouds to his disciples St. John, St.Peter and St. James. (Archive Photos)

JESUS CHRIST, ARTICLES ON

The Son of God, who became man, is considered in several articles, principally: JESUS CHRIST (IN THE BIBLE) and JESUS CHRIST (IN THEOLOGY). The latter article has a section devoted to specific questions of special interest, some of which are treated also in separate articles (e.g., THEANDRIC ACTS OF CHRIST; IMPECCABILITY OF CHRIST; HISTORICAL JESUS). See also CHRISTOLOGY. Mysteries of the life, death, and resurrection of Christ are treated in individual articles (ASCENSION OF JESUS CHRIST; RESURRECTION OF CHRIST [IN THE NEW TESTAMENT]; PASSION OF CHRIST [IN THE BIBLE]; VIRGIN BIRTH). Topics of special importance in the development of Christological doctrine are treated in CHRISTOLOGY, CONTROVERSIES ON (PATRISTIC) and in separate articles, e.g., MONOPHYSITISM; NESTORIANISM; for later controversies, see ASSUMPTUS-HOMO THEOLOGY; SUBSISTENCE (IN CHRISTOLOGY); INCARNATION, NECESSITY OF THE. The principal articles on the incarnation are INCARNATION; HYPOSTATIC UNION; HYPOSTATIC UNION, GRACE OF. The principal articles on the salvific work of Christ are REDEMPTION (IN THE BIBLE); REDEMPTION (THEOLOGY OF). Related articles are SACRIFICE OF THE CROSS; SATISFACTION OF CHRIST; ATONEMENT; RECAPITULATION IN CHRIST; SOTERIOLOGY.

[G. F. LANAVE]

JESUS CHRIST (IN THE BIBLE)

Although there is an abundance of information about Jesus Christ in the Bible, there are difficulties in interpreting and evaluating it because of the nature of the Biblical writings. This article, therefore, begins with a discussion of the problems involved in using the Bible as a source of information about Jesus, His life, His work, and the meaning of His person. Secondly, taking into account the nature of the Biblical sources, it attempts to determine what conclusions can be reached regarding the main events of Jesus' life, what was the content of His personal teaching, and what Jesus Himself thought about His person and work. Lastly, it seeks to determine the Apostolic Church's interpretation of the person and work of Jesus by listing the titles with which the early Church spoke of Him.

The Biblical Sources and Their Value

Within the 1st century after Jesus' death only two Latin authors made undisputed mention of Him. Tacitus (*Ann.* 15.44) said that the Christians were named for a *Christus* who had been condemned to death by Pontius Pilate. Pliny the Younger (Letter to Trajan: *Epist.* 10.69) said that the Christians sang hymns to a certain *Christus*

At the Church of the Holy Sepulcher in Jerusalem a nun crouches to touch the stone at the 12th Station of the Cross, Golgotha, where Jesus died. The site is controlled by the Greek Orthodox, Roman Catholic, and Armenian Orthodox churches. (AP/Wide World Photos)

as to a God. The Jewish author Flavius Josephus (*Ant.* 20.9.1) mentioned the martyrdom of James, "a brother of Jesus who is called the Christ." One must turn to the Bible for any further 1st-century information about Jesus.

The Old Testament cannot be expected to give any direct historical information about Jesus. Furthermore, recent studies of the nature of Old Testament prophecy have shown that messianic prophecies do not give the detailed information that many Christian apologists have sought there (*see* MESSIANISM). The Old Testament is indispensable, however, for an understanding of the categories and terms in which both Jesus and the Apostolic Church expressed themselves. There remains only the New Testament as a source for the life of Jesus and the meaning of His work and person.

Apostolic Tradition. Since the New Testament is the product of the Apostolic Church, it can be expected to reflect the concerns of the Church at that time. The Christians of the 1st decade after Jesus continued to live as good Jews—as Jews, however, who were convinced that the expected MESSIAH had come, although in a totally unexpected way. The DAY OF THE LORD had arrived, the

Jesus Christ, illustration. (Archive Photos)

"Pietá," painting by Titian, in the Academy at Venice.

SPIRIT OF GOD had been poured out on the world (Acts 2.1–11). Their enthusiasm drove them to try to share this conviction by recounting what had happened and by explaining its meaning, at first to their fellow Jews, later to the pagans. Thus the Apostolic Church, bursting with a message that would change the world, produced a brief preaching outline of significant facts drawn from Jesus' life that served ultimately as the basic outline of the Gospels.

Although they continued to frequent the Temple (Acts 2.46), the Christians were conscious of a certain but as yet undefined distinctness from Judaism shown by their continuing "steadfastly in the teaching of the apostles and in the communion of the breaking of bread and in prayers" (Acts 2.42) in their homes. Innumerable new problems arose as the Christians became more conscious of this distinctness and of the universal character of their movement in its spread to the Gentile world. How did the everyday living of the Christian life differ from the life

of the Jew and of the pagan? For answers they searched their memories for what Jesus had said. Instruction might be drawn from parallel situations on which Jesus had spoken or from the example of His actions. The moral teaching of the Old Testament and a deeper search into the meaning of Christianity could give principles to live by. This didactic activity of the early Church, as well as controversies with Jews and pagans, preserved the memory of many sayings and incidents from Jesus' life. These tended to be single isolated incidents, cut off from the framework of chronology and geography since these details contributed little to the problems of practical Christian living. The sayings of Jesus did not need to be exact quotations; often they were not since they were drawn from memories and not from stenographic reports. The words of Jesus could and needed to be adapted to the Christian needs. The incidents were sometimes stripped of detail that did not serve a purpose. In time such sayings and incidents were collected together, not on the basis of

"The Transfiguration," from "The Gospel According to the Four Evangelists," written in Armenia, 13th century.

"Christ Among the Doctors," oil painting on wood panel by Bernardino Luini, showing Jesus as a young man, c. 1515–1530. (©National Gallery Collection; By kind permission of the Trustees of the National Gallery, London/CORBIS.)

chronology or topography, but on mnemonic and topical principles. Gradually a tradition grew about what Jesus had done and said. Practical, kerygmatic (*see* KERYGMA), didactic, apologetic, and liturgical concerns determined the form and content of this tradition, which developed against the background of Old Testament thinking and in Jewish categories of thought and modes of expression. *See* FORM CRITICISM, BIBLICAL; TRADITION (IN THE BIBLE).

Role of Faith in the Apostolic Tradition. Those who formulated and preserved the tradition just described were conscious of the necessity that it be based on historical occurrence. See, e.g., 1 Cor 15.14–15: "If Christ has not risen, vain is our preaching, vain too is your faith. Yes, and we are found false witnesses as to God, in that we have borne witness against God that he raised Christ." But the bare recital of historical occurrences is ambiguous. Other men had been reported raised from the dead for whom no one claimed divinity. Other men had

been executed and no one claimed that they had thereby redeemed the world. Yet the early Christians attached such significance to the death and Resurrection of Jesus. *See* RESURRECTION OF CHRIST, 1; REDEMPTION (IN THE BIBLE). Historical fact needs interpretation. St. Paul tried to use human wisdom to substantiate his interpretation at Athens and found it inadequate (Acts 17.22–33). Having profited from this experience, he told the Corinthians, "I . . . did not come with pretentious speech or wisdom, announcing unto you the witness to Christ. . . . My speech and my preaching were not in the persuasive words of wisdom, but in the demonstration of the Spirit and of power, that your faith might rest, not on the wisdom of men, but on the power of God" (1 Cor 2.1, 4–5). Therefore in early Christian tradition the bare facts of historical occurrence were always coupled with an interpretation drawn from faith. To substantiate the validity of the interpretation an appeal was made to the action of the Holy Spirit, who bore witness to what had happened through

Christ being nailed to cross, engraving. (©Bettmann/CORBIS)

group of disciples and taught them by His words and actions in a way accommodated to their mentality and designed to make a deep impression upon them and to be an aid to memory. This was the method used by other Jewish teachers of His day, when it was the custom that a man's teaching be passed on orally. (2) The Apostles, enlightened and strengthened by the Resurrection of Jesus and the possession of the Holy Spirit, proclaimed first and foremost the death and Resurrection of the Lord, then other events of His life and His teaching. They necessarily used the various forms of speech that suited their purposes and fitted the mentality of their hearers, interpreting the words and deeds of Jesus according to their hearers' needs. (3) Finally, for diverse reasons, the data of faith began to be preserved in the written word rather than by oral tradition. Pastoral considerations occasioned the writing of the Epistles; the death of the witnesses of Christ's death and Resurrection occasioned the writing of the Gospels. Thus, great diversity is to be found in the New Testament as a result of the different points of view and purposes of the different human authors, the different needs of the specific bodies of Christians to which each writing was directed, and finally, the fact that the diverse interests and methods of preaching and teaching of the early Church had left their marks on the tradition upon which these writings were based. "Unless the exegete, then, pays attention to all those factors which have a bearing on the origin and composition of the Gospels, and makes due use of the acceptable findings of modern research, he will fail in his duty of ascertaining what the intentions of the sacred writers were, and what it is that they have actually said" [Instruction of the Pontifical Biblical Commission (May 14, 1964) on *The Historical Truth of the Gospel,* authorized English translation, *The Catholic Biblical Quarterly* 26 (1964) 305–312].

Nevertheless a surprising unity runs through the diversity of the New Testament. This unity is not due to any preconceived master plan of a human editorial board, but to the work of the Holy Spirit, who both directed the development of the early Christian tradition and inspired the various human authors to write as they did.

Problem for the Theologian. Since the theologian's task is that of faith seeking understanding, he applies the principles of human reason to the data of faith in order to understand better the content of faith and to express better his insights. To do this he necessarily works within the framework of some philosophical system of human thought. He finds his first difficulty in the fact that he cannot presuppose that the New Testament writers worked from the same set of philosophical presuppositions as his own. The New Testament writers worked from a Jewish frame of reference that is dynamically oriented (often called existential), not from a static or essential one.

the Resurrection and ASCENSION OF JESUS CHRIST: He had been seated at the right hand of the Father as messianic Lord and Christ. Thus the earliest formulations of faith in the divinity of Jesus were in these terms (Acts 2.32–36; Rom 1.4). The early churchmen insisted on the effects of the Holy Spirit because they were tangible and could be substantiated by experience and historical witness, and thus these in turn confirmed the truth of the witness of the Holy Spirit to the person and meaning of Jesus in SALVATION HISTORY. Consequently, everything handed down about Jesus' works and words was colored by the post-Resurrection faith. Everything was seen in retrospect and reported with the understanding that the Apostles had later, not necessarily with the understanding they had at the time the events happened.

New Testament Based on Apostolic Tradition. The New Testament writings reflect their origins in the early Church. To assess their content and its historical trustworthiness, the reader must keep in mind the three stages of tradition through which the teachings and life of Jesus have come down to us. (1) Jesus chose a special

"The Agony in the Garden," painting on wood panel by Giovanni Bellini, c. 1465. (© National Gallery Collection; By kind permission of the Trustees of the National Gallery, London/CORBIS)

Therefore the theologian can expect, for example, no discussion of the concepts of person and nature as applied to God, no formulated doctrine of the Holy TRINITY. Consequently, both those who deny any teaching on three Persons in one God in the New Testament and those who try to find there such a philosophical formulation of the doctrine are victims of the same error of thinking, viz., the projection of a foreign frame of reference upon the New Testament. The theologian's first task is to understand the New Testament within the sacred authors' frame of reference (principally the work of the Biblical theologian) and then translate these understandings into the framework and expression of a different set of philosophical presuppositions (principally the work of the systematic theologian). He gains much understanding from this latter effort, but the New Testament does not do this task for him. Secondly, the theologian must be aware that the New Testament writers are at the beginning of the process of finding ever more precise and adequate terminology. To read later theological precision into the terminology of the New Testament writer would be to do him an injustice and lose much of his meaning. Finally, the theologian must remain aware of the practical orientation of the New Testament and not expect to find worked out answers to the theoretical problems that claim his attention.

Problem for the Historian. According to modern historical method, the historian must first establish with considerable accuracy the sequence of events for the period his work is to cover. For this the indispensable guidelines are chronology and topology. Having established the sequence of events, he must proceed to point out the interrelation of cause and effect between the events, including the stages of psychological development of the principal personalities involved.

As soon as the historian attempts to apply this modern historical method to a biography of Jesus he finds that the New Testament, his only source of information, does not share his high regard for chronology and topology. Each Evangelist goes his own way except for a broad fourpoint outline: (1) the witness of the Baptist; (2) a public ministry in Galilee; (3) a journey to Jerusalem; and (4) the death and Resurrection there. But even this outline is developed with disproportionate emphasis on various points (e.g., compare Mark and Luke on the journey to Jerusalem) and is evidently schematic. John mentions several journeys to Jerusalem, while the SYNOPTIC GOS-

PELS mention only one, although the saying "Jerusalem, Jerusalem! . . . How often would I have gathered thy children together" (Mt 23.37; Lk 13.34) seems to imply a considerably earlier ministry there. Any attempt at a detailed sequence of events of Jesus' life will be a tissue of hundreds of hypotheses for which more or less support can be found in the sources, but which more often reflect only the arbitrary preference of the biographer for the order of one inspired author against that of another equally inspired author. Historians who have proceeded in this way have worked from the unexamined presupposition that the Evangelists were using the same historical method as they. Those who have denied any historical value to the contents of the Gospels because of the impossibility of establishing a detailed sequence of events in Jesus' life seem to be working from the presupposition that history can be written only according to modern historical method. Today it is recognized more and more that there is much valid historical detail to be found in the Gospels, but each pericope must be judged on its own merits, and one must be content with much less certitude regarding the detailed order of the historical events than was formerly supposed. This does not contradict the inspired nature of the texts.

Before the historian can begin to assess the historical trustworthiness of the individual pericopes of the Gospel material he must determine to what extent the early churchmen's post-Resurrection faith and their application of the traditions about Jesus to the practical needs of the early Church have modified the historical content of these traditions. In such an assessment full consideration must be given to the facts that the New Testament authors, who were responsible for preserving and applying the traditions about Jesus, were conscious that their work would be in vain if there were no historical basis for their teaching, that they were men of faith who had accepted the witness of the Holy Spirit, and that it was their office to present the traditions about Jesus in such a way that they could be the basis for a living Christian faith and activity. Finally, the Christian historian must remember that it transcends the power of the strict historical method alone to establish the validity of the interpretation based on faith that the tradition about Jesus put on the historical facts that it contains. In this regard the historical method can establish only motives of credibility. (*See* JESUS CHRIST, BIOGRAPHICAL STUDIES OF.)

The Historical Jesus

Once the difficulties inherent in the sources have been taken into account, it is possible to assert a great deal concerning the life and teachings of Jesus.

Outline of Main Events in the Life of Jesus Christ. It is possible to group the following events into a rough

biographical outline without claiming to give an exhaustive listing of facts that can be established by modern historical method.

Family Background and Early Life. Although born in Bethlehem before the death of HEROD THE GREAT (d. 4 B.C.), Jesus grew up in Nazareth in Galilee (*see* INFANCY NARRATIVES). JOSEPH, the carpenter, was popularly accepted as His father. His mother's name was Mary (*see* MARY, BLESSED VIRGIN, I). James, Joseph (or Joses), Simon, and Jude were the names of close relatives, called simply BROTHERS of Jesus in the New Testament. We have no information about His early training. No doubt He spoke Aramaic. His later activity in the synagogues indicates He could read the Old Testament in Hebrew. He could have known some Greek, but there is no evidence that Greek thought influenced Him.

Public Life in Galilee. At about the age of 30 Jesus was baptized by JOHN THE BAPTIST (*see* BAPTISM OF THE LORD; TEMPTATIONS OF JESUS). He did not become a follower of John, but went back to Galilee and lived a life in many respects like that of the RABBIS. He spoke in the synagogues, debated with the SCRIBES, sometimes using their methods of exposition of the Scriptures, and gathered disciples and taught them. In other respects His life was in marked contrast to that of a rabbi. He often taught in the open, in the streets, by the Sea of Galilee, in the fields. He associated freely with the classes of people the rabbis made a point of avoiding—women, children, tax collectors, sinners, the poor "people of the land" who had no knowledge of the Law. The enthusiasm of the crowds was due in large part to His miraculous healing activity and His concern to relieve suffering. His usual method of teaching on His own authority and the main burden of His teaching were different from those of the rabbis. The result was that the rabbis did not accept Him as one of their own, but were often in open hostility to Him.

There is no way of knowing the precise length of this period of His life. The Synoptics mention only one Passover, whereas the Fourth Gospel mentions at least three without making any claim that the listing is exhaustive. Perhaps this period extended over three or four years or even longer.

Ministry in Jerusalem. An important turning point in Jesus' life was His final journey to Jerusalem. On this occasion He openly confronted the highest authorities of Judaism and forced a showdown by His authoritative entry into the city and Temple and by His bold activities and teaching there. He ate a last supper with His disciples, after which He was arrested, tried by the Jewish authorities, found guilty of blasphemy, and turned over to the Roman authorities on charges of sedition; He died on a

Friday afternoon by crucifixion and was buried. These events occurred while Pontius Pilate was governor of Judea, a post he held from A.D. 26 to 36. One can only conjecture about a more precise date for His death. (*See* PASSION OF CHRIST, I.)

Nothing relating to Jesus can be more firmly established by the historical method than the early Christian conviction that Jesus rose from the dead. This conviction is not the particular experience of a few enthusiasts or a particular theological opinion of a few Apostles that carried the day, but is found wherever there were early Christian witnesses and communities, no matter how varied their emphasis in teaching might be. The Resurrection, however, as a mystery of faith cannot be proved by the modern historical method alone, but it can be shown to be most reasonable.

Characteristics of Jesus as Man. A historical study of the ''Man, Christ Jesus'' (1 Tm 2.5) has much more to offer than the meager outline just presented. Although the Gospels tell us nothing about the external appearance of Jesus, He could hardly have been repulsive. He must have been physically strong to stand up under the heat, cold, hunger, journeys, incessant activity, and the importunity of the crowds. The ease with which He turned to nature and the ways of men for illustrations in His teaching show Him to have been sensitive, appreciative, and observant of His surroundings. Yet the traditions about Jesus show practically no interest in these aspects of His personality.

The Gospels are made up almost exclusively of a series of vignettes in which a procession of very real and very different people come into contact with Jesus. He went out to them, met them, spoke to them, and interacted with them. Out of these accounts of the interplay of personalities emerges a dynamically attractive and distinctive historical person.

He was approachable and open to fishermen, farmers, Scribes, Pharisees, tax collectors, public sinners, officials in government, members of the Sanhedrin, and children. If they were hesitant, He invited them to come. He was adaptable to the demands they made on Him. This indicates a deep concern for the welfare of each individual who came into contact with Him, a willingness to become genuinely involved with the concerns of the people, and a capacity for great self-sacrifice.

He showed Himself to be a man of perception and penetrating insight into inner thoughts and motivations. Every scene described in the Gospels shows Jesus dealing with the situation according to the kind of person He encountered. He saw through His opponents, disarmed their objections, answered their unspoken questions, or

forced them to give the answer for themselves. He forgave the paralytic's sins, although only a cure was explicitly requested. He often healed the sick, sometimes put them off to test them, or He refused, as He did at Nazareth, if He failed to find the acceptance of Him that He called faith. He was often at hand to help when the well-disposed were hesitant to ask.

He reacted to each situation with honest and appropriate emotion. He showed pity and compassion to the sufferer, such as the blind and the lame; the confused, such as Nicodemus; the self-disgusted sinner, such as the woman who bathed His feet with tears; the inadequate rich young man; and the superficial. He was encouraging to the sincere, demanding upon the self-interested, sometimes impatient with the obtuse disciples who were slow to understand, angry with the obstinate Pharisees and the perverse demons. There was no sham in Him, and He left no room for it in others. His behavior was often at variance with what was expected because of prejudice or unthinking convention, e.g., eating with tax collectors. Those who only imperfectly understood His purposes and goals could not sway Him. He fled from the crowds that tried to make Him king. He rebuked Peter when Peter tried to dissuade Him from a role of suffering. He refused the request of James and John because it was based on a false notion of His kingdom. He set His face resolutely toward Jerusalem, although His disciples tried to dissuade Him. He obviously had a different set of values, which He would not compromise, a consciousness of what He had to do, and a clear sense of goals from which He could not be turned aside.

The overall impression to be gathered from the Gospels is that of an extraordinarily endowed, powerful, well-poised, and attractive personality, whose psychological balance and good sense no one can question. But there hangs over Jesus a sense of mystery, a sense of unmistakable otherness that no amount of analysis of human traits can explain. It is the secret both of His influence and of His rejection.

The Teaching of Jesus. While Jesus knew, and on occasion used, the methods of the rabbis, more often His teaching was wonderfully direct, clear, simple, and within the grasp of His hearers, without appeal to the authority of tradition or even of Scripture. His manner of speaking was concrete, living, striking. At other times His words were paradoxical, hyperbolic, provocative of thought, and calling for a reexamination of conventional positions. (*See* PARABLES OF JESUS.)

Jesus' Jewish contemporaries found their God and their self-identity in God's great acts of the past and in the hope for future restoration of their life and character. The present was looked upon as a time of preserving what

God had done, summed up in the covenant Law, and of waiting for the fulfillment of the promises. Consequently the present was relatively insignificant. What was startlingly new about Jesus' proclamation was that the present had become significant because "the time is fulfilled, and the kingdom of God is at hand. Repent and believe" (Mk 1.15).

The hope for the future had been summed up in the catchword, KINGDOM OF GOD, i.e., reign of God, the time of God's final interventions. With the appearance of Jesus, this definitive rule of God was at hand. Old methods of teaching designed to preserve, explain, and apply the covenant Law were no longer adequate. There was no longer time for procrastination in declaring oneself. To repent past duplicity and to submit to the present activity of God whatever may be its consequences were the "faith" that Jesus demanded. God and His will were inescapable present realities in the person, teaching, and activity of Jesus. The old era was drawing to a close. The Scribes and PHARISEES, the guardians of the Law, rebelled because they saw Jesus' teaching as an attack on the Law and tradition. The demons cried out because they sensed an encroachment on their sphere of power. His own relatives and neighbors thought Him mad. But the disinherited of this world marveled, and those of good will praised God.

What was Jesus' attitude toward the Law, the study and observance of which was the prime religious practice of His fellow Jews? From a superficial reading of the Gospels His attitude seems ambiguous. On the one hand, He showed respect for the Pharisees, the recognized men of the Law, by being a guest in their homes. He said of them, without trace of irony, "The Scribes and the Pharisees have sat on the chair of Moses. All things, therefore, that they command you, observe and do" (Mt 23.2–3). He sent the healed leper to the priests as the Law prescribed. He told the crowds, "Do not think that I have come to destroy the Law or the Prophets. I have not come to destroy, but to fulfill" (Mt 5.17). At other times He vehemently condemned certain interpretations and extensions of the Law and refused to conform His actions to them, e.g., the interpretations of what constituted work forbidden on the Sabbath. He ignored Mosaic prescriptions about ritual cleanliness and dietary restrictions (Mk 7.15). On the question of divorce He pronounced against an explicit Mosaic prescription explaining that "by reason of the hardness of your heart he [Moses] wrote you that commandment" (Mk 10.5).

In the SERMON ON THE MOUNT Jesus contrasted His understanding of the Law with what "was said to the ancients." It was a question not only of murder, adultery, etc., but even of wrath, the lustful look, the "legal" di-

vorce, the mere oath (by which one word is singled out above others as true), the degree of retaliation that falls within the limits of the Law, the kind of love that excludes the enemy—all these were equally against the Law.

To understand Jesus' attitude toward the Law it is necessary to consider the more fundamental concern of Jesus already alluded to. From many passages, especially in John, but also in the Synoptics, it is seen that the driving force of Jesus' life was the will of God. "My food is to do the will of him who sent me" (Jn 4.34). The Law had validity only insofar as it was an expression of God's will. Therefore those human interpretations and extensions of the Law that limited, misunderstood, or went beyond God's will had to be repudiated. Even the Old Testament itself, in which God at times accommodated Himself to human weakness and convention, was an imperfect expression of God's will. If Jesus was to "fulfill the Law" in the sense of bringing it to the achievement of its inner purpose, these imperfections had to be removed.

The strongest denunciations were reserved for that duplicity that sought by a misuse of casuistry to keep the external letter of the Law, but at the same time to leave the way open for a noncommittal attitude toward the will of God. Often associated with this duplicity was the attempt to define virtue in terms of external observance and the extension of such observance to minutiae never intended to be covered by the Law, e.g., the paying of "tithes on mint and anise and cummin," while leaving "undone the weightier matters of the Law, right judgment and mercy and faith" (Mt 23.23).

The will of God embraces more than what is expressed in the Commandments. When the rich young man came with the question, "What shall I do to gain eternal life?" Jesus listed the Commandments for him, and He looked upon him with love when he said he had always kept them. But one thing was still lacking in him: that commitment to God's will implied in rejecting the concerns of this life and throwing in his lot with Jesus (Mk 10.17–22). Consequently, as indispensable as keeping the Commandments might be, Jesus summed up the conditions for entry into the kingdom of God in the words, "He who does the will of my Father in heaven shall enter the kingdom of heaven" (Mt 7.21). This is the justice that "exceeds that of the Scribes and Pharisees" (Mt 5.20).

Jesus' Self-consciousness. How did Jesus Himself think of His person and mission? Many hesitate to ask this question either because they consider it impossible to answer or because they think it too human, especially if it implies a development of understanding on Jesus' part. But the question cannot be ignored. The Gospel portrait of the historical Jesus shows Him as having a clear idea of His mission, of goals from which He refused to be turned aside. It is permissible and necessary to ask how He thought of these goals. Concern for the psychological and human aspect of Jesus does not detract from faith in His divinity. The New Testament writers who spoke most realistically of His growth in knowledge (Lk 2.52) did not hesitate to proclaim Jesus' divinity. Finally, an answer to this question is a necessary prerequisite for a solution to the further question of the continuity between the historical Jesus and the Christ of faith. One can approach the question by summarizing the meaning and significance of the titles that Jesus applied to Himself.

Messiah. Perhaps Jesus never spoke of Himself as the Messiah, and He was most cautious when others applied the title to Him. According to a popular misconception, the Messiah was to establish the political sovereignty of Israel over the whole world. Jesus knew this was not His mission. Therefore, as soon as Peter recognized Him as Messiah, He modified the idea by stressing the need for His suffering (Mk 8.27–33). By this He implicitly laid claim to the Old Testament title, Servant of the Lord. When the high priest asked Him if He were the Messiah, He qualified His answer by a reference to the exalted Son of Man of Daniel (Mk 14.62; cf. Dn 7.13).

Jesus' reluctance to use the title was not shared by the first Christians. By the end of the Apostolic age the term CHRIST (χριστός, the Greek translation of the Hebrew *mašîaḥ,* messiah) had lost its character as a title and was considered part of the personal name, Jesus Christ. The early Church must have found no better title by which to present the meaning of Jesus to the Jews as the fulfillment of the destiny of Israel. It had the further advantage of emphasizing the transcendent kingly nature and rule of Jesus in the kingdom He had established. The danger of political misunderstanding was no longer present since Jesus was no longer physically present. Thus, the confession of faith that first distinguished the Christian was "Jesus is the Christ."

Servant of the Lord. Deutero-Isaiah described a mysterious figure called simply the Servant. The essential characteristic of this Servant of Yahweh is that he suffers vicariously for the many who deserve to suffer and by so doing establishes the right relationship between God and men. In regard to the possible connection between the suffering Servant and Jesus' self-consciousness, two related questions must be asked: did Jesus see a place for suffering in the fulfillment of His mission, and did He explain the meaning of such suffering in terms of the Servant concept?

There are a number of statements attributed to Jesus in the Gospels that either imply or state that Jesus foresaw suffering and even violent death as part of His mission. Some of these (Mk 2.20; Lk 13.33; Mt 12.40) may reflect concerns of the early Church or the theology of the Evangelists. Both Mark and Luke, however, have the saying about the special baptism with which Jesus must be baptized, and from the context of Mark it is clear that this refers at least to a painful death (Mk 10.38; Lk 12.50).

The strongest argument, however, for the assertion that Jesus foresaw a painful death is found in the triple prediction of the Passion found in each of the Synoptic Gospels. Although it is possible or even likely that some details in these predictions were drawn from the actual event, the strong rebuke administered to Peter, "Get behind me, satan" (Mt 8.33), makes sense only as a response to Peter's incomprehension of the fact that Jesus the Messiah must suffer.

Concerning the question of Jesus' use of the Servant concept to explain the purpose of His suffering, it must be admitted that only Luke explicitly cites the Isaian poems in a saying of Jesus placed just before the agony in the garden (Lk 22.37; cf. Is 53.12). More significant, however, are certain allusions to the Servant poems in sayings of Jesus that are generally considered authentic. According to all the Gospels, Jesus used the Last Supper as the occasion for explaining the meaning of His approaching death. In blessing the cup of wine, He spoke of His blood that was to be "poured out for the many" (Mk 14.24), a probable allusion to Is 52.13–53.12, where the Servant is said to pour out his life and where the recipients of the Servant's blessings are four times designated as "the many." An even clearer allusion to the same poem is found in the saying of Jesus that "the Son of Man also has not come to be served but to serve, and to give his life as a ransom for many" (Mk 10.45).

From Acts and the Christological hymn in Phil 2.5–11 it is seen that the early Church used the Servant concept to explain the significance of Jesus' death; but this approach soon fell into disuse. Thus the most plausible historical reconstruction of the use of the Servant theology seems to be that Jesus used allusion or even direct reference to the Servant to explain His understanding of the purpose of His life and to modify the popular misconceptions associated with the term Messiah. The early Church followed His example and found this concept useful while still in a Jewish environment, but less effective in a Gentile one.

Prophet. On several occasions after Jesus had worked wonders, His contemporaries referred to Him as a PROPHET (Lk 7.16). Jesus accepted the title when He applied to Himself the saying, "A prophet is not without honor except in his own country" (Mk 6.4). This title may have contributed to His consciousness of the necessity of His suffering since throughout the Old Testament the prophet was a man of unmerited suffering. However, both Jesus and the early Church found this title inadequate as an explanation of Jesus.

There was also a great deal of speculation about a special prophet—"the Prophet"—who would come to usher in messianic times. The current speculation pictured him in various ways: a great prophet of the past as ELIJAH returned, a prophet who is the forerunner of God Himself in His final intervention or the forerunner of the Messiah. While certain elements of the crowds speculated about whether Jesus was this Prophet (Mk 8.28), it seems that Jesus never so considered Himself. In the Synoptics John the Baptist is described as fulfilling this expectation. John the Evangelist, perhaps, saw some truth in this explanation of the role of Jesus.

Son of Man. The title by which Jesus regularly referred to Himself was SON OF MAN, used approximately 80 times in the Gospels and almost always on the lips of Jesus. It is applied to Him by another only once—by Stephen in Acts 7.56. Thus the Evangelists preserve the memory that Jesus used this title to describe Himself, but the early Christians made little use of it to express their faith in Jesus.

Aramaic *bar nāšā'* (literally, son of man) meant simply a man. While this meaning can be a satisfactory explanation of the term in many cases of the Gospel usage, the Old Testament background gives the reason for Jesus' predilection for the term. In the Old Testament the Aramaic expression for son of man or its Hebrew equivalent is most commonly used to mean an individual member of the human race with special emphasis on the weakness of man, prone to suffering, in contrast to the strength of God. Thus it is used regularly by God to address the prophet Ezekiel. In Dn 7.13, however, the term is applied to an apocalyptic figure that represents the messianic kingdom of God, a transcendent figure coming on the clouds of heaven surrounded by the exalted symbols of divine majesty. Thus the ambiguity of the term made it possible for Jesus to put into it the meaning He wished. It connoted high exaltation while leaving room for a conception of Himself as the Suffering Servant, and it had not the disadvantage of arousing mistaken political hopes. The ambiguity of the term forced the early Church to explain the two poles of the paradox, and this was done by applying different titles to Jesus and abandoning the title Son of Man. Thus began the theological process that culminated some centuries later in the formulation of the Church's faith in Jesus as true God and true Man.

Son of God. The early Church professed its faith in the divinity of Jesus by the confession, "Jesus is the SON OF GOD." All the books of the New Testament contain this confession in one form or another. It is the key to the understanding of Mark's Gospel (see MARK, GOSPEL ACCORDING TO ST.), the climax of which is the exclamation of the centurion, "Truly this man was the Son of God" (Mk 15.39). Mark draws up his account of Jesus' life to lead the reader to make these words of the centurion his own profession of faith.

It is doubtful that Jesus ever made an explicit claim to be divine during His public life. Such a claim by one who was so obviously a man would have been dismissed as madness. Upon the supposition that Jesus was conscious of being divine, what course was open to Him other than that described by Mark? Jesus worked wonders for which there was no human explanation; He forgave sin; He taught in a way that indicated He was more than man, drawing the authority for His teaching from Himself and not from anything outside Himself, not even from the Scriptures. According to Matthew, Luke, and John, Jesus carefully depicted His unique relationship to God by the way He referred to Him as "my Father." He indicated that He was conscious of a unity of will and activity with God. His actions and words would be enigmatic if considered those of a simple man, no matter how highly endowed by God. His life, death, and Resurrection were all preparation for the reception of the witness of the Holy Spirit that Jesus was the Son of God. Thus the Evangelists were being faithful to a key fact of Jesus' life and person when they made explicit something that from the nature of things Jesus could only imply during His public life. Historical research can show the reasonableness of faith in the divinity of Jesus. It cannot be a substitute for this act of faith.

Christological Titles Originating in the Apostolic Church

The cautious and sometimes mysterious self-revelation of Jesus during His earthly ministry was succeeded by the full flowering of Christian faith in Him. The titles bestowed upon Him reflect the faith of the Church in His divinity and His exalted role with regard to mankind and all the world.

Lord. Closely associated with the titles Christ and Son of God was that of LORD. The disciples had called Jesus Lord in the secular sense of master. With the Easter experience they saw a much deeper meaning in this term. The risen Christ had received divine honors that made Ps 109(110).1 applicable to Him: "The Lord said to my Lord: Sit at my right hand till I make your enemies your footstool." This is the most frequently quoted Old Testament passage in the New Testament. The Easter experience showed that the title Lord could be used of Jesus in the same sense that it was used as a substitute for the name YAHWEH in the Jewish liturgy, for Jesus in His messianic kingship exercised the kingship of Yahweh (*see* KINGSHIP IN THE ANCIENT NEAR EAST). Passages in the Old Testament referring to Yahweh and titles of honor for God (except Father) could be applied to Jesus because the divine name Lord had been given to Him (Phil 2.9–11).

The same term was an apt one also in the Hellenistic world. There the term Lord was used as a title for divinities and also to express the imperial power of the emperor, to whom divine worship was shown, especially in the eastern parts of the Roman Empire. Thus for the Christian of pagan origin Lord expressed Jesus' supreme rule over all creation as well as over the people of God. Compared to the lordship of Jesus, all other lordships were insignificant. For St. Paul the essentially Christian confession of faith is, "Jesus is Lord" (Rom 10.9; 1 Cor 12.3).

Savior. When God rescued men from sin and death, He was often called SAVIOR in the Old Testament; so, too, were the divinely commissioned men through whom He worked. This title seems to have been transferred to Jesus at an early date, but became popular only in the later New Testament writers, e.g., Luke and the PASTORAL EPISTLES. Because of the connotations the word had in the Hellenistic world, which was looking for savior gods, and especially in pagan ruler worship, this title was a rich one combining certain aspects of the title Lord with the Old Testament idea of delivery from sin and death. It may have been found more useful than the Suffering Servant concept to explain the meaning of the death of Jesus to the Gentile world.

The Word. Although the title Word of God for Jesus became a favorite one in patristic times and the center of the Christological controversies of that period, it is found only in the Johannine writings of the New Testament, i.e., in Jn 1.1, 14; 1 Jn 1.1; and Rv 19.13. While John states clearly the preexistence of Jesus, his main purpose in using this title is to point out Jesus as the revelation of the Father. God's revelation can be found in the word because He created by the word (Gn 1.3–31) and communicated Himself to man in the prophetic word spoken under divine impulse, an action that reached its climax finally and perfectly in the words and actions of Jesus. Jesus is the perfect revelation of God because He is the Word (personified) made flesh. Thus each saying or action of Jesus is a "sign" because it reveals God to man. Secondarily, John may have chosen this title for Jesus because he saw in Him the fulfillment of Hellenistic speculation on the λόγος. [*See* LOGOS, 1; JOHN, GOSPEL ACCORDING TO ST.; REVELATION, CONCEPT OF (IN THE BIBLE).]

High Priest. Later Jewish speculation expected an eschatological mediator who would bring to perfection the role of the Levitical HIGH PRIEST; this is clear especially in the writings of the QUMRAN COMMUNITY. In Ps 109(110) the king is given a priestly role "according to the order of Melchisedec" (v. 4), and this Psalm was interpreted as referring to the expected kingly Messiah. Whether the two lines of priestly speculation based on Aaron and Melchisedec had any influence on one another is difficult to determine. The Epistle to the HEBREWS made the high priestly function of Jesus central to the understanding of Him. By coming as the perfect high priest, of the order of Melchisedec and not of Aaron, He combined in Himself and surpassed both priestly expectations. Jesus was the perfect high priest offering once and for all the perfect sacrifice, thus becoming the perfect mediator between God and man because He was both God and man (Heb 4.1–14–10.18). No other New Testament writing so stressed the humanity of Jesus on the one hand, or so clearly stated His divinity on the other.

God. This title is rarely used of Jesus in the New Testament, and in most of the places where it seems to be used (the text being uncertain) there are difficulties of interpretation. The theological controversies of the patristic period have had their repercussions on the transmission of the New Testament text. Jesus is rarely called God in the New Testament because the New Testament writers preferred to reserve that title for the Father and to apply to Jesus titles that described His functions—Lord, Son of Man, Son of God, and Logos—all of which, however, contain the idea of the divinity of Jesus. The only incontrovertible instances where Jesus is given the title God are found in Jn 1.1;20.28; and Heb 1.8. While there are controversies about whether Paul called Jesus God, e.g., in Rom 9.5, where it is probable that he did, there can be no doubt that Paul believed Jesus to be preexistent and divine. He simply preferred the titles Lord and Son of God to express this idea. The few instances of the use of God as a title for Jesus come from the late New Testament writings and are evidence of the beginnings of the theological reflection that characterized the patristic period.

See Also: TRANSFIGURATION; PAROUSIA, 1

Bibliography: B. RIGAUX, "L'Historicité de Jésus devant l'exégèse récente," *Revue biblique* 65 (1958) 481–522. J. M. ROBINSON, *A New Quest of the Historical Jesus* (Naperville, Illinois 1959). E. STAUFFER, *Jesus and His Story,* tr. R. and C. WINSTON (New York 1959). H. E. TÖDT, *Der Menschensohn in der synoptischen Überlieferung* (Gütersloh 1959). J. A. T. ROBINSON, *Jesus and His Coming* (London 1957). C. H. DODD, *Historical Tradition in the Fourth Gospel* (Cambridge, England 1963). O. CULLMANN, *The Christology of the New Testament,* tr. S. C. GUTHRIE and C. A. M. HALL (rev. ed. Philadelphia 1963). L. CERFAUX, *Christ in the Theology of St. Paul,* tr. G. WEBB and A. WALKER (New York 1959). J. BONSIRVEN, *The Theology of the New Testament,* tr. S. F. L. TYE (Westminster, Maryland 1963). R. BULTMANN, *Theology of the New Testament,* tr. K. GROBEL, 2 v. (New York 1951–55). V. TAYLOR, *The Person of Christ in New Testament Teaching* (New York

"The Flagellation of Christ" by Caravaggio, 1607, Musee des Beaux-Arts, Rouen, France. (©Archivo Iconografico, S.A./CORBIS)

1958). A. SCHWEITZER, *The Quest for the Historical Jesus*, tr. W. MONTGOMERY (New York 1968). G. BORNKAMM, *Jesus of Nazareth*, tr. I. and F. MCLUSKEY (New York 1961). E. P. SANDERS, *Jesus and Judaism* (Philadelphia 1985). J. P. MEIER, *A Marginal Jew*, 3 vols. (Garden City, New York 1991, 1994, 2001). N. T. WRIGHT, *Jesus and the Victory of God* (Philadelphia 1996). For additional bibliography *see* JESUS CHRIST, BIOGRAPHICAL STUDIES OF.

[R. ORLETT]

JESUS CHRIST (IN THEOLOGY)

"The theology of Jesus Christ" in this article refers to the effort of Christian thinkers, subsequent to the New Testament writers, to arrive at a deeper understanding and to draw out the full consequences of the divinely revealed truth of the INCARNATION. The subject therefore prescinds so far as possible from the closely allied mysteries of Christ's preexistence as God (*see* TRINITY, HOLY) and of His principal activities on earth as savior of man-kind [*see* REDEMPTION (THEOLOGY OF)], founder of the Christian community [*see* CHURCH, II (THEOLOGY OF)], and source of Christian holiness (*see* SACRAMENTAL, THEOLOGY). This article is divided into three major parts. The first traces classical christological dogma as it developed in the patristic era. The second describes its development in the context of scholasticism, both medieval and modern. This section of the article will close with an account of the paradigm shift in christology in the twentieth century. The third part deals with individual questions of special importance in christology.

The Formation of Classical Dogma

By the close of the New Testament period, as Pliny the Younger observed, Christians were singing hymns to Christ as to a god. They imaged Jesus as the Son of Man who at his Second Coming would exercise the divine prerogative of judgment. They pictured him as Lord, seated at God's right hand, having received the name at which every knee should bend and now pouring forth the gift of God's Spirit. They found in him the pattern according to which God had created the universe and the goal toward which God intended it. On two occasions in the fourth Gospel (Jn 1.1; 20.28) and once in the Letter to the Hebrews (1.8) Jesus is called "God."

In all of this, the New Testament suggests that in the context of their liturgical experience, the religious imagination of early Christians was so being shaped that they found themselves placing the man Jesus together with the one he called Father on the other side of the line which for Jews separates the transcendent Creator of the universe from all else. In worship they were experiencing an exigence to broaden the term "God" to somehow include Jesus as well.

Confessing Jesus as divine is one thing. Thinking through what this involves is another, and this task the New Testament bequeathed to subsequent generations. Two specific questions presented themselves. First, how can the Father be one, the Son another, both be divine, and yet there be only one God? Second, if the man Jesus be confessed as truly divine, how is the union of the divine and the human in him to be conceived without slighting one or the other? The literature of the patristic era documents a centuries-long process of trial and error in which first the one, then the other of these questions was addressed and out of which the classical dogmas of the Councils of Nicea (325 A.D.), Chalcedon (451 A.D.), and III Constantinople (681 A.D.) emerged.

Early controversies: denying the problem. Viewed schematically, the simplest solution to the problem posed by confessing the man Jesus as divine is to deny one term or the other of the tension. It was Jesus' humanity, not his divinity, that first proved problematic. This issue came to the fore in Gnosticism, a highly complex religious movement which had originated before Christianity had appeared and which culminated during the 3d century A.D. in the form, and under the more familiar name, of MANICHAEISM. Convinced that flesh is radically antagonistic to spirit, Gnostics conceived salvation as deliverance from the sordidness of the material world. Their myths pictured a heavenly redeemer sent from above to impart true knowledge, the liberating message that human beings' destiny lies in the realm of the spiritual and divine. They found a true incarnation of the redeemer inconceivable. Hence the New Testament accounts of the conception, birth, sufferings, and death of Jesus were not to be taken at face value. In various ways Gnostics affirmed that the mortal career of Christ was an illusion: he only "seemed" to be a man, he only "appeared" to suffer and die. Hence their position is known as Docetism (from the Greek verb meaning "to

Scene from the "Legend of the Holy Cross" by Piero della Francesca, Church of S. Francesco, Arezzo, Italy.

seem"). Some early form of this movement may have been known to the authors of Luke and John. Irenaeus of Lyons wrote extensively against its later, more developed forms. Ignatius of Antioch uttered a passionate warning against Docetism on his way to martyrdom:

> Be deaf, therefore, when anyone speaks to you apart from Jesus Christ, who was of the family of David and of Mary, who was truly born, both ate and drank, was truly crucified under Pontius Pilate, was truly crucified and died in the sight of those in heaven and on earth and under the earth. . . . But if, as some affirm who are without God—that is, are unbelievers—His suffering was only a semblance (but it is they who are merely a semblance), why am I a prisoner, and why do I even long to fight with the beasts? In that case I am dying in vain. [*Trall.* 9–10, tr. K. Lake, Loeb Classical Library (New York 1912—)]

The other extreme lay in denying the divinity of Christ. This was the charge leveled by Tertullian against the Ebionites, a second-century offshoot of Jewish Chris-

"The Baptism of Christ" by Andrea Pisano, panel of the first bronze doors of the Baptistery at Florence, 1336.

tianity living in Palestine. Their persistence in archaic imagery and thought-forms drew criticism from Eusebius as well; in his *Church History* (3.27), Eusebius reports that they denied the preexistence of Christ and imaged him as a messianic being especially created by God.

Arian crisis. A fierce storm arose at the beginning of the fourth century when ARIUS, a presbyter of Alexandria, resolved the ambiguities attendant upon previous Word christologies by affirming that strictly speaking the Word was not divine at all but rather God's first creature. He is the most exalted of God's creatures, authorized by God to be His agent in the work of creation, and adopted as His Son. The WORD, then, is specifically different from the Father. He is a secondary deity, subordinate in nature to, not the equal of, the Father. With this position Arius brought to its logical conclusion the subordinationism generated by various Greek philosophical assumptions in earlier thinkers like Tertullian and Origen for whom, although both Father and Son were divine, the Son, or Word, was less divine than the Father. Arius' position, in effect, undercut the reality of the Incarnation, undermined the salvific efficacy of Christ's mediatorship, and dissolved the Trinity. In response, the Council of Nicea (325 A.D.) affirmed the full divinity of Christ.

Apollinaris and the soul of Jesus. Nicea secured the full divinity of Jesus Christ but left unresolved the problem of the relationship between the divine and the human in him. This problem came to the fore with APOLLINARIS, bishop of Laodicea and a staunch defender of Nicea in the confusing period that followed that council. Though a resolute anti-Arian, Apollinaris nevertheless borrowed some elements of Arius's teaching to formulate a theory of the Incarnation that would exclude from Jesus the presence of a human soul. His motives were beyond reproach. Utterly convinced of Christ's true and complete divinity, Apollinaris reasoned that if Christ were to be one, He could not simultaneously possess a true and complete humanity. Two wholes, Apollinaris contended, cannot form one whole; two beings already perfect, God and man, cannot coalesce into unity. To ensure ontic unity in Jesus, therefore, the divinity and humanity must be thought of as complementing each other, one component contributing what the other is incapable of supplying. Hence Apollinaris theorized that the Word took a human body without a human soul, and that in Christ the Word substituted for the spiritual soul. The Incarnation, therefore, is adequately described as the union of the Word with living flesh.

These metaphysical reasonings seemed to find confirmation in the necessity of postulating in Christ total sinlessness and utter conformity to the divine will. If a human intellect and a human will were to be permitted to Christ, He could not be denied freedom of decision, and consequently there would be grave risk of His escaping, so to speak, the divine control. Made dependent on the good will of Jesus' humanity, the divine plan for the Redemption of the human race might have gone awry if a humanly free Jesus had refused to cooperate. To safeguard Christ's ethical goodness and to ensure the certainty of Redemption, therefore, Apollinaris argued that Christ was subject to transience only in His organic material being. His spiritual thinking and willing, on the contrary, were unalterable, for they were divine. He had but a single intellect, a single will, a single consciousness, and these were His deity. Thus Christ was a "heavenly human" insofar as He derived His flesh from Mary, but His thinking and willing He possessed from eternity.

Despite its good intentions, Apollinaris' position rendered Christ less than human by denying him a spiritual, rational, immortal soul. On this position, the Incarnation and redemption were drained of relevance. If Christ had no human soul, he was not like us. An alien to the human race, he could be neither the exemplar of humankind nor the model of every virtue. If he assumed no human soul, his presence among us could not redeem, purify, and divinize our human souls. This was the line of criticism set down tirelessly by the Cappadocian Fathers.

"Christ Converses with Nicodemus." (©Historical Picture Archive/CORBIS)

GREGORY OF NAZIANZUS [*Epistulae* 101; *Patrologia Graeca* 37:182–183] expressed this argument succinctly in a letter to Cledonius against Apollinaris.

An official condemnation was pronounced at the Synod of Rome in A.D. 382 under Pope Damasus I: "We condemn those who claim that in his human flesh the Word of God dwelt in place of a rational and intellective soul. Rather, instead of substituting for a rational and intellective soul, the Word and Son of God Himself assumed and thereby saved a soul like ours (that is, a rational and intellective soul) but without sin" (H. Denzinger, *Enchiridion symbolorum* 159). Apollinarianism was also condemned by name at the Ecumenical Council at Constantinople in A.D. 381.

At the close of the fourth century. In the closing years of the fourth century, the elements of the christological problem proper were in place. Against the Docetists, the Church had established the reality of Christ's flesh; against Arius, his full divinity; and, in opposition to Apollinaris, his possession of a truly human soul. Implicit in these affirmations was a notice that however the union of God and humankind in Jesus was to be understood, no solution involving either a dilution of his humanity or a dissipation of his divinity was to be accepted. This insight, however, remained negative. The crucial question still remained: how was the union of divinity and humanity in Jesus to be positively understood. This was the intricate question that largely focused attention from the fifth to the seventh centuries. In summary, one may say that an answer was arrived at in three successive movements, each of which culminated in an ecumenical council: Ephesus, Chalcedon, and III CONSTANTINOPLE. These councils dealt in turn with the challenges of NESTORIANISM, MONOPHYSITISM, and MONOTHELITISM, seeking in each case to balance the conflicting views of the rival schools of thought in the Eastern church of the era, at Antioch and Alexandria.

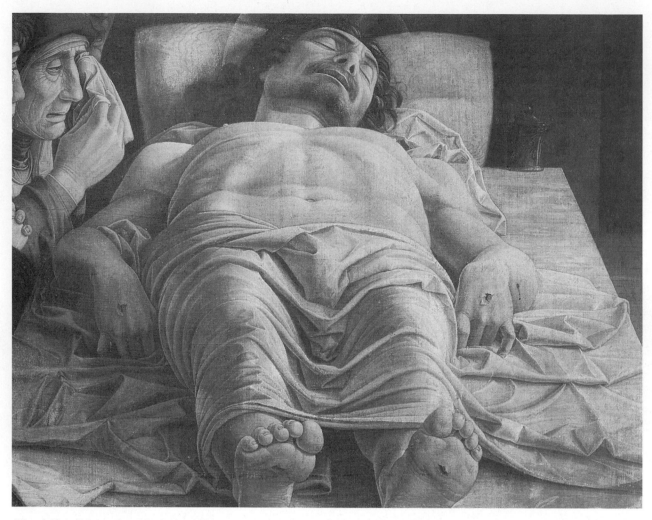

"Dead Christ" by Andrea Mantegna, 1466, Pinacoteca di Brera, Milan, Italy. (©Archivo Iconografico, S. A./CORBIS)

Theodore of Mopsuestia. Apollinarianism took Alexandrian theology to an extreme and drew a sharp reaction from the school of Antioch; the latter placed emphasis on the human nature of Christ. The two most important Antiochene theologians were DIODORE OF TARSUS and his pupil THEODORE OF MOPSUESTIA; only the latter's thought has been amply preserved. Theodore objected strongly to the Alexandrian "Word-flesh" theology. He argued that if Christ were a divine nature imprisoned in a human body, then he would have been immune from all its weaknesses and defects, such as hunger, thirst, and fatigue, since these defects are not intrinsic to the body but come from imperfections of the soul that presides over it. Theodore concluded that the Word took not only a body but a complete human being, composed of a body and an immortal soul. As for the Apollinarian argument that the human soul is sinful, Theodore suggested that divine grace kept Christ's soul free from all taint of sin. Hence Theodore of Mopsuestia's scheme

may be designated as a "Word-man" rather than a "Word-flesh" scheme. He proposes a human nature, complete and independent, that grows in knowledge and experience. He most often describes Christ in his earthly life as the "man assumed" by the Word. Though Theodore gives the impression of positing a duality between the Word and Christ, he rejects the idea of two Sons and argues that the distinction of natures does not prevent their being one individual.

Theodore's chief weakness lay in accounting for the unity of Christ. His best effort appeals to the image of indwelling. The Word dwelt in the humanity as in a temple. In support of this he cites Jn 2.19, where Christ identifies his body with the Temple. Thus the God-man is a unity for Theodore. "The Son is unique," he declares, "because of the perfect conjunction of natures operated by the divine will" (*Hom. cat.* 3.10; *Studi e Testi* 145:67). Again, "we point to difference of natures [*physeis*], but

"The Crown of Thorns," from the *"The Bible,"* engraving by Gustave Dore, 1866. (©Chris Hellier/CORBIS)

to unity of person [*prospon*]'' (*De incarn.* 11; *Patrologia Graeca* 66.983).

One hundred years after his death, the doctrine of Theodore of Mopsuestia was condemned by Pope Vigilius in 548, and by the Second Council of Constantinople in 553. These condemnations stemmed from events set in motion by Theodore's pupil Nestorius.

Nestorius. In 427, Emperor Theodosius II elected NESTORIUS, a presbyter of Antioch, as patriarch of the imperial See of Constantinople. Nestorius promptly became embroiled in controversy. Being educated in the Antiochene school, which emphasized the distinction of the two natures in Christ, Nestorius protested against giving the Virgin Mary the title of THEOTOKOS, Mother of God. She should be called either ''Mother of the man'' or ''Mother of Christ,'' but not ''Mother of God.'' Nestorius strongly objected to attributing human properties to the Word, emphatically denying that the Word participated in the sufferings of Christ's human nature. There was a union, but not a union of essence, between God and man. It was rather a ''conjunction'' which was described as ''perfect,'' ''exact,'' and ''continuous.'' ''The man'' was the temple in which ''the God'' dwelt.

The most remarkable feature of Nestorius' teaching is his description of the two natures in the God-man as a single *prosopon*. By this term he seemed to have meant an individual considered from the point of view of his outward aspect or form. According to Nestorius, ''It is Christ who is the *prospon* of the union.'' He took it for granted on philosophical grounds that for a nature to exist in reality, it had to possess a *prosopon*. Hence, the reality of the two natures in Christ demanded that each continue to exist in its own *prosopon* as well as in the ''*prosopon* of union,'' the latter resulting from the coalescence of the divine and human natures but identical with neither the *prosopon* of the Word nor that of the humanity.

Cyril of Alexandria. Nestorius found a bitter and brilliant opponent in CYRIL OF ALEXANDRIA. In Cyril's view, Nestorius's attack on the title Theotokos for the Virgin Mary meant that Nestorius divided Christ into two, the divine Word and an ordinary human being who because of his moral excellence was favored with an exceptionally full indwelling of the Word. From Cyril's viewpoint, Nestorius rendered the Incarnation an illusion and robbed Christ's sufferings of redemptive significance.

None of this, modern scholars have recognized, was what Nestorius intended, but the Antiochene weakness in articulating the unity of Christ left him vulnerable to such a negative reading. Antiochene theology began with the concrete human being whom it confessed to be one with the divine Word; this theology has often been named an *assumptus-homo* theology for its emphasis on the human being whom the Word assumed as his own. Alexandrian theology, on the other hand, began with the divine Word who became human. The subject of this union is the divine self of the Logos. Even after the Incarnation, there is only one subject in Christ. This subject, the Word, assumed human nature physically and not through some moral act of the will. It follows that the actions of Christ as both God and human have one subject, the Logos. One can therefore legitimately say: ''The Logos became human and suffered''; and also, in answer to the phrase over which the controversy began: ''Mary is the Theotokos—the Mother of God.''

Cyril began his attack on Nestorius with a sharp exchange of letters. He also sent his account of Nestorius's thinking to Pope Celestine, who called a synod at Rome that quickly decided against Nestorius. The pope entrusted Cyril with the task of calling Nestorius to order. Among the letters Cyril sent Nestorius was one that listed twelve propositions, provocative in language and unacceptable from an Antiochene perspective, to which Nestorius was to submit. Nestorius refused, and the Emperor Theodosius convened an Ecumenical Council at EPHESUS in 431. The proceedings of this council were highly irregular and confused. Taking advantage of the delay of the Antiochenes, Cyril had an assembly of bishops favorable to himself condemn Nestorius and canonize Cyril's second letter to the latter, in which the phrase ''Theotokos'' occurred, as an official commentary on the faith of Nicea. When John of Antioch and his bishops finally arrived, they held a council of their own and condemned Cyril. Eventually the papal legates endorsed Cyril's meeting, and thus Nestorius was condemned. After two years of mutual excommunication, the Antiochenes and Alexandrians were reunited through the acceptance by both sides of a creedal formula contained in a letter of John of Antioch to Cyril. The formula spoke of the ''union of two natures'' in ''one *prosopon*,'' while emphasizing the distinctness of the natures after the union. It also identified the subject in Christ as the eternal Word.

Monophysitism. Tension between the two schools erupted once again in 448, when Flavian, patriarch of Constantinople, found the archimandrite EUTYCHES guilty of heresy. Eutyches refused to accept the creedal formula mutually agreed upon in 433 and stubbornly insisted on the phrase ''after the union, one incarnate nature,'' a phrase that he had received from Cyril and that had originated, unbeknownst to Cyril, with Apollinaris. While in Cyril's usage the phrase simply meant that Christ was a single concrete individual, human and divine, Eutyches seemed to take it to mean that, though there were two natures before the Incarnation, after the

Incarnation there was but one, the human being absorbed into the divine.

After his condemnation, Eutyches fled to Alexandria, where Dioscorus had succeeded Cyril as patriarch. Flavian reported the proceedings of the trial to Rome, and Pope Leo responded approvingly with a dogmatic letter known as the "Tome of Leo" in which he affirmed the completeness of each of Christ's two natures. Meanwhile, however, Dioscorus engineered a meeting in 449, which was subsequently known as the "Robber Synod of Ephesus." At this meeting, he refused to allow a reading of Leo's Tome, rehabilitated Eutyches, condemned Flavian on a technicality, and deposed other major Antiochene bishops from their sees.

Upon the accidental death of Emperor Theodosius, however, his sister Pulcheria assumed the throne, and she and her husband, Marcian, began undoing the mischief Dioscorus had wrought. In 451, with Pope Leo's reluctant consent, they convened the Fourth Ecumenical Council, first at Nicea and then closer to the capital at Chalcedon. The definition of faith at which this council eventually arrived marks a climax to the development of christological doctrine in the ancient church. Reiterating the creeds of both Nicea and I Constantinople, it confesses Christ as one and the same, complete in divinity and complete in humanity. Four times over it affirms this, balancing Nicea's confession of Christ's full divinity with an equally strong affirmation of his complete humanity: he is truly human, *homoousios* with us, composed of a rational soul and a body, like us in all things except sin. Summing up the two sets of attributes, divine and human, it predicates of the Son, the definition of faith introduces a technical term; he exists in two *physeis* (natures), and these are neither changed nor confused, nor are they divided or separated. Reaffirming Christ's unity, it states that these natures come together in one *prosopon* and one HYPOSTASIS or person.

Chalcedon thus articulated the dogma of the HYPOSTATIC UNION, the union of the two natures in the one person of Christ, and this dogma, with its terms of "substance," "person," and "nature," would come to provide subsequent Catholic christological reflection with its starting point, terms, and framework.

Monothelitism, adoptionism. Alexandrians interpreted Chalcedon as a victory for Nestorius and rejected it, and the eventual Monophysite schism proved to be permanent. Seeking reconciliation, Chalcedon's defenders stressed Chalcedon's compatibility with Cyril's thought, and this led to a condemnation of the writings of Theodore of Mopsuestia and two other Antiochenes, Ibas of Edessa and Theodoret of Cyr, at II Constantinople in 553. Meanwhile the difficulties raised by Apollinaris

regarding a possible conflict between the human and divine wills in Christ persisted, leading some to propose that there was in Christ a single energy (Monenergism) and, as Patriarch Sergius of Constantiople had it, only one will (Monothelitism). The Third Council of Constantinople, however, meeting in 681, rejected this Alexandrian view and drew out the implications of Chalcedon's two natures by affirming in Christ the existence of two natural operations and two wills. It thus reaffirmed that the union of the human nature with the divine subject in no way diminishes the fullness of Christ's humanity.

In the following century, an adoptionist position emerged briefly in Spain. Its proponents held that with respect to his human nature Jesus could only be regarded as God's adopted son, not his true Son. A synod in Frankfurt in 794 rejected this position and repeated that the human nature of Christ had its foundation in the divine subject, the Second Person of the Trinity. Thus concluded the formation of a body of classical patristic conciliar doctrine that proved a stable possession throughout the Middle Ages and beyond.

[W. P. LOEWE/J. J. WALSH]

Scholasticism, Medieval and Modern

Western Christendom in the Middle Ages saw the development of schools and eventually universities, and the latter provided the context for the flourishing of such theologians as THOMAS AQUINAS, BONAVENTURE, and DUNS SCOTUS. Anselm of Canterbury had identified their task as *fides quaerens intellectum*, faith seeking understanding. Taking classical doctrine developed in the patristic era as a given, the medieval doctors sought to develop a methodical, systematically ordered, metaphysically coherent account of its intelligibility. Not surprisingly, philosophical differences among them yielded differences in their accounts of Christ's inner constitution in the hypostatic union and of the perfections that accrued to his humanity because of it, namely, his holiness and fullness of grace, his sinlessness, freedom, and human knowledge. If it can be said that medieval theologians thus focused on what Christ is and what he has, post-Tridentine theologians then turned to a third point, what he wrought for our redemption, devoting their efforts to systematic understandings of Christ's satisfaction and merit. Soteriology thus emerged as a closely connected but separable sequel to christology.

Medieval issues. The most fundamental issue explored by medieval theologians was the inner constitution of Christ. They sought some a degree of understanding of how it was that the divine Person of the Word brings it about that two natures, human and divine, make up a substantial unity while each remains itself, wholly unchanged. On this issue, philosophical differences came forcefully into play. In Thomas Aquinas' position, there exists a real distinction between nature or essence, on the one hand, and existence on the other. A person is constituted when a particular kind of nature, namely, an intellectual nature, receives its own proper existence. Christ's human nature, however, lacked its own proper existence, and hence there was in him no human person. In its place was communicated an "existence of union," that is, a created participation in the proper existence of the divine Word. In this manner, Aquinas safeguarded the unity of Christ's person. Duns Scotus took another route to the same end. His philosophical background lay in the idealist tradition, and he denied the distinction of essence and existence. In his thought, to be a person consists in the negative attribute of a nature not being assumed by another subject. In Christ's case, since his human nature was assumed by the Word, there was no human person. The advantage of Thomas's solution lies in the intimate union it reveals between the human nature of Christ and the Second Person of the Trinity. The advantage of Duns Scotus's view is that it safeguards the fullness of Christ's humanity in every way. These, very briefly, are only two of many interpretations offered by theologians as they probed the central mystery of their faith in search of a richer and deeper understanding of the revelation of the living God. [*See* HYPOSTATIC UNION; PERSON (IN THEOLOGY); NATURE.]

Adoration. If Christ is both God and man, what should be one's religious posture with respect to him? In his ANATHEMAS drawn up before the Council of Ephesus, St. Cyril of Alexandria rejected the Nestorian notion of "co-veneration" of the man Jesus with the Logos. Cyril set it down as Catholic teaching that the Word-made-flesh was to be worshiped with a single ADORATION. This is based on Christ's own teaching recorded in John's Gospel, where He requires that the same worship be given to the Incarnate Son as to the Father: ". . . that all men may honor the Son even as they honor the Father" (Jn 5.23). Paul repeats this teaching when he writes to the Philippians "that at the name of Jesus every knee should bend of those in heaven, on earth and under the earth" (Phil 2.10).

Hence, Scripture and the Fathers make it quite clear that one should worship the God-man. But, another question can be asked: Can one worship the humanity of Christ? The humanity of Christ is a creature; it is not God. The medieval theologians, despite their differences on the question of the inner constitution of Christ, commonly held that the humanity of Christ is to be worshiped in itself though not for its own sake. The humanity of Christ, in such an act of worship, is the material object adored, but it is not the motive for the adoration. It is worshiped

as the visible manifestation of the Second Person; and it is only the Second Person of the Trinity who is formally worshiped.

Christ's holiness, sinlessness, and freedom. A lack of common understanding of what was meant by sanctity led to controversy on Christ's holiness. Theologians in the Thomist line distinguished between substantial and accidental sanctity in the created order, while uncreated sanctity could be attributed to God alone. Created sanctity is defined as union of the creature with God. If this relationship is in the substantial order, as is true of Christ by virtue of the hypostatic union, then one can say that his humanity possesses substantial sanctity. Duns Scotus, however, seems to have understood substantial sanctity as identical to God's uncreated sanctity, and thus he rejected the Thomist position.

If Christ's substantial sanctity was a matter of dispute, his possession of accidental sanctity, that is, sanctifying grace, the reality by which a created human soul participates in the very nature of God, was not. (It is called "accidental" not in the sense that it could be lacking to Christ; that would be impossible; but in the sense that its principle is sanctifying grace, which, ontologically speaking, is an accident as opposed to a substance.) Taking their lead from John— "And the Word was made flesh and dwelt among us . . . full of grace and truth. . . . And of his fullness we have all received, grace for grace" (Jn 1.14, 16)—theologians ascribed sanctifying grace in its fullness to the human soul of Christ. Though the human nature of Christ is holy by reason of its intimate relation to the Word, yet this does not give the human nature as such a share in the divine nature. As head of His Mystical Body, the Church, it is also fitting that Christ possess the fullness of the grace that flows to the members.

The negative side of Christ's holiness is his sinlessness. Scripture attests to this many times. "He did no sin; neither was deceit found in His mouth" (1 Pt 2.22). "For we have not a high priest who cannot have compassion on our infirmities, but one tried as we are in all things except sin" (Heb 4.15). And Jesus Himself challenges His enemies: "Which of you can convict me of sin?" (Jn 8.46). Chalcedon had taught that he is "like us in all things except sin," and the Council of Florence (1442) taught that he "was conceived, was born, and died without sin" (H. Denzinger, *Enchiridion symbolorum* 1347). Besides the fact of Christ's sinlessness, it was also commonly taught that he was absolutely incapable of sinning. This followed from the hypostatic union. All actions are attributable to the person, and in the case of Christ, the person is the divine Word, making it inconceivable that he could sin. It followed further that being impecccable,

Christ was also free from concupiscence, the human inclination to sin, since this is the result of original sin.

If Christ was incapable of sinning, the question then arose, how was this compatible with his human freedom? The solution that would concede only one will in Christ had been rejected at the third Council of Constantinople in 680. This solemn definition posited two really distinct, physically free wills in Christ. In this it merely confirmed what is implied in Scripture where Christ prays in His agony: "Father, if it is possible, let this cup pass away from me; yet not as I will, but as thou willest" (Mt 26.39; cf. Lk 22.42). Again, in John's Gospel one finds Christ saying: "For I have come down from heaven, not to do my own will, but the will of Him who sent me" (Jn 6.38). Here the path to an answer lay through analysis of the concept of freedom. Freedom of choice is intrinsic to the earthly human condition, but the choice of evil is an abuse of that freedom. Hence being incapable of choosing evil rendered Christ free in a more basic sense, in that he enjoyed perfectly and without hindrance the freedom to achieve the destiny and fulfillment for which humankind is made, union with God.

Christ's human knowledge. Medieval theologians attributed three kinds of human knowledge to Christ. The Gospels say that Jesus "advanced in wisdom" (Lk 2.52). The Epistle to the Hebrews states that Jesus "learned obedience from the things that he suffered" (Heb 5.8). At face value, these texts say that Jesus did experience a definite progression in learning. Aquinas affirmed that, like all human beings, Christ acquired ordinary experiential knowledge. This was the kind of knowledge by which he came to know the world around him and the society of his day as he grew up. The Franciscans Bonaventure and Duns Scotus, and later the Jesuit Suarez, denied this kind of knowledge in Christ, since they thought it superfluous in light of the other sources of human knowledge he enjoyed.

Second, Aquinas and his contemporaries attributed infused human knowledge to Christ. This was a knowledge not acquired through ordinary sense experience but directly implanted or poured in by God. This seems to have first been proposed by Alexander of Hales (d. 1245). Thomas argued to this kind of knowledge on the basis of the principle that Christ's humanity must be as perfect as possible, to which was added the consideration that as redeemer, Christ ought to have been equipped with the knowledge that would facilitate his mission. Thus it was fitting, for example, that he be able to predict the future.

Third, it was taught that from the moment of his conception, Christ enjoyed the BEATIFIC VISION, that face-to-face knowledge of God otherwise reserved for the saints in heaven that constitutes ultimate fulfillment and happiness for human beings. That Christ had such knowledge is perhaps implied in such texts from the Scriptures as: "Not that anyone has seen the Father except him who is from God; he has seen the Father" (Jn 6.46). "I speak what I have seen with my Father" (Jn 8.38). And Jesus prays at the Last Supper: "Just Father, the world has not known thee, but I have known thee" (Jn 17.25). Although the Fathers of the Church apparently did not consider the question as such, they did frequently write of the perfection of Christ's knowledge. Moreover, it was taught that it was precisely through the Beatific Vision as knowledge of the Triune God that Christ humanly knew his divine identity as the Second Person. Obvious questions arose: how was this possession of the Beatific Vision to be reconciled with the ignorance implied in Christ's growth in experiential knowledge? And how was it to be reconciled with the reality of Christ's suffering in the Passion? With regard to the first, recourse was had to the limited character of the Beatific Vision. Christ's human intellect is a created thing and therefore finite. It could not possibly comprehend God to the extent that God comprehends Himself. Jesus, in His human intellect, does not grasp God totally and at once in a single act. This is a limitation common to all created intellects enjoying the beatific vision. Furthermore, it was held that the vision of God is nonconceptual. It is not knowledge that is expressed in what we now know as concepts. Hence it does not remove the possibility of knowledge coming from sense experience. Sense experience may well be the means of conceptualizing discursively what is grasped in the Beatific Vision. To this problem and to the difficulties offered by indications of certain ignorances in Jesus revealed in the Gospels, Duns Scotus suggested that Jesus' knowledge from the vision of God was potential knowledge. By way of contemplation He would realize this potential knowledge when His Father's will required it.

With regard to the question of the reality of Christ's suffering, Thomas made a distinction between the soul considered according to its essence and the soul considered according to its parts and powers. Thus Christ would have enjoyed the Beatific Vision in the essence of his soul even while suffering the Passion in his soul's parts and powers.

Modern manuals. Late in the 19th century, Jesuits of the Roman school sought a return to medieval scholasticism as an antidote to modernity's turn to the subject, and Pope Leo XIII commended Thomas Aquinas as the model for Catholic theology. In this context, the neoscholastic manual of christology, modeled after a tract composed by the Jesuit Cardinal Franzelin, came into common usage and dominated Catholic clerical education until shortly after Vatican II. Catholic seminarians marched through a logically ordered sequence of courses. Fundamental theology established that Christ was from God and had established the Catholic Church, so that whatever the Church taught was to be believed. A course on the one God (*De Deo Uno*) established the existence of God and God's general attributes. There followed a course on the Trinity (*De Deo Trino*), and then the course on christology (*De Verbo Incarnato*).

In one fundamental way, these neoscholastic tracts differed from their medieval antecedents. The basic unit of a medieval Summa was the *quaestio*, and the goal was enhanced understanding of the truths of faith. The basic unit of the manual, however, was the thesis; its goal was certitude, and the path to certitude lay through proving the thesis. The proof in turn often consisted in an appeal to authority, be the authority that of a council or of Scripture.

The course on christology commonly fell into three parts. First, since the triune character of God had already been established, the first issue to arise was how it was possible for the divine Second Person to become incarnate. In response, one worked out the metaphysics of person and nature as elements in the hypostatic union. Second, the ramifications for Christ's human nature of being assumed by a divine Person were deduced in terms of his human intellect (experiential and infused knowledge and the Beatific Vision) and his will (impeccability, freedom, fullness of grace). Third, an account of how the agent of redemption, thus equipped, performed his task was offered, generally with some version of satisfaction theory, sometimes with a fuller treatment of Christ's triple office as prophet, priest, and king.

Within this neoscholastic context old debates resurfaced, a new question suggested itself, and hesitations about traditional positions developed. As for old debates, medieval theologians had split on the question of the primary purpose of the Incarnation. Rupert of Deutz had been the first to assert that the Word would have become incarnate even if Adam had not sinned. Thomas Aquinas prudently disagreed. For him, scripture indicated that as a matter of fact Christ had come to redeem the human race, and regarding what might have otherwise occurred we have no data on the basis of which to speculate. Scotus, however, taught the opposite, positing the glorification of Christ as the primary purpose of the Incarnation. Thus the party lines were set for succeeding generations. The issue arose again in modern times with the publication in 1867 by a French Capuchin of a dissertation defending the Thomist view, and debate continued into the twentieth century along traditional lines, while a version of the Scotist view would live on beyond the demise of neoscholasticism in the theology of Karl Rahner.

An even more ancient debate revived when a new question came to be entertained. Scholastic theology was metaphysical in its treatment of person, natures, operations, and wills. It was settled doctrine that in Christ there was one person in whom were joined two natures, two operations, and two wills. But modern culture posed a new question: what did all this mean psychologically, in terms of Christ's consciousness? One approach, suggested by Déodat de Basly, revived the Antiochene theology of the assumed humanity, positing a fully human psychological ego in Christ. It followed that Christ humanly knew himself to be divine only through the Beatific Vision. On the other hand, the Alexandrian emphasis on the Word as subject of all Christ's activities found expression in those theologians who posited that the divine Word experienced himself humanly in all his conscious human acts. Yet proponents of this position disagreed philosophically among themselves on the meaning of consciousness and its relation to reflective knowledge.

Misgivings arose among neoscholastic theologians regarding the scope of human knowledge traditionally ascribed to Christ. Thomas had defended the role of experiential, acquired knowledge in Christ against those who found it superfluous because of the infused knowledge and Beatific Vision that he enjoyed. In conceiving Christ's knowledge, however, Thomas appealed to a principle of perfection: as the humanity of the Son of God, Christ's humanity ought to enjoy every perfection possible. It followed from this principle, for Thomas, that Christ knew all that could be known, that no ignorance could be ascribed to Christ, and that he did not learn from other people. Indeed, Christ freely assumed only those human weaknesses necessary for his redemptive passion and death, while from other defects, such as susceptibility to disease, he was free. Later commentators followed up on Thomas with claims that during his lifetime Christ already knew modern mathematics, science, and languages. Others, however, reacted against such exaggerations by setting reasonable limits to his human knowledge. They allowed as infused only that knowledge necessary to his mission, and they acknowledged in Christ an experiential knowledge fully subject to the conditions of the time and place in which he lived.

Paradigm shift. The year 1951 marked the fifteen-hundredth anniversary of the Council of Chalcedon. The scholarship generated by that occasion marked a turning point in Catholic christology. What became clear first of all was a gap between the dogma of Chalcedon and the christology of the neoscholastic manuals. Chalcedon unambiguously affirmed the full humanity of Jesus. The manuals, however, as well as their medieval antecedents, exhibited a ''neochalcedonianism'' hearkening back to the period directly after Chalcedon when Alexandrian emphases in interpreting that dogma had prevailed.

A number of critiques of the neoscholastic manuals of christology began to be voiced. With regard to method, the question was raised whether the ''high, descending'' approach that simply and unproblematically took the divinity of Christ, the Son of God and Second Person of the Trinity, as its starting point was not inappropriate to a cultural situation in which the very existence of God was no longer self-evident. Was there not a need to render some account of how belief in Christ's divinity had arisen and developed, rather than simply taking that belief as given? With regard to content, the manuals were found to have narrowed the christology of Thomas Aquinas and other medieval scholastics. Whereas Thomas pursued a full exploration of the New Testament narrative of the various mysteries of the life of Christ, the manuals were content to deal with Christ's humanity under the abstract metaphysical rubric of nature. The manuals thus presented a christology that took no account of the specific shape and events of Jesus' life, of how his life issued in his crucifixion, or of his resurrection. Finally, besides what the manuals took for granted and what they omitted, a problem of language was noted. Simple repetition of the terminology of ''one divine person in two natures'' in an age which had come to construe the notion of person psychologically rather than metaphysically engendered on the popular level what Karl Rahner called a ''crypto-monophysitism.'' People faithfully recited the orthodox formula, but they tended to imagine Jesus in docetic or Apollinarian fashion as a historical figure whose consciousness was divine though his outward form was human, so that he obviously was capable of reading minds, predicting the future, and exercising miraculous powers over nature.

Precisely out of faithfulness to Chalcedon, Catholic christology set about recovering the full humanity of Christ. In the 1950s and 1960s, this movement operated on two fronts, the one philosophical and the other biblical. Karl Rahner, for example, drew upon his contemporary reinterpretation of Thomism to forge a theological anthropology capable of dispelling any crudely mythological understanding of the Incarnation. On his view, the hypostatic union effected the supreme and gracious fulfillment of the universal call to self-transcendence into the holy mystery of God that constitutes humanity as such. Similar philosophical resources enabled Bernard Lonergan to meet the difficulties attending the traditional language of a single divine, and hence not human, person in Christ. Transposing the Chalcedonian terms into the realm of human interiority, he showed how the Chalcedonian formula calls for a full, free, and developing human subjectivity in Jesus coherent with the contemporary,

psychologically informed understanding of what it means to be human. Meanwhile, on the biblical front, exegetes began to highlight in the gospel portraits of Christ precisely those human features—ignorance, sorrow, anger, weariness, and the like—which the dogmatic textbooks with their principle of perfection had tended to explain away.

Meanwhile, scholarly developments in other fields were making ever more evident the inadequacies and poverty of the neoscholastic manuals. In France ''la nouvelle théologie'' had set about recovering the riches of patristic theology. Burgeoning liturgical scholarship was restoring the centrality of Christ's Paschal Mystery to Christian sacramental life and spirituality. The 1964 *Instruction* of the Pontifical Biblical Commission marked the full emancipation of Catholic biblical scholars, and within a short time they had joined the forefront of their field. Their practice of source, form, and redaction criticism rendered available the prehistory and variety of New Testament christologies, while newer sociological and literary methods of analysis and interpretation facilitated the appropriation of those christologies in the contemporary church.

If the project of recovering the full humanity of Jesus began as a self-corrective movement within the paradigm of the neoscholastic manual christology, that wineskin burst when, in the mid-1970s, Catholic theologians as diverse as Walter Kasper, Hans Küng, and Edward Schillebeeckx began drawing on the results of the so-called New Quest for the Historical Jesus, a project initiated in the 1950s among German Protestant exegetes trained by Rudolf Bultmann. With this development, the ahistorical classicism of the manuals yielded fully to the historical consciousness of modernity.

This profound shift in horizon bestowed a new shape on Catholic christologies. Whereas the christology of the manuals was basically commentary on Chalcedon, the new christologies offer a genetic and evaluative account of the entire christological tradition with a view toward mediating the revelatory and redemptive import of Jesus Christ into the contemporary situation. Very often they begin with the question of the historical Jesus, offering some account of what can be known of Jesus' earthly career by historical means and taking a position on the theological significance of these historical data. Proceeding next to Jesus' resurrection, they take a position on the nature and knowability of this event and of its significance both in relation to Jesus' life and death and to such anthropological constants as human hope and the quest for meaning. Having secured the factors accounting for the genesis of Christian faith, namely, Jesus' earthly career remembered in light of his resurrection, the new christologies survey the development and diversity of the christologies of the New Testament and then proceed to reconstruct the development of the classical dogmas of the patristic era.

Within this new christological paradigm, the dogmas of the patristic councils find themselves relocated as particular moments within the ongoing tradition, normative moments to be sure, but no longer defining the entire christological enterprise. Thus relocated, classical dogma requires interpretation, while that interpretation in turn comprises only one task within a more broadly conceived christological project. It should be noted that in the post-neoscholastic situation there exists a pluralism of philosophical foundations and methodological options among theologians. These come into play in the new christologies to render the meaning and significance of classical dogma a less than secure possession. Specifically, one not uncommonly finds the formulae of both Nicea and Chalcedon interpreted as confessions of the unique presence of God in the man Jesus, a line of interpretation which some find helpful in relation to other issues posed by contemporary culture, while others regard it as regressive to a pre-Nicene stage of development if not an outright denial of classical dogma.

The first task of the new christologies as we have been surveying them is retrospective, a critical determination of what the tradition has been in the past. Next, having reviewed the tradition, they face a second major task as a further question arises. Given what the tradition has been, what should the christological tradition be in the present? At this point, as theologians seek to discover and articulate what it means for God's salvation to be mediated through Jesus Christ here and now, soteriology rejoins christology.

As the church recognizes inculturation as necessary to its self-constitution, the variety of cultural and social contexts that concretely determine the present situation comes to the forefront. Within this variety, each specific context presents its own conditions for both the intelligibility of the gospel and for the significance of its saving message. Sin and redemption are concrete realities, and their shape varies among cultures and societies. For this reason also contemporary christologies exhibit a pluralistic character.

Bibliography: O. CULLMANN, *The Christology of the New Testament*, tr. S. C. GUTHRIE and C. A. M. HALL (rev. ed. Philadelphia, Pa. 1963). R. GARRIGOU-LAGRANGE, *Christ the Savior*, tr. B. ROSE (St. Louis, Mo. 1950). R. GUARDINI, *The Lord*, tr. E. C. BRIEFS (Chicago, Ill. 1954). M. J. SCHEEBEN, *The Mysteries of Christianity*, tr. C. VOLLERT (St. Louis, Mo. 1946), esp. 313–465. P. FREDRIKSEN, *From Jesus to Christ: The Origins of the New Testament Images of Jesus* (New Haven, Conn. 1988). A. GRILLMEIER, *Christ in Christian Tradition*, v. 1, *From the Apostolic Age to Chalcedon (451)*, tr. J. BOWKER (2d ed., rev. Atlanta, Ga. 1975). B. STUDER, *Trinity and Incarnation: The Faith of the Early Church*, tr. M. WESTERHOFF, ed. A. LOUTH (Collegeville, Minn. 1993). L. D. DAVIS, *The First Seven Ecumenical Councils (325–787): Their History and Theology* (Collegeville, Minn. 1983). B. LONERGAN, *The Way to Nicea: The Dialectical Development of Trinitarian Theology*, tr. C. O'DONOVAN (Philadelphia, Pa. 1976). K. RAHNER, "Current Issues in Christology," *Theological Investigations* 1, tr. C. ERNST (Baltimore, Md. 1961) 149–200. W. KASPER, *Jesus The Christ*, tr. V. GREEN (New York 1976). H. KÜNG, *On Being a Christian*, tr. E. QUINN (Garden City, N.Y. 1976). E. SCHILLEBEECKX, *Jesus: An Experiment in Christology*, tr. H. HOSKINS (New York 1979).

[W. P. LOEWE/J. J. WALSH]

Special Questions

Theology has a number of foci of special interest in its study of Jesus Christ and His work. Certain of these, although they may have been treated in the historical portion of this article and elsewhere, receive specific treatment here.

1. BEATIFIC VISION

The human knowledge of Christ includes the beatific, or intuitive, vision of God. This is today common and certain doctrine. See the decree of the Holy Office, June 5, 1918 (H. Denzinger, *Enchiridion symbolorum* 3645–46), and Pius XII, *Mystici Corporis Christi* in *Acta Apostolicae Sedis* 76 (H. Denzinger, *Enchiridion symbolorum* 3812). Both scholastic theologians of the past and modern theologians teach that Christ in His humanity (i.e., in His human intellect, from the very first instant of the Incarnation) had the immediate vision of God. The main difficulty lies in explaining the coexistence in Christ of the vision and His Passion.

The fact of Christ's vision of God may not be explicitly stated in Scripture, but a solid foundation for a theological proof is found in Jn 1.18 and 3.11, and in Mt 11.27. Christ had a knowledge of the Father that no one else ever had, not even Moses (see, e.g., Ex 24.9–11) or Isaiah (Is 6.1–5). The Fathers, however, do not give any unambiguous statement of Christ's vision of God, except, no doubt, St. Augustine, in an indirect way, when saying that He is the only one who saw God when in the flesh (*Divers. quaest.* 60; *Patrologia Latina* 40:60).

The theological reason is mainly twofold: Christ's mission and the HYPOSTATIC UNION. He was to be, as man, the revealer of the Father; this function, which He discharged in His human nature, supposes that He knew the Father by His human (not only by His divine) knowledge (see St. Thomas Aquinas, *Summa theologiae* 3a, 9.1 ad 1). As the head and fountain of all grace, He had to have the fullness of grace, including the vision (*ibid.* 3a, 9.2). Yet the reason is not cogent. His function as revealer did not require that He have the vision from the first instant of the Incarnation; nor is the vision expressible in human concepts and terms and so does not serve immediately for that function. Furthermore, only in the fullness of His glory is Christ the source of glory for His members.

Perhaps more stringent is the proof from the hypostatic union: the two, hypostatic union and vision, of necessity go together. The scholastics of former times said so on the basis of the principle of perfection: Christ must have had all the time all perfections He could have, including the vision. Modern theologians introduce into the argument a new element drawn from the psychology of Christ. Christ's self-awareness as a Divine Person in His human nature includes the beatific, or immediate, vision of God. Here again there is a twofold approach in conceiving the connection between His self-awareness and the beatific vision. One starts from the vision and shows that only in the vision Christ-man sees that He is, as He always was, the eternal Son of the Father (cf. H. Bouëssé). Another takes its starting point in Christ's self-awareness: He knows, as is clear from the Gospels, that He and the Father are one (Jn 10.30): He is aware of being God. In this very self-awareness He is aware of the Father and of the Spirit: He has an immediate vision of God (cf. K. Rahner).

Here, Rahner insists, one has some clue to the difficulty, or the mystery, of Christ being both *viator* and *comprehensor,* not being exempt from suffering though having the vision. His vision of God is identical with His self-awareness as Son of God, i.e., it is the awareness of Himself as subject, not as object. That is why, Rahner suggests, this intuitive vision of God can be immediate without being beatific. This explanation seems simpler than the more common one, namely, that it is by a special dispensation, a sort of permanent miracle, demanded by Christ's mission to save men by His Passion and death (and Resurrection), that the glory of the vision did not all the time transform and beatify His humanity, as it did at the Transfiguration.

Christ's vision of God, it is common teaching, was not comprehensive with regard to its primary object, the divine essence; it was limited because it was human. Nor did it extend, as to its secondary objects, to all that the divine knowledge comprehends, but only to what pertains to the object of God's vision-knowledge (*scientia visionis*), not to the object of the knowledge of simple understanding (*simplicis intelligentiae*); and here it extends particularly, if not exclusively, to all that pertains to His mission and men's salvation.

See Also: BEATIFIC VISION, 6, 7; JESUS CHRIST, ARTICLES ON.

Bibliography: A. MICHEL, *Dictionnaire de théologie catholique,* ed. A. VACANT et al., (Paris 1903–50) 8.1:1273–74; 14.2:1651–53. Ibid. Tables générales 2:2583–86, 2650–54. K. RAHNER, *Lexikon für Theologie und Kirche,* ed. J. HOFER and K. RAHNER (Freiburg 1957–65) 5:955; in H. VORGRIMLER, *Dogmatic versus Biblical Theology* (London 1964) 241–267. C. CHOPIN, *Le Verbe incarné et rédempteur* (Tournai 1963) 98–100. J. GALOT, *Nouvelle revue théologique* 70 (1960) 648–649.

[P. DE LETTER]

2. DEATH

Christ came to save all men from sin and its consequences through His Passion, death, and Resurrection: this is the faith one professes in the Credo. Death, a violent death, the death of the cross, was an essential part of His redemptive mission. To be considered are the fact and the manner, the reason and meaning, and various aspects of Christ's death, in the plan of salvation.

Fact. The gospel, the New Testament, and the early Christian tradition bear witness to the fact that Christ actually suffered and died (and rose again from death). Historically His Passion and death came about through the opposition of the Jewish leaders of the time to His spiritual messianic mission—their opposition and rejection of the God-Man symbolizing the rejection of the Holy One of God by sinful mankind. With the Fathers of the Church, one may see here how God's providence allows the wickedness of men and uses it as a way toward the fulfillment of His designs. Even so, the death of Christ is not only a historical fact but also a mystery.

Manner. Death was not for Christ, as it is for other men, a natural necessity and a penal consequence of sin. He, the Sinless One, was not bound by the law of death that in the present divine economy is for men a sequel to sin (cf. Rom 5.12). His hypostatic union and beatific vision well might have, perhaps should have, excluded for Him the possibility of dying (freely); but for the purpose of men's Redemption, He took a passible and mortal human nature so as to be able to suffer and die for men. Why did the way of men's salvation decreed by the Father include the death of Our Savior (when apparently it could have been accomplished otherwise)? Because of the very meaning and purpose of His redemptive mission.

Reason. Christ came, as second Adam and new head of the human race, summing up in Himself men's entire history, to restore what was lost by the first Adam (cf. Rom ch. 5). The fall of men in Adam meant the loss of the life of grace and of the original gifts that were to be its sacramental sign—freedom from CONCUPISCENCE and from death. With sin, death and disorder entered into the world. Fallen man could not redeem himself, yet for the honor of mankind no less than for His own glory God willed—according to what theologians call the principle of immanent reparation—that one of the human race should offer condign satisfaction for sin. Only through the insertion into human history of the Son of God made man could one of the race make good what Adam undid. In that manner, St. Thomas says, the Incarnation was "necessary" for men's Redemption (*Comp. theol.* 200). Christ came and freely took upon Himself the penalty of sin—death and suffering—and by so doing He made satisfaction for the sin of man. Being God and man, He could do what only a man can do: suffer and die; and do what only God can do: have a hold on and restore the whole of our human nature and race. (No single merely human individual could do so; if Adam could so act, for the worse, it was because he happened to be the head of the race.) By the very fact of His Passion and death, Christ restored to men's nature the lost gifts, including freedom from death, and so worked men's Redemption. By dying He killed death. He rose from the dead, and so shall we.

Meaning. This basic concept of traditional and contemporary SOTERIOLOGY, expressed here after the teaching of St. Thomas (cf. *Comp. theol.* 227–230), manifests the meaning of Christ's violent death on the cross. He suffered and died in order to "repair" our fallen nature, by freely taking upon Himself the penalty of sin. He died a violent death because in our fallen race reparation of sin implies suffering unto death, and because, as theologians say, on account of the perfect harmony of His humanity, suffering and death could come to Him only from external violence. He died the death of the cross of His own free will (though His human nature shrank from it; cf. Mt 26.39) in obedience to the Father's plan of salvation and out of love for men. His death freely accepted led to a life of glory; it was a paschal mystery, a passage to life. It was also the highest revelation of God's love: by dying out of love for sinful men, Christ gave them the highest proof of love a man can give (cf. Jn 15.13) and so told them, not in words but in deeds, that God is love (1 Jn 4.8).

Various aspects. The complex richness of the mystery of Christ's death is proposed in the various theologies of the Redemption systematizing the teaching of the Church and that of Scripture and tradition. These are complementary, as it were, so many of its facets. Christ's death on the cross meant condign *satisfaction* for the sins of mankind: the offer to God of a more precious gift and greater glory than had been rejected by the offense of sin. By dying freely, out of love for God and men, Christ *merited* our Redemption and all graces included in it, removing the obstacle to grace that is sin. He *expiated* our sins by freely taking up suffering and death; He bore our sins, not by substituting for us sinners, but by doing on our behalf, as the new head of the race, what no one else could do, viz, offer *vicarious* satisfaction. He thus *liberated* us

from the slavery of sin and of the prince of this world, setting us free from sin and death, turning our own death into a sharing in His paschal mystery. By restoring grace and with it the pledge of all the original gifts, He *repaired* our fallen human nature and so *reconciled* us with the Father. His death was the *sacrifice* offered in expiation and reconciliation; it was the visible and effective sacrament of our reunion with and rededication to God, the efficacious sign of our restoration to grace, its acceptance being sanctioned in His Resurrection. The paschal mystery of Christ's death and Resurrection is made permanent in both the heavenly liturgy (cf. Heb 7.24–25) and in the memorial of the Passion and Resurrection that is the Eucharistic Sacrifice. It equally reveals the transformation of death for those who die in Christ: Christian death is no longer a mere natural necessity or a penalty of sin; it is a means of satisfying for sin and the way to enter upon glory. Both Christ's death and that of the Christian are inconceivable without the Resurrection.

See Also: CRUCIFIXION, THEOLOGICAL SIGNIFICANCE OF; DEATH (THEOLOGY OF); EXPIATION (IN THEOLOGY); REDEMPTION (THEOLOGY OF); REPARATION; RESURRECTION OF CHRIST, 2; SACRIFICE OF THE CROSS; SATISFACTION OF CHRIST.

Bibliography: J. LEBRETON, *Dictionnaire de la Bible,* suppl. ed. L. PIROT (Paris 1928) 4:1045–62. K. RAHNER, *On the Theology of Death,* tr. C. D. HENKEY (*Quaestiones disputatae* 2; New York 1961). F. BOURASSA, *Sciences ecclésiastiques* 15 (1963) 351–381. R. FEUILLET, *Revue biblique* 66 (1959) 481–513. L. MALEVEZ, *Revue du clergé africain* 18 (1963) 3–26.

[P. DE LETTER]

3. DIVINITY

Christ's divinity is in a true sense the basis of the Christian faith: with it stands or falls the religion named after Him. Of this central mystery this article (1) states the meaning as expressed in the Credo, (2) sketches the growth in the awareness of the Church, from Scripture to Credo, and (3) indicates the bearing on Christ's mission and men's salvation.

Meaning of the faith. When the Catholic Church confesses that Jesus Christ is God, it states a mystery beyond men's comprehension, yet it knows definitely what it means and does not mean to say. Christ is truly God: He is not a divinized or heavenly creature, as Gnostics said; or the first and greatest of God's creatures, Word of God, as Arius held; or a God subordinate to the Father, as Semi-Arians said. He is not a man adopted as son of God, however unique and excellent adoptionists fancied His adoption to be. He is not a mere man, God's minister of salvation, as Socinians and Unitarians felt compelled to say. Nor is the Jesus of history different from the Christ of faith, a man made into God by a process of APOTHEO-SIS, as Modernists and liberals once said and the de-mythologizers of the New Testament say today. The Church repudiates all such attempts at eluding the mystery, as it also discarded the view of ancient modalists, who, misunderstanding the Trinity, believed that Christ is not only consubstantial but identical with the Father.

The Church believes that Jesus Christ is true God, Son of God made man, the Second Person of the Trinity, who took unto Himself a human nature and so exists not only in the divine but also in a human nature: one divine Person in two natures. The man who in His earthly life was known as Jesus of Nazareth was not a human person made one, as Nestorius said, in a unique way of moral unity, with the Person of the Son of God. He was God, Son of the Father, made man for men's salvation.

Reason and history are unable to prove the mystery as a fact. The eyewitnesses of Christ's life saw the man in Jesus but did not see God; they saw only signs, the miracles, and on the strength of them believed in the divine power He claimed. Historical evidence about Christ's life, death, and Resurrection can make His divinity reasonably acceptable or credible; it cannot prove it with logical stringency. To accept the divinity of Christ requires a free assent of faith assisted by the light of grace and justified before reason by guarantees of its truthfulness. Only so can one enter into the mystery of Christ's divinity. No wonder rationalism rejects it and endeavors to explain ''rationally'' the facts of the life of Christ and of the history of Christianity.

Growth of the faith. The starting point of the faith is Scripture, God's message of salvation to men. It may be doubted whether the Old Testament writers ever suspected that the Messiah, the Savior of men, was to be more than a man chosen and elected by the God of Israel for the salvation of His people. Even though they knew He was to be the Son of God, filled with His sevenfold spirit (Is 11.1–3), this need not mean nor could it have meant to the monotheists of Israel that He was God.

In the New Testament, the revelation of Christ's divinity was gradual, discreet, and mainly indirect. One never meets a blunt statement: Christ is God. It had to be so if that faith was to find entrance with the Jews. Christ's own testimony about Himself was explicit as to His being the Messiah and in continuity with the Old Testament expectation, though He repudiated a temporal messianic kingdom for a higher spiritual one. With regard to His divinity, His testimony was more implicit than explicit, more indirect than forthright. His works and miracles more than His words were to prove to men that He had divine power, even in another way than others had who worked miracles before. He meant to suggest that He had

the power to forgive sins to the very people who thought that God alone forgives sins (Mt 9.6). In St. John's Gospel, Christ's testimony about His divinity is more definite, yet even here more indirect than plain. He never says in so many words, ''I am God,'' but He says that He is one with the Father (Jn 10.30), a Son of God in a unique sense, in more than the messianic sense of the phrase (cf. Jn 5.18; 16.25–28; 20.17). He claims for Himself the prerogatives of the divine nature and confirms that claim in deeds. He has power over the Sabbath (Mk 2.28; 3.1–5), the power to give life (Jn 10.10), the power to judge (Jn 5.27). All power is given Him in heaven and on earth (Mt 28.18). He claims preexistence with God the Father from the beginning, before He came down to earth (Jn 8.58). He claims for Himself unity in being and power with the Father and mutual immanence with the Father (Jn 14.10). In men's religion He claims a central place, the same as that of God the Father; to believe in Him and to abide in Him means to believe and abide in God (cf. Jn 15.7–8). Thus in word and deed Jesus testified He was the Son of the Father equal with Him in divinity. How shocking this was to Jewish ears is apparent from their reaction. They understood His testimony in the way He intended it and accused Him of blasphemy. Nor did the disciples understand it in any other way, but they believed.

The Church of apostolic times shared the faith of the eyewitnesses of Christ's life, death, and Resurrection. The very titles of Yahweh and His attributes were given to Christ, Lord of all, and not merely Messiah (cf. Jn 20.28; Acts 10.36). Doxologies meant to be addressed to God alone were addressed also to Christ (cf. Rom 16.27). St. Paul is a witness to the faith in Christ's preexistence as the eternal Son of God, participating in the divine nature, though appearing among men in the form of a slave (Phil 2.6). If He nowhere explicitly calls Him God (except perhaps Rom 9.5), but only Lord and Savior, it was because to his mind God was synonymous with Father. More definite is St. John's intention of teaching that Christ Jesus is the Word incarnate: Word of God, true God, made flesh to dwell among us (Jn 1.1, 14). John is explicit about the Incarnation and the divinity of Christ. This faith of the Church is explicitly referred to Christ's testimony in word and deed—His life, death, and Resurrection.

When later the Church expressed its faith in Christ, inherited from the Apostles, it said in its Credo: ''I believe in one Lord Jesus Christ, only begotten Son of God, born from the Father before all times . . . consubstantial with the Father . . . who for us men and our salvation . . . was incarnate by the Holy Spirit from the Virgin Mary, and became man'' (H. Denzinger, *Enchiridion symbolorum* 150). It could not say more explicitly that

Jesus Christ is truly God, Son of God become man for men's salvation.

It was the task of the Fathers of the Church and of the early councils to formulate the mystery of Christ, true God and true man, in accurate and technical terms, the mystery of the INCARNATION and of the HYPOSTATIC UNION.

Christ's mission and men's salvation. The Son of God became man so that the sons of men might become sons of God (cf. St. Augustine, *Epist.* 140.3.9; *Patrologia Latina* 33:541). The Word was made flesh so that men might be deified (St. Athanasius, *Inc.* 54). These words express Christ's mission: He came for men's salvation and divinization. But unless He was truly God, the Fathers reason, He could not divinize men; nor would they become in Christ adoptive sons of God if He were not the true Son of God [cf. St. Athanasius, *Adv. arian.* 3.24; see É. Mersch, "Filii in Filio," *Nouvelle revue théologique* 65 (1938) 551–582, 681–702, 809–830].

Christ could not be men's Savior and the agent of their divinization unless He were the new head of the race, the second Adam, head of the Mystical Body, in which membership is through grace. He could not be such if He were a mere man. Only a God-Man, St. Thomas reasons, could remake fallen nature (cf. *Comp. theol.* 200) or take unto Himself the entire human race to make it into His Body (cf. *Summa theologiae* 3a, 7) and the new people of God. Thus the divinity of Christ is the ontological foundation both of His mission as men's Savior and of their salvation and deification as God's adopted sons.

Faith in Christ's divinity, then, is the cornerstone of the Christian faith. No doubt the mystery that the man Jesus is truly God baffles one's understanding. Yet, from the Church's teaching on this, faith and the work of its doctors seeking some understanding of that faith, one comes to have some insight into the mystery. The doctrine on Christ, or Christology, explains how the Divine Person of the Son of God subsists in two natures, divine and human, both of these unaltered and undiminished in the hypostatic union. Christ is true God and true man. And the Church's teaching on men's salvation in Christ, or soteriology, shows that only one of the human race who is truly God could, by immanent reparation, save men from the Fall and its consequences and divinize them so as to make them into sons of God by regenerating adoption. Men's faith in the divinity of Christ, therefore, is postulated by their faith in the history of their salvation through Him. Thus, for those who believe in Christ, the theology of Christ Our Savior shows that the mystery of His divinity, for all its exalted transcendence, in the context of the Christian faith stands to reason.

Bibliography: J. LEBRETON, *Dictionnaire de la Bible,* suppl. ed., L. PIROT (Paris 1928) 4:1025–34. A. MICHEL, *Dictionnaire de théologie catholique,* ed. A VACANT et al. (Paris 1903–50) 8.1:1172–1213. *Ibid.,* Tables générales 2:2548–2655. K. RAHNER, *Lexikon für Theolgie und Kirche,* ed. J. HOFER and K. RAHNER (Freiburg 1957–65) 5:954. K. ADAM, *The Son of God,* tr. P. HEREFORD (London 1934). L. CERFAUX, *Christ in the Theology of St. Paul,* tr. G. WEBB and A. WALKER (New York 1959). J. GUITTON, *The Problem of Jesus,* tr. A. G. SMITH (New York 1955). A. GEORGE, *Revue biblique* 72 (1965) 185–209.

[P. DE LETTER]

4. HUMANITY

Jesus Christ was truly man. His humanity is not only a fact of observation or of history; it is also a mystery of faith. Hence the twofold question: What do we believe of the humanity of Christ? What does this faith mean in Christology and soteriology?

We believe that Christ was (and is) a real and perfect man, one of the race of Adam. He had a real and complete human nature, including a real human body like ours, not only the appearance of a body, as Docetists and Manichees both in ancient and medieval times fancied. For them the flesh was evil. Nor was it a celestial body, whether ethereal, as the Gnostic Valentine said, or created in heaven by the Holy Spirit, as imagined by the Priscillianists (6th century) and the Anabaptists (16th century). Christ's humanity included a human soul like ours. The WORD did not take the place of His soul (as Arius said) or substitute for the "rational" soul (as Apollinaris held). His human nature was complete with all the potencies of the sense and bodily life, no less than with its human spiritual faculties of mind and will. (Monothelites excluded the latter.) He was born a real man from a human mother, the Virgin Mary, of Adam's race (but—a sign of the mystery—He was conceived and born miraculously). Thus He was consubstantial with us. Yet—and here lies the mystery of Christ's humanity— His human nature, perfect and complete, was not a human person distinct from the Divine Person of the Word, as Nestorius implied when he refused to call Mary the MOTHER OF GOD; it was the human nature of a Divine Person. This point of our faith enwraps the humanity of Christ in full mystery. The Son of God is this man known as Jesus of Nazareth.

The foundation of this faith lies in what the Gospels and other New Testament writings say of Christ's life and death (and Resurrection). Christ is presented there as an individual man, who was born and died, who lived a human life, felt hunger and thirst, loved and wept, prayed and obeyed. To His contemporaries these facts showed Jesus as a true man. This by itself may not exclude Docetism. But Christ said He came to die and give His life for our Redemption; were He not a true man, He would have been deceiving, not redeeming, us. His human life included true human knowledge and a human will distinct from the divine will. To interpret the facts of Christ's life and message in a Docetist sense, or in the sense of His having an incomplete human nature, would basically ruin the witness of the Gospels as reliable documents. Moreover, the place that the tradition of the Church gives to the humanity of Christ in its faith in Christ and the Redemption supposes faith in His real and complete humanity.

Faith in Christ, Son of God made man for our salvation, includes belief in His humanity. Our Redemption by His Passion, death, and Resurrection supposes that Christ's human nature was real and one like ours from the race of Adam. The Son of God became man that as man, by immanent reparation, He might restore our fallen nature. Redemption supposes that He took a complete human nature. "What was not taken on [by the Word] cannot be healed. . ." (St. Gregory of Nazianzus, *Epist.* 101; *Enchiridion patristicum* 1018). In a word, unless Christ's humanity was real and complete, our Redemption could not be real and the restoration of our fallen nature complete.

Our faith in Christ, the God-Man, supposes that His humanity is not a human person (the mystery). For if it were, and if there were a duality of persons in Christ, then the Divine Person would not really *be* man but only united with a man; Christ would not be what our faith says He is. Theology may struggle to "explain" the hypostatic union and to show why His humanity is not a human person (*see* HYPOSTATIC UNION); it remains true that there is a mystery of Christ's humanity, real and complete and yet not a person, that is implied in our faith in the Incarnation.

Two consequences must be noted here. Christ as man is the natural, and not the adoptive, Son of God, because He is solely a Divine Person, not a human person. Christ's humanity is worthy of adoration, because it is the humanity of a Divine Person, and adoration goes to the Person.

One providential fact, symbolic of the mystery of Christ's humanity, is our ignorance of His human appearance. To His contemporaries this was known, but it veiled the mystery of the Person. To us this ignorance symbolizes the mystery of His humanity.

See Also: JESUS CHRIST, ARTICLES ON; MYSTERY (IN THEOLOGY); THEANDRIC ACTS OF CHRIST.

Bibliography: A. MICHEL, *Dictionnaire de théologie catholique,* ed. A VACANT et al. (Paris 1903–50) 8.1:1148–64. *Ibid.* Tables générales 2:2548–2655. K. RAHNER, *Lexikon für Theologie und Kirche,* ed. J. HOFER and K. RAHNER (Freiburg 1957–65) 5:954–955. R. GUARDINI, *The Humanity of Christ,* tr. R. WALLS (New York 1964). B. LEEMING, *The Irish Theological Quarterly* 22 (1955) 293–312.

[P. DE LETTER]

5. NATURAL DEFECTS

The doctrine of the HYPOSTATIC UNION implies that an ontologically perfect, concrete human nature was assumed by the Second Person of the Trinity. But a human nature qua human nature is created and composed, and thus a limited and imperfect nature, susceptible to certain deficiencies and weaknesses (i.e., *defectus*) by this very fact. Thus, in respect to Christ's own concrete human nature, the question arises whether and to what extent it was subjected to those infirmities of both body and soul that are characteristic of human nature *in communi.*

Scripture, while it, of course, says nothing explicitly about the ontological necessity or nonnecessity of this question, clearly testifies to the historical fact that, by reason of Christ's voluntary acceptance of all that in any way would fittingly contribute to His accomplishing the end of the Incarnation, viz, mankind's Redemption, His human nature was exposed to all those natural infirmities that are not in themselves directly sinful. The Synoptic Gospels in their descriptions of Christ's Passion and death, St. John's Gospel in its preoccupation with asserting Christ's true humanity (probably against the already rising heretical Docetist theories that argued Christ had only the fictitious appearance of a body that could suffer and undergo death), and many texts of St. Paul in their insistence on the efficacy of Christ's suffering for our salvation—all these can be seen as summarized in 4.14–5.10 of the Epistle to the HEBREWS: "For we have not a high priest who cannot have compassion on our infirmities, but one tried as we are in all things except sin. . . . And he, Son though he was, learned obedience from the things that he suffered, and when perfected, he became to all who obey him the cause of eternal salvation . . ." (cf. the 12th of the anathemas of St. Cyril against Nestorius, H. Denzinger, *Enchiridion symbolorum* 263).

Further theological determinations and explicitations are presented by St. Thomas (*Summa theologiae* 3a, 14, the bodily defects assumed by the Son of God; 15, the defects of soul assumed by Christ). He formulates the principles implied in Scripture: (1) Because the human nature of Christ was assumed by the Divine Person of the Word, it could, by this very fact, have been preserved immune from those defects intrinsic to human nature *in communi* by reason of the human nature's ontological structure; (2) but the Divine Person Incarnate voluntarily chose not to enjoy this due immunity in order to accomplish in a superabundant and most suitable fashion the purposes of His becoming man. Thus, Christ would (*a*) satisfy for the sins of mankind by undergoing the punishment due to sin, such as hunger, thirst, fatigue, pain, and death; (*b*) confirm the faith of mankind in the truth of the Incarnation; and (*c*) give the Christian an example of those virtues of patience and endurance he ought to imitate in his own life.

Finally, St. Thomas derives from these two a third principle whereby it is possible to judge whether or not a specific human deficiency was assumed by the divine Word: Christ accepted all those infirmities of nature that are not actually repugnant to the dignity of the Divine Person, and are truly fit and suitable (*convenientes*) to either the principal or secondary purpose of the Incarnation. Such deficiencies, voluntarily endured and not allowed to be obliterated either by the divine nature itself or by the beatific vision enjoyed by the human nature, became meritorious for mankind's salvation.

Thus specifically, Christ assumed those bodily defects that are common to all human nature as consequences of original sin, but not those that are present only in some men as consequences of particular causes, for instance, sickness or disease. In Christ's soul there was no sin or any irrational inclination to sin (*fomes peccati*), no error or privative ignorance, although His soul was truly passible, i.e., subject both to bodily passions and to the animal or psychological passions, i.e., the sensitive appetites (*see* PROPASSIONS OF CHRIST).

See Also: IMPECCABILITY OF CHRIST.

Bibliography: K. ADAM, *The Christ of Faith,* tr. J. CRICK (New York 1957) 210–232. R. GARRIGOU-LAGRANGE, *Christ the Savior,* tr. B. ROSE (St. Louis, Mo. 1950) 401–419. E. HUGON, *The Mystery of the Incarnation,* tr. a nun of St. Dominic's Priory, Carisbrooke (London 1925) 233–243. F. LAKNER, *Lexikon für Theologie und Kirche,* ed. J. HOFER and K. RAHNER (Freiburg 1957–65) 3:188–189. L. LERCHER, *Institutiones theologiae dogmaticae* (5th ed. Barcelona 1951) 3:124–135. B. J. LONERGAN, *De Verbo incarnato* (Rome 1961) 146–180. A. MICHEL, *Dictionnaire de théologie catholique,* ed. A VACANT et al. (Paris 1903–50) 8.1:1155–64, 1327–28. A. SCHLITZER, *Redemptive Incarnation* (3d rev. ed. Notre Dame, Ind. 1962). B. M. XIBERTA Y ROQUETA, *Enchiridion de Verbo Incarnato* (Madrid 1957), Index Doctrinarium 22.

[D. R. GRABNER]

6. KNOWLEDGE

Christ being God and man had both a divine and a human knowledge. His divine knowledge was infinite, one with that of the Father and the Spirit; and because of the COMMUNICATION OF IDIOMS this man Christ could be said to have an infinite knowledge. This article deals only with Christ's human knowledge, which, though unique, was not infinite. It examines (1) the teaching of the faith based on Scripture; (2) its theological systematization, viz, Christ's threefold human knowledge (the vision, infused knowledge, and experimental knowledge); and (3) the objection to such knowledge from Christ's ignorance of the Last Day.

Faith about Christ's Human Knowledge. It is a doctrine of the faith, though not defined, that besides the divine there was in Christ human knowledge. This is a consequence of His real and complete humanity: His human mind and sense faculties had their own operations, as is attested abundantly in the Gospels. It is, moreover, postulated by His mission to preach to men in human concepts and words the message of salvation. The Gospels exalt the excellence of Christ's human knowledge. As a 12-year-old child, He astonishes people by His knowledge (Lk 2.40, 47), and later, during His ministry, all are wondering at His teaching (Mt 7.28–29; 13.54–55). He knows distant things (Mk 13.42); He reads the hearts of men (Lk 6.8; 7.39–40; Mk 2.6–8). He foretells the future—His Passion, the fall of Jerusalem, and His Second Coming. St. John calls Him full of grace and truth (Jn 1.14). St. Paul says that in Him are "hidden all the treasures of wisdom and knowledge" (Col 2.3).

Christ Himself says that He draws His teaching from His knowledge of the Father (Mt 11.27; cf. Jn 1.18; 3.11–36). He speaks of what He has seen with the Father. Besides, He observed men and things, as is shown in His parables. He learns from experience what obedience means (Heb 5.8). He learns what was said by the Prophets of the Old Law. He asks questions and wonders at the answers He is given (Mk 5.31; Jn 11.34; Mt 8.10).

Accordingly, from Holy Scripture Christ's human knowledge appears as excellent and exceptional, multiple too—some of it He derives from His contact with the Father; some He learns from experience. On one occasion, however, He says (Mk 13.32) that He does not know about the Day of Judgment—this raises the problem of His "ignorance."

Christ's threefold human knowledge. Theology has systematized the teaching of Scripture on Christ's human knowledge (the Fathers did little more than take up the problem of His "ignorance"). Theologians have done so on the basis of two principles: (1) the principle of perfection, meaning that Christ, being the most perfect of all men, had to have all possible perfection of human knowledge (possible in His concrete situation); and (2) the principle of equipment for His mission, meaning that He had to have the knowledge of God and men needed for His mission as Word-Incarnate Redeemer. Hence theologians say that He had the beatific vision, infused knowledge, and acquired knowledge.

Beatific Vision. Concerning the beatific vision of Christ, see part 1 of this article. One remark is to be made here. The sharing of Christ's human intellect in the vision, a connatural consequence of the hypostatic union, was not immediately serviceable for His mission as revealer of the mystery of salvation, because the vision is inexpressible in human concepts. But it was the reason for Christ's infused knowledge.

Infused Knowledge. The fact of this knowledge in Christ is commonly held by theologians. They distinguish, in the knowledge that Scripture says Christ derived from His contact with the Father, the vision of God (without species and ineffable) and the infused knowledge, or knowledge by infused species (expressible in human concepts and words). The distinction may be implicit in Scripture (cf. Jn 7.16; Mt 11.27).

The nature of this infused knowledge is akin to that of angelic knowledge. Angels know not by acquired but by infused species; this is their natural way of knowing. For Christ's human intellect, infused knowledge was not natural but supernatural, either absolutely, in the case of supernatural mysteries, or relatively, in the case of objects that can also be known naturally. The first is per se infused, the second infused per accidens.

The reason for this knowledge in Christ is not any imperfection or insufficiency in His immediate vision of God; rather it is the very perfection of this vision. Because vision knowledge is incommunicable in human terms, and Christ's mission entailed the communication to men of divine mysteries, a communicable knowledge of these mysteries was necessary. And so Christ's vision connaturally postulates as its complement the infused knowledge of the mysteries of salvation. The specific reason for the existence of infused knowledge in Christ is derived from His mission rather than from the principle of perfection.

The extension of Christ's infused knowledge is conceived differently, depending on the reason given for its existence. St. Thomas Aquinas (*Summa theologiae* 3a, 11.5), on the basis of the principle of perfection, says that by infused knowledge Christ knew all that pertains to human learning and all that men know through divine revelation (not, however, the divine essence, object of the vision). He adds that infused knowledge (unlike the vision) is not actual all the time but only habitual. Today theologians incline to explain the extension of Christ's infused knowledge from the purpose and nature of His mission; this was a coming in lowliness, not in glory, and did not require the knowledge of all human learning (infused per accidens) but only of all that pertains to men's salvation (mainly infused per se). This was necessary and sufficient for Christ to discharge His mission. In this latter supposition, Christ's infused knowledge was mainly, if not exclusively, supernatural, or per se infused; in that of St. Thomas, His infused knowledge of human learning was natural in substance but supernatural *quoad modum* (angelic), or infused per accidens.

Acquired Knowledge. The fact of Christ's experiential, or acquired, knowledge is considered certain by theologians today. (It was not so in the past; for fear of having to admit real progress in His knowledge, some postulated a complete infused knowledge and allowed only new manifestation of knowledge.) Since His humanity was complete and included sense faculties and a human intellect, to deny acquired knowledge in Christ seems to tend to Docetism. And without His having this knowledge, many sayings in the Gospels hardly have meaning.

The extension of this knowledge is conceived in different ways. St. Thomas, on the a priori principle of perfection, teaches that Christ knew by acquired knowledge all that could be known by the agent intellect (*Summa theologiae* 3a, 12.1). Some commentators went so far as to say He knew all about mathematics, the sciences, languages, etc. (A. Lépicier). This, however, goes against the very nature of Christ's experiential knowledge, which, like that of anyone else, was limited and restricted. Nor did His mission require such a knowledge. Today it is commonly said that Christ's acquired knowledge was perfect in keeping with the concrete circumstances of His time and place, age and mission, and His dealings with people for His redemptive and prophetic mission.

The question of Christ's progress in knowledge causes no difficulty today and is commonly answered in the affirmative. It is of the nature of acquired knowledge to grow with observation and experience and to become more perfect. And cf. Lk 2.40, 52. Nor is there any difficulty about the question as to whether or not Christ learned from other people. St. Thomas (*Summa theologiae* 3a, 12.3–4) held that, because it is unbecoming for the first mover in any field of action to be moved by inferiors, Christ could not have been taught by others. What he said applies no doubt to the message of salvation that Christ learned from none but His Father. But it lies in the nature of one's acquired human knowledge, including that of Christ, that one learn from others; men are naturally social and dependent on one another to acquire the knowledge necessary for a human way of living. Jesus, then, learned from His parents, as later He also received, in answer to His questions, information that He did not yet know from experience. This in no way is contrary to the perfection of Christ's acquired knowledge.

Unity and Harmony of Christ's Threefold Knowledge. Christ's divine knowledge did not make unnecessary or meaningless His human knowledge. So also the three kinds of human knowledge in Christ, required by what Scripture and revelation say of the God-Man, did not hinder or exclude but rather complemented one another. The three were required on different grounds and existed on different levels, while uniting in one human consciousness for the purpose of Christ's mission.

The vision, though always in act, could coexist with infused and acquired knowledge, because it existed on a different level and was not conditioned by any created species. (But the mystery remains: Christ is both *comprehensor* and *viator*). Both infused and acquired knowledge depend on species, but on species of different origin: one depends on species infused by God, the other on species acquired through sense experience. Because the first kind of species pertains to objects that per se do not come within sense experience, they do not apparently stand in the way of acquired knowledge. A difficulty may arise, not easily soluble, as to whether the exercise of one of these two kinds of knowledge can go together with that of the other. Perhaps, as has been suggested, the experience of mystics in whom the more perfect mystical knowledge does no longer hinder (as it did in a less perfect stage) ordinary sense experience and experiential knowledge may be a hint that the perfect infused knowledge in Christ did not hinder His acquired knowledge. In the case of a knowledge infused per accidens, this should not hinder but rather help the cognate acquired knowledge.

Moreover, because the three kinds of knowledge in Christ referred to different objects, they complemented one another. His vision knowledge, ineffable and incommunicable, was the spring of His communicable infused knowledge of the mystery of salvation. Without being perfected by the latter, it was complemented by the infused knowledge, which made His mission as revealer of the Father possible. This infused knowledge, in turn, was in need of the acquired knowledge, because it was to be communicated to particular persons in the particular concepts and words of a particular language, to be learned from experience and intercourse with people. To that extent it was conditioned for its effective communication by Christ's experiential knowledge.

The three kinds of knowledge were the acts and possession of one human intellect and one human awareness; they were distinct, not separated. Their perfect harmony, however, remains mysterious; it is part of the very mystery of Christ.

Christ's ignorance of the Last Day. The text of Mk 13.32 was a problem in the time of the Fathers. Some seemed to say that Christ had no human knowledge of the Last Day, e.g., St. Gregory of Nyssa. Others, such as St. John Chrysostom and most of the Latin Fathers, rejected the supposition of a real ignorance in Christ. St. Augustine proposed the solution that has become universally accepted: Christ had no communicable knowledge of the Last Day, because it did not pertain to His mission to reveal it. Augustine said this in the context of the question about human infirmities taken on by Christ; his solution here too has prevailed: Christ took all of these infirmities, except ignorance, which is not only a consequence but

also a principle of sin (*Divers. quaest.* 83.60). According to the scholastic systematization of Christ's threefold human knowledge, one should say then that Christ knew the Last Day in His vision knowledge, not in His infused knowledge.

A century after St. Augustine, the error of the Agnoetae, e.g., Themistius, categorically affirmed Christ's human ignorance of the day. It was condemned by Pope St. Gregory (H. Denzinger, *Enchiridion symbolorum* 474). Since then, both East and West have rallied to the teaching of St. Augustine.

Bibliography: A. MICHEL, *Dictionnaire de théologie catholique,* ed. A. VACANT et al. (Paris 1903–50) 14.2:1628–65. *Ibid.,* Tables générales 2:2548–2655. ''Wissen Christi,'' *Lexikon für Theologie und Kirche,* ed. J. HOFER and K. RAHNER (Freiburg 1957–65) v. 10. C. CHOPIN, *Le Verbe incarné et rédempteur* (Tournai 1963), 93–102. A. DOOLAN, *The Irish Ecclesiastical Record* 93 (1960) 249–254. J. GALOT, *Nouvelle revue théologique* 82 (1960) 113–131; condensed in *Theology Digest* 12 (1964) 48–52. B. LEEMING, *Irish Theological Quarterly* 19 (1952) 135–147, 234–253.

[P. DE LETTER]

7. WILL

Just as there are two complete and perfect natures in Christ, one divine, the other human, there are two wills in Christ, one divine, the other human. This is a doctrine of faith, and its denial was declared to be heretical by the Third Council of Constantinople (680–681), presided over by Pope Agatho through his legates, and confirmed in its acts by his successor, Pope Leo II. ''According to the teaching of the holy Fathers, we proclaim that there are two natural wills in Him [Christ], and two natural operations, neither divided nor changed, neither separated nor intermingled'' (H. Denz, *Enchiridion symbolorum* 556).

The occasion of this doctrinal declaration of the Church was the theologico-political attempt by Sergius, patriarch of Constantinople, to reconcile Monophysites (who held one nature in Christ) with orthodox Catholics. (*See* MONOTHELETISM.) The theory that in Christ there is only one principle of operation was sufficiently ambiguous to be satisfactory to Monophysites, while Catholics might be led to acknowledge the single principle of operation as the Divine Person, operating through two natures. It even drew a timid and controverted approbation from Pope HONORIUS I (d. 638). Monotheletism, although clearly condemned, continued to count adherents among Orientals as late as the Middle Ages.

Existence and nature of human will. Sacred Scripture testifies to the existence of a human will in Christ that is distinct from His divine will. His words ''not my will but thine be done'' (Lk 22.42) were addressed to His Father. Moreover, works of honor are attributed to Christ, such as prayer, obedience, merit, which cannot proceed from the divine will, since they are manifested to a superior. They can proceed only from a created will. In His Incarnation the Son of God assumed a perfect human nature, at the same time retaining His perfect divine nature. But there is no human nature without the human will, just as there is no divine nature without the divine will. St. Thomas adds: "Whatever was in the human nature of Christ was moved at the bidding of the divine will, yet it does not follow that in Christ there was no movement of the will proper to human nature" (*Summa theologiae* 3a, 18.1 ad 1). By this one is to understand that the human will is no useless appendage but an operating faculty in the human nature of Christ.

The WILL is defined as the intellectual appetite—an inclination to the good apprehended by the intellect. As human, the will is colored by the operation of the human intellect. Its operation is twofold, one with regard to the end, the other with regard to the means to the end. The human will is necessarily moved by the concept of HAPPINESS, of perfect goodness, as well as by goods that are desired in themselves, such as health. This function of the will denominates the *will as nature*. With regard to the means to the end, to created goods as distinguished from the absolute and perfect good, the will is in control of its movement. Hence this operation denominates the *will as reason*. Both of these functions are essential to the human will, and therefore must have been in Christ.

Freedom of will in Christ. Christ certainly enjoyed freedom of will, as is evident from the fact that the proper act of the *will as reason* is to choose, and this is also the proper act of free will. Not only had Christ free will, but He enjoyed perfect freedom (cf. Jn 10.17–18). The fact that His will was perfectly subject to the divine will in no way impaired its own proper motion and tendency. This conformity to the divine will was rather the guarantee of the perfect freedom of Christ, giving it its special value, so that having its own activity, it exercised it under and in accord with the divine influence. This is true of all human activity that is morally good. It befitted Christ in a special fashion, for He was not only sinless but impeccable.

Christ did not exercise free will where other men did not exercise it, i.e., in desire for the end, happiness, in the operation of His will as nature, in His love of the divine essence clearly seen in the beatific vision. Yet it was always within His power, under the efficacious motion of God, to turn toward this or that created good, which, because of its inherent limitation, cannot fully satisfy the aspiration of His will toward the complete and unalloyed good. This is the root of human freedom.

Impeccability of Christ. By reason of the hypostatic union, His possession of the beatific vision from the first instant of His conception, and the immutable fullness of grace, Christ's will not only always factually conformed to the divine will, but, more than this, it could not defect from this conformity; Christ could not sin. It is a common fallacy that the inability to sin in some fashion curtails freedom. The erroneous foundation of this assumption is exposed by a little reflection that the power to choose indifferently good or evil (the apparent good) is really a sign of deficiency in the faculty whose object is the good as apprehended by reason.

While the choice between good and evil was not open to Christ, it was always within His power, under the efficacious motion of God, to turn toward this or that created good, which, because of its limitations, could not fully satisfy the aspirations of the will toward the perfect and absolute good. And yet in spite of all this, we are still forced to admit that Christ's impeccability presents a serious problem when considered in relation to His obedience to His Father's command.

Harmony of human and divine wills in Christ. Because He was truly man, Christ had a sensible nature and therefore a sensitive appetite. Because He was perfect man, His sensitive appetite never escaped, anticipated, or rebelled against the control of His reason. Therefore, because of this rational control, the sensible appetite in Christ is called the will in an extended sense. The field of the sensible appetite is sensible pleasure and pain. So theologically speaking, one can distinguish in Christ four wills: divine will, human will as reason, human will as nature, human will as sensuality. There was perfect harmony between the divine will and the human will as reason. Its perfect conformity was proof of its perfection. On the other hand, the will as nature and the will of sensuality, because of their natures, allowed by the Son of God to do what belonged to them (*Summa theologiae* 3a, 18.6), shrank from sensible pain and bodily hurt, as foreseen in His Passion. So Christ's words in the Garden of Olives, "Father, if it is possible, let this cup pass away from me; yet not as I will, but as thou willest" (Mt 26.39), expressed first of all the movement of the will of sensuality and the will as nature, then the absolute conformity of His will as reason to the divine will.

The natural shrinking of the will as sensuality and the will as nature from the suffering of the Passion, and the eager desire of Christ's will as reason joyfully to embrace that suffering in complete obedience to the command of the divine will, did not constitute civil war within Christ. The salvation of the human race, the reason for the divine command, is a good beyond the scope of the sense appetite. Will as nature could love this goal as a good, but was incapable of ordering the Passion to it as a means to the end. Only the will as reason could do that. Nor was the will as reason impeded or retarded by the movement of the will of sensuality and the will as nature. So, just as the human will has its most proper operation, free choice, though it is perfectly subject to the divine will, so too the sense appetite and the will as nature in Christ have their full and proper operation in their perfect subjection to the will as reason. Both properly fly from sorrow and pain, but with the limitation of that flight to the demands of reason. So proclaimed the Third Council of Constantinople: "The human will is compliant, and not opposing or contrary; as a matter of fact, it is even obedient to His divine and omnipotent will" (H. Denzinger, *Enchiridion symbolorum* 556).

Bibliography: THOMAS AQUINAS, *Summa theologiae* 3a, 18–20. A. MICHEL, *Dictionnaire de théologie catholique*, ed. A. VACANT et al. (Paris 1903–50) 8.1:1160–64, 1267–69, 1290–1312. M. JUGIE, *ibid.* 10:2307–23. *Sacrae theologiae summa* (Madrid 1961) 3:1.408–447. H. RAHNER and A. GRILLMEIER, *Lexikon für Theologie und Kirche* (Freiburg 1957–65) 7:570–572. R. GARRIGOU-LAGRANGE, *Christ the Savior*, tr. B. ROSE (St. Louis, Mo. 1950) 439–486. W. R. FARRELL, *Companion to the Summa*, 4 v. (New York 1942) 4:99–104. C. HÉRIS, *The Mystery of Christ*, tr. D. FAHEY (Westminster, Md. 1950) 63–69.

[J. R. GILLIS]

8. POWER AND THEANDRIC ACTS

The power of Christ considered here is not His divine power that as Son of God He has in common with the Father and the Spirit and that He exercises independently of His humanity in such activity as pertains to creation, but the power of His humanity. Because of its being the "joined instrument" of the Word, Christ's human nature has, besides its own power, natural and supernatural (through grace), a unique instrumental virtue, or power. The actions of the second power are called theandric in the strict sense of the term.

Christ's own human power. The power of Christ's humanity operative in those actions in which His human nature acts as chief cause, either in natural activity, such as walking, eating, speaking, or in supernatural operations, such as acts of infused virtues (e.g., fortitude, temperance) does not essentially differ from that of another man—except on two points. First, because of the unique perfection of His humanity and His sanctifying grace, these operations too have a unique perfection. Second, this activity is the human or supernatural (created) activity of a Divine Person.

These actions, however, are not theandric, because in them Christ's humanity acts as chief cause. They may, however, be called theandric in a broad sense, not only because of the special divine, natural or supernatural, help that guides them, but specifically because they pertain to the Person of the Word in virtue of the HYPOSTATIC UNION.

His power in theandric actions. Theandric in the strict sense are those actions of Christ in which His humanity acts as the joint instrument of the Word, His divine Person and nature being the principal cause. The "instrumental virtue" added to His humanity by the hypostatic union is a power that enables it to be the instrument of the Word in theandric actions. Though not infinite, and therefore not omnipotent, because His humanity is finite, it yet extends to effects that are beyond purely human or created causality.

This unique power of Christ's humanity is manifested mainly in two kinds of activity: in working miracles and in dispensing sanctifying grace. In both of these activities, the two natures of Christ are active: the divine nature as principal cause and the human nature as instrumental cause. The activity of His humanity is here raised in its conjoint activity with the Word so as to be actually the subordinate and instrumental cause of divine effects. In this sense, Christ's humanity has a unique power. When other persons or creatures are assumed by God as ministers or instruments to work miracles or give grace, their instrumental causality differs from that of Christ's humanity. They are separated instruments, persons or things distinct from the Person of the chief cause; Christ's humanity is the permanently joined instrument of the Word, the principal cause. Because of this aspect of the hypostatic union, Christ's human will and activity coincide with the divine will in a manner other created wills cannot. His instrumental causality in the dispensation of grace has an excellence that transcends that of any minister or Sacrament of grace.

Different theological concepts of this instrumental virtue have been proposed. Some reduce it to the moral causality of an infallibly efficacious intercession, after Scotus and G. Vázquez, in reference to Jn 11.41. Others, more commonly and more aptly, see it as an instrumental efficiency of Christ's humanity. This latter concept fits better such texts as Lk 6.19 and 8.46, where a power is said to go out from Jesus, or Jn 15.5, about the vine and the branches. When this instrumental efficient causality is conceived as physical (analogically) or intentionally perfective, i.e., as the expression of a divine command or will, then Christ's working of miracles or granting of grace appears as something unique, in the sense that His human will, being the human will of the Word, of necessity coincides freely with His divine will, and so the man-Christ works miracles and grants grace on His personal authority.

This instrumental power of Christ's humanity in giving grace is also manifested in the giving of the Holy Spirit; the Apostles receive the Spirit when Jesus breathes over them through the human words that He pronounces.

Another element of the power of Christ is His prayer, which has a unique power of intercession.

See Also: THEANDRIC ACTS OF CHRIST.

Bibliography: A. MICHEL, *Dictionnaire de théologie catholique,* ed. A. VACANT et al. (Paris 1903–50) 8.1:1312–23. PIUS XII, *Mystici Corporis Christi* in *Acta Apostolicae Seids* 35 (1943) 50. B. RAIGNEAU-JULIEN, *Revue thomiste* 55 (1955) 615–628. C. CHOPIN, *Le Verbe incarné et rédempteur* (Tournai 1963) 105–108.

[P. DE LETTER]

9. MESSIANIC CONSCIOUSNESS

This question deals with a fact and not the conditions for its possibility. Whether Jesus actually attributed to Himself messianic prerogatives is the point under consideration, not how He was able to do so or what type of knowledge this presupposed. The method employed will be biblical rather than apologetical. It may not, however, be amiss to note that the Apostolic proclamation of Jesus as MESSIAH presupposed His own assertion of the same. Even the hypothesis tracing this kerygma to an erroneous acceptance of His Resurrection must admit that predisposition was necessary for His followers to witness such "apparitions." This in turn has its most plausible explanation in His own pretensions before death. To investigate the function He attributed to Himself either directly or by acquiescing in the titles that others gave Him, recourse will be had above all to the Synoptics.

Although the Old Testament gave the Messiah the traits of king [Ps 2, 109 (110)], prophet (Dt 18.15; Is 42.1–9; 49.1–6; 52.13–53.12), and transcendent figure of the last days (Dn 7.13), all these were not, at the proper time, combined immediately and with ease so as to represent to people's minds a single historical individual. Even Jesus' Apostles were not exempt from a popular conception emphasizing the first to the exclusion of the second (Mk 8.31–33; Mt 16.21–23); a distinction was also made on occasion between the Messiah and the Prophet (Jn 1.21, 25; 7.40–41).

It will be recalled that the Gospel narratives in their present form were not the first books of the New Testament to be written. They presuppose an oral and written tradition; there are differences of perspective between them and other parts of the New Testament. One of the titles, SON OF MAN, given to Jesus most frequently in John and the Synoptics, appears almost never in the rest of the New Testament. Conversely, *Christ* is used in the Synoptics to refer directly to Jesus only rarely and with qualifying restrictions, though it is His normal title elsewhere.

To speak of His messianic consciousness is to inquire into His way of identifying Himself in terms of functions He fulfilled. These are described variously and can be analyzed in His titles. *Messiah*: both in the Greek text and in the Latin version, this rendering of the Hebrew is most infrequent. When it does appear, Jesus is not represented as using it (Jn 1.41; 4.25). *Son of David*: a messianic title; those seeking aid apply it to Him (Mk 10.47–48; Mt 20.30–31; Lk 18.38–39). Emphasizing the already popular regal qualities of the Messiah, the title SON OF DAVID only too easily lent itself to misinterpretation. Jesus explicitly approved its application to Himself only at the end of His public life and teaching (Mt 21.9, 15–17); He did not hesitate to point out its incompleteness as a means of designating the Messiah (Mk 12.35–37; Mt 22.41–46; Lk20.41–44).

Christ: if the kerygmatic discourses in the Acts of the Apostles apply the title CHRIST to Jesus without hesitation and the Pauline Epistles treat it almost like a personal name, the Gospels are different in this regard. When it is attributed to Him, He does not receive it with perfect equanimity. Not His usual way of referring to Himself, when He does accept it, it is an adaptation to the form of questions put by others (Mk 14.61–62; Mt 26.63–64; Lk 22.66–69), or an accommodation to their usage (Mk 8.30; Mt 16.17–20; Lk 9.20–22). This often introduces the whole into a prophetic context of approaching suffering and death (Mk 8.31; Lk 9.22; Mt 16.21), or else into the apocalyptic frame of reference of Dn 7 (Mk 14.62; Mt 26.64; Lk 22.69).

Son of Man (cf. Dn 7.13): although the title is employed almost exclusively by Jesus in reference to Himself before His Resurrection, its biblical meaning is not always messianic (Ps 8.5). Still the repeated usage in the third person (with the definite article in the Greek text), when a subject is speaking of himself, is unusual and calculated to draw attention to the speaker. In the Synoptics, the title serves to designate Jesus in His functions, some exercised in the present and others to be fulfilled in the future.

The Son of Man as pictured in the first group has characteristics that are antithetical. Lord of the Sabbath (Mk 2.28; Mt 12.8; Lk 6.5), forgiver of sins (Mk 2.10; Mt 9.5–6; Lk 5.24), the Son of Man is already endowed with superhuman prerogatives. But He lacks what even the foxes and birds possess (Lk 9.58; Mt 8.20) and is subjected to misunderstanding and accusations on the part of men (Mt 11.19; Lk 7.34).

The future role of the Son of Man is likewise twofold. Again it will be both one of ignominy and suffering (Mt 17.22; Mk 10.45; Lk 11.30; Mt 12.40), as well as one of transcendence and glory (Mk 13.26–27; 14.62; Mt 26.64). The prophetic and the apocalyptic are thus introduced.

While announcing the presence of the KINGDOM OF GOD ushered in by John, Jesus gradually revealed His own identity as Messiah in terms of present and future endurance and action. This messianic secret He did not tell to all (Mk 4.11), or to the unprepared. The progressive steps in its revelation were psychologically capable of transforming an excessively political concept of God's Anointed into a more spiritual and religious one. Whereas He is not represented by the Synoptics as rejecting strictly messianic titles, He did not accept them, in the traditions these Gospels represent, immediately at the outset of His preaching without qualification and clarification. The designation He Himself chose to use included in its meaning the simultaneous verification of opposites in the present, together with emphasis on a future when He would realize in Himself transcendent apocalyptic glory through and after suffering as Yahweh's Servant (see SUFFERING SERVANT, SONGS OF). Before His death and Resurrection, He was already the Messiah and conscious of so being, but His messianic work was as yet incomplete. This temporal element in His progressive verification and manifestation of messianic properties was better expressed with a term that did not connote immediately the idea of triumph complete from the start. In this perspective certain messianic titles, with the associations they had at the time, were more likely to confuse than convey the desired message. Their avoidance and the choice of another term capable of progressive development and explanation are hardly coincidental in the Synoptics.

See Also: JESUS CHRIST, IN THE BIBLE; MESSIAH; MESSIANISM.

Bibliography: A. MICHEL, *Dictionnaire de théologie catholique,* ed. A. VACANT et al. (Paris 1903–50), Tables générales 2:2551–53, 2598–2605, 2621–23. H. GROSS et al., *Lexikon für Theologie und Kirche,* ed. J. HOFER and K. RAHNER (Freiburg 1957–65) 7:336–342. A. Vögtle, *ibid.* 7:297–300. A. VÖGTLE and R. SCHNACKENBURG, *ibid.* 7:922–940, *Encyclopedic Dictionary of the Bible,* tr. and adap. L. HARTMAN (New York 1963) 1142–56, 1510–25. E. DHANIS, "De filio hominis in Vetere Testamento et in iudaismo," *Gregorianum* 45 (1964) 5–59, R. BULTMANN, *Theology of the New Testament,* tr. K. GROBEL, 2 v. (New York 1951–55).

[C. J. PETER]

10. PSYCHOLOGICAL UNITY

No more is intended in what follows than an exposition of the general positions taken by Catholic theologians. First, however, some explanation is necessary about the point under consideration. That Jesus Christ is unique in His divine personality and dual in His natures is an article of faith; whatever He did, whatever He endured, it was God the Son who was acting and suffering. This faith has its origin in Christ's revelation of His own ontological unity, that of a subject with attributes both divine and human. But to communicate this mystery of His unity to others in word and deed, He had first somehow to come to know it Himself.

If He enjoyed a variety of types of intellectual knowledge, how was it that He recognized Himself as the common subject of them all? Did He know Himself as such only as an object of contemplation in the vision of God? Or was He aware of this fact in other ways as well? Was the ego of the Suffering Servant divine or human? If the first, was the Word of God conscious of Himself in the pain experienced through and in and by virtue of His body and soul? Christ's subjective unity as grasped in His life of sense experience, intellection, and affection is what will be discussed here. What were the psychological conditions presupposed by His revelation of His oneness? How did that experience or knowledge arise?

Presuppositions. Constants appear in most Catholic attempts to answer these questions. The first is that in Jesus of Nazareth the one Person is that of the Word, who alone became incarnate and was man. The Father and Holy Spirit could not be conscious of themselves in His humanity since it belonged to or was united to the Person of neither of them. Second, no operation of the Son through the divine nature is proper to Him alone. Furthermore, a complete and perfect humanity in Christ is in no way impeded by either of the foregoing. If unconscious suffering is not real for man, neither is it for Him. Finally He had a special knowledge, usually reserved for the blessed in the final phase of God's kingdom, the vision of God. In this He saw the Word and His own human nature. He recognized that He was God the Word made man and realized that the ultimate subject of His human activity was the eternal Son of God.

Theologians discuss whether or not He *experienced* the same divine subject in acts of human knowledge other than beatific. When He was hungry, thirsty, tired, scourged, and crucified, was His divine Ego aware of itself in a human way precisely because of and in this sense experience? Was the Word conscious of Himself in all the acts of sensation, knowledge, and love realized in His humanity?

Here profound differences appear, based on philosophical conceptions of CONSCIOUSNESS. These are probably as much as any other the reason for the diverse theological opinions. Consciousness is proposed as the exercise of introspection or reflection in which the feeling, knowing, loving subject becomes the object of explicit consideration. As such it could not properly speaking be found in God, who knows Himself without reflecting on any prior act of cognition or volition. If not this, then consciousness is the self-presence or awareness a subject necessarily has of itself in every psychological act. Such experience provides the prerequisite data for introspection and for scientific studies of the subject as such. In addition, there is disagreement as to whether an ontological unity of person is compatible with a plurality of psychological egos. Must the latter be really identified with the person?

Theology of the assumed humanity. This theory is preoccupied with preserving the psychological integrity of the manhood in Jesus. What was present through reflection on acts of knowing and loving was a human ego. In this His situation was like that of other men. But He was different, since His Person was not human but divine. In His purely human or natural acts, He was present to Himself without being aware of the fact that He was the eternal Son of God. The latter He was and realized full well in an act of human knowledge that was supernatural, namely, the vision of God. Knowing Himself as the Word, He was nevertheless not strictly conscious of so being in acts other than the beatific vision. What He was conscious of in such activity was what appeared to Him in introspective reflection; that was a human ego, as His human nature was complete and the principle of His human actions. The subject of that ego was recognized as a Divine Person only through the beatific vision.

Theology of God-with-Us. The distinguishing characteristic of this theology, which embraces a number of different opinions, is that it maintains that Christ is conscious of His divine Ego through and by virtue of human acts other than the vision of God. What He experienced in such activity is not a human ego but the divine Ego of the Word. That experience of the eternal Word, however, is not described by all in the same way. It may take place in an act of reflection on one that precedes it; or it may be presupposed by and offer the grounds for such reflection. In either case, the reality experienced is divine though present in a human way. So too, though a divine Ego is experienced or falls within the field of human consciousness, the vision of God may be a necessary complement to it for Christ's *assertion* of identity between the subject He experienced and what He knew of God's own Son.

See Also: COMMUNICATION OF IDIOMS; HYPOSTATIC UNION; INCOMMUNICABILITY; PERSON (IN THEOLOGY); THEANDRIC ACTS OF CHRIST.

Bibliography: A. MICHEL, *Dictionnaire de théologie catholique,* ed. A. VACANT et al. (Paris 1903–50), Tables générales 2:2650–54. K. RAHNER, *Lexikon für Theologie und Kirche,* ed. J. HOFER and K. RAHNER (Freiburgh 1957–65) 5:959–961. "Wissen Christi," *ibid.,* v. 10. P. GALTIER, *L'Unité du Christ* (2d ed. Paris 1939). P. PARENTE, *L'Io di Cristo* (2d ed. Brescia 1955). B. J. LONERGAN, *De constitutione Christi ontologica et psychologica* (3d ed. Rome 1961). H. DIEPEN, *La Théologie de L'Emmanuel* (Bruges 1960).

[C. J. PETER]

11. PROPHET, PRIEST, AND KING

In treating of the incarnate Word's principal activity of REDEMPTION, many theologians prefer to propound the doctrine by considering the three messianic offices or functions of Christ, which can fittingly be said to comprehend His whole work as Redeemer and Mediator: (1) the prophetic or magisterial office, (2) the sacerdotal office, and (3) the kingly office. A detailed study of these three is ordinarily preceded by general considerations of the concept of Redemption, i.e., the unique restitution of the ORIGINAL JUSTICE mankind possessed before the Fall.

Prophetic or magisterial office. The scriptural teaching (especially of St. John) concerning Jesus as the LOGOS or WORD of the Father and the many related themes (e.g., wisdom, light, truth) stress the fact that man's attaining Redemption or salvation requires his coming to know God and God's positive will as revealed in sacred history. Thus Jesus must, first of all, be the concrete manifestation of God's will for man, i.e., of the divine precepts and promises: "Now this is everlasting life, that they may know thee, the only true God, and him whom thou hast sent, Jesus Christ" (Jn 17.3; cf. Heb 1.1–5).

The infallible efficacy of Christ's teaching power (*magisterium*) in bringing mankind to that indispensable knowledge of faith that is necessary for salvation derives ultimately from the fact that He is a Divine Person and thus uniquely enabled to know and make known the eternal MYSTERY of the Father's will: "All things have been delivered to me by my Father; and no one knows the Son except the Father; nor does anyone know the Father except the Son, and him to whom the Son chooses to reveal him" (Mt 1 1.27).

The infallible magisterium of the Church, by reason of Christ's authentic delegation of power and mission to teach given to the Apostles and their successors, is thus ultimately a participation in Christ's unique teaching power.

Sacerdotal office. The consideration of Christ in His priesthood, perhaps more than in any other aspect, brings out the totality of His mediatorship between God and man. As eternal High Priest, He offers Himself as a perfectly dedicated and consecrated Victim in a sacrifice of adoration, praise, thanksgiving, petition, and vicarious reparation, an infinitely pleasing sacrifice to God the Father. Thus He restores that intimate union between God and man that had been destroyed through sin.

The principal treatment in Scripture of Christ's priesthood and sacrifice is the Epistle to the HEBREWS, in which the author, through a detailed comparison of the New Covenant with the Old Covenant, shows the infinite superiority of the one over the other; he insists that Christ, called to this task by a unique vocation of God and taken from among men, whose lot He has shared in all things except sin, exercises a priesthood and offers a sacrifice that has a once-for-all and eternal efficacy: "It was fitting that we should have such a high priest, holy, innocent, undefiled, set apart from sinners, and become higher than the heavens" (Heb 7.26; see whole section 4.14–7.28).

Kingly office. At His trial, Jesus answered Pilate's question as to whether or not He was a king: "Thou sayest it; I am a king. This is why I was born, and why I have come into the world, to bear witness to the truth" (Jn 18.37). The Synoptic Gospels, preoccupied with announcing the Good News of the coming of the Kingdom of God, give a certain stress to the theme of Christ's kingship, to which they add, however, a number of other related themes. The general truth that these themes all illustrate in their own way is that into the hands of Jesus, as the Lamb of God, have been entrusted all "blessing and honor and glory and dominion, forever and ever" (Rv 5.13). For a great number of relevant scriptural texts, see the Mass and Office for the feast of Christ the King.

Bibliography: I. SOLANO, *Sacrae theologiae summa* (Madrid 1961) 3:1, 694–791. A. MICHEL, *Dictionnaire de théologie catholique,* ed. A. VACANT et al. (Paris 1903–50) 8.1:1345–59. O. CULLMANN, *The Christology of the New Testament,* tr. S. GUTHRIE and C. HALL (Philadelphia, Pa. 1959). A. GRAHAM, *The Christ of Catholicism* (New York 1947) 214–260. C. V. HÉRIS, *The Mystery of Christ,* tr. D. FAHEY (Westminster, Md. 1950). A. SCHLITZER, *Redemptive Incarnation* (2d ed. Notre Dame, Ind. 1956) 184–307.

[D. R. GRABNER]

12. PRIMACY

The primacy of Christ is taught by St. Paul in Col 1.18: ". . . that in all things he [Christ] may have the first place." The following article outlines the historical development of this doctrine.

Early Christian writers considered Christ's primacy mainly in such partial, concrete aspects as His kingship and priesthood. Only St. Irenaeus took as his central theological viewpoint God's plan to sum up all things in Christ (*see* RECAPITULATION IN CHRIST). St. Jerome and St. Maximus, however, pointed out that the universe tends toward Christ as its goal, and many other Fathers, including the Cappadocians, stressed Christ's role as exemplar of the cosmos.

Rupert of Deutz, a medieval theologian, first asserted that the Word would have become man even if Adam had not sinned. This thesis was rejected by most scholastics for a reason given in a sermon of St. Augustine (*Serm.* 175, *Patrologia Latina* 38:945–949): without the disease,

there is no need for a physician; without sin, no need for a redeemer. St. Thomas took a prudent stand: "We do not know what God would have done had He not foreseen sin" (*In 1 Tim.* 1.4). Yet because of Augustine's authority, he conceded that there probably would have been no Incarnation without a prior sin (*Summa theologiae* 3a, 1.3). Duns Scotus, however, pointed out that although Christ is certainly man's Redeemer, His role in the universe cannot be reduced to the Redemption exclusively. He would exist as man, then, even without the sin of Adam (*In 3 sent.* 7.3, Vivès ed., 14:354–355).

Scotists continued to hold this view, and Thomists the opposite one. L. Molina, seeking to reconcile these positions, taught that Redemption from sin and the glory of Christ were "equally first" as reasons for the Incarnation (*Concordia,* Paris 1876, 477–490). This solution clearly transferred the controversy from the hypothetical question (whether Christ *would* have come) to the question of fact: how does the Incarnation fit into the divine plan? Yet it was not widely accepted; most theologians continued to insist that one of Molina's "equally first" reasons for the Incarnation was in fact prior to the other.

Interest in the subject gradually waned, and it lay dormant until 1867, when Hilary of Paris, a Capuchin, published a dissertation defending the Thomistic view. A lively controversy then arose, in which several questions were clearly distinguished for the first time: the relation of Christ's humanity to other creatures, the primary reason for the Incarnation, the order of the divine intentions, and the effect of sin on God's plan.

The traditional division of opinion was still apparent and continues to this day. Thomists maintain a "relative" primacy, resulting from an adjustment in God's plan brought about by sin. In this view, the angels and man's first parents before the Fall belong to a different economy from that of redeemed mankind; the former partake of the "grace of God"; the latter, of the "grace of Christ." Molinists continue to propose a "middle way," in which Christ's glory and man's Redemption are "equally first" in God's plan. Scotists set forth the doctrine of Christ's "absolute" primacy, which allows for only one economy, based on the Incarnation. According to traditional Scotism, the God-Man was originally destined to come as a glorious king, but the Fall caused a modification of the divine plan and brought about the "passible mode" of the Incarnation.

A recent adaptation of Scotism, worked out by J. F. Bonnefoy, OFM (1897–1958), and accepted in its broad outlines by such independent theologians as K. Rahner and C. Davis, rejects even this modification in the divine plan. It maintains that out of many possible worlds, God chose to create one in which sin, although neither willed nor positively permitted by Him, would set the stage for a redemptive Incarnation. Even in God's primitive plan, which remains forever unchanged, Christ is here envisioned as one who will enter history in the passible flesh of sinful mankind, suffer, die, and thus enter into the glory prepared for Him by His Father (Lk 24.26).

As developed by Bonnefoy, the doctrine of Christ's primacy now has the following structure. Its basic premise is the revealed datum that Christ's human nature, by reason of its intimate union with the Godhead, occupies the first place among creatures. From this fact is deduced the corollary that the Incarnation was willed by God "in the first place" and all other created realities only "after"—i.e., in dependence upon—Christ's human nature.

This dependence is said to consist in a threefold causal bond: Christ as man is (1) the meritorious cause of all other creatures and events, (2) the exemplar whose perfections are imitated in all other creatures, and (3) the proximate goal toward which the entire created order tends. Mary, as Christ's mother and noblest of all mere creatures, is "second" in God's plan; angels and the rest of mankind are then willed as the Body of Christ, as sharers in His glorified life. The material universe, finally, is envisioned as the "home" of Jesus, Mary, and other men. The order of actual creation is thus the opposite of the order in God's plan, as is to be expected in the work of an intelligent agent.

See Also: INCARNATION.

Bibliography: J. F. BONNEFOY, *Christ and the Cosmos,* tr. M. D. MEILACH (Paterson 1965), contains full bibliography. I. M. ROCCA and G. M. ROSCHINI, *De ratione primaria existentiae Christi et Deiparae . . .* (Rome 1944). U. LATTANZI, *Il primato universale di Cristo secondo le s. Scritture* (Rome 1937). F. M. RISI, *Sul motivo primario dell'Incarnazione del Verbo . . . ,* 4 v. (Rome 1897–98).

[M. D. MEILACH]

13. THE HISTORICAL JESUS

The question of the historical Jesus arises once biblical scholarship has made apparent the theological character of the NT witness to Jesus as the Christ. Given the New Testament theological articulations of Jesus' religious significance as grasped by Christian faith, what can be known about Jesus through the lenses made available by the modern discipline of critical history? This question has given rise to the so-called Quest for the Historical Jesus, an ongoing scholarly movement that has unfolded in three distinct phases.

The first phase, commonly referred to as the "old quest," began in the late eighteenth century with the German deist H. S. Reimarus and ran until 1906, the year in which A. Schweitzer published a magisterial summary and critique of the movement. After a hiatus of almost half a century, a "new quest" took its impetus from a programmatic lecture delivered in 1953 by E. Käsemann. Three years later G. Bornkamm's *Jesus of Nazareth* provided the basis of a consensus that would hold sway until 1985. In that year E. P. Sanders' *Jesus and Judaism* offered the sort of retrospective critique that Schweitzer had provided for the "old quest," and the same year saw the organization of a group known as the Jesus Seminar under the leadership of R. Funk and J. D. Crossan. A "third quest" has emerged in which such figures as J. P. Meier, N. T. Wright, and M. Borg play a prominent role. Profound conflict regarding what sources are relevant to historical inquiry into Jesus' earthly career and regarding what methods are most appropriate for obtaining historical knowledge of Jesus from those sources marks this phase of research. The result has been widely varying historical portraits of Jesus of Nazareth.

From the outset of the "old quest," a major ambiguity attendant upon the project became apparent. Within the context of the Enlightenment prejudice against religious traditions, H. S. Reimarus, and after him figures like D. F. Strauss and B. Bauer, sought to wield history as a weapon with which to discredit the Christian church. On their account, the real Jesus was the historical Jesus, and the discrepancy between the historical Jesus and Jesus as the Church confessed him undermined the plausibility of that confession. To the Christ of faith they opposed the real, historical Jesus. At the same time, liberal figures in the "old quest," like A. von Harnack, took a similar tack, though with a different goal. Their goal was not to discredit Christianity but to reconcile it with modernity, and to this end they appealed to the historical Jesus as the basis and norm of Christian faith. Thus Harnack sought contemporary relevance by proposing the historical Jesus and his simple message as the essence of Christianity, while dismissing the patristic doctrines about Jesus' divine status and inner constitution as a cultural husk whose day had passed.

The same maneuver toward the same goals can be observed among some exegetes as well as systematic theologians in the period of the "third quest" as well. For these scholars the historical Jesus is the real Jesus, and the real Jesus ought to be the basis and norm of Christian faith. This apparently commonsense approach masks, however, an ambiguity. There is no doubt that the real Jesus is the Jesus who lived two thousand years ago. This is the Jesus about whom historians inquire. This is also the Jesus whom Christians confess as Christ, Lord, Son of God. But when Reimarus, Harnack, and now scholars like Funk identify the historical Jesus with the real Jesus, they are claiming that historical inquiry has an exclusive franchise on the objective truth about Jesus. Such a claim is inflated, on two scores. First, the difference between the historical Jesus and the Christ of faith is epistemological, not substantive. The two terms refer, not to two different entities, but to one and the same entity grasped according to two distinct modes of knowing, each with its own scope, operations, and conditions for objectivity. Hence, to restrict the reality of Jesus to what can be grasped by historical method betrays a positivist constriction of human knowing. On the other hand, a refusal in principle to engage the significance of what historical research proffers constitutes fideism.

Furthermore, an analysis of what constitutes a historical portrait of Jesus discloses why no such portrait can of itself provide the basis and norm of Christian faith. The goal of arriving at a historical portrait of Jesus involves one in three distinguishable sets of historical operations. First, there is the question of determining what data are relevant as possible sources of historical information about Jesus. Answering that question imposes such tasks as determining dates for the possibly relevant sources, ascertaining the literary relationships among them, and delving into their prehistory. Conventionally, these have been the tasks that have defined source and form-critical analysis of the New Testament and related documents. Second, there is the task of extricating from the sources a set of more or less probable facts about Jesus—what he actually did and said. This task has been pursued through the application of such criteria as the principles of embarrassment, dissimilarity, multiple attestation, and coherence, though these criteria have themselves been subject to critique and refinement, and alternative procedures have also been proposed. Third, once such a set of facts has been established, they become data for the further question of what they add up to, what image renders them historically intelligible within the world of the first century. Though logically distinct from and posterior to the second question, in practice there is an interplay between image and facts. One commonly begins with some image, or several, as a hypothesis and then employs it or them as a heuristic guiding one's critical probe of the sources for determining the facts about Jesus; in the process that initial hypothesis is confirmed, revised, or replaced.

Thus, the historical Jesus refers to a complex construct that rests on a set of more or less probable judgments about what sources are relevant and to what degree. There follows a second set of judgments, again of greater or lesser probability, determining what Jesus actually said and did. Those judgments, in turn, supply the data for yet another judgment regarding what image or images best renders the facts constituted by the second set of judgments historically intelligible. The historical Jesus, concretely, is always someone's historical Jesus

and always in principle subject to revision. Hence, appeals to the historical Jesus as the real Jesus that should norm Christian faith are misguided.

On the positive side, the project of historical inquiry about Jesus serves christology as a strong counterweight to the perennial tendency toward docetism. It provides a vivid reminder that the one whom his disciples came to confess as Christ, Lord, and Son of God first encountered them as one like them in all things except sin, as a first-century Jew among his fellow Jews. Furthermore, when historical reconstructions of Jesus' earthly career are drawn into the horizon of Christian faith, the coherence of these images and narratives with the transformative values appropriated in the tradition's confession of Jesus as the Christ may come to light. Then, in a manner analogous to the initial formation of the christological tradition, these historical constructs may provide the material for new christological symbols and postcritical narratives that function to disclose both Jesus' identity as the self-presence of God to the community and the values inherent in a response of faith to this Jesus as the Christ.

Bibliography: A. SCHWEITZER, *The Quest for the Historical Jesus*, tr. W. MONTGOMERY (New York 1968). G. BORNKAMM, *Jesus of Nazareth*, tr. I. and F. MCLUSKEY (New York 1961). E. P. SANDERS, *Jesus and Judaism* (Philadelphia, Pa. 1985). J. CROSSAN, *The Historical Jesus: The Life of a Mediterranean Jewish Peasant* (San Francisco, Calif. 1991). J. MEIER, *A Marginal Jew*, 3 vols. (Garden City, N.Y. 1991, 1994, 2001). N. T. WRIGHT, *Jesus and the Victory of God* (Philadelphia 1996). M. POWELL, *Jesus as a Figure in History* (Louisville 1998).

[W. P. LOEWE]

14. CHRIST AND THEOLOGIES OF LIBERATION

Historical consciousness recognizes the historical process and all the societies and cultures it has brought forth as the product of human agency. Humankind therefore faces the task of assuming responsibility for history itself. Theologically, this requires reconceiving sin and grace as factors in conflict not only in the lives of individuals but in the dynamics of globalization presently at work in the economies, politics, and cultures of every human society. In this context, a theological discernment of "the signs of the times" becomes a crucial dimension of proclaiming the gospel.

Against this background, the full significance of the projects of liberation theologies and their European counterpart, political theology, stands forth. Latin American liberation theology began with the insight that the poverty endemic to the peoples of Central and South America is more than an unfortunate state of affairs. Rather, situations in which a wealthy elite in service to neocolonial economic powers control the political institutions of society and maintain their status by violent means if necessary stand opposed to God's will. Such situations are sinful. In addition, in Latin America the societies in question have been culturally Catholic, and the Church has been complicit in creating and sustaining them.

Hence, liberation theology begins with a call to repentance. Theologically, this translates into the exercise of a hermeneutics of suspicion that asks what elements of the Christian tradition may have contributed to the present sinful situation. With regard to christology, two traditional images of Christ come under criticism. First, popular devotion to the suffering Christ has functioned ambiguously. Concentration on Christ's suffering apart from his resurrection fosters a christology of resignation that serves to reconcile victims of social injustice to their state in life; the element of protest implicit in the image of Christ suffering remains latent. Second, the image of the imperial, conquering Christ too easily colludes with the imperialist projects of the colonial and neocolonial eras in Latin America, inducing docility in those whom such projects oppress and exploit.

Liberation christologies begin from within the faith of the Church, but rather than starting from the classic dogmas of Christ's divinity and inner constitution, they seek to historicize those dogmas through recourse to narratives that explicate the redemptive significance of belief in Jesus as Son of God and Son of Man. Hence, they commonly appeal to the historical Jesus and his praxis as the starting point and basis of their christological narratives. This appeal differs significantly, however, from the maneuver noted above, in which the historical Jesus refers epistemologically to Jesus as reconstructed by historical-critical methods and in which such reconstructions are accorded a normative basis for critique of Christian belief. The historical Jesus, for liberation theologians, refers rather to Jesus as a historical subject and to the account of his praxis that emerges from a reading of the Synoptic Gospels, in some cases augmented by results of the "new quest," from the perspective of the impoverished and oppressed peoples of Latin America. This is a reading from faith to faith quite different from the positivist reductions of Enlightenment authors and their successors.

As the Son of God in history, Jesus proclaimed and enacted the reign of God, and this commitment placed Him in solidarity with the economically exploited, politically oppressed, and socially marginalized among his people. His ministry assumed a conflictual character that eventually led to His death. Jesus called twelve disciples to his inner circle, signaling that the time of Israel's renewal was at hand. He cured the ill, including those among them who were ritually unclean, and He proclaimed God's forgiveness to prostitutes and sinners. He challenged scribes and Pharisees and denounced the

wealthy. Finally, He unmasked the violent, murderous character of the anti-reign and the system it sustained and, celebrating a final meal with his disciples, He poured himself out in loving trust of the Abba-God whose reign He proclaimed. Though the establishment condemned and executed him, God raised Him up and made him a life-giving Spirit to those who would find in following him the gift and task of liberation from the idols of this world. In Jesus' life, death, and resurrection they discover God's salvation urging them to continue Jesus' struggle for justice in the sure hope that not even death can overcome the power of self-sacrificing love.

Bibliography: I. ELLACURIA and J. SOBRINO, eds., *Mysterium Liberationis: Fundamental Concepts of Liberation Theology* (Maryknoll, N.Y. 1993). J. SOBRINO, *Jesus the Liberator: A Historical-Theological Reading of Jesus of Nazareth*, tr. P. BURNS and F. MCDONAGH (Maryknoll, N.Y. 1993).

[W. P. LOEWE]

15. FEMINIST CHRISTOLOGIES

The women's movement began with a challenge to the taken-for-granted character of the cultural and social place commonly assigned to women. Rather than reflecting the natural order of things, women's relegation to inferior and dependent status derives from patriarchy, an unjust system of relations in which males dominate the social order. Patriarchy, in turn, finds cultural expression in androcentrism, which accords universality to male experience, so that reality comes to be defined from a male perspective.

Applying the analytic concepts of patriarchy and androcentrism to the Christian tradition, feminist theologians find that Jesus' maleness has become entangled in an androcentric set of dualisms that associate the male with spirit, rationality, and power and the female with matter, emotion, and weakness. Hence, it comes to seem self-evident that women be excluded from roles of leadership and decision making within a hierarchically ordered ecclesial community. At the same time, Jesus' redemptive passion becomes a warrant for women to accept not only their subordinate role but even, in the extreme, the violent abuse that can accompany it.

For Christian feminists, the tradition is ambiguous, not simply oppressive, and hence they pursue a hermeneutics of remembrance. Like liberation theologians, they highlight the iconoclastic Christ of the Synoptic Gospels whose proclamation and enactment of the reign of God brought wholeness and liberation to the marginalized and oppressed of society. Without claiming that Jesus was a feminist, they note within all four gospel narratives the ways in which Jesus transgressed the social code of his day. Thus, Jesus healed and exorcized women; he formed friendships with women, called them to discipleship, taught them, and included them in His entourage as He pursued His itinerant ministry. Further, His address to God as "Abba" subverted patriarchal conceptions of both God and human fatherhood. In contrast to Peter and the male disciples who fled upon Jesus' arrest, the women were faithful to Jesus to the end. The empty-tomb narratives portray women as the first to hear the good news of Jesus' resurrection, and Mary Magdalen is the first to see the risen Lord.

Pushing behind the gospel narratives, feminist biblical scholars find indications that the early Jesus movement was a community of equals in which women exercised leadership roles conjointly with men, functioning as apostles, prophets, and heads of household churches. Soon, however, the mores of the Hellenistic world prevailed, and the same Paul who numbered women among his co-workers and declared that in Christ there is neither male nor female, also admonished women to cover their heads and be silent in church.

Classical dogma also yields liberating insights. In rejecting subordinationism and confessing Christ's co-equality in divinity with the Father, the Council of Nicea (325) limned the mystery of ultimate reality as no isolated and monadic supreme monarch but as constituted by a community of persons with relationship at its very heart. Human beings, it would then follow, created in the image of God, are fundamentally relational and achieve their humanity through participation in community. The Council of Chalcedon (451), in turn, so distinguished person from nature that the former is never reducible to the latter, an insight that counters every form of sexism and racism.

Yet according to feminist theologians, the mysteries of Trinity and Incarnation find androcentric expression when Christians weekly profess belief "in one God, the Father almighty . . . and in His only Son, Jesus Christ." Despite the constant doctrine of the divine transcendence, the dominant imagery of God in the Christian tradition has been male and so fosters the androcentric dualism that devalues women and deprives the tradition of the insights generated by women's experience. To overcome this imbalance, feminist theologians turn to scriptural passages that ascribe maternal concern to God and that image divine creativity and redemptive activity as birthing; at the same time, they trace out a trajectory that continues this feminine imagery for God and Christ in patristic literature and in the writings of medieval doctors and mystics.

The biblical wisdom tradition plays a central role in the feminist project of recovery and reconstruction. Starting from the Greek literature of the late Old Testament period that personifies the divine wisdom in the figure of a woman, Sophia, who is preexistent agent of creation, and continuing in the New Testament, where Jesus is portrayed as both Sophia's emissary and her embodiment, the wisdom tradition offers a resource for constructive rearticulations of the mysteries of Trinity and Incarnation that bring balance to the dominant Logos tradition.

Bibliography: R. RUETHER, *Sexism and God-Talk: Toward a Feminist Theology* (Boston, Mass. 1983). E. A. JOHNSON, *She Who Is: The Mystery of God in Feminist Theological Discourse* (New York 1992). A. CARR, *Transforming Grace: Christian Tradition and Women's Experience* (New York 1988). E. SCHÜSSLER FIOREN-ZA, *In Memory of Her: A Feminist Theological Reconstruction of Christian Origins* (New York 1983); *Jesus Miriam's Child, Sophia's Prophet* (New York 1994).

[W. P. LOEWE]

16. JESUS CHRIST AND WORLD RELIGIONS

At the Second Vatican Council the Roman Catholic church adopted a new stance of ecumenical openness not only to other Christian communities but to the great world religions as well. The council's "Declaration on the Relationship of the Church to Non-Christian Religions" affirmed the genuine holiness and truth to be found in Hinduism and Buddhism. It expressed high esteem for Islamic belief and worship, and it recognized the special ties and common heritage that bind Christians to Jews. With respect to all, the council urged dialogue and collaboration.

With this stance of openness and appreciation toward other world religions, the council was retrieving an ancient stream of Christian tradition. Patristic writers like Justin Martyr had expressed an inclusive universality whereby Christians recognized in both Judaism and Hellenistic philosophical culture the work of God's Logos. More typically, however, in the context of Christendom an exclusive attitude came to prevail, emblemized in the famous phrase of the Fourth Lateran Council (1215) "*extra ecclesiam, nulla salus.*"

Distinctively, contemporary cultural factors fostered the council's revival of a more inclusive tradition. Foremost among these is globalization, the process carried out by international economic networks and electronic communications media rendering different cultures immediately present and interactive with one another. Interaction becomes interpenetration as geopolitical and economic factors unleash new waves of migration, so that temples and mosques are taking their place on the Western landscape among the more familiar synagogues and churches; religious communities formerly distant and strange to one another now find themselves neighbors. Globalization, in turn, hastens the end of Eurocentric classicism, while contemporary anthropology suggests an empirical understanding of human cultures as constructs based on particular, historically generated sets of meanings and values, an understanding congenial to Vatican II's acknowledgment of other religions and their beliefs as responses to the questions posed by "the profound mysteries of human existence."

Recognition of religious authenticity in other world religions requires development in the Christian understanding of the salvific role of Jesus Christ. How is this central Christian belief to be conceived when no historical mediation of the Christ-event to the majority of the world's population can be discerned, when universal conversion to the Church seems an unlikely possibility, and when God's saving grace is acknowledged outside of Christianity?

Karl Rahner addressed this issue in a manner particularly congenial to the stance expressed in the council's declaration. On the one hand, he argued, God's efficacious will to save is universal, so that being human is as such conditioned by a "supernatural existential"; if human beings find their authentic humanity in fidelity to the unrestricted desire they experience to know the real and love the good, the secret of that desire, its origin and goal, is the lure of Holy Mystery, God's own self-offer in grace. Furthermore, human beings are intrinsically historical and social, requiring a mediation of grace that meets these dimensions of their humanity. Thus, on wholly inner-Christian grounds Rahner could conclude to the likelihood that it is precisely through the world religions as historically and socially constituted that God's saving grace is mediated to most of humankind. Yet this in no way relativizes either the Christ-event or the Church, for in the plan of salvation history Christ becomes, in scholastic terms, the final cause of the grace mediated through the world religions, while the Church functions as sacrament rendering present and explicit the meaning of the grace operating anonymously, as it were, in the world religions.

Rahner's position and variants on it break with Christian exclusivism, recognizing salvific efficacy in other religions. At the same time, they maintain intact the basic Christian narrative of salvation history, the story of preparation for Christ, His Incarnation, death, and Resurrection, His continuing presence in the Church until the Second Coming. Other religions now find a place in this story as mediators of the grace that heads toward Christ and is available in its fullness in the Church. Much as in Justin Martyr, Christianity now, in a sense, includes the other religions, recapitulating, correcting, and fulfilling them. Other religions have value, but that value is ultimately constituted by Christ and imperfect in comparison with the Christian Church. In this sense, Hinduism, Buddhism, and Islam join Judaism as *praeparatio evangelica,*

even if the preparatory period is now likely to perdure until the *eschaton.*

Once religious authenticity is recognized in other religions, however, further questions arise. If in other religions God's salvation is indeed being mediated through savior figures other than Christ, what becomes of the Christian confession that He and He alone is universal savior? Similarly, on what grounds does one decide *a priori* that all other religions are in some way deficient and imperfect in comparison to Christianity? Do not the dogmatic assumptions of even an inclusive Christian approach to other world religions betray an unconscious hubris and lingering traces of Western cultural imperialism? Does not Christian inclusivism therefore ultimately reduce to the former exclusivism?

Among Catholic theologians, issues such as these have animated the work of R. Panikkar, P. Knitter, and R. Haight. On the position toward which they head, Jesus is one savior among others, decisive for Christians and deserving their total religious commitment, and also relevant to all other human beings. The savior figures of other religions are similarly decisive for their devotees and relevant to all, so that each religion remains itself while open to learn from the distinctive religious experience and insights of the others.

This position involves, in the work of all three, a radical christological revision. Pannikar, for example, elaborates a distinction between Christ and Jesus: Christ symbolizes the expressive dimension of ultimate reality, a non-dualistic theandric principle, and while Jesus' identity is fully constituted as the embodiment of Christ, Christ is in no way exhausted in that embodiment. Hence, while one may say that Jesus is Christ, one may not say simply that Christ is Jesus, for Christ is also Krishna and many others.

In the name of completely open dialogue, Knitter has espoused moving beyond the christocentrism of positions like Rahner's, first to a theocentrism like that expressed in the mission of self-understanding of the historical Jesus, and ultimately, since not all religions are theistic, to a soteriocentrist stance. New Testament passages that clearly express an exclusive view of Jesus as the sole savior can be ascribed to various cultural conditioning factors, and such passages are to be regarded as confessional, performative language rather than declarative assertions. To say, for example, that Jesus is Lord is always to say that Jesus is Lord for me, not that He is universally Lord. With regard to the Incarnation, both Knitter and Haight argue that Johannine symbolism must not be allowed to overpower the dynamic and evolving diversity of New Testament expressions of Jesus' religious significance, nor must such symbolism be literalized.

This linguistic requirement holds especially for the interpretation of the classical dogmas of Nicea and Chalcedon, whose point, Haight asserts, reduces to the saving presence of God in the man Jesus, such that Jesus is the symbol of God for Christians. From this perspective, contemporary interpretations of the Chalcedonian formula like Rahner's become dogmatically arbitrary when they assert that the Incarnation can occur but once.

A declaration from the Congregation for the Doctrine of the Faith in 2000, *Dominus Iesus*, met such revisionist christologies with a firm reiteration of traditional Catholic belief. Other theologians, notably Jacques Dupuis, find in the classic Christology and Trinitarian theology of the Christian tradition ample resources for addressing issues of religious pluralism and interreligious dialogue. First, Chalcedonian dogma suggests recognition of the historical and cultural particularity of both Jesus and the Church. While affirming that the identity of Jesus is that of the eternal Son of God, Chalcedon stressed that in the Incarnation the Son became fully human, "like us in all things except sin." Under contemporary cultural conditions, in which the empirical counts for as much as the essential, faith does not cease to recognize in Jesus the Incarnate Son. Faith also, however, perceives him as a first-century Jew with all the limitations of experience and knowledge implied by that ancient and alien cultural particularity. By His *kenosis,* the Son of God accepted the conditions of human historicity.

The same holds for the movement issuing from Him. The Church's expression of the mystery of grace that constitutes it is always subject to historical limitation and, precisely as the expression of mystery, that understanding and expression will always remain imperfect, analogous, and subject to development. Because the Church's identity and redemptive mission is always realized through concrete historical experience, it follows that at any moment the Church only exists as culturally embodied and thereby also limited.

If the Chalcedonian dogma of the hypostatic union bespeaks the human particularity and limitation of both Jesus and the Church, Nicea and I Constantinople suggest positive principles for Christian engagement with the world religions. The First Council of Constantinople confessed the full divinity of the Holy Spirit. Christians discern in their authentic religious experience, in their desire to love the Lord their God with their whole hearts, the gift of God's Holy Spirit, the Spirit whose love in turn illumines their minds to recognize God as triune and to recognize in Jesus and His Church the mediators of God's love to them. Yet by that same principle Christians may discern the operation of God's Holy Spirit in the authentic religious experience mediated by the other world religions as well.

This stance in no way implies a simple relativism. For all the historical particularity of Jesus and His Church, Christians will also recall Nicea's doctrine that given the full divinity of the Son, whatever can be said of the Father can also be said of the Son and vice versa, save what is proper to being precisely Father or Son. In that case, recalling the imperfect and analogous character of their understanding of the truth of God as triune mystery, Christians will advance into dialogue open to discerning in other world religions the operation of the Spirit who is always Spirit of both the Father and the Son and to enriching their understanding of the triune divine mystery from the experience and insights of other traditions.

In dialogue with other world religions, Christians encounter interpretations of Jesus in conflict with their own. In Judaism the Talmud reflects polemical antagonism, portraying Jesus as the illegitimate son of Mary and a Roman soldier, who performed wonders by black magic and was rightfully executed as a sorcerer. The contemporary scene reflects a softening of these harsh attitudes. Among some Jewish scholars there is a movement to reclaim Jesus as one of their own people. They stress, for example, his affinities with the Pharisaic movement of His day as well as His resonances with the classical prophetic tradition. For all this, however, Jews stand firm in rejecting Christian claims to a messianic title for Jesus. In their view, the messianic day of salvation clearly did not arrive with Jesus' advent. Rather, history continues as before, bloodily unredeemed, and Israel's sufferings have only intensified at the hands of those who claim to follow Jesus in the Christian churches.

Islam honors Jesus a son of the virgin Mary, a miracle-working prophet raised up by God to confirm the Torah and to prepare the way for a greater prophet yet to come. Jesus died a natural death, not at the Romans' hands on the cross. With their confession of Jesus' divinity, Christians crudely betray the utter transcendence of Allah.

Hindus like M. Gandhi have discerned in Jesus' teaching strong affinities with the way of *bhakti,* loving devotion and surrender to God. Yet they strongly reject the claim that in Jesus alone the divine has become incarnate even while they seem to devalue any incarnation as an occurrence in history and hence in the realm of the ultimately unreal.

In such conflicts over Jesus and His religious significance, two things should also be noted. First, each contested issue also points to areas of common conviction, and, second, each can provide a stimulus to refined Christian self-understanding. With the experience of prophecy, for example, Judaism, Christianity, and Islam intersect, while Jewish resistance to Christian messianic claims can dislodge any naive and triumphalistic realized eschatology in favor of heightened attention to authentic redemptive praxis. Hindu devotion, in turn, can illumine the significance of contemporary reconstructions of the teaching of the historical Jesus.

Bibliography: K. RAHNER, ''Jesus Christ in Non-Christian Religions,'' in *Foundations of Christian Faith,* tr. W. DYCH (New York 1978) 311–321. R. PANIKKAR, *The Unknown Christ of Hinduism* (rev. ed.; Maryknoll, N.Y. 1981). P. KNITTER, *No Other Name? A Survey of Christian Attitudes toward the World Religions* (Maryknoll, N.Y. 1985). R. HAIGHT, *Jesus Symbol of God* (Maryknoll, N.Y. 1999). J. DUPUIS, *Toward a Christian Theology of Religious Pluralism* (Maryknoll, N.Y. 1997).

[W. P. LOEWE]

JESUS CHRIST, BIOGRAPHICAL STUDIES OF

Biographical studies of Jesus Christ represent primarily not a question of historiography about the presence and reliability of authentic documents on the event of His having lived a human life but rather a double theological problem: the knowability of the historical Incarnation (epistemology of the Incarnation) and the significance of this event for the Christian. This article follows along the ages the unfolding of these two inseparably connected problems in five sections: (1) Lives of Jesus based on simple faith, (2) Jesus and the critics, (3) Lives of Jesus in the English-speaking world, (4) the Catholic development from apologetics to Christology, and (5) the imaginative Lives of Jesus.

Based on Simple Faith. The canonical Gospels, besides their kerygmatic and liturgical purpose, reveal a true historical interest in the earthly life of Jesus, a biographical interest that must, however, be measured by the standard of contemporary thinking. Christians have always desired to know more about the full human reality of the life of Jesus, not only as far as it concerns their own historical origin but also because this earthly life of the Lord determines the true and full reality of their own Christian existence. The same attitude is evident in the apocryphal writings that tried to fill in the blank spaces in Jesus' life, especially in its early stages, and thereby distorted His teaching with many, mostly Gnostic, additions [see W. Bauer, *Das Leben Jesu im Zeitalter der neutestamentlichen Apokryphen* (Tübingen 1909) and J. Walterscheid, *Das Leben Jesu nach den neutestamentlichen Apokryphen* (Düsseldorf 1953)]. Beginning with Origen [see R. M. Grant, *The Earliest Lives of Jesus* (London 1961)] and Melito of Sardes, a more historical realism can be observed in the desire to identify actual locations in Christ's early life. Moreover, the account (*c.*

A.D. 400) of Egeria's pilgrimage to the Holy Land (*see* PILGRIMAGES, 2), the work of archdeacon Theodosius, *De situ terrae sanctae* (both given in *Corpus scriptorum ecclesiasticorum latinorum* 39:35–101, 135–150), and other similar writings (see B. Altaner, *Patrology,* tr. H. Graef 261–262) show that Christianity even at that early age understood itself as the continuation and historical unfolding of Christ.

In Early Christianity. Tatian's DIATESSARON (*c.* 170–180) was the first attempt to reconstruct the life of the Lord according to the Gospels. It had an enormous success in the Orient, and in some churches it even replaced the individual Gospels in the liturgy. Of doubtful authenticity, however, is the work of Ammonius of Alexandria (*c.* 220), who completed Matthew with marginal notes from the other Gospels (*Patrologia Graeca*, ed. J. P. Migne, 85:1381–92). In any case, this work was employed by Victor, Bishop of Capua (d. 554), as the basis for his *Ammonii Alexandrini evangelicae harmoniae interprete Victore episcopo capuano,* in which he used the Vulgate text (*Patrologia Latina*, ed. J. P. Migne, 68:255–359).

A Spanish priest, C. V. Aquilinus Juvencus, approached the subject more freely by writing the life of Jesus, *Historiae evangelicae libri IV,* in the form of 3,211 hexameters. Caelius Sedulius first wrote the five books of his *Paschale Carmen* in verse, then completed it as *Opus Paschale* in prose (*Patrologia Latina* 19:354–752). In the early Middle Ages the same romantic approach is shown in CAEDMON's poetry (*c.* 680) and in CYNEWULF's *The Christ* [*c.* 750; see A. S. Cook, *The Christ of Cynewulf: A Poem in Three Parts: The Advent, the Ascension and the Last Judgment* (Boston 1910)]. Then there are the *HELIAND* (*c.* 850) in 6,000 verses [for the text see O. Behaghel (Tübingen 1958)]; the *Liber evangeliorum theodisce conscriptus* (between 863 and 871) by Otfrid of Weissenburg, OSB; the *Cantilena de miraculis Christi* (1063) by Ezzo von Bamberg, which became the song of the Crusaders; and the *Xristos Paschon* (11th century), a dramatic presentation in 2,640 verses of Christ's death and Resurrection.

The Oriental Church, even in more recent times, showed no similar interest in the earthly life of Jesus. Oriental piety is centered more in the risen and eschatological Lord who is present in the liturgical performance of the mysteries and the life of the Church. On the other hand, Islam presents a picture of Jesus that is concerned with details of his earthly life. It draws on two traditions, the Jesus portrayed in the Qur'ān, and Jesus the wandering ascetic pictured in hundreds of pious tales in later Arabic literature (eighth century Iraq). Many of the details in the Qur'ān and in these stories have parallels in the

Jesus healing the sick. (©Bettmann/CORBIS)

Gnostic Gospels. (see, T. Khalidi, *The Muslim Jesus*, Harvard University Press 2001).

In the Middle Ages. The CRUSADES and the typically FRANCISCAN SPIRITUALITY with its devotion toward the humanity of Jesus created a new attitude: pious meditation on the individual events in His life. The *Meditationes vitae Christi* of the 13th or 14th century had profound influence on art and literature until the 17th century. For a long time the work was attributed to St. BONAVENTURE, but its author was most likely a certain Johannes a Caulibus (or Laudibus), although his authorship of it has recently been contested. The *Vita Jesu Christi e quatuor evangeliis et scriptoribus orthodoxis concinnata* by the Carthusian LUDOLPH OF SAXONY (1300–78) had 88 Latin editions and was translated into many modern languages. Almost as popular, especially in Italy, was the work *De gestis Domini Salvatoris* (15 v. 1338–47) by the Augustinian Simon Fidati of Cascia.

More scholarly interest is revealed in PETER COMESTOR's (d. 1179) *Historia scholastica* (*Patrologia Latina* 198:1053–1722), which includes a life of Jesus, and in Guyart des Moulin's *Bible Historiale* (1291–94). Moreover, the great scholastics dedicated a special part of their Christologies to the mysteries of the life of Jesus (see, e.g., St. Thomas Aquinas, *Summa theologiae* 3a, 31–57).

From the 15th to the 17th Century. In this period the Gospel harmonies served as basic patterns for the lives of Jesus. Some examples are: Jean GERSON (d. 1429), *Monotessaron* (printed in 1471); Cornelius JANSEN (the Elder), Bishop of Ghent, *Concordia evangelica seu vita Jesu Christi ex quatuor evangeliis in unum caput congesta* (Douai 1571); Antonius Bruich, *Monotessaron breve* (Cologne 1539), noteworthy because of the author's keen sense for the truly historical; William of Branteghem, a Carthusian from Antwerp, *Jesu Christi vita iuxta quatuor evangelistarum narrationes* (Antwerp 1537), with several French translations; and Sebastian Barradas, SJ, *Commentaria in concordiam et historiam evangelicam* (Coimbra 1599). Christian Andrichomius, a priest of Delft, Holland, published under the pseudonym Christianus Crucis his *Vita Jesu Christi ex quatuor evangeliis breviter contexta* (Antwerp 1578). The Spanish theologian Alfonso SALMERÓN, SJ, edited his *Commentaria in evangelicam historiam* (Madrid 1598). Late products of the same type were George Heser, SJ (d. 1686), *Vitae D.N. Jesu Christi monotessaron evangelicum,* and M. Azibert, *Synopsis evangeliorum historica seu vitae D.N. Jesu Christi quadruplex et una narratio* (Albi 1897).

Of the Protestant contributions especially noteworthy is Andreas OSIANDER's *Harmonia evangelica graece et latine* (Basel 1537). Osiander, who firmly believed in

Chapel of Nativity. (Archive Photos)

the verbal inspiration of the Scriptures, reconstructed the life of Jesus with much care by using exclusively the words of the Bible. Other Protestant harmonies are: M. Chemnitz, *Harmonia quatuor evangelistarum,* continued and published by his student P. Leyser (1593–1611); J. Clericus (Amsterdam 1699); N. Toinard (Paris 1707); and J. J. Griesbach, *Synopsis evangeliorum Matthaei, Marci et Lucae* (Halle 1774–76, 4th ed. 1822). In the 20th century a number of Catholic authors attempted Gospel harmonies with varying degrees of success: S. Hartdegen (in English, Paterson, New Jersey, 1942), R. Cox (in English, Auckland 3d ed. 1954), A. Tricot (in French, Tournai 2d ed. 1946), and J. Bover (in Spanish, Barcelona 1943).

The meditative types of the lives of Jesus were restored under the influence of St. IGNATIUS OF LOYOLA. In his spiritual exercises the 2d and 3d weeks were consecrated to meditations on the life of Christ. N. Avancini's (d. 1611) *Vita et doctrina Jesu Christi* had more than 50 editions. P. de Ribadeneira, *Vida y misterios de Cristo Nuestro Senor,* Luis de la Puente, *Meditaciones de los misterios de nuestra S. Fe* (Valladolid 1605, followed by more than 400 editions), and many other similar writings emphasized the meaning of Christ's earthly life for the Christian's own life.

The age of the Reformation, besides making a greater use of vernacular languages, introduced a more acute sense of the historical. Examples in this category are: Ludovico Filcaja, *Vita del nostro Salvatore Jesu Christo* (Venice 1548); Laurence Forer, SJ, professor at Ingol-

"Salvator Mundi," oil painting on wood panel by Andrea Previtali showing Christ as Savior of the World, 1519. (©National Gallery Collection; by kind permission of the Trustees of the National Gallery, London/CORBIS)

stadt and Döllingen, *Das Leben und Leiden Jesu Christi* (Munich 1637); Bernard de Montereuil, SJ, *Vie du Sauveur du monde Jésus-Christ, tirée du text des IV évangiles reduite en un corps d'histoire* (Paris 1639, reed. many times); G. S. MENOCHIO, the well-known exegete, *Historia sacra della vita . . . del nostro redentore Gesù Cristo* (Rome 1633); and Nicholas Letourneaux, *Histoire de la vie de N.S. Jésus-Christ* (Paris 1678; somewhat Jansenistically infected). Sebastian Le Nain de Tillemont, the famous French Church historian, wrote as an introduction to his monumental work on the first six Christian centuries a very solid and critical life of Jesus. The greatest success of the 17th century was Martinus Linus von Cochem, OFMCap, *Leben und Leiden Jesu Christi* (Frankfurt 1677), which from the fourth edition (1860) on was entitled *Das grosse Leben Christi*. Still being reprinted in the early part of the 20th century, it has had some 260 editions.

In the 18th Century. A. CALMET presented his excellent *Histoire de la vie et des miracles de Jésus-Christ* (Paris 1720) as a worthy contribution of his exegetical research. The outstanding life of Jesus published in that century was the *Histoire de la vie de N.S. Jésus-Christ depuis son Incarnation jusqu'à son Ascension* (3 v. Avignon 1774) by F. de Ligny (1709–88). This work, often reissued and translated into English, was regarded as a classic in France until J. E. Renan's superseded it.

The most original life of Jesus from this period was written by Clemens M. Brentano. It was based on the visions of Anna Catherina EMMERICH (1774–1824). The Passion story was published first (Sulzbach 1833), then came the three volumes of *Das Leben Jesu* (ed. K. E. Schmöger, Regensburg 1858–60), and finally the collection of all visions, which included the life of Mary, appeared under the title *Das arme Leben und bittere Leiden unseres Herren Jesu Christi* (Regensburg 1881, 5th ed. 1920; English tr. 2d ed. London 1907).

Jesus and the Critics. A revolutionary change came about between 1774 and 1778 when G. E. LESSING published the *Wolfenbüttel Fragmenten* of an unknown author [English tr. by A. Voysey, a deist, *The Object of Jesus and His Disciples as Seen in the New Testament* (1879)]. The "Fragments" were parts from the *Apologie oder Schutzschrift für die vernünftige Verehrer Gottes,* by Hemann Samuel REIMARUS (1694–1768), a teacher of Oriental languages in Hamburg. In Reimarus's writing, which he himself did not dare to publish, the postulates of DEISM (of English origins and propagated on the Continent by Voltaire, J. J. Rousseau, and by the Encyclopedists) confronted, for the first time, the historical reality of the Incarnation. According to Reimarus, Jesus was merely a man whose doctrine did not go, in its content,

Christ ascending from tomb, painting. (©Bettmann/CORBIS)

beyond the Jewish-apocalyptic expectations of the kingdom of God; His Resurrection was a fraud perpetrated by the Apostles.

Earlier Rationalists. J. S. Semler's immediate answer (Halle 1779) could not stop the growing flow of rationalistic attacks on the real life of Jesus. K. H. G. Venturini's (1768–1849) *Natürliche Geschichte des grossen Propheten von Nazareth* (3 v. 1800; 2d ed. 4 v. Jena 1805) is full of exaggerations. He proposed a frivolous view of the Nativity, and according to him Jesus was crucified by the disillusioned populace and brought back to life by His friends after His apparent death. Venturini alluded to an ESSENE affiliation of Jesus, a theory that was taken up by Salvator in his *Life of Jesus* (2 v. Paris 1838). A much milder, more esthetic approach was shown in J. G. von HERDER (1744–1803), *Vom Erlöser des Menschen nach unseren drei ersten Evangelien* (Riga 1796) and *Von Gottes Sohn der Weltheiland nach Johannes Evangelium* (Riga 1797). Herder was the first to insist that any historical harmonization between John and the Synoptics must be regarded as impossible. H. E. G. Paulus

Detail of a fresco showing "Christ in Glory," 1157–1188, the Panteon de los Reyes, Colegiata de San Isodoro, Leon, Spain. (©Archivo Iconografico, S.A./CORBIS)

(1761–1851) in his *Das Leben Jesu als Grundlage einer reinen Geschichte des Urchristentums* (2 v. Heidelberg 1828) mercilessly eliminated everything that is miraculous or supernatural.

Later Rationalists. F. D. E. SCHLEIERMACHER's (1768–1834) mild resistance to these rationalistic interpretations in his Berlin University lectures on the life of Jesus (1831–32, ed. posthumously by Rüterich, Berlin 1864) was soon followed by the most extreme and logical explosion of rationalistic thought. D. F. STRAUSS (1808–74), who had attended Schleiermacher's lectures, published *Das Leben Jesu kritisch bearbeitet* (2 v. Tübingen 1835; English tr. *The Life of Jesus Critically Examined,* from the 4th German ed., London 1846, 3d ed. 1898). Influenced by G. W. F. HEGEL, Strauss first proposed the myth theory: although Jesus of Nazareth was a historical person, in the preaching of His disciples the true facts of His life and teachings were completely covered by Old Testament messianic dreams and other mythological imaginations; unintentionally the Gospel story became nothing else but a presentation of primitive Christian ideology that resembled history. Later, Strauss published a somewhat milder version of his ideas in *Das Leben Jesu für das deutsche Volk bearbeitet* (Leipzig

1863). However, in answering the publication of Schleiermacher's lectures, he returned to his extreme views in *Der Christus des Glaubens und der Jesus der Geschichte* (Berlin 1865).

The uproar of criticism from all over Germany quickly revealed the weak points of Strauss's rationalism. He had completely neglected sound and serious textual criticism and interpreted the Gospel history entirely on the basis of his philosophical presuppositions. One of his most renowned critics was J. A. W. Neander (1789–1850) in *Das Leben Jesu Christi* (Hamburg 1837; English tr. *The Life of Jesus Christ,* London 1851). Another leader of the *Vermittlungs-Theologie* who was strongly critical of Strauss was J. P. Lange (1802–84); he published a life of Jesus in three volumes (1844–47; English tr. 4 v. 1872).

In France, J. E. RENAN (1823–92) published, as the first volume of his *Histoire des origines du Christianisme,* his *La Vie de Jésus-Christ* (Paris 1863; English tr. London 1864). In Germany, Renan was not taken seriously, and his book was not translated into German until 1895. Actually, his *Life of Jesus* was a literary rather than a scholarly achievement. Renan proposed a legend hypothesis in order to do away with the miraculous and supernatural. According to him, Jesus was a likeable, peace-loving, good rabbi, and only the contradictions of His contemporaries turned Him into an apocalyptic revolutionary. In answering Renan, more than 95 books were published in France; one of the best was *Jésus-Christ, son temps, sa vie, son oeuvre* (2 v. Paris 1865; English tr. London 1869) by E. D. de Pressensé (1824–91), a conservative Protestant. Also, the Catholic A. J. A. GRATRY answered in *Jésus-Christ, réponse à M. Renan* (Paris 1864).

Liberal School. The rationalistic bias of Strauss and Renan and of many other authors of the same trend had a greater impact on the public mind than on the scholarly theological research that was represented by the so-called liberal school in Germany. Basing themselves on the substantial historical reliability of Mark, the liberals tried to understand psychologically the personality of Jesus, especially His messianic consciousness. The main representatives were K. T. Keim (1825–78), *Die Geschichte Jesu von Nazara* (3 v. Zürich 1867–72; English tr. 6 v. London 1873–83), a moderately rationalistic work that rejected the Resurrection and insisted on the priority of Matthew; K. A. von Hase (1800–90), *Geschichte Jesu* (Leipzig 1876), the first survey of previous lives; H. J. HOLTZMANN (1832–1910); and B. Weiss (1827–1918), *Leben Jesu* (2 v. 1882), of which the English translation, *The Life of Jesus* (Edinburgh 1883), was a standard book in its time.

The school of comparative religion tried to explain the phenomenon of Christianity as a natural development arising from the contemporary religious situation, from Hellenism, from Oriental influences, and especially from Esserie-apocalyptic speculations. Among its main representatives were: A. Hilgenfeld (1823–1907); O. Pfeiderer (1839–1908); and especially W. BOUSSET (1865–1920), who endeavored to deduce Christianity from Hellenistic influences on Jewish religious thinking in his *Jesus* (Halle 1904; English tr. London and New York 1906) and particularly in his *Kyrios Christos* (Göttingen 1913, 3d ed. 1926). A modern representative of this trend is R. OTTO, *Reich Gottes und Menschensohn* (Munich 1934, 3d ed. 1954; English tr. Boston 1943, repr. 1957).

Toward the end of the 19th century the eschatological school came into prominence. J. Weiss (1863–1914) in his *Die Predigt Jesu vom Reiche Gottes* (Göttingen 1892) made the first attempt at a consistent eschatology: Jesus was not a moral preacher as the liberals thought; He announced the imminent coming of the eschatological kingdom of God in which He would be revealed as the true Messiah. A. Schweitzer (1875–1965), in his studies on the lives of Jesus, *Von Reimarus zu Wrede* (Tübingen 1902) and *Geschichte der Leben Jesu Forschung* [Tübingen 1906, 6th ed. 1951; English tr. *The Quest for the Historical Jesus* (London 1954)], developed the concepts of "interim ethics" and "imminent parousia." For the later development of the eschatological school, see W. G. Kümmel, *Verheissung und Erfüllung* (Zürich 1945; English tr. *Promise and Fulfillment,* London 1957). Kümmel rejected not only Schweitzer's views but also the more moderate "realized eschatology" of C. H. Dodd and T. W. Manson and the "center eschatology" of O. Cullmann, and he insisted on God's active presence in Christ.

Form Criticism School. The problem of MESSIANISM, not yet fully answered, was forced to retreat in favor of an even more basic question, raised by Biblical FORM CRITICISM. W. Wrede (1859–1906) in his *Das Messiasgeheimnis in den Evangelien* (Göttingen 1901) overthrew the Marcan hypothesis that sought to derive all early Christology from Mark. After the publication of M. Köhler's (1835–1917) *Der sogenannte historische Jesus und der geschichtliche, biblische Christus* (Leipzig 1892; rev. E. Wolf, Munich 1953, 2d ed. 1956; English tr. Philadelphia 1964), it became more and more axiomatic that there was an insurmountable abyss between the Christ of faith, presented in the Gospels, and the Jesus of history, of whom we have very little information.

The principles of the form criticism proposed by H. GUNKEL for the Old Testament were first applied to the Gospels by M. Dibelius and R. Bultmann. They endeavored to show that these accounts had been formed and shaped by the faith consciousness of the primitive Chris-

tian community. Events and teachings were selected and emphasized according to their existential meaning for Christian life (*Sitz im Leben*). K. L. Schmidt in his *Rahmen der Geschichte Jesu* (Berlin 1919) pointed out that even the chronological and topographical data of the Gospel stories were chosen and arranged in order to illustrate doctrinal tenets.

Bultmann, by pushing this method to its extremes, reduced one's total knowledge of the historical existence of Jesus to a merely subjective belief in His call to conversion. The only really meaningful thing for Christian existence in the life of Jesus is that one perceives God's eschatological call for decision. All the rest of the Gospel stories stems from mythological attempts for a human realization of this call. In order to make the essential message of the Gospels acceptable to modern man, the Gospels must be demythologized (*see* DEMYTHOLOGIZING). "I do indeed think that we can now know almost nothing concerning the life and personality of Jesus, since the early Christian sources show no interest in either and are, moreover, fragmentary and often legendary; and other sources about Jesus do not exist" [*Jesus and the Word* (London 1934) 8; from the German *Jesus,* Berlin 1926, 2d ed. 1951].

Dibelius was less radical than Bultmann. In his *Jesus* (Tübingen 1926; 3d ed. Berlin 1960; English tr. 1949) and also in his earlier *Die Botschaft von Jesus Christus* (1935; English tr. 1939), he tried to recognize a historical process in the life of Jesus. Still, also for him everything is centered on the actuality of the kingdom of God that in Jesus came irresistibly and closely upon us.

Reaction. The post-Bultmannian Protestant research worked hard to overcome the extreme conclusions of the master. G. Bornkamm, in his *Jesus von Nazareth* (Stuttgart 1956, English tr. New York and London 1960), still had a rather negative outlook: for him the Jesus of history can be known only as a sign, not as a reality. E. Käsemann ["Das Problem des historischen Jesus," *Zeitschrift für Theologie und Kirche* 51 (1954) 125–153 and "Neutestamentliche Fragen von heute" *ibid.* 54 (1957) 1–21] and E. Fuchs ["Die Frage nach dem Historischen Jesus" *ibid.* 53 (1956) 210–229, and "Glaube und Geschichte im Blick auf die Frage nach dem historischen Jesus," *ibid.* 54 (1957) 117–156] insisted emphatically that the Christ of faith could not be divorced from the Jesus of history. Along this line most of the modern scholars, such as N. A. Dahl, H. Riesenfeld, G. Ebeling, J. Jeremias, H. Diem, have prepared the way for a more positive view and have tried to free the exegesis from the contamination of philosophical presuppositions. A faith without fact, without a person at its center, means mere DOCETISM. All of Bultmann's critics have agreed that the problem must be restated. New methods were already proposed by W. Grundmann, *Die Geschichte Jesu Christi* (Berlin 1957), and especially by E. Stauffer, *Jesus: Gestalt und Geschichte* [Bern 1957; English tr. London 1960; see also his *Die Botschaft Jesu* (Bern 1959)]. H. Conzelmann, *Die Religion in Geschichte und Gegenwart* 621) thinks that, against the basic conclusion of the form criticism, it is now generally accepted that the faith of the primitive community was not exclusively based on the Easter events but rather went back substantially to the historical life of Jesus. H. W. Bartsch, although accepting the continuity between the life and teachings of Jesus and the KE-RYGMA of the primitive community, still does not wish to base the Christian faith on the Jesus of history [*Das historische Problem des Leben Jesu* (Munich 1960)].

Other Non-Catholic Works. In France, there are two recent standard works on the life of Jesus: M. Goguel's *Jésus-Christ* (Paris 1930; English tr. *The Life of Jesus*, New York 1933, repr. 1960), with an excellent chapter, "The Life of Jesus in Research" (37–69), with full bibliographical information; and C. de Guignebert's *Jesus* (Paris 1933; English tr. New York 1935, repr. 1956), which is completely rationalistic.

The best work of Jewish scholarship on the life of Jesus is J. Klausner's *Jesus of Nazareth* (Hebrew original, 1925; German tr. Berlin 2d ed. 1952; English tr. New York 1953). An interesting attempt was made by A. Robert, *Jesus of Nazareth: The Hidden Years* (English tr. from the Fr., New York 1962), to understand the human religious life of Jesus from its devout Jewish background.

The English-Speaking World. The problems in the research on the life of Jesus in Germany affected also the English-speaking world. However, English and American scholars refused to accept the extreme conclusions of the 19th-century rationalism or those of the 20th-century form criticism. There were exceptions; e.g., C. C. Hennel, a retired London merchant, in his book, *An Enquiry concerning the Origins of Christianity* (London 1838), followed the lines proposed by Strauss. (Strauss himself wrote the foreword to the German translation of 1840.) In his *Myth, Magic and Morals: A Study of Christian Origins* (London 1909) and *The Historical Christ* (London 1914), F. C. Conybeare claimed that Paul's fictitious Christ of the faith who appears in the Gospels and in the dogmas of the Church is entirely different from the Jesus who lived in reality. In the United States, J. MacKinnon Robertson (1856–1933), *Christianity and Mythology* (1900) and *Jesus and Judas* (1927), and W. B. Smith (1850–1934), *The Pre-Christian Jesus* (1906), are the representatives of radical views.

Before World War II. Among the lives of Jesus written in English in the 19th century are: F. W. Farrar, *Life of Christ* (London 1874), an impressive Christian answer to Renan, which in one year had 12 editions; J. C. Geikie, *The Life and Words of Christ* (2 v. London 1877); A. Edersheim, *The Life and Times of Jesus the Messiah* (2 v. London 1883), erudite but at times lacking in critical judgment; and W. SANDAY, *Outline of the Life of Christ* (Edinburgh 1909, a reprint of his article from J. Hastings and J. A. Selbia, eds., *Dictionary of the Bible*).

Several works on the life of Christ appeared in the 20th century before World War II: E. Digges la Touche, *The Person of Christ in Modern Thought* (London 1912); T. J. Thorburn, *Jesus the Christ: Historical or Mythical?* (Edinburgh 1912); A. C. Headlam, *The Life and Teaching of Jesus Christ* (1923); A. W. Robinson, *The Christ and the Gospels* (1924); J. Warschauer, *The Historical Life of Jesus* (London 1927), based on A. Schweitzer's principles; S. J. Case, *The Historicity of Jesus* (Chicago 1912); and *Jesus: A New Biography* (Chicago 1927), written in a truly Christian spirit and judged by J. M. Robinson to be the best available; C. Gore, *Jesus of Nazareth* (1919); B. W. Bacon, *Jesus the Son of God* (1930); F. C. Burkitt, *Jesus Christ* (1932); B. S. Easton, *Christ and the Gospels* (1930), and *What Jesus Thought* (1938).

Since World War II. Among the lives of Christ published since 1945 are: V. Taylor, *The Life and Ministry of Jesus* (1945); G. S. Duncan, *Jesus, Son of Man: Studies in a Modern Portrait* (1947); C. J. Cadoux, *Life of Jesus* (1948); E. J. Goodspeed, *Life of Jesus* (1950); H. E. W. Turner, *Jesus, Master and Lord* (2d ed. 1954); H. R. Fuller, *The Mission and Achievement of Jesus* (1954); W. E. Bundy, *Jesus and the First Three Gospels* (1955); L. F. Church, *The Life of Jesus* (1957); and J. Knox, *Jesus, Lord and Christ* (1958).

Critical Works. The English answer to the messianic problem was given by the school of realized eschatology, represented by scholars such as C. H. Dodd in his *History and the Gospel* (1938), W. Manson in his *Jesus the Messiah* (1943), and T. W. Manson in his *The Servant Messiah: A Study of the Public Ministry of Jesus* (1953). According to these scholars Jesus understood Himself in the sense of a synthesis of the concepts of the SON OF MAN and that of the Servant of the Lord (*see* SUFFERING SERVANT, SONGS OF THE) combined with the idea of the presence of the kingdom of God.

In regard to the problems raised by form criticism, the extreme conclusions were not accepted by scholars in England or the United States. Some exceptions were A. E. J. Rawlinson, F. C. Grant, and especially W. E. Bundy in his *Jesus and the First Three Gospels* (1955). In a symposium [see *Expository Times* 53 (1941–42) 60–66,175–177, 248–251] V. Taylor, T. W. Manson, and C. J. Cadoux, though agreeing that it is impossible to write a real biography of Jesus, still rejected the Bultmannian exaggerations in this regard. Also, G. V. Jones, *Christology and Myth in the New Testament* [(London 1956) 14–16, English bibliography], and H. E. W. Turner, *Jesus, Master and Lord* (London 2d ed. 1954) are on the conservative and constructive side.

In fact, all over the world the-life-of-Jesus research seems to have taken a more positive turn. J. M. Robinson, *A New Quest of the Historical Jesus* (London 1959; German tr. *Kerygma und der historische Jesus,* Zurich 1960, with more recent bibliography) rejects the attempts of the school of realized eschatology and of E. Stauffer and thinks that the problem has to be reformulated on an existentialist basis. According to Stauffer the historian mediates and builds a bridge for his generation to persons who lived in the past. He can do this on the basis of the Gospels also in regard to Jesus. Thus, by using the historicocritical method properly one can arrive at the very words of Jesus and so reach beyond the understanding of the primitive Church to the true understanding that Jesus had of His own existence. E. Käsemann may be correct, however, in his "The Problem of the Historical Jesus," *Essays on New Testament Themes* (London 1964) 15–47, in saying that a historian may state the existence of the riddle of Jesus but he will never be able to answer and solve it.

Catholic Development from Apologetics to Christology. Lives of Jesus written by Catholics in the 19th century and the first decade of the 20th, which were based on the assumption of the full historical value of the Gospels, are still of value despite the valid observations of form criticism. Worthy of mention are: P. J. Schegg, *Sechs Bücher des Lebens Jesu* (2 v. Freiburg 1874–75); P. Naumann, *Das Leben unseres Herren und Heilandes Jesus Christus* (3 v. Prague 1875–77); J. Grimm, *Das Leben Jesu nach den vier Evangelien* (7 v. Regensburg 1876–99); P. H. J. Coleridge, *The Life of Our Life* (London 1869); J. N. Sepp and D. B. HANEBERG, *Das Leben Jesu* (7 v. 1843–46, 4th ed. Munich 1898); A. J. Maas, *The Life of Christ according to Gospel History* (4th ed. St. Louis 1891; repr. 1954); *Christ in Type and Prophecy* (New York 1893–96); and "Jesus Christ," *The Catholic Encyclopedia*, ed. C. G. Herbermann et al. 8:374–385.

In French, E. Bougaud, *Jésus-Christ* (Paris 1884), and P. Didon, OP, *Jésus-Christ* (2 v. Paris 1891; English tr. New York 1891), are both more devotional than scholarly, yet the latter is based on serious research. The real answer to Renan was given by H. C. Fouard, *La Vie de N.S. Jésus-Christ* (2 v. Paris 1880, 21st ed. 1911; English tr. 1891). Equally thorough and scholarly is É. P. LE CAMUS, *La Vie de N.S. Jésus-Christ* (2 v. Paris 1883; English tr. 1908).

Apologetical Works. Noteworthy achievements among the more recent apologetical lives of Jesus are: H. Felder, *Jesus Christus* (2 v. Paderborn 1911–14; English tr. *Christ and the Critics,* London 1924); A. Meyenberg, *Leben Jesu Werk* (3 v. Luzern 1922–32); and L. C. Fillion, *Jésus-Christ* (3 v. Paris 1922; English tr. St. Louis 1928–29). Deserving of special mention are: L. de GRANDMAISON, *Jésus-Christ,* (2 v. Paris 1928, 23d ed. 1941); M. Lepin, *Jésus-Christ, sa vie et son oeuvre* (Paris 1912) and *Le Christ Jésu, son existence historique et sa divinité* (Paris 1929), both still ranking among the best; M. J. LAGRANGE, *L'Évangile de Jésus-Christ* (Paris 1929, 2d ed. 1954), which unites modern criticism with Catholic orthodoxy; and J. LEBRETON, *The Life and Teaching of Jesus Christ, Our Lord* (French ed. 2 v. Paris 1931, 2d ed. 1947; English tr. London 1935, repr. 1950). J. Sickenberger, *Das Leben Jesu nach den vier Evangelien* (Münster 1933), is somewhat outdated; J. Christiani, *Jésus-Christ, fils de Dieu* (3 v. Lyons 1934); and A. GOODIER's *The Public Life of Jesus* (3 v. London 1930) and *The Passion and Death of Jesus* (London 1933) are devotional rather than scholarly.

Interesting among the most modern publications are: F. M. Willam, *Das Leben Jesu im Lande und Volke Israel* (10th ed., Freiburg 1960–61; English tr. St. Louis 1944), which paints an excellent portrait of Jesus' contemporary settings; J. Pickl, *Messias König Jesus* (Munich 1939; English tr. St. Louis 1946), which gives a good picture of Roman military life and guerrilla warfare and conveys new insights into the Passion of Jesus; and W. Beilner, *Christus und die Pharisaer* (Vienna 1959), which elaborates on another important aspect on a solid exegetical basis. More comprehensive lives are: G. Ricciotti, *The Life of Christ* (Milan 1941; English tr, Milwaukee 1947); H. Daniel-Rops, *Jesus and His Times* (New York 1956, from the French); and A. FERNÁNDEZ TRUYOLS, *The Life of Christ* (Madrid 1954; English tr. Westminster, Maryland 1958). The most recent work by an American Catholic is F. J. Sheen, *Life of Christ* (New York 1958).

Theological Works. After the modernistic assumptions of a gradual and purely human development of Jesus' messianic consciousness had been rejected, Catholic authors, in treating the psychological problem of the life of Jesus, were more concerned about the Chalcedonian orthodoxy of the metaphysical divine sonship than about the reality of a truly human historical existence. The turn is marked by P. Galtier, *L'Unité du Christ* (Paris 1939). R. Guardini, *Der Herr* (Würzburg 11th ed. 1959; English tr. *The Lord,* Chicago 1937, 5th ed. 1954); K. Adam, *Jesus Christus* (Düsseldorf 8th ed. 1949; English tr. *The Christ of Our Faith,* New York 1957); and A. Graham, *The Christ of Catholicism* (London 1947) fully acknowledge the modern theological and psychological problem of the life of Jesus without sacrificing Catholic orthodoxy. The reinterpretation of Jesus' consciousness of His own divinity—for which, according to K. Rahner and J. Galot, the beatific vision does not seem any more to be a *conditio sine qua non*—makes it possible to accept a real, human, historical progress in His life. How much of this life can be reconstructed on the basis of Biblical and archeological research remains another problem. But according to H. Vögtle (*Lexikon für Theologie und Kirche*, ed. J. Hofer and K. Rahner, 5:923) a minimalistic evaluation of the cognoscibility of the historical facts of Jesus' human life can be much more erroneous than the basic confidence in the truly historical value of the Gospel narratives.

The theological problem here lies, perhaps, not so much in going back beyond the Christ of faith to the Jesus of history—for here the answer depends entirely on the different ecclesiological conceptions—as in the transition from the Jesus of history to the Christ of faith. What was the basis on which the Apostles recognized and accepted this Man as the Messiah and, ultimately, as the trinitarian Son of God? Was their faith and the subsequent faith of the Church founded on the life of Jesus that was exposed to everybody, to all human observation and judgment? Or is the historical human life of Jesus to be regarded as the visible sacramental presence of which the inner mystery—now and then flashing through the mortal exterior in the strange aura of miraculous phenomena—cannot be comprehended by merely human intelligence but solely by the faith that is a grace given by God?

The rationalistic refusal to accept the Jesus of history in order to save the transcendent God of reason; the liberal attempts to consider the life of Jesus as a purely human and moral phenomenon so as to save Jesus the man in His admirable human reality; or Bultmann's concern to save the divine reality of Jesus by demythologizing the Gospel and reducing the divine in Him to mere subjectivity; or all the other Protestant theories that change the full reality of the Incarnation of the Word to a mere "word event" (*Wortereignis*)—all are ultimately rooted in the confusion over the radical theological problem of a true ontological encounter between God and man in the mystery of the Incarnation. In the Incarnation, as Rahner states, not only is an individual human nature assumed by the Son of God, but also the whole of human history is assumed by Him. As the historical Jesus He became part of man's mortal history, and through His death, Resurrection, and Ascension He transcended it and became the Lord of history. Only after a due clarification of such essentially theological problems, and particularly those concerning the dynamic, personal, social, and ontological structure of the Incarnation, will it be possible to reconsider successfully the hitherto somewhat Monophysiti-cally—either too divinely or too humanly—conceived life of Christ.

Imaginative Lives of Jesus. T. Ziolkowski divides the fictionalizing biographies into two principal groups. There is the group that he calls "modern apocrypha," a blend of scholarship, fiction, and literary forgery, that claim to be based on documents, newly discovered, that throw new light on the life of Jesus—notably on the so-called Silent Years before he began his public ministry. A notable example of this kind of fictional biography is *La vie inconnue de Jésus Christ* by Nicolas Notovitch (1894). Notovitch, a Russan war correspondent, alleged to have discovered an ancient "Life of Saint Issa, Best of the Sons of Men," during his travels to Tibet in 1887. Another example of this kind of apocrypha is *Der Benan-Brief* published by Ernst von der Planitz (1910), based on the letter allegedly written by Benan, a priest at Memphis, who described how Jesus' reputation as a great healer dates from the time he was studying medicine in Egypt.

The second group of fictionalized biographies had precedents in the early Latin poets, the mystery plays of the Middle Ages, and modern literature that aimed to make the figure of Jesus appealing to contemporary audiences and had as their purpose pious meditation on his life. In more recent times the most widely circulated was Ernest Renan's *Vie de Jésus* (1863) "whose critical insufficiency is matched only by its aesthetic charm" (Ziolkowski). Although Renan manifested an anti-Christian bias, his work owed its popularity in large part to the fact that many moderns are more interested in the human reality of Jesus than in His divinity—although in a way that does not necessarily exclude faith in His divinity. Giovanni Papini argued in his introduction to his *Story of Christ* (*Storia di Cristo*, Florence, 1921), perhaps the greatest success since Renan, that since every generation has its own concerns it is necessary to translate the Gospel into their terms. Papini was followed by a series of "Jesus books" as varied as the points of view of their authors: F. Timmermann, *Das Jesuskind in Flandern* (1923); Emil Ludwig, *Der Menschensohn* (1928); D. Mereshkowksi, *Jesus the Unknown* (1932) and *Jesus Who Is to Come* (1934); Shalom Asch, *The Nazarene* (1939); Edzar Schaper (converted to Catholicism in 1952), *Das Leben Jesu* (1936); and Fulton Oursler, *The Greatest Story Ever Told* (1949). For all its factual detail Jim Bishop's effort to describe *The Day Christ Died* (1957) as if he were a journalist reporting the day's news from Jerusalem is a fictional account. Two of the most imaginative (and popular) fictionalizing biographies in the mid-twentieth century were Robert Graves's *King Jesus* (1946) and Nikos Kazantzakis's *The Last Temptation of Christ* (1953). Despite Graves's claim that "every important element in the story is based on some tradition however tenuous'' and that he took pains to verify the historical background, it reflects his pagan sympathies. Kazantakis makes no pretense at historical accuracy. His is a bold and highly personal interpretation of Jesus. ''That part of Christ's nature which was profoundly human,'' he writes in the prologue, ''helps us to understand him, and love him and to pursue his Passion as though it were our own.''

It should be noted that these fictionalizing biographies must be distinguished from another genre that Ziolkowski calls ''fictional transfigurations.'' The latter are works of fiction that take Jesus' life as a pattern for an entirely modern plot much as James Joyce did with Odysseus in his *Ulysses*. Among Ziolkowski's examples are such twentieth-century novels as Thomas Mann's *The Magic Mountain*, John Steinbeck's *Grapes of Wrath*, Ignazio Silone's *Bread and Wine*, and Nikos Kanzantzakis' *The Greek Passion*. The parallels are essentially formal. Often the Christ-figure in works of this genre has little resemblance to the moral values and religious attitudes of the Jesus of the Gospels.

Bibliography: J. M. BELLAMY, *Les Biographies nouvelles de N.S. Jésus-Christ et les commentaires récents de l'Évangile* (Vannes 1892). W. SANDAY, *The Life of Christ in Recent Research* (New York 1908). W. D. MACKENZIE, J. HASTINGS, ed., *Encyclopedia of Religion and Ethics*, 13 v. (Edinburgh 1908–27) 7:505–551. H. WEINEL, *Jesus im 19. Jahrhundert* (3d ed. Tübingen 1914). G. BALDENSPERGER, ''Un Demi-siècle de recherches sur l'historicité de Jésus,'' *Revue de théologie et de philosophie* 12 (1924) 161–210, F. M. BRAUN, *Où en est le problème de Jésus?* (Paris 1932). J. KLAUSNER, *Encyclopedia Judaica: Das Judentum in Geschichte und Gegenwart*, 10 v. (Berlin 1928–34) 9:52–77. E. F. SCOTT, ''Recent Lives of Jesus,'' *Harvard Theological Review* 26 (1934) 1–32. H. ANDERSON, *Jesus and the Christian Origins: A Commentary on Modern Viewpoints* (New York 1964). A. PATON and L. POPE, ''The Novelist and Christ,'' *The Saturday Review of Literature* (Dec. 4, 1954). R. DETWEILER, ''Christ and the Christ Figure in American Fiction,'' *The Christian Scholar* (Summer 1964). T. ZIOLKOWSKI, *Fictional Transfigurations of Christ* (Princeton 1972).

[C. H. HENKEY/EDS.]

JESUS CHRIST, ICONOGRAPHY OF

The early Christians had images of Christ made for their own veneration despite the Biblical prohibition (Ex 20.4) against the making of images. Eusebius of Caesarea wrote that in his own day images of Christ and the Apostles going back to apostolic times still existed (*Ecclesiatical History* 7.18). According to Irenaeus (*Adversus haereses* 1.25.6), the heretical Gnostics and Carpocratians venerated or worshiped effigies of Jesus, Pythagoras, Plato, and Aristotle. An image of Jesus, together with those of Abraham and Orpheus, was venerated in the *lararium* of the Emperor Alexander Severus.

It is not possible to determine if any of these images were intended to represent the true likeness of Christ. However, one can assume that the anthropomorphic representation of Christ was not posterior to, but was either contemporary with, or even anterior to, the representation of Christ by symbols. This wound appears to be true even in the face of the opposition of Church Fathers such as Irenaeus, Eusebius, and Epiphanius to the making of such images. Also, the Council of Elvira (*c.* 315) had condemned the making of religious pictures (*Picturas in ecclesia esse non debere, ne quod colitur et adorabitur in parietirus dipingatur*).

Physical Types. Each period created the type of Christ it desired, since neither the New Testament nor patristic literature provides a physical description of Jesus. In general, there are two types, one based on Ps 44(45).3, ''Fairer in beauty are you than the sons of men; grace is poured out upon your lips''; and the other on Is 53.2, ''There is in him no stately bearing to make us look at him, nor appearance that would attract us to him.'' In the *Acts of the Martyrs,* which probably reflects a popular tradition, Christ always appears as youthful and beautiful (*Acta Andr. et Matth.* 33; *Mart. Mt.* 13).

From the very beginning, these two types were further divided into subcategories. The young, beardless Christ was represented as a lad with short, curly hair (sarcophagus, Musée Lapidaire, Arles, early 4th century; strigillated Christ, Peter sarcophagus, Lateran Museum, Rome, late Tetrarchian period, 300–310; clipeus sarcophagus, Lateran Museum), as a boy with long, curly hair (statuette of seated Christ, Museo Nazionale, Rome *c.* 360; Christ on a sarcophagus of Junius Bassus, Vatican Grotto), as an older but still youthful man with short, curly hair (mosaic of Christ between Archbishop Ecclesius and S. Vitale, Ravenna, 6th century), and as a youth with long hair (arcade sarcophagus, Lateran Museum, *c.* 350–360; Ascension on an ivory relief, National Museum, Munich, *c.* 400; mosaic of the Good Shepherd, Mausoleum of Galla Placidia, Ravenna, *c.* 440; mosaic of Christ and Apostles in the squinch of the baptistery, S. Lorenzo, Milan, 355–397).

The youthful types of the beardless Christ were derived from the image of the Good Shepherd, which was always represented as a youth according to the custom of entrusting boys with the task of tending sheep. This type was dominant in antiquity to the 5th century, in Ravenna to the 7th century. It occurs in representations of Christ as Orpheus, Christ as the Thaumaturge, and even in those of Christ as Teacher and Pantocrator. The image persisted in the West through the Ottonian period, after which it appeared only sporadically: mosaics, St. Mark's, Venice, end of the 13th century; Timoteo Viti (1467–1523), Art

"Head of Christ Crowned with Thorns," oil painting on wood panel after Guido Reni, c. 1640–1749.

Master of the Aachen Altar, Christ appearing to Mary, 1485. (©Archivo Iconografico, S.A./CORBIS)

Gallery, Brescia; Bernardino Luini (1470–1532), Ambrosian Gallery, Milan; Giovanni Antonio Boltraffio (1467–1516), Carrara Academy, Bergamo. An older but still beardless type appears in "The Redeemer" by RAPHAEL (Municipal Art Gallery, Brescia). A heroic beardless Christ dominates the Last Judgment in the Sistine Chapel by MICHELANGELO.

The bearded type of Christ appeared at the turn of the 4th century concurrently with the appearance of the historical representation of New Testament scenes and persons. Since the 5th century this has been the major mode of representation of Christ in both East and West, except in Ravenna and in the Carolingian and Ottonian West. In addition to the beard, the style of which changes from period to period, Christ wears long hair, parted in the middle. Although the Nazarenes did wear their hair long, in contrast to the Romans, it was not the intent of the artist to show an ethnic type of Christ. Rather, it was traditional for Prophets and angels, creatures more than

human, to be represented as wearing the hair long; moreover, philosophers and teachers continued to wear their hair long, and even retained their beards, after the custom had gone out of existence. The aim was to invest the image of Christ with something of the transcendental.

The bearded type, in its turn, was subdivided into a full-bearded one and another wearing only cheek and chin beard, with the upper lip clean-shaven. The fully bearded type, which became typical in the East after the 8th century and also dominant in the West after the Ottonian period, was used originally for representations of Christ as the True Philosopher (polychrome fragment of a frieze sarcophagus, Museo Nazionale, Rome, *c.* 300), as the Miracle-Worker (Jona sarcophagus, Lateran Museum, end of 3d century), as Christ in Majesty or the Law-Giver (mosaic of Christ between SS. Cosmas and Damian, apse of SS. Cosmas and Damian, Rome, 6th century; sarcophagus fragment, Museum of S. Sebastiano, Rome,

Bronze crucifix, detail showing head and shoulders of the Christ figure, Ottonian, 11th century. (Marburg-Art Reference, Art Resource, NY)

c. 370), and as Pantocrator (Daphni, Greece, *c.* 1100; wall painting of Christ Blessing, Boiana, near Sofia, 1259).

The second type, which is rare, appears in the following works: a 5th-century mosaic of *Traditio Legis,* S. Costanza, Rome; Crucifixion fresco, S. Maria Antiqua, Rome, 8th century; Master of the Lyversberger Passion, ''Jesus Crowned with Thorns,'' Cologne Art Gallery, 15th century; Hans Holbein the Elder (*c.* 1465–1524), ''The Crucifixion,'' Augsburg Museum; Master of Mary's Life, ''Crucifixion,'' Munich Art Gallery, 15th century; George Minne, wood engraving,''The Baptism of Christ,'' 20th century.

It has been suggested that these types of Christ were derived from pagan deities such as Zeus, Eros, Apollo, or Asklepios. But it is highly unlikely that the early Christians would have utilized these pagan types for the exemplification of Christ. There exists a legend of a painter who, having sought to depict an image of Christ according to a type of Zeus, was punished by having his hands withered by God (*Theod. lect.* 15). Moreover, the bearded and beardless types were not products of specific geographic areas of the Roman world representing ethnic types. The so-called Syrian and Semitic types of Christ were not developed in Syria and Palestine, and the con-

trasting youthful type was not a Western innovation; for the types of Christ did not depend so much on external influences as on the concept of Christ held in each period or area.

Thematic Types. The earliest representations, which have to do specifically with the theme of salvation and resurrection, depict Christ in a completely nonpersonalized manner; there are no distinctive traits of character or individuality in countenance or in the conformation of the body. Rather, images reflect a compromise between the classical ideal of physical beauty (*kalos kagathos*) and the description in Ps 44(45).3.

At this stage of the development of Christian society, when persecution was rife and there were forebodings of doom of the empire, the ordinary believer was profoundly concerned with the assurance of his own salvation and the provision of a basis for hope of a resurrection and eternal life. Christ was for him a symbol of salvation. Thus the various representations of Christ on the painted walls of the catacombs corresponded to those passages in the Bible and in the writings of the early Church Fathers where the hope of redemption is expressed (Ex 34.23, 37.24; Is 40.11) Christ thus appears as a Good Shepherd as early as the 2d century, as Orpheus in the 3d century, and as the True Philosopher (Tertullian, *Apol.* 46–47). He might appear as Orpheus, since the story of the latter was considered analogous to that of the Good Shepherd. Orpheus, like Christ, had been able to charm with his music (redeem) the wild beasts (sinners, lost souls), and also, like Christ, to descend into Hades to redeem a soul incarcerated there.

As the Good Shepherd, Christ was represented wearing a *tunica exomis* and carrying a sheep on his shoulders or surrounded by sheep; as Orpheus he was dressed as a Phrygian; and as the True Philosopher, He wore at first, as Cynic philosopher, the pallium with breast and shoulder uncovered; but later, as a specifically Christian philosopher, a pallium that covered the entire body, and sandals. The portrait of the True Philosopher as Cynic corresponded to the description in Is 53.2.

As a result of the Christological controversies that took place from the 4th to the 7th century, a deliberate attempt was made to stress the human nature of Christ, if not the actual, historical Person. The task was difficult since neither the Gospels nor any other historical writings furnish a description of the real Christ. Descriptions of Christ, however, existed in legendary works. In the 8th century, John of Damascus described Jesus as being handsome and tall, with hair slightly curled, eyebrows very arched and meeting in the middle of the forehead; His face oval, complexion pale olive, and hair and beard the color of ripe corn. A 13th-century text, probably derived from a contemporary Greek source, is written in the form of a letter by Publius Lentulus, ''president'' of the people of Jerusalem, to Tiberius Caesar, in which Christ is described as tall, with fair long hair flowing down to the shoulders. ''It is slightly crisp and curled, parted in the middle and falling on either side as in the custom of the Nazarenes. His cheeks are somewhat rosy, the nose and mouth are well shaped, the beard is thick and the color of a ripe hazel nut, like the hair it is short and parted in the middle.'' His eyes are blue, at times flashing with sudden fire. ''No man has ever heard Him laugh but often men have seen Him weep. . . . He is as handsome as a man can be.''

It is likely that the handsome images produced in the Gothic period, e.g., the Beau Dieu at Amiens and the Beau Christ at Rheims, are based on such a description as that in the letter of Lentulus, which had some currency during the period. St. Thomas Aquinas in his commentary on Psalm 44(45) stated that Christ possessed physical beauty of the highest order. Finally, according to Syrian legends, Christ had black eyes and a black beard.

Acheiropoietic Images. There are several ''acheiropoietai,'' or images made without the intervention of human hands; but from the existing evidence concerning them, these images no more correspond among themselves than do the descriptions that have come down. Perhaps the two most famous are the so-called Mandylion of Edessa, supposedly produced by Christ Himself for Abgar (preserved at S. Silvestro, Rome), and the veil of Veronica, supposedly an impress made by Christ Himself (preserved in the treasury of St. Peter's, Rome). Another legend relates that a portrait begun by St. Luke was completed by angels (now venerated at the chapel of the Sancta Sanctorum, Rome); there is also a portrait supposed to have been given by St. Peter to the Roman senator Pudens (exposed on Easter Sunday at S. Prassede, Rome).

A resolution to difficulties surrounding the acheiropoietic images can be found in the statement made by St. Augustine that ''the image of Christ according to the flesh has been created and modified by countless conceptions, all varying. His true likeness is unknown to us'' (*Conf.*). St. Irenaeus also had said that ''the physical features of Jesus are unknown.'' Moreover, the New Testament had declared specifically (2 Cor 5.16) that we no longer know Christ according to the flesh. In the 4th century a true portrait of Christ would have been unthinkable (Epiphanius, *Panarion haereseon* 27.6.9).

Majestas Domini. Christian artists of the 4th and 5th centuries sought to represent the majesty of Christ. In one book of the New Testament, the Revelation, they found an image of Christ more mysterious than that of either the

German 13th-century stained glass panel depicting Christ. (Marburg-Art Reference, Art Resource, NY)

liturgy or the other books of the New Testament. In the Revelation the apparitions are closest to the ancient theophanies of Isaiah, Ezekiel, and Daniel. Illustrated Apocalypses that appeared from the 5th century on offer a magnificent history of the majesty of Christ.

In the West the vision of the Lord surrounded by four winged creatures was detached from the total setting of the Apocalypse; it was made purely Christological and called *Majestas Domini*. In the 2d century, Irenaeus, Bishop of Lyons, saw in the central figure of Ezechiel's vision the Logos and in the tetramorphic cherubim the modes of operation of the Logos that were later fulfilled in the Apocalypse: ''It is clear that the creator of the universe, the Logos, He who is seated on the cherubim, had delivered to us the Gospel under four forms'' (*Adversus haereses, Patrologia Graeca* 7:1039). The four creatures resembling lion, ox, man, and eagle were generally interpreted as the four Evangelists. From Irenaeus the interpretation passed into the exegetical works of the Latin Church Fathers where it was available for the programming of artistic representations. According to the theologians of the Middle Ages, who called them *sacramenta* of Christ, they signified four aspects of His nature corresponding to the four principal moments of His earthly existence: Birth, Death, Resurrection, and Ascension. The

"The Dead Christ," bronze sculpture by Giuseppe Sammartino, *1753.* (©Mimmo Jodice/CORBIS)

compact formula was expressed in a sermon on the Ascension by Honorius of Autun: *Christus erat homo nascendo, vitulus moriendo, leo resurgendo, aquila ascendendo* (*Patrologia Latina,* 172:956). The distich summed up epigrammatically Christ's earthly career from birth through death and resurrection to final divinization and reunion with the Godhead.

Though it originated in the East, the figure of Christ surrounded by the four living creatures was given definitive form in the Carolingian period. A representation of Christ in Majesty appeared in the Evangelistary of Gudohin (751–754, Autun Library); He is flanked by angels in a large central clipeus and surrounded by the symbols of the four Evangelists. In the art of the Carolingian renaissance the image of Christ was patterned after the youthful figure in the mosaics and sarcophagi of the early Christian period. He is represented in this manner in the Evangelistary of Godescalc (Bibliothèque Nationale, Paris), a masterpiece of apocalyptic art. In ivories of the same period the imperial figure of Christ is shown seated in the midst of the four winged creatures. The type was maintained in the Romanesque period, as in the apsidal fresco of S. Clemente de Tahull.

The Christ in Majesty of Western art was derived from the Byzantine Pantocrator. But whereas the Pantocrator was always represented as a bust at the top of cupolas within the church, the *Majestas Domini* shows Christ seated on a throne either in the apse or on the tympanum of a portal. The portal was considered symbolic of the entranceway to revelation. The *Majestas Domini*

in the portal tympanum greeted the pilgrim and the faithful. Suger said to the visitors at St. Denis that the beauty that illumines souls must direct them toward the light of which Christ is the true gateway (*Christus janua vera*).

In the 12th century the type became universal throughout the West. All of the exemplars represented the Majesty of the Lord and were enhanced with the figures of the Apocalypse and Old Testament visions. The fully developed type is found in 12th-century French sculpture, as at Moissac, Chartres, and Charlieu, and in Limoges enamels, all of which display a common image of Christ. Derived from successive redactions of apsidal frescoes of the preceding period, representations of the period from 1140 to 1160 are especially homogeneous.

In its beginnings monumental sculpture had translated mainly hieratic and frontal models, but the fiercely linear image of the miniatures, for example, gradually was ennobled. The frontal figure of the Byzantine Pantocrator was given classical qualities and made more supple. Though in Germany and Italy the type of Christ remained little changed from its Byzantine prototype, in France it acquired a new expressiveness and beauty. The last Majesties of Gothic sculpture reflect a humanizing tendency that is at a considerable remove from he hieratic tradition.

With the creation of the image of the Pantocrator and its Western derivatives, Christian art reached the acme of its representation of Christ as the Logos. Thereafter, it was concerned only with the Son of Man, subject to all the infirmities. The suffering Christ, the *vir dolorum* spoken of by Isaiah (53.3), was depicted as human in His frailty, reviled, spat upon, mocked, wilting under the blows of the scourges, bent under the weight of the cross, exhausted and *in extremis* on Calvary, and finally agonizing and dying on the cross.

The Dead Christ. The representation of the dead Christ, however, appeared at an earlier time in history. The change was brought about, probably during the Christological controversies in the Church from the 4th to the 7th century, by the necessity of emphasizing Christ's human nature, the reality of which had been denied by the Docetists. Eastern Christian art went straight to the heart of the problem by representing a dead Christ on the cross (Greek Psalter, 1066, British Museum, manuscript Add. 19352, fol. 87b; mosaic of the Crucifixion in the monastery of Daphni, Greece, 11th century).

The image of the dead Christ was revived by Nicetas Stethatos "Pectoratos" (*Antidialogus and Dialexis*), in accordance with the ritual of the Zeon of the Byzantine Church and the aphthartodocetic doctrine on which it is based. Christ was depicted with bent head (Jn 19.30) and closed eyes but without any mark of suffering or of the scourging on His body, and with two separate jets, one of blood and the other of water, gushing out of His side wound to imply that the body was not in a state of decomposition. This representation was attacked by Cardinal Humbert as a representation of the antichrist, but it spread westward and appeared in Italy in the 13th century (Coppo di Marcovaldo, panel crucifix, Palazzo Communale, San Gimignano). On the whole, however, Western artists refrained from the representation of an incorruptible body of Christ, and by and large they painted a fully dead Christ on the Cross, as in the many Luccan and Pisan Crucifixions of the 13th century.

Man of Sorrows. Christ portrayed as the Man of Sorrows seems at an opposite pole from triumphant representations of Christ in the earlier Middle Ages, and is also strikingly different in conception from the active Christ of Renaissance art.

In the 11th and 12th centuries the concept of a triumphant Christ was pervasive, and the High Middle Ages produced an idealized representation that is best seen in the Beau Dieu of Amiens. In the late 14th century appeared the fully developed type of the Man of Sorrows; it was frequently represented in the art of the 15th and early 16th centuries. In one class of representations Christ is shown standing with the crown of thorns on His head and pointing with His right hand to the wound in His side. The tragic crown of thorns replaced the actual royal crown in certain representations of Christ in the 12th century; subsequently it became an attribute of all representations of the suffering Christ, whether as the crucified or as the Man of Sorrows. Another class shows him seated on a rock or wooden block, wearily supporting His head with the right hand (sculpture, Heiligkreuzkirche, Gmünd, early 15th century). This type, the Christ in Distress, was influenced by the developed medieval iconography of the Patriarch Job on the dungheap, wearied by extreme physical suffering and the psychic torment of false comforters. A third class of representations is to be found in Italian art, where Christ stands in the tomb or is seated on it, with the Virgin and St. John or angels supporting Him.

In works of art from northern Europe the countenance of Christ as Man of Sorrows is filled with deep grief (Conrad von Einbeck, 1416, Moritzkirche, Halle). The suffering and sorrowful aspect of Christ was made explicit in a 15th-century painting by an anonymous Spanish master. His head is crowned with thorns, His brow is knit in anguish, and two large tears are on His eyelids, paralleled by two thin streams of blood on His cheeks. An inscription around the frame reads: *O vos omnes qui transitis per viam, [attendite] et videte si este dolor similis sicut dolor meus.* Albrecht Dürer returned

The Crucifixion of Jesus Christ, sculpture by Bernini, in the Spanish monastery of El Escorial. (©Adam Woolfitt/CORBIS)

to the subject several times during his career. In a final version of the Man of Sorrows in "The Small Passion" (1511), he depicted a tragic, isolated, and abject figure of Christ, with head in hand and face almost completely hidden in dark shadow cast by the lowered head. Dürer's was the climactic representation of the figure of the Man of Sorrows.

Humanity of Christ. The concept of the humanity of Christ was carried forward in Renaissance and baroque art. If God may not die, He may not despair either. Only man is subject to both despair and death. In the 17th century an awesome Christ appears in the art of Pacheco, Zurbarán, and Velázquez, who attempt to render the moment when He cried out: "My God, my God, why hast thou forsaken me?" (Mt 27.46). Christ is shown looking up to heaven in anguish, surrounded by the gloom of that "darkness at noon" in the image of the *Cristo agonizante.* The Veronica image of the suffering Christ provided a source for the Spanish painters Zurbarán and Velázquez in their creating of the *Cristo agonizante;* they transferred the visage to that of the crucified Christ to express the moment of "despair."

Christ's Humanity is shown also through His compassion for the multitude and for children. Rembrandt in particular depicted the tender Christ of the Gospels ("Disciples of Emmaus," 1648, Louvre, Paris; "Christ Healing the Sick," known also as "The Hundred Guilder Print," *c.* 1642; "The Raising of Lazarus," Rijksmuseum, Amsterdam). The 19th-century painter Fritz von Uhde, in whose works the influence of socialism is visible, depicted the Christ of the Poor in his "Suffer the Little Children to Come unto Me" ("Lasset die Kindlein zu mir kommen," 1884, Museum der bildenden Kunste, Leipzig) and "Come, Lord, Be Our Guest" ("Komm, Herr Jesu, sei unser Gast," 1885, National-galerie, Berlin). The type of Christ appearing in Protestant art is related to the idealized description in the letter of Lentulus. The exception is the ethnic Christ of Rembrandt.

Christus Coelestis Medicus. In the 17th and 18th centuries, in part due to increased respect for the medical profession following upon improvement in the science of healing, a new type of Christ was created, which appears mostly in German art, although the earliest representation appears in Dutch art in 1510. Christ as Apothecary is shown behind a counter and surrounded by the paraphernalia of the druggist's profession. This image had been prepared by the mystical speculations of such writers as J. V. Andreae (1586–1654), J. Arndt (1555–1621), and J. Boehme (1575–1624), but the seed for it may be found in the NT (Mt 9.12, Mk 2.17, and Lk 5.31) and also in the OT (Is 53.5). Tertullian, among the early Church Fathers, also makes reference to it (*Adv. Marcionem* 3.17.11).

Sacred Heart of Jesus. The Heart of Jesus image, or *Caritate Christi,* intended to demonstrate Christ's all-consuming love for man, is based in general on the scriptural texts that speak of His compassion for man, and specifically on the vision of St. Margaret Mary Alacoque (1674). Past images of Christ shown pointing or looking at the wound of His side, or even spreading the gash, as in a Vision of St. Bernard by the Master of the Peringsdorfer Altar (Germanisches Museum, Nuremberg), contributed to the creation of the new image in which Christ is shown usually in half-length, pointing to a flaming heart in which the lance wound is shown, inscribed in a crown of thorns, surmounted by a cross. Though frequently repeated, this representation retains only the long hair and beard of the Pantocrator and otherwise is an example of the decline of Christian art. As a conceptual image of Christ's love for man, it is aesthetically inferior to the compassionate Christ.

The Ethnic Christ of the Missions. The images of Christ that have come out of the missionary fields of Asia, Africa, and the Americas reveal no new concept of Our Lord, except ethnically. It is still the long-haired, bearded type of the West with, however, native features. If Christ, despite His Hebraic race, is to be conceived as representing universal human nature, the insistence of each people to look upon Him merely as representing one of their own kind is not an acceptable solution to the problem. His image should rise above all race so that in it one should be able to say that in Him "there is neither Greek nor Jew, circumcision or uncircumcision."

In the 20th century, images of the Suffering Christ by G. Rouault and of the Crucified Christ by G. Sutherland and R. Lebrun are in the tradition of powerful representation by GRÜNEWALD and a host of German, Spanish, and French masters from Gothic to baroque times.

See Also: TRINITY, HOLY, ICONOGRAPHY OF; GOD THE FATHER, ICONOGRAPHY OF; HOLY SPIRIT, ICONOGRAPHY OF; CRUCIFIXION (IN ART); TREE OF JESSE; MARY, BLESSED VIRGIN, ICONOGRAPHY OF; LAST SUPPER, ICONOGRAPHY OF; DESCENT OF CHRIST INTO HELL; PENTECOST, ICONOGRAPHY OF; APOCALYPSE, ICONOGRAPHY OF; JOHN THE BAPTIST, ST., ICONOGRAPHY OF; APOSTLES, ICONOGRAPHY OF; SACRAMENTS, ICONOGRAPHY OF; HOLY NAME, ICONOGRAPHY OF; SACRED HEART, ICONOGRAPHY OF; ICON.

Bibliography: J. E. WEIS-LIEBESDORF, *Christus- und Apostelbilder* (Freiburg 1902). F. DE MÉLY, "Le Christ achéropoïète de Sainte-Praxède," *Bulletin de la Société nationale des antiquités de France* (1903) 182–183. P. LAUER, "Images achéropites du Christ," *ibid.* 229–. G. STUHLFAUTH, *Die ältesten Porträts Christi und der Apostel* (Berlin 1918). L. HEILMAIER, "Der jugendliche Christus in der altchristlichen Volkskunst," *Die christliche Kunst* 15 (1918–19) 236–. J. SAUER, *Die ältesten Christusbilder* (Berlin 1920). R. EISLER, *Orpheus the Fisher* (London 1921). J. SAUER, *Die ältesten Christusbilder* (Berlin 1923). G. E. MEILLE, *Christ's Likeness in History and Art* (London 1924). W. ROTHES, *Christus, des Heilands Leben, Leiden, Sterben und Verherrlichung in der bildenden Kunst* (Cologne 1924). V. SCHULZE, "Die Christus Statue in Panéas," *Zeitschrifte für die neutestamentliche Wissenschft und die Kunde der älteren Kirche* 24 (Giessen-Berlin 1925) 51–55. H. LECLERCQ, *Dictionnaire d'archéologie chrétienneet de liturgie,* ed. F. CABROL, H. LECLERCQ and H. I. MARROU, 15 v. (Paris 1907–53) 7.2:2393–2468. E. PANOFSKY, "Imago Pietatis," in *Festschrift für Max J. Friedländer* (Leipzig 1927). K. HORN, *Das Christusbild unserer Zeit* (Berlin 1929). F. WALTER, *Wie sah Christus aus? Ein Jerusalemfund* (Munich 1930). H. PREUSS, *Das Bild Christi im Wandel der Zeiten* (Leipzig 1932). H. PRIEBE, *Das Christusbild in der Kunst des 19. und 20. Jahrhundert* (Berlin 1932). L. TANDELLI, *Enciclopedia Italiana di scienzi, littere ed arti,* 36 v. (Rome 1929–39) 16:856–880. C. C. DOBSON, *The Face of Christ* (Milwaukee 1933). W. F. A. VITTER, *Die Entwicklung des Christusbildes in Literatur und Kunst in der frühchristlichen und frühbyzantinischen Zeit* (Bonn 1934). G. VAN DER OSTEN, *Der Schmerzensmann* (Berlin 1935). J. KOLLWITZ, "Christus als Lehrer und die Gesetzübergabe an Petrus in der konstantinischen Kunst Roms," *Römische Quartalschrift für christliche Altertumskunde und für Kirchengeschichte*

44 (Freiburg 1936) 45–66. E. PETERSON, "Le Christ Imperator," *Questions liturgiques et paroissiales* 23 (1938) 282–287. G. DE JERPHANION, "L'Image de Jésus-Christ dans l'art chrétien," *Nouvelle Revue théologique* 65 (Tournai-Louvain-Paris 1938) 257–283. P. MORNAND, *Visage du Christ* (Paris 1938), illus. F. VAN DER MEER, *Maiestas Domini: Théophanies de l'Apocalypse dans l'art chrétien* (Paris 1938). F. GERKE, *Christus in der spätantiken Plastik* (Berlin 1940). J. KOLLWITZ, *Oströmische Plastik der theodosianischen Zeit* (Berlin 1941). The Society for the Propagation of the Gospel, *Son of Man* (Westminster, MD 1946), pictures and carvings by Indian, African, and Chinese artists. F. MADER and R. HOFFMANN, *Christus in der Kunst* (Munich 1947). J. KOLLWITZ, "Das Bild von Christus dem König und Liturgie der christlichen Frühzeit," *Theologie und Glaube* 35 (Paderborn 1947–48) 95–117. P. DONCOEUR, *Le Christ dans l'art français* (Paris 1948). W. MERSMANN, *Der Schmerzensmann* (Düsseldorf 1952). H. P. L'ORANGE, *Studies on the Iconography of Cosmic Kingship in the Ancient World* (Oslo 1953) 124–197. *Reallexikon zur deutschen Kunstgeschichte*, v.3 (Stuttgart 1954). E. KITZINGER, "The Cult of Images in the Age before Iconoclasm," *Dumbarton Oaks Papers*, 8 Harvard University (Cambridge, MA 1954) 83–151. F. OSLENDER and L. SCHREYER, eds., *Das Antlitz Christi* (Hamburg 1956). *Imago Christi* (Antwerp 1958), exhibition catalogue. T. BURCKHARDT, *Principes et méthodes de l'art sacré* (Lyons 1958) 107–137. L. SCHREYER, *Das Christusbild und die Kunst des 20. Jahrhunderts* (Salzburg 1960). C. IHM, *Die Programme der christlichen Apsismalerei vom 4. Jahrhundert bis zur Mitte des 8. Jahrhunderts* (Wiesbaden 1960). J. JOBÉ, *Ecce Homo* (New York 1962). H. AURENHAMMER, *Lexikon der Christlichen Ikonographie*.

[L. P. SIGER; L. A. LEITE]

JESUS PRAYER

A method of meditation that consists in the control of breath and bodily movement accompanied by the repetition of the name of Jesus to bring about an absorption in the presence of God. It postulates concentration of consciousness through an intensive exercise of those bodily organs in which spiritual potentialities are supposedly located. The method demands that, in a sitting position, subjects control their breathing and flex their muscles, concentrating on the heartbeat and repeating continually, "Lord Jesus Christ, have mercy on me," while the will is relaxed in acts of forgiveness, mercy and hope in God. Its aim is not ecstasy, but a liberation of the understanding for the peaceful acceptance of union within the Word of God or the Silent Nameless One.

The origin of this kind of prayer is unknown, though hypotheses postulate the influence of ancient Indian Chakras technique on the Greek Fathers. In EVAGRIUS PONTICUS and MACARIUS THE EGYPTIAN there are traces of this practice; and THEODORET OF CYR speaks of prayerful breath control (*Patrologia Graeca*, 83:589), while Diadochus of Photice, HESYCHIUS OF JERUSALEM, GREGORY SINAITES, and Peter the Hagiorite (d. 734) mention different forms of the prayer "Jesus Christ, Son of God, have mercy on us."

In his *Philocalia* (Venice 1782) NICODEMUS THE HAGIORITE cites 38 spiritual treatises that mention the Jesus Prayer, and in modern times the archimandrite Paissy VELITCHKOVSKY popularized this kind of devotion as a Russian spiritual practice.

There is a trace of a similar kind of prayer in the West with BERNARD OF CLAIRVAUX (Sermones), Hugh of Balma, BERNARDINE OF SIENA.

Bibliography: J. HAUSHERR, "La Méthode d'oraison hésychast," *Orientalia Christiana Analecta*, 9 (Rome 1927) 101–209. I. BRYANCHANINOV, *On the Prayer of Jesus: From the Ascetic Essays . . .* , tr. FATHER LAZARUS (London 1952). G. WINKLER, "The Jesus Prayer as a Spiritual Path in Greek and Russian Monasticism," in *The Continuing Quest for God: Monastic Spirituality in Tradition and Transition*, ed. W. SKUDLAREK (Collegeville, Minn. 1982), 100–113. K. WARE, "The Origins of the Jesus Prayer: Diadochus, Gaza, Sinai," in *The Study of Spirituality*, eds. C. JONES, G. WAINWRIGHT, E. YARNOLD (New York 1986) 175–184. R. F. SLESINSKI, "The Philosophical Presuppositions of the Jesus Prayer," *Following the Star from the East: Essays in Honour of Archimandrite Boniface Luykx*, ed. A. M. CHIROVSKY (Ottawa 1992) 203–214. N. CORNEANU, "The Jesus Prayer and Deification," *Saint Vladimir's Theological Quarterly* 39:1 (1995) 3–24. K. VOGT, "The Coptic Practice of the Jesus Prayer: A Tradition Revived," in *Between Desert and City: The Coptic Orthodox Church Today*, eds. N. VAN DOORN-HARDER and K. VOGT (Oslo 1997) 111–120. J. B. TRAPNELL, "The Mutual Transformation of Self and Symbol: Bede Griffiths and the Jesus Prayer," *Horizons* 23 (1996) 215–241.

[F. X. MURPHY/EDS.]

JEURIS, PAULINE, ST.

In religion Sr. Marie Amandine, called by the Chinese, 'the laughing foreigner'; martyr, religious of the Franciscan Missionaries of Mary; b. Dec. 28, 1872, Herkla-Ville, Belgium; d. July 9, 1900, Taiyüan, China. Without a doubt Pauline's family was pious—four of the seven siblings entered religious life. Following her mother's death (ca. 1879), the children were separated into several homes when her father was forced to seek work in a neighboring village. At age 15, Pauline became a secular Franciscan tertiary. Later she followed her sister Rosalie (Sr. Marie Honorine) into the novitiate at Antwerp and was herself imitated by their sister Mathilde. Now known as Sr. Marie Amandine, she was trained in Marseilles, France, as a nurse in preparation for service in the hospital Bp. Francisco Fagolla wished to establish in Shanxi. En route to her assignment, she met with Sr. Marie Honorine who was stationed in Colombo, Sri Lanka (then Ceylon). She undertook her work with joy until she fell seriously ill. Soon after her recovery the mission was besieged by the Boxers. Having died singing the Te Deum, she was beatified as a martyr with her religious sisters by Pope Pius XII, Nov. 24, 1946, and canonized, Oct. 1, 2000, by Pope John Paul II with Augustine Zhao Rong and companions.

Feast: July 4.

Bibliography: G. GOYAU, *Valiant Women: Mother Mary of the Passion and the Franciscan Missionaries of Mary*, tr. G. TELFORD (London 1936). M. T. DE BLARER, *Les Bse Marie Hermine de Jésus et ses compagnes, franciscaines missionnaires de Marie, massacrées le 9 juillet 1900 à Tai–Yuan–Fou, Chine* (Paris 1947). L. M. BALCONI, *Le Martiri di Taiyuen* (Milan 1945). *Acta Apostolicae Sedis* 47 (1955) 381–388. *L'Osservatore Romano*, Eng. Ed. 40 (2000): 1–2, 10. 5503.

[K. I. RABENSTEIN]

JEWEL, JOHN

Bishop of Salisbury and first official apologist of the new Elizabethan Church; b. Buden, Devonshire, England, May 24, 1522; d. Monkton Fairleigh, near Wiltshire, Sept. 23, 1571. After being educated at Merton and Corpus Christi Colleges, Oxford, he became a fellow of Corpus Christi in 1542, and a renowned teacher. With Mary Tudor's accession (1553), those suspected of Protestantism were dismissed from Oxford. Jewel lost his fellowship. Seeking refuge in Frankfort, he supported John Foxe in his controversy with John Knox. Later he met Peter Martyr Vermigli in Strasbourg, and together they visited Zurich and Padua. Their letters, written between 1553 and 1555, provide a valuable source of historical data. Upon the accession of Elizabeth I (1558), Jewel returned to England and was sent in 1559 as disputant to refute the Roman Catholics at the Conference of Westminster. On Jan. 21, 1560 he was consecrated bishop of Salisbury, and he soon challenged the Catholics on three different occasions to show that certain Catholic practices could be proved by Scripture or the writings of the Fathers. His *Apologia ecclesiae Anglicanae* (1562), the first official pronouncement of the position of the Church of England, was answered by Thomas Harding (1516–72), a Louvain exile and former chaplain of Bishop Stephen Gardiner. For three years a bitter controversy continued between the students at Louvain and the Protestant divines in England, during which theological works gave way to political tracts. Jewel's writings were published in 1609 by Richard Bancroft, Archbishop of Canterbury, and later edited by J. Ayre (4 v. London 1845–50).

Bibliography: J. JEWEL, *An Apology of the Church of England,* tr. J. E. BOOTY (Ithaca, N.Y. 1963). W. M. SOUTHGATE, *John Jewel and the Problem of Doctrinal Authority* (Cambridge, Mass. 1962). M. CREIGHTON, *The Dictionary of National Biography from the Earliest Times to 1900* 10:815–819. F. L. CROSS, *The Oxford Dictionary of the Christian Church* 726. M. SCHMIDT, *Die Religion in Geschichte und Gegenwart* 3:663–664.

[M. A. FRAWLEY]

JEWISH PHILOSOPHY

Jewish philosophy may be described as the explication of Jewish beliefs and practices by means of general philosophical concepts and moral norms. It must thus be seen in a twofold manner: as an outgrowth of the Biblical-rabbinic tradition on which Judaism rests and as a part of the history of philosophy at large. Whereas the Biblical and rabbinic writings developed within the Jewish community, Jewish philosophy flourished whenever Jewish thinkers participated in the philosophical speculations of an outside culture. And though significant differences, both religious and philosophical, distinguish ancient and medieval from much of modern Jewish thought, the subject matter of Jewish philosophy may generally be divided into three parts. As interpretation of Jewish tradition, Jewish philosophy concentrates on topics such as the election of Israel, the prophecy of Moses, the Law (Torah) and its eternity, and Jewish conceptions of the Messiah and the afterlife. As religious philosophy, it investigates those philosophical notions common to Judaism, Christianity, and Islam, such as the existence of God, the divine attributes, creation, prophecy, the human soul, and the principles of human conduct. Finally, as philosophy, it studies notions that are primarily of philosophical interest, such as the structure of logical arguments, the constitution of the world, and the divisions of being.

Chronologically, Jewish philosophy may be divided into three phases: (1) its early development in the Diaspora community of the Hellenistic world, (2) its flourishing in both Islamic and Christian lands in the Middle Ages, and (3) its modern period, which began in the 18th century and has continued to today. The remainder of this article sketches the details of this chronology.

Early Development. Jewish philosophy developed in the Hellenistic world, where, from 200 B.C. to A.D. 100, Jewish thinkers of the DIASPORA produced a Jewish philosophical literature in Greek.

Of the Hellenistic writers, PHILO JUDAEUS is the only one the majority of whose works are extant. Writing largely in the form of commentaries on the Pentateuch, Philo proposed to show that Biblical thought, allegorically interpreted, is identical with Greek philosophical teachings. For Philo, God is one, self-sufficient, incorporeal, and possessed of infinite power and goodness. He created the world out of a preexistent matter by means of the ideas and patterns contained in an intermediate being, the logos, also created by God. According to other Philonic usages, logos may refer also to the ideas existing in the mind of God and the ideas embodied in the world.

Man, in Philo's view, is composed of a body rooted in the world of sense and a soul directed toward the world of spirit. He attains his ultimate happiness through control of his desires and through contemplation, particularly the contemplation of God. Philosophical speculation finds its culmination in the mystical intuition of God.

Whereas Philo influenced Fathers of the Christian Church, he had no direct successor among the Jews. Thus Jewish philosophy lay dormant until the Middle Ages.

Medieval Period. The first contribution of the medieval phase, which was part of a cultural revival in the Islamic East, was that of SA'ADIA BEN JOSEPH, head of the rabbinical academy at Sura (near Baghdad). Influenced by the MU'TAZILITES, a branch of the Mutakallimūn (Muslim rational theologians), and making use of Platonic, Aristotelian, and Stoic notions, Sa'adia set out to formulate a Jewish KALĀM.

Kalām. He wrote his major work, *Kitāb al-Amanāt wal-I'tiqadāt (Beliefs and Opinions),* to resolve the doubts of his contemporaries and to turn them from belief on the basis of religious authority alone to belief confirmed by rational speculation. In the true *kalām* fashion, he begins his demonstrations with proofs for the creation of the world, which, in turn, lead to the demonstration of the existence of God, the creator. Affirming that the world was created in time, out of nothing, and by a creator distinct from it, Sa'adia refutes 12 cosmogonic theories that he considers incorrect. He establishes the unity of God by philosophical arguments and polemicizes against dualists and Trinitarians. He appears to hold that God is known through negative predication, teaching that multiple attributes are ascribed to God because of the shortcomings of human language, not because of any multiplicity in Him.

God communicates with men through prophets whose mission is attested by miraculous occurrences. Prophecy is productive of the Law. Following *kalām* distinctions, Sa'adia divides the Law into rational laws, which are also discoverable by human reason, and traditional laws, which are the result of God's will.

Human freedom is the central doctrine of Sa'adia's philosophy of man. Though God is omnipotent and omniscient, man possesses freedom of choice, as is shown by sense experience and confirmed by doctrines of human responsibility. Hence God is just in rewarding and punishing man.

Neoplatonism. Although *kalām* teachings did influence later Jewish philosophers, Sa'adia remained the major representative of this school. Already in his day, however, Jewish philosophy had begun to turn in a Neoplatonic direction. Influenced by Neoplatonic works such as the *Theology of Aristotle,* Jewish Neoplatonists inquired how the world emanated from God and how man

Moses Mendelssohn. (Archive Photos)

may return to Him. Their solutions emphasized the voluntary nature of emanation and the fact that, in his return to God, man can never become united with the godhead.

ISAAC ISRAELI, author also of medical treatises, is best known as a philosopher for his *Book of Definitions* and *Book of Elements,* which have been preserved in Hebrew and Latin translations. According to Isaac, the world emanated from God through His power and will, with primary matter and first form preceding intellect, the souls, and the world. Human life has as its goal union with supernal wisdom, a union that is preceded by the purification and illumination of the soul.

By far the most important Jewish Neoplatonist was Solomon ibn Gabirol, known in the Latin world as AVICEBRON or Avicebrol, with whom the setting of Jewish philosophy shifted from the Islamic East to Spain and the Islamic West. Known among his people for his magnificent Hebrew poems—among them his cosmogonic poem, The Royal Crown—Gabirol achieved fame in the Christian world through the Latin translation of his major philosophical work, *Fons vitae (Fountain of Life).*

Metaphysical in nature, without Biblical and rabbinic citations, the *Fountain of Life* is primarily an exposition of Gabirol's doctrine of matter and form. Beginning with an account of emanation, Gabirol holds that the world proceeded from the First Essence, God. The first emanation is the Divine Will, which emphasizes the voluntary, as opposed to the necessary, emanation of the world from God. From Divine Will emanates primary matter and first form; these, according to Gabirol, are the constituent principles of all created beings, the intelligences included. Gabirol's notion that even intelligences are composed of matter and form became the subject for an extensive debate among Christian philosophers of the 13th and 14th centuries.

The 11th and 12th centuries saw two philosophers who, virtually unknown outside Judaism, greatly influenced their own people. Baḥyā ibn Pāqūdā (fl. 1080–90; *Enciclopedia filosofica,* 1:562) wrote a much-read ethical treatise, *Duties of the Heart,* in which he describes ten spiritual qualities—the highest being the love of God—and gives practical directions for attaining them.

The *Kuzari* (*c.* 1140) of Judah Ben Samuel Ha-Levi was another widely read work. Using as his framework the story of the conversion of the King of the Khazars to Judaism, ha-Levi sets down his *apologia* for the Jewish religion in the form of a dialogue. Rejecting the philosophical conception of God as the first cause, ha-Levi describes Him as the God of Abraham, Isaac, and Jacob, who reveals Himself in historical events. The author devotes a special portion of his book to the election of Israel, which he understands as the result of a special divine emanation and which culminates in prophecy. In spite of the generally anti-rationalistic tenor of his views—in which he parallels the Muslim ALGAZEL—ha-Levi, at times, uses *kalām* and other philosophical arguments.

The first Jewish philosopher to write in Hebrew was Abraham bar Ḥiyya, a younger contemporary of ha-Levi. Neoplatonic in orientation, he is noteworthy for his attempt to develop a philosophy of history.

Aristotelianism. By the middle of the 12th century Jewish philosophy was ready to begin its next phase. Under the influence of ALFARABI, AVICENNA, and AVEMPACE, it turned in an Aristotelian direction. Abraham ben David ha-Levi, otherwise known as Ibn Daud (*c.* 1110–80), discussed a number of problems in Aristotelian physics and metaphysics and their application to religious teachings in his *Exalted Faith,* which also contains an extensive critique of Ibn Gabirol.

Jewish Aristotelianism reached its climax, however, with Moses MAIMONIDES, the Rabbi Moses of the Latins. The towering figure of medieval Jewish thought, Maimonides discussed some philosophical issues in his legal writings, but the full and technical exposition of his views is found in his *Guide of the Perplexed.*

Addressing students of philosophy who had become vexed by literal interpretations of certain scriptural pas-sages, Maimonides devoted his *Guide* to explaining the inner meaning of the Law. To provide a correct conception of God is the first part of this task. Beginning with the interpretation of Biblical anthropomorphic and anthropopathic terms applied to God, Maimonides shows that such terms must be understood either as attributes of action or as negative attributes. He rejects the use of positive attributes in describing God. Before setting down his proofs for existence, unity, and incorporeality of God, Maimonides undertakes an extensive critique of the views of the Mutakallimūn, judging their proofs of these same attributes incorrect since based on faulty philosophical methods. Besides demonstrating the existence of God as the prime mover and the first cause, Maimonides uses the notions of necessary and contingent being to show that God is a being necessary through Himself. Maimonides maintains that human reason alone cannot prove whether the world had a beginning in time or is eternal. He accepts creation because the arguments for it are more convincing and because it is the teaching of Scripture. Prophecy occupies a central position in Maimonides's thought. A prophet must possess physical, moral, and intellectual perfection as well as a well-developed imagination. In prophecy an emanation proceeding from God through the intermediacy of the Active Intellect affects the rational and imaginative faculties of the prophet. In his political function the prophet, particularly Moses, is the bearer of the Law. The final purpose of the Law is to produce correct opinions about God in all believers and to instill those moral norms that are prerequisites to understanding. Many Biblical commandments, according to Maimonides, serve to eradicate idolatrous practices.

After Maimonides, the setting of Jewish philosophy shifted to Christian lands—Christian Spain, southern France, and Italy—and its language became Hebrew. Under the influence of AVERROËS, most of whose commentaries on Aristotle had been translated into Hebrew, Jewish philosophy turned in a more strictly Aristotelian direction. Shem Tob Falqera (d. 1290), Joseph ibn Kaspi (1279–c. 1340), and Moses of Narbonne (d. after 1362) wrote commentaries on Maimonides's *Guide* as well as a variety of general philosophical works, including supercommentaries on Averroës.

Among 13th-century philosophers, Hillel ben Samuel of Verona defended individual immortality against Averroës's doctrine of the unity of the intellect, whereas Isaac Albalag developed a doctrine of the double truth (*see* INTELLECT, UNITY OF; DOUBLE TRUTH, THEORY OF).

By far the most important post-Maimonidean was LEVI BEN GERSON (also known as Gersonides), astronomer, Biblical exegete, and commentator on Averroës. In his major work, the *Wars of the Lord,* Gersonides investigated, in true scholastic fashion, problems that he considered had been treated insufficiently or solved unsatisfactorily by Maimonides. Showing an affinity to Averroës, Gersonides described God in Aristotle's phrase as "Thought Thinking Itself" rather than as the ineffable Neoplatonic One. Similarly, holding that analytic distinctions do not introduce real distinctions in the things to which they are applied, Gersonides held that positive attributes may be predicated of God. Differing again from Maimonides, Gersonides affirmed that the creation of the world can be philosophically demonstrated. The world was created by God out of an unformed, eternally existing matter and is not, as the Neoplatonists thought, the result of emanation. In line with his more Aristotelian views, Gersonides held that God knows and guides the world only insofar as it is subject to general laws.

Reaction. The reaction to Jewish Aristotelianism came with Hasdai ben Abraham CRESCAS, who, in his *Light of the Lord,* undertook a critique of certain of Aristotle's physical and metaphysical views. Affirming, against Aristotle, that the existence of an actual infinite (in particular, infinite space) is possible, Crescas rejected the Aristotelian proofs for the existence of God as the first mover and the first cause, but retained the proof for God as a necessary being. For Crescas, goodness is the primary attribute of God, who created the world by His will and out of love. Crescas saw the goal of human life as the love of God rather than the contemplation of God. The precepts of the Law, for him, become means of loving God. Unlike other Jewish philosophers, however, Crescas denies the freedom of the human will.

Medieval Jewish philosophy drew to a close with such writers as Simon ben Ẓemaḥ Duran (1361–1444); Joseph ALBO, author of the *Book of Principles;* and Isaac ABRABANEL.

Modern Period. Modern Jewish thought differs from ancient and medieval in that many modern Jewish thinkers brought a liberal interpretation of Judaism to their investigations. In addition, reflecting modern philosophical movements, they developed their thought along rationalist, idealist, neo-Kantian, pragmatic, and existentialist lines.

Historians of philosophy sometimes consider Baruch SPINOZA the first Jewish philosopher in the modern world. However, although it is true that Spinoza was influenced by medieval Jewish philosophers, particularly Maimonides and Crescas, he can hardly be placed within the mainstream of the Jewish philosophical tradition. When he undertakes to separate philosophy from religion in his *Theologico-Political Treatise,* he attempts in the process to invalidate the claims of Scripture as understood by Jewish tradition. Moreover, the pantheistic system developed in his *Ethics,* with its identity of God and nature, cannot be said to be in harmony with Jewish beliefs.

The first modern Jewish philosopher was Moses Mendelssohn (1729–86). A true philosopher of the Enlightenment, he relegated speculation about God, the world, and man to philosophy and considered Judaism largely as revealed legislation (*see* ENLIGHTENMENT, PHILOSOPHY OF).

Of the more recent philosophers, Hermann Cohen (1842–1918) is worthy of note. Basing himself on Kantian thought, Cohen saw in Judaism, with its emphasis on the unity of God, moral law, and Messianic expectations, the ideal embodiment of the Religion of Reason. In his later years Cohen emphasized the more personal elements of religion, such as man's awareness of his transgressions and the need for reconciliation with God. (*See* KANTIANISM.)

With Franz Rosenzweig (1886–1929) and Martin BUBER (1878–1965), Jewish philosophy entered its existentialist phase. Rejecting the categories of speculative philosophy, Buber makes the more personal aspects of human life the subject of his investigations. Developing his dialogical philosophy, Buber describes two types of relations: "I-It," the relation between man and objects; "I-Thou," the relation between man and man. A special relation is that between the "I" and the "Eternal Thou," God. Man, according to Buber, can establish an "I-Thou" relation even with objects. The community rather than the isolated life of the individual is the proper setting for human life. In his writings, Buber draws heavily on Scripture and the Hasidic literature. The present mood of Jewish philosophy appears to be existentialist to a large extent. (*See* EXISTENTIALISM, 6.)

See Also: ARABIAN PHILOSOPHY; SCHOLASTICISM, 1.

Bibliography: Texts in translation. *Three Jewish Philosophers* (Meridian Bks.; New York 1960), contains *Philo: Selections,* ed. H. LEWY; *Suadya: Selections from Book of Doctrines and Beliefs,* ed. A. ALTMANN; *Jehuda Halevi: Selections from Kuzari,* ed. I. HEINEMANN. *Philo,* tr. F. H. COLSON and G. H. WHITAKER, 10 v. (*Loeb Classical Library*; 1929–62). S. IBN GABIROL, *Fountain of Life* [*Fons vitae,*] tr. from Lat. text of C. BAEUMKER by H. E. WEDECK (New York 1962). I. ISRAELI, *Works,* tr. with comments and an outline of his philosophy, A. ALTMANN and S. M. STERN (Oxford 1958). SAADIA GAON, *The Book of Beliefs and Opinions,* tr. S. ROSENBLATT (Yale Judaica Ser 1; New Haven 1948). BAHYA BEN JOSEPH IBN PAKUDA, *Duties of the Heart,* tr. M. HYAMSON, 2 v. (2d ed. New York 1962). JUDAH HA-LEVI, *The Kuzari,* tr. H. HIRSCHFELD (New York 1964). M. MAIMONIDES, *Guide of the Perplexed,* tr. with introd. and nn. S. PINES, introd. essay L. STRAUSS (Chicago 1963). H. A. WOLFSON, *Crescas' Critique of Aristotle* (Cambridge, MA 1929). J. ALBO, *Sefer ha-'Ikkarim (Book of Principles),* ed. and tr. I. HUSLK, 4 v. in 5 (Philadelphia 1929–30), Hebrew and English

M. I. BUBER, *I and Thou* (2d ed. New York 1958). Studies. G. VAJDA, *Jüdische Philosophie* (Bern 1950), 2 bibliog; "Les Études de philosophie juive du moyen âge 1950–1960," *Die Metaphysik im Mittelalter,* ed. P. WILPERT (Miscellanea Mediaevalia 2; Berlin 1963) 126–135. J. GUTTMANN, *Philosophies of Judaism: The History of Jewish Philosophy from Biblical Times to Franz Rosenzweig,* tr. D. W. SILVERMAN (New York 1964). H. A. WOLFSON, *Philo: Foundations of Religious Philosophy in Judaism, Christianity and Islam,* 2 v. (Cambridge, MA 1947). I. HUSIK, *A History of Medieval Jewish Philosophy* (2d ed. New York 1930; pa. 1958). S. H. BERGMAN, *Faith and Reason: An Introduction to Modern Jewish Thought,* tr. and ed. A. JOSPE (Washington 1961). J. B. AGUS, *Modern Philosophies of Judaism* (New York 1941). L. STRAUSS, *Persecution and the Art of Writing* (Glencoe, IL 1952); *Philosophie und Gesetz* (Berlin 1935).

[A. HYMAN]

JEWS, POST-BIBLICAL HISTORY OF THE

The history of the Jewish people is primarily the history of its religious development and, at the same time, in the Old Testament period, the history of man's salvation. From the time God made Israel His chosen people through His covenant with them on Mount Sinai, the Torah, or the Mosaic Law, has been regarded by the Jewish people as the center of its life, and ever since the Babylonian Exile the Jews have considered the study and fulfillment of this Law their principal duty.

The history of the Jews reveals its real and deep meaning only if one concentrates attention on the religious element in it. The same is true of the post-Biblical era, which for the Jewish people on the whole was an almost uninterrupted period of suffering and persecution. Even the unfriendly attitude Christendom has shown the Jews throughout the centuries must be considered here. The objective, chronological presentation here of the most important events in the history of the Jews is neither tendentious nor accusatory. The external happenings in this history, frightful though they frequently were, especially in recent times, have always been subservient to the very special plan of God, whose call and gifts of grace to Israel are, according to the testimony of Saint Paul (Romans 12.29), irrevocable. Justice can be done to the history of the Jews only if it is primarily regarded as the expression of God's inscrutable government of the world. For the Biblical era of the history of the Jews, *see* ISRAEL, 3.

The post-Biblical era is reviewed here in a survey of the six main periods of the Jewish history: (1) the Roman and Byzantine period (A.D. 67–622), (2) the Islamic period (622–1096), (3) the period of the Crusades and the Spanish Inquisition (1096–1492), (4) the period of the Renaissance and the Reformation (1492–1650), (5) the beginning of the modern era (1650–1750), and (6) the emancipation (1750–1948). For the period since 1948, *see* ISRAEL (STATE OF).

Roman and Byzantine Period (67–622). The history of the Jews in this period was marked by their first revolt against Rome (67–70), which brought about the destruction of Jerusalem; by their second revolt under BAR KOKHBA (132–35), which ended in the complete devastation of Palestine; and by the survival of the Jews in the Babylonian and other Diasporas.

First Revolt. The ever increasing tension between the Jews and the Roman authorities in Palestine reached its breaking point when the tyranny of the Roman governor Gessius Florus (64–66) provoked the Jews to open, armed rebellion against Rome. The military preparations on the Jewish side were supervised by Joseph ben Mattathiah, who later, under the name of Flavius JOSEPHUS, left to future generations, together with other historical writings, a description of this revolt in his *Jewish War.* The Jewish military forces, however, could not withstand the legions of the Roman General Vespasian and, after heavy losses, withdrew to Jerusalem. A siege of several months followed; the city was conquered by Vespasian's son Titus in the year 70 and, together with its Temple, utterly destroyed. The Roman soldiers, after inflicting a terrible massacre on the population, led thousands of Jews away into slavery.

The national catastrophe of the year 70 made a renewal of religious life imperative for the Jews. From now on emphasis was placed on the so-called academies. While Jerusalem was still under siege, Rabbi JOHANAN BEN ZAKKAI, with wise foresight, had obtained permission from Titus to settle with his disciples at Jamnia, which now became the new seat of the SANHEDRIN. Even after the year 70 the Jews of Palestine retained a certain amount of local autonomy, which the Romans sanctioned by conferring on Gamaliel (II), the head of the Jamnia academy, the title of patriarch. The main concern at this time of the doctors of the Law, among whom Rabbi AKIBA BEN JOSEPH was outstanding, was in the field of HALAKAH, i.e., the interpretation of the various prescriptions of the Law that would assure for the future that the observance of the commandments of the Torah would hold the first place in the life of the Jewish people.

Second Revolt. Meanwhile the hand of Rome lay heavy on the land, and there were several uprisings among the Jews, sometimes, as in 115, extending into the DIASPORA; all of them were cruelly suppressed. The limit was reached in 132, when the Emperor Hadrian decided to erect a heathen sanctuary on the site of the ruined Temple. The whole population rose up in protest under the leadership of Simeon bar Koziba, called Bar Kokhba by his disciples. For three years he held the country under his control. But the conquest of Bether by the Roman legions put an end to this last attempt to regain national independence. The population of Judea was decimated, and the remnant of the religious and national life sought refuge in the mountains of Galilee, while strictly enforced laws made every practice of the Jewish religion liable to severe penalties.

Under the Emperor Antoninus Plus (138–61) conditions became better for the Jews, and they even received a certain amount of local autonomy. The interest of the leading Jewish academies was now concentrated on the codification of all the extra-Biblical traditions, which until then had been handed down only orally, but which, on account of the unfavorable conditions of the time, were in danger of being entirely lost. This work is mainly contained in the MISHNAH, completed by the Patriarch Rabbi JUDAH HA-NASI c. 200. The gradual dissolution, however, of Palestinian Judaism could not be checked, and with the abolition of the patriarchate in 425, its whole political life was practically extinguished.

Babylonian Diaspora. In Mesopotamia, where, ever since the first (Babylonian) destruction of Jerusalem (587 B.C.) there had been a Jewish colony that constantly grew in importance, the political situation, first under the Parthians and then under the Sassanians, was considerably better than in Palestine. The Jews were subject to a so-called exilarch who was acknowledged as their official head and whose authority extended to all the Jewish communities in the Persian Empire; they thus enjoyed considerable autonomy. Academies for the study of the Law were established in the chief centers of Jewish life. The most important of these were the academies of Sura and Pumbedita, which were founded by two famous doctors of the Law, Rab and Samuel (175–254). The heads of the Babylonian school, who later had the title of gaon, were regarded as the highest religious authority in Judaism.

The discussions of the scholars both in Palestine, especially in the academies of Caesarea and Tiberias, and in Babylonia concerning the religious decisions of the Mishnah were in turn codified and resulted in the two TALMUDS, the one of Palestine, inaccurately called the Jerusalem Talmud, and the other of Babylonia; the former was completed toward the end of the 4th and the latter toward the beginning of the 6th century. From this time on, the norms of the Talmud formed the supreme guide for the whole religious life of JUDAISM. At the same time other ancient traditions were likewise being constantly recorded, and these came down to us in the MIDRASHIC LITERATURE, which is partly of a halakic-juridical character and partly of a haggadic-edifying character (*see* HAG-

GADAH). All these writings constitute what is known as the ancient rabbinical literature.

Jewish Diaspora in Other Countries. Besides those in Mesopotamia, Egypt, and Asia Minor, there were Jewish communities also in most of the commercially important places of the Roman Empire. The catastrophes that the Jewish nation suffered in Palestine did not, on the whole, seriously affect the juridical status of the Jews in the Diaspora. They were the only people in the empire who, for recognized religious reasons, did not have to take part in the official state worship.

During the first Christian centuries the cleft widened between Judaism and rising Christianity. The latter, despite periodic waves of persecution, grew stronger and stronger and, thanks to the well-organized activity of its missionaries, made considerable progress everywhere. Since the Christians who were converted from paganism soon vastly outnumbered the Judaeo-Christians, the formulation of Christian doctrine had to be adapted to the mentality of these converts from the heathen world; hence, there appeared a more and more noticeable alienation between Judaism and Christianity, which subsequently had a decisive influence on the relations between the two religions throughout the centuries. [See R. Wilde, *The Treatment of the Jews in the Greek Christian Writers of the First Three Centuries* (Washington 1949).]

With the Edict of MILAN, which Constantine the Great issued in 313, the way was opened for Christianity to become the official religion of the state. Consequently the juridical status of the Jews was changed, and against them a large number of legal enactments, based on a quite definite theological bias, were made, whereby the Jews were limited more and more in their freedom of action and increasingly discriminated against in their social life.

There was a short period of relief for them under Julian the Apostate (361–63), who even considered the ideea of rebuilding the Temple of Jerusalem. But under Theodosius II (408–50) the reaction had already set in, and the regulations against the Jews in the Theodosian Code remained, from then on, a fixed part of all the subsequent laws that regulated Jewish life in Christian countries.

The invasion by the barbarians made the Jewish communities share in the common misery, but even in the new states that were eventually founded by these invaders, whose rulers were now converted to Christianity, the general situation of the Jews was hardly improved. The popes of Rome, particularly Gregory the Great (590–604), objected to the persecutions and forced conversions of the Jews, yet even the canonical regulations continued to limit the freedom of the Jews more and more.

Especially oppressive were the conditions in the Byzantine Empire, where the Jews were accused of being in collusion with the enemies of the country, particularly the Persians. Thus, Emperor Heraclius (610–42), in whose reign Jerusalem was conquered by the Persians, forbade all practice of the Jewish religion. At that time in Europe too the expulsion of the Jews had already begun, as in France under King Dagobert (626). The condition of the Jews was very bad also in Spain, where in the last centuries of Visigothic domination the influence of the regulations that were made in the provincial synods of Toledo rendered the exercise of Jewish worship practically impossible.

Islamic Period (622 to 1096). Despite certain discriminatory legislation, the Jews generally prospered in the lands conquered by the Muslims, and in the mutually beneficial symbiosis between Judaism and ISLAM the Jewish medieval culture reached its greatest heights, especially in Spain.

Jewish-Arabic Symbiosis. A new era began for Judaism with the appearance of Islam on the scene of history and with the establishment of the caliphate (*see* CALIPH). At the height of the Islamic power, the caliphate was able, though after several internal ruptures, to subject to Arab hegemony under the law of the Prophet all the nations from India to the Atlantic Ocean and from Arabia to the borders of the Pyrenees.

MUḤAMMAD, who had borrowed much from Judaism and whose initial success in Arabia was due largely to the great religious influence of the Jews on the peninsula and to the spiritual preparation that this had made possible, had hoped that the Jews would embrace his religious system with open arms. Their resolute opposition, however, led also in Islam to laws of segregation, which resulted especially in laying on the Jews, as well as on the Christians, heavy financial burdens and in relegating them to a merely tolerated position at the edge of the Dâr el-Islâm (the Muslim world). However, it protected them, as well as the Christians, from forced conversion, since it regarded each group as a ''People of the Book,'' that is, a community that participated in a stage on the road of divine revelation.

In spite of this legislation, which, moreover, came into full force only after the decline of Muslim supremacy, the position of the Jews in the Islamic countries was more favorable, to a greater or lesser degree, than it had been under Christian rule. To earn a living they now turned more and more to trade—a development that was greatly fostered by their international connections, whereas until then agriculture and small industry had been their main occupations. In cultural matters a certain symbiosis developed between the Jews and the Arabs,

which was furthered by the relationship between the two groups in language (both Hebrew and Arabic being Semitic languages) and in the sphere of religious concepts and which led to a new efflorescence in Jewish intellectual life.

The Jews very soon adopted Arabic as their everyday language, and this aroused in them a new interest in Hebrew, the language of their own sacred literature. Thus, this became the age of the first great Hebrew grammarians. The position of the exilarch was confirmed by the caliphs who resided in Baghdad, near ancient Babylon, and the Babylonian academies received a fresh impetus, so that their heads, called geonim (plural of gaon), were able, through their circular letters, to direct Jewish life throughout the world. (*See* RESPONSA, JEWISH.)

Through the Arabs, Jewish scholars became acquainted also with the ideas of ancient philosophy, from which until then they had kept aloof—with the exception of Philo, who had but little influence on official Jewish thought. For the first time Jewish theology now left the way of purely inner meditation on the treasures of tradition and adopted the system of the Islamic theologians, the *KALĀM,* which is the interpretation of revealed truths with the help of philosophical principles.

In the second half of the 8th century there became noticeable in Judaism a certain opposition to the Talmudic practices as they were handed down and carried out by the Babylonian academies. Taking up ancient concepts and the tendencies of several sects, the adherents of this movement, who gathered around Anan ben David of the exilarch family, denied the binding force of the oral traditions that were codified in the Talmud. They called themselves Benê Mikrā (Sons of the Scriptures), a term with which the word Karaism is related, because they accepted only the Sacred Scriptures as their sole law. The Karaites met a resolute opponent in Gaon SA'ADIA BEN JOSEPH (882–942), the first Jewish religious philosopher. With the death of Sa'adia the decline of the centers of Jewish learning in Mesopotamia set in, which coincided with the fall of the caliphate of Baghdad; in the 11th century the office of the exilarch, after it was combined for a short time in a personal union with that of the gaon, disappeared. The centers of Jewish learning in Palestine were restored to new vigor for a short period under the Egyptian Fatimid Dynasty, but the conquest of Jerusalem by the Crusaders in 1099 put an end to all Jewish life in the Holy Land.

Spanish Period. The Jewish-Arabic symbiosis reached its climax in Spain, where, after the conquest of Toledo by the Muslim army in 711, a development began that culminated in the 10th century with the establishment of the caliphate of Córdoba. Jewish scholars and wealthy Jews occupied prominent positions, such as those held by Hasdai Ibn Shaprut at the court of Córdoba and by Samuel ha-Nagid in Granada. Religious philosophers, mystics, scholars, and poets could freely develop their genius, and so in Spain there was a new flowering of Hebrew literature. The great work of religious philosophy by Solomon ben Judah ibn Gabirol (1020–50), who was called Avicebron by the scholastics, became universally known. Ibn Paqūda (c. 1080) wrote *The Duties of the Heart,* a widely circulated work that many generations of Jews used as a source of spiritual direction. Moses ben Jacob IBN EZRA (c. 1100) left to posterity a large number of elegiac poems. Judah ben Samuel ha-Levi, who lived about the same time, was the greatest poet of the era. In his *Songs of Sion* the intense longing of the Jewish people for the days of their past glory finds eloquent expression, and in his *Kuzari* he left them a highly prized apologia of Judaism. Abraham ben Meïr IBN EZRA was a gifted poet also, but he is better known for his valuable commentary on the Scriptures.

The greatest personality of this period is without doubt Moses ben Maimon (1135–1204) or MAIMONIDES, as he is also called. He was concerned primarily with proving that faith and reason do not contradict each other. For this purpose he made use of the categories of Aristotelian philosophy, which at that time was enjoying the increasing and special interest also of the Muslim philosophers. In his *Guide to the Perplexed* Maimonides endeavored to solve the seeming contradictions between religion and philosophy. His most important work is the *Mishneh Torah* (Repetition of the Law) or *Yad Hazaka* (Strong Hand), a clear, systematic summary of the whole of Talmudic erudition. In the *Book of Knowledge,* a commentary on the Talmud, Maimonides sets forth his well-known 13 basic dogmas of Judaism.

However, in Spain too the situation of the Jews grew worse with the *Reconquista,* the reconquest of the country by the Christian princes.

Period of the Crusades and Spanish Inquisition (1096 to 1492). After a few centuries of relative freedom following the Carolingian revival, the Jews suffered from restrictive laws and active persecution in western Europe during the era of the Crusades and the later Middle Ages; these reached their climax in the Spanish Inquisition.

West-European Jewish Communities. After the disturbances of the so-called migration of the nations, Charlemagne, at the beginning of the 9th century, was the first to reunite under a single rule the countries that were later called France, Germany, and Italy. The condition of the Jews in these lands was now noticeably improved. New Jewish communities were formed in various places, and the previously existing ones took on new life and played

an important role in the development of commercial relations. On the whole, the situation remained unchanged, in spite of repeated attacks by ecclesiastics, in the states that evolved from the Carolingian monarchy.

The Jewish communities enjoyed far-reaching rights of self-government, and in the 10th century important Jewish schools arose for the first time in western Europe. One of the foremost authorities was Rabbi Gershom ben Judah, ''the Light of the Exile'' (c. 1000), who taught at Mainz and adapted the norms of Old Testament and Talmudic law to the changed conditions of the European Jews, as, for instance, by his prohibition against polygamy. Rabbi Shelomoh ben Yiṣḥaq of Troyes, more commonly known as RASHI, who lived at this time (1040–1105), was the greatest commentator on the Bible and Talmud that Judaism ever produced. In Italy, too, there were everywhere growing Jewish communities that displayed a vigorous intellectual life.

The Crusades. A sudden change, however, was brought in the conditions of the Jews by the Crusades. In a frightful manner the ill-will against the Jews that had been fostered by religious motives through the centuries now burst forth in violence and deepened more and more the chasm that separated Christians and Jews.

In the First Crusade (1096) it was especially the Jewish communities of the Rhineland that had to suffer, and in the Second Crusade (1146–47) the same outrages were repeated there in spite of the courageous intervention of Saint Bernard of Clairvaux on behalf of the persecuted Jews. This age, too, witnessed the first appearance of the calumny of Jewish ''ritual murder,'' i.e., the allegation that the Jews murdered Christians in order to obtain blood for the Passover and other rituals. This libel raged on for centuries despite all the papal counter-declarations and prohibitions. During the Third Crusade (1189) the measures taken to protect the Jews by the German princes proved more successful, but now it was mainly the Jewish communities in England that had much to suffer.

The Crusades brought with them a complete revolution in the way of Jewish life. Everywhere the ancient anti-Jewish laws were again enforced and augmented by new regulations, even in the field of Canon Law. Where it had not yet been the custom, the Jews were ordered to live in separate districts or GHETTOS and to wear a distinctive costume (the ''Jewish hat'' and the ''yellow patch''). As Christians now began to engage in commerce on a constantly increasing scale, the Jews were more and more forced out of this livelihood. Since the Third Council of the Lateran (1179) renewed in full rigor the prohibition against taking interest on loans, the Jews, for whom this law did not apply, were forced more and more into the pawn and loan business, which, besides the old-clothes trade, was practically the only way left open for them to earn a living. On the other hand, numerous chain reactions of anti-Jewish outrages were provoked. Practically all social contact between Jews and Christians ceased, and Jewry, which, in keeping with the admonitions of such Fathers of the Church as Augustine and John Chrysostom, was allowed a bare subsistence at the edge of the Christian community, began to live a life entirely of its own. The situation lasted practically until the era of the emancipation. These various regulations and phenomena did not manifest themselves uniformly everywhere; there were great differences in the various countries. From this time on, expulsions of the Jews took place periodically. They began in France, where, however, at the payment of much money, the Jews were allowed to come back several times. England followed suit in 1290, and here the expulsion remained in effect for several centuries. Jews were forced to listen to Christian sermons and religious discussions, their own literature was strictly censured, and the Talmud was made a forbidden book and frequently burned in the public squares.

The Spanish Tragedy. At the beginning of the 13th century, with the victories of the Christian princes in all parts of Spain except the enclave of Granada, the *Reconquista* of this country was practically complete. But the importance of the Jews in every field was too great to allow at once a rigorous enforcement of the anti-Jewish laws. Nevertheless, the Inquisition was soon introduced in Spain, and in 1265 the great Jewish scholar Moses ben Nahman, called also NAHMANIDES, was among those who were forced to leave the country.

In the inner-Jewish sector a battle now began over the question of the recognition or the condemnation of the writings of Maimonides. As early as the middle of the 12th century Abraham ben David of Posquières had violently opposed the great teacher's use of philosophical principles in the exposition of divine revelation, and in the 13th century Rabbi Solomon ben Abraham had condemned his writings at Montpellier and handed them over to the Inquisition. In Spain itself the strict Talmudic system had been recently strengthened through the efforts of Rabbi Solomon ben Adret (*c.* 1235–1310), but the viewpoint of Maimonides found adherents in Hasdai ben Abraham CRESCAS (1340–1410) and his disciple Joseph ALBO (*c.* 1388–1444), the author of the *Book of the Principles of Faith.*

In the field of religious legislation the ideas of Maimonides gained the upper hand. In the spirit of his *Mishneh Torah,* Rabbi Jacob ben Asher (*c.* 1300) wrote his *Arba Turim,* a commentary on the Talmud that later formed the basis for the *Shulḥan Aruch* of Rabbi Joseph ben Ephraim CARO (1488–1575). The latter work, with

the glosses of Rabbi Moses Isserles of Cracow (1520–75) which was adapted to conditions in central and eastern Europe, has remained the basis of all the rabbinical interpretations of the Talmud.

Increasing external difficulties and the internal religious struggle caused an ever larger group of Jews to turn to the mysticism of the CABALA, which likewise went back to ancient traditions and which began its irrepressible march of triumph through the Jewish world after the still mysterious ''discovery'' of the ZOHAR by the Spanish-Jewish mystic, Moses de Leon (1260–1305).

The general situation of the Jews in Spain now noticeably deteriorated; in 1391 and in 1412 excesses of cruelty ensued, and a large number of Jews, known as MARRANOS, submitted, through fear, to the pretense of being baptized. When, toward the end of the 15th century, the kingdoms of Castile and Aragon were united, the Inquisition was reactivated, primarily against the Marranos, under the leadership of Tomás de TORQUEMADA, and in 1492 a decree was issued that all the Jews who refused to be baptized would have to leave Spain within three months. This spelled the end, after more than 1,000 years, of Spanish Judaism. Many refugees first migrated to neighboring Portugal, but six years later they were expelled from this country too; others went to Turkey, where they were given asylum, or to other lands in the Mediterranean area, where numerous communities were founded of so-called Sephardic Jews, speaking their Spanish dialect of Ladino.

Period of the Renaissance and Reformation (1492 to 1650). Although the humanism of the Renaissance did not result in any noticeably humane treatment of the Jews in Europe, and the disturbances that accompanied the Reformation added to their sufferings, both the Ashkenazi Jews of Poland and the Sephardic Jews of the Mediterranean lands and western Europe were able to preserve and develop their typically Jewish way of life.

General Situation. In Germany, after the massacres in the period of the Crusades, when numerous Jews fled from this country to eastern Europe (bringing with them their German dialect, Yiddish), conditions became somewhat stabilized, although ominous warnings of danger were ever present. As imperial *Kammerknechte* (chamberlains), the Jews were placed under the direct protection of the emperor, but they had to pay a heavy tax for this privilege. Later on, in 1355, the right to collect this tax was given to the local princes by the Golden Bull of Charles IV. Yet this did not protect the Jews from the constantly recurring bloody outrages and pillages, such as occurred in 1298 (under Rindfleisch), from 1336 to 1339 (the ''Armleder'' massacres), in 1337 (the ''desecration of the hosts'' incident in Deggendorf, Bavaria), in 1348 to 1349 (the outbreak of the Black Death and the accusation of poisoning of wells), and in 1421 (the "Vienna Geserah," ritual murder accusation). In 1434 the Council of Basel renewed the old anti-Jewish regulations as part of the Church's Canon Law, and the Franciscan friar JOHN CAPISTRAN took it on himself to aid the execution of these laws everywhere, which caused a new outbreak of serious persecution.

At the beginning of the Reformation the situation of the Jews looked as if it would improve. But when Luther had to admit that his expectations for their conversion had come to naught, the benevolence that he had first shown the Jews out of reverence for the people of God now turned into a grim hostility that found expression in a series of anti-Jewish pamphlets. One positive aspect of the Reformation, in the eyes of the Jews, was the revival of interest in the study of Hebrew, which brought renowned Christian scholars in contact with learned Jews.

The Catholic Counter Reformation, too, led to a renewal in the strict application of the laws against the Jews. These laws now affected the Italian Jews also, who, despite their relatively small number, had played a significant role in the cultural sphere because of their contact with the Renaissance. In Italy, for instance, the first Jewish printing press was set up and the first Hebrew books were printed. But because of the inauspicious omens of renewed persecution, the centers of Jewish life moved to other countries where better conditions prevailed.

Polish Judaism. In the period of the Crusades Jewish settlements were fostered by the dukes of Great Poland, since those nobles saw in this a chance to bring their country into the network of international commerce. In spite of the resolute resistance of the clergy, Boleslas of Kalisz issued a statute in 1264 that was very favorable to the Jews. Later on, King Casimir the Great (133–370) admitted into his realm a large number of Jews who had fled from the persecution that had broken out after the Black Death. With a few interruptions, this favorable situation lasted under the Lithuanian Jagiellos. During the reign of Sigismund III (1588–1632) the condition of the Jews in Poland deteriorated as a result of the anti-Jewish propaganda of the Jesuits, though the Jewish communities there had grown so strong and were so well organized that they withstood these attacks with ease.

In Poland the autonomous Jewish system of community government reached the peak of its development. Every community of importance was directed by a kahal, a body of notables elected yearly that conducted all the administrative affairs. Juridical matters were entrusted to the rabbis, and a court of appeals met every year in Lublin at the time of the annual fair in that city and in conjunction with the assembly of the various kahals. The highest court of appeals in Poland was the Council of the Four Countries (Great Poland, Little Poland, Podolia-Galicia, and Volhynia); in Lithuania there was the Council of the Great Communities.

The kahal was especially interested in education. In every community there was a *heder* (elementary school), and in many of them there was also a *yeshivah* (Talmudic academy); in both of these, exclusively Jewish disciplines were taught and studied, which soon assured to the Polish Jews great intellectual superiority and to their leading rabbis undeniable authority.

The Sephardic Sphere. The immigration of the Jews from Spain into Turkey continued long after 1492 with a flow of Marranos who had found more and more unbearable the activities of the informers and secret police that the Inquisition encouraged. Many *Españolos,* such as Don Joseph Nassi, reached positions of great influence at the Sublime Porte (the Ottoman imperial court).

In 1517 the Turks occupied Egypt also and thereby became the rulers of Palestine as well. Groups of refugees, therefore, now migrated to the Holy Land, new communities arose in the cities of Jerusalem, Hebron, Tiberias, and especially Safed (in Galilee). Safed became the seat of a new school of the cabalists. Its founder, Jacob Berab, who had settled there in 1534, was followed in 1538 by Rabbi Joseph Caro, the author of the *Shulḥan Aruch,* and by his close friend, Solomon Alkabeṣ. Among the great sages in the cabalistic school of Safed were Rabbi Isaac LURIA (1534–72) and his disciple and brother-in-law, Moses Cordovero (d.1570). Luria's teachings, with their pronounced messianic spirit, found an able propagandist in his disciple, Ḥayyim Vidal Calabrese.

Under the pressure of the Jewish expulsion from Spain and of the consequent sufferings, messianic movements were started in various places. Their beginnings are connected with the names of David Reubeni and Solomon Molcho. Later on, their climax was reached in the person of Shabbatai Ṣevi of Smyrna (1626–76). Many respectable Jewish personalities, among whom were learned rabbis, hailed Shabbatai as the promised Messiah. Even after his conversion to Islam, the messianic movement did not fully die out but provoked heated discussions in the Jewish communities. On lines similar to those of Shabbatai Ṣevi was the movement in Poland that was inspired by Jacob Frank (d. 1791), who eventually was converted to Christianity. (*See* SHABBATAIÏSM.)

An important new wave of immigration started in the 17th century when Marranos from Portugal found refuge in Holland. The Dutch, who had shaken off the Spanish domination toward the end of the 16th century, showed the refugees, whom they let settle wherever they wished, a toleration that was most unusual in those days. A large Jewish community arose in Amsterdam, which soon reached a very flourishing state under the leadership of such renowned Ḥakamim (sages) as Manasseh ben Israel. Amsterdam also was the home of the great Jewish thinkers Gabriel (Uriel) ACOSTA (d. 1640) and Baruch SPINOZA (d. 1677), both of whom, however, came in conflict with the rabbinic authorities and fell under the ban of the synagogue. After the Dutch revolution of 1649 some Portuguese Jews from Holland settled in England—for the first time since the expulsion in 1290. Colonies of Marranos were established also at Bordeaux and other places in southern France, where they were known as "new Christians." Genuine Jewish communities did not exist in France till 1648, when Alsace-Lorraine was incorporated in the French kingdom.

Beginning of the Modern Era (1650 to 1750). From the middle of the 17th to the middle of the 18th century the situation of the Jews in Poland grew more desperate, but they found spiritual consolation in the pietist movement of HASIDISM; in the rest of Europe the Jews suffered the usual series of persecutions.

Economic Situation in Eastern Europe. In the 17th century the position of the Jews in Poland became more and more untenable, although up to that time they had lived there in relatively tolerable circumstances. The revolt of the Cossacks under Bogdan Chmielnicki in 1648 destroyed hundreds of Jewish communities in the Ukraine and in Volhynia and caused numerous deaths, and the subsequent wars and disturbances brought much misery on all the other Jewish settlements in Poland. Meanwhile the tax burden weighed ever heavier on the Jews there. The Polish merchants and artisans were gradually driving the Jews out of business, and many of these were obliged to live as tenant farmers on the estates of the nobility, which in turn aroused the hatred of the exploited peasantry against them, so that bloody outrages occurred constantly.

Religious Reaction: Ḥasidism. The Jewish reaction to these oppressive conditions arose from within, on the religious level. Since the late medieval period, and especially since Isaac Luria, the influence of the cabala on the life of all Jewry had constantly grown. On the other hand, it was precisely in Poland, the center of Jewish learning, that opposition arose against the tendency of the Talmudists to stress exclusively man's intellectual faculties.

On this background appeared, about 1730, the figure of Rabbi Israel ben Eliezer, called Ba'al Shem Tov, who became the founder of the Ḥasidim (the devout). The teaching of Ba'al Shem (Master of the Name, i.e., of God), which was set forth by means of popular stories, emphasized, without at all calling in question the tradi-

tional doctrines, the absolute superiority of the life of piety expressed by devout prayers of the heart and an ardent love of God, all based on the Lurian cabala. Under Ba'al Shem's successor, Rabbi Dov Ber of Mezhirich (d. 1773), the Ḥasidic movement received a firm structure and continued to spread, especially in Podolia, Galicia, and Volhynia, despite the strong opposition of the Mitnagdim (opponents), whose spokesman was the greatest Talmudist of his time, Gaon Rabbi Ella of Vilna (1720–97). In the following generation Ḥasidism split up into numerous local groups, each of which at times were under the leadership of a Tzaddik ("saintly" miracle-working rabbi). Ḥasidism was the last great religious movement in Judaism.

Situation in Germany and Austria. In the Germanic countries, too, the Jews had hard times during the 16th and 17th centuries. Pogroms and outrages were their constant lot. At the beginning of the 16th century the old communities of Frankfurt am Main and Worms suffered hardships because of the so-called Fettmilch revolt. In 1670 the Jews of Vienna, some of whom as financiers had rendered valuable services to the Hapsburg emperors during the Thirty Years' War, became victims of a decree of expulsion. In Bohemia, which, especially in Prague, had the largest Jewish community in the Hapsburg countries, the attempt was made to limit the number of the Jews by the so-called family-control law which permitted only the oldest son of a family to marry.

Emancipation (1750–1948). After their emancipation, which was largely the result of the 18th-century Enlightenment and the French Revolution, the Jews adapted themselves to the new conditions with various degrees of success. But the waves of modern anti-Semitism finally broke over them with such fury that they were almost annihilated by the Nazis. An indirect outcome of this was the establishment in Palestine by the Zionists of the Jewish State of Israel.

The Enlightenment and the French Revolution. While the old structure of the regulations concerning the Jews remained unchanged, the liberal ideas that were broadcast in France, especially by the Encyclopedists, made themselves felt more and more. The first Jew of this time who made contact with modern thought was the Berliner Moses Dessau, better known as Moses Mendelssohn (1728–86). Being an important philosopher himself, he endeavored by all means to have his fellow believers, who had remained almost completely unaffected by the intellectual movements of the modern age, to join the general stage of cultural development achieved by their contemporaries. He was practically the first Jew who wrote in High German, and he translated the Bible into this language—a very bold enterprise at that time, because it made him look like a heretic in the eyes of the strictly tradition-minded rabbis.

The first real civic emancipation of the Jews, which liberated them after centuries from the ghettos and made them equal to their fellow men, with full human rights, was a result of the French Revolution. The effective legal measures, however, met with stubborn opposition from the Christian population, especially in Alsace. At the invitation of Napoleon, the so-called Great Synagogue met at Paris in 1807 to settle the relations between the Jews and the State. The emperor applied the consistorial system to the Jews also, and thus put an end to the old autonomy of their communities. In the countries occupied by Napoleon, such as Italy, Holland, and Westphalia, the Jews were likewise given civil rights. In other countries the development was much slower and not without setbacks.

Reactions within the Jewish Communities. The emancipation and its forerunners caused a complete revolution within Judaism. The traditional framework of Jewish life, which had remained practically unchanged for centuries, now collapsed in western Europe and along with it was shattered the Jewish system of instruction and education. At this time there came into being a new type of Jew, who, while retaining his Jewish faith, was also a full-fledged citizen of this or that country and consequently became more and more assimilated to the life and culture of his non-Jewish environment. Since many progressive Jews thought that their emancipation was proceeding too slowly, this period saw the so-called Baptism Movement widely affecting various social strata among the Jews who looked upon Baptism as an entrance ticket into Christian society.

This development, which, within a few years, transplanted the Jews from the Middle Ages into the modern world, advanced so fast that it took some time until there were aroused in Judaism the counterforces for stemming the constant loss in the ranks of the Jews. Endeavors were now made to adapt, by means of suitable reforms, the religious institutions of Judaism, particularly those connected with synagogue service, to the changed conditions of the time. The leaders of the movement in Germany were Samuel Holdheim (1806–60), Abraham Geiger (1810–74), and Ludwig Philippson (1811–89). Such attempts at reform provoked violent opposition from those who were attached to the traditional forms. The latter found a militant spokesman in Rabbi Moses Sofer-Schreiber of Pressburg (1773–1839), who opposed on principle any kind of innovation. A conservative, conciliatory movement, which later gained the upper hand in most of the Jewish communities in Germany, was represented by Zacharias Frankel (1801–75), the founder of

the Jewish theological seminary of Breslau, the first modern institution for the education of rabbis, while Samson Raphael Hirsch became the spiritual father of the new German-Jewish orthodoxy that recognized the necessity of modern education while holding fast to the old. In this period of intellectual innovation the "Science of Judaism" was born under the *Altmeister* Leopold Zunz (1794–1886), the historian Heinrich Graetz (1817–91), as well as under several others.

Progressive civil emancipation of the Jews made some advances in certain countries, but only the year 1848 brought the decisive change. The real, or at least theoretically and legally granted equality was effected in Germany with the founding of the German Empire in 1870 to 1871, and in the Austrian countries with the Austro-Hungarian settlement in 1867.

In Russia. Russia received its Jewish population through the various partitions of Poland (in 1792, 1793, and 1795), and the Russian government anxiously watched the Jews to keep them within the boundaries of the newly annexed lands ("settlement area"). Under Alexander I (1801–25) some liberal measures in their favor were attempted, such as the Jewish Statute of 1804, but these largely remained dead letters. Under Nicolaus I (1825–55) a 25-year term of military service was introduced for the Jews, in order to further their "assimilation" (i.e., Baptism). Among cultured Jews, the Enlightenment, which in Russia and Poland they adopted in a typically Jewish form called the HASKALAH, made great progress and stimulated the growth of neo-Hebrew literature. During the reign of Alexander II (1855–81) certain civil rights and cultural possibilities were granted to the Jews, but when the reactionary party was victorious under Alexander III (1891–94), a real reign of terror began; in 1881 to 1882 a series of bloody pogroms broke out, which were followed by oppressive anti-Jewish measures.

Anti-Semitism. After the emancipation, opposition against the Jews adopted a new shape: modern anti-semitism that aimed at forcing the Jews out of the positions they already had achieved and preventing them from making further progress in social life. This anti-Semitism was strongly promoted by the fact that many Jews, in making good use of the opportunities offered by liberalism and the nascent industrial revolution, had won for themselves leading positions in economic life.

In Germany the soul of the movement was the Protestant minister Adolf Stöcker, who was appointed court preacher in Berlin (1878). In Austria, Canon Rohling, a theology professor of Prague, zealously propagated anti-Semitism by his writings. Karl Lueger, who later became mayor of Vienna, founded the Christian Socialist party, which made anti-Semitism a part of its program, while, in the so-called Greater-Germany Camp, Georg von Schönerer was the exponent of his party's anti-Semitic principles. In France the journalist Edouard Drumont was the mouthpiece of the anti-Semites whose agitation led to the Dreyfus affair. This led the Jews, in turn, to reflect on the hazardous nature of their "equality" and to stand a sponsor of Zionism in the person of the Viennese journalist Theodore Herzl.

In America. The pogroms in Russia, the anti-Semitic movements in the other countries, and the lack of possibility for economic progress produced, from 1880 on, the great wave of Jewish immigration, especially from eastern Europe, to America. Here, since the 18th century, a Portuguese-Jewish community had already existed, and this had later been increased by other Jewish settlers, particularly from Germany. The Jewish population in America soon made its importance felt in the economic sphere and showed a remarkable growth in cultural life. In the field of Jewish science and religious reform, all the movements brought over from Europe underwent further independent development in America, and in their variety have given to American Judaism its characteristic features.

In Palestine. Under the influence of the Zionist movement and its forerunners, emigrants, at first from Russia, began to settle in Palestine. In its beginnings this emigration was strongly promoted by Baron Edmond de Rothschild. The great pogroms of 1903 in Kishinev and Homel again drove numerous refugees into all the countries that would receive them.

In the Muslim World. In the Islamic countries the Jews remained for a long time within the framework of their traditional structure. The Damascus Affair of 1840, when the libel of so-called ritual murder caused a persecution of the Jews, cast a glaring light on their real situation and called to their defense leading European Jews, such as Sir Moses Montefiore, the English philanthropist, and Adolphe Crémieux, cofounder of the Paris *Alliance Israélite Universele.* The occupation of Algiers by France in 1830 changed the lot of the Jews in this country also. The *Alliance* instituted a lively cultural activity, and in 1870 the Algerian Jews were granted French citizenship by the *Lex Crémieux.* Likewise in Tunisia, when it was formed into a French protectorate in 1881, the Jews were given civil equality with the Muslims though in Morocco they were not freed from their medieval ghettos until 1912, and then only partially. In Egypt the way to the same development was prepared by the English Protectorate in 1882, but in other Arab countries, such as Yemen, the Jews still remained without civic rights.

World War I and Its Consequences. It was again mainly the Russian Jews who suffered the consequences

of the war; they were herded from the border areas into the interior of the country on the pretext that they were conspiring with the enemy. Although the revolution of 1917 brought them freedom, the Jewish communities, especially in the Ukraine, were again sorely afflicted in the ensuing struggles between the "Reds" and the "Whites."

In the countries newly established by the peace treaty of 1918 to 1919 the Jewish problem had to receive new solutions. An agreement for the protection of minorities was drawn up, and a committee of the League of Nations was entrusted with the execution of its stipulations. The largest number of Jews (almost three million) lived in the newly organized state of Poland, where they were able to preserve, in spite of some tendencies toward assimilation, their individual character as a people with its own language (Yiddish) and its own cultural institutions. Thanks to this situation, the traditional way of life of the Ashkenazi Jews was retained longer in Poland than elsewhere. Polish Judaism thus formed a large reservoir of native Jewish forces. The equality granted to the Jews by the constitution in Poland, as well as in Rumania and Hungary (*Numerus clausus*), was quite limited in practice, whereas Czechoslovakia, under President Masaryk, presented a praiseworthy exception in this regard.

In Soviet Russia the Jews in particular suffered in the economic upheaval that the new regime brought with it, which necessitated a change to entirely new means of gaining a livelihood. The attempt to establish the Jewish autonomous region of Biro-Bidyan in the far-eastern part of the Soviet Union met with but little response. Yiddish culture was still flourishing to some extent in Russia during the first years after the revolution, until under Stalin all genuinely Jewish life was made impossible.

In Germany: The Beginning of the End. In the German Reich, where the Jews played a certain role during the political revolution of 1918 and where, in the so-called Weimar Republic, the way was prepared for an organic symbiosis between the Jews and the non-Jewish population, the anti-Semites again appeared on the scene. In 1922 the Jewish minister of foreign affairs, Walter Rathenau, fell a victim to their machinations, and in 1923 Adolf Hitler managed the first *Putsch* in Munich, assisted by the anti-Semites of General Ludendorff's "Old Guard." Hitler's book *Mein Kampf,* which incorporated and systematized all the old anti-Semitic theories and slogans, became the modern Bible of anti-Semitism, and when Hitler came to power in 1933 as the leader of his NSDAP (German National Socialist Labor party), the stage was set for the greatest catastrophe in the history of the Jewish people; six million people were its victims solely because they were Jews. It will take Judaism a long time to recover from this enormous massacre, but its inner power is unbroken, and the establishment of the State of Israel in 1948, despite the outrageous injustice that was thereby done to the non-Jewish inhabitants of Palestine, has given a new proof of its vitality.

Bibliography: S. W. BARON, *A Social and Religious History of the Jews,* 8 v. (2d ed. New York 1952–58; index 960). S. M. DUB-NOW, *Weltgeschichte des jüdischen Volkes,* 10 v. (Berlin 1925–29). H. H. GRAETZ, *History of the Jews,* ed. and tr. B LÖWY, 6 v. (Philadelphia 1945). M. MARGOLIS and A. MARX, *A History of the Jewish People* (New York 1927; repr. pa. 1958). L. FINKELSTEIN, ed., *The Jews: Their History, Culture and Religion,* 2 v. (3d ed. New York 1960).

[K. HRUBY]

JIMÉNEZ DE ENCISO, SALVADOR

Bishop of Popayán, Colombia; b. Málaga, Spain, 1765; d. Popayán, Feb. 13, 1841. Jiménez came to America with the Archbishop of Charcas (Sucre), José Antonio de San Alberto. He graduated from the University of Charcas with degrees in theology and law before returning to Spain where he became a canon in Córdoba and Málaga.

On Feb. 14, 1815, Ferdinand VII presented Jiménez as a candidate for the episcopate of Popayán. Pius VII appointed him on March 13, 1815, and he was consecrated in Madrid. He assumed possession of his episcopate by proxy on May 7, 1818, and entered it on Aug. 6, 1818. When the troops of the cause of independence, victorious at the battle of Boyacá (Aug. 7, 1819), approached Popayán, Jiménez withdrew to Pasto and excommunicated the supporters of the republic from there. The vice president of the republic, Gen. Francisco de Paula Santander, then declared the See of Popayán to be vacant, a measure approved by the congress on Aug. 31, 1821. In Pasto, Jiménez arranged an armistice between the royalists and the republican troops commanded by General Sucre. When Bolívar wrote to him (Jan. 31, 1822) that several bishops had supported the independence movement, he did not reply, but his intervention brought the Pasto fighters, who upheld the king's cause, to sign a capitulation agreement with Bolívar.

Jiménez then requested his passport in order to return to Spain, but Bolívar replied (June 10, 1822) that a bishop could not leave his church for political reasons, and asked him, in the name of the Colombian government, to remain. The prelate, believing that the independence of Colombia was now an accomplished fact, returned to Popayán and gave his obedience to the new government (Sept. 22, 1822). Bolívar then wrote to Santander, praising the bishop's decision: "The bishop of Popayán will be very useful to us because he is sensitive to the best interests of Colombia." Jiménez wrote to Pius VII on behalf of the new republic, asking him to attend to its needs as soon as possible: "I shall not conceal from Your Holiness that there are also some weeds in the fertile field of the Church in Colombia; but the good seed is more abundant, and I should even venture to say that in the history of mankind's revolutions, no other can be said to have inflicted fewer wounds on the sacrosanct religion of our Lord Jesus Christ" (P. de Leturia, *Relaciones entre la Santa Sede e Hispanoamérica,* 3:268). In 1833, Jiménez wished to return to Spain because he was vexed with several influential persons in Popayán, but again the government dissuaded him.

During his episcopate Jiménez restored the seminary and began the construction of the new cathedral. He consecrated various bishops of Colombia and Ecuador. He maintained friendly relations with the Colombian government, in spite of its frequent meddlings in ecclesiastical matters. Because of the scarcity of clergy, he was often forced to ordain as priests persons who had not completed the necessary studies and nor possessed the required moral qualities.

Bibliography: R. VARGAS UGARTE, *El episcopado en los tiempos de la emancipación sudamericana* (Buenos Aires 1945). P. DE LETURIA, *El ocaso del patronato real la América española: La acción diplomática de Bolívar ante Pío VII . . .* (Madrid 1925). G. GARCÍA-HERRERA, *Un obispo de historia: El obispo de Popayán, don Salvador Ximénez de Enciso y Cobos Padilla* (Málaga 1961).

[J. M. PACHECO]

JOACHIM OF BRANDENBURG

The name of two imperial electors (father and son) of the 15th and 16th centuries.

Joachim I, Catholic elector; b. Feb. 21, 1484; d. Stendal, July 11, 1535. He inherited the electorate of Brandenburg upon the death of his father, John, on Jan. 9, 1499, and soon restored sorely needed law and order. In 1506 he founded the University of Frankfurt-an-der-Oder, and in 1524 he added the county of Ruppin to the family holdings. His hostility to the teachings of Martin Luther prolonged the influence of Catholicism in Brandenburg until the reign of his son Joachim II. In his political alignments and alliances, such as the Swabian League, he followed a proimperial, propapal policy. In 1530 he was among the few Catholic princes ready to go to war for these convictions. Not only was he intolerant of Protestantism, but as early as 1510 he had banished the Jews from his lands. Upon his death in July 1535, he divided Brandenburg between his two sons, Joachim II and John, in violation of the *Dispositio Achillea's* provision for the establishment of primogeniture.

Joachim II, Protestant elector; b. Jan. 9, 1505; d. Kopenick, Jan. 3, 1571. In 1535 he received only the old and middle marks of Brandenburg with the title of elector, while his brother John inherited the new mark and the title of margrave. John immediately embraced Lutheranism, but not until 1539 did Joachim II allow Lutheran preachers to enter Brandenburg. Joachim did not break with Rome at once. Rather, he followed the example set by Henry VIII in England. Monasteries and convents were closed, and the bishops came under state control. This new settlement was approved by the Emperor Charles V in 1541. Joachim's main reason for embracing the reform faith seems to have been the desire for personal wealth resulting from the confiscation of church lands, rather than religious conviction. By the time Joachim died in 1571, Brandenburg was one of the principal Protestant strongholds in Germany. In 1537 he gained a claim to Silesia (the duchies of Liegnitz, Brieg, and Wohlau) for the Hohenzollern family. This claim was later to be the basis upon which Frederick the Great relied in 1740 when he annexed the three Silesian duchies.

Bibliography: J. JANSSEN, *History of the German People at the Close of the Middle Ages,* tr. M. A. MITCHELL and A. M. CHRISTIE, 17 v. (London 1896–1925). F. VOIGT, *Geschichte des brandenburgish-preussischen Staates* (3d ed. Berlin 1878). J. HEIDEMANN, *Die Reformation in der Mark Brandenburg* (Berlin 1889), J. LORTZ, *Die Reformation in Deutschland,* 2 v. (Freiburg 1939–40). F. L. CARSTEN, *The Origins of Prussia* (Oxford 1954). H. HOLBORN, *A History of Modern Germany: The Reformation* (New York 1959). S. SKALWEIT, *Lexicon für Theologie und Kirche* 5:974–975.

[J. G. GALLAHER]

JOACHIM OF FIORE

Cistercian mystic; b. Celico, near Cosenza, Italy, *c.* 1130; d. Fiore, Calabria, 1201 or 1202. As a young man, Joachim of Fiore (Flora, Floris) made a pilgrimage to the Holy Land, witnessing en route (probably at Constantinople) the horrors of an epidemic. This experience, together with his visit to the Thebaid anchorites and a Lenten retreat in Jerusalem, changed his life. Returning to Sicily, he withdrew to the Cistercian monastery at Sambucina, but without taking the habit, and devoted himself to lay preaching until ecclesiastical disapproval led him to make profession at the Cistercian monastery in Corazzo, where he was ordained in 1168. Elected abbot (1177–78), he appealed to Lucius III, who authorized him to spend a year and a half writing at the monastery in Casamari. In 1191 he left the Cistercians to found at San Giovanni, in Fiore, a more austere branch of the order, which was approved in 1196. In 1202(?) he publicly submitted all his works to the judgment of the Holy See but died before any judgment was passed. Contemporaries testified to his love of Christ, his fervor at Mass, his inspiring eloquence in preaching. Gentle and pure, he loved all creatures and lived in utter poverty.

Joachim's entire doctrine is reducible to his teaching on the Trinity and on history. Opposing Peter Lombard, Joachim held the unity of the Trinity to be not *vera et propria,* but *collectiva et similitudinaria,* a thesis that was condemned by Lateran IV (1215) as tritheistic. The same tritheistic tendency appeared in Joachim's developmental theology of history, which moves from the Age of the Father (Old Testament), characterized by fear and servile obedience (this was the age of the married and the old), to the Age of the Son (New Testament), which was characterized by faith and filial obedience (this was the age of the clergy and the young), to the Age of the Holy Spirit, due to begin about 1260, which Joachim believed would be characterized by love and liberty (this was the age of monks and infants). The visible Church of the second age was to be absorbed by the spiritual Church of the third; the clergy and hierarchy were to have a place in the spiritual order; the active life was to be absorbed by the contemplative; Jews were to be converted, Greeks and Latins reconciled; wars were to cease, universal love would reign, and the theology of the beatitudes would endure to the end of the world, the *evangelium aeternum* of the Revelation (14.6).

This doctrine was taken up by the Spiritual Franciscans, that is, the Joachimites, mixed with ideas from the Apocrypha, and carried far beyond Joachim's intentions. With the condemnation of Gherardo of Borgo San Donnino's *Introductorium in evangelium aeternum* by Alexander IV (1256), the teaching of Joachim himself was condemned. It was revived in a modified form by PETER JOHN OLIVI and UBERTINO OF CASALE, and by many German writers of the Reformation, and with COLA DI RIENZO it resulted in the political messianism familiar to later times. Joachim's concept of history, developmental and tripartite, is also familiar through Hegel, Schilling, and many contemporary thinkers.

After Joachim's death, a multitude of works, largely pseudo-prophetical, appeared under his name, making his canon difficult to establish. Unquestionably authentic and most important are *Concordia novi et veteris testamenti* (Venice 1519); *Expositio in Apocalypsim* (Venice 1527); and *Psalterium decem chordarum* (Venice 1527). Of probable or doubtful authenticity are *Tractatus super quattuor evangelia,* ed. Ernesto Buonaiuti (Rome 1930); *De articulis fidei,* ed. *idem* (Rome 1936); *Liber figurarum,* ed. Leone Tondelli (Turin 1939; tr. 1953); *De vita et regula S. Benedicti,* ed. C. Baraut in *Analecta sacra Tarraconensia* 24 (Barcelona 1951) 33–122; *De septem sigillis,* ed. Marjorie Reeves and Beatrice Hirsch-Reich, in *Recherches de théologie ancienne et médiévale* 21 (1954): 24–247; and *Adversus Judaeos,* ed. Arsenio Frugoni (Rome 1957). Very doubtful is the authenticity of the *Liber contra Lombardum,* ed. C. Ottaviani (Rome 1934).

See Also: FRANCISCAN SPIRITUALS.

Bibliography: *Acta Sanctorum* (Antwerp 1643—; Venice 1734—; Paris 1864—) May 7:87–141. E. JORDAN, *Dictionnaire de théologie catholique,* 15 v. (Paris 1903–50) 8.2:1426–58. J. RATZINGER, *Lexikon für Theologie und Kirche,* 10 v. (Freiburg 1957–65) 5:975–976. F. EHRLE, *Wetzer und Welte's Kirchenlexikon,* v. 6 (2d ed. Freiburg 1889) 1471–80; "Die Spiritualen, ihr Verhältnis zum Franziskanerorden und zu den Fraticellen," *Archiv für Literatur- und Kirchengeschichte des Mittelalters,* 7 v., ed. H. DENIFLE and F. EHRLE 1:509–569; 2:108–164, 249–336; 3:553–623; 4:1–200. M. W. BLOOMFIELD, "Joachim of Flora: A Critical Survey . . . ," *Traditio* 13 (1957): 249–311. F. RUSSO, "Rassegna Gioachimito-Dantesco," *Miscellanea Francescana* 38 (1938): 65–83; *Bibliografia gioachimita* (Florence 1954); *Gioacchino da Fiore e le fondazioni florensi in Calabria* (Naples 1959). E. BUONAIUTI, *G. da Fiore: I tempi, la vita, il messaggio* (Rome 1931). D. L. DOUIE *The Nature and Effect of the Heresy of the Fraticelli* (Manchester 1932). H. GRUNDMANN, *Neue Forschungen über Joachim von Fiore* (Marburg 1950). M. REEVES, *The Influence of Prophecy in the Later Middle Ages: A Study in Joachimism* (Oxford 1969). B. MCGINN, "The Abbot and the Doctors: Scholastic Reactions to the Radical Eschatology of Joachim of Fiore," *Church History* 40 (1971): 30–47. D. C. WEST and S. ZIMDARS- SWARTZ, *Joachim of Fiore: A Study in Spiritual Perception and History* (Bloomington 1983).

[M. F. LAUGHLIN]

Manuscript folio from "Expositio in Apocalypism" (Cod. Vat. Lat. 4860), by Joachim of Fiore.

JOAN, POPESS, FABLE OF

Concerns a woman alleged to have been pope in the 9th, 10th, or 11th centuries. It is based on a 13th-century tale found in the writings of such chroniclers and preachers as the Dominicans John de Mailly and Stephen de Bourbon, and the 13th-century Franciscan author of the *Chronica minor* (*Monumenta Germaniae Scriptores* 24:184), but especially the Polish Dominican MARTIN OF TROPPAU. Martin's account (*Monumenta Germaniae Scriptores* 22:428), the one most widely circulated and accepted, declared that LEO IV (d. 855) was succeeded by a John Anglicus, pope for two and a half years, who was, in fact, a woman. Joan, educated in Athens, was returning to Mainz dressed as a man when she stopped off at Rome and so impressed all by her learning that she became a curial notary, a cardinal, and finally pope. Her sex was discovered when, during a procession, she gave birth to a child in the road between the Colosseum and St. Clement's, or in the church itself. Her punishment and death are variously described. An ancient statue of a pagan priest with a serving boy, discovered and set up near St. Clement's, and an inscription variously resolved and interpreted, were both considered to refer to Popess Joan.

Pius V ordered both destroyed (according to Jakobclerus who wrote a guidebook to Rome in 1575). That the story was accepted is evident from the fact that her statue was included among the popes in the cathedral of Siena (*c.* 1400). Hus reproached the Council of CONSTANCE (1415) with Popess Joan, whose existence no one denied. The domination of the 10th-century popes by the women of the house of Theophylactus is one of several explanations given for the development of the fable. Its falsity was recognized first by J. AVENTINUS (d. 1534) and by O. Panvinio, R. BELLARMINE, and D. Blondel, all in the 16th century.

Bibliography: Sources. *Monumenta Germaniae Scriptores* (Berlin 1826–) 22:428; 24:184, 243, 514. *Liber Pontificalis,* ed. L. DUCHESNE (Paris 1958) 2:xxvi–xxvii. Literature. F. SPANHEIM, *Histoire de la papesse Jeanne,* 2 v. (3d ed. The Hague 1736). J. J. I. VON DÖLLINGER, *Die Papstfabeln des Mittelalters* (2d ed. Stuttgart 1890). F. X. SEPPELT, *Geschichte der Päpste von den Anfängen bis zur Mitte des 20. Jh* (Leipzig 1931–41) 2:238–240. J. QUÉTIF and J. ÉCHARD, *Scriptores Ordinis Praedicatorum* (Paris 1719–23) 1.1:367. E. VACANDARD, *Études de critique et d'histoire religieuse,* 4 v. (Paris 1909–23) 4:13–39. *Revue d'histoire ecclésiastique* 20 (Louvain 1924) 296*, 5401. G. SCHWAIGER, *Lexikon für Theologie und Kirche,* ed. J. HOFER and K. RAHNER, 10 v. (2d ed. Freiburg 1957–65) 5:984–985. H. FUHRMANN, *Die Religion in Geschichte und Gegenwart,* 7 v. (3d ed. Tübingen 1957–65) 3:803.

[C. M. AHERNE]

Joan of Arc drives out camp followers in a scene from the "Vigils of Charles VII," 1431.

JOAN OF ARC, ST.

Jeanne la Pucelle, national patroness of France; b. Domremy, Lorraine (Department, Meuse), France, Jan. 6, 1412; d. Rouen, France, May 30, 1431.

Except for her piety, nothing in "Jeannette's" early years distinguished her from other children of the countryside. When she was about 13, her "voices," which she kept secret for almost five years, revealed her mission, the deliverance of the French Kingdom from English control. The treaty of Troyes (May 20, 1420), had made the English king, Henry V, king of France, setting aside the legitimate heir, the future Charles VII. The madness of Charles VI, French military reverses, and the alliance between England and Burgundy had prepared for this shattering event. After the successive deaths of Henry V and Charles VI, the duke of Bedford, regent of France for his nephew, HENRY VI, undertook to complete the conquest of the kingdom by tracking down the Dauphin (Charles

VII), who had taken refuge beyond the Loire, and by putting Orléans under siege.

Joan secretly left her home in January of 1429, succeeded in obtaining an escort from the captain of Vaucouleurs, who had remained faithful to the king of France, and was presented to Charles VII at Chinon (Feb. 25, 1429). Having had Joan examined by theologians at Poitiers, Charles consented to follow her advice and reassembled his army. With Joan in command they marched on Orléans and in eight days (May 8, 1429) ended the siege that had lasted eight months. After the brilliant victory of Patay (June 18), she opened the road to Reims, where Charles was crowned in the cathedral on July 17.

The coronation rallied the people of France, who until then had been hesitant in their support of Charles; it marked the end of English victories. But unfortunately the apathetic and ill-advised king opposed Joan's further plans. When at length she again went into action, hoping to relieve Compiègne, besieged by the Burgundians, Joan was taken prisoner (May 23, 1430). She was sold to the English, who, in placing her on trial for heresy, sought at once to remove a formidable adversary and to discredit the king who owed her his crown. The trial was held in Rouen, presided over by the bishop of Beauvais, Pierre Cauchon, the former rector of the University of Paris and a staunch champion of the English. After months of interrogation (Feb. 21 to May 24, 1431) and artifice, in which Cauchon tricked Joan into an admission of guilt, the judge sentenced her to death as a relapsed heretic. On May 30 she was excommunicated, turned over to the secular arm, and burned at the stake. Engulfed by the flames, Joan protested her innocence and the holiness of her mission.

Even during her lifetime, Joan was hailed as a saint because of both the preternatural character of her deeds and the purity of her life. She was solemnly rehabilitated by the Church after a seven-year trial (1449–56), during which 115 witnesses were heard; she was beatified April 19, 1909, and canonized May 9, 1920.

Feast: May 30.

Bibliography: Sources. P. TISSET and Y. LANHERS, *Procès de Jeanne d'Arc* (Paris 1960). J. E. J. QUICHERAT, *Procès de condamnation et de réhabilitation de Jeanne d'Arc*, 5 v. (Paris 1841–49). P. DONCOEUR and Y. LANHERS, eds., *Documents et recherches relatifs à Jeanne la Pucelle*, 5 v. (Paris 1952–61). P. DONCOEUR, *La Minute française des interrogatoires de Jeanne d'Arc* (Paris 1952). C. QUINTAL and D. RANKIN, *Letters of Joan of Arc* (Pittsburgh 1969). Literature. W. P. BARRETT, ed. and tr., *The Trial of Joan of Arc* (New York 1932). R. BRASILLACH, *Le procès de Jeanne d'Arc* (Paris 1941). G. BORDONOVE, *Jeanne d'Arc et la Guerre de Cent ans* (Paris 1994). O. BOUZY, *Jeanne d'Arc, mythes et réalités* (Paris 1999). R. CARATINI, *Jeanne d'Arc: De Domrémy à Orléans et du bûcher à la légende* (Paris 1999). M. DAVID-DARNAC, *Histoire véridique et merveilleuse de la Pucelle d'Orléans* (Paris 1965) tr. as *The True Story of the Maid of Orleans*, tr. P. DE POLNAY (London 1969); *Le Dossier de Jehanne* (Paris 1968). A. LANG, *The Maid of France* (London 1913). N. MARGOLIS, *Joan of Arc in History, Literature, and Film* (New York 1990). R. M. J. PERNOUD, *The Retrial of Joan of Arc*, tr. J. M. COHEN (New York 1955); *Jeanne d'Arc par ellemême et par ses témoins* (Paris 1975) tr. as *Joan of Arc by Herself and Her Witnesses*, tr. E. HYAMS (New York 1982); *La Libération d'Orléans* (Paris 1969); with G. BAÏLAC and G. GAUCHER, *Jeanne et Thérèse* (Paris 1984); with M.-V. CLIN, *Jeanne d'Arc* (Paris 1986) tr. as *Joan of Arc: Her Story*, tr. J. DUQUESNAY ADAMS, ed. B. WHEELER (New York 1999); *Jeanne d'Arc et la guerre de Cent Ans* (Paris 1990); *La spiritualité de Jeanne d'Arc* (Paris 1992); *Réhabilitation de Jeanne d'Arc* (Monaco 1995); with J. TULARD and J. PERNOUD, *Jeanne d'Arc, Napoléon: le paradoxe du biographe* (Monaco 1997); *Réhabilitation de Jeanne d'Arc* (Monaco 1995). V. M. SACKVILLE-WEST, *Saint Joan of Arc* (New York 1991). P. DE SERMOISE, *Jeanne d'Arc et la mandragore* (Monaco 1983); *Les missions secrètes de Jehanne la Pucelle* (Paris 1970) tr. as *Joan of Arc and Her Secret Missions*, tr. J. TAYLOR (London 1973). *Memorial du Vᵉ centenaire de la réhabilitation de Jeanne d'Arc, 1456–1956* (Paris 1958). K. SULLIVAN, *The Interrogation of Joan of Arc* (Minneapolis 1999). B. WHEELER and C. T. WOOD, eds., *Fresh Verdicts on Joan of Arc* (New York 1996).

[R. PERNOUD]

JOAN OF AZA, BL.

Mother of St. DOMINIC; b. castle of Aza, in Old Castile, Spain, *c.* 1140; d. Calaruega, *c.* 1190–1203. She married Felix de Guzman of Calaruega and bore him four children. The two eldest, Bl. Mannes (d. *c.* 1230; feast: July 30) and Antonio having become clerics, Joan visited the shrine of St. DOMINIC OF SILOS to pray for another child. When her prayer was heard, she resolved in gratitude to name the child Dominic. According to tradition, she dreamed that "she bore a dog in her womb and that it ran with a burning torch in its mouth to set the world aflame." This is the origin of the symbolic dog representing the Dominican Order. Joan's fourth child, a daughter, became the mother of two sons who entered the order. Joan is buried at Peñafiel; her cult was confirmed in 1828.

Feast: Aug. 8.

Bibliography: *Année Dominicaine*, August 1 (Lyons 1898) 31–48. M. C. DE GANAY, *Les Bienheureuses dominicaines* (2d ed. Paris 1924) 13–21. L. BERRA, A. MERCATI and A. PELZER, *Dizionario ecclesiatico*, 3 v. (Turin 1954–58) 2:135. A. BUTLER, *The Lives of the Saints*, ed. H. THURSTON and D. ATTWATER, 4 v. (New York 1956) 3:283–284.3.

[M. J. FINNEGAN]

JOAN OF FRANCE (VALOIS), ST.

Foundress of the Franciscan Annunciades; b. Paris, 1464; d. Bourges, France, Feb. 4, 1505. Joan, the sister of Charles VII, was deformed from birth, and because of her infirmity was despised by her father, Louis XI. When she was only two months old, she was betrothed to the duke of Orléans, and at the age of five she was sent to his chateau to be trained in court etiquette. Joan was a devout child with a lively horror of sin. She wanted to enter a cloister, but her desire met with only derision and abuse. She was once apparently granted a vision in which it was revealed to her that someday she would flee the world she feared and found a religious community. However, the marriage was solemnized when she was 12. The duke treated her with utmost contempt, and when he succeeded to the throne he had the marriage annulled, pensioning off his unwanted wife. Free at last, Joan devoted herself entirely to prayer and good works. Her Franciscan confessor wanted her to found a Poor Clare monastery, but she preferred the active works of charity. With a group of 10 devout women she founded the Franciscan

Annunciades. The rule was approved in 1501, and a year later she erected a second monastery at Bourges, dedicated to the care of the sick as well as to the ordinary austerities of monastic life. Joan adopted the name of Sister Gabriella Marie and made profession in the community, but resided in her own palace until the time of her death. She was buried in the habit along with her royal crown. In 1617 the canonization process was opened. Briefs of Popes ALEXANDER VII, INNOCENT X, and CLEMENT XI styled her "saint" without undertaking formal canonization proceedings, and in 1775 PIUS VI authorized the cult.

Feast: Feb. 4.

Bibliography: A. BUTLER, *The Lives of the Saints,* ed. H. THURSTON and D. ATTWATER, 4 v. (New York 1956) 1:252–253. A. DESTEFANIS, *Louis XII et Jeanne de France* (Avignon 1975). J.-F. DRÈZE, *Raison d'Etat, raison de Dieu: politique et mystique chez Jeanne de France* (Paris 1991). A. M. C. FORSTER, *The Good Duchess: Joan of France* (London 1950). A. REDIER, *Jeanne de France* (Le Puy, France 1946).

[M. J. DORCY]

JOAN OF ORVIETO, BL.

Dominican tertiary and mystic; also known as Giovanna or Vanna; b. Carnaiola, near Orvieto, Italy, 1264; d. Orvieto, July 23, 1306. Having refused a proposed marriage, she entered the Third Order of St. Dominic; Bl. JAMES OF BEVAGNA was her spiritual director. She received the stigmata and frequently entered into ecstasy. Her special devotions were to the holy angels and the Passion of Christ. Distinguished for her care of the poor, she was venerated by the townspeople, who, despite all her efforts to the contrary, honored her as a saint. Reportedly, the best way to be assured of her prayers was to do her an injury. BENEDICT XIV approved her cult in 1754.

Feast: July 23.

Bibliography: M. C. DE GANAY, *Les Bienheureuses dominicaines* (2d ed. Paris 1924) 109–120. A. BUTLER, *The Lives of the Saints* (New York 1956) 3:171–172. G. GIERATHS, *Lexikon für Theologie und Kirche,* 10 v. (2d, new ed. Freiburg 1957–65) 5:984.

[M. J. FINNEGAN]

JOAN OF PORTUGAL, BL.

Eldest child and heiress to Alfonso V, king of Portugal; b. Lisbon, Feb. 6, 1452; d. Aveiro, Portugal, May 12, 1490. Despite family pressure to contract an advantageous marriage alliance, Joan, devout from her earliest years, resolved to maintain her virginity and to join a convent. She remained briefly in the cloister of Odivellas before entering the Dominican convent of Jesus at Aveiro. There in 1475 she assumed the Dominican habit; however, she was not professed, nor did she give up control of her property; this was in deference to her father's desire to maintain a clear line of succession to Portugal's throne. She died, apparently of a fever, and was buried in the cloister of Aveiro, which is today a museum. At the request of King Pedro, she was beatified by INNOCENT XII on April 4, 1693.

Feast: May 12.

Bibliography: M. PINHEIRA, *Vita, Acta Sanctorum* May 7:711–749. F. CORREIA DE LACERDA, *Virtvosa vida, e sancta morte da princesa dona Ioanna* (Lisbon 1674). *Crónica da fundação do Mosteiro de Jesus, de Aveiro e memorial da infanta santa Joana, filha del Rei Dom Alfonso V,* ed. A. G. DA R. MADAHIL (Aveiro 1939). M. C. DE GANAY, *Les Bienheureuses dominicaines* (Paris 1913). A. BUTLER, *The Lives of the Saints,* ed. H. THURSTON and D. ATTWATER, 4 v. (New York 1956) 2: 291–292. A. G. DA R. MADAHIL, *Iconografia da infanta santa Joana* (Aveiro 1957). R. F. DOS SANTOS, *Rumos cruzados* (Fátima 1968).

[A. O'MALLEY]

JOAN OF SANTA LUCIA, BL.

Virgin; b. Bagno, Romagna, Italy, September 4 (year unknown); d. there January 16 or 17, c. 1105. She became a nun in the CAMALDOLESE convent of S. Lucia at Bagno. Her remains were transferred to the town's parish church in 1287. Later the town ascribed the cessation of a plague to her intercession and made her its patroness in 1506. Her cult was confirmed in 1823. There is a fresco of Bl. Joan and Agnes in the Camaldolese church at Bagno.

Feast: Sept. 4 (Bagno); Feb. 13 (Camaldolese).

Bibliography: *Acta Sanctorum* Jan. 2:423–424. A. M. ZIMMERMANN, *Kalendarium Benedictinum: Die Heiligen und Seligen des Benediktinerorderns und seiner Zweige* 3:13–14.

[M. R. P. MC GUIRE]

JOAN OF SIGNA, BL.

Virgin and recluse; b. Signa, near Florence, Italy, c. 1245; d. near Signa, Nov. 9, 1307. At the age of 23 she became a recluse in a cell in the neighborhood of Signa. She remained there for 40 years and had a reputation for working miracles. Her cult gained considerable impetus in 1348, when the cessation of an epidemic was attributed to her intercession; her cult was confirmed in 1798. She is claimed by the FRANCISCAN ORDER as a tertiary and also by the VALLOMBROSAN MONKS, the CARMELITES, and the AUGUSTINIANS, although the BOLLANDISTS hold there is no evidence of her connection with any order.

Feast: Nov. 7 (Florence); Nov. 17 (FRANCISCANS).

Bibliography: *Vitae* ed. in *Archivum Franciscanum historicum* 10 (1917) 367–386. *Acta Sanctorum* 544 Nov. 4 (1925) 280–288. Gruppo archeologico signese, *Vita e miracoli della beata Giovanna da Signa*, ed. M. BENELLI and R. VANNINI (Signa 1995). A. BUTLER, *The Lives of the Saints* (New York 1956) 4:374–375. J. BAUR, *Lexikon für Theologie und Kirche*, 10 v. (2d, new ed. Freiburg 1957–65) 5:985.

[C. R. BYERLY]

JOANA ANGÉLICA DE JESÚS

Brazilian nun, heroine of Independence; b. Salvador, Bahía, Dec. 11, 1761; d. there, Feb. 20, 1822. She was the daughter of José Tavares de Almeida and Caetana Maria de Silva, both Bahians of Portuguese ancestry. In 1782 she entered the Conceptionist Franciscan convent of Lapa in her native city. She made her profession as one of the Reformed Nuns of Our Lady of Conception on May 18, 1783. She held the positions of clerk (1797), vicar (1812), and, finally, abbess (1817), a post to which she returned in 1821. She was exercising her duties as abbess when the struggle broke out in the city between the Portuguese troops, under the command of General Madeira de Melo, and the Brazilians, led by Brigadier Freitas Guimarães. The fighting moved from street to street. On Feb. 20, 1822, the Portuguese soldiers, convinced that Brazilian soldiers were using the tower of the convent of Lapa as a vantage point from which to shoot at the Portuguese, decided to invade it. The abbess opposed this bravely; she appeared in the door of the cloister, impeding the entrance of the invaders and exclaiming: ''Go back, bandits! Respect the house of the Lord. Before carrying out your infamous plan, you will pass over my dead body.'' She was not able to deter the fury of the soldiers, who forced their entrance by means of bayonets and killed the abbess. The chaplain of the convent, Daniel Nunes da Silva, who also tried to oppose the entry, suffered a number of wounds but survived. Nothing was found in the convent to justify the violence.

Bibliography: B. J. DE SOUZA, *Joanna Angélica: A primeira heroína da independência do Brasil* (Bahia 1922). A. L. DE SOUZA, *Bahianos ilustres, 1564–1925* (Salvador 1949).

[A. J. LACOMBE]

JOANNES ANDREAE

The most distinguished and successful lay canonist of the Middle Ages; b. probably at Bologna, *c.* 1270; d. Bologna, July 7, 1348. There is no evidence that Joannes was illegitimate, as many biographers assert and there is no reason to doubt the validity of his parents marriage, even though his father did become a priest when Joannes was about eight years old. Having been taught the rudiments of grammar by his father and theology by the Dominican JOHN OF PARMA, Joannes entered the University of Bologna, where he studied Canon Law under Aegidius de Fuscariis, GUIDO DE BAYSIO, and Marsilius de Mantighellis and civil law under Martinus Syllimanus. He received his doctorate in Canon Law between 1296 and 1300. Shortly thereafter he married Mylantia, the daughter of Bonincontro dall'Ospedale, the vicar of the bishop of Bologna. They had four sons and three daughters. Two of his sons chose ecclesiastical careers, while the other two, Bonincontro and Federico, became successful lay canonists. His daughters married jurists. Joannes also adopted the famous canonist Joannes Calderini. First and foremost a teacher, he spent almost his entire life as professor of Canon Law in Bologna, although he did teach for a short time in Padua from 1307 to 1309 and again in 1319. Highly esteemed by popes and civil leaders, he carried out several diplomatic missions on behalf of Bologna and of the papal legate. Joannes died of the plague and was buried in the church of St. Dominic in Bologna. With his death the classical period of Canon Law came to a close (*see* CANON LAW, HISTORY OF, 4).

Many of his works are to a large extent compilations, in which Joannes gathered together, from the works of preceding canonists, all that was important for the benefit and convenience of his students. He was not a mere compiler; he made judicious selections, not hesitating to criticize when necessary, and from them he developed his own doctrine. Furthermore, his concern for questions of authorship and chronology ranks him as the first historian of Canon Law, to whom succeeding generations owe a great debt.

Two of his commentaries, the *Apparatus* on the *Liber Sextus* of BONIFACE VIII (1301) and the *Apparatus* on the *Clementines* (1322), were accepted as the *GLOSSA ORDINARIA*. Two minor treatises on marriage law *Summa super quarto libro Decretalium* and *Lectura super arboribus consanguinitatis et affinitatis,* enjoyed considerable popularity in the Middle Ages.

His greatest achievement was his *Novella Commentaria* series, comprising the *Novella* on the Decretals of GREGORY IX (*c.* 1338), the *Quaestiones Mercuriales* (1338–40), and the *Novella* on the *Liber Sextus* (1342–46). These works are similar in structure and method to Guido de Baysio's *Rosarium*. In them Joannes supplemented the text of the decretals with glosses indicating later canonical enactments found in the *Liber Sextus,* the *Clementines,* and the *Extravagantes,* and he enriched the *Glossa ordinaria* by gathering together all that he found useful in the various apparatuses of his predecessors and contemporaries. The *Quaestiones Mercuri-*

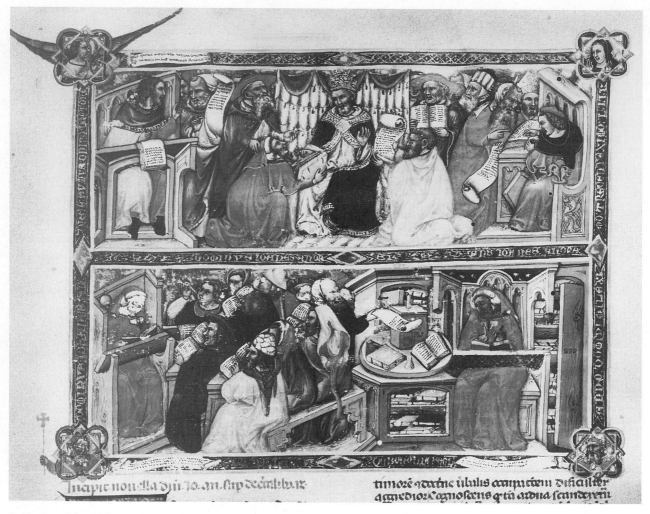

Beginning of the Prologue to Joannes Andreae's "Novella," dated 1353, in the Bibliotheca Apostolica Vaticana, Rome (Cod. Vat. Lat. 1456, fol. 1r).

ales is a dual work, comprising a *Novella commentaria* on the title *De regulis iuris* of the *Liber Sextus* and a collection of more than 100 *quaestiones disputatae* composed by Joannes Andreae and many others. *The Quaestiones* are arranged according to the various rules of law, supplement the commentary, and serve as illustrations of the rules.

Joannes did not publish a *Novella* on the *Clementines,* although the beginnings of such a commentary may perhaps be seen in an apparatus of additions (*Apostillae,* 1324–30) recently discovered in a Vatican MS. His last work, and one of his best, was the *Additiones* to the *Speculum* of William DURANTI (the Elder, 1346–47). It is similar in style and structure to the *Novella commentaria.*

Bibliography: S. STELLING–MICHAUD, *Dictionnaire de droit canonique,* ed. R. NAZ, 7 v. (Paris 1935–) 6:89–92. F. K. V. SAVIGNY, *Geschichte des römischen Rechts in Mittelalter,* 7 v. (2d ed. Heidelberg 1934–51) 6:98–125. S. KUTTNER, "J. A. and His 'Novella' on the Decretals of Gregory IX," *The Jurist,* 24 (1964) 393–408; "The Apostillae of J. A. on the Clementines," in *Études d'histoire du droit canonique dédiées à Gabriel Le Bras,* 2 v. (Paris 1965) 1:195–201. G. ROSSI, "Contributi alla biografia del canonista Giovanni d'Andrea," *Rivista trimestrale di diritto e procedura civile,* 11 (1957), 1451–1502.

[C. M. ROSEN]

JOANNES DE DEO

Canonist, b. Silves, Portugal, end of 12th century; d. Lisbon, March 15, 1267. He studied under Zoen, Archpriest of Bologna, later bishop of Avignon (after 1240), to whom he dedicated several works. As professor in the University of Bologna he published many treatises with valuable information about decretists and decretalists.

His *Principium decretalium* is very important for the history of the *Compilationes.* Among his early works are the *Casus decretalium, Breviarium decretorum, Distinctiones super toto iure canonico, Arbor versificata,* and *Chronica,* all of which were mentioned in *Liber iudicum* (1238). Later appeared the *Apparatus decretorum* (before 1241), *Epistulae canonicae de decimis* (May 30, 1240), *Notabilia cum summis super titulis decretalium* (dedicated to Cardinal Gil Torres, Sept. 1241), *Casus Legum canonizatarum* (Sept. 1, 1241), and the *Summa super quattuor causis decretorum* (1243), which is a continuation of the *Summa Huguccionis,* and contains a list of all his earlier works. The *Liber dispensationum,* published Aug. 28, 1243 and dedicated to Dominican and Franciscan friars, with a list of his earlier works, was submitted to Innocent IV for correction. It is a complete recension, some parts of which had been published before the election of the pope. In the dedication (after 1248) of the *Liber Cavillationum* (dated Sept. 2, 1246) to Cardinal William, and of the *Liber quaestionum* to Cardinal Ottaviano Ubaldino (Sept. 6, 1248), he lists the *Liber pastoralis* (August 1244) dedicated to Cardinal William of Sant' Eustachio and the *Liber poenitentiarius* dedicated to the Bishop of Lisbon (Oct. 28, 1247). The above lists do not mention other authentic works: *Concordantiae decretorum cum titulis decretalium, De electione, Principium decretalium, De abusibus contra canones* (an appendix to the *Liber poenitentiarius*), *Liber opinionum,* which was submitted for correction to Innocent IV in October 1251, and the *Summula super decimis ecclesiasticis,* a letter urging the Dominicans to preach about the duty of paying tithes, with the addition of a prologue and further considerations on the same subject addressed to Alexander IV and the cardinals. Even if some of these works are not very original, they are valuable for their rich indication of sources.

Joannes de Deo was appointed judge several times, even by Popes Innocent IV and Alexander IV. Upon his return to Portugal, he was archdeacon of Santarém in Lisbon in March 1260, and was appointed judge and arbiter in lawsuits. One of them concerned the Monastery of S. Cruz in Coimbra, and in it Pedro Julião, the famous philosopher and later Pope John XXI, was also involved.

Bibliography: A. D. DE SOUSA COSTA, *Um mestre português em Bolonha no século XIII* (Braga 1957). A. VAN HOVE, *Commentarium Lovaniense in Codicem iuris canonici 1,* v.1–5 (Mechlin 1928—) 1:477, 480, 484–486.

[A. D. DE SOUSA COSTA]

JOANNES DE LIGNANO

Jurist and canonist, son of Count Giacomo degli Oldrendi; b. Milan, *c.* 1320; d. Feb. 16, 1383. He studied law at the University of Bologna and by 1350 had earned his doctorate *in utroque iure.* Intensely devoted to the Church and a leading political figure in Bologna, he played an important role in settling the disputes between the papacy and Bologna that broke out during the last 30 years of his life. Peace was finally achieved in 1377, and in 1378 Joannes was appointed the first vicar-general of the pope at Bologna. As a sign of gratitude, Bologna conferred honorary citizenship upon him. During the Western Schism he defended the election of Urban VI, particularly by means of his tract *De Fletu Ecclesiae* (1378–79).

His writings embrace canon and civil law, philosophy, theology, astronomy, and astrology. His principal canonical works are: *Commentaria in Decretales, Commentaria in Decretum, Commentaria in Clementinas, De beneficiorum ecclesiasticorum pluralitate* and *De interdicto ecclesiastico.* His most important works, *De bello* (on war) and *De pace* (on peace), are a systematic exposition and a synthesis of all the problems regarding war and peace, taking into consideration canon, civil, and feudal law. Because of these two works, Joannes is considered the creator of the juridic doctrine on war and the precursor of public international law.

Bibliography: S. STELLING-MICHAUD, *Dictionnaire de droit canonique,* ed. R. NAZ, 7 v. (Paris 1935–65) 6:111–112. J. F. V. SCHULTE, *Die Geschichte der Quellen und der Literatur des kanonischen Rechts,* 3 v. in 4 pts. (Stuttgart 1975–80) 2:257–261. G. ERMINI, "I trattati della guerra e della pace di Giovanni da Legnano," *Studi e memorie per la storia dell'Università di Bologna,* 8 (1924) 1–154.

[C. M. ROSEN]

JOANNES FAVENTINUS

Canonist; b. Faenza, Italy; d. Faenza, 1187. Faventinus (John of Faenza) was a student and professor at the school of Bologna, which he left about 1174 to return to his native city. His best known work is a *Summa* on the Decretum of GRATIAN, likely composed while he was still at Bologna. Although he borrows heavily from his predecessors, as he himself confesses, especially from the *Summae* of RUFINUS and of Stephen of Tournai, he is important for the fact that he made these works as well as the teaching of other early decretists widely known. He has been rated as the most-used and best of the Bolognese canonists before Huguccio. More than 40 manuscripts have survived. All later commentators on the *Decretum* refer to his work. He comments only briefly on the *De poenitentia* and the *De consecratione.* His references to the more recent papal legislation are few, with nothing on that of Alexander III. He is quite conversant with Lombard and Roman law and the commentaries on the latter. His later *Glossae,* perhaps begun at Bologna and continued at Faenza, reveal a more mature and independent thinker.

Bibliography: A. STICKLER, *Dictionnaire de droit canonique,* ed. R. NAZ, 7 v. (Paris 1935–65) 6:99–102. S. KUTTNER, *Repertorium der Kanonistik* (Rome 1937) 11, 143–145. J. F. V. SCHULTE, *Die Geschichte der Quellen und der Literatur des kanonischen Rechts,* 3 v. in 4 pts. (Stuttgart 1875–80) 1:137–140.

[T. P. MCLAUGHLIN]

JOANNES LAPUS CASTILIONEUS

Lay canonist and teacher, b. Florence, Italy, d. June 27, 1381. He received his doctorate in law (1353) from Bologna, where he was a student of John Calderini and John of Lignano. He was professor of law in Florence until 1378. During this time he held important positions in the city government and was head of the Guelph party. He was sent on missions to Urban V and Gregory XI. He was accused of wanting to see Florence under the temporal power of the papacy and was forced to flee the city. His property was sold, and a reward was offered for his death or arrest and return to Florence. In spite of this, he won the favor of Charles of Durazzo and became professor of law in Padua. When Charles was crowned king, Castilioneus was appointed personal representative to the pope, who named him consistorial lawyer and senator. His principal works are *Allegationes Iuris, Tractatus hospitalitatis,* the first treatment of the privileges and juridic import of works of charity and *Repetitiones.*

Bibliography: J. VIRET, *Dictionnaire de droit canonique,* ed. R. NAZ, 7 v. (Paris 1935–65) 6:110–111. J. F. V. SCHULTE, *Die Geschichte der Quellen und der Literatur des kanonischen Rechts,* 3 v. in 4 pts. (Stuttgart 1875–80) 2:270–272.

[H. A. LARROQUE]

JOANNES PARVUS

French theologian (also known as Jean Petit); b. Caux, France, *c.* 1360; d. Hesdin, France, July 15, 1411. His addresses on the various aspects of the WESTERN SCHISM *c.* 1403 made him a well-known member of the theological faculty of the University of Paris, but his teaching on TYRANNICIDE won him even greater notoriety. On Nov. 23, 1407, Louis, Duke of Orléans, brother of King Charles VI of France, was assassinated in Paris. His cousin, John the Fearless, Duke of Burgundy, who was responsible for the crime, retired to his domains in Flanders and summoned Joannes Parvus to Amiens to prepare his vindication. Before the king and a carefully selected assemblage in Paris, Parvus delivered on March 8, 1408, an ostentatiously learned apologia in defense of his patron's role in the assassination, the *Justificatio ducis Burgundiae* [J. Gerson, *Opera omnia,* ed. L. E. Dupin (5 v. Amsterdam 1706) 5:15–42].

His method of argumentation can be reduced to the following syllogism: it is licit to put to death one who is guilty of high treason and has become a tyrant; the Duke of Orléans was guilty of treason and was a tyrant; therefore, he deserved death, and the Duke of Burgundy was not guilty of murder or complicity. In proof of his major premise Parvus chose the main texts in favor of tyrannicide from Scripture, Aristotle, Seneca, St. Augustine, C. SALUTATI, and especially from JOHN OF SALISBURY and THOMAS AQUINAS. Few texts apodictically supported his thesis, and historical and doctrinal truths suffered at his hands. Despite strong reaction, John the Fearless obtained letters of pardon from the king, and Parvus left Paris for the estate of his patron in Hesdin, where he wrote three answers to attacks on his *Justificatio.* There he died, regretting, it was said, his defense of such a thesis. Gerson found heresy in seven propositions he drew from the *Justificatio,* and the bishop of Paris along with the inquisitor of France condemned the work and nine propositions said to be found in it, on Feb. 23, 1414. After the appeal of the Duke of Burgundy, the antipope JOHN XXIII established a papal commission of investigation, but Gerson's assault on Parvus's *Justificatio* was relentless. At the Council of CONSTANCE he strove to secure conciliar support for the condemnation by the bishop of Paris until both parties agreed, by the terms of the Treaty of Arras, Feb. 23, 1415, to end the discussion by their envoys at the council. After the withdrawal of John XXIII from the council, Gerson disregarded this stipulation and publicly upheld the condemnation. On July 6, 1415, the council enacted a general condemnation of tyrannicide without naming Joannes Parvus. His opponents insisted on conciliar censure of the nine propositions drawn from his *Justificatio,* but the commission on matters of faith annulled, on Jan. 16, 1416, the condemnation of the bishop of Paris, and a final attempt to have the council declare Parvus a heretic, along with John of FALKENBERG (d. 1435), proved futile. In Paris on Nov. 3, 1418, the Duke of Burgundy had the condemnation of Parvus by the bishop of Paris withdrawn, while at this same time the king and the University of Paris repudiated the opponents of the duke and his apologist, ending the conflict.

Bibliography: J. D. MANSI, *Sacrorum Conciliorum nova et amplissima collectio,* 31 v. (Florence-Venice 1757–98) 2:731–873. B. BESS, "Die Lehre vom Tyrannenmord auf dem Konstanzer Konzil," *Zeitschrift für Kirchengeschichte* (Stuttgart 1876—) 36 (1902) 1–61. C. KAMM, "Der Prozess gegen die *Justificatio ducis Burgundiae* auf der Pariser Synode, 1413–1414," *Römische Quartalschrift für Christliche Altertumskunde und für Kirchengeschichte* (Freiburg 1887—) 26 (1912) 3–19, 27–57, 97–113, 159–186.

A. COVILLE, *Jean Petit* (Paris 1932). A. TEETAERT, *Dictionnaire de théologie catholique,* ed. A. VACANT et al., 15 v. (Paris 1903–50) 12.1:1338–44. G. SANTINELLO, *Enciclopedia filosofica,* 4 v. (Venice–Rome 1957) 3:1343–44. L. BOEHM, *Lexicon für Theologie und Kirche,* eds. J. HOFER and K. RAHNER, 10 v. (2d new ed. Freiburg 1957–65) 5:1069.

[J. M. O'DONNELL]

JOANNES TEUTONICUS (ZEMECKE)

Glossator; b. second half of 12th century; d. Halberstadt, April 25, 1245 or 1246. He was provost of the Collegiate Chapter of St. Maria. He studied civil law (under Azo) and Canon Law in Bologna and taught there probably until 1220. He is one of the most important glossators of his day and from 1210 to 1220 was among the outstanding scholars of Bologna.

His works include the *Apparatus* for the constitutions of the Fourth Lateran Council, written immediately after the publication of these constitutions; the *Compilatio IV antiqua,* composed in 1215–16 and presented to Pope Innocent III but not approved by him, thus slow to win recognition; the *Apparatus* for the *Compilatio IV antiqua,* which was composed at the same time as the collection itself, and which became in practice the *GLOSSA ORDINARIA* on *Compilatio IV antiqua, Apparatus* for *Compilatio III antiqua,* composed about 1217 and making thorough use of the preceding; glosses on *Compilatio V antiqua,* which, however, are scattered and do not amount to an *apparatus;* glosses on the *Arbor consanguinitatis et affinitatis;* and *Quaestiones* contained in various collections, notably, as *QQ. dominicales,* in the Klosterneuburg Collection.

But there is no doubt that his chief work is the *Glossa ordinaria* on the Decretum of GRATIAN. This glossary was elaborated between 1212 and 1215 but was certainly not published until after the conclusion of the Fourth Lateran Council; between 1216 and 1217 it was again revised, especially in respect of certain allegations against the *Compilatio IV antiqua.* The *apparatus* begins with the words *Tractaturus Gratianus de iure canonico primo incipit a simplicioribus.* . . In it Joannes collates the basic doctrines of the Decretum and the decretals, relying mainly on the *Apparatus Ordinaturus Magister,* on the *Summa* of HUGUCCIO, on the *Apparatus* of ALANUS ANGLICUS, and on the *Apparatus* of Laurentius Hispanus. These must be regarded as his chief sources and are sometimes even cited verbatim. His own glosses played a significant role; in them he often expressed his own doctrine in a polemical form. However, he is not generous in his credits (i.e., in ascribing the individual glosses to the original authors) and many glosses appear as his own, although they have been taken over, often literally, from others. This basic and not unduly prolix commentary on the Decretum was soon adopted by the school of Bologna and by juridical practice as the standard *apparatus* and was used as such.

The only threat to its dissemination and importance was the appearance of the decretals of GREGORY IX (1234; however, it is a point to Joannes's merit that no new *apparatus* was composed; his was taken over and merely revised by BARTHOLOMEW OF BRESCIA and brought up to date in form and content. In this revision it survived, was disseminated, and entered into the later printed editions. *The Glossa ordinaria* of Joannes is even today a basic source for research on the history of Canon Law in the field of classical Canon Law. What Joannes has failed to include, especially from Huguccio and Laurentius, but from others as well, was added later in repeated essays, among which the *Apparatus* of Johannes de Phintona and the *Rosarium* of GUIDO DE BAYSIO deserve special mention.

Bibliography: J. F. V. SCHULTE, *Die Geschichte der Quellen und der Literatur des kanonischen Rechts,* 3 v. in 4 pts. (Stuttgart 1875–80) 1:172–175. S. KUTTNER, *Repertorium der Kanonistik* (Rome 1937), *passim.* S. KUTTNER, ''Bernardus Compostellanus antiquus,'' *Traditio,* 1 (1943) 291–292, 305 n.82, 323 n.16; ''Joannes Teutonicus, das vierte Laterankonzil und die Compilatio Quarta,'' *Miscellanca Giovanni Mercati,* 6 v. (Rome 1946) 5:608–634. A. GARCÍA, ''El Concilio IV de Letrán y sus comentarios,'' *Traditio,* 14 (1958) 493–498. S. STELLING-MICHAUD, *Dictionnaire de droit canonique,* ed. R. NAZ, 7 v. (Paris 1935–65) 6:120–122.

[A. M. STICKLER]

JOB, BOOK OF

This masterpiece of Old Testament (OT) wisdom literature will be discussed under the following headings: Plan, Content, and Integrity; Rhythm and Structural Features; Author, Date, Canonicity, and Setting; and Teaching.

Plan, Content, and Integrity. Job is a complex mosaic of rich and evocative poetry. It has, however, a detailed plan carefully elaborated by its author:

1. Prose Introduction: the affliction of Job (ch. 1–2).
2. Three Cycles of Dialogue between Job and his friends (ch. 3–28).
   a. Opening Plaint: Job curses the day of his birth (ch. 3).
   b. First (ch. 4–14), Second (ch. 15–21), and Third (ch. 22–27) Cycles of Dialogue between Eliphaz, Bildad, Zophar, and Job.
   c. Encomium of Wisdom, accessible only to God (ch. 28).
3. Job's Review of His Case before God (ch. 29–31).

4. The Intervention of Elihu (ch. 32–37).

5. The Lord's Response to Job (ch. 38–42.6).

6. Prose Conclusion: the restoration of Job (ch.42.7–17).

1. Prose Introduction. The introduction (ch. 1–2), with its scenes at the heavenly court, its recurrent series of disasters, and the persevering integrity of Job, is presented as a setting for the poetry to follow. Whatever facts or popular tales may underlie the narrative, the biblical writer clearly meant to pose in unmistakable terms the problem of the sufferings of the just and the relation of these sufferings to the plan of the Creator.

2. Three Cycles of Dialogue. The dialogue, using the freedom proper to poetry, enlarges on various aspects of the problem of suffering and makes it plain that a complete answer to it is beyond the reach of the speakers, including Job himself.

a. Job, who in the prose is a model of patient perseverance (see Jas 5.11), here (ch. 3) prepares the way for the remonstrances of his friends by wishing he had perished at birth.

b. In three rounds of speeches (ch. 4–27) the friends of Job probe into the reason for his misfortunes, which they attribute to his fault. They counsel him to pray for forgiveness. Job insists both on the extremity of his misery and on the absence of any wrongdoing that would justify the imputations of his friends. The speeches are not intended each to counter the arguments of the preceding; and the progression is not a matter of logic. Thus, in the first cycle Eliphaz (ch. 4–5) suggests the chastening effect of affliction and the certainty of Job's restoration if he prays for it. Job's reply (ch. 6–7) calls for death, rebukes the timidity of his friends, and turns to God in complaint, rather than in penitence. Then Bildad (ch. 8) and Zophar (ch. 11) declare that Job's future is sure to be visibly in harmony with his guilt or innocence before God. Following Bildad, Job (ch.9–10) acknowledges God's might, wishes that he had an arbiter before God, and asks why his Creator afflicts His own handiwork. In ch. 12–14, Job protests that God's might can be seen at times to bring about destruction, and that his friends are using unworthy arguments on God's behalf; he then turns to God and asks again why he is being chastised. The end of this speech (ch. 14) describes before God the pitiful condition of all mankind, guilt-stained and confronted with death. The two later cycles add more asperity than argument. In the second cycle, the friends (ch. 15, 18, 20) all make the point that the wicked do not remain unpunished. Job first protests (ch. 16–17) that God is allowing his friends to wrong him; then, in

a famous passage (ch. 19), he appeals to the vindication he still expects from God, by whom he has been struck; and finally (ch. 21) he denies outright that the punishment of the wicked is visibly evident from experience. The third cycle (ch. 22–27) has suffered damage in transmission, after Eliphaz's renewed plea to Job to repent (ch. 22), so that the progress of the debate, and even the identity of the speakers, becomes difficult to follow. Many arrangements for these chapters have been proposed. The reader may take ch. 23–24 as spoken by Job, with the warning that verses 24.13–24 are textually of extraordinary difficulty. If Bildad is given ch. 25 and Job ch. 26, a panegyric of God's creative might, then Zophar's last speech may be found in 27.13–21 and Job's response to this in 27.2–12. In any case, Job is still maintaining his innocence in 27.5–6, and the positions are unchanged as the dialogue closes. Decreasing proportions observable in the three cycles make it unlikely that any sizable number of verses belonging to the third cycle has been lost.

The encomium of wisdom (ch. 28) has often been thought to be distinct in authorship from the rest of Job. Its message is that wisdom, which is of transcendent value, cannot be discovered by any creature, but is known fully only to the Creator. The final line (28.28) sees man's wisdom in the fear of the Lord and the avoidance of evil—qualities attributed to Job in the prose introduction (1.8, 2.3). There seems no adequate reason to deny this poem to the original author of Job; it draws from the dialogue the only general conclusion that can be drawn from it and balances very well Job's bitter outcry of ch. 3. This would be the only place in the poetry where the author speaks in his own name (at least in 28.28).

3. Job's Review of His Case. In ch. 29–31, Job reviews his life without reference to the debate. His past blessings are contrasted with the wretched state of those whose sons now revile him (29.1–30.8), his present sorrows are feelingly described (30.9–31), and his examination of a blameless conscience leads him at last to call upon the Almighty to enter into judgment with him (31.1–40). The text of this section is well preserved, though verses 31.38–40, for example, are out of place.

4. Elihu's Intervention. If the Almighty does not at once answer Job's final plea (31.35–37), this is due, in the Book as we have it, to the intervention of Elihu (ch. 32–37). There is widespread agreement that these chapters differ in effectiveness from the rest of Job. Elihu is a youth who, in a series of monologues with prolonged and wordy introductions, impetuously takes issue with all the preceding speakers. Many see his chief contribution in the appraisal (33.13–32, 36.8–15) of the chastening value of affliction, although this was already spoken of by Eliphaz (ch. 4–5). Elihu's final description of God's hidden majesty (36.22–37.24) is impressive and prepares for the appearance of the Lord in ch. 38. Yet this entire section is seemingly an afterthought in the arrangement of the Book, and it is most easily explained as the work of a subsequent inspired poet.

5. The Lord's Response to Job. The speech of the Lord (38.1–41.26) can be seen to balance, in structure and intent, the final plea of Job (ch. 29–31), to which it is the reply. Job only is addressed; Elihu and the three friends are ignored. After pointing to the marvels of His creation in the earth, the sea, and the heavens (38.2–38), the Lord takes up the wonders of His providence for birds and beasts (38.39–39.30). There is a brief exchange with Job (40.1–5); the Lord concludes His discourse by introducing (40.7–14) two fabulous examples of His creative art: behemoth (40.15–24), and LEVIATHAN (40.25–41.26). Job then humbly repents (42.1–6) his presumption. Some have supposed that the behemoth and leviathan passages are later additions. They are, however, integral to this section of the Book, and there is every reason to attribute them to its original author.

6. Prose Conclusion. The conclusion (42.7–17) provides a resolution to the theme of the Book; it finds Job, by God's favor, restored to fully twice the benefits he had enjoyed before his affliction and interceding with God for his friends. This by no means represents the culmination of the sacred writer's understanding of the problem he has broached; rather, it is his expression of faith in the abiding goodness and justice of the Lord, in the only terms through which in his day Old Testament man could concretely relate those attributes to the case of Job. That the conclusion is by the author of the poetry has sometimes been denied, but it is so closely tailored to the requirements of the case that no alternative is really plausible.

Job is for the most part well preserved in Hebrew (for ch. 24–28, see above), but the difficulties of its unusual diction are not the only problems of detail. The LXX is a kind of abridged poetic approximation of it, rather than a systematic rendering into Greek; since the days of Origen, omissions in it have been eked out from the rendering of Theodotion. A pre-Christian Targum of Job in Aramaic found in fragmentary state in a cave near Khirbet Qumran has proved to be a close rendering of the Hebrew, with the third cycle presented in the customary order.

Rhythm and Structural Features. Job employs the normal "didactic" meter of other Hebrew poetry, with two (occasionally three) hemistichs of three or four stresses each to the full verse line. These lines are grouped into recognizable larger units that may vary from couplets (two full lines) to seven-line stanzas. There is a standard length for a normal speech in the dialogue, so that the stanzas are woven into a pattern of between 20 lines (ch. 8) and 24 lines (ch. 3), but they are usually of 22 or 23 lines. This norm is borrowed from alphabet acrostics (as in Lamentations, some Psalms). Longer discourses in the first cycle are multiples of such patterns. Job's speech, or its initial pattern, always exceeds the preceding speech of a friend by a minimal number of lines. Eliphaz speaks in five-line stanzas, Bildad in 3s, Zophar in 6s. Job's speeches are more varied: patterns built on 3s and 4s after Eliphaz, others on 5s and 6s after Zophar. In the later cycles, the speeches are systematically diminished in length; otherwise, the same conventions are observed. Job's final plea (ch. 29–31) is of 33 + 22 + 40 lines, with ch. 31 especially complex; the Lord's reply in ch. 38–41 is of 36 + 34 (= 70) + 50 lines, including in the last grouping the 33-line description of Leviathan, in alternating 6s and 5s.

Author, Date, Canonicity, and Setting. The unknown author of Job lived in Palestine, probably in the 6th or 5th century B.C. His work shows a knowledge of various Psalms (cf. Ps 8.5 with Jb 7.17 and Ps 38[39].14 with Jb 10.20) and shares common problems with Jeremiah (Jer 12.1–4, 20.14–18). His language is tinged with Aramaic (this is more pronounced in the Elihu passages) and with Arabic; in part, this may be deliberate local coloring. Though perhaps earlier than the final editing of Proverbs, Job, in its teaching on God's dealings with the individual (see "Teaching" below), stands intermediate between Proverbs and the later books of Ecclesiastes and Wisdom as a preparation for New Testament doctrine. That Job belongs in the canon of inspired OT books is a constant datum of Christian and Jewish tradition. Babylonian compositions, such as "I will praise the lord of wisdom," and the so-called Theodicy, which share many elements of the problem treated in Job, are neither directly related to it nor truly comparable in form or content. The technique of Jb 31, with its disclaimer of a series of faults ("negative confession"), is a commonplace in Egyptian literature, but the parallel is of little significance. A Syro-Canaanite mythological coloring in some of the descriptions in Job (Rahab: 9.12; Leviathan and the sea: 3.8, 7.12, 26.13) echoes themes from that pagan culture.

Teaching. The Book of Job includes majestic descriptions of the omniscience and omnipotence of God; these are the attributes impressed on Job himself (40.1–5, 42.1–6). Job's own earlier testimony to them (9.2–24, 12.7–25, 23.1–17) is inadequate as long as he maintains that his human, created justice gives him a claim on God for an explanation of his own case. The praises of God in ch. 25–26 (and again by Elihu in 36.22–37.24) combine with the Lord's description of His created works in ch. 38–41 to inculcate this lesson.

In the book as a whole, Job learns first, under the prodding of his friends, that the theory they all shared—that a man's justice regularly goes hand in hand with visible mundane gifts from God—is false. Ultimately, he learns that the limited human justice to which he clings vanishes into inconsequence before the majesty of God; whatever there is of it is God's, who will use it, as He uses Job's sufferings, for what He will. When Job accepts this, the mystery is not removed, but the way for God's bounty is open to the full (42.7–17). Neither does the New Testament remove the mystery, but the Crucifixion and the Resurrection of the Son of God give to both suffering and justice their ultimate meaning for the man of faith.

The much-discussed passage Jb 19.25–27 has been used as early as the time of Clement of Rome (*1 Clem.* 26.3) as an evidence for the doctrine of the resurrection of the body. The Hebrew text has real obscurities, however, and the versions do not agree. The Vulgate rendering of it is luminous with St. Jerome's Christian faith on the subject, and it is this rendering which is employed by St. Augustine (*Patrologia Latina,* ed. J. P. Migne, 271 v., indexes 4 v. [Paris 1878–90] 41.779). On the other hand, St. John Chrysostom's statement that Job had no clear idea of the resurrection of the dead (*Patrologia Graeca,* ed. J. P. Migne, 161 v. [Paris 1857–66] 57.396) is well known. This judgment is so much more in conformity with the actual data of the text, with the tenor of the argument in the book as a whole, and with the progress in understanding of individual retribution that can be traced throughout the OT that it would seem to command acceptance. The Job of the book bears witness to a crucial stage in that progress, but though he wishes for the possibility of a return from the nether world (Jb 14.13–17), it is not given to him to affirm it.

Angels in the Book of Job are the exalted servants of God, in whom He can yet find fault (4.18, 15.15). The SATAN of the introduction is not the devil, but a member of the heavenly court; loyal to God and distrustful of Job, he is imagined for purposes of the story.

Bibliography: E. J. KISSANE, *The Book of Job* (New York 1946). E. P. DHORME, *Le Livre de Job* (Études Bibliques; Paris 1926). C. WESTERMANN, *Der Aufbau des Buches Hiob* (Tübingen 1956). F. HORST, *Hiob* (Biblischer Kommentar, Altes Testament 16; Neukirchen 1960–) 4 fasc; HANS STRAUSS, v. XVI/2 (Neukirchener Verlag 1996). H. H. ROWLEY, "The Book of Job and Its Meaning," *Bulletin of the John Rylands Library* 41 (1958–59) 167–207. A. LE-FÈVRE, *Dictionnaire de la Bible,* suppl. ed. L. PIROT et al. (Paris 1928–) 4:1073–98, esp. "Étude Doctrinale" 1088–98. R. A. F. MACKENZIE, "The Purpose of the Jahweh Speeches in the Book of Job," *Biblica* 40.1–2 (1959) 435–445. P. W. SKEHAN, "Strophic Patterns in the Book of Job," *Catholic Biblical Quarterly* 23 (1961) 125–142; "Job's Final Plea (Job 29–31) and the Lord's Reply (Job 38–41)," *Biblica* 45 (1964) 51–62. R. A. F. MACKENZIE and R. E. MURPHY, in *The New Jerome Bible Commentary* (Englewood Cliffs, N.J. 1990) 466–488. A. SCHÖKEL, *Job* (Madrid 1981). P. DHORME, *A Commentary on the Book of Job* (London 1967).

[P. W. SKEHAN]

JOCELIN OF BRAKELOND

English Benedictine, chronicler of BURY-ST.-EDMUNDS; flourished late 12th century. His account of this distinguished Benedictine house under the rule of Abbot SAMSON (1182–1211) provided Carlyle with materials for the sympathetic second book of *Past and Present.* When Jocelin served his novitiate (1173) at St.-Edmunds, Samson of Tottington was novice master. In 1182 Samson became abbot and for six years thereafter Jocelin served as his chaplain—an office that kept him in close association with a model administrator. Jocelin's history covers the years 1173 to 1202. It is forthright, familiar, clear, and convincing. David Knowles has observed that in Jocelin's pages "the daily life of the cloister is mirrored with a fidelity found in no other medieval chronicle" [*Monastic Sites from the Air* (Cambridge, Eng. 1952) 14]. Jocelin was guest master in 1198 and almoner in 1212. The date of his death is unknown, but it must have been sometime after April 1215.

Bibliography: T. ARNOLD, ed., *Cronica,* in *Memorials of St. Edmund's Abbey,* 3 v. [*Rerum Britannicarum medii aevi scriptores,* 244 v. (1890–96) 1:209–336]. H. E. BUTLER, ed. and tr., *The Chronicle* (New York 1949). T. E. TOMLIN, ed. and tr., *Monastic and Social Life in the Twelfth Century as Exemplified in the Chronicles of Jocelyn de Brakelond* (London 1844). T. CARLYLE, *Past and Present* (2d ed. New York 1843). D. KNOWLES, *Saints and Scholars* (Cambridge, Eng. 1962) 63–69.

[A. R. HOGUE]

JOCELIN OF GLASGOW

Scottish Cistercian, bishop; d. Melrose Abbey, 1199. Jocelin became prior and then abbot of MELROSE ABBEY (1170). In 1174 he was elected bishop of Glasgow and immediately asserted his see's independence of YORK by going to CLAIRVAUX for his consecration, which he received at the hands of the papal legate, Archbishop ESKIL OF LUND (1175). Resistance to the claims of York over the Scottish Church marked his entire episcopate and in 1181, when ROGER DE PONT L'ÉVÊQUE, Archbishop of York, placed Scotland under an interdict, it was Jocelin who, at the request of the Scottish King William the Lion, went to Rome to secure absolution from the interdict. Not only did he succeed in this, but he also brought back the GOLDEN ROSE as a present from Pope Lucius III to William. As part of his resistance to York he promoted Jocelin of Furness's life of St. KENTIGERN, the patron of Glasgow. He largely rebuilt the cathedral at Glasgow. He was buried at Melrose.

Bibliography: *Chronica de Mailros,* ed. J. STEVENSON (Edinburgh 1835). C. L. KINGSFORD, *The Dictionary of National Biography From the Earliest Times to 1900,* 63 v. (London 1885–1900) 10:833–834.

[D. NICHOLL]

JOCELIN OF WELLS

Bishop, royal servant; d. Wells, England, Nov. 19, 1242. Jocelin came of a landed family from the neighborhood of Wells, Somerset, and was the younger brother of Hugh, bishop of Lincoln (1209–35). The two brothers rose quickly in the royal service and by 1203 or 1204 Jocelin was one of the justiciars at Westminster as well as a canon of Wells. On his election as bishop of Bath and Glastonbury by the canons of Bath and Wells (1205–06) he became involved in the ancient dispute between Bath and GLASTONBURY ABBEY (*see* SAVARIC OF BATH) which was not settled until 1217 when Jocelin, in return for certain manors, surrendered his claim over Glastonbury and the see was henceforth known as BATH AND WELLS. In 1208 Jocelin left England because of the interdict resulting from the disputed appointment of Abp. STEPHEN LANGTON, but he returned in 1213 and was henceforth active in the service of both King JOHN and HENRY III as justiciar and custodian of castles. His name appears in the preamble of MAGNA CARTA. Along with his brother Hugh he founded St. John's Hospital at Wells. He reorganized the constitution of his chapter and its prebends and rebuilt much of the cathedral, the present nave and choir as well as the west façade being his work. He is buried in the choir in a striking tomb.

Bibliography: C. L. KINGSFORD, *The Dictionary of National Biography From the Earliest Times to 1900,* 63 v. (London 1885–1900) 10:835–836. J. LENEVE, *Fasti Ecclesiae Anglicanae 1300–1541* (1716) 1:130–131. H. WHARTON, *Anglia sacra . . . ,* 2 pts. (London 1691) 1:563–564, 582–583. J. H. ROBINSON, *Somerset Historical Essays* (Oxford 1921).

[D. NICHOLL]

JOCHAM, MAGNUS

Noted moral theologian; b. Rieder-bei-Immenstadt, March 23, 1808; d. Freising, March 4, 1893. Jocham is referred to also with the pseudonym "Johannes Clericus." He was engaged in pastoral work from 1841 to 1878, thus providing himself with valuable experience for his later work as professor of moral theology at the Freising lyceum. In this position, which he assumed in 1878, he soon developed a keen interest in Thomistic moral theology. Much stimulated by the organic unity of dogma and moral in St. Thomas's *Summa theologiae,* and relying to a great extent upon J. M. SAILER and J. B. HIRSCHER, he produced his *Moral-theologie oder die Lehre vom Christl. Leben nach den Grundsätzen der Kath. Kirche* (Sulzbach 1852–54). This is a moral theology in the sense of a doctrine of sacramental fulfillment and was directed against the rationalism and moralism current at the time. Jocham also contributed much by means of numerous translations, as well as the composition of many pastoralascetical treatises.

Bibliography: M. JOCHAM, *Memoiren eines Obskuranten* (Kempten 1896). P. HADROSSEK, *Die Bedeutung des Systemgedankens für die Moraltheologie in Deutschland seit der Thomas-Renaissance* (Munich 1950).

[E. LEWIS]

JOCISM

The movement of young workers founded by Joseph CARDIJN (1882–1967) as a curate in Belgium, named the Jeunesse Ouvrière Chrétienne (JOC) and extended first in Belgium and France and then throughout the world in a variety of specialized movements, e.g., the Jeunesse Agricole Chrétienne (JAC) and the Jeunesse Étudiante Chrétienne (JEC). Its characteristic organization of small groups for the apostolate of "like to like" and its method of formation (see-judge-act) were widely adopted and praised by Pius XI and succeeding popes. Paul VI elevated the founder to the college of cardinals in 1965. The concept of a Catholic youth movement that would be autonomous, socially oriented, and aimed at the development of all aspects of young factory workers was a radical innovation in Catholic circles of the time. The whole weight of tradition had been paternalistic and pietistic. By 1918, however, Belgian Catholics were becoming aware of the disastrous effects of the neglect of the social problems resulting from industrialization. Socialism had filled the vacuum, and the working class had largely abandoned traditional religion. To satisfy working-class aspirations it was necessary to direct an appeal specifically to this social class and to create working-class organizations under working-class leadership with working-class goals. This necessity was seen clearly by Cardijn, a true pioneer.

[J. N. MOODY]

JOEL, BOOK OF

The second of the MINOR PROPHETS. The Book of Joel can be divided into two parts. Two sermons in which Joel calls the people to prayer and repentance to avert a severe locust plague constitute the first part (1.2–2.17). For his first sermon the prophet seems to use a liturgical framework. After picturing the ravages of the locusts (1.2–12), he urges the priests to assemble the community for a solemn fast (1.13–14), and finally he recites the prayer for the occasion (1.15–20). The second sermon opens with a cry to sound the alarm in Zion and a description of the oncoming locusts as an army (2.1–11). An urgent, moving call to repentance follows (2.12–14); the sermon then ends with a renewal of the command to assemble the community for a solemn fast (2.15–17).

The second part (2.18–4.21) opens quietly. Yahweh responds to Israel's repentance, in an oracle announcing the end of the locusts (2.18–20). The prophet replies with a hymn of thanksgiving (2.21–24); Yahweh's response continues with promises of prosperity (2.25–27). Suddenly, Joel's vision of the future unfolds the final, climactic DAY OF THE LORD (YAHWEH). The description is striking, resembling apocalyptic rather than prophetic literature. The heralds, or symptomatic signs, of that final, messianic Day of Yahweh will be the pouring out of the Spirit (3.1–2) and astronomical, cosmic disturbances (3.3–5) from which Mt. Zion will be a refuge for those who call upon the name of the Lord. The judgment and destruction of the nations in the Valley of Jehoshaphat (merely a symbolic name, "Yahweh judges") will then take place (4.1–17). A dramatic scene then pictures the nations assembling from every side to war against Yahweh and His people in the Valley of Jehoshaphat. Yahweh's judgment on them is an execution, accompanied by dreadful cosmic disorders. Peace and calm then return in the description of the new earth of the messianic age, a peaceful, marvelous country (4.18–21). Judah and Jerusalem will remain continually with Yahweh, who dwells in Zion. The elements in Joel's vision of the final day of Yahweh, taken together, indicate that the work belongs to a literature in the process of transition from simple prophetic to apocalyptic.

Debate continues over the unity of authorship. For various reasons, many recent critics favor a literary unity, e.g., A. Bentzen (1940), A. Lods (1950), A. Weiser (1940), and A. S. Kapelrud (1948). Others hold for a duality of authorship. According to B. Duhm (1911), a Deutero-Joel would have written ch. 3 and 4. Duhm was followed by G. Hölscher (1914), O. Eissfeldt (1934), W. Baumgartner (1947), J. Trinquet (1953), and T. H. Robinson (1938). Robinson would apparently demand a further special author for 4.4–8. The interpretation of the first two chapters is closely connected with this question of the unity of authorship.

The figurative interpretation sees the locust plague as a military invasion or political catastrophe—one of the signs of the Day of Yahweh. Many favoring this interpretation understand as lying in the future the disaster that is described as present, the future being a historical or an eschatological one. The real or "literal" interpretation sees in these chapters a description of an actual locust plague. However, some of these "realists" regard the plague as eschatological: the historical locusts figured in the plagues in Egypt, but the disaster was placed among the final disorders that would herald the Day of Yahweh. Others prefer to interpret this description of an actual locust plague as present. Even here there is a division of opinion. Some commentators maintain that since these passages are concerned with a historical present, whatever is eschatological must be due to a Deutero-Joel. Others claim that this present actual locust plague is viewed in a prophetic perspective that sees the plague as a symptomatic sign of the Day of Yahweh.

Scholarly opinion regarding the date of Joel is fairly unanimous: *c.* 400 B.C. This date is based on a combination of factors, e.g., the absence of any reference to Jewish kings or to Babylon, the position of the priests and elders as heads of the community, and a strong similarity to several books regarded as late.

Joel's message envisions a final onslaught against Jerusalem, an eschatological conflict between Yahweh and the nations (*see* Ez ch. 38–39; Zec ch. 14). Yahweh will intervene with cosmic disorders, slaughtering His enemies. This catastrophic divine intervention will usher in the final age, an entirely new age in which God's people will be forever at peace.

Bibliography: R. PAUTREL, *Dictionnaire de la Bible,* suppl. ed. L. PIROT, et al. (Paris 1928—) 4:1098–1104. *Encyclopedic Dictionary of the Bible* (New York 1963) 1173–75. A. ROBERT and A. FEUILLET, *Introduction à la Bible* (Tournai 1959) 1:576–578. L. H. BROCKINGTON, in *Peake's Commentary on the Bible,* ed. M. BLACK and H. H. ROWLEY (New York 1962) 438a–540d.

[J. MORIARITY]

JOHANAN BEN ZAKKAI

Jewish religious and political leader who laid the foundations of a new epoch in JUDAISM after the Roman destruction of Jerusalem; b. Palestine, around the beginning of the Christian era; d. there, *c.* A.D. 80. Johanan studied under both Hillel and Shammai, but he was influenced more by the former. Later, as one of the leading PHARISEES in Jerusalem, he engaged in frequent controversy with the SADDUCEES. Because of the fanatical attachment of the Sadducean priests and the ZEALOTS for the Temple, he foretold its destruction several years before the event (*Yoma* 39b). At the beginning of the Jewish revolt of 66–70 he at first remained in Jerusalem; but later, during the siege, he escaped from the doomed city, carried out by his disciples, according to tradition, in a coffin (*Git.* 56). Vespasian received him kindly and allowed him to establish a Jewish academy at Jabneh (Jamnia) even before the fall of Jerusalem (A.D. 70). From then to the revolt of BAR KOKHBA (132–135), Jabneh and its academy formed the spiritual center of Palestinian Jewry. Thanks to the leadership of Johanan, "the state was changed into an academy, the royal dynasty into a patriarchate, and the Sanhedrin left the Temple site and continued independently in Jabneh" [H. J. Schoeps, *Ausfrühchristlicher Zeit* (Tübingen 1950) 168]. Johanan was one of the tannaitic teachers whose sayings are frequently cited in the TALMUD. He was held in such high esteem that the rare title of Rabban (our teacher) was bestowed on him.

Bibliography: J. NEUSNER, *A Life of Rabban Johanan ben Zakkai* (Studia Post-Biblica 6; Leiden 1962). H. REVEL, *Universal Jewish Encyclopedia* ed., J. SINGER (New York 1901–06) 6:164–166. *Jewish Encyclopedia* (New York 1939–44) 7:214–217. *Encyclopedia Judaica* (Berlin 1928–34) 9:222–227. K. SCHUBERT, *Lexikon für Theologie und Kirche*, ed. J. HOFER and K. RAHNER (Freiburg 1957–65) 5:981. E. LOHSE, *Die Religion in Geschichte und Gegenwart* (Tübingen 1957–65) 3:800.

[M. J. STIASSNY]

JOHANNES CORNUBIENSIS

Theologian; b. Cornwall, between 1125 and 1130; d. 1199 or 1200. He was a student of THIERRY OF CHARTRES in the arts before 1155 and of PETER LOMBARD, MAURICE OF SULLY, and ROBERT OF MELUN (HEREFORD) in theology before 1160. He returned to England by 1173 and taught theology, probably at Oxford. About 1155 he translated from the Welsh and commented upon the *Prophetia Merlini,* or Book of the Seven Kings [C. Greith, *Spicilegium Vaticanum,* (Frauenfeld 1838) 82–106]. From 1177 to 1179 he wrote an important Christological treatise [*Patrologia Latina*, ed. J. P. Migne, 217 v., indexes 4 v. (Paris 1878–90) 199:1043–86; "The *Eulogium ad Alexandrum papam tertium* of John of Cornwall," *Mediaeval Studies* 13 (1951) 253–300]. Unauthentic are another Christological treatise [*Patrologia Latina*, 177:295–316; "The So-Called *Apologia de Verbo incarnato,*" *Franciscan Studies* (1956) 102–143; 17 (1957) 85], the *De canone mystici libaminis* [*Patrologia Latina*, 177:455–470], an *Argumentum et quaestio* [extracts in E. Rathbone, "John of Cornwall, a Brief Biography," *Recherches de théologie ancienne et médiévale*, 17 (1950) 40–60], and an unprinted *Abbreviatio Sententiarum Petri Lombardi.*

Bibliography: R. F. STUDENY, *John of Cornwall, an Opponent of Nihilianism: A Study in the Christological Controversies of the Twelfth Century* (Vienna 1939). A. M. LANDGRAF, *Introducción a la historia de la literatura teológica de la escolástica incipiente* (Barcelona 1956). J. C. DIDIER, *Dictionnaire de théologie catholique*, ed. A. VACANT et al., 15 v. (Paris 1903–50) Tables générales 2:2460–61. L. OTT, *Lexikon für Theologie und Kirche*, ed. J. HOFER and K. RAHNER, 10 v. (2d, new ed. Freiburg 1957–65) 5:1022.

[J. N. GARVIN]

JOHANNINE COMMA

In 1 John 5.7–8 there appears a striking reference to the Catholic doctrine of the Trinity. "For there are three who bear witness [in heaven: the Father, the Word, and the Holy Spirit; and these three are one. And there are three that bear witness on earth]: the Spirit, and the water, and the blood; and these three are one" (CCD translation). The bracketed phrases appear in the Clementine-Vulgate version of the Bible, the official version of the Sacred Scriptures for the Latin rite of the Church. Among scholars these phrases are commonly called the "Johannine Comma." On the basis of manuscript evidence scholars seriously question their authenticity.

The Comma is absent in all the ancient Greek manuscripts of the New Testament with the exception of four rather recent manuscripts that date from the 13th to 16th centuries. The Comma is lacking in such ancient Oriental versions as the Peshitta, Philoxenian, Coptic, Ethiopic, and Armenian. While the majority of the Latin manuscripts of 1 John do contain the Comma, the earlier and better manuscripts, both of the Old Latin and Vulgate versions, lack it. The earliest manuscript in which it appears dates from the 9th century.

The Fathers of the East do not quote or refer to the Johannine Comma in their Christological controversies. This omission indicates that the Comma was not part of the biblical text of their time, for they surely would have used it had it been in the text. Some 4th-century Latin writers, while referring to 1 John 5.8b and giving this a Trinitarian interpretation, failed to give any indication that they knew of the existence of the Comma as a scriptural passage.

The development of the Comma can be followed in the ecclesiastical writers of the late 4th and 5th centuries, especially in Spain and Africa. Apparently, it developed as a result of the Trinitarian interpretation of the triad: spirit-water-blood found in 1 John 5.8b. By way of a gloss on the sacred text it eventually found its way into the text itself. It is first mentioned as a scriptural quotation by Priscillian of Avila (d. 380), or perhaps his disciple Instantius, in the *Liber Apologeticus*. Since the 5th century it has been part of the material that the Church has used in its Trinitarian teaching and has appeared with increasing frequency in the Latin manuscripts of 1 John.

Due to the overcritical spirit that was prevalent in the late 19th and early 20th centuries, the Church considered it necessary in its decree of the Holy Office of January 13, 1897, to caution its scholars against rashly rejecting or doubting the authenticity of this passage. However, in a decree of June 2, 1927, the Holy Office clarified its earlier statement in declaring that scholars may be inclined to doubt or reject the authenticity of the Johannine Comma subject to any forthcoming judgment of the Church. No scholar any longer accepts its authenticity. But even though the Comma is not a biblical passage, it is a firm witness to the fact that the faith of the 5th-century Christian was fully Trinitarian.

Bibliography: R. E. BROWN, *The Epistles of John* (The Anchor Bible 30; New York 1982) 775–87. I. H. MARSHALL, *The Epistles of John* (The New International Commentary on the New Testament; Grand Rapids 1978) 235–39. R. SCHNACKENBURG, *The Johannine Epistles. A Commentary*, tr. R. and I. FULLER (New York 1992) 235–38. Further detailed bibliography can be traced in the references found in these commentaries, especially Brown's detailed bibliography (see *The Epistles*, 786–87).

[C. DRAINA/F. J. MOLONEY]

JOHANNINE WRITINGS

The Johannine Gospel

The Gospels were not literal accounts of the ministry of Jesus. While John drew on an authentic tradition of Jesus' words and deeds, various influences had modified that tradition in the six or seven decades separating Jesus from the evangelist. Then, even after the evangelist had shaped the tradition into a written composition (perhaps in several editions), the work was redacted further (probably at a time when the evangelist was dead). Until recent times, much scholarly attention has been paid to the traditions that may have formed the Gospel of John, and attempts have been made to isolate the stages of redaction that produced the Gospel as we now have it. These concerns are still present in Johannine scholarship (Painter, Schnelle, Labahn), but more attention is currently dedicated to the narrative power of the final narrative (Culpepper, Stibbe, Moloney).

It is not universally accepted that the first "Johannine Writing" to appear was the Gospel of John, but that is the majority position, and it is adopted for this article. Today few scholars would identify either the source of the Johannine tradition or the evangelist as the apostle, John the Son of Zebedee. They pay greater attention to the failure of John to use the term "apostle" (in the technical sense), to the constant stress on "disciple," to the rivalry between the Johannine "disciple whom Jesus loved" and Peter (who in other NT works appears as the most famous of the Twelve apostles), and to the lack of anything approaching apostolic authority in the community situation envisaged in the Johannine epistles. All these factors make better sense if the Johannine community could not trace its origins to one of the Twelve—a lack that led Johannine theology to exalt love by Jesus rather than apostolic commissioning as the most essential factor. The disciple whom Jesus loved may best be seen as an unknown companion of Jesus during the ministry, perhaps insignificant when compared with the first-ranked members of the Twelve, but a figure whose subsequent history and role in the origins of the Johannine community gave him a major symbolic significance for this group. The majority of scholars has come to distinguish him from the evangelist, a second-generation Christian who may have been his disciple. Whoever he may have been, a historical figure who knew Jesus of Nazareth, and who became the founding figure and storyteller of a later Christian community, is a major source for the so-called Johannine writings.

Johannine community history. Differences in theology and tone that separate John from the Synoptics are often explained through the peculiar history of the Johannine community. With variations, that history as proposed by a number of scholars (J. L. Martyn, R. E. Brown, G. Richter—with variations) may be synopsized thus. The forebears were Jews who believed in Jesus as the Messiah and the royal Son of God, a Christology similar to that found in the Synoptic Gospels. Presumably a disciple, later known as the one whom Jesus loved, would have been among this group. We may find traces of them in John 1 in which the first disciples are Galileans who use traditional titles for Jesus. The advent of other believers of less traditional backgrounds changed the Johannine orientation. Part of this advent may be exemplified in Jn 4:39–42 in which a large number of Samaritans accept Jesus—something unheard of in the other Gospels.

This second strain presumably brought a different set of Israelite concepts through which they interpreted Jesus. For instance, while in the Synoptics Jesus is presented as a wisdom teacher using parables and only occasionally associated with divine Wisdom (Mt 11:19; Lk 11:49), in John there is little by way of parables and Jesus is consistently described in language echoing the OT portrait of personified divine Wisdom: a figure with God at the creation, coming into the world to give life and knowledge, dwelling among people, seeking them out and inviting them to eat. While in Matthew and Luke, Jesus is insistently shown to be descended from David, for John a Moses imagery is far more important. David became king by divine appointment and thereafter was treated by God as His representative and son; Moses spoke to God on the mountain and was shown by Him the divine plan to be revealed to the people when he came down. The Johannine Jesus is a Son who came down from God and who does and says only what He had seen and heard when He was with God (Jn 5:19; 8:38). The similarity to Moses is obvious; yet Moses had first to ascend to God's presence, while the Johannine Son of Man was already with God and had only to descend (3:13). Thus the Johannine Jesus combines aspects of divine Wisdom with the Moses imagery. The Samaritans would be a possible source for part of this imagery since they rejected Davidic claims and based their theology on Mosaic revelation. But the Johannine contact with the original traditions concerning Jesus always remains an important influence. The Johannine Son of Man may have to descend, but he also must be lifted up on a cross (3:14; 8:28; 12:32–34). It is interesting that in Jn 8:48 the christological claims of Jesus are rejected by "the Jews" with the charge that He is a Samaritan.

In any case, several relevant facts are clear. Among the four Gospels, only John describes an Incarnation in which a figure who had been with God comes into the world and becomes flesh. The Johannine Jesus can speak of a life He had with the Father before the world began (17:5). Using the divine "I am" (8:58), He states that He is one with the heavenly Father (10:30) and in Him God is intimately present and visible (10:38, 14:9–10). None of this appears in the other Gospels. Correspondingly, John describes extreme Jewish hostility toward Jesus on the basis of this exalted Christology because Jesus makes Himself equal to God (5:28; 10:33). Mention is made of synagogue trials and expulsions (9:22,34; 12:42; 16:2), an understandable procedure if the Jewish authorities thought that the disciples of Jesus had departed from the cardinal principle of Israel: "The Lord our God is One" (Dt 6:4). Undergoing such trials plausibly explains why much of John is cast in the legal language of confession, testimony, and witness (e.g., 1:19–20; 5:30ff.), and why debates over the meaning of Scripture are technical (6:31–33; 10:34–36). Inevitably such a history would have made the expelled Johannine Christians more emphatic about their Christology of a divine Word become flesh, and so they would have had contempt for other believers in Jesus who were unwilling to go so far (6:60–66; 8:31ff.;12:42–43).

Attention must also be given to the world in which the Gospel was written. The Gospel of John is not a gnostic document, but it most likely finally appeared in Asia Minor (the traditional location of Ephesus remains the best contender), where a number of religious influences were present. The mixture of the decaying traditional Greek religions, largely taken over and added to by Roman religious strains, and the influence of religions coming from the East produced a unique religious atmosphere. These were the major elements in the eventual development of Gnosticism, a form of religion also strongly influenced by early Christianity. There are many elements in the Gospel of John that deliberately address this new world. Johannine Christianity had its origins within Judaism, but the Gospel of John also makes much of "knowledge" (17:3), revelation (1:18), ascent and descent (3:13; 6:62), and certain expressions appear that were important in later Gnosticism (for example, τα ιδια and 'ο λογος). Perhaps the greatest sign of genius in the composition of the Gospel of John is its loyalty to the Christian tradition, but its telling the story of Jesus in a new way that it might be better understood in a new world.

Literary skill of the evangelist. As the point just made indicates, the tone and emphases given to the Jesus tradition in John have been shaped by the community's life, but the effectiveness of the Gospel in communicating the resultant Christology stems from the techniques of the narrative. Those techniques have been studied from the vantage point of modern literary criticism (e.g., Culpepper; Stibbe, Moloney), and we are now much more conscious of the extraordinary blending of message and vehicle in John. If there were synagogue trials that forced the Johannine Christians to decide for or against Jesus and thus to be judged, the Gospel itself is meant to make the reader decide about Jesus. The dramatic technique of having Jesus confront the *dramatis personae* of the Gospel face to face, one to one, inevitably involves the reader in a confrontation.

The Christology of a stranger who has come from above into an alien world is conveyed by having Jesus misunderstood by the Gospel characters who try to evaluate Him in the categories familiar to their own lives. An important narrative strategy of the author is found in the Prologue (1:1–18). Only the reader has access to this exalted presentation of who Jesus is (the pre-existent Logos, the unique revelation of God, the bringer of life to those who accept him in faith, the fulfillment of God's gifts, made flesh in the person of Jesus Christ). Having read this first page, the readers can understand Jesus better than the characters in the story, who have not read the Prologue, and are thus often found "misunderstanding" the words of Jesus (for example, 2:19–20; 3:3–5;

4:13–15; 5:17–18; 6:32–34). The readers have no such option. Enticed into participation in the drama by outguessing the Gospel characters, the reader may find that they may also misunderstand Jesus. This leads them to be challenged by Him as the evangelist intends (20:31). The solemn conclusion to the Gospel makes it clear that the evangelist does not write the story for the sake of the story, but to lead his readers into deeper faith. The exalted and quasi-poetic language of Jesus' self-revelation is entirely fitting for a figure from above who speaks of another world and is very similar in tone to the OT speeches of divine Wisdom and strikes a chord with the newer religions, emerging at the turn of the first Christian century. The characterizations found in John (Nicodemus, the Samaritan Woman, the Blind Man, Pilate) are increasingly seen as reflecting the evangelist's intention of personifying an array of attitudes that will speak to the readers' life situation.

Traditional Johannine questions, such as sources, history of religion background to the Gospel, and stages of redactional activity, continue to be pursued. Sources have been delineated (R. Fortna, W. Nicol; Langbrandter, Labahn), but the issue is somewhat relativized if the sources came from the same community tradition ultimately reflected in the Gospel. The thesis of John's dependence on the Synoptics has been strongly revived (F. Neirynck, M. E. Boismard; U. Schnelle, M. Lang), but has not won the day.

The Johannine Epistles

It is likely, but not certain, that the three Epistles were by one author. Most scholars would distinguish him from the evangelist. One might plausibly posit a Johannine school of writers consisting of the evangelist, the epistolary "presbyter," and the final redactor of the Gospel—all distinct from but perhaps disciples of the disciple whom Jesus loved. That sequence may also reflect the dating of the composition: the main edition of the Gospel in the 90s, the Epistles c. 100, and the redaction of the Gospel shortly afterward. None of this is certain, as we do not have the scientifically controllable data to come to firm final conclusions.

While 2–3 John fit the letter format perfectly, 1 John has no aspect of that format and is not an epistle or letter. Serving as a treatise on the interpretation of Johannine thought as found in the Gospel, 1 John is best understood if both the author (with his adherents) and those whom he attacks as secessionists (1 Jn 2:19) considered John as their sole authoritative Gospel (*hē angelia* of 1:5 and 3:11?). The complete absence in 1 John of references to the Jews and the synagogue suggests that that phase of Johannine life is long past, but now the high Christology

that caused the struggle with the Jews has become a source of conflict within the community. One group, attacked by the writer, seems to have put little emphasis on the human career of Jesus, on how He "walked," and on His death. For them it was enough that the Word entered the world: this was the divine salvific intervention. Correspondingly, they would have attributed little salvific importance to what the disciples of Jesus did in their lives once they had received God's light and life by faith.

Since the Gospel was written in struggle with the Jews, there is a danger that the elements in the Gospel that highlight Jesus' humanity might drop from view. He speaks as a divine figure who knows all things (Jn 2:25; 6:6) and apparently He does not need to petition God for assistance in His actions (11:41–42; 12:27–28). In the Gospel, life and light are offered by Jesus during the ministry (and thus before His death on the cross) to those who believe in Him (4:10; 5:40; 6:47); the only sin stressed is the failure to believe (9:41). Thus it is not inconceivable that the secessionists could have read John in this light to support their theology. Insistently, in order to correct them the author of 1 John has to argue from what was at the "beginning" (1 Jn 1:1; 2:7, 13, 24; 3:11), apparently a period of the Jesus tradition antedating the Gospel and (in the epistolary author's view) presupposed by the evangelist. For that reason, 1 Jn 1:1–4 comments on the Prologue of John but puts stress on witnesses who could constitute a chain of contact with the earthly Jesus—a chain in which the writers of the Johannine school would undoubtedly be prominent—as a guide to the importance of Jesus in the flesh. Throughout, 1 John stresses the importance of how Jesus walked, his salvific death, and the ethical behavior of the believer in view of further divine judgment—themes close the Synoptic theology and a confirmation of the insight advocated above that Johannine beginnings were not unlike the origins of the Synoptic tradition.

In struggling with the secessionists, the epistolary author never seems to have apostolic authority or the authority against error ascribed to the presbyter bishops emerging in the churches described in Acts and the Pauline Pastorals. The supreme authority is the anointing (presumably by the Spirit; 1 Jn 2:27) which would guide the believer. Since the secessionists could also appeal to the Spirit for their teaching (and the author could respond only that their Spirit was the spirit of deceit; 4:1–6), apparently the secession was successful and spread widely (prompting the fear expressed in 2 Jn). A possible interpretation of 3 John is that in one Johannine community Diotrephes decided on the necessity of supreme local pastoral authority in order to fight the secession, much to the distress of the epistolary author, who regarded such assumption of primacy as a violation of Johannine tradition. His may have been a rear guard resistance, however, for the redactor of the Gospel (21:15–17) recognizes human pastoral authority over the sheep.

If there are strains in the Johannine Epistles that would heighten similarity between the Johannine Christians and other churches attested in the NT, the secessionists may have been a bridge in the other direction to the Gnostics, who were the first to comment on the Gospel and almost made it their own work in the 2d century. Indeed, the issue of the relation of John to Gnosticism needs elaboration in this direction. As has already been mentioned in the above discussion of the development of the Gospel, John is not a gnostic work but that, having its roots in Jewish Wisdom speculation, it had outlooks that Gnostics could find harmonious. Such compatibility seems to have made John suspect in more traditional 2d century Christian circles (whence a relative silence about the Gospel), until Irenaeus, *Adversus Haereses,* used 1 John to show how John could be read in an orthodox manner. The ultimate contribution of 1 John may have been to save John for the larger Church.

The Johannine Revelation

Only Revelation names its author as "John" (Rv 1:1, 4, 9; 22:8). Paradoxically, this document, which should also be dated about the same time as the other Johannine writings (toward the end of the 1st century), is universally regarded as *not* belonging to the same "school" that produced the Gospel and the Epistles of John. The fierce traditional end-time eschatology of the Revelation (Rv 17–22) cannot be related to the important realized eschatology of the Gospel (e.g., Jn 3:16–21; 5:24–25; 6:50, 58), even though an end-time eschatology is also found in the Gospel (e.g., 5:28–29; 6:40, 54). Similarly, the Christology of Revelation, especially its understanding of the crucifixion as the slain and vindicated Lamb (Rv 5:6–14), is very different from the Johannine understanding of the crucifixion of Jesus as a "lifting up/exaltation" (Jn 3:14; 8:28; 12:32–33). The Johannine use of "the Lamb of God" (Jn 1:29, 36) cannot support the weight of an argument associating the two writings. The glory of God and the means by which the Son of God will be glorified are crucial to the Gospel, yet absent from Revelation, which has a quite different understanding of the vindication of the crucified Jesus. From the time of Irenaeus, the association of the Gospel, and subsequently the Epistles, with John the Son of Zebedee, led Christian tradition to associate the only book signed by an author named "John" with the Gospel and the Epistles. While often regarded as part of "the Johannine writings," the Revelation and the other Johannine writings have little in common.

See Also: JOHN, EPISTLES OF ST.; JOHN, GOSPEL ACCORDING TO ST.; REVELATION, BOOK OF.

Bibliography: M. É. BOISMARD and A. LAMOUILLE, *Synopse des quatre Evangiles. III: l'Évangile de Jean* (Paris 1977). R. E. BROWN, *The Gospel According to John,* 2 v. (Garden City 1966, 1970); *The Community of the Beloved Disciple* (New York 1979). O. CULLMAN, *The Johannine Circle* (Philadelphia, Pa. 1976). R. A. CULPEPPER, *The Johannine School* (Missoula, Mont. 1975); *Anatomy of the Fourth Gospel* (Philadelphia, Pa. 1983). M. DE JONGE, *Jesus: Stranger from Heaven and Son of God* (Missoula, Mont. 1977). R. FORTNA, *The Gospel of Signs* (Cambridge 1970); *The Fourth Gospel and its Predecessor: From Narrative Source to Present Gospel* (Edinburgh 1989). E. HAENCHEN, *John,* 2 v., *Hermeneia* (Philadelphia, Pa. 1984). E. KÄSEMANN, *The Testament of Jesus According to John 17* (Philadelphia, Pa. 1968). R. KYSAR, *The Fourth Evangelist and His Gospel* (Minneapolis, Minn. 1975); "The Fourth Gospel. A Report on Recent Research," *Aufstieg und Niedergang der römischen Welt* II 25/3 (1985) 2389–2480. B. LINDARS, *The Gospel of John* (London 1972). M. W. G. STIBBE, *John* (Sheffield 1993). F. J. MOLONEY, *The Gospel of John* (Collegeville, Minn. 1998). J. L. MARTYN, *History and Theology in the Fourth Gospel* (rev. ed. Nashville, Tenn. 1979); *The Gospel of John in Christian History* (New York 1978). W. MEEKS, *The Prophet-King* (Leiden 1967). U. SCHNELLE, *Antidocetic Christology in the Gospel of John: An Investigation of the Place of the Fourth Gospel in the Johannine School* (Minneapolis 1992). W. LANGBRANDTNER, *Weltferner Gott oder Gott der Liebe. Der Ketzerstreit in der johanneischen Kirche. Eine exegetisch-religionsgeschichtliche Untersuchung mit Berücksichtigung der koptisch-gnostischen Texte aus Nag-Hammadi* (Bern 1977). F. NEIRYNCK, *Jean et les Synoptiques* (Louvain 1979). M. LANG, *Johannes und die Synoptiker. Eine redaktionsgeschichtliche Analyse von Joh 18–20 vor dem markinischen und lukanischen Hintergrund* (Göttingen 1999). W. NICOL, *The Semeia in the Fourth Gospel* (Leiden 1972). M. LABAHN, *Jesus als Lebensspender. Unsertsuchungen zu einer Geschichte der johanneischen Tradition anhand ihrer Wundergeschichten* (Berlin 1999). J. PAINTER, *The Quest for the Messiah. The History, Literature and Theology of the Johannine Community* (2d ed. Edinburgh 1993) G. RICHTER, *Studien zum Johannesevangelium* (Regensburg 1977). R. SCHNACKENBURG, *The Gospel According to St. John,* 3 v. (New York 1968, 1980, 1982). D. M. SMITH, *Johannine Christianity: Essays on Its Setting, Sources, and Theology* (Columbia, S.C. 1984). *John Among the Gospels. The Relationship in Twentieth-Century Research* (Minneapolis, Minn. 1992). **Epistles.** Commentaries by R. E. BROWN (Garden City 1982); R. BULTMANN (Philadelphia 1973); J. L. HOULDEN (New York 1973); I. H. MARSHALL (Grand Rapids, Mich. 1978); S. S. SMALLEY (Waco, Tx. 1984); R. SCHNACKENBURG (New York 1992); D. RENSBERGER (Nashville, Tenn. 1997).

[R. E. BROWN/F. J. MOLONEY]

JOHN, APOSTLE, ST.

The brothers James the Greater [*see* JAMES (SON OF ZEBEDEE), ST.] and John were sons of Zebedee (Mt 4.21). This evidence points to the possibility that their mother was Salome (cf. Mt 27.56 with Mk 15.40). Further speculation flows from this identification. A comparison of the last two passages (Mt 26.56 and Mk 15.40) with Jn 19.25 indicates that the mother of the brothers may have been the sister of Mary, the mother of Jesus, and that, therefore, the brothers may have been cousins of Jesus. Zebedee and his sons were fishermen, and in Lk 5.10 it is said that the brothers were partners of Simon Peter. The common order of the names, James and John, may indicate that John was the younger. Acts 4.13 characterizes John as uneducated. Such evidence, however weak, warns against crediting too much literary and theological creativity to John, the son of Zebedee.

If the unnamed disciple of Jn 1.35–40 was John, then he was once a disciple of John the Baptist and first met Jesus in the Jordan Valley. There is a reasonable possibility that the unnamed disciple of 1.35–40 should be identified with the Beloved Disciple of the Fourth Gospel. The step from that identification to the further identification of the Beloved Disciple with John, the Son of Zebedee, is at best speculative, and based upon later patristic and ecclesial traditions. John, James, Peter, and Andrew were the first four disciples called in Galilee (Mk 1.16–20), and these four names appear first in all lists of the TWELVE. John, along with Peter and James, was one of the three disciples most closely associated with Jesus, witnessing the raising of Jairus's daughter (Mk 5.37), the Transfiguration (Mk 9.2), and the agony in the garden (Mk 14.33). Too much should not be made of these associations, however. Mark has deliberately established an inner group among "the Twelve," and he associated this group with important moments of revelation in the Gospel of Mark. John and James were ready to call down fire from heaven against the Samaritan towns that did not accept Jesus (Lk 9.54). This fiery disposition (see also Mk 9.38–39) may account for the name given to them by Jesus, Boanerges or "sons of thunder" (Mk 3.17). Their request for the highest rank in the kingdom (Mk 10.35–41) was met by Jesus with a demand for willingness to suffer martyrdom. If John is to be identified with the beloved disciple of the Fourth Gospel, further information concerning him is available from that source; *see* JOHN, GOSPEL ACCORDING TO ST.

According to Lk 22.8, Peter and John were the two sent to prepare the Last Supper; this association of Peter and John is found also in Acts, e.g., 1.13. Peter and John encountered the lame beggar at the Temple and were subsequently arrested and released (Acts ch. 3–4); Peter and John went to Samaria to communicate the Holy Spirit (8.14–25); when Paul visited Jerusalem for the second time after his conversion, he found John along with Peter and James (the brother of the Lord) as the three principal figures in the Jerusalem church (Gal 2.9). A final Biblical reference to John is in Rv 1.9 if, as is customary (Justin, *Dial.* 81), the visionary John is identified with the son of Zebedee; this John was in adverse circumstances at Patmos, off the coast of Asia Minor. The identification of

John, the Son of Zebedee with the John of the Apocalypse, however, is most unlikely.

For these later years of John's life we are dependent on inferences about the authorship of the Johannine writings and on patristic tradition. A very plausible report is that of Irenaeus (*Adv. Haer.* 2.22.5), a tradition he had from Polycarp of Smyrna who knew John: John lived at Ephesus in Asia Minor until the time of Trajan. The common opinion, drawn from Irenaeus and other 2d-century witnesses, is that on Patmos John wrote the Apocalypse (perhaps late in the reign of Domitian, 81–96) and at Ephesus, the Epistles and the Gospel (perhaps early in the reign of Trajan, 98–117). Modern literary criticism, however, would require at least the positing of several editings and the use of secretaries to preserve authorship by John and yet account for the diversities in style and thought of the five Johannine writings.

The more likely scenario is that an ex-disciple of John the Baptist was the foundational figure and inspiration of a so-called "Johannine Community." He is the "author" of the Fourth Gospel (see Jn 1.35–40; 21:24). Other "Johannine Communities" developed from the original group, and divisions among them eventually led to the writing of the Johannine Epistles. They were not written by the Beloved Disciple, who had died by this time (see Jn 21.20–23). But they continued the same theological tradition as they faced new difficulties, and as the originally unified community began to divide (see 1 Jn 2.19). Revelation comes from another figure, also called "John" (a common name), identified as "the presbyter" (see Rv 1.1, 4, 9; 21.2; 22.8).

An ancient cult of John at Ephesus is attested to by the ruins of an impressive basilica.

Contrary to Irenaeus, there is a tradition that John died an early death; it has no real value. Tertullian (*Praescrip. Haer.* 36) says that John was brought from Ephesus to Rome and cast into a cauldron of boiling oil before the Latin Gate, but was miraculously preserved. This tradition is seemingly not historical, and the feast (May 6) has been omitted from the general calendar. Among stories told of John may be made of his unwillingness to associate with the heretic Cerinthus in the public baths (Irenaeus, *Adv. Haer.* 3.3.4), his raising a dead man to life (Eusebius, *Hist. Eccl.* 5.18.14), his reclaiming a robber for Christ (Clement of Alexandria, *What Rich Man* 42), and his repeating of the instruction: "Little children, love one another" (Jerome, *On Gal.* 6.10).

Of Docetic or Gnostic origins are several *Acts of John* (by Leucius, by Prochorus) and an *Apocryphon of John;* the former stresses the virginity of John. A legend of the assumption of John developed in Encratite circles.

Of the four Evangelistic figures based on Ez 1.10 and Rv 4.7, John is depicted as an eagle because of the theological heights of the Prologue. The late use of the chalice in Johannine iconography may reflect Mt 20.23 ("You will drink my cup"), combined with the legend that when John was given a poisoned cup, the poison came out in the form of a serpent. There is a custom in Europe of a "cup of charity" drunk in honor of John. The practice of celebrating John's feast (Dec. 27) immediately after that of Stephen is ancient, originating before the 5th century. Sometimes John and James were honored together; but in this feast, perhaps through confusion, the James who was honored was the brother of the Lord, and not the brother of John.

The data provided above lists all the possible appearances of John, the Son of Zebedee, in the New Testament, and the major subsequent reflection upon that data. Several family and apostolic links have been suggested in this listing. None of them are certain, and most are based upon a tendency to render more certain data that remains outside our scientific control. John, the Son of Zebedee, was certainly one of the first disciples of Jesus, the brother of James (see Mk 3.17). He was also one of "the Twelve," a historical group of foundational disciples of Jesus whom Jesus gathered around himself during his public ministry. The long association of the name of John the Son of Zebedee with the Gospel of John, this link was first made late in the second century by Ireneus. He was anxious to save the Fourth Gospel from becoming the Gospel of the Gnostics. The earliest use of the Fourth Gospel is found in Gnostic writings. His apostolic ministry and his death in either Jerusalem or (more likely) Ephesus, remain in the realms of speculation. We only have the witness of later interested parties for such detail.

Bibliography: In addition to the bibliography provided in the entry under the Gospel according to St. John, see M.-E. BOISMARD, *Le Martyre de Jean l'Apôtre* (Paris 1996). R. E. BROWN, *The Community of the Beloved Disciple* (New York 1979). J. H. CHARLESWORTH, *The Beloved Disciple. Whose Witness Validates the Gospel of John?* (Valley Forge 1995). R. A. CULPEPPER, *John, the Son of Zebedee: The Life of a Legend* (Columbia 1994). J. P. MEIER, "The Circle of the Twelve: Did It Exist During Jesus' Public Ministry?" *Journal of Biblical Literature* 116 (1997) 635–672.

[R. E BROWN/F. J. MOLONEY]

JOHN, EPISTLES OF

Three canonical works come under this rubric: 1 John, a general letter addressed as a warning to a particular area, but applicable to all Christians; 2 John, a letter addressed to the "elect lady," which is probably a reference to a church, and it is also generally applicable; 3 John, a letter addressed to Gaius. In 2 and 3 John the author is identified as the "presbyter" or "elder." These two epistles are of about the same length, each probably written on one papyrus sheet.

This article discusses the questions of authorship, the relationship between the Epistles and the Fourth Gospel, and then gives attention to the literary form and the message of 1–3 John. It concludes with some suggestions concerning the historical situation in early Christian communities reflected in the Gospel of John and the Johannine Epistles.

The Authorship of the Epistles. Polycarp of Smyrna (*Phil.* 7), writing between A.D. 115 and 140, seems to cite 1 Jn 4.2–3; and Papias, *c.* 140, is said by Eusebius (*Historia Ecclesiastica* 3.39.17) to have cited 1 John. Therefore there has been no real doubt about the canonicity of 1 John. The MURATORIAN CANON, *c.* 200, mentions two Epistles of John; and Irenaeus cites both 1 and 2 John and ascribes them, along with the Gospel, to John the Apostle. Beginning with Clement of Alexandria and Origen references to three epistles are found. Both Eusebius (*Historia Ecclesiastica* 3.25.3) and Jerome (*Vir. illus.* 9.18) suggest that 2 and 3 John were written by one other than John the Apostle who wrote the Fourth Gospel and 1 John. By the end of the 4th century, 2 and 3 John found their way into canonical acceptance both in the West and the East, except at Antioch. They are not found in the Syriac PESHITTA.

The Council of Trent settled the canonicity of 1, 2, and 3 John; it did not settle the question of authorship, disputed even in antiquity. Since 2 and 3 John are so much alike and claim the same author, there is no real reason to doubt their common authorship. But did this "presbyter" also write 1 John? There are many parallels in thought between 2 John and 1 John, although the phrasing is not always the same. In 1 Jn 1.7 the phrase "walk in light" occurs, while 2 John 4 has "walking in the truth." Both Epistles (1 Jn 2.7–8; 2 Jn 5) mention a new commandment that is also old because it existed from the beginning. The connection between love and keeping the commandments is similar in both (1 Jn 2.4–5; 2 Jn 6). Both (1 Jn 4.2; 2 Jn 7) stress the importance of confessing that Jesus Christ has come in the flesh. Thus whether or not the same scribe is responsible for the writing, it seems clear that these Epistles belong to the same school of thought, and thus to the same author in the Biblical sense, i.e., the person responsible for the message.

The Epistles and the Fourth Gospel. The author of the Gospel looks back upon a period when those who confessed that Jesus was the Christ had been cast out of the Synagogue (see 9.22; 12.42; 16.2). After the destruction of Jerusalem by the Romans in A.D. 70, the surviving Jews, who largely belonged to a group described in the

Gospels as the Pharisees, worked hard to re-establish its religious practice which, for the Jews (then and now), is intimately associated with all aspects of everyday life. But Jewish-Christians had also survived. Gradually these two different forms of Judaism went their separate ways. The Fourth Gospel is one piece of evidence of this process that would have gradually taken place across the Mediterranean world. However, the final separation of the communities behind the Epistles of John from their Jewish roots was long since past. The problems with people "outside" the Johannine communities had been resolved, for better or for worse. The Epistles face an inevitable further stage in the story of the people for whom they were written: problems were emerging within the communities. There was a breakdown among members of different communities that looked to the Gospel of John for their story of Jesus. Thus, "Johannine" communities existed with differing interpretations of their founding tradition, the Gospel of John. The author of 1 John can write: "They went out from us, but they were not of us; for if they had been of us, they would have continued with us; but they went out, that it might be plain that they all are not of us" (1 Jn 2.19. See also 2 Jn 7).

As is evident from the language and theological solutions proposed to overcome early Christian crises, the Gospel and the Epistles come from the same theological background. But the Epistles reflect a situation where the original group is spreading (and dividing) into a number of communities. A Christian leader addresses his fellow Christians in an attempt to dissuade them from following the behavior and beliefs of others who, in his opinion, are in error and have "gone out" from the founding community. The presence of different communities is especially clear in 3 John where the author of the Epistle, an "Elder," a senior figure in a Christian community, pleads with the leader of another community, Gaius, to disregard the thought and behavior of a third party, Diotrephes (3 Jn 9–10). At least three groups are involved.

Throughout 1 John the author writes negatively of the group who "went out" (see 1 Jn 2.19). The first part of the Epistle is dedicated to an attack upon some who do not share his ideas. He writes accusingly: "If we say that we have fellowship with him while we are walking in darkness, we lie and do not do what is true" (1.6). The same spirit lies behind a series of further affirmations: "If we say that we have no sin, we deceive ourselves, and truth is not in us" (1.8); "If we say that we have not sinned, we make him a liar, and his word is not in us" (1.10). A similar form of attack is phrased differently: "The one who says 'I know him' but disobeys his commandments is a liar, and the truth is not in that person" (2.4); "The one who says he abides in him ought to walk

in the same way in which he walked" (2:6). These examples, drawn from the first pages of the Epistle, are but a sample. The list could go on, as the writer continually attacks "whoever says. . ." (2.4, 9, 11) or "everyone who. . ." (2.23; 3.4, 8). Such angry polemic is directed against people who are divided from the author.

The Problem of a Principle of Love. A fundamental belief of the Christian tradition which has its origin in the Gospel of John is that God is love (see 1 Jn 4.8, 16). This belief comes from the Gospel's insistence that the presence of Jesus in the human story is the result of God's love: "God so loved the world that he gave his own only Son" (Jn 3.16). The mission of the Son was to make the Father known (see Jn 4.34; 5.36; 15.13; 17.3–4). This takes place in the loving self-gift of Jesus on the Cross. There the love of God can be seen as generations of believers gaze upon the one whom they have pierced (Jn 19.37). The mission of Jesus has consequences for those who regard themselves as his disciples. They are called to a unity of love (see Jn 13.34–35; 15.12, 17; 17.11, 20–23). A loving God has called disciples who are to love one another as he has loved them: "You did not choose me, but I chose you and appointed you that you should go and bear fruit and that your fruit should abide" (Jn 15.16).

For the author of 1 John, this central feature of John's Gospel had not become a reality in the lives of the subsequent members of those communities who looked back to the story of Jesus as it had been passed down to them in the Gospel of John. The author seeks the fruits which should be visible (see Jn 15.5), but abiding fruits that should flow from the initiative of God in choosing his disciples are hard to find among some. But not all is anger and pain. The members of the communities are reminded of fundamental principles of the Gospel of John. The author faces the inevitable difficulty of looking to a document from the past as he tries to make it relevant to his present situation.

The Epistles of John are proof that this was already a problem within the short period of time that had elapsed between the production of the Gospel of John and the writing of the Epistles. The author of 1 John presupposes that the recipients of this letter are on his side, but he may have some doubts. They may have been wavering, and this could explain the harshness of his stance against all who had a different understanding of the Gospel. The author of the Epistle looks back to the Johannine tradition in the Christian Church. But the tone of the document indicates that one of the central elements in the Gospel's teaching on discipleship is not being lived. No doubt he writes in the hope of restoring the mutuality of love demanded by the teaching of Jesus. However, he risks the establishment of a community where like-minded people love one another, but have little affection or concern for those outside the boundaries of their community.

A Letter? Unlike 2 and 3 John, 1 John can only be called a "letter" in a general sense. As we shall see below, the two later Epistles (2 and 3 John) follow the stereotyped form of a letter in antiquity. From the many examples of letters still available from that time, scholars have been able to trace the common structure of a letter. Ancient letters began with a standard form of introduction, in which the writer was introduced, the addressee named and an initial greeting exchanged. This was generally followed by a word of thanksgiving to the gods, and then the body of the letter. At the beginning and end of this main section, were found stereotyped expressions of good will and indications of the purpose of the letter. It would close with a formula of farewell.

There are hints of these forms in 1 John (cf. 2.1, 5.21), and the author continually addresses himself to a very specific audience. But this is hardly enough to call it a stereotypical letter from antiquity. Indeed, its literary form is unique and, as we will see, the uniqueness comes from the loyalty of the author to the tradition that formed him: the Gospel of John. The majority of the so-called "epistles" in the Christian Scriptures are motivated by something other than everyday events, business matters, or personal greetings and family communications. They are what we might call theological tracts, even though they use the overall shape of a letter. Paul's Epistle to the Romans is an outstanding example of a letter which is only loosely associated with the letter-form, but which must be regarded as an authentic letter. Paul writes to persuade the Romans of the importance of God's all-embracing offer of salvation, made through the death and resurrection of Jesus. It is this effort to persuade which gives the Epistle its lasting value.

The letter-form has been transcended by the passion of early Christian authors to convince the recipients of the importance of what God had done in and through Jesus Christ. 1 John communicates between an author who has things he wishes to teach readers who might be losing confidence in their beliefs. A "rhetoric of persuasion" is at play across the document and generates the unique literary form of 1 John.

The Shape and Message of 1 John. The structure and argument of 1 John parallel the founding Gospel of John. This further indicates that the people to whom this letter was written were part of the tradition that produced the Gospel of John. The readers received a document restating in a letter-tract form the major theological arguments of the Gospel. The author has modeled the Epistle upon the structure of the Gospel, with a prologue (1.1–4.

See Jn 1.1–18), the body of the Epistle in two parts ([a] 1.5–3.10. See Jn 1.19–12.50. [b] 3.11–5.12. See Jn 13.1–20.19) and a conclusion (5.13–21. See Jn 20.30–31).

The Prologue (1.1–4) recalls Jn 1.1–18. It too tells of the "beginnings" of the Christian story: Jesus who revealed the word of life. But it also looks back to another "beginning," to the original community which lived in fellowship with the Father and the Son. In the first part of the Gospel's account of the ministry of Jesus (Jn 1.19–12.50), Jesus lived and proclaimed his message within the context of hostile rejection. So also the first central section of the Epistle, which could be given the description, "God is light and we must walk in the light as Jesus walked" (1.5–3.10), is also at times hostile. It insists that Christians live as Jesus lived, and attacks the false ideas and way of life of some who have left the community. In the second central section, to which we could give the title, "We must love one another as God has loved us in Jesus Christ" (3.11–5.12), the hostility softens, but does not disappear. Recalling Jn 13.1–17.26, the author develops the theme of the centrality of true love and true faith as the basis for Christian confidence. The Epistle concludes (5.13–21) with an assurance that true believers can pray with confidence, in the midst of difficulties and conflicts, and rest in God's unfailing protection.

As is obvious from this schematic presentation of the First Epistle of John, the pain and anger generated by division among Johannine Christians have not impoverished the power and comfort of the Christian message. The author's presentation of God, Jesus and the Christian response to the action of God in his Son, is not dissipated. The Christian tradition which first found expression in the story of Jesus in the Gospel of John remains strongly present in the First Epistle of John. The very way the author organized his Epistle, following the overall shape of the Gospel, is an indication of his loyalty to that tradition.

A Passionate Voice. Despite the polemical voice that rings through 1 John, our reading these pages should focus, not so much on the so-called errors of the opponents, but on the passion which generated the Epistle. For all his one-sidedness, the author has produced within this short document a remarkable synthesis of some of the essential elements of the Christian tradition:

> Jesus' teaching about God as Father, and especially in his association of this teaching with the themes of love (1 Jn 3.1; 4.7–12, 14; 5.1–2).
> Fellowship with God means fellowship with the Father and the Son (1.3; 2.22–25).
> The importance of the human Jesus of Nazareth as the Christ, the Son of God (2.22; 3.23; 4.2; 5.6),

and that his death on the cross atones for our inevitable sinfulness (2.2; 3.16; 4.10; 5.6).

The tension between the gifts of the "now" and the need to wait for a "not yet" (2.18, 28; 3.2–3).

The experience of the Spirit (3.24; 4.4, 6, 13) grounded in some form of initiation rite, possibly baptism (2.20, 27; 3.9; 5.18).

The emphasis on the importance of faith for salvation, for knowledge of God through the acceptance of Jesus as the Christ (3.23; 4.16; 5.1, 4–5, 10–12).

The ethical teaching of the love of God and the love of our neighbor (see 2.15–17; 3.17; 4.20; 21; 5.21).

A New Way of Stating Truths. These elements of the Christian tradition have been recast in a letter-form, using the language and imagery of the Gospel of John.

Developing the theme of "light" in the Gospel of John (see Jn 1.4–5, 7–9; 3.19–21; 8.12; 9.5; 11.9; 12.35–36, 46), the author of the Epistle claims that God is light (1.5) and love (4.8, 16). The person born of God (2.29; 3.9; 4.7; 5.1, 4, 18) walks in the light (2.9). Those born of God are children of God (3.1), and derive their life from God (5.11–13).

The realm opposed to God is one of darkness and death, characterized by hatred, falsehood, murder and unbelief. The dualism of the Fourth Gospel continues in 1 John.

Ways of speaking about Jesus found in the Gospel of John remain. Jesus is even called "the word" (1.1. See Jn 1.1–2). But especially significant is the use of the two titles "the Christ" and "the Son of God" which are so important for correct faith, according to the Gospel's conclusion (Jn 20.31). The close identification between God and Jesus (see Jn 1.1–2) is repeated as the Epistle comes to a close: "This is the true God and eternal life" (1 Jn 5.20).

To be saved is to have "eternal life" and to be a child of God (3.1; 5.11–13, 20. See Jn 17.3, 12; 5.19–30), even though the believer must still wait for the coming of the end time (2.18; 3.2. See Jn 5.27–29; 6.40, 44).

The Holy Spirit in the community is the gift of God (3.24; 4.13; see Jn 14.26).

The commandments of God and of Christ must be obeyed, especially the love command (3.11, 23). The Gospel commands that the disciples love one another as Jesus has loved them, so that the world might know that they are his disciples (see Jn 13.34–35). This ideal command becomes more practical in 1 John. Mutual love, reflecting the love of God and obeying the command of the Son, is to be shown to our fellow believer (4.7–21), and should be seen in the way we walk as Jesus walked (2.6).

These indications demonstrate a robust understanding of both foundational Christian beliefs which have their roots in the life and teaching, death and resurrection of Jesus, and the articulation of those beliefs in the Gospel of John.

2 and 3 John: True Letters. From Christianity's earliest years, believers and critics have wondered why such short (and somewhat fractious) documents as 2–3 John have become part of the Christian Scriptures. They were addressed to a local situation in an attempt to deal with conflicts in these communities, but they were quickly associated with the figure of John, the author of a Gospel. They were thus seen as part of a tradition deserving a place in "the Johannine Writings." 2 and 3 John correspond reasonably well with the widely attested form of a First Century Hellenistic letter. The following indicates how the three basic elements of these letters appear in 2 and 3 John.

2 John

Opening formula (vv. 1–3)
Sender—addressee— greeting (vv. 1–3)

Body of the Letter (vv. 4–12)
Expression of joy—transition to the body of the letter (v. 3)
Request concerning the commandment to love (vv. 5–6)
Warning against the Antichrists and their teaching (vv. 7–11)
Promise of a visit, closing the body of the letter (v. 12)

Concluding Formula (v. 13)

3 John

Opening formula (vv. 1–2)
Sender—addressee—greeting (vv. 1–2)

Body of the Letter (vv. 3–14)
Expression of joy—transition to the body of the letter (vv. 3–4)
Request for hospitality and support (vv. 5–8)
The hostility of Diotrephes (vv. 9–10)
An appeal to do good and a recommendation for Demetrius (vv. 11–12)
Promise of a visit, closing the body of the letter (vv. 13–14)

Concluding formula (v. 15)

Message. We only hear one side of the argument, but these documents allow us to eavesdrop upon a conversation between a significant figure within the communities ("the Elder") and a community (2 Jn: the elect lady and her children) or the leader of one of the communities, another "Elder" (3 Jn: Gaius). 2–3 John are not theological tracts, but reflect the Elder's concern for the ongoing faith of early Christian communities. They thus afford us access to the sometimes difficult experiences of an emerging Christian Church.

In 2 John 7 the author of the Epistle, in a way reminiscent of 1 Jn 2.19, warns the community of those who have left them. Not only have they departed from a once unified community; they have also departed from the teachings the author would regard as true Christian belief. Such dangerous deceivers and antichrists must be shunned if they approach the community to which 2 John is written. For the moment that is all the author wishes to tell his fellow-believers. He will explain the situation when he comes to visit them in the near future. The situation in 3 John is more local, personal, and bitter, written to Gaius, a senior figure in a community (also an "Elder"), who deserves praise for the way he has made wandering fellow Christians welcome. His acceptance of itinerant believers, however, is to be contrasted with the attitude and arrogance of a certain Diotrephes who has refused to welcome the emissaries of the letter-writer, and has also refused to accept his authority. But all is not lost, as the author can recommend another Christian, Demetrius, who is true. Divisions are hardening, as some are "in" and others are "out." But this arrogance is not only to be laid at the door of Diotrephes, who rejects the letter-writer's emissaries and his authority (3 Jn). It was also the position advocated by the author of 2 John as he instructed his "beloved lady and her children" to avoid the dangerous influence of the deceivers and the antichrists: "If any one comes to you and does not bring this doctrine, do not receive him into the house or give him any greeting" (2 Jn 11).

The Story of the Gospel and Epistles of John. Many scholars believe that a single tradition, which can be called "the Johannine tradition," lies behind the Gospel of John and 1, 2 and 3 John. There were those who believed that Jesus was the Christ, the Son of God (Jn 20.31), but who found it difficult to love one another as Jesus had loved them (see Jn 13.34–35; 15.12). The Gospel already reflects the tensions which existed in an early Christian community as it developed an understanding of Jesus which became steadily more distant from the community's origins within Judaism (see, for example 6.60–66). A missionary activity, initially among the Samaritans (see 4.1–42), and a physical journey of a community which had its origins in Israel, but which seems to have finally settled in Asia Minor, led to the development of its tradition. The community could no longer locate Jesus within the strictly Jewish categories of other early Christian communities. They came to speak of Jesus as "the Christ," "the Son of God," "I AM," "the Word," and they told of Jesus' claims to be one with God, whom he called his Father (see, for example, 5.19–30; 10.30, 38).

The community and the local Synagogue inevitably suffered a complete and final separation (see 9.22; 12.42;

16.2). Once this took place, the tradition developed with a greater sense of independence. These early Christians no longer used only Jewish categories to understand Jesus, but moving into the broader Greco-Roman world of Asia Minor saw the need to tell the old story in a new way. The presentation of the person and role of Jesus Christ in the Prologue to the Fourth Gospel (1.1–18) and the final prayer of Jesus (17.1–26) are good examples (but not the only examples) of such writing. These well-known and much-loved passages have their roots in the Jewish story of Jesus and the earliest years of the tradition, but they re-tell the traditional story that it might make sense in a new world. This was not a simple process. The addition of John 21 indicates that there may have been some misunderstanding of the nature of the community. This is clarified by the account of the miraculous draft of many fish into the one boat (21.1–14). Its attention to Peter, the pastor and shepherd, and the Beloved Disciple who also follows Jesus (vv. 15–24) shows that there were concerns over authority in the community.

The Epistles continue this story. Difficulties with the Synagogue long since past, the threat of opposition from outside the community seemed to have disappeared. The Elder focuses his attention upon internal difficulties. Already in 1 John the author of the Epistle presents an argument which is aimed at supporting his fragile community in the face of some ex-members of the community who have left them (see 1 Jn 2.19). They are regarded as the antichrists (2.18), purveyors of a false ethic (see 1.8–10; 2.15–17; 3.4–10; 5.2), rejecting the importance of mutual love within the community (see 2.9–11; 3.14–18, 4.7–12, 20–21). They do not regard the historical Jesus as the Christ and the Son of God (2.22–23, 3.23; 4.2–3; 5.5–6), and they seem to have difficulty with the traditional understanding of the end of time (3.2–3; 4.17). Such teaching and practice are contrary to the tradition which the author insists communities had received "in the beginning" (1.1; 2.7, 13–14, 24). As we have seen, the structure and argument in 1 John can be interpreted as a loose commentary upon the Fourth Gospel. It certainly presupposes a knowledge of that story of Jesus, and the Christian traditions which flow from it.

Toward the end of the first Christian Century, there were a several communities which looked back to the story of Jesus as it is told in the Gospel of John. There they found inspiration and guidance in their Christian lives. No specific audience is indicated in 1 John. It was probably written for the central community where a division had already taken place over different interpretations of the original tradition. These interpretations disturbed the remnant that remained faithful to the tradition defended by the author. The situation of 2 and 3 John, understood as brief letters from the same author as 1 John, now

NEW CATHOLIC ENCYCLOPEDIA **901**

calling himself "the Elder," are indications of his campaign to protect other communities from the teachings of missionaries coming from the breakaway group. 2 John warns a Church against admitting them; 3 John attempts to get help for the itinerant brethren who had the support of the Elder. They were probably missionaries sympathetic to the position of the Elder, moving about among the early Christian communities, spreading the warning and defending the tradition. Strong personalities emerged, especially the Elder and Diotrephes. Originally from the same tradition, but leaders of geographically separate communities, Diotrephes took seriously the warnings of 2 John 10–11. He would not admit anyone into his community, not even the emissaries of the Elder, whose authority he refused to accept (3 Jn 9–10). Yet the Elder still has support from the community of elect lady (2 Jn 1.1–2, 13), Gaius (3 Jn 1–4, 15), and Demetrius (3 Jn 11–12).

We can only speculate about the subsequent history of the emerging interpretations of the tradition that originated in the Gospel of John. A lack of teaching authority leads the author of 1 John to point to the need to test the spirits (1 John 4.1–6), a method of identifying truth which would hardly be effective in a faith community attempting to establish a body of doctrine. But the belief that Jesus of Nazareth is the Christ, the Son of God who atones for our sins, becomes fundamental to the emerging Christian Church. The same could be said for the Elder's defense of a traditional understanding of the end of time. We have a very one-sided presentation of those who have left the original community. But their ethics, their idea of community, their understanding of the end-time and of Jesus Christ, as presented by the Elder, look very like an early stage of what eventually flowered in second-century GNOSTICISM. This powerful religious tradition, which had many different representatives, understood Jesus as a revealing figure who imparted a saving "knowledge" (Greek: γνῶσις). His humanity and his death faded in importance. The Gnostics regarded some people as "illuminated" by knowledge, and considerable ambiguity surrounded their ethical behavior. Gnosticism faltered as the Christian Church gradually asserted itself, with the support of secular authority, as the dominant belief system. It could be suggested that neither the one-sided Christianity of the Elder nor the early Gnosticism of Diotrephes lived beyond the second century.

Bibliography: A. E. BROOKE, *A Critical and Exegetical Commentary on the Johannine Epistles* (Edinburgh 1912). R. E. BROWN, *The Community of the Beloved Disciple* (New York 1979). C. H. DODD, *The Johannine Epistles* (New York 1946). D. RENSBERGER, *1 John, 2 John, 3 John* (Abingdon New Testament Commentaries; Nashville 1997). R. SCHNACKENBURG, *The Johannine Epistles. A Commentary* (New York 1992). S. S. SMALLEY, *1, 2, 3 John* (Word Biblical Commentary 51; Waco 1984). B. F. WESTCOTT, *The Epistles of St John: The Greek Text with Notes* (3d ed. 1892; repr. Abingdon 1966).

[F. J. MOLONEY]

JOHN, GOSPEL ACCORDING TO

After a discussion of the unity of the Fourth Gospel, this article considers the questions of historical tradition in the Gospel, influences on the Gospel, its destination and purpose, the date of its writing, the problem of authorship. It concludes by proposing an outline of the Gospel.

Unity of the fourth Gospel. Is John as it now stands the work of one man? The solution commonly accepted before the advent of criticism was that this Gospel was the work of John, son of Zebedee, composed shortly before his death. Leaving the problem of the author's identity for a later section, we note here that there are indications of more than one hand in the Gospel. The Prologue has a formal poetic style and theological stresses, e.g., the personified Word, not found elsewhere in the Gospel. Coming after 20.30–31, ch. 21 is clearly an addition, narrating Resurrection appearances totally independent of those narrated in ch. 20 and exhibiting a Greek style somewhat different from the rest of the Gospel. Within the body of the Gospel there are breaks in sequence difficult to reconcile as the work of one writer, e.g., one ending for the public ministry in 10.40–42 and another ending in 12.37–43; two endings for the farewell discourse of Jesus in 14.31 and 18.1; unattached speeches that ill fit the context, such as 3.31–36 and 12.44–50. There is no need to dwell on the problem of the story of the adulteress (7.53–8.11), which is certainly not Johannine in style, does not fit the context, and is missing in the early Greek MSS. (It was an independent morsel of Gospel tradition that in later witnesses was inserted in John or sometimes in Luke; according to Tridentine norms it is inspired Scripture.) All this has led scholars to posit that, besides an author or evangelist who was chiefly responsible for the tradition of John, there was a subsequent editor (or a series of editors), perhaps the evangelist's disciple(s), who added material to the body of the Gospel narrative, material stemming in one way or another from the author.

Source Theory. Many critics suggest that, leaving aside the editorial additions, even the body of the Gospel is not a unity but is a combination of sources. The most articulate formulation of this theory is that of R. Bultmann, who posits three sources that were combined by the evangelist. First, there was, according to him, a collection of revelatory discourses. Composed originally in Aramaic, this source began with the Prologue and con-

The Virgin of Humility and Saint Jerome translating the Gospel of John, diptych by Benedetto di Bindo, 15th century. (©Philadelphia Museum of Art/CORBIS)

tained poetic discourses wherein a revealer from heaven announced himself under the formula, "I am . . ." (Jn 6.35; 10.7, 11; 15.1) and demanded faith in himself as the condition for man's salvation. Bultmann connects the GNOSTICISM of these discourses with the thought of the Mandaeans, a syncretistic baptizing sect living in Iraq, somehow related to John the Baptist (*see* MANDAEAN RELIGION). Second, there was a collection of Jesus' miraculous signs. Written in Greek with strong Semitic affinities, this source had as an introduction the call of the first disciples (1.35–51) and enumerated the signs done by Jesus (2.11; 4.54; 20.30). Finally, there was a narrative of the Passion and Resurrection.

For Bultmann, the first and second sources had no real historical value as a memory of the actual words and deeds of Jesus. The evangelist combined them, Christianized the Gnosticism, and made the composite work the vehicle of a personal, somewhat existential theology. His

hand may be seen in certain additions to the sources. For Bultmann, a final stage in the composition of the Gospel was the work of "the ecclesiastical redactor," a primitive censor who adapted the evangelist's work to make it acceptable to orthodox authorities in the Church. The redactor corrected the antisacramental tenor of the original by adding sacramental references ("water" in 3.5; the Eucharist in 6.51–58; the Eucharist and Baptism in 19.34). He adapted the Evangelist's realized eschatology [*see* ESCHATOLOGY (IN THE BIBLE)] by adding references to the second coming of Christ (5.28–29), and he harmonized John with the Synoptic tradition.

This analysis is ingenious and has some valid insights, e.g., the poetic style of the discourses; but it is open to serious objections. For instance, realized eschatology and a hope for the second coming are not mutually exclusive, and the corrective aspect of the final editing is highly questionable. There are no satisfactory contemporary literary parallels for the sources that Bultmann posits. Moreover, the same stylistic peculiarities are rather uniform throughout the Gospel, as shown by E. Schweizer and E. Ruckstuhl; yet it would be logical to expect different styles to be evident in the remnants of the different sources. C. H. Dodd has shown that miraculous sign and discourse in John are not artificially juxtaposed, but that the discourse is a most necessary explanation of the sign.

Redaction Theory. If the source theory is rejected, there is another more plausible explanation of the composition of John. This is the redaction theory: that underlying the body of the Gospel there is a series of redactions, oral and literary. M. E. Boismard suggests that the one evangelist was responsible for these redactions, as might well happen if the same material was preached over and over again for a long time. This theory would explain different theological emphases within John, e.g., realized and final eschatology, and less and more specific sacramentalism. It would also explain the repetitiveness of John where there seem to be different versions of the same material (e.g., 5.19–25 and 5.26–30; 14.1–31 and 16.4–33). If such redactions stem from the same evangelist at different periods, the unity of Johannine style would still be respected. According to this theory, the evangelist himself may have given written form to one or more of these editions; but as seen above, the final form of the Gospel would not be the work of the evangelist but the work of an editor who acted not as a censor but as the completer of the evangelist's work. This theory would do justice both to the evidence of the Gospel itself and to tradition, for there is a suggestion in the early witnesses (MURATORIAN Canon, Toletan Latin Preface, *Acts of John* by Prochorus) that others were associated with John in producing this Gospel.

It is not possible for the modern scholar to reconstruct perfectly the various editions of the evangelist or always to detect the hand of the final editor(s). Various scholars (J. Bernard, F. Hoare, Bultmann) have rearranged John to get a better sequence, e.g., by transposing ch. 5 and 6, and by putting 10.1–18 after 10.19–29.

Today the tendency is to comment on the Gospel as it has been given to us. The meaning thus obtained is more likely to be loyal to the author's intent than is a modern subjective and often tendentious rearrangement. The advent of a greater attention to the importance of narrative as such, and the development of a number of approaches to biblical narratives, has tipped the balance even further against the earlier interest in sources and reordering the material. Source critical study continues (see U. Schnelle; J. Painter) but the majority of contemporary Johannine scholars, especially those writing in English, devote their attention to the structure and message of the narrative as we have received it in the canonical text (see M. W. G. Stibbe, T. Brodie, F. J. Moloney).

Historical Tradition in the fourth Gospel. If unity is posited for John, the question must still be asked whether the body of the Gospel as it stems from the evangelist represents independent historical tradition. It has been maintained by some critics that the evangelist borrowed and adapted his historical framework from the SYNOPTIC GOSPELS and that what is peculiar to John may be explained either as deliberate alteration of Synoptic details for theological purposes, or else as invention.

Today this approach has lost ground for three reasons. First, it is now seriously contested that John borrowed from the Synoptic tradition; P. Gardner-Smith and Dodd have made a careful study of the relationship between the two traditions as regards the words and deeds of Jesus. In scenes shared by the two traditions, such as the healing of the royal official's son (Jn 4.46–54) and the multiplication of the loaves (Jn 6.1–13), it is almost impossible to explain the differences in John on any pattern of deliberate alteration. Many of the details peculiar to John have every mark of being primitive. Thus it seems that there must be posited for John a tradition independent of the Synoptic tradition, a tradition that in some details will be more primitive, in some details more advanced. Such a position also rules out the ancient theory that John was written to supplement the Synoptic Gospels.

Second, there has been external verification or support for some of the material found in John alone. The pool of BETHESDA in Jn 5.2 has been excavated in Jerusalem and has been found to have five porticoes, just as John describes it. Its name appears in the copper scroll from Qumran. The stone pavement of the Lithostrotos (19.13) may have been uncovered under the fortress Antonia (*see* PRAETORIUM). As A. Guilding has reconstructed the synagogue lectionary, the texts read in the synagogue at a particular feast were often those that underlie Jesus' discourse on that feast as reported in John, e.g., 6.35–50, on the Passover. P. Borgen shows that a discourse such as 6.35–50 fits all the rules of rabbinic exegesis prevailing in Jesus' own time. These and many other discoveries indicate that the author of the Gospel had an accurate knowledge of Palestine and its customs before the destruction of A.D. 70.

Third, some of the arguments against Johannine historicity have been weakened in recent years. A prime example is the argument that the abstract language of dualism in John, e.g., light and darkness in 3.19–21, could not possibly stem from the Palestine of Jesus' time, but belongs to the Gnostic or Hellenistic world of the 2d century. But this language has recently been found in the Dead Sea Scrolls of Qumran, showing that it was current at least among one group of Jews before and during Jesus' time. A proper understanding of John's theological purpose explains other difficulties. For example, in 11.49 the author does not mistakenly think that the high priesthood was an annual office; he is emphasizing the significant character of "that year" in which Jesus died.

Although there is an increasing tendency to admit that the fourth Gospel contains independent historical tradition, there is widespread overconfidence in the other direction, that John cannot be used as a biographical guide in reconstructing the life of Christ. The standard lives of Christ have been written by fitting Synoptic material into Johannine chronology. This procedure is objectionable on several accounts. First, often the Synoptic Gospels themselves do not give the words and deeds of Jesus in their historical order; many once independent stories have been fitted into their existing sequence according to logic or theology rather than chronology. Second, there is no guarantee that John's chronology is complete. The whole basis for thinking that Jesus had a two- or three-year ministry is that John mentions three Passovers (2.13; 6.4; 11.55). However, the reason for mentioning these Passovers is theological (20.30–31); they are significant for the narrative. There is no guarantee that there were not more Passovers in the ministry of Jesus that were not mentioned because they had no significance. Moreover, in the final editing of John there has been rearrangement, and the present Johannine sequence is not necessarily always historical. One must recognize, then, the limitations imposed on the use of the historical tradition preserved in John, but this must not be overstated. Recent work on the historical Jesus (J. P. Meier; F. J. Moloney) has turned more regularly to John, and often concluded in favor of the basic historicity of many elements in the Johannine account. (*See* JESUS CHRIST, BIOGRAPHICAL STUDIES OF.)

Influences on the fourth Gospel. Complementary to the previous problem is that of influences on the Gospel. Those who do not accept the historical character of the Johannine tradition often suggest Gnostic or Hellenistic influences on the Evangelist.

Gnostic Influence. The "History of Religions School," prominent early in the 20th century, brought forward the possibility of Gnostic influence on John, and W. Bauer and Bultmann have been prominent defenders of this theory. Until recently there were very few examples of 2d-century Gnosticism, and so it was possible to think that John might fit into this sphere. The discovery of Gnostic documents at Chenoboskion (*see* CHENOBOSKION, GNOSTIC TEXTS OF) has changed the picture. Neither the *Gospel of Truth* nor the *Gospel of Thomas* is

close to John in thought. Both betray indirect knowledge of John, but their Gnosticism is more developed than anything in John. At most, it may be said that John, like the Dead Sea Scrolls, exhibits a dualism and a vocabulary that is pre-Gnostic but that was funneled into later Gnosticism.

Nor has Bultmann's Mandaean hypothesis won any real following. The oldest extant forms of Mandaean theology are to be dated late in the Christian period. It is possible that sectarians of John the Baptist were among the forebears of the Mandaeans; but as far as can safely be reconstructed, the peculiarly Gnostic aspect of Mandaean theology is the product of later syncretism. The most important single factor in Bultmann's theory concerns the Gnostic redeemer-myth, but there is no clear evidence of the existence of this myth at a period early enough to have influenced John.

Hellenistic Influence. It has also been suggested, in varying degrees, e.g., by B. W. Bacon, Dodd, and C. K. Barrett, that John betrays Hellenistic influence. A distinction must be made here. There was already considerable Hellenistic influence on pre-Christian Judaism. This is exemplified in the speculations on personified Wisdom in Sirach and the Book of Wisdom and in the theology of sectarian Judaism as seen at Qumran and among the Samaritans. There is no doubt that this Hellenistic strain within Judaism had its indirect influence on John. Our problem concerns direct Hellenistic influence. In writing in Greek every one of the evangelists made an inevitable adaptation of the message of Jesus; but the question is whether John adopted Greek patterns and vocabulary on a large scale in order to interpret Jesus to the Greek world. For instance, it has been suggested that John reflects a popular Platonism in his distinctions between what is above and what is below (3.31), between the real heavenly bread and natural bread (6.32). Some have thought that the "Word" of the Prologue is an adaptation of the Stoic λόγος. Each suggestion could be discussed in detail, but in general, there is today a strong tendency to recognize that the basis of such thought can be found in Palestinian Judaism. The "Word" is far closer to personified Wisdom and to the Jewish notion of God's creative word than it is to anything in Stoicism. Even the parallels suggested between Philo and John are explicable mostly in terms of common OT background and milieu rather than in terms of direct influence. The HERMETIC literature has also been suggested as having parallels to John. Once again there is the difficulty of dating, since the body of Hermetic literature is post-Johannine, and earlier stages have to be imaginatively reconstructed. The parallels between John and the Dead Sea Scrolls are closer than those between John and Hermetism.

Palestinian Judaism. Thus it may be said that in many ways it is neither Gnosticism nor the Hellenistic world, but Palestinian Judaism, that remains the most plausible influence on Johannine thought and expression, an influence that fits with the theory that John gives us an independent, reliable tradition about Jesus of Nazareth. The standard currents of OT thought are found in John. Jesus is presented as the Messiah, the elect Servant of Yahweh, the King of Israel, the Prophet. While the number of explicit OT citations in John is relatively low, there are many implicit references to OT personages and scenes: to the first chapters of Genesis (Jn 1–2.10); to Abraham (8.31–58); to Isaac (3.16); to Jacob (4.5–12); to Moses (1.17; 5.46; etc.); to the events of the Exodus, such as the manna (6.31–59), the water from the rock (7.38), the bronze serpent (3.14), and the Tent of Meeting (1.14); to the judges (10.35); to the theme of the royal shepherd (ch. 10). Jewish institutions are the theme of ch. 2 to 4; Jewish feasts are the theme of ch. 5 to 10. The Aramaic features that underlie John's Greek are so strong that some scholars have suggested that John was originally composed in Aramaic. H. L. Strack, P. Billerbeck, A. Schlatter, and Dodd have pointed out the echoes in John of patterns that are found also in rabbinic Judaism.

The strongest objection to explaining John in terms of Palestinian Judaism remains; it is the difference between Johannine thought and expression and that of the Synoptics. Contemporary scholarship is pointing out that many of the Johannine characteristics may have had their origins in Palestinian Judaism, but they have been deliberately used in the Gospel of John because they addressed the syncretistic religious world into which the Gospel was proclaimed at the end of the First Christian Century.

Yet, if both represent historical tradition, if both come from the background of the Palestine in which Jesus lived, how can they be so different? It is because Jesus speaks so differently in John from the way he speaks in the Synoptics that scholars have posited some extraneous influence on John. No complete solution of this problem has yet been forthcoming, but today the problem is being studied more seriously in terms of both traditions being faithful to Jesus. An important factor that we must recognize is that John highlights strains in the tradition about Jesus that are present also in the Synoptic tradition, but only in muted form. John capitalizes on the divine "I am" drawn from the use of ἐγό εἰμι in the Septuagint (LXX) of Deutero-Isaiah (Is 43.10–11, 25) and perhaps from the Wisdom literature. This usage is seen once in Mk 6.50. The Hour of Jesus' return to the Father in death, Resurrection, and Ascension is important in John (2.4; 7.30; 12.23; 13.1; 17.1), but it is only incidental in the Synoptic tradition (Mk 14.35, 41). Only occasionally does Jesus speak as divine Wisdom in the Synoptics (Mt 11.9; Lk 11.49), but He does so all through John. The figures of bread and water that Jesus uses to describe Himself and His revelation (John ch. 6; 4; 7.37–39) are used of Wisdom in the OT [Prv 9.5; Dt 8.3; Is 55.1–3; Sir 24.18–20; Ps 35(36).9]. Perhaps one of the best indications that the Johannine Jesus is not exclusively Johannine is the so-called Johannine Logion in Mt 11.25–30 and in Lk 10.21–22, where the Synoptic Jesus speaks like the Johannine Jesus.

Another factor contributing to a solution is a better appreciation of each of the four evangelists as a theologian. Something of John's theology has gone into his picture of Jesus, but so has something of the theology of the other three evangelists gone into each of their portraits of Jesus. Even though Clement of Alexandria early designated St. John's as the spiritual Gospel and though John is known as "the theologian," his way of presenting Jesus in the Gospel differs from the Synoptic way only in degree, not in kind. It is now believed that each evangelist interpreted Jesus in his own way; consequently, differences among the Gospels are less startling than when it was thought that the evangelists were giving strictly objective and coldly factual portraits of Jesus. If one allows interpretative freedom to the evangelist and recognizes that he is expounding a different KERYGMA than that expounded in the Synoptics it may be held that Johannine singularities do not necessitate the positing of a major extraneous, non-Jewish influence on the Gospel according to John, but the presence of the unique and new features of the Johannine telling of the Gospel account indicates that in this Gospel we have a telling of the old story in a new way.

Destination and purpose of the Gospel. Scholars have argued about the group to which John was directed, and the most important suggestions will be given below. That there are persuasive arguments for more than one group makes it likely that the Gospel had more than one purpose. It may be that some of the diversity of purpose reflects the different redactions by the Evangelist and the editor(s).

Apologetic against Sectarians of the Baptist. In the Prologue there are several references in which it seems that the writer wishes to prevent anyone from claiming too much glory for John the Baptist. Because of this, it has been suggested that one of the chief purposes of the Gospel was to refute exaggerated claims of the followers of John the Baptist. Bultmann's theory of Mandaean influence on John also gives attention to the followers of John the Baptist; indeed, he has suggested that the Prologue was originally a hymn in praise of John the Baptist.

In evaluating this theory, one recognizes that there was a group of John the Baptist's followers who never accepted Christianity. The pseudo-Clementine writings (c. 200) portray these sectarians as asserting that John the Baptist, not Jesus, was the Messiah. We should note, however, that there is not the slightest evidence that these sectarians were originally Gnostic; neither is it safe to use the Mandaean writings to reconstruct their theology. Some of the negations about John the Baptist in John do seem to be an apologetic refutation of the putative claims of the sectarians in John's time as far as we can reconstruct these claims from other sources. Thus Jn 1.8–9 insists that Jesus, not John the Baptist, was the light; and if the BENEDICTUS was originally a hymn to John the Baptist, Lk 1.78 might suggest that the baptist's followers thought of him as the light. Also worth mentioning is the insistence that Jesus existed before John the Baptist, not vice versa, and that therefore Jesus is greater (1.30). In John, John the Baptist denies that he is the Messiah (1.20) and indicates that Jesus is (3.28–30). Nevertheless, John does not deprecate the baptist but regards him as a uniquely important witness sent by God (1.6, 31; 5.31–40). In summation, it is an exaggeration to see the apologetic against the sectarians of John the Baptist as playing a predominant role in the Gospel, even though it is important. If anything, there may have been difficulties in the early Church with the ex-disciples of John the Baptist. John never speaks negatively of John the Baptist, but Acts 18.24–19:7 indicates that there were some who knew the baptism of John the Baptist, but not Christian Baptism. How were they to be handled? (see C. Niemand)

Polemic against "the Jews." Jesus addressed Himself to His Palestinian Jewish contemporaries in order to persuade them that His was a special role in bringing God's reign (kingdom) into time. Therefore, in any Gospel that preserves a historical tradition one may expect a certain apologetic addressed to the Jews. John is stronger, however, in this respect than the Synoptic Gospels, since the perfection of Jewish institutions (purifications, Temple, worship) and feasts (Sabbath, Passover, Tabernacles, Dedication) is the theme on which the Johannine account of the ministry is organized. It is for this reason that W. C. van Unnik and J. A. T. Robinson have advanced the theory that the primary and almost exclusive purpose of the Gospel was a missionary effort directed to the Diaspora Jews.

It seems that John was not addressed to Palestinian Jews. The term "the Jews" is a hostile one throughout most of John. It is clear that the term is not an ethnic designation, for in ch. 9 the blind man and his parents are contrasted to "the Jews," even though the family is obviously Jewish. "The Jews" often appears in John when the Synoptics speak of the chief priests, the Pharisees, and the Sanhedrin authorities (also cf. Jn 11.47 with

18.14); it may be said that for John "the Jews" refers to the Jewish authorities, especially those in Jerusalem, who are hostile to Jesus. Why does the evangelist give them a title that is clearly anachronistic in the ministry of Jesus? By the time of the writing of John, the Jews in general had become hostile to the followers of Jesus. No longer was there a practical hope for the conversion of the Jews, for synagogue and Church were locked in struggle, and a bitter polemic was developing on both sides. By using the title "the Jews" to refer to those who were hostile to Jesus during the ministry, John was associating the Jews of his own time with them as their descendants. Obviously such terminology ill befitted any missionary effort addressed to Palestinian Jews.

However, as R. Schnackenburg has insisted, the general tenor of John toward even the non-Palestinian Jews can scarcely be called missionary. The hostile debates between Jesus and "the Jews" in Jn 5–12 reflect opposite theological positions. Many of the members of the Johannine community would have been ethnic Jews, but they believed that Jesus was the Christ, the Son of God (see Jn 20.30–31), the only one who has come from God to make God known (see Jn 1.18; 3.13–14). Jesus' opponents ("the Jews") will not accept this claim. They have rejected the suggestion that anyone except Moses has made God known (see Jn 9.28–29). For John, "the Jews" represent a closed religious system. For John, Jesus does not "replace" the traditions of Israel. He is the consummate gift of God, perfecting the former gift of the Law, given through Moses (see Jn 1.16–17). This is most clear in that section of the Gospel where the conflict between Jesus and "the Jews" is most intense, Jn 5–10. Jesus does not abolish the Jewish celebrations of Sabbath (Jn 5), Passover (Jn 6), Tabernacles (Jn 7.1–10.21), and Dedication (Jn 10.22–39). The theology, language, and ritual of the Jewish celebrations are rendered christological, and thus perfected in Jesus Christ. This is the root of the conflict between Jesus and "the Jews" (see Moloney, *Signs and Shadows*).

Encouragement to Jewish Christians. There is one exception that fits in with this picture of a general polemic against hostile Judaism. Before the destruction of the Temple, official Judaism had tolerated Jewish Christians within the synagogue. In the decades following the Jewish War, and into the 2d century, there was a gradual parting of the ways between two pre-war Jewish sects: Pharisaic Judaism and Christian Judaism. It has long been claimed that a formal curse against Christians was recited publicly as part of the Eighteen Benedictions, so that failure to pronounce it would betray a Jew of Christian leanings. Under the leadership of Gamaliel II at Jamnia, it has been claimed that this blessing was used to eliminate Jews who accepted Jesus as the Messiah from the Synagogue (J. L. Martyn; R. E. Brown). Recent scholarship has shown that this so-called "blessing" (*birkat ha-minim*) cannot be reconstructed as a direct attack upon the Christians. Nor can it be clearly associated with Gamaliel II (P. van der Horst). It is also clear that in some places Jews and Christians continued a close association well into the 2d century (J. M. Lieu). Nevertheless, behind the Gospel of John lies an experience of expulsion (see Jn 9:22; 12:42; 16:2, where the Greek word ἀπέλαση is found). There is no need to link this with any formal post-war decision from the Jewish leadership at Jamnia. However local the parting of the ways over the christological claims made for Jesus by the Christians, the pain of separation from the Synagogue is still felt by the readers of the Gospel of John. Undoubtedly many of the Jewish Christians were torn between their ties to their brethren and their faith in Jesus. It is most probable that one of the principal purposes of the fourth Gospel was to encourage such Jewish Christians. The arrangement of the first part of the Gospel is designed to show them that, although they leave Judaism, they have in Jesus a perfection of all that they hold dear by way of institutions and feasts. In the Gospel narratives those who believe in Jesus are distinguished from the hostile "Jews," and indeed the blind man in ch. 9 is a hero who is excommunicated from the synagogue for his faith (9.22, 34). On two other occasions, John anachronistically mentions excommunication (12.42; 16.2), showing that it was a major issue when the Gospel was being written. In 12.42–43 we have a criticism of those who believe in Jesus but are afraid to confess it publicly for fear of the Jews, and in 19.38 we see how Joseph and Nicodemus overcome their fear and acknowledge their adherence to Jesus' cause. The Gospel was written, in part, to help the Jewish Christians at the end of the century to do likewise.

Encouragement to Christians in General. The purpose of the Gospel is expressed in Jn 20.31: "That you may believe that Jesus is the Messiah, the Son of God, and that believing you may have life in his name." If the first half of this statement reflects some of the apologetic motifs we have seen above, the second half shows a desire to confirm those who already believe in Jesus. By the time John was written, there was a well-organized Christian community with a sacramental and liturgical life. What was the connection between all of this and Jesus of Nazareth? Was He merely a figure of historical interest who had founded a religion that now stood on its own? The fourth Gospel is a resounding "no" to this question. Its message is that Jesus is as vital a source of life to His followers at the end of the century as He was when He walked through Palestine. Only through belief in Him can a man have eternal life; the Church exists not as a substitute for Jesus but as a community rooted in belief in

Jesus. The Johannine image for the Church is the vine and branches (ch. 15), for the branches cannot live apart from the vine, which is Jesus. John recognizes a sacramental system, but he shows that the Sacraments are ways in which Jesus gives life. During His lifetime His miracles were signs of life-giving activity; in the Gospel John often gives these miraculous signs a secondary sacramental import to show that Sacraments have taken the place of miracles as life-giving acts. In ch. 3 the suggestion that sight and entry into the Kingdom can only take place by means of the spirit and water has baptismal background. Ch. 6 the multiplication of the loaves symbolizes the Eucharist. Similar sacramental background is found in the gift of the blood and water in 19:34–35.

A particular aspect of rooting the life of the Church in Jesus is seen in the presentation of the PARACLETE (ch. 14–16). The Apostolic generation was dying out, and this was producing a crisis in the Church (2 Pt 3.4). Without those who had been eyewitnesses commissioned to preach Jesus, how would Jesus' presence be kept alive in the Church? The other NT writings know of the Spirit as a charismatic force, of the Spirit's role at Baptism, etc.; but it is John above all that shows the Paraclete as the continuation of Jesus' activity in the Church. The key to the Paraclete passages in John is that the activities predicated of the Paraclete have previously been predicated of Jesus, so that the Paraclete is the answer to how Jesus will remain active in the Church when the last human links in the chain of eyewitnesses connecting the Church to Jesus have been broken. Jesus has given His Spirit to the Church to teach, to guide, to be with it forever.

The Johannine emphasis on realized eschatology can also be understood against this background of Church life. As the apostolic generation died out, the failure of Jesus to return became a problem. Many had understood that this generation would not die out before Jesus returned (Mt 24.34), and there seems to have been a special hope that Jesus would return before John died (Jn 21.22–23). Without ever losing the primitive hope of the return of Jesus, John has its own solution to the problem: an emphasis on the fact that many of the things that Christians expected at the end of time were already here, at least in part. There was no need to wait for the second coming in order to face judgment, or to receive eternal life (3.18–21; 5.24–25), or to become children of God, since human beings were already begotten from above through the Spirit at Baptism (3.5), or even to have the presence of Jesus, since he was among them in His Paraclete. In these aspects and in many others the Gospel is a great work of theology, developing a historical tradition about the words and deeds of Jesus in order to give new depth to the faith and life of Christians.

Encouragement for the Gentiles. In particular, John shows the Gentile Christians that their conversion was part of God's plan in sending His Son. By the use of irony, Jn 7.35 hints that ultimately Jesus will go to the Gentiles (''the Greeks'') to teach them. In 10.16 there is an insistence that the Good Shepherd will lay down His life for sheep that are not of the fold of Israel in order to bring them into His flock. By unconscious prophecy, Caiphas (11.52) predicts that Jesus will die not only for the nation of Israel, but for all God's scattered children. Finally, the public ministry of Jesus reaches its climax when, after He has been rejected by the Jews, the whole world begins to come to Him (12.19) and the Gentiles seek after Him (12.20–21). This is the sign that the hour of His glorification has come (12.23); and when in that hour He is lifted up on the cross in return to His Father, He draws all men to Himself (12.32). This theme of ''gathering'' is symbolically acted out at the cross. There Jesus gives the Beloved Disciple to his Mother, and vice-versa. As he dies, he gives the Spirit, blood and water to the new community, standing at the foot of the cross (19:25–37)

Date of writing. The plausible range for the dating of John has narrowed according to recent scholarly views, and a range between A.D. 90 and 110 has the widest following. It is to be stressed that this is a range for the actual writing of John in its final, complete form; as has been seen, the basic tradition behind John may have taken its form earlier, and some parts of John may have been written long before the final form.

Latest Date. The latest plausible date is *c.* 110. The arguments formerly proposed for a late 2d-century dating (A. Loisy, 150–160) have lost their force, e.g., the proposed similarities between John and Gnosticism, the dependency of John on the Synoptics. One argument for late dating must be discussed, namely, that John was not known by any early 2d-century writer. It is quite clear that after *c.* 170 John was known to Tatian, Theophilus of Antioch, Irenaeus, and others. The discussion about the earlier part of the century is centered around Ignatius of Antioch and Justin. J. W. Sanders, followed by Barrett, questions whether these authors used John; but in detailed studies, C. Maurer and J. S. Romanides strongly maintain dependence on John. In the most complete study ever done on the use of John in the 2d century, F. M. Braun finds ample reason to affirm that John was accepted in orthodox circles in Egypt, Rome, Syria, and Asia Minor from the early years of the century.

Although the arguments for late dating have now lost their force, new arguments for early dating have appeared. In 1935 C. H. Roberts published an Egyptian papyrus fragment (P[52]) of John ch. 18 that is dated between 135 and 150. Since few scholars think that John was composed in Egypt or that this papyrus was the autograph, one must allow time between the writing of John and its wide circulation in Egypt. Papyrus Egerton 2, a composite work of *c.* 150 drawing on both John and the Synoptics, is another mid-century Egyptian witness to John. There are two long papyri texts of John from the end of the 2d century in the Bodmer collection (P[60,75]). Since these reflect different textual traditions (P[66] is closer to Codex Sinaiticus; P[75] is closer to Codex Vaticanus), one must allow time between the writing of John and this development. All these witnesses make a date of much later than 110 for the Johannine autograph very unlikely.

The positing of an independent historical tradition for John has also led to an earlier dating. This tradition must have come out of Palestine not much later than 70, for the flight of the Christian community from Palestine during the first Jewish revolt and the thoroughness of the destruction at that time make it unlikely that material for a genuine historical tradition could have been gathered after that date. Working on probabilities, we may suppose that the author composed or collected his tradition in Palestine before 70, or outside Palestine within a generation after 70. If we allow another generation for editorial process, we reach a date of *c.* 110 at the latest for final writing.

Earliest Date. The earliest plausible date is less certain, but it is probably *c.* 90. There have been some suggestions (W. F. Albright, E. R. Goodenough) of a very early date, before 70. Recently, J. A. T. Robinson has claimed that John was the first of the Gospels, written well before the fall of Jerusalem. Too early a date cannot be reconciled with the literary process posited from internal analysis. The argument from silence for an early date is weak; e.g., Goodenough argues that John 7.42 betrays ignorance of the virginal birth of Jesus at Bethlehem, and that therefore John is earlier than Matthew or Luke. In 7.42 we probably have an example of Johannine irony in which, as in 4.12, the speakers in their ignorance actually formulate a true statement about Jesus. Similarly, Robinson claims that the words of the chief priests and the Pharisees in 11.48 show that the Romans had not yet destroyed the holy place and the nation. This is also typical Johannine irony. They decide to slay Jesus (see 11.53), but as the Gospel is read and heard in a Christian community, the holy place and the nation have been destroyed by the Romans, and the risen Jesus is alive.

One internal argument that is helpful for determining the earliest plausible date for John is the question of the expulsion from the synagogue mentioned above. The experience of the Johannine Christians evidenced by 9.22, 12.42, and 16.2 may not have been universal, but the gradual parting of the ways between two pre-war Jewish sects does seem to have been an active issue before the mid-80s. No date before 90 seems likely. The plausible range of 90 to 110 thus arrived at agrees with the earliest tradition (Irenaeus) that John was written as the last of the Gospels, during the reign of Trajan (98–117).

Authorship of the Fourth Gospel

External attestation. In this discussion we note that the concept of authorship in antiquity was broader than our modern identification of author and writer. For the ancients, attribution of a work to an author did not preclude a free use of secretaries, editors, and schools of writers. The author is the man who stands behind the tradition. The major tradition that has come down within the Christian Church is that the author of this Gospel was John, son of Zebedee, who published it in his last years at Ephesus. This tradition is found at the end of the 2d century in Irenaeus (*Adv.haer.* 3.1.1.), the Muratorian Canon, Clement of Alexandria, and others. The evidence of Irenaeus is important because he claims to have it from Polycarp of Smyrna, who knew John; but this evidence is contested in four grounds. First, there is a curious silence about John's presence at Ephesus in works where one might expect to find it mentioned: Paul to the Ephesians, Ignatius to the Ephesians, Polycarp's writing, the life of Polycarp, and Papias.

Second, Irenaeus might have been wrong about Polycarp's relation to John the Apostle. He says (*Adv.haer.* 5.33.4) that Papias heard John, but Papias himself does not confirm this. Was there another John whom both Papias and Polycarp knew? It should be noted that Irenaeus claims to have known Polycarp but not Papias. Third, there is a tradition that John the Apostle died early. It is found in a late extract of Philip of Side (430), in George Hamartolus (9th century), and in some 5th- and 6th-century martyrologies. It probably results from an overliteral interpretation of Mk 10.39 and from a confusion of names (John the Baptist with John of Zebedee; James, the brother of the Lord, with James of Zebedee).

Fourth, it has been suggested that it was another John at Ephesus who wrote the Gospel—Elder, or Presbyter, John. Papias (Eusebius, *Hist. Eccl.* 3.39.4) says that he got information about Christian origins from the sayings of the elders: what Andrew, Peter, Philip, Thomas, James, *John,* and Matthew said—clearly members of the Twelve; what the disciples (of the Lord), Aristion and *Elder John,* say. The difference of tenses seems to indicate that the first group was dead and the second group alive when Papias made the inquiry (100–140). That there were two Johns involved is the most obvious meaning. Later, Dionysius of Alexandria and Eusebius, in their desire to remove the Apocalypse with its MILLENARIAN-ISM from the canon of the Scriptures, attributed it, but not the fourth Gospel, to Elder John. (For the presbyter, or elder, of 2 and 3 John in relation to the Gospel, *see* JOHN, EPISTLES OF ST.).

In summation, Irenaeus's evidence is not infallible, but it is still far from disproved. There were ancient denials of apostolic origin for John on the part of some anti-Montanists and of the ALOGOI. But these were sectarians who disliked John's doctrine, and they are no witness to any widespread doubt in the Church about Johannine authorship.

Internal Evidence. Was Irenaeus right? It is impossible to give a certain answer. The majority of contemporary scholars do not regard it as a significant question. Most who have pursued the matter conclude that the author was a founding figure in the community, probably a disciple of Jesus, but not the son of Zebedee or one of the Twelve Apostles. John the Evangelist fails to pay any attention to the term "apostle" in the technical sense, favoring the use of the expression "disciple," with a particular focus upon the "Beloved Disciple." Indeed, there is an apparent rivalry between Peter and the Beloved Disciple, unresolved until the addition of ch. 21. There is a complete lack of any sense of apostolic ministry in John, and the only commandments that are found are to love (13.34–35; 15.12, 17) and to believe (14.1, 11, 12). These factors make better sense if the Johannine community could not trace its origins to one of the Twelve —a lack that led Johannine theology to exalt love and belief rather than an apostolic commissioning as the essential factor in the cohesion of the community. This lacuna is remedied by Peter's commissioning as the shepherd in 21:15–19. However, dating the Epistles of John after the Gospel indicates that the lack of more formal institutional authority led to the disintegration of the Johannine community.

From the story of the Gospel itself, however, an interesting anonymous figure emerges. An active character in the story is never named. He is generally called "the other disciple" (see 18.15, 16; 20.3, 4, 8), but eventually becomes "the other disciple... whom Jesus loved" (see 20.2). This is "the Beloved Disciple" (see 13.23; 19.26), the author of the Gospel (21.20, 23, 24). The narrative of the Gospel bears traces of its "author." He was a disciple of Jesus, a founding figure in a community whose Gospel we today call the Gospel of John. His desire to keep his name out of the account of the life of Jesus was respected, even after he had died.

His death is presupposed by 21.20–23. The addendum to the Gospel (ch. 21) provides information about the later situation of the Johannine community. As Peter "follows" Jesus (21.19), he looks back to the Beloved Disciple who is, in turn, following (v. 20). He enquires about the destiny of this other important figure (v. 21). Jesus tells Peter that he is not to concern himself whether or not the Beloved Disciple will live on until Jesus returns (v. 22), but the narrator then adds a further explanatory comment to the words of Jesus (v. 23). Jesus did not say that the Beloved Disciple would not die, but that whether or not he would die was not Peter's concern. This comment is called for because "the rumor spread in the community that this disciple would not die" (v. 23), but that is not exactly what Jesus had said. The community had to be taught exactly what Jesus meant. What was the problem? The Beloved Disciple was no longer alive as ch. 21 was being written, and his death had to be explained.

The weight of the evidence, briefly summarized above, is against the Beloved Discple and Apostle John being one and the same figure, but it should not worry us that we cannot be certain. The authority of the Gospel of John comes from its message, not from the apostolicity of its author. The important thing about the Gospel is that it has stood the test of time. After two thousand years of Christian history we continue to read this life-story of Jesus. The author (see 21.24) was diligent in keeping his name out of the story, even when it appears that he may have been an active participant (see 1.35–40; 13.23–25; 18.15–16; 19.25–27; 20.2, 3, 8; 21.7, 20, 24). Oceans of scholarly ink have been spilt attempting to put it back again. Perhaps the ultimate fruitlessness of the search for certainty should teach us to respect the desire of the original author, and respect the work he has left us.

Outline of the Gospel. Outlines of John are notoriously unsatisfactory because, while there are broadly defined sections and themes, the sections overlap and the themes are stated briefly, left, and then picked up again and further developed later in the narrative. Many rich themes are merely stated, and not thoroughly worked through. The Gospel of John contains a great deal of "self-contained allusiveness" (E. C. Hoskyns).

Many outlines or structures of the Gospel of John are determined by scholarly discussion of the sources behind the Gospel, or the way various redactional stages have shaped the material. The following outline is determined by the belief that, whatever the sources and the redaction history of the Gospel, the finished product is to be read as a coherent narrative and theological unity.

I. THE PROLOGUE (1.1–18). This hymn informs the reader of who Jesus is (pre-existent Logos become flesh in the person of Jesus the Christ, the perfection of God's gifts to humankind, the unique revelation of God who brings life to all who believe in him). Armed with this knowledge, unavailable to the characters in the story, the reader is called into judgment as each encounter between Jesus and those characters takes place.

II. THE BOOK OF SIGNS (1.19–12.50). The public ministry of Jesus is told. In this section of the Gospel, Jesus calls and forms disciples, teaches, works miracles, encounters opposition, and challenges the characters in the story, and especially the reader of the story.

A. The first days of Jesus (1.19–51). Set within a context of four days (see vv. 24–28, 29–34, 35–42, 43–51), John the Baptist gives witness to Jesus over the first two days, and the first disciples move toward Jesus, expressing partially correct faith. They are finally challenged by Jesus to a deeper faith, and promised the sight of "greater things" (vv. 50–51).

B. From Cana to Cana (2.1–4.54). Framed between two Cana miracles (2.1–12; 4.43–54), and marked by two comments (2.23–25; 4.31–38), a series of episodes tell of a variety of responses to Jesus. These responses serve as examples of false, partial, and perfect faith, first among Jews, and then from the Samaritans.
1. The first miracle at Cana (2.12)
2. Jesus and "the Jews" (2.12–22)
3. The narrator's comment on faith (2.23–25)
4. Jesus and Nicodemus (3.1–21)
5. Jesus and John the Baptist (3.22–36)
6. Jesus and the Samaritan woman I (4.1–15)
7. Jesus and the Samaritan woman II (4.16–30)
8. Jesus comments on his mission (4.31–38)
9. Jesus and the Samaritan villagers (4.39–42)
10. The second miracle at Cana

C. The feasts of "the Jews" (5.1–10.42). Within a context of increasing hostility, Jesus claims to perfect the Jewish celebrations of Sabbath, Passover, Tabernacles, and Dedication.
1. Jesus and the Sabbath (5.1–47)
2. Jesus and the Passover (6.1–71)
3. Jesus and Tabernacles I (7.1–8.59)
4. Jesus and Tabernacles II (9.1–10.21)
5. Jesus and Dedication (10.22–42)

D. Jesus turns toward "the hour" (11.1–12.50). The resurrection of Lazarus triggers the decision that Jesus must die for the nation, and not only for the nation, but to gather into one the children of God who are scattered. The arrival of the final Passover is noted as Jesus is anointed, enters Jerusalem, is sought by the Greeks, and makes a final attempt to have "the Jews" walk in the light of his revelation of God on the cross.
1. A resurrection that will lead to death (11.1–54)

2. The hour has come (11.55–12.36)

3. Conclusion of the ministry and the Book of Signs

III. THE BOOK OF GLORY (13.1–20.29). The second half of the Gospel moves toward the fulfillment of Jesus' promise that he would be "lifted up" (see 3.14; 8.28; 12.32–33) on a cross. In Johannine theology, this act of self-gift is a consummate act of love (see 15.13) and is thus the time and the place where the glory of God can be seen, and the means by which the Son of God is glorified (see 11.4). The focus on "glory" emerges from the events, discourses, and prayer of Jesus' final evening with the disciples, and then from the unique Johannine narrative of Jesus' death and resurrection.

A. The last discourse (13.1–17.26). This carefully constructed description of events and words of Jesus from his last night with the disciples states and re-states themes around the command to love (15.12–17), in the midst of rejection and hated (15.1–11, 15.18–16.3).

1. Making God known: the footwashing and the morsel (13.1–38)

2. Living after Jesus' departure (14.1–31)

3. To abide, to love, and to be hated (15.1–16.3)

4. Living after Jesus' departure (16.4–33)

5. Making God known: Jesus' final prayer (17.1–26)

B. The Passion (18.1–19.42). A further carefully constructed narrative tells the traditional story of the arrest, trials, crucifixion, death, and burial of Jesus, but it focuses upon this moment is Jesus' royal enthronement, making God known and establishing a community.

1. Jesus and his enemies in a garden (18.1–11)

2. Jesus' appearance before "the Jews" (18.12–27)

3. Jesus before Pilate (18.28–19.16a)

4. The crucifixion of Jesus(19.16b–37)

5. Jesus buried in a garden with his new-found friends (19.38–42)

C. The Resurrection (20.1–29). Scenes at the tomb, and then in the house return to the faith response of those who encounter Jesus (see 2.1–4.54)

1. Scenes at the tomb (20.1–18)

   a. Visits to the empty tomb (20.1–10)

   b. Jesus appears to Mary Magdalene (20.11–18)

2. Scenes in the house

   a. Jesus appears to the disciples, but not Thomas (20.19–23)

   b. Jesus appears to the disciples, including Thomas (20.24–29)

IV. THE CONCLUSION TO THE GOSPEL (20.30–31)

V. EPILOGUE: Further resurrection appearances deal with matters left unresolved by the original Gospel: who belongs to the community of Jesus, and the respective roles of Peter and the Beloved Disciple (21.1–25)

1. The miraculous draft of fishes on the Sea of Tiberias (21.1–14)

2. Jesus, Peter, and the Beloved Disciple (21.15–24)

3. A second conclusion to the Gospel (21:25)

Bibliography: General. Commentaries: C. K. BARRETT, *The Gospel According to St. John* (2d ed. London 1978). J. H. BERNARD, *A Critical and Exegetical Commentary on the Gospel According to St. John,* 2 v. (*International Critical Commentary,* New York 1929). G. R. BEASLEY-MURRAY, *John* (*Word Biblical Commentary* 36, Waco, Tx. 1987). J. BECKER, *Das Evangelium des Johannes,* 2 v. (*Ökumenischer Taschenbuchkommentar zum Neuen Testament 4/1–2,* Gütersloh and Würzburg 1979–1981). R. BULTMANN, *The Gospel of John: A Commentary,* tr. G. R. BEASLEY-MURRAY (Oxford 1971). T. L. BRODIE, *The Gospel According to John: A Literary and Theological Commentary* (New York 1993). R. E. BROWN, *The Gospel According to John,* 2 v. (Anchor Bible 29–29a, New York 1966–1970). D. A. CARSON, *The Gospel According to John* (Grand Rapids, Mich. 1991). E. HAENCHEN, *John 1–2,* 2 v. (Philadelphia, Pa. 1984). E. C. HOSKYNS, *The Fourth Gospel* (2d ed. London 1947). R. H. LIGHTFOOT, *St. John's Gospel: A Commentary* (Oxford 1956). B. LINDARS, *The Gospel of John* (New Century Bible, London 1972). F. J. MOLONEY, *The Gospel of John* (Sacra Pagina 4, Collegeville, Minn. 1998). R. SCHNACKENBURG, *The Gospel According to St. John,* 3 v. (London/New York 1968–82). U. SCHNELLE, *Das Evangelium nach Johannes* (Theologischer Handkommentar zum Neuen Testament 4, Leipzig 1998). M. W. G. STIBBE, *John* (Readings: A New Biblical Commentary, Sheffield 1993). Other Studies: R. E. BROWN, *The Community of the Beloved Disciple* (New York 1979). C. KOESTER, *Symbolism in the Fourth Gospel* (Minneapolis, Minn. 1995). R. KYSAR, *The Fourth Evangelist and His Gospel: An Examination of Contemporary Scholarship* (Minneapolis, Minn. 1975). R. KYSAR, "The Fourth Gospel: A Report on Recent Research," in W. HAASE and H. TEMPORINI, eds., *Aufstieg und Niedergang der römischen Welt Teil II: Principat. Religion* (Berlin 1979–) 25:2389–2480. M. LABAHN, *Jesus als Lebenspender. Untersuchungen zu einer Geschichte der johanneischen Tradition anhand ihrer Wundergeschichten* (Beihefte zue Zeitschrift für die neutestamentliche Wissenschaft 98, Berlin 1999). W. LANGBRANDTNER, *Weltferner Gott oder Gott der Liebe. Der Ketzerstreit in der johanneischen Kirche. Eine exegetisch-religionsgeschichtliche Untersuchung mit Berücksichtigung der koptisch-gnostischen Texte aus Nag-Hammadi* (Beiträge zue biblischen Exegese und Theologie 6, Bern 1977). F. J. MOLONEY, *The Johannine Son of Man* (2d ed. Biblioteca di Scienze Religiose 14, Rome 1978); "Where Does One Look? Reflections on Some Recent Johannine Scholarship." *Salesianum* 62 (2000) 223–251. C. NIEMAND, *Die Fusswashungserzählung des Johannesevangeliums. Untersuchungen zur ihrer Entstehung und Überlieferung im Urchristentum* (Studia Anselmiana 114, Rome 1993). J. PAINTER, *The Quest for the Messiah: The History, Literature and Theology of the Fourth Gospel* (2d ed. Edinburgh 1993). U. SCHNELLE, *Antidocetic Christology in the Gospel of John: An Investigation of the Place of the Fourth Gospel in the Johannine School* (Minneapolis, Minn. 1992). M. W. G. STIBBE, *John as Storyteller: Narrative Criticism and the Fourth Gospel* (Society for New Testament Studies Supplement Series 73, Cambridge 1992). On the unity of the Gospel. E. SCHWEI-

ZER, *Ego eimi* (Göttingen 1939). E. RUCKSTUHL, *Die literarische Einheit des Johannes-evangeliums* (Fribourg 1951). B. NOACK, *Zur Johanneische Tradition* (Copenhagen 1954). D. M. SMITH, *Johannine Christianity. Essays on Its Setting, Sources, and Theology* (Columbia 1984); M.-É. BOISMARD, "S. Luc et la rédaction du Quatrième Évangile," *Revue biblique* 69 (1962) 185–211. D. M. SMITH, *The Composition and Order of the Fourth Gospel* (New Haven, Conn. 1965). On historical tradition in the Gospel. P. GARDINER-SMITH, *Saint John and the Synoptic Gospels* (Cambridge, Eng. 1938). C. H. DODD, *Historical Tradition in the Fourth Gospel* (Cambridge, Eng. 1963). R. E. BROWN, "The Qumrân Scrolls and the Johannine Gospel and Epistles," *Catholic Biblical Quarterly* 17 (1955) 403–419, 559–574; "The Problem of Historicity in John," *ibid.* 24 (1962) 1–14; D. M. SMITH, *John Among the Gospels: The Relationship in Twentieth-Century Research* (Columbia, S.C. 2001). J. P. MEIER, *A Marginal Jew: Rethinking the Historical Jesus,* 2 v. (New York 1991–1994). F. J. MOLONEY, "The Fourth Gospel and the Jesus of History." *New Testament Studies* 46 (2000) 42–58. On influences on the fourth Gospel. H. ODEBERG, *The Fourth Gospel Interpreted in Its Relation to Contemporaneous Religious Currents in Palestine and the Hellenistic-Oriental World* (Chicago, Ill. 1960, reprint of 1929 edition). R. H. STRACHAN, *The Fourth Gospel: Its Significance and Environment* (London 1941). F. M. BRAUN, *Jean le théologien,* v. 1 (Paris 1959) treats subject of John and Gnosticism, v. 2 (1964) treats subject of John and Judaism. C. H. DODD, *The Interpretation of the Fourth Gospel* (Cambridge, Eng. 1960), esp. 3–130. G. QUISPEL, "L'Évangile de Jean et la Gnose," *L'Évangile de Jean* (Louvain 1958) 197–208. R. E. BROWN, "The Gospel of Thomas and St. John's Gospel," *New Testament Studies* 9 (1962–63) 155–177; H. KOESTER, "The History of Religions School, Gnosis and the Gospel of John," *Studia Theologica* 40 (1986) 115–36; K.-W. TRÖGER, "Ja oder Nein zur Welt. War der Evangelist Christ order Gnostiker?" *Theologische Versuche* 7 (1976) 61–80; M. J. J. MENKEN, *Old Testament Quotations in the Fourth Gospel* (Kampen 1996); A. OBERMANN, *Die christologische Erfüllung der Schrift im Johannesevangelium. Eine Untersuchung zur johanneischen Hermeneutik anhand der Schriftzitate* (*Wissenschaftliche Untersuchungen zum Neuen Testament 2. Reihe* 83. Tübingen 1996). J. H. CHARLESWORTH, *John and the Dead Sea Scrolls* (New York 1990). On destination and purpose of the Gospel. E. L. ALLEN, "The Jewish Christian Church in the Fourth Gospel," *Journal of Biblical Literature* 74 (1955) 88–92. K. L. CARROLL, "The Fourth Gospel and the Exclusion of Christians from the Synagogues," *Bulletin of the John Rylands Library* 40 (1957) 19–32. J. A. T. ROBINSON, "The Destination and Purpose of St. John's Gospel," *New Testament Studies* 6 (1959–60) 117–131. W. C. VAN UNNIK, "The Purpose of St. John's Gospel," *Studia Evangelica* (1957) 1:382–411. A. WIND, "Destination and Purpose of the Gospel of John," *Novum Testamentum* 14 (1972) 26–69. R. SCHNACKENBURG, "Die Messiasfrage im Johannesevangelium," *N.T. Aufsätze. für J. Schmid* (Regensburg 1963) 240–264. C. K. BARRETT, *The Gospel of John and Judaism* (London 1975). F. MANNS, *L'Évangile de Jean à la lumière du Judaïsm* (*Studia Biblica Franciscani analecta,* Jerusalem 1991). J. ASHTON, "The Identity and Function of the *Ioudaioi* in the Fourth Gospel," *Novum Testamentum* 27 (1985) 40–75. J. L. MARTYN, *History and Theology in the Fourth Gospel* (2d ed. Nashville, Tenn. 1979); F. J. MOLONEY, *Signs and Shadows: Reading John 5–12* (Minneapolis, Minn. 1996). On the date of writing. J. N. SANDERS, *The Fourth Gospel in the Early Church* (Cambridge, Eng. 1943). C. MAURER, *Ignatius von Antiochien und das Johannesevangelium* (Zürich 1949); J. S. ROMANIDES, "Justin Martyr and the Fourth Gospel," *Greek Orthodox Theological Review* 4 (1958–59) 115–134. E. R. GOODENOUGH, "John: A Primitive Gospel," *Journal of Biblical Literature* 64

(1945) 145–182. W. F. ALBRIGHT, *The Archaeology of Palestine* (rev. ed. Baltimore, Md. 1960) 243–249. J. A. T. ROBINSON, *The Priority of John* (London 1985). M. WILES, *The Interpretation of the Fourth Gospel in the Early Church* (Cambridge 1960). J. M. LIEU, *Image and Reality: The Jews in the World of Christians in the Second Century* (Edinburgh 1996). P. W. VAN DER HORST, "The Birkat ha-minim in Recent Research," *The Expository Times* 105 (1994) 363–68. On the authorship of the Gospel. H. P. V. NUNN, *The Authorship of the Fourth Gospel* (Oxford 1952). M. HENGEL, *The Johannine Question* (Philadelphia, Pa. 1989). R. A. CULPEPPER, *John, the Son of Zebedee: The Life of a Legend* (*Studies on Personalities of the New Testament,* Columbia 1994). J. H. CHARLESWORTH, *The Beloved Disciple: Whose Witness Validates the Gospel of John?* (Valley Forge, Pa. 1995)

[R. E. BROWN/F. J. MOLONEY]

JOHN III DUCAS VATATZES, BYZANTINE EMPEROR

In Byzantine Church, St.; b. *c.* end of 12th century; d. Nicaea, Oct. 30, 1254. The son-in-law of Emperor Theodore I Lascaris, he ascended the throne in 1222 at Nicaea, the Byzantine capital during the Latin occupation of Constantinople (1204–61). After the death of his first wife, he married Constance (Anne), daughter of the German Emperor FREDERICK II. Throughout much of his reign he carried on unionistic negotiations with Rome, chiefly with the object of recovering Constantinople. Generally considered one of the greatest of the Byzantine emperors, he pursued an effective economic policy and made significant territorial gains, largely at the expense of the Latins, all of which led to a regeneration of the empire and prepared the way for the reconquest of Constantinople. His interest in learning and his charitable measures made him so popular that soon after his death he was honored as St. John the Merciful.

Feast: Nov. 4.

Bibliography: H. G. BECK, *Kirche und theologische Literatur im byzantinischen Reich* (Munich 1959) 672–674. F. DÖLGER, *Corpus der griechischen Urkunden des Mittelalters und der neueren Zeit,* series A, *Regesten* (Munich 1924–32) 3:1709–1822. *Bibliotheca hagiographica Graeca,* ed. F. HALKIN, 3 v. (Brussels 1957) 1:34–35. G. OSTERGORSKY, *History of the Byzantine State,* tr. J. HUSSEY, from 2d German ed. (Oxford 1956) 386–395.

[G. T. DENNIS]

JOHN, KING OF ENGLAND

Reigned 1199 to Oct. 19, 1216; b. Oxford, England, Dec. 24, 1167; d. Newark, England. The youngest son of King HENRY II of England and Eleanor of Aquitaine, he was called John Lackland since his father did not at first grant him an appanage on the Continent. Upon the death

John, King of England, engraving. (©UPI/CORBIS)

of his brother King RICHARD I the Lion–Hearted, John became King of England and lord of the ''Angevin empire'' in France, even though his young nephew Arthur had by right of primogeniture a stronger claim to the throne. John eventually had Arthur murdered (1203).

John's marriage in 1200 to Isabella of Angoulême, who was betrothed to Hugh of Lusignan, led to a judicial action initiated by the Lusignans at the court of King PHILIP II AUGUSTUS, their common suzerain in France. This action resulted in open warfare between John and his feudal overlord (Philip) and John's ultimate forfeiture and loss of NORMANDY as well as of the Angevin possessions on the Continent (roughly Brittany, the Loire country, and Aquitaine) to the French Crown. After the death of Abp. HUBERT WALTER (1205) a disputed election to Canterbury was settled in Rome by Pope INNOCENT III, who chose STEPHEN LANGTON for the see. This led to a quarrel between Innocent and John when the King refused to recognize Langton. After two years of dispute Innocent placed England under interdict; then in 1209 he excommunicated the King. In 1212 he deposed him, released his subjects from their oath of allegiance, and threatened to elect a new king. Philip Augustus was already preparing an invasion of England to execute the papal sentence when John, faced with the united opposition of Innocent, Philip Augustus, and various of his own dissatisfied bar-

ons, decided to capitulate to the Pope. He submitted to the papal demands on May 12, 1213, and three days later accepted the Kingdom of England as a fief of the Apostolic See in return for an annual tribute to his new suzerain. While this capitulation earned him the future protection of the Pope and undermined both the Capetian justification for aggression and the baronial justification for rebellion, it did not reconcile the barons to John's despotic government and arbitrary scutages, or to his military ineptitude, which led to the brilliant French victory at Bouvines in 1214. In June 1215 a considerable number of barons, with the moral support of Langton, met the King in arms at Runnymede and exacted his agreement to MAGNA CARTA, which severely limited his exercise of the royal authority and placed the Crown under the control of an oligarchic committee of his vassals. John, however, as a papal vassal, enjoyed the support of Innocent III, who annulled Magna Carta. In the course of the civil war precipitated by this maneuver and the French invasion that followed in its wake, King John died of a surfeit of peaches, leaving the throne and the confusion to his young son, King HENRY III of England.

Bibliography: GERVASE OF CANTERBURY, *Gesta Regum,* ed. W. STUBBS [*Rerum Britannicarum medii aevi scriptores,* 244 v., 73.2. (1879)]. RALPH OF COGGESHALL, *Chronicon Anglicanum,* ed. J. STEVENSON [*Rerum Britannicarum medii aevi scriptores,* 244 v., 66, (1875)]. WALTER OF COVENTRY, *Memoriale,* ed. W. STUBBS, 2 v. [*Rerum Britannicarum medii aevi scriptores,* 244 v., (1872, 1873)]. ROGER OF WENDOVER, *Flores Historiarum,* v. 1–3 of *Chronica Majora,* ed. H. R. LUARD [*Rerum Britannicarum medii aevi scriptores,* 244 v., 57, (1872–83)]. *Annales Monastici,* ed. H. R. LUARD, 5 v. [*Rerum Britannicarum medii aevi scriptores,* 244 v., 36, (1864–69)] v.1 *De Margam, Theokesberia, et Burton,* v.3. *De Dunstaplia et Bermundeseia.* K. NORGATE, *John Lackland* (London 1902). Z. N. BROOKE, *The English Church and the Papacy from the Conquest to the Reign of John* (Cambridge, Eng. 1931). C. E. PETIT–DUTAILLIS, *The Feudal Monarchy in France and England . . . ,* tr. E. D. HUNT (New York 1964). S. PAINTER, *The Reign of King John* (Oxford 1949). A. L. POOLE, *From Domesday Book to Magna Carta, Oxford History of England,* ed. G. N. CLARK, 14 v. (2d ed. Oxford 1955) 3. J. T. APPLEBY, *John, King of England* (New York 1959). W. L. WARREN, *King John* (New York 1961).

[J. BRÜCKMANN]

JOHN III SOBIESKI, KING OF POLAND

Reigned 1674 to 1696; b. Olesko, Galicia, June 2, 1624; d. Wilanow, June 17, 1696. Through his mother, he inherited the Zolkiewski fortune; through his father, the enormous Sobieski estates. He was one of the wealthiest nobles in Poland. Later, he augmented his fortune through his marriage to Marie Kazimiera d' Arquien, the widow of John Zamoyski. After completing his education on his family estates and at the University of Cracow, he traveled widely in western and southern Europe. He fought in the Cossack insurrection (1648) and helped expel the Swedes from Poland. He was rapidly advanced in the army for his services to King John Casimir and in 1665 became the commander in chief. His first exploit in the latter capacity was, with an army raised chiefly at his own expense, to suppress an insurrection of the Cossacks who were assisted by the Turks and Tatars. Later he led the Poles against a Turkish invasion, which he turned back with a crowning victory at Chocim (1673) in which the Turks lost some 20,000 men and a great many guns. The coincidental popularity of his victories at the time of King Michael Wisniowiecki's death contributed greatly to his election as king.

Sobieski attempted to strengthen the power of the monarch and to transform Poland into a hereditary monarchy as a way of stemming the decline of the state. He was encouraged in this by his wife, who sought to recast the Polish constitution according to the patterns set by Louis XIV. However, the opposition of the nobility proved too strong for them to overcome. In the end Sobieski failed in his program to reform the constitution.

Sobieski was more successful in his foreign policy. One of his greatest ambitions was the union of Christian Europe in a crusade to drive the Turks out of Europe; he partially realized this through the organization of the Holy League and to this he sacrificed other more specifically Polish interests. When in 1683 the Turks laid siege to Vienna, which the Emperor Leopold had abandoned, Sobieski, at the request of the papal nuncio, gathered a force of some 25,000 Poles and marched to the relief of the city. These troops were joined by some 28,000 troops from the Holy Roman Empire and some 23,000 men raised among the peoples of the Austrian Empire, to form a combined Christian force of some 76,000 men led by Sobieski against the Turks, who were led by Kara Mustapha and whose forces numbered from 115,000 to 210,000 men. On Sept. 12, 1683, he personally led his Polish cavalry in the charge that decided the battle. The resulting relief of Vienna and the liberation of Hungary were the crowning achievements of his career. Henceforth Turkey ceased to be a serious threat to Christian Europe. Sobieski did not see the culmination of the war, however, since he died three years before the Treaty of Karlowitz was signed.

A devout Catholic and a stanch defender of the Church, Sobieski promoted the cause of the Eastern Catholic Church within his realms. At the same time, he spurred on the reform of the Orthodox Church, assisted the Protestants and scrupulously protected the rights of the Jews. After his reign began the long decline that culminated in Poland's partition.

John III Sobieski, King of Poland. (Archive Photos)

Bibliography: J. B. MORTON, *Sobieski, King of Poland* (London 1932). O. HALECKI, *A History of Poland* (3d ed. New York 1961). *Cambridge History of Poland,* v.1., ed. W. F. REDDAWAY et al. (Cambridge, Eng. 1941—). R. DYBOSKI, *Ten Centuries of Poland's History* (Warsaw 1937). A. TAMBORRA, *Enciclopedia cattolica,* ed. P. PASCHINI et al. (Rome 1949–54) 6:598–599.

[E. KUSIELEWICZ]

JOHN III SCHOLASTICUS, PATRIARCH OF CONSTANTINOPLE

Patriarchate: Jan. 31, 565, to 577; pioneer canonist of the Byzantine Church; b. Sirimis, near Antioch, 503 or 525–530; d. Aug. 31, 577. John, son of a cleric, entered the law profession, was ordained rather late in life, and served as *APOCRISIARIUS* for the patriarch of Antioch at Constantinople. He was appointed patriarch of Constantinople by JUSTINIAN I and was consecrated probably on Feb. 1, 565. He succeeded Eutychius, who was exiled for opposing the edict favoring aphthartodocetism. John seems to have accepted the honor on condition that he would not subscribe to the edict until it had been accepted by the other patriarchs, especially by Anastasius of Antioch.

He became a close friend of Justin II, who became emperor on Nov. 14, 565, and he took an active part in the new ruler's efforts to win over the MONOPHYSITES during the first six years of his reign. To cure the schisms within the heretics' ranks first, the patriarch found himself in the curious position of acting for the emperor as arbiter for two groups of heretical bishops, the tritheists and other Monophysite sects. When Justin decided on persecution, John was commissioned to carry it out, showing no mercy. But when he consecrated a patriarch for Alexandria, he was reprimanded by the patriarch of Antioch (Theophan., *Conf.* 6062).

While still at Antioch, John had compiled the earliest systematic, Byzantine collection of canons (ecclesiastical legislation) that has been preserved. He used as the basis an anonymous collection of canons under 60 headings prepared in Antioch *c.* 545 with an appendix of 21 laws of emperors on Church matters. John's collection rearranged the work under 50 titles and added 68 canons from those of St. BASIL, as he himself says (Joannis Scholastici, *Synagoga L titulorum* 5.10). After coming to Constantinople, John composed his so-called *Collection of 87 Chapters.* It is a collection of excerpts, some word for word, others summarized, taken from Justinian's *novels* pertaining to ecclesiastical affairs. About 570 John gave both these works a final revision. He also published a Catechetical Treatise or *Mystagogia,* which JOHN PHILOPONUS controverted. Many Byzantinists have attempted to identify John with the chronicler JOHN MALALAS, but E. Stein and V. Beneěevič reject the identification.

Bibliography: H. G. BECK, *Kirche und theologische Literatur im byzantinischen Reich* (Munich 1959) 422–423. A. FLICHE and V. MARTIN, eds., *Histoire de l'église depuis les origines jusqu'à nos jours* (Paris 1935–) v. 4. E. STEIN. *Histoire du Bas-Empire,* translated by J. R. PALANAQUE, 2 v. in 3 (Paris 1949–59) 2:687–689. F. DÖLGER, in *Lexikon für Theologie und Kirche,* ed. J. HOFER and K. RAHNER, 10 v. (2d new ed. Freiburg 1957–65) 5:1080–81. L. PETIT, *Dictionnaire de théologie catholique,* ed. A. VACANT et al., 15 v. (Paris 1903–50; Tables générales 1951–) 8.1:829–831. HERMAN, *Dictionnaire de driot canonique,* ed. R. NAZ, 7 v. (Paris 1935–65) 6:118–120. J. SCHOLASTICUS, *Synagoga L titulorum,* ed. V. BENEŠEVIČ (Munich 1937). E. SCHWARTZ, *Die Kanonessammlung des Johannes Scholastikos* (Munich 1933).

[M. J. HIGGINS]

Scholasticus and appointed *sacellarius* (in the early Byzantine period the official in charge of funds for the care of the poor). He was famous for his asceticism and was chosen to succeed EUTYCHIUS I shortly before the death of Emperor Tiberius II. He was present in his official capacity when Tiberius solemnly proclaimed MAURICE coemperor and successor, and he blessed the wedding of Maurice and Tiberius's daughter. Though Tiberius himself had crowned Maurice when he raised him to the imperial rank, in keeping with customary procedure, when Maurice co-opted his 4-year-old son, Theodosius, it was John the Faster who crowned the boy. This was a most unusual procedure, introduced, no doubt, because the monarch wished to make the succession more secure.

It was the patriarch who, according to John of Nikiu, led the opposition to Maurice's restoration of Chosroes II to the throne of Persia and forced a postponement of longer than a year. When the emperor advocated clemency toward two men accused of sorcery, the patriarch insisted on the death sentence. John, however, is supposed to have favored tolerance of the Monophysites.

Maurice had a very high personal regard for John because of his asceticism and charity; and esteem for the prelate's virtue may have influenced the emperor as much as self-interest when he supported the patriarch against Pope GREGORY I in the dispute over the title "ecumenical." The Byzantine Church canonized John and commemorated him on September 2. Of the various works on Confession ascribed to him, only the sermon on penitence (*Patrologia Graeca,* ed. J. P. MIGNE, 88:1937–78) may be authentic.

Bibliography: THEOPHYLACTUS SIMOCATTES, *Historiae,* ed. C. DE BOOR (BT; 1887) 1.1.2:22; 1.10:2–3; 1.11:14–21; 7.6:1–5. THEOPHANES THE CONFESSOR, *Chronographia,* ed. C. DE BOOR, 2 v. (Leipzig 1883–85) 6074.23–24; 6082.26–27; 6086, cf 6087; 8–10, cf. 28. *Synaxarium ecclesiae Constantinopolitanae. Propylaeum ad Acta sanctorum novembris,* ed. H. DELEHAYE (Brussels 1902) September 2:2. *The Chronicle of John, Bishop of Nikiou,* tr. R. H. CHARLES (London 1916). M. J. HIGGINS, *The Persian War of the Emperor Maurice,* v.1 (Washington 1939) 43–45. H. G. BECK, *Lexikon für Theologie und Kirche,* ed. J. HOFER and K. RAHNER, 10 v. (2d, new ed. Freiburg 1957–65) 5:1065–66.

[M. J. HIGGINS]

JOHN IV THE FASTER, PATRIARCH OF CONSTANTINOPLE

Consecrated April 12, 582; d. Sept. 2, 595. John is known chiefly for his part in the controversy over the title "ecumenical patriarch" (*see* BYZANTINE CHURCH, HISTORY OF). According to the synaxary and the patriarchal lists, he was born in Constantinople, earned his living as a coinmaker, and was ordained deacon by JOHN III

JOHN VII GRAMMATICUS, PATRIARCH OF CONSTANTINOPLE

A leading iconoclastic theologian during the second phase of iconoclasm (815–843); b. Constantinople, *c.* end of 8th century; d. near Constantinople, between 843 and 863. He was of Armenian origin, and his literary talents earned him the name of Grammaticus, although he was often called by other epithets based on his supposed knowledge of magic. He was ordained about 806. His first open attack on the veneration of images came in 813 when the iconoclast Byzantine Emperor LEO V attained the throne. At his request John compiled a handbook of Biblical and patristic texts against the cult of images; it was used in the iconoclastic council of 815, but is no longer extant. Too young to be named patriarch, he was appointed to the palace clergy and took charge of the education of the future Byzantine Emperor THEOPHILUS. Upon the accession of his pupil (829), John was promoted to *syncellus* and was also sent on embassies to Bagdad. On Jan. 21, 837, he was named patriarch and he immediately began a violent persecution of the orthodox, especially among the bishops and well-known monks. The death of Theophilus in January of 842 signaled the end of iconoclasm, and the Empress THEODORA (2) had John deposed. Excommunicated in March 843, he died in prison sometime before 863.

Bibliography: P. J. ALEXANDER, *The Patriarch Nicephorus of Constantinople* (Oxford 1958). V. LAURENT, *Catholicisme* 6: 513–515, with complete bibliography.

[G. T. DENNIS]

JOHN X CAMATEROS, PATRIARCH OF CONSTANTINOPLE

Episcopate: Aug. 5, 1198 to April or May 1206. As chartophylax John was already highly placed in the patriarchal chancery before his accession to patriarch. He was respected for his knowledge of classical literature and proficiency in philosophy and rhetoric. His two letters to Pope Innocent III, written early in his patriarchate (1199 and 1200), focus primarily on the Roman primacy and more briefly on the *FILIOQUE;* they constitute an important addition to the Byzantine Orthodox view that the papal claims to universal primacy were ecclesiastically indefensible.

Rome's primacy, according to the patriarch, was always understood in regional terms and was based historically on the city's political importance as the capital of the empire, rather than on St. Peter. In terms of its relationship to the other churches and patriarchates, Rome was in effect "first in rank as among sisters of equal honor." As we should expect, John's subsequent alleged submission to Innocent (based on the evidence of western sources) is unlikely, given his earlier exegesis of primacy.

The most important of John's synodal decisions concerned the teaching of Michael Glycas who had earlier written against the incorruptibility of the Eucharistic ele-

ments. The synod responded by censuring Glycas posthumously and by repeating the anathema issued by the Church in 1157 on a related Eucharistic controversy. The patriarch's literary output was otherwise modest. A response to several dogmatic questions posed by Narses of Lampron survives as well as a homily on the feast of the Epiphany and three treatises on the procession of the Holy Spirit, addressed in part to Hugh Etherianus of Pisa.

John lived to see the latinization of his church and the dismemberment of the Byzantine Empire by the fourth crusade (April 1204). Theodore I Lascaris, the imperial successor to the Angeli, urged him to join his government at Nicaea but he refused. He died a refugee-exile at Didymoteichon (June 1206).

Bibliography: F.R. GAHBAUER, *Die Pentarchietheorie im Zeitalter des Grossen Schismas* (Frankfurt am Main 1993) 199–208. V. GRUMEL et. al., *Les regestes des Actes du Patriarcat de Constantinople* 8 fascicules (Paris, 1932–79) fasc.3, nos.1193–1204. A. PAPADAKIS and A. TALBOT, "John X Camaterus Confronts Innocent III: An Unpublished Correspondence," *Byzantinoslavica* 33 (1972) 26–41. J. SPITERIS, *La Critica Byzantina del Primato Romano nel secolo XII* (Rome 1979) 248–399, 324–331.

[A. PAPADAKIS]

JOHN XI BECCUS, PATRIARCH OF CONSTANTINOPLE

Artisan of the union of Oriental and Western churches; b. Nicaea between 1230 and 1240; d. St. George, Bithynia, March 1297.

Recipient of an excellent Byzantine education, John became a functionary in the Constantinopolitan patriarchate in 1263 and was named chartophylax (archivist and assistant chancellor) by Patriarch Arsenius (1254–66), then the great skeuophylax or sacristan of the patriarchate. In the dispute between Patriarch Arsenius and Emperor MICHAEL PALAEOLOGUS, Beccus followed Arsenius but eventually was won over to the emperor's side. Michael entrusted him with important diplomatic missions, sending him in 1268 to Kral (King) Stephen Uroš of Serbia, and to St. LOUIS IX at Tunis on the eve of the crusading French king's death (1270).

When Pope GREGORY X accepted the emperor's overtures toward a union of the Greek and Latin Churches and assembled the bishops in a synod to demonstrate the advantages of such a move, Beccus opposed the project and was imprisoned on charges that he eventually proved to be calumnious. In prison, however, he made a study of the Greek and Latin theology, particularly with regard to the FILIOQUE or the double procession of the Holy Spirit from the Father and the Son, in keeping with the opinions of NICEPHORUS Blemmydes. As a consequence he recognized the primacy of the Bishop of Rome as well as the orthodoxy of the filioque and found himself bound in conscience to work for the reunion of the Churches. This union was solemnly proclaimed at the Council of LYONS in 1274 in the presence of Pope Gregory X and the Greek ambassadors. The patriarch of Constantinople opposed the move and abdicated; and John Beccus, returned to imperial favor, was elected patriarch in 1275.

Kindly and charitable, he used his office to care for the poor while working feverishly to have the union achieved at Lyons accepted in the Greek churches; and in a synod, he, with his clergy, abjured the schism, recognized the pope's jurisdiction over the universal Church while respecting Byzantine rites and customs, and admitted the double procession of the Holy Spirit. However, he was opposed by members of his clergy and the imperial family and particularly by the violently anti-Latin monasteries. To counter this opposition he called a second synod in which he excommunicated whoever would not recognize "the Roman Church as mother and head of all the Churches, and the mistress who teaches the orthodox faith."

The demands of Pope NICHOLAS III (1277–80) for an unconditional submission of the Greek Church to Rome provoked a new and grave crisis in the already difficult relations between Rome and Byzantium.

Abandoned by both the emperor and the higher clergy, Beccus abdicated in 1279. He was recalled by the emperor to participate in negotiations relative to the union with ambassadors of the pope; he was reinstated in 1280, but found the task of imposing the union most difficult, particularly when the emperor attempted to achieve it by force. In 1282 Pope MARTIN IV (1281–85) denounced the union for political motives and excommunicated both the emperor and the Greek Church. Michael Palaeologus died that same year, and the rise of ANDRONICUS II and the rupture of relations with Rome forced Beccus to resign once more. He was exiled to Broussa and gave himself over to a violent polemic particularly against his successor, George of Cyprus, who took the name Gregory. At the Synod of Blachernae in 1284 he upheld the double procession of the Holy Spirit and attacked Gregory violently. He was deported to the fortress of St. George on the Gulf of Nicomedia, but continued his attacks on Gregory, eventually securing his abdication (1289). Though reduced to poverty, he steadfastly refused to buy his liberty by compromise and died in exile.

Among his writings, which are mainly polemical and circumstantial, are a letter to Pope John XXI (1277) and another to Pope Nicholas III (1278); a profession of faith;

Epigraphai, or a collection of patristic texts on the procession of the Holy Spirit, later controverted by Gregory PALAMAS; a tract on the peace and union of the ancient and new Roman Churches, which deals with the theological thought of authors of the patristic age and later writers, including PHOTIUS, John Phurnes, and Nicholas of Methone (revised several times); three books on the procession of the Holy Spirit and four books addressed to Constantine Meliteniotes; and *Antirrhetikos* against George Moschampar and one encyclical letter against GREGORY II CYPRIUS. His writings bring a new historical viewpoint into play. Of all the Greek theologians he manifested the greatest erudition and constraining logic in dealing with theological arguments favoring the union of the Churches and the antiquity of the doctrine of the double procession of the Holy Spirit. Spread widely by his followers at the end of the 13th century, his writings occasioned a movement that prepared the way for the reunion at the Council of FLORENCE in 1439.

Bibliography: *Opera omnia, Patrologia Graeca,* ed. J. P. MIGNE, 161 v. (Paris 1857–66) 141. H. LAEMMER, *Scriptorum Graeciae orthodoxae bibliotheca selecta* (Freiburg 1864). L. PETIT, *Dictionnaire de théologie catholique,* ed. A. VACANT et al., 15 v. (Paris 1903–05) 8.1:656–660. L. BRÉHIER, *Dictionnaire d'histoire et de géographie ecclésiastiques,* ed. A BAUDRILLART et al. (Paris 1912—) 7:354–364. V. LAURENT, *Lexikon für Theologie und Kirche,* ed. J. HOFER and K. RAHNER, 10 v. (2d, new ed. Freiburg 1957–65) 5:1008–09. *Échos d'Orient,* 25 (1926) 316–319. H. G. BECK, *Kirche und theologische Literatur im byzantinischen Reich* (Munich 1959) 677–683. J. DRÄSEKE, *Zeitschrift für wissenschaftliche Theologie* NS 15 (1907) 231–253. R. SOUARN, *Échos d'Orient,* 3 (1899) 229–237. D. J. GEANAKOPLOS, *Emperor Michael Palaeologus and the West, 1258–1282* (Cambridge, Mass. 1959). G. HOFMANN, *Orientalia Christiana periodica,* 11 (1945) 141–164.

[L. VEREECKE]

JOHN XIV CALECAS, PATRIARCH OF CONSTANTINOPLE

Flourished 1334 to 1347; b. Apros, Asia Minor, *c.* 1283; d. Constantinople, Dec. 29, 1347. Of a modest family, Calecas entered the Constantinopolitan clergy and was favored by the Grand Domesticus, later Emperor JOHN VI CANTACUZENUS, who selected him for patriarch in 1334 despite the fact that Calecas was married and the father of a family. In 1341 he held a synod that censured BARLAAM OF CALABRIA, and forbade further discussion of the Hesychast question on the light that appeared on Mt. Thabor during the Transfiguration. On the death of ANDRONICUS III (1341), Anne of Savoy became regent for John V Palaeologus. Calecas supported her, and broke with Cantacuzenus, who encouraged the Hesychast monks and Gregory PALAMAS to disobey the orders of the synod of 1341. Calecas held a second synod (1342) that condemned Palamas and imprisoned him. Anne of Savoy attempted to reconcile Calecas and Palamas and, on failing, had Calecas deposed by a synod in February 1347. On taking power in March, Cantacuzenus confirmed the deposition. Calecas was imprisoned and exiled to Didymotichus, but returned to die in Constantinople at the end of the year.

Of John's writings, besides his polemical treatises and encyclical condemning Barlaam (1341), the collection of his disciplinary, dogmatic, and canonical decisions is an important source for the history of the period. The collection of Sunday sermons attributed to him is rather the Homilary of Constantinople begun by Patriarch John IX Agapetus (1111–34) and used by succeeding patriarchs. Accounts of his life by his enemies John Cantacuzenus and Nicephorus Gregoras are prejudicial.

Bibliography: *Patrologia Graeca*, ed. J. P. MIGNE, 161 v. (Paris 1857–66) 150:891–903; 152:1215–84. *Acta et diplomata graeca medii aevi,* eds. F. MIKLOSICH and J. MÖLLER, 6 v. (Vienna 1860–90) 2:168–243. H. G. BECK, *Kirche und theologische Literatur im byzantinischen Reich* (Munich 1959) 728–729. J. M. HOECK, *Lexikon für Theologie und Kirche*, ed. J. HOFER and K. RAHNER, 10 v. (2d, new ed. Freiburg 1957–65) 5:1047–48. J. GOUILLARD, *Dictionnaire d'histoire et de géographie ecclésiastiques*, ed. A. BAUDRILLART et al. (Paris 1912—) 11:378–380. M. JUGIE, *Catholicisme* 2:377–378.

[F. CHIOVARO]

JOHN I, POPE, ST.

Pontificate: Aug. 13, 523 to May 18, 526; b. Tuscany, d. Ravenna. The liquidation of the ACACIAN SCHISM was viewed by the Emperor JUSTIN I and his nephew Justinian as a necessary preliminary step to long–range plans aimed at consolidating and restoring the Roman Empire. A year after the restoration of communion with Rome, an imperial decree closing all Arian churches in Constantinople and dismissing all Arians from employment in the imperial services indicated that a harder line would be followed toward Ostrogothic Italy, since a considerable number of King THEODORIC's coreligionists living in Constantinople had to bear the brunt of the new measure. Theodoric retaliated by altering his policy of conciliation and toleration toward Catholics. Pope John I had been a supporter of Laurentius who had made peace with Symmachus. At the time of his election he was a senior deacon but elderly and infirm. He was summoned to Ravenna to head an embassy to Constantinople to secure a reversal of the imperial policy and to obtain permission for those who had been forcibly converted to Catholicism to revert to Arianism. The pope undertook to plead the first request, but refused the second. He was received in the capital on the Bosporus (Oct. or Nov. 525) with the utmost honors; a large delegation came out as far as the 15th milestone with candles and crosses to greet him, and the emperor prostrated himself before him "as if he were Peter in person." The pope solemnly celebrated Christmas and crowned the emperor once again in a festal coronation. He celebrated Easter (April 19, 526) with great solemnity in HAGIA SOPHIA, in the presence of the patriarch, the clergy, and the imperial court. The pope occupied a throne of honor on the right–hand side of the basilica, above that of the patriarch, and read the prayers aloud in Latin. Pope John remained in Constantinople for five months, successfully negotiating the return of the Arian churches, but was unable to secure satisfaction on the other points demanded by the king, thus making his diplomatic mission a failure, despite all the honors paid to him.

Suspecting that the Roman aristocracy was plotting with Constantinople against him, King Theodoric put two prominent members, the Christian philosopher BOETHIUS and his father-in-law Symmachus, to death as a warning. When Pope John returned to Ravenna, he was imprisoned with his suite and died shortly thereafter, probably from maltreatment (starvation). He was regarded as a martyr and was interred in St. Peter's. The pope brought back with him from Constantinople rich gifts from the Emperor Justin I, which were distributed among the Roman basilicas. In 526 the canonist DIONYSIUS EXIGUUS drew up his Paschal Cycle according to the Alexandrian usage, which Rome had adopted; he began the practice of numbering years from the Incarnation, abandoning the unwieldy custom of designating them according to the era of Diocletian; this new method gradually gained acceptance under the name, the Christian Era.

Feast: May 27.

Bibliography: *Patrologia latina* 63:529–534, spurious letters. *Clavis Patrum latinorum,* ed. E. DEKKERS (Streenbrugge 1961)1685. *Liber pontificalis,* ed. L. DUCHESNE (Paris 1886–1958) 1.275–278; 3:90–91. H. LÖWE, "Theoderich der Grosse und Papst Johann I," *Historisches Jahrbuch der Görres–Gesellschaft* 72 (Munich 1953) 83–100. H. JEDIN, *History of the Church* (New York 1980) 2:625. J. N. D.KELLY, *Oxford Dictionary of Popes* (New York, 1986) 54–55. J. RICHARDS, *Popes and Papacy the Early Middle Ages* (London 1979) 109–113; 118–1120. R. AUBERT, *Dictionnaire d'histoire et de géographie ecclésiastiques,* 26 (Paris 1997). G. SCHWAIGER, *Lexikon für Theologie und Kirche,* 3d. ed. (Freiburg 1996).

[J. CHAPIN]

JOHN II, POPE

Pontificate: Dec. 31, 532 to May 8, 535. The death of Pope BONIFACE II was followed by a vacancy in the papacy of two months, during which attempts were made by all aspirants to bribe their way into the papacy. When the elderly Roman priest Mercurius was finally elected, he took the name of John II. He considered it inappropriate to keep Mercury, the name of a pagan deity, and thus became the first pope to change his name. He obtained from the Gothic king Athalaric confirmation of the decree of the Roman Senate banning simony in papal elections. This is the last known *senatus consultum* of that body and had been enacted a few years earlier. The king ordered it to be engraved on marble and set up in the atrium of St. Peter's. He added a provision that if a disputed election had to be referred for arbitration to Ravenna, the Roman clergy and the people were to be fined 3,000 *solidi,* and the amount would be given to the poor.

In a dogmatic decree defining the faith of Chalcedon, published in 533 after a religious conference in Constantinople, the emperor JUSTINIAN I incorporated the theopaschite formula favored by the Scythian monks, which he had already inserted in the profession of faith found at the beginning of his great code (528). The "sleepless" monks of Constantinople (Acoemeti), the chief opponents among the orthodox to use the formula, felt themselves threatened by the emperor's acts and appealed to the pope. Justinian dispatched his edict to the pope, the Senate, and the Roman people, requesting that the pope approve the formula and condemn the recalcitrant monks, even though Pope Hosmisdas had rejected the formula.

John II attempted to persuade the monks to abandon their opposition, but when this failed, he excommunicated them as Nestorians (March 24, 534). He wrote to the emperor informing him of the fact, and sanctioned use of the formula. The emperor's letter to the pope, *Reddentes honorem* (June 6, 533), was incorporated in the Code of Justinian together with the pope's reply. It contained remarkably deferential language with respect to the Apostolic See, acknowledged as "the head of all the Churches." The emperor was anxious to inform them of "all that concerns the state of the Church." He referred to "the authority of your see," which he claimed that he was eager to increase, and he praised Rome as the center of unity and criterion of orthodoxy. These comments were not incompatible with the looser view of the Roman primacy entertained at Byzantium and generally in the East, as subsequent events demonstrated. John II was in correspondence with St. CAESARIUS OF ARLES regarding Bp. Contumeliosus of Riez in Provence, who was accused of various crimes. The pope ordered him to be confined in a monastery. Pope John was buried in the portico of St. Peter's. Four of his letters are extant.

Bibliography: *Clavis Patrum latinorum,* ed. E. DEKKERS (Streenbrugge 1961) 1692. *Patrologia Latina* ed. J. P. MIGNE (Paris 1878–90) 66:17–32. *Senatus consultum* of 530, E. SCHWARTZ, *Acta conciliorum oecumenicorum* 4.2 (Berlin 1914) 97. *Liber pontificalis,* ed. L. DUCHESNE (Paris 1886–1958) 1:285–286; 3:91. R. U. MONTINI, *Le tombe dei papi* (Rome 1957). E. FERGUSON, ed., *Encyclopedia of Early Christianity* (New York 1997) 1:621. H. JEDIN, *History of the Church* (New York 1980) 2:444–445. J. N. D. KELLY, *Oxford Dictionary of the Popes* (New York 1986) 57–58. J. RICHARDS, *Popes and Papacy in the Early Middle Ages* (London 1979) 126–127. R. AUBERT, *Dictionnaire d'histoire et de géographie ecclésiastiques,* 25 (Paris 1995) s.v. "Innocent, évêque de Maronée en Thrace." R. AUBERT, *Dictionnaire d' histoire et de géographie ecclésiastiques,* 26 (Paris 1997). J. SPEIGL, "Formula Iustinianus. Kircheneinigung mit kaiserlichen Glaubensbekenntnissen (Codex Iustinianus I 1, 5–8)," *Ostkirchliches Studien* 44 (1995) 105–34.

[J. CHAPIN]

JOHN III, POPE

Pontificate: July 17, 561 to July 13, 574. Following the death of PELAGIUS I, Catelinus, son of the *vir illustris* Anastasius, was elected pope, but he had to wait for four months for imperial confirmation before he could be consecrated. The pope took the name John III. During his reign the Lombards invaded Italy. It is not known whether the Byzantine General Narses was responsible for inviting them. His critics said that he did so out of anger over his recall by Emperor JUSTINIAN I at the request of the Italians, who were suffering from his exactions. The withdrawal of Narses facilitated the Lombard conquest of the backbone of the peninsula under King Alboin. One result of the invasion was to hasten the end of the schism over the THREE CHAPTERS (572) that separated Milan and the northern Italian sees from the apostolic see. Bishop Laurentius II of Milan, unable to occupy his see because of the Lombards, thought it best to reconcile with Rome in the face of the barbarian onslaught. However, the archbishop of AQUILEIA refused to be reconciled. When the barbarians reached Aquileia, the patriarch and his flock fled to the island of Grado, imitating the Venetians who had fled to the islands from the hordes of Attila in the fifth century. The pope persuaded Narses to return from Naples to defend Rome, but owing to strife between the Byzantine commander and the Romans, the pope took up residence in the cemetery of Praetextatus on the Via Appia until the death of Narses (*c.* 572) to avoid entanglement in the quarrel. John III was buried in St. Peter's.

Bibliography: *Clavis Patrum latinorum,* ed. E. DEKKERS (Streenbrugge 1961) 1704. *Monumenta Germaniae Historica* (Berlin 1826–) division: Epistolae 1 (1891) 230. *Liber pontificalis,* ed. L. DUCHESNE (Paris 1886–92, 1958) 1:305–307, 3:92. H. LECLERCQ, *Dictionnaire d'archéologie chrétienne et de liturgie,* ed. F. CABROL, H. LECLERCQ, and H. I. MARROU (Paris 1907–53) 13:1:1221–22. O. BERTOLINI, *Roma di fronte a Bisanzio e ai Longobardi* (Bologna 1941). R. U. MONTINI, *Le Tombe dei papi* (Rome 1957) 112. H. JEDIN, *History of the Church* (New York 1980) 2:629. J. N. D. KELLY, *Oxford Dictionary of the Popes* (New York 1986) 64. J. RICHARDS, *Popes and Papacy in the Early Middle Ages* (London

1979) 162–166. R. AUBERT, *Dictionnaire d'histoire et de géographie ecclésiastiques,* 26 (Paris 1995).

[J. CHAPIN]

JOHN IV, POPE

Pontificate: August 640 to Oct. 12, 642; d. Rome. He was a Dalmation by birth, son of Venantius (probably consultor to the exarch of Ravenna). He redeemed Christian captives taken by the Slavs in the Balkans and he endowed a chapel at the Lateran baptistery with relics. In a letter written to the Celtic clergy in England while he was pope-elect, John censured both PELAGIANISM and the Celtic custom of keeping Easter on the 14 of Nisan (Bede, *Hist. Eccl.* 2.19). Early in 641 he assembled a synod that condemned MONOTHELITISM (Mansi 10:607e). Later he informed PYRRHUS, Patriarch of Constantinople, that he rejected the ecthesis published by Emperor HERACLIUS in 638 because it proclaimed a single Will in Christ (Mansi 11:9b). John's epistle to Emperor Constantine III upheld the orthodoxy of Pope HONORIUS I (625–38), explaining that Honorius had understood the unity of Will in Christ as meaning that in His sinless humanity there was no place for opposition between the law of the members and the law of the mind (see Rom 7.23).

Bibliography: E. JAFFÉ, *Regesta pontificum romanorum ab condita ecclesia ad annum post Christian natum 1198,* ed. P. EWALD 1:227–228; 2:698–739. *Liber pontificalis,* ed. L. DUCHESNE, v. 1-2 (Paris 1886–92), v. 3 (Paris 1958) 1:330; 3:94. *Patrolgia Latina,* ed. J. P. MIGNE, 217 v., indexes 4 v. (Paris 1878–90) 80:601–608. C. J. VON HEFELE, *Histoire des conciles d'après les documents originaux,* tr. and continued by H. LECLERCQ, 10 v. in 19 (Paris 1907–38) 3.1:390–398. H. K. MANN, *The Lives of the Popes in the Early Middle Ages from 590 to 1304,* 18 v. (London 1902–32) 1.1:351–368. J. HALLER, *Das Papsttum,* 5 v. (2d, rev. ed. Stuttgart 1950–53) 1:314–317. F. X. SEPPELT, *Geschichte der Päpste von den Anfängen bis zur Mitte des 20. Jh.,* (Munich) 2:57–59. J. N. D. KELLY, *Oxford Dictionary of Popes* (New York 1986), 72–73

[H. G. J. BECK]

JOHN V, POPE

Pontificate: July 23, 685 to Aug. 2, 686; d. Rome. He was of a Syrian family, the son of Cyriacus. While a deacon, as recorded in his epitaph, John had been one of Pope Agatho's legates to the sixth ecumenical Council of CONSTANTINOPLE III (680–681). He was canonically elected in the Lateran basilica and then installed in the Lateran palace, in accord with the recent decree of the Emperor CONSTANTINE IV Pogonatus to Pope Benedict II (Dölger Reg. 252). John, in synod, cassated the ordina-

tion of the bishop of Sassari, Sardinia, by Citonatus, Archbishop of Cagliari in Sardinia, and decreed that the irregularly consecrated bishop be again subject to the provincial authority of the bishop of Rome rather than to that of Cagliari.

Bibliography: E. JAFFÉ, *Regesta pontificum romanorum ab condita ecclesia ad annum post Christian natum 1198,* ed. P. EWALD 1:242. *Liber pontificalis,* ed. L. DUCHESNE, v. 1-2 (Paris 1886–92), v. 3 (Paris 1958) 1:366–367; 3:96. H. K. MANN, *The Lives of the Popes in the Early Middle Ages from 590 to 1304,* 18 v. (London 1902–32) 1.2:64–67. F. DÖLGER, *Corpus der griechischen Urkunden des Mittelalters und der neueren Zeit,* series A, *Regesten* (Munich 1924–32) 1.1:252–254. J. GAY, "Quelques remarques sur les papes grecs et syriens avant la querelle des iconoclastes (678–715)," *Mélanges Schlumberger* (Paris 1924) 1:40–54. E. CASPAR, *Geschichte de Papsttums von den Anfängen bis zur Höhe der Weltherrschaft,* 2v. (Tübingen 1930–33) 2:620–631. O. BERTOLINI, *Roma di fronte a Bisanzio e ai Longobardi* (Bologna 1941). J. HALLER, *Das Papsttum,* 5 v. (2d, rev. ed. Stuttgart 1950–53) 1:342–344. F. X. SEPPELT, *Geschichte der Päpste von den Anfängen bis zur Mitte des 20. Jh.,* (Munich) 2: 78–82. J. N. D. KELLY, *Oxford Dictionary of Popes* (New York 1986), 80–81.

[H. G. J. BECK]

JOHN VI, POPE

Pontificate: Oct. 30, 701, to Jan. 11, 705; d. Rome. Of Greek descent, John succeeded in quelling the revolt of the Italian militia against the imperial exarch, Theophylactus, who had moved from Sicily to Rome. John's negotiations with the Lombard Gisulf, Duke of Benevento, resulted in the liberation of captives taken during Gisulf's invasion of the Campania and the withdrawal of the Beneventan troops. The only extant letter of John's pontificate (Eddius, *Vita s. Wilfredi,* ch. 54) originated from a four-month Roman synod of 704 that referred the dispute between the exiled WILFRID OF YORK, Bosa, Bishop of York, and JOHN OF BEVERLEY, Bishop of Hexham, to the jurisdiction of Archbishop BRITHWALD OF CANTERBURY, with the provision that should an appeal be lodged from the decision of Canterbury all concerned would be obliged to appear in Rome.

Bibliography: *Liber pontificalis,* ed. L. DUCHESNE (Paris 1886–92) 1:383–384; 3:98. P. JAFFÉ, *Regesta pontificum romanorum ab condita ecclesia ad annum post Christum natum 1198,* ed. P. EWALD (2d ed. Leipzig 1881–88; repr. Graz 1956) 1:245–246. EDDIUS STEPHANUS, *The Life of Bishop Wilfrid,* ed. and tr. B. COLGRAVE (New York 1927). BEDE, *A History of the English Church and People,* tr. L. SHERLEY-PRICE (Harmondsworth 1955) bk. 5, ch. 19. H. K. MANN, *The Lives of the Popes in the Early Middle Ages from 590 to 1304* (London 1902–32) 1.2:105–108. O. BERTOLINI, *Roma di fronte a Bisanzio e ai Longobardi* (Bologna 1941); "I Papi e le relazioni politiche di Roma con i ducati Longobardi di Spoleto e di Benevento," *Rivista di storia della Chiesa iri Italia* 9 (1955) 1–57. J. HALLER, *Das Papsttum* (Stuttgart 1950–53)1:342–344. F. X. SEPPELT, *Geschichte der Päpste von den Anfängen bis zur Mitte*

Pope John VII, contemporary mosaic portrait now in the Grotto of St. Peter's in Rome, early 8th century.

des 20. Jh. (Munich 1955) 2:85. J. GODFREY, *The Church in Anglo-Saxon England* (Cambridge, Eng. 1962). R. AUBERT, *Dictionnaire d'histoire et de géographie ecclésiastiques* 26 (Paris 1997). J. N. D. KELLY, *Oxford Dictionary of Popes* (New York 1986) 83.

[H. G. J. BECK]

JOHN VII, POPE

Pontifcate: Mar. 1, 705 to Oct. 18, 707; d. Rome. John was of Greek ancestry, the son of that Plato whose epitaph records his restoration of the imperial palaces at Rome. John's own building activity at St. Peter's, St. Eugenia's, and S. Maria Antiqua is noted by the *Liber pontificalis.* During his reign King Aribert II (701–712) of the Lombards restored to the Roman Church its patrimony in the Cottian Alps. Emperor JUSTINIAN II, probably in 706, dispatched two bishops from Constantinople to request a Roman synod that would indicate which of the 102 canons decreed by the QUINISEXT SYNOD in 692 were objectionable to the Holy See. Pope SERGIUS I (687–701) had earlier rejected all of them, but John returned the canons without emendation. His contemporary biographer censured him for this; but the papal action may well have been an indication that the question was no longer open. Two contemporary likenesses of John are extant: one in

mosaic, in the Grotto of St. Peter's, Rome; the other in a painting in S. Maria Antiqua, Rome.

Bibliography: *Liber pontificalis,* ed. L. DUCHESNE (Paris 1886–92)1:385–387; 3:98–99. P. JAFFÉ, *Regesta pontificum romanorum ab condita ecclesia ad annum post Christum natum 1198,* ed. P. EWALD (2d ed. Leipzig 1881–88; repr. Graz 1958) 1: 246–247. C. J. VON HEFELE, *Histoire des conciles d'après les documents originaux,* tr. H. LECLERC (Paris 1907–38) 3.1:578–581. H. K. MANN, *The Lives of the Popes in the Early Middle Ages from 590 to 1304* (London 1902–32)1.2:109–123. E. CASPAR, *Geschichte de Papsttums von den Anfängen bis zur Höhe der Weltherrschaft* (Tübingen 1930–33) 2:630–637. J. HALLER, *Das Papsttum* (2d ed. Stuttgart 1950–53)1:343–344. F. X. SEPPELT, *Geschichte der Päpste von den Anfängen bis zur Mitte des 20. Jh.* (Munich 1955) 2:85–95. G. SCHWAIGER, *Lexikon für Theologie und Kirche,* ed. J. HOFER and K. RAHNER (Freiburg 1957–65) 5:987–988. R. AUBERT, *Dictionnaire d'histoire et de gèographie ecclésiastiques,* 26 (Paris 1997). A. GUILLOU, ''Nom du pape Jean VII (705–708), commanditaire d'un ambon à Sainte–Marie–Antique,'' *Recueil des inscriptions grecques médiévales d'Italia* (Rome 1996) 123–4. V. NOE, ''L'oratorio mariano di Giovanni VII,'' *La Madonna della Basilica Vaticana* (1994) 21–24. P.J. NORDHAGEN, ''Icons Designed for the Display of Sumptuous Votive Gifts,'' *Dumbarton Oaks Papers* (Washington, DC 1987) 453–60. J. OSBORNE, ''Early Medieval Wall Paintings in the Catacomb of San Valentino,'' *Papers of the British School at Rome* (London 1981) 82–90. I. ŠEVČENKO, ''Three Paradoxes of the Cyrillo–Methodian Mission,'' *Ideology, Letters and Culture in the Byzantine World* (London 1982) n.4. J. N. D. KELLY, *Oxford Dictionary of Popes* (New York 1986) 84–85.

[H. G. J. BECK]

JOHN VIII, POPE

Pontificate: Dec. 14, 872 to Dec. 16, 882. The son of the Roman, Gundo, he was an archdeacon of the Roman Church for twenty years before he succeeded ADRIAN II in the Papal See, despite the opposition of FORMOSUS. In his ten-year pontificate John was compelled to contend with the EASTERN SCHISM, Roman intrigue, the treachery of Italian princes, contention for the imperial throne, and Saracen invasion: in short, the entire gamut of troubles characteristic of his violent epoch. Although no contemporary biography was written, a long series of letters (*Monumenta Germaniae Historica: Epistolae* 7:1–133) and a lengthy *Register* of his acts (*Regesta pontificum romanorum ab condita ecclesia ad anum post Christum natum 1198* 1:376–422; 2:704, 746) trace in detail a complicated and action-filled pontificate. John supported the missionary work of (St.) Methodius (*see* CYRIL AND METHODIUS, SS) among the Slavs. At first John forbade the Slavonic language for use in their liturgy, but later approved it. Although intrigue and violence against Methodius and his Slavic colleagues by German and Hungarian princes and churchmen crushed the use of the Slavonic liturgy in Moravia, it survived among the BULGARS. Other problems prevented John from effectively seizing the opportunity offered by King BORIS I of bringing the Bulgarian Church under the direct jurisdiction of Rome rather than Constantinople. He did, however, manage to preserve the Church of Croatia for the West. In 879 John recognized PHOTIUS as patriarch of Constantinople. John has been condemned for his early indulgent treatment of Photius, but it is more realistic to recognize that the pope continuously received false intelligence from the East and, throughout the affair of Photius, was distracted by problems at home.

In the West the most harassing of John's troubles was with the Saracen pirates who, in alliance with petty Italian princes, kept invading, occupying, pillaging, retreating, and returning to Italy throughout John's pontificate. The pope's natural ally in Italy against such an enemy was the Roman Emperor: John supported Emperor LOUIS II and on the death of Louis (875) named Charles the Bald emperor, crowning him in Rome on Christmas Day, 875. In February 876 Charles became king of Italy also, and he and John joined forces against the Saracens and allied Italian princes. Before his help could be of much use, however, Charles died (October 877). Pope John favored Boso, duke of Arles, to succeed to the Empire, but Boso was reluctant to fight for the crown. Staving off the pressures of Guido III of Spoleto and Adalbert of Tuscany, John crowned Charles III the Fat emperor in 881. John, in effect, was his own general and admiral; he fortified Rome, founded a pontifical navy, and defended the coasts. He was still repelling invaders when he died in 882. Pope John's ten-year pontificate seems incredibly eventful, and he emerges as one of the better popes in the centuries between Gregory I and Gregory VII.

Bibliography: *Liber pontificalis,* ed. L. DUCHESNE (Paris 1886–92) 2:221–223. H. K. MANN, *The Lives of the Popes in the Early Middle Ages from 590 to 1304* (London 1902–32) 3:231–352. A. LAPÔTRE, *Le Pape Jean VIII* (Paris 1895). A. FLICHE and V. MARTIN, eds., *Histoire de l'église depuis les origines jusqu'à nos jours* (Paris 1935—) 6:413–439. F. DVORNIK, *Byzantine Missions among the Slavs. SS. Constantine-Cyril and Methodius* (New Brunswick 1970). F. E. ENGREEN, "Pope J. VIII and the Arabs," *Speculum* 20 (1945) 318–330. F. DVORNIK, *The Photian Schism* (Cambridge, Eng. 1948). F. X. SEPPELT, *Geschichte der Päpste von den Anfängen bis zur Mitte des 20. Jh.* (Munich 1955) 2:305–329, 434. *Dictionnaire de théologie catholique,* ed. A. VACANT et al. (Tables générales, Paris 1951—) 2442–43. M. M. GAREJO-GUEMBE, "Die Erfahrungen der Zeit des Photios für den heutigen ökumenischen Dialog zwischen Orthodox und Katholizismus," *Orthodoxes Forum* (St. Ottilien 1993) 179–86. R. HAUGH, *Photius and the Carolingians: The Trinitarian Controversy* (Belmont, Mass. 1975). A. GEROSTERGIOS, *Photius the Great* (Belmont, Mass. 1980). TH. GRANIER, "Napolitains et Lombards aux VIIIe–Xie siècles. De la guerre des peuples à la 'guerre des saints' en Italie du Sud," *Mélanges de l'École Moyen Âge-Temps Modernes* (Roma 1996) 403–50. J. MEIJER, *A Successful Council of Union: A Theological Analysis of the Photian Synod of 879–880* (Thessalonikē 1975). N. STAUBACH, "Herkules an der 'Cathedra Petri'," in *Iconologia sacra. Mythos, Bildkunst und Dichtung in der Religions- und Sozialgeschichte Al-*

teuropas. Festschrift für Karl Hauck zum 75. Geburstag (Berlin/New York 1994) 383–402. H. TAVIANI-CAROZZI, "La vision impériale de l'Occident médiéval: un témoinage lombard du Xe siècle," in *Histoire et société. Mélanges offerts à George Duby* (Aix-en Provence 1992) 179–92. G. VISMARA, *Impium foedus. Le origini della "Respublica christiana,"* (Milano 1974). J. N. D. KELLY, *Oxford Dictionary of Popes* (New York 1986) 110–111.

[C. E. SHEEDY]

JOHN VIII, ANTIPOPE

Pontificate: January 844. Virtually nothing is known of the deacon John, except that he was acclaimed pope upon the death of Pope Gregory IV (827–844). Gregory died in January, and the people of Rome rioted, seized the Lateran and proclaimed John the new pope. The city's aristocracy put down the uprising and forced John to leave the Lateran; they then elected the archpriest Sergius (844–847) as pope. The emperor Lothair (840–855) subsequently recognized the election through his son Louis, who served as an envoy in Rome. Nothing certain is known of John's fate, though some sources report that he was confined to a monastery.

Bibliography: L. DUCHESNE, ed. *Liber Pontificalis* (Paris 1886–92; repr. 1955–57) 2.86–87. P. JAFFÉ, *Regesta pontificum Romanorum* (Leipzig 1885–88; repr. Graz 1956) 1.327. F. X. SEPPELT, *Geschichte der Päpste von den Anfängen bis zur Mitte des zwanzigsten Jahrhunderts* (Munich 1954–59) 2.221. J. N. D. KELLY, *The Oxford Dictionary of Popes* (New York 1986) 103. R. AUBERT, *Dictionnaire d'histoire et de géographie ecclésiastiques* (Paris 1997) 26:1160.

[P. M. SAVAGE]

JOHN IX, POPE

Pontificate: December 897 or January 898 to January–April 900. John, a Roman who was a Benedictine monk and was ordained priest by Pope FORMOSUS, was elected pope despite strong opposition from a rival candidate, Sergius, bishop of Caere (later Pope SERGIUS III), who was a leader of the party opposed to Pope Formosus. John enjoyed the support of Emperor LAMBERT OF SPOLETO in this disputed election. As pope, John's chief concern was to continue the effort begun by his predecessor, Pope THEODORE, aimed at ending the strife that had dominated Rome since the trial of Pope Formosus in 897. The issues causing that strife were addressed in two councils held at Rome and at Ravenna in 898; Lambert of Spoleto, who had been crowned emperor by Formosus, lent his support to this effort. The acts of the council that had tried Formosus' corpse were nullified. Provisions were made for pardoning all those who had acted against Formosus except Sergius and his close followers, who were deposed and excommunicated. All of Formosus' acts, including his ordinations, were declared valid with the exception of his coronation of Arnulf of Germany as emperor; however, his coronation of Lambert was validated. The prohibition of transfer of bishops from one see to another was confirmed. In an effort to regularize papal elections the provisions of the *Constituto Romana* of 824 agreed upon between Pope EUGENIUS II and Emperor Lothair I were reaffirmed. This agreement provided that the pope was to be elected by cardinal bishops and clergy meeting in the presence of the Senate and the people, but required that the consecration of a newly elected pope must be held in the presence of an imperial legate. Also reconfirmed were the provisions of the *Constituto Romana* defining the rights and responsibilities of both pope and emperor in the governance of the Papal State in terms that guaranteed the territorial integrity and limited autonomy of the Papal State while reserving to the emperor the right to intervene in the internal affairs of the Papal State in the interests of keeping order. In effect, in order to gain an effective protector for the Papal State, John IX was willing to turn back the clock by accepting an arrangement that many of his predecessors had resisted.

John's concerns reached beyond affairs in the Papal State and Italy. His legates played a decisive role in a council in Constantinople in 899 that worked out solutions to the final, unsettled issues involved in the longstanding quarrel centering on Patriarch PHOTIUS. It also allowed a reconciliation not only between Rome and Constantinople but among the factions in the East that emerged from the Photian affair. In an effort to repair the damage done to the missionary establishment of Methodius in Moravia by rival German clergymen seeking to dominate that land, John IX responded favorably to a request from the Moravian ruler to create an independent church organization for Moravia. He was called upon to adjudicate a disputed episcopal election in the West Frankish kingdom.

But these actions paled in the face of the crisis emerging in Italy. John's hope of having found a reliable protector disappeared suddenly with the death of Lambert in 898. Italy suffered increasing chaos involving several factors: rivalry of powerful princes, especially Berengar of Friuli and Louis of Provence, for the kingship of Italy and the imperial title; Magyar invasions of the north; Greek and Saracen incursions in the south; the efforts of local potentates unrestrained by any higher authority to carve out private lordships. Soon after the death of John IX partisan strife again took center stage, creating an opportunity for a Roman official, Theophylactus, and his family to seize control of the papal office and the Papal State.

Bibliography: Sources. *Le Liber Pontificalis,* ed. L. DUCHESNE, 3 v., 2nd ed. (Paris 1955–1957), 2: 232. *Regesta Pontificum Romanorum ab condita ecclesia ad annum post Christum MCXCVIII,* ed. P. JAFFÉ, 2 v., 2nd ed. (Leipzig 1885–1888), 1: 442–443. J. D. MANSI, *Sacrorum conciliorum, nova et amplissima collectio,* 54 v. (Paris 1901–1920; reprinted Graz, 1960–1961), 18A: 109–234. *Papsturkunden 896–1048,* ed. H. ZIMMERMANN v. 1, *896–996* 2nd ed. rev., Denkschriften, Österreichische Akademie der Wissenschaft, Philosophische-Historische Klasse 174 (Vienna 1989) 13–23. E. DÜMMLER, *Auxilius und Vulgarius: Quellen und Forschungen zur Geschichte des Papsttums im Anfange des zehnten Jahrhunderts* (Leipzig 1866). E. DÜMMLER, *Gesta Berengarii Imperatoris. Beiträge zur Geschichte Italiens im Anfange des zehnten Jahrunderts* (Halle 1871) (In these two studies, Dümmler edits and comments on the main texts that emerged from the quarrel over Formosus' trial, including the tracts by Auxilius and Eugenius Vulgarius). **Literature.** L. DUCHESNE, *The Beginnings of the Temporal Sovereignty of the Popes, A.D. 754–1073,* tr. A. H. MATTHEW (London 1908) 167–216. C. J. HEFELE, *Histoire des conciles d'après les documents originaux,* tr. H. LECLERCQ, v. 4, part 2 (Paris 1911) 708–719. J. DUHR "La concile de Ravenna, 895. La réhabilitation du pape Formose," *Recherches de science religieuse,* 22 (1932) 541–579. F. X. SEPPELT, *Geschichte des Papsttums. Eine Geschichte der Päpste von den Anfängen bis zum Tod Pius X,* v. 2: *Das Papsttums im Frühmittelalter. Geschichte des Päpste von Regierungsantritt Gregors des Grossen bis zum Mitte des 11. Jahrhundert,* (Leipzig 1934) 333–335. A. FLICHE, *L'Europe occidentale de 888 à 1125,* Histoire générale: Histoire du Moyen Âge 2 (Paris 1941) 41–59, 110–131. É. AMANN and A. DUMAS, *L'Église au pouvoir des laïques (888–1037),* Histoire de la Église depuis les origines jusqu'a nos jours, ed. A. FLICHE and V. MARTIN, 7 (Paris 1948) 26–28, 115–116. F. DVORNIK, *The Photian Schism: History and Legend* (Cambridge 1948). W. HARTMANN, *Die Synoden der Karolingerzeit im Frankenreich und in Italien,* Konziliengeschichte, ed. W. BRANDMÜLLER (Paderborn 1987) 388–396. P. LLEWELLYN, *Rome in the Dark Ages* (London 1993) 286–315.

[R. E. SULLIVAN]

JOHN X, POPE

Pontificate: March or April 914 to May or June 928; b. John of Tossignano, Romagna. Bishop of Bologna and archbishop of Ravenna, *c.* 905 to 914. John owed his office to the family of THEOPHYLACTUS; but the account of LIUTPRAND OF CREMONA, suggesting an affair with the influential THEODORA, wife of Theophylactus, as the cause of John's preferment, is improbable. John was determined to rid southern Italy of the Saracens, and to this end formed an alliance between the Byzantine Emperor CONSTANTINE VII, Berengar I (whom he crowned as emperor December 915), and other Italian princes. In the campaign that followed, the pope himself took part, and by August 915 the Saracens had been driven from their stronghold on the Garigliano River. During the difficult years of his pontificate, John strove to establish the temporal authority of the Holy See. He approved the strict rule of CLUNY, which had just been founded (910), and promoted the conversion of the Normans and the interests of the Church in Spain and the Slavic areas. He sent legates to the Synod of Hohenaltheim (916), which prepared the way for the close union of Church and State in Germany. He unfortunately approved of Hugh, the five–year–old son of Count Heribert, as archbishop of Reims in order to secure the release of King Charles the Simple, whom Heribert held in prison. A schism between Rome and Constantinople over the allowing of marriage for the fourth time ended during his pontificate. Whether John conferred the imperial title on Simeon, Czar of Bulgaria (893–927), is uncertain. John's pontificate ended in tragedy. After the murder of Berengar in 924, the pope formed an alliance with King Hugh of Italy, thus arousing the enmity of MAROZIA, daughter of Theophylactus and Theodora. John was deposed and imprisoned in April 928, and afterward smothered by order of Marozia.

See Also: CRESCENTII.

Bibliography: P. JAFFÉ, *Regesta pontificum romanorum ab condita ecclesia ad annum post Christum natum 1198*, ed. S. LÖWENFELD, 882-1198. *Liber pontificalis*, ed. L. DUCHESNE 2:240–241. H. K. MANN, *The Lives of the Popes in the Early Middle Ages from 590 to 1304* 4:149–187. C. J. VON HEFELE, *Histoire des conciles d'après les documents originaux*, tr. H. LECLERCQ 4.2:734–750. A. FLICHE and V. MARTIN, eds., *Histoire de l'église depuis les origines jusqu'à nos jours* 7:34–38. J. HALLER, *Das Papsttum* 2:199, 546–549. R. AUBERT, *Dictionnaire d'histoire et de géographie ecclésiastiques* 26 (Paris 1997), s.v. "Jean X, pape." H. FUHRMANN, "Die Synode von Hohenaltheim (916)—quellenkundlich betrachtet," *Deutsches Archiv für Erforschung des Mittelalters* (Kön–Wien 1987), 440–68. R. KATÎÎ, "Methodii doctrina," *Slovo* (Zagreb 1986), 11–44. I. NICHOLAS PATRIARCH OF CONSTANIOPLE, *Letters [913–25]* (Washington, DC 1973). R. SAVIGNI, "Sacerdozio e regno in età post–carolingia: l'episcopato di Giovanni X, arcivescovo di Ravenna (905–914) e Papa (914–928)," *Rivista di Storia della Chiesa in Italia* (Roma 1992), 1–29. H. WOLTER, *Lexikon für Theologie und Kirche* 3d. ed. 5 (Freiburg 1996) s.v. "Hohenaltheim, Synode v. [916]." H. ZIMMERMANN, *Lexikon für Theologie und Kirche* 3d ed. 5 (Freiburg 1996), s.v. "Johannes X." J. N. D. KELLY, *Oxford Dictionary of Popes* (New York 1986), 121–122.

[S. MCKENNA]

JOHN XI, POPE

Pontificate: March 931 to Jan. 936; d. Rome. Upon the death of STEPHEN VII in 931, MAROZIA, of the House of THEOPHYLACTUS, obtained the papacy for her son John, a youth in his early twenties and a cardinal priest at the church of Santa Maria in the Trastevere. The *Liber pontificalis* and LIUTPRAND OF CREMONA assert that John XI was the son of Marozia and SERGIUS III but this is open to question. Undoubtedly John was Marozia's son, possibly by her first marriage with Alberic of Spoleto by whom she had another son, Alberic II. As pope, John was dominated by his mother. When Marozia married her

third husband, Hugh of Provence, King of Italy, in 932, John XI witnessed the ceremony. As a result of the Roman revolt (932) led by Alberic, King Hugh sought refuge in Pavia. Marozia was taken prisoner, and Alberic, master of the city, had himself proclaimed Prince of Rome. He ruled the city effectively for the next 20 years. John XI became Alberic's prisoner and exercised spiritual duties only. Even in these Alberic interfered, as is evidenced by the creation of Artold, Archbishop of Rheims (933) and Theophylactus, Patriarch of Constantinople. At the request of St. ODO OF CLUNY, John granted many privileges to CLUNY and its dependent daughterhouses. His pontificate was marked by cordial relations with the Byzantine Emperor. John was buried in St. John Lateran.

See Also: CRESCENTII.

Bibliography: P. JAFFÉ, *Regesta pontificum romanorum ab condita ecclesia ad annum post Christum natum 1198*, ed. S. LÖWENFELD 1:454–455; 2:706, 746–747. *Liber pontificalis*, ed. L. DUCHESNE 2:243. L. DUCHESNE, *The Beginnings of the Temporal Sovereignty of the Popes, A.D. 754–1073* (London 1908). H. K. MANN, *The Lives of the Popes in the Early Middle Ages from 590 to 1304* 4: 191–204. J. HALLER, *Das Papsttum* 2:201–204. F. X. SEPPELT, *Geschichte der Päpste von den Anfängen bis zur Mitte des 20. Jh.* 2:355–357, 434–435. G. SCHWAIGER, *Lexikon für Theologie und Kirche*[2] 5:990. R. AUBERT, *Dictionnaire d'histoire et de géographie ecclésiastiques* 26 (Paris 1997), s.v. "Jean XI, pape." R. BENERICETTI, *La cronologia dei Papi dei secoli IX–XI secondo le carte di Ravenna* (1999), 39. J. N. D. KELLY, *Oxford Dictionary of Popes* (New York 1986), 123.

[M. A. MULHOLLAND]

JOHN XII, POPE

Pontificate: Dec. 16, 955 to May 14, 964; b. Rome, *c.* 936. Before his death in 954, Alberic II of Spoleto, the undisputed master of Rome, made the nobles swear to elect his only son, Octavian, to the papacy at the death of Agapetus II. As pope, Octavian changed his name to John. Even if this immature pontiff, scarcely 18, were not guilty of all the vices attributed to him by LIUTPRAND (*Monumenta Germaniae Historica: Scriptores* 3:340–346), there is sufficient unbiased evidence to prove that he was unworthy of his office. In 959, attempting to recover former papal lands from King Berengarius II, John appealed for help to OTTO I. The German king willingly obliged, and late in 961 his army appeared in Italy. On Feb. 2, 962, John crowned Otto emperor and Otto's wife, (St.) Adelaide, empress, in St. Peter's Basilica, beginning the long association of the imperial title with the German kingdom (*see* HOLY ROMAN EMPIRE). Otto issued the *Privilegium Ottonianum*, promising to make the pope the temporal ruler of almost three-fourths of Italy. On the other hand, the pope had to recognize the emperor's suzerainty over the STATES OF THE CHURCH and agree that future popes were not to be consecrated until they had taken an oath of fealty to the emperor. The pope resented these terms, and when Otto left the city, began to plot against him. The emperor, therefore, returned on November 3, but John escaped to Tivoli with the papal treasury. On November 6, Otto summoned a synod in St. Peter's, and there the pope was accused of gross misconduct; he was ordered to appear in person and clear himself of these charges. When John refused, he was deposed on December 4 and replaced by a Roman lay official, LEO VIII. Many in Rome opposed this high-handed action and John easily regained control of the city (early 964) after Otto's departure. He punished many of his enemies and declared the acts of Leo VIII null and void. John died suddenly under circumstances that, according to Liutprand, were just as scandalous as his life.

See Also: CRESCENTII.

Bibliography: P. JAFFÉ, *Regesta pontificum romanorum ab condita ecclesia ad annum post Christum natum 1198*, ed. S. LÖWENFELD (Graz 1956) 1:463–467. *Liber pontificalis*, ed. L. DUCHESNE (Paris 1886–92) 2:246–249. H. K. MANN, *The Lives of the Popes in the Early Middle Ages from 590 to 1304* (London 1902–32) 4:241–272. E. AMANN, *Dictionnaire de théologie catholique*, ed. A. VACANT et al., (Paris 1903–50) 8.1:619–626. A. FLICHE and V. MARTIN, *Histoire de l'église depuis les origines jusqu'à nos jours* (Paris 1935—) 7:44–55. P. BREZZI, *Roma e l'Impero medioevale, 774–1252* (Bologna 1947). J. HALLER, *Das Papsttum* (Stuttgart 1950–53) 2:204–215, 549–555. W. ULLMANN, "The Origins of the Ottonianum," *Cambridge Historical Journal* 11 (Cambridge, Eng. 1953) 114–128; *The Growth of Papal Government in the Middle Ages* (London 1955). P. E. SCHRAMM, *Kaiser, Rom und Renovatio* (Darmstadt 1957). H. BEUMANN, "Die Gründung des Bistums Oldenburg und die Missionspolitik Ottos des Grossen," *Ausgewählte Aufsätze aus des Jahren 1966–1986. Festgabe zu seinem 75. Geburtstag* (1987) 177–92. G. GRESSER, *Biographisch-Bibliographisches Kirchenlexikon* 6 (1993), s.v. "Otger (Otgar, Otkerius), Bischof von Speyer." K. HAMPE, "Die Berufung Ottos des Grossen nach Rom durch Papst Johann XII," in *Historische Aufsätze Karl Zeumer zum sechzigsten Geburtstag als Festgabe dargebracht von Freunden und Schüer* (Frankfurt 1987) 153–63. E. D. HEHL, "Die angeblichen Kanones der röischen Synode vom Febuar 962," *Deutsches Archiv für Erforschung des Mittelalters* (Köln-Wien 1986) 620–8. E. D. HEHL, *Lexikon für Theologie und Kirche* 5 (Freiburg 1996), s.v. "Johannes XII." H. PLATELL, "Théophylacte," *Catholicisme hier aujourd'hui demain* (Paris 1996) 119–20. T. STRUVE, *Lexikon des Mittelalters*, 7 (München-Zurich 1994–1995), s.v. "Privilegium Ottonianum." J. N. D. KELLY, *Oxford Dictionary of Popes* (New York 1986) 126–127.

[S. MCKENNA]

JOHN XIII, POPE

Pontificate: Oct. 1, 965 to Sept. 6, 972; b. Rome, probably a cousin of Alberic II of Spoleto and brother of Crescentius. John was the bishop of Narni when he was chosen as pope by OTTO I. Noble opposition in Rome, re-

senting the imperial election and John's attempts to curb their power, rebelled in December 965 and took the Pope to the Campagna as a prisoner. However, early in 966 John escaped and, aided by Otto's army, returned to Rome in November. The CRESCENTII had remained loyal and gradually became the leaders of the Roman aristocracy. John's remaining years were spent in peace since Otto stayed in Italy until 972. The pope and the emperor encouraged the extension of the CLUNIAC REFORM. Together they presided at a synod in Ravenna, April 967, where laws were passed against clerical marriage (*see* CELIBACY, CLERICAL HISTORY OF); but the times were not propitious for so sweeping a reform. The pope conferred the imperial crown on the 12–year-old OTTO II on Christmas Day 967; on April 14, 972, he married the young emperor to the Byzantine princess Theophano, whom he also crowned as empress. In 962 John XII, at Otto's request, had approved the erection of the metropolitan See of Magdeburg, but opposition in the German hierarchy prevented the erection. By 968, John XIII had succeeded, and he consecrated Adalbert its first and most important archbishop. Magdeburg with its suffragan sees became the headquarters for the conversion of the Slavs. John died in Rome and was buried in St. Paul-Outside-the-Walls.

Bibliography: P. JAFFÉ, *Regesta pontificum romanorum ab condita ecclesia ad annum post Christum natum 1198*, ed. S. LÖWENFELD 1:470–477. *Liber ponficialis*, ed. L. DUCHESNE 2:252–254. C. J. VON HEFELE, *Histoire des conciles d'après les documents originaux*, tr. H. LECLERCQ 4.2:825–832. P. BREZZI, *Roma e l'Impero medioevale* (Bologna 1947). H. K. MANN, *The Lives of the Popes in the Early Middle Ages from 590 to 1304* 4:282–304. J. HALLER, *Das Papsttum* 2:215–218, 554–555. P. E. SCHRAMM, *Kaiser, Rom und Renovatio* (2d. ed. Darmstadt 1957). G. SCHWAIGER, *Lexikon für Theologie und Kirche*[2] 5:990–991. R. AUBERT, *Dictionnaire d'histoire et de géographie ecclésiastiques* 26 (Paris 1997), s.v. "Jean XIII, pape." E. D. HEHL, "Meresburg—eine Bistumgründung unter Vorbehalt. Gelübde, Kirchenrecht und politischer Spielraum im 10. Jahrhundert," *Frühmittelalterliche Studien* (Berlin 1997), 96–119. LIUDPRAND OF CREMONA, "Relatio de legatione Constantinopolitana (The Mission to Constantinople)," *The Journal of Ecclesiastical History* (Cambridge 1994). J. N. D. KELLY, *Oxford Dictionary of Popes* (New York 1986), 129–130.

[S. MCKENNA]

JOHN XIV, POPE

Pontificate: November or December 983 to Aug. 20, 984; b. Peter Canepanova. Bishop of Pavia and archchancellor for Italy, he was chosen pope by OTTO II. A letter to Alo, Archbishop of Benevento, the only extant document of his pontificate, reveals his concern for the reform of the Church. When Otto II died at Rome, Dec. 7, 983, the Empress Theophano was forced to leave the city to defend the claim of her three-year-old son, OTTO III. John was now at the mercy of the CRESCENTII and their antipope, Boniface VII, who returned to Rome from Constantinople. He was deposed and imprisoned in the Castel Sant' Angelo in April 984, and died from either hunger or poison.

Bibliography: L. JAFFÉ, *Regesta pontificum romanorum ab condita ecclesia ad annum post Christum natum 1198*, ed. S. LÖWENFELD (Graz 1956) 1:484–485. *Liber pontificalis*, ed. L. DUSHESNE (Paris 1958) 2:259. H. K. MANN, *The Lives of the Popes in the Early Middle Ages from 590 to 1304* (London 1902–32) 4:330–338. A. FLICHE and V. MARTIN eds. *Historie de l'église depuis les origines jusqu'à nos jours* (Paris 1935–) 7:62–63. J. HALLER, *Das Papsttum*, (2d, rev. ed. Stuttgart 1950–53) 2:217, 555. R. AUBERT, *Dictionnaire d'histoire de géographie ecclésiastiques*, 26 (Paris 1997). R. BENERICETTI, *La cronologia dei Papi dei secoli IX–XI secondo le carte di Ravenna* (1999) 50. J. N. D. KELLY, *Oxford Dictionary of the Popes* (New York 1986) 132–133.

[S. MCKENNA]

JOHN XV, POPE

Pontificate: August 985 to March 996. The son of a Roman priest named Leo, he was elected pope after the forcible removal of the legitimate Pope JOHN XIV and the eleven-month reign (until July 985) of the usurper, Boniface VII. He owed his election (which took place some time between Aug. 6 and Sept. 5, 985) to the influence of John Crescentius II, who as PATRICIUS ROMANORUM continued to hold political sway over Rome. John sought at times to evade this domination of the CRESCENTII and succeeded, to a limited degree, in restoring impeded papal authority during his ten-year pontificate. He enjoyed friendly contacts with the Empire's regents, namely, Emperor OTTO I's widow, St. Adelaide, and Emperor OTTO II's widow, Theophano. Through his legate, Leo of Trevi, he brought about the Peace of Rouen (991), which settled the quarrel between King Ethelred II of England and Duke Richard of Normandy; he confirmed the peace with a papal bull.

John brought papal authority to bear on the dispute over the archdiocese of Reims precipitated by Hugh Capet, king of France, who had made Arnulf, nephew of Duke Charles of Lorraine, the archbishop there in 989. Charles, an opponent of Hugh Capet, had imprisoned the archbishop; subsequently Capet held a synod at Saint-Basle near Reims, which deposed Arnulf (991). Capet considered him a traitor and chose as his successor Gerbert of Aurillac (the future SYLVESTER II). The pope objected to this deposal, and in 995 his legate presided over a council at Mouzon (995)—attended only by the German bishops—which condemned and suspended Gerbert in turn. When Capet died (October 996) Arnulf was finally released from imprisonment and restored to his see.

About 990 John received Poland as a papal fief from Duke Mieszko of Poland. He initiated the practice of papal CANONIZATION OF SAINTS, and on Jan. 31, 993, solemnly canonized Bp. ULRIC OF AUGSBURG at a Roman synod held in the Lateran and proclaimed the canonization in a papal bull of February 3 to the French and German bishops. John has been considered a promoter of the CLUNIAC REFORM. His dictatorial manners and his tendency to favor his relatives, however, provoked criticism and opposition among the Roman clergy that John Crescentius II utilized to force the pope to flee to Tuscany. There John successfully sought the support of the young OTTO III, and as the king progressed toward Rome (996) for his imperial coronation, Crescentius was forced to seek peace with the pope. John returned to Rome but died before the imperial party reached the city.

Bibliography: P. JAFFÉ, *Regesta pontificum romanorum ab condita ecclesia ad annum post Christum natum 1198*, ed. S. LÖWENFELD (Graz 1956) 1:486–489; 2:707–708. *Liber pontificalis*, ed. L. DUCHESNE (Paris 1886–92) 2:260; 3. K. G. VON ZMIGROD-STADNICKI, *Die Schenkung Polens an Papst Johannes XV* (Fribourg 1911). F. SCHNEIDER, "Johann XV., Papst, u. Ottos III. Romfahrt," *Mitteilungen des Instituts für österreichische Geschichtsforschung* 39 (1923) 193–218. *Dictionnaire de théologie catholique*, ed. A. VACANT et al. (Tables générales 1951—) 2444. R. AUBERT, *Dictionnaire d'histoire et de géographie ecclésiastiques* 26 (Paris 1997), s.v. "Jean XV, pape." F. X. BISCHOF, "Die Kanonisation Bischof Ulrichs auf der Lateransynode des Jahres 993," in *Bischof Ulrich von Augsburg, 890–973. Seine Zeit—sein Leben—sein Verehrung. Festschrift aus Anlaß des tausendjährigens Jubiläs seiner Kanonisation im Jahre 993* (1993) 197–222. K. GÓRICH, *Lexikon für Theologie und Kirche* 5 (Freiburg 1996), s.v. "Johannes XV." CHR. LÜBKE, *Lexikon des Mittelalters* 6 (München-Zürich 1992/1993), s.v. "Mieszko I. Fürst von Polen." L. MUSSET, "Un millénaire oublié: la remise en place de la hiéarchie épiscopale en Normandie autour de 990," in *Papautés, monarchisme et théories politiques. Études d'histoire médiévale offertes à Marcel Pascaut* (Lyon 1994) 563–73. G. WOLF, "Die Kanonisationsbulle von 993 für den hl. Oudalrich von Augsburg und Vergleichbares," *Archiv für Dipolmatik Schriftgeschichte, Siegelkunde und Wappenkunde* 40 (Köln-Wien 1994, 85–104). J. N. D. KELLY, *Oxford Dictionary of Popes* (New York 1986) 133–134.

[W. M. PLÖCHL]

JOHN XVI, ANTIPOPE

Pontificate: February or March 997 to May 998. He probably died in 1001. John Philagathos was a Greek born in Rossano (Calabria). He was Otto II's chancellor for Italy from 980 to 982, when the emperor appointed him abbot of Nonantola (near Modena). In 987 he was one of young Otto III's (983–1002, emp. 996) tutors. The following year he was appointed bishop of Piacenza, which Pope John XV temporarily raised to an archbishopric for him at the request of Otto. Also in 987 John Philagathos headed the king's court in Pavia, and he was chancellor for Italy again in 991–92. In 994 he was sent to Constantinople to find a Byzantine princess to wed Otto III. Having made progress in this mission, he returned to Italy with the Byzantine ambassador Bishop Leo of Synada in November 996. However, the month before John and Leo arrived, Crescentius II Nomentanus had used the emperor's absence from Rome to revolt against Otto's rule. Crescentius had expelled Pope Gregory V (996–99) and set himself up as dictator of the city.

Upon his return, John went to northern Italy, where he was in contact with both Otto (in Aachen) and Crescentius. It is difficult to understand John's position in this divisive situation, but for reasons that remain obscure, he went to Rome and was named Pope John XVI in February or March 997. Some scholars see in John's actions a conspiracy with the Byzantines; others consider him a victim of Crescentius' intrigues and perhaps of his own ambition. Whatever the truth, he had become involved in a dangerous political situation that quickly worsened. In March 997, Gregory V excommunicated him, removing him as abbot of Nonantola and archbishop of Piacenza. Additionally, Crescentius had usurped for himself all temporal power in the city and the Papal States. These actions left John with little spiritual authority and no political resources of his own. That summer he received messages from Otto, and a letter from Abbot Nilus of Rossano (ca. 910–1004); both criticized his actions and called for him to step down. John attempted to contact Otto and seemed ready to submit to his demands, but Crescentius jailed the imperial messengers who were sent to negotiate with the antipope.

Finally, when Otto marched on Italy in December 997, John fled Rome for Campagna. After the emperor and Pope Gregory V entered Rome in February 998, Crescentius was seized and soon beheaded. Troops were sent to search for John, whom they captured and imprisoned in a Roman monastery. Later he was blinded, mutilated on the nose, ears, and tongue, and paraded through the streets of Rome on a donkey. Abbot Nilus protested these actions, but to no avail. At a Lenten synod in 998, Gregory formally deposed John and confined him to a monastery where he later died.

Bibliography: L. DUCHESNE, ed. *Liber Pontificalis* (Paris 1886–92; repr. 1955–57) 2.261–64. P. JAFFÉ, *Regesta pontificum Romanorum* (Leipzig 1885–88; repr. Graz 1956) 1.495–96. M. P. VINSON, ed. and trans. *The Correspondance of Leo Metropolitan of Synada and Syncellus* (Washington, DC 1985). B. PLATINA, *De vita Christi ac omnium pontificum* 143, ed. G. GAIDA, in *Rerum italicarum scriptores* 3.1, ed. L. A. MURATORI (Città di Castello and Bologna 1913–32) 174–75. H. K. MANN, *The Lives of the Popes in the Early Middle Ages* (London 1902–32) 4.389–90, 415–46. H. ZIMMERMAN, *Papstabsetzungen des Mittelalters* (Graz, Vienna, Cologne 1968) 105–18. A. NITSCHKE, "Der mißhandelte Papst: Folgen ottonischer Italienpolitik," in *Staat und Gesellschaft in Mittelalter*

und *Früher Neuzeit: Gedenkschrift für J. Leuschner* (Göttingen 1983) 40–53. J. N. D. KELLY, *The Oxford Dictionary of Popes* (New York 1986) 135–36.

[P. M. SAVAGE]

JOHN XVII, POPE

Pontificate: May 16 to Nov. 6, 1003. He was a native of Rome, called John Sicco, and a member of the party of the CRESCENTII before his election. After the death of SYLVESTER II, John was made pope by the *patricius* Crescentius III (d. 1012), who had exercised great influence over Roman affairs since the death of OTTO III in January 1002. Before he had taken orders he had been married and was father of three sons, who also became ecclesiastics. There exist no reports of the activities of his short pontificate, except the fact that he was obviously a puppet of the Crescentii.

Bibliography: J. HALLER, *Das Papsttum,* 5 v. (2d, rev. ed. Stuttgart 1950–53) 2:229, 562. R. POUPARDIN, "Note sur la chronologie de Jean XVII," *Mélanges d'archéologie et d'histoire* 21 (1901) 387–390. P. JAFFÉ, *Regesta pontificum romanorum ab condita ecclesia ad annum post Christian natum 1198,* ed. S. LÖWENFELD 1:501. E. AMANN, *Dictionnaire de théologie catholique,* ed. A. VACANT et al., 15 v. (Paris 1903–50; Tables générales 1951–) 8.1:629. G. SCHWAIGER, *Lexikon für Theologie und Kirche,* ed. J. HOFER and K. RAHNER, 10 v. (2d, new ed. Freiburg 1957–65); suppl., *Das Zweite Vatikanische Konzil: Dokumente und Kommentare,* ed. H. S. BRECHTER et al., pt. 1 (1966) 5:992. R. AUBERT, *Dictionnaire d'histoire et de géographie ecclésiastiques* 26 (Paris 1997), s.v. "Jean XVII (XVIII), pape." R. BENERICETTI, *La cronologia dei Pape dei secoli IX–XI secondo le carte di Ravenna* (1999), 55. J. N. D. KELLY, *Oxford Dictionary of Popes* (New York 1986), 138.

[W. M. PLÖCHL]

JOHN XVIII, POPE

Pontificate: Dec. 25, 1003 to June or July 1009; b. Joannes Fasanus, Rome; d. Abbey of St. Paul–Outside–the–Walls, Rome. Prior to his election he was *cardinalis s. Petri.* He was elected through the influence of Crescentius III (d. 1012), but he was less dependent on the Roman patrician family of CRESCENTII than his predecessor, JOHN XVII, had been. He somewhat strengthened papal authority by the restoration of the episcopal See of Merseburg in 1004. In 1007 he confirmed the foundation of the bishopric of BAMBERG, which had been erected by Emperor HENRY II. He also conferred the PALLIUM on Abp. Meingaudus of TRIER and Elphege (d. 1012) of CANTERBURY. He bestowed papal protection on the abbey of SAINT-BENOÎT-SUR-LOIRE, and he definitely opposed the pretensions of Abp. Letericus of SENS and

Bp. Fulco of ORLÉANS, who tried to abrogate the papal privileges of that monastery. It is noteworthy that John was recognized in Constantinople as the bishop of Rome, for his name appears on the DIPTYCHS of the BYZANTINE CHURCH. John at length retired to ST. PAUL-OUTSIDE-THE-WALLS and lived there as a monk. He is buried at the same monastery.

Bibliography: J. HALLER, *Das Papsttum* 2:229, 242–247, 562. F. X. SEPPELT, *Geschichte der Päpste von den Anfängen bis zur Mitte des 20. Jh.* 2:401. P. JAFFÉ, *Regesta pontificum romanorum ab condita ecclesia ad annum post Christum natum 1198*, ed. S. LÖWENFELD 501–503. E. AMANN, *Dictionnaire de théologie catholique*, ed. A. VACANT et. al. 8.1:629–630. R. AUBERT, *Dictionnaire d'histoire et de géographie ecclésiastiques* 26 (Paris 1997), s.v. "Jean XVIII (XIX), pape." R. BENERICETTI, *La cronologia dei Papi dei secoli IX–XI secondo le carte di Ravenna* (1999), 56–57. W. ZIEZULEWICZ, "Monastic Forgery in an Age of Reform: A Bull of Pope John XVIII for Saint–Florent–de–Saumur (April 1004)," *Archivum Historicum Societatis Iesu* (Roma 1985), 7–42. J. N. D. KELLY, *Oxford Dictionary of Popes* (New York 1986), 138–139.

[W. M. PLÖCHL]

JOHN XIX, POPE

Pontificate: April 19, 1024 to 1032. Romanus, as he was named, came from the family of the TUSCULANI, successors to the CRESCENTII in providing the Church with popes. He adopted, during the pontificate of his brother BENEDICT VIII, the title *Consul, dux et senator omnium Romanorum,* with no special claim to this title except Emperor HENRY II's approval. After the death of his brother, Romanus, although still a layman, took possession of the papacy as a family inheritance and, despite canonical regulations, received all the orders on one day, taking the name John XIX. At Easter 1027 he crowned CONRAD II emperor. In ecclesiastical affairs he was dominated by Conrad, especially in the interminable controversies between the patriarchs of AQUILEIA and GRADO and between the bishop of Constance and the abbot of Reichenau. On the other hand, he prevented Conrad's interference in Rome and made Tusculum supreme in the States of the Church. John could hardly contribute much to the reform of the Church and showed himself an inconsistent administrator, interested chiefly in financial gain; e.g., he made demands of money for hierarchial posts. According to RODULPHUS GLABER, John even planned to recognize the patriarch of Constantinople as ecumenical in exchange for money but is supposed to have been dissuaded by WILLIAM OF SAINT–BÉNIGNE of Dijon. The name of the pope was omitted from the diptychs of the Byzantine Church since John's time, a fact that may indicate that Glaber's statement and other exaggerated charges made against the pope are false. Among his positive achievements were the support he gave to GUIDO OF AREZZO, the CLUNIAC REFORM, and—at least indirectly—the Truce of God. He was buried in St. Peter's.

Bibliography: Sources. J. M. WATTERICH, ed., *Pontificum romanorum . . . vitae,* 2 v. (Leipzig 1862) 1:70, 75, 708–711. P. JAFFÉ, *Regesta pontificum romanorum ab condita ecclesia ad annum post Christum natum 1198,* ed. S. LÖWENFELD (repr. Graz 1956) 1:514–519. R. GLABER, *Les Cinq livres de ses histoires,* ed. M. PROU (Paris 1886) 93–94. *Liber ponfiticalis,* ed. L. DUCHESNE (Paris 1886–92) 2:269; 3:132. L. SANTIFALLER, "Chronologisches Verzeichnis der Urkunden Papst Johanns XIX," *Römische historische Mitteilungen* 1 (1956–57) 35–76. W. KÖLMEL, *Rom und der Kirchenstaat im 10. und 11. Jahrhundert* (Berlin 1935). P. BREZZI, *Roma e l'Impero medioevale* (Bologna 1947). A. FLICHE and V. MARTIN, eds., *Histoire de l'église depuis les origines jusqu'à nos jours* (Paris 1935) 7:87–89. L. SANTIFALLER, *Zur Geschichte des ottonischsalischen Reichskirchensystems* (2d ed. Vienna 1964). F. X. SEPPELT, *Geschichte der Päpste von den Anfängen bis zur Mitte des 20. Jh.* (Munich 1954–59) 2:408–412. G. SCHWAIGER, *Lexikon für Theologie und Kirche,* ed. J. HOFER and K. RAHNER (Freiburg 1957–65) 5:992. R. AUBERT, *Dictionnaire d'histoire et de géographie ecclésiastiques* 26 (Paris 1997). R. BENERICETTI, *La cronologia dei Papi dei secoli IX–XI secondo le carte di Ravenna* (1999), 60–62. G. TURRI, "Guido d'Arezzo o Guido di Pomposa," in *Palestra del Clero* (1994) 527–32. H. WOLFRAM, "Die Gesandtschaft Konrads II. nach Konstantinopel (1027/29)," *Mitteilungen des Instituts für Österreichische Geschichtsforschung* (1992) 161–74. J. N. D. KELLY, *Oxford Dictionary of Popes* (New York 1986) 141–142.

[G. RILL]

JOHN XX, POPE

There was no pope of this name. Because of confusion in the writings of MARIANUS SCOTUS, copied by subsequent authors, a mythical Pope John reigned four months between BONIFACE VII (d. 985). and JOHN XV, who thereby was designated, erroneously, as John XVI and so on. The several popes named John in the 10th and 11th centuries have since been correctly numbered, but JOHN XXI (PETER OF SPAIN) and JOHN XXII bear numbered names that they themselves assumed.

Bibliography: *Annuario Pontificio* (Rome 1912–), footnote under John XXI and esp. see under John XIV. É. AMANN, *Dictionnaire de théologie catholique,* ed. A. VACANT et al. (Paris 1903–50; Tables générales 1951–) 8.1:632–633. G. SCHWAIGER, *Lexikon für Theologie und Kirche,* ed. J. HOFER and K. RAHNER (Freiburg 1957–65) 5:992.

[A. O'MALLEY]

JOHN XXI, POPE

Pontificate: Sept. 16, 1276, to May 20, 1277; b. Petrus Juliani or Petrus Hispanus, Lisbon, Portugal, before *c.* 1205; d. Viterbo, Italy. Little is known about Peter. His short tenure as pope has made it virtually impossible to assess the impact of his reign. The two major tasks of his papacy, the restoration of the Eastern Church to the Western Church and a crusade, were incomplete at the time of his death. By contrast, Peter's work in the academic arena is much better known. Peter himself was an energetic man who made significant contributions in the fields of philosophy, theology, medicine, and logic. He is particularly remembered in the history of philosophy for his ordering of an investigation into the teaching of Averroism at the University of Paris. The action ultimately culminated in the condemnations of 1277.

There is virtually no information regarding Peter's early life. The currently accepted theory is that he was born before 1205, although scholars have suggested later dates. There is consensus, however, that Peter was born in Lisbon, Portugal, that he was the son of a man named Julianus, that he was baptized Peter Juliani and that he was probably tied to a noble family. In terms of his academic formation, Peter probably attended the cathedral school in Lisbon and by 1220 he was studying at the University of Paris. His teachers in theology were more likely Alexander of Hales, William of Auxerre, and William of Auvergne. By 1231 it would appear that Peter had traveled to northern Spain where he taught logic and composed a famous logical treatise that was entitled *Tractatus.* In 1235, Peter was probably studying medicine in both Toulouse and Montpellier.

By Jan. 11, 1245, Peter was in Siena, Italy where he taught medicine. He remained there for roughly five years and then he likely returned to Portugal. While there, Peter served as the dean of the Church of Lisbon and as archdeacon of Vermoim in the diocese of Braga. In March 1254, Peter attended the Cortes (Diet) of Leiria and in 1257 he was given the office of prior of Santa Maria at Guimarães. In 1263, Peter had been appointed *magister scholarum* of the Cathedral School of Lisbon. His activities between the years 1264–1272 are not known. In 1272 Pope Gregory X summoned Peter to become his court physician at Viterbo. It was during this period that Peter probably compiled his medical treatise *Thesaurus pauperum.* By the end of March or in early April 1273, Peter was selected to be the archbishop of Braga and on June 5 of that same year Pope Gregory X appointed him cardinal-bishop of Frascati (Tusculum). In June 1273, Peter accompanied Gregory to the General Council of Lyons in June 1273.

There is some evidence that suggests that that Peter returned to the University of Paris for a short stay in 1274. Nevertheless, he continued to govern the See of Braga until May 23, 1275. Peter's friend and patron Pope Gregory X died on Jan. 10, 1276. Gregory was succeeded by the remarkably short reigns of Innocent V and Adrian V and after the latter's death, Peter was elected pope. On Sept. 13, 1276 Peter was mistakenly crowned John XXI instead of XX. His reign as pope is commonly viewed as a political compromise between French and Italian factions. His most important deeds were the issuance of the bull *Relatio nimis implacida* in which he ordered the bishop of Paris, Étienne Tempier, to investigate errors being taught at the University of Paris. The bull led to attacks on Latin Averroism, a few positions regarding courtly love by Andrew Campellanus, and some ideas relating to St. Thomas' thought. In a second bull, *Flumen aque vive,* John ordered Bishop Tempier to purify the doctrines of the Parisian masters. John's pontificate ended abruptly when the roof of his study collapsed on him on May 14, 1277. He died from his injuries on May 20, 1277.

Peter was an able scholar and on one occasion he referred to himself as "doctor in liberal arts, rector of the philosophical sublimity, honor of the medical faculty and past master in the science of the soul." The description is apt but there are questions concerning the authorship of his *Summulae logicales.* According to one tradition of scholarship the work may have been written by a Dominican friar named Peter Alfonsi of Spain. The more popular view, however, is that the man who became Pope John XXI was the author of the *Summulae logicales* which is more properly called *Tractatus.* In addition to the *Tractatus,* Peter probably wrote a second logical treatise titled *Syncategoremata.* In the field of medicine, Peter's *Thesaurus pauperum* achieved great notoriety and has overshadowed his 14 other works on medicine that include commentaries on Hippocrates, Galen, and Isaac. As rector of philosophical sublimity, Peter is credited with having commented on Aristotle's *De Anima, Historia animalium, De morte et vita, De causis longitudinis et brevitatis vitae,* and *De sensu et sensato.* Apparently Peter wrote two commentaries on pseudo-Denys the Areopagite that reflect some influence from *De coelesti hierarchia,* Neoplationism, and St. Augustine. Finally, as a past master of the science of the soul, Peter argued for an Augustinian view of God's role in illuminating the intellect in ordinary cognition in his work *Scientia libri de anima.*

Bibliography: Soources. JOHN XXI, *Summulae logicales,* ed. I. M. BOCHEŃSKI (Turin 1947); *Tractatus, called afterwards Summule Logicales,* ed. L.M. DE RIJK (Leiden 1972); *Expositio librorum beati Dionysii,* ed. M. ALONSO (Lisbon 1957); *Scientia libri de anima,* ed. id. (Madrid 1941); *Comentario al "De anima" de Aristoteles,* ed. id. (Madrid 1944); *Expositio libri De anima. De morte et vita et De causis longitudinis et brevitatis vitae. Liber naturalis de rebus principalibus,* ed. id. (Madrid 1952); *Thesaurus pauperum,* ed. and tr. L. DE PINA, and M. H. DA ROCHA PEREIRA (Oporto 1955); *Regimen sanitatis,* ed. M. H. DA ROCHA PEREIRA (Figueira da Foz 1960); *Die Ophthalmologie: Liber de oculo,* ed. and tr. A. M. BERGER (Munich 1899); *Le Registre de Jean XXI,* ed.

L. CADIER (Paris 1898); *The Summulae logicales of Peter of Spain,* ed. and tr. J. P. MULLALLY (Notre Dame, Ind. 1945). **Literature.** R. STAPPER, *Papst Johannes XXI* (Münster 1898). L. THORNDIKE, *A History of Magic and Experimental Science* (New York 1923–58) 2:488–516. M. GRABMANN, *Handschriftliche Forschungen und Funde zu den philosophischen Schriften des Petrus Hispanus, Sitzungsberichte der Bayerischen Akademie der Wissenschaften zu München* 9 (Munich 1936). J. FERREIRA, "As *Sümulas logicais* de Pedro Hispano e os seus comentadores," *Colectânea de Estudos* 3 (1952) 360–393; "Introduçâo ao estudo do *Liber de anima* de Pedro Hispano," *Revista filosófica* 3 (Coimbra 1954) 177–198; *Presença do Augustinismo avicenizante na teoria dos intelectos de Pedro Hispano* (Braga 1959); "L'Homme dans la doctrine de Pierre d'Espagne," in *L'Homme et son destin* (Actes du Premier Congrès International de Philosophie médiévale; Louvain-Paris 1960) 445–461. L.M. DE RIJK, "On the Genuine Text of Peter of Spain's *Summule Logicales I,*" *Vivarium* 6 (1968) 1–34; "On the Genuine Text of Peter of Spain's *Summule Logicales IV,*" *Vivarium* 7 (1969) 120–162; "On the Life of Peter of Spain, the author of the *Tractatus,* called afterwards *Summule Logicales*" *Vivarium* 8 (1970) 123–154. M. DE ASUA, "El Comentario de Pedro Hispano Sobre el *De Animalibus.* Transcripcion de las quaestiones sobre la controversia entre medicos y filosofos," *Patristica et mediaevalia* 16 (1995) 45–66; A. D'ORS "Petrus Hispanus O.P. Auctor Summularum," *Vivarium* 35 no. 1 (1997) 21–71; M. DE ASUA "Los Problemata o Quaestiones de animalibus de Pedro Hispano," *Stromata* 54 (1998) 267–302

[J. A. SHEPPARD]

JOHN XXII, POPE

Pontificate: Aug. 7, 1316, to Dec. 4, 1334; b. Jacques Duèse (or d'Euze) in Cahors, southern France, *c.* 1245; d. Avignon. Born into a rich bourgeois family, he studied canon and Roman law at Montpellier and Orléans. Bishop of Fréjus from 1300, he was appointed chancellor of Charles II and then Robert of Naples (1308–10); he was consecrated bishop of Avignon in 1310, cardinal-priest of S. Vitale in 1312, and cardinal bishop of Porto in 1313, his last stage before the See of St. Peter. At the age of 72, he was elected to the papacy after a two-year vacancy and not before he encouraged rumors about his precarious physical condition. Eventually, John ruled the Church for 18 consecutive years, during which he established the papal court at Avignon.

John XXII continued the reorganization of the Church along the centralizing lines fixed in the previous century and increased the papal treasury through strengthening apostolic control over church offices and benefices. He promulgated the *Liber Septimus,* the collection of decretals of his predecessor, Clement V, also known as CLEMENTINAE; his own judicial decisions, the *EXTRAVAGANTES COMMUNES,* were the last addition to CANON LAW until the 16th century. Although he was personally austere, energetic, and kindly, his strong family affections and local patriotism brought charges of nepo-

tism. Indeed, of the 28 cardinals he nominated, 20 were from southern France, three of them his nephews.

In the political sphere, John continued the strong alliance with the western kings and submitted the papacy to the interests of Edward II and Edward III, both in the internal arena of England and in their protracted conflict with Scotland. In France, as well, he tried to strengthen the monarchy in the critical transition period between the Capetians and the Valois.

Less successful was John's long conflict with Emperor Louis IV, the Bavarian. Following a disputed election to the German crown (1314), the pope admonished the two contenders to settle their dispute amicably. Papal moderation, however, changed radically once Louis of Bavaria defeated Frederick of Austria (1322), for the victorious king appointed an imperial vicar in Italy and gave political support to the pope's enemy, Galeazzo VISCONTI of Milan. Employing the precedent established by INNOCENT III, John declared that the imperial election lay with the papacy and ordered Louis to annul his former acts and to renounce the imperial dignity until a papal decision was issued. The German response came in the Declaration of Nuremberg, which formally denied the papal claims (Nov. 16, 1323). These were condemned once again in the Sachsenhausen Appellation (May 22, 1324), which declared John a heretic because of his declarations on evangelical poverty. At this stage the conflict between pope and emperor-elect lost its original, political essence and became a war between two well-defined ideological factions. To fortify his position, Louis gave asylum to MARSILIUS OF PADUA and JOHN OF JANDUN, the authors of the *Defensor pacis,* who championed the independent status of secular princes and declared the ecumenical council superior to the pope. John retaliated by excommunicating Louis, but the latter was crowned emperor in Rome by the senator Sciarra COLONNA (Jan. 17, 1328). Louis thereupon charged John with being an usurper and oppressor of the Church, deposed him, and brought about the election of the Franciscan Spiritual Peter of Corbara, as antipope NICHOLAS V (May 12). These extremist measures, however, proved short lived. After Louis returned to Germany (1329), Peter submitted to the pope, who had excommunicated him and subsequently imprisoned him in Avignon. Louis tried unsuccessfully to negotiate a reconciliation with the papal curia. Still, the radical Franciscans (among them the English philosopher WILLIAM OCKHAM) together with Marsilius of Padua continued their vigorous antipapal campaign from the imperial court in Munich.

The critical role of the FRANCISCANS during the conflict between *regnum et sacerdotium* hints at their own clash with the papal curia during John's pontificate.

Throughout the 13th century, the order had enjoyed papal protection, which brought about, *inter alia,* the nomination of a special coordinator between the order and the Holy See, as well as papal formal ownership of Franciscan wealth as a means of safeguarding the order's allegiance to evangelical poverty. Still, the many conflicts within the ranks of the order between the Spirituals, who favored strict adherence to St. Francis's rule of poverty, and the Conventuals, who held to a broader interpretation, led to continuous papal intervention. Shortly after his accession, John took action against the Spirituals and imprisoned their delegates at Avignon. In a series of decrees, the pope ordered them to resume obedience to their superiors (*Quorundam exigit,* Oct. 7, 1317). He condemned the most extreme champions of evangelical poverty, such as the FRATICELLI and BEGUINES (*Sancta Romana,* Dec. 30, 1317), and the Tuscan Spirituals, who had taken refuge in Sicily (*Gloriosam ecclesiam,* Jan. 23, 1318). Twenty-five Spirituals were handed over to the INQUISITION, which put four of them to the stake. In order to undermine their ideological foundations, John condemned the *Postilla super Apocalypsim,* a treatise written by the undisputed leader of the Spirituals, PETER JOHN OLIVI. Up to this point, the pope had confronted the tenets and way of life of the most radical Franciscans. Two years later, however, he began a frontal attack against the order as a whole, condemning the Franciscan doctrine of evangelical poverty, (*Ad conditorem canonum,* Dec. 8, 1322) and made it heretical to assert that Christ and the Apostles had not owned goods (*Cum inter nonnullos,* Nov. 12, 1323) (*see* POVERTY CONTROVERSY). The pope later deposed and excommunicated the minister-general, MICHAEL OF CESENA (*Quia vir reprobus,* Nov. 16, 1329), who, together with the proctor of the order, BONAGRATIA OF BERGAMO, and William Ockham, had fled from Avignon and joined forces with the emperor. John eventually succeeded in submitting the Franciscan Order to apostolic obedience. The Perpignan Chapter chose Gerald Odonis as minister-general in place of Cesena, thus facilitating a reconciliation with the papal curia (1331).

The protracted conflict with the Franciscans exposed John to criticism, but it did not challenge his status as Vicar of God on Earth and ultimate speaker of Catholic orthodoxy. The controversy over the BEATIFIC VISION, however, threatened the theological foundations of the papacy, for criticism came no longer from members of a monastic order suspected of a biased approach, but from the masters of the faculty of theology in Paris. During the winter of 1331–32, John XXII preached four sermons on the beatific vision. Although not yet defined as dogma, traditional doctrine maintained that the souls of the saints, who were in paradise, enjoyed the full vision of God immediately after their deaths. The pope, however, claimed that since an individual is composed of body and soul, his final reward is deferred until their reunion at the resurrection on the Day of Judgment. The University of Paris condemned these theories in the autumn of 1333, and it was supported by most theologians whom the pope consulted. On his deathbed, John retreated to some degree, acknowledging that the souls of the blessed see God and the divine essence face to face as clearly as their condition permits. He stated that his former position was only a personal opinion. The pope's capitulation to the theological tenets of the university can be regarded as a reflection of the changing balance of power in Christendom on the eve of the Conciliar Movement.

John set up foreign missions and established bishoprics in Anatolia, Armenia, Iran, and India. A patron of learning, he founded the papal library at Avignon (*see* VATICAN LIBRARY) and the University of Cahors.

Bibliography: *Lettres de Jean XXII,* ed. A. FAYEN, 2 v. in 3 (Rome 1908–12); *Lettres secrètes et curiales de Pape Jean XXII . . . ,* ed. A. L. COULON and S. CLÉMENCET (Paris 1906–); *Lettres communes . . . ,* ed. G. MOLLAT and G. DE LESQUES, 16 v. in 15 (Bibl. des Écoles franç. ser. 3; Paris 1904–47). G. MOLLAT, *The Popes at Avignon,* tr. J. LOVE (New York 1963). J. E. WEAKLAND, ''Administration and Fiscal Centralization under Pope John XXII, 1316–1334,'' *Catholic Historical Review* 54 (1968) 39–54, 285–310; ''Pope John XXII and the Beatific Vision Controversy,'' *Annuale Mediaevale* 9 (1968) 76–84. M. D. LAMBERT, ''The Franciscan Crisis under John XXII,'' *Franciscan Studies* 10 (1972) 123–143. K. E. SPIERS, ''Pope John XXII and Marsilius of Padua on the Universal Dominion of Christ,'' *Medioevo* 6 (1980) 471–478. S. MENACHE, ''The Failure of John XXII's Policy toward France and England,'' *Church History* 55:4 (1986) 423–437. R. LAMBERTINI, ''*Usus* and *usura:* Poverty and Usury in the Franciscans' Responses to John XXII's *Quia vir reprobus,''* *Franciscan Studies* 54 (1994)185–210. S. KINSELLA, ''The Poverty of Christ in the Medieval Debates between the Papacy and the Franciscans,'' *Laurentianum* 36:3 (1995) 477–509. M. DYKMANS, ''Nouveaux textes de Jean XXII sur la vision beatifique,'' *Revue d'histoire ecclesiastique* 66:2 (1971) 401–417. C. TROTTMAN, ''Vision béatifique et intuition d'un objet absent: des sources franciscaines du nominalisme aux defenseurs scotiste de l'opinion de Jean XXII sur la vision différée,'' *Studi Medievali* ser. 3, 34:2 (1994) 653–715.

[S. MENACHE]

JOHN XXIII, POPE, BL.

Pontificate, Oct. 28, 1958, to June 3, 1963; Angelo Giuseppe Roncalli, b. Sotto il Monte, Bergamo, Italy, Nov. 25, 1881; d. Rome, Italy, June 3, 1963.

Prepapal Career

He was the third of 13 children, the first son, of pious peasants, Giovanni Battista and Marianna Giulia (Mazzola) Roncalli, who rented land as sharecroppers (*mezzadri*). Besides working in the fields, Angelo attended the elementary school in the town, took lessons from a priest in the neighboring town of Carvico, went to a "college" in Celana, and at 12 entered the diocesan minor seminary at Bergamo. There he came under the influence of the progressive leaders of the Italian Catholic social movement, especially of Bp. Camillo Guindani of Bergamo and two zealous laymen, Count Stanislao Medolago-Albani and Niccolò Rezzara. A scholarship of the Cerasoli Foundation in 1901 enabled Roncalli to become a student at the Roman Seminary (Apollinare), where Umberto Benigni deepened his knowledge of church history. He interrupted his education for a year to serve as a volunteer in the 73d Infantry Regiment of the Italian Army, thereby shortening the period of compulsory military training. After taking the doctorate in theology, he was ordained on Aug. 10, 1904, in the church of S. Maria in Monte Santo.

Early Priesthood. As he was beginning graduate studies in Canon Law, he was appointed secretary of the new bishop of Bergamo, Count Giacomo Radini-Tedeschi, a far-sighted, social-minded prelate, whom Roncalli served faithfully for more than nine years, gaining experience in all forms of Catholic action and an understanding of the problems of the working class. At the same time he taught apologetics and ecclesiastical history, and later also patrology, at the diocesan seminary. In that era of violent reaction against MODERNISM he was falsely accused of such errors by some integralists; actually, in his teaching he tended to avoid controversial questions. He published several brief monographs—one in commemoration of the great Church historian Baronius, *Il card. Cesare Baronio, per il centenario della sua morte* (Monza 1908; repub. Rome 1961), and two on local history, *Gli inizi del seminario di Bergamo e S. Carlo Borromeo* (1910; rev. Bergamo 1939) and *La 'Misericordia Maggiore' di Bergamo e le altre istituzioni di beneficenza amministrate dalla Congregazione di Carità* (Bergamo 1912). As diocesan assistant to the Women's Catholic Action and a member of various diocesan committees, he became concerned also in political problems and favored Catholic involvement in national affairs.

In 1915, when Italy entered World War I, Roncalli was recalled to, the army and was assigned to military hospitals in Bergamo first as a sergeant in the medical corps and then as a lieutenant in the chaplains' corps; he also ministered to the soldiers on the battlefields of the Piave and to the sick during the epidemic of Spanish influenza. In his leisure time he wrote *In Memoria di Monsignore Giacomo Radini-Tedeschi, vescovo di Bergamo* (Bergamo 1916), a laudatory and cautious biography. After the war he resumed the duties of spiritual adviser to the Union of Catholic Women and the Union of Catholic Youth, was appointed spiritual director of the diocesan

Pope John XXIII. (©Bettmann/CORBIS.)

seminary, and at his own expense, opened a hostel and clubhouse for young men studying in Bergamo (Casa dello Studente). At the request of Bp. Luigi Marelli, he established the Opera di Sant'Alessandro to coordinate the various educational activities of the diocese.

In 1920 he helped to organize the first national Eucharistic Congress to be held in Italy after the war. A year later he was invited to Rome by Benedict XV, named director of the Society for the Propagation of the Faith in Italy, and given the task of centralizing the administration of the society first on the national level and then on the international. He collaborated in the writing of the motu proprio *Romanorum Pontificum* (May 3, 1922) by which Pius XI raised the society to papal status, transferred its headquarters from Lyons to Rome, and placed it under the Congregation for the PROPAGATION OF THE FAITH. Roncalli was a member of the General High Council, which coordinated the work of this association with that of other bodies supporting the missions.

Diplomat in the Near East. In 1925 Roncalli was appointed titular archbishop of Areopolis and apostolic visitator to Bulgaria and was consecrated on March 19 in the church of SS. Ambrose and Charles (San Carlo al Corso) in Rome. Accompanied by a Belgian Benedictine, Constantine Bosschaerts, he promptly took up residence in the politically troubled capital, Sofia, and concerned himself with the problems of the Eastern-rite Catholics, who constituted a small, scattered minority of about 4,000 among the predominantly Orthodox population. He visited the remote and impoverished communities of refugees from Macedonia and Thrace and selected a young native priest, Kyril Kurteff, as apostolic administrator (later exarch). He had fewer anxieties over the 40,000 Catholics of the Latin rite, who were better organized but were unfortunately dependent on the political and ecclesiastical support of France. He introduced retreats for isolated priests, presided over the first congress of Bulgarian Catholics at Yambol, and personally assisted the victims of the earthquake of 1928 with money from Rome. Since the state church was Orthodox, he was watched with suspicion by its ecclesiastical leaders. When the king or czar, Boris III, contrary to his promises, had his marriage with Giovanna di Savoia, Catholic daughter of King Victor Emmanuel III of Italy, repeated according to the Orthodox rite in 1930 and had their first child baptized by the Orthodox metropolitan in 1933, Roncalli protested to no avail. He was successful, however, in securing the government's consent to the establishment of an apostolic delegation in 1931.

On Nov. 24, 1934, Roncalli was named apostolic delegate to Turkey and Greece, and on the 30th he was transferred from the titular see of Areopolis to that of Mesembria (in Bulgaria). He succeeded in closing the breach that existed between the delegation and the local clergy of the Latin rite. As administrator of the Vicariate Apostolic of ISTANBUL, Roncalli had immediate jurisdiction over the approximately 10,000 Catholics of the Latin rite, who were for the most part foreigners and were decreasing in number. Amid trying circumstances he fostered harmony among the different national colonies in the city. Not only was his presence as apostolic delegate officially ignored and barely tolerated by the Turkish government, but he had to contend with the antireligious reforms of Kemal Atatürk's secular and nationalistic republic and to witness the closing of many Catholic schools, the cessation of Catholic publications, and the laying aside of clerical garb and religious habits in public. With characteristic optimism he took a benevolent view of the new constitution and tried to demonstrate to the Turkish rulers the purely spiritual and supranational nature of the Church's activity. To show his respect for the government and people of Turkey, he introduced the use of the Turkish language into divine worship and official documents. Eventually he won the personal esteem of some of the highest Turkish statesmen. One of his many conciliatory gestures toward the Orthodox was the visit that he paid to the Ecumenical Patriarch Benjamin, in the Phanar on May 27, 1939; he was courteously received.

During World War II, when Istanbul became a center of international espionage and intrigue, Roncalli provided the Holy See with much valuable information that he obtained from diplomats as well as public sources. Among the former he cultivated a useful friendship with the German ambassador to Turkey Franz von Papen, who was a Catholic. He made every effort to pacify the French of his flock, who bitterly resented Italian participation in the disastrous war against their fatherland, and he helped many persecuted Jews fleeing from central and eastern Europe.

In Greece, where he was confronted with the confusion existing among the 50,000 Catholics of the country, he eventually succeeded in bringing about greater unity of action among the bishops of the Latin, BYZANTINE, and ARMENIAN CHURCHES. He was never able, however, to achieve the desired *modus vivendi* with the Greek government, which, under the pressure of the Orthodox churchmen, enacted anti-Catholic legislation concerning marriages, conversions, and publications, and obstructed his efforts to found a seminary for Latin Catholics. During the war he was impeded in his relations with the Greeks by having the same nationality as the army of occupation, but he kept aloof from political disputes and tried to act as a mediator between the opposing parties. He aided the starving regardless of their religion, and he went to Rome to urge the Holy See to persuade the British to relax the blockade of Greek ports in order that desperately needed food supplies and medicines might be imported. Upon his return he negotiated with the representatives of the Axis for the required guarantees; he also intervened frequently to prevent or repair injustices. He visited both the occupying and the captured troops, and he set up in Istanbul an office for the location of prisoners of war and missing persons. After August 1942, he was unable to maintain further contact with the Catholics of Greece because of the military operations.

Nuncio in Paris. Meanwhile in France Charles de Gaulle's provisional government at Paris requested the Holy See to recall the nuncio Valerio Valeri, who had been accredited to Henri Pétain's government at Vichy. Pius XII chose Roncalli for the difficult post, and the nuncio, appointed on Nov. 22, 1944, arrived in Paris on December 30. Unobtrusively he labored to repair the spiritual divisions that had been embittered by the war and its consequences. When the leaders of the Resistance accused at least half of the French bishops of collaboration with the Nazis and when the government called for the removal of 33, the nuncio investigated and in the end advised only three bishops to resign. He also obtained the government's consent to 27 episcopal nominations within his first three years, and in 1945 he successfully recommended to the pope three archbishops for the cardinalate.

He pleaded for the humane treatment and prompt repatriation of the German prisoners of war who were detained in France for several years, and he arranged for the transfer of several hundred theological students among them to one camp at Le Caudrey (near Chartres), where their preparation for the priesthood could be continued.

Throughout the continual succession of unstable governments that followed De Gaulle's withdrawal from public life, Roncalli remained on friendly terms with whatever politicians came to power. He won the admiration of the Socialist Vincent Auriol, president of the Republic, and of the radical Édouard Herriot, president of the National Assembly, and he enjoyed the confidence of Catholics such as Georges Bidault and Robert Schuman; but he never attempted to become intimate with the members of the Mouvement Républicain Populaire. When the government grant to private schools, begun under the Vichy régime, was suspended in 1945, he cooperated with the French episcopate in presenting the Church's claim to a fair share of the funds; eventually (1951) his efforts were rewarded to some extent by the concession of a small annual subsidy for each pupil. To his regular duties, he added those of first permanent observer of the Holy See at the United Nations Educational, Scientific, and Cultural Organization (UNESCO) for 19 months, and he addressed the sixth and seventh general assemblies in 1951 and 1952.

Roncalli traveled widely, made a pilgrimage to LOURDES almost every year, and in 1950 made a journey to Algeria and other parts of North Africa. In his dealings with the French bishops, he was not hasty in judging new experiments in the apostolate and he was tolerant of discussion in the intellectual sphere and patient with innovations in the pastoral ministry. Thus he viewed Cardinal Emanuel SUHARD'S novel plan to evangelize the dechristianized masses (Mission de France) hopefully, and he attentively observed the activities of the WORKER-PRIESTS among the proletariat; this movement was severely restricted by the Holy See several months after his final departure from France. After he became pope, it was completely suppressed by a decree of the Holy Office dated July 3, 1959.

Patriarch of Venice. Roncalli was made a cardinal priest (Jan. 12, 1953), and given the titular church of Santa Prisca on the Aventine. He received the red biretta (and the grand cross of the Legion of Honor) from President Auriol in the Elysée Palace on January 15. Although he had at first been destined for a position in the Roman CURIA, he was offered the patriarchate of VENICE after the death of the incumbent, and he gladly accepted. Appointed on January 15, he arrived in the city on March 15, where he soon won the affection of his clergy and people.

During his five years in Venice, he wrote brief, frequent circular letters on topics of current importance; visited all the parishes and showed his concern for the working class; established 30 new parishes and built a new minor seminary; and developed various forms of Catholic action. Concerned about moral laxity in the city, he prevented the projected transfer of the gambling casino from the Lido to the center of town, and he forbade the clergy to visit the biennial festival of art in 1954 because of some improper pictures exhibited there; two years later he was able to revoke the prohibition and even to attend the exhibition himself. As president of the Tri-Venetian Episcopal Conference, he compelled the left-wing faction of the Christian Democrats to suspend publication of their weekly, *Il Popolo Veneto;* in a letter dated Christmas 1955, the Episcopal Conference denounced the proposed "opening to the Left." On Aug. 16, 1956, Roncalli issued a pastoral letter in which he rebuked those who persisted in advocating this policy at any cost. Nevertheless when the Italian Socialist party held its national convention at Venice in February 1957, he exhorted his flock to welcome the delegates, who appeared to him to desire to promote the ideals of social peace and justice; some of the right-wing Christian Democrats then protested his action. In 1958 he completed the fifth and last volume of *Gli Atti della Visita Apostolica di S. Carlo Borromeo a Bergamo (1575),* the collection of historical documents that he had been editing since 1909 (with the collaboration of a Bergamask priest, Pietro Forno, for v.1 and 2) and had published at intervals (Florence, 1936, 1937, 1938, 1946, 1958) in the series "Fontes Ambrosiani."

Pontificate

After PIUS XII'S death (Oct. 9, 1958), Roncalli was summoned to the conclave, which opened October 25 and was attended by 51 cardinals (of whom 17 were Italian); Roncalli was elected on October 28 and crowned on November 4. He kept as his private secretary Loris Capovilla, who bad served him in that capacity at Venice, and he appointed Domenico TARDINI pro-secretary (soon cardinal secretary) of state; this office had been vacant since 1944. After Tardini died on July 30, 1961, the pope appointed Cardinal Amleto Cicognani his successor. With only 52 members in the College of Cardinals, including 12 more than 80 years old, Pope John held his first consistory on Dec. 15, 1958, at which, annulling in part the regulation of Sixtus V (1586) and Canon 231 of the Code of Canon Law by which a maximum of 70 members was fixed, he created 23 new cardinals. In the second consistory (Dec. 14, 1959) he added eight more; the third (March 28, 1960) announced the elevation of ten prelates, of whom seven were named and three were reserved *in pectore.* In the fourth consistory (Jan. 16, 1961), four new cardinals were created, and in the last (March 19, 1962), ten. The total was then the highest in history—87 (plus the three never revealed)—and the representation the most international.

In another consistory (Jan. 25, 1959) the pope proposed to the cardinals three major undertakings: a diocesan synod for Rome, an ecumenical council for the universal Church, and a revision of the Code of CANON LAW (preceded by the promulgation of the Code of Oriental Law). The synod, the first in the history of Rome, was solemnly opened by the pope in the Basilica of St. John Lateran on Jan. 24, 1960; he addressed it at St. Peter's on the following three days and closed it there on January 31. Its decrees, promulgated by the apostolic constitution *Sollicitudo omnium ecclesiarum,* were designed to remedy the ills of the Church in a city that had grown from 400,000 inhabitants in 1900 to more than two million in 1960 and that had only 220 secular and 360 religious priests.

Vatican Council II. The ecumenical council, which he decided to call the Second Vatican Council, is undoubtedly the major achievement of John's pontificate, although it was not completed before his death (*see* VATICAN COUNCIL II). Attributing the idea of convoking such an assembly to a sudden inspiration from the Holy Ghost, he prescribed as its immediate task the renewal of the religious life of Catholics and the bringing up to date of the teaching, discipline, and organization of the Church, with the ultimate goal being the unity of Christians. At the solemn opening of the council on Oct. 11, 1962, he delivered a memorable discourse, and on the next two days he received the members of the 86 extraordinary missions sent by governments and international bodies and the 39 non-Catholic observers and guests who had accepted invitations to the council. Although he did not attend the general congregations or normally interfere with the deliberations, he intervened on November 21 at a critical point by deciding that the schema on revelation, which had been rejected on the preceding day by somewhat less than the required majority of two-thirds, should not be discussed further but should be revised by a special mixed commission. This encouraged the majority who were in favor of change; hence it was a turning point in the first session. He closed the first period of the council on December 8 with an allocution in which he announced the creation of a new commission, charged with following and directing the conciliar activities during the nine-month recess. On Jan. 6, 1963, he sent to each father of the council a letter, *Mirabilis ille,* in which he gave directives for the continuation of the work during the interval and recommended local collaboration.

Law and Liturgy. John took the first step toward revision of the Code of Canon Law by announcing the cre-

ation of a pontifical commission on March 28, 1963. Earlier modifications of ecclesiastical law had been introduced by his *motu proprio Suburbicariis sedibus* (April 11, 1962), removing all power of jurisdiction over the SUBURBICARIAN sees from the cardinal bishops who bear their titles and entrusting the government of these dioceses to the bishops of the place; thus he freed the cardinals of distracting responsibilities and enabled them to devote their undivided attention to curial affairs. Four days later by the *motu proprio Cum gravissima* he decreed that the episcopal dignity would henceforth be conferred on all cardinals, regardless of their rank within the College. Moreover, by the *motu proprio Summi Pontificis electio* (Sept. 5, 1962) he modified Pius XII's dispositions regarding the vacancy of the Holy See. He also made the patriarchs of the Eastern churches who were not cardinals adjunct members of the Congregation for the ORIENTAL CHURCH. Finally, he added another office to the Roman Curia by elevating to that rank, by the *motu proprio Boni Pastoris* (Feb. 22, 1959), the papal commission for cinema, radio, and television; he laid down new rules for its functioning and put Abp. Martin J. O'Connor, rector of the NORTH AMERICAN COLLEGE in Rome, at its head.

John manifested his determination to enhance the sacred liturgy by the *motu proprio Rubricarum instructum* (July 25, 1960), approving a new code of rubrics for the Breviary and Missal. He also permitted the distribution of Holy Communion to the sick in the afternoon (Oct. 21, 1961). Several times he warned against exaggerations and excesses in the worship of the saints. He chose the schema on the liturgy as the first topic to be treated by Vatican Council II, and he ordered that the name of St. Joseph be inserted in the Canon of the Mass after that of the Blessed Virgin Mary (Nov. 13, 1962). Finally, in response to the direct appeal of the Greek Melkite patriarch Maximos IV Sayegh, he rescinded (April 5, 1960) the decision of the Holy Office forbidding the use of the vernacular in the Byzantine rite (specifically, the use of English in Birmingham, Alabama).

Encyclical Letters. John issued seven encyclical letters: *Ad Petri cathedram* (June 29, 1959), treating the triple theme of truth, unity, and peace, which are to be acquired and developed under the inspiration of charity; *Sacerdotii Nostri primordia* (July 31, 1959) on the centenary of the death of St. Jean Marie Baptiste VIANNEY, Curé d'Ars, with regard to all aspects of the contemporary life of priests; *Princeps Pastorum* (Nov. 28, 1959) on the 40th anniversary of the apostolic letter *Maximum illud* on the missions (development of a native hierarchy and clergy, collaboration of other countries, education of the clergy, apostolate of the laity, etc.); MATER ET MAGISTRA (dated May 15, 1961, pub. July 15) on recent developments of the social question in the light of Christian doctrine; *Aeterna Dei* (Nov. 11, 1961) on the 15th centenary of the death of St. Leo the Great; *Paenitentiam agere* (July 1, 1962) on the necessity of penance to ensure the success of Vatican Council II; and *PACEM IN TERRIS* (April 11, 1963), addressed to all men of good will, on peace among all nations based on truth, justice, charity, and liberty and on the right organization of society for the attainment of this end. He also issued an encyclical epistle, *Grata recordatio* (Sept. 29, 1959), on the recitation of the rosary.

Canonizations. John canonized the following saints: Carlo da Sezze and Joaquina de VEDRUNA Y DE MAS (April 12, 1959), Gregory BARBARIGO (May 26, 1960), Juan de Ribera (June 12, 1960), Maria Bertilla BOSCARDIN (May 11, 1961), Martin de PORRES (May 6, 1962), Pierre Julien EYMARD, Antonio Maria Pucci, and FRANCESCO MARIA OF CAMPOROSSO (Dec. 9, 1962), and Vincent PALLOTTI (Jan. 20, 1963). He declared the following to be blessed: Elena GUERRA (April 26, 1959), Marguerite d' Youville (May 3, 1959), Innocenzo of Berzo (Nov. 12, 1961), Elizabeth SETON (March 17, 1963), and Luigi Maria Palazzolo (March 19, 1963). He also declared St. LAWRENCE OF BRINDISI to be a doctor of the Church (March 19, 1959).

Ecumenism and Diplomacy. During John's pontificate notable advances were made in ecumenical relations (*see* ECUMENICAL MOVEMENT). Catholic theologians conferred with the Orthodox at Rhodes in August 1959, when the executive committee of the WORLD COUNCIL OF CHURCHES met there. The Secretariat for Promoting CHRISTIAN UNITY was instituted by the motu proprio *Superno Dei nutu* (June 5, 1960) and Cardinal A. Bea was appointed president. Two papal envoys were sent to the patriarch of Constantinople, Athanagoras, on June 27, 1961. For the first time the Catholic Church was represented at an assembly of the World Council of Churches, when in November 1961 five official observers designated by Bea's secretariat went to New Delhi. In consideration of the Jews the pope commanded that the epithets "perfidis (Judaeis)" and "(judaicam) perfidiam" in the Roman liturgy of Good Friday be deleted.

During his pontificate a very large number of statesmen were received in audience. The pope's visit to Pres. Antonio Segni (May 11, 1963) was the first made by a pope to the Quirinal since the establishment of the Republic of ITALY. Secret negotiations with the Soviet Union resulted in the release of Josyf Slipyi, Ukrainian metropolitan of Lvov, who had been confined in Siberia and who arrived in Rome on Feb. 9, 1963. Attempts to procure the liberation of other Catholic prelates imprisoned behind the Iron Curtain, especially Cardinal József

Mindszenty, archbishop of Esztergom, ended in failure. John's efforts for world peace included an appeal to the heads of the governments involved (Sept. 10, 1961) when international tension was rapidly mounting over the Berlin Crisis; he appealed to the French and to the revolutionaries on June 3, 1962, during the civil war in Algeria; and he appealed again to the rulers of the most powerful countries on Oct. 25, 1962, begging them to continue to treat with each other in regard to Cuba. The International Balzan Foundation awarded him its Peace Prize for 1962; the four Soviet members of the foundation's general council concurred in this decision, and Nikita Khrushchev approved of their action.

Other Accomplishments. As bishop of Rome, John XXIII displayed unremitting care of his diocese; he made frequent appearances in the parishes, hospitals, and educational and charitable institutions of the city. He also traveled farther than any pope since Pius IX, going by automobile to the summer villa of the Roman Seminary at Roccantica (Sept. 10, 1960) and by train to Loreto and Assisi (Oct. 4, 1962) to pray for the forthcoming ecumenical council. To improve the education of candidates for the priesthood, he elevated the Lateran Athenaeum to the status of a pontifical university on May 17, 1959; on March 7, 1963, he did the same for the Athenaeum Angelicum, now known as the Pontifical University of St. Thomas Aquinas. In order to promote the study of Latin among seminarians and other students, he issued the apostolic constitution *Veterum sapientia* (Feb. 22, 1962). He sought means to strengthen the Church in Latin America and frequently expressed his concern for the "Church of Silence" in eastern Europe and eastern Asia. He also fostered the growth of the missions; besides writing the encyclical *Princeps Pastorum,* he consecrated 14 bishops for Africa, Asia, and Oceania in St. Peter's on May 8, 1960, and 14 more on May 21, 1961.

Pope John appeared in public for the last time at his window in the Vatican on May 22, 1963. Shortly thereafter he began to succumb to a gastric cancer from which he had suffered for about a year. Having endured a prolonged agony, he died on June 3 (Pentecost Monday). As the world mourned, his body was buried in a simple tomb in the crypt of St. Peter's. On Nov. 18, 1965, Paul VI announced initiation of procedures looking to the beatification and ultimate canonization of his two immediate predecessors, John XXIII and Pius XII.

Character. A man of evangelical simplicity and unaffected humility, John XXIII was never ashamed of his lowly origins and always remained closely attached to his native soil and his rustic family. His diary, *Journey of a Soul* [tr. by D. White (New York 1965)], published posthumously, reveals a profound interior life and an unwavering trust in Divine Providence. One of his favorite apothegms was *Voluntas Dei, pax nostra.* He was a highly cultured man, versed in history, archeology, and architecture, fond of literature (especially Manzoni), art, and music; he could speak French, Bulgarian, Russian, Turkish, and modern Greek, in addition to Italian and Latin. Gifted with an agreeable disposition and a ready wit, he was characteristically open and affable, understanding and compassionate, jovial and calm, familiar in audiences, hospitable, and a lively conversationalist.

Throughout his life he valued the care of souls above any other occupation. He disliked the bureaucracy of the Roman Curia, demythologized the papacy, and diminished the cult of the pontifical personality. He allowed as much freedom of thought and action as possible to others and recognized the limitations of his own knowledge and ability. He perceived the need of reform and his pontificate is regarded as a turning point in the history of the Catholic Church. Considered by some, because of his advanced age and ambiguous reputation at the time of his election, to be merely a transitional pontiff, John XXIII instead initiated a new age. As part of the Jubilee Year 2000 events, he was beatified by Pope John Paul II on September 3 together with Pope Pius IX.

Bibliography: *Scritti e discorsi, 1953–1958,* 4 v. (Rome 1959–62); *Discorsi, messaggi, colloqui del Santo Padre Giovanni XXIII,* 5 v. (Vatican City 1961–64). *Souvenirs d'un nonce: Cahiers de France, 1944–1953* (Paris 1963); *Encyclicals of Pope John XXIII* (Washington 1965). *Acta et documenta Concilio oecumenico Vaticano II apparando,* ser.2, v.1 *Acta summi pontificis Ioannis XXIII* (Vatican City 1964). *Wit and Wisdom of Good Pope John,* comp. H. FESQUET, tr. S. ATTANASIO (New York 1964). U. GROPPI and J. S. LOMBARDI, *Above All a Shepherd: Pope John XXIII* (New York 1959). A. LAZZARINI, *Pope John XXIII,* tr. M. HATWELL (New York 1959). F. X. MURPHY, *John XXIII Comes to the Vatican* (New York 1959). R. ROUQUETTE, ''Le Mystère Roncalli,'' *Études* 318 (1963) 4–18, Eng. tr. *Catholic Mind* 62 (Apr. 1964) 4–12. E. E. HATES, *Pope John and His Revolution* (London 1965). V. BRANCA and S. ROSSO-MAZZINGHI, ed. *Angelo Giuseppe Roncalli: dal patriarcato di Venezia alla cattedra di San Pietro* (Florence 1984). G. ALBERIGO, ed. *Giovanni XXIII: transizione del papato e della Chiesa* (Rome 1988). P. HEBBLETHWAITE, *Pope John XXIII, Shepherd of the Modern World* (Garden City, NY 1985).

[R. TRISCO]

JOHN XXIII, ANTIPOPE

Pontificate (Pisan obedience): May 17, 1410 to May 29, 1415. Born Baldassare Cossa into an impoverished family of Neapolitan aristocrats (ca. 1370), he died in Florence on either June 23, 1419 or (see Esch) on December 27. There are few reliable facts concerning Cossa's early life, though there is a tradition that he left a military career in favor of church service. He studied canon law at Bologna and entered the papal curia of Boniface IX (1389–1404). Cossa became archdeacon of Bologna in 1396, and in 1402 Boniface named him cardinal deacon of St. Eustachio and appointed him legate to Bologna and Romagna. From 1403 to 1408 he lived in Bologna, where his administrative and financial abilities brought that region of Italy back under the control of the Papal States. During the Great SCHISM, Cossa was one of the cardinals who broke with GREGORY XII (1406–15) in May 1408, when the latter showed that he had no intention of ending the Schism (Gregory named four new cardinals, thus signaling his desire to continue his line of the papacy). Cossa went to Pisa where he and most of Gregory's and antipope Benedict XIII's cardinals called for a council to end the Schism. Together with Peter of Candia, he took the leading role in organizing the Council of Pisa and was largely responsible for engineering Peter's election as Antipope Alexander V (1409–10). After Alexander' death in the following year, and in spite of rumors (now largely considered false) that Cossa had poisoned him, the Pisan cardinals met at Bologna and unanimously elected Cossa to be Alexander's successor. He took the name John XXIII.

John's election did little to change the nature of the Schism; there were still three active claimants to the papacy: John, Benedict XIII (1394–1417), and Gregory XII. While John had by far the widest political support (England, France, and many Italian and German states), he was still politically vulnerable, especially in Italy. He had also acquired the reputation of being a worldly, unscrupulous, and ambitious man of questionable moral character (he was considered tyrannical as papal legate in Bologna, and was rumored to have had numerous romantic liaisons). In Italy, King Ladislaus of Durazzo-Naples (1386–1414) continued to press his claim to much of the Papal States, and John depended on Louis II of Anjou for protection. After Louis defeated Ladislaus at Roccasecca (May 19, 1411), John entered Rome on April 12, 1411. Here John called a council (April 29, 1412–March 1413), ostensibly to continue church reform, but it only managed to condemn (Feb. 10, 1413) the writings of the English reformer John Wycliff (ca. 1325–84). John also created several new cardinals, among whom were Francisco Zarabella, Pierre d'Ailly, Guillaume Fillastre, and Robert Hallam. In August 1412, John excommunicated the Bohemian reformer Jan Hus (ca. 1369–1415) because he was preaching against the antipope's pseudo-crusade against Ladislaus (John granted indulgences to all who contributed money to the cause).

Soon John was forced to come to terms with Ladislaus because his protector, Louis of Anjou, had returned to France. For a brief time the two were allies, but in May

1413 Ladislaus again attacked Rome, and John had to flee with his cardinals. They went to Florence, where John asked for the support of the German king Sigismund (1410–37; emp. 1433). Sigismund saw this appeal as an opportunity to hold a general council and to end the schism. In exchange for his support, Sigismund forced John to call a council in the king's territory. On Dec. 9, 1413 John issued a bull convoking a council to be held at Constance in November the following year. In spite of Ladislaus' death on Aug. 6, 1414, John was compelled by his cardinals to travel to Constance, where he opened the council on Nov. 5, 1414.

John hoped that as pope he could dominate the proceedings and convince the council to ratify the decisions made at the Council of Pisa, thus eliminating BENEDICT XIII and GREGORY VII, and leaving John as legitimate pope. But his hopes came to naught in February and early March 1415, when the Germans, English, and French insisted that all three rival popes should abdicate. During the night of March 20 John fled Constance for Schaffhausen, in Duke Frederick of Austria's territory. Soon Sigismund declared war against the duke, and John was compelled to flee again, this time to Burgundy. But the Duke of Burgundy refused him safe conduct, and John had to retire to Freiburg instead (April 29, 1415). These actions further inflamed opposition to him at the council, and he was formally deposed in the 12th session (May 29, 1415).

In the meantime, Sigismund had captured Freiburg and brought John back to the council. Here he officially ratified the council's decisions, declared them infallible, and renounced his right to the papacy. Again known as Baldassare Cossa, he remained in captivity for three years. Sigismund handed him over to Louis III of Bavaria (a well-known enemy of Cossa), who kept him as a prisoner in Rudolfzell, Gottleiben, Heidelberg, and Mannheim until well after Dec. 28, 1417, the time that the council had decreed his release. He was set free sometime in 1418. Cossa then went to Florence and formally submitted to the council's pope, MARTIN V (1417–31). On June 23, 1419 Martin appointed Cossa cardinal bishop of Tusculum-Frascati, but he died six months later. Cossa's magnificent tomb, which displays the papal crest, is in the baptistery at Florence. It was commissioned by Cosimo de Medici and includes work by Bartolomeo di Michelozzo and Donatello.

JOHN XXIII is generally considered one of the more worldly and opportunistic popes of the Great Schism. He showed little concern for spiritual matters, and some of his actions, particularly during his battles with Ladislaus and the Council of Constance, support this judgment. But John's deep involvement in the political, administrative, and financial aspects of ecclesiastical life often led to a positive outcome for the papal court. His policies concerning the Papal States were surprisingly effective; and, given the circumstances of Italian politics, it is difficult to see how he could have more circumspectly protected his interests in Rome or solidified control of the Papal States. Furthermore, the circumstances of his deposition raise a difficult question: can a council suspend and depose the pope under whose authority it has been convened if he is unwilling? For these reasons and others, current scholarship is mitigating some of the negative interpretations of John XXIII's reign.

Bibliography: L. DUCHESNE, ed. *Liber Pontificalis* (Paris 1886–92; repr. 1955–57) 2:507–20, 543–45, 554–55. J. D. MANSI, *Sacrorum conciliorum nova et amplissima collectio* (Florence and Venice 1759–98; repr. Graz 1960–61) 27:506–715. *Acta concilii Constanciensis,* ed. H. FINKE and J. HOLLENSTEINER (Münster 1986–28). DIETRICH OF NIEHEIM, *De schismate libri tres,* ed. G. ERLER (Leipzig 1890); and *De vita ac factis constanciensibus Johannis Papae XXIII,* in *Magnum oecumenicum Constanciense Concilium,* ed. H. VON DER HART (Frankfurt 1697–1742) 2:335–459. B. PLATINA, *De vita Christi ac omnium pontificum* 213 (208) ed. G. GAIDA, in *Rerum italicarum scriptores* 3:1, ed. L. A. MURATORI (Città di Castello and Bologna 1913–32) 304–12. C. J. VON HEFELE and H. LECLERCQ, *Histoire des conciles d'après les documents originaux* (Paris 1907–38) v. 7. J. BLUMENTHAL, "Johan XXIII: seine Wahl un seine Persönlichkeit," *Zeitschrift für Kirchengeschichte* 21 (1901) 488–516. E. J. KITTS, *In the Days of the Councils* (London 1908); *Pope John XXIII and Master John Hus* (London 1910; New York 1978). H. G. PETER, *Die Informationen Papst Johanns XXIII und dessen Flucht von Konstanz bis Schaffhausen* (Freiburg 1926). F. X. SEPPELT, *Geschichte der Päpste von den Anfängen bis zur Mitte des zwanzigsten Jahrhunderts* (Munich 1956) 4:241–53. R. BÄUMER, *Lexikon für Theologie und Kirche* (Freiburg 1957–65) 5:995. L. R. LOOMIS, *The Council of Constance* (New York 1961). H. JEDIN and J. DOLAN, eds. *Handbook of Church History* (New York 1965–81) 4:448–68. J. SMITH, *The Great Schism, 1378: The Disintegration of the Papacy* (New York 1970). A. ESCH, "Das Papsttum unter der Herrschaft der Neapolitaner," in *Festschrift für Hermann Heimpel,* v. 2 (Gottingen 1972) 713–800. L. WALDMÜLLER, "Materialien zur Geschichte John XXIII, 1410–1414," *Annuarium historiae conciliorum* 7 (1975) 229–237. C. M. D. CROWDER, *Unity, Heresy, and Reform: 1378–1460* (London 1977). R. CONDON, *A Trembling upon Rome: A Work of Fiction* (New York 1983). A. LANDO, *Il papa deposto, Pisa 1409* (Torino 1985). J. N. D. KELLY, *The Oxford Dictionary of Popes* (Oxford and New York 1986) 237–39 for additional bibliography. W. BRANDMÜLER, "Infeliciter electus fuit in Papam," in *Ecclesia et Regnum: Festschrift F.J. Schmale* (Bochum 1989) 309–22. W. BRANDMÜLER, *Das Konzil von Konstanz* (Paderborn 1991). For additional bibliography see A. FRENKEN, *Lexikon des Mittelalters* (Munich 1991) 5:546–47; and *Dictionnaire d'histoire et de géographie ecclésiastiques* (Paris 1997) 26:1171–72.

[P. M. SAVAGE]

JOHN BACONTHORP

Known as *Doctor resolutus;* b. Baconsthorpe, Norfolk, England, *c.* 1290; d. London, *c.* 1348. After joining the order, he studied at the Oxford Whitefriars under Robert Walsingham (d. 1310) and at Paris under Guy Terrena (d. 1342). He lectured on the *Sentences* (ed. Lyons 1484) and became a master in theology at Paris before Whitsun 1323. As regent master he delivered *Quodlibeta* 1–2 at the University of Paris and *Quodlibeta* 3 at the Carmelite school in 1330. He was lecturer in Cambridge by 1330. Between 1327 and 1333 he was provincial of the order in England.

Agostino NIFO called Baconthorp *princeps Averroistarum.* But in fact he accepted none of the heterodox teachings of AVERROËS, such as the eternity of the world or the unicity of the intellect. To him Averroës was "the worst of heretics." However, Baconthorp was an outstanding commentator on Aristotle and Averroës; his interpretations of Averroës, which were more benign than those of Thomas Aquinas, were highly valued by the Averroists of the Renaissance.

Baconthorp denied the real distinction between the soul and its powers, as well as that between active and passive intellects, insisting that these are but two aspects of the same power. In explaining knowledge he eliminated intelligible species as useless and absurd. For him, the essence of a material substance is intelligible in itself; it does not need an agent intellect to render it actually intelligible. Rejecting many doctrines of St. Thomas, he adopted positions widely held in his day. For him, essence and existence are really distinct, not as different things, but as different modes of being; essence corresponds to potential being, and existence to actual being. In theology Baconthorp was an ardent advocate of the IMMACULATE CONCEPTION promulgated by DUNS SCOTUS and the Franciscans. He defended the attempt of THOMAS BRADWARDINE to reconcile human freedom with divine sovereignty and the primacy of divine causality. An outstanding theologian and philosopher, he exercised great influence on the Carmelite school up to the 17th century.

His commentaries on Aristotle's *Metaphysics, De anima,* and *Ethics* are no longer extant. He also wrote commentaries on Matthew and Paul; on Augustine's *De Trinitate* and *De civitate Dei;* on Anselm's *De incarnatione Verbi* and *Cur Deus homo;* and various *Opuscula.* His three *Quodlibeta* were printed in Venice, 1527.

Bibliography: B. M. XIBERTA Y ROQUETA, *De scriptoribus scholasticis saeculi XIV ex ordine Carmelitarum* (Louvain 1931) 167–240. A. B. EMDEN, *A Biographical Register of the University of Oxford to A.D. 1500,* 3 v. (Oxford 1957–59) 1:88–89. A. DI S. PAOLO, *Dictionnaire d'histoire et de géographie ecclésiastiques,* ed. A. BAUDRILLART et al. (Paris 1912—) 6:87–90. É. H. GILSON, *History of Christian Philosophy in the Middle Ages* (New York 1955).

[A. MAURER]

JOHN BAPTIST OF THE CONCEPTION, ST.

Trinitarian reformer, writer, mystic; b. Almadóvar del Campo, Spain, July 10, 1561; d. Córdoba, Feb. 14, 1613. Juan García early evidenced remarkable spirituality and love for recollection. He studied philosophy with the Discalced Carmelites at Almadóvar and theology at the Universities of Baeza and Toledo. He entered the Trinitarian Order in 1580. Admired for outstanding virtue, mortification, and prayerfulness, he was professed (1581) and made official preacher at La Guardia and Seville.

When the general chapter approved the establishment of houses for the primitive observance of John de Matha (1594), John Baptist was made superior at Valdepeñas. His sanctity, self-effacement, and love for God enabled him to overcome opposition to his "reform" as foretold by St. TESESA OF AVILA. He thought of his work as a restoration rather than reform, adding the use of sandals and other austerities to the original rule. A prolific writer, he wrote on all phases of theology, but with special emphasis on mysticism; his works fill nine volumes. Winning the support of Pope CLEMENT VIII (1599), King PHILIP III, and others, he established 19 houses of the Discalced friars before his death. His Discalced Trinitarians today form the surviving branch of the Trinitarian Friars founded by JOHN OF MATHA (1213) and FELIX OF VALOIS (1198). He was beatified by PIUS VII in 1819 and canonized by Paul VI on May 25, 1975.

Feast: Feb. 14.

Bibliography: ANTONINO DE LA ASUNCÍON, *Diccionario de escritores trinitarios* (Rome 1899) 1:182ff. JUAN DEL SAGRADO CORAZÓN, *Santo y Reformador* (Córdoba 1959). P. MEDRANO HERRERO, *San Juan Bautista de la Concepción, escritor* (Ciudad Real, Spain 1994); *Valores literarios de San Juan Bautista de la Concepción* (Ponce, P.R. 1994). J. PUJANA, *Trinidad y experiencia mística en San Juan Bautista de la Concepción* (Salamanca 1983); *San Juan Bautista de la Concepcion: Carisma y mision* (Madrid 1994). A. BUTLER, *The Lives of the Saints,* ed. H. THURSTON and D. ATTWATER, 4 v. (New York 1956) 1:339–340.

[P. M. DONOVAN]

JOHN BASSANDUS, BL.

Religious reformer and diplomat; b. Besançon, France, 1360; d. in the monastery of Collemaggio, near Aquila, Italy, Aug. 26, 1445. He entered the Augustinian monastery in Besançon in 1378, joined the CELESTINES in Paris in 1390, and was sent to found a monastery in Amiens, where he was spiritual director of St. COLETTE. He was prior in Paris and provincial of France five times from 1411 to 1441, traveling in Italy, Spain, and England for the visitation of Celestine houses. Charles VII of France sent him on an unsuccessful mission to persuade AMADEUS OF SAVOY (antipope Felix V) to resign his claims to the tiara. Jean GERSON, his friend, dedicated his *De susceptione humanitatis Christi* to him. In 1443, Eugene IV called on him to reform Collemaggio. St. JOHN CAPISTRAN gave his funeral oration, and his third successor at Collemaggio wrote his vita (*Acta Sanctorum*, Aug. 5:870–892). His relics are in Aquila.

Feast: Aug. 26.

Bibliography: B. HEURTEBIZE, *Dictionnaire d'histoire et de géographie ecclésiastiques* 6:1263–64.

[J. PÉREZ DE URBEL]

JOHN BENINCASA, BL.

Servite hermit; b. Florence, Italy, 1376; d. Monticelli, Italy, May 9, 1426. He entered the SERVITES at Montepulciano while still very young and at the age of 25 was permitted to embrace the life of a hermit on Mount Montagnata, near Siena, and later in a cave near Monticelli. The local population had great admiration for the rigorous asceticism he practiced in his lonely retreat, and they often sought him out for spiritual advice. His death was reputed to have been announced by the spontaneous ringing of the local church bells. He was buried at Monticelli, and his cult was approved on Dec. 19, 1829. Although he has the same family name, he is not related to (St.) Catherine of Siena.

Feast: May 11.

Bibliography: *Acta Sanctorum*, May 7:651–652. L. RAFFAELLI, *Vita breve del beato Giovanni Benincasa da Firenze* (Rome 1927). A. BUTLER, *The Lives of the Saints* (New York 1956) 2:275.

[B. J. COMASKEY]

JOHN BLUND

English philosopher and theologian; b. *c.* 1180; d. 1248 (place unknown). Blund studied and taught the arts first at Paris, then at Oxford. He left Oxford at the dispersal of masters and scholars in 1209 and went to Paris for his theological course, becoming master *c.* 1220. At the great dispersion of the University of Paris in 1229, he returned to England with other English masters and resumed teaching theology at Oxford. On Aug. 26, 1232, he was elected archbishop of Canterbury; but his election was contested and finally annulled by Gregory IX because of his irregularity in holding two benefices with the cure of souls without a dispensation. However, as canon

St. John Baptist of the Conception.

and prebendary of Chichester, and also possessing both benefices, restored to him by papal bull in 1233, he was appointed chancellor of York in 1234.

Henry of Avranches claims that Blund was the most distinguished Aristotelian of his day and was the first to lecture on the newly discovered books of ARISTOTLE at Paris and Oxford. Indeed his *Tractatus de anima* shows his truly vast knowledge of Aristotle; its chief inspiration, however, was AVICENNA. Blund followed Avicenna closely but not blindly, arranging the matter as best suited himself, inserting new elements from other sources, and retaining his full freedom to dissent from his model whenever he had reason to do so. Against Avicenna and the generally accepted view at the time, he firmly maintained that the heavenly bodies are not animate, and so are moved by their natures, not by their souls. With Aristotle, he defined the soul as "the perfection of a body endowed with organs having in it the capacity of life" (*De anim.* 412a 27–28), following the Greek-Latin version but substituting *perfectio* for *actus* and omitting *prima*. (There was indeed a long tradition coming down from CALCIDIUS for the use of *perfectio* in the definition of the soul.) Blund's definition became current in the first quarter of the 13th century (cf., e.g., ROLAND OF CREMONA and WILLIAM OF AUVERGNE). With Avicenna he stressed the substantiality of the soul; and to safeguard its immortality, which he vigorously defended, he upheld its absolute simplicity and spirituality and denied its hylomorphic composition. He taught the unity of soul in one individual. Yet there were other influences at work: Calcidius, BOETHIUS, NEMESIUS OF EMESA, JOHN DAMASCENE, ADELARD OF BATH, and WILLIAM OF CONCHES, and perhaps also the *De naturis rerum* of his older contemporary ALEXANDER NECKHAM. His chapter on memory is dependent mainly on St. AUGUSTINE, and that on free will on St. ANSELM OF CANTERBURY. On the other hand, traces of Blund's influence may easily be detected in Alexander Neckham's latest work, the *Speculum speculationum,* and in the *Summa de creaturis* of St. ALBERT THE GREAT. Blund's treatise *De anima* belongs to a period of transition and reflects the interests and controversies of the time. It is an attempt to join Eastern philosophy with Western thought: a good illustration of the teaching of the faculty of arts in the first decade of the 13th century and a striking example of the penetration of Aristotle and Avicenna into the Paris and Oxford schools.

The *Tractatus de anima* is extant in three MSS; an edition is in preparation by D. A. Callus. The theological writings have not survived.

Bibliography: *The Shorter Latin Poems of Master Henry of Avranches Relating to England,* ed. J. C. RUSSELL and J. P. HIERONIMUS (Cambridge, Mass. 1935) 127–136. J. C. RUSSELL, *Dictionary of Writers of 13th Century England* (New York 1936) 56–58. D. A. CALLUS, "Introduction of Aristotelian Learning to Oxford," *Proceedings of the British Academy,* 29 (1943) 241–252; "The Treatise of John Blund *On the Soul*" in *Autour d'Aristote: Recueil d'études . . . offert à Mgr. A. Mansion,* (Louvain 1955) 471–495. O. LOTTIN, *Psychologie et morale aux XII et XIII siécles,* 6 v. in 8, (Louvain 1942–60) 3:606, 610–617. A. B. EMDEN, *A Biographical Register of the University of Oxford to A.D. 1500,* 3 v. (Oxford 1857–59) 1:206.

[D. A. CALLUS]

JOHN BONUS OF MILAN, ST.

Bishop; b. Camogli, Italy, end of sixth century; d. Jan. 2 (3?), 660. John (Giovanni) Camillus the Good was bishop of Milan from 649 until his death. The name Camillus derived from Camogli, where he was born of a noble family; the cognomen Bonus became attached to him in his own time because of his great prudence, magnanimity, and especially his easy friendship with and love of neighbor. He fought strenuously against Monothelitism and had a part in the LATERAN COUNCIL of 649. His cult grew only after the discovery and translation of his relics by Bp. Aribert of Milan in the 11th century. His remains are at present in the cathedral of Milan, brought there by Charles BORROMEO in 1582.

Feast: Jan. 10.

Bibliography: *Acta Sanctorum* Jan 1:622–623. *Analecta Bollandiana* 15 (1896) 356–358. *Bibliotheca hagiographica latina antiquae et mediae aetatis,* 2 v. (Brussels 1898–1901; suppl. 1911) 1:4354. A. TAMBORINI, I santi milanesi (Milan 1927) 46–51. F. MANTUANO, *La leggenda del beato Zannebono da Mantua* (Mantua 1971, rep. of 1512 ed.).

[W. A. JURGENS]

JOHN BURIDAN

Philosopher and precursor of modern science; b. probably Bethune, northern France, toward the end of the thirteenth century; d. after 1358. Few definite facts are known about his life. Except for at least one trip to the Papal Curia at Avignon, his entire career was spent at the University of Paris, where, according to HENRY OF KALKAR, he taught for about 50 years. In 1328 he was a master of arts and rector of the university, a post he held again in 1340. In 1342 Pope Clement VI conferred on him a canonry in the church of Arras. In 1348 the bishop of Paris made him chaplain of the church of St. André-des-Arcs. His name headed the list of 22 Parisian masters from Picardy presented to the pope in 1349. He served as a delegate from the "Picard nation," drawing up in 1347 a statute relating to the administration of finances and to the organization of religious offices for that nation, and in 1357 and 1358, reestablishing peace between the "Picard nation" and the "English nation." The last year in which the name of Buridan is mentioned is 1358; possibly he died soon after that date.

Buridan's philosophy is known chiefly through his commentaries. He wrote *Quaestiones in artem veterem* (on the *Isagoge* of Porphyry, the *Categories,* and *On Interpretation*) and *Quaestiones in Analytica priora et posteriora, Quaestiones in Topica,* and *Quaestiones super libro De elenchis.* Under the title of *Summa logicae* he reshaped the *Summulae logicales* of Peter of Spain (*see* JOHN XXI), adapting them to nominalist ideas. His natural philosophy is contained in commentaries and questions on the physical treatises of Aristotle: *Physics, De caelo et mundo, De generatione et corruptione, Meteorologica, De anima, Parva naturalia, De motibus animalium,* and *De physiognomia.* He wrote similar elaborations of Aristotle's *Metaphysics, Nicomachean Ethics,* and *Politics.* Aside from certain indications of relative chronology, the dates of these treatises cannot be determined. He also wrote minor independent works devoted to particular questions. When the royal order of March 1, 1474, ordering the confiscation of all nominalist books was revoked in 1481, there was a revival of interest in Buridan's views; repeated printings were made of his principal works at the end of the fifteenth century and the beginning of the sixteenth century.

Buridan was a leading figure in the nominalist current of the fourteenth century, although the exact extent of his faithfulness to WILLIAM OF OCKHAM is a matter of debate. In spite of the judgments of censure passed by the university in 1326, 1339, and 1340 against certain nominalist positions, Buridan's authority was not affected. He was prudently careful to disassociate himself from the extreme NOMINALISM of such men as NICHOLAS OF AUTRECOURT and JOHN OF MIRECOURT. Against Nicholas he defended the principle of causality and its application in proving the existence of God; and he engaged in a polemic with John about the distinction between substance and accidents. Although, like Ockham, he tended to enlarge the field of probable truths at the expense of demonstrable truths and to separate more concisely the domain of faith from that of philosophical thought, he maintained his independence on many points, for example, on the idea of science, *suppositio,* local motion, and time. In the doctrine of the will, he professed an intellectual determinism: the choice between two goods is inevitably determined by the one that is superior to the other; freedom consists only in the power to suspend this choice by a supplementary thought.

Buridan is important mainly for his physical theories, particularly his explanation of local motion by the theory of IMPETUS, which he applied to the motion of the celestial spheres as well as to motion in the sublunary world. Because of this and related theories about the nature of weight and the acceleration of falling bodies, and by his acceptance of Ptolemy's system of astronomy, Buridan is considered a forerunner of LEONARDO DA VINCI, Nicolaus COPERNICUS, and Galileo GALILEI.

Otherwise, his nominalism found a more immediate area of expansion into the new universities, particularly German, which were being founded in growing numbers during this period, and where his former students, now professors (such as ALBERT OF SAXONY and MARSILIUS OF INGHEN), spread his philosophical ideas.

Bibliography: *Iohannis Buridani Quaestiones super libros quattuor de caelo et mundo,* ed. E. A. MOODY (Cambridge, Mass. 1942). E. FARAL, "Jean Buridan: Notes sur les manuscrits, les éditions et le contenu de ses ouvrages," *Archives d'histoire doctrinale et littéraire du moyen-âge* 21 (1946): 1–53; "Jean Buridan, maître ès arts de l'Université de Paris," *Histoire littéraire de la France* 38 (1949): 462–605. G. SARTON, *Introduction to the History of Science,* 3 v. in 5 (Baltimore 1927–48) 3.1: 540–546. A. C. CROMBIE, *Augustine to Galileo: The History of Science, 400–1650* (Cambridge, Mass. 1953). R. TATON, ed., *A History of Science,* v. 1 *Ancient and Medieval Science,* tr. A. J. POMERANS (New York 1963). M. CLAGETT, *The Science of Mechanics in the Middle Ages* (Madison 1959). P. M. M. DUHEM, *Le Système du monde: Histoire des doctrines cosmologiques de Platon à Copernic* (5 v. Paris 1913–17; repr. 10 v. 1954–59). A. MAIER, *Die Vorläufer Galileis im 14. Jahrhundert* (Rome 1949); *Zwei Grundprobleme der scholastischen Naturphilosophie: Das Problem der intensiven Grösse. Die Im-*

petustheorie (2d ed. Rome 1951); *An der Grenze von Scholastik und Naturwissenschaft* (2d ed. Rome 1952); *Metaphysische Hintergründe der spätscholastischen Naturphilosophie* (Rome 1955); *Zwischen Philosophie und Mechanik* (Rome 1958). M. E. REINA, *Il problema del linguaggio in Buridano* (Vicenza 1959); *Note sulla psicologia di Buridano* (Milan 1959).

[H. BASCOUR]

JOHN CANTIUS, ST.

Theologian; b. Kanti near Oswiecim, Poland, June 23, 1390; d. Cracow, Poland, Dec. 24, 1473. He enrolled at the University of CRACOW in 1413 and received the master's degree in liberal arts in 1417. From 1421 to 1429 he was rector of the school of the TEMPLARS at Miechów. After returning to the university, he taught in the school of philosophy, of which he was dean in 1432 and again 1437–38. In 1443 he obtained the degree of master in theology. He made a pilgrimage to JERUSALEM and journeyed several times to Rome. As the 16 extant manuscript volumes of his lectures show, he was a devoted and conscientious professor, but he became noted more for his sanctity than for the brilliance and originality of his teaching. A man of great mortification, he was also very considerate of the destitute. His biographies, mostly popular, abound with examples of his holiness and miracles, actual and legendary. Beatified in 1690, he was declared patron of Poland and Lithuania in 1737 by CLEMENT XII and canonized in 1767. He was buried in the church of St. Anne at Cracow.

Feast: Dec. 23 (formerly Oct. 20).

Bibliography: *Podreczna encyklopedia Kościelna,* v.17–18 (Warsaw 1909) 336–337. *Acta Sanctorum* Oct. 8:1042–1106. F. JAROSZEWICZ, *Matka Świetych Polska* (Cracow 1767; repr. in 4 pts. Poznań 1893). P. SKARGA, *Żywoty Świetych Pańskich* [*Kraków: 1723*] z dod. Ks. Stagraczynskiego (Chicago 1905) 393–397. A. ZAHORSKA, *Ilustrowane Zywoty Swietych Polskich* (Potulice, Poland 1937) 264–273. M. RECHOWICZ, *Świety Jan Kanty i Benedykt Hesse w świetle krakowskiej kompilacji teologicznej z XV wieku* (Lublin 1958). R. M. ZAWADZKI, ed., *Catalogus codicum manu s. Ioannis Cantii scriptorum qui in Bibliotheca Apostolica Vaticana asservantur* (Cracow 1997).

[L. SIEKANIEC]

JOHN CAPISTRAN, ST.

Franciscan theologian, preacher, and papal diplomat; b. Capestrano, Abruzzi Province, Italy, June 24, 1386; d. Ilok, Yugoslavia, Oct. 23, 1456. He was the son of a baron named Anthony, who came across the Alps in 1382 with the army of Louis I of Anjou; his mother was of the Amici family in Abruzzi. He was assigned a tutor at the age of six. His father and his brothers were killed during the struggle between the partisans of Louis II of Anjou (d. 1399) and of Ladislas of Naples (d. 1414). In 1401 he went to PERUGIA, where he studied civil and canon law from c. 1406, becoming in 1411 the adviser to the rector of the *Sapienza,* and in 1413, judge for the quarter of Santa Susanna (*Archivum Franciscanum historicum* 55:39–77), in which position he dealt severely with the FRATICELLI. When he sided with the populace, he was imprisoned by Braccio of Montone (d. 1424) after the battle of San Egidio. As a result of this event a religious crisis arose in this worldly man, who was already married to the daughter of the Count of San Valentino, although the marriage had not yet been consummated.

Religious Vocation. Once out of the Brufa prison, he joined the Observant FRANCISCANS at Perugia on Oct. 4, 1415, and became a humble and unpretentious novice under the direction of his master, the lay brother Onuphrius of Seggiano. Professed on Oct. 5, 1416, he studied theology and was admitted to Holy Orders c. Nov. 14, 1418 (*Archivum Franciscanum historicum* 49:77–82), after which he preached against the Fraticelli. In 1422 he was in Rome for the jubilee, and MARTIN V authorized him on November 11 to establish five residences. He preached during Lent of 1423 at SIENA, and he spent 1425 working with BERNARDINE OF SIENA, hearing confessions while Bernardine preached. In 1426 Bernardine was accused of HERESY for his devotion to the name of Jesus, and Capistran came from Aquila and successfully defended him before Martin V. He continued to preach against the Fraticelli and returned to Rome in 1429 to represent the Franciscan Observants, who looked to him for leadership when the papacy called a general chapter to resolve the split in the order. After being appointed assistant (1430) to the new minister general William of Casale (d. 1442), Capistran saw his *Constitutiones Martinianae* approved by the chapter of Assisi in June 1430; but when the Conventual FRANCISCANS obtained the bull *Ad statum* in August, the attempted reform and unification failed. By 1431 the Observants were granted their own provincial vicars, and in 1433 the care of the holy places in Palestine was entrusted to them. Capistran opposed events in Ferrara in 1434, defended in vain the Angevin cause in Naples as papal legate from 1435 to 1436, and in December of 1436 obtained for the members of the Third Order the right to live in common. In 1437 he assisted with the Colettine reform of the POOR CLARES at Ferrara, defended the Venetian JESUATI, and preached during Advent and the following Lent at Verona, as well as completing three valuable treatises. He visited the Holy Land at the end of 1439, and the years from 1440 to 1442 were spent in Milan preaching and writing. In late 1442 and early 1443 he was Franciscan visitor in Burgundy and in Flanders, where he worked to prevent Philip the Good from joining

the antipope Felix V (Amadeus VIII of Savoy); he also tried in vain to attract St. COLETTE and her followers to the Observants and deposed two unworthy provincial ministers (*Archivum Franciscanum historicum* 35:113–132, 254–295).

Franciscan Administrator. The Padua chapter of 1443 saw the final failure of the attempted unification of the Order, and Capistran became, for the first time, vicar general of the Cismontane family of the Observants, promulgating on Sept. 23, 1443, his *Ordinationes montis Alverniae.* He reconciled Aquila with Alphonse V of Aragon, drew up a course of studies dated Feb. 6, 1444, preached the crusade in Sicily, and after Easter 1445 obtained the Ara Coeli as the main house for the Observants. The bull *Ut sacra* (Jan. 11, 1446) sanctioned the independence, which was already an accomplished fact, of the two Observant groups within the order.

Appointed to the Ara Coeli community by the next vicar-general, James Primadicci (d. 1460), Capistran became vicar provincial of Abruzzi and worked for the canonization of Bernardine of Siena. In that same period he founded several convents and monasteries, reformed the Poor Clares of Perugia, wrote a *Vita s. Bernardini,* and received into the Third Order James Franchi, whose writings provide valuable insights into Capistran's career.

When once again elected vicar general at Bosco di Mugello, Florence, in 1449, he ousted the Fraticelli from Sinalunga and from Massa Fermana. In Rome on May 24, 1450, he saw the canonization of St. Bernardine, and late that same year he visited the Province of Liguria. He preached in Venetia during the early months of 1450 and at Venice during Lent.

Apostolate to Central Europe. In 1451 Pope NICHOLAS V, at the request of Emperor Frederick III and the urging of Enea Silvo Piccolomini, the future PIUS II, sent Capistran to Austria to preach against the HUSSITES. He left on April 28 with 12 confreres, and on May 30 he received Wiener Neustadt as his mission. His efforts at conversion of the Jews, reform of the Franciscan Conventuals, and propagation of the Observants met with success, but although he spared no effort by word and pen to convert the Hussites, he could not enter Prague. On May 27, 1452, his commissioner general, Mark Fantuzzi of Bologna, succeeded him as vicar general, and he himself was promoted to commissioner general for Austria, Styria, Hungary, and Bohemia. He continued to correspond with Rome in order to prevent any attack on the bulls of EUGENE IV in favor of the Observants, especially after CALLISTUS III succeeded Nicholas V in 1455.

On Crusade. The critical situation on the Turkish front led Piccolomini in July 1454 to urge that Capistran be given the additional mission of preaching the crusade, and at the end of May the following year Capistran proceeded to Hungary, where plans were prepared for battles at Györ and at Budapest. In January 1456 he undertook an energetic campaign to win back the schismatics, and during the following months he recruited crusaders whom he led to Belgrade at the beginning of July. If the naval attack on the 14th must be credited to John Hunyadi, Capistran alone was responsible for the victory of the 21st, thanks to his courage and his devotion to the name of Jesus. Hunyadi died of the plague at Zemun on Aug. 11, 1456, and Capistran was ill when he left for Slankemen (letters to the pope, dated July 23 and Aug. 27). He arrived at Ilok on Sept. 1, 1456; he remained there until his death. A last missive dated Oct. 21 prescribed that all his books and personal possessions be returned to Capestrano.

Cult. Popular veneration began soon after his death, as is evidenced by the paintings of Bartolomeo Vivarini in 1459 (Louvre and oratory of Gagliano-Aterno) and of Sebastian of Casentino (Museum of Aquila). The process of canonization began as early as 1457, but his cause, promoted by the zealous JAMES OF THE MARCHES and John of Tagliacozzo, was opposed by Cardinal John of CARVAJAL (d. 1469). Biographies of Capistran were numerous from 1459 to 1463 (*Studi francescani* 53:299–344). In 1514 his cultus was permitted in the Diocese of Sulmona, and in 1622 was extended to the Franciscan Order. The canonization proceedings begun in 1625 were resumed in 1649 and were continued until Capistran was finally canonized with PASCHAL BAYLON and three others by ALEXANDER VIII on Oct. 16, 1690. In 1880 his feast was extended to the universal Church. He is honored with the title "apostle of Europe" (*Studi francescani* 53:252–274), and the West is his debtor for his efforts in delaying the Turkish advance in the mid–15th century.

Feast: March 28; Oct. 23 in Abruzzi, Austria, and Hungary).

Bibliography: A. STANKO, *The Miracles of St. John Capistran* (New York 2000) 429–441, bib. F. BANFI, "Le fonti per la storia di S. Giovanni da Capestrano" *Studi francescani* 53 (1956), 299–344. S. DAMIAN and F. DE MARCHIS, "Giovanni da Capestrano, 1386–1456: Il mistero delle sue reliquie: Contributo per una ricerca di storia francescana con le ultime acquisizioni documentali," *Vita Minorum* 64 (1993) 226–41, 331–49. P. PETRECCA, *San Giovanni da Capestrano* (Florence 1992).

[J. CAMBELL]

JOHN CHRYSOSTOM, ST.

Patriarch of Constantinople, Father and Doctor of the Universal Church, patron of preachers; b. Antioch, *c.* 349; d. Comana in Pontus, Sept. 14, 407. The surname Chrysostom first occurs in the sixth century and has practically supplanted his given name.

Life. A vivid and true image of John emerges both from his own works and, especially for the period after his elevation to the See of Constantinople (397), from the contemporary *Dialogue* of PALLADIUS. The older ecclesiastical historians, SOCRATES and, more reliably, SOZOMEN, give important accounts; later pre-Bollandist biographers, more interested in hagiography than history, offer collections of anecdotes and legends. C. Baur provides a definitive modern biography.

At Antioch. Fourth-century Antioch was a center of culture, heresy, and schism. Pagans were numerous and powerful in the government and the schools; the majority of bishops had been at least semi-Arians; the Catholics themselves were separated by a schism between Bishops Paulinus and Meletius. There John was born and reared. His father, Secundus, was a high-ranking army officer, probably a Latin and a Christian; his Greek mother, Anthusa, was widowed at the age of 20 shortly after John's birth. Renouncing remarriage, she reared her son with great courage and piety. In his treatise *On the Priesthood* John pays her a signal tribute as a great Christian mother. She sent John to study philosophy under Andragathius and rhetoric in the school of the distinguished pagan sophist and rhetorician Libanius.

His parentage and classical training combined to produce in him the strong will and firmness of the Roman, tempered by the versatile and vivacious spirit of the Greek. At the age of 18, still a catechumen, John came under the influence of Meletius. He directed John to the monastic school of DIODORE, who initiated him in the literal and grammatical exegesis of the school of Antioch. The following Easter (*c.* 368) Meletius baptized John and three years later ordained him lector. Although John lived an ascetical life at home, he longed to become a monk; after four years with Meletius and Diodore he moved to the nearby mountains. For another four years he studied and prayed there under the direction of an old hermit. The next two years he lived alone in a cave, studying the Scriptures and practicing indiscreet austerities, which impaired his health and forced his return to Antioch. As soon as he had sufficiently recovered, John resumed his duties as lector. In 381 he was ordained deacon by Meletius, and for five years assisted at liturgical functions, cared for the poor, the sick, and the widows, and helped in instructing the catechumens. It was probably toward the end of this period that he wrote his famous work *On the Priesthood,* a classic on the importance and dignity of the pastoral office.

In 386 FLAVIAN, successor to Meletius, ordained John a priest, and he began his remarkable career as preacher, exegete, and moralist. The next year he proved his eloquence and rapport with his people when tax-burdened Antioch revolted to protest a new levy. Rioters pulled down the statues of the imperial family and dragged them through the streets. Chrysostom met the crisis in a series of sermons (*De statuis; Patrologia Graeca*, ed. J. P. Migne [Paris 1857–66] 49: 15–222) in which he exhorted and consoled his now penitent hearers and restrained them from further excesses born of remorse and despair. Bishop Flavian hurried to the capital, winning the emperor's clemency, and John was able to report the happy outcome in his Easter sermon of 387.

John preached at Antioch for twelve fruitful years. There he produced the bulk of his literary legacy, which has proved so rich a source of theological and historical knowledge. Although a polemicist, apologist, and dogmatist of some stature, he owes his place as a DOCTOR OF THE CHURCH chiefly to the continuous explanation of Scripture that he presents in his magisterial commentaries.

Bishop of Constantinople. Nectarius, Patriarch of Constantinople, died in 397. Many vied to succeed him; but the Emperor ARCADIUS, at the suggestion of his minister Eutropius, selected John as the new Patriarch. Chrysostom was lured to the capital by a ruse and consecrated bishop on Feb. 26, 398.

Immediately he was plunged into a morass of ecclesiastical and political intrigue. Nectarius had wasted church revenues; John curbed expenses, opened hospitals, and alleviated the misery of the poor. Since Nectarius had likewise permitted clerical laxity, John had to institute reforms. He ousted one deacon for murder, another for adultery. His clergy were forbidden to keep virgins and deaconesses in their houses, a practice that had occasioned much scandal (*see* VIRGINES SUBINTRODUCTAE). Monks who preferred aimless wandering to cenobitic discipline were confined to their monasteries. Worldly widows were ordered to remarry or show the decorum proper to their state.

These reforms alienated many of the clergy, but were popular with the people and generally approved at court. The people also applauded John's good services when the imperial minister, Eutropius, fell into disgrace (399) and General Gainas revolted (400). When Eutropius fled to the cathedral for sanctuary, John excoriated his abuse of power, but defended his right to asylum and thus temporarily saved his life. When Gainas demanded a church for his Arian Goths and highborn hostages to guarantee his usurped consulship, John intervened. He refused the church and saved the hostages from death, but not from exile. Gainas was soon declared a public enemy and fled. After these events, Empress Eudoxia completely dominated the vacillating Emperor Arcadius.

John's influence was now at its peak, but he had his tragic flaw. Although he was usually peaceful and patient, his zeal for God, Church, and justice often led him to blunt speech and action offensive to those in high places. His excoriation of luxury and extravagances delighted many who heard him, but the attacks were intolerable to the upper classes. The ladies at court especially resented his rebukes and convinced Eudoxia that John's onslaughts were aimed at her. Thenceforth she collaborated with his foes.

In 401 John's zeal for the Church took him to Ephesus, where he presided over a synod that deposed six bishops found guilty of simony. Although Constantinople enjoyed a *de facto* hegemony as a patriarchate over Ephesus, and John presided at the express invitation of several bishops, his jurisdiction was questioned and he made more enemies. On his return to Constantinople he found that a guest, Bishop SEVERIAN OF GABALA, had stirred trouble among the local clergy. Severian, a favorite at court, protested to Eudoxia when John asked him to return to his own diocese. To prevent an open rift with the court and schism in the Church, John agreed to let him stay; but Severian, who coveted the capital see, thereafter worked successfully with other disaffected bishops and courtiers to destroy John.

The cabal found an unscrupulous leader in THEOPHILUS, Patriarch of Alexandria. Jealous for the eastern primacy of his own see, he had reluctantly consecrated John bishop instead of his own Egyptian candidate. In 401 he had excommunicated and exiled as Origenists some Nitrian monks who had offended him. Led by the TALL BROTHERS (Dioscorus, Ammon, Eusebius, and Euthymius), they arrived in the capital, where John gave them shelter, but prudently withheld ecclesiastical fellowship pending settlement of their case. They appealed to the emperor, who summoned Theophilus to the capital to appear before a synod over which Chrysostom would preside. Theophilus was slow to obey the summons, but quick to mount a counterthrust: he decided to oppose the synod that was to judge him with another that would judge John. But agents sent to Antioch failed to find grounds against John. EPIPHANIUS OF CONSTANTIA also demanded the expulsion of the Nitrian monks and John's signature on a synodal decree condemning Origen, but returned home when he recognized that Theophilus was making him his tool. Theophilus enlisted aid at court, where Severian and other foes seem to have falsified John's published sermons to make it appear that he had slandered the empress. John often preached on the vanity and luxury of women, and Eudoxia was easily convinced that John had referred to her as Jezebel.

Meanwhile 40 bishops, summoned by imperial rescript, waited for Theophilus to arrive, but John protested against convening the synod on canonical grounds: Theophilus must first be heard by a synod in his own province; further, such schisms among bishops were a scandal to the Church.

On his arrival in 403 Theophilus convened the illegal Synod of the OAK, and presided over 36 bishops, of whom at least 29 were his Egyptian suffragans. The others included Severian and some bishops John had deposed at Ephesus. When summoned to defend himself against 46 charges, John refused to appear or to recognize a synod in which not only his accusers, but even his judges were his bitter foes. He ignored a second and third summons and was declared deposed. Arcadius ratified the deposition, and three days later John was spirited from the capital under military guard. That very night an accident occurred in the palace—probably the empress had a miscarriage—and this Eudoxia connected with the injustice committed in Chrysostom's case. She saw to his immediate recall and, after some delay, John returned amid general rejoicing.

Late in 403 a silver statue of Eudoxia was erected in the square facing the cathedral. The noise of the celebration disturbed the Divine Liturgy, and from his pulpit John complained bitterly. Eudoxia took this as a public insult. A new insult was alleged in early 404 when Chrysostom, preaching on John the Baptist, was reported to have said "Again Herodias rages . . . again she demands the head of John on a platter." The text survives (*Patrologia Graeca* 59:485), but may well be spurious. Again his enemies urged his exile, but Arcadius only forbade him to enter the cathedral, and at Easter some 3,000 catechumens assembled at the Baths of Constantine to be baptized. Soldiers broke up the service and the baptismal waters ran red with blood. Two attempts on John's life failed. Tension ran high, riots threatened, and Arcadius finally decreed exile. On June 24, 404, yielding only to force, John left Constantinople for the last time.

Exile and Death. Scarcely was he on board ship when the cathedral and senate house went up in flames. John and his followers (Johnites) were accused of setting the fire to cover their theft of the church treasures. An inventory showed nothing missing. When the Johnites refused to recognize John's successors (the aged Arsacius and, shortly after, Atticus, both of whom had been among his accusers at the Synod of the Oak), their property was confiscated and they were exiled.

Before leaving Constantinople, John had written to Pope INNOCENT I to protest his deposition and to request a trial. Theophilus also sent a report. After hearing witnesses on both sides, Innocent refused to recognize John's deposition. A synod of Latin bishops who examined the matter declared the Synod of the Oak invalid.

Through Innocent and the Western Emperor Honorius they requested Arcadius first to restore Chrysostom and then to have the case decided by a general synod of Greeks and Latins to meet at Salonika, but the synod never convened.

On arrival at the capital, the papal envoys, including five bishops, were jailed, treated ignominiously, and finally sent back to Rome. Innocent then broke off communion with Theophilus, Atticus, and all of Chrysostom's chief opponents. The schism endured until, after John's death, atonement was made and John's name was restored to the diptychs at Alexandria, Antioch, and Constantinople.

For three years John's place of exile was Cucusus, a frontier outpost in Armenia. Despite the dangers and remoteness of the place, friends still visited him, and he kept up a correspondence with the faithful at Antioch and Constantinople. Angered by his persistent popularity and influence in the capital, his foes persuaded Arcadius to send John to more remote Pityus, 600 marine miles from Constantinople across the Black Sea, but the trip had to be made overland, across six mountain ranges and numerous streams. His guard forced him to march bareheaded in sun and rain. Worn out with hardship and fever, he died at Comana in Pontus, uttering as his last words, "Glory to God for all things."

In 438 Theodosius II brought his body to Constantinople and solemnly buried it in the Church of the Apostles. In 1204 the Venetians plundered the city and sent his relics to Rome, where his grave is still shown in the choir chapel of St. Peter's.

Feast: Jan. 27.

Character and Eloquence. Iconography gives no authentic portrait of Chrysostom, but tradition reveals him as an ascetic, unimposing yet dignified. His intellect was lively and penetrating, although not given to speculation. Although dauntless in the fight for justice, John went out with mercy to the poor and sinners. His rich imagination infused his sermons with power and variety. Like a true Greek, he loved proportion, but his choleric temperament often blazed forth in deep and vehement feeling.

He was not an orator in the classic mold. His homilies seem poorly structured, roving from point to point and filled with repetitions, but they have an interior, spiritual unity. He was often interrupted with applause and tears. This rapport made him feel free to say whatever he wished and his audience willing to hear whatever he had to say. Few orators ever roused more enthusiasm or exercised so complete a mastery over their audience.

Works. John's stature in ecclesiastical history derives less from his administrative ability than from his talents as writer and preacher. Few Greek Fathers have left so extensive a literary legacy of writings in the form of treatises, homilies, and letters.

Treatises. These deal with monastic, ascetical, and apologetical topics and are published in *Patrologia Graeca* 47, 48, 50, and 52. Most noteworthy are two exhortations *Ad Theodorum lapsum,* the one (*Patrologia Graeca* 47:277–308) addressed to a fallen monk, the other (*ibid.* 309–316) to his fellow student THEODORE OF MOPSUESTIA, who planned to return to the world and marry; *Adversus subintroductas* (*ibid.* 495–574), condemning the custom of priests having virgins as housekeepers; *De sacerdotio* (*ibid.* 623–692), on the greatness and dignity of the pastoral office; *Contra Judaeos et Gentiles* (*Patrologia Graeca* 48:813–838), demonstrating to Jews and Gentiles that Christ is God; *Quod nemo laeditur* (*Patrologia Graeca* 52:459–480), written in exile, proving that no man can be harmed unless he cooperates with those who would harm him.

Homilies. Here belong the commentaries on Scripture, groups of sermons on special subjects, and single homilies. (1) Commentaries on the Old Testament include 67 homilies on Genesis and eight sermons on Genesis, ch. 1 to 3 (*Patrologia Graeca* 53, 54), which may be a first recension; 59 on selected Psalms (*Patrologia Graeca* 55), which interpret Psalms 4 to 12, 43 to 49, 108 to 117, and 119 to 150. Those on the New Testament include 90 homilies on Matthew (*Patrologia Graeca* 57, 58); 88 on John (*Patrologia Graeca* 59), probably in a second recension; 55 on Acts (*Patrologia Graeca* 60), also in two recensions; there are more than 200 homilies on the Pauline Epistles (*Patrologia Graeca* 59–63), as well as a running elucidation of the text of Galatians (*Patrologia Graeca* 61:611–682), which is probably a recension made by a later editor from a series of homilies. (2) Among the groups on special subjects must be mentioned 21 homilies *De statuis* (*Patrologia Graeca* 49:15–222) delivered during the revolt at Antioch; two on the fall of Eutropius (*Patrologia Graeca* 52:391–414); eight against Judaizing Christians (*Patrologia Graeca* 48:843–942); twelve against the Anomoean Arians on the incomprehensible nature of God (*ibid.* 701–812); and eight baptismal catecheses discovered on Mt. Athos in 1955 by A. Wenger. (3) There are numerous single homilies, on the occasion of his ordination (*Patrologia Graeca* 48:693–700), before his exile (*Patrologia Graeca* 52:427–430), and on his recall (*ibid.* 443–448); also sermons on moral subjects and on certain feasts and saints.

Letters. Best known of some 236 letters are two to Pope Innocent I and 17 to the deaconess Olympias; the rest, addressed to more than 100 persons, give an intimate picture of his exile (*Patrologia Graeca* 52).

Spurious Works. These include a synopsis of Old Testament and New Testament (*Patrologia Graeca* 56:313–386); the Liturgy of St. Chrysostom, which in its present form postdates his death, although he may have contributed to earlier versions; an incomplete commentary on Matthew, the *Opus imperfectum,* existing only in Latin, which seems to be the work of a fifth-century Arian.

Exegete and Doctor. As an exegete Chrysostom, like his teacher Diodore, followed the school of Antioch and was the most important exponent of its historico-grammatical method. Alexandrian allegory was foreign to him. He used allegory only when the inspired writer suggested it; even then it was the simple kind, which sees a reality through a type. He employed his deep insight into the meaning of Scripture to find applications for the lives and conduct of his flock. His exegesis was never far removed from instruction in morality and exhortation to the life of virtue.

Chrysostom was no speculative theologian. He felt that few were attracted to the Church by the profundity of her dogma; it was the moral teaching of the Gospels, the ideal of Christian charity, the hope that God would rescue them in their miseries that brought men into the Church. His task was to keep them there as worthy members of Christ. Nonetheless his works are rich in doctrine, and from the first he stood forth as an important witness to the faith. He clearly taught the duality of natures in Christ, but made no attempt to explain the oneness of person. His many clear statements on the Real Presence and sacrificial role of Christ in the Eucharist have won for him the name of Doctor of the Eucharist. He was not always clear on the nature and transmission of original sin, but Augustine rightly exonerates him of Pelagian error (*Patrologia Latina*, ed. J. P. Migne [Paris 1878–90] 44:656). He never referred to Mary as Θεοτόκος, a name suspect at Antioch. Neither did he call her Χριστοτόκος or ἀνθρωποτόκος, but stood apart from this controversy. He spoke explicitly of her perpetual virginity, but elsewhere implied that she was guilty of at least imperfections. As St. Thomas Aquinas observed, here Chrysostom has gone too far (*Summa theologiae* 3a, 27.4 ad 3).

Efforts to find in his works an unequivocal witness to the practice of private confession to a priest have failed. He often spoke of confession, but meant either public confession or that made to God alone in which the sinner judged himself guilty and God forgave him. He clearly acknowledged the primacy of Peter, but nowhere accorded the same primacy to the pope. Possibly this was because in the schism at Antioch neither Meletius nor Flavian was in union with Rome until John, on his accession to the See of Constantinople, obtained letters of ecclesiastical communion with Rome for both Flavian and himself. When he was deposed, he did ask Innocent I to intervene in his favor and to maintain communion with him, but this was not a recognition of papal primacy. He sent the same request to the bishops of Milan and Aquileia. The problem of papal primacy as now understood in the Church may never have occurred to him. For him the Church was one: schisms that divided it were just as bad as heresies that altered its faith. (For the so-called Liturgy of St. John Chrysostom, *see* BYZANTINE RITE.)

Bibliography: Complete editions. *Opera graece,* ed. H. SAVILE, 8 v. (Eton 1610–12), best text; *Patrologia Graeca* ed. J. P. MIGNE (Paris 1857–66) v. 47–64, repr. of B. DE MONTFAUCON, 13 v. in 24 (Paris 1835–39). Translations. *Lettres à Olympias,* ed. and tr. A. M. MALINGREY (*Sources Chrétiennes,* ed. H. DE LUBAC et al. [Paris 1941] 13; 1947); *Huit catéchèses baptismales inédites,* ed. A. WENGER (*ibid.* 50; 1957); *Commentary on St. John,* ed. T. A. GOGGIN, 2 v. (*The Fathers of the Church: A New Translation,* ed. R. J. DEFERRARI et al. 33, 41; 1957, 1960); *Baptismal Instructions,* ed. P. W. HARKINS (*Ancient Christian Writers,* ed. J. QUASTEN et al. [Westminster, Md.-London 1946–] 31; 1963). Literature. D. BURGER, *Complete Bibliography of Scholarship on the Life and Works of St. John Chrysostom* (Evanston 1964). J. QUASTEN, *Patrology* (Westminster, Maryland 1950–) 3:424–482; E. VENABLES, *A Dictionary of Christian Biography,* ed. W. SMITH and H. WACE (London 1877—87) 1:518–535. H. LIETZMANN, *Paulys Realenzyklopädie der klassischen Altertumswissenschaft,* ed. G. WISSOWA et al. 9.2 (Stuttgart 1916) 1811–28; repr. in *Texte und Untersuchungen zur Geschichte der altchristlichen Literatur* 67 (Berlin 1958) 326–347. C. BAUR, *John Chrysostom and His Time,* tr. M. GONZAGA, 2 v. (Westminster, Md. 1960–61). R. E. CARTER, "The Chronology of St. John Chrysostom's Early Life," *Traditio* 18 (1962) 357–364. F. H. CHASE, *Chrysostom: A Study in the History of Biblical Interpretation* (Cambridge, Eng. 1887). B. GIORGIATIS, *Die Lehre des Johannes Chrysostomos über die heiligen Schriften* (Athens 1947). A. MOULARD, *Saint Jean Chrysostome, le défenseur du mariage et l'apôtre de la virginité* (Paris 1923). E. BOULARAND, *La Venue de l'homme à la foi d'après saint Jean Chrysostome* (*Analecta Gregoriana* 18; Rome 1939). H. KEANE, "The Sacrament of Penance in St. John Chrysostom," *The Irish Theological Quarterly* 14 (1919) 305–317. G. FITTKAU, *Der Begriff des Mysteriums bei Johannes Chrysostomus* (Bonn 1953). E. MICHAUD, "L'Ecclésiologie de s. Jean Chrysostome," *Revue internationale de théologie* 11 (1903) 491–620. L. MEYER, *Saint Jean Chrysostome, maître de perfection chrétienne* (Paris 1933). G. G. CHRISTO, *Martyrdom According to John Chrysostom: "To Live Is Christ, To Die Is Gain"* (Lewiston, NY 1997). J. N. D. KELLY, *Golden Mouth: The Story of John Chrysostom: Ascetic, Preacher, Bishop* (Ithaca, NY 1995). F. VAN DE PAVERD, *St. John Chrysostom, the Homilies on the Statues: An Introduction* (Rome 1991). R. A. KRUPP, *Shepherding the Flock of God: The Pastoral Theology of John Chrysostom* (New York 1991). M. A. SCHATKIN, *John Chrysostom as Apologist* (Thessalonike 1987). R. L. WILKEN, *John Chrysostom and the Jews: Rhetoric and Reality in the Late Fourth Century* (Berkeley, Calif. 1983).

[P. W. HARKINS]

JOHN CLIMACUS, ST.

Abbot, ascetic, and writer on the spiritual life (also known as Ἰωάννης ὁ τῆς κλίμακος and John the Scho-lastic); b. 579; d. 649. Details of his life are unknown. His *Heavenly Ladder,* Κλῖμαξ τοῦ παραδείσου, was one of the most widely used Greek handbooks of the ascetic life. Its popularity with lay as well as monastic readers is attested by the existence of 33 illustrated Greek manuscripts, plus an uncounted number of copies without illustration—so large a number of manuscripts being responsible for the fact that there is as yet no critical edition. The work was translated into Latin, Syriac, Arabic, Armenian, and Church Slavonic, as well as a number of modern languages.

The *Ladder,* written while the author was abbot of the monastery at Mt. Sinai, shows striking psychological insight, stemming from his acute powers of observation and deep knowledge of the spiritual life. As the title indicates, the ascetic life is portrayed in the form of a ladder that the monk must ascend, each step on the ladder representing a virtue that must be acquired or a vice that must be eradicated. There are 30 steps, representing the 30 years of the hidden life of Christ, before the beginning of His public ministry. Each step is the subject of a chapter in which the author describes the virtue or vice in question and shows the way in which it is to be acquired or eliminated.

After undergoing discipline as a novice, the monk has to gain a solid footing on each step as he masters in succession such qualities as obedience, meekness, chastity, temperance, poverty, humility, and discretion or comes in his progress to the steps at which he has to deal with malice, slander, sloth, gluttony, avarice, vainglory, pride, etc. As the monk toils upward he has to fight off the attacks of demons who seek to tear him from the ladder and hurl him into the abyss. Finally the monk, if he passes successfully through all trials, reaches step 30, titled Faith, Hope, and Charity, and there receives the crown of glory from the hand of Christ.

John Climacus was evidently familiar with the works of earlier ascetic writers, and, though his treatment and point of view are his own, his book shows similarities in method and arrangement to the collection of sayings of holy men preserved in a Latin translation of a Greek original under the title *Verba seniorum.* The *Ladder* had widespread and important influence on later Greek ascetic writers, especially the Hesychasts (*see* HESYCHASM), and was popular in monasteries in Slavic countries. SYMEON THE NEW THEOLOGIAN was especially indebted to his lifelong study of the *Ladder.*

Feast: March 30.

Bibliography: *Patrologia Graeca,* ed. J. P. MIGNE (Paris 1857–66) 88:632–1161. JOHN CLIMACUS, *Ladder of Divine Ascent,* tr. L. MOORE, intro. M. HEPPELL (New York 1959); *Scala paradisi,* ed. P. TREVISAN, 2 v. (Turin 1941). L. PETIT, *Dictionnaire de théolo-*

Manuscript from "Heavenly Ladder," by St. John Climacus.

gie catholique, ed. A. VACANT, 15 v. (Paris 1903–50; Tables générales 1951–) 8.1:690–693. J. R. MARTIN, *The Illustrations of the Heavenly Ladder of John Climacus* (Princeton Studies in MS Illumination 5; Princeton 1954). J. CHRYSSAVGIS, *Ascent to Heaven: The Theology of the Human Person according to Saint John of the Ladder* (Brookline, Mass. 1989). J. MACK, *Ascending the Heights: A Layman's Guide to the Ladder of Divine Ascent* (Ben Lomond, Calif. 1999).

[G. DOWNEY]

JOHN COLOMBINI, BL.

Founder of the JESUATI; b. Siena, *c.* 1304; d. Monte Amiata, Italy, July 31, 1367. John was a merchant, a member of the Sienese senate, and a magistrate. In 1342 he married Biagia Cerretani. After reading the biography of St. MARY OF EGYPT he began to lead an ascetic life. He provided for his wife, gave his goods to the poor, and dedicated himself to the care of the sick. Disciples gathered about him, and he obtained approbation of his congregation from URBAN V in 1367. He was buried in Siena. His cult spread locally, and GREGORY XIII beatified him. Colombini's writings included 114 *Letters,* reflecting affective spirituality, the *Laudi spirituali,* of which only the "Diletto Gesú Cristo chi ben t'ama" has been authenticated, and a vita of Peter Petroni, now lost.

Feast: July 31.

Bibliography: A. BERTOLI, ed., *Le lettere del b. G. Colombini* (Lanciano 1925). *Acta Sanctorum* July 7:344–420. A. BUTLER, *The Lives of the Saints,* ed. H. THURSTON and D. ATTWATER, 4 v. (New York 1956) 3:228–230.

[M. G. MC NEIL]

JOHN DA PIAN DEL CARPINE

Better known as John of Plano Carpini, the first European to give detailed information on the Mongols; b.

probably Piano della Maggione (formerly Pian di Carpini), near Perugia, *c.* 1180; d. probably Italy, Aug. 1, 1252. An early companion of St. Francis, John became a Franciscan warden in Saxony in 1222, and provincial of Germany in 1228. On April 16, 1245, he left Lyons as head of one of the three embassies sent by Innocent IV to contact the Mongols and deliver to them the letters *Dei Patris immensa* and *Cum non solum.* His mission successfully accomplished, John wrote a voluminous report—*Istoria Mongalorum quos nos Tartaros appellamus.* The first part of this work is a masterly description of the country of the Mongols, the customs of the inhabitants, their character, and their history. It is a sober, objective, concise report, a masterpiece of its kind. The second part of the *Istoria* is a short record of the journey to Mongolia undertaken in the company of BENEDICT THE POLE. In Mongolia John assisted at the enthronement of the Great Khan Güyük (Aug. 24, 1246), by whom he was received on several occasions. He left the Khan's court on November 13, and almost six months later he reached the Khan's uncle Batu, in the region of the Volga. Via Kiev and Hungary he returned to Lyons in November 1247. Soon afterward John was installed as archbishop of Bar (Antivari). The journey of this sexagenarian monk to the Mongols ranks among the finest journeys of exploration; his report is one of the best sources on the Mongols of the 13th century.

Bibliography: F. SORELLI, "Per Regioni Diverse: Fra Giovanni da Pian del Carpine," in *I Compagni di Francesco e la Prima Generazione Minoritica* (Spoleto 1992), 259–83. P. DAFFINA, *Giovanni di Pian di Carpine* (Spoleto 1989), bibliography.

[D. SINOR]

JOHN DAMASCENE, ST.

Surnamed Chrysorrhoas or the Golden Speaker, Oriental monk, Father of the Church; b. Damascus, *c.* 645; d. near Jerusalem, *c.* 750.

Life. John's family was the well-to-do Manṣūr family; his grandfather and father had occupied ministerial posts, first under the Byzantine and, after 636, under the Arab rulers of Damascus. Under the care of Cosmas, a ransomed Sicilian prisoner, he received a well-rounded Greek education and a knowledge of Arabic as well as of the Islamic religion. He achieved a position of trust in the Muslim court, but because of the Caliph Abd al-malik's (685–705) hostility toward Christians he resigned his post (*c.* 700). With Cosmas he became a monk at Mar Saba near Jerusalem, and was ordained by Patriarch John V of Jerusalem (705–735) before the outbreak of the controversy over iconoclasm. John taught in the monastery, preached in Jerusalem, and counseled various bishops on questions of faith, devoting himself in particular to the composition of theological tracts. According to information in the vita he reedited his writings toward the end of his life; this statement is supported by evidence in MSS tradition.

Iconoclasm. John's career is inseparably connected with the controversy over ICONOCLASM in which he supported the veneration of images with theological arguments, and because he lived outside the Byzantine realm he was able to oppose the iconoclastic-minded emperor with vehemence. The story that his hand was cut off and miraculously healed by the Mother of God is legendary. He was dead before the Iconoclastic Synod of 754, which condemned him with a fourfold anathema. His orthodoxy was vindicated by the seventh general council (Nicaea II) in 787; and he has been considered a saint since the end of the 8th century.

John was buried in the monastery of Mar Saba, where the body seems to have been located until the 12th century, when, apparently, it was removed to Constantinople and venerated there from the 13th to the 15th century. Despite evidence provided by several vitae, one of which was written by the Patriarch John of Jerusalem (d. 966), and all of which depend upon an Arabic source, as well as other information supplied in ecclesiastical and profane documents, the chronology of his life and particularly the date of his death is uncertain. The latter is usually ascribed to 749, following S. Vailhé. The Acts of the synod of 754 record John as already dead (*Sacrorum Conciliorum nova et amplissima collectio,* 13:356) and an Arabic menologion says that at his death he was 104 years old (*Patrologia Graeca,* 94:501). Other Arabic sources describe him and the poet al Aḥtal (b. *c.* 640) as friends and table companions of Prince Yazīd I (b. *c.* 642). Hence it is assumed that he was of a similar age and his dates are given as 645 to 750.

Dogmatic Writings. John left a literary heritage of which J. Hoeck has claimed 150 titles as authentic works. His principal dogmatic work is Πηγὴ γνώσεως (Source of knowledge), which is usually considered to include a trilogy, although the title refers properly only to the first part. In its present form this work is prefaced with a dedicatory letter to Cosmas, John's adopted brother who became bishop of Maiuma near Gaza *c.* 743. Part one, called the *Dialectica,* is a philosophical propaedeutic, or preparation for the faith, in 68 chapters, depending largely on patristic citations and strongly influenced by the Isagoge of the Neoplatonist Porphyry. Part two is a history of heresies that recapitulates the 80 chapters of the *Panarion* of EPIPHANIUS OF CONSTANTIA (SALAMIS) and adds 20 further chapters taken bodily from other sources. The chapters dealing with Islam (100), iconoclasm (102), and

Miniature detail of St. John Damascene composing a sermon, 11th century, from "Menologian of Basil II".

the Aposchites (103) do not seem to be authentic. This entire section is also found as chapter 34 of the *Doctrina patrum.* Part three is the *Ekthesis,* or *Exposition of the Orthodox Faith,* in 100 chapters and treats of God, creation, anthropology, Christology, soteriology, and eschatology, with an appendix that deals with ascetical questions.

This *Exposition* was translated into Latin in the 12th century and divided into four books modeled on the scholastic structure of the Sentences of Peter Lombard. The principal sources of the first and third sections are the Epitome of THEODORET OF CYR, GREGORY OF NAZIANZUS, EULOGIUS OF ALEXANDRIA, NEMESIUS OF EMESA, PSEUDO-DIONYSIUS, LEONTIUS OF BYZANTIUM, MAXIMUS THE CONFESSOR, and ANASTASIUS SINAITA. Originally this work seems to have consisted of the *Dialectica* and the *Exposition* and only in the second redaction was it made into a trilogy by Damascene himself. His other dogmatic writings include an *Institutio elementaris,* or elementary introduction to dogma, written for Bp. John of Laodicea, several *Professiones fidei,* tracts against the Nestorians, Jacobites, Monothelites, Manichees, and Islamites, and three celebrated *Discourses against the Iconoclasts* (726–730) in which he defends classical doctrine in favor of the veneration of images, but demonstrates his own independent thinking.

Ascetical and Exegetical Works. Among Damascene's moral and ascetic writings are treatises on sacred fasting, the eight spirits of evil, and the virtues and vices, as well as a number of prayers. It is probable that he had a hand in structuring the collection of maxims and devotional texts known as the *Sacra Parallela.* In his exegetical writings Damascene prepared a commentary on the Pauline Epistles borrowing freely from St. John Chrysostom. But the authenticity of the homilies on the Hexaemeron attributed to him is doubtful.

Hagiography. John devoted much of his preaching to hagiographical encomiums in praise of SS. Anastasia, Barbara, John Chrysostom, and Elias (unedited) and accounts of the sufferings of the martyrs, including Artemius and Catherine (lost); of doubtful authenticity are the passions of Paraskeue and Meletius of Antioch. He produced a masterful story in the edifying account of the life of BARLAAM AND JOASAPH, whose authenticity, though long disputed, seems now established. Of his sermons on the mysteries of the liturgy and the saints, at least 13 are authentic; some are still unedited and several have been attributed to John of Euboea.

Mariology. His Marian sermons are most famous, in particular three homilies for August 15 preached on the site of Mary's dormition at Gethsemane. In the second of these, the celebrated passage referring to the deposit of Mary's clothing in the Blachernae convent in Constantinople has long been recognized as an interpolation. The sermon on Mary's nativity was delivered in the Sanctuary of the Sheep pool, the legendary place of Mary's birth. John is renowned likewise as a hymn writer; at least eight of the *Canones,* or poems made of nine odes each differing in metrical structure, which celebrate the principal feasts of the Lord, are authentic, and a number of the hymns in the so-called *Octoechos* are of his authorship.

John is credited with an Easter Table (*Paschalion*) and the composition or redaction of the monastic *Typicon* of Mar Saba. Under his name there are a large number of pseudoepigraphica, some of which may be the remains of lost works.

Sources. Characteristic of John's writings is a traditionally carefree plagiarizing of authors without reference to sources. Thus in his *Exposition of the Faith* he combined the greater part of the anthropology and psychology of Nemesius of Emesa with the pseudo-Cyrillian tract on the Trinity; in his *passio* of Artemius he embodied part of the lost church history of Philostorgius; in the Barlaam romance, the Apology of Aristides and a section of the Prince's Mirror of Agapetus; and in his Christmas Sermon, a religious conversation held at the Sassanid court. His use of Chrysostom's commentaries on St. Paul and his embodiment of the *Panarion* of Epiphanius in his history of heresies has been mentioned. G. Richter has unearthed various strata in the *Dialectica;* but the investigation of his sources is difficult and still in need of attention. John frequently repeated entire sentences and even paragraphs of his own writings, even within the same work.

Evaluation. John Damascene was certainly the most significant, however, not the most independent, theological thinker in an age little distinguished for creativity. Starting with the principle that he desircd to say nothing of his own creation and did not wish to pass beyond traditional bounds, he tried to adapt himself to the whole patristic learning without indulging in originality. In his principal work, the *Exposition,* which he put together out of many diversely oriented sources, he did not achieve the closed circle of the Latin scholastic *Summae.* In his art of compilation by means of selection and omission together with inserted commentaries, he managed to achieve a high degree of intellectual autonomy and a compositional technique that, considering the limitations of Byzantine systematic thinking, deserve esteem. His learning and works were conditioned by an environment that was not conducive to the elaboration of the Christian faith. While his theological influence on both East and West has often been exaggerated, the mass of MSS, editions, and whole or partial translations of his works—among the oldest are Syriac (*c.* 800), Arabic, Armenian, and ancient Bulgarian (10th century), Georgian (11th century), and Latin (12th century)—demonstrate the high appraisal given him by posterity.

Essentially a Chalcedonian, John Damascene was considered in the West the principal witness of Greek theology. He was rated as one of the greater Byzantine dogmaticians and an Oriental writer of considerable versatility, although a critique of his accomplishment according to current standards of scholarship demands a negative evaluation.

Feast: March 27.

Bibliography: M. JUGIE, *Dictionnaire de théologie catholique,* ed. A. VACANT et al., 15 v. (Paris 1903–50; Tables générales 1951–) 8.1:693–751, doctrine and bibliog. J. NASRALLAH, *Saint Jean de Damas* (Harissa 1950). J. M. HOECK, "Stand und Aufgaben der Damaskenos-Forschung," *Orientalia Christiana periodica* 17 (1951) 5–60; *Bibliotheca hagiographica Graeca,* ed. F. HALKIN, 3 v. (Brussels 1957) 3:884–885. H. G. BECK, *Kirche und theologische Literatur im byzantinischen Reich* (Munich 1959) 476–486. H. PERI, *Der Religionsdisput der Barlaam-Legende* (Salamanca 1959). I. DICK, *Proche-Orient chrétien,* 12 (1962) 209–223, 319–332; 13 (1963) 114–129. B. HEMMERDINGER, "La Vita arabe de saint Jean Damascène et *Bibliotheca hagiographica Graeca,* 884," *Orientalia Christiana periodica* 28 (1962) 422–423. L. SWEENEY, "John Damascene's *Infinite Sea of Essence,*" *Studia Patristica,* v. 6 (Texte und Untersuchungen zur Geschichte der altchristlichen Literatur 81; Berlin 1962) 248–263. B. KOTTER, *Die Überlieferung der "Pege gnoseos" des hl. Johannes von Damaskos* (Studia patristica et byzantina 5; Ettal 1959). G. RICHTER, *Die Dialektik des Johannes von Damaskos* (Ettal 1964). M. GORDILLO, *Orientalia Christiana periodica* 27 (1961) 162–170. G. D. DRAGAS, "Exchange or Communication of Properties and Deification: Antidosis or Communicatio Idiomatum and Theosis," *Greek Orthodox Theological Review,* 43, no. 1–4 (Spring-Winter 1998) 377–399. K. PARRY, *Depicting the Word: Byzantine Iconophile Thought of the Eighth and Ninth Centuries* (Leiden 1996). T. F. X. NOBLE, "John Damascene and the History of the Iconoclastic Controversy," in *Religion, Culture, and Society in the Early Middle Ages,* ed. T. F. X. NOBLE and J. J. CONTRENI (Kalamazoo, Mich. 1987) 95–116. D. J. SAHAS, *John of Damascus on Islam: The "Heresy of the Ishmaelite"* (Leiden 1972).

[B. KOTTER]

JOHN DE BRITTO, ST.

Missionary and martyr; b. Lisbon, Mar. 1, 1647; d. Oriyûr, India, Feb. 4, 1693. De Britto, of the high nobility, was educated as a page with the royal Prince (later Peter II). He entered the Jesuits in December 1662 and was ordained in January 1673. He arrived in Goa in September 1673, and after preparation, went to his mission in southeast India (Madura, Tanjore, Marava, the Cauvery delta). He followed the ascetic, withdrawn life of a sannyasi missionary that R. de NOBILI had led, thus having access to both Brahmins and the lower castes. His labors were successful, although handicapped by war and other disasters. After a period spent farther south (1679–85), he returned to Marava and was imprisoned (July 17, 1686), tortured, and expelled from the country. In September 1687, he returned to Portugal but was not allowed to go to Rome to report in person. In March 1689, he left again for India, where he was visitor of the Jesuit mission (1691). He had great success, converting many to Christianity, including the feudal chief of Siruvalli. The chief then dismissed all his wives except the first. Among those dismissed was the niece of the Prince of Marava. The prince, with Brahmin support, began a persecution. He had the missionary brought before him and sent him to Oriyûr, where he was beheaded. John was beatified Feb. 17, 1852, and canonized June 22, 1947.

Feast: Feb. 4 (Jesuits).

Bibliography: A. DE BIL, *Dictionnaire d'histoire et de géographie ecclésiastiques* 10:771–772. C. A. MORESCHINI, *San Giovanni de Britto* (Florence 1943). A. BESSIÈRES, *Le Nouveau François–Xavier* (Toulouse 1946). A. SAULTIÈRE, *Red Sand* (Madura 1947). A. NEVETT, *John de Britto and His Times* (Anand, India 1980).

[J. WICKI]

JOHN DE GRANDISSON

Bishop of Exeter; b. Ashperton, Herefordshire, England, 1292; d. Chudleigh, Devon, July 16, 1369. He was studying civil law, probably at Oxford, by *c.* 1306. Between 1313 and 1317 he studied theology at Paris under Jacques Fournier, later Pope BENEDICT XII. By 1322 he was a papal chaplain. He returned to Oxford for study in 1326–27, the year that he became bishop of EXETER by papal provision. A diligent diocesan, he finished the reconstruction of the nave of his cathedral and built St. Radegunde's Chapel, where he is buried. He founded the College of Ottery St. Mary in 1337. Concerned over the effect of papal PROVISION in England, he informed Pope CLEMENT VI in 1342 that at the council of the Province of Canterbury held in London "no small wonder arose at the burdensome and hitherto unknown multitude of apostolic provisions." In 1349 the Bishop presented his views concerning provision to King Edward III. He composed a *Legenda de sanctis* and a life of Thomas BECKET, copies of which are in Exeter Cathedral Library, and in 1337 compiled an *Ordinale* for the regulation of services performed in his cathedral. He willed his large library to his cathedral church, the collegiate churches of Ottery, Crediton, and Bosham, the Black Friars of Exeter, and Exeter College.

Bibliography: F. C. HINGESTON–RANDOLPH, ed., *Register of John de Grandisson . . . ,* 3 v. (Exeter 1894–99). J. N. DALTON, ed., *Ordinale,* 2 v. Henry Bradshaw Society (London 1891—) 37, 38; 1909). W. HUNT, *The Dictionary of National Biography From the Earliest Times to 1900,* 63 v. (London 1885–1900) 8:371–372. W. A. PANTIN, *The English Church in the 14th Century* (Cambridge, Eng. 1955). A. B. EMDEN, *A Biographical Register of the University of Oxford to A.D. 1500,* 3 v. (Oxford 1957–59) 2:800–801.

[V. MUDROCH]

JOHN DE GREY (GRAY)

Bishop of Norwich, justiciar of Ireland; b. Norfolk, England; d. Saint-Jean-d'Audely, near Poitiers, France, Oct. 18, 1214. First mentioned in 1198 in the service of Prince John (*see* JOHN, KING OF ENGLAND), he rose rapidly in the ecclesiastical hierarchy once John succeeded King RICHARD I, the Lion-Heart on the English throne (1199). By March 1200 he had become archdeacon of Cleveland, and a month later he is mentioned as archdeacon of Gloucester. On September 24 of the same year he was consecrated bishop of Norwich. He evidently enjoyed the royal favor, and when HUBERT WALTER, the Archbishop of Canterbury, died in 1205, King John had him elected to CANTERBURY. This election, however, was disputed, and Pope INNOCENT III sought to resolve the matter by suggesting the election, instead, of STEPHEN LANGTON. King John refused to recognize Langton's election, and this precipitated the disastrous quarrel between king and pope that plagued the greater part of King John's reign. During this period John de Grey continued to function as justiciar at court and as itinerant royal judge except while in Ireland, where he served as justiciar (1209–13). There he distinguished himself by his attempts to increase English influence northward and westward and to reform Irish coinage, law, and administration along English models, as well as to raise money and troops for the king. His devotion and loyalty to the cause of the king earned him both an early excommunication by the pope and a special exclusion from the general absolution that followed John's submission to Innocent in 1213. Later that year, however, John de Grey went to Rome and received not only a full pardon but also the papal favor to such an extent that it was feared in England that he would return there as Innocent's special agent to subject the kingdom to papal rule. In 1214 Innocent provided for his election to Durham, over the protest of the monastic chapter there, but John de Grey died on his way back to England before taking possession of his new see. He was the uncle of Abp. WALTER DE GRAY.

Bibliography: A. L. POOLE, *From Domesday Book to Magna Carta* (2d ed. Oxford History of England 3; 1955). W. L. WARREN, *King John* (New York 1961).

[J. BRÜCKMANN]

JOHN DE OFFORD

Chancellor of England, archbishop-elect of Canterbury; d. Tottenham Court, May 20, 1349. The alternate form "Ufford" derives from the assumption that he was a son of Robert Ufford, Earl of Suffolk, but the evidence points to his being of the family of Offord, whose estate at Offord Dameys, Huntingdonshire, he administered until 1332. His younger brother Andrew frequently appears in the records as envoy and commissioner to foreign courts and held various minor posts in church and state. John was a doctor of civil law by 1334, probably of Cambridge, where he is commemorated as a benefactor. He had entered the royal service before 1328 and soon won King EDWARD III's confidence. For the next 20 years he was constantly employed in private and political negotiations with the pope and the French king in France, Brabant, and Flanders. He is said to have added eloquence, sagacity, shrewd counsel, and dependability to legal acumen, and this brought him rapid promotion to high office. In 1342 he became keeper of the privy seal and later of the great seal also. In 1344 he was installed as dean of Lincoln Cathedral, and in 1345 he was appointed lord chancellor of the kingdom. Although by then aged and paralytic, and despite his strong support of the stringent measures taken against papal PROVISION, Offord was nominated to the See of CANTERBURY by the King, who rejected the cathedral chapter's election of THOMAS BRADWARDINE. Offord was papally provided to the see on Sept. 24, 1348, and took custody of the temporalities in December. But he died before receiving the pallium or consecration. He was buried by night at Christ Church, Canterbury.

Bibliography: H. WARTON, *Anglia sacra,* 2 v. (London 1691) 1:42, 60, 118, 794. T. RYMER, *Foedera, conventions, litterae... inter reges Angliae et alios quosvis imperators, reges, pontifices... ab A.D. 1101 ad nostra usque tempora...* (to 1654), 20 v. (London 1704–35). W. F. HOOK, *Lives of the Archbishops of Canterbury,* 12 v. (London 1860–84) 4:73, 103. C. L. KINGSFORD, *The Dictionary of National Biography from the Earliest Times to 1900,* 63 v. (London 1885–1900) 14:901–902. A. B. EMDEN, *Biographical Register of the Scholars of the University of Cambridge before 1500* (Cambridge, Eng. 1963) 431–433.

[J. H. BAXTER]

JOHN DE RIDEVALL

Franciscan writer, fl. 1331 to 1340. He was the 54th lector at the Franciscans' Oxford Convent, 1331–32, and was also known as John of Musca. He became a doctor of theology c. 1331. A number of theological and philosophical works are attributed to him. He wrote a *Commentarius super Fulgencium* (Venice, St. Mark's manuscript 139, codex, F. 121–136) in which, like NICHO-LAS TREVET and the Franciscan, JOHN OF WALES, he considers classical mythology as a reservoir of moralizing subject matter for the use of preachers. A similar commentary, *Ovidii metamorphoseos fabule ccxviii moraliter exposite* (Cambridge, Eng., Public Library 1:11, 20 F. 162–199) is now usually ascribed to Peter Bersuire rather than to John. Books 1, 2, 3, 6, and 7 of John's commentary on St. Augustine's *De civitate Dei* are extant (Manuscripts Oxford C.C.C. 186 and 187, by Jo. Rydevallis or Rydewall, Friar Minor). There is a commentary on the Apocalypse, *Lectura super Apocalypsi,* at St. Mark's, Venice (Classification 1, manuscript 139, folios 110–119). A commentary on the letter of Valerius to Rufinus, *In Valerium ad Rufinum de uxore non ducenda* (Manuscripts Cambridge, Public Library, Mm 1, 18, 5), often ascribed to John, shows a similarity to John of Wales.

Bibliography: J. DE RIDEVALL, *Fülgentius metaforalis: Ein Beitrag zur Geschichte der antiken Mythologie im Mittelalter,* ed. H. LIEBESCHÜTZ (Leipzig 1926). C. L. KINGSFORD, *The Dictionary of National Biography From the Earliest Times to 1900,* 63 v. (London 1885–1900) 16: 1164–65. A. G. LITTLE, *The Grey Friars in Oxford* (Oxford 1892). B. SMALLEY, "J. Ridewall's Commentary on De civitate Dei," *Medium Aevum,* 25 (1956) 140–153. F. STEGMÜLLER, *Repertorium biblicum medii aevi,* 7 v. (Madrid 1949–61) 3: 4882–86. A. B. EMDEN, *A Biographical Register of the University of Oxford to A.D. 1500,* 3 v. (Oxford 1957–59) 3:1576.

[J. J. SMITH]

JOHN DE SACROBOSCO

Astronomer, applied mathematician; b. Paris, late 12th century, d. mid-13th century (1244 or 1256). Also known as John of Hollywood. Extant historical documents from his own time do not mention the name of Sacrobosco; his fame began only as a result of the growing popularity of his works. He is recognized as an early promoter of the ongoing project to describe nature mathematically. Franciscan and Dominican theologians took interest in Sacrobosco and wrote numerous commentaries on his *De Sphaera.* A 1271 commentary on *De Sphaera* by Robertus Anglicus identifies the author of the work as "Johannes de Sacrobosco Anglicus" suggesting an English origin. Historians seeking Sacrobosco's place of birth etymologically variously suggest England, Scotland, and Ireland. Most follow the early English tradition, although lacking a satisfactory etymological explanation for Sacrobosco or Hollywood. The popular suggestion of *Halifax* has since proven incorrect as *fax* refers to hair, not wood. His grave, apparently destroyed in the French Revolution, lay in the monastery of Saint-Mathurin in Paris. The epitaph recognized Sacrobosco as a famous astronomer and a *computista*—an expert in time calculations. A 1297 commentary on *De Sphaera* connects Sacrobosco to the University of Paris, where he was likely on faculty from about 1221.

Four extant treatises can be attributed to Sacrobosco with some degree of certainty. In the popular textbook, *Algorismus*, he demonstrates the use of what he terms ''Arabic'' numerals for arithmetic, ushering the use of Indo-Arabic numerals into the university curriculum. His most notable work, *Tractatus de Sphaera*, is divided into four chapters concerning (1) the structure of the universe, (2) the circles of the celestial sphere, (3) the observable implications of the foregoing for the rotation of the heavens, and (4) the motion of planets, theories of Sun and Moon, and the cause of eclipses. *De Sphaera* follows a Ptolemaic model, but innovates in its explanation for the phenomenon of procession. While *Algorismus* cannot be dated, *de Sphaera* seems to have been composed during Sacrobosco's career at the University of Paris and an early manuscript dates to 1240. *De Sphaera* remained in constant print for two centuries, the last edition being published in 1674 at Antwerp. It is significantly shorter than Sacrobosco's *Compotus*, a general treatise on ecclesiastical and civil time reckoning written between 1232 and 1235. In the *Compotus*, Sacrobosco proposes reforms to the Julian calendar that would eliminate the effects of accumulated errors and bring stability to the dates of the equinoxes. The *Tractatus de quadrante* is a brief work describing the Old Quadrant and its use. A number of spurious works exist, such as the *Theorica planetarum* and commentaries on Aristotle's *De Caelo* and *De generatione et corruptione*.

Bibliography: O. PEDERSEN, ''In Quest of Sacrobosco,'' *Journal for the History of Astronomy* 16 (1985), 175–221. W. R. KNORR, ''Sacrobosco's *Quadrans*: Date and Sources,'' *Journal for the History of Astronomy* 28 (1997), 197–222. J. MORETON, ''John of Sacrobosco and the Calendar,'' *Viator* 25 (1994), 229–244. L. THORNDIKE, *The Sphere of Sacrobosco and its Commentators* (Chicago 1949).

[J. H. BARLOW]

JOHN DE SAINT-POL

Archbishop of Dublin, chancellor of Ireland; b. Owston, West Riding, Yorkshire, England, *c.* 1295; d. Dublin, Ireland, Sept. 9, 1362. The Saint-Pol family had originally come from Guienne, France. Some time before 1330 John had received a papal dispensation from the disabilities of illegitimacy, but in 1339 the bishop of Winchester was directed by Rome to affirm his legitimacy, new evidence having come to light. John was already a clerk in the royal chancery by 1318, and in 1330 he was licensed to hold the numerous ecclesiastical BENEFICES he ac-

quired in various dioceses. From Jan. 13 to Feb. 17, 1334, as well as several times thereafter, he was guardian of the great seal in the absence of the chancellor of England, and on April 29, 1337, he was created master of the rolls. Imprisoned in 1341 by King EDWARD III on grounds of misadministration, he was released through the help of Abp. JOHN STRATFORD and in 1343 regained a position at the chancery. On Sept. 4, 1349, he was named archbishop of Dublin by papal PROVISION. In 1351 the new Archbishop was ordered by Pope CLEMENT VI to proceed against certain heretics who, fleeing from the persecution of Bp. Richard Lederede of Ossory (fl. 1350), had obtained protection from Alexander Bicknor, John's predecessor as archbishop. John disputed the right of RICHARD FITZRALPH, Archbishop of ARMAGH, to use the title PRIMATE OF IRELAND, until Edward revoked (1353) the royal letters in favor of Armagh and had the whole case removed to Rome. From 1350 to 1356 John was also chancellor of Ireland; in 1358 he was made a member of the privy council. He used his influence at Dublin in attempting to win a general amnesty for English and Irish rebels. As archbishop he enlarged Holy Trinity Cathedral (now called Christ Church), tried to secure numerous privileges for the see, and played a part in developing its liturgy. He held a provincial synod at Dublin in Lent of 1351 and a number of his decrees, issued on this occasion and later, for the regulation of diocesan affairs, are extant. He was buried in his cathedral.

Bibliography: ''Provincial and Diocesan Decrees of the Diocese of Dublin . . . ,'' *Archivium Hibernicum*, ed. A. GWYNN, 11 (1944) 34–37, 84–90. A. BELLESHEIM, *Geschichte der katholischen Kirche in Irland,* 3 v. (Mainz 1890–91) 1:519–520. E. I. CARLYLE, *The Dictionary of National Biography From the Earliest Times to 1900,* 63 v. (London 1885–1900) 17:662–663. A. B. EMDEN, *A Biographical Register of the University of Oxford to A.D. 1500,* 3 v. (Oxford 1957–59) 3:1629–30. G. J. HAND, ''The Psalter of Christ Church, Dublin,'' *Reportorium novum,* 1.2 (1956) 313; ''Cambridge University Additional Manuscript 710,'' *ibidem* 2.1 (1958) 21. W. HAWKES, ''The Liturgy in Dublin, 1200–1500: Manuscript Sources,'' *ibidem* 36–37.

[B. J. COMASKEY]

JOHN DE SECCHEVILLE (SÈCHEVILLE)

English scholastic philosopher, diplomat; b. of noble Exeter family; d. between 1279 and 1292. De Seccheville, called also John of Siccavilla, of Sackville, or of Driton, was a master of arts by 1245, possibly of Oxford. He studied at Paris, where he was rector of the faculty of arts of the university in 1256. He took part in the university's struggle against the MENDICANTS and was a member—along with men such as WILLIAM OF SAINT-AMOUR—of the delegation the university sent to Rome during these troubles. In 1258, during the Barons' War, he was back in England, where he served as secretary to the Duke of Gloucester. In 1259 he served as an intermediary between King Henry III of England and the King of France in their peace negotiations. He seems to have returned to Paris after that. In 1263, when the University of Paris was dispersed, John probably resided at Oxford for a time; but it was at Paris (*c.* 1263) that he wrote his chief work, the *De principiis naturae,* which seems to favor the Averroistic theses concerning monopsychism, eternity of time, and eternity of generation and motion (*see* AVERROISM). He was in London in 1265 and seems not to have left England again. He remains one of the chief representatives of the Averroistic current at the University of Paris during the second half of the 13th century.

Bibliography: JOHN DE SECCHEVILLE, *De principiis naturae,* ed. R. M. GIGUÈRE (Montreal 1956). J. C. RUSSELL, *Dictionary of Writers of 13th Century England* (New York 1936) 76–77. A. B. EMDEN, *A Biographical Register of the Scholars of the University of Oxford to A.D. 1500,* 3 v. (Oxford 1957–59) 3:1661–62.

[T. C. CROWLEY]

JOHN DISCALCEATUS, BL.

Franciscan friar; b. Saint-Vougay, Brittany, France, *c.* 1280; d. Quimper, France, Dec. 15, 1349. From his youth he devoted himself to works of charity; and after he was ordained (*c.* 1303) in the Diocese of RENNES, he led a life of poverty and austerity, devoted to the cure of souls. He was so attracted by FRANCISCAN spirituality that in 1316 he joined that order. He is said to have gone barefoot for more than 13 years—hence the name *Discalceatus*—and led an exemplary life of charity and self-denial, giving to the poor the very clothes he wore. He died of the plague. For the many miracles attributed to him, he was popularly proclaimed a saint, but his cult has never been approved by the Church, although he is commemorated in the Franciscan order.

Feast: Dec. 15.

Bibliography: F. M. PAOLINI, *Un Document inédit du XIV^esiècle sur la vie de St. Jean Discalcéat* (Rome 1910). *Acta Ordinis Fratrum Minorum* 29 (1910) 12–28; 33 (1914) 161–163. W. LAMPEN, *Collectanea Franciscana* 26 (1956) 421–424. W. FORSTER, *Lexikon für Theologie und Kirche,* ed. J. HOFER and K. RAHNER, 10 v. (2d, new ed. Freiburg 1957–65) 5:1028.

[S. OLIVIERI]

JOHN GILBERT

Dominican theologian, bishop, treasurer of England; d. London, July 28, 1397. Without family influence, he rose to high administrative office by his ability, in Church and state, becoming bishop of Bangor (1372–75), Hereford (1375–89), and Saint David's (1389–97) and serving as treasurer of England from October 1386 to May 1389 and August 1389 to 1391. He proved himself to be an efficient and conscientious official. He studied at Oxford before 1366 and later at Paris. In 1378 he was chancellor of the University of Oxford. As friar and theologian he opposed John WYCLIF both at Oxford and at the 1382 synod of Blackfriars. One of the ablest diplomats in the royal service, he took part in important embassies on both ecclesiastical and secular business from 1373 to 1395. He was occupied with administrative reforms between 1380 and 1388. Though at times associated with John of Gaunt, he appears to have been trusted by both Richard II and the opposing baronial factions.

Bibliography: *Registrum Johannis Gilbert, Episcopi Herefordensis,* ed. J. H. PARRY (Canterbury and York Society; London 1915) 1375–89. T. F. TOUT, *Chapters in the Administrative History of Mediaeval England,* 6 v. (Manchester 1923–35) 3:413, 454–460. É. PERROY, *L'Angleterre et le Grand Schisme d'Occident* (Paris 1933). A. B. EMDEN, *A Biographical Register of the University of Oxford to A.D. 1500,* 3 v. (Oxford 1957–59) 1:765–766.

[M. M. CHIBNALL]

JOHN GUALBERT, ST.

Abbot, founder of the VALLOMBROSANS; b. Florence, Italy, *c.* 995; d. S. Michele Arcangelo Abbey, Passignano, Italy, July 12, 1073. A member of the Visdomini family, John was a knight until the murderer of one of his kinsmen asked his forgiveness on Good Friday. He spared the man's life and was soon after professed as a Benedictine monk at S. Miniato, Florence. Seeking a more austere life, he went to CAMALDOLI sometime before the death of St. ROMUALD (d. 1027). But John wished to found an order aimed directly at promoting Church reform, and *c.* 1030 he withdrew to VALLOMBROSA to lead an eremitic life. In 1038 he founded a monastery there, which he placed under the BENEDICTINE RULE but with special statutes. He made provision for *CONVERSI* in order to free the choir monks from manual labor. Vallombrosans soon reformed or founded other communities, such as those of S. Salvi, Moscheta, and Passignano, to which hospices were attached for the care of the poor and the sick. All these houses were placed under the authority of a single abbot general. John's reforms brought him into bitter conflict with the archbishop of Florence, Peter Mezzabarba, the notorious simoniac. John is buried at Passignano. In 1193 he was canonized by Pope CELESTINE III.

Feast: July 12.

Bibliography: Two lives of John and prayers attributed to him, *Acta Sanctorum* July 3:297–433. S. CASINI, *Storia di S. Gio-*

St. John Gualbert, four scenes from his life, 14th-century altarpiece, Italian school, in Santa Croce, Florence.

vanni Gualberto Fiorentino (Florence 1934). B. QUILICI, *Giovanni Gualberto e la sua riforma monastica* (Florence 1943). E. LUCCHESI, *S. Giovanni Gualberto. Dai boschi d'Italia alle foreste del Brasile* (Florence 1959). A. SALVINI, *S. Giovanni Gualberto, fondatore di Vallombrosa* (Livorno 1972). G. SPINELLI and G. ROSSI, eds., *Alle origini di Vallombrosa* (Novara 1984).

[B. HAMILTON]

JOHN ITALUS

Byzantine philosopher and humanist; b. Southern Italy, *c.* 1025; d. after 1082. A student at Constantinople under Michael Psellus (*c.* 1049), he succeeded his master at the university there early in 1055 and became a close friend of Emperor MICHAEL VII DUCAS. He reached the height of his career in the 1070s, but his popularity as a teacher earned him many enemies, particularly among the Byzantine clergy. His lectures dealt with the teachings of Plato and the Neoplatonists, and he wrote commentaries on Plato, on Aristotle's logic, on Proclus, and on IAMBLICHUS. In 1077 nine theses reputed to be taken from his teachings were condemned by a synod in Constantinople. Finally, on March 13, 1082, Italus and his doctrines were solemnly condemned by a second synod, and he was banished to a monastery when the sentence was confirmed by Emperor Alexius I Comnenus (March 20). Most modern scholars believe that he was not guilty of doctrinal error, but that it was his devotion to Platonic philosophy and his overemphasis in the employment of logic and reason to explain dogma that brought down the wrath of the Church upon him. Although his works were publicly burned, some MSS are still extant.

Bibliography: *Opuscula selecta,* ed. G. CERETELI (Tiflis 1924–26). *Quaestiones quodlibetales,* ed. P. JOANNOU (Ettal 1956). P. STEPHANOU, *Jean Italos, philosophe et humaniste* (Orientalia Christiana Anulecta 134; 1949) *Lexikon für Theologie und Kirche,* ed. J. HOFER and K. RAHNER, 5:1043. V. GRUMEL, *Les Regestes des actes du patriarcat de Constantinople* (Kadikoi-Bucharest 1935—) 1.3:907, list of theses condemned in 1077. P. JOANNOU, *Die Il-*

luminationslehre des Michael Psellos und Joannes Italos (Ettal 1956). F. MASAI, *Pléthon et le platonisme de Mistra* (Paris 1956) 284–297.

[G. T. DENNIS]

JOHN JOSEPH OF THE CROSS, ST.

Religious; b. Ischia, in the Gulf of Naples, Aug. 15, 1654; d. Naples, March 5, 1734. Leaving his well-to-do parents at the age of 16, John Joseph became the first Italian to join the Alcantarines, a strict reform group within the Franciscan Order newly introduced into Italy by friars from Spain. When only 21 years old, he was entrusted with the building of a new house of the reform at Piedimonte di Alife. It was only under obedience that he received Holy Orders in 1677. After his ordination to the priesthood he was appointed master of novices. In this office he showed himself unusually gifted in the art of spiritual direction, and throughout his life he was much sought after as a confessor. He served two terms as guardian, and when the first Alcantarine province was erected in Italy in 1702, he was chosen to head it. He successfully guided the new province through its first stormy years, when disputes between the Spanish and Italian factions within the reform movement threatened the very existence of the Alcantarines in Italy.

John Joseph vigorously embraced the almost repellent austerities that typified the Alcantarine reform in its early days and sought to emulate in every detail the life and virtues of St. Peter of Alcántara, its founder. He wore a number of spiked crosses under his rough habit, scourged himself daily, and for the last 30 years of his life abstained from all liquids. He died at the friary of Santa Lucia del Monte. He was buried there, and his tomb immediately became a place of popular pilgrimage. He was beatified by Pius VI in 1789 and canonized by Gregory XVI in 1839.

Feast: March 5.

Bibliography: DIODATA DEL'ASSUNTA, . . . *Vita di B. Gio Guiseppe della Croce* (Naples 1789). LÉON DE CLARY, *Lives of the Saints and Blessed of the Three Orders of St. Francis,* 4 v. (Taunton, Eng. 1885–87) 1:349–368. A. BUTLER, *The Lives of the Saints,* rev. ed. H. THURSTON and D. ATTWATER (New York 1956) 1:490–493.

[C. LYNCH]

JOHN KLENKOK

Theologian, opponent of the Sachsenspiegel; b. Buken, Hanover; d. Avignon, June 17, 1374. John became *doctor utriusque iuris,* probably at Bologna, before he joined the AUGUSTINIANS in Herford where a document of 1346 calls him *clericus OESA.* He was sent to Oxford where he received a D.D. in 1359. In 1363 and 1367–68, he was provincial of the province of Saxony. John criticized certain articles of the Sachsenspiegel, the medieval civil law of eastern Germany, which he felt were opposed to human and divine law. The inquisitor Walter Kerlinger, OP, asked for his opinion in writing but misused the confidence by turning over the treatise, called the *Decadicon,* to the magistrate of Magdeburg instead of to the proper ecclesiastical authorities (1369). A great outcry followed, and John called on Bp. Albert of Halberstadt to appoint two Austin masters, Rudolf Block and Jordan of Saxony, to be his judges. Both decided against him. In 1370 Klenkok was a professor at Prague and an intimate friend of Bp. John of Neumarkt, chancellor of the empire. A year later he sent Gregory XI at Avignon a revision of his *Decadicon,* in which 21 articles of the Sachsenspiegel were held condemnable. Gregory responded in 1374 by denouncing 14 articles, which became known in German law as *articoli reprobari.* Klenkok was made papal penitentiary. As such he opposed JOHN MILÍČ, the Bohemian nationalist and foe of the mendicants. Both died at Avignon in June 1374. John wrote commentaries on the Apocalypse, the letters of St. John, and the Lombard, but only the *Decadicon* has been published.

Bibliography: H. BÜTOW, ''Zur Lebensgeschichte des Augustinermönches Johannes Klenkok,'' *Historische Vierteljahrschrift* 29 (1934–35) 541–575. D. TRAPP, ''Augustinian Theology of the 14th Century,'' *Augustiniana* 6 (1956) 223–239; ''Notes on John Klenkok,'' *Augustinianum* 4 (1964) 358–404. A. B. EMDEN, *A Biographical Register of the University of Oxford to A.D. 1500,* 3 v. (Oxford 1957–59) 2:1057. A. ZUMKELLER, ''Manuskripte von Werken der Autoren des Augustiner- Eremitenordens in mitteleuropäischen Bibliotheken,'' 521–534. B. OCKER, ''Johannes Klenkok: A Friar's Life, c. 1310–1374,'' *Transactions of the American Philosophical Society 83, part 5:* VII-116 (Philadelphia 1993).

[F. ROTH]

JOHN KYNYNGHAM

Carmelite theologian (also known as John Cunningham); b. Suffolk, England; d. York, England, May 12, 1399. He entered the CARMELITE ORDER at Ipswich, had moved to Oxford by 1372, and served as provincial prior of the English Carmelites from 1393 till his death. He was one of a number of Carmelite confessors to John of Gaunt and he witnessed that prince's will, in which he is described as ''mestre Johan Kynyngham doctour en theologie.'' Kynyngham was an early (*c.* 1373) and vigorous opponent of John WYCLIF, and as a member of the council assembled at Black Friars, London, in 1382 to condemn 24 propositions taken from the writings of Wyclif, he was called upon to preach the final sermon to the assembly. He was present also for the trial of Henry CRUMPE in 1392, and on November 1 of the same year he preached before Richard II, who later summoned Kynyngham to a council scheduled to begin on Jan. 27, 1399, for the discussion of the WESTERN SCHISM. He died in the Carmelite friary at York where he is buried.

Bibliography: Kynyngham's three *Ingressus* against Wyclif: *Fasciculi Zizaniorum magistri Johannis Wyclif cum tritico,* ed. W. W. SHIRLEY, [*Rerum Britannicarum medii aevi scriptores,* 244 v., 5, (1858)] 4–104. C. DE VILLIERS, *Bibliotheca carmelitana,* ed. G. WESSELS, 2 v. in 1 (Rome 1927) 2:9, 21–23. C. L. KINGSFORD, *The Dictionary of National Biography From the Earliest Times to 1900,* 63 v. (London 1885–1900) 11:361–362. J. CROMPTON, "Fasciculi Zizaniorum," *The Journal of Ecclesiastical History* (London 1950—) 12 (1961) 35–45, 155–166. J. A. ROBSON, *Wyclif and the Oxford Schools* (Cambridge, Eng. 1961) 162–170. A. B. EMDEN, *A Biographical Register of the University of Oxford to A.D. 1500,* 3 v. (Oxford 1957–59) 2:1077.

[K. J. EGAN]

JOHN LE MOINE

Cardinal and canonist; b. Crécy-en-Ponthieu (northern France), *c.* 1250; d. Avignon, 1313. He studied philosophy and theology in Paris and was also a doctor *in utroque iure.* For a time an auditor of the Rota, he was dean of the Church of Bayeux from 1288 to 1292. Celestine V named him cardinal, which is why authors often refer to him simply as *Cardinalis.* Under Boniface VIII he became vice chancellor of the Roman Church. He was also called to fulfill important diplomatic missions, particularly during the great controversies between Philip IV (the Fair) of France and the Holy See. As a canonist, John is known above all for his *Apparatus* (1301) on the LIBER SEXTUS of Boniface VIII (1298), of which there are many manuscripts and printed editions (e.g., Paris 1535; Venice 1585, 1602). He also glossed some later constitutions of Boniface VIII and Benedict XI. A sagacious jurist, experienced in controversies, quick to reconcile opposing issues, he developed an important theory on the constitution and rights of the College of Cardinals.

Bibliography: G. A. DIGARD, *Philippe le Bel et le Saint-siège de 1285 à 1304,* 2 v. (Paris 1936) 1:140–142, 157–159. A. VAN HOVE, *Commentarium Lovaniense in Codicem iuris canonici 1,* v. 1–5 (Mechlin 1928—) 1:474–476. B. TIERNEY, *Foundations of the Conciliar Theory* (Cambridge, Eng. 1955) 180–191, 208–209. *Dictionnaire de droit canonique,* ed. R. NAZ, 7 v. (Paris 1935–65) 6:112–113.

[P. LEGENDRE]

JOHN LE ROMEYN

Archbishop of York; b. *c.* 1230; d. Bishop Burton, near Beverley, Yorkshire, England, March 10, 1296. He was the illegitimate son of the Italian-born treasurer of York and a servant woman. A dispensation from illegitimacy was obtained (*c.* 1237), thus enabling him to be ordained. Romeyn received a master of arts degree from Oxford in 1256 and was the recipient of a number of livings. By 1270 he was at Paris, where he took a doctorate in theology (1276). Elected archbishop of YORK (Oct. 29, 1285), Romeyn was consecrated at Rome on Feb. 10, 1286. His episcopal career was stormy. He antagonized King Edward I by trying secular cases in his episcopal court, and he quarreled with the influential Anthony BEK, bishop of Durham, and formerly keeper of the king's wardrobe. In the course of this controversy, which centered on judicial appeals from the consistory court of Durham to York, Romeyn appealed his case to Rome and eventually excommunicated Bek (1292). Edward, in turn, imprisoned the Archbishop in the Tower, charging that the excommunication infringed on the royal prerogative. In 1293 Romeyn was released on promise to pay 4,000 marks. His register reveals that, in spite of this involvement in Church-State affairs, Romeyn concerned himself with his own province: his clergy was encouraged to study theology in the chancellor's school at York, and he rebuilt the nave of York Minster. During his tenure the chapter houses at York and Southwell were built, and the choir of Ripon extended. Romeyn's body was interred in York Minster.

Bibliography: JOHN LE ROMEYN, *Register,* ed. W. BROWN (Surtees Society 123, 128; London 1913–16). C. M. FRASER, *A History of Antony Bek, Bishop of Durham 1283–1311* (Oxford 1957) 47–48, 53, 57, 94 96, 111, 113–114, 147–148, 228. D. KNOWLES, *The Religious Orders in England,* 3 v. (Cambridge, Eng. 1948–60) 1:89–90, 93. D. L. DOUIE, *Archbishop Pecham* (Oxford 1952) 69, 112, 230–234, 322. A. B. EMDEN, *A Biographical Register of the University of Oxford to A.D. 1500,* 3 v. (Oxford 1957–59) 2:1134–35.

[B. F. BYERLY]

JOHN LOBEDAU, BL.

Franciscan; b. Toruń (Pomerania), probably after 1231; d. Chelmno, Oct. 9, 1264. Having entered the Franciscan convent (founded in 1239) in his native city, subject to the province of Bohemia and Poland, he was transferred in 1258 to the newly founded convent of St. James at Chelmno. Pious, learned, animated with zeal for souls, he was the confessor and spiritual director of JUTTA OF SANGERHAUSEN, a relative of Anno, the grand master of the TEUTONIC KNIGHTS (1257). He was buried at Chelmno, and miracles reputedly obtained through his intercession established him as the protector of sailors and fishermen. Hymns testify to an early cult. He is represented holding a book and surrounded by a bright light. His cult, approved Oct. 31, 1638, is limited to Poland; his name is not in the Franciscan liturgical calendar.

Feast: Oct. 9.

Bibliography: F. SCHEMBEK, *Żywot b. Jana Prussaca* (Toruń, Poland 1627); Lat. tr., *Acta Sanctorum* Oct. 4:1097–1100. *Scriptores rerum Prussicarum,* ed. T. HIRSCH et al., 5 v. (Leipzig 1861–74) 2:392–396. A. DU MONSTIER, *Martyrologium franciscanum* (2d ed. Paris 1753). L. LEMMENS, "Annales minorum Prussicorum," *Archivum Franciscanum historicum* 6 (1913) 702–704. C. KROLLMANN, ed., *Altpreussische Biographie* (Königsberg 1936–) v.1. J. L. BAUDOT and L. CHAUSSIN, *Vies des saints et des bienheureux selon l'ordre du calendrier avec l'historique des fêtes* 10:253–254.

[J. CAMBELL]

JOHN LUTTERELL

English scholastic theologian and philosopher; d. Avignon, July 17, 1335. Before 1304 he obtained a papal dispensation from the impediment of illegitimacy, in view of his ordination to sacred orders, and again on Sept. 1, 1331, probably in prospect of the bishopric of Salisbury. About 1317 he acquired his doctor's degree of divinity at Oxford, was elected chancellor of the university on Oct. 10, 1317, and successfully prosecuted the dispute of the university with the Dominicans. He may be the author of many documents on this question, collected by Richard of Bury in his *Liber epistolaris* [*Formularies which bear on the history of Oxford c. 1204–1420,* ed. H. E. Salter et al. (Oxford 1942) 1.4–5, 14–66, 71–79]. When Cardinal Gaucelm de Jean visited England *c.* 1318, John Lutterell was appointed by the university to conduct the dispute before him. In 1322 he became the central figure in a conflict with the masters and scholars of the university; this was so serious that the chapter of Lincoln warned it could lead to a general schism. He was deposed as chancellor in September 1322. At the invitation of his friend at Avignon, Master Stephen de Kettelbergh, he was at the papal court there from late summer of 1323 to May 13, 1325, when he was recalled to England. John XXII explained his prolonged stay as attributable to papal proceedings against "a certain pestiferous doctrine." There is no doubt that the teaching of WILLIAM OF OCKHAM was meant, since Lutterell had just finished examining Ockham's commentary on the *Sentences,* from which he denounced 56 propositions as "against true and sane doctrine" [J. Koch, "Neue Aktenstücke zu dem gegen Wilhelm von Ockham in Avignon geführten Prozess," *Recherches de théologie ancienne et médiévale,* 7 (1935) 353–380; 8 (1936) 79–93, 168–197]. He was also one of the masters of theology who condemned 51 articles of Ockham in 1326 [A. Pelzer, "Les 51 articles de Guillaume Occam censurés, en Avignon, en 1326," *Revue*

d'histoire ecclésiastique, 18 (1922) 240–70]. In 1328–29 he was again in Avignon, and in 1332–33 he was among the masters of theology who condemned theological errors of DURANDUS OF SAINT-POURÇAIN and THOMAS WALEYS.

Lutterell was esteemed for his skill as a stylist. His doctrines are known from his *Libellus contra doctrinam Guilelmi Occam,* written in 1323–24. Between 1327 and 1333 he wrote a treatise at Avignon, *Epistola de visione beatifica,* defending the singular view of John XXII. He is said to have written also *In vesperies magistrorum* and *Praelectiones Oxonienses.* He held several benefices and in the years 1325 to 1334 he received 32 papal mandates [*Calendar of Entries in the Papal Registers relating to Great Britain and Ireland, Papal Letters,* 2 (London 1895), *passim*].

Bibliography: A. B. EMDEN, *A Biographical Register of the University of Oxford to A.D. 1500,* 3 v. (Oxford 1957–59) 2:1181–82. F. HOFFMANN, *Die erste Kritik des Ockhamismus durch den Oxforder Kanzler Johannes Lutterell* (Breslau 1941); *Die Schriften des Oxforder Kanzlers Iohannes Lutterell* (Leipzig 1959). G. N. BUESCHER, *The Eucharistic Teaching of William Ockham* (Washington 1950), xix–xxvii, 145–150.

[S. GIEBEN]

JOHN MALALAS

In Syriac *Malel,* or "rhetorician," Byzantine historian; fl. mid-sixth century. Nothing definite is known of his life, but he seems to have been a native of Antioch, and was probably of Syrian origin. He may be identical with the Patriarch JOHN III Scholasticus (565–577). His *Chronicle* recounts the history of the world from creation to 565 A.D. and embraces Biblical history, Greek mythology, and the history of Eastern peoples, as well as the political history of Greece, Rome, and the early Byzantine Empire. Malalas was an uncritical compiler, with a taste for the anecdotal and trivial, e.g., his description of the personal appearance of the heroes of the Trojan War. But he had access to many sources now lost, in particular a history of his native Antioch, on which he supplies much priceless information. His tone is one of extremely naïve Christian apologetic. Used with critical discrimination, his *Chronicle* is a valuable source for the history of his own time. He wrote a simple, unclassical Greek, with no literary pretensions, but he could tell a good story well. The Greek text survives in a slightly abbreviated form in a single manuscript, but an Old Slavonic translation made in the 10th or 11th century preserves a fuller version. His *Chronicle* was copied or excerpted, directly or indirectly, by all subsequent Byzantine writers of universal history.

Bibliography: *Ioannis Malalae chronographia,* ed. L. DINDORF (Bonn 1831). *The Chronicle of J. M., bks. VIII–XVIII,* trs.,

M. SPINKA and G. DOWNEY (Chicago 1940). *Die römische Kaisergeschichte bei Malalas*, ed. A. SCHENK VON STAUFFENBERG (Stuttgart 1931), critical text of bks. 9–12. G. MORAVCSIK, *Byzantinoturcica*, 2 v. (2d ed. Berlin 1958) 1:329–334, full bibliog. K. WEIERHOLT, *Studien im Sprachgebrauch des Malalas* (Oslo 1963).

[R. BROWNING]

JOHN MILÍČ

Ascetic, Bohemian reform preacher; b. Kroměříž, Czechoslovakia, *c.* 1305; d. Avignon, June 29, 1374. After being educated in Prague, he became registrar at the court of Emperor CHARLES IV (1358–60) and then an official of the chancery (1360–62). Under the influence of the Archbishop of Prague, ERNEST OF PARDUBICE, he became a priest and later a canon of Prague. Inspired by the reform spirit on one hand and disgusted by the corruption of the clergy on the other, he renounced all dignities, and from December 1363 he lived in absolute poverty and preached penance.

John inaugurated the DEVOTIO MODERNA in Bohemia with VOJTĚCH RAŇKŮV in an attempt to materialize true reform under the guidance of John of Jenštein, Archbishop of Prague. Each day Milíč preached in Latin for the clergy in St. Nicholas Church and then for the people in St. Egid's; after the death of Conrad of Waldhausen (1369) he preached daily in St. Vitus Cathedral. He was an ardent proponent of daily Communion as an integral part of the reform. Milíč was one of those who urged a vernacular translation of the Bible for the use of the laity. Because of prevailing corruption of morals he awaited the end of the world and predicted an imminent coming of Antichrist. When he thus preached in Rome, in 1367, he was imprisoned by the INQUISITION as a heretic. There he wrote his *Libellus de Anti-Christo* in 1368. Pope URBAN V, to whom he sent his ideas on the urgency of Church reform in a special memorandum, permitted him to return to Prague. There he resumed his preaching, in both German and Czech. He founded a house called Jerusalem for reformed women sinners. In 1373, once again accused of heresy, he went to AVIGNON to justify himself before Pope GREGORY XI and was allowed to preach to the cardinals. Milíč is characterized as one of the forerunners of the HUSSITES, but he radically opposed reform carried on outside the Church. His Latin works *Gratiae Dei* and *Abortivus* are still unpublished.

Bibliography: *Vitae sanctorum et aliorum quorundam pietate insignium*, ed. J. PERWOLF, et al., 7 v. (Fontes rerum Bohemicarum 1; Prague 1873–1932) 401–436. H. HURTER, *Nomenclator literarius theologiae catholicae*, 5 v. in 6 (3d ed., Innsbruck 1903–13) 2:663. O. ODLOZILIK, *Jan Milíčz Kroměříže* (Prague 1924). A. HYMA, *The Christian Renaissance: A History of the "De-*

votio Moderna" (New York 1925). S. H. THOMPSON, "Learning at the Court of Charles IV," *Speculum*, 25 (1950) 1–20. F. DVORNIK, *The Slavs in European History and Civilization* (New Brunswick, N.J. 1962).

[J. PAPIN]

JOHN OF ACTON

Priest and noted English canonist; d. November 1349. He received a doctor of civil law degree from Oxford *c.* 1311 and a doctor of Canon Law degree from Cambridge before 1330. While at Cambridge he engaged in a fictitious *quaestio disputata* with M. Walter Elveden *c.* 1335 (Gonville and Caius College, Cambridge, MS 483, flyleaf). A canon of Lincoln by papal provision in 1329, he became rector of Willingham by Stow, Lincolnshire, in 1330, and an official of the Court of York in 1335.

He is chiefly known for his famous gloss, composed *c.* 1333 to 1335, on the Legatine Constitutions of the 13th century Legates, Otto and Ottobuono. In this he performed a valuable service for the Church in England, providing a comprehensive gloss on every significant word of the constitutions of 1237 (Otto) and 1268 (Ottobuono). He shows a wide knowledge of the classic sources and commentators of Canon Law, although, as Maitland has noted, he is a little too human to be strictly scientific: his gloss often is a growl against greedy prelates, hypocritical friars, rapacious officials, and papal exactions. The gloss has been printed twice, and many manuscripts survive. In 1346, three years before his death, he also wrote a *Septuplum,* a two-part work of moral theology that has not yet been edited.

Bibliography: JOHN OF ACTON, *Constitutiones legatime, seu legatine regionis Anglicane,* as appendix to W. LYNDWOOD, *Provinciale seu Constitutiones Angliae,* 2 pts. (Oxford 1679). S. LEE, *The Dictionary of National Biography From the Earliest Times to 1900,* 63 v. (London 1885–1900) 1:67. F. W. MAITLAND, *Roman Canon Law in the Church of England* (London 1898). A. B. EMDEN, *A Biographical Register of the University of Oxford to A.D. 1500,* 3 v. (Oxford 1957–59) 1:11–12; *Biographical Register of the Scholars of the University of Cambridge before 1500* (Cambridge, Eng. 1963) 2. L. BOYLE, "The Curriculum of the Faculty of Canon Law at Oxford in the First Half of the 14th Century," in Oxford Historical Society, *Oxford Studies Presented to Daniel Callus* (Oxford 1964).

[L. E. BOYLE]

JOHN OF ANTIOCH

Fifth century bishop of Antioch; d. *c.* 441. Little is known of the early life of John of Antioch, before his consecration as bishop of that see in 428, except that he was a friend and fellow student of NESTORIUS. When the latter began to preach his ideas on the THEOTOKOS, John, as bishop of Antioch, urged him not to stir up trouble, and claimed that the title had been sanctioned by the early Fathers. Once the disturbance began, however, John sided with Nestorius. Summoned to the Council of EPHESUS by imperial order, John sent word that he and his suffragans would not be able to reach Ephesus in time for the opening session. As a result, the Antiochians were not present on June 22, 431, when the council condemned and deposed Nestorius. On June 26, John of Antioch arrived at Ephesus, was incensed at the reports of council proceedings, and began a rival synod that vindicated Nestorius and condemned CYRIL OF ALEXANDRIA as an Apollinarian. On July 10, the original council repeated its denunciation of Nestorius, and, on July 17, excommunicated John and his adherents. John appealed to the Emperor, who ratified the decisions of both assemblies, deposing Cyril and Nestorius.

As a result of the council, the Antiochene Church broke away from the rest of Christianity, although it seems that both John of Antioch and Cyril were sincerely desirous of reunion. In April 433, the schism was healed when John and Cyril were reconciled. John had sent to Alexandria a profession of faith probably drawn up by THEODORET OF CYR. Cyril accepted the formula and, in turn, John agreed to the condemnation of Nestorius.

This reconciliation caused violent reactions in the Byzantine Church. Those who leaned toward Nestorius's views thought that John had betrayed their cause and espoused heresy. Toward these, John at first adopted a policy of conciliation. Meanwhile, others criticized him for not stamping out NESTORIANISM. Eventually, the Church at EDESSA, a Nestorian stronghold, renounced its ties with Antioch and began the East Syrian Nestorian Church. At this point John tried to use civil and military force to end the schism but died soon afterward.

John corresponded with PROCLUS OF CONSTANTINOPLE, Cyril of Alexandria, and Emperor THEODOSIUS II on the subjects of Proclus's letter to the Armenians and the orthodoxy of THEODORE OF MOPSUESTIA. Some of John's letters on the Nestorian controversy are preserved among the correspondence of Proclus and of Cyril of Alexandria.

Bibliography: Letters *Patrologia Graeca*, ed. J. P. MIGNE, 161 v. (Paris 1857–66) 77:131–132, 163–166, 167–174, 247–250, 329–332, 365, 877–878; 83:1440–46. *Synodicon adversus tragoedium Irenaei, Patrologia Graeca*, 84:550–864. *Acta conciliorum oecumenicorum* (Berlin 1914—) 1.1:93–96, 119; 1.4:79, 33; 1.5:124–135; 1.7:84, 146, 151–161; 3; 4. M. LE QUIEN, *Oriens Christianus* (Leipzig-Wiesbaden 1904—) 2 721. O. BARDENHEWER, *Geschichte der altkirchlichen Literatur*, 5 v. (Freiburg 1913–32) 4:362. 370–371. W. KRAATZ, *Texte und Untersuchungen zur Geschichte der altchristlichen Literatur* (Berlin 1882—) 26.2:191–200, on Nestorius. P. T. CAMELOT, *Éphèse et Chalcédoine* 54, 70–72, 209–211. *Histoire de l'église depuis les origines jusqu'à nos jours*, eds. A. FLICHE and V. MARTIN *Histoire de l'église depuis les origines jusqu'à nos jours* (Paris 1935—) 4:163–191. J. DANIÉLOU and H. I. MARROU, *The First Six Hundred Years*, tr. V. CRONIN, of *The Christian Centuries* (New York 1964—) 1:345–348. B. ALTANER, *Patrology*, tr. H. GRAEF from 5th German ed. (New York 1960) 329. J. QUASTEN, *Patrology*, 3 v. (Westminster, Md. 1950–53) 3:118, 130.

[J. F. KRASTEL]

JOHN OF APPLEBY

Ecclesiastical lawyer, dean of St. Paul's, London (1365–89); b. perhaps at Appleby, Westmorland, date unknown; d. between Sept. 24 and Oct. 1, 1389. A bachelor of civil law by 1349, he had a doctorate in this subject by 1359, possibly from Oxford. He was not John of Appleby, bachelor of civil law, Archdeacon of Carlisle (1364), and brother of Thomas, Bishop of Carlisle. He was active as a lawyer, and in 1361 the convent of Durham retained him as adviser, a position he held until his death. In 1363, while an advocate at the papal Curia, he obtained a reservation of the deanery of St. Paul's. Archbishops WILLIAM WITTLESEY and SIMON OF SUDBURY employed his services. He was present at the condemnation of John WYCLIF's doctrines at the Blackfriars' synod (London 1382). Twice in 1372 King Edward III used him on diplomatic missions; in 1389 he was a member of the famous court of chivalry that affirmed the right of Sir Richard le Scrope of Bolton to bear the arms "azure, a bend gold." He was a great pluralist. In his will he remembered the parish church and poor of Appleby and asked to be buried in St. Paul's cathedral.

Bibliography: *North Country Wills*, ed. J. W. CLAY, 2 v., Durham Surtees Society (Durham 1908–12) v. 2. A. B. EMDEN, *A Biographical Register of the University of Oxford to A.D. 1500*, 3 v. (Oxford 1957–59) 1:40–41. I. J. CHURCHILL, *Canterbury Administration*, 2 v. (New York 1933) 1:29 n., 501 n.; 2:3. J. LENEVE, *Fasti Ecclesiae Anglicannae 1300–1541* (1716) v.5.

[F. D. BLACKLEY]

JOHN OF AVILA, ST.

Preacher, spiritual director, and mystical writer; b. Almodóvar del Campo (New Castile), Spain, 1500 (1499); d. Montilla (Córdoba), May 10, 1569. He was born of a wealthy and pious family and received an excellent education. At the age of 14 he was sent to the University of Salamanca to study law, but he soon abandoned this profession in favor of training in philosophy and theology. These he studied at Alcalá, where he was a student of Domingo de Soto. John's parents died leaving him the sole heir of the family fortune, but after his ordination he distributed his inheritance to the poor and prepared to become a missionary in America. In 1527 he went to Seville from whence he hoped to journey to Mexico, but there Abp. Hernando de Contreras persuaded him to stay and work for the faith in Spain.

As a missionary in Andalusia for nine years, he attracted great crowds by his magnificent preaching and was in great demand for confession and spiritual direction. However, his strong pleas for reform and his denunciation of vice in high places won him the enmity of certain influential persons. He was accused before the Inquisition, but the charges were easily refuted and he was declared innocent in 1533. From Seville he went to Córdoba and then to Granada in 1537 where he collaborated with Abp. Gaspare Avalos in the organization of the university there.

John of Avila's greatest work was as a reformer of clerical life in Spain. He became the center of a circle of disciples, secular priests of devout life who dedicated themselves to the spiritual direction and teaching of youths in the colleges that John founded. Outstanding among these clerical schools was the University of Baeza, which became a model for seminaries and for the schools of the Jesuits. Among the many saintly persons who enjoyed the friendship and spiritual direction of John of Avila were St. John of God, St. Francis Borgia, St. Teresa of Avila, and Louis of Granada, who wrote a biography of John. He is especially revered by the Jesuits with whom he had a close relationship and whose work he particularly encouraged. The spread of the Society of Jesus in Spain was greatly facilitated by his friendship and support.

His *Audi filia* is a masterwork on Christian perfection and a singularly fine example of the mystical literature of the period. His other writings include many sermons and letters of spiritual direction that are considered classics of Spanish literature. Not long after his death his writings were collected and translated into other languages. A critical and annotated edition of John's works was published in 1952 by Luigi Sala Balust. John of Avila was beatified by Leo XIII on April 15, 1894 and canonized by Paul VI on May 31, 1970.

Feast: May 10.

Bibliography: *Obras. completas,* ed. L. SALA BALUST, 2 V. (BAC; 1952–53); *Lettres de direction,* ed. and tr. J. M. DE BUCK (Louvain 1927). *Certain selected spiritual epistles, 1631* (Ilkley, Eng. 1977). L. DE ODDI, *Life of the Blessed Master John of Avila,* ed. J. G. MACLEOD (New York 1898), tr. from Ital. Baudot-Chaussin 13:37–45. C. M. NANNEI, *La Doctrina cristiana de San Juan de Avila: Contribución al estudio de su doctrina catequética* (Pamplona 1977). J. GAUTIER, *Catholicisme* 6:417–419. *Vidas del padre maestro Juan de Avila, Luis de Granada, Luis Muñoz,* ed. L. S. BALUST (Barcelona 1964).

[J. C. WILLKE]

JOHN OF BASTONE, BL.

Sylvestrine monk; b. early 13th century; d. Fabriano, Italy, March 24, 1290. John joined SILVESTER GUZZOLINI as a teacher of grammar in Fabriano and was later ordained. He lived for 60 years as a Sylvestrine BENEDICTINE in the monastery of Monte Fano. His cult was approved by Pope CLEMENT XIV in 1772, and his relics are kept in the church of San Benedetto near Fabriano. Andreas Jacobi (d. 1326) of Fabriano, a confrere of John, wrote a vita that is published along with the *Acta canonizationis* (Rome 1772) and edited in altered form by J. Mercati (Camerino 1613).

Feast: March 24.

Bibliography: G. GUIDI, *Brevi notizie. . . del b. Giovanni del Bastone* (Fabriano 1916). *Bibliotheca hagiographica latina antiquae et mediae aetatis,* 2 v. (Brussels 1898–1901; suppl. 1911) 4335. A. M. ZIMMERMANN, *Kalendarium Bendictinum: Die Heiligen und Seligen des Benediktinerorderns und seiner Zweige,* 4 v. (Metten 1933–38) 1: 367–370. A. M. ZIMMERMANN, *Lexikon für Theologie und Kirche,* ed. J. HOFER and K. RAHNER, 10 v. (2d, new ed. Freiburg 1957–65); suppl., *Das Zweite Vatikanische Konzil: Dokumente und Kommentare,* ed. H. S. BRECHTER et al., pt. 1 (1966) 5:1006.

[C. R. BYERLY]

JOHN OF BEVERLEY, ST.

Anglo-Saxon bishop of Hexham and York; b. Harpham, Humberside; d. Beverley, England, May 7, 721. He was of noble birth and was a disciple of HILDA at WHITBY and later of Abp. THEODORE OF CANTERBURY. Consecrated bishop of Hexham in 687, he ordained BEDE deacon in 692 and priest in 703. In 705 he was translated to YORK as successor to WILFRID OF YORK. John resigned this see in 720, consecrating Wilfrid the younger as his successor. He retired to the monastery he had founded in Beverley and died shortly afterward. His cult became very popular in the north of England, and his shrine at Beverley was a place of pilgrimage and sanctuary all through the Middle Ages. Bede, the main source for his life, tells a number of delightful stories of the miracles he performed. His relics are still at Beverley Minster.

Feast: May 7; Oct. 25 (translation).

Bibliography: W. HUNT, *The Dictionary of National Biography from the Earliest Times to 1900* 10:872–873. BEDE, *Ecclesiastical History* 4.23; 5.2, 3, 24. FOLCARDO, *The Historians of the*

Church of York and Its Archbishops, ed. J. RAINE (*Rerum Britannicarum medii aevi scriptores* 71; 1879) 239–260.

[B. COLGRAVE]

JOHN OF BICLARO

Bishop of Gerona, historian; b. Scallabis, Lusitania, Portugal, *c.* 540, of Catholic Visigothic nobility; d. Gerona?, after 621. He was a contemporary of ISIDORE OF SEVILLE (*Vir. ill.,* 44). On his return to Spain *c.* 576, after 16 years of study in Constantinople, he was exiled to Arian Barcelona because of his faith. After the death of Leovigild (569–586) John founded the monastery of Biclaro (location unknown). As its abbot, he also wrote a rule, no longer extant. He attended councils in Saragossa in 592, Toledo in 597 and 610, Barcelona in 599, and Egara in 614. His chronicle (567–590) continued that of VICTOR OF TUNNUNA, whose erroneous chronology he adopted until 583. On firsthand information John described the politically active reign of Leovigild, to whom he was loyal despite religious differences. In his work John reported on the rebels exiled to far parts of Spain; the rebellion of Leovigild's Catholic son HERMENEGILD in Seville (579–584); the conversion to Catholicism of King Reccared and the Visigoths in 587; attacks by the Franks in Visigothic Gaul; and Byzantine, Lombard, and North African history. He gave the regnal years for both Byzantine and Visigothic rulers but did not use the Spanish Era. Isidore's comprehensive work supplanted John's chronicle.

Bibliography: *Monumenta Germaniae Historica, Auctores antiquissimi* (Berlin 1826—) 11:207–220. *Juan de Biclaro,* ed. J. CAMPOS (Madrid 1960). O. BARDENHEWER, *Geschichte der altkirchlichen Literatur,* 5 v. (Freiburg 1913–32) 5:396–398. B. SÁNCHEZ ALONSO, *Historia de la historiografía española* (2d ed. Madrid 1947–) v. 1. H. BRAUNERT, *Lexikon für Theologie und Kirche,* ed. J. HOFER and K. RAHNER, 10 v. (2d, new ed Freiburg 1957–65) 5:1010.

[E. P. COLBERT]

JOHN OF BRIDLINGTON, ST.

The last Englishman to be canonized until modern times; b. Thwing, York, *c.* 1320; d. Bridlington, 1379. He studied at Oxford for three years (1335–38) before entering the CANONS REGULAR OF ST. AUGUSTINE at St. Mary, Bridlington, near Thwing. In 1361 he was elected prior. He was venerated as a saint during his lifetime, and was canonized by Boniface IX, Sept. 24, 1401. The prophecies under his name are now known to have been written by John Erghome.

Feast: Oct. 21 (formerly Oct. 10).

Bibliography: Sources. *Acta Sanctorum* Oct. 5:135–144; Oct. Suppl. 42. P. GROSJEAN, *Analecta Bollandiana* 53 (1935) 101–129. Literature. C. L. KINGSFORD, *The Dictionary of National Biography from the Earliest Times to 1900* 10:888. J. S. PURVIS, *St. John of Bridlington* (Bridlington, Eng. 1924). A. O. GWYNN, *The English Austin Friars* (London 1940) 134–138, 220–221. D. KNOWLES, *The Religious Orders in England* 2:117–118. A. B. EMDEN, *Biographical Register of the Scholars of the University of Cambridge before 1500* 1:265.

[T. P. DUNNING]

JOHN OF BROMYARD

English Dominican preacher; from the name Bromyard it is conjectured that he was born in Herefordshire, England; d. 1352(?). Probably a student at Oxford, he was licensed to hear confessions in the Hereford diocese from 1326 to 1352. He prepared his *Opus trivium,* or *Distinctiones Bromyard,* a compilation from the divine, canonical, and civil laws, as a handbook for preachers. A revised and augmented version of this work, entitled *Summa praedicantium,* was a voluminous source of moral and anecdotal sermon materials arranged in alphabetical form. The *Summa* was highly esteemed during the later Middle Ages. It was multiplied in manuscripts and went through many printed editions (the first, at Basel, 1474), and served for years as a manual for preachers. The prologue to the *Summa* indicates its relationship to the *Opus trivium.* Bromyard further prepared notes for sermons, entitled also *Distinctiones.* The *Summa* was formerly ascribed to another John Bromyard (d. after 1397), who was at one time chancellor of Cambridge, prior of the Dominican priory of Hereford, and member of the 1382 London Black Friars council, which condemned the errors of John WYCLIF. From internal textual evidence, contemporary allusions in the *Summa,* and a sermon of Bp. John de SHEPEY OF ROCHESTER preached in 1354, it is now clear that the later Bromyard was not the author.

Bibliography: A. B. EMDEN, *A Biographical Register of the University of Oxford to A.D. 1500,* 3 v. (Oxford 1957–59) 1:278. G. R. OWST, *Preaching in Medieval England* (Cambridge, Eng. 1926); *Literature and Pulpit in Medieval England* (2d ed. New York 1961) 224, 595.

[A. DABASH]

JOHN OF CARAMOLA, BL.

Cistercian brother, ascetic; b. Toulouse, France; d. Sagittario, Italy, Aug. 26, 1339. John was a native of the city of Toulouse, but he led the austere life of a hermit for several years in the remote wilderness on Mt. Caramola in Lucania, Italy. During the whole period of Lent, he allowed himself bread sufficient for only one small meal. He lived in close communion with God and was reputedly endowed with the gift of prophecy. Because of a severe illness during a very cold winter, he went to the CISTERCIAN monastery of Santa Maria of Sagittario at Chiaramonte to seek assistance. There he continued his austere penitential practices as a lay brother. His diet consisted of small amounts of bread and water; his bed was so small that he could not lie in a normal position. The monks testified that they never saw him sleeping. He edified his confreres by his observance of silence; contemplation was his great occupation. After his death many miracles were attributed to his intercession: e.g., the infirm were cured by touching his incorrupt body, which led to his popular veneration.

Feast: Aug. 26.

Bibliography: *Acta Sanctorum* August 5:854–862. *Bibliotheca hagiographica latina antiquae ct mediae aetatis,* 2 v. (Brussels 1898–1901; suppl. 1911) 1:4369. A. M. ZIMMERMANN, *Kalendarium Benedictinum: Die Heiligen und Seligen des Benediktinerorderns und seiner Zweige,* 4 v. (Metten 1933–38) 2:625–626. S. LENSSEN, *Hagiologium cisterciense,* 2 v. (Tilburg 1948–49; suppl. 1951)1:194. F. UGHELLI, *Italia sacra,* ed. N. COLETI, 10 v. in 9 (2d ed. Venice 1717–22) 7:91–93.

[M. B. MORRIS]

JOHN OF CHÂTILLON, ST.

Abbot and bishop; b. Châtillon, Bretagne, France, *c.* 1098; d. Quingamp, Feb. 1, 1163. He is sometimes called Jean de Craticula (of the grate) because of the iron grating around his tomb. His parents were Breton. He is often confused with a CISTERCIAN contemporary of the same name whom St. BERNARD sent to found a monastery at Bégard in the Diocese of Tréquier. John became bishop of Aleth and transferred that see to the isle of Aaron, which he renamed Saint-Malo. He was a strict, zealous abbot of the Saint-Croix monastery of the CANONS REGULAR OF ST. AUGUSTINE, at Quingamp. He found himself involved in endless litigation when, as bishop, he attempted to replace monks from MARMOUTIER with the canons regular in his cathedral.

Feast: Feb. 1.

Bibliography: *Acta Sanctorum,* Feb. 1:250–254. F. M. DUINE, *Catalogue des sources hagiographiques* (Paris 1922). A. M. ZIMMERMANN, *Kalendarium Benedictinum: Die Heiligen und Seligen des Benediktinerorderns und seiner Zweige* 1:154. A. BUTLER, *The Lives of the Saints* 1:229–230. A. M. ZIMMERMANN, *Lexikon für Theologie und Kirche,* 10 v. (2d, new ed. Freiburg, 1957-65) 5:1022–23.

[E. J. KEALEY]

JOHN OF DUKLA, ST.

(Polish: Jan); observant Franciscan priest; b. *c.* 1414 in Dukla in the Central Beskid Mountains of Galicia in the southeastern extremity of Poland; d. Sept. 29, 1484 at Lviv (Lvov), now in the western Ukraine; canonized June 10, 1997.

John of Dukla was born into a middle-class family. He studied at the Jagiellonian University of Krakow, which had been founded by Queen St. Hedwig. After living as a hermit in Dukla, John became a Franciscan at Lemberg (1440), where he was ordained and served for a time as guardian. About this time he realized that he must share the fruit of his contemplation with souls seeking salvation. At the instigation of John of Capistrano, he became a member of the Observant Franciscans (Bernardines) in 1463. Thereafter, John was a successful missioner in Galicia, especially among the Ruthenian schismatics and the German burghers of Lviv. Impassioned preaching, pastoral zeal, ardent prayer, patience, and charity were hallmarks of his sanctity. Blinded in old age, he continued to hear confessions and preached by having others read his sermons. Originally, his remains were buried in the cemetery of Lviv. In 1945 the body was translated to Rzeszow, then to the church of the Franciscans at Dukla. Although John was beatified in 1733 by Pope Clement XII, his canonization had been delayed due to the partition of Poland. He is one of the patrons of Poland and Lithuania.

Feast: July 10 (formerly Sept. 28 and Oct. 1).

Bibliography: *L'Osservatore Romano,* English edition, no. 26 (1997) 8, 11; no. 27 (1997) 6–8, 11.

[K. I. RABENSTEIN]

JOHN OF DUMBLETON

Oxford philosopher; fl. 1338–49. A native of Dumbleton in Gloucestershire in the diocese of Worcester, he is first mentioned as a fellow of Merton College in the scrutinies of 1338–39. He was named a foundation fellow of Queen's College in the founder's statutes of Feb. 10, 1340. By this date he had completed his regency in arts and was enrolled in the faculty of theology, intending to take Holy Orders. However, he returned to Merton where he remained at least until 1348. He is assumed to have died of the plague around 1349, a "bachelor of sacred theology." His fame rests largely on his unpublished *Summa logicae et philosophiae naturalis,* begun after 1335 and ending abruptly in part nine of ten projected. This work is also known as *Summa theologiae maior, Summa philosophiae,* and *In philosophiam moralem lib.*

X. Other works attributed to him by Leland, Tanner, Coxe, Poole, and Duhem are insufficiently established. An Ockhamist in logic and natural philosophy, he also accepted enthusiastically the mathematical theorem of THOMAS BRADWARDINE and tried to apply it to new problems of intension and remission of velocities, densities, illumination, and certitude. Although largely unsuccessful in this, he prepared the way for the completely mathematical approach of RICHARD OF SWYNESHED.

See Also: OCKHAMISM; SCIENCE (IN THE MIDDLE AGES).

Bibliography: A. B. EMDEN, *A Biographical Register of the Scholars of the University of Oxford to A.D. 1500,* 3 v. (Oxford 1957–59) 1:603. J. A. WEISHEIPL, ''Place of John Dumbleton in the Merton School,'' *Isis* 50 (1959) 439–454.

[J. A. WEISHEIPL]

JOHN OF EGYPT, ST.

Hermit of Lycopolis, b. Lycopolis (modern Asyut), *c.* 300; d. near Lycopolis, 394. A carpenter, he entered a monastery between the ages of 25 and 30, and after several years there he became a hermit in a cave on Mt. Lykos, where he remained until his death some 40 years later. John, who communicated with visitors only through a window, was sought for spiritual advice and was reputed to have the gift of prophecy, so that he was known as the Seer. Legend credits him with having foretold the victories of the Roman Emperor THEODOSIUS I over Maximus and Eugenius, as well as the death of the Emperor himself (395).

Feast: Mar. 27; Oct. 17 (Coptic Church).

Bibliography: PALLADIUS OF HELENOPOLIS, *Historia Lausiaca, Patrologia Graeca* 34:1107–15, new ed. by A. J. FESTUGIÈRE in *Historia Monachorum in Aegypto (Subsidia hagiographica* 34; 1961) 9–35. *Bibliotheca hagiographica Graeca* 3:34.

[G. T. DENNIS]

JOHN OF EPHESUS

Sixth century Monophysite bishop and Church historian; b. near Amida (DIARBEKR), *c.* 507; d. 586. John of Ephesus, known also as John of Asia or of Amida, began his career as a monk. Because of the anti-Monophysite decrees of JUSTIN I (521) he was forced to lead a nomadic life. Going to Constantinople, he gained the favor of Empress THEODORA (1) and, through her, of JUSTINIAN I. He became ''titular'' bishop of Ephesus (*c.* 542) and was sent to convert the pagans of the mountainous areas of Lydia and Caria in Asia Minor. His efforts were most successful; more than 70,000 persons were baptized, pagan temples were destroyed, and Christian churches and monasteries were built in their places. Under JUSTIN II John's fervent Monophysitism led to his imprisonment. After being released, he wandered about until his death.

John of Ephesus is the most important early historian in the Syriac language. He wrote an *Ecclesiastical History* in three volumes, tracing Church history from the time of Julius Caesar to 585. Only the third volume is extant (years 571–585). He was also the author of *Lives of the Eastern Saints* (*c.* 568), which contains 58 sketches of the lives of Oriental monks and ascetics.

Bibliography: *Lives of the Eastern Saints,* ed. and tr. E. W. BROOKS, 17 v. (Paris 1923–25). *Patrologia orientalis,* ed. R. GRAFFIN and F. NAU (Paris 1903—) 17.1; 18.4; 19.2. *Corpus scriptorum Christianorum orientalium* (Paris-Louvain 1903) 105. E. STEIN, *Histoire du Bas-Empire,* tr. J. R. PALANQUE, 2 v. in 3 (Paris 1949–59) 371–372, 683–684, 829–831. H. RAHNER, *Lexikon für Theologie,* ed. J. HOFER and K. RAHNER, 10 v. (2d, new ed. Freiburg 1957–65) 5:1030. B. ALTANER, *Patrology,* tr. H. GRAEF from 5th German ed. (New York 1960) 258. E. TISSERANT, *Dictionnaire de théologie catholique,* ed. A. VACANT et al. (Paris 1903–50) 8.1:752–753. L. DUCHESNE, *L'Église au VIᵉ siècle* (Paris 1925) 276–280.

[J. F. KRASTEL]

JOHN OF FALKENBERG

Polish Dominican, polemicist, b. Danzig, Pomerania, *c.* 1365; d. Legnica, Poland, *c.* 1435. He entered the Order of Preachers and spent his novitiate at Kammin in his native Pomerania. In 1385 he was master of theology at the studium in Vienna, in 1408 he was preaching in Prague, and in 1411 he functioned as inquisitor at Magdeburg. In opposition to the Dominican Master General Leonard de Datis, Falkenberg declared himself a supporter of GREGORY XII (1406–15), the Pope in Rome during the WESTERN SCHISM. In 1406 Falkenberg attacked Matthew of Cracow. In the long altercation between the Teutonic Knights and the Polish King, he allied himself with the former; in a violent tractate (or *Satira*), *De monarchia mundi,* written in 1410, he defended the cause of the Knights against the king. During the Council of CONSTANCE he maintained the morality of tyrannicide as advocated by Joannes Parvus and wrote his *Tres tractuli* in answer to Gerson, Peter of Ailly, and others who condemned the works of Parvus. Nicholas, Archbishop of Gniezno, insisted that the council examine the *De monarchia* and a conciliar committee ordered it burned (1417). A chapter of the Dominican Order at Strasbourg in 1417 also condemned the work and sentenced Falkenberg to life imprisonment. The Poles and Lithuanians at Constance continued to urge the council as a whole to condemn Falkenberg for heresy, but Pope Martin V refused to ratify any such sentence, saying that he confirmed only what the council had done *conciliariter circa materiam fidei.* However, when the pope returned to Rome (May 1418), he took Falkenberg with him and kept him in confinement until 1424.

Bibliography: J. QUÉTIF and J. ÉCHARD, *Scriptores Ordinis Praedicatorum* (New York 1959) 1.2:760–761. B. BESS, "Johannes Falkenberg, O.P. und der preussisch-polnische Streit vor dem Konstanzer Konzil," *Zeitschrift für Kirchengeschichte* 16 (1896) 385–464. G. SOMMERFELDT, "Johann Falkenberg," *Zeitschrift für katholische Theologie* 39 (1915) 803–805. H. FINKE, ed., *Acta concilii Constanciensis* 4:249–254, 352–432. H. J. SCHROEDER, *Disciplinary Decrees of the General Councils* (St. Louis 1937) 451. H. TÜCHLE, *Lexikon für Theologie und Kirche,* ed. J. HOFER and K. RAHNER (Freiburg 1957–65) 5:1031–32. *The Council of Constance,* tr. L. R. LOOMIS, ed. J. H. MUNDY and K. M. WOODY (New York 1961).

[M. J. FINNEGAN]

JOHN OF FECKENHAM

Alias Howman, Marian abbot of Westminster; b. Feckenham, Worcestershire, *c.* 1512; d. Wisbech Castle, Cambridgeshire, *c.* October 1584. Of a yeoman family, he was educated probably at the almonry school at the Benedictine abbey of Evesham; he was professed there, taking—as was then usual—the name of his hometown. Sent to the Benedictine Oxford college, Gloucester Hall, Feckenham graduated Bachelor of Divinity in 1539. His monastery was dissolved by Henry VIII in January of 1540 after which he became, in succession, chaplain to the two religiously conservative bishops, Bell of Worcester and Bonner of London. Like them he accepted the royal supremacy, but rejected Protestantism and for this he was imprisoned (1551–53). At the accession of the Catholic Queen Mary he was released, reconciled to the Church, and made dean of St. Paul's, London, in January of 1554. He played a minor part in the restoration of Catholicism. By November 1556 Westminster Abbey was restored as a monastery to a group of some 20 former monks, mostly former colleagues at Gloucester Hall, and Feckenham was elected abbot. Cardinal Reginald Pole intended to introduce there the reformed observance of the Cassinese Congregation and to make Westminster the seedbed for the gradual restoration of reformed Benedictines, Cistercians, and Augustinian Canons throughout England. But very little of this program had been achieved when Pole and Queen Mary died in November of 1558. Feckenham spoke in the House of Lords against the Elizabethan Bills of Supremacy, First Fruits, and Uniformity. By June of 1559 the Westminster community was dispersed by royal orders, and on May 20, 1560 Feckenham was sent to the Tower for opposing Elizabe-

than policies. He remained in custody for the rest of his life. Although he was accused of wavering in his Catholicism, the truth seems to be that he was always eager to attend Protestant sermons so as to debate afterward with the preachers and that he was willing (the royal ecclesiastical supremacy apart) to accept Elizabeth as the rightful queen, all papal bulls to the contrary notwithstanding. He is important as the only Marian prelate to have left any body of theological writings.

Bibliography: H. AVELING, *Dictionnaire d'histoire et de géographie ecclésiastiques,* ed. A. BAUDRILLART et. al. (Paris 1912—) D. KNOWLES, *The Religious Orders in England,* 3 v. (Cambridge, Eng 1948–60) 3:421–443.

[H. AVELING]

JOHN OF FREIBURG (RUMSIK)

Dominican, moralist, canonist, lector at Freiburg im Breisgau; b. Haslach(?), date unknown; d. March 10, 1314, Freiburg. He wrote a *Summa Confessorum* (1280–98) that made pastoral theology a science by relating its material to speculative moral principles, especially those of St. THOMAS AQUINAS. This work, the classic in its genre, was inspired by the *Summa de poenitentiis* of St. RAYMOND OF PEÑAFORT. Many manuscripts, an alphabetically arranged German version by Berthold Huenlin, OP (11 ed. between. 1472–98), and a French extract, *La règle des marchands,* attest its opportuneness. John also wrote a *Manuale,* an epitome of his *Summa,* a *Confessionale* for less skilled confessors, *Additiones* to Raymond's *Summa,* a *Tabula* to the text and gloss of the same *Summa,* a *Quaestiones causales* (1280), and perhaps a commentary on the *Sentences.*

Bibliography: J. QUÉTIF and J. ÉCHARD, *Scriptores Ordinis Praedicatorum* (New York 1959) 1.1:523–526. M. D. CHENU, *Dictionnaire de théologie catholique,* ed. A. VACANT et al. (Paris 1903–50) 8.1:761–762. W. MÜLLER, *Lexikon für Theologie und Kirche,* ed. J. HOFER and K. RAHNER (Freiburg 1957–65) 5:1033–34.

[W. A. HINNEBUSCH]

JOHN OF GOD, ST.

Founder of the Brothers Hospitallers; b. John Ciudad, in Montemor-o-Novo, Portugal, March 8, 1495; d. Granada, Spain, March 8, 1550. John Ciudad, as a youth, was a shepherd in the service of the bailiff of the count of Oroprusa in Castile. In 1522 he enlisted in a company of soldiers raised by the count, and fought in wars between the Spaniards and French, and later, in Hungary, against the Turks. While a soldier, he gave up the practice of his religion and lived an immoral life.

At about the age of 40 he left the military life and returned to Spain, where he became a shepherd. He became remorseful over his sinful life while a soldier and attempted to enter Africa to ransom captives and, possibly, to become a martyr. Assured by a confessor that his wish for martyrdom was ill founded, he returned to Spain. In 1538 he opened a small shop in Granada, where he sold books and religious pictures. Here, influenced by a sermon of St. JOHN OF AVILA, he became very extreme in his conduct, running about the city praying for mercy. For some months he was committed to a lunatic asylum. Through the counsel of John of Avila, he recovered and devoted himself to the care of the sick poor.

In Granada he rented a house, which he supported by his own labor and in which he cared for the abandoned sick of the city. He soon attracted others to the work, and his apostolate of the sick won the approval of the archbishop of Granada. John was an able administrator; he operated his hospital in a businesslike way and was consulted on the setting up of homes for the sick in other parts of the country.

He had no thought, it seems, of founding a religious community. His work drew others into the care of the sick. The bishop of Tuy, who gave him the name John of God, prescribed a habit for him and his companions. A rule, bearing his name, was drawn up after he died, and his followers were approved as a religious congregation in 1571 by PIUS V. Final approval was given to the order in 1596 by SIXTUS V.

John was canonized by ALEXANDER VIII in 1690, although the bull was not issued until the following year, by INNOCENT XII. In 1886 LEO XIII declared St. John, with St. CAMILLUS DE LELLIS, patron of hospitals and the sick. In 1930 PIUS XI declared him patron of nurses. He is also honored by booksellers and printers. Generally St. John is pictured with the symbol of a pomegranate surmounted by a small cross; the pomegranate stands for the city of Granada and refers to the legendary visitation he received from the Child Jesus, who told him, "Thou wilt find thy cross in Granada."

Feast: March 8.

Bibliography: *Acta Sanctorum* March 1 (1668) 814-60. A. BUTLER, *The Lives of the Saints,* ed. H. THURSTON and D. ATTWATER, 4 v. (New York 1956) 1:517–520. PIUS XI, "Expedit plane" (apostolic letter, August 28, 1930) *Acta Apostolicae Sedis* S 23 (1931) 8–9. M. GÓMEZ-MORENO, *Priniclas históricas de San Juan de Dios* (Madrid 1950), N. MCMAHON, *St. John of God* (New York 1953). W. CROSS, *St. John of God: Patron Saint of Hospitals, the Sick, Nurses and All Who Look After the Sick* (London 1977). R. D. RUMBAUT, *John of God: His Place in the History of Psychiatry and Medicine* (Miami, Fla. 1978). P. DREYFUS, *Saint Jean de Dieu: le père de l'hôpital moderne / Paul Dreyfus* (Paris 1995), includes extensive bibliography. A. DE GOUVEIA, *Vida e morte de S. João de Deus: seguida das cartas do Santo e da sua iconografia,* ed. M. CADAFAZ DE MATOS, tr. M. DE ANDRADE (Lisbon 1996). ORDEN HOSPITALARIA DE SAN JUAN DE DIOS, *Iconografia: San Juan de Dios in México, América Central* (Mexico City 1997).

St. John of God.

[T. J. MUNN]

JOHN OF GORZE, ST.

Abbot and monastic reformer (known also as Jean de Vandières); b. Vandières, France, late 9th century; d. *c.* 975. He was the son of a wealthy landowner and, according to his biographer, John, Abbot of Saint-Arnulf (d. 977), he studied for a time at METZ and later at the Abbey of SAINT-MIHIEL in the Moselle Valley. Upon the death of his father and his mother's remarriage, John was forced to interrupt his studies to care for his ancestral estate and the education of his younger brothers, but he resumed his studies at Toul, under the direction of Bernerus the Deacon. Already cherishing a desire for the more perfect life, he made a pilgrimage to Rome and visited MONTE CASSINO. Upon his return he met the deeply spiritual Einold, archdeacon of Toul, and spent some time under his direction. In 933 Einold and John with five companions went to the Abbey of GORZE to reestablish monastic discipline there according to the wish of ADALBERO, bishop of Metz. Einold became abbot and John, his loyal supporter, functioning as procurator, was busy with the physical restoration of the monastery, which had suffered from the ravages of the Normans, as well as with the spiritual reform of the monks. In 953 John went to CÓRDOBA, where he spent 3 years as the envoy of OTTO I to the UMAY-YAD CALIPH Abd-er-Rahman III (d. 961). After the death of Einold, John became abbot and played a leading role in the monastic reform movement of which Gorze was the center. The exact date of John's death is not known, but it is known that he died in the 40th year of his monastic profession.

Feast: Feb. 27 or March 7.

Bibliography: *Acta sanctorum* Feb. 3:691–721. *Monumenta Germaniae Historica: Scriptores* (Berlin 1826) 4:335–377. A. D'HERBOMEZ, ed., *Cartulaire de l'abbaye de Gorze* (Paris 1898) 169–206. A. M. ZIMMERMANN, *Kalendarium Benedictinum* (Metten 1933–38) 1:258–261. L. H. COTTINEAU, *Répertoire topobibliographique des abbayes et des prieurés* (Mâcon 1935–39) 1:13033–04. *Histoire de l'église depuis les origines jusqu'à nos jours* 7:420–421. *Vies des saintes et des bienheuruex* 2:574–578. S. HILPISCH, *Lexikon für Theologie und Kirche* ed. J. HOFER and K. RAHNER (Freiburg 1957–65) 5:1038. R. GAZEAU, *Catholicisme* 6:437–438. E. SACKUR, *Die Cluniacenser*, 2 v. (Halle 1892–94), 1:146–150, 2:358–361.

[H. DRESSLER]

JOHN OF HOVEDEN

John of Hoveden (present-day Howden in Yorkshire) is the name of several illustrious men in the 13th century. The most famous was an English religious poet, d. after 1275. It is difficult to determine the facts of his life. He may be the astrologer of that name, who is known to have been born in London. The poet reputedly studied at the University of OXFORD, and although the official records of the school do not report his attendance, his scientific outlook as reflected in his poetical works tends to corroborate an Oxford education. It is certain that by 1268 he was a clerk of Queen Eleanor of Provence, wife of King HENRY III of England and mother of King EDWARD I. It seems that he was one of the first prebendaries of the collegiate church of Howden, where he undertook to rebuild the choir and was eventually buried. It is known that he was made canon and prebendary of the king's free chapel in Bridgnorth Castle, Salop; some aver that he had vacated this position by 1275; others claim that he still held it in 1284 but not in 1291. The mystical poetry of Hoveden was of an uncommonly high order, original and wide-ranging. His masterpiece was undoubtedly the *Philomena*, a work of 4,000 lines on the birth, Passion, and Resurrection of Christ. His eight other Latin poems include the *Canticum amoris*, which is a kind of preliminary sketch of the *Philomena*, and the 723-stanza *Quinquaginta cantica salvatoris*. The *Quindecim gaudia BMV*

dwells on the 15 joys of Mary; the very similar *Cythara* treats of the love and Passion of Christ. The *Quinquaginta salutationes* is on the sorrows of Mary. The *Viola* praises the Virgin in 250 verses, while the short work *Lyra* is especially interesting because in its musical setting it is a *conductus duplex* in the manner of the Notre-Dame school. Hoveden's only surviving poem in Anglo-Norman is the *Rossignol* (see L. W. Stone), addressed to Queen Eleanor and on the same theme as the *Philomena*. He is also credited with a scientific treatise, *Practica chilindri* (ed. E. Brock, *Essays on Chaucer,* Chaucer Society 1868).

As a religious poet of 13th-century England, Hoveden belongs in the front rank beside JOHN PECKHAM. An inheritor of the Bernardine and Franciscan tradition of spirituality (*see* FRANCISCAN SPIRITUALITY), he was a precursor of the great 14th-century mystics, and Richard ROLLE DE HAMPOLE especially shows Hoveden's influence (*see* HYMNOLOGY).

Bibliography: Works. C. BLUME, ed., "Johannis de Hovedene *Philomena,*" *Hymnologische Beiträge* 4 (Leipzig 1930). *The Poems of John of Hoveden*, ed. F. J. E. RABY (Surtees Society 154; London 1939). L. W. STONE, "Jean de Howden, poète anglo-normand du XIIIᵉ siècle," *Romania* 69 (1946–47) 496–519. **Literature.** F. J. E. RABY, "John of Hoveden," *Laudate* 12 (1935) 87–. F. J. E. RABY, *A History of Christian-Latin Poetry from the Beginnings to the Close of the Middle Ages* (2d ed. Oxford 1953) 389–395. A. B. EMDEN, *A Biographical Register of the University of Oxford to A.D. 1500,* 3 v. (Oxford 1957–59) 2:974–975. J. SZÖVÉRFFY, *Die Annalen der lateinischen Hymnendichtung. Ein Handbuch,* 2 v. (Berlin 1964–65) 2:82, 259–262.

[M. J. HAMILTON]

JOHN OF JANDUN

Averroist master of arts at Paris; b. Jandun, Ardennes, France, *c.* 1275; d. Todi, Italy, 1328. He studied arts at the University of Paris, where he taught and became an intimate friend of MARSILIUS OF PADUA. In 1316 he obtained a canonry at Senlis. The foremost advocate of Latin Averroism in his day, he described himself as "a mimic of Aristotle and AVERROËS" [*In Metaph.* (Venice 1525) folio 84]. In his commentaries on Aristotle's *De anima* (Venice 1473), *Physics* (Venice 1488), *De caelo et mundo* (Venice 1501), *Parva naturalia* (Venice 1505), and *Metaphysics* he strongly defended all the basic teachings of Latin Averroism, especially the eternity of the world and motion, unicity of the human intellect, denial of personal immortality, and personal responsibility in moral actions (*see* AVERROISM, LATIN; INTELLECT, UNITY OF; SCHOLASTICISM, 1). Unlike SIGER OF BRABANT and BOETHIUS OF SWEDEN, he explicitly taught the doctrine of a double truth and gave greater weight to truths demonstrated by reason than to truths revealed by faith (*see* DOUBLE TRUTH, THEORY OF). While teaching in Paris he collaborated with or at least gave some kind of assistance to Marsilius of Padua in the composition of *Defensor pacis*. When authorship of this antipapal work became known in 1324, he was forced to leave Paris with Marsilius. In 1326 he sought the protection of LOUIS IV the Bavarian, together with Marsilius of Padua, WILLIAM OF OCKHAM, and MICHAEL OF CESENA. In 1327 many propositions extracted from *Defensor pacis* were condemned by JOHN XXII; John of Jandun was explicitly mentioned in the bull of condemnation. Louis IV nominated him bishop of Ferrara in 1328, but it is doubtful that he was ever consecrated.

Besides commenting on the works of Aristotle, he wrote *De laudibus Parisius, Quaestiones de formatione foetus, Quaestiones de gradibus et pluralitate formarum, Tractatus de specie intelligibili, Duo tractatus de sensu agente,* and a commentary on Averroës' *De substantia orbis.*

While professedly admitting all the truths of faith, he adamantly denied that reason could prove that the higher faculties of man's soul—the possible intellect, the agent intellect, and the will—are immaterial and spiritual. Similarly, he believed in creation *ex nihilo,* although this doctrine seemed to him to be absolutely incomprehensible. He remarked, "I believe that this is true, but I do not know how to prove it; good for those who do" (*sed demonstrare nescio; gaudeant qui hoc sciunt*). Because of many such remarks, it is impossible to know whether John scoffed at Christian faith or merely sneered at the simplicity of theologians who pretended to prove what they held only on faith.

Bibliography: A. POMPEI, *Enciclopedia filosofica,* 4 v. (Venice-Rome 1957) 2:760–761. N. VALOIS, "Jean de Jandum et Marsile de Padoue," *Histoire littéraire de la France,* 33 (1906) 528–623. E. GILSON, *History of Christian Philosophy,* 522–524. E. SANTOVITO, *Enciclopaedia cattolica,* ed. P. PASCHINI et al., 12 v. (Rome 1949–54) 6:566. B. NARDI, *Sigieri di Brabante nel pensiero del Rinascimento italiano* (Rome 1945). U. CHEVALIER, *Répertoire des sources historiques du moyen-âge. Biobibliographie,* 2 v. (2d ed. Paris 1905–07) 2426. S. MCCLINTOCK, *Perversity and Error: Studies on the Averroist John of Jandun* (pa. Bloomington, Ind. 1956).

[J. A. WEISHEIPL]

JOHN OF JERUSALEM

Fourth century Palestinian bishop; d. 417. John succeeded Cyril as bishop of Jerusalem in 387. His relations with JEROME and RUFINUS OF AQUILEIA were excellent at first—all shared in enthusiasm for ORIGEN. In 393, however, EPIPHANIUS OF SALAMIS, following his emissary,

the monk Atarbius to Palestine, preached a thunderous sermon against Origen in John's own church and presence. While Rufinus was unimpressed and John indignant, Jerome joined Epiphanius in attacking John. John denied the Bethlehem monks access to the holy places in Jerusalem and refused to baptize their converts or bury their dead. In the fall of 396 Jerome published his virulent broadsheet, *To Pammachius, against John of Jerusalem* [*Patrologia Latina,* ed. J. P. Migne, 217 v., indexes 4 v. (Paris 1878–90) 23:371–412].

THEOPHILUS OF ALEXANDRIA, whose sympathies then lay with John and Rufinus, effected a reconciliation at Easter in 397. When the quarrel between Jerome and Rufinus flared up again, John held aloof; he attended Paula's funeral in 404. When PELAGIUS, whose ally Caelestius had already been condemned at Carthage, came to Palestine, John received him kindly, whereas Jerome was hostile; AUGUSTINE sent Orosius to Bethlehem to alert the monks. Pelagius confronted Orosius at a Jerusalem diocesan synod in July 415. Orosius (*Lib. Apol.* 3–7) alleged that Pelagius taught a doctrine opposed by Augustine; but "I," said John, "am Augustine here." There was, apparently, interpreter trouble; but verbal agreement was reached, to Orosius's annoyance, on the formula, "God can enable the earnest man to avoid sin," and John declared Pelagius innocent. In December John attended the metropolitan synod at Diospolis, where Pelagius was again acquitted. John is probably the bishop of Jerusalem mentioned in Egeria's *Pilgrimage.*

Arabic Manuscripts of Mount Sinai, edited by A. S. ATIYA, lists unpublished sermons of John (codex 309). The evidence very slightly favors John's authorship of the *Mystagogical Catecheses* ascribed in most manuscripts to his predecessor Cyril. The tenth century Munich manuscript attributes them to John, and three other manuscripts attribute them to "Cyril and John." While the converse often happens, the works of famous men are not easily attributed to unknown authors. John may have simply borrowed his predecessor's *Mystagogiae;* or if they are his own, they may be quite heavily indebted to Cyril. It is probable that the need to complete Cyril's prebaptismal catecheses, which originally, at least in some manuscripts, circulated alone, was felt, John's *Mystagogiae* were added, and either (W. TELFER) the difference in authorship was not always copied or (T. SCHERMANN) scribes gradually displaced John's name in the manuscripts by that of the famous catechist.

Bibliography: W. J. SWAANS, *Muséon* 55 (1942) 1–43. W. J. SWAANS and RICHARD, *Mélanges de science religieuse* 5 (1948) 282, support John's authorship. P. PEETERS, *Analecta Bollandiana* (1943) 270–271, doubts Cyril's authorship. J. QUASTEN, *Patrology,* 3 v. (Westminster, Md. 1950—) 3:362–367 and *St. Cyril of Jerusalem's Lectures on the Christian Sacraments,* ed. F. L. CROSS, Society for Promoting Christian knowledge (London 1951) consider the case for John still unproved. J. FERGUSON, *Pelagius: A Historical and Theological Study* (Cambridge, Eng. 1956). F. CAVALLERA, *Saint Jérôme*, 2 v. *Spicilegium sacrum Lovaniense* (Louvain 1922) 1, 2; 1:193–227; 323–329; 2:31–36, 91–96. T. SCHERMANN, *Theologische Revue*, 10 (1911) 575–579. A. S. ATIYA, *A Hand List of Arabic manuscripts and Scrolls Microfilmed at the Library of the Monastary of St. Catherine* (Baltimore 1955).

[A. A. STEPHENSON]

JOHN OF JESUS MARY

Or Juan de San Pedro y Ustarroz, educator and mystical writer; b. Calahorra, Logrono, Spain, Jan. 27, 1564; d. Montecompatri, May 29, 1615. He was the son of the famous physician, Diego de San Pedro. He came to know the Discalced Carmelites while studying at Salamanca. He took the habit and was later professed at Pastrana (Jan. 30, 1583). Soon afterward he was appointed professor at the Colegio Complutense. Nicholas Doria chose him for the same office in the newly founded convent of Genoa, Italy, where he was ordained priest in 1590. He accompanied Doria to Cremona for the general chapter of the Carmelite Order (1593) that decreed the separation of the Reform from the old Order of Carmel. On his return from the general chapter, he was appointed master of novices at St. Ann's of Genoa (1593–98) and was later transferred to the novitiate of La Scala in Rome, where he served first as assistant to the master of novices (1599–1601), then as master of novices (1601–11). He took an active part in the foundation of the Italian Congregation. At its first general chapter (1605), he was elected second definitor and procurator general (1608–11); he finally became general in 1611. Completing his term as general in 1614, he retired to the convent of St. Sylvester in Montecompatri.

Almost all his writings deal with the proper spiritual formation of religious, both superiors and subjects; his published writings number 65. These appeared together in a three-volume collection, first published in Cologne (1622), and again in Florence (1771–74).

Bibliography: FLORENCIO DEL NIÑO JESÚS, *El ven. P. fr. Juan de Jesús María* (Burgos 1919). E. A. PEERS, *Studies of the Spanish Mystics*, 3 v. (London 1960) v.3. PIER GIORGIO DEL SACRO CUORE, *La contemplazione secondo il Ven. P. Giovanni di Gesù Maria* (Cremona, Italy 1950).

[O. RODRÍGUEZ]

JOHN OF LA ROCHELLE (DE RUPELLA)

Franciscan philosopher and theologian; b. La Rochelle, France, *c.* 1190–1200; d. Paris(?), Feb. 8, 1245.

The first clear reference is a listing of him as a friar and master of theology (1238). It is probable that he was already a master or at least licensed in theology when he entered the order. Before coming into intimate association with ALEXANDER OF HALES, John seems to have planned and partly written a *Summa theologicae disciplinae,* as may be concluded from the introduction to his *Summa* on the Articles of Faith. Much of the material in this *Summa* was later incorporated into the so-called "*Summa* of Alexander of Hales." To this period likewise belongs the Tract on the Soul and the Virtues, and perhaps several of the commentaries on Scripture [confer F. Stegmüller, *Repertorium biblicum medii aevi*, 7 v. (Madrid 1949–61) 3:4888–4915].

Under the guidance and inspiration of Alexander, John achieved maturity as a theologian. After 1236 he was the faithful companion and helper of this "monarch of theologians." Together they were the principal counselors of the ministers provincial in the deposition of ELIAS OF CORTONA in 1239 [*Analecta Franciscana* 1:18; *Archivum Franciscanum historicum*, 33 (1940) 221–225]. In 1241–42 they wrote an explanation of the Franciscan Rule in collaboration with two other masters [*Expositio quatuor magistrorum super regulam fratrum minorum*, ed. L. Oliger (Rome 1950)]. Their Disputed Questions are so intermingled that it is sometimes difficult to distinguish those of Alexander from those of John. On his part, John made considerable use of Alexander's Gloss on the Sentences, with material also from PHILIP THE CHANCELLOR, to produce a *Summa de anima,* justly regarded as the first scholastic text of psychology [ed. T. Domenichelli (Prato 1882)].

This close collaboration bore fruit in the *Summa* of Theology that bears the name of Alexander; book 1, on God, and book 3, on the Incarnation and Passion, law, grace, and faith, were almost beyond doubt written by John of La Rochelle. At the same time, as a preacher he attained independent fame [confer *Eleven Marian Sermons,* ed. K. Lynch (St. Bonaventure, N.Y. 1961)]. His last known sermon was before the Roman Curia at Lyons on Dec. 4, 1244. John, like Alexander, died the following year.

Bibliography: V. DOUCET, "Prolegomena" to Alexander of Hales, *Summa theologica,* book 3 in v.4 (Quaracchi-Florence 1948); "Prolegomena" to Alexander of Hales, *Glossa in quatuor libros Sententiarum Petri Lombardi* (Bibliotheca Franciscana Scholastica Medii Aevi 12–15; Quaracchi-Florence 1951–57). P. MICHAUD-QUANTIN, "Une Division 'augustinienne' des puissances de l'âme au Moyen-âge," *Revue des études augustiniennes*, 3 (1957) 235–248. E. GILSON, *History of Christian Philosophy*, 683–685.

[I. C. BRADY]

JOHN OF LA VERNA, BL.

Franciscan priest; b. Fermo, near ANCONA, Italy, 1259; d. La Verna, Aug. 9, 1322. Ascetical even as a child, at ten he joined the Augustinian canons and at 13 the Franciscans. After residing in hermitages in the Marches of Ancona and Fermo, he settled in a hermit's cell at La Verna (Alvernia) c. 1290. He received graces of rapture, infused knowledge, and prophecy. His mystical experiences, described in part in the FIORETTI, included visions of the Sacred Heart, the Blessed Virgin, St. FRANCIS, and St. LAWRENCE. Though he opposed the Franciscan SPIRITUALS, he befriended and gave the last rites to their partisan, the poet JACOPONE DA TODI. In his last years John preached throughout Tuscany, and in 1311 he testified in favor of the PORTIUNCULA indulgence. He wrote the one-page, mystical *De gradibus animae,* but his authorship of the Preface of St. Francis is disputed. His cult was approved in 1880.

Feast: Aug. 13.

Bibliography: *Acta Sanctorum* August 2:453–474. *Fioretti di San Francesco,* ch. 49–53; English ed. R. BROWN (Garden City, NY 1958) 155–168, 211–213, 305–307, 329, 332, 343, 347, 349. *I fioretti del B. Giovanni della Verna,* ed. G. MELANI (La Verna 1959). L. OLIGER, "Il B. Giovanni della Verna," *La Verna* (Arezzo 1913) 116–155. A. BUTLER, *The Lives of the Saints,* ed. H. THURSTON and D. ATTWATER, 4 v. (New York 1956) 3:324–325. D. CRESI, "Il prefazio di S. Francesco," *Studi francescani* 35 (1960) 95–102. GIOVANNI DA SETTIMO, *Vita del B. Giovanni della Verna,* ed. G. MELANI (La Verna 1962).

[R. BROWN]

JOHN OF LANGTON

Bishop, chancellor of England; b. perhaps at Church Langton, Leicestershire; d. Chichester, July 19, 1337. Langton may have been from a landed family and the brother of bishop Walter Langton of Coventry and Lichfield (1296–1321). He obtained his Master of Arts probably at Oxford, to which he left a sum of money for poor students. Langton's early career was spent in the royal chancery where he was competent as an official, but not outstanding as an individual. He was keeper of the rolls before 1286, chancellor for EDWARD I from 1292 to 1302 and for EDWARD II from 1307 to 1310. In 1298 he was the minority candidate for the See of Ely, but despite royal support, did not obtain the bishopric; in 1305, however, he was elected and became bishop of CHICHESTER. During the troubled reign of Edward II he was a moderate and a peacemaker, belonging to the Middle Party and helping to negotiate the Treaty of Leake in 1318. He did not take an active part in the overthrow of Edward II and retired from politics after the coronation of Edward III.

Bibliography: C. L. KINGSFORD, *The Dictionary of National Biography From the Earliest Times to 1900,* 63 v. (London 1885–1900) 11:561–562. T. F. TOUT, *Chapters in the Administrative History of Mediaeval England,* 6 v. (New York 1920–33). K. EDWARDS, "The Political Importance of the English Bishops During the Reign of Edward II," *English Historical Review* (London 1886—) 59 (1944) 311–347; "The Social Origins and Provenance of the English Bishops During the Reign of Edward II," *Transactions of the Royal Historical Society,* 5th series 9 (1959) 51–79. A. B. EMDEN, *A Biographical Register of the University of Oxford to A.D. 1500,* 3 v. (Oxford 1957–59) 2:1099–1100.

[F. D. BLACKLEY]

JOHN OF LICHTENBERG

German Dominican Thomist; flourished 1307 to 1313. Sometimes known as Picardi, a family name or sobriquet, and Teutonicus, he lectured at the Dominican priory in Cologne before 1307. As bachelor in theology at Paris (1307–08), he wrote a commentary on the *Sentences* (Vienna, Biblical Naturalist Manuscript Latin 1114). His studies were interrupted when he was elected provincial of the German province (1308–10), but he returned to Paris in 1310 to become master in theology. He was in the retinue of HENRY VII, Holy Roman Emperor, during his journey to Italy in 1311–12. Named bishop of Regensburg by CLEMENT V in 1313, he did not take possession of the see since the cathedral chapter had already elected another. At an unknown date he discussed and determined 36 *Quaestiones* at the priory in Cologne (Vat. lat. 859). He was one of the earliest and more important members of the early Thomistic school in Germany.

Bibliography: J. P. MÜLLER, *Lexikon für Theologie und Kirche,* ed. J. HOFER and K. RAHNER, 10 v. (2d, new ed. Frieburg 1957–65) 5:1056–57. J. QUÉTIF and J. ÉCHARD, *Scriptores Ordinis Praedicatorum,* 5 v. (Paris 1719–23) 1.2:523–526. A. LANDGRAF, "Johannes Picardi de Lichtenberg und seine *Quaestiones Disputatae*," *Zeitschrift für katholische Theologie* (1922) 510–555. M. GRABMANN, "Forschungen zur Geschichte der ältesten deutschen Thomistenschule des Dominakanerordens" in his *Mittelalterliches Geistesleben,* 3 v. (Munich 1926–56) 1:4104–20. A. FRIES, "Codex Vaticanus Latinus 1114 und der Sentenzenkommentar des Johannes von Lichtenberg," *Archivum Fratrum Praedicatorum,* 7, (1937) 305–319.

[J. F. HINNEBUSCH]

JOHN OF LODI, ST.

Benedictine; b. Lodi, Lombardy, Italy, c. 1025–30; d. Gubbio, Sept. 7, 1105. After an excellent education in the liberal arts, he abandoned society for a strict eremitical life. Already a priest, he joined the group of hermits at FONTE AVELLANA (c. 1065) and became the assistant and traveling companion of the elderly (St.) PETER DAMIAN (d. 1072). Shortly after Damian's death he prepared a reliable biography of his master, who had addressed two of his writings to him (*Opusc.* 44 and *Ep.* 6.10), and who had entrusted him with the critical revision of his literary works. After 1080 John became prior of the hermitage in Fonte Avellana. In 1104 he was elected bishop of Gubbio, but he died in the first year of his office and was buried in the cathedral of Gubbio.

Feast: Sept. 7.

Bibliography: *Bibliotheca hagiographica latina antiquae ct mediae aetatis,* 2 v. (Brussels 1898–1901; suppl. 1911) 1:4409–10. A. POTTHAST, *Bibliotheca historica medii aevi* (2d ed. 1896; repr. Graz 1954) 2:1400. F. NEUKIRCH, *Das Leben des Petrus Damiani* (Göttingen 1875). A. M. ZIMMERMANN, *Kalendarium Benedictinum: Die Heiligen und Seligen des Benediktinerorderns und seiner Zweige,* 4 v. (Metten 1933–38) 3:25, 27. J. L. BAUDOT and L. CHAUSSIN, *Vies des saints et des bienheueux selon l'ordre du calendrier avec l'historique des fêtes,* ed. by The Benedictines of Paris, 12 v. (Paris 1935–56) 9:148–149. K. REINDEL, "Studien zur Ueberlieferung der Werke des Petrus Damiani," *Deutsches Archiv für Erforschung des Mittelalters* 15 (1959) 23–102. U. CHEVALIER, *Répertoire des sources historiques du moyen-âge. Biobibliographie,* 2 v. (2d. ed. Paris 1905–07) 1204.

[F. DRESSLER]

JOHN OF MATERA, ST.

Also known as John of Pulsano, Benedictine, founder and abbot; b. Matera, Kingdom of Naples, 1070; d. Pulsano, June 20, 1139. Following what he considered divine commands, John spent much of his life journeying from one religious house to another seeking an environment conducive to his severe mortifications. Having lived some years as a hermit, he founded a small monastery at Ginosa (not far from Matera), which was dispersed by the NORMANS. He then joined WILLIAM OF VERCELLI, but he left that community when fire destroyed its buildings. When preaching in Bari, he narrowly escaped being burned as a heretic. Finally he settled at Pulsano near Monte Gargano in Apulia (*c.* 1130), where he attracted a small group of followers (the now extinct Benedictine Congregation of Pulsano), whom he governed, until his death, according to a strict interpretation of the BENEDICTINE RULE.

Feast: June 20.

Bibliography: *Acta Sanctorum* June 5:33–50. G. J. GIORDANO, *Croniche de Monte Vergine* (Naples 1649) 520–527. A. F. PECCI, *Vita S. Iohannis a Mathera abbatis, Pulsanensis Congregationis fundatoris* (Putineani 1938); rev. B. DE GAIFFER, *Analecta Bollandiana* 57 (1939) 174–176.

[E. J. KEALEY]

JOHN OF MATHA, ST.

Founder of the Trinitarians; b. Faucon (Provence), France, June 23, 1160; d. Rome, Italy, Dec. 17, 1213. He studied and was ordained at Paris and there, presumably, founded the TRINITARIANS in 1197, obtaining approval of his order from INNOCENT III in 1198 or soon after. The order, whose principal houses were at Cerfroid (Dept. Aisne, France) and Rome, devoted itself to ransoming Christians carried into slavery in Africa by the Muslims. John propagated his institute in Italy and Spain as well as France. His alleged connection with FELIX OF VALOIS is unhistorical, and details of his life are very uncertain since the early Trinitarians failed to preserve their archives. Hence the above few facts about John's life are all that can be known with certainty. Stories of his many miracles and of his personal journeys to Africa are largely the invention of 15th and 16th century Trinitarians. John's relics were taken to Madrid in 1655, and in that year and again in 1694 his cult was officially pproved.

Feast: Feb. 8.

Bibliography: P. DESLANDRES, *L'Ordre des Trinitaires,* 2 v. (Paris 1903). G. ANTIGNANI, *Vita di Giovanni de Matha e ripercussioni della sua opera nei tempi* (Siena 1982). R. CASTAÑO, *Nacido para la liberación: San Juan de Mata* (Córdoba 1985). A. BUTLER, *The Lives of the Saints,* rev. ed. H. THURSTON and D. ATTWATER, 4 v. (New York 1956) 1:276–278, indicates the deficiencies in the early history of the Trinitarians.

[A. G. BIGGS]

JOHN OF MECKLENBERG, ST.

First bishop of Mecklenberg and martyr, of Anglo-Saxon ancestry; d. Nov. 10, 1066. The ancient historians of Iceland testify that he was one of several foreign missionaries who preached the faith in that country. John returned to the Continent at the request of Abp. ADALBERT I of Bremen-Hamburg, but it is not clear whether the archbishop sent him to Iceland in the first place. Although of advanced age, John was made the first bishop of Mecklenberg sometime after 1055 and was sent to the Slavic tribes (*see* SLAVS), including the Wends in Saxony. During an uprising there in 1066 he was captured with many other Christians. When he would not abjure the faith, his hands and feet were amputated; he was decapitated and his head, impaled on a spike, was offered to the tribal god Redigast. John of Mecklenberg is falsely called the first American martyr because the territory Viendland (land of the Wends) is erroneously identified as Vinland, the reputed Norse settlement in North America.

Feast: Nov. 10.

Bibliography: *Acta Sanctorum* November 4:564–566. *Monumenta Germaniae Scriptores* (Berlin 1825–) 29:413. J. FISCHER, "Kann Bischof Johannes aus Irland († 1066) mit Recht als erster Märtyrer Amerikas bezeichnet werden?" *Zeitschrift für katholische Theologie* 24 (1900) 756–758. K. SCHMALTZ, *Kirchengeschichte*

Mecklenburgs, 3 v. (Schwerin 1935–52) v.1. H. FUHRMANN, *Lexikon für Theologie und Kirche,* ed. J. HOFER and K. RAHNER, 10 v. (2d, new ed. Freiburg 1957–65) 5:1060.

[V. A. SCHAEFER]

JOHN OF MIRECOURT

Cistercian scholastic theologian of French origin (de Mirecuria, Vosges), often referred to simply as the white monk (*monachus albus*); flourished Paris 1345–47. He studied theology at Paris. In 1345 he was a bachelor of theology and wrote a commentary on the *Sentences.* In 1347 Parisian masters of theology censured 63 propositions from this commentary; later the chancellor, acting on the advice of the masters, condemned 41 of these [*Chartularium universitatis Parisiensis,* ed. H. Denifle and E. Chatelain, 4 v. (Paris 1889–97) 2:610–614]. To each of these university actions John reacted with an apology justifying his position [*Recherches de théologie ancienne et médiévale* 5 (1933) 40–78; 192–204]. Two versions of the commentary are extant, but the second seems to be an anonymous compilation based on the first. Neither version has been published. It is most likely that John never became a master in theology.

Two themes are dominant through the commentary, namely, the difficulty of attaining human certitude and the capacity of nature in moral matters. For John, there is little hope of more than mere probability because (1) it is rarely possible to reduce proofs to the basic first principle that contradictories cannot be true at one and the same time, since sense knowledge is deceptive, and (2) God can always intervene miraculously. For him, probability characterizes any statement not known with certainty, or believed by faith, or determined by the Church, or proposed by one whose statement ought not be negated or its opposite affirmed. John's insistence on the probable character of most human knowledge led him to maintain many absurd views as at least equally probable. Agreeing that God's existence is not a *per se nota* proposition, he maintained that assent to demonstrations of His existence is less meritorious than assent to articles of faith based on charity. He held that God can by His absolute power (*potentia absoluta*) command man to hate Him. Moreover, God can be said to be the cause of sin, provided "cause" is restricted to permissive causality. John and many of his contemporaries, notably NICHOLAS OF AUTRECOURT, defended disturbingly extreme views for two reasons. They wanted to guarantee unquestionable certitude in knowledge, and they wished to emphasize the unlimited freedom of God. In his two Apologies John carefully explained that he wished to prove merely that outside the data of faith, very few demonstrations are more than probable.

John was influenced by WILLIAM OF OCKHAM, ROBERT HOLCOT, and THOMAS OF BUCKINGHAM; some historians maintain that he was also influenced by the *De causa Dei* of THOMAS BRADWARDINE. He had considerable influence on PETER OF AILLY and the development of late medieval NOMINALISM in theology.

Bibliography: JOHN OF MIRECOURT, *Commentary on the Sentences* (Paris), Biblical Naturalist Manuscript Latin, 15882 (folio 1–184: book 1): Manuscript Latin 15883 (folio 1–94: book 2; folio 95–133: book 3; folio 134–150: book 4). A. BIRKENMAJER, *Ein Rechtfertigungsschreiben Johanns von Mirecourt, Beiträge zur Geschichte der Philosophie und Theologie des Mittelalters,* 20.5; (1922). K. MICHALSKI, "Die vielfachen Redaktionen einiger Kommentare zu Petrus Lombardus," *Miscellanea Ehrle* (Rome 1924) 1:219—. A. POMPEI, *Enciclopedia filosofica,* 4 v. (Venice-Rome 1957) 2:762.

[J. R. O'DONNELL]

JOHN OF MONTE CORVINO

First Western missionary to China, founder of the medieval Franciscan mission in China; b. Monte Corvino (Salerno); d. *c.* 1330. In 1289 this Franciscan, already an experienced missionary conversant with the Persian and Armenian languages, and the bearer of letters to the pope from certain Eastern rulers, was in turn entrusted by Pope NICHOLAS IV with various letters, including one to the Mongol great Khan at Khanbalik (Peking). In 1291 John set out through Persia, passed a year in India, where he made about 100 converts, and followed the sea route up the China coast, thence to the Mongol capital. One of his two companions, Nicholas of Pistoia, OP, died in India. The other, Peter Lucalongo, a merchant, remained with the friar, and the two reached Khanbalik in 1294. Khan Timor Olcheitu (Chen Tsung) received them courteously. For a number of years John labored alone, overcoming with his tact the hostility he encountered from Nestorian clergy. At Tenduk, northwest of Khanbalik, the ruler, Prince George, a convert from NESTORIANISM, supported the establishment of a mission, which did not, however, outlast George's lifetime. The letters to the West that John dispatched in 1305 and 1306 resulted in his being named archbishop by Clement V (1307). Franciscan suffragans were named to consecrate him and further develop the mission. Meanwhile, on land donated by Peter Lucalongo, John built three churches in Khanbalik. He also baptized more than 6,000 converts, translated the New Testament and Psalter into the native speech, probably Uighur or Mongol in Uighur characters, and trained a native boys' choir that delighted the Khan. He had also made contacts with the Alans resident in the capital and personally served a church of the Armenian rite. On his death at the age of 82, he was mourned by non-Christians and Christians alike.

See Also: MISSIONS, HISTORY OF (MEDIEVAL).

Bibliography: *Sinica franciscana,* v. 1, ed. A. VAN DEN WYNGAERT (Quaracchi-Florence 1929). A. C. MOULE, *Christians in China before the Year 1550* (New York 1930). K. S. LATOURETTE, *A History of Christian Missions in China* (New York 1929). A. VAN DEN WYNGAERT, *Notes sur Jean de Mont Corvin* (Lille 1924), also in *La France franciscaine,* 6 (1923) 135–186. J. RICHARD, ''Essor et déclin l'église catholique de Chine au XIVᵉ siècle,'' *Bulletin de la société des missionsétrangères de Paris* (Hong Kong 1962).

[M. W. BALDWIN]

JOHN OF MONTE MARANO, ST.

Bishop and patron of the city of Monte Marano, Province of Avellino, Italy; fl. late 11th century. Said to have been a BENEDICTINE monk, he was nominated bishop on request of the faithful of the city by GREGORY VII in 1074 and consecrated at Benevento. He was outstanding for his charity to the poor, for whom he labored with his own hands, and according to a legendary vita he also performed miracles. His body is preserved with great honors in the cathedral of Monte Marano, and his cult was confirmed in 1906. A tradition with no historical foundation makes him a disciple of WILLIAM OF VERCELLI, founder of the Abbey of Monte Vergine.

Feast: Aug. 17.

Bibliography: F. UGHELLI, *Italia sacra,* ed. N. COLETI, 10 v. in 9 (2d ed. Venice 1717–22) v.8. J. MABILLON, *Acta sanctorum ordinis S. Benedicti* 9:874–876. *Acta Sanctorum,* Aug. 3:510–513. *Bibliotheca hagiographica latina antiquae et mediae aetatis* 1:4414. A. M. ZIMMERMANN, *Kalendarium Benedictinum: Die Heiligen und Seligen des Benediktinerorderns und seiner Zweige* 2:585–586. J. L. BAUDOT and L. CHAUSSIN, *Vies des saints et des bienheureux selon l'ordre du calendrier avec l'historique des fêtes* 8:302. *Rivista storica benedettina* 1 (1906) 324; 2 (1907) 362. A. M. ZIMMERMANN, *Lexikon für Theologie und Kirche*² 5:1062.

[A. LENTINI]

JOHN OF MONTFORT, BL.

Nobleman from Voralberg, Knight Templar, crusader; d. Famagusta, Cyprus, 1177, 1200, or 1248. He was wounded in a battle at Jerusalem against the Saracens and died as a result, after having been taken to Cyprus. His body was translated to the abbey church of Beaulieu, Nicosia, where it was venerated until the Turkish conquest (1571). The native Cypriots have venerated him as blessed. Through the counts of Montfort he was commemorated also in the region of Langnau, Switzerland.

Feast: May 24 (formerly May 25 on Cyprus).

Bibliography: *Acta Sanctorum,* May 5:273. A. M. ZIMMERMANN, *Kalendarium Benedictinum: Die Heiligen und Seligen des Benediktinerorderns und seiner Zweige* 2:220–221. J. HACKETT, *A History of the Orthodox Church of Cyprus* (London 1901). M. KERVRAN, *Les grandes heures de Jean de Montfort et de Jeanne la Flamme* (Mayenne 1981).

[M. A. HABIG]

JOHN OF MONTMIRAIL, BL.

Cistercian monk; b. 1165; d. Longpont Abbey, Sept. 29, 1217. An impetuous and loyal knight in the service of King PHILIP II AUGUSTUS OF FRANCE, he converted to a less worldly life and established a hostel near his castle, where he himself cared for the sick. In 1210 he left his wife and children to become a CISTERCIAN monk at the Abbey of Longpont in the diocese of Soissons. There he distinguished himself by his extraordinary devotion to the virtues of obedience and humility. His relics were translated to the abbey church in 1253, and he was honored as early as 1491 in the Cistercian martyrology. His cult was approved July 19, 1891.

Feast: Sept. 29 (Italian Cistercians and in the Dioceses of Soissons and Châlons-sur-Marne).

Bibliography: *Acta Sanctorum* September 8 (1863) 186–235. U. CHEVALIER, *Répertoire des sources historiques du moyen-âge. Biobibliographie,* 2 v. (2d. ed. Paris 1905–07) 2:2448. A. M. ZIMMERMANN, *Kalendarium Benedictinum: Die Heiligen und Seligen des Benediktinerorderns und seiner Zweige,* 4 v. (Metten 1933–38) 3:115–118. A. DIMIER, ''Le Bienheureux Jean de Montmirail moine de Longpont,'' *Mémoires de la fédération des sociétés savantes de l'Aisne* 7 (1960–61) 182–191. J. L. BAUDOT and L. CHAUSSIN, *Vies des saints et des bienheueux selon l'ordre du calendrier avec l'historique des fêtes,* ed. by The Benedictines of Paris, 12 v. (Paris 1935–56) 9:613–615. K. SPAHR, *Lexikon für Theologie und Kirche,* ed. J. HOFER and K. RAHNER, 10 v. (2d, new ed. Freiburg 1957–65) 5:1063.

[M. STANDAERT]

JOHN OF NAPLES

Dominican Thomist theologian; b. Naples, Italy, of noble parents; fl. 1310 to 1336; d. Naples. He entered the order in that city at the priory of San Domenico Maggiore, where THOMAS AQUINAS had entered and spent the last years of his life. Sent to the University of Paris, he met HARVEY NEDELLEC, DURANDUS OF SAINT–POURÇAIN, Meister ECKHART, John of Parma (fl. 1313), and PETER OF LA PALU. He read the *Sentences* during the academic years 1310 to 1312 and received license to incept in December 1315. He taught as a master in Paris until 1317. In his fidelity to Aquinas he stands in sharp contrast to Durandus of Saint–Pourçain. The general chapter of the order that met in Metz in June 1313 appointed John to the commission entrusted with examining the teaching of Durandus. In 1316–17 he and Peter of La Palu compiled a list of 235 errors in the writings of Durandus. In one of his quodlibetal questions he publicly maintained the right to teach all the doctrines of Aquinas despite the condemnation of Étienne TEMPIER in 1277.

The general chapter of Pamplona in 1317 assigned him as lector in the Dominican *Studium* in Naples; he taught there for many years. He was frequently consulted concerning current controversies, notably the absolute poverty of Christ in the Franciscan poverty controversy, the state of the blessed before the Last Judgment as viewed by JOHN XXII, and the affair of MICHAEL OF CESENA. Deeply concerned with the canonization of Aquinas, he presented hearsay testimony on Aug. 1, 1319, to commissioners entrusted with promoting Aquinas's beatification and canonization. In 1323 as substitute for William of Tocco, procurator general and promoter of the cause, he went to Avignon with witnesses and officials for the second process of inquiry. Illness prevented him from delivering his panegyric prepared for July 14, 1323. He was present at the general chapter of Bordeaux in 1324 that elected Barnabas of Vercelli master general of the order. He was named executor of Bartholomew of Capua's will on March 14, 1325. A document concerning this will, dated June 9, 1336, is the last known evidence of his activities.

His commentary on the *Sentences* is no longer extant. His *Quaestiones variae 42 disputatae* (ed. Naples 1618) were disputed at Paris, as were his 13 *Quodlibeta* and 8 sermons. Because of his personal devotion and fidelity to St. Thomas, his activities are a significant witness to the development of THOMISM among Italian Dominicans.

Bibliography: J. QUÉTIF and J. ÉCHARD, *Scriptores Ordinis Praedicatorum* 1.2:567. J. P. MÜLLER, *Lexikon für Theologie und Kirche*[2] 5:1064–65. P. GLORIEUX, *La Littérature quodlibétique* 1:159–173. M. GRABMANN, "La scuola tomistica italiana nel XIII e principio del XIV secolo," *Rivista di filosofia neoscolastica* 15 (Milan 1923) 138–143. C. J. JELLOUSCHEK, "Johannes v. Neapel und seine Lehre vom Verhältnisse zwischen Gott und Welt," *Xenia Thomistica* (Rome 1925) 2:75. J. KOCH, "Durandus de S. Porciano, OP," *Beiträge zur Geschichte der Philosophie und Theologie des Mittelalters* 26 (Münster 1927). T. KAEPPELI, "Giovanni Regina di Napoli," *Archivum Fratrum Praedicatorum* 10 (Rome 1940) 48–71. A. ISZAK, *Enciclopedia filosofica* 2:765.

[P. GLORIEUX]

JOHN OF NEPOMUC, ST.

Patron of the Czechs, alleged martyr; b. John (Ivan) Wölflin at Nepomuc (or Pomuk), Bohemia, March 20, c. 1350; d. Prague, 1393. A canon of the Prague cathedral, he advanced to the post of vicar-general of the Archdiocese of Prague (1389) while John of Jenštein was archbishop (1378–1400). Nepomuc has traditionally been considered "the patron of the seal of confession" for supposedly, as spiritual director of Queen Sophie, he refused to reveal anything when the king, WENCESLAUS IV of Bohemia, demanded his confirmation of Sophie's suspected adultery. The whole incident, however, is probably legendary, for it is unthinkable that the queen's confessor could have been anyone closely connected with the archbishop, who had distinguished himself as a determined opponent of the king ever since they had both assumed office in 1378. More historically accurate is the account of Nepomuc's death. In 1393 the king and archbishop were currently clashing over the Benedictine Abbey of Kladruby, which Wenceslaus had intended to confiscate once the old abbot died and to use as the basis for a new diocese he wished to found. However, when the abbot died, Nepomuc, as vicar–general, immediately confirmed the appointment of a new abbot on March 10, 1393. At a subsequent conference of king and archbishop, the choleric Wenceslaus flew into a rage, seized three of the archbishop's counselors, including Nepomuc, and ordered them to be tortured. (Exactly what information he sought is not known.) When the king recovered from his fit of anger, two of the counselors were released without grave ill effects. Nepomuc, however, was in such poor condition that he was dispatched by being thrown into the River Vltava. When his body was retrieved, he came to be popularly regarded as a martyr. It was especially during the Counter Reformation in Bohemia that Nepomuc was established as a great national martyr and patron by the Catholics of Bohemia (in much the same way that John HUS became the hero of the Protestants of Bohemia). In 1729, despite more than three centuries of controversy over the cause and details of his death, Nepomuc was canonized by Pope BENEDICT XIII. However, in 1961 the Sacred Congregation of Rites suppressed his feast in the calendar of the universal Church [*Ephemeredes liturgicae,* 75 (1961) 424].

Feast: May 16 (local churches).

Bibliography: *Acta Sanctorum,* May 3 (1680) 668–80. F. M. BARTOS, *Jan Nepomucky svetec temna* (Prague 1921). J. WEISSKOPF, *Johannes von Pomuk* (Munich 1948). *Lexikon für Theologie und Kirche,* ed. J. HOFER and K. RAHNER, 10 v. (2d, new ed. Freiburg 1957–65) 5:1065. A. BUTLER, *The Lives of the Saints,* rev. ed. H. THURSTON and D. ATTWATER, 4 v. (New York 1956) 2:332–333. P. DE VOOGHT, "J. de Pomuk," *Revue d'histoire ecclésiastique,* 48 (1953) 777–795. *Hussiana* (Louvain 1960) 400–441. Schlossmuseum Gobelsburg, *Barocke Volksfrömmigkeit. Andachtsgraphik, Votivbilder, Zeugnisse d. Volksverehrung des hl. Johann v. Nepomuk. Ausstellung. Katalog,* ed. L. SCHMIDT (Vienna 1971). *Johannes von Nepomuk: ein Text–BildBand,* ed. J. NEUHARDT (Graz 1979). H. L. ZOLLNER, *Johannes von Nepomuk zu*

Ehren: die Ettlinger Schlosskapelle. . . (Karlsruhe 1992). V. VLNAS, *Jan Nepomucký, ceská legenda* (Prague 1993), cult.

[B. B. SZCZESNIAK]

JOHN OF OTZUN

Also known as Hovhannes IV Otznetzi, Armenian Catholicos, called the Philosopher for his theological and canonical works; b. Otzun, 650; d. Dwin, 729. Esteemed for holiness and learning, he was chosen Catholicos in 718. Soon afterward he held a national synod at Dwin to reform the liturgy and discipline of the Armenian Church. In 726 he presided over a synod at Manzikert, which discussed the doctrine and union with the SYRIAN (Jacobite) Church, and was the recipient of a letter from the Patriarch of Constantinople, Germanus I (715–730), urging the Armenian Monophysites to accept union with the Byzantine Church on the strength of the Christology of St. CYRIL OF ALEXANDRIA. His chief writings are: (1) a discourse (or pastoral letter) at the synod of Dwin insisting on preserving Armenian ecclesiastical traditions; (2) a treatise on the Incarnation (*Contra Phantasticos*), stressing the two natures in Christ; (3) a work against the PAULICIANS; (4) a reform of the Armenian Breviary; and (5) a collection of canonical works. Without mentioning the Council of CHALCEDON, his teaching generally follows its doctrines, although he sometimes employs different terms to emphasize various aspects of CHRISTOLOGY.

Bibliography: *Domini Joannis Philosophi Ozniensis, Armeniorum Catholici opera,* ed. and tr. J. B. AUCHER, Latin and Armenian eds., (Venice 1834). V. INGLISIAN, ''Die Armenische Literatur,'' *Armenische und Kaukasische Sprachen,* v. 7 of *Handbuch der Orientalistik,* ed. B. SPULER et al., (Leiden 1963) 174–175. A. GRILLMEIER and H. BACHT, *Das Konzil von Chalkedon:Geschichte und Gegenwart,* 3 v. (Würzburg 1951–54) 2:407–417. H. G. BECK, *Kirche und theologische Literatur im byzantinischen Reich* (Munich 1959) 474.

[G. T. DENNIS]

JOHN OF OXFORD

Bishop of Norwich, jurist; d. June 2, 1200. The son of Henry of Oxford, sheriff in 1154–55, John began his early career *c.* 1154–56 within the framework of family influence in Oxford, and *c.* 1160 he became rural dean of Oxford. It is clear that by 1163–64 John was engaged in royal administration. He was deeply involved in negotiations resulting from the archbishop Thomas BECKET dispute and perhaps presided at Clarendon in January 1164 (*see* CLARENDON, CONSTITUTIONS OF). He was ubiquitous in the service of King HENRY II in the years 1164 to 1170:

on missions to Pope ALEXANDER III (in 1164, 1166, and 1169–70), to King LOUIS VII of France, to Philip of Flanders, and to Emperor FREDERICK I; in dealings with the papal legates in 1169; and in Becket's company on the latter's return from exile in 1170. His intrusion as dean of Salisbury in 1165 at Henry's wish but against the commands of both pope and archbishop (in November 1166 he was finally appointed by papal *COLLATIO*), together with his participation at the schismatical council of Würzburg on May 23, 1165, resulted in his excommunication by Becket at Vézelay on Whitsunday 1166. And, despite his subsequent reconciliation with the pope, John remained for the Becket party the former usurper dean and notorious *jurator.* Before and after his elevation to the bishopric of Norwich in 1175 (elected Nov. 26; consecrated Dec. 14) he was among the most active executants of Henry II's policies: in the Saxon and Sicilian marriage affairs of 1166 and 1176; in judicial business; as an archjusticiar of the realm in 1179; and as participant at many royal councils. His work as bishop is recorded in his *acta* and charters and in the decretals and commissions he received as a papal judge delegate. He was present at the Third LATERAN COUNCIL of 1179 and set out on crusade with King RICHARD I in 1190 but was absolved by the pope from his crusading oath on reaching Italy. Various writings have been, without clear evidence, attributed to him, and Daniel de Morley's *Liber de naturis* was dedicated to him.

Bibliography: R. W. EYTON, *Court, Household and Itinerary of King Henry II* (London 1878). W. H. HUTTON, *The Dictionary of National Biography From the Earliest Times to 1900,* 63 v. (London 1885–1900) 15:1517. R. FOREVILLE, *L'Église et la royauté en Angleterre sous Henri II Plantagenet* (Paris 1943), *passim.* A. B. EMDEN, *A Biographical Register of the University of Oxford to A.D. 1500,* 3 v. (Oxford 1957–59) 2:1414.

[C. DUGGAN]

JOHN (QUIDORT) OF PARIS

Dominican theologian, polemicist, and defender of THOMISM; b. Paris, between 1240 and 1269; d. Bordeaux, Sept. 22, 1306. Although little documentation is available, it is probable that he received his arts education from the University of Paris before entering the Dominican Order at Saint-Jacques at an early age [J. Quétif and J. Échard, *Scriptores Ordinis Praedicatorum,* 5 v. (Paris 1719–23) 1:500]. Prior to 1284 he strongly defended the doctrines of THOMAS AQUINAS in his *Correctorium "Circa"* [ed. J. P. Müller (Rome 1941)], replying to the *Correctorium fratris Thomae* by WILLIAM DE LA MARE (*see* CORRECTORIA). Between 1284 and 1286 he commented on the *Sentences* as a bachelor of theology. From this commentary sixteen propositions were extracted from his teaching on the Eucharist and reported to the master general of the order as erroneous. He defended himself successfully in his *Apologia, c.* 1287, but his studies at the university were postponed. He acquired fame as a preacher in Paris, where he was sometimes called *Praedicator Monoculus.* He continued to defend basic Thomistic teachings under attack in *Tractatus de unitate formarum* (ed. Venice 1513). In 1302 he wrote his celebrated *De petestate regis et papali* [ed. J. Leclercq, (Paris 1942)], which discusses the distinction and limitations of civil and papal authority. On June 26, 1303, he signed an appeal to the council against BONIFACE VIII [*Chartularium universitatis Parisiensis*, ed. H. Denifle and E. Chatelain, 4 v. (Paris 1989–97) 2:634]. In 1304 he received his license to incept as a master of theology at the university. In that year he presented a *Determinatio* on the question of how the real Body of Christ exists in the Eucharist (ed. London 1686). While he admitted the traditional teaching that the substance of bread is converted into the substance of Christ's Body, namely, TRANSUBSTANTIATION, he insisted that this doctrine was not defined by the Church, and therefore not necessarily the only explanation. He suggested as equally tenable a second possibility, whereby the substance of bread is assumed by the person of Christ (*suppositum Verbi*) and remains together with the Body of Christ. This theory, which later came to be known as consubstantiation, or impanation, attracted much attention among the Reformers of the 16th and 17th century. John's view was examined and censured by a commission of four bishops, numerous theologians, and canonists. Perpetual silence was imposed on him under pain of excommunication, and he was suspended from teaching and preaching (*Chartularium universitatis Parisiensis*, 2:656). He appealed his case to CLEMENT V, who was then at Bordeaux, but died before receiving a decision.

Substantially Thomistic on all controverted doctrines of Aquinas in his day, he was an original thinker who did not simply repeat the views of St. Thomas. His contribution to ecclesiology and political philosophy is significant in the development of Thomism. Among his metaphysical doctrines, the notion of *esse* has attracted most attention, but contemporary scholars are not unanimous in their evaluation of it. Nevertheless, he is one of the most significant representatives of the early Thomistic school in France.

Bibliography: P. GLORIEUX, *Répertoire des maîtres en théologie de Paris au XIIIᵉ siècle* (Paris 1933–34) 1:189–193. A. J. HEIMAN, ''Essence and *Esse* according to Jean Quidort,'' *Mediaeval Studies*, 15 (1953) 137–146; ''Two Questions concerning the *Esse* of Creatures in the Doctrine of J. Q.,'' *An Étienne Gilson Tribute*, ed. C. J. O'NEIL (Milwaukee 1959) 51–67. P. STELLA, *Enciclopedia filosofica*, 4 v. (Venice–Rome 1957) 2:763. F. J. ROENSCH, *Early Thomistic School* (Dubuque 1964). J. P. MÜLLER, *Lexikon für Theologie und Kirche*, ed. J. HOFER and K. RAHNER, 10 v. (2d, new ed. Freiburg 1957–65) 5:1068. E. GILSON, *History of Christian Philosophy, passim.*

[A. J. HEIMAN]

JOHN OF PARMA, BL.

Franciscan minister general, 1247 to 1257; b. 1208?, Parma; d. 1289. John was born in the anti-imperial city of Parma. After entering the Franciscan Order in the 1230s, he lived most of his life beyond the confines of his native city. Sent to study at the Franciscan *studium generale* in Paris, he was appointed as a lector of theology in various *studia* of the Order, in Bologna (*c.* 1241) then in Naples (*c.* 1243–45). In 1245, upon the deaths of ALEXANDER OF HALES and JOHN OF LA ROCHELLE, John found himself called back to Paris, this time as lector in theology for the friars. When in July 1245 the minister general of the Franciscan Order, Crescentius of Jesi, decided not to attend the First Council of Lyons (whose primary aim was to excommunicate Emperor Frederick II), INNOCENT IV asked John to represent the friars. At the General Chapter of 1247, the friars chose him as minister general, replacing the irascible Crescentius. John immediately set out on a visitation of the provinces of England, France and Spain.

During his time in Naples, John had absorbed the eschatological ideas of JOACHIM OF FIORE, and became one of the leading proponents of them. The Franciscan chronicler, SALIMBENE, refers to John as a *maximus joachita.* This current of eschatological thinking was highly critical of the actions of Frederick II toward the Church and the moral corruption of the ecclesiastical hierarchy; it also envisioned a leading role to be played by both the Friars Minor and Preacher—the prophesied *viri spirituales* of Joachim of Fiore—in the eschatological events of an end-time fast approaching. John was instrumental in bringing these ideas—and the associated pseudo-Joachim texts—northward. Indeed the well-known fascination with Joachite ideas of HUGH OF DIGNE and his circle of adherents at Hyères can be traced directly to John.

One of the key elements in the eschatological scenario propounded by Joachim and the Franciscan Joachites was the reunion of the Latin and Greek Churches. Thus, it was not simply John's knowledge of Greek, but more especially, his belief in the critical importance of this latter event that prompted Innocent IV to call him back from his visitation in early 1249 to lead a delegation of friars to Nicaea in order to explore the possibility of a reunion between Rome and the Greek Church in exile led by its emperor, John Vatatzès. John and his companions (among whom was another *maximus joachita*, Gerard of

Borgo San Donnino) were responsible for drafting the interpolations to the *Vaticinium Sibillae Erithreae*, an apocalyptic text that predicted the return of the Greek Empire and Church from exile in Nicaea to Constantinople and the demise of the Hohenstaufen line as the necessary preludes to the last days. In addition, the *Vaticinium* anticipates the friars serving not simply as missionaries to but bishops of a renewed Church in the East, activities already strongly promoted within the Order itself by the minister general.

When the mission foundered in mid-1250 with no concrete results, John returned to the West. He addressed himself to the critical issue facing the Franciscan community in this period: how to balance the needs of food, clothing and housing of an ever-growing Order with its vocation of total poverty. Determined that the deeds of the friars match their ideals, at successive general chapters in 1251 and 1254, John led the opposition of many within the community to *Ordinem vestrum*—the bull of Innocent IV granted to the Order in 1245 that had opened the door to the possibility of greater laxities among the friars in their observance of poverty.

John struck a humble posture on behalf of the Minors at the University of Paris during the controversies with the secular masters, calming the situation by publicly promising to abide by the strictures imposed by the masters limiting the mendicants to one chair of theology. But in 1255 when it was learned that an inflammatory book fiercely critical of the papacy and hierarchy, predicting their demise in a new Age of the Spirit—the famous *Liber introductorius* to the works of Joachim of Fiore—had actually been written by a Franciscan, Gerard of Borgo San Donnino, John rallied to the defense of his embattled confrère. In doing so, he became inextricably associated with the radical ideas of the book.

ALEXANDER IV demanded that John resign as minister general at a special chapter in Rome on Feb. 2, 1257; he was replaced by the young theologian, BONAVENTURE of Bagnoregio. The latter put Gerard and his companions on trial the following year for heresy, resulting in their perpetual imprisonment, but John suffered only the humiliation of his deposition. A few years later, however, probably in 1261 or 1262, John himself was put on trial by Bonaventure for, according to Angelo Clareno, having written a "little book," whose identity has never been determined. Only the timely intervention of Cardinal Ottobono in his behalf spared the former general from a fate similar to the other Franciscan Joachites. He was allowed to retire, under house arrest, to the quiet of the hermitage of Greccio. There he remained for nearly the rest of his days until, in 1289, having received permission to leave the hermitage, he set out again for his beloved East. But

John died en route shortly afterwards in the town of Camerino in the Marches of Ancona.

Bibliography: SALIMBENE, *Cronica, I*, ed. G. SCALIA (Turnhout 1998), 453–477. A. CLARENO, *Liber chronicarum sive tribulationum ordinis minorum*, ed. G. BOCCALI (S. Maria degli Angeli 1999), 354–388. R. BROOKE, *Early Franciscan Government* (Cambridge 1959). P. ALEXANDER, "The Diffusion of Byzantine Apocalypses in the Medieval West and the Beginnings of Joachimism," in *Prophecy and Millenarianism. Essays in Honour of Marjorie Reeves*, ed. A. WILLIAMS (Essex 1980), 53–106. A. FRANCHI, *La svolta politico- ecclesiastica tra Roma e Bisanzio* (1249–1254). *La legazione di Giovanni da Parma. Il ruolo di Federico II* (Rome 1981).

[M. F. CUSATO]

JOHN OF RAGUSA

Theologian and churchman, active at the Council of BASEL; b. Ragusa, *c.* 1390 to 1395; d. Lausanne, 1443. John (Stojković) entered the Dominican Order in his native city and studied at Paris, receiving his doctor's degree in 1420. In 1423 he was envoy of that university to the Synod of Pavia. Here he was papal preacher, but he protested when the assembly was dissolved. In the interval, and definitely in 1429, before the opening of the Council of Basel, he served as procurator-general of the Dominicans at the Holy See. Most of John's subsequent history is connected with the Council of Basel. In 1431, Cardinal G. Cesarini being impeded, John was delegated to open the Council and he delivered the inaugural sermon; he left an account of the early activities of the assembly. In 1433 John, one of several theologians named to negotiate with the Hussites, debated at great length with one of their leaders, John Rokycana, on the reception of Communion under one or both species. In 1435 and 1437 he was ambassador of the Council to Constantinople to urge the cause of reunion and was instrumental in having the Eastern Emperor and the patriarch send a delegation to Basel for this purpose. On a mission in 1438 to the Emperor Albert II, he spoke in behalf of the council, showing conciliarist leanings. Upon his return to the council he joined the dissident party. In 1438 he was made bishop of Ardijsch, and in 1440 cardinal priest of San Sisto by the antipope Felix V. John's writings include a treatise on the Church, the sermon on Communion under both species, the history of the early work of the Council of Basel, a treatise on reunion of the Hussites, an unfinished account of his travels in the East and on reunion with the Greeks, and a concordance of indeclinable words in Sacred Scripture.

Bibliography: B. ALTANER, "Zur Geschichte der Handschriftensammlung des Kardinals Johannes von Ragusa," *Historisches Jahrbuch der Görres-Gesellschaft* 47 (1927) 730–732. A. WALZ, "I cardinali domenicani: Note bio-bibliografiche," *Memorie Domeni-*

cane 57 (1940) 32. G. THILS, "Le *Tractatus de Ecclesia* de Jean de Raguse," *Angelicum* 17 (1940) 219–244. K. BINDER, "Der *Tractatus de Ecclesia* Johanns von Ragusa und die Verhandlungen des Konzils von Basel mit den Husiten," *ibid.* 28 (1951) 30–54. B. DUDA, *Joannis Stojković de Ragusio, O. P.: Doctrina de cognoscibilitate Ecclesiae* (Rome 1958). R. ROGOSIC, *Lexikon für Theologie und Kirche*, ed. J. HOFER and K. RAHNER (Freiburg 1957–65) 5:1073–4.

[J. F. HINNEBUSCH]

JOHN OF RAVENNA

Archbishop; b. *c.* 812; d. after 863. Traditionally it has been held that John was the first archbishop of Dalmatia and Croatia; but many scholars now doubt this attribution and think that he has been confused with Pope JOHN IV, a native of Dalmatia, or with Pope JOHN X, who reorganized the hierarchy of Dalmatia and Croatia and subjected the area to Split *c.* 925. As archbishop of RAVENNA from 850 to 861, John was a partisan of Emperor LOUIS II and a troublemaker for both LEO IV and NICHOLAS I. He fraudulently seized the property of Leo's subjects, oppressed clergy and laity alike, and even murdered a papal legate. In all this he was helped by his brother Gregory, Duke of Emilia. A visit to Ravenna by Leo to reprimand him was of no avail [P. Jaffé, *Regesta pontificum romanorum ab condita ecclesia ad annum post Christium natum 1198*], and later, under Nicholas, deputations came to Rome to protest against John's continued oppressions. The pope tried to dissuade him by legates and letters, but John continued to excommunicate his opponents and seize property, even papal property, arbitrarily. He also acted *ultra vires* in sentencing clerics directly subject to Rome. Summoned to Rome in 861 to give an account of his misdeeds, he refused to go, was found contumacious by the pope, and excommunicated [J. D. Mansi, *Sacrorum Concillorum nova et amplissima collectio*, 31 v. (Florence-Venice 1757–98) 15:658; *Liber pontificalis*, ed. L. Duchesne, v.1–2 (Paris 1886–92), v.3 (Paris 1958) 2:168]. John enlisted the help of Louis and with the Emperor's ambassadors went to Rome, but he failed to reverse the decision. Nicholas himself visited Ravenna to restore the properties appropriated by the archbishop. In all, John was condemned by three successive synods at Rome, and when he was rebuffed at a second appeal for help to Emperor Louis, he was forced to make his peace with a synod at Rome in November of 861 [*Patrologia Latina*, ed. J. P. Migne, 217 v., indexes 4 v. (Paris 1878–90) 106:787–792]. He swore fidelity and obedience to the pope and purged himself of heresy, but his repentance was short-lived, and he had to be deposed again in 863 for siding with Gunther, Archbishop of Cologne (d. 873), and Thiergaud of Trier in their conflict with the papacy over the divorce of King LOTHAIR II.

Bibliography: *Liber pontificalis*, ed. L. DUCHESNE, v.1–2 (Paris 1886–92), v.3 (Paris 1958) 2:157–158. F. DVORNIK, *The Slavs: Their Early History and Civilization* (Boston 1956). A. MERCATI and A. PELZER, *Dizionario ecclesiastico*, 3 v. (Turin 1957–58) 2:172. F. BULIĆ and J. BERVALDI, *Kronotaksa spljetskih nadbiskupa* (Zagreb 1913) 116–132. R. ROGOSIĆ, *Lexikon für Theologie und Kirche*, ed. J. HOFER and K. RAHNER, 10 v. (2 d, new ed. Freiburg 1957–65) 5:1073–74. T. SCHIEFFER, "Nikolaus I," *ibidem* 7:976–977.

[T. P. HALTON]

JOHN OF RÉÔME, ST.

Monastic founder, abbot; b. Courtangy, France, *c.* 450; d. Jan. 28, *c.* 539–44. He took the monastic habit at Lérins. Recalled by his own bishop, he founded at Réôme (now Ménétreux, commune of Corsaint) a monastery later called Saint-Jean-de-Réôme or Moûtier-Saint-Jean-en-Auxois. He introduced into his monastery the rule of MACARIUS OF EGYPT, under which he had lived at LÉRINS. He was one of the pioneers of the monastic life in Burgundy, enjoying a great reputation for sanctity and for working miracles. His remains were preserved from the Saracens (731) and the Vikings (888); and again in 1793 the principal relics escaped the Revolutionaries. His biography was written by Jonas of Susa.

Feast: Jan. 28.

Bibliography: *Vita, Monumenta Germaniae Historica: Scriptores rerum Merovingicarum* 3:502–517. *Bibliotheca hagiographica latina antiquae et mediae aetatis* 1:4424–31. A. BUTLER, *The Lives of the Saints* 1:187. T. PAYR, *Lexikon für Theologie und Kirche²* 5:1074. P. VIARD, *Catholicisme* 6:433–434.

[T. P. HALTON]

JOHN OF RIPA

Italian Franciscan theologian known as *Doctor difficilis* and *Doctor supersubtilis;* flourished Paris, 1357–68. Although his family name was Plantadossi, he was called Joannes de Ripa or de Marchia because he belonged to the Franciscan friary of Ripatransone in the Marche of Ascoli near Piceno. It is not possible to assign exact dates for his academic activities, although it is most probable that he lectured on the *Sentences* at the University of Paris *c.* 1357 and remained there as professor until after 1368. His basic formation and outlook were Scotistic, but he manifested more originality and independence than most in the development of SCOTISM. It is unlikely that he was ever personally censured for his teachings, although some of his followers were, namely, Louis of Padua (flourished 1362–64) and John of Bâle (flourished 1381–85). Three major works of John are extant: *Lectura super primum Sententiarum* [ed. A. Combes, (Paris 1961)], *Conclusiones circa primum librum Sententiarum* [ed. A. Combes, (Paris 1957)], and *Determinationes* [ed. A. Combes, (Paris 1957)]. Parts of a commentary on the other books of the *Sentences* also are extant. Other treatises have been attributed to him, but they are spurious, or wrongly catalogued, or simply lost.

In the commentary on the *Sentences* John tried to make as clear as possible the character of the beatitude communicated by God to His creatures. The problem was fundamentally Augustinian and was made more explicit by DUNS SCOTUS; it was concerned with reconciling the immensity of God and the finiteness of creatures. John carefully examined the nature of God's immensity, especially in relation to man's sanctification. Employing a philosophy based on the "intension and remission of forms," he saw in man a *potentia vitalis* as a basis for sanctity and beatific knowledge by way of presence rather than of physical information. In the *Determinationes,* however, he went out of his way to refute the tenet that God is somehow the formal cause of creatures.

The influence of John of Ripa is difficult to assess. He was a disciple of Duns Scotus, yet he often disagreed with him. His teaching is reflected in the fourteen articles of the Franciscan Louis of Padua that were condemned in 1362 [*Chartularium universitatis Parisensis*, ed. H. Denifle and E. Chatelain, 4 v. (Paris 1889–97) 3:95–97].

Bibliography: A. COMBES, "Jean de Vippa, Jean de Rupa ou Jean de Ripa," *Archives d'histoire doctrinale et littéraire du moyen-âge* (Paris 1926—) 14 (1939) 253–290; "Présentation de J. de R.," *ibidem* 31 (1956) 145–242; *Jean Gerson, commentateur dionysien* (Études de philosophie médiévale 30; Paris 1940). P. VIGNAUX, "Dogme de l'Incarnation et métaphysique de la forme chez J. de R.," *Mélanges offerts à Étienne Gilson* (Toronto 1959) 661–672. Z. KALUZA, "La nature des écrits de Jean de Ripa" *Traditio* 43 (1983) 257–98. F. RUELLO, *La théologie naturelle de Jean de Ripa* (Paris 1992), bibliograpy; *La pensée de Jean de Ripa: Immensité divine et connaisance théologique* (Fribourg 1990); "Le projet théologique de Jean de Ripa" *Traditio* 49 (1994) 127–70.

[J. R. O'DONNELL]

JOHN OF RODINGTON

Franciscan scholastic; b. Rodington (Rodendon, Rodin, etc.) on the river Roden, *c.* 1290; d. Bedford, 1348? He may have entered the Friars Minor at Stamford, and he is listed as the fifty-sixth lector of the order at Oxford, where he had become master of theology; his regency probably dates between *c.* 1325 and 1328. There is some indication that he also taught at Paris [*Beiträge zur Geschichte der Philosophie und Theologie des Mittelalters* (Münster 1891—) supplement 3.2:1158], and it is known that he visited Basel in July of 1340. Sometime

thereafter he became the ninteenth minister provincial of the English Franciscans. It is affirmed without great evidence that he died in 1348, a victim of the Black Death; one list states he is buried at Bedford. Besides his *Sentences* he left a *quodlibet* "On Conscience," and may also have written one "On Faith." According to some, he was a follower of DUNS SCOTUS; yet in the question published by B. Nardi (from *In 1 sent.* 3.3), John upholds the earlier, Augustinian position on divine ILLUMINATION. Despite its title, "On Conscience" considers the whole basis of the moral life, citing AUGUSTINE as the primary authority, together with RICHARD OF SAINT-VICTOR and St. ANSELM OF CANTERBURY. John opposes, rather than accepts, WILLIAM OF OCKHAM. (*See* AUGUSTINIANISM; SCOTISM.)

Bibliography: E. GILSON, *History of Christian Philosophy* 762–63. J. LECHNER, "Die Quästionen des Sentenzenkommentars des Johannes von Rodington, O. F. M.," *Franziskanische Studien,* 22 (1935) 232–248; "Kleine Beiträge zur Geschichte des englischen Franziskaner-Schrifttums im Mittelalter," *Philosophisches Jahrbuch der Görres-Gesellschaft*, 53.3 (1940) 375. B. NARDI, *Soggetto e oggetto del conoscere nella filosofia antica e medievale* (2d ed. Rome 1952) 70–92. A. B. EMDEN, *A Biographical Register of the University of Oxford to A.D. 1500*, 3 v. (Oxford 1957–59) 3:1583–84.

[I. C. BRADY]

JOHN OF SAINT-SAMSON

Carmelite lay brother and mystic; b. Sens, France, Dec. 29, 1571; d. Rennes, Sept. 14, 1636. His name in the world was Jean du Moulin. He was born of well-to-do parents, but the mishandling of an eye disease when he was three years old left him blind for life. He received a good education, became acquainted with literature and history, and learned to understand and speak Latin. He also learned to play various musical instruments well. In 1589, his parents having died, he turned to Christ, and he began a wandering existence until 1597, when he took up residence in Paris. Apparently, he quickly became well acquainted with the works of many spiritual writers, especially of the mystics of the Low Countries and the Rhineland. About 1600 he came into contact with the Paris Carmelites of the Place Maubert, where he was able to fire a small circle of young religious with enthusiasm for the spiritual life and mysticism. In 1606 he joined the Carmelites at Dol in Brittany. He lived there for six years in great poverty and underwent various severe trials. Now spiritually mature, he entered the reform of Touraine under the name of John of Saint-Samson.

The leaders of this movement tested him thoroughly and minutely respecting his virtues and his spiritual reading, enlisting the help of doctors of the Sorbonne and of men of outstanding spiritual prestige. He stood the test with conspicuous success. From this time until his death, he assisted in the spiritual formation of numerous generations of novices, and he was the spiritual adviser of many others. Hence in the reform of Touraine, he exercised great influence, especially as a master of the spiritual life.

His writings exhibit a very complex character. They form the residue of conferences, instructions, and counselings, all reflecting his personal experience and prayer. Some he dictated himself, but more often they were committed to writing later, and subjects are not treated systematically and comprehensively. Moreover, John employed the difficult terminology of his favorite authors, Jan van RUYSBROECK and HENRY OF HERP. His works, comprising some 60 treatises and contemplations, along with a number of letters, were published in 1658 and 1659 by Donatien de Saint-Nicolas. Unfortunately, the editor recast the text and destroyed much of its vividness. A critical edition is needed.

According to John of Saint-Samson, the queen of the spiritual life is love, which is directed to Christ, the "Bien-Aimé." Love brings with it as an inseparable partner, detachment (humility, mortification, suffering, etc.) in all stages of the spiritual life. Love looks to the All of God, detachment to the nothingness of the creature. Love makes the soul steadily more contemplative; detachment causes it to turn steadily further away from the non-divine. Thus the spiritual life looks to nothingness and to the All at the same time. The soul reaches this state fully only in the hereafter, but some foretaste of it is experienced in the highest mystical grace. Then the soul knows itself as one with God, who is the All, and loses all psychological consciousness of created being and of itself.

Love and detachment govern the spiritual life. Love strives toward interior and exterior conformity to the divinity and the humanity of Christ. Moreover, the mind must live by this divine and human life, must lose itself completely in the Person of the God-Man, to the last degree of identification with Christ and in Christ. In this striving, the life of prayer, particularly aspirative prayer, occupies an important place. This frequently repeated, brief lifting of the mind and heart to God reaches its fullest scope only when the soul has progressed to some degree in the spiritual life. Love thereby becomes strengthened and purified, and recollection becomes more profound. As long as recollection is not complete, this kind of prayer retains its worth. In combination with detachment, John emphasizes two traditionally Carmelite values, solitude and silence, both of which are helpful in excluding all contact with the non-divine. Furthermore, John has many beautiful texts dealing with Marian mysticism.

The mystics of the Low Countries were very popular in France about 1600. From them, especially from Ruysbroeck and Herp, John took over, in addition to terminology, certain fundamental theological ideas: their teaching on the Trinity, exemplarism, the structure of the soul, recollection, and Trinitarian mysticism. John is one of the most important writers of the so-called abstract school, which assumes the possibility of a union of the soul with the Divine Nature, a union that is direct, without intermediacy or distinction (at least it is so experienced). Another characteristic of John's doctrine deserving of mention is the emphasis on self-annihilation (*anéantissement*) and pure love (*amour pur et désinteressé*). Both attain their zenith in the highest mystical grace; yet it appears from the texts that John did not assume or advocate a complete *anéantissement* or a complete *amour pur*.

Bibliography: DONATIEN DE S. NICOLAS, *Les Oeuvres spirituelles et mystiques du divin contemplatif F. Jean de S. Samson*, 2 v. (Rennes 1658–59). MATHURIN DE S. ANNE, *Vita, theoremata et opuscula insignis mystae venerabilis fratris Ioannis a S. Samsone* (Lyons 1654). S. M. BOUCHEREAUX, *La Réforme des Carmes en France et Jean de St.-Samson* (Paris 1950). P. W. JANSSEN, *Les Origines de la réforme des Carmes en France au XVIIe siècle* (The Hague 1963). SERNIN-MARIE DE S. ANDRÉ, *La vie du V. F. Jean de Saint-Samson, religieux carme de la Réforme de Touraine* (Paris 1881).

[P. W. JANSSEN]

JOHN OF ST. THOMAS

Thomistic theologian and philosopher; b. Portugal?, July 9, 1589; d. Saragossa, Spain, July 17, 1644.

John was the son of Peter Poinsot, nobleman secretary to Archduke Albert of Austria, cardinal and viceroy to Portugal, and later governor of the Netherlands under Philip II of Spain. With his brother Luis, who became a Trinitarian and taught theology at Coimbra from 1637 to 1655, John received his baccalaureate in arts at Coimbra in 1605. At the same Jesuit school, he began his theological course under two Trinitarians. After one year of study he moved to the Netherlands and attended Louvain where he studied under Thomas de Torres, a Spanish Dominican. He entered the Order of Preachers after he received his *Baccalaureus Biblicus*.

John of St. Thomas began his theological teaching in 1620, after spending several years as an *artium lector*. Having taught at Piacenza and Madrid, he was made associate professor at the University of Alcalá, where he lectured to classes larger than any then assembled in Spain. After about a decade he succeeded to the principal theological chair at Alcalá. During all this time he exercised with justice and charity the office of qualificator of the Supreme Council of the Spanish Inquisition. Despite accusations to the contrary, he seems not to have assisted the Jansenist heretics. However, he did refuse to allow the professors at Louvain to be condemned on insufficient evidence before Philip IV, who held civil jurisdiction over that university. For Philip, he performed the difficult function of confessor and adviser. He was at his king's side in battle, yet at the same time he corrected the text of his theological treatise on the *Gifts of the Holy Spirit.*

John of St. Thomas died either from fever, or from poison administered by courtiers envious of his influence for good over the king. His influence had been widespread through his efforts with the king and through letters and minor writings such as his *Compendium* of Catholic doctrine; this last was published first in Madrid in 1640, and after seven Spanish editions, translated into Italian, Latin, Gaelic, and Polish. John also wrote a directory for a good confession for Philip IV, and, just before he died, a treatise on preparation for a happy death.

His first major work, the *Cursus Philosophicus,* which was reprinted (at least in part) 16 times between 1631 and 1930, is in two sections, the first of which is available in English. That first section, including both formal and material logic, has been the basic source of much recent traditional and contemporary Catholic teaching on the art of logic. The second section, *Philosophia Naturalis,* accurately represents Thomistic philosophical teaching on corporeal being and psychology.

His *Cursus Theologicus,* published five times before the current Solesmes edition, follows the order of the questions, but not the articles, of the *Summa Theologiae.* After prefatory treatises on the nature of theology, its certitude against opponents, and its order, John of St. Thomas discussed basic theological problems in the light of the thinking of the post-Reformation period, although not that of the Counter Reformation. For the most part he was in doctrinal agreement with Capreolus and Cajetan (Tomaso de Vio), but he did advance some unique opinions, e.g., that the quintessential characteristic of the Deity is in knowing rather than in being. Some of his treatises, such as the *Gifts of the Holy Spirit* (New York 1951), rise above both classroom technique and commentary, and become autonomous presentations, classical in both content and style.

The style of John of St. Thomas is simple and clear. He preferred austere lucidity, and he made his own the words of St. Jerome: "I have written for the strong not the squeamish."

Bibliography: J. QUÉTIF and J. ÉCHARD, *Scriptores Ordinis Praedicatorum.* (Paris 1719–23) 2.2:538–539. H. HURTER, *Nomenclator literarius theologiae catholicae* (Innsbruck 1926) 3:915–916. J. M. RAMIREZ, *Dictionnaire de théologie catholique,* ed. A. VACANT et al., (Paris 1903—50) 8.1:803–808. D. RAMIREZ, "Vita Johannis a Sancto Thoma," in JOHN OF ST. THOMAS, *Cursus Theologicus,* ed. BENEDICTINES OF SOLESMES (Paris 1930–53) 1:xxxv–xliii. E. J. FURTON, *A Medieval Semiotic: Reference and Representation in John of St. Thomas' Theory of Signs* (New York 1995). John Poinsot issue, *The Thomist* 58 (1994): 543–615.

[D. HUGHES]

JOHN OF SALERNO, BL.

Also known as Giovanni (John) Guarna; Dominican preacher; b. Salerno, Italy, *c.* 1190; d. Florence, Aug. 9 (or Sept. 10), 1242. After receiving the habit from (St.) DOMINIC at Bologna, he was delegated by him to introduce the order into Florence. He founded the priory of Santa Maria Novella in that city and the monastery of the Dominican nuns at Ripoli. GREGORY IX commissioned him to preach against the PATARINES, a Manichaean sect, especially in Florence, and to reform the Diocese of Chiusi. PIUS VI beatified him in 1783.

Feast: Aug. 9.

Bibliography: *Acta Sanctorum,* Sept. 3:626–636. *Analecta Bollandiana* 7 (1888) 85–95. *Année Dominicaine,* 23 v. (Lyons 1883–1909) Aug. 1:477–485. G. GIERATHS, *Lexikon für Theologie und Kirche,* 10 v. (2d, new ed. Freiburg 1957–65) 5:1079.

[A. H. CAMACHO]

JOHN OF SALISBURY

Political theorist, historian, philosopher, humanist of the twelfth century renaissance, and Bishop of Chartres; b. Old Sarum, near Salisbury, *c.* 1115; d. Chartres, October 25, 1180.

Life. Though little is known about his background, John's writings contain a large amount of biographical material and historical information. After undergoing his formative training in England, John began his higher education at Mont-Saint-Geneviève in Paris in 1136 under Peter ABELARD, ROBERT OF MELUN, and a teacher known only as Alberic. In 1137 finding himself insufficiently prepared in grammar, he went to study under WILLIAM OF CONCHES, whom he calls the greatest grammarian since BERNARD OF CHARTRES. After three years of study, presumably at Chartres, John continued his education at Paris where he also tutored younger students. At some point he also studied under THIERRY OF CHARTRES, GILBERT DE LA PORRÉE, ROBERT PULLAN, and Adam of the Little Bridge. His writings mention some of his notable life-long friends and acquaintances, who included PETER OF CELLE, Thomas BECKET, and Nicholas Breakspear—later Pope ADRIAN IV.

In 1147 John returned to England, where he served in the household of THEOBALD Archbishop of Canterbury for the next twenty years. As the bishop's consultant, confidant, friend, secretary, and advisor, John became familiar with the most powerful men in the realm. He represented the Archbishop on the continent, even at Rome, where he was attached to the papal court. In 1148 he attended the Church Council of Reims, where BERNARD OF CLAIRVAUX and others challenged the orthodoxy of Gilbert Bishop of Poitiers. Because of his support for Theobald and later for Becket in their conflicts with King Henry II, John twice found himself in exile from England. He spent most of the seven years (1163–70) of the second exile at the Abbey Church of Saint Rèmi. John returned to England after his friend Thomas Becket was murdered (December 29, 1170) and remained there until his election as Bishop of Chartres in 1176. After being consecrated at Sens by Maurice Bishop of Paris, John returned to Chartres and took up the duties of the bishopric. He attended the Third Lateran Council of 1179. He died on October 25, 1180 and was buried at the abbey church of Notre Dame de Josaphat in Chartres.

Works and Thought. John read widely. He moves freely from the writings of the Church Fathers and Scripture to "pagan" poetry, and he uses any story or example that makes his point. Although John wrote both poetry and prose, the great bulk of his literary output lay in his letters, where he demonstrates the full range of his rhetorical skills. John's early works include his philosophical treatises. *Entheticus, De dogmatic philosophorum* also called the *Entheticus Major* (c. 1155), the *Metalogicon* (c. 1157), and the *Policraticus* (1157–59).

The first of these is a satire of princes and courtiers, in which contemporary people are compared to ancient poets and philosophers. It is a good example of the esteem that twelfth century humanists had for the ancient non-Christian world.

The *Metalogicon* is a book written against a clerk whom John calls Cornificius and his group of educational reformers, the Cornificians. Before turning his focus to logic, especially that of Aristotle (the Organon), John presents a defense of the traditional curriculum, the trivium (grammar, rhetoric, and logic). John argues against the Conifician program that sought to shorten the course of study so students could advance onto their careers. In this work John offers the reader a wealth of information about himself and the schools in the first half of the twelfth century. It includes accounts of his teachers, his courses of study, and recollections about the teaching style of his teachers' teachers, like Bernard of Chartres, who instructed William of Conches and Gilbert de la Porrée.

The *Policraticus* is a work of political philosophy in which John adds to what he had begun in the *Entheticus*, by offering a more sustained and organized discussion of the art of government. John desires to harmonize ancient political philosophy—most notably Aristotle—with Patristic and medieval Church teachings, and he creates an abstract framework for governing society and for making people better human beings and better Christians. Philosophy is presented as a tool to aid people in bringing about the reign of God. John outlines the traits, not only of good and bad princes, but of church officials as well. He chastises clerics and priests and presents a powerful call for reform of abuses within the Church. He calls tyranny—private, public, and ecclesiastical—an evil that we have the right to oppose, and he justifies the execution of tyrannical kings. Since the *Policraticus* was written during one of John's exiles from the court of Theobald, not surprisingly John attempts to analyze the relationship between Church and state. Interestingly, although John was loyal to Church authority in its struggle with the secular authority, he devises a plan of government that offers a large measure of autonomy to the state to govern without the oversight of ecclesiastical authority.

John's later writings include the *Historia pontificalis* (1163–64) in which John offers a mostly first-hand account of life in the papal court from 1148 to 1151. It presents to the reader a unique view of the pontiffs and the papal curia. John also wrote two biographies; *The Life of Saint Anslem* (1163), written at the request of Becket, and the *Life of Thomas Becket* (1171–73), which was composed shortly after the archbishop's martyrdom.

Bibliography: *Sources: Entheticus de Dogmatic philosophorum (Entheticus Major)*, ed. R. E. PEPIN, *Traditio* 31 (1975) 127–193. *Metalogicon*, ed. J. B. HALL and K. S. B. KEATS-ROHAN, (Turnhout, Brepols 1991). *Policraticus*, ed. C. C. J. WEBB, 2 vols., (Oxford 1909); English trans. C. NEDERMAN, (Cambridge 1990). *Life of Thomas Becket*, ed. J. C. ROBERTSON and J. B. SHEPPARD, *Materials for the History of Archbishop Thomas Becket, II Rerum Britannicarum medii aevi scriptores*, vol. 67 (1876) 301–322. *The Life of Saint Anslem, Patrologia Latina*, ed. J. P. MIGNE (Paris 1878–90) 199 1009–1040. *Historia Pontificalis*, ed. M. CHIBNALL (London 1956, Nachdruck 1986). *The Letters of John of Salisbury, Volume I, The Early Letters (1153–61)*, ed. W. J. MILLOR, H. E. BUTLER and C. N. L. BROOKE (London 1955). *The Letters of John of Salisbury, Volume II, The Later Letters (1163–1180)*, ed. W. J. MILLOR and C. N. L. BROOKE (Oxford 1979). Literature. K. L. FORHAN, "A Twelfth-Century 'Bureaucrat' and the Life of the Mind: The Political Thought of John of Salisbury," *Proceedings of the PMR Conference* (Villanova, Pennsylvania 10, 1985), 65–74. H. LEIBESCHÜTZ, *Medieval Humanism in the Life and Writings of John of Salisbury* (Nendeln, Lichtenstein 1968). C. C. J. WEBB, *John of Salisbury* (London 1932). M. WILKS, ed., *The Life and Times of John of Salisbury* (Oxford 1984). C. NEDERMAN, "Aristotelianism in John of Salisbury's Policraticus," in *Journal of the History of Philosophy, XXI*, 1983, 203–229; "Aristotelian Ethics and John of Salisbury's Letters," *Viator, XVIII*, 1987, 161–173. K. S. B. KEATS-ROHAN, "The Chronology of John of Salisbury's Studies in France," *Studi medievali, XXVIII*, 1987, 193–203.

[P. ELLARD]

JOHN OF SCYTHOPOLIS

Sixth century Byzantine priest and bishop of Scythopolis in Palestina II for a period probably after 536 but before about 548. He is not to be confused with John the Grammarian. A *scholastikos,* or lawyer, and a very learned man, John of Scythopolis composed several important theological works, all but one of which are lost: a work against the Monophysites, attacked before 512 by the strict Dyophysite, Basil of Cilicia, now lost; after about 518, a work against SEVERUS OF ANTIOCH, extant in a fragment defending the formula of two energies in Jesus Christ; and finally, the first long scholia on the works of PSEUDO-DIONYSIUS the Areopagite, later incorporated into the less extensive scholia of MAXIMUS the Confessor but preserved also in a Syriac translation. The scholia defend both the authenticity and orthodoxy of the corpus of Pseudo-Dionysius. John's Christology is Neochalcedonian, that is, defends the agreement of the formulas of the Council of CHALCEDON (451) with the Christology of CYRIL OF ALEXANDRIA.

Bibliography: H. U. VON BALTHASAR, "Das Scholienwerk des Johannes von Scythopolis." *Scholastik,* 15 (1940) 16–38. C. MOELLER, "Le Chalcédonisme et le néo-chalcétonisme," A. GRILLMEIER and H. BACHT, *Das Konzil von Chalkedon: Geschichte und Gegenwart,* 3 v. (Würzburg 1951–54) 1:674–676.

[D. B. EVANS]

JOHN OF SPAIN (HISPANUS)

Philosopher; d. Toledo, 1166. A converted Jew, he lived principally in Toledo and became bishop of Segovia in 1149, and then archbishop of Toledo. He is often confused with JOHN OF SEVILLE (HISPALENSIS). Although lacking originality in thought, he adroitly synthesized the ideas of others and made observations concerning differences among the schools from a historical viewpoint. Collaborating with his disciple DOMINIC GUNDISALVI, he promoted the spread of philosophy in Europe by translating Arab texts and elaborating original works. Among the fruits of this collaboration, the following are the most noteworthy: (1) *Tractatus de anima,* ed. J. T. Muckle, "The Treatise De anima of Dominicus Gundisalvus," manuscript 2 (1940); (2) *Liber de causis,* ed. from the Arab-Latin text by O. Bardenhewer, *Die pseudoaristotelische Schrift über das reine Gute bekannt unter dem Namen Liber de causis. . .* (Freiburg 1882); (3) *Liber de causis primis et secundis,* ed. R. De Vaux, in *Notes et textes sur l'avicennisme latin* (Paris 1934).

Bibliography: M. ALONSO, "Traducciones del árabe al latín por Juan Hispano (Ibn Dawud)," *Al-Andalus,* 17 (1952) 129–151; *Temas filosóficos medievales (Ibn Dāwād y Gundisalvo)* (Comillas 1959).

[D. CABANELAS]

JOHN OF STERNGASSEN

Dominican theologian and mystic; d. Cologne, after 1327. Often said to have been an immediate disciple of St. THOMAS AQUINAS, he was a contemporary of Meister ECKHART and a brother of Gerard, author of the popular *Pratum animarum.* As master in theology he taught in the priories at Strassburg and notably at Cologne, where he lived from 1310 onward. Some sermons and sayings survive in German. His principal work, a commentary on the *Sentences,* was discovered by M. GRABMANN. This work clearly shows him to be an avowed Thomist. He frequently refers to Aquinas as *doctor noster.* Like his brother and NICHOLAS OF STRASSBURG, he did not subscribe to the Neoplatonic tendencies of many of his German confreres, but followed closely the Aristotelianism of St. Thomas. Only on the question of the real distinction between essence and existence in creatures did he depart from authentic Thomistic teaching, preferring the intentional distinction proposed by HENRY OF GHENT.

Bibliography: J. QUÉTIF and J. ÉCHARD, *Scriptores Ordinis Praedicatorum,* 5 v. (Paris 1719–23) 1.1:700. C. TESTORE, *Enciclopedia filosofica,* 4 v. (Venice-Rome 1957) 2:769–770. M. GRABMANN, *Mittelalterliches Geistesleben,* 3 v. (Munich 1925–56) 1:392–400. F. STEGMÜLLER, *Repertorium commentariorum in Sententias Petri Lombardi,* 2 v. (Würzburg 1947) 1:244–245.

[J. J. PRZEZDZIECKI]

JOHN OF THE CROSS, ST.

Founder (with St. Teresa) of the Discalced Carmelites, Doctor of the Church, renowned for his poetry and writings in ascetical-mystical theology; b. Fontiveros, Spain, June 24, 1542; d. Ubeda, Dec. 14, 1591.

Life. Gonzalo de Yepes, John's father, was disowned by his wealthy family of silk merchants for marrying a humble silk weaver, Catalina Alvarez. When forced to adapt to surroundings of poverty and hard work, Gonzalo died young, shortly after the birth of John, his third son.

John received his elementary education in Medina del Campo at an institution for the children of the poor, in which he was also fed and clothed. Besides his elementary studies, he was introduced to various crafts through apprenticeships. At 17 he found work at a hospital in Medina and was also able to enroll in the Jesuit College, where he received solid training in the humanities.

In 1563, he entered the Carmelite Order in Medina and changed his name to Fray Juan de Santo Matía. After his novitiate and profession of vows, he went for studies to his order's College of San Andrés at Salamanca.

He enrolled at the university in Salamanca in the school of arts from 1564 to 1567 and in the theological course from 1567 to 1568. In the school of arts, he attended classes in philosophy; in theology, he probably heard the lectures of Mancio de Corpus Christi, OP, on the *Summa* of St. Thomas. An indication of Fray Juan's talents is evident in his appointment as prefect of studies while still a student. As prefect his duties were to teach class daily, defend public theses, and assist the regent master in resolving objections.

He was ordained in 1567, and while in Medina to sing his first Mass, he met Teresa of Avila, who had begun a reform within the order. She spoke to him of her plan to restore the Carmelite Primitive Rule for the friars as well as the nuns. Fray Juan, who had been longing for a life of deeper solitude and was thinking about transferring to the Carthusians, promised to adopt this life. With two others he made profession of the Carmelite Primitive Rule at Duruelo, Nov. 28, 1568, and changed his name to Fray John of the Cross. The new life in keeping with the Primitive Rule was austere and predominantly contemplative. But the active apostolate was not excluded; it consisted mainly of preaching and hearing confessions. The friars of this new reform wore sandals and were soon referred to as Discalced Carmelites.

At Duruelo Fray John was appointed subprior and novice master. Later he was named rector of a newly established house of studies in Alcalá. In the spring of 1571, Teresa was ordered to govern the Convent of the Incarnation and to reform its 130 nuns. Realizing the need of a prudent, learned, and holy confessor at the Incarnation, she obtained permission from the apostolic visitor to have Fray John as confessor.

While he was confessor there, the reform grew rapidly. But the attitude of the Carmelite Order toward the reform began to change mainly due to a conflict of jurisdiction. In 1575, in a chapter at Piacenza, it was determined to stop the expansion of the reform of the order.

On the night of Dec. 2, 1577, some Carmelites seized Fray John, took him to Toledo, and demanded a renunciation of the reform. He refused, maintaining that he had remained at the Incarnation by order of the nuncio. They declared him a rebel and imprisoned him. He lived nine months in a cell 6 feet wide and 10 feet long, with no light other than what came through a slit high up in the wall. During this imprisonment he composed some of his great poems. In August 1578, in a perhaps miraculous way, he escaped; eventually he journeyed to a monastery of Discalced in southern Spain.

The following years were given to administration: he was prior on several occasions, rector of the Carmelite College in Baeza, and vicar provincial of the southern province. In 1588 he was elected major definitor, becom-

St. John of the Cross.

ing a member of the reform's new governing body, headed by Father Doria.

During these years as superior he did most of his writing. He also devoted much time to the guidance of lay people as well as giving spiritual direction to the Carmelite friars and nuns.

His deep life of prayer is evident in the splendid descriptions of *The Spiritual Canticle* and *The Living Flame of Love*. He once admitted: "God communicates the mystery of the Trinity to this sinner in such a way that if His Majesty did not strengthen my weakness by a special help, it would be impossible for me to live."

Toward the end of his life, a controversy arose within the reform. Father Doria desired to abandon jurisdiction over the nuns founded by St. Teresa and also to expel Father Gratian, a favorite confessor of Teresa, from the reform. As a member of the governing body, Fray John of the Cross opposed Doria in both matters. For obvious reasons John was not elected to any office in the chapter of 1591. He was instead sent to a solitary monastery in southern Spain. While there, he heard news of the efforts being made to expel him also from the reform.

In mid-September, he noted a slight fever caused by an ulcerous inflammation of the leg. As the sickness grew worse, he was obliged to leave the solitude he so loved for the sake of medical attention. He chose to go to Ubeda rather than Baeza because "in Ubeda, nobody knows me." The prior of Ubeda received him unwillingly and complained of the added expense. On the night of December 13, John of the Cross died, repeating the words of the psalmist: "Into your hands, O Lord, I commend my spirit."

In 1592 his body was transferred to Segovia. He was beatified by Clement X in 1675, canonized by Benedict XIII in 1726, and declared a Doctor of the Church by Pius XI in 1926.

Writings. The saint's major treatises are *The Ascent of Mount Carmel—The Dark Night, The Spiritual Canticle,* and *The Living Flame of Love.* These writings have greatly influenced studies in spiritual theology. Pius XI, in proclaiming St. John of the Cross a Doctor of the Church, stated that they are rightly looked upon as a code and guide for the faithful soul endeavoring to embrace a more perfect life.

The Ascent of Mount Carmel—The Dark Night, beginning as a commentary on the poem *The Dark Night,* is a treatise on how to reach perfection (union with God). The poem, St. John says, refers to the path of perfection as a dark night for three reasons: the soul on this path must mortify its appetites, journey in faith, and receive God's communication. These reasons involve privation just as night involves a privation of light. The *Ascent* has three books and the *Dark Night,* two.

Book One of the *Ascent* discusses the mortification of all voluntary, inordinate appetites because these appetites are contrary to the perfect love of God. It frequently refers as well to the active night (or purification) of the senses, teaching that a man must acquire the habit of using his sense faculties only for God's honor and glory, out of love for Christ and in imitation of Him.

Books Two and Three of the *Ascent* treat the journey in faith, especially as it is in the active purification of the spirit. The soul must walk in the darkness of faith to reach union with God, and deprive itself of everything contradicting full adherence to God and to the law of Christ and of His Church. In the active night (or purification) of the spirit, a man must endeavor to purge his spiritual faculties through the theological virtues. The saint explains how each of these virtues purifies its respective faculty of whatever is not for God's glory, and unites it to God. In these two books he has especially in mind souls receiving contemplation; hence, in seeking to purify their spiritual faculties they must also turn aside in prayer from particular knowledge in order to receive through a general, loving attentiveness to God in faith the general, loving

knowledge of God, which is the meaning of contemplation.

The two books of the *Dark Night* describe how God purifies the soul passively. The discussion of God's communication is limited to that communication called purgative contemplation. Because this contemplation is dark and painful to the soul it is called a night.

Book One of the *Night* deals with the defects of beginners, the signs of initial contemplation, and the benefits of the passive purification of the senses. Book Two gives a vivid picture and analyses of the purgative contemplation that God infuses in the passive night of the spirit.

Through these active and passive purifications, the soul reaches union with God, ridding itself of everything out of conformity with His will. In this union, it habitually employs all its faculties, appetites, operations, and emotions in God, so that in its activity it resembles God; this union is called "the union of likeness."

The Spiritual Canticle comprises a poem (a loving colloquy between the soul and Christ) and its commentary. The stanzas of the poem are like outpourings of that love which arose from the abundant mystical knowledge communicated by God to the soul of the saint. They recount the history of his love of Christ and its forward movement, and mark the degrees and stages of his spiritual life. In its general plan the poem dwells on four main aspects of the life of divine love: (1) the anxious loving search for the Beloved; (2) the first encounter with Him; (3) perfect union with Him; (4) the desire for that perfect union that will be had in glory.

The chief elements of the commentary include: a general summary of the content of each stanza, a detailed explanation of each verse, and frequent doctrinal explanations of the thought.

The Living Flame of Love is also a poem with a commentary. This poem is the song of a soul that has reached a highly perfect love within the state of transformation. The state of transformation in God is the loftiest attainable on earth. It is equivalent to the state called "spiritual marriage" in the *Canticle* and "the divine union" in the *Ascent-Night:* a habitual union with God through the likeness of love. The four stanzas of the *Living Flame* refer to transient, intense actual unions (in contradiction to the habitual union) experienced by one advanced within this state of transformation.

The commentary, like that of the *Canticle,* gives a general summary of each stanza, a detailed explanation of each verse, and many doctrinal explanations.

In his major works, therefore, St. John of the Cross writes mainly of how one reaches perfection (or union with God), and of the life of divine union itself. In brief, this union is reached through the practice of the theological virtues, which purify the soul and unite it with God. The life of union with God is a life of perfect faith, hope, and charity.

His remaining writings include relatively few letters, various maxims and counsels, and about ten poems. These minor works deal chiefly with the same themes as the major works.

Feast: Nov. 24.

Bibliography: *The Collected Works of Saint John of the Cross,* trans. K. KAVANAUGH and O. RODRIGUEZ, rev. ed. (Washington, D.C. 1991). K. KAVANAUGH, *John of the Cross: Doctor of Light and Love* (New York 1999). C. THOMPSON, *The Poet and the Mystic: A Study of the Cantico Espiritual of San Juan de la Cruz* (Oxford 1977). R. HARDY, *Search for Nothing: The Life of John of the Cross* (New York 1982). I. MATTHEW, *The Impact of God: Soundings from St. John of the Cross* (London 1995). E. PACHO et al, *Introdccion a la lectura cde San Juan de la Cruz* (Salamanca 1991). S. PAYNE, *John of the Cross and the Cognitive Value of Mysticism: An Analysis of Sanjuanist Teaching and Its Philosophical Implications for Contemporary Discussions of Mystical Experience* (Dordrecht 1990). F. RUIZ et al, *God Speaks in the Night,* trans. K. KAVANAUGH (Washington, D.C. 1991, repr. 2000). G. TAVARD, *Poetry and Contemplation in Saint John of the Cross* (Athens, Ohio 1988). K. WOJTYŁA, *Faith according to St. John of the Cross,* trans. J. AUMANN (San Francisco 1981).

[K. KAVANAUGH]

JOHN OF THORESBY

Archbishop of York, chancellor of England; b. probably North Thoresby, Lindsey, England; d. Bishopthorpe, Yorkshire, Nov. 6, 1373. He studied at Oxford, where he was a bachelor of civil law by 1341. He was made bishop of SAINT DAVIDS in Wales by papal PROVISION in 1347, was translated to WORCESTER in 1351, and finally, was translated to York in 1352, though he was enthroned there only in 1354. In the royal service from 1330, he was a notary in the chancery (1336), master of the rolls (1341), keeper of the privy seal (1345–47), and chancellor of England (1349–56). He was one of the guardians of the kingdom during King EDWARD III's absence in France (1355). As archbishop he first settled the dispute between CANTERBURY and YORK as to the right to bear the cross: it was decided that each primate was to be allowed to bear his cross erect in the other's province (April 20, 1353). This was confirmed by the pope on Feb. 22, 1354, who directed at the same time that the archbishop of York should be styled "Primate of England" while the archbishop of Canterbury should be called "Primate of All England." Thoresby laid the foundation of the new choir in York Minster in 1360 and built the lady-chapel at the east end. By his direction a "catechism" or commentary in English on the Creed, the Lord's Prayer, and the Ten Commandments was drawn up (1357) for his parish priests by John de Traystek (or Garrick), a monk of St. Mary's, York.

Bibliography: JOHN OF THORESBY, *Lay Folks' Catechism,* ed. T. F. SIMMONS and H. E. NOLLOTH, Early English Text Society (London 1901) 118. W. A. PANTIN, *The English Church in the 14th Century* (Cambridge, Eng. 1955). A. B. EMDEN, *A Biographical Register of the University of Oxford to A.D. 1500,* 3 v. (Oxford 1957–59) 3:1863–64. M. MCKISACK, *The Fourteenth Century, 1307–1399* (Oxford 1959). C. L. KINGSFORD, *The Dictionary of National Biography From the Earliest Times to 1900,* 63 v. (London 1885–1900) 19:760–762.

[V. MUDROCH]

JOHN OF VALENCE, ST.

Bishop; b. diocese of Lyons, France; d. Valence, March 21, 1146. John became a priest and a canon of the Lyons cathedral. He resolved to enter CÎTEAUX but decided to substitute a pilgrimage to the shrine of SANTIAGO DE COMPOSTELA. On his return he had a dream in which Christ complained: "He ought to be Mine, not as a pilgrim, but as a dweller in My house." John then entered Cîteaux (1114) and in 1118 was sent to found the monastery of Bonnevaux (*Bona Vallis*) on the Loire, from which he established four daughter-houses. In 1141 John was elected bishop of Valence, where, while maintaining a rigorous way of life for himself, he actively alleviated the sufferings of widows, orphans, and the poor, and in other ways promoted social justice. His cultus was confirmed in 1901.

Feast: April 26.

Bibliography: See the life by John's contemporary and eyewitness, GIRARDUS, *Vita s. Johannis episcopi Valentinensis* in E. MARTÈNE and U. DURAND, *Thesaurus novus anecdotorum* 3:1693–1702. *Bibliotheca hagiographica latina antiquae et mediae aetatis* 4446. A. M. ZIMMERMANN, *Kalendarium Benedictinum: Die Heiligen und Seligen des Benediktinerorderns und seiner Zweige* 1:364–366.

[J. R. SOMMERFELDT]

JOHN OF VERCELLI, BL.

Dominican master general; b. Mosso Santa-Maria, Biella (prov. Vercelli), *c.* 1200; d. Montpellier, Nov. 30, 1283. As a secular priest, he studied and taught civil and Canon Law at Paris, and later at Vercelli. Received into the order by JORDAN OF SAXONY (*c.* 1230), he became prior of Vercelli (1245), vicar-general for Hungary (1255), prior of San Nicolo at Bologna (1256), provincial of Lombardy (1257–64), and finally sixth master general

(1264–83). As general he visited personally, and on foot, almost all the houses of the order, except those of Spain, urging perfect observance of the constitutions and traditions of the order; presided at 20 general charters and sent many encyclical letters [ed. *Monumenta Ordinis Fratrum Praedicatorum historica* 5 (1900) 63–129]; and built the famous *Arca* into which he translated the body of St. DOMINIC. Among the eminent Dominicans whom he consulted were Peter de Tarantaise (INNOCENT V), ALBERT THE GREAT, and THOMAS AQUINAS. He declined the patriarchate of Jerusalem (1278). Pius X approved his cult Sept. 7, 1803.

Feast: Dec. 1.

Bibliography: J. P. MOTHON, *Vita del b. Giovanni da Vercelli,* Ital. tr. L. CHINA (Vercelli 1903). D. A. MORTIER, *Histoire des maîtres généraux de l'ordre des Frères Prêcheurs,* 8 v. (Paris 1903–20) 2:1–170, G. D. D'OLDENICO, "Dei rapporti tra Giovanni Garbella da Vercelli sesto Maestro Generale dei Domenicani con Giovanni Gersen Abate di S. Stefano di Vercelli nei riguardi della Imitazione di Cristo," *Memorie Domenicane* 68 (1951) 201–211; "B. Giovanni Garbella da Vercelli sesto Maestro Generale Domenicano," *ibid.* 69 (1952) 259–265. A. P. FRUTAZ, *Lexikon für Theologie und Kirche,* ed. J. HOFER and K. RAHNER, 10 v. (2d, new ed. Freiburg 1957–65) 5:1094. J. L. BAUDOT and L. CHAUSSIN, *Vies des saints et des bienheueux selon l'ordre du calendrier avec l'historique des fêtes,* ed. by The Benedictines of Paris, 12 v. (Paris 1935–56) 12:48–51.

[S. L. FORTE]

JOHN OF WALDBY

Preacher, writer; d. shortly after 1372. John must be distinguished from his younger relative, archbishop ROBERT WALDBY OF YORK. He was ordained acolyte Dec. 16, 1334, and had received his D.Th. from Oxford by 1354, probably the year he became provincial of the AUGUSTINIANS in England. Five of his works are extant while at least nine others are lost. All were originally sermons but were changed into devotional reading texts. His collection of seven homilies on the *Our Father* treat the seven capital sins. In his collection of five sermons on the *Ave Maria* covering the principal feasts of Our Lady, he defends the Immaculate Conception. His name and ideas received wide circulation through the *Mirour of Life* of William of Nassington, who claimed to have based his work on John's *Our Father*, but there is little similarity to John's extant text. The collection of 12 sermons on the *Apostles Creed* was dedicated to Thomas de la Mare, future abbot of ST. ALBAN's, and prior of TYNEMOUTH PRIORY where the Austins taught Latin. John's *Novum opus dominicale* is extant; the *Misercordiae Domini* long assigned to Richard ROLLE DE HAMPOLE is now credited to him. His main sources were St. Bernard and especially Augustine, almost all of whose works were available to

John in the Austin library in York. John must be counted among the mystical writers of England.

Bibliography: A. B. EMDEN, *A Biographical Register of the University of Oxford to A.D. 1500,* 3 v. (Oxford 1957–59) 3:1957–58. B. HACKETT, *Sanctus Augustinus, vitae spiritualis magister,* 2 v. (Rome 1959) v. 2. A. O. GWYNN, *The English Austin Friars* (London 1940) 114–123. G. R. OWST, *Literature and Pulpit . . .* (New York 1961).

[F. ROTH]

JOHN OF WALES

Bolognese canonist of the classical period, of whom nothing is known other than that he was a native of Wales. He wrote an *apparatus* to the *Compilatio tertia antiqua* (1210–15), and put together and glossed what is known as the *Compilatio secunda antiqua* between 1210 and 1212 or 1215. This compilation is, in fact, the third in time of the five "received" collections of decretal letters prior to the great compilation commissioned by Gregory IX in 1234 (*see* QUINQUE COMPILATIONES ANTIQUAE), but it became known as the "second" or "intermediate" since it contained decretals after those in the *Breviarium,* or *Compilatio prima,* of Bernard of Pavia (1191–92) and before the official collection of Innocent III's decretals known as *Compilatio tertia* (1210). John's fellow exiles GILBERTUS ANGLICUS and ALANUS ANGLICUS had made collections of decretals to supplement *Compilation prima* before 1210; but although these collections had been superseded by Innocent's *Compilatio,* there was still a demand for the extra documents they contained. Of all the attempts made to arrange these documents of Gilbertus and Alanus systematically in a single collection, only that of John was accepted by the schools as *Compilatio secunda.* The center of his compilation depends on Gilbertus and Alanus; the system is that of the five books of the *Compilatio prima.* In all there are 106 titles divided into 331 chapters, embracing texts prior to the *Decretum* and many decretals of Clement III (1187–91) and Celestine III (1191–98), as well as decretals omitted from *Compilatio prima,* such as some of Alexander III and Lucius III [ed. A. Friedberg, *Quinque Compilationes Antiquae* (Leiden 1876) 66–104].

Bibliography: F. GILLMANN, "Johannes Galensis als Glossator . . . ," *Archiv für katholisches Kirchenrecht,* 105 (1925) 488–565. "Des Johannes Galensis Apparat zur Compilatio III in der Universitäts-bibliothek Erlangen," *ibidem* 118 (1938) 174–222. G. POST, "Additional Glosses of Johannes Galensis and Silvester in the Early Tancred or So-called Laurentius Apparatus to Compilatio III," *ibidem* 119 (1939) 364–375. A. VAN HOVE, *Commentarium Lovaniense in Codicem iuris canonici 1,* v.1–5 (Mechlin 1928—) 1:356, 444, 445. A. M. STICKLER, *Historia iuris canonici latini: v. 1, Historia fontium* (Turin 1950) 234. S. KUTTNER, "Bernardus Compostellanus antiquus," *Traditio* 1 (1943)

310. G. OESTERLÉ, *Dictionnaire de droit canonique,* ed. R. NAZ, 7 v. (Paris 1935–65) 6:105–106.

[L. E. BOYLE]

JOHN OF WALES

English theologian (known also as Waleys, Guallensis, de Wells); d. Paris, April 3?, 1285. He was a bachelor in theology before entering the FRANCISCANS and was made the sixth lector in the Oxford friary *c.* 1257–58. As a regent master in Paris (1281–83), he was known as *arbor vitae,* and was appointed (1282) one of the five masters in theology to examine the doctrines of PETER JOHN OLIVI. In the same year he was employed by archbishop JOHN PECKHAM to negotiate peace between the English and the Welsh. At his death he was respected and admired for his practical wisdom and piety. Among his writings, some of which were translated into Catalan and Italian and published as often as 12 times between 1470 and 1520, are: a *Communiloquium* of informal discourses; a *Compendiloquium,* which is a biographical history of philosophy; a *Breviloquium* of the four cardinal virtues as illustrated in the lives of great men of antiquity; a *Moniloquium* for the use of young preachers; a *Legiloquium* on the Ten Commandments; a *Summa de penitentia;* and a treatise on the seven deadly sins.

Bibliography: J. SWANSON, *John of Wales: A Study of the Works and Ideas of a Thirteenth-Century Friar* (Cambridge 1989). W. A. PANTIN, "John of Wales and Medieval Humanism," in *Medieval Studies Presented to Aubrey Gwynn* (Dublin 1961) 297–319.

[J. A. WEISHEIPL]

JOHN OF WALES

English Franciscan theologian, lector at the Oxford friary *c.* 1349; flourished 1349–78. He took part in the riot against the university chancellor in March 1349. He lectured for many years at the London Friary before receiving the degree of master by order of Urban V in January 1367, and again in September 1368. Having received the doctorate in theology, he was appointed papal chaplain in April 1372, and envoy of the king to the Roman Curia in September 1377. In 1378 his London hospice was robbed of horses, books, money, and plate, but these were returned by order of the king.

Bibliography: A. G. LITTLE, *The Grey Friars in Oxford* (Oxford 1891) 78, 175, 311–312. *The Dictionary of National Biography From the Earliest Times to 1900,* 63 v. (London 1885–1900) 20:1140. P. É. D'ALENÇON, *Dictionnaire de théologie catholique,* ed. A. VACANT et al. (Paris 1903–50) 8.1:763–764. W. LAMPEN, *Lexikon für Theologie und Kirche,* ed. J. HOFER and K. RAHNER, 10 v. (2d, new ed. Freiburg 1957–65) 5:1040–41. A. B. EMDEN, *A Bio-*

graphical Register of the University of Oxford to A.D. 1500, 3 v. (Oxford 1957–59) 3:2008.

[J. A. WEISHEIPL]

JOHN PARENTI

Franciscan minister general, 1227 to 1232; b. probably at Civita Castellana; b. and d. dates unknown. He was a Roman citizen and doctor of laws who joined the order soon after its establishment. In 1219 he was made provincial minister of Spain. His policies as minister general advanced the development of the Friars Minor into an educated and efficient order. Two notable events occurred in 1230: the translation of the relics of St. FRANCIS to the basilica in ASSISI and the acquisition of the bull *Quo elongati,* and GREGORY IX's exposition of the Rule. In 1232 Parenti resigned under pressure from the friars supporting ELIAS OF CORTONA.

Bibliography: THOMAS OF ECCLESTON, *Tractatus de adventu Fratrum Minorum in Angliam,* ed. A. G. LITTLE (2d ed. Manchester 1951). GRATIEN DE PARIS (E. BADIN), *Histoire . . . de l'ordre des frères mineurs au XIIIᵉ siècle* (Paris 1928). R. B. BROOKE, *Early Franciscan Government* (Cambridge, Eng. 1959).

[R. B. BROOKE]

JOHN PAUL I, POPE

Pontificate Aug. 26–Sept. 28, 1978; b. Albino Luciani, Oct. 17, 1912, Forno di Canale, Italy. He was born into a poor family. His father, a Socialist Party organizer, was at one point forced to migrate to Switzerland for work. After studies in the minor seminary at Feltre and the major seminary at Belluno, young Luciani was ordained a priest on July 7, 1935. Fr. Luciani earned a doctorate in theology at the Gregorianum in Rome in 1937, and served briefly as a parish priest at Forno di Canale and Agerdo. From 1937 to 1947 he was professor of theology, canon law, and history of sacred art at the Belluno seminary, for a time serving also as vice-rector. Popular as a preacher and a catechist, his book *Catechism Crumbs* went through several editions. While continuing to teach, he also became in 1947 pro-chancellor of the diocese, then named vicar-general. In 1958 he was named to the see of Vittorio-Veneto and ordained bishop by John XXIII at St. Peter's. He participated in VATICAN COUNCIL II, and his commitment to its spirit of renewal was expressed in a pastoral letter to his diocese in 1967, "Notes on the Council."

Bishop Luciani, named Patriarch of Venice in 1969, was created cardinal by Pope Paul VI at the consistory of March 5, 1973, with San Marco, Piazza Venezia, as his titular church. In 1976 he published *Illustrissimi,* an imaginative book of letters he addressed to famous literary and historical figures, including Jesus. In the conclave that met in August 1978 to elect a successor to Paul VI, Cardinal Luciani was elected the first day, on the fourth ballot. His election was surprising because of its swiftness and was welcomed because of his warmth and simplicity. He did away with the traditional papal coronation and was installed as the supreme pastor by receiving the archiepiscopal pallium on Sept. 3, 1978; the pope referred to the ceremony as the inauguration of his pastoral ministry. The program Pope John Paul outlined the day after his election proposed the following: to continue to put into effect the heritage of Vatican II; to preserve the integrity of church discipline in the lives of priests and faithful; to remind the entire Church that the first duty is evangelization; to continue the ecumenical thrust, without compromising doctrine but without hesitancy; to pursue with patience but firmness the serene and constructive dialogue of Paul VI for pastoral action; to support every laudable and worthy initiative for world peace.

The pope did not live to carry out this program; the Church and the world were shocked by his sudden death after barely a month in office. But John Paul I had long suffered from poor health, although illness was kept secret and not revealed until after his death. His physical condition and the pressures of the office, not a fanciful assassination plot, joined to bring his pontificate to an abrupt end. The "September Papacy" had brought fulfillment to the longing in people's hearts for a person and a leader who radiated joy, holiness, and simple goodness. His passing left the hope that the response to his brief pontificate would be remembered by his successors and by every pastor in the Church.

Bibliography: J. CORNWELL, *A Thief in the Night: The Mysterious Death of Pope John Paul I* (New York 1989). P. HEBBLETHWAITE, *The Year of Three Popes* (Cleveland 1979).

[T. C. O'BRIEN]

JOHN PAUL II, POPE

The first Slavic pope ever and the first non-Italian elected to the See of Peter in four and a half centuries, John Paul II's personality, pastoral method, and magisterium left indelible marks on world Catholicism. As the Council of Trent and the Counter-Reformation popes defined the Church's relationship to an emerging modern world, the Second VATICAN COUNCIL as authoritatively interpreted by John Paul II may well define Catholicism's relationship to whatever follows the "modern world" in the twenty-first century and beyond.

Early Life. Karol Józef Wojtyła was born on May 18, 1920 in Wadowice, a provincial Galician town near Kraków. His father, Karol, was a retired army officer; his mother, Emilia Kaczorowska, had previously borne another son, Edmund, and a daughter who died shortly after birth. Emilia Wojtyła died in 1929; young Karol, "Lolek" to his family and friends, was just finishing the third grade. Three and a half years later, his brother Edmund, a doctor, died of scarlet fever contracted from a patient. Lolek and his father lived by themselves for the next nine years. The son would later write that his father's piety, austerity, and interest in Polish literature and history constituted "my first seminary."

Wojtyła received an excellent classical elementary and secondary education in Wadowice, where he was a star student and a fine athlete and outdoorsman. During high school he immersed himself in the classics of Polish Romantic literature and became deeply involved in the theater under the influence of an avant-garde director, Mieczysław Kotlarczyk.

In 1938, Wojtyła moved with his father to Kraków to begin studies in Polish philology at the Jagiellonian University. His undergraduate career was interrupted by the Second World War. Shortly after conquering Poland, the Nazis closed the university and shipped many of its professors to the Sachsenhausen concentration camp. Polish cultural life went underground for the duration of the war.

The War Years. From 1939 to 1945, Wojtyła was heavily engaged in various forms of cultural resistance to the German Occupation of his homeland. He continued his studies when the Jagiellonian University reconstituted itself underground. With his mentor, Mieczysław Kotlarczyk, he founded the Rhapsodic Theatre, a clandestine troupe whose experimental productions of Polish classics helped keep alive the national memory the Nazis were determined to erase. He joined UNIA, a broad-based, clandestine resistance movement which included armed cadres and a unit devoted to saving Polish Jews from the Holocaust; UNIA worked to lay the cultural, social, and political foundations for a postwar Christian democratic Poland. Young Wojtyła also took an active role in his parish, leading one of the original Living Rosary groups of young men; here he encountered the lay mystic Jan Tyranowski, who introduced him to the writings of St. JOHN OF THE CROSS and St. TERESA OF AVILA. As all these activities were strictly banned by the Occupation, Wojtyła lived for more than five years at the daily risk of his life.

From 1940 to August of 1944, Wojtyła was also a manual laborer, first as a quarryman and blaster and later as a worker in the Solvay chemical factory on the outskirts of Kraków; the experience marked him for life. After his father's death in February 1941, Karol struggled to discern his vocation, torn between his love for the theater and the academic life and an increasing sense that he was being called to the priesthood. After a period of intense reflection (during which he explored the possibility of entering the Carmelites, only to be told that they were accepting no new novices during the war), it became clear to him that God intended him for the priesthood. The heroic archbishop of Kraków, Adam Stefan SAPIEHA, accepted him as a candidate and for two years Wojtyła lived a double life, continuing his manual work and his resistance activities while beginning his philosophy and theology studies in the clandestine seminary that Sapieha had created in defiance of the Occupation. In August 1944, when the Gestapo attempted to arrest the young men of Kraków to forestall a repetition of the Warsaw Uprising, Sapieha took his clandestine seminarians into his home, which functioned as an underground seminary until the Soviet Army drove the Germans from Kraków in January 1945. Daily life with the "prince-archbishop," as Sapieha (son of a noble Polish-Lithuanian family) was known, provided Wojtyła with his model of the priest and bishop as *defensor hominis,* the defender of the rights of his people.

The Young Priest. On Nov. 1, 1946, Cardinal Sapieha ordained Wojtyła to the priesthood and then sent him to Rome to obtain his doctorate in theology at the Pontifical University of St. Thomas Aquinas, the "Angelicum." After living at the Belgian College for two years and exploring the Belgian and French worker-priest experiments during vacations, Wojtyła completed a dissertation on *The Doctrine of Faith According to St. John of the Cross* under the direction of Reginald GARRIGOU-LAGRANGE, O.P. Garrigou's single criticism of the dissertation, that Wojtyła did not use the phrase "divine object" of God, indicated that the young Polish priest-scholar was beginning to move beyond the NEO-SCHOLASTICISM then dominating Catholic intellectual life.

After six months of service in the country parish at Niegowić, Father Wojtyła was assigned by Cardinal Sapieha to St. Florian's Church in Kraków, a parish frequented by Catholic intellectuals and professionals. His task was to form a new student chaplaincy for the students of the Jagiellonian University, the Kraków Academy of Fine Arts, and the Kraków Polytechnic: a front-line post in the struggle with Poland's new communist regime for the soul of Polish youth. Father Wojtyła became an immensely successful student chaplain and a pastoral pioneer. He encouraged his students to participate actively in the Mass; he formed choirs, directed theatrical groups,

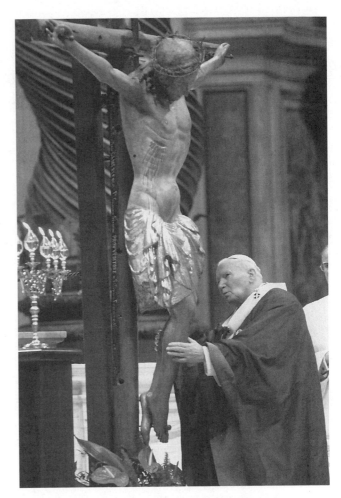

Pope John Paul II embraces the legs of Jesus Christ on a wooden crucifix during Day of Pardon Mass in St. Peter's Basilica, Vatican City, 2000. (AP/Wide World Photos)

and provided off-campus opportunities for the kind of philosophical and theological studies that were difficult or impossible in the Marxist-dominated academic environment of Kraków. Defying both clerical convention and communist restrictions on organizing youth groups, he took young men and women into the countryside for skiing, hiking, camping, and kayaking trips that were also opportunities for pastoral care. His young friends called him *Wujek,* "Uncle," a kind of Stalin-era *nom de guerre;* as the circle of students expanded, they came to call themselves Wojtyła's *Środowisko,* or "milieu." The friendships formed in these years endured throughout Wojtyła's life. As he formed young professionals into mature Christians, they were forming him into one of the most dynamic priests of his generation and igniting his interests in modern problems of sexual ethics, marriage, and family life.

Amidst this intense pastoral activity, Father Wojtyła wrote numerous essays and poems (the latter published

Pope John Paul II (right) with Tibet's exiled spiritual leader, Dalai Lama, at the Interreligious Assembly, St. Peter's Square, Vatican, Rome, Italy, 1999. (Arturo Mari/AP/Wide World Photos)

pseudonymously) for the independent Kraków Catholic newspaper *Tygodnik Powszechny* (Universal Weekly). He also composed a play, *Our God's Brother,* which explored the temptations of revolutionary violence through Kotlarczyk's "inner theater" dramatic method. The play was loosely based on the life of Albert CHMIELOWSKI, a Polish painter who founded a religious community dedicated to the homeless.

Scholar and Bishop. In 1953, Wojtyła completed his habilitation doctorate under instructions from Archbishop Eugeniusz Baziak. His dissertation explored the moral philosophy of the German phenomenologist, Max Scheler, and marked the beginning of Wojtyła's intellectual combination of THOMISM and PHENOMENOLOGY. One of the dissertation readers, Professor Stefan Swieżawski, encouraged the young philosopher to join the faculty of the Catholic University of Lublin (KUL), the only Catholic institution of higher education behind the iron curtain. Archbishop Baziak approved the arrangement and Karol Wojtyła was appointed instructor in philosophical ethics at KUL, where he would shortly rise to full professor. Wojtyła maintained his relationship to KUL for decades, participating in a distinctive philo-

sophical project in which the truth of reality and morals would be probed through a disciplined reflection on the human person. The KUL philosophers proposed to challenge Marxism and other distorted modern ideologies on their own intellectual ground: what was authentic human liberation? On this basis, Wojtyła would eventually develop a complex philosophical anthropology rooted in an analysis of human moral agency.

While commuting weekly to KUL, where he was a magnetic teacher, confessor, and counselor, Father Wojtyła continued his pastoral work in Kraków, adding a ministry to healthcare professionals to his ongoing work with students, and teaching social ethics in the Kraków seminary. In 1958, Pope Pius XII appointed him Titular Bishop of Ombi and Auxiliary Bishop of Kraków. Wojtyła was ordained bishop in Wawel Cathedral on Sept. 29, 1958, and added a new load of episcopal duties to his academic work at KUL and his pastoral activities. In conversation with his graduate students and other lay friends, Bishop Wojtyła prepared his first book, *Love and Responsibility,* in which he discussed sexual ethics and the beauty of sexual love with a frankness startling in its time and place.

The Second Vatican Council. When the Ante-Preparatory Commission appointed by Pope John XXIII wrote the world's bishops inviting suggestions for agenda of the Second Vatican Council, Bishop Wojtyła, the forty-year-old auxiliary of Kraków, responded with a philosophical essay urging that the council propose Christian humanism as the Church's response to the civilizational crisis of the mid-twentieth century. Defective ideas of the human person, Wojtyła argued, were at the root of a century of fear that had already produced two world wars, three totalitarian systems, unprecedented slaughter, and the greatest persecution of the Church in history. Reconstituting the Church as an evangelical movement proclaiming the truth about the human person was, in his judgment, the crucial intellectual and pastoral task of the Council—a vision congruent with John XXIII's historic opening address to the bishops on Oct. 11, 1962. That vision would guide Wojtyła's participation in and implementation of Vatican II for more than forty years.

Wojtyła attended all four periods of the Council, taking an increasingly active role. Entering the council as a very junior auxiliary bishop, he participated in the third and fourth periods (and the crucial intercession between the third and fourth periods) as the archbishop of Kraków, a post to which he was nominated by Pope Paul VI on Dec. 30, 1963. His formal interventions at the council were on themes he had stressed during his priestly ministry: the universal call to holiness, the baptismal dignity

A rally to celebrate the Jasna Góra Shrine's 600th anniversary. (©Bettmann/CORBIS)

of all Christians, the lay vocation in the world as an expression of the triple *munus* of Christ, and religious freedom as the first of human rights. Wojtyła's largest contribution to Vatican II came in helping draft and then defend *Gaudium et spes,* the "Pastoral Constitution on the Church in the Modern World." Work on this document during the early 1965 intercession and the fourth period of Vatican II brought Wojtyła into contact with important Western theologians, including Yves CONGAR and Henri de LUBAC, the latter becoming a good friend.

During the later periods of the council, Wojtyła began work on *Osoba y czyn* (Person and Act), his major philosophical work, which was intended to provide a secure philosophical foundation for the council's anthropology and teaching on religious freedom. In it, he utilized the resources of both a renewed Thomism and phenomenology.

Archbishop of Kraków. With the entire Polish Church, Wojtyła celebrated the millennium of Polish Christianity in 1966. In 1970, after completing a guidebook to the Vatican Council's 16 documents, *Sources of Renewal,* he began planning an extensive implementation of Vatican II, aimed at enabling his entire archdiocese to relive the conciliar experience. After two years of preparation, the Synod of Kraków began in May 1972 and was completed in June 1979. Five hundred discussion groups brought religious, clergy, and laity together to learn the council's teaching and apply it to the pastoral life of the archdiocese.

Named cardinal in 1967, Wojtyła's priorities as archbishop included a vigorous defense of religious freedom (which involved an ongoing battle with the communist regime over the construction of new churches and the public expression of Catholic faith); the development of the seminary and a faculty of theology to replace the Jagiellonian University faculty of theology, which had been closed by the regime in 1954; support for family life (including the establishment of an Institute of Family Life and diocesan-wide marriage-preparation programs); youth ministry; outreach to intellectuals; a broad-ranging ministry of charity; and extensive parish visitations. In carrying out these projects, Wojtyła exemplified the local bishop as pastor, teacher, and defender of the rights of his people.

Cardinal Wojtyła collaborated closely with Cardinal Stefan WYSZYŃSKI, Primate of Poland. The two men had different sensibilities, and Wojtyła's ecclesiology was more reflective of Vatican II than Wyszyński's. But the communist regime was completely unsuccessful in its ongoing attempts to drive a wedge between the two Polish cardinals, both of whom were determined to maintain the Church's unity against an implacable foe. Wojtyła also did what he could to support the hard-pressed Church in Czechslovakia; he and one of his auxiliary bishops clandestinely ordained priests for service underground in Czechoslovakia.

During his 14 years as archbishop of Kraków, Wojtyła became one of the best-known and most highly respected churchmen in the world. In addition to his work as a cardinal with various dicasteries of the Roman Curia, he participated in the meetings of the Synod of Bishops in 1969, 1971, 1974, and 1977, serving as *relator* of the 1974 synod on evangelization. Wojtyła was also elected by his episcopal peers as a member of the Synod Council. In 1968, a Kraków-based theological commission organized by Cardinal Wojtyła sent a lengthy memorandum on the Church's marital ethic to Pope Paul VI, who was then preparing the encyclical *Humanae vitae*; the memorandum proposed a thoroughly humanistic understanding of human sexuality as the foundation for the Church's sexual ethic and teaching on contraception.

Wojtyła visited the United States and Canada in 1969, and returned to the United States in 1976 for the International Eucharistic Congress. He also led the Polish delegation to the 1973 International Eucharistic Congress in Australia. In April 1974, he gave a major philosophical paper at the International Thomistic Congress in Italy, drawing the admiration of the German philosopher Joseph Pieper, among others. Paul VI invited Cardinal Wojtyła to deliver the 1976 Lenten retreat for the pope and his closest Curial collaborators; Wojtyła's retreat conferences were later published as a book, *Sign of Contradiction.*

The Year of Three Popes. Paul VI died on Aug. 6, 1978; Wojtyła traveled to Rome with Cardinal Wyszyński for the conclave that elected Albino Luciani of Venice as Pope John Paul I on August 25. On September 29, after celebrating his twentieth episcopal anniversary with friends, he received the news of John Paul I's death the previous night. Over the next several days,

Wojtyła wrote his last poem, "Stanisław," a meditation on the first martyr-bishop of Kraków. On October 8, at the church of St. Stanisław in Rome, he preached at a memorial Mass for John Paul I, citing Jn 21.15 and the capacity for a greater love of Christ as the prime requisite of Peter's successor.

On October 16, the second day of the second conclave of 1978, Karol Wojtyła was elected the 263rd successor to St. Peter. Taking the name John Paul II, he immediately broke precedent by receiving the first homage of the College of Cardinals standing, rather than sitting on a faldstool as tradition dictated. Like John Paul I, he declined coronation with the tiara. The homily at his installation Mass on October 22 was punctuated by the antiphon, "Be not afraid! Open the doors to Christ!"—a proclamation of robust faith and a call to a new Christian humanism that would characterize his pontificate for more than two decades.

JOHN PAUL II AND THE WORLD

Pope John Paul II had a greater impact on contemporary history than any pope in centuries. Yet his capacity to shape the world of his times was not mediated through the normal instruments of power. Rather, his papacy embodied a new, "post-Constantinian" approach to politics that was anticipated by the Second Vatican Council. The council's Declaration on Religious Freedom had broken the Church free from the embrace of political authority by asserting that the Catholic Church would no longer accept coercive state power as a buttress for its truth claims or a support for its evangelical mission. This new vision of the Church's relationship to the worlds of power—an ecclesiology of public engagement in which the Church sought to teach the nations, not rule the nations—had a decisive influence on the pontificate of John Paul II, and through him, on the history of the late twentieth century.

The Framework. The intellectual framework for John Paul II's public witness and diplomacy, and his distinctive view of the history of his times, may be found in his two addresses to the General Assembly of the United Nations.

In his first U.N. address on Oct. 2, 1979, John Paul characteristically began his analysis of world politics with the dignity of the human person: any legitimate politics, he proposed, "comes *from man,* is exercised *by man,* and is *for man.*" Human progress was to be measured, not only by material standards, but in the realm of the human spirit; that was why the 1948 Universal Declaration of Human Rights was a "milestone on the long and difficult path of the human race." Violations of human rights, not weapons stockpiles, were at the root of the world's division into Cold War camps and the primary threat to world peace. The cause of peace was thus the cause of human rights, and the first of human rights was religious freedom. To deny anyone the freedom to search for the truth, to adhere to it, and to express it publicly was profoundly dehumanizing, because the search for truth was of the very essence of humanity. Religious believers, agnostics, and atheists should be able to agree on this as a matter of shared humanistic conviction. Rightly understood, religious freedom was not a sectarian matter.

In this 1979 address, which challenged both communist regimes and the instrumental view of politics frequently encountered in the West, John Paul II explicitly committed the Catholic Church to the cause of human freedom and the defense of basic human rights as the primary goals of its engagement with world politics, a commitment that had been implicit in Pope John XXIII's 1963 encyclical PACEM IN TERRIS, and in Vatican II's "Declaration on Religious Freedom." Sixteen years later, on Oct. 8, 1995, the pope deepened that commitment in a second address to the U.N. General Assembly, which was marking its fiftieth anniversary in a world dramatically changed from 1979.

In that address, John Paul II vigorously defended the universality of human rights, a concept then being challenged by authoritarian regimes in Asia, by Islamic activists, and by some western intellectuals. The universal reach of the quest for freedom, the pope argued, was a key to understanding this quest as "one of the great dynamics of human history." Moreover, the global character of the human striving for freedom bore empirical witness that there is a universal human nature and a universal moral law; this moral logic built into human beings was the basis for a genuine dialogue between individuals, nations, and cultures. The "universal moral law written on the human heart is precisely [the] kind of 'grammar' which is needed" if the world was to engage in a serious conversation about the human future: if a "century of violent coercion," as the pope put it, was to be followed by a "century of persuasion." The world had yet to learn to "live with diversity"; yet difference was enriching, for "different cultures are but different ways of facing the question of the meaning of human existence." If humanity could learn "not [to] be afraid of man," then men and women would eventually come to see that "the tears of this century have prepared the ground for a new springtime of the human spirit."

The Challenge to Communism. As his 1979 U.N. address made clear, John Paul II intended to be a global public defender of human rights: he would challenge the material power of totalitarian and authoritarian regimes with the weapons of the human spirit and of culture, those products of man's spiritual nature that create national

identities. This "culture first" strategy of change was first tested in the pope's native east central Europe.

The Soviet authorities quickly discerned that the election of a Polish pope created a profound challenge to the post-Yalta order in Europe. As restive and persecuted Catholic minorities in Lithuania and Ukraine began to assert themselves more vigorously in the wake of John Paul's election, and as the pope ignited a revolution of conscience in Poland that spread throughout the Soviet external empire, the Kremlin's worst fears began to be realized.

John Paul II's epic nine-day pilgrimage to Poland in June 1979 was a primary, even decisive, catalyst in the decade-long process that led to the collapse of European communism ten years later. In some 40 homilies and addresses, John Paul returned to his Polish countrymen their authentic history and culture, giving them tools of resistance that communism could not blunt. One-third of the Polish nation saw the pope in person, and virtually everyone else saw him on television or heard him on radio. The visit, a moment of catharsis for a people oppressed since 1939, was also a moment of moral clarification in which tens of thousands of people made the personal decision to resist the communist culture of the lie and to take the "risk of freedom," as the pope would call it at the U.N. in 1995.

The results of that revolution of conscience came swiftly. Solidarity, a free-trade union movement that was also a de facto political opposition, was born in August 1980 in Gdańsk. In December 1980, the Soviet Union was on the verge of launching an invasion of Poland to crush the new independent union and execute its leaders. On Dec. 16, 1980, having been made aware of this threat through his own informants and through United States intelligence sources, John Paul II wrote an unprecedented personal letter to Soviet president Leonid Brezhnev, urging full respect for the integrity of Poland and the rights of its people and signaling his nonnegotiable support for Solidarity. It seemed to many observers that there was an obvious connection between the pope's relationship to Solidarity and the attempt on his life that took place on May 13, 1981 in St. Peter's Square, when he was shot by a professional assassin with links to Warsaw Pact intelligence services.

John Paul condemned the imposition of martial law in Poland on Dec. 13, 1981, which included the mass arrests of Solidarity leaders. During his 1983 pilgrimage to his homeland, he urged the Polish authorities to enter a dialogue with the Solidarity leadership as the precondition to national renewal. In 1987, as the Polish economy and regime slowly crumbled, John Paul returned to Poland to help lay the moral foundations for the free society whose emergence he anticipated, an expectation that was vindicated two years later when Solidarity swept the available seats in the first semi-free elections in Poland in decades.

During the 1980s, the pope urged Catholic leaders throughout east central Europe to be vigorous defenders of religious freedom and other basic human rights. His support had a marked effect on Cardinal Frantiśek Tomáśek of Prague, who was transformed from a rather mute figure into the grand old man of the democratic resistance to communism in Czechoslovakia. John Paul also inspired a revitalized Catholic resistance in Slovakia, where numerous Catholic clergy and laity emerged from underground to take leading roles in the resistance. As these events were unfolding, the Lithuanian Catholic Committee for the Defense of Believers Rights intensified its activity despite harsh Soviet repression, and activists for religious freedom became more vocal among the Greek Catholics of Ukraine. John Paul's apostolic letter of Dec. 31, 1980, *Egregiae Virtutis,* naming SS. CYRIL AND METHODIUS, apostles of the Slavs, as co-patrons of Europe was an unmistakable signal to Catholics throughout central and eastern Europe that the pope would bend every effort to re-link the two halves of Catholic Europe. The pope's increasing prestige as a global moral leader brought him into contact with Soviet dissidents in the mid-1980s. In 1985, human rights activist Elena Bonner left a secret meeting with John Paul in the Vatican in tears, saying "He's the most remarkable man I have ever met. He is all light. He is a source of light." Some three years later, John Paul counseled Bonner's husband, Soviet physicist and human rights campaigner Andrei Sakharov, as he tried to clarify his political responsibilities in the U.S.S.R.

Mikhail Gorbachev, the last leader of the Soviet Union, visited John Paul II in the Vatican on Dec. 1, 1989, symbolically marking the end of 70 years of fierce Soviet anti-Catholic propaganda and persecution. In the mid-1990s, Gorbachev publicly conceded what was obvious to the Catholic people of central and eastern Europe throughout the 1980s: that John Paul II had been the pivotal figure in the complex events that led to the collapse of communist regimes in 1989. That the pope did this not by issuing anathemas or by calling princes to repentance in the snow but by igniting a revolution of conscience that ultimately produced a nonviolent political revolution demonstrated in action the morally driven approach to world politics that he had outlined to the United Nations in 1979.

John Paul II was less successful in engaging communist regimes in Asia. More than two decades of efforts to open a line of dialogue with the People's Republic of China were largely frustrated, although diplomatic contacts between the Holy See and the PRC took place. In November 1983, the pope wrote a private letter to Chinese leader Deng Xiaoping, underscoring the Church's respect for Chinese culture and requesting a formal dialogue; Deng Xiaoping never answered and his successors persistently blocked the pope's efforts to visit any part of China. Holy See relations with Vietnam were also difficult during the pontificate, although some progress was made in the 1990s on the appointment of bishops.

The Challenge to Free Societies. John Paul II quickly discerned that the quest for human freedom had not been completely vindicated, much less secured, by the Revolution of 1989. On May 1, 1991, his third social encyclical, CENTESIMUS ANNUS, analyzed the dramatic events of the recent past while scouting the terrain of public life in the democracies of the future. Describing the free and virtuous society as an interlocking complex of three parts—democratic polity, free economy, public moral culture—the pope argued that the last was the foundation of the entire edifice. Democracy and the free economy were not machines that could run by themselves. Absent the disciplines and direction given by a vibrant public moral culture, democracy and the free economy would self-destruct; as the pope put it in perhaps the most controversial sentence of the encyclical, "a democracy without values easily turns into open or thinly disguised totalitarianism."

The totalitarianism John Paul had in mind was not a recrudescence of fascism or communism, but a gross utilitarianism which drove genuine moral discourse out of public life. A democracy without transcendent moral reference points would have to resolve its differences on the basis of power alone, the pope warned. And that would spell the end of democracy. In his 1992 encyclical VERITATIS SPLENDOR, the pope deepened his challenge to free societies, arguing that a mutual recognition of the obligations of the moral law was the most secure foundation on which to build democratic equality and to safeguard the rights of the less powerful. John Paul returned to this theme in the encyclical EVANGELIUM VITAE (1995), chastising democracies that erect moral wrongs into "rights" as "tyrant states." The democratic future was profoundly threatened, the pope wrote, if those whom the strong deemed weak, inconvenient, or burdensome could be put beyond the boundaries of legal protection through the legalization of abortion and euthanasia.

The urgency of these life issues for the democratic future was underlined by the World Conference on Population and Development, held in Cairo in September 1994. The U.S. government and several of its European allies, coordinating their efforts with the U.N. Fund for

Population Activities and the International Planned Parenthood Federation, intended that the Cairo conference would declare abortion as a basic human right on a par with religious freedom or freedom of speech. John Paul II, amidst the difficulties caused by a broken femur and hip-replacement surgery in April 1994, led a worldwide effort against this proposal, deploying all the assets of Vatican diplomacy while conducting a vigorous public campaign through the media in defense of the rights of women and the rights of the unborn. It was a striking example of the pope's enduring conviction that the word of truth, spoken clearly and forcefully enough, can bend the shape of history in humane directions. The Cairo conference refused to endorse the notion of abortion as a basic human right. Few doubted that it would have done so absent the intervention of John Paul II, exercising the power of moral witness.

John Paul II and Latin America. When John Paul was elected in 1978, Latin America was both the demographic center of world Catholicism and an arena of turmoil, confusion, and violence. During his first pilgrimage abroad in January of 1979, the pope spoke to the Third General Conference of the Conference of Latin American Bishops Conferences (CELAM) in Puebla, Mexico. In a lengthy address he criticized those aspects of LIBERATION THEOLOGY which portrayed Jesus as the "subversive man of Nazareth." A Church fully engaged in the struggle for justice in Latin America was an evangelical imperative; a partisan Church, the pope insisted, was an evangelical impossibility. These themes were later developed in two instructions from the Congregation for the Doctrine of the Faith, on "Certain Aspects of the Theology of Liberation" (1984) and on "Christian Freedom and Liberation" (1987). The pope's 1979 visit to Mexico, which had been governed as a secularist one-party state for decades, gave the local Church an unprecedented opportunity to express itself publicly. Tremendous popular support set in motion a process in which the Church was gradually freed to assume the kind of culture-forming role that John Paul II had urged at Puebla. In 2000, one-party rule in Mexico ended, and a new future for Mexican Catholicism opened up.

The pope's sharpest personal confrontation with certain distorted theologies of liberation came in Nicaragua in 1983. There, the Marxist Sandinista government (which included several priests), attempted to disrupt the pope's Mass in Managua and to drown out his homily. The pope's efforts were vindicated, however, in the democratic transitions in Central America of the late 1980s. Those transitions, effected through popular votes, put an end to the civil wars in Nicaragua and El Salvador, which had led to a crude persecution of the Church in the former

and the murder of the Archbishop Oscar ROMERO in the latter.

The problems of democratic transition also framed John Paul's important pilgrimage to Chile in 1987. Chile had been ruled for 14 years by a military dictatorship led by General Augusto Pinochet. Human rights abuses were widespread; the Chilean Church had responded by creating a Vicariate of Solidarity which sought to rebuild civil society in the country. Beginning in 1978, the Holy See, at John Paul II's initiative, had successfully mediated a border dispute between Chile and Argentina which threatened to result in war, and the pope had considerable credibility with both the Pinochet regime (which included many serious Catholics) and the Chilean democratic opposition. The pope and his Chilean collaborators designed a pilgrimage built around the theme of civil reconciliation. During the pilgrimage, John Paul defended the Church's role as promoter of human rights, signaling to both the government and the democratic opposition that a nonviolent transition to democracy was imperative. The pilgrimage was marred by a violent demonstration which threatened to disrupt the pope's Mass in Santiago; the pope refused to leave the venue and the Mass was completed, despite a riot in which the government seemed not entirely innocent. Eighteen months after the pilgrimage, a national plebiscite rejected continuing military rule and set Chile firmly on the road to democracy.

A year later, John Paul defied the efforts of Paraguayan dictator Alfredo Stroessner to block his meeting with that country's democratic dissidents. As in Chile, the pope stressed the moral cleansing of society as the foundation of building authentic democracy. Less than nine months after the pope's visit, General Stroessner was overthrown in a military coup, which led to general elections in 1989 and a democratic transition that the local Church supported throughout the 1990s, despite difficult political and economic conditions.

As with Poland in 1979, John Paul's epic pilgrimage to Cuba in January of 1998 sought to restore to a hard-pressed people their authentic history and culture. This reclamation of national culture would, it was hoped, create the foundations of civil society and enable Cuba to move beyond communist dictatorship and re-enter the community of the western hemisphere. The Castro regime was reasonably cooperative during the papal visit, which saw the first public display of the national Marian icon, Our Lady of Charity of El Cobre, in 40 years. In the years immediately following the papal pilgrimage, however, change in Cuba was much slower than either the Holy See or the local Church had anticipated.

In 1978, when John Paul II was elected pope, virtually all of Latin America was ruled by authoritarian regimes of one sort or another; economic stagnation was epidemic; and Central America was beset by chaos and war. Within two decades, Latin America had made a remarkable transition to democratic governments and free economies, although widespread poverty and some political instability remained. While the changes in Latin America had multiple causes, it was clear that John Paul's ability to inspire an engaged Church that was not a partisan Church had had a considerable impact on Latin American public life.

Papal Diplomacy Under John Paul II. Even as John Paul II explored the possibilities of a post-Constantinian papacy that engaged the world of power through moral witness and argument, the diplomacy of the Holy See continued. By 2000, the Holy See had formal diplomatic relations at the ambassadorial level with 172 countries, and was represented at the United Nations, the European Community, and a host of other international agencies and organizations. John Paul's annual New Year meetings with the diplomatic corps accredited to the Holy See provided an opportunity to drive home the message that all politics, including international politics, had an irreducible moral component.

A singularly dramatic accomplishment of John Paul II's diplomacy was the completion of a "Fundamental Agreement" between the Holy See and the State of Israel on Dec. 30, 1993; ambassadors were exchanged the following year. The Fundamental Agreement was the result of a complex 18-month-long negotiation in which the pope's personal commitment to full diplomatic relations between the Holy See and the Jewish state played a decisive role.

John Paul's diplomacy also suffered frustrations. Through both formal and informal means, the pope tried to help create conditions for a peaceful resolution of the crisis of Yugoslavia. These efforts did not meet with notable success. John Paul was determined to go to Sarajevo as a witness for peace as the city was being destroyed by shelling, but a scheduled 1994 visit was canceled because of the threat of violence against pilgrims. When the pope did manage to get to shattered Sarajevo in 1997, officials discovered and defused a bomb, evidently intended to destroy his motorcade, along the road into the city.

In 1982, the pope was confronted by a diplomatic conundrum: could he make a long-planned pilgrimage to Great Britain during the Falklands/Malvinas War, which was being fought against Argentina, a Catholic country? John Paul's solution was instinctively pastoral: to fulfill his commitment to Great Britain, to go on pilgrimage to Argentina the following month, and to urge peace and reconciliation in both countries. The 1989–90 Gulf crisis was a trying time for the pope, who for months urged a

negotiated diplomatic resolution to Iraq's invasion and subjugation of Kuwait. In 1992, addressing the U.N. Food and Agricultural Organization in Rome, John Paul spoke of a duty of humanitarian intervention in situations where genocide was impending or underway; the pope did not specify on whom this duty fell or how it was to be carried out. As with the Gulf War, the question of a papal development of the Church's traditional just-war doctrine was, evidently, being left for a future pontificate. In 1979 in Ireland, in Latin America throughout the 1980s, and in 1985–86 in the Philippines, the pope had urged a kind of "preferential option for nonviolence" in resolving sectarian conflict and in effecting democratic transitions. The relationship of this option to the Church's traditional approach to interstate conflict, in which the restoration of justice was the primary imperative, was also a topic for future theological development.

Throughout his pontificate, John Paul II, whose contempt for the Yalta division of Europe into Cold War camps dated back to the late 1940s, spoke frequently about the urgency of rebuilding a Europe that could breathe with both its "lungs," east and west. This personal passion matched the Holy See's longstanding commitment to European unification through such instruments as the Common Market and the European Union [EU]. In later years, however, the pope sharply criticized the tendency of EU bureaucracies and the European Parliament to enshrine a host of dubious lifestyle rights in European law; the Holy See also grew increasingly concerned about the way in which issues of abortion, euthanasia, and the technological means of human reproduction were being resolved in western European states. These concerns raised questions about the future of the Holy See's commitment to European integration.

John Paul II also dealt with the worlds of power through an unprecedented informal diplomacy. With the pope's encouragement, although without any formal linkage to the Holy See, the SANT' EGIDIO Community, a Rome-based Catholic renewal movement, successfully mediated the Mozambican civil war in a series of negotiations during the 1990s. Similar Sant' Egidio efforts took place in Algeria and the Balkans, although without measurable success. John Paul II also sent Cardinal Roger Etchegaray, the French president of the Pontifical Council for Justice and Peace, as a personal, unofficial representative to conflict situations in Africa, Latin America, Asia and Oceania. The cardinal described this informal diplomacy, aimed at getting conflicted parties in conversation with one another, as a "politics of presence" that was a "reinforcement and extension of the spiritual mission" of the pope.

THE POPE AND THE CHURCH

Immediately after his election, John Paul announced that the program of his pontificate would be the full implementation of the Second Vatican Council. Like Pope John XXIII, John Paul II believed that the council was a "new Pentecost" in which the Holy Spirit was preparing the Church for a "springtime of evangelization" in its third millennium. That conviction set the framework for the pope's governance of the Church, his magisterium, and his distinctive papal style.

An Evangelical Church. The most visible expression of John Paul's vision of the Church as a dynamic evangelical movement proposing to the world the truth of the human condition was his wide-ranging program of pastoral pilgrimages, of which there were 94 between January 1979 and June 2001. The pope took seriously the injunction of Luke 22.32, that Peter's distinctive mission was to strengthen his brethren in the faith. Interpreting this mandate literally while marrying it to the modern transportation and communications revolutions, John Paul II traveled to virtually every corner of the planet. His global evangelism drew the largest crowd in human history in Manila in January 1995, and as the pontificate unfolded, statisticians suggested that John Paul II had been seen in person by more human beings than any man who ever lived. The impact of this new style of papal witness was multiplied by the broadcast media, as radio and television brought the Successor of Peter into billions of homes.

In line with his evangelical priorities, John Paul moved quickly to address one of the most deeply contentious issues in post-conciliar Catholicism, devoting 129 general audience addresses between 1979 and 1984 to an innovative "theology of the body" which sought to explain the Church's sexual ethic (and meet the challenge of the sexual revolution) on the basis of a humanistic reading of human sexuality and a fresh analysis of biblical texts. In a similarly conflicted area, John Paul worked to open a new dialogue between the Church and natural science. In 1981, he established a papal commission to re-examine the Galileo case; the commission report, issued in 1992 and endorsed by the pope, openly admitted that the Church had made an "objective error" in the Galileo controversy.

The pope's commitment to Vatican II teaching on the "universal call to holiness" impelled him to restructure the process of beatification and canonization in 1983. The apostolic constitution *Divinus Magister Perfectionis* shifted the paradigm of the process from legal procedure to scholarly historical investigation. The result was an unprecedented number of beatifications and canonizations during the pontificate, as the pope sought to give public expression to the Church's teaching that sanctity was available to everyone.

WORLD YOUTH DAYS, which drew millions of young people from all over the planet for a week of catechesis and liturgical celebrations with the Bishop of Rome, were another John Paul II innovation and quickly became a signature event in the pontificate. The first international WYD, held in Buenos Aires in 1987, was followed by similar meetings in Santiago de Compostela (1989), Częstochowa (1991), Denver (1993), Manila (1995), Paris (1997), and Rome (2000). The Rome WYD, which drew two million young people to its closing Mass, was the largest pilgrimage in European history. The pope's magnetic attraction for the young, which involved a profound challenge to lead lives of moral heroism, continued even as he aged.

John Paul's leadership in more traditional Church events should also be understood in an evangelical and conciliar framework. The 16 general, regional, and local Synods of Bishops he summoned and attended, like the post-synodal apostolic exhortations he wrote as a reflection on the deliberations of a Synod general assembly, were intended to provide interpretive keys to the renewal of Catholic life as proposed by Vatican II. The Extraordinary Synod of 1985, marking the twentieth anniversary of the Council, was of particular importance for its stress on the Council's COMMUNIO ecclesiology, its critique of political and ideological interpretations of Vatican II., and its commissioning of the Catechism of the Catholic Church. Of special note as well were the Synods (and subsequent apostolic exhortations) on the family, the priesthood, the sacrament of reconciliation, the lay vocation in the world, the priesthood, and the consecrated life. While few, including the pope, were entirely satisfied with the Synod process, the pontificate unmistakably established the SYNOD OF BISHOPS as a permanent feature of Catholic life.

John Paul's was also one of the most important legislative pontificates in history. Following the intentions of John XXIII, he completed a thorough reform of canon law, issuing the new Code of CANON LAW for Latin-rite Catholicism in 1983. The apostolic constitution promulgating the new code, *Sacrae disciplinae leges,* stressed its incorporation of the ecclesiology of Vatican II. A new Code of Oriental Canon Law for eastern Catholic Churches was issued in 1990. In addition to these legislative accomplishments, the pope also reorganized the Roman Curia to reflect the council's concerns in the 1988 apostolic constitution *Pastor Bonus.* In 1996, he issued *Universi Dominici Gregis,* which reformed the process for the election of a pope by suppressing election by acclamation and delegation, stressing the personal responsibility of the cardinal-electors, and providing for election by simple majority after two weeks of inconclusive ballots under the traditional two-thirds majority rule.

In another apostolic constitution, *EX CORDE ECCLESIAE* (1990), John Paul sought to strengthen the Catholic identity of all Catholic institutions of higher education, as he had done in *SAPIENTIA CHRISTIANA,* a 1979 apostolic constitution regulating pontifical universities and pontifical faculties in the sacred sciences. *Ex Corde Ecclesiae* caused considerable controversy in the United States, even as the pope changed the terms of debate over the distinctive character of Catholic colleges and universities. *Sapientia Chistiana* and *Ex Corde Ecclesiae* were important moments in the pope's continuous effort to strengthen Catholic intellectual life as an integral part of what he came to call, in the 1990s, the "new evangelization," which put considerable emphasis on the evangelization of culture.

The pope's reform of Vatican press relations was also evangelically inspired. John Paul II recognized the crucial importance of the media. His 1984 decision to appoint Joaquín Navarro–Valls, a Spanish layman and veteran foreign correspondent, as papal spokesman and head of the Holy See Press Office helped move the Vatican into the modern communications age. An online Vatican Information Service began transmitting daily bulletins in 1991. According to Navarro, John Paul II saw the "dialectic with world opinion" available through the media as an instrument for reforming the Church and shaping the world political agenda, as in the months before the Cairo world population conference in 1994.

The multiple strands of John Paul's effort to get the Church to experience itself as a vibrant evangelical movement were woven into a complex tapestry during the Great Jubilee of 2000, which the Pope frequently described as the interpretive key to his pontificate. After opening the Holy Door of St. Peter's on Christmas Eve, 1999, John Paul undertook an extensive biblical pilgrimage in several phases to Mount Sinai, the Holy Land, Athens, and Damascus. The Iraqi government made it impossible for the pope to begin this pilgrimage in Ur, home of Abraham, the Church's "father in faith," so John Paul celebrated a day of recollection in honor of Abraham in the Vatican audience hall. Symbolizing the universal call to holiness, there were special jubilee days in Rome for consecrated religious men and women, the sick, health-care workers, artists, permanent deacons, the Roman Curia, craftsmen, priests, scientists, migrants and itinerant people, journalists, prisoners, young people, intellectuals, the elderly, bishops, families, athletes, parliamentarians and government workers, the world of agriculture, the armed forces and police, laity, the dis-

abled, and the entertainment world. In June 2000, Rome hosted the forty-seventh International Eucharistic Congress. On the First Sunday of Lent during the jubilee year, the pope, presiding at a Mass in St. Peter's Basilica, publicly asked God's forgiveness for the sins Christians had committed against the Gospel and against their neighbors in the first two millennia—a "cleansing of the Church's conscience" which John Paul believed essential to preparing for the twenty-first century springtime of evangelization. The Christian witnesses of the twentieth century, the greatest century of persecution in history, were honored at a special ecumenical service at the Roman Coliseum on May 7. During the Jubilee, the pope beatified a host of martyrs (from Brazil, the Philippines, Poland, Thailand, Mexico, and Vietnam), two popes (Pius IX and John XXIII), and two of the child visionaries of Fatíma (Francisco and Jacinta Marto). The first saint canonized during the jubilee was Sister Faustina KOWALSKA, the Polish mystic whose devotion to the merciful Christ had spread throughout the world. In October 2000, John Paul canonized 120 martyrs of China, the Philadelphia heiress and foundress Katherine DREXEL, and Josephine BAKHITA, a former Sudanese slave.

The Great Jubilee of 2000, which drew an estimated twenty-seven million pilgrims to Rome, was solemnly closed on Jan. 6, 2001. As John Paul had intended, it had been a celebration of the evangelical future, not simply a commemoration of the past.

Magisterium. Unlike previous councils, Vatican II had provided no interpretive keys to its teaching through doctrinal definitions, creeds, canons, or anathemas. The extensive magisterium of John Paul II, which marks his as one of the great teaching pontificates in history, offered the Church keys for the authentic interpretation of Vatican II and its implementation.

In addition to issuing seven apostolic constitutions, John Paul II wrote thirteen encyclicals and ten postsynodal apostolic exhortations, touching virtually every major issue on the post-Vatican II Catholic agenda. His inaugural encyclical, *REDEMPTOR HOMINIS*, was the first encyclical ever on Christian anthropology and offered the Church and the world a set of program notes for the pontificate to follow; *Redemptor hominis* was also the first panel in a Trinitarian triptych of encyclicals that came to include *DIVES IN MISERICORDIA* and *DOMINUM ET VIVICANTEM*. Two encyclicals, *Veritatis splendor* and *FIDES ET RATIO*, defended the human capacity to know the truth of things, including the moral truth of things. The pope's social doctrine was developed in three encyclicals: *LABOREM EXERCENS, SOLLICITUDO REI SOCIALIS*, and *Centesimus annus. UT UNUM SINT* was the first encyclical ever devoted entirely to ecumenism. *REDEMPTORIS MISSIO* recommitted the Church to the mission *ad gentes* in a distinctively dialogical mode: "The Church proposes; she imposes nothing." *Evangelium vitae* was a passionate defense of the right to life from conception until natural death. Other encyclicals honored SS. Cyril and Methodius (*SLAVORUM APOSTOLI*) and the Blessed Virgin at the end of the 1986-87 Marian Year (*REDEMPTORIS MATER*).

Following the lead of Paul VI in *Evangelium nuntiandi*, John Paul sought to complete the work of general assemblies of the Synods of Bishops with post-synodal apostolic exhortations addressing key issues of the post-Vatican II period: *Catechesi tradendae* (catechetics), *Familiaris consortio* (marriage and family life), *Reconciliatio et Paenitentia* (the sacrament of penance), *Christifideles laici* (the lay vocation in the world), *Pastores dabo vobis* (the ministerial priesthood and priestly formation), and *Vita consecrata* (consecrated life). John Paul also issued apostolic exhortations after the pre-jubilee regional synods for Africa, Asia, North and South America.

The Pope also wrote a large number of apostolic letters, among the most important of which were *Dominicae cenae* (the Eucharist), *Salvifici doloris* (redemptive suffering), *Euntes in mundum* (the millennium of Christianity among the eastern Slavs), *Mulieris dignitatem* (women in the modern world), *TERTIO MILLENNIO ADVENIENTE* (announcing the Great Jubilee of 2000), *Dies Domini* (on sanctifying time and the Lord's Day), and *Novo millennio ineunte* (concluding the Great Jubilee of 2000). Among some Catholics in North America and western Europe, the apostolic letter *Ordinatio sacerdotalis*, which reaffirmed that the Church was not authorized to ordain women to the ministerial priesthood, caused controversy.

John Paul II also devised new forms of the papal magisterium, writing extensive letters to families, children, artists, and the elderly. John Paul's theology of the body should also be considered among the most important developments in his papal magisterium.

Ecumenism and Interreligious Dialogue. With the pontificate of John Paul II, the Catholic Church entered fully into the ecumenical movement, and in doing so reconfigured the world movement for Christian unity.

The pope laid particular emphasis on ecumenism with the Christian East, in the hope that the wounds of a millennium of Christian division (formally opened in 1054), could be healed on the threshold of the third millennium of Christian history. While the pope did not bring that great dream of ecclesial reconciliation to fruition, in part because of the reluctance (and, in some cases, hostility) of Orthodox leaders and theologians, he did advance Catholic ecumenism *ad orientem* in numerous ways: visiting Ecumenical Patriarch Dimitrios I at the

Phanar in 1979, hosting Dimitrios in Rome in 1987 and his successor, Bartholomew I, in 1995; through his pilgrimages to Romania (1999), the Holy Land (2000), Greece and Damascus (2001) and Ukraine (2001); and in the encyclical *Ut unum sint,* which seemed to propose a return to the status quo before 1054. The difficulties of dialogue with Orthodoxy were amplified by the post-communist resurgence of the once-heavily-persecuted eastern Catholic Churches in the former Soviet Union and its satellites.

More tangible progress was made during the pontificate with the Oriental Orthodox churches (sometimes known as MONOPHYSITE or pre-Chalcedonian churches), as the pope signed or re-affirmed common Christological declarations with the Armenian Apostolic Church, the Coptic Orthodox Church, and the Syrian Orthodox Church, and also with the Assyrian Church of the East. John Paul II formed a close spiritual friendship with the Armenian Catolicos, Karekan I Sarkissian, who died in 1999.

John Paul also bent considerable efforts toward closing breaches in western Christianity dating back to the REFORMATION. At the pope's insistence, a meeting with other Christian leaders and an ecumenical prayer service were part of virtually every papal pilgrimage throughout the world. The once-promising Anglican-Roman Catholic dialogue ran into considerable difficulties, however, when parts of the Anglican Communion decided to admit women to the ministerial priesthood, a decision which raised questions about Anglican understandings of apostolicity and sacramentality. The pontificate saw some advances in the Lutheran-Catholic dialogue, including a historic "Joint Declaration on Justification by Faith" in 1999, but without the cause of full ecclesial communion being much advanced. John Paul's global evangelism and his vigorous defense of the right to life created new possibilities for ecumenical dialogue with evangelical and pentecostal Protestantism, even as the Catholic insistence on the centrality of the life issues to contemporary Christian witness created further ecumenical difficulties with liberal Protestant communities.

In 1995, the general secretary of the World Council of Church told a Roman audience that a new ecumenical paradigm was needed, in which the various Christian communities would abandon the quest for a common creed, a common baptism, and a common Eucharist while working together on issues of the environment, peace, and world poverty. Thus John Paul's insistence that Christian unity must be unity in the truth that Christ bequeathed his Church made the Catholic Church the principal institutional defender of the classic goals that had launched the modern ecumenical movement in 1910.

Building on Vatican II's declaration *Nostra aetatae,* Catholic-Jewish relations entered a new phase with the pontificate of John Paul II. The pope's historic 1986 visit to the Synagogue of Rome, his steady condemnations of the sin of anti-Semitism, the establishment of diplomatic relations between the Holy See and the State of Israel, and the pope's Holy Land pilgrimage laid the foundation for what some observers saw as a new, theologically oriented Catholic-Jewish dialogue in the twenty-first century.

In 1985, at the invitation of King Hassan II, John Paul addressed a large gathering of Muslim young people in Casablanca. During his jubilee pilgrimage to Damascus in 2001, he became the first pope to visit a mosque. The dialogue with Islam, however, was made more difficult because of Muslim persecution of Christians in the Holy Land, Asia, and Africa, which the pope sharply challenged during a visit to Sudan in 1993. The pope also met on several occasions with the Dalai Lama, and was enthusiastically received by Hindus in India in 1986.

On Oct. 27, 1986, the pope gathered several dozen world religious leaders at Assisi for an unprecedented World Day of Prayer for Peace. "Being together to pray," John Paul insisted, was not syncretism. Criticism of the event from some curial elements continued long afterwards.

Internationalizing the Curia. The pope drew his closest collaborators in Rome from throughout the world Church, accelerating the internationalization of the Roman Curia that had begun under Paul VI. Among the pope's closest advisers were a German (Cardinal Joseph Ratzinger, prefect of the Congregation for the Doctrine of the Faith from November 1981), an African (Cardinal Bernardin Gantin of Benin, prefect of the Congregation for Bishops from 1984 to 1998), a Slovak (Cardinal Jozef Tomko, general secretary of the Synod of Bishops from 1979 to 1985, and prefect of the Congregation for the Evangelization of Peoples [Propaganda Fidei] from 1985 until 2001). A Spaniard (Eduardo Martínez Somalo), an Australian, (Edward Cassidy), an Italian (Giovanni Battista Re), and an Argentine (Leonardo Sandri) served the Pope in the crucial post of Sostituto (Deputy for Ordinary Affairs of the Secretariat of State), in effect the papal chief-of-staff. In 1998, an American, James Harvey, was named Prefect of the Papal Household, and by 2001, 19 of the 24 heads of Roman dicasteries were non-Italians.

After Paul VI's Secretary of State, the Frenchman Jean Villot, died in 1979, two Italian papal diplomats were appointed to this most senior post in the Roman Curia: Agostino CASAROLI (1979–1990) and Angelo Sodano (from 1990). The pope's choice of Casaroli, architect of the Ostpolitik of Paul VI (about which Cardinal

Wojtyła had had serious doubts), surprised some. But the Polish pope, with his vigorous public defense of religious freedom, and the Italian curialist, devoted to the discretions of diplomacy, made an effective team in confronting European communism. An Italian (Achille Silvestrini, later Prefect of the Congregation for the Oriental Churches), and a Frenchman, Jean-Lous Tauran, served John Paul as Secretary for Relations with States, or foreign minister of the Holy See. Father Roberto Tucci, S.J., the president of Vatican Radio, played an invaluable role as impresario of the pope's foreign travels for more than 15 years.

The pope's willingness to go against the grain of bureaucratic convention led to several distinctive episcopal appointments during his pontificate: a convert from Judaism as archbishop of Paris (Jean-Marie Lustiger); a former U.S. Navy chaplain who had been a diocesan bishop for just a few months as archbishop of New York (John O'CONNOR); and, in the latter years of the pontificate, intellectually accomplished and publicly assertive younger bishops who had not followed the conventional career path as leaders of major sees.

Between 1979 and 2001, John Paul II created 201 cardinals. On six occasions, he called the College of Cardinals into extraordinary consistory to discuss various problems of Catholic life, a practice that had lain fallow for 400 years. By 2001, John Paul had created over 90 percent of the electorate that would eventually choose his successor.

Controversies. Ecumenical Councils have always been followed by controversy, and the pontificate of John Paul II, an expression of Vatican II, was no exception.

In 1982, the pope intervened in the governance of the Society of Jesus, appointing a personal delegate to lead the Society after the incapacitation of its general, Father Pedro ARRUPE. Father Arrupe's successor, Father Pieter-Hans Kolvenbach, was elected in 1983; opinions differed widely on whether the papal intervention had led to a successful reformation of the Church's largest and most prestigious male religious order.

The situation of post-conciliar Catholic theology was another arena of controversy. On Dec. 15, 1979, at the order of the Congregation for the Doctrine of the Faith, Father Hans Küng's ecclesiastical mandate to teach as a professor of Catholic theology was withdrawn; in 1987, CDF wrote the Chancellor of the Catholic University of America that Father Charles Curran was to be considered no longer suitable to teach Catholic theology. In both cases, action followed extensive and public dissent by the theologians in question and lengthy consultations with Vatican officials. Public action was taken against four other theologians in the first 22 years of the pontificate. The pope's theological critics, however, remained in control of many theological faculties in the West, suggesting that frequently heard charges of repression were overwrought.

John Paul II and Cardinal Ratzinger made considerable efforts to reconcile Archbishop Marcel LEFEBVRE and his followers. In 1984, the pope granted an indult allowing more widespread use of the TRIDENTINE rite in the 1962 Roman Missal. But the core of the Lefebvrist dissent was not liturgical, but rather theological: among other matters, the French archbishop disdained the Council's ecclesiology and refused to accept Vatican II's *Declaration on Religious Freedom.* His refusal to be mollified by the 1984 indult made clear that he considered Vatican II an act of infidelity of which liturgical change was but one manifestation. Dissent became crisis when, on June 30, 1988, Lefebvre, after lengthy and fruitless negotiations and a plea from the pope, ordained four new bishops without authorization. On July 1, Cardinal Gantin signed a decree stating that, as Lefebvre had committed a schismatic act, he, the four bishops he ordained, and the retired bishops who had taken part in the ordinations had automatically incurred excommunication. Any Catholic supporting Lefebvre would also incur excommunication. On July 2, the pope issued an apostolic letter, *Ecclesia Dei,* creating a commission to reconcile those of Lefebvre's supporters who did not wish to follow the Frenchman into schism.

While criticism of the pope from self-styled progressive Catholics received extensive media attention, John Paul II was also criticized, if less vocally, by Catholics who welcomed his strong evangelical presence and his vigorous exercise of the papal magisterium, but who thought him lax in his governance of the Church: too willing to countenance theological dissent, insufficiently energetic in reforming the episcopate, the priesthood, and the religious orders. The pope, committed to what he termed the "method of persuasion," had, it seems, a different ecclesiological vision and a different strategy, based on the conviction that what was true to the vision of Vatican II would endure and flourish, while what was false would wither and eventually die of its own implausibility.

A Different Kind of Pope. Determined to remain himself, John Paul II gave a distinctive personal stamp to the Office of Peter. Every year he hosted a seminar at Castel Gandolfo, the papal summer residence, for humanities scholars or scholars in the natural sciences; some participants were agnostics or atheists. With the exceptions of those times when he was in hospital or on vacation (two more innovations: a pope being treated in a

hospital, and a pope spending time hiking in the Italian Alps), he invited guests for lunch or dinner every day, drawing information about the Church and the world from a diverse set of personalities. The pope also maintained an extensive, informal correspondence, outside official channels, with interlocutors throughout the world. Friends and colleagues became accustomed to unexpected phone calls announcing that "the Holy Father would like to speak with you."

John Paul also reorganized the procedures for the quinquennial *AD LIMINA* visit that all diocesan bishops make to Rome in order to spend more time with the bishops individually and in national or regional groups. *Ad limina* visits under Paul VI gave the visiting bishop one opportunity to meet the pope; John Paul met each bishop four times, in a private session, at Mass, over a meal, and by delivering a discourse to the bishop's national or regional group (the discourse was given to each bishop individually in written form after 1995). By one knowledgeable estimate, 40 percent of the pope's official schedule was devoted in any given year to meetings with bishops. John Paul II also took his title as Primate of Italy with greater seriousness than any pope in centuries, making dozens of pastoral visits throughout the Italian peninsula and personally visiting some three hundred Roman parishes.

The pope's determination that the Vatican itself should reflect the realities of the world Church was manifest in the vast number of audiences he granted to an extraordinary range of groups, including chefs, hairdressers, and kayakers. John Paul changed the ambience of the Vatican in other ways. In 1994, he opened a convent for contemplative nuns inside Vatican City, a new feature of Vatican life which demonstrated the pope's conviction that prayer must be at the heart of the ministry of service exercised by the apostolic see. In 1988, John Paul dedicated a shelter for the homeless within the walls of the Vatican. During his pontificate, the pope also created two new pontifical academies: the Pontifical Academy for the Social Sciences and the Pontifical Academy for Life.

From 1994 on, John Paul suffered from an increasing number of physical burdens. He was most visibly effected by a form of Parkinson's disease and a hip replacement that left him walking with pain. Yet the pope's charisma did not diminish, as the jubilee year amply demonstrated. In a world tempted to think of the elderly and disabled as disposable, the pope's witness to the dignity of human life was magnified by his evident physical suffering.

Enduring Accomplishments. As he led the Church into the third millennium of its history, ten enduring accomplishments of the pontificate of John Paul II could be identified. He had revitalized the papacy as an office of evangelical witness. He had secured the legacy of Vatican II in its fullness as an epic spiritual event at which the Church, guided by the Holy Spirit, had engaged modernity through an enriched sense of its own unique nature and mission. He had been the pivotal figure in the collapse of European communism. He had identified the moral challenges facing free societies in the twenty-first century. He had put ecumenism at the heart of the Church's consciousness. He had created the possibility of a new religious dialogue between Catholicism and living Judaism. He had modeled a truth-centered method of interreligious dialogue, demonstrating that humanity's deepest convictions could be in conversation not conflict. He had proposed a compelling Christian response to the sexual revolution in his theology of the body. He had made clear, in the *Catechism of the Catholic Church*, that the Church could still advance a comprehensive account of its faith and hope, and he had positioned the Catholic Church as the principal institutional defender of the claims of human reason. He had given unmeasurable inspiration to tens, perhaps hundreds, of millions of human beings. His inaugural call, "Be not afraid!" had changed the course of world history by changing the direction of individual lives.

Bibliography: POPE JOHN PAUL II, *Crossing the Threshold of Hope* (New York 1994). K. L. SCHMITZ, *At the Center of the Human Drama: The Philosophical Anthropology of Karol Wojtyła/Pope John Paul II* (Washington 1993). G. WEIGEL, *Witness to Hope: The Biography of Pope John Paul II* (New York 1999; rev. ed. 2000), contains bibliography.

[G. WEIGEL]

JOHN PAUL II CULTURAL CENTER

The cultural center that takes its name and inspiration from Pope John Paul II is located in Washington, DC. The center features state-of-the-art exhibits and interactive media activities designed to provide visitors an experience that inspires faith, promotes religious values, and fosters respect for diverse cultural backgrounds. The five main galleries explore (1) the history of the Church and the papacy; (2) how faith is celebrated around the world; (3) the relationship between the human and the physical world; (4) ways that God's presence is expressed in art; and (5) world cultures and their relationship to the Catholic Church.

Works by Christian artists from around the world and from the collection of the Vatican Museum are displayed. The permanent collection highlights Marian themes. Another component integral to the center is the Intercultural Forum. Scholars research and study themes related to the impact of the papacy on world cultures and the promotion of values relating to the dignity of the human person. Facilities include a library, auditorium, and conference rooms. The inspiration for the center is Pope John Paul's call for renewed evangelization in the new millennium.

The multi-million dollar project was initiated by Cardinal Adam Maida, archbishop of Detroit, and designed by Leo A. Daly, architect, engineer, and interior designer, and Edwin Schlossberg, Inc., exhibit designer. It opened during the Jubilee Year 2000 on a 14-acre site adjacent to the Basilica of the National Shrine of the Immaculate Conception and the Catholic University of America in northeast Washington, DC.

[G. M. BUGARIN]

JOHN PAUL II INSTITUTE ON MARRIAGE AND FAMILY

The John Paul II Institute for Studies on Marriage and Family, with headquarters at the Pontifical Lateran University in Rome, has as its purpose study and research that highlight the uniqueness and importance of the Church's mission to the family. The Synod of Bishops (Fifth General Assembly, 1980) had called for the creation of theological centers devoted to the study of the Church's teaching on marriage and the family. Pope John Paul II responded in October 1982 by issuing *Magnum Matrimonii Sacramentum,* an apostolic constitution that serves as the charter of the Institute. The Institute is empowered to grant degrees, and its president is appointed by the Holy Father.

It was Pope John Paul II's stated intention that the work of the Institute be spread throughout the world, and thus it established extensions in Spain (Valencia), Mexico (Mexico City-Guadalajara), and the United States (Washington, D.C.). The last was founded by the invitation of James Cardinal Hickey, archbishop of Washington, and the request of Virgil C. Dechant, supreme knight of the Knights of Columbus, to serve American and other English-speaking students. The Congregation for Catholic Education gave it the status of a pontifical faculty August 22, 1988.

The curricula of the John Paul II Institute encompass the full range of studies required for a complete theological education in the areas of marriage and family: philosophy, theological method, systematic and spiritual theology, Christian ethics and moral theology, public policy, canon law, biblical theology, and the life sciences. The programs of study seek to foster in students the theological competency necessary for the exercise of a variety of Christian ministries, including counseling, pastoral and missionary work in the specialized areas of marriage and family, and for religious leadership positions, especially in family life bureaus. In particular, the Institute prepares its students for work in Christian education, research, and publication, especially as members of the faculties of seminaries, theological schools, and departments of religious studies. In addition, the Institute enables persons anticipating professional service in education, health care, social work, community and public interest organizations, law, and public life to understand more fully the theological basis of their vocations.

The American extension is located at 487 Michigan Avenue, NE, Washington, DC 20017.

[C. A. ANDERSON]

JOHN PECKHAM (PECHAM)

English Franciscan theologian, archbishop of Canterbury, known as *Doctor ingeniosus;* b. Patcham, Sussex, *c.* 1220–25; d. Mortlake Manor, Surrey, Dec. 8, 1292. Peckham received his early schooling probably at Lewes, then studied at Paris in the faculty of arts (1245–50), possibly under ROGER BACON; he completed these studies at Oxford. Peckham entered the order in *c.* 1250 and returned to Paris, where he studied theology, becoming a master in 1269. If not an immediate disciple of BONAVENTURE, Peckham was at least strongly influenced by his doctrines. With THOMAS AQUINAS, he took an active part in the POVERTY CONTROVERSY.

While at Paris he wrote *Tractatus pauperis* (1270) and some of his quodlibets. Among his disciples was THOMAS OF CANTELUPE, later bishop of Hereford. Peckham left Paris *c.* 1271–72 for Oxford, where he is said to have introduced the *disputatio de quolibet.* Chosen minister provincial of England in 1275, he participated in the general chapter of Padua (1276) and was made the first Franciscan Magister S. Palatii at Rome in 1277. During these years he tried to prevent "the spread of Averroism and THOMISM" [A. B. Emden, *A Biographical Register of the University of Oxford to A.D. 1500,* 3 v. (Oxford 1957–59)].

On Jan. 28, 1279, he was elected archbishop of Canterbury and primate of England by NICHOLAS III, succeeding ROBERT KILWARDBY. Peckham was noted for his zeal for ecclesiastical discipline and the rights of the Church. At Oxford on Oct. 29, 1284, he renewed the prohibitions issued by Kilwardby in 1277; on April 30, 1286, he condemned a number of opinions of RICHARD KNAPWELL. In 1290 he preached the Crusade.

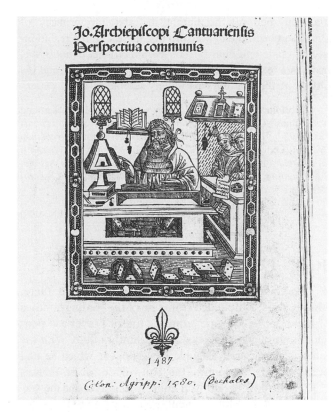

Woodcut frontispiece to "Perspectiva Commuis," by John Peckham, Paris, 1511 Edition.

Among Peckham's more than 50 writings are those on science and philosophy: *Perspectiva communis, Summa de esse et essentia,* and *Tractatus de anima;* on the Bible: *Collectarium S. Bibliae I–IV, Postilla Threnorum;* on theology: *In 1 sent.* and *Tractatus de Trinitate;* numerous *Quaestiones disputatae;* and four quodlibets. On Franciscan spirituality Peckham is noted for three treatises on poverty: *Tractatus pauperis, Tractatus de paupertate contra R. de Kilwardby OP,* and *Defensio fratrum mendicantium,* a satiric poem of dubious authenticity. His liturgical and pastoral writings include *Constitutiones provinciales of Reading and Lambeth; Acta episcopatus; Officium SS. Trinitatis,* a poetic composition; and some religious hymns.

Peckham was one of the best representatives and defenders of AUGUSTINIANISM against the rising forces of ARISTOTELIANISM. He taught the immediate evidence of the existence of God, approved the argument of ANSELM OF CANTERBURY, and denied the possibility of eternal creation. In psychology he accepted only a virtual distinction between the soul and its faculties, and held that immortality can be proved by irrefutable arguments. In addition, he accented the autodeterminism of the will and its primacy over the intellect. Peckham also disputed Thomas's notion of the unicity of the substantial form in man. In theology he taught the absolute primacy of Christ, a twofold real sonship in Christ, and the real identity of grace and charity. His *Perspective communis* was used as a textbook in optics in many universities, and his Office of the Trinity was widely adopted.

Bibliography: I. BRADY, "John Peckham and the Background of Aquinas' De Aeternitate Mundi," in *Saint Thomas Aquinas 1274–1974* (Toronto 1974) 141–178. D. L. DOUIE, *Archbishop Pecham* (Oxford 1952). A. P. ESTEVEZ, *La Materia, de Avicena a la Escuela Franciscana (Avicena, Averroes, Tomas de Aquino, Buenaventura, Pecham, Marston, Olivo, Mediavilla, Duns Escoto)* (Maracaibo, Venezuela 1998).

[A. EMMEN]

JOHN PELINGOTTO, BL.

Franciscan tertiary; b. Urbino, Italy, 1240; d. there, June 1, 1304. Descended from one of the leading families of the area, he led an exemplary life of prayer and penance both inside and outside his family circle. With his father's permission he gave up trade, for which he had been trained, and joining the Third Order of St. Francis *c.* 1255, he devoted himself entirely to prayer and the service of God. In 1300 he went on pilgrimage to Rome for Pope BONIFACE VIII's Jubilee Year, and L. Wadding (*Annales Ordinis Minorum* 4:38–42) relates that people pointed him out as "the holy man from Urbino." After his death, according to his own wish, he was buried in the church of San Francesco in his native city. His cult was approved by BENEDICT XV on Nov. 12, 1918.

Feast: June 2.

Bibliography: *Acta Sanctorum* June 1:144–151. *Acta Apostolicae Sedis* 10 (1918) 513–516, decree approving cult. *Acta ordinis Fratrum Minorum* 37 (1918) 218–221; 38 (1919) 11–12, 28–31, 49–51. *Archivum Franciscanum historicum* 14 (1921) 27.

[S. OLIVIERI]

JOHN PHILOPONUS

Alexandrian theologian and philosopher of the sixth century, known also as John the Grammarian. He was a disciple of Ammonius of Hermias. The name Philoponus means lover of work; the philoponoi were members of a confraternity whose task it was to look after places of worship.

Philoponus wrote treatises on the Astrolabe and the Arithmetic of Nichomachus of Gerosa and two treatises on grammar that had some influence as lexicons. He also wrote commentaries on the following works of Aristotle: the *Categories, Prior* and *Posterior Analytics,* four books of the *Physics, Generation and Corruption, Generation of Animals,* the *Metaphysics,* the *Meteors,* and the *Soul,* of which only William of Moerbeke's translation of the third book is authentic. His theological and philosophical treatises include On the Eternity of the World Against Proclus, On the Creation of the World, the Arbiter, the Relation of the Whole and Its Parts, On Images Against Iamblichus, On Easter, and On the Resurrection. Many of his works are not extant.

The commentaries, although Aristotelian in terminology, are Platonic in character, often mixed with Stoic and occasionally Christian notions. Moreover, they reflect the opinions of Ammonius to such an extent that they often appear to be little more than an edition of his teachings. It may be that Philoponus, a Christian, was used to prevent the closing of the school at Alexandria, as had already happened at Athens.

In the Categories Philoponus insists that all possible beings will sometime be realized in being. In the Physics he attributes a real and efficient causality to the demiurge; all generation requires divine causality. Creatures exercise no really efficient causality but are, at best, instrumental causes. He considered the Neoplatonists pantheists and asserted an exaggerated pluralism against them. Following the Stoics, he granted three dimensions to primary matter. The soul is a mover of the body; the agent intellect is within the soul. Genus and species have no reality outside the mind. Logic is necessary in both the speculative and practical disciplines to distinguish between truth and falsity, good and evil.

The theological works are clearly Monophysitic; his exaggerated pluralism and the doctrine of the relation of the whole and parts allowed him no alternative. When these doctrines were applied to the Trinity, a sort of verbal tritheism resulted; nowhere, however, does Philoponus say that there are three gods. He attacked the primacy of the Roman See and called Leo the Great a Nestorian. In discussing the whole and its parts, Philoponus asserted that the totality is not a sum total of the parts, but the resulting reality of the composite; outside the reality of the individual the term parts is meaningless. Nature, hypostasis, substance, essence, and individual are in reality one and the same thing. Consequently, in Christ there is only one nature, a composite nature. This, Philoponus claimed, was the teaching handed down from ancient times. He was reprimanded at the Council of Constantinople III (680). Through the Arabian philosophers and WILLIAM OF MOERBEKE some of Philoponus's teachings reached the West; but with the exception of his doctrine of the agent intellect and the kinetic theory of IMPETUS, his influence was not great.

Bibliography: Works. Commentaries on Aristotle in *Commentaria in Aristotelem Graeca,* 13–17 (Berlin 1887–1901).

Τονικά παραγγέλματα, ed. W. DINDORF (Leipzig 1825). Περί τῶν διαφόρως τονουμένων καί διάφορα σῆμαινόντων, ed. P. EGENOLFF (Breslau 1880). "On the Astrolabe," *The Astrolabes of the World,* tr. R. W. T. GUNTHER, 2 v. (Oxford 1932) 61–81. *De Aeternitate Mundi Contra Proclum,* ed. H. RABE (Leipzig 1899). *De Opificio Mundi,* ed. G. REICHHARDT (Leipzig 1897). H. REINER, "Der Metaphysik-Kommentar des Joannes Philoponos," *Hermes* 82.4 (1954) 480–482. *Paulys Realencyklopädie der klassischen Altertumswissenschaft,* ed. G. WISSOWA et al. (Stuttgart 1893—). Literature. G. FURLANI, "Sei scritti Antetriteistica in lingua Siriaca," *Patrologia orientalis,* ed. R. GRAFFIN and F. NAU (Paris 1903—) 14:685–772. "Il trattato di Giovanni Filopono sul rapporto tra le parte e gli elemente ed il tutto e le parte tradotto dal Siriaco," *Atti del Reale Istituto Veneto di scienze, lettere ed arti.* 86.2 (1921–22). "L'Anatema di Giovanni d'Alessandria contro Giovanni Filopono," *Atti della Reale Academia delle scienze di Torino* 55 (1919–20) 188–194. "Unità e dualità di natura secondo Giovanni il Filopono," *Bessarione* 27 (1923) 58–65. A. SANDA, *Opuscula Monophysitica Joannis Philoponi* (Beirut 1930), contains Latin text of *Arbiter,* an epitome of *Arbiter,* Solution of doubtful questions, Treatise to Sergius's *On Totality and Parts,* Treatise on difference, number and division, Letter to Justinian. H. D. SAFFREY, "Le Chrétien Jean Philopon et la Survivance de l'école d'Alexandrie," *Revue des études grecques* (Paris 1888—) 78 (1954) 396–410. T. HERMANN, "Johannes Philoponos als Monophysit," *Zeitschrift für die neutestamentliche Wissenschaft und die Kunde der älteren Kirche,* 29 (1930) 209–264. E. ÉVRARD, "Les Convictions religieuses de Jean Philopon et la date de son commentaire aux Météorologiques," *Académie royale de Belgique: Bulletin de la classe des lettres et des sciences morales et politiques,* 5th ser. 39.3 (1953) 299–357. G. VERBEKE, "Guillaume de Moerbeke, traducteur de Jean Philopon," *Revue philosophieque de Louvain,* 49 (1951) 222–235. M. DE CORTE, "Le Commentaire de Jean Philopon sur le troisième livre du Traitè de l'âme," *Bibliothèque de la faculté de philosophie et lettres de l'Université de Liège,* fasc. 65 (Paris 1934), see corrections by A. MANSION in *Mélanges Auguste Pelzer* (Louvain 1947) 325. S. SAMBURSKY, "Philoponus' Interpretation of Aristotle's Theory of Light," *Osiris* 13 (1958) 114–126. M. STEINSCHNEIDER, "Johannes Philoponos bei den Arabern," *Mémoires de l'Académie des sciences de S. Petersbourg* 13 (1869) 152–176. Several important articles by S. PÉTRIDÈS et al., in *Échos d'Orient,* 4 (1900–01) 225–231; 7 (1904) 341–348; 14 (1911) 277–278; 33 (1934) 181—. "Third Council of Constantinople," see J. D. MANSI, *Sacrorum Concillorum nova et amplissima collectio,* 31 v. (Florence-Venice 1757–98) 11:501C.

[J. R. O'DONNELL]

JOHN PRANDOTA OF CRACOW, BL.

Bishop; b. Białaczów, Poland, early 13th century; d. Cracow, Poland, Sept. 21, 1266. A descendant of the noble Odroważ family, he became bishop of CRACOW in 1242, and he did much to secure, in 1253, the canonization of St. STANISLAUS, his martyred predecessor in that see. He drove the heretical Flagellants out of his diocese (*see* FLAGELLATION). When Duke CONRAD OF MASOVIA seized church property, Prandota excommunicated him. A respected leader of the Polish magnates, the bishop worked together with Boleslav V the Chaste (d. 1279) and his saintly wife, KINGA, for the welfare of Little Po-

land. Prandota was an ideal bishop of his time, combining sanctity with political sagacity and moral leadership. His cult ended in the 17th century because of a misunderstanding of Pope URBAN VIII's bull on the veneration of saints (*see* SAINTS, DEVOTION TO THE).

Feast: Sept. 21.

Bibliography: *Acta Sanctorum* Sept. 6:279–288. *Monumenta Poloniae historica,* 6 v. (LVOV 1864–93) 4:439–500. *Bibliothecas hagiographica latina antiquae et mediae aetatis* 4421. A. ZAHORSKA, *Ilustrowane Zywoty Swietych Polskich* (Potulice, Pol. 1937) 170–180. Z. SZOSTKIEWICZ, "Katalog biskupów obrz. łac. przedrozbiorowej Polski," *Sacrum Poloniae millenium* 1 (1954) 540. B. STASIEWSKI, *Lexikon für Theologie und Kirche*[2] 5:1072.

[L. SIEKANIEC]

JOHN SCOTUS ERIUGENA

Theologian, translator, known variously as John the Scot, Erigena, and Scottigena; b. Ireland, *c.* 810; d. probably in England, *c.* 877. Arriving between 845 and 847 at the palace school of Charles the Bald, at Quierzy near Laon, he taught grammar and dialectics. Earliest factual information concerns his involvement in the controversy concerning predestination that began in 849 and continued with varying degrees of intensity until 860. In 851 Pardulus of Laon urged HINCMAR OF REIMS to consult John about the question; at that date John must have attained a certain eminence as a theologian. In his *De predestinatione* (*Patrologia Latina* 122: 355–440), completed in 851, he insisted that there is but one predestination to good and that no one is compelled by God's foreknowledge to do evil. Through FREE WILL, a gift of God, man may sin, but he is not predestined to do so, since evil is not a physical reality. If one knows the simple rules of dialectics, he would know that a twofold predestination is a rational impossibility. Attacked by PRUDENTIUS OF TROYES and FLORUS OF LYONS, this work was condemned at the councils of Valencia (855) and Langres (859). John's work as teacher of the LIBERAL ARTS is reflected principally in the *Annotationes in Marcianum Capellam,* ed. C. E. Lutz (Cambridge, Mass. 1939), completed about 859–860.

Translations. A new phase in his life and thought began when Eriugena was commissioned by Charles around 860 to make a new translation of the works of PSEUDO-DIONYSIUS (*Patrologia Latina* 122:1029–1194; *Dionysiaca,* 2 v. Bruges 1937–1950). Equipped, most probably, with a rudimentary knowledge of Greek learned in Ireland, he perfected his knowledge in France. In 827 the Byzantine Emperor Michael Balbus sent a copy of Dionysius's works to Louis the Pious, who immediately commissioned Hilduin, Abbot of Saint-Denis, to translate them into Latin. The imperfection of this translation, or transliteration, prompted Charles to ask Eriugena to prepare a better translation. This influential translation, completed between 860 and 862, consisted of four works (*De divinis nominibus, Theologia mystica, De hierarchia caelestia,* and *De hierarchia ecclesiastica*) and ten letters together with two prefaces. Charles then commissioned Eriugena to translate the commentaries (*Ambigua*) of MAXIMUS THE CONFESSOR (*Patrologia Latina* 122:1193–1222). This translation, composed between 862 and 864, consisted of a preface, two poems, and 67 chapters, of which only the first five and beginning of the sixth have been printed. He translated also *Sermo de imagine* (περὶ κατασκευῆς ἀνερώπου) of Gregory of Nyssa and *Sermo de fide* (Ἀγκυρατός) of Epiphanius about 865. This contact with Greek sources provided Eriugena with a new appreciation of dialectics and Platonic thought "longeque a modernis sensibus remotum."

Later Works. The result was a new period of personal, creative writing: commentaries on the Gospel of St. John (*Patrologia Latina* 122:283–348), Pseudo-Dionysius [*Patrologia Latina* 122:125–284; H. F. Dondaine, *Archives d'histoire doctrinale et litéraire du moyen-âge* 18 (1950–1951) 245–302], and *De divisione naturae* (*Patrologia Latina* 122:441–1022). This last, sometimes called *Perifiseon,* or περὶ φύσεως μερισμοί, is his most important original work. Composed between 862 and 866, it was dedicated to Wulfad, later archbishop of Bourges. Written in the form of a dialogue between a master, designated by N (*Nutritor*), and a disciple, A (*Alumnus*), it drew heavily from Greek and Latin Platonic sources, notably Pseudo-Dionysius, St. AUGUSTINE, Maximus, and ORIGEN. It is divided into five books. Book one deals with God, His unknowability, and man's language in speaking about Him; book two deals with various divisions of being, created and uncreated; book three considers creatures as theophanies of God; book four is concerned mainly with man, his creation, life in Paradise, and the Fall; book five is devoted to the return of all things to God through Christ.

De divisione naturae apparently was used by AMALRIC OF BÈNE and DAVID OF DINANT to interpret Aristotle in the 13th century. The work was condemned at the Council of Paris in 1210; and, on Jan. 23, 1225, Honorius III ordered all copies to be burned publicly, under pain of excommunication and suspicion of heresy. When Eriugena's works were first printed at Oxford in 1681, the *De divisione naturae* was placed on the INDEX OF FORBIDDEN BOOKS because of the pantheistic implication of its expressions.

Reason and Revelation. Eriugena was always motivated by a profound passion for truth. "There is no death worse than ignorance of truth," he wrote, "and no pit deeper than promulgation of what is really false." Human reason, in its present state, is clouded as a result of original sin, but it is still capable of attaining truths from the contemplation of creatures seen. The infallible source of truth is divine revelation unfolded in the Scriptures. Both rational and revealed truths are theophanies, for they are both manifestations of God. Consequently Eriugena was convinced that there can be no conflict between *ratio vera* and divine revelation. Since God embodied a hidden truth in the words of Sacred Scripture, it is prudent for reason to begin with the word of God: "Ratiocinationis exordium ex divinis eloquiis assumendum esse aestimo." Eriugena used several analogies to press this point: Scripture is a banquet tempting reason to eat, a holy sepulcher into which Peter (symbolizing faith) entered before John (symbolizing reason) to seek the Lord. Therefore reason should begin by accepting God's revelation and pursue its task under the inspiration of grace.

Following tradition, Eriugena recognized four senses of Scripture: literal, spiritual, historical, and allegorical. Of these Eriugena preferred the spiritual and allegorical, insisting that works (*agere*) and knowledge (*scire*) must culminate in theology. Although the Scriptures are divinely inspired and many earlier writers have interpreted them, the excellence of reason must not be underestimated. Priority of nature is of greater dignity than priority of time. Since the Fathers interpreting Scripture are prior in time and reason is prior by nature, reason has the greater dignity. Eriugena recognized a hierarchy of guides in the attainment of truth: Scripture, reason, and the authority of the Fathers. In seeking ultimate truth reason exercises an activity that the Greeks called "philosophizing." For Eriugena, as for St. AUGUSTINE before him, true philosophy does not differ from true religion. "What is philosophy but an expounding of the rules of religion whereby man humbly adores and rationally seeks God, the highest cause and source of everything." Thus in *De predestinatione* Eriugena could identify true philosophy and true religion; in his *Annotationes in Martianum Capellam* he said, "No one enters heaven except through philosophy."

For Eriugena, the disciple of Pseudo-Dionysius and Maximus, the formal structure of philosophy is dialectical, consisting of division, definition, demonstration, and resolution. The formal, logical structure perceived in thought is also found in physical reality. Thus the division of concepts corresponds to the division of natures.

Division of Natures. In *De divisione naturae* Eriugena presented a number of divisions according to which being may be classified, the most important of which is his division of natures into four types or stages: (1) nature that creates and is not created ("natura creans et non creata"), (2) nature that is created and also creates ("natura creata et creans"), (3) nature that is created and does not create ("natura creata et non creans"), (4) nature that is not created and does not create ("natura non creata et non creans").

Nature that creates and is not created is God Himself. Since being is whatever can be grasped by sense and intellect, God must be said to transcend all being (*supra ens, supra bonum*). As far as knowledge is concerned, He is more properly nonbeing, nothing. He is, in fact, the nothingness from which all things are made (Gn 1.2), since apart from Him there is nothing from which anything can be made. None of the CATEGORIES OF BEING can be predicated of God, who is ineffable and incomprehensible, even to Himself. Although unknowable and ineffable, God expresses himself through theophanies, which are divine ideas, revelation, and creation. Following Pseudo-Dionysius, Eriugena distinguished three theologies, or approaches to knowledge of God: affirmative, negative, and transcendent. Affirmative theology is limited to the positive statements that can be said of God, such as that He is one substance (οὐσία) and three Persons (ὑποστάσεις). Negative theology consists of all the negations that must be said of God, such as incorporeal, ineffable, and incomprehensible. Transcendent theology is marked by the use of such transcendent terms as supersubstantial, superessential, and superdesirable. According to the Scriptures, the Father generated the Son and "Catholic faith obliges one to profess that the Holy Spirit proceeds from the Father *and* the Son, or from the Father *through* the Son." Since the exact Trinitarian formula is difficult to determine, according to Eriugena, it is better not to venture any rash conjecture. For him, God reveals Himself as the Father of all when He creates everything in the Word and distributes His graces through the Holy Spirit.

Nature that is created and also creates is the theophany of divine ideas existing in the Word. These ideas are eternal because they are created in the Word and, in a certain sense, are coeternal with God; but precisely because they are created and come from God, they are not fully coeternal. Here Eriugena's dialectics faltered. As he interpreted divine ideas, they were a fulfillment and completion of God Himself. They are the first theophanies of creation, needing only to be divided into lower genera, species, and individuals. This division is properly the work of the Holy Spirit. The image of the Trinity, therefore, is manifested not only in the Scriptures, but also in things, e.g., essence, power, and activity.

Nature that is created and does not create is the world of immaterial and material creatures made from the nothingness that is God. For Eriugena, God is made (*factus est*) in His creatures and these constitute three vast regions: purely immaterial substances (angels), composite substances of spirit and matter (man), and purely material substances (world). Being in all His creatures, God is, in a sense, their essence, even though creatures are not divine. While Eriugena's language is often pantheistic, he insists on the absolute transcendence of God beyond all being (*supra ens*). Created nature constitutes a hierarchy, and angels within that hierarchy also constitute a hierarchy of essences. The nature of each angel is determined by its position in the hierarchy. Each angel receives intellectual illumination from above and diffuses it below. Man, the lowest intellectual creature, receives intellectual illumination from angels and God. Before Adam's fall, man, although corporeal, was not divided into male and female; nor was reproduction achieved through intercourse. Original sin, according to Eriugena, divided man sexually and individually. In his fall, man carried all lower creatures with him to disorder, to further division, and to fatal dissension. Creatures had their true and perfect being in the mind of God, in divine ideas. In the mind of God, man had perfect knowledge of all things. After the fall of Adam, man can gather knowledge only gradually and with great difficulty from the divided, fragmented, and fleeting impressions of sense. From sensory impressions of the world man must form the unity of images and ideas whereby God can once more be known. Objects of sense also existed originally as ideas in the mind of God and as such their existence was perfect. But after the fall, they too became further divided into a conglomeration of intelligible qualities. Now they are only imperfect theophanies revealing something of God.

Nature that is not created and does not create is the return of all things to God. The return begins at the moment sensible things reach their ultimate division, for even divided qualities unite to form a corporeal substance. Man's final division comes with death, when his soul departs and his body disintegrates. The return of all things to God is possible only through Christ's redemptive act and redeeming grace. The return of man to God does not take place instantaneously, but gradually. Death must be followed by the final resurrection when the body returns to the soul, becoming spiritual and sexless. Then body and soul will return to their ideal state in the mind of God. The whole terrestrial sphere will be brought back to Paradise in the mind of God. In the end there will be only God. This does not mean the annihilation of all things, but the restoration of all things to "real being" in the divine nothingness. All men will become pure spirits. The blessed will have an "intellectual vision" in the darkness of the Godhead. The wicked will be punished by being deprived of knowledge; they will suffer the worst punishment possible—ignorance of the truth.

See Also: SCHOLASTICISM; PHILOSOPHY, HISTORY OF; DIALECTICS IN THE MIDDLE AGES; PANTHEISM.

Bibliography: É. H. GILSON, *History of Christian Philosophy in the Middle Ages* (New York 1955) 113–128. M. CAPPUYNS, *Jean Scot Érigène, sa vie, son oeuvre, sa pensée* (Louvain 1933). M. DAL PRA, *Scoto Eriugena e il neoplatonismo medievale* (2d ed. Milan 1951); *Enciclopedia filosofica* 4:473–478. F. VERNET, *Dictionnaire de théologie catholique,* ed. A. VACANT et al. 15 v. (Paris 1903–50) 5.1:401–434. L. SCHEFFCZYK, *Lexikon für Theologie und Kirche,* 5:1082–83. W. N. PITTENGER, "The Christian Philosophy of John Scotus Erigena," *Journal of Religion* 24 (1944). H. F. DONDAINE, "Saint Thomas et Scot Érigène," *Revue des sciences philosophiques et théologiques* 35 (1951) 31–33. K. G. MOORE, "Johannes Scotus Erigena on Imagination," *Journal of Psychology* 23 (1947) 169–178. J. J. O'MEARA, *Eriugena* (Oxford 1988). D. MORAN, *The Philosophy of John Scottus Eriugena: A Study of Idealism in the Middle Ages* (Cambridge 1989). D. CARABINE, *John Scottus Eriugena* (New York 2000).

[L. E. LYNCH]

JOHN STRATFORD

Archbishop of Canterbury, chancellor of England; b. Stratford-on-Avon; d. Mayfield, Sussex, Aug. 23, 1348. He was educated at Oxford, where by 1312 he was doctor of civil law. The demand for his legal skill gained him many benefices in the Church as well as civil offices, including that of royal envoy at the papal Curia in AVIGNON, where King EDWARD II charged him to secure the election of ROBERT BALDOK as bishop of WINCHESTER in 1323. Instead John secured his own appointment to Winchester by papal PROVISION, much to the king's indignation. Though he was later readmitted to the king's favor, it was Stratford who drafted the six articles giving reasons for Edward II's deposition in 1327, and he was one of the bishops who obtained the king's consent to abdication. For the next decade Stratford was a leading actor on the political scene, serving as chancellor (1330–34, 1335–37, 1340) and in 1333 becoming archbishop of Canterbury. But in late 1340 he strongly objected to the foreign policy of EDWARD III, who returned from Flanders, removed Stratford's brother, ROBERT STRATFORD, from the chancellorship, and initiated a propaganda war upon Archbishop Stratford throughout England. Stratford replied on December 29 by comparing himself to the persecuted Thomas BECKET. When the king attempted to try Stratford in the court of exchequer, the archbishop insisted on taking his place in Parliament, thus vindicating the right of peers not to be tried outside of Parliament. Within a year (October 1341) Stratford was reconciled to the king, whom he continued to advise until his own death. He was always more a politician than a pastor.

Bibliography: T. F. TOUT, *Chapters in the Administrative History of Mediaeval England,* 6 v. (New York 1920–33) v. 3. M. MC-

KISACK, *The Fourteenth Century, 1307–1399* (Oxford 1959). A. B. EMDEN, *A Biographical Register of the University of Oxford to A.D. 1500,* 3 v. (Oxford 1957–59) 3:1796–98.

[D. NICHOLL]

JOHN THE ALMSGIVER, ST.

Patriarch of Alexandria, 610 to 617 or 619; b. Amathus, Cyprus; d. there, 619. He was the son of Epiphanius, the governor of Cyprus, and Honesta. John married early and had a number of children, all of whom died in infancy. Later, as a widower and friend of SOPHRONIUS (patriarch of Jerusalem), John MOSCHUS, and Leontius of Neapolis, John was elected patriarch of Alexandria by acclamation in 610 and set about reforming the discipline of the clergy and laity. He built monasteries and churches, established refuges for the Syrians dispossessed by the Persians, and strenuously urged the rich of Alexandria to participate in his work for the poor. When the imperial official Nicetas confiscated the Church's revenues for military purposes, John forced him to make restitution. When the Persians occupied Egypt, he fled to his ancestral home in Cyprus, where he died. His remains were translated several times and finally came to rest at Presbourg on Jan. 23, 1632. John wrote a vita of Bishop Tychon of Amathus in Cyprus; his own vita was written by Leontius of Neapolis.

Feast: Jan. 23 and Nov. 12 (Greek Church).

Bibliography: *Acta Sanctorum,* Jan. 3:108–148. *Three Byzantine Saints: Contemporary Biographies of St. Daniel the Stylite, St. Theodore of Sykeon, and St. John the Almsgiver,* tr. E. A. S. DAWES and N. H. BAYNES (Crestwood, N.Y. 1996). *Leontios von Neapolis Leben des hl. Johannes,* ed. H. GELZER (Freiburg 1893), Greek original and French tr. in *Vie de Syméon le Fou; Vie de Jean de Chypre,* ed. A. J. FESTUGÈRE and L. RYDÉN (Paris 1974). H. G. BECK, *Kirche und theologische Literatur im byzantinischen Reich* (Munich 1959) 459–460. H. DUCKWORTH, *St. John the Almsgiver* (Oxford 1901). H. DELEHAYE, *Analecta Bollandiana,* 26 (1907) 244–245; *ibid.* 45 (1927) 5–74, vita by Sophronius. *Bibliotheca hagiographica Graeca,* ed. F. HALKIN, 3 v. (Brussels 1957) 3:886–889.

[F. CHIOVARO]

JOHN THE BAPTIST, ST.

Christ's precursor, son of the priest ZACHARY and Mary's kinswoman St. ELIZABETH.

Birth and Infancy. The Gospel of Luke provides details of John's annunciation, birth, and infancy. The archangel GABRIEL appeared to Zachary while he was performing his priestly duty in the Temple and announced that Elizabeth would conceive a son in her old age (Lk 1.11). The form used corresponds to that employed in the OT in foretelling the births of the famous men (Jgs 13.2–20). Gabriel told Zachary to give his promised son the name of John, which means "Yahweh is gracious" (Lk 1.13). The child would be filled with the Holy Spirit from his mother's womb and become an ascetic of Israel. He would lead many of the sons of Israel to their Lord and would walk in the power and spirit of Elias (1.14–17). In his canticle called the BENEDICTUS ZACHARY sings of his son as "prophet of the Most High" (1.76). John was born six months before Christ (1.36), according to tradition in the town of Ain Karim, about three-and-a-half miles west of Jerusalem. During the visit of Mary to Elizabeth the unborn John leapt with messianic joy in his mother's womb (1.44). Luke also relates that John spent his youth in the desert (1.80).

Ministry. John appeared in the region of the JORDAN as an ascetic and a preacher of penance (Mt 3.1–6; Mk 1.1–6; Lk 3.1–6; Jn 1.19–28). With his preaching of baptism for the forgiveness of sins, the Kingdom of God began to unfold. As PRECURSOR OF THE MESSIAH, his principal task was to announce the arrival of Jesus Christ as Messiah and to baptize him. He appeared not as a priest, like his father, but as a preacher clothed in camel's hair, the traditional garb of the prophets; ELIJAH, whom John resembles in many ways, is described as wearing the same ascetic clothing (2 Kgs 1.8). For centuries the people had honored this sign of the prophet, but false prophets had caused it to fall into disrepute, so that to wear it was to invite sarcasm (Zec 13.3–4).

John came as "a voice crying in the desert" (Is 40.3–4). All four Evangelists identify the Isaian "voice" with the Baptist. According to the Fourth Gospel the Baptist categorically denied that he was Elijah or the expected Prophet or the Messiah (Jn 1.19–23). But he was indeed the last of the OT prophets, one sent by God to announce the baptism of repentance and the arrival of the Kingdom in Christ. He preached a moral reform designed to prepare the Jews for the advent of the Messiah. Their interior conversion was to be visibly proclaimed by baptism with water and a confession of sin. Jesus' submission to John's baptism indicated his acknowledgement of the truth of John's mission but by that very act supplanted John's baptism (Mt 3.13–17; Mk 1.9–11; Lk 3.21–22; Jn 1.32–34). (*See* BAPTISM OF CHRIST.)

The message of John's sermons is rather forbidding and severe (Mt 3.7–12; Mk 1.7–8; Lk 3.7–18). More important is the imminent coming of the Messiah and the impending judgment he would bring: "the axe is laid to the root of the trees" (Lk 3.9). But Luke (3.10–14) insists also on the positive and humane aspects of the Baptist's message. No profession is denied salvation; all are called

John the Baptist. (Archive Photos)

primarily to practice justice and charity toward their fellow man.

In John's Gospel the Baptist describes himself as the friend of the Bridegroom who must decrease as Christ must increase (Jn 3.25–30); he proclaims Jesus as the Lamb of God, and a few of John's disciples follow Jesus (Jn 1.35–37).

The Disciples of John the Baptist. John gathered around him a group of disciples (Mt 11.2; Lk 7.18–19) who remained faithful to him until his death. He taught them a special way of prayer (Lk 11.1) and fasting. The apostles Andrew and John had been disciples of the Baptist before joining Christ (Jn 1.35–40). The Synoptic Gospels record a dispute between the disciples of the Baptist and those of Christ over fasting (Mt 9.14 and parallels), and John's Gospel refers to a dispute between the disciples of the Baptist and those of Jesus over baptism (Jn 3.25–28). The Baptist, however, seems to have counseled his disciples to follow Jesus (Mt 11.2–6; see below).

Later (A.D. 53), Paul met Apollos and about 12 Ephesians who had received the baptism of John and apparently formed their own religious community at Ephesus (Acts 18.24; 19.1–7). The Fourth Gospel seems to contain a polemic against the disciples of the Baptist (Jn 1.6–8), which suggests that they existed as a separate

"Salome Receiving the Head of Saint John the Baptist," painting by Guercino, Museo Civico, Rimini, Italy. (© Archivo Iconografico, S. A./Corbis-Bettmann)

group, distinct from the Christian Church, even up to the end of the first century.

Imprisonment and Death. The Evangelists further describe how "all the country of Judea went out to him, and all the inhabitants of Jerusalem" (Mk 1.5; Mt 3.5; Lk 3.7). Josephus (*Ant.* 18.5.2), as well as the Evangelists, records the reaction of HEROD ANTIPAS, who, fearing an uprising, had the Baptist imprisoned. John had fearlessly denounced Herod's sinful marriage with HERODIAS, his brother's wife. In turn, Herodias instigated her daughter Salome to request John's death; to please her Herod had John beheaded, although he had regarded him as a religious and just man (Mt 14.3; Mk 6.17–20). While in prison, John had sent a delegation of his disciples to ask Jesus if He was the Messiah. According to some critics, John had found it difficult to accept a meek and merciful Messiah rather than an Elijah-like figure. In answer, Jesus pointed to his fulfillment of the OT messianic expecta-

tion, especially as described by Isaiah (35.5; 61.1). He then took the occasion to eulogize John as "a prophet, yes, more than a prophet. . . . Among those born of women there has not arisen a greater than John the Baptist" (Mt 11.9–11; Lk 7.18–28).

John the Baptist and Qumran. Many scholars think that the QUMRAN community of the Judean desert had an important influence on the Baptist. Some claim that John belonged to the community (e.g., J. Steinmann); others suggest that a common eschatological expectation in the area of the Judean desert is sufficient to explain the similarities (e.g., P. Benoit).

These similarities are striking. The Baptist stands against a specific background, that of the messianic expectation of the Judean desert. The Qumran community was a priestly one; John, too, came from a priestly family that manifested intense messianic hopes. Both John and the sectarians of Qumran found inspiration in the text of

Is 40.3. John preached a baptism of repentance, and while the Qumran community practiced ritual ablutions, there is no indication that they attached any moral significance to these. Yet the Qumran ritual was frequently repeated, whereas that of John was apparently administered only once. John announced a second baptism with the Holy Spirit and with fire (Lk 3.16), that is, an eschatological judgment; the Qumran ascetics, too, preached a second baptism that would be the work of the Spirit of God and would be eschatological (1QS 4.20–22). A striking difference, however, between John the Baptist and the Qumran community is the universality present in John's preaching in contrast to the closed character of the Qumran group, which regarded all outsiders as "sons of darkness."

Since John spent many years in the desert (Lk 1.80) and since there are marked similarities between John and the Qumranites, it seems probable that he knew the Qumran community. It has even been suggested that as a child he had been educated by them. Certainly, it appears that an influence was at work, for the discoveries at Qumran shed light upon the figure of John the Baptist and upon the general eschatological expectation that existed in the Judean desert. Whether there was a more immediate influence is not ascertainable. But he certainly was not a member of the Qumran community during his active ministry, for his missionary life was not in keeping with the rule of this community.

Iconography. The first representation of John, dating from the beginning of the second century, is found in the Catacombs of St. Callistus in Rome. It depicts the baptism of Christ by John. Evidence of a cult of the Baptist is not apparent before the fourth century, when Constantine built the Lateran Basilica and dedicated it to St. John the Baptist. In the sixth century the baptism of Christ by John was sculptured in bas relief on the ivory throne of Bishop Maximian, at present in the Archiepiscopal Museum at Ravenna. Throughout the Middle Ages and Renaissance and to the present, the Baptist has been the subject of paintings, sculptures, bronzes, and frescoes by the greatest of the artists. Statues of him are found on the Cathedrals of Chartres, Amiens, and Reims. In the Peruzzi Chapel of the church of S. Croce in Florence there is a series of frescoes by Giotto depicting John's life.

Bibliography: *Encyclopedic Dictionary of the Bible,* tr. L. HARTMAN (New York 1963) 1179–81. J. MICHL et al., *Lexikon für Theologie und Kirche*[2] (Freiburg 1930–38) 5:1084–89. P. VIELHAUER, *Die Religion in Geschichte und Gegenwart*[3] 3:804–808. J. STEINMANN, *Saint John the Baptist,* tr. M. BOYES (New York 1958). P. BENOIT "Qumrân et le N. T.," *New Testament Studies* 7 (1960–61) 276–296. J. DUPONT "L'Ambassade de Jean-Baptiste," *Nouvelle revue théologique* 83 (1961) 805–821, 943–959. A. FEUIL-LET, "Lea Trouvailles de Qumrân: Saint Jean-Baptiste et les hommes du désert," *Cahiers Évangiles* 27 (1957) 33–38.

[M. E. MCIVER]

JOHN THE BAPTIST, ST., ICONOGRAPHY OF

The iconography of St. John the Baptist is manifest in both cyclic representations of his life and in noncyclic representations.

Cyclic. The figure of John the Baptist was represented in Christian art as early as the 2d century. In the first stage he was represented only in relation to Christological scenes, especially to the scene of the Baptism of Christ (sarcophagus from Basilica Petronilla, Rome). As early as the 5th century, artists depicted various scenes of the life of John the Baptist on the basis of Biblical texts as well as apocryphal literature and legends. Consequently there existed a rich narrative cycle of the life of the saint already by the 11th century, and in the 13th century it came to include almost 20 scenes (frescoes of Braunschweig cathedral). The important scenes of the life of John the Baptist are: (1) the annunciation to Zacharias in the Temple; (2) the Visitation; (3) the birth and the naming; (4) the Circumcision; (5) the flight of Elizabeth, his mother, and young John to the mountain; (6) John the Baptist going into the wilderness; (7) the preaching in the wilderness; (8) the axe laid on the foot of a tree; (9) John the Baptist and the people of Israel receiving baptism from him; (10) John the Baptist bearing witness to Christ; (11) the baptism of Christ; (12) John the Baptist before Herod and Herodea; (13) arrest and imprisonment of John the Baptist; (14) the feast of Herod; (15) beheading of John the Baptist; (16) burial of the saint by his disciples; (17) burning of the bones of the saint; (18) quenching of the ashes; (19) discovery of the head of John the Baptist.

Noncyclic. In the early Church he soon became an object of veneration of the faithful and was ranked with the 12 Apostles and the four Evangelists. In the ivory sculpture on Maximianus's cathedra in Ravenna (6th century) he is represented with the four Evangelists, holding the symbol of the Lamb of God. In middle Byzantine art he was represented in the scene of the Last Judgment as an intercessor side by side with the Virgin Mary (Deësis). In the illustration to the apocryphal *Gospel of Nicodemus,* he was represented as foretelling the Descent of Christ into Hell. In the Italian Renaissance, artists invented a religious-genre motif of John the Baptist as a young boy dressed in camel fur and holding a cross-staff. Donatello represented the saint as an idealized youth (Museo Na-

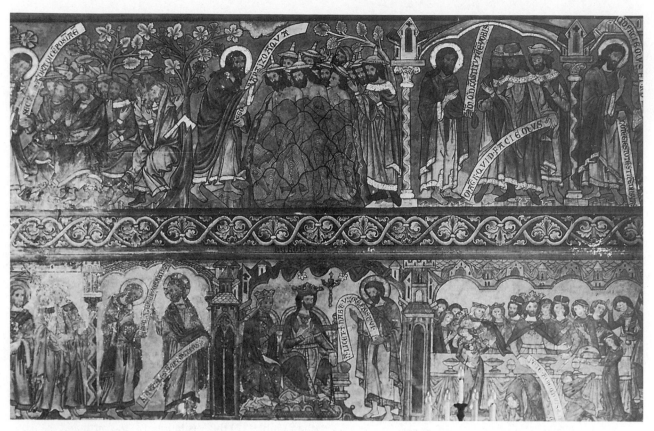

Life of St. John the Baptist, 13th-century fresco cycle in the cathedral church of St. Blasius, Braunschweig, Germany.

zionale, Florence) and in a very realistic manner (Siena cathedral). In the 16th century John the Baptist came to be represented as a playmate of Christ. This was a favorite motif in the series of Raphael's Madonna portraits (e.g., the Alba Madonna; National Gallery, Washington). In the baroque period, especially in the areas of Westphalia and the Lower Rhine, there arose a fervent veneration of the saint as a healer of illnesses of the head and neck. The so-called *Johannesschüssel*, the head of the saint on a charger, became a very popular motif of the period (paintings of Pordenone and Luini).

Bibliography: W. HARING, ''The Winged St. John the Baptist,'' *Art Bulletin* 5 (1922) 34–40. H. LECLERCQ, *Dictionnaire d'archéologie chrétienne et de liturgie,* ed. F. CARROLL, H. LECLERQ and H. I. MARROU, 15 v. (Paris 1907–53) 7.2:2167–84. G. KAFTAL, *Iconography of the Saints in Tuscan Painting* (Florence 1952) 550–560. L. RÉAU, *Iconographie de l'art chrétien,* 6 v. (Paris 1955–59) 2.1:431–463.

[S. TSUJI]

JOHN THE DEACON OF NAPLES

Hagiographer; b. Naples, *c.* 880; place and date of death unknown. A student of the priest AUXILIUS, he had become deacon of Southern Gennaro in Naples by 906; in that year he took part in the translation of the relics of St. Sosius from Miseno to Naples. While still young he compiled a lively chronicle of the bishops of Naples from 762 to 872 [*Monumenta Germaniae Historica, Scriptores rerum Langobardicarum* (Berlin 1826—) 424–435; also L. A. Muratori, *Rerum italicarum scriptores, 500–1500,* 25 v. in 28 (Milan 1723–51) 1.2:291–318]. He is best known for his hagiographical works dealing with St. Severinus [*Acta Sanctorum* January 1:497–499], St. Januarius (*Acta Sanctorum* September 6:874–878), St. Sosius (*Acta Sanctorum* September 6:879–884), the Forty Martyrs of Sebaste, a Latin translation (*Acta Sanctorum* March 2:22–25), and St. Procopius (*Rerum italicarum scriptores, 500–1500,* 1.2:269–273).

Bibliography: D. MALLARDO, ''Giovanni diacono napoletano,'' *Rivista di storia della Chiesa iri Italia,* 2 (1948) 317–337; 4 (1950) 325–358.

[G. T. DENNIS]

JOHN THE DEACON OF ROME (HYMMONIDES)

Author of the vita of GREGORY THE GREAT; b. *c.* 824; d. before 882. Probably a monk of MONTE CASSINO, he belonged to the court of CHARLES THE BALD for some time and subsequently (after 875) was a member of the entourage of Pope JOHN VIII (872–882). At John's request he wrote the *Vita Gregorii Magni* [*Patrologia Latina*, ed. J. P. Migne 217 V., indexes 4 v. (Paris 1878–90) 75:59–242], which is considered the best biography written in the period. For this work he used Gregory's register, quoting it extensively, and these extracts are still important for the study of PAPAL REGISTERS, particularly Gregory's. John is reputed to be the author of several other works, some of which are extant. He planned an extensive history of the Church for which his friend ANASTASIUS THE LIBRARIAN translated fragments for the Greek writings of Nicephorus, GEORGE SYNCELLUS, and THEOPHANES, but the plan was never realized. At the request of GAUDERICH OF VELLETRI he began a *Vita s. Clementis Romani,* but this work is lost. He rewrote in verse the apochryphal *Coena Cypriani* (ed. A. Lapôtre), attributed to St. CYPRIAN. John's authorship of the *Epistola ad Senarium* remains doubtful; however, his authorship of the *Commentary of St. John Chrysostom* on the Pentateuch is more probable. It is believed that he contributed to the account of Pope ADRIAN II in the LIBER PONTIFICALIS, and that he acted as papal secretary to JOHN VIII.

Bibliography: A. LAPÔTRE, "Le Souper de Jean Diacre," *Mélanges d'archéologie et d'histoire* 21 (1901) 305–385. M. MANITIUS, *Geschichte der lateinischen Literatur des Mittelalters,* 3 v. (Munich 1911–31) 1:689–695. G. ARNALDI, "Giovanni Immonide e la cultura a Roma al tempo di Giovanni VIII," *Bullettino dell'Istituto storico italiano per il medio evo e Archivio Muratoriano* 68 (1956) 33–89.

[J. J. MUZAS]

JOHN THE GRAMMARIAN, OF CAESAREA

Flourished in early 6th century, in Palestine, Byzantine theologian. Between 514 and 518 he wrote an Apology in defense of the Trinitarian definition of the Council of Chalcedon. Apart from three fragments that have been identified among the fragments of Eulogius of Alexandria by C. Moeller, his original work in Greek is lost. However, the moderate Monophysite theologian SEVERUS of Antioch, who was patriarch of that see from 512 to his deposition in 518 and was subsequently active as a writer, composed an elaborate attack on John's Apology entitled *Contra impium Grammaticum,* which is preserved in Syriac translation. This work contains forty-four extensive passages from John's work, including numerous patristic texts that John employed to support his exposition. John was an acute theological thinker who wished to give a strict but clear interpretation of the central teaching of the Council of Chalcedon. At the same time, he wished to establish an essential harmony between the definition of CYRIL OF ALEXANDRIA, including the ideas expressed in his *Anathematisms,* and that of the Council of Chalcedon. Relying heavily on the Trinitarian teachings and terminology of the great Cappadocian Fathers, he was the first to state formally that the human nature of Christ can never be thought of without hypostasis, since at no time did it exist alone without the Logos. He maintained in precise terms that the two natures of Christ were united by a hypostatic union in one hypostasis. John has been characterized by B. Altaner as the first important exponent of NeoChalcedonian Christology.

Bibliography: J. LEBON, *Contra Impium Grammaticum* (*Corpus scriptorum Christianorum orientalium,* 93, 101, 111; 1929–1938; repr. 1952). C. MOELLER, "Trois fragments grecs de l'Apologie de Jean le Grammairien pour le concile de Chalcédoine," *Revue d'histoire ecclésiastique,* 46 (1951) 683–688. H. G. BECK, *Kirche und theologische Literatur im byzantinischen Reich* (Munich 1959) 285, 377, 388, with bibliography. B. ALTANER, *Patrology,* tr. H. GRAEF from 5th German ed. (New York 1960) 613–614, with bibliography.

[M. R. P. MCGUIRE]

JOHN THE SILENT, ST.

Called the Hesychast or Sabaite; 6th-century Armenian monk and bishop of Colonia; b. Nicopolis, 454; d. Jan. 8, 559. John's biography was written by CYRIL OF SCYTHOPOLIS, who described him as the son of a rich family. At 18, on the death of his parents, John abandoned his fortune and founded a monastic settlement in a wilderness, which he directed for a number of years. He was chosen bishop of Colonia in Armenia; but after a short time he fled to Jerusalem, where he was received into the monastery of St. Sabas and lived in perpetual silence.

Feast: May 13.

Bibliography: *Acta Sanctorum* May 3:230–236, 14*–18*. *Bibliotheca hagiographica Graeca* 897, 898. E. SCHWARTZ, ed., *Kyrillos von Skythopolis* (*Texte und Untersuchungen zur Geschichte der altchristlichen Literatur* 49.2; 1939) 201–222. G. GARITTE, *Analecta Bollandiana* 72 (1954) 75–84.

[P. ROCHE]

JOHN VINCENTIUS, ST.

Benedictine bishop and hermit; d. probably Dec. 12, 1012. At first a bishop in the district around RAVENNA, he later became a hermit on Monte Pirchiriano in Piedmont, where, after the fashion of St. ROMUALD and the CAMALDOLESE, he gathered around himself a colony of hermits known as Santa-Maria delle Celle. On this spot in 987 he built the chapel in honor of St. Michael, which by the year 1000 had grown into the Abbey of San Michele di Chiusa. Later, in 1006, he played a part in the foundation of San Solutore in Turin. In 1154 his remains were translated to the parish church of Sant' Ambrogio.

Feast: Dec. 21.

Bibliography: *Chronicon monasterii s. Michaelis Clusini* in *Monumenta Germaniae Historica: Scriptores* 30.2:961–964. F. SAVIO, *Gli Antichi Vescovi d'Italia*, v.1 *Il Piemonte* (Turin 1898). A. M. ZIMMERMANN, *Kalendarium Benedictinum: Die Heiligen und Seligen des Benediktinerorderns und seiner Zweige* 3:466–468.

[P. L. HUG]

JOHN WELLES

English theologian; d. Perugia, 1388. He was a Benedictine of RAMSEY ABBEY and was ordained on June 7, 1365. He studied at Oxford (Gloucester College), becoming master in theology by 1377, and served as head of Gloucester College for many years. He became an active and bitter opponent of John WYCLIF when the Oxford reformer attacked monastic orders as *religiones privatae*. Welles, known as the "Hammer of Heretics," was one of the 12 doctors who examined the writings of Wyclif at Oxford in 1380. He took a prominent part in the council at Blackfriars, London, convened by archbishop William COURTENAY for suppression of Wyclifite teachings in 1382. In 1387 the provincial chapter of English Black Monks appointed him to transact its business on the Continent and to plead for the release of Cardinal ADAM EASTON from the papal prison in Rome. He died the following year in Perugia and was buried in the church of Santa Sabina. He was author of many sermons, letters, and polemical treatises, including: *De socii sui ingratitudine, Pro religione privata, Super cleri praerogativa,* and *Super Eucharistiae negotio.*

Bibliography: *Fasciculi Zizaniorum,* ed. W. W. SHIRLEY, *Rerum Britannicarum medii aevi scriptores,* 244 v. (London 1858–96) 5:239–241, 287, 499. H. B. WORKMAN, *John Wyclif,* 2 v. (Oxford 1926) 2:123–124. *The Dictionary of National Biography From the Earliest Times to 1900,* 63 v. (London 1885–1900) 20:1139–40. A. B. EMDEN, *A Biographical Register of the University of Oxford to A.D. 1500,* 3 v. (Oxford 1957–59) 3:2008.

[J. A. WEISHEIPL]

JOHN AND PAUL, SS.

Roman martyrs named in the Canon of the Mass. According to the legendary *passio,* John and Paul were brothers, officials at the imperial court, whom JULIAN THE APOSTATE (361–363) had put to death as Christians by the Roman officer Terentianus. They were allegedly decapitated in their home on the Caelian hill and secretly buried in the basement. On the death of Julian, the new Emperor Jovian then constructed a basilica over the site of their martyrdom. Excavations beneath the Basilica of Saints Giovanni e Paolo in Rome were interpreted by Germano di S. Stanislao at the beginning of the 20th century, and more recently by G. de Sanctis, as indicative of the historical existence of the two saints. However, the complexity of the manuscript tradition of the *passio* and its authenticity have been studied by outstanding hagiographers who deny its historical worth: FRANCHI DE' CAVALIERI considered the *passio* a plagiarism on the Acts of Saints Juventinus and Maximinus; Lanzoni and H. Delehaye thought the original title of the basilica referred to John the Baptist and the Apostle St. Paul. A. Prandi's judgment (1953) still seems to be the most authentic: the archeological remains beneath the present church are a remarkable specimen of what was a large pagan home apparently used for Christian services, over which the original basilica was built in the fifth century; but the archeological evidence provides no clear or undisputable link between the monument and the saints. John and Paul were greatly honored in England; a council at Oxford in 1222 made their feast a holy day of obligation in Great Britain. Because of the generosity of Cardinal Francis Spellman of New York, whose titular church it was, the remains of the ancient house beneath the present basilica have been almost totally restored.

Feast: June 26.

Bibliography: G. DI S. STANISLAO, *La casa Celimontana dei SS. Martiri Giovanni e Paolo* (Rome 1894); cpf. *Analecta Bollandiana,* 14 (1895) 332. G. DE SANCTIS, *I Santi Giovanni e Paolo martiri celimontani* (Rome 1962); cpf. B. DE GAIFFIER, *Analecta Bollandiana,* 82 (1964) 439–440. E. GASDIA, *La casa paganocristiana del Celio* (Rome 1937). A. PRANDI, *Il complesso monumentale della basilica celimontana* (Vatican City 1953). V. L. KENNEDY, *The Saints of the Canon of the Mass* (Vatican City 1938) 131–137. P. FRANCHI DE' CAVALIERI, *Note agiografiche* (*Studi e Testi,* 9; 1902) 53–65. F. L. CROSS, *The Oxford Dictionary of the Christian Churh* (London 1957) 738.

[V. RICCI]

JOHNSON, GEORGE

Professor, administrator; b. Toledo, Ohio, Feb. 22, 1889; d. Washington, D.C., June 4, 1944. He was the son of Henry and Kathryn (McCarthy) Johnson. After studying at St. John's University, Toledo, (M.A., 1912), and St. Bernard's Seminary, Rochester, N.Y., he was sent to the North American College, Rome, Italy, where he was ordained in 1914. He served for two years as secretary to Bp. Joseph Schrembs and then left to obtain his doctorate in education (1919) at The Catholic University of America, Washington, D.C. He was then diocesan superintendent of schools at Toledo until 1921, when Bp. Thomas J. Shahan appointed him professor of education at Catholic University, a post he held until his death.

In addition to his teaching, he served (1923–27) as assistant at neighboring St. Anthony parish, where he was in charge of the parochial school. He was also director of the Campus School of The Catholic University from its inception in 1935. In 1928–29 Johnson was appointed director of the Department of Education of the National Catholic Welfare Conference and secretary general of the National Catholic Educational Association. These posts, which he held until his death, gave him national influence on American education and led to appointments on several presidential committees. When the Commission on American Citizenship was founded at Catholic University by the American hierarchy in 1938, Johnson was named to its executive committee. In 1943 he was made director of this commission. He wrote the commission's statement of principles, *Better Men for Better Times* (1943), as well as a study of Catholic elementary school curricula, three textbooks on Bible and Church history, and several periodical articles. In November 1942 he was named domestic prelate by Pius XII.

[E. KEVANE]

JOHNSON, ROBERT, BL.

Priest, martyr; b. Shropshire, England; d. hanged, drawn, and quartered at Tyburn (London), May 28, 1582. Johnson entered the German College in Rome on Oct. 1, 1571, but completed his seminary studies at the English College in Douai. Following his ordination at Brussels (April 1576), he labored in London for six years interrupted only by a pilgrimage to Rome (1579) and imprisonment. He was arrested July 12, 1580 and imprisoned at the Poultry Counter until he was transferred to the Tower of London (December 5). Johnson endured the rack (December 16), then was thrust into an underground dungeon until his trial (November 14) at which he was found guilty on the fictitious charge of conspiring against the king at Rome and Rheims. On November 20, he was condemned. He was executed with BB. Thomas FORD and John SHERT, who were also implicated in the same "plot." He was beatified by Pope Leo XIII.

Feast of the English Martyrs: May 4 (England).

See Also: ENGLAND, SCOTLAND, AND WALES, MARTYRS OF.

Bibliography: R. CHALLONER, *Memoirs of Missionary Priests,* ed. J. H. POLLEN (rev. ed. London 1924; repr. Farnborough 1969). J. H. POLLEN, *Acts of English Martyrs* (London 1891).

[K. I. RABENSTEIN]

JOHNSON, THOMAS, BL.

Carthusian priest, martyr; starved to death at Newgate Prison, London, Sept. 20, 1537. Thomas, a monk at the London Charterhouse, had already seen the deaths of many of his Carthusian brothers, including the priors SS. John HOUGHTON, Robert LAWRENCE, and Augustine WEBSTER (d. 1535), as well as others. On May 18, 1537, the 38 remaining monks of the London Charterhouse were required to take the Oath of Supremacy. Frs. Thomas Johnson, Richard Bere, and Thomas Green, as well as John Davy and the lay brothers Robert Salt, William Greenwood, Thomas Redyng, Thomas Scryven, Walter Pierson, and William Horne were imprisoned at Newgate for refusing to recognize King Henry VIII as supreme head of the Church in England. There they were chained to posts with their hands behind them and left to die. St. Thomas More's former ward, Margaret Giggs Clement, bribed the jailer to allow her access to the prisoners to feed them. This continued for some time until authorities questioned the monks' continued survival without food. Seven died June 6–16 (Greenwood, Davy, Salt, Pierson, Green, Scryven, and Redyng). Thereafter it appears Cromwell ordered that the remaining monks be fed so that they could stand for execution, but it is believed that Johnson was eventually starved to death. He was beatified by Pope Leo XIII on Dec. 9, 1886.

Feast of the English Martyrs: May 4 (England).

See Also: ENGLAND, SCOTLAND, AND WALES, MARTYRS OF.

Bibliography: R. CHALLONER, *Memoirs of Missionary Priests,* ed. J. H. POLLEN (rev. ed. London 1924; repr. Farnborough 1969). J. H. POLLEN, *Acts of English Martyrs* (London 1891).

[K. I. RABENSTEIN]

JOLENTA OF HUNGARY, BL.

Widow, Poor Clare nun; b. Hungary, *c.* 1235; d. Gniezno, Poland, *c.* 1298–99. Jolenta (Yolande, Helena) was a grandniece of St. HEDWIG, a niece of St. ELIZABETH OF HUNGARY, and a sister of SS. MARGARET OF HUNGARY and KINGA of Poland. Her father was King Bela IV of Hungary and her mother, Mary, a daughter of the Emperor of Constantinople. At the age of five, Jolenta was placed under the care of her sister Kinga, queen of Po-

Niccolò Jommelli. (©Archivo Iconografico, S.A./CORBIS.)

land, wife of Boleslas V the Chaste. Jolenta married Duke Boleslas VI the Pious of Kalisz. After the duke died in 1279 and two daughters had married, she and her youngest daughter joined her widowed sister Kinga in the POOR CLARE convent at Stary Sacz. Later Jolenta moved to the Poor Clare convent she and her husband had founded at Gniezno, and there held the office of abbess. Originally authorized by URBAN VIII, Jolenta's cult was approved by LEO XII in 1827. Prior to 1961 her feast was observed by all three branches of the First Order of St. Francis.

Feast: June 15.

Bibliography: LÉON DE CLARY, *Lives of the Saints and Blessed of the Three Orders of St. Francis,* 4 v. (Taunton, England 1885–87) v.2. A. BUTLER, *The Lives of the Saints,* ed. H. THURSTON and D. ATTWATER, 4 v. (New York 1956) 2:550. M. A. HABIG, *Franciscan Book of Saints* (Chicago 1959) 421–423.

[M. A. HABIG]

JOMMELLI, NICCOLÒ

Composer of opera and sacred music in classical style; b. Aversa, near Naples, Sept. 10, 1714; d. Naples, Aug. 25, 1774. After basic music training under the Aversa cathedral choirmaster, Mazillo, and contact with contemporary musicians such as Feo, Durante, and Leo, he produced his first opera, *L'Errore amoroso,* in 1737. In 1741, while under the tutelage of Padre Giovanni Martini, he began writing sacred works of artistic importance. Following further opera composition in Venice and Vienna, he was appointed assistant *maestro di cappella* of St. Peter's in 1750, and three years later, *Kapellmeister* to the Duke of Württemberg at Stuttgart. It was during his 15-year stay in Germany that his style underwent a distinct change. From the flowing Neapolitan idiom of his Italian compositions, he turned toward placing more emphasis on harmonic complexity, frequent and free use of modulation, and instrumental accompaniment. Because of these innovations he is sometimes called the Italian Glück. His sacred works include Masses, motets, oratorios, Te Deums, Offertory hymns, and sequences. His most famous, *Miserere,* for two voices, was completed just before his death.

Bibliography: R. EITNER, *Quellen-Lexikon der Musiker und Musikgelehrten,* 10 v. (Leipzig 1900–04; New York 1947) 5:294–299, listing of church music. O. URSPRUNG, *Die katholische Kirchenmusik* (Handbuch der Musikwissenschaft 8; Postdam 1931). A. MONDOLFI, *Die Musik in Geschichte und Gegenwart,* ed. F. BLUME (Kassel-Basel 1949–) 7:142–154. J. O. CARLSON, *Selected Masses of Niccolò Jommelli* (Ph.D. diss. University of Illinois 1974). W. HOCHSTEIN, *Die Kirchenmusik von Niccolò Jommelli (1714–1774)* (Hildesheim 1984). M. P. MCCLYMONDS, *Niccolò Jommelli: The Last Years, 1769–1774* (Ann Arbor 1980); "Niccolò Jommelli," in *The New Grove Dictionary of Music and Musicians,* ed., S. SADIE (New York 1980) 9:689–695. D. E. MONSON, "Niccolò Jommelli," in *International Dictionary of Opera,* ed., C. S. LARUE, (Detroit 1993) 653–56. N. SLONIMSKY, ed. *Baker's Biographical Dictionary of Musicians* (New York 1992) 862–63. A. L. TOLKOFF, *The Stuttgart Operas of Niccolò Jommelli* (Ph.D. diss. Yale University 1974).

[M. CORDOVANA]

JÓN ÖGMUNDSSON, ST.

Also known as Ogmund; first bishop of Hólar, Iceland; b. Breidabolsstadur, 1052; d. April 23, 1121. He went abroad, perhaps as far as Rome, and brought back Saemund the Learned, founder of the famous Icelandic school at Oddi. Jón was priest of Breidabolsstadur when the decision was made to divide Iceland into two dioceses. He built a new church at Hólar and started a school there for future priests. Jón has left a permanent mark on the Icelandic language, as he was responsible for renaming the days of the week to remove their pagan associations. He was canonized in 1201, and devotion to him has survived in Iceland to the present day.

Feast: March 8.

Bibliography: *Byskupa sögur,* 3 v. (Reykjavík 1948; reprint 1953). *Origines Islandicae,* ed. and tr. G. VIGFÚSSON and F. Y. POWELL, 2 v. (Oxford 1905). J. HELGASON, "Jón Ögmundsson . . . ,"

Norvegia sacra, 5 (1925) 1–34. J. C. F. HOOD, *Icelandic Church Saga* (London 1946). E. KRISTJÁN, *Um Hóladómkirkju* (Hólar 1993).

[D. C. C. POCHIN MOULD]

JONAH, BOOK OF

Written in clear, simple language, this difficult and profound little book has long been the subject of lively discussion. This article covers the structure and content; authorship, sources, and date; and literary genre and theological purpose.

Structure and Content. Although traditionally listed among those of the MINOR PROPHETS, the book is not, strictly speaking, a prophetical book but a story of late date concerning a particular mission of Jonah (Hebrew: *yōnâ,* ''dove''). The book falls into two parts (ch. 1–2 and ch. 3–4), each part consisting of two scenes.

Part I. The first part prepares the reader for the impact of the second. God commissioned Jonah to go to Nineveh to preach repentance, but Jonah rebelled— presumably against the idea of preaching salvation to non-Israelites—and sailed toward Spain. God sent a storm that was about to destroy the ship. When the mariners discovered that Jonah had occasioned their danger by his disobedience, they threw him into the sea, which immediately became calm. A ''large fish'' swallowed Jonah. After three days God commanded the fish to vomit him safely on dry land.

Part II. At the second order to preach, Jonah obeyed. The Ninevites heard him, repented, and were pardoned, but Jonah was angry because of Nineveh's good fortune. The story ends in a confrontation of God and Jonah. Having lost the shade from the plant that God had miraculously provided for him, Jonah was indignant enough to die. God forced Jonah to see reason by a rhetorical question: If you are so upset about losing so small a thing, which you did nothing to procure, is there not much greater reason for my being concerned over Nineveh and all its inhabitants who are also objects of my loving care?

Author, Sources, and Date. This anonymous writing exhibits dependence on earlier Biblical books. The pseudonym of the hero alludes to the historical Jonah, son of Amittai, an 8th-century Galilean prophet from Gath-hepher (modern Khirbet ez-Zurrâ') in Zebulun (2 Kgs 14.25). The storm recalls Ez 26–28, especially ch. 27, where the technique is reversed: In Ezekiel, God hurls a storm against His enemies but in Jonah, against His own prophet. In Ezekiel, ship and crew sink; but in Jonah, pagan mariners and their ship survive while Jonah is cast into the sea. The author of the Book of Jonah develops

Jonah Thrown in the Sea, from the ''Great Bible of Demeter Nekcsei-Lipocz.''

Jeremiah's theology of divine pardon for repentant sinners (cf. Jon 3.10b and Jer 18.7–8; 26.3), and God's universal love (cf. Jon 1.2 and Jer 1.5). Ancient commentators generally considered the 8th-century prophet Jonah both hero and author of the book. However, the literary and theological dependence already noted, in addition to considerations of language, of history, and of mentality, indicate a post-Exilic period as the time of composition. Philological examination reveals late Hebrew and Aramaisms but probably no Greek influence. The author speaks of Nineveh (destroyed 612 B.C.) as no longer existing except in popular imagination. Moreover, in the people's minds it had become a colossal city (Jon 3.3), whereas archeologists have shown ancient Nineveh to have been only three miles wide. Finally, the author's liberal attitude toward pagans seems to be a reaction against a too-nationalistic view of God's providence. These data drawn from the story itself point to a post-Exilic writer probably of the Ezra-Nehemiah period (middle of the 5th century). He probably wrote before the Greek period, certainly before Sirach (cf. Sir 49). Because the canticle (Jon 2.3–10) is probably without Aramaisms and any apparent connection with the context, it is generally considered an insertion. Some judge it a mosaic of psalm pieces, some of which may be as late as the

3rd century B.C.; others consider it an original and unified composition.

Literary Genre and Theological Purpose. Scholars today do not consider Jonah a historical narrative but an edifying story. The unknown writer artfully, ironically compounds familiar scriptural material, with perhaps some folklorish elements, to make a didactic fiction, a MIDRASH. The "sign of Jonah" mentioned in the Gospels (Mt 12.38–41; Lk 11.29–32), if correctly transmitted, is no argument for the historicity of Jonah. Neither Jesus nor the Gospel writers were treating of literary or historical criticism, but were citing a familiar example somewhat as people today allude to Cinderella or the Prodigal Son. The author's purpose is to warn his Jewish contemporaries against their extreme nationalism. He accomplishes this by a satire in which every narrow-minded Israelite of the day would see himself reflected in the person of Jonah. In the first part of the book Jonah is a recalcitrant prophet; in the last chapter, the incarnation of the particularist spirit. Criticizing this spirit furthers the author's purpose. When Jonah was the beneficiary of divine mercy, he prayed; but when Ninevites were objects of the same mercy, he was angry enough to die. Theologically broad-minded, the author teaches that God rules the world, that His providence extends to all men. Tension between the spirit of particularism and universalism should be resolved in favor of the latter because the mercy of God waits for all who repent no matter what their nation.

Bibliography: A. ROBERT and A. TRICOT, *Guide to the Bible*, tr. E. P. ARBEZ and M. P. MCGUIRE, 2 v. (Tournai-New York 1951–55; v. 1, rev. and enl. 1960) 1:345–346. L. DENNEFELD, *Dictionnaire de théologie catholique* 8.2:1497–1504. H. G. MITCHELL, et al., *Aggai, Zachariah, Malachi, and Jonah* (New York 1912). E. SELLIN, *Das Zwölfprophetenbuch* (Leipzig 1929). T. H. ROBINSON and F. HORST, *Die zwölf Kleinen Propheten* (*Handbuch zum Alten Testament* 14; 2d ed. 1954). A. R. JOHNSON, "Jonah II. 3–10: A Study in Cultic Phantasy," *Studies in Old Testament Prophecy,* ed. H. H. ROWLEY (Edinburgh 1950) 82–102. S. H. BLANK, "'Doest Thou Well to Be Angry?' A Study in Self-Pity," *Hebrew Union College Annual* 26 (1955) 29–41. J. HOWTON, "The Sign of Jonah," *Scottish Journal of Theology* 15 (1962) 288–304. S. R. DRIVER, *An Introduction to the Literature of the Old Testament* (11th ed. rev. and enl. New York 1905) 321–25. A. FEUILLET, *Le Livre de Jonas* (2d ed. Paris 1957). Popular presentation. A. JONES, *Unless Some Man Show Me* (New York 1951) 48–68.

[J. M. LANE]

JONAH, SIGN OF

The answer that Jesus gave when His adversaries asked Him for a sign in proof of His heavenly mission as recounted in Mt 12.38–42; 16.1–4; and Lk 11.29–32. These three passages create a problem because they give different explanations of what He meant by the sign that He offered, "the sign of Jonah." The matter is further complicated by the partial parallel in Mk 8.11–12. The solution seems to be that the words and deeds of Jesus were not always recorded by the Evangelists exactly as they were spoken or done, but they were often given new meanings in the inspired KERYGMA OF THE APOSTLES, and these different interpretations were then recorded in the Gospels. *See* FORM CRITICISM, BIBLICAL.

Gospel accounts. In Mk 8.11–12 it is stated that when the PHARISEES demanded of Jesus a sign from heaven as a means of embarrassing Him, He became angry and answered simply: "A sign shall not be given to this generation."

According to Luke, when Jesus was asked for a sign (Lk 11.16), He first said, "This generation is an evil generation; it demands a sign, but no sign will be given it but the sign of Jonah" (11.29); then He adds this explanation: "Even as Jonah was a sign to the Ninevites, so will the Son of Man be to this generation. . . . The men of Nineveh will rise up in judgment with this generation and condemn it; for they repented at the preaching of Jonah, and behold, a greater than Jonah is here" (11.30, 32).

According to Mt 12.38–42, when "certain of the SCRIBES and Pharisees" asked Jesus for a sign (v. 38), He first said in answer: "An evil and adulterous generation demands a sign, but no sign will be given it but the sign of Jonah the prophet" (v. 39); this is parallel with Lk 11.29. Then He added a first explanation of the sign: "Even as Jonah was in the belly of the fish three days and three nights, so will the Son of Man be three days and three nights in the heart of the earth" (v. 40); this is unique to Matthew. Finally a second explanation is given: "The men of Nineveh will rise up in the judgment with this generation and will condemn it; for they repented at the preaching of Jonah, and behold, a greater than Jonah is here" (v. 41); this is parallel to Lk 11.32.

According to Mt 16.1–4, in a context that is similar partly to Mk 8.10–12 (a boating scene) and partly to Lk 12.54–55 (signs of the weather), when "the Pharisees and SADDUCEES. . . asked Him to show a sign from heaven" (Mt 16.1), He answered: "An evil and adulterous generation demands a sign, but no sign will be given it but the sign of Jonah" (v. 4); this is parallel to Lk 11.29 and Mt 12.39. In this passage no explanation of the sign is given.

Original logion and kerygmatic explanations. Most exegetes are now agreed that the original logion (saying) of Jesus was as in Mt 12.39; 16.4; Lk 11.29, i.e., simply that no sign at all would be given to the present wicked generation except the sign of Jonah—with no explanation of the sign. It is therefore certain that the sign concerns the future, after the present generation is dead; this is clear from the future tense of the verb δοθήσεται (will be given) and from the fact that the sign of Jonah is not mentioned in Mk 8.11–12 (the present generation will not see any sign, not even the sign of Jonah). Actually, Jonah gave no "sign" to the Ninevites.

The two explanations of the sign that are given in the Gospels, viz, the Ninevites converted by Jonah testifying against the present generation on Judgment Day (Mt 12.41; Lk 11.32) and the comparison between Jonah's salvation from the belly of the fish and the Resurrection of Jesus from the dead (Mt 12.40, a passage that presupposes the Resurrection as already having happened), although not originally spoken by Jesus to His adversaries, are inspired interpretations of the Apostolic preaching that give a key for solving the puzzle of the sign of Jonah. Since the kerygmatic explanations of this sign connect it with the Resurrection and the Last Judgment, it can be explained best as designating the PAROUSIA of the risen Christ coming in judgment. Other interpretations, viz, that the sign of Jonah is the preaching of Jesus on repentance and the coming judgment, or the entire ministry of Jesus, or solely His Resurrection, do not do justice to all the passages concerned. The notion that takes the meaning of Jonah's name (Heb. *yônâ*, dove) as the basis for an interpretation whereby the "sign of the dove" would refer to Jesus under the symbol of a dove cannot be taken seriously.

Bibliography: *Encyclopedic Dictionary of the Bible* (New York 1963) 1200–02. A. VÖGTLE, *Lexikon für Theologie und Kirche,* ed. J. HOFER and K. RAHNER (Freiburg 1957–65) 5:1116–17. J. HOWTON, "The Sign of Jonah," *Scottish Journal of Theology* 15 (1962) 288–304. O. GLOMBITZA, "Das Zeichen des Jona," *New Testament Studies* 8 (1962) 359–366.

[J. M. LANE]

JONAH BEN JIȘHAQ, JEHUDAH

Learned Jewish convert; b. Safed, Galilee, Oct. 28, 1588; d. Rome, May 26, 1668. During his extensive travels in Europe as a rabbi he was converted to Catholicism in Poland and took the name of John the Baptist. Later he was sent by the King of Poland to Constantinople for the purchase of precious stones. There, however, he was arrested on the charge of espionage and would have been executed had not the Venetian ambassador interceded for him and enabled him to go to Italy. In Italy, where he was known as Giovanni Battista, he taught Hebrew and Aramaic, first at Pisa and then at the College of the Propaganda, Rome. One of his students at Rome was G. BARTOLOCCI (1613–87), who received much help from

Jonah in preparing his masterpiece, the *Bibliotheca magna rabbinica de scriptoribus et de scriptis hebraicis* (4 v. Rome 1675–94). Jonah himself published a Hebrew translation from the Latin of the four Gospels, with a preface by Pope Clement IX (Rome 1668).

Bibliography: E. LEVESQUE, *Dictionnaire de la Bible,* ed. F. VIGOUROUX, 5 v. (Paris 1895–1912) 1.2:1514. F. X. E. ALBERT, *The Catholic Encyclopedia,* ed. C. G. HERBERMANN et al., 16 v. (New York 1907–14) 2:350.

[L. F. HARTMAN]

JONAS, JUSTUS (JODOCUS KOCH)

Lutheran theologian at Wittenberg and reformer of Halle; b. Nordhausen, Germany, June 5 or 6, 1493; d. Eisfeld, Oct. 9, 1555. Jonas studied in Erfurt (Bachelor of Arts 1507, Master of Arts 1510) and at Wittenberg. In 1518 he returned to Erfurt as lecturer in law. In 1521 he became professor of Canon Law at Wittenberg and accompanied Martin Luther to Worms. An Erasmian humanist, he was won over to theology and scriptural studies. His activity as a theologian included collaboration on Luther's Bible translation, a commentary on the *Acts,* a translation of Melanchthon's *Loci* and of Luther's *De servo arbitrio,* a contribution to the Augsburg Confession, participation in the Marburg Colloquy with Ulrich Zwingli, and the composition of an influential church order for Zerbst. His activity as a reformer included the introduction of the Reformation in Naumburg and service as visitor in Ducal Saxony after the death of Duke George (1539), Protestant leader in Halle (1541–46), evangelical preacher in Hildesheim (1547), court preacher for Duke Ernest in Coburg (1552), organizer of the Lutheran Church in Regensburg (1552), and superintendent at Eisfeld (1553–55).

Bibliography: *Der Briefwechsel der Justus Jonas,* ed. G. KAWERAU, 2 v. (Halle 1884–85). W. DELIUS, *Justus Jonas, 1493–1555* (Berlin 1952). *Die Religion in Geschichte und Gegenwart*[3], 7 v. (3d ed. Tübingen 1957–65) 3:856. M. E. LEHMANN, *Justus Jonas, Loyal Reformer* (Minneapolis 1963).

[L. W. SPITZ]

JONAS OF BOBBIO

Hagiographer; b. Susa, in Piedmont, *c.* 600; d. after 665. He entered the abbey of BOBBIO in 618, about three years after the death of the Irish missionary abbot, COLUMBAN. Here Jonas served as secretary to abbots ATHALA OF BOBBIO (d. 626) and BERTULF OF BOBBIO (d. 639). He also knew another companion of St. Columban, St. EUSTACE OF LUXEUIL. Jonas spent three years

(639–642) as a missionary with St. AMANDUS in the north of France. From his writings it is evident that he traveled extensively; at the request of Clotar III he visited Chalon-sur-Saône. After 650 Jonas seems never to have returned to Bobbio. In 652 and 653 he served temporarily as abbot of Saint-Amand-les-Eaux and was still alive in 665. Most of our information about Jonas comes from the autobiographical asides in his writings. Jonas's works include a life of Bishop VEDAST OF ARRAS, [*Monumenta Germaniae Historica, Scriptores rerum Merovingicarum* (Berlin 1826—) 3:406–413] and a life of abbot JOHN OF RÉOMÉ (*Monumenta Germaniae Historica, Scriptores rerum Merovingicarum* 3:505–517). His principal work, a life of St. Columban, undertaken on orders from Bertulf, was completed only after the abbot's death (*Monumenta Germaniae Historica, Scriptores rerum Merovingicarum* 4:61–152). The first of its two books is an account of the founder based on information Jonas gathered in his travels and on interviews with those who knew the saint. The second book is primarily an account of St. Columban's successors: Athala and Bertulf at Bobbio, Eustace at LUXEUIL. As a hagiographer Jonas reflects the shortcomings of the age and the genre: disregard for chronology, preoccupation with the miraculous, and decadence in language and grammar. On the other hand, Jonas did make an effort to ascertain facts, and generally shows himself a reliable reporter.

Bibliography: H. LECLERCQ, *Dictionnaire d'archéologie chrétienne et de liturgie,* ed. F. CARBOL, H. LECLERCQ and H. I. MARROU, 15 v. (Paris 1907–53) 7,2:2631–41. W. WATTENBACH *Deutschlands Geschichtsquellen im Mittelalter. Vorzeit und Karolinger,* Hefte 1–4, ed. W. LEVISON and H. LÖWE (Weimar 1952–63) 1:133–134.

[B. L. MARTHALER]

JONAS OF ORLÉANS

Frankish bishop, theological writer; b. Aquitaine, before 780; d. Orléans, 843. Jonas, whose name is connected with the questions of veneration of images and Church-State relations, succeeded THEODULF as bishop of Orléans in 818 and governed that see for 25 years during the reigns of LOUIS THE PIOUS and CHARLES THE BALD. He was active in the reform synods of 825 to 837. He opposed his fellow bishops AGOBARD OF LYONS and EBBO OF REIMS. Jonas left three treatises [*Patrologia Latina,* ed. J. P. Migne, 217 v., indexes 4 v. (Paris 1878–90) 106:117–387]: *De institutione laicali,* on the moral duties of married persons; an untitled work on the duties of monarchs, given the title *De institutione regia* by later editors; and *De cultu imaginum,* on the veneration of images. *De institutione laicali* and *De institutione regia* are companion pieces, similar in approach and style. Jonas

wrote the first at the request of Matfrid, Count of Orléans. The second was written for the instruction of Pepin, young King of Aquitaine, son of Louis the Pious. Neither contains much original material. Jonas followed the typical pre-scholastic practice of employing a chain of passages from Scripture and the Fathers, with only transitional and connective comment. In the treatise for Matfrid, Jonas discusses, among other things, the dominant vices of the laity: delay of repentance, with the presumptuous hope of getting into Purgatory; receiving Holy Communion only at the great feasts; postponement of Extreme Unction for the dying; excessive preoccupation with gambling, hunting, and dogs; and cursing, lying, and worldliness. In the treatise for King Pepin, Jonas explains what it is to be a king, what the king must do and avoid, what is properly his office. The king must reward good citizens, punish criminals, suppress crime, and care for the poor. His justice will be a support to the throne, while injustice will overthrow it. *De cultu imaginum* was written on commission of Emperor Louis against the views of bishop CLAUDIUS OF TURIN. It is in three books: on images, on the veneration of the cross, and on pilgrimages and the invocation of saints. Jonas apparently tried to steer a middle course between ICONOCLASM and image worship. He held that IMAGES properly are for the adornment of churches, for commemoration, and for the instruction of the faithful. He rejected excessive and superstitious cults amounting to adoration.

Bibliography: JONAS OF ORLÉANS, *Les Idées politico-religieuses . . . ,* ed. J. REVIRON (Paris 1930). M. MANITIUS, *Geschichte der lateinischen Literatur des Mittelalters,* 3 v. (Munich 1911–31) 1:374–380. W. WATTENBACH *Deutschlands Geschichtsquellen im Mittelalter. Vorzeit und Karolinger,* Hefte 1–4, ed. W. LEVISON and H. LÖWE (Weimar 1952–63) 3:311ff. Beih. 9. A. GARCIA MARTINEZ, ''El primer tratado político-religioso del siglo IXe tratado de institutione regia del obispo aquitano Jonas de Orléans,'' *Crisis* 4 (Madrid 1957) 239–264.

[C. E. SHEEDY]

JONATUS, ST.

Benedictine; d. *c.* 691. He was a disciple of St. AMANDUS, the Apostle of the Belgians, by whom he was summoned to come from the Abbey of Elnon to serve as abbot over the monks of the double monastery of Marchiennes, near Douai. The nuns of this house were governed by St. Rictrudis.

Feast: Aug. 1.

Bibliography: *Acta Sanctorum,* Aug. 1:70–75. J. L. BAUDOT and L. CHAUSSIN, *Vies des saints et des bienheureux selon l'ordre du calendrier avec l'historique des fêtes* (Paris 1935–56) 8:12. *Miraculum,* ed. E. SACKUR, in *Neues Archiv der Gesellschaft für ältere deutsche Geschichtskunde* 15 (1890) 448–452. A. M. ZIMMER-

MANN, *Kalendarium Benedictinum: Die Heiligen und Seligen des Benediktinerorderns und seiner Zweige,* 4 v. (Metten 1933–38) 2:523–525.

[O. L. KAPSNER]

JONES, EDWARD, BL.

Priest, martyr; b. Diocese of St. Asaph, Wales; d. hanged, drawn, and quartered in Fleet Street, London, England, May 6, 1590. When Jones, raised as an Anglican, was convicted of the truth of the Catholic faith, he migrated to Rheims where he was received into the Church in 1587 and ordained priest the following year. He immediately returned to England to exercise his ministry. He was arrested (1590) in a Fleet Street shop by a man pretending to be a Catholic, imprisoned in the Tower of London, and tortured into admitting his priesthood. At his trial he skillfully pled that a confession elicited under duress was not legally sufficient to ensure a conviction. Although the court complimented him on his courageous bearing, he was nevertheless convicted of high treason for entering England as an illegally ordained priest. He was executed immediately—across from the grocer's shop where he had been captured. Jones was beatified by Pius XI on Dec. 15, 1929.

Feast of the English Martyrs: May 4 (England).

See Also: ENGLAND, SCOTLAND, AND WALES, MARTYRS OF.

Bibliography: R. CHALLONER, *Memoirs of Missionary Priests,* ed. J. H. POLLEN (rev. ed. London 1924; repr. Farnborough 1969), I, 168–69. J. H. POLLEN, *Acts of English Martyrs* (London 1891).

[K. I. RABENSTEIN]

JONES, JOHN ST.

Franciscan priest and martyr; *alias* Buckley; b. Clynog Fawr, Caernarvonshire, June 1559; d. St. Thomas Waterings, Southwark, July 12, 1598. He joined the Franciscans at Pontoise (France) or at Rome, where in 1591 he was certainly a member of the community at the convent of S. Maria in Ara Coeli. In 1592 he left for the English mission and appears to have worked mostly in London, where he became a close friend of Henry GARNET, who praised his religious spirit and zeal. Arrested in 1597, he was kept a prisoner for a year, during which time he or John Gerard reconciled John RIGBY to the Church. He was indicted in February of 1598 along with Robert Barnes, a Wiltshire gentleman, and Jane Wiseman of Braddocks, Essex. Probably for lack of evidence, the

trial was postponed until June 30. The charge against Jones was that, as a priest ordained overseas, he had returned to minister in his native country; his two codefendants were charged with sheltering him. Present in court was Richard Topcliffe, the pursuivant, who had assured his agent, Nicholas Jones, that he would give him Barnes's property in return for his assistance in securing the priest's condemnation. The chief witness against the prisoners was Nicholas Jones's wife, Anne Bellamy, the betrayer of Robert Southwell. In spite of a brilliant defense, Barnes was condemned; Jane Wiseman, who refused to plead, was sentenced to *peine forte* (the death suffered by Margaret CLITHEROW); Jones was found guilty of exercising his priesthood contrary to statute. The place chosen for Jones's execution was St. Thomas Waterings on the Old Kent Road, once the first halting place of pilgrims from London to the shrine of St. Thomas à Becket in Canterbury. Because the hangman forgot his rope, the execution was delayed an hour. Jones prayed, and addressing the waiting crowd, he protested that he had never in his life entertained any thought of treason against his queen or country and declared that Topcliffe's cruelty had ''been sufficient to make [the Queen] odious to all priests in the kingdom.'' His head was displayed in Southwark and his members in the Lambeth and Newington roads. He was beatified by Pius XI on Dec. 15, 1929 and canonized on Oct. 25, 1970, as one of the Martyrs of ENGLAND, SCOTLAND, AND WALES.

Feast: July 12; Oct. 25; May 4.

Bibliography: *Publications of the Catholic Record Society* 5:14, 362–375. J. E. PAUL, *Blessed John Jones* (Postulation pamphlet; London 1960). A. BUTLER, *The Lives of the Saints* (New York 1956) 3:87. J. GILLOW, *A Literary and Biographical History or Bibliographical Dictionary of the English Catholics from 1534 to the Present Time* (New York 1961) 3:657–660. R. CHALLONER, *Memoirs of Missionary Priests,* ed. J. H. POLLEN (rev. ed. London 1924).

[G. FITZ HERBERT]

JONES, WILLIAM AMBROSE

Bishop, missionary; b. Cambridge, New York, July 21, 1865; d. Philadelphia, Pennsylvania, Feb. 17, 1921. After joining the Augustinians in 1886 at Villanova, Pennsylvania, he made his religious profession on Feb. 6, 1887, and was ordained in Philadelphia by Archbishop Patrick J. Ryan in 1890. Having been assigned first to parishes in Philadelphia and Atlantic City, New Jersey, he was master of novices and clerics at Villanova from 1896 to 1899. Following the Spanish–American War an appeal was made for American clerics to go to Cuba, and Jones was sent to Havana in January of 1899 to take charge of an old church called San Agustín (Spanish Augustinians had been in Cuba since the early 17th century). Two years later he opened the Colegio San Augustín, and in 1903 he assumed care of the church known as El Cristo. Jones's Cuban mission later developed into three parishes and a pontifical university (St. Thomas of Villanova, which was confiscated by the Castro government in April 1961). In 1906 he was appointed bishop of San Juan, Puerto Rico. When he was consecrated in Havana on Feb. 24, 1907, he became the second American bishop in Puerto Rico, succeeding James H. Blenk, SM (1899–1906).

[A. J. ENNIS]

JONG, JOHANNES DE

Cardinal (1946), ecclesiastical historian; b. Nes, Ameland Island, Netherlands, Sept. 10, 1885; d. Amersfoort, Netherlands, Sept. 8, 1955. After ordination (1908) he studied in Rome, where he received a Doctorate in Philosophy from the Academy of St. Thomas Aquinas (1910) and a Doctorate in Sacred Theology from the Gregorian University (1911). In 1914 he became professor of ecclesiastical history in the major seminary in Rijsenburg, and in 1931, rector. His lectures there resulted in a textbook, *Handboek voor de Kerkgeschiedenis* (2 v., 1929–31; 5th ed. in 5 v., revised by R. Post and G. Abbink, 1962–). De Jong was appointed coadjutor (1935) to archbishop J. H. G. Jansen of Utrecht and succeeded to the archdiocese upon Jansen's resignation (1936). During the German occupation of the Netherlands (1940–45) non-Catholics as well as Catholics acknowledged De Jong as the leader in resistance to encroachments on liberty. The archbishop's protests against the dissolution of the Catholic Worker's Association (1941) and the persecution of Jews clearly manifested this leadership. De Jong, in poor health since 1944, retired in 1951 and was succeeded by Bernard Alfrink, who had become his coadjutor a few weeks previously.

Bibliography: H. W. F. AUKES, *Kardinaal de Jong* (Utrecht 1956), with a list of De J.'s writings.

[A. G. WEILER]

JORDAN, EDWARD BENEDICT

Professor, author; b. Dunmore, Pennsylvania, Dec. 17, 1884; d. Washington, D.C., July 19, 1951. He was the son of Patrick F. and Bridget (O'Hara) Jordan. After completing his undergraduate studies at St. Thomas College, Scranton, Pennsylvania (1903) and Mt. St. Mary's College, Emmitsburg, Maryland (1905), he attended the Propaganda University, Rome, receiving the Doctorate in

Sacred Theology in 1909. He was ordained the same year, and appointed to the faculty of Mt. St. Mary's College, where from 1910 to 1921 he served successively as professor of biology, professor of education, and vice president. In 1921 he came to Washington, D.C., as an instructor in the department of education at The Catholic University of America. He was promoted to the rank of associate professor in 1926, named a domestic prelate by Pius XI in 1936, and became head of the department in 1941. He served also as dean of the Catholic Sisters College after 1936 and was made national director of the International Federation of Catholic Alumnae in 1943. That same year he was appointed vice rector of The Catholic University, a post he held until his death. Jordan's writings included translations of Franz de Hovre's works, *Philosophy and Education* (1931) and *Catholicism in Education* (1934). At a time when the views of John Dewey and his school were influencing American education, these treatises provided Catholic teachers and students with useful expositions of fundamental principles. Jordan also wrote monographs on the theory of evolution and the philosophy of education.

[E. KEVANE]

JORDAN, FRANCIS MARY OF THE CROSS

Religious founder; b. Gurtweil (Baden), Germany, June 16, 1848; d. Tafers, Switzerland, Sept. 8, 1918. After seminary studies in Freiburg im Breisgau, he was ordained (1878). Interest in Oriental studies led to his extended visit to the Holy Land (1880). Upon returning to Rome he founded the SALVATORIANS to combat modern evils and to circumvent the religious restrictions imposed by the KULTURKAMPF. Jordan and two other priests pronounced their religious vows on Dec. 8, 1881. At this time the founder, whose baptismal name was John Baptist, took the name Francis Mary of the Cross. Jordan's original aim was to form a loosely knit group of priests, but he deferred to the wishes of Rome and reorganized his society into a congregation of priests and brothers. As superior general until 1915, Jordan witnessed the spread of the Salvatorians to several countries. He visited the U.S. and established the first permanent foundation in this country at St. Nazianz, Wisconsin. In 1883 Jordan organized a community of religious women whose superior was Mother Petra Streitel. This group was the nucleus of the FRANCISCAN SISTERS OF THE SORROWFUL MOTHER, organized into a new congregation in 1885. In 1888 Jordan cooperated with Mother Mary of the Apostles to found the Sisters of the DIVINE SAVIOR, who were to aid the Salvatorians in their labors. The *decretum super scripta* in Jordan's cause for beatification was issued in 1956.

Bibliography: F. M. JORDAN, *Exhortations and Admonitions,* tr. W. HERBST (2d ed. St. Nazianz, Wisconsin 1946). P. PFEIFFER, *Father Francis Mary of the Cross Jordan,* tr. W. HERBST (St. Nazianz, Wisconsin 1936).

[R. MOLLEN]

JORDAN, THE

Forming one of the world's most remarkable watercourses, the Jordan Valley traverses the entire length of Palestine from north to south. The etymology of the word Jordan is uncertain; some scholars favor an Indo-Aryan origin composed of *yor-don,* ''year–river,'' i.e., ''perennial river,'' but most hold that it is derived from the Semitic *yārad,* ''to descend,'' which is more descriptive, for no valley or river descends deeper than the Jordan (*yardēn* in Hebrew).

Geology and Geography. The wide, arid Jordan depression is part of the larger geological trough known as the Great Rift Valley, which runs from northern Syria, through the Jordan Valley, the DEAD SEA, the Araba in the south, down through the Gulf of Aqaba and the RED SEA, to Lake Nyasa in East Africa—a distance of more than 3,000 miles. Some 30 million years ago, probably during the Miocene Age when the main mountain–forming changes occurred in the Near East, two parallel faults in the earth's crust developed, and as the hills shoved higher on either side, the depression between these faults continued sinking along the same line of weakness. In Palestine a large inland sea formed, which for a time extended even into the trans–Jordan region. However, because of the elevation of the Wādi el-'Arabah in the south it did not join with the Gulf of Aqaba. After the last Pluvial period in Palestine, the water flooding the valley receded to the three natural basins of the valley floor, thus creating the present Lake Huleh, the Sea of GALILEE, and the Dead Sea. These bodies of water are of markedly different altitudes, and each is fed in turn by the waters of the Jordan River flowing into the valley from the region of Mount Hermon.

The streams that cascade from the slopes and foothills of this majestic mountain meet in the marshy area approximately seven miles above Lake Huleh to form the Jordan proper. Lake Huleh is a small, triangular body of water 230 feet above sea level; it serves as the river's first pause on its rapid descent southward. Although well known to Jesus and the Apostles, who traveled as far north as CAESAREA PHILIPPI (ancient Paneas), the lake is not mentioned in the Bible. From Lake Huleh to the Sea

Francis Mary of the Cross Jordan.

of Galilee, which lies 695 feet below sea level, is a distance of not more than ten miles. The river tumbles and cascades vigorously, cutting a gorge in the black basalt rock left by volcanic activity of previous ages and then flows through a delta into the Sea of Galilee. This beautiful lake, which for the Christian evokes such vivid memories of the Master and his fishermen Disciples, measures 13 miles long and about seven miles wide.

Leaving the lake and the verdant Galilean countryside the Jordan descends swiftly again. The valley is now called by the Arabs *el-Ghor,* which may best be translated as ''the canyon.'' In the central strip the ancient sea bed lies exposed and has been severely eroded, so that *qaṭṭarah* hills (mounds and gullies of whitish–gray marl and clay) create the very real effect of typical badlands. The river itself has cut a deep channel through this alluvial deposit, and here in the ''river bottom'' one finds a sort of jungle inhabited by wild life, which in ancient times included large animals such as the lion (Jer 49.19). It is still heavily thicketed and is called in Arabic *ez-Zor* (the thicket). As one goes further south the valley narrows. The rapid waters of the Jordan swirl and twist as though trying to escape the destiny that awaits them in the Dead Sea. From the Sea of Galilee to the Dead Sea is a distance of 65 miles, but the Jordan, looping constantly, covers more than three times that distance.

Pilgrims baptised in Jordan River, Galilee. (©Richard T. Nowitz/CORBIS)

From the east the Jordan is joined by two important tributaries, the Yarmuk and the Jaboc (Jabbok). These streams, which today are used extensively for irrigation by the Hashemite Kingdom of Jordan, equal the Jordan proper in volume of water. Both are perennial and flow through mighty canyons of their own. Below the Jaboc the valley widens again until at JERICHO it is some 12 miles across. Owing to the high temperatures of the Jericho Plain, caused by the sub-sea level situation, tropical fruits and vegetables respond readily to irrigation. The Jordan River meanders through this plain and finally forms a sizeable delta as it dumps its muddy waters into the deep, salty reservoir of the Dead Sea. The Dead Sea is 1,286 feet below sea level—the lowest point on the surface of the earth.

History and Typology. There is abundant evidence that in prehistoric times the Jordan Valley was dotted by large and small settlements and that a thriving civilization flourished. Archeological surveys made of numerous sites by Nelson Glueck, especially on the eastern side of the valley and at the delta junctures of the Jordan tributaries, as well as the truly astonishing excavations at Tell es–Sulṭān (ancient Jericho) under the direction of Kathleen Kenyon, have dramatized the importance of this val-

ley in man's first efforts toward an agricultural and sedentary way of life. The primitive settlement at Jericho, the oldest known city in the world, dates back to *c.* 7800 B.C. (plus or minus 210 years), as evidenced by carbon–14 tests.

The Jordan is referred to more than 200 times in the Bible. It is particularly with the conquest of Canaan by the Israelite tribes, as popularly told in the Book of JOSHUA, that the Jordan enters historically and symbolically into the life of Israel. The story of Moses and the Exodus is continued in the account of the Israelites crossing miraculously dry-shod through the Jordan River, storming the walled city of Jericho, and entering into the land of promise. However, it was only in the Christian era that the full typology of the Jordan was developed. The early Church Fathers, particularly of the Alexandrian school, insisted that the crossing of the Jordan into the land of promise is as deeply symbolic of Christian initiation as the crossing of the Red Sea out of the land of bondage. The story of Elijah (2 Kgs 2.11) and the account of Naaman the Syrian (2 Kgs 2.12) were frequently used in a baptismal context.

Turning to the New Testament, the Gospels begin with the scene of JOHN THE BAPTIST, a man from the desert near the Jordan, preaching repentance and baptizing the people in the river. The Christian rite of Baptism owes much to the practice of the Baptist and the ascetical communities in the area. *See* BAPTISM (IN THE BIBLE). Today there is a little shrine-chapel on the banks of the Jordan not far from Jericho that commemorates the BAPTISM OF CHRIST by John.

Also, an allusion to the Jordan as a symbol of redemption is made in Matthew ch. 19–20 (also possibly in Jn 10.40–42, where Jesus, like Josue, waits three days before crossing the Jordan to raise his friend Lazarus): Jesus, traveling from Galilee to Jerusalem for the last time, proceeds slowly through the territories on the far side of the Jordan, then crosses the river at Jericho and ascends to the Holy City, where the Passover would be realized fully in His own death and Resurrection.

Bibliography: *Encyclopedic Dictionary of the Bible,* tr. and adap. by L. HARTMAN (New York 1963), from A. VAN DEN BORN, *Bijbels Woordenboek* 1205–08. K. HÖPF, *Lexikon für Theologie und Kirche*[2], ed. J. HOFER and K. RAHNER, 10 v. (2d, new ed. Freiburg 1957–65) 5:1118–19. F. M. ABEL, *Géographie de la Palestine,* 2 v. (Paris 1933–38) 1:161–178. D. BALY, *The Geography of the Bible* (New York 1957) 193–216. E. G. KRAELING, *Rand McNally Bible Atlas* (2d ed. New York 1962) 25–27. C. KOPP, *The Holy Places of the Gospels,* tr. R. WALLS (New York 1963) 99–103. J. DANIÉLOU, *The Bible and the Liturgy* (South Bend, Ind. 1956) 86–113, for typology.

[J. W. RAUSCH]

JORDAN, THE CATHOLIC CHURCH IN

The Hashemite Kingdom of Jordan is a small Arab country of the Middle East, bordered on the south and east by Saudi Arabia, on the northeast by Iraq, and on the north by Syria and the Israeli-occupied Golan Heights. To the west, the Jordan River provides a natural boundary with Israel and separates Jordan from the Israeli-occupied West Bank, which has been claimed as a Palestinian homeland since the mid-20th century. Largely comprised of arid desert that stretches westward from Saudi Arabia, Jordan's landscape rises to highlands in the west before descending to the Great Rift Valley lining the Jordan River. Al'Aqabah, a port city, is located in the south, on the coast of the gulf of 'Aqaba. Despite the limited supply of fresh water, the country's rainy season allows for the production of wheat, barley, olives, and citrus fruits, while natural resources include phosphates, potash, and small amounts of shale oil. Among Jordan's main exports are fertilizers, phosphates, and manufactured goods.

After gaining independence from Great Britain in 1946, Jordan instituted a parliamentary government with

---

Capital: Amman.
Size: 37,737 sq. miles.
Population: 4,998,560 in 2000.
Languages: Arabic; English is widely understood among the upper classes.
Religions: 4,598,678 Muslims (92%), 69,971 Catholics (1%), 74,970 Protestants (1.5%), 32,490 others.

---

a hereditary monarch. The vast majority of the population is Arab, though there are small groups of Circassians and Armenians. Most residents of Jordan are Sunni Muslim.

Catholics in Jordan are divided between Greek Orthodox, the majority, and Latin-rite. Ecclesiastically, a vicariate for the Latin-rite located in Amman is governed by the Patriarchate of Jerusalem, with its seat at Palestine, while the Melkite Greek Catholic Church's Archdiocese of Petra and Filadelfia is located in Amman. A large part of the Promised Land of Biblical times as well as all of ancient Edom, Galaad, and Moab lies within the borders of the country. The spiritual capital of Jordan is the Old City of Jerusalem, sacred to Muslims and Christians alike. Wadi Al-Kharrar, a site on the east bank of the Jordan River that is thought by many Christian historians to be the site of the baptism of Jesus, was prepared by the Jordanian government and opened to the public as part of Jubilee 2000.

Until the 20th century, the lands of Jordan spanned both sides of the Jordan River, its western boundary extending to the Dead Sea. Amman, the nation's capital, was known in OT times as Rabbah or Rabbath-Ammon, capital city of the AMMONITES, and in the Greco-Roman period as Filadelfia, the southernmost city of the DECAPOLIS. In 1998 archeologists working in Ayla discovered the remains of what was judged to be the oldest Christian church in the world, a Roman structure that dated to A.D. 350. In A.D. 636 the region was invaded by the Muslims; the OTTOMAN TURKS assumed control from 1517 to 1918. Between 1918 and 1949 the lands east of the JORDAN RIVER were known as the Emirate—later the Kingdom of Transjordan—while those to the west, together with the modern State of Israel (created in 1948), formed the British-mandated territory of PALESTINE.

On May 25, 1946, Jordan gained its independence from Great Britain. Between 1953 and 1999 the country was ruled by King Hussein, who guided the nation through several turbulent decades as pressures from the world's superpowers and the age-old tensions between Arab nations flared. In 1989 Hussein instituted parliamentary elections, after which the government grew increasingly liberal. In 1994 Jordan signed an historic peace treaty with Israel. Praised by the pope, the agree-

ment ended decades of armed conflict. Reconciliation of the status of the West Bank had yet to be decided, although the Vatican signed an agreement of recognition and enumeration of rights with Palestinian leader Yasser Arafat in February 2000.

Although Islam was declared the official state religion, Jordan's 1952 constitution guaranteed the freedom of most religious faiths and of the right to worship in the three recognized faiths: Islam, Christianity, and Judaism. In 1976 Pope Paul VI's visit to the holy sites in Jordan did much to encourage stronger relations between King Hussein and the Vatican. In 1980 the Church was given the right to teach the faith in its own schools, and in 1997 the government began providing Christian education in public schools where it was requested. While Christian religious tribunals and other church-run programs operating in Jordan were extended the same rights and freedoms as were Islamic ones, evangelization activities were prohibited as in violation of Islamic law. In addition to Roman Catholics, Jordan had groups of Greek Orthodox, Greek Melkite Catholics, Armenian Orthodox, and Maronite Catholics living within its borders. A number of small evangelical Christian churches were denied classification by the Ministry of Justice as legitimate religions. Jordan established diplomatic relations with the Holy See in 1994; in 2000 there were 64 Catholic parishes located within the country.

On Feb. 8, 1999, King Hussein died and was succeeded by his son, Abdullah II. The following September

The Treasury is the first building a visitor sees coming through the Siq, a canyon, which leads to Petra, Jordan. (©Wolfgang Kaehler/
CORBIS)

the new Jordanian king traveled to the Vatican for an audience with Pope John Paul II, during which time a papal visit to Jordan was planned. On March 20, 2000, the pope arrived in Amman as part of a trip to the Holy Land. During a Latin-rite mass in Amman that was attended by over 35,000 people, the Pope honored both St. John the Baptist, the patron saint of Jordan, and the late King Hussein for his efforts in advancing the Middle East peace process. He also spoke of his wish that all believers realize themselves to be ''one people and one single family'' and acknowledged each of the Catholic community's leaders by commending their ''noble tradition of respect for all religions.'' As a country with large-scale external debt (estimated at $8.4 billion in 1998), Jordan was among those nations receiving the help of Pope John Paul II in encouraging wealthy nations to forgive a portion of these payments.

Bibliography: *Bilan du Monde* 2:540–545. Jordan Ministry of Economy, Department of Statistics, *First Census of Population and Housing* (Amman 1962—).

[A. A. DI LELLA/EDS.]

JORDAN FORZATÈ, BL.

B. Padua, Italy, *c.* 1158; d. Venice, 1248. After studying law, he became a CAMALDOLESE monk and was later prior of San Benedetto Novello in Padua, which he began rebuilding in 1195. GREGORY IX appointed him (1231) examiner in the canonization process for ANTHONY OF PADUA. During FREDERICK II's struggle with the popes, Jordan, as *doctor decretalium* (*see* DECRETALISTS) of the city council of Padua, played a crucial role in the quarrel. Imprisoned by Ezzelino III of Romagna in 1237, he was freed by Frederick two years later and took refuge in Aquileia. He went finally to the monastery Della Celestia in Venice. His body was moved in 1810 to the cathedral of Padua.

Feast: Aug. 7 (Padua, Treviso, Praglia).

Bibliography: *Acta Sanctorum,* Aug. 2:200–214. C. I. BERNARDI, *Il beato Giordano F.* (Treviso 1930). I. ROSA, *Il beato Giordano F.* (Padua 1932). *The Book of Saints* (4th ed. New York 1947) 343.

[M. CSÁKY]

JORDAN OF GIANO

Franciscan chronicler; b. Giano, in the valley of Spoleto, Italy, *c.* 1195; d. Magdeburg, Germany (where he is buried), after 1262. He entered the order in 1217 or 1218, when he was probably already a deacon. Toward the end of September 1221 he went to Germany with CAESARIUS OF SPEYER; he was ordained in 1223, and from 1224 to 1239, was custos of the order in Thuringia. In 1230 and again in 1238 he was sent by his superiors to Rome, becoming involved in the difficulties with ELIAS OF CORTONA. In 1241 he was provincial vicar of Bohemia-Poland, where he lived through the Tartar invasion, of which he gave a good account in his letters. In 1242 he was provincial vicar of Saxony. The provincial chapter commissioned him (1262) to put into writing his recollections of the foundations of the order in Germany. His chronicle, dictated to Brother BALDWIN OF BRANDENBURG, runs from 1207 to 1262 and was continued as the provincial chronicle of Saxony until the end of the 15th century. Although partly anecdotal, betraying the weaknesses and lacunae that often mar the efforts of old age, it is still an important source for the early history of the order.

Bibliography: *Chronica,* ed. H. BOEHMER (Paris 1908). *Monumenta Germaniae Historica, Scriptores* (Berlin 1826—) 28:208–211. E. J. AUWEILER, *The ''Chronica fratris Jordani a Giano''* (Washington 1917). L. HARDICK, ed., *Nach Deutschland und England* (Werl 1957).

[L. HARDICK]

JORDAN OF QUEDLINBURG

Augustinian scholar and author; b. Quedlinburg, Saxony, Germany, *c.* 1300; d. Vienna, Austria, 1380. He was a student of HENRY OF FRIEMAR, of Hermann of Halle (d. 1334), and of Prosper of Reggio (*c.* 1318). He lectured in the Augustinian monasteries of Erfurt and Magdeburg and in other German houses of the order, including the provincial of Saxony from 1341 to 1351, where he was instrumental in the reorganization of the AUGUSTINIANS and in their transformation into a MENDICANT ORDER. The difficulties of this undertaking are partly recorded in his writings. However, his chief influence lies in his spirituality, for he was considered to be a master of the spiritual life. He deplored the ascetic exaggerations that were typical of his times; his writings reflect the strong influence of German MYSTICISM on his thought. He was also renowned as a preacher, and collections of his sermons were widely used during the late Middle Ages. Perhaps his most important work, one of the most celebrated ascetical treatises of the 14th century, was the *Vitasfratrum* (Rome 1587), which influenced the spiritual reform of the order and provides valuable evidence of its early history. It is disputed whether he lived and died in Vienna; indeed, some scholars have placed his death in Vienne, France. However, many important Augustinians connected with him were members of the Viennese convent, attracted there by the new University of VIENNA, founded in 1365.

Bibliography: Works. *Liber vitasfratrum,* ed. R. ARBESMANN and W. HÜMPFNER (New York 1943). *Opus postillarum et sermonum de tempore* (Strasbourg 1483). *Sermones de sanctis* (Paris 1484). *Collectanea seu Speculum Augustinianum* (Paris 1686). *Tractatus de spiritu libertatis* (lost). *Expositio dominicae orationis* (manuscript). **Literature.** R. LIEVENS, *J. van Quedlinburg in de Nederlanden* (Ghent 1958). F. RENNHOFER, *Die Augustiner-Eremiten in Wien* (Würzburg 1956). A. ZUMKELLER in *Sanctus Augustinus vitae spiritualis magister,* 2 v. (Rome 1959) v.2. E. SAAK, "Quidlibet christianus. Saints and Society in the Sermons of Jordan of Quedlinburg OESA," in *Models of Holiness in Medieval Sermons* (Louvain-la-Neuve 1996) 317–338; "The Creation of Augustinian Identity in the Later Middle Ages, Parts I and II," *Augustiniana* 49 (1999) 109–164, 251–286.

[W. M. PLÖCHL]

JORDAN OF SAXONY, BL.

Second master general of the Order of Preachers; b. date unknown, apparently in the ancient Diocese of Mainz; d. in shipwreck returning from the Holy Land, Feb. 13, 1237. Jordan received the Dominican habit in Paris on Ash Wednesday, 1220, where he was a lecturer at the University of Paris. In 1221 he was named provincial of the Lombardy Province, the greatest province of the Order at that time. Less than a year later he succeeded St. Dominic as master general. He travelled frequently between Paris and Bologna, the two most important seats of European learning, visiting the convents of the various provinces, strengthening and enlarging them. In these travels he drew many vocations to the Order through his preaching and teaching. He is said to have brought more than 1,000 candidates into the Order himself.

His literary work is accepted as that of a master of letters. He is renowned for the spiritual letters of direction he addressed to Bl. Diana d'Andalo and her community at the Monastery of St. Agnes in Bologna. These letters are still used by spiritual directors. His influence left a deep impression on the constitutions of the Order of Preachers. He was the outstanding historian of the early days of the Order and the first biographer of St. Dominic. Historians continue to use his *Libellus de principiis Ordinis Praedicatorum.* His 15 years as master general enabled him to develop most of the machinery needed for the governing of provinces and to perfect the general government of the entire Order.

Jordan initiated the Dominican tradition of singing the *Salve Regina* at the end of the Dominican liturgical day, as well as at the side of a dying friar. The possibility of his identification with Jordanus Nemorarius, the mathematician, has been discussed by historians, most of whom reject it.

Feast: Feb. 15.

Bibliography: M. ARON, *Saint Dominic's Successor* (St. Louis 1955). G. VANN, *To Heaven with Diana! A Study of Jordan of Saxony and Diana d'Andalo, with a Translation of the Letters of Jordan* (New York 1960). H. C. SCHEEBEN, *Beiträge zur Geschichte Jordans von Sachsen* (Quellen und Forschungen zur Geschichte des Dominkanerordens in Deutschland 35; Vechte 1938). B. ALTANER, *Die Briefe Jordans von Sachsen, des zweiten Dominikanergenerals, 1222–37* (Quellen und Forschungen zur Geschichte des Dominikanerordens in Deutschland 20; Leipzig 1925).

[E. M. ROGERS]

JORIS, DAVID

Visionary Dutch religious leader who combined elements of pacifist, revolutionary, and spiritualist Anabaptist teachings and whose followers (Jorists) survived in Holland and North Germany into the 17th century; b. Bruges or Ghent, Flanders, 1501?; d. Basel, Switzerland, Aug. 25, 1556. A painter of stained-glass windows, he joined the Anabaptist movement early. While rejecting revolution, he nevertheless accepted the apocalyptic expectations of the revolutionaries. Mystic visions led him to claim to be the "third David," sent to complete the work of the second (Christ). After years of persecution, he and many of his followers found refuge in Basel (1543), where he used an assumed name (Jan van Brugge) and pretended adherence to the Reformed faith. He continued his prolific production of mystical writings, which were published in Holland (*Wonder Book,* 1542, 1551). After his death, disputes among his adherents led to an investigation that resulted in the exhumation of his corpse, which was burned at the stake in 1559. This led to the saying, "If Basel would burn her heretics alive, she would not have the trouble of digging them up." His Basel adherents, who recanted, were not molested.

Bibliography: R. H. BAINTON, *David Joris, Wiedertäufer und Kämpfer für Toleranz im 16. Jahrhundert* (Leipzig 1937); *The Travail of Religious Liberty* (Philadelphia 1951). G. H. WILLIAMS, *The Radical Reformation* (Philadelphia 1962). E. HAMMERSCHMIDT, *Lexikon für Theologie und Kirche,* J. HOFER and K. RAHNER, 10 v. (2d, new ed. Freiburg 1957–65) 5:1122.

[G. W. FORELL]

JORNET E IBARS, TERESA, BL.

Foundress of the LITTLE SISTERS OF THE POOR AND AGED; b. Aytona (Lérida), Spain, Jan. 9, 1843; d. Liria (Valencia), Aug. 26, 1897. Teresa, the daughter of pious peasants, joined the Poor Clares, but ill health soon compelled her to return home. With the cooperation of Saturnino López Novoa, a priest, she founded her religious congregation to provide care and solace for the aged. Together with ten companions, Teresa of Jesus (as she was known in religion) took the habit at Barbastro (Huesca) but soon transferred the mother-house to Valencia, where it remains. She continued as superior general until her death, by which time the institute had 103 houses. By 1961 it had 3,079 members and 201 houses and had spread to several countries, including the U.S. Papal approval came in 1887. Teresa was noted for her affability, kindness, and devotion to the Blessed Virgin Mary. She was beatified April 27, 1958.

Feast: Aug. 26.

Bibliography: E. PIETROMARCHI, *La Beata Teresa de Jesus: Jornet e Ibars* (Rome 1958). *Acta Apostolicae Sedis* 50 (1958) 322–325. J. L. BAUDOT and L. CHAUSSIN, *Vies des saints et des bienheureux selon l'ordre du calendrier avec l'historique des fêtes* 13:196–197.

[I. BASTARRIKA]

JOSAPHAT KUNCEVYČ, ST.

"Apostle of Union" and martyr; b. Włodzimir, then in the Polish Province of Wolyn, *c.* 1580–82; d. Witebsk, Nov. 12, 1623. Sent to Wilno as an apprentice tradesman, he came under the influence of those clergy adhering to the Union of BREST, entered a Basilian monastery (1604), and was ordained in 1609. He achieved quick advancement in his order through his ability as a speaker and the example of his zealous religious life. His success in winning adherents to the cause of the Union brought him the bishopric of Witebsk in 1617, with the right of succession to the archbishopric of Polotsk. In his new capacity, his efforts on behalf of the Union were so successful that within a short time the greater part of the Orthodox within Lithuania were won to the Union and the position of the Church greatly improved; however, as a result of the efforts of Peter Sahaidachny, the leader of the Cossacks, a new Orthodox hierarchy was named in Lithuania and a more effective opposition to the activities of the Eastern Catholics was organized, directed primarily against Kuncevyč and his followers. Despite the fact that King Sigismund III wavered in his support of the Eastern Catholics during this phase of the struggle with the schismatics, Kuncevyč succeeded in holding his own and even in having Meletiĭ SMOTRYTS'KYĭ, the newly named Orthodox archbishop of Polotsk, deposed. Shortly thereafter, Kuncevyč suffered a martyr's death at the hands of an enraged mob during a sharp outbreak against the Eastern Catholics of Witebsk. His remains were recovered from the Dnieper River and interred at Biala, in Podlasie. Kuncevyč was beatified in 1643 and canonized in 1867.

Feast: Nov. 12 (formerly 14).

Bibliography: S. *Josaphat Hieromartyr, documenta romana beatificationis et canonizationis,* ed. A. G. WELYKYJ, 2 v. (Rome 1952–55). N. CONTIERI, *Vita di S. Giosafat arcivescovo e martire Ruteno dell' ordine di S. Basilio il Grande* (Rome 1867). G. HOFFMANN, "Der hl. Josaphat," *Orientalia Christiana,* 1 (1923) 297–320; 3 (1924–25) 173–239. A. GUÉPIN, *Un Apôtre de l'union des églises au XVIIᵉ siècle: St. Josaphat et l'église gréco-slave en Pologne et en Russie,* 2 v. (Rome 1897). T. BORESKY, *Life of St. Josaphat* (New York 1955). *Acta Apostolicae Sedis,* 15 (1923) 49–63. A. BUTLER, *The Lives of the Saints,* rev. ed. H. THURSTON and D. ATTWATER, 4 v. (New York 1956) 4:337–340. *Cambridge History of Poland,* ed. W. F. REDDAWAY et al., 2 v. (Cambridge, Eng. 1941–50) v.1.

[E. KUSIELEWICZ]

JOSCIO, BL.

Monk at SAINT-BERTIN, near Saint-Omer, diocese of Arras, France, also known as Josbert, Joscius, or Valbebertus; d. there, apparently Nov. 30, 1163 (or 1186). According to legendary material incorporated into the *Speculum Maius* by VINCENT OF BEAUVAIS (8.116), five roses were said to have sprouted from Joscio's head at his death. Each carried a letter of the name Maria. THOMAS OF CANTIMPRÉ in his *Bonum universale de apibus* (2.29) calls the monk "Josbert" and reports that this miraculous phenomenon took place at Déols (Berry). The monk's grave was under the small choir altar at Saint-Bertin, and the miracle was depicted in the ambulatory of the choir. He received his own feast at Saint-Bertin's in 1619.

Feast: Nov. 30.

Bibliography: *Acta Sanctorum,* Oct. 11 (1864) 793. A. M. ZIMMERMANN, *Kalendarium Benedictinum: Die Heiligen und Seligen des Benediktinerordens und seiner Zweige* 3:375–376. J. L. BAUDOT and L. CHAUSSIN, *Vies des saints et des bienheureux selon l'ordre du calendrier avec l'historique des fêtes* 11:1003–04. A. M. ZIMMERMANN, *Lexikon für Theologie und Kirche*² 5:1124.

[M. R. P. MCGUIRE]

JOSEPH, ST.

Husband of the Blessed Virgin Mary and father of Jesus Christ by right of marriage and by spiritual and legal ties. The name that he bore, in honor of the Patriarch JOSEPH, son of Jacob, was quite common in his time; cf. Joseph of Arimathea (Mt 27.57), Joseph Barsabbas (Acts 1.23), Joseph Barnabas (Acts 4.36), etc. Except for incidental references to Joseph as being regarded as the father of Jesus (Mt 13.55; Lk 3.23; Jn 1.45; 6.42), the only NT information on Joseph is given in Mt, ch. 1 and 2, and Lk, ch. 1 and 2. On the historical value of these chapters, *see* INFANCY NARRATIVES.

Life. In Mt 1.6–16, where Joseph's father is called Jacob, his ancestry is traced back to King David through the latter's son Solomon; but in Lk 3.23–32, where Joseph's father is called Heli, his ancestry is traced back to David through the latter's son Nathan. The two lines of descent are thus completely different, except for their convergence at Salathiel and Zorobabel (Mt 1.12; Lk 3.27). The obvious purpose of both lists is to show that Jesus, by being the legal son of Joseph, had a right to be called the "Son of David" (Mt 15.23), a recognized title of the Messiah (Mt 22.42).

Although Joseph was apparently living in Nazareth at the time when he was betrothed to Mary (Lk 1.26–27), he was probably a native of Bethlehem, or at least he owned property there. It was primarily for the sake of property taxes that he was obliged to be registered in the Roman census at Bethlehem, for the Romans would not have been interested in his Davidic descent as such (Lk 2.4). In Mt 13.55 Jesus is called "the son of the τέκτων," while in the parallel passage of Mk 6.3 Jesus Himself is called "the τέκτων." It is possible that the oral tradition represented in Matthew attributed to Joseph what was originally, as in Mark, attributed only to Jesus. But there is no good reason why both father and son should not have had the same trade. In any case, it is commonly taken for granted that Joseph was a τέκτων. This Greek word, like the corresponding Latin word *faber,* signifies in itself no more than "craftsman, artisan," and could be used of a worker in stone or metal as well as in wood. Yet in actual usage it almost always designated a woodworker, i.e., either a carpenter or cabinetmaker.

Art and popular imagination have usually pictured Joseph as an old man. But this is surely a false idea. The rabbis at the time of Christ commonly taught that men should marry between the ages of 13 and 19, and Joseph, as a "just" (i.e., law-abiding) man, would no doubt have conformed to this practice. Since the Gospels never suggest that he was still living during the public ministry of Jesus, he most likely died before he was 50 years old.

Marriage with Mary. At the time of Jesus' conception and birth Mary was "betrothed" to Joseph (Mt 1.18; Lk 1.27; 2.5). Hebrew "betrothal" was more than engagement in the modern sense, but less than full marriage. It consisted in a formal contract that made the man and woman husband and wife. Conjugal infidelity on the part of the "betrothed" woman was regarded as adultery in the strict sense. The betrothal ceremony was followed after several months by the "wedding," the ceremony in which the man received the woman into his house and consummated the marriage. As related in Mt 1.18–25, Joseph noticed that Mary, while thus betrothed to him, had become pregnant. The Evangelist forewarns the reader that this had happened "by the Holy Spirit." But the whole point of the story is that Joseph himself did not yet

Stone monument of St. Joseph, Montreal. (©Jan Butchofsky-Houser/CORBIS)

know the cause of her pregnancy. "Joseph, her husband, being a just man, and not wishing to expose her to reproach, was minded to put her away privately." The Greek word, δίκαιος, that is here translated as "just," is the equivalent of the Hebrew word, ṣaddîq, that designates a man who is very conscientious in the observance of the Law, which in the present case would not allow him to consummate a marriage with a woman who had been guilty of adultery during the time of her betrothal.

Historically, Joseph's conduct, when he learned of Mary's pregnancy, has had three principal interpretations: (1) that he actually suspected Mary of adultery [e.g., Augustine, *Epistolae* 153.4, 9 (*Corpus scriptorum ecclesiasticorum latinorum* 44:2.3, 405)]; (2) that he surmised she was the mother of the Messiah, and he wished to withdraw in humility [e.g., Bernard, *Hom. super "Missus est"* 2.14 (*Patrologia Latina,* ed. J. P. Migne, 217 v., indexes 4 v. (Paris 1878–90) 183:68)]; (3) that he was subjected to agonizing perplexity [e.g., F. Suárez, *In 3,* q. 29, disp. 7.2, 6; *Op. om.* (Paris 1860) 19.1190]. Tradi-

The angel reassures St. Joseph, detail of a mosaic in the Santa Maria Maggiore, Rome.

tionally, the third supposition has by far prevailed; namely, that in his uncertainty Joseph strove to obey the law concerning adulterous wives by arranging for a divorce, but that at the time his evident conviction that Mary was somehow innocent led him to decide "to put her away privately" as the only way out of the dilemma. This would have been the type of divorce whereby the reason for it did not have to be revealed.

After an angel of the Lord revealed to him in a dream the sacred mystery of the virginal conception of Jesus and commanded him "to take Mary as his wife," he was at once faithful to the responsibility that he had assumed at his betrothal to her, and "he took unto him his wife"; that is, he went through with the second, "wedding," ceremony, whereby he took her into his house. The Evangelist, however, immediately warns the reader that he did not consummate the marriage: "He did not know her till she brought forth her first-born son." The only purpose of the latter statement is to insist that Mary was a virgin at the birth of Jesus. It says nothing, one way or the other, regarding the relations between Joseph and Mary after the birth of Jesus. The Catholic doctrine of the perpetual virginity of Mary is based on tradition that goes back to the earliest age of the Church. Although never consummated, the marriage of Joseph and Mary was unquestionably a genuine marriage. On the problem of how Mary could have contracted a true marriage when she, as often supposed by Catholic theologians, had a vow of perpetual virginity, a supposition based erroneously on Lk 1.34, *see* MARY, BLESSED VIRGIN, II (IN THEOLOGY.)

Joseph and the Child Jesus. The commonly held notion that Joseph and Mary arrived at Bethlehem on the day before Jesus was born is almost certainly wrong. The phrase used in Lk 2.6, that Jesus was born "while they were there," clearly implies that they had been there for some days before His birth. Moreover, the four-day journey from Nazareth to Bethlehem at a time when Mary would have been so close to term supposes unbelievable carelessness on the part of both Joseph and Mary. The statement that "there was no room for them in the inn" at Bethlehem need not imply that they had been turned away by a hardhearted innkeeper. It might just as well mean that the "inn," a stockade with open alcoves like the modern Near-Eastern khan, was regarded by them as an unfitting place for Mary to give birth to her Son. They therefore withdrew to a cave (rather than a stable) that was ordinarily used as a refuge for cattle, and here Mary laid her newborn Babe on the stone shelf that otherwise served as a feeding trough for the animals.

Luke speaks of Jesus' "parents" (Lk 2.27, 41, 43),"His father and mother" (2.33), and in Mary's words, "'Thy father and I'" (2.48), thus linking Joseph with Mary as a true, though evidently equally virginal, parent of Jesus. As the legal father of Jesus, Joseph exercised the right of naming his Child (Mt 1.21, 25) and, in the opinion of some authors, was the one who circumcised Him at home (Lk 2.21). He was also present at the Purification and Presentation in the temple (Lk 2.22). If the account in Mt ch. 2 is to be harmonized chronologically with this, the visit of the Magi to the Holy Family at Bethlehem must have taken place more than 40 days after the birth of Jesus, because at the departure of the Magi Joseph was warned by an angel to flee with Mary and Jesus into "Egypt"—probably the frontier between Palestine and Egypt, south of ancient Judah (Mt 2.13). Some time later he was told, again in a dream by an angel, to return to the land of Israel (Mt 2.20). Prudently, fearing the tyranny of Herod's son Archelaus, Joseph went, not to his own town of Bethlehem, as he had first intended, but to Mary's town of Nazareth (Mt 2.22). There Jesus was subject to him as well as to Mary (Lk 2.51). Each year Joseph and Mary went to Jerusalem for the Feast of the Passover. When Jesus was 12 years old he accompanied them on this journey (for the first time?). When the boy Jesus had remained behind and was found after three days in the temple, Joseph, like Mary, did not understand the deeper messianic import of His words, that they should have known that He would be "at His Father's" (Lk 2.41–50). This is the last that is known of Joseph from the Gospels. Whatever else legends have imagined is of value only as a token of Christian piety.

Bibliography: U. HOLZMEISTER, *De Sancto Ioseph Quaestiones Biblicae* (Rome 1945); "De Nuptiis S. Ioseph," *Verbum*

Adoration of the Magi, detail of ivory book cover from Metz, late 9th or early 10th century, with Joseph standing behind the chair.

Domini (Rome 1921–) 25 (1947) 145–149. D. BUZY, *Saint Joseph* (Paris 1952).

[F. L. FILAS]

JOSEPH, ST., DEVOTION TO

The devotion to St. Joseph as emphasizing his position in the Holy Family originated relatively late in Church history. The chief reason for this delay was undoubtedly the fear that Joseph's unique role as virginal husband of Mary and father of Jesus by spiritual ties might have caused misunderstanding about the dogmas of Mary's perpetual virginity and Jesus' miraculous origin in Mary.

Influence of Apocryphal Legends. The apocryphal legends of Christ's childhood also played a key role in thwarting the full appreciation of Joseph's true dignity. The chief sources for these tales were the *Protoevangel of James*, the *Gospel of Thomas*, the *Coptic History of Joseph the Carpenter*, the *Gospel of Pseudo-Matthew*, and the *Gospel of the Nativity of Mary*, composed with mutual interdependence from before A.D. 150 onward. These pious tales expanded on Christ's childhood, adding bi-

zarre miracles and even irreverent fantasies. Uncritical use of the legends in medieval drama, art, and poetry helped keep their stories alive, though it handed them down to us in more romantic form. The legends make four principal claims concerning St. Joseph: his *miraculous* selection as a *mere guardian* of Mary; and his *advanced age* as a *widower*.

To make sure that Joseph could not be considered the natural father of Jesus, the legends attributed to him an advanced age when sexual powers would be least imperative. Yet if Joseph had been so old, he could not have appeared to be the natural father of Jesus in the public eye, as was part of his vocation to protect the reputation of Jesus and Mary. The legends had another reason for representing the age of St. Joseph. It was necessary to depict him as a widower with six children from an earlier marriage, as an attempt to explain the gospel references to the "brethren of Jesus" (Mt 12.46; Jn 2.12; 7.10). The legends claimed that Joseph was miraculously selected, but they shrank from using the gospel term "husband." They proposed the miracle of Joseph's blooming staff as a sign of his divine selection. This prodigy was patently modeled on the miracle of Aaron's blooming staff in Nm 17.19–24. Apart from the gross impropriety of setting up

Betrothal of Mary and Joseph, detail of a fresco by Giotto in the Arena Chapel at Padua, first quarter of the 14th century.

the young maiden Mary for the public scrutiny that the legends claim was exercised, much like that turned upon a slave on the block, to narrate so manifest a miracle would have been unfit, since such an event would have contradicted the obscurity that we know surrounded the Incarnation. The special providence of God certainly brought Joseph and Mary together, but the circumstances of the legendary miracle are in such bad taste or appear so artificially contrived that they make the event incredible. In paintings and statues of St. Joseph the lily as an emblem of purity replaced the staff for many centuries, first occurring perhaps in the "Espousal," a fresco painted by Giotto between 1303–06 at Padua.

History of the Devotion. Former claims of an independent devotion early manifested toward St. Joseph in the Eastern Church cannot be allowed, since Joseph was grouped there with Patriarchs of the Old Testament. He was pictured at best as the aged guardian and widower, only incidentally on the scene and never intimately shar-

ing in the mysteries of Christ's childhood. Moreover, it is no longer justified to claim that the Carmelites brought the devotion from the East in the 12th century.

The first known independent commemoration of St. Joseph occurs in an 8th-century martyrology from an unknown church in northern France or Belgium, listing the saint on March 20 as "spouse of Mary" (*Analecta Bollandiana* 72 [1954], 357–362). In the early 800s martyrologies such as those from the Benedictine monastery at Reichenau list March 19 as the day of St. Joseph's death. The definitive explanation for the choice of March 19 still remains to be found. During the Middle Ages the desire to know more of Jesus and Mary led to the first recognition of St. Joseph; this was an embryonic form of the independent devotion. First observances of March 19 as a feast, not a mere commemoration, seem to have occurred among the Servites by the year 1324, although evidence suggests equally early observances among the Franciscans and at Bologna.

The Franciscans Peter John Olivi (d. 1298) and his near contemporary, Ubertino de Casale, appraised Joseph's greatness in terms that suggest that they were far ahead of their times, but the great publicizers of the devotion were John Gerson (d. 1429), St. Bernardine of Siena (d. 1444), and later St. Teresa of Ávila (d. 1582). The feast of St. Joseph had not been celebrated widely until its introduction at Rome in about 1479 by Sixtus IV. This seems to have stimulated its spread to at least 70 known European cities by the time of the Council of Trent. In 1522 the Dominican Isidore de Isolani published the first essay toward a scholarly theology of St. Joseph. After the saint's steady rise in popular esteem and in the liturgy, a momentous event in the history of the devotion occurred in Pius IX's proclamation of St. Joseph as Patron of the Universal Church, Dec. 8, 1870. Worldwide devotion to St. Joseph is centered at St. Joseph's Oratory, Montreal, Canada, founded by Brother André, CSC, in 1904.

Theology. Josephology is the name for the theological study of St. Joseph's dignity, mission, and prerogatives. Fundamental to the saint's position is the fact of his true, virginal marriage to the Mother of God. Jesus is the fruit of this marriage not because He was generated by means of it, but because He was received and reared within it according to God's reason for bringing it into existence (cf. St. Thomas Aquinas, *In 4 Sent.* 30 2.2 ad 4). Mary's parenthood was shared with Joseph, since Mary belonged to Joseph as his wife (see Augustine, *De Cons. Evang.* 2.1; *Corpus scriptorum ecclesiasticorum Latinorum* 43.3.4:83: Francis de Sales, *The Spiritual Conferences,* Burns, Oates, London, 1909, no. 19, 367); since they owned everything in common as husband and wife (e.g., Suárez, *In 3,* 29.8.1.4; Vivès, 123; Cornelius a Lapide, *In Isaiam,* 8; *Comment. in Script. Sac.,* Vivès, Paris, 11, 214); and since the procreation of the Child Jesus in Joseph's wife, even though virginal, belonged to Joseph's marriage. Normally, a mutual moral bond arises between father and son because of physical generation, because such generation calls for the rearing of the child (St. Thomas Aquinas, *In 4 Sent.* 26.1.1). In the case of St. Joseph this parental and therefore paternal moral bond between father and son was miraculously present without generation of Jesus by Joseph. Hence, it presents an example of a unique fatherhood in an analogous and wide sense, but still a true fatherhood in the moral order. Thus, Jesus belonged to Joseph's family by right of Joseph's marriage to Christ's mother, and by Joseph's fatherly love, authority, and watchful service—all implied in the traditional title of "foster father of Jesus." Joseph appeared publicly as if he were the natural father of Jesus, thus shielding the virginity of Mary and the reputation of Jesus. It is to be noted that this public opinion (referred

19th-century stained glass window depicting a scene from the life of Jesus featuring St. Joseph the Carpenter. (©Marc Garanger/CORBIS)

to in the title, "putative father of Jesus") does not of itself create a fatherly relationship. The genealogies (Mt 1.1–16; Lk 3.23–28) were traced through St. Joseph and thus recognized him as the already constituted direct legal ancestor of Christ (hence, his title of "legal father of Jesus"). Joseph's actions in naming Jesus and in protecting, accepting, and supporting both Mary and her Child indicated that Joseph was the head of their household. His authority was acknowledged as such (especially by Mary in Lk 2.48 and by Luke in 2.51: "subject to *them*"). "Adoptive father of Jesus" in the strict sense is not a correct title of St. Joseph, because Jesus belonged to Joseph's own family and was not adopted into it.

Augustine presents the entire modern doctrine on the fatherhood of St. Joseph even though he does not develop it fully (cf. Filas, *Joseph and Jesus,* 21–61, for other analyses of patristic opinion). In his classic text, "Every good of marriage was fulfilled in the parents of Christ: offspring, loyalty, and the sacrament" (*Corpus scriptorum ecclesiasticorum Latinorum* 42.8.2:225), Augustine asserts that the marriage is not merely potentially but is actually fruitful, so that from the union of Joseph and Mary the Child Jesus somehow drew his origin. Since "conjugal intercourse did not take place" (*ibid.*), the origin of the Child was influenced not in the physical but exclusively in the moral order. The same idea recurs almost as a theme throughout much of *Sermon 51* (esp. 10–21; *Patrologia Latina*, ed. J. P. Migne, 271 v., indexes 4 v. [Paris 1878–90] 38: 342–351): "Just as she was virginally the wife, so was he virginally the husband; and just as she was virginally the mother, so was he virginally the father . . . . Why was Joseph father? Because the certainty of his fatherhood is in proportion to his virginity." Here Augustine equivalently originated a new title for Joseph, "virginal father of Jesus" (cf. *Enchirid. Indulg.* no. 477), signifying that Joseph himself was a virgin, and that he received Christ within his virginal marriage with a selfless paternal love. All this can be called the Augustinian tradition and is fully developed in Suárez (*In 3,* 29.8), with the significant innovation that Joseph shared with Mary a true though subordinate role of cooperating in the order of the hypostatic union. Suárez (d. 1617) emphasizes that Joseph is father of Jesus in every way short of physical generation. This would make Joseph at least a moral cause removing obstacles to the Incarnation, or, more positively, a moral dispositive cause of the Incarnation according to the following reasoning: Joseph's holiness and Joseph's consent to the marriage as virginal brought about the circumstances that in God's plan were required for the Incarnation, namely, the virginal marriage receiving Christ within it, and the superlative holiness that should have fittingly existed in the head of the Holy Family.

From Joseph's position as husband and father, therefore, there "arise all his dignity, grace, holiness and glory. . . . Since the bond of marriage existed between Joseph and the Blessed Virgin, there can be no doubt that more than any other person he approached that supereminent dignity by which the Mother of God is raised far above all created natures" (Leo XIII, *Quamquam Pluries,* Aug. 15, 1889). Although liturgical rank does not indicate the relative holiness of a saint, one can say that in accordance with these words the Church in practice venerates St. Joseph as second in holiness and dignity only to Mary. In this sense he receives a cultus of *protodulia,* i.e., "first veneration" in degree above all other saints except Mary. The words of Jesus (Mt 11.11; Lk 7.28) concerning John the Baptist do not militate against this preeminence. They are to be interpreted as hyperbolical praise of John as the greatest Prophet of the Old Testament. Since all theological evidence points to the uniqueness of Mary's Immaculate Conception, no sound grounds exist for claiming that Joseph was conceived without original sin. Whether or not he was purified of original sin in his mother's womb is uncertain, since no arguments are conclusive. It is theologically agreed as a certain minimum that because of his exceptional intimacy with Jesus and Mary he never committed grievous sin after his marriage to Our Lady. While some theologians do not admit his complete freedom from semideliberate venial sin and from concupiscence, others hold as more likely a lifelong confirmation in grace as well as those two added privileges, believing them necessary to give Joseph the holiness befitting his exalted vocation. An impressive number of Catholic theologians (such as Suárez, St. Francis de Sales, Lepicier, Jugie, and Llamera) present the assumption of St. Joseph (i.e., the belief that his glorified body is now in heaven with his soul) as a probable opinion of several centuries' standing. Joseph's intimacy with the body of Christ in the family life at Nazareth and his spiritual likeness to Mary are the strongest reasons to suppose that if anyone, at least he in addition to Mary was granted this privilege (also cf. Mt 27.52).

Patronage and Feast. St. Joseph is Patron of the Universal Church because "this is his numberless family, scattered throughout all lands, over which he rules with a sort of paternal authority, because he is the husband of Mary and the father of Jesus Christ" (Leo XIII, *Quamquam Pluries*). In the Litany of St. Joseph he is also invoked as patron of workmen, families, virgins, the sick, and the dying. In papal documents and by popular acclaim he has been hailed also as patron of prayer and the interior life, of the poor, of those in authority, fathers, priests and religious, travelers, and because of his closeness to Our Lady, as patron of devotion to Mary. He was officially declared patron of Mexico (1555), Canada (1624), Bohemia (1655), the Chinese missions (1678), and Belgium (1689). In 1937 Pius XI chose him as patron in the Church's campaign against atheistic communism, in the encyclical *Divini Redemptoris*. On March 19, 1961, John XXIII proclaimed him heavenly protector of Vatican Council II.

March 19 is celebrated as a feast of the first class, the principal feast of St. Joseph, spouse of the Blessed Virgin, Confessor, and Patron of the Universal Church. According to 1917 *Codex iuris canonicis* c.1247.1, it is a holy day of obligation, but an indult releasing the United States from earlier Church law was granted by the Holy See to the Third Plenary Council of Baltimore in 1884 because of the difficulty of observing holy days in a non-Catholic environment. The Feast of St. Joseph the Worker on May 1 was promulgated by Pius XII in 1955. Thereafter, the Solemnity of St. Joseph, formerly called the Feast of St. Joseph's Patronage and observed on the third Wednesday after Easter, was suppressed. By indult the Mass of Joseph the Worker may be said on Labor Day in the United States and Canada. The choice of May 1 was made to counteract atheistic communism's celebration of May Day, and to emphasize the dignity of labor, Christian ideals in labor relations, and the example of St. Joseph as a workman. The Feast of the Holy Family (on the first Sunday after Epiphany) commemorates the hidden life that Jesus shared with Mary and Joseph. In that sense it is a feast of St. Joseph. Ever since 1815 petitions have been sent to the Holy See from hundreds of bishops and thousands of layfolk asking for the inclusion of St. Joseph's name in the *Confiteor, Suscipe Sancta Trinitas, Communicantes,* and *Libera Nos Quaesumus* of the Mass. The inclusion would be a means of granting him an honor more aptly proportioned to his dignity as head of the Holy Family and Patron of the Universal Church, for he would be recognized as such in the liturgy. By a decree of John XXIII dated Nov.13, 1962, and effective December 8 of the same year, the name of St. Joseph was finally inserted into the *Communicantes.*

Bibliography: F. L. FILAS, *The Man Nearest to Christ: Nature and Historic Development of the Devotion to St. Joseph* (Milwaukee 1944); *Joseph and Jesus* (Milwaukee 1952); *Joseph Most Just* (Milwaukee 1956); *St. Joseph and Daily Christian Living* (New York 1959); *Joseph: The Man Closest to Jesus* (Boston 1962). R. GAUTHIER, *La Paternité de Saint Joseph* (Montreal 1958). U. HOLZMEISTER, *De Sancto Ioseph quaestiones biblicae* (Rome 1945). A. H. LEPICIER, *Saint Joseph: Époux de la très sainte Vierge* (Paris 1933). J. MUELLER, *The Fatherhood of St. Joseph,* tr. A. DENGLER (St. Louis 1952). H. RONDET, *Saint Joseph,* tr. and ed. D. ATTWATER (New York 1956). J. SEITZ, *Die Verehrung des hl. Joseph: In ihrer geschichtlichen Entwicklung bis zum Konzil von Trient dargestellt* (Freiburg 1908). B. LLAMERA, *Saint Joseph,* tr. M. ELIZABETH (St. Louis 1962).

[F. L. FILAS]

JOSEPH II, HOLY ROMAN EMPEROR

Reigned 1765 to 1790; b. Vienna, Mar. 13, 1741; d. there, Feb. 20, 1790. As the eldest son of Emperor Francis I and MARIA THERESA, he was carefully educated. At an early age he showed keen intelligence but also a changeable, imprudent character, lack of sympathy, and a pronounced tactlessness, especially with inferiors. In 1764 he was elected emperor and coregent in Austria with his mother. In reality, at this time he could play an independent role only in military affairs. He successfully insisted upon the participation of Austria in the first partition of Poland (1772) and later obtained the territory of Bucovina, which Turkey ceded voluntarily (1775). However, a plan for the acquisition of Bavaria was frustrated by FREDERICK II OF PRUSSIA in 1778, 1779, and again in 1785. Toward the end of his reign Joseph allowed Russia

Engraving of Joseph II, Holy Roman Emperor.

to draw him into a hapless war against Turkey (1782–92); after severe reverses, his troops conquered Belgrade (1789) but were forced to evacuate it at the conclusion of the Treaty of Sistova on Aug. 4, 1791.

Plans for Church Reform. Imbued from youth with the ideals of the ENLIGHTENMENT, he submitted to his mother such a radical plan for the transformation of the Catholic monastic orders that it was unacceptable even to Prince Wenzel von KAUNITZ. Joseph welcomed the dissolution of the Society of Jesus and eagerly collaborated in a scheme for its liquidation in Austria. He also supported the introduction and execution of Kaunitz's new State-Church system and regretted that his mother was too frightened to carry it out fully. One of his first executive acts as a sole and absolute ruler (1780) was to ask for a perusal of all the legislative proposals that Maria Theresa had not acted upon because of religious scruples. At the same time he informed the qualified expert in ecclesiastical affairs, Councilor Franz Joseph HEINKE, of a program of innovations he intended to introduce into the Austrian Church. This plan was so little thought out that

Heinke dissuaded him from executing some of his ideas; for example, the appointment of a primate of Austria.

The emperor then sought to effect his reforms in another direction. First he severed all jurisdictional ties between national monasteries and their superior generals residing abroad. Then he put the correspondence of the Austrian bishops, which until that time had been free, under state control. Particularly vicious was the demand of the emperor, inspired by Kaunitz, that the pope should grant him the right to nominate the bishops of his Italian provinces, as was the case in the other parts of the empire. Should the Holy See not accede to this demand, the emperor threatened to exercise his ancient sovereign rights and appoint the Catholic bishops in Lombardy himself. Pius VI resolved to journey to Vienna to try by personal talks to divert the monarch's intentions. He arrived on March 22, 1782, and diplomatically succeeded in eliminating Chancellor Kaunitz from the discussions. Kaunitz, however, sent his master an ultimatum, demanding control of the negotiations and, having obtained it, refused every important concession. To avoid more extreme developments, the pope conceded to the emperor the right to nominate the Italian bishops, but as a papal privilege. This was confirmed by a concordat on Jan. 20, 1784, after the emperor's visit to Rome on Dec. 23, 1783. The chancellor nearly succeeded in having the bishop of Laibach (Ljubljana), *persona non grata* with the pope, appointed archbishop; only the bishop's death frustrated this plan.

Monasteries and Parishes. More spectacular were Joseph II's innovations within the Austrian Church. First, all contemplative orders were suppressed, for the reason that contemplative life is useless to the world and therefore cannot be agreeable to God. Secondly, it was enacted that members of any and all monasteries could be used to remedy cases of pastoral need. These two measures showed Joseph's lack of understanding of monastic life in general and resulted in the suppression of 876 monasteries and convents within the empire. The money realized by the sale of their properties, often squandered irresponsibly, formed a *patrimonium ecclesiasticum* to provide pensions for monks expelled from their houses, salaries for clergymen, and funds for new parishes—774 in all. Through this new system of salaries, the clergy became ecclesiastical civil servants to look after the interests of the state in a domain not directly accessible to secular civil servants. Thirdly, it was established as a policy that no foreign bishops should have jurisdiction of an Austrian diocese, and similarly no Austrian diocese should include non-Austrian territory.

Seminary Legislation. Since the clergy had been reduced to servants of the Josephinist state, the state had to take care of the education of priests and to provide buildings for that purpose. Maria Theresa had already put the study of theology under strict state supervision. In 1783 Joseph II established in all of Austria 12 general seminaries to replace the episcopal seminaries and the corresponding institutions of the religious orders. In the new institutions, administered by rectors appointed by the state, the students of theology received an education for the priesthood penetrated by enlightened and anti-Church ideas, but neglecting the most elementary moral training. The emperor himself found reason to reproach the administration of the general seminary in Prague in 1787 on this point. An outstanding interference in the ecclesiastical domain was the Josephinist Marriage Act of Jan. 16, 1783, which separated the marriage contract from the Sacrament; abolished several ecclesiastical marriage impediments, replacing them with impediments formulated by the state; and assigned complete jurisdiction over matrimonial affairs to the state in contradiction to canons of the Council of Trent.

Since Joseph II enforced these innovations with his accustomed haste and harshness and without consideration for tradition, the new rules aroused the resentment and growing resistance of the people and finally led to a national revolution in Hungary and Belgium. The emperor, already weakened by tuberculosis, could no longer cope with such opposition. He was forced to apply for help from the pope he had treated so badly. Finally, toward the end, he withdrew most of his political reforms in despair over the failure of his actions, without, however, being able to restore peace to his dominions. Joseph II was denied a harmonious family life. He held a true affection for his first wife, Isabella, daughter of the duke of Parma, but she died when he was 22 years old. His second marriage to Josepha (d. 1767), daughter of Charles Albert, elector of Bavaria, was a political maneuver and was unhappy. He left no children and was succeeded by his brother, Leopold II (reigned 1790–92), formerly the grand duke of Tuscany (1765–90).

Bibliography: P. P. MITROFANOV, *Joseph II, seine politische und kulturelle Tätigkeit,* 2 v. (Vienna 1910). F. MAASS, *Der Josephinismus: Quellen zu seiner Geschichte in Österreich 1760–1790,* 5 v. (Vienna 1951–61) v.2–3. E. WOLF, 3:862–864. S. K. PADOVER, *The Revolutionary Emperor Joseph the Second* (New York 1934). RGG³-Die Religion in Geschichte und Gegenwart (Tübingen 1957–65). F. FEJTÖ, *Un Habsbourg révolutionnaire: Joseph II* (Paris 1953). M. C. GOODWIN, *The Papal Conflict with Josephinism* (New York 1938). E. BENEDIKT, *Kaiser Joseph II* (2d ed. Vienna 1947).

[F. MAASS]

JOSEPH I, PATRIARCH OF CONSTANTINOPLE

Flourished 1267 to 1275 and 1282 to 1283; b. Asia Minor, *c.* 1200; d. Constantinople, March of 1283. A priest and chaplain at the imperial court of Nicaea, Joseph, upon the death of his wife, entered the monastery of Mt. Galesios between Smyrna and Ephesus. However, he continued to take part in ecclesiastical affairs and was excommunicated by the Patriarch Arsenius Autorianus for interference with the patriarch's jurisdiction. But Arsenius was deposed soon after; and after a short incumbency of Germanus III, Joseph was enthroned as patriarch on Jan. 18, 1267. He proved an intransigent opponent of the reunion projects of Emperor MICHAEL VIII PALAEOLOGUS and was aided in his opposition by the controversialist Job Jasites. In defiance of the reunion achieved at the Council of LYONS (1274), Joseph took an oath never to recognize the Roman Church unless it gave up its errors or a panorthodox council ruled on the question. Joseph was urged to this position by the emperor's sister Eulogia. He wrote a *Confession* in support of his oath; and when the Emperor Michael persuaded him to reconsider the problem, Joseph retired from the patriarchate because of his oath (1275). He was reinstated by the Emperor ANDRONICUS II on Dec. 31, 1282 and, on his death, was hailed as a confessor by the emperor. His letters and testament are unedited, but several excerpts of an anti-Latin work on the FILIOQUE are contained in a manuscript attributed to Joseph II.

Feast: Oct. 30.

Bibliography: F. DÖLGER, *Lexikon für Theologie und Kirche,* ed. J. HOFER and K. RAHNER, 10 v. (2d, new ed. Freiburg 1957–65) 5:1127–28. L. PETIT, *Dictionnaire de théologie catholique,* ed. A. VACANT et al., 15 v. (Paris 1903–50) 8.2:1541–42. V. LAURENT, "Le Serment anti–latin du patriarche Joseph Ier," *Échos d'Orient,* 26 (1927) 396–407. *Byzantinische Zeitschrift* 30 (1929–30) 489–496, his excommunication. H. G. BECK, *Kirche und theologische Literatur im byzantinischen Reich* (Munich 1959) 676–677. J. CARELLIUS, ed., *Confessio,* in *Nuova raccolta d'opuscoli scientifici e filologici,* ed. F. MANDELLI, v. 23 (Venice 1755) 20–23. L. BRÉHIER, *Le Monde byzantin,* 3 v. (Paris 1947–50) 1:392–411. G. OSTROGORSKY, *History of the Byzantine State,* tr. J. HUSSEY from 2d German ed. (Oxford 1956) 411, 433. D. J. GEANAKOPLOS, *Emperor Michael Palaeologus and the West, 1258–1282* (Cambridge, Mass. 1959).

[F. CHIOVARO]

JOSEPH CALASANCTIUS, ST.

Founder of the Clerks Regular of Religious Schools (PIARISTS); b. Peralta de la Sal, near Barbastro, Aragon, Spain, Sept. 11, 1556; d. Rome, Italy, Aug. 25, 1648. He studied law and theology at the universities of Lérida and Valencia, and was ordained in 1583. He went to Rome in 1592 and became associated with Cardinal Marc'-Antonio Colonna. He also became a member of various confraternities, which better acquainted him with the problems of the laity. He was convinced of the need for religious and secular education for the children of the poor, and opened the first free public school in Europe, at the Church of Santa Dorothea, in 1597. An increasingly large number of students required Calasanctius to enlist more teachers. CLEMENT VIII encouraged and financially assisted the new institution; PAUL V continued this help and recognized the foundation of Calasanctius as a formal religious congregation in 1617. Other schools were opened, and in 1621 the teachers were given the full privileges of a religious order. Calasanctius was named superior general and was later confirmed in this appointment for life.

The order enjoyed a rapid growth in Italy and in neighboring countries. Before the death of Calasanctius the order was organized in six provinces, with 500 members in 37 houses. Partly because of its rapid growth, internal dissension arose and Calasanctius suffered grave opposition from some of his own brethren. External attacks frequently centered on the nature of the work done by the Piarists. Free education of the poor was an idea that was novel and suspect at the time, for many believed that the poorer classes, once educated, would no longer pursue their former occupations, to the detriment of society. Moreover, the friendship of Calasanctius and GALILEO, and the fact that many young Piarists were educated by the great scientist, contributed to further misunderstandings.

Calasanctius's troubles culminated in 1643 when URBAN VIII ordered the deposition of the generalate, and at the age of 86 Calasanctius stood trial before the Holy Office. He saw the destruction of his work in 1646 when INNOCENT X reduced the order to a simple federation of independent religious houses. With the patience of Job, to whom he was likened, Calasanctius never lost hope that the Piarists would be restored to their original status as a full religious order. This hope was fulfilled only after his death. In 1656 ALEXANDER VII partially reestablished the Piarists as a congregation of simple vows, and the order was completely reinstituted in 1669 by CLEMENT IX. Calasanctius was beatified in 1748 and canonized in 1767. He was declared "the heavenly patron of all Christian schools" by PIUS XII.

Feast: Aug. 25 (formerly 27).

Bibliography: JOSEPH CALASANCTIUS, *Florilegium Calasanctianum,* ed. L. PICANYOL (Rome 1958). *Epistolario,* ed. L. PICANYOL, 9 v. (Rome 1950–56). J. DE C. BAU, *Biografía crítica de San José de Calasanz* (Madrid 1949). S. GINER GUERRI, *El proceso* *de beatificación de San José de Calasanz* (Madrid 1973). TERESA OF AVILA, *Calasanz Teresian Reader: Selection of Teresian Sentences and Sayings That Deeply Influenced the Spirituality of Her Devoted Reader, Saint Joseph Calasanz,* ed. L. GRACIA (New York 1987). J. TIMON-DAVID, *Vie de saint Joseph Calasanct, fondateur des écoles pies,* 2 v. (Marseille 1884). C. S. DURRANT, *The Life of Saint Joseph Calasanctius* (Los Angeles 1954). F. GIORDANO, *Il Calasanzio e l'origine della scuola popolare* (Genoa 1960). J. C. HEIDENREICH, *Der hl. Joseph Calasanz* (Vienna 1907). A. SAPA, *Teologia spirituale e pedagogica di san Giuseppe Calasanzio* (Florence 1951). R. BRANCA, *Avventura del Calasanzio* (Cagliari 1967). G. SÁNTHA, *Ensayos críticos sobre S. José de Calasanz y las escuelas Pías* (Salamanca 1976). M. A. ASIAIN, *La experiencia cristiana de Calasanz* (Salamanca 1980).

[L. A. IRANYI]

JOSEPH OF CUPERTINO, ST.

Conventual Franciscan friar whose ecstatic flights earned him the title the "flying friar"; b. Cupertino (Lecce), June 17, 1603; d. Osimo, Sept. 18, 1663. He desired religious life and entered the Capuchin Order as a lay brother but was dismissed. His mother appealed to two uncles, both Conventuals, who brought him into their order as a tertiary. His simplicity and obedience won him acceptance to the clerical state in 1625. Despite his poor progress in theological studies, he was ordained in 1628. Joseph was sent to Grotella, where his life of miracles and ecstasies began. For ten years the surrounding countryside witnessed the wonders of this friar. Authorities tried to hide him and forbade his presence at public office and the gatherings of the friars. He was denounced to the Inquisition at Naples in 1638, freed after three examinations, but sent to his general in Rome. Here he was taken to visit Pope URBAN VIII. At the sight of the Holy Father, Joseph went into ecstasy and rose from the ground till the command of his general called him to his senses. He was assigned to the Sacro Convento, Assisi, where the mystic phenomena ceased. Two years later, the ecstasies returned. His fame soon spread beyond Italy and pilgrims came to witness his ecstatic flights. One group, including the Spanish ambassador, saw him take flight over their heads to the high altar. The Duke of Brunswick, a Lutheran, became a Catholic after twice witnessing Joseph in ecstasies at Mass. Pope INNOCENT X ordered Joseph into retirement with the Capuchins at Pietrarubbia and later at Fossombrone. In 1657 Pope ALEXANDER VII allowed him to return to the Conventuals at Osimo. He spent the remainder of his life in seclusion. He was beatified by Benedict XIV in 1753, and canonized by Clement XIII on July 16, 1767.

Feast: Sept. 18.

Bibliography: G. PARISCIANI, *L'inquisizione e il caso S. Guiseppe da Copertino: Con appendice di documenti inediti*

(Padua 1996). H. THURSTON, *The Physical Phenomena of Mysticism,* ed. J. H. CREHAN (London 1952).

[R. J. BARTMAN]

JOSEPH OF LEONESSA, ST.

Capuchin preacher and missionary; b. Leonessa, Italy, Jan. 8, 1556; d. Amatrice, Italy, Feb. 4, 1612. St. Joseph was the son of a nobleman, Giovanni Desiderii, and Francesca Paolini, who had him baptized as Euphranius. At 15, both parents having died, he lived with his uncle Battista, a professor in Viterbo, who educated him. On Jan. 1, 1573, he joined the Capuchin Order and changed his name to Joseph. When or where he was ordained is not known, but after ordination he preached with much success in Abruzzi and the neighboring regions. At his request, he was sent to preach to the infidels. He departed on Aug. 1, 1587, for Constantinople, where he ministered to galley slaves and preached in the city. Eventually he was imprisoned, but upon his release he took up the same tasks. Later, he was seized in an attempt to enter the royal palace to preach to the sultan and was condemned to death. After hanging by hooks through his hand and foot for three days, he was miraculously released. He returned to Italy, where he again became known for his preaching and love for the poor and sick, working many miracles, before dying after an operation for cancer. His body, buried first in Amatrice, was transferred to Leonessa. He was beatified on June 19, 1737, by CLEMENT XII; canonized on June 29, 1746, by BENEDICT XIV; and declared on Jan. 12, 1952, the patron of the Capuchin missions in the Turkish Republic by PIUS XII.

Feast: Feb. 4.

Bibliography: *Lexicon Capuccinum* (Rome 1951) 865–867. A. BRENNAN, *Saint Joseph of Leonessa* (London 1912). GIACINTO DA BELMONTE, *Vita di St. Giuseppe da Leonessa* (Rome 1896). I. MAUSOLF, *Round Table of Franciscan Research* 14 (1948) 1–23.

[V. WYDEVEN]

JOSEPH OF METHONE

Byzantine scholar, prounionist, and bishop; b. John Plusiadenus, probably in Candia, Crete, *c.* 1429; d. Methone, Aug. 9, 1500. He was well educated in Latin, Greek, and theology, an excellent copyist, and a specialist in ecclesiastical music. He was ordained before 1455. Like most Cretans, John Plusiadenus in his earlier years was a strong anti-unionist, but was converted by studying the acts of the Council of FLORENCE, and became one of 12 Byzantine priests who officially supported the union, for which they were generally boycotted as religious and national traitors. In an encyclical and a dialogue he tried in vain to justify the group's position, and eventually they had to ask for financial aid from Venice and the pope. Cardinal BESSARION selected Joseph as "head of the Churches" in the Orient and "vice-Protopapas" (*c.* 1466–67 to *c.* 1481). He probably resided in Italy, chiefly in Venice, employed in copying manuscripts from 1472 to *c.* 1492, when he was elected to the See of Methone with the name of Joseph. He was in Venice again in 1497, in Rome at Christmas 1498, and was about to visit Crete when he was informed of the impending Turkish attack on Methone. He hastened to his see and was killed there, cross in hand, by the onrushing Turks.

Plusiadenus is best known for his consistent support of the union of Florence, notably in his *Defensio synodi Florentinae*, a patristic defense of the five main elements in the decree of union, written after 1455, and often printed under the name of Gennadius [*Patrologia Graeca*, ed. J. P. Migne, 161 v. (Paris 1857–66) 154:1109–1394]. He also wrote *Sermo apologeticus pro synodo Florentina adv. Marcum Ephesium* (*Patrologia Graeca*, 154:1023–94); *Disceptatio de differentiis inter Graecos et Latinos* (*c.* 1460; *Patrologia Graeca*, 154:959–1023); and poetry, sermons, and other minor works, as well as ecclesiastical music.

Bibliography: M. MANOUSSAKAS, "Recherches sur la vie de Jean Plousiadénos," *Revue des études Byzantines*, 17 (1959) 28–51. L. PETIT, *Dictionnaire de théologie catholique*, ed. A. VACANT et al., 15 v. (Paris 1903–50) 8.2:1526–29. M. CANDAL, "La Apologia," *Orientalia Christiana periodica*, 21 (1955) 36–57.

[J. GILL]

JOSEPH OF THE HOLY SPIRIT

Discalced Carmelite theologian and writer (name in the world, Joseph Barroso); b. Braga, Portugal, Dec. 26, 1609; d. Madrid, Jan. 27, 1674. He is commonly known as the "Portuguese" to distinguish him from his homonym the "Andalusian." He was professed in the Discalced Carmelites in Lisbon (May 30, 1632) and after ordination was instrumental in the establishing of foundations at Braga (1635), Nahia (1653), and Cascaes. Because of his fame as a preacher the King of Portugal offered him a bishopric, which he refused out of humility; he was never consecrated bishop, as some authors have stated, but was a professor of theology for many years. He was transferred to the general's house of St. Hermenegild in Madrid where he died, esteemed for his holiness. Here his body was venerated until the exclaustration of religious orders in Spain (1835). He wrote two works of importance. One was the *Cadena Mistica* (Madrid 1678), the first attempt to codify the spirituality of the

Teresian school. It remains useful even today, since the author had access to many writings and manuscripts no longer available. His other work, *Enucleatio mysticae theologiae*, was published posthumously (Cologne 1684).

Bibliography: "Vita et opera," in *Enucleatio mysticae theologiae S. Dionysii Aropagitae,* crit. ed. ANASTASIO A S. PAULO (Rome 1927); introduction is the best biography. J. HEERINCKX, "Doctrina mystica Iosephi a Sp. Sancto Lusitani, O. C. D.," *Antonianum* 3 (1928) 485–493. SIMEON S. FAMILIA, "Mystical Chain of Carmel," *Spiritual Life* 8 (1962) 99–106.

[O. RODRIGUEZ]

JOSEPHINISM

The Austrian State-Church system of the period of ENLIGHTENMENT, the rules of which were worked out by the Imperial Chancellor, Prince Wenzel Anton von Kaunitz, approved by Empress MARIA THERESA, and implemented by her son JOSEPH II to such an extent that the whole System took its name from him.

Principles of Reform. In contradistinction to the preceding Hapsburg State-Church system, Josephinism did not take the papal privileges as the legal basis for papal interference in Church affairs, but the sovereign power of the State to which, it was thought, the Church and its ministers also were subject. Hence, even those ecclesiastical reforms effected by the Josephinist State for the material benefit of the Church, e.g., increase in parishes, demarcation of dioceses, better remuneration of the clergy, and reorganization of theological studies, were dictated in the first place by reasons of state: pastoral care was held to be inseparable from the safety of the State. But improvements in ecclesiastical administration cannot by themselves evoke and further internal spiritual life, as every real reform in Church matters testifies. Not only is the purely secular purpose of the State unable to do this, but besides, the interference of Josephinism in the intimate organization of the Church was liable to weaken the supernatural life to the vanishing point, if not to kill it. A standard example is the suppression, on principle, of the contemplative orders, judged and condemned from a purely utilitarian standpoint in complete misunderstanding of their spiritual purpose. Hence, the first real reform of Austrian Catholicism that began in the first half of the 19th century took place without Josephinist influences in its spiritual regeneration.

Influence of Prince Kaunitz. In the 1760s Prince Kaunitz recognized during his negotiations with the Roman Curia that the latter was unwilling to forego the immunity of Church property without corresponding compensation from the State. He, therefore, in 1767 issued ordinances for Austrian Lombardy, a territory under his immediate administration, restricting on essential points Church property rights, endangering the free movement of Church personnel, and imperiling the independence of the Church from the State. When, notwithstanding Church protests, Maria Theresa confirmed these ordinances, Kaunitz submitted to her on June 15, 1768, a set of secret instructions to his supreme administrative body in Milan, which was to put the relation between State and Church on an entirely new basis. The Church was to be subject to the State in all mixed questions. The State was to obtain all Church property. It was even to control the spiritual activity of the clergy, since, so the document declared, "the ruler is vitally interested in keeping dogma in harmony with the gospel and in adapting the discipline of the clergy and the outward forms of religion to the needs of the commonweal." The instructions further prevented the formation of a "corpus ecclesiasticum," as in France, so that all churchmen stood before the State as individual persons. Herewith there was erected a State-Church system differing unfavorably from Gallicanism in its pressure on the Church. Another protest, this time from the Pope, was disregarded by the Empress. In 1769 the system was extended to the whole monarchy, and in the last decade of the reign of the Empress it was applied especially against the monastic orders.

Summit and Decline. While Maria Theresa hesitated to draw the last consequences from the new State-Church system, her successor, Joseph II, knew no such restraints. He isolated the Austrian Church from Rome and subjected her internally to so far-reaching a control that the whole system, though already in use for 12 years, was named after him. His enforced innovations were bound to wound the feelings of the people. Everywhere disturbances broke out, so that his successor, Leopold II, promised kindly to examine the complaints of the bishops. But when quiet had been restored to the state, the Josephinist system was confirmed on all essential points on March 17, 1791. Under Emperor Francis II (I) the situation remained unchanged; Josephinism was introduced in 1816 even in the newly gained Italian territories. A formal papal condemnation was threatening. But after a journey to Rome in 1819, the Emperor tried to reestablish peace with the Church. To that effect he had Prince Klemens Wenzel von Metternich conduct negotiations with the papal nuncio in Vienna from 1832 to 1836, but they were interrupted by the unexpected death of Francis, March 2, 1835. After 1848, many churchmen, especially among the younger clergy, were won over to the idea of freeing the Church from the yoke of the State. The last phase of the emancipation came when the young Emperor Francis Joseph I, through the ordinances of April 18

and 23, 1850, abolished the Josephinist Church-State system.

Bibliography: F. MAASS, ed., *Der Josephinismus: Quellen zu seiner Geschichte in Österreich 1760–1850,* 5 v. (Fontes rerum Austriacarum II.71–75; Vienna 1951–61). M. C. GOODWIN, *The Papal Conflict with Josephinism* (New York 1938). F. VALJAVEC, *Der Josephinismus* (2d ed. Vienna 1945), with reservations. E. WINTER, *Geschichte des Josefinismus* (Berlin 1962), anti-Catholic. E. WOLF, *Die Religion in Geschitchte und Gegenwart,* 7 v. (3d ed. Tübingen 1957–65) 3:866–867.

[F. MAASS]

JOSEPHINUM, THE PONTIFICAL COLLEGE

The Pontifical College Josephinum was officially founded by Rev. John Joseph Jessing (1836–1899) on Sept. 1, 1888 in Columbus, Ohio. He established it as a bilingual German-English institution to prepare candidates for the priesthood who would serve the growing German-American immigrant population in the United States. In 1875 Jessing had opened an orphanage for boys in Pomeroy, Ohio, where he was pastor of Sacred Heart Catholic Church from 1870 until 1877, at which time he and the orphanage moved to Columbus, the state's capitol. By means of appeals in the German-language newspaper *Ohio Waisenfreund* ("Orphan's Friend"), first published on May 2, 1873, Jessing raised funds first for the orphans, then later for needy students when the seminary was founded in 1888. With each passing year, classes were added with the result that by the time of Jessing's death in 1899 a faculty of philosophy and theology complemented the first six years of classical studies. All costs associated with the training of seminarians were provided by the bilingual (German and English) institution. The name "Josephinum" dates back to the May 5, 1886 edition of the *Ohio Waisenfreund* where it appeared as another name for "St. Joseph's Orphan Home."

Jessing was born in Münster, Germany. After combat service in the Westphalian Artillery (1864–1866), he immigrated to the United States in 1867 where he entered Mt. St. Mary's Seminary, Cincinnati, in 1868. Upon ordination to the priesthood in 1870 for the diocese of Columbus, he was immediately appointed pastor in Pomeroy. Both his newspaper and seminary were inspired by his objective to sustain the language and Catholic faith of fellow German-speaking immigrants in the United States. Monsignor Jessing created a domestic prelate in 1896, and saw the first class of six men ordained to the priesthood on June 29, 1899, shortly before his death (Nov. 2).

In an effort to ensure the ethnic and missionary character of the Josephinum, Jessing initially offered the title to the institution and its future direction to the *Deutsch-Americanischer Priester-Verein* (German-American Priests' Association), founded in St. Louis in 1887. Failing to secure their patronage, Jessing entered into negotiations with the Holy See. The Congregation for the Propagation of the Faith accepted his proposal and designated the Josephinum a pontifical institution on Dec. 12, 1892. In the original constitutions accepted by Rome, the apostolic delegate in the United States (now the apostolic nuncio) was named the ordinary of the Pontifical College Josephinum and was given the task of assigning the priests ordained there to various U.S. dioceses. This provision was later changed, and since the 1960s all students are affiliated with particular dioceses or religious communities into which they are incardinated upon ordination.

The orphanage division was closed in 1932, followed by the high school in 1967. After more than a century, the Josephinum, is the only pontifical college in the United States, under the direct supervision of the Holy See's Congregation for Catholic Education, and was accredited by the Association of Theological Schools in 1970, and by the Higher Learning Commission in 1976. The Josephinum maintains its missionary spirit, but its emphasis on German-language ministry has given way to a program of formation for service among Spanish-speaking peoples in the United States. The student body, about a hundred in 2000, includes candidates from Ugandan and Burmese dioceses. The full-time faculty, made up of diocesan and religious priests, religious women and laity, numbers more than thirty.

Bibliography: L. J. FICK, *The Jessing Legacy*, (Columbus, OH 1988). R. P. CLOONEY, ed., *The Spirit of John Joseph Jessing: Priest, Orphan's Friend, Visionary* (Columbus, OH 1999).

[J. F. GARNEAU]

JOSEPHITES

(SSJ, Official Catholic Directory #0700); a congregation of priests and brothers, officially designated St. Joseph's Society of the Sacred Heart (SSJ), but popularly known as Josephite Fathers or Josephite Missionaries.

Origin. The Josephite society, numbering more than 250 priests and brothers in 1963, was founded in 1866 at Mill Hill, London, England, by Herbert VAUGHAN, later cardinal archbishop of Westminster. Vaughan's plan to found a society of missionary priests was encouraged by Cardinal Nicholas Wiseman, who recalled that St. Vincent Pallotti had declared that England would not be rewon to the Catholic Church until she resumed her pre-Reformation practice of sending priests to the foreign missions.

In 1871, when Vaughan asked Pius IX for a mission field for his new society, the pope suggested that the first Josephites be sent to the U.S. to work among the more than four million recently emancipated African Americans. The suggestion was an answer to the appeal of the American hierarchy who, during the Second Plenary Council of Baltimore in 1866, begged for priests who would devote themselves to the service of black Americans. In December 1871 four priests from Mill Hill arrived in Baltimore, Md., to begin work.

Within the next two decades, more missionaries came from Mill Hill to the U.S., but experience showed that the African-American missions could be served better by an American community. Thus, in 1893, by mutual consent of Cardinal Vaughan and Cardinal James Gibbons of Baltimore, an American community was established under the direction of Gibbons. The original community, St. Joseph's Society for Foreign Missions of Mill Hill, or MILL HILL MISSIONARIES, continued to flourish both in England and on the Continent and in many mission areas of the world. The American community, under the original four Josephites, formed the new Society of St. Joseph, which received the decree of praise in 1932, officially establishing it as a pontifical society.

Development. The society was founded to work exclusively within the African-American community. The original members dedicated themselves by vow to this particular vocation. In the years following 1871, missions were established in Washington, D.C.; Richmond and Norfolk, VA.; Charleston, SC; and Louisville, KY. In the 20th century, the work spread, with the greatest concentration of Josephites in Florida, Alabama, Mississippi, Louisiana, and Texas. The generalate is in Baltimore, MD.

Bibliography: *The Colored Harvest* (Baltimore 1888–1960) superseded by the *Josephite Harvest* (Baltimore 1960–). J. T. GILLARD, *The Catholic Church and the American Negro* (Baltimore 1930); *Colored Catholics in the U.S.* (Baltimore 1941). JOSEPHITE FATHERS, *Society of St. Joseph of the Sacred Heart, 1893–1943* (Baltimore 1943). F. M. DEVRES, *Remembered in Blessing: The Courtfield Story* (London 1955).

[M. J. O'ROURKE/EDS.]

JOSEPHUS, FLAVIUS

Jewish historiographer and cultural apologist whose main works, *The Jewish War* and *Jewish Antiquities,* are of great value for the history of the Jews; b. Jerusalem, between Sept. 13, A.D. 37 and March 16, 38; d. place and date unknown, probably *c.* 101.

Life. Josephus [in MSS Ἰωσηπ(π)ος or Ἰωσιπ(π)ος] was the son of Matthias, a "priest of the first course," who was himself descended from the Hasmonaeans in both the paternal and the maternal line. He was educated for public office from an early age; between his 16th and 19th year he acquired personal experience of the doctrines and practices of Pharisees, Sadducees, and Essenes, and also spent some time in the wilderness of Judea with an ascetic solitary. On his return to Jerusalem, he became a member of the Pharisee group and entered public life. He went to Rome, *c.* 63–64, on a successful embassy and made friends in Nero's circle and even with the pro-Jewish Empress Poppaea. Upon returning to Palestine on the eve of the Jewish revolt, Josephus appears to have supported his party's position on the inexpediency of revolt. However, to maintain power after Cestius Gallus's defeat, the Pharisees had to show signs of militancy, so they sent Josephus to take command in Galilee. For this period there are two inconsistent accounts. In *The Jewish War* (*De bello Judaico,* hereafter, *B.J.*), he portrays himself as the general in command of the revolt in Galilee. In his autobiography (*Vita*), written years later, Josephus replies to Justus of Tiberias, who accused him of causing the revolt of Tiberias against Rome, and explains that he was sent to restrain, not to command, the revolt; in this account, the relationship between his actions and his motives is more complex. He organized the defense of the region but temporized with both Zealot and Roman; when, however, Vespasian started subjugating Galilee, Josephus opposed him resolutely. He skillfully defended Jotapata for a while and finally, by an unprepossessing stratagem, surrendered to Vespasian. The prisoner then prophesied that Vespasian would become emperor, which helped his chances of survival.

If his earlier motives are unclear, subsequently at least, he was sincerely convinced that Rome would conquer and that it would be better that the Romans should destroy only the Jewish ZEALOTS, not the whole people and religion, of which he remained a sturdy apologist. In Vespasian's entourage, as a prisoner and talisman, he observed the subjugation of Galilee and Judea. On Vespasian's departure from Alexandria for Rome, Josephus returned to Palestine in the suite of Titus, and witnessed the siege of Jerusalem, taking notes, interrogating deserters, and helping in negotiations between besiegers and besieged. From the final carnage he succeeded in saving several friends and relatives and some scrolls.

After the war he received compensation for the loss of his property in Jerusalem by the gift of other estates in Palestine. However, he followed Titus to Rome, became a citizen, and devoted himself to literary studies. Vespasian dismissed a charge that he was implicated in a Jewish revolt in Cyrene. Josephus received a pension and seems to have become the official war historian. Between 75 and 79, he composed *The Jewish War,* which

he offered to Vespasian; Titus praised it and ordered its publication. Henceforward, under Vespasian, Titus, and Domitian, his life was one of ease.

He was married at least three times, and twice divorced. It is not clear whether he already had a wife, left in Jerusalem during the siege (*B.J.* 5.419), but in any case he married, at Vespasian's command, a captive Jewess from Caesarea. Later, a lady from Alexandria bore him three children, of whom one, Hyrcanus, survived. These women being each in her turn divorced, a Cretan Jewess of distinguished family bore him two further children, Justus and Simonides Agrippa.

Under Domitian, Josephus had a literary patron, one Epaphroditus, who was either a freedman of Nero who died in 96, or a grammarian who, according to the Souda, lived until the days of Nerva. In either case, Josephus's literary activity ceases about this date; the latest events implied are the death of Agrippa (between 92 and 95) and the 13th year of Domitian (A.D. 94). The circumstances of his death are not known. Eusebius's (*Ecclesiastical History* 3.9.2) tells us that a statue was erected in Rome in Josephus's honor. Perhaps this still survives (in the Ny Carlsberg Glyptotek, Copenhagen).

The Jewish War. Immediately after the Jewish revolt Josephus composed, in Aramaic, an account of it for the Jews of Adiabene and Mesopotamia and for the native populations of Parthia, Babylonia, and Arabia, in order to dissuade them from attacks on Rome. Between 75 and 79, he finished the seven books of his work on the same subject in Greek.

Josephus wrote *The Jewish War* for diffusion in the Greco–Roman world to show the greatness of the Roman victory and the folly of further sedition. He joined with these congenial emphases the theme that it was the "Jewish tyrants," i.e., the Zealots, who were responsible, an exculpation that was very timely for both the Pharisees and the Jews of the Diaspora. Josephus insists that his account of the fighting, in contrast with other histories now lost, is that of an eyewitness who took notes on the doings of both sides during the war. He further acknowledges the help he derived from the field commentaries of Vespasian and Titus and from critical remarks by King Agrippa. His relationship to his rivals' histories is not clear. This main part of his work is of great historical value. He prefaced it with an ill-proportioned history of the Jews from the days of Antiochus Epiphanes until the start of the war. This may be divided, on bases of style, content, and sources, into three parts. The first covers events from 170 B.C. until Archelaus's deposition in A.D. 6. Until the rise of Antipater, Herod's father, the account is brief, but from then until the accession of Archelaus the fortunes of that dynasty are detailed. Here Josephus uses the *Uni-*

versal History of Nicolaus of Damascus, a non–Jewish, pro–Herodian source composed before A.D. 14. Josephus, or some intermediary, has reworked this source, especially in its account of the Maccabean period. The second part is the account of the three Jewish sects. This derives from a Jewish ethnographic writing used by Philo and perhaps Hippolytus. The third part is an account of the procuratorial period that is jejune up to the time of Felix (A.D. 52–60) but thenceforward abundant.

The Jewish Antiquities. The 20 books of the Ἰουδαϊκὴ Ἀρχαιολογία were modeled, in their title and number, on *The Roman Antiquities* of Dionysius of Halicarnassus. *The Jewish Antiquities* is a history of the Jews from Creation to the start of the Jewish revolt, and a piece of cultural propaganda showing the Greeks how the Jew's God–given constitution made their nation prosper. This apologetic motive accounts for numerous modifications and additions that the Biblical sources undergo, and for a sustained anti-Samaritan note. A 21st book, *Life,* a revised account of Josephus's conduct in the Galilean campaign with introductory and concluding biographical material, was appended to *The Jewish Antiquities.* The entire work was finished after Agrippa II's death. The date of completion given, A.D. 94, may refer to this edition of *The Jewish Antiquities* or to an earlier one finished before the *Life,* in its present form, was projected. The value of *The Jewish Antiquities* depends on the value of the sources available to its author. In delimiting these, however, certainty has not yet been attained. Some scholars see Josephus as an academic historian critically selecting details from several sources, although occasionally revealing his own bias. Others hold that he merely abridged the offerings of some two or three late sources, which already reflected selectivity and bias in dealing with the events. This latter solution, in itself probably extreme, merely shifts the question of value to the sources of Josephus's putative precursors.

Specifically, in the period covered by the Hebrew OT it is possible that Josephus had not read all the numerous Hellenistic historians whom he cites. He will have found many citations from them in one or two Jewish historical school texts, and these texts could also be the source of the Alexandrian exegetical material that he uses. But almost certainly he used the Hebrew OT and Greek Septuagint (often in the Lucianic text–type) directly and not merely in such a school text's adaptations of the paraphrases of Demetrius or Artapanus. Again, Josephus's clear stylistic affinity with such historians as Dionysius of Halicarnassus and Nicolaus of Damascus implies that he read them; he could surely utilize their contents as well as their style. Besides, his own education would have familiarized him with much of the traditional Jewish material that he used. Josephus, or his immediate

source, clearly lacked information about the period from the end of the Persian empire to the start of the Maccabean revolt. Little but the *Alexander Romance,* the *Epistle of Aristeas,* and Polybius was drawn upon. For the revolt itself, he had a shorter form of 1 Maccabees; but not, it seems, 2 Maccabees. Thereafter, Strabo and Nicolaus of Damascus, together with Jewish tradition, whether oral or written, are his ultimate sources.

For his account of King Herod it has been suggested that Josephus used Nicolaus of Damascus only indirectly, in an anti-Herodian Jewish redaction. Josephus himself, however, especially after Agrippa II's death, could well be responsible for some of these anti–Herodian elements. It is doubtful that he had direct access to Herod's *Memoirs* or to the biography, sympathetic to Herod, of a certain Ptolemy. The differences between the account of Herod in *The Jewish Antiquities* and that in *The Jewish War* show that Josephus either secured new sources or made different use of the old ones. In favor of his direct use here of Nicolaus—and this would affect the analysis of the sources of all the second half of *The Jewish Antiquities*—it is significant that, after the point where Nicolaus's *History* stops, Josephus's information is scanty until he reaches the period of Agrippa I. Thenceforward he is better informed. Some material will have come from Agrippa II; some, from what Josephus himself had seen and heard. In Rome he had access to Roman decrees; not all those that he cites will have been found in his sources. His account of Gaius's assassination, the accessions of Claudius and Nero, and of Parthian and Adiabenian history follows closely that of a Roman patrician historian, probably Cluvius Rufus.

The Jewish Antiquities contains a much discussed passage, the so–called *Testimonium Flavianum,* seemingly one of the earliest non–Christian references to Jesus Christ. Internal arguments for a lack of authenticity are inconclusive, but formal and external evidence suggests that it has undergone glossing [see J. P. MEIER, *Catholic Biblical Quarterly* 52 (1991) 76–103]. The Greek text of *The Jewish Antiquities,* of which a Byzantine *Epitome* also exists, was translated into Latin at the order of Cassiodorus, but there is no evidence for any Latin translation of the *Life.*

Against Apion. This inadequate but now standard title derives from Eusebius and St. Jerome. Origen (*C. Celsum* 1.16, 4.11; ed. P. Kotschau, *Die griechischen christlichen Schriftsteller der ersten drei Jahrhunderte* 1.68, 281) and Eusebius (*Ecclesiastical History* 3.9.4., etc.; ed. E. Schwartz, *Die griechischen christlichen Schriftsteller der ersten drei Jahrhunderte,* 2.222, etc.) usually call it "*On the Antiquity of the Jews*" and this title is supported by the text of the work. Porphyry [*De*

Abstinentia 4.14 (ed. A. Nauck, Teubner ser., 251)] says *Against Apion* came in part from Josephus's *To the Greeks*. It was composed after *The Jewish Antiquities*, but still during the life of Epaphroditus; Josephus wrote it, in two books, in reply to criticism of *Antiquities*. It presents and refutes the anti–Jewish propaganda current in the Hellenistic world (*see* ANTI–SEMITISM). First, the relatively greater antiquity of the Jews is demonstrated, and the silence of certain Greek writers on this subject is explained. Then, current accusations against Jewish history, religion, and morals are refuted, and finally there is a brief exposition of Moses and his laws, and a comparison with Greek law and theology. The value of *Against Apion* as a source of observations on Jewish history by lost historians and especially of fragments of the anti–Jewish polemicists—Manetho, Chaeremon, Lysimachus, Apollonius Molon, and Apion himself—is inestimable. In its day, however, its originality must have been small. It shows traces of deriving from an Alexandrian Jewish tradition of academic polemic, and many of the citations may have been commonplaces of this tradition.

In his apologetic works, Josephus appears to represent no one school of Judaism. His own training was Pharisaic and Palestinian, but his apologetic, HAGGADAH, and HALAKAH, contain many characteristics of Alexandrian Judaism. His relationship, literary and ideological, with Philo merits further study.

Recent Developments. The last quarter of the 20th century was a period of especially intensive activity in Josephus scholarship. In that period appeared two important research tools: a complete concordance to Josephus's writings and a compendious, annotated bibliography of the relevant secondary literature. New translations of commentaries on the historian's works in English, French, and German were in progress. L. H. Feldman authored numerous studies on Josephus's depiction of Biblical characters as compared with their portrayal in Scripture itself and elsewhere in Jewish–Christian tradition. Authors like T. W. Franxman and C. T. Begg investigated the Josephan reworking of selected Scriptural segments in detail. In line with a wide tendency in Biblical studies, Josephus's stance toward women has likewise underwent considerable scrutiny in these years. Several volumes of collected essays were published in the 1980s and 1990s, offering investigations of a wide range of special questions in the Josephan corpus. All indications were that the renaissance of Josephus studies that marked the end of the second millennium would continue into the third.

Bibliography: Editions, Translations, Commentaries, Tools. *Opera*, ed. B. NIESE, 7. v. (Berlin 1887–95) ; Eng. tr. H. ST. J. THACKERAY et. al., 10 v. (Loeb Classical Library; 1926–1965) ; Fr. tr. E. NODET (Paris 1990–). S. MASON et al., *Commentary on Flavius Josephus* (Leiden 1999–). L. H. FELDMAN, *Josephus and Modern Scholarship (1937–1980)* (Berlin 1984); *Josephus: A Supplmentary Bibliography* (Berlin 1986). K. H. RENGSTORF, *A Complete Concordance to Flavius Josephus*, 4 v. (Leiden 1973–1983). **Studies.** H. W. ATTRIDGE, *The Interpretation of Biblical History in the "Antiquitates Judaicae" of Flavius Josephus* (Harvard Dissertations in Religion 7; Missoula, MT 1977). C. T. BEGG, *Josephus' Account of the Early Divided Monarchy*, (Bibliotheca ephemeridum theologicarum Lovaniensium 108; Leuven 1993) 212–420; *Josephus' Story of the Later Monarchy* (Bibliotheca ephemeridum theologicarum Lovaniensium 155; Leuven 2000). P. BILDE, *Flavius Josephus between Jerusalem and Rome* (Sheffield 1988). C. A. BROWN, *No Longer Be Silent: First Century Jewish Portraits of Biblical Women. Studies in Pseudo– Philo's "Biblical Antiquities" and Josephus's "Jewish Antiquities"* (Louisville 1992). S. J. D. COHEN, *Josephus in Galilee and Rome: His Vita and Development as a Historian* (Leiden 1979). L. H. FELDMAN, *Studies in Josephus' Rewritten Bible* (Journal for the Study of Judaism in the Persian, Hellenistic, and Roman Period Sup 58; Leiden 1998); *Josephus's Interpretation of the Bible* (Hellenistic Culture and Society 27; Berkeley, CA 1998). L. H. FELDMAN and G. HATA, eds., *Josephus, The Bible and History* (Leiden 1989). L. H. FELDMAN and J. R. LEVISON, eds., *Josephus' "Contra Apionem": Studies in Its Character & Context with a Latin Concordance to the Portion Missing in Greek* (Arbeiten zur Geschichte des antiken Judentums und des Urchristentums 34; Leiden 1996). R. K. GNUSE, *Dreams and Dream Reports in the Writings of Josephus: A Traditio–Historical Analysis* (Arbeiten zur Geschichte des antiken Judentums und des Urchristentums 36; Leiden 1996). K.–S. KRIEGER, *Geschichtsschreibung als Apologetik bei Flavius Josephus* (Tübingen/Basel 1994). B. MAYER–SCHÄRTEL, *Das Frauenbild des Josephus: Eine socialgeschichtliche und kulturanthropologische Untersuchung* (Stuttgart 1995). S. MASON, *Flavius Josephus on the Pharisees: A Composition–Critical Study* (Leiden 1991). S. MASON, ed., *Understanding Josephus: Seven Perspectives* (Sheffield 1998). E. NODET, *Le Pentateuque de Flavius Josephus* (Paris 1996). F. PARENTE and J. SIEVERS, eds., *Josephus & the History of the Greco–Roman Period: Essays in Memory of Morton Smith* (Leiden 1994). B. SCHRÖDER, *Die "vaterlichen Gesetze', Flavius Josephus als Vermittler von Halachah an Griechen und Römer* (Tübingen 1996). S. SCHWARTZ, *Josephus and Judean Politics* (Columbia Studies in the Classical Tradition 18; Leiden 1990). P. SPILSBURY, *The Image of the Jew in Flavius Josephus' Paraphrase of the Bible* (Tübingen 1998); G. E. STERLING, *Historiography and Self-Definition. Josephos, Luke—Acts and Apologetic Historiography* (Novum Testamentum Sup 64; Leiden 1992). E. C. ULRICH, *The Qumran Text of Samuel and Josephus* (Harvard Semitic Monographs 19; Missoula, MT 1978). P. VILLALBA I VARNEDA, *The Historical Method of Flavius Josephus* (Arbeiten zur Geschichte des antiken Judentums und des Urchristentums 19; Leiden 1986).

[J. STRUGNELL/C. T. BEGG]

JOSHUA, BOOK OF

The first book of the Bible after the Pentateuch; it stands at the beginning of the collection that the classical division of the Hebrew Bible calls the Earlier Prophets (*see* PROPHETIC BOOKS OF THE OLD TESTAMENT). It is named after the man who figures most prominently in its pages. The overriding theme of the book, namely, the idea that the land of Canaan had been won by the Israel-

Illumination from the Book of Joshua.

ites ultimately because of Yahweh's promise to the Patriarchs and His special help to Joshua, determined its structure and its literary forms. The theme of conquest by Yahweh's will and power also points to the period of the 13th–12th centuries B.C. as the time during which the traditions that make up the material of the book began to form.

Structure. The Book of Joshua falls naturally into three parts. Chapters 1–12 are concerned with the conquest of Canaan, and ch. 13–21 with the partitioning of the land among the Israelite tribes, while ch. 22–24 contain certain supplements. Although the differences that set off these three sections are such as to suggest that they were at one time independent literary units, a final editor has connected them into a further unity that must be read as a whole. The following summary of the three parts will provide a concise view of the content of the whole book.

First Part (ch. 1–12). Chapter 1 introduces the theme of conquest by linking Joshua to Moses and by describing the Israelite tribes in Transjordan on the verge of attempting entry into Canaan. Chapter 2 shows the scouts sent by Joshua gathering information about the land around Jericho to assess its strength and weakness, so that plans may be laid for an attack in that area as soon as the cross-

ing of the Jordan has been managed. In ch. 3 the crossing of the river is made by the special help of Yahweh, who dries up its waters when the priests who carry the ark wade in. In ch. 4 after memorializing the wonderful event by two sets of 12 stones. Joshua camps at Galgal east of Jericho, where he sets up a third group of 12 stones. Chapter 5 says that, in preparation for the holy war in the offing. Joshua, at Yahweh's command, took care of the matter of circumcision, which the Israelites had neglected during the desert years. The climax of this alert is the celebration of the Passover at Galgal and Joshua's vision of a mysterious captain of the host of Yahweh.

Chapter 6 tells about the capture of JERICHO as the result of special help from Yahweh through the relentless marching and trumpeting of the priests. In the general destruction of the city the harlot Rahab's house and family are spared because of the help she had given earlier to the Israelite scouts. Chapter 7 tells about the disastrous defeat suffered by the Israelites at AI and accounts for it by pointing to the disobedience of Achan, who had kept part of Jericho's doomed property for himself. When Achan, his family, and all his possessions are destroyed as a punishment for this crime, Ai falls easily to Joshua's strategy (8.1–29). The high point of this first phase of the conquest that carried the Israelites into central Canaan comes at Mt. Ebal, where a sacrifice is offered and the law is proclaimed in the form of blessings and curses (8.30–35).

Chapter 9 is an account of Israel's agreement with the clever Gibeonites, natives who trick Joshua into sparing their lives by pretending to be travelers from a distant land who had heard of the power of Joshua's God and want to join up with God's people. Because this agreement is sealed by oath, it has to be honored even when the trick is discovered. So the Gibeonites are spared, but they are forced to become slaves. Chapter 10 tells of a coalition of five Canaanite chieftains and their defeat by Joshua at GIDEON. This victory is accomplished, like those at Jericho and Ai, by the special help of Yahweh. Chapter 10 concludes with a description of Joshua's conquests in Canaan's southland. Chapter 11 tells about another coalition, this time among the northern Canaanites, to oppose Joshua's march, and about his victory over them at Hazor and other northern cities. Chapter 12 sums up the whole work of the conquest by listing the kings whose cities had been invaded and taken by Joshua.

Second Part (ch. 13–21). These chapters are for the most part a description of the way in which the conquered land was partitioned among the Israelite tribes. This unit of the book contrasts sharply with the first 12 chapters. In the first part of the book, Joshua is in the full vigor of his military power, and all opposition seems to crumble beneath his march. In this second part he is an old man, and a very large part of Canaan remains unconquered.

Chapter 13 tells of the settling of the tribes of REUBEN, Gad, and half of Manasseh in Transjordan. In ch. 14 attention is given to the problems of the tribes attempting to settle west of the Jordan, with a special note about Caleb, who had been Joshua's fellow scout in the earlier years when Moses was still leading the Israelites (Nm 14.5–7). Caleb receives the hilly land around Hebron, which still remains to be taken from the native Anakim. Chapter 15 details the boundaries of JUDAH. Then, after a further note about Caleb's victory over the Anakim at Hebron and about his daughter's successful request for some property of her own, a list of Judean cities is given, which shows the writer's close knowledge of that area. In ch. 16–17 the settling of the Joseph tribes, EPHRAIM and the other half of Manasseh, west of the Jordan, is recounted. In ch. 18 the work of conquest is said to be complete, and Joshua sets up headquarters at Shiloh to direct the work of settling the remaining seven Israelite tribes. Land is assigned to the tribes of BENJAMIN, SIMEON, ZEBULUN, ISSACHAR, ASHER, NAPHTALI, and DAN. Chapter 20 lists the cities of ASYLUM, or refuge, throughout Canaan, where a person may find safety if he has committed unintended homicide. Chapter 21 lists the cities allotted to members of the priestly tribe of Levi, who had not received a special territory of their own.

Third Part (ch. 22–24). The supplements are among the most important parts of the whole book (their place in the book's general teaching will be considered later). Chapter 22 tells about Joshua's blessing on the members of the Transjordanian Israelite tribes who helped in conquering Canaan west of Jordan. Chapter 23 gives Joshua's final exhortation to his people. Chapter 24 continues this appeal in more detail. At SHECHEM he reviews the SALVATION HISTORY of the Israelites since Abraham, and they renew their COVENANT with YAHWEH, who has been the author of these great saving events in their past. The book concludes with a note about Joshua's death and burial and another about the reburial of the bones of Joseph, which had been brought along when the Israelites escaped from Egypt, and a final word about the death and burial of the priest Eleazer.

Literary Forms. The wide variety of the materials that entered into the Book of Joshua points to a variety of literary forms in which that material is cast. The Book of Joshua belongs to the category of historical narrative. But the sense in which it is a history has to be carefully qualified.

Etiological. After ch. 1, which has the form of an introduction to the whole book, the literary form that has been operative in the writing of much of ch. 2–9 is that of the etiological story. *See* ETIOLOGY (IN THE BIBLE). The etiological story is a special kind of narrative about a person or place. It is not simply a record of what happened at a certain place or to a certain person. It is a narrative built up in such a way as to explain the reason (or cause, α'ιτία) why a place or person has such and such a name, or why certain objects are found in a certain place. The ultimate purpose of the etiological story is, of course, deeper. The etiological story of Adam's being taken from the 'ădāmâ (farm land) in Gn 2.7 is not so much interested in explaining the first man's name as in saying something about his God-given task of working the land. The strictly historical value of the etiological story varies from one such story to the next, depending on the nearness of the storyteller to the event he is describing. In the case of the Book of Joshua there are good reasons for holding that the traditions about Jericho, Ai, Gibeon, etc., began to form at a time not far removed from the actual period of the conquest of Canaan in the 13th–12th centuries B.C. The narratives in Jos 4.3, 5–9, 20–24; 5.9; 6.25–26; 7.26: 8.28–29; 9.27 show the characteristics of the etiological story as it appears elsewhere in the Bible. The passage in 4.1–9 invites the Israelites of a later, more settled period to connect the big stones of the Jordan Valley with Joshua's crossing of the Jordan by the power of

Yahweh at a critical point in their earlier history. This function of the story in the text is more important than the information about the actual reason why the stones are there at all.

Epical. The literary form characteristic of ch. 10–11 is the epic, or saga, in which the central figure, Joshua, is presented in heroic proportions. The whole work of the conquest is attributed to him in such a way as to put into almost complete obscurity the contributions of any other men. The work of the conquest is presented as coming off without any great difficulty. This triumphalism and the centering of attention so predominantly on Joshua is certainly the result of the hyperbolizing and simplifying tendencies proper to the saga. The battle of Gibeon in ch. 10, where at Joshua's command the sun and moon "stop" while he gains a total victory over the enemy, is perhaps the clearest instance of the epic form in the book. The poetic quality of 10.12–13 and the enthusiastic conclusion in 10.14—"Never before or since was there a day like this"—heightens the impression that the writer is consciously hyperbolizing his hero. If we are dealing here with the epic form, the problem of the so-called miracle of the sun and moon may be an unreal problem. *See* SUN MIRACLES (IN THE BIBLE). The passage in 10.28–43, in its account of the campaign in southern Canaan, shows Joshua moving easily from one triumph to another. The whole thing comes off without a hitch because it is all happening at the command of Yahweh and by His help. This would seem to be the theological point of the epic story in this case. The picture presented in other parts of the book from ch. 13 through 21 shows that Joshua had far from finished the work of conquest. Such a picture points up the epic nature of these narratives in ch. 10–11 by way of contrast. In 11.23 it is stated: "Thus Joshua captured the whole country, just as the Lord had foretold to Moses. Joshua gave it to Israel as their heritage, apportioning it among the tribes. And the land enjoyed peace." Yet, a little further on in the book (13.1) God says to Joshua, "Though now you are old and advanced in years, a very large part of the land still remains to be conquered."

Geographical. Chapters 13–21 are heavily geographical. These long lists of place names can be boring to the modern reader, although they have not ceased to stimulate and challenge the archeologist and the cartographer. Whether or not one may speak of a special geographical form, it seems that these accounts were not set down merely for the sake of mapping out the story of the conquest and partitioning of Canaan. The repeated mention of these cities serves, like the memorial stones in the Jordan Valley, to remind the Israelites of Yahweh's favor and protection during the critical days when they were struggling to get a firm grip on the land He had promised them. In the more settled period of the Israelite monarchy and during the sad years of exile when the land had been lost, the believing Israelite could reflect on these long lists of cities and recall how dear his land really was. In some ways this section of the book, e.g., in 13.1, counteracts by its realism some of the exaggerations proper to the heroic stories in ch. 2–12. In other ways, the picture of Israel's possession of Canaan is also exaggerated in ch. 13–21. According to 13.1–7 Yahweh tells Joshua to portion out lands of which some, for instance those in the far north, probably never belonged to the Israelites at any time. These chapters were intended to give the Israelites who would read them not only a picture of what had happened but also a hope for the future that was nourished by the loving recital of the names of these cities. Yahweh had given them the land, so their faith convinced them; it must be a good land, fertile and spacious.

Deuteronomic. The supplementary ch. 22–24 that close the Book of Joshua are written in the style of Deuteronomy. The farewell discourse of Joshua in ch. 23 is similar in form to that of Moses in Dt 31.26–29. Joshua, in his old age, reviews the history of his people and promises that Yahweh will continue to protect them if they obey Him faithfully. He warns of terrible punishment in the event of disobedience. Characteristic of this discourse form is its tone of serious exhortation. It is addressed to the hearts of its readers and makes its appeal over and over. The plea to "remember" what Yahweh has done in the past and to be aware "today" of what He will do in the future is a part of this style. Chapter 24 duplicates ch. 23 to a large extent. It may well be that ch. 24, with its specific reference to Shechem, is the older of the two accounts of Joshua's farewell address. In ch. 24, too, the style of Deuteronomy can be felt in the review of salvation history, the reminder of Yahweh's faithful love, the exhortation to fear and obey Him, the warning against disobedience. Chapter 24 differs from ch. 23 mainly by being more specific geographically; it places the discourse at Shechem. It also leads more explicitly than ch. 23 to the renewal of the covenant. Chapter 24 is written in the style of Deuteronomy ch. 29–30. Because of the detail about Shechem, between Mt. GARIZIM and Mt. Ebal, Jos 24.1–15 may be an expansion by the DEUTERONOMISTS of the material in Jos 8.30–35, which already speaks of the sacrifice and the renewal of the covenant at those mountains in central Canaan in the early stages of the conquest.

Origin. The ancient Jewish and early Christian tradition that Joshua himself wrote this book has been universally abandoned. In Jos 24.26 the recording of laws in a book of the Law of the Lord is indeed attributed to Joshua, and in 5.1 (in the Hebrew text but not in translations) the writer speaks of "our crossing" the Jordan River; also, the "us" in 5.6 might imply that the writer was there. But these texts, in view of the tendency of the Israelites to identify themselves with the corporate personality of their ancestors, cannot be read as clear indications that Joshua wrote the book. The variety of literary elements that make up its contents shows that it was not written by one author but by many compilers. If Joshua wrote any of it, today it would seem impossible to isolate what he may have written. Rather, a rough history of the compilation of these materials can be sketched over a long period of time from the events that lie at the book's source (*c.* 1200 B.C.) to the time of the exile (*c.* 550 B.C.). The frequent repetition of the statement that some situation or other has continued "until this day" (4.9; 5.9; 6.25; etc.) heightens the impression that much of the material in this book took written shape long after the events described.

The idea was put forward for a while in recent times that the Book of Joshua formed the sixth book of a HEXATEUCH and that its contents could be analyzed in the same way as the PENTATEUCH into the four classical documents or traditions (Yahwist, Elohist, Deuteronomist, Priestly). But studies, by M. Noth especially, gave a new direction to this question. He developed the idea that the Book of Joshua belongs, not to the Pentateuch, but to a Deuteronomic corpus of writings running from Deuteronomy through Kings. The analysis of the formation of this book is now commonly made within the larger framework of the whole Deuteronomic corpus. Centering the attention here on the part of this corpus that is the Book of Joshua, the following reconstruction of its formation can be suggested.

Benjaminite traditions preserved at Galgal, along with scattered traditions from other parts of Palestine, were collected and organized in written form by a Judean about 900 B.C. to produce much of what is now in ch. 2–12. Chapters 13–21, which deal with the partitioning of the land, present a geography of Palestine that reflects various periods of Israelite history from David (d. 970 B.C.) to Josia (d. 609 B.C.). The merging of these materials into the actual unit that is ch. 13–21 took place about 600 B.C. The Deuteronomist editors who did this work in the process of incorporating the Book of Joshua within the whole Deuteronomic corpus left traces of their editorial activity in ch. 1, which consciously connects the Book of Joshua with Deuteronomy. Also in Jos 8.30–35 such traces are to be found in repeated references to the Law and in the writer's concern to link the position of Joshua with that of Moses. Chapter 23 is best read as a Deuteronomist's reworking of the more detailed account in ch. 24.

Doctrine. If the Book of Joshua is a history, it is above all a religious history. Events are narrated in such a way as to make a point. The writer is concerned to present a teaching about Yahweh's action in Israel's life. A summary of this teaching can be given as follows.

The conquest of Canaan was due to Yahweh's power and His special guidance of Joshua, rather than to any purely human effort. Israel's possession of the land was the manifestation of Yahweh's loving fidelity to the Patriarchs, who had received His promise that their children would in fact one day possess this land. Continued possession of the land would depend on Israel's fidelity to Yahweh through obedience to the law of Sinai. Chapter 23 sums up the doctrine of the whole book with a special emphasis on its moral lesson: "If you transgress the covenant of the Lord, your God, which he enjoined on you, and serve other gods and worship them, the anger of the Lord will flare up against you and you will quickly perish from the good land which he has given you" (23.16).

From the standpoint of its doctrine, as well as that of its relevance for the modern world, the Book of Joshua poses some problems that seem far more troublesome than the historical problem raised by the archeology of Jericho and Ai. A major one is the book's attitude toward the wars of extermination that the writer attributes to the command of Yahweh. In what sense did Yahweh will and command the killing of the men, women, and children of Canaan? Joshua's way of waging war was of a piece with the customs of warfare in ancient Egypt, Mesopotamia, Moab, and Europe. Yahweh manifests and accomplishes His will in a wide variety of ways, sometimes through the sinful actions of men in war. According to the Bible's way of speaking, what later theologians call God's permissive will is spoken of in terms of divine commands. Against this background one may understand the "divine commands" underlying Joshua's wars of extermination. Yahweh permitted Joshua's objectively immoral killings in order to accomplish His purpose of punishing the Canaanites for their idolatry, fulfilling His promise to give Canaan to the Israelites, and removing from them some of the danger of idolatrous worship. The author of the book, precisely in order to insist on the fact that these divine purposes were being accomplished in the actions of Joshua, expressed Yahweh's permissive will as divine command. The author neither denied nor affirmed the guilt of Joshua for these massacres; possibly because such a judgment would not have served his purpose in writing the book, possibly because the writer simply did not know what judgment to make. It has been said that know what judgment to make. It has been said that modern men must not too quickly point an accusing finger at Joshua or at the writer of the book that bears his name, since men have developed or allowed to develop ways of making war that have proved far more destructive of human life than anything known in the ancient world. This is true. But it does not remove the problem of the link between Joshua's wars of extermination and the will of God. Perhaps one of the greatest values of the book for the modern world is precisely its function in stimulating thought about this intense modern problem.

Bibliography: Commentaries. F. M. ABEL, *Le Livre de Josué* (*Bible de Jérusalem* 6; 1950). D. BALDI, *Giosuè* (Turin 1952). F. NÖSTSCHER, *Das Buch Josue* (Echter Bibel: Die Hl. Schrift in deutscher Ubersetzung Würzburg 1947). M. NOTH, *Das Buch Josua* (2d ed. *Handbuch Zum Alten Testament* 1:7; 1953). Articles. P. AU-VRAY, *Dictionnaire de la Bible,* supplement ed. L. PIROT, et al. (Paris 1928–) 4:1131–41. J. SCHARBERT, *Lexikon für Theologie und Kirche,* ed. J. HOFER and K. RAHNER, 10 v. (2d, new ed. Freiburg 1957–65) 5:1145–46. *Encyclopedic Dictionary of the Bible,* translated and adapted by L. HARTMAN (New York, 1963) 1218–22. L. ROST and W. WERBECK, *Die Religion in Geschichte und Gegenwart,* 7 v. (3d ed. Tübingen 1957–65) 3:873–874.

[M. STRANGE]

JOSHUA, SON OF NUN

Joshua, son of Nun and protagonist of the Book of Joshua, is the most prominent of several Biblical persons who bore the name Joshua in the Old Testament period. The meaning of his name (Heb. $y^eh\hat{o}\check{s}\hat{u}a$' and in post–exilic times $y\bar{e}\check{s}\hat{u}a$'), ''Yahweh saves,'' is not exploited in the Book of Joshua, as it is exploited implicitly in Nm 13.16 and much more clearly later in Sir 46.1. In the Septuagint he is called 'Ιησοῦς, JESUS.

Biblical Portrait. In the book that bears his name, Joshua overshadows all the other human figures in the story of the conquest and division of the Holy Land. In ch. 1 he is seen as the man who, by Yahweh's will, steps into the role of Moses, whose death is described in the closing chapter of Deuteronomy. The continuity of leadership and Yahweh's presence with Moses are thus established in the early history of Israel.

The book pictures Joshua as a man fearless in battle, not because of his own strength and courage, but because of the powerful presence of Yahweh. Convinced that Israel's success in the struggle for possession of Canaan would be due entirely to the will of Yahweh, Joshua took drastic steps when he thought Yahweh's will was being opposed. The death of Achan and his family in ch. 7 exemplifies this uncompromising side of his character.

In ch. 8 Joshua is seen as an expert military strategist whose ability is attributed to the guidance of Yahweh. In ch. 9 he appears as a man true to his own promised word even though the promise had been spoken as the result of a trick on the part of the Gabaonites. In ch. 10 he thrills to his victory over the AMORRITE KINGS, but he gives credit to Yahweh as the one who fought and conquered for Israel. He killed these chiefs in a way that was in keeping with the chilling description of his war policies in Jos 10.40—sparing no one, but the massacre of every living soul. At times he needed encouragement in face of great opposition (Jos 11.6).

In general, the first part of the book (ch. 1–12) presents Joshua's work of conquering Canaan as coming off without any doubt of the outcome. The setback at AI was remedied as soon as the offending Achan was destroyed. The general picture in Yahweh's name and by His power, moving easily from one triumph to another throughout the whole land of Canaan. As will be seen, this picture must be altered when the life of Joshua is examined from a critical historical point of view.

The second part of the book (ch. 13–21), which deals with the division of the land among the Israelite tribes, does not add much to the earlier chapters' portrait of Joshua, except a stress on his wisdom and fairness in seeing to the distribution of the land.

The farewell addresses in the supplementary conclusions to the book (ch. 22–24) show Joshua as a man deeply concerned about the people's loyalty and obedience to Yahweh and deeply aware of Yahweh's own fidelity in making good all His promises. In the summary of salvation history that is given in ch. 24 Joshua appears as a leader who had a remarkable respect for the people's freedom to choose between Yahweh and the other gods.

Other books of the Old Testament help to fill in the picture of Joshua. According to Ex 17.9–10, Joshua was Moses' attendant and the commander of the Israelite battle forces in the desert skirmishes before Sinai. In Ex 24.13–14 Joshua is placed in close association with Moses during the latter's communion with Yahweh. In Nm 11.27–29 Joshua is shown as jealous for Moses when he thinks that Moses' position as prophet is being threatened by the prophetic spirit stirring among the people. In Nm 14.5–7 Joshua, along the Caleb, get credit for giving the right advice about marching in against the land they have scouted, though this advice went unheeded. In Nm 28.18–23 the authority of Moses passes on to Joshua, who is described as a man fit for this role. According to 32.6–15 Caleb and Joshua were the only ones among the men who came out of Egypt who would actually enter the promised land because they were faithful to Yahweh. According to Dt 1.37–38 Moses, who admitted that he himself would not enter, considered it his mission to encourage Joshua, whose work it would be to lead the desert–born generation into their possession. When Dt 34.7–9 describes the transfer of Israel's allegiance from Moses to Joshua, the new leader is said to be full of the spirit of wisdom. In 1 Chr 7.27 it is stated that a Joshua, son of Nun, belonged to the Joseph tribe of Ephraim, an interesting fact in connection with the special treatment given by Joshua to the Joseph tribes (Joshua ch. 17). According to Jos 19.49–50 Joshua's hometown, Timnath–serah, which later was to be his burial place (Jos 24.30), lay in the mountains of Ephraim. In Sir 46.1–6 Joshua is praised for his ability as a soldier, his prophetic activity, and in a general way for living up to his name as a savior of his people.

This Old Testament portrait of Joshua is carried over to the New Testament and given a new dimension in Heb 4.8–11; with the same Greek name, he is compared with the new Jesus who leads His people all the way to the perfect rest as Joshua had done in his imperfect way.

Criticism of the Biblical Portrait. An analysis of the literary forms of the Book of Joshua and of the archeological facts about such cities as Jericho leads to an alteration of the Biblical portrait of Joshua. The epic or saga form, which is prominent in the Book of Joshua, is characterized by its hyperbolizing and simplifying tendencies. Its simplifying tendency is seen when it attributes the whole work of the conquest to Joshua, thereby playing down or neglecting altogether any other human agents. Its hyperbolizing tendency is evident when it pictures the conquest as a triumphant movement from one victory to another without any doubt of the final outcome. In Jos 11.23 this side of the picture is summed up by saying that Joshua conquered the whole land and then distributed it among the various tribes of Israel. However, the statement in Jos 13.1 about the amount of work that remained to be done even when Joshua was an old man fits the setting supposed by the Book of Judges and points up the exaggerating tendencies of the first 12 chapters of the Book of Joshua.

If one ask what Joshua really had to do with the conquest, no fully satisfactory answer can be given. That a man whom the Bible calls Joshua, son of Nun, had something important to do with the Israelite people's entry into Canaan in the 13th century B.C. seems beyond reasonable questioning. Exodus and Numbers show that Moses was concerned about his successor. Deuteronomy records the tradition about the way the problem of succession was handled. As far as the actual conquest is concerned, the Book of Joshua places most of his activity in central Palestine, which fits the statement of 1 Chr 7.27 that Joshua belonged to the Joseph tribe of Ephraim. The saga form would build on a core of fact. If central Palestine was the scene of Joshua's real battles and victories, the Israelite storyteller could start with this fact and expand it into a picture of Joshua taking over the whole of Canaan. The statement in Jos 13.1 that even when Joshua's battles were all over "very much" of the land still remained to be conquered provides a sobering balance in the attempt to answer the question about what really happened. The

archeological problem about Jericho's apparent nonhabitation during the whole period in which Joshua's activity must be placed (the second half of the 13th century B.C.) further complicates the historical question. Only conjectural answers can be given. While one can affirm Joshua's importance in the conquest phase of Israel's history, it must be admitted that an exact delineation of his activity is impossible.

Joshua's Place in Salvation History. More important and possible than determining exactly what Joshua did is an understanding of his place in the theology of the Old Testament writers. Joshua stands forever in the shadow of Moses. This fact does not diminish him. It highlights his indispensable role as the man who led the people all the way into the Holy Land. Through Joshua's activity as well as that of Moses, Yahweh's loving fidelity was manifested as He saved His people from Egypt and the desert and brought them into the land He had promised to Abraham, Isaac, and Jacob.

Iconography. The many events narrated in the Book of Joshua gave artists copious material to work with. Such scenes as Joshua's crossing the Jordan, his siege and capture of Jericho and Ai, and victory over the Amorrite kings are frequently represented. Among the best–known cycles of these scenes are the 4th–century mosaics in St. Mary Major, Rome; the famous Joshua Scroll in the Vatican Library from *c.* A.D. 800 and the 13th–century Psalter of St. Louis in the Bibliothèque Nationale, Paris.

Bibliography: H. H. ROWLEY, *From Joseph to Joshua* (London 1950). J. SCHARBERT, *Lexikon für Theologie und Kirche*[2], ed. J. HOFER and K. RAHNER, 10 v. (2d, new ed. Freiburg 1957–65) 5:1145. *Encyclopedic Dictionary of the Bible,* tr. and adap. by L. HARTMAN (New York 1963), from A. VAN DEN BORN, *Bijbels Woordenboek,* 1212–18. For additional bibliography *see* JOSHUA, BOOK OF. Iconography. L. RÉAU, *Iconographie de l'art chrétien,* 6 v. (Paris 1955–59) 1.2:219–227. K. KÜNSTLE, *Ikonographie der christlichen Kunst,* 2 v. (Freiburg 1926–28) 1:301–302.

[M. STRANGE]

JOSIPPON

A medieval Hebrew chronicle of Jewish history from Adam to the end of the first Jewish revolt, consisting essentially of a partly abbreviated, partly expanded translation of *Hegesippus,* the free Latin version of Flavius Josephus's *Jewish War.* Josippon means "the Little Josippus," Josippus (like Hegesippus) being a Latin form of the historian's name. Because of the inadequacy of published information on the MS tradition of the text and its earliest versions, little is certain about the compiler, his sources, and the original extent of his work.

In its vulgate form, *Josippon* starts with an introduction covering Jewish history from Adam to the Seleucids, with digressions on Roman, Persian, and Macedonian history. The OT, Josephus's *Antiquities,* and Jewish legend have all contributed to this section, which contains in addition a form of the Alexander Romance dependent upon the 12th-century redaction of Leo the Archpresbyter's Latin version of Pseudo-Callisthenes. This last is demonstrably a later addition to the original work. The remainder of the book treats of Jewish history from the Machabean period until A.D. 73. The author's basic source here is *Hegesippus,* with additions from the Latin translations of Josephus's other works—his *Life,* of which no Latin version existed, is not used. Other details are taken from 2 Maccabees, which Josephus himself never used, and still others from Jewish oral tradition.

The unknown author claims to be Flavius JOSEPHUS (ben Mattathiah), but confuses him with Joseph ben Gorion (cf. *Hegesippus* 3.3.2, ed. V. Ussani, *Corpus scriptorum ecclesiasticorum latinorum* 66.187.12–14), and so calls himself Joseph ben Gorion. Occasionally, Pseudo-Josephus, forgetting his role, expressly cites Josephus.

Internal evidence suggests southern Italy as the place of composition, and some form of *Josippon* is attested there *c.* A.D. 950. Thereafter it rapidly gained popularity, being often cited by Jewish scholars and translated into other languages used by the Jews. It was well known not only among Jews; a 10th-century Arabic version by Zakariya ibn Sa'īd was used by Muslim historians and, in part, by Christians of Egypt. From the Arabic an Ethiopic version was made (probably 12th–14th century) and was highly regarded by the Ethiopic church, which until the 16th century had no text of Maccabees. A Slavonic version also was made, and translations into French, German, and English show its popularity among Christians.

Bibliography: The poorer two of the three Hebrew text-types have been published. The Mantuan *editio princeps* was reprinted by D. Günzburg and A. Kahana (Berdiczew 1896–1913); all other printings give the Constantinople vulgate text. A critical edition is by D. FLUSSER. M. KAMIL, *Des Josef Ben Gorion (Josippon) Geschichte der Juden (Zēna 'Ayhūd)* (New York 1938), contains the Ethiopic text and a comparison with the Arabic. On the Arabic, which, like the Slavonic, still needs scientific editing, see also G. GRAF, *Geschichte der christlichen arabischen Literatur,* 5 v. (*Studi e Testi* 118, 133, 146, 147, 172; Vatican City 1944–53) 1:221–223. Literature. S. W. BARON, *A Social and Religious History of the Jews,* 8 v. (2nd ed. New York 1952–58; index 1960) 6:189–195, 417–421. E. SCHÜRER, *A History of the Jewish People in the Time of Jesus Christ,* tr. J. MACPHERSON et al., 5 v. (Edinburgh 1897–98) 1.1:165–166.

[J. STRUGNELL]

JOUARRE-EN-BRIE, ABBEY OF

French abbey of Benedictine nuns, Diocese of Meaux. The foundation of Jouarre-en-Brie between 630 and 634 was sponsored by Bl. Adon, former treasurer to King Clotaire II. Originally it was a double monastery for monks and nuns, the former coming from LUXEUIL. The nuns eventually took over the entire foundation. The abbess enjoyed full seignorial authority over the abbatial domains. In Carolingian times the abbey was a famous school for girls of the nobility. From 1225 to 1690 the abbess, always of the highest nobility, exercised a quasi-episcopal authority over the parishes on her estates, appointing the pastors and maintaining a chapter of 12 canons in the abbey, who served as chaplains. The abbey was sacked three times during the Hundred Years' War. The ruined and depopulated house was reformed in 1523, but the subsequent religious wars precipitated another decline. Abbess Charlotte of Bourbon, who had been forced to enter the convent by her family, escaped in 1572 and embraced Protestantism. Early in the 17th century the church and convent were magnificently rebuilt by Abbess Jeanne of Lorraine. Later Abbess Henriette of Lorraine was involved in a famous debate with Bishop BOSSUET of Meaux and was forced to relinquish many of her privileges. The French Revolution suppressed the abbey in 1791. The church was destroyed but the convent was reoccupied by Benedictine nuns in 1837.

Bibliography: J. B. BOSSUET, *Oeuvres complètes,* 48 v. (Paris 1828–31) 30:187–323. H. THIERCELIN, *Le monastère de Jouarre, son histoire jusqu'à la Révolution* (Paris 1861). U. CHEVALIER, *Répertoire des sources historiques du moyen-âge. Topobibliographie,* 2 v. (Paris 1894–1903) 1:1577. *L'Abbaye royale Notre-Dame de Jouarre,* 2 v. (Paris 1961). L. H. COTTINEAU, *Répertoire topobibliographique des abbayes et prieurés,* 2 v. (Mâcon 1935–39) 1:1489–90.

[L. J. LEKAI]

JOUBERT, EUGÉNIE, BL.

Religious of the Holy Family of the Sacred Heart; b. Feb. 11, 1876, Ysingeaux, France; d. July 2, 1904, Liège, Belgium. In 1895, Joubert joined the new congregation of the *Soeurs de la Sainte-Famille de Sacré-Coeur,* founded at Puy by Mère Marie Ignace Melin. She taught catechism to small children at Saint-Denis and Aubervilliers to carefully prepare them for their First Confession and Communion until her health failed. From that time she was assigned to Liège, where she died at age 28 after a two-year illness. She is known for her devotion to the Sacred Heart and her practice of the "Little Way." Joubert was beatified by John Paul II, Nov. 20, 1994.

Bibliography: J. BOUFLET, *Le charisme et la catéchèse* (Paris 1998).

[K. I. RABENSTEIN]

JOURNET, CHARLES

Swiss cardinal and theologian; b. Vernier near Geneva, Jan. 26, 1891, d. Fribourg, April 15, 1975. After classical studies in Geneva and Mariahilf College, Schwyz, and St. Michael's College, Fribourg, he entered the diocesan major seminary in Fribourg. Ordained to the priesthood on July 15, 1917, he was appointed professor of dogmatic theology in the same seminary on Sept. 25, 1924, and remained on the faculty until 1970. In 1926 he founded with F. Charrière the theological journal *Nova et vetera,* of which he remained the editor for most of his career. In 1965 he was named titular archbishop and cardinal. He was a member of the preconciliar theological commission for VATICAN COUNCIL II and made several significant interventions during the council. In addition to his theological teaching and writing he was also active in other pastoral activities in both Geneva and Fribourg, where he is remembered for his humility and gracious wit. He maintained a lifelong friendship and correspondence with Jacques Maritain.

Journet is customarily identified with the THOMISM practiced by J. MARITAIN, E. GILSON, and the French Dominicans generally. Indeed, he describes his masterwork as "a comprehensive work in which I hope to explain the church, from the standpoint of speculative theology, in terms of the four causes from which she results—efficient, material, formal and final. This work is to be in four books" (*The Church of the Word Incarnate. An Essay in Speculative Theology,* v. 1, *The Apostolic Hierarchy,* tr. by A. H. C. Downes [New York 1955] xxv). Unfortunately only this first volume appeared in English. The original French, *L'Église du Verbe incarné* was published in Paris by Desclée de Brouwer et Cie. in 1941, 1951, and 1969. While remaining deeply indebted to St. Thomas, he posed significant challenges to the NEO-SCHOLASTICISM of his time. Although ecclesiology was his speciality, Cardinal Journet's works indicate his other interests: *L'Esprit du Protestantisme* (Paris 1925) and *L'Union des Églises* (Paris 1927); mysticism and the knowledge of God, *The Dark Knowledge of God,* tr. J. F. Anderson (London 1948) and *Introduction à la Théologie* (Paris 1947); and *The Primacy of Peter from the Protestant and from the Catholic Point of View,* tr. John Chapin (Westminster, Md., 1954); and the Christian-Muslim dialogue, *Théologie de l'Église* (Paris 1958) and "Qui est membre de l'Église," *Nova et vetera,* 36 (1961) 199–203; and *The Meaning of Evil,* tr. Michael Barry

(New York 1963), which are still significant. Journet and Yves Congar carried on a prolonged discussion about the status of the sinner in the holy Church from 1953 when Congar reviewed v. 2 of *La Théologie du Verbe incarné.* These reviews and other remarks by Congar have been collected in Journet's *Sainte Église* (Paris 1963) 618–669. According to Journet, as late as 1965, "the church is indeed not without *sinners,* but it is without *sin.*" See his "Il carattere teandrico della Chiesa fonte di tensione permanente," in G. Baraúna, ed., *La Chiesa del Vaticano II* (Florence 1965) 361. Congar, on the other hand, expressed what is today the more commonly accepted view that the Church itself is sinful, thus avoiding awkward distinctions between sinful member and holy Church, which end up making the Church not a real, historical People of God, but an imaginary construct.

Cardinal Journet will be justly remembered for his contributions to the theological model of the Church as the MYSTICAL BODY OF CHRIST. His Thomistic background enabled him to maintain the balance between the Church's visible and invisible dimensions, which had been so severely sundered in previous theology. Likewise, his Thomistic sacramental insight enabled him to understand that the ecclesial institution and structure form the *sacramentum* of the more mystical inner life of grace of the Church. His ECCLESIOLOGY was a significant contribution to the spirit and theology which matured at Vatican II.

Journet is perhaps found by the generation after his death to be too conceptualist, too "scholastic," too beholden to abstract thought. His true spirit, however, is better indicated by the dedication of his masterwork not only to the Doctors Augustine and Thomas but also to the Virgin Catherine of Siena, and especially by a quotation from the Persian Bisthami, which concludes his *The Dark Knowledge of God* (122): "For thirty years I travelled in search of God, and when, at the end of this time, I opened my eyes, I saw that it was He Who sought me. A voice cried to me: O Abu Yazid, what is it you desire? I replied: I desire to desire nothing, for I am the desired and You are He Who desires!"

Bibliography: S. JAKI, *Les tendances nouvelles de l'ecclésiologie* (Rome 1957). D. M. DOYLE, "Journet, Congar, and the Roots of Communion Ecclesiology," *Theological Studies,* 58 (Sept. 1997) 461–479. P.-M. EMONET, "Le Cardinal Journet: Portrait intérieur (Chambray-les-Tours 1983). L. MÉROZ, *Le Cardinal Journet, ou La sainte théologie* (Lausanne 1981). P. CHENAUX, ed., *Charles Journet (1891–1975): Un théolgien en son siècle: Actes du colloque de Genève, 1991* (Fribourg 1992).

[R. KRESS/D. M. DOYLE]

JOY

Understood in a strict sense, a pleasant state of quiescence in which the will rests satisfied in a good object (thing, person, action) that has been desired and is now possessed or has been accomplished (rational or spiritual joy). Such joy is proper to rational creatures because it requires an intellectual, reflexive awareness that the good has been attained; joy is distinguished from delight (*delectatio*), which can be experienced by nonrational creatures and by man in his nonrational faculties (Thomas Aquinas, ST 1a2ae, 31.3). In a broader sense, the feeling of pleasure or delight that is experienced when the sensitive appetite has attained a good for which it has been striving may be called joy (sensible joy). From this point of view, joy may be considered either as the pleasurable end product (as described above) or the passion (emotion) of joy from which the pleasant experience proceeds. Thus joy is one of the 11 basic passions (emotions) listed by St. Thomas (ST 1a2ae, 23.1 and 4). More precisely it is the third of the concupiscible (i.e., mild or ordinary) passions. Its object is a simple good, i.e., a good apprehended on a nonintellectual level without reference to difficulty involved in its attainment. Its product or termination is a pleasant state of quiescence in the good that is possessed.

Joy is also one of the fruits of the Holy Spirit listed by St. Paul (Gal 5.22). These fruits are derivatives of human actions performed under the influence of the virtues and of the gifts of the Holy Spirit that cause a certain intimate delight in the soul of the doer. Joy as a fruit of the Holy Spirit corresponds to the gift of understanding (ST 2a2ae, 8.8).

Either rational or sensible joy is morally good when the object, the possession of which causes the joy, is morally acceptable and has been attained by good means. Conversely, joy is morally bad if it is occasioned by an object that is morally bad or has been attained by evil means.

The highest and most complete joy of which man is capable is the spiritual joy resulting from the blessed vision of God.

Bibliography: THOMAS AQUINAS, *Summa theologiae* 1a2ae 23, 25, 31; 2a2ae 28. *Dictionnaire de théologie catholique*, ed. A. VACANT Tables générales 2673–74. E. SCHICK and A. AUER, *Lexikon für Theologie und Kirche*, ed. J. HOFER and K. RAHNER, 10 v. (2d, new ed. Freiburg 1957–65) 4:361–363. G. MANISE, F. ROBERTI et al., *Dictionary of Moral Theology*, ed. P. PALAZZINI et al., tr. H. J. YANNONE et al., from 2d Ital. Ed. (Westminster, MD 1962) 663–664. P. NOBLE *L'Amitié avec Dieu* (new ed. Paris 1932).

[P. CURRAN]

JOYEUSE, HENRI, DUC DE

Comte du Bouchage, Capuchin Friar Minor, known in religion as Ange de Joyeuse, a notable figure in the civil and religious life of France at the end of the 16th and beginning of 17th centuries; b. Couiza, Languedoc, September or October, 1562; d. Rivoli, Sept. 28, 1608. He was the third son of Guillaume de Joyeuse, lieutenant general for the king in Languedoc. His family was stanchly Catholic and loyalist, a fact that greatly influenced his career. In 1577 he entered the College of Navarre and from there, following his two elder brothers, joined the *mignons,* the exclusive circle of friends surrounding Henri III. He was appointed Grand Master of the Royal Wardrobe in 1579, and won distinction that year in a military engagement at La Fère. The king influenced him to marry Catherine de Nogaret de la Valette, sister of the Duke of Épernon. From this marriage a daughter was born. As governor of Anjou, in 1585 Joyeuse took the town of Angers without loss from Condé's troops, for which he was awarded the governorship of Touraine, Maine, and Perche. His wife died in August of 1587, and he, having never become attached to a worldly career, entered the Capuchins in Paris the next month. The year following his profession in 1588, he was ordained, and he went to Italy to study theology. He returned to France, but was drawn from the cloister to partake actively in the Wars of Religion.

After the death of his three brothers, the people of Toulouse desired a Joyeuse to lead them. Cardinal François de Joyeuse, Archbishop of Narbonne, refused on the ground of military inexperience; it was left to Père Ange, now rightful duke of Joyeuse, to become leader of the League in Languedoc. Ange accepted in 1592, provided that he received papal approval. Meanwhile he began reorganizing the local forces of the League. His position was eventually regularized by Clement VIII, who sanctioned his exclaustration and transference to the company of priests of the Order of Malta. In 1596 he was reconciled to Henry IV, who appointed him Lieutenant-governor of Languedoc and marshal of France. He reentered the Capuchins on March 25, 1599. His remaining years were spent in the apostolate and in the office of provincial, to which he was appointed twice. He was much appreciated as a preacher and spiritual adviser, his teaching being influenced evidently by Benedict of Canfield (William Benedict FITCH). In 1608, while attending the general chapter of his Order in Rome, he was elected a definitor general, the first non-Italian to be so promoted. He died on the way back to France and was buried in the Rue St. Honoré, Paris.

Bibliography: J. BROUSSE, *The Lives of Ange de Joyeuse and Benet Canfield,* ed. T. A. BIRRELL from R. ROCKWOOD'S tr. of 1623

(New York 1959). FATHER CUTHBERT, *The Capuchins,* 2 v. (London 1928). L. DE GONZAGUE, *Le Père Ange de Joyeuse, Frère Mineur Capucin, Maréchal de France, 1563–1608* (Paris 1928). AGATHANGE DE PARIS, *Un Cas de jurisprudence pontificale: Le P. Ange de Joyeuse, Capucin et Maréchal de France* (Assisi 1936). *Lexicon Capuccinum* (Rome 1951) 73–74 gives full bibliography.

[C. REEL]

JUAN DE LOS ANGELES

Franciscan Observant, mystical theologian, court preacher; b. probably near Oropesa (Ávila), 1536; d. Madrid?, 1609. Juan de Los Angeles (Martinez) studied at the University of Alcalá, and after joining the Friars Minor sometime before 1562 was transferred to the Province of San José (Madrid). He spent the rest of his life preaching, confessing, writing, and traveling on foot in Spain and abroad. He was spiritual director to the Infanta, Sor Margarita de la Cruz (a nun) and preacher to the royal chapter of her mother, the Empress Maria. In 1601, having served as guardian of San Antonio in Guadalajara (1595) and of San Bernardino in Madrid (1598), he was elected provincial minister of San José, but resigned in 1603 because of ill health. He remained active, however, until his death. His writings may be classified as Neoplatonic, affective, and psychological; they deal with such problems as the absorption of the soul in God, love without knowledge (which he seems to admit), active and passive recollection, kinds of ecstasy, mystical phenomena, and spiritual enslavement to Mary. His works, which are numerous and have appeared in many editions and translations, include: *Triunfos del amor de Dios* (Medina 1589–90), *Conquista del reino de Dios* (Madrid 1595), *Lucha espiritual y amorosa* (Madrid 1600), *Tratado de las soberanos misterios . . . de la misa* (Madrid 1604), *Cofradia y devoción de las esclavas y esclavos de . . . Virgen María* (Alcalá 1608?), and the *Manual de vida perfecta* (Madrid 1608).

Bibliography: JUAN DE LOS ANGELES, *Obras místicas,* ed. J. SALA, 2 v. (Madrid 1912–17); *Fray Juan de los Angeles (Antología),* ed. J. DOMÍNGUEZ BERRUETA (Madrid 1940). M. MENÉNDEZ-PELAYO, *Historia de las ideas estéticas en España* (4th ed. Madrid 1928—) 3. J. DOMÍNGUEZ BERRUETA, *Fray Juan de los Angeles* (Madrid 1927). A. TORRÓ, *Fray Juan de los Angeles, místico-psicólogo,* 2 v. (Barcelona 1924). F. DE ROS, *Dictionnaire de spiritualité ascétique et mystique. Doctrine et histoire,* ed. M. VILLER et al., (Paris 1932—) 2.2:2015–16; "La Vie et l'oeuvre de Jean Anges," *Mélanges offerts au R. P. Ferdinand Cavallera* (Toulouse 1948) 405–423. *Místicos Franciscanos españoles,* 3 v. (Madrid 1948–49) 3:461–701. E. A. PEERS, *Spanish Mysticism; A Preliminary Survey* (New York 1924); *Studies of the Spanish Mystics,* 2 v. (London 1927–30) 1:347–405.

[M. F. LAUGHLIN]

JUAN DIEGO, BL.

According to tradition, the name of the Native Mexican to whom the Virgin Mary appeared at Tepeyac, a hill outside of Mexico City, on Dec. 9, 1531. According to this same tradition, Juan Diego's given name was Cuauhtlatoatzin, and he was born around 1474 in Cuautitlán, about 20 kilometers north of Tenochtitlán (Mexico City). He was married but had no children. When he and his wife were baptized in 1524, he took the name Juan Diego, and his wife the name María Lucía. The earliest written account (1649) of the apparitions, the *Nican Mopohua,* calls him a *macehualli* (poor Indian). In 1666 when a formal ecclesiastical inquiry was made into the apparitions, Juan Diego was described as being devout and religious even before his conversion. After this, he was said to have walked weekly to Tenochtitlán to attend Mass and receive catechetical instruction. When his wife died in 1529, he went to live with his uncle, Juan Bernardino. Juan Diego was 57 at the time of the apparitions and from then on he lived in a small room attached to the chapel that housed the image of OUR LADY OF GUADALUPE, as its custodian. He is said to have received special permission from the bishop to receive communion three times a week. He died on May 30, 1548 at 78 years of age.

Juan Diego was recognized as blessed by means of an equivalent beatification on May 6, 1990, at the Basilica of Our Lady of Guadalupe in the presence of Pope John Paul II with the reading of a decree from the Sacred Congregation for the Causes of Saints. It recognized that public devotion to Juan Diego was a long tradition, approved an obligatory memorial for the archdiocese of Mexico City and an optional memorial for other dioceses. The decree set December 9, the date of the first apparition, as the day for the memorial.

Although there are written accounts from the 16th century that mention both the shrine and devotion to the Virgin of Guadalupe, the first written mention of Juan Diego is in the above cited *Nican Mopohua.* This so called *silencio guadalupano* of over a century has led some, including the abbot of the Basilica of Guadalupe, Msgr. Guillermo Shulemberg Prado, and the Vincentian historian Stafford Poole, to question the historicity of Juan Diego. This view caused a certain amount of controversy in 1996 and led to the resignation of the abbot. In 2000, Asunción Garcia Samper of the Center of Guadalupe Studies published a book proving the historicity of Bl. Juan Diego, as a nobleman. This information will be used during Juan Diego's now-advanced cause for canonization.

Feast: Dec. 9.

Bibliography: V. ELIZONDO, *Guadalupe: Mother of the New Creation* (Maryknoll, NY 1997). R. NEBEL, *Santa María Tonantzin*

Pilgrims on their knees in front of the shrine to Our Lady of Guadalupe, where Juan Diego claimed to have had visions of the Virgin Mary in 1531. (©Hulton Getty/Liason Agency)

Virgen de Guadalupe: Continuidad y transformación religiosa en México. tr. C. W. BUSTILLOS (Mexico City 1995). Center of Guadalupe Studies, *El Mensajero de la Virgen* (Mexico City 2000). S. POOLE, *Our Lady of Guadalupe: The Origins and Sources of a Mexican National Symbol, 1531–1797* (Tucson 1995). *The Story of Guadalupe: Luis Laso de la Vega's Huei tlamahuicoltica of 1649,* ed. and tr. L. SOUSA, S. POOLE, and J. LOCKHART (Stanford 1998).

[J. A. RUBIO]

JUANA DE LA CRUZ

Franciscan tertiary and mystic, often referred to as "Madre" or "Santa." b. Juana Vázquez Gutiérrez, daughter of Juan Vázquez and Catalina Gutiérrez, in Azaña, near Toledo, in 1481; d. 1534. At the age of 15 she entered the beaterio of Santa Maria de la Cruz near the town of Cubas, between Madrid and Toledo. This was a religious house of women, founded as a result of apparitions of the Virgin Mary, which followed the rule of the Secular Third Order of Saint Francis. It would later become a cloistered monastery and follow the rule of the Regular Third Order of Saint Francis until 1970 when it adopted the Rule of Saint Clare. In 1509, when she was 28, Juana was elected abbess and embarked upon a program of refounding and spiritual leadership that, with few interruptions, lasted until her death in 1534.

Her influence is most evidenced in her spiritual teachings especially in her sermons which were eventually written down and comprise the book *El libro del conorte* (The Book of Consolation). These sermons reflect a stylized form that includes a novel retelling of a gospel pericope, descriptions of allegorical pageants that take place in heaven on major feasts, and interpretations pertinent to those seeking spiritual growth. People of all classes, including Cardinal Cisneros, the confessor to Queen Isabella, and the Emperor, came to hear her.

In 1621 Mother Juana's beatification process was officially opened in Rome. She was declared "venerable" in 1630, but the official process was never concluded. The cause for her formal canonization was reopened in 1986 and is still in process.

Bibliography: I. GARCIA DE ANDRES, *La Santa Juana, Grande y Legitima Maestra Franciscana* (Separata de "Vedad y Vida" 1994). R. SURTZ, *The Guitar of God: Gender, Power and Authority in the Visionary World of Mother Juan de la Cruz* (Philadelphia 1990); *Writing Women in Late Medieval and Early Modern Spain: The Mothers of Teresa of Avila* (Philadelphia 1995).

[G. SCHINELLI]

JUBILEE YEAR

Israelite institution to be kept on every seventh Sabbath year by restoring alienated lands, freeing Hebrew slaves, and abstaining from sowing and harvesting. (On this "fallow" and on "slave-release," *see* SABBATH YEAR.) In the OT the jubilee year is treated only in Lv 25.8 to 25.55, with secondary references in Lv 27.17 to 27.21 and Nm 36.4.

Meaning of the Name. The jubilee year is called *šᵉnat hayyôbēl* (the *yôbēl*) in Lv 25.13, 28, 40, 50, *hayyôbēl* (the *yôbēl*) in Lv 25.15, 28, 30, and simply *yôbēl* in 25.10 to 25.12. In Ex 19.13 the word *yôbēl* (?Phoenician "ram") stands for the ram's horn (*qeren yôbēl*) blown as a trumpet (*šôpār*), as is clear from Jos 6.5 to 6.13. According to the common explanation, therefore, the jubilee year was called *šᵉnat hayyôbēl* (year of the ram's horn) because it was inaugurated by the blowing of a ram's horn trumpet. However, in the only passage that mentions this manner of opening the jubilee year (Lv 25.9) the horn that is blown is called simply a *šôpar* (trumpet), not a *yôbēl*.

Hence, some scholars hold that originally the term *yôbēl* as used in *šᵉnat yôbēl* has no connection with the ram's horn trumpet, but was a synonym for *dᵉrôr* (release, LXX *áphesis*) used in Lv 25.10; Ez 46.17 (*šᵉnat dᵉrôr*, year of release; Is 61.1 *áphesis*; so now Lemche, Carmichael; Ringe; Kutsch. *ybl Die Religion in Geschichte und Gegenwart*, 7 v. (3d ed. Tübingen 1957–65). The late Greek loanword ιωβηλαῖος, from Heb. *yôbēl*, should have produced a Latin loanword in the form of *jobelaeus;* but by a mistaken etymology, as if the word were connected with Latin *jubilum* (backwoods gaiety, joyous shouting), the word turned out in Latin as *jubilaeus*, whence English jubilee.

Legislation. According to Lv 25.8, the jubilee year is to be celebrated on every seventh SABBATH year, and it is thus expressly stated as ending a cycle of 49 years; when it is called "the 50th year" in 25.10, this should be understood as merely a round number, since two fallow years in a row would hardly be plausible (*pace* Josephus). The jubilee year, though a joyful homecoming, is to begin on the Day of Atonement (25.9).

Legislation for the jubilee year, a uniformizing development of various seventh-year laws, aims essentially to protect the small farmer against monopolizing landholders, by contriving that all land shall ultimately remain forever in the same "family." But counterproductively this means "the few important clans to whom each plot was assigned" (presumably by Joshua— and to be retrieved by the returnees from exile). But repurchase-right of a wealthier brother (*go'el* Lv 25.25–28) could over some generations result in huge monopolistic landholdings.

The precept given in 25.10, 13, "Every one of you shall return to your own estate and family," may have referred originally to an ancient homecoming celebration. But in 25.14 to 25.17, 25.23 to 25.31, this is interpreted to mean that title to a foreclosed mortgage is to be regained in the jubilee year, in (or after) the seventh seventh-year debt release called *šᵉmiṭṭâ* in Dt 15.1 to 15.9, and akin to Ex 21.2.8 in the Covenant Code. Apparently the final redactor of the Jubilee law judged that an indenture terminated after only seven years was so impractical that the social-justice aim would be better served by imposing as a last resort a definitive manumission in the seventh-seventh year (Lv 25.40–41). Similarly for the prohibition of retaining, beyond a certain period, any pledge or gage, such as fields (mortgages or nonliving gages) or children (live gages: 2 Kgs 4.1; Neh 5.5), preference is indicated for the six- or seven-year limit (cf. Dt 15.1), but in the legislation for the jubilee year a period seven times as long is tolerated as more realistic (Lv 25.35–55).

Recent researches on the growth of biblical-era cities force reevaluation of the real-life status of the small farmer reduced by debt to a tenant-"slave," who is plainly the proximate concern of the jubilee law. It has been assumed that he continues to occupy and till the same plot, but now for an absentee owner. But sociological statistics (V. Fritz 1995, F. Frick 1977, both titled *The City in Ancient Israel*; Lemche, *Early Israel* 1985) on the proportion of the total "agrarian" population living in cities make it likely that many of those working either their own or an absentee-owner's farm really lived in one of the 48 major cities (*all* called "levitical!"). As much as one fourth of the 16-hour work day might have been required simply to plod an ox to work and back. This would hold also for both small-*owners* and free hired laborers. On the other hand, the new "owner" may well have lived on his acquired property, either alongside or without his (''slave'') tenant.

At least in its present form the legislation on the jubilee year, which was drawn up by the Pentateuchal PRIESTLY WRITERS, is postexilic. For the framing of a festive calendar, a sort of moral unity of the separate cases of debt servitudes, pictured as expiring on the seventh Sabbath year after the first entry into the Holy Land (cf. 25.2), was visualized from the viewpoint of the end of the Exile. To this liturgical framework belong such casuistic ramifications as Lv 25.32 to 25.34; 27.17 to 27.21; Nm 36.4. The primary theological value is inculcated in Lv 25.23: only God is the true owner of all the land, which He decrees is to be utilized as private property, yet is to be managed (nowadays taking into account that small farming is uneconomical), so that all the world's population may have reasonable access to its resources.

See Also: HOLY YEAR.

Bibliography: R. DE VAUX, *Ancient Israel, Its Life and Institutions,* tr. J. MCHUGH (New York 1961) 175–77. T. SEIDL, *Lexikon für Theologie und Kirche,* ed. W. KASPAR et al. (Freiburg 1993–2001), 5: 854–56. C. WRIGHT, *Anchor Bible Dictionary* 5 (1992), 857–61. D. BERGANT, ''Jubilee,'' *Bible Today* 37 (1999) 342–48. E. NEUFELD, ''Socio-economic Background of Yobel and Šᵉmitta,'' *Rivista degli Studi Orientali* 33 (1958) 53–124. A. MEIN-HOLD, ''Jubeljahr,'' *Theologische Realenzyklopädia* 17 (1988) 280–81; ''Zur Beziehung Gott, Volk, Land im Jobel-Zusammenhang,'' *Biblische Zeitschrift* 29 (1985) 245–61. ERHARD S. GERSTENBERGER, *Leviticus* (Gottingen 1993) 337–64. K. ELLIGER, *Leviticus* (Tübingen, Mohr 1966). C. CARMICHAEL, ''The Sabbath/Jubilee Cycle and the Seven-Year Famine in Egypt,'' *Biblica* 80 (1999) 224–39. N. C. HABEL, *The Land Is Mine: Six Biblical Land Ideologies* (Minneapolis 1995). J. FAGER, *Land Tenure and the Biblical Jubilee* (Sheffield 1993). K. HENREY, ''Land Tenure in the OT,'' *Palestine Exploration Quarterly* 34 (1986) 5–15. Y. AMIT, ''The Jubilee Law—an Attempt at Instituting Social Justice,'' in H. REVENTLOW et al., eds., *Justice and Righteousness* (Sheffield 1992) 47–59. S. RINGE, *Jesus, Liberation, and the Biblical Jubilee,* Overtures to Biblical Theology 19 (Philadelphia 1985). *Encyclopedic Dictionary of the Bible,* tr. and adap. by L. HARTMAN (New York 1963), from A. VAN DEN BORN, *Bijbels Woordenboek* 1224–25. R. NORTH, *The Biblical Jubilee: After Fifty Years* (Rome 2000). *Sociology of the Biblical Jubilee (Analecta biblica* 145 & 4: 2000 &1954). M. WEINFELD, *Social Justice in Ancient Israel* (Minneapolis 1995). N. LEMCHE, *Early Israel* (Leiden 1985); ''Andurarum and mišarum,'' *Journal of Near Eastern Studies* 38 (1979) 11–22; ''Manumission of Slaves—The Fallow Year—The Sabbatical Year—The Jubilee Year,'' *Vetus Testamentum* 26 (1976) 38–59. S. HOENIG, ''Sabbatical Years and the Year of Jubilee,'' *Jewish Quarterly Review* 59 (1969) 222–36. D. CHARPIN, ''L'andurarum à Mari,'' *Mari* 6 (1990) 253–70. E. CORTESE, ''L'anno giubilare . . . ,'' *Rivista Biblica* 29 (1981) 129–46.

[R. NORTH]

ISBN 0-7876-4011-5

9 780787 640118